D1286645

Ben Hodges / Scott Denny

THEATRE WORLD®

Volume 68 / 2011–2012

THEATRE WORLD®
Volume 68
Copyright © 2013 by Ben Hodges

Published in 2013 by Theatre World Media
Distributed by Applause Theatre & Cinema Books
An Imprint of Hal Leonard Corporation
7777 West Bluemound Road
Milwaukee, WI 53213

Trade Book Division Editorial Offices
33 Plymouth Street, Montclair, NJ 07042

Printed in the United States of America
Book design by Tony Meisel

ISBN 978-1-47688-677-0

ISSN 1088-4564

www.applausebooks.com

To Brian Stokes Mitchell

Whose incredible diversity and success onstage and tireless philanthropy offstage is an inspiration to all performers everywhere. His devotion to this publication and the Theatre World Awards organization is unmatched and will always be appreciated by all who benefit from them.

Acknowledgements

Theatre World would like to extend a very special thank you to all the New York and regional press agents, theatre marketing departments, and theatre photographers for their constant and steadfast support of this publication as well as for the endless resources that they provide to the editorial staff.

Our gratitude is eternally extended to our contributing photographers: Joan Marcus, Carol Rosegg, Paul Kolnik, Richard Termine, Gerry Goodstein, T. Charles Erickson, Monique Carboni, Dixie Sheridan, Paula Court, Michal Daniel, Robert J. Saferstein, Peter James Zielinski, David Alkire, Richard Anderson, Pavel Antonov, Miranda Arden, Catherine Ashmore, Pier Baccaro, Jim Baldassare, Erin Balino, SuzAnne Barabas, Armin Bardel, Brian Barenio, Stan Barouh, Rachelle Beckerman, Derrick Belcham, Chris Bennion, Stephanie Berger, Kevin Berne, Rick Berubé, Rose Billings, Marc Bovino, Jay Brady, Michael Brosilow, Harry Butler, Nino Fernando Campagna, Owen Carey, Roy Chicas, Jonathan Christman, Meagan Cignoli, Bradley Clements, Larry Cobra, Peter Coombs, Arthur Cornelius, Gregory Costanzo, Sandra Coudert, Lindsey Crane, Amanda Culp, Julie Curry, Whitney Curtis, Ellie D'Eustachio, Blaine Davis, Robert Day, Manuel Navarro de la Fuente, Joe del Tufo, Phile Deprez, Jeff Derose, Henry DiRocco, Lisa Dozier, Erik Ekroth, Aaron Epstein, Eric Y. Exit, Felix Photography, Benoit Fontaine, Joshua Frachisseur, Tim Fuller, Marc Garvin, Drew Geraci, Gili Getz, Gion, Ronald L. Glassman, Jenny Graham, Larry Gumpel, Aric Gunter, Steven Gunther, Raymond Haddad, Sabrina Hamilton, Jeremy Handelman, John Haynes, Murray Head, Susan Helbock, Michael Henninger, Ben Hider, Albert Hirshon, Justin Hoch, Nikola Horejs, Ken Howard, Lyn Hughes, Ken Huth, James David Jackson, Ken Jacques, Ryan Jensen, Rafael Jordan, Kristie Kahns, Thom Kaine, Jon Kandel, Dermot Kelly, Jennifer Maufrais Kelly, Sue Kessler, Ben King, Johnny Knight, Alex Koch, Ed Kreiger, Stephen Kunken, Michael Kwlechinski, Michael Lamont, Liz Lauren, Chang W. Lee, Corky Lee, Kantu Lentz, Stuart Levine, Geraint Lewis, James Leynse, Alexandria Marlin, Roger Mastroianni, Douglas McBride, Dave McCracken, Jeff McCrum, Steve McNicholas, Ari Mintz, Gustavo Monroy, Meghan Moore, David Morgan, Jerry Naunheim Jr., Doug Nuttelman, Erik Pearson, Ry Pepper, Johan Persson, Pierre, Ves Pitts, Eduardo Placer, Stephen Poff, Michael Portantiere, Leah Prater, Jaime Quinoñes, Patrick Redmond, Justin Richardson, Alyssa Ringler, John Roese, Mark Rohna, Suzi Sadler, Craig Schwartz, Darron Setlow, The Shaltzes, Kim T. Sharp, Bev Sheehan, Steve Shevett, Erika Sidor, Michelle Sims, Jonathan Slaff, Richard Hubert Smith, Gil Smith, Owen Smith, Diane Sobolewski, Hong Sooyeon, Squid Ink Creative, Theresa Squire, Marcus Stern, Noah Strone, Ben Strothmann, Scott Suchman, Stephen Sunderlin, Evan Sung, Daniel Talbott, Steve Tanner, Eran Tari, Brandon Thibodeaux, Ned Thorne, Stephen B. Thornton, Shirin Tinat, Ali Tollervey, Dominick Totino, Mark Turek, Sandy Underwood, Goran Veljic, Pascal Victor, Levi Walker, Bree Michael Warner, Sturgis Warner, Jon Wasserman, Lee Wexler, Drew Wingert, Nicholas Woods, Scott Wynn, Jordana Zeldin, and Tom Zuback.

Equally, we are extrememly grateful for our New York press agents: The Acting Company: Paula Raymond; Janet Appel; Jim Baldassare; Boneau/Bryan-Brown: Chris Boneau, Adrian Bryan-Brown, Jim Byk, Jackie Green, Kelly Guiod, Linnae Hodzic, Kevin Jones, Amy Kass, Holly Kinney, Emily Meagher, Aaron Meier, Christine Olver, Joe Perrotta, Amanda Sales, Heath Schwartz, Michael Strassheim, Susanne Tighe; Jill Bowman; John Capo; Bruce Cohen; Cohn Dutcher: Dan Dutcher, Candace Newson; Peter Cromarty; DARR Publicity: David Gibbs, David Gersten and Associates: David Gersten, Shane Marshall Brown, Bill Evans, Jim Randolph; Helene Davis; Lauren Fitzgerald; Merle Frimark; Karen Greco; The Hartman Group: Michael Hartman, Leslie Baden Papa, Nicole Capatasto, Tom D'Ambrosio, Juliana Hannett, Alyssa Hart, Bethany Larsen, Matt Ross, Frances White, Wayne Wolfe; Ellen Jacobs; Judy Jacksina; The Karpel Group: Bridget Kaplinski; Keith Sherman and Associates: Keith Sherman, Scott Klein, Bret Oberman, Glenna Freedman, Dan Demello, Logan Metzler; Jeffrey Richards and Associates: Irene Gandy, Elon Rutberg, Alana Karpoff, Diana Rissetto; Ryan Hallett; Beck Lee; Jenny Lerner; Lincoln Center Theater: Philip Rinaldi, Barbara Carroll, Amanda Dekker; Kevin McAnarney; Miller Wright and Associates: Miller Wright, Dan Fortune, Danielle Grabianowski; Maya PR: Penny Landau; Emily Owens; O + M Company: Rick Miramontez, Dusty Bennett, Molly Barnett, Philip Carrubba, Jaron Caldwell, Sam Corbett, Jon Dimond, Richard Hillman, Yufen Kung, Jillian Lawton, Chelsea Nachman, Patrick O'Neil, Felicia Pollack, Alexandra Rubin, Andy Snyder, Elizabeth Wagner; Paper Mill Playhouse: Shayne Austin Miller; Patrick Paris; Pearl Theatre Company: Aaron Schwartzbord; Polk and Company: Matt Polk; The Public Theater: Candi Adams, Sam Neuman, Josh Ferri, Julie Danni; The Publicity Office: Marc Thibodeau, Michael Borowski, Jeremy Shaffer, Matt Fasano; Scotti Rhodes; Katie Rosin; Audrey Ross; Richard Kornberg and Associates: Richard Kornberg, Don Summa, Billy Zavelson, Danielle McGarry; Rubenstein Communications Inc.: Howard Rubenstein, Amy Jacobs, Tom Keaney, Elyse Weissman; Sam Rudy Media Relations: Sam Rudy, Robert Lasko, Dale Heller; Pete Sanders; Susan L. Schulman; Brett Singer; Jonathan Slaff; Spin Cycle: Ron Lasko; Springer Associates: Gary Springer, Joe Trentacosta; Sun Productions: Stephen Sunderlin; Type A Marketing: DJ Martin; Walt Disney Theatricals: Adrianna Douzous, Dennis Crowley, Ryan Hallet, Brendan Padgett; The Wooster Group: Clay Hapaz; Blake Zidell; and Lanie Zipoy.

Our gratitude is also eternally extended to our contributing regional theatre staff and press personnel who have contributed time and efforts for their company's listing: Mark Siano (ACT- A Contemporary Theatre), Kirsty Gaukel (Actors Theatre of Louisville), Lauren Pelletier (Alley Theatre), Kathleen Covington (Alliance Theatre), Christine Miller (American Conservatory Theater), Katalin Mitchell (American Repertory Theater), Maura Roche, Leigh Goldenberg (Arden Theatre Company), Greta Hays (Arena Stage), Ashley Pettit (Arkansas Repertory Theatre), Charlie Siedenburg (Barrington Stage Company), Amanda Leslie, Christina Webb (Barter Theatre), Terence Keane (Berkeley Repertory Theatre), Colleen Hughes (Berkshire Theatre Group: Berkshire Theatre Festival), Stephanie Dennis (Bristol Riverside Theatre), Marilyn Langbein (California Shakespeare Theater), Heather Jackson (CENTERSTAGE), Nancy Hereford, Shannon Smith (Center Theatre Group), Anne Marie Wilharm (Chicago Shakespeare Theater), Connie Yeager (Cincinnati Playhouse in the Park), Lisa Craig (Cleveland Play House), Kelsey Guy (Dallas Theater Center), Amanda Curry (Delaware Theatre Company), Alexandra Griesmer (Denver Center Theatre Company), Jeff Carpenter (5th Avenue Theater), Audra Lange, Elizabeth Lafelice (Florida Studio Theatre), Lauren Beyea (Ford's Theatre), Marci Tate (Georgia Shakespeare Festival), Dawn Kellogg (Geva Theatre Center), Amanda ReCupido (Goodman Theatre), Elisa Hale (Goodspeed Musicals), Seena Hodges (Guthrie Theater), Rebecca Curtiss (Huntington Theatre Company), Jonathan Billig (Illinois Theatre Center), Richard Roberts (Indiana Repertory Theatre),

Laura Muir (Kansas City Repertory Theatre), Deanna Chew (La Jolla Playhouse), Steven Scarpa (Long Wharf Theatre), Valerie Galloway Chapa (Lyric Stage), Dan Bauer (McCarter Theatre), Dan Berube (Merrimack Repertory Theatre), Michael Klein (Music Theatre of Wichita), Scott Miller (New Line Theatre), Heather Millen (North Carolina Theatre), Samara Harand, Cathy Taylor, Leeann Torske (Northlight Theatre), Mike Hausberg (The Old Globe), Heather Latiri (Olney Theatre Center), Amy Richard (Oregon Shakespeare Festival), Kelly Stevens (Paper Mill Playhouse), Jonathan White (Pasadena Playhouse, State Theatre of California), Stephanie Dennis (Philadelphia Theatre Company), Margie Romero (Pittsburgh Public Theater), Connie Mahan (PlayMakers Repertory Company), Natalie Genter-Gilmore (Portland Center Stage), Megan Doane (Portland Stage Company), Katie Puglisi (Repertory Theatre of St. Louis), Ana Zavala (San Jose Repertory Theatre), Sarah Meals (Seattle Repertory Theatre), Katherine Colwell (Shakespeare Theatre Company), Katherine Tucker (Signature Theatre), BethAnne George (South Coast Repertory), Kristen Goodman (STAGES ST. LOUIS), Kelsey Munson (Steppenwolf Theatre), Patrick Finlon (Syracuse Stage), Marilyn Busch (Trinity Repertory Company), Stephanie Coen (Two River Theater Company), Morgan Vaughan (Virginia Stage Company), Patricia Blaufuss (Westport Country Playhouse), and Stephen Padla (Yale Repertory).

The editors of *Theatre World* would also like give very special thanks to: John Cerullo (Group Publisher, Hal Leonard Performing Arts Publishing Group), the staff at Hal Leonard Performing Arts Publishing Group: Jamie Nelson (Publicity and Marketing Assistant), Carol Flannery (Editorial Director), Clare Cerullo (Production Manager), Marybeth Keating, (Associate Editor); the staff of Ouest restaurant; Gerard Alessandrini; Beth Allen, Bob Anderson; Epitacio Arganza; Elvira, Kenneth, Bryan, J.R., Arlene, Daryl, and Kayden Autencio; Feliciano Baltazar; Joel Banuelos; Jason Baruch and Sendroff and Baruch LLP; Seth Barrish, Lee Brock, Eric Paeper, and The Barrow Group Theater Company/The Barrow Group School; Jed Bernstein and the Commercial Theater Institute; Wayne Besen and Truth Wins Out; Micah-Shane Brewer and Drew Ogle; Fred Cantor; Fred Caruso; Jason Cicci, Monday Morning Productions, and Summer Stage New York; June Clark; Richard Cohen; Sue Cosson; Susan Cosson; Kimberly Courtney Esq.; Robert Dean Davis; Carol and Nick Dawson; Bob and Brenda Denny; Jamie deRoy; Tim Deak; Diane Dixon; Jetaun Dobbs; Eleanor Speert, Allan Hubby, and the staff of the Drama Book Shop; Craig Dudley; the staff of the Duplex Cabaret and Piano Bar; Sherry Eaker; Ben Feldman Esq. and Beigelman, Feiner, and Feldman, P.C.; Emily Feldman; David Fritz; Christine and David Grimsby; the Estates of the late Charles J. Grant Jr. and Zan Van Antwerp; Helen Guditis and the Broadway Theater Museum; Brenda Saunders-Hampden Esq.; Brad Hampton; Laura Hagan; Al and Sherry Hodges; Michael Humphreys Esq.; Charlie and Phyllis Hurt; Gretchen, Aaron, Eli, and Max Kerr; Sofia Khalid; Jane, Lynn, Kris, and Leslie Kircher; the staff of Macy's Parade and Entertainment Group; Andrew Kirtzman, Luke Escamilla, and The Madison Fire Island Pines; Bob Levine; David Lowry; Stuart Marshall; Kenneth Marzin; Joaquin Matias Esq.; Heath McCormack; Michael Messina; Barry Monush and Screen World; Ted Chapin, Howard Sherman; Jason Bowcutt, Shay Gines, Nick Micozzi, and the staff and respective voting committees of the New York Innovative Theatre Awards; Barbara O'Malley; Petie Dodrill, Craig Johnson, Rob Johnson, Dennis Romer, Katie Robbins, Dean Jo Ann VanSant, Ed Vaughan, the late Dr. Charles O. Dodrill and the staff of Otterbein College/Otterbein College Department of Theatre and Dance, P.J. Owen; William Craver and Paradigm; Bernadette Peters; John Philip Esq. and Andrew Resto; Frank Politano Esq.; Angie and Drew Powell; Kay Radtke; Carolyn, David, Glenna, and Jonas Rapp; Charlotte St. Martin and the League of American Theatres and Producers; Andrea Evans Young and the SFX Archive; P.J. McAteer, Mario Priola, and the staff of the Sip-n-Twirl; Susan Stoller; Henry Grossman, Michael Riordan, John Sala, Mark Snyder, Martha Swope; Renée Isely Tobin and Bob, Kate, Eric, Laura, and Anna, Tobin; Bob Ost and Theater Resources Unlimited Inc.; Tom Lynch, Kati Meister, Erin Oestreich, Steven Bloom, Mary Botosan, Randall Hemming, Barry Keating, Jane Stuart, and the board of directors of The Theatre World Awards Inc.; Peter Filichia, Harry Haun, Howard Kissel, Matthew Murray, Frank Scheck, Michael Sommers, Linda Winer, and the voting committee of The Theatre World Awards Inc.; Jack Williams, Steven Smith, and the staff of the University of Tennessee at Knoxville; Hugo Uys; Wilson Valentin; Laura and Michael Viade; Kathie Packer and the Estate of the late Frederic B. Vogel; Sarah and Bill Willis; the Estate of John A. Willis; George Wilson; Seth and Wolkofsky and Adeena Gabriel; Shane Frampton; and Doug Wright.

Contents

Broadway   **9**

Color Photo Highlights   10
Season Overview   25
Productions That Opened This Season   28
Productions That Played Through / Closed This Season   84
Special Events   112

Off-Broadway   **119**

Photo Highlights   120
Season Overview   122
Productions That Opened This Season   124
Productions That Played Through / Closed This Season   188
Special Events   197

Off-Broadway Company Series   **203**

Photo Highlights   204
Company Series Listings   206

Off-Off-Broadway   **269**

Season Overview   270
Off-Off-Broadway Listings   272

Professional Regional Companies   **341**

Season Overview   342
Regional Company Listings   344

Theatrical Awards   **405**

Theatre World Awards   409
Major New York Awards   422

Regional and Other Theatrical Awards   430

Longest-Running Shows   **449**

Broadway   450
Off-Broadway   459

Obituaries   **463**

Index   **471**

Contributors' Biographies   **533**

Editor's Note

This is the sixty-eighth continuous volume of *Theatre World* since it was first published in 1945. It is also the sixth for which I have served as editor in chief and the second that has been published under our own Theatre World Media imprint. All of the *Theatre World* editors and designers continue to improve and expand the quantity and quality within these pages with each passing year, and I am confident that the volume you have before you is the most complete, as well as the most beautifully produced, in our history.

Theatre World is the oldest, most comprehensive annual pictorial and statistical record of the American theatre, and now the most current. There is more information on the American theatre within these pages than can be gleaned from any other resource, even in the Age of the Internet. Despite the rise of online resources, none of them have remotely approached the completeness of *Theatre World*. Ironically, the Internet has only increased the availability of this publication, as more and more theatre students, fans, industry professionals, and historians are finding out about *Theatre World*, as well as finding out that this is the only comprehensive resource of the entire American theatre season available—in *any* format.

Much of the information within these pages is fleeting. Theatre producers and press agents are understandably focused on the immediate task in front of them of producing a show—or a season—with precious little time for archiving their production information or photographs for posterity. Theatre is an immediate art, and therefore it becomes the job of *Theatre World* to capture this snapshot of our collective American culture each year before it recedes into the past. That is precisely why our mission to chronicle each and every season is so important, from Broadway, to Off-Broadway, to Off-Off-Broadway and regional theatre.

With respect to the edition currently before you, I am particularly proud of our successful efforts to include more and more regional theatres within these covers, and there are in fact more regional companies within these pages than ever before. The increasing completeness of information on Off-Off-Broadway theatre productions is also unprecedented in any medium. (And of course there are more Off-Off-Broadway productions—and of an increasing quality—than Broadway and Off-Broadway combined.) Our Major Theatrical Awards section is doubtless unmatched, as is most certainly our comprehensive obituary section. We also continue the newly revived tradition of seasoned industry professionals introducing each respective venue: Adam Feldman for Broadway; Linda Buchwald for Off-Broadway; Shay Gines for Off-Off-Broadway; and Rob Weinert-Kendt for regional theatre. These essays provide the proper analysis and overview of each respective geographically located theatre season, and add to the ongoing *Theatre World* narrative, now more than a half-century old.

Above all, however, *Theatre World* is known as an incomparable photographic record of the theatre. Many even consider this our most attractive quality, and feature us as a coffee table book to fascinate and entice readers with the diversity and breadth of the photographs within our pages. More than 800 photographs are included here, providing not only an indelible and unprecedented visual record of the theatrical season, but also a reference for producers, directors, designers, and actors to the roles or productions that they—or others— have created.

Many of us got into show business because we liked to tell (as well as hear) good stories. We have all come together in this publication to tell our collective story of the 2011–2012 theatre season. It is one in which so many took part, from Syracuse to San Diego. We hope you enjoy reading each chapter of each volume as much as we have enjoyed creating them for you, and whether you are a performer, crewperson, member of the audience, we always hope that you enjoy the show.

—Ben Hodges, Editor in Chief

Also by Ben Hodges

The Commercial Theater Institute Guide to Producing Plays and Musicals
(Applause Theatre and Cinema Books)

Forbidden Acts: Pioneering Gay & Lesbian Plays of the Twentieth Century
(Applause Theatre and Cinema Books)

The American Theatre Wing Presents The Play That Changed My Life: America's Foremost Playwrights on the Plays That Influenced Them
(Applause Theatre and Cinema Books)

Outplays: Landmark Gay and Lesbian Plays of the Twentieth Century
(Alyson Books)

Also by Theatre World Media

Screen World Volume 62: The Films of 2010

Screen World Volume 63: The Films of 2011

BROADWAY

June 1, 2011–May 31, 2012

Top: Paul Gross and Kim Cattrall in Private Lives. *Opened at the Music Box Theatre November 17, 2011 (photo by Cylla von Tiedemann)*

Center: Raúl Esparza and the Company of Leap of Faith. *Opened at the St. James Theatre April 26, 2012 (photo by Joan Marcus)*

Bottom: Frank Langella and Adam Driver in the Roundabout Theatre Company production of Man and Boy. *Opened at the American Airlines Theatre October 9, 2011 (photo by Joan Marcus)*

Above: A scene from Spider-Man Turn Off the Dark. *Opened at the Foxwoods Theatre June 14, 2011 (photo by Jacob Cohl)*

Left: Sierra Boggess and Tyne Daly in the Manhattan Theatre Club production of Master Class. *Opened at the Samuel J. Friedman Theatre July 7, 2011 (photo by Joan Marcus)*

Top: The Ensemble of Follies. *Opened at the Marquis Theatre September 12, 2011 (photo by Joan Marcus)*

Left: Samuel L. Jackson and Angela Bassett *in* The Mountaintop. *Opened at the Bernard B. Jacobs Theatre October 13, 2011 (photo by Joan Marcus)*

Below: Marlo Thomas and Lisa Emery in George is Dead, *one of the three short plays in* Relatively Speaking. *Opened at the Brooks Atkinson Theatre October 20, 2011 (photo by Joan Marcus)*

Above: Jennifer Lim and Gary Wilmes in Chinglish. *Opened at the Longacre Theatre October 27, 2011 (photo by Michael McCabe)*

Left: The Company in Godspell. *Opened at the Circle in the Squre November 7, 2011 (photo by Jeremy Daniel)*

Above left: Judith Light and Rachel Griffiths in the Lincoln Center Theater production of Other Desert Cities. *Opened at the Booth Theatre November 3, 2011 (photo by Joan Marcus)*

Above right: Nina Arianda and Hugh Dancy in the Manhattan Theatre Club production of Venus in Fur. *Opened at the Samuel J. Friedman November 8, 2011; transferred to the Lyceum Theatre February 7, 2012. (photo by Joan Marcus)*

Bottom right: Hugh Jackman with (l-r) Kearran Giovanni, Emily Tyra, and Lara Seibert in Hugh Jackman Back on Broadway. *Opened at the Broadhurst Theatre November 10, 2011 (photo by Joan Marcus)*

Above left: Patti LuPone and Mandy Patinkin in An Evening with Patti LuPone and Mandy Patinkin. *Opened at the Ethel Barrymore Theatre November 21, 2011 (photo by Joan Marcus)*

Above right: Laura Osnes and Jeremy Jordan in Bonnie and Clyde. *Opened at the Gerald Schoenfeld Theatre December 1, 2011 (photo by Nathan Johnson)*

Bottom: Hamish Linklater, Alan Rickman, Lily Rabe (standing), Hettienne Park, and Jerry O'Connell (foreground) in Seminar. *Opened at the John Golden Theatre November 20, 2011 (photo by Jeremy Daniel)*

Above: Dulé Hill and Tracie Thoms in Stick Fly. *Opened at the Cort Theatre December 8, 2011 (photo by Richard Termine)*

Right: David Turner, Jessie Mueller, and Harry Connick Jr. in On a Clear Day You Can See Forever. *Opened at the St. James Theatre December 11, 2011 (photo by Paul Kolnik)*

Top: Ato Blankson-Wood, Alex Wyse, Teddy Toye, Alexander Aguilar, and Jared Zirilli in Lysistrata Jones. *Opened at the Walter Kerr Theatre December 14, 2011 (photo by Joan Marcus)*

Left: David Alan Grier (center) and the Company of The Gershwins' Porgy and Bess. *Opened at the Richard Rodgers Theatre January 12, 2012 (photo by Michael Lutch)*

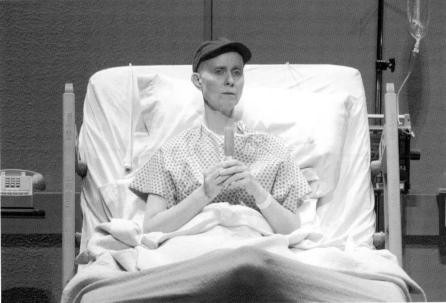

Above: Jim Dale, Carla Gugino, and Rosemary Harris in the Roundabout Theatre Company production of The Road to Mecca. *Opened at the American Airlines Theatre January 17, 2012. (photo by Joan Marcus)*

Right: Cynthia Nixon in the Manhattan Theatre Club production of Wit. *Opened at the Samuel J. Friedman Theatre January 26, 2012 (photo by Joan Marcus)*

Above: Steve Kazee and Cristin Milioti in Once. Opened at the Bernard B. Jacobs Theatre March 18, 2012 (photo by Joan Marcus)

Left: Peter Nolan and the Company of the Stratford Shakespeare Festival production of Jesus Christ Superstar. Opened at the Neil Simon Theatre March 22, 2012 (photo by Joan Marcus)

The Company of Newsies
The Musical. *Opened at the
Nederlander Theatre
March 29, 2012.
(photo by Deen Van Meer)*

John Larroquette (center)
and the Company in Gore
Vidal's The Best Man.
*Opened at the Gerald
Schoenfeld Theatre
April 1, 2012
(photo by Joan Marcus)*

*Above: Michael Cumpsty
and Tracie Bennett in* End of
the Rainbow. *Opened at the
Belasco Theatre April 2, 2012
(photo by Carol Rosegg)*

*Left: Elena Roger (center) and
the Company in* Evita.
*Opened at the Marquis Theatre
April 5, 2012
(photo by Richard Termine)*

Above: David Rossmer, Adam
Chanler-Berat, Carson Elrod
(center), and the Company in Peter
and the Starcatcher. Opened at the
Brooks Atkinson Theatre April 15,
2012 (photo by Joan Marcus)

Right: Oliver Chris, Tom Edden, and
James Corden One Man,
Two Guvnors. Opened at the Music
Box Theatre April 18, 2012
(photo by Joan Marcus)

Left: Richard Fleeshman (back), Da'Vine Joy Randolph, and Caissie Levy in Ghost The Musical. *Opened at the Lunt-Fontanne Theatre April 23, 2012 (photo by Joan Marcus)*

Above: Blair Underwood and Nicole Ari Parker in A Streetcar Named Desire. *Opened at the Broadhurst Theatre April 22, 2012. (photo by Ken Howard)*

Left: Frank Wood, Annie Parisse, Christina Kirk, Jeremy Shamos, Damon Gupton, and Crystal A. Dickinson in the Playwrights Horizons production of Clybourne Park. *Opened at the Walter Kerr Theatre April 19, 2012 (photo by Nathan Johnson)*

The Ensemble of Nice Work If You Can Get It. *Opened at the Imperial Theatre April 24, 2012 (photo by Joan Marcus)*

Michael Esper, Dick Latessa, Linda Lavin, and Kate Jennings Grant in the Vineyard Theatre production of The Lyons. *Opened at the Cort Theatre April 23, 2012 (photo by Carol Rosegg)*

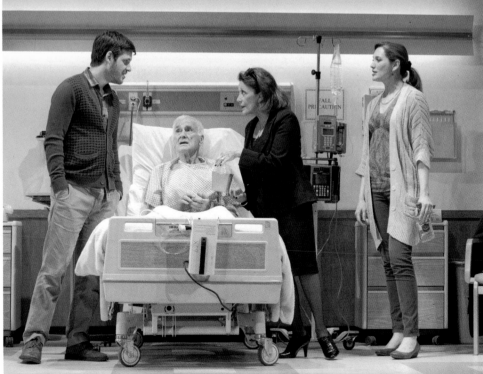

Top: *Spencer Kayden, Ben Daniels, and Patricia Kalember in the Roundabout Theatre Company production of* Don't Dress for Dinner. *Opened at the American Airlines Theatre April 26, 2012* (photo by Joan Marcus)

Left: *John Lithgow and Margaret Colin in the Manhattan Theatre Club production of* The Columnist. *Opened at the Samuel J. Friedman Theatre April 25, 2012* (photo by Joan Marcus)

2011-2012 Broadway Season:
Singular Sensations

By Adam Feldman, Associate Theatre Editor, *Time Out New York*

Casual observers of the 2011-12 Broadway season could be forgiven, at times, for thinking they were seeing double. Two George Gershwin shows! Two Andrew Lloyd Webber shows! Two Alan Menken shows! Two dramatic portraits of gay icons in decline! Two revivals with *Sex and the City* alumnae! Two new musicals starring newcomer Jeremy Jordan! Two old musicals about Jesus!

On closer inspection, however, the season's fare turns out to have been remarkably varied. General trends may be identified: a majority of the season's new musicals were adapted from films, for example, and its most artistically significant work tended to have roots Off-Broadway or at regional theatres. But the style and content of the offerings ranged widely. Broadway's buffet seemed intent on providing something for every palate: From comic-book diversion to touching romance, from Bible lessons to Jazz Age dazzle, from ribald farce to classic family drama, from biting racial inquiry to seafaring adventure.

Although the superhero musical *Spider-Man: Turn Off the Dark* was arguably the most spectacular production in Broadway history, and certainly the most expensive, its official opening in June—the season's first—was something of an anticlimax. From the beginning of its rehearsal period the previous October, the show had fought a tidal wave of controversy, feverish gossip and barely disguised Schadenfreude. Injuries related to its aerial stunts had made *Spider-Man* the subject of national news, and word of mouth was poisonous. Despite the major names involved (including U2's Bono and the Edge, who wrote the score), the project seemed doomed to flop.

Theatre critics had written about *Spider-Man* in February—breaking with the custom of waiting for an official opening night, on grounds that the show's preview period seemed indefinite—and had depicted it as a fiasco. Since then, however, the show had changed radically. Its original auteur, Julie Taymor, was tossed overboard; so was most of its ambitious but confusing second act. Philip William McKinley took over as director, and Roberto Aguirre-Sacasa, a playwright whose background included a stint with Marvel Comics, was brought in to refashion the book along more conventional lines.

When the show finally opened in June, after a short break for retooling and a record-shattering 182 preview performances, the reaction reflected exhaustion with the drawn-out *Spider-Man* saga. Critics fried the show again, but in somewhat cooler pans. (*Spider-Man* fared poorly with the Tony nominating committee as well; only its extravagant sets and costumes were nominated.) Audiences didn't care: In defiance of nearly all predictions, the new *Spider-Man* was a hit, catching tourists like eager flies.

The other two original musicals that opened on Broadway in the remainder of 2011 were less fortunate. *Bonnie and Clyde*, which featured rising young talents Jeremy Jordan and Laura Osnes as the notorious 1930s crime duo of Bonnie Parker and Clyde Barrow, earned lukewarm notices (though kinder ones than its prolific composer, the frequent critical whipping boy Frank Wildhorn, had received earlier in the year for *Wonderland*). Douglas Carter Beane and Lewis Flinn's *Lysistrata Jones* was a randy, peppy update of Aristophanes' sexual-protest comedy, set in the world of college basketball; it moved to the Walter Kerr Theatre after a summer run Off-Broadway, but mixed-to-favorable reviews didn't give it much of a bounce in sales. Both shows opened in December and closed after less than a month.

The rapid demise of *Bonnie and Clyde* proved good news indeed for *Newsies The Musical*. Adapted by Broadway fixture Harvey Fierstein from a 1992 live-action Disney musical film, and featuring an expanded version of the movie's rousing Alan Menken–Jack Feldman score, the show debuted at New Jersey's Paper Mill Playhouse in October. Jeremy Jordan gave a dynamic star turn in that production as the scrappy teenage instigator of an 1899 newsboy strike; with *Bonnie and Clyde* behind him, the actor was free to headline *Newsies* again at the Nederlander

Theatre in March. (This made him the first performer in living memory to originate leading roles in two new Broadway musicals in a single season.)

Directed by Jeff Calhoun and livened by Christopher Gattelli's acrobatic choreography, *Newsies* was a family-friendly crowd-pleaser in the *Annie* tradition of well-polished scruff, tied to an inspirational David-and-Goliath message. The 2011-12 season's other major musical success, *Once*, had also started as a film, but was cut from entirely different cloth.

Moody, modern, and bittersweet, *Once* told of two lonely people—an Irish man and a Czech woman, both unnamed—who meet in Dublin, connect through music, and change each other in unexpected ways. Enda Walsh's script and John Tiffany's staging struck an elegant balance between naturalism and theatricality. The cast of thirteen, led by an appealingly wounded Steve Kazee and an enchantingly quirky Cristin Milioti, doubled as an onstage band. When the production began previews in December at the East Village's New York Theatre Workshop, audiences were captivated by its poignant story and Celtic soul.

In a highly unusual move, the show announced its impending Broadway transfer before the Off-Broadway version had officially opened or been reviewed. Skeptics wondered whether the show's charm could survive in a larger venue, but *Once*—whose adult emotionality and somber whimsy marked it apart from any other musical on Broadway—soon emerged as the sleeper hit of the year. In June, it was rewarded with eight Tony Awards, including those for Best Musical, Best Director of a Musical, and Best Actor in a Musical.

Two less accomplished new tuners based on popular movies opened in the spring as well. The love-after-death thriller *Ghost the Musical* was a London import that, like *Spider-Man*, featured new music by rock-pop songwriters (Glen Ballard and Eurythmics' Dave Stewart) and relied heavily on impressive special effects; critics and audiences alike found it sappy, and it lasted only four months. *Leap of Faith* starred Raúl Esparza as the evangelical flimflam artist played by Steve Martin in the 1992 film, and offered a gospel-tinged score by Glenn Slater and *Newsies* composer Alan Menken. The final show of the season to open, *Leap of Faith* was also the fastest of the season to close; it shuttered after just nineteen performances.

Nestled among the spring's movie adaptations was one other new musical: *Nice Work If You Can Get It*, a retro romp built—like 1983's *My One and Only* and 1992's *Crazy for You*—around songs from the treasured catalog of George and Ira Gershwin. (Joe DiPietro's book borrowed its bones from the 1926 Gershwin musical *Oh, Kay!*) Matthew Broderick starred as a well-heeled Prohibition-era playboy; Kelli O'Hara was his romantic foil, a spunky bootlegger. Following up on her 2011 production of *Anything Goes*, director-choreographer Kathleen Marshall laid on the showbiz glitz. Although some reviewers found Broderick's performance listless, veteran troupers Judy Kaye and Michael McGrath delivered vivid comedic character turns (and won Tony Awards for their merry troubles).

Broadway got a second dose of the Gershwin boys in the spring with *The Gershwins' Porgy and Bess*, a controversial revival of the brothers' classic 1935 folk opera, set in the hardscrabble African-American slums of South Carolina. Directed by Diane Paulus, whose exuberantly tangled 2009 revival of *Hair* returned to Broadway in the summer of 2011 as part of its national tour, *Porgy and Bess* encountered pointed resistance before it even began.

In an August interview with the *New York Times* before the production's premiere at the American Repertory Theater in Massachusetts, Paulus and two of her principal collaborators on the project—leading lady Audra McDonald and playwright Suzan-Lori Parks—discussed changes they were considering making to *Porgy and Bess* in the interest of dramatic economy, as well as to reflect modern attitudes toward race in a piece that had been criticized as insensitive. No less an eminence than Stephen Sondheim took umbrage; in a stingingly sarcastic public letter to the *Times*, the composer criticized the "arrogance" of suggesting that the opera needed editing (and bristled at the inclusion of the Gershwin name in the production's official title, which he considered a slight to co-librettist DuBose Heyward).

Around the same time, one of Sondheim's own masterpieces, 1971's ravishing *Follies,* returned to Broadway for a limited run, in a revival that had debuted in May at the Kennedy Center in Washington, D.C. Bernadette Peters, Jan Maxwell, Danny Burstein, and Ron Raines played the unhappy central couples in Sondheim and James Goldman's darkly dazzling pageant. (The cast of forty-one also notably included British stage star Elaine Paige, who sang "I'm Still Here.") After forty years, *Follies*'s vivisection of American nostalgia remained sharp—even if the musical had itself become, ironically, the object of nostalgia among musical-theatre connoisseurs. Critics showered praise on Eric Shaeffer's lavish production, and the engagement was extended through January.

When *Porgy and Bess* opened at the Richard Rodgers Theatre at the start of 2012, critics were divided about the alterations that Paulus and Parks had made to the work, including the replacement of sung recitative with spoken dialogue and the choice to give the disabled beggar Porgy (Norm Lewis) a cane instead of his customary goat cart. (One idea floated in the *Times* interview—that of a more hopeful ending—had apparently been abandoned.) But everyone agreed that Audra McDonald gave a heart-piercing performance as the agonized Bess, with some singling out supporting players Phillip Boykin and David Alan Grier for praise. At the Tony Awards in June, *Porgy and Bess* beat out *Follies* as Best Revival of a Musical, and McDonald took home the prize for Best Actress in a Musical (her fifth Tony Award).

Four other musical revivals vied for audiences in the 2011-12 season—a distinct uptick from 2010-11, which had offered only two. The weirdest was *On a Clear Day You Can See Forever,* Alan Jay Lerner and Burton Lane's 1965 musical about reincarnation and extrasensory perception. In this heavily rewritten version of a famously strange show, Harry Connick Jr. played a 1970s psychiatrist who falls for a 1940s jazz singer who is the female past-life identity of his current gay male patient. Jessie Mueller made a promising debut as the singer, but the revisions to *On a Clear Day* made what was already a curio even curiouser, and the revival closed quickly.

Collectors of Broadway trivia will remember 2012 as the year when Jesus Christ appeared in three musicals running simultaneously on the Great White Way: in a cameo appearance in *The Book of Mormon,* and as the central figure in concurrent revivals of *Godspell* and *Jesus Christ Superstar.* Both of the latter had made their first New York appearances in 1971, and both showed signs of age.

Godspell, an assortment of mostly comic vignettes based on parables from the New Testament, opened at Circle in the Square Theatre in November, in a version that retained Stephen Schwartz's catchy score (reorchestrated for a more *Glee*-ful sound) and interpolated new material developed by director Daniel Goldstein and his actors. But critics complained that the irreverence of *Godspell*'s approach to the Bible no longer seemed fresh, and that, despite a mostly buoyant young cast, the production often resembled a bumptious megachurch youth-ministry service.

Jesus Christ Superstar encountered a similar problem when it was born again at the Neil Simon Theatre in March. Directed by Des McAnuff, the revival was a hit in 2011 at Canada's Stratford Shakespeare Festival. But on Broadway, McAnuff's nearly humorless production—though strikingly designed and powerfully sung—inspired few new followers to Andrew Lloyd Webber and Tim Rice's rock opera, whose storytelling and media satire seemed too thin to support so stately a treatment. Both *Godspell* and *Jesus Christ Superstar* closed at a loss in the summer, one week apart. (Given its sheer volume of flops with spiritual themes—not just the two Jesus musicals but also *Ghost, Leap of Faith,* and *On a Clear Day*—2011-12 may go down in history as the season when Broadway found religion, and promptly lost it again.)

Jesus Christ Superstar overlapped with the first Broadway revival of another Lloyd Webber–Rice collaboration: *Evita,* the team's 1978 musical about the meteoric rise and fall of Argentine first lady Eva Perón. The production was an import of director Michael Grandage's 2006 West End staging—complete with its Argentine-born leading lady, Elena Roger, who had earned rave reviews in London. Her interpretation of the role was received coldly in New York, however, and her vocal power was compared unflatteringly to that of the show's original Broadway

star, Patti LuPone. The revival's primary commercial draw turned out to be the handsome pop singer Ricky Martin as *Evita*'s acerbic narrator, Ché; screaming fans regularly greeted Martin at the stage door. (The revival ended its run when he departed it in January 2013.)

The strapping Aussie movie star Hugh Jackman inspired even greater fan frenzy in the fall when he flaunted his megawatt charisma in the Vegas-style *Hugh Jackman, Back on Broadway,* a sold-out concert run that was widely hailed as a triumph of musical-theatre showmanship. A few blocks away, with less flash, *Evita*'s original Broadway costars reunited for *An Evening with Patti LuPone and Mandy Patinkin,* a master class–style presentation in which the actor-singers put their distinctive stamps on songs from a variety of musicals, backed by a single piano. (A two-week run of the likeable one-man show *Shatner's World: We Just Live in It* featured only a brief sample of *Star Trek* star William Shatner's unique musical stylings.)

Turning our attention to the non-musical side of the season, we find that all four of the works that wound up in contention for Best Play at the 2011-12 Tonys emerged from Off-Broadway productions in previous seasons. The eventual winner, Bruce Norris's *Clybourne Park,* had premiered at Playwrights Horizons in February 2010. Written in reply to Lorraine Hansberry's groundbreaking 1959 drama, *A Raisin in the Sun,* Norris's incisive, bitterly humorous play examined America's shifting dialogue about race by looking at real-estate negotiations for a Chicago-area house in two different periods (1959 in the first act, 2009 in the second).

After *Clybourne Park* won the 2011 Pulitzer Prize and earned acclaim in a London production, producers prepared to bring it to Broadway for a limited run with its sterling original Off-Broadway ensemble. Offstage drama briefly threatened to scuttle the show in January 2012, when lead producer Scott Rudin pulled out of the project after an acrimonious personal dispute with Norris; Jujamcyn Theaters president Jordan Roth stepped in to fund a production that helped give intellectual heft to the season.

Another delayed transfer from the 2009-2010 Off Broadway season was *Venus in Fur,* a sexually charged two-hander by David Ives. In its 2010 run at Classic Stage Company, the play had earned its leading lady, Nina Arianda, an ecstatic burst of a-star-is-born reviews. The nonprofit Manhattan Theatre Club gave her a chance to reprise her pyrotechnical performance in the fall, opposite a new co-star, Hugh Dancy; the production transferred to a commercial run at the Lyceum Theatre in February, and won Arianda a Tony for Best Actress in a Play.

Peter and the Starcatcher opened on Broadway in April on the heels of a 2011 run at New York Theatre Workshop. Adapted by Rick Elice from a popular children's book, this swashbuckling prequel to *Peter Pan* soared on the directorial pixie dust of its tongue-in-check story-theatre staging by Roger Rees and Alex Timbers; on Tony night, it swept all four awards for creative design, and Christian Borle snagged a Best Featured Actor trophy for his delicious hamming as the future Captain Hook.

Lincoln Center Theater, which chipped in to produce *Clybourne Park,* also brought one of its own shows to the Great White Way in the fall. *Other Desert Cities,* which had premiered Off-Broadway at Lincoln Center's Mitzi E. Newhouse Theater in the previous season, marked the Broadway debut of playwright Jon Robin Baitz; burnished with tart one-liners, this family-politics drama was lit by a starry cast that included stage vets Stockard Channing, Stacy Keach, and Judith Light (who won a Featured Actress Tony). The formidable Linda Lavin, who had originated Light's role, passed on repeating it in order to play a gorgon-like Jewish mother in the season's fifth Off-Broadway transfer of a play: Nicky Silver's acid-tipped dark comedy *The Lyons,* which opened at the Vineyard Theatre in October and transferred to the Cort Theatre for a three-month run in April.

In a salutary sign of increasing diversity on Broadway—and, perhaps, of ongoing changes in audience demographics—the fall season offered three new dramas by nonwhite authors, including two African-American women. Katori Hall's *The Mountaintop* starred Samuel L. Jackson as Dr. Martin Luther King Jr. and Angela Bassett as a mysterious visitor to his hotel room on the eve of his assassination; Lydia R. Diamond's *Stick Fly* looked at class- and race-based conflicts within a wealthy black family in Martha's Vineyard. David Henry Hwang, the only Asian-

American playwright with Broadway on his résumé, returned to the Street with *Chinglish*, an intercultural comedy-drama about an American businessman in China.

Relatively Speaking—a triptych of comedic one-acts on Jewish-family themes by Woody Allen, Elaine May, and Ethan Coen—was pitched at a more old-fashioned Broadway crowd. Marlo Thomas was praised for her comically grotesque performance in the May piece, but the show was largely dismissed as creaky. Rounding out the fall collection of new plays was Theresa Rebeck's *Seminar*, in which the sonorous Alan Rickman played the instructor of a weekly writing class struggling through internal rivalries. Generally well-reviewed, the play enjoyed a six-month run; it closed in May, without Rickman, a week after receiving no Tony nominations.

The Tony for Best Actor in a Play was captured by another English actor, James Corden, for his rollicking comic turn in the hit farce *One Man, Two Guvnors*, which opened at the Music Box Theatre in May after a 2011 London run. Adapted by Richard Bean from Carlo Goldini's commedia-flavored 1743 farce (whose action it relocated to 1960s England), the show delighted audiences with expertly executed slapstick; Corden's semi-improvisational interactions with the crowd added mightily to the fun.

A more divisive British import was Peter Quilter's *End of the Rainbow*, which starred Tracie Bennett as a decrepit, sex-crazed, and pill-ravaged Judy Garland in the final stretch of the singer's career. Admirers praised Bennett's performance, which included multiple musical numbers, as a wonder of stamina; detractors found the show's treatment of Garland demeaning. Two other biodramas opened in April, too. Eric Simonson's short-lived *Magic/Bird* dealt with the professional rivalry and off-court friendship of basketball stars Magic Johnson and Larry Bird. David Auburn's *The Columnist*, the playwright's first Broadway offering since his Pulitzer Prize–winning 2000 drama *Proof*, starred John Lithgow as Joseph Alsop, an influential conservative political columnist (and closeted homosexual) of the Cold War period.

The 2011-12 season's selection of play revivals began in a biographical vein in July with Manhattan Theatre Club's resurrection of *Master Class*, Terrence McNally's 1995 portrait of opera eminence Maria Callas. Critics mostly found that the earthy Tyne Daly, cast against type as the play's glamorously catty version of La Divina, played the role with sensitivity; opinion was divided about the underlying quality of the play. In January, MTC served up another 1990s vehicle for a strong leading lady with its revival of *Wit*, Margaret Edson's Pulitzer-winning 1999 drama about a proud, cruel English professor confronting terminal cancer. Cynthia Nixon received respectful notices in the demanding central role.

In contrast with the MTC's busy season, Broadway's other nonprofit powerhouse, Roundabout Theatre Company, kept a low profile with a slate of three modest revivals. In October, Frank Langella and Adam Driver opened in Terence Rattigan's

ethical drama *Man and Boy* (1963); in January, the luminous Rosemary Harris played opposite Carla Gugino in Athol Fugard's searching *The Road to Mecca* (1987); and in April, the Roundabout offered the first Broadway production of *Don't Dress for Dinner* (1987), a French farce by Marc Comoletti, whose *Boeing-Boeing* had taken off in a 2008 production.

Most of the season's play revivals came with mass-culture stars attached, with varying results. A November mounting of Noël Coward's *Private Lives*, starring Nixon's *Sex and the City* costar Kim Cattrall, closed at the end of December. An all-black production of Tennessee Williams's *A Streetcar Named Desire* in April (following in the footsteps of 2008's African-American take on *Cat on a Hot Tin Roof*) offered the comely Blair Underwood and Nicole Ari Parker as Stanley Kowalski and Blanche DuBois; ticket sales were spotty, and a planned extension of the limited engagement was canceled.

The dramatic revival that enjoyed the longest run was *Gore Vidal's The Best Man*, a 1960 political thriller about backroom dealings at a presidential convention. (Producer Jeffrey Richards had also revived it in 2000.) Larded with A-list names—including James Earl Jones, Angela Lansbury, John Larroquette and Candice Bergen—the production opened in April for what would eventually be 185 performances.

In terms of prestige and profitability, however, no revival could compete with the juggernaut that was *Death of a Salesman*. Directed by the legendary Mike Nichols, this revival of Arthur Miller's everyman tragedy featured a strong ensemble cast led by Philip Seymour Hoffman (as a palpably drained Willy Loman), and presented itself as a throwback to a classy Broadway of yesteryear: Its set reproduced Jo Mielziner's original 1949 design, and its official press photos were in black and white. Audiences and most critics applauded; tickets were scarce, and the production won Tonys for Best Revival and Best Director of a Play.

In other ways, the Broadway of old continued to fade slowly into history. In deference to the dead, theatre marquees were dimmed twice: for director-producer Theodore Mann and longtime theatre critic Howard Kissel. Among many other theatre luminaries lost during the season were Tom Aldredge, Jeffrey Ash, Doris Belack, Stephen Douglass, William Duell, Peter Falk, Leo Friedman, Ben Gazzara, Ulu Grosbard, Eiko Ishioka, Jerry Leiber, Harry Morgan, John Neville, Patricia Neway, Alice Playten, Cliff Robertson, Bradshaw Smith, Tony Stevens, Margaret Tyzack, Jane White, Judd Woldin, and John Wood.

The new Broadway, meanwhile, was evolving in multiple directions. If the box-office success of *Spider-Man: Turn Off the Dark* suggested that audiences wanted the brightest and loudest bangs for their bucks, the parallel triumph of *Once* proved that others were open to a very different variety of modern-day musical theatre. What these two shows had in common is that they were unlike any other. Stealing periodic looks in the rear-review mirror, Broadway continued to drive ahead with productions that seemed one-of-a-kind.

Jeremy Jordan made recent Broadway history starring in two musicals within the same season, Bonnie & Clyde *and* Newsies The Musical. *Jordan received a 2012 Theatre World Award for his performance in* Bonnie & Clyde *(photo by Nathan Johnson)*

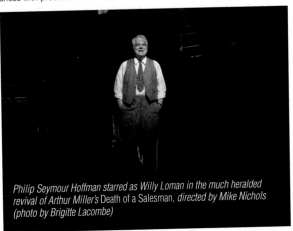

Philip Seymour Hoffman starred as Willy Loman in the much heralded revival of Arthur Miller's Death of a Salesman, *directed by Mike Nichols (photo by Brigitte Lacombe)*

Spider-Man: Turn Off the Dark

Foxwoods Theatre; First Preview: November 28, 2010; Opening Night: June 14, 2011; 182 previews, 400 performances as of May 31, 2012

Music & lyrics by Bono and The Edge, book by Julie Taymor, Glen Berger, and Roberto Aguirre-Sacasa; Produced by Michael Cohl & Jeremiah J. Harris, Land Line Productions, Hello Entertainment/David Garfinkle/Tony Adams, Sony Pictures Entertainment, Norton Herrick & Herrick Entertainment, Billy Rovzar & Fernando Rovzar, Stephen Bronfman, Jeffrey B. Hecktman, Omneity Entertainment/Richard G. Weinberg, James L. Nederlander, Terry Allen Kramer, S2BN Entertainment, Jam Theatricals, Mayerson/Gould/Hauser/Tysoe Group, Patricia Lambrecht, Paul McGuinness, in arrangement with Marvel Entertainment; Original Direction, Julie Taymor; Creative Consultant, Philip Wm. McKinley; Choreography & Ariel Choreography, Daniel Ezralow; Additional Choreography, Chase Brock; Sets, George Tsypin; Lighting, Donald Holder; Costumes, Eiko Ishioka; Sound, Jonathan Deans; Projections, Kyle Cooper; Masks, Julie Taymor; Hair, Campbell Young Associates, Luc Verschueren; Makeup, Judy Chin; Aerial Design, Scott Rogers; Aerial Rigging, Jaque Paquin; Projection Coordinator/Additional Content Design, Howard Werner; Prosthetics Design, Louie Zakarian; Arrangements & Orchestrations, David Campbell; Music Supervision, Teese Gohl; Music Producer, Paul Bogaev; Music Director, Kim Grigsby; Music Coordinator, Antoine Silverman; Vocal Arrangements, David Campbell, Teese Gohl, Kimberly Grigsby; Additional Arrangements/Vocal Arrangements, Dawn Kenny, Rori Coleman; Associate Set Design, Rob Bissinger; Resident Director, Keith Batten; Resident Choreographer, Jason Snow; Production Stage Managers, C. Randall White & Kathleen E. Purvis; Casting, Telsey + Company; Marketing Director, Len Gill; Marketing, Keith Hurd; Associate Producer, Anne Tanaka; Production Management, Juniper Street Productions (Hillary Blanken, Kevin Broomell, Guy Kwan, Ana Rose Greene, Alexandra Paull, Joseph DeLuise) & MB Productions (Mike Bauder, Sonya Duveneck); General Management, Alan Wasser, Allan Williams, Aaron Lustbader, Mark Shacket; Executive Producers, Glenn Orsher, Stephen Howard, Martin McCallum, Adam Silberman; Technical Director, Fred Gallo; Company Manager, Marc Borsak; Second Assistant Stage Managers, Sandra M. Franck, Andrew Neal, Jenny Slattery, Michael Wilhoite; Sub Stage Managers, Theresa A. Bailey, Valerie Lau-Kee Lai, Bonnie Panson; Associate Company Manager, Thom Mitchell; Assistant Company Manager, Lisa Guzman; Vocal Coach, Don Lawrence; Dialect Coach, Deborah Hecht; Acting Coach, Sheila Grey; Assistant Creative Consultant/Assistant Director, Eileen F. Haggerty; Assistant Director, Dodd Loomis; Assistant Choreographer, Cherice Barton; Production Aerial Supervisor, Angela Phillips; U.K. Casting, Gillian Hawser; Set Design Creative Team: Arturs Virtmanis (pop-up and dimensional design) Baiba Baiba (illustration and graphics) Sergei Goloshapov (cityscape graphics); Assistant Set Design Team: Anita La Scala (first assistant set design), Sia Balabanova, Rafael Kayanan (graphic art), Nathan Heverin (pop-ups), Eric Beauzay, Catherine Chung, Rachel Short Janocko, Damon Pelletier, Daniel Zimmerman (model makers), Robert John Andrusko, Toni Barton, Larry W. Brown, Mark Fitzgibbons, Jonathan Spencer, Josh Zangen (draftsmen), Tijana Bjelajac, Szu-Feng Chen, Heather Dunbar, Mimi Lien, Qin (Lucy) Lu, Robert Pyzocha, Chsato Uno, Frank McCullough (assistant set design), Lily Twining (pre-visualization); Associate Design: Mary Nemecek Peterson (costumes), Angela Johnson (makeup), Vivien Leone (lighting), Brian Hsieh, Keith Caggiano (sound); Assistant Design: Angela M. Kahler, Katie Irish (costumes), Caroline Chao, Carolyn Wong, Michael Jones (lighting), Sarah Jakubasz (video), Cory McCutcheon (hair); Costume Shoppers, Jennifer Adams, Dana Burkart, Cathy Parrott, Jen Raskopf; Assistant to the Lighting Designer, Porsche McGovern; Automated Light Programmer, Richard Tyndall; Video Programmer, Phil Gilbert; Puppet and Mask Supervisor, Louis Troisi; Assistant Mask and Puppet Coordinator, Curran Banach; Automated Flying Programmer, Jason Shupe; Production Properties Supervisor, Joseph P. Harris Jr.; Associate Properties Supervisor, Timothy M. Abel; Crew: Jack Anderson (production carpenter), Andrew Elman, Dave Fulton, Hugh Hardyman, Kris Keene, Matthew J. Lynch, Mike Norris, Geoffrey Vaughn (assistant carpenters), Randall Zaibek, James Fedigan (production electricians), Ron Martin (head electrician), Jason Lindahl, Chris Herman (production video electricians), Simon Matthews (production

sound engineer), John Sibley (head sound engineer), Dan Hochstine (assistant sound engineer); Martin Garcia, Gonzalo Brea (E-stop personnel), Michael D. Hannah (production wardrobe supervisor), Christel Murdock, Sonya Wysocki (assistant wardrobe supervisors), Robert Belopede, Diana Calderazzo, Jackie Freeman, Rachel Garrett, Lyle Jones, Carrie Kamerer, Rosemary Keough, Shannon McDowell, Leslie Moulton, Daniel Mura, Kyle O'Connor, Michael Piscitelli, Jack Scott, Kyle Stewart, Ron Tagert, Arlene Watson, Cheryl Widner (dressers), Alejandra Rubinos (seamstress), William Hamilton (laundry), John James (hair supervisor), Cory McCutcheon (assistant hair supervisor), Therese Ducey, Brian Hennings (hairstylists), Angela Johnson (production makeup supervisor), Tiffany Hicks (assistant makeup supervisor), Ben Nabors, Matt Kazman, Nora Tennessen (video crew); Technical Production Assistants, Sue Barsoum, Steve Chazaro, Kate DellaFera, Sonya Duveneck, Ania Parks, Alexandra Paull, Melissa Spengler, Kim Straatemeier; Production Assistants, Allison Cottrell, Hannah Dorfman, Amanda Johnson, Gregory Murray, Samantha Preiss, Danya Taymor, Raynelle Wrights; Costume Interns, Yingshi June Lin, Tomke Von Gawinski; Physical Therapist, Heidi Green; Official Athletic Trainer, Prime Blueprint/Dr. Edyth Heus; Consulting Producer, Jeffery Auerbach; Producing Consultant, Carl Pasbjerg; Executive Assistants: Jamie Forshaw (Mr. Cohl), Stella Morelli (Mr. Harris), Tricia Olson (Mr. Orsher); General Management Associates, Mark Barna, Jake Hirzel; General Management Office, Hilary Ackerman, Nina Lutwick, Dawn Kusinski, Jennifer O'Connor; Marketing Director, Len Gill; Marketing Associate, Mary Caitlin Barrett; Advertising, Serino/Coyne, Nancy Coyne, Sandy Block, Angelo Desimini; Website & Internet Marketing, Situation Marketing, Damian Bazadona, John Lanasa, Jeremy Kraus, Victoria Gettler; National Public Relations, Ken Sunshine/Sunshine, Sachs & Associates; Press, O+M Company, Rick Miramontez, Andy Snyder, Jaron Caldwell, Elizabeth Wagner, Sam Corbett; Cast recording: Interscope Records 001578202

CAST Peter Parker/Spider-Man **Reeve Carney**; Arachne **T.V. Carpio**[*1]; Mary Jane Watson **Jennifer Damiano**[*2]; Mrs. Gribrock **Isabel Keating**; Flash (A Bully) **Matt Caplan**[*3]; Kong (A Bully) **Luther Creek**; Meeks (A Bully) **Christopher W. Tierney**; Boyle (A Bully) **Dwayne Clark**; Uncle Ben **Ken Marks**; Aunt May **Isabel Keating**; MJ's Father **Jeb Brown**[*4]; Normon Osborn/Green Goblin **Patrick Page**; Emily Osborn **Laura Beth Wells**[*5]; J. Jonah Jameson **Michael Mulheren**; Gangsters **Matt Caplan**[*3], **Dwayne Clark**, **Luther Creek**; Buttons (A Reporter) **Ken Marks**; Bud (A Reporter) **Matt Caplan**[*3]; Stokes (A Reporter) **Jeb Brown**[*4]; Maxie (A Reporter) **Isabel Keating**; Travis (A Reporter) **Luther Creek**; Robertson (A Reporter) **Dwayne Clark**; Viper Executives **Jeb Brown**[*4], **Luther Creek**, **Dwayne Clark**, **Ken Marks**; The Sinister Six: Carnage **Collin Baja**[*6]; Electro **Emmanuel Brown**[*7]; Kraven the Hunter **Christopher W. Tierney**; The Lizard **Brandon Rubendall**[*8]; Swarm **Gerald Avery**[*9]; Swiss Miss **Sean Samuels**[*10]; Marbles **Laura Beth Wells**[*5]; Exterminator Flyer **Craig Henningsen**; Green Goblin Flyer **Collin Baja**[*6]; Citizens, Weavers, Students, Lab Assistants, Reporters, Puppeteers, Spider-Men, Secretaries, Soldiers **Gerald Avery**[*9], **Collin Baja**[*6], **Marcus Bellamy**, **Emmanuel Brown**[*7], **Jeb Brown**[*4], **Matt Caplan**[*3], **Dwayne Clark**, **Luther Creek**, **Craig Henningsen**, **Dana Marie Ingraham**, **Ayo Jackson**, **Isabel Keating**, **Natalie Lomonte**, **Ken Marks**, **Kristen Martin**, **Jodi McFadden**, **Bethany Moore**, **Kristen Faith Oei**, **Jennifer Christine Perry**, **Brandon Rubendall**[*8], **Sean Samuels**[*10], **Dollar Tan**, **Christopher W. Tierney**, **Laura Beth Wells**[*5]; Ensemble Aerialists **Kevin Aubin**, **Gerald Avery**[*9], **Collin Baja**[*6], **Marcus Bellamy**, **Jessica Leigh Brown**, **Luther Creek**, **Daniel Curry**, **Erin Elliott**, **Craig Henningsen**, **Dana Marie Ingraham**, **Ayo Jackson**, **Ari Loeb**, **Natalie Lomonte**, **Kristen Martins**, **Jodi McFadden**, **Bethany Moore**, **Kristen Faith Oei**, **Jennifer Christine Perry**, **Brandon Rubendall**[*8], **Sean Samuels**[*10], **Christopher W. Tierney**; Swings[*11] **Kevin Aubin**, **Jessica Leigh Brown**, **Daniel Curry**, **Erin Elliott**, **Joshua Kobak**, **Megan Lewis**, **Ari Loeb**, **Kevin C. Loomis**, **Kyle Post**, **Joey Taranto**; Peter Parker/Spider-Man at certain performances **Matthew James Thomas**

UNDERSTUDIES Kevin Aubin (Gangster, Carnage, Kraven, The Lizard, Swiss Miss), Collin Baja (Boyle), Marcus Bellamy (Swarm), Jeb Brown (Osborne/

Green Goblin), Jessica Leigh Brown (Mrs. Gribrock, Aunt May, Maxie, Emily, Marbles), Matt Caplan (Peter Parker/Spider-Man, Viper Executive), Luther Creek (MJ's Father), Daniel Curry (Gangster, Carnage, Kraven, The Lizard, Swiss Miss), Joshua Kobak (Meeks, Kraven), Megan Lewis (Arachne, Mrs. Gribrock, Aunt May, Maxie, Emily, Marbles), Ari Loeb (Gangster, Electro, Kraven, The Lizard, Swarm, Swiss Miss), Kevin C. Loomis (Jameson, Uncle Ben, MJ's Father, Buttons, Bud, Stokes, Travis, Robertson, Viper Executive), Ken Marks (Jameson), Kristen Martin (Mary Jane), Jodi McFadden (Arachne), Kyle Post (Flash, Boyle, Kong, Meeks, Gangster, Buttons, Bud, Stokes, Travis, Robertson, Viper Executive), Brandon Rubendall (Carnage, Swiss Miss), Sean Samuels (Boyle), Dollar Tan (Electro), Joey Taranto (Flash, Boyle, Kong, Meeks, Gangster, Bud, Travis, Robertson, Viper Executive), Laura Beth Wells (Mrs. Gribrock, Aunt May)

*Succeeded by: 1. Christina Sajous (11/15/11), Katrina Lenk (5/29/12) 2. Rebecca Faulkenberry (11/10/11) 3. Matthew Wilkas (1/31/12) 4. Timothy Warmen (8/9/11) 5. Emily Shoolin (1/31/12) 6. Adam Roberts (9/13/11) 7. Maxx Reed (3/20/12) 8. Julius C. Carter (1/31/12) 9. Drew Heflin (12/20/11), Gerald Avery (5/22/12) 10. Reed Kelly (1/31/12) 11. Additional replacements since opening: Adam Ray Dyer (Ensemble Aerialist/Swing), Elizabeth Judd (Ensemble Aerialist), Heather Lang (Ensemble Aerialist/Swing), Leon Le (Ensemble Aerialist/Swing)

ORCHESTRA Kimberly Grigsby (Conductor); Charles duChateau (Associate Conductor/Keyboard); Zane Carney, Matt Beck, Ben Butler (Guitar); Aiden Moore, Richard Hammond (Basses); Jon Epcar (Drums); Billy Jay Stein (Keyboard); John Clancy (Percussion); Bill Ruyle (Hammered Dulcimer/Percussion); Antoine Silverman (Concert Master); Christopher Cardona (Viola/Violin); Anja Wood (Cello); Don Downs, Tony Kadleck (Trumpets); Theresa MacDonnell (French Horn); Marcus Rojas (Trombone/Tuba) Aaron Heick (Reeds)

MUSICAL NUMBERS The Myth of Arachne; Behold and Wonder; Bullying by Numbers; No More; D.I.Y World; Venom; Bouncing Off the Walls; Rise Above; Pull the Trigger; Picture This; A Freak Like Me Needs Company; If the World Should End; Sinistereo; Spider-Man!; Turn Off the Dark; I Just Can't Walk Away; Boy Falls From the Sky; I'll Take Manhattan; Finale–A New Dawn

2011-2012 AWARDS Outer Critics Circle Awards: Outstanding Set Design (George Tsypin), Outstanding Costume Design (Eiko Ishioka); Richard Seff Award: Patrick Page

World premiere of a new musical presented in two acts.

SYNOPSIS Drawing from more than 40 years of Marvel comic books for inspiration, *Spider-Man Turn Off the Dark* spins a new take on the mythic tale of Peter Parker, a teenager whose unremarkable life is turned upside-down when he's bitten by a genetically-altered spider and wakes up the next morning clinging to the ceiling. As he discovers he has been endowed with astonishing powers, and also great responsibility, Peter learns to navigate the perilous and peculiar demands of being a web-slinging superhero.

Patrick Page

Reeve Carney (photos by Joan Marcus)

T.V. Carpio

Patrick Page and Reeve Carney

The Company

The Company

Reeve Carney and Jennifer Damiano

Reeve Carney and Jennifer Damiano

Samuel J. Friedman Theatre; First Preview: June 14, 2011; Opening Night: July 7, 2011; Closed September 4, 2011; 26 previews, 67 performances

Written by Terrence McNally; Produced by Manhattan Theatre Club (Lynne Meadow, Artistic Director; Barry Grove, Executive Producer) by special arrangement with Max Cooper, Maberry Theatricals, Marks-Moore-Tunbull Group, and Ted Snowdon; Director, Stephen Wadsworth; Sets, Thomas Lynch; Costumes, Martin Pakledinaz; Lighting, David Lander; Sound, Jim Gottlieb; Wigs, Paul Huntley; Production Stage Manager, Susie Cordon; Stage Manager, Allison Sommers; Company Manager, Seth Shepsle; Music Director, Bradley Moore; Voice Coach, Kate Wilson; Italian Coach, Corradina Caporello; Opera Style Coach, Robert Morrison; Opera Voice Coach, Marlena Malas; Makeup Design, Angelina Avallone; Assistant Directors, Mary Birnbaum, David Paul; Assistant to the Playwright, Tom Klebba; Associate Set Design, Charlie Corcoran; Assistant Costume Design, Sarah Cubbage; Associate Lighting Design, Ben Pilat; Associate Sound Design, Marc Polimeni; Crew: Matt Maloney (spotlight), John Fullum (flyman), Vaughn Preston (automation operator), Natasha Steinhagen (hair/makeup supervisor), Savannah Leville (dresser), Lisa Schwartz (production assistant); For MTC: General Manager, Florie Seery; Artistic Producer, Mandy Greenfield; Director of Artistic Development, Jerry Patch; Marketing, Debra Waxman-Pilla; Production Manager, Joshua Helman; Director of Casting, Nancy Piccione; Artistic Line Producer, Lisa McNulty; Development, Lynne Randall; Artistic Consultant, Daniel Sullivan; Artistic Operations, Amy Gilkes Loe; Finance, Jessica Adler; Associate General Manager, Lindsey Brooks Sag; Subscriber Services, Robert Allenberg; Telesales, George Tetlow; Education, David Shookhoff; Associate Production Manager, Bethany Weinstein; Assistant Production Manager, Kevin Service; Prop Supervisor, Scott Laule; Assistant Properties Supervisor, Julia Sandy; Props Carpenter, Peter Grimes; Costume Supervisor, Erin Hennessy Dean; Press, Boneau/Bryan-Brown, Chris Boneau, Aaron Meier, Christine Olver, Emily Meagher

CAST Sharon Graham **Sierra Boggess**; Stagehand **Clinton Brandhagen**; Emmanuel Weinstock **Jeremy Cohen**; Maria Callas **Tyne Daly**; Sophie De Palma **Alexandra Silber**; Anthony Candolino **Garrett Sorenson**

UNDERSTUDIES Jacqueline Antaramian (Maria Callas), Brian Calì (Stagehand, Anthony Candolino), Leah Edwards (Sharon Graham, Sophie De Palma), Dan K. Kurland (Emmanuel Weinstock)

Revival of a play presented in two acts. Originally presented by the Philadelphia Theatre Company March 1, 1995, and subsequently at the Mark Taper Forum in Los Angeles and the Eisenhower Theatre at the Kennedy Center. The original Broadway production opened at the John Golden Theatre November 5, 1995, and closed June 29, 1997, playing 598 performances (see *Theatre World* Vol. 52, page 25).

SYNOPSIS Terrence McNally's play about Maria Callas takes us to one of her famous master classes, where, late in her own career, she dares the next generation to make the same sacrifices and rise to the same heights that made her the most celebrated, the most reviled and the most controversial singer of her time.

Garrett Sorenson and Tyne Daly

Clinton Brandhagen and Tyne Daly

Jeremy Cohen and Alexandra Silber (photos by Joan Marcus)

St. James Theatre; First Preview: July 5, 2011; Opening Night: July 13, 2011; Closed September 10, 2011; 11 previews, 67 performances

Book and lyrics by Gerome Ragni & James Rado, music and orchestrations by Galt MacDermot; Produced by The Public Theater (Oskar Eustis, Artistic Director; Joey Parnes, Interim Executive Director; Mandy Hackett, Associate Artistic Director), Nederlander Productions Inc., Carl Mollenberg/WenLarBar Productions, Rebecca Gold/Myla Lerner, Rick Costello, Joy Newman & Daivd Schumeister, Paul G. Rice/Paul Bartz, Debbie Bisno, Christopher Hart Productions, John Pinckard, Terry Schnuck, Joey Parnes, by special arrangement with Elizabeth Ireland McCann; Associate Producers, Jenny Gersten, S.D. Wagner, John Johnson; Director, Diane Paulus; Choreography, Karole Armitage; Sets, Scott Pask; Costumes, Michael McDonald; Lighting, Kevin Adams; Sound, Acme Sound Partners; Orchestrations, Galt MacDermot; Music Supervisor, Nadia DiGiallonardo; Music Director, David Truskinoff; Music Coordinator, Seymour Red Press; Wigs, Gerrad Kelly; Production Supervisor, Nancy Harrington; Production Stage Manager, William Joseph Barnes; Casting, Jordan Thaler & Heidi Griffiths; Marketing, Allied Live Inc.; Tour Booking, Broadway Booking Office NYC; General Management, Joey Parnes, John Johnson, Kim Sellon, S.D. Wagner; Company Manager, Jennifer R. Graves; Stage Manager, Chris Zaccardi; Assistant Stage Manager, Kathryn McKee; Assistant Company Manager, Kit Ingui; Dance Captain, John Moauro; Associate Design: Paul Weimer (set), Joel Silver (lighting), Lisa Zinni (costumes), David Thomas (sound); Assistant Lighting, Andy Fritsch; Management Associates, Kristen Luciani, Nate Koch; Casting Associate, Amber Wakefield; Crew Supervisors: Larry Morley (production carpenter), Mike Smanko (production properties), Genevieve Headrick (production electrician), Jim Wilkinson (production sound), Rob Bevenger (wardrobe supervisor), Lisa Ann Fraley (hair supervisor); Advertising, SpotCo; Interactive Marketing, Situation Interactive; Press, O+M Company, Rick Miramontez, Molly Barnett, Elizabeth Wagner; Cast recording: Sh-K-Boom/Ghostlight Records 4467

CAST Dionne **Phyre Hawkins**; Berger **Steel Burkhardt**; Woof **Matt DeAngelis**; Hud **Darius Nichols**; Claude **Paris Remillard**; Sheila **Caren Lyn Tackett**; Jeanie **Kacie Sheik**; Crissy **Kaitlin Kiyan**; Mother/Buddahdalirama **Allison Guinn**; Dad/Margaret Mead **Josh Lamon**; Hubert/John Wilkes Booth **Lee Zarrett**; Abraham Lincoln **Lulu Fall**; Tribe **Shaleah Adkisson, Nicholas Belton, Marshal Kennedy Carolan, Mike Evariste, Lulu Fall, Nkrumah Gatling, Allison Guinn, Sara King, Josh Lamon, John Moauro, Christine Nolan, Emmy Raver-Lampman, Arbender Robinson, Cailan Rose, Jen Sese, Lee Zarrett**; Tribe Swings **Emily Afton, Larkin Bogan, Corey Bradley, Laura Dreyfuss, Trey Fountain, Tanesha Ross**

MUSICIANS David Truskinoff (Conductor/Keyboard), Jared Stein (Assistant Conductor/Keyboard), Josh Weinstein (Guitar), Frank Canino (Bass), Daniel Block (Woodwinds), Elaine Burt, Ronald Buttacavoli & Robert Millikan (Trumpets), Charles Gordon (Trombone), Sean Ritenauer (Percussion), Wayne Dunton (Drums)

MUSICAL NUMBERS Aquarius; Donna; Hashish; Sodomy; Colored Spade; Manchester England; I'm Black; Ain't Got No; Sheila Franklin; I Believe in Love; Ain't Got No (reprise); Air; The Stone Age; I Got Life; Initials; Going Down; Hair; My Conviction; Easy to Be Hard; Don't Put It Down; Frank Mills; Hare Krishna; Where Do I Go; Electric Blues; Oh Great God of Power; Black Boys; White Boys; Walking in Space; Minuet; Yes I's Finished on Y'alls Farmlands; Four Score and Seven Years Ago/Abie Baby; Give Up All Desires; Three-Five-Zero-Zero; What a Piece of Work Is Man; Good Morning Starshine; Ain't Got No (reprise); The Flesh Failures; Manchester/Eyes Look Your Last; Flesh Failures/Let the Sun Shine In

SETTING New York City, the late 1960s. Return engagement (and national tour) of the revival of the rock musical presented in two acts. This production was previously presented at the Delacorte Theater as part of Joe's Pub in the Park September 22-24, 2007 (see *Theatre World* Vol. 64, page 186) which led to a full production at the Delacorte July 22–September 14, 2008; subsequently making a commercial transfer to the Al Hirschfeld Theatre March 31, 2009–June 27, 2010,

playing 519 performances (see *Theatre World* Vol. 65, pages 66 & 228.) Originally produced Off-Broadway at the Public Theater October 17–December 10, 1967; reopened at the midtown discothèque Cheetah December 22, 1968–January 28, 1968. The show transferred to the Biltmore Theatre April 29, 1968, closing July 1, 1972 after 1,750 performances (see *Theatre World* Vol. 24, pages 59 and 11).

SYNOPSIS *Hair* depicts the birth of a cultural movement in the 60s and 70s that changed America forever. The musical follows a group of hopeful, free-spirited young people who advocate a lifestyle of pacifism and free-love in a society riddled with intolerance and brutality during the Vietnam War. As they explore sexual identity, challenge racism, experiment with drugs and burn draft cards, the tribe in *Hair* creates an irresistible message of hope that continues to resonate with audiences 40 years later.

The Tribe

The Tribe (photos by Joan Marcus)

Marquis Theatre; First Preview: August 7, 2011; Opening Night: September 12, 2011; Closed January 22, 2012; 38 previews, 152 performances

Book by James Goldman, music and lyrics by Stephen Sondheim; Produced by the John F. Kennedy Center for the Performing Arts (David M. Rubenstein, Chairman; Michael M. Kaiser, President; Max A. Woodward, Vice President), Nederlander Presentations Inc., Adrienne Arsht, HRH Foundation; Executive Producer, Allan Williams; Director, Eric Schaeffer; Choreography, Warren Carlyle; Music Director, James Moore; Sets, Derek McLane; Costumes, Gregg Barnes; Lighting, Natasha Katz; Sound, Kai Harada; Hair and Wigs, David Brian Brown; Makeup, Joseph Dulude II; Production Stage Manager, Arthur Gaffin; Associate Director, David Ruttura; Orchestrations, Jonathan Tunick; Dance Music Arrangements, John Berkman; Music Coordinator, John Miller; Casting, Laura Stanczyk Casting; Production Manager, Juniper Street Productions, Hillary Blanken, Guy Kwan, Ana Rose Greene, Joseph DeLuise; General Management, Alan Wasser Associates, Allan Williams, Mark Shacket, Aaron Lustbader; Company Manager, Kimberly Kelly; Casting Associates, Meryl Ballew, Tony Tilli, Alicai Newkirk, Anika Chapin, Kate Freeman, Sarah Johnson; Stage Manager, Laurie Goldfelder; Assistant Stage Manager, Jamie Greathouse; Assistant Company Manager, Michael Altbaum; Assistant Choreographer/Dance Captain, Sara Edwards; Assistant Dance Captain, Amos Wolff; Associate Design: Erica Hemminger Shoko Kambara (set), Matthew Pachtman (costumes), Yael Lubetzky (lighting), Jana Hoglund (sound), Richard Orton (hair and wigs); Assistant Design: Brett Banakis (set), Irma Escobar, Sky Switser (costumes), Joel Shier (lighting); Costume Interns, Elise Tollefsen, Molly Deale; Moving Lights Programmer, Marc Polimeni; Crew: Fred Gallo (production carpenter), Scott "Gus" Poitras (head carpenter), David J. Elmer (flyman), Randall Zaibek, James Fedigan (production electricians), Eric Norris (head electrician), Stephen Long (assistant electrician), Matthew Elias Hodges (production properties supervisor), Jeremy Lydic (properties coordinator), Andrew Meeker (head properties supervisor), Patrick Pummill (production sound engineer), Elizabeth Coleman (deck audio), Rick Kelly (wardrobe supervisor), Lolly Totero (Ms. Peters' dresser), Christina Ainge, Jenny Barnes, Gary Biangone, Cathy Cline, Cece Cruz, Ron Fleming, Patti Luther, Danny Paul, Phillip Rolfe, Kelly Saxon, Julienne Schubert-Blechman, Franc Weinperl (dressers), Richard Orton (hair supervisor), Mitchell Beck (assistant hair supervisor), Chelsea Roth, Danny Koye (hair dressers), Melissa Hansen, Johnny Kruger, Lee Micklin, Lindsey Turteltaub (production assistants); Assistant to Mr. Miller, Nichole Jennino; Rehearsal Pianist, Mat Eisenstein; Rehearsal Drummer, Rich Rosenzweig; Music Department Intern, Anthony DeAngelis; NIDA Production Secondment (Sound), Remy Woods; Marketing Services, Type A Marketing, Anne Rippey, John McCoy, DJ Martin, Robin Steinthal; Advertising/Digital Outreach and Website, Serino/Coyne, Sandy Block, Greg Corradetti, Robert Jones, Danielle Boyle, David Barrineua, Jim Glaub, Chip Meyrelles, Laurie Connor, Kevin Keating, Whitney Manalio Creighton, Mark Seeley; Press, Boneau/Bryan-Brown, Adrian Bryan-Brown, Heath Schwartz, Michael Strassheim; Cast recording: PS Classics 1105

CAST Sally Durant Plummer **Bernadette Peters**; Young Sally **Lora Lee Gayer**; Sandra Crane **Florence Lacey**; Young Sandra **Kiira Schmidt**; DeeDee West **Colleen Fitzpatrick**; Young DeeDee **Leslie Donna Flesner**; Solange LaFitte **Mary Beth Peil**; Young Solange **Ashley Yeater**; Hattie Walker **Jayne Houdyshell**; Young Hattie **Jenifer Foote**; Roscoe **Michael Hayes**; Stella Deems **Terri White**; Young Stella **Erin N. Moore**; Max Deems **Frederick Strother**; Heidi Schiller **Rosalind Elias**; Young Heidi **Leah Horowitz**; Emily Whitman **Susan Watson**; Young Emily **Danielle Jordan**; Theodore Whitman **Don Correia**; Carlotta Campion **Elaine Page**; Young Carlotta **Pamela Otterson**; Phyllis Rogers Stone **Jan Maxwell**; Young Phyllis **Kirsten Scott**; Benjamin Stone **Ron Raines**; Buddy Plummer **Danny Burstein**; Dimitri Weismann **David Sabin**; Young Buddy **Christian Delcroix**; Young Ben **Nick Verina**; Kevin **Clifton Samuels**; Buddy's Blues "Margie" **Kiira Schmidt**; Buddy's Blues "Sally" **Jenifer Foote**; Ensemble **Lawrence Alexander, Brandon Bieber, John Carroll, Leslie Donna Flesner, Jenifer Foote, Leah Horowitz, Suzanne Hylenski, Danielle Jordan, Amanda Kloots-Larsen, Brittany Marcin, Erin N. Moore, Pamela Otterson, Clifton Samuels, Kiira Schmidt, Brian Shepard, Amos Wolff, Ashley Yeater**;

Swings **Matthew deGuzman, Sara Edwards**

UNDERSTUDIES Brandon Bieber (Roscoe, Young Buddy), Don Correia (Buddy Plummer), Sara Edwards (Buddy's Blues "Margie", Buddy's Blues "Sally", Dee Dee West), Colleen Fitzpatrick (Phyllis Rogers Stone, Solange LaFitte), Leslie Donna Flesner (Young Heidi), Jenifer Foote (Dee Dee West, Sandra Crane, Solange LaFitte), Danielle Jordan (Emily Whitman, Young Sally), Joseph Kolinski (Benjamin Stone, Buddy Plummer, Dimitri Weismann, Max Deems, Theodore Whitman), Florence Lacey (Carlotta Campion, Sally Durant Plummer), Kiira Schmidt (Young Phyllis), Brian Shepard (Young Ben), Jessica Sheridan (Carlotta Campion, Dee Dee West, Hattie Walker, Heidi Schiller, Sandra Crane, Stella Deems), Amos Wolff (Kevin)

ORCHESTRA James Moore (Conductor); Marvin Laird (Associate Conductor/ Keyboard); Vincent J. Fanuele (Assistant Conductor); Rick Dolan (Concert Master); Ashley Horn, Robert Shaw, Una Tone, Karl Kawahara, Kiku Enomoto (Violins); Kenneth Burward-Hoy, David Creswell (Violas); Laura Bontrager, Sarah Hewitt-Roth (Celli); Ray Kilday (Bass); Barbara Biggers (Harp); Todd Groves, Dave Noland, Les Scott, Rick Heckman, Chad Smith (Woodwinds); Trevor Neumann, Matthew Peterson, Jeremy Miloszewicz (Trumpets); William DeVos (French Horn); Keith O'Quinn, Dan Levine, Vincent J. Fanuele (Trombones); Charles Descarfino (Percussion); Rich Rosenzweig (Drums); Greg Utzig (Guitar)

MUSICAL NUMBERS Beautiful Girls; Don't Look at Me; Waiting for the Girls Upstairs; Rain on the Roof; Ah, Paris! ; Broadway Baby; The Road You Didn't Take; In Buddy's Eyes; Who's That Woman?; I'm Still Here; Too Many Mornings; The Right Girl; One More Kiss; Could I Leave You?; Loveland; You're Gonna Love Tomorrow; Love Will See Us Through; The God-Why-Don't-You-Love-Me Blues; Losing My Mind; The Story of Lucy and Jessie; Live, Laugh, Love

2011-2012 AWARDS Tony Award: Best Costume Design of a Musical (Gregg Barnes); Drama Desk Awards: Outstanding Revival of a Musical, Outstanding Actor in a Musical (Danny Burstein), Outstanding Costume Design (Gregg Barnes); Outer Critics Circle Awards: Outstanding Revival of a Musical, Outstanding Actor in a Musical (Danny Burstein); Drama League Award: Distinguished Revival of a Musical

SETTING A party on the stage of the Weismann Theatre. Tonight. Revival of a musical presented in two acts. Originally produced on Broadway at the Winter Garden Theatre April 4, 1971–July 1, 1972, playing 522 performances (see *Theatre World* Vol. 37, page 42). A previous Broadway revival celebrating the show's thirtieth anniversary played the Belasco Theatre April 5–July 14, 2001, playing 117 performances (see *Theatre World* Vol. 57, page 34). This revival played the John F. Kennedy Center for the Performing Arts' Eisenhower Theatre May 7-June 19, 2011 with most of this cast. Following the Broadway engagement, the show played Center Theatre Group's Ahmanson Theatre in Los Angeles May 9–June 9, 2012 (see page 362 in this volume).

SYNOPSIS When former members of the "Weismann Follies" reunite on the eve of their theater's demolition, two couples remember their past and face the harsher realities of the present. Reminiscing of their younger selves and the years gone by, the crumbling theater brings back memories for both couples of good times and bad. *Follies* echoes the songs, exuberance and romance of the vaudeville days between the two World Wars.

Elaine Paige and the Male Ensemble

Jan Maxwell and the Company

Don Correia, Susan Watson, Jayne Houdyshell, and Mary Beth Peil

Jenifer Foote, Danny Burstein, and Kiira Schmidt

Rosalind Elias and Leah Horowitz (photos by Joan Marcus)

Kirsten Scott, Nick Verina, Lora Lee Gayer, and Christian Delcroix

Man and Boy

American Airlines Theatre; First Preview: September 9, 2011; Opening Night: October 9, 2011; Closed November 27, 2011; 35 previews, 57 performances

Written by Terence Ratigan; Produced by the Roundabout Theatre Company (Todd Haimes, Artistic Director; Harold Wolpert, Managing Director; Julia C. Levy, Executive Director); Director, Maria Aitken; Sets, Derek McLane; Costumes, Martin Pakledinaz; Lighting, Kevin Adams; Original Music and Sound, John Gromada; Hair and Wigs, Paul Huntley; Dialect Coach, Stephen Gabis; Production Stage Manager, Nevin Hedley; Production Management, Aurora Productions; Casting, Jim Carnahan and Kate Boka; General Manager, Denise Cooper; Stage Manager, Bryce McDonald; Company Manager, Carly DiFulvio; Assistant Director, G.D. Kimble; Makeup, Joe Dulude II; Associate Design: Shoko Kambara (set), Matthew Pachtman (costumes); Assistant Design: Erica Hemminger (set), Pete Bragg (lighting), Matthew Walsh (sound); Production Properties Supervisor, Peter Sarafin; Assistant Production Properties, Matt Hodges; Crew: Glenn Merwede (production carpenter), Brian Maiuri (production electrician), Robert W. Dowling II (running properties), Dann Wojnar (sound operator), Susan J. Fallon (wardrobe supervisor), Vangeli Kasluris, Kat Martin (dressers), Dale Carman (wardrobe dayworker), Manuela Laporte (hair and wig supervisor), Kristen Torgrimson (production assistant); Assistant to Mr. Langella, Joshua Pilote; For Aurora Productions: Gene O' Donovan, Ben Heller, Stephanie Sherline, Jarid Sumner, Rebecca Zuber, Anita Shah, Liza Luxenberg, Steven Dalton, Eugenio Saenz Flores, Isaac Katzanek, Melissa Mazdra; Roundabout Staff: Sydney Beers (General Manager), Greg Backstrom (Associate Managing Director); David B. Steffen (Director of Marketing and Sales Promotion); Lynne Gugenheim Gregory (Director of Development); Gene Feist (Founding Director), Scott Ellis (Associate Artistic Director); Greg McCaslin (Education Director), Sydney Beers (General Manager), Susan Neiman (Director of Finance), Antonio Palumbo (IT Director), Wendy Hutton (Director of Database Operations), Charlie Gabowski Jr. (Director of Sales Operations); Advertising, SpotCo; Interactive Marketing, Situation Interactive; Press, Boneau/Bryan-Brown, Adrian Bryan-Brown, Matt Polk, Jessica Johnson, Amy Kass

CAST Carol Penn **Virginia Kull**; Basil Anthony **Adam Driver**; Sven Johnson **Michael Siberry**; Gregor Antonescu **Frank Langella**; Mark Herries **Zach Grenier**; David Beeston **Brian Hutchison**; Countess Antonescu **Francesca Faridany**

UNDERSTUDIES John Hickok (Sven Johnson, Mark Herries), Vayu O'Donnell (Basil Anthony, David Beeston), Allison Jean White (Carol Penn, Countess Antonescu)

SETTING Place: A basement apartment in Greenwich Village, New York. Time: Continuous, roughly between 6 p.m. and 8:30 p.m. on an autumn night in 1934. Revival of a play presented in two acts. Originally presented at the Brooks Atkinson Theatre November 12–December 28, 1963, playing 54 performances (see *Theatre World* Vol. 20.)

SYNOPSIS At the height of the Great Depression, ruthless financier Gregor Antonescu's business is dangerously close to crumbling. In order to escape the wolves at his door, Gregor tracks down his estranged son Basil in the hopes of using his Greenwich Village apartment as a base to make a company-saving deal. Can this reunion help them reconcile? Or will this corrupt father use his only son as a pawn in one last power play? *Man and Boy* is a gripping story about family, success and what we're willing to sacrifice for both.

Adam Driver, Frank Langella, Michael Siberry, and Zach Grenier

Virginia Kull, Frank Langella, and Adam Driver (background)

Frank Langella (photos by Joan Marcus)

The Mountaintop

Bernard B. Jacobs Theatre; First Preview: September 22, 2011; Opening Night: October 13, 2011; Closed January 22, 2012; 24 previews, 117 performances

Written by Katori Hall; Produced by Jean Doumanian, Sonia Friedman Productions, Ambassador Theatre Group (Howard Panter, Rosemary Squire), Raise the Roof 7 (Elaine Krauss, Harriet Leve, Jennifer Manocherian), Ted Snowdon, Alhadeff Productions (Marleen Alhadeff, Kenny Alhadeff)/Lauren Doll, B Square + 4 Productions (Barbara and Buddy Freitag)/Broadway Across America (John Gore), Jacki Barlia Florin/Max Cooper-Wendy Federman, Ronnie Planalp/Carl Moellenberg-Deborah Taylor, Marla Rubin Productions/Blumenthal Performing Arts (Tom Gabbard), in association with Scott Delman; Director, Kenny Leon; Original Music, Branford Marsalis; Set and Projections, David Gallo; Costumes, Constanza Romero; Lighting, Brian MacDevitt; Sound, Dan Moses Schreier; Hair and Wigs, Charles G. LaPointe; Casting, Jim Carnahan; Production Management, Aurora Productions; Production Stage Manager, Jimmie Lee Smith; Associate Producer, Patrick Daly; Company Manager, Brig Berney; General Manager, Richards/Climan Inc.; Stage Manager, Kenneth J. McGee; Assistant Director, Kamilah Forbes; Dialect Coach, Kate Wilson; Special Effects, Jeremy Chernick; Associate Design: Evan F. Adamson (set), Steve Channon (projections/animation), Jennifer Schriever (lighting), David Bullard (sound); Assistant Design: Angela M. Kahler (costumes), Peter Hoerburger (lighting); Design Studio Manager, Sarah Zeitler; Projection Research Director, Jan Price Frazier; Set Design Interns, Pamela Lee, Ga Hyun Bae; Projection Design Interns, Samantha Shoffner, Tess James; Prosthetic Design, Adam Bailey; Crew: Brian Munroe (production carpenter), Dan Coey (production electrician), John Dory (production sound engineer), Peter Sarafin (production props coordinator), Buist Bickley (assistant production props), Moira MacGregor Conrad (wardrobe supervisor), Askia Won Ling Jacob (dresser), Carole Morales (hair supervisor), Paula Wise (production assistant); Personal Assistants: Volney McFarlin (Mr. Jackson), Alex Van Praag (Ms. Bassett), JaMeeka Holloway (Ms. Hall), Victoria Dunn (Mr. Leon); Advertising and Marketing, SpotCo, Drew Hodges, Jim Edwards, Tom Greenwald, Vinny Sinato, Jim Aquino, Laura Ellis, Sara Fitzpatrick, Kristen Bardwil, Nick Pramik, Caroline Newhouse, Kristen Rathbun, Julie Wechsler; For Aurora Productions: Gene O'Donovan, Ben Heller, Stephanie Sherline, Jarid Sumner, Liza Luxemberg, Anita Shah, Rebecca Zuber, Steven Dalton, Eugenio Saenz Flores, Isaac Katzanek, Melissa Mazdra; For Richards/Climan Inc.: David R. Richards, Tamar Haimes, Michael Sag, Kyle Bonder, Jessica Fried, Jaqueline Lolek; Press, O+M Company, Rick Miramontez, Philip Carrubba, Molly Barnett, Sam Corbett, Andy Snyder

CAST Dr. Martin Luther King Jr. **Samuel L. Jackson**; Camae **Angela Bassett**

STANDBYS Billy Eugene Jones (Dr. King), Rosalyn Coleman (Camae)

SETTING The action takes place April 3, 1968. Room 306, Lorraine Motel, Memphis, Tennessee. Broadway premiere of a new play presented without intermission. Developed at Lark Play Development Center in New York City. World premiere produced in London by Theatre 503 in June 2011. The production transferred to Trafalgar Studios in the West End in July 2009.

SYNOPSIS *The Mountaintop* is a gripping reimagining of events the night before the assassination of civil rights leader Dr. Martin Luther King, Jr., as he retires to Room 306 in the now famous Lorraine Motel in Memphis, after delivering his legendary "I've Been to the Mountaintop" speech to a massive church congregation. When room service is delivered by a young woman, whose identity we puzzle over, King is forced to confront his past, as well as his legacy to his people.

Samuel L. Jackson and Angela Bassett

Angela Bassett (photos by Joan Marcus)

Relatively Speaking

Brooks Atkinson Theatre; First Preview: September 20, 2011; Opening Night: October 20; Closed January 29, 2012; 35 previews, 109 performances

Three one-act comedies: *Talking Cure* by Ethan Coen; *George Is Dead* by Elaine May; *Honeymoon Motel* by Woody Allen; Produced by Julian Schlossberg, Letty Aronson, Edward Walson, LeRoy Schecter, Tom Sherak, Daveed D. Frazier, and Roy Furman; Director, John Turturro; Set, Santo Loquasto; Costumes, Donna Zakowska; Lighting, Kenneth Posner; Sound, Carl Casella; Casting, Cindy Tolan; Production Stage Manager, Ira Mont; Production Management, Aurora Productions (Gene O;Donovan, Ben Heller, Stephanie Sherline, Jarid Sumner, Liza Luxenberg, Anita Shah, Rebecca Zuber, Steven Dalton, Eugenio Saenz Flores, Isaac Katzanek, Melissa Mazdra; Associate Producer, The Weinstein Company; Company Manager, Bruce Klinger; General Management, Richards/Climan Inc. (David R. Richards, Tamar Haimes, Michael Sag, Kyle Bonder, Jessica Fried, Jacqueline Kolek; Stage Manager, Matthew Lacey; Associate Design: Jenny B. Sawyers (set), John Viesta (lighting); Assistant Design: Erika Ingrid Lilienthal (costumes), Josh Liebert (sound); Production Assistant, Kate Croasdale; Casting Associates, Adam Caldwell, Ann Davidson; Casting Assistant, Cynthia Degros; Assistant to the Director, Nathan Brewer; Crew: Jason Clark (production carpenter), Ben Horrigan (deck automation carpenter), Manuel Becker (production electrician), Jay Penfield (lighting programmer), Wallace Flores (production sound), Kathy Fabian/Propstar (props coordinator), Carrie Mossman (associate props coordinator), John Tutalo (head props), Tim Ferro, Mary Wilson, Sarah Bird, Cassie Dorland, John Estep (props artisans), Kay Grunder (wardrobe supervisor), Kim Prentice (dresser), Carmel Vargyas (hair supervisor); Assistant to Mr. Schlossberg, Ruth Better; Assistant to Ms. May, Chantal Ribeiro; Assistant to Mr. Turturro, Cameron Bossert; Advertising, Serino/Coyne; Marketing Service, Type A Marketing/Anne Rippey, John McCoy, Robin Steinthal; Press, Boneau/Bryan-Brown, Chris Boneau, Joe Perrotta, Kelly Guiod

CAST *Talking Cure*: Doctor **Jason Kravits**; Patient **Danny Hoch**; Attendant **Max Gordon Moore**; Father **Allen Lewis Rickman**; Mother **Katherine Borowitz**; *George Is Dead*: Carla **Lisa Emery**; Doreen **Marlo Thomas**; Michael **Grant Shaud**; Nanny **Patricia O'Connell**; Funeral Director **Allen Lewis Rickman**; Assistant Funeral Director **Max Gordon Moore**; *Honeymoon Motel*: Jerry Spector **Steve Guttenberg**; Nina Roth **Ari Graynor**; Eddie **Grant Shaud**; Judy Spector **Caroline Aaron**; Fay Roth **Julie Kavner**; Sam Roth **Mark Linn-Baker**; Rabbi Baumel **Richard Libertini**; Dr. Brill **Jason Kravits**; Sal Buonacotti **Danny Hoch**; Paul Jessup **Bill Army**

UNDERSTUDIES Grant Shaud (Patient, Jerry Spector), Max Gordon Moore (Patient, Sal Buonacotti, Paul Jessup), Bill Army (Attendant, Assistant Funeral Director), Julia Brothers (Mother, Carla), Katherine Borowitz (Doreen, Judy Spector, Fay Roth), Elizabeth Shepherd (Nanny), Jason Kravits (Funeral Director), Sarah Sokolovic (Nina Roth), Allen Lewis Rickman (Dr. Brill)

World premiere of three one-act plays presented with a pause after *Talking Cure* and an intermission after *George Is Dead*.

SYNOPSIS *Relatively Speaking* is comprised of three one-act comedies, each springing from different branches of the family tree. In *Talk Therapy*, Ethan Coen uncovers the sort of insanity that can come only from family. *George is Dead* explores the hilarity of death. *Honeymoon Motel* invites you to the sort of wedding day you won't forget.

Grant Shaud, Marlo Thomas, and Lisa Emery in George is Dead

Ari Graynor and Steve Guttenberg in Honeymoon Hotel

Jason Kravits and Danny Hoch in Talking Cure *(photos by Joan Marcus)*

Johnny Wu, Angela Lin, Christine Lin, Gary Wilmes, and Jennifer Lim

Stephen Pucci and Jennifer Lim (photos by Michael McCabe)

Stephen Pucci, Gary Wilmes, Angela Lin, and Larry Lei Zhang

Chinglish

Longacre Theatre; First Preview: October 11, 2011; Opening Night: October 27, 2011; Closed January 29, 2012; 19 previews, 101 performances

Written by David Henry Hwang; Produced by Jeffrey Richards, Jerry Frankel, Jay and Cindy Gutterman/Cathy Chernoff, Keni Koenigsberg/Lily Fan, Joseph and Matthew Deitch, Dasha Epstein, Ronald and Mac Frankel, Barry and Carole Kaye, Mary Lu Roffe, The Broadway Consortium, Ken Davenport, Filerman Bensinger, Herbert Goldsmith, Jam Theatricals, Olympus Theatricals, Playful Productions, David and Barbara Stoller, Roy Gottlieb, Mary Casey, Hunter Arnold, in association with the Goodman Theatre; Director, Leigh Silverman; Sets, David Korins; Costumes, Anita Yavich; Lighting, Brian MacDevitt; Sound, Darron L West; Projections, Jeff Sugg, Shawn Duan; Technical Supervision, Hudson Theatrical Associates; Casting, Telsey + Company, Jordan Thaler and Heidi Griffiths, Adam Belcuore; Cultural Advisors, Joanna C. Lee, Ken Smith; Mandarin Chinese Translations, Candace Chong; Production Stage Manager, Stephen M. Kaus; Associate Producer, Jeremy Scott Blaustein; General Management, Richards/Climan Inc.; Company Manager, Elizabeth M. Talmadge; Stage Manager, Jillian M. Oliver; Assistant Producer, Michael Crea; Assistant Director/Script Coordinator, Johnson Henshaw; Dramaturg, Oskar Eustis; Assistant to the Playwright, Liz Dengel; Dialect Coach, Kate Wilson; Associate Design: Rod Lemmond (set) Ariel Benjamin (lighting), Carles Coes (sound); Assistant to the Set Designer, Jame Weinman; Assistant Costume Designers, Nancy A. Palmatier, Sarah Smith; Projection Consultant, Daniel Brodie; Moving Lights Programmer, Sean Beach; Production Properties Manager, Heather Thompson; Crew: Edward Diaz (production carpenter), Scott DeVerna (advance electrician), Jim vanBergen (advance sound), Kathy Fabian (production props), McBrien Dunbar (automation operator), Elle Xu-Bustin (sound/video operator), Sid King (associate props coordinator), Cassie Dorland (assistant props coordinator), Barry Doss (wardrobe supervisor), Bryen Shannon (dresser), Linda Rice (hair and makeup supervisor), Carly J. Price (production assistant); For Richards/Climan Inc.: David R. Richards, Tamar Haimes, Michael Sag, Kyle Bonder, Jessica Fried, Jaqueline Kolek; For Hudson Theatrical Associates: Neil A. Mazzella, Sam Ellis, Irene Wang, Walter Murphy, Corky Boyd; Advertising and Online, Serino/Coyne (Greg Corradetti, Tom Callahan, Robert Jones, Danielle Boyle, Jim Glaub, Laurie Connor); Interactive Marketing, Broadway's Best Shows, Andy Drachenberg, Christopher Pineda; Press, Jeffrey Richards Associates, Irene Gandy, Alana Karpoff, Ryan Hallett

CAST Daniel Cavenaugh **Gary Wilmes**; Peter Timms **Stephen Pucci**; Minister Cai Guoliang **Larry Lei Zhang**; Xi Yan **Jennifer Lim**; Miss Qian/Prosecutor Li **Angela Lin**; Miss Zhao **Christine Lin**; Bing/Judge Xu Geming **Johnny Wu**

UNDERSTUDIES Tony Carlin (Daniel Cavenaugh), Angela Lin (Xi Yan), Vivian Chiu (Miss Zhao, Miss Qian/Prosecutor Li), Brian Nishii (Peter Timms, Bing/Judge Xu Geming, Minister Cai Guoliang)

2011-2012 AWARD Theatre World Award: Jennifer Lim

SETTING The present. An American assembly room and the city of Guiyang, China. Broadway premiere of a new play presented in two acts. Developed at the Lark Play Development Center in association with the Public Theater. World premiere at the Goodman Theatre (Robert Falls, Artistic Director; Roche Schulfer, Executive Director) in Chicago June 18–July 31, 2011 (see *Theatre World* Vol. 67, page 345).

SYNOPSIS *Chinglish* is a new comedy about the misadventures of miscommunication. It is the story of an American businessman desperate to launch a new enterprise in China. There are only three things standing in his way: He can't speak the language. He can't learn the customs. And he's falling in love with the one woman he absolutely can't have.

Other Desert Cities

Booth Theatre; First Preview: October 12, 2011; Opening Night: November 3, 2011; 25 previews, 241 performances as of May 31, 2012

Written by Jon Robin Baitz; Produced by Lincoln Center Theater (André Bishop, Artistic Director; Bernard Gersten, Executive Producer) in association with Bob Boyett; Director, Joe Mantello; Sets, John Lee Beatty; Costumes, David Zinn; Lighting, Kenneth Posner; Sound, Jill BC DuBoff; Original Music, Justin Ellington; Production Stage Manager, James FitzSimmons; Casting, Daniel Swee; Company Manager, Matthew Markoff; Associate Design: Jacob Climer (costumes), David Snaderson (sound); Assistant Design: Kacie Hultgren (set), Anthony Pearson (lighting); Props Coordinator, Buist Bickley; Makeup, Angelina Avallone; Crew: John Weingart (production carpenter), Beth Berkeley (production sound), David Karlson (production electrician), Ryan Rossetto (wardrobe supervisor), Charlie Catanese (Mary Ann Oberpriller (dressers), John McNulty (hair supervisor), Katherine Wallace (production assistant); Wigs, Paul Huntley; Poster Art, James McMullan; For LCT: Adam Siegel (Managing Director), Jeff Hamlin (Production Manager), Hattie K. Jutagir (Executive Director of Development and Planning), David S. Brown (Director of Finance), Linda Mason Ross (Director of Marketing), Kati Koerner (Director of Education), Graciela Daniele, Nicholas Hutner, Jack O'Brien, Susan Stroman, Daniel Sullivan (Associate Directors), Bartlett Sher (Resident Director), Anne Cattaneo (Dramaturg and Director, LCT Directors Lab), Ira Weitzman (Musical Theatre Associate Producer), Paige Evans (Artistic Director/LCT3); Advertising, Serino/Coyne, Jim Russek, Roger Micone, Becca Goland-Van Ryn, Alexandra Rubin; Press, Philip Rinaldi, Barbara Carroll, Amanda Dekker

CAST Polly Wyeth **Stockard Channing**[1]; Brooke Wyeth **Rachel Griffiths**[2]; Lyman Wyeth **Stacy Keach**; Trip Wyeth **Thomas Sadoski**[3]; Silda Grauman **Judith Light**

UNDERSTUDIES[4] Lauren Klein (Polly Wyeth, Silda Grauman), Jack Davidson (Lyman Wyeth), Liz Wisan (Brooke Wisan), Matthew Risch (Trip Wyeth)

*Succeeded by: 1. Lauren Klein (3/14/12), Stockard Channing (4/8/12) 2. Elizabeth Marvel (3/6/12) 3. Matthew Risch (12/8/11), Thomas Sadoski (12/27/11), Justin Kirk (1/10/12), Matthew Risch (3/27/12), Thomas Sadoski (5/8/12) 4. Additional Understudies: Jennifer Harmon (Polly Wyeth, Silda Grauman), Karen Walsh (Brooke Wyeth), Jed Orlemann (Trip Wyeth), Robbie Collier Sublett (Trip Wyeth)

2011-2012 AWARDS Tony Award: Best Performance by an Actress in a Featured Role in a Play (Judith Light); Drama League Award: Distinguished Production of a Play; Drama Desk Award: Outstanding Featured Actress in a Play (Judith Light)

SETTING Time: Christmas 2004, and the last scene March 2010. Place: The Wyeth home, Palm Springs, California. Broadway premiere of a new play presented in two acts. Orignally presented Off-Broadway at Lincoln Center Theatre's Mitzi Newhouse Theatre January 13–February 27, 2011 (see *Theatre World* Vol. 67, page 207).

SYNOPSIS In *Other Desert Cities*, Brooke Wyeth, a once promising novelist, returns home after a six year absence to celebrate Christmas in Palm Springs with her parents, former members of the Reagan inner-circle, her brother, and her aunt. When Brooke announces that she is about to publish a memoir focusing on an explosive chapter in the family's history, the holiday reunion is thrown into turmoil and the Wyeths are both bound together and torn apart as they struggle to come to terms with their past.

Rachel Griffiths, Stockard Channing, Stacy Keach, and Thomas Sadoski

Rachel Griffiths and Stacy Keach

Rachel Griffiths and Thomas Sadoski (photos by Joan Marcus)

Godspell

Circle in the Square Theatre; First Preview: October 13, 2011; Opening Night: November 7, 2011; 30 previews, 235 performances as of May 31, 2012

Conceived and originally directed by John-Michael Tebelak, music and new lyrics by Stephen Schwartz; Produced by Ken Davenport, Hunter Arnold, Broadway Across America, Luigi Caiola, Rose Caiola, Edgar Lansbury, Mike McClernon, The Tolchin Family, Guillermo Weichers and Juan Torres, and The People of Godspell; Director, Daniel Goldstein; Choreography, Christopher Gattelli; Music Director, Charlie Alterman; Sets, David Korins; Costumes, Miranda Hoffman; Lighting, David Weiner; Sound, Andrew Keister; Casting, Telsey + Company; Special Effects Design, Chic Silber; Orchestrations and Vocal Arrangements, Michael Holland; Music Coordinator, John Miller; Production Stage Manager, David O'Brien; Production Management, Juniper Street Productions (Hillary Blanken, Joseph DeLuise, Guy Kwan, Ana Rose Greene); General Management, The Charlotte Wilcox Company (Matthew W. Krawiec, Dina S. Friedler, Seth Marquette, Regina Mancha, Margaret Wilcox, Chantel Hopper, Ryan Smillie, Stephen Donovan); Associate Producers, Dennis Grimaldi Productions, Todd Miller, Pivot Entertainment Group, Chris Welch, Cedric Yau; Stage Manager, Stephen R. Gruse; Assistant Stage Manager, Colleen Danaher; Makeup, Ashley Ryan; Associate Director, Kate Pines; Associate Choreographer, Bethany Pettigrew; Assitant to the Choreographer, Brendan Naylor; For Telsey Casting: Bernard Telsey, Will Cantler, David Vaccari, Bethany Knox, Craig Burns, Tiffany Little Canfield, Rachel Hoffman, Justin Huff, Patrick Goodwin, Abbie Brady-Dalton, David Morris, Cesar A Rocha, Andrew Femenella, Karyn Casl, Kristina Bramhall; Associate Design: Amanda Stephens (set), Katie Irish (costumes), Joel Shier (lighting), Michael Bogden (sound), Aaron Waitz (special effects); Assistant Design: Sarah Cubbage, Rebecca Lasky, Sara Tosetti (costumes), Rob Ross (lighting), Don Foley (special effects); Crew: Neil McShane (production electrician), Marc Polimeni (moving lights programmer), George Wagner (production property master), Robert Dagna (prop crew), Jake Hall (deck audio), James Hall (wardrobe supervisor), Jason Blair, Kate Sorg (dressers); Assistant to Mr. Schwartz, Michael Cole; Assistant to Mr. Miller, Jennifer Coolbaugh; Synthesizer Programmer, Randy Cohen; SDC Observer, Katie Lupica; Production Assistants, Megan E. Coutts, Kendra Stockton; Paper Mill Playhouse Casting, Alison Franck; Advertising, Serino/Coyne, Greg Corrandetti, Sandy Block, Ryan Cunningham, Joaquin Esteva, Nehanda Loiseau; Website, Davenport Theatrical Enterprises, Jamie Lynn Ballard; Music Preparations, Joann Kane Music Services, Russ Bartmus; For Davenport Theatricals: Ken Davenport (President), Matt Kovich (Vice President), Blair Ingenthron (Assistant to Mr. Davenport), Jamie Lynn Ballard (Creative Director/Web Design), Kristin Johnson (Director of Marketing), Steven Tartick (Director of Online Marketing), Jennifer Ashley Tepper (Director of Promotions), Ben Skinner (Marketing Associate), Marie Grossman (Management Associate), Jody Bell (Director of Group Sales), Jennie Marks (Group Sales Associate), Jane Caplow (Director of Creative Development), Philip Lakin (Street Promotions Manager); Press, The Publicity Office, Jeremy Shaffer, Marc Thibodeau, Michael Borowski; Cast recording: Sh-K-Boom/Ghostlight Records 84456

CAST Jesus **Hunter Parrish**[*1]; John and Judas **Wallace Smith**; Ensemble **Uzo Aduba**, **Nick Blaemire**, **Celisse Henderson**, **Morgan James**, **Telly Leung**, **Lindsay Mendez**[*2], **George Salazar**, **Anna Maria Perez de Tagle**

UNDERSTUDIES Joaquina Kalukango[*3], Eric Michael Krop, Corey Mach, Julia Mattison

*Succeeded by: 1. Corbin Bleu (4/17/12) 2. Hannah Elless (5/22/12) 3. Amina S. Robinson

ORCHESTRA Charlie Alterman (Conductor/Piano/Keyboard), Matt Hinkley (Associate Conductor/Guitar/Keyboard), Michael Aarons and Thad DeBrock (Guitars), Steve Millhouse (Bass), Shannon Ford (Drums)

MUSICAL NUMBERS Prologue; Prepare Ye; Save the People; Day by Day; Learn Your Lessons Well; Bless the Lord; All for the Best; All Good Gifts; Light of the World; Turn Back, O Man; Alas for You; By My Side; We Beseech Thee; Beautiful City; On the Willows; Finale

Revival of a musical presented in two acts. Originally presented at the Cherry Lane Theatre May 17, 1971, transferred to the Promenade Theatre and closed June 13, 1976, playing 2,124 performances (see *Theatre World* Vol. 27, page 114). Opened on Broadway at the Broadhurst Theatre June 22, 1976, transferred to the Plymouth Theatre September 15, 1976, and finally the Ambassador Theatre January 12, 1977 where it closed September 4, 1977, playing 527 performances (see *Theatre World* Vol. 33, page 12). The show was revived Off-Broadway at the Theatre at St. Peter's Church August 2–October 7, 2000 (see *Theatre World* Vol. 57, page 118). This production, its first Broadway revival, was produced in part by "The People of Godspell" which was comprised of a community of hundreds of micro-investors, the first time a Broadway musical has been funded in this manner.

SYNOPSIS Based on "The Gospel According to St. Matthew," *Godspell* uses improvisation and contemporary themes to illustrate the parables, bringing these lessons to life through the grand tradition of musical theatre.

Hunter Parrish

Celisse Henderson

Uzo Abuda and the Company

The Company

Telly Leung, Wallace Smith, and Lindsay Mendez

The Company

Nick Blaemire (center) and the Company (photos by Jeremy Daniel)

Hugh Dancy and Nina Arianda

Nina Arianda (photos by Joan Marcus)

Hugh Dancy

Venus in Fur

Samuel J. Friedman Theatre; First Preview: October 13, 2011; Opening Night: November 8, 2011; On hiatus December 19, 2011–February 6, 2012; Transferred to the Lyceum Theatre February 7, 2012; 37 previews, 171 performances as of May 31, 2012

Written by David Ives; Produced by Manhattan Theatre Club (Lynne Meadow, Artistic Director; Barry Grove, Executive Producer) by special arrangement with Jon B. Platt, Scott Landis, and Classic Stage Company; Director, Walter Bobbie; Sets, John Lee Beatty; Costumes, Anita Yavich; Lighting, Peter Kaczorowski; Sound, Acme Sound Partners; Fight Direction, Thomas Schall; Production Stage Manager, Winnie Y. Lok; Casting, Nancy Piccione and James Calleri; Company Manager, Erin Moeller; Stage Manager, Carlos Maisonet; Mary Mill Directing Fellow, Ross Evans; Makeup, Angelina Avallone; Vocal Coach, Deborah Hecht; Associate Set, Kacie Hultgren; Assistant Costumes, Nicole Jescinth Smith; Assistant Lighting, Gina Scherr; Associate Sound, Jason Crystal; Hair/Makeup Supervisor, Natasha Steinhagen; Lighting Programmer, Jay Penfield; Production Assistant, Samantha Flint; For MTC: General Manager, Florie Seery; Artistic Producer, Mandy Greenfield; Director of Artistic Development, Jerry Patch; Marketing, Debra Waxman-Pilla; Production Manager, Joshua Helman; Director of Casting, Nancy Piccione; Artistic Line Producer, Lisa McNulty; Development, Lynne Randall; Artistic Consultant, Daniel Sullivan; Artistic Operations, Amy Gilkes Loe; Finance, Jessica Adler; Associate General Manager, Lindsey Brooks Sag; Subscriber Services, Robert Allenberg; Telesales, George Tetlow; Education, David Shookhoff; Associate Production Manager, Bethany Weinstein; Assistant Production Manager, Kevin Service; Prop Supervisor, Scott Laule; Assistant Properties Supervisor, Julia Sandy; Props Carpenter, Peter Grimes; Costume Supervisor, Erin Hennessy Dean; Press, Boneau/Bryan-Brown, Chris Boneau, Aaron Meier, Christine Olver, Emily Meagher

CAST Vanda **Nina Arianda**; Thomas **Hugh Dancy**

UNDERSTUDIES Mark Alhadeff (Thomas), Victoria Mack (Vanda), Liv Rooth (Vanda – replacement)

2011-2012 AWARD Tony Award: Best Performance by an Actress in a Leading Role (Nina Arianda)

SETTING A rehearsal room in Manhattan; the present. Transfer of an Off-Broadway play presented without intermission. Originally presented at Classic Stage Company (Brian Kulick, Artistic Director; Jessica R. Jenen, Executive Director) January 13–March 28, 2010 (see *Theatre World* Vol. 66, page 216). Miss Arianda won a Theatre World Award for her performance in that production.

SYNOPSIS Vanda is a preternaturally talented young actress determined to land the lead in Thomas' new play based on the classic erotic novel, *Venus in Fur*. Her emotionally charged audition for the gifted but demanding playwright/director becomes an electrifying game of cat and mouse, blurring the lines between fantasy and reality, seduction and power, love and sex.

Nina Arianda and Hugh Dancy

Hugh Jackman Back on Broadway

Broadhurst Theatre; First Preview: October 25, 2011; Opening Night: November 10, 2011; Closed January 1, 2012; 18 previews, 61 performances

Produced by Robert Fox and The Shubert Organization (Philip J. Smith, Chairman; Robert E. Wankel, President); Direction and Choreography, Warren Carlyle; Music Director, Patrick Vaccariello; Scenic Consultant, John Lee Beatty; Costume Design, William Ivey Long, Lighting, Ken Billington; Sound, John Shivers; Video Design, Alexander V. Nichols; General Management, Bespoke Theatricals (Maggie Brohn, Amy Jacobs, Devin Kendell, Nina Lannan); Company Manager, Heidi Neven; Hair, Edward J. Wilson; Casting, Tara Rubin Casting (Tara Rubin, Eric Woodall, Merri Sugarman, Dale Brown, Kaitlin Shaw, Lindsay Levine); Production Stage Manager, Kim Vernace; Stage Manager, Charles Underhill; Associate Director, Angie Canuel; Technical Supervision, Neil A. Mazzella/Hudson Theatrical Associates; Orchestrations, August Eriksmoen, Micheal Gibson, Larry Hochman, Mark Hummel, Michael John LaChiusa, Jim Laev, Richard Mann, Richard Marx, JJ McGeehan, Danny Troob, Patrick Vaccariello, Don Walker, Harold Wheeler; Associate Design: John Demous, Anthony Pearson (lighting), Martha Bromelmeier (costumes), David Patridge (sound); Assistant to the Lighting Designer, Brandon Baker; Moving Light Programmer, David Arch; Synthesizer Programmer, Jim Abbott; Crew: Jimmy Maloney Jr. (production electrician), Ronald Schwier (head electrician), Fran Rapp (production carpenter), Michael Van Nest (followspot), David Patridge (head sound), Kathleen Gallagher (wardrobe supervisor), Geoffrey Polischuck (Mr. Jackman's dresser), Rose Keough (dresser); Booking Agency for Mr. Jackman, WME Entertainment; Press Representation for Mr. Jackman, Rogers & Cowan Inc.; Writing Consultant for Mr. Jackman, John Macks; Assistant to Mr. Jackman, Irving Milgrom; Assistant to Mr. Fox, Sarah Richardson; Piano Vocal Score Preparation, Tim Brown; Music Copying, Kaye-Houston Music Inc.; Advertising and Online Marketing, SpotCo (Drew Hodges, Jim Edwards, Tom Greenwald, Y. Darius Suyama, Caraline Sogliuzzo, Sarah Fitzpatrick, Kristen Bardwil, Meghan Ownbey, Marc Mettler, Matt Wilstein); Press, Boneau/Bryan-Brown, Adrian Bryan-Brown, Jackie Green, Kelly Guiod

CAST Hugh Jackman; Ensemble **Robin Campbell**, **Kearran Giovanni**, **Anne Otto**, **Lara Seibert**, **Hilary Michael Thompson**, **Emily Tyra**; Vocalists **Clifton Bieundurry**, **Olive Knight**; Didgeridoo Players **Paul Boon**, **Nathan Mundraby**

ORCHESTRA Partick Vaccariello (Conductor); Jim Laev (Associate Conductor/Piano/Synth); Martin Agee (Concert Master); Fritz Krakowski, Dan Ianculovici (Violins); Peter Prosser, Vivian Israel (Celli); Ben Kono, Adam Kolker, David Young, Ron Jannelli (Reeds); Trevor Neumann, Scott Wendholt (Trumpets); Tim Albright, Jack Schatz (Trombones); Brian Brake (Drums); Paul Nowinski (Bass); JJ McGeehan (Guitars)

2011-2012 AWARD Tony Award: Special Award (Hugh Jackman)

A theatrical concert of pop and Broadway standards performed in two acts.

SYNOPSIS Accompanied by an 18-piece orchestra, Hugh Jackman performs a personal selection of his favorite musical numbers that reflect on the stage and film star's remarkable life and career, from *The Boy from Oz* to Hollywood.

Emily Tyra, Anne Otto, Hugh Jackman, Robin Campbell,and Kearran Giovanni

Hugh Jackman (photos by Joan Marcus)

Emily Tyra, Hugh Jackman, Lara Seibert, and Kearran Giovanni

Lara Seibert, Kearran Giovanni, Hugh Jackman, Robin Campbell, and Anne Otto

Private Lives

Music Box Theatre; First Preview: November 6, 2011; Opening Night: November 17, 2011; Closed December 31, 2011; 12 previews, 53 performances

Written by Noël Coward; Produced by Duncan C. Weldon and Paul Elliott, Theatre Royal Bath, Terri and Timothy Childs, Sonia Friedman Productions, Bill Ballard and David Mirvish; Director, Richard Eyre; Set and Costumes, Rob Howell; Lighting, David Howe; Music Supervisor and Composer, Matthew Scott; Sound, Jason Barnes (U.K.), Chris Cronin (U.S.); Associate Director, Anna Ledwich; Fight Director, Alison De Burgh; Movement Director, Scarlett Mackmin; U.K. Production Manager, Patrick Molony; U.S. Production Manager/Technical Supervisor, Juniper Street Productions; General Management, Alan Wasser, Allan Williams, Mark Shacket; Company Manager, Cathy Kwon; Production Stage Manager, Howard Jepson; Hair, Campbell Young Associates, Luc Verschueren; Stage Manager, Olivia Roberts; Dialect Coach, Jill McCulloch; Associate Lighting, Vivien Leone; Crew: Bobby Hentze (production carpenter), Jon Lawson (production electrician), Jill Johnson (production props), Rafe Carlotto (production sound), Doug Petitjean (wardrobe supervisor), Laura Beattie (star dresser), Julie Tobia (dresser), Rick Carato (hair supervisor), Dennis Maher (house carpenter), William K. Rowland (house electrician), Kim Garnett (house props), Brian Maher (house flyman); For Alan Wasser Associates: Aaron Lustbader; For Juniper Street Productions: Hillary Blanken, Guy Kwan, Joseph DeLuise, Ana Rose Greene; Advertising and Marketing, aka (Clint Bond Jr., Andrew Danner, Pippa Bexon, Kevin Hirst, Adam Jay, Janette Roush, Meghan Bartley, Sara Rosenweig, Trevor Sponseller, Erin Rech, Jen Taylor); Press, Boneau/Bryan-Brown, Adrian Bryan-Brown, Jackie Green, Kelly Guiod

CAST Sybil **Anna Madeley**; Elyot **Paul Gross**; Victor **Simon Paisley Day**; Amanda **Kim Cattrall**; Louise **Caroline Lena Olsson**

UNDERSTUDIES Christy Bruce (Sybil, Amanda, Louise), Dylan Scott Smith (Elyot, Victor)

SETTING Act 1: A hotel terrace in Deuville, France; Act 2: Amanda's apartment in Paris, late in the evening a few days later; Act 3: Amanda's apartment, the next morning. Revival of a comedy presented in three acts with one intermission after Act 1. Originally produced on Broadway at the Times Square Theatre January–September 1931. This production, its seventh major New York revival, previously played in London and Toronto. The most recent revival played the Richard Rodgers Theatre, starring Alan Rickman and Lindsay Duncan, April 28–September 1, 2002 (see *Theatre World* Vol. 58, page 56).

SYNOPSIS Glamorous, rich and reckless, Amanda and Elyot have been divorced from each other for five years. Now both are honeymooning with their new spouses in the South of France. When, by chance, they meet again across adjoining hotel balconies, their insatiable feelings for each other are immediately rekindled. They hurl themselves headlong into love and lust without a care for scandal, new partners or memories of what drove them apart in the first place… for a little while, anyway.

Paul Gross and Anna Madeley

Paul Gross and Kim Cattrall (photos by Cylla von Tiedemann)

Paul Gross and Kim Cattrall

Kim Cattrall and Simon Paisley Day

Hamish Linklater, Hettienne Park, Lily Rabe, and Jerry O'Connell

Hettienne Park and Jerry O'Connell (photos by Jeremy Daniel)

Hamish Linklater and Lily Rabe

Seminar

John Golden Theatre; First Preview: October 27, 2011; Opening Night: November 20, 2011; Closed May 6, 2012; 26 previews, 191 performances

Written by Theresa Rebeck; Produced by Jeffrey Finn, Jill Furman, John N. Hart Jr. and Patrick Milling Smith, Roy Furman, David Ian, David Mirvish, Amy Nauiokas, James Spry; Director, Sam Gold; Sets and Costumes, David Zinn; Lighting, Ben Stanton; Original Music and Sound, John Gromada; Casting, MelCap Casting (David Caparelliotis, Mele Nagler); Production Manager, Peter Fulbright/Tech Production Services (Mary Duffe, Colleen Houlehen, Sheena Crespo); Production Stage Manager, Charles Means; Associate Producers, Matthew Schneider, Wake Up Marconi, Jamie Kaye-Phillips, Charles Stone/Ben Limberg; Executive Producer/General Management, 101 Productions Ltd. (Wendy Orshan, Jeffrey M. Wilson, David Auster, Elie Landau); Company Manager, Barbara Crompton; Stage Manager, Lisa Buxbaum; Assistant Director, Portia Krieger; Associate Design: Josh Zangen (set), Jacob A. Climer (costumes), Ken Ellott (lighting), Alex Neumann (sound); Assistant Costumes, Matthew Simonelli; Assistant to the Set Designer, Michael Simmons; Assistant to the Costume Designer, Stefanie Genda; Production Props, Buist Bickley; Prop Shopper, Sarah Gosnell; Prop Painter, Emily Walsh; Prop Upholstery, Julia Sandy; Crew: Paul Wimmer (production carpenter), Thomas Lawrey (production electrician), Rob Presley (head props), Wayne Smith (head sound), Terry McGarty (house carpenter), Thomas Anderson (house flyman), Sylvia Yoshioka (house electrician), Leah Nelson (house properties), Robert Guy (wardrobe supervisor), John Robelen, Tree Sarvay (dressers); Advertising/Digital Outreach/Website/Marketing, Serino/Coyne; Press, The Publicity Office, Marc Thibodeau, Michael Borowski, Jeremy Shaffer

CAST Douglas **Jerry O'Connell**; Martin **Hamish Linklater**[*1]; Kate **Lily Rabe**[*2]; Izzy **Hettienne Park**; Leonard **Alan Rickman**[*3]

Succeeded by: 1. Justin Long (4/3/12) 2. Zoe Lister-Jones (4/3/12) 3. Jeff Goldblum (4/3/12)

STANDBYS Rocco Sisto (Leonard), Christina Pumariega (Kate and Izzy), Matthew Greer (Martin and Douglas)

2011-2012 AWARD Theatre World Award: Hettienne Park

World premiere of a new play presented without intermission.

SYNOPSIS In *Seminar*, four aspiring young novelists sign up for private writing classes with Leonard, an international literary figure. Under his recklessly brilliant and unorthodox instruction, some thrive and others flounder, alliances are made and broken, sex is used as a weapon and hearts are unmoored. The wordplay is not the only thing that turns vicious as innocence collides with experience in this provocative new comedy.

Alan Rickman (center) and the Company

Patti LuPone

Mandy Patinkin (photos by Joan Marcus)

An Evening with Patti LuPone and Mandy Patinkin

Ethel Barrymore Theatre; First Preview: November 6, 2011; Opening Night: November 21, 2011; Closed January 13, 2012; 6 previews, 57 performances

Conceived by Mandy Patinkin and Paul Ford; Produced by Staci Levine, The Dodgers, Jon B. Platt, Jessica R. Jenen; Director, Mandy Patinkin; Music Director, Paul Ford; Dance Consultant, Ann Reinking; Featuring music and lyrics by Stephen Sondheim, Richard Rodgers & Oscar Hammerstein II, Jerome Kern & Johnny Mercer, Frank Loesser, Kern & Hammerstein II, John Kander & Fred Ebb, Vincent Youmans & Hammerstein II, Murray Grand, Jule Styne, Styne & Sondheim, Sir Andrew Lloyd Webber & Tim Rice, Howard Ashman & Alan Menken; Design, David Korins; Lighting, Eric Cornwell; Sound, Daniel J. Gerhard; Costumes, Jon Can Coskunses; Production Stage Manager, Matthew Aaron Stern; Production Manager, Aurora Productions (Gene O'Donovan, Ben Heller, Stephanie Sherline, Jarid Sumner, Liza Luxenberg, Anita Shah, Anthony Jusino, Steven Dalton, Eudenio Saenz Flores, Isaac Katzanek, Melissa Mazdra); Company Manager, Jennifer Hindman Kemp; General Manager, Richards/Climan Inc. (David R. Richards, Tamar Haimes, Michael Sag, Kyle Bonder, Jessica Fried, Jaqueline Kolek); Executive Producer, Groundswell Theatricals Inc. (Staci Levine, Tim Hurley, Richard Cerato); Stage Manager, Laura Skolnik; Producer Associate, Tim Hurley; Assistant Dance Consultant, Jim Borstelmann; Associate Scenic Design, Rod Lemmond; Assistant Lighting Design, Cory Pattak; Assistant to the Lighting Designer, Amy Francis Schott; Assistant to the Sound Designer, Alexis Parsons; Crew: Craig Caccamise (production electrician), Phil Lojo, Paul Delcioppo (production sound engineers), Dan Hochstine (assistant sound engineer), Mark Fiore (head sound mixer), Brian Renoni (lead followspot), Lyle Jones (wardrobe supervisor), Ruth Carsch (hair and wig supervisor), Georgia Theodosis (draper), Sean Beach (moving light programmer); Publicist for Miss LuPone, Philip Rinaldi; Assistant to Miss LuPone, Pamela Lyster; Advertising/Marketing/Digital Outreach and Website, Serino/Coyne (Greg Corradetti, Sandy Block, Andrei Olenik, Kim Hewski, Jon Erwin, Brian Wright, Jim Glaub, Chip Meyrelles, Laurie Connor, Kevin Keating, Whitney Creighton, Crystal Chase); Press, Boneau/Bryan-Brown, Adrian Bryan-Brown, Susanne Tighe, Christine Olver

CAST Patti LuPone and Mandy Patinkin

ORCHESTRA Paul Ford (Music Director, Piano), John Beal (Bass)

MUSICAL NUMBERS Another Hundred People; When; A Cockeyed Optimist; Twin Soliloquies; Some Enchanted Evening; Some Enchanted Evening (reprise); Getting Married Today; Loving You; A Cockeyed Optimist (reprise); I'm Old Fashioned; I Have the Room Above Her; Baby It's Cold Outside; Everybody Says Don't; A Quite Thing; It Takes Two; I Won't Dance; I Want a Man; April in Fairbanks; Old Folks; Everything's Coming Up Roses; The God-Why-Don't-You-Love-Me Blues; The Hills of Tomorrow; Merrily We Roll Along; Old Friends; Oh What a Circus; Don't Cry for Me Argentina; Somewhere That's Green; In Buddy's Eyes; You're a Queer One, Julie Jordan; If I Loved You; If I Loved You (reprise); What's the Use of Wond'rin; If I Loved You (reprise); You'll Never Walk Alone

Broadway premiere of a musical concert presented in two acts.

SYNOPSIS Patti LuPone and Mandy Patinkin reuinite on Broadway for *An Evening with Patti LuPone and Mandy Patinkin*. The two Broadway legends who first appeared together giving Tony Award winning performances in *Evita*, bring their critcally acclaimed theatre concert, a funny, passionate, intimate, and unique musical love story told eniterly through a masterful selection of some of the greatest songs ever written for the stage.

Bonnie & Clyde

Gerald Schoenfeld Theatre; First Preview: November 4, 2011; Opening Night: December 1, 2011; Closed December 30, 2011; 33 previews, 36 performances

Book by Ivan Menchell, lyrics by Don Black, music by Frank Wildhorn; Produced by Kathleen Raitt, Jerry Frankel, Jeffrey Richards, Barry Satchwell Smith, Michael A. Jenkins, Howard Caplan, Bernie Abrams/Michael Speyer, Howard Kagan, Barry and Carole Kaye, Terry Schnuck, Nederlander Presentations, Corey Brunish/Brisa Trinchero, Alden Badway Podell/The Broadway Consortium, Patty Baker, Bazinet & Company, Uniteus Entertainment, Ken Mahoney, Jeremy Scott Blaustein, in association with Stageventures 2011 Limited Partnership, Infinity Stages, Robert G. Bartner/Ambassador Theatre Group, BGM, Broadway Across America, Michael D. Coit, Mary Cossette, Ronald Frankel, Lloyd Fruge, Bruce Robert Harris/Jack W. Batman, Cynthia Stroum, DSM/Gabriel Kamel, Irving Welzer; Director and Choreography, Jeff Calhoun; Music Supervision/Arrangements/Orchestrations, John McDaniel; Music Director, Jason Howland; Set and Costumes, Tobin Ost; Lighting, Michael Gilliam; Sound, John Shivers; Projection, Aaron Rhyne; Casting, Telsey + Company; Hair and Wigs, Charles LaPointe; Makeup, Ashley Ryan; Fight Director, Steve Rankin; Technical Supervisor, Neil A. Mazzella/Hudson Theatrical Associations; Production Stage Manager, Paul J. Smith; Associate Director, Coy Middlebrook; Music Contractor, David Lai; General Management, Bespoke Theatricals (Maggie Brohn, Amy Jacobs, Devin Keudell, Nina Lannan); Associate General Manager, David Roth; Company Manager, Doug Gaeta; Associate Company Manager, Roseanna Sharrow; Stage Manager, Megan Schneid; Assistant Stage Manager, Jason Brouillard; Assistant Directors, Corey Brunish, J. Scott Lapp; Fight Captain, Daniel Cooney; Assistant to the Director, Nick Stimler; SDCF Mike Ockrent Directing Fellow, Alex Lippard; Assistant Producer, Michael Crea; Dialect Coach, Shane Ann Younts; Makeup Design, Ashley Ryan; Associate Design: Christine Peters (set), Leslie Malitz (costumes), Warren Flynn (lighting), Leah Loukas (hair), Ned Stresen-Reuter (projections), David Patridge (sound); Assistant Design: Brian Kalin, Frank McCullough (set), Christian DeAngelis (lighting), Daniel Durkin (projection), Automated Lighting, Warren Flyn; Video Programmer, Benjamin Keightley; Assistant to Mr. Wildhorn, Nicholas Cheng; Music Preparation, Music Ink/Christopher Deschene, Tony Finno, John W. Lowell, Peter Foley; Synthesizer Programmer, Randy Cohen; Assistant Fight Director, Shad Ramsey; Crew: Don Oberpriller (production carpenter), Tim McWilliams (house carpenter), Glenn Ingram (house flyman), Karl Schuberth (fly automation), Mark Diaz (deck automation), Jimmy Maloney (production electrician), Brad Robertson (head electrician), Leslie Ann Kilian (house electrician), Peter Guernsey, Marc Schmittroth (followspots), Kevin Kennedy (advance sound), Emiliano Pares (production properties), Brian Schweppe (head properties), Steve McDonald, Neil Rosenberg (house properties), Susan Checklick (wardrobe supervisor), Meredith Benson, Jake Fry, Jennifer Hohn, Franklin Hollenbeck, Tamara Kopko, Keith Shaw (dressers), Pat Marcus (hair supervisor), Carrie Rohm (hair assistant), Vanessa Brown (children's guardian), Dan Urlie (costume shopper), Eric Mendez (costume intern), Michael Rico Cohen, Aaron Elgart (production assistants); Tutoring, On Location Education/Alan Simon, Jodi Green; General Management Associates, Libby Fox, Danielle Saks; Advertising, Serino/Coyne; Website Design/Online Marketing, Situation Interactive; Interactive Marketing Service, Broadway's Best Shows; Press, Jeffrey Richards Associates, Irene Gandy, Alana Karpoff, Ryan Hallett, Elon Rutberg; Cast recording: Broadway Records BR-CD000112

CAST Bonnie Parker **Laura Osnes**; Clyde Barrow **Jeremy Jordan**; Young Bonnie **Kelsey Fowler**; Emma Parker **Mimi Bessette**; Minister/First Penitentiary Guard/Detective Alcorn **Daniel Cooney**; Young Clyde **Talon Ackerman**; Cumie Barrow **Leslie Becker**; Henry Barrow **Victor Hernandez**; Buck Barrow **Claybourne Elder**; First Judge/Bank Teller/Captain Frank Hamer **Tad Wilson**; Ted Hinton **Louis Hobson**; Blanche Barrow **Melissa van der Schyff**; Elanore **Garrett Long**; Trish **Marissa McGowan**; Stella **Alison Cimmet**; Sheriff Schmid **Joe Hart**; Bud **Matt Lutz**; Preacher/Second Judge **Michael Lanning**; Shopkeeper/Deputy Johnson **Jon Fletcher**; Governor Ferguson **Leslie Becker**; Ensemble **Alison Cimmet, Daniel Cooney, Jon Fletcher, Michael Lanning, Garrett Long, Matt Lutz, Marissa McGowan,**

Tad Wilson; Swings **Katie Klaus, Sean Jenness, Cassie Okena, Justin Matthew Sargeant**

UNDERSTUDIES Rozi Baker (Young Bonnie), Alison Cimmet (Blanche Barrow, Cumie Barrow, Emma Parker, Governor Ferguson), Daniel Cooney (Preacher, Sheriff Schmid), Jon Fletcher (Clyde Barrow), Sean Jenness (Henry Barrow, Preacher), Katie Klaus (Blanche Barrow), Garrett Long (Blanche Barrow, Cumie Barrow, Emma Parker, Governor Ferguson), Matt Lutz (Buck Barrow, Ted Hinton), Marissa McGowan (Bonnie Parker), Cassie Okenka (Bonnie Parker), Justin Matthew Sargent (Buck Barrow, Bud, Clyde Barrow, Ted Hinton), Jack Tartaglia (Young Clyde), Tad Wilson (Preacher, Sheriff Schmid)

ORCHESTRA Jason Howland (Conductor/Piano), Jeff Tanski (Associate Conductor/Synthesizer), Cenovia Cummins (Violin), Clint DeGanon (Drums), Chris Lightcap (Bass), Brian Koonin (Guitar 1), Gordon Titcomb (Guitar 2/Banjo/Pedal Steel), Rob Jacoby and Dan Willis (Woodwinds)

MUSICAL NUMBERS Picture Show; This World Will Remember Us; You're Goin' Back to Jail; How 'Bout a Dance; When I Drive; God's Arms Are Always Open; You Can Do Better Than Him; You Love Who You Love; Raise a Little Hell; This World Will Remember Us (reprise); Made in America; Too Late to Turn Back Now; That's What You Call a Dream; What Was Good Enough for You; Bonnie; Raise a Little Hell (reprise); Dyin' Ain't So Bad; God's Arms Are Always Open (reprise); Picture Show (reprise); Dyin' Ain't So Bad (reprise)

2011-2012 AWARDS Theatre World Award: Jeremy Jordan

SETTING Texas, and other parts of the south and Midwest; early 1930s. New York premiere of a new musical presented in two acts. World premiere at La Jolla Playhouse (Christopher Ashley, Artistic Director; Michael S. Rosenberg, Managing Director) November 10–December 20, 2009 (see *Theatre World* Vol. 66, page 375). Subsequently produced at Asolo Repertory Theatre (Michael Donald Edwards, Producing Artistic Director; Linda DiGabriele, Managing Director) November 16–December 19, 2010.

SYNOPSIS In Depression-era Texas, a young Bonnie Parker falls in love with Clyde Barrow, a criminal on the run from the law. Their love affair soon spirals out of control, as Bonnie & Clyde commit a series of bank robberies. As their notoriety — and body count — rises, the ill-fated lovers find themselves racing to the top of the Public Enemies list.

Jeremy Jordan and Laura Osnes

Meliisa Van Der Schyff and Laura Osnes

Melissa Van Der Schyff, Claybourne Elder, Jeremy Jordan, and Laura Osnes

Jeremy Jordan and Laura Osnes (photos by Nathan Johnson)

Jeremy Jordan, Joe Hart, and Louis Hobson

Claybourne Elder and Jeremy Jordan

Jeremy Jordan and Laura Osnes

Stick Fly

Cort Theatre; First Preview: November 18, 2011; Opening Night: December 8, 2011; Closed February 26, 2012; 24 previews, 85 performances

Written by Lydia R. Diamond; Produced by Nelle Nugent, Alicia Keys, Samuel Nappi, Reuben Cannon, Jay H. Harris/Catherine Schreiber, Huntington Theatre Company, Dan Frishwasser, Charles Salameno, Sharon A. Carr/Patricia Klausner/ Rick Danzansky, Daveed D. Frazier/Mark Thompson, in association with Joseph Sirola, Cato and Nicole June/Matthew and Shawna Watley, Eric Falkenstein, Kenneth Teaton; Director, Kenny Leon; Original Music and Orchestrations, Alicia Keys; Set, David Gallo; Costumes, Reggie Ray; Lighting, Beverly Emmons; Sound, Peter Fitzgerald; Casting, MelCap Casting (Mele Nagler, David Caparelliotis, Lauren Port, Felicia Rudolph, Christina Wright); Production Stage Manager, Robert Bennett; Production Management, Aurora Productions; General Manager, Peter Bogyo; Associate Producers, Sarahbeth Grossman, Michael Maso, Erika Rose; Company Manager, Chris Morey; Stage Manager, lark hackshaw; Hair, Gregory Bazemore; Assistant Director, Kamilah Forbes; Associate Design: Evan F. Adamson (set), Greg Guarnaccia and Judith Daitsman (lighting), Megan Henninger (sound); Assistant Costume Designers, Richard Gross, Maggie Dick; Voice Coach, Kate Wilson; Crew: Edward Diaz (production carpenter), Scott DeVerna (production electrician), Vera Pizzarelli (production properties), Jens McVoy (production sound engineer), Lonnie Gaddie (house properties), Eileen Miller (wardrobe supervisor), Anita Ali Dais, Richard Gross (dressers), Michael Block (production assistant); Assistant to the General Manager, Lily Alia; Scenic Studio Manager, Sarah Zeitler; Scenic Studio Coordinator, Jan Price Frazier; Assistants to Mr. Gallo, Smantha Shoffner, Tabitha Pease; Costume Intern, Sankara McCain; Production Props Coordinator, Kathy Fabian/Propstar; Assoicate Props Coordinators, Carrie Mossman, Timothy Ferro; Props Artisans, Cassie Dorland, John Estep, Gloria Sun, Mary Wilson, Kelly Kuykendall, Holly Griffin; For Aurora Productions: Gene O'Donovan, Ben Heller, Stephanie Sherline, Jarid Sumner, Liza Luxenberg, Anita Shah, Anthony Jusino, Steven Dalton, Eugenio Saenz Flores, Isaac Katznek, Melissa Mazdra; Advertising, aka; Marketing and Promotions, Walker Internaltion Communications Group, Donna Walker-Kuhne, Cherine Anderson, Toni Isreal; Website and Social Media, Bay Bridge Productions; Press, Boneau/Bryan-Brown, Chris Boneau, Heath Schwartz, Emily Meagher

CAST Cheryl **Condola Rashad**; Taylor **Tracie Thoms**; Spoon (Kent) LeVay **Dulé Hill**; Flip (Harold) LeVay **Mekhi Phifer**; Joe LeVay **Ruben Santiago-Hudson**; Kimber **Rosie Benton**

UNDERSTUDIES Jerome Preston Bates (Joe LeVay), Don Guillory (Spoon LeVay, Flip LeVay), Gretchen Hall (Kimber), Zakiya Young (Cheryl, Taylor)

SETTING The LeVay Home, Martha's Vineyard; 2005; Not Oak Bluffs. New York premiere of a new play presented in two acts. Developed at Chicago Dramatists and produced by Congo Square Theatre. The East Coast premiere was produced by the McCarter Theatre Center September 7–October 14, 2007 (see *Theatre World* Vol 64, page 317). A further developemental production was produced jointly by Arena Stage and the Huntington Theatre Company January 1–March 28, 2010 (see *Theatre World* Vol. 66, pages 347 and 373).

SYNOPSIS It was a relaxing weekend on Martha's Vineyard ... until the baggage got unpacked. Meet the LeVays. When two adult sons independently choose to introduce their girlfriends to the parents on the same weekend, sibling rivalries flare, opinions clash, class distinctions divide and family secrets unravel.

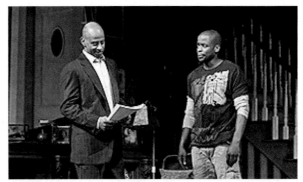
Ruben Santiago-Hudson and Dulé Hill

Condola Rashad, Mekhi Phifer, and Roise Benton

Ruben Santiago-Hudson, Condola Rashad, Mekhi Phifer, Roise Benton, Tracie Thoms, and Dulé Hill (photos by Richard Termine)

On a Clear Day You Can See Forever

St. James Theatre; First Preview: November 12, 2011; Opening Night: December 11, 2011; Closed January 29, 2012; 29 previews, 57 performances

Music by Burton Lane, lyrics and original book by Alan Jay Lerner, new book by Peter Parnell; Produced by Tom Hulce and Ira Pittelman, Liza Lerner, Broadway Across America, Joseph Smith, Michael McCabe, Bernie Abrams/Michael Speyer, Takonkiet Viravan/Scenario Thailand, Michael Watt, Jacki Barlia Florin-Adam Blanshay/Chauspeciale/Astrachan & Jupin, Paul Boskind and Martian Entertainment, Brannon Wiles, Carlos Arana/Christopher Maring; Re-conceived and Directed by Michael Mayer; Choreography, Joann M. Hunter; Orchestrations, Doug Besterman; Music Director/Vocal and Instrumental Music Arrangements, Lawrence Yurman; Set, Christine Jones; Costumes, Catherine Zuber; Lighting, Kevin Adams; Sound, Peter Hylenski; Wigs and Hair, Tom Watson; Casting, Jim Carnahan, Stephen Kopel; Music Coordinator, John Miller; Associate Producers, Stage Ventures 2011 Limited Partnership; Associate Producer, Austin Regan; Associate Choreographer, Scott Taylor; Production Stage Manager, Lisa Iacucci; Technical Supervision, Hudson Theatrical Associates; General Manager, The Charlotte Wilcox Company (Seth Marquette, Dina S. Friedler, Matthew W. Krawiec, Regina Mancha, Margaret Wicox, Chantel Hopper, Ryan Smillie, Stephen Donovan); Company Manager, James Lawson; Assistant Company Manager, Fracesca De La Vega; Producing Associate for Mr. Pittelman and Mr. Hulce, Christopher Manning; Executive Assistant to Mr. Pittelman, Dorothy Evans; Casting Associates, Carrie Gardner, Jillian Cimini, Michael Morlani, Lexie Pregosin; Stage Manager, Rachel A. Wolff; Assistant Stage Manager, Steve Henry; Technical Supervisor, Sam Ellis; Assistant Choreographer/Dance Captain, Patrick O'Neill; Keyboard Programmer, Karl Mansfield; Music Preparation, Anixter Rice Music Services; Additional Orchestrations, Larry Blank; Associate Design: Ed Coco (set), Ryan Park (costumes), Joel E. Silver (lighting), Keith Caggiano (sound); Assistant Design: Brett Banakis, Jonathan Collins, Michael Riha (set), Patrick Bevilacqua, David Newll (costumes), Paul Toben (lighting); Assistant to Ms. Zuber, Leon Dobkowski; Moving Lights Programmer, Victor Seastone; Makeup Design, Ashley Ryan; Crew: Todd Frank (head carpenter), Chris Pravata (deck carpenter), Robert N. Valli (deck automation), Greg Husinko (production electrician), Nicholas Keslake (head electrician), Kathy Fabian/Propstar (production properties coordinator), Timothy Ferro (associate props coordinator), Mary Wilson, Carrie Mossman, Cassie Dorland, John Estep, Sarah Bird, Jessica Provencale (prop artisans), Eric Castaldo (head propmaster), Phil Lojo, Paul Delcioppo (production sound), Jesse Stevens (sound engineer), Bill Ruger (assistant sound engineer), Patrick Bevilacqua (wardrobe supervisor), Tom Bertsch (assistant wardrobe supervisor), Sara Darneille, Joe Hickey, Savan Leveille, Kimberly Mark, Del Miskie, Derek Moreno, Claire Verlaet, Libby Villanova, Sandy Vojta (dressers), Victoria Grecki (Mr. Connick's dresser), Joshua Gericke (hair supervisor), Kevin Maybee (assistant hair supervisor); Rehearsal Musicians, David Hahn, Paul Pizzuti; Production Assistants, Samantha Preiss, Taylor Michael; Assistant to Mr. Miller, Jennifer Coolbaugh; Specialty Prop Construction, Aardvark Interiors, Cigar Box Studios, Mike Billings; Flame Treatment, Turning Star Inc.; Advertising/Digital Outreach and Website, Serino/Coyne, Sandy Block, Scott Johnson, Tom Callahan, Robert Jones, Ryan Cunningham, Jamie Caplan, Jim Glaub, Chip Meyrelles, Laurie Connor, Kevin Keating, Ryan Greer, Whitney Creighton, Crystal Chase; Marketing, Type A Marketing/Anne Rippey, Elyce Henkin, Sarah Ziering; Press, The Hartman Group, Michael Hartman, Leslie Papa, Whitney Holden Gore

CAST Dr. Mark Bruckner **Harry Connick Jr.**; David Gamble **David Turner**; Anton/Dr. Leo Kravis/Mr. Van Deusen/Gene Miller/Wesley Porter (1974) **Paul O'Brien**; Vera/Mrs. Hatch/Mrs. Lloyd/Radio Singer **Lori Wilner**; Muriel Bunson **Sarah Stiles**; Hannah **Alex Ellis**; Paula **Alysha Umphress**; Roger/Sawyer/Radio Singer **Tyler Maynard**; Alan/Wesley Porter (1944) **Zachary Prince**; Preston/Announcer/Radio Singer/Stage Manager **Benjamin Eakeley**; Dr. Sharone Stein **Kerry O'Malley**; Leora Kahn/Club Vedado Singer/Betsy Rappaport/Cynthia Roland/Radio Singer **Heather Ayers**; Melinda Wells **Jessie Mueller**; Maurice **Drew Gehling**; Ensemble **Kendal Hartse**, **Grasan Kingsberry**; Swings **Patrick O'Neill**, **Christianne Tisdale**; Standby for Harry Connick Jr. **Sean Allan Krill**

UNDERSTUDIES Heather Ayers (Dr. Sharone Stein), Benjamin Eakeley (Warren Smith), Alex Ellis (Muriel Bunson), Kendal Hartse (Betsy Rappaport, Club Vedado Singer, Cynthia Roland, Leora Kahn, Radio Singer), Philip Hoffman (Anton, Dr. Leo Kravis, Gene Miller, Maurice, Mr. Van Deusen, Wesley Porter [1974]), Tyler Maynard (David Gamble), Zachary Prince (David Gamble, Warren Smith), Christianne Tisdale (Betsy Rappaport, Club Vedado Singer, Cynthia Roland, Dr. Sharone Stein, Leora Kahn, Mrs. Hatch, Mrs. Lloyd, Radio Singer, Vera), Alysha Umphress (Melinda Wells, Muriel Bunson)

ORCHESTRA Lawrence Yurman (Conductor); David J. Hahn (Associate Conductor/Keyboards); Geoff Burke, Charlie Pillow, Don McGeen (Woodwinds); Gregory L. Gisbert, Kevin Bryan (Trumpets); Dion Tucker, Joe Barati (Trombones); Patrick Pridemore (French Horn); Jack Cavari (Guitar); Neal Caine (Bass); Paul Pizzuti (Drums); Javier Diaz (Percussion); Karl Mansfield (Keyboards); Anna Reinserman (Harp); Sylvia D'Avanzo, Louise Owen (Violins); Amy Ralske (Cello)

MUSICAL NUMBERS Hurry! It's Lovely Up Here; She Isn't You; Open Your Eyes; Open Your Eyes (reprise); Hurry! It's Lovely Up Here (reprise); Wait 'Til We're Sixty-Five; Wait 'Til We're Sixty-Five (reprise); You're All the World to Me; Who Is There Among Us Who Knows; Who Is There Among Us Who Knows (reprise); On the S.S. Bernard Cohn; Love With All the Trimmings; Open Your Eyes (reprise); Melinda; Go to Sleep; Ev'ry Night at Seven; Too Late Now; Love With All the Trimmings (reprise); When I'm Being Born Again; (S)he Wasn't You; What Did I Have That I Don't Have; Come Back to Me; Too Late Now (reprise); On a Clear Day You Can See Forever; Finale

2011-2012 AWARD Theatre World Award: Jessie Mueller

SETTING New York City, 1974. Revival of a musical (reconceived and revised) presented in two acts. The original Broadway production, starring John Cullum and Barbara Harris, was produced at the Mark Hellinger Theatre October 17, 1965–June 11, 1966 playing 280 performances (see *Theatre World* Vol. 22, page 20). This version of the show was originally presented by New York Stage and Film Company and the Powerhouse Theatre at Vassar in July 2010, and received a further developmental lab production at the Vineyard Theatre in 2011.

SYNOPSIS Love blooms in unexpected places in the delightfully reimagined world of *On a Clear Day You Can See Forever*. Still in love with his deceased wife, Dr. Mark Bruckner, a dashing psychiatrist and professor, unknowingly takes on the case of his life with David Gamble, a quirky young florists' assistant. While putting David under hypnosis to help him quit smoking so he can move in with his perfect boyfriend Warren, Dr. Bruckner stumbles upon what he believes to be David's former self – a dazzling and self-possessed 1940's jazz singer Melinda Wells. Instantly intrigued by Melinda, Dr. Bruckner finds himself swept up in the pursuit of an irresistible (and impossible) love affair with this woman from another time and place, who may or may not have ever existed.

Harry Connick Jr.

Jessie Mueller and Harry Connick Jr.

Jessie Mueller (right) and the Company

David Turner and Drew Gehling

David Turner

Jessie Mueller (photos by Paul Kolnik)

Harry Connick Jr., Jessie Mueller, and David Turner

Lysistrata Jones

Walter Kerr Theatre; First Preview: November 12, 2011; Opening Night: December 14, 2011; Closed January 8, 2012; 34 previews, 30 performances

Book by Douglas Carter Beane, music, lyrics, orchestrations, and arrangements by Lewis Flinn; Prouduced by Paula Herold, Alan Wasser, Joseph Smith, Michael McCabe, John Breglio, Takonkiet Viravan/Scenario Thailand, Hilary A. Williams, Broadway Across America (John Gore, CEO), James G. Robinson, in association with Tony Meola, Martin McCallum, Marianne Mills; Director and Choreograpy, Dan Knechtges; Music Director, Brad Simmons; Sets, Allen Moyer; Costumes, David C. Woolard and Thomas Charles LeGalley; Lighting, Michael Gottlieb; Sound, Tony Meola; Hair, Mark Adam Rampmeyer; Associate Choreographer, Jessica Hartman; Casting, Cindy Tolan, Adam Caldwell; Production Stage Manager, Lois L. Griffing; Music Coordinator, Dean Sharenow; Production Management, Juniper Street Productions, Hillary Blanken, Joseph DeLuise, Guy Kwan, Ana Rose Greene; General Management, Alan Wasser Associates, Allan Williams, Aaron Lustbader, Mark Shacket; Company Manager, John E. Gendron; Stage Manager, Thomas Recktenwald; Assistant Stage Manager, Neveen Mahmoud; Assistant Company Manager, Meredith Morgan; Media Design, Howard Werner/Lightswitch; Assistant Director, Nick Eilerman; Associate Design: Jonathan Collins (set), Matthew Pachtman (costumes), Craig Stelzenmuller (lighting), Zach Williamson (sound); Assistant to the Costume Designers, Joseph Blaha; Assistant Lighting Designer, Jeremy Cunningham; Moving Light Programmer, David Arch; Video Programmer, Phil Gilbert; Crew: Fred Gallo (production carpenter), David Cohen (head carpenter), David J. Elmer (advance carpenter), Susan Barras (production props), Andrew Meeker (head props), Rick Baxter (production electrician), Sandra Paradise (head electrician), Joshua Maszle (production sound engineer), Christina Devany (deck audio), Scott Westervelt (wardrobe supervisor), Scotty R. Cain, Jessica Dermody, Angela Simpson (dressers); Brandalyn Fulton (makeup consultant), Jennifer Bullock (hair supervisor; Music Copyist/Assistant to Mr. Flinn, Alex Vorse; Dance Captain, Charlie Sutton; Production Assistant, Cody Renard Richard; Technical Production Assistant, Colyn Fiendel; General Management Associates, Mark Barna, Christopher D'Angelo, Jake Hirzel, Lane Marsh; General Management Office, Hilary Ackerman, Nina Lutwick, Jennifer O'Connor; Marketing, Type A Marketing, Anne Rippey, Elyce Henkin, Allison Morrow, David Loughner; Advertising/Digital Outreach and Website, Serino/Coyne (Sandy Block, Greg Coradetti, Roger Micone, Ryan Cunningham, Jim Glaub, Chip Meyerelles, Laurie Connor, Whitney Creighton, Mark Seeley, Kevin Keating, Ryan Greer); Press, The Hartman Group, Michael Hartman, Tom D'Ambrosio, Frances White; Cast recording: Broadway Records BRCD00312

CAST 'Uardo **Alexander Aguilar**; Tylis **Ato Blankson-Wood**; Lampito **Katie Boren**; Robin **Lindsay Nicole Chambers**; Hetaira **Liz Mikel**; Lysistrata Jones **Patti Murin**; Cleonice **Kat Nejat**; Mick **Josh Segarra**; Myrrhine **LaQuet Sharnell**; Xander **Jason Tam**; Harold **Teddy Toye**; Cinesias **Alex Wyse**

UNDERSTUDIES Alexander Aguilar (Mick), LaVon Fisher-Wilson (Hetaira), Libby Servais (Lampito, Lysistrata Jones, Myrrhine, Robin), Charlie Sutton ('Uardo, Cinesias, Harold, Xander), Barrett Wilbert Weed (Cleonice, Lampito, Myrrhine, Robin) and Jared Zirilli ('Uardo, Cinesias, Mick, Tyllis)

THE *LYSISTRATA* BAND Brad Simmons (Conductor/Keyboard 1), Chris Haberl (Associate Conductor/Keyboard 2), Freddy Hall (Guitar), Alan Stevens Hewitt (Bass), Marques Walls (Drums), Wilson Torres (Percussion), Biti Strauchn (Vocalist/Percussion), Randy Cohen (Keyboard and Electronic Drum Programmer)

MUSICAL NUMBERS Picture Show; This World Will Remember Us; You're Goin' Back to Jail; How 'Bout a Dance; When I Drive; God's Arms Are Always Open; You Can Do Better Than Him; You Love Who You Love; Raise a Little Hell; This World Will Remember Us (reprise); Made in America; Too Late to Turn Back Now; That's What You Call a Dream; What Was Good Enough for You; Bonnie; Raise a Little Hell (reprise); Dyin' Ain't So Bad; God's Arms Are Always Open (reprise); Picture Show (reprise); Dyin' Ain't So Bad (reprise)

Broadway premiere of a new musical presented in two acts. Developed and first presented in New York at The Gym at Judson. Originally produced by Dallas Theatre Center (Kevin Moriarty, Artistic Director; Heather M. Kitchen, Executive Director) under the title *Give It Up!* January 15–February 14, 2010 (see *Theatre World* Vol. 66, page 358). New York premiere produced by Transport Group (Jack Cummings III, Artistic Director; Lori Fineman, Executive Director) May 15–June 24, 2011 (see page 124 in this volume).

SYNOPSIS The Athens University basketball team hasn't won a game in 30 years. But when spunky transfer student Lysistrata Jones dares the squad's fed-up girlfriends to stop 'giving it up' to their boyfriends until they win a game, their legendary losing streak could be coming to an end. In this boisterous new musical comedy, Lyssie J. and her girl-power posse give Aristophanes' classic comedy a sexy, modern twist and take student activism to a whole new level.

Liz Mikel and the Company

Josh Segarra and Patti Murin

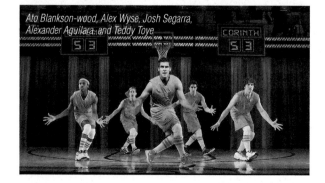

Ato Blankson-wood, Alex Wyse, Josh Segarra, Alexander Aguilara, and Teddy Toye

Lindsa Nicole Chambers, LaQuet Sharnell, Patti Murin, Katie Boren, and Kat Nejat

Kat Nejat, Lindsay Nicole Chambers, Patti Murin, LaQuet Sharnell, and Katie Boren

The Company

Patti Murin and Jason Tam

Josh Segarra (photos by Joan Marcus)

Audra McDonald and Phillip Boykin

Joshua Henry and Nikki Renée Daniels

Norm Lewis and the Company

The Gershwins' **Porgy and Bess**

Richard Rodgers Theatre; First Preview: December 17, 2011; Opening Night: January 12, 2012; 28 previews, 161 performances as of May 31, 2012

Music and lyrics by George Gershwin, DuBose and Dorothy Heyward, and Ira Gershwin; Adapted by Suzan-Lori Parks and Diedre L. Murray; Produced by Jeffrey Richards, Jerry Frankel, Rebecca Gold, Howard Kagan, Cheryl Wiesenfeld/Brunish Trinchero/Meredith Lucio-The Broadway Consortium, Joseph & Matthew Deitch, Mark S. Golub & David S. Golub, Terry Schnuck, Freitag Productions/Heni Koenigsberg-Michael Filerman, The Leonore S. Gershwin 1987 Trust, Universal Pictures Stage Productions, Ken Mahoney, Judith Resnick, Norman Tulchin/Robert G. Bartner/ATG, Paper Boy Productions (Wil Dombrowski, Bruston Kade Manuel), Christopher Hart, Michael A. Alden-Dale Badway, Broadway Across America (John Gore, CEO; Thomas McGrath, Chairman), Irene Gandy, Will Trice, American Repertory Theater; Director, Diane Paulus; Choreography, Ronald K. Brown; Orchestrations, William David Brohn and Christopher Jahnke; Sets, Riccardo Hernandez; Costumes, ESosa; Lighting, Christopher Akerlined; Sound, Acme Sound Partners; Wigs/Hair/Makeup, J. Jared Janas and Rob Greene; Music Supervisor, David Loud; Music Director and Conductor, Constantine Kitsopoulos; Music Coordinator, John Miller; Casting, Tesley + Company; Associate Director/Production Stage Manager, Nancy Harrington; Technical Supervision, Hudson Theatrical Associates, Neil A. Mazella, Sam Ellis, Irene Wang, Walter Murphy, Corky Boyd; Company Manager, Bruce Klinger; General Management, Richards/Climan Inc. (David R. Richards, Tamar Haimes, Michael Sag, Kyle Bonder, Jessica Fried, Jacqueline Kolek); Associate Producers, Ronald Frankel, James Fuld Jr., Allan S. Gordon, INFINITY Stages, Shorenstein Hays-Nederlander Theatres LLC, David & Barbara Stoller, Michael & Jean Strunsky, Theresa Wozunk; Stage Manager, Julie Baldauff; Assistant Stage Manager, Sharika Niles; Assistant Company Manager, Caitlin Fahey; Assistant Director, Mia Walker; Assistant Choreographer, Arcell Cabuag; Dance Captain/Fight Captain, Lisa Nicole Wilkerson; Assistant Producer, Michael Crea, Dialect Coach, Denise Woods; Fight Director, J. Steven White; Music Preparation, Larry Abel, Music Preparation International; Assistant to the Orchestrators/Music Assistant, Neil Douglas Reilly; Assistant to Mr. Miller, Nichole Jennino; Music Assistant, Nehemiah Luckett; Associate Design: Maruti Evans (set), Cathy Parrott (costumes), Caroline Chao (lighting), Jason Crystal (sound); Assistant to Mr. Akerlind, Seth Reiser; Lighting Programmer, Warren Flynn; Video Programmers, C. Andrew Bauer, Daniel Brodie; Production Assistant, Christopher Windom; Crew: Francis Rapp (production carpenter), Tim Rossi (head carpenter), Ronald Knox (flyman), Jimmy Maloney (production electrician), William Walters, John Carton, Brian Frankel (followspot operators), Worth Strecker (production properties supervisor), Justin Rathbun (sound engineer), James Wilkinson (deck audio), Darin Stillman (advance sound), Jesse Galvan (wardrobe supervisor), Vangeli Kaseluris, Kurt Keilmann, Angela Lehrer, Ylena Nunez, Kate Sorg (dressers), Thomas Augustine (hair supervisor), Brendan O'Neal (hair dresser); Assistant to Ms. Murray, Randal Eng; Advertising, Serino/Coyne, Greg Corradetti, Tom Callahan, Danielle Boyle, Peter Gunther, Drew Nebrig; Website/Online Marketing, SpotCo, Michael Crowley, Meghan Ownbey; Interactive Marketing, Broadway's Best Shows, Andy Drachenberg, Christopher Pineda; Press, Jeffrey Richards Assoicates, Irene Gandy, Alana Karpoff, Ryan Hallett, Elon Rutberg; Cast recording: PS Classics 1206

CAST Clara **Nikki Renée Daniels**; Jake **Joshua Henry**; Mariah **NaTasha Yvette Williams**; Sporting Life **David Alan Grier**; Mingo, the Undertaker **J.D. Webster**; Serena **Bryonha Marie Parham**; Robbins **Nathaniel Stampley**; Porgy **Norm Lewis**; Crown **Phillip Boykin**; Bess **Audra McDonald**; Detective **Christopher Innvar**; Policeman **Joseph Dellger**; The Strawberry Woman **Andrea Jones-Sojola**; Peter, the Honey Man **Phumzile Sojola**; The Crab Man **Cedric Neal**; Fisherman **Roosevelt André Credit**, **Trevon Davis**, **Wilkie Ferguson III**; Women of Catfish Row **Allison Blackwell**, **Heather Hill**, **Alicia Hall Moran**, **Lisa Nicole Wilkerson**; Swings **Carmen Ruby Floyd**, **David Hughey**, **Julius Thomas III**

UNDERSTUDIES Sumayya Ali (Bess, Clara, Serena, Strawberry Woman), Allison Blackwell (Mariah), Trevon Davis (Jake), Joseph Dellger, Wilkie Ferguson III (Robbins, The Crab Man), Carmen Ruby Floyd (Mariah), Gavin Gregory (Crown, Sporting Life), Heather Hill (Strawberry Woman), David Hughey (A Fisherman, Jake, Robbins, Sporting Life), Andrea Jones-Sojola (Clara, Serena), Alicia Hall Moran (Bess), Phumzile Sojola (Robbins), Nathaniel Stampley (Crown, Porgy), Julius Thomas III (A Fisherman, Mingo, Peter, The Crab Man)

ORCHESTRA Constantine Kitsopoulos (Conductor); Paul Masse (Associate Conductor/Piano/Celeste); Belinda Whitney (Concert Master); Katherine Fink, Lynne Cohen, Steve Kenyon, Jonathan Levine, Jill M. Collura (Woodwinds); Nick Marchione, Dan Urness (Trumpets); Keith O'Quinn (Trombone); Jennifer Wharton (Bass Trombone/Tuba); R.J. Kelley, Eric Davis (French Horns); Orlando Wells, Karl Kawahara, Philip Payton (Violins); Crystal Garner, Liuh-Wen Ting (Violas); Sarah J. Seiver, Summer Boggess (Cellos); Bill Ellison (Bass); Charles Descarfino (Drums/Percussion)

MUSICAL NUMBERS Overture; Summertime; A Woman Is a Sometime Thing; Crap Game; Gone, Gone, Gone; My Man's Gone Now; Leaving for the Promised Land; It Takes a Long Pull; I Got Plenty of Nothing; I Hates Your Strutting Style; Bess, You Is My Woman Now; Oh I Can't Sit Down; Entr'acte; It Ain't Necessarily So; What You Want With Bess?; Oh, Doctor Jesus; Street Cries; I Loves You, Porgy; Oh, The Lord Shake the Heaven; A Red Headed Woman; Clara, Don't You Be Downhearted; There's a Boat That's Leaving Soon; Where's My Bess?; I'm On My Way

2011-2012 AWARDS Tony Awards: Best Revival of a Musical, Best Performance by an Actress in a Leading Role in a Musical (Audra McDonald); Drama Desk Awards: Outstanding Actress in a Musical (Audra McDonald), Outstanding Sound Design of a Musical (Acme Sound Partners); Outer Critics Circle Award: Outstanding Actress in a Musical (Audra McDonald); Drama League Awards: Distinguished Performance (Audra McDonald), Founders Award for Excellence in Direction (Diane Paulus); Fred and Adele Astaire Awards: Excellence in Choreography on Broadway (Ronald K. Brown), Best Female Dancer on Broadway (Lisa Nicole Wilkerson); **Theatre World Award:** Phillip Boykin

SETTING Time: Late 1930s. Place: Catfish Row and Kittawah Island in Charleston, South Carolina. Revival of a musical/opera presented in two acts. Originally premiered at the Alvin Theatre October 10, 1935–January 25, 1936. This production marked the seventh major New York revival. This production was first presented at the American Repertory Theatre (Diane Paulus, Artistic Director; Diane Borger, Producer), August 17, 2011 (see page 350 in this volume).

SYNOPSIS The Gershwins' classic musical *Porgy and Bess* is set in Charleston's fabled Catfish Row, where the beautiful Bess struggles to break free from her scandalous past, and the only one who can rescue her is the crippled but courageous Porgy. Threatened by her formidable former lover Crown, and the seductive enticements of the colorful troublemaker Sporting Life, Porgy and Bess' relationship evolves into a deep romance that triumphs as one of theater's most exhilarating love stories.

David Alan Grier and the Company

Wilkie Ferguson, Joshua Henry, Trevon Davis, and Roosevelt André

Audra McDonald and Norm Lewis (photos by Michael Lutch)

NaTasha Yvette Williams, David Alan Grier, and the Company

The Road to Mecca

American Airlines Theatre; First Preview: December 16, 2011; Opening Night: January 17, 2012; Closed March 4, 2012; 34 previews, 56 performances

Written by Athol Fugard; Produced by the Roundabout Theatre Company (Todd Haimes, Artistic Director; Harold Wolpert, Managing Director; Julia C. Levy, Executive Director) by special arrangement with Signature Theatre Company; Director, Gordon Edelstein; Sets, Michael Yeargan; Costumes, Susan Hilferty; Lighting, Peter Kaczorowski; Original Music and Sound, John Gromada; Hair and Wigs, Paul Huntley; Production Stage Manager, Roy Harris; Production Management, Aurora Productions; Casting, Jim Carnahan and Stephen Kopel; General Manager, Denise Cooper; Stage Manager, Denise Yaney; Company Manager, Carly DiFulvio; Assistant Director, Alexander Greenfield; Associate Design: Lauren Rockman (set), Marina Reti (costumes); Assistant Design: Mikiko Suzuki MacAdams (set), Peter Hoerburger (lighting), Keri Thibodeau (lighting), Matthew Walsh (sound); Assistants to Mr. Yeargan, Jinsun Kim, Chien-Yu Peng, A. Ram Kim; Production Props Supervisor, Peter Sarafin; Prop Shoppers, Matt Hodges, Buist Bickley; Crew: Glen Merwede (production carpenter), Brian Maiuri (production electrician), Robert W. Dowling II (running properties), Dann Wojnar (sound operator), Susan J. Fallon (wardrobe supervisor), Kat Martin (dresser), Dale Carman (wardrobe dayworker), Manuela Laporte (hair and wig supervisor), Trisha Henson (production assistant); For Aurora Productions: Gene O' Donovan, Ben Heller, Stephanie Sherline, Jarid Sumner, Anthony Jusino, Anita Shah, Liza Luxenberg, Steven Dalton, Eugenio Saenz Flores, Isaac Katzanek, Melissa Mazdra; Roundabout Staff: Sydney Beers (General Manager), Greg Backstrom (Associate Managing Director); David B. Steffen (Director of Marketing and Sales Promotion); Lynne Gugenheim Gregory (Director of Development); Gene Feist (Founding Director), Scott Ellis (Adams Associate Artistic Director); Greg McCaslin (Education Director), Sydney Beers (General Manager), Susan Neiman (Director of Finance), Wendy Hutton (Director of Audience Services), Charlie Gabowski Jr. (Director of Sales Operations); Advertising, SpotCo; Interactive Marketing, Situation Interactive; Press, Boneau/Bryan-Brown, Adrian Bryan-Brown, Matt Polk, Jessica Johnson, Amy Kass

CAST Miss Helen **Rosemary Harris**; Elsa Barlow **Carla Gugino**; Marius Byleveld **Jim Dale**

UNDERSTUDIES Martin LaPlatney (Marius LePlatney), Gordana Rashovich (Miss Helen), Karen Walsh (Elsa Barlow)

SETTING A small Karoo village of New Bethesda, South Africa; autumn 1974. Broadway premiere of a play presented in two acts. World premiere at the Yale Repertory in 1984. Off-Broadway premiere at the Promenade Theatre March 29–September 11, 1988, playing 172 performances (see *Theatre World* Vol. 44, page 67).

SYNOPSIS *The Road to Mecca* tells the story of an elderly woman who has spent the years since her husband's death transforming her home into an intricate and dazzling work of art. The reclusive Miss Helen has become depressed and appears increasingly unable to care for herself. Pastor Marius Byleveld, who embodies the village's conservative values, is determined to get Miss Helen into an old-age home. Her friend Elsa, a young teacher from Cape Town who is deeply suspicious of the patriarchal traditions Byleveld represents, is just as determined that Miss Helen remain free.

Jim Dale and Rosemary Harris

Rosemary Harris and Carla Gugino

Rosemary Harris and Carla Gugino (photos by Joan Marcus)

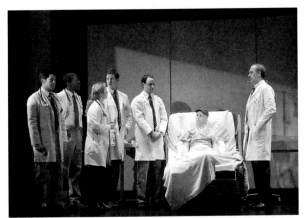

Pun Bandhu, Chiké Johnson, Jessica Dickey, Zachary Spicer, Greg Keller, Cynthia Nixon, and Michael Countryman

Cynthia Nixon and Carra Patterson

Cynthia Nixon and Suzanne Bertish (photos by Joan Marcus)

Wit

Samuel J. Friedman Theatre; First Preview: January 5, 2011; Opening Night: January 26, 2012; Closed March 17, 2012; 24 previews, 61 performances

Written by Margaret Edson; Produced by Manhattan Theatre Club (Lynne Meadow, Artistic Director; Barry Grove, Executive Producer); Director, Lynne Meadow; Sets, Santo Loquasto; Costumes, Jennifer von Mayrhauser; Lighting, Peter Kaczorowski; Sound, Jill BC DuBoff; Specialty Staging Consultant, J. David Brimmer; Production Stage Manager, Barclay Stiff; Projections, Rocco DeSanti; Wigs, Paul Huntley; Makeup, Angelina Avallone; Stage Manager, Kelly Beaulieu; Company Manager, Erin Moeller; Mary Mill Directing Fellow, Kel Haney; Assistant Design: Antje Ellerman (set), Leslie Bernstein (costumes), Gina Scherr (lighting), Janie Bullard (sound); Costume Intern, Heather Carey; Crew: Marc Polimeni (lighting programmer), Sean Kane (spotlight operator), Vaughn Preston (automation operator), Natasha Steinhagen (hair/makeup supervisor), Aaron Elgart, McKenzie Murphy (production assistants); Specialty Staging Assistants, Dan O'Driscoll, Turner Smith, Rin Allen, Mitchell McCoy; For MTC: General Manager, Florie Seery; Artistic Producer, Mandy Greenfield; Director of Artistic Development, Jerry Patch; Marketing, Debra Waxman-Pilla; Production Manager, Joshua Helman; Director of Casting, Nancy Piccione; Artistic Line Producer, Lisa McNulty; Development, Lynne Randall; Artistic Consultant, Daniel Sullivan; Artistic Operations, Amy Gilkes Loe; Finance, Jessica Adler; Human Resources, Darren Robertson; Associate General Manager, Lindsey Brooks Sag; Subscriber Services, Robert Allenberg; Telesales, George Tetlow; Education, David Shookhoff; Associate Production Manager, Bethany Weinstein; Assistant Production Manager, Kevin Service; Prop Supervisor, Scott Laule; Assistant Properties Supervisor, Julia Sandy; Props Carpenter, Peter Grimes; Costume Supervisor, Erin Hennessy Dean; Associate Production Manager, Bethany Weinstein; Assistant Production Manager, Kevin Service; Assistant Properties Supervisor, Julia Sandy; Props Carpenter, Peter Grimes; Advertising, SpotCo; Press, Boneau/Bryan-Brown, Chris Boneau, Aaron Meier, Christine Olver, Emily Meagher

CAST Vivian Bearing, Ph.D. **Cynthia Nixon**; Harvey Kelekian, M.D./Mr. Bearing **Michael Countryman**; E.M. Ashford, D. Phil **Suzanne Bertish**; Susie Monahan, R.N., B.S.N. **Carra Patterson**; Lab Technicians/Sudents/Fellows **Pun Bandhu**, **Jessica Dickey**, **Chiké Johnson**, **Zachary Spicer**; Jason Posner, M.D. **Greg Keller**

UNDERSTUDIES Jessica Dickey (Susie Monahan), Elizabeth Norment (Vivian Bearing, E.M. Ashford), Irene Sofia Lucio (Lab Technicians/Students/Fellows), Stephen Schnetzer (Harvey Kelekian/Mr. Bearing), Zachary Spicer (Jason Posner)

SETTING Time: 1995. Place: A university hospital. Broadway premiere of an Off-Broadway play presented without intermission. Originally produced at South Coast Repertory (David Emmes, Producing Artistic Director; Martin Benson, Artistic Director) January 24, 1995. The original New York production starring Kathleen Chalfant was first presented at Long Wharf Theatre in New Haven, Connecticut (Doug Hughes, Artistic Director; Michael Ross, Managing Director) in November 1997, and then presented by MCC Theater (Bernard Telsey and Robert LuPone, Artistic Directors) September 9–December 13, 1998, playing 93 performances. The show transferred to Union Square Theatre December 18, 1998–April 9, 2000, playing 522 performances (see *Theatre World* Vol. 55, page 106).

SYNOPSIS *Wit* follows a brilliant and exacting poetry professor as she undergoes experimental treatment for cancer. A scholar who devoted her life to academia, she must now face the irony and injustice of becoming the subject of research.

Shatner's World: We Just Live In It...

Music Box Theatre; First Preview: February 14, 2012; Opening Night: February 16, 2012; Closed March 4, 2012; 2 previews, 17 performances

Written by William Shatner; Produced by Innovation Arts and Entertainment, Larry A. Thompson Organization, Adam Troy Epstein, Seth Keyes, Josh Sherman, Larry A. Thompson; Director, Scott Faris; Sets, Edward Pierce; Lighting, Ken Billington; Sound, Peter Fitzgerald; Technical Supervisor, Aurora Productions (Gene O'Donovan, Ben Heller, Stephanie Sherline, Jarid Sumner, Liza Luxenberg, Anita Shah, Anthony Jusino, Steven Dalton, Eugenio Saenz Flores, Isaac Katzanek, Aneta Feld, Melissa Mazdra; General Management, Bespoke Theatricals (Devin Keudell, Amy Jacobs, Maggie Brohn, Nina Lannan); Production Stage Manager, Paul J. Smith; Company Manager, Heidi Nevin; Production Assistants, Aaron Elgert, Alison Harma; Associate Lighting, Anthony Pearson; Production Electrician, Neil McShane; Assistant to Mr. Shatner, Kathleen Hays; Assistant to Mr. Thompson, Robert J. Endara II; For Innovation Arts and Entertainment: Adam Epstein (CEO), Seth Keyes (VP/Director of Programming), Todd Rossi and Julie Chepy (Co-Vice Presidents/Event Marketing & Venue Logistics), Jaymes Kaiser and Nancy Rebek(Tour Directors/Marketing & Event Logistics), Jason Merder (Director of Production), Linsey Proper (Director of Accounting), Gina Knapik (Director of Design and Creative Production), Christy Warren (Director of Patron Communication and Ticketing), Emily Dehm and Melissa Buckley (Project Managers), Kate Terwilliger (Junior Designer), Josh Sherman (Innovation Touring Group President); General Management Associates, Steve Dow, Libby Fox, David Roth, Danielle Saks; Advertising, SpotCo (Drew Hodges, Jim Edwards, Tom Greenwald, Stacey Maya); Press, Boneau/Bryan-Brown, Adrian Bryan-Brown, Jackie Green, Michael Strassheim

CAST William Shatner

World premiere of a solo performance piece performed with one intermission. The production embarked on a national tour following its Broadway engagement.

SYNOPSIS William Shatner take audiences on a voyage through his life and career, from Shakespearean stage actor to internationally known icon and raconteur, known as much for his unique persona as for his expansive body of work on television and film.

William Shatner (photos by Joan Marcus)

Arthur Miller's **Death of a Salesman**

Ethel Barrymore Theatre; First Preview: February 14, 2012; Opening Night: March 15, 2012; 30 previews, 75 performances as of May 31, 2012

Written by Arthur Miller; Produced by Scott Rudin, Stuart Thompson, Jon B. Platt, Columbia Pictures, Jean Doumanian, Merritt Forrest Baer, Roger Berlind, Scott M. Delman, Sonia Friedman Productions, Ruth Hendel, Carl Moellenberg, Scott & Brian Zeilinger, Eli Bush; Director, Mike Nichols; Sets, Jo Mielziner; Costumes, Ann Roth; Lighting, Brian MacDevitt; Sound, Scott Lehrer; Hair and Wigs, David Brian Brown; Makeup, Ivana Primorac; Original Music, Alex North; Music Supervisor, Glen Kelly; Scene Design Preparation, Brian Webb; Casting, MelCap Casting; Fight Director, Thomas Schall; Production Stage Manager, Jill Cordle; Production Management, Aurora Productions; General Manager, Stuart Thompson Productions, Patrick Gracey; Company Manager, Jennifer Hindman Kemp; Assistant Director, Kathy Hendrickson; Vocal Coach, Grace Zandarski; Associate Design: Matthew Pachtman (costumes), Jennifer Schriever (lighting), Will Pickens (sound); Assistant to the Lighting Designer, Coby Chasman-Beck; Crew: Dan Coey (production electrician), Jen Dunlap (production props), Michael Hill (moving lights programmer), Jason Clark (head carpenter), Andrew Meeker (head properties), Mike Hyman (head electrician), David Stollings (sound engineer), Kay Grunder (wardrobe supervisor), Mitchell Beck (hair supervisor), Kimberly Prentice, Kelly Saxon, Claire Verlaet (dressers), Ariel C. Osborne, Amy Steinman (production assistants); For Stuart Thompson Productions: David Turner, Kevin Emrick, Christopher Taggart, Andrew Lowy, Brittany Weber, James Yandoli; For Scott Rudin: Steven Cardwell, Donald Devcich, Jessica Held, Adam Klaff, Kim Lessing, Julie Oh, Nick Reimond, Jason Sack, Dan Sarrow; For Aurora Productions: Gene O'Donovan, Ben Heller, Stephanie Sherline, Jarid Sumner, Liza Luxenberg, Anita Shah, Anthony Jusino, Steven Dalton, Eugenio Saenz Flores, Isaac Katzanek, Aneta Feld, Melissa Mazdra; Advertising, Serino/Coyne; Press, Boneau/Bryan-Brown, Chris Boneau, Jim Byk, Kelly Guiod

CAST Willy Loman **Philip Seymour Hoffman**; Linda Loman **Linda Emond**; Biff Loman **Andrew Garfield**; Happy Loman **Finn Wittrock**; Bernard **Fran Kranz**; The Woman **Molly Price**; Charley **Bill Camp**; Ben **John Glover**; Howard Wagner **Remy Auberjonois**; Jenny **Kathleen McNenny**; Stanley **Glenn Fleshler**; Miss Forsythe **Stephanie Janssen**; Letta **Elizabeth Morton**; Second Waiter **Brad Koed**

UNDERSTUDIES Kathleen McNenny (Linda Loman), Brad Koed (Biff Loman, Happy Loman, Bernard), Glenn Fleshler (Willy Loman), Julian Gamble (Ben, Charley), Thomas Michael Hammond (Howard Wagner, Stanley, Second Waiter), Meredith Holzman (The Woman, Miss Forsythe, Letta)

MUSICIANS David Loud (Conductor), Katherine Fink (Flute, Alto Flute), Sarah Seiver (Cello), Don Downs (Trumpet, Flugelhorn), Mark Thrasher (Clarinet, Bass Clarinet)

2011-2012 AWARDS Tony Awards: Best Revival of a Play, Best Direction of a Play (Mike Nichols); Drama Desk Awards: Outstanding Revival of a Play, Outstanding Direction of a Play (Mike Nichols), Outstanding Lighting Design (Brian MacDevitt); Outer Critics Circle Award: Outstanding Revival of a Play; Drama League Award: Outstanding Revival of a Play; **Theatre World Award:** Finn Wittrock

SETTING Time: The late 1940s. Place: Willy Loman's house and yard and various places in New York City and Boston. Revival of a play with music presented in two acts. Originally produced at the Morosco Theatre February 10, 1949–November 18, 1950, playing 742 performances (see *Theatre World* Vol. 5). This production marked the fourth major revival on the Broadway. The most recent revival was the Goodman Theatre production which played the Eugene O'Neill Theatre February 10–November 7, 1999, starring Brian Dennehy (see *Theatre World* Vol. 5, page 91).

Andrew Garfield and Finn Wittrock (photos by Brigitte Lacombe)

SYNOPSIS Arthur Miller's Tony Award and Pulitzer Prize-winning masterpiece *Death of a Salesman* returns to Broadway in a new production directed by Mike Nichols with sets based on the designs of original set designer Jo Meilziner. Salesman Willy Loman finds his career crumbling and his relationships with his wife and sons severly tested in Miller's dream-like meditation on the cost of the American dream.

Finn Wittrock, Andrew Garfield, Linda Emond, and Philip Seymour Hoffman

Bill Camp, Linda Emond, Finn Witrock, and Andrew Garfield

Once

Bernard B. Jacobs Theatre; First Preview: February 28, 2012; Opening Night: March 18, 2012; 23 previews, 85 performances as of May 31, 2012

Book by Enda Walsh, music and lyrics by Glen Hansard and Markéta Irglová; Based on the motion picture written and directed by John Carney; Produced by Barbara Broccoli, John N. Hart Jr., Patrick Milling Smith, Frederick Zollow, Brian Carmody, Michael G. Wilson, Orin Wolf, The Shubert Organization (Philip J. Smith, Chairman; Robert E. Wankel, President), Robert Cole (Executive Producer), in association with New York Theatre Workshop (James C. Nicola, Artistic Director; William Russo, Managing Director); Director, John Tiffany; Movement, Steven Hoggett; Music Supervision and Orchestrations, Martin Lowe; Sets and Costumes, Bob Crowley; Lighting, Natasha Katz; Sound, Clive Goodwin; Dialect Coach, Stephen Gabis; Casting, Jim Carnahan, Stephen Kopel; Production Stage Manager, Bess Marie Glorioso; Production Manager, Aurora Productions; Vocal Supervisor, Liz Caplan Vocal Studios; Music Coordinator, John Miller; Company Manager, Lisa M. Poyer; Associate Company Manager, Susan Keappock; Stage Manager, Ana M. Garcia; Assistant Stage Manager, Katherine Shea; Associate Producers, Charles Stone, Ben Limberg; Movement Associate, Yasmine Lee; Associate Music Supervisor, Rob Preuss; Music Captain, David Abeles; Dance Captain, J. Michael Zygo; Czech Diction and Translation, Suzanna Halsey; Assistant Design: Frank McCullough (set), Peter Hoerburger, Yael Lubetzky (lighting), Brian Walters (sound); Crew: Rebecca O'Neill (production carpenter), Michael Pitzer (production electrician), Reg Vessey (production props), Philip Lojo/Paul Delcioppo (production sound engineer), Eric Norris (head electrician), Dan Hochstine (sound engineer), Reid Hall (instrument technician), Matt Hodges (props supervisor), Lisa Buckley (U.K. props), Sean Beach (lighting programmer), Jason Choquette (advance production sound), Jeffery Wallach (NYTW costume liaison), Kathleen Gallagher (wardrobe supervisor), Cailin Anderson, Katie Chihaby (dressers); Child Guardian, Lisa Schwartz; Tutor, On Location Education, Muriel Kester; Production Assistants, Brandon Bart, Amanda Hutt, Eric Love, Ryan McCurdy, Danese C. Smalls; Assistant to Mr. Hart, Maximillian Traber, Assistant to Mr. Smith, Catherine Waage, Assistant to Mr. Cole and Mr. Zollo, Timothy Flateman; For Aurora Productions: Gene O'Donovan, Ben Heller, Stephanie Sherline, Jarid Sumner, Liza Luxenberg, Anita Shah, Anthony Jusino, Steven Dalton, Eugenio Saenz Flores, Isaac Katzanek, Aneta Feld, Melissa Mazdra; Advertising/Website and Online Marketing/Marketing and Promotions, SpotCo (Drew Hodges, Jim Edwards, Tom Greenwald, Tom McCann, Laura Ellis, Sara Fitzpatrick, Marc Mettler, Michael Crowley, Meghan Ownbey, Nick Pramik, Kristen Rathbun, Julie Wechsler, Caroline Newhouse); Press, Boneau/Bryan-Brown, Adrian Bryan-Brown, Matt Polk, Christine Olver; Cast recording: Masterworks Broadway 88691948242

CAST-MUSICIANS Eamon (*Guitar, Piano, Melodica, Harmonica*) **David Abeles**; Andrej (*Electric Bass, Ukulele, Tambourine, Cajon, Guitar*) **Will Connolly**; Réza (*Violin*) **Elizabeth A. Davis**; Guy (*Guitar*) **Steve Kazee**; Da (*Mandolin*) **David Patrick Kelly**; Girl (*Piano*) **Cristin Milioti**; Baruška (*Piano, Accordion, Tambourine, Melodica*) **Anne L. Nathan**; Švec (*Banjo, Guitar, Mandolin, Drum Set*) **Lucas Papaelias**; Ivanka **Ripley Sobo** or **Mckayla Twiggs**; Bank Manager (*Violin, Accordion, Cello, Guitar, Mandolin*) **Andy Taylor**; Ex-Girlfriend (*Violin*) **Erikka Walsh**; Billy (*Guitar, Ukulele, Cajon, Snare Drum*) **Paul Whitty**; Emcee (*Guitar*) **J. Michael Zygo**

UNDERSTUDIES Joanne Borts (Baruška), Samuel Cohen (Da, Eamon, Emcee), Brandon Ellis (Andrej, Bank Manager, Billy, Eamon, Švec), Andrea Goss (Ex-Girlfriend, Girl, Réza), Ben Hope (Andrej, Emcee, Guy, Švec), Erikka Walsh (Girl, Réza), J. Michael Zygo (Billy, Guy)

MUSICAL NUMBERS Leave; Falling Slowly; North Strand; The Moon; Ej, Pada, Pada, Rosicka; If You Want Me; Broken Hearted Hoover Fixer Sucker Guy; Say It to Me Now; Abandoned in Bandon; Gold; Sleeping; When Your Mind's Made Up; The Hill; Gold (A capella); The Moon (reprise); Falling Slowly (reprise)

2011-2012 AWARDS Tony Awards: Best Musical, Best Book of a Musical (Enda Walsh), Best Direction of a Musical (John Tiffany), Best Performance by a Leading Actor in a Musical (Steve Kazee), Best Orchestrations (Martin Lowe), Best Scenic Design of a Musical (Bob Crowley), Best Lighting Design of a Musical (Natasha Katz), Best Sound Design of a Musical (Clive Goodwin); Drama Desk Awards: Outstanding Musical, Outstanding Lyrics (Glen Hansard and Markéta Irglová), Outstanding Director of a Musical (John Tiffany); Outer Critics Circle Awards: Outstanding New Broadway Musical, Outstanding Director of a Musical (John Tiffany), Outstanding Book of a Musical (Enda Walsh); New York Drama Critics Circle Award: Best Musical; Drama League Award: Distinguished Production of a Musical; Lucille Lortel Awards (for its Off-Broadway run): Outstanding Musical, Outstanding Choreographey (Steven Hogget), and Outstanding Lighting Design (Natasha Katz)

Transfer of the new Off-Broadway musical presented in two acts. Originally developed at the American Repertory Theatre in Cambridge, Massachusettes (Diane Paulus, Artistic Director; Diane Borger, Producer) April 2011. The Off-Broadway premiere was presented at the New York Theatre Workshop November 15, 2011–January 15, 2012 (see page 236 in this volume).

SYNOPSIS Based on the 2007 Academy Award-winning film, *Once* tells the story an Irish musician and a Czech immigrant drawn together by their shared love of music. Over the course of one fateful week, their unexpected friendship and collaboration evolves into a powerful but complicated romance, heightened by the raw emotion of the songs they create together. Brought to the stage by an award-winning team of visionary artists and featuring an ensemble cast of gifted actor/musicians, *Once* is a musical celebration of life and love: thrilling in its originality, daring in its honesty... and unforgettable in every way.

Cristin Milioti and Steve Kazee

Paul Whitty and Elizabeth A. Davis

Steve Kazee and Cristin Milioti

Anne L. Nathan, Will Connolly, Cristin Milioti, Elizabeth A. Davis,
and Lucas Papaelias

Steve Kazee, Anne L. Nathan (background), and Cristin Milioti

Steve Kazee and the Company (photos by Joan Marcus)

Elizabeth A. Davis and Cristin Milioti

The Company

Mark Cassius, Marcus Nance, Jeremy Kushnier, Josh Young, Sandy Winsby, and Aaron Walpole

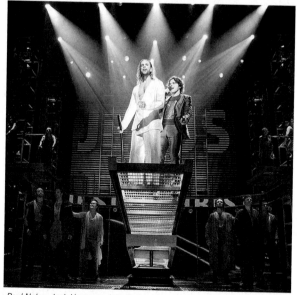

Paul Nolan, Josh Young, and the Company

Jesus Christ Superstar

Neil Simon Theatre; First Preview: March 1, 2012; Opening Night: March 22, 2012; 24 previews, 79 performances as of May 31, 2012

Lyrics by Tim Rice, music by Andrew Lloyd Webber; Produced by The Dodgers and The Really Useful Group, Latitude Link, Tamara and Kevin Kinsella, Pelican Group, Waxman-Dokton, Joe Cocoran, Detsky/Sokolowski/Kassie, Florin-Blanshay-Fan/Broadway Across America, Rich/Caudwell, Shin/Coleman, TheatreDreams North America LLC; Presented by the Stratford Shakespeare Festival; Director, Des McAnuff; Choreography, Lisa Shriver; Music Direction and Supervision, Rich Fox; Sets, Robert Brill; Costumes, Paul Tazewell; Lighting, Howell Binkley; Sound, Steve Canyon Kennedy; Video, Sean Nieuwenhuis; Fight Director, Daniel Levinson; Stunt Coordinator, Simon Fon; Music Coordinator, John Miller; Production Stage Manager, Frank Hartenstein; Company Manager, Kimberly Kelley; Technical Supervisor, Hudson Theatrical Associates, Neil A. Mazella, Sam Ellis, Irene Wang; New York Casting, Tara Rubin Casting; Stratford Casting, Beth Russell; Associate Producers, Lauren Mitchell, Nederlander Presentations Inc.; Executive Producer, Sally Campbell Morse; General Management, Dodger Management Group; Stage Manager, Brian Scott; Assistant Stage Manager, Kelly A. Martindale; Assistant Company Manager, Michael Altbaum; Associate Technical Supervisor, John Tiggeloven; Technical Production Assistant, Caitlin McInerney; Assistant Director, Lezlie Wade; Associate Choreographer, Bradley "Shooz" Rapier; Assistant Choreographer, Marc Kimelman; Dance Captain, Matthew Rossoff; Assistant Dance Captain, Krista Leis; Fight Captain, Julius Sermonia; Associate Design: Steven Kemp (set), Katie Irish (costumes), Ryan O'Gara (lighting), Walter Trarbach, Andrew Keister (sound); Assistant Design: Brandon Kleiman, Angrette McCloskey, Dustin O'Neill (set), Angela Kahler (costumes), Amanda Zieve (lighting), Jana Hoglund (sound), Davida Tkach (video); Costume Shopper, Dana Burkart; Casting Associates, Dale Brown, Merri Sugarman, Eric Woodall, Stephanie Yankwitt, Kaitlin Shaw, Lindsay Levine; Crew: Edward Diaz (production carpenter), Ben Horrigan (automation flyman), Jae Day (advance electrician), Keith Buchanan (production electrician), Walter Trarbach (production sound engineer), Julie Randolph (production sound mixer), Matt Walsh (deck soundman), Emiliano Pares (production props), Pete Drummond (head props), Scott Westervelt (production wardrobe supervisor), Angela Simpson (assistant wardrobe supervisor), Meredith Benson, Maria Cecilia Cruz, Hilda Garci-Suli, Hecto Lugo, Polly Noble, Ryan Oslak, Julienne Schubert-Blechman, Roy Seiler (dressers), Gerry Altenburg, Erica Croft-Fraser (production wig supervisors), Heather Wright (hair supervisor), Carrie Rohm (assistant hair supervisor), Tim Miller (hair dresser), Courtney James, Ryan Mekenian (production assistants); For the Dodgers: Michael David (President), Sally Campbell Morse (Executive Producer), Lauren Mitchell (Director of Creative Development), Pamela Lloyd (Director of Business Administration), Jessica Ludwig (Director of Marketing), Paula Maldonado (Director of Finance), Jeff Parvin (Production Manager), Flora Johnstone (Associate General Manager); For Really Useful Group: Andrew Lloyd Webber, Madeleine Lloyd Webber (Directors), Mark Wordsworth (Chairman), Barney Wragg (Managing Director); Promotions, Red Rising Marketing, Michael Redman, Nicole Pando; Advertising, Serino/Coyne, Scott Johnson, Sandy Block, Marci Kaufman, Ryan Cunningham, Sarah Marcus; Web Design, Situation Interactive; Press, Boneau/Bryan-Brown, Adrian Bryan-Brown, Susanne Tighe, Emily Meagher

CAST Jesus Christ **Paul Nolan**; Judas Iscariot **Josh Young**; Mary Magdalene **Chilina Kennedy**; Pontius Pilate **Tom Hewitt**; King Herod **Bruce Dow**; Caiaphas **Marcus Nance**; Annas **Aaron Walpole**; Simon Zealotes **Lee Siegel**; Peter **Mike Nadajewski**; Thaddeus **Matt Alfano**; Matthew, Priest **Mark Cassius**; Bartholomew **Ryan Gifford**; James the Lesser, Priest **Jeremy Kushnier**; Thomas **Jaz Sealey**; John **Jason Sermonia**; James **Julius Sermonia**; Phillip **Jonathan Winsby**; Andrew, Priest **Sandy Winsby**; Jonah/Swing **Nick Cartell**; Elizabeth **Mary Antonini**; Ruth **Karen Burthwright**; Mary (Martha's Sister) **Jacqueline Burtney**; Sarah **Kaylee Harwood**; Martha, Maid by the Fire **Melissa O'Neil**; Rachel **Laurin Padolina**; Esther **Katrina Reynolds**; Swings **Krista Leis, Matthew Rossoff, Matt Stokes**

UNDERSTUDIES Nick Cartell (Annas, Jesus, Judas), Mark Cassius (Annas), Kaylee Harwood (Mary Magdalene), Jeremy Kushnier (Jesus, Judas, Pilate), Mike Nadajewski (Herod), Melissa O'Neil (Mary Magdalene), Matt Stokes (Caiaphas, Herod, Pilate), Jonathan Winsby (Jesus), Sandy Winsby (Caiaphas, Pontius Pilate)

ORCHESTRA Rick Fox (Conductor/Piano/Organ); Matt Gallagher (Associate Conductor/Keyboards); Sonny Paladino (Assistant Conductor/Keyboards); David Mann (Reeds); Dave Trigg, Jeff Wilfore (Trumpets); Nathan Mayland (Trombone/Tuba); Kate Dennis, William DeVos (French Horns); Kevin Ramessar (Guitar 1); Larry Saltzman (Guitar 2); Francisco Centeno (Bass); Clint DeGanon (Drums); Joseph Passaro (Percussion)

MUSICAL NUMBERS Overture; Heaven on Their Minds; What's the Buzz; Strange Thing; Mystifying; Everything's Alright; This Jesus Must Die; Hosanna; Simon Zealotes; Poor Jerusalem; Pilate's Dream; The Temple/Make Us Well; Everything's Alright (reprise); I Don't Know How to Love Him; Damned for All Time/Blood Money; The Last Supper; Gethsemane; The Arrest; Peter's Denial; Pilate and Christ; Herod's Song; Could We Start Again Please?; Judas' Death; Trial by Pilate/39 Lashes; Superstar; Crucifixion; John 19:41

2011-2012 AWARDS Theatre World Award: Josh Young

SETTING Bethany, Jerusalem, Pontius Pilate's palace, the garden of Gethsemane, house of Herod, Golgotha. Revival of a rock opera presented in two acts. Originally a concept recording, the show was officially presented as a concert on July 11, 1971 in Pittsburgh. The original Broadway production opened at the Mark Hellinger Theatre October 12, 1971 and ran until July 1, 1973 playing 711 performances (see *Theatre World* Vol. 28, page 12). The musical was first revived at the Longacre Theatre November 23, 1977–February 12, 1978 playing 96 performances (see *Theatre World* Vol. 34, page 23). A second revival played the Ford Center for the Performing Arts (now the Foxwoods Theatre) April 16–September 3, 2000 playing 161 performances (see *Theatre World* Vol. 56, page 39).

SYNOPSIS Andrew Lloyd Webber and Tim Rice's classic rock opera returns to Broadway in a new production from Canada's Stratford Festival. The rock opera examines the final days of Jesus Christ leading up to his crucifixion as seen through the eyes of his betrayer Judas.

Josh Young

Chilina Kennedy, Paul Nolan, and Josh Young

Bruce Dow and the Company (photos by Joan Marcus)

Paul Nolan, Lee Siegel, and the Company

Newsies The Musical

Nederlander Theatre; First Preview: March 15, 2012; Opening Night: March 29, 2012; 16 previews, 72 performances as of May 31, 2012

Music by Alan Menken, lyrics by Jack Feldman, book by Harvey Fierstein; Based on the 1992 Disney film written by Bob Tzudiker and Noni White; Produced by Disney Theatrical Productions under the direction of Thomas Schumacher; Director, Jeff Calhoun; Choreography, Christopher Gattelli; Music Supervision/Incidental Music/Vocal Arrangements, Michael Kosarin; Orchestrations, Danny Troob; Sets, Tobin Ost; Costumes, Jess Goldstein; Lighting, Jeff Croiter; Sound, Ken Travis; Projections, Sven Ortel; Hair and Wigs, Charles G. LaPointe; Fight Direction, J. Allen Suddeth; Casting, Telsey + Company, Justin Huff; Associate Producer, Anne Quart; Technical Supervision, Neil Mazzella and Geoffrey Quart; Production/Company Manager, Eduardo Castro; Production Stage Manager, Thomas J. Gates; Music Director/Dance Music Arrangements, Mark Hummel; Music Coordinator, John Miller; Associate Director, Richard J. Hinds; Associate Choreographer, Lou Castro; Assistant Company Manager, Emily Powell; Stage Manager, Timothy Eaker; Assistant Stage Manager, Becky Fleming; Production Coordinator, Kerry McGrath; Dance Captain, Ryan Steele; Assistant Dance Captain, Michael Fatica; Fight Captain, Kevin Carolan; Associate Music Director, Steven Malone; Additional Orchestrations, Steve Margoshes, Dave Siegel; Dialect and Vocal Coach, Shane Ann Younts; Music Production Assistant, Brendan Whiting; Music Preparation, Anixter Rice Music Services; Electronic Music Programming, Jeff Marder; Rehearsal Musicians, Paul Davis, Mat Eisenstein; Production Assistants, Bryan Bradford, Patrick Egan, Aaron Elgart, Mark A. Stys, Amanda Tamny; Associate Design: Christine Peters (set), Mike Floyd, China Lee (costumes), Cory Pattak (lighting), Alex Hawthorn (sound); Assistant Design: Jerome Martin, John Raley (set), Wilburn Bonnell (lighting), Lucy Mackinnon (projections), Leah Loukas (hair and wigs); Moving Light Programmer, Victor Seastone; Projection Programmer, Florian Mosleh; Assistant to the Projection Designer, Gabe Rives-Corbett; Assistant Fight Director, Ted Sharon; Technical Supervision, Troika Entertainment; Technical Associates, Irene Wang, Sam Ellis; Technical Production Assistant, Canara Price; Crew: Sam Mahan (advance carpenter), Eddie Bash (head carpenter), Karl Schuberth (automation), Michael Allen (carpenter), James Maloney (production electrician), Brad Robertson (associate production electrician), Emiliano Pares (production properties), Brian Schweppe (head properties), Michael Critchlow (assistant properties), Phil Lojo, Paul DelCioppo (production sound), Cassy Givens (head sound), Gabe Wood (sound assistant), Rick Kelly (wardrobe supervisor), Jenny Barnes, Gary Biangone, Franklin Hollenbeck, Phillip Rolfe, Keith Shaw, Franc Weinperl (dressers), Frederick Waggoner (hair supervisor), Amanda Duffy (hairdresser); Associate to Mr. Menken, Rick Kunis; Assistant to John Miller, Jennifer Coolbaugh; Assistant to Mr. Calhoun, Derek Hersey; Children's Guardian, Vanessa Brown; Children's Tutoring, On Location Education, Nancy Van Ness, Beverly Brennan; Advertising, Serino/Coyne; For Disney Theatricals: David Schrader (EVP and Managing Director), Ron Kollen (SVP International), Fiona Thomas (VP International, Europe), James Thane (VP International, Australia), Dana Amendola (VP Operations), Joe Quenqua (VP Publicity), Jack Eldon (VP Domestic), June Heindel (VP Human Resources), Chris Montan (Executive Music Producer), Steve Fickinger (VP Creative Development), Anne Quart (VP Production), Andrew Flatt (SVP Marketing), Bryan Dockett (VP National Sales), Jonathan Olson (SVP Business and Legal Affairs), Mario Iannetta (VP Finance/Business Development), Steven Downing (VP Theatrical Merchandise); Press, Dennis Crowley, Michelle Bergmann

CAST Jack Kelly **Jeremy Jordan**; Crutchie **Andrew Keenan-Bolger**; Race **Ryan Breslin**; Albert/Bill **Garett Hawe**; Specs **Ryan Steele**; Henry **Kyle Coffman**; Finch **Aaron J. Albano**; Elmer **Evan Kasprzak**; Romeo **Andy Richardson**; Mush **Ephraim Sykes**; Katherine **Kara Lindsay**; Darcy **Thayne Jasperson**; Nuns **Julie Foldesi**, **Carpathia Jenkins**, **Laurie Veldheer**; Morris Delancey **Mike Faist**; Oscar Delancey **Brendon Stimson**; Wiesel/Stage Manager/Mr. Jacobi/Mayor **John E. Brady**; Davey **Ben Fankhauser**; Les **Lewis Grasso** or **Matthew J. Schechter**; Joseph Pulitzer

John Dossett; Seitz **Mark Aldrich**; Bunsen **Nick Sullivan**; Hannah **Laurie Veldheer**; Snyder **Stuart Marland**; Medda Larkin **Carpathia Jenkins**; Scabs **Tommy Bracco**, **Jess LeProtto**, **Alex Wong**; Spot Conlon **Tommy Bracco**; Governor Roosevelt **Kevin Carolan**; Citizens of New York **Aaron J. Albano**, **Mark Aldrich**, **Tommy Bracco**, **John E. Brady**, **Ryan Breslin**, **Kevin Carolan**, **Kyle Coffman**, **Mike Faist**, **Julie Foldesi**, **Garett Hawe**, **Thayne Jasperson**, **Evan Kasprzak**, **Jess LeProtto**, **Stuart Marland**, **Andy Richardson**, **Ryan Steele**, **Brendon Stimson**, **Nick Sullivan**, **Ephraim Sykes**, **Laurie Veldheer**, **Alex Wong**; Swings **Caitlyn Caughell**, **Michael Fatica**, **Jack Scott**, **Stuart Zagnit**

UNDERSTUDIES Mark Aldrich (Governor Roosevelt), John E. Brady (Joseph Pulitzer), Ryan Breslin (Davey), Caitlyn Caughell (Katherine, Medda Larkin), Mike Faist (Jack Kelly), Julie Foldesi (Medda Larkin), Garett Hawe (Crutchie, Davey), Evan Kasprzak (Bunsen, Seitz), Stuart Marland (Joseph Pulitzer), Andy Richardson (Crutchie), Brendon Stimson (Jack Kelly), Nick Sullivan (Mayor, Mr. Jacobi, Snyder, Stage Manager, Wiesel), Laurie Veldheer (Katherine), Stuart Zagnit (Bunsen, Wiesel/Stage Manager/Mr. Jacobi/Mayor, Governor Roosevelt, Seitz, Snyder); Standby for Katherine: Madeline Trumble

ORCHESTRA Mark Hummel (Conductor); Steven Malone (Associate Conductor/Keyboard); Mat Eisenstein (Assistant Conductor/Keyboard); Tom Murray, Mark Thrasher (Woodwinds); Trevor D. Neumann (Trumpet/Flugel); Dan Levine (Trombone); Brian Koonin (Guitar); Ray Kilday (Bass); Paul Davis (Drums); Ed Shea (Percussion); Mary Rowell (Violin); Deborah Assael-Migliore (Cello)

MUSICAL NUMBERS Santa Fe (prologue); Carrying the Banner; The Bottom Line; That's Rich; I Never Planned on You/Don't Come a-Knocking; The World Will Know; The World Will Know (reprise); Watch What Happens; Seize the Day; Santa Fe; King of New York; Watch What Happens (reprise); The Bottom Line (reprise); Brooklyn's Here; Something to Believe In; Seize the Day (reprise); Once and for All; Seize the Day (reprise); Finale

2011-2012 AWARDS Tony Awards: Best Choreography (Christopher Gattelli), Best Original Score Written for the Theatre (Alan Menken and Jack Feldman); Drama Desk Awards: Outstanding Choreography (Christopher Gattelli), Outstanding Music (Alan Menken); Outer Critics Circle Awards: Outstanding New Score Broadway or Off-Broadway (Alan Menken and Jack Feldman), Outstanding Choreographer (Christopher Gattelli)

SETTING Place: Lower Manhattan. Time: Summer, 1899. Broadway premiere of a new musical presented in seventeen scenes in two acts. World premiere at Paper Mill Playhouse in Millburn, New Jersey (Mark S. Hoebee, Producing Artistic Director; Todd Schmidt, Managing Director) September 25–October 16, 2011 (see page 392 in this volume).

SYNOPSIS *Newsies* is the rousing tale of Jack Kelly, a charismatic newsboy and leader of a ragged band of teenaged 'newsies,' who dreams only of a better life far from the hardship of the streets. But when publishing titans Joseph Pulitzer and William Randolph Hearst raise distribution prices at the newsboys' expense, Jack finds a cause to fight for and rallies newsies from across the city to strike for what's right.

The Company

Jeremy Jordan (center) and the Company

The Company

Aaron J. Albano, Jess LeProtto, and the Company

Kara Lindsay and Jeremy Jordan

The Company (photos by Deen Van Meer)

Gore Vidal's **The Best Man**

Gerald Schoenfeld Theatre; First Preview: March 6, 2012; Opening Night: April 1, 2012; 31 previews, 69 performances as of May 31, 2012

Written by Gore Vidal; Produced by Jeffrey Richards, Jerry Frankel, INFINITY Stages, Universal Pictures Stage Productions, Barbara Manocherian/Michael Palitz, Ken Mahoney/The Broadway Consortium, Kathleen K. Johnson, Andy Sandberg, Fifty Church Street Productions, Larry Hirschhorn/Bennu Productions, Patty Baker, Paul Boskind and Martian Entertainment, Wendy Federman, Mark S. Golub & David S. Golub, Cricket Hooper Jiranek, Stewart F. Lane & Bonnie Comley, Carl Moellenberg, Harold Thau, Will Trice; Director, Michael Wilson; Sets, Derek McLane; Costumes, Ann Roth; Lighting, Kenneth Posner; Original Music and Sound, John Gromada; Projections, Peter Nigrini; Hair, Josh Marquette; Casting, Telsey + Company, Will Cantler; Technical Supervision, Hudson Theatrical Productions; Production Stage Manager, Matthew Farrell; Company Manager, Brig Berney; General Manager, Richards/Climan Inc.; Associate Producer, Stephanie Rosenberg; Stage Manager, Kenneth J. McGee; Assistant Director, David Alpert; Assistant Producer, Michael Crea; SDC Observer, Jessica Rose McVay; Makeup, Angelina Avallone; Dialect Coach, Kate Wilson; Associate Design: Aimee B. Dombo (set), Matthew Pachtman (costumes), John Viesta (lighting), Alex Neumann (sound), C. Andrew Bauer (projections); Assistant Design: Erica Hemminger (set), Dan Scully (projections); Assistant to Ms. Roth, Irma Escobar; Projection Programmer, Benjamin Keightley; Sound Intern, Chet Miller; Crew: Robert Griffin (production carpenter), McBrien Dunbar (carpenter/deck automation), James Maloney (production electrician), Brian Maiuri (associate production electrician), Jay Penfield (electrician), Wayne Smith (production sound engineer), Peter Sarafin (production properties coordinator), Buist Bickley (assistant props coordinator), Linda Lee (wardrobe supervisor), Laura Beattie, Kimberly Butler, Maeve Fiona Butler, Andrea Gonzalez, Daniel Paul, Lolly Totero (dressers), Carole Morales (hair/wig supervisor), Linda Rice (assistant hair supervisor), Lori Lundquist, Shelley Miles, Sean Lyons (production assistants); Assistant to Mr. Bagert, Matthew Masten; For Richards/Climan Inc.: David R. Richards, Tamar Haimes, Michael Sag, Kyle Bonder, Jessica Fried, Ashley Rodbro; For Hudson Theatrical Associates: Neil A. Mazzella, Sam Ellis, Irene Wang, Walter Murphy, Corky Boyd, Jillian Oliver; Advertising, Serino/Coyne; Press, Jeffrey Richards Associates, Irene Gandy, Alana Karpoff, Ryan Hallett

CAST *The Party*: Former President Arthur "Artie" Hockstader **James Earl Jones**; Mrs. Sue-Ellen Gamadge, *Chairman of the Women's Division* **Angela Lansbury**; Senator Clyde Carlin **Dakin Matthews**; *The Candidates*: Secretary William Russell **John Larroquette**; Alice Russell, *his wife* **Candice Bergen**; Dick Jensen, *his campaign manager* **Michael McKean**; Catherine, *a campaign aide* **Angelica Page**; Senator Joseph Cantwell **Eric McCormack**; Mabel Cantwell, *his wife* **Kerry Butler**; Don Blades, *his campaign manager* **Corey Brill**; *The Visitors*: Dr. Artinian, *a psychiatrist* **Bill Kux**; Sheldon Marcus **Jefferson Mays**; *The Press*: John Malcolm, *the News commentator* **Sherman Howard**; Howie Annenberg, *a reporter from the Philadelphia Inquirer* **Fred Parker**; Frank Pearson, *a reporter from New York Daily Mirror* **Tony Carlin**; Barbara Brinkley, *a reporter from United Press International* **Donna Hanover**; Mitch Graham, *a reporter from the Washington Post* **James Lecesne**; *The Hotel Staff*: Bellboy **Curtis Billings**; Cleaning Woman **Amy Tribbey**; Security **Tony Carlin**; Additional Press, Hotel Staff, Campaign Workers, and Delegates **Curtis Billings, Tony Carlin, Olja Hrustic, Bill Kux, James Lecesne, Fred Parker, Amy Tribbey**

UNDERSTUDIES Curtis Billings (Frank Pearson, Security, Howie Annenberg, Mitch Graham), Tony Carlin (Senator Joseph Cantwell, News Commentator), Donna Hanover (Alice Russell, Mrs. Sue-Ellen Gamadge), Sherman Howard (Secretary William Russell, Dick Jensen), Olja Hrustic (Assistant to Barbara Brinkley, Cleaning Woman), Bill Kux (Senator Clyde Carlin, Bellboy, Photographer, Campaign Worker, Bell Person, Cameraperson), James Lecesne (Dick Jensen, Sheldon Marcus, Dr. Artinian, Additional Hotel Staff, Reporter), Dakin Matthews (Former President Arthur Hockstader), Angelica Page (Mabel Cantwell, Alice

Russell), Fred Parker (Don Blades, News Commentator), Amy Tribbey (Barbara Brinkley, Mrs. Cantwell, Catherine, Additional Hotel Staff, Reporter, Mabel Cantwell)

2011-2012 AWARDS Drama Desk Award: Outstanding Sound Design in a Play (John Gromada); Outer Critics Circle Award: Outstanding Featured Actor in a Play (James Earl Jones)

SETTING Time: July, 1960. Place: The Presidential Convention, Philadelphia, Pennsylvania. Revival of a play presented in three acts with two intermissions. Originally presented at the Morosco Theatre March 31, 1960–July 8, 1961, playing 520 performances (see *Theatre World* Vol. 16, page 82). The play was previously revived at the Virginia Theatre (now the August Wilson Theatre) September 17–December 30, 2000, playing 121 performances (see *Theatre World* Vol. 57, page 12)

SYNOPSIS A play about power, ambition, political secrets, ruthlessness and the race for the presidency, Gore Vidal's *The Best Man* is set at the national convention where two candidates are vying for their party's nomination during the primary season. It's an inside look at the dirt-digging, double-dealing, triple-crossing chicanery of presidential electioneering and what could be more fun in a presidential campaign season than these theatrical fireworks.

John Larroquette, James Earl Jones, Jefferson Mays, and Michael McKean

Kerry Butler, Eric McCormack, and Angela Lansbury *(photos by Joan Marcus)*

Michael Cumpsty, Tracie Bennett, and Tom Pelphrey

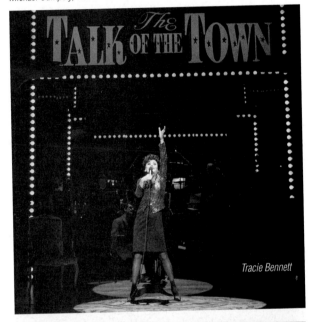
Tracie Bennett

Tracie Bennett and Tom Pelphrey (photos by Carol Rosegg)

End of the Rainbow

Belasco Theatre; First Preview: March 19, 2012; Opening Night: April 2, 2012; 16 previews, 68 performances as of May 31, 2012

Written by Peter Quilter; Produced by Lee Dean, Laurence Meyers, Joey Parnes, Ellis Goodman, Chase Mishkin, Shadowcather Entertainment/Alhadeff Productions, National Angels U.S. Inc., Charles Diamond/Jenny Topper, Myla Lerner/Barbara and Buddy Freitag, Spring Sirkin/Candy Gold, Hilary Williams, S.D. Wagner, John Johnson, in association with the Guthrie Theater (Joe Dowling, Director); Director, Terry Johnson; Sets and Costumes, William Dudley; Lighting, Christopher Akerlind; Sound, Gareth Owen; Orchestrations, Chris Egan; Musical Arrangements, Gareth Valentine; Music Director, Jeffrey Saver; Music Coordinator, Seymour Red Press; Casting, Pat McCorkle; Production Stage Manager, Mark Dobrow; General Management, Joey Parnes Productions, S.D. Wagner, John Johnson, Kim Sellon, Kit Ingui, Nathan V. Koch; U.K. General Manager for Lee Dean, Mardi Metters; Stage Manager, Racel Zack; Assistant Stage Manager, Don Noble; Company Manager, Kim Sellon; Assistant Company Manager, Kit Ingui; Associate Lighting, Caroline Chao; Associate Sound, Joanna Lynne Staub; Assistant Director, Benjamin Shaw; Dialect Coach, Kate Wilson; Crew: Larry Morley (production carpenter), Mike Smanko (production properties), Dan Coey (production electrician), Michael Hill (moving lights programmer), Joanna Lynne Staub (production sound/A1), Liz Coleman (deck sound/A2), Roberto Bevenger Gonzalez (wardrobe supervisor), Julian Andres Arango, Del Miskie (dressers), Jon Jordan (hair supervisor); U.K. Technical Director, Leigh Porter; Music Copyist, Emily Grishman; Production Assistants, Sarah Howell, Bethany Wood; Management Assistant, Chie Morita; Management Intern, Emily DaSilva; Advertising/Marketing/Sales, aka (Elizabeth Furze, Scott A. Moore, Andrew Damer, Pippa Bexon, Bashan Awuart, Mary Littell, Adam Jay, Janette Roush, Shane Marshall Brown, Erin Rech, Jen Taylor); Press, O+M Company, Rick Miramontez, Andy Snyder

CAST Judy Garland **Tracie Bennett**; Anthony **Michael Cumpsty**; Mickey Deans **Tom Pelphrey**; BBC Interviewer/Porter/ASM **Jay Russell**

STANDBYS Sarah Uriarte Berry (Judy Garland), Erik Heger (Mickey Deans), Don Noble (Anthony, BBC Interviewer/Porter/ASM)

MUSICIANS Louis Bruno (Bass), Wayne Goodman (Trombone), Richard Rosensweig (Drums), Edward Salkin (Woodwind), David Stahl (Trumpet)

MUSICAL NUMBERS Overture; Heaven on Their Minds; What's the Buzz; Strange Thing; Mystifying; Everything's Alright; This Jesus Must Die; Hosanna; Simon Zealotes; Poor Jerusalem; Pilate's Dream; The Temple/Make Us Well; Everything's Alright (reprise); I Don't Know How to Love Him; Damned for All Time/Blood Money; The Last Supper; Gethsemane; The Arrest; Peter's Denial; Pilate and Christ; Herod's Song; Could We Start Again Please?; Judas' Death; Trial by Pilate/39 Lashes; Superstar; Crucifixion; John 19:41

2011-2012 AWARDS Drama Desk Award: Outstanding Actress in a Play (Tracie Bennett); Outer Critics Circle Award: Outstanding Actress in a Play (Tracie Bennett); **Theatre World Award:** Tracie Bennett

SETTING The Ritz Hotel, London; December 1968. New York premiere of a new play with music presented in two acts. Originally presented in the U.K. at Royal & Derngate, Northampton (Laurie Sansom, Artistic Director; Martin Sutherland, Executive Director) and subsequently in the West End at Trafalger Studios. American premiere presented by the Guthrie Theater (Joe Dowling, Artistic Director) January 28–March 11, 2012.

SYNOPSIS Judy Garland is about to make her comeback… again. In a London hotel room preparing for a series of concerts, with both her new young fiancé and her adoring accompanist, Garland struggles to get "beyond the rainbow" with her signature cocktail of talent, tenacity, and razor-sharp wit. This savagely funny drama offers unique insight into the inner conflict that inspired and consumed one of the most beloved figures in American popular culture. End of the Rainbow features some of Garland's most memorable songs, performed with the show-stopping gusto for which she will always be remembered.

Evita

Marquis Theatre; First Preview: March 14, 2012; Opening Night: April 5, 2012; 26 previews, 65 performances as of May 31, 2012

Lyrics by Tim Rice, music by Andrew Lloyd Webber; Produced by Hal Luftig, Scott Sanders Productions, Roy Furman, Yasuhiro Kawana, Allan S. Gordon/Adam S. Gordon, James L. Nederlander, Terry Allen Kramer, Gutterman Fuld Chernoff/Pittsburgh CLO, Thousand Stars Productions, Adam Blanshay, Adam Zotovich, Robert Ahrens, Stephanie P. McClelland, Carole L. Haber, Richardo Hornos, Carol Fineman, Brian Smith, Warren & Jâlé Trepp; Licensor, The Really Useful Group; Director, Michael Grandage; Choreography, Rob Ashford; Music Supervisor/Conductor, Kristen Blodgette; Sets and Costumes, Christopher Oram; Lighting, Neil Austin; Sound, Mick Potter; Wigs and Hair, Richard Mawbey; Projections, Zachary Borovay; Casting, Telsey + Company; Technical Supervisor, Christopher C. Smith; Production Stage Manager, Michael J. Passaro; Associate Director, Seth Sklar-Heyn; Associate Choreographer, Chris Bailey; Orchestrations, Andrew Lloyd Webber and David Cullen; Dance Arrangements, David Chase; Music Coordinator, David Lai; General Management, Bespoke Theatricals (Amy Jacobs, Maggie Brohn, Devin Keudell, Nina Lannan); Associate General Manager, David Roth; Company Manager, Nathan Gehan; Assistant Company Manager, Kate Egan; Stage Manager, Pat Sosnow; Assistant Stage Manager, Jim Athens; Dance Captain, Jennie Ford; Assistant Dance Captain, Matt Wall; Associate Design: Bryan Johnson (U.S. set), Richard Kent (U.K. set), Barry Doss (costumes), Dan Walker (lighting), Anthony Smolenski (sound), Driscol A. Otto (projections); Assistant Design: David Woodhead, Andrew Riley, Simon Anthony Wells (U.K. scenic assistants), Christina Cocchiara, Robert J. Martin (costumes), Kristina Kloss (lighting), Daniel Vatsky (projections); Lighting Programmer, Rob Halliday; Assistant to the Hair Designer, Susan Pedersen; Makeup, Jason Goldsberry; Synthesizer Programmer, Stuart Andrews; Assistant Synthesizer Programmer, Dave Weiser; Music Copyist, Rob Meffe; Crew: Donald J. Oberpriller (production carpenter), David Elmer (fly automation), Jimmy Maloney (production electrician), Kevin Barry (associate production electrician), Brian Aman (head followspot), Paul Delcioppo, Phil Lojo (production sound), George Huckins (head sound), John Dory (assistant sound), Vera Pizzarelli (production props/head props), Douglas Petitjean (wardrobe supervisor), Deirdre LaBarre (assistant wardrobe supervisor), Scott Cain (Mr. Martin's dresser), Jeannie Naughton (Ms. Roger's dresser), Erick Medinilla (Mr. Cerveris' dresser), Tracy Diebold, Jake Fry, Adam Giradet, Tanya Guercy-Blue, Samantha Lawrence, Kathleen Mack, Jay Woods (dressers), Wanda Gregory (hair supervisor), Rick Caroto, Jenny Pendergraft, Emilia Martin (hair assistants); Children's Guardian, Bridget Mills; Projection Research, Sheila Maniar; Costume Production Assistant, Carly J. Price; Costume Shoppers, Adam Adelman, Edgar Conteras; U.K. Costume Design Liaison, Stephanie Arditti; Production Assistants, Lee Micklin, Derric Nolte, Michael Ulreich; SDC Observer, Stephen Kaliski; Associate to Mr. Luftig, Brian Smith; Assistant to Mr. Sanders, Jamie Quiroz; Children's Tutoring, On Location Education/Alan Simon, Jodi Green; Marketing Services, Type A Marketing/Anne Rippey, Elyce Henkin, Melissa Cohen; Advertisng/Website and Online Marketing, SpotCo; Press, The Hartman Group, Michael Hartman, Leslie Baden Papa, Whitney Holden Gore; Cast recording: Masterworks Broadway 542435

CAST Che **Ricky Martin**; Eva **Elena Roger**; Eva (at Wed. eve and Sat. mat. Performances) **Christina DeCicco**; Magaldi **Max Von Essen**; Perón **Michael Cerveris**; Mistress **Rachel Potter**; Child **Maya Jade Frank** or **Isabela Moner**; Ensemble **Ashley Amber, George Lee Andrews, Eric L. Christian, Kristine Covillo, Colin Cunliffe, Margot de la Barre, Bradley Dean, Rebecca Eichenberger, Melanie Field, Constantine Germanacos, Laurel Harris, Bahiyah Hibah, Nick Kenkel, Brad Little, Erica Mansfield, Emily Mechler, Sydney Morton, Jessica Lea Patty, Aleks Pevec, Rachel Potter, Kristie Dale Sanders, Timothy Shew, Johnny Stellard, Alex Michael Stoll, Daniel Torres**; Swings **Wendi Bergamini, Jennie Ford, Michaeljon Slinger, Matt Wall**

UNDERSTUDIES Bradley Dean (Perón), Christina DeCicco (Eva), Constantine Germanacos (Migaldi), Laurel Harris (Eva), Brad Little (Perón), Emily Mechler (Mistress), Sydney Morton (Mistress), Jessica Lea Patty (Eva), Daniel Torres (Che), Max Von Essen (Che), Matt Wall (Migaldi)

ORCHESTRA Kristen Blodgette (Conductor); Associate Conductor: William Waldrop (Associate Conductor/Keyboard); James Ercole, Kathleen Nester (Woodwinds); James de la Garza, Alex Holton (Trumpets); Tim Albright (Trombone); Shelagh Abate (French Horn); Michael Aarons (Guitar); Jeff Cooper (Bass); Bill Lanham (Drums); Dave Roth (Percussion); Andrew Einhorn (Keyboard);: Eddie Monteiro (Keyboards/Accordion); Victor Costanzi, Katherine Livolsi-Landau, Suzy Perelman (Violin); David Blinn (Viola); Mairi Dorman-Phaneuf (Cello)

MUSICAL NUMBERS Requiem; Oh, What a Circus; On This Night of a Thousand Stars; Eva, Beware of the City; Buenos Aires; Goodnight and Thank You; The Art of the Possible; Charity Concert; I'd Be Surprisingly Good for You; Another Suitcase in Another Hall; Peron's Latest Flame; A New Argentina; On the Balcony of the Casa Rosada; Don't Cry for Me Argentina; High Flying, Adored; Rainbow High; Rainbow Tour; The Chorus Girl Hasn't Learned; And the Money Kept Rolling In; Santa Evita; Waltz for Eva and Che; You Must Love Me; She is a Diamond; Dice Are Rolling; Eva's Final Broadcast; Montage; Lament

SETTING Junin and Buenos Aires, Argentina; 1934-1952. Revival of a musical presented in two acts. World premiere presented in London at the Prince Edward Theatre June 25, 1978 (directed by Hal Prince and starring Elaine Page). The original Broadway production, also directed Prince, and starring Patti LuPone and Mandy Patinkin, opened at the Broadway Theatre September 25, 1979 and closed June 26, 1983, playing 1,567 performances (see *Theatre World* Vol. 36, page 17). Ms. Roger starred in the 2006 West End revival, which was directed by Mr. Grandage.

SYNOPSIS Eva Perón used her beauty and charisma to rise meteorically from the slums of Argentina to the presidential mansion as First Lady. She won international acclaim and adoration from her own people as a champion of the poor, while glamour, power and greed made her one of the world's first major political celebrities. *Evita* tells Eva's passionate and tragic story through Tim Rice and Andrew Lloyd Webber's most dazzling and beloved score.

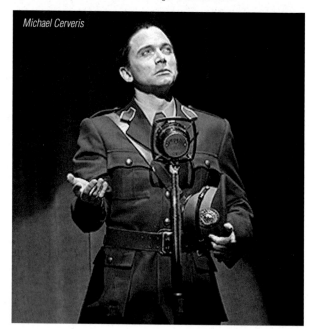

Michael Cerveris

Ricky Martin and the Company

Michael Cerveris and Elena Roger

Michael Cerveris and the Company

Max von Essen and Elena Roger (photos by Richard Termine)

Elena Roger and the Company

Elena Roger and the Company

Tug Coker, Peter Scolari, and Francois Battiste

Kevin Daniels and Tug Coker (photos by Joan Marcus)

Kevin Daniels, Deirdre O'Connell, and Tug Coker

Magic/Bird

Longacre Theatre; First Preview: March 21, 2012; Opening Night: April 11, 2012; Closed May 12, 2012; 24 previews, 37 performances

Written by Eric Simonson; Produced by Fran Kirmser, Tony Ponturo, W. Scott McGraw, John Mara Jr., Tamara Tunie/Jeffrey Donovan, Friends of Magic Bird, in association with the National Basketball Association (David J. Stern, Commissioner); Director, Thomas Kail; Sets, David Korins; Costumes, Paul Tazewell; Lighting, Howell Binkley; Media Design, Jeff Sugg; Sound, Nevin Steinberg; Casting, Telsey + Company; Hair and Wigs, Charles G. LaPointe; Dialect Coach, Stephen Gabis; Technical Supervisor/Production Manager, David Benken; General Management, Bespoke Theatricals (Maggie Brohn, Amy Jacobs, Devin Keudell, Nina Lannan); Production Stage Manager, J. Philip Bassett; Associate Producers, Rachel Weinstein, Richard Redmond & William Bloom; Company Manager, Doug Gaeta; Associate Production Management, Rose Palombo, Martin Pavloff; Associate General Manager, Danielle Saks; Stage Manager, Gregory T. Livoti; Assistant Director, Patrick Vassel; Original Music, Nevin Steinberg; Associate Design: Rod Lemmond (set), Kara Harmon (costumes), Ryan O'Gara (lighting), Jason Crystal (sound), Daniel Brodie (media); Assistant Design: Amanda Stephens (set), Joe Doran (lighting), Janie Bullard and David Thomas (sound); Assistants to the Scenic Designer, Sarah Muxlow, Emily Inglis; Video Programmer, Patrick Southern; Moving Lights Programmer, Sean Beach; Crew: David M. Cohen (production/head carpenter), Wilbur Graham (house carpenter), Andre Grey (flyman), Jeff Zink (advance rigger), Michael LoBue (production electrician), Brent Oakley (head electrician), Ric Rogers (house electrician), Brian Collins (moving light/video technician), Jason Crystal (sound engineer), Jacob White (production/head properties), John Lofgren (house properties), Susan Checklick (wardrobe supervisor), Carrie Kamerer, Paul Ludick (dressers), Amy Neswald (hair supervisor), Rebecca Spinac, Matthew Lutz (production assistants); For Kirmser Ponturo Group: Courtney Bottomley, Amanda Zoch (production associates), Joe Favorito (sports outreach), Jason Howard (website); Marketing Outreach, Walk Tall Girl Productions; Advertising, SpotCo (Jim Edwards, Drew Hodges, Tom Greenwald, Beth Watson, Nora Tillmanns); Marketing and Press, Kirmser Ponturo Group

CAST Earvin "Magic" Johnson **Kevin Daniels**; Larry Bird **Tug Coker**; Pat Riley/Red Auerbach/Jerry Buss/Tom/Bob Woolf **Peter Scolari**; Dinah Bird/Patricia Moore/Shelly/Georgia Bird **Deirdre O'Connell**; Willy/Bryant Gumble/Jon Lennox/Ron Baxter **Francois Battiste**; Henry Alvarado/Cedric Maxwell/Norm Nixon/Frank/Michael Cooper/Jeff **Robert Manning Jr.**

UNDERSTUDIES Anthony Holiday (Earvin "Magic" Johnson, Willy/Bryant Gumble/Jon Lennox/Ron Baxter, Henry Alvarado/Cedric Maxwell/Norm Nixon/Frank/Michael Cooper/Jeff), Gregory Jones (Larry Bird, Pat Riley/Red Auerbach/Jerry Bus/Tom/Bob Woolf), Anne-Marie Cusson (Dinah Bird/Patricia Moore/Shelly/Georgia Bird)

SETTING 1979-1992. World premiere of a new play presented in two acts.

SYNOPSIS At the heart of one of the fiercest rivalries in sports history, two of the greatest basketball players of all-time battled for three championships, bragging rights, and the future of their sport in the 1980s. Johnson and Bird electrified the nation on the court, reinvigorated the NBA, and turned their rivalry into one of the greatest and most famous friendships in professional sports.

Peter and the Starcatcher

Brooks Atkinson Theatre; First Preview: March 28, 2012; Opening Night: April 15, 2012; 18 previews, 53 performances as of May 31, 2012

Written by Rick Elice; Based upon the novel by Dave Berry and Ridley Pearson; Produced by Nancy Nagel Gibbs, Greg Schaffert, Eva Price, Tom Smedes, Disney Theatrical Productions, Suzan & Ken Wirth/DeBartolo Miggs, Catherine Schreiber/ Daveed Frazier & Mark Thompson, Jack Lane, Jane Dubin, Allan S. Gordon/Adam S. Gordon, Baer & Casserly/Nathan Vernon, Rich Affannato/Peter Stern, Brunish & Trinchero/Laura Little Productions, Larry Hirschhorn/Hummel & Greene, Jamie deRoy & Probo Productions/Radio Mouse Entertainment (M. Kilburg Reedy & Jason E. Grossman), Hugh Hysell/Avram Freedberg & Marybeth Dale, New York Theatre Workshop; Directors, Roger Rees and Alex Timbers; Music and Arrangements, Wayne Barker; Movement, Steven Hoggett; Sets, Donyale Werle; Costumes, Paloma Young; Lighting, Jeff Croiter; Sound, Darron L West; Music Direction and Additional Arrangements, Marco Pagula; Technical Supervisor, David Benken; Production Supervisor, Clifford Schwartz; Casting, Jim Carnahan, Jack Doulin, Tara Rubin; General Management, 321 Theatrical Management (Nina Essman, Marcia Goldberg); Production Management, David Benken, Rose Palombo; Company Manager, Tracy Geltman; Assistant Stage Manager, Brent McCreary; Dramaturg, Ken Cerniglia; For Disney Theatrical, Daniel Posener; Assistant Director, Lillian King; Movement Associate, Patrick McCollum; Fight Director, Jacob Grigorlia-Rosenbaum; Associate Design: Michael Carnahan (set), Matthew Pachtman (costumes), Joel Silver (lighting), Charles Coes (sound); Assistant Lighting Designers, Cory Pattak, Andy Fritsch; Assistants to Designers: Craig Napoliello (prop sculptor), Stephen Dobay (set), Hannah Davis (rendering painter), David Mendizabal (costume), Grant Yeager (lighting); Crew: Patrick Eviston (production carpenter), Michael Muery (advance carpenter), Brian GF McGarity (production electrician), Jerry Marshall (production props), Rob Bass (sound engineer), Timothy Rogers (Vari Light programmer), Jessica Dermody (wardrobe supervisor), Jim Hodun, Jamie Englehart (dressers), Brandon Dailey (hair stylist), J. Jared Janas (hair consultant), McKenzie Murphy, Smantha Preiss (production assistants); Advertising and Marketing, Serino/Coyne; Press, O+M Company, Rick Miramontez, Molly Barnett, Ryan Ratelle, Chelsea Nachman

CAST Fighting Prawn **Teddy Bergman**; Black Stache **Christian Borle**; Mrs. Bumbrake **Arnie Burton**; Boy **Adam Chanler-Berat**; Slank/Hawking Clam **Matt D'Amico**; Smee **Kevin Del Aguila**; Prentiss **Carson Elrod**; Alf **Greg Hildreth**; Lord Aster **Rick Holmes**; Captain Scott **Isaiah Johnson**; Molly **Celia Keenan-Bolger**; Ted **David Rossmer**

UNDERSTUDIES Betsy Hogg (Molly, Ted, Mrs. Bumbrake), Orville Mendoza (Smee, Alf, Fighting Prawn, Slank/Hawking Clam, Mrs. Bumbrake), Jason Ralph (Boy, Prentiss, Ted, Fighting Prawn, Captain Scott), John Sanders (Black Stache, Lord Aster, Captain Scott, Mrs. Bumbrake, Smee), Carson Elrod (Black Stache), Isaiah Johnson (Lord Aster, Slank/Hawking Clam, Alf)

MUSICIANS Marco Paguia (Conductor), Deanne Prouty (Drums/Percussion), Randy Cohen (Keyboard and Electronic Percussion Programmer)

2011-2012 AWARDS Tony Awards: Best Performance by an Actor in a Featured Role in a Play (Christian Borle), Best Scenic Design of a Play (Donyale Werle), Best Costume Design of a Play (Paloma Young), Best Lighting Design of a Play (Jeff Croiter), Best Sound Design of a Play (Darron L West)

Broadway premiere of a new play with music presented in two acts. World premiere presented Off-Broadway at the New York Theatre Workshop (James C. Nicola, Artistic Director; William Russo, Managing Director) March 9–April 24, 2011 with most of this cast (see *Theatre World* Vol. 67, page 216). Originally presented as a "Page to Stage" workshop production at La Jolla Playhouse (Christopher Ashley, Artistic Director; Michael S. Rosenberg, Executive Director) February 13–March 8, 2009 (see *Theatre World* Vol. 65, page 331).

SYNOPSIS In this innovative and imaginative new play, based on *The New York Times* best selling Disney-Hyperion novel by Dave Barry and Ridley Pearson, a company of twelve actors plays more than a hundred unforgettable characters, all on a journey to answer the century-old question: How did Peter Pan become The Boy Who Never Grew Up? This epic origin story of one of popular culture's most enduring and beloved characters proves that an audience's imagination can be the most captivating place in the world.

The Company

Adam Chanler-Berat, Christian Borle, and the Company

Kevin Del Aguila and Christian Borle (photos by Joan Marcus)

One Man, Two Guvnors

Music Box Theatre; First Preview: April 6, 2012; Opening Night: April 18, 2012; 13 previews, 51 performances as of May 31, 2012

Written by Richard Bean; Based on *The Servant of Two Masters* by Carlo Goldoni; Songs by Grant Olding; Produced by National Theatre of Great Britain (Nicholas Hytner, Director; Nick Starr, Executive Director), Bob Boyett, National Angels, Chris Harper, Tim Levy, Scott Rudin, Roger Berlind, Harriet Newman Leve, Stephanie P. McClelland, Broadway Across America, Jam Theatricals, Daryl Roth, Sonia Friedman, Harris Karma Productions, Deborah Taylor, Richard Willis; Director, Nicholas Hytner; Physical Comedy Director, Cal McCrystal; Set and Costumes, Mark Thompson; Lighting, Mark Henderson; Sound, Paul Arditti; Associate Director and Choreographer, Adam Penford; Original U.K. Casting, Alastair Coomer; U.S. Casting, Tara Rubin Casting; Music Director, Charlie Rosen; Production Stage Manager, William Joseph Barnes; Technical Supervisor/Production Management, David Benken; National Theatre Technical Producer, Katrina Gilroy; National Theatre Administrative Producer, Robin Hawkes; General Management, James Triner; Associate Production Manager, Rose Palombo; Company Manager, Elizabeth M. Talmadge; Stage Manager, Chris Zaccardi; Assistant Stage Manager, Liz Bates; Music Director, Charlie Rosen; U.K. Production Manager, Anna Anderson; Associate Design: Peter Eastman (set), Daryl Stone (costumes), Tom Snell (U.K. lighting), Michael Jones (U.S. lighting), John Owens (U.K. sound), Drew Levy (U.S. sound); Moving Light Programmer, Marc Polimeni; Crew: Cambell Young Associates (hair coordinator), John McPherson (head carpenter), Michael Shepp (advance rigger), , Jon Lawson (production electrician), Lucas Indelicato (head sound engineer), Denise J. Grillo (production properties coordinator), Kevin Crawford (assistant props), Raymond Panelli (wardrobe supervisor), Susan Cerceo (assistant wardrobe supervisor), Karen Gilbert, Chip White (dressers), Kathryn Guida, Scott Tucker (stitchers/laundry), Carmel Vargyas (hair supervisor), Kevin R. Maybee (hairdresser), Morgan Holbrook, Katie McKee, James C. Steele, Michael Tosto (production assistants); Management Assistant, Megan Bowers; Advertising and Marketing, SpotCo.; Press, Boneau/Bryan-Brown, Adrian Bryan-Brown, Jessica Johnson, Christine Olver

CAST Henry Dungle **Martyn Ellis**; Dolly **Suzie Toase**; Lloyd Boateng **Trevor Laird**; Charlie "the Duck" Clench **Fred Ridgeway**; Pauline Clench **Claire Lams**; Alan Dangle **Daniel Rigby**; Francis Henshall **James Corden**; Rachel Crabbe **Jemima Rooper**; Stanley Stubbers **Oliver Chris**; Gareth **Ben Livingston**; Alfie **Tom Edden**; Ensemble **Eli James, Ben Livingston, Sarah Manton, Stephen Pilkington, David Ryan Smith, Natalie Smith**; *The Craze*: **Jason Rabinowitz** (Lead Vocals), **Austin Moorehead** (Lead Guitar), **Charlie Rosen** (Music Director/Bass), **Jacob Colin Cohen** (Drums/Percussion)

UNDERSTUDIES Brian Gonzales (Francis), Eli James (Stanley), Natalie Smith (Rachel), Ben Livingston (Charlie, Harry), Sarah Manton (Dolly, Pauline), Stephen Pilkington (Alan, Alfie), David Ryan Smith (Lloyd, Gareth), Liz Baltes (Female Ensemble), Charlie Rosen (Lead Guitar, Drums, Lead Vocals), Matt Cusack (Bass, Lead Vocals), Zach Jones (Lead Vocals, Drums)

2011-2012 AWARDS Tony Award: Best Leading Actor in a Play (James Corden); Drama Desk Awards: Outstanding Actor in a Play (James Corden), Outstanding Featured Actor in a Play (Tom Edden), Outstanding Music in a Play (Grant Olding); Outer Critics Circle Awards: Outstanding New Broadway Play, Outstanding Direction of a Play (Nicholas Hytner), Outstanding Actor in a Play (James Corden)

SETTING The seaside town of Brighton, England. 1963. U.S. premiere of a new comedy with music presented in two acts. World premiere at the National Theatre's Lyttelton Theatre May 24–September 19, 2011. The show embarked on a U.K. tour for five weeks then to London for an open-ended run on the West End at the Adelphi Theatre November 21, 2011, and subsequently transferred to the Theatre Royal Haymarket March 2, 2012.

SYNOPSIS In *One Man, Two Guvnors*, Francis Henshall, always-famished and easily-confused, agrees to work for a local gangster as well as a criminal in hiding, both of whom are linked in a tangled web of schemes and romantic associations... none of which Francis can keep straight. So he has to do everything in his power to keep his two guvnors from meeting while trying to eat anything in sight along the way. Falling trousers, flying fish heads, star-crossed lovers, cross-dressing mobsters and a fabulous on-stage band are just some of what awaits in this deliriously new play from across the pond.

Suzie Toase, Oliver Chris, James Corden, and Jemima Rooper

James Corden, Suzie Toase, Claire Lams, Oliver Chris, Jemima Rooper, Daniel Rigby, Trevor Laird, Martyn Ellis, and Fred Ridgeway

Charlie Rosen, Austin Moorehead, Jacob Colin Cohen, and Jason Rabinowitz as "The Craze" (photos by Joan Marcus)

Jeremy Shamos, Damon Gupton, Crystal A. Dickenson

Damon Gupton, Annie Parisse, Crystal A. Dickinson, and Jeremy Shamos

Frank Wood, Annie Parisse, Christina Kirk, Jeremy Shamos, Damon Gupton, and Crystal A. Dickinson (photos by Nathan Johnson)

Clybourne Park

Walter Kerr Theatre; First Preview: March 26, 2012; Opening Night: April 19, 2012; 19 previews, 49 performances as of May 31, 2012

Written by Bruce Norris; Produced by Jujamcyn Theatres, Jane Bergère, Roger Berlind/Quintet Productions, Eric Falkenstein/Dan Frishwasser, Ruth Hendel/ Harris Karma Productions, JTG Theatricals, Daryl Roth, Jon B. Platt, Center Theatre Group (Michael Ritchie, Artistic Director; Edward L. Rada, Managing Director; Douglas C. Baker, Producing Director) in association with Lincoln Center Theater (Andre Bishop, Artistic Director; Bernard Gersten, Executive Director; Adam Siegel, Managing Director) and Playwrights Horizons (Tim Sanford, Artistic Director; Leslie Marcus, Managing Director; Carol Fishman, General Manager); Director, Pam McKinnon; Set, Daniel Ostling; Costumes, Ilona Somogyi; Lighting, Allen Lee Hughes; Sound, John Gromada; Hair and Wigs, Charles LaPointe; Casting Alaine Alldaffer; Production Management, Aurora Productions; Production Stage Manager, C.A. Clark; General Manager, Bespoke Theatricals (Amy Jacobs, Nina Lannan, Maggie Brohn, Devin Keudell); Executive Producer, Red Awning; Company Manager, Heidi Neven; Associate Casting Director, Lisa Donadio; Stage Manager, James Latus; Assistant Director, Kimberly Faith Hickman; Associate Design: Jessica Wegener Shay (costumes), Xavier Pierce (lighting), Chris Cronin (sound), Leah Loukas (hair); Assistant Lighting Design, Miriam Crowe; Crew: Chad Heulitt (production carpenter), Michael Pitzer (production electrician), Faye Armon (production props supervisor), Jill Johnson (production props), Ed Chapman (production sound engineer), Christine Ainge (wardrobe supervisor), Ron Fleming, Francine Schwartz-Brown (dressers), Pat Marcus (hair supervisor), Brenda Sabakt-Davis (scenic consultant); For Aurora Productions: Gene O' Donovan, Ben Heller, Stephanie Sherline, Jarid Sumner, Anthony Jusino, Anita Shah, Liza Luxenberg, Steven Dalton, Eugenio Saenz Flores, Isaac Katzanek, Melissa Mazdra; Advertising and Marketing, Serino/ Coyne; Press, O+M Company, Rick Miramontez, Joyce Friedmann, Ryan Ratelle, Andy Snyder, Michael Jorgensen

CAST Francine/Lena **Crystal A. Dickinson**; Jim/Tom/Kenneth **Brendan Griffin**; Albert/Kevin **Damon Gupton**; Bev/Kathy **Christina Kirk**; Betsy/ Lindsey **Annie Parisse**; Karl/Steve **Jeremy Shamos**; Russ/Dan **Frank Wood**

UNDERSTUDIES April Yvette Thompson (Francine/Lena), Richard Thieriot (Jim/Tom/Kenneth, Russ/Dan), Brandon J. Dirden (Albert/Kevin), Carly Street (Bev/Kathy, Betsy/Lindsey), Greg Stuhr (Russ/Dan)

2011-2012 AWARDS Tony Award: Best Play; **Theatre World Award:** Crystal A. Dickinson

SETTING A house at 406 Clybourne Street in the Clybourne Park area of Chicago (the fictional home in Lorraine Hansbury's play, *A Raisin in the Sun*). Time: Act One: 1959. Act Two: 2009. Broadway premiere of a new play presented in two acts. This production was previously presented at Playwrights Horizons January 29–March 21, 2010 (see *Theatre World* Vol. 66, page 237). This production was subsequently produced at Center Theatre Group January 25–February 26, 2012, prior to its Broadway engagement. The play received the 2011 Pulitzer Prize for Drama.

SYNOPSIS *Clybourne Park* is the wickedly funny and fiercely provocative new play about race, real estate and the volatile values of each. *Clybourne Park* explodes in two outrageous acts set 50 years apart. Act One takes place in 1959, as nervous community leaders anxiously try to stop the sale of a home to a black family. Act Two is set in the same house in the present day, as the now predominantly African-American neighborhood battles to hold its ground in the face of gentrification.

Nicole Ari Parker and Blair Underwood

Daphne Rubin-Vega and Blair Underwood

Nicole Ari Parker, Dapne Rubin-Vega, and Blair Underwood (photos by Ken Howard)

A Streetcar Named Desire

Broadhurst Theatre; First Preview: April 3, 2012; Opening Night: April 22, 2012; 23 previews, 45 performances as of May 31, 2012

Written by Tennessee Williams; Produced by Stephen C. Byrd, Alia M. Jones, Anthony Lacavera; BET Networks, Henry G. Jarecki, Simon Says Entertainment, Dacap Productions, in association with Linda Davila, Patricia and Thomas Bransford, and Theatre Venture Inc.; Director, Emily Mann; Original Music, Terence Blanchard; Sets, Eugene Lee; Costumes, Paul Tazwell; Lighting, Edward Pierce; Sound, Mark Bennett; Casting, Telsey + Company, Will Cantler; Fight Direction, Rick Sordelet; Vocal and Dialect Coach, Beth McGuire; Hair and Wigs, Charles G. LaPointe; Technical Supervision, Jake Bell, Production Services Ltd.; Production Stage Manager, Lloyd Davis Jr.; General Manager, Roy Gabay; Company Manager, Bruce Kagel; Associate Producers, Daryl Roth, Paulette Martin-Carter, Keisha and Troy Dixon, Socrates Marquez, Randolph Sturrup, Ellen Krass, Renee Hunter, Stephen Vallentine, Walter White, Jacqui Lee, Stephen Johnson, George Williams, Linden Rhoads, Antony Detre, Consortium Ventures, Jessica Isaacs, William Nettles; Assistant Stage Manager, Hilary Austin; Associate Director, Jade King Carroll; Assistant Director, Shannon Cameron; Assistant to the Director, Pat Golden; Assistant Composers, Mark Strand, Joshua Johnson; Associate Design: Nick Francone (set), Sara Tosetti (costumes), Jonathan Spencer (lighting), Leon Rothenberg and Danny Erdberg (sound); Assistant Costume Design, Sarah Cubbage; Props Coordinator, Kathy Fabian/Propstar; Props Associates, Carrie Mossman, Cassie Dorland Crew: Thomas Hague (lighting programmer), Charles J. Deverna, Brendan C. Quiqley (production electrcians), Brian McGarty and Richard Howrad (production carpenters), J. Marvin Crosland (head props), Wallace Flores (production sound engineer), Laura Koch (house props), Moira Conrad (wardrobe supervisor), Catherine Dee, Anita Ali Davis (dressers), Jamie Stewart (hair and wig supervisor), Coleen M. Sherry, Trey Johnson (production assistants); For Roy Gabay Productions: Mandy Tate, Daniel Kuney, Chris Aniello, Katrina Elliott, Marg Gagliardi, Lily Alia; Group Sales and Marketing, Walker Communications Group Inc, Donna Walker-Kuhne, Cherine Anderson; Advertising, aka; Press, Springer Associates, Gary Springer, Joe Trentacosta

CAST Stella **Daphne Rubin-Vega**; Eunice **Amelia Campbell**; Mexican Woman/Neighbor **Carmen de Lavallade**; Stanley **Blair Underwood**; Harold Mitchell (Mitch) **Wood Harris**; Blance **Nicole Ari Parker**; Steve **Matthew Saldívar**; Pablo **Jacinto Taras Riddick**; Young Collector **Aaron Clifton Moten**; Doctor **Count Stovall**; Matron **Rosa Evangelina Arredondo**

UNDERSTUDIES Rosa Evangelina Arredondo (Blanche, Stella), Morocco Omari (Stanley, Mitch, Steve, Pablo, Doctor), Danielle Lee Greaves (Eunice, Mexican Woman/Neighbor, Matron), J. Mallory McCree (Young Collector)

SETTING French Quarter, New Orleans. 1952. Revival of a classic drama presented in two acts. Originally presented on Broadway at the Ethyl Barrymore Theatre, starring Marlon Brando, Jessica Tandy, and Kim Hunter, December 3, 1947–December 17, 1949, playing 855 performances (see *Theatre World* Vol. 4, page 48). This production marked the eighth major New York revival of the play. The most recent revival was produced by the Roundabout Theatre at Studio 54, starring Natasha Richardson, John C. Reilly, and Amy Ryan, April 26–July 3, 2005 (see *Theatre World* Vol. 61, page 75.)

SYNOPSIS Tennessee Williams' sultry drama, *A Streetcar Named Desire*, set against the sexy backdrop of New Orleans' gritty French Quarter, tells the tale of former school teacher and socialite Blanche DuBois, as she's forced to move in with her sister Stella and her brut of a husband Stanley. But the fragile, Blanche quickly gets a gritty life lesson in the seamy, steamy underbelly of 1950's New Orleans.

Ghost The Musical

Lunt-Fontanne Theatre; First Preview: March 15, 2012; Opening Night: April 23, 2012; 39 previews, 44 performances as of May 31, 2012

Book and lyrics by Bruce Joel Rubin, music and lyrics by Dave Stewart and Glen Ballard; Based on the Paramount Pictures film written by Bruce Joel Rubin; "Unchained Melody" written by Hy Zaret and Alex North, courtesy of Frank Music Corp.; Produced by Colin Ingram, Hello Entertainment/David Garfinkle, Donovan Mannato, MJE Productions, Patricia Lambrecht, Adam Silberman, in association with Coppel/Watt/Withers/Bewick, Fin Gray/Michael Melnick, Mayerson/Gould Hauser/Tysoe, Richard Chaifetz and Jill Chaifetz, Jeffrey B. Hecktman, Land Line Productions, Gilbert Productions/Marion/Shahar, Fresh Glory Productions/Bruce Cargnegie-Brown, by special arrangement with Paramount Pictures; Director, Matthew Warchus; Design, Rob Howell; Choreography, Ashley Wallen; Lighting, Hugh Vanstone; Illusions, Paul Kieve; Sound, Bobby Aitken; Music Supervisor/Arrangements/Orchestrations, Christopher Nightingale; Video and Projection Design, Jon Driscoll; Additional Movement Sequences, Liam Steel; Music Director, David Holcenberg; Associate Director, Thomas Caruso; Casting, Tara Rubin Casting (U.S.), David Grindrod (U.K.); Production Stage Manager, Ira Mont; General Management, Bespoke Theatricals (Nina Lannan, Devin Keudell, Maggie Brohn, Amy Jacobs); Production Management, Aurora Productions (Gene O'Donovan, Ben Heller, Stephanie Sherline, Jarid Sumner, Liza Luxenberg, Anita Shah, Anthony Jusino, Steven Dalton, Eugenio Saenz Flores, Isaac Katzanek, Aneta Feld, Melissa Mazdra); Company Manager, Shaun Moorman; Associate Company Manager, Roseanna Sharrow; Associate General Manager, Steve Dow; Stage Manager, Julia P. Jones; Assistant Stage Manager, Matthew Lacey; Consulting Stage Manager U.K., Natalie Wood; Dance Captain/Fight Captain, James Brown III; Assistant Dance Captain, Afra Hines; Fight Director, Terry King; Hair/Wigs and Makeup Design, Campbell Young Associates; For Colin Ingram: Simon Ash (Associate General Manager), Louise Waldron (Financial Controller), Daisy Campey (Production Assistant); For Hello Entertainment: Adam Silberman (Executive Producer), Michael Lowen (CFO), Clay Martin (Executive Assistant), PJ Miller (Special Projects Manager); Associates for Tara Rubin: Eric Woodall, Merri Sugarman, Dale Brown, Stephanie Yankwitt, Kaitlin Shaw, Lindsay Levine; Associates for David Grindrod: Will Burton, Stephen Crockett; Associate Design: Rosalind Coombes & Paul Weimer (set), Daryl A. Stone (costumes), Tim Lutkin & Joel Shier (lighting), Simon King & Garth Helm (sound), Gemma Carrington & Michael Clark (video & projections), Joanie Spina (illusionist); Assistant Costume Design, Rachel Attridge; Costume Design Assistant, Audrey Nauman; Crew: Francis Rapp (head carpenter), John Croissant (fly automation carpenter), Joel DeRuyter (deck automation carpenter), Mike Cornell (head electrician), Randall Zaibek, Jimmy Fedigan (production electricians), Steve Long (moving light technician), David Arch (moving light programmer), David Bornstein (production property master), Lisa Buckley, Lizzie Frankl (U.K. props supervisors), Christina Gould (props shopper), Mike Wojchik (production sound engineer), Colle Bustin (assistant sound engineer), Ben Evans (production sound mixer-U.K.), Drew Levy (advance sound), Jason Lindahl (production video technician), Chris Kurtz (video technician), Terri Purcell (wardrobe supervisor), Nanette Golia (associate wardrobe supervisor), Michael Berglund, Ken Brown, Tina Clifton, Margian Flanagan, Jaymes Gill, Joby Horrigan, Peggie Kurz, Marcia McIntosh, Duduzile Mitall, Lisa Preston, Jessica Scoblick (dressers), Susan Corrado (hair supervisor), Monica Costea (assistant hair supervisor), Lisa Acevedo (hairdresser); Associate Music Director U.K., Laurie Perkins; Music Technology, Phij Adams; Music Technology Associate, Andy Grobengieser; Digital Arrangements and Programming, Ned Douglas; Video System Consultant, Alan Cox; Video/Projections Programmers, Laura Frank, Emily Harding; Special Effects Coordinators, Randall Zaibek, Jimmy Fedigan; Music Coypying, Emily Grishman (U.S.), Tom Kelly (U.K.); Vocal Coach, Deborah Hecht; Production Assistants, Kate Croasdale, Cody Renard Richard, Kristen Togrimson; SDC Directing Intern, Stephen Brotebeck; SDC Observer, Ryan Emmons; General Management Associates, Libby Fox, Danielle Saks; Advertising/Marketing/Online and Digital Interactive, SpotCo (Drew Hodges, Jim Edwards, Tom Greenwald, Stephen Sosnowski, Nora Tilmanns, Nick Pramik, Kristen Rathbun, Julie Wechsler, Caroline Newhouse, Kristen Bardwil, Corey

Caissie Levy and Richard Fleeshman

Caissie Levy, Richard Fleeshman, and Bryce Pinkham

Richard Fleeshman

Spinney, Rebecca Cohen, Marisa Delmore, Sara Fitzpatrick, Marc Mettler, Jennifer Sacks, Christina Sees, Matt Wilstein, Stephen Santore); Press, The Hartman Group, Michael Hartman, Juliana Hannett, Emily McGill; Cast recording: Surfdog Records 530628

CAST Sam Wheat **Richard Fleeshman**; Molly Jensen **Caissie Levy**; Oda Mae Brown **Da'Vine Joy Randolph**; Carl Bruner **Bryce Pinkham**; Willie Lopez **Michael Balderrama**; Subway Ghost **Tyler McGee**; Hospital Ghost **Lance Roberts**; Clara/Officer Wallace **Moya Angela**; Louise/Nun **Carly Hughes**; Bank Assistant **Jennifer Noble**; Minister/Detective Beiderman **Jason Babinsky**; Mrs. Santiago **Jennifer Sanchez**; Orlando **Daniel J. Watts**; Ortisha **Vasthy Mompoint**; Bank Officer/Nun **Alison Luff**; Ensemble **Moya Angela**, **Jason Babinsky**, **Jeremy Davis**, **Sharona D'Ornellas**, **Josh Franklin**, **Albert Guerzon**, **Jeremy Davis**, **Sharona D'Ornellas**, **Josh Franklin**, **Albert Guerzon**, **Afra Hines**, **Carly Hughes**, **Alison Luff**, **Tyler McGee**, **Vasthy Mompoint**, **Jennifer Noble**, **Joe Aaron Reid**, **Lance Roberts**, **Constantine Rousouli**, **Jennifer Sanchez**, **Daniel J. Watts**; Swings **Mike Cannon**, **Stephen Carrasco**, **Karen Hyland**, **Jesse Wildman**

UNDERSTUDIES Moya Angela (Oda Mae Brown), Jason Babinsky (Carl Bruner), Mike Cannon (Willie Lopez), Stephen Carrasco (Hospital Ghost), Josh Franklin (Sam Wheat), Afra Hines (Clara, Louise), Carly Hughes (Oda Mae Brown), Alison Luff (Molly Jensen), Vasthy Mompoint (Clara, Louise), Jennifer Noble (Molly Jensen), Joe Aaron Reid (Willie Lopez), Constantine Rousouli (Carl Bruner, Sam Wheat), Daniel J. Watts (Hospital Ghost, Subway Ghost)

ORCHESTRA David Holcenberg (Conductor); Andy Grobengieser (Associate Conductor/Keyboard 2); Deborah Abramson (Keyboard 1); Eric Davis, J.J. McGeehan (Guitars); Randy Landau (Bass); Howard Joines (Drums); John Reid (Trumpet); Bruce Eidem (Trombone); Hideaki Aomori (Woodwinds); Zohar Schondorf (Horn); Elizabeth Lim-Dutton (Concert Master); Cenovia Cummins, Jim Tsao, Robin Zeh (Violins); Jonathan Dinklage, Hiroko Taguchi (Violin/Viola); Jeanne LeBlanc (Cello)

MUSICAL NUMBERS Here Right Now; Unchained Melody; More; Three Little Words; You Gotta Go; Are You a Believer?; With You; Suspend My Disbelief/I Had a Life; Rain/Hold On; Life Turns on a Dime; Focus; Talkin' 'Bout a Miracle; Nothing Stops Another Day; I'm Outta Here; Unchained Melody (reprise)

2011-2012 AWARDS Drama Desk Award: Outstanding Set Design (Jon Driscoll, Rob Howell, Paul Kieve); Outer Critics Circle Award: Oustanding Lighting Design (Hugh Vanstone)

SETTING New York City, modern day. U.S. premiere of a new musical presented in two acts. World premiere at the Manchester Opera House in March 2011. The show opened in the West End at the Piccadilly Theatre July 19, 2011.

SYNOPSIS *Ghost The Musical* is a timeless fantasy about the power of love. Walking back to their apartment one night, Sam and Molly are mugged, leaving Sam murdered on a dark street. Sam is trapped as a ghost between this world and the next and unable to leave Molly, who he learns is in grave danger. With the help of a phony storefront psychic, Oda Mae Brown, Sam tries to communicate with Molly in the hope of saving and protecting her.

Da'Vine Joy Randolph, Richard Fleeshman, and Jeremy Davis

Caissie Levy and Richard Fleeshman

Bryce Pinkham and the Company (photos by Joan Marcus)

Da'Vie Joy Randolph and the Company

Linda Lavin and Dick Latessa

Kate Jennings Grant and Michael Esper (photos by Carol Rosegg)

Michael Esper and Gregory Woodall

The Lyons

Cort Theatre; First Preview: April 5, 2012; Opening Night: April 23, 2012; 21 previews, 44 performances as of May 31, 2012

Written by Nicky Silver; Produced by Kathleen K. Johnson and the Vineyard Theatre; Director, Mark Brokaw; Sets, Allen Moyer; Costumes, Michael Krass; Lighting, David Lander; Original Music and Sound, David Van Tieghem; Production Management, Aurora Productions; Fight Director, Thomas Schall; Production Stage Manager, Robert Bennett; Casting, Henry Russell Bergstein; General Manager, Niko Companies Ltd.; Associate Producer, Jonathan Tessero; Stage Manager, Lois Griffing; Production Assistant, Jessica Johnstone; Assistant to the Producer, Judy Crozier; Assistant Director, Sam Pinkleton; Associate Sound Design, David Sanderson; Assistant Design: Warren Karp (set), Brenda Abbandandolo (costumes), Travis McHale (lighting), Emma Wilk (sound); Crew: Ed Diaz (production carpenter), Scott Deverna (production electrician), Lonnie Gaddy (production properties), Rob Brenner (advance properties supervisor), Jim Van Bergen (sound board engineer), Eileen Miller (wardrobe supervisor), Annie Sunai (costume shopper), Tessa Dunning (property coordinator); Ms. Lavin's Makeup, J. Roy Helland; Ms. Lavin's hair, Antonio Soddu; For Niko Companies: Manny Kladitis, Jeffrey Chrzczon, Jason T. Vanderwoude; For Aurora Productions: Gene O'Donovan, Ben Heller, Stephanie Sherline, Anita Shah, Jarid Sumner, Anthony Jusino, Liza Luxenberg, Steven Dalton, Eugenio Saenz Flores, Isaac Katzanek, Anita Field, Melissa Mazdra; Advertising and Marketing, aka (Scott A. Moore, Liz Furze, Joshua Lee Poole, Jennifer Sims, Adam Jay, Janette Roush, Sara Rosenzweig, Erin Rech, Jen Taylor, Flora Pei); Press, Sam Rudy Media Relations

CAST Rita Lyons **Linda Lavin**; Ben Lyons **Dick Latessa**; Lisa Lyons **Kate Jennings Grant**; Curtis Lyons **Michael Esper**; Nurse **Brenda Pressley**; Brian **Gregory Woodell**

UNDERSTUDIES Richard Gallagher (Curtis, Brian), Tim Jerome (Ben), Eva Kaminsky (Lisa/Nurse), John Wernke (Curtis, Brian)

SETTING A hospital room and an empty apartment; the present. Broadway premiere of a new play presented in two acts. World premiere at the Vineyard Theatre (Douglas Aibel, Artistic Director; Jennifer Garvey-Blackwell, Executive Producer; Sarah Stern, Co-artistic Director; Rebecca Habel, Managing Director) October 11, 2011 (see page 261 in this volume).

SYNOPSIS *The Lyons* is a funny and edgy work about Rita Lyons, the indomitable matriarch of a family at a major crossroads: her husband is dying, her son's in a dubious relationship, her daughter's struggling to stay sober and on top of it all, she can't settle on a new design for the living room.

Kate Jennings Grant and Linda Lavin

Nice Work If You Can Get It

Imperial Theatre; First Preview: March 29, 2012; Opening Night: April 24, 2012; 27 previews, 42 performances as of May 31, 2012

Music and lyrics by George Gershwin and Ira Gershwin, book by Joe DiPietro; Inspired by material by Guy Bolton and P.G. Wodehouse; Produced by Scott Landis, Roger Berlind, Sonia Friedman Productions, Roy Furman, Standing CO Vation (Chris Bensinger, Richard Winkler, Jamie deRoy, Michael Filerman, Dennis Grimaldi, Remmel T. Dickinson, Bruce R. Harris, Jack W. Batman), Candy Spelling, Freddy DeMann, Ronald Frankel, Harold Newman, Jon B. Platt, Raise the Roof 8 (Jennifer Manocherian, Elaine Krauss, Jean Doumanian, Harriet Newman Leve), Takonkiet Viravan, William Berlind/Ed Burke, Carole L. Haber/Susan Carusi, Buddy and Barbara Freitag/Sanford Robertson, Jim Herbert/Under the Wire (Jacki Barlia Florin, Douglas Denoff, Margot Astrachan), Emanuel Azenberg, The Shubert Organization (Philip J. Smith, Chairman; Robert E. Wankel, President); Director and Choreography, Kathleen Marshall; Music Supervision and Arrangements, David Chase; Music Director, Tom Murray; Sets, Derek McLane; Costumes, Martin Pakledinaz; Lighting, Peter Kaczorowski; Sound, Brian Ronan; Hair and Wigs, Paul Huntley; Makeup, Angelina Avallone; Projections, Alexander V. Nichols; Casting, Jay Binder, Jack Bowdan; Orchestrations, Bill Elliott; Music Coordinator, Seymour Red Press; Associate Director, Marc Bruni; Associate Choreographer, David Eggers; Technical Director, Neil Mazzella/Hudson Theatrical Associates; General Management, 101 Productions Ltd. (Wendy Orshan, Jeffrey M. Wilson, Elie Landau, Ron Gubin, Chris Morey); Production Stage Manager, Bonnie L. Becker; Company Manager, Thom Clay; Production Manager, Tech Production Services, Peter Fulbright, Mary Duffe, James Kolpin; Stage Manager, Charles Underhill; Assistant Stage Manager, Scott Rowen; Associate Company Manager, Kevin Beebee; Dance Captain, Jason DePinto; Assistant Dance Captain, Kaitlyn Davidson; SDC Observer, Lorna Ventura; Associate Tech Supervisors, Sheena Crespo, Irene Wang; Associate Design: Shoko Kambara (set), Amy Clark (costumes), Paul Toben (lighting), Cody Spencer (sound); Assistant Design: Erica Hemminger (set), Leon Dobrowski, Justin Hall, Heather Lockard, Amanda Seymour (costumes), Sarah Jakubasz (lighting), Jessica Weeks (sound), Jorge Vargas (makeup); Props Coordinator, Kathy Fabian/Propstar; Assistant Props Coordinators, Carrie Mossman, Mike Billings; Crew: Paul Wimmer (production carpenter), Richard Force (assistant carpenter/automation), Walter Bullard (house carpenter), Jimmy Maloney Jr. (production electrician), Tom Lawrey (associate production electrician), Jason Wilcozs (head electrician), Josh Weitzman (moving lights programmer), Paul Dean (house electrician), Alexander V. Nichols (video programmer), Christian DeAngelis (assistant video programmer), Neil Rosenberg (production props supervisor), John Tutalo (head props), Heidi Brown (house props), Chris Sloan (advance sound), Louis Igoe (sound operator), David Dignazio (sound associate), Karen L. Eifert (wardrobe supervisor), Irma Escobar (assistant wardrobe supervisor), Dani Berger, Mark Richard Caswell, Fran Curry, Suzane Delahunt, Lauren Galitelli, Gayle Palmieri, Geoffrey Polischuck, Mark Trezza (dressers), Nathaniel Hathaway (hair/makeup supervisor), Bary Ernst, Kevin Phillips (hair/makeup assistants); Assistant to the Costume Designer, Valerie Marcus Ramshur; Music Copying, Emily Grishman Music Preparation, Katharine Edmonds; Music Department Production Assistant, James Ballard; Keyboard Programmer, Randy Cohen; Scenic Studio Assistant, Paul DePoo; Production Assistants, Julie DeVore, Lauren Hirsh, Johnny Milani; Advertising/Marketing/Digital Outreach and Website, Serino/Coyne; Press, Boneau/Bryan-Brown, Chris Boneau, Heath Schwartz, Michael Strassheim; Cast recording: Shout Factory 13740

CAST Jeannie Muldoon **Robyn Hurder**; Jimmy Winter **Matthew Broderick**; Billie Bendix **Kelli O'Hara**; Duke Mahoney **Chris Sullivan**; Cookie McGee **Michael McGrath**; Chief Berry **Stanely Wayne Mathis**; Senator Max Evergreen **Terry Beaver**; Duchess Estonia Dulworth **Judy Kaye**; Eileen Evergreen **Jennifer Laura Thompson**; Millicent Winter **Estelle Parsons**; *The Chorus Girls*: Olive **Cameron Adams**; Dottie **Kimberly Fauré**; Midge **Stephanie Martignetti**; Alice **Samantha Sturm**; Rosie **Kristen Beth Williams**; Flo **Candice Marie Woods**; *The Vice Squad*: Elliot **Clyde Alves**;

Slim **Robert Hartwell**; Fletcher **Barrett Martin**; Edgar **Adam Perry**; Floyd **Jeffrey Schecter**; Vic **Joey Sorge**; Standby for Duke, Cookie, Chief Berry, Senator **Michael X. Martin**; Standby for Duchess, Millicent **Jennifer Smith**; Swings **Kaitlyn Davidson, Jason DePinto**

UNDERSTUDIES Cameron Adams (Billie Bendix), Kimberly Fauré (Eileen Evergreen, Jeannie Muldoon), Stephanie Martignetti (Billie Bendix), Jeffrey Howard Schecter (Chief Berry, Cookie McGee), Joey Sorge (Jimmy Winter) and Kristen Beth Williams (Duchess Estonia Dulworth, Eileen Evergreen, Jeannie Muldoon)

ORCHESTRA Tom Murray (Conductor); Shawn Gough (Associate Conductor/Piano/Accordion); Joseph Joubert (Assistant Conductor/Piano/Keyboards); Paul Woodiel (Violin); Ralph Olsen, Todd Groves, Richard A. Heckman, Jay Brandford (Woodwinds); Robert Millikan, Brian Pareshi, Shawn Edmonds (Trumpets); Clint Sharman, Jason Jackson, Jack Schatz (Trombones); Eric Poland (Drums); Andrew Blanco (Percussion); James Hershman (Guitar); Richard Sarpola (Bass)

MUSICAL NUMBERS Overture, Sweet and Lowdown; Nice Work If You Can Get It; Nice Work If You Can Get It (reprise); Demon Rum; Someone to Watch Over Me; Delishious; I've Got to Be There; I've Got to Be There (reprise); Treat Me Rough; Let's Call the Whole Thing Off; Do It Again (lyrics by Buddy DeSylva); 'S Wonderful; Fascinating Rhythm; Lady Be Good; But Not for Me; By Strauss; Sweet and Lowdown (reprise); Do, Do, Do; Hangin' Around With You; Looking for a Boy; Blah, Blah, Blah; Let's Call the Whole Thing Off (reprise); Will You Remember Me?; I've Got to Be There (reprise); I've Got a Crush on You; Blah, Blah, Blah (reprise); Looking for a Boy (reprise); Delishious (reprise); Someone to Watch Over Me (reprise); They All Laughed

2011-2012 AWARDS Tony Awards: Best Performance by an Actor in a Featured Role in a Musical (Michael McGrath), Best Performance by a Actress in a Featured Role in a Musical (Judy Kaye); Drama Desk Awards: Outstanding Book of a Musical (Joe DiPietro), Outstanding Featured Actor in a Musical (Michael McGrath), Outstanding Featured Actress in a Musical (Judy Kaye); Outer Critics Circle Awards: Outstanding Featured Actor in a Musical (Michael McGrath), Outstanding Featured Actress in a Musical (Judy Kaye)

SETTING Time: July 1927. Place: Long Island, New York. World premiere of a new musical presented in fourteen scenes in two acts.

SYNOPSIS Featuring some of George and Ira Gershwin's best loved songs, *Nice Work If You Can Get It* is a new musical that tells the story of Billie Bendix, a bootlegger who meets wealthy playboy Jimmy Walker on the weekend of his nuptials. Mayhem ensues.

Matthew Broderick and Kelli O'Hara

Kelli O'Hara and Matthew Broderick

Matthew Broderick and the Company

Matthew Broderick and the Company

Chris Sullivan and Robyn Hurder

Terry Beaver, Estelle Parsons, Kelli O'Hara, and Matthew Broderick

The Company (photos by Joan Marcus)

The Columnist

Samuel J. Friedman Theatre; First Preview: April 4, 2012; Opening Night: April 25, 2012; 23 previews, 42 performances as of May 31, 2012

Written by David Auburn; Produced by Manhattan Theatre Club (Lynne Meadow, Artistic Director; Barry Grove, Executive Producer); Director, Daniel Sullivan; Sets, John Lee Beatty; Costumes, Jess Goldstein; Lighting, Kenneth Posner; Original Music and Sound, John Gromada; Projections, Rocco DiSanti; Hair and Wigs, Charles G. LaPointe; Casting, David Caparelliotis; Production Stage Manager, Jane Grey; Stage Manager, Denise Yaney; Company Manager, Erin Moeller; Mary Mill Directing Fellow, Rachel Slaven; Fight Director, Thomas Schall; Makeup, Barry Berger; Dialect Coach, Charlotte Fleck; Assistant Design: Kacie Hultgren (set), Chloe Chapin (costumes), Nick Solyom (lighting), Alex Neumann (sound), Ido Levran (projections); Crew: Vaughn Preston (automation operator), Alex Fogel (lightboard programmer), John Fullum (flyman), Richard Klinger (deck hand), Robin Baxter (hair and makeup supervisor), Patrick Bevilacqua (wardrobe supervisor), David Oliver (dresser), Alex Mark (production assistant); For MTC: General Manager, Florie Seery; Artistic Producer, Mandy Greenfield; Director of Artistic Development, Jerry Patch; Marketing, Debra Waxman-Pilla; Production Manager, Joshua Helman; Director of Casting, Nancy Piccione; Artistic Line Producer, Lisa McNulty; Development, Lynne Randall; Artistic Consultant, Daniel Sullivan; Artistic Operations, Amy Gilkes Loe; Finance, Jessica Adler; Associate General Manager, Lindsey Brooks Sag; Subscriber Services, Robert Allenberg; Telesales, George Tetlow; Education, David Shookhoff; Associate Production Manager, Bethany Weinstein; Assistant Production Manager, Kevin Service; Prop Supervisor, Scott Laule; Assistant Properties Supervisor, Julia Sandy; Props Carpenter, Peter Grimes; Costume Supervisor, Erin Hennessy Dean; Associate Production Manager, Bethany Weinstein; Assistant Production Manager, Kevin Service; Assistant Properties Supervisor, Julia Sandy; Props Carpenter, Peter Grimes; Advertising, SpotCo; Press, Boneau/Bryan-Brown, Chris Boneau, Aaron Meier, Christine Olver, Emily Meagher

CAST Joseph Alsop **John Lithgow**; Andrei **Brian J. Smith**; Susan Mary Alsop **Margaret Colin**; Stewart Alsop **Boyd Gaines**; Abigail **Grace Gummer**; Halberstam **Stephen Kunken**; Philip **Marc Bonan**

UNDERSTUDIES Marc Bonan (Andrei), Charlotte Maier (Susan Mary Alsop), Anthony Newfield (Joseph Alsop), Brian J. Smith (Philip), Adria Vitlar (Abigail), Tony Ward (Stewart Alsop, Halberstam)

SETTING Washington, D.C. and other locations; mid-twentieth century. World premiere of a new play presented in two acts.

SYNOPSIS *The Columnist* is based on the real-life syndicated political columnist Joseph Alsop. Columnists are kings in midcentury America and Alsop wears the crown. Joe is beloved, feared and courted in equal measure by the Washington political world at whose center he sits. But as the '60s dawn and America undergoes dizzying change, the intense political drama Joe is embroiled in becomes deeply personal as well.

John Lithgow and Boyd Gaines

John Lithgow and Grace Gummer

Margaret Colin

John Lithgow and Brian J. Smith

Don't Dress for Dinner

American Airlines Theatre; First Preview: March 30, 2012; Opening Night: April 26, 2012; 32 previews, 41 performances as of May 31, 2012

Ben Daniels, Spencer Kayden, and Patricia Kalember

Written by Marc Camoletti, adapted by Robin Hawdon; Produced by the Roundabout Theatre Company (Todd Haimes, Artistic Director; Harold Wolpert, Managing Director; Julia C. Levy, Executive Director) in association with Damian Arnold; Director, John Tillinger; Sets, John Lee Beatty; Costumes, William Ivey Long; Lighting, Ken Billington; Sound, David Van Tieghem; Hair and Wigs, Paul Huntley; Fight Director, Thomas Schall; Production Stage Manager, Barclay Stiff; Production Management, Aurora Productions; Casting, Jim Carnahan, Carrie Gardner, Stephen Kopel, Laura Stanczyk; General Manager, Denise Cooper; Company Manager, Carly DiFulvio; Stage Manager, Kelly Beaulieu; Assistant Director, Jessica Creane; Associate Design: Kacie Hultgren (set), Cathy Parrot (costumes), John Demous (lighting), Dave Sanderson (sound); Director of William Ivey Long Studios, Donald Sanders; Costume Intern, Emily Winokur; Makeup, Angelina Avallone; Makeup Assistant, Valentina Celada; Tango Instuctor, Dardo Galletto; Production Properties Supervisor, Peter Sarafin; Assistant Production Properties, Buist Bickley; Crew: Glenn Merwede (production carpenter), Brian Maiuri (production electrician), Robert W. Dowling III (running properties), Dann Wojnar (sound operator), Susan J. Fallon (wardrobe supervisor), Dale Carman, Kat Martin (dressers), Jillian Tilley (wardrobe dayworker), Manuela Laporte (hair and wig supervisor), Davin De Santis (production assistant); For Aurora Productions: Gene O' Donovan, Ben Heller, Stephanie Sherline, Jarid Sumner, Anthony Jusino, Anita Shah, Liza Luxenberg, Steven Dalton, Eugenio Saenz Flores, Isaac Katzanek, Melissa Mazdra; Roundabout Staff: Sydney Beers (General Manager), Greg Backstrom (Associate Managing Director); Thomas Mygatt (Director of Marketing and Sales Promotion); Lynne Gugenheim Gregory (Director of Development); Gene Feist (Founding Director), Scott Ellis (Adams Associate Artistic Director); Greg McCaslin (Education Director), Sydney Beers (General Manager), Susan Neiman (Director of Finance), Daniel V. Gomez (Director of Information Technology), Wendy Hutton (Director of Audience Services), Charlie Gabowski Jr. (Director of Sales Operations); Advertising, SpotCo; Interactive Marketing, Situation Interactive; Press, Boneau/Bryan-Brown, Adrian Bryan-Brown, Matt Polk, Jessica Johnson, Amy Kass

Adam James, Jennifer Tilly, and Ben Daniels (photos by Joan Marcus)

CAST Bernard **Adam James**; Jacqueline **Patricia Kalember**; Robert **Ben Daniels**; Suzette **Spencer Kayden**; Suzanne **Jennifer Tilly**; George **David Aron Damane**

UNDERSTUDIES Tom Galantich (Robert), Frances Mercanti-Anthony (Jacqueline, Suzette, Suzanne), James Andrew O'Connor (Bernard, George)

2011-2012 AWARD Outer Critics Circle Award: Outstanding Featured Actress in a Play (Spencer Kayden)

SETTING 1960: A country home northwest of Paris. Broadway premiere of a comedy presented in two acts. Originally produced in Paris where it ran for over two years, the play opened in the West End at the Apollo Theatre in March 1991, transferred to the Duchess Theatre where it ran for six years. Mr. Tillinger directed a production of the show at the Royal George Theatre in Chicago in November 2008 featuring Ms. Kayden and Ms. Kalember.

SYNOPSIS *Don't Dress for Dinner* is an affair—or three!—to remember. Bernard's plans for a romantic rendezvous with his mistress are complete with a gourmet caterer and an alibi courtesy of his friend, Robert. But when Bernard's wife learns that Robert will be visiting for the weekend, she decides to stay in town for a surprise tryst of her own… setting the stage for a collision course of hidden identities and outrageous infidelities. The cook is Suzette, the lover is Suzanne, the friend is bewildered, the wife is suspicious, the husband is losing his mind and everyone is guaranteed a good time at this hilarious romp through the French countryside.

Spencer Kayden, Patricia Kalember, Jennifer Tilly, and David Aaron Damane

Leslie Odom Jr. and Kecia Lewis-Evans

Jessica Phillips and Raúl Espaza

Leap of Faith

St. James Theatre; First Preview: April 3, 2012; Opening Night: April 26, 2012; Closed May 13, 2012; 24 previews, 20 performances

Music by Alan Menken, book by Janus Cercone and Warren Leight, lyrics by Glenn Slater; Based on the motion picture *Leap of Faith*, produced by Paramount Pictures Corporation and written by Janus Cercone; Produced by Michael Manheim, James D. Stern, Douglas L. Meyer, Marc Routh, Richard Frankel, Tom Viertel, Steven Baruch, Annette Niemtzow, Daryl Roth, Robert G. Bartner, Steven and Shanna Silva, Endgame Entertainment, Patricia Monaco, Debi Coleman, Dancap Productions Inc., Steve Kaplan, Relativity Media LLC, Rich/Caudwell, Center Theatre Group, in association with Michael Palitz, Richard J. Stern, Melissa Pinkly/Celine Rosenthal, Independent Presenters Network, Diana Buckhantz, Pamela Cooper, Vera Guerin, Leading Investment Co. Ltd., Christina Papagjika, Victor Syrmis, Semlitz/Glaser Productions, and Jujamcyn Theatres; Director, Christopher Ashley; Choreography, Sergio Trujillo; Music Supervision, Michael Kosarin; Sets, Robin Wagner; Costumes, William Ivey Long; Lighting, Don Holder; Sound, John Shivers; Video Coordinator, Shawn Sagady; Wigs and Hair, Paul Huntley; Makeup, Angelina Avallone; Casting, Telsey + Company; Orchestrations, Michael Starobin, Joseph Joubert; Vocal and Incidental Music Arrangements, Michael Kosarin; Dance Music Arrangements, Zane Mark; Music Director, Brent-Alan Huffman; Music Coordinator, John Miller; Associate Director, Beatrice Terry; Associate Choreographer, Edgar Godineaux; Production Supervisor, Steven Zweigbaum; General Management, Frankel Green Theatrical Management (Richard Frankel, Laura Green, Joe Watson); Technical Supervision, Neil A. Mazzella/Hudson Theatrical Associates; Associate Producers, Broadway Across America (John Gore, CEO); Company Manager, Kathy Lowe; Associate Company Manager, Sammy Ledbetter; Technical Supervisor, Sam Ellis; Production Supervisor, Steven Zweigbaum; Stage Manager, Joseph Sheridan; Assistant Stage Manager, Marisha Ploski; Assistant Choreography, Dionne Figgins; Dance Captain, Ian Paget; Assistant Dance Captain, Manoly Farrell; Illusion Design, Afterglow Group LLC/Peter Samelson; Associate Design: David Peterson (set), Martha Bromelmeier (costumes), Jeanne Koenig (lighting), David Patridge (sound), Giovanna Calabretta, Edward J. Wilson (wigs); Assistant Design: Atkin Pace (set), Brenda Abbandandolo (costumes), Heather Graff, Karen Spahn (lighting); Assistants to William Ivey Long, Brian Mear, Donald Sanders, Jennifer Raskopf; Associate General Manager, Joshua A. Saletnik; Company Management Assistant, Katie Pope; Company Management Intern, Mike McLinden; SDC Observer, Lindsey Hope Pearlman; Synthesizer Programmer, Jeff Marder; Music Copying, Anixter Rice Music Services, Russ Anixter, Don Rice; Rehearsal Musicians, Perry Cavari, Jesse Kissel; Music Production Assistant, Scott Wasserman; Crew: Todd Frank (head carpenter), Chris Pravata, Robert Valli (assistant carpenters), James Maloney (production electrician), Ron Schwier (associate production electrician), Ross Feilhauer (advance electrician), Ron Schwier (head electrician), Aland Henderson (moving light programmer), Kevin Kennedy (advance production sound engineer), David Patridge (head sound engineer), Peter Karrer (assistant sound engineer), Eric Castaldo (head props), Dan Mueller (video programmer), Robert Guy (wardrobe supervisor), Kimberly Baird (assistant wardrobe supervisor), Kevin O'Brien (Mr. Esparza's dresser), Renée Borys, Susan E. Cook, Sara Darneille, Victoria Grecki, David Grevengoed, Josephn Hickey, Dawn Marcoccia, Kimberly Mark, Barbara Morse, Melanie Olbrych, Shonté Walker (dressers), Edward J. Wilson (hair and wig supervisor), Jeanette Harrington (assistant hair and wig supervisor); Daniel Koye, Cheryl Thomas, Alison Wadsworth (hairdressers), Lawrence Copeland, T.J. Kearney, Deanna Weiner (production assistants); Turtoring On Location Education, Lisa Chasin, Irene Karasik; Children's Guardian, Rachel Maier; Assistants, Karen Bove (Mr. Stern), Melissa Pinsly (Mr. Routh), Tania Senewiratne (Mr. Viertel), Sonja Soper (Mr. Baruch); Advertising/Digital Outreach and Website, Serino/Coyne; Press, Boneau/Bryan-Brown, Chris Boneau, Jackie Green, Kelly Guiod; Cast recording: Sh-K-Boom/Ghostlight Records 84465

CAST Ida Mae Sturdevant **Kecia Lewis-Evans**; Isaiah Sturdevant **Leslie Odom Jr.**; Ornella Sturdevant **Krystal Joy Brown**; Jonas Nightingale **Raúl Esparza**; Brother Zak **Bryce Ryness**; Sam Nightingale **Kendra Kassebaum**; Brother Amon **C.E. Smith**; Brother Carl **Dennis Stowe**; Marla McGowan **Jessica Phillips**; Emma Schlarp **Roberta Wall**; Jake McGowan **Talon Ackerman**; Susie Raylove **Michelle Duffy**; Amanda Wayne **Dierdre Friel**; Angels of Mercy **Hettie Barnhill**, **Ta'Rea Campbell**, **Lynorris Evans**, **Bob Gaynor**, **Lucia Giannetta**, **Angela Grovey**, **Tiffany Janene Howard**, **Grasan Kingsberry**, **Fletcher McTaggart**, **Eliseo Román**, **Bryce Ryness**, **C.E. Smith**, **Dennis Stowe**, **Betsy Struxness**, **Virginia Ann Woodruff**; Townspeople **Michelle Duffy**, **Dierdre Friel**, **Bob Gaynor**, **Louis Hobson**, **Ann Sanders**, **Danny Stiles**, **Betsy Struxness**, **Roberta Wall**; Offstage Vocalists **Maurice Murphy**, **Terita Redd**; Swings **Malony Farrell**, **Maurice Murphy**, **Ian Paget**, **Terita Redd**

UNDERSTUDIES Kyle Brenn (Jake McGowan), Ta'Rea Campbell (Ornella Sturdevant), Michelle Duffy (Marla McGowan, Sam Nightingale), Angela Grovey (Ida Mae Sturdevant), Louis Hobson (Jonas Nightingale), Grasan Kingsberry (Isaiah Sturdevant), Maurice Murphy (Isaiah Sturdevant), Terita Redd (Ornella Sturdevant), Bryce Ryness (Jonas Nightingale), Ann Sanders (Marla McGowan), Betsy Struxness (Sam Nightingale), Virginia Ann Woodruff (Ida Mae Sturdevant)

ORCHESTRA Brent-Alan Huffman (Conductor); Jason Michael Webb (Associate Conductor/Piano/Synthesizer); Jeff Marder (Assistant Conductor/Hammond B3/Synthesizer); Rick Dolan (Concert Master); Gregory Thymius, Charles Pillow, Dave Noland, Roger Rosenberg (Woodwinds); Matthew Peterson, Gregory L. Gisbert, Jeremy Miloszewicz (Trumpets/Flügels);: Timothy Sessions (Trombone/Bass Trombone); Una Tone, Shinwon Kim (Violins); Richard Brice (Viola); Sarah Hewitt-Roth (Cello); Lynn Keller (Electric Bass); David Spinozza (Guitar); Perry Cavari (Drums/Percussion)

MUSICAL NUMBERS Rise Up!; Fox in the Henhouse; Fields of the Lord; Step Into the Light; Walking Like Daddy; Lost; I Can Read You; Like Magic; I Can Read You (reprise); Dancin' in the Devil's Shoes; King of Sin; Dancin' in the Devil's Shoes (reprise); Rise Up! (reprise); Long Past Dreamin'; Are You on the Bus?; Like Magic (reprise); People Like Us; Last Chance Salvation; If Your Faith Is Strong Enough; Jonas' Soliloquy; Leap of Faith

SETTING The St. James Theatre, New York, and Sweetwater, Kansas; the present. New York premiere of a new musical presented in two acts. World premiere presented at Center Theatre Group's Ahmanson Theatre (Michael Ritchie, Artistic Director; Charles Dillingham, Managing Director) September 11–October 24, 2010 (see *Theatre World* Vol. 67, page 334) with most of this company.

SYNOPSIS Based on the motion picture of the same name, *Leap of Faith* tells the story of Jonas Nightingale, an electrifying performer and rabble-rouser who's planning to take the whole town for a ride. But when a small-town girl stops him in his tracks, the hustler may just discover something to believe in.

Raúl Esparza (photos by Joan Marcus)

Raúl Esparza and the Company

Raúl Esparza and the Company

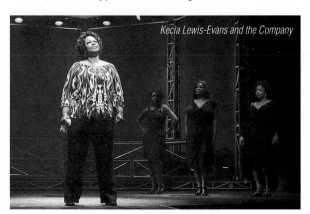

Kecia Lewis-Evans and the Company

PLAYED THROUGH/CLOSED THIS SEASON

The Addams Family

Lunt-Fontanne Theatre; First Preview: March 8, 2010; Opening Night: April 8, 2010; Closed December 31, 2011; 35 previews, 725 performances

Book by Marshall Brickman & Rick Elice, music by Andrew Lippa; Based on characters created by Charles Addams; Produced by Stuart Oken, Roy Furman, Michael Leavitt, Five Cent Productions, Stephen Schuler, Decca Theatricals, Scott M. Delman, Stuart Ditsky, Terry Allen Kramer, Stephanie P. McClelland, James L. Nederlander, Eva Price, Jam Theatricals (Arny Granat, Jerry Mickelson, Steve Traxler)/Mary Lu Roffe, Pittsburgh CLO/Jay & Cindy Gutterman/Mort Swinsky, Vivek Tiwary/Gary Kaplan, The Weinstein Company/Clarence LLC, Adam Zotovich/Tribe Theatricals (Carl Moellenberg, Wendy Federman, Jamie deRoy, Larry Hirschhorn) in special arrangement with Elephant Eye Theatrical; Direction/Design, Phelim McDermott & Julian Crouch; Choreography, Sergio Trujillo; Creative Consultant, Jerry Zaks; Lighting, Natasha Katz; Sound, Acme Sound Partners, Puppetry, Basil Twist; Hair, Tom Watson; Makeup, Angelina Avallone; Special Effects, Gregory Meeh; Orchestrations, Larry Hochman; Music Director, Mary-Mitchell Campbell; Dance Arrangements, August Eriksmoen; Vocal Arrangements & Incidental Music, Andrew Lippa; Casting, Telsey + Company; Marketing, Type A Marketing; Music Coordinator, Michael Keller; Production Management, Aurora Productions; General Management, 101 Productions Ltd.; Production Supervisor 2009-2011, Beverly Randolph; Company Manager, Tracy Geltman; Production Stage Manager, Scott Taylor Rollison; Stage Manager, Allison A. Lee; Assistant Stage Manager, Zac Chandler; Associate Directors, Heidi Miami Marshal, Steve Bebout; Associate Choreographer, Dontee Kiehn; Associate Company Manager, Chris D'Angelo; Associate Design: Frank McCullough (set), MaryAnn D. Smith, David Kaley (costumes), Yael Lubetzky (lighting), Jason Crystal (sound), Jeremy Chernick (special effects), Ceili Clemens (puppets); Automated Lighting, Aland Henderson; Assistant Design: Lauren Alvarez, Jeffrey Hinchee, Christine Peters (set), Sarah Laux (costumes), Joel Shier (lighting), Jorge Vargas (makeup); Costume Assistant, Jennifer A. Jacob; Assistant in Puppetry, Meredith Miller; Music Preparation, Kaye-Houston Music Inc.; Electronic Music Programmer, James Abbott; Additional Orchestrations, August Eriksmoen, Danny Troob; Additional Drum & Percussion Arrangements, Damien Bassman; Advertising, Serino/Coyne, Sandy Block, Angelo Desimini; Interactive Marketing, Situation Interactive; Press, The Publicity Office, Marc Thibodeau, Jeremy Shaffer, Michael S. Borowski, Matthew Fasano; Cast recording: Decca 001428002

CAST *The Addams Family*: Gomez Addams **Roger Rees**; Morticia Addams **Bebe Neuwirth**[*1]; Uncle Fester **Brad Oscar**; Grandma **Jackie Hoffman**; Wednesday Addams **Rachel Potter**; Pugsley Addams **Adam Riegler**; Lurch **Zachary James**; *The Beineke Family*: Mal Beineke **Adam Grupper**; Alice Beineke **Heidi Blickenstaff**; Lucas Beineke **Jesse Swenson**; *The Addams Ancestors*: **Becca Ayers, Tom Berklund, Mo Brady, Erick Buckley, Stephanie Gibson, Matthew Gumley, Fred Inkley, Lisa Karlin, Reed Kelly, Allison Thomas Lee, Jessica Lea Patty, Liz Ramos, Logan Rowland, Courtney Wolfson**; Standby for Gomez Addams and Mal Beineke **Merwin Foard**; Swings **Jim Borstelmann, Michael Buchanan, Colin Cunliffe**[*2], **Valerie Fagan, Dontee Kiehn, Tess Soltau, Samantha Sturm, Charlie Sutton**

UNDERSTUDIES For Gomez: Jim Borstelmann; For Morticia: Stephanie Gibson, Becca Ayers; For Uncle Fester: Jim Borstelmann, Erick Buckley; For Wednesday: Jessica Lea Patty, Lisa Karlin, Courtney Wolfson; For Grandma: Becca Ayers, Valerie Fagan; For Pugsley: Logan Rowland; For Lurch: Fred Inkley, Tom Berklund; For Mal: Fred Inkley; For Alice: Valerie Fagan, Becca Ayers; For Lucas: Colin Cunliffe, Mo Brady

*Succeeded by: 1. Brooke Shields (6/28/11) 2. Mike Cannon

ORCHESTRA Mary-Mitchell Campbell (Conductor), Marco Paguia (Associate Conductor/Keyboard 1), Victoria Paterson (Concert Master/Violin), Sean Carney (Violin), Hiroko Taguchi (Viola), Allison Seidner (Cello), John Chudoba, Bud Burridge (Trumpet), Robert Stuttmann (Trombones/Tuba), Erica Von Kleist (Reed 1), Charles Pillow (Reed 2), Frank Santagata (Reed 3), Zohar Schondorf (French Horn), Damien Bassman (Drums), Dave Kuhn (Bass), Dave Pepin (Keyboard 2), Jim Hershman (Guitars), Billy Miller (Percussion)

MUSICAL NUMBERS Overture; When You're an Addams; Pulled; Where Did We Go Wrong; One Normal Night; Morticia; What If; Full Disclosure; Waiting; Full Disclosure – Part 2; Entr'acte; Just Around the Corner; The Moon and Me; Happy/Sad; Crazier Than You; Let's Not Talk About Anything Else But Love; In the Arms; Live Before We Die; Tango de Amor; Move Toward the Darkness

SETTING The Addams Family mansion in Central Park, New York City. New York premiere of a new musical presented in two acts. World premiere (out-of-town tryout) at the Ford Center for the Performing Arts Oriental Theatre in Chicago, Illinois, November 13, 2009–January 10, 2010.

SYNOPSIS Based on the beloved *The New Yorker* cartoon characters created by American cartoonist Charles Addams, *The Addams Family* is a new musical comedy about the ghoulish clan that lives by its own rules in a haunted mansion. The macabre family is put to the test when daughter Wednesday falls for the normal "boy next door," Lucas Beineke. When the Beineke family comes to dinner, Gomez, Morticia, Wednesday, Pugsley, Fester, Grandma, and Lurch are sent headlong into a night that will change the family forever.

Brooke Shields, Zachary James, Rachel Potter, and Jesse Swenson (photo by Jeremy Daniel)

Anything Goes

Stephen Sondheim Theatre; First Preview: March 10, 2011; Opening Night: April 7, 2011; 32 previews, 477 performances as of May 31, 2012

Music and lyrics by Cole Porter, original book by P.G. Wodehouse, Guy Bolton, Howard Lindsay and Russell Crouse; Revised book by Timothy Crouse and John Weidman; Produced by the Roundabout Theatre Company (Todd Haimes, Artistic Director; Harold Wolpert, Managing Director; Julia C. Levy, Executive Director) Director and Choreographer, Kathleen Marshall; Musical Supervisor/Vocal Arrangements, Rob Fisher; Sets, Derek McLane; Costumes, Martin Pakledinaz; Lighting, Peter Kaczorowski; Sound, Brian Ronan; Additional Orchestrations, Bill Elliott; Original Orchestrations, Michael Gibson; Dance Arrangements, David Chase; Music Director, James Lowe; Music Coordinator, Seymour Red Press; Hair & Wigs, Paul Huntley; Makeup, Angelina Avallone; Production Stage Manager, Peter Hanson; Casting, Jim Carnahan & Stephen Kopel; Associate Director, Marc Bruni; Associate Choreographer, Vince Pesce; Technical Supervisor, Steve Beers; Executive Producer, Sydney Beers; Director of Marketing & Sales Promotion, David B. Steffen/Thomas Mygatt; Director of Development, Lynne Gugenheim Gregory; Founding Director, Gene Feist; Associate Artistic Director, Scott Ellis; Company Manager, Doug Gaeta/Karl Baudendistel; Assistant Company Manager, David Solomon; Stage Manager, Jon Krause; Assistant Stage Manager, Rachel Bauder; Dance Captain, Jennifer Savelli; Assistant Dance Captain, Justin Greer; Assistant Choreographer, David Eggers; Music Preparation, Emily Grishman, Katharine Edmonds; Synthesizer Programer, Bruce Samuels; Associate Design: Sara Jean Tosetti (costumes), Paul Toben (lighting), Giovanna Calabretta (hair & wigs); Assistant Design: Erica Hemminger (set), John Emmett O'Brien (sound); Costume Design Assistant, Carisa Kelly; Assistant to the Costume Designer, Justin Hall; Music Department Interns, Molly Gachignard, Ian Weinberger; Costume Interns, Hannah Kittel, Shannon Smith, Heather Mathiesen; Crew: Shannon Slaton (production sound engineer/mixer), Paul Ashton (automation operator), William Craven (flyman), Josh Weitzman (production electrician/moving lights programmer), John Wooding, Jocelyn Smith (assistant production electricians), Dorian Fuchs, Erika Warmbrunn, Jessica Morton (follow spots), Jocelyn Smith, Francis Elers (deck electricians), Andrew Forste (house props), Dan Mendeloff, Nelson Vaughn (props run crew), Carrie Mossman (associate production props), Mike Billings, Tim Ferro, Cathy Small, Mary Wilson (prop artisans), Nadine Hettel (wardrobe supervisor), Suzanne Delahunt, Tara Delahunt, Kevin Mark Harris, Julien Havard, Emily Meriweather, Pamela Pierzina, Stacy Sarmiento (dressers), Nathaniel Hathaway (hair and wig supervisor), Monica Costea, Heather Wright (hair and wig assistants); SDC Oberver, Adam Cates; Production Assistants, Rachel Baudner, Hannah Dorfman; Advertising, SpotCo; Interactive Marketing, Situation Interactive; Roundabout Staff: Jim Carnahan Director of Artistic Develpoment/Casting, Greg McCaslin (Education), Susan Neiman (Finance), Antonio Palumbo (IT Director), Charlie Garbowski Jr. (Ticketing Sales); Press, Boneau/Bryan-Brown, Adrian Bryan-Brown, Matt Polk, Jessica Johnson, Amy Kass; Cast recording: Sh-K-Boom/Ghostlight Records 84452

CAST Elisha J. Whitney **John McMartin**[*1]; Fred, *a bartender* **Josh Franklin**[*2]; Billy Crocker **Colin Donnell**[*3]; Reno Sweeney **Sutton Foster**[*4]; Captain **Walter Charles**[*5]; Ship's Purser **Robert Creighton**; Crew **Clyde Alves**[*6], **Ward Billeisen**, **Daniel J. Edwards**, **Josh Franklin**[*2], **Kevin Munhall**, **Adam Perry**[*7], **William Ryall**, **Anthony Wayne**[*8]; A Reporter **Anthony Wayne**[*8]; A Photographer **Clyde Alves**[*6]; Henry T. Dobson, *a minister* **William Ryall**; Luke **Andrew Cao**; John **Raymond J. Lee**; *Angels:* Purity **Shina Ann Morris**; Chastity **Kimberly Fauré**[*9]; Charity **Jennifer Savelli**; Virtue **Joyce Chittick**[*10]; Hope Harcourt **Laura Osnes**[*11]; Mrs. Evangeline Harcourt **Jessica Walter**[*12]; Lord Evelyn Oakleigh **Adam Godley**[*13]; Erma **Jessica Stone**; Moonface Martin **Joel Grey**; Old Lady in Wheelchair **Linda Muggleston**[*14]; FBI Agents **Adam Perry**[*7], **Kevin Munhall**; Quartet **Ward Billeisen**, **Josh Franklin**[*2], **Daniel J. Edwards**, **William Ryall**; Ship's Passengers **Clyde Alves**[*6], **Ward Billeisen**, **Nikki Renée Daniels**[*15], **Daniel J. Edwards**, **Josh Franklin**[*2], **Tari Kelly**, **Linda Muggleston**[*14], **Kevin Munhall**, **Adam Perry**[*7], **William Ryall**, **Anthony Wayne**[*6], **Kristen Beth Williams**[*16]; Swings[*17] **Margot de la Barre**, **Justin Greer**

UNDERSTUDIES Clyde Alves[*6] (Purser), Joyce Chittick[*10] (Erma), Robert Creighton (Moonface Martin), Nikki Renée Daniels[*15] (Hope Harcourt), Daniel J. Edwards (John, Luke), Josh Franklin[*2] (Billy Crocker, Lord Evelyn Oakleigh), Justin Greer (Purser), Tari Kelly (Reno, Erma), Linda Muggleston[*14] (Mrs. Evangeline Harcourt), William Ryall (Captain, Elisha J. Whitney), Kiira Schmidt (Reno)

Succeeded by: 1. John Horton (5/1/12) 2. Derek Hanson (Jan. 2012) 3. Bill English (1/24/12), Colin Donnell (2/21/12), Bill English (3/2/12), Colin Donnell (4/3/12), Bill English (5/1/12) 4. Tari Kelly (8/22/11), Sutton Foster (8/30/11), Stephanie J. Block (11/4/11), Sutton Foster (11/24/11), Stephanie J. Block (3/15/12) 5. Ed Dixon (5/1/12) 6. Brandon Bieber 7. Brandon Rubendall 8. Lawrence Alexander 9. Kearran Giovanni, Brittany Marcin (3/3/12) 10. Hayley Podschun, Kaitlin Mesh (5/22/11) 11. Erin Mackey (11/13/11) 12. Kelly Bishop (8/9/11), Julie Halston (1/17/12) 13. Robert Petkoff (1/13/12) 14. Leslie Becker 15. Mary Michael Patterson 16. Kiira Schmidt, Janine DiVita 17. Michelle Lookadoo, Vanessa Sonon

ORCHESTRA James Lowe (Conductor), David Gursky (Associate Conductor/ Piano), James Ercole, Ronald Jannelli, Ralph Olsen, David Young (Reeds), Earl Gardner, Ken Rampton, Stu Satalof (Trumpets), Larry Ferrell, Robert Fornier, Wayne Goodman/Larry Farrell (Trombones), Jeffrey Carney (Bass), John Redsecker (Drums), Bill Hayes (Percussion), Eric Davis (Guitar)

MUSICAL NUMBERS I Get a Kick Out of You; There's No Cure Like Travel; Bon Voyage; You're the Top; Easy to Love; Easy to Love (reprise); The Crew Song; Friendship; There'll Always Be A Lady Fair (Sailor's Chantey); Friendship (reprise); It's De-lovely; Anything Goes; Public Enemy #1; Blow, Gabriel, Blow; Goodbye, Little Dream, Goodbye; Be Like the Bluebird; All Through the Night; The Gypsy in Me; Buddie, Beware; Finale

SETTING A smoky Manhattan bar and onboard a luxury ocean liner; 1930s. Revival of a musical presented in two acts. The original Broadway production, starring Ethyl Merman, was presented at the Alvin (Neil Simon) Theatre and the 46th Street (Richard Rodgers) Theatre November 21, 1934–November 16, 1935. The musical was first revived Off-Broadway at the Orpheum Theatre May 15– December 9, 1962 and incorporated songs from the film version and songs from other Cole Porter musicals (see *Theatre World* Vol. 18, page 164). Lincoln Center Theater revived and revised the musical at the Vivian Beaumont Theater October 19, 1987–September 3, 1989 (starring Patti LuPone), playing 784 performances (see *Theatre World* Vol. 44, page 92). This new revival is based on the Lincoln Center revival version.

SYNOPSIS Cole Porter's classic musical *Anything Goes* returns to Broadway for its second major revival. When the S.S. American heads out to sea, etiquette and convention head out the portholes as two unlikely pairs set off on the course to true love… proving that sometimes destiny needs a little help from a crew of singing sailors, an exotic disguise and some good old-fashioned blackmail.

Stephanie J. Block and the Company

Raúl Esparza, Tom Riley, and Lia Williams

Lia Williams and Noah Robbins

Arcadia

Ethel Barrymore Theatre; First Preview: February 26, 2011; Opening Night: March 17, 2011; Closed June 19, 2011; 20 previews, 108 performances

Written by Tom Stoppard; Produced by Sonia Friedman Productions, Roger Berlind, Stephanie P. McClelland, Scott M. Delman, Nicholas Quinn Rosenkranz, Disney Theatrical Group, Robert G. Bartner, Olympus Theatricals, Douglas Smith, in association with Janine Safer Whitney; Director, David Levaux; Set, Hildegard Bechtler; Costumes, Gregory Gale; Lighting, Donald Holder; Sound, David Van Tieghem; Hair, David Bryan Brown; Music, Corin Buckeridge; Casting, Jim Carnahan; Advertising and Marketing, aka; U.S. General Management, 101 Productions Ltd.; U.K. General Management, Sonia Friedman Productions; Production Stage Manager, Ira Mont; Technical Supervisro, Peter Fulbright; Dialect Consultant, Elizabeth Smith; Choreographer, Jodi Moccia; Company Manager, David van Zyll de Jong; Makeup, Naomi Donne; Stage Manager, Matthew Lacey; Assistant Director, Jawson Lawson; Associate Design, Colleen Kesterson (costumes), John Viesta (lighting), David Sanderson (sound); Assistant Design: Luke Smith (U.K. set), Evan Adamson & Frank McCullough (U.S. set), Caroline Chao & Michael P. Jones (lighting); Assistants to Mr. Gale, Julia Broer, Jennifer A. Jacob; Assistant to Mr. Holder, Anna Cecilia Martin; Crew: Rich Cocchiara (production carpenter), Michael LoBue (production electrician), Darin Stillman (production sound), Dylan Foley, Robert Presley (advance props), Robert Guy (wardrobe supervisor), Renee Borys, Kevin O'Brien (dressers), Rick Caroto (wig and hair supervisor), Jason Pelusio (production assistant); Press, Boneau/Bryan-Brown, Adrian Bryan-Brown, Aaron Meier, Emily Meagher

CAST Thomasina Coverly **Bel Powley**; Septimus Hodge **Tom Riley**; Jellaby **Edward James Hyland**; Ezra Chater **David Turner**; Richard Noakes **Byron Jennings**; Lady Croom **Margaret Colin**; Captain Brice, RN **Glenn Fleshler**; Hannah Jarvis **Lia Williams**; Chloë Coverly **Grace Gummer**; Bernard Nightingale **Billy Crudup**; Valentine Coverly **Raúl Esparza**; Gus Coverly/Augustus Coverly **Noah Robbins**

UNDERSTUDIES Bianca Amato (Hannah Jarvis, Lady Croom), Jack Cutmore-Scott (Augustus Coverly, Gus Coverly, Septimus Hodge), Alyssa May Gold (Chloë Coverly, Thomasina Coverly), Baylen Thomas (Bernard Nightingale, Valentine Coverly), Ray Virta (Captain Brice, RN, Ezra Chater, Jellaby, Richard Noakes)

SETTING The room on the garden front of a very large country house in Derbyshire, England; 1809 and the present day. Revival of a play presented in two acts. Mr. Levaux's production previously played the West End prior to this Broadway engagement. World premiere produced at the Royal National Theatre in London April 13, 1993. Lincoln Center Theater produced the New York premiere at the Vivian Beaumont Theater March 31–August 27, 1995 playing 173 performances (see *Theatre World* Vol. 51, page 47). Mr. Crudup appeared as "Septimus" in that production, and won a 1995 Theatre World Award for his Broadway debut.

SYNOPSIS Thomasina, a gifted pupil, proposes a startling theory, beyond her comprehension. All around her, the adults, including her tutor Septimus, are preoccupied with secret desires, illicit passions, and professional rivalries. Two hundred years later, academic adversaries Hannah and Bernard are piecing together puzzling clues, curiously recalling those events of 1809, in their quest for an increasingly elusive truth.

Grace Gummer and Billy Crudup (photos by Carol Rosegg)

Baby It's You!

Broadhurst Theatre; First Preview: March 26, 2011; Opening Night: April 27, 2011; Closed September 4, 2011; 33 previews, 148 performances

Book by Floyd Mutrux & Colin Escott, conceived by Floyd Mutrux; Produced by Warner Brothers Theatre Ventures (Gregg Maday, Executive Vice President/Lead Producer) and American Pop Anthology (Jonathan Sanger, Producer) in association with Universal Music Group and Pasadena Playhouse (Sheldon Epps, Artistic Director; Stephen Eich, Executive Director); Directors, Floyd Mutrux & Sheldon Epps; Choreography, Birgitte Mutrux; Music Director, Shelton Becton; Set, Anna Louizos; Costumes, Lizz Wolff; Lighting, Howell Binkley; Sound, Carl Casella; Projections, Jason H. Thompson; Hair & Wigs, David H. Lawrence; Casting, Telsey + Company; Production Stage Manager, Joshua Halperin; Music Supervisor & Arrangements, Rahn Coleman; Orchestrations, Don Sebesky; Music Coordinator, John Miller; Marketing, Type A Marketing, Anne Rippey; Advertising, SpotCo; Technical Director/Production Management, Brian Lynch; General Management, Alan Wasser, Allan Williams, Aaron Lustbader; Consulting Producer, Richard Perry; For Warner Brothers: Barry Meyer (Chairman & CEO), Alan Horn (President & COO); For Warner Theatre Ventures: Raymond Wu (SVP/Development/Operations; Laura Valan (CFO), Mark Coker (SVP Finance); For American Pop Anthology: Gerald Katell (Executive Producer), Artie Ripp (Historical Consultant); Company Manager, Matthew Sher; Casting, Telsey + Company; Stage Manager, Matthew Aron Stern; Assistant Stage Manager, Jason Brouillard; Assistant Company Manager, Maia Sutton; Assistant Choreographer, Tyrone A. Jackson; Associate Design: Aimee B. Dombo, Jeremy W. Foil (Set), Sarah Sophia Lidz (costumes), Ryan O'Gara (lighting), Wallace Flores (sound), Oslyn Holder (makeup); Assistant Design: Melissa Shakun (set), Amanda Bujak (costumes), Josh Liebert, Robert Hanlon (sound), Jeff Teeter, Resa Deverich (projections), Linda Rice (hair); Costume Design Assistant, Elizabeth Van Buren; Assistant to Mr. Binkley, Michael Rummage; Automated Lighting/Moving Lighting Programmer, David Arch; Music Copying, Emily Grishman, Katharine Edmonds; Synthesizer Programmer, Karl Mansfied; Music Clearances, Jill Myers Music, Projection Image Clearances, Jay Floyd; Crew: Brian McGarity (house carpenter), Chris Kluth (production carpenter), Robert Hentze (automation), Brian Bullard (flyman), Charlie DeVerna (house electrician), Keith Buchanan (production electrician), Patrick Harrington (spotlight), Matthew Mellinger (projection programming), Ronnie Vitelli (house props), George Wagner (production props), James Wilinson (production sound supervisor), Ty Lackey (production sound engineer), James Hall (wardrobe supervisor), Renee Kelly (hair supervisor), Jason Blair, Kay Gowenlock, Franklin Hollenbeck, Ginny Housel, Susan Kroeter, Ylena Nunez, Kathreine Sorg (dressers), Patricia Marcus, Richard Fabris (hairstylists); Assitant to John Miller, Jennifer Coolbaugh; Assitant to Mr. Epps, Courtney Harper; Assistant to Mr. Mutrux, Ashley Mutrux; Press, The Hartman Group, Michael Hartman, Wayne Wolfe, Nicole Capatasto; Cast recording: Universal/Verve Music Group VRVB001570402

CAST Florence Greenberg **Beth Leavel**; Luther Dixon **Allan Louis**; Jocko, Chuck Jackson, Ronald Isley, Gene Chandler **Geno Henderson**; Micki, Romantic, Dionne Warwick **Erica Ash**; Mary Jane Greenberg, Lesley Gore **Kelli Barrett**; Beverly, Ruby **Kyra Da Costa**; Millie **Erica Dorfler**; Street Singer **Jahi A. Kearse**; Doris, Romantic **Crystal Starr**; Bernie Greenberg, Milt Gabler **Barry Pearl**; Shirley **Christina Sajous**; Stanley Greenberg, Murray Schwartz, Kingsman **Brandon Uranowitz**

STANDBYS Erica Ash (Shirley), Alison Cimmet (Florence), Erica Dorfler (Beverly/Ruby, Doris/Romantic, Shirley), Berlando Drake (Beverly/Ruby, Micki/Romantic/Dionne Warwick, Shirley), Adam Heller (Bernie/Milt), Jahi A. Kearse (Jocko/Jacskon/Isley/Chandler), Annette Moore (Millie, Beverly/Ruby, Micki/Romantic/Warwick, Doris/Romantic), Zachary Prince (Stanley/Scwartz/Kingsman), Ken Robinson (Jocko/Jackson, Isley/Chandler, Luther), Chelsea Morgan Stock (Lesley Gore, Mary Jane)

ORCHESTRA Shelton Becton (Coductor/Synth 1), Joel Scott (Associate Conductor/Synth 2), Tom Murray (Reeds), Ravi Best (Trumpet/Flugel), Raymond Pounds (Drums), Francisco Centeno (Electric Bass), Michael Aarons (Guitar), Charlie Descarfino (Percussion)

MUSICAL NUMBERS Mr. Lee; Book of Love; Rockin' Robin; Dance With Me; Mama Said; Yakety Yak; Get a Job; The Stroll; I Met Him on a Sunday; Dedicated to the One I Love; Sixteen Candles; Tonight's the Night; Dedicated to the One I Love (reprise); Since I Don't Have You; Big John; He's So Fine; Soldier Boy; Shout; Twist And Shout; Mama Said; Mr. Bassman; Duke of Earl; Foolish Little Girl; It's My Party; Our Day Will Come; The Dark End of the Street; Rhythm of the Rain; You're So Fine; Hey Paula; Louie, Louie; You Really Got a Hold on Me; Baby It's You; Any Day Now; A Thing of the Past; Don't Make Me Over; Walk on By; Baby It's You (reprise); Tonight's the Night (reprise); Dedicated to the One I Love (reprise); I Say a Little Prayer; Shout (reprise); Twist and Shout

SETTING 1958-1965. Passaic, New Jersey and New York City. New York premiere of a new musical presented in two acts. World premiere produced at Pasadena Playhouse November 13–December 20, 2009.

SYNOPSIS *Baby It's You!* Is inspired by the true story of Florence Greenberg, the woman who changed the recording world forever. Before Motown and the British Invasion, Greenberg took the male-dominated music industry by storm, revolutionizing pop music and becoming the most influential and successful female record company president ever. After discovering one of the greatest girl-groups of all time, The Shirelles, at her daughter's high school, Greenberg packed the girls in her car, drove across the George Washington Bridge to New York City, and embarked on a trailblazing journey from New Jersey housewife to record mogul, creating the independent house of hits that was Scepter Records.

Crystal Starr, Christina Sajous, Beth Leavel, Erica Ash, and Kyra Da Costa

Crystal Starr, Erica Ash, Kyra Da Costa, Geno Henderson, and Christne Sajous (photos by Ari Mintz)

Bengal Tiger at the Baghdad Zoo

Richard Rodgers Theatre; First Preview: March 11, 2011; Opening Night: March 31, 2011; Closed July 3, 2011; 23 previews, 108 performances

Written by Rajiv Joseph; Produced by Robyn Goodman, Kevin McCollum, Jeffrey Seller, Sander Jacobs, Ruth Hendel/Burnt Umber, Scott Zeilinger, Brian Zeilinger, Center Theatre Group, Stephen Kocis/Walt Grossman; Director, Moisés Kaufman; Sets, Derek McLane; Costumes, David Zinn; Lighting, David Lander; Sound, Acme Sound Partners and Cricket S. Myers; Music, Kathryn Bostic; Casting Bonnie Grisan & MelCap Casting; Production Stage Manager, Beverly Jenkins; Original Fight Director, Bobby C. King; Technical Supervisor, Brian Lynch; General Management, Richards/Climan Inc.; Company Manager, Lizbeth Cone; Stage Manager, Alex Lyu Volckhausen; Production Assistants, Erica Christensen, Dwayne K. Mann, Johnny A. Milani; Assistant Director, Timothy Koch; Arabic Coach, Fajer Al-Kaisi; Translations/Cultural Consultants, Raida Fahmi, Ammar Ramzi; Associate Design: Brett Banakis (set) Jacob Climer (costumes), Heather Graf (lighting), Jason Crystal (sound); Assistant Lighting, Ben Pilat; Crew: McBrien Dunbar (head carpenter/automation), Cletus Karamon (head electrician), Justin Rathbun (head sound operator), Jay Pennfield (moving light programmer), Geroge Wagner (props supervisor), Ron Groomes (head props), Moira MacGregor-Conrad (wardrobe supervisor), Tree Sarvay (dresser); Additional Fight Direction, Ron Piretti; Fight Captain, Brad Fleischer; Gunshot Blood Effects, Hero Props/Seán McArdle; Hair & Makeup Supervisor-Special Effects, Adam Bailey; Assistant to Mr Williams, Rebecca Erwin Spencer; Advertising, SpotCo; Press, Sam Rudy Media Relations, Sam Rudy, Dale Heller

CAST Tiger **Robin Williams**; Tom **Glenn Davis**; Kev **Brad Fleischer**; Musa **Arian Moayed**; Iraqi Teenager, Hadia **Sheila Vand**; Iraqi Man, Uday **Hrach Titizian**; Iraqi Woman, Leper, Arabic Vocals **Necar Zadegan**

UNDERSTUDIES Understudies: Hend Ayoub (Hadia, Iraqi Teenager, Iraqi Woman, Leper), Corey Brill (Kev, Tom), Daoud Heidami (Iraqi Man, Musa, Uday), Sherman Howard (Tiger)

SETTING Baghdad; 2003. New York premiere of a new play presented in two acts. World premiere presented by Center Theatre Group (Michael Ritchie, Artistic Director; Charles Dillingham, Managing Director) at the Mark Taper Forum in Los Angeles April 14–May 30, 2010 (see *Theatre World* Vol. 66, page 356). Developed at the Lark Play Development Center in New York City.

SYNOPSIS In *Bengal Tiger At The Baghdad Zoo*, a tiger haunts the streets of present day Baghdad seeking the meaning of life. As he witnesses the puzzling absurdities of war, the tiger encounters Americans and Iraqis who are searching for friendship, redemption and a toilet seat made of gold.

Robin Williams (photos by Carol Rosegg)

Robin Williams, Brad Fleischer, and Glenn Davis

Arian Moayed and Sheila Vand

Billy Elliot

Imperial Theatre; First Preview: October 1, 2008; Opening Night: November 13, 2008; Closed January 8, 2012; 40 previews, 1,312 performances

Music by Elton John, book and lyrics by Lee Hall; based on the Universal Pictures/Studio Canal film *Billy Elliot* with screenplay by Lee Hall and direction by Stephen Daldry; Produced by Universal Pictures Stage Productions, Working Title Films, Old Vic Productions, in association with Weinstein Live Entertainment & Fidelity Investments; Director, Stephen Daldry; Choreography, Peter Darling; Associate Director, Julian Webber; Sets, Ian MacNeil; Costumes, Nicky Gillibrand; Lighting, Rick Fisher; Sound, Paul Arditti; Producers, Tim Bevan, Eric Fellner, Jon Fin, Sally Greene; Executive Producers, David Furnish, Angela Morrison; Musical Supervision and Orchestrations, Martin Koch; Music Director, David Chase; Associate Choreographer, Kathryn Dunn; Assistant Choreographer, Nikki Belsher; General Manager, Bespoke Theatricals; Hair/Wigs/Makeup, Campbell Young; U.K. Associate Design: Paul Atkinson (set), Claire Murphy (costumes), Vic Smerdon (lighting/programmer); John Owens (sound); Adult Casting, Tara Rubin; Children's Casting, Nora Brennan; Resident Director, B.T. McNicholl; Production Stage Manager, Bonnie L. Becker; Music Contractor, Michael Keller; Production Supervisors, Arthur Siccardi, Patrick Sullivan; General Management, Nina Lannan Associates/Devin Keudell; U.K. Casting, Pippa Ailion; Company Manager, Greg Arst; Associate Company Manager, Carol. M. Dune; Assistant Company Manager, Ashley Berman; Stage Manager, Scott Rowen; Assistant Stage Managers, Charlene Speyerer, Andrew C. Gottlieb; Supervising Dialect Coach (U.K.), William Conacher; Resident Dialect Coach, Ben Furey; Resident Director, Mark Schneider; Resident Choreographers, Sara Brians, Kurt Froman;

The Company (photos by Carol Rosegg)

Peter Mazurowski, Emily Skinner, and the Ballet Girls

Fight Director, David S. Leong; Dance Captains, Robbie Roby, Michaeljon Slinger, Cara Kjellman, Alison Levenberg; Fight Captain, Jason Babinsky; Choreographic Supervision, Ellen Kane; Staging and Dance Assistant, Lee Proud; U.S. Associate Design: Brian Russman (costumes), Daniel Walker (lighting), Tony Smolenski IV (sound); Moving Lights, David Arch; Music Copying, Emily Grishman Music Preparation; Ballet Instructors, Finis Jhung, Francois Perron; Acrobat Instructor, Hector Salazar; Marketing, Allied Live and aka; Advertising, SpotCo; Press, The Hartman Group; London Cast recording: Decca Broadway B0006 130-72

CAST Billy[*1] **Tade Biesinger** or **Jacob Clemente** or **Joseph Harrington** or **Peter Mazrowski**; Mrs. Wilkinson **Emily Skinner**; Dad **Gregory Jbara**[*2]; Grandma **Carole Shelley**[*3]; Tony **Will Chase**[*4]; George **Joel Hatch**[*5]; Michael[*6] **Cameron Clifford** or **Neil McCaffrey**[*6]; Debbie **Lilla Crawford**; Small Boy[*6] **Alex Dreier** or **Zachary Maitlin**; Big Davey **Brad Nacht**[*7]; Lesley **Stephanie Kurtzuba**; Scab/Posh Dad **Drew McVety**; Mum **Laura Marie Duncan**; Mr. Braithwaite **Thommie Retter**; Tracey Atkinson **Ruby Rakos**[*8]; Older Billy/Scottish Dancer **Stephen Hanna**; Mr. Wilkerson **Brad Bradley**; Pit Supervisor **Autin Lesch**; Tall Boy/Posh Boy[*9] **Ben Cook** or **Tade Biesinger** or **Joseph Harrington** or **Peter Mazrowski**; Clipboard Woman **Liz Pearce**; "Expressing Yourself" Dancers **Michael Arnold**, **Kevin Bernard**, **Jason Babinsky**, **Brad Bradley**, **Jeremy Davis**, **C.K. Edwards**, **Stephanie Kurtzuba**, **David Larsen**, **Nicholas Sipes**, **Grant Turner**; Ensemble[*10] **Michael Arnold**, **Kevin Bernard**, **Brad Bradley**, **Laura Marie Duncan**, **C.K. Edwards**, **Eric Gunhus**, **Stephen Hanna**, **Aaron Kaburick**, **Stephanie Kurtzuba**, **David Larsen**, **Merle Louise**, **Austin Lesch**, **Brad Nacht**, **Liz Pearce**, **Thommie Retter**, **Grant Turner**, **Christopher Brian Williams**, **Thad Turner Wilson**, **Katrina Yaukey**; Ballet Girls[*11] **Ali Brier**, **Ava DeMary**, **Eboni Edwards**, **Makenzi Rae Fischbach**, **Marina Micalizzi**, **Ruby Rakos**, **Kendra Tate**, **Holly Taylor**, **Kayla Vanderbilt**; Swings[*12] **Stephen Carrasco**, **Jeremy Davis**, **Cara Kjellman**, **David Koch**, **Alison Levenberg**, **Robbie Roby**, **Michaeljon Slinger**, **Ryan Steele**, **Heather Tepe**, **Natalie Wisdom**, **Caroline Workman**

*Succeeded by: 1. Jacob Clemente departed July 3, 2011; Giuseppe Bausilo alternated July 3-November 6, 2011; Myles Erlick added as an alternate September-November 2011; Julian Elia alternated November 8, 2001 until closing 2. Daniel Jenkins (9/6/11) 3. Katherine McGrath (9/6/11) 4. Patrick Mulvey (7/15/11) 5. William Youmans (9/6/11) 6. Jack Broderick (9/27/11) 7. Danny Rutigliano 8. Annabelle Kempf 9. Giuseppe Bausilo, Miles Erlick, Julian Elia 10. Danny Rutigliano, Nicholas Sipes 11. Brianna Fragomeni, Maria May 12. Olivia Alboher, Ian Liberto

ORCHESTRA Shawn Gough (Conductor/Resident Musical Director); Annbritt Duchateau (Associate Conductor/Keyboards); Joesph Joubert (Assistant Conductor/Keyboards); Ed Salkin, Rick Heckman, Mike Migliore, Jay Brandford (Reeds); James Dela Garza, John Dent, Alex Holton (Trumpets); Dick Clark, Jack Schatz (Trombones); Larry DiBello, Eva Conti (French Horns); JJ McGeehan (Guitar); Randy Landau (Bass); Gary Seligson (Drums); Howard Joines (Percussion)

MUSICAL NUMBERS The Stars Look Down; Shine; We'd Go Dancing; Solidarity; Expressing Yourself; Dear Billy (Mum's Letter); Born to Boogie; Angry Dance; Merry Christmas Maggie Thatcher; Deep Into the Ground; He Could Go and He Could Shine; Electricity; Once We Were Kings; Dear Billy (Billy's Reply); Company Celebration

SETTING A small mining town in County Durham, Northeast England, 1984–1985. Act 1: The eve of the Miner's Strike. Act 2: Six months later. American premiere of a musical presented in two acts. World premiere at the Victoria Palace Theatre (London), March 31, 2005 where it is still running.

SYNOPSIS Set behind the political backdrop of England's coal miner strike, *Billy Elliot The Musical* is a funny, heart-warming and feel-good celebration of one young boy's dream to break free from the expectations of his middle class roots. Based on the enormously popular film, this powerful new musical is the story of a boy who discovers he has a special talent for dance.

The Book of Mormon

Eugene O'Neill Theatre; First Preview: February 24, 2011; Opening Night: March 24, 2011; 28 previews, 493 performances as of May 31, 2012

Book, music, and lyrics by Trey Parker, Robert Lopez, and Matt Stone; Produced by Anne Garefino, Scott Rudin, Roger Berlind, Scott M. Delman, Jean Doumanian, Roy Furman, Important Musicals LLC, Stephanie P. McClelland, Kevin Morris, Jon B. Platt, Sonia Friedman Productions; Executive Producer, Stuart Thompson; Directors, Casey Nicholaw and Trey Parker; Choreography, Casey Nicholaw; Music Direction/Vocal Arrangements, Stephen Oremus; Sets, Scott Pask; Costumes, Ann Roth; Lighting, Brian MacDevitt; Sound, Brian Ronin; Hair, Josh Marquette, Casting, Carrie Gardner; Production Stage Manager, Karen Moore; Orchestrations, Larry Hochman & Stephen Oremus; Dance Music Arrangements, Glen Kelly; Music Coordinator, Michael Keller; Production Management, Aurora Productions; General Mangement, Stuart Thompson Productions/David Turner; Company Manager, Adam J. Miller; Makeup, Randy Houston Mercer; Associate Director, Jennifer Werner; Associate Choreographer, John MacInnis; For Scott Rudin Productions: Eli Bush, Steven Cardwell, Max Grossman, Adam Klaff, Joshua Mehr, Allie Moore, Matt Nemeth, Jill Simon, Nora Skinner; Stage Manager, Rachel S. McCutchen; Assistant Stage Manager, Michael P. Zaleski; Assistant Company Manager, Megan Curren; Dance Captain, Graham Bowen; Assistant Dance Captain, Asmeret Ghebremichael; Associate Design: Frank McCullough (set), Matthew Pachtman, Michelle Matland (costumes), Benjamin C. Travis (lighting), Ashley Hanson (sound); Assistant Design: Lauren Alvarez, Christine Peters (set), Carl Faber (lighting); Costume Design Assistant, Irma Escobar; Associate Music Director, Adam Ben-David; Keyboard Programmer, Randy Cohen; Drum Programmer, Sean McDaniel; Rehearsal Pianist, Brian Usifer; Music Copying, Emily Grishman Music Preparation, Katharine Edmonds; Crew: Mike Martinez (production carpenter), Dan Coey (production electrician), Drayton Allison (head electrician), Chris Sloan (production sound engineer), David Arch (moving lights), Damian Caza-Cleypool (lead front electrics), Jason McKenna (sound engineer), Andrew Lanzarotta (deck automation), Scott Dixon (fly automation), Ken Keneally (production props), Pete Sarafin (props coordinator), Dolly Williams (wardrobe supervisor), Fred Castner (assistant wardrobe supervisor), Tod L. McKim (hair supervisor), D'Ambrose Boyd, Micheal Harrell, Eugene Nicks, Melanie McClintock, Jeff McGovney, Virginia Neinenger, Veneda Treusdale (dressers), Joel Hawkins, Mathew Wilson (hair dressers), Sara Cox Bradley, Derek DiGregorio (production assistants); Music Department Assistant, Matthew Aument; Casting Associate, Jillian Cimini; For Stuart Thompson: Stuart Thompson, David Turner, Marshall B. Purdy, Cassidy Briggs, Kevin Emrick, Geo Karapetyan, Brittany Levasseur, Andrew Lowy, Christpher Taggart; For Aurora Productions: Gene O'Donovan, W. Benjamin Heller II, Stephanie Sherline, Jarid Sumner, Liza Luxenberg, Jason Margolis, Ryan Stanisz, Melissa Mazdra; Advertising, Serino/Coyne; Marketing/Web Interactive, aka, South Park Digital Studios/aka; Press, Boneau/Bryan-Brown, Chris Boneau, Jim Byk, Christine Olver; Cast recording: Sh-K-Boom/Ghostlight Records 84446

CAST Mormon **Jason Michael Snow**; Moroni/Elder McKinley **Rory O'Malley**; Elder Price **Andrew Rannells**; Elder Cunningham **Josh Gad**; Missionary Training Center Voice/Price's Dad/Joseph Smith/Mission President **Lewis Cleale**; Cunningham's Dad **Kevin Duda**; Mrs. Brown **Rema Webb**[*1]; Guards **John Eric Parker**, **Tommar Wilson**; Mafala Hatimbi **Michael Potts**; Nabulungi **Nikki M. James**; General **Brian Tyree Henry**; Doctor **Michael James Scott**; Ensemble **Scott Barnhardt**, **Justin Bohon**, **Darlesia Cearcy**, **Kevin Duda**, **Asmeret Ghebremichael**, **Brian Tyree Henry**, **Clark Johnson**, **John Eric Parker**, **Benjamin Schrader**, **Michael James Scott**, **Brian Sears**, **Jason Michael Snow**, **Lawrence Stallings**, **Rema Webb**[*1], **Maia Nkenge Wilson**, **Tommar Wilson**; Swings[*2] **Graham Bowen**, **Ta'rae Campbell**, **Tyson Jennette**, **Nick Spangler**

UNDERSTUDIES Scott Barnhardt (Elder McKinley), Ta'Rea Campbell (Nabulungi), Kevin Duda (Elder Price, Mission President, Price's Dad), Asmeret Ghebremichael (Nabulungi), Tyson Jennette (Mafala Hatimbi), John Eric Parker (Mafala Hatimbi), Benjamin Schrader (Elder Cunningham, Mission President, Price's Dad), Brian Sears (Elder McKinley), Nick Spangler (Elder Price); Standby for Elder Price: Nic Rouleau; Standby for Elder Cunningham: Jared Gertner or Will Blum

*Succeeded by: 1. Tamika Sonja Lawrence (3/27/12) 2. Douglas Lyons, Matthew Marks, Allison Semmes, Valisa LeKae

ORCHESTRA Stephen Oremus (Conductor/Keyboard), Adam Ben-David (Associate Conductor/Keyboard), Jake Schwartz (Guitars), Dave Phillips (Bass), Sean McDaniel (Drums/Percussion), Bryan Cook (Reeds), Raul Agraz (Trumpet), Randy Andos (Trombone), Entcho Todorov (Violin/Viola)

MUSICAL NUMBERS Hello!; Two By Two; You And Me (But Mostly Me); Hasa Diga Eebowai; Turn It Off; I Am Here For You; All American Prophet; Sal Tlay Ka Siti; Man Up; Song List; Making Things Up Again; Spooky Mormon Hell Dream; I Believe; Baptize Me; I Am Africa; Joseph Smith American Moses; Tomorrow Is a Latter Day

World premiere of a new musical presented in two acts.

SYNOPSIS Created by the writers of *South Park* and the composer of *Avenue Q*, *The Book of Morman* tells the tale of an unlikely pair of Mormon missionaries who have their faith and their sanity tested when they venture from Salt Lake City to AIDS-ravaged Uganda in the hopes of converting villagers with the story of Joseph Smith and the founding of the Mormon Church. The problem is, only one of them has actually read the book.

Michael James Scott, Asmeret Ghebremichal, Rema Webb, Lawrence Stallings, Maia Nkenge Wilson, Darlesia Cearcy, and Josh Gad

*Nikki M. James, Andrew Rannells, Josh Gad, and the Company
(photos by Joan Marcus)*

Robert Sean Leonard, Nina Arianda, and Jim Belushi

Jim Belushi and Nina Arianda

Liv Rooth, Jim Belushi, Bill Christ, Danny Rutigliano, and Frank Wood (photos by Carol Rosegg)

Born Yesterday

Cort Theatre; First Preview: March 31, 2011; Opening Night: April 24, 2011; Closed June 26, 2011; 28 previews, 73 performances

Written by Garson Kanin; Produced by Philip Morgaman, Anne Caruso, Vincent Caruso, Frankie J. Grande, James P. MacGilvray, Brian Kapetanis, Robert S. Basso, in association with Peter J. Puleo; Director, Doug Hughes; Set, John Lee Beatty; Costumes, Catherine Zuber; Lighting, Peter Kaczorowski; Original Music/Sound, David Van Tieghem; Hair/Wigs, Tom Watson; Casting, Jay Binder; Fight Director, J. David Brimmer; Production Stage Manager, Tripp Phillips; Technical Supervisor, Larry Morley; Company Manager, Brig Berney; General Management, Richards/Climan Inc. (David R. Richards, Tamar Haimes, Michael Sag, Kyle Bonder, Cesar Hawas; Press, Stage Manager, Jason Hindelang; Assistant Director, Alexander Greenfield; Fight Captain, Fred Arsenault; Makeup, Ashley Ryan; Associate Design: Kacie Hultgren (set), David Sanderson (sound); Assistant Design: Patrick Bevilacqua, Nicole Moody, Ryan Park (costumes); Jake DeGroot (lighting); Lighting Programmer, David Sanderson; Assistant Fight Director, Turner Smith; Crew: Edward Diaz (production carpenter), Shannon M.M. January (production electrician), Jens McVoy (production sound), Scott DeVerna (head electrician), Lonnie Gaddy (head props), Scott Laule, Buist Bickley (props coordinators), Dave Levenberg (props supervisor), Patrick Bevilazqua (wardrobe supervisor), Carmel A. Vargyas (hair supervisor), Erin Byrne, Lo Marriott, Steve Chazaro, Claire Verlaet (dressers), Robbie Peters, John Bantal (production assistants); Assistant to Mr. Belushi, Laura Marriott; Advertising/Digital Outreach/Online Media/Video Production/Website, Serino/Coyne; Marketing, Type A Marketing/Anne Rippey, Michael Porto, John McCoy; Press, Richard Kornberg & Associates, Don Summa, Billy Zavelson, Danielle McGarry

CAST Helen, *a maid* **Jennifer Regan**; Paul Verrall **Robert Sean Leonard**; Eddie Brock **Michael McGrath**; Bellhop **Fred Arsenault**; Another Bellhop/Bootblack **Danny Rutigliano**; A Third Bellhop/Barber **Bill Christ**; Harry Brock **Jim Belushi**; Assistant Manager **Andrew Weems**; Billie Dawn **Nina Arianda**; Ed Devery **Frank Wood**; Manicurist **Liv Rooth**; Senator Norval Hedges **Terry Beaver**; Mrs. Hedges **Patricia Hodges**

UNDERSTUDIES Liv Rooth (Billie Dawn), Bill Christ (Harry Brock), Fred Arsenault (Paul Verrall), Robert Emmet Lunney (Ed Devery, Assistant Manager, Bellhops, Barber, Bootblack), Danny Rutigliano (Eddie Brock), Andrew Weems (Senator Hedges), Jennifer Regan (Mrs. Hedges)

SETTING Washington D.C.; 1946. Act I: September; Act II: About two months later; Act III: Later that night. Revival of a play presented in three acts with one intermission and one brief pause between Acts II & III. Originally produced on Broadway at the Lyceum Theatre and subsequently Henry Miller's Theatre February 4, 1946–December 31, 1949 (starring Judy Holliday and Paul Douglas) playing 1,642 performances (see *Theatre World* Vol. 2, page 66). The show had a previous revival at the 46th Street (Richard Rodgers) Theatre January 18–June 11, 1989 (starring Ed Asner and Madeline Kahn) playing 153 performances (see *Theatre World* Vol. 45, page 23).

SYNOPSIS *Born Yesterday* is the timeless and timely story of a not-so-dumb-blonde, her less-than-honest brute of a boyfriend, and the no-nonsense reporter who helps her uncover some of the dirtiest little secrets in Washington.

Catch Me If You Can

Neil Simon Theatre; First Preview: March 11, 2011; Opening Night: April 10, 2011; Closed September 4, 2011; 32 previews, 166 performances

Book by Terrence McNally, music by Marc Shaiman, lyrics by Scott Wittman & Marc Shaiman; Based on the DreamWorks Motion Picture; Produced by Margo Lion, Hal Luftig, Stacey Mindich, Yasuhiro Kawana, Scott and Brian Zeilinger, The Rialto Group, The Araca Group, Michael Watt, Barbara and Buddy Freitag, Jay & Cindy Gutterman/Pittsburgh CLO, Elizabeth Williams, Johnny Roscoe Productions/Van Dean, Fakston Productions/Solshay Productions, Patty Baker/Richard Winkler, Nederlander Presentations, Inc. and Warren Trepp; Produced in association with Remmel T. Dickinson, Paula Herold/Kate Lear, Stephanie P. McClelland, Jamie deRoy, Barry Feirstein, Rainerio J. Reyes, Rodney Rigby, Loraine Boyle, Amuse Inc., Joseph & Matthew Deitch/Cathy Chernoff, Joan Stein/Jon Murray and The 5th Avenue Theatre; Director, Jack O'Brien; Choreography, Jerry Mitchell; Music Director, John McDaniel; Arrangements, Marc Shaiman; Orchestrations, Marc Shaiman & Larry Blank; Set, David Rockwell; Costumes, William Ivey Long; Lighting, Kenneth Posner; Sound, Steve Canyon Kennedy; Casting, Telsey + Company; Wigs & Hair, Paul Huntley; Associate Director, Matt Lenz; Associate Choreographers, Joey Pizzi, Nick Kenkel; Production Stage Manager, Rolt Smith; Music Coordinator, John Miller; Technical Supervisor, Chris Smith/Smitty; Associate Producers, Brian Smith, T. Rick Hayashi; General Manager, The Charlotte Wilcox Company; Keyboard Programmer, Synthlink LLC, Jim Harp; Company Manager, James Lawson; Assistant Company Manager, Katrina Elliott; Stage Manager, Andrea O. Saraffian; Assistant Stage Manager, Lisa Ann Chernoff; Dance Captain, Nick Kenkel; Associate Design: Michael Todd Potter (set), Martha Bromelmeier (costumes), Aaron Spivey (lighting), Andrew Keister, Walter Trabach (sound), Giovanna Calabretta, Edward J. Wilson (hair & wig); Assistant Design: Ann Bartek, Charles Corcoran, Todd Edward Ivins, Dick Jaris (set), Rachel Attridge (costumes), Kathleen Dobbins (lighting); Assistant to Mr. Rockwell, Anne Colice; Rockwell Studio Leader, Barry Richards; Rockwell Studio Support, T.J. Greenway; William Ivey Long Studio Director, Donald Sanders; Moving Light Programmer, Paul J. Sonnleitner; Makeup Consultant, Joseph Dulude II; Crew: Randall Zaibek, James Fedigan (production electricians), Mike Pilipski (production props supervisor), Donald J. Oberpriller (production carpenter), Michael Cornell (head electrician), Sandy Paradise (assistant electrician), Daniel Tramontozzi (sound engineer/board operator), Brett Bingman (assistant sound engineer), Peter Drummond (head props), Jacob White (assistant props), Douglas Petitjean (wardrobe supervisor), Deirdre LaBarre (assistant wardrobe supervisor), Edward J. Wilson (hair supervisor), Steven Kirkham (assistant hair supervisor); Music Tech Associate, Scott Riessett; Music Preparation, Joann Kane Music Service/Russ Bartmus, Mark Graham; Rehearsal Pianists, Jason Sherbundy, Seth Farber; Assistants to the Composer & Lyricist, Richard Read; Assistant to John Miller, Nichole Jennino; Production Assistants, Holly Coombs, Carly J. Price; For Charlotte Wilcox: Seth Marquette, Matthew w. Krawiec, Dina S. Friedler, Regina Mancha, Steve Supeck, Margaret Wilcox, Ryan Smilie, Stephen Donovan; Advertising, SpotCo; Online Marketing, Situation Interactive; Press, The Hartman Group, Michael Hartman, Leslie Papa, Alyssa Hart; Cast recording: Sh-K-Boom/Ghostlight Records 84449

CAST Frank Abagnale Jr. **Aaron Tveit**; Agent Branton **Joe Cassidy**; Agent Dollar **Brandon Wardell**; Agent Carl Hanratty **Norbert Leo Butz**; Agent Cod **Timothy McCuen Piggee**; Frank Abagnale Sr. **Tom Wopat**; Paula Abagnale **Rachel de Benedet**; Cheryl Ann **Rachelle Rak**; Brenda Strong **Kerry Butler**; Roger Strong **Nick Wyman**; Carol Strong **Linda Hart**; The Frank Abagnale Jr. Players **Joe Cassidy, Alex Ellis, Jennifer Frankel, Lisa Gajda, Bob Gaynor, Kearran Giovanni, Grasan Kingsberry, Michael X. Martin, Aleks Pevec, Timothy McCuen Piggee, Rachelle Rak, Joe Aaron Reid, Angie Schworer, Sabrina Sloan, Sarrah Strimel, Charlie Sutton, Brandon Wardell, Katie Webber, Candice Marie Woods**; Standby for Frank Abagnale Jr. **Jay Armstrong Johnson**; Swings **Sara Andreas, Will Erat, Nick Kenkel, Kristin Piro**

UNDERSTUDIES Joe Cassidy (Agent Carl Hanratty), Alex Ellis (Brenda Strong), Will Erat (Agent Carl Hanratty, Roger Strong), Jennifer Frankel (Carol Strong), Lisa Gajda (Carol Strong), Bob Gaynor (Frank Abagnale Sr.), Michael X. Martin (Frank Abagnale Sr., Roger Strong), Rachelle Rak (Paula Abagnale), Angie Schworer (Paula Abagnale), Brandon Wardell (Frank Abagnale Jr.), Katie Webber (Brenda Strong)

ORCHESTRA John McDaniel (Conductor), Lon Hoyt (Associate Conductor/Keyboard), Todd Groves, Rick Heckman, Alden Banta (Woodwinds), Dave Trigg, Trevor Neumann (Trumpets), Alan Ferber (Trombone), Larry Saltzman (Guitar), Vincent Fay (Bass), Clint de Ganon (Drums), Joseph Passaro (Percussion), Jason Sherbundy (Keyboards), Brian Koonin (Keyboard/Guitar), Rick Dolan (Concert Master), Belinda Whitney (Violin), Clay Reude (Cello)

MUSICAL NUMBERS Live in Living Color; The Pinstripes Are All That They See; Someone Else's Skin; Jet Set; Live in Living Color (reprise); Don't Break the Rules; The Pinstripes Are All That They See (reprise); Butter Outta Cream; The Man Inside the Clues; Christmas Is My Favorite Time of Year; My Favorite Time of Year; Doctor's Orders; Live in Living Color (reprise); Don't Be a Stranger; Little Boy, Be a Man; Seven Wonders; (Our) Family Tree; Fly, Fly Away; Good-Bye; Strange But True

New York premiere of a new musical presented in two acts. World premiere at the 5th Avenue Theatre in Seattle, Washington (David Armstrong, Executive Producer and Artistic Director; Bernadine Griffin, Managing Director; Bill Berry, Producing Director) July 23–August 16, 2009 (see *Theatre World* Vol. 66, page 363).

SYNOPSIS *Catch Me If You Can* captures the astonishing true story of Frank Abagnale Jr., a world-class con artist who passed himself off as a doctor, a lawyer, and a jet pilot — all before the age of 21. With straight-arrow FBI agent Carl Hanratty on Frank's trail, we're off on a jet-setting, cat-and-mouse chase, as a jazzy, swinging-sixties score keeps this adventure in constant motion. In the end, Agent Hanratty learns he and Frank aren't so very different after all, and Frank finds out what happens when love catches up to a man on the run.

Norbert Leo Butz (photo by Joan Marcus)

Chicago

Ambassador Theatre; First Preview: October 23, 1996; Opening Night: November 14, 1996; 25 previews, 6,451 performances as of May 31, 2012

Lyrics by Fred Ebb, music by John Kander, book by Fred Ebb and Bob Fosse; Based on the play by Maurine Dallas Watkins; Production based on the 1996 City Center *Encores!* production; Original production directed and choreographed by Bob Fosse; Produced by Barry & Fran Weissler in association with Kardana/Hart Sharp Productions and Broadway Across America; Director, Walter Bobbie; Choreography, Ann Reinking in the style of Bob Fosse; Supervising Music Director, Rob Fisher; Music Director, Leslie Stifelman; Sets, John Lee Beatty; Costumes, William Ivey Long; Lighting, Ken Billington; Sound, Scott Lehrer; Orchestrations, Ralph Burns; Dance Arrangements, Peter Howard; Script Adaptation, David Thompson; Musical Coordinator, Seymour Red Press; Hair/Wigs, David Brian Brown; Casting, Duncan Stewart (current), Jay Binder (original); Technical Supervisor, Arthur P. Siccardi; Dance Supervisor, Gary Chryst; Production Stage Manager, Rolt Smith; Executive Producer, Alecia Parker; General Manager, B.J. Holt; Company Manager, Rina L. Saltzman; Stage Managers, Terrence J. Witter, Mindy Farbrother, Scott Farris; Associate General Manager, Matthew Rimmer; Assistant Director, Jonathan Bernstein; Assistant Choreographer, Debra McWaters; Dance Captain, David Kent; Associate Lighting Design, John McKernon; Assistant Set Design, Eric Renschler, Shelley Barclay; General Management Associate, Stephen Spadaro; Crew: Kevin Woodworth (wardrobe supervisor), Jenna Brauer (hair supervisor), Joseph Mooneyham (production carpenter), James Fedigan (production electrician), Luciano Fusco (head electrician), Michael Guggino

Amra-Faye Wright and the Company

Carol Woods (photos by Jeremy Daniel)

(front lite operator), John Montgomery (production sound engineer), Fred Phelan (production props), Sue Setpnik, Kathy Dacey, Cleopatra Matheos, Rick Meadows, Patrick Rinn (dressers); Costume Assistant, Donald Sanders; Assistant to Mr. Billington, Jon Kusner; Assistant to Mr. Leher, Thom Mohrman; Music Preparation, Chelsea Music Services; Advertising, SpotCo; Press, The Publicity Office, Jeremy Shaffer; Cast recording: RCA 68727-2

CAST Velma Kelly **Amra-Faye Wright**[*1]; Roxie Hart **Christie Brinkley**[*2]; Amos Hart **Raymond Bokhour**[*3]; Matron "Mama" Morton **Carol Woods**[*4]; Billy Flynn **Brent Barrett**[*5]; Mary Sunshine **R. Lowe**; Fred Casely **James Harkness**[*6]; Sergeant Fogarty **Adam Zotovitch**; Liz **Nicole Bridgewater**; Annie **Jill Niklaus**[*7]; June **Donna Marie Asbury**; Hunyak **Nili Bassman**; Mona **Dylis Croman**; Go-To-Hell-Kitty **Melissa Rae Mahon**; Harry/Martin Harrison **Peter Nelson**; Aaron/"Me and My Baby" Specialty **Ryan Worsing**; Doctor/Judge **Jason Patrick Sands**; The Jury/"Me and My Baby" Specialty **Michael Cusumano**; Bailiff/Court Clerk **Greg Reuter**[*8]

UNDERSTUDIES Melissa Rae Mahon (Roxie), Dylis Croman (Roxie), Donna Marie Asbury (Velma), Jason Patrick Sands (Billy), Jason Patrick Sands (Amos, Fred), Adam Zotovich (Amos), Nicole Bridgewater ("Mama" Morton, Velma), David Kent/Brian Spitulnik (Fred Casely, "Me and My Baby"), J. Loeffelholtz (Mary Sunshine); Jennifer Dunne, David Kent, Sharon Moore, Brian Spitulnik (All other roles); Eddie Bennett, Jennifer Dunne (Swings)

*Succeeded by: 1. Nikka Graff Lanzarone (7/5/11), Amra-Faye Wright (9/5/11), Bahiyah Hibah (11/1/11), Amra-Faye Wright (2/2/12), Terra C. MacLeod (5/7/12) 2. Charlotte d'Amboise (6/24/11), Kara DioGuardi (9/6/11), Charlotte d'Amboise (11/1/11), Bianca Marroquin (1/16/12), Christie Brinkley (4/6/12), Tracy Shayne (4/28/12) 3. Chris Sullivan (6/20/11), Raymond Bokhour (12/19/11), Chris Sullivan (1/2/12), Raymond Bokhour (2/2/12) 4. Roz Ryan (5/7/12) 5. Christopher Sieber (6/23/11), Tony Yazbeck (8/29/11), John O'Hurley (11/1/11), Brent Barrett (12/19/11), Marco Zunino (1/16/12), Tony Yazbeck (3/5/12), 6. Brian O'Brien 7. Cristy Candler 8. Amos Wolff. Temporary cast members from the season: Kate Dunn (Hunyak), Gabriela Garcia (Annie), T.W. Smith (Mary Sunshine), Tonya Wathen (Annie/Hunyak/Swing), D. Micchiche (Mary Sunshine)

ORCHESTRA Leslie Stifelman (Conductor); Scott Cady (Associate Conductor/Piano); Seymour Red Press, Jack Stuckey, Richard Centalonza (Woodwinds); Glenn Drewes, Darryl Shaw (Trumpets); Dave Bargeron, Bruce Bonvissuto (Trombones); John Johnson (Assistant Conductor/Piano/Accordion); Jay Berliner (Banjo); Dan Peck (Bass/Tuba); Marshall Coid (Violin); Ronald Zito (Drums/Percussion)

MUSICAL NUMBERS All That Jazz; Funny Honey; Cell Block Tango; When You're Good to Mama; Tap Dance; All I Care About; A Little Bit of Good; We Both Reached for the Gun; Roxie; I Can't Do It Alone; My Own Best Friend; Entr'acte; I Know a Girl; Me and My Baby; Mister Cellophane; When Velma Takes the Stand; Razzle Dazzle; Class; Nowadays; Hot Honey Rag; Finale

SETTING Chicago, Illinois. The late 1920s. A musical vaudeville presented in two acts. This production originally opened at the Richard Rodgers Theatre; transferred to the Shubert on February 12, 1997; and transferred to the Ambassador on January 29, 2003. For original production credits see *Theatre World* Vol. 53, page 14. The original Broadway production ran June 3, 1975–August 27, 1977 at the 46th Street Theatre (now the Richard Rodgers Theatre where this revival first played) playing 936 performances (see *Theatre World* Vol. 32, Page 8). On August 27, 2011 *Chicago* became the fourth longest-running production in Broadway history, and the longest-running American musical. The show celebrated its fifteenth year on Broadway November 14, 2011.

SYNOPSIS Murder, media circus, vaudeville, and celebrity meet in this 1920s tale of two of the Windy City's most celebrated felons and their rise to fame amidst a razzle dazzle trial.

Ghetto Klown

Lyceum Theatre; First Preview: February 21, 2011; Opening Night: March 22, 2011; Closed July 10, 2011; 25 previews, 95 performances

Written by John Leguizamo; Produced by WestBeth Entertainment (Arnold Engelman, Camron Cooke, Juliana Slaton, Jenni Muller), Daveed D. Frazier, and Nelle Nugent; Executive Producer, Arnold Engelman; Associate Producers, Insurgent Media, Camron Cooke, Kenneth Treaton; Director, Fisher Stevens; Set, Happy Massee; Lighting, Jen Schriever; Sound, Peter Fitzgerald; Projections, Aaron Gonzalez; Technical Supervision, Hudson Theatrical Associates; Production Consultant, Christopher Cronin; Movement Consultant, Marlyn Ortiz; Publicity, Blanca Lasalle, Creative Link; Online Marketing, Bay Bridge Productions; Production Stage Manager, Arabella Powell; Company Manager, John E. Gendron; Stage Manager, Chelsea Antrim; Associate Lighting, Peter Hoerburger; Assistant to Ms. Schriever, John Wilder; Moving Light Programmer, Sean Beach; Assistant Sound, Megan Henninger; Assistant Projections, Eric T. Sutton; Wardrobe Stylist, Young-Ah Kim; Crew: Adam Braunstein (production carpenter), Jonathan Cohen (production electrician), James Maloney (advance electrician), Wallace Flores (production sound), Kathy Fabian and Tim Ferro/Propstar (props coordinators), Leah Nelson (production props), Danny Paul (wardrobe supervisor); Assistant Director, Micha Frank; Assistant to Mr. Stevens, Zara Duffy; Graphic Design, KRL Creative/Kim Lyle; Key Art, Billi Kid; Advertising, Neil Turton; Press, Boneau/ Bryan-Brown, Jackie Green, Kelly Guiod

Performed by **John Leguizamo**

New York premiere of a solo performance play presented in two acts. *Ghetto Klown* was showcased in earlier incarnations in Philadelphia, New Haven, Santa Fe, Louisville, La Jolla, Toronto, and Montreal; an "unplugged" version of the show played at the Royal George Theatre in Chicago under the title *John Leguizmo Warms Up* prior to his Broadway engagement.

SYNOPSIS *Ghetto Klown* is the next chapter in John Leguizamo's popular personal and professional story. It is his fifth one-man play, his third on Broadway, and follows in the uninhibited tradition of his *Mambo Mouth, Spic-O-Rama, Freak,* and *Sexaholix…a Love Story.* In Leguizamo's trademark style, the piece explodes with energy, heating up the stage with vivid accounts of the colorful characters who have populated his life. He takes audiences from his adolescent memories in Queens to the early days of his acting career and on to the sets of major motion pictures and his roles opposite some of Hollywood's biggest stars.

John Leguizamo (photo by Carol Rosegg)

The House of Blue Leaves

Walter Kerr Theatre; First Preview: April 4, 2011; Opening Night: April 25, 2011; Closed June 25, 2011; 21 previews, 72 performances

Written by John Guare; Produced by Scott Rudin, Stuart Thompson, Jean Doumanian, Mary Lu Roffe/Susan Gallin/Rodger Hess, The Araca Group, Scott M. Delman, Roy Furman, Ruth Hendel, Jon B. Platt, Sonia Friedman Productions/ Scott Landis; Director, David Cromer; Original Songs, John Guare; Set, Scott Pask; Costumes, Jane Greenwood; Lighting, Brian Macdevitt; Sound, Fitz Patton & Josh Schmidt; Hair/Wigs, Tom Watson; Casting, MelCap Casting; Fight Direction, Thomas Schall; Production Stage Manager, Barclay Stiff; Production Management, Aurora Productions; General Management, Stuart Thompson Productions/Marshall B. Purdy; Company Manager, Chris Morey; Stage Manager, Kelly Beaulieu; Assistant Director, Michael Padden; Dialect Coach, Howerd Samuelson; Associate Design: Christine Peters, Lauren Alvarez (set), Moria Clinton (costumes), Jennifer Schriever (lighting), Joshua Reid, Joanna Lynne Staub (sound); Hair Stylist for Mr. Stiller, Lori Guidroz; Makeup Consultants, Naomi Donne, Alicce Lane; Marketing, aka; Advertising, Serino/Coyne; Press, Boneau/Bryan-Brown, Chris Boneau, Heath Schwarth, Michael Strassheim

CAST Artie Shaughnessy **Ben Stiller**; Ronnie Shaughnessy **Christopher Abbot**; Bunny Flingus **Jennifer Jason Lee**; Bananas Shaughnessy **Edie Falco**; Corrina Stroller **Alison Pill**; Head Nun **Mary Beth Hurt**; Second Nun **Susan Bennett**; Little Nun **Halley Feiffer**; Policeman **Jimmy Davis**; White Man **Tally Sessions**; Billy Einhorn **Thomas Sadoski**; Understudies **Jim Bracchitta** (Artie), **Katie Kreisler** (Bananas, Head Nun, Second Nun), **Susan Bennett** (Bunny), **Amelia McClain** (Corrinna, Little Nun), **Jimmy Davis** (Ronnie)

SETTING A cold apartment in Sunnyside, Queens; October 4, 1965. Revival of a black comedy presented in two acts. The original New York production opened Off-Broadway at the Truck and Warehouse Theatre February 10, 1971 (with Mr. Stiller's mother Anne Meara as "Bunny") playing 337 perfomances (see *Theatre World* Vol. 27, page 98). The play was previously revived at Lincoln Center's Mitzi E. Newhouse Theater February 28, 1986 (featuring Mr. Stiller as "Ronnie" in his New York debut) and transferred to the Vivian Beaumont Theatre on April 29, 1986 and subsequently the Plymouth Theatre October 14, 1986, where it closed March 15, 1987 after 398 performances (see *Theatre World* Vol. 42, pages 43 & 97).

SYNOPSIS Set on the day of Pope Paul VI's visit to New York City, *The House of Blue Leaves* is a satirical take on celebrity, religion, and the frequent merging of the two. Artie Shaughnessy, a Central Park zookeeper, is trying to cope with a schizophrenic wife, an impatient girlfriend, and a bomb-making son who is AWOL from the Army, all the while dreaming of getting a blessing from the Pope to escape his lower-middle class existence and become a singer and songwriter.

Ben Stiller and Edie Falco (photo my Joan Marcus)

How to Succeed in Business Without Really Trying

Al Hirschfeld Theatre; First Preview: February 26, 2011; Opening Night: March 27, 2011; Closed May 20, 2012; 30 previews, 473 performances

Music & lyrics by Frank Loesser, book by Abe Burrows, Jack Weinstock, & Willie Gilbert; Based on the book by Shepherd Mead; Produced by Broadway Across America, Craig Zadan, Neil Meron, Joseph Smith, Michael McCabe, Candy Spelling, Takonkiet Viravan/Scenario Thailand, Hilary A. Williams, Jen Namoff/Fakston Productions, Two Left Feet Productions/Power Arts, Hop Theatricals, LLC/PaulChau/Daniel Frishwasser/Michael Jackowitz and Michael Speyer-Bernie Abrams/Jacki Barlia Florin-Adam Blanshay/Arlene Scanlan/TBS Service; Director & Choreographer, Rob Ashford; Music Director/Arrangements, David Chase; Set, Derek McLane; Costumes, Catherine Zuber; Lighting, Howell Binkley; Sound, Jon Weston; Hair & Wigs, Tom Watson; Orchestrations, Doug Besterman; Music Coordinator, Howard Joines; Production Stage Manager, Michael J. Passaro; Associate Director, Stephen Sposito; Associate Choreographer, Christopher Bailey; Assistant Choreographers, Sarah O'Gleby, Charlie Williams; Casting, Tara Rubin; Production Manager, Juniper Street Productions; Marketing, Type A Marketing, Anne Rippey; General Management, Alan Wasser, Allan Williams, Mark Shacket; Associate Producers, Stage Ventures, 2010 Limited Partnership; Executive Producer, Beth Williams; Company Manager, Penelope Dalton; Stage Manager, Pat Sosnow; Assistant Stage Manager, Jim Athens; Assistant Company Manager, Cathy Kwon; Dance Captain, Sarah O'Bleby; Assistant Dance Captain, Matt Wall; SDC Traube Fellow, Sara-Ashley Bischoff; Associate Design: Shoko Kambara (set), Ryan O'Gara (lighting), Jason Strangfeld (sound); Assistant Design: Brett Banakis (set), Sean Beach, Amanda Zieve (lighting), Michael Eisenberg (sound); Scenic Design Assistant, Paul Depoo; Costume Design Intern, Peter Dolhas; Moving Lights Programmer, Eric Norris; Makeup Design, Ahsley Ryan; Aerial Design, Sonja Rzepski; Stunt Coordinator, Mike Russo; Erik Hansen (production carpenter), Scott "Gus" Poitras (automation carpenter), James J. Fedigan, Randall Zaibek (production electricians), Brian Dawson (head electrician) Christopher Pantuso (production props supervisor), Jim Cane; (assistant props supervisor), Paul Delcioppo, Phil Lojo (production sound engineers), Charles Grieco (deck audio), Debbie Cheretun (wardrobe supervisor), Brendan Cooper (assistant wardrobe supervisor), Sandy Binion, Barry Hoff (star dressers), Shana Albery, Joshua Burns, Kristin Farley, Anthony Hoffman, Jeffrey Johnson, Nesreen Mahmoud, Icey Parks (dressers), Katie Beatty (hair supervisor), Carla Muniz, Brendan O'Neal (hair dressers); Keyboard Programmer, Randy Cohen; Music Preparation, Anixter Rice Music Service; For Alan Wasser: Mark Shacket, Aaron Lustbader; For Type A: Michael Porto, Elyce Henkin, Sarah Ziering; For Juniper Street: Hilary Blanken, Guy Kwan, Joseph DeLuise, Kevin Broomell, Ana Rose Grene; General Management Associates, Lane Marsh, Steve Greer; Advertising, Serino/Coyne; Press, The Hartman Group, Michael Hartman, Wayne Wolfe, Matt Ross, Nicole Capatasto; Cast recording: Decca Broadway DCAUB001564502

CAST The Voice of the Narrator **Anderson Cooper**; J. Pierpont Finch **Daniel Radcliffe**[*1]; Mr. Gatch **Nick Mayo**; Mr. Jenkins **Charlie Williams**[*2]; Mr. Johnson/TV Announcer **Kevin Covert**; Mr. Matthews **Ryan Watkinson**[*1]; Mr. Peterson **Marty Lawson**; Mr. Tackaberry **Joey Sorge**[*3]; Mr. Toynbee **David Hull**[*4]; Mr. Andrews **Barrett Martin**[*5]; J.B. Biggley **John Larroquette**[*6]; Rosemary Pilkington **Rose Hemingway**; Mr. Bratt **Michael Park**; Smitty **Mary Faber**; Miss Jones **Ellen Harvey**; Miss Krumholtz **Megan Sikora**[*7]; Bud Frump **Christopher J. Hanke**[*8]; Mr. Twimble/Wally Womper **Rob Bartlett**; Hedy LaRue **Tammy Blanchard**; Mr. Davis **Justin Keyes**[*9]; Meredith **Stephanie Rothenberg**[*10]; Kathy/Scrub Woman **Cameron Adams**[*11]; Miss Grabowski/Scrub Woman **Paige Faure**; Nancy **Tanya Birl**; Lily **Samantha Zack**; Mr. Ovington **Cleve Asbury**; Swings[*12] **Erica Mansfield, Sarah O'Gleby, Michaeljon Slinger, Matt Wall**

UNDERSTUDIES Cameron Adams (Rosemary Pillkington), Cleve Asbury (Mr. Twimble, Wally Womper), Rob Bartlett (J.B. Biggley), Kevin Covert (Mr. Twimble, Wally Womper), Paige Faure (Hedy La Rue, Smitty), Dave Hull (J. Pierrepont Finch), Justin Keyes (Bud Frump, J. Pierrepont Finch), Erica Mansfield (Miss

Jones), Nick Mayo (Bert Bratt), Michael Park (J.B. Biggley), Stephanie Rothenberg (Rosemary Pillkington), Megan Sikora (Hedy La Rue, Miss Jones, Smitty), Joey Sorge (Bert Bratt), Charlie Williams (Bud Frump)

Succeeded by: 1. Darren Criss (1/3/12), Nick Jonas (1/24/12) 2. Charlie Sutton 3. Timothy J. Alex 4. Taylor Frey 5. Andrew Madsen 6. Beau Bridges (1/3/12) 7. Shannon Lewis 8. Michael Urie (1/24/12) 9. Robert Hager 10. Synthia Link 11. Abby Church 12. Holly Ann Butler, J. Austin Eyer, Ian Liberto, Karl Warden

ORCHESTRA David Chase (Conductor), Matt Perri (Associate Conductor/Keyboard/Piano), Steve Kenyon, Lawrence Feldman, Mark Thrasher (Reeds), Nicholas Marchione, Scott Wendholt (Trumpets), John Allred, George Flynn (Trombones), David Peel (Horn), Paul Pizzuti (Drums), Neal Caine (Bass), Scott Kuney (Guitars), Erik Charlston (Percussion), Grace Paradise (Harp)

MUSICAL NUMBERS Overture; How to Succeed; Happy To Keep His Dinner Warm; Coffee Break; Company Way; Company Way (reprise); Rosemary's Philosophy; A Secretary Is Not a Toy; Been a Long Day; Been a Long Day (reprise); Grand Old Ivy; Paris Original; Rosemary; Act I Finale; Cinderella Darling; Happy To Keep His Dinner Warm (reprise); Love From a Heart of Gold; I Believe in You; Pirate Dance; I Believe in You (reprise); Brotherhood of Man; Finale

SETTING The new Park Avenue office building of The World Wide Wicket Company in New York City; 1961. Revival of a musical presented in two acts. Originally produced on Broadway at the 46th Street (Richard Rodgers) Theatre starring Robert Morse October 14, 1961–March 6, 1965 playing 1,417 performances (see *Theatre World* Vol. 18, page 26). The musical was revived at the Richard Rodgers Theatre starring Matthew Broderick March 23, 1996–July 14, 1996 playing 548 performances (see *Theatre World* Vol. 54, page 42).

SYNOPSIS The 1961 Tony and Pulitzer Prize-winning musical comedy satire about the world of big business returns to Broadway in this 50th Anniversary revival. Daniel Radcliffe stars as J. Pierpont Finch, a young window washer, who with the help of the titular book, rises to the top of the World Wide Wicket Company in New York City.

Daniel Radcliffe, Rob Bartlett, and the Company

John Larroquette and Tammy Blanchard (photos by Ari Mintz)

David Furr and Santino Fontana

Brian Bedford and Charlotte Parry

Santino Fontana, Charlotte Parry, original cast member Sara Topham, and David Furr (photos by Joan Marcus)

The Importance of Being Earnest

American Airlines Theatre; First Preview: December 17, 2010; Opening Night: January 13, 2011; Closed June 26, 2011; 30 previews, 189 performances

Written by Oscar Wilde; Produced by the Roundabout Theatre Company (Todd Haimes, Artistic Director; Harold Wolpert, Managing Director; Julia C. Levy, Executive Director); Director, Brian Bedford; Set & Costumes, Desmond Heeley; Lighting, Duane Schuler; Sound, Drew Levy; Original Music, Berthold Carrière; Hair & Wigs, Paul Huntley; Dialect Consultant, Elizabeth Smith; Production Stage Manager, Robyn Henry; Production Management, Aurora Productions; Casting, Jim Carnahan, Carrie Gardner, Kate Boka; General Manager, Rebecca Habel; Director of Development, Lynne Gugenheim Gregory; Founding Director, Gene Feist; Associate Artistic Director; Company Manager, Carly DiFulvio; Stage Manager, Bryce McDonald; Assistant Director, Robert Beard; Makeup, Angelina Avallone; Associate Design: Michael Carnahan (set), Devon Painter (costumes), Justin Partier (lighting), Will Pickens (sound); Assistant Set Design, Rachel Nemec, Shana Burns; Assistant Makeup Artist, Jorge Vargas; Assistant to Mr. Heeley, Ren LaDassor; Production Props Supervisor, Peter Sarafin; Production Consultant, Campbell Baird; Period Movement Consultant, Frank Ventura; Crew: Glenn Merwede (production carpenter), Brian Maiuri (production electrician), Robert W. Dowling II (running properties), Dann Wojnar (sound operator), Mike Allen (flyman), Susan J. Fallon (wardrobe supervisor), Lauren Gallitelli, Kat Martin (dressers), Dale Carman (wardrobe day crew), Manuela Laporte (hair and wig supervisor), Yolanda Ramsay (hair and wig assistant), Sara Cox Bradley (production assistant); Roundabout Staff: Director of Artistic Development/Casting, Jim Carnahan; Director of Education, Greg McCaslin; Associate Managing Director, Greg Backstrom; General Manager, Sydney Beers; Director of Finance, Susan Neiman; IT Director, Antonio Palumbo; Director of Marketing and Sales Promotion, David B. Steffen; Director of Ticketing Sales, Charlie Garbowski Jr.; Press, Boneau/Bryan-Brown, Adrian Bryan-Brown, Matt Polk, Jessica Johnson, Amy Kass

CAST Lane **Paul O'Brien**; Algernon Moncreiff **Santino Fontana**; John Worthing **David Furr**; Lady Bracknell **Brain Bedford**; Gwendolen Fairfax **Jessie Austrian**; Cecily Cardew **Charlotte Parry**; Miss Prism **Jayne Houdyshell**; Rev. Canon Chasuble **Brian Murray**; Merriman **Tim MacDonald**; Servant **Amanda Lee Cobb**

UNDERSTUDIES Sean Arbuckle (John Worthing, Algernon Moncrief), Amanda Lee Cobb (Gwendolyn Fairfax, Cecily Cardew), Colin McPhillamy (Merriman, Lane, Servant), Paul O'Brien (Rev. Canon Chasuble), Sandra Shipley (Lady Bracknell, Miss Prism); Replacements during the run: Richard Gallagher (John Worthing, Algernon Moncrief, Servant), Jefrey Heyenga (Rev. Canon Chausuble, Merriman, Lane)

SETTING Algernon Moncrieff's rooms in Picadilly. The garden at the Manor House, Wooton. Morning room at the Manor House, Woolton. Late nineteenth century. Revival of a play presented in three acts with two intermissions. The Stratford Shakespeare Festival presented Mr. Bedford's acclaimed production May 9–October 30, 2009. This production maked the 8th major New York revival since the plays Broadway debut in 1895.

SYNOPSIS One of the funniest comedies in the English language – and a critique of the conventions and hypocrisies of so-called polite society that remains stingingly pertinent even today – *The Importance of Being Earnest* centers on dashing men-about-town John Worthing and Algernon Moncrieff, who pursue fair ladies Gwendolen Fairfax and Cecily Cardew. Matters are complicated by the imaginary characters invented by both men to cover their on-the-sly activities – not to mention the disapproval of Gwendolen's mother, the formidable Lady Bracknell.

Jersey Boys

August Wilson Theatre; First Preview: October 4, 2005; Opening Night: November 6, 2005; 38 previews, 2,714 performances as of May 31, 2012

Book by Marshall Brickman and Rick Elice, music by Bob Gaudio, lyrics by Bob Crewe; Produced by Dodger Theatricals (Michael David, Edward Strong, Rocco Landesman, Des McAnuff), Joseph J. Grano, Pelican Group, Tamara Kinsella and Kevin Kinsella, in association with Latitude Link, Rick Steiner and Osher/Staton/ Bell/ Mayerson Group; Director, Des McAnuff; Choreography, Sergio Trujillo; Musical Director, Vocal Arrangements/Incidental Music, Ron Melrose; Sets, Klara Zieglerova; Costumes, Jess Goldstein; Lighting, Howell Binkley; Sound, Steve Canyon Kennedy; Projections, Michael Clark; Hair/Wigs, Charles LaPointe; Fight Director, Steve Rankin; Assistant Director, West Hyler; Production Supervisor, Richard Hester; Production Stage Manager, Michelle Bosch; Orchestrations, Steve Orich; Music Coordinator, John Miller; Technical Supervisor, Peter Fulbright; Casting, Tara Rubin (East), Sharon Bialy, Sherry Thomas (West); Company Manager, Sandra Carlson; Associate Company Manager, Tim Sulka; Associate Producers, Lauren Mitchell and Rhoda Mayerson; Executive Producer, Sally Campbell Morse; Promotions, HHC Marketing; Stage Manager, Brendan M. Fay; Assistant Stage Manager, Pamela Remler Dialect Coach, Stephen Gabis; Dance and Fight Captain, Peter Gregus; Music Technical Design, Deborah Hurwitz; Senior Associate General Manager, Jennifer F. Vaughan; Associate General Manager, Flora Johnstone; Production Manager, Jeff Parvin; Associate Company Manager, Tim Sulka; Technical Supervision, Tech Production Services, Peter Fulbright; Music Technical Design, Deborah N. Hurwitz; Associate Director, West Hyler; Assistant Director, Holly-Anne Ruggiero; Second Assistant Director, Alex Timbers; Associate Choreographers, Danny Austin, Kelly Devine; Associate Music Supervisor, Michael Rafter; Fight Captain, Erik Bates; Associate Design: Nany Thun Todd Ivins (set), Alejo Vietti (costumes), Patricia Nichols (lighting), Andrew Keister (sound), Jason Thompson (projections); Assistant Design: Sonoka Gozelski, Matthew Myhrum (set), China Lee, Elizabeth Flauto (costumes), Sarah E.C. Maines (lighting), Chris Kateff (projections); Marketing, Dodger Marketing; Advertising, Serino/Coyne; Press, Boneau/Bryan-Brown, Susanne Tighe, Heath Schwartz; Cast recording: Rhino R2 73271

CAST French Rap Star/Detective #1/Hal Miller/Barry Belson/Police Officer/ Davis **Kris Coleman**[1]; Stanley/Hank Majewski/Crewe's PA/Joe Long **Erik Bates**; Bob Crewe/others **Peter Gregus**[2]; Tommy DeVito **Dominic Nolfi**[3]; Nick DeVito/Stosh/Billy Dixon/Norman Waxman/Charlie Calello/others **Miles Aubrey**; Joey/Recording Studio Engineer/others **Russell Fischer**; Gyp De Carlo/others **Mark Lotito**; Mary Delgado/Angel/others **Cara Cooper**; Church Lady/Miss Frankie Nolan/Bob's Party Girl/Angel/Lorraine/others **Jessica Rush**; Bob Gaudio **Ryan Jesse**[4]; Frankie's Mother/Nick's Date/Angel/Francine/others **Sara Schmidt**; Nick Massi **Matt Bogart**; Frankie Valli **Jarrod Spector** (evenings)/**Dominic Scaglione Jr.** (matinees); Thugs **Ken Dow**, **Joe Payne**; Swings **Jared Bradshaw**, **Brad Bass**, **Katie O'Toole**, **Nathan Scherich**, **Jake Speck**, **Taylor Sternberg**

UNDERSTUDIES Eric Bates (DeVito, Crewe), Russell Fischer (Valli), Miles Aubrey (Massi, Gyp), John Hickman (Gaudio, Massi, Gyp, Crewe), Taylor Sternberg, (Valli), Jake Speck (Gaudio, Massi, DeVito)

*Succeeded by: 1. John Edwards (7/5/11) 2. Courter Simmons (1/10/12), Peter Gregus (3/6/12) 3. Andy Karl (10/11/11) 4. Quinn VanAntwerp (10/11/11)

MUSICIANS Andrew Wilder (Conductor/Keyboards); Deborah Hurwitz (Associate Conductor/Keyboards); Stephen "Hoops" Snyder (Keyboards); Joe Payne (Guitars); Ken Dow (Bass); Kevin Dow (Drums); Matt Hong, Ben Kono (Reeds); David Spier (Trumpet)

MUSICAL NUMBERS Ces Soirées-La (Oh What a Night); Silhouettes; You're the Apple of My Eye; I Can't Give You Anything But Love; Earth Angel; Sunday Kind of Love; My Mother's Eyes; I Go Ape; (Who Wears) Short Shorts; I'm in the Mood for Love/Moody's Mood for Love; Cry for Me; An Angel Cried; I Still Care; Trance; Sherry; Big Girls Don't Cry; Walk Like a Man; December; 1963 (Oh What a Night); My Boyfriend's Back; My Eyes Adored You; Dawn (Go Away); Walk Like a Man (reprise); Big Man in Town; Beggin'; Stay; Let's Hang On (To What We've Got); Opus 17 (Don't You Worry 'Bout Me); Bye Bye Baby; C'mon Marianne; Can't Take My Eyes Off of You; Working My Way Back to You; Fallen Angel; Rag Doll; Who Loves You

SETTING New Jersey, New York, and across the U.S., 1950s–now. A new musical presented in two acts. For original production credits see *Theatre World* Vol. 62, page 34. World Premiere produced by La Jolla Playhouse, October 5, 2004.

SYNOPSIS "How did four blue-collar kids become one of the greatest successes in pop music history? You ask four guys, you get four different answers." *Jersey Boys* is the story of the legendary Four Seasons, blue-collar boys who formed a singing group and reached the heights of rock 'n' roll stardom.

The Company

Andy Karl (photos by Joan Marcus)

Jerusalem

Music Box Theatre; First Preview: April 2, 2011; Opening Night: April 21, 2011; Closed August 21, 2011; 21 previews, 141 performances

Written by Jez Butterworth; Produced by Sonia Friedman Productions, Stuart Thompson, Scott Rudin, Roger Berlind, Royal Court Theatre Productions, Beverly Bartner/Alice Tulchin, Dede Harris/Rupert Gavin, Broadway Across America, Jon B. Platt, 1001 Nights/Stephanie P. McClelland, Carole L. Haber/Richard Willis, Jacki Baria Florin/Adam Blanshay; Presented by The Royal Court Theatre; Director, Ian Rickson; Sets & Costumes, Ultz; Lighting, Mimi Jordan Sherin; Sound, Ian Dickinson (Autograph); Original Music, Stephen Warbeck; U.K. Casting, Amy Ball; U.S. Casing, Jim Carnahan; Production Stage Manager, Jill Cordle; Production Management, Aurora Productions; General Management, Stuart Thompson Productions/David Turner; U.K. General Management, Sonia Friedman Productions; Company Manager, Christopher D'Angelo; Stage Manager, Kenneth McGee; U.K Stage Managers, Cath Bates, Maddy Grant; Associate Design: Josh Zangen, Ryan Trupp (set); Katie Irish (costumes); Steve Andrews [U.K], D.M. Wood [U.S] (lighting); Joanna Lynne Staub (sound); Assistant Lighting [U.S.], Gordon Olson; U.K. Production Management, Paul Handley; U.K. Costume Supervisors, Iona Kenrick, Rana Fowler; Crew: Jim Fossi (production carpenter), Brendan Quigley (production electrician), Eric Norris (light board programmer), Scott Monroe (production props), Beth Berkeley (production sound), Dennis Maher (house carpenter), Kim Garnett (house props), William K. Rowland (house electrician), Kay Grunder (wardrober supervisor), Kimberly Prentice, Chip White (dressers), Hannah Gore, Jason Pelusio (production assistants); Dialect Coach, Charmian Hoare; U.S. Vocal Coach, Andrew Wade; Advertising, aka; Press, Boneau/Bryan-Brown, Chris Boneau, Jim Byk, Christine Olver

CAST Phaedra **Aimeé-Ffion Edwards**; Ms. Fawcett **Sarah Moyle**; Mr. Parsons **Harvey Robinson**; Johnny 'Rooster' Byron **Mark Rylance**; Ginger **Mackenzie Crook**; The Professor **Alan David**; Lee **John Gallagher Jr.**; Davey **Danny Kirrane**; Pea **Molly Ranson**; Tanya **Charlotte Mills**; Wesley **Max Baker**; Marky **Aiden Eyrick** or **Mark Page**; Dawn **Geraldine Hughes**; Troy Whitworth **Barry Sloane**; Frank Whitworth **Jay Sullivan**; Danny Whitworth **Richard Short**

UNDERSTUDIES Frances Mercanti-Anthony (Dawn, Ms. Fawcett), James Riordan (The Professor, Wesley), Harvey Robinson (Ginger), Richard Short (Davey, Troy Whitworth), Jay Sullivan (Lee, Mr. Parsons), Libby Woodbridge (Pea, Phaedra, Tanya)

SETTING Flintrock, Wiltshire, England 2011. American premiere of a new play presented in three acts with one intermission after act 1 and a short pause between Acts 2 & 3. Originally presented at the Royal Court Theatre (London) July 13–August 22, 2009 and transferred to the Apollo Theatre January 28–April 24, 2010.

SYNOPSIS In the woods of South West England, Johnny 'Rooster' Byron, former daredevil motorcyclist and modern-day Pied Piper, is a wanted man. The council officials want to serve him an eviction notice, his son wants to be taken to the country fair, a stepfather wants to give him a serious kicking and a motley crew of friends wants his ample supply of drugs and alcohol.

Mark Rylance

Mackenzie Crook (photos by Joan Marcus)

John Gallagher Jr

The Lion King

Minskoff Theatre; First Preview: October 15, 1997; Opening Night: November 13, 1997; 33 previews, 6,038 performances as of May 31, 2012

Music by Elton John, lyrics by Tim Rice, additional music and lyrics by Lebo M, Mark Mancina, Jay Rifkin, Julie Taymor, Hans Zimmer; book by Roger Allers and Irene Mecchi, adapted from screenplay by Ms. Mecchi, Jonathan Roberts and Linda Woolverton; Produced by Walt Disney Theatrical Productions (Peter Schneider, President; Thomas Schumacher, Executive VP); Director, Julie Taymor; Choreography, Garth Fagan; Orchestrations, Robert Elhai, David Metzger, Bruce Fowler; Music Director/Conductor, Karl Jurman; Original Music Director, Joseph Church; Sets, Richard Hudson; Costumes/Masks/Puppets, Julie Taymor; Lighting, Donald Holder; Masks/Puppets, Michael Curry; Sound, Tony Meola/ Steve Canyon Kennedy; Hair/Makeup, Michael Ward; Projections, Geoff Puckett; Technical Director, David Benken; Casting, Jay Binder; Company Manager, Thomas Schlenk; Associate Company Manager, Christopher A. Recker; Associate Producer, Anne Quart; Production Stage Manager, Ron Vodicka; Stage Managers, Carmen I. Abrazado, Antonia Gianino, Arabella Powell, Tom Reynolds; Resident Director, Darren Katz; Resident Dance Supervisor, Ruthlyn Salomons; Associate Design: Peter Eastman (set), Mary Nemecek Peterson (costumes), Louis Troisi (mask & puppets), John Shivers (sound), Carole Hancock (hair & wigs), Jeanne Koenig (lighting); Assistant Design: Marty Vreeland (lighting); Executive Music Producer, Chris Montan; Vocal Arrangements, Lebo M; Music Coordinator, Michael Keller; Dance Captains, Garland Days, Willa Noel-Montague; Fight Captain, Ray Mercer; Assistant Choreographers, Norwood J. Pennewell, Natalie Rogers; South African Dialect Coach, Ron Kunene; For *The Lion King* Worldwide: Doc Zorthian (Production Supervisor), Myriah Perkins (Senior Production Manager), Thomas Schlenk (Production Manager), Michael Height (Production Manager), John Stefaniuk (Associate Director), Marey Griffith (Associate Choreographer), Clement Ishmael (Music Supervisor), Celise Hicks (Dance Supervisor), Aland Henderson (Automated Lighting), Kelly Archer (Production Coordinator), Zachary Baer (Management Assistant); Advertising, Serino/Coyne; Interactive Marketing, Situation Marketing, Damian Bazadonna, Lisa Cecchini, Miriam Gardin; Press, Disney Theatricals, Dennis Crowley, Lindsay Braverman; Cast recording: Walt Disney 60802-7

CAST Rafiki **Tshidi Manye**; Mufasa **Alton Fitzgerald White**; Sarabi **Jean Michelle Grier**; Zazu **Cameron Pow**[*1]; Scar **Gareth Saxe**[*2]; Young Simba **Judah Bellamy** or **Aubrey Omari Joseph**[*3]; Young Nala[*4] **Shaylin Becton** or **Khail Toi Bryant**; Shenzi **Bonita J. Hamilton**; Banzai **James Brown-Orleans**; Ed **Enrique Segura**; Timon **Fred Berman**; Pumbaa **Tom Alan Robbins**[*5]; Simba **Clifton Oliver**[*6]; Nala **Chanteé Schuler**; Ensemble Singers[*7] **Alvin Crawford, Lindiwe Dlamini, Bongi Duma, Jean Michelle Grier, Joel Karie, Ron Kunene, Sheryl McCallum, S'bu Ngema, Nteliseng Nkhela, Selloane A. Nkhela, L. Steven Taylor, Vusi Sondiyazi**; Ensemble Dancers[*8]: **Sant'gria Bello, Camille M. Brown, Gabriel Croom, Christopher Freeman, Nicole Adell Johnson, Lisa Lewis, Charity de Loera, Jaysin McCollum, Ray Mercer, Jennifer Harrison Newman, Torya, Philip W. Turner, Camille Workman**; Season Swings **Garland Days, Angelica Edwards, Kenny Ingram, Brian M. Love, Dennis Johnston, Willa-Noel Montague, Matthew S. Morgan, James A. Pierce III, Chondra La-Tease Profit, Jacqueline René, Arbender J. Robinson, Natalie Turner**; Standbys **Jim Ferris** (Timon, Pumbaa, Zazu), **Thom Christopher Warren** (Scar, Pumbaa, Zazu)

*Succeeded by: 1. Jeff Binder 2. Patrick R. Brown (1/6/12) 3. Niles Fitch 4. Nia Ashleigh or Imani Dia Smith 5. Ben Jeffrey 6. Adam Jacobs (8/29/11), Dashaun Young (5/16/12) 7. Derrick Davis, Trista Dollison, Ian Yuri Gardner, Andrea Jones, Jason Veasey, Rema Webb 8. Donna Michelle Vaughn, Zach Law Ingram, Keisha Laren Clarke Gray, Charlaine Katsuyoshi, Rhea Roderick

MUSICIANS Karl Jurman (Conductor); Cherie Rosen (Associate Conductor/ Keyboard Synthesizer); Ted Baker, Paul Ascenzo (Synthesizers); David Weis (Wood Flute/Flute/Piccolo); Francisca Mendoza (Concertmaster/Violin); Krystof Witek, Avril Brown (Violins); Ralph Farris (Violin/Viola); Eliana Mendozza, Bruce Wang (Cellos); Robert DeBellis (Flute/Clarinet/Bass Clarinet); Patrick Milando, Alexandra Cook, Greg Smith (French Horns); Rock Ciccarone (Trombone); Morris Kainuma (Bass Trombone/Tuba); Tom Barney (Upright & Electric Bass); Tommy Igoe (Assistant Conductor/Drums); Kevin Kuhn (Guitar); Rolando Morales-Mantos (Assistant Conductor/Percussion); Valerie Dee Naranjo, Tom Brett (Percussion/Mallets); Junior "Gabu" Wedderburn (Percussion)

MUSICAL NUMBERS Circle of Life; Morning Report; I Just Can't Wait to Be King; Chow Down; They Live in You; Be Prepared; Hakuna Matata; One by One; Madness of King Scar; Shadowland; Endless Night; Can You Feel the Love Tonight; King of Pride Rock/Finale

A musical presented in two acts. For original production credits see *Theatre World* Vol. 54, page 20. Originally opened at the New Amsterdam Theatre and transferred to the Minskoff Theatre June 13, 2006.

SYNOPSIS Based on the 1994 Disney animated feature film, *The Lion King* tells the story of the adventures of Simba, a young lion cub, as he struggles to accept the responsibilities of adulthood and his destined role as king.

The Company

Adam Jacobs (photos by Joan Marcus)

Mamma Mia!

Winter Garden Theatre; First Preview: October 5, 2001: Opening Night: October 18, 2001; 14 previews, 4,403 performances as of May 31, 2012

Book by Catherine Johnson, music, lyrics, and orchestrations by Benny Andersson, Björn Ulvaeus, some songs with Stig Anderson; Produced by Judy Craymer, Richard East and Björn Ulvaeus for Littlestar Services Limited, in association with Universal; Director, Phyllida Lloyd; Sets and Costumes, Mark Thompson; Lighting, Howard Harrison; Sound, Andrew Bruce & Bobby Aitken; Wigs, Paul Huntley; Choreography, Anthony Van Laast; Musical Supervision/ Orchestrations, Martin Koch; Associate Musical Director/Supervisor, David Holcenberg; Musical Coordination, Michael Keller; Associate Director, Robert McQueen; Associate Choreographer, Nichola Treherne; Dance Supervisor, Janet Rothermel; Resident Director, Martha Banta; Technical Supervisor, Arthur Siccardi; General Manager, Bespoke Theatricals, Devin Keudell, Maggie Brohn, Amy Jacobs, Nina Lannan; Company Manager, J. Anthony Magner; Associate Company Manager, Ryan Conway; Production Stage Manager, Sherry Cohen; Stage Managers, Dean R. Greer, Michael Pule; Casting, Tara Rubin; Synthesizer Programmer, Nicholas Gilpin; Associate Design: Nancy Thun (set U.S.), Jonathan Allen (set U.K.), Lucy Gaiger, Scott Traugott (costumes), Josh Marquette (hair), Brian Buchanan, David Patridge (sound); Music Transcription Anders Neglin; Dance Captains, Tony Gonzalez, Janet Rothermel; Advertising, Serino/Coyne; Press, Boneau/Bryan-Brown; London Cast recording: Polydor 543 115 2

CAST Sophie Sheridan **Liana Hunt**; Ali **Catherine Ricafort**; Lisa **Halle Morris**; Tanya **Judy McLane**; Rosie **Jennifer Perry**; Donna Sheridan **Lisa Brescia**; Sky **Corey Greenan**[1]; Pepper **Matthew Mindlin**[2]; Eddie **Andrew Chappelle**; Harry Bright **Clarke Thorell**[3]; Bill Austin **Patrick Boll**; Sam Carmichael **John Dossett**[4]; Father Alexandrios **Bryan Scott Johnson**; Ensemble[5] **Deana Aguinaga, Meredith Akins, Brent Black, Timothy Booth, Natalie Bradshaw, Allyson Carr, Felicity Claire, Mark Dancewicz, Michelle Dawson, Annie Edgerton, Stacia Fernandez, Natalie Gallo, Corey Greenan, Albert Guerzon, Bryan Scott Johnson, Carol Linnea Johnson, Monica Kapoor, Alison Luff, Corinne Melançon, Paul Heesang Miller, Gerard Salvador, Sharone Sayegh, Allison Strong, Laurie Wells, Blake Whyte**; Season Swings **A.J. Fisher, Eric Giancola, Jon-Erik Goldberg, Tony Gonzales, Lauren Sambataro, Janet Rothermel, Ryan Sander, Leah Zepel**

UNDERSTUDIES Brent Black (Bill, Sam, Father Alexandrios), Natalie Bradshaw (Sophie, Ali), Timothy Booth (Harry, Bill, Sam), Felicity Claire (Lisa, Sophie), Mark Dancewicz (Pepper), Stacia Fernandez (Tanya, Rosie), Tony Gonzalez (Sky, Eddie, Father Alexandrios), Albert Guerzon (Eddie), Bryan Scott Johnson (Harry, Bill), Monica Kapoor (Ali, Lisa), Corinne Melançon (Donna, Tanya), Ryan Sander (Sky, Eddie), Gerard Salvador (Pepper), Sharone Saygh (Lisa), Corey Greenan (Sky)

*Succeeded by: 1. Jordan Dean (6/6/11) 2. Jacob Pinion (6/6/11) 3. David Beach (6/6/11) 4. David Hemphill (6/6/11) 5. Annie Edgerton, Jennifer Noth

ORCHESTRA Rob Preuss (Conductor/Keyboard 1); Steve Marzullo (Associate Conductor/Keyboard 2); Sue Anschutz (Keyboard 3); Myles Chase (Keyboard 4); Doug Quinn, Jeff Campbell (Guitars); Paul Adamy (Bass); Ray Marchica (Drums); David Nyberg (Percussion)

MUSICAL NUMBERS Chiquitita; Dancing Queen; Does Your Mother Know?; Gimme! Gimmie! Gimmie!; Honey, Honey; I Do, I Do, I Do, I Do; I Have a Dream; Knowing Me Knowing You; Lay All Your Love on Me; Mamma Mia; Money Money Money; One of Us; Our Last Summer; Slipping Through My Fingers; S.O.S.; Super Trouper; Take a Chance on Me; Thank You For the Music; The Name of the Game; The Winner Takes All; Under Attack; Voulez-Vous

SETTING Time: A wedding weekend. Place: A tiny Greek island. A musical presented in two acts. For original production credits see *Theatre World* Vol. 58, Page 27). The show celebrated its tenth year on Broadway October 18, 2011.

SYNOPSIS *Mamma Mia!* collects a group of hit songs by the Swedish pop group ABBA and shapes them around the story of a single mother coping with her young daughter's marriage on a picturesque Greek isle. While the daughter plans her future with the love of her life, her mother is haunted by three different men who may or may not be her daughter's father.

Jordan Dean and the Company

John Hemphill, David Beach, and Patrick Boll (photos by Joan Marcus)

Mary Poppins

New Amsterdam Theatre; First Preview: October 14, 2006; Opening Night: November 16, 2006; 30 previews, 2,306 performances as of May 31, 2012

Music and lyrics by Richard M. Sherman and Robert B. Sherman, book by Julian Fellowes, new songs and additional music/lyrics by George Stiles and Anthony Drewe; based on the stories of P.L. Travers and the 1964 Walt Disney Film; Produced and co-created by Cameron Mackintosh; Produced for Disney Theatrical Productions by Thomas Schumacher; Associate Producers, Todd Lacy, James Thane; Director, Richard Eyre; Co-Direction/Choreography, Matthew Bourne; Sets/Costumes, Bob Crowley; Lighting, Howard Harrison; Co-choreographer, Stephen Mear; Music Supervisor, David Caddick; Music Director, Brad Haak; Orchestrations, William David Brohn; Sound, Steve Canyon Kennedy; Dance/Vocal Arrangements, George Stiles; Associate Director, Anthony Lyn; Associate Choreographer, Geoffrey Garratt;; Makeup, Naomi Donne; Casting, Tara Rubin; Technical Director, David Benken; Production Stage Manager, Mark Dobrow; Resident Choreographer, Tom Kosis; Company Manager, Dave Ehle; Assistant Company Manager, Laura Eichholz; Associate GM, Alan Wasser; Stage Manager, Jason Trubitt; Assistant Stage Managers, Valerie Lau-Kee Lai, Michael Wilhoite, Terence Orleans Alexander; Dance Captain, Brian Collier, Suzanne Hylenski, Dialect/Vocal Coach, Deborah Hecht; Wigs, Angela Cobbin; Illusions, Jim Steinmeyer; Technical Director, David Benken; Production Supervisor, Patrick Eviston; Production Manager, Jane Abramson; Flying, Raymond King; Automation, Steve Stackle, David Helk; Properties, Victor Amerling, Tim Abel, Joe Bivone, John Saye; Keyboard Programming, Stuart Andrews; Music Contractor, David Lai; Dance Captains, Brian Collier, Geoffrey Goldberg, Kelly Jacobs; Music Copyist, Emily Grisham Music Preparation; Advertising, Serino/Coyne; Press, Disney Theatricals, Dennis Crowley, Michelle Bergmann; London Cast recording: Disney Theatricals 61391-7

Andrew Keenan-Bolger and Valerie Boyle

Steffanie Leigh and Gavin Lee (photos by Joan Marcus)

CAST Bert **Gavin Lee**; George Banks **Karl Kenzler**; Winifred Banks **Megan Osterhaus**[*1]; Jane Banks[*2] **Rozi Baker** or **Rachel Resheff** or **Brigid Harrington**; Michael Banks[*3] **David Gabriel Lerner** or **Lewis Grosso** or **Anthony Scarpone-Lambert**; Katie Nanna/Annie **Kristine Carbone**; Policeman **Corey Skaggs**; Miss Lark **Kate Chapman**[*4]; Admiral Boom/Bank Chairman **Jonathan Freeman**[*5]; Mrs. Brill **Valerie Boyle**; Robertson Ay **Andrew Keenan-Bolger**[*6]; Mary Poppins **Ashely Brown**[*7]; Park Keeper/Mr. Punch **James Hindman**; Neleus **Nick Kepley**[*8]; Queen Victoria/Miss Smythe/Miss Andrew **Ruth Gottschall**[*9]; Von Hussler/Jack-In-A-Box **Tom Souhrada**; Northbrook **Chad Seib**; Bird Woman **Ann Arvia**; Mrs. Corry **Janelle Anne Robinson**; Fannie **Amber Owens**; Annie **Catherine Brunell**; Valentine **Barrett Davis**[*10]; Ensemble[*11] **Tia Altinay, David Baum, Catherine Brunell, Kristin Carbone, Barrett Davis, Elizabeth DeRosa, Case Dillard, James Hindman, Nick Kepley, Tyler Maynard, Kathleen Nanni, Brian Ogilvie, Amber Owens, T. Oliver Reid, Janelle Anne Robinson, Laura Schutter, Chad Seib, Corey Skaggs, Tom Souhrada, Kevin Samuel Yee**; Season Swings **Julie Barnes, Pam Bradley, Kathy Calahan, Brian Collier, Geoffrey Goldberg, Suzanne Hylenski, Kelly Jacobs, Rommy Sandhu, James Tabeek, Jen Taylor**

*Succeeded by: 1. Blythe Wilson, Megan Osterhaus 2. Annie Baltic or Camille Mancuso or Kara Oates 3. Reese Sebastian Diaz or Noah Marlowe or Tyler Merna 4. Emily Harvey 5. Ed Dixon, Jonathan Freeman 6. Shua Potter, Andrew Keenan-Bolger, Dennis Moench 7. Laura Michelle Kelly (7/19/11), Steffanie Leigh (10/11/11) 8. Garrett Hawe, Josh Assor 9. Jessica Sheridan, Ruth Gottschall 10. Eric Hatch, Barrett Davis 11. Josh Assor, Emily Harvey, Koh Mochizuki, Chuck Rea, Christopher Shinn, Jesse Swimm, Nic Thompson, Garrett Hawe, Sam Kiernan, Dominic Roberts

ORCHESTRA Brad Haak (Conductor); Dale Rieling (Associate Conductor/2nd Keyboard); Milton Granger (Assistant Conductor/Piano); Peter Donovan (Bass); Dave Ratajczak (Drums); Daniel Haskins (Percussion), Nate Brown (Guitar/Banjo/E-Bow); Russell Rizner, Shelagh Abate (Horns); John Sheppard, Jason Covey (Trumpets); Marc Donatelle (Trombone/Euphonium); Jeff Caswell (Bass Trombone/Tuba); Meryl Abt (Clarinet); Alexandra Knoll (Oboe/English Horn); Brian Miller (Flutes); Stephanie Cummins (Cello)

MUSICAL NUMBERS Chim Chim Cher-ee; Cherry Tree Lane (Part 1); The Perfect Nanny; Cherry Tree Lane (Part 2); Practically Perfect; Jolly Holiday; Cherry Tree Lane (reprise); Being Mrs. Banks; Jolly Holiday (reprise); A Spoonful of Sugar; Precision and Order; A Man Has Dreams; Feed the Birds; Supercalifragilisticexpialidocious; Temper; Temper; Chim; Chim; Cher-ee (reprise); Cherry Tree Lane (reprise); Brimstone and Treacle (Part 1); Let's Go Fly A Kite; Good For Nothing; Being Mrs. Banks (reprise); Brimstone and Treacle (Part 2); Practically Perfect (reprise); Chim Chim Cher-ee (reprise); Step in Time; A Man Has Dreams; A Spoonful of Sugar (reprise); Anything Can Happen; A Spoonful of Sugar (reprise); A Shooting Star

SETTING In and around the Banks' household somewhere in London at the turn of the last century. American premiere of a new musical presented in two acts. For original production credits, see *Theatre World* Vol. 63, page 41. Originally produced in London at the Prince Edward Theatre on December 15, 2004.

SYNOPSIS Based on the Walt Disney classic film and the novels by P.L. Travers, *Mary Poppins* is the story of the Banks family and how their lives change after the arrival of nanny Mary Poppins at their home at 17 Cherry Tree Lane in London.

Memphis

Shubert Theatre; First Preview: September 23, 2009; Opening Night: October 19, 2009; 30 previews, 1,088 performances as of May 31, 2012

Book and lyrics by Joe DiPietro, music and lyrics by David Bryan; Based on a concept by George W. George; Produced by Junkyard Dog Productions (Randy Adams, Kenny Alhadeff, Sue Frost), Barbara and Buddy Freitag, Marleen and Kenny Alhadeff, Latitude Link, Jim and Susan Blair, Demos Bizar Entertainment (Nick Demos & Francine Bizar), Land Line Productions, Apples and Oranges Productions, Dave Copley, Dancap Productions Inc., Alex and Katya Lukianov, Tony Ponturo, 2 Guys Productions, Richard Winkler, in association with Lauren Doll, Eric and Marsi Gardiner, Linda and Bill Potter, Broadway Across America (John Gore, CEO; Thomas B. McGrath, Chairman; Beth Williams, COO & Head of Production), Jocko Productions, Patty Baker, Dan Frishwasser, Bob Bartner/Scott and Kaylin Union, Loraine Boyle/Chase Mishkin, Remmel T. Dickinson/Memphis Orpheum Group (Pat Halloran), ShadowCatcher Entertainment/Vijay and Sita Vashee; Director, Christopher Ashley; Choreographer, Sergio Trujillo; Music Producer/Music Supervisor, Christopher Jahnke; Associate Producers, Emily and Aaron Alhadeff, Alison and Andi Alhadeff, Ken Clay, Joseph Craig, Ron and Marjorie Danz, Cyrena Esposito, Bruce and Joanne Glant, Matt Murphy; Sets, David Gallo; Costumes, Paul Tazewell; Lighting, Howell Binkley; Sound, Ken Travis; Projections, David Gallo & Sandy Sagady; Hair & Wigs, Charles G. LaPointe; Fight Director, Steve Rankin; Casting, Telsey + Company; Associate Choreographer, Kelly Devine; Orchestrations, Daryl Waters & David Bryan; Musical Director, Kenny J. Seymour; Dance Arrangements, August Eriksmoen; Music Contractor, Michael Keller; Production Stage Manager, Arturo E. Porazzi; General Manager, Alchemy Production Group, Carl Pasbjerg & Frank Scardino; Production Management, Juniper Street Productions; Company Manager, Jim Brandeberry; Associate Director, Beatrice Terry; Associate Choreographer, Edgar Godineaux; Stage Manager, Gary Mickelson; Assistant Stage Managers, Christine Viega, Alexis Shorter; Associate Company Manager, Michelle Tamagwa; Junkyard Dog Associate, Kristel J. Brown; Associate to the General Managers, Amanda Coleman; Dance/Fight Captain, Jermaine R. Rembert; Assistant Dance Captain, Candice Monet McCall; Assistant Fight Director, Shad Ramsey; Dramaturg, Gabriel Greene; Dialect Coach, Stephen Gabis; Makeup, Angelina Avellone; Associate Design: Steven C. Kemp (set), Rory Powers (costumes), Mark Simpson (lighting), Leah Loukas (hair); Assistant Design: Maria Zamansky (costumes), Alex Hawthorn (sound), Steve Channon (projections); Assistants to Desginers: Kara Harmon (costumes), Amanda Zieve (lighting); Moving Light Programmer, David Arch; Projection Programmer, Florian Mosleh; Music Copying, Christopher Deschene; Keyboard Programmer, Kenny J. Seymoure; Advertising/Marketing, aka; Press, The Hartman Group, Michael Hartman, Juliana Hannett, Frances White; Cast recording: Rhino 523944

CAST White DJ/Mr. Collins/Gordon Grant **David McDonald**; Black DJ **Rhett George**[*1]; Delray **J. Bernard Calloway**[*2]; Gator **Derrick Baskin**; Bobby **Will Mann**[*3]; Wailin' Joe/Reverend Hobson **Robert Hartwell**; Ethel **Monette McKay**; Felicia **Montego Glover**; Huey **Chad Kimball**[*4]; Mr. Simmons **John Jellison**; Clara **Elizabeth Ward Land**; Buck Wiley/Martin Holton **Justin Patterson**; Perry Como/Frank Dryer **Jamison Scott**; Mama **Nancy Opel**[*5]; Ensemble[*6] **Felicia Boswell, Sam J. Cahn, Preston W. Dugger III, Hilary Elk, Bryan Fenkart, Bahiyah Sayyed Gaines, Rhett George**[*1], **Gregory Haney, Robert Hartwell, Tiffany Janene Howard, John Jellison, Elizabeth Ward Land, Kevin Massey, David McDonald, Paul McGill, Monette McKay, Andy Mills, Justin Patterson, Ephraim M. Sykes, Jamison Scott, Dan'yelle Williamson** Swings[*7] **Tyrone A. Jackson, Candice Monet McCall, Sydney Morton, Jermaine R. Rembert**

UNDERSTUDIES Elizabeth Ward Land, Betsy Struxness (Mama); Bryan Fenkart, Kevin Massey, Justin Patterson (Huey); Ashley Blanchet, Dan'yelle Williamson (Felicia); Rhett G. George, Robert Hartwell (Bobby, Delray); David McDonald, Justin Patterson (Mr. Simmons)

*Succeeded by: 1. Antoine L. Smith 2. Christopher Jackson (1/24/12), J. Bernard Calloway (2/28/12) 3. James Monroe Inglehart (8/2/11) 4. Adam Pascal (10/25/11) 5. Cass Morgan (10/15/11), Nancy Opel (2/14/12) 6. Ahshley Blanchet, Darius Barnes, Bryan Langlitz, Carmen Shavone Borders, Angela C. Brydon, Lauren Lim Jackson, 7. Sasha Hutchings

THE *MEMPHIS* BAND Kenny J. Seymour (Conductor/Keyboard 1), Jason Michael Webb (Associate Conductor/Keyboard 2), John Putnam (Guitars), George Farmer (Bass), Clayton Craddock (Drums), John Walsh (Trumpet), Birch Johnson (Trombone), Scott Kreitzer & Ken Hitchcock (Reeds)

MUSICAL NUMBERS Underground; The Music of My Soul; Scratch My Itch; Ain't Nothin' But a Kiss; Hello, My Name is Huey; Everybody Wants to Be Black on a Saturday Night; Make Me Stronger; Colored Woman; Someday; She's My Sister; Radio; Say a Prayer; Crazy Little Huey; Big Love; Love Will Stand When All Else Falls; Stand Up; Change Don't Come Easy; Tear the House Down; Love Will Stand/Ain't Nothin' But a Kiss (reprise); Memphis Lives in Me; Steal Your Rock 'n' Roll

SETTING Time: The 1950s. Place: Memphis, Tennessee and New York City. New York premiere of a new musical presented in two acts. World premiere produced as a joint venture at North Shore Music Theatre in Beverly, Massachusetts September 23–October 12, 2003 and at TheatreWorks in Palo Alto, California January 24–February 15, 2004. The show played LaJolla Playhouse August 19–September 28, 2008 and at 5th Avenue Theatre in Seattle January 27–February 15, 2009 prior to its Broadway debut (see *Theatre World* Vol. 65, pages 319 and 330).

SYNOPSIS Inspired by actual events, *Memphis* takes place in the smoky halls and underground clubs of the segregated 1950s. A young white DJ named Huey Calhoun who wants to change the world falls in love with everything he shouldn't: rock and roll and an electrifying black club singer who is ready for her big break. *Memphis* is an original story about the cultural revolution that erupted when his vision met her voice, and the music changed forever.

Adam Pascal (photo by Joan Marcus)

Million Dollar Quartet

Nederlander Theatre; First Preview: March 13, 2010; Opening Night: April 11, 2010; Closed June 12, 2011; 34 previews, 489 performances

Book by Colin Escott & Floyd Mutrux; Original concept and direction by Floyd Mutrux; Inspired by Elvis Presley, Johnny Cash, Jerry Lee Lewis, and Carl Perkins; Produced by Relevant Theatricals (Gigi Pritzker and Ted Rawlins), John Cossette Productions, American Pop Anthology, Broadway Across America (John Gore, CEO; Thomas B. McGrath, Chairman; Jennifer Costello, Associate Producer; Sara Skolnick, Associate Producer), James L. Nederlander; Director, Eric Schaeffer; Musical Arrangements/Supervisor, Chuck Mead; Set, Derek McLane; Costumes, Jane Greenwood; Lighting, Howell Binkley; Sound, Kai Harada; Hair & Wigs, Tom Watson; Associate Music Supervisor, August Eriksmoen; Casting, Telsey + Company; Marketing Director, Carol Chiavetta; Marketing, Allied Live LLC; Production Stage Manager, Robert Witherow; Production Manager, Juniper Street Productions, Hilary Blanken, Kevin Broomell, Guy Kwan, Ana Rose Greene, Sue Semaan; General Management, Alan Wasser, Allan Williams, Mark Shacket, Dawn Kusinski; Company Manager, Jolie Gabler; Assistant Director, David Ruttura; U.K. Consulting Producers, Joseph Smith, Michael McCabe; Japan Consulting Producer, TBS Services Inc.; Stage Manager, Carolyn Kelson; Assistant Stage Manager, Erik Hayden; Associate Design: Shoko Kambara (set), Moria Clinton (costumes), Ryan O'Gara (lighting); Assistant Lighting Designers, Amanda Zieve, Sean Beach; Music Contractor, Michael Keller; Additional Arrangements, Levi Kreis; Advertising, SpotCo; Press, Boneau/Bryan-Brown, Adrian Bryan-Brown, Aaron Meier, Amy Kass

CAST Carl Perkins **Robert Britton Lyons**; Johnny Cash **Lance Guest**; Jerry Lee Lewis **Jared Mason**; Elvis Presley **Eddie Clendening**; Jay Perkins (Bass Player) **Corey Kaiser**; Fluke (Drummer) **Larry Lelli**; Sam Phillips **Hunter Foster**; Dyanne **Victoria Matlock**

UNDERSTUDIES Christopher Ryan Grant (Johnny, Sam), Erik Hayden (Elvis, Carl), James Moye (Sam); Steve Benoit (Elvis), Nicolette Hart (Dyanne), Dan Mills (Carl), Randy Redd (Jerry Lee), Billy Woodward (Elvis, Johnny)

MUSICAL NUMBERS Blue Suede Shoes; Real Wild Child; Matchbox; Who Do You Love? Folsom Prison Blues; Fever; Memories Are Made of This; That's All Right; Brown Eyed Handsome Man; Down By the Riverside; Sixteen Tons; My Babe; Long Tall Sally; Peace in the Valley; I Walk the Line; I Hear You Knocking; Party; Great Balls of Fire; Down By the Riverside (reprise); Hound Dog; Riders in the Sky; See You Later Alligator; Whole Lotta Shakin' Goin On

SETTING Time: December 4, 1956. Place: Sun Records, Memphis, Tennessee. New York premiere of a new musical presented without intermission. After closing, the production transferred Off-Broadway at New World Stages (see page 136 in this volume).

SYNOPSIS On December 4, 1956, an auspicious twist of fate brought Johnny Cash, Jerry Lee Lewis, Carl Perkins, and Elvis Presley together. The place was Sun Records' storefront studio in Memphis. The man who made it happen was Sam Phillips, the "Father of Rock and Roll," who discovered them all. The four young musicians united for the only time in their careers for an impromptu recording that has come to be known as one of the greatest rock jam sessions of all time.

Bobby Cannavale and Chris Rock (photo by Joan Marcus)

The Motherf**ker with the Hat

Gerald Schoenfeld Theatre; First Preview: March 15, 2011; Opening Night: April 11, 2011; Closed July 17, 2011; 28 previews, 117 performances

Written by Stephen Adly Guirgus; Produced by Scott Rudin, Stuart Thompson, Public Theater Productions, LAByrinth Theater Company, Fabula Media Partners LLC, Jean Doumanian, Ruth Hendel, Carl Moellenberg, Jon B. Platt, Tulchin Bartner/Jamie deRoy; Director, Anna D. Shapiro; Sets, Todd Rosenthal; Costumes, Mimi O'Donnell; Lighting, Donald Holder; Sound, Acme Sound Partners; Original Music, Terence Blanchard; Casting, Jordan Thaler & Heidi Griffiths; Production Stage Manager, Charles Means; Production Management, Aurora Productions; General Management, Stuart Thompson Productions/Marshall B. Purdy; Company Manager, Kathy Lowe; Stage Manager, Antonia Gianino; Fight Choreographer, Steve Arboleda; Assistant Director, Cat Miller; Assistant to Mr. Guirgis, Japhet Balaban; Associate Design, Valerie Ramshur (costumes), Caroline Chao (lighting), David Thomas (sound); Assistants to Mr. Rosenthal, Kevin Depinet, Shaun Renfro; Assistant Lighting, Michael P. Jones; Makeup, Cookie Jordan; Crew: Todd Frank (production carpenter), Timothy McWilliams (house carpenter), Glenn Ingram (automation), James Maloney (production electrician), Justin Freeman (head electrician), Leslie Ann Kilian (house electrician), Michael Farfalla (sound engineer), John Tutalo (head props), Heidi L. Brown (head props), Sarah Bird (prop shopper), Susan Checklick (wardrobe supervisor), Paul Ludick (dresser), Jule DeVore (production assistant); Advertising & Marketing, aka; Press, Boneau/Bryan-Brown, Chris Boneau, Heath Schwartz, Kelly Guiod

CAST Veronica **Elizabeth Rodriguez**; Jackie **Bobby Cannavale**; Ralph D. **Chris Rock**; Victoria **Annabella Sciorra**; Cousin Julio **Yul Vázquez**

UNDERSTUDIES Rosál Colon (Veronica, Victoria), Ron Cephas Jones (Ralph D.), Alfredo Narciso (Jackie, Cousin Julio)

SETTING New York City, present day. World premiere of a new play presented in two acts. Developed at Ojai Playwrights Conference and at LAByrinth Theatre Company.

SYNOPSIS *The Motherfucker with the Hat* is a new high-octane, verbal cage match about love, fidelity, and misplaced haberdashery from playwright Stephen Adly Guirgis. Jackie and Veronica have been in love since the 8th grade. But now, Jackie is on parole and living clean and sober under the guidance of his sponsor, Ralph D, while still living and loving with his volatile soul mate Veronica who is fiercely loving, but far from sober. Still, their love is pure. And true. Nothing can come between them – except a hat.

Robert Britton Lyons, Eddie Clendening, and Lance Guest (photo by Joan Marcus)

The Normal Heart

John Golden Theatre; First Preview: April 19, 2011; Opening Night: April 27, 2011; Closed July 10, 2011; 10 previews, 86 performances

Written by Larry Kramer; Produced by Daryl Roth, Paul Boskind and Martian Entertainment in association with Gregory Rae and Jayne Baron Sherman/Alexander Fraser; Directors, Joel Grey & George C. Wolfe; Set, David Rockwell; Costumes, Martin Pakledinaz; Lighting, David Weiner; Projections, Batwin + Robin Productions Inc.; Original Music & Sound, David Van Tieghem; Casting, Telsey + Company; Technical Supervisor, Tech Production Services, Peter Fulbright, Mary Duffe, Colleen Houlehen, Kaitlyn Anderson; PSM, Karen Armstrong; Marketing, Serino/Coyne/Leslie Barrett; General Management, 101 Productions Ltd.; Company Manager, Ron Gubin; Stage Manager, Matthew Farrell; Associate Design: Richard Jaris (set) David J. Kaley (costumes), Michael P. Jones (lighting), David Sanderson (sound), Bob Peterson (projections); Moving Light Programmer, Marc Polimeni; Video Programmer, Paul Vershbow; Makeup, Joseph Dulude II; Crew: Peter Malbuisson (production carpenter), Michale S. LoBue (production electrician), Kathy Fabian (production properties supervisor), Andrew Meeker (head props), Nick Borisjuk (head sound operator), Barry Doss (wardrobe supervisor), Jamie Engelhart, Bryen Shannon (dressers), David Cohen, Brian Gold (production assistants); Advertising and New Media Marketing, Serino/Coyne; Assistants to Ms. Roth, Greg Raby, Megan Smith; Press, O+M Company, Rick Miramontez, Molly Barnett, Andy Snyder, Sam Corbett

CAST Craig Donner/Grady **Luke MacFarlane**; Mickey Marcus **Patrick Breen**; Ned Weeks **Joe Mantello**; David **Wayne Alan Wilcox**; Dr. Emma Brookner **Ellen Barkin**; Bruce Niles **Lee Pace**; Felix Turner **John Benjamin Hickey**; Ben Weeks **Mark Harelik**; Tommy Boatwright **Jim Parsons**; Hiram Keeble/Examining Doctor **Richard Topol**

UNDERSTUDIES Jordan Baker (Dr. Emma Brookner), Jon Levenson (Ben Weeks, Examining Doctor, Hiram Keebler, Mickey Marcus, Ned Weeks), Lee Aaron Rosen (Bruce Niles, Craig Donner, David, Grady, Tommy Boatwright)

SETTING Between July 1981 and May 1984 in New York City. Broadway premiere of the revival of an Off-Broadway play presented in two acts. Originally presented at The Public Theater April 21, 1985–January 5, 1986 playing 294 performances (see *Theatre World* Vol. 41, page 114). The Worth Street Theatre revived the play at the Public Theater in (in Anspacher Hall where the original production performed in 1985) April 21–June 29, 2004 (see *Theatre Word* Vol. 60, page 123).

SYNOPSIS *The Normal Heart* dramatizes the outbreak of the AIDS crisis in New York and one group of gay men's fight to win recognition of their plight from a seemingly indifferent media and mayor. The action, centered on the irascible, enemy-making firebrand Ned Weeks, is largely drawn from Larry Kramer's own experiences founding — and eventually losing control of — the Gay Men's Health Crisis, now the world's largest private organization assisting people living with AIDS.

The Company (photo by Joan Marcus)

The People in the Picture

Studio 54; First Preview: April 1, 2011; Opening Night: April 28, 2011; Closed June 19, 2011; 30 previews, 60 performances

Book and lyrics by Iris Rainer Dart, music by Mike Stoller and Artie Butler; Additional music and lyrics by Mark Warshavsky; Produced by the Roundabout Theatre Company (Todd Haimes, Artistic Director; Harold Wolpert, Managing Director; Julia C. Levy, Executive Director) in association with Tracy Aron, Al Parinello and Stefany Bergson; Director, Leonard Foglia; Musical Staging, Andy Blanenbuehler; Music Director, Paul Gemignani; Sets, Riccardo Hernandez; Costumes, Ann Hould-Ward; Lighting, Howell Binkley and James F. Ingalls; Sound, Dan Moses Schreier; Projections, Elaine J. McCarthy; Hair & Wigs, Paul Huntley; Makeup, Angelina Avallone; Orchestrations, Michael Starobin; Dance Arrangements, Alex Lacamoire; Dialect Coach, Kate Wilson; Fight Director, Rick Sordelet; PSM, Peter Wolf; Production Manager, Aurora Productions; Casting, Jim Carnahan & Stephen Kopel; General Manager, Rebecca Habel; Executive Producer, Sydney Beers; Company Manager, Karl Baudendistel; Stage Manager, Brian Bogin; Assistant Company Manager, Laura Stuart; Assistant Director, Cat Williams; Associate Musical Stager/Dance Captain, Rachel Bress; Fight Captain, Brad Bradley; Music Copying, Emily Grishman, Katharine Edmonds; Music Contractor, Bruce Eidem; Synthesizer Programmer, Randy Cohen; Advertising, SpotCo; Press, Boneau/Bryan-Brown, Adrian Bryan-Brown, Matt Polk, Jessica Johnson, Amy Kass; Cast recording: Kritzerland Records

CAST Doovie Feldman **Hal Robinson**; Moishe Rosenwald **Alexander Gemignani**; Chayesel Fisher **Joyce Van Patten**; Yossie Pinsker **Chip Zien**; Avram Krinsky **Lewis J. Stadlen**; Chaim Bradovsky **Christopher Innvar**; Jenny **Rachel Resheff**; Bubbie/Raisel **Donna Murphy**; Red **Nicole Parker**; Hoodlums **Jeremy Davis, Jeffrey Schecter**; Hollywood Girls **Emilee Dupré, Shannon Lewis, Jessica Lea Patty, Megan Reinking**; Rabbi Velvel **Hal Robinson**; Dobrisch **Megan Reinking**; Dr. Godblum **Louis Hobson**; Young Red **Andie Mechanic**; Jerzy **Paul Anthony Stewart**; Rachel **Maya Goldman**; Swings **Brad Bradley, Rachel Bress**; Understudies **Brad Bradley, Emilee Dupré, Maya Goldman, Louis Hobson, Andie Mechanic, Jessica Lea Patty, Jeffrey Schecter, Lori Wilner, Stuart Zagnit**

ORCHESTRA Paul Gemignani (Musical Director); Mark Mitchell (Associate Conductor/Keyboard); Larry Lelli (2nd Associate Conductor/Drummer, Small Percussion); Sylvia D'Avanzo (Concert Master/1st Violin); Deborah Assael (Cello); Steven Lyons (Oboe, EH, FL, Clarinet, Tenor); Don McGeen (Clarinet, Bass Clarinet, Bassoon, Baritone); Greg Thymius (Flute, Piccolo, Alto Sax, Soprano Sax); Dominic Derasse (Trumpet 1, Flugal Horn, Cornet); Bruce Eidem (Trombone, Euphonium); Phil Granger (Trumpet 2, Flugal Horn, Librarian); Randy Cohen (Synthesizer, Accordion); John Beal (Bass)

MUSICAL NUMBERS Prologue; Bread and Theatre; Matryoshka; Before We Lose the Light/The Dybbuk; Remember Who You Are; Hollywood Girls; Remember Who You Are (reprise); And God Laughs; Oyfen Pripitchik; Red's Dilemma; For This; Oyfen Pripitchik (reprise); Prologue, We Were Here; Now and Then; Ich, Uch, Feh; Selective Memory; Saying Goodbye; Child of My Child; Remember Who You Are (reprise); Bread and Theatre (reprise)/We Were Here (finale)

SETTING New York City 1977 and Warsaw, Poland 1935-1946. World premiere of a new musical presented in two acts.

SYNOPSIS Once the darling of the Yiddish Theatre in pre-war Poland, now a grandmother in New York City, Bubbie has had quite a life. But what will it all mean if she can't pass on her stories to the next generation? Though her granddaughter is enchanted by her tales, her daughter Red will do anything to keep from looking back. *The People in the Picture* celebrates the importance of learning from our past, and the power of laughter.

The Phantom of the Opera

Majestic Theatre; First Preview: January 9, 1988. Opening Night: January 26, 1988; 16 previews, 10,126 performances as of May 31, 2012

Music and book by Andrew Lloyd Webber, lyrics by Charles Hart; additional lyrics and book by Richard Stilgoe; Based on the novel by Gaston Leroux; Produced by Cameron Mackintosh and The Really Useful Theatre Company; Director, Harold Prince; Musical Staging/Choreography, Gillian Lynne; Orchestrations, David Cullen, Mr. Lloyd Webber; Design, Maria Björnson; Lighting, Andrew Bridge; Sound, Martin Levan; Original Musical Director and Supervisor, David Caddick; Musical Director, David Lai; Production Supervisor, Peter von Mayrhauser; Casting, Tara Rubin; Original Casting, Johnson-Liff Associates; General Manager, Alan Wasser; Production Dance Supervisor, Denny Berry; Associate Musical Supervisor, Kristen Blodgette; Associate General Manager, Allan Williams; Technical Production Managers, Jake Bell; Company Manager, Steve Greer; Production Stage Manager, Craig Jacobs; Stage Managers, Bethe Ward, Brendan Smith; Assistant Company Manager, Katherine McNamee; Assistant to Mr. Prince, Ruth Mitchell; Associate Set, Dana Kenn; Associate Costumes, Sam Fleming; Associate Lighting, Debra Dumas; Associate Sound, Paul Gatehouse; Sculptures Consultant, Stephen Pyle; Pro Tools Programmer, Lee McCutcheon; Dance Captain, Laurie V. Langdon; Marketing, Type A Marketing; Advertising, Serino/Coyne; Press, The Publicity Office, Marc Thibodeau, Michael S. Borowski, Jeremy Shaffer; London Cast recording: Polydor 831273

CAST The Phantom of the Opera **Hugh Panaro**; Christine Daae **Sara Jean Ford**[1]; Christine Daae (alt.) **Marni Rabb**; Raoul, Vicomte de Chagny **Sean MacLaughlin**[2]; Carlotta Giudicelli **Liz McCartney**[3]; Monsieur André **George Lee Andrews**[4]; Monsieur Firmin **David Cryer**[5]; Madame Giry **Marilyn Caskey**[6]; Ubaldo Piangi **Evan Harrington**[7]; Meg Giry **Heather McFadden**[8]; Monsieur Reyer/Hairdresser **Jim Weitzer**; Auctioneer **John Kuether**; Jeweler (Il Muto) **Frank Mastrone**; Monsieur Lefevre/Firechief **Kenneth Kantor**; Joseph Buquet **Richard Poole**; Don Attilio **John Kuether**; Passarino **Jeremy Stolle**; Slave Master[9] **James Zander**; Slave Master (Sat. Mat.) **Nicholas Cunningham**; Solo Dancer[9] **James Zander** or **Nicholas Cunningham**; Page **Susan Owen**; Porter/Fireman **Chris Bohannon**[10]; Spanish Lady **Melanie Field**[11]; Wardrobe Mistress/Confidante **Michele McConnell**[12]; Princess **Elizabeth Welch**; Madame Firmin **Kris Koop**; Innkeeper's Wife **Mary Illes**; Marksman **Paul A. Schaefer**; Ballet Chorus of the Opera Populaire[13] **Dara Adler, A manda Edge, Polly Baird, Kara Klein, Gianna Loungway, Mabel Modrono, Jessica Radetsky, Carly Blake Sebouhian, Dianna Warren**; Ballet Swing **Laurie V. Langdon**; Swings **Scott Mikita, James Romick, Janet Saia, Jim Weitzer, Stephen Tewksbury, Greg Mills, Carrington Vilmont, Kelly Jeanne Grant**

*Succeeded by: 1. Trista Moldovan (12/9/11) 2. Kyle Barisich (6/4/11) 3. Michelle McConnell (7/11/11) 4. Aaron Galligan-Stierle (9/5/11) 5. Kevin Ligon (9/5/11) 6. Cristin J. Hubbard (10/31/11) 7. David Gaschen (8/22/11), Christian Šebek (9/2/11) 8. Jessica Bishop (7/4/11), Heather McFadden (1/16/12) 9. Harlan Bengel, Darius Crenshaw, Kfir, Justin Peck 10. Stephen Tweksbury 11. Kimilee Bryant 12. Satomi Hofman 13. Jessica Bishop, Paloma Garcia-Lee

ORCHESTRA David Caddick, Kristen Blodgette, David Lai, Paul Schwartz, Tim Stella, Norman Weiss (Conductors); Joyce Hammann (Concert Master), Alvin E. Rogers, Gayle Dixon, Kurt Coble, Jan Mullen, Karen Milne (Violins); Stephanie Fricker, Veronica Salas (Violas); Ted Ackerman, Karl Bennion (Cellos); Melissa Slocum (Bass); Henry Fanelli (Harp); Sheryl Henze, Ed Matthew, Melanie Feld, Matthew Goodman, Atsuko Sato (Woodwinds); Lowell Hershey, Francis Bonny (Trumpets); William Whitaker (Trombone); Daniel Culpepper, Peter Reit, David Smith (French Horn); Eric Cohen, Jan Hagiwara (Percussion); Tim Stella, Norman Weiss (Keyboards)

MUSICAL NUMBERS Think of Me; Angel of Music; Little Lotte/The Mirror; Phantom of the Opera; Music of the Night; I Remember/Stranger Than You Dreamt It; Magical Lasso; Notes/Prima Donna; Poor Fool He Makes Me Laugh; Why Have You Brought Me Here?/Raoul I've Been There; All I Ask of You; Masquerade/Why So Silent?; Twisted Every Way; Wishing You Were Somehow Here Again; Wandering Child/Bravo Bravo; Point of No Return; Down Once More/Track Down This Murderer; Finale

SETTING In and around the Paris Opera House, 1881–1911. A musical presented in two acts with nineteen scenes and a prologue. For original production credits see *Theatre World* Vol. 44, page 20. The show became the longest running show in Broadway history on January 9, 2006. Now in its twenty-fourth year, the musical surpassed the 10,000 performance mark on February 11, 2012.

SYNOPSIS A disfigured musical genius haunts the catacombs beneath the Paris Opera and exerts strange control over a lovely young soprano.

Hugh Panaro and Trista Moldovan

The Company (photos by Joan Marcus)

Priscilla Queen of the Desert

Palace Theatre; First Preview: February 28, 2011; Opening Night: March 20, 2011; 23 previews, 497 performances as of May 31, 2012

Book by Stephan Elliott and Alan Scott, based on the Latent Image/Specific Films motion picture distributed by Metro-Godwyn-Mayer Inc.; Produced by Bette Midler, James L. Nederlander, Garry McQuinn, Liz Koops, Michael Hamlyn, Allan Scott, Roy Furman/Richard Willis, Terry Allen Kramer, Terri and Timothy Childs, Ken Greiner, Ruth Hendel, Chugg Entertainment, Michael Buckley, Stewart F. Lane/Bonnie Comley, Bruce Davey, Thierry Suc/TS3, Bartner/Jenkins, Broadway Across America/Heni Koenigsberg, Myla Lerner/Debbie Bisno/Kit Seidel/Rebecca Gold, Paul Boskind and Martian Entertainment/Kevin Spirtas-Scott Mauro Productions/MAS Music Arts & Show, David Mirvish; Produced in association with MGM On Stage, Darcie Denkert and Dean Stolber; Associate Producer, Ken Sunshine; Executive Producer, Aleica Parker; Director/Development for the Stage, Simon Phillips; Choreography, Ross Coleman; Music Supervision & Arrangements, Stephen "Spud" Murphy; Production Supervision, Jerry Mitchell; Bus Concept & Production Design, Brian Thompson; Costumes, Tim Chappel & Lizzy Gardiner; Lighting, Nick Schlieper; Sound, Jonathan Deans & Peter Fitzgerald; Orchestratrions, Stephen "Spud" Murphy & Charlie Hull; Music Director, Jeffrey Klitz; Musical Coordinator, John Miller; Casting, Telsey + Company; Associate Director, Dean Bryant; Associate Choreographer, Andrew Hallsworth; Advertising, SpotCo; Marketing, Nick Pramik; Technical Supervisor, David Benken; Production Stage Manager, David Hyslop; Flying, Flying by Foy; Makeup, Cassie Hanlon; General Manager, B.J. Holt; Company Manager, Thom Clay; North America-International Associate Producer, Clare Rainbow; International Associate Producer, Kristen Hann; Associate Technical Supervisor, Rose Palombo; Stage Manager, Mahlon Kruse; Assistant Stage Manager, Megan Schneid; Associate General Manager, Hilary Hamilton; General Management Associate, Stephen Spadaro; Assistant Company Manager, Tammie Ward; Dance Captain, Eric Sciotto; Assistant Dance Captain, Joshua Buscher; Assistant to Ms. Parker, Marilyn Stout; Assistant to Mr. Holt, Katharine Hayes; Associate Design: Bryan Johnson (set), Brian J. Bustos (costumes), Michael P. Jones (lighting), Richard Mawbey (wigs); Assistant Design: Katie Irish, Mike Floyd (costumes), Carolyn Wong (lighting), Benjamin Moir (makeup); Bus Visual Animation Sequences Design, Brian Thomson; Animators, Jamie Clennett, Kenji Oates; Photoshoppers, Pip Runciman, Micka Agosta; LED Web Content, Chris Twyman; Dialect Coach, Gillian Lane-Plescia; Crew: Patrick Eviston (head carpenter), Michael Shepp Jr. (automation), Jeff Zink (assistant carpenter), Jon Lawson (production electrician), Patrick Ainge (head electrician), Jesse Hancox (assistant electrician), Chris Herman (moving lights and video programmer), Garth Helm (production sound), Steve Henshaw (head sound), Jerry Marshall (production props), James Cariot (assistant props), Meghan Carsella (wardrobe supervisor), Meghan Bowers (assistant wardrobe supervisor, Justen Brosnan (hair and makeup supervisor); Additional Synthesizer Programming, Jeff Marder;Music Copying, Martine Monroe; Advertising/Website/Online Marketing, SpotCo; Press, Boneau/Bryan-Brown, Adrian Bryan-Brown, Joe Perrotta, Michael Strassheim; Cast recording: Rhino Records 081227977733

CAST Divas **Jacqueline B. Arnold, Anastacia McCleskey, Ashley Spencer**[*1]; Tick (Mitzi) **Will Swenson**; Miss Understanding **Nathan Lee Graham**; Marion **Jessica Phillips**[*2]; Benji[*3] **Luke Mannikus** or **Ashton Woerz**; Farrah/Young Bernadette **Steve Schepis**; Bernadette **Tony Sheldon**; Adam (Felicia) **Nick Adams**; Shirley **Keala Settle**[*4]; Jimmy **James Brown III**[*5]; Bob **C. David Johnson**[*6]; Cynthia **J. Elaine Marcos**; Frank **Mike McGowan**; Ensemble[*7] **Thom Allison, Jacqueline B. Arnold, James Brown III, Kyle Brown, Nathan Lee Graham, Gavin Lodge, J. Elaine Marcos, Anastacia McCleskey, Mike McGowan, Jeff Metzler, Jessica Phillips, Steve Shepis, Keala Settle, Ashley Spencer, Bryan West, Tad Wilson**; Swings **Joshua Buscher, Ellyn Marie Marsh, Eric Sciotto, Amaker Smith, Esther Stilwell**

UNDERSTUDIES Thom Allison (Bernadette, Jimmy, Miss Understanding), James Brown III (Miss Understanding), Kyle Brown (Frank), Joshua Buscher (Farrah, Young Bernadette), Gavin Lodge (Bernadette, Frank, Tick [Mitzi]), Luke Mannikus (Benji), Ellyn Marie Marsh (Cynthia, Diva, Marion, Shirley), Mike McGowan (Bob), Jeff Metzler (Young Bernadette), Steve Schepis (Adam [Felicia]), Eric Sciotto (Tick [Mitzi]), Amaker Smith (Jimmy), Esther Stilwell (Cynthia, Diva, Marion, Shirley), Bryan West (Adam [Felicia]), Tad Wilson (Bob), Ashton Woerz (Benji)

Succeeded by: 1. Lisa Howard 2. Julie Reiber 3. Gaten Matarazzo, Sebastian Thomas 4. Alysha Umphress 5. Anthony Wayne 6. Adam LeFevre 7. Todd A. Horman, Lisa Howard, Alysha Umphress, Anthony Wayne, Branch Woodman

ORCHESTRA Jeffrey Klitz (Conductor), Jeff Marder (Associate Conductor), David Mann (Woodwinds), Ed Hamilton (Guitar), Barry Danielian (Trumpet), Michael Davis (Trombone), Luico Hopper (Bass), Warren Odze (Drums), Roger Squitero (Percussion)

MUSICAL NUMBERS It's Raining Men; What's Love Got to Do With It?; I Say a Little Prayer; Don't Leave Me This Way; Material Girl; Go West; Holiday; Like a Virgin; I Say a Little Prayer (reprise); I Love the Nightlife; True Colors; Sempre Libre; Color My World; I Will Survive; Thank God I'm a Country Boy; A Fine Romance; Thank God I'm a Country Boy (reprise); Shake Your Groove Thing; Pop Muzik; A Fine Romance (reprise); Girls Just Wanna Have Fun; Hot Stuff; MacArthur Park; Boogie Wonderland; The Floor Show; Always on My Mind; Like a Prayer; We Belong; Finally Medley

SETTING Sydney and Alice Springs, Australia, and the roads between. U.S. premiere of a new musical presented in two acts. World premiere in Sydney in 2006, and subsequently in Melbourne, New Zealand, and London (where it continues to play at the Palace Theatre in the West End. Mr. Sheldon starred in the production in Sydney, Melbourne, and London. Most of this cast performed the show in Toronto at the Princess of Wales Theatre October 12, 2010–January 2, 2011 as a pre-Broadway tryout.

SYNOPSIS Based on the Academy Award winning film, *Priscilla Queen of the Desert* follows a trio of friends (who happen to be drag queens) as they hop aboard a battered old bus searching for love and friendship in the middle of the Australiian outback and end up finding more than they could ever have dreamed. The musical features a score of pop and dance music favorites.

Will Swenson, Tony Sheldon, Nick Adams, and the Company (photos by Joan Marcus)

Steve Landes

Rain: A Tribute to The Beatles on Broadway

Brooks Atkinson Theatre+; First Preview: October 19, 2010; Opening Night: October 26, 2010; Closed July 31, 2011; 8 previews, 300 performances

Produced by Annerin Production, Magic Arts & Entertainment/NewSpace/Tix Productions, Nederlander Presentations Inc., and RAIN; Set, Scott Christensen, Todd Skinner; Video, Darren McCaulley, Mathieu St-Arnaud; Lighting, Stephan Gotschel; Sound, Abe Jacob; General Management, NIKO Companies and Steve Boulay; Band Management, Mark Lewis; Production Supervisor, Theatrical Services Inc., Arthur Siccardi, Pat Sullivan; Marketing, Bruce Granath; For NIKO: Manny Kladitis, David Loughner, Jason T. Vanderwoude; Marketing & Original Press, Merle Frimark Associates; Production Manager, Scott Christensen; Company Manager, Jesse White/Robert Tevyaw; Production Stage Manager, Lurie Horns Pfeffer; Costume Coordinators, Robin Robinson, Russ Lease; Sound Assistant, Joshua D. Reid; Production Sound Operator, Jim vanBergen; Monitor Mixer, Craig Van Tassel; Sound System Consultants, Acme Sound Partners; Video Technician, Brandon Epperson; Show Electrician/Board Operator, Michael Cornell; Electric Advisor, Jimmy Fedigan; Wardrobe Supervisor, Allison Goodsell; Backline, Ted Pallas; Graphics, Gary Hewitt, Wedge.a&d; Media Design, Paul J. Toth; AdvanceHD.com; Press Associates, Amy Katz, Twilla Duncan; Advertising, SpotCo; Tour Direction, The Road Company; For Annerin Productions: Jeff Parry (CEO/Producer), Ralph Schmidtke (COO), Stu Peterson (CFO), Jenna DeBoice (Prod. Assistant), Kate McConney (Administration); Magic Arts & Entertainment/NewSpace/Tix Productions: John W. Ballard (President), Lee D. Marshall (Producer), Joe Marsh (Producer), Steve Boulay (COO), Bruce Granath (Marketing), Mary Ann Porcaro (Operations Manager); Press, The Hartman Group

CAST Joe Bithorn (Vocals, Lead Guitar, Guitar Synth, Sitar), **Ralph Castelli** (Drums, Percussion, Vocals), **Joey Curatolo** (Vocals, Bass, Piano, Guitar), **Steve Landes** (Vocals, Rhythm Guitar, Piano, Harmonica)

ALTERNATES Mark Beyer (Keyboard, Percussion), Graham Alexander (Vocals, Bass, Piano, Guitar), Joe Bologna (Drums, Percussion, Vocals), Douglas Cox (Drums, Percussion, Vocals), Jim Irizarry (Vocals, Rhythm Guitar, Piano, Harmonica), David Leon (Vocals, Rhythm Guitar, Piano, Harmonica), Mark Lewis (Keyboard, Percussion), Jimmy Pou (Vocals, Lead Guitar, Guitar Synth), Mac Ruffing (Vocals, Bass, Piano, Guitar), Chris Smallwood (Keyboard, Percussion), Tom Teeley (Vocals, Lead Guitar, Guitar Synth, Sitar)

MUSICAL NUMBERS Across The Universe; All My Loving; All You Need Is Love; And I Love Her; Blackbird; Come Together; A Day In The Life; Day Tripper; Eleanor Rigby; The End; Get Back; Girl; Give Peace A Chance; A Hard Day's Night; Hello Goodbye; Hey Jude; I Am The Walrus; I Feel Fine; I Saw Her Standing There; I Want To Hold Your Hand; I'm Happy Just To Dance With You; I've Just Seen A Face; Let It Be; Mother Nature's Son; Norwegian Wood (This Bird Has Flown); Revolution; Rocky Raccoon; Sgt. Pepper's Lonely Hearts Club Band; Strawberry Fields Forever; This Boy (Ringo's Theme); Till There Was You; Twist And Shout; Two Of Us; We Can Work It Out; With A Little Help From My Friends; Yesterday

Broadway premiere of a revue/concert presented in two acts.

SYNOPSIS With the goal of delivering a perfect note-for-note performance, *Rain* performs the music of the Beatles live, with the same respect a classical musician treats Mozart. The show covers songs ranging from the early days of the band's appearances on The Ed Sullivan Show through the Abbey Road years, including historical film footage and television commercials, plus live cameras zooming in for close-ups of the band.

+ The production originally opened at the Neil Simon where it played through January 15, 2011, went on haitus for three weeks, and reopened at the Brooks Atkinson Theatre February 8, 2011.

Ralph Castilli (photos by Joan Marcus)

Rock of Ages

Helen Hayes Theatre+; First Preview: March 20, 2009 Opening Night: April 7, 2009; 22 previews, 1,229 performances as of May 31, 2012

Book by Chris D'Arienzo; Produced by Matthew Weaver, Carl Levin, Barry Habib, Scott Prisand, Corner Store Fund, in association with Janet Billig Rich, Hillary Weaver, Toni Habib, Paula Davis, Simon & Stefany Bergson/Jennifer Maloney, Charles Rolecek, Susanne Brook, Israel Wolfson, Sara Katz/Jayson Raitt, Max Gottlieb/John Butler, David Kaufman/Jay Franks, Michael Wittlin, Prospect Pictures, Laura Smith/Bill Bodnar; Director, Kristin Hanggi; Choreography, Kelly Devine; Music Supervision, Arrangements & Orchestrations, Ethan Popp; Music Director, Henry Aronson; Music Coordinator, John Miller; Original Arrangements, David Gibbs; Set, Beowulf Boritt; Costumes, Gregory Gale; Lighting, Jason Lyons; Sound, Peter Hylenski; Projections, Zak Borovay; Hair & Wigs, Tom Watson; Makeup, Angelina Avallone; Casting, Telsey + Company; Production Stage Manager, Matthew DiCarlo; Vocal Coach, Liz Caplan Vocal Studios; Associate Choreographer, Robert Tatad; Associate Director/Stage Manager, Adam John Hunter; Associate Producer, David Gibbs; General Management, Roy Gabay; Technical Supervisor, Peter Fulbright/Tech Production Services Inc. (Colleen Houlehen, Mary Duffe, Miranda Wigginton); Company Manager, Daniel Kuney; Associate Company Manager, Chris Aniello; Stage Manager, Justin Scribner; Assistant Stage Manager, Heather J. Weiss; Associate Director, Adam John Hunter; Resident Director, Adam Dannheisser; Associate Design: Jo Winiarski (set), Grant Wilcoxson (lighting), Karl Ruckdeschel (costumes), Daniel Brodie (projections), Keith Caggiano (sound); Assistant Design: Maiko Chii, Alexis Distler, Buist Bickley (set), Julia Broer & Colleen Kesterson (costumes), Driscoll Otto, Sean Beach (lighting), Drew Levy (sound), Austin Switser (projections); Associate Choreography, Robert Tatad; Creative Advisor, Wendy Goldberg; Script Supervisor, Justin Mabardi; Synthesizer Programmer, Randy Cohen; Music Copying/Preparation, Firefly Music Service/Brian Hobbs; Rehearsal Pianist, Keith Cotton; Dance Captain, Jennifer Rias; Advertising and Marketing, aka; Press, The Hartman Group; Cast recording: New Line Records

CAST Lonny/Record Company Man **Mitchell Jarvis**[*1]; Justice/Mother **Michele Mais**; Dennis/Record Company Man **Adam Dannheisser**; Drew **Dan Domenech**; Sherrie **Rebecca Faulkenberry**[*2]; Father/Stacee Jaxx **MiG Ayesa**[*3]; Regina/Candi **Josephine Rose Roberts**; Mayor/Ja'Keith Gill/Strip Club DJ/Ensemble **André Ward**; Hertz **Paul Schoeffler**[*5]; Franz **Cody Scott Lancaster**; Waitress/Ensemble **Erika Hunter**[*6]; Reporter/Ensemble **Emily Williams**[*7]; Sleazy Producer/Joey Primo/Ensemble **Jeremy Woodard**[*8]; Young Groupie/Ensemble **Tessa Alves**; Offstage Vocals **Cassie Silva**, **Tony LePage**; Swings[*9] **Jennifer Foote**, **Tony LePage**, **Ralph Meitzler**, **Michael Minarik**, **Justin Matthew Sargent**, , **Cassie Silva**, **Valerie Stanois**, **Becca Tobin**

*Succeeded by: 1. Genson Blimline (12/19/11) 2. Emily Padgett (11/7/11), Ashley Spencer (5/11/12) 3. Jeremy Woodward (10/3/11) 5. Bret Tuomi, Paul Schoeffler 6. Katie Webber (12/19/11) 7. Neka Zang (4/3/12) 8. Joey Calveri (10/3/11) 9. Jennifer Rias, Lindsay Janisse, Josh Sassanella

ROCK OF AGES **BAND** Henry Aronson (Conductor/Keyboard), Joel Hoekstra (Guitar 1), Tommy Kessler (Guitar 2), Jon Weber (Drums), Winston Roye (Bass)

MUSICAL NUMBERS We Built This City; Nothin' but a Good Time; Keep on Loving You; Just Like Paradise; I Wanna Rock; Too Much Time on My Hands; Renegade; I Hate Myself for Loving You; Oh Sherrie; Waiting for a Girl Like You; Shadows of the Night; Don't Stop Believing; Heaven; The Search is Over; We're Not Gonna Take It; High Enough; The Final Countdown; I Want to Know What Love Is; Harden My Heart; Here I Go Again; To Be With You; Every Rose Has Its Thorn; Hit Me With Your Best Shot; Can't Fight This Feeling; Wanted Dead or Alive; Cum on Feel the Noize; Any Way You Want It; Heat of the Moment; Sister Christian; More Than Words

SETTING Los Angeles and Hollywood, 1987. Transfer of the Off-Broadway musical presented in two acts. World premiere at the Vanguard Hollywood January 26–February 18, 2006. Previously presented at New World Stages October 1, 2008–January 4, 2009. For original production credits, please see *Theatre World* Vol. 65, pages 69 and 152.

SYNOPSIS *Rock of Ages* is an explosive new musical with a heart as big as 80's rock hair. In 1987 on the Sunset Strip, as a legendary rock club faces its demise at the hands of eager developers, a young rocker hoping for his big break falls for a small town girl chasing big dreams of her own, and they fall in love to the greatest songs of the era. An arena-rock love story, *Rock of Ages* is told through the hits of some of the 80's greatest rockers including Journey, Bon Jovi, Styx, Reo Speedwagon, Pat Benatar, Joan Jett, Warrant, Night Ranger, Extreme, Foreigner, Survivor, Quarterflash, Damn Yankees, Twisted Sister, Poison, Asia and Whitesnake.

+The show originally opened at the Brooks Atkinson Theatre and temporarily closed January 9, 2011 for a ten week hiatus before reopening at the Helen Hayes Theatre March 24, 2011.

The Company

Jeremy Woodard (photos by Paul Kolnik)

Sister Act

Broadway Theatre; First Preview: March 24, 2011; Opening Night: April 20, 2011; 28 previews, 461 performances as of May 31, 2012

Music by Alan Menken, lyrics by Glenn Slater, book by Cheri Steinkellner & Bill Steinkellner; Additional Book Material by Douglas Carter Beane; Based on the Touchstone Pictures Motion Picture written by Joseph Howard; Presented by Whoopi Goldberg & Stage Entertainment in association with the Shubert Organization and Disney Theatrical Productions; Producers, Whoopi Goldberg, Joop Van Den Ende, Bill Taylor, Rebecca Quigley; Director, Jerry Zaks; Choreography, Anthony Van Laast; Set, Klara Zieglerova; Costumes, Lez Brotherston; Lighting, Natasha Katz; Sound, John Shivers; Casting, Telsey + Company; Wigs and Hair, David Brian Brown; Production Management, Aurora Productions; Production Supervisor, Steven Beckler; Orchestrations, Doug Besterman; Dance Arrangements, Mark Hummel; Music Director, Brent-Alan Huffman; Music Coordinator, John Miller; Music Supervisor, Vocal & Incidental Music Arrangements, Michael Kosarin; Original Production Depeveloped in Association with Peter Schneider & Michael Reno; Associate Producer for Whoop Inc., Tom Leonardis; Director of Creative Development, Ulrike Burger-Brujis; General Manager, 321 Theatricals; Executive Producer, Beverley D. Mac Keen; For 321: Nina Essman, Nancy Nagel Gibbs, Marcia Goldberg; For Aurora: Gene O'Donovan, W. Benjamin Heller II, Stephanie Sherline, Jarid Sumner, Liza Luxenberg, Jason Margolis, Ryan Stanisz, Melissa Mazdra; Company Manager, Roeya Banuazizi; Associate Company Manager, Eric Cornell; Production Stage Manager, Steven Beckler; Stage Manager, Jason Trubitt; Assistant Stage Manager, Mary MacLeod; Associate Director, Steve Bebout; Assistant Director, Stephen Edlund; Script Assistant, Paul Downs Colaizzo; Associate Choreographer, Ben Clare; U.S. Associate Choreographer, Janet Rothermel; Associate Design: Andrew D. Edwards (set), Diane Williams (costumes U.K), Amy Clark (costumes U.S.), Yael Lubetzky (lighting), David Patridge (sound); Assistant Design, Marina Reti (costumes), Jonathan Spencer (lighting), Moving Light Programmer, Hilary Knox; Makeup Consultant, Milagros Medina-Cerdeira; Crew: Fran Rapp (production carpenter), Patrick Shea (deck automation), Steve Schroettnig (fly automation), J. Michael Pitzer (production electrician), Jeremy Wahlers (head electrician), Justin McClintock (follow spot), Emiliano Pares (production props), Brian Schweppe (prop master), Anmaree Rodibaugh (assistant props), Kevin Kennedy (production sound), George Huckins (sound engineer), Pitsch Karrer (assistant sound engineer), Eddie Harrison (wardrobe supervisor), Jennifer Griggs-Cennamo (assistant wardrobe), Wanda Gregory (hair supervisor), Ashley Leitzel-Reichenbach (assistant hair), Maeve Fiona Butler, Cat Dee, Kathleen Gallagher, Viictoria Grecki, Tim Greer, Sue Hamilton, Gayle Palmieri, Geoffrey Polischuk, Erin Brooke Roth, Chris Sanders (dressers); House Crew: Charles Rasmussen (carpenter), George D. Milne (electrician), Rick DalCortivo (properties), Thomas Cole Jr (flyman); Music Preparation, Russell Anixter, Donald Rice; Electronic Music Design, Andrew Barrett/Lionella Productions LLC; Rehearsal Musicians, Aron Accurso (piano), Steven Malone (piano), Richard Mercurio (drums); Music Interns, Adam Overett, Brendan Whiting; Prod. Assistants, Kathryn Ambrose, Chirstopher Michael Borg, Rebecca Peterson, Jamie Ware; Assistant to John Miller, Jennifer Coolbaugh; Advertising/Website/Interactive Media, SpotCo; Marketing, aka; For Stage Entertainment: Bill Taylor (CEO), Rebecca Quigley (Executive Producer), Beverley D. MacKeen (Executive Director); Press, The Hartman Group, Michael Hartman, Tom D'Ambrosio, Michelle Bergmann; Cast recording (London): Sh-K-Boom/Ghostlight Records 84446

CAST Deloris Van Cartier **Patina Miller**[1]; Michelle **Rashidra Scott**; Tina **Aléna Watters**; Curtis Jackson **Kingsley Leggs**; Joey **John Treacy Egan**; Pablo **Caesar Samayoa**; TJ **Demond Green**; Ernie **Blake Hammond**[2]; Eddie Souther **Chester Gregory**; Joey Finnochio **Blake Hammond**[3]; Cop **Alan H. Green**[4]; Mother Superior **Victoria Clark**[5]; Monsignor O' Hara **Fred Applegate**; Mary Robert **Marla Mindelle**; Mary Patrick **Sarah Bolt**; Mary Lazarus **Audrie Neenan**; Mary Martin-of-Tours **Wendy James**[6]; Mary Theresa **Madeleine Doherty**; Waitress **Holly Davis**; Ensemble[7] **Jennifer Allen, Charl Brown, Holly Davis, Christina DeCicco, Madeleine**

Doherty, Alan H. Green, Blake Hammond, Wendy James, Kevin Ligon, Marissa Perry, Corbin Reid, Rashidra Scott, Jennifer Simard, Lael Van Keuren, Roberta B. Wall, Aléna Watters; Swings[8] **Natalie Bradshaw, Carrie A. Johnson, Louise Madison, Ernie Pruneda, Lance Roberts**

UNDERSTUDIES Jennifer Allen (Mary Lazarus, Mother Superior), Charl Brown (Eddie Souther, Pablo, TJ), Holly Davis (Mary Patrick), Christina DeCicco (Mary Robert), Alan H. Green (Curtis Jackson, Eddie Souther), Blake Hammond (Joey, Monsignor O' Hara), Wendy James (Mother Superior), Kevin Ligon (Joey, Monsignor O' Hara), Marissa Perry (Mary Patrick), Ernie Pruneda (Pablo, TJ), Corbin Reid (Deloris Van Cartier, Michelle, Tina), Lance Roberts (Curtis Jackson), Rashidra Scott (Deloris Van Cartier), Lael Van Keuren (Mary Robert, Michelle, Tina), Roberta B. Wall (Mary Lazarus)

Succeeded by: 1. Raven-Symoné (3/27/12) 2. Chris Bohannon 3. Danny Stiles, Aaron Kaburick 4. Melvin Abston 5. Carolee Carmello (11/19/11) 6. Trisha Rapier 7. Kimberly Marable, Trisha Rapier, Chelsea Morgan Stock, Chris Bohannon, Danny Stiles, Aaron Kuburick, Melvin Abston, Jessica Sheridan 8. Jacqui Graziano, T. Oliver Reid

ORCHESTRA Michael Kosarin (Conductor); Brent-Alan Huffman (Associate Conductor/Keyboards); Aron Accurso (Assistant Conductor/Keyboards); Suzanne Ornstein (Concert Master); Mineko Yajima, Eric DeGioia, Kristina Musser (Violins); Roger Shell (Cello); Andrew Sterman, Marc Phaneuf, Jacqueline Henderson (Woodwinds); Craig Johnson, Scott Harrell (Trumpets); Gary Grimaldi, Jeff Nelson (Trombones); John Benthal (Guitar); Dick Sarpola (Bass); Rich Mercurio (Drums); Michael Englander (Percussion)

MUSICAL NUMBERS Take Me to Heaven; Fabulous, Baby!; Here Within These Walls; It's Good to Be a Nun; When I Find My Baby; I Could Be That Guy; Raise Your Voice; Take Me to Heaven (reprise); Sunday Morning Fever; Lady in the Long Black Dress; Haven't Got a Prayer; Bless Our Show; The Life I Never Led; Fabulous, Baby! (reprise); Sister Act; When I Find My Baby (reprise); The Life I Never Led (reprise); Sister Act (reprise); Spread the Love Around

SETTING Philadelphia; 1978. New York premiere of a new musical presented in two acts. Originally produced by Pasadena Playhouse (Pasadena, California) October 24–December 23, 2006 and subsequently at the Alliance Theatre (Atlanta, Georgia) January 17–February 25, 2007 (see *Theatre World* Vol. 63, page 305). The London production opened on the West End at the London Palladium June 2, 2009–October 30, 2010 starring Ms. Miller.

SYNOPSIS When disco diva Deloris Van Cartier witnesses a murder, she is put in protective custody in the one place cops are sure she won't be found — a convent! Disguised as a nun, she finds herself at odds with both the rigid lifestyle and an uptight Mother Superior. Using her unique disco moves and singing talent to inspire the choir, Deloris breathes new life into the church and community, but in doing so blows her cover. Soon the gang is giving chase, only to find themselves up against Deloris and the power of her new found Sister Hood.

The Company (photos by Joan Marcus)

War Horse

Vivian Beaumont Theatre; First Preview: March 15, 2011; Opening Night: April 14, 2011; 33 previews, 470 performances as of May 31, 2012

Based on the novel by Michael Morpurgo, adapted by Nick Stafford, in association with Handspring Puppet Company; Produced by Lincoln Center Theater (André Bishop, Artistic Director; Bernard Gersten, Executive Producer) and the National Theatre of Great Britain (Nicholas Hytner, Director of the National; Nick Star, Executive Director) in association with Bob Boyett and War Horse LP; Presented by the National Theatre of Great Britain; Directors, Marianne Elliott & Tom Morris; Sets, Costumes, and Drawings, Rae Smith; Puppet Design, Fabrication, and Direction, Adrian Kohler with Basil Jones for Handspring Puppet Company; Lighting, Paule Constable; Director of Movement & Horse Sequences, Toby Sedwick; Animation & Projection Design, 59 Productions; Music, Adrian Sutton; Songmaker, John Tams; Sound, Christopher Shutt; Music Pliska; Associate Puppetry Director, Mervyn Millar; Stage Manager, Rick Steiger; Casting, Daniel Swee; NT Technical Producer, Katrina Gilroy; NT Producer, Chris Harper; NT Associate Producer, Robin Hawkes; NT Marketing, Alex Bayley; Boyett Theatricals Producer, Tim Levy; Fight Director, Thomas Schall; Dialect Coach, Gillian Lane-Plescia; Vocal Coach, Kate Wilson; Hair & Wigs, Paul Huntley; General Manager, Adam Siegel; Production Manager, Jeff Hamlin; Development, Hattie K. Jutagir; Marketing, Linda Mason Ross; Musical Theatre Associate Producer, Ira Weitzman; Finance, David S. Brown; Education, Kati Koerner; LCT Directors Lab/Dramaturg, Anne Cattaneo; LCT3 Artistic Director, Paige Evans; House Manager, Rheba Flegelman; Company Manager, Matthew Markoff/Jessica Perlmeter Cochrane; Assistant Company Manager, Rachel Scheer; Associate Director, Drew Barr; Puppetry Associate, Matt Acheson; Movement Associate, Adrienne Kapstein; Assistant Stage Managers, Lisa Iacucci, Amy Marsico; Associate Design: Frank McCullough (U.S. set), Johanna Coe (U.K. costumes), Sarah Laux (U.S. costumes), Nick Simmons (U.K. lighting), Karen Spahn (U.S. lighting), John Owens (U.K. sound); U.S. Assistant Sound, Bridget O'Connor; U.K. Puppetry Technician, Ed Dimbleby; Automated Light Programmer, Benjamin Pearcy; Props, Faye Armon; Fight Captain, Ian Lassiter; Makeup, Cynthia Demand; Incidental Music: Gary Maurer (Engineer), Steve Cohen (Copyist), Jim Lake (Trumpet/Coronet), Angela Gosse (Trumpet/Coronet), Judy Yin-Chi Lee (Horn/Alto Horn), Hitomi Yakata (Trombone/Euphonium), Richard Heckman (Clarinet/Flute); Advertising, Serino/Coyne; Press, Philip Rinaldi, Barbara Carroll, Amanda Dekker

CAST *The Horses*: Joey as a foal **Stephen James Anthony**[1], **David Pegram**, **Leenya Rideout**; Joey **Joby Earle**[2], **Ariel Heller**[3], **Alex Hoeffler**, **Jeslyn Kelly**, **Jonathan David Martin**, **Prentice Onayemi**, **Jude Sandy**, **Zach Villa**[4], or **Enrico D. Wey**; Topthorn **Joby Earle**[2], **Joel Reuben Ganz**, **Ariel Heller**[3], **Alex Hoeffler**, **Tom Lee**, **Jonathan Christopher MacMillan**, **Jude Sandy**, **Zach Villa**[4], or **Enrico D. Wey**; Coco **Joby Earle**[2], **Joel Reuben Ganz**, **Alex Hoeffler**, **Jeslyn Kelly**, **Tom Lee**, **Jonathan David Martin**, **Zach Villa**[4], or **Enrico D. Wey**; Heine **Sanjit De Silva**[5], **Bhavesh Patel**[6]; *The People*: Song Woman **Kate Pfaffl**[7]; Song Man **Liam Robinson**[8]; Lieutenant James Nicholls **Stephen Plunkett**[9]; Arthur Narracott **T. Ryder Smith**[10]; Billy Narracott **Matt Doyle**[11]; Albert Narracott **Seth Numrich**[12]; Ted Narracott **Boris McGiver**[13]; Chapman Carter **Austin Durant**[14]; Allan Elliot Villar; John Greig **Joby Earle**[2], **Joel Reuben Ganz**, **Alex Hoeffler**, or **Jonathan David Martin**; Rose Narracott **Alyssa Breshnahan**; Priest Peter Hermann[15]; Captain Charles Stewart **Brian Lee Huynh**; Seargeant Thunder **Richard Crawford**; Private David Taylor **David Pegram**[16]; Paulette **Cat Walleck**[17]; Soldat Schnabel **Zach Appelman**[18]; Hauptmann Friedrich Müller **Peter Hermann**[15]; Soldat Klausen **Elliot Villar**; Doctor Schweyk **Sanjit De Silva**[5]; Oberst Strauss **Bhavesh Patel**[6]; Sergeant Fine **Zach Appelman**[18]; Unteroffizier Klebb **Stephen Plunkett**[9]; Emilie **Madeleine Rose Yen**; Taff **Sanjit De Silva**[5]; Manfred **Austin Durant**[14]; Matron Callaghan **Leenya Rideout**[19]; Annie Gilbert **Hannah Sloat**; Veterinary Officer Martin **Ian Lassiter**[20]; Goose **Joby Earle**[2], **Jonathan Christopher MacMillan** or **Jude Sandy**; Understudies **Harlan Bengel**, **Geoffrey Allen Murphy**, **Isaac Woofter**

Succeeded by: 1. Hunter Canning (1/12/12) 2. Lute Brewer (1/12/12) 3. Leah Hofman (1/12/12) 4. Joel Ruben Ganz (1/12/12) 5. Tommy Schrider (1/12/12) 6. Nat McIntyre 7. Jessica Tyler Wright (4/24/12) 8. Jack Spann (1/12/12) 9. Sanjit De Silva 10. David Manis (1/12/12) 11. Stephen James Anthony (1/12/12) 12. Andrew Durand (1/12/12) 13. Andy Murray (1/12/12) 14. Anthony Cochrane (1/12/12) 15. David Lansbury (1/12/12) 16. Matt Dickson 17. Tessa Klein (1/12/12) 18. Ben Graney 19. Katrina Yaukey 20. Michael Braun, Ben Horner

SETTING Devon, England and France, 1914. U.S. premiere of a play with music presented in two acts. World premiere at the National Theatre's Olivier Theatre in South Bank, London October 17, 2007–February 14, 2008 and a second run September 10, 2008–March 18, 2009. The production transferred to the West End at the New London Theatre April 3, 2009 where it continues to run.

SYNOPSIS In Devon at the outbreak of World War I, Joey, young Albert Narracott's beloved horse, is sold to the cavalry and shipped to France. Joey serves in the British and German armies, befriends Topthorn (another army horse), and gets caught up in enemy fire. Death, disease and fate take him on an extraordinary odyssey, serving on both sides before finding himself alone in a no man's land. But Albert cannot forget Joey, and, still not old enough to enlist in the army, he embarks on a dangerous mission to find and bring him back to Devon.

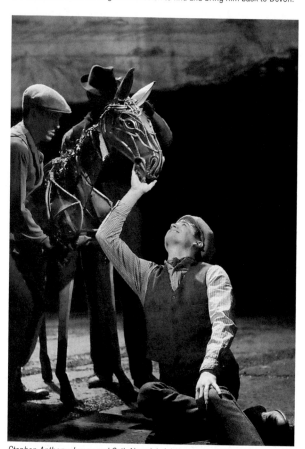

Stephen Anthony James and Seth Numrich (photos by Paul Kolnik)

Wicked

Gershwin Theatre; First Preview: October 8, 2003; Opening Night: October 30, 2003; 25 previews, 3,560 performances as May 31, 2011

Book by Winnie Holzman, music and lyrics by Stephen Schwartz; Based on the novel by Gregory Maguire; Produced by Marc Platt, Universal Pictures, The Araca Group, Jon B. Platt and David Stone; Director, Joe Mantello; Musical Staging, Wayne Cilento; Music Supervisor, Stephen Oremus; Orchestrations, William David Brohn; Sets, Eugene Lee; Costumes, Susan Hilferty; Lighting, Kenneth Posner; Sound, Tony Meola; Projections, Elanie J. McCarthy; Wigs/Hair, Tom Watson; Technical Supervisor, Jake Bell; Arrangements, Alex Lacamoire, Stephen Oremus; Dance Arrangements, James Lynn Abbott; Music Coordinator, Michael Keller; Special Effects, Chic Silber; Production Supervisor, Thom Widmann; Music Director, Bryan Perri; Dance Supervisor, Mark Myars; Associate Director, Lisa Leguillou; Casting, Bernard Telsey; Production Stage Manager, Marybeth Abel; Stage Manager, Jennifer Marik; Assistant Stage Managers, Christy Ney, Shawn Pennington; Company Management, Susan Sampline; Associate Company Manager, Adam Jackson; General Management, 321 Theatrical Management; Executive Producers, Marcia Goldberg and Nina Essman; Fight Director, Tom Schall; Flying, Paul Rubin/ZFX Inc.; Dressing/Properties, Kristie Thompson; Makeup, Joe Dulude II; Assistant Director, Paul Dobie; Assistant Choreography, Corinne McFadden-Herrera; Music Preparation, Peter R. Miller; Synthesizer Programming, Andrew Barrett; Advertising, Serino/Coyne; Press, The Hartman Group; Cast recording: Decca B 0001 682-02

Jackie Burns (photos by Joan Marcus)

CAST Glinda **Katie Rose Clarke**[*1]; Witch's Father/Ozian Official **Michael DeVries**[*2]; Witch's Mother **Kristen Gorski-Wergeles**[*3]; Midwife **Kathy Santen**; Elphaba **Teal Wicks**[*4]; Nessarose **Jenny Fellner**[*5]; Boq **Etai BenShlomo**[*6]; Madame Morrible **Kathy Fitzgerald**[*7]; Doctor Dillamond **Tom Flynn**; Fiyero **Richard H. Blake**[*8]; The Wonderful Wizard of Oz **Tom McGowan**[*9]; Chistery **Mark Shunkey**; Ensemble[*10] **Aaron J. Albano, Nova Bergeron, Jerad Bortz, Michael DeVries, Maia Evwaraye-Griffin, Kristina Fernandez, Kristen Leigh Gorski, Lindsay K. Northen, Rhea Patterson, Nathan Peck, Eddie Pendergraft, Alexander Quiroga, Josh Rouah, Kathy Santen, Mark Shunkey, Heather Spore, Stephanie Torns, Brian Wanee, Betsy Webel, Robin Wilner**; Standbys **Jennifer Dinoia**[*11] (Elphaba), **Laura Woyasz**[*12] (Glinda); Season Swings **Anthony Galde, Brian Munn, Desi Oakley, Briana Yacavone, Jonathan Warren, Alicia Albright, Todd Anderson, Catherine Charlebois, Kevin Jordan, Ryan Patrick Kelley, Kelly Lafarga, Mark Myers, Amanda Rose, Libby Servais**

*Succeeded by: 1. Chandra Lee Schwartz (9/27/11) 2. Sean McCourt (February 2012), Michael DeVries (March 2012), John Schiappa (5/22/12) 3. Lindsay Janisse 4. Jackie Burns (9/27/11) 5. Cristy Candler (8/2/11), Jenny Fellner (11/8/11) 6. Taylor Trench (1/24/12), Etai BenShlomo (4/24/12) 7. Randy Danson (12/13/11) 8. Kyle Dean Massey (8/16/11), Richard H. Blake (9/6/11) 9. P.J. Benjamin (2/7/12), Adam Grupper (4/24/12) 10. Al Blackstone, Caroline Bowman, Zach Hannah, David Hull, Lindsay Janisse, Jesse JP Johnson, Colby Q. Lindeman, Sean McCourt, Jonathan McGill, Amanda Rose, Constantine Rousouli, John Schiappa, Bud Weber 11. Caroline Bowman 12. Kate Fahrner

ORCHESTRA Brian Perri (Conductor); David Evans (Associate Conductor/Keyboards); Ben Cohn (Assistant Conductor/Piano/Synthesizers); Christian Hebel (Concertmaster); Victor Schultz (Violin); Kevin Roy (Viola); Dan Miller (Cello); Konrad Adderly (Bass); John Moses, John Campo, Tuck Lee, Helen Campo, Chad Smith (Woodwinds); Jon Owens, Tom Hoyt (Trumpets); Dale Kirkland, Douglas Purviance (Trombones); Theo Primis, Chad Yarbrough (French Horn); Paul Loesel (Keyboards); Ric Molina, Greg Skaff (Guitars); Andy Jones (Percussion); Matt VanderEnde (Drums); Laura Sherman (Harp)

MUSICAL NUMBERS No One Mourns the Wicked; Dear Old Shiz; The Wizard and I; What Is This Feeling?; Something Bad; Dancing Through Life; Popular; I'm Not That Girl; One Short Day; A Sentimental Man; Defying Gravity; No One Mourns the Wicked (Reprise); Thank Goodness; The Wicked Witch of the East; Wonderful; I'm Not That Girl (Reprise); As Long as You're Mine; No Good Deed; March of the Witch Hunters; For Good; Finale

SETTING The Land of Oz. A musical presented in two acts. World premiere presented in San Francisco at the Curran Theatre May 28–June 29, 2003. For original production credits see *Theatre World* Vol. 60, page 34.

SYNOPSIS *Wicked* explores the early life of the witches of Oz, Glinda and Elphaba, who meet at Shiz University. Glinda is madly popular and Elphaba is green. After an initial period of mutual loathing, the roommates begin to learn something about each other. Their life paths continue to intersect, and eventually their choices and convictions take them on widely different paths.

The Company

SPECIAL EVENTS

Camelot

Shubert Theatre; June 13, 2011

Book and lyrics by Alan Jay Lerner, music by Frederick Loewe; Based upon *The Once and Future King* by T.H. White; Original production directed and staged by Moss Hart; Produced by the Irish Repertory Theatre (Charlotte Moore, Artistic Director; Ciarán O'Reilly, Producing Director); Adapted and directed by Charlotte Moore; Music Director, Mark Hartman; Lighting, Mark Simpson; Sound Engineer, Greg Freedman; Music Assistant, Ben Boecker; Stage Managers, Arthur Atkinson, Pamela Brusoski, Christine Lemme; Vocal Coach, Bruce Barnes; Rehearsal Pianist, Kevin B. Winebold; Event Consultants, Carla Capone, Joanne Shia; Lighting Programmer, David Arch; Production Assistants, Jason Brubaker, Julie Lira, Marina Peirano; Irish Rep Staff: Maureen Cavanaugh (Development Director), Fiona Whelan (Membership Manager), Melissa L. Pelkey (Marketing Manager), David Friedman (Business Manager), Jeffrey Wingfield (Box Office Manager), Cynthia Jankowski (Production Coordinator), Deirdre Higgins (Wardrobe Supervisor), Kara Manning (Literary Manager); Press, Shirley Herz, Bob Lasko

CAST Narrator **Ciarán O'Reilly**; Sir Dinidan **Ciarán Sheehan**; Sir Lionel **Christopher Lynn**; Merlyn **James A. Stephens**; Arthur **Jeremy Irons**; Guenevere **Melissa Errico**; Nimue **Victoria Mallory**; Lancelot **James Barbour**; Squire Dap **Rory Duffy**; Pellinore **Brian Murray**; Sir Sagamore **Dewey Caddell**; Mordred **Josh Grisetti**; Morgan Le Fey **KT Sullivan**; Tom of Warwick **Jacob Clemente**; The King's Court **Michael A. Alden, Anthony Aloise, Sean Bell, Jason Blaine, Ben Boecker, Danya Bowers, Bill Brooks, Susan Burcham, Sean Casserly, Matt Castle, Kerry Conte, Sarah Cooney, Dashira Cortes, Mike Cruz, Dan Debenport, Scott Denny, Natalie Douglas, Beth Eunice, Katie Fabel, Bonnie Fraser, Frank Galgano, Stephanie Granade, Rita Harvey, Katherine Heaton, A.J. Irvin, Danny Katz, Matt Leahy, Robyn Elizabeth Lee, David Levinson, Harold Lewter, John Anthony Lopez, Michael Jennings Mahoney, Alyssa Malgeri, Gregory McDonald, Helen McTernan, Brian J. Nash, Mary Orzano, Georgia Osborne, Marcie Passley, Robyn Payne, Lisa Riegel, Shanna Sharp, Becca Shimkin, Emily Skeggs, Sami Skow, Ryan Speakman, Tom Stajmiger, Kevin B. Winebold, Darryl Winslow, Jennifer Wren**

ORCHESTRA Mark Hartman (Conductor); Jeff Schiller (Flute/Piccolo); Leslie Godfrey (Oboe/English Horn); Ed Nishimura (Clarinet); Joseph d'Auguste (Clarinet/Flute); Jeremy Clayton (Bassoon); RJ Kelly (Horn 1); Eric C. Davis (Horn 2); Benjamin Brody (Horn 3); Timothy Wendt (Trumpet 1); Colin Brigstocke (Trumpet 2); Jason Wiseman (Trumpet 3); Lane Schneier (Trombone 1); Nadav Nirenberg (Trombone 2); Joe Choroszewski (Percussion); Nicholas DiFabbio (Guitar/Lute/Mandolin); Karen Lindquist (Harp); Blair Lawhead (Violin/Concertmaster); Kate Light, Antonio Nelson, Jessica Nelson (Violin 1); Una Tone, Chris Marchant (Violin 2); David Cerruti, Armand Alpyspaev (Viola); Melanie Mason, Allison Seidner (Cello); Steve Millhouse (Bass)

MUSICAL NUMBERS Overture; I Wonder What the King Is Doing Tonight?; The Simple Joys of Maidenhood; Camelot; Guenevere's Welcome; Camelot (reprise); Follow Me; Camelot (reprise); C'est Moi; The Lusty Month of May; How to Handle a Woman; The Jousts; Before I Gaze at You Again; Propositions; Madrigal/If Ever I Would Leave You; The Seven Deadly Virtues; What Do the Simple Folk Do?; The Persuasion; Fie On Goodness; I Loved You Once in Silence; Guenevere; Finale Ultimo

SETTING In and around Camelot and a battlefield in France; a long time ago. Concert version of a revival of a musical presented without intermission. The original Broadway production was presented at the Majestic Theatre December 3, 1960–January 5, 1963, playing 873 performances (see *Theatre World* Vol. 17, p. 49).

SYNOPSIS The Irish Repertory presents a ninety-minute concert version of the beloved classic Lerner and Loewe musical for their annual Gala Benefit. *Camelot* defined an age with its lush romantic score that soars above the legendary tale of idealism, passion and betrayal. King Arthur has created a utopian land of chivalry and civil rule. But when his beloved Queen Guenevere and Sir Lancelot, his most trusted knight, succumb to their passion for one another, he faces a terrible dilemma that will rock his kingdom to its very core.

Melissa Errico and Jeremy Irons in Camelot *(photo by James Higgins)*

Broadway Bares XXI: Masterpiece

Roseland Ballroom; June 19, 2011

Produced by Broadway Cares/Equity Fights AIDS, Michael Graziano, Kimberly Russell; Executive Producer, Jerry Mitchell; Director, Josh Rhodes; Associate Director, Paul Rhodes; Lighting, Philip S. Rosenberg; Set, Mary Houston; Projections, Brian Beasley, Michael Clark, Aaron Rhyne, Daniel Robinson; Costume Coordination, Craig Lowrey; Hair & Wig Coordination, Danny Koye; Makeup Design and Coordination, The M•A•C Pro Team; Sound, Acme Sound Partners; Production Manager, Nathan Hurlin; Production Stage Manager, Jennifer Rogers; Presenting Sponsor, M•A•C Viva; Sponsors, 1-800-Postcards, Absolut Vodka, aussieBum, CAA, Club H Fitness, Element New York Times Square West, Get Gay Chauffeur, Here Media, Logo, The New York Times, Next Magazine, PMD Promotion, Showtime Networks, United Airlines, Zarley Family Foundation; Choreographers, Armando Farman Jr., James Harkness, Nick Kenkel, Dontee Kiehn, Stephanie Lang, Melissa Rae Mahon, Barry Morgan, Rachelle Rak, Josh Rhodes, Jon Rua, Michael Lee Scott, Mark Stuart, Lee Wilkins; Production Manager, Nathan Hurlin; Production Stage Manager, Jennifer Rogers; Production Supervisor, Richard Hester; Associate Producers, Trisha Doss, Colyn Fiendel; Associate Production Manager and Props, Michael Palm; Stage Managers, Zach Chandler, Michael Rico Cohen, Casey Cook, Richard Costabile, Kimothy Cruise, Aurora De Lucia, Matt DiCarlo, Christopher Economakos, Veronica Falborn, Colyn Fiendel, Theresa Flanagan, Bess Marie Glorioso, Marci Glotzer, Michail Haynes, Caskey Hunsader, Kelly Ice, Trey Johnson, Samuel-Moses Jones, B. Bales Karlin, Terri K. Kohler, Talia Krispel, Melissa Magliula, Rachel Maier, Kate McDoniel, Joanne E. McInerney, Ellen Mezzera, Christopher R. Munnell, Jason Pelusio, Samantha Preiss, Jason Quinn, Megan Scneid, Lisa Susanne Schwartz, David Sugarman, Ron Tal, Sarah Testerman, Jason Trubitt, Alex Lyu Volckhausen; Opening Number *Going, Going, Gone*: Music by Matthew Sklar, Lyrics by Chad Beguelin; Dialogue by Hunter Foster, Dance Arrangement by David Chase, Orchestrations/Vocal Arrangements/Music Direction by Lynn Shankel, Beth Leavel (Auctioneer-Singer), Julia Burrows, Pamela Bob, Danny Calvert, Miles Johnson, Ryan Speakman, Kay Trinidad (Vocalists); Closing Number *The Final Masterpiece*: Lon Hoyt (Music Director), Patina Miller (Vocalist), Danny Calvert, Rosie Colosi, Scott Guthrie, Rashidra Scott, Laurie Sheppart, Alena Watters

(Background Vocals); Music Editors, Lee Wilkins, Brent Lord; Rotation Masters, Christopher Sieber, Jen Cody; Book and Scenes, Hunter Foster; Assistant Director, Sydney Christopher Berens; Press, Boneau/Bryan-Brown

THE COMPANY *Special Guests*: Beth Leavel, Roger Rees, Rory O'Malley, Jim Parsons, Michael Reidel, Judith Light, Patina Miller; *Dancers*: Chip Abbott, Cesar Abreu, Scott Ahearn Meredith Akins, John Alix, Megan Allen Matt Anctil, Sara Andreas, Beckley Andrews, Sara Antkowiak-Maier, Michael Apuzzo, Ashley Arcement, Dave August, Heather Lea Bair, Sean Baptiste, Jim Becker, Alec Bell, Danielle Hannah Bensky, Samantha Berger, Guto Bittencourt, Christina Black, Michael Blatt, Thomas Bradfield, Mo Brady, Steve Bratton, Giselle Lorenz Brock, Summer Broyhill, Larry Bullock, Joshua Buscher, Daniel Byrd, Samuel J. Cahn, Danny Calvert, Allyson Carr, Katie Cass, Kristy Cavanaugh, Anthony Cefala, Adam Chandler, Andrew Chappelle, Olivia Cipolla, Rosie Colosi, David Contreras, Kevin Covert, Gabriel Croom, Chris Crowthers, Holly Cruz, Nicholas Cunningham, Michael Cusumano, Christine Danelson, Taryn Darr, Barrett Davis, Anthony Decarlis, Kristin DeCesare, Robin De Jésus, Zachary Denison, Robert Lee Dillard, Mark Donaldson, Michelle Dowdy, Jennifer Dunne, Yurel Echezarreta, Trevor Effinger, Hillary Elliott, Alex Ellis, Lynann Escatel, Daniel Lynn Evans, Armando Farfan Jr., Wilkie Ferguson, Rosie Lani Fiedelman, Russell Fischer, Adam Fleming, Andrea Fornarola, Jen Frankel, Danielle Froelich, Paloma Garcia-Lee, Leah Gerstel, Stephanie Gibson, Greer Gisy, Andrew Glaszek, David Gray, Jessica Green, Katy Grenfell, Jenny Gruby, Tony Guerrero, Scott Guthrie, Aaron Hanmilton, Elinor Harrison, Afra Hines, Daxfurth Houston, Timothy Hughes, Lauren Lim Jackson, Laura Johnson, Naomi Kakuk, Lisa Karlin, Laura Keller, Reed Kelly, Nick Kenkel, Grasan Kingsberry, Stephanie Klemons, Caitlin Krause, Christopher Michael Lacey, Anton Harrison Lamon, Leah Landau, Nikka Graff Lanzarone, John Paul LaPorte, Marina Lazzaretto, Kenny Lear, Allison Thomas Lee, Adam Lendermon, Aaron J. Libby, Ryan Lyons, Karl Maier, Nalina Mann, Renee Marino, Danny Marr, Gina Mazzarella, Patrick McCollum, Richard Meeker, Kaitlin Mesh, Chris Messina, Brant Michaels, Denise Marie Miller, Andy Mills, Marla Mindelle, Brian Patrick Murphy, Peter Nelson, Melissa Oropesa, Ryan Overberg, Kate Pazakis, Brandon Perayda, Adam Perry, Marissa Perry, William Michael Peters, Annie Petersmeyer, Kristin Piro, Meghan Pool, Jessica Press, Alexander Quiroga, Eddie Rabon, Matthew Ragas, Antuan Raimone, John Raterman, Madeline Reed, Ian M. Richardson, Alex Ringler, Robbie Roby, Mark Roland, Marissa Rosen, Brandon Rubendall, Celia Mei Rubin, Julius Anthony Rubio, Naomi Rusalka, Mike Russo, Alison Ryan, Amy Ryerson, Marcos Santana, Kimberly Schafer, Rashidra Scott, Shanna Sharp, Ray Sheen, Laurie Sheppard, Robb Sherman, Evan Siegel, Matthew Skrincosky, Michaeljon Slinger, George Smallwood, Alexandra C. Smith, Justin Smith, Beau Speer, Derek St. Pierre, Meghan Starr, Taylor Sternberg, Molly Winter Stewart, Gregory Stockbridge, Chad Stone, Sarrah Strimel, Mark Stuart, Charlie Sutton, James Tabeck, Rickey Tripp, Sheldon Tucker, Laura Volpacchio, Ryan Watkinson, Alena Watters, Anthony Wayne, Katie Webber, Micki Weiner, Steven Wenslawski, Kristen Beth Williams, Randy Witherspoon, Jacob Wood, Jody Cole Wood, Ryan Worshing, Samantha Zack

The Company in a number inspired by Peter Paul Rubens at Broadway Bares XXI

THE PROGRAM Lot 21: Going, Going, Gone; Lot 22: Washington Crossing the Delaware; Lot 23: American Gothic; Lot 24: Andy Warhol; Lot 25: The African Mask; Lot 26: The Mona Lisa; Lot 27: Pablo Picasso; Lot 28: Peter Paul Rubens; Lot 29: René Magritte; Lot 30: The Scream; Lot 31: Claude Monet; Lot 32: The Sculpture; Lot 33: Keith Haring; Lot 24: The Final Masterpiece

FUNDRAISING Event Total: **$1,103,172**; Strip-a-thon Team Winner: "Going, Going, Gone" number ($35,909); Runners Up: "American Gothic" number ($35,909), "Munch and Degas" team ($26,597); Strip-a-thon Individual Winner: Reed Kelly ($420,795); Male Runners-up: Steve Bratton ($13,200), Andrew Glaszek ($7,326); Female Runners-up: Madeline Reed ($5,391), Kristen Beth Williams ($4,094)

SYNOPSIS A variety burlesque show presented without intermission. Since its inception in 1992, choreographer and director Jerry Mitchell – then in the ensemble of *The Will Rogers Follies* – put six of his fellow dancers up on the bar at an infamous "watering hole" in New York City's Chelsea district and raised $8,000 for Broadway Cares, the twenty-one editions of Broadway Bares have grown beyond all expectations, raising more than $8.6 million for Broadway Cares/Equity Fights AIDS.

Matthew Skrincosky, Justin Smith, Dave August, and Alex Ringler in a number inspired by Pablo Picasso at Broadway Bares XXI

8

Eugene O'Neill Theatre; September 19, 2011

Written by Dustin Lance Black; Presented by the American Foundation for Equal Rights (Dustin Lance Black, Bruce Cohen, Chad H. Griffin, Jonathan D. Lewis, Kenneth B. Mehlman, Michele Reiner, Rob Reiner, Adam Umhoefer) and Broadway Impact (Gavin Creel, Jenny Kanelos, Rory O'Malley, Ben Pelteson) in association with Alan Wasser Associates and The Jujamcyn Theaters (Jordan Roth, President; Paul Libin, Executive Vice President); Director, Joe Mantello; Set, Scott Pask; Lighting, Benjamin Travis; Projections, Howard Werner; Sound, Brian Ronan; Researcher, Kate Sullivan Gibbens; Production Stage Manager, William Joseph Barnes; Production Management, Aurora Productions; Company Manager, John E. Gendron; Casting, Telsey + Company; General Management, Alan Wasser, Allen Williams, Aaron Lustbader, Lane Marsh; Executive Producers, Jenny Kanelos, Adam Umhoefer; Stage Managers, James Fitzsimmons, Linda Marvel; Associate Sound, Chris Sloan; Ticketing/Fundraising, Annie Mullaly Weir; Hair and Makeup, Mark Adam Rampmeyer, Brandalyn Fulton, Pat Marcus, Wanda Gregory; Advertising, SpotCo; Press, Boneau/Bryan-Brown, Chris Boneau, Michael Strassheim

John Lithgow, Morgan Freeman, Christine Lahti, and Ellen Barkin in 8
(photo by Jenny Anderson)

CAST *The Court:* Chief Judge Vaughn R. Walker **Bob Balaban**; Theodore B. Olson, *lawyer for the Plaintiffs* **John Lithgow**; David Boies, *lawyer for the Plaintiffs* **Morgan Freeman**; Charles J. Cooper, *lawyer for the Defense* **Bradley Whitford**; Court Clerk **Kate Shindle**; *The Plaintiffs:* Kris Perry **Christine Lahti**; Sandy Stier **Ellen Barkin**; Jeff Zarrillo **Matt Bomer**; Paul Katami **Cheyenne Jackson**; Spencer Perry, *son of Plaintiff* **Jay Armstrong Johnson**; Elliot Perry, *son of Plaintiff)* **Ben Rosenfeld**; *Witnesses for Plaintiffs:* Dr. Nancy Cott **Yeardley Smith**; Dr. Gregory M. Herek **K. Todd Freeman**; Dr. Ilan Meyer **Anthony Edwards**; Dr. Gary Segura **Stephen Spinella**; Ryan Kendall **Rory O'Malley**; *Witnesses for Defense:* David Blankenhorn **Rob Reiner**; William Tam **Ken Leung**; *Other Characters:* Evan Wolfson **Larry Kramer**; Maggie Gallagher **Jayne Houdyshell**; Broadcast Journalist **Campbell Brown**

SETTING June 16, 2010; The U.S. District Court for the Northern District of California San Francisco. World premiere of a staged reading of a new play presented without intermission. Presented as a benefit for the American Foundation for Equal Rights (AFER) and Broadway Impact.

SYNOPSIS *8* portrays the closing arguments of Perry v. Schwarzenegger, a federal trial that led to the overturn of Proposition 8—an amendment eliminating rights of same-sex couples to marry in California. It was created by Dustin Lance Black in light of the court's denial of a motion to release a video recording of the trial and to give the public a true account of what transpired in the courtroom. The play is written in the style of verbatim theatre reenactment, using transcripts from the trial, journalist records, and media interviews from the plaintiffs, defendants and proponents involved.

Broadway Flea Market and Grand Auction

Times Square; September 25, 2011

Produced by Broadway Cares/Equity Fights AIDS (Tom Viola, Executive Director); Producing Director, Michael Graziano; Production Manager, Nathan Hurlin; Auctioneers, Lorna Kelly and Tasha Lwarence; Auction Host, Bryan Batt; Celebrity Autograph Table and Photo Booth Host, Jim Caruso; Silent Auction Hosts, Michael Goddard and Kristen Wyatt; Flash Auction Host, Susan Blackwell; Event Sponsors, *The New York Times*, Juniors Restaurant, and United Airlines

CELEBRITY AUTOGRAPH AND PHOTO BOOTH PARTICIPANTS Josh Gad, Nikki M. James, Andrew Rannells and Rory O'Malley from *The Book of Mormon*; Colin Donnell, Sutton Foster, Adam Godley and Joel Grey from *Anything Goes*; Patina Miller from *Sister Act*; Danny Burstein, Jayne Houdyshell, Ron Raines and Terri White from *Follies*; Nick Adams and Tony Sheldon from *Priscilla Queen of the Desert*; Jackie Hoffman, Brad Oscar and Roger Rees from *The Addams*

Family, Rose Hemingway from *How to Succeed In Business Without Really Trying*, Hunter Parrish, Telly Leung, Lindsay Mendez and Anna Maria Perez de Taglé from *Godspell*, Seth Numrich from *War Horse*, Judith Light and Thomas Sadoski from *Other Desert Cities*; Bryan Batt, Charles Busch, Bobby Cannavale, Jason Danieley, Joyce DeWitt, Michael Emerson, Ana Gasteyer, Montego Glover, Jonathan Groff, Megan Hilty, Beth Leavel, Marin Mazzie, Laura Osnes, Patrick Page, Adam Pascal, Carrie Preston, Anthony Rapp, Alice Ripley

FUNDRAISING TOTAL $547,658

TOP FUNDRAISING TABLES *Wicked* ($15,367): *Follies* ($14,819); TDF ($11,635); Broadway Beat ($10,580); *The Phantom of the Opera* ($9,313); *The Book of Mormon* ($9,229); *How to Succeed in Business Without Really Trying* ($9,192); *Spider-Man: Turn Off the Dark* ($7,697); United Scenic Artists Local 829 ($7,346); *War Horse/Lincoln Center Theater* ($7,217)

SYNOPSIS Twenty-fifth annual flea market and auction benefit for Broadway Cares/Equity Fights AIDS. This free event open to the public offers a chance for fans to purchase autographed show memorabilia, posters, playbills, rare costume sketches, and several other show related items, as well as a silent auction and flash auctions. The event ends with the live Grand Auction that includes walk-on roles in such hits as *Chicago, Jersey Boys, The Lion King, Mamma Mia!, Memphis, Priscilla Queen of the Desert, Rock of Ages, Sister Act*, and Cirue du Soleil's *Zarkana*, as well as other special autographed and celebrity items from Broadway's top stars. This year the event extended beyond its usual West 44th street location to include the Times Square pedestrian plaza on Broadway between West 43rd and West 44th Street. In all, 63 auction booths and tables represented a wide range of the theatrical community on Broadway and off. One of the most popular events at the Flea Market includes the Celebrity Autograph Table and Photo Booth, where fans can meet the celebrities in exchange for contributions. Since its debut in 1987, twenty-five editions of this event have raised $9,185,327 for the social services provided by The Actors Fund and hundreds of AIDS and family service organizations BC/EFA supports each year.

Kirsten Wyatt, Susan Blackwell, and Michael Goddard at the Broadway Flea Market (photos by Peter James Zielinski)

Company members from Billy Elliot the Musical *at the Broadway Flea Market*

The Visit

Abassador Theatre; November 30, 2011

Music by John Kander, lyrics by Fred Ebb, book by Terrence McNally; Based on the play *Der Besuch der alten Dame* by Friedrich Dürrenmatt, adapted by Maurice Valncy; Produced by The Actors Fund (Tim Pinckney, Producer) and the Vineyard Theatre (Douglas Aibel, Artistic Director; Jennifer Garvey-Blackwell, Executive Director); Consulting Producer, Steven Yuhasz; Director, Carl Andress; Music Director, Jon Kalbfleisch; Choreography, Ann Reinking; Music Supervisor/Vocal and Dance Arrangements, David Loud; Orchestrations, Michael Gibson; Additional Orchestrations, Larry Hochman; Lighting, John McKennon; Sound Supervisor, Patrick Weaver; Makeup, Nathan Johnson; Production Stage Manager, Jason A. Quinn; Marketing, Elizabeth Findlay, Adam Jay, aka; Casting, Stuart Howard and Paul Hardt; Music Coordinator, John Monaco; Press, The Publicity Office, Jeremy Shaffer

CAST Anton Schell **John Cullum**; The Mayor **Mark Jacoby**; Claire Zachanassian **Chita Rivera**; Annie **Linda Balgord**; Young Anton **D.B. Bonds**; Louis Perch **Matthew Deming**; Benny **Alan H. Green**; Rudi **James Harms**; The Priest **Michael Hayward-Jones**; Lenny **Howard Kaye**; Evgeny **Doug Kreeger**; Young Clair **Mary Ann Lamb**; The Doctor **Jerry Lanning**; Jacob Chicken **Ryan Lowe**; Matilda **Karen Murphy**; Kurt **Brian O'Brien**; Karl **Kevin Reed**; The Policeman **Hal Robinson**; The Schoolmaster **Jeremy Webb**; Ottilie **Dana Steingold**; Townspeople **Brianne Moore**, **Joy Hermalyn**, **Rebecca Strimaitis**

MUSICAL NUMBERS Out of the Darkness; At Last; I Walk Away; I Know Claire; A Happy Ending; You, You, You; I Must Have Been Something; Look at Me; A Masque; Testimony; Winter; Yellow Shoes; Chorale; A Confession; I Would Never Leave You; The One-Legged Tango; Back and Forth; The Only One; Fear; A Car Ride; Winter (reprise); Love and Love Alone; In the Forest Again; Finale

SETTING Brachen, Switzerland; mid-1950s. Broadway premiere of a musical presented as a staged concert in two acts. The musical, originally developed as a vehicle for Angela Lansbury, was scheduled to open on Broadway March 15, 2001, but Lansbury withdrew due to the illness and subsequent death of her husband. Chita Rivera was signed as her replacement and the musical had its world premiere at the Goodman Theatre, directed by Frank Galati and choreographed by Ann Reinking, October 1, 2001, co-starring John McMartin. The Signature Theatre in Arlington, Virginia produced the show May 27–June 22, 1008, directed by Mr. Galati, choreographed by Ms. Reinking, and starring Ms. Rivera, Mr. Jacoby, and George Hearn. This staged concert was presented as a benefit for The Actors Fund and the Vineyard Theatre.

SYNOPSIS Claire Zachanassian was driven from her hometown in disgrace when she was 17, having been betrayed by her lover Anton Schell. Several decades and seven husbands later, Zachanassian has become the richest woman in the world, yet her hometown has fallen on hard times. When Zachanassian returns with an offer to save the town, salvation comes with an outrageous price tag.

Chita Rivera and John Cullum in The Visit *(photo by Bruce Glikas)*

Gypsy of the Year

New Amsterdam Theatre; December 5 & 6, 2011

Presented by Broadway Cares/Equity Fights AIDS; Producers, Michael Graziano, Kimberly Russell, Tom Viola; Director, Valerie Lau-Kee Lai; Lighting, Paul Miller; Sound, Kurt Fischer, Marie Renee Foucher; Production Manager, Nathan Hurlin; Production Stage Manager, Jason Trubitt; Associate Producer, Trisha Doss; Stage Managers, Terence Orleans Alexander, Eileen Arnold, Jerry Dee Lame, Derric Nolte, Joshua Pilote, Kat Purvis, Jennifer Rogers, Ashley Singh, David Sugarman; Assistant Director, Barrett Davis; Assistant Lighting, Nick Flinn; Automated Lights, Marc Polemeni; Host, Seth Rudetsky; Special Guest, Carol Channing; Presenters, Jan Maxwell, Patrick Page, Beth Leavel, Danny Burstein, Nick Adams, Michele Mais, Russell Fischer, Judith Light; Final Presenters: Bernadette Peters, Hugh Jackman, Daniel Radcliffe; Judges: Stephanie J. Block, Jeff Calhoun, Kim Cattrall, Nikki M. James, Paul Libin, Tony Sheldon; Broadway Flea Market and Grand Auction Winner Guest Judges: Stephanie Toups and Karen Walter; Opening Number: Rommy Sandhu (Creator/Director), Ben Cohn (Creator/Music Director), Patricia Birch (Original Choreographer), Vanessa Brown (Dialogue), Scott T. Stevens (Company Manager), Julie Barnes and Bobby Petska (Assistant Choreography), Bryan Crook and Ethan Popp (Orchestrations), Brett Macias (Copyist), Michael McGoff (Stage Manager), Timothy Eaker (Assistant Stage Manager), Brian Hemesath and Jared B. Leese (Costumes); Associate Musical Director, Chris Haberl; Opening Number Stage Managers, Colyn W. Fiendel, Johnny Milani, Veronica Falborn; Opening Number Costumes, Brian Hemesath; Press, Boneau/Bryan-Brown

Walter Bobbie, Daniel Douglas, Tom Harris, Barry Bostwick, and James Canning from the 1971 Broadway cast of Grease *at Gypsy of the Year*

HIGHLIGHTS Opening Number: The original 1972 Broadway cast of *Grease* reuniting for a 40-year anniversary tribute, featuring Barry Bostwick (Danny), Carole Demas (Sandy), Adrienne Barbeau (Rizzo), Don Billet (Vince Fontaine), Walter Bobbie (Roger), James Canning (Doody), Daniel Douglas (Burger Palace Boy), Katie Hanley (Marty), Tom Harris (Eugene), Ilene Kristen (Patty), Alan Paul (Teen Angel/Johnny Casino), Joy Rinaldi (Pink Lady), Mews Small (Frenchy), and joined by original director Tom Moore, co-creator Jim Jacobs, Julie Barnes, Brian Barry, Ward Billeisen, Patrick Boyd, Tommy Bracco, Kimberly Faure, Evan Kasprzak, Becca Kloha, Sae La Chin, Dustienne Miller, Vasthy Mompoint, Shina Ann Morris, Jesse Swimm, Vanessa Sonon, Anthony Wayne, Joshua Woodie; *NEWSical the Musical* ("Liza & Lady Gaga"), written by Rick Crom, directed by Mark Waldrop, music direction by Ed Goldschneider; *Chicago* ("Chicago Now and Forever"), written, directed, and choreographed by Melissa Rae Mahon, co-written by Brian O'Brien, music direction by Leslie Stifelman; *Spider-Man: Turn Off the Dark* ("Good As New"), choreographed by Marcus Bellamy, Emanuel Brown, Dana Marie Ingraham, Ayo Jackson, Ari Loeb, and Natalie Lomonte; *Mamma Mia!* ("Mamma Mia: ____!"), written by the company, directed by David

Beach and Gerard Salvador; *Follies* ("A Farewell to Follies"), written by Brandon Bieber, Jenifer Foote, Jan Maxwell, and Amos Wolff, directed and choreographed by Bradon Bieber, music direction by Brad Gardner; *SILENCE! The Musical* ("Silence! Night!"), written by Hunter Bell and Brian J. Nash, directed by Lucia Spina; *National Tours* ("Every Day I'm Shufflin'"), directed and choreographed by Shea Sullivan; *The Phantom of the Opera* ("I Wonder As I Wander"), created by Kris Koop Ouellette and Marni Raab, music direction by Kristen Blodgette; *Mary Poppins* ("Junior Edition"), written by Tom Souhrada, directed by James Hindman; *Memphis* ("What's Goin' On"), directed and choreographed by Tyrone A. Jackson, music direction by Jason Michael Webb; *Naked Boys Singing* ("Forever Naked"), written by Dave August, Michael Munoz, and Aubrey Grant, directed by Dave August, music direction by Jeff Biering and Chris Kong; *How to Succeed in Business Without Really Trying* ("Do the F**ing Show"), written by Daniel Radcliffe, directed by Nick Mayo, choreography by David Hull, music direction by Larry Goldberg; *The Awesome 80s Prom* ("Pzazz 101: How to Make it Big in Show Biz"), written by Wade Dooley, directed by Isaac Klein; *The Lion King* ("In Your Left Ear"), written by Camille Brown, directed and choreographed by Ray Mercer, music direction by Bongi Duma; *Anything Goes* ("June"), written and directed by William Ryall, music direction by James Lowe; *The Addams Family* ("Curtain Speech"), written by Steve Bebout and Adam Riegler, directed by Steve Bebout; *Sister Act* ("The Broadway Confession Session"), written and directed by Lance Roberts, choreography and music direction by Charl Brown; Finale: *Billy Elliot* ("Don't Let The Sun Go Down On Me"), written and directed by Eric Gunhus, choreography by Sara Brians, music direction by Richard Rockage, featuring Julian Elia and more than 80 current and former cast members (including nine of the boys who have played Billy) reuniting on stage

COMPETETION Winner: *Billy Elliot*; First Runner-up: *Mary Poppins*

FUNDRAISING Total for 53 participating Broadway, Off-Broadway, and National Touring Companies: **$4,895,253**; Top Fundraisers: Broadway Musicals: *How to Succeed in Business...* (Top Fundraiser: $325,935), *The Book of Mormon* (1st Runner-up: $315,968), *Wicked* (2nd Runner-up $240,809), *Spider Man: Turn Off the Dark* (3rd Runner-up: $197,285), *Follies* (4th Runner-up: $186,405); Broadway Plays: *Other Desert Cities* (Top Fundraiser: $77,712); Off-Broadway: *Rent* (Top Fundraiser: $43,300); National Tours: *Wicked* Munchkinland Company (Top Fundraiser: $326,902), *Wicked* Emerald City Company (1st Runner-up: $316,299), *Mary Poppins* (2nd Runner-up: $169,709), *Jersey Boys* (3rd Runner-up: $157,831)

SYNOPSIS 23rd annual talent and variety show presented without intermission. The *Gypsy of the Year Competition* is the culmination of a period of intensive fundraising where New York's most talented "gypsies," chorus members from Broadway and Off-Broadway shows, join in a competition variety show as six weeks of intensive fundraising by the community comes to a close. Since 1989, twenty-three editions of the *Gypsy of the Year* have raised a combined total of $49,031,973 for Broadway Cares/Equity Fights AIDS.

Leslie Uggams and the cast of Anything Goes *at Gypsy of the Year (photos by Peter James Zielinski)*

She Loves Me

Stephen Sondheim Theatre; December 5, 2011

Book by Joe Masteroff, music by Jerry Bock, lyrics by Sheldon Harnick; Based on a play by Miklos Laszlo; Produced by the Roundabout Theatre Company (Todd Haimes, Artistic Director; Harold Wolpert, Managing Director; Julia C. Levy, Executive Director) and Benefit Concert Reading Co-Chairs Michael T. Cohen and Amanda and Gary Wolf; Director, Scott Ellis; Music Director, Paul Gemignani; Musical Staging, JoAnn Hunter; Set, Derek McLane; Costumes, Jeff Mahshie; Lighting, Peter Kaczorowski; Sound, Brian Ronan; Projections, Elaine J. McCarthy; Orchestrations, Don Walker; Additional Orchestrations, Michael Starobin; Additional Dance Arrangements, David Dabbon; Production Stage Manager, Lori M. Doyle; Associate Director, David Solomon; Casting, Jim Carnahan and Stephen Kopel; Technical Supervisor, Steve Beers; Executive Producer, Sydney Beers; Associate Managing Director, Greg Backstrom; Director of Marketing and Sales Promotion, David B. Steffen; Director of Development, Lynne Gugenheim Gregory; Founding Director, Gene Feist; Adams Associate Artistic Director, Scott Ellis; Underwritters, Susanne and Douglas Durst, Beryl Snyder and Steven Trost, Diane and Tom Tuft, Margot Adams; Production Stage Manager, Lori M. Doyle; Music Contractor, Bruce Eidem; Synthesizer Programmer, Randy Cohen; Music Copying, Emily Grishman, Katharine Edmonds; Company Manager, Karl Baudendistel; Deck Stage Manager, Rachel Bauder; Assistant Stage Manager, Steven Howard Kaplan; Assistant Design: Erica Hemminger (set), Kyle Lacolla (costumes), Peter Hoerburger (lighting), Shawn Boyle, Shawn Duan (projections); Assistant Musical Staging, Scott Taylor; Props, Propstar; Production Assistants, Zachary Baer, Christina Pezzello, Betsy Selman; Hair Supervisor, Nathaniel Hathaway; Wardrobe Supervisor, Kimberly Butler; Automation Operator, Paul Ashton; Flyman, William Craven; Deck Carpenters, Donald Roberts, John Patrick Nord; Sound Mixer, Shannon Slaton; Spot Operators, Dorion Fuchs, Erika Warmbrunn, Jessica Morton; Deck Electricians, Jocelyn Smith, Francis Elers; Properties Crew, Dan Mendeloff, Nelson Vaughn; Press, Boneau/Bryan-Brown, Adrian Bryan-Brown, Matt Polk, Jessica Johnson, Amy Kass

CAST Ladislav Sipos **Michael McGrath**; Arpad Laszlo **Rory O'Malley**; Ilona Ritter **Jane Krakowski**; Steven Kodaly **Gavin Creel**; Georg Nowack **Josh Radnor**; Mr. Maraczek **Victor Garber**; Customers **Jane Brockman, Rachel de Benedet, Rebecca Eichenberger, Gina Ferrall, Jessica Vosk**; Amalia Balash **Kelli O'Hara**; Keller **Jim Walton**; Headwaiter **Peter Bartlett**; Bus Boy **Jeffrey Schecter**; Ensemble **Jane Brockman, Rachel de Benedet, Rebecca Eichenberger, Gina Ferrall, Rob Lorey, Jeffrey Schecter, Jessica Vosk, Jim Walton**

ORCHESTRA Paul Gemignani (Conductor); Sylvia D'Avonzo (Concertmistress/Violin); Sean Carney, Suzy Perelman (Violin); Roger Shell (Cello); Greg Thymius (Woodwinds 1); Julie Ferrara (Woodwinds 2); Don McGeen (Woodwinds 3); Dominic Derasse (Trumpet); Sara Della Posta (French Horn); Mark Mitchell (Keyboard 1); Tony Geralis (Keyboard 2); Bill Schimmel (Accordion); Jennifer Hoult (Harp); Paul Pizutti (Drums); Joe Pasarro (Percussion); John Beal (Bass)

MUSICAL NUMBERS Overture; Good Morning, Good Day; Sounds While Selling; Days Gone By; No More Candy; Three Letters; Tonight at Eight; I Don't Know His Name; Perspective; Goodbye Georg; Will He Like Me?" Illona; I Resolve; A Romantic Atmosphere; Dear Friend; Entr'Acte; Try Me; Where's My Shoe; Vanilla Ice Cream; She Loves Me; A Trip to the Library; Grand Knowing You; Twelve Days to Christmas; Finale

SETTING Time/Place: Budapest, 1934. Staged concert version of a revival of a musical presented in two acts. The original Broadway production was presented at the Eugene O'Neill Theatre April 23, 1963– January 11, 1964, playing 301 performances (see *Theatre World* Vol. 19, page 94). The Roundabout Theatre Company revived the show (with Mr. Ellis as the director) at the Criterion Center Stage Right June 10–August 1, 1993, and then transferred the production to the Brooks Atkinson Theatre October 7, 1993–June 19, 1994, playing a total of 354 performances at both venues (see *Theatre World* Vol. 50, page 17).

SYNOPSIS The Roundabout Theatre Company presents a one-night only benefit concert of one of their most successful musical revivals from the past as a celebration of their 20th anniversary of producing on Broadway. *She Loves Me* follows two feuding clerks in a European parfumerie who secretly find solace in their anonymous romantic pen pals, little knowing their respective correspondents are actually each other.

Broadway Backwards 7

Al Hirschfeld Theatre; March 5, 2012

Created, written, and directed by Robert Bartley; Produced by The Lesbian, Gay, Bisexual & Transgender Community Center and Broadway Cares/Equity Fight AIDS: Executive Producer, Tom Viola; Producers, Michael Graziano, Danny Whitman, Timothy Sullivan; Music Direction, Mary-Mitchell Campbell; Choreographers, Stephanie Klemmons, Patrick O'Neill; Arrangements/Orchestrations, Ron Abel, Matt Aument, Wayne Barker, Mary-Mitchell Campbell, Will Curry, Sam Davis, Anthony DeAngelis, Oran Eldor, Joel Fram, Brad Gardner, Steven Gross, Chris Haberl, Chris Littlefield, Rob Meffe, Andrew Resnick, Tim Rosser, Adam Wachter, Lawrence Yurman; Lighting, Ryan O'Gara; Costumes, Philip Heckman; Lighting, Ryan O'Gara; Production Manager, Nathan Hurlin; Production Stage Manager, Matthew DiCarlo; Company Manager, Scott T. Stevens; Associate Producer, Trisha Doss; Associate Production Manager, Christopher DeLuise; Special Events Officer for The Center, Amanda DeMeester; Associate Music Director, Tim Rosser; Assistant Music Director, Tom Galaher; Stage Manager, Kimberly Russell; Assistant Stage Managers, Zac Chandler, Nathan K. Claus, Susan Davison, Colyn Fiendel, Trey Johnson, Tara Kelly, Angela F. Kiessel, David E. Liddel, Ellie MacPherson, Andrea Jo Martin, Kathleen Munroe, Cathy O'Neal, Joshua Pilote, Jeff Siebert, Anna Trachtman; Assistant to the Director, Bailey Lawrence; Production Assistant, Sarah Rae Mitchel; Dance Captains, Tony Howell, Shonté Walker; Special Material, Robert Bartley, Danny Whitman; Additional Music Preparation, Enrico de Trizio, Jess Glover, Kat Sherrell, Adam Wiggins; Music Copyists, Doug Houston, Anne Kaye; Lighting Programmer, Eric Norris; Assistant Lighting, Sean Beach; Associate Costumes, Matthew Kilgore; Hair and Makeup, Dyana Aives, Michael Serapiglia, Bobbie Clifton Zlotnik; Presenting Sponor, Lifetime Networks; Sponsors, HBO, *The New York Times*, United Airlines, DIRECTV, Here!, Marriott Marquis, John's Pizzaria, Mercer, Bloomberg, Get Gay Chauffeur, *Next Magazine*; Press, Boneau/Bryan-Brown

CAST Bryan Batt, Sierra Boggess, Jim Brochu, Betty Buckley, Charles Busch, Dan Butler, Mario Cantone, Len Cariou, Jenn Colella, Cicily Daniels, Robin De Jesús, Nancy Dussault, Harvey Evans, Anthony Federov, Barrett Foa, Shawna Hamic, Jackie Hoffman, LaChanze, Telly Leung, Jessie Mueller, Adam Pascal, Andrew Rannells, Brian Charles Rooney, Jason Michael Snow, Elizabeth Stanley, George Takei, Bruce Vilanch

Elizabeth Stanley and Sierra Boggess in Broadway Backwards
(photos by Peter James Zielinski)

ORCHESTRA Mary-Mitchell Campbell, Joel Fram, Brian Usifer, Lawrence Yurman (Conductors); Tom Gallaher, Dan Green, Tim Rosser (Piano); Randy Landau (Bass); Jay Mack (Drums); Summer Boggess (Cello); Steve Lyon, Dave Noland (Reeds); Jim Hershman (Guitar); Colin Brigstocke, Dan Urness (Trumpets)

MUSICAL NUMBERS "Wouldn't It Be Loverly" (*My Fair Lady*): Robin De Jesús; "Life With Harold" (*The Full Monty*): Bryan Batt; "Go the Distance" (*Hercules*): LaChanze; "Hernando's Hideaway" (*The Pajama Game*): The Ensemble; "Tonight at 8" (*She Loves Me*): Nancy Dussault; "If He Walked Into My Life" (*Mame*): Charles Busch; "The Boy Friend" (*The Boy Friend*): Dan Butler and Ensemble; "The Music That Makes Me Dance" (*Funny Girl*): Andrew Rannells; "I Still Believe" (*Miss Saigon*): Barrett Foa and Telly Leung; "I Just Want to Dance" (*Jerry Springer: The Opera*): Jason Michael Snow, Cicily Daniels, and Ensemble; "I Know Him So Well" (*Chess*): Anthony Federov and Brian Charles Rooney; "Easy As Life" (*Aida*): Adam Pascal; "It's Never Too Late to Fall in Love" (*The Boy Friend*): Jim Brochu and Harvey Evans; "What Did I Have That I Don't Have (*On a Clear Day You Can See Forever*): Mario Cantone; "She Wasn't You/Come Back to Me" (*On a Clear Day You Can See Forever*): Jessie Mueller; "The Game" (*Damn Yankees*): Jenn Colella, Jackie Hoffman, and Ensemble; "Something Wonderful" (*The King and I*); Len Cariou; "Old Fashioned Wedding" (*Annie Get Your Gun*): Robin De Jesús and Jason Michael Snow; "I Am What I Am" (*La Cage aux Folles*): Shawna Hamic and Ensemble

SYNOPSIS Seventh annual benefit concert presented in two acts. *Broadway Backwards* reinterprets the songs of musical theater by featuring women singing songs originally written for men and men singing songs written for women. By keeping the lyrics intact, including the pronouns, each song takes on an entirely new dimension. It's Broadway in a whole new key. This year's concert raised a record-breaking total of $329,000 for both Broadway Cares and the LGBT Center.

Jim Brochu and Harvey Evans in Broadway Backwards

Easter Bonnet Competition

Minskoff Theatre; April 23 & 24, 2012

Written by David Beach and Danny Whitman; Presented by Broadway Cares/Equity Fights AIDS; Producers, Michael Graziano, Kimberly Russell, and Tom Viola; Director, Kristin Newhouse; Sound, Alain Van Achte; Lighting, Martin E. Vreeland; Production Manager, Nathan Hurlin; Production Stage Manager, Valerie Lau-Kee Lai; Stage Managers, Terence Orleans Alexander, Bess Marie Glorioso, Joshua Pilote, Alexis R. Prussack, Michael Pule, Kat Purvis, David Sugarman, Jason Trubitt, Nancy Elizabeth Vest; Co-Producer, Timothy Sullivan; Associate Producer, Trisha Doss; Associate Production Manager, Christopher DeLuise; Assistant Director, Alex Lyu Volckhausen; Assistant Lighting, Gette Leve; Vocie of God, David Massenheimer; Ticketing, Cat Domiano, Skip Lawing; Volunteer Coordination, R. Keith Bullock, Trisha Doss, Kimberly Russell; Poster and Playbill Art, Justin, "Squigs" Robertson; Playbill Design and Graphics, Carol A. Ingram; Hosts: Stockard Channing, Judith Light, Stacy Keach, Gavin Creel, Rory O'Malley, Raven-Symoné, Jeremy Jordan, Nick Jonas, Michael Urie, Rob Bartlett, Corbin Bleu, Lindsay Mendez, George Salazar, Tshidi Manye, Ron Kunene; Special Guests/Award Presentations: Ricky Martin, Audra McDonald, Eric McCormack; Judges: Nina Arianda, Hugh Dancy, Celia Keenan-Bolger, Adam Chanler-Berat, Megan Hilty, Lisa Lampanelli, Carrie Roberts, Frank Wood, Mark Anderson; Broadway Flea Market and Grand Auction Winner Guest Judge: Karen Walter; Judge Introductions: Jerry O'Connell and Corbin Bleu; Sponsors, *The New York Times* and United Airlines; Press, Boneau/Bryan-Brown

HIGHLIGHTS Opening Number (inspired by *Smash*): written by David Beach and Stacia Fernandez, directed and choreographed by Rommy Sandhu, musical direction and arrangements by Ben Cohn, associate musical direction by Dan Green and Andy Collopy, orchestrations by Ben Cohen and Jesse Vargas, associate choreography by Allison Plamondon; Opening number performed by Tia Altinay, Barrett Davis, Suzanne Hylenski, Jess Le Protto, Michelle Loucadoux, Cara Massey, Elaine Matthews, Dustienne Miller, Kathleen Nanni, Felicity Stiverson, Jesse Swimm, James Tabeek, Nicky Venditti, Anissa Wiley; featuring Andre Garner, Blair Goldberg, T. Oliver Reid, Bret Shuford, Matthew Stocke, Marguerite Willibanks, Linda Balgord; The Gershwins' *Porgy and Bess*: ("It Ain't Necessarily So"), created by Sumayya Ali, Allison Blackwell, Joshua Henry, Heather Hill, and Lisa Nicole Wilkerson; *The Awesome 80s Prom* ("Pzazz 101 with Mary Shennanbargger"), written by Wade Dooley, directed by Isaac Klein; *Avenue Q* ("Monday Night on Avenue Q"), written by Jed Resnick, directed by Marissa Heiser, music direction and arrangements by Andrew Graham; *Anything Goes* ("Anything Goes"), written by Dave Solomon and Julie Halston, directed by Brandon Rubendall, Dave Solomon, and Raymond J. Lee, choreography by Brandon Rubendall; *Spider-Man: Turn Off the Dark* ("Kiss of the Spider-Man"), written and directed by David Marquez, music direction by Charles duChateau; *The Phantom of the Opera* ("Phantom Abbey"), written by Trista Moldovan, directed by Kris Koop Ouellette and Andrew Glant-Linden, choreography by Nicholas Cunningham; Dancers Responding to AIDS ("Boys, Boys, Boys"), written, directed, and choreographed by Ray Mercer; *Jersey Boys* ("The Hunger Games: Jersey Boys Audition"), written, directed, and choreographed by David Marquez, co-written, music direction, and arrangements by Bob Bray; Scenic Bonnets of Broadway, directed by Scott T. Stevens (included bonnets from *Other Desert Cities*, *Once*, and *Death of a Salesman*; *The Book of Mormon* ("The Golden Plates"), written by Rachelle Ferrell, directed and music direction by Sean McDaniel; *The Lion King* ("Hallelujah Harlem!"), concept, direction, and choreography by Kenny Ingram, music direction by Peter Candela; *Mamma Mia!* ("Rang De Bassanti – The Color of Patriotism"), written, directed, and choreographed by Monica Kapoor with introduction by Stacia Fernandez, musical direction by Jeff Campbell; *Mary Poppins* ("Junior Bloody Classic Plays"), written and directed by Tom Souhrada and James Hindman, musical direction by Milton Granger and Brian Taylor; *Chicago* ("All That Jazzy"), written and directed by Brian O'Brien, music direction by Leslie Stifelman and Melissa Rae Mahon; Finale ("Help Is On the Way" by David Friedman– the official anthem of BC/EFA), music direction by Mary-Mitchell Campbell, sung by Titus Burgess

BONNET PRESENTATION Winner: *The Lion King*; First Runner-up: *Mary Poppins*

BONNET DESIGN AWARD *Mamma Mia!* (Created by Glen Russo, Rodd Sovar, Monica Kapoor, Don Lawrence, Lisa Brescia, John Maloney)

FUNDRAISING Total for 51 participating Broadway, Off-Broadway, and National Touring Companies: **$3,677,855**; Top Fundraising Award (Overall): *The Book of Mormon* ($286,725); Broadway Musical: *Spider-Man: Turn Off the Dark* (First Runner-up: $231,997), *Wicked* (Second Runner-up: $204,777), *The Phantom of the Opera* (Third Runner-up: $144,899), *How to Succeed in Business…* (Fourth Runner-up: $144,179); Broadway Play: *Other Desert Cities* (Top Fundraiser: $71,965); National Touring Shows: *Wicked* – Emerald City Company (Top Fundraiser: $280,504), *Wicked* – Munchkinland Company (First Runner-up: $166,434), *Les Misérables* (Second Runner-up: $158,816), *American Idiot* (Third Runner-up: $141,661), *Mamma Mia!* (Fourth Runner-up: $128,033); Off-Broadway: *Rent* (Top Fundraiser: $38,265), *Avenue Q* (First Runner-up: $30,094)

SYNOPSIS Twenty-sixth annual talent and variety show presented without intermission. The *Easter Bonnet Competition* is the two-day spectacular that features the companies of Broadway, Off-Broadway, and touring productions singing, dancing, performing comedic sketches, and donning hand-crafted original Easter bonnets. This Broadway tradition is the culmination of six intensive weeks of fundraising efforts by Broadway, Off-Broadway, and national touring companies. Since 1987, the twenty-six editions of the *Easter Bonnet Competition* have raised over $49 million for Broadway Cares/Equity Fights AIDS, which in turn has supported programs at the Actors Fund including the AIDS Initiative, The Phyllis Newman Women's Heath Initiative, The Al Hirschfeld Free Heath-Clinic, as well as over 400 AIDS and family service organizations across the country.

Christy Brinkley and the Company of Chicago at the Easter Bonnet Competition (photos by Monica Simoes)

The Company of Mamma Mia! *at the Easter Bonnet Competition*

OFF-BROADWAY

June 1, 2011–May 31, 2012

Top: Judy Gold in The Judy Show – My Life As a Sitcom. *Opened at DR2 July 6, 2011 (photo by T. Charles Erickson)*

Center: David Josefsberg and Courtney Balan in Rated P for Parenthood. *Opened at the Westside Theatre–Upstairs February 29, 2012 (photo by Carol Rosegg)*

Bottom: Patti Murin, LaQuet Sharnell, Kat Nejat, Liz Mikel, Lindsay Chambers, and Katie Boren in the Transport Group's Lysistrata Jones. *Opened at the Judson Memorial Church Gymnasium Basketball Court June 5, 2011 (photo by Carol Rosegg)*

The Company of Voca People. Opened at the Westside Theatre–Upstairs July 12, 2010 (photo by Leon Sokoletski)

A scene from Traces. Opened at Union Square Theatre August 8, 2011 (photo by Michael Menke)

The Company of the Off-Broadway revival of Rent. Opened at New World Stages August 11, 2011 (photo by Joan Marcus)

Rinde Eckert in the Culture Project's And God Created Great Whales. Opened at 45 Bleecker February 12, 2012 (photo by Steve Gunther)

Jenn Harris and Brent Barrett in SILENCE! The Musical. Opened at Theatre 80 St. Marks July 9, 2011 (photo by Carol Rosegg)

Jay Stratton, Amy Landon, and Jim Brochu in the Peccadillo Theater Company's *The Man Who Came to Dinner. Opened at the Theatre at St. Clements December 4, 2011 (photo by Carol Rosegg)*

Susan Pourfar and Russell Harvard in Tribes. *Opened at the Barrow Street Theatre March 4, 2012 (photo by Gregory Costanzo)*

Jason Butler Harner and Cory Michael Smith in Cock. *Opened at the Duke on 42nd Street May 17, 2012 (photo by Joan Marcus)*

Megan Hill and Steven Boyer in Hand to God. *Opened at the Ensemble Studio Theatre October 31, 2011 (photo by Gerry Goodstein)*

Mary Testa and the Company of Transport Group's Queen of the Mist. *Opened at the Judson Memorial Church Gymnasium November 6, 2011 (photo by Carol Rosegg)*

The Off-Broadway Season:
A Profitable Season

Linda Buchwald, Contributing Editor, *TDF Stages* and *StageGrade*

The biggest winner of the 2012 Tony Awards was the Off-Broadway nonprofit theatre company New York Theatre Workshop. Its productions of *Once* and *Peter and the Starcatcher* were nominated for a combined twenty Tony Awards. *Once*, based on the 2007 movie of the same name, opened at the New York Theatre Workshop on December 6, 2011. That same day, a Broadway transfer was announced. The musical was directed by John Tiffany, with book by Enda Walsh, movement by Steven Hoggett, and score by the stars of the film, Glen Hansard and Marketa Irglova. Steve Kazee and Cristin Milioti played the Irish musician and Czech immigrant who bond over their love of music.

The reviews for the New York Theatre Workshop production, which were published after the transfer announcement, were mostly positive, though not unanimously so. *New York Times*' Ben Brantley gave a mixed review, but even he changed his tune reviewing the Broadway production, writing, "When I first saw the musical *Once* at the New York Theatre Workshop last December, it registered as a little too twee, too conventionally sentimental, for the East Village. Yet on Broadway—at the Bernard B. Jacobs Theatre to be exact, where *Once* opened on Sunday night—what is essentially the same production feels as vital and surprising as the early spring that has crept up on Manhattan." The Off-Broadway production won Lucille Lortel Awards for outstanding musical, outstanding choreographer, and outstanding lighting design (Natasha Katz), and a Special Citation Obie Award for Tiffany, Hoggett, and orchestrator Martin Lowe. The Broadway production not only won eight Tony awards, including best new musical, but recouped its commercial investment after only twenty-one weeks, faster than any Tony-winning best musical in a decade.

Peter and the Starcatcher, from the 2010-2011 Off-Broadway season, was the other biggest winner on Tony night. The prequel to *Peter Pan* adapted by Rick Elice and directed by Roger Rees and Alex Timbers did not win best new play, but it did receive five awards, more than any other play that season.

The 2011-2012 New York Theatre Workshop season began with *The Select (The Sun Also Rises)*, Elevator Repair Service's take on Ernest Hemingway's *The Sun Also Rises*, and the last in its trilogy of adaptations of classic American works. The play opened on September 11, 2011, and did not receive the type of accolades given to Elevator Repair Service's *Gatz* (a Public Theater production from the previous season). The reviews were very mixed, with many critics failing to be swept up by the material as they were with *Gatz*, but the production did win Lucille Lortel and Obie Awards for outstanding sound design by Matt Tierney and Ben Williams. The Elevator Repair Service also won a Special Citation Obie Award.

The New York Theatre Workshop had more success, at least as far as critics were concerned, with *An Iliad*, an adaptation of Homer's *Iliad* created by Lisa Peterson and Denis O'Hare. O'Hare and Stephen Spinella alternated performances in the one-man anti-war show, which had two opening nights, on March 6 and 7, 2012, respectively. *An Iliad* won a Lucille Lortel Award for Outstanding Solo Show and both actors were nominated for Drama Desk Awards for Outstanding Solo Performance. Peterson, O'Hare, Spinella, and sound designer Mark Bennett, who also wrote original music, won a Special Citation Obie Award.

The other theatre to have one of its Off-Broadway productions transfer to Broadway during the 2011-2012 season was The Vineyard Theatre, but it was not a financial success. (Other Broadway plays that originated Off-Broadway were from previous seasons: Classic Stage Company's *Venus in Fur* and Playwright Horizons' *Clybourne Park* were seen in 2009-2010 and Lincoln Center Theatre's *Other Desert Cities* in 2010-2011, but they further illustrate the trend of major Off-Broadway companies producing work that can transfer to Broadway.) Nicky Silvers' *The Lyons* opened at the Vineyard on October 11, 2011. Linda Lavin turned down the chance to reprise roles in two Broadway transfers, *Follies* and *Other Desert Cities*, to originate the role of Rita Lyons, the matriarch of the Lyons

family, who have gathered in Ben Lyons' hospital room to say goodbye. The show was praised for Silvers' dialogue and especially Lavin's performance. *The Lyons* opened on Broadway in April 2012 and critics largely thought the rewrites had improved the play, but though it had no trouble filling the Vineyard over its two extensions, it had much more difficulty finding an audience for the 1,082-seat Cort Theatre. After poor grosses and no Tony wins and only one nomination (for Lavin, who also won an Obie Award for the performance), the show closed on July 1, 2012.

Another powerhouse female performance came from Mary Testa in *Queen of the Mist*, a Transport Group production, which opened at the Gym at Judson on November 6, 2011. Testa played Anna Edson Taylor, who set out to be the first woman to ride Niagara Falls in a barrel at the age of sixty-three, in the new Michael John LaChiusa musical. Testa was awarded a Special Drama Desk for her three-decade career, including her *Queen of the Mist* performance.

Also receiving a Special Drama Desk was Nick Westrate for his versatile roles in three Off-Broadway shows: *Unnatural Acts* (Classic Stage Company), *Love's Labor's Lost* (The Public Theater), and *Galileo* (Classic Stage Company). And the cast of *Sweet and Sad*—Jon DeVries, Shuler Hensley, Maryann Plunkett, Laila Robins, Jay O. Sanders, and J. Smith-Cameron—received a Drama Desk and Obie for ensemble performance. The play was the second part of Richard Nelson's political trilogy about the Apple family at the Public Theater.

Other plays recognized for both acting and writing were *Sons of the Prophet* and *4000 Miles*. *Sons of the Prophet* was Stephen Karam's second play for Roundabout Stage Company, having made his New York debut with *Speech and Debate* at Roundabout Underground. His *Sons of the Prophet* opened at the Laura Pels Theatre on October 20, 2011. The play about a Lebanese family received positive reviews and Karam was the recipient of the Drama Desk's new Sam Norkin Off-Broadway Award. The play won Lucille Lortel Awards for Outstanding Play and Santino Fontana won a Lucille Lortel Award and Obie Award for his performance as Joseph Douaihy, a former runner sidelined by injury. Chris Perfetti played his brother Charles and received a Theatre World Award.

4000 Miles debuted at The Duke on 42nd Street as part of Lincoln Center's LCT3 program, which produces new work by new playwrights, in June 2011. Amy Herzog's play about a twenty-one-year-old staying with his ninety-one-year-old grandmother after a tragedy on a bike trip was well-received, and Lincoln Center Theater transferred it to its Mitzi E. Newhouse Stage, where it opened on April 2, 2012, to even stronger reviews. Gabriel Ebert and Mary Louise Wilson received Obie Awards for their performances and the play was named the best new American play by the Obie Awards.

Playwrights Horizons' season was dominated by young playwrights: Itamar Moses' *Completeness*, Leslye Headland's *Assistance* (a film was also released of her play *Bachelorette*, seen at Second Stage Uptown in 2010), and Dan LeFranc's *The Big Meal*. It is not surprising that as part of *New York Magazine*'s "Reasons to Love New York 2012," number forty was "Because It's Finally a Good Time to Be a Young Playwright."

While young playwrights like Karam and Herzog were gaining recognition, three young, successful actors—Zach Braff, Zoe Kazan, and Jesse Eisenberg—had their plays produced at major Off-Broadway theatre companies. Charles Isherwood wrote about the trend in the *New York Times* article "Theater Talkback: When Actors Write the Words": "I can't recall another similar flurry in the more than a dozen years I've been reviewing... The trend, if trend it becomes, of name actors making waves as writers for the New York theatre does raise potentially troubling questions. Are producers and artistic directors intentionally (or unconsciously) trying to exploit the authors' notoriety as actors to attract audiences to plays that they might not produce if they were written by unknowns?"

Braff, known for his role on the television show *Scrubs*, wrote *All New People*, which opened at Second Stage on July 25, 2011. He is no stranger to writing, having written the 2004 indie hit film *Garden State*. The play starred Justin Bartha as the depressed Charlie, who finds himself in a New Jersey beach house with a strange collection of characters played by Krysten Ritter, Anna Camp, and David

Wilson Barnes. The play was criticized for lack of believability and clichés, though it was largely agreed that Second Stage gave it a fine production directed by Peter DuBois, who also directed *Sons of the Prophet*. *New York Magazine*'s Scott Brown gave the play a scathing review, causing *Scrubs* creator Bill Lawrence to send him a defense of the play.

Kazan is also a screenwriter. Her film *Ruby Sparks*, in which she also starred, was released around the same time as her play *We Live Here*, in which she did not appear. *We Live Here* opened at New York City Center Stage I on October 12, 2011, as part of Manhattan Theatre Club's season. As was the case with *All New People*, Sam Gold's—who had a busy season also directing *Seminar* on Broadway and the Off-Broadway Roundabout revival of *Look Back in Anger*—slick production was better received than the play itself about a family preparing for a wedding as old, painful secrets are revealed.

Eisenberg, star of *The Social Network*, was the only one of the three to actually star in his play, alongside Justin Bartha, apparently the go-to actor for young stars making their playwriting debut. *Asuncion*, about how a pair of liberal roommates reveal their own racism as a Filipina woman comes to stay with them, opened at the Cherry Lane Theatre on October 27, 2011, and was slightly better received than the other two. In fact, Cherry Lane Theatre is producing another one of Eisenberg's plays in the 2012-2013 season.

The 2011-2012 Off-Broadway season was not only notable for new work, but for new theatre spaces. The Signature Theatre Company opened the doors of its new home at the Pershing Square Signature Center, a seventy-five thousand square foot theatre complex designed by Frank Gehry with three theatre spaces: a café, a lobby, and a bookshop. The space's inaugural play was Edward Albee's *The Lady From Dubuque*, part of the company's Legacy Program, which honors a playwright who has been in residence at the Signature with the premiere of an early play.

The rest of the season included three Athol Fugard shows: *Blood Knot*, *My Children! My Africa!*, and *The Train Driver*—as part of the company's Residency One; an immersive look at one playwright—and Katori Hall's *Hurt Village*, Will Eno's *Title and Deed*, and Kenneth Lonergan's *Medieval Play* as part of its Residency Five, which provides five-year residencies for playwrights.

Atlantic Theatre Company, which had been using Classic Stage Company and other theatre spaces for its shows during its remodel, reopened its Linda Gross Theater with *Storefront Church*, which officially opened on June 11, 2012. It is

John Patrick Shanley's final play in the "Church and State trilogy," which included *Doubt*, generally considered to be a far superior play.

The season saw two major musical revivals. Much was made of MCC's attempt to rework the 1988 Broadway flop *Carrie*. Stafford Arima's modern take set out to fix the problems that made the musical based on the Stephen King novel a failure, but when it opened on March 1, 2012, at the Lucille Lortel Theatre, critics once again tore the musical apart, though this time for different reasons, including lack of blood. An extension through April 22 was announced before opening, but was later canceled, and the show closed on April 8, but the show will live on in a cast recording.

Another major Off-Broadway musical revival was *Rent*, which opened at New World Stages on August 11, 2011, not even three years after the original production closed on Broadway. This was a new production, but it was directed by the show's original helmer Michael Greif and once again starred a cast of young unknowns, but they did not experience the rise to fame of the original cast and the show closed on September 9, 2011. New World Stages also saw the coming and going of the Broadway musical *Million Dollar Quartet*, which transferred on July 28, 2011, and ran there for nearly a year before closing on June 24, 2012. But *Avenue Q* continues to play at New World Stages, where it has been since October 2009.

Perhaps the biggest surprise of commercial Off-Broadway was *Silence! The Musical*, which unlike *Carrie*, proved that musicals based on horror films can be successful. But maybe the key is to be funny. The unauthorized *Silence of the Lambs* parody opened at Theatre 80 on July 9, 2011, where it received positive reviews. It then transferred to the 9th Space Theatre at PS 122 and then to the Elektra Theatre. It was supposed to close on December 30, 2012, but producers announced that performances would resume on January 18, 2013.

If any show proves that a show can make an impact Off-Broadway without transferring to Broadway, it is *Tribes*. The play about a young deaf man named Billy who lives with his hearing family opened at the Barrow Street Theatre on March 4, 2012, and was recognized for David Cromer's production in the round, as well as the ensemble performances. Russell Harvard, who played Billy, received a Theatre World Award and Susan Pourfar, who played his girlfriend, was the winner of the Theatre World Awards' Dorothy Loudon Award for Excellence in the Theatre, as well as an Obie. Remarkably, the show, which kept extending, recouped its investment in November 2012—a rare feat for any play, on or Off-Broadway.

Jesse Eisenberg and Justin Bartha in Mr. Eisenberg's play Asuncion, *presented by Rattlestick Playwrights Theater in association with the Cherry Lane Theatre. Opened at the Cherry Lane Theatre October 27, 2011 (photo by Sandra Coudert)*

Stephen Spinella and Denis O'Hare alternated performances in New York Theatre Workshop's production of the solo-actor play An Iliad, *created by Mr. O'Hare and Lisa Peterson. Opened at New York Theatre Workshop March 6 and 7, 2012 (photo by Joan Marcus)*

Sex on the Beach

Roy Arias Theatre; First Preview: May 12, 2011; Opening Night: June 2, 2011; Closed September 2, 2011

Written by Roy Arias; Produced by Roy Arias Studios and Theatres; Director, Alfred Preisser; Set, Samantha Shoffner; Costumes, Mia Stephenson; Lighting, Tracy Wertheimer; Marketing, HHC Marketing; Press, David Gersten and Associates

CAST La Caramelo/ Brazo E' Niño /Esperanza **Roy Arias**; Vocalist **Natalia Peguero**

SETTING Cuba, the Dominican Republic, and Puerto Rico. Off-Broadway premiere of a new solo performance play with musical interludes presented without intermission. A Spanish language version of the play was previously presented in 2006.

SYNOPSIS In the sea of contradictions that is the Spanish Caribbean, three characters of different gender and circumstances find that the best way to leave their respective countries is through practicing the oldest profession. The transvestite La Caramelo, the hustler Brazo E' Niño and the Cuban escort Esperanza fight their demons in hilarious and dramatic ways by confronting the choices that have taken them to where they are and the dreams they are still not ready to give up.

Roy Arias in Sex on the Beach (photo courtesy of the production)

My Sinatra

Midtown Theatre at HA!; Opening Night: June 4, 2011; Transferred to Downstairs at Sofia's January 18, 2012; 300 performances as of May 31, 2012

Written by Cary Hoffman with additional material by Paul Linke; Produced by UNCLES, LLC in association with John Capie and Stuart Plosky; Musical Director, Alex Nelson; Script Consultant, Randal Myler; Production Designer, Jay Ryan (Midtown Theatre), Keith A. Truax (Sofia's); Video, James Daher; General Manager, Brierpatch Productions (Midtown Theatre), Jennifer Ehrenberg Sofia's); Production Designer, Keith A. Truax; PSM, Patrick Goss; Company Manager, Heather Moss; Board Operator, Nicholas Allen; Sound Consultant, Larry Nachsin; Marketing, Leanne Schanzer Promotions; Press, Beck Lee Media Blitz

Performed by **Cary Hoffman**

Off-Broadway premiere of an autobiographical solo performance play with music presented in two acts. The production previously played over sixteen months of sold-out performances as a cabaret show at The Triad.

SYNOPSIS This one man show starring Cary Hoffman explores Hoffman's own life as a Sinatra idolizer with the ability to channel his voice. Hoffman highlights the story with performances of over twenty of Sinatra's greatest hits.

Cary Hoffman in My Sinatra (photo by Stephen Sorokoff)

Lysistrata Jones

Judson Memorial Church Gymnasium; First Preview: May 15, 2011; Opening Night: June 5, 2011; Closed June 24, 2011; 20 previews, 20 performances

Book by Douglas Carter Beane, music and lyrics by Lewis Flinn; Produced by Transport Group (Jack Cummings III, Artistic Director; Lori Fineman, Executive Director); Director/Choreography, Dan Knechtges; Set, Allen Moyer; Costumes, David Woolard and Thomas Charles LeGalley; Lighting, Michael Gottlieb; Sound, Tony Meola; Music Director, Brad Simmons; Orchestrations, Lewis Flinn; Casting, Cindy Tolan; Associate Choreography, Jessica Hartman; PSM, Wendy Patten; Production Manager, Charles Hubbard; Stage Manager, Donald Peter Butchko; Props, Susan Barras; Assistant to the Musical Director, Kristen Rosenfeld; Associate Design: Warren Karp (set), Zach Williamson (sound); Assistant Design: Ryan Seelig (lighting), Gian-Murray Ginino (sound); Wardrobe Supervisor, Cailin Anderson; Sound Engineer, Josh Maszle; Dance Captain, Teddy Toye; Lightboard Programmer, Josh Newman; Spots, Adam Blodgett, Liam Nelligan; SDC Observer, Liz Piccoli; Production Assistants, Cody Renard Richard, Chad Gneiting, Jan Rosenberg; Press, Richard Kornberg and Associates, Don Summa/Hartman Public Relations, Michael Hartman

CAST Uardo **Alexander Aguilar**; Tyllus **Max Kumangai** (May 15-June 12)/ **Ato Bankson-Wood** (June 15-24); Lampito **Katie Boren**; Robin **Lindsay Nicole Chambers**; Heterai **Liz Mikel**; Lysistrata Jones **Patti Murin**; Cleonice **Kat Nejat**; Mick **Josh Segarra**; Myhrinne **LaQuet Sharnell**; Xander **Jason Tam**; Harold **Teddy Toye**; Cinesius **Alex Wyse**

THE BAND Brad Simmons (Conductor/Keyboards/Vocals), Biti Stauchr (Vocals/Percussionist), Marques Walls (Drums), Alan Stevens Hewitt (Bass), Freddy Hall (Guitar)

MUSICAL NUMBERS Opening-Right Now; Change the World; No More Giving It Up!; Lay Low; I Don't Think So; You Go Your Way; Where Am I Now; Writing on the Wall; Hold On; Don't Judge a Book; Right Now Operetta; When She Smiles; Give It Up!

New York premiere of a new musical presented in two acts. World premiere at Dallas Theatre Center (under the title Give It Up!) January 15–February 14, 2010 (see Theatre World Vol. 66, page 358). The production transferred to Broadway later in the season (see page 52 in this volume).

SYNOPSIS The Athens University basketball team hasn't won a game in 30 years. But when spunky transfer student Lysistrata Jones dares the squad's fed-up girlfriends to stop "giving it up" to their boyfriends until they win a game, their legendary losing streak could be coming to an end. Lyssie and her girl-power posse give the Aristophanes' classic Greek comedy a riotous new twist, staged on an actual basketball court.

Patti Murin, LaQuet Sharnell, Kat Nejat, Liz Mikel (front, center), Lindsay Chambers, and Katie Boren in Lysistrata Jones *(photo by Carol Rosegg)*

Sam's Romance

Actors Temple Theatre; First Preview: May 11, 2011; Opening Night: June 5, 2011; Closed July 31, 2011; 15 previews, 41 performances

Written by Paul Manuel Kane; Produced by Janozak Productions; Director, Hillary Spector; Sets/Lighting, Josh Iacovelli; Costumes, Elizabeth Flores; Sound, Kristin Worall; Press, David Gersten and Associates

CAST Natalie **Oni Brown**; Rose **Lee Anne Hutchison**; Sam **Ed Kershen**; Joe **Todd Licea**; Luba **Neva Small**

SETTING 1953; New York. Off-Broadway premiere of a new play presented without intermission.

SYNOPSIS He is Jewish and she is black. He is 50, she is 20. Its 1953 in New York. Oy! *Sam's Romance* is an edgy comedy about connections. People who make the wrong connection. People who don't connect no matter how they try. And, people who never connect but go on living with great expectations of connecting.

Desperate Writers

Union Square Theatre; First Preview: May 17, 2011; Opening Night: June 6, 2011; Closed June 25, 2011; 21 previews, 23 performances

Written by Joshua Grenrock and Catherine Schreiber; Produced by Carnagie Hill Productions and James Spry; Director, Kay Cole; Sets, Lauren Halpern; Costumes, Stephen Donovan; Lighting, Jeremy Pivnick; Sound, Michael Eisenberg; Production Supervisor, Production Core, James E. Cleveland; Production Manager, Katy Ross; PSM, Bernita Robinson; General Manager, Tom Smedes; Casting, Jay Binder, Jack Bowdan; Executive Producer, Lynn Shaw; Advertising/Marketing, The Pekoe Group; Company Manager, Meredith Morgan; ASM, Michael Joseph Ormond; Assistant Production Manager, Ronald Grimshaw; Technical Director, Peter Fry; Master Electrician, The Lighting Syndicate; Production Electrician, John Anselmo; Associate Design: Biran Ireland (set), Joshua Reid (sound); Assistant Design: William Noguchi (set), Oliver Wason (lighting); Sound Engineer, Criag Freeman; Prop Supervisor, Faye Armon; Assistant Props, Katie Fleming, Ariele Hertzoff; Light Board Programmer/Operator, Daniel Dansby; Wardrobe Supervisor/Deck Crew, Rayneese Primrose; Deck Crew, Michael Hertzer; Production Assistants, Katie Hong, Molly Kaufhold, Carlton Hall; Graphics, Buddha-Cowboy Production, Ty Donaldson; Press, Richard Kornberg and Associates, Billy Zavelson

CAST Ashley **Maddie Corman**; David **Jim Stanek**; Vanessa **Pauletta Washington**; Brandon/Wagner/Trevor/Rick/Husband/Voice of Ed **Kelsey Nash**; Carol/Waitress/Tina **Angel Desai**; Nikki/Sycophant #1/Laura/House Buyer/Wife **Susan Louise O'Connor**; Sycophant #2/Marty/Jackson/House Buyer/Zeno **Vayu O'Donnell**; Jessica Vane **Catherine Schreiber**; Danny Burke **Christopher Durham**; Leo Goldberg **Bob Ari**

UNDERSTUDIES Marguerite Simpson (Ashley, Carol et al, Nikki et al), Beth Glover (Jessica, Vanessa), Michael Zlabinger (David, Rick et al, Jackson et al), Stephen Berger (Burke, Goldberg)

SETTING Los Angeles, California. Halloween 2007. New York premiere of a new play presented without intermission. World premiere at Edgemar Theater (Santa Monica, California) in 2008.

SYNOPSIS A couple of desperate writers, with the baby clock ticking and their home about to be sold out from under them, are driven to desperate measures to get their script read, bought and made in this hilarious, fast-paced, screwball comedy, that pokes fun at the crazy film biz.

Angel Desai, Kelsey Nash, Susan Louise O'Connor, Jim Stanek, Vayu O'Donnell, and Maddie Corman in Desperate Writers *(photo by Carol Rosegg)*

Angelina Ballerina the Musical

Dicapo Opera Theatre†; Opening Night: June 18, 2011; Temporarily Closed May 20, 2012; 79 performances as of May 31, 2012

Book and lyrics by Susan DiLallo, music by Ben Morss, based on the the books and characters created by Katharine Holabird, with illustrations by Helen Craig; Produced by Vital Theatre Company in association with HIT Entertainment; Director/Choreographer, Sam Viverito; Music Director, Michael Borth; Set, Kyle Dixon; Costumes, Elisabeth Vastola; Lighting, Josh Bradford; Sound, Martin Peacock; PSM, Shani Colleen Murfin; Assistant Director, Shani Colleen Murfin; Press, Stephen Sunderlin

CAST Gracie **Carole Ashley**[*1]; Dad **Ronn Burton**[*2] or **Brett Ricci**; Viki **Tiffany Wiesend**[*3]; Miss Mimi **Alexis Field**[*4] or **Harmony Livingston**[*5]; Serena **Jessica Freitas**[*6] or **Amy White**[*7]; Alice **Maggie Gomez Madonia**[*8]; Angelina **Lauren Nestor** or **Kara Jones**[*9]; AZ **Wesley Tunison**[*10]; Swings **Johnny Machesko**[*11], **Stefanie O'Connell**[*12]

*Succeeded by: 1. Abby Bernbaum or Kristin Guerin (1/15/12) 2. Nicholas Kochanov (10/21/11) 3. Molly Stoller or Amanda Vacrelotti (1/15/12) 4. Amima Camille (1/15/12) 5. Katie Sexton (1/15/12) 6. Megan Roup (9/17/11), Jessica Frietas (1/15/12), Ashley Talluto (4/14/12) 7. Sarah Blodgett (9/17/11) 8. Jennifer Margulis (10/21/11), Hannah Owens or Shannon Walsh (1/15/12) 9. Theresa Renee (1/15/12) 10. Roberto Araujo (9/17/11), Jimmy Larkin (1/15/12), Tommy McKeirnan (5/4/12) 11. Matt Paessler (10/21/11), Jake Primmerman (1/15/12),

Matt Paessler (5/4/12) 12. Amanda Varcelotti and Jeanine Wacker (10/21-11/26), Joyce Paulino (10/21/11), Ruthie Stephens (1/15/12)

Off-Broadway transfer of a musical for young audiences presented without intermission. World premiere at Vital Theatre October 2, 2010–January 2, 2011. The production transferred to Union Square Theatre January 9–March 13, 2011 and took a brief sabbatical prior to opening at the Dicapo Opera Theatre.

SYNOPSIS Angelina and her friends, and even their teacher, are all aflutter because a special guest is coming to visit Camembert Academy! Angelina and her friends will perform all types of dance, including hip-hop, modern dance, the Irish jig and of course, ballet and they are excited to show off their skills to their famous visitor. Angelina is the most excited of all, but will she get the starring moment she hopes for?

†The production played at Dicapo until September 11, 2011; transferred to the Theatre at St. Peter's Church September 18–October 17, 2011; returned to Vital Theatre Company (McGinn/Cazale Theatre) October 21, 2011–April 22, 2012; transferred to Florence Gould Hall for three performances in May 6-20, 2012. The production was slated to continue its run at Riverside Theatre on July 8, 2012.

Amber Courtney, Amanda Yachachak, Whitney Meyer, Cassie Okenka, and Erik Restivo in Angelina Ballerina The Musical *(photo by Sun Productions)*

No Child...

Barrow Street Theatre; First Perormance: June 5, 2011; Official Opening Night: June 19, 2011; Closed August 14, 2011; 59 performances

Written by Nilaja Sun; Produced by Scott Morfee and Tom Wirtshafter; Director, Hal Brooks; Originally produced by Epic Theatre Ensemble; Original Set, Narelle Sissons; Original Costumes, Jessica Gaffney; Original Lighting, Mark Barton; Original Sound, Ron Russell; Original Stage Manager, Tom Taylor; General Mangement, Michael Page and Amy Dalba; Press, O+M Company, Jon Dimond

Performed by **Nilaja Sun**

Return engagement of a solo-performance play presented without intermission. World premiere at the Beckett Theatre on Theatre Row May 10–June 4, 2006. Off-Broadway premiere presented at the Barrow Street Theatre July 26, 2006–June 3, 2007 playing 311 performances (see *Theatre World* Vol. 63, page 129). Following the initial Off-Broadway run, Ms. Sun toured the production nationally and internationally to great acclaim.

SYNOPSIS *No Child...* is a tour-de-force exploration of the New York City public school system by the multi-award winning actress and teaching-artist Nilaja Sun, who fearlessly transforms with rapid-fire precision into the teachers, students, parents, administrators, janitors, and security guards who inhabit our schools and shape the future of America. *No Child...* is an insightful, hilarious, and touching master class for anyone who is concerned about the state of our education system and how we might fix it.

Nilaja Sun in No Child... *(photo by T. Charles Erickson)*

The Eyes of Babylon

59E59 Theater B; First Preview: June 14, 2011; Opening Night: June 19, 2011; Closed July 3, 2011; 8 previews, 16 performances

Written by Jeff Key; Produced by Semaphore Projects and The Mehadi Foundation as part of the 2011 Americas Off Broadway Festival; Director, Yuval Dadadi; Lighting, Lee Terry; Sound, Chris Comfort; Stage Manager, Kate Simko; Producer, Jennilyn Merten; Assistant Sound, William Neal; Soundboard Operator, Tyler Easter; Propsmaster, Heather Cooper; Production Assistant/Wardrobe, Vicky Zhang; Marketing, Shira Dentz; Web Design, Davina Pallone; Assistant to the Producer, Lucy Spain; Press, Karen Greco

Performed by **Jeff Key**

New York premiere of a new solo-performance play presented without intermission. Originally presented in Los Angeles at the Tamarind Theatre October 25, 2004–January 13, 2005.

SYNOPSIS U.S. Marine Jeff Key transforms his Iraq journal into a gritty, humorous and poetic solo-performance about going to war as a 34-year-old gay man at the heady start of the Iraq invasion only to find the war is not what it seems and the greatest battle is with himself.

Jeff Key in The Eyes of Babylon *(photo courtesy of The Mehadi Foundation)*

Pins and Needles: A New Revolutionary Musical in Brooklyn

Irondale Center; Opening Night: June 22, 2011; Closed July 9, 2011; 9 performances

Music and lyrics by Harold Rome, Gene Raskin, Josh White, Leadbelly, Jim Garland, Earl Robinson, Yip Harburg, and members of the company; Scenes and sketches by Arthur Arent, Melanie Joseph, Lynn Nottage, Sara Zatz/Ping Chong & Co., and members of the company; Produced by The Foundry Theatre (Melanie Joseph, Artistic Producer; James Morrison, Producer; Sherrine Azab, Associate Producer) and performed by FUREE – Families United for Economic Equality (Valery Jean, Executive Director); Director, Ken Rus Schmoll; Music Director, Richard Harper; Choreography, Camille A. Brown; Sets and Costumes, Arnulfo Maldonado; Lighting, Sara Sidman; Sound, Greg Tobler; Props Coordinator, Deborah Gaouette; PSM, Heather Arnson; Stage Manager, Alejandra Duque; Line Producer, Evan O'Brient; FUREE Project Producer, Monica L. Williams; Assistant Choreographer, Francine Elizabeth Ott; Assistant Costumes/Wardrobe Supervisor, Brieanna Lewis; Assistant Lighting, Keri Thibodeau; ASM, Ashley Rossetti; Production Manager/Technical Director, David Nelson; Master Electrician, Jake Heinrichs/The Lighting Syndicate; Production Electrician/Spot Op, Jon Degaetano; Audio Supervisor/Mixer, Dylan Carrow; Run Crew, Ella Metuki, Janette Valenzo Venegas; Graphic Designer, Christopher Abueg; Documentarians, Ujju Aggarwal and Michael Premo

CAST Shannon Barber, Stephen Barnes, Cynthia Butts, Marilyn Charles, Donna Douglas, Latisha Douglas, Earlyn Kizzy Ferguson, Ermiyas Harper, Yosef Harper, Debbie Howell, Wanda Imasuen, Euston James, Cory Jeminez, Jackie Phillip, Valerie Phillips, Nova Strachan, Marsha Zeigler

MUSICIANS Richard Harper (Piano/Keyboard), Billy "Spaceman" Patterson (Guitar), Al MacDowell (Bass), Warren Smith (Drums), Yuri Yamashita (Percussion)

SONGS AND SCENES: Sing Me a Song With Social Significance; The City Grows; Landlord; Free and Equal Blues; In a Public Assistance Office; Chain Store Daisy; There's a Man Goin' Round Takin' Names; Call It Un-American; Doing the Reactionary; Mene Mene Tekel; I Don't Want Your Millions Mister; Workers Rights; Not Cricket to Picket; We Got Rights Too; Nobody Makes a Pass at Me; I've Got the Nerve to Be in Love; What Good Is Love?; Activists Born; Sitting On Your Status Quo

Revised version of a classic musical revue presented in two acts. The original production was presented at the Labor Stage Theatre (formerly the Princess Theatre) and subsequently the Windsor Theatre November 27, 1939–June 22, 1940 playing 1,108 performances.

SYNOPSIS From 1937 to 1941, *Pins and Needles* was a hit musical comedy revue running on Broadway written for and performed by members of The International Ladies Garment Workers' Union, who sang out for all the people fighting for jobs, housing, a minimum wage, immigrants' rights and economic justice. FUREE presents a new adaptation, utilizing material form the original along with new sketches and songs, satirizing our own contemporary reactionaries and aiming to connect theater and social justice in a way that is entertaining more than message-based.

Members of FUREE (Families United for Racial and Economic Equality) in Pins and Needles *(photo by Ari Mintz)*

The Devil's Music: The Life and Blues of Bessie Smith

St. Luke's Theatre; First Preview: June 7, 2011; Opening Night: June 22, 2011; Closed September 2, 2012; 7 previews, 124 performances

Written by Angelo Parra; Produced by Penguin Rep Theatre (Joe Brancato, Artistic Director; Andrew M. Horn, Executive Director) and Edmund Gaynes, in association with Lizanne and Don Mitchell; Concept/Musical Staging/Direction, Joe Brancato; Set, Michael Schweikardt; Costumes, Patricia E. Doherty; Lighting, Jeff Croiter; Sound, Jack Kennedy; Music Director/Arrangements, Miche Braden; PSM, C. Renee Alexander; General Management, Jessimeg Productions; Production Manager, Josh Iacovelli; Associate Lighting, Cory Pattak; Production Assistants, Patrick Scheid, Jamil Chokachi; Wardrobe Supervisor, Courtney Irizarry; Master Electrician, Jared Welch; Set Construction, Ken Larson; Graphic Designer, Richard Harper; Press, David Gersten and Associates

CAST AND MUSICIANS Bessie Smith **Miche Braden**; Pickle/Bass **Jim Hankins**; Piano **Aaron Graves**; Saxaphone **Anthony E. Nelson Jr.** or **Keith Loftis**

SETTING Monday, October 4, 1937 and the Saturday night, nine days earlier; A buffet flat in Memphis, Tennessee. Off-Broadway premiere of a new biographical musical presented without intermission. World premiere at Penguin Rep Theatre in Stony Point, New York.

SYNOPSIS Sexy and racy, blues singer Bessie Smith was the definition of a Red Hot Mamma and the most successful entertainer of her time. On the eve of her tragic death in 1937, Bessie takes center stage in *The Devil's Music: The Life and Blues of Bessie Smith* and tells the story of her amazing life and career, her loves and losses.

Jim Hankins (on bass), Miche Braden, Aaron Graves (on piano), and Keith Loftis (on saxophone) in The Devil's Music: The Life and Blues of Bessie Smith *(photo by John Quilty)*

The Rap Guide to Evolution

SoHo Playhouse; First Preview: June 17, 2011; Opening Night: June 26, 2011; Closed November 6, 2011; 13 previews, 120 performances

Written by Baba Brinkman; Produced by Dovetail Productions (Sharon Levy, Producer); Director, Dodd Loomis; Projections, Wendall K. Harrington; Set, Derek Stenborg; Sound, Ken Travis; Lighting, Jason Boyd; Music Producer, DJ Jamie Simmonds; General Management, Foster Entertainment; Stage Manager, Nicole Press; Video Programmer, Paul Vershbow; Projection Associate, Erik Pearson; Projection Assistant, Kristen Robinson; Projection Graphics, Bo Eriksson; Projection Intern, Jason Gallaher; Sound Operator, Joseph Riordan; Production Assistant, Megan Riordan; Advertising and Marketing, The Peko Group; Soho Playhouse Artistic Director, Darren Lee Cole; Soho Playhouse Executive Director, Faith A. Mulvhill; Press, Blake Zidell & Associates

Performed by **Baba Brinkman** with DJ **Jamie Simmonds**

U.S. premiere of a new solo performance play with music presented without intermission. World premiere at the 2009 Edinburgh Fringe Festival.

SYNOPSIS *The Rap Guide to Evolution* seems to speak for itself: Canadian Baba Brinkman creates an entire hip-hop show about evolution, combining the wit, poetry and charisma of a great rapper with the accuracy and rigor of a scientific expert. But The Rap Guide not only uses hip-hop as a vehicle to communicate the facts of evolution; Brinkman also accomplishes the (more surprising) feat of illuminating the origins and complexities of hip-hop culture with Darwin as his inspiration.

Baba Brinkman in The Rap Guide to Evolution *(photo by Yuval Binur)*

The Magdalene

Theatre at St. Clement's; First Preview: June 14, 2011; Opening Night: June 27, 2011; Closed July 13, 2011; 15 previews, 17 performances

Music by James Olm, book and lyrics by J.C. Hanley and James Olm; Inspired by the Gospels of Mary and Thomas; Produced by Emerald Green Productions and Angelo Fraboni Productions; Director, Richard Burk; Creative Consultant, Richard Maltby Jr.; Sets/Lighting, Sean McIntosh; Costumes, Darrell Wagner; Sound, Carl Casella; General Manager, Peter Bloch; Casting Lewis & Fox Casting; PSM, Jessie Vacchiano; ASM, Michael O'Donnell; Company Manager, Alexandra Bernson; Sound Board, Jordan Maltby; Master Electrician, Lance Robinson; Advertising and Marketing, The Pekoe Group; Press, Richard Kornberg and Associates

CAST Mary Magdalene **Lindsie VanWinkle**; Levi/Jean Doresse **Devin Desantis**; Peter/John Wesley **Xander Chauncey;** Annas/Pope Gregory **John Antony**; Roman Soldier/Emperor Constantine **Patrick Oliver Jones**; The Little Girl/The Little Lamb **Faith Annette Engen**; Yeshua **Shad Olsen**; Jacob **Osborn Focht**; Rivkah **Evangelia Kingley**; Pilatus **Eugene Barry-Hill**; Older Woman **Caleb Damscroder**; Ensemble **Caleb Damscroder, Laura Huizenga, Jillian Schochet**; Swing **Lyle Colby Mackston**

UNDERSTUDIES Patrick Oliver Jones (Pilatus), Caleb Damscroder (Levi), Laura Huizenga (Little Girl)

MUSICIANS Barbara Lee (Conductor/Piano), Bob Jones (Bass), Darrell Smith (Drums), B.J. Gandolfo (Alternate Pianist)

MUSICAL NUMBERS What Did You See In Me?; Closer to God; Set Me As A Seal; Something Greater; Jerusalem!; Yeshua! Yeshua!/Seeds of Wisdom; We Are Blessed; Song of Songs; Who Are You? – Part I; What Is He? – Part II; The Waters Of The River; Strength And Retribution – Part I; Strength And Retribution – Part II; The Assault; The Assault; We Are Blessed (reprise); Two Lives; Set Me As A Seal (reprise); I Am With You; Mary, The Magdalene

World premiere of a new musical presented without intermission.

SYNOPSIS Inspired by the Gnostic Gospels of Mary and Thomas, *The Magdalene* is a stirring love story that includes information left out when the Bible was compiled in AD 325. Mary Magdalene, dismissed for almost 2000 years as a "penitent prostitute," may well have been not only a disciple of Jesus, but placed in a position above the other Apostles. Why was a powerful female figure downgraded as the church was created? Why was sexuality expunged from the most important Biblical figures? And what was the real personal connection between Mary and Jesus? These themes have inspired a thrilling new musical that takes a modern look at the world's greatest story of faith and love.

Lindsie VanWinkle and Shad Olsen in The Magdelene
(photo by Peter James Zielenski)

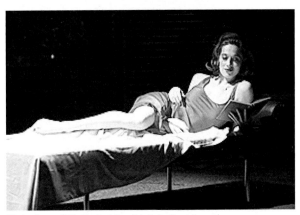

Marina Squerciati in Manipulation *(photo by Carol Rosegg)*

Manipulation

Cherry Lane Theatre; First Preview: June 21, 2011; Opening Night: June 28, 2011; Closed August 21, 2011; 7 previews, 63 performances

Written by Victoria E. Calderon; Produced by the Cherry Lane Theatre (Angelina Fiordellisi, Executive Director); Director, Will Pomerantz; Sets, Bill Stabile; Costumes, Alejo Vietti; Lighting, Kirk Bookman; Sound, Jeremy Lee; Casting, Stephanie Klapper; ; General Management, Niko Companies Ltd. (Manny Kladitis, Jeffrey Chrzczon, Jason T. Vanderwoude); Technical Director, Jay Janicki; PSM, Brian Meister; ASM, Brian Rardin; Production Assistant, Angela Hesterman; Original Direction, Marilyn Fried; Associate Design: Dana Lauren Kenn (set), China Lee (costumes), Steve O'Shea (lighting), Sam Kusnetz (sound); Fight Instructor, Rick Sordelet; Fight Captain, John-Patrick Driscoll; Puppet Design, Bela Schenková; Puppet Builders, ANPU Theatre; Puppet Master, Brendan McMahon; Assistants to Ms. Calderon, Mara McKevitt, Dimitri Hamlin; Puppet Maintenance, Lake Simons; Projection Supervison, Sam Kusnetz; Head Carpenter, Daniel Thomas; Sound/Light Board Operator, Alexander Fisher; Wardrobe Supervisor, AraBella C. Fischer; Marketing, Leanne Schanzer Promotions; Advertising, Hofstetter + Partners/Agency 212; Press, Shirley Herz, Bob Lasko

CAST Beatriz **Saundra Santiago**; Cristina **Marina Squerciati** Mauricio **Robert Bogue**; Luis **Rafi Silver**; Dr. Lublitz **Jeremy Stiles Holm**; Poeta **Brendan McMahon**; Alejandro **Gabriel Furman**

UNDERSTUDIES John-Patrick Driscoll (Mauricio, Alejandro, Poeta), Gabriel Furman (Luis), Brendan McMahon (Dr. Lublitz), Elizabeth Norment (Beatriz), Michele Vazquez (Cristina)

SETTING Latin America; today. World premiere of a new play presented without intermission.

SYNOPSIS In *Manipulation*, Cristina seemingly has it all. And yet, her husband torments her with infidelity while her mother condones it, encouraging Cristina to behave in the same sordid way. She seeks professional help from a psychiatrist, be he is determined to take advantage of her troubles and satisfy his own lewd intentions. Has Cristina lost all control of her life, mind and body? Or can she turn the tables and cut the ties that bind her? This provocative modern interpretation of an overlooked biblical story ends with a shocking twist that's as seductive as it is dark and dangerous.

Cirque du Soleil: Zarkana

Radio City Music Hall; First Preview: June 9, 2011; Opening Night: June 29, 2011; Closed October 8, 2011

Written and directed by François Girard; Produced by Cirque du Soleil (Guy Laliberté, Founder; Daniel Lamarre (President & CEO); Artistic Guides, Guy Laliberté, Gilles Ste-Croix; Director of Creation, Line Tremblay; Set and Props, Stéphane Roy; Costumes, Alan Hranitelj; Composer/Music Director, Nick Littlemore; Choreographers, Debra Brown, Jean-Jacques Pillet, Olena Koliadenko; Lighting, Alain Lortie; Image Content, Raymond St-Lean; Sound, Steven Dubuc; Acrobatic Performance Design, Florence Pot; Rigging and Acrobatic Equipment Design, Danny Zen; Makeup, Eleni Uranis; Musical Consultant, Sir Elton John; Dramaturge, Serge Lamothe; Guangzhou Cranes Act, Vilen Golovko; Clown Master, René Bazinet; Storyboard Illustrator, Robert Massicotte; Director of Content for New Creations/Casting/Performance and Trends, Fabrice Becker; Casting, Line Giasson, Céline Lavallée; Executive Producer, Aldo Giampaolo; Production Manager, Robert Lemoine; PSM, Sylvain Auclair; Technical Director, David Churchill; Company Manager, George Anthony Agbuya; Production Coordinator, Irina Besschetnaya; Artistic Director, Ann-Marie Corbeil; General Stage Manager, Carolyn Wyld; Stage Managers, Noémie Dubé-Dupuis, Matt Watkins; ASM, Katie McNiff, Operations Production Manager, David Lee Dovell; Operations Technical Director, Byron Shaw; Marketing/Promotions, Allied Live LLC; Advertising/Interactive, SpotCo; New York Press, The Publicity Office, Marc Thibodeau

ARTISTS Zark/Singer **Garou**; Lia/Singer **Cassiopée**; Backup Singers **Paul Bisson, Meetu Chilana**; Aerial Duet **Di Wu, Jun Guo**; Banquine **Ekaterina Aleshina, Yury Baramzin, Konstantin Besschetnyy, Valeriy Chernyy, Vladimir Fromin, Denis Gircha, Nikolay Glushchenko, Alexey Gribtsov, Sergey Kholodkov, Pavel Koreshkov, Dmitry Kukva, Dmitry Shilov, Dima Sidorenko, Halina Starevich, Alexandre Zaitsev**; Clowns (Hocus and Pocus) **Daniel Passer, Wayne Wilson**; Flag Manipulation **Frederico Pisapia, Giuseppe Schiavo, Marco Senatore, Vincenzo Schiavo**; Grand Volant (Catchers) **Alexander Romanyuta, Artem Ledovskikh**; Grand Volant (Flyers) **Maria Boldyreva, Dmitry Denisov, Yakov Dryda, Andriy Marchuk, Ganna Myrgorodska, Denis Pankov, Valerii Pereshkura, Sergey Poletskyy, Maksym Sautin, Petr Serdioukov, Artem Skabelkin**; Handbalancing **Anatoliy Zalevskiy**; Juggling **Masha Choodu**; Ladders **Anastasia Dvoretskaya, Victoria Dvoretskaya, Dmitry Dvoretskiy**; Movers, Aerial Hoops (White Clowns) **Kristina Besschetnaya, Anne De Lottinville, Julie Dionne, Evelyne Lamontagne, Dany Rabello, Masha Terentieva**; Movers, Cyr Wheel (White Clowns) **Elijah Brown, Tom Cholot, Jason Nious, Olivier Lefébure, Jérémie Robert, Ghislain Ramage,**

Lysanne Richard, Philippe Trépanier; Russian Bar **Carole Demers**, **Johnny Gasser**, **Yuri Kreer**; Sand Painting (Oracle) **Erika Chen**; Wheel of Death/High Wire **Ray Navas Velez**, **Rudy Navas Velez**; High Wire **Roberto Navas Yovany**, **Rony Navas Velez**; *Musicians*: Bandleader/Keyboard 1 **Steve Bach**; Bass/Percussion **Peter Fand**; Drum Set **Jakubu Griffin**; Drum Set/Percussion **Aaron Guidry**; Guitar **Joe Hundertmark**; Keyboard 2/Piano **Keith Paraska**

World premiere of a theatrical variety show and acrobatic circus presented with one intermission.

SYNOPSIS *Zarkana* is a visual vortex set in a slightly twisted musical and acrobatic fantasy universe where, little by little, chaos and craziness give way to festivity and love regained. The story is about a magician in an abandoned theatre who has lost his love and his magic. As he cries and begs the gods for her return, he is plunged into a world inhabited by surreal creatures. The diverse cast of international artists transports the audience into a fantastical and suspenseful world, blurring the boundaries between the real and imaginary.

The finale of Cirque du Soleil's Zarkana *(photo by Jeremy Daniel)*

The Berenstain Bears Live!
In Family Matters, the Musical

Manhattan Movement and Arts Center†; First Preview: June 25, 2011; Opening Night: July 3, 2011; 5 previews, 77 performances as of May 31, 2012 (weekend performances)

Book, music, and lyrics by Michael Borton, additional book material by Michael Slade; Adapted from the children's book series by Stan and Jan Berenstain; Produced by Matt Murphy; Director/Choreography, Devanand Janki; Orchestrations, R. MacKenzie Lewis; Music Director, Daniel Green; Sets, Luke Hegel-Cantarella; Costumes, Lora LaVon; Lighting, David Ojala; Properties Master, Alexandra Gieger; Casting, Cindi Rush; Stage Manager, Kristine Schlachter; Associate Director/Choreographer, Nancy Renée Braun; Company Manager, Matt Franzetti; Creative Development Associate, Nick Brennan; Graphic Design, Ari Rosenbaum; Production Intern, Christina Pezzello; MMAC Executive Artistic Director, Rose Caiola; Technical Director, David Ojala; Marketing, Davenport Theatrical Enterprises; Press, Springer Associates, Joe Trentacosta

CAST Papa Bear **Ryan Scarlata**; Mama Bear **Laurie Geigel**; Brother Bear **Alex Goley**; Sister Bear **Jill Kurzner**; Lizzie/Dr. Grizzly/Gran **Rori Nogee**; Freddy/Gramps **Ben Thorpe**; Swings **William Bailey**, **Danielle Defassio**

MUSICAL NUMBERS Another Day in Bear Country; I'm Dreaming; Hello; It's Not Fair; Fluff on Your Tummy; Ballad of Wily Fox; Phooey; Let's Hide the Evidence; Step Up to the Starting Line; Family Matters

New York premiere of a new musical for young audiences presented without intermission. The production ended a thirty-five week national tour prior to this engagement.

SYNOPSIS In *The Berenstain Bears LIVE! in Family Matters, the Musical*, Papa Bear can't stop eating junk food, Brother Bear's grades are slipping, and Sister Bear still has a lot to learn about talking to strangers. Thankfully, we can always depend on Mama Bear and her loving patience to help set things right. After all, this is one bear tree house where family truly matters!

†Transferred to the Marjorie S. Deane Little Theatre November 5, 2011.

A scene from The Berenstain Bears LIVE! In Family Matters, the Musical *(photo by Aaron Epstein)*

MoLoRa

Joan Weill Center for Dance at Alvin Ailey Citigroup Theatre; First Performance: June 30, 2011; Official Opening Night: July 6, 2011; Closed July 24, 2011; 22 performances

Created and directed by Yael Farber, adapted from Aeschylsus's *Oresteia* trilogy; Produced by Farber Foundry Theatre Company (South Africa) and Culture Project's Women Center Stage (Alan Buchman, Artistic Director; Nan Richardson, Executive Director; Vanessa Sparling, Managing Director; Manda Martin, Lead Producer); Executive Producer for the Farber Foundry, ArKtype/Thomas O. Kriegsman; Assistant Producer, Kendall Karg; Set, Larry Leroux and Leigh Colombick; Costumes, Natalie Lundon and Johny Mathole; Lighting, Caleb Wertenbaker; Instrument and Song Arrangements, The Ngqoko Cultural Group; U.S. Assistant Director/Company and Stage Manager, Damon Krometis; South African Assistant Director/Dramaturgical Contributor, Yana Sakelaris; ASM, Johanna Thelin; Vocal Coaching Assistant, Dorothy Ann Gould; Technical Director, Jay Janicki; South African Production Coordinator, Leigh Colombick; Master Carpenter, Evan True; Master Electrician, Adrian Kozlow; Sound Operator, Joel Wilhemi; Lighting Operators, Michael Swan, Josh Monroe; Seamstress, Virginia Sweeney; Artwork, Christy Briggs; For Culture Project: Jayashri Wyatt (Director of Productions), Victoria Andújar (Administrative Director and Special Assistant to Mr. Buchman), Elisa Lavery (Senior Marketing Associate), Jennifer Joyce (Senior Development Associate), Winter Miller (Development Associate), Jae Hee Byun (Box Office/Development Assistant), Nurit Schwarzbaum (Bookkeeper); Press, O+M Company

CAST Klytemnestra **Dorothy Ann Gould**; Elektra **Jabulile Tshabalala**; Orestes **Sandile Matsheni**; Chorus and Musicians (Ngqoko Cultural Group) **Tandiwe Lungisa**, **Tsolwana B. Mpayipheli**, **Nofenishala Mvotyo**, **Nopasile Mvotyo**, **Nokhaya Mvotyo**, **Nosomething Ntese**, **Nogcinile Yekani**

SONGS Blood Has Been Spilt; Destroyer of Peace; A Respected Clan Amongst the Xhosas; Sleep, My Child; You in Johannesburg; Father of the Leading Initiate; Village Name in Lady Frere, Republic of South Africa; Blessing From the Ancestors; Morning Star (Rises From the Dark); My Dream; We Are From Ngqoko; Gathering of Ancestors; The Joker; Handicapped

New York premiere of a play with music presented without intermission. Originally presented at the Market Theatre in Johannesburg, South Africa in 2007.

SYNOPSIS Set after the fall of apartheid, *MoLoRa* reimagines the ancient Greek Oresteia to tell the story of her own country's painful and extraordinary transition to democracy. As Klytemnestra and Elektra – mother and daughter, perpetrator and victim – sit to face each other in an open hearing, *MoLoRa* reenacts a watershed moment in world history, illuminating the universal and excruciating choice for any victim: to seek revenge or choose forgiveness.

Jabulile Tshabalala in MoLoRa *(photo by Ruphin Couzyer)*

The Judy Show: My life as a Sitcom

DR2; First Preview: June 30, 2011; Opening Night: July 6, 2011; Closed November 27, 2011; 6 previews, 151 performances

Written by Judy Gold and Kate Moira Ryan; Produced by Daryl Roth and Eva Price in association with Jamie Cesa, Lynn Shaw, Tom Smedes, Bruce Robert Harris, and Jack W. Batman; Director, Amanda Charlton; Original Music, Judy Gold; Lyrics, Kate Moira Ryan and Judy Gold; Additional Material, Eric Kornfeld and Bob Smith; Music Director, Kris Kukul; Sets and Projections, Andrew Boyce; Lighting, Paul Toben; Sound, Alex Neumann and Janie Bullard; Stylist, Emily DeAngelis; Marketing, HHC Marketing; PSM, Scott Pegg; Production Manager, Joshua Scherr; Associate Producers, Alexander Fraser, Jeremy Katz; General Management, Maximum Entertainment Productions (Avram Freedburg, Mary Beth Doyle, Eva Price); Assistant Director, Ethan Heard; Company Manager, Taylor James; Associate General Manager, Holly Sutton; Production Assistant, Nicole M. Smith; Assistant Lighting, Daniel O'Brien; Voiceover, Joe Plummer; Web Mistress, Dana Friedman; Assistants to Ms. Roth, Greg Raby, Megan Smith; Advertising, Hofstetter + Partners; Press, Keith Sherman and Associates, Brett Oberman, Logan Metzler

Performed by **Judy Gold**

World premiere of a new autobiographical solo performance play with music presented without intermission.

SYNOPSIS Building on the success of her show *25 Questions for a Jewish Mother*, funny-woman Judy Gold returns to the stage in this hilarious look at her life through the lens of the classic sitcoms of her youth. With multimedia, original music, laughter, and love, Judy shows us how she balances family and ambition with a little help from our favorite TV shows of the 70s, 80s, and 90s.

Judy Gold in The Judy Show: My Life As a Sitcom
(photo by T. Charles Erickson)

Eva the Chaste

Clurman Theatre on Theatre Row; First Preview: July 6, 2011; Opening Night: July 8, 2011; Closed July 24, 2011; 2 previews, 15 performances

Written by Barbara Hammond; Produced by Fallen Angel Theatre Company (Aedín Moloney, Artistic Director); Director, John Keating; Set, Melissa Shakun; Costumes/Graphic Design, Eileen Connolly; Lighting, Jessica Burgess; Sound, Mark Parenti; Stage Manager, Katharine Sarah Fergerson; Production Manager, Ruth Kavanagh; Music, Kevin Conneff & Paddy Moloney (The Chieftains); Assistant Director, Rachel Hip-Flores; Production Assistant, Miki Bourne; Photographer, Ryn Wilson; Press, Source Communications, Ken Frydman

CAST Eva **Aedín Moloney**

World premiere of a new solo performance play presented without intermission.

SYNOPSIS *Eva the Chaste* immerses the audience in the pivotal passions and pressing responsibilities of a woman whose twenty-year sprint away from her past comes crashing to a close as dawn breaks over Dublin Bay. *Eva the Chaste* explores the profound and unpredictable bond between a mother and a daughter; the grasp for life at the approach of death; and the road to hell – shining, smooth, and paved with good intentions.

Aedin Maloney in Eva the Chaste *(photo by Ira Peppercorn)*

SILENCE! The Musical

Theatre 80†; First Preview: June 24, 2011; Opening Night: July 9, 2011; 8 previews, 247 performances as of May 31, 2012

Music and lyrics by Jon Kaplan and Al Kaplan, book by Hunter Bell; Adapted from the screenplay *Silence! The Musical* by Jon and Al Kaplan; Based on the 1991 film *The Silence of the Lambs* directed by Jonathan Demme and screenplay by Ted Tally, adapted from the Tom Harris novel; Produced by Victoria Lang, Rich Affannato, and Donna Trinkoff in association with Scott Kirschenbaum, Theater Mogul, Neil Gobioff, and Terry Schnuck with John Arthur Pinckard; Director/Choreography, Christopher Gattelli; Music Supervisor/Additional Orchestrations, Mark Hartman; Music Director/Orchestrations, Brian J. Nash; Sets, Scott Pask; Costumes, David Kaley; Lighting, Jeff Croiter; Sound, Carl Casella; Projections, Richard H. DiBella; PSM, Ritchard Druther; Production Manager, Josh Iacovelli; Casting, Cindi Rush; General Manager, Tom Smedes; Associate Producers, Mark Hartman, Dan McMillan, Brian J. Nash; Graphic Design, Christie Scanlan; Social Media, Bryce Norbitz; Company Manager, Alexandra Agosta; ASM, Jana Llynn; Assistant Director, Kate Wetherhead; Associate Lighting, Grant Yeager; Props, Troy David, Carrie Mossman; Wigs, J. Jared Janas and Rob Greene; Wardrobe Supervisor, Dustin Cross; Sound Operator, Anthony Trentinella; Production Assistants/Crew, Sean Barrett, Lisa Carroll, Regina Stephenson; Assistant to the Director, Brendan Naylor; Assistant to Mr. Hartman, Ben Boecker; Advertising, Hofstetter + Partners/Agency 212; Press, Jim Randolph; Cast recording: Sh-K-Boom/Ghostlight Records 84455

CAST Dr. Hannibal Lecter **Brent Barrett**[*1]; Clarice Starling **Jenn Harris**; Jame Gumb, aka "Buffalo Bill," et al **Stephen Bienskie**; Dr. Chilton, et al **Harry Bouvy**; Ardelia Mapp, et al **Deidre Goodwin**; Sgt. Pembry, et al **Jeff Hiller**[*2]; Jack Crawford, et al **Howard Kaye**; Catherine Martin, et al **Lucia Spina**[*3]; Dream Hannibal **Callan Bergmann**; Dream Clarice **Ashlee Dupré**; Standbys[*4] **Pamela Bob**, **Doug Trapp**

*Succeeded by: 1. David Garrison (10/25/11) 2. Topher Nuccio (10/25/11) 3. Annie Funke (1/12/12), Kimberly Stern (3/28/12) 4. Added 10/25/11 for the open-ended run

BAND Brian J. Nash (Conductor/Keyboard 1), Nate Patten (Keyboard 2), Dan McMillan (Percussion), Dorothy Martin (Second Associate Conductor)

MUSICAL NUMBERS Silence!; Thish Ish It; The Right Guide; If I Could Smell Her Cunt; Papa Shtarling; It's Agent Shtarling; Are You About a Size 14?; My Daughter Is Catherine; Quid Pro Quo; I'd Fuck Me; It's Me!; Catherine Dies Today; Papa Shtarling (reprise); Put the Fucking Lotion in the Basket; We're Going In!; Bill's Death (In the Dark With a Maniac); Finale (Silence Reprise)

Off-Broadway premiere of a new musical presented in two acts. Orignally based on a 2003 internet musical comprised of nine songs, the show evolved into a stage production which premiered August 12, 2005 as part of the New York International Fringe Festival. The show made its London debut October 19, 2009 for a two week run at the Barons Court Theatre, and a revised version, directed and choreographed by Mr. Gattelli, was presented at Above The Stag Theatre in London January 19–February 28, 2010.

SYNOPSIS In the Academy Award-winning film *The Silence of the Lambs*, rookie FBI agent Clarice Starling matches wits with the brilliant but insane cannibal, Dr. Hannibal Lecter, to catch the serial killer known only as Buffalo Bill. Clarice must face her own demons and race the clock to unlock Lecter's clues before another innocent girl is killed and skinned by Bill. Now, the hair-raising has been turned on its ear and retold in the only way it can be – as a musical. A singing chorus of floppy eared lambs narrates the action; Buffalo Bill gleefully dances a hoedown while kidnapping hapless Catherine Martin; and even Dr. Lecter, scary as ever, sings about the life he'd like to lead someday outside the prison walls.

†The production ended its eight-week limited engagement September 26, 2011; due to popular demand the production was extended and transferred to the 9th Space Theatre at PS 122 on October 25, 2011 (with an official opening on November 15, 2011) for an open-ended run.

Jenn Harris and the Company of SILENCE! The Musical *(photo by Carol Rosegg)*

Voca People

Westside Theatre-Upstairs†; First Preview: June 23, 2011; Opening Night: July 12, 2011; Closed September 2, 2012; 16 previews, 409 performances

Created and directed by Lior Kalfo; Music Director and Arrangements, Shai Fishman; Produced by Doron Lida, Revital Vilnai-Kalfo, Leeorna Solomons, and Eva Price; Musical Staging, Naomi Perlov; Lighting, Roy Milo; Sound, Naor Ben Meir; Costumes, Hana Yefet; PSM, Andrew J. White; ASM, Naomi Anhorn; Production Manager, Joshua Scherr; Associate Production Manager, Adrian White; Casting, Joy Dewing, Clemmons/Dewing Casting; General Management, Maximum Entertainment (Avram Freedberg, Mary Beth Dale, Eva Price, Holly Sutton, Taylor James); Company Manager, Holly Sutton; Assistant Director, Tom Shwartzberg; Assistant Musical Director, Karen Dryer; Creative Consultant, Lee Overtree; Voca People Marcom Manager, Ornit Egosi; International Production Manager, Ronen Sharon; Sound Engineer, Kim Fuhr-Carbone; Master Electrician, John Anselmo; U.S. Associate Sound Design, Matt Kraus; Rehearsal Director, Naomi Perlov; Production Vocal Supervisor, Liz Caplan Vocal Studios; Comic Advisors, Ino Ben David and Boaz Ben David; Makeup, Rinat Alony, Sigal Kedem; Prop Design, Nitzan Raphali; Marketing, Leanne Schanzer Promotions; Advertising/Digital, aka; Press, Keith Sherman and Associates, Scott Klein, Brett Olberman, Bill Coyle, Logan Metzler

CAST Bari-Tone **Ryan Alexander**[1]; Captain Beat-On **Mercer Boffey**[2]; Alta **Laura Dadap**[3]; Mezzo **Emily Drennan**; Scratcher **Tiago Grade**, Soprana **Chelsey Keding**; Tubas **Jermaine Miles**[4]; Tenoro **Jonathan Shew**[5]; Swings **Christine Paterson, Gavriel Savit**[6]

*Succeeded by: 1. Jacob Schniedier 2. Michael Feigenbaum 3. Adi Kozlovsky or Katie Bland 4. Christopher David Lukos 5. Nick Anastasia, Omer Shaish 6. Bryant Vance,

U.S. premiere of a theatrical event combining comedy, a ccapella singing, and beat box entertainment presented without intermission.

SYNOPSIS The *Voca People* have landed! Direct from the far side of the sun to the wild side of musical comedy, this innovative, international, and intergalactic musical sensation features over seventy a cappella and beat box versions of the popular songs performed by eight snow-white ruby-lipped aliens with perfect harmony. No instruments, no sound effects – just eight incredible talents breathing life into the greatest music on earth.

†The production closed at the Westside Theatre January 8, 2012 and transferred to New World Stages – Stage 2 February 16, 2012.

A scene from Voca People *(photo by (photo by Leon Sokoletski)*

Brownsville Bred

59E59 Theater B; First Preview: July 14, 2011; Opening Night: July 17, 2011; Closed July 31, 2011; 4 previews, 12 performances

Written by Elaine Del Valle; Produced by Pamela Moller Kareman, The Schoolhouse Theater, and Theatre 808 (Simon W. MacLean and Carey Macaleer, Producers); Director, Pamela Moller Kareman; Sets, Jason Bolen; Lighting, David Pentz; Sound, Matt Stine; PSM, Lionel A. Christian; Production Manager/ Producer, Quinn Cassavale; Additional Sponsorship, Al Eskanazy Productions, Urban Latino Media, and Fania Records; Press, Karen Greco

Performed by **Elaine Del Valle**

Off-Broadway premiere of a new play presented without intermission. Developed at Wynn Handman Studios and Nuyorican Poets Café and originally produced at The Schoolhouse Theatre in Croton Falls, New York in October 2010.

SYNOPSIS *Brownsville Bred* is the spirited tale of a young Nuyorican girl growing up in the 1980s in one of the most dangerous neighborhoods in NYC. Elaine Del Valle leads the audience on a hilarious and harrowing journey through poverty, crime and drug addiction, emerging through hope, family and a good dose of salsa. Beginning at the Langston Hughes Projects and chronicling her journey out of Brownsville, Del Valle's story is at once frightening, exhilarating and ultimately triumphant.

Elaine Del Valle in Brownsville Bred *(photo by Ron Marotta)*

A Strange and Separate People

Studio Theatre on Theatre Row; First Preview: July 14, 2011; Opening Night: July 19, 2011; Closed July 30, 2011

Written by Jon Marans; Produced by Stacy Shane/ManUnderdog Productions; Executive Producer, Daryl Roth; Director, Jeff Calhoun; Sets and Costumes, Clint Ramos; Lighting, Ryan O'Gara; Sound, Jill BC DuBoff; General Management, Daryl Roth Theatricals/Adam Hess; PSM, Julie DeRossi; Production Manager, Kirk Extrell; Company Manager, Kyle Provost; Graphic Design, Adrian Sie; Casting, Stephanie Klapper; ASM, Aaron Elgart; Press, Kevin P. McAnarney

CAST Phyllis Berman **Tricia Paoluccio**; Jay Berman **Jonathan Hammond**; Stuart Weinstein **Noah Weisberg**

SETTING Phyllis and Jay's Upper West Side apartment and other locations in New York City; the present. Off-Broadway premiere of a play presented without intermission. World premiere at Penguin Repertory Theatre in Stony Point, New York (Joe Brancato, Artistic Director; Andrew M. Horn, Executive Director) October 6, 2005.

SYNOPSIS In *A Strange and Separate People*, Orthodox couple Jay and Phyllis have managed to find a precarious equilibrium in their complicated personal and religious lives. That delicate balance is severely tested when Stuart, a handsome, cocky, charismatic, and newly Orthodox gay doctor invades their lives. The three intelligent, opinionated people, who have a deep love of religion, learning, and questioning authority, ferociously clash in a contemporary story of betrayal and new beginnings.

Noah Weisberg and Jonathan Hammond in A Strange and Separate People *(photo by Michael Portantiere)*

The Parting Glass

Barrow Street Theatre; Opening Night: July 20, 2011; Closed July 31, 2011; 12 performances

Written by Dermot Bolger; Produced by axis: Ballymun as part of Culture Ireland's "Imagine Ireland" year-long celebration; Producer, Niamh Ni Chonchubhair; Director, Mark O'Brien; Set, Robert Ballagh; Costumes, Marie Tierney; Lighting, Conleth White

CAST Eoin **Ray Yeates**

SETTING Dublin Airport, 2010. Off-Broadway premiere of a solo performance play presented without intermission. World premiere at axis: Ballymun (Dublin, Ireland) June 1-11, 2010. Previously played Off-Off Broadway at PS 122 as part of the 2010 undergroundzero Festival July 21-25, 2010.

SYNOPSIS On a magical night in the Dublin airport, Eoin waits with a headful of memories, and the hopes and dreams of an Irish emigrant trying to make sense of his journey home. Set on the night Thierry Henry's left hand dashed Ireland's

World Cup dreams, *The Parting Glass* is about the return of a man to the land of his youth, to witness the Celtic Tiger turn to ashes, to say goodbye to his past, and find hope in his future. *The Parting Glass* is a universal story of friendship, family and fatherhood. Losing was never this much fun.

Ray Yeates in The Parting Glass *(photo by Tom Lawlor)*

The Patsy and Jonas

Duke on 42nd Street; First Preview: July 15, 2011; Opening Night: July 24, 2011; Closed August 13, 2011

The Patsy written by Barry Conners; *Jonas* written by David Greenspan; Produced by Transport Group (Jack Cummings III, Artistic Director; Lori Fineman, Executive Director); Director, Jack Cummings III; Sets and Costumes, Dane Laffery; Lighting, Mark Barton; Sound, Michael Rasbury; Dramaturgy, Kristina Corcoran Williams; Stage Manager, Theresa Flanagan; Production Manager, Charles Hubbard; Company Manager, Wendy Patten; Associate Set Design, Scott Tedmon-Jones; Assistant Design: Max Krembs (sound), Jessica Emerson (set); Production Assistant, Julia Berman; Graphic Designer, Christiaan Rule; Artwork, Drew Demavich; Assistant to the Artistic Director, Joshua W. Kelley; Arts Administration/Marketing Intern, Lianne DiFabbio; Press, Richard Kornberg and Associates, Don Summa

Performed by **David Greenspan**

Revival (*The Patsy*) of a six-character play presented as a solo-performance piece presented without intermission; World premiere (*Jonas*) of a monologue presented as a double bill with *The Patsy* on selected performances with an intermission. *The Patsy* was originally presented at the Booth Theatre December 22, 1925–July 1926, playing 245 performances.

SYNOPSIS David Greenspan playfully resurrects the 1925 Cinderella story of a girl who is a little less beautiful and a little less loved and her fractious, gossipy family. Filled with familial intrigue, marital sparring, lovers in pursuit, country club scandals and labors of the heart, *The Patsy* explores one family's aspirations of wealth, status, and love in pre-depression America through one astonishing and virtuosic performer. *Jonas*, a one-act monologue written and performed by Greenspan, is a darkly funny and mercurial exploration of doppelgangers past and present and lives real and imagined.

David Greenspan in The Patsy (photo by Carol Rosegg)

Alma Cuervo and Danny Aielo in The Shoemaker (photo by Ben Hider)

The Shoemaker

Acorn Theatre on Theatre Row; First Preview: July 14, 2011; Opening Night: July 24, 2011; Closed August 14, 2011; 11 previews, 16 performances

Written by Susan Charlotte; Producers, Danny Aiello and Susan Charlotte; Co-Producers, Louis Baldonieri and Mary Davis; Produced by Cause Celebrè; Director, Antony Marsellis; Set, Ray Klausen; Costumes, Theresa Squire; Lighting/Sound, Bernie Dove; Wardrobe, David Toser; PSM, Anita Ross; Stage Manager, C. Renee Alexander; Marketing, Tracey Miller & Associates; Assistant to the Producer, Brendan Hill; Press, Springer Associates

CAST Guiseppe **Danny Aiello**; Hilary **Alma Cuervo**; Louise **Lucy DeVito**; Offstage Voices **Michael Twaine**

SETTING Hell's Kitchen, New York. World premiere of a new play presented in two acts. A one-act version of the show was produced in 2001. (This production was accidentally listed in *Theatre World* Vol. 67 as opening in 2010. The editors regret this error).

SYNOPSIS *The Shoemaker* is a compelling drama that focuses on a shoemaker, an Italian Jew, on a devastating day that has become a turning point in American history. As each hour passes he confronts yet another part of his past, present and an uncertain future.

The Yellow Brick Road

Lucille Lortel Theatre; First Preview: July 19, 2011; Opening Night: July 27, 2011; Closed August 19, 2011; 9 previews, 39 performances

Book by Mando Alvarado and Tommy Newman, lyrics and music by Jaime Lozano and Tommy Newman; Inspired by *The Wonderful Wizard of Oz* by L. Frank Baum; Produced by Theatreworks USA (Barbara Pasternack, Artistic Director; Ken Arthur, Producing Director) by special arrangement with Lucille Lortel Foundation; Director, Devanand Janki; Choreography, Devanand Janki and Robert Tatad; Set, Roger Hanna; Costumes, Sydney Maresca; Lighting, Jeff Croiter; Sound, Carl Casella; Musical Arrangements, Jaime Lozano; Music Direction/Additional Arrangements, Zachary Dietz; Orchestrations, Salomon Lerner and Jaime Lozano; Puppet Design and Supervisor/Prop Supervisor, Lake Simons; PSM, Byron F. Abens; Associate Lighting, Cory Pattak; Assistant to Lighting Designer, Andrew Dorman; Production Manager, Bob Daley; Production Assistant, Wells Thorne; Carpenter, Scott Girshek; Production/Master Electrician, Sheila Donovan; Puppet Consultant, Eric Wright; Props, Josh Yocum; Wardrobe Amy Elizabeth Bravo; Follow Spot, Shane Arthur; Press, The Publicity Office, Jeremy Shaffer

CAST Mother/Carnival Gloria/Monkey/Wizard **Lexi Rhoades**; Dora **Virginia Cavaliere**; Uncle Chelo/Pico/Scarecrow **Ryan Duncan**; Uncle Chaparro/Chico/Frank/Mountain Lion **Cedric Leiba Jr.**; Tino/Rico/Bob/Iron Chef **Frank Viveros**; La Curandera/LaBruja/Bouncer **Natalie Toro**

UNDERSTUDIES Joshua Cruz (Scarecrow/Iron Chef/Mountain Lion), Veronica Reyes (Wizard/Dora/La Bruja)

MUSICAL NUMBERS Y Todo Que Estar Bien (Everything Has to Be Perfect); Way Out There; You Were Born in the Twilight; Vamos a Bailar y Cantar! (Festival!); El Camino Amarillo (The Yellow Brick Road); En Mi Cabeza (In My Head); It's in the Pot; A Pint-Sized Lion; Powerless; Los Espejos (The Mirrors); I've Got What You Need; Powerless (reprise); The Gifts; Way Out There (reprise); Finale

World premiere of a new musical for young audiences presented without intermission.

SYNOPSIS *The Yellow Brick Road* is a salsa and merengue-infused musical inspired by *The Wizard of Oz*. In Chicago, Dora's mother and father are working very hard to prepare an exciting quinceanera for her. But Doris feels caught between the expectations of her heritage and her desire to be like any other American teenager, and doesn't understand why the tradition is so important to her family. With a little help from a mysterious woman and her enchanted gift, Dora is swept up into a grand tornado that drops her (and her little chiuahua, too) in a magical world where she must slip on the ruby zapatillas and take a journey of self-discovery down the yellow brick road.

Ryan Duncan, Virginia Cavaliere, Cedric Leiba Jr., and Frank Viveros in The Yellow Brick Road *(photo by Jeremy Daniel)*

A Jew Grows in Brooklyn

Queens Theatre; Opening Night: July 28, 2011; Closed August 21, 2011; 17 performances

Written by Jake Ehrenreich; Produced by Queens Theatre in the Park in association with GFour Productions; Director, Jon Huberth; Current Set Design, Luke Hadsall; Original Set Design, Joseph Egan; Music Director, Katya Stanislavskaya; Original Music Direction, Eylsa Sunshine; Lighting, Anjeanette Stokes; Musical Consultant, Larry Cohen; Creative Consultant, Lisa Ehrenreich; Press, Michelle Tabnick, Sydney Pratt

Performed by **Jake Ehrenreich**; Musicians **Katya Stanislavskaya** or **Larry Cohen** (Keyboards/Vocals), **Jon Hurley** (Guitar/Bass/ Vocals), **Jeff Bruce** (Drums/Vocals)

Return engagement of an autobiographical solo performance show with live music presented without intermission. For synopsis and previous production history, please see second listing on page 182 in this section.

Jake Ehrenreich in A Jew Grows in Brooklyn *(photo by Carol Rosegg)*

Million Dollar Quartet

New World Stages – Stage 4; First Preview: n/a; Opening Night: July 28, 2011; Closed June 24, 2012; 412 performances

Book by Colin Escott & Floyd Mutrux; Original concept and direction by Floyd Mutrux; Inspired by Elvis Presley, Johnny Cash, Jerry Lee Lewis, and Carl Perkins; Produced by Relevant Theatricals, John Cossette Productions, American Pop Anthology, Broadway Across America, and James L. Nederlander; Director, Eric Schaeffer; Musical Arrangements/Supervisor, Chuck Mead; Set, Derek McLane; Costumes, Jane Greenwood; Lighting, Howell Binkley; Sound, Kai Harada; Hair & Wigs, Tom Watson; Associate Music Supervisor, August Eriksmoen; Casting, Telsey + Company; Marketing, Type A Marketing; PSM, Robert Witherow; Production Manager, Juniper Street Productions; General Management, Alan Wasser, Allan Williams, Lane Marsh; Stage Manager, Carolyn Kelson; Company Manager, Mark Barna; Assistant Director, David Ruttura; U.K. Consulting Producers, Joseph Smith, Michael McCabe; Japan Consulting Producer, TBS Services Inc.; Associate Design: Shoko Kambara (set), Moria Clinton (costumes), Ryan O'Gara (lighting), Jana Hoglund (sound); Assistant Lighting, Michael Rummage; Carpenter, Joseph DeLuise; Electricians, Thomas Dyer, John DeLustro; Sound Engineer, Reece Nunez; Deck Stage Hand, Alexandra Paull; Moving Light Programmer, David Arch; Wardrobe/Hair Supervisor, Megan Moore; Music Contractor, Michael Keller; Additional Arrangements, Levi Kreis; Advertising/Website/Online Marketing, The Marketing Division; Press, Boneau/Bryan-Brown, Adrian Bryan-Brown, Aaron Meier, Amy Kass, Joe Perrotta

CAST Carl Perkins **Robert Britton Lyons**; Johnny Cash **Lance Guest**; Jerry Lee Lewis **David Abeles**[*1]; Elvis Presley **Eddie Clendening**; Jay Perkins (Bass Player) **Corey Kaiser**; Fluke (Drummer) **Don Peretz**; Sam Phillips **James Moye**[*2]; Dyanne **Victoria Matlock**

UNDERSTUDIES Christopher Ryan Grant[*3] (Johnny, Sam), Erik Hayden (Elvis, Carl), Dan Mills (Carl), Randy Redd[*4] (Jerry Lee), Megan Reinking (Dyanne), Robert Shaw (Elvis)

*Succeeded by: 1. Eric Stang (10/17/11), Randy Redd (5/14/12) 2. Curt Bouril (5/16/12) 3. Johnny Kinnaird 4. Luke Holloway

SETTING Time: December 4, 1956. Place: Sun Records, Memphis, Tennessee. Transfer of the Broadway musical presented without intermission. The production originally played the Nederlander Theatre April 11, 2010–June 12, 2011 playing 489 performances (for more information, including musical numbers, please see page 103 in this volume).

SYNOPSIS Inspired by true events, *Million Dollar Quartet* captures the infectious spirit, freewheeling excitement and thrilling sounds of a singular moment when four of the music industry's most extraordinary talents, all in their creative prime, came together for one of the most memorable nights in music history.

Eric Stang, Victoria Matlock, Eddie Clendening, James Moye, Lance Guest, and Robert Britton Lyons in Million Dollar Quartet *(photo by Joan Marcus)*

Soldier's Song

Poet's Den Theater; First Preview: July 21, 2011; Opening Night: July 28, 2011; Closed August 27, 2011; 5 previews, 15 performances

Book, music, and lyrics by Jim Cohen and Joanne Lee Drexler Cohen; Produced by Raphael Benavides Productions; Director, Angelica Page (Torn); Music Director, Natalie Tenenbaum; Sets, Daniel Allen Nelson; Costume Consultant, Daniel James Cole; Lighting, Jane Masterson; Stage Manager, Haydee Leyva; ASM, Sylvie Preston; Technical Supervisor, Mark Benavides; Assistant Director, Gina Bonati; Marketing, HHC Marketing; Press, James Sliman

CAST José **J.W. Cortes**; Erica **Christiana Little**; Ashley **Melody Allegra Berger**; Raúl **Noah Chase**

UNDERSTUDIES Jeffrey Hernández (José, Raúl), Cari Jones (Erica, Ashley)

MUSICIANS Natalie Tenenbaum (Conductor), Jeffrey Hernández, Jerry Nelson Soto

MUSICAL NUMBERS Road Back Home; Mi Corazon; Staycation; Dreaming of You; Good Man/Good Horse; Friendship Anthem; You're My Love; Blackberry Blues; She's Just Lunch; Stay Awhile; As Long As It Takes; Soldier's Song; Courage Walks With a Soldier; A Really Good Bet; A New Song; As Long As It Takes (reprise); Anniversary Song Bouquet

SETTING San Juan, Iraq, and South Carolina; the last decade. World premiere of a new musical presented in two acts.

SYNOPSIS In *Soldier's Song*, the poor but handsome and talented Jose is an aspiring singer/songwriter performing at a nightclub in Puerto Rico when he meets the elegant and wealthy Erica. They fall in love and continue an incredible four-month love affair until Jose is sent off to serve in Iraq. Before he goes, Erica promises that she will wait for him as long as it takes.

J.W. Cortes in Soldier's Song

The Pretty Trap

Acorn Theatre on Theatre Row; First Preview: August 2, 2011; Opening Night: August 3, 2011; Closed August 21, 2011; 2 previews, 15 performances

Written by Tennessee Williams; Produced by Cause Célèbre (Susan Charlotte, Artistic Director) in association with Mary J. Davis; Director, Antony Marsellis; Set, Ray Klausen; Lighting and Sound, Bernie Dove; Costumes, David Toser; PSM, Anita Ross; Stage Manager, C. Renee Alexander; Assistant to the Producer, Brendan Hill; Associate Lighting, John Burkland; Assistant Design: Leah Farrelly (set), Rachel O'Conner (sound); Properties Master, Ricola Wille; Master Electrician, Dennis Grimaldi; Production Consultant, Matthew Anastasio; Wardrobe, Courtney Irizarry; Graphic Design, Ken Krug; Accounting, Ira Schall; Legal, M. Graham Coleman, Esq.; Press, Springer Associates, Joe Trentacosta

CAST Amanda Wingfield **Katharine Houghton**; Tom Wingfield **Robert Eli**; Laura Wingfield **Nisi Sturgis**; Gentleman Caller **Loren Dunn**

New York premiere of a one-act version of a classic play presented without intermission. Presented in repertory with *The Shoemaker*. Cause Célèbre previously presented a reading of the play featuring Kathleen Turner in 2005.

SYNOPSIS Before Tennessee Williams wrote his masterpiece, *The Glass Menagerie*, he wrote a one-act version called *The Pretty Trap*. In celebration of the centennial year of Tennessee Williams, Cause Célèbre presents a fully-staged production of the long-buried piece about a mother awaiting the arrival of her daughter's gentleman caller. Ms. Houghton's aunt, Katharine Hepburn, famously played "Amanda" in a 1973 television version of the *The Glass Menagerie*.

Katharine Houghton, Nisi Sturgis, Robert Eli, and Loren Dun in The Pretty Trap *(photo by Ben Hider)*

Traces

Union Square Theatre; First Preview: July 29, 2011; Opening Night: August 8, 2011; Closed September 2, 2012

Created, devised, and presented by Les 7 Doigts de la Main/7 Fingers (Montreal, Canada); Produced by Fox Theatricals (Kristin Caskey and Mike Isaacson), Tom Gabbard, Amanda DuBois, The Denver Center for the Performing Arts, Nassib El-Husseini, and Tom Lightburn; Direction/Choreography, Shana Carroll and Gypsy Snider; Acrobatic Design, Sébastien Soldevila; Lighting, Nol van Genuchten; Costumes, Manon Desmarais; Set & Props Original Design, Flavia Hevia; Set and Props Adaptation/Music & Soundscape/Video, Les 7 Doights de la Main; Prop Adaptation, Bruno Tassé; General Management, DR Theatrical Management, Seth A. Goldstein, Adam Hess; N.Y. Production Management, Production Core; Stage Manager, Valérie Ménard; Production Supervisor, James E. Cleveland; Head Coach (Acrobatics), Jerôme Le Baut; Aerial Strap, Isabelle Chassé; Hand

Balancing, Samuel Tétreault; Skateboards, Yann Fily-Paré; Single Wheel, Ethan Law; Piano, Sophie Houle; Fox Theatricals Associate Producer, Megan Larche; Associate General Manager, Danielle Karliner; Master Electrician, John Anselmo Jr.; Deck Carpenter, Evan Hernandez; Audio Engineer, Kim Carter; Wardrobe Supervisor, Karli Brae; For Les 7 Doigts de la Main: Nassib El-Husseini (CEO), Shana Carroll, Isabelle Chassé, Patrick Léonard, Sébastien Soldevila, Gypsy Snider, Samuel Tétreault (Founding Members/Artistic Directors), Tina Diab (Touring/Development Director), Richard Gagnon (Administrative Director), Céline Boucher (Accounting Director), Luc Paradis (Production Director), Yves Touchette (Technical Director), Sophie Picard (Operations Director), Marion Bellin (Communication), Anna Cassel (Touring), Vincent Houle (Production); Advertising and Marketing, aka; Press, The Hartman Group, Michael Hartman, Matt Ross, Nicole Capatasto

CAST **Mason Ames**, **Valérie Benoît-Charbonneau**, **Mathieu Cloutier**, **Bradley Henderson**, **Philippe Normand-Jenny**, **Xia Zhengqi**, **Florian Zumkehr**; Standbys **Lucas Boutin**, **Francisco Cruz**, **Gisle Henriet**, **Geneviève Morin**, **Tarek Rammo**, **Philip Rosenberg**

New York premiere of a theatrical circus/street performance piece with acrobatics, dance, physical comedy, music, and multimedia presented without intermission.

SYNOPSIS If the world ended tomorrow, what would you leave behind? In *Traces*, the human body is pushed to its limits as a group of friends leave their mark in a run-down warehouse through acrobatics, music, and dance. Fusing the traditions of circus with the energy of street performance, *Traces* is an explosive display of raw emotion and physicality in an intimate urban setting. When it counts, will you leave it all on the stage?

Les 7 Doights de la Main in Traces *(photo by Michael Menke)*

Henry V

Shabazz Center; First Preview: August 3, 2011; Opening Night: August 10, 2011; Closed September 4, 2011; 4 previews, 21 performances

Written by William Shakespeare; Produced by the Classical Theatre of Harlem (Ty Jones, Producing Director); Director, Jenny Bennett; Set, Anka Lupes; Lighting, Colin D. Young; Composition and Sound, Patricia Ju; Costumes, Rachel Dozier-Ezell; PSM, Katrina Lynn Olson; ASM, Meg Friedman; Sound Board Operator, Melissa Hamm; Light Board Operator, Anthony Lalor; Wardrobe, Stephanie Wilson; Deck Crew, Aaron Austin, Derrick Harris, Jamie Chung; Producing Assistant, Anthony Lalor; Future Classics Administrator, Otis Ramsey Zoe; Marketing, Art Meets Commerce; Press, Alessandro Chillé

CAST Henry V **Ty Jones**; Alice, Canterbury, Nym, Gower, Le Fer **Carine Montbertrand**; Montjoy **Chantal Nchako**; Princess Katherine, York **Fedna Jacquet**; Pistol, Lord Scroop, Burgundy **Glenn Gordon**; Dauphin, Cambridge,

Bates **Jeremy J. Tardy**; Bedford, Governor Harfleur **Kalon Hayward**; Gloucester, Orleans **Karim Sekou**; Westmoreland **Kwasi Osei**; Bardolph, Constable of France **Lelund Durond**; Duke of Exeter, Sir John Falstaff **Michael Early**; Michael Williams, Bishop of Ely, MacMorris **Paulo Quiros**; King of France, Mistress Quickly, Erpingham **Stephanie Berry**; Boy **Tremayne "Trey" Rollins**; Fluellen, Gray, Bretagne **Warren Jackson**

Revival of a classical play in a new adaptation presented without intermission. The production played additional performances at East River Park Amphitheater August 27-29.

SYNOPSIS As young King Henry V takes the throne, his dying father's advice to "busy giddy minds with foreign quarrels" ringing in his ears. His reputation as a fun-loving lad who's lived among the common folk inspires love from commoners and disregard from his enemies. CTH's explores the thoughtful, funny, and belligerent diplomacy of Henry V, and what it means for a king to bear the burdensome expectations of the crown – and the people to bear the expectations of the king – as Henry V works to win the hearts of all.

Fedna Jacquet and Ty Jones in Henry V *(photo by Ruth Sovronsky)*

HotelMotel

Gershwin Hotel; First Preview: August 4, 2011; Opening Night: August 10, 2011; Closed October 10, 2011; 6 previews, 64 performances

Two plays: *Pink Knees On Pale Skin* written and directed by Derek Ahonen, and *Animals & Plants* written and directed by Adam Rapp; Produced by The Amoralists (James Kautz, Artistic Director & Co-Founder; Derek Ahonen, Associate Artistic Director & Co-Founder; Matthew Pilieci, Acting Company Director & Co-Founder) and The Gershwin Hotel; Sets, Alfred Schatz; Costumes, Jessica Pabst; Lighting, Keith Parham; Sound/Composer/Pianist, Phil Carluzzo; Associate Sound, Eric Shimelonis; Props, Master, Judy Merrick; Special Effects, Jeremy Chernick; Assistant Costumes, Katie Hartsoe; Artwork, Danika Novogorodoff; Producer, Shoshona Currier; Associate Producer, Kelcie Beene; PSM, Jaimie Van Dyke; Dramaturg, Michael Swift; Director of Production, Sean Bauer; General Manager, Anthony Francavilla; Literary Manager, David Carter; Marketing, Seena Hodges; Development, Caroline Gibbs; Assistant Director, Gretchen Hollis; Dramaturg, Michael Swift; Assistant Directors, Gretchen Hollis, Paul Terkel; Production Assistants, Sea McHale, Golda Kelly Ryan, Rebecca Fong, Hunter Macnare; Press, David Gibbs/DARR Publicity

CAST *Pink Knees On Pale Skin*: Dr. Sarah Bauer **Sarah Lemp**; Leroy **Jordan Tisdale**; Robert Wyatt **James Kautz**; Caroline Wyatt **Vanessa Vache**; Theodore Williams **Byron Anthony**; Allison Williams **Anna Stromberg**;

Norman **Nick Lawson**; *Animals and Plants*: Dantly **William Apps**; Burris **Matthew Pileci**; Cassandra **Katie Broad**; Buck **Brian Mendes**

UNDERSTUDIES Paul Terkel (Norman, Theodore), Selene Beretta (Dr. Sarah Bauer), Sarah Roy (Allison)

SETTING *Pink Knees On Pale Skin*: The back room of the Gershwin Hotel. *Animals and Plants*: A motel room in Boone, North Carolina. World premiere (*Pink Knees On Pale Skin*) and New York premiere (*Animals and Plants*) of two one-act plays presented with one intermission.

SYNOPSIS Set at the Gershwin hotel with only 20 audience members at each performance, *HotelMotel* is The Amoralists' most penetrating theatrical experience yet. In *Pink Knees On Pale Skin* the Wyatt and the Williams families are meeting with Dr. Sarah, aka the Orgy Counselor, to participate in an organized orgy held in a discrete hotel room. But on this particular night, Dr. Sarah has designed a self destructive twist, guaranteed to unleash chaos upon all involved. In *Animals and Plants*, two drug runners are snowbound in a cheap motel room at the foot of the Appalachian Mountains. As they wait for their connection, they are visited by a mysterious young woman who may or may not figure into their future. While the snow mounts and the night slips into darkness, the money disappears, a long-time friendship is tested, and all three of their lives will be changed forever.

Sarah Lemp, Nick Lawson, and Jordan Tisdale in Pink Knees on Pale Skin, *one of the two plays in* HotelMotel *(photo by Monica Simoes)*

My Mother's Italian, My Father's Jewish, and I'm Still in Therapy

Midtown Theater at HA!; First Preview: August 5, 2011; Opening Night: August 10, 2011; Closed August 31, 2011; 4 previews, 18 performances

Written by Steve Solomon; Produced by Off Broadway Booking, Steve Solomon, and Abby Koffler, in association with Midtown Theater; Director, Andy Rogow; Booking Manager, Orin Wolf; Press, Springer Associates, Joe Trentacosta

Performed by **Steve Solomon**

New York premiere of a sequel solo performance play presented in two acts. Mr. Solomon's original show *My Mother's Italian, My Father's Jewish, and I'm in Therapy* opened at the Little Shubert Theatre December 8, 2006, tranferred to the Westside Theatre (Downstairs) May 4, 2007, and closed August 24, 2008, playing 684 performances (see *Theatre World* Vol. 63, page 155).

SYNOPSIS The comedy chaos continues in this critically acclaimed sequel to Steve Solomon's original smash hit. *Still in Therapy* takes us back to Steve's wacky childhood growing up with his twin sister "The Smoker." The audience follows along in this wonderfully funny journey about growing up, mixed marriages, ex-wives, dogs, cats, dieting and dozens of other side-splitting situations.

Steve Solomon in My Mother's Italian, My Father's Jewish, and I'm Still in Therapy *(photo courtesy of William Morris Endeavor)*

Rent

New World Stages – Stage 1; First Preview: July 14, 2011; Opening Night: August 11, 2011; Closed ; 32 previews, 333 performances as of May 31, 2012

Book, music, and lyrics by Jonathan Larson; Produced by Jeffrey Seller, Kevin McCollum, Allan S. Gordon; Director, Michael Greif; Choreography, Larry Keigwin; Music Supervision and Additional Arrangements, Tim Weil; Set, Mark Wendlend; Costumes, Angela Wendt; Lighting, Kevin Adams; Sound, Brian Ronan; Projections, Peter Nigrini; Original Concept/Additional Lyrics, Billy Aronson; Dramaturg, Lynn M. Thomson; Music Arrangements, Steve Skinner; Musical Director, Will Van Dyke; Casting, Telsey + Company; Marketing, Allied Live; General Manager, John S. Corker; Technical Supervisor, Brian Lynch; PSM, Monica A. Cuoco; Stage Manager, Stephen Ravet; Production Supervisor, Brian Lynch; Company Manager, Andrew Jones; Wigs and Makeup, Barry Lee Moe; Assistant Director, Billy Porter; Associate Choreographer, Nicole Wolcott; Dance Captain, Marcus Paul James; Associate Design: Lisa Zinni (costumes), Jeremy Cunningham (lighting), Dan Scully (projections); Scene Design Assistants, Brett J. Banakis, Jonathan Collins, Rachel Nemec; Assistant Desgin: Abigail Hahn (costumes), Michael Berger (lighting), Cody Spencer (sound); Music Coordinator, Michael Keller; Music Copying, Kaye-Houston Music; Projection Programmer, Ben Keightley; Projection Editor, Dan Vatsky; Moving Light Programmer, Jay Penfield; Production Prop Supervisor, George Wagner; Properties, John Bryant; Production Electrician, Tom Dyer; Production Projections, Chris Herman; Carpenter, Michael Demyan; Head Electrician, Daniel O'Brien; Sound Engineer, Louis Igoe; Assistant Sound, Nate Putnam, Jessica Weeks; Wardrobe Supervisor, Desiree Eckert; Wardrobe Assistant, Karle J. Meyers; Director Assistants, Andy Senor Jr., Adam Kantor; Production Assistants, Katherine Young, Sarah Fujiwara; Advertising, SpotCo; Website, Pit Bull Interactive; Press, Richard Kornberg and Associates, Don Summa

CAST Mark Cohen **Adam Chanler-Berat**[1]; Roger Davis **Matt Shingledecker**[2]; Mrs. Cohen, Coat Vendor and others **Morgan Weed**; Tom Collins **Nicholas Christopher**[3]; Benjamin Coffin III **Ephraim Sykes**[4]; Joanne Jefferson **Corbin Reid**; The Man, Mr. Grey and others **Ben Thompson**[5]; Angel Dumott Schunard **MJ Rodriguez**; Mimi Marquez **Arianda Fernandez**; Maureen Johnson **Annaleigh Ashford**[6]; Mr. Jefferson, Paul and others **Marcus Paul James**; Mrs. Jefferson, Homeless Woman and others **Tamika Sonja Lawrence**[7]; Steve, Gordon, Waiter and others **Michael Wartella**[8]; Alexi Darling, Mrs. Davis and others **Margot Bingham**; Swings **Xavier Cano**, **Sean Michael Murray**, **Genny Lis Padilla**

UNDERSTUDIES Sean Michael Murray (Mark, Roger, Benjamin), Michael Wartella (Mark, Angel), Ben Thompson[5] (Roger, Tom Collins), Marcus Paul James (Tom Collins, Benjamin), Xavier Cano (Benjamin, Angel), Margot Bingham (Joanne, Mimi), Tamika Sonja Lawrence[7] (Joanne), Genny Lis Padilla (Maureen), Morgan Weed (Maureen)

*Succeeded by: 1. Josh Grisetti (1/20/12) 2. Justin Johnson (1/20/12) 3. Brandon Victor Dixon (12/1/11) 4. Rashad Naylor (1/20/12) 5. Aaron LaVigne (1/7/12) 6. Emma Hunton (1/13/12) 7. Shaleah Adkisson (3/9/12) 8. Taylor Trensch (5/28/12)

THE BAND Will Van Dyke (Conductor/Keyboards), Michael Gacetta (Associate Conductor/Keyboards), Mark Vanderpoel (Bass), Alec Berlin (Guitar), Carter McLean (Drums)

MUSICAL NUMBERS Tune Up/Voice Mail #1; Rent; You Okay Honey?; One Song Glory; Light My Candle; Voice Mail #2; Today 4 U; You'll See; Tango Maureen; Life Support; Out Tonight; Another Day; Will I?; On the Street; Santa Fe; I'll Cover You; We're Okay; Christmas Bells; Over the Moon; La Vie Boheme/I Should Tell You; Seasons of Love; Happy New Year; Voice Mail #3; Voice Mail #4; Without You; Voice Mail #5; Contact; I'll Cover You (reprise); Halloween; Goodbye, Love; What You Own; Voice Mail #6; Your Eyes/Finale

SETTING New York City, East Village; mid 1990s. Revival of a musical presented in two acts. Originally workshopped in 1994 at New York Theatre Workshop, the show had its world premiere at NYTW January 26, 1996. The show production transferred to Broadway to the Nederlander Theatre April 29, 1996, running until September 7, 2008 playing 5,124 performances (see *Theatre World* Vol. 52, pages 58 & 97). Tragedy occurred when the 35 year old author, Jonathan Larson, died of an aortic aneurysm following the final dress rehearsal of his show January 24, 1996. In place of the first scheduled preview on January 25, the company sang the score for Mr. Larson's friends and family at the theatre.

SYNOPSIS *Rent* returns in a new production directed by Michael Greif who directed the show's original Off-Broadway and Broadway productions. *Rent* is about being young and learning to survive in NYC, falling in love, finding your voice, and living for today. *Rent* made a lasting mark on Broadway with songs that rock and a story that resonates.

MJ Rodriguez, Matt Shingledecker, Nicholas Christopher, and Adam Chanler-Berat in Rent *(photo by Joan Marcus)*

Herman Kline's Midlife Crisis

Beckett Theatre on Theatre Row; First Preview: August 7, 2011; Opening Night: August 14, 2011; Closed September 3, 2011; 6 previews, 18 performances

Written by Josh Koenigsberg; Produced by At Play Productions, Kelcie Beene, and Anthony Francavilla; Director, Sherri Eden Barber; Set, Anne Allen Goelz; Costumes, Whitney Locher; Lighting, Jeffrey Small; Sound, Zane Birdwell; Assistant Lighting, Christopher Staebell; PSM, Carly Levin; Stage Manager, Catherine Lynch; Press, Sam Rudy Media Relations

CAST Dr. Herman Kline **Adam LeFevre**; Liz Kline **Kathryn Kates**; Lauren Axelrod **Mary Quick**; Ernie Santos **Bobby Moreno**

SETTING Riverdale, New York; the present. U.S. premiere of a new play presented in three scenes without intermission.

SYNOPSIS Some men get a red Porsche. Some men get a new wife. Herman Kline got something different. Prominent NYC trauma doctor Herman Kline is struggling with the tedium of career and marriage. But that's all about to change when he makes a startling discovery while tending to a patient in the ER. *Herman Kline's Midlife Crisis* is a dark, bittersweet – and ultimately heartbreaking new comedy about the bizarre ways in which we deal with our own mortality.

Kathryn Kates and Adam LeFevre in Herman Kline's Midlife Crisis *(photo by Robert J. Saferstein)*

Tricks the Devil Taught Me

Minetta Lane Theatre; First Preview: July 29, 2011; Opening Night: August 18, 2011; Closed August 28, 2011; 24 previews, 13 performances

Written and directed by Tony George; Produced by Maddy Bassi, Circa 1440 Inc., and Idle Mind Ltd.; Set, Eli Kaplan-Wildmann; Costumes, Asa Benally; Lighting, Scott Davis; Sound, Walter Trarbach; Casting, Stuart Howard, Paul Hardt; PSM, Andrew Zachary Cohen; ASM, Travis Acreman; General Manager, Laura Heller; Production Manager, Shannon Case; Associate Producers, Diana Browning, Katy Graves, Mary Hill, Melissa and Santa Claire Hirsch, Deanna Hoerauf, Sealy Hutchings, Sally and Douglas Pendergras, Amy Ward, Kathy Young; Assistant Set, Katie White; Assistant Costumes, Nina Vartanian; Props, Katie White; Sound Supervisor, Dave Horowitz; Wardrobe, Asa Benally; Advertising/Marketing, Davenport Theatrical Enterprises; Press, Pete Sanders, JS2 Communications

CAST Betty **Beth Grant**; Don/Clark/Franklin **Peter Bradbury**; Jeremy/Young Don **T.J. Linnard**; Lorraine **Jodie Lynne McClintock**; Kim/Young Betty **Julie Jeseneck**; Renee **Mary Testa**; Elizabeth **Desiree Rodriguez**

SETTING A small town in West Texas; 1987-2010. World premiere of a new play presented in two acts.

SYNOPSIS Don and Betty have been married for 22 years, almost as long as they have had their son, Jeremy. But there is whispering behind closed doors, and the once invisible imperfections begin to poison the air. Right and wrong are swept up in a whirlwind of lies, hope and haunting memories. Perfume of whiskey sweetens the smell of prayer as the supporting cast reaches for their own versions of salvation. Will the faithful be saved, or have they run out of time?

Peter Bradbury and TJ Linnard in Tricks the Devil Taught Me
(photo by Carol Rosegg)

Septimus & Clarissa

Baruch Performing Arts Center; Opening Night: September 7, 2011; Closed October 8, 2011; 28 performances

Written by Ellen McLaughlin, based on *Mrs. Dalloway* by Virginia Woolf; Created and choreographed in collaboration with the ensemble; Produced by Ripe Time (Rachel Dickstein, Artistic Director; Wesley Middleton, Producing Director) and Melanie Hopkins; Direction and Development, Rachel Dickstein; Original Score, Gina Leishman; Set/Properties, Susan Zeeman Rogers; Costumes, Oana Botez-Ban; Lighting, Keith Parham; Sound, Jane Shaw; PSM, Lori Amondson; ASM, Jennifer Caster; Music Supervisor, Rinde Eckert; Voice and Dialect Coach, Ginger Eckert; Casting, Geoff Josselson; Production Supervisor, Production Core/James E. Cleveland; Production Manager, Rob Reese; Assistant Production Manager, Andrew Scott Rosenfeld; Technical Director, Kurtis Kash Rivers; Assistant Design: Amanda Clegg Lyon (lighting), Ien DeNio (sound); Assistant to Set and Props Designer, Will Barrios; Music Assistant, Danielle De Matteo; Production Assistqnt, Chris Johnson; Props Master, Rachel Schapira; Wardrobe Supervisor, Abby Barker; Master Electrician, John Anselmo Jr.; Board Programmer/Operator, Zachary Ciaburri; Graphic Design, Adrien Goulet; Press, Blake Zidell & Associates

CAST Evans, Peter Walsh (in past) and others **Craig Baldwin**; Clarissa Dalloway (in past) and others **LeeAnne Hutchison**; Sally Seton (in past) and others **Ellen McLaughlin**; Peter Walsh, Dr. Holmes, and others **Tom Nelis**; Miss Kilman, Aunt Helena, and others **Susan Pellegrino**; Septimus Warren Smith **Tommy Schrider**; Lucrezia Warren Smith, Elizabeth Dalloway **Miriam Silverman**; Richard Dalloway, Dr. Bradshaw, and others **Henry Stram**

MUSICIANS (recorded) Doug Wieselman (Clarinets), Charlie Bunham (Violin), Marika Hughes (Cello), Gina Leishman (Piano/Glass), Kenny Wollensen (Percussion)

World premiere of a new play with music presented in two acts.

SYNOPSIS Looking through the eyes of a veteran on the verge of suicide and a socialite whose past comes back to haunt her, *Septimus & Clarissa* tells a shocking and relevant story of war and its aftermath through a feast of words, images,

movement and sound. This visceral exploration of Woolf's groundbreaking novel dives deep into the tensions of post-WWI London to expose the darkness that lurks beneath the fragile surface of peace.

Henry Stram and Ellen McLaughlin in Septimus and Clarissa
(photo by Richard Finkelstein)

Cymbeline

Barrow Street Theatre; First Preview: August 27, 2011; Opening Night: September 8, 2011; Closed January 15, 2012; 10 previews, 150 performances

Written by William Shakespeare; Presented by Fiasco Theater, conceived by Jessie Austrian, Noah Brody, and Ben Steinfeld; Produced by Theatre for a New Audience (Jeffrey Horowitz, Artistic Director; Dorothy Ryan, Managing Director), Scott Morfee, Jean Doumanian, Tom Wirtshafter, The Somerled Charitable Foundation (Robert and Wendy Macdonald), Burnt Umber Productions (Judi Krupp and Bill Gerber), Christian Chadd Taylor, Marc & Lisa Biales/Ted Snowdon; Directors, Noah Brody and Ben Steinfeld; Set, Jean-Guy Lecat; Costumes, Whitney Locher; Lighting, Tim Cryan; Fabulous Trunk Design/Fabrication, Jacques Roy; Properties, Caite Hevner; PSM, Christina Lowe; Casting, Deborah Brown; Vocal & Text Consultant, Cicely Berry; Fight Director, Noah Brody; Music Director, Ben Steinfeld; Fight Consultant, J. Allen Suddeth; Production Supervisor, Production Core/James E. Cleveland; General Management, Michael Page and Amy Dalba; General Manager Theatre for a New Audience, Theresa Von Klug; ASM, Shane Schnetzler; Production Manager, Joshua Sherr; Technical Director, Kurtis Rivers; Assistant Director, Michael Perlman; Assistant Design: Pierre LeBon (set), Haley Lieberman (costumes), Lucrecia Bricendo (lighting); Master Electrician, John Anselmo Jr.; Advertising, Ann Murphy; Press, Bruce Cohen Group Ltd.

CAST Imogen **Jessie Austrian**; Posthumus/Roman Captain **Noah Brody**; Pisanio/Philario/Caius Lucius/Guiderius **Paul L. Coffey**; Cymbeline/Cloten/Cornelius **Andy Grotelueschen**; Iachimo/Arviragus **Ben Steinfeld**; Queen/Frenchman/Belaria **Emily Young**

UNDERSTUDIES Ellen Adair (Imogen Queen, Queen/Frenchman/Belaria), Patrick Mulryan (Posthumas/Roman Captain, Pisanio/Philario/Caius Lucius, Cybeline/Cloten/Cornelius, Iachimo/Arviragus)

SETTING Commercial extension of the Off-Broadway premiere of a new version of a classic play presented in two acts. The production was previously presented by Theatre for a New Audience at the New Victory Theatre January 13-31, 2011 (see *Theatre World* Vol. 67, page 235). World premiere at Access Theater Gallery September 25–October 2, 2009 (see *Theatre World* Vol. 66, page 268).

SYNOPSIS As dizzyingly eventful a drama as Shakespeare ever conceived, *Cymbeline* tells of a beautiful princess separated from her beloved, the cruel step-mother who tries to kill her, a credulous husband duped by an adversary, an exiled nobleman who kidnaps a king's sons and a Roman invasion of Britain. In this lightning-paced production, a plain white cloth becomes a sail, a bed sheet, and a toga and a "fabulous" trunk becomes a bed, a throne and a cave. The transformations are magical and playful and true to the play, deepening its themes of illusion, deception and belief.

Ben Steinfield, Emily Young, and Paul L. Coffey in Cymbeline *(photo by Gerry Goodstein)*

Harry & Eddie: The Birth of Israel

St. Luke's Theatre†; First Preview: August 25, 2011; Opening Night: September 8, 2011; Closed December 18, 2011; 6 previews, 55 performances

Written by Mark Weston; Produced by Jessimeg Productions; Director/Sound Design, Bob Spiotto; Sets and Lighting/Production Manager, Josh Iacovelli; Costumes, Lydia Gladstone; General Management, Jessimeg Productions; Associate General Manager, Julia Beardsley; Assistant General Managers, Catherine Fowles, Marie-Elena Ortiz; Production Assistants, Dustin Cross, Britt Johnson; Graphic Design, Frank Dain; Sound Engineer, Jaclyn Zolezzi; Theatre Operator, Edmund Gaynes; Co-Artistic Director, Pamela Hall; Sales, Bill Fitzgerald; Press, Susan L. Schulman

CAST Eddie Jacobson **Rick Grossman**; Bluma Jacobson **Lydia Gladstone**; Harry S. Truman **Daniel Hicks**

SETTING May 24, 1948 at a B'nai Brith function in Washington, D.C., shifting to Kansas City, and other locations from 1900 to May 1948. World premire of a new play presented without intermission. A staged reading of the show was presented at Hofstra University in conjunction with Hoftra's "Israel at 60: A Celebration" in 2008.

SYNOPSIS Eddie Jacobson, a Jewish haberdashery salesman, and Harry Truman initially bonded during World War I where the Missouri men were put in charge of a struggling army canteen. The success of that venture leads to their joining forces after the war to open a haberdashery store in Kansas City, MO. When the depression hit and their store failed, Harry went into politics and Eddie went back on the road as a traveling salesman. In 1948, as the Zionists were struggling to convince President Truman to support the United Nation's recognition of Israel, Eddie was asked to push their unlikely friendship to the breaking point.

†Transferred to Actors Temple Theatre October 12, 2012.

Dan Hicks, Rick Grossman, and Lydia Gladstone in Harry & Eddie: The Birth of Israel *(photo by Carol Rosegg)*

The Lapsburgh Layover

Ars Nova; First Preview: August 31, 2011; Opening Night: September 12, 2011; Closed September 24, 2011; 9 previews, 11 performances

Written by Justin Jain, Dave Johnson, Leah Walton, and Bradley K. Wrenn; Presented by The Berserker Residents; Produced by Ars Nova (Jason Eagan, Artistic Director, Jeremy Blocker, Managing Director); Development and Director, Oliver Butler; Set, Lisi Stoessel; Costumes, Sydney Maresca; Lighting, Brian Tovar; Sound, M.L. Dogg; Puppets, Dorothee Senechal; PSM, Donald Butchko; Stage Manager, Catherine Anne Tucker; Production Manager, Joshua Kohler; Production Assistant, Andrew Rosenfeld; Properties Manager, Eric Beauzay; Associate Design: Jacquelyn Marolt (set), John Kemp (sound); Assistant Lighting, John Wilder; Technical Director, Aneta Feld; Prop Associate, Kathryn Vega; Wardrobe Supervisor, Kathryn McGaughey; Sound Board Operator, Andy Smart; Electricians, Max Doolittle, Richard Chamblin, Matthew Reifsteck, Melissa Shippers, Joseph Wolflau; Carpenters, P.J. Landers, Kevin Rees, Andy Smart, Greg Westby; Run Crew, Rachel E. Parks; Graphics, Trevor Martin; For Ars Nova: Associate Artistic Director, Emily Shooltz; General Manager, Ann Marshall; Development, Cameron Kroll; Artisic Coordinator, Jocelyn Florence; Marketing, Claire Graves; Facilities Manager, José Reyes; House Manager, Elizabeth Irwin; Casting Consultant, David Caparelliotis; Press, Seven17 PR, Bridget Klapinski,

CAST **Justin Jain**, **Dave Johnson**, **Leah Walton**, **Bradley K. Wrenn**

Bradley K. Wrenn, Justin Jain, and Dave Johnson in The Lapsburgh Layover *(photo by Ben Arons)*

World premiere of a new play presented without intermission.

SYNOPSIS *The Lapsburgh Layover* centers on the citizens of the tiny, isolated city Lapsburgh, who have prepared a theatrical entertainment to help some American tourists pass the time while their international flight refuels. As the piece is performed, it reveals not only Lapsburgh's many charms, but also darker forces lurk just beyond the borders.

Invasion!

Flea Theater; First Preview: September 6, 2011; Opening Night: September 13, 2011; Closed October 1, 2011; 7 previews, 27 performances

Written by Jonas Hassen Khemiri, translated by Rachel Willson-Broyles; Produced by The Play Company (Kate Loewald, Founding Producer; Lauren Weigel, Executive Producer) in association with the Flea Theater (Jim Simpson, Artistic Director; Carol Ostrow, Producing Director); Director, Erica Schmidt; Set, Antje Ellerman; Costumes, Oana Botez Ban; Lighting, Mattew Richards; Sound, Bart Fasbender; PSM, Larry K. Ash; Fight Choreography, J. Steven White; Casting, Judy Henderson; Production Supervisor, Production Core, James E. Cleveland; Artistic Associate, Melissa Hardy; Production Manager, Adrian White; ASM, Kate Michael Gibson; Props Supervisor, Starlet Jacobs; Technical Director, Jack Blacketer; Master Electrician, Ben Tevelow; Production Head Audio, Graham Johnson; Assistant Production Manager, Kim Negrete; Lighting Programmer/Board Operator, Melissa Shippers; Wardrobe Supervisor, AraBella Fischer; Audio Programmer, William Neal; Production Assistant, Brian Simmons; Arabic Translator and Coach, Omar Khalifah; Marketing Consultant, Rohi Mirza Pandya; Graphic Design, Noah Scalin; Press, Sam Rudy Media Relations, Dale Heller

CAST Actor A **Andrew Ramcharan Guilarte**; Actor C **Francis Benhamou**; Actor D **Bobby Moreno**; Actor B **Nick Choksi**

Encore presentation of a new play presented without intermission. Previously presented at Walkerspace February 9–March 21, 2011 (see *Theatre World* Vol. 67, page 159).

SYNOPSIS *Invasion!* is a subversive comedy that centers on 'Abulkasem,' a name that bears seemingly magical powers, and a series of characters who assume the name for their own reasons. Who is 'Abulkasem'? Is he a character in a fairy tale, or an international super-spy? Is she a renowned auteur director? Does he/she pose a clear and present danger? And is there more than one? That all depends on who you ask.

Andrew Guilarte and Francis Benhamou in Invasion! *(photo by Carol Rosegg)*

Dally with the Devil

Beckett Theatre on Theatre Row; First Preview: September 10, 2011; Opening Night: September 14, 2011; Closed October 8, 2011; 3 previews, 26 performances

Written by Victor L. Cahn; Presented by Rachel Reiner Productions; Director, Eric Parness; Set, Jisun Kim; Costumes, Michelle Eden Humphrey; Lighting, Pamela Kupper; Sound/Composer, Nick Moore; Props Master, Lauren Madden; Casting, Stephanie Klapper; Production Manager, Nicole Godino; PSM, Sean McCain; ASM, Veronica Graveline; Technical Director, Matt Vieira; Assistant Costumes, Ashley Sweetman; Marketing Consultant, Marie Reynolds; Logo, Billy Mitchell; Press, Springer Associates, Joe Trentacosta

CAST Charlotte **Erika Rolfsrud**; Irene **Elizabeth Norment**; Megan **Elizabeth A. Davis**

World premiere of a new play presented without intermission.

SYNOPSIS Just in time for election season, *Dally With The Devil* focuses on three women immersed in political intrigue: two officials from opposing campaigns competing to use a powerful blogger to influence the outcome of a Senatorial election. As charges escalate, tactics shift, and the battle swerves in unexpected directions. *Dally With The Devil* is filled with power plays, blackmail, and plenty of media spin…it's politics as usual.

Erika Rolfsrud, Elizabeth A. Davis, and Elizabeth Norment in Dally With The Devil *(photo by Jon Kandel)*

Play It Cool

Acorn Theatre on Theatre Row; First Preview: September 2, 2011; Opening Night: September 14, 2011; Closed October 8, 2011; 16 previews, 29 performances

Conceived by Larry Dean Harris, book by Martin Casella and Larry Dean Harris, lyrics by Mark Winkler, music by Phillip Swann, additional music by Jim Andron, Michael Cruz, Marilyn Harris, Emilio Palame, Larry Steelman; Produced by Mary's Hideaway LLC; Director, Sharon Rosen; Choreography, Marc Kimelman; Music Director, David Libby; Music Supervisor/Arrangements, Joseph A. Baker; Set, Thomas A. Walsh; Costumes, Therese Bruck; Lighting, Deb Sullivan; Sound, Carl Casella and Peter Fitzgerald; Hair and Wigs, Josh Schwartz; PSM, Jane Pole; ASM, Megan J. Alvord; Casting Consultant, Michael Cassara; General Manager, Roy Gabay Productions, Mandy Tate, Daniel Kuney, Chris Aniello, Mark Gagliardi, Vic Kelman; Company Manager, Bruce Kagel; Production Supervisor, Production Core/James E. Cleveland; Production Manager, Katy Yonally; Assistant Production Manager, Ron Grimshaw; Assistant to the Producer, Alyson Cermak; Dance Captain, Michael Buchanan; Associate Set, Veronica Kimmel; Assistant Design: Paula Dal Santo (set), Meghan Gaber (costumes), Porsche McGovern (lighting); Master Electrician, The Lighting, Syndicate; Technical Director, Paul Frydrychowski; Assistant Technical Director, Kurtis Rivers; Props Master/Deck Crew, Leah Farrelly; Props Assistant, Ricola Wille; Production Electrician, Jake Heinrichs; Production Sound/Head Mixer, Adam Rigby; Wardrobe, Meghan Gaber; Hair and Wigs Supervisor, Josh Schwartz; Spot Op, Gifford Williams; Production

Assistants, Alyson Cermak, Matthew Laderoute, Matt Allamon; Advertising and Marketing, HHC Marketing; Press, Kevin P. McAnarney

CAST Henry **Michael F. McGuirk**; Lena **Robyn Hurder**; Mary **Sally Mayes**; Will **Michael Buchanan**; Eddie **Chris Hoch**

MUSICIANS David Libby (Conductor/Piano), Dan Fabricatore (Bass), Dan Gross (Drums)

MUSICAL NUMBERS Club Life/Welcome; Scattin' in the Moonlight; Happy Ending; In My Drag; Whatever It Takes; Welcome to Hollywood; Baby's On Third; Future Street; Curvy Time Bomb; Turn Up the Heat; Hip to Your Tricks; How Do I Go Home Tonight?; Jazz Is a Special Taste; The Lesson; Like Jazz; In a Lonely Place; Whatever It Takes (reprise); Play It Cool/Brand New Day; Like Jazz (reprise); Play It Cool (reprise)

SETTING Mary's Hideway, a little club off Sunset. Hollywood; June, 1953. Off-Broadway premiere of a new musical presented in two acts. World premiere presented at Celebration Theatre (Hollywood) June 8–July 28, 2006. New York premiere presented at the TBG Theater September 22–October 5, 2008 as part of the 2008 New York Music Theatre Festival; subsequently presented at National Alliance for Musical Theatre Festival of New Musicals in 2010.

SYNOPSIS Sexy… sultry…repressive – Hollywood 1953, an underground nightclub where everyone's got a secret. At Mary's Hideway, it was a place for sizzling jazz and for the ambitious people who are finding the courage to be who they are. It is the noir time of the '50s, and the laws governing gay and lesbian clubs produced every glance that had a double meaning and the words that were innuendo. Here everything had to be done to the strict code. These are some of the people who had the guts to break the rules.

Michael Buchanan, Michael F. McGuirk, Sally Mayes, and Robyn Hurder in Play It Cool *(photo by Joan Marcus)*

Conni's Avant Garde Restaurant: The Mothership Landing

Irondale Center; Opening Night: September 15, 2011; Closed September 25, 2011; 8 performances

Written by Conni's Avant Garde Restaurant; Produced by Irondale Center (Jim Niesen, Artistic Director; Terry Greiss, Executive Director) and Conni's Restaurant; Director, Paul Bargetto; Set, David Barber; Lighting, Jeanette Yew; Stage Manager, Diana Egizi; Consulting Director, Cynthia Croot; Technical Director, Michaelangelo DeSerio; Press, Lucy Walters-Maneri

CAST Melody Bates, Stephanie Dodd, Connie Hall, Deborah Philips, Jeffrey Fracé, Jerusha Klemperer, Justin Badger, Kelly Hayes, Peter Lettre, Peter Richards, Rachel Murdy, David Barber

A experimental theatre and dining event presented in five acts/courses.

SYNOPSIS Conni's Avant Garde Restaurant is a group of bold (if fictional) theatrical performers, devoted to the ongoing celebration of the work of Conni Convergence, the beloved icon of stage and screen. Hailed as "devilish dinner theatre," the event transforms Irondale's raw theatre space into a lush banquet hall—complete with a visible kitchen—where each night, guests are treated to a gourmet-dining experience, with food carefully prepared on the premises and served with charismatic flourish by self-proclaimed geniuses of the avant-garde theater.

Peter Lettre, Rachel Murdy, and Justin Badger in Conni's Avant Garde Restaurant *(photo by Diana Chester)*

Crane Story

Cherry Lane Theatre; First Preview: September 6, 2011; Opening Night: September 15, 2011; Closed October 1, 2011; 8 previews, 13 performances

Written by Jen Silverman; Produced by The Playwrights Realm (Katherine Kovner, Artistic Director) in association with Cherry Lane Theatre (Angelina Fiordellisi, Artistic Director); Director, Katherine Kovner; Producing Director, Stephanie Ybarra; Set, Michael Locher; Costumes, Moria Clinton; Lighting, Ji-Youn Chang; Composer/Sound, Nathan A. Roberts; Puppets, Puppet Kitchen; Props, Layna Fisher; Movement Design, Miki Orihara, Masumi Kishimoto; Dramaturg, Christine Scarfuto; Casting, Paul Davis/Calleri Casting; PSM, Joanne E. McInerney; Production Manager, Aaron Verdery; ASM, Ryan C. Durham; Associate Set, Lauren Rockman; Technical Director, Janio Marrero; Light Board, Sam Gordon; Sound Operator, Leo Martin; Production Assistant, Maximillian Daley; Wardrobe Assistant, Faye Richards; Press, Bruce Cohen

CAST Ishida **Louis Ozawa Changchien**; Skell **Susan Hyon**; Crane **Christine Toy Johnson**; Cassis **Angela Lin**; Junpei **Jake Manabat**; Theo **Barret O'Brien**; Drowned Man **David Shih**

SETTING Japan: Tokyo and Okayama; also the Underworld. World premiere of a new play presented in two acts.

SYNOPSIS Told with an ensemble of actors, puppets, and live music, *Crane Story* is about a young woman who travels back to Japan to find the soul of her dead brother and put it to rest. Along her journey, she falls in love, and encounters many magical worlds and creatures, like the Librarian of the Dead and a talking Crane.

Louis Ozawa Changchien and Angela Lin in Crane Story *(photo by Erik Pearson)*

Seed

National Black Theatre; First Preview: September 6, 2011; Opening Night: September 16, 2011; Closed: October 9, 2011; 9 previews, 31 performances

Written by Radha Blank; Presented by the Classical Theatre of Harlem (Ty Jones, Producing Director) and the Hip-Hop Theater Festival (Clyde Valentín, Executive Director; Kamilah Forbers, Artistic Director; Darren Sussman, Chair); Associate Producer, Travis LeMont Ballenger; Director, Niegel Smith; Set, Ken Larson; Lighting, Colin D. Young; Costumes, Emily DeAngelis; Sound, Luqman Brown; Projections, Kate Freer; Wigs, Cookie Jordan; Company Manager, Tiffany Vega; Associate Producer, Travis LaMont Ballenger; PSM, Marci Skolnick; ASM, Alex Brouwer; Marketing, Hip-Hop Theater Festival, Donna Walker-Kuhne; Technical Director, Daniel Thomas, Kelvin Productions LLC; General Manager, Aaron Grant, Kelvin Productions LLC; Production Manager, Vincent J. DeMarco; Kelvin Productions LLC; Company Manager, Tiffany Vega; Props, Raphael Mishler; Press, Cheryl Dunkin & Company, Pitch Control PR, John Wyszniewski

CAST Latonya **Jocelyn Bioh**; Che-Che **Khadim Diop**; Anne Colleen Simpson **Bridgit Antoinette Evans**; Twan **Jaime Lincoln Smith**; Rashawn **Pernell Walker**

World premiere of a new play presented in two acts. Developed at the Washington D.C. Hip-Hop Theater Festival and Arena Stage's New Play Institute.

SYNOPSIS *Seed* explores themes of abandonment, poverty, class differences, and byproducts of the crack epidemic that swept through Harlem in the 1980s & 90s. *Seed* follows burnt-out social worker Anne Colleen Simpson, who decides to leave the field on a high note, with a book detailing her career. When Chee-Chee, a gifted twelve-year-old from the projects collides into her life, she's forced to confront his young mother and the shadows of her past. Anne and Chee-Chee develop an unlikely friendship that leads to an explosive encounter threatening both their futures.

Arias with a Twist Deluxe

Abrons Arts Center; First Preview: September 14, 2011; Opening Night: September 18, 2011; Closed October 16, 2011; 5 previews, 25 performances

Khadim Diop in Seed *(photo by Ruth Sovronsky)*

Created by Joey Arias and Basil Twist; Produced by Tandem Otter Productions (Basil Twist, Artistic Director; Barbara Busackino, Producer) and Abrons Arts Center; Director/Design, Basil Twist; Lighting, Ayuma "Poe" Saegusa; Sound, Greg Duffin; Projections, Daniel Brodie; Original Songs, Alex Gifford; Artistic Advisor/Costume Design, Manfred Thierry Mugler; Musical Arrangements and Production, Eliot Douglass and Jean Houle Francoise; Costume Execution, Fritz Masten; Voice Overs, Edgar Oliver and David Ilku; Technical Director, David Ojala; PSM, Neelam Vaswani; ASM, Carmen Torres; Sound Engineer and Operator, Masako Kataoka; Lighting Supervisor/Follow Spots, Hanne Reilly; Assistant Lighting Supervisor, James Goodin; Glover, Sandy Schiller; Wigs, Barry Hendrickson; Puppet Build Captains, Millie Taylor and Ceili Clemens; Press, Richard Kornberg and Associates

CAST Joey Arias; Puppeteers **Jamie Moore**, **Chris DeVille**, **Amanda Villalobos**, **Kirsten Kammermeyer**, **Matt Leabo**, **Lindsay Abromaitis-Smith**

Revised and expanded version of a solo performance revue/exotic fantasy of song and puppetry presented without intermission. The original production was presented by HERE at the Dorothy B. Williams Theatre June 12–December 31, 2008 playing 181 performances (see *Theatre World* Vol. 65, page 137).

SYNOPSIS This deliriously madcap fantasy revue, engorged from a world tour with all the beloved song stylings of Joey Arias enveloped in Basil Twist's eye-popping theatrical enchantments that took New York by storm in 2008 returns with deluxe twists in a more lavish production. Androgonous star Arias in the show that combines an out-of-this-world plot with familiar and original songs.

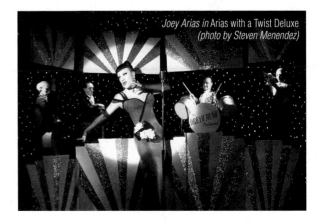

Joey Arias in Arias with a Twist Deluxe *(photo by Steven Menendez)*

Kithless in Paradise

Lion Theatre on Theatre Row; First Preview: September 13, 2011; Opening Night: September 20, 2011; Closed October 9, 2011; 4 previews, 21 performances

Written by Molly Moroney; Produced by Bill Norett/Cyrano Players Inc.; Director, Niki Flacks; Sets, Raul Abrego; Costumes, Rebecca Lustig; Lighting, Josh Scherr; Sound, Kimberly Carbone; PSM, Kristine Ayers; ASM, Kelly Ruth Cole; Production Supervisor, Production Core/James E. Cleveland; General Management, Cesa Entertainment Inc.; Associate General Manager, Diane Alianiello; Assistant Lighting, John Anselmo Jr.; Marketing and Advertising, The Pekoe Group; Press, Springer Associates, Joe Trentacosta

CAST Sandy Loring **Jill Melanie Wirth**; Phil Barrett **Brit Herring**; Polly Barrett **Tracy Newirth**; Tim McCall **David Wirth**; Janice McCall **Liz Forst**; Ken Loring **Bob Manus**

SETTING The home of Tim and Janice McCall in San Francisco; 2009. World premiere of a new play presented in two acts.

SYNOPSIS Some people have it all -- endless supplies of cash, a chic circle of friends and the perfect marriage. The McCalls and Barretts share a life in the lap of luxury and decades of friendship. A rollicking, lavish dinner party that promises to be full of laughter, wine and nostalgia takes a foul turn when a guest pushes the boundaries of friendship too far. Secrets spill forth, leaving all to question the tenuous binds that hold marriage, kith & kin, and life-long friendships together.

Jill Melanie Wirth, Brit Herring, Tracy Newirth, David Wirth), Liz Forst, and Bob Manus in Kithless in Paradise *(photo by Carol Rosegg)*

Chix 6

Queens Theatre; Opening Night: September 27, 2011; Closed October 30, 2011; 35 performances

Book, music, and lyrics by Lourds Lane, additional book by D.J. Salisbury; Produced by Queens Theatre (Ray Cullom, Artistic Director), Ready, Fire, Aim Productions, Nederlander-Browne, Dan Frishwasser, in association with Wendy Timmons/Jennifer Salwell; Executive Producers, Aldo Scrofani and Heather Provost; Director, D.J. Salisbury; Music Supervisor, Wendy Bobbitt Cavett; Choreography, Ron DeJesus; Set, Beowulf Boritt; Costumes, Chris March; Lighting, Ryan O'Gara; Sound, Peter Fitzgerald; Video/Projections, David Gallo; Flying Sequence Design, Paul Rubin; Circus Sequence Design/Lead Flyman, Bobby Hedglin-Taylor; Casting, Scott Wojcik and Gayle Seay; General Management, Theatre Management Associates, Aldo Scrofani, Maria Di Dia, Tara Troutman, Joe Polack, Byan Byrd, Reagan Copeland; PSM, Patty Grabb; Stage Manager, Meg Friedman; Production Manager, Keith A. Truax; Associate Producers, Stu Sternbach, John Fletcher; Company Manager, Bobby Driggers;

Associate Director, Thom Christopher Warren; Associate Choreography/Assistant Director, Ann Cooley; Associate Aerial Sequence Design, Aaron Verdery; Associate Design: Alexis Distler (set), Caite Hevner (projections), Ty Lacke, Ricky Lighthall, Megan Henninger (sound); Assistant Design: Tim Brown (projections), Victoria Miller (sound); Casting Associate, Gretchen Ferris; Production Properties, Joshua Yocom; Production Electrician, Tom Dyer; Master Electrician, Eric Shoenberger; Spot Ops, Christian Doran, Jana Matoli; Deck Sound, Harvey Neil; Head Props, Becky Malkemes; Wardrobe Supervisor, Erica Giles; Dresser, Jamie Sellers; Moving Lights Programmer, Mike Barczys; Projection Programmer, Paul Vershbow; Assistant Projections Programmer, Alan Edwards; Design Interns, Matt Lefferts, Franklin Winerib

CAST Lightning Girl **Ellenore Scott**; Mi Roar **CJ Tyson**; Jay Champ **Brian Gallagher**; Katie White **Carrie Manolakos**; Blaze **Celina Carvajal**; Seven **Nicolette Hart**; Mama-Mazing **Danielle Lee Greaves**; Interviewer **Josh Sassanella**; Rise **Lourds Lane**; Lola Touché **Molly Tynes**

UNDERSTUDIES Erica Sweany (Katie, Blaze, Lola, Lightning Girl), Kelly Carey (Rise, Mama-Mazing, Seven), Josh Sassannella (Jay, Mi Roar)

BAND Julie McBride (Keyboards), Britt Lightning (Guitar), Julia Adamy (Bass), Sarah Vasil (Drums)

MUSICAL NUMBERS Who's Stronger Now; She Deserves the Light; Held While Flying; My Art; In Your Pocket; Babe; Most Gorgeous Creature; Misfit; Amor; To My Angels; You Call, WE Come; We're Here; The Waking Hour; What Are You Doing Right Now?; The Only Thing Constant; Victory; My Art (reprise); The Circus Song; I Hate Your Guts; Mama's Looking for a Sex Slave; Waking Hour (reprise); Finesse/Lioness; Waking Hour (reprise #2); Held While Flying; My Life; I Will Start the Fire Now

World premiere of a new rock musical presented in two acts.

SYNOPSIS *Chix 6* tells the story of Katie, a comic book artist trapped in an unhealthy relationship with Jay, a narcissistic musician who will do whatever it takes to get ahead. When Jay's emotional games become too much to bear, Katie's creations – a quintet of strong, sassy, superheroines – come to life, leaping off the page to teach the vulnerable artist how to be strong and make changes in her life.

The Company in Chix 6 *(photo courtesy of Lourds Lane)*

Lidless

Walkerspace; First Preview: September 20, 2011; Opening Night: September 28, 2011; Closed October 15, 2011; 7 previews, 16 performances

Written by Frances Ya-Chu Cowhig; Produced by Page 73 Productions (Liz Jones and Asher Richelli, Executive Directors; Michael Walkup, Associate Director); Director, Tea Alagi ; Set, Scott Bradley; Lighting, Tyler Micoleau;

Sound and Original Music, Daniel Kluger; Costumes, Jessica Pabst; Fight Choreography, Thomas Schall; PSM, Shayna O'Neill; Casting, Jack Doulin; Production Supervision, McBrien Dunbar; General Management, Brierpatch Productions; ASM, Kate Rourke; Assistant Director, Ann Marie Dorr; Assistant Set/Prop Master, Starlet Jacobs; Assistant Lighting, Marika Kent; Assistant Costumes, Katie Hartsoe; Casting Associate, Jenn Haltman; Casting Assistant, Ashley Monroe; Technical Director, Caleb Hammons; Master Electrician, Timothy Parrish; Company Manager, Christopher A. Singleton; Light Board Operator, Max Doolittle; Audio Supervisor, Brandon Wolcott; Marketing Consultant, Jess Burkle; Graphic Design, Noah Scalin; Producing Associate, Oren Stevens; Press, David Gersten and Associates

CAST Rhiannon **Emma Galvin**; Riva/Zakiyah **Maha Chehlaoui**; Alice **Danielle Skraastad**; Lucas **Thom Rivera**; Bashir **Laith Nakli**

SETTING Time: 2004, and fifteen years later. Place: Guantánamo Bay, and Minnesota. New York premiere of a new play presented without intermission. World premiere at University of Texas Department of Theatre and Dance in 2009.

SYNOPSIS Fifteen years after serving at Guantanamo Bay, Alice has medicated away her memories of Gitmo and nested with her husband and daughter in the Midwest. But when Bashir, a former Gitmo detainee, finds his way to Alice's flower shop, his demands force Alice to reconcile their shared past, splintering the civilian life she's so carefully arranged. *Lidless* explores the nature of trauma, the conflicting eroticism and brutality of violence, and the blurry line between revenge and redemption.

Danielle Skraastad and Laith Nakli in Lidless *(photo credit Richard Termine)*

The Nightmare Story

Irondale Center; Opening Night: October 5, 2011; Closed October 28, 2011; 25 performances

Written, directed, created, and presented by PigPen Theatre Company; Produced by Irondale Center (Jim Niesen, Artistic Director; Terry Greiss, Executive Director); Lighting, Bart Cortright; Scenic and Puppet Design, Lydia Fine

CAST **Alex Falberg**, **Arya Shahi**, **Ben Ferguson**, **Curtis Gillen**, **Daniel Weschler**, **Matt Nuemberger**, **Ryan Melia**

Off-Broadway premiere of a new play with music and puppetry presented without intermission. World premiere in the 2010 New York International Fringe Festival. The production was also presented at the Barrow Street Theatre for three performances January 25-29, 2012.

SYNOPSIS A boy's beloved mother shows symptoms of the mythical "Nightmare Disease". Now he must journey into the unknown to find a cure... before it's too late. PigPen Theatre Company, which began at Carnegie Mellon University in 2008, combines storytelling, music, puppetry, and shadow-play in this new theatrical piece.

Alex Falberg, Curtis Gillen, and Arya Shahi in The Nightmare Story *(photo by Bart Cortright)*

Any Given Monday

59E59 Theater B; First Preview: October 6, 2011; Opening Night: October 12, 2011; Closed November 6, 2011; 6 previews, 27 performances

Written by Bruce Graham; Produced by Act II Playhouse (Bud Martin, Producing Artistic Director; Howie Brown, Managing Director); Associate Producer, The Active Theater; Director, Bud Martin; Sets, Dirk Durossette; Lighting, Paul Miller; Costumes, Bobby Pearce; Sound, Jacob Subotnick; Casting, Cindi Rush; PSM, Kerri J. Lynch; Production Manager, Joshua Scherr; Company Manager, Kyle Provost; ASM, Trisha Henson; Associate Director, Nathaniel Shaw; Props Master, Jeena Yoon; Master Electrician, John Anselmo; Associate Casting, Michele B. Weis; Management Assistants, Emily Havlik, Sean Daniels; General Management Consultant, DR Theatrical Management, Adam Hess, Seth Goldstein, Heather Schings, Aaron Thompson, Kyle Provost, Danielle Karliner, Jodi Schoenbrun Carter; Strategic Marketing, aka, Liz Furze, Scott Moore, Elizabeth Findlay, Sara Rosenzweig; Marketing Associate, Scott Lupi; Act II Business Manager, Beth Dietzler; Act II Director of Communications and Education, Bill D'Agostino; Act II Production and Company Manager, Andy Shaw; Act II PSM, Marguerite Price; Press, Keith Sherman and Associates, Brett Oberman

CAST Sarah **Lauren Ashley Carter**; Mickey **Michael Mastro**; Risa **Hillary B. Smith**; Lenny **Paul Michael Valley**

New York premiere of a new play presented in two acts. World premiere co-produced by Theatre Exile (Center City, Pennsylvania; Joe Canuso, Producing Artistic Director) and Act II Playhouse (Ambler, Pennsylvania) in February 12, 2010.

SYNOPSIS Lenny is a great guy, a good teacher, an excellent father, and a loving husband. When Lenny's wife leaves him for a smooth-talking lothario who builds Walmarts, his life is shattered. While Lenny consoles himself with pizza and Monday Night Football, his best friend Mick takes matters into his own hands. Now Lenny must decide what he will stand up for and who he will stand up to. How far is too far to get back to happily-ever-after?

Lauren Ashley Carter and Michael Mastro in Any Given Monday *(photo by Carol Rosegg)*

Beyond Words

Urban Stages; First Preview: October 7, 2011; Opening Night: October 12, 2011; Closed October 30, 2011; 4 previews, 17 performances

Written and conceived by Bill Bowers; Produced by Urban Stages (Frances Hill, Founding Artistic Director); Director, Scott Illingworth;Set, Roman Tatarowicz; Costumes, Michael Growler; Lighting, Lee Terry; Sound, David Margolin Lawson; Stage Manager, Laura Lindsay; Program Cover, Sondra Graff; For Urban Stages: Rachel Sullivan (Program Director), Olga Devyatisilnaya (Company Manager), Antoinette Mullins (Development/Marketing), Peter Napolitano (Producing Associate); Press, Springer Associates, Joe Trentacosta

Performed by **Bill Bowers**

World premiere of a new solo performance piece presented in eleven scenes without intermission.

SYNOPSIS *Beyond Word*, a collection of mime, music, and monologues, is a poignant journey that continues Bowers' ongoing investigation of silence in our culture. Set against the backdrop of small town America, *Beyond Words* takes the audience on a funny and poignant journey of sound and silence. One of the most acclaimed mimes in America today, Bill Bowers' eloquent movement evokes the deepest truths of the human condition.

Bill Bowers in Beyond Words *(photo by Yoshio Itagaki)*

Stop the Virgens

St. Ann's Warehouse; Opening Night: October 12, 2011; Closed October 22, 2011; 8 performances

Co-Created by Karen O and KK Barrett; Produced by The Creators Project and St. Ann's Warehouse (Susan Feldman, Artistic Director); Director, Adam Rapp; Production Design, KK Barrett; Choreography, Mariangela Lopez; Music Director, Sam Spiegel; Choir Director and Conductor, Debra Barsha; Costumes, Christian Joy; Makeup and Hair, Mike Potter; Projections, Darrel Maloney; Lighting, Keith Parham; Sound, Andrees Velasquez; Line Producer, Laura Roumanos; Executive Producers, Eddy Moretti, Mark Subias; Casting, Stephanie Klapper; Production Manager, Jeremiah Thies; Sound Engineer, Jamie McElhinney; Costumes Consultant, Jedssica Pabst; Set Associate, Christopher Heilman; Special Effects, Jeremy Chernick; Stage Manager, Richard A. Hodge; Associate Director, Lila Neugebauer; Dramaturg, Michael Swift; Producing Associate, Michael Bulger; ASMs, Rosy Garner, Emily Paige Ballou; Monitor Engineer, Duncan Cutler; Costume Assistant, Katie Hartso; Lighting Assistant, Amada Clegg; Projection Assistants, Joe Cantalupo, Olivia Sebesky; Hair and Makeup Assistant, Nicole Bridgeford; Illustrations, Sonny Gerasimowicz; For St. Ann's: Alex Berg (Finance), Marilynn Donini (External Affairs), Bill Updegraff (Marketing), Erik Wallin (General Manager), Owen Hughes (Production Manager), Kristyn R. Smith (Technical Director); Press, Blake Zidell and Associates

Karen O and the Company in Stop the Virgens *(photo by James Medcraft)*

CAST Narrator **Karen O**; Sentinel 1 **Lili Taylor**; Sentinel 2 **Eliza Ladd**; Virgens **Katie Broad, Britney Coleman, Natalie Kuhn, Molly McAdoo, Jeanna Phillips, Leah Roth, Jennae Alexa Ruiz Santos**; Virgen Acolyte Chorus **Kimberly Arce, Emma March Barash, Ardis Barrow, Dinah Berkeley, Lydian Blossom, Veracity Butcher, Drew Citron, Amber Coartney, Hannah Corrigan, Caitlin Davis, Morgan Everitt, Rachel Flynn, Rebecca Fong, Danielle Frimer, Josephine Edwards Ganner, Leslie Gauthier, Laura Gourdine, Kate Hamilton, Laura Hankin, Ellen Haun, Lauren Hayes, Julia Hirsch, Nadia Hulett, Katherine Kerrick, Caitlin Marz, Eizabeth May, Tara Novie, Brittany Parker, Elly Smokler, Caitlin Savlor Stephens, Shaina K. Taub**

BAND Nick Zinner (Music Director/Guitar), Mark Ramos-Nisita (Keyboard), Patrick Keeler (Drums), Jack Lawrence (Bass), Brian Chase (Percussion), Jason Grisell (Guitar/Vocals), Gillian Rivers (Violin), Yuiko Kamakari (Viola), Justin Kantor (Cello), Ian Young (Saxophone), Frank London (Trumpet)

World premiere of a new multimedia rock musical/opera presented without intermission.

SYNOPSIS *Stop the Virgens*, a psycho opera by Yeah Yeah Yeah vocalist Karen O, is an assault on the tragic joys of youth, fever dreams drenched in visual seduction, a cathartic spell spun through a cycle of nine songs.

La Strada

TBG Theater; Opening Night: October 22, 2011; Closed December 4, 2011; 39 performances

Written by Federico Fellini, Tullio Pinelli, and Ennio Flaiano, based on film directed by Fellini; Adapted by Gerard Vázquez; Produced by La Strada Theater Company (Luis Carlos de La Lombana, Artistic Director and Executive Producer); Co-Producers, Nacho Blanco, Martín Fernandez Lombana, Jazmin Blanco; Directors, René Buch and Jorge Merced; Production Design, Jason Sturm; Costumes, Kanako Hiyama; Lighting/Technical Director, Pope Jackson; Music, Luis Carlos de La Lombana, Caridad Martos; Music Consultant, Zulema Clares; Stage Choreography, Mike Yahn; State Manager, Karina Alós; Supertitles, Betsy Pujols; Clown Consultant, Audrey Crabtree; Light Operator, Gabriel García

CAST Zampanó **Luis Carlos de La Lombana**; Gelsomina **Nanda Abella**; The Fool/Scarf (a clown) **Israel Ruiz**; Hat (a clown) **Winston Estevez**; Coat (a clown)/Tavern Keeper **María Peyramaure** or **Adela Maria Bolet**; Violin and clown **Stephanie Davis**; Trumpet and clown **Jennifer Harder**

The Company of La Strada *(photo courtesy of Luis Carlos de La Lombana)*

Off-Broadway premiere of a play with music presented in Spanish with English titles in two acts. Previously presented at Theater IATI February 23–March 6, 2011.

SYNOPSIS La Strada Company presents a return engagement of its award-winning stage production of Fellini's *La Strada*. In need of help for his street entertainment, Zampano offers money to a poor woman in exchange for her daughter Gelsomina, a young woman whose innocence borders on mental retardation. Together they set out on a journey through several villages, presenting a spectacle of brute force leavened with comic interludes. In spite of his abuses, Gelsomina starts to develop an intense devotion towards him.

Sistas: The Musical

St. Luke's Theatre; First Preview: September 29, 2011; Opening Night: October 23, 2011; 11 previews, 116 performances as of May 31, 2012

Written by Dorothy Marcic; Produced by Hinton Battle and Jenkay LLC (Jay Harris and William Franzblau); Directors, Keneth Ferrone; Associate Director, Ed Staudenmayer; Musical Director, Nicholas Cheng; Additional Arrangements, Germono Toussaint; Choreography, Lauren Lim Jackson; Associate Choreographer, Renée Marino; Sets/ASM, Josh Iacovelli; Costumes, Tricia Barsamian; Lighting, Kia Rogers; Casting, Jamibeth Margolis; General Manager, Sherra Johnston; PSM, Joshua Quinn; Marketing, Leanne Schanzer; Advertising, Hofstetter + Partners/Agency 212; For St. Luke's Theatre: Edmund Gaynes (Operator), Pamela Hall (Co-Artistic Director), Jessimeg Productions (General Manager), Julia Beardsley (Associate General Manager), Catherine Fowles, Maria-Elena Ortiz (Assistant General Managers), Bill Fitzgerald (Sales); Press, Sam Mattingly, SM Communications

CAST Roberta **Jennifer Fouché**; Heather **Amy Goldberger**; Gloria **Tracey Conyer Lee**; Simone **April Nixon**; Tamika **Lexi Rhoades**

MUSICIANS Nicholas Cheng (Keyboard), Matt Cusack (Bass), Brian Adler (Percussion)

MUSIC CREDITS A Good Man Is Hard To Find; A Woman's Worth; Ain't Gonna Let Nobody Turn Me Around; Beautiful; Control; God Bless the Child; Golden; Hot Stuff; I Am Not My Hair; I Have Nothing; I'm Gonna Make You Love Me; I Will Survive; Images; Just Fine; You Keep Me Hangin' On; Let's Wait a While; Milkshake; My Man; Nowhere to Run; Oh Happy Day; R.E.S.P.E.C.T; Say a Little Prayer; Shoop Shoop Song; Single Ladies (Put a Ring on It); Society's Child; Stormy Weather; Strange Fruit; Sweet Talkin' Guy; Tain't Nobody's Business If I Do; Take My Hand Precious Lord; That's Why Darkies Were Born; Tyrone; We Are Family; You Gotta Be

Off-Broadway premiere of a new musical presented without intermission. The world premiere was presented as part of the 2011 New York Musical Theatre Festival.

SYNOPSIS *Sistas* tells of the struggles, joys, and triumphs of being black and of being a woman in America. Told through the life and experiences of one woman and the women in her family, the story segues from the days of Jim Crow to the present and covers topics from segregation and the women's movement to the meaning of love and control. The narrative is stitched with songs that capture the mood and issues of each period and time. In the end, the women find strength in each others' stories and arrive at a way to best honor the memory of their beloved Grandma - a seminal figure in their development as strong and accomplished women.

Amy Goldberger, April Nixon, Tracy Conyer Lee, Jennifer Fouche, and Lexi Rhoades in Sistas: The Musical (photo by Russ Rowland)

Say Goodnight Gracie

The Life, Laughter and Love of George Burns

St. Luke's Theatre; First Preview: October 14, 2011; Opening Night: October 30, 2011; Closed January 8, 2012; 8 previews, 29 performances

Written by Rupert Holmes; Produced by William Franzblau and Jay Harris; Incidental Music, Rupert Holmes; Design Manager, Elaine Smith; Sound, Carl Casella; Script and Music Supervision, Teressa Esposito; PSM, Josh Iacovelli; General Manager, Sherra Johnston; Marketing, Leanne Schanzer Promotions; Advertising, Hofstetter + Partners; For St. Luke's Theatre: Edmund Gaynes (Operator), Pamela Hall (Co-Artistic Director), Jessimeg Productions (General Manager), Julia Beardsley (Associate General Manager), Catherine Fowles, Maria-Elena Ortiz (Assistant General Managers), Bill Fitzgerald (Sales); Press, Peter Cromarty and Company

CAST George Burns **Joel Rooks**; Voice of Gracie Allen **Didi Conn**

Joel Rooks in Say Goodnight Gracie
(photo by Scott Myers)

Revival of a solo performance play presented without intermission. Originally presented on Broadway at the Helen Hayes Theatre October 10, 2002–August 24, 2003 playing 364 performances. Mr. Rooks was the understudy to Frank Gorshin in that production (see Theatre World Vol. 59, page 28).

SYNOPSIS In Say Goodnight Gracie, audiences take a guided tour through an American century told through the eyes of George Burns, who savored each day from his impoverished youth on the lower East side, to his career in Vaudeville, his marriage to Gracie Allen, their rise to success on stage, screen, radio and TV, and finally George's second time around.

Hand to God

Ensemble Studio Theatre; First Preview: October 27, 2011; Opening Night: October 31, 2011; Closed December 18, 2011; Encored February 29–April 1, 2012; 4 previews, 74 performances

Written by Robert Askins; Produced by Ensemble Studio Theatre (William Carden, Artistic Director; Paul Alexander Slee, Executive Director) and EST/ Youngblood (Graeme Gillis and RJ Tolan, Co-Artistic Directors); Director, Mortitz von Stuelpnagel; Sets, Rebecca Lord-Surratt; Costumes, Sydney Maresca; Lighting, Matthew Richards; Sound, Chris Barlow; Puppet Design, Marte Johanne Ekhougen; Fight Director, Robert Westley; Properties Master, Deb Gaouette; Technical Director, Derek F. Dickinson; PSM, Michele Ebel; ASM, Joshua Hernandez; Season Producer, Web Begole; Assistant Season Producer, Stephen Brown; Marketing, Ryan Hugh McWilliams; Casting, Tom Rowan; Graphic Designer, Ian Robinson; Light Board Programmer, Erik Herskowitz; Sound Board Engineer/Operator, Emily Auciello; Master Electrician, Sarah Abigail Hoke-Brady; Wardrobe Supervisor, Kaitlin Binnie; Carpenters, Neil Becker, Mayur Deshmukh, Peter Dubin, Blake Raphael; Finance Director, Randee Smith; Associate Director of EST Sloan Project/Literary Manager, Linsay Firman; EST Going to the River, Elizabeth Van Dyke; Press, Bruce Cohen

CAST Jason/Tyrone **Steven Boyer**; Margery **Geneva Carr**; Jessica **Megan Hill**; Timothy **Bobby Moreno**; Pastor Greg **Scott Sowers**

World premiere of a new play presented in two acts. Developed at Southampton Arts MFA program in Theatre in Film at Stony Book University in 2011.

SYNOPSIS Christian Puppet Ministries are, in fundamentalist Christian congregations, normally a great way to teach children about the Bible. Each child gets a puppet, and each puppet gets its own personality. But in Hand to God, children can be fooled by Satan's tricks. For even within the sanctuary of the Christian Puppet Ministry of Cypress, Texas, the devil lurks; Hand to God tells that story.

Steven Boyer and Megan Hill in Hand to God (photo by Gerry Goodstein)

A Charity Case

Clurman Theatre on Theatre Row; First Preview: October 28, 2011; Opening Night: November 2, 2011; Closed November 21, 2011; 5 previews, 25 performances

Written and directed by Wendy Beckett; Produced by Pascal Productions; Set, David L. Arsenault; Lighting, Travis McHale; Costumes, Theresa Squire; Sound, Ian Wehrle; Composer, Felicity Wilcox; Casting, Judy Henderson; PSM, Scott Pegg; ASM, Michal Salonia; General Manager, Adam Fitzgerald; Production Supervisor, Production Core, James E. Cleveland; Production Manager, Amanda Raymond; Marketing and Advertising, The Pekoe Group; Press, Glenna Freedman Public Relations

CAST Faith **Alison Fraser**; Deidre **Alysia Reiner**; Harper **Jill Shackner**

World premiere of a new play presented without intermission.

SYNOPSIS Is it possible to find yourself when you don't understand where you came from? A young girl struggles to come of age while caught in an endless tug of war between her loyalty to the imperfect woman who took her in and her curiosity about the troubled woman who gave her away. *A Charity Case* delves deeply into the entanglements between a biological mother, an adoptive mother and their 17-year-old daughter.

Jill Shackner and Alison Fraser in A Charity Case
(photo by Kevin Thomas Garcia)

How Much Is Enough? Our Values in Question

St. Ann's Warehouse; Opening Night: November 3, 2011; Closed November 27, 2011; 22 performances

Written by Krik Lynn, created with and directed by Melanie Joseph; Produced by St. Ann's Warehouse (Susan Feldman, Artistic Director); Presented by The Foundry Theatre (Melanie Joseph, Artistic Producer; Evan O'Brient, Producer); Set/Lighting/Projections, Jeanette Oi-Suk Yew; Sound, Kristyn R. Smith; Dramaturg, Morgan Jenness; PSM, Sarah Elizabeth Ford; Assistant Director/Co-Producer, Sherrine Azab; Associate Lighting/Projections, Tracy Wertheimer; Production Manager, Ana Mari de Quesada; Sound Mixer, Stowe Nelson; Video Operator, Phillip Gulley; Graphic Designer, Anita Merk; Translations, Alejandra Duque, Luis Lopez, Telesh Lopez; For St. Ann's: Alex Berg (Finance), Marilynn Donini (External Affairs), Bill Updegraff (Marketing), Erik Wallin (General Manager), Owen Hughes (Production Manager), Kristyn R. Smith (Technical Director); Press, Blake Zidell and Associates

CAST Carlo **Noel Joseph Allain**; Marissa **Mia Katigbak**; Freddie **Carl Hancock Rux**; The Googler **Mohammad Yousuf**

New York premiere of a new theatrical piece with audience participation presented World premiere at ArtsEmerson in Boston in August 2011.

SYNOPSIS *How Much is Enough?* explores notions of "value" – in all its poetic iterations – quantitatively through our relations to money and qualitatively by asking what we hold dear. The piece is built entirely out of questions posed by three performers (and a live "googler" on the computer) to audience members, to each other, to the universe, and then some, about how we live our lives, what plans we've made for the future and what advice we can offer one another as we attempt to create lives of value. Equal parts town hall meeting, party, guide for the perplexed, *How Much is Enough?* gathers its greatest theatricality from the most interesting people in the theater – those who usually sit in the dark.

A scene from How Much Is Enough: Our Values in Question
(photo courtesy of The Foundry Theatre)

The Fartiste

Sofia's Downstairs Theater; First Preview: October 9, 2011; Opening Night: November 4, 2011; Closed November 27, 2011; 15 previews, 20 performances

Book by Charlie Schulman, music and lyrics by Michael Roberts; Produced by The Schulberts (Michael Roberts and Charlie Schulman) and Robert Dragotta; Director, John Gould Rubin; Choreography, Richard Move; Music Director, Rachel Kaufman; Sets, Andreea Mincic; Costumes, Kristina Makowski; Lighting, Joyce Liao; Sound, Betsy Rhodes; Casting, Stephanie Klapper; PSM, Fran Rubenstein; ASM/Understudy, Kaitlyn Hickey; Vocal Sound Effects Design, Steve Scott; Dance Captain, Rachel Kopf; General Management, Laura Heller; Technical Director, Scott A. Blackburn; Production Manager, Bernie Dove Design; Company Manager, Mandy Tate; Assistant to the Director, Kristina Mueller; Assistant to the Choreographer, Maximilian Cappelli-King; Associate Producers, Diane Procter/Ratter Productions LLC and Stephen Hanks; Set Design Assistant, Jonathan Cottle; Master Electrician, John Burkland; Electrician, Jeff Englander; Wardrobe Supervisor, Rodney Harper; Sound Engineer/Mixer, Stowe Nelson; Production Assistants, Laurel Fox, Francesca Conlon, Alex Elmalah; Website, Sari Schorr, Jonathan A. Sindall; Advertising/Online Marketing, Davenport Theatricals; Marketing, Leanne Schanzer Promotions; Press, JS 2 Communications, Pete Sanders, Ross Matsubara, Jaclyn York

CAST Joseph Pujol **Kevin Kraft**; Nini/Rose/Jane/Marie **Rachel Kopf**; Charles Ziedler/Henri Toulouse-Lautrec **Herndon Lackey**; Elizabeth/Joseph's Father/Can-Can Dancer **Analisa Leaming**; La Goulou/Antoinette **Lindsay Roginski**; Vocal "Effectiste" **Steven Scott**; Aristide Bruant **Nick Wyman**

BAND Rachel Kaufman (Music Director/Keyboard), Ben Rauch (Assistant Music Director/Keyboard 2), Howie Gordon (Drums)

MUSICAL NUMBERS Overture; The Great Pujol; What Kind of Man Is He; We Live For Art; More; Give Em What They Want

SETTING 1890s; Paris. Off-Broadway premiere of a new musical comedy presented without intermission. World premiere at the 2006 New York International Fringe Festival.

SYNOPSIS *The Fartiste* is a strange (but true!) story about the uniquely talented Joseph Pujol, whose musical derriere propelled him to being the highest-paid performer at the illustrious Moulin Rouge. Full of romance, hilarious characters, sweet melodies, and a chorus of Can-Can dancers, *The Fartiste* is an outrageous comedy for the whole family.

(Kneeling, center): Kevin Kraft, (l-r back): Analisa Leaming Lindsay Roginski, Herndon Lackey, Rachel Kopf, and Nick Wyman in The Fartiste
(photo by Carol Rosegg)

Iron Curtain

Baruch Performing Arts Center; Opening Night: November 5, 2011; Closed December 4, 2011; 29 performances

Book by Susan DiLallo, music by Stephen Weiner, lyrics by Peter Mills; Produced by Prospect Theater Company (Cara Reichel, Producing Artistic Director; Melissa Hubert, Managing Director) by special arrangement with Fireboat Productions; Director, Cara Reichel; Choreography, Christine O'Grady; Music Supervision and Orchestrations, Remy Kurs; Sets, Brian Prather; Costumes, Sidney Shannon; Lighting, Doug Harry; Sound, Andy Leviss; Music Director, Brandon Sturiale; Stage Manager, Kat West; General Manager, Gretchen Margaroli; Technical Director, Anthony Carpenter; ASM, Taylor Marun; Assistant Director, Rory Sullivan; Assistant Choreographer, Jennifer DiDonato; Production Assistants, Andrew B. Blake, Michelle Karst; Associate Set, Alexander Woodward; Assistant Costumes, Rachel Guilfoyle; Sound Engineer, Stephanie Riddle; Production Electrician/Programmer, Rob Lilly; Wardrobe Supervisor, Jeffrey Potter-Watts; Prop Artisan, Marina Guzman; Spots, Morgan Fox, Stephanie Holser; Dance Captain, Sara Brophy

CAST Shirley Dooley **Maria Couch**; Masha **Jenn Gambatese**; Howard Katz **Todd Alan Johnson**; Hildret Heinz **Bobbi Kotula**; Murray Finkel **David Perlman**; Sergei Schmearnov **Aaron Ramey**; Yevgenyi Onanov **Gordon Stanley**; Ballerina and others **Sara Brophy**; Border Guard and others **Ronn Burton**; Yury the Hotel Clerk and others **Clint Carter**; Nikita Khrushchev and others **John Fico**; Olga and others **Andrea McCullough**; Producer and others **James Patterson**; Travel Agent and others **Robby Sharpe**; Threshing Maiden and others **Aubrey Sinn**; Swing **Jennifer Margulis**

BAND Brandon Sturiale (Conductor/Piano), Steven Cuevas (Keyboard 2/Violin), Pat Swoboda (Bass), James Pingenot (Percussion), Brad Mulholland (Reed 1), Giuseppe Fusco (Reed 2), John Blevins (Trumpet), Darius Jones (Trombone)

MUSICAL NUMBERS Overture/Prologue; The Pitch; The Sorriest Team Around; The Ministry of Musical Persuasion; Missing; Life in the Lapov Luxuary; The Sorriest Team Around (reprise); Harvest Moon; Missing (reprise); We'll Make It; The Party Line; We Made It; Act One Finale; That's Capital; Half A World Away; Five Year Plan; A Frau Divided; If Not For Musicals; Eleven O'Clock Number; Finale

Revival of a musical presented in two acts. Previously presented at the National Alliance for Musical Theatre's Festival of New Musicals in 2009. Developed at the Eugene O'Neill Theater Center in 2008 and further developed at Village Theatre in Issaquah, Washington (Robb Hunt, Executive Producer; Steve Tomkins, Artistic Director).

SYNOPSIS Prospect's hit musical is back in a brand-new production – and it's louder, faster, and funnier than ever! This uproarious original comedy is set during Broadway's Golden Age of the 1950s. The hapless songwriting team of Howard Katz and Murray Finkel finally get their big break when they are kidnapped by the KGB, taken to Russia, and forced to fix the world's worst communist propaganda musical. Will they choose fame or freedom?

Jenn Gambatese (center) with (clockwise l-r): Sara Brophy, Robby Sharpe, James Patterson, Ronn Burton, and Clint Carter in Iron Curtain
(photo by Gerry Goodstein)

Puberty Rites...not a bootleg experience

Castillo Theatre; First Preview: October 27, 2011; Opening Night: November 6, 2011; Closed November 20, 2011; 9 previews, 11 performances

Written by Elaine Jackson; Produced by Woodie King Jr.'s New Federal Theatre in association with the Castillo Theatre (Dan Friedman, Artistic Director; Diane Stiles, Managing Director); Director, A. Dean Irby; Sets/Technical Director, Anthony Davidson; Costumes, Ali Turns; Lighting, Shirely Prendergast; Sound, Bill Toles; Stage Manager Bayo; ASM/Props, Rosita Timm; Casting, Lawrence Evans; Master Electrician/Light Board Operator, Antoinette Tynes; Wardrobe Supervisor, Lora Jackson; Sound Board Operator, Frank Camera; Production Crew, Erich Loetterle, Dani'Q; Company Manager, Patricia White; Graphic Design, Sean O'Halloran; Advertising, Charlie Silver/Miller Advertising; Press, David Gersten and Associates/Rogers Media Associates, Charles Rogers

CAST Keesha **Yasha Jackson**; Vesna **Arielle Uppaluri**

SETTING Early spring; Northern California outside of Keesha's apartment overlooking Ravenswood High School. Off-Broadway premiere of a new play presented in four scenes in two acts without intermission.

SYNOPSIS *Puberty Rites…not a bootleg experience* is a poignant "coming of age" drama. An elemental heritage bonds two girls to an American heritage at the beginning of the 21st Century, Keesha, from her struggling Black world and Vesna, from her White world of physical privilege. Both face emotional poverty as they confront each other and their inherited past and future. Their personal secrets threaten to destroy them and their dreams.

Arielle Uppaluri and Yasha Jackson in Puberty Rites *(photo by Gerry Goodstein)*

Queen of the Mist

Judson Memorial Church Gymnasium; First Preview: October 18, 2011; Opening Night: November 6, 2011; Closed December 4, 2011; 21 previews, 28 performances

Words and music by Michael John LaChiusa; Produced by Transport Group (Jack Cummings III, Artistic Director; Lori Fineman, Executive Director); Director, Jack Cummings III; Choreography, Scott Rink; Musical Direction, Chris Fenwick; Orchestrations, Michael Starobin; Set, Sandra Goldmark; Costumes, Kathryn Rohe; Lighting, R. Lee Kennedy; Sound, Walter Trarbach; Wigs, Paul Huntley; Casting, Nora Brennan; PSM, Wendy Patten; Production Manager, Charles Hubbard; Stage Manager, Theresa Flanagan; Associate Director, Gregg Wiggans; Dramaturg, Kristina Cocoran Williams; Assistant Choreographer, Megan Kelley; Props/Assistant Set Design, Aaron Sheckler; Music Coordinator, Seymour Red Press; Music Preparation, Brian Allan Hobbs/FireFly Music Service; Assistant to the Musical Director, Kristen Rosenfeld; Associate Design: Warren Karp (set), Zach Williamson (sound); Associate Sound, Matt Walsh; Associate Wigs, Giovanna Calabretta; Assistant Lighting Design, Robert Eshleman; Wardrobe Supervisor, Keith Schneider; Wardrobe Assistants, Shana Albery, Ricardo Fernandez, Faye Richards, Ramsey Scott; Sound Engineer, Dave Horowitz; Casting Assistant, Jen Rogers; Production Assistants, Julia Berman, Glenda DeAbreu, Mike Desposito, Rachel Gordon; Graphic Designer, Christiaan Rule; Press, Richard Kornberg and Associates, Don Summa; Cast recording: Sh-K-Boom/Ghostlight Records 84460

CAST Anna "Annie" Edson Taylor **Mary Testa**; Mr. Frank Russell (Anna's Manager) **Andrew Samonsky**; Jane (Anna's Sister) **Theresa McCarthy**; Man with his Hand Wrapped in a Handkerchief **Tally Sessions**; Carrie Nation **Julia**

Murney; Mike Taylor (a Soldier) **Stanley Bahorek**; A New Manager **D.C. Anderson**

MUSICIANS Chris Fenwick (Keyboard 1), Mark Mitchell (Keyboard 2), David Byrd Marrow (French Horn), Susan French (Violin), Martha Hyde (Woodwinds), Jeffrey Levine (Bass), Anik Oulianine (Cello)

MUSICAL NUMBERS Opening; There Is Greatness In Me; A Letter to Jane/The Tiger; Charity; Glorius Devel/The Waters; The Barrel/Cradle or Coffin; Types Like You; Do the Pan!; Floating Cloud/Cradle or Coffin (reprise); Laugh at the Tiger; On the Other Side; Act One Finale; The Quintessential Hero; The Quintessential Hero; Million Dolla' Momma; Expectations; Bookings (Part One); Break Down the Door; The Green; Bookings (Part Two); Postcards; The Fall (Act Two Finale)

SETTING Early 1900s; Western New York State, Niagra Falls: Jane's home, the Niagra River, Anna's kitchen, the Pan-American Exposition in Buffalo, a saloon, a burlesque house, Anna's postcard booth, a hotel room, a lecture hall. World premiere of a new musical presented in two acts.

SYNOPSIS *Queen of the Mist* is based on an astounding and outrageous true story, about Anna Edson Taylor, who, in 1901, set out to be the first woman to shoot Niagara Falls in a barrel of her own design. Navigating both the treacherous Falls and a fickle public with a ravenous appetite for sensationalism, this unconventional heroine vies for her legacy in a world clamoring with swindling managers, assassins, revolutionaries, moralizing family, anarchists and activists. Convinced that there is greatness in her and determined not to live as ordinary, she sets out to tempt her fate.

Mary Testa (in tub), Stanley Bahorek, D.C. Anderson, and Tally Sessions in Queen of the Mist *(photo by Carol Rosegg)*

Three British Solos

Shadow Boxing · The Maddening Rain · Bunny

59E59 Theater C; First Preview: November 1, 2011; Opening Night: November 6, 2011; Closed November 20, 2011; 12 previews, 33 performances (4 previews, 11 performances each)

Three solo performance plays presented as part of the 2011 Brits Off Broadway; Produced by 59E59 (Elysabeth Kleinhans, President and Artistic Director; Peter Tear, Executive Producer); Included: *Shadow Boxing* by James Gaddas; Presented by Cross Cut; Director/Lighting, Donald Pulford; Sound, Anthony Januszewski; Management, TimeWontWait; AEA Stage Manager, Jess Johnston; *The Maddening Rain* by Nicholas Pierpan; Presented by Darbourne Luff and Upstart Theatre; Producers, Tom Mansfield, Richard Darbourne and David Luff Director, Matthew Dunster; Design, Alison McDowall; Lighting, Emma Chapman; Sound, David Sharrock; Video, The Bidd Group; Production Technician, Mishi Bekesi; AEA Stage Manager, Jess Johnston; *Bunny* by Jack Thorne; Presented by nabokov; Producer, Mark Cartwright; Director, Joe Murphy; Design, Hannah Clark; Video, Ian William Galloway; Illustrations, Jenny Turner; Lighting, Ric Mountjoy; Assistant Director, Kirsty Patrick Ward; New York Marketing Consultant, Vicky Graham; AEA Stage Manager, Jess Johnston; 59E59 Production Manager, James Sparnon; Press, Karen Greco

CAST *Shadow Boxing:* Flynn **Jonny Collis-Scurll**; *The Maddening Rain:* Actor **Felix Scott**; *Bunny:* Katie **Rosie Wyatt**

U.S. premieres of three solo performance plays presented in repertory, each without intermission.

SYNOPSIS Three British solo shows kick off the 2011 Brits Off Broadway festival at 59E59. *Shadow Boxing* tells the story of Flynn, the son of a boxer who couldn't win, who becomes a successful fighter through utter dedication. But is his gruelling training merely an avoidance tactic? In *The Maddening Rain*, a broker torn between Chilean lithium deals and reuniting with his first love, battles his way through the tough worlds of love and finance. *Bunny* focuses on feisty 18-year-old Katie, who is thrust on a white-knuckle ride through one extraordinary evening when her boyfriend is attacked on the street. Amidst the baying for blood and the longing for love, Katie is forced to decide her future.

Rosie Wyatt in Bunny, *one of the* Three British Solos *(photo by Joel Fildes)*

The Company in Freckleface Strawberry The Musical *(photo by Carol Rosegg)*

Freckleface The Musical

Manhattan Movement and Arts Center; Opening Night: November 8, 2011; Closed July 1, 2012; 133 performances (Saturday and Sunday performances)

Book by Gary Kupper and Rose Caiola, music and lyrics by Gary Kupper; Based on the children's book *Freckleface Strawberry* by Julianne Moore; Produced by Manhattan Movement and Arts Center Productions, Rose Caiola; Director, Buddy Crutchfield; Choreography, Gail Pennington Crutchfield; Music Director/ Additional Arrangements, Dave Keyes; Set, Adam Koch; Costumes, Fabio Toblini and Holly Cain; Lighting/Sound/Production Manager, Bernie Dove; Co-Lighting, John Burlak; General Manager, Laura Heller; PSM, Neal Kowalsky; ASM, Erin Person; Casting, Cindi Rush; Assistant Director, Pamela Edington; Assistant Choreographer, Shelby Kaufman; Assistant to the Choreographer, Christopher B. Williams; Music Arrangements, Gary Kupper, Chris Hajian; Assistant Sound/ Audio Engineer, Bick Gosset; Marketing and Advertising, Davenport Theatricals; Press, Pete Sanders/JS2 Communications

CAST Strawberry **Francesca McGrory**; Ballet Girl/Francine **Bridget Riley**; Jake **Matthew Hooper**; Mother/Teacher/Jane **Sarah Haines**; Emily **Ashley Tobias**; Harry/Don Fontaine **William Bailey**; Danny/Little Brother **Wesley Tunison**; Swings **Amanda Yachechak**, **Michael Bradshaw Flynn**

MUSICAL NUMBERS Opening, Look At Me, Little Freckleface Strawberry, I Like Danny, I Hate Freckles, Freckleface Gangster Vaudeville, Perfect, Lonely Girl, I Can Be Anything, We Wanna Be Like Them, Kid In the Mask, Creative Minds, Be Yourself, Basketball, Lonely Girl (reprise), Hey It's Me, Once Upon A Time, When You Got Friends, Different, Happily Ever After

Return engagement of a new musical for young audiences presented without intermission. World premiere at New World Stages October 1, 2010–April 24, 2011 (see *Theatre World* Vol. 67, page 139).

SYNOPSIS *Freckleface The Musical* chronicles the life of seven-year-old Strawberry being teased by her schoolmates for having bright red hair and freckles. She feels different from everyone else and does anything to get rid of them — from scrubbing them with soap and even wearing a ski mask to school. Strawberry goes on a journey and discovers that all people are different. She ultimately learns to accept herself for all of who she is, freckles and all.

Iphigenia in Tauris

Lion Theatre on Theatre Row; Opening Night: November 8, 2011; Closed December 4, 2011; 32 performances

Written by Euripides, adapted by Louis Markos; Produced by the Leonidas Loizides Theatre Company; Producer/Director, Leonidis Loizides; Sets, Georgio Stefano; Costumes, Pantelis Mitsi; Original Music and Sound, Neophytos Stratis; Assistant Director, Eftychia Papadopoulou

CAST Iphigenia **Eftychia Papadopoulou**; Orestes **Alexis Mouyiaris** or **Francesco Andolfi**; Athena/Chorus **Alesandra Nahodil**; King Thoas **Taso Mikroulis**; Pylades/Messenger **Daniel Rodas**; Herdsman/Servant **Michael Iakovou**; Leader of the Chorus **Julia Peterson**; Chorus **Stephanie Valkanas**

New York premiere of a new adaptation of a classic play presented in Greek without intermission. This production toured the United States prior to this engagement.

SYNOPSIS In *Iphigenia in Tauris*, an exiled brother is driven mad by guilt and remorse; a sister is saved from the sacrificial knife of her father to serve as high priestess in a barbaric land. Swept together in a net of fate they must then concoct a daring escape in attempt to avert the tragedies that pursue them. *Iphigenia in Tauris* is the most modern and compelling of Greek dramas.

Nina Conti: Talk to the Hand

59E59 Theater A; First Preview: November 8, 2011; Opening Night: November 10, 2011; Closed November 13, 2011; 2 previews, 5 performances

Created by Nina Conti and Bill Dare; Presented by Pleasance Theatre as part of the 2011 Brits Off Broadway; Produced by 59E59 (Elysabeth Kleinhans, President and Artistic Director; Peter Tear, Executive Producer); Technical Supervisor, Meredith Brown; Production Manager, James Sparnon; Press, Karen Greco

Performed by **Nina Conti**

U.S. premiere of a solo performance play with puppets presented without intermission.

SYNOPSIS Nina Conti bravely goes where no ventriloquist has gone before. Joined by the sassy Granny and the sardonic Monkey, Nina is off on a seat-of-her-pants adventure that grants the audience access to her uncensored mind, constance lashings of warmth, technical brilliance, and vibrant wit.

Standing On Ceremony: The Gay Marriage Plays

Minetta Lane Theatre; First Preview: November 7, 2011; Opening Night: November 13, 2011; Closed December 18, 2011; 7 previews, 41 performances

Conceived by Brian Shipper; Included: *The Revision* by Jordan Harrison, *This Flight Tonight* by Wendy MacLeod, *My Husband* by Paul Rudnick, *On Facebook* by Doug Wright, *A Traditional Wedding* by Mo Gaffney, *Strange Fruit* by Neil LaBute, *The Gay Agenda* by Paul Rudnick, *London Mosquitoes* by Moisés Kaufman, *Pablo & Andrew at the Altar of Words* by José Rivera; Produced by Joan Stein, Richard Frankel, Annette Niemtzow, Fakston Productions (Ken Fakler and Dan Stone), Harley Medcalf, Jon Murray/Harvey Reese, in association with Diana Buckhantz and Niclas Nagler; Director, Stuart Ross; Executive Producer, Joe Watson; Associate Producers, Luigi Caiola, Rebecca Falcon, Mary C. Solomon; Production Supervisor, David Gallo Design; Set, Sarah Zeitler; Lighting, Josh Starr; Sound, Sound Associates; Costume Consultant, Frank Torre; General Management, Frankel Green Theatrical Management, Joe Watson; Production Manager, Production Core, James E. Cleveland; PSM, Seth Sklar-Heyn; Casting, Tara Rubin; ASM, Sarah Butke; Company Manager, Kathy Lowe; Assistant Company Manager, Katie Pope; Associate Production Manager, Katy Yonally; Assistant Production Manager, Ron Grimshaw; Technician, Molly Kaufhold; Marketing, Leanne Schanzer Promotions; Advertising, Serino Coyne; Press, O+M Company, Rick Miramontez, Molly Barnett, Sam Corbett, Andy Snyder

CAST **Craig Bierko, Mark Consuelos, Polly Draper, Harriet Harris, Beth Leavel, Richard Thomas**; Standbys **Donna Lynne Champlin, Matt Sullivan**

New York premiere of nine short plays presented without intermission. The show began as a series of benefits in Los Angeles. A portion of the ticket sales was donated to Freedom to Marry and other marriage equality organizations. On November 7, the Tectonic Theater Project (Moisés Kaufman, Artistic Director; Greg Reiner, Executive Director) partnered with *Standing on Ceremony* to present *Standing on Ceremony: The National Event*, in which the play was produced at more than 40 theaters across the country.

SYNOPSIS *Standing On Ceremony: The Gay Marriage Plays* is an exciting, provocative evening of nine short plays and monologues by some of America's most illustrious playwrights. Responding to the ongoing battle for marriage equality throughout the United States, these American writers have created an evening that is at once as insightful and stirring as it is funny and heartwarming.

Nina Conti and Monkey in Nina Conti: Talk to the Hand

Harriet Harris and Mark Consuelos in Standing On Ceremony: The Gay Marriage Plays *(photo by Joan Marcus)*

The Sugarhouse at the Edge of the Wilderness

Connelly Theater; First Preview: November 8, 2011; Opening Night: November 15, 2011; Closed December 4, 2011; 5 previews, 19 performances

Written by Carla Ching; Produced by Ma-Yi Theater Company (Ralph B. Peña, Artistic Director; Jorge Z. Ortoll, Executive Director; Suzette Porte, Associate Director); Director, Daniella Topol; Music and Lyrics, Carla Ching and Christopher Larkin; Set, Clint Ramos; Costumes, Theresa Squire; Lighting, Japhy Weideman; Sound, Shane Rettig; Video, Alex Koch and David Tennent; Dramaturg, Jon Kern; PSM, Danielle Buccino; Production Manager, Layhoon Tan; Assistant Director, Dennis Gupta; ASM, Kristine Ayers; Fight Choreographer, Bjorn DuPaty; Associate Set, Craig Napoliello; Assistant Design: Amanda Jenks (costumes), Zachary Ciaburri (costumes), Kate Brown (sound); Technical Director, Rory Mulholland; Specialty Scenery, Paper Mache Monkey Art and Design; Master Electrician, Paul Jones; Audio Supervisor, Dylan Carrow; Prop Coordinator, D. Schuyler Burks; Wardrobe Supervisor, Matthew Hundley; Board Operator, Collin Barnum; Press, Sam Rudy Media Relations

CAST Greta **Ali Ahn**; Baba Yaga, Ma, Hettie **Cindy Cheung**; Miles **Bjorn DuPaty**; Han **Christopher Larkin**; Opal **April Matthis**; Doc **David Spangler**

World premiere of a new play with music presented in two acts.

SYNOPSIS *The Sugar House at the Edge of the Wilderness*, a fractured adaptation of the classic fairy tale Hansel and Gretel, is about today's constantly shifting notions of family, home, parenthood and children. When their father dies and their mother goes on a grief pilgrimage, Chinese adoptees Greta and Han are sent to live with their ex-rockstar uncle and his young girlfriend. Wrestling with the wilds of New York and their grief, Greta gets in trouble with the law and Han runs away to play music on the street. On the edge of the wilderness, Greta and Han must ask themselves: If I can't go home, where do I go?

Ali Ahn and Christopher Larkin in The Sugar House at the Edge of the Wilderness *(photo by Web Begole)*

Burmese Days

59E59 Theater B; First Preview: November 9, 2011; Opening Night: November 16, 2011; Closed December 4, 2011; 8 previews, 22 performances

Written by George Orwell, adapted and directed by Ryan Kiggell; Presented by aya theatre company as part of the 2011 Brits Off Broadway; Produced by 59E59 (Elysabeth Kleinhans, President and Artistic Director; Peter Tear, Executive Producer); Producer, Elisa Terren; Set/Costumes, George Moustakas; Lighting, Anna Sbokou; Sound, Helen Atkinson; Assistant Director, Claire Moyer; Assistant Costumes, Jonathan Van Veek; Casting Associate, Annalie Powell; Burmese Dance Choreography, Shwe Min Thar Than Win; AEA Stage Manager, Amy Kaskeski; Press, Karen Greco

CAST Elizabeth, Ma Kin **Charlotte Allam**; Ellis, Veraswami **Amerjit Deu**; MacGregor, Sammy **Ryan Kiggell**; Ko Ba Sein, Westfield, Ko S'la, Verrall **Zak Shukor**; Mrs. Lackersteen, Ma Hla May **Elisa Terren**; U Po Kyin, Flory **Jamie Zubairi**

U.S. premiere of a new play presented in two acts.

SYNOPSIS Based on George Orwell's first novel, *Burmese Days* is an uncompromising look at the underbelly of the British Empire. Love, friendship and morality are tested against the bitter reality of life in colonial Burma. This compelling account of British colonialism was inspired by Orwell's service in the Burmese Military Police.

Elisa Terren and Jamie Zubairi in Burmese Days *(photo by Carol Rosegg)*

Henry V

Irondale Center; Opening Night: November 22, 2011; Closed December 10, 2011; 14 performances

Written by William Shakespeare; Produced by Irondale Ensemble Project (Jim Niesen, Artistic Director; Terry Greiss, Executive Director); Director, Jim Niesen; Set/Lighting, Ken Rothchild; Costumes, Hilarie Blumenthal; Technical Director/Production Manager, Michaelangelo DeSerio; Acting Coach, Barbara Mackenzie-Wood; Stage Manager, Maria Knapp; ASM, Josie McAdam; Master Electrician, Nolan Kennedy; Carpenter, Stephen Brenman; Wardrobe, Jennifer Donnelly; Electricians, Thomas Kelley, Norman Lander; For Irondale: David Dean (Development Consultant), Amanda Hinkle (Director of Education), Jordon Rosin (Volunteer Coordinator), Jenna Weinberg (Admin Assistant); Press, Lucy Walters Maneri

CAST Chorus, Pistol, King of France, Sir Thomas Grey, Captain Macmorris **Michael-David Gordon**; Archbishop of Cantebury, Nym, Chorus, Sir Thomas Erpingham, Michael Williams, Duke of Burgandy **Terry Greiss**; Bardolph, Montjoy, Captain Jamy **Michael Kendrick**; Bishop of Ely, Chorus, Richard Earl of Cambridge, Constable of France, Captain Fluellen, Duke of York **Gabriel King**; Attendant, Lord Scroop of Masham, Boy, John Bates **Ben Matthews**; Katherine (matinees), Translator, Attendant to Montjoy **Alex Miyashiro**; Duke of Exeter, Chorus, Alice, Alexander Court **Patrena Murray**; Henry V **Matt Neurnberger**; Hostess Quickly, Duke of Gloucester, Katherine **Scarlet Maressa Rivera**; Earl of Westmorland, Lewis the Dauphin, Gower, Chorus **Damen Scanton**; Musician **Dan Weschler**

Revival of a classic play in a new adaptation presented without intermission.

SYNOPSIS Irondale Ensemble presents *Henry V*, part of the 1599 Project, a series of fast and furious chamber productions of Shakespeare classics performed by an ensemble of eight actors. This "Henry" focuses on the affect that war has on all participants – those who fight the wars and those who lead them.

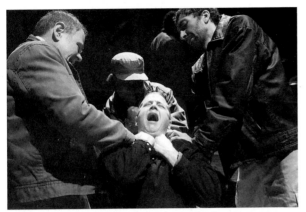

Terry Greiss, Patrena Murray, Michael Kendrick (kneeling), and Damen Scranton in Irondale Ensemble's Henry V *(photo by Gerry Goodstein)*

The Door

59E59 Theater C; First Preview: November 22, 2011; Opening Night: November 29, 2011; Closed December 11, 2011; 6 previews, 16 performances

Written by Tony Earnshaw; Presented by New Ways in association with Unfit Productions U.K. Ltd. as part of the 2011 Brits Off Broadway; Produced by 59E59 (Elysabeth Kleinhans, President and Artistic Director; Peter Tear, Executive Producer); Director, Anna Adams; AEA Stage Manager, Jess Johnston; For Unfit Productions: Chris Westgate (Founder), Tom Cobley, Tony Earnshaw; Press, Karen Greco

CAST Boyd **Tom Cobley**; Ryan **Chris Westgate**

U.S. premiere of a new play play presented without intermission. Previously presented in the U.K. at the Maidenhead Festival, the Elbridge Festival, the Leatherhead Theatre, and the Edinburgh Fringe Festival in 2010.

SYNOPSIS Two men wait in a room with only each other and a banging door for company. They talk, bicker, argue and joke. But these men are not strangers; they have history. Somebody died - but who was responsible?

Tom Cobley and Chris Westgate in The Door *(photo by Tony Earnshaw)*

The Canterbury Tales Remixed

SoHo Playhouse; First Preview: November 23, 2011; Opening Night: December 4, 2011; Closed February 5, 2012; 5 previews, 59 performances

Written by Baba Brinkman, based on the stories by Chaucer; Produced by SoHo Playhouse; Director, Darren Lee Cole; Music and Tuntablism, Jamie Simmonds; Projections, Erik Pearson; Lighting, Rome Brown; Associate Projections, Don Cieslik; Projection Assistants, Erik Brinkman, Asher Jay; PSM, Nicole Press; Production Manager, Jon Johnson; Special Thanks, Rick Everett, Wendall Harrington, Paul Vershbow; Press, Springer Associates, Joe Trentacosta

Performed by **Baba Brinkman** with DJ **Jamie Simmonds**

Program: Prologue, Gilgamesh, Pardoner's Tale, The Merchant's Tale, Wife of Bath, Beowulf

World premiere of a new solo performance play with music presented without intermission. Brinkman previously presented earlier versions of some of these tales in his solo shows *The Rap Canterbury Tales* at the Edinburgh Fringe in 2004 and *Rapconteur* at the Edinburgh Finge in 2010.

SYNOPSIS *The Canterbury Tales Remixed* brings Geoffrey Chaucer's timeless *Canterbury Tales* to vivid life in an entertaining virtuoso performance linking today's hip-hop lyrics with the greatest stories ever told. Just like the most heart-wrenching songs by Eminem or Kanye West, these ancient tales are infused with lust, betrayal, infidelity, greed, jealousy, ambition, and the endless struggles between men and women seeking happiness.

Baba Brinkman in The Canterbury Tales Remixed *(photo by Ben Hider)*

The Man Who Came to Dinner

Theatre at St. Clement's; First Preview: November 25, 2011; Opening Night: December 4, 2011; Closed December 18, 2011; 8 previews, 13 performances

Written by Moss Hart and George S. Kaufman; Produced by the Peccadillo Theatre Company (Dan Wakerman, Artistic Director; Kevin Kennedy, Managing Director; Tim Hurley, General Manager; Director, Dan Wackerman; Set, Harry Feiner; Lighting, Jimmy Lawlor; Costumes, Amy Pedigo-Otto; Wigs, Sarah Levine; PSM, Andrea Wales; ASM, Michael Alifanz; Production Manager, Andrew T. Chandler; Casting, Michael Cassara; Technical Director, Carlo Adinolfi; Properties, Carlos Aguilar; Marketing Director, Leah Michalos; Graphic Design, Dick Larson; Social Media, Stefanie Petersen; Production Assistant, Jeffrey Nielsen; Wardrobe Supervisor, Hannah Rose; Wardrobe/Hair, Tiffany Provencher; Marketing, Hugh Hysell; Press, Jim Randolph

CAST Henderson, Radio Technician, Deputy **Dave Bobb**; Sheridan Whiteside **Jim Brochu**; Michaelson, Expressman, Deputy **Ray Crisara**; Ernest Stanley

Ira Denmark; Richard Stanley **Scott Evans**; Sarah **Thursday Farrar**; Sandy **Kevin Fugaro**; June Stanley **Jenna Gavigan**; Harriet Stanley **Kristin Griffith**; Baker, Westcott, Plainclothes Man **Einar Gunn**; Lorraine Sheldon **Cady Huffman**; Daisy Stanley **Susan Jeffries**; Maggie Cutler **Amy Landon**; Nurse Preen **Kristine Nevins**; Professor Metz **John Seidman**; Mrs. McCutcheon **Carolyn Seiff**; Banjo **Joseph R. Sicari**; Choir Boy **Jackson Stenborg**; Bert Jefferson **Jay Stratton**; Dr. Bradley **Tony Triano**; Mrs. Dexter **Susan Varon**; John **Reggie Whitehead**; Parolee, Radio Technician, Expressman **DaRon Lamar Williams**; Beverly Carlton **John Windsor-Cunningham**

SETTING Masalia, Ohio. 1939; The home of Mr. and Mrs. Ernest Stanley. Act One: Scene 1: A December morning. Scene 2: About a week later. Act Two: Another week-Christmas Eve. Act Three: Christmas morning. Revival of a classic comedy presented in three acts with one intermission between Acts One and Two. The original Broadway production was presented at the Music Box Theatre October 16, 1939–July 12, 1941 playing 739 performances.

SYNOPSIS In this hilarious comedy satire, celebrated critic and radio personality Sheridan Whiteside slips on an icy doorstep while on a December lecture tour. Confined for several weeks of recovery at the Midwestern home of the utterly conventional Mr. and Mrs. Stanley, he proceeds to turn the family's life inside out with his incessant demands, long-distance phone calls and parade of eccentric celebrity guests.

Jim Brochu (left, in wheelchair) and the Company in The Man Who Came to Dinner *(photo by Carol Rosegg)*

Neighbourhood Watch

59E59 Theater A; First Preview: November 30, 2001; Opening Night: December 7, 2011; Closed January 1, 2012; 8 previews, 31 performances

Written and directed by Alan Ayckbourn; Presented by the Stephen Joseph Theatre (Scarborough, England –Chris Monks, Artistic Director; Stephen Wood, Executive Director) as part of the 2011 Brits Off Broadway; Produced by 59E59 (Elysabeth Kleinhans, President and Artistic Director; Peter Tear, Executive Producer); Design, Pip Leckenby; Lighting, Mick Hughes; Stage Manager, Andy Hall; AEA Stage Manager, Kelly Hess; Touring and Programming Director, Amanda Saunders; Production Manager, Adrian Sweeney; Head of Communications, Ruth Puckering; Press, Karen Greco

CAST Dorothy **Eileen Battye**; Rod **Terence Booth**; Luther **Phil Cheadle**; Martin **Matthew Cottle**; Gareth **Richard Derrington**; Amy **Frances Grey**; Magda **Amy Loughton**; Hilda **Alexandra Mathie**

U.S. premiere of a new play presented in two acts. World premiere at the Stephen Joseph Theatre September 13, 2011. Following this run, the production made its London premiere at the Tricycle Theatre April 11, 2012.

SYNOPSIS In *Neighbourhood Watch*, Ayckbourne's 75th play, things are not right on The Bluebell Hill Development. Theft, petty crime, vandalism, all the ills of modern suburban existence are on the increase. Newcomers Martin and his sister Hilda are the crime wave's latest victims and resolve to take action. After all, the law of the land, all that's right and proper and even God Himself are surely on their side.

Matthew Cottle and Frances Grey in Neighborhood Watch *(photo by Karl Andre)*

Balls...the Musical?

Lion Theatre on Theatre Row; First Preview: December 7, 2011; Opening Night: December 8, 2011; Closed December 18, 2011; 1 preview, 14 performances

Created by Bret Carr, Mick Bonde, Brandon Ellis, Michael "Tuba" McKinsey, and Nick Verina; Produced by Blue Balls Inc. in association with JAKK Productions; Director, Kasey Marino; Music Director/Arrangements/Pianist, Sonny Paladino; Choreographer/Assistant Director, Abby Lee; Lighting, Timothy Parrish; Sound, Jessica Pazz; PSM, Joshua Pilote; General Management, Brierpatch Productions; Press, Charlie Siedenberg

CAST Bret **Bret Carr**; Mick **Mick Bonde**; Burger **Nikkieli Demone**; Brandon **Brandon Ellis**; Will **Will Ray**

Off-Broadway premiere of a satirical musial revue presented without intermission. Previously presented at the 2011 New York Musical Theatre Festival.

SYNOPSIS Take an unruly quintet of testosterone laden performers; brilliant talent on the piano, add in the reinterpretation of a few old musical theater "chestnuts", and POW! you get a hilarious hour and a half of entertainment! Bridged with heartfelt moments, *Balls* unabashedly celebrates its own inappropriateness and examines the role of the straight male in musical theatre!

Nikkieli Demone, Will Ray, Brandon Ellis, Mick Bonde, and Bret Carr in Balls...the Musical? *(photo courtesy of the production)*

James X

Theatre at 45 Bleecker; First Preview: December 6, 2011; Opening Night: December 9, 2011; Closed December 18, 2011; 3 previews, 12 performances

Written by Gerard Mannix Flynn; Produced by Gabriel Byrne, Liam Neeson, Culture Project (Alan Buchman, Artistic Director); Presented by Farcry Production and Maedhbh McMahon as part of Imagine Ireland, Culture Ireland's year of Irish Arts in America; Director, Gabriel Byrne; For Culture Project: Jayashri Wyatt (Director of Productions), Victoria Andújar (Administrative Director and Special Assistant to Mr. Buchman), Elisa Lavery (Senior Marketing Associate), Jennifer Joyce (Senior Development Associate), Winter Miller (Development Associate), Jae Hee Byun (Box Office/Development Assistant), Nurit Schwarzbaum (Bookkeeper); Press, Richard Kornberg and Associates

Performed by **Gerard Mannix Flynn**

U.S. premiere of a solo performance play presented without intermission. World premiere presented in Dublin in 2009.

SYNOPSIS An Irish government tribunal of inquiry into institutions responsible for cruel and inhumane treatment of children is in session. In the foyer, James X, one of those children, now a man anxiously prepares to offer the testimony which he hopes will unshackle him from the past. As he waits, James is confronted with the fact that the tribunal he is about to go before is part of the very same system that made prisoners of children like him and sighting this truth prompts him to tell the story that will really, finally set him free.

Gerard Mannix Flynn in James X *(photo by Riona McMonagle)*

Farm Boy

59E59 Theater B; First Preview: December 7, 2011; Opening Night: December 13, 2011; Closed January 1, 2012; 7 previews, 22 performances

Written by Michael Morpurgo, adapted and directed by Daniel Buckroyd; Presented by New Perspectives Theatre Company (Daniel Buckroyd, Artistic Director; Chris Kirkwood, General Manager) as part of the 2011 Brits Off Broadway; Produced by 59E59 (Elysabeth Kleinhans, President and Artistic Director; Peter Tear, Executive Producer); Composer, Matt Marks; Lighting, Mark Dymock; Stage Manager/Production Manager, Mandy Ivory-Castile; AEA Stage Manager, Amy Kaskesi; Tractor Construction, Tim Brierley; Tractor Painting, Susan Winters; Illustrations, Robert Day; New Perspectives Finance Officer, Tim Bowness; New Perspectives Associate Director, Tilly Branson; Associate Fundraiser, Tilly Branson; Marketing and Administration, Kayleigh Hunt; U.S. Press, Karen Greco

CAST Grandson **Richard Pryal**; Grandfather **John Walters**

U.S. premire of a new play presented without intermission.

SYNOPSIS Award-winning writer Michael Morpurgo's compelling sequel to his acclaimed novel *War Horse* is a moving account of the changing face of the English countryside and a beautifully-crafted reminder that stories really can reach out across the generations. This magical tale of the bonds between grandfather and grandson is brought to life in this delightful show combining drama, storytelling and original music.

John Walters and Richard Pryal in Farm Boy *(photo by Carol Rosegg)*

Peter Pan

Theater at Madison Square Garden; Opening Night: December 14, 2011; Closed December 30, 2011; 24 performances

Written by Sir James M. Barrie; Lyrics by Carolyn Leigh, music by Moose Charlap; Additional lyrics by Betty Comden and Adolph Green; Additional music by Jule Styne; Produced by McCoy Rigby Entertainment, Nederlander Presentations, Albert Nocciolino, Larry Payton, Michael Filerman, Heni Koenigsberg, and La Mirada Theatre for the Performing Arts; Original Broadway production conceived, directed and choreographed by Jerome Robbins; Director, Glenn Casale; Tour Direction, Tour Group Ltd, L. Glenn Poppleton; Choreography, Patti Colombo; Orchestration/Musical Supervision and Direction, Keith Levenson; General Management, McCoy Rigby Entertainment; Set, John Iacovelli; Costumes, Shigeru Yaji; Lighting, Michael Gilliam; Sound, Julie Ferrin; Flying Sequences, Paul Rubin; Casting, Julia Flores; Wigs, Mitchell Hale; Fight Director, Sean Boyd; PSM, Michael McEowen; Production Supervision, Buck Mason; Company Manager, Michael Sanfilippo; Stage Manager, William Alan Coats; ASM, Cambria Larson; Assistant Company Manager, Carla Rugg; Producing Consultant, K. Lee Harvey; Assistant Choreographer/Dance Captain, Rod Roberts; Fight Captain, Clark Roberts; Assistant to the Director, Kenn McLeod; Associate Production Managers, Gina Farina, Theresa Flemming; Master Carpenter, Dan Sylvia; Head Electrician, Gary Weintraub; Head Sound, Timothy Schmidt; Wardrobe Supervisor, Donna MacNaughton; Props Master, Deborah H. Malcolm; Wig and Hair Master, Katie McCoy; Flyman, Leon Lobsinger; Electronic Music Design, Notion Music Inc.; Tour Marketing and Press, Anita Dloniak and Associations; National Press, John Thomas

CAST Mrs. Darling/Mermaid/Wendy (Grown-Up) **Kim Crosby**; Wendy Darling **Krista Buccellato**; John Darling **Cade Cannon Ball**; Michael Darling **Julia Massey** or **Jordyn Davis**; Liza/Tiger Lily **Jenna Wright**; Nana/Bill Jukes/Crocodile **Clark Roberts** Mr. Darlin/Capatian Hook **Tom Hewitt** Peter Pan **Cathy Rigby**; Curly **Shanon Mari Mills**; 1st Twin **JC Layag**; 2nd Twin **Marc Andrew Nuñez**; Slightly **Dane Wagner**; Tootles/Jane **Carly Bracco**; Smee

James Leo Ryan; Cecco **Steven Strafford**; Starkey **Michael A. Shepperd**; Pirates and Indians **J. David Anderson, Seth Belliston, Jasmine Ejan, Shannon Stoeke, John J. Todd, Andrew Wilson**; Swings **Melissa Roberts, Rod Roberts**

UNDERSTUDIES Shanon Mari Mills (Peter Pan, Mrs. Darling/Mermaid/Grown-Up Wendy); Shannon Stoeke (Mr. Darling/Captain Hook, Starkey), Steven Stafford (Mr. Smee), Carly Bracco (Wendy), Melissa Roberts (Wendy, Twins 1 & 2, Tootles/Jane, Curly), Jordyn Davis (John Darling), Jasmine Ejan (Liza/Tiger Lily), JC Layag (Slightly), Rod Roberts (Nana, Crocodile, Bill Jukes, Cecco)

MUSICIANS Keith Levenson (Conductor), Bruce Barnes (Assistant Conductor/Keyboard 1), Tommy Bradford (Drums/Percussion), Kelly Ann Lambert (Keyboard 2)

MUSICAL NUMBERS Tender Shepherd; I Gotta Crow; Neverland; I'm Flying; Pirate March; A Princely Scheme; Indians!; Wendy; I Won't Group Up; Another Princely Scheme; Ugg-a-Wugg; Distant Melody; I Gotta Crow (reprise); Tender Shepherd (reprise); I Won't Group Up (reprise); Neverland (reprise)

SETTING The Nursery of the Darling Residence, Neverland, Marooner's Rock, The Home Underground, and The Pirate Ship. National touring company of a revival of a musical presented in seven scenes in two acts. The original Broadway production played the Winter Garden Theatre October 20, 1954–February 26, 1955 playing 155 performances (see *Theatre World* Vol. 11, page 25). The musical has played five Broadway revivals in 1981, 1990, 1991, and 1998-99, and a summer 1999 return engagement.

SYNOPSIS Olympic gymnast Cathy Rigby returns to her signature Tony-nominated and Emmy Award-winning role as the boy who won't grow up in a new national tour of *Peter Pan*. Rigby starred in the 1990, 1991, and 1998-99 Broadway revivals, and toured the country extensively in the role through 2006, including the Theater at Madison Square Garden in December 2005. The internationally-known tale recounts the adventures of the three Darling children as they fly away from their nursery into the magic and wonder of Never Land. There, they encounter Captain Hook, villainous pirates, a crocodile, Indians and the fairy Tinker Bell.

Cathy Rigby in Peter Pan
(photo by Craig Schwartz)

Kissing Sid James

59E59 Theater C; First Preview: December 13, 2011; Opening Night: December 18, 2011; Closed January 1, 2012; 7 previews, 15 performances

Written by Robert Farquhar; Presented Red Lion Theatres and Cracking Up Productions as part of the 2011 Brits Off Broadway; Produced by 59E59 (Elysabeth Kleinhans, President and Artistic Director; Peter Tear, Executive Producer); Director, Jason Lawson; Set, Heather Wolensky; Costumes, Kate Klinger; Lighting, Jay Scott; Sound, Christopher Ash; Associate Lighting, Josh Starr; AEA Stage Manager, Jess Johnston; General Managers, Henry Filloux-Bennett, Nicholas Thompson; U.S. Press, Karen Greco

CAST Eddie **Alan Drake**; Crystal **Charlotte McKinney**

U.S. premiere of a new play presented in two acts.

SYNOPSIS Eddie and Crystal, two lonely hearts, throw caution to the wind and decide to spend a festive weekend together in an English seaside town. Hoping to find love amongst warm beer and cold chips, the mismatched lovers fight to find some common ground. But should Eddie have stayed at home to play scrabble with his mum?

Charlotte McKinney and Alan Drake in Kissing Sid James
(photo by Carol Rosegg)

It's Always Right Now, Until It's Later

St. Ann's Warehouse; Opening Night: January 3, 2012; Closed January 29, 2012; 24 performances

Written by Daniel Kitson; Produced by St. Ann's Warehouse (Susan Feldman, Artistic Director); Design, Susannah Henry and Daniel Kitson; Technical Director, Jon Meggat; Lighting, Rob Pell-Walpole and Daniel Kitson; For St. Ann's: Alex Berg (Finance), Marilynn Donini (External Affairs), Bill Updegraff (Marketing), Erik Wallin (General Manager), Owen Hughes (Production Manager), Kristyn R. Smith (Technical Director); Press, Blake Zidell and Associates

Performed by **Daniel Kitson**

U.S. premiere of a new solo performance show presented without intermission. Created at the Invisible Dot and Battersea Arts Centre in July 2010 and first presented August 11, 2010 at the Edinburgh Fringe Festival. The production also played The National Theatre's Lyttelton Theatre October 7-21, 2010 and a return engagement December 19-22, 2011 prior to this U.S. premiere.

SYNOPSIS St. Ann's Warehouse welcomes Daniel Kitson back after last year's hit show, *The Interminable Suicide of Gregory Church*. A new show about everything and nothing, *It's Always Right Now, Until It's Later* is about every single one of us, the past in our pockets, the future in our hearts and us, ourselves, very much stuck, trapped forever, in the tiny eternal moment between the two.

Daniel Kitson in It's Always Right Now, Until It's Later *(photo by Pavel Antonov)*

Leo

Clurman Theatre on Theatre Row; First Preview: January 6, 2012; Opening Night: January 15, 2012; Closed February 5, 2012; 8 previews, 22 performances

Created by Circle of Eleven (Berlin); Based on an original idea by Tobias Wegner; Produced by The Carol Tambor Theatrical Foundation (Carol Tambor, Chairman; Kent Lawson, President; Marilynn Tammi, Vice President) and Circle of Eleven; Director, Daniel Brière; Creative Producer, Gregg Parks; Set/Lighting, Flavia Hevia; Video, Heiko Kalmbach; Animation, Ingo Panke; Costumes, Heather McCrimmon; Choreography, Juan Kruz de Garaio Esnaola; Chief Executive Edinburgh Fringe Festival, Kath M. Mainland; Press, Karen Greco

Performed by **Tobias Wegner**

U.S. premiere of a new physical and multimedia theatre piece presented without intermission. World premiere at the 2011 Edinburgh Fringe Festival where it won "Best of Edinburgh Award."

SYNOPSIS *Leo* is a surprising and hilarious show that defies the laws of gravity. An ingenious combination of stage design and video projections, *Leo* creates an unexpected environment in which our hero is forced to adapt to this surprising situation. Follow *Leo*, in a logic-defying, fantastic adventure!

Tobias Wegner in Leo *(photo by Heiko Kalmbach)*

The Picture Box

Beckett Theatre on Theatre Row; First Preview: January 12, 2012; Opening Night: January 15, 2012; Closed January 29, 2012; 4 previews, 15 performances

Written by Cate Ryan; Produced by The Negro Ensemble Company (Charles Weldon, Artistic Director); Director, Charles Weldon; Set, Patrice Davidson; Costumes, Mark Caswell; Lighting, Ves Weaver; PSM, Femi Heggie; Press, Kevin McAnarney

CAST Mackie **Arthur French**; Josephine **Elain Graham**; Carrie **Jenniver Van Dyck**; Bob **Malachy Cleary**; Karen **Marisa Redanty**

SETTING Long Island; Election Day, 2008. World premiere of a new play presented without intermission.

SYNOPSIS From the deep south to the northeast, a young black man comes to work at the home of a white family on New York's Long Island. This young man becomes the "caretaker" of the little girl who lives in the home. She has been emotionally abandoned by her mother through her mother's second marriage. The trust of this estranged child creates a bond with her caretaker that spans a lifetime. Love and caring comes in all forms.

Arthur French and Jennifer Van Dyck in The Picture Box *(photo by Carmen L. deJesus)*

The Fall to Earth

59E59 Theater B; First Preview: January 13, 2012; Opening Night: January 18, 2012; Closed February 5, 2012; 5 previews, 20 performances

Written by Joel Drake Johnson; Produced by InProximity Theatre Company (Laurie Schaefer and Jolie Curtsinger, Co-Artistic Directors); Director, Joe Brancato; Set, James J. Fenton; Lighting, Todd Wren; Costumes, Patricia Doherty; Original Music and Sound, Sean Hagerty; Props, Jon Knust; Casting, Cindi Rush; Scenic Construction, Ken Larson Company; PSM, Michael Palmer; ASM, Angela Perez; Assistant Set, Christopher Thompson; Production Manager, Jeremy Karafin; For InProximity: Michael Poignand (Associate Producer), Jenna Gottlieb (Associate Producer); Press, Karen Greco

CAST Fay **Deborah Hedwall**; Terry **Amelia Campbell**; Rachel **Jolie Curtsinger**

New York premiere of a play presented without intermission. World premiere at Steppenwolf Theatre March 25–May 9, 2004

SYNOPSIS Kenny lived his life in secret. His mother and sister travel to an unfamiliar town looking for answers. With the help of a local policewoman they uncover tragic truths about him, their family and themselves.

Deborah Hedwall and Jolie Curtsinger in The Fall to Earth *(photo by John Quilty)*

Bob

New York Live Arts; Opening Night: January 19, 2012; Closed January 28, 2012; 10 performances

Created by Will Bond, text adapted by Jocelyn Clarke; Conceived and directed by Anne Bogart; Produced by SITI Company (Anne Bogart and Tadashi Suzuki, Founders); Set, Neil Patel; Lighting, Brian H. Scott; Soundscape, Darron L West; Costumes, James Schuette; Original Lighting, Mimi Jordan Sherin; Original Stage Manager, Megan Wanlass; For SITI Company: Megan Wanlass (Executive Director), Michelle Preston (Deputy Director), Vanessa Sparling (General Manager), Tina Mitchell (Artistic Associate); Press, Jenny Lerner

Performed by **Will Bond**

Revival of a solo performance play presented without intermission. World premiere at the Wexner Center for the Arts February 1998. New York premiere at New York Theatre Workshop April 22–May 31, 1998 (see *Theatre World* Vol. 54, page 97).

SYNOPSIS SITI Company returns to New York and begins its presenting partnership with the newly formed New York Live Arts with its Obie Award-winning *Bob*, a solo show that revolves around the life and times of internationally known avant-garde theater director, Robert Wilson. Acclaimed as a genius, he rides the fast track of the ever-shrinking global art scene. He uses his own history and everyone around him as fodder for his grandiose staged spectacles. Through *Bob*, you'll experience a creative crisis in the making and see where American pop culture and high culture collide. Bob is not meant to be a realistic portrait of Robert Wilson the man, rather a dip into an engaging perspective about family, art, and American Culture.

Will Bond in Bob *(photo courtesy of SITI Company)*

Seth Rudetsky's DISASTER! A 1970's disaster movie…musical

The Triad; Opening Night: January 22, 2012; Closed March 25, 2012; 7 performances (Sunday evenings)

Concept and co-written by Seth Rudetsky and Jack Plotnick; Co-creator of original concept and additional material by Drew Geraci; Produced by Off The Aisle; Director/Choreography, Denis Jones; Music Director, Steve Marzullo; Sets, Colin McGurk; Costumes, Brian Hemesath; Stage Manager, Tom Kosis; Assistant Director, Barry Busby; ASM, Jeremy Geller; Press, Springer Associates, Joe Trentacosta

CAST Ted **Seth Rudetsky**; Scott **Paul Castree**; Maury **Tom Riis Farrell**; Shirley **Kathy Fitzgerald**[*1]; Jackie **Lauren Kennedy**[*2]; Sister Mary Downey **Anika Larsen**; Marianne **Carrie Manolakos;** Levora **Lacretta Nicole**; Ben/Lisa **Clark Oliver**; Chad **Zak Resnick**; Tony **Clif Thorn**; Ensemble **Sherz Aletaha, Saum Eskandini, Spring Groove**[*3]**, Jennifer Knox, Kevin Loreque**; Understudy **Drew Geraci**

*Succeeded by: 1. Annie Golden 2. Felicia Finley 3. Lindsay Nicole Chambers

MUSICIANS Steve Marzullo (Keyboard), Matt Brown (Guitar), Jim Donica (Bass), Greg Joseph (Drums)

SETTING Summer 1979; New York City. World premiere of a new parody musical presented in two acts.

SYNOPSIS A tribute to such films as *The Poseidon Adventure, Airport, Earthquake,* and *The Swarm, Disaster!* starts on a summer night in 1979. All the hottest New York City A-Listers are putting on their platform shoes and polyester disco shirts and heading to the grand opening of Manhattan's first floating casino and discotheque. Little do they know that their night of boogie fever, Farrah Fawcett-feathered-hair and Bella Abzug hats will turn into….DISASTER!

Philoktetes **Seth Moore**; Carrier **Tommy Crawford**; Shade of Herakles **Victor Joel Ortiz**; Shade of Dejanira **Kate Michaud**; *Ajax*: Sheep **Dave Brown**, **Charlotte Bydwell**, **Alexander Cook**, **Ugo Chukwu**, **Victoria Haynes**, **Miles Jacoby**, **Erik Olson**, **Liz Tancredi**; Ajax **Grant Harrison**; Agamemnon **Sean McIntyre**; Menelaus **Alex Grubbs**; Odysseus **Bobby Foley**; Eurysakes **Tony Vo**; Tekmessa **Allison Buck**; Carrier **Tommy Crawford**; Philoktetes **Seth Moore**; *Elektra*: Orestes **Erik Olson**; Shade of Agamemnon **Sean McIntyre**; Elektra **Betsy Lippitt**; Chrysothemis **Charlotte Bydwell**; Clytemnestra **Akyiaa Wilson**; Aegisthus **Nate Washburn**; *Antigone*: Antigone **Katherine Folk-Sullivan**; Polyneices **Yoni Ben-Yehuda**; Creon **Stephen Stout**; Ismene **Cleo Gray**; Haemon **Matt Barbot**; Blind Seer **Holly Chou**; Carrier **Tommy Crawford**

New York premiere of new adaptations of seven classic plays presented with two meal breaks. Workshopped at Oregon Shakespeare Festival and in New York at Exit, Pursued by a Bear Theater Company, the show premiered at the The Hypocrites in Chicago September 6–October 23, 2011.

SYNOPSIS In *These Seven Sicknesses*, Sophocles' seven surviving plays combine to create a stunning portrait of the human condition, where the intermingling of chance and fate yields disquieting results. A witty and relevant interpretation of the classics, *These Seven Sicknesses* is an epic examination of the past and a window on the present.

Seth Rudetsky and Lauren Kennedy in Disaster! *(photo by Drew Geraci)*

These Seven Sicknesses

Flea Theater; First Preview: January 19, 2012; Opening Night: January 29, 2012; Closed March 4, 2012; 8 previews, 24 performances

Written by Sean Graney, based on the seven surviving plays of Sophocles; Produced the Flea Theater (Jim Simpson, Artistic Director; Carol Ostrow, Producing Director; Beth Dembrow, Managing Director); Director, Ed Sylvanus Iskandar; Set, Julia Noulin-Merat; Costumes, Loren Shaw; Lighting, Carl Wiemann; Sound, Patrick Metzger; Fight Director, Michael Wieser; Music Director, David Dabbon; Dramaturg, Greg Vanhorn; Stage Management, Edward Herman, Kara Kaufman; Production Voice/Speech Coach, Amy Jo Jackson; Assistant Set, John Jalandoni; Assistant Costumes, Maeve Kelly; Assistant Dramaturg, Sarah Wansley; Graphic Design, David Prittie; Assistant to Set Design, John Jalandoni; Resident Directors, Tom Costello, Ben Kamine; Technical Director, Liz Blessing; Development, Penn Genthner; Marketing and Membership, Christopher Massimine; Company Manager, Sarah Wansley; Assistant Technical Director, Kyle Crose; Marketing Assistant, Crystal Arnette; Press, Ron Lasko/Spin Cycle

CAST *Prologue*: Orderly **Will Turner**; Nurse 1 **Glenna Grant**; New Nurse **Tiffany Abercrombie**; Nurse **Eloise Eonnet**; Nurse 3 **Marie Claire Roussel**; Nurse 4 **Jenelle Chu**; Nurse 5 **Olivia Stoker**; *Oedipus*: Sick Woman **Cameran Hebb**; Oedipus **Jeff Ronan**; Antigone **Katherine Folk-Sullivan**; Creon **Stephen Stout**; Blind Seer **Holly Chou**; Jocasta **Satomi Blair**; Carrier **Tommy Crawford**; Ismene **Cleo Gray**; Polyneices **Yoni-Ben Yehuda**; Eteokles **Bobby Foley**; *In Trachis*: Dejanira **Kate Michaud**; Hyllus **Miles Jacoby**; Carrier **Tommy Crawford**; Philoktetes **Seth Moore**; Iole **Liz Tancredi**; Herakles **Victor Joel Ortiz**; *In Colonus*: Antigone **Katherine Folk-Sullivan**; Oedipus **Ugo Chukwu**; Creon **Stephen Stout**; Polyneices **Yoni Ben-Yehuda**; Ismene **Cleo Gray**; Blind Seer **Holly Chau**; Carrier **Tommy Crawford**; *Philoktetes*: Odysseus **Bobby Foley**; Neoptolemus **Alex Herrald**;

Katherine Folk-Sullivan and Jeff Ronan in These Seven Sicknesses *(photo by Laura June Kirsch)*

Myths and Hymns

West End Theatre; Opening Night: January 31, 2012; Closed February 26, 2012; 28 performances

Music and lyrics by Adam Guettel, additional lyrics by Ellen Fitzhugh; New narrative by Elizabeth Lucas; Produced by Prospect Theater Company (Cara Reichel, Producing Artistic Director; Melissa Hubert, Managing Director); Director, Elizabeth Lucas; Choreography, Wendy Seyb; Sets, Ann Bartek; Costumes, Emily Morgan DeAngelis; Lighting, Herrick Goldman; Sound, Janie Bullard; Musical Director, Katya Stanislavskaya; Stage Manager, Kristine Ayers; Music Supervisor/Additional Arrangements, Robert Meffe; Original Orchestrations, Bruce Coughlin; Production Manager, Damon Whitten; Company Manager, B.J. Evans; Props Coordinator, Morgan Fox; Technical Director, Tim Adams; ASM, Kristin Dwyer; Associate Lighting, Susan M. Nicholson; Master Electrician, Nicolo DePierro; Sound Mixer, Alex Fisher; Audio Engineer, Carrie Cook; Wardrobe Supervisor, Stephanie Holser; Dance Captain, Lucas Steele

CAST Woman **Linda Balgord**; Daughter **Anika Larsen**; Husband **Bob Stillman**; Son **Lucas Steele**; Trickster **Ally Bonino**; Lover **Matthew Farcher**; Shapeshifter **Donell James Foreman**

BAND Katya Stanislavskaya (Conductor/Piano), Adam Waddell (Violin), Alden Terry (Bass), Jay Mack (Percussion), Jonathan Russ (Guitar), Allison Seidner (Cello)

MUSICAL NUMBERS *Part 1: Reality*: Link; *Part 2: Joyful Beginnings*: Hero and Leander; At the Sounding; Prometheus; Pegasus; *Part 3: Loss of the Spirit*: There's a Shout; Come to Jesus; Saturn Returns; Jesus the Mighty Conqueror; *Part 4: Loss of the Body*: Icarus; Children of the Heavenly King; There's A Land; Life Is But a Dream; *Part 5: Loss of the Mind or Time Passes Anyway*: Sisyphus; How Can I Lose You? Migratory V; *Part 6: Bargaining With God*: Awaiting You; The Great Highway; Build a Bridge; Saturn Returns (reprise); *Part 7: Return to Grace*: Migratory V (reprise)

Revival of a theatrical song cycle presented in seven parts without intermission. The original production (under the title *Saturn Returns*) was presented Off-Broadway at the Public Theater March 24–April 26, 1998 (see *Theatre World* Vol. 54, page 96).

SYNOPSIS As a daughter returns to move her ailing mother out of the family home, the two wrestle with the ghosts of their father and husband, brother and son, re-living and confronting their mythologized past. Director Elizabeth Lucas's original concept brings a character-driven context to Adam Guettel's celebrated song cycle, illuminating the intricate relationships amongst a single family.

Bob Stillman, Linda Balgord and Ally Bonino in Myths and Hymns *(photo by Richard Termine)*

Tokio Confidential

Atlantic Stage 2; Opening Night: February 5, 2012; Closed February 19, 2012; 19 performances

Book, music, and lyrics by Eric Schorr; Produced by Scandal Productions; Director, Johanna McKeon; Choreography, Tricia Brouk; Music Director, Mark Hartman; Set, David Barber; Lighting, Joel Silver; Costumes, Jacob Climer; Sound, Carl Casella; Video/Projections, Darrel Maloney; Orchestrations, Zak Sandler; Wigs, Ashley Ryan; Casting, Judy Bowman; PSM, Jess Johnston; Production Supervisor, Production Core; Company Manager, Danielle Karliner; General Management Consultant, DR Theatrical Management (Seth A. Goldstein, Adam Hess, Aaron Thompson, Heather Schings, Kyle Provost, Danielle Karliner); ASM, Hilary Austin; Assistant Director, Samuel Stonefield; Assistant Choreographer, Ljuba Castot; Associate Production Manager, Josh Morgan; Assistant Company Manager, Mickey McGuire; Technical Director, Kevin Mullins; Assistant Technical Director, Jason Slack; Assistant Lighting, Mary Ellen Stebbins; Scene Design

Assistants, Catherine Jacot Guillarmo, Thomas George; Noh Advisors, Master Kansuke and Shuhei Kinoshita; Master Electrician, John Anselmo; Associate Master Electrician, Derek Raynor; Advertising, Hofstetter+Parnters/Agency 212; Marketing, Sozo Media, Rika Iino; Press, Keith Sherman and Associates, Scott Klein, Brett Oberman, Bill Coyle, Logan Metzler

CAST Ernest Osmond **Jeff Kready**; Akira/Waki Priest **Austin Ku**; Horiyoshi/Customs Officer/Rickshaw Driver/Michimori **Mel Sagrado Maghuyop**; Ralph Archer **Benjamin McHugh**; Sachiko/Kozaisho **Manna Nichols**; Ulysses S. Grant **Mike O'Carroll**; Isabella Archer **Jill Paice**

ORCHESTRA Mark Hartman (Conductor/Keyboard), Danny Weller (Bass), Chris Reza (Reed 1), Danny Rivera (Reed 2)

MUSICAL NUMBERS Restless Spirits; Journey With Me; The Power of Suggestion; Are You Prepared For That?; Indelible; Tale of the Yoshiwara; Shifting Ground; A Reluctant Soldier; Magic Needles; Hototogisu; Draw the Line; The Jurisdiction of Affection; Looking-back Willow; At Sea; Ukiyo; The Spider; Beautiful Brevity; Finale

SETTING Time: 1879-1880, Japan. World premiere of a new musical presented in two acts.

SYNOPSIS Isabella Archer, a young American war widow crosses an ocean in search of a lost love – and is about to cross a line from which she can never return. *Tokio Confidential* is a journey across the boundaries between pleasure and pain, art and artifice, the secrets of the flesh and the sins of the heart.

Mel Maghuyop, Jill Paice, and Benjamin McHugh in Tokio Confidential *(photo by Ellis Gaskell)*

Chekhovek

ArcLight Theatre; First Preview: February 1, 2012; Opening Night: February 7, 2012; Closed March 4, 2012; 6 previews, 34 performances

Based on short stories written by Anton Chekhov, from translations by Constance Garnett; Adapted and directed by Melania Levitsky; Produced by The Actors' Ensemble, GoShow Entertainment, and William Goins; Set, David L. Arsenault; Lighting, Natassia Jimenez; Costumes, Erica E. Evans; PSM, Jessa Nicole Pollack; ASM, Jeanne Travis; Music, Jonathan Talbott; General Manager, Adam Fitzgerald; Carpenter, Daniel Moss; Electrician, Xander Duffy; Marketing and Advertising, The Pekoe Group; Press, Bruce Cohen

CAST Eddie Allen, David Anderson, Elizabeth Fountain, Rob Leo Roy, Celia Schaefer; Musician Jonathan Talbott

New York premiere of a new play presented in two acts. World premiere (under the title *Virtue, Desire, Death, and Foolishness*) produced by Walking the dog Theatre Company in Hudson, New York in 2009.

SYNOPSIS In *Chekhovek*, five actors and one musician bring nine of Anton Chekhov's best known and most theatrical short stories to life in the new comedy that presents an array of flawed, intense and quite human characters from *The Lady with the Dog*, *Death of a Government Clerk*, *The Ninny*, *A Blunder*, *The Huntsman*, *The Chemist's Wife*, *The Black Monk*, *Vanka*, *The Chorus Girl*, and *Gusev*.

David Anderson and Elizabeth Fountain in Chekhovek *(photo by Dan Region)*

Psycho Therapy

Cherry Lane Theatre; First Preview: January 19, 2012; Opening Night: February 7, 2012; Closed February 25, 2012; 17 previews, 21 performances; Encored April 8-May 26, 2012; 55 performances

Written by Frank Strausser; Produced by Barbara Ligeti and Wishing Well Productions by special arrangement with the Cherry Lane Theatre (Angelina Fiordellisi, Executive Director); Original Director, Alex Lippard (uncredited in playbill; Encore Director, Michael Bush; Set, Michael V. Moore; Costumes, Amanda Bujak; Lighting, Jeff Croiter; Sound, Amy Altadonna; Composer, Allison Leyton-Brown; Fight Director, Christian Kelly-Sordelet; Logo Design, Sean Day Michael; Casting, Jeffery Passero; La Vie Productions, General Manager; PSM, Marci Skolnick; ASM, Nathan K. Claus; Production Supervisor, Production Core/James E. Cleveland; Associate Producer, Christine De Lisle; Advertising and Marketing, The Pekoe Group; Press, Sam Rudy Media Relations

CAST Dorian **Jeffrey Carlson**[1]; Nancy **Jan Leslie Harding**; Philip **Laurence Lau**; Lily **Angelica Page**[2]

*Succeeded by: 1. Alexander Cendese 2. Lois Robbins (February 18 and 25 matinee performances), Gabrielle Miller (4/8/12)

SETTING Los Angeles; The present. Off-Broadway premiere of a new play presented without intermission. Previously presented at the 2009 Midtown International Theatre Festival.

SYNOPSIS Lily's fiancée Phillip blows off couples therapy and Dorian, her hot young ex-boyfriend, jumps in to fill the void. When the trio ends up on the couch together, only therapist Nancy Winston can untangle the kinks.

Jan Leslie Harding, Laurence Lau, Angelica Page, and Jeffrey Carlson in Psycho Therapy *(photo by Carol Rosegg)*

And God Created Great Whales

Theatre at 45 Bleecker; First Preview: February 7, 2012; Opening Night: February 12, 2012; Closed March 25, 2012; 5 previews, 37 performances

Created, composed, and written by Rinde Eckert; Produced by Culture Project (Allan Buchman, Artistic Director; Nan Richardson, Executive Director; Vanessa Sparling, Managing Director) in association with Elisha Wiesel; Director, David Schweizer; Sets and Lighting, John Torres and Caleb Wertenbaker (based on original designs by Kevin Adams); Costumes, Clint Ramos; Sound, Rinde Eckert; PSM, Scott Pegg; ASM, Elliot Meyers; Tour Booking, Sue Endrizzi Morris; For Culture Project: Manda Martin (Associate Artistic Director), Jayashri Wyatt (Director of Productions), Victoria Andújar (Administrative Director and Special Assistant to Mr. Buchman), Jake Platt (Technical Director), Alex Mallory and Rebecca Schwartz (Assistant Producers), Elisa Lavery (Senior Marketing Associate), Jennifer Joyce (Senior Development Associate), Mary Moore (Box Office); Press, Richard Kornberg and Associates

CAST Nathan **Rinde Eckert**; Olivia **Nora Cole**

Revival of a play with music presented without intermission. Commissioned and originally produced by The Foundry Theatre in June 2000.

SYNOPSIS *And God Created Great Whales* is a haunting musical adventure that delves into the psyche of a composer who is trying to create an opera based on Herman Melville's *Moby Dick*. Desperately fighting against a disease that is eating away at his mind, he must rely on a tape recorder to remind him of yesterday's instructions to himself. Rinde Eckert displays his full creative force in this frenzied, funny, romantic, and moving play.

Rinde Eckert and Nora Cole in And God Created Great Whales
(photo by Caleb Wertenbaker)

Neimah Djourabchi and Bonnie Sherman in The Inexplicable Redemption
of Agent G *(photo by Peter James Zielinski)*

The Inexplicable Redemption of Agent G

Beckett Theatre on Theatre Row; First Preview: February 7, 2012; Opening Night:
February 14, 2012; Closed March 4, 2012; 7 previews, 18 performances

Written by Qui Nguyen; Produced by Ma-Yi Theater Company (Ralph B. Peña,
Artistic Director; Jorge Z. Ortoll, Executive Director; Suzette Porte, Associate
Director) in association with Vampire Cowboys (Qui Nguyen and Robert Ross
Parker, Artistic Directors; Abby Marcus, Managing Director; Nick Francone,
Producing Director); Director/Film and Animation Director, Robert Ross Parker;
Sets and Lighting, Nick Francone; Costumes, Jessica Wegener Shay; Original
Music and Sound, Shane Rettig; Video, Matt Tennie; Puppet Desing, David
Valentine; Choreography, Jamie Dunn; PSM, Danielle Buccino; ASM, Kelly
Ruth Cole; Production Manager, Katherine Gloria Tharp; Fight Choreography,
Qui Nguyen; Assistant Design: Kristina Makowski (costumes), Heather Smaha
(lighting), Kate Brown (sound), Spike McCue (video); Technical Director, Rudy
Guerrero; Scenery, Randy Lee Hartwig; Audio Supervisor/Board Operator, Kevin
Feustel; Prop Coordinator, Kristine Ayers; Wardrobe Supervisor, Kyle Skillin;
Fight/Dance Captain, Bonnie Sherman; Crew, A.J. Jackson, Will Hansen, Laura
Krassowski, Evan Roby, Matt Creeden, Mauli Delaney, Jeffrey Nielsen; Program
Cover, Jeremy Arambulo; Additional Video, Luke Harlan; Press, Sam Rudy Media
Relations

CAST Hung **Neimah Djourabchi**; Dinh, Tien, Pimp, Gookie Monster, David
Henry Hwang **Jon Hoche**; San **Brooke Ishibashi**; Molly, Abby **Bonnie
Sherman**; Qui **Temar Underwood**

Off-Broadway premiere of a new play with martial arts and multimedia presented
without intermission. World premiere Off-Off Broadway at the Icubator Arts Project
March 24–April 16, 2011 (see *Theatre World* Vol. 67, page 298).

SYNOPSIS It's been 10 years since Agent G has last been in Vietnam where
his family and friends were all viciously slain. He's now come back looking for
answers and a good bit of revenge, however forces are at hand trying to stop him
as well as the playwright from finishing this brutal task.

Poetic License

59E59 Theater B; First Preview: February 9, 2012; Opening Night: February 15,
2012; Closed March 4, 2012; 6 previews, 20 performances

Written by Jack Canfora; Produced by The Directors Company (Michael Parva,
Artistic/Producing Director) in association with New Jersey Repertory Company
(SuzAnene Barabas, Artistic Producer; Gabor Barabas, Executive Producer);
Director, Evan Bergman; Set Design/Prop Master, Jessica L. Parks; Costumes,
Patricia E. Doherty; Lighting, Jill Nagle; Sound, John Emmett O'Brien; Casting,
Judy Henderson; PSM, Rose Riccardi; ASM, Katharine S. Fergerson; General
Manager, Leah Michalos; Business/Marketing Director, R.K. Greene; Resident
Master Director, Nagle Jackson; Dramatuge, Melissa Page; Technical Director,
Aneta Feld; Wardrobe Supervisor, Amber Paul; Master Carpenter, James Sullivan;
Press Consultant, Joe Trentacosta; Press for 59E59, Karen Greco

CAST Katherine Greer **Natalie Kuhn**; Edmund **Ari Butler**; Diane Greer **Liza
Vann**; John Greer **Geraint Wyn Davies**

SETTING Place: The living room of a house near the campus of a Northeastern
college. Time: Roughly autumn, roughly now. New York premiere of a new
play presented without intermission. World premiere at New Jersey Repertory
Company.

SYNOPSIS John Greer is a professor at a renowned university, a beloved father,
and he is about to be named Poet Laureate. He owes much of his success to
his wife, Diane, who aggressively shepherds his career. But when their daughter
and her new boyfriend return home for the weekend, hidden secrets emerge that
threaten to destroy the image he has cultivated in both his public and private lives.
Poetic License is a biting drama set against the cut-throat, "publish or perish"
world of academia, and explores how one person's past can shape his art, his
family and, in this case, his future.

Geraint Wyn Davies, Ari Butler, and Liza Vann in Poetic License
(photo by Carol Rosegg)

Sally and Tom (The American Way)

Castillo Theatre; Opening Night: February 17, 2012; Closed March 25, 2012; Encored April 20–May 6, 2012; 25 performances

Book and lyrics by Fred Newman, music by Annie Roboff; Produced by the Castillo Theatre (Dan Friedman, Artistic Director; Diane Stiles, Managing Director); Director, Gabrielle L. Kurlander; Sets and Video, Joseph Spirito; Costumes, EmilieCharlotte; Lighting, NickKolin; Wigs/Makeup, Karine Ivey; Choreography, Lonné Moretton; Musical Director, Michael Walsh; Music Arrangements/Sound, David Belmont; Stage Manager, Ben Rodman; Producer, John Rankin III; Assistant Directors, Antoine Joyce, David Nackman; Assistant Producers, Shereen Brown, Kimberly Chin, Nick Maccarone; Wardrobe Supervisors, Shereen Brown, Jessy Cheng, Xinyue Guan, Chandra Jawalaprasad; Electricians, Eric Loetterle, Ramik Rivers, Jamie Spear, Skekth Williams; Lighting Operators, Michael Conrad, Stephano Dubuc; Sound Operators, Emmanuel Nunez, Liam Riordan, Jamie Spear, Dawn Winbush; Production Coordinator, Andy Allis; Sales and Marketing, Gail Peck

CAST James T. Callender **Sean Patrick Gibbons**[1]; James Madison **Jacqueline Salit** or **David Nackman**; Madison Hemings **Brian D. Hills**; Thomas Jefferson **Adam Kemmerer**[2]; Sally Hemings **Ava Jenkins**

*Succeeded by: 1. David Nackman (4/20/12) 2. Thaddeus Pearson (4/20/12)

Sean Patrick Gibbons, Ava Jenkins, Brian D. Hills, Jacqueline Salit in
Sally and Tom (The American Way) *(photo by Ronald L. Glassman)*

ORCHESTRA Michael Walsh (Keyboards), David Belmont (Guitar, Percussion), Don Hulbert (Flute), Premik Russell Tubbs (Brass, Reeds), Zsaz Rutkowski (Cello), Gerry McCord (Bass), Arnie Wise (Drums), Ursel Schlict (Piano), Eric Udel (Bass)

MUSICAL NUMBERS I'm a Yankee Doodle Mercenary; I'll Always Be Thought of That Way; Jefferson's Declaration; I'll Never Be Free; Is It Constitutional?; Enslaved by the Color of Our Skin; Rich and Poor Hypocrisy; The Coward's Song; The American Way; The Beginning of America's Night

SETTING Richmond and Monticello, Virginia; 1789–1802. Revival of a musical presented in five scenes in two acts. The original production was presented at the Castillo Theatre October 7–December 4, 2005 (see *Theatre World* Vol. 62, page 223).

SYNOPSIS *Sally and Tom (The American Way)* examines the 30-year relationship between Thomas Jefferson and his slave Sally Hemings, a relationship that produced six children and embodies the wrenching conflict between democracy and slavery, and its legacy of racism that continues to shape America to this day.

Call Me Waldo

June Havoc Theatre; First Preview: February 14, 2012; Opening Night: February 22, 2012; Closed March 11, 2012; 8 previews, 20 performances

Written by Rob Ackerman; Produced by the Working Theater (Mark Plesent, Producing Artistic Director; Nicholas Betito, General Manager); Director, Margarett Perry; Sets and Lighting, David L. Arsenault; Costumes and Props, Hannah Kochman; Sound, Don Tindall; Production Supervisor, Production Core/James L. Cleveland; PSM, Trisha Henson; ASM, Rebecca Spinac; Stage Management Sub, Eileen Arnold; Development Consultant, Adam J. Thompson; Literary Manager, Dina Vovsi; Press, Sam Rudy Media Relations

CAST Lee/Waldo **Matthew Boston**; Gus **Brian Dykstra**; Sarah **Rita Rehn**; Cynthia **Jennifer Dorr White**

SETTING Bethpage, Long Island. Off-Broadway premiere of a new play presented without intermission. This production played its world premiere engagement at the Kitchen Theater in Ithaca, New York (Rachel Lampert, Artistic Director; Stephen Nunley, Managing Director) January 18–February 5, 2012.

SYNOPSIS Lee Fountain is an ordinary electrician: his boss doesn't appreciate him, his wife keeps correcting him, and his life seems to have lost all meaning. But when Lee starts channeling the spirit of Ralph Waldo Emerson, everyone wakes up. *Call Me Waldo* shows us how one person's poetic yearnings can change everyone and everything - even our imperfect world.

Brian Dykstra, Rita Rehn, and Matthew Boston in Call Me Waldo
(photo by Lia Chang)

Early Plays

St. Ann's Warehouse; First Preview: February 15, 2012; Opening Night: February 22, 2012; Closed March 11, 2012; 7 previews, 20 performances

Based on the Glenciarn plays (*Moon of the Caribbees*, *Bound East for Cardiff*, and *The Long Voyage Home*) written by Eugene O'Neill; Produced by the Wooster Group (Elizabeth LeCompte, Artistic Director) and New York City Players (Richard Maxwell, Artistic Director); Presented by St. Ann's Warehouse (Susan Feldman, Artistic Director); Director/Composer, Richard Maxwell; Set, Jim Clayburgh and Elizabeth LeCompte; Costumes, Enver Chakartash; Lighting, Aron Deyo and Michael McGee; Sound, Bobby McElver; Projections, Andrew Schneider; Production Manager/Additional Set/Sound Operator, Bozkurt Karasu; Stage Manager, Teresa Hartmann; Assistant Director, Nicholas Elliott; Musicians, Bobby McElver, Brian Mendes, Andrew Schneider; Technical Director, Bill Kennedy; Production Staff for The Wooster Group, Snadra Garner, Cynthia Hedstrom, Jason Gray Platt, Jamie Poskin; Video Blog, Zbigniew Bzymek; Press, Blake Zidell and Associates

CAST *Moon of the Caribbees*: Driscoll **Ari Fliakos**; Smitty **Kevin Hurley**; Cocky **Keith Connolly**; Big Frank/Paul/Lamps **Jim Fletcher**; Yank **Brian Mendes**; Davis **Andrew Schneider**; Olson/Max **Bobby McElver**; Paddy/Chips **Lakpa Bhutia**; The Donkeyman **Alex Delinois**; Bella **Kate Valk**; Pearl **Victoria Vazquez**; The First Mate **Enver Chakartash**; *Bound East for Cardiff*: Yank **Brian Mendes**; Driscoll **Ari Fliakos**; Cocky **Keith Connolly**; Davis **Andrew Schneider**; Scotty **Lakpa Bhutia**; Olson/Paul **Bobby McElver**; Smitty **Kevin Hurley**; Ivan **Jim Fletcher**; The Captain **Enver Chakartash**; The Mate **Alex Delinois**; *The Long Voyage Home*: Fat Joe **Jim Fletcher**; Nick **Kevin Hurley**; Mag/Kate **Kate Valk**; Driscoll **Ari Fliakos**; Olson **Bobby McElver**; Cocky **Keith Connolly**; Ivan **Lakpa Bhutia**; Freda **Victoria Vazquez**; One of the Roughs **Enver Chakartash**; The Rough **Alex Delinois**

World premiere of an adaptation of three early one-act plays presented with original music and songs without intermission.

SYNOPSIS The Wooster Group invited Richard Maxwell of New York City Players to adapt and direct Eugene O'Neill's early "Glencairn" plays—*Bound East for Cardiff* (1914), *The Long Voyage Home* (1917) and *The Moon of the Caribbees* (1918). *Early Plays* takes O'Neill's tales of sailors on and off the ocean as a base to explore themes of longing and eternity. Dark episodes showing the underside of turn-of-the-century maritime life—brawls, dances and carousing—are staged with a quotidian grace allowing these simple stories to resonate emotionally.

Brian Mendes and Ari Fliakos in Early Plays *(photo by Zbigniew Bzymek)*

Same River

Irondale Center; Opening Night: February 23, 2012; Closed March 3, 2012; 7 performances

Devised and presented by the Strike Anywhere Performance Ensemble (Leese Walker, Artistic/Producing Director); Production Desing and Lighting, Joe Doran; Costumes, Erin Schultz; Sound, Rolf Sturm; Video, Jonathan Carr; Stage Manager, Amanda Hinkle; Technical Director, Michaelangelo DeSerio; Production Assistant, Meredith Cody; Installation Artists, Haifa Bint-Kadi, Jeanne Wilkinson; Education Coordinator, Amanda Hinkle; Light Board Operator, Dennis Yueh-Yeh Li; Sound Engineer, Ian Axness; Video Engineer, Jonathan Carr; Build Crew, Steve Brenman, Mike Faba, Omar Jaslin, Norman Lander, Nolan Kennedy; Irondale Center Press, Press, Lucy Walters-Maneri

CAST **Donna Bouthillier**, **Rob Henke** (Trumpet), **Nolan Kennedy**, **Damen Scranton**, **Rolf Sturm** (Guitar), **Leese Walker**

World premiere of a improvisational theatrical piece with music, multimedia, and art installation presented without intermission.

SYNOPSIS *Same River* is an improvised, interdisciplinary performance based on interviews with local residents about fracking. Strike Anywhere uses the collected information and personal stories to create a high-quality, improvised performance with social and political significance. As hydro-fracking is poised to affect NYC's water supply, *Same River* brings the upstate war over this controversial method of drilling downstream and provides a forum for meaningful dialogue, empathy, awareness and local action.

Donna Bouthillier in Same River *(photo by Lorenzo Ciniglio)*

Rated P for Parenthood

Westside Theatre-Upstairs; First Preview: February 8, 2012; Opening Night: February 29, 2012; Closed April 8, 2012; 24 previews, 46 performances

Book and lyrics by Sandy Rustin, music and lyrics by Dan Lipton and David Rossmer; Produced by Andrew Asnes, Timothy Schmidt, Evan Fleischer, Eve Chilton, in association with Jed Bernstein, Charlotte Cohn, Larry Hirschhorn/Joe and Sandi Black; Director, Jeremy Dobrish; Choreography, Rachel Bress; Set, Steven Capone; Costumes, Emily DeAngelis; Lighting, Michael Gottlieb; Sound, Jill BC DuBoff and David Sanderson; Casting, Cindi Rush; Projections, Chris Kateff and Richard DiBella; Prop Master, Jeena Yoon; Orchestrations and Arrangements, David Rossmer and Dan Lipton; Music Director, Meg Zervoulis; PSM, Cambra Overend; Production Supervisor, Production Core/James L. Cleveland; Assoicate Producer, Richard Hornos; General Management, DR Theatrical Management, Adam Hess, Seth Goldstein; Company Manager, Kyle Provost; Associate Director, Gina Rattan; Associate Choreographer, Parker Esse; Production Manager, Jared

Goldstein; ASM, Bryn Magnus; Keyboard Programmer, Randy Cohen; Music Copyist, Matt Aument; Dance Captain, Natalie Charle Ellis; Assistant Design: Matthew Hundley (costumes), Robert W. Sambrato (lighting); Associate Casting, Michele B. Weiss; Assistant Production Manager, Taylor Michael; Wardrobe, Charlotte Lily Gaspard; Production Assistant, Jean Marie Hufford; Audio Technician, David Weigant; Assistant Company Managers, Julie DeRossi, Mickey McGuire; Marketing Director, Above the Title Entertainment; Marketing Associate, Scott Lupi; Marketing Assistant, Amelia Bienstock; Advertising and Marketing, aka; Press, O+M Company, Rick Miramontez, Elizabeth Wagner

CAST Woman 1 **Courtney Balan**; Man 2 **Chris Hoch**; Man 1 **David Josefsberg**; Woman 2 **Joanna Young** Understudies **Natalie Charle Ellis**, **Spencer Moses**

MUSICIANS Meg Zervoulis (Conductor/Keyboard), Vincent Livolsi (Percussion), Nathan A. Roberts (Guitar)

SCENES & SONGS *Prelude*; *Push It on Out*; Photo Fiasco; *Little Boy*; The Babysitters; *Tick Tock*; The First Talk; Interview With a Headmaster; Mind Over Playground; *Prayer for Ellie*; *Parent Teacher Conference*; Thumb Sucker; You Can't Handle the Tooth; The Second Talk; *Man in a Uniform*; *Homework*; Supervision; *Wild Romance*; The Last Talk; *The Game*; *Morning Love Song*; The Sandwich Artist; *Driving in D Minor*; School Supplies; Prom Night; *To Be Continued…*

Off-Broadway premiere of a new musical revue presented without intermission. World premiere produced by Midtown Direct Rep at the South Orange Performing Arts Center May 5-8, 2011.

SYNOPSIS *Rated P for Parenthood* chronicles every stage of modern-day parenting, from conception to college, with giant doses of heart and humor. A versatile cast of four takes the audience through the ups and downs of childrearing - from the sublime to the ridiculous - in a series of comic and musical vignettes.

(Front): Joanna Young, David Josefsburg, (back): Courtney Balan, and Chris Hoch in Rated P for Parenthood *(photo by Carol Rosegg)*

Tribes

Barrow Street Theatre; First Preview: February 16, 2012; Opening Night: March 4, 2012; Closed ; 19 previews, 99 performances as of May 31, 2012

Written by Nina Raine; Produced by Scott Morfee, Jean Doumanian, Tom Wirstshafter, Patrick Daly, Jennifer Manocherian, Barbara Manocherian, Christian Chadd Taylor, Burnt Umber Productions (Judi Krupp and Bill Gerber), Marc and Lisa Biales, and Roger E. Kass; Director, David Cromer; Set, Scott Pask; Costumes, Tristan Raines; Lighting, Keith Parham; Projections, Jeff Sugg; Sound, Daniel Kluger; Prop Design and Coordination, Kathy Fabian/Propstar; Hair and Makeup, Leah J. Loukas; PSM, Richard A. Hodge; Dialect Coach, Stephen Gabis; Casting, Pat McCorkle; General Manager, Michael Page; Associate General Manager, Amy Dalba; Production Management, Production Core/James L. Cleveland; Production Manager, Katy J. Yonally; Technical Director, Peter Fry; ASM, Rosy Garner; Assistant Design: John Zuiker (set), Caitlin Conci (costumes), Ryan Metzler (lighting), Patrick Southern (projections), Nathan Wheeler (sound); Assistant Production Manager, Maggie Davis; Assistant Technical Director, Sergio Murania; Assistant Director, Seth Sikes; Production Assistant, Xander Duffy; ASL Interpreter, Candace Broecker-Penn; ASL Consultant, Alexandria Wailes; Piano Coach, Daniel Kluger; Master Electrician, The Lightning Syndicate; Mainstage Programmer, Bill Growney; Audio Head, Colin Whitely; Scenic Charge, Jacquelyn Marlot; Projections Operator, Josh Kohler; Prop Running Crew, Matt Allamon; Artwork, Fraver; Advertising, aka; Press, O+M Company, Rick Miramontez, Molly Barnett

CAST Daniel **Will Brill**; Billy **Russell Harvard**; Christopher **Jeff Perry**; Sylvia **Susan Pourfar**; Ruth **Gayle Rankin**; Beth **Mare Winningham**

UNDERSTUDIES Thomas Dellamonica (Billy, Daniel), Meghan Mae O'Neill (Ruth, Sylvia)

2011-2012 AWARDS Drama Desk Award: Outstanding Play; New York Drama Critics Circle Award: Best Foreign Play; Off-Broadway Alliance Award: Best New Play; Obie Award: Susan Pourfar (Performance); **Theatre World Award**: Russell Harvard; **Dorothy Loudon Award**: Susan Pourfar

U.S. premiere of a new play presented in two acts. Commissioned and first presented by the English Stage Company at the Royal Court Theatre on October 14, 2010.

SYNOPSIS In *Tribes*, Billy was born deaf, into a hearing family, and raised inside the fiercely idiosyncratic and unrepentantly politically incorrect cocoon of his parent's house. He has adapted brilliantly to his family's unconventional ways, but they've never bothered to return the favor. It's not until he meets Sylvia, a young woman on the brink of deafness, that he finally understands what it means to be understood. Yes, Billy's family can hear, but will they ever listen?

Jeff Perry and Russell Harvard in Tribes *(photo by Gregory Costanzo)*

Eternal Equinox

59E59 Theater C; First Preview: March 1, 2012; Opening Night: March 7, 2012; Closed March 31, 2012; 6 previews, 26 performances

Written by Joyce Hokin Sachs; Produced by Grove Theater Center (Kevin Cocran, Artistic Director; Charles Johanson, Executive Director); Director, Kevin Cochran; Set, Leonard Ogden; Costumes, Tracy Christensen; Lighting, David Darwin; Sound, Hunter Stephenson; Stage Manager, Amanda-Mae Goodridge; ASM, Michal Salonia; Wardrobe Supervisor, Brie Furches-Howell; Assistant to the Producers, Anthony Subietas; Photographer, Eric Johanson; Press, Karen Greco

CAST Vanessa Bell **Hollis McCarthy**; Duncan Grant **Michael Gabriel Goodfriend**; George Mallory **Christian Pedersen**

SETTING The studio space at Charleston, the summer home of Vanessa Bell and Duncan Grant in Sussex. Autumn, 1923. New York premiere of a new play presented in five scenes in two acts. World premiere presented at Grove Theater Center (Burbank, California) June 27–July 25, 2009. An earlier version of the play (entitled *Equinox*) opened at the Odyssey Theatre in Los Angeles in 2006.

SYNOPSIS British painters Duncan Grant and Vanessa Bell are packing up their summer retreat when the work is interrupted by the surprise visit of George Mallory, the dashing explorer and moutaineer, who is about to leave on his third Everest expedition. Since both Duncan and Vanessa have had an affair with George in earlier years, the visit is filled with uneasy questions as the three sort out their art, sex, conquests, and loves. *Eternal Equinox* is a romantic comedy about the very uncommon romantic lives of the Bloomsbury Group artists.

Christian Pedersen, Hollis McCarthy, and Michael Gabriel Goodfriend in Eternal Equinox *(photo by Eric Johanson)*

Flight

DR2; First Preview: March 2, 2012; Opening Night: March 7, 2012; Closed April 1, 2012; 5 previews, 27 performances

Written by Michael Wallerstein; Produced by the Alchemy Theatre Company (Robert Saxner, Producing Artistic Director) in association with Playwrights' Playground (Gary Garrison, Founder); Director, Padraic Lillis; Set and Costumes, Lea Umberger; Lighting, Sarah Sidman; Sound, Elizabeth Rhodes; Casting, Laura Stanczyk; PSM, Carly Levin; ASM, Catherine Lynch; Marketing and Advertising, DR Theatrical Management; Press, Kevin McAnarney

CAST Andrew **Jonathan Walker**; Judith **Maria Tucci**; Linda McCartney **Maddie Corman**

World premiere of a new play presented without intermission.

SYNOPSIS *Flight* dramatizes a man's search for truth, love and his identity against the backdrop of his mother's deterioration and haunting memories of her past with both confronting what she's never shared or made peace with. Funny, tender, and distressing, *Flight* touches in surprising and challenging ways.

Jonathan Walker, Maddie Corman, and Maria Tucci in Flight *(photo by Michael Schwartz)*

Saint Joan

Access Theater; First Preview: March 7, 2012; Opening Night: March 9, 2012; Closed May 13, 2012; 2 previews, 57 performances

Written by George Bernard Shaw; Produced by Bedlam Theatre Company (Eric Tucker and Andrus Nichols, Co-Artistic Directors); Director, Eric Tucker; Stage Manager, Sarah Nochenson; ASM, Samantha Steinmetz; Dramaturg, Katherine Goodland; Associate Producer, Kate Hamill; Artitic Associates, Tina Packer, Alan Altschuler; Press, Ron Lasko/Spin Cycle

CAST Joan of Arc **Andrus Nichols**; All Other Roles **Eric Tucker**, **Tom O'Keefe**, **Ted Lewis**

SETTING France; 15th Century. Revival of a classic play presented in six scenes and a prologue with two intermissions.

SYNOPSIS Considered by many to be Shaw's greatest play and one of the greatest plays ever written, *Saint Joan* earned him the Nobel Prize in 1925. In this stripped down, boldly theatrical, four person production we witness the Joan of Arc that Shaw intended – not a saint, a witch, or a madwoman – but a farm girl who is anything but simple; an illiterate intellectual, a true genius whose focus on the individual rocked the Church and State to their core.

Andrus Nichols in Saint Joan. *(photo by Michael Mallard)*

The Maria Project

59E59 Theater B; First Preview: March 6, 2012; Opening Night: March 11, 2012; Closed April 1, 2012; 7 previews, 22 performances

Written and developed by Marcella Goheen; Produced by Pure Projects Inc. in association with Uncle Frank Productions; Director, Larry Moss; Technical Director, Perchik Kreiman-Miller; Footage Editor, Thavisouk Phrasavath; Editor, Edward Einhorn; Assistant Editor, Erin McCaffrey; PSM, Megan E. Coutts; Outreach Coordinator, Juliet Griego; Assistant to Ms. Goheen, Karly Restrapo; Founders, Marcia Otero Salazar and Francisco De Salazar; Advisor, James McLaren; Press, Karen Greco

Performed by **Marcella Goheen**

Off-Broadway premiere of a new solo performance play/docudrama presented without intermission.

SYNOPSIS As a child, Marcella Goheen was told a dark, haunting secret regarding the shocking truth about the mysterious death of her grandmother Maria. Using documentary footage, music and storytelling, follow Marcella as she uncovers three generations of lost family history and gives a voice to the silenced Maria Salazar.

Marcella Goheen in The Maria Project *(photo by Carol Rosegg)*

Teresa's Ecstasy

Cherry Lane Theatre; First Preview: March 4, 2012; Opening Night: March 14, 2012; Closed April 1, 2012; 9 previews, 16 performances

Written by Begonya Plaza; Produced by Avila Productions LLC by special arrangement with the Cherry Lane Theatre (Angelina Fiordellisi, Founding Artistic Director); Producer, Jim Weiner; Executive Producer, Jack Sharkey; Director, Will Pomerantz; Set, Adrian W. Jones; Costumes, Suzanne Chesney; Lighting, Scott Clyve; Sound, Jane Shaw; Original Music, Albert Carbonell; Stage Manager, Michael Alifanz; ASM, Matt Hundley; Production Manager, Duane Pagano; General Management, Boat Rocker Entertainment; Associate Producers, Ashley Fellman, Alena Chinault; Assistant Set Design, Katherine Akiko Day; Assistant to the General Manager, Stephanie Wilder; Advertising and Marketing, Lawrence Weiner and Associates; Graphic Design, Christy Briggs; Graphic Production, Charles Flores; Press, Karen Greco

CAST Carlotta **Begonya Plaza**; Andrés **Shawn Elliott**; Becky **Linda Larkin**

SETTING Barcelona. The Present Day. World premiere of a new play presented in two acts.

SYNOPSIS *Teresa's Ecstasy* is a sexually charged look at politics, religion and ultimately love. Carlotta's return to Barcelona has two purposes. It's a stopover on the way to Avila, where she is researching an article on St. Teresa, a 16th century nun. It's also to serve her husband Andres with divorce papers. Over a sumptuous lunch of wine and gazpacho, Andres fights to rekindle their relationship. But Carlotta is on a quest for the divine, and in the process of discovering the mystical *Teresa's Ecstasy*, she discovers herself.

Shawn Elliott, Begonya Plaza, and Linda Larkin in Teresa's Ecstasy *(photo by Carol Rosegg)*

Innocent Flesh

Actors Temple Theatre; First Preview: March 1, 2012; Opening Night: March 15, 2012; Closed May 27, 2012; 6 previews, 42 performances

Written by and directed by Kenyetta Lethridge; Produced by MZL LLC in association with Diana C. Zollicoffer, Michael Mann, and Kenyetta Lethridge; Sets and Lighting, Josh Iacovelli; Original Music, Jwyanza Kalonji Hobson and Ken Christiansen; Sound, Pennix McGee; Choreography, Angelina Prendergast; Production Manager, Paul Bourgeois; Co-Producer, Brad Guerrero; General Management, Jessimeg Productions, Edmund Gaynes, Julia Beardsley, Catherine Fowles; Photos, Diana C. Zollicoffer; Graphic Design, Frank Dain; Advertising, Epstein-O'Brien Advertising; Theatre Operator, Edmund Gaynes; Co-Artistic Director, Pamela Hall; Press, Edward Callaghan and John Wegorzewski, Alchimia Public Relations and Marketing

CAST Candace **Dapne Gabriel**; Danna **Clara Gabrielle**; Lisa **Jameelah Nuriddin**; Lupita **Angelina Prendergast**

SETTING The time is now. Or maybe there is no time at all. A sort of surreal space in time. New York premiere of a new play presented in two acts. World premiere at the Zephyr on Melrose (Los Angles) January 24–February 16, 2012 prior to this engagement.

SYNOPSIS *Innocent Flesh* is a new play that melds together some of Lethridge's own personal experiences as a teacher and researcher over the years to tell the sad reality of these four young girls and the hardships they face as underage prostitutes in America. Written in a multi-layered style that uses poetry, dance, and a modern take on the classic Greek Chorus, the play unveils the secrets of how girls from all walks of life can find themselves on the streets, selling their bodies to men.

(Seated): Jameelah Nuriddin, Angelina Prendergast, Daphne Gabriel, (standing): Clare Gabrielle, and Crystal Boyd in Innocent Flesh *(photo courtesy of the production)*

The Maids

Theatre at St. Clement's; First Preview: March 6, 2012; Opening Night: March 15, 2012; Closed April 1, 2012; 6 previews, 22 performances

Written by Jean Genet, translated by Bernard Frechtman; Produced by Red Bull Theater (Jesse Berger, Artistic Director; Wendy Anderson, Director of Artistic and Strategic Development; Renee Blinkwolt, General Manager); Sets, Dane Laffrey; Costumes, Sara Jean Tosetti; Lighting, Peter West; Sound, Brandon Wolcott; Properties, Morgan Fox; PSM, Damon W. Arrington; Production Supervisor, Production Core/James L. Cleveland; Line Producer, Evan O'Brient; Dramaturg, Mirabelle Ordinaire; Assistant Director, Deborah Wolfson; Fight Director, David Anzuelo; Voice and Speech Coach, Deborah Hecht; ASM, Kristine Ayers; Associate Lighting, Nick Flynn; General Manager, Renee Blinkwolt; Production Manager, Ron Gimshaw; Assistant Production Manager, Dave Upton; Technical Director, Peter Fry; Production Assistant, Brett Wulfson; Assistant Producer, Ben Prusiner; Master Electrician, John Anselmo; Production Audio Head, Nathan Wheeler; Associate Artistic Director, Craig Baldwin; Bull Session Curator, George Mayer; ASL Coordinator, Robbie Berry; Press, David Gersten and Associates

CAST Claire (a housemaid) **Jeanine Serralles**; Solange (a housemaid, her sister) **Ana Reeder**; Madame (their mistress) **J. Smith-Cameron**

Revival of a classic play in a presented without intermission.

SYNOPSIS Revenge tragedy meets film noir in this seductively playful and incendiary masterpiece from Jean Genet. House-maid sisters Solange and Claire spend their days dreaming of escape, while their bourgeois employer Madame floats through life on champagne bubbles - until fantasies turn deadly in this thrilling psychological kaleidoscope of a play. Set in a phantasmagoric world of masks and mirrors, ceremonies and sensuality, heightened language and beautiful gesture, *The Maids* is ritualistic exploration of class, the nature of identity, and the power of imagination.

Anna Reeder and Jeanine Serralles in The Maids *(photo by Carol Rosegg)*

Tin Pan Alley

Actors Temple Theatre; First Preview: February 25, 2012; Opening Night: March 19, 2012; Closed July 29, 2012; 11 previews, 50 performances

Conceived, directed, choreographed by Gene Castle; Produced by Edmund Gaynes in association with David Gersten; Music Director, Erik James; Sets and Lighting, Josh Iacovelli; Costumes, Dustin Cross; Creative Consultant, Jane Actman; General Management, Jessimeg Productions, Edmund Gaynes, Julia Beardsley, Catherine Fowles; PSM, Paul Bourgeois; Assistant to the Director, Catherine Fowles; Production Assistant, Jocelyn Brown; Advertising, Epstein-O'Brien Adverstising; Graphic Design, Courtney Russell Smith; Co-Artistic Director, Pamela Hall; Director of Sales, Bill Fitzgerald; Press, David Gersten and Associates

CAST **Loni Ackerman**, **Brad Bradey**, **Gene Castle**, **Karla Shook**; Piano and additional vocals **Erik James**

MUSICAL NUMBERS Let Me Sing and I'm Happy; Yankee Doodle Dandy; On the Banks of the Wabash; Daisy; Bird in a Gilded Cage; The Sidewalks of New York; After the Ball; At a Georgia Camp Meeting; Maple Leaf Rag; The Streets of New York; Oh You Beautiful Doll; Nobody; Some of These Days; Let Me Call You Sweetheart; The Entertainer; Alexander's Ragtime Band; St. Louis Blues; Too Much Mustard; Over There; I Didn't Raise My Boy to Be a Soldier; Till We Meet Again - Richard Whiting; Goodbye Broadway, Hello France; When Johnny Comes Marching; Oh By Jingo, Oh By Gee; He Loves and She Loves; It Had to Be You; Ain't We Got Fun; Let's Do It; Blue Skies; Button Up Your Overcoat; Birth of the Blues; Black Bottom; Charleston; Charleston; Five Foot Two; Give My Regards to Broadway; Swanee; When the Red Red Robin; Second Hand Rose; If You Knew Susie, Like I Know Susie; You Made Me Love You; Let Yourself Go

World premire of a new musical revue presented without intermission.

SYNOPSIS *Tin Pan Alley* is a musical revue of the golden age of American popular music from the 1890s through the 1930s. With simple tunes, it sings and dances its way through the music that has become part of our collective memory.

Ben Rauch (on piano), Loni Ackerman, Gene Castle, Karla Shook, and Brad Bradley in Tin Pan Alley (The Original iTunes) (photo by Carol Rosegg)

Him

SoHo Playhouse; First Preview: March 10, 2012; Opening Night: March 21, 2012; Closed March 24, 2012; 11 previews, 3 performances

Written and directed by Clifford Streit; Produced by ; Sets and Lighting, Josh Iacovelli; Costumes, Dustin Cross; Sound, Juni Li; Stage Manager, Jonathan Santos; Press, Ron Lasko/Spin Cycle

CAST Matthew **Todd Alan Crain**; Nick **Jon Fleming**; Margo **Lindsay Goranson**; Rana **Georgia X. Lifsher**; Troy **James Sautter**; James **Julian Mercer**

Off-Broadway premiere of a new play presented in two acts. Previously played at the Cherry Lane Studio Theatre December 9, 2011–January 8, 2012.

SYNOPSIS In *Him*, hunky actor Nick Cooper has just landed his breakthrough film role and the offers from Hollywood's A-list are pouring in. The only problem: Nick is gay and his viper of an agent wants to keep him in the closet. Nick is happy to play along in spite of the vocal opposition of his boyfriend Matthew. But all hell breaks loose when a Latina bombshell is brought in to 'play' Nick's girlfriend.

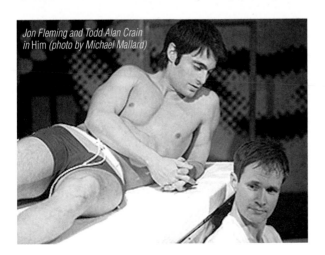

Jon Fleming and Todd Alan Crain in Him (photo by Michael Mallard)

My Occasion of Sin

Urban Stages; First Preview: March 16, 2012; Opening Night: March 21, 2012; Closed April 15, 2012; 3 previews, 24 performances

Written by Monica Bauer; Produced by Urban Stages (Fraces Hill, Artistic Director; Peter Napolitano, Producing Director); Set, Roman Tatarowicz; Costumes, Anna Lacivita; Lighting, Deborah Constantine; Sound, Sean Hagerty; Projections, Kevin R. Frech; PSM, Debra Stunich; Technical Director/Builder, Eric Zoback; Master Electrician Meghan Santelli; Prop Master, Kire Tosevski; Costume Associate, Amy Pedigo; Lighting Assistants, Michelle Tobias, Timothy Huth; Stagehand, Mike Holmes; Social Media, Elizabeth Polland; For Urban Stages: Rachel Sullivan (Program Director), Olga Devyatisilnaya (Company Manager), Antoinette Mullins (Development and Marketing), Press, Springer Associates, Joe Trentacosta

CAST Mary Margaret Irzandowsky **Rosebud Baker**; Helen Hollewinski **Janice Hall**; Luigi Wells **Royce Johnson**; George Hollewinski **Scott Robertson**; Vivian Strong **Danielle Thompson**

SETTING A segregated city in 1969. World premiere of a new play with music presented without intermission.

SYNOPSIS Inspired by true events that led to one of the worst race riots in the author's birthplace of Omaha, Nebraska, *My Occasion of Sin* centers on two men from very different backgrounds: Luigi, a black jazz drummer and George, a white music store owner who plays accordion. The two are thrown together by fate, finding common ground in their love of music. Mary Margaret and Vivian, two young girls from opposite sides of the segregated city, drink in the new jazz scene for reasons of their own. Music seems to unite and uplift everyone around. Soon, occasions of sin, where fear, mistrust and racism fester, are inescapable. Violence erupts, changing everyone's lives forever.

Royce Johnson, Janice Hall, and Scott Robertson in My Occasion of Sin (photo by Ben Hider)

Elephant Room

St. Ann's Warehouse; Opening Night: March 22, 2012; Closed April 8, 2012; 19 performances

Created by Steve Cuiffo, Trey Lyford, and Geoff Sobelle; Produced by St. Ann's Warehouse (Susan Feldman, Artistic Director; Andrew D. Hamingson, Executive Director); Director, Paul Lazar; Set, Mimi Lien; Costumes, Christal Weatherly; Lighting, Christopher Kuhl; Sound, Nick Kourtides; Stage Manager, Jill Beckman; General Manager, Dorit Avganim; Production Manager/Technical Director, Thomas Snyder; Loxodontics, The Puppet Kitchen; Assistant Technical Director, Ian Guzzone; Associate Set, Amy Rubin; ASM, Zane Johnston; Lighting Assistant,

Adam Blumenthal; Sound Operator, Susan Adelizzi; Deck Hand, Sean Meehan; Wardrobe, Becka Landau; St. Ann's General Manager, Erik Wallin; Press, Blake Zidell and Associates

CAST Dennis Diamond **Geoff Sobelle**; Daryl Hannah **Trey Lyford**; Louie Magic **Steve Cuiffo**

New York premiere of a theatrical piece with magic presented without intermission. Originally co-produced and presented by Philadelphia Live Arts Festival and Arena Stage Washington, DC (Molly Smith, Artistic Director; Edgar Dobie, Managing Director) in September 2-17, 2011 and January 20–February 26, 2012. Commissioned by Center Theatre Group, Los Angeles.

SYNOPSIS *Elephant Room* examines the childlike wonder of three deluded illusionists who choose to live their off-center lives by sleight of hand. Three magicians. Two acts. One show. Zero boring stuff. Sub-zero intelligence. It's time to make it all add up… in the *Elephant Room*. Illusionists Dennis Diamond, Louie Magic, and Daryl Hannah invite you to a place of secrets. Of mystery. The place between the back of your mind and the tip of your tongue. Let's pretend it's a room – a real room. And you're really here. In the *Elephant Room*.

Trey Lyford, Steve Cuiffo, and Geoff Sobelle in Elephant Room
(photo by Pavel Antonov)

The Underbelly Diaries

Studio Theatre on Theatre Row; Opening Night: March 22, 2012; Closed April 7, 2012; 9 performances

Written by Aaron Berg; Director, Dwight McFee; Production Design/Stage Manager, Alexa Carroll; Assistant Stage Manager/Board Operator, Michelle Marcus; Assistant Board Operator, Maurice Williams; Creative Consultant, Mark Breslin; Press, Pete Sanders

Performed by **Aaron Berg**

New York premiere of a new solo performance play presented without intermission. Previously presented at the Toronto Fringe Festival and engagements in Los Angeles and San Francisco.

SYNOPSIS He was from a prominent Jewish family. He became a steroid-addicted bodybuilder, a male stripper, and a stud for hire for men and women. *The Underbelly Diaries* is a frank, honest and funny look at capitalism and the American dream personified.

The Soap Myth

Black Box Theatre at the Steinberg Center; First Preview: March 23, 2012; Opening Night: March 26, 2012; Closed April 22, 2012; 4 previews, 32 performances

Written by Jeff Cohen; Produced by the National Jewish Theatre (Arnold Mittelman, Producing Artistic Director); Director, Arnold Mittelman; Sets, Heather Wolensky; Costumes, David Withrow; Lighting, Jay Scott; PSM, Alan Fox; ASM, Miriam Hyfler; General Manager, Edward Einhorn; Casting, Cindi Rush; Composer, Leon Levitch; Music Curator, Brett Werb; Technical Director, Wyatt Kuether; Historic Consultants, Irving Roth, David G. Marwell; Wardrobe Supervisor, Katie Laine Harrison; Graphic Design, Clinton Corbett; Web Design, Denise Young; Adminsitrative Assistant, Susana Perez; Marketing Assistant, Rebecca Joy Fletcher; Board Operator, Berit Johnson; Props, Emily Roencrantz; Production Assistant, Addison O'Donnell; Press, Richard Kornberg and Associates

CAST Annie Blumberg **Andi Potamkin**; Comic, Daniel Silver, Smirnov, Mazur, Neely **Donald Corren**; Esther Fineman, Brenda Goodsen **Dee Pelletier**; Milton Saltzman **Greg Mullavey**

SETTING Summer 2001 and earlier; New York City. Off-Broadway premiere of a new play presented without intermission. An earlier version was presented by Dog Run Rep in 2009 at South Street Seaport.

SYNOPSIS The horrific possibility that the Nazis turned Jews into soap is the catalyst for *The Soap Myth*. Cohen's lead characters, a survivor and a young investigative journalist, go on a collision course to ascertain how much fact is needed for something not to be fiction.

Andi Potamkin and Greg Mullavey in The Soap Myth *(photo by Richard Termine)*

Out of Iceland

Walkerspace; First Preview: March 24, 2012; Opening Night: April 1, 2012; Closed April 22, 2012; 7 previews, 19 performances

Written by Drew Larimore; Produced by Alfred R. Kahn in association with Culture Project (Allan Buchman, Artistic Director); Director, Josh Hecht; Set, Narelle Sissons; Lighting, Paul Whitaker; Costumes, Jennifer Caprio; Original Music, Ryan Rumery; Sound, Ryan Rumery and M. Florian Staab; Press, David Gersten and Associates

CAST Caroline Miller **Jillian Crane**; Hal Tinker **Michael Bakkensen**; Thor **Lea DeLaria**

Off-Broadway premiere of a new play presented without intermission.

SYNOPSIS In *Out of Iceland*, Caroline Miller, an established writer from New York, is at a loss for words when she falls off an Icelandic volcano and awakes on the couch of a complete stranger. Hal Tanker is the misplaced cowboy in charge of the grounds who nurses her back to health. Then there's Thor, Iceland's flamboyant troll who crawled out of the television one night to warn her about something – or did she imagine that? When their truck mysteriously disappears in the middle of "The Middle," Hal and Caroline must face their biggest fears in a long night in one of the most mystical places on earth.

Lea DeLaria in Out of Iceland *(photo by Richard Termine)*

Naked Boys Singing!

Kirk Theatre on Theatre Row; First Preview: March 22, 2012; Opening Night: April 5, 2012; 6 previews, 25 performances as of May 31, 2012 (Thursdays through Saturdays)

Written by Stephen Bates, Marie Cain, Perry Hart, Shelly Markham, Jim Morgan, David Pevsner, Rayme Sciaroni, Mark Savage, Ben Schaechter, Robert Schrock, Trance Thompson, Bruce Vilanch, Mark Winkler; Produced and new show conception by Tom and Michael D'Angora; Co-Directors, Tom D'Angora and Michael Duling; Set and Projections, Susannah Bohlke; Lighting, KJ Hardy; Costumes, Mina Ha; Music Director, Alex LeFevre; Choreography, Alex Ringler; Stage Manager, Scott Delacruz

CAST Jon-Paul Mateo, Alex Ringler, Ryan Obermeier, David San Angelo, Ricky Schroeder, Steph Stanek, Christopher Trepinski

MUSICAL NUMBERS Gratuitous Nudity, Naked Maid, The Bliss of a Bris, Window to Window, Fight the Urge, Robert Mitchum, Jack's Song, Members Only, Perky Little Porn Star, Kris Look What You've Missed, Muscle Addiction, Nothin' But the Radio On, The Entertainer, Window to the Soul, Finale/Naked Boys Singing!

A new and revised production of an Off-Broadway musical revue presented without intermission. The original production closed earlier this season after 3,069 performances (see page 194 in this volume).

SYNOPSIS In *Naked Boys Singing!*, each of the six boys performs a solo tune that celebrates the male anatomy with playful wit and unabashed explicitness. Whether extolling the anxiety of a high school locker room or the celebrating the joys of performing in the buff, every penile synonym known to man is referenced in the show. The boys also perform together in ensemble pieces that get crowds roaring.

David San Angelo, Ryan Obermeier, Alex Ringler, Christopher Trepinski, Steph Stanek, and Ricky Schroeder in Naked Boys Singing! *(photo by Michael D'Angora)*

To Kill a Kelpie

Theatre 80 and Theatre at St. Luke's; Opening Night: April 6, 2012; Closed April 15, 2012; 12 performances

Written by Matthew McVarish; Produced by Stop the Silence and Poorboy Theatre Company; Supported by Creative Scotland in association with the Moira Anderson Foundation; Executive Producer, Dr. Pamela Pine; Director/Dramaturge/Set, Sandy Thomson; Composer and Sound, Alex Attwood; Graphic Design, Rick Richardson; Associate Producer, Mark Williams; General Managers, Stop the Silence and Inbrook; Production Managers, Lauren Brown and Jacob Wilkins; Poorboy Theatre Coordinator, Christy Johansen; Press, Inbrook & Anni Dori Public Relations

CAST Dubhghall Tomas **Allan Lindsay**; Fionnghall **Matthew McVarish**; Voice of Caoimhe **Jen Lowrie**; Voice of Alethea **Eildh McCormick**; Understudy **Jeremiah Reynolds**

SETTING Scotland. Inside Alexander's Croft and outside on the banks of the Loch; over two days. New York premiere of a new play presented in three acts with one intermission. The production toured the United States in 2011.

SYNOPSIS When twin brothers, Dougal and Fin, reunite following the death of their uncle, they share the day they have always hoped would, and would never, happen. Retelling his gruesome tales of a child-devouring monster – The Kelpie – the men talk to the wee boys they once were, shedding stoicism and sobriety in an isolated Scottish croft. With the rambunctious humour of those who have lived the unlivable, *To Kill a Kelpie* journeys through a family album filled with life shaping events and conflicting memories, deftly handling huge themes and fine details with an equal measure of care.

Julius Caesar

Baruch Performing Arts Center; Opening Night: April 9, 2012; Closed April 22, 2012; 12 performances

Written by William Shakespeare; Produced by The Acting Company (Margot Harley, Co-Founder and Producing Director) in association with the Guthrie Theater (Joe Dowling, Director); Director, Rob Melrose; Set, Neil Patel; Costumes, Candice Donnelly; Lighting, Michael Chybowski; Sound, Cliff Caruthers; Video, Shawn Sagady; Fight Director, Felix Ivanoff; Voice and Speech Consultant, Andrew Wade; Text Editing, Rob Melrose and Ian Belknap; Props, Olivia Gagne; Casting, Pat McCorkle; PSM, Richard Costabile; ASM, Meg Friedman; Staff Repertory Director, Adriana Baer; Production Manager/Technical Director, Daniel B. Chapman; Lighting Director, Annie Wiegand; Wardrobe Supervisor, Mariela Novoa; Sound Supervisor, Mark Van Hare; Prop Supervisor, Olivia Gagne; Touring Company Manager, Ken Samuels; Resident Company Manager, Joseph Parks; For The Acting Company: Gerry Cornez (Development and Communications), Nancy Cook (General Manager), Ian Belknap (Associate Artistic Director); Press, Judy Katz Public Relations, Sean Katz

CAST Marullus/Trebonius/Messala **Ray Chapman**; Flavius, Cinna **Whitney Hudson**; Julius Caesar **Bjorn DuPaty**; Casca **Kevin Orton**; Calpurnia **Kaliswa Brewster**; Marc Antony **Zachary Fine**; Soothsayer/Cinna the Poet **Caleb Carlson**; Marcus Brutus **William Sturdivant**; Caius Cassius **Sid Solomon**; Lucius **Ernest Bentley**; Metellus Cimber/Octavius Caesar **Joseph Midyett**; Decius Brutus/Lepidus **Noah Putterman**; Portia/Popilius **Kathleen Wise**

Bjorn DuPaty and William Sturdivant (foreground) with Noah Putterman, Ray Chapman, and Kevin Orton in Julius Caesar *(photo by Heidi Bohnenkamp)*

New York premiere of a new touring production of a classical play presented in with one intermission. This production premiered at the Guthrie Theater January 14, 2012.

SYNOPSIS *Julius Caesar* is a classic story of pride and envy, arrogance and honor, opportunity and tragic strategic errors. Written in one of his most productive times of Shakespeare's life, *Julius Caesar* blends the historic events of the reign of this iconic roman emperor with tragic elements and .compelling language creating of Shakespeare's greatest tragedies.

Federer Versus Murray

59E59 Theater C; First Preview: April 4, 2012; Opening Night: April 10, 2012; Closed April 22, 2012; 7 previews, 16 performances

Written and directed by Gerda Stevenson; Produced by Communicado Productions (Gerry Mulgrew, Artistic Director) as part of Scotland Week; Design, Jessica Brettle; Lighting, Simon Wilkinson; Technical Manager, Naomi Stalker; Sound, Jamie Wilson; Producer, Lorna Duguid; Stage Manager, Amy Kaskeski; Press, Karen Greco

CAST Flo **Gerda Stevenson**; Jimmy **Dave Anderson**; Saxophonist **Ben Bryden**

U.S. premiere of a new play presented without intermission. Originally presented at Lunchtime Theatre (Glasgow).

SYNOPSIS Comedy and tragedy collide in *Federer versus Murray*, a powerful new play about bereavement and war on three levels: the private war between a couple in a long-term marriage, the public war of rivalry within sport, and political war between nations. A beautiful study of human strength and fragility told through the lives of two very ordinary people, this moving and genuinely funny play unfolds as the (Switzerland versus Scotland) Wimbledon Tennis Semi-Final plays out on television.

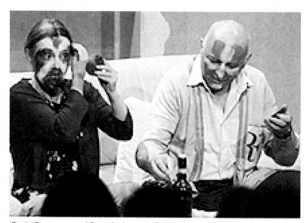

Gerda Stevenson and Dave Anderson in Federer Versus Murray
(photo courtesy of Communicado Theatre Company)

A Slow Air

59E59 Theater B; First Preview: April 4, 2012; Opening Night: April 12, 2012; Closed April 29, 2012; 8 previews, 19 performances

Written and directed by David Harrower; Produced by Tron Theatre Company (Andy Arnold, Artistic Director) as part of Scotland Week; Set and Costumes, Jessica Brettle; Lighting, Dave Shea; Sound, Daniel Padden; Company Stage

Manager, Suzanne Goldberg; Production Manager, Jo Masson; Stage Manager, David Sneddon; Chief Electrician, Mark Hughes; Head of Sound, Barry McCall; Technical Stage Manager, Karen Bryce; 59E59 Production Manager, Jim Sparnon; AEA Stage Manager, Jess Johnston; Press, Karen Greco

CAST Athol **Lewis Howden**; Morna **Susan Vidler**

U.S. premiere of a new play presented without intermission. World premiere at the Tron Theatre (Glasgow) May 11-21, 2011 as part of the Mayfesto Festival and subsequently at the Edinburge Fringe in the Traverse Theatre August 5-29, 2011.

SYNOPSIS Morna, a house-cleaner for well-off families in Edinburgh, shares her Dalry flat with her son. Her elder brother, Athol, owner of a floor tiling company and father of two grown children, lives near Glasgow airport with his wife Evelyn. Like any brother and sister they have fond and not-so fond memories of their upbringing, differing views on their parents, and definite opinions about each other. They haven't spoken to each other in fourteen years. When Morna's son Joshua travels west to make contact with Athol, he sets off, for all of them, a remarkable and life-changing series of events.

Susan Vidler and Lewis Howden in A Slow Air *(photo by John Johnston)*

You Better Sit Down:
Tales from My Parents' Divorce

Flea Theatre; First Preview: April 7, 2012; Opening Night: April 12, 2012; Closed May 6, 2012; 4 previews, 26 performances

Written by Anne Kauffman, Matthew Maher, Caitlin Miller, Jennifer R. Morris, Janice Paran, and Robbie Collier Sublett; Conceived by Jennifer R. Morris; Produced by The Civilians (Steven Cosson, Artistic Director; Marion Friedman Young, Managing Director) and The Flea Theater (Jim Simpson, Artistic Director; Carol Ostrow, Producing Director; Beth Dembrow, Managing Director); Director, Anne Kauffman; Set, Mimi Lien; Lighting, Ben Stanton; Costumes, Sarah Beers; Sound, Leah Gelpe; Projections, Caite Hevner; PSM, Megan Schwarz Dickert; ASM, Danielle Teague-Daniels; Dramaturg, Janice Paran; Graphic Design, Jaime Vallés; Associate Design: Caite Hevner (set), Alejandro Fajardo (lighting), Arshan Gailus (sound); Props, Kate Foster; Lightboard Operator/Wardrobe, Elana McKelahan; Sound and Projections Operator, Jim Armstrong; For The Civilians: Ian Daniel (Associate Artistic Director), Sarah Benvenuti (Devleopment Director), Rosalind Grush (Development and Communications Associate); For The Flea Theater: Liz Blessing (Technical Director), Penn Genthner (Development), Chris Massimine (Marketing and Membership), Sarah Wansley (Company Manager), Kyle Crose (Assistant Technical Director); Press, Ron Lasko/Spin Cycle

CAST Mary Anne **Caitlin Miller**; Janet **Robbie Collier Sublett**; Beverly **Jennifer R. Morris**; John, Finde **Matthew Maher**

New York premiere of a new play presented without intermission. World premiere presented by Williamstown Theatre Festival August 17, 2011.

SYNOPSIS Four members of The Civilians sat their parents down and asked them for the real story behind their divorces. Each actor assumes the role of their own mother or father (or in one case, both) in a show crafted entirely from those verbatim interviews. *You Better Sit Down: Tales from My Parents' Divorce* is shockingly candid, unexpectedly hilarious, and proves that what we want to know about our parents' lives and what we actually should know are two totally different things.

Robbie Collier Sublett, Jennifer R. Morris, Matthew Maher, Caitlin Miller in You Better Sit Down: Tales from My Parents' Divorce *(photo by Joan Marcus)*

In Masks Outrageous and Austere

Theatre at 45 Bleecker; First Preview: April 6, 2012; Opening Night: April 16, 2012; Closed May 13, 2012; 9 previews, 28 performances

Written by Tennessee Williams; Produced by Culture Project (Allan Buchman, Founder and Artistic Director), Victor Syrmis, and Carl Rumbaugh; Executive Producers, Allan Buchman, Roy Gabay; Director, David Schweizer; Set, James Noone; Costumes, Gabriel Berry; Lighting, Alexander V. Nicholas; Original Music and Sound, Dan Moses Schreier; Video and Projections, Darrel Maloney; Wigs and Makeup, Cookie Jordan; Dramaturg, Joe E. Jeffreys; Production Supervisor, Production Core/James E. Cleveland; Casting, Billy Hopkins; Company Manager, Katrina Elliott; PSM, Scott Pegg; General Management, Roy Gabay, Daniel Kuney; Associate Producer, Justin Matson; Stage Manager, Christine Catti; Production Manager, Amanda Raymond; Assistant Production Manager, Maggie Davis; Associate Media Producer, Marisa Kronenberg; Assistant Director, Eddie Prunoske; Associate Costumes, Andrea Hood; Assistant Design: Adrienne Carlile (set), Adam Godbout (set), Christian DeAngelis (lighting), Joshua D. Reid (sound), Dan Scully (projections); Casting Associate, Ashley Ingram; Technical Director, Pete Fry; Prop Supervisor, Jennie Marino; Production Electrician, John Anselmo; Production Audio, Joshua D. Reid; Video/Projections Supervisor, Joe Cantalupo; Lighting Programmer, Bridget Chervenka; Video Programmer, Benjamin Keightley; Wardrobe Supervisor, Andrea Dockhorn; Dresser, Matt Hundley; Hair and Makeup Artist, Aaron Kinchen; Electrics/Video Operator, KJ Hardy; Sound Engineer, Meghan Zugibe; Stage Management PA/Deckhand, Patrick John Moran; Production Assistants, Cameron Bartell, Jake Blagburn, Kenneth Faust, Kalen Larson; Consultant, Richard Lewis; Marketing, Two Sheps That Pass…, Vera Shepps Scholl and Amy Long; LA Video Shoot Producer, Ron Dempsey; Consultant/NYC Video Shoot Producer, Eric Marciano; Gun Wrangler, Len Francavilla; GM Associates, Mandy Tate, Lily Alia, Chris Aniello, Mark Gagliardi, Bruce Kagel; Press, O+M Company, Rick Miramontez, Richardd Hillman, Michael Jorgensen

CAST Gideon **Ward Horton**; Gideon **Scot Charles Anderson**; Gideon **Kaolin Bass**; Billy Foxworth **Robert Beitzel**; Jerry **Sam Underwood**; Peg Foyle **Pamela Shaw**; Joey **Christopher Halladay**; Clarissa "Babe" Foxworth **Shirley Knight**; Mrs. Gorse-Bracken **Alison Fraser**; Playboy **Connor Buckley**; Mac **Jermaine Miles**; Interpreter **Jonathan Kim**; Kennelsworth **Buck Henry**; Dr. Lester G. Syme **Austin Pendleton**; Standby for Babe **Maude Mitchell**

UNDERSTUDIES Tina Alexis Allen (Babe, Matron, Peg), Dana Watkins (Billy, Joey, Playboy), Ward Horton (Jerry), Tunde Somade (Mac, Gideons)

SETTING Place: A sundeck facing the ocean. Time: Late August, 1983. Act I: Scene One: Near sundown. Scene Two: Afternoon, the next day. Act II: Scene One: Early dusk that same day. Scene Two: Twilight. World premiere of an uproduced play with multimedia presented in four scenes in two acts.

SYNOPSIS Tennessee Williams goes for broke in his final full-length play, exploring the surreal, the nefarious, and the erotic in ways never before attempted by the great American master. The richest woman in the world, her gay husband, and his young lover are thrust into a mystery world, defined by disorientation and paranoia, where they are held captive by omnipotent corporate forces. A cast of bizarre characters enters an increasingly threatening environment, and tensions reach a fever pitch as trust among the three protagonists begins to disintegrate.

Alison Fraser and Shriley Knight in In Masks Outrageous and Austere (photo by Carol Rosegg)

Festen

St. Ann's Warehouse; Opening Night: April 20, 2012; Closed April 29, 2012; 10 performances

Adapted for the stage by Thomas Vinterberg and Mogens Rukov; Produced by TR Warszawa (Poland) and St. Ann's Warehouse (Susan Feldman, Artistic Director); Director, Grzegorz Jarzyna; Set, Małgorzata Szcz niak; Costumes, Magdalena Maciejewska; Lighting, Jacqueline Sobiszewski; Music, Paweł Mykietyn, Piotr Domi ski; Supertititles, Agnieszka Tuszy ska; Assistant Director, Paweł Kulka; Production Manager, Małgorzata Cichulska; Communications, Justyna Konczewska; Stage Manager, Karolina G bska; Electricians, Krzysztof Krawczy ski, Elliot Janetopoulos; Sound Engineers, Piotr Domi ski, Charles Shell; Wardrobe, El bieta Kołtonowicz, Elizabeth Sargent; Makeup, Monika Fetela; Prop Master, Grzegorz Zielski; Set Builder, Andrzej Tuszewicz; Stagehands, Tadeusz Tomaszewski, Paul Birkelo; Assistant Company Manager/Translator, Dominika Laster

CAST Helge **Jan Peszek**; Else **Ewa Dałkowska**; Christian **Andrzej Chyra**; Helene **Danuta Stenka/Katarzyna Herman**; Michael **Marek Kalita**; Mette

Agnieszka Podsiadlik; Pia **Magdalena Cielecka**; Michelle **Aleksandra Popławska**; Helmut **Mariusz Benoit**; Grandmother **Danuta Szaflarska**; Grandfather **Zygmunt Malanowicz**; Lars **Wojciech Kalarus**; Kim **Redbad Klijnstra**; Aunt **Magdalena Kuta**; Uncle Leif **Cezary Kosi ski**; Gbatokai **Carlos Ferreira**; Poul **Stanisław Spara v ski**; Bent **Marek K pi ski**; Waiter **Jan Dravnel**; Dorothe **Antoninia Kalita**; Kasper **Konstanty Kosi ski**; Pianist **Andrzej Winnicki**

American premiere of a new play performed in Polish with English supertitles in two acts.

SYNOPSIS *Festen* revolves around the weekend-long gathering of a wealthy landowner's family. His youngest son, Christian, makes a dinner speech accusing the father of molesting him and his twin sister throughout childhood. (The sister has recently committed suicide, and her ghost haunts Christian and the other relatives.) The festivities turn into a nightmare of accusations and counter-accusations. Amidst the feast's finery, lies are exposed and the guests are suspended between doubt and indignation. But it is left to the closing scene to determine whether the accusations are the product of Christian's fevered imagination or an expression of literal truth.

The Company in Festen (photo by Marc Enguerand)

The Merchant of Venice

Clurman Theatre on Theatre Row; First Preview: April 14, 2012; Opening Night: April 22, 2012; Closed May 13, 2012; 7 previews, 20 performances

Written by William Shakespeare; Produced by Theater Breaking Through Barriers (Ike Schambelan, Artistic Director); Director, Ike Schambelan; Sets and Lighting, Bert Scott; Costumes, Kristine Koury; Assistant Costumes, Caitlin Cisek; Prop Design, Segolene Marchand Lazzaro; Assistant Director, Christina Roussos; Stage Manager, Brooke Elsinghorst; ASM, Christine Julia Massoud; Production Manager, Nicholas Lazzaro; Wardrobe Supervisor, Jamie Bertoluzzi; Wigs and Makeup, Erin Kennedy Lunsford; Original Song, Nicholas Viselli; Company Administrator, Joan Duddy; Marketing, Michelle Tabnick; Graphic Design, Jane O'Wyatt; Financial Consultant, Sherri Kotimsky; Fundraising Consultant, Sue Ferziger; Press, Shirley Herz Associates, Bob Lasko

CAST Antonio, Tubal, Sal **Melanie Boland**; Bassanio, Sal, Portia's servant **Gregg Mozgala**; Gratiano, Balthazar, Sal **David Harrell**; Lorenzo, Duke, Leonardo, Jailer, Sal, Portia's servant **Stephen Drabicki**; Portia, Launcelot Gobbo, Sal **Pamela Sabaugh**; Nerissa, Jessica, Sal, Servants **Mary Theresa Archbold**; Shylock, Morocco, Old Gobbo, Aragon, Stephano **Nicholas Viselli**

Revival of a classic play presented in two acts.

SYNOPSIS Theater Breaking Through Barriers' take on Shakespeare's classic *The Merchant of Venice* features seven actors, including five with disabilities. A comedy about four contracts and four outcasts, the play follows a Christian merchant and his relationship with a Jewish moneylender. The contracts deal with flesh, rings, caskets, and livery; and the play asks how you respond to a broken deal: with justice or mercy.

The City Club

Minetta Lane Theatre; First Preview: April 3, 2012; Opening Night: April 23, 2012; Closed June 1, 2012; 23 previews, 17 performances

Book by Glenn M. Stewart, music and lyrics by James Compton, Tony De Meur, and Tim Brown; Produced by Glenn M. Stewart, Mitchell Maxwell, Donna Stewart, and Carol Castelli; Director, Mitchell Maxwell; Choreography, Lorin Latarro; Music Supervisor/Orchestrations, James Compton; Sets, Rob Bissinger; Costumes, David C. Woolard; Lighting, David F. Segal; Sound, Carl Casella; Hair and Wigs, Charles G. LaPointe; Casting, Michael Cassara; Fight Director, Rick Sordelet; Music Director, Jonathon Lynch; Music Coordinator, John Miller; PSM, Jason A. Quinn; Production Manager, Juniper Street Productions, Hillary Blanken, Joseph DeLuise, Ana Rose Greene, Guy Kwan; General Management, Carol Castelli; ASM, Jennifer Rogers; Company Manager, Christian Fitzgerald; Assistant to the General Manager, Julia Izumi; Assistant to John Miller, Jennifer Coolbaugh; Makeup Design, Cookie Jordan; Dance Captain, Kaitlin Mesh; Fight Captain, Patrick O'Neill; Associate Design, Josh Liebert; Assistant Design: Anita LaScala (set), Carolyn Hoffmann (costumes), Jacob Platt (lighting); Production Carpenter, Joseph DeLuise; Head Carpenter, Josh Bradford; Production Electrician, Tom Dyer; Associate Production Electrician, Ben Hagen; Light Programmer, Colin Scott; Light Board Operator, Antoine Thrower; Follow Spot, Jason Cook; Production Property Master, Meghan Abel; Show Carpenter/Head Props, John Panichello; Production Sound/FOH Mixer, Adam Rigby; Wardrobe Supervisor, Chadd McMillan; Hair Supervisor, Sarah Levine; Production Assistant, Lindsey Alexander; Marketing, Brylin Marketing; Advertising, Hofstetter & Partners/Agency 212; Press, Judy Jacksina Company

CAST Parker Brown **Kenny Brawner**; Charles Davenport (Chaz) **Andrew Pandaleon**; Prince Royale/Tough/Governor **Robert J. Townsend**; Candy **Emily Tyra**; Rose **Autumn Guzzardi**; Lily **Kaitlin Mesh**; Crystal LaBelle **Kristen Martin**; Jake Olson/Frances **Patrick O'Neill**; Lieutenant/Doc **Peter Bradbury**; Madelaine Bondurant (Maddy) **Ana Hoffman**; Swings **Nikkieli Demone, Kelcy Griffin**

UNDERSTUDIES Autumn Guzzardi (Crystal), Nikkieli Demone (Parker), Kelcy Griffin (Maddy), Patrick O'Neill (Chaz), Robert J. Townsend (Lieutenant/Doc), Emily Tyra (Rose)

BAND Jonathon Lyncy (Conductor/Trumpet), Kenny Brawner (Piano), Vincent Fay (Bass), Mike Milgliore (Reeds), Frank Pagano (Drums)

MUSICAL NUMBERS Dark Streets; Hot, Sweet, & Blonde; Love's the Thing; Blood on the Ground; Life on the Layaway Plan; Can't Get Off This Train; Saturday Night; Send Me Your Kiss; Talking to the Devil; A Real Good Woman; Lollipop Man; You're Falling in Love with Me; Why Did It Have to Be You; Boogie Woogie Fever; Fix You Like the Doctor; Let 'em Roll; It Ain't Right; Too Much Juice; It Don't Make No Never Mind; The Game of Life; Dark Streets (reprise)

SETTING The City Club; 1934. American premiere of a new jazz and blues musical presented in two acts. World premiere at the Edinburgh Fringe Festival in 2004.

SYNOPSIS *The City Club* is a twisting noir morality tale of intrigue, murder, corruption, and sex. Charles "Chaz" Davenport is a young privileged scion of a corrupt family whose vice grip on their city is as tight as it is inescapable. Obsessed with music and the people who write it, play it, sing it and worship it, Chaz opens The City Club, a Mecca of pure and unbridled musical genius,

opportunity, and escape. The club's success attracts his father's enemies who bring with them extremely creative and effective revenge tactics. The universe inside the club spirals as low as city outside. Absinthe becomes the drink of choice, heroine the desired high and women the most valuable form of currency. The forces of good and evil battle it out to a great blues and jazz score.

The Company in The City Club *(photo by Carol Rosegg)*

Macbeth

Judson Memorial Church Gymnasium; First Preview: April 18, 2012; Opening Night: April 25, 2012; Closed May 6, 2012; 10 previews, 24 performances

Written by William Shakespeare; Produced by Aquila Theatre (Peter Meineck, Artistic Director); Director and Design, Desiree Sanchez Meineck; Lighting, Peter Meineck; Staff Director, Eric Mercado; Technical Director, Amy Carr; Office Manager, Lindsay Beecher; Artistic and Producing Associate, Kimberly Pau Donato; Press, David Gersten and Associates

CAST Lady Macduff/Rosse **Rachel Barrington**; Witch 3/Ensemble **Janet Dunson**; Banquo/Captain/Porter/Messenger/Murderer 2 **Peter F. Gardiner**; Macduff/Duncan/Murderer 1 **James Lavender**; Malcolm/Fleance **Aaron McDaniel**; Witch 1/Ensemble **Alexandra Milne**; Lady Macbeth/Boy **Rebecca Reaney**; Macbeth **Guy Oliver-Watts**; Witch 2/Ensemble **Mary Werntz**

Guy Oliver-Watts in the Aquila Theatre's Macbeth *(photo by Richard Termine)*

SETTING Scotland and England; mid eleventh century. New York premiere of a new revival of a classic play presented in five acts with one intermission.

SYNOPSIS Aquila's *Macbeth* is a tension-filled, sexually charged, and visceral production that places Shakespeare's language at its core. Performed by a cast of American and British actors with extensive credits with the Royal Shakespeare Company, Royal National Theatre, West End, major regional, London and New York theatre, this superb cast brings Shakespeare's intoxicating language to vivid life.

Color Between the Lines

Irondale Center; Opening Night: April 26, 2012; Closed May 24, 2012; 21 performances

Created and presented by Irondale Ensemble Project; Music and songs by Nolan Kennedy and Michael-David Gordon, Terry Greiss, Taifa Harris, Ben Mathews, Alex Miyashiro, Patrena Murray, Scarlet Maressa Rivera, Damen Scranton, Victoria L. Ward; Producer and Director, Jim Niesen; Executive Director, Terry Greiss; Sets and Lighting, Ken Rothchild; Costumes, Hilarie Blumenthal; Musical Director/Sound, Nolan Kennedy; Musical Staging/Choreography, Antwayn Hopper and Natasha Soto-Arbors; Acting Coach, Barbara Mackenzie Wood; Directing Associate, Bella Loudon; Dance Captain, Alex Miyashiro; Production Manager and Technical Director, Micahelangelo DeSerio; Stage Manager, Maria Knapp; ASM, Josie McAdam; Sound Mixer, Jack Flachbart; Lead Carpenter, Steven Brenman; Dramaturgical Support, Prithi Kanakamedala, Josie McAdam; Director of Education, Amanda Hinkle; Development Consultant, David Dean; Individual Gifts Consultant, David Garvoille; Press, Lucy Walters Maneri

CAST **Michael-David Gordon**, **Terry Greiss**, **Nolan Kenndey**, **Ben Mathews**, **Alex Miyashiro**, **Patrena Murray**, **Scarlet Maressa Rivera**, **Damen Scranton**, **Victoria L. Ward**

World premiere of a series of musical vingettes presented without intermission.

SYNOPSIS *Color Between the Lines* is an original work devised by the Irondale ensemble and developed as part of the borough's first public history project to explore the abolitionist movement in Brooklyn. The whole project, also known as 'In Pursuit of Freedom,' brings to life this fascinating story while teasing out the relevance of the subject for contemporary audiences. The show tells and sings the stories of Brooklynites, black and white, who went about living their lives with dignity and perseverance, who signed the petitions, raised the money, opened the schools, started the businesses and came together to change the direction of a nation.

The Company in Color Between the Lines *(photo by Gerry Goodstein)*

Eavesdropping on Dreams

Cherry Lane Studio; First Preview: April 20, 2012; Opening Night: April 29, 2012; Closed May 19, 2012; 9 previews, 18 performances

Written by Rivka Bekerman-Greenberg; Produced by Barefoot Theatre Company (Francisco Solorzano, Producing Artistic Director; Nicole Haran, Co-Artistic Director); Director, Ron Cohen; Set, Niluka Hotaling; Lighting, Eric Nightengale; Costumes, Victoria Malvagno; Sound, Adam Stone; PSM, Michael Denis; ASM, Kristina Mueller; Casting, Judy Keller; Associate Producers, Samantha Fontana, Judy Keller; Assistant Costumes, Jennie West Alexander; Graphic Design, Adam Dalton; Press, Sam Rudy Media Relations

CAST Rosa **Lynn Cohen**; Renee **Stephanie Roth Haberle**; Shaina **Aidan Koehler**; Yakov, Rumkowski **Mike Shapiro**; Hans, SS Officer **Christopher Whalen**

World premiere of a new play presented without intermission.

SYNOPSIS *Eavesdropping on Dreams* is about three generations in one family and their struggles with coming to terms with the aftermath of the Holocaust. Shaina Eberkohn, a 25 year-old medical student, searches for clues about her family's lost history. Her mother, who is paralyzed by her own demons, opposes Shaina's obsession. And Shaina's grandmother, a survivor of the Lodz ghetto and Auschwitz, refuses to help. All three are caught in a web comprised of vague memories, distant emotions, and nightmarish dreams. As they struggle to make sense of it all, they uncover a harrowing secret that unlocks their mysterious past.

Lynn Cohen in Eavesdropping on Dreams *(photo by Francisco Solorzano)*

Fat Camp

American Theatre of Actors–Chernuchin Theatre; First Preview: April 12, 2012; Opening Night: April 29, 2012; Closed May 13, 2012; 21 previews, 17 performances

Book by Randy Blair and Tim Drucker, music by Matthew roi Berger, lyrics by Randy Blair; Produced by Eleven Entertainment/Michael Minarik and the Dodgers; Director, Casey Hushion; Music Director/Arrangements and Orchestrations, Jason DeBord; Choreography, Kelly Devine; Set, Beowulf Boritt; Costumes, David C. Woolard; Lighting, Jason Lyons; Sound, Matt Kraus; PSM, Rachel A. Wolff; ASM, Steve Henry; Casting, Michael Cassara; General Manager, Dodger Management Group, Jennifer F. Vaughan, Flora Johnstone, Lauren Freed, Jeff Parvin; Company Manager, John Gendron; Assistant Musical Director, Jodie Moore; Additional Orchestrations, Adam Blau; Associate Director, Dontee Kiehn; Assistant Director, Alex Bisker; Technical Director, Peter J. Davis; Props Coordinator, Buist Bickley; Associate Design: Jo Winiarski (set), Peter Hoerburger (lighting), Mike Tracey (sound); Assistant Costumes, Joey Blaha; Automated Lighting Programmer, Tim Rogers; Assistant to Mr. Lyons, Jamie Roderick; Production Assistants, Taylor Michael, Samantha Saltzman; Master Carpenter, Mason Merriam; Carpenter, Kristen Rosengren; Electricians, Nick DeFrange, Anthony Gleason; Sound Engineer, Alex Ritter; Wardrobe, Meg Schadl; Advertising, Serino Coyne; Marketing, Dodger Marketing; Dance Captain, Nancy Renée Braun; Press, The Hartman Group, Leslie Baden Papa, Whitney Holden Gore

CAST Aspen **Nancy Renée Braun**; Titus **Michael Buchanan**; Sandy **Janet Dickinson**; Robert **Daniel Everidge**; Taylor **Molly Hager**; Dapne **Carly Jibson**; Anshel **Cale Krise**; Mike **Marcus Neville**; Darnell **Larry Owens**; Britta **Kate Weber**; Ashley **Tracy Weiler**; Brent **Jared Zirilli**; Campers **Charles Barksdale, Bridie Carroll, Jennifer Foster, Michael Mendez**

UNDERSTUDIES Nancy Renée Braun (Sandy, Ashley), Michael Mendez (Robert, Ansel), Jennifer Foster (Taylor), Bridie Carroll (Daphne, Britta), Michael Buchanan (Mike, Brent), Charles Barksdale (Darnell)

BAND Jason DeBord (Conductor/Keyboard), Kenny Brescia (Guitar), Steve Bartosik (Drums), John Lang (Bass)

The Company in Fat Camp *(photo by Chad Batka)*

MUSICAL NUMBERS Welcome to Tomorrow; Can't Take Away My Summer; Taylor & Daphne; Brent von Bingenberger; Anshel's Song; Hungry for It; Candymen; First Kiss; Picture Take Me; Top of the World; All On You; Thinner; Take Back Your Summer; Cannonball; Hanging On; One Shot; Feels A Little Bit Like Love

Off-Broadway premiere of a new musical presented in two acts. World premiere at the 2009 New York Musical Theatre Festival.

SYNOPSIS *Fat Camp* is the story of a rock 'n' roll rebel and the place where he proves he's more than meets the eye: Camp Overton. This clever and quirky comedy, a smash hit at the New York Musical Theatre Festival where it won "Best of Fest," is a delicious new musical about first love, second chances and lasting friendships.

Macbeth

47th Street Theatre; First Preview: April 20, 2012; Opening Night: April 29, 2012; Closed May 26, 2012; 7 previews, 22 performances

Written by William Shakespeare; Produced by Epic Theatre Ensemble (Melissa Friedman, Artistic Director; Ron Russell, Executive Director); Director, Ron Russell; Set, Mikiko Suzuki MacAdams; Costumes, Alixandra Gage Englund; Lighting, Cat Tate Starmer; Sound, Ron Russell; Multimedia, Steven Boling; Movement Director, Will Pomerantz; Fight Director, David Anzuelo; Assistant Director, James Watkins; PSM, Erin Maureen Koster; Stage Manager, Molly Minor Eustis; Production Manager, Jee Han; Technical Director, Joie Bauer; Assistant Design: Daisy Long (lighting), Chien Yu Peng and Yasuko Tokunaga (set); Carpenters, Zachary Buzik, Philip Ross, Mateo Solano; Scenic Charge, Anna Hewit; Painters, Matthew Laiosa, A. Ram Kim; Master Electrician, The Lighting Syndicates; Board Operators, James Watkins, Tim Pracher-Dix, Will Doughty; For Epic Theatre Ensemble: James Wallert (Associate Artistic Director), Robert Chelimsky (Managing Director), Heather Cohn (Director of Development), S. Brian Jones (Education Programs Director), Will Pomerantz (Associate Director of Artistic Development); Press, Glenna Freedman Public Relations

CAST Lady Macbeth **Melissa Friedman**; Ross **Devin E. Haqq**; Banquo **Rhett Henckel**; Macbeth **Ty Jones**; Malcolm **Scott Kerns**; Witch #1 **Aimé Donna Kelly**; Lady Macduff **Lori E. Parquet**; Witch #2 **Julian Rozzell Jr.**; Macduff **Godfrey L. Simmons Jr.**; Witch #3 **James Wallert**; Duncan **Richard Easton**

Revival of a classic play with multimedia presented in two acts.

Ty Jones and Melissa Friedman in Epic Theatre Ensemble's Macbeth *(photo by Carol Rosegg)*

SYNOPSIS Things are going along fine. You're on your way up the ladder. Then the bottom falls out. You and your family struggle along— when suddenly someone appears and says you can have it all back…you just have to do this one little thing. How far would you go to get back what you thought fate had promised you? The Epic ensemble presents a brutal and darkly funny exploration of the banality of evil in Shakespeare's classic thriller.

Headstrong

Ensemble Studio Theatre; First Preview: April 18, 2012; Opening Night: April 30, 2012; Closed May 27, 2012; 7 previews, 32 performances

Written by Patrick Link; Presented by Ensemble Studio Theatre (William Carden, Artistic Director; Paul Alexander Slee, Executive Director) with the Alfred P. Sloan Foundation Science & Technology Project (Doron Weber, Vice President of Programs); Director, William Carden; Sets, Jason Simms; Costumes, Suzanne Chesney; Lighting, Chris Dallos; Sound, Janie Bullard; Video, David Tennent; Technical Director, Derek Dickinson; Assistant Costumes, Jessica Pitcairn; Properties Manager, Kate Stack; PSM, Danielle Buccino; ASM, Kelly Ruth Cole; Assistant Director, Francesca Di Cesare; Season Producer, Web Bogole; EST/Sloan Project Director, Graeme Gillis; EST Sloan Associate Director/Literary Manager, Linsay Firman; Assistant Season Producer, Stephen Brown; Casting, Tom Rowan; Finance Director, Randee Smith; Development Director, Miriam Gardin; Literary Associate, Samantha Sembler; Development Associate, Heather Gallagher; Sound and Video Operator, Emily Auciello; Wardrobe Supervisor, Eileen Lalley; Master Electrician, Stephen Brown; Run Crew, Sarah Dowling, Sean Willkens; Scenic Artist, Kira Nehmer; Marketing Manager/Graphic Design/Box Office, Ryan Hugh McWilliams; Press, Bruce Cohen and Rich Kelley

CAST Duncan Troy **Ron Canada**; Dr. Moses Odame **Tim Cain**; Nick Merritt **Alexander Gemignani**; Sylvia Green **Nedra McClyde**

World premiere of a new play presented without intermission.

SYNOPSIS *Headstrong* is the story of a long-retired NFL linebacker who played with the greats and tackled them to the ground. When his son-in-law, a Pro Bowler himself, dies under strange circumstances, he and his widowed daughter struggle with their own culpability, and whether the brain trauma he suffered in life was the price of football greatness.

Nedra McClyde and Ron Canada in Headstrong *(photo by Gerry Goodstein)*

Evolution

59E59 Theater C; First Preview: April 26, 2012; Opening Night: May 2, 2012; Closed May 20, 2012; 6 previews, 20 performances

Written by Patricia Buckley, music by Marc Mellits; Produced by Absolute Uncertainty and Kristi McKay in association with Interart Theatre and Nicola Murphy; Director, Michele Chivu; Set and Video, Jim Findlay; Costumes, Anna Alisa Belous; Lighting, Thomas Dunn; Sound, Will Pickents; Stage Manager, David A. Vandervliet; Prop Master, Jeffrey Potter-Watts; Additional Dramaturgy, Leslie Noble; Associate Lighting, Laura J. Eckelman; Production Manager/Technical Director, Andy Theodorou; Video Programmer, David Tennant; Video Operator, Matt Daurio; Master Electrician, Laura Shoch; Set Construction, Paul Smithyman, Florencia Paoppi, Janio Marrero, Stefan Karfakis; Electrician, Matt Daurio; Associate Producers, Cherry Lane Theatre, Milesquare Theatre; Fiscal Sponsor, The Redhouse Arts Center; Press, Karen Greco

CAST Minnie, Pammy, Mother, Sherry **Patricia Buckley**; Voices **Karel Blakeley, Bill Morris, Leslie Noble, Lynnea Harding, Erin Whylan**

SETTING Coastal America. The present. Off-Broadway premiere of a new play presented without intermission. Developed at the Cherry Lane Theatre 2012 Mentor Project (Angelina Fiordellisi, Founding Artistic Director).

SYNOPSIS Scientific fact and family history collide in Evolution, which combines the paleontology of whale evolution with the contemporary tale of a woman's extraordinary transformation and her family's attempts - by turns comic, tragic and poetic - to prevent it. Evolution creates a world in which past, present and future exist simultaneously, and considers the question 'How Should We Respond To Change?'

Patricia Buckley in Evolution *(photo by Russ Rowland)*

A Jew Grows in Brooklyn

Jacqueline Kennedy Onassis Theater; Opening Night: May 2, 2012; 30 performances as of May 31, 2012

Written by Jake Ehrenreich; Produced by Door to Door Generations; Director, Jon Huberth; Creative Consultant, Lisa Ehrenreich; Music Director, Katya Stanislavskaya; Current Set Design and Construction, Luke Hadsall; Sound Engineer, Mark Goodell; Musical Consultant, Larry Cohen; Lighting, Anjeanette Stokes; Production Manager, Jeffrey C. Stevenson; General Management, Krista Robbins; Original Set Design, Joseph Egan; Original Music Direction, Eylsa Sunshine; Graphic Design, Ron Slanina; Marketing and Advertising, Leanne Schanzer; Press, Glenna Freedman Public Relations

Performed by **Jake Ehrenreich**

MUSICIANS Katya Stanislavskaya or Larry Cohen (Keyboards/Vocals), Jon Hurley (Guitar/Bass/ Vocals), Jeff Bruce (Drums/Vocals)

Return engagement of an autobiographical solo performance show with live music presented without intermission. World premiere at the Chernuchin Theatre at American Theatre of Actors April 10, 2006 (see *Theatre World* Vol. 62, page 127). That production transferred to the Lamb's Theatre June 7, 2006, and then transferred to 37 Arts October 11, 2006 where it closed June 10, 2007 after 304 performances. The production subsequently toured over twenty-five cities.

SYNOPSIS *A Jew Grows in Brooklyn* is the story of a baby boomer, the son of survivors who grew up in 1960s Brooklyn and wanted nothing more than to be American. Along the way, Ehrenreich, backed by a trio of musician/singers, performs the popular music of both his and his parent's generations, and demonstrates, from adolescence in Brooklyn, to the classic Catskills, how survivors learn to laugh again. With the help of a visual multi-media set, he weaves philosophy into personal history as he recreates his journey from denial to acceptance to rebirth.

Jake Ehrenreich in A Jew Grows in Brooklyn *(photo by Carol Rosegg)*

American Jornalero

INTAR; First Preview: May 3, 2012; Opening Night: May 7, 2012; Closed June 3, 2012; 4 previews, 21 performances

Written by Ed Cardona Jr. Produced by INTAR (Lou Moreno, Artistic Director; John McCormack, Executive Director) as part of TeatroStageFest 2012; Director, Mariana Carreño King; Set. Raul Abrego; Lighting, María Cristina Fusté; Costumes, Harry Nadal; Sound, Julian Mesri; Stage Manager, David Apichell; ASM, Laura Kathryne Gomez; Fight Director, David Anzuelo; Assistant Director, Jordana de la Cruz; Assistant Set and Lighting, Irmaris Sanchez-Diaz; Master Electrician, Ivan Salinas; For INTAR: Jose Sanchez (Facilities/Office Manager), Jeff Berzon (Financial Manager), Billy Hopkins (Casting Consultant), Lucy Thurber (HPRL Director); Press, David Gersten and Associates

CAST Luis **Bernardo Cubría**; Michigan **Bobby Plasencia**; Montezuma **David Crommett**; Mark **Joel Ripka**; Marcelo **Jose Joaquin Perez**; Toby **Quinlan Corbett**

SETTING Queens, New York. 2006. Off-Broadway premiere of a new play presented without intermission. Originally workshopped at the Working Theatre (Mark Pleasant, Artistic Director).

SYNOPSIS In *American Jornalero*, a group of immigrant day laborers waiting to be picked up for work collide with two citizen vigilantes fashioning themselves on the Minuteman Project.

Bernardo Cubria and Jose Joaquin Perez in American Jornalero *(photo by Carol Rosegg)*

Heat Wave: The Jack Cole Project

Queens Theatre in the Park; First Preview: May 3, 2012; Opening Night: May 9, 2012; Closed May 20, 2012; 5 previews, 13 performances

Conceived, directed, and choreographed by chet Walker; Produced by Queens Theatre (Roy Cullom, Artistic Director, Scott Mohon, Managing Director) in association with Walkerdance (Chet Walker, Artistic Director); Music Direction and Arrangements, Rick Hip-Flores; Set, Kelly James Tighe; Costumes, Brad Musgrove; Lighting, Paul Miller; Projections, Erik Scanlon; Contributing Choreographer, Ray Hesselink; Dance Supervisor, Bill Hastings; Casting, Michael Cassara; Assistant to Mr. Walker/Dance Captain, Emanuel Abruzzo; PSM, Melissa M. Spengler; ASM, Andrea Jo Martin; Project Manager, Jude Domski; Master Electrician/Light Board Operator, Steve Wolf; Master Carpenter, Sarah Schetter; Costume Shop Supervisor/Draper, Erica Giles; Electricians, Kirk Fitzgerald, Tom Lombardo, Temisha Johnson, Christine Cruz; Scenic Carpenter, AJ Mattioli, Matt Dinsick; Sound Board Operator, Mike Lawler; Spotlight Operators, AJ Mattioli, Kirk Fitzgerald; Wig Design, Steven Perfidia Kirkham; Milliner and Crafts Artist, Sarah Riffle; Wig Technician, Ashley Miller; Wardrobe, Erica Giles, Grace Trimble, Ali Valcarcel; Co-Dance Captain, Rosi Lani Fiedelman; Casting Associate, Anika Chapin; Director of Marketing and Communications, Ed Kiley; Marketing Assistant, Sydney Pratt; Development Jonathan Park; Advertising, Hofstetter + Partners/Agency 212; Press, JS2 Communications, Pete Sanders, Jaclyn York, Dennis Mihalsky

CAST Featured Performer **David Elder**; Ensemble **Emanuel Abruzzo, Colin Bradbury, Rosi Lani Fiedelman, Andrew Fitch, Leeds Hill, Nadine Isenegger, Kristine Piro, Rachelle Rak, Matt Rivera, Lindsay Roginski, Joshua Schulteis, Jena Vanelslader**; Swings **Philip Northington, Naomi Rusalka**

MUSICIANS Rick Hip-Flores (Conductor/Piano), Stefan Schatz (Drums), Steve Smyth (Trumpet/Flugelhorn), Debbie Kennedy (Bass), Tom Olin (Reeds)

World premiere of a new musical revue presented in two acts.

SYNOPSIS *Heat Wave* pays tribute to dancer-choreographer Jack Cole (1911-1974), featuring recreations of more than two dozen Cole numbers from such films as *Kismet*, *Les Girls*, and *There's No Business Like Show Business*, as well as new pieces choreographed in Cole's inimitable style. Cole, considered the father of theatrical jazz and musical theatre dance, was known for his signature knee slides, struts, and slinky sexuality, and his works influenced a new generation of dancers and choreographers, including Bob Fosse, Gwen Verdon and Michael Bennett.

Jena Van Elslander, David Elder, Lindsay Roginski, and Kristin Piro in
Heat Wave: The Jack Cole Project *(photo by Carol Rosegg)*

Take What Is Yours

59E59 Theater B; First Preview: May 3, 2012; Opening Night: May 9, 2012;
Closed May 27, 2012; 6 previews, 20 performances

Concieved by Erica Fae, written by Erica Fae and Jill A. Samuels; Produced by anecdota; Director, Jill A. Samuels; Sound, Kristin Worrall; Costumes, Alixandra Gage Englund; Projectins, Tal Yarden; Set Design Concept, Jill A. Samuels; Set Consultant, Deb O; Lighting, Alison Brummer; Associate Producer, Kate Hamill; National Advisor, Rebecca Otto; Stage Manager, Stephanie Armitage; Technical Director, Grant Neale; Assistant Lighting, Sean Conlin; Set Construction, Ariel Boles, Greg Squared, Jill A. Samuels, Deb O, Truman Clarke McCasland; Scenic Painter, Danielle Baskin; Sound Board Operator, Christopher Day; Press, Karen Greco

CAST Alice **Erica Fae**; The Man **Wayne Maugans**; Guard/Gandor **Adrian Jevicki**; Guard **David Riley**; Nurse **Courtney Stallings**

Off-Broadway premiere of a new play presented without intermission. Previously presented as a solo performance piece at Interborough Repertory Theatre June 14–July 2, 2010.

SYNOPSIS *Take What Is Yours* is the little-known true story of how American women fought and won the right to vote. Composed in the words of Alice Paul, the National Woman's Party ,and documents of the time, this stunning new production weaves virtuosic performances with striking visuals and a richly-layered sound score into a moving and inspiring story.

Wayne Maugans and Erica Fae in Take What Is Yours
(photo by Augustinus Tjahaya)

Travelers

59E59 Theater A; Opening Night: May 10, 2012; Closed May 13, 2012; 5 performances

Two chamber operas *The Wandering Scholar* and *S vitri* by Gustav Holst; *The Wandering Scholar* libretto by Clifford Bax after a book by Helen Waddell with chamber orchestrations, Benjamin Britten and Imogen Holst; *S vitri* libretto by Holst, after an episode in *The Mahabharata*; Produced by The Little Opera Theatre of NY (Philip Shneidman, Founder and Artistic Director; Stephanie Altman Dominus, Managing Director); Conductor, Richard Cordova; Director, Philip Shneidman; Set, Neil Patel; Costumes, Lara de Bruijn; Lighting, Amanda Clegg Lyon and Natalie Robin; PSM, Aaron Heflich Shapiro; Production Manager, Andy Theodorou; ASM, Jenna Bauman; Assistant Set, Caleb Levengood; Props, Jeff Protter-Watts; Associate Music Director, Catherine Miller; Artistic Adminstrator, Dennis Blackwell; Public Relations, Paula Mlyn and Lee Streby; Press, Karen Greco

CAST *The Wandering Scholar*: Louis, a farmer **Ron Loyd**; Alison, his wife **Sharin Apostoulou** or **Maria Alu**; Father Philippe **Jeffrey Tucker**; Pierre, a wandering scholar **Benjamin Robinson**; *S vitri*: Satyav n, a woodman **Rufus Müller**; S vitri, his wife **Heather Johnson** or **Toby Newman**; Death **Michael Scarcelle**; Ensemble (both shows) **Lily Arbisser**, **Suzanne Chadwick**, **Helen Gabrielsen**, **Jessica Grigg**, **Katherine Howell**, **Keiko Kai**, **Julie Marie Miller**, **Leandra Ramm**

ORCHESTRA Richard Cordova (Conductor); Philip Wharton (Concertmaster); Sean Carney, Mioi Takeda, Carla Fabiani (Violins); Denise Cridge, Corey Ramey (Violas); Melanie Mason, Paul Wolfram (Cellos); Troy Rinker (Bass); Clare Hoffman (Flute); Margaret Lancaster (Flute/Piccolo); Pascal Archer (Clarinet); Keve Wilson (Oboe/Horn); Mike Sayre (French Horn); Gili Sharett (Bassoon); Lynette Wardle (Harp); Matt Smallcomb (Percussion)

Off-Broadway premieres of two chamber operas presented without intermission.

SYNOPSIS *Travelers: Operas by Gustav Holst* is comprised of two short English chamber operas, one a tale of comic hypocrisy, the other a tale of pure devotion. *The Wandering Scholar* is an amusing tale of a young wife, a Priest, and a traveling scholar; and what the husband finds when he returns home. *S vitri* is a mythic tale of love to the lover, the child to the mother, the song to the singer, a wife to her husband.

Miracle on South Division Street

St. Luke's Theatre; First Preview: April 25, 2012; Opening Night: May 13, 2012; Closed July 29, 2012; 9 previews, 45 performances

Written by Tom Dudzick; Produced by Penguin Rep (Joe Brancato, Artistic Director; Andrew M. Horn, Executive Director) and Morton Wolkowitz; Director, Joe Brancato; Set and Lighting, Josh Iacovelli; Costumes, Gail Cooper-Hecht; Sound, Chris Rummel; PSM, Michael Palmer; Casting, Cindi Rush; Associate Producers, Barry and Helene Lewis, Joseph Grosso; ASM, Jamil Chokachi; Wardrobe Supervisor, Courtney Irizarry; Production Crew, Paul Bourgeois, Justin Holcomb, Jonathan Santos, Curtis Shaw; Set Construction, Ken Larson; Theatre Operator, Edmund Gaynes; Co-Artistic Director, Pamela Hall; Theatre General Management, Jessimeg Productions, Julia Beardsley, Catherine Fowles; Sales, Bill Fitzgerald; Technical Director, Josh Iacovelli; Press, David Gersten and Associates

CAST Jimmy Nowak **Rusty Ross**; Ruth Nowak **Andrea Maulella**; Clara Nowak **Peggy Cosgrave**; Beverly Nowak **Liz Zazzi**

SETTING Clara Nowak's kitchen, in a run-down working class neighborhood of Buffalo, NY. Early autumn, 2010. Off-Broadway premiere of a new play presented without intermission. World premiere at Penguin Rep Theatre (under the title *Our Lady of South Division Street*) May 15–June 14, 2009.

SYNOPSIS *Miracle on South Division Street* is a new comedy about family, faith and adjusting to life's surprises. Her neighborhood may be depressed but not Clara Nowak. She and her three grown children tend a shrine built to commemorate the miraculous vision her father had in his barbershop in 1942. Clara has never lost her faith even if her kids have their doubts. That is, not until a deathbed confession reveals a long-hidden family secret, and all heck breaks loose on South Division Street.

Rusty Ross, Peggy Cosgrave, and Liz Zazzi in Miracle on South Division Street *(photo by Aaron Pepis)*

Cock

Duke on 42nd Street; First Preview: May 1, 2012; Opening Night: May 17, 2012; 18 previews, 17 performances as of May 31, 2012

Written by Mike Bartlett; Produced by Stuart Thompson, Jean Doumanian, Royal Court Theatre, William Berlind, Scott Delman, Dena Hammerstein, Jon B. Platt, Scott Rudin, Ted Snowdon, and True Love Productions; Director, James Macdonald; Set and Costumes, Miriam Buether; Lighting, Peter Mumford; Sound, Darron L West; Casting, Cindy Tolan; PSM, Martha Donaldson; Production Manager, Aurora Productions, Gene O'Donvan, Ben Heller, Stephanie Sherline, Jarid Sumner, Anthony Jusino, Anita Shah, Liza Lexemberg, Steven Dalton, Eugenio Saenz Flores, Isaac Katzanek, Janel D'Ammassa, Melissa Mazdra; General Management, Davenport Theatrical Enterprises, Ken Davenport, Jennifer Collins Ritter, Ryan Lympus; Company Manager, Pam Dickler; Associate Producers, Kevin Emrick, Patrick Daly; ASM/Understudy, Nilanjana Bose; Dialect Coach, Kate Wilson; Assistant Director, Stella Powell-Jones; Production Assistant, B. Bales Karlin; Assistant Design: Kina Parks (set), Dale Knoth (lighting), Sarah Cubbage (costumes), M. Florian Staab (sound); Wardrobe Supervisor, Caitlin Brown; Production Electrician, Tom Dyer; Production Carpenter, Vadim Malinskiy; Casting Associate, Adam Caldwell; Advertising and Marketing, SpotCo; Press, Boneau/Bryan-Brown, Chris Boneau, Susanne Tighe, Christine Olver

CAST John **Cory Michael Smith**; M **Jason Butler Harner**; W **Amanda Quaid**; F **Cotter Smith**

U.S. premiere of a new play presented without intermission. World premiere presented by the English Stage Company at the Royal Court Theatre November 13, 2009.

SYNOPSIS Royal Court Theatre's Olivier Award-winning production of Mike Bartlett's play *Cock* arrives Off-Broadway with an American cast. *Cock* involves a rather unusual love triangle. When John and his boyfriend of seven years take a break, the last thing he expects is to suddenly meet the woman of his dreams. Now he has a big choice to make.

Cory Michael Smith, Cotter Smith, Jason Butler Harner, and Amanda Quaid in Cock *(photo by Joan Marcus)*

Old Jews Telling Jokes

Westside Theatre–Downstairs; First Preview: May 1, 2012; Opening Night: May 20, 2012; 23 previews, 13 performances as of May 31, 2012

Created by Peter Gethers and Daniel Okrent; Produced by Daniel Okrent, Peter Gethers, Richard Frankel, Tom Viertel, Steven Baruch, and Marc Routh; Director, Marc Bruni; Original Internet Series Creators and Producers, Sam Hoffman, Tim Williams, Eric Spiegelman; Set and Video, David Gallo; Costumes, Alejo Vietti; Lighting, Jeff Croiter; Sound, Peter Fitzgerald; Animation, Steve Channon; Music Supervision and Arrangements, Adam Wachter; Title Song, Adam Gwon; Casting, Tara Rubin; General Management, Frankel Green Theatrical Management, Richard Frankel, Laura Green, Joe Watson, Grant A. Rice; Production Supervision, Production Core/James E. Clevaland; PSM, William H. Lang; Stage Manager, Sarah Butke; Company Manager, Bobby Driggers; Assistant Company Manager, Kendall Booher; Creative Consultant, Stuart Ross; Production Manager, Amanda Raymond; Assistant Production Manager, Josh Morgan; Production Administrative Assistant, Laura Archer; Technical Director, Peter Fry; Master Electrician, The Lighting Syndicate, Doug Filomena; Onsite Master Electrician, Patrick Dugan; Associate Design: Evan Adamson (set), China Lee (costumes); Assistant Design: Wilburn Bonnell (lighting), Megan Henninger (sound); Video Assistant, Sheryl Liu; Gallo Design Studio Assistant, Shayla Spradley; Lighting Programmer, Matthew Taylor; Prop Master, Joshua Yocum; Wig Master, Leah Loukas; Automation Supervisor, Ry Pepper; Wardrobe/Production Technician, Molly Kaufhold; Head Video, Joe Cantalupo; Production Assistants, Kenny Faust, Scott Andrews, S.M. Payson; Marketing, Leanne Schanzer; Advertising, Serino Coyne; Press, Boneau/Bryan-Brown, Chris Boneau, Jackie Green, Amy Kass

CAST Morty **Lenny Wolpe**; Bunny **Marilyn Sokol**; Nathan **Todd Susman**; Debbi **Audrey Lynn Weston**; Reuben **Bill Army**; Pianist **Donald Corren**

STANDBYS Donald Corren (Morty, Nathan), Suzanne Grodner (Bunny, Debbi), Garth Kravits (Reuben/Pianist)

World premiere of a comedy and sketch revue with music presented without intermission.

SYNOPSIS Get ready for an outrageous evening of one-liners, double-entendres, and hysterical routines sure to triple you over with laughter! *Old Jews Telling Jokes* showcases five actors in a revue that pays tribute to and reinvents classic jokes of the past and present. Think you've heard them all before? Not this way. The show also features comic songs, brand new and satisfyingly old, as well as tributes to some of the giants of the comedy world and to the brilliant raconteurs from the *Old Jews Telling Jokes* website, which inspired the show. If you've ever had a mother, visited a doctor, or walked into a bar with a priest, a rabbi and a frog, *Old Jews Telling Jokes* will sit in the dark, give you a second opinion, and ask you where you got that.

Audrey Lynn Weston, Marilyn Sokol, Lenny Wolpe, Todd Susman, and Bill Army in Old Jews Telling Jokes *(photo by Joan Marcus)*

She's of a Certain Age

Beckett Theatre on Theatre Row; First Preview: April 26, 2012; Opening Night: May 20, 2012; Closed June 10, 2012; 28 previews, 32 performances

Short plays written by Susan Charlotte: *Did You Know My Husband?*, *Living for Design*, *Come On*, and *Sundown*; Produced by Cause Célèbre (Susan Charlotte, Artistic Director) in association with Mary J. Davis; Director, Antony Marsellis and Christopher Hart; Set, James Wolk; Lighting, Dennis Parichy; Sound, Andy Cohen; PSM, C. Renee Alexander; Stage Manager, Bernita Robinson; Company Manager, Brendan Hill; Costume Consultant, Liz Covey; Accountant, Ira Schall; Graphic Design, Ken Krug; Assistant Set, Sarah Harris; Set Construction, Ken Larson; Production Assistant, Brandon Brown; Accounting, Ira Schall; Legal, M. Graham Coleman, Esq.; Press, Pucci/Hunt PR, Maria Pucci, Christina Wyeth

CAST Sylvia **Rosemary Prinz**; Dottie **Lois Markle**; Julia **Drea De Niro**; Jim **Robert Newman**

Lois Markle and Rosemary Prinz in She's of a Certain Age *(photo by Ben Hider)*

SETTING A luxury high rise building, midtown Manhattan. Thanksgiving 2010, Independence Day 2010, Valentine's Day 2011. World premiere of four short plays presented without intermission.

SYNOPSIS How old is a woman of a certain age? Word has it that the age keeps changing and getting older! Three women and one man, ranging in age from forty to eighty, face the challenges presented by different stages in life with humor and humanity.

Here I Go

59E59 Theater C; First Preview: May 22, 2012; Opening Night: May 24, 2012; Closed June 3, 2012; 2 previews, 10 performances

Written by David Todd, conceived and directed by Luke Leonard; Produced by Monk Parrots (Luke Leonard and Joey LePage, Producing Artistic Directors); Associate Director, Shaun Patrick Tubbs; Production Design, Luke Leonard; Lighting/Technical Director, Eric Nightingale; Costumes, Jennifer Skura; Sound, Michael Howell; Light Operator, John Harmon; Associate Director for Monk Parrots, Jennifer Skura; Communications Administrator, John Harmon; Speical Events Adminstrator, Jessica Pohlman; Press, Karen Greco

CAST The Man **Michael Howell**; Lynette, age 60 **Natalie Leonard**; Lynette, age 26 **Jessica Pohlman**; Lynette, age 16 **Mariah Ilardi-Lowy**; Lynette, age 8 **Gates Loren Leonard**; The Voice of Lynette **Julie Nelson**

New York premiere of a new play presented without intermission. Workshopped at Dixon Place June 23, 2011.

SYNOPSIS A woman considering suicide is visited by a pet horse and versions of herself at various ages while a man tries to take her hand. Will she go? *Here I Go* hitches the emotional gamut of classic, country music with a romanticized depiction of Lynette, a cowgirl in her 60s contemplating suicide. Accusation and acceptance are major themes that prompt questions related to loss and sacrifice in *Here I Go*.

Gates Loren Leonard, Michael Howell, and Natalie Leonard in Here I Go *(photo by Corey Torpie)*

Jukebox Jackie: Snatches of Jackie Curtis

Ellen Stewart Theatre at LaMama; First Preview: May 24, 2012; Opening Night: May 30, 2012; Closed June 10, 2012; 5 previews, 12 performances

Conceived and directed by Scott Wittman, collaged by Scott Whitman and Tony Zanetta; Produced by LaMama ETC (Mia Yoo, Artistic Director) as part of the Queer New York International Arts Festival; Design, Scott Pask; Costumes,

Rita Ryack; Lighting, Aaron Spivey; Projections, Caite Hevner; Staging, Joey Pizzi; Music Director/Arrangements, Lance Horne; Collage, Scott Wittman and Tony Zanetta; PSM, Jason A. Quinn; Stage Manager, Sarah Tschirpke; Staging Associate, Chad Luke Schiro; Jackie's Trunk Design and Creation, Tom Hooper; Graphic Design, Tim Hailand and Kissane Viola; Assistant Design: Orit Jacoby Carroll (set), Joel Shire (lighting), Jessica De La Cruz (costumes); Press, Sam Rudy Media Relations

CAST Justin Vivian Bond, Bridget Everett, Cole Escola, Steel Burkhardt; Special appearances (certain performances) Penny Arcade, Jayne County, Cherry Vanilla, Agosto Machado

MUSICIANS (Lance Horne and The Colored Girls) Lance Horne, Matt Aronoff, Matthew Bauder, Dave Berger, Mike Jackson, Steve Welsh

World premiere of a revue with poetry, music, and dance presented without intermission.

SYNOPSIS *Jukebox Jackie: Snatches of Jackie Curtis* is a collage of scenes, poetry, music and dance culled from the works of Jackie Curtis, who performed as both a man and a woman throughout his career in the 60s, 70s and 80s, stating, "I'm not a boy, not a girl, not a faggot, not a drag queen, not a transsexual. I'm just me, Jackie." The four performers embody the the different sides of Jackie through different stages of Jackie's life.

Justin Vivian Bond and Cole Escola in Jukebox Jackie: Snatches of Jackie Curtis *(photo by Mat Szwajkos)*

I Am a Tree

Theatre at St. Clement's; First Preview: May 25, 2012; Opening Night: May 31, 2012; Closed June 30, 2012; 5 previews, 24 performances

Written by Dulcy Rogers; Produced by United Pies, Inc.; Director, Allan Miller; Set and Props, Neil Patel; Lighting, Yael Lubetzky; Sound, Jason Crystal; Stage Manager, Christine Lemme; General Management, Melanie Hopkins; Production Management, Bethany Weinstein; General Management Associate, BJ Evans; Stage Management Sub, Melanie T. Morgan; Graphic Design, Gabriel Aronson; Production Sound Engineer, Nathan McKinney; Production Electrician, Mitchell Ost; Scenic Painter, Holly Griffin; Scenic Crew, Porter Fulman, Andrew Castle, Stefano Pennisi; Electrics Crew, Andrew Balmer, Brett Maughan, Eliza Gujardo, Victoria Loye, Alison Ostendorf, Steven Materno; Lighting Programmer, Curtis Lee; Marketing, The Pekoe Group; Press, Karen Greco

CAST Claire, Aurelia, Lillian, Lou Dulcy Rogers

New York premiere of a new solo performance play presented without intermission. World premiere at the Lillian Theatre at the Elephant Stages (Los Angeles) June 11–July 17, 2010.

SYNOPSIS Thirty-something year old Claire discovers she has family members she never knew existed. Desperate to find out about the mother she barely knew, she embarks on an odyssey to find these relatives, hoping they will give her the answers she needs. But what she ends up finding is three wildly eccentric aunts, who have three very different perspectives on what her mother was like, what actually happened to her and why.

Spiegelworld: Empire

Spiegelworld Tent at 265 West 45th Street; First Preview: May 22, 2012; Opening Night: May 31, 2012; Closed September 2, 2012; 16 previews, 163 performances

Created by Spiegelworld; Produced by Ross Mollison and David J. Foster; Presented by Related Companies and Boston Properties; Director, Wayne Harrison; Choreography, John O'Connell; Music Producer, Jamie Siegel; Costumes, Angus Strathie; Production Design, Josh Zangen; Art Director, Matthew Hodges; Lighting, Martin Kinnane; Sound, Matt Kraus; Project Manager, Joshua Scherr; Production Manager, Nate Terracio; PSM, Lara Tenenbaum; Press, O+M Company

CAST Oscar (Clown/MC) Jonathan Taylor; Fanny (Clown/MC) Anne Goldmann; Vocalist (Miss Purple) Lena Hall; Trio Bingo - Banquine Olena Lomaga, Anastasiia Pemiakova, Anastasiia Gavrylenko; Roller-Skating Roma Hervida, Sven Rauhe; Aerial Sphere and Hula Hoops Elena Lev; Chair Balancing Vladamir Malachkin; Spintop on Driftwood & Branch Balancing Rigolo; Risley Tariku Degefa, Yonas Alemu; Hand to Hand/Adagio Ludivine Furnon, Martin Charrat; Wheel Master Yasuaki Yoshikawa

World premiere of a new theatrical circus, burlesque, cabaret, and variety show presented without intermission.

SYNOPSIS Spiegelworld returns to New York City for a summer-only engagement of *Empire*, an all-new show headlined by some of the sexiest, most daring artists ever to arrive on Broadway. Gravity defying. Sanity defying. So close, you can almost touch them! The antique spiegeltent that popped up at Times Square is furnished with beveled mirrors, plush velvet seating booths and the most intimate stage in town. *Empire* smashes through the borders of comedy, circus, variety and burlesque to take over Broadway for the summer. Step inside and get ready to be shocked and awed by *Empire*!

A scene from Spiegelworld: Empire *(photo by Thom Kaine)*

PLAYED TROUGH / CLOSED THIS SEASON

The Accidental Pervert

layers Theatre*; First Preview: December 4, 2009; Opening Night: January 23, 2010; 13 previews, 244 performances as of May 31, 2012 (Fridays and Saturday evenings only)

Written by Andrew Goffman; Director, Charles Messina; Choreography, Sherri Norige; Audio/Visual Design, Andrew Wingert; Dramaturg, Liza Lentina; Production Coordinator, Gina Ferranti; Lighting, Shannon Epstein; Set/Technical Director, Anthony Augello; Graphic Design, Robert Tallon; Dialogue Coach, Stanley Harrison; Creative Assistant, Christy Benati; House Manager, Carlo Rivieccio; Press, Judy Jacksina

Performed by **Andrew Goffman**

Off-Broadway debut of a solo performance play presented without intermission. Originally workshopped at the 45th Street Theatre and eventually played Off-Off-Broadway at the Triad Theatre.

SYNOPSIS *The Accidental Pervert* is the true accounting of one boy's odyssey to manhood via a childhood dominated by pornography, an addiction accumulated after the boy happens upon his father's collection of XXX-Rated video tapes in a bedroom closet. Goffman takes his audience on a hilarious and self-deprecating journey into a world of his addiction to pornography until the age of 26, when he met his wife.

*The production transferred to the 13th Street Repertory July 15, 2011.

Andrew Goffman in The Accidental Pervert *(photo by Drew Wingert)*

Avenue Q

New World Stages – Stage 3; First Preview: October 9, 2009; Opening Night: October 21, 2010; 14, previews, 1,089 performances as of May 31, 2012

Music and lyrics by Robert Lopez and Jeff Marx, book by Jeff Whitty; Produced by Kevin McCollum, Robyn Goodman, Jeffrey Seller, Vineyard Theatre & The New Group; Director, Jason Moore; Choreography, Ken Roberson; Music Supervision/Orchestrations/Arrangements, Stephen Oremus; Music Director, Andrew Graham; Puppets Conception/Design, Rick Lyon; Set, Anna Louizos; Costumes, Mirena Rada; Lighting, Howell Binkley; Sound, Acme Sound Partners; Animation, Robert Lopez; Incidental Music, Gary Adler; Casting, Cindy Tolan; General Manager/Marketing/Advertising, Davenport Theatrical Enterprises; Production Manager, Travis Walker/ Autonomous Production Services; PSM, Christine M. Daly; Stage Manager/Dance and Puppet Captain, James Darrah; ASM, Michael

Liscio Jr.; Company Manager, Ryan Lympus/Jennifer Collins Ritter; Resident Director, Evan Ensign; Associate Design: Todd Potter (set), Ryan O'Gara (lighting), Karl Ruckdeschel (costumes); Assistant Lighting, Sooyeon Hong; Lighting Programmer, Chris Herman; Keyboard Programming, Mark Hartman, Jim Abbott, Randy Cohen; Music Copying, Emily Grishman/Alex Lacamoire; Animation/Video Production, Sound Associates Inc.; Sound & Video Design Effects, Brett Jarvis; Press, Sam Rudy Media Relations; Broadway cast recording: RCA 82876-55923-2

CAST Princeton/Rod **Adam Kantor**[*1]; Brian **Nicholas Kohn**; Kate Monster/Lucy the Slut & others **Veronica Kuhn**; Nicky/Trekkie Monster/Bad Idea Bear & others **Rob Morrison**; Christmas Eve **Hazel Ann Raymundo**; Gary Coleman **Haneefah Wood**; Mrs. T./Bad Idea Bear & others **Ruthie Ann Miles**[*2]; Ensemble **Kate Lippstreu**, **Jed Resnick**; Swings[*3] **Jasmin Walker**, **Michael Liscio Jr.**

*Succeeded by: 1. Jeffrey David Sears (12/26/11), Darren Bluestone 2. Lexie Fridell 3. Added: Lisa Helmi Johnson ("Christmas Eve" Vacation Swing, Jan. 2012)

ORCHESTRA Andrew Graham (Conductor/keyboard); Karl Mansfield (Associate Conductor/keyboard); Patience Higgins (reeds); Joe Choroszewski (drums)

MUSICAL NUMBERS Avenue Q Theme; What Do You Do With a BA in English?/It Sucks to be Me; If You Were Gay; Purpose; Everyone's a Little Bit Racist; The Internet Is for Porn; Mix Tape; I'm Not Wearing Underwear Today; Special; You Can Be as Loud as the Hell You Want (When You're Making Love); Fantasies Come True; My Girlfriend Who Lives in Canada; There's a Fine, Fine Line; It Sucks to Be Me (reprise); There Is Life Outside Your Apartment; The More You Ruv Someone; Schadenfreude; I Wish I Could Go Back to College; The Money Song; For Now

SETTING An outer borough of New York City; the present. A musical presented in two acts. Originally presented Off-Broadway March 19, 2003 at the Vineyard Theatre (see *Theatre World* Vol. 59, page 179). Transferred to Broadway at the John Golden Theatre July 10, 2003–September 13, 2010, playing 2,534 performances (see *Theatre World* Vol. 60, page 25 for original Broadway credits). This unprecedented transfer back to Off-Broadway marked the first time a Broadway musical has moved to an Off-Broadway theatre.

SYNOPSIS *Avenue Q* is about real life: finding a job, losing a job, learning about racism, getting an apartment, getting kicked out of your apartment, being different, falling in love, promiscuity, avoiding commitment, and internet porn. Twenty and thirty-something puppets and humans survive life in the big city and search for their purpose in this naughty but timely musical that features "full puppet nudity!"

The Awesome 80s Prom

Webster Hall; First Preview: July 23, 2004 (Friday evenings only); Opening Night: September 10, 2004 (Fridays and Saturdays); 428 performances as of May 31, 2012 (Saturdays only)

Written and produced by Ken Davenport; Co-Authored by The Class of '89 (Sheila Berzan, Alex Black, Adam Bloom, Anne Bobby, Courtney Balan, Mary Faber, Emily McNamara, Troy Metcalf, Jenna Pace, Amanda Ryan Paige, Mark Shunock, Josh Walden, Noah Weisberg, Brandon Williams, Simon Wong and Fletcher Young); Director, Ken Davenport; Choreography, Drew Geraci; Costumes, Randall E. Klein; Lighting, Martin Postma; Production Stage Manager, Carlos Maisonet; Associate Producers, Amanda Dubois, Jennifer Manocherian; General Manager, Davenport Theatricals; Company Manager, Nicole Gehring; ASM, Kathryn Galloway; Casting, Daryl Eisenberg; Press, David Gersten & Associates

CAST Johnny Hughes (The DJ) **Dillon Porter**[*1]; Lloyd Parker (The Photographer) **Alex Fast**[*2]; Dickie Harrington (The Drama Queen) **Bennett Leak**[*3]; Michael Jay (The Class President) **Craig Jorczak**[*4]; Mr. Snelgrove The Principal) **Thomas Poarch**; Molly Parker (The Freshman) **Pamela Macey**; Inga Swanson (The Swedish Exchange Student) **Lindsay Ryan**[*5]; Joshua "Beef" Beefarowski (A Football Player) **Michael Barra**[*6]; Whitley Whitiker (The

Head Cheerleader) **Jessica West Regan**; Nick Fender (The Rebel) **Brandon Marotta**; Heather #1 (A Cheerleader) **Joanne Nosuchinsky**; Heather #2 (The Other Cheerleader) **Kate Wood Riley**; Kerrie Kowalski (The Spaz) **Missy Diaz**[7]; Melissa Ann Martin (Head of the Prom Committee) **Lauren Schafler**; Louis Fensterpock (The Nerd) **Daryl Embry**; Blake Williams (Captain of the Football Team) **Chris Cafero**; Mrs. Lascalzo (The Drama Teacher) **Andrea Biggs**; Feung Schwey (The Asian Exchange Student) **Anderson Lim**; The Mystery Guest **CP Lacey**

*Succeeded by: 1. Craig Jorczak (alt.), Jared Thompson (April 2012) 2. Zachary Sciranka 3. Wade Dooley (7/23/11) 4. Alex Fast 5. Paige Grimard 6. Andrew Arena (Jan. 2012) 7. Emily Tarpey (May 2012). Temporary replacements: Jennifer Peters (Heather #1/#2), Megan Gerlach (Heather #1/#2), Ashley Campana (Kerrie), Allison Carter Thompson (Heather #1)

SETTING Wanaget High's Senior Prom, 1989. An interactive theatrical experience presented without intermission

SYNOPSIS The Captain of the Football Team, the Asian Exchange Student, the Geek, and the Head Cheerleader are all competing for Prom King and Queen. The audience decides who wins while moonwalking to retro hits from the decade.

Reid Skidmore and David Wendell Boykins in Black Angels Over Tuskegee *(photo by Alexandra Martin)*

Black Angels Over Tuskegee

Actors Temple Theatre†; First Preview: January 29, 2010; Opening Night: February 15, 2010; 6 previews, 282 performances as of May 31, 2012 (Saturday and Sunday performances)

Written and directed by Layon Gray; Produced by The Black Gents of Hollywood, Edmund Gaynes, and The Layon Gray Experience; Set, Josh Iacovelli; Costumes, Jason McGee; Lighting, David Boykins & Graham Kindred; Sound, Aidan Cole; Fight Choreography, Diego Villada; General Management, Jessimeg Productions, Julia Beardsley; PSM, Nilton Emillio; Technical Operator, Jonathon Santos; Choreography/Movement, Layon Gray; Set Dressing/Props, Gayle Lowe; Assistant to Writer, Jackie Coleman; Assistant to Director, Maria Canidy; Casting, Karrie Moore; Advertising, Epstein-Obrien; Press, David Gersten & Associates

CAST Man **Thaddeus Daniels**; Quenten Dorsey **Layon Gray**; Abraham Dorsey **Thom Scott II**; Theodore Franks **Ananias Dixon**; Elijah Sams **Delano Barbosa**; Jerimah Jones **Melvin Huffnagle**; Percival Nash **David Roberts**; Major Roberts **Steve Brustein**

UNDERSTUDIES Reginald L. Barnes (Jerimah), Derek Shaun (Jerimah), Lamman Rucker (Elijah), Jeantique Oriol (Elijah), Rob Morgan (Man), Craig Colasanti (Major Roberts), Andrew Mathews, Tobias Truvillion

New York premiere of a new play presented in two acts. World premiere presented at the Whitmore Lindley Theatre Center in North Hollywood October 10–19, 2008 and January 31–March 1, 2009.

SYNOPSIS In *Black Angels Over Tuskegee*, which is based on true events, six men explore their collective struggle with Jim Crow, their intelligence, patriotism, dreams of an inclusive fair society, and brotherhood as they become the first African American fighter pilots in the U.S. Army Air Forces.

†The production originally opened at the Theatre at St. Luke's and transferred to the Actors Temple Theater on June 5, 2011.

Blue Man Group

Astor Place Theatre; Opening Night: November 7, 1991; 11,269 performances as of May 31, 2012

Created and written by Matt Goldman, Phil Stanton, and Chris Wink; Produced by Blue Man Productions; Directors, Marlene Swartz and Blue Man Group; Artistic Directors, Caryl Glaab and Michael Quinn; Artistic/Musical Collaborators, Larry Heinemann and Ian Pai; Set, Kevin Joseph Roach; Costumes, Lydia Tanji and Patricia Murphy; Lighting, Brian Aldous, Matthew McCarthy; Sound, Raymond Schilke, Jon Weston; Computer Graphics, Kurisu-Chan; Video, Caryl Glaab, Dennis Diamond; Resident Music Director, Josh Matthews; PSM, Patti McCabe; Company Manager, Akia Squitieri; Stage Managers, Bernadette Castro, Jenny Lynch; Resident General Manager, Leslie Witthohn; General Manager of North American Productions, Alison Schwartz; Performing Directors, Chris Bowen; Randall Jaynes, Matt Ramsey; Blue Man Captain, Isaac Eddy; Original Executive Producer, Maria Di Dia; Casting, Deb Burton; Press, O+M Company

CAST (rotating) **Gideon Banner, Chris Bowen, Matt DiLoreto, Isaac Eddy, Josh Elrod, Mark Frankel, Randall Jaynes, General Judd, Colin Hurd, Peter Musante, Matt Ramsey, Brian Scott, Pete Simpson**

MUSICIANS (rotating) Dan Dobson, Zach Eichenhorn, Christina Files, Geoff Gersh, Jerry Kops, Jeff Lipstein, Josh Matthews, Mack Price, Anthony Riscica, Tom Shad, Clem Waldmann

An evening of performance art presented without intermission. For original production credits see *Theatre World* Volume 48, Page 90.

SYNOPSIS The three-man new-vaudeville Blue Man Group combines comedy, music, art, and multimedia to produce a unique form of entertainment.

Channeling Kevin Spacey

St. Luke's Theatre; First Preview: April 17, 2011; Opening Night: May 15, 2011; 8 previews, 109 performances as of May 31, 2012 (Saturday and Sunday performances)

Written by Elan Wolf Farbiarz and Cory Terry; Presented by Wolf & William Productions; Director, Elan Wolf Farbiarz; General Manager, Jessimeg Productions, Edmund Gaynes, Julia Beardsley; Stage Manager/Technical Director, Josh Iacovelli; Graphics, Micah Logsdon; Photography, Kent Meister and Warren Chow; Assistant General Manager, Catherine Fowles, Emily Ciotti; House Manager, Scott Layman; Original Press, John Capo

CAST Charlie **Justin R.G. Holcomb**; Multiple Characters **Jamil Chokachi**

Off-Broadway premiere of a new play presented without intermission. World premiere at the 2008 Winnipeg Fringe Festival. U.S. premiere at Broward Center for the Performing Arts (Ft. Lauderdale) in 2010.

SYNOPSIS In *Channeling Kevin Spacey* we meet Charlie, a meek pushover stuck in a dead end job and a loveless relationship. After a particularly soul-squashing day at work, Charlie has an epiphany and resolves to change his life. Fans of Kevin Spacey and Al Pacino are in for a treat as Charlie's adventure channels the characters of both actors, triggering devastating and hilarious confrontations.

The Complete Performer

SoHo Playhouse Huron Club; Opening Night: December 19, 2009; 123 performances as of May 31, 2012 (Saturday performances)

Written by Ted Greenberg, and Mike Motz; Producer, Matt Wayne; Director/Writing Consultant, Steve Rosenfield; Lighting/Stage Manager, Kate August; Production Design, Bestar Mujaj and Matt Wayne; Choreographer, Mike Motz; Website, Stephen Bittrich; Graphics, Jessica Disbrow Talley, Wade Dansby; Technical Director, Bestar Mujaj; Props, Saz Freymann, Ien Denio; Press, Lanie Zipoy

CAST The Complete Performer **Ted Greenberg**; Guest Mascot **Matt Wayne**; Mascot Trainer **Mike Motz**; Audience **Olga Wood**, **Samantha Chapman**

Return engagement of a mostly one-man comedy presented without intermission. Previously presented at the 2008 New York International Fringe Festival and November 8–December 27, 2008 at Soho Playhouse (see *Theatre World* Vol. 65, page 155.)

SYNOPSIS *The Complete Performer* is a mostly one-man comedy show, featuring *The Late Show with David Letterman's* Emmy Award-winning writer Ted Greenberg and his crowd-rousing mascot. The show combines stand-up, mind reading, magic, a half-time show and full-frontal nudity. *The Complete Performer* is a quintessential New York theatre experience.

Danny and Sylvia: The Danny Kaye Musical

St. Luke's Theatre; First Preview: May 6, 2009; Opening Night: May 13, 2009; Closed April 27, 2012; 5 previews, 351 performances (Sunday performances)

Book and lyrics by Robert McElwaine, music by Bob Bain; Presented by Hy Juter and Edmund Gaynes; Director, Pamela Hall; Choreographer, Gene Castle; Sets, Josh Iacovelli; Lighting, Garaham Kindred; Costumes, Elizabeth Flores; Music Director, David Fiorello; General Manager, Jessimeg Productions; Production Stage Manager, Josh Iacovelli; Associate General Manager, Julia Beardsley; Props, Robert Pemberton; Press, Susan L. Schulman

CAST Danny Kaye **Brian Childers**; Sylvia Fine **Kimberly Faye Greenberg**

MUSICIAN David Fiorello (piano)

MUSICAL NUMBERS Another Summer, At Liberty, at the Club Versailles, At the London Palladium, Can't Get That Man Off My Mind, Danny Kaminsky, I Can't Live Without You, If I Knew Then, If I Needed a Guy, I'm a Star, Just one Girl, La Vie Paree, Now Look What You Made Me Do, Requiem for Danny Kaminsky, She's Got a Fine Head on My Shoulders, Sylvia's Song, Tummler, We've Closed On Opening Night, We Make a Wonderful Team, What Shall We Say, You Got A Problem With That, Anatole of Paris, The Maladjusted Jester, Melody in 4F, One Life to Live, Tchaikovsky, Dinah, Minnie the Moocher, Ballin' the Jack, P.S. One Four Nine

SETTING 1936 to 1948 in New York, Hollywood and London. Off-Broadway premiere of a musical presented in two acts.

SYNOPSIS *Danny and Sylvia* takes a look at the famous couple from the time the young undisciplined comic Danny Kaminsky meets aspiring songwriter Sylvia Fine at an audition in the 1930s. Under Sylvia's guidance as mentor, manager, and eventually, wife, Kaye rises from improvisational comic to international film star. The musical explores their inspired collaboration and the romance and conflict that made them such a volatile and successful couple.

The Fantasticks

Snapple Theater Center – Jerry Orbach Theater; First Preview: July 28, 2006; Opening Night: August 23, 2006; 27 previews, 2,305 performances as of May 31, 2012

Book and lyrics by Tom Jones, music by Harvey Schmidt, suggested by the play *Les Romanesques* by Edmond Rostand; Produced by Terzetto LLC, Pat Flicker Addiss, and MARS Theatricals (Amy Danis/Mark Johanness); Director, Tom Jones;

Original Staging, Word Baker; Sets and Costumes, Ed Wittstein; Lighting, Mary Jo Dondlinger; Sound, Dominic Sack; Casting, Terzetto LLC; Musical Director, Robert Felstein; Choreography/Musical Staging, Janet Watson; Production Stage Manager, Shanna Spinello/Paul Blankenship; ASMs, Michael Krug, Brandon Kahn, Paul Blankenship; Associate Director, Kim Moore; Associate Producers, Carter-Parke Productions and Patrick Robustelli; Production Supervisor, Dan Shaheen; Original Press, John Capo–DBS Press; Cast recording: Sh-K-Boom/Ghostlight 84415

CAST The Narrator (El Gallo) **Edward Watts**[1]; The Boy (Matt) **Matt Leisey**[2]; The Girl (Luisa) **Juliette Trafton**; The Boy's Father (Hucklebee) **Dan Sharkey**; The Girl's Father (Bellomy) **Bill Bateman**; The Old Actor (Henry) **MacIntyre Dixon**[3]; The Man Who Dies (Mortimer) **Michael Nostrand**; The Mute **Matt Dengler**[4]; At the Piano **Robert Felstein**; At the Harp **Jacqueline Kerrod**

STANDBYS Tom Flagg (Hucklebee/Henry/Mortimer), Charles West (El Gallo/Hucklebee/Bellomy), Ann Markt[5] (The Mute/Luisa), Matt Dengler[4] (Matt)

*Succeeded by: 1. Bradley Dean (7/25/11), Ed Watts (11/7/11), Jeremiah James (5/8/21) 2. Aaron Carter (11/7/11) 3. Tom Flagg, MacIntyre Dixon 4. Matt Leisey 5. Addi McDaniel, Heidi Giberson

MUSICAL NUMBERS Overture, Try to Remember, Much More, Metaphor, Never Say No, It Depends on What You Pay, Soon It's Gonna Rain, Abduction Ballet, Happy Ending, This Plum is Too Ripe, I Can See It, Plant a Radish, Round and Round, They Were You, Try to Remember (reprise)

Revival of the musical presented in two acts. *The Fantasticks* is the world's longest running musical and the longest running Off-Broadway production ever. The original production opened at the Sullivan Street Playhouse on May 3, 1960–January 13, 2002, playing over 17,000 performances (for original credits, see *Theatre World* Vol. 16, page 167).

SYNOPSIS *The Fantasticks* tells the story of a young boy and girl who fall madly in love at the hands of their meddling fathers, but soon grow restless and stray from one another. The audience uses its imagination to follow El Gallo as he creates a world of moonlight and magic, then pain and disillusionment, until the boy and girl find their way back to one another.

Ed Watts in The Fantasticks (photo by Carol Rosegg)

Jim Stanek and George Morfogen in Freud's Last Session
(photo by Carol Rosegg)

Freud's Last Session

Marjorie S. Deane Little Theatre†; First Preview: July 9, 2010; Opening Night: July 22, 2010; Closed July 22, 2012; 8 previews, 775 performances

Written by Mark St. Germain, suggested by "The Question of God" by Dr. Armand M. Nicholi Jr.; Produced by Carolyn Rossi Copeland, Robert Stillman, and Jack Thomas; Presented by Barrington Stage Company (Julianne Boyd, Artistic Director; Richard M. Parison Jr., Producing Director); Director, Tyler Marchant; Set, Brian Prather; Costumes, Mark Mariani; Lighting, Clifton Taylor; Sound, Beth Lake; Advertising/Marketing, The Pekoe Group; Casting, Pat McCorkle; PSM, Kate J. Cudworth; Production Managers, Wheeler Kincaid, Cedric Hill; General Management, CRC Productions; Company Manager, Robert E. Schneider; Assistant Set, Alexander Woodward; Assistant Lighting, Greg Guarnaccia; Press, Jim Randolph

CAST Sigmund Freud **Martin Rayner**[*1]; C.S. Lewis **Mark H. Dold**[*2]; Standby **Tuck Milligan**

*Succeeded by: 1. George Morfogen (3/16/12), Martin Rayner (5/2/12) 2. Jim Stanek (3/16/12), Mark H. Dold (5/2/12)

SETTING September 3, 1939; Freud's Study at 20 Maresfield Gardens, Hampstead, NW London. New York premiere of a new play presented without intermission. Originally produced at Barrington Stage Company (Sheffield, Massachusettes) June 10-28, 2009 (see *Theatre World* Vol. 66, page 349).

SYNOPSIS *Freud's Last Session* centers on legendary psychoanalyst Dr. Sigmund Freud, who invites the young, rising academic star C.S. Lewis to his home in London. Lewis, expecting to be called on the carpet for satirizing Freud in a recent book, soon realizes Freud has a much more significant agenda. On the day England enters World War II, Freud and Lewis clash on the existence of God, the joy of love, the purpose of sex, and the meaning of life — just a few weeks before Freud's own death.

†The production closed at the Deane Little Theatre on October 2, 2011 and transferred to New World Stages — Stage 5, resuming performances October 7, 2011.

Fuerza Bruta: Look Up

Daryl Roth Theatre; First Preview: October 11, 2007; Opening Night: October 24, 2007; 14 previews, 1,604 performances as of May 31, 2012

Created and directed by Diqui James; Produced by Live Nation Artists Events Group, Fuerzabruta, Ozono, and Stephen Shaw; Executive Producer, Steve Howard; Composer/Musical Director, Gaby Kerpel; Lighting, Edi Pampin; Sound, Hernan Nupieri; Costumes, Andrea Mattio; Automation, Alberto Figueiras; General Coordinator, Fabio D'Aquila; Production, Agustina James; Technical Director, Alejandro Garcia; Marketing, Eric Schnall; Casting, James Calleri; Set-up Technical Supervisor, Bradley Thompson; General Manager, Laura Kirspel; PSM, Jeff Benish; Production Coordinator/ASM, E. Cameron Holsinger; Special Effects, Rick Sordelet; Press, Rogers & Cohen, Lauren Wilsman

CAST Freddy Bosche, Hallie Bulleit, Daniel Case, Alvaro Colom, Dusty Giamanco, Christina Glur, Khadija Griffith, John Hartzell, Michael Hollick, Michele Jongeneel, Joshua Kobak, Angelica Kushi, Gwyneth Larsen, Liam Lane, Tamara Levinson, Rose Mallare, Brooke Miyasaki, Jon Morris, Marlyn Ortiz, Jessica Osborne, Kepani Salgado-Ramos, Dario Vaccaro; Swings Jason Novak, Kira Morris, Andy Pellick, Jeslyn Kelly, Ilia Castro

U.S. premiere of a theatrical experience piece with music presented without intermission. Originally presented in Buenos Aries, and subsequently in Lisbon, London, and Bogata. Since 2005, Fuerza Bruta has played over 2,500 shows in over 20 cities worldwide.

SYNOPSIS The creators of the long running hit *De La Guarda* push the boundaries of theatrical creativity, motivation, and innovation in their new work featuring a non-stop collision of dynamic music, visceral emotion, and kinetic aerial imagery. *Fuerza Bruta: Look Up* breaks free from the confines of spoken language and theatrical convention as both performers and audience are immersed in an environment that floods the senses, evoking pure visceral emotion in a place where individual imagination soars.

Deni Yang in The Gazillion Bubble Show *(photo courtesy of the production)*

Gazillion Bubble Show

New World Stages — Stage 2†; First Preview: January 17, 2007; Opening Night: February 15, 2007; 2,101 performances as of May 31, 2012

Created and staged by Fan Yang; Produced by Castle Talent Inc., Fan Yang, and Neodus Company, Ltd.; Artistic Director, Jamie Jang; Show Director, Steve Lee; Sets, Fan Yang; Lighting, Jin Ho Kim; Sound, Joon Lee; Gazilllion Bubbles FX, Special Effects, Alex Cheung; Theatrical Special Effects, CITC/Gary and Stephanie Crawford; Original Music, Kyu Hyung Lee, Workspace Co., Ltd.; Laser Design, Abhilash George; Lumalaser, Tim Ziegenbein; Lighting Effects, David Lau; Special Effects Inventor, Dragan Maricic; Production Stage Manager, Yeung Jin Son; Stage Manager, Min Song; Technical Director, Alan Kho; General Manager, Daryl Roth Theatricals; Marketing, HHC Marketing; Marketing Director, Chermaine Cho; Press, Springer Associates, Joe Trentacosta, Gary Springer

Performed by **Ana Yang, Fan Yang, Jano Yang, Deni Yang**, or **Melody Yang**

New York premiere of an interactive theatrical event presented without intermission. Fan Yang's wife, Ana, performed the show in 2008 while he toured with the production across the globe. Later, his brother, Jano, joined the production. On September 24, 2010 (with an official opening night of November 5, 2010), the show was subtitled *The Next Generation* as his son, Deni, was featured. In 2011, Fan's daughter, Melody, joined the rotating cast of family performers.

SYNOPSIS The first interactive stage production of its kind, complete with fantastic light effects and lasers, Fan Yang and his family blend art and science to dazzle audiences with his jaw-dropping masterpieces of bubble artistry that defy gravity and logic as we know it.

†The production originally opened on Stage 3 and moved to Stage 2 in September, 2009.

ImaginOcean

New World Stages – Stage 5; First Preview: March 17, 2010; Opening Night: March 31, 2010; Closed September 4, 2011; 11 previews, 440 performances

Book by John Tartaglia, music & lyrics by William Wade; Presented by Philip Katz, Michael Shawn Lewis, and John Tartaglia; Director/Musical Staging, Donna Drake; Set, Robert Andrew Kovach; Puppet Design & Fabrication, The Puppet Kitchen; Music Recording, Yellow Sound Lab/Matthias Winter & Michael Croiter; Recording Engineer, Matthias Winter; Advertising, Hofstetter+Partners/Agency 212; Marketing, HHC Marketing; Casting, Melanie Lockyer; Development Consultant, Georgianna Young; PSM, Emilie Bray Schoenfeld; General Manager, The Splinter Group (Seth A. Goldstein, Heather Schings, William Goldstein); Production Assistant, Beth Rolfs); Creative and Website, Michael Naylor; Assistant to the Director/Producers, Daniel Seth; Study Guide/Educational Outreach, Thru the Stage Door; Press, Betsy Braun

CAST *Puppeteers:* Tank **James W. Wojtal Jr.**; Bubbles **Stacey Weingarten**; Dorsel **Ryan Dillon**; Ripple/Leonard **Lara Maclean**; Baby Jellyfish/Arrows/Others **Carole D'Agostino**; Spirit of Friendship/Jellyfish/Arrow/Others **Nate Begle**; Spirit of Friendship/Jellyfish/Arrows/Others **Jonathan Carlucci**; Puppet Wrangler/Swing **Brian T. Carson**; *Voice:* Tank/Dorsel/Leonard **John Tartaglia**; Bubbles/Arrow **Donna Drake**; Ripple/Baby Jellyfish **Michael Shawn Lewis**; Spirit of Friendship **Meladi Montano** (speaking), **Cathlene Grant** (singing)

MUSICIANS (recorded) Randy Andos (Trombone), Michael Croiter (Drums), Joe Fiedler (Trombone), Brian Koonin (Guitar), MaryAnn McSweeney (Acoustic/Electric Bass), Kristy Norter (Reeds/Winds), Clay Ruede (Cello), Denise Stillwell (Violin/Viola), William Wade (Piano/Orchestrations); Back-up Vocals: Camilo Castro, Heather Curran, Gavin Esham, Nick Gaswirth, Samantha Grenell-Zaidman, Amy Jones, Tyrick Jones, Ruperta Nelson, Krista Severeid, Michael Yeshion; Children's Chorus: Willow Bennison, Allegra Berman, Nadia Filanovsky, Cathlene Grant, Savannah Henry, Ashley Laird, Meldi Montano, Delainah Perkins, Miranda Powell, Lila Smith-Marooney; "Which Way to Turn" Soloist: Nick Gaswirth

MUSICAL NUMBERS On Our Way; Jellyfish Jive; On Our Way (reprise); Which Way to Turn; Imagination; Just a Stone's Throw Away; The Treasure; Finale

SETTING The Ocean Floor. New York premiere of a puppet theatre musical presented without intermission. A previous version debuted November 20, 2009 on Royal Caribbean International's revolutionary cruise ship, *Oasis of the Seas*.

SYNOPSIS A one-of-a-kind live black-light puppet show, John Tartaglia's *ImaginOcean* is a magical undersea adventure for kids of all ages. Tank, Bubbles and Dorsel are three best friends who just happen to be fish, and they're about to set out on a remarkable journey of discovery. And it all starts with a treasure map. As they swim off in search of clues, they'll sing, dance, and make new friends, including everyone in the audience. Ultimately they discover the greatest treasure of all: friendship.

A scene from ImaginOcean *(photo by Aaron Epstein)*

Love, Loss, and What I Wore

Westside Theatre – Downstairs; First Preview: September 21, 2009; Opening Night: October 1, 2009; Closed March 25, 2012; 11 previews, 1,013 performances

Written by Nora Ephron and Delia Ephron; Based on the book by Ilene Beckerman; Produced by Daryl Roth; Director, Karen Carpenter; Sets, Jo Winiarski; Costumes, Jessica Jahn; Lighting, Jeff Croiter; Sound, Walter Trarbach; Casting, Tara Rubin; Makeup, Maria Verel; Stage Management, Zoya Kachadurian, Nancy Elizabeth Vest, Bess Marie Glorioso; Production Manager, Shannon Case; General Manager, Adam Hess; Associate Producer, Alexander Fraser; Associate General Manager, Jodi Schoenbrun Carter; Advertising, Eliran Murphy Group; Marketing, Leanne Schanzer Promotions; Assistant Design: Carla Cruz (set), Sarah James (costumes), Grant Yeager (lighting); Propmaster, Buist Bickley; Wardrobe Supervisor, Ren LaDassor; Production Carpenter, Colin McNamara; Press, O+M Company, Rick Miramontez, Molly Barnett

CAST *June 1–July 3:* **Emme, Susan Sullivan, Julie Halston, Ashley Austin Morris, Emily Bergl, Didi Conn** (filled in for Ms. Halston June 8–11); *July 6–August 7:* **Anita Gillette, Aisha de Haas, Alison Fraser, Marla Maples, Zuzanna Szadkowski**; *August 10–September 4:* **Marylouise Burke, Ann Harada, Yeardley Smith, Emmanuelle Chriqui, Roslyn Ruff**; *September 7–October 2:* **Zuzanna Szadkowski, Joyce Van Patten, Ashley Austin Morris, Janel Maloney, Adriane Lenox**; *October 5–30:* **Zuzanna Szadkowski, La La Anthony, Samantha Mathis, Dee Hoty, Concetta Tomei**; *November 2–December 4:* **Zuzanna Szadkowski, Maddie Corman, Eve Plumb, Amanda Setton, Jenny Allen**; *December 7–30:* **Daisy Eagan, Myra Lucretia Taylor, Sonia Manzano, Loretta Swit, Emily Dorsch**; *January 4–29:* **Lillias White, Nancy Dusault, Veanne Cox, Katie Lee, Fern Mallis**; *February 1–26:* **Dawn Wells, Robin Strasser, Quincy Tyler Bernstine, Alexandra Silber, Zuzanna Szadkowski**; *February 29–March 25:* **Sierra Boggess, Ally Walker, Erica Watson, Joyce Van Patten, Karyn Quackenbush**

Off-Broadway commercial transfer of a collection of monologues and scenes presented without intermission. Previously presented in 2008 at the DR2 Theatre. The production rasied $175,000 (in-kind and cash donations) to benefit Dress for Success, a charity that provides work clothing and job support for low-income women. 120 actresses in 30 casts performed in the show through the run, wearing 126 black dresses, 52 tubes of lipstick, 125 pairs of shoes, and over 200 pairs of Spanx. Since opening Off-Broadway, the show has been produced on six continents, and the five cast members from December embarked on a five-city national tour January 3–March 4, 2012.

SYNOPSIS Based on the best-selling book by Ilene Beckerman as well as on the recollections of the Ephrons' friends, this collection of stories (performed by a five-member all-star rotating cast who perform the piece in four-week cycles) dares to ask "Can't we all just stop pretending anything is ever going to be the new black?" *Love, Loss, and What I Wore* opens the closet on this and other sartorial queries by using clothing and accessories as a metaphor for matters far deeper than the average walk-in closet.

Lillias White, Veanne Cox, Eve Plumb, Katie Lee, and Nancy Dussault in Love, Loss, and What I Wore *(photo by Carol Rosegg)*

Miss Abigail's Guide to Dating, Mating and Marriage!

Downstairs Cabaret Theatre at Sofia's; First Preview: October 7, 2010; Opening Night: October 24, 2010; Closed June 30, 2012; 22 previews, 396 performances

Written by Ken Davenport and Sarah Saltzberg; Inspired by the book by Abigail Grotke; Presented by Ken Davenport; Director, Ken Davenport; Set, Hilary Noxon; Lighting, Graham Kindred; Costumes, Abbi Stern; Production Manager, Jeramiah Peay; Associate Producers, Lily M. Fan, Todd Miller; General Management, Davenport Theatrical Enterprises/Matt Kovich; Casting, Daryl Eisenberg; Production Stage Manager, Carlos Maisonet; Theme Song, Matt Kovich (music and lyrics), Doug Katsaros (orchestrations); Company Manager, Melissa Heller; Production Supervisor/Technical Director, Katie Takacs; Marketing & Advertising, Davenport Media Enterprises; Assistant Company Manager, Lindsey Freeman; Press, The Morris + King Company

CAST Miss Abigail **Eve Plumb**[1]; Paco **Manuel Herrera**[2]

*Succeeded by: 1. Joyce DeWitt (6/1/11), Laurie Birmingham (10/15/11), Christine Pedi (10/29/11) 2. Mauricio Perez (2/2/12), Eddie Gutierrez (5/1/12), Isaac Cruz (6/19/12)

New York premiere of a new play presented without intermission. World premiere developmental production at the David A Strasz Jr. Performing Arts Center (Tampa, Florida) June 9–July 3, 2010, featuring Laurie Birmingham and Mauricio Perez.

SYNOPSIS *Miss Abigail's Guide to Dating, Mating, & Marriage* is the story of Miss Abigail, the most sought-after relationship expert to the stars (think Dr. Ruth meets Emily Post), and her sexy sidekick Paco, as they travel the world teaching Miss Abigail's outrageously funny "how-to's" on dating, mating, and marriage! Let Miss Abigail take you back to a simpler time, before booty calls and before speed-dating . . . back when the divorce rate wasn't 50% and when 'fidelity' was more than an investment firm!

Eddie Gutierrez and Christine Pedi in Miss Abigail's Guide to Dating, Mating and Marriage! *(photo by Jeremy Daniel)*

My Big Gay Italian Wedding

St. Luke's Thetare; First Preview: May 5, 2010; Opening Night: May 22, 2010; Closed August 20, 2011; 11 previews, 215 performances (Thursday, Friday, Saturday performances)

Written by Anthony J. Wilkinson; Produced by Dina Manzo & Sonia Blangiardo in association with Anndee Productions, Eileen Caruso, Donna DiCrescento, Frank Levinson, Dina Manzo, Dolores Naso; Director, Teresa A. Cicala; Choreography, J. Austin Eyer; Original Music, David Boyd; Sets, Rob Santeramo; Costumes, Philip Heckman; Lighting, Graham Kindred; General Manager, Davenport Theatrical Enterprises, Matt Kovich; Production Manager, Jeramiah Peay; Casting, Daryl Eisenberg; Production Stage Manager, C.J. Thom III; Assistant Stage Manager, Kelly Ice; Wardrobe Supervisor, Megan Opalinski; Marketing, HHC Marketing; Press, Keith Sherman & Associates, Brett Oberman

CAST Anthony Pinnunziato **Anthony J. Wilkinson**; Andrew Polinski **Marty Thomas**[1]; Lucia **Liz Gerecitano**; Angela Pinnunziato **Randi Kaplan**; Rodney Erik Ransom[2]; Father Rosalia **Chad Kessler**; Aunt Toniann **Kim Sozzi**[3]; Gregorio **Adam Shorsten**; Connie **Meagan Robar**; Joseph Pinnunziato **Joe Scanio**; Mario **Stephen Mark Lukas**[4]; Frankie **Billy Yoder**[5]; Maria **Marissa Rosen**; Maurizio Legrande **Brett Douglas**; Ensemble/Male Understudy **Joey Murray**; Ensemble/Female Understudy **Leah Gerstel**

*Succeeded by: 1. Chase Coleman 2. Gay Pride Month Guest Stars: Farrah Moans (June 2-4), Hedda Lettuce (June 9-11), Mimi Imfurst (June 16-18), Stacy Lane Matthews (June 23-25) 3. Guest Star: Judy Torres (July 15-16) 4. Tommaso Antico 5. Mike Russo

Revised version of a play with music presented in two acts. The original production premiered Off-Broadway at the Actors Playhouse November 14, 2003, transferred to Theatre Four (Julia Miles Theatre) where it closed August 21, 2004, playing 76 performances on a weekend schedule (see *Theatre World* Vol. 60, page 107). The revised and updated version was first presented as a benefit September 12, 2009 at the St. George Theatre in Staten Island.

SYNOPSIS *My Big Gay Italian Wedding* focuses on two gay men as they plan their wedding and the people around them, including an overbearing Italian mother, a jealous ex-boyfriend, the wedding planner from Hell, and an assortment of family and friends.

The Company of My Big Gay Italian Wedding *(photo courtesy of the production)*

Naked Boys Singing!

New World Stages – Stage 2; First Preview: July 2, 1999; Opening Night: July 22, 1999; Closed January 28, 2012; 3,069 performances (Thursday and Saturday performances)

Written by Stephen Bates, Marie Cain, Perry Hart, Shelly Markham, Jim Morgan, David Pevsner, Rayme Sciaroni, Mark Savage, Ben Schaechter, Robert Schrock, Trance Thompson, Bruce Vilanch, Mark Winkler; Conceived and directed by Robert Schrock; Produced by Jamie Cesa, Carl D. White, Hugh Hayes, Tom Smedes, Jennifer Dumas; Choreography, Jeffry Denman; Music Director, Jeffrey Biering; Original Musical Director and Arrangements, Stephen Bates; Set/Costumes, Carl D. White; Lighting, Aaron Copp; Production Stage Manager, Scott DelaCruz/Tara Nachtigall; Assistant Stage Manager, Dave August; Dance Captain, Craig Lowry; Original Press, Peter Cromarty; Press, David Gersten; L.A. Cast recording: Café Pacific Records

CAST Naked Maid **Gregory Stockbridge**; Radio **Aubrey Grant**; Robert Mitchum **Nimmy Weisbrod**; Entertainer **Anthony Romeo**; Bris **Zachary Clause**[1]; Porn Star **Tony Neidenbach**; Muscle Addiction **Michael Munoz**; Window **Dave August**; Swings **Garret D. Smith**[2], **Craig Lowry**; Piano: **Jeffrey Biering**

*Succeeded by: 1. Chris Layton (August 2011) 2. Kenny Lear (August 2011)

MUSICAL NUMBERS Gratuitous Nudity, Naked Maid, The Bliss of a Bris, Window to Window, Fight the Urge, Robert Mitchum, Jack's Song, Members Only, Perky Little Porn Star, Kris Look What You've Missed, Muscle Addiction, Nothin' But the Radio On, The Entertainer, Window to the Soul, Finale/Naked Boys Singing!

The Company of Naked Boys Singing

A musical revue presented without intermission. For original production credits see *Theatre World* Vol. 56, page 114. Originally opened at The Actors Playhouse; transferred to Theatre Four (Julia Miles Theatre) March 17, 2004; transferred to the John Houseman Theater September 17, 2004; transferred to the 47th Street Theatre November 12, 2004; transferred back to the Julia Miles Theatre May 6, 2005; transferred to New World Stages October 14, 2005. At the conclusion of its run, the show had played eight different theaters (including three at New World Stages), employed 235 company members (including 71 actors–two of which were porn stars), and hosted 2,032 bachelorette parties. 562 performances were stopped because audience members were taking pictures. A newly conceived version of the show utilizing six actors and produced by Tom and Michael D'Angora (based on their successful Provincetown production) opened at the Kirk Theatre on Theatre Row on April 5, 2012, a mere two months after the original production closed (see listing earlier in this section).

SYNOPSIS The title says it all! Caution and costumes are thrown to the wind in this musical revue featuring an original score and a handful of hunks displaying their special charms as they celebrate the splendors of male nudity in comedy, song, and dance.

NEWSical the Musical

Full Spin Ahead!/End of the World Edition

Kirk Theatre; First Preview: December 13, 2010; Opening Night: January 9, 2011; 31 previews, 655 performances as of May 31, 2012

Created and written by Rick Crom; Produced by Elyse Pasquale and Tom D'Angora in association with Annette Niemtzow and Adam Weinstock, Director, Mark Waldrop; Music Director/Arrangements/Accompanist, Ed Goldsheider; Set/Projections, Jason Courson; Costumes, Davdi Kaley; Lighting, Josh Starr; Wigs, J. Jared Janas and Rob Greene; Production Stage Manager/General Manager, Scott F. Delacruz; Production Assistant/Board Operator, Ryan Obermeier; Wardrobe, Christine Massoud; Marketing, Meri Krassner/S.R.O. Marketing; Graphics/Web Design, Michael Duling; Original Press, John Capo; Press, Project Publicity/Len Evans; Cast recording: CD Baby

CAST **Christina Bianco, Christine Pedi**[1], **John Walton West**[2], **Michael West**; Understudies **Amy Griffin, Tommy Walker**[3]

Succeeded by: 1. Leslie Kritzer (3/25/11), Christine Pedi (4/24/11) 2. Tommy Walker (4/6/12) 3. Ryan Knowles (4/6/12)

Christine Pedi, John Walton West, Michael West, and Christina Bianco in Newsical the Musical *(photo by Stephen Sorokoff)*

A new edition of a musical revue presented in two acts. Originally presented at the John Houseman Studio January 9, 2004 for an eight-week limited engagment. The show re-opened as an Off-Broadway production at Upstairs at Studio 54 September 17, 2004, closing April 17, 2005 after 215 performances (see *Theatre World* Vol. 61, page 125). A revised edition of the show returned to the 47th Street Theatre December 9, 2009–March 21, 2010 playing 121 performances (see *Theatre World* Vol. 66, page 155). The newest version, entitled *The End of the World Edition*, officially opened February 1, 2012.

SYNOPSIS The Drama Desk nominated *NEWSical the Musical* is back again lampooning current events, headlines, newsmakers, celebrities, and politicians. With songs and material being updated on a regular basis, composer-lyricist Rick Crom's topical musical comedy is an ever-evolving mockery of all the news that is fit to spoof!

Richard Shoberg and Catherine Russell in Perfect Crime
(photo courtesy of John Capo)

Perfect Crime

Snapple Theater Center – Anne L. Bernstein Theater†; Opening Night: April 18, 1987; 10,282 performances as of May 31, 2012

By Warren Manzi; Presented by The Actors Collective in association with the Methuen Company; Director, Jeffrey Hyatt; Set, Jay Stone, Warren Manzi; Costumes, Nancy Bush; Lighting, Jeff Fontaine; Sound, David Lawson; Production Stage Manager, Kim Moore; Press, John Capo–DBS Press

CAST Margaret Thorne Brent **Catherine Russell**; Inspector James Ascher **Richard Shoberg**; W. Harrison Brent **John Hillner**; Lionel McAuley **George McDaniel**; David Breuer **Patrick Robustelli**; Understudies **Andrea Leigh, Don Noble**

SETTING Windsor Locks, Connecticut. A mystery presented in two acts. For original production credits see *Theatre World* Vol. 43, page 96. The production hit the milestone 10,000th performance on September 25, 2011 and celebrated its 25th anniversary on April 18, 2012. Catherine Russell has only missed four performances since the show opened in 1987, and on April 18, 2009, she was inducted into the Guinness Book of Records for "Most Performances by a Theater Actor in the Same Role" for not missing a day of work in twenty-two years. *Perfect Crime* is the longest running play in the history of New York theatre.

SYNOPSIS Margaret Brent is an accomplished Connecticut psychiatrist and potential cold-blooded killer. When her wealthy husband turns up dead, she gets caught in the middle of a terrifying game of cat and mouse with a deranged patient and the handsome but duplicitous investigator assigned to the case. As the clock ticks to the final chilling revelation, a mounting set of secrets and indiscretions leads to a shocking turns of events. Did Margaret Brent commit the perfect crime?

†The show originally opened at the Courtyard Playhouse (39 Grove Street); transferred to: Second Stage Uptown (now the McGinn-Cazale Theatre) August–October 1987; 47th Street Theatre: October–December 1987; Intar 53 Theater on 42nd Street (now demolished): January–April 1988; Harold Clurman Theatre (now demolished): May 1988–August 1990; 47th Street Theatre: August–December 1990; Theatre Four (now the Julia Miles Theatre): January 1991–September 1993; 47th Street Theatre: September 1993–January 1994; The Duffy Theatre at Broadway and 46th (now demolished): February 1994–May 2006; Snapple Theater Center: May 22, 2006–present.

Pinkalicious, The Musical

Bleecker Street Theatre†; Opening Day: November 1, 2008; 373 performances as of May 31, 2012 (Saturday and Sunday performances)

Book and lyrics by Elizabeth Kann & Victoria Kann, music & lyrics by John Gregor; Produced by Vital Theatre Company (Stephen Sunderlin, Artistic Director; Linda Ames Key, Education Director; Mary Kate Burke, Associate Producer); Director, Teresa K. Pond; Original Director, Suzu McConnell-Wood; Choreography, Dax Valdes; Music Director, Jad Bernardo; Set, Mary Hamrick; Costumes, Colleen Kesterson & Randi Fowler; Props, Dan Jagendorf & Kerry McGuire; PSM, Kara M. Teolis; Stage Managers, Nataliya Vasilyeva and Katie Gorman; Casting, Bob Cline; Company Manager, Cadien Dumas; Press, Stephen Sunderlin

CAST Peter Pinkerton **Jonny Beauchamp**[*1] or **Travis Nunes**[*2]; Pinkalicious **Megan MacPhee**[*3] or **Amber Dickerson**; Dr. Wink/Alison **Rori Nogee** or **Kyla Schoer**[*4]; Mr. Pinkerton **Ryan Albers**[*5] or **John Bauchman** or **Ryan Speakman**[*6]; Mrs. Pinkerton **Joanna Hernandez** or **Melanie Dusel**; Understudy **Holly Buczek**

*Succeeded by: 1. Peej Mele 2. Jake Mendes, Gred Gorenc 3. Christina Rose Rahn, Danielle Gaines, Kara Jones 4. Mychal Phillips 5. Todd Zehrer 6. Matheiu Whitman

A musical for young audiences presented without intermission. World premiere presented at the McGinn/Cazale Theatre January 13–February 25, 2007, and extended at Soho Playhouse March 3–May 25, 2007 (see *Theatre World* Vol. 63, page 291). The show re-opened at New World Stages January 12–May 25, 2008 (see *Theatre World* Vol. 64, page 268) and encored August 2–September 21, 2008.

SYNOPSIS Pinkalicious can't stop eating pink cupcakes despite warnings from her parents. Her pink indulgence lands her at the doctor's office with Pinkititis, an affliction that turns her pink from head to toe - a dream come true for this pink loving enthusiast. But when her hue goes too far, only Pinkalicious can figure out a way to get out of this predicament.

†After the abrupt closing of Bleecker Street Theatre on October 14, 2010, the show played the Cherry Lane Theatre October 16-23, 2010, the Theatre at St. Peter's to November 6–December 5, 2010, the Vineyard Theatre December 11, 2010–March 11, 2011, and finally the Manhattan Movement & Arts Center on April 2, 2011 to the present.

Quantum Eye: Magic and Mentalism

Theatre 80 St. Marks; Opening Night: February 9, 2007; 597 performances as of May 31, 2012 (Saturday performances)

Created by Sam Eaton; Produced and directed by Samuel Rosenthal; Original Music, Scott O'Brien; Art Design, Fearless Design; Assistant Producer, Mimi Rosenthal; Artwork, Glenn Hidlago; Wardrobe, Larry the Tailer

Performed by **Sam Eaton**

Programme: A Gulity Conscience, One Card, Fourth Dimension, Reading Minds, Animal Instinct, Digimancy, Mental Sketch, Transmission, An Unusual Talent, Mnemoncis, Strange News

A mentalist/magic show presented without intermission. The show was workshopped and made open to the public from August 2006, and officially opened at the WorkShop Theatre's Jewel Box Theatre. The show relocated to the Soho Playhouse Huron Club on June 15, 2007, then to the Snapple Theater Center on November 24, 2007. The production moved to the Bleecker Street Theatre Downstairs on February 14, 2009–October 14, 2010 when Bleecker Street abruptly closed. The show then played various venues before making a new home at Theatre 80 on January 15, 2011.

SYNOPSIS *The Quantum Eye* is Sam Eaton's entertaining and fascinating exploration of mentalism, magic, perception and deception, where extraordinary ability and humor blend with the audience to make for a unique performance every time. His masterful use of prediction, manipulation, memorization and calculation will amaze and entertain audiences. It is an extraordinary blend of 21st Century mentalism and Victorian-era mystery. Join Sam on a journey past the limits of possibility in a show that you will never forget.

Sleep No More

McKittrick Hotel; First Preview: March 7, 2011; Opening Night: April 13, 2011; Still playing as of May 31, 2012

Created by Punchdrunk; Produced by Emursive (Randy Weiner, Arthur Karpati, and Jonathan Hochwald) in association and Rebecca Gold Productions and Douglas G. Smith; Directors, Felix Barrett and Maxine Doyle; Design, Felix Barrett, Livi Vaughan, Beatrice Minns; Choreography, Maxine Doyle; Sound, Stephen Dobie; Lighting, Felix Barrett, Euan Maybank, Austin R. Smith; Costumes, David Israel Reynoso, Becka Landau; Assistant Designers, Zoe Franklin, Lucia Rosenwald; Associate Choreographer, Conor Doyle; Senior Event Manager, Carolyn Rae Boyd; Production Consultant, Colin Nightingale; Supervising Producer, Vance Garrett

CAST Macbeth/Porter **Eric Jackson Bradley** or **Nicholas Bruder**; Macduff/Bellhop/Mr. Bargarran **Luke Murphy** or **John Sorensen-Jolink**; Lady Macbeth/Agnes Naismith **Sophie Bortolussi** or **Tori Sparks**; Lady Macduff/Matron **Isadora Wolfe** or **Lucy York** or **Alli Ross**; Banquo/J. Fulton **Gabriel Forestieri** or **Jeffery Lyon**; Bald Witch/Catherine Campbell **Kelly Bartnik** or **Hope T. Davis**; Boy Witch/Speakeasy Barman **Jordan Morley** or **Paul Singh**; Constance DeWinter/Matron/Hecate (swing) **Maya Lubinsky**; Malcolm **Rob Najarian** or **Adam Scher** or **Benjamin Thys**; Duncan **Phil Atkins**; Maximilian Martell **Nicholas Atkinson** or **Alexander Silverman**; Hecate **Careena Melia**; Porter/Orderly/Malcolm/Macduff/Speakeasy Barman **Matthew Oaks**; Sexy Witch/Nurse Shaw **Ching-I Chang**; Sexy Witch/Nurse Shaw/Lady Macbeth **Stephanie Eaton**; Violet **Elizabeth Romanski**

SWINGS Natalie Thomas (Lady Macbeth, Bald Witch, Agnes Naismith), Marla Phelan (Sexy Witch/Matron/Agnes Naismith/Catherine Campbell), Ted Johnson (J. Fulton/Speakeasy Barman/Bellhop/Mr. Bargarran/Orderly/Porter), Conor Doyle (Boy Witch)

New York premiere of an immersive theatre and performance installation. Originally presented in London at the Beaufoy Building in 2003 and in 2009 in collaboration with American Repertory Theatre in Boston at the Old Lincoln School in Brookline. Nearly the entire company performs every performance, but all alternate roles. Listed above are the actors who most often play the specific role, though many have played other roles as well.

SYNOPSIS London's Punchdrunk expands their 2003 film noir-inspired *Sleep No More*, based on *Macbeth*, and creates a unique theatrical experience in three former Chelsea Warehouses which have been converted into the fictional "McKittrick Hotel." *Sleep No More* takes a non-linear approach to its storytelling, allowing theatergoers to freely explore the environment, where scenes, tableaux and scenarios play out, conjuring the world and themes of Shakespeare's bloody tale. The audience, in mask, moves at their own pace, creating a unique journey for each theatre goer, as they navigate up and down stairs, through dimly lit furniture cluttered rooms and corridors, and dim passages.

A scene from Sleep No More *(photo by Olivia Polermo)*

Stomp

Orpheum; First Preview: February 18, 1994; Opening Night: February 27, 1994; 7,681 performances as of May 31, 2012

Created/Directed by Luke Cresswell and Steve McNicholas; Produced by Columbia Artists Management, Harriet Newman Leve, James D. Stern, Morton Wolkowitz, Schuster/Maxwell, Galin/Sandler, and Markley/Manocherian; Lighting, Mr. McNicholas, Neil Tiplady; Casting, Vince Liebhart/Scot Willingham; Executive Producers, Richard Frankel Productions/Marc Routh; Associate Producer, Fred Bracken; General Manager, Richard Frankel Productions/Joe Watson; PSM, Paul Botchis; ASM, Elizabeth Grunewald; Technical Director, Joseph Robinson; Company Manager, Tim Grassel; Assistant Company Manager, Maia Watson; Press, Boneau/Bryan-Brown, Jackie Green, Joe Perrotta

CAST (rotating) **John Angeles, Alan Asuncion, Michelle Dorrance, Marivaldo Dos Santos, Dustin Elsea, Fritzlyn Hector, Brad Holland, Anthony Johnson, Ryan Johnson, Lance Liles, Lisa La Touche, Stephanie Middleton, Keith Middleton, Jason Mills, Joeseph Russomano, Carlos Thomas, Fiona Wilkes, Nicholas V. Young**

A percussive performance art piece presented with an intermission. For original production credits see *Theatre World* Vol. 50, page 113.

SYNOPSIS *Stomp* is a high-energy, percussive symphony, coupled with dance, played entirely on non-traditional instruments, such as garbage can lids, buckets, brooms and sticks.

A scene from Stomp

SPECIAL EVENTS AND ADDITIONAL PRODUCTIONS

The Old Masters

Metropolitan Museum of Art; June 20 & 27, 2011; 2 performances

Written by Simon Gray; Director, Michael Rudman; Originally produced by John Martello and Elliot Martin; Casting, Jack Doulin

CAST Fowles **Rufus Collins**; Mary **Shirley Knight**; Joseph Duveen **Brian Murray**; Nicky Mariano **Heidi Schreck**; Bernard Berenson **Sam Waterston**

SETTING Berenson's villa in Florence, Italy; 1930s. New York premiere of a new play in staged reading presented in two acts. This cast performed the U.S. premiere of the play at the Long Wharf Theatre January 19–February 13, 2011 (see *Theatre World* Vol. 67, page 353).

SYNOPSIS *The Old Masters* deals with the renowned art historian Berenson and art collector Lord Duveen, longtime associates who meet for a final, explosive encounter. Unfolding in the looming shadow of the rise of Italian Fascism, the two giants conduct an epic battle over the intrinsic value of art and money, connoisseurship and profits, as they debate a putative Renaissance masterpiece, *The Adoration of the Shepherds*.

Celebrity Autobiography: Gay Pride Edition

Grammercy Theatre; June 25, 2011

Created and developed by Eugene Pack and Dayle Reyfel; Producer/General Manager, Angelo Fraboni Productions; Producer, Peter Martin; Autobiography Authors: Susan Lucci, Justin Bieber, Cher, Dolly Parton, Ivana Trump, Madonna, Elizabeth Taylor; Presented by Barefoot Wine; Press, Spin Cycle/Ron Lasko

CAST **Mario Cantone**, **Rachel Dratch**, **Daisy Eagan**, **Sharon Gless**, **Kristen Johnston**, **Eugene Pack**, **Dayle Reyfel**, **Mo Rocca**, **Michael Urie**

Staged readings of texts from celebrity autobiographies presented without intermission.

SYNOPSIS *Celebrity Autobiography*, which originated in Los Angeles and was later adapted for a Bravo TV special, features actors reading selections from the autobiographies of the famous and infamous. This special edition coincided with New York's Gay Pride celebration. *Celebrity Autobiography* has played a succesful three-year run at the Triad Theatre, and toured nationally.

Lincoln Center Festival – Theater Events

Nigel Redden, Director

Royal Shakespeare Company in Residency Co-presented by the Park Avenue Armory and Ohio State University; Presented on a full-scale replica of the Elizabethan thrust stage in Stratford-Upon-Avon at the Park Avenue Armory's Wade Thompson Drill Hall; Artistic Director, Michael Boyd; In repertory July 6-August 14, 2011

As You Like It Director, Michael Boyd; Design, Tom Piper; Lighting, Wolfgang Gobbel; Choreography, Struan Leslie; Music, John Woolf; Sound, Andrew Franks; Fight Director, Terry King; **Cast:** Charles Aitken (Oliver), Peter Peverley (Jaques/Dennis), Jonjo O'Neill (Orlando), Larrington Walker (Adam), James Tucker (Duke Frederick), Mariah Gale (Celia), Katy Stephens (Rosalind), Richard Katz (Touchstone), Ansu Kabia (Le Beau), David Carr (Charles), Debbie Korley (Hisperia), Clarence Smith (Duke Ferdinand), Dharmesh Patel (Lord Amiens/ William), James Howard (First Lord), David Rubin (Lord), Forbes Masson (Jaques), Geoffrey Freshwater (Corin), Dyfan Dwyfor (Silvius), Sophie Russell (Audrey), James Traherne (Sir Oliver Martext), Christine Entwisle (Phoebe)

Romeo and Juliet Director, Rupert Goold; Design, Tom Scutt; Lighting, Howard Harrison; Music and Sound, Adam Cork; Projections and Video, Lorna Heavey; Choreography, Georgina Lamb; Fight Director, Terry King; **Cast:** David Carr (Escalus), Jonjo O'Neill (Mercutio), James Howard (Paris), David Rubin (Montague), Simone Saunders (Lady Montague/Lady), Sam Troughton (Romeo), Oliver Ryan (Benvolio), Gruffudd Glyn (Balthasar), Peter Peverley (Abraham/Friar John/Watchman), Richard Katz (Capulet), Christine Entwisle (Lady Capulet), Mariah Gale (Juliet), Joseph Arkley (Tybalt), Noma Dumezweni (Nurse), Dyfan Dwyfor (Peter), Patrick Romer (Cousin Capulet/Apothecary/Constable), James Traherne (Sampson/Watchman), Dharmesh Patel (Gregory), Forbes Masson (Friar Laurence), Debbie Korley (Lady), Kirsty Woodward (Lady)

King Lear Director, David Farr; Design, Jon Bausor; Lighting, Jon Clark; Music, Keith Clouston; Sound, Christopher Shutt; Movement, Ann Yee; Fight Director, Kate Waters; **Cast:** Greg Hicks (King Lear), Kelly Hunter (Goneril), Katy Stephens (Regan), Samantha Young (Cordelia), John Mackay (Duke of Albany), Clarence Smith (Duke of Cornwall), Brian Doherty (King of France), Ansu Kabia (Duke of Burgundy/Herald), Darrell D'Silva (Earl of Kent), Geoffrey Freshwater (Earl of Gloucester), Charles Aitken (Edgar), Tunji Kasim (Edmund), Larrington Walker (Old Man/Knight), Phillip Edgerley (Curan/Doctor/Knight), Sophie Russell (Fool), James Tucker (Oswald), Christopher Saul (Lear's Gentleman), Adam Burton (Messenger/Captain/Knight), Paul Hamilton (Cornwall's Man/Knight), James Howard (Knight), Hannah Young (Nurse)

The Winter's Tale Director, David Farr; Design, Jon Bausor; Lighting, Jon Clark; Music, Keith Clouston; Sound, Martin Slavin; Choreography, Arthur Pita; Director of Puppetry, Steve Tiplady; Aerial Consultant, Lyndall Merry; **Cast:** Joseph Arkley (Archidamus), John Mackay (Camillo), Greg Hicks (Leontes), Darrell D'Silva (Polixenes), Kelly Hunter (Hermione), Alfie Jones and Sebastian Salisbury (Mamillius), Hannah Young (Emilia), Simone Saunders (Lady/Dorcas), Kirsty Woodward (Lady/Mopsa), David Rubin (Antigonus), Adam Burton (Sicilian Lord), Gruffudd Glyn (Sicilian Lord/Young Shepherd), Noma Dumezweni (Paulina), Phillip Edgerley (Cleomenes), Sam Troughton (Dion/Paulina's Steward), Paul Hamilton and Oliver Ryan (Servants), Mr. Arkley (Officer), Tunji Kasim (Officer/Florizel), Patrick Romer (Mariner/Time/Servant), Larrington Walker (Old Shepherd), Brian Doherty (Autolycus), Samantha Young (Perdita)

Julius Caesar Director, Lucy Bailey; Sets and Video, William Dudley; Costumes, Fotini Dimou; Lighting, Oliver Fenwick; Movement, Sarah Dowling; Music Django Bates; Sound, Fergus O'Hare; Associate Design, Nathalie Maury; Fight Director, Philip d'Orleans; Video System Design, Alan Cox; **Cast:** Greg Hicks (Julius Caesar), Noma Dumezweni (Calphurnia), Hannah Young (Portia), Tunji Kasim (Lucius/Romulus), Joseph Arkley (Remus/Octavius Caesar/Artemidorus), Sam Troughton (Marcus Brutus), John Mackay (Cassius), Oliver Ryan (Casca), Brian Doherty (Decius Brutus), Gruffudd Glyn (Cinna), David Rubin (Trebonius), Adam Burton (Metellus Cimber), Paul Hamilton (Caius Ligarius), Christopher Saul (Cicero/Lepidus), Patrick Romer (Publius/Murullus/Cinna the Poet), Phillip Edgerley (Popilius/Flavius/Antony's Servant), Darrell D'Silva (Mark Antony), Larrington Walker (Soothsayer/Octavius's Servant), Samantha Young (Soothsayer's Acolyte), Kirsty Woodward (Caesar's Servant/Priestess), Simone Saunders (Calphurnia's Servant)

The Temple of the Golden Pavilion by Amon Miyamoto and Chihiro Ito; Based on the novel by Yuko Mishima; Adaptation, Serge Lamothe; Director, Amon Miyamoto; Music, Yutaka Fukuoka; Choreography, Shuji Onodera; Sets, Boris Kudlicka; Costumes, Ayako Maeda; Lighting, Yuji Sawada; Sound, Koichi Yamamoto; Projections, Yasunori Kakegawa, Satoshi Kuriyama; **Cast:** Go Morita (Mizoguchi), Sousuke Takaoka (Kashiwagi), Shunsuke Daito (Tsurukawa), Noriko Nakagoshi (Uiko/Beautiful Woman/Flower Arrangement Teacher), Choei Takahashi (Mizoguchi's Father/Master Zenkai), Rei Okamoto (Mizoguchi's Mother), Osamu Kaou (Deacon), Tetsuroh Sagawa (Master Dosen), Fuyuki Yamakawa (Phoenix); Enemble: Ikkou Tamura, Daiichiro Yuyama, Kouhei Wakaba, Matsuri Hashimoto, Naoya Oda, Takahiro Kato, Agatha Okada, Hitomi Miwa; U.S. premiere of a play presented in two acts; Frederick P. Rose Hall; July 21-24, 2011

The Silver Tassie by Sean O'Casey; Presented by Druid Theater Company (Galway, Ireland); Director, Garry Hynes; Set and Costumes, Francis O'Connor; Movement, David Bolger with Vanessa Lefrancois; Lighting, Davy Cunningham; Sound, John Leonard; Composer/Music Director, Elliot Davis; Music Consultant, Philip Chevron; Casting, Maureen Hughes; Production Manager, Eamonn Fox; Company Manager, Sarah Lynch; Stage Managers, Danny Erskine, Noodles H. O'Lurie, Paula Tierney; Technical Manager, Barry O'Brien; **Cast:** Eamon Morrissey (Sylvester Heegan/The Corporal), John Olohan (Simon Norton/The Staff-Wallah), Clare Dunne (Susie Monican), Marion O'Dwyer (Mrs. Foran), Ruth Hegarty (Mrs. Heegan/The Sister of the Ward), Liam Carney (Teddy Foran), Garrett Lombard (Harry Heegan), Charlie Murphy (Jessie Taite), Raymond Scannell (Barney Bagnal), Christopher Doyle, Gerard Kelly, Elliot Harper, Adam Welsh (Soldiers in France), Bush Moukarzel (The Visitor), Mr. Harper (Surgeon Forby Maxwell); Young Chorus: Jordan Bolli-Thompson, Lara Connaughton, John Gaughan, Miriam Ward; U.S. premiere of a revival of a 1928 play with music presented in four acts with one intermission; Gerald W. Lynch Theater at John Jay College; July 24-31, 2011.

Garret Lombard (center) and the Company of Druid's The Silver Tassie, *presented as part of the Lincoln Center Festival (photo by Stephanie Berger)*

Broadway Barks 13

Shubert Alley; July 9, 2011

Script by Richard Hester; Presented by Shubert Alley and Broadway Cares/ Equity Fights AIDS; Produced by Richard Hester, Patty Saccente, and Scott T. Stevens; Executive Producers/Hosts, Mary Tyler Moore and Bernadette Peters; Stage Managers, Michelle Bosch, Brendan Fay, Meg Friedman, Kelly Kinsela, Talia Krispel, Peter Lawrence, Jason Pelusio, Joshua Pilote, Michelle Reupert, Jennifer Rogers, Kimberly Russell, David Sugarman; Shelter Coordinator, Barbara Tolan; Sound Equipment, John Grasso; Sound Design and Engineer, Lucas Rico Corrubia; Sound Assistants, Lucas Rico Corrubia Jr., Rebecca Heroff Corrubia; Poster and Playbill Cover Artwork, Justin 'Squigs' Robertson; Website, David Risley; Program Design and Layout, Tracy Lynn Putman; Booth Theatre Crew, Adam Bruanstein, Susan Goulet; Press, Judy Katz & Associates

GUEST STARS Nick Adams, Nina Arianda, Heidi Blickenstaff, Steel Burkhardt, Kerry Butler, Norbert Leo Butz, Bobby Cannavale, Reeve Carney, Victoria Clark, Jennifer Damiano, Paige Davis, Matt DeAngelis, Sutton Foster, Adam Godley, Joel Grey, John Benjamin Hickey, Jackie Hoffman, Nikki M. James, Isabel Keating, Josh Lamon, Beth Leavel, Joe Mantello, Michael McGrath, Judy McLane, John McMartin, Patina Miller, Michael Mulheren, Bebe Neuwirth, Rory O'Malley, Brad Oscar, Patrick Page, Andrew Rannells, Paris Remillard, Elizabeth Rodriguez, Annabelle Sciorra, Kacie Sheik, Alexandra Silber, Will Swenson, Aaron Tveitt, Yul Vázquez

SYNOPSIS A star-studded dog and cat adopt-a-thon benefiting New York City animal shelters and adoption agencies, this annual event, produced by Broadway Cares/Equity Fights AIDS and sponsored by the ASPCA and PEDIGREE with additional sponsorship by the New York Times, helps many of New York City's shelter animals find permanent homes by informing New Yorkers about the plight of the thousands of homeless dogs and cats in the metropolitan area.

Sutton Foster at Broadway Barks 13 *(photo by Peter James Zielinski)*

Hero: The Musical

David H. Koch Theater; Opening Night: August 23, 2011; Closed September 3, 2011; 14 performances

Book and lyrics by A Reum Han, music by Sang Joon Oh; Presented by ACOM International; Director, Ho Jin Yun; Music Director, Moon Jyung Kim; Choreography, Ran Young Lee; Sets, Dong Woo Park; Costumes, Ji Yeon Kim; Lighting, Yun Young Koo; Sound, Do Kyung Kwon; Makeup and Hair, Hee Sun Yang; Props, Hee Jung Im; Orchestrations, Peter Casey; General Managers, Steven M. Levy, Leonard Soloway; U.S. Press, Richard Kornberg and Associates

CAST Sung Hwa Chung (An Chuggun), Sung Gee Kim (Ito Hirobumi), Sung Eun Lee (Sorhui), Mi Do Jeun (Lingling); Ensemble: Sung Hyuk Moon, Hwee Cho, Jin Woong Lim, Eui UK Jeong, Yong Hee Lim, Gi Young Chang, Young Wan Kim, Hong Seok Suh

SETTING 1909-1910, Russia, Korea, and Japan. U.S. premiere of a new musical presented in Korean with English surtitles in two acts. World premiere in Seoul, Korea in 2009.

SYNOPSIS *Hero: The Musical* tells the epic story of activist An Chunggun who sacrificed his life in the fight to preserve Korean independence and attain peace in Asia. Chunggun was executed in Japan on March 26, 1910 after facing trial for his involvement in the assassination of Japanese leader Ito Hirobumi, who is considered instrumental in the Japanese invasion of Korea. Over a century later, Chunggun's body remains in Japan, but his legacy as a hero lives on in his homeland of Korea.

Sung Hwa Chung (center) and the Company in Hero: The Musical *(photo by Kwan-Hee Ryu)*

Hedwig and the Angry Inch

New World Stages – Stage 2; October 31, 2011

Book by Jon Cameron Mitchell, music and lyrics by Stephen Trask; Presented by Broadway Cares/Equity Fights AIDS (Tom Viola, Executive Director); Producer, Trisha Doss; Director, Aaron Mark; Music Director/Keyboards/Guitar, Matt Hinkley; Sound, Evan Schultz; Production Supervisor, Nathan Hurlin; PSM, Michael McGoff; ASM, David S. Cohen

CAST Hedwig/Tommy Gnosis **David Brian Colbert**; Yitzhak **Petra DeLuca**; *The Angry Inch*: Krzyzhtof (Lead Guitar) **Sean Driscoll**; Schlatko (Drums) **Kevin Garcia**; Schlepkyk (Rhythm Guitar) **Justin Goldner**; Jakek (Bass) **Charlie Rosen**

Revival of a rock musical presented without intermission as a benefit for Broadway Cares/Equity Fights AIDS. Colbert and DeLuca previously performed the show for BC/EFA in 2005, 2006, and 2009. The original production played at the Jane Street Theater February 14, 1998–April 9, 2000 playing 857 performances (see *Theatre World* Vol. 54, page 149).

SYNOPSIS Hedwig, a transsexual punk rock singer from East Berlin, lands in America after a botched sex change operation. The "internationally ignored song stylist barley standing before you," shares her outrageous and unexpectedly hilarious life story with the audience while touring America with her band, the Angry Inch.

Desdemona

Frederick P. Rose Hall at Lincoln Center; November 2-3, 2011; 2 performances

Written by Toni Morrison; Presented as part of the 2011 White Light Festival (Jane Moss, Artistic Director) in association with Wiener Festwochen, Théâtre Nanterre-Amandiers, Cal Performances, spielzeit'europa of the Berliner Festspiele, Barbican, Arts Council London, and London 2012 Festival; Director, Peter Sellars; Music and Vocals, Rokia Traoré; Lighting, James F. Ingalls

CAST Desdemona **Tina Benko**; Barbary **Rokia Traoré**; Ensemble Vocals **Fatim Kouyaté, Kadiatou Sangaré, Bintou Soumbonou**; Musicians **Mamah Diabaté** (Ngoni), **Mamadyba Camara** (Kora)

New York premiere of a theatrical piece with music presented without intermission.

SYNOPSIS Inspired by Shakespeare's *Othello*, this intimate and profound new work is a musical-dramatic collaboration between Nobel laureate Toni Morrison, director Peter Sellars, and Malian singer-songwriter Rokia Traoré. Actress Tina Benko and Traoré, representing Othello's Desdemona and her African nurse Barbary, meditate in poetry and song on violence, womanhood, and the transcendent power of love.

Four Quartets

Clark Studio Theater at Lincoln Center; November 8-12, 2011; 6 performances

Poetry by T.S. Eliot, music by Beethoven; Conceived and created by Stephen Dillane and Katie Mitchell; Presented by the Donmar Warehouse as part of the 2011 White Light Festival (Jane Moss, Artistic Director); Director, Katie Mitchell; Set, Vicki Mortimer; Lighting, Jon Clark; Assistant Director, Dan Ayling

CAST Stephen Dillane (Actor); Musicians (The Miró Quartet): **Daniel Ching** (Violin), **Tereza Stanilav** (Violin), **Joshua Gindele** (Cello), **John Largess** (Viola)

Revival of a solo-poetry performance followed by a chamber music presentation performed with one intermission. Originally presented at the Donmar Warehouse (London), in January 2009, Dillane and the Miró Quartet presented the performance at the Baryshnikov Arts Center December 2-3, 2009 as part of Lincoln Center's Great Performers series.

SYNOPSIS Stephen Dillane reunites with the Miró Quartet in *Four Quartets*, a piece that combines T.S. Eliot's sprawling poetry meditation on time, love, and morality with Beethoven's String Quartet in A minor, Op.132, which inspired Eliot's poem.

Cotton Club Parade

New York City Center; November 18-22, 2011; 6 performances

Conceived by Jack Viertel; Music and lyrics by Duke Ellington; Selected text by Langston Hughes; Additional songs by Jimmy McHugh, Dorothy Fields, and Harold Arlen; Presented by City Center *Encores!* (Arlene Shuler, President and CEO) and Jazz at Lincoln Center (Daryl Waters, Director; Laura Johnson, Executive Producer); Director/Choreography, Warren Carlyle; Music Director, Wynton Marsalis; Scenic Consultant, John Lee Beatty; Costume Consultant, Toni-Leslie James; Lighting, Peter Kaczorowski; Sound, Scott Lehrer; Casting, Laura Stanczyk; Company Manager, Michael Zande; PSM, Peter Lawrence; Associate Musical Director, Daryl Waters; Music Supervisor, Kay Niewood; Press, Helene Davis

CAST Alexandria "Brinae Ali" Bradley, Everett Bradley, Andrew "Dr. Ew" Carter, Carla Cook, Nicolette DePass, Brandon Victor Dixon, DeWitt Fleming Jr., Carmen Ruby Floyd, Jared Grimes, Jeremiah "Showtyme" Haynes, Rosena Hill, Rachael Hollingsworth, Kendrick Jones, Monroe Kent, Tony winner Adriane Lenox and T. Oliver Reid, with Shani "Virgo" Alston, Jason E. Bernard, Tanya Birl, Braxton Brooks, Christopher Broughton, Chanon Judson, Karine Plantadit, Monique Smith, Daniel J. Watts, Joseph Monroe Webb, Christian Dante White, J.L. Williams

MUSICIANS *Jazz at Lincoln Center Orchestra*: Wynton Marsalis (Music Director/Trumpet); Daryl Waters (Associate Music Director/Conductor); Ryan Kisor, Kenny Rampton, Marcus Printup (Trumpets); Vincent Gardner (Trombone/Sousaphone); Chris Crenshaw, Wayne Goodman (Trombones); Sherman Irby, Ted Nash, Walter Blanding, Victor Goines, Joe Temperley (Reeds); James Chirillo (Guitar/Banjo); Dan Nimmer (Piano); Carlos Henriquez (Bass); Ali Jackson (Drums)

World premiere of a new musical revue presented without intermission.

SYNOPSIS *Cotton Club Parade* is a celebration of Duke Ellington's years at the famed Harlem nightclub in the 1920s and '30s, when the joint was jumping with revues featuring big band swing and blues, dancers, singers, comedians and novelty acts. With Ellington's music as the centerpiece, this production re-imagines one of the composer's Cotton Club floor shows.

Joshua Henry and the Company of Cotton Club Parade *(photo by Joan Marcus)*

QUILT – A Musical Celebration and Reflection on 30 Years

Avery Fisher Hall; November 28, 2012

Book by Jim Morgan, Merle Hubbard, and John Schak; Music by Michael Stockler, lyrics by Jim Morgan; Executive Producer/Design, Faisal Al-Juburi; Event Co-chairs, Tony Kushner, Regan Hofmann; Director, David Esbjornson; Benefit Host, Whoopi Goldberg; Music Director, Jesse Vargas; Lighting, Paul Miller

CAST **Michael Urie**, **Nikki M. James**, **Bruce Vilanch**, **Jon Secada**, **James Naughton**, **Elizabeth Hubbard**, **Richard Thomas**, **Constantine Maroulis**, **Dapne Rubin-Vega**, **Bobby Steggert**, **Steven Cupo**, **Anthony Rapp**, **Heather Raffo**, *The Book of Mormon* **cast members**

Revival of a musical presented without intermission. Presented as a benefit for Friends In Deed, God's Love We Deliver, Hispanic Federation, International AIDS Prevention Initiative, The NAMES Project Foundation, and Rosie O'Donnell's "Rosie's Theater Kids." The piece was originally presented in 1992 at the University of Maryland and the Smithsonian Institute to coinside with the display of the NAMES PROJECT AIDS Memorial Quilt in the Washington D.C. National Mall. This benefit marked the first high profile New York production of the piece.

SYNOPSIS *QUILT – A Musical Celebration* is a musical featuring monologues and original songs based on stories for, from, and about the NAMES PROJECT AIDS memorial quilt, which began in 1987. *QUILT* commemorates the victims and survivors of this disease and the ones left behind. This production commemorated the twenty-fifth anniversary of the founding of the Quilt, and the thirtieth anniversary of the HIV/AIDS crisis. Pieces of the quilt representing New York City artists in the fields of theatre, music, and fashion were on display at Lincoln Center while the benefit was presented.

A Chanukah Charol

New World Stages – Stage 2; December 11 & 18, 2011, January 2 & 8 2012; 4 performances

Written by Jackie Hoffman and Michael Schiralli; Inspired by Patrick Stewart's *A Christmas Carol*; Presented by Time Out NY Lounge/New World Stages; Director, Michael Schiralli; Press, David Gersten and Associates

Performed by **Jackie Hoffman**

World premiere of a new solo-performance, pseudo-autobiographical show presented without intermission.

SYNOPSIS In her all new holiday show, this kvetching comedienne is forced to examine her life when she is visited by the Ghosts of Chanukah Past, Present and Future, and even Molly Picon! What she finds on her quest for fame is that she is a dark desperate diva who would give Scrooge a run for his money.

Christmas Eve with Christmas Eve

Midtown Theatre at HA! Comedy Club; December 12, 2011

Conceived and written by Gary Adler, Ann Harada, and Alan Muraoka; Presented by Broadway Cares/Equity Fights AIDS; Director, Alan Muraoka; Choreography, Mark Myars; Music Director, Gary Adler

CAST Christmas Eve **Ann Harada**; Brian **Jordan Gelber**; As Themselves **Al Blackstone**, **Adam Fleming**, **Daniel Jenkins**, **Andrew Keenan-Bolger**, **Marc Kudisch**, **Norm Lewis**, **Jose Llana**, **Raymond J. Lee**, **Telly Leung**, **Austin Miller**, **Patrick Page**, **Howie Michael Smith**

Third edition of a musical revue benefit performance presented without intermission. Presented as a benefit for Broadway Cares/Equity Fights AIDS. Originally presented in 2009, this benefit raised more than $6,600.

SYNOPSIS Christmas Eve, the beloved, opinionated, heavily-accented therapist from *Avenue Q*, makes her holiday fantasies come true in this evening of song and comedy. Christmas Eve and her guests both skewer and pay tribute to great romantic duets and iconic moments of Broadway. No lyricist will be spared as Harada reinterprets the Broadway songbook with the help of talented, hilarious, and gorgeous leading men, including a special appearance from *Avenue Q's* favorite closeted-gay Republican, Rod.

Ann Harada and the Company in Christmas Eve with Christmas Eve *(photo by Peter James Zielinski)*

Rapp Reads Rapp: *Nocturne*

Symphony Space; December 12, 2011

Written by Adam Rapp; Presented by Royal Family Productions (Chris Henry, Artistic Director/Co-Founder; Katie Avebe, Executive Director/Co-Founder); Co-Founders, Mary Bernardi, Andy Theodorou; Press, Springer Associates, Joe Trentacosta

Performed by **Anthony Rapp**

Benefit reading revival of a play presented in two acts. Proceeds from the event supported Royal Family Productions, a non-profit theatre company. World premiere presented at American Repertory Theatre (Cambridge, Massachusetts) October 15, 2000. The New York premiere at the New York Theatre Workshop in collaboaration with A.R.T. May 4, 2001 (see *Theatre World* Vol. 57, page 96).

SYNOPSIS Adam Rapp's highly acclaimed play *Nocturne* centers on a former piano prodigy who recounts the tragic events that tore his family apart. With a keen eye for human relationships and a deft ear for language, Rapp explores the aftershock of this unimaginable event. *Nocturne* is a devastating, elegant, and gripping dissection of the American dream. In this benefit performance, his brother Anthony Rapp performs a reading of the play as a solo-performance piece.

Twilight: The Musical

New World Stages – Stage 2; January 16, 2012

Created by Ashley Griffin, music and lyrics by Jeremy Ezell, Ashley Griffin, Sean Mahoney, David Mallumud, and Michael Sutherland; Presented by Liz Ulmer Theatricals and Dreamcatcher Entertainment; Director, Gabriel Barre; Choreography, Matthew Neff; Music Director, David John Madore; Costumes, Erica Giles; Lighting, Reuben Rosenthal; PSM, Kelly Ruth Cole; Sound/Technical Director, Kevin Feustel; Casting, Michael Cassara; Makeup, Matthew Allen; Assistant Music Director/Keyboards, Martin Landry; Assistant Director, Misti B. Wills

CAST Edward **Colin Hanlon**; Bella Swan **Meghann Fahy**; Jacob **Jared Zirilli**; Mike/Sam/Carlyle/Werewolf/Charlie/Bill Compton/Bio Teacher **Jeffry Denman**; Angela/Rosalie/Hermione/Leah/Esme **Jenna Leigh Green**; Alice/Jessica/Renesmee/Jane **Lauren Lopez**; Eric/Emmett/Harry Potter/Seth/Dracula **Jason Michael Snow**; Tyler/Ben/Jasper/Ron/Lestat **Olli Haaskivi**; Dancers **Eddie Gutierrez, Lindsay Dunn, Michael McArthur, Kaitlin Mesh, Clifton Samuels**

Benefit concert reading of a new musical presented in two acts. Proceeds supported Blessings in a Backpack, a program designed to feed elementary school children in need of food on weekends.

SYNOPSIS A parody of the *Twilight* books and films, this musical examines our culture of obsession through the story of teenage outsider Bella Swan who risks everything when she embarks on a star-crossed romance with Vampire Edward Cullen.

Love Letters

Westside Theatre; February 13, 2012

Written by A.R. Gurney; Presented by The Actors Fund (Joseph Benincasa, President and CEO); Producer, Tim Pinckney; Director, Tom Cianfichi

CAST Andrew Makepeace Ladd III **Bryan Batt**; Melissa Gardner **Patricia Clarkson**

Benefit performance of a revival of a play presented without intermission. Proceeds supported The Actors Fund. Batt and Clarkson, both New Orleans natives and dear friends, previously performed the play to benefit a struggling historic theatre in their hometown.

SYNOPSIS A unique and imaginative theatre piece, *Love Letters* is made up of letters exchanged over a lifetime between two people who grew up together, went their separate ways, but continued to share confidences through correspondence. Beginning with birthday party thank-you notes and summer camp postcards, *Love Letters* follows Andy and Melissa through college, marriage and careers as they share a life and love in writings.

Bryan Batt and Patricia Clarkson in Love Letters *(photo by James Liles)*

The Best of Jim Caruso's Cast Party

Town Hall; February 23, 2012

Created and hosted by Jim Caruso; Presented by Scott Siegel as a benefit for The Actors Fund; Director, Rick Hinkson; Musical Director, Billy Stritch; Stage Manager, Jennifer Marie Russo; Press, Springer Associates, Joe Trentacosta

CAST Linda Lavin, Marilyn Maye, Jane Monheit, Stephanie J. Block, Janis Siegel, David Ippolito, Julia Murney, Lisa Lampanielli, Paulo Szot, Liz Mikel, Marcus Monroe, Rudi Macaggi, John Bucchino, Erich Bergen, Frank Wildhorn, Laura Osnes, Aaron Weinstein, Holly Near, Paul Loesel, Terri Klausner, Andrew Nemr and Cats Paying Dues Company

MUSICIANS Billy Stritch (Piano), Daniel Glass (Drums), Tom Hubbard (Bass)

A musical revue and variety show presented in two acts. Part of the proceeds from the show supported The Actors Fund.

SYNOPSIS Entertainer and host Jim Caruso brings his weekly star-studded open-mic night at Birdland to Town Hall for the second year as one-night only special benefit production. Caruso brings some of his famous friends as well as his devoted and talented regulars to the stage, performing a "Neo-Ed Sullivan Show" with singing, dancing, comedy, musicians, clowns, and variety acts. *Jim Caruso's Cast Party*, now in ninth year every Monday night at Birdland, has become an institution where newbies and famous veterans take the spotlight.

Stephanie J. Block and Julia Murney in
The Best of Jim Caruso's Cast Party *(photo courtesy of Jim Caruso)*

Broadway Bears XV

B.B. King Blues Club & Grill; March 18, 2012

Presented by Scott T. Stevens for Broadway Cares/Equity Fights AIDS; Production Manager, Michael Palm; Music Director, Michael Lavine; Opening Number Lyrics, Douglas Braverman; Stage Manager, Bess Marie Glorioso; Program/Poster, Carol A. Ingram; Press, Boneau/Bryan-Brown

TALENT Host **Bryan Batt**; Auctioneer **Lorna Kelly**; Opening Number **Christine Pedi** and **Kurt Peterson**, and **Michael Lavine**; Presenters and Special Guest Stars **Seth Numrich, Tony Sheldon, Nick Adams, Harvey Evans, Kurt Peterson, Jeremy Jordan, Patrick Page, Danny Burstein, Norm Lewis, Faith Dane, Hunter Ryan Herdlicka, Zach James, Donnie Kehr, Ilene Kristen, Rebecca Luker, Andrea McArdle, Michele McConnell, Judy McLane, Laura Osnes, Justin Matthew Sargent, Jennifer Smith**

HIGHEST BIDS Joey from *War Horse* ($20,000), designed by Barak Stribling and Jamie Filippelli, signed by Seth Numrich; **Simba** from *The Lion King* ($18,000), designed by Katie Falk, Ilya Vett, and Islah Abdul-Rahim, signed by Julie Taymor; **J. Pierrepont Finch** from *How to Succeed in Business Without Really Trying* ($11,000), designed by Amy Micallef, signed by Daniel Radcliffe, Darren Criss, and Nick Jonas; **Felicia, Bernadette, and Mitzi** from *Priscilla Queen of the Desert* ($4,500/$3,400/$3,000), a trio of bears designed by Amy Micallef, signed by Nick Adams, Tony Sheldon, and Will Swenson; **Dragonfly Showgirl** from *Follies* ($8,000), designed by Polly Isham Kinney and Judith E. Marsh, signed by Bernadette Peters, Danny Burstein, Jan Maxwell, and Gregg Barnes; **The Divine Miss M** from *Bette Midler's Clams on the Half Shell Revue* ($7,000), designed by Kevin Phillips, signed by Bette Midler; **Shimbleshanks** from *Cats* ($5,500), designed by Therese Stadelmeier-Tresco, signed by Betty Buckley; **Cogsworth** from *Beauty and the Beast* ($5,250), designed by Zoë Morsette, signed by Ann Hould-Ward and Alan Menken; **Hugh Jackman as Peter Allen** from *Hugh Jackman Back on Broadway* ($5,000), designed by Matthew Hemesath, signed by Hugh Jackman; **Elphaba** from *Wicked* ($4,750), designed by John Henson, signed by Susan Hilferty, Gregory Maguire, and Stephen Schwartz; **Elder Price and Elder Cunningham** from *The Book of Mormon* ($3,000), two bears designed by Robin McGee, signed by Josh Gad, Andrew Rannells, Trey Parker, and Matt Stone; **Franki Valli** from *Jersey Boys* ($3,000), designed by Rosi Zingales, signed by Frankie Valli; **Newsie** from *Newsies* ($3,000), designed by Cailin Anderson, signed by Jeremy Jordan and Alan Menken

SYNOPSIS Broadway Cares presents the fifteenth and grand finale edition of a grand auction of Broadway inspired teddy bears featuring special entertainment. A total of 52 teddy bears, donated by the North American Bear Company and transformed into uniquely costumed, handmade, one-of-a-kind, collectibles, raised a record-setting $198,300 through online, telephone, and live bids. Proceeds went to Broadway Cares/Equity Fights AIDS. The cumulative fundraising total for the fifteen editions of *The Broadway Bears* auctions reached a remarkable $2,048,427 from 643 bears.

Little Shop of Horrors

Lucille Lortel Theatre; March 19, 2012

Music by Alan Menken, book and lyrics by Howard Ashman; Based on the film by Roger Corman; Presented by Friends in Theater Company and Story Pirates; Producer, Philip Accorso; Director, David Lefkowich; Music Director, Jonathan Rose; Choreography, Curtis Holbrook; Costumes, Jennifer Caprio; Sound, Derek Baird; Production Manager, Meryl Ballew

CAST Seymour **Tom Deckman**; Audrey **Kenita Miller**; Audrey II **Carmen Ruby Floyd**; Orin **Brian Sears**; Mushnik **Skipp Sudduth**; Crystal **Eleasha Gamble**; Ronette **Dan'yelle Williamson**; Chiffon **LaQuet Sharnell**;

Ensemble **Phillip Claflin, Sean Clark, Sheena DiMatteo, Michael Hull, Kristen Marie, Jenna Miller, Darcy Wright, Michael Yeshion**

Benefit performance of a revival of a musical presented in two acts. Proceeds benefitted the Make-A-Wish Foundation of Metro and Western New York, a non-profit organization that has given hope, strength, and joy to children with life-threatening medical conditions since 1980. The original production played Off-Broadway at the Orpheum Theatre July 27, 1982–November 1, 1987 playing 2,209 performances (see *Theatre World* Vol. 39, page 76).

SYNOPSIS In this musical based on the 1960s cult horror film, nerdy Seymour, a down-and-out skid row floral assistant, becomes an overnight sensation when he discovers an exotic plant with a mysterious craving for fresh blood. Soon "Audrey II" grows into an ill-tempered, foul-mouthed, R&B-singing carnivore who offers him fame and fortune in exchange for feeding its growing appetite, finally revealing itself to be an alien creature poised for global domination!

The Broadway Beauty Pageant

Symphony Space; March 19, 2012

Conceived by Jeffery Self and Ryan J. Davis; Produced by the Ali Forney Center (Carl Siciliano, Director), Ryan J. Davis, Jeffrey Self, Wil Fisher, and Matthew Oberstein; Presented by Time Warner NYC, HBO, and The Corcoran Group; Director, Ryan J. Davis; Musical Director, Christopher Denny; Choreography, Erin Porvaznika; Lighting, Brian Tovar; Host: Tovah Feldshuh; Judges: Jackie Hoffman, Michael Musto, Tonya Pinkins; Opening Number "Beautiful Boy" written by Gerard Alessandrini, performed by Brett Barrett; Special performances from past winners Frankie James Grande, Michael Cusumano, Anthony Hollock; Press, O+M Company, Jaron Caldwell

CONTESTANTS Andrew Chappelle (Mr. *Mamma Mia!* – WINNER), **Wilkie Ferguson III** (Mr. *Porgy and Bess*), **Corey Mach** (Mr. *Godspell*), **Jesse Swimm** (Mr. *Mary Poppins*), **Anthony Wayne** (Mr. *Priscilla Queen of the Desert*)

SYNOPSIS The sixth annual *Broadway Beauty Pageant*, formerly titled *Mr. Broadway*, features male cast members representing their respective Broadway shows, competing for the title crown through talent, interview, and swimsuit competitions. The contestants go head to head in front of a panel of celebrity judges, but the final vote up to the audience. This event is presented as a benefit for the Ali Forney Center, the nation's largest and most comprehensive organization dedicated to LGBT youth.

Nothing Like a Dame

Gerald Lynch Theatre; March 26, 2012

Created by Phyllis Newman; Presented by The Actors Fund (Joseph Benincasa, President and CEO); Producer, Tim Pinckney; Director, Richard Roland; Music Director, Glen Roven

CAST Polly Bergen, Andréa Burns, Mario Cantone, Countess Luann de Lesseps, Lauren Flanigan, Hunter Ryan Herdlicka, Jackie Hoffman, David M. Lutken, Marilyn Maye, Alexandra Silber, Elaine Stritch, Talise Trevigne, Bruce Vilanch; Musicians **Glen Roven** (Piano), **Buddy Williams** (Drums), **Garry Haase** (Bass), **Irwin Fisch** (Synthesizer)

SYNOPSIS The seventeenth edition of *Nothing Like a Dame* was themed "Their Favorite Things," based on the *Playbill.com* feature series. Through engaging stories and songs, favorite performers from stage and screen take the audience on a journey of their favorite shows and performances, highlighting those unforgettable nights in the theatres that have influenced their careers. This annual production raised $60,000 for the Phyllis Newman Women's Health Initiative.

OFF-BROADWAY Company Series
June 1, 2011–May 31, 2012

Top: Seth Numrich, Noah Galvin, and Libby Woodbridge in Yosemite. *Opened at Rattlestick Playrights Theater January 26, 2012 (photo by Sandra Coudert)*

Center: Orlagh Cassidy, Rachel Pickup, Aedín Moloney, and Annabell Hagg in Dancing at Lughnasa. *Opened at the Irish Repertory Theatre October 30, 2011 (photo by Carol Rosegg)*

Bottom: Nikiya Mathis, Cherisse Booth, Angela Lewis, and LeRoy McClain in Playwrights Horizons/Women's Project co-production of Milk Like Sugar. *Opened at the Peter Jay Sharp Theatre November 10, 2011 (photo by Ari Mintz)*

George Dvorsky, Christiane Noll, Sal Viviano, and Jenn Colella in the York Theatre Company revival of Closer Than Ever. Opened at the Theatre at St. Peter's June 20, 2012 (photo by Carol Rosegg)

Gabriel Ebert and Mary Louise Wilson in Lincoln Center Theater's 4000 Miles. Opened at the Mitzi E. Newhouse Theater April 2, 2012 (photo by Erin Baino)

Marin Mazzie and Molly Ranson in Manhattan Class Company's Carrie. Opened at the Lucille Lortel Theatre March 1, 2012 (photo by Joan Marcus)

Kevin Spacey in The Bridge Project's production of Richard III. Opened at Brooklyn Academy of Music's Harvey Theatre January 10, 2012 (photo by Joan Marcus)

Steve Kazee and Cristin Milioti in Once. Opened at New York Theatre Workshop December 6, 2011 (photo by Joan Marcus)

Jonathan Louis Dent, Chris Perfetti, Santino Fontana, and Yusef Bulos in Roundabout Theatre Company's Sons of the Prophet. *Opened at the Laura Pels Theatre October 20, 2011 (photo by Joan Marcus)*

Laila Robins and Jane Alexander in the Signature Theatre Company production of Edward Albee's *The Lady from Dubuque. Opened at Pershing Square Signature Center's End Stage Theatre March 5, 2012 (photo by Joan Marcus)*

Betsy Wolfe, Lin-Manuel Miranda, Colin Donnell, Celia-Keenan Bolger, and Adam Grupper in the City Center Encores production of Merrily We Roll Along. *Opened at New York City Center February 8, 2012 (photo by Joan Marcus)*

Sebastian Arcelus and Marc Kudisch in The Blue Flower. *Opened at Second Stage November 9, 2011 (photo by Ari Mintz)*

Hunter Bell, Jeff Bowen, Susan Blackwell, and Heidi Blickenstaff in Now. Here. This. *Opened at the Vineyard Theatre March 28, 2012 (photo by Carol Rosegg)*

Mark Doherty, Warren Kelly, Anne Newhall, and Lori Gardner in Blame It on Beckett *(photos by Kim T. Sharp)*

Leopold Lowe and Peter Brouwer in Lost on the Natchez Trace

Buzz Roddy and Brian Wallace (video image) in Lifeline

Abingdon Theatre Company

Nineteenth Season

Artistic Director, Jan Buttram; Managing Director, Samuel J. Bellinger; Associate Artistic Director & Literary Manager, Kim T. Sharp; General Manager, Amanda Kate Joshi; Casting, William Schill; Development Director, Heather Henderson; Technical Director/Production Manager/Facilities Manager, John Trevellini; Rental Associate, Jerry Bradley; Marketing/Advertising Associate, Rachel Carter; Casting Associate, Hannah Davis; Playwright Outreach Coordinator, Bara Swain; Playwright Group Coordinator, Frank Tangredi; Maintenance, Braulio Miranda; Sunday Series Coordinator, David Flora; Artistic Director Emeritus, Pamela Paul; Development Interns, Dawn Marie Perry, Joseph Dineen; Marketing Intern, Grace Vasquez; Literary Interns, Katherine Jamison, Diana Lea Mai, Vincent Scott; Press, Shirley Herz Associates, Bob Lasko

STUDIO PRODUCTIONS

Blame It on Beckett by John Morogiello; Director, Jackob G. Hofmann; Sets, Andrew Lu; Costumes, Kimberly Matela; Lighting, Duane Pagano; Sound, David Margolin Lawson; PSM, Mark Hoffner; ASM, Joseph Dineen; Graphic Design, Anthony J. Merced, Grace Vasquez; House Manager, Patricia Crowe; **Cast:** Mark Doherty (Jim Braschi), Lori Gardner (Heidi Bishop), Warren Kelley (Jim Foley), Anne Newhall (Tina Fike)

Dorothy Strelsin Theatre; First Preview: October 7, 2011; Opening Night: October 16, 2011; Closed October 31, 2011; 9 previews, 11 performances. World premiere of a new play presented in eight scenes in two acts. Synopsis: Set in a literary office of a regional theatre, *Blame It on Beckett* centers on an intern struggling to balance her artistic integrity against the demands of her personal and professional life.

Lost on the Natchez Trace by Jan Buttram; Director, Kate Bushmann; Sets, Andrew Lu; Costumes, Catherine Siracusa and Sidney Levitt; Lighting, Travis McHale; Sound, David Margolin Lawson; Fight Choreographer, Rick Sordelet; PSM, Genevieve Ortiz; ASM, Joseph Dineen; Dramaturg, Julie Hegner; House Manager, Patricia Crowe; Box Office, Rachel Carter; Graphic Design, John Boudreau Designs, **Cast:** Peter Brouwer (Malcolm Jeters), Leopold Lowe (Tom)

Dorothy Strelsin Theatre; First Preview: February 3, 2012; Opening Night: February 12, 2012; Closed February 26, 2012; 9 previews, 11 performances. Setting: Time: October 1825, near dawn; Place: Swampland along the Natchez Trace. World premiere of a new play presented without intermission. Synopsis: When slave auctioneer Malcolm Jeters falls from his mule in Mississippi's Natchez Trace, he is left stranded, injured and starving. Tom, a runaway slave, discovers him, offering a sliver of hope in the vast swampland. The meeting triggers a desperate negotiation for Malcolm's rescue. Who will pay the highest price?

Lifeline by Frank Tangredi; Director, Jules Ochoa; Sets, David Arsenault; Costumes, Kimberly Matela; Lighting, Travis McHale; Sound, Ian Wehrle; PSM, Mark Hoffner; ASM, Kristin Bodall; House Manager, Patricia Crowe; Box Office, Rachel Carter; Graphic Design, John Boudreau Designs; Casting, Hannah Davis; Projection Design, Connor Lynch; Video Design and Editor, Glen Kasper; Camera for Video Segments, Mike Herron; Audio for Video Segments, Brian Miklas; Video Makeup Artist, Julia Langer; **Cast:** Brian Wallace (Ken Salmon), Buzz Roddy (Pete Viatale), Lori Gardner (Wendy Salmon), Brit Whittle (Seamus Cudahy), Carole Monferdini (Phyllis Salmon)

Dorothy Strelsin Theatre; First Preview: March 9, 2012; Opening Night: March 18, 2012; Closed April 1, 2012; 9 previews, 13 performances. Setting: Time: The present; Place: The living room of of the furnished rented basement of Pete's house in a suburb of New York City. World premiere of new play presented without intermission. Synopsis: When good-hearted Pete rents his basement to depressed, unstable Ken, there seems to be a potential for a wonderful friendship. But, as he delves into Ken's world, Pete uncovers problems that might not be solved with a game of poker and a six-pack.

The Actors Company Theatre (TACT)

Nineteenth Season

Co-Artistic Directors, Scott Alan Evans, Cynthia Harris, & Jenn Thompson; Artistic Director Emeritus, Simon Jones; Executive Director, Scott Alan Evans; General Manager, Cathy Bencivenga; Development, Anna Hayman; Development Associate, Jessica Lechtenberg; Resident Casting Director, Kelly Gillespie; Press, O+M Company, Richard Hillman

Children by A.R. Gurney; Based on the short story "Goodbye, My Brother" by John Cheever; Director, Scott Alan Evans; Set, Brett Banakis; Lighting, Bradley King; Costumes, Haley Lieberman; Sound, Stephen Kunken; Props, Lauren Madden; PSM, Robert V. Thurber; ASM, Michael Friedlander; Dramaturge, Stephanie Walter; Assistant Director, Lauren Miller; **Cast:** Darrie Lawrence (Mother), Margaret Nichols (Barbara), Richard Thieriot (Randy), Lynn Wright (Jane)

Beckett Theatre on Theatre Row; First Preview: October 18, 2011; Opening Night: October 27, 2011; Closed November 20, 2011; 9 previews, 24 performances. Setting: The terrace of a summer house on an island off the coast of Massachusetts; Fourth of July weekend, 1970. Revival of a play presented without intermission. Originally presented in London at the Mermaid Theatre in 1974, Manhattan Theatre Club first produced the New York premiere October 20–November 14, 1976, featuring Swoosie Kurtz, Holland Taylor, and Nancy Marchand (see *Theatre World* Vol. 33, page 132). This production marked the play's first major New York revival. Synopsis: As a wealthy family celebrates the holiday in their ancestral summer home, an estranged son unexpectedly arrives. Traditions are questioned, secrets revealed, and the course of the future changes for them all. This early work by A.R. Gurney crackles with repressed feelings, witty repartee, and everything we've come to expect from this preeminent chronicler of the American WASP.

Lost in Yonkers by Neil Simon; Director, Jenn Thompson; Set, John McDermott; Costumes, David Toser; Lighting, Martin E. Vreeland; Sound, Toby Jaguar Algya; Props, Lauren Madden; PSM, Jack Gianino; ASM, Michael Friedlander; Assistant Director, Lauren Miller; **Cast:** Cynthia Harris (Grandma Kurnitz), Alec Beard (Louie), Dominic Compertore (Eddie), Stephanie Cozart (Gert), Matthew Gumley (Jay), Russell Posner (Arty), Finnerty Steeves (Bella)

Beckett Theatre on Theatre Row; First Preview: March 13, 2012; Opening Night: March 22, 2012; Closed April 14, 2012; 9 previews, 24 performances. Setting: A two-bedroom apartment over Kurnitz Kandy Store in Yonkers, New York, 1942. Revival of a play presented in two acts in eight scenes. The world premiere was presented at the Stevens Center for the Performing Arts (Winston-Salem, NC) December 30, 1990 and subsequently in New York at the Richard Rodgers Theatre February 21, 1991–January 3, 1993, playing 780 performances (see *Theatre World* Vol. 47, page 25), starring Kevin Spacey, Irene Worth, and Mercedes Ruehl. Synopsis: *Lost in Yonkers* chronicles the story of two young brothers left in the care of the dysfunctional extended family they hardly know. Hard-hearted Grandma Kurnitz extols her own punishing brand of tough love while their tender and mentally challenged Aunt Bella offers unintended lessons in courage and resolve. As a war rages halfway across the world, a subtler generational battle is waged in the Kurnitz home, echoing the growing pains and hard truths of a nation and a family.

SALON SERIES – STAGED READINGS AT TACT STUDIO

Canaries Sometimes Sing by Frederick Lonsdale; Director, Stuart Ross; Music, Amir Khosrowpour; Stage Manager, Eileen Arnold; **Cast:** Mark Alhadeff (Geoffrey Lyme), Margot White (Ann Lyme), Ron McClary (Ernest Melton), Kelly McAndrew (Elma Melton); September 16-19, 2011; 5 performances

Kibitzer by Edward G. Robinson and Jo Swerling; Director, Gregory Salata; Music, David Broom; PSM, Meredith Dixon; **Cast:** John Plumpis (Lazarus), Ron McClary (Meyer), Richard Ferrone (Kikapoupolos), Jack Koenig (Sarnov/Briggs), Jeffrey C. Hawkins (Marks/Hanson), James Prendergast (James Livingston), Justine Salata (Josie), Matt Faucher (Bill/Phillips/Reporter), Geoffrey Malloy (Emil Schmidt); December 2-5, 2011; 5 performances

Darrie Lawrence, Lynn Wright, Margaret Nichols, and Richard Thieriot in Children *(photos by Stephen Kunken)*

The Sacred Flame by W. Somerset Maugham; Director by Rebecca Patterson; Music, Amir Khosrowpour; PSM, Ryan Gohsman; **Cast:** Nora Chester (Mrs. Tabret), Elisabeth Ahrens (Nurse Wayland), Scott Schafer (Dr. Harvester), Jeffrey C. Hawkins (Maurice), James Murtaugh (Major Liconda), Molly Wright Stuart (Stella), David Ian Lee (Colin), Becky Baumwoll (Alice); January 20-23, 2012; 5 performances

Roly Poly by Lenox Robinson; Director, Drew Barr; Music, Alex Burtzos; PSM, D.C. Rosenberg; **Cast:** Ron McClary (John Loiseau), Dana Smith-Croll (Mrs. Katherine Loiseau), Margaret Nichols (Kitty Carre-Lamadon), James Saba (Dick Carre-Lamadon), Nora Chester (Sister Beatrice), Letitia Lange (Sister Margaret), Darrie Lawrence (Countess de Breville), James Prendergast (Count de Breville), John Plumpis (Mr. Cornudet), Mary Bacon (Elizabeth Rousset "Roly Poly"), Alec Beard (A German Lieutenant), Jake Green (George/Bob/Peter/etc.); May 18-21, 2012; 5 performances

Russell Posner, Matthew Gumley, and Cynthia Harris in Lost in Yonkers

Atlantic Theater Company

Twenty-sixth Season

Artistic Director, Neil Pepe; Managing Director, Jeffory Lawson; School Director, Mary McCann; Associate Artistic Director, Christian Parker; Artistic Leadership Associate, Jaime Castañeda; Literary Associate, Abigail Katz; General Manager, Jamie Tyrol; Production Manager, Michael Wade; Company Manager, Teresa Gozzo; Operations Manager, Steven Eheart; Business Manager, Chris Kam; Development Director, Cynthia Flowers; Individual Giving/Special Events, Chloe Hughes; Development Associate/Institutional Giving, Nick Luckenbaugh; Capital Giving, Julia Lazarus/Oliver Dow, Ben Lasser; Marketing Director, Ryan Pointer; Marketing and Membership Associate, Courtney Kochuba; Director of Education and Recruitment, Heather Baird; School Associate Director, Lorielle Mallue; Director of Student Affairs, Clayton Early; School Artistic Director, Alison Beatty; Acting School and Stage 2 Production Manager, Andrew Pape/Chris Batstone; School Resident Designer, Gabe Evansohn; Education Coordinator/Box Office, Frances Tarr; Casting, Telsey + Company; Student Affairs, Clayton Early; Press, Boneau/Bryan-Brown, Chris Boneau, Joe Perrotta, Kelly Guiod

Bluebird by Simon Stephens; Director, Gaye Taylor Upchurch; Sets, Rachel Hauck; Costumes, Sarah Holden; Lighting, Ben Stanton; Sound, Darron L West; Original Music, Mark Bennett; Dialect Coach, Stephen Gabis; PSM, Kasey Ostopchuck; ASM, Molly Minor Eustis; Casting, MelCap Casting; Assistant Director, Tom Costello; Assistant Design: Carolyn Mraz (set), Amelie Chunleau (costumes); Production Assistant, Brittany Kramer; Sound Supervisor, David Arnold; Technical Director, Grant Bowen; Master Electrician, David Sexton; Props, Alexandra Geiger; **Cast:** Simon Russell Beale (Jimmy MacNeill), Tobias Segal (Guvnor/Billy Lee), Kate Blumberg (Janine), Mary McCann (Clare), Todd Weeks (Richard/Enthusiastic Man), Michael Countryman (Robert/Man), Charlotte Parry (Angela), John Sharian (Andy), Mara Measor (Girl)

Atlantic Stage 2; First Preview: August 9, 2011; Opening Night: August 22, 2011; Closed September 9, 2011; 13 previews, 22 performances. American premiere of a play presented without intermission. World premiere at the Royal Court Theatre (London) in December 1998. Synopsis: Jimmy MacNeill is a London taxi driver who seems to draw personal stories and confessions from his passengers without even trying. But through each new fare, Jimmy's own life and secret burdens unfurl. *Bluebird* illuminates big questions about how we transcend our own mistakes, and the value and cost of intimacy.

Dreams of Flying Dreams of Falling by Adam Rapp; Director, Neil Pepe; Sets, Andrew Boyce and Takeshi Kata; Costumes, Theresa Squire; Lighting, Tyler Micoleau; Original Music and Sound, David Van Tieghem; PSM, Erin Maureen Koster; ASM, Rhonda Picou; Assistant Director, Akeem Baisden-Folkes; Associate Sound, Brandon Wolcott; Assistant Design, Nicole Wee (costumes), James Naylor (lighting); Production Electrician, The Lighting Syndicate; Wardrobe Supervisor, Katja Andreiev; Board Operator, Megan Caplan; Props, Desirée Maurer; Sound Supervisor, David Arnold; Deck Crew Chief, Casey Krueger; **Cast:** Christine Lahti (Sandra Cabot), Quincy Tyler Bernstine (Wilma), Reed Birney (Dr. Bertram Cabot), Cotter Smith (Dirk Von Stofenberk), Katherine Waterston (Cora Cabot), Betsy Aidem (Celeste Von Stofenberg), Shane McRae (James Von Stofenberg)

East 13th Street Theatre (Classic Stage Company); First Preview: September 13, 2011; Opening Night: October 3, 2011; Closed October 30, 2011; 24 previews, 32 performances. Setting, An opulent Connecticut home. World premiere of a new play presented without intermission. Synopsis: In this surreal new play, something is not right in the world. The sky is a strange color, and there are geese bombarding the Connecticut home of Sandra and Bertram Cabot. *Dreams of Flying Dreams of Falling* lifts the veil on the lives of two wealthy American families, and shows us how even the most polished among us can behave like animals.

Happy Hour Three short plays (*End Days, City Lights, Wayfarer's Inn*) by Ethan Cohen; Director, Neil Pepe; Sets, Riccardo Hernandez; Costumes, Sarah Edwards; Lighting, Jason Lyons; Sound, David Van Tieghem; Stage Manager, Alison DeSantis; ASM, Lauren Kurinskas; Assistant Director, Akeem Baisden-Folkes; Assistant Design: Maruti Evans (set), Summer Lee Jack (costumes), Grant Wilcoxen (lighting), Janie Bullard (sound); Technical Director, Jason Pardine; Wardrobe Supervisor, Katja Andreiev; Hair and Makeup, Amanda Miller; Board Operator, Robert Ross; Props Master, Christine Goldman; Sound Supervisor, David A. Arnold; Production Electrician, The Lighting Syndicate; Deck Crew Chief, Joe Petrosino; **Cast:** *End Days*: Gordon MacDonald (Hoffman), Clark Gregg (Koch), Lenny Venito (Bartender), Ana Reeder (Female Voice), Rock Kohli (Slava), Joey Slotnick (Man in Parka); *City Lights*: Joey Slotnick (Ted), Aya Cash (Kim), Cassie Beck (Marci), Rock Kohli (Cabbie); *Wayfarer's Inn*: Clark Gregg (Buck), Lenny Venito (Tony), Susan Hyon (Japanese Waitress), Ana Reeder (Gretchen), Amanda Quaid (Lucy)

Peter Norton Space; First Preview: November 16, 2011; Opening Night: December 5, 2011; Closed December 31, 2011; 22 previews, 32 performances. World premiere of three one-act plays presented with one intermission and one pause. Synopsis: In *Happy Hour*, an embittered barfly has a theory—or two—about what the world has become. A lonely young man and lonely young woman can't see how right they are for each other. His motel room is so ugly a business traveler wants to end it all. Your life could be worse—and these three one-act comedies show you how.

CQ/CX by Gabe McKinley; Director, David Leveaux; Sets, David Rockwell; Costumes, Jess Goldstein; Lighting, Ben Stanton; Original Music and Sound, David Van Tieghem; Projections, Peter Nigrini and C. Andrew Bauer; Stage Manager, Jenna Woods; ASM, Jamie Lynne Sullivan; Associate Design: Dick Jaris, T.J. Greenway (set), China Lee (costumes); Assistant Design: David Sexton (lighting), Ben Truppin-Brown (sound), Lianne Arnold (projections); Technical Director, Jason Paradine; Electrician, The Lighting Syndicate; Deck Crew Chief, Christine Goldman; Deck Crew, Andrew Trow; Wardrobe Supervisor, Katja Andreiev; Board Operator, Jes Halm; Props, Susan Barras; Prop Artisan, Lillian Clements; Sound Supervisor, David A. Arnold; Video Supervisor, Dustin O'Neill; **Cast:** David Pittu (Junior), Tim Hopper (Ben), Peter Jay Fernandez (Gerald Haynes), Kobi Libii (Jay Bennett), Arliss Howard (Hal Martin), Steve Rosen (Jacob Sherman), Sheila Tapia (Monica Soria), Larry Bryggman (Frank King)

Peter Norton Space; First Preview: January 25, 2012; Opening Night: February 15, 2012; Closed March 11, 2012; 24 previews, 30 performances. World premiere of a new play presented in two acts. Synopsis: Jay, an up-and-coming black reporter at *The New York Times*, finds his dreams of becoming a famous journalist come crashing down as he becomes the center of a plagiarism scandal. In this new play inspired by real events, truth becomes slippery and racial tensions reach a boiling point. *CQ/CX* raises difficult questions about the state of our media culture, the meaning and price of journalistic integrity, and the collateral damage of unchecked ambition and compounded lies.

Simon Russell Beale and Kate Blumberg in Bluebird *(photo by Kevin Thomas Garcia)*

Teddy Cañez, Xochitl Romero, Carmen Zilles, and Alfredo Narciso in Chimichangas and Zoloft *(photo by Ahron Foster)*

Chimichangas and Zoloft by Fernanda Coppel; Director, Jaime Castañeda; Set, Lauren Halpern; Costumes, Jessica Wegener Shay; Lighting, Grant W.S. Yeager; Sound, Broken Chord; Dialect Coach, Violence Consultant, J. David Brimmer; Doug Paulson; PSM, Michael Alifanz; ASM, Catherine M. Lynch; Casting, MelCap Casting; Projection Consultant, Dustin O'Neill; Assistant Director, Sash Bischoff; Assistant Design: Brian Ireland (set), Ashley Rose Horton (costumes), Charlie Winter (lighting); SFX Makeup Consultant, Erin Kennedy Lunsford; Production Assistant, Ashley K. Singh; Sound Supervisor, David A. Arnold; Technical Director, Dylan Luke; Master Electrician, Gregory Barrett; Props, Christine Goldman; Wardrobe Supervisor, Erica Smith; Board Operator, Aaron Dayton; **Cast:** Zabryna Guevara (Sonia Martinez), Carmen Zilles (Jackie Martinez), Xochitl Romero (Penelope Lopez), Alfredo Narciso (Alejandro Lopez), Teddy Cañez (Ricardo Martinez)

Atlantic Stage 2; First Preview: May 23, 2012; Opening Night: June 3, 2012; Closed June 24, 2012; 13 previews, 24 performances. Setting: Los Angeles, California. World premiere of a new play presented without intermission. Synopsis: Suffering from a profound sense of disappointment after her 40th birthday, Sonia flees her family and goes on a binge of prescription Zoloft and greasy chimichangas. Sonia's daughter Jackie and her best friend Penelope hatch a plan to lure Sonia back home, while their fathers struggle with a secret association of their own. This irreverent story examines the search for happiness and the mysteries of sexuality through the eyes of two brazen teenagers.

Storefront Church Written and directed by John Patrick Shanley; Sets, Takeshi Kata; Costumes, Alejo Vietti; Lighting, Matthew Richards; Sound, Bart Fasbender; Wigs, Charles LaPointe; Dialects, Shane Ann Younts; PSM, Alison DeSantis; ASM, Jamie Lynne Sullivan; Assistant Director, Julie DeLaurenti; Associate Design: China Lee (set), Leah Loukas (wigs); Assistant Design: Sebastien Grouard (set), G. Benjamin Swope (lighting), Sam Kusnetz (sound); Technical Director, Roy Howington; Props, Susan Barras; Sound Supervisor, David A. Arnold; Production Electrician, The Lighting Syndicate; Wardrobe Supervisor, Katja Andreiev; Board Operator, Robert Sambrato; Deck Crew, Katherine Pursell; **Cast:** Bob Dishy (Ethan Goldklang), Zach Grenier (Reed Van Druyten), Giancarlo Esposito (Donaldo Calderon), Tonya Pinkins (Jessie Cortez), Ron Cephas Jones (Chester Kimmich), Jordan Lage (Tom Raidenberg)

Linda Gross Theater; First Preview: May 16, 2012; Opening Night: June 11, 2012; Closed July 1, 2012; 31 previews, 24 performances. Setting: Time: December 2009. Place: New York. World premiere of a new play presented in two acts. This production marked the first to return to Atlantic's main stage after a two-year, $8.3 million dollar renovation. Synopsis: *Storefront Church* centers on a Bronx borough President who is forced by the mortgage crisis into a confrontation with a local minister. The question they confront is one that faces us all: What is the relationship between spiritual experience and social action?

ATLANTIC FOR KIDS

The True Story of the 3 Little Pigs! Book and lyrics by Robert Kauzlaric, music by Paul Gilvary and William Rush; Adapted from the children's book by Jon Scieszka and Lane Smith; Director, Anya Saffir; Choreography, Alison Beatty; Music Director/Pianist, Nate Weida; Sets and Lighting, Gabe Evansohn; Costumes, Katja Andreiev; Puppets, Katey Parker; Production Coordinator, Beth Stegman; Production Manager, Andrew Pape; Guitarist, Emil McGloin; **Cast:** Max Bisantz (Maxwell), Paul Eddy (Rocky), Janna Emig (Julia), Jessica Frey (Lillian Magill), Benjamin Katz (Dr. Billy), Michael R. Piazza (Alexander T. Wolfe), Rebecca Schoffer (Martha), Chloe Wepper (Judge Juris Prudence). New York premiere of a new musical for children presented without intermission; East 13th Street Theatre (Classic Stage Company); October 8-30, 2011; 17 performances

The Hundred Dresses Book by G. Riley Mills, music and lyrics by Ralph Covert; Adapted by from the novel by Eleanor Estes; Originally presented by Chicago Children's Theatre; Director and Choreography, Alison Beatty; Arrangements, Tim Splain; Music Director/Keyboard, Brandon Sturiale; Arrangements, Timothy Splain; Sets and Lighting, Gabe Evansohn; Costumes, Katja Andreiev; Production Coordinator, Beth Stegman; Production Manager, Chris Batstone; Assistant Director, Akeem Baisden-Folkes; **Cast:** David Bernstein (Willie), Janna Emig (Miss Mason), Kim Fischer (Jack), Stephanie Hsu (Maddie), Daniel Johnsen (Jan Petronski/Old Man Svensen), Jeanna Phillips (Peggy), Marisa Parry (Cecile), Rebecca Schoffer (Wanda Petronski). New York premiere of a new musical for kids presented without intermission; Peter Norton Space; February 19–March 11, 2012; 15 performances

Shane McRae and Katherine Waterston in Dreams of Flying Dreams of Falling *(photo by Kevin Thomas Garcia)*

Anna Reeder, Amanda Quaid, and Clark Gregg in Happy Hour *(photo by Doug Hamilton)Hamilton)*

Brooklyn Academy of Music

Founded in 1861

Chairman of the Board, Alan H. Fishman; Vice Chairmen of the Board, Wiliam I. Campbell and Adam E. Max; President, Karen Brooks Hopkins; Executive Producer, Joseph V. Melillo

2011 NEXT WAVE FESTIVAL (29TH ANNUAL)

Awakening *A Musical Meditation on the Anniversary of 9/11* Presented by Kronos Quartet (Janet Cowperthwaite, Managing Director; Laird Rodet, Associate Director) with the Brooklyn Youth Chorus (Dianne Berkun, Conductor/Artistic Director); Sets and Lighting, Laurence Neff; Audio, Brian Mohr; Technical Associate, Calvin L. Jones; Composers, Dmitri Yanov-Yanovsky, Ram Narayan, Einstürzende Neubauten, John Oswald, Michael Gordon, Osvaldo Golijov, Gustavo Santaolalla, Terry Riley, Aulis Sallinen, Vladimir Martynov; Arrangements, Kronos, Ljova (Lev Zhurbin), Jacob Garchik, Paola Prestini, Vladimir Martynov; For Kronos: Sidney Chen (Artistic Administrator), Scott Fraser (Sound Designer), Christina Johnson (Communications); Kronos Quartet: David Harrington (Violin/Artistic Director), John Sherba (Violin), Hank Dutt (Viola), Jeffrey Zeigler (Cello)

Program: Part 1: Awakening; Oh Mother, the Handsome Man Tortures Me; Lullaby; Raga Mishra Bhairavi: Alap; Part II: Armenia; Spectre; Selections from *The Sad Park*; Part III: Darkness 9/11; One Earth, One People, One Love; Tusen Tankar; Winter Was Hard; The Beatitudes

Howard Gilman Opera House; September 21– September 24, 2011; 4 performances. New York premiere of a theatrical musical concert presented in three parts without intermission. Synopsis: Kronos Quartet returns to BAM with a heartfelt program comprising of twelve original and traditional compositions that reflect upon those instances where traditional language fails, and music steps in to restore equilibrium in the midst of imbalance.

To the Ones I Love Presented by Compagnie Thor; Co-produced by Théâtre de la Place and Théâtre de Namur; Choreography/Sets, Thierry Smits; Music, J.S. Bach; Sound, Maxime Bodson; Co-Set Design/Lighting/Technical Coordinator, Thomas Beni; Costumes, Luc Gering; Choreographer Assistant, Benjamin Bac; Sound Technician, Benoit Ausloos; Dancers: Rudi Cole, Daudet Grazaï, Christian D. Guerematchi, Alpha Sanneh, Dean Lee, Damien Chevron, Christophe Jeannot, Alexandre Gbeblewoo, Pascal Beugre-Tellier

Harvey Theater; September 29–October 1, 2011; 3 performances. U.S. premiere of a theatrical dance piece presented without intermission. Synopsis: A provocative merging of traditional and contemporary modern dance, Belgian choreographer Thierry Smits new work celebrates the male physique's beauty, power, and capacity for expression and pays homage to movement at its purest, unencumbered by narrative and infused with artfully woven elements of hip-hop, martial arts, African dance, and ballet.

The Threepenny Opera Text and lyrics by Bertolt Brecht, music by Kurt Weill; Adapted from Elizabeth Hauptmann's German version of John Gay's *The Beggar's Opera*; Presented by Berliner Ensemble; Director/Stage and Light Concept, Robert Wilson; Music Directors, Hans-Jörn Brandenburg and Stefan Rager; Costumes, Jacques Reynaud; Co-director, Ann-Christin Rommen; Set Co-design, Serge von Arx; Costume Co-design, Yashi Tabassomi; Dramaturgy, Jutta Ferbers and Anika Bárdos; Lighting, Andreas Fuchs and Ulrich Eh; **Cast:** Jürgen Holtz (Jonathan J. Peachum), Traute Hoess (Celia Peachum), Stefanie Stappenbeck (Polly Peachum), Stefan Kurt (Macheath), Axel Werner (Brown), Anna Graenzer (Lucy Brown), Angela Winkler (Jenny), Georgios Tsivanoglou (Filch), Ulrich Brandhoff (Walt Dreary), Martin Schneider (Matt of the Mint), Boris Jacoby (Crooked Finger Jack), Winfried Goos (Sawtooth Bob), Dejan Bu in (Jimmy), Jörg Thieme (Ed), Uli Pleßmann (Smith), Heinrich Buttchereit (Reverend Kimball), Anke Engelsmann (Betty), Ruth Glöss (Old Prostitute), Ursula Höpfner-Tabori (Dolly), Marina Senckel (Vixer), Gabriele Völsch (Molly), Gerd Kunath (A riding messenger), Walter Schmidinger (A voice)

Howard Gilman Opera House; October 4-8, 2011; 5 performances. U.S. premiere of a new production of a classic musical presented in German with English titles in three acts with one intermission. Synopsis: Robert Wilson joins the world-renowned Berliner Ensemble in a bold new production of Brecht and Weill's seminal work. Wilson places the story of Peachum, Polly, and Macheath in a bewitching setting informed equally by the striking designs of German Expressionist cinema and the shattering, seductive world of Weimar-era cabaret.

Angela Winkler in The Threepenny Opera *(photo by Lesley Leslie-Spinks)*

The Speakers Progress Written and directed by Sulayman Al-Bassam; Presented by S Theatre (Kuwait); Design, Sam Collins; Composition and Sound, Lewis Gibson; Lighting, Marcus Doshi; Costumes, Abdullah Al Awadhi; Artistic Producer/Script Editor, Georgina Van Welie; Assistant Director, Nigel Barrett; Technical Director, Saad El Shaarawy; Production Manager, Aude Albiges; Surtitles, Dana Mikhail; Stage Manager, Nigel Barrett; Company Manager, Wafa Al Fraheen; **Cast:** Amal Omran (The Girl-Boy), Carole Abboud (The Lady), Faisal Al Ameeri (The Ruler/The Clown), Fayez Kazak (The Mullah), Sulayman Al-Bassam (The Speaker), Nicolas Daniel (The Drunken Uncle), Nassar Al Nassar (The Uncle's Sidekick), Nowar Yousef (The Lady's Maid), Sa'ad El Farraj (The Actor from The Golden Era via video)

Harvey Theater; October 6-8, 2011; 3 performances. U.S. premiere of a new play presented in English and Arabic with English titles without intermission. Synopsis: In an unnamed totalitarian state, all forms of theater have been banned. When a condemned 1960s production of *Twelfth Night* is discovered, it becomes the focal point for political resistance blogs and underground social networks. A dark satire on decades of hopelessness and political inertia that have fed recent revolts across the Arab region, *The Speaker's Progress* is a daring metaphor for the mechanisms of dissent.

Water Stains on the Wall Concept, set, and choreography by Lin Hwai-Min (Artistic Director); Presented by Cloud Gate Dance Theatre of Taiwan; Music, Toshio Hosokawa; Lighting, Lulu W.L Lee; Costumes, Lin Ching-Ju; Projections, Ethan Wang; Associate Artistic Director, Lee Ching-Chun; Music Consultant, Liang Chun-Mei; Chi Kung Master, Hsiung Wei; Martial Arts Master, Adam Chi Hsu; Calligraphy Master, Huang Wei-Jong; International Representative, Wang Jaw-Hwa; Project Managers, Wang Shu-Chen, Liu Yi-Ling; Project Coordinator, Lin I-Hsuan; Technical Director, Lee Wan-Ling; Production Manager, Li Chia-Nung; Senior Stage Manager, Kuo Yuan-Hsien; Stage Supervisors, Chen Chih-

Feng, Lin Ching-Kai; Lighting Supervisor, Lin Szu-Chen; Wardrobe, Hsu Wen-Wen; Dancers: Chou Chang-Ning, Huang Pei-Hua, Lee Ching-Chun, Tsai Ming-Yuan, Chiu I-Wen, Ko Wan-Chun, Lin Chia-Liang, Liu Hui-Ling, Su I-Ping, Wang Chih-Hao, Wong Lap-Cheong, Yang I-Chun Yu Chien-Hung, Hou Tang-Li, Huang Mei-Ya, Lee Tzu-Chun, Lin Hsin-Fang

Howard Gilman Opera House; October 12-15, 2011; 4 performances. New York premiere of a new theatrical dance piece presented without intermission. Synopsis: *Water Stains on the Wall* is a choreographic exploration of the beauty and aesthetics of calligraphy through chi kung, internal martial arts, modern dance, and meditation.

Symphony for the Dance Floor by Daniel Bernard Roumain (DBR); Director, D.J. Mendel; Photography and Video, Jonathan Mannion; Choreography, Millicent Johnnie; Lighting, Miriam Crowe; Costumes, Adia Whitaker; Additional Music, Lord Jamar, Cynthia Hopkins, Dave Archuletta; Assistant Director, Jordana Toback; Production Manager, Annie March; Co-producers, Nicole Borrelli Hearn, Rika Iino; MC/DJ, Lord Jamar; Vocalist, Cynthia Hopkins; Principal Dancers, Veleda Roehl, Andre Zachery, Leah Mitchell; Company Dancers, Alicia Dellimore, Alison Dellimore, Elizabeth Lucrezio, Stephanie Mas, Stephanie Padila

Harvey Theater; October 13-15, 2011; 4 performances. New York premiere of a theatrical fusion of music, art, and movement presented without intermission. Synopsis: Acclaimed composer-violinist Daniel Bernard Roumain (DBR) returns with an invigorating new production fueled by his inimitable mash-up of pop, hip-hop, and classical music, augmented with live dance, photography and video, rap, and performance art, structured in four movements that follow traditional symphonic form.

Haze Presented by Beijing Dance Theater (Han Jiang; Producer and Text); Choreography, Wang Yuanyuan; Composition, Henryk Górecki and Biosphere; Set, Tan Shaoyuan; Lighting, Han Jiang; Sound/Music Arrangements, Liu Bo; Costumes, Zhong Jiani; Scenery Production, Wang Pu; Video Production/Text, Liu Tang; Stage Manager, Chen Xiaji; Lighting Assistant, Liu Zhao; Rehearsal Mistress, Xle Yang; Operations Manager, Zhang Yu; Artistic Director Assistant, Wang Chao; Company Manager, E. John Pendleton; Production Manager, Patrice Thomas; General Manager, JPH Consulatants; Dancers: Wu Shanshan, Zhang Xiaochuan, Lu Yahui, Yuan Jiaxin, Qiu Jingjing, Sun Rong, Feng Linshu, Cai Tieming, Liu Wei, Yan Xiaoqiang, Xie Ming, Yin Fang, Wang Hao, Zhu Ke, Wei Tushan, Zheng Jie, Guo Mingfu

Harvey Theater; October 19-22, 2011; 4 performances. U.S. premiere of a theatrical dance piece presented without intermission. Synopsis: Beijing Dance Theater channels the tension between China's complex struggle with centuries-old traditions and its headlong rush into the future. Synthesizing classical ballet and dance theater, Wang has crafted a work of courage and rapturous beauty in response to modern economic and environmental crises. Adding a rarely seen dimension to the movement, the dancers rise and fall in a world of shadows and ghostly stillness, creating an unsparing revelation of a culture in the grip of social and spiritual uncertainty.

Cries and Whispers by Ingmar Bergman; Presented by Toneelgroep Amsterdam; Director, Ivo van Hove; Scenography, Jan Versweyveld; Dramaturgy, Peter van Kraaij; Video, Tal Yarden; Costumes, Wojciech Dziedzic; Sound, Roeland Fernhout; **Cast:** Roeland Fernhout (Joakim/Doctor), Janni Goslinga (Karin), Hugo Koolschijn (Frederik/Priest), Chris Nietvelt (Agnes), Halina Reijn (Maria), Karina Smulders (Anna)

Harvey Theater; October 25-29, 2011; 5 performances. U.S. premiere of a play based on a film presented in two acts. Synopsis: In a sterile grey room, an artist lies dying. Her video diaries flicker on screens, offering consoling images of an ersatz immortality as her estranged sisters hover about, removed. Ivo van Hove transports us to a collective soul bound by the most tenuous compassion. On a stage transfigured by grief, gripping performances drive this modern adaptation of Bergman's unflinching 1972 film about the will to live and the astounding human capacity for empathy amid the debris of damaged life.

Roeland Fernhout and Halina Reijn in Cries and Whispers
(photo by Jan Versweyveld)

I don't believe in outer space Written, directed, and presented by William Forsythe and the Forsythe Company; Music, Thom Willems; Sound, Niels Lanz; Graphics, Dietrich Krüger; Costumes, Dorothee Merg; Lighting, Tanja Rühl; Dramaturgy, Freya Vass-Rhee; Managing Director, Vera Battis-Reese; Assistant Sound and Video, Mara Brinker; Artistic Assistant/Ballet Master, Thierry Guiderdoni; Technical Production/Stage Supervisor, Dirk Heymann; Makeup/Sylist, Roerita Kuster; Accompanist, David Morrow; Technical Production, Ulf Naumann; Producer, Julian Gabriel Richter; Press/Marketing, Mechthild Rühl; Physiotherapist, Holger Tietz; Ballet Trainer, Yannick Sempey; Stage/Tour Manager, Paul Viebeg; Dancers: Yoko Ando, Cyril Baldy, Esther Balfe, Dana Caspersen, Katja Cheraneva, Brigel Gjoka, Amancio Gonzalez, John Johnson, David Kern, Fabrice Mazliah, Roberta Mosca, Tilman O'Donnell, Jone San Martin, Yasutake Shimaji, Elizabeth Waterhouse, Riley Watts, Ander Zabala

Howard Gilman Opera House; October 26-29, 2011; 4 performances. New York premiere of a theatrical dance piece presented without intermission. Synopsis: *I don't believe in outer space* is a darkly comic exploration of absence made present. Tragic themes from the lyrics of pop songs pervade the evening, placed into changing, outlandish contexts as one choreographic element among many. All the while, 18 phenomenal dancers mingle in freakish scenes, balancing as virtuosic bodies on the edge of an abyss. This is the beyond, the boundlessness of the universe, but only if you believe in it.

69°S Created by Phantom Limb in collaboration with David Harrington and Kronos Quartet, developed with Tony Taccone; Producer, Thomas O. Kriegsmann/ArKtype in association with Beth Morrison Projects; Director, Sophie Hunter; Music/Puppets, Erik Sanko; Sets, Jessica Grindstaff; Choreography, Andrea Miller; Video, Shaun Irons, Lauren Petty; Costumes, threeASFOUR; Lighting, Andrew Hill; Recorded Performance, Kronos Quartet; Production Manager, Dave Shelley; Technical Director/Lighting Supervisor, John Finen; Stage Manager, Randi Rivera; Sound/Musical Treatment, Martin J.A. Lambeek; Contributing Sound, Tei Blow, Zachary Layton, Andy Green; Collaborating Architect, Gia Wolff; String Arrangements, Jacob Garchick; Kronos Quartet Engineer, John Kilgore; Skeleton Key Recording, Andy Green and Bryce Gogin; Choreography Assistant, Francesca Romo; Lighting Concept, André Pronk; Documentation, Tommy Bertelsen; Boatswain, Gregory Kozatek; Puppetry Consultant, Liam Hurley; Dramaturgy, Christie Evangelisto; **Cast:** Kira Rae Blazek, Sabrina D'Angelo, Takemi Kitamura, Rowan Magee, Aaron Mattocks, Carlton Ward; Musicians (*Skelton Key*): Benjamin Clapp, Craig LeBlang, Erik Sanko, Bob Vaccarelli

Harvey Theater; November 2-5, 2011; 4 performances. New York premiere of a new play with puppetry, multimedia, and live music presented without intermission. Synopsis: Sixty-nine degrees south latitude, threshold of Antarctica, foreboding and cold. In an attempt to cross the continent, explorer Ernest Shackleton and crew have been shipwrecked, and they emerge before us in the snow. Junk-rock band Skeleton Key performs live as the puppets – animated by ghostly figures on stilts – navigate the forsaken plain. A cryptic geologic language accompanies their journey, composed of field recordings layered over a gripping minimalist score. As astral projections bathe the audience in a long polar night, hope rises with the sun and a darkly beautiful vision of the Antarctic future unfolds in this tale of survival at the end of the earth.

Phantom Limb in 69° S *(photo by Pavel Antonov)*

Brooklyn Babylon Music by Darcy James Argue, Animation and live painting by Danijel Zezelj; Produced by Beth Morrison Projects; Video and Projections, Jim Findlay; Costumes, Paloma Young; Sound Engineer, Justin Balch; Lighting, Scott Bolman; Directorial Consultation, Isaac Butler; Video Engineer, James Daher; Assistant Lighting, Nicholas Houfek; Stage Manager, Lindsey Turteltaub; Production Supervisor, Production Core, James Cleveland; Production Manager, Jared Goldstein; Executive Assistant, Brian Rady; Company Manager, James Daniel; *Secret Society:* Darcy James Argue (Conductor); Erica von Kleist (Piccolo, Flute, Alto Flute, Alto Sax, Soprano Sax); Rob Wilkerson (Flute, Clarinet, Soprano Sax, Alto Sax); Sam Sadigursky (Clarinet, Tenor Sax); John Ellis (Clarinet, Bass Clarinet, Tenor Sax); Josh Sinton (Clarinet, Bass Clarinet, Contrabass Clarinet, Baritone Sax); Seneca Black, Tom Goehring, Matt Holman, Nadje Noordhuis, Ingrid Jensen (Trumpet, Flugelhorn); Mike Fahie (Trombone, Euphonium); Ryan Keberle (Trombone); James Hirschfeld (Trombone, Tuba); Jennifer Whaton (Bass Trombone, Tuba); Sebastian Noelle (Acoustic Guitar, Electric Guitar); Gordon Webster (Piano, Electric Piano, Melodica); Matt Clohesy (Contrabass, Electric Bass); Ted Poor (Drum Set, Percussion)

Harvey Theater; November 9-12, 2011; 4 performances. World premiere of a musical and multimedia performance piece presented without intermission. Synopsis: In a future Brooklyn, a the tallest tower in the world is being built. All it needs is a carousel on top, spinning over the city below. Conjuring the seductive majesty of Fritz Lang's *Metropolis* and the gritty social narrative of Walker Evans' photography, acclaimed artist Zezelj joins forces with composer Argue and his steampunk-jazz big band Secret Society to tell this story of extravagance and urban ambition. The result is a feast for the senses: Zezelj paints live onstage alongside his own projected animation as Secret Society scores the rise of this dystopian city.

Canyon Created by John Jasperse and the Company; Commissioned for BAM 2011 Next Wave and the Wexner Center for the Arts; Choreography/Costumes, John Jasperse; Composer, Hahn Rowe; Visual Design, Tony Orrico; Lighting/Production Manager, James Clotfelter; Live Sound Mix, Dave Cook; Additional Costumes, Reid Bartelme; **Cast:** Lindsay Clark, Erin Cornell, Kennis Hawkins, Burr Johnson, James McGinn; Musicians: Olivia De Prato (Violin), Ha-Yang Kim

(Cello), Doug Wieselman (Bass Clarinet), Hahn Rowe (Violin, Guitar, Electronics)

Harvey Theater; November 17-20, 2011; 4 performances. New York premiere of a dance piece with live music presented without intermission. Synopsis: In his latest work, Jasperse tackles wonder and the ineffable-the transformative power of losing oneself in visceral experience-where the supremacy of the intellect is humbled into a state of awe. *Canyon* plays with engineered disorientation, sensory overload, spaciousness, fractured connectivity, and rapture.

The Infernal Comedy: Confessions of a serial killer Written and directed by Michael Sturminger; Music direction and concept by Martin Haselböck, based on an idea by Birgit Hutter and Haselböck; Presented by Muikkonzept; Costumes, Birgit Hutter; Music, Christophe Willibald Gluck, Luigi Boccherini, Antonio Vivaldi, Wolfgang Amadeus Mozart, Franz Joseph Haydn, Carl Maria von Weber; **Cast:** John Malkovich (Actor); Sopranos (Alternating, two in each performance): Marie Arnet, Kirsten Blaise, Louise Fribo, Martene Grimson; Orchester Wiener Akademie: Martin Haselböck (Conductor); Ilia Korol, David Drabek, Piroska Batori, Maria Kaluzhskikh, Inigo Aranzasti, Christiane Bruckmann-Hiller, Gerlinde Sonnleitner, Anna-Maria Sonnleitner, Diana Kiendl-Samarovski, Veronika Schulz-Eckart, Thomas Trsek, Katarzyna Brzoza, Agnes Petersen, Florian Hasenburger (Violins); Peter Aigner, Éva Posvanecz, Martina Reiter (Viola); Balázs Máté, Nikolay Gimaletdinov, Michal Stahel (Cello); Walter Bachkönig, Jan Krigovsky, Alexandra Dienz (Double Bass); Christian Gurtner (Flute); Gonzalo Ruiz, Peter Wuttke (Oboe); Peter Rabl, Ronald Sebesta (Clarinet); Mrs. Laszlo Zoltanne Vörös, Rainer Johannsen (Bassoon); Hermann Ebner, Ferenc Varga (Horn)

Howard Gilman Opera House; November 17-19, 2011; 4 performances. New York premiere of a theatrical/chamber music/operatic piece presented without intermission. Synopsis: "Does Jekyll know about Hyde?" asks serial killer turned writer Jack Unterweger before strangling a soprano with a brassiere. Though himself dead, Unterweger has returned to tell the audience his story. Two singers, accompanied by the virtuoso early-music ensemble Orchester Wiener Akademie, perform live opera arias in an inspired counterpoint, providing both a soundtrack to and a deliciously ironic commentary on Unterweger's disturbing confessions.

John Malkovich in The Infernal Comedy *(photo by Nathalie Bauer)*

Supernatural Wife Based on *Alkestis* by Euripides, translated by Anne Carson; Presented by Big Dance Theater; Created in collaboration with the cast; Co-directors, Paul Lazar and Annie-B Parson; Choreography, Annie-B Parson; Sound, Jane Shaw; Set, Joanne Howard; Video, Jeff Larson; Lighting, Joe Levasseur; Costumes, Oana Botez-Ban; Music, David Lang, Brunk, Carter Burwell, Richard Howgill, Jane Shaw; Choral/Vocal Music, Chris Giarmo; Production Manager, Aaron Rosenblum; Technical Director, Josh Higgason; Sound Assistant, Jamie McElhinney; Project Producer, Estelle Woodward Arnal; Silent Movie Text, Rainer Maria Rilke; **Cast:** Molly Hickok, Tymberly Canale, Chris Giarmo, Elizabeth DeMent, Aaron Mattocks, Pete Simpson; Additional Cast: Paul Lazar (Admetos' father on video/Silent Movie Performer), Simon Eskin (Child's Voice), Hope Hickok (Silent Movie Performer); Interns: Anna Brenner, Hayden Gilbert, Stiven Luka, Rebecca Goodman, Carolyn Defrin, Chinaza Uche, Eva Claycomb, Janna Avner

Harvey Theater; November 29–December 3, 2011; 5 performances. New York premiere of a dance/theater adaptation of a play presented without intermission. Synopsis: In a feverish blend of drama, music, dance, and live video, Big Dance Theater presents a moving adaptation of Euripides' mysterious tragicomedy *Alkestis*. In the wake of his wife's decision to die in his stead, King Admentus finds that to love the dead is endless tears. *Supernatural Wife* revisits the power of tragedy while thoroughly subverting its theatrical and emotional conventions.

Tudo Isto É Fado Produced and programmed by Leticia Montalvo and Lian Calvo Serrano (Curator); Presented by Tempest Entertainment; *Lisboa Soul* (December 2): Tour Manager, Helder Moutinho; Singers: Rodrigo, Beatriz Da Conceição, YAMI, Vânia Cristina, Ritinha Lobo, Michaela Vaz; Guitars: Ricardo Parreira, Marco De Oliveira, Manuel De Oliveira; Keyboards: Carlos Eduardo Fernandes Garcia; Drummer: Mario Marques; *Carmané* (December 2): Lighting, Paulo Mendes; Sound, Aldredo Almeida, Maria Joao Castanheira; Manager, Paulo Salgado; Vocals: Camané; Portueguse Guitar: Jose Manuel Neto; Guitar: Carlos Manuel Proenca; Double Bass: Paulo Paz; *Deolinda* (December 3): Tour Manager, Nelson Gomes; Sound, Sergio Milhano; Lighting, Frederico Rompante; Vocals: Ana Bacalhau; Double Bass: Ze Pedro Leitão; Guitar: Pedro da Silva Martins, Luis Jose Martins; *Amália Hoje* (December 3): Manager, John Gonçalves; Stage Technician, Joaa Pedrosa; Sound, Jorge Pina, Nuno Ruas; Vocals: Sonia Tavares; Keyboards: Nuno Gonçalves; Guitars/Vocals: Paulo Praça; Guitar: Israel Pereira; Drums: Mario Barreiros; Bass Guitar: Carl Minneman

Howard Gilman Opera House; December 2-3, 2011; 2 performances. U.S. premiere of four musical performances presented over two days, each performance with intermission. Synopsis: With smoldering intensity and a yearning heart, *Tudo Isto É Fado* peers into the poetry and seductive sounds of Fado, Portugal's soulful national song style in a special two-day presentation.

Krapp's Last Tape by Samuel Beckett; Presented by the Gate Theatre Dublin (Michael Colgan, Director) in association with David Eden Productions (Erica Charpentier, General Manager, Michael Michelson, Production Manager); Director, Michael Colgan; Lighting, James McConnell; Company Stage Manager, Catherine Buffrey; Touring Manager/Gate Deputy Director, Pádraig Heneghan; Touring Assistant, Rowena Burke; Production Coordinator, Valerie Keogh; Gate Theatre Head of Production, Teerth Chungh; Gate Production Manager, Jim McConnell; Gate Press and Marketing, Jennifer Higgins, Caroline Kennedy; Wardrobe Supervisor, Kiki Beamish; **Cast:** John Hurt (Krapp)

John Hurt in Krapp's Last Tape *(photo by Richard Termine)*

Harvey Theater; December 6-18, 2011; 15 performances. U.S. premiere of a new revival of a play presented without intermission. Synopsis: A tragedy for a lone actor, a tape recorder, and many bananas, *Krapp's Last Tape* is one of Beckett's most personal stage works. Featuring discreet details from the writer's own life, this dramatization of the messy truths of memory and time illuminates the predicament we face when we become strangers to our former selves. Krapp is an embittered and dyspeptic man who marks the occasion of his 69th birthday by revisiting his 39-year-old self. Veering from outrage to contemplation, Krapp exhibits the ticks and tocks of a beaten man whose spirit unravels in the misery of lost time as the tapes unspool.

Merce Cunningham: The Legacy Tour Presented by the Merce Cunningham Dance Company; Choreography, Merce Cunningham; Founding Music Director, John Cage; Music Director, Takehisa Kosugi; Director of Choreography, Robert Swinston; Executive Director, Trevor Carlson; Director of Production, Davison Scandrett; Company Manager, Jennifer Goggans; Sound Engineer/Music Coordinator, Jesse Stiles; Lighting Director, Christine Shallenberg; Wardrobe Supervisor, Anna Finke; Assistant Production Manager, Carrie Wood; Production Assistant/Carpenter, Pepper Fajans; Touring Manager, Jeff Donaldson-Forbes; Archivist, David Vaughan; Program A: *Roaratorio* (December 7): Décor, Mark Lancaster; Music, John Cage; Lighting, Mark Lancaster and Christine Shallenberg; Restaging, Patricia Lent; Program B: *Second Hand* & *Biped* (December 8); *Second Hand*: Music, John Cage; Costumes, Jasper Johns; Lighting, Richard Nelson; Piano, David Behrman; *Biped*: Music, Gavin Bryars; Décor, Shelley Eshkar, Paul Kaiser; Costumes, Suzanne Gallo; Lighting, Aaron Copp; Musicians: Gavin Bryars (Double Bass/Synthesizer), Loren Dempster (Cello), John King (Electric Guitar), Takehisi Kosugi (Violin/Percussion); Program C: *Pond Way, RainForest, Split Sides* (December 9-10); *Pond Way*: Music, Brian Eno; Décor, Roy Lichtenstein; Costumes, Suzanne Gallo; Lighting, David Covey; Restaging, Robert Swinston; *RainForest*: Music, David Tudor; Décor, Andy Warhol; Lighting, Aaron Copp; Musicians, John King, Takehisa Kosugi; Restaging, Robert Swinston and Jennifer Goggans; *Split Sides*: Music, Radiohead, Sigur Rós; Décor, Robert Heishman, Catherine Yass; Costumes, James Hall; Lighting, James F. Ingalls; Musicians, John King, Takehisa Kosugi; **Dancers:** Brandon Collwes, Dylan Crossman, Emma Desjardins, Jennifer Goggans, John Hinrichs, Daniel Madoff, Rashaun Mitchell, Marcie Munnerlyn, Krista Nelson, Silas Riener, Jamie Scott, Robert Swinston, Melissa Toogood, Andrea Weber

"Split Sides", one of the pieces in Merce Cunningham: The Legacy Tour *(photo by Tony Dougherty)*

Howard Gilman Opera House; December 7-10, 2011; 4 performances. Revivals of contemporary dance programs, Program A presented without intermission, Program B presented with one intermission; Program C presented with two intermissions. Synopsis: *The Legacy Tour* offers audiences a final chance to see six major large scale works from legendary choreographer Merce Cunningham, whose seven-decade long career established a bold repertoire as beloved as it was immensely influential.

WINTER-SPRING SEASON

Richard III by William Shakespeare; Produced by BAM, The Old Vic, and Neal Street as part of The Bridge Project; Director, Sam Mendes; Sets, Tom Piper; Costumes, Catherine Zuber; Lighting, Paul Pyant; Projections, Jon Driscoll; Sound, Gareth Fry; Music, Mark Bennett; Music Coordinator and Direction, Curtis Moore; Fight Director, Terry King; Artistic Associate, Gaye Taylor Upchurch; Casting, Daniel Swee, Maggie Lunn; International Tour Producer, Claire Béjanin; Associate Director, Bruce Guthrie; Production Manager, Dominic Fraser; Production Co-Co-coordinator, Audrey Hoo; PSM, Richard Clayton; ASMs, Jenefer Tait, Samantha Watson; Electrician, Andrew Furby; Projection Engineer, Pradeep Dash; Associate Design: Jonathan Lipman (costumes), Dan Large (lighting), Ross Chatfield (sound); Associate Composer, Matthew Henning; Production Carpenter, Tom Humphrey; Wardrobe Dresser, Dean Nichols; Wigs Mistress, Anna Morena; Tour Press, Jo Allan; Flying Effects, High Performance; Additional Wigs, Campbell Young; **Cast:** Kevin Spacey (Richard, *Duke of Gloucester, later King Richard III*), Chandler Williams (George, *Duke of Clarence, brother to Richard and Edward IV*), Howard W. Overshown (Brackenbury/Lord Mayor of London), Jack Ellis (William, *Lord Hastings, Lord Chamberlain*), Annabel Scholey (Lady Anne), Haydn Gwynne (Queen Elizabeth, *wife of King Edward IV*), Isaiah Johnson (Lord Rivers, *brother of Queen Elizabeth*/Scrivner), Nathan Darrow (Lord Grey, *son of Queen Elizabeth/ Henry, Earl of Richmond*), Gavin Stenhouse (Marquess of Dorset, *son of Queen Elizabeth*), Chuk Iwuji (Duke of Buckingham), Michael Rudko (Lord Stanley, *Earl of Derby*), Gemma Jones (Queen Margaret, *widow of King Henry VI*), Gary Powell (First Murderer/Sir Francis Lovel), Jeremy Bobb (Second Murderer/Sir William Catesby), Andrew Long (King Edward IV/Bishop of Ely), Maureen Anderman (Duchess of York, *mother of King Edward IV, Richard, and Clarence*), Katherine Manners (Young Richard Duke of York, *son of King Edward IV*), Hannah Stokely (Young Edward Prince of Wales, *son and heir of King Edward IV*), Stephen Lee Anderson (Sir Richard Ratcliffe), Simon Lee Phillips (Sir James Tyrrel/Duke of Norfolk); Musicians: Curtis Moore (Keyboards, Vocals, Percussion), Hugh Wilkinson (Percussion)

Harvey Theater; Opening Night: January 10, 2012; Closed March 4, 2012; 55 performances. Revival of a classic play presented in five acts with one intermission. Synopsis: At the climax of the Wars of the Roses, Richard watches his brother ascend the throne of England and confides in us-with all the profound bitterness of an outcast born with a hunchback and malformed leg-his intention to seize the crown. Navigating an imposing assemblage of some of Shakespeare's greatest female characters, Richard lusts for power, assuring his own bloody rise and fall. This production marked the final installment of The Bridge Project, a three-year transatlantic partnership uniting BAM, The Old Vic, and Neal Street, mounting classic productions with artists from both the U.K. and U.S., and touring these productions across the globe.

Kevin Spacey and Annabel Scholey in The Bridge Project production of Richard III *(photo by Joan Marcus)*

'Tis Pity She's a Whore by John Ford; Presented by Cheek by Jowl (Beth Byrne, Executive Director; Roisin Caffrey, General Manager) in co-production with the Barbican (London), Les Gémeaux/Sceaux/Scène Nationale, and Sydney Festival; Director, Declan Donnellan; Design, Nick Ormerod; Associate Director/ Movement, Jane Gibson; Lighting, Judith Greenwood; Music/Sound, Nick Powell; Associate Director, Owen Horsley; Production Manager, Simon Bourne; Costume Supervisor, Angie Burns; Company Manager, Linsey Hall; Technical Stage Manager, Dougie Wilson; Deputy Stage Manager, Clare Loxley; Lighting Technician, Kristina Hjelm; Sound Technician, Mark Cunningham; Wardrobe Manager, Victoria Youngson; ASM (Tour), Rosina Webb; ASM (Rehearsals/Paris), Tilly Stokes; American Stage Manager, R. Michael Blanco; **Cast:** Suzanne Burden (Hippolita), David Collings (Florio), Ryan Ellsworth (Donado), Jimmy Fairhurst (Gratiano), Jack Gordon (Giovanni), Nyasha Hatendi (Friar), Jack Hawkins (Soranzo), Lizzie Hopley (Putana), Peter Moreton (Cardinal/Doctor), David Mumeni (Grimaldi), Laurence Spellman (Vasques), Lydia Wilson (Annabella)

Front (l-r): Lizzie Hopley, Lydia Wilson, Peter Moreson, Jack Hawkins; Back (l-r): Ryan Ellswoth, Suzanne Burden, David Collings, David Mumeni, Jack Gordon, Nysha Hatendi in Cheek by Jowl's 'Tis Pity She's a Whore *(photo by Manuel Harlan)*

Harvey Theater; Opening Night: March 20, 2012; Closed March 31, 2012; 12 performances. U.S. premiere of a new revival of a play presented without intermission. Synopsis: Cheek by Jowl returns to BAM with John Ford's *'Tis Pity She's a Whore*, one of the most controversial plays in the English theatrical canon. Siblings Giovanni and Annabella are of noble birth and madly in love. Full of the idealism of youth, their passion is all-consuming-and can only bring about their ruin. With the men of Parma ready to fight and kill for Annabella's hand, religion, morality, and madness all collide as the brother and sister's terrible secret is revealed.

Being Shakespeare by Jonathan Bate; Co-Produced by Ambassador Theatre Group (Howard Panter (CEO and Creative Director; Adam Speers, Executive Producer; Evann White, Producer), Act Productions Limited (Roger Wingate, Chairman; J. Alan Davis, Managing Director), Robert Bartner and Norman Tulchin; Director/Design, Tom Cairns; Lighting, Bruno Poet; Music and Sound, Ben Ringham and Max Ringham; Company Manager, Maralyn Sarrington; Production Manager, Dominic Fraser; American Stage Manager, Peter Wolf; Associate Design: David Sadler (lighting), Avgoustos Psillas (sound); Design Assistant, Stephanie Williams; For Ambassador: Sarah Gimblett (Creative Assistant), Vicky Hawkins (General Manager), Zareen Walker (Production Coordinator), Claire Kehoe (Production Assistant), Neil Rutherford (Head of Casting), Peter Kavanagh (Business Affairs Director), Hannah Levin (Production Marketing); For Act Productions: Karen Marshall (Director of Administration), Anna Collins (Creative and Development Coordinator), Pauline Morrison (Finance), Luci Lyne (Administration and Production); **Cast:** Simon Callow

Harvey Theater; Opening Night: April 4, 2012; Closed April 14, 2012; 10 performances. U.S. premiere of a new solo performance play presented with one intermission. Synopsis: In a tour-de-force performance, veteran actor Simon Callow assumes the daunting challenge of illuminating the man behind the legend in this compelling one-man play. Channeling Macbeth and Henry V, musing over Shakespeare's childhood, Callow leaps from anecdote to soliloquy, using the famous Seven Ages of Man speech from *As You Like It* as his guide to consider how a glovemaker's son could have gone on to write the world.

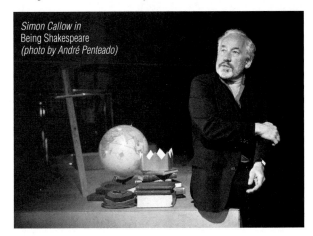

*Simon Callow in
Being Shakespeare
(photo by André Penteado)*

Three Sisters by Anton Chekhov; Presented by Maly Drama Theatre of St. Petersburg; Director Lev Dodin; Music, P. Grundstrem, Nicola Paganini, Iakov Prigogiy, Henry Sayers, Petr Chaikovsky, A. Shishkin; Design, Alexander Borovsky; Lighting, Damir Ismagilov; Director's Assistant, Valery Galendeev; Assistant Director, Elena Solomonova; Dancing Coach, Yuri Vasilkov; Military Consultant, Colonel Nikolay Morozov; Head of Music, Mikhail Alexandrov; Technical Director, Evgeny Nikoiforov; Set Supervisor/Stagehand, Sergey Ivanov; Stagehands, Vladimir Tretiakov, Pavel Toporov, Michail Andreev; Igor Tupikin, Pavel Efimov, Maxim Romashina; Costume Technology, Rafael Mamalimov; Wardrobe, Maria Fomina, Natalia Selezneva, Galina Ivanova; Props, Svetlana Tretiakova, Alla Onatieva; Sound Crew, Yuri Vavilov, Tatiana Shepeleva; Makeup, Alla Nudel; Musicians, Alexander Abuchovich, Ksenia Vassilieva; Stage Manager, Nathalia Sollogub; U.S. Representative, David Eden Productions; **Cast:** Alexander Bykovsky (Andrey Prozorov), Ekaterina Kleopina (Natasha, *his fiancée, later his wife*), Irinia Tychinina (Olga), Elena Kalinina (Masha), Ekaterina Tarasova (Irina), Sergey Vlasov (Feodor Kulygin, *high school teacher married to Masha*), Igor Chernevich (Alexander Vershinin, *lieutentant-colonel in charge of a battery*), Sergey Kuryshev (Nicolai Tuzenbach, *baron, lieutenant in the army*), Alexander Koshkarev (Vassili Soleny, *staff captain*), Alexander Zavyalov (Ivan Chebutikin, *army doctor*), Danila Shevchenko (Alexey Fedotik, *sub-lieutenant*), Stanislav Nikolsky (Vladimir Rode, *sub-lieutenant*), Sergey Kozyrev (Ferapont, *door-keeper at local council offices, an old man*), Natalia Akimova (Anfisa, *nurse*), Elena Solomonova (Maid), Anatoly Kolibyanov (Soldier)

Harvey Theater; Opening Night: April 18, 2012; Closed April 28, 2012; 10 performances. U.S. premiere of a new revival of a play presented in Russian with English titles in four acts with one intermission. Synopsis: Maly Drama Theatre returns with Chekhov's great, tragicomic story of women contending with disillusioned life in a small Russian town. *Three Sisters* follows the Prozorov sisters and their brother Andrey who are forced to leave Moscow for life in a provincial town. Following the death of their father, the family bravely confronts the tragic discrepancies between yearnings and reality, and a saga unfolds about the vital importance of staying true to oneself while struggling with the burden of everyday life.

The Caretaker by Harold Pinter; Presented by Theatre Royal Bath Productions (Danny Moar, Producer) and Liverpool Everyman and Playhouse; Director, Christopher Morahan; Sets, Eileen Diss; Costumes, Dany Everett; Lighting, Colin Grenfell; Sound, Tom Lishman; Fight Director, Bret Yount; Assistant Director, Will Wrightson; Production Manager, Sean Pritcard; Casting, Siobhan Bracke; General Manager/Tour Marketing/Press, CAPA; Company Manager, Terence Dale; For Theatre Royal Bath: Stephen Ross (Chairman), Gabby Akbar (Finance Director), Eugene Hibbert (General Manager), Nicky Palmer (Production Administrator), Simon Friend (Associate Producer); **Cast:** Alex Hassell (Mick), Alan Cox (Aston), Jonathan Pryce (Davies); Understudies: Gareth Williams (Davies), Liam Reilly (Mick, Aston)

Harvey Theater; Opening Night: May 3, 2012; Closed June 17, 2012; 45 performances. New York premiere of a new revival of a play presented in two acts. Synopsis: A pair of working-class brothers allows a homeless man to stay in their decrepit London flat, an act of compassion that sparks a cycle of cruelties, delusions, and shifting loyalties in a desperate struggle over territory. Pinter's first great success, *The Caretaker* powerfully displays his sharp intelligence, masterful and spare use of language, and uncompromising exploration of life's menace and comedy.

Jonathan Pryce, Alex Hassell, and Alan Cox in The Caretaker
(photo by Richard Termine)

Wear it like a crown Presented by Cirkus Cirkör; Director, Tilde Björfors; Music and Lyrics, Rebekka Karijord; Costumes, Anna Bonnevier; Lighting, Ulf Englund; Dramaturgy, Camilla Damkjaer; Choreography, Molly Saudek, Cilla Ross; Film and Projections, Johan Bååth; Hair and Makeup, Helena Andersson; Props/Décor, Tomas Helsing; Director's Assistant, Hanna Reinius; Circus Rigging, Ulf Poly Nylin, Anders Freudendahl; Constructor, Joel Jedström; Sound Technician, Alex Angleflod; Tour Leader, Camilla Hammarström; Props, Patric Martinsson; Costume Assistant, Rebecka Vestergren-Ahlin; Prop Assistant, Sara Brobert; Technical Assistants, Petter Ekström, Joakim Ekström; Photography, Mattias Edwall, Mats Bäcker; Managing Producer/Graphic Design, Anna Lindqvist; English Translation, Johanna Majzner; Technical Production, Stefan Karlström; International Relations, Lars Wassrin; **Cast:** Henrik Agger (Wizard of Wonder),Louise Bjurholm (Miraculous and Supernatural), David Eriksson (Marvel of the Century), Fouzia Rakez (Wild Weird and Wonderful), Jesper Nikolajeff (Nerves of Steel), Anna Lagerkvist (Mistress of Mayhem)

Howard Gilman Opera House; Opening Night: June 1, 2012; Closed June 3, 2012; 4 performances. U.S. premiere of a theatrical circus presented with one intermission. Synopsis: An arresting tableau of theatrics passes from shadows into light in *Wear it like a crown* from Sweden's Cirkus Cirkör. Consisting of six interlocking stories of solitary dreamers who yearn to connect with the world by way of juggling, knife-throwing, daredevil acrobatics, dance, and mime, Cirkus Cirkör rekindles the narrative possibilities of traditional vaudeville while leaping forward with a new circus aesthetic. Anchored by the lush folk-inflected chamber pop of Norwegian chanteuse Rebekka Karijord, *Wear it like a crown* explores a world in which magic and redemption are possible.

City Center *Encores!*

Nineteenth Season

Artistic Director, Jack Viertel; President & CEO of City Center, Arlene Shuler; Senior Vice President & Managing Director, Mark Litvin; *Encores!* General Management Associate, Patrick Bell; Scenic Consultant, John Lee Beatty; Music Coordinator, Seymour Red Press; Company Manager, Michael Zande; Casting; Jay Binder, Jack Bowdan; Press, Helene Davis; Encores Artistic Associates: John Lee Beatty, Jay Binder, Walter Bobbie, David Ives, Kathleen Marshall

Merrily We Roll Along Music and lyrics by Stephen Sondheim, book by George Furth; Based on the play by George S. Kaufman and Moss Hart; Originally directed on Broadway by Harold Prince; Director and Adaptation, James Lapine; Musical Staging, Dan Knechtges; Music Director, Rob Berman; Costume Consultant, Ann Hould-Ward; Lighting, Ken Billington; Sound, Dan Moses Schreier; Projections, Wendall K. Harrington; Hair and Wigs, Tom Watson; PSM, Peter Lawrence; Orchestrations, Jonathan Tunick; Stage Manager, Jim Woolley; ASM, Bryan Rountree; Associate Musical Director/Choral Preparation, Ben Whiteley; Associate Director, Wes Grantom; Assistant Director, Emmy Frank; Assistant Staging, DJ Gray; Dance Captain, Charlie Sutton; Fight Director, Rick Sordelet; Associate Projections, Daniel Brodie; Assistant Scenic Consultants, Kacie Hultgren, Charles Murdoch Lucas; Assistant Costumes, Abigail Hahn; Assistant Lighting, Anthony Pearson; Assistant Sound, Nicholas Pope; Projections Photography, Peter Cunningham; Assistant Musical Director, Josh Clayton; Cast recording: PS Classics 1208; **Cast:** Colin Donnell (Franklin Shepard), Celia Keenan-Bolger (Mary Flynn), Lin-Manuel Miranda (Charley Kringas), Adam Grupper (Joe Josephson), Betsy Wolfe (Beth Spencer), Elizabeth Stanley (Gussie Carnegie), Zachary Unger (Franklin Shepard Jr), Andrew Samonsky (Tyler), Ben Crawford (Terry), Mylinda Hull (Scotty), Rachel Coloff (Dory), Joshua Dela Cruz (Ru), Michael Winther (Jerome), Pearl Sun (KT), Patricia Noonan (Meg), Whit Baldwin (Bunker/Dancer), Jessica Vosk (TV Newswoman), Marja Harmon (Makeup Artist), Charlie Sutton (Photographer/Dancer), Sean McKnight (Dancer), Karl Warden (Dancer), Michael X. Martin (Mr. Spencer), Colleen Fitzpatrick (Mrs. Spencer), Bernard Dotson (Minister), Kenita R. Miller (Audition Girl), Leah Horowitz (Evelyn); Ensemble: Whit Baldwin, Rachel Coloff, Ben Crawford, Joshua Dela Cruz, Bernard Dotson, Colleen Fitzpatrick, Marja Harmon, Leah Horowitz, Mylinda Hull, Michael X. Martin, Sean McKnight, Kenita R. Miller, Patricia Noonan, Andrew Samonsky, Pearl Sun, Charlie Sutton, Zachary Unger, Jessica Vosk, Karl Warden, Michael Winther; Orchestra: Rob Berman (Conductor); Richard Brice, David Blinn, Shelly Holland-Moritz, David Creswell (Violas); Roger Shell, Deborah Assael (Celli); John Beal (Double Bass); Joshua Rosenblum (Piano); Danny Percefull (Synthesizer); James Hershman (Guitar); David Roth (Percussion); Steven Kenyon, Lino Gomez, Todd Groves, Richard Heckman, John Winder (Woodwinds); Russ Rizner (French Horn); Donald Downs, Glenn Drewes, Brian Pareschi (Trumpets); Bruce Bonvissuto (Trombone); Marcus Rojas (Tuba); Richard Rosensweig (Percussion)

Musical Numbers: Overture; Merrily We Roll Along; That Frank; Old Friends; Like It Was; Franklin Shepard, Inc.; Old Friends; Growing Up; Not a Day Goes By; Now You Know; Entr'acte; Musical Husbands; It's a Hit!; The Blob; Growing Up; Good Thing Going; Bobby and Jackie and Jack; Not a Day Goes By; Opening Doors; Our Time

New York City Center; Opening Night: February 8, 2012; Closed February 19, 2012; 15 performances. Setting: Bel Air, California and New York City; 1976-1957. Revival of a musical in staged concert format presented in nine scenes in two acts. The original production of *Merrily We Roll Along* opened at the Alvin (Neil Simon) Theatre on November 16, 1981, playing 52 previews and 16 performances (see *Theatre World* Vol. 38, page 16). Synopsis: Sondheim and Furth's legendary musical, which runs backwards in time from 1976 to 1955, examines the lives of three people whose friendship is tested by time, events, ambition and fate. It charts the rise of a songwriting team during the years of Sondheim's own young career, and features some of his most brilliant and bruising songs.

Lin-Manuel Miranda, Celia Keenan-Bolger, and Colin Donnell in Merrily We Roll Along *(photo by Joan Marcus)*

Pipe Dream Music by Richard Rodgers, book and lyrics by Oscar Hammerstein II; Based on the novels *Cannery Row* and *Sweet Thursday* by John Steinbeck; Director, Marc Bruni; Music Director, Rob Berman; Choreography, Kelli Barclay; Costume Consultant, Toni-Leslie James; Lighting, Ken Billington; Sound, Scott Lehrer; Concert Adaptation, David Ives; Orchestrations, Robert Russell Bennett; Dance Arrangements, John Morris; PSM, Peter Lawrence; Stage Manager, Jim Woolley; ASM, Bryan Rountree; Associate Musical Director, Mark Mitchell; Assistant Director, Ross Evans; Assistant Choreographer, Matthew Kilgore; Dance Assistant, Kristyn Pope; Associate Lighting, James Milkey; Associate Costumes, Nicky Toboloski; Assistant Scenic Consultant, Hannah Davis; Assistant Costumes, Josh Quinn; Wigs and Hair, Robert-Charles Vallance; Assistant Wigs and Hair, Sara Bender; Music Consultant, Bruce Pomahac; Assistant Music Director, Josh Clayton; Cast recording: Sh-K-Boom/Ghostlight Records 84463; **Cast:** Will Chase (Doc), Stephen Wallem (Hazel), Analisa Leaming (Millicent Henderson), Tom Wopat (Mac), Laura Osnes (Suzy), Leslie Uggams (Fauna), James Moye (Jim Blaikey), James Clow (Ray Busch), Steve Routman (George Herman), Richard Pruitt (Eddie), Philip Hernández (Joe), Linda Mugleston (Agnes), Lora Lee Gayer (Mabel), Monica L. Patton (Marjorie), Jessica Hershberg (Emma), Charlie Sutton (Dream Doc), Jay Lusteck (Sonny Boy), Martín Solá (Esteban), Jack Doyle (Dr. Dormody); *The Flophouse Gang, Bear Flag Café Girls, and People of Cannery Row*: Matthew Bauman, Jack Doyle, Lora Lee Gayer, James Harkness, Jessica Hershberg, Emily Hsu, Cara Kjellman, Denis Lambert, Analisa Leaming, Jay Lusteck, Linda Mugleston, Shannon M. O'Bryan, Monica L. Patton, Richard Pruitt, Vincent Rodriguez III, Kelly Sheehan, Martín Solá, Charlie Sutton, Nicholas Ward, Victor James Wisehart; Orchestra: Rob Berman (Conductor); Suzanne Ornstein [Concertmistress], Belinda Whitney, Mineko Yajima, Maura Giannini, Laura Seaton, Christoph Franzgrote, Lisa Matricardi, Robert Zubrycki, Kristina Musser (Violins); Shelly Holland-Moritz, David Creswell (Violas); Roger Shell, AnjaWood (Celli); John Beal (Double Bass); David Gursky (Piano); Susan Jolles (Harp); Steven Kenyon, Lino Gomez, David Gould, Melanie Feld, John Winder (Woodwinds); Russ Rizner, David Byrd-Marrow (French Horns); Tony Kadleck, Glenn Drewes, John Dent (Trumpets); Bruce Bonvissuto, Randy Andos (Trombones); Marcus Rojas (Tuba); Billy Miller (Percussion)

Musical Numbers: Overture; All Kinds of People; The Tide Pool; Everybody's Got a Home But Me; All Kinds of People (reprise); A Lopsided Bus; Bums' Opera; Fauna's Song; A Lopsided Bus (reprise); The Man I Used to Be; Sweet Thursday; Suzy Is a Good Thing; Sweet Thursday (reprise); All at Once You Love Her; Entr'acte; The Happiest House on the Block; The Party That We're Gonna Have Tomorrow Night; We Are a Gang of Witches; Will You Marry Me?; Thinkin'; All at Once You Love Her (reprise); How Long?; The Next Time It Happens; Finale: Sweet Thursday

New York City Center; Opening Night: March 28, 2012; Closed April 1, 2012; 7 performances. Setting: Cannery Row, Monterey County, California, in the 1950s. Revival of a musical in stage concert format presented in fifteen scenes in two acts. The original production of *Pipe Dream* opened at the Shubert Theatre on November 30, 1955, playing 246 performances (see *Theatre World* Vol. 12, page 70). Synopsis: Outcasts yearning for a better life populate the bordellos and flophouses of a 1950s California seaside town in Rodgers and Hammerstein's *Pipe Dream*. At the heart of the story is the unlikely romance between Doc, a marine biologist, and Suzy, a vagrant who has recently taken up residence at a local brothel. This rare gem has not seen on the American stage in more than two decades.

Leslie Uggams and the Company of Pipe Dream *(photo by Ari Mintz)*

Gentlemen Prefer Blondes Music by Jule Styne, lyrics by Leo Robin, book by Anita Loos and Joseph Fields; Adapted from the novel by Anita Loos; Director, John Rando; Music Director, Rob Berman; Choreography, Randy Skinner; Costume Consultant, David C. Woolard; Lighting, Peter Kaczorowski; Sound, Scott Lehrer; Concert Adaptation, David Ives; Original Orchestrations, Don Walker; PSM, Peter Lawrence; Stage Manager, Jim Woolley; ASM, Derric Nolte; Associate Music Director/Choral Preparation, Joel Fram; Assistant Director, Stephen Sposito; Associate Choreographer, Sara Brians; Dance Assistant, Jeremy Benton; Wigs, Mark Adam Rampmeyer; Associate Scenic Consultant, Kacie Hultgren; Assistant Scenic Consultant, Claire Bretschneider; Assistant Costumes, Joseph S. Blaha; Assistant Lighting, Keri Thibodeau; Assistant Music Director, Josh Clayton; Original Dance Arrangements, Trude Rittman; Original Vocal Arrangements, Hugh Martin; Cast recording: Masterworks Broadway 547099; **Cast:** Brennan Brown (Steward/Mr. Robert Lemanteur/Gus Esmond Sr.), Rachel York (Dorothy Shaw), Megan Hilty (Lorelei Lee), Clarke Thorell (Gus Esmond Jr.), Sandra Shipley (Lady Phyllis Beekman), Simon Jones (Sir Francis Beekman), Deborah Rush (Mrs. Ella Spofford), Aaron Lazar (Henry Spofford), Stephen R. Buntrock (Josephus Gage), Luke Hawkins (Frank of the Olympic Team), Eric Bourne (George of the Olympic Team), Megan Sikora (Gloria Stark), Steven Boyer (Pierre the Chief Steward/ Louis Lemanteur), Anna Aimee White (First Show Girl), Kristyn Pope (Second Show Girl/Fifi), Shannon M. O'Bryan (Zizi), Arlo Hill (Maitre d'), Phillip Attmore & Jared Grimes (Attmore & Grimes); *Ship Passengers, Olympians, Club Patrons and People of Paris:* Callan Bergmann, Charissa Bertels, Sam Bolen, Eric Bourne, Kyle Brown, Robin Campbell, Brandon Davidson, Christine DiGiallonardo, Luke Hawkins, Arlo Hill, Michael Marcotte, Nick McGough, Shannon M. O'Bryan, Lindsay O'Neil, Kristyn Pope, Lindsay Roberts, Heath Saunders, Kelly Sheehan, Jessica Vosk, Anna Aimee White, Matt Zimmerman; Orchestra: Suzanne Ornstein, [Concertmistress], Belinda Whitney, Mineko Yajima, Maura Giannini, Christoph Franzgrote, Kristina Musser, Lisa Matricardi, Eric DeGioia, Robert Zubrycki (Violins); David Blinn, Crystal Garner (Violas); Roger Shell, Deborah Assael (Celli); John Beal (Double Bass); Jay Berliner (Guitar); Steven Kenyon, David

Young, Ronald Jannelli, David Weiss, John Winder (Woodwinds); Russ Rizner (French Horn); Donald Downs, Glenn Drewes, Ken Rampton (Trumpets); Bruce Bonvissuto, Randy Andos (Trombones); Nicholas Archer (Piano); Billy Miller (Percussion)

Musical Numbers: Overture; It's High Time; Bye, Bye Baby; I'm Just a Little Girl from Little Rock; I Love What I'm Doing; Just a Kiss Apart; The Practice Scherzo; It's Delightful Down in Chile; Sunshine; In the Champ de Mars; I'm A' Tingle, I'm A' Glow; You Say You Care; Finaletto; Entr'acte; Mamie Is Mimi; Coquette; Diamonds Are a Girl's Best Friend; Gentlemen Prefer Blondes; Homesick; Keeping Cool with Coolidge; Button Up with Esmond; Finale

New York City Center; Opening Night: May 9, 2011; Closed March 12, 2011; 7 performances. Setting: New York, Paris, and at sea. 1924. Revival of a musical in stage concert format presented in nine scenes in two acts. The original production of *Gentlemen Prefer Blondes* opened at the Ziegfeld Theatre on December 8, 1949, playing 740 performances (see *Theatre World* Vol. 4, page 47). Synopsis: *Gentlemen Prefer Blondes* follows the madcap adventures of the original "dumb blonde," Lorelei Lee, as she sets sail for Europe with her best friend Dorothy Shaw. The gold-digging Lorelei is the only girl in the world who can stand on a stage with a spotlight in her eye and still see a diamond inside a man's pocket. *Gentlemen Prefer Blondes* made a star of Carol Channing on Broadway and later cemented Marilyn Monroe's status as an American film icon and sex symbol in the 1953 screen version.

Megan Hilty in Gentlemen Prefer Blondes *(photo by Joan Marcus)*

Classic Stage Company

Forty-fifth Season

Artistic Director, Brian Kulick; Executive Director, Greg Reiner; General Manager, Jeff Griffin; Associate Artistic Director, Tony Speciale; Development, Audrey Carmeli; Company Manager, John C. Hume; Marketing and Communications, Meghan Zaneski; Audience Services, Gina Cimmelli; Education Manager, Kathleen Dorman; Business Manager, Jen Soloway; Casting, James Calleri; Production Supervisor, James E. Cleveland/Production Core; Production Manager, Adrian White; Art Direction and Design, Michael Yuen; Artistic Associates, Craig Baldwin, Rachel Chavkin, Jimmy Maize; Press, The Publicity Office, Marc Thibodeau

The Cherry Orchard by Anton Chekhov, translated by John Christopher Jones; Director, Andrei Belgrader; Choreography, Orlando Pabotoy; Sets, Santo Loquasto; Costume, Marco Piemontese; Lighting, James F. Ingalls; Original Music and Sound, Christian Frederickson and Ryan Rumery; Hair, Paul Huntley; PSM, Joanne E. McInerney; Assistant Production Manager, Josh Morgan; Props Master, Starlet Jacobs; Prop Assistants, Sarah Bird, Jeffery Petersen; Assistant Directors, Alex Correra and Lily Whitsitt; Associate Set Design, Antje Ellerman; Assistant Design: Michelle Ridley, Luana Busetti (costumes), Steve Maturno (lighting), M. Florian Staab (sound); Electricians, The Lighting Syndicate, Desi Fischer; Technical Director, Jack Blacketer; Audio Supervisor, Nicholas Gorczynski; Board Operator, Katie Hong; Animal Wrangler, John Paul Venuti; **Cast:** John Turturro (Lopakhin), Elisabeth Waterston (Dunyasha), Michael Urie (Epikhodov), Katherine Waterston (Anya), Dianne Wiest (Ranevskaya), Juliet Rylance (Varya), Daniel Davis (Gaev), Roberta Maxwell (Charlotta), Ken Cheeseman (Pischik), Slate Homgren (Yasha), Alvin Epstein (Fiers), Josh Hamilton (Trofimov), Michael Wieser (Station-Master/Servant), Ben Diskant (Post Office Clerk/Servant), Bentley (Charlotta's Dog)

East 13th Street Theatre; First Preview: November 16, 2011; Opening Night: December 4, 2012; Closed January 8, 2012; 17 previews, 34 performances. Revival of a classic play presented in four acts with one intermission. Synopsis: First presented in 1904 at the Moscow Art Theatre, *The Cherry Orchard* was Chekhov's final play, and this new production completes CSC's acclaimed Chekhov Cycle, which included *The Seagull*, *Uncle Vanya*, and *Three Sisters*, which were presented over the last five seasons. Madame Ranevskaya and her family are blind to the winds of change that are about to overtake them and their cherished cherry orchard, as their estate faces auction to pay the mortgage.

John Turturro, Alvin Epstein, Daniel Davis, and Dianne Wiest in The Cherry Orchard *(photo by Carol Rosegg)*

Galileo by Bertolt Brecht, translated by Charles Laughton; Director, Brian Kulick; Choreography, Tony Speciale; Sets, Adrianne Lobel; Costumes, Oana Botez-Ban; Lighting, Justin Townsend; Original Music and Sound, Christian Frederickson and Ryan Rumery; Projections, Jan Hartley; PSM, Joanne E. McInerney; ASM, Kelly McGrath; Assistant Production Manager, Melissa Shippers; Technical Director,

Kevin Mullins; SDC Observer, Ryder Thompson; Associate Sound Design, M. Florian Staab; Assistant Design: AraBella Fischer (costumes), Christopher Thielking (lighting); Electricians, The Lighting Syndicate, Rebecca McCoy; Scenic Artist, Starlet Jacobs; Props Supervisor, Sven Nelson; Board Operator, Katie Hong; Deck Crew, Romo Hallahan, James Monahan; **Cast:** Andy Phelan (Andrea/The Prince), F. Murray Abraham (Galileo), Amanda Quaid (Virginia), Nick Westrate (Ludovico), Steven Rattazzi (Priuli/The Ballad Singer/Boy), Steven Skybell (Sagredo/Cardinal Bellarmin), Jon Devries (The Old Cardinal/Federzoni), Robert Dorfman (Cardinal Barberini), Aaron Himelstein (The Little Monk); Understudy: Mark Junek

East 13th Street Theatre; First Preview: January 12, 2011; Opening Night: February 3, 2011; Closed March 6, 2011; 23 previews, 26 performances. Revival of a classic play presented in two acts. Synopsis: *Galileo* explores the question of a scientist's social and ethical responsibility, as the brilliant scientist Galileo must choose between his life and his life's work when confronted with the Inquisition.

F. Murray Abraham and Steven Skybell in Galileo *(photo by Joan Marcus)*

A Midsummer Night's Dream by William Shakespeare; Director, Tony Speciale; Choreography, George De La Peña; Set, Mark Wendland; Costumes, Andrea Lauer; Lighting, Tyler Micoleau; Original Music, Christian Frederickson and Ryan Rumery; Sound, M. Florian Staab; Fight Choreography, Carrie Brewer; PSM, Chandra LaViolette; ASM, Megan Griffith; Associate Production Manager, Josh Morgan; Technical Director, Nick Warren Grey; Assistant Technical Director,

Casey Kruger; Assistant Director, Andrew Zox; Associate Costume Design/Makeup Design, Amy Wright; Assistant Design: Rachel Nemec, Jon Collins (set), Aaron Crosby (costumes), Marika Kent (lighting); Wigs, Charles LaPointe; Wardrobe Supervisor, AraBella Fischer; Assistant Fight Choreography, Judi Lewis Ockler; Projections, Brett J. Banakis; Fight and Dance Captain, Chad Lindsey; Electricians, The Lighting Syndicate, Desi Fischer; Audio Supervisor, Nicholas Gorczynski; Board Operator, Megan Caplan; Deck Crew, Courtney Smith; Wardrobe, Genevieve White; **Cast:** Anthony Heald (Theseus/Oberon), Bebe Neuwirth (Hippolyta/Titania), Christina Ricci (Hermia), Taylor Mac (Egeus/Puck), Nick Gehlfuss (Lysander), Jordan Dean (Demetrius), Halley Wegryn Gross (Helena), Rob Yang (Peter Quince/Peaseblossom), Steven Skybell (Nick Bottom), David Greenspan (Francis Flute/Cobweb), Erin Hill (Robin Starveling/First Fairy), Chad Lindsey (Tom Snout/Mustardseed), James Patrick Nelson (Snug/Moth); Understudies: Mark Junek, Morgan Rosse

East 13th Street Theatre; First Preview: April 4, 2012; Opening Night: April 29, 2012; Closed May 20, 2012; 27 previews, 25 performances. Revival of a classic play presented in two acts. Synopsis: "Jack shall have Jill; Naught shall go ill" promises Puck, the hobgoblin of the night, and how can things be anything but grand when Tony Award-winner Bebe Neuwirth plays Titania, the queen of the fairies, in Shakespeare's immortal comic romp.

Bebe Neuwirth (center) and the Company in A Midsummer Night's Dream *(photo by Joan Marcus)*

ADDITIONAL EVENTS

The Young Company: Much Ado About Nothing by William Shakespeare; Presented in association with the Graduate Acting Program of Columbia School for the Arts; Director/Sound, Jimmy Maize; Set, Amanda Rehbein; Lighting, Christopher Thielking; Costumes, Oana Botez-Ban; Music Direction/Arrangements, Jonathan Camuzeaux; Dramaturgy, Lezlie Cross; Stage Manager, Michelle Cote; Cast: Itohan Aghayere, Daniel Bielisnki, Sarah Eismann, Melissa Graham, Kate Flanagan, Danielle Faitelson, Matthew Michael Hurley, Eddie Ray Jackson, Dave Klasko, Daniel Levitt, Adam Lubitz, Blaze Mancillas, Natalia Miranda Guzman, Jensen Olaya; Musicians: Max Johnson, Max Robinson, Michael Rosengarten, Willis Wilson; March 5-16, 2012; 11 performances.

Open Rehearsal Series: Monday Night *Antony & Cleopatra* by Wiliam Shakespeare; April 16: with Stephanie Roth Haberle and Sam Tsoutsouvas, directed by Brian Kulick; April 23: with Laila Robins, directed by Craig Baldwin; April 30: with Kim Cattrall, directed by Brian Kulick

Irish Repertory Theatre

Twenty-fourth Season

Artistic Director, Charlotte Moore; Producing Director, Ciarán O'Reilly; Business Manager, Dave Friedman; Development Director, Maureen Cavanaugh/Gretchen H. Page; Membership Manager, Fiona Whelan; Marketing Manager, Melissa L. Pelkey; Box Office, Jeffrey Wingfield; Audience Services, Jared Dawson; Literary Manager, Kara Manning; Casting, Deborah Brown; Production Coordinator, Cynthia Jankowski; Master Carpenter, Donal O'Reilly; Master Electrician, Tom Dyer; Set Construction, Ken Larson; Wardrobe Supervisor, Deirdre Higgins; Press, Shirley Herz and Bob Lasko

NOCTÚ Presented by Ériu Dance Company; Conceived and directed by Breandán de Gallaí; Presented as part of Imagine Ireland; Lighting, Michael O'Connor; Costumes, Nikki Connor; Original Music, Joe Csibi; Additional Music, Mary Coughlan, Godfrapp, Beoga, Kate Bush, Seán O'Brien, Juan D'Areinzo, Björk, West Ocean Quartet, Cake, Imelda May, Leonard Cohen, Madeleine, Peyroux, Igor Stravinsky, Talking Heads; Script Consultant, Seán de Gallaí; PSM, Caesar Arroyo; **Cast:** Jack Anderson, Peta Anderson, Ellen Bonner, Orlagh Carty, Joseph Comerford, Niamh Darcy, Gyula Glaser, James Greenan, Kyla Marsh, Megan McElhatton, Ashlene McFadden, Kienan Melino, Nick O'Connell, Katrina O'Donnell, Aislinn Ryan, Callum Spencer

Ériu Dance Company in NOCTÚ *(photos by Carol Rosegg unless noted)*

Program/Music: Warmup – "Miss Brown to You"; Stretch/Get Into Costume – "Deer Stop"; Senior Ceilí Invention – "Chu Chullain's Despair"; Aisling's Dream – "Night of the Swallow"; Shadow Dolls – music by Joe Scibi; Hornpipe – "Hornpipes"; Tango – "La Cumparsita"; Violently Happy – music by Björk; Anxiety – "Some Vague Utopia, 3rd Mvt.; Olsín's Dance – "I Will Survive"; Patrick's Dance – "Dance Me to the End of Love"; The Triumvirate – "Getting Some Fun Out of Life"; Firebird – "The Firebird Suite: Infernal Dance"; UnderWorld – music by Joe Csibi; Reprise 1 – "UnderWorld"; Reprise 2 – "Burning Down the House" and "Night of the Swallow"

Francis J. Greenberger Mainstage; First Preview: September 6, 2011; Opening Night: September 12, 2011; Closed October 2, 2011; 7 previews, 25 performances. U.S. premiere of a theatrical dance piece presented without intermission. Synopsis: *NO TÚ*, a new departure for the Irish dance show genre, pushes the boundaries of the Irish dance aesthetic and explores new expression possibilities, allowing the audience to get under the skin of those who perform and get a glimpse of what matters to them.

Dancing at Lughnasa by Brian Friel; Director, Charlotte Moore; Choreography, Barry McNabb; Set, Antje Ellermann; Costumes, Linda Fisher and Jessica Barrios; Lighting, Richard Pilbrow and Michael Gottlieb; Sound, M. Florian Staab; Music, Ryan Rumery and Christian Frederickson; Hair and Wigs, Robert-Charles

Vallance; Dialects, Stepen Gabis; Props, Deidre Brennan; PSM, Pamela Brusoski; ASM, Rebecca C. Monroe; Light Board Programmer, Megan Peti; Scenic Painters, Dave Bhulai, Jonny Lombardo; Seamstress, Fran Bradfield; Production Assistant, Jason Brubaker; **Cast:** Michael McMonagle (Michael), Annabel Hägg (Chris), Jo Kinsella (Maggie), Rachel Pickup (Agnes), Aedín Moloney (Rose), Orlagh Cassidy (Kate), John Tyrrell (Jack), Kevin Collins (Gerry)

Francis J. Greenberger Mainstage; First Preview: October 20, 2011; Opening Night: October 30, 2011; Closed January 29, 2012; 11 previews, 98 performances. Setting: The Mundy family home, outside the village of Ballybeg, County Donegal, Ireland; August-September, 1936. Twentieth anniversary revival of a play presented in two acts. World premiere presented at the Abbey Theatre in Dublin in 1990; transferred to London's National Theatre in 1991. The Broadway production played the Plymouth Theatre October 24, 1991–October 25, 1992, playing 421 performances (see *Theatre World* Vol. 48, page 10). Synopsis: *Dancing at Lughnasa*, a memory play is told through the eyes of Michael, who recounts the late summer days as a seven-year old boy at his Aunt's cottage. Set during Lughnasadh, the Celtic harvest festival, love briefly seems possible for three of the Mundy sisters, and the family welcomes home the frail elder brother, returning from life as a missionary in Africa. As the summer ends, the family foresees the sadness and economic privations under which they will suffer as all hopes fade.

Orlagh Cassidy, Aedin Moloney, Jo Kinsella, Michael Countryman, Rachel Pickup, and Annabel Hagg in Dancing at Lughnasa

A Child's Christmas in Wales in Concert by Dylan Thomas, arranged and directed by Charlotte Moore; Music Director, John Bell; Costumes; David Toser; Lighting, Michael O'Connor; PSM, April Ann Kline; ASM, Jason Brubaker; **Cast:** Edwin Cahill, Howard McGillin, Ashley Robinson, Danielle Erin Rhodes, Beverly Ward; Musician: John Bell (Piano)

Musical Numbers: Deck the Halls; Take My Hand, Tomorrow's Christmas; God Rest Ye Merry, Gentlemen; Ring Out the Bells!; Carol Medley: I Saw Three Ships/Bring a Torch, Jeanette Isabella/Joseph Dearest, Joseph Mild/The Holly and the Ivy; All Through the Night; Open Your Eyes; I Don't Want a Lot For Christmas; And the Soft Snow Falls; The Greatest Gift of All; Miss Fogarty's Christmas Cake; Little Jack Horner; A-Soaling; Aunts and Uncles Come to Dinner; Five Verses of "A Winter's Tale" by Dylan Thomas; Walking in the Snow; Dylan Thomas is a Fool; Hark the Herald Angels Sing; Silent Night; Calon Lân; Take My Hand, Tomorrow's Christmas (reprise); Medley of Favorites: White Christmas/I'll Be Home for Christmas/Baby It's Cold Outside/Have Yourself a Merry Little Christmas/It's the Most Wonderful Time of the Year

W. Scott McLucas Studio; First Preview: December 7, 2011; Opening Night: December 11, 2010; Closed December 31, 2011; 6 previews, 21 performances. Revival of a theatrical concert with text and music presented without intermission. Synopsis: A holiday favorite, the iconic piece features traditional and contemporary Christmas music interwoven within the classic story of the legendary snowy

Christmas Day in Wales. The Irish Rep first produced *A Child's Christmas in Wales* in December 2000, and revived the production in 2007 and 2008. This version, which contained revised musical material, was also presented last season.

Danielle Erin Rhodes, Edwin Cahill, Howard McGillin (seated), Beverly Ward, and Ashley Robinson in A Child's Christmas in Wales in Concert

Beyond the Horizon by Eugene O'Neill; Director, Ciarán O'Reilly; Set, Hugh Landwehr; Costumes, Linda Fisher and Jessica Barrios; Lighting, Brian Nason; Original Music, Ryan Rumery; Sound, M. Florian Staab; Hair and Wigs, Robert-Charles Vallance; Props, Deirdre Brennan; Dialect Coach, Stephen Gabis; PSM, April Ann Kline; ASM, Rebecca C. Monroe; Assistant Lighting, Luamar Cervejeira; Scene Drop, Alice Carroll; Scenic Painters, Dave Bhulai, Jonny Lombardo; Light Board Programmer, Colin J. Scott; Hair Assistant, Sara Bender; Prop Assistant, Sven Henry Nelson; **Cast:** Lucas Hall (Robert Mayo), Rod Brogan (Andrew Mayo), Wrenn Schmidt (Ruth Atkins), John Thomas Waite (Captain Dick Scott), Johanna Leister (Kate Mayo), David Sitler (James Mayo), Patricia Conolly (Mrs. Atkins), Aimée Laurence (Mary), Jonathan Judge-Russo (Ben), John Thomas Waite (Dr. Fawcett)

Wrenn Schmidt and Lucas Hall in Beyond the Horizon

Francis J. Greenberger Mainstage; First Preview: February 15, 2012; Opening Night: February 26, 2012; Closed April 15, 2012; 12 previews, 50 performances. Setting: The Mayo household and farm in rural Eastern Massachusetts; 1907-1916. Revival of a classic play presented in six scenes in two acts. Originally produced on Broadway at the Morosco Theatre February 2, 1920, playing 111 performances. Synopsis: O'Neill's first full-length riveting drama pits brother against brother for the heart of one woman. Robert Mayo, a romantic young poet is about to embark on the voyage of his dreams. His brother Andrew is a contented farmer with a passion for the land. On the eve of Robert's departure, when their neighbor, the beautiful Ruth declares her love for one over the other, the brothers trade lives with heart-breaking consequences. The farmer goes to sea and the poet tends the land.

Give Me Your Hand by Paul Durcan, based on his poetry; Conceived by Dermot Crowley; Director, Richard Twyman; Original Music and Technical Direction, Jamie Beamish; Video Filming and Editing, Daniel Grixti; PSM, Pamela Brusoski; **Cast:** Dermot Crowley, Dearbhla Malloy

W. Scott McLucas Studio; First Preview: March 7, 2012; Opening Night: March 11, 2012; Closed April 1, 2012; 6 previews, 22 performances. New York premiere of a new theatrical piece presented without intermission. Synopsis: Paul Durcan has taken some of the most famous paintings in the world, and interpreted them with his own unique voice. Two of Ireland's most eminent actors take an imaginative stroll through the National Gallery and re-discover everyone from Van Gogh and Van Eyck, to Rubens and Gainsborough, through the unique prism of the author's imagination.

Dermot Crowey and Dearbhla Molloy in Give Me Your Hand

Man and Superman by George Bernard Shaw; Co-presented by Gingold Theatrical Group (David Staller, Founder and Artistic Director); Director/Adaptation, David Staller; Sets, James Noone; Costumes, Theresa Squire; Lighting, Kirk Bookman; Sound, M. Florian Staab; Hair and Wigs, Robert-Charles Vallance; Props, Sven Henry Nelson; PSM, Elis C. Arroyo; ASM, Arthur Atkinson; Assistant Lighting, Greg Solomon; Assistant to Mr. Noone, Adrienne Carlile; Assistant to Mr. Vallance, Sara Bender; Light Board Programmer, Colin J. Scott; Costume Assistant, Fay Koplovitz; Scenic Painters, Dave Bhulai, Jonny Lombardo; **Cast:** Janie Brookshire (Ann), Max Gordon Moore (Jack), Will Bradley (Octavius), Jonathan Hammond (Mendoza), Brian Sgambati (Straker), Margaret Loesser Robinson (Violet), Laurie Kennedy (Mrs. Whitefield), Paul O'Brien (Malone), Zachary Spicer (Hector), Brian Murray (Ramsden)

Francis J. Greenberger Mainstage; First Preview: April 26, 2012; Opening Night: May 6, 2012; Closed July 1, 2012; 11 previews, 57 performances. Setting: 1905; England, Spain, Hell, and Granada. Revival of a classic play presented in six scenes in two acts. Originally presented at London's Royal Court Theatre May 23, 1905. The New York premiere opened at Hudson Theatre in September 5, 1905, playing 192 performances. Synopsis: *Man and Superman* involves Jack Tanner, determined not to marry his ward, Ann Whitefield, who is equally determined to land him. Ann chases Jack from London, across the channel, into the mountains of Spain, and even to Hell and back in the famous dream scene *Don Juan in Hell*.

New Girl in Town Music and lyrics by Bob Merrill, book by George Abbott; Based on Eugene O'Neill's *Annie Christie*; Director, Charlotte Moore; Music Direction, John Bell; Choreography, Barry McNabb; Sets, James Morgan; Costumes, China Lee; Lighting, Mary Jo Dondlinger; Sound, Zachary Williamson; Hair and Wigs, Robert-Charles Vallance; Props, Rich Murray; Dialect Coach,

Will Bradley, Jonathan Hammond, Max Gordon Moore, Brian Murray, Paul O'Brien, Margaret Loesser Robinson,and Janie Brookshire in Man and Superman *(photo by James Higgins)*

Stephen Gabis; Video, Richard DiBella; PSM, Christine Lemme; ASM, Arthur Atkinson; Orchestrations, Josh Clayton; Light Board Programmer, Megan L. Peti; Assistant Costumes, Sarah Bertolazzi; Hair Assistant, Sara Bender; Scenic Drop Painter, Alice Carroll; Scenic Painters, Dave Bhulai, Jonny Lombardo; Production Assistant, Jason Brubaker; **Cast:** Cliff Bemis (Chris Christopherson), Danielle Ferland (Marthy), Margarett Loesser Robinson (Anna), Patrick Cummings (Matt), Dewey Caddell (Larry/Ensemble), Abby Church (Pansy/Ensemble), Matt Gibson (Patrick/Ensemble), Kimberly Dawn Neumann (Pearl/Ensemble), Alex Puette (Oscar/Ensemble), Amber Stone (Lily/Ensemble), Stephen Zinnato (Charlie Clancy/Ensemble); Musicians: John Bell (Conductor/Keyboard), Jeremy Clayton (Reeds), Don Peretz (Percussion), Nick Russo (Guitar/Banjo)

Musical Numbers: Roll Yer Socks Up; Anna Lilla; On the Farm; Flings; It's Good to Be Alive; Look at 'Er; It's Good to Be Alive (reprise); Yer My Friend, Aintcha?; Did You Close Your Eyes?; At the Check Apron Bal; Ven I Valse; Sunshine Girl; Sunshine Girl (reprise); If That Was Love; Did You Close Your Eyes? (reprise); Look at 'Er (reprise); Chess and Checkers

Francis J. Greenberger Mainstage; First Preview: July 18, 2012; Opening Night: July 26, 2012; Closed September 14, 2012; 9 previews, 53 performances. Setting: 1926; The waterfront, New York City. Revival of a musical presented in eleven scenes in two acts. Originally produced on Broadway at the 46th Street (Richard Rodgers) Theatre May 14, 1957–May 24, 1958, playing 431 performances (see *Theatre World* Vol. 13, page 118). Synopsis: Anna, a woman with a checkered past, joins her father, Old Chris Christopherson, Captain of a coal barge shuttling between Boston and New York. On a foggy July 4th night, a sailor is pulled from the dark waters of the Atlantic. As the fog clears, Anna's and Matt Burke's eyes meet and their lives are changed forever.

The Ensemble in New Girl in Town

Keen Company

Twelfth Season

Artistic Director, Carl Forsman; Executive Director, Damon Chua; Production Manager, Josh Bradford; Resident Director, Jonathan Silverstein; Development Director, Joanna Sheehan; Education Director (Keen Teens), Blake Lawrence; Marketing Director, Abigail Rose Solomon; Graphic Design, Chris Jamros, J Media; Social Media Coordinator, Jenny Donheiser; Crew, Geoff Barnes, David Bogosian, Alan Brinks, Lee C. Bush, Jessica Halem, Demetrios, Jacks, Timothy Parrish, Dave Polato, Kia Rogers, Laura Schoch; Press, David Gersten and Associates

Lemon Sky by Lanford Wilson; Director, Jonathan Silverstein; Sets, Bill Clarke; Costumes, Jennifer Paar; Lighting, Josh Bradford; Sound, Obediah Eaves; Technical Director, Marshall Miller; Stage Manager, Jeff Meyers; ASM, Kristina Teschner; Fight Choreographer, Paul Molnar; Dialect Coach, Charley Layton; Assistant Director, Caleb Eigsti; Casting, Calleri Casting; Props Design, Ricola Wille; Associate Lighting, Peter Hoerburger; Assistant Costumes, Amanda Jenks; Master Electrician, Jeffrey Toombs; Sound Engineer, Colin Whitely; **Cast:** Keith Nobbs (Alan), Kellie Overbey (Ronnie), Kevin Kilner (Douglas), Amie Tedesco (Penny), Alyssa May Gould (Carol), Logan Riley Bruner (Jerry), Zachary Mackiewicz (Jack)

Keith Nobbs and Kevin Kilner in Lemon Sky (photo by Richard Termine)

Clurman Theatre on Theatre Row; First Preview: September 13, 2011; Opening Night: September 27, 2011; Closed October 22, 2011; 14 previews, 28 performances. Setting: One of the thousands of homes in the suburbs of San Diego, California; this one is in El Cajon, California, a city surrounded by low mountains; 1970 and the late 1950s. Revival of a play presented in two acts. Originally presented at Studio Arena Theatre (Buffalo, New York) March 26, 1970, featuring Christopher Walken, Charles Durning, and Kathy Bates. The production transferred Off-Broadway to the Playhouse Theatre May 17-31, 1970, playing 8 previews and 16 performances (see *Theatre World* Vol. 26, pages 136 and 214). Synopsis: In *Lemon Sky*, Wilson recounts a personal story in autobiographical detail: his journey, at age 17, to California to live with his estranged father's second family.

Painting Churches by Tina Howe; Director, Carl Forsman; Set, Beowulf Boritt; Costumes, Jennifer Paar; Lighting, Josh Bradford; Original Music and Sound, Ryan Rumery; Props, Ricola Wille; Stage Manager, Jeff Meyers; Props, Ricola Wille; Technical Director, Marshall Miller; ASM, Diane Healy; Casting, Calleri Casting; Assistant Director, Dorit Katzenelenbogen; Fight Choreography, Paul Molnar; Draper, Marie Stair; Hair Design, Antonio Soddu; Assistant Design: Jared Rutherford (set), Amanda Jenks (costumes), Daisy Long (lighting), Florian Staab (sound); Assistant Production Manager, Michael Lapinsky; House Manager, Caleb Eigsti; Wardrobe Supervisor, Jamie Bertoluzzi; Master Electrician, Jeffrey Toombs;

Crew, Cressa Amundsen, Jen Brinker, Lee C. Bush, Kia Rogers, Samuel Payne, Demetrius Jacks, Geoffrey Barnes, Jesse Wilson, Joe Truman, Mary Stazewski, Chris Haag, Kevin Strano, Adam Mark Bishop, Scott Basten, Laura Schoch; **Cast:** Kathleen Chalfant (Fanny), John Cunningham (Gardner), Kate Turnbull (Margaret)

Clurman Theatre on Theatre Row; First Preview: February 14, 2012; Opening Night: March 6, 2012; Closed April 7, 2012; 21 previews, 35 performances. Revival of a play presented in five scenes in two acts. Setting: The living room of the Churches' townhouse in the Beacon Hill area of Boston, a few years ago. World premiere produced by Second Stage at the South Street Theatre, featuring Marian Seldes and Frances Conroy, January 25–February 27, 1983, playing 12 previews and 18 performances. The production transferred to the Lamb's Theatre, featuring Seldes, George Martin, and Elizabeth McGovern, November 22, 1983–May 20, 1984, playing 9 previews and 206 performances (see *Theatre World* Vol. 39, page 119; Vol. 40, page 68). Synopsis: *Painting Churches* concerns an elderly couple, Fanny and Gardner Church, who are packing and about to move to a beach home on Cape Cod. Their daughter, Margaret, an artist who lives in New York, has arrived to help them pack and paint their portrait. Over the course of several days, Margaret sees her role in the parent-child relationship changing.

Kathleen Chalfant and John Cunningham in Painting Churches (photo by Carol Rosegg)

KEEN TEENS

World premiere productions of new plays performed by high school students; Included: *Wayward Loafers of Gooseberry High* by Michael Mitnick, directed by Christopher Mirto; *Letters to Kurt* by Janine Nabers, directed by Cat Miller; *Drama Geeks vs. Zombie Cheerleaders* by Kathryn Walat, directed by Portia Krieger; Lion Theatre at Theatre Row; May 18-20, 2012

Kate Turnbull and Kathleen Chalfant in Painting Churches (photo by Carol Rosegg)

Labyrinth Theater Company

Twentieth Season

Artistic Directors, Stephen Adly Guirgis, Mimi O'Donnell, and Yul Vázquez; Managing Director, Danny Feldman; General Manager, Robert A. Sherrill; Development, Yasmine Falk; Communications Manager, Willie Orbison; Education, Monique Carboni; Production Manager, Rosie Cruz; Founding Artistic Directors, John Ortiz, Philip Seymour Hoffman; Press, O+M Company, Rick Miramontez, Elizabeth Wagner, Chelsea Nachman

The Atmosphere of Memory by David Bar Katz; Original Songs by Adam Schlesinger (music) and David Bar Katz (lyrics); Director, Pam MacKinnon; Set, David Gallo; Costumes, Emily Rebholz; Lighting, Dans Maree Sheehan; Sound, Brendan Connelly; Stage Manager, C.A. Clark; Technical Director, Richard A. Montgomery II; ASM, Travis Acreman; Additional Casting, Judy Bowman; Props Master, Samantha Shoffner; Associate Set Design, Sarah Zeitler; Assistant Costume Design, Sarah Bertolozzi; Wardrobe Supervisor, Ryan Dodson; Light and Sound Operator, Jason Bielsker; Deck Crew, Matthew White; Production Assistants, Mia Mountain, Amy Russell; **Cast:** Ellen Burstyn (Claire), Max Casella (Jon), Kelley Curran (Helen), David Deblinger (Tom/Steve), John Glover (Murray), Charles Goforth (Shrink/Mike), Paul Kandel (Jack), Kelley Rae O'Donnell (Interviewer), Melissa Ross (Esther), Sidney Williams (Narrator/Rex)

Bank Street Theater; First Preview: October 15, 2011; Opening Night: October 30, 2011; Closed November 20, 2011; 15 previews, 22 performances. World premiere of a new play presented in two acts. Synopsis: Playwright Jon Stone has found the courage to write his masterpiece: a play about his upbringing. But when his actual mother is cast to play his mother on stage and his estranged father remembers the family history differently, Jon is forced to rewrite, not only his play, but his past as well. Playwright Katz imagines a world where the boundaries between life and art, fact and fiction, are as blurry as *The Atmosphere of Memory* itself.

John Glover and Ellen Burstyn in The Atmosphere of Memory
(photo by Monique Carboni)

Ninth and Joanie by Brett C. Leonard; Director, Mark Wing-Davey; Sets, David Meyer; Costumes, Mimi O'Donnell; Lighting, Bradley King; Sound, David Bullard; Stage Manager, Rhonda Picou; Technical Director, Paul Bradley; Special Effects, Jeremy Chernick; Associate Director, Scott Illingworth; Assistant Technical Director, Jason Goedken; ASM, Andrea Wales; Fight Choreographer, David Anzuelo; Child Casting, Lois Drabkin; Master Electrician, Dan Mullins; Props Master, Morgan Fox; Associate Set Design, Carolyn Mraz; Assistant Design: Alexis Forte (costumes), Gertjan Houben (lighting); Light and Sound Operator, Matthew White; Scenic Charge, Katie Fry; Makeup Effects, Erin Kennedy Lunsford; Production Assistant, Sarah Bessey; **Cast:** Rosal Colón (Isabella), Kevin Corrigan (Rocco), Dominic Fumusa (Michael), Bob Glaudini (Charlie), Samuel Mercedes (Carlito)

Bank Street Theater; First Preview: April 5, 2012; Opening Night: April 18, 2012; Closed May 6, 2012; 13 previews, 21 performances. Setting: 1986, South Philadelphia. 9th Street. World premiere of a new play presented in two acts. Synopsis: An Italian-American family gathers to mourn a departed matriarch. Old questions of loyalty and legacy, love and loss, cast a shadow across three generations as they are forced to confront a violent past and an uncertain future in this provocative new drama.

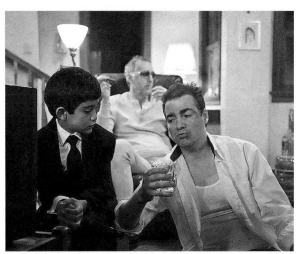

Samuel Mercedes and Kevin Corrigan (front), and Bob Glaudini in Ninth and Joanie *(photo by Kate Edwards)*

READINGS AND SPECIAL EVENTS

Barn Series Twelfth annual new play reading series; Bank Street Theater; Included: *The Power of Duff* by Stephen Belber, directed by Cat Miller (September 18-19, 2011); *Fuente Ovejuna: A Disloyal Adaptation* by Cusi Cram from the play by Lope De Vega, directed by Suzanne Agins (September 22 & 29, 2011); *Busted* by Florencia Lozano, directed by Jill DeArmon (November 6-7, 2011); *Deep Trees* by Andrea Ciannavei, directed by Scott Illingworth, featuring Bobby Cannavale, Salvatore Inzerillo, and Lili Taylor (December 5, 2011); Two one-act plays: *Antidote* by Bob Glaudini, directed by Lola Glaudini, featuring John Diehl, Marco Greco, and Gregg Henry; presented with *Snapshot* by Brett C. Leonard (December 14-15, 2011); *Ask/Tell* by David Bar Katz, directed by Philip Seymour Hoffman (December 18-19, 2011); *Mentor* by Webb Wilcoxen, directed by Jill DeArmon, featuring Florencia Lozano and Nyambi Nyambi (January 28-29, 2012); *Between You, Me & The Lampshade* by Raúl Castillo, directed by Felix Solis, featuring David Anzuelo, Audrey Esparza, Lyle Friedman, Alex Flores, and Daphne Rubin-Vega (February 2-3, 2012); *Bathroom Bolero* by Scott Hudson, directed by Padraic Lillis, featuring Florencia Lozano, Kristina Poe, and Sidney Williams (June 1, 2012); *The Restlessness of Desire* by Kristina Poe, directed by Liza Colón, featuring Elizabeth Canavan, Bobby Cannavale, Linda Larkin, Richard Petrocelli, Elizabeth Rodriguez, and Scott Sowers (June 2-3, 2012)

Celebrity Charades 2011: Down and Derby Labyrinth's Annual Gala-Speed Charades Competition; Sponsored by Appleton Estate Jamaica Rum, *GQ* Magazine, and Raymond Weil; Featuring: Bob Balaban, Bobby Cannavale, Philip Seymour Hoffman, John Ortiz, Chris Rock, Cynthia Rowley, Kristen Wiig, Josh Charles, Tom Colicchio, Padma Lakshmi, Jesse L. Martin, Daphne Rubin-Vega, Michelle Trachtenberg, Yul Vázquez, Evan Rachel Wood, David Zayas; Presentation of the 2011 Dave Hoghe Award: Labyrinth's former Co-Artistic Directors Philip Seymour Hoffman and John Ortiz in honor of their outstanding leadership and continued dedication to Labyrinth Theater Company; Highline Ballroom; November 14, 2011

Lincoln Center Theater

Twenty-seventh Season

Artistic Director, André Bishop; Executive Producer, Bernard Gersten; Managing Director, Adam Siegel; Production Manager, Jeff Hamlin; General Manager, Jessica Niebanck; Development, Hattie K. Jutagir; Finance, David S. Brown; Marketing, Linda Mason Ross; Education, Kati Koerner; Associate Directors, Graciela Danielle, Nicholas Hytner, Jack O'Brien, Susan Stroman, Daniel Sullivan; Resident Director, Bartlett Sher; Dramaturg and Director of Director of LCT Directors Lab, Anne Cattaneo; Musical Theatre Associate Producer, Ira Weitzman; LCT3 Director, Paige Evans; Casting, Daniel Swee; House Manager, William Cannon (Newhouse), Nikki Vera (Claire Tow); Associate General Manager, Meghan Lantzy; Associate Production Manager, Paul Smithyman; Press, Philip Rinaldi, Barbara Carroll, Amanda Dekker

Blood and Gifts by J.T. Rogers; Director, Bartlett Sher; Sets, Michael Yeargan; Costumes, Catherine Zuber; Lighting, Donald Holder; Sound, Peter John Still; Stage Manager, Jennifer Rae Moore; Company Manager, Jessica Perlmeter Cochrane; Dialect Coach, Deborah Hecht; Fight Director, Thomas Schall; Hair and Wigs, Jon Carter; ASM, Emily Glinick; Assistant Company Manager, Rachel Scheer; Assistant Director, Kristin Flanders; Associate Design: Mikiko Suzuki MacAdams (set), Caroline Chao (lighting); Assistant Design: Chien-Yu Peng (set), Amelia Dombrowski, David Newell, Ryan Park (costumes), Carolyn Wong, Marihan Mehelba (lighting), Benjamin Furiga (sound); Props Coordinator, Faye Armon; Props Assistants, Lillian Clements, Marina Guzman; Wardrobe Supervisor, Sheri Maher; Dressers, Audrey Maher, Linda McAllister; Production Assistant, B. Bales Karlin; **Cast:** Michael Aronov (Dmitri Gromov), Jeremy Davidson (James Warnock), Gabriel Ruiz (Colonel Afridi), Andrés Munar (Military Clerk/ CIA Analyst), Jefferson Mays (Simon Craig), Bernard White (Abdullah Khan), Pej Vahdat (Saeed), Paul Niebanck (Soldier/Administrative Aide), Andrew Weems (Political Speech Writer), Liv Rooth (Congressional Staffer), John Procaccino (Walter Barnes), Robert Hogan (Senator Jefferson Birch), Rudy Mungaray, J. Paul Nicholas (Mujahideen, Clerks, Aides); Understudies: Andrew Weems (Gromov and Craig), Paul Niebanck (Warnock), J. Paul Nicholas (Afridi and Khan), Rudy Mungaray (Clerk, Soldier, Political Speech Writer, Administrative Aide, CIA Analyst), Adria Vitlar (Congressional Staffer), Tony Campisi (Barnes and Birch)

Jeremy Davidson, Gabriel Ruiz, and Jefferson Mays in Blood and Gifts *(photo by T. Charles Erickson)*

Mitzi E. Newhouse Theater; First Preview: October 27, 2011; Opening Night: November 21, 2011; Closed January 8, 2012; 26 previews, 56 performances. Setting: 1981 to 1991. Pakistan, America, and Afghanistan. U.S. premiere of a new play presented in two acts. World premiere produced by the Royal National Theatre (London) in 2010. A shorter version of the play appeared as part of the Tricycle Theatre (London) 12-play epic *The Great Game Afghanistan* in 2009. Synopsis: *Blood and Gifts* tells the story of the secret spy war behind the official Soviet-

Afghan War of the 1980s. Spanning a decade, the play follows CIA operative Jim Warnock as he struggles to stop the Soviet Army's destruction of Afghanistan. The ground constantly shifts for Jim and his counterparts in the KGB and British and Pakistani secret service as the political and personal alliances between the men keep changing. As the outcome of the entire Cold War comes into play, Jim and a larger-than-life Afghan warlord find the only person they can trust is each other. *Blood and Gifts* tells the story of the unknown men who shaped one of the greatest historical events of recent history, the repercussions of which continue to shape our world.

Bernard White, Andrew Weems, Pej Vahdat, Andres Munar, J. Paul Nicholas, and Jeremy Davidson in Blood and Gifts *(photo by T. Charles Erickson)*

4000 Miles by Amy Herzog; Director, Daniel Aukin; Sets, Lauren Halpern; Costumes, Kaye Voyce; Lighting, Japhy Weideman; Original Music and Sound, Ryan Rumery; Stage Manager, Kasey Ostopchuck; ASM, Kelly Stillwell; Company Manager, Josh Lowenthal; Assistant Company Manager, Rachel Scheer; Assistant Director, Judy Merrick; Associate Design: Brian Ireland (set), Natalie Robin (lighting); Assistant Design: Sarah Gosnell (costumes), Amanda Lyon (lighting), M. Florian Staab (sound); Production Electrician, Josh Rich; Production Sound, Stephen Bettridge; Props Coordinator, Faye Armon; Props Assistant, Nicole Laemmie; Wardrobe Supervisor, Sheri Maher; **Cast:** Gabriel Ebert (Leo), Mary Louise Wilson (Vera Joseph), Zoë Winters (Bec), Greta Lee (Amanda); Understudies: Reggie Gowland (Leo), Susan Blommaert (Vera Joseph), Julia Lawler (Bec), Melanie Arii Mah (Amanda)

Gabriel Ebert and Zoë Winters in 4000 Miles *(photo by Erin Baiano)*

Mitzi E. Newhouse Theater; First Preview: March 15, 2012; Opening Night: April 2, 2012; Closed July 1, 2012; 20 previews, 94 performances. Setting: Time: September of a recent year; Place: Greenwich Village. Off-Broadway return engagement of a new play presented without intermission. World premiere produced at the Duke on 42nd Street under the auspices of the LCT3 Series June 6–July 9, 2011 (see *Theatre World* Vol. 67, page 208). *4000 Miles* was written in the Soho Rep Writer/Director Lab. Synopsis: After losing his best friend while they were on a cross-country bike trip, 21 year-old Leo seeks solace with his feisty 91 year-old grandmother in her West Village apartment. *4000 Miles* examines how these two outsiders find their way in today's world.

Gabriel Ebert and Mary Louise Wilson in 4000 Miles *(photo by Erin Baiano)*

LCT3 – THE STEINBERG NEW WORKS PROGRAM

All-American by Julia Brownell; Director, Evan Cabnet; Sets, Lee Savage; Costumes, Jessica Wegener Shay; Lighting, Japhy Weideman; Sound, Jill BC DuBoff; Stage Manager, Charles M. Turner III; ASM, Courtney James; Company Manager, Josh Lowenthal; Assistant Director, Lee Kasper; Assistant Design: Kristina Makowski (costumes), Zachary Ciaburri (lighting), Ben Truppin-Brown (sound); Props Coordinator, Faye Armon; Props Assistant, Marina Guzman; Technical Director/Deck Crew, Ernie Johns; Head Electrician, Nathan Winner; Light Board Operator, Kate Conover; Sound Board Operator, Bill Grady; Wardrobe Supervisor, Alex Bartlett; Deck Crew, Jesse Froncek; Dresser, Elizabeth Goodrum; Script Assistant, Julia Meltzer; LCT3 Representatives, Scott Arnold, Rhonda Lipscomb, Stephen McFarland; **Cast:** C.J. Wilson (Mike Slattery), Meredith Forlenza (Katie Slattery), Harry Zittel (Aaron Slattery), Sarah Steele (Natasha Gordon), Rebecca Creskoff (Beth Slattery), Brock Harris (Jake Myers)

Meredith Forlenza and C.J. Wilson in All-American
(photo by Gregory Costanszo)

Duke on 42nd Street; First Preview: October 24, 2011; Opening Night: November 7, 2011; Closed November 19, 2011; 15 previews, 16 performances. Setting: Time: Fall, 2011; Place: Palo Alto, California. World premiere of a new play presented without intermission. Synopsis: *All-American* is the story of a modern American family: suburban dad and former NFL star Mike Slattery works hard to make his daughter Katie the star quarterback at her new school while ignoring her brainy twin brother Aaron. But Katie isn't sure she wants to keep playing, and Mike's wife Beth isn't sure she wants to keep playing along.

Slowgirl by Greg Pierce; Director, Anne Kaufman; Sets, Rachel Hauck; Costumes, Emily Rebholz; Lighting, Japhy Weideman; Sound, Leah Glepe; Stage Manager, Charles M. Turner III; ASM, Maggie Swing; Company Manager, Josh Loenthal; Assistant Director, Caitlin O'Connell; Assistant Design: Carolyn Mraz (set); Katie Harsoe (costumes), Dani Clifford (lighting), Sam Kusnetz (sound); Fight Director, Jeff Barry; Props, Faye Armon; Light Board Operator, Nathan Winner; Sound Board Operator, Charles Shell; Wardrobe Supervisor, Alex Bartlett; **Cast:** Sarah Steele (Becky), Željko Ivanek (Sterling)

Claire Tow Theater (Inaugural Production in the new home for LCT3); First Preview: June 4, 2012; Opening Night: June 18, 2012; Closed August 5, 2012; 16 previews, 52 performances. Setting: Time: A week in late April, the present. Place: Sterling's house outside the tiny town of Los Angeles, Costa Rica. World premiere of a new play presented in four scenes without intermission. Synopsis: *Slowgirl* is the story of a teenager who flees to her reclusive uncle's retreat in the Costa Rican jungle to escape the aftermath of a horrific accident. The week they spend together forces them both to confront who they are as well as what it is they are running from.

Željko Ivanek and Sarah Steele in Slowgirl *(photo by Erin Baiano)*

MCC Theater (Manhattan Class Company)

Twenty-sixth Season

Artistic Directors, Robert LuPone, Bernard Telsey, and William Cantler; Executive Director, Blake West; General Manager, Ted Rounsaville; Company Manager/Assistant General Manager, Jenna Chase; Literary Manager/Dramaturg, Stephen Willems; Development, Erica Lynn Schwartz; Marketing, Ian Allen; Development Associate, Glenn Grieves; Marketing Associate, Sarah Rushakoff; Education/Outreach, Alex Sarian; Youth Company Acting Lab Director, Jennifer Shirley; Youth Company Playwriting Diector, Lucy Thurber; Production Manager, B.D. White; Resident Playwright, Neil LaBute; Producing Special Arrangements, The Lucille Lortel Theatre Foundation; Casting, Telsey + Company; Lead Reader, Jennie Contuzzi; Press, O+M Company, Rick Miramontez, Jon Dimond, Jaron Caldwell, Molly Barnett

The Submission by Jeff Talbott; Director, Walter Bobbie; Set, David Zinn; Costumes, Anita Yavich; Lighting, David Weiner; Original Music, Ryan Rumery and Christian Frederickson; Sound, Ryan Rumery; Projections, Darrel Maloney; PSM, Timothy R. Semon; Stage Manager, Sean M. Thorne; Production Assistant, Tyler Gabbard; Assistant Director, Ross Evans; Props Master, Karin White; Fight Director, Thomas Schall; Associate Sound, M. Florian Staab; Assistant Design: Tim McMath, Michael Simmons (set), Erica Evans, Nicole Jescinth Smith (costumes), David Sexton (lighting); Technical Director, Nicholas Warren Gray; Master Electrician, Sheila Donovan; Sound Supervisor, Bill Grady; Light Board Operator and Programmer, Dan Mullins; Deck Carpenter, Alex Camus; Wardrobe Supervisor, Dara Fargotstein; Sound Board Operator, Chip Barow; **Cast:** Jonathan Groff (Danny), Will Rogers (Trevor), Eddie Kaye Thomas (Pete), Rutina Wesley (Emilie)

Lucille Lortel Theatre; First Preview: September 8, 2011; Opening Night: September 27, 2011; Closed October 22, 2011; 18 previews, 34 performances. Setting: Time: One year, October to October. World premiere of a new play presented without intermission. Synopsis: Shaleeha G'ntamobi's stirring new play about an alcoholic black mother and her card sharp son trying to get out of the projects has just been accepted into the nation's preeminent theater festival. Trouble is, Shaleeha G'ntamobi doesn't exist, except in the imagination of wannabe-playwright Danny Larsen, who created her as a kind of affirmative-action nom-de-plume. But a nom-de-guerre may prove more useful as the lies pile up, shaky alliances are forged, and everyone dear to Danny must decide whether or not to run for cover as the whole thing threatens to blow up in his lily white face.

Jonathan Groff, Eddie Kaye Thomas and Will Rogers in The Submission
(photos by Joan Marcus)

Wild Animals You Should Know by Thomas Higgins; Director, Trip Cullman; Sets, Andromache Chalfant; Costumes, Jenny Mannis; Lighting, David Weiner; Sound, Fitz Patton; PSM, Kelly Glasgow; Stage Manager, Rachel Motz; Production Assistant, Angela F. Kiessel; Assistant Director, David Mendizábal; Props Master, Karin White; Projections, Joe Cantalupo; Assistant Design: Valerie Bert (costumes), David Sexton (lighting); Technical Director, Nicholas Warren Gray; Master Electrician, Sheila Donovan; Sound Supervisor, Bill Grady; Light Board Operator and Programmer, Dan Mullins; Deck Carpenter, Alex Camus; Wardrobe Supervisor, Dara Fargotstein; Sound Board Operator, Chip Barrow; **Cast:** John Behlmann (Rodney), Patrick Breen (Walter), Gideon Glick (Jacob), Jay Armstrong Jones (Matthew), Alice Ripley (Marsha), Daniel Stewart Sherman (Larry)

Lucille Lortel Theatre; First Preview: November 4, 2011; Opening Night: November 20, 2011; Closed December 11, 2011; 17 previews, 22 performances. Setting: Time: The present. Place: The suburbs. World premiere of a new play presented without intermission. Developed at Ojai Playwrights Conference (Robert Egan, Artistic Director). Synopsis: Matthew and Jacob are an unlikely pair of friends. Matthew is a soccer star, full of brio and teenage swagger. Jacob is, well, not. Beneath the surface the two are locked in an innocently erotic game of cat and mouse. When Matthew's reluctant father, Walter, is wrangled by his wife Marsha into chaperoning the boys' trip to a wilderness scout camp, he finds himself drawn into their adolescent game. But Matthew has secretly decided just how far he's willing to go for his final act of scouting and everyone might do well to heed the scouts' motto: Be Prepared.

Daniel Stewart Sherman, Gideon Glick, John Behlmann, Patrick Breen, and Jay Armstrong Johnson in Wild Animals You Should Know

Carrie Music by Michael Gore, lyrics by Dean Pitchford, book by Lawrence D. Cohen; Based on the novel by Stephen King; Director, Stafford Arima; Choreography, Matt Williams; Music Direction/Arrangements, Mary-Mitchell Campbell; Sets, David Zinn; Costumes, Emily Rebholz; Lighting, Kevin Adams; Sound, Jonathan Deans; Projections, Sven Ortel; Wigs, Leah J. Loukas; Fight Director, Rick Sordelet; Special Effects, Matthew Holtzclaw; Orchestrations, Doug Besterman; Vocal Design, AnnMarie Milazzo; PSM, Amber White; Stage Manager Jamie Hill; Production General Manager, Reed Ridgley; Dance Captains, Mackenzie Bell, Jake Boyd; Fight Captain, Ben Thompson; Production Assistants, Lindsey Alexander, Travis Brendle, Angela F. Kiessel; Associate Director, Todd Underwood; Associate Choreographer, Jenn Rapp; Associate Music Director, Paul Staroba; Assistant Music Director, Adam Wachter; Music Preparation, Anixter Rice Music Service; Synthesizer Programmer, Randy Cohen; Props Master, Karin White; Assistant Design: Michael Simmons (set), Katie Hartsoe, Sarah Bertolozzi (costumes), Pete Bragg (lighting), Joshua D. Reid (sound), Lucy Mackinnon (projections); Prom Dress Construction, Anne Wingate; Wig and Wardrobe Supervisor, Melinda Basaca; Wardrobe Crew, Desiree Eckert; Lighting Intern, William Noguchi; Projection Programmer, Florian Mosleh; Projection Intern, Gabe

Rives-Corbett; Technical Director, Nicholas Warren Gray; Assistant Technical Director, Conor Loughran; Master Electrician, Sheila Donovan; Production Sound, Bill Grady; Sound Mixer, Carin Ford; Light Board Programmer, Jay Penfield; Light Board Operator, Dan Mullins; Follow Spot/Deck Carpenter, Alex Camus; Carpenters, Ernie Johns, Mike Zally, Andrew Merkel, Jason Laughlin, Newell Kring, Lance Harkins, Jesse Froncek, James White, Wally Lugo; Electricians, Sam Gordon, Jes Halm, Mitch Ost, Amanda Lemen, Richard Ponce, Annie Wiegant, Robert Sambrato, Jake Simon-Gersuk, Dylan Uremovich; Rehearsal Pianist, Tim Rosser; Cast recording: Sh-K-Boom/Ghostlight Records 86660; **Cast:** Marin Mazzie (Margaret White), Molly Ranson (Carrie White), Christy Altomare (Sue Snell), Carmen Cusack (Lynn Gardner), Jeanna De Waal (Chris Hargensen), Derek Klena (Tommy Ross), Ben Thompson (Billy Nolan), Wayne Alan Wilcox (Mr. Stephens), Corey Boardman (George), Blair Goldberg (Norma), F. Michael Haynie (Freddy), Andy Mientus (Stokes), Elly Noble (Helen), Jen Sese (Frieda); Standbys/ Understudies: Anne Tolpegin (Margaret White, Lynn Gardner), Mackenzie Bell (Lynn, Chris, Frieda, Helen, Norma), Corey Boardman (Tommy), Jake Boyd (Tommy, Mr. Stephens, Freddy, George, Stokes), Blair Goldberg (Chris), Andy Mientus (Billy), Elly Noble (Sue, Carrie), Jen Sese (Carrie); Band: Mary-Mitchell Campbell (Conductor/Keyboard 1), Paul Staroba (Associate Conductor/Keyboard 1), Adam Wachter (Keyboard 2), Craig Magnano (Guitar 1), Dillon Kondor (Guitar 2), Brian Hamm (Bass), Damien Bassman (Drums and Percussion), Alisa Horn (Cello)

Musical Numbers: In; Carrie; Open Your Heart; And Eve Was Weak; The World According to Chris; Evening Prayers; Dreamer In Disguise; Once You See; Unsuspecting Hearts; Do Me a Favor; I Remember How Those Boys Could Dance; A Night We'll Never Forget; You Shine; Why Not Me; Stay Here Instead; When There's No One; The Prom; Carrie (reprise); Epilogue

Lucille Lortel Theatre; First Preview: January 31, 2012; Opening Night: March 1, 2012; Closed April 8, 2012; 34 previews, 46 performances. Setting: Chamblerlain, Maine; the present. Revised version of a musical presented in two acts. The original production of *Carrie* was presented at the Virginia (August Wilson) Theatre April 28–May 15, 1988 (opened May 12), playing 16 previews, 5 performances (see *Theatre World* Vol. 44, page 36). Synopsis: MCC Theater unites the original authors of the legendary 1988 Broadway production with Stafford Arima in a newly reworked and re-imagined version of the now cult musical *Carrie*. Carrie White is a misfit. At school, she's an outcast who's bullied by the popular crowd, and virtually invisible to everyone else. At home, she's at the mercy of her loving but cruelly over-protective mother. But Carrie's just discovered she's got a special power, and if pushed too far, she's not afraid to use it.

Molly Ranson and the Company in Carrie

Manhattan Theatre Club

Fortieth Season

Artistic Director, Lynne Meadow; Executive Producer, Barry Grove; General Manager, Florie Seery; Artistic Producer, Mandy Greenfield; Director of Artistic Development, Jerry Patch; Director of Artistic Operations, Amy Gilkes Loe; Artistic Line Producer, Lisa McNulty; Director of Casting, Nancy Piccione; Development, Lynne Randall; Marketing, Debra Waxman-Pilla; Finance, Jessica Adler; Associate General Manager, Lindsey Brooks Sag; Subscriber Services, Robert Allenberg; Telesales/Telefunding, George Tetlow; Education, David Shookhoff; Production Manager, Joshua Helman; Company Manager, Julia Baldwin/Samantha Kindler; Properties Supervisor, Scott Laule; Costume Supervisor, Erin Hennessy Dean; Lighting/Sound Supervisor, Jeff Dodson; Wardrobe Supervisor, Katherine Harber; Press, Boneau/Bryan-Brown, Chris Boneau, Aaron Meier, Christine Olver, Emily Meagher

We Live Here by Zoe Kazan; Director, Sam Gold; Sets, John Lee Beatty; Costumes, David Zinn; Lighting, Ben Stanton; Original Music and Sound, Ryan Rumery; Fight Direction, Thomas Schall; PSM, David. H. Lurie; Casting, David Caparelliotis; Stage Manager, Gregory T. Livoti; Jonathan Alper Directing Fellow, Reginald L. Douglas; Associate Design: Kacie Hultgren (set), Jacob A. Climer (costumes), Janie Bullard (sound); Assistant Design: Erick L. Sundquist (costumes), Brandon D. Mitchell (lighting); Makeup, Angelina Avallone; **Cast:** Amy Irving (Maggie), Betty Gilpin (Dinah), Mark Blum (Lawrence), Jeremy Shamos (Sandy), Jessica Collins (Althea), Oscar Isaac (Daniel); Understudies: Jessica Love (Maggie)

City Center Stage I; First Preview: September 22, 2011; Opening Night: October 12, 2011; Closed November 6, 2011; 22 previews, 31 performances. Setting: New England; Summer, the present. World premiere of a new play presented in two acts. Synopsis: Allie Bateman's wedding is Sunday. When her younger sister Dinah returns to their parents' home for the festivities, she brings more than anyone expected: a new boyfriend, whose hidden history resurrects passions and painful memories for the whole family. Over one emotionally charged weekend, the Batemans must acknowledge and accept loss to gain hope for regeneration.

Betty Gilpin, Oscar Isaac, Amy Irving, Mark Blum, Jessica Collins, and Jeremy Shamos in We Live Here *(photo by Joan Marcus)*

Close Up Space by Molly Smith Metzler; Director, Leigh Silverman; Sets, Todd Rosenthal; Costumes, Emily Rebholz; Lighting, Matt Frey; Sound, Jill BC DuBoff; Hair, Paul Huntley; PSM, Martha Donaldson; Stage Manager, Katrina Hermann; Jonathan Alper Directing Fellow, Lila Neugebauer; Assistant Design: Sean Renfro (set), Sarah Laux (costumes), Natalie Robin (lighting), Janie Bullard (sound); Fight Director, Thomas Schall; Russian Coach, Madeleine George; Dialect Coach, Charlotte Fleck; SDC Observer, Kevin Bigger; **Cast:** David Hyde Pierce (Paul), Jessica DiGiovanni (Bailey), Michael Chernus (Steve), Rosie Perez (Vanessa Finn

Adams), Colby Minfie (Harper); Understudies: Molly Camp (Harper/Bailey), Opal Alladin (Vanessa), Tony Ward (Paul/Steve)

City Center Stage I; First Preview: December 1, 2011; Opening Night: December 19, 2011; Closed January 29, 2012; 21 previews, 46 performances. Setting: Late autumn, this year; the office of Tandem Books, a small publishing house in New York City. World premiere of a new play presented without intermission. Developed at the Eugene O'Neill Theater Center and Chautauqua Theatre Company in 2010. Synopsis: Paul Barrow, an obsessive book editor on a major deadline, has just about had it with his assistant who's been camping in the office, a famous author threatening to bail on him, and an intern who is no help at all. But when his fiery daughter shows up and lambasts him in Russian, Paul faces a glaring personal error that can't be corrected with red ink.

Jessica DiGiovanni, David Hyde Pierce, and Michael Chernus in Close Up Space *(photo by Joan Marcus)*

Rosie Perez and David Hyde Pierce in Close Up Space *(photo by Joan Marcus)*

Alexis Bledel and Brian Hutchison in Regrets *(photo by Carol Rosegg)*

Regrets by Matt Charman; Director, Carolyn Cantor; Sets, Rachel Hauck; Costumes, Ilona Somogyi; Lighting, Ben Stanton; Sound, Jill BC DuBoff; Fight Director, Thomas Schall; PSM, Hannah Cohen; Stage Manager, Eileen Ryan Kelly; Jonathan Alper Directing Fellow, Kevin Bigger; Wigs, Charles G. LaPointe; Makeup, Angelina Avallone; Clarinet Coach, Maureen Hurd Hause; Vocal Coach, Judylee Vivier; Associate Sound, David Sanderson; Assistant Design: Carolyn Mraz (set), Sanghee Kim (costumes), Brandon D. Mitchell (lighting); **Cast:** Alexis Bledel (Chrissie Meyers), Curt Bouril (Robert Hanratty), Ansel Elgort (Caleb Farley), Brian Hutchison (Ben Clancy), Adriane Lenox (Mrs. Duke), Lucas Caleb Rooney (Gerald Driscoll), Richard Topol (Alvin Novotny); Understudies: Thursday Farrar (Mrs. Duke), George Hampe (Caleb/Robert), Fredric Lehne (Ben/Gerald/Alvin), Brianne Moncrief (Chrissie)

City Center Stage I; First Preview: March 8, 2012; Opening Night: March 27, 2012; Closed April 29, 2012; 22 previews, 47 performances. Setting: 1954; Pyramid Lake, Nevada. World premiere of a new play presented in two acts. Synopsis: Caleb Farley is the youngest man ever to show up at Mrs. Duke's cabins, a ramshackle retreat in the Nevada desert and one of the few places men can go to secure a quick divorce. Caleb claims he fled his Hollywood home for the same reason as the other men in camp – to shed the lives and wives they've known and begin anew. But in an era of heightened fears and political distrust, accusations that Caleb is hiding more than just a broken heart test each man's loyalty: to country and to one another.

Mint Theater Company

Twentieth Season

Producing Artistic Director, Jonathan Bank; General Manager/Finance and Production Manager, Sherri Kotimsky; Development Associate/Production Dramaturgy, Heather J. Violanti; Audience Relations and Marketing, Adrienne Scott; Development Consultant, Ellen Mittenthal; Assistant Production Manager, Wayne Yeager; Graphics, Hey Jude Graphics; Videographer, Joshua Paul Johnson; Casting, Amy Schecter; Advertising and Marketing, The Pekoe Group; Press, David Gersten & Associates

Temporal Powers by Teresa Deevy; Director, Jonathan Bank; Sets, Vicki R. Davis; Costumes, Andrea Varga; Lighting, Jeff Nellis; Sound, Jane Shaw; Properties, Joshua Yocom; Additional Dramaturgy and Dialects, Amy Stoller; PSM, Lisa McGinn; ASMs, Lauren McArthur, Andrea Jo Martin; Illustrations, Stefano Imbert; Fight Director, Michael Chin; Assistant Costumes, Oga Mills; Assistant Lighting/Programmer, Rachel Szymanski; Wardrobe Supervisor, Leah Mitchell; Assistant to the Director, Natalia Schwein; Board Operator, Shannon Epstein; Scenic Charge, Julia Hahn-Gallego; Carpenters, Carlton Hall, Daniel Halliday; Production Assistant, Renee Jackson; **Cast:** Aidan Redmond (Michael Donovan), Rosie Benton (Min Donovan), Eli James (Moses Barron), Wrenn Schmidt (Lizzie Brennan), Fiana Toibin (Daisy Barron), Con Horgan (Ned Cooney), Bairbre Dowling (Maggie Cooney), Paul Carlin (Jim Slattery), Robertson Carricart (Father O'Brien)

Mint Theatre; First Preview: August 3, 2011; Opening Night: August 29, 2011; Closed October 9, 2010; 24 previews, 43 performances. Setting: Afternoon in the early autumn of 1927, a few hours later, and the next day. American premiere of a 1932 drama presented in three acts with two intermissions. Synopsis: *Temporal Powers* tells the moving story of a great love straining under the weight of conflicting passions. Desperate and destitute, Michael and Min Powers take refuge for the night in a crumbling ruin. Buried within the walls could be the answer to their prayers — money for a fresh start — if only they could agree to use it. What follows is a fierce moral struggle that no one can win.

Aidan Redmond and Rosie Benton in Temporal Powers
(photos by Richard Termine)

Rutherford & Son by Githa Sowerby; Director, Richard Corley; Sets, Vicki R. Davis; Costumes, Charlotte Palmer-Lane; Lighting, Nicole Pearce; Composer and Sound, Ellen Mandel; Sound, Jane Shaw; Props, Joshua Yocom; Dialects and Dramaturgy, Amy Stoller; Wigs, Gerard Kelly; PSM, Allison Deutsch; ASM, Andrea Jo Martin; Assistant to the Director, Jesse Marchese; Assistant Costumes, Matthew Keating; Assistant Lighting/Programmer, Carla Linton; Wardrobe Supervisor, Leah Mitchell; Board Operator, Robert Mendoza; Production Assistant, Josephine Ronga; Carpenters, Daniel Halliday, Eric Nightengale; **Cast:** Robert Hogan (John Rutherford), Eli James (John, his son), James Patrick Nelson (Richard, *his son*), Sara Surrey (Janet, *his daughter*), Sandra Shipley (Ann, *his sister*), Allison McLemore (Mary, *young John's wife*); David Van Pelt (Martin), Dale Soules (Mrs. Henderson)

Mint Theatre; First Preview: February 4, 2012; Opening Night: February 27, 2012; Closed April 8, 2012; 23 previews, 43 performances. Setting: Living room of John Rutherford's home in Northern England; an evening in December early 1910s, two days later, and one night later. Revival of a play presented in three acts with two intermissions. Originally presented at the Royal Court Theatre in London February 1, 1912. The Mint Theatre previously presented the play with most of this cast in September 2001. Synopsis: *Rutherford & Son* tells the story of a father determined to do whatever it takes to ensure the success and succession of the family glassworks, now in danger of shattering. Rutherford rules home and business with an iron fist, a tyrant who inspires fear in his workers and hatred in his grown children. His eldest son, working in secret, has discovered a process that could save the firm, but refuses to share it with his father unless he gets his price.

David van Pelt and Sara Surrey in Rutherford and Son

Love Goes to Press by Martha Gellhorn and Virginia Cowles; Director, Jerry Ruiz; Sets, Steven C. Kemp; Costumes, Andrea Varga; Lighting, Christian DeAngelis; Sound, Jane Shaw; Props, Joshua Yocum; Additional Dramaturgy and Dialects, Amy Stoller; PSM, Samone B. Weissman; ASM, Catherine Costanzo; Illustration, Stefano Imbert; Assistant Costumes, Kaitlyn Day; Assistant Sound, Ben Truppin-Brown; Wardrobe Supervisor, Leah Mitchell; Board Operator, Roselle Rosado; Production Assistants, Josephine Ronga, Sophie Frankle; **Cast:** David Graham Jones (Leonard Lightfoot), Jay Patterson (Tex Crowder), Curzon Dobell (Hank O'Reilly), Rob Breckenridge (Joe Rogers), Bradford Cover (Major Philip Brooke-Jervaux), Ned Noyes (Corporal Cramp), Margot White (Daphne Rutherford), Angela Pierce (Jane Mason), Heidi Armbruster (Annabelle Jones), Thomas Matthew Kelley (Major Dick Hawkins), Peter Cormican (Captain Sir Allastair Drake)

Mint Theatre; First Preview: May 26, 2012; Opening Night: June 18, 2012; Closed July 29, 2012; 23 previews, 43 performances. Setting: A press camp in Poggibonsi, Italy; three days in February, 1944. Revival of a play presented in four scenes in three acts with two intermissions. World premiere in London at the Embassy Theatre in 1946. The Broadway premiere played the Biltmore Theatre January 1-4, 1947, playing only 5 performances (see *Theatre World* Vol. 3, page 67). This production marked the play's first revival. Synopsis: *Love Goes To Press* is a sharp-tongued comedy about women war correspondents that had them rolling in the aisles in London in 1946. The play paints a delicious portrait of two smart, funny, brave, ambitious and complex women working just miles from the front lines (as the authors did), surrounded by less competent, less adventurous men.

The New Group

Sixteenth Season

Artistic Director, Scott Elliott; Executive Director, Geoffrey Rich; General Manager, Elisabeth Bayer; Director of Development, Jamie Lehrer; Associate Artistic Director, Ian Morgan; General Manager, Elisabeth Bayer; Manager of Institutional Giving, James Gittins; Manager of Individual Giving and Events, Brandon Suisse; Marketing Manager, Laura Padilla; Artistic Associate, Matthew Klein; Production Supervisor, Peter R. Feuchtwanger/PRF Productions; Casting, Judy Henderson, Kimberly Graham; Graphic Design, Rogers Eckersley Design; Program Designs, Jakub Kupiszewski; House Manager, Alaina Sciascia; Press, Bridget Klapinski, Seven17 PR

Burning by Thomas Bradshaw; Director, Scott Elliott; Set, Derek McLane; Costumes, Clint Ramos; Lighting, Peter Kaczorowski; Sound, Bart Fasbender; Projections, Wendall K. Harrington; Assistant Director, Marie Masters; Dialect Coach, Doug Paulson; Fight Direction, David Anzuelo; PSM, Valeria A. Peterson; Props Supervisor, Michelle Davis; Associate Costumes, Julia Broer; Assistant Design: Shoko Kambara (set), Marika Kent (lighting), William Neal (sound), Connor Lynch (projections); Carpenters, Tom Goehring, Michael Zally, Michael McGee; Video Operator, Nicholas Lazzaro; Projection Programmer, Colin Scott; Electricians, Tom Dyer, Laurence Austin Bransgrove; Audio, David Arnold, Erin Ballantine; Wardrobe Supervisor, Kristi Koury; Production Assistants, Rachel Anderson, Kari Nelson; **Cast:** Jeff Biehl (Paul, Heinz, Priest, Funeral Director), Reyna de Courcy (Karin), Barrett Doss (Gretchen), Hunter Foster (Older Chris), Andrew Garman (Jack), Drew Hildebrand (Michael), Evan Johnson (Chris), Danny Mastrogiorgio (Simon), Andrew Polk (Noah), Larisa Polonsky (Josephine), Adam Trese (Donald), Vladimir Versailles (Franklin), Stephen Tyrone Williams (Peter)

Acorn Theatre on Theatre Row; First Preview: October 26, 2011; Opening Night: November 14 2011; Closed December 17, 2011; 19 previews, 34 performances. World premiere of a new play presented in two acts. Synopsis: In intersecting stories spanning two eras, a contemporary black painter who hides his race goes to Germany for a show, only to find that the gallery owner has misinterpreted his work. In the '80s a homeless teenager comes to New York to become an actor and is taken in by two gay men, who are producing a new play. Titillating, taboo-testing and psychosexually insightful, this tale of ambition and self-invention opens the conceits of the worlds of art and theatre.

Barrett Doss and Stephen Tyrone William in Burning

Russian Transport by Erika Sheffer; Director, Scott Elliott; Set, Derek McLane; Costumes, Ann Hould-Ward; Lighting, Peter Kaczorowski; Sound, Bart Fasbender; Dialect Coach, Doug Paulson; Fight Director, David Anzuelo; Assistant Director, Marie Masters; PSM, Valerie A. Peterson; Russian Consultant, Vera Berlyavsky; Props Supervisor, Matt Frew; Associate Costumes, Christopher Vergara; Assistant Design: Shoko Kambara (set), Marika Kent (lighting), William Neal (sound);

Lighting Programmer, Jeff Englander; Carpenters, John A. Martinez, J. Michael Zally; Electricians, Tom Dyer, Laurence Austin Bransgrove; Audio, David Arnold, Sam Kusnetz; Wardrobe Supervisor, Kristi Koury; Production Assistants, Kateria Madison, Nelson Patino Jr., David Shaw; **Cast:** Janeane Garofalo (Diana), Daniel Oreskes (Misha), Morgan Spector (Boris), Sarah Steele (Mira), Raviv Ullman (Alex)

Acorn Theatre on Theatre Row; First Preview: January 17, 2012; Opening Night: January 30, 2012; Closed March 24, 2012; 13 previews, 56 performances. Setting: The Russian Jewish community of Sheepshead Bay, Brooklyn; the present. World premiere of a new play presented in two acts. Synopsis: *Russian Transport* captures the complex layers of one particular immigrant experience. Diana and Misha, an immigrant couple, run a struggling car service while trying to carve out the American Dream for their teenagers. When Diana's sexy, mysterious brother arrives to stay with them, family loyalty is tested. For Alex and Mira, Uncle Boris is an exciting addition to their home, but soon Alex is pulled into his Uncle's dangerous world.

Sarah Steele, Janeane Garofalo, and Raviv Ullman in Russian Transport

An Early History of Fire by David Rabe; Director, Jo Bonney; Set, Neil Patel; Costumes, Theresa Squire; Lighting, Lap Chi Chu; Sound, Ken Travis; Dialect Coach, Doug Paulson; Fight Direction, David Anzuelo; Assistant Director, Sash Bischoff; PSM, Valerie A. Peterson; Props Supervisor, Matt Frew; Associate Design: Caleb Levengood (set), Nick Kolin (lighting); Assistant Costume Design, Amanda Jenks; Carpenters, John A. Martinez, J. Michael Zally; Electricians, Tom Dyer, Laurence Austin Bransgrove; Audio, David Arnold; Wardrobe Supervisor, Kristi Biglin; Production Assistants, David Shaw, Amanda Beckett; **Cast:** Gordon Clapp (Pop), Erin Darke (Shirley), Jonny Orsini (Terry), Devin Ratray (Benji), Dennis Staroselsky (Jake), Theo Stockman (Danny), Claire van der Boom (Karen)

Acorn Theatre on Theatre Row; First Preview: April 5, 2012; Opening Night: April 30, 2012; Closed May 26, 2012; 24 previews, 28 performances. Setting: Early fall around 1962 in a medium sized town in the Midwest. World premiere of a new play presented in two acts. Synopsis: *An Early History of Fire* is set at the tipping point of the early 1960s. In a Midwestern town, Danny's days are defined by friendship and loyalty – but the bigger world encroaches in the form of Karen, back from college in the east, alluring and unsettling because of all she has learned. Awhirl in longing and eyeing a chance for radical change, Danny struggles against the grip of his immigrant father, who mourns a vanished world of lost prestige while clinging to his only son.

New Victory Theater

Sixteenth Season

President, Cora Cahan; Executive VP, Lisa Lawer Post; VP of Development, Deborah Anne Trimble; VP of Finance, Kim Dobbie Neuer; VP of Operations, Jack Dobson; Director of Artistic Programming, Mary Rose Lloyd; Director of Institutional Giving, Katherine Freedman; Director of Digital Services, Lilaia Kairis; Directors of Education, Courtney J. Boddie (School), Lindsey Buller Maliekel (Public); Director of Facilities, Robert Saracena; Director of IT, Cohn; Director of Marketing and Communications, Lauren P. Fitzgerald; Directors of Operations, Melinda Berk (New Victory), Alma Malabanan-McGrath (New 42nd Street Studios/Duke on 42nd Street); Director of Production, David Jenson; Director of Public Relations, Laura Kaplow-Goldman/Allison Mui Mitchell; Director of Ticket Operations, Robin Leeds

The Little Prince by Antoine de Saint-Exupéry, adapted by Rick Cummins and John Scoullar; Presented by Bristol Riverside Theater (Bristol, PA; Susan D. Atkinson, Founding Director; Keith Baker, Artistic Director; Amy Kaissar, Managing Director); Director, Susan D. Atkinson; Set, Tom Gleeson; Costumes, Millie Hiibel; Puppets, Michael Schupbach; Lighting, Ryan O'Gara; Sound, William Neal; Production Manager, William S. Crandall; Technical Director, Stephen Hungerford; PSM, Kate Simko; Puppet Construction, Monkey Boys Productions; **Cast:** Leonard C. Haas (Aviator), Eileen Cella (Little Prince), Michael Schupbach (Fox), Carol Anne Raffa (Rose/Various Puppets), Robert Smythe (Men in Planets/Various Puppets)

New Victory Theatre; October 1-16, 2011; 11 performances. New York premiere of a play with puppetry presented without intermission. Synopsis: Bristol Riverside Theatre presents a touching new stage adaptation of the enchanting French fable by Saint-Exupéry in which life-size puppets share the stage with actors.

The Bristol Riverside Theatre production of The Little Prince *(photo by Leila Ghaznavi)*

White by Andy Manley; Presented by Catherine Wheels Theatre Company (Scotland); Director, Gill Robertson; Design, Shona Reppe; Music, Danny Krass; Lighting/Production Manager, Craig Fleming; Stage Manager, Suzie Normand; Producer, Paul Fitzpatrick; Projects Manager, Louise Gilmour Wills; **Cast:** Andy Manley (Cotton), Ian Cameron (Wrinkle)

Studio 3A/B New 42nd Street Studios; October 13–November 13, 2012; 41 performances. U.S. premiere of a contemporary theatre piece with music presented without intermission. Synopsis: Cotton and Wrinkle, lovingly care for their orderly white world, working hard to hide any hint of hue. But keeping things pigment-free proves problematic for the beanie-wearing buddies." Will they allow for some color in their monochrome world?

The Complete World of Sports (abridged) Created and presented by the Reduced Shakespeare Company (Sonoma, California); Company Founder, Daniel Singer; Directors, Reed Martin and Austin Tichenor; Sound, Zach Moore, Jason Weber, Joe Winkler; Costumes, Julia Kwitchoff; General Manager, Jane Martin; Company Manager/Wardrobe/Props, Alli Bostedt; Stage Manager, Elaine Randolph; Wardrobe Supervisor, Jenni Schwaner Ladd; Props, Elizabeth Bazzano, Matt Rippy; Backdrop, Dottie Marshall English, Scott Loebl; **Cast:** Reed Martin, Matt Rippy, Austin Tichenor

New Victory Theatre; October 21-November 6, 2011; 15 performances. New York premiere of a new comedy presented with one intermission. Synopsis: The lunacy of sports collides with ludicrous wit in *The Complete World of Sports (abridged)* by the Reduced Shakespeare Company, exploring every sport ever known to man – from "Neanderthal in the Middle" to Quidditch.

Reed Martin, Austin Tichenor, and Matt Rippy in The Complete World of Sports (abridged) *(photo by John Burgess)*

Untapped! Created and presented by Raw Metal Dance (Brisbane, Australia); Director/Design, Andrew Fee; Choreography, Andrew Fee and the Company; Costumes, Lucy Chambers; Lighting/Stage Manager, Troy Kelly; Sound, Jamie Taylor; General Manager, Jess Chambers; **Cast:** Dancers: Andrew Fee, Daniel Sintes, Matthew Sintes, Reece Hopkins, Sam Windsor; Musicians: Jeremy O'Connor (Bass), Andrew Keppie (Guitar), Joel Warden (Drums), Jonathan Grant (Beatbox)

New Victory Theatre; November 11-27, 2011; 16 performances. U.S. premiere of a theatrical dance piece presented without intermission. Synopsis: *Untapped!* is a raucous, adrenaline-fueled mash-up of funk, tap and acrobatics featuring an all-boy crew of daredevil performers and musicians.

A scene from Untapped! *(photo courtesy of Raw Metal Dance)*

Bai Xi Presented by Cirque Shanghai (China); Executive Producer, Haiping Ge; Producer, Gary Fjelstad; Director, Miao Miao Chen; Choreography, Brenda Didier; Costumes, Jay Cochran; Lighting, Matt Saunier; Sound/Stage Manager, Lucas Bonewits; Music Editor, Jian Min Huang; Graphics, Max Painter; Operations, Qing Hu; **Cast:** Congcong Cai, Qi Chen, Jianbin Feng, Jian Gao, Shiting Huang, Xueping Huang, Zhiwei Huang, Guangbo Liu, Guangying Liu, Wenwei Liu, Yunming Liu, Jiali Luo, Jie Pang, Wenhua Su, Yushi Su, Huiyuan Tang, Yizhu Wu, Famin Xie, Hailin Zhang, Yehai Zhou, Yuhua Zhu

New Victory Theatre; December 2–January 1, 2012; 28 performances. New York premiere of a theatrical circus presented without intermission. Synopsis: From climbing a three-story tower of chairs to balancing en pointe on a man's head, this supremely gifted cadre of contortionists, aerialists, and gymnasts perform an astounding array of contemporary and traditional circus feats. The company of *Bai Xi* thrills audiences with strength, beauty, and the uncanny ability to make the impossible look effortless.

Stella Den Haag Theatre Company (Netherlands) in Rumplestiltskin, *part of the* ZOEM! New Dutch Theater Festival *(photo by Robert Benschop)*

Rumplestiltskin Text by Hans van den Boom; Presented by Stella Den Haag (Den Haag, Netherlands) as part of New Victory's *Zoem! New Dutch Theater* series; Director, Erna van den Berg; Music Director, Marielle Woltring; Sets, Nele Ceustermans; Costumes, Doreien De Jonge; Lighting, Reier Pos; Sound, Peter Kerkvliet; Technical Team, Gercho Kolthof, Tjarko Van Heese; Equity Stage Manager, Lindsay Stares; **Cast:** Titus Boonstra (Rumplestiltskin), Annemarie de Bruijn (Desirée van der Laan); Rik Engelgeer (Prince Edward); Rienus Krul (Frans Joseph Waldhoorn), Rosa Mee (Esmiralda)

Duke on 42nd Street; January 6-8, 2012; 5 performances. U.S. premiere of a play with music presented in English without intermission. Synopsis: In this artful and eerie rendition of the fairy tale known to Dutch children as "Niemand Weet, Niemand Weet," live music, storytelling, and drama intertwine to turn this classic story into an enthralling, contemporary play.

Miss Ophelia Based on the book *Ophelia's Shadow Theatre* by Michael Ende; Presented by Het Filiaal (Utrecht, Netherlands) as part of of New Victory's *Zoem! New Dutch Theater* series; Director, Ramses Graus; Set, Joris van Oosterwijk; Artistic Director/Direction Coach, Monique Corvers; Music Director/Sound, Gábor Tarján; Costumes, Joost van Wijmen; Production Manager, Aafje Roth; Sound/Lighting Technician, Laurens Schoonheim; Management, Marjolein van Bommel; **Cast:** Ramses Graus, Mirthe Klieverik

Duke on 42nd Street; January 13-15, 2012; 5 performances. U.S. premiere of a puppet theatre piece presented without intermission. Synopsis: Two performers use storytelling, puppetry and music to dramatize the tale of Ophelia, an ordinary person, who upon discovering a shadow that belongs to no one, experiences something extraordinary.

Hands Up! Created and performed by Leo Petersen; Presented by Lejo (Amersfoort, Netherlands) as part of New Victory's *Zoem! New Dutch Theater* series; Production Manager, Hanna De Mink

Studio 3A/B New 42nd Street Studios; January 21-22, 2012; 6 performances. U.S. premiere of a puppet theatre piece presented without intermission. Synopsis: Using just his hands, an animated soundtrack, and simple props, Lejo, a regular on the Dutch version of *Sesame Street,* conjures a vast collection of kooky, quirky, and clever characters in this wordless puppetry production.

Wuthering Heights, Restless Souls Written by Jeroen Olyslaegers, based on the novel by Emily Brontë; Translated from Dutch by Rina Vergano; Presented by Theater Artemis (Den Bosch, Netherlands) and Theater Antigone (Kortrijk, Belgium) as part of New Victory's *Zoem! New Dutch Theater* series; Director, Floor Huygen; Set/Stage Manager, Michiel van Cauwelaert; Sound, Florentijn Boddendijk and Remco de Jong; Dramaturg, Peter Anthonissen; Costumes, Marike Kamphuis; Production/Wardrobe Manager, Jasper Willems; Equity Stage Manager, Mary-Susan Gregson; Technical Stage Manager/Lighting, Marq Claessens; Management, Maurice Dujardin; **Cast:** Alejandra Theus (Cathy), Joris Smit (Heathcliff), Fabian Jansen (Hindley), An Hackselmans (Nelly), Daan van Dijsseldonk (Edgar), Roos Van Vlaenderen (Isa)

New Victory Theatre; January 27-29, 2012; 4 performances. U.S. premiere of a play without intermission. Synopsis: Performed on a spare set evoking the wild and mysterious nature of the moors, this contemporary stage adaptation exposes the timeless nature and inescapable power of the Emily Brontë classic love story.

Brazil! Brazil Created and directed by Toby Gough, co-created by Dr. Hana Al Hadad; Presented by World Stage Productions (Salvador de Bahia, Brazil) and Broadway Asia International; Choreography, Marcos Santana; Original Music, Rhythm Carnival; Video, Tracking Productions; Costumes, Fabio Toblini, Holly Cain; Lighting, Ryan O'Gara; Sound, Sam Kusnetz; Props, Faye Armon; Production Manager, Jay Janicki; Scenic Elements, Toby Gough, Faye Armon, Katelyn Schroeder; Production Supervisor, Heather Hadly; General Management, Gena Chavez; Executive Producers, Simone Genatt Haft, Marc Routh; **Cast:** Gianne Abbott, Igor Alisson, Mickey Beigi, Ananias Explosion, John Farnworth, Paloma Gomes, Jonathas, Jay Super Jump, Arthur Mansilla, Pururu Mao No

Couro, Carlinhos Pajeú, Tedy Santana, Marcelo Santolis, Kiko Souza, André Tigáná

New Victory Theatre; February 10-26, 2012; 17 performances. U.S. premiere of a physical theatre piece presented without intermission. Synopsis: This South American celebration blends the rhythms of Rio Carnaval with acrobatics and soccer-inspired street dance.

A scene from Brazil! Brazil! *(photo by Kenny Mathieson)*

The Adventures of Tom Sawyer Adapted by Laura Eason from the novel by Mark Twain; Presented by Actors Theatre of Louisville, The Repertory Theatre of St. Louis, Kansas City Repertory Theatre, and Hartford Stage; Director, Jeremy B. Cohen; Sets, Dan Ostling; Costumes, Lorraine Venberg; Lighting, Robert Wierzel; Sound, Broken Chord; Fight/Movement Director, Tommy Rapley; PSM, Mary R. Hounour; ASMs, Michelle Gutierrez, Don Hovis; Wardrobe, Michael Prusik; Audio, Jeffrey Keirsey; Assistant Design: Daniel Stratton (set), Adam Greene (lighting), Daniel Kluger (sound); **Cast:** Joseph Adams (Muff Potter/Ensemble), Justin Fuller (Joe Harper/Ensemble), Tim McKiernan (Tom Sawyer), Michael Nichols (Injun Joe/School Master/Ensemble), Robbie Tann (Huckleberry Finn/Ensemble), Hayley Treider (Becky Thatcher), Nate Trinrud (Sid Sawyer/Doc Robinson/Ensemble), Nance Williamson (Aunt Polly/Widow Douglas/Ensemble)

New Victory Theatre; March 2-11, 2012; 10 performances. New York premiere a play presented without intermission. Synopsis: Twain's beloved novel comes to life in this splendid theatrical adaptation by Lookingglass Theatre co-founder, Laura Eason. Loyal to Twain's original text, this production captures the thrill of mischief-making, the fickleness of first love and the cold shivers that linger after a graveyard adventure goes awry.

Lucky Duck Book by Bill Russell and Jeffrey Hatcher, music by Henry Krieger, lyrics by Bill Russell; Based on "The Ugly Duckling" by Hans Christian Andersen; Presented by Coterie Theatre (Kansas City, Missouri); Director, Jeff Church; Music Director, Anthony T. Edwards; Choreography, Ernie Nolan; Set, Ryan J. Zirngibl; Costumes, Georgianna Buchanan; Lighting, Jarrett Bertoncin; Sound, David Kiehl; Props, Ron Megee; PSM, Amy M. Ables Owen; Technical Director/Master Carpenter, Scott Hobart; Company Manager, Mara Franke; Dialects, Erika Bailey; **Cast:** Kip Niven (King Armand), Seth Golay (Drake), Julie Shaw (Mrs. Mallard/Goosetella/Queen), Emily Shackelford (Mildred/Pig/Priggy), Katie Karel (Millicent/Wren/Verblinka/Chicken Little), Jennie Greenberry (Serena), Francisco Villegas (Rudy Rooster/Narrator/Mr. Baa/Cop/Model), Greg Krumins (Free Range Chicken/Carl/Pig/Model), Tosin Morohunfola (Free Range Chicken/Clem/Pig/

Tim McKiernan, Casey Predovic, and Louisa Krause in The Adventures of Tom Sawyer *(photo by T. Charles Erickson)*

Model), Tim Scott (Wolf); Musicians: Anthony T. Edwards (Conductor/Keyboards), Andy Burns (Percussion), Jim Whitney (Bass), David Deitweiler (Reeds)

New Victory Theatre; March 16-25, 2012; 10 performances. New York premiere of a musical presented without intermission. Synopsis: Krieger (*Dreamgirls*), Russell (*Side Show*) and Hatcher (*Tuesdays with Morrie*) collaborate on this satirical, rags-to-runway musical geared especially for the elementary school set. *Lucky Duck* puts a musical modern spin on the classic Hans Christian Andersen.

The Company in Lucky Duck *(photo by Robert Schrader)*

Ahhh HA! Choreographed and directed by Robin Lane; Presented by Do Jump! (Portland Oregon); Costumes, Katherine Salzman, Daniela Steiner; Puppets, Geahk Burchill; Composers, Ralph Hutley, Joe Janiga, Courtney von Drehle, Joan Szymko; Choral Music, Conspirare; Conductor, Craig Hella Johnson; Lighting/Stage Manager/Rigging, Tad Shannon; ASM, Joceline Wynn; Rehearsal Directors, Nicolo Kehrwald, Wendy Cohen; Video/Sound Engineer, Yalcin Erhan; Projections/Rigging, T.C. Smith; Water Animation, Daniel Lane; Lead Rigging, Mike Mesa; Technical Director/Rigging, David Saintey; Company Manager/Marketing and Promotions, Janine Twining; Photography and Graphic Design, Jeff Freeman; Graphics and Web Design, Kristen Raine; Executive Director, Kim Montagriff; **Cast:** Curtis Carlyle (Juggler & Diabolo Boy), Shersten Finley (Aerialist & Actorbat), Lindsay Fischer (Aerialist & Actorbat), Jeff George (Actor, Dancer &

The members of Do Jump!
in Ahhh HA!
(photo by Jeffrey Freeman)

Forsyth (Mrs. Van Amersfoort), Claire Jones (Mother), Deborah Kennedy (Aunty Pie), John Leary (Jesus), Steve Meyer (Musician), Yael Stone (Eliza), Matthew Whittet (Thomas)

New Victory Theatre; April 20-29, 2012; 8 performances. U.S. premiere of a play presented in two acts. Synopsis: Thomas Klopper takes amazing journeys through his imagination, where tropical fish swim in Amsterdam's canals, hailstorms rage in mid-summer, and every so often, Jesus stops by. *The Book of Everything* is about finding your own voice, struggling with big ideas and facing fears.

John Leary, Matthew Whittet, and the Company in The Book of Everything
(photo by Heidrun Lohr)

Plop! Based on the picture book *The Terrible Plop* by Ursula Duborsarsky; Presented by Windmill Theatre (Adelaide, Australia); Director, Sam Haren; Design, Geoff Cobham; Stage Manager, Emma O'Neill; Illustrator, Andrew Joyner; Composer/Musician, DJ Tr!p (Tyson Hopprich); **Cast:** Nathan O'Keefe, Nadia Rossi

Studio 3A/B New 42nd Street Studios; April 26–May 13, 2012; 24 performances. U.S. premiere of an interactive play presented without intermission. Synopsis: Adelaide's Windmill Theatre brings *Plop!*, a participatory play for young children that is filled with tricks and traps, gadgets and gizmos, rhythm and rhyme, and a chance for everyone to dance.

8cho Aerial Tango Presented by Brenda Angiel Aerial Dance Company (Buenos Aries, Argentina); Director/Choreographer, Brenda Angiel; Orchestra Direction, Composition, and Arrangements, Juan Pablo Arcangeli and Martín Ghersa; Lighting, David Ferri; Costumes, Caroline Ferraiuolo and Pilar Belmonte; Choreographic Assistant, Cristina Tziouras; Tango Consultants, Valencia Batiuk, Martín Ojeda, Juan Malizia, Damian Esell, Cesar Peral, Marcos Ayala; Production Manager/Main Rigger, Andrés Puertas; Rigger, Alejo Gago; **Cast:** Dancers: Lucas Coria, Mauro Dann, Viviana Finkelstein, Amparo González Sola, Juan Iglesias, María Luján Minguez, Cristina Tziouras; Musicians: Joaquin Apesteguia (Guitar), Juan Pablo Arcangeli (Contrabass), Martín Ghersa (Drums, Vibraphone), Adolfo Maria Trepiana (Bandoneón), Pablo Borghi (Violin), Ulises Avedaño Montes (Piano), Alejandro Guyot (Vocalist)

New Victory Theatre; May 4-20, 2012; 15 performances. New York premiere of a dance-theater piece presented without intermission. Synopsis: Set in a sultry Argentine nightspot, seven dancers perform solo, in pairs and as an ensemble, experimenting with speed and space to create surreal thrills. Accompanied by a six-piece orchestra and vocalist, they leap, lunge, swirl and swivel in midair, on the walls—even upside down—combining the familiar with the fantastical.

Actorbat), Yoji Hall (Aerialist & Actorbat), Nicolo Kehrwald (Aerialist & Actorbat), Mike Mesa (Juggler & Diabolo Boy), Kailee McMurran (Dancer, Aerialist & Actorbat), Tony Palomino (Dancer & Actorbat), Jack Stocklynn (Actorbat), Brittany Walsh (Aerialist & Actorbat), Tia Monet Zapp (Aerialist & Actorbat); Musicians (Klezmocracy): Ralph Huntley (Keyboards), Joe Janiga (Drums), Courtney Von Drehle (Saxophone, Slide Guitar, Accordion)

New Victory Theatre; March 30–April 14, 2012; 15 performances. New York premiere of a physical theatre production presented without intermission. Synopsis: Aerialists that act! Comedians that fly! Acrobats that dance! Do Jump!'s multi-talented ensemble enthralls audiences with their incredible physical skill, hilarious comedy, and moments of heart-stopping beauty, all set to live music by the Afro-Hebrew ensemble Klezmocracy. *Ahhh HA!* is a journey from the sublime to the ridiculous and back again, fusing athletics with aesthetics, choreography with creativity and theater with illusion to create a whole new world of wonder.

The Book of Everything Based on the Dutch novel *Het Boek van alle dingen* by Guus Kuijer, adapted by Richard Tulloch; Presented by Belvoir Street Theatre and Kim Carpenter's Theatre of Image (Sydney, Australia) Director, Neil Armfield; Set & Costumes, Kim Carpenter; Choreography, Julia Cotton; Composer, Iain Grandage; Lighting, Nigel Levings; Sound, Steve Francis; Assistant Director, Eamon Flack; Production Manager, Christopher Mercer; Head Mechanist, Damion Holling; Lighting Supervisor, Suzy Brooks; Sound Supervisor/Operator, Michael Toisuta; Stage Manager, Rebecca Anderson; ASM, Courtney Wilson; Company Manager, Annelies Crowe; Cast: Alison Bell (Margot), Peter Carroll (Father/Bumbiter), Julie

New York Gilbert & Sullivan Players

Thirty-seventh Season

Artistic Director & General Manager, Albert Bergeret; Managing Director, David Wannen; Music by Sir Arthur Sullivan and Librettos by Sir William S. Gilbert; Associate Manager, Joseph Rubin; Costumes, Gail Wofford; Lighting, Brian Presti; Technical Director/Production Stage Manager, David Sigafoose; Assistant Stage Manager, Annette Dieli; Head of Wardrobe, Corey Groom; Administratve Intern, Joseph Rubin; Assistant Music Director, Andrea Stryker-Rodda; Orchestra Manager, Larry Tietze; Press, Peter Cromarty

Season Orchestra: Violin: Robert Lawrence, Valery Levy, Peter Vandewater, Nicholas Szucs, Barney Stevens, Jeff Ellenberger, Paula Flatow, Ellen Gronnuingen, Carla Fabiani, Ellen Gronningen, Andrea Andros; Viola: Carol Benner, Carol Landon; Cello: Robert Tennen, Susan Poliacik; Bass: Deb Spohnheimer; Flute: Laura George, Melanie Bradford, Karla Moe, Lucy Goeres; Oboe: Nancy Ranger; Clarinet: Larry Tietze, Joan Porter; Bassoon: Susan Shaw, Andrea Herr, James Jeter, Paul Stebbins; French Horn: Stephen Quint, Heidi Garson, Peter Hirsch; Trumpet: Terry Szor, Richard Titone, John Thomas; Trombone: Steve Shulman, Paul Geidel, Joe Stanko; Percussion: Michael Osrowitz

The Grand Duke *or The Statuatory Duel* Director/Conductor, Albert Bergeret; Choreography/Co-director, David Auxier; **Cast:** Stephen O'Brien (Rudolph), Daniel Greenwood (Ernest Dummkopf), Richard Alan Holmes (Ludwig), James Mills (Dr. Tannhuser), Quinto Ott (The Prince of Monte Carlo), Chris-Ian Sanchez (Viscount Mentone), Louis Dall'Ava (Ben Hashbaz), David Auxier (Herald), Sarah Caldwell Smith (The Princess of Monte Carlo), Angela Christine Smith (The Baroness von Krakenfeldt), Charlotte Detrick (Julia Jellicoe), Melissa Attebury (Lisa), Sarah Hutchison (Olga), Amy Maude Helfer (Gretchen), Elizabeth Cernadas (Bertha), Rebecca O'Sullivan (Elsa); Ensemble: Caítlín Burke, Brooke Collins, Michael Connolly, Carol Davis, Victoria Devany, Michael Galante, Alan Hill, Daniel Lockwood, David Macaluso, Marcie Passley, Lucian Russell, Matthew Wages, Lauren Wenegrat, Emily Wright, Adam Yankowy

Symphony Space; November 13, 2011; 1 performance. Setting: A public square of Speisesaal, and a hall in the Grand Ducal Palace; 1910. Revival of an operetta presented in two acts. Synopsis: The tangled plot of *The Grand Duke* involves an acting troupe engaged in a conspiracy to overthrow the miserly and mean spirited grand duke of a small German duchy.

The Pirates of Penzance *or The Slave of Duty* Director/Conductor, Albert Bergeret; Co-director, David Auxier; Choreography, Bill Fabris; Assistant Conductor, Joseph Rubin; Set, Lou Anne Gilleland; **Cast:** James Mills (Major-General Stanley), David Wannen (The Pirate King), David Macaluso (Samuel), Daniel Greenwood or Paul Betz (Frederic), David Auxier (Sergeant of Police), Sarah Caldwell Smith (Mabel), Cáitlín Burke (Edith), Amy Maude Helfer (Kate), Jennifer Piacenti (Isabel), Angela Christine Smith (Ruth); Ensemble: Meredith Borden, Elisabeth Cernadas, Michael Connolly, Louis Dall'Ava, Katie Hall, Alan Hill, Michael Galante, Sarah Hutchison, Lance Olds, Rebecca O'Sullivan, Quinto Ott, Monique Pelletier, Chris-Ian Sanchez, Matthew Wages, Emily D. Wright, Adam Yankowy

Symphony Space; December 28, 2011–January 1, 2012; 6 performances. Setting: A rocky seashore on the coast of Cornwall, a ruined chapel by moonlight. Revival of an operetta presented in two acts. Synopsis: *The Pirates of Penzance* centers on the dilemma of Frederic who, as a child, was mistakenly apprenticed to the pirates until his twenty-first birthday. Helping Frederic to deal with his predicament are the brash Pirate King, Ruth (the pirate maid-of-all-work), romantic Mabel, and the stuffy Major-General Stanley.

Patience *or Bunthorne's Bride* Director/Conductor, Albert Bergeret; Co-director/Choreography, David Auxier; **Cast:** David Wannen (Colonel Calverley), Matthew Wages (Major Murgatroyd), Daniel Greenwood (Lieut. The Duke of Dunstable), James Mills (Reginald Bunthorne), David Macaluso (Archibald Grosvenor), Dana Mooney (Mr. Bunthorne's Solicitor), Erika Person (The Lady Angela), Melissa Attebury (The Lady Saphir), Meredith Borden (The Lady Ella), Caitlin Burke (The Lady Jane), Sarah Caldwell Smith (Patience); Ensemble: Paul Betz, Elisabeth Cernadas, Brooke Collins, Louis Dall'Ava, Lauren Frankovich, Michael Galante, Katie Hall, Amy Maude Helfer, Alan Hill, Sarah Hutchison, James LaRosa, Stephen O'Brien, Rebecca O'Sullivan, Quinto Ott, Marcie Passley, Monique Pelletier, Chris-Ian Sanchez, Angela Christine Smith, Eric Werner, Adam Yankowy

Symphony Space; March 11, 2012; 1 performance. Setting: Exterior of the Castle Bunthorne; Revival of an operetta presented in two acts. Synopsis: *Patience* features the sweet and vivacious village milkmaid who cannot comprehend the infatuation of all the other ladies in town with Reginald Bunthorne, a self-styled disciple of the aesthetic movement. Bunthorne's only true interest is Patience, the one woman who does not fall for his overblown pretensions.

Iolanthe *or the Peer and the Peri* Director/Conductor, Albert Bergeret; Co-director/Choreography, David Auxier; Set, Jack Garver; **Cast:** Stephen O'Brien (The Lord Chancellor), Richard Alan Holmes (The Earl of Mountararat), Cameron Smith (The Earl Tolloller), David Wannen (Private Willis), Daniel Greenwood (Strephon), Angela Christine Smith (Queen of the Fairies), Erika Person (Iolanthe), Amy Maude Helfer (Leila), Lauren Pastorek (Celia), Sonja O'Brien (Fleta), Laurelyn Watson Chase (Phyllis); Ensemble: Paul Betz, Elisabeth Cernadas, Brooke Collins, Louis Dall'Ava, Lauren Frankovich, Michael Galante, Katie Hall, Alan Hill, Sarah Hutchison, David Macaluso, James Mills, Rebecca O'Sullivan, Quinto Ott, Marcie Passley, Monique Pelletier, Chris-Ian Sanchez, Sarah Caldwell Smith, Matthew Wages, Eric Werner, Emily D. Wright

Symphony Space; March 19-20, 2012; 2 performances. Setting: An Arcadian landscape and the Palace Yard, Westminster; between 1700 and 1882. Revival of an operetta presented in two acts. Synopsis: *Iolanthe* centers on the burning question, can a man who is half-fairy find happiness in a world where to marry a mortal is a capital offense?

Stephen O'Brien and Angela Christine Smith in The Grand Duke
photo by William Reynolds)

New York Theatre Workshop

Twenty-ninth Season

Artistic Director, James C. Nicola; Managing Director, William Russo; Associate Artistic Director, Linda S. Chapman; General Manager, C. Barrack Evans; Development, Alisa Schierman; Education, Bryn Thorsson; Finance and Administration, Rachel McBeth; Casting, Jack Doulin; Production/Facilities Manager, Brian Garber; Literary Associate, Geoffrey Jackson Scott; Artistic Administrator, Rachel Silverman; Artistic Associates, Wayne Barker, Alex Lewin; Individual Giving and Board Relations, Norma Scheck; Marketing, Rebekah Paine; Associate Director of Development, Brenna C. Thomas; Technical Director, Paul Bradley; Press, Richard Kornberg and Associates, Don Summa

The Select (The Sun Also Rises) Based on the novel by Ernest Hemingway; Created and Co-produced by Elevator Repair Service (John Collins, Artistic Director; Victoria Vazquez, Managing Director and Education Director; Ariana Smart Truman, Producer; B.D. White, Production Manager); Director, John Collins; Sets and Costumes, David Zinn; Lighting, Mark Barton; Sound, Matt Tierney and Ben Williams; PSM/Assistant Director/Light Board, Sarah Hughes; ASM, Danielle Buccino; Additional Costumes, Colleen Werthmann; Dance and Movement Coach, Katherine Profeta; Assistant Lighting, Dans Maree Sheehan; Sound Engineer, Jason Sebastian; Assistant to the Set Designer, Michael Simmons; ERS Company Manager, Lindsay Hockaday; Production Electrician, John Anselmo Jr.; Assistant Technical Director, Brendon Rigimbal; Costume Shop Manager, Jeffrey Wallach; Sound Technicians, Jason Sebastain, Matt Tierney, Ben Williams; Light Board Programmer, Jay Penfield; Scenic Artist, Katherine Fry; Wardrobe, Jeffrey Wallach; Stagehand, Lou Dileo; ERS Development and External Relations, Edward McKeaney; **Cast:** Mike Iveson (Jake Barnes), Matt Tierney (Robert Cohn), Kate Scelsa (Frances, others), Ben Williams (Bill Gorton, Zizi, others), Pete Simpson (Mike Campbell, others), Kaneza Schaal (Georgette, the concierge, the drummer, Belmonte, others), Vin Knight (Count Mippipopolous, Braddocks, Montoya, others), Lucy Taylor (Brett Ashley), Frank Boyd (Harvey Stone, Harris, others), Susie Sokol (Pedro Romero, others)

East 4th Street Theatre; First Preview: August 19, 2011; Opening Night: September 11, 2011; Closed October 23, 2011; 21 previews, 21 performances. World premiere of a new play presented in two acts. Synopsis: *The Select (The Sun Also Rises)* is the tale of young expatriates living in early 20th century Europe in which journalist Jake Barnes, his former lover Lady Brett Ashley, and the writer Robert Cohn cope with post-war realities and enter the 'age of anxiety' following the end World War I. Elevator Repair Service stages the novel, to complete a trilogy of staging classic American literature, following their lauded productions of *Gatz* and *The Sound and the Fury*.

The Company in The Select (The Sun Also Rises) *(photo by Rob Strong)*

Once Book by Enda Walsh, music and lyrics by Glen Hansard and Markéta Irglová; Based on the motion picture written and directed by John Carney; Director, John Tiffany; Movement, Steven Hoggett; Music Supervision and Orchestrations, Martin Lowe; Sets and Costumes, Bob Crowley; Lighting, Natasha Katz; Sound, Clive Goodwin; Dialect Coach, Stephen Gabis; Vocal Supervisor, Liz Caplan Vocal Studios; Casting, Jim Carnahan, Stephen Kopel; PSM, Bess Marie Glorioso; ASM, Katherine Shea; Assistant Director, Kareem Fahmy; Movement Associate, Yasmine Lee; Assistant Music Supervisor, Rob Preuss; Scenic Design Assistant, Frank McCullough; Lighting Design Assistant, Yael Lubetzky; Sound Design Assistant, Brian Walters; Sound Supervisor, David Fowler; Props Master, Matt Hodges; U.K. Props, Lisa Buckley; Czech Translation, Suzanna Halsey; Production Assistant, Lisa Schwartz; Production Electrician, John Anselmo Jr.; Sound Board Operator, David Fowler; Light Board Programmer, Rosey Cruz; Light Board Operator, Lou Dileo; Sound Crew, Reid Hall, Riley Kubly, Michael Curran; Charge, Katherine Fry; Scenic Artists, Tacy Flaherty, Sarah Trieckel; Wardrobe Supervisor, Jeffrey Wallach; Wardrobe, Cailin Anderson; Deck Crew, Brandon Bart; Welder, Lukas Bridgeman; Cast recording: Masterworks Broadway 88691948242; **Cast-Musicians:** David Abeles (Eamon), Claire Candela (Ivona), Will Connoly (Andrej), Elizabeth A. Davis (Reza), Steve Kazee (Guy), David Patrick Kelly (Da), Cristin Milioti (Girl), Anne L. Nathan (Baruska), Lucas Papelias (Svec), Andy Taylor (Bank Manager), Erikka Walsh (Ex-Girlfriend), Paul Whitty (Billy), J. Michael Zygo (Emcee)

Elizabeth A. Davis and Cristin Milioti in Once *(photo by Joan Marcus)*

Musical Numbers: Leave; Falling Slowly; North Strand; The Moon; Ej, Pada, Pada, Rosicka; If You Want Me; Broken Hearted Hoover Fixer Sucker Guy; Say It to Me Now; Abandoned in Bandon; Gold; Sleeping; When Your Mind's Made Up; The Hill; Gold (A capella); The Moon (reprise); Falling Slowly (reprise)

East 4th Street Theatre; First Preview: November 15, 2011; Opening Night: December 6, 2011; Closed January 15, 2012; 23 previews, 47 performances. World premiere of a new musical presented without intermission. The musical had a workshop developmental production at the American Repertory Theatre in Cambridge, Massachusetts (Diane Paulus, Artistic Director; Diane Borger, Producer) in April, 2011. The production transferred to Broadway February 28, 2012 (see page 60 in this volume). Synopsis: *Once* tells the story an Irish musician and a Czech immigrant drawn together by their shared love of music. Over the course of one fateful week, their unexpected friendship and collaboration evolves into a powerful but complicated romance, heightened by the raw emotion of the songs they create together.

An Iliad by Denis O'Hare and Lisa Peterson; Based on Homer's *The Iliad* translated by Robert Fagles; Director, Lisa Peterson; Sets, Rachel Hauck; Costumes, Marina Draghici; Lighting, Scott Zielinski; Original Music and Sound, Mark Bennett; PSM, Donald Fried; ASM, James C. Steele; Assistant Director, Jessi D. Hill; Scenic Design Assistant, Carolyn Mraz; Lighting Design Assistants, Bradley King, Dante Olivia Smith; Associate Sound/Sound Crew, Charles Coes; Sound Design Assistant, Jake Zerrer; Music Assistant, Zach Redler; Props Master, Allie Geiger; Greek Advisor, Claire Catenaccio; Production Assistant, Marcy Reed; Production Electrician, John Anselmo Jr.; Sound Supervisor, Toby Algya; Milltone Tongue Drum, Larry Miller; Sound Board, Ben Truppin-Brown; Light Board Programmer, Rosey Cruz; Light Board Operator, Lou DiLeo; Scenic Painter, Tacy Flaherty; Scenic Charge, Katherine Fry; Wardrobe Supervisor, Jeffrey Wallach; Costume Crew, Katie Chihaby, Julian Kroboth; Master Carpenter, Lukas Bridgeman; **Cast:** Denis O'Hare or Stephen Spinella (The Poet – in repertory), Brian Ellingsen (Bassist)

East 4th Street Theatre; First Preview: February 15, 2012; Opening Nights: March 6 and 7, 2012; Closed April 1, 2012; 21 previews, 31 performances. New York premiere of a solo performance play presented without intermission. Developed as part of the Usual Suspects Program at NYTW, the play received developmental readings at Vassar and Dartmouth, and was developed in part with the Sundance Institute Theatre Program. World premiere at Seattle Repertory Theatre (Jerry Manning, Producing Artistic Director; Benjamin Moore, Managing Director) April 9–May 16, 2010 (see *Theatre World* Vol. 66, page 390). Subsequently produced at the McCarter Theatre Center (Emily Mann, Artistic Director; Tim Shields, Managing Director; Mara Isaacs, Producing Director) October 19–November 7, 2010 (see *Theatre World* Vol. 67, page 354).

Food and Fadwa by Lameece Issaq and Jacob Kader; Co-presented by Noor Theatre (in residence at NYTW); Director, Shana Gold; Set, Andromache Chalfant; Costumes, Gabriel Berry; Lighting, Japhy Weideman; Sound, Jane Shaw; Original Music, Jane Shaw, Amir ElSaffar, and George Ziadeh; PSM, Lindsey Turteltaub; Dramaturgy, Nancy Vitale; Assistant Director, Noelle Ghoussaini; Music Consultation, George Ziadeh and Amir ElSaffar; Design Assistants: Rebecca Lord-Surratt (set), Whitney Adams (costumes), Justin Partier (lighting), Emma Wilk (sound); Props Master, Starlet Jacobs; Fight Director, Scott Barrow; Dialect Coach, Laith Nakli; Assistant Props, Cat Green; Assistant Dramaturg, Anna Umansky; Production Assistant, Katie Lindsay; Sound Supervisor, Toby Algya; Light Board Programmer, Alex Fabozzi; Light Board Operator, Lou DiLeo; Sound Crew, Leo A. Martin IV, Nicholas Pope; Scenic Charge, Katherine Fry; Scenic Painter, Tacy Flaherty, Daina Cramer; Wardrobe Supervisor, Jeffrey Wallach; Master Carpenter, Luckas Bridgeman; Production Electricians, John Anselmo Jr., Rosie Cruz; **Cast:** Maha Chehlaoui (Dalal Faranesh), Nasser Faris (Baba), Lameece Issaq (Fadwa Faraesh), Kathryn Kates (Aunt Samia), Arian Moayed (Emir Azzam), Heather Raffo (Hayat Johnson), Haaz Sleiman (Youssif Azzam)

East 4th Street Theatre; First Preview: May 18, 2012; Opening Night: June 7, 2012; Closed June 24, 2012; 24 previews, 37 performances. World premiere of a new play presented in two acts. Synopsis: Fadwa Faranesh is an unmarried, 30-something Palestinian woman living in Bethlehem in the politically volatile West Bank. Known for her delectable cooking and deep-seated sense of duty to her family and aging father, our kitchen maven insists on continuing the preparations for the wedding of her younger sister despite constraints of daily life under occupation. In *Food and Fadwa* politics blend with family tensions to create a humorous and heartbreaking meal of a play that melds the fight a Palestinian family wages to hold onto its traditional culture with its need to celebrate love, joy, and hope.

Denis O'Hare in An Illiad *(photo by Joan Marcus)*

Heather Raffo, Haaz Sleiman, Lameece Issaq, Aryan Moayed, Kathryn Kates, and Maha Chehlaoui in Food and Fadwa *(photo by Joan Marcus)*

Pan Asian Repertory Theatre

Thirty-fifth Season

Artistic Producing Director, Tisa Chang; Communications Director, Abby Felder; Artistic Associate, Ron Nakahara; Workshop Instructor, Ernest Abuba; Fight Choreographer, Michael G. Chin; Outreach Associate/House Manager, Danny Gomez; Box Office, Amanda Jornov; Sound Coordinator, Phillip Rudy; Sound Operator, Claire Bacon; Wardrobe, Sarah Melane and Keiko Obremski; Webmaster, Auric Abuba; Production Manager/Technical Director, Jay Janicki; Set Execution, The Ken Larson Company; Box Office Manager, Monet Hurst-Mendoza; Bookkeeper, Rosemary Kahn; Graphics, Ramon Gil & Katelyn Davis; Advertising, Miller Advertising; Photo Archivist, Corky Lee; Press, Keith Sherman and Associates

Shanghai Lil's Book and lyrics by Lilah Kan, music by Louis Stewart, re-envisioned by Tisa Chang; Director, Tisa Chang; Choreography, Susan Ancheta; Sets, Gian Marco Lo Forte; Costumes, Kate Mincer; Lighting, Jiyoun Chang; Orchestrations, Kevin Kasca; Music Direction/Additional Orchestrations, Sarah Brett England; Stage Manager, Elis C. Arroyo; ASM, A.J. Dobbs; Props/Assistant to Sets, Jennifer McDuffee; Dance Captain, Rebecca Lee Lerman; **Cast:** Whitney Kam Lee (Chase), Christine Toy Johnson (Lil), Leanne Cabrera (Sara), Timothy Ng (Jerry), Rebecca Lee Lerman (Hyacinth), Lisa Villamaria (Peony), Jaygee Macapugay (Mei-Mei); Musicians: Sarah Brett England (Piano), Shoshana Seid-Green (Synthesizer)

Musical Numbers: Dream Time Hour; Uncertain Times; Growing Up Is So Exciting; It's Really a Home; Tango; Is It Really Possible; The Sneezing Jingle; At Shanghai Lil's; Ballroom Waltz; It's Time to Dance; Jerry's Farewell; War Duet; Farewell Reprise; I'm Confused By My Feelings for Him; Tai Chi Ballet; Moon Song; Patriot's Salute; Finale

West End Theatre; First Preview: November 11, 2011; Opening Night: November 16, 2011; Closed November 27, 2011; 7 previews, 13 performances. Setting: A San Francisco Chinatown nightclub during World War II. A revised version of a musical presented in two acts. The original world premiere production was presented by Pan Asian Repertory April 22, 1997 (see *Theatre World* Vol. 53, page 165). Synopsis: In a world where the American musical embodies the optimism of boy-meets-girl romance and the American Dream, a cast of Asian American performers charm their audience at Lil's nightclub with song, dance and comedy in spite of the looming specter of WWII and internment.

Stella Rising by Napaua Davoy; Presented as part of NewWorks 2012; Director, Karine Plantadit; Music for *Someday* and *Or Is It Me* by Andrei Kondakov; Music for *The Last Thing on My Mind* by Tom Paxton; Lighting, Jiyoun Chang; Costumes, Jennifer Anderson; Stage Manager, Jun Li; **Cast:** Napaua Davoy (Narrator, *Stella's second daughter*/Stella, *Hawaiian-Chinese war bride in various ages*/Dad, *Stella's husband from Oklahoma*/Billie Jan, *deceased daughter*/Grandmother, *Dad's mother*/Mephistopheles/Police Officer/Candy, *Middle daughter*/Stacy, *youngest daughter*/Louella, *Stella's niece*)

Musical Numbers: The Yellow Butterfly; The Overture; Tokyo Suite; Why So Many Children; You Can't Go Home; The Strength of Religion; Someday; Darling, Don't Leave Me; The Transformation Aria; Getting My Groove On; Tiny Yellow Butterfly; Lahaina; The Last Thing On My Mind; Or Is It Me

West End Theatre; Opening Night: March 8, 2012; Closed March 17, 2012; 9 performances. Setting: 1947-present; Japan, Southeast Texas, California, and Hawaii. New York premiere of a new solo performance play with music presented without intermission. Synopsis: *Stella Rising* is a humorous and poignant rendering, based on the author's turbulent "east vs. west/mother vs. daughter" experience, as life's traumas change the family in the most unexpected ways. This one-woman show, spanning 70 years of history, is presented through dialogue, dance, and original songs ranging from Blues to Jazz to Opera, and ultimately reveals a brighter side of Alzheimer's.

Napua Davoy in Stella Rising (photos by Corky Lee)

BAUDELAIRE: La Mort Created, conceived, and scripted by Ernest Abuba, Anna Gheesling, Shigeko Sara Suga, and Minouche Waring; Presented as part of NewWorks 2012; Director/Choreography, Shigeko Sara Suga; Sets, Gian Marco Lo Forte and Justin West; Lighting, Marie Yokoyama; Costumes, Keiko Obremski; Stage Manager, Jun Li; ASM, Ada Chau; English Translations, James McGowan, Richard Howard, Michael Field, F.P. Sturm, Jackson Matthews, Roy Campbell, Robert Lowell, Algernon Charles Swinburne; Script Support, Annel Martinez and Dominique Amiot; **Cast:** Ernest Abuba (Baudelaire, *a Man*), Shigeko Sara

Rebecca Lee Lerman. Lisa Villamaria. Leanne Cabrera in Shanghai Lil's

Suga (Entity), Anna Gheesling (Entity), Tiffany Chen (Entity), Paola Irun (Entity replacement), Tim Liu and Aaron Chieu (Kuroko); Musicians: Yukio Tsuji (Music Director/Shakuhachi Player/Percussionist), Arturo Martinez (Flamenco Guitar)

West End Theatre; Opening Night: March 23, 2012; Closed April 1, 2012; 8 performances. World premiere of a theatrical dance piece presented without intermission. Synopsis: Inspired by Baudelaire's masterpiece "Les Fleur du Mal", *BAUDELAIRE: La Mort* is dance theatre that fuses Butoh, Flamenco and French poetry in a visceral and lyrical exploration of life's beginnings and endings.

Aaron Chieu, Tiffany Chen, Ernest Abuba, Shigeko Sara Suga, and Tim Liu in Baudelaire: LaMort

Rangoon by Mayank Keshaviah; Director, Raul Aranas; Sets, Kaori Akazawa; Costumes, Carol A. Pelletier; Lighting, Victor En Yu Tan; Dramaturg, Snehal Desai; Sound Coordinator, Phillip Rudy; Stage Manager, April Ann Kline; ASM, Miriam Hyfler; **Cast:** Faizul Khan (Dhiraj Patel), Sunita S. Mukhi (Seema Patel), Adeel Ahmed (Vinay Patel), Anita Sabherwal (Tejal Patel), James Rana (Chetan Patel), Krishen Mehta (Motilal Patel), Kylie Delre (Marge), Juan Luis Acevedo (Orlando), Daniel Robert Sullivan (Randy)

Clurman Theatre on Theatre Row; First Preview: May 25, 2012; Opening Night: May 31, 2012; Closed June 17, 2012; 7 previews, 23 performances. Setting: The suburban and rural South, 2004. World premiere of a new play presented in two acts. Synopsis: In this contemporary play that spans from Burma to the American south, a family of Indian émigrés must deal with seductions of American life while keeping its heritage alive.

Adeel Ahmed, Anita Sabherwal, Sunita S. Mukhi, Faizul Khan, and James Rana in Rangoon *(photos by Corky Lee)*

Pearl Theatre Company

Twenty-eighth Season

Artistic Director, J.R. Sullivan; Managing Director, David Roberts; Production Manager/Technical Director, Gary Levinson; Dramaturg, Kate Farrington; Marketing and Press, Aaron Schwartzbord; Development Manager, Tiffany Kleeman Baran; Audience Services Manager, Justin Dewey; Artistic Administrator, Sarah Wozniak; Business Manager, Michael Levinton; Costume Shop Manager, Anna Light/Niki Hernandez-Adams; Education, Carol Schultz; Development Consultant, David Bury and Associates; Technology Consultants, Marathon Consulting

The Bald Soprano by Eugene Ionesco, translated by Donald M. Allen; Director, Hal Brooks; Set, Harry Feiner; Costumes, Barbara A. Bell; Lighting, Stephen Petrilli; Sound, M.L. Dogg; PSM, Erin Albrecht; Production Assistant, Abbey Bay; Dialects, Amy Stoller; Props, Joshua Yocom; Wigs, Amanda Miller; Wardrobe Supervisor, Sally Hall; Cutter/Draper, Anna Gerdes; Milliner, Arnold Levine; Carpenters/Electricians, Nia Adams, A.J. Cote, Kevin Mullins, Jason Slack; **Cast:** Rachel Botchan (Mrs. Smith), Bradford Cover (Mr. Smith), Brad Heberlee (Mr. Martin), Jolly Abraham (Mrs. Martin), Robin Leslie Brown (Mary), Dan Daily (The Fire Chief); Understudies: Carol Schultz (Mrs. Smith, Mary), Michael Aguirre (Mr. Smith), Musa Bacon (The Fire Chief), Julie McKay (Mrs. Martin), Craig Mungavin (Mr. Martin), Abbey Bay (Swing)

City Center Stage II; First Preview: September 13, 2011; Opening Night: September 25, 2011; Closed October 23, 2011; 13 previews, 29 performances. Setting: An English evening in an English interior. Revival of a classic play presented without intermission. Synopsis: The Smiths live in a typical house on a typical street, cheerfully entertaining typical friends and typical neighbors— in a world that's anything but typical. Ionesco's game-changing absurdist comedy tumbles us into a bizarre and brilliant comic universe, where time is out of joint, language has misplaced its meaning, and identity itself is up for grabs.

Bradford Cover and Rachel Botchan in The Bald Soprano *(photo by Jacob J. Goldberg)*

Richard II by William Shakespeare; Director, J.R. Sullivan; Set, Harry Feiner; Costumes, Martha Hally; Lighting, Stephen Petrilli; Sound, Jane Shaw; Voice and Text Direction, Dudley Knight; Fight Director, David Ian Lee; Movement Coach, Kali Quinn; PSM, Dale Smallwood; Production Assistant, Kristin Bodall; Production Intern, Meggan White; Props, Joshua Yocom; Wardrobe Supervisor, Sally Hall; Costume Intern, Sydney Davis; Stitchers, Teddy Ricker, Mary Margaret Powers; Cutter/Draper, Anna Gerdes; Carpenters, Jason Slack, Kevin Mullins, A.J. Cote, Dan Berardi, Robert Dutiel; **Cast:** Jolly Abraham (Queen/Harry Percy), Robin Leslie Brown (Green/Duchess of Gloucester/Gardener's Assistant/Murderer 1), Wayne T. Carr (Duke of Aumerle/Lord Willoughby/Keeper of the Prison),

Christ (Edmund, *Duke of York*), Dominic Cuskern (Lord Marshal/York's Servant/Lord Salisbury/Abbot of Westminster/Groom), Grant Goodman (Henry Bolingbroke, *Duke of Hereford*), Simon Kendall (Bushy/Sir Stephen Scroop/Lord Fitzwater/Murderer 2), Dan Kremer (John of Guant, *Duke of Lancaster*/Gardener), Sean McNall (Richard II), Chris Mixon (Thomas Mowbray, *Duke of Norfolk*/Earl of Northumberland), Charlie Francis Murphy (Bagot/Lord Berkeley/Welsh Captain/Sir Pierce of Exton), Carol Schultz (Bishop of Carlisle/Lady Attending the Queen/Duchess of York); Apprentices: Michael Aguirre, Virginia Bartholomew, Rob Benson, Kristin Bodall, Connor Carew, Lee Chrisman, Josh Doucette, Maggie Fales, Meera Rohit Kumbhani, Drew Lewis, Craig Mungavin, Kevin Shimko.

City Center Stage II; First Preview: November 8, 2011; Opening Night: November 20, 2011; Closed December 24, 2011; 14 previews, 35 performances. Setting: The late 14th century, England. Revival of a classic play in five acts presented with one intermission. Synopsis: Corruption, ambition, and greed stalk the nation—and threaten to destroy its future. In *Richard II*, Shakespeare chronicles the shattering fall of one king and the meteoric rise of another in a raw and powerful tale of a country—and a soul—in chaos.

Sean McNall and Jolly Abraham in Richard II *(photo by Gregory Costanzo)*

The Philanderer by George Bernard Shaw; Director, Gus Kaikkonen; Set, Jo Winiarski; Costumes, Sam Fleming; Lighting, Stephen Petrilli; Sound, Jane Shaw; Fight Director, Rod Kinter; PSM, Erin Albrecht; Production Assistant, Emily Rolston; Props, Carlos Aguilar; Wigs, Gerard Kelly; Production Intern, Meggan White; Wardrobe Supervisor, Preesa Adeline-Bullington; Costume Shop Intern, Elly Sumner; Draper, Anna Gerdes; Board Operator, Victoria Loye; Carpenters, Pete Fry, Katie Meade, Kevin Mullins; **Cast:** Bradford Cover (Leonard Charteris), Rachel Botchan (Grace Tranfield), Karron Graves (Julia Craven, *Colonel Craven's elder daughter*), Dominic Cuskern (Joseph Cuthbertson), Dan Daily (Colonel Daniel Craven, *Grace's father*), Chris Mixon (Dr. Percy Paramore), Shalita Grant

(Sylvia Craven, *Colonel Craven's younger daughter*), Chris Richards (Page Boy and Butler); Understudy: Chris Richards (Leonard); Apprentices: Chris Cornwell, Andrew Goldwasser, Rocio Mendez, Emily Rolston, Chris Wright, Kimberly Wong

City Center Stage II; First Preview: January 10, 2012; Opening Night: January 22, 2012; Closed February 19, 2012; 14 previews, 29 performances. Setting: 1897. Act I Scene 1: A flat in Ashley Gardens in the Victoria District of London, past ten at night; Scene 2: The Library of the Ibsen Club, the next day at noon; Act II Scene 1: The same, ten minutes later; Scene 2: Sitting room in Dr. Paramore's Office in Saville Row, immediately after. Revival of a classic play presented in four scenes in two acts. Synopsis: Leonard Charteris has two big problems—called Grace and Julia. He can't quite win the heart of one or break free of the other. And he's fairly sure it's all Henrik Ibsen's fault. Shaw's pert and playful satire serves up a wise and wicked portrait of the perilous joys of love in a modern age.

A Moon for the Misbegotten by Eugene O'Neill; Director, J.R. Sullivan; Set, Jo Winiarski; Costumes, Rachel Laritz; Lighting, Jaymi Lee Smith; Sound, Lindsay Jones; Fight Director, Rod Kinter; Assistant to the Director, Ryan Krause; PSM, Dale Smallwood; Production Assistant, Norah Scheinman; Production Intern, Katie Meade; Dialect Design, Amy Stoller; Props, Sara Swanberg; Assistant Design: Jared Rutherford (set), Benjamin Weill (lighting), Will Pickens (sound); Costume Design Assistant, Jenny Clark; Wardrobe Supervisor, Preesa Adeline Bullington; Draper, Anna Gerdes; Board Operator, Victoria Love; **Cast:** Kim Martin-Cotton (Josie Hogan), Sean McNall (Mike Hogan, *her* brother), Dan Daily (Phil Hogan, *her father*), Andrew May (James Tyrone Jr.), Kern McFadden (T. Stedman Harder)

City Center Stage II; First Preview: March 6, 2012; Opening Night: March 18, 2012; Closed April 15, 2012; 14 previews, 29 performances. Setting: Connecticut, September 1923. Act I: The Farmhouse, around noon; Act II: 11 o'clock that night; Act III: Later; Act IV: Dawn of the following morning. Revival of a play presented in four acts with two intermissions after Acts I and II. The original production was produced at the Bijou Theatre May 2–June 29, 1957, playing 68 performances (see *Theatre World* Vol. 13, page 115). The play has had four major Broadway revivals, most recently at the Brooks Atkinson Theatre April 9–June 10, 2007 (see *Theatre World* Vol. 63, page 69.) Synopsis: They meet on a barren patch of earth, in the glow of an autumn moon. The jaded James Tyrone is on the edge of despair; the fiercely passionate Josie Hogan is lonely beyond endurance. But on this night, under this moon, hope sparks between them. In O'Neill's bittersweet elegy, two wounded hearts experience the power of redemption—and the saving grace of love.

Kim Martin-Cotton and Andrew May in A Moon for the Misbegotten *(photo by Jacob J. Goldberg)*

Playwrights Horizons

Forty-first Season

Artistic Director, Tim Sanford; Managing Director, Leslie Marcus; General Manager, Carol Fishman; Director of New Play Development, Adam Greenfield; Director of Musical Theatre/Literary Associate, Kent Nicholson; Casting, Alaine Alldaffer; Production Manager, Christopher Boll; Development, Beth Nathanson; Controller, Jack Feher; Marketing, Eric Winick; Director of Ticket Central, Ross Peabody; School Director, Helen R. Cook; Company Manager, Caroline Aquino; Technical Director, Brian Coleman; Press, The Publicity Office, Marc Thibodeau, Michael S. Borowski, Jeremy Shaffer

Completeness by Itamar Moses; Director, Pam MacKinnon; Sets and Costumes, David Zinn; Lighting, Russell H. Champa; Original Music and Sound, Bray Poor; Projections and Video, Rocco DiSanti; PSM, Charles Turner III; ASM, Katrina Hermann; Assistant Design: Tim McMath, F. Michael Simmons (set), Jacob Climer (costumes), Justin Partier (lighting), Ido Levran (video and projections); Assistant Technical Director, Marc Vogt; Carpenters, Steven Bert, Will Duty, David Nelson; Scenic Artists, Carolyn Bonanni, Samantha Yaeger; Automation, Nick DeFrange; Props Supervisor, Desireé Maurer; Prop Assistants, Sarah Engelke, Julie Jentzen, Kathleen Stack; Costume Supervisor, Tiia E. Torchia; Wardrobe, Katie Chihaby; Lighting Supervisor, Douglas Filomena; Light Board, Sam Punia; Audio Supervisor, Dylan Carrow; Audio Operator, Sarah Gates; Costume Assistant, Sarah Reever; **Cast:** Karl Miller (Elliot), Aubrey Dollar (Molly), Meredith Forlenza (Lauren/Katie/Nell), Brian Avers (Don/Clark/Franklin)

Mainstage Theatre; First Preview: August 19, 2011; Opening Night: September 13, 2011; Closed: September 25, 2011; 24 previews, 15 performances. Setting: A university campus. New York premiere of a new play presented in two acts. World premiere at South Coast Repertory Theater, Costa Mesa, California (Marc Masterson, Artistic Director) April 17–May 8, 2011 (see *Theatre World* Vol. 67, page 370). Synopsis: In *Completeness*, when computer scientists Elliot builds a computer program to help molecular biologist Molly with her research project, the variables in their evolving relationship shift as rapidly as the terms of their experiment. This deft and imaginative new ROM-comedy shows that even the most sophisticated algorithm may freeze in the face of life's infinite possibilities.

Aubrey Dollar and Karl Miller in Completeness *(photo by Joan Marcus)*

Milk Like Sugar by Kirsten Greenidge; Co-presented by Women's Project Theater (Julia Crosby, Artistic Director) and La Jolla Playhouse (Christopher Ashley, Artistic Director; Michael Rosenberg, Managing Director); Director, Rebecca Taichman; Sets, Mimi Lien; Costumes, Toni-Leslie James; Lighting, Justin Townsned; Original Music and Sound, Andre Pluess; Alaine Alldaffer, Telsey + Company; PSM, Kyle Gates; ASM, Allison Cottrell; Assistant Design: Mar Urrestarazu (set), Josh Quinn (costumes), Christopher Kuhl (lighting), Nick Borisjuk (sound); Carpenters, Will Duty, Joel Howell, Caroline Blackford; Scenic Artists, Samantha Yaeger, Carolyn Bonanni; Deck Carpenter, John Underwood;

Props Supervisors, Desireé Maurer, Kathleen Stack; Prop Carpenter, Jason Craig; Prop Assistant, Sarah Engelke; Costume Supervisor, Tiia E. Torchia; Wardrobe, Katie Chihaby; Lighting Supervisor, Douglas Filomena; Light Board, Bridget Chervchenka; Audio Supervisor, Dylan Carrow; Audio Operator, Daniel Spitaliere; Graphics, Bradford Louryk; Artwork Photography, Aaron Epstein; Marketing Consultant, Marcia Pendelton; **Cast:** Cherise Boothe (Talisha), Angela Lewis (Annie), Nikiya Mathis (Margie), LeRoy McClain (Antwoine), J. Mallory-McCree (Malik), Adrienne C. Moore (Keera), Tonya Pinkins (Myrna)

Peter Jay Sharp Theatre; First Preview: October 13, 2011; Opening Night: November 11, 2011; Closed November 27, 2011; 22 previews, 31 performances. New York premiere of a new play presented without intermission. World premiere presented at La Jolla Playhouse August 30–September 25, 2011. Synopsis: With potential for more but nowhere to put it, sixteen-year-old Annie's got a choice: honor the pregnancy pact she made with her friends, or find the path to a brighter future. In this observant new play, Kirsten Greenidge finds savage humor and gritty poetry in one inner-city girl's struggle to carve out a life beyond the only one she knows.

Tonya Pinkins and Angela Lewis in Milk Like Sugar *(photo by Ari Mintz)*

Maple and Vine by Jordan Harrison; Director, Anne Kauffman; Sets, Alexander Dodge; Costumes, Ilona Somogyi; Lighting, David Weiner; Original Music and Sound, Bray Poor; PSM, Willam H. Lang; ASM, Ryan Gohsman; Assistant Design: Alexander Woodward (set), Sangree Kim (costumes), Phil Kong, William Noguchi (lighting), Jana Hoglund (sound); Wigs, Charles LaPointe; Automation Operator, Nick DeFrange; Deck Carpenter, Adam Walck; Props Crew, Jessica Provenzale (supervisor), Jason Craig (carpenter), Jung Griffin (artisan), Kathleen Stack (assistant), Julie Jentzen (assistant); Wardrobe, Katie Chihaby; Lighting Supervisor, Douglas Filomena; Light Board, Sam Punia; Audio Supervisor, Dylan Carrow; Audio Operator, Sarah Gates; Scenic Artists, Samantha Yaeger, Kathryn Veillette; Graphic Design, Rogers Eckersley; **Cast:** Marin Ireland (Katha), Peter Kim (Ryu), Trent Dawson (Dean), Jeanine Serralles (Ellen/Jenna), Pedro Pascal (Roger/Omar)

Mainstage Theatre; First Preview: November 19, 2011; Opening Night: December 7, 2011; Closed: December 23, 2011; 20 previews, 19 performances. Setting: The Present. New York premiere of a new play presented in two acts. World premiere at Actors Theatre of Louisville's Humana Festival March 4–April 3, 2011 (see *Theatre World* Vol. 67, page 318). Originally developed by The Civilians. Synopsis: Katha and Ryu have become allergic to their 21st-century lives. After they meet a charismatic man from a community of 1950s re-enactors, they forsake cell phones and sushi for cigarettes and Tupperware parties. In this compulsively authentic world, Katha and Ryu are surprised by what their new neighbors – and they themselves – are willing to sacrifice for happiness.

Marin Ireland, Jeanine Serralles, Trent Dawson, and Peter Kim in Maple and Vine *(photo by Joan Marcus)*

Assistance by Leslye Headland; Director, Trip Cullman; Sets, David Korins; Costumes, Jessica Pabst; Lighting, Ben Stanton; Sound, Jill BC DuBoff; Choreography, Jeffry Denman; PSM, Kyle Gates; ASM, Vanessa Coakley; Associate Set Design: Amanda Stephens; Assistant Design: Katie Hartsoe (costumes), Alejandro Fajardo (lighting), Emma Wilk (sound); Assistant to the Set Designer, James Weinman; Deck Carpenter, Adam Walck; Props Crew: Jessica Provenzale (supervisor), Kathleen Stack, Julie Jentzen, Ellie Bye (assistants); Costume Supervisor, Tiia E. Torchia; Wardrobe, Katie Chihaby; Lighting Supervisor, Douglas Filomena; Light Board, Sam Punia; Audio Supervisor, Dylan Carrow; Audio Operator, Leo A. Martin IV; Costume Assistant, Sarah Reever; Scenic Artists, Samantha Yaeger, Kira Nehmer; Carpenters, Will Duty, Stephen Bert, Caroline Blackford, Joel Howell, Ben Morris; **Cast:** Michael Esper (Nick), Virginia Kull (Nora), Lucas Near-Verbrugghe (Vince), Sue Jean Kim (Heather), Amy Rosoff (Jenny), Bobby Steggert (Justin)

Mainstage Theatre; First Preview: February 3, 2012; Opening Night: February 28, 2012; Closed: March 11, 2012; 23 previews, 46 performances. Setting: An office below Canal Street, New York. The present. New York premiere of a new play presented without intermission. World premiere presented by IAMA Theatre Company (Los Angeles) in 2008. Synopsis: For these young assistants, life is an endless series of humiliations at the hands of their hellacious boss, a powerful uber-magnate. In rare moments of calm, Nick and Nora and their co-workers question whether all their work will lead to success—or just more work. *Assistance* is a biting, high-octane satire about our attraction to power and what we're willing to sacrifice to stay in its orbit.

Michael Esper and Virginia Kull in Assistance *(photo by Joan Marcus)*

The Big Meal by Dan LeFranc; Director, Sam Gold; Sets and Costumes, David Zinn; Lighting, Mark Barton; Sound, Leah Gelpe; PSM, Alaina Taylor; ASM, Katrina Herrmann; Assistant Design: Michael Simmons (set), Jacob Climer (costumes), Christopher Kuhl (lighting), Emma Wilk (sound); Deck Carpenter, John Underwood; Props Crew, Jessica Provenzale (supervisor), Kathleen Stack (assistant), Jason Craig (carpenter); Costume Supervisor, Tiia E. Torchia; Wardrobe Jenna Glendye; Lighting Supervisor, Douglas Filomena; Light Board, Holly Burnell; Audio Supervisor, Dylan Carrow; Audio Operator, Daniel Spitaliere; Graphics, Bradford Louryk; Costume Assistant, Sarah Reever; Scenic Artist, Carolyn Bonanni; Carpenters, Will Duty, Joel Howell; **Cast:** Anita Gillette (Woman 1), Tom Bloom (Man 1), Jennifer Mudge (Woman 2), David Wilson Barnes (Man 2), Phoebe Strole (Woman 3), Cameron Scoggins (Man 3), Rachel Resheff (Girl), Griffin Birney (Boy), Molly Ward (Server)

Peter Jay Sharp Theater; First Preview: March 1, 2012; Opening Night: March 21, 2012; Closed April 8, 2012; 23 previews, 46 performances. Setting: New York premiere of a new play presented without intermission. World premiere at American Theater Company (Chicago) February 7, 2011. Synopsis: Somewhere in America, in a typical suburban restaurant on a typical night, Sam and Nicole meet. And sparks fly, setting in motion an expansive tale that traverses five generations of a modern family, from first kiss to final goodbye. A stunning, big-hearted play that spans nearly eighty years in a single sitting, *The Big Meal* tells the extraordinary story of an ordinary family.

David Wilson Barnes, Cameron Scoggins, Phoebe Strole, Jennifer Mudge, and Anita Gillette in The Big Meal *(photo by Joan Marcus)*

Rapture, Blister, Burn by Gina Gionfriddo; Director, Peter DuBois; Sets, Alexander Dodge; Costumes, Mimi O'Donnell; Lighting, Jeff Croiter; Sound, M.L. Dogg; PSM, Lisa Ann Chernoff; ASM, Allison Cottrell; Assistant Design: Colin McGurk, Kenichi Takahashi (set), Cathy Parrott (costumes), Cory Pattak (lighting), John Kemp (sound); Automation, Adam Walck; Deck Carpenter, Julie Jentzen; Costume Supervisor, Tiia E. Torchia; Wardrobe, Anna Flaglor; Lighting Supervisor, Douglas Filomena; Props Crew, Jessica Provenzale (supervisor), Julie Jentzen, Kathleen Stack (assistants); Scenic Artist, Caroline Bonanni; Costume Assistant, Sarah Reever; Audio Supervisor, Dylan Carrow; Audio Operator, Leo A. Martin IV; Show Art Illustration, Sam Hendricks; Carpenters, Carolyn Blackwell, Eric Brooks, Will Duty, Joel Howell, Timothy Reynolds; **Cast:** Kellie Overbey (Gwen), Amy Brenneman (Catherine), Lee Tergesen (Don), Virginia Kull (Avery), Beth Dixon (Alice)

Mainstage Theatre; First Preview: May 18, 2012; Opening Night: June 12, 2012; Closed July 1, 2012; 30 previews, 22 performances. Setting: A college town in New England, summer. World premiere of a new play presented in two acts. Synopsis: After grad school, Catherine and Gwen chose polar opposite paths. Catherine built a career as a rockstar academic, while Gwen built a home with her husband and children. Decades later, unfulfilled in polar opposite ways, each woman covets the other's life, commencing a dangerous game of musical chairs – the prize being Gwen's husband. *Rapture, Blister, Burn* is an unflinching look at gender politics in the wake of 20th century feminist ideals.

Primary Stages

Twenty-seventh Season

Founder and Executive Producer, Casey Childs; Artistic Director, Andrew Leynse; Managing Director, Elliot Fox; Associate Artistic Director, Michelle Bossy; Literary Manager, Tessa LaNeve; Development, Jessica Sadowski Comas; Marketing, Elizabeth Kandel; General Manager, Toni Marie Davis; Production Supervisor, Peter R. Feuchtwanger; Casting, Stephanie Klapper; Press, O+M Company, Rick Miramontez, Philip Carrubba (*Olive and the Bitter Herbs, Motherhood Out Loud*)/ Keith Sherman and Associates, Brett Oberman (*Rx, The Morini Strad*)

Olive and the Bitter Herbs by Charles Busch; Produced in association with Daryl Roth and Bob Boyett; Director, Mark Brokaw; Set, Anna Louizos; Costumes, Suzy Benzinger; Lighting, Mary Louise Geiger; Original Music and Sound, John Gromada; Props Coordinator, Kathy Fabian/Propstar; PSM, William H. Lang; ASM, Trisha Henson; Assistant Design: Aimee Dombo, Adam Karavatakis, Melissa Shakun (set), Patrick Chevillot (costumes), Amanda Clegg Lyon (lighting), Janie Bullard (sound); Associate Props, Carrie Mossman; Assistant Director, Sam Pinkleton; Carpenters, Bruno Fontaine, Josh Vasquez; Upholstery/ Soft Goods, Mary Wilson, Kathry Vega; Prop Carpenter, John Estep; Electrician, Tom Dyer; Light Board Programmer, Evan Purcell; Audio, David A. Arnold, Erin Ballentine; Board Operator, Jennifer Campos; Wardrobe Supervisor, Michelle Ridley; Production Assistants, Paula Clarkson, Allison Douglass; **Cast:** Marcia Jean Kurtz (Olive), Julie Halston (Wendy), David Garrison (Robert), Dan Butler (Trey), Richard Masur (Sylvan)

59E59 Theater A; First Preview: July 26, 2011; Opening Night: August 16, 2011; Closed September 4, 2011; 20 previews, 21 performances. Setting: Olive's apartment living room in the East Thirties, in Manhattan. World premiere of a new play presented in two acts. Synopsis: Actress Olive Fisher sees a ghost in her mirror, her radiator's broken, the couple next door stinks up her apartment with exotic cheeses, and the highlight of her long career was a sausage commercial in the 80s. While she's not the most popular tenant, her neighbors invite themselves over and she finds herself hosting a Passover Seder. But are Olive's guests there to see her or the mysterious man in her mirror? *Olive and the Bitter Herbs* is a comedy about connecting to the people in our lives – those with us and those who have passed on.

David Garrison, Dan Butler, Marcia Jean Kurtz, Richard Masur, and Julie Halston in Olive and the Bitter Herbs

Motherhood Out Loud Conceived by Susan Rice and Joan Stein; Scenes: *Squeeze, Hold, Release* by Cheryl L. West; *Next to the Crib* by Brooke Berman; *New in the Motherhood* by Lisa Loomer; *Queen Esther* by Michele Lowe; *Baby Bird* by Theresa Rebeck; *If We're Using a Surrogate Why Am I the One with Morning Sickness* by Marco Pennette; *Nooha's List* by Lameece Issaq; *My Almost Family* by Luanne Rice; *Michael's Date* by Claire LaZebnik; *Threesome* by Leslie

Ayvazian; *Bridal Shop* by Michele Lowe; *Stars and Striped* by Jessica Goldberg; *Elizabeth* by David Gale; *Report on Motherhood* by Beth Henley; *My Baby* by Annie Weisman; Director, Lisa Peterson; Set, Rachel Hauck; Costumes, David C. Woolard; Lighting, Christopher Kuhl; Sound, Jill BC DuBoff; Projections, Jan Hartley; Animation, Emily Hubley; Dramaturgy, Janice Paran; PSM, Donald Fried; Casting, Stephanie Klapper/Telsey + Company; ASM, James Steele; Assistant Design: Carolyn Mraz (set), Joseph S. Blaha (costumes), Adam Blumenthal (lighting), Ben Truppin-Brown (sound); Assistant Director, Kaytlin McIntyre; Carpenters, John A. Martinez, J. Michael Zally; Electricians, Tom Dyer, Yuriy Nayer; Audio, David A. Arnold, Erin Ballentine; Board Operator, Jennifer Campos; Projection Operator, Patrick Metzger; Wardrobe Supervisor, Michelle Ridley; Marketing and Promotions, The Pekoe Group; **Cast:** Mary Bacon (Actor A), Saidah Arrika Ekulona (Actor B), Randy Graff (Actor C), James Lecesne (Actor D)

59E59 Theater A; First Preview: September 20, 2011; Opening Night: October 4, 2011; Closed October 29, 2010; 14 previews, 26 performances. New York premiere of a new play presented in fifteen short scenes without intermission. World premiere presented at Hartford Stage (Michael Wilson, Artistic Director; Michael Stotts, Managing Director) February 24–March 21, 2010 (see *Theatre World* Vol. 66, page 372). Synopsis: When entrusting the subject of motherhood to a collection of celebrated American writers, the result is a joyous, moving, hilarious, and thrilling theatrical play. *Motherhood Out Loud* shatters traditional notions about parenthood, celebrates the deeply personal truths that span and unite generations, and reveals with illuminating insight the humor, raw emotions and rocky roads we experience in life.

Saidah Arrika Eulona, Mary Bacon, and Randy Graf in Motherhood Out Loud

Rx by Kate Fodor; Director, Ethan McSweeny; Set, Lee Savage; Costumes, Andrea Lauer; Lighting, Matthew Richards; Original Music and Sound, Lindsay Jones; Prop Supervisor, Faye Armon; PSM, Jennifer Rae Moore; ASM, B. Bales Karlin; Assistant Design: D. Schuyler Burks (set), Joseph S. Blaha (costumes), Wilburn Bonnel (lighting), Anthony Mattana (sound); Prop Assistant, Marina Guzman; Carpenters, John A. Martinez, J. Michael Zally; Electricians, Tom Dyer, Laurance A. Bransgrove; Light Board Programmer, Colin Scott; Production Audio, David A. Arnold; Board Operator, Jennifer Campos; Wardrobe Supervisor, Michelle Ridley; Assistant Director/SDC Observer, Elyzabeth Gorman; Production Assistant, Sarah Johnson; **Cast:** Marin Hinkle (Meena Pierotti, *Managing Editor, Piggies, American Cattle & Swine Magazine*), Stephen Kunken (Phil Gray, *Schmidt Phama researcher*), Michael Bakkensen (Simon, *Meena's boss*), Marylouise Burke (Frances, *a widow in need of new underwear*), Paul Niebanck (Richard, *a marketing executive*/Ed, *Schmidt Pharma researcher*)

59E59 Theater A; First Preview: January 24, 2012; Opening Night: February 7, 2012; Closed March 3, 2012; 14 previews, 26 performances. Setting: A Midwestern city. The present. World premiere of a new play presented without intermission. Synopsis: Meena Pierotti's job is making her unhappy. Luckily, there's a pill for that. Well, not yet. Meena has joined the clinical trial for a new drug targeting workplace depression. The trial gets messy, however, when she falls in love with her doctor, who himself is trying to enroll in a drug trial targeting heartbreak.

The Morini Strad by Willy Holtzman; Produced in association with Jamie deRoy, Barry Feirstein, and Dan Frishwasser; Director, Casey Child; Set, Neil Patel; Costumes, David C. Woolard; Lighting, M.L. Geiger; Original Music and Sound, Lindsay Jones; Projections, Jan Hartley; PSM, Sarah Melissa Hall; ASM, Christine D'Amore; Music Consultant, Louise Beach; Prop Master, Tessa Dunning; Assistant Design: Ameyalli Ruiz Alacon (set), Joseph S. Blaha (costumes), Nicholas Colin (lighting), Anthony Mattana (sound), Nemo Leach (projections); Carpenters, John A. Martinez, J. Michael Zally; Electricians, Tom Dyer, Laurence Austin Bransgrove; Light Board Programmer, Colin Scott; Production Audio, David A. Arnold; Production Video, Michael Curran; Board Operator, Jennifer Campos; Wardrobe Supervisor, Michelle Ridley; Projection Operator, Scott Basten; Assistant Director, Benjamin Kern; Production Assistants, Lisa Haedrich, Amy Puleo; **Cast:** Mary Beth Peil (Erica), Michael Laurence (Brian), Hanah Stuart (Violinist)

59E59 Theater A; First Preview: March 20, 2012; Opening Night: April 3, 2012; Closed April 28, 2012; 14 previews, 26 performances. Setting: The recent past. Manhattan, Upper Fifth Avenue. New York premiere of a new play presented without intermission. Commissioned and originally produced by Pittsburgh's City Theatre Company (Tracy Brigden, Artistic Director; Mark R. Power, Managing Director) November 6–December 12, 2010. Synopsis: Inspired by the true story of concert violinist Erica Morini and her legendary Stradivarius, *The Morini Strad* is a delicate duet between Erica, a former child prodigy, and Brian, an independent violin maker she hires to restore and then sell her beloved Strad. As Brian makes the arrangements, the question of what will become of the priceless instrument threatens to destroy their unexpected friendship. Through classical music and fiery confrontations, Brian and Erica must face the choices they've made about their music and their lives.

Mary Beth Peil and Michael Laurence in The Morini Strad *(photos by James Leynse)*

The Public Theater

Fifty-sixth Season

Artistic Director, Oskar Eustis; Executive Director, Joey Parnes/Patrick Willingham; General Manager, Andrea Nellis/Steven Showalter; Associate Artistic Director, Mandy Hackett; Associate Producer, Maria Goyanes; Development, Sandra E. Davis; Marketing, Nella Vera; Communications, Candi Adams; Casting, Jordan Thaler, Heidi Griffiths; Capital Projects, Adrienne Dobsovits; Director of Joe's Pub, Shanta Thake; Director of Musical Theatre Initiative, Ted Sperling; Director of Shakespeare Initiative, Barry Edelstein; Under the Radar, Mark Russell; Special Projects, Eric Louie; Master Writer Chair, Suzan-Lori Parks; Director of Production, Ruth E. Sternberg; Information Technology, Robert Cohn; Ticket Services, Jimmy Goodsey; Press, Sam Neuman

Shakespeare in the Park

All's Well That Ends Well by William Shakespeare; Director, Daniel Sullivan; Set, Scott Pask; Costumes, Jane Greenwood; Lighting, Peter Kaczorowski; Original Music, Tom Kitt; Sound, Acme Sound Partners; Hair and Wigs, Tom Watson; Fight Director, Thomas Schall; Choreography, Mimi Lieber; Vocal Coach, Shane-Ann Younts; PSM, James Latus; Stage Managers, Buzz Cohen, M. William Shiner; Assistant Director, Nelson T. Eusebio III; Recorded Musicians: Mary-Mitchell Campbell (Piano), Damien Bassman (Percussion), Mairi Dorman (Cello), Christian Hebel (Violin), Katherine Livolsi (Violin), Erin Benim (Viola); Associate Design: Orit Jacoby Carroll (set), Jessica Ford (costumes), Gina Scherr (lighting), Jason Crystal (sound); Assistant Costume Design, Moria Clinton; Assistant Choreographer, Cilda Shaur; Crew (both productions): Reece Nunez (audio engineer), Jake Scudder (house sound engineer), Jess Bauer, Alex Neumann (A2), Andrea Hood (assistant costume supervisor), Sydney Ledger (wardrobe supervisor), Isaac Grnya (hair/wig supervisor), Kate Mitchell (costume day work/change-over crew supervisor), Rachel Brown, Charlotte Gaspard, T. Michael Hall, Vivian Pavlos (wardrobe crew), Raquel Bianchini (hair/wig crew), Liz Lee, Kate Milazzo, Joel Wilbur (costume day work/change-over crew), Zach Murphy (production electrician), A.J. Jackson (master electrician), Loren Pratt, Alex Taylor (assistant electricians), Tim Kaufman (light board operator/programmer), Brandon Voight (lead lamp), Daniel Garrison, Tim Harrison, A.J. Jackson, Rob Reese (follow spots), Sara Swanberg (props crew chief), David Schneider (lead props artisan), Luis Torres (set run crew), Rich Holst (automation run crew), Aaron Treat (scene shop supervisor), Hugh Morris-Stan (charge painters), Laura Krassowski, Cory Rodriguez, Max Ward (scenic painters); **Cast:** Tonya Pinkins (Countess of Rousillion), André Holland (Bertram), Reg Rogers (Parolles), Annie Parisse (Helena), Dakin Matthews (Lafew), Aleque Reid (Maudlin), Jordan Lund (Rinaldo), David Manis (Lavatch), Caitlin O'Connell (Isbel/A Widow), John Cullum (King of France), Lorenzo Pisoni (First Brother Dumaine), Michael Hayden (Second

André Holland and Tonya Pinkins (center), and the Company in All's Well That Ends Well *(photo by Joan Marcus)*

Brother Dumaine), Joe Forbrich (Duke of Florence), Kristen Connolly (Diana), Zoey Martinson (Mariana), Katie Meister (Third Daughter), Katie Wieland (Fourth Daughter), Carson Elrod (Interpreter), Lucas Caleb Rooney (A French Gentleman); Ensemble: Bill Army, Lauren Ferguson, Edena Hines, Zoey Martinson, Adam McNulty, Katie Meister, Charlie Francis Murphy, Aleque Reid, Benjamin Thys, Brendan Titley, Katie Wieland, Roger Yeh

Delacorte Theater; First Preview: June 11, 2011; Opening Night: June 26, 2011; Closed June 27, 2011; 9 previews, 13 performances. Setting: Rousillion and Florence, Italy. Revival of a classic play presented in two acts in repertory with *Measure for Measure*. Synopsis: *All's Well That Ends Well* is a fairytale for grown-ups. This beguiling fable follows the low-born Helena, one of Shakespeare's most resourceful heroines, as she inventively surmounts obstacle after impossible obstacle in order to win the love of the aristocratic and haughty Count Bertram.

Measure for Measure by William Shakespeare; Director, David Esbjornson; Sets, Scott Pask; Costumes, Elizabeth Hope Clancy; Lighting, Peter Kaczorowski; Original Music and Sound Score, John Gromada; Sound, Acme Sound Partners; Hair and Wigs, Charles LaPointe; Vocal Coach, Shane-Ann Younts; PSM, M. William Shiner; Stage Managers, Buzz Cohen, James Latus, Sean M. Thorne; Assistant Director, Peter Francis James; Recorded Musicians: Greg Talenfeld (Guitar), Bill Ruyle (Drums); Associate Design: Orit Jacoby Carroll (set), Gina Scherr (lighting), Jason Crystal (sound); Assistant Costume Design, Lena Sands; Assistant Original Music and Sound Score, Alexander Sovronsky; Fight Consultant, Lisa Kopitsky; Production Assistants (both productions): Megan Alvord, Samantha Flint, Kristen Gibbs, Taylor Michael; **Cast:** Lorenzo Pisoni (Vincentio), Michael Hayden (Angelo), John Cullum (Escalus), Dakin Matthews (Provost), Danai Gurira (Isabella), André Holland (Claudio), Kristen Connolly (Juliet), Reg Rogers (Lucio), Annie Parisse (Mariana), Zachary Unger/Benjamin Perry Wenzelberg (Boys), Joe Forbrich (Peter), Caitlin O'Connell (Francisca), Tonya Pinkins (Mistress Overdone), Carson Elrod (Pompey), David Manis (Elbow), Lucas Caleb Rooney (Froth/Barnardine), Jordan Lund (Abhorson); Ensemble: Bill Army, Charlie Francis Murphy, Carra Patterson, James Rees, Benjamin Thys, Brendan Titley, Katie Tuminelly, Roger Yeh

Delacorte Theater; First Preview: June 6, 2011; Opening Night: June 30, 2011; Closed July 30, 2011; 9 previews, 13 performances. Revival of a classic play presented in two acts in repertory with *All's Well That Ends Well*. Synopsis: *Measure for Measure* sweeps from the corridors of national power to the intimate confines of the bedroom, and from the convent's chapel to the executioner's block. It is Shakespeare at his grittiest: a bracing and bawdy glimpse of what happens when those in power allow their basest human impulses to range unchecked.

Danai Gurira, Dakin Matthews, Annie Parisse, Michael Hayden, and Lorenzo Pisoni in Measure for Measure *(photo by Joan Marcus)*

MAINSTAGE PRODUCTIONS

The Agony and the Ecstasy of Steve Jobs Created and written by Mike Daisey; Director, Jean-Michele Gregory; Sets/Lighting, Seth Reiser; PSM, Pamela Salling; Sound System Design, Gabriel Bennett; Production Assistant, Hannah Jagoe; Sound Operator, Laura Brauner; Production Electrician, Zach Murphy; Master Electrician/Light Board Operator, Tim Kaufman; Assistant Master Electrician, Laura Krassowski; Scene Shop Supervisor, Aaron Treat; Charge Painter, Hugh Morris-Stan; Electricians, Danielle Colburn, Thad Horst, A.J. Jackson, Ashley Lewis, Heidi O'Connell, Meredith Pompeani, Loren Pratt, Michael Rivera, Kevin Scott, Brandon Voight, Max Ward; Scene Construction/Load-In Crew, Stephanie Lee, Thomas Ibbitson, Matt Miccucci, Jason Paradine, Peter Russo, Mike Sakolsky, Greg Thayer, Luis Torres; **Cast:** Mike Daisey (Performer)

Martinson Theater; First Preview: October 11, 2011; Opening Night: October 17, 2011; Closed December 4, 2011; Encore Extension January 31–March 18, 2012; 7 previews, 97 performances. New York premiere of a new solo performance play presented without intermission. World premiere at the Time-Based Art Festival in Portland, Oregon in September 2010. Synopsis: Mike Daisey turns his razor-sharp wit to America's most mysterious technology icon in this hilarious and harrowing tale of pride, beauty, lust, and industrial design. He illuminates how the CEO of Apple and his obsessions shape our lives, while sharing stories of his own travels to China to investigate the factories where millions toil to make iPhones and iPods. Daisey's dangerous journey shines a light on our love affair with our devices and the human cost of creating them.

Mike Daisey in The Agony and the Ecstasy of Steve Jobs *(photo by Joan Marcus)*

King Lear by William Shakespeare; Director, James MacDonald; Sets, Miriam Buether; Costumes, Gabriel Berry; Lighting, Christopher Akerlind; Sound, Darron L West; Fight Director, Thomas Schall; Vocal Consultant, Elizabeth Smith; PSM, James Latus; Stage Manager, Buzz Cohen; Assistant Director, Ian Hersey; Associate Design: Tristan Jeffers (set), Sydney Gallas (costumes), Charles Coes (sound); Assistant Design: Benjamin M. Zawacki (costumes), Sooyeon Hong (lighting); Costume Design Interns, Rebecca Joy Wallace, Catherine Wuest; Production Assistants, Michelle Scalpone, Amy K. Witherby; Production Audio, Matt Hubbs; Sound Board, Ann-Marie Dalenberg; Wardrobe Supervisor, T.

Michael Hall; Wardrobe Crew, Charlotte Gaspard, Elizabeth Lee, Heather Stanley; Production Electrician, Zach Murphy; Assistant Master Electrician, Brandon Voight; Light Board Programmer/Operator, Tim Kaufman; Props Run Crew, Sara Jean Swanberg; Props Carpenter, David Schneider; Prop Artisans, Claire Karoff, Raphael Mishler; Scene Shop Supervisor, Aaron Treat; Charge Painter, Hugh Morris-Stan; Production Carpenter, Jason Paradine; Scene Run Crew, Nick Moodey, Luis Torres; Production Crew, Cory Rodriguez, Bob Vesce; Hair and Makeup, Cookie Jordan; **Cast:** Sam Waterston (Lear), Enid Graham (Goneril), Kelli O'Hara (Regan), Kristen Connolly (Cordelia), Richard Topol (Duke of Albany), Frank Wood (Duke of Cornwall), Michael Izquierdo (King of France), Che Ayende (Duke of Burgundy), Michael McKean (Earl of Gloucester), Arian Moayed (Edgar), Seth Gilliam (Edmund), John Douglas Thompson (Earl of Kent), Bill Irwin (Fool), Michael Crane (Oswald), Herb Foster (Old Man), Craig Bockhorn (A Gentleman); Che Ayende, Craig Bockhorn, Herb Foster, Michael Izquierdo (Knights, Servants, Soldiers, Attendants)

Newman Theater; First Preview: October 18, 2011; Opening Night: November 2, 2011; Closed November 20, 2011; 22 previews, 16 performances. Revival of a classic play presented in two acts. Synopsis: *King Lear* is one of the towering works of world literature. In no other play is Shakespeare's tragic vision more terrifyingly clear – and nowhere in his canon does he create a richer or more complex set of characters. When King Lear divides his kingdom among his three daughters, he sets in motion a cascade of violence that sweeps the civilized world to the brink of chaos, and Lear to the edge of madness.

Michael McKean and Sam Waterston in King Lear *(photo by Joan Marcus)*

Gob Squad's Kitchen (You've Never Had It So Good) Created by Gob Squad (U.K./Germany), devised by the company; Co-produced by Volksbuehne am Rosa-Luxemburg-Platz Berlin, donaufestival Niederoesterreich, Nottingham Playhouse and Fierce!; Video, Miles Chalcraft; Sound, Jeff McGrory; Tour/Stage Manager, Sophia Simitzis, Mat Hand; PSM, Elizabeth Moreau; Gob Squad Production Manager Christina Runge; Gob Squad U.K. Producer, Ayla Suveren; Gob Squad Design Assistant, Chasper Bertschinger; Gob Squad Management, Eva Hartmann; Assistant Production Manager, Catherine Barricklow; Production Assistant, Amy Witherby; Props Master, Claire Karoff; Assistant Props, Raphael Mishler; Production Audio, Emma Wilk; Production Electrician, Zach Murphy; Master Electrician/Board Operator, Michael Cecchini; Electricians, Lois Catanzaro, Danielle Colburn, Thad Horst, A.J. Jackson, Ashley Lewis, Heidi O'Connell, Meredith Pompeani, Loren Pratt, Michael Rivera, Kevin Scott, Brandon Voight; Scene Shop Supervisor, Aaron Treat; Charge Painter, Hugh Morris-Stan; Deck Carpenter, Nick Moody; Production Intern, Christopher Buchegger; **Cast:** Johanna Freiburg, Sean Patten, Sharon Smith, Berit Stumpf, Sarah Thom, Bastian Trost, Simon Will, Erik Pold, Nina Tecklenburg, Laura Tonke

Newman Theater; First Preview: January 19, 2012; Opening Night: January 23, 2012; Closed February 5, 2012; 6 previews, 17 performances. Return engagement of an interactive multimedia theatrical piece presented without intermission. Previously presented at the Public January 6-8, 2011 as part of the Under the Radar Festival. Synopsis: It's 1965, and everything is about to happen. The German/British collective Gob Squad invites you to take the hand of the King of Pop himself, Andy Warhol, and take a trip back to where it all began. *Gob Squad's Kitchen* reconstructs Warhol's films on a journey back to the underground cinemas of New York City in 1965. In the uncertain quest to illuminate the past for a new generation, Gob Squad reflects on the nature of authenticity, our future, and the hidden depths beneath the shiny surfaces of modern life.

No Place to Go by Ethan Lipton; Director, Leigh Silverman; Music, Ethan Lipton, Eben Levy, Ian M. Riggs, Vito Dieterle; Lighting, Ben Stanton; Sound Consultant, Acme Sound Partners; PSM, William H. Lang; Production Manager, Elizabeth Moreau; Assistant Production Manager, Catherine Barricklow; Production Assistant, Rebecca Goldstein-Glaze; Production Audio, Malachy Kronberg and Jon Shriver; Sound Engineers, Joel Bikema, Thanasis Psarros, Jon Shriver; Master Electrician/Light Board, Jason L. Miller; Electricians, Zack Shepard, Chris Thielking, John Wilder; Scene Shop Supervisor, Aaron Treat; **Cast:** Ethan Lipton (Performer), Vito Dieterle (Saxaphone), Eben Levy (Guitar), Ian M. Riggs (Bass)

Joe's Pub; First Preview: March 14, 2012; Opening Night: March 21, 2012; Closed April 8, 2012; 6 previews, 17 performances. World premiere of a solo performance play with music presented without intermission. Synopsis: The company where he's worked for the past 10 years is moving to another planet, and playwright Ethan Lipton doesn't want to go. Part love letter to his co-workers, part query to the universe, part protest to his company and country, *No Place to Go* delivers a hilarious, irreverent and personal musical ode to the unemployed in this unforgettable evening.

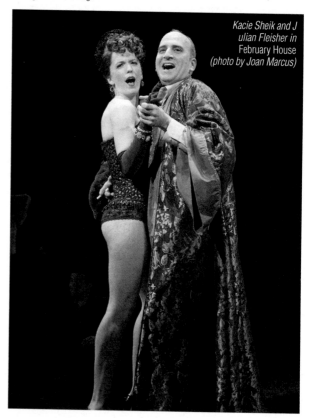

Kacie Sheik and Julian Fleisher in February House *(photo by Joan Marcus)*

Gatz Text from *The Great Gatsby* by F. Scott Fitzgerald; Created by Elevator Repair Service (John Collins, Artistic Director; Ariana Smart Truman, Producer); Director, John Collins; Associate Director, Steve Bodow; Set, Louisa Thompson; Costumes, Coleen Werthmann; Lighting, Mark Barton; Sound, Ben Williams; PSM, Sarah Hughes; Stage Manager, Elizabeth Moreau; Production Manager, Andy Knapp; Assistant Prop Master, Sara Swanberg; Assistant Design: Ana Schumacher, Campbell Ringel (costumes), Dans Maree Sheehan (lighting), Gabriel Bennett (sound); Production Assistant, Amy Witherby; FOH Engineer, Jason Sebastian; Production Audio, John Kemp; Wardrobe Supervisor, T. Michael Hall; Production Electrician, Zach Murphy; Master Electrician, Loren Pratt; Assistant Master Electrician, Michael Cecchini; Light Operators, Tim Harrison, Laura Krassowski; Light Board Operator, Sarah Hughes; Lead Props Artisans, Lily Clements, Raphael Mishler; Scene Shop Supervisor, Aaron Treat; Charge Painter, Hugh Morris-Stan; Scene Construction, Joseph Mathers, Jason Paradine, Kevin Kelly, Stephanie Lee, Peter Russo, Greg Thayer; Electricians, Andrew Balmer, Lois Catanzaro, Carson Gross, Thad Horst, Brandon Jaffe, Meghan Kennedy, Laura Krassowski, Curtis Lee, Heidi O'Connell, Meredith Pompeani, Kevin Scott, Stephanie Shecter, Christopher Thielking; **Cast:** Scott Shepherd (Nick), Jim Fletcher (Jim), Kate Scelsa (Lucille), Susie Sokol (Jordan), Victoria Vazquez (Daisy), Gary Wilmes (Tom), Frank Boyd (George), Laurena Allan (Myrtle), Annie McNamara (Catherine), Vin Knight (Chester), Ben Williams (Michaelis), Mike Iveson (Ewing), Ross Fletcher (Henry C. Gatz); Understudies: Lindsay Hockaday, Matt Tierney

Martinson Hall; First Preview: March 14, 2012; Opening Night: March 18, 2012; Closed May 13, 2012; 3 previews, 29 performances. Encore production of a play presented in four acts with two intermissions and one dinner break. ERS premiered the theatrical event in May 2006 at the Kunsten Festival des Arts in Brussels. The U.S. premiere played the Walker Arts Center in Minneapolis in September 2006. The Public Theater presented the show October 3–November 28, 2011 (see *Theatre World* Vol. 67, page 222). Synopsis: One morning in the low-rent office of a small business, an employee finds a copy of *The Great Gatsby* in the clutter of his desk and starts to read it out loud. After a series of strange coincidences, it's no longer clear whether he's reading the book or the book is transforming him. *Gatz* is a theatrical and literary tour de force, not a retelling of the Gatsby story but an enactment of the novel itself. Over the course of six-and-a-half hours, Fitzgerald's American masterpiece is delivered word for word, startlingly brought to life by a low-rent office staff in the midst of their inscrutable business operations.

Scott Shepherd and the Company in Gatz *(photo by Joan Marcus)*

February House Music and lyrics by Gabriel Kahane, book by Seth Bockley; Produced in association with the Long Wharf Theatre (Gordon Edelstein, Artistic Director; Joshua Borenstein, Managing Director); Director, Davis McCallum; Choreography, Danny Mefford; Music Director, Andy Boroson; Sets, Riccardo Hernandez; Costumes, Jess Goldstein; Lighting, Mark Barton; Sound, Leon Rothenberg; Orchestrations, Gabriel Kahane; Vocal/Dialect Coach, Deborah Hecht; PSM, Cole Bonenberger; Stage Manager, Marisa Levy; Production

Manager, Elizabeth Moreua; Assistant Production Manager, Catherine Barricklow; Assistant Costume Master, Andrea Hood; Assistant Audio Supervisor, Malachy Kronberg; Prop Master, Kathryn Vega; Assistant Design: Maruti Evans (set), Trevor Bowen (costumes), Ryan Seelig (lighting), David Corsello (sound); Production Assistant, Jared Oberholtzer; Stage Mangement Intern, Samantha Frener; Music Intern, Benjamin M. Bonnerna; FOH Engineer, Ann-Marie Dalenberg; Deck Sound, Toni Portacci; Production Audio, Josh Davis, John Kemp; Wardrobe Supervisor, Judy McFarland; Wardrobe Crew, Kate Robards; Wig/Hair Supervisor, Samantha Weiner; Production Electrician, Zach Murphy; Master Electrician, Alex Tylor; Assistant Master Electrician, Carson Gross; Light Board Programmer, Victoria Loye; Light Board Operator, Heather Smaha; Follow Spots, Ron Gimshaw, Ashley Lewis; Prop Run Crew, Ellie Bye; Scene Shop Supervisor, Aaron Treat; Charge Painter, Hugh Morris-Stan; Scenic Artist, Max Ward; Deck Carpenter, Emily Scanlan; Cast recording: Story Sound Records 8; **Cast:** Stanley Bahorek (Benjamin Britten), Ken Barnett (Peter Pears), Ken Clark (Reeves McCullers), Julian Fleisher (George Davis), Stephanie Hayes (Erika Mann), Erik Lochtefeld (W.H. Auden), Kacie Sheik (Gypsy Rose Lee), A.J. Shively (Chester Kallam), Kristen Sieh (Carson McCullers); Understudy: Josh Lamon (George Davis); Musicians: Andy Boronson (Keyboard), Andy Stack (Banjo, Guitar), Tema Watstein (Violin), Jane O'Hare (Cello), Jay Hassler (Flute, Clarinet, Bass Clarinet), Aaron Irwin (Flute, Clarinet, Bass Clarinet)

Musical Numbers: Light Upon the Hill; George Comes Through; A Room Comes Together; Shall We Live Here?; Refugee Blues; Coney Island; Awkward Angel; Chester's Etiquette; Refugee Blues II; Wanderlust; Discontent; A Little Brain; Goodnight to the Boardinghouse; A Certain Itch; Awkward Angel (reprise); It Is Time for the Destruction of Error; You Sit in Your Chair; Ride Out the Light; Discontent (reprise); Georgia; Funeral Blues; California; Light Upon the Hill (reprise); Goodnight to the Boardinghouse (reprise)

Martinson Theater; First Preview: May 8, 2012; Opening Night: May 22, 2012; Closed June 17, 2012; 15 previews, 32 performances. Setting: 7 Middagh Street, Brooklyn Heights, New York; 1940-1941. World premiere of a new musical presented in two acts. New York Stage and Film Company and the Powerhouse Theater at Vassar presented a developmental production in July 2011. Synopsis: Carson McCullers. Benjamin Britten. W.H. Auden. Gypsy Rose Lee. Visionary and flamboyant editor George Davis transforms a dilapidated Brooklyn boardinghouse into a bohemian commune for these leading lights of 1940s New York. The residents of 7 Middagh Street create a tumultuous and remarkable makeshift family searching for love, inspiration, and refuge from the looming war in Europe. Inspired by true events, this powerful and funny new musical (the first commission of the Public's Music Theater Initiative) mixes elements of classical operetta, jazz, and musical comedy with modern folk-pop.

PUBLIC LAB (FIFTH SEASON)

Sweet and Sad Written and directed by Richard Nelson; Sets and Costumes, Susan Hilferty; Lighting, Jennifer Tipton; Sound, Scott Lehrer and Will Pickens; PSM, Pamela Salling; Stage Manager, Maggie Swing; Production Manager, Elizabeth Moreau; Company Manager, Rebecca Sherman; Assistant Director, David Chapman; Costume Supervisor, Andrea Hood; Prop Master, Amelia Freeman-Lynde; Assistant Lighting, Alan C. Edwards; Sound Board, Ann-Marie Dalenberg; Wardrobe Supervisor, T. Michael Hall; Production Electrician, Alex Taylor; First Electrician, Laura Krassowski; Light Board Operator/Programmer, Tim Harrison; Props Run Crew, Lily Perlmutter; Props Shopper, Elijah McStotts; Scene Shop Supervisor, Aaron Treat; **Cast:** Jay O. Sanders (Richard Apple), Maryann Plunkett (Barbara Apple), Laila Robins (Marian Apple Platt), J. Smith-Cameron (Jane Apple Halls), Jon DeVries (Benjamin Apple), Shuler Hensley (Tim Andrews)

Anspacher Theater; First Preview: September 6, 2011; Opening Night: September 11, 2011; Closed September 25, 2011; 5 previews, 17 performances. Setting: Sunday, September 11, 2011 between 2pm and 4pm in the dining room of the Apple's house on Center Street in Rhinebeck, New York. World premiere of a new play presented without intermission. Synopsis: The Apple Family finds themselves together again for the first time since Election Night, 2010. Marian, reeling from a personal tragedy, now lives with her sister Barbara; sister Jane is back with her boyfriend Tim, their brother Richard has come up from Manhattan, and Uncle Benjamin prepares for his first dramatic performance in years. Over Sunday brunch on the tenth anniversary of 9/11, the Apples find themselves talking about loss, memory, remembrance and the meaning of compensation.

The Company in Sweet and Sad *(photo by Joan Marcus)*

Love's Labor's Lost by William Shakespeare; Director, Karin Coonrod; Set, John Conklin; Costumes, Oana Botez-Ban; Lighting, Brian H. Scott; Music, Tony Geballe; Vocal Coach, Robert Perillo; PSM, Lori Lundquist; Stage Manager, Maggie Swing; Assistant Director, Devin Brain; Assistant to the Director, Jaclyn Biskup; Dramaturg, Emily Madison; Production Manager, Elizabeth Moreau; Assistant Production Manager, Catherine Barricklow; Costume Supervisor, Andrea Hood; Assistant Costume Design, AraBella Fischer; Props Master, Paper Maché Monkey; Wardrobe Supervisor, Judy McFarland; Wardrobe, Beth DuBon; Production Electrician, Chris Thielking; Light Board Programmer, Danielle Colburn; Light Board Operator, Tim Harrison; Props Run Crew, Matt Frew; Scene Shop Supervisor/Crew, Aaron Treat; **Cast:** Hoon Lee (Ferdinand), Nick Westrate (Berowne), Keith Eric Chappelle (Longaville), Jorge Chacon (Dumaine), Renee Elise Goldsberry (Princess of France), Rebecca Brooksher (Rosaline), Samira Wiley (Maria/Moth), Michelle Beck (Katharine), Robert Stanton (Boyet/Anthony Dull), Reg E. Cathey (Don Adriano de Armaod), Mousa Kraish (Costard), Steven Skybell (Holofernes), Francis Jue (Sir Nathaniel/Marcade), Stephanie DiMaggio (Jaquenetta)

Anspacher Theater; First Preview: October 18, 2011; Opening Night: October 31, 2011; Closed November 6, 2011; 15 previews, 9 performances. Revival of a classic play presented without intermission. Synopsis: The King of France and his best buds swear off romance and withdraw into their studies…until three some girls show up. As the young couples stumble their way toward love, the others in their circle – a pedantic school master, a Spanish dandy, a streetwise con-man, and a cop with a few screws loose – work through their own mad dilemmas. In the end, the real world intrudes and brings everyone back to earth.

Titus Andronicus by William Shakespeare; Director, Michael Sexton; Sets, Brett J. Banakis; Costumes, Caitlin O'Connor; Lighting, Mark Barton; Music and Sound, Brandon Wolcott; Fight Director, Thomas Schall; PSM, M. William Shiner; Stage Manager, Alaina Taylor; Assistant Director, Lisa Szolovits; Assistant to the Director, Emilie Soffe; Text Coach, Ian Hersey; Costume Supervisor, Andrea Hood; Props Master, Paper Maché Monkey; Assistant Design: Adrianne Carney (costumes), Ryan Seelig (lighting), Nathan Wheeler (sound); Scenic Design Assistant, Sofia Pia Belenky; Production Assistant, Chris Borg; FOH Engineer, Malachy Kronberg; Wardrobe Supervisor, T. Michael Hall; Production Electrician, Alex Taylor; Electrician, Thad Horst; Light Board Programmer, Daniellle Colburn; Light Board Operator, Timothy Harrison; Scene Shop Supervisor, Aaron Treat;

Charge Painter, Hugh Morris-Stan; Set/Props Run Crew, Luis Toress; **Cast:** Frank Dolce (A Boy/Mutius/Young Lucius/Alarbus), Jacob Fishel (Saturninus), Daoud Heidami (Bassianus/Publius/Aemilius/Nurse/Messenger/A Goth), Jay O. Sanders (Titus Andronicus), Sherman Howard (Marus Andronicus), Rob Campbell (Lucius), Patrick Carroll (Quintus/Chiron), William Jackson Harper (Martius/Demetrius), Jennifer Ikeda (Lavinia), Stephanie Roth Haberle (Tamora), Ron Cephas Jones (Aaron)

Anspacher Theater; First Preview: November 29, 2011; Opening Night: December 13, 2011; Closed December 18, 2012; 15 previews, 8 performances. Revival of a classic play presented in two acts. Synopsis: Titus is Rome's greatest general and the head of a noble Roman family. When his armies vanquish the Goths, their defeated queen unleashes a fury that rocks Titus's city, devastates his children, and shatters his sense of self. The cycle of revenge is shocking, bloody, and all-encompassing, but expressed through poetry and theatricality as vivid, energized, and thrilling as anything in Shakespeare's later works.

Sherman Howard, Ron Cephas Jones, Jay O. Sanders, Rob Campbell, and Jacob Fishel in Titus Andronicus *(photo by Joan Marcus)*

The Total Bent Book and lyrics by Stew, music by Stew and Heidi Rodewald; Director, Joanna Settle; Sets, Andrew Lieberman; Costumes, Gabriel Berry; Lighting, Adam Silverman; Sound, Obadiah Eaves, Acme Sound Partners; Choreography, David Neumann; PSM, M. William Shiner; Stage Manager, Kelly Glasow; Dance Captain, Eddie R. Brown III; Assistant Director, Nicole A. Watson; Script Supervisor, Johnson Henshaw; Vocal Coach, Barbara Maier; Props, Amelia Freeman-Lynde; Associate Design, Andrea Hood (costumes), Mike Inwood (lighting); Assistant Set Design, Kristin Ellert, Eric Southern; Pre-Production Sound Design, Wilheim Stegmeier; FOH Engineer, Ann-Marie Dalenberg; Deck Sound, Jess Bauer; Production Audio, Malachy Kronberg; Wardrobe Supervisor, T. Michael Hall; Wardrobe, Elizabeth Lee, Adrian Boyes; Production Electrician, Alex Taylor; Light Board Operator, Alex Taylor; Light Board Programmer, Danielle Colburn; Scene Shop Supervisor, Aaron Treat; Charge Painter, Hugh Morris-Stan; **Cast:** Kenny Brawner (Deacon Charlie), Eddie R. Brown III (Abee), David Cale (Byron), Harriett D. Foy (Your Imaginary Friend), Vondie Curtis Hall (Joe Roy), William Jackson Harper (Marty Roy), Damian Lemar Hudson (Deacon Oennis), Julian Rozzell Jr. (Andrew), Kenny Brawner (Musician)

Anspacher Theater; Opening Night: February 24, 2012; Closed March 18, 2012; 24 performances. Co-commissioned by Berkeley Repertory Theatre (Tony Taccone, Artistic Director; Susan Medak, Managing Director). Synopsis: Stew and Heidi Rodewald (*Passing Strange*) return to the Public with a new musical about a black gospel prodigy from down south and a white music producer from South London who meet in a recording studio just south of the Twilight Zone, as they both desperately seek their own versions of transcendence, salvation, and a hit record. Divine inspiration, fantastical visions, and one legendary music-producer father frame this electrifying new musical about the complicated space between the sacred and the profane.

Rattlestick Playwrights Theater

Seventeenth Season

Artistic Director, David Van Asselt; Managing Director, Brian Long; Finance Manager, Lori Singleton; Literary Managers, Denis Butkus, Julie Kline, Daniel Talbott; Literary Associates, Brian Miskell, Diana Stahl, Sanford Wilson; Production Manager, Eugenia Furneaux-Arends; Technical Director, Katie Takacs; Marketing & Development Associates, Allison Altaman, Lisa Anderson, Emily Daly, Kirsten Egenes, Breanna Foister, Zoe Geltman, Rosa Gilmore, Christina Hurtado, Everett Irving, K.C. Luce, Heidi Pointet, Samantha Strelitz; Press, O+M Company, Rick Miramontez, Richard Hillman

The Wood by Dan Klores; Director, David Bar Katz; Set, John McDermott; Costumes, Kalere A. Payton; Lighting, Joel Moritz; Sound, Janie Bullard; Projections, Steve Channon; PSM, Jamie Wolfe; ASM, Sam Horwith; Props, Nina Alexander; Hair and Makeup, Erin Kennedy Lunsford; Paint Charge, Eugenia Furneaux; Assistant Director, Scott Illingworth; Carpenters, Alex Anderson, Jeffrey Cuismano; Nick Monroy, Adam Piotrowicz; Assistant to the Playwright, Eric Krugley; Associate Projections, Caite Hevner; Projection Assistant, Tess James; Haitian Consultant, Cybil Charlier; Additional Originial Music, Bob Golden; Electrician, The Lighting Syndicate; Casting, Judy Bowman; Graphic Design, Achilles Lavidis; Program Design, Allison Altman; **Cast:** Michael Carlsen (Justin Volpe), Melanie Charles (Micheline Louima/Nurse), David Deblinger (Tommy/Cop), Kim Director (Alice McAlary), Thomas Kopache (Dave Hecht/Editor/Cop/George Marks), Vladimir Versailles (Abner Louima), John Viscardi (Mike McAlary), Sidney Williams (Doctor/EMS Worker/Bill Roche)

Rattlestick Theater 224 Waverly; First Preview: September 1, 2011; Opening Night: September 15, 2011; Closed October 9, 2011; 7 previews, 25 performances. World premiere of a new play presented without in two acts. Synopsis: *The Wood* is a fast-paced, insider's look at Mike McAlary, the larger-than-life columnist for the *Daily News* and the *New York Post* and his missionary zeal to ferret out the truth. A Pulitzer Prize-winner for his exposé of the New York police torture of Haitian immigrant Abner Louima in 1997, McAlary died of colon cancer on Christmas Day 1998 at the age of 41.

John Viscardi, Vladimir Versailles, and Melanie Charles in The Wood *(photo by Sandra Coudert)*

Asuncion by Jesse Eisenberg; Presented by special arrangement with the Cherry Lane Theatre (Angelina Fiordellisi, Artistic Director); Director, Kip Fagan; Set, John McDermott; Costumes, Jessica Pabst; Lighting, Ben Stanton; Sound, Bart Fasbender; Casting, Calleri Casting; PSM, Melissa Mae Gregus; ASM, Michael Denis; Fight Director, Thomas Schall; Props Master, Andrew Diaz; Photographer, Heather Phelps-Lipton; Graphic Design, Achilles Lavidis; Assistant Director, Stefanie Abel Horowitz; Assistant Costumes, Kaitlin E. Hartsoe; Lighting Programmer, Holly Burnell; Assistant Production Manager, Judy Merrick; Assistant Technical Director, Stephan McKenny; Carpenters, Nick Monroy, Adam Piotrowicz, Jeffrey Cuismano; **Cast:** Remy Auberjonois (Stuart), Justin Bartha (Vinny), Jesse Eisenberg (Edgar), Camille Mana (Asuncion)

Cherry Lane Theatre; First Preview: October 12, 2011; Opening Night: October 27, 2011; Closed December 18, 2011; 13 previews, 58 performances. Setting: An apartment, off-campus in Poughkeepsie, New York. World premiere of a new play presented in two acts. Synopsis: Edgar and Vinny are not racist. In fact, Edgar maintains a blog condemning American imperialism and Vinny is three-quarters into a PhD in Black Studies. When a young Filipina woman named Asuncion becomes their new roommate, the pair has a perfect opportunity to demonstrate how open-minded they truly are. Eisenberg's hilarious and heartbreaking new comedy explores the complicated ways we exploit culture and politics for our own needs.

Remy Aberjonois and Jesse Eisenberg in Asuncion *(photo by Sandra Coudert)*

Horsedreams by Dael Orlandersmith; Director, Gordon Edelstein; Set, Takeshi Kata; Costumes, Kaye Voyce; Lighting, Marcus Doshi; Sound, Ryan Rumery; PSM, Sunneva Stapleton; ASM, Andrew Slater; Props Master/Scenic Artist, Andrew Diaz; Assistant Director, Desdemona Chiang; Assistant Design: Sebastien Grouard, Chika Shimizu (set), Janie Bullard (sound); Scenic Artists, Eugenia Furneaux, John McDermott; Set Construction, Ken Larson Company; Electrician, The Lighting Syndicate; Casting, Calleri Casting; Graphic Design, Achilles Lavidis; Program Design, Lisa Anderson; **Cast:** Roxanna Hope (Desiree), Michael Laurence (Loman), Matthew Schechter (Luka), Dael Orlandersmith (Mira)

Rattlestick Theater 224 Waverly; First Preview: November 9, 2011; Opening Night: November 17, 2011; Closed December 11, 2011; 7 previews, 25 performances. World premiere of a new play presented without intermission. Synopsis: *Horsedreams* explores the breakdown of the family unit as a result of addiction. After his wife, Desiree, dies of an accidental overdose, Loman faces the harsh reality of raising their son, Luka, alone.

Yosemite by Daniel Talbott; Director, Pedro Pascal; Set, Raul Abrego; Costumes, Tristan Raines; Lighting, Joel Moritz; Sound, Janie Bullard; PSM, Michael Denis; ASM, Sam Horwith; Props Master, Andrew Diaz; Assistant Technical Director, A.J. Coté; Assistant Director, Evan Caccioppoli; Assistant Costumes, Caitlin Conci; Scenic Artists, Eugenia Furneaux, Judy Merrick, Ashley Pridemore; Carpenters, Devon Brown, Kyle Marchant, Nick Monroy, Adam Piotrowicz; Set Construction, Ken Larson Company; Electrician, The Lighting Syndicate; Custom Knit Wear, Debi Barton; Fight Director, David Anzuelo; **Cast:** Kathryn Erbe (Julie), Noah Galvin (Jer), Seth Numrich (Jake), Libby Woodbridge (Ruby)

Rattlestick Theater 224 Waverly; First Preview: January 18, 2012; Opening Night: January 26, 2012; Closed March 3, 2012; 7 previews, 31 performances. World premiere of a new play presented without intermission. Synopsis: *Yosemite* tells the story of three siblings who are sent out into the snow-silent woods in the

Sierra Nevada foothills to dig a hole that will be deep enough to bury a family secret. As they dig, they search for a way to escape or be rescued from their lives as the snow continues to fall and the world sinks in around them.

Michael Laurence, Roxana Hope, and Matthew Schechter in Horsedreams *(photo by Sandra Coudert)*

Seth Numrich, Kathryn Erbe, Noah Galvin, and Libby Woodbridge in Yosemite *(photo by Sandra Coudert)*

Massacre (Sing to Your Children) by Jose Rivera; Director, Brian Mertes; Set, Andromache Chalfant; Costumes, Caitlin O'Connor; Lighting, Austin Smith; Sound, Daniel Baker; Props Master, Andrew Diaz; PSM, Melissa Mae Gregus; ASM, Sam Horwith; Props Designer, Andrew Diaz; Special Effects, Jeremy Chernick; Makeup, Erin Kennedy Lunsford; Masks, Julian Crouch, Caitlin O'Connor; Fight Director, Rick Sordelet; Composer of "Hole in the Ground", Saskia Lane; Assistant Technical Director, A.J. Coté; Assistant Director, Shelley Carter; Set Construction, Ken Larson Company; Electrician, The Lighting, Syndicate; Marketing Consultant, WiT Media; Graphic Design, Achilles Lavidis; Program Design, Lisa Anderson; **Cast:** Jojo Gonzalez (Panama), Denis Butkus (Erik), Brendan Averett (Hector), Sona Tatoyan (Lila), William Jackson Harper (Eliseo), Jolly Abraham (Janis), Dana Eskelson (Vivy), Anatol Yusef (Joe)

Dana Ekelson, Sona Tatoyan, William Jackson Harper, and Brendan Averett in Massacre (Sing to Your Children) *(photo by Sandra Coudert)*

Rattlestick Theater 224 Waverly; First Preview: April 4, 2012; Opening Night: April 12, 2012; Closed May 12, 2012; 7 previews, 31 performances. World premiere of a new play presented in two acts. Synopsis: In a small New Hampshire town, seven friends conspire to murder their mysterious neighbor Joe. On the night of the killing, as they confront the many meanings of their crime and finally relax and laugh and love again…there's a knock on their door.

3C by David Adjmi; Co-produced by piece by piece productions (Wendy vanden Heuvel, Artistic Director) and Rising Phoenix Repertory (Daniel Talbott, Artistic Director); Director, Jackson Gay; Set, John McDermott; Costumes, Oana Botez; Lighting, Tyler Micoleau; Sound, Matt Tierney; Choreography, Deney Terrio; Hair and Makeup, Jon Carter; Violence Consultant, J. David Brimmer; General Management, Snug Harbor Productions, Steven Chaikelson/Kendra Bator; PSM, Tom Taylor; ASM, Julie DeRossi; Assistant General Manager/Company Manager, Evan O'Brient; Assistant Director, Chet Siegel; Assistant Choreographer, Erin Porvaznika; Assistant Design: Andrew Diaz, Maikiko Suzuki MacAdams (set), Karen Boyer (costumes), Marika Kent (light), Janie Bullard (sound); Props Master, Andrew Diaz; Assistant Technical Directors, A.J. Coté, Philip Rossi; Electrician, The Lighting, Syndicate, Doug Filomena; Assistant to Mr. Adjmi, Philip Gates; Wardrobe Supervisor, AraBella C. Fischer; Stage Crew, Holly Burnell, Michael Denis; Advertising and Marketing, The Pekoe Group; Press, Richard Kornberg and Associates, Don Summa; **Cast:** Hannah Cabell (Linda), Anna Chlumsky (Connie), Bill Buell (Mr. Wicker), Jake Silbermann (Brad), Kate Buddeke (Mrs. Wicker), Eddie Cahill (Terry)

Rattlestick Theater 224 Waverly; First Preview: June 6, 2012; Opening Night: June 21, 2012; Closed July 14, 2012; 7 previews, 31 performances. Setting: Santa Monica, California; 1978. World premiere of a new play presented without intermission. Synopsis: Ex-serviceman Brad lands in L.A. to start a new life after the Vietnam War. When he winds up trashed in Connie and Linda's kitchen after a wild night of partying, the three strike a deal for an arrangement that has hilarious and devastating consequences for everyone. *3C* is a terrifying yet amusing look at a culture that likes to amuse itself, even as it teeters on the brink of ruin.

Roundabout Theatre Company

Forty-sixth Season

Artistic Director, Todd Haimes; Managing Director, Harold Wolpert; Executive Director, Julia C. Levy; Associate Artistic Director, Scott Ellis; Founding Director, Gene Feist; Artistic Development/Casting, Jim Carnahan; Development, Lynne Gugenheim Gregory; Marketing/Sales Promotion, David B. Steffen/Thomas Mygatt; Education, Greg McCaslin; General Manager, Sydney Beers; Associate Managing Director, Greg Backstrom; General Manager of the Steinberg Center, Rachel E. Ayers; Finance, Susan Neiman; Database Operations, Wendy Hutton; Sales Operations, Charlie Garbowski Jr.; Production Manager, Aurora Productions; Press, Boneau/Bryan-Brown, Jessica Johnson, Matt Polk, Amy Kass

Sons of the Prophet by Stephen Karam; Produced in association with Huntington Theatre Company in Boston (Peter DuBois, Artistic Director; Michael Maso, Managing Director); Director, Peter DuBois; Sets, Anna Louizos; Costumes, Bobby Frederick Tilley II; Lighting, Japhy Weideman; Sound, M.L. Dogg; Production Stage Mananger, Leslie Sears; Company Manager, Nicholas Caccavo; Casting, Carrie Gardner; Artistic Consultant, Robyn Goodman; Stage Manager, Morgan R. Holbrook; Assistant Directors, Chris Carcione (1st), Michelle Kurchuk (2nd); Associate Lighting, Justin A. Partier; Assistant Design: Hilary Noxon (set), Sarah Reever (costumes), Gary Slootskiy (lighting), John Kemp (sound); Master Technician, Nicholas Wolff Lyndon; Props, Matt Hodges; Wardrobe Supervisor, Amy Kitzhaber; Carpenters, Rebecca O'Neill, Martin Perrin; Electricians, Tom Dyer, Karissa Riehl; Sound Supervisor, Bridget O'Connor; Automation Programmer, Adam Lang; Lighting Programmer, Colin Scott; Deck, Sarah K. Conyers; Movement Consultant, Michael G. Chin; **Cast:** Santino Fontana (Joseph), Joanna Gleason (Gloria), Chris Perfetti (Charles), Yusef Bulos (Bill), Dee Nelson (Dr. Manor, Ensemble), Charles Socarides (Timothy), Lizbeth Mackay (Mrs. McAndrew, Ensemble), Jonathan Louis Dent (Vin); Understudies: Dan McCabe (Timothy, Charles, Joseph), Jared McNeill (Vin), Thomas Ryan (Bill)

Laura Pels Theatre; First Preview: September 28, 2011; Opening Night: October 20, 2011; Closed January 1, 2012; 26 previews, 82 performances. Setting: July 2006–March 2007; Northeastern and Central Pennsylvania. Co-world premiere of a new play presented without intermission. Previously presented at the Huntington Theatre Company April 1–May 1, 2011 (see *Theatre World* Vol. 67, page 348). Synopsis: If to live is to suffer, then Joseph Douaihy is more alive than most. With unexplained chronic pain and the fate of his reeling family on his shoulders, Joseph's health, sanity, and insurance premium are on the line. In an age when modern medicine has a cure for just about everything, *Sons of the Prophet* is a funny and honest take on how we cope with wounds that just won't heal. **2012 Theatre World Award:** Chris Perfetti

Chris Perfetti and Yusef Bulos in Sons of the Prophet

Look Back in Anger by John Osborne; Director, Sam Gold; Sets, Andrew Lieberman; Costumes, David Zinn; Lighting, Mark Barton; Sound, Bray Poor; Hair, Josh Marquette; Dialects, Stephen Gabis; Fight Director, Thomas Schall; PSM, Megan Smith; Company Manager, Nicholas Caccavo; Casting, Carrie Gardner; Stage Manager, Shane Schnetzler; Assistant Director, Craig Baldwin; Assistant Design: Jacob A. Climer (costumes), Mike Inwood (lighting), Charles Coes (sound); Props, Matt Hodges; Master Technician, Nicholas Wolff Lyndon; Wardrobe Supervisor, Amy Kitzhaber; Hair Supervisor, Stacy Shneiderman; Carpenters, Rebecca O'Neill, Adam Lang; Electricians, Tom Dyer, Karissa Riehl; Production Sound, Bridget O'Connor; Assistant Technician, Marc Grimshaw; Dresser, Brittany Vaughan; Production Assistant, Paul Brewster; **Cast:** Matthew Rhys (Jimmy Porter), Adam Driver (Cliff Lewis), Sarah Goldberg (Alison Porter), Charlotte Parry (Helena Charles); Understudies: Adam Greer (Jimmy, Cliff), Jennifer Joan Thompson (Alison, Helena)

Laura Pels Theatre; First Preview: January 13, 2012; Opening Night: February 2, 2012; Closed April 8, 2012; 24 previews, 75 performances. Setting: The Porters' one-room flat in the Midlands, England; April and a few months later, mid-1950s. Revival of a play presented in three acts with one intermission. Originally premiering in London at the Royal Court Theatre May 8, 1956, the production moved to Broadway and opened at the Lyceum Theatre October 1, 1957, transferred to the John Golden Theatre March 17, 1958 where it closed September 20, 1958, playing 407 performances (see *Theatre World* Vol. 14, page 17). Synopsis: Often regarded as a pivotal theatrical work of the last century, *Look Back in Anger* is a shocking and vibrant drama about four people struggling to live together and love each other.

Santino Fontana and Joanna Gleason in Sons of the Prophet
(photos by Joan Marcus)

Sarah Goldberg and Adam Driver in Look Back in Anger

Sarah Goldberg and Matthew Ryhs in Look Back in Anger

The Common Pursuit by Simon Gray; Director, Moisés Kaufman; Sets, Derek McLane; Costumes, Clint Ramos; Lighting, David Lander; Original Music and Sound, Daniel Kluger; Dialect Coach, Deborah Hecht; Fight Director, Thomas Schall; General Manager, Nicholas J. Caccavo; PSM, Bryce McDonald; Casting, Carrie Gardner, Stephen Kopel; Company Manager, Sherra Johnston; Stage Manager, Sara Cox Bradley; Assistant Director, Whitney Mosery; Assistant Design: Dede Ayite (costumes), Davida Tkach (lighting), Alex Neumann (sound), Master Technician, Nicholas Wolff Lyndon; Associate Master Technician, Marc Grimshaw; Props, Jen Dunlap; Wardrobe Supervisor, Amy Kitzhaber; Dresser, Brittany Vaughan; Carpenters, Rebecca O'Neill, Adam Lang; Electricians, Tom Dyer, Ben Hagen; Sound Supervisor, Bridget O'Connor; Automation Operator, Adam Lang; Lighting Programmer, Colin Scott; Observer to the Director, Bejmamin Viertel; Production Assistant, Kristen Torgrimson; **Cast:** Josh Cooke (Stuart Thorne), Kristen Bush (Marigold Watson), Jacob Fishel (Martin Musgrove), Tim McGeever (Humphry Taylor), Lucas Near-Verbrugghe (Nick Finchling), Kieran Campion (Peter Whetworth); Understudies: Stephanie Fieger (Marigold), Spencer Plachy (Stuart, Peter), Grant James Varjas (Martin, Humphry, Nick)

Laura Pels Theatre; First Preview: May 4, 2012; Opening Night: May 24, 2012; Closed July 29, 2012; 21 previews, 59 performances. Setting: Act I Scene 1: Stuart's room in Cambridge, the college years; Act I Scene 2: Stuart's office in Holborn, early summer, nine years later; Act II Scene 1: Stuart and Martin's office, three years later; Act II Scene 2: Martin's office, late autumn, a few years later;

Epilogue: same as Scene 1. Revival of a play presented in four scenes and an epilogue in two acts. The play had its world premiere in the U.K. at the Lyric Theatre, Hammersmith July 3, 1984, and the American premiere at the Long Wharf Theatre in 1985. The original New York production played Off-Broadway at the Promenade Theatre October 19, 1986–August 23, 1987, playing 19 previews and 352 performances (see *Theatre World* Vol. 43, page 72). Synopsis: *The Common Pursuit* chronicles twenty years in the lives of six friends, from their ambitious collegiate days to their surprising discoveries in the real world. Idealistic Cambridge student Stuart Thorne enlists some of his classmates to help him launch a new literary magazine. With the pursuit of great literature as their common thread, they become lifelong friends. But when damaging secrets crop up and business demands creep in, Stuart is faced with some unexpected decisions.

ROUNDABOUT UNDERGROUND

Suicide, Incorporated by Andrew Hinderaker; Director, Jonathan Berry; Sets, Daniel Zimmerman; Costumes, Jessica Wegener Shay; Lighting, Zach Blane; Sound and Original Music, Chad Raines; PSM, Jenna Woods; Casting, Carrie Gardner; Production Manager, Michael Wade; General Manager, Rachel E. Ayers; Roundabout Underground Producer, Robyn Goodman; Associate Producers, Jill Rafson, Josh Fiedler; Company Manager, Nicholas Caccavo; ASM, Jamie Lynne Sullivan; Associate Production Manager, Joel Krause; Technical Director, Chris Soley; Props, Meghan Buchanan; Assistant Director, Michael Perlman; Assistant Design: Marina Reti, David Arsenault (set), Ashley Rose Horton (costumes), Greg Solomon (lighting), Leo A. Martin IV (sound); Board Operator, Rob Sambrato; Wardrobe Supervisor, Ashley Rose Horton; Electrician, Danielle Clifford; Sound Supervisor, Erin Ballentine; Production Assistant, Karen Hashley; **Cast:** Gabriel Ebert (Jason), Toby Leonard Moore (Scott), Corey Hawkins (Perry), Jake O'Connor (Tommy), James McMeniamin (Norm), Mike DiSalvo (Officer)

Black Box Theatre at the Steinberg Center for Theatre; First Preview: October 14, 2011; Opening Night: November 2, 2011; Closed December 23, 2011; 21 previews, 59 performances. New York premiere of a new play presented without intermission. World premiere at Chicago's Gift Theatre Company in June 2010. Synopsis: The right words can be hard to find, especially when they're your last. This provocative and darkly funny play takes us to an unorthodox writing service that specializes in crafting the perfect suicide note, where a subversive new employee is suspected of the unthinkable. Could he actually be helping his client find happiness? *Suicide, Incorporated* is about the business of rewriting your ending.

Jake O'Connor and Gabriel Ebert in Suicide, Incorporated

Second Stage Theatre

Thirty-third Season

Artistic Director, Carole Rothman; Executive Director, Casey Reitz; Associate Artistic Director, Christopher Burney; General Manager, Dean A. Carpenter; Finance Director, Janice B. Cwill; Administrative Manager, John Mackessy; Finance/ Management Associate, Catharine Guiher; Management Associate, Christy Ming-Trent; Annual Fund Director, Karen Goldfeder; Individual Giving Manager, Daniel McCoy; Development Associates, Willa Vail, Solimar Colon; Events and Special Projects, Lee Ann Gullie; Marketing and Communications Director, Laura DiLorenzo; Sales Director, Noel Hatem; Marketing Associate, Nathan Leslie; Ticket Services Manager, Greg Turner; Production Manager, Jeff Wild; Casting, MelCap Casting (Mele Nagler, David Caparelliotis, Lauren Port); Technical Director, Robert G. Mahon III; House Manager, Joshua Schliefer; Director of Play Development, Kyle Frisina; Press, The Hartman Group, Tom D'Ambrosio, Michelle Bergmann

The Blue Flower by Jim Bauer and Ruth Bauer; Director, Will Pomerantz; Choreography, Chase Brock; Sets, Beowulf Boritt; Costumes, Ann Hould-Ward; Lighting, Donald Holder; Sound, Dan Moses Schreier; Projections and Film Supervision, Aaron Rhyne; Films, Jim Bauer and Ruth Bauer; Music Supervision, Dominick Amendum; Orchestrations, Jim Bauer; Casting, MelCap Casting; PSM, Diane DeVita; Stage Manager, Neil Krasnow; Production Assistant, Robert Peters; Assistant Director/Drama League Directing Fellow, Amanda Friou; Assistant Choreographer, Joshua Christopher; Production Electrician, John Tees; Audio Master, Mark Huang; Music Department Assistant, Jacob Combs; Associate Design: Michael Jones (lighting), David Bullard (sound), Ned Stresen-Reuter (projections); Assistant Design: Alexis Distler (set), Abigail Hahn (costumes), Caroline Chao, Marihan Mehelba, Carolyn Wong (lighting), Dan Durkin (projections); Video Programmer, Erik Trester; Hair and Makeup, David Lawrence; Props, Susan Barras; Wardrobe and Wigs, Cornelia Wall; Wardrobe Supervisor, Ashley Farra; Light Board Programmer, Anup Aurora; Light Board, Sarah Bullock; Sound Board, Nicholas Pope; Deck Audio, Kortney Barber; Film Editing, Matt Stone; Film Cinematography, Jamie Moere, Joseph Vitagliano; **Cast:** Sebastian Arcelus (Franz), Marc Kudisch (Max), Meghan McGeary (Hannah), Joseph Medeiros (Typewriter Man), Julia Osborne (Gramophone Girl), Graham Rowat (Mr. O). Aaron Serotsky (Sewing Machine Man), Tael Wicks (Maria); Understudies: Emilee Dupré (Hannah, Gramophone Girl), Michael Roberts McKee (Sewing Machine Man, Typewriter Man), Joseph Medeiros (Franz), Julia Osborne (Maria), Aaron Serotsky (Max, Mr. O); Musicians: Dominick Amendum (Conductor/Piano), Summer Boggess (Cello), Patrick Carmichael (Drums), Lou Garrett (Guitars), Steve Gilewski (Bass), Damian Primis (Bassoon), Carl Riehl (Accodion), John Widgren (Pedal Steel Guitar), Paul Staroba (Associate Conductor)

Second Stage; First Preview: October 14, 2011; Opening Night: November 9, 2011; Closed November 27, 2011; 33 previews, 21 performances. Off-Broadway premiere of a new musical Originally presented in the 2004 New York Music Theatre Festival by the Prospect Theater Company. World premiere at American Repertory Theatre December 8, 2012 (see Theatre World Vol. 67, page 322). Synopsis: Influenced by Expressionism, Dadaism, and the politics of the day, *The Blue Flower* explores the romantic, tumultuous relationships between three artists and a scientist, as they create a world of art, revolution, and passion in a story told through music that blends 1920's Berlin cabaret with the lyricism of American country and western.

How I Learned to Drive by Paula Vogel; Director, Kate Whoriskey; Sets, Derek McLane; Costumes, Jenny Mannis; Lighting, Peter Kaczorowski; Original Music and Sound, Rob Milburn and Michael Bodeen; PSM, Bryce McDonald; Stage Manager, Sara Cox Bradley; Production Assistant, Jillian Anderson; Assistant Director, Jenna Worsham; Dialect Coach, Kate Wilson; Movement Consultant, Warren Adams; Production Electrician, John Tees; Audio Master, Mark Huang; Assistant Design: Shoko Kambara (set), Valerie Bert (costumes), Brandon Mitchell (lighting), John Kemp (sound); Props, Susan Barras; Wardrobe Supervisor, Ashey Farra; Wigs, Erin Kennedy Lunsford; Wig Supervisor, Sarah Levine; Automation,

Brayn McGuckin; Deck Carpenter, Rob Boyle; Light Board Programmer, Anup Aurora; Light Board, Sarah Bullock; Sound Board, Kortney Barber; **Cast:** Elizabeth Reaser (Li'l Bit), Norbert Leo Butz (Peck), Kevin Cahoon (Male Greek Chorus), Jennifer Regan (Female Greek Chorus), Marnie Schulenburg (Teenage Greek Chorus)

Second Stage; First Preview: January 24, 2012; Opening Night: February 13, 2012; Closed March 11, 2012; 24 previews, 31 performances. Revival of a new play presented without intermission. World premiere at the Vineyard Theatre February 27–April 13, 1997 playing 18 previews and 29 performances (see Theatre World Vol. 53, pages 108). The production transferred to the Century Theatre May 6, 1997–April 19, 1998, playing 450 performances (see Theatre World Vol. 54, page 70). Synopsis: *How I Learned to Drive* explores the complex relationship between Li'l Bit and her Uncle Peck, as a series of driving lessons progresses from innocence to something much darker.

Kevin Cahoon, Marnie Schulenburg, Norbert Leo Butz, Jennifer Regan, and Elizabeth Reaser in How I Learned to Drive *(photo by Joan Marcus)*

Lonely, I'm Not by Paul Weitz; Director, Trip Cullman; Set, Mark Wendland; Costumes, Emily Rebholz; Lighting, Matt Frey; Projections, Aaron Rhyne; Sound, Bart Fasbender; PSM, Lori Ann Zepp; Stage Manager, Ashley J. Nelson; Production Assistant, Katie Kavett; Assistant Director, Jess Chayes; Production Electrician, John Tees; Audio Master, Mark Huang; Associate Projections, Ned Stresen-Reuter; Assistant Design: Brett J. Banakis (set), Katie Hartsoe (costumes), Sarah Lurie (lighting), Sam Kusnetz (sound), Bart Bortright (projections); Projection Programmer, Matthew Mellinger; Props, Susan Barras, Bryan McGuckin; Wardrobe Supervisor, Ashley Farra; Deck Carpenter, Rob Boyle; Light Board, Jes Halm; Sound Board, Kortney Barber; **Cast:** Topher Grace (Porter), Olivia Thirlby (Heather), Maureen Sebastian (Carlotta/Wendy/Claire), Christopher Jackson (Little Dog/Barista/Waiter), Lisa Emery (Grace/Yana/Administrator), Mark Blum (Rick/Decter)

Second Stage; First Preview: April 10, 2012; Opening Night: May 7, 2012; Closed June 3, 2012; 33 previews, 31 performances. World premiere of a new play presented without intermission. Synopsis: Porter has been married and divorced, earned seven figures as a corporate "ninja" and had a nervous breakdown, all at an early age. After four years without a job or a date, Porter decides to give life another shot, and he meets an ambitious young businesswoman who is overcoming her own obstacles to emotional success.

Olivia Thirlby and Topher Grace in Lonely, I'm Not
(photo by Joan Marcus)

Dogfight Music and lyrics by Benj Pasek and Justin Paul, book by Peter Duchan; Based on the Warner Brothers film and screenplay by Bob Comfort; Director, Joe Mantello; Choreography, Christopher Gattelli; Music Director, Bryan Perri; Set and Costumes, David Zinn; Lighting, Paul Gallo; Sound, Fitz Patton; Hair, Josh Marquette; Orchestrations, Michael Starobin; Vocal Arrangements, Justin Paul; Music Coordinator, Michael Keller; PSM, Diane DiVita; Stage Manager, Jenna Woods; Associate Director, Grady McLeod Bowman; Makeup, Ashley Ryan; Production Electrician, John Tees; Audio Master, Mark Huang; Associate Design: Jacob A. Climer (costumes), Craig Stelzenmuller (lighting), Joshua D. Reid (sound); Assistant Design: Brett Banakis (set), Hannah Dubrow (lighting); Props, Susan Barras; Fight Director, Thomas Schall; Marine Consultant, John Robison; Automation, Bryan McGuckin; Music Assistant, Greg Kenna; Cast recording: Sh-K-Boom/Ghostlight Records **Cast:** Annaleigh Ashford (Marcy), Becca Ayers (Mama), Nick Blaemire (Bernstein), Steven Booth (Gibbs), Dierdre Friel (Chippy), Adam Halpin (Stevens), F. Michael Haynie (Fector), Derek Klena (Eddie Birdlace), Lindsay Mendez (Rose Fenny), James Moye (Lounge Singer), Josh Segarra (Boland); Understudies: Steven Booth (Eddie, Bernstein, Fector), Dierdre Friel (Marcy, Mama), Adam Halpin (Eddie, Boland, Lounge Singer), F. Michael Haynie (Bernstein), Robert Lenzi (Boland, Stevens, Lounge Singer, Gibbs), Jen Sese (Rose, Marcy, Chippy, Gibbs); Musicians: Bryan Perri (Conductor), Michael Blanco (Bass), Sean Carney (Violin), Alisa Horn (Cello), Dillon Kondor (Guitar), Drew Simpson (Drums)

Second Stage; First Preview: June 27, 2012; Opening Night: July 16, 2012; Closed August 19, 2012; 24 previews, 39 performances. Setting: San Francisco,

Lindsay Mendez, Derek Klena, and the Company in Dogfight
(photo by Joan Marcus)

November 21, 1963. World premiere of a new musical presented in two acts. Synopsis: On the eve of their deployment, three young Marines set out for one final boys' night of debauchery. But when Corporal Eddie Birdlace meets Rose, an awkward and idealistic waitress he enlists to win a cruel bet with his fellow recruits, she rewrites the rules of the game and teaches him the power of compassion.

SECOND STAGE UPTOWN SERIES

The Bad Guys by Alena Smith; Director, Hal Brooks; Set, Jason Simms; Costumes, Jessica Pabst; Lighting, Seth Reiser; Sound, Ryan Rumery; PSM, Kyle Gates; Stage Manager, Colleen M. Sherry; Assistant Design: Fredrick Simmons (set), Stephanie Levin (costumes), Sarah Lurie (lighting), M. Florian Staab (sound); Scenic Charge, A. Ram Kim; Production Electrician, John Tees; Production Carpenter, Martin Perrin; Production Sound, M.L. Dogg; Props, Susan Barras; Lighting Programmer, Sarah Bullock; Light Board, Chris Steckel; Sound Board, Emily Auciello; Wardrobe Supervisor, Samantha Guinan; Production Assistant, Heather Englander; Stage Management Intern, Paula Clarkson; **Cast:** Michael Braun (Fink), Roe Hartrampf (Whit), James McMenamin (Noah), Tobias Segal (Jesse), Raviv Ullman (Paul)

McGinn/Cazale Theatre; First Preview: May 22, 2012; Opening Night: June 4, 2012; Closed June 17, 2012; 14 previews, 13 performances. World premiere of a new play presented without intermission. Synopsis: Five childhood buddies reunite on a late-summer afternoon for some beer, grilling and weed, but deep within their friendship lurk ghosts that rock the patio beneath them. Bitingly comic and ruthlessly recognizable, this is the story of a generation at war with itself over what it means to "man up."

Tobias Segal, Michael Braun, Raviv Ullman, and Roe Hartrampf in The Bad Guys *(photo Joan Marcus)*

Warrior Class by Kenneth Lin; Director, Evan Cabnet; Set, Andromache Chalfant; Costumes, Jessica Pabst; Lighting, Japhy Weideman; Sound, Jill BC DuBoff; PSM, Lori Ann Zepp; Stage Manager, Ashley J. Nelson; Assistant Design: Sarah Lurie (lighting/board programmer), Rebecca Lord-Surratt (set), Anthony Mattana (sound); Scenic Charge, A. Ram Kim; Production Electrician, John Tees; Production Carpenter, Steve Rosenberg; Production Sound, M.L. Dogg and Erin Ballantine; Props, Susan Barras; Sound Board, Daniel Carlyon; Wardrobe Supervisor, Sammi Guinan; Production Assistant, Chris Steckel; **Cast:** Louis Ozawa Changchien (Julius), Katharine Powell (Holly), David Rasche (Nathan)

McGinn/Cazale Theatre; First Preview: July 11, 2012; Opening Night July 23, 2012; Closed August 11, 2012; 12 previews, 27 performances. World premiere of a new play presented without intermission. Synopsis: When Assemblyman Julius Lee makes a bid for Congress, the ghosts of his college days come back to haunt him. Nothing reveals true colors like a sprint to the finish, when friends become enemies and allies can turn on a dime. *Warrior Class* is a political battle of race, romance, forgiveness and debt.

Signature Theatre

Twenty-first Season

Inaugural Season at the Pershing Square Signature Center

Founding Artistic Director, James Houghton; Executive Director, Erika Mallin; Associate Artistic Director, Beth Whitaker; General Manager, Adam Bernstein; Director of Development, Kirsten Hughes/Meghan Pressman; Director of Marketing/Audience Services, David Hatkoff; Director of Production, Paul Ziemer; Literary Director, Christie Evangelisto; Associate General Manager, Kendra Ramthun; Company Manager, Daniel Hoyos; Artistic Line Producer, Rob Marcato; Casting, Telsey + Company, Will Cantler; Associate Production Manager, Layhoon Tan; Technical Director, Seth Marion; Costume Shop Supervisor, Vanessa Watters; Lighting Supervisor, Jake Heinrichs; Playwrights-in-Residence: Edward Albee (Legacy), Athol Fugard (Residency One), Annie Baker, Will Eno, Katori Hall, Kenneth Lonergan, Regina Taylor (Residency Five); Press, Boneau/Bryan-Brown, Chris Boneau, Heath Schwartz, Emily Meagher

RESIDENCY ONE: ATHOL FUGARD SERIES

Blood Knot Written and directed by Athol Fugard; Set, Christopher H. Barreca; Costumes, Susan Hilferty; Lighting, Stephen Strawbridge; Sound, Brett Jarvis; Original Music, Doug Wieselman; Dialects, Barbara Rubin; Fight Director, Rick Sordelet; PSM, Pamela Salling; ASM, Maggie Swing; Dramaturg, Christie Evangelisto; Assistant Director, Joseph Ward; Assistant Design: Lianne Arnold (set), Marina Reti (costumes), Alan Edwards (ligiting), Stephanie Riddle (sound), Properties, Sarah Bird, Dana Lewman; Production Carpenter, Allison Nowicki; Production Electrician, Desi Fischer; Light Board Programmer/Operator, Bridget Chervenka; Wardrobe Supervisor, Abby Barker; Production SVC, Sarah Gates; Deck Carpenter, Kara Aghabekian; Production Assistant, Lily Perlmutter; **Cast:** Scott Shepherd (Morris), Colman Domingo (Zachariah)

Alice Griffin Jewel Box Theatre; First Preview: January 31, 2012; Opening Night: February 16, 2012; Closed March 11, 2012; 20 previews, 28 performances. Setting: Korsten, a Coloured location on the outskirts of Port Elizabeth, South Africa. 1961. Revival of a play presented in two acts. Originally produced on Broadway at the John Golden Theatre December 10, 1985–March 6, 1986, playing 13 previews and 96 performances (see *Theatre World* Vol. 42, page 22). Synopsis: Between patchwork walls in a one-room shack, two biracial South African brothers grapple with poverty and isolation. Morris is light-skinned enough to pass for white, but dark-skinned Zach feels imprisoned by his job at a whites-only park. When they find themselves on some dangerous new ground, they must come face to face with the blood knot between them.

Scott Shepherd and Colman Domingo in Blood Knot
(photos by Joan Marcus unless otherwise noted)

My Children! My Africa! by Athol Fugard; Director, Ruben Santiago-Hudson; Sets, Neil Patel; Costumes, Karen Perry; Lighting, Marcus Doshi; Sound, Robert Kaplowitz; Music, Bobby McFerrin; Dialects, Ron Kunene and Barbara Rubin; PSM, Amanda Michaels; ASM, Hannah Woodward; Dramaturg, Kirsten Bowen; Assistant Director, Awoye Timpo; Assistant Design: Caleb Levengood (set), Pamela Mieser (costumes), Milim Sung (lighting), Jessica Paz (sound); Props, Matt Hodges, Sarah Bird; Production Carpenter, Jeremy DeLuca; Production Electricians, Jay Sterkel, Sean Linehan; Light Board Programmer/Operator, Tim Parrish; Wardrobe Supervisor, Abby Barker; Production SVC, Sarah Gates; Deck Carpenter, Stephen Ehrlich; Production Assistant, Lily Perlmutter; **Cast:** James A. Williams (Mr. M [Anela Myalatya]), Allie Gallerani (Isabel Dyson), Stephen Tyrone Williams (Thami Mbikwana)

Stephen Tyrone Williams and Allie Gallerani in My Children! My Africa!

Romulus Linney Courtyard Theatre; First Preview: May 1, 2012; Opening Night: May 24, 2012; Closed June 17, 2012; 24 previews, 25 performances. Setting: A classroom in a small Eastern Cape Karoo town in the autumn of 1984. Revival of a play presented in two acts. Originally produced by The Market Theatre (Johannesburg), June 1989. New York premiere presented by New York Theatre Workshop December 2, 1989–January 14, 1990, playing 45 perforamances (see *Theatre World* Vol. 46, page 91). Synopsis: Mr. M, an idealistic teacher, seeks to provide a future for his gifted student Thami by forming a debate team with Isabel, a spirited student from the local white school. But outside the classroom Mr. M's hopes for Thami are challenged by their generational divide and increasing political unrest. *My Children! My Africa!* is an honest and unflinching portrait of a country on the brink of revolution, and is a testament to the power and potential of youth, hope, and ideas.

The Train Driver Written and directed by Athol Fugard; Sets, Christopher H. Barreca; Costumes, Susan Hilferty; Lighting, Stephen Strawbridge; Sound, Brett Jarvis; Original Music, Doug Wieselman; Dialects, Barbara Rubin; PSM, Linda Marvel; Dramaturg, Dirsten Bowen; Assistant Director, Joseph Ward; Associate Costumes, Marina Reti; Assistant Design: Vincent Richards, Nina Caussa (set), Hyun Seung Lee (lighting); Production Electrician, Jay Sterkel; Props, Sarah Bird, Dana Lewman; Light Board Programmer/Operator, Stephanie Palmer; Wardrobe Supervisor, Abby Barker; Project Manager, Josh Sturnam; Production SVC, Sarah Gates; Deck Carpenter, Stephen Ehrlich; Scenic Paint Charge, Carolyn Bonanni; Production Assistant, Emily Hayes; Assistant to Mr. Fugard, Gabriel Weissman; **Cast:** Leon Addison Brown (Simon Hanabe), Ritchie Coster (Roelf Visagie)

Romulus Linney Courtyard Theatre; First Preview: August 14, 2012; Opening Night: September 9, 2012; Closed September 23, 2012; 32 previews, 15 performances. Setting: The graveyard of Shukuma, a squatter camp on the outskirts of Port Elizabeth. New York premiere of a new play presented without intermission. World premiere at The Fugard Theatre in Cape Town, South Africa in March 2010. U.S. premiere produced in Los Angeles at The Fountain Theatre

October 16–December 12, 2010. Synopsis: Roelf, a train driver, has spent weeks searching for the identities of a mother and child he unintentionally killed with his train. After a fruitless journey through shanty towns, he encounters an old gravedigger named Simon who helps the desperate man unburden his conscience. Based on a true story, *The Train Driver* is a soulful exploration of guilt, suffering and the powerful bonds that grow between strangers.

Leon Addison Brown in The Train Driver *(photo by Richard Termine)*

RESIDENCY FIVE – NEW PLAYS FROM FIVE RESIDENT PLAYWRIGHTS OVER FIVE YEARS

Hurt Village by Katori Hall; Director, Patricia McGregor; Sets and Projections, David Gallo; Costumes, Clint Ramos; Lighting, Sarah Sidman; Sound, Robert Kaplowitz; Hair/Wigs/Makeup, Cookie Jordan; Additional Music, Luqman Brown; Fight Director, Rick Sordelet; Dialect Coach, Kate Wilson; PSM, Jane Pole; ASM, Megan J. Alvord; Dramaturg, Kirsten Bowen; Assistant Director, Molly Murphy; Associate Design: Tabitha Pease (set), Caite Hevner (projections), Jessica Paz (sound); Assistant Design: Dede Ayite (costumes), Dan Hansell (lighting); Jookin' Consultant, U-Dig Dance Academy/Daniel Price; Fight Captain, Charlie Hudson III; Production Carpenter, Jeremy DeLuca; Production Electrician, Jay Sterkel; Production SVC, Dave Horowitz; Props, Kathy Fabian, Cassie Dorland; Deck Carpenter, Stephen Ehrlich; Projections Programmer, Timothy Brown; Light Board Programmer/Operator, Tim Parrish; AV Operator, Dave Horowitz; Wardrobe Supervisor, Sally Hall; Wigs and Makeup Supervisor, Gina Leone; Production Assistant, Alyson Cermak; **Cast:** Joaquina Kalukango (Cookie), Marsha Stephanie Blake (Crank), Tonya Pinkins (Big Mama), Corey Hawkins (Buggy), Saycon Sengbloh (Toyia), Nicholas Christopher (Cornbread), Charlie Hudson III (Ebony), Lloyd Watts (Skillet), Ron Cephas Jones (Tony C)

Romulus Linney Courtyard Theatre; First Preview: February 7, 2012; Opening Night: February 27, 2012; Closed March 25, 2012; 24 previews, 32 performances. Setting: The end of summer, Hurt Village in Memphis, Tennessee; Second Bush Dynasty. World premiere of a new play presented in two acts. Synopsis: It's the end of a long summer in Hurt Village, a housing project in Memphis. A government Hope Grant means relocation for many of the project's residents, including Cookie, a thirteen year-old aspiring rapper, along with her mother Crank and great-grandmother Big Mama. As the family prepares to move, Cookie's father Buggy unexpectedly returns from a tour of duty in Iraq. Ravaged by the war, Buggy struggles to find a position in his disintegrating community, along with a place in his daughter's wounded heart. **2012 Theatre World Award:** Joaquina Kalukango

Tonya Pinkins (front, center) with (l-r) Marsha Stephanie Blake, Nicholas Christopher, Saycon Sengbloh, Joaquina Kalukango, and Corey Hawkins in Hurt Village

Title and Deed by Will Eno; Presented in association with Gare St Lazare Players Ireland (Conor Lovett and Judy Hegart Lovett, Artistic Directors; Maura O'Keeffe, Producer); Director, Judy Hegarty Lovett; Set, Christine Jones; Costumes, Andrea Lauer; Lighting, Ben Stanton; PSM, Donald Fried; Assistant Design: Ioannis Sochorakis (set), Amy Wright (costumes), David Sexton (lighting); Production/Deck Carpenter, Allison Nowicki; Production Electrician, Desi Fischer; Props, Sarah Bird; Sound Operator, Marshall York; Light Board Programmer/Operator, Dave Polato; Wardrobe Supervisor, Katherine Harber; Production Assistant, Maegen Sacco; **Cast:** Conor Lovett (Man)

Alice Griffin Jewel Box Theatre; First Preview: May 8, 2012; Opening Night: May 20, 2012; Closed June 3, 2012; 15 previews, 35 performances. Setting: The theatre, a room. U.S. premiere of a new solo performance play presented without intermission. World premiere at the Kilkenny Arts Centre (Ireland) in August 2011. Synopsis: A nameless traveler from a far off place searches for connection and solace in an unknown country in this funny and sad meditation on mortality, loneliness, innocence, home, family, love, funerals, words, and the world.

Medieval Play Written and directed by Kenneth Lonergan; Sets, Walt Spangler; Costumes, Michael Krass; Lighting, Jason Lyons; Sound, David Van Tieghem; Fight Director, J. David Brimmer; PSM, David H. Lurie; Stage Manager, Andrew C. Gottlieb; Dramaturg, Christie Evangelisto; Assistant Director, Elizabeth Carlson; Assistant Design: Jisum Kim (set), Robert Croghan (costumes), Grant Wilcoxen (lighting), Brandon Wolcott (sound); Production Carpenter, Rory Mulholland; Production Electricians, Kevin Johnson, Austin Smith; Production SVC/Sound Operator, Anthony Luciani; Props, Sarah Bird, Matt Hodges; Deck Carpenter, Philip Cruise Warren; Automation, Jeff Cusimano; Props Carpenter, Ahsley Crokett; Light Board Programmer/Operator, Bridget Chervenka; First Hand, Judi Olson; Wardrobe Supervisor, Sally Hall; Wardrobe Crew, Kyle Skillin; Armor

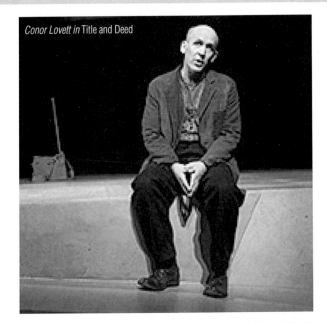

Conor Lovett in Title and Deed

Workers, Bob Knapp, Jon Vogt; Production Assistants, Amanda Kosack, Mauli Delaney, Lily Perlmutter; **Cast:** Josh Hamilton (Sir Ralph), Tate Donovan (Sir Alfred), C.J. Wilson (Sir Lionel, 2nd Cardinal, Sir Niccolo Galeazzo, Doctor, Death), Kevin Geer (Sir Simon, 1st Cardinal, Dietrich, Pope Gregory XI), John Pankow (Cardinal Robert of Geneva-afterwards Pope Clement VII, Illuminator, Jaques, 1st Diner, Herald), Anthony Arkin (Bartolomeo Prignano-afterwards Pope Urban VI, Tree, Elderly Cardinal, Servant), Heather Burns (Catherine of Siena, 2nd Harlot, 2nd Diner), Halley Feiffer (Margery, 1st Harlot, Emilia, Jester, Queen Joanna, Beatrice)

Irene Diamond Stage; First Preview: May 15, 2012; Opening Night: June 7, 2012; Closed June 25, 2012; 27 previews, 20 performances. Setting: Various locations in France and Italy, 1376-1378. World premiere of a new play presented in two acts. Synopsis: Two French mercenary knights set out on a quest for relative moral redemption against the classic comic background of late 14th century ecclesiastical politics. A story of friendship, love, noble feats of arms, indiscriminate brutality, the progressive refinement of medieval table manners and the general decline of the chivalric ideal at the onset of the Great Papal Schism of 1378.

LEGACY PROGRAM – EDWARD ALBEE

The Lady from Dubuque by Edward Albee; Director, David Esbjornson; Set, John Arnone; Costumes, Elizabeth Hope Clancy; Lighting, David Lander; Sound, John Gromada; Fight Director, Rick Sordelet; PSM, David H. Lurie; Stage Manager, Andrew C. Gottlieb; Dramaturg, Christie Evangelisto; Hair and Makeup Consultant, Erin Kennedy Lunsford; Associate Set, John Farrell; Assistant Design: Shawn McColloch (costumes), Travis McHale (lighting), Janie Bullard (sound); Props, Matt Hodges, Sarah Bird; Production Carpenter, Rory Mulholland; Production Electrician, Austin Smith; Production SVC, Ken Hypes; Light Board Programmer/Operator, David Polato; Sound Operator, Marshall York; Wardrobe Supervisor, Kalere Payton; Deck Carpenter, Dale Drupla; Assistant to Mr. Albee, Jakob Holder; Production Assistant, Amanda Kosack; Directing Observer, Paige Kiliany; **Cast:** Michael Hayden (Sam), Laila Robins (Jo), C.J. Wilson (Fred), Catherine Curtain (Lucinda), Thomas Jay Ryan (Edgar), Tricia Paoluccio (Carol), Peter Francis James (Oscar), Jane Alexander (Elizabeth)

End Stage Theatre; First Preview: February 14, 2012; Opening Night: March 5, 2012; Closed April 15, 2012; 25 previews, 46 performances. Setting: A house in the suburbs. Now. Revival of a play presented in two acts. Originally presented on Broadway at the Morosco Theatre January 31–February 9, 1980, playing 8 previews and 12 performances (see *Theatre World* Vol. 36, page 38). Synopsis: At a late night party, Sam and Jo entertain their friends with a round of Twenty Questions and another round of drinks. When an unexpected guest and her mysterious companion arrive, the question "Who are you?" gains a whole new and desperate meaning.

Catherine Curtain, C.J. Wilson, Thomas Jay Ryan, Laila Robins, Jane Alexander, and Michael Hayden in Edward Albee's The Lady from Dubuque

Josh Hamilton, Tate Donovan, and Halley Feiffer in Medieval Play

Michael Hayden and Laila Robins in Edward Albee's The Lady from Dubuque

Soho Rep

Thirty-sixth Season

Artistic Director, Sarah Benson; Executive Director, Tania Carmargo; Producer, Caleb Hammons; Literary & Humanities Manager, Raphael Martin; Production & Facilities Manager, Robbie Saenz de Viteri; Development Associate, Teff Nichols; Artistic and Producing Assistant, Eric Shethar; Development Consultant, Jennie Greer; Management Consultant, Michael Bodel; Writer/Director Lab Co-Chairs, Jenny Schwartz and Ken Russ Schmoll; Box Office, William Burke; Management Assistant, Heather Gallagher; Graphic Design, Omnivore; Website, Bad Feather; Founding Artistic Directors, Marlene Swarz and Jerry Engelbach; Press, Blake Zidell and Associates

Elective Affinities by David Adjmi; Presented in association with piece by piece productions (Wendy vanden Heuvel) and Rising Phoenix Repertory (Daniel Talbott, Artistic Director); Director, Sarah Benson; Set, Louisa Thompson; Costumes, Susan Hilferty; Lighting, Mark Barton; Sound, Matt Tierney; PSM, Tom Taylor; Casting, Jack Doulin; General Management, Snug Harbor Productions, Steven Chaikelson, Kendra Bator; ASM, Kate Croasdale; Assistant Director, Kathryn Kozlark; General Management Assistant, Christina Macchiarola; Casting Assistant, Ashley Monroe; Assistant Set, Katherine Akiko Day; Props Master, Lily Fairbanks; Location Scouts, Tom Sexton, Geoffrey Booth; Run Crew, Gabel Eiben; Catering, Gillie Holme; Alice's Butlers, David McDonald, George Crowley; Alice's Catering Staff, Joyce Hata, David Moradi, Tobias Wilson; House Manager, Wayne Petro; Website, Josh Levine; **Cast:** Zoe Caldwell (Alice Hauptmann)

American Irish Historical Society; First Preview: November 17, 2011; Opening Night: December 1, 2011; Closed December 18, 2011; 8 previews, 13 performances. U.S. premiere of an interactive solo-performance play presented without intermission. World premiere at Royal Shakespeare Company in October 2005; transferred to the Soho Theatre (London) April 2006. Developed at the Royal Court Theatre in the U.K., and Lincoln Center Theater and the Pearl Theatre in the U.S. (featuring Marian Seldes). Synopsis: This unique site-specific event invites audiences into the apartment of a witty octogenarian offering a funny and savage portrait of cultured life, along with tea and sandwiches. *Elective Affinities* promises to initiate a vital discourse about what it means to be civilized.

Zoe Caldwell in Elective Affinities *(photos by Julia Cervantes)*

The Ugly One by Marius von Mayenburg; Co-presented by The Play Company ((Kate Loewald, Founding Producer; Lauren Weigel, Executive Director), in association with John Adrian Selzer; Director, Daniel Aukin; Translation, Maja Zade; Set, Eugene Lee; Costumes, Theresa Squire; Lighting, Matt Frey; Sound, Matt Tierney; Props, Starlet Jacobs; PSM, Davin De Santis; ASM, Brittany Kramer; Casting, Jack Doulin; Assistant Design: Patrick Lynch (set), Amanda Jenks (costumes), Sarah Lurie (lighting), Jara Belmonte (props); Casting Assistant, Ashley Monroe; Production Assistant, Casey Griffin; Wardrobe Supervisor, Grace Trimble; Set Construction, Joseph Silovsky; Electrics, The Lighting Syndicate; Lighting Programmer, Heather Smaha; Audio, Jason Sebastian; Sound Board Operator, Cooper Gardner; **Cast:** Steven Boyer (Karlmann), Andrew Garman (Scheffler), Lisa Joyce (Fanny), Alfredo Narciso (Lette)

Soho Rep (Walkerspace); First Preview: February 1, 2012; Opening Night: February 7, 2012; Closed February 26, 2012; 6 previews, 21 performances. New York premiere of a new play presented without intermission. Synopsis: Lette is a successful engineer who is also unspeakably ugly. His plastic surgeon is reluctant to operate - Lette's face is so ugly it will have to be rebuilt from scratch. The surgeon's efforts are rewarded, however, when Lette emerges from the operation an Adonis. His life changes overnight: his wife finds him irresistible, he becomes an overnight star at his company and he is fawned upon wherever he goes. But this dream life soon becomes a nightmare, as Lette's surgeon begins to offer his face to anyone who can pay.

Alfredo Narciso and Steven Boyer in The Ugly One

Uncle Vanya by Anton Chekhov, adapted by Annie Baker; Presented in association with John Adrian Selzer; Director, Sam Gold; Set, Andrew Lieberman; Costumes, Annie Baker; Lighting, Mark Barton; Sound, Matt Tierney; Props, Kate Foster; Fight Director, Thomas Schall; Literal Translation, Margarita Shalina; PSM, Christina Lowe; ASM, Shane Schnetzler; Casting, Jack Doulin; Technical Director, Dave Ogle; Assistant Director, Knud Adams; Stage Management Assistant, Claire Dyrud; Associate Design: Amanda Seymour (costumes), Mike Inwood (lighting); Assistant Design: Ika Avaliani (set), Janie Bullard (sound); Assistant Fight Director, Ian Lassiter; Wardrobe Supervisors, Ali Valcarcel and Grace Trimble; Master Electrician, Karen Walcott; Lighting Programmer, Sarah Lurie; Board Operator, Cooper Gardner; Wigmaker and Makeup Artist, Amanda Miller; Lightbox Letter Fabrication, Fred Foster; Map Fabrication, Ika Avaliani; Knitting Consultant, Rita Bobry; Production Assistants, Adam Blodgett, Daniel Roberts; SDC Observer, Charlie Birns; **Cast:** Reed Birney (Vanya), Maria Dizzia (Yelena), Georgia Engel (Marina), Peter Friedman (The Professor), Matthew Maher (Waffles), Rebecca Schull* (Maria), Michael Shannon (Astrov), Paul Thureen (Yefim), Merritt Wever (Sonya); *Succeeded by Roberta Maxwell (7/24/12)

Soho Rep (Walkerspace); First Preview: June 7, 2012; Opening Night: June 17, 2012; Closed August 26, 2012; 11 previews, 66 performances. World premiere of a new adaptation of a classic play presented in two acts. Synopsis: Longtime academic Vanya comes to question his devotion to an aging professor, whose wife Vanya loves even as she is drawn to the enigmatic Doctor Astrov. Playwright Barker and director Gold team up to stage an intimate and immersive adaptation of the Chekhov masterpiece. Gold's concept for *Uncle Vanya* places the audience and the cast together inside an A-frame house constructed within Soho Rep's home.

READINGS

Writer/Director Lab Reading Series Downtown's premiere program for new plays; Included: *How to Get Into Buildings* by Trish Harnetiaux, directed by Jeremy Bloom (April 2, 2012); *Sprawl* by Joshua Conkel, directed by Jen Wineman (April 9, 2012); *Cockfight* by Peter Gil-Sheridan, directed by Anna Brenner (April 16, 2012); *Really Really Really Really Really* by Jackie Sibblies Drury, directed by David F. Chapman (May 7, 2012)

Theatre for a New Audience

Thirty-second Season

Artistic Director, Jeffrey Horowitz; Board Chairman, Theodore Rogers/Henry Christensen III; Managing Director, Dorothy Ryan; General Manager, Theresa von Klug; Development, James L. Lynes; Education, Katie Miller; Finance, Elizabeth Lees; Capital Campaign Director, Rachel Lovett; Associate Artistic Director, Arin Arbus; Associate General Manager, Christopher Jenkins; Associate Education, Carie Donnelson; Associate Finance, Andrew Zimmerman; Development Associate, Daniel Bayer; Capital Associate, Elizabeth Carena; Assistant General Manager, Courtney F. Caldwell; Associate to the Artistic Director, Danya Taymor; Literary Advisor, Jonathan Kalb; Production Manager, B.D. White; Resident Director of Voice, Andrew Wade; Press, Bruce Cohen

Cymbeline by William Shakespeare; Created and presented by Fiasco Theater; Co-Produced by Scott Morfee, Jean Doumanian, Tom Wirtshafter, The Somerled Charitable Foundation, Burnt Umber Productions, Christian Chadd Taylor, Marc & Lisa Biales/Ted Snowdon

Barrow Street Theatre; First Preview: August 27, 2011; Opening Night: September 8, 2011; Closed January 15, 2012; 10 previews, 150 performances. Commercial transfer of a new version of a classic play presented in two acts. The U.S. premiere of this production was presented last season at the New Victory Theatre. For complete listing information, see page 141 in this volume.

Fragments Texts by Samuel Beckett (*Rough for Theatre I; Rockaby; Act Without Words II; Neither; Come and Go*); Produced in association with Baryshnikov Arts Center; Presented by C.I.C.T/Théâtre des Bouffes du Nord; Directors, Peter Brook and Marie-Hélène Estienne; Lighting, Philippe Vialatte; Company Manager, Thomas Becelewski; Technical Manager, Jean Dauriac; PSM, Christopher C. Dunlop; Lighting Supervisor, Wilburn Bonnell; Lighting Operator, Megan Kaplan; Deck/Wardrobe Crew, Caitlin Dixon; **Cast:** Jos Houben, Kathryn Hunter, Marcello Magni

Baryshnikov Arts Center; First Preview: November 9, 2011; Opening Night: November 13, 2011; Closed December 4, 2011; 5 previews, 24 performances. New York premiere of an absurdist theatre piece presented in English without intermission. Created in French in October 2006 at Théâtre des Bouffes du Nord with the collaboration of Lilo Bauer; revived in English in co-production with the Young Vic Theatre in London. Synopsis: Brook and Estienne interpret five Beckett shorts to form a cumulative story, much of which is hidden, either whispered beyond our hearing, or evoked with the broadest brush strokes by characters that either speak in riddles or don't speak at all. Ambiguity and uncertainty—going nowhere and everywhere fast—reign in this dramatic collection, inviting the audience to fill in the particulars, to supply its own insight.

Marcello Magni in Fragments
(photo by Pascal Victor/ArtComArt)

Jeff Brooks, Darryl Winslow, Michael Iannucci, Jesse Means, David Skeist, and Kristine Zbornik in Shlemiel the First *(photo by Gerry Goodstein)*

Shlemiel the First Conceived and adapted by Robert Brustein, lyrics by Arnold Weinstein, music composed, adapted, and orchestrated by Hankus Netsky; Based on the play by Isaac Bashevis Singer; Co-produced by National Yiddish Theatre – Folksbiene (Zalmen Mlotek, Artistic Director; Bryna Wasserman, Executive Director; Motl Didner, Associate Artistic Director), NYU Skirball Center for the Performing Arts (Jay Olivia, Executive Producer; Michael Harrington, Senior Director), and Peak Performances at Montclair State University (Jedediah Wheeler, Artistic Director; Jill Dombrowski, Executive Producer; Jessica Wasilewski, Associate Producer); Director/Choreography/Editorial Supervision, David Gordon; Arrangements/Additional Music/Music Direction, Zalmen Mlotek; Sets, Robert Israel; Costumes, Catherine Zuber; Lighting, Jennifer Tipton; Sound, David Meschter; Costume Supervisor, Haley Lieberman; Casting, Cindi Rush and Deborah Brown; PSM, Ed Fitzgerald; ASM, Marci Skolnick; Associate Music Director, Michael Larsen; Assistant to the Choreographer, Daniel Gwitzman; Assistant Lighting, Laura Eckelman; Props, Jeremy Lydic; Wardrobe, Dara Fargotstein, Anjia Jalac; Master Electrician, Stephanie Shechter; Spot Ops, Sammy Gordon, Amanda Lemen; Sound Operator, Ethan Blade; Deck Crew, Megan Caplan; **Cast:** Amy Warren (Tryna Ritza), Michael Iannucci (Shlemiel), Kristine Zbornik (Gittel, Sender Shlamazel, Yenta Pesha), Darryl Winslow (Mottel, Moishe Pipik, Chaim Rascal), Jesse Means (Zeinvel Schmeckel, Man in House), David Skeist (Mendel Scmendrick), Bob Ader (Dopey Petzel, Zalman Tippish), Jeff Brooks (Gronam Ox), Stephen Cain, Brandon Lavon Hightower, Amanda A. Lederer, Brandon Monokian, Aaron Netsky (Ensemble); The Shlemiel Band: Zalmen Mlotek (Piano/Conductor), Michael Larsen (Piano/Conductor Alternate), Yaeko Miranda Elmaleh (Violin), Daniel Linden (Trombone), Nick Morrison (Banjo/Mandolin/Guitar), Dmitri "Zisl" Slepovitch (Clarinet), Grant Smith (Drums/Percussion), Ezra Weller (Trumpet), Jim Whitney (Bass)

Musical Numbers: Wake-Up Song; Shlemiel's Song; We're Talking Chelm; Yenta's Blintzes; Beadle With a Dreydl; I'm Going to Die; Missionary Tour; Geography Song; My One and Only Shlemiel; Rascal's Song; My One and Only Shlemiel (reprise), Meshugah; Twos; The Screen Song; Can This Be Hell?; Matters of the Heart; Wisdom; We're Talking Chelm (reprise)

Jack H. Skirball Center for the Performing Arts at NYU; First Preview: December 13, 2011; Opening Night: December 15, 2011; Closed December 31, 2011; 2 previews, 21 performances. Setting: The legendary town of Chelm. Revival of a Klezmer musical presented in two acts. World premiere co-produced by American Music Theatre Festival (Philadelphia) and American Repertory Theatre at A.R.T in 1994 and subsequently played New York, San Francisco, and Los Angeles (see *Theatre World* Vol. 50, page 161). This revival was first produced in January 2010 at the Montclair State University. Synopsis: *Shlemiel the First* takes place in a village of fools, where Sclemiel, a half sad-sack clown, half accidental messiah, charms with his childlike innocence. The musical, playfulness and unapologetic, turns an already absurd world hilariously, and redemptively, topsy-turvy.

The Broken Heart by John Ford; Director, Selina Cartmell; Sets, Antje Ellermann; Costumes, Susan Hilferty; Lighting, Marcus Doshi; Composer and Sound, David Van Tieghem; Choreography, Annie-B Parson; Voice Director, Andrew Wade; Dramaturg, Jonathan Kalb; Fight Director, J. Allen Suddeth; Casting, Deborah Brown; PSM, Linda Marvel; ASM, Sid King; Dance Captain, Margaret Loesser Robinson; Assistant Director, Danya Taymor; Assistant Choreographer, Tymberly Canale; Dance Coach, Luke Miller; Associate Costumes, Marina Reti; Assistant Design: Phillip Tokarsky (set), Becky Lasky, Sara James (costumes), Milim Sung, Jeremy Cunningham (lighting), Sam Kusnetz (sound); Prop Master, Claire Karoff; Assistant Production Manager/Technical Director, Megan Caplan; Assistant Technical Director/Crew, Ernie Johns; Wardrobe, Dara Fargotstein, Caitlin Dixon; Sound Supervisor/Operator, Chip Barrow; Sound Crew, Dave Hunter; **Cast:** Philip Goodwin (Amyclas), John Keating (Armostes/Phulas), Andrew Weems (Bassanes), Bianca Amato (Calantha), Robert Langdon Lloyd (Crotolon), Margaret Loesser Robinson (Euphrania/Philema), Olwen Fouéré (Grausis), Saxon Palmer (Ithocles), Justin Blanchard (Nearchus), Jacob Fishel (Orgilus), Annika Boras (Penthea), Ian Holcomb (Prophilus), Tom Nelis (Tecnicus), Molly Yeh (A Musician)

Duke on 42nd Street; First Preview: February 4, 2012; Opening Night: February 12, 2012; Closed March 4, 2012; 8 previews, 25 performances. Setting: Legendary Sparta. Off-Broadway premiere of a 1629 comic-tragedy presented in two acts. Synopsis: A long feud between two Spartan families has ended with the loving engagement of their children, Penthea and Orgilus. Penthea's father, however, dies before the wedding can take place, and her twin brother, Ithocles, forces her into a socially advantageous match with a jealous older man. Ithocles returns to Sparta a war hero and falls in love with the Princess Calantha, hoping for precisely the joy he has deprived his sister. When Origlus takes his revenge, Calantha cannot stand aloof.

The Taming of the Shrew by William Shakespeare; Director, Arin Arbus; Sets, Donyale Werle; Costumes, Anita Yavich; Lighting, Marcus Doshi; Composer, Michael Friedman; Voice Director, Andrew Wade; Dramaturg, Jonathan Kalb; Choreographer, Doug Elkins; Movement Consultant, B.H. Barry; Casting, Deborah Brown; PSM, Renee Lutz; ASM, Marjorie Ann Wood; Technical Director, Megan Caplan; Props Master, Meghan Buchanan; Wigs, Erin Kennedy Lunsford; Assistant Design: Erica Evans, Nicole Smith (costumes), Milim Sung, Jeremy Cunningham (lighting); Assistant to the Director, Emily Ernst; Sound Supervisor, Chip Barrow; Light Board Operator, Sam Gordon; Wardrobe Supervisor, Dara Fargotstein; Production Carpenter/Assistant Technical Director, Ernie Johns; **Cast:** Varín Ayala (Biondello), Denis Butkus (Lucentio/Sugarsop), Paul L. Coffey (The Lord), Matthew Cowles (Christopher Sly/The Merchant), Olwen Fouéré (The Hostess/Widow), Andy Grotelueschen (Petruchio), John Christopher Jones (Grumio/Nathaniel), John Keating (Tranio), Robert Langdon Lloyd (Baptista Minola/Joseph), Peter Maloney (Curtis/The Tailor/Vincentio), Jonathan Mastro (Piano Player), Saxon Palmer (Hortensio), John Pankow (Gremio), Kathryn Saffell (Bianca Minola), Maggie Siff (Katharina Minola)

Duke on 42nd Street; First Preview: March 18, 2012; Opening Night: April 1, 2012; Closed April 21, 2012; 14 previews, 22 performances. Setting: The American Frontier in the late 19th century; Padua and Verona (within the play). Revival of a classic play presented in two acts. Synopsis: Arbis frames Shakespeare's classic comedy against the backdrop of the Wild West, as a traveling acting toupe performs the play as part of a comic experiment that a wealthy Lord conducts upon a drunken tinker. In the play, Shakespeare depicts a rough world where everyone is out for themselves — scheming, deceiving and hiding beneath disguises. Forced to marry a brash young gold-digger so that her sweeter, younger sister may marry for love, the temperamental Katherine proves to be more than Petruchio bargained for.

Annika Boras and Jacob Fishel in The Broken Heart *(photo by Gerry Goodstein)*

Maggie Siff and Andy Grotelueschen in The Taming of the Shrew *(photo by Henry Grossman)*

Vineyard Theatre

Thirty-first Season

Artistic Director, Douglas Aibel; Co-Associate Artistic Director, Sarah Stern; Executive Director, Jennifer Garvey-Blackwell; Managing Director, Rebecca Habel; External Affairs, Jonathan K. Waller; Development, Veronica R. Bainbridge; Management Associate, Dennis Hruska; Audience Services, Cody Andrus; Development Associate, Erica Mann; Marketing/Graphic Design Associate, Eric Pargac; Production Managers, Ben Morris, David Nelson; Education, Eric Dente; Literary Associate, Miriam Weiner; Casting Associate, Henry Russell Bergstein; Education Instructor, Dax Valdes; Literary Fellow, Louise Gough; Shank Playwriting Fellow, Krista Knight; Press, Sam Rudy and Dale Heller

The Lyons by Nicky Silver; Director, Mark Brokaw; Sets, Allen Moyer; Costumes, Michael Krass; Lighting, David Lander; Original Music and Sound, David Van Tieghem; Fight Director, Thomas Schall; PSM, Roy Harris; ASM, Denise Yaney; Assistant Director, Sam Pinkleton; Props Master, Tessa Dunning; Associate Design: Warren Karp (set), Ben Pilat (lighting); Assistant Design: Brenda Abbandandolo (costumes), Emma Wilk (sound); Master Carpenter/Deck Supervisor, Eric Brooks; Wardrobe Supervisor, Jessica Moy; Light and Sound Operator, Lisa Hufnagel; Deck Crew, Rebecca Key; Production Assistants, Colyn Fiendel, Jessica Johnstone, Michael Karns **Cast:** Linda Lavin (Rita Lyons), Dick Latessa (Ben Lyons), Kate Jennings Grant (Lisa Lyons), Brenda Pressley (Nurse), Gregory Wooddell (Brian)

Gertrude and Irving Dimson Theatre; First Preview: September 22, 2011; Opening Night: October 11, 2011; Closed November 20, 2011; 19 previews, 40 performances. Setting: Act I: A hospital room; Act II Scene 1: A meeting hall; Scene 2: An empty apartment; Scene 3: A hospital room. World premiere of a new dark comedy presented in four scenes in two acts. This production transferred to Broadway April 23, 2012 (see page 77 in this volume). Synopsis: *The Lyons* is an outrageously funny and stirring work about a family grappling with the impending death of its patriarch. When Ben's wife and grown children gather to say goodbye, they learn that despite being a family, each of them is utterly isolated. Afraid of closeness and afraid of solitude, they are propelled into foreign territory - human connection.

Kate Jennings Grant and Linda Lavin in The Lyons

Outside People by Zayd Dohrn; Co-produced by Naked Angels (Andy Donald, Artistic Director; Renee Blinkwolt, Managing Director); Director, Evan Cabnet; Set, Takeshi Kata; Costumes, Jessica Wegener Shay; Lighting, Ben Stanton; Sound, Jill BC DuBoff; PSM, Charles M. Turner III; ASM, Courtney James; Assistant Production Manager, Meredith Pompeani; Assistant Director, Lee Kasper; Props Master, Lily Fairbanks; Assistant Design: Kina Park (set), Kristina Makowski (costumes), Alejandro Fajardo (lighting), Ben Truppin-Brown (sound); Mandarin Consultant, Li Jun Li; British Dialect Coach, Gillian Lane-Piescia; Master Carpenter/Deck Supervisor, Eric Brooks; Wardrobe Supervisor, Jessica Moy; Light Operator, Lisa Hufnagel; Sound Operator, Collin Priddy-Barnum; Deck Carpenter, Rebecca Key; Production Assistant, Amy Lynch; **Cast:** Matt Dellapina (Malcolm), Li Jun Li (Xiao Mei), Nelson Lee (David), Sonequa Martin-Green (Samanya)

Gertrude and Irving Dimson Theatre; First Preview: December 21, 2011; Opening Night: January 10, 2012; Closed February 4, 2012; 15 previews, 28 performances. Setting: Beijing, China; the present. World premiere of a new play presented without intermission. Synopsis: *Outside People* is a dark comic story of a young American man, Malcolm, who falls in love with a young Chinese woman, Xiao Mei. But as his eyes open to the subtle social, political, and economic forces that inform their relationship, he must confront his complex place in the foreign culture of Beijing, the friendship that brought him there, and his own deepest fears and desires.

Li Jun Li, Nelson Lee, Sonequa Martiin-Green, and Matt Dellapina in Outside People *(photos by Carol Rosegg)*

NOW. HERE. THIS. Book by Hunter Bell and Susan Blackwell; Music, lyrics, and co-vocal arrangements by Jeff Bowen; Based on a collaboration by Hunter Bell, Michael Berresse, Susan Blackwell, Heidi Blickenstaff, Jeff Bowen, and Larry Pressgrove; Director/Choreographer, Michael Berresse; Music Director/Co-Vocal Arrangements/Co-Orchestrations, Larry Pressgrove; Co-Orchestrations, Rob Preuss; Music Coordinator, Howard Joines; Sets, Neil Patel; Costumes, Gregory Gale; Lighting, Jeff Croiter and Grant Yeager; Sound, Acme Sound Partners; Projections, Richard DiBella; PSM, Martha Donaldson; ASM, Tom Reynolds; Assistant Production Manager, Meredith Pompeani; Assistant Director, Ashley Van Buren; Props Master, Lily Fairbanks; Associate Design: Caleb Levengood (set), Colleen Kesterson (costumes), Sooyean Hong (lighting), Alex Ritter (sound), Chris Kateff and Emma Wilk (projections); Master Carpenter/Deck Supervisor, Eric Brooks; Scenic Charge, Carolyn Bonanni; Sound Supervisor, Dave Arnold; Wardrobe Supervisor, Jessica Moy; Lights and Projection Operator, Lisa Hufnagel; Sound Engineer; Hugh Bascom; Deck Carpenter/Spot Operator, Rebecca Key; Production Assistant, Howie Tilkin; Carpenter, Tim Mele; Honorary Executive Producer, Iliana Guibert; Cast recording: Sh-K-Boom/Ghostlight Records 84466; **Cast:** Hunter Bell (Hunter), Susan Blackwell (Susan), Jeff Bowen (Jeff), Heidi Blickenstaff (Heidi), Roger Rees (Museum Voice Over); Musicians: Larry Pressgrove (Keyboard), Chris Biesterfeldt (Guitar), Joe Mowatt (Percussion/Drums), Steve Count (Guitar/Bass)

Musical Numbers: Prologue: What Are the Odds?; I Wonder; Dazzle Camouflage; Archer; I Rarely Schedule Nothing; Members Only; That'll Never Be Me; Kick Me; Then Comes You; The Amazing Adventures of the "Doc" Wibert S. Pound; That Makes Me Hot; Golden Palace; Get Into It; This Time; Finale

Gertrude and Irving Dimson Theatre; First Preview: March 7, 2012; Opening Night: March 28, 2012; Closed April 28, 2012; 21 previews, 34 performances. World premiere of a new musical presented without intermission. Developed at the Eugene O'Neill Theatre Center's Cabaret and Performance Conference in 2009. The musical was presented as Vineyard's Developmental Lab production June 4-19, 2011 (see *Theatre World* Vol. 67, page 236). Synopsis: *NOW. HERE. THIS.* marks the return of the ultra-talented team behind the Obie Award-winning musical *[title of show]* which premiered at The Vineyard in 2006, and went on to an acclaimed, Tony-nominated Broadway run in 2008. The six original collaborators are back and all delving into life's big questions with inimitable humor and humanity. The show explores birds, bees, reptiles, early man, ancient civilizations and outer space. Also, loneliness, friendship, hoarding, hiding, laughing, living and dying. And middle school. And dinosaurs.

DEVELOPMENTAL LAB

The Landing Book and lyrics by Greg Pierce; Music by John Kander; Director, Walter Bobbie; Music Director, David Loud; **Cast:** Julia Murney; David Hyde Pierce, Jake Bennett Siegfried, Paul Anthony StewaGertrude and Irving Dimson Theatre; May 15–June 3, 2012; 19 performances. Developmental production of a new musical presented without intermission. Synopsis: *The Landing* is a new beautiful and haunting triptych musical, comprised of three distinct and gripping stories that invite audiences into worlds where the characters confront what it means to get what they think they want.

Hunter Bell, Jeff Bowen, Susan Blackwell, and Heidi Blickenstaff in Now. Here. This.

Women's Project Theater

Thirty-fourth Season

Producing Artistic Director, Julie Crosby, PhD.; Associate Artistic Director, Megan E. Carter; Director of Marketing, Deane Brosnan; General Manager, Lisa Fane; Group Outreach, Kimberly Faith Hickman; Assistant Manager, Diana Bilbao; Directors Lab Liaison, Daniella Topol; Playwright-in-Residence, Andrea Kuchlewska; Production Manager, Aduro Productions (Carolyn Kelson & Jason Janicki); Casting, Alaine Alldaffer & Lisa Donadio; Financial Services, Patricia Taylor; Interns, Haley Bierman, Sasha Diamond, Emma Goidel, Rachel Marcus, Kate Prendergast; Creative Agency, The Pekoe Group; Website, Kurt Johns; IT Consultant, Daniel Pardes; Graphic Design, Christy Briggs, Heather Honnold; Press, Bruce Cohen

Milk Like Sugar by Kirsten Greenidge; Co-presented by Playwrights Horizons (Tim Sanford, Artistic Director; Leslie Marcus, Managing Director; Carol Fishman, General Manager) and La Jolla Playhouse (Christopher Ashley, Artistic Director; Michael Rosenberg, Managing Director); Director, Rebecca Taichman; Sets, Mimi Lien; Costumes, Toni-Leslie James; Lighting, Justin Townsned; Original Music and Sound, Andre Pluess; Casting, Alaine Alldaffer, Telsey + Company; Press, The Publicity Office; Production Manager, Christopher Boll; PSM, Kyle Gates; ASM, Allison Cottrell; **Cast:** Cherise Boothe (Talisha), Angela Lewis (Annie), Nikiya Mathis (Margie), LeRoy McClain (Antwoine), J. Mallory-McCree (Malik), Adrienne C. Moore (Keera), Tonya Pinkins (Myrna)

Peter Jay Sharp Theatre; First Preview: October 13, 2011; Opening Night: November 11, 2011; Closed November 27, 2011; 22 previews, 31 performances. New York premiere of a new play presented without intermission. For complete credits, please see listing under Playwrights Horizons in this section.

How the World Began by Catherine Trieschmann; Director, Daniella Topol; Presented in association with South Coast Repertory (Marc Masterson, Artistic Director; Paula Tomei, Managing Director); Set and Costumes, Clint Ramos; Lighting, Brian H. Scott; Sound, Darron L West; PSM, Jack Gianino; Stage Manager, Julie DeVore; Dramaturgy, Megan E. Carter; Assistant Director, Jessi D. Hill; Production Assistants, Diana Bilbao and Sophie Blumberg; Assistant Design: Craig Napoliello (set), Julia Broer (costumes), Bradley King (lighting), Eben Hoffer (sound); Wardrobe Supervisor, Anna Estelle Flaglor; Props Apprentice, Abbey L. Bay; Sound Board Operator, Joseph Wolfslau; Master Electrician, Adrian Kozlow; Master Carpenter, Danny Thomas; **Cast:** Justin Kruger (Micah Staab), Adam LeFevre (Gene Dinkel), Heidi Schreck (Susan Pierce)

Heidi Schreck and Justin Kruger in How the World Began
(photo by Carol Rosegg)

Peter Jay Sharp Theatre; First Preview: December 28, 2011; Opening Night: January 8, 2012; Closed January 29, 2012; 5 previews, 26 performances. Setting: Place: Plainview, Kansas. Time: The Present. New York premiere of a new play presented without intermission. World premiere at South Coast Repertory September 15–October 16, 2011. Synopsis: Susan, a high school biology teacher, leaves Manhattan for a teaching job at a makeshift high school in a rural Kansas town recently devastated by a tornado. But when she makes an off-handed remark regarding the origins of life, she unleashes community outrage and the particular distress of a disturbed young boy. *How the World Began* invites audiences to consider their own beliefs and their perhaps unspoken opinions of others.

We Play for the Gods Written, directed, and produced by the 2010-2012 Women's Project Lab (Playwrights: Charity Ballard, Alexandra Collier, Andrea Kuchlewska, Dominique Morisseau, Kristen Palmer, Melisa Tien, Stefanie Zadravec; Producers: Stephanie Ybarra (Lead), Elizabeth R. English, Manda Martin; Directors: Jessi D. Hill, Sarah Rasmussen, Mia Rovegno, Nicole A. Watson); Set, Jennifer Moeller; Costumes, Moria Sine Clinton; Lighting, Scott Bolman; Sound, Stowe Nelson; PSM, Zac Chandler; Production Manager, Elizabeth Moreua; Assistant Design: Akiko Kosaka (set), Christopher Metzger (costumes), Oliver Wason (lighting), Erik Skovgaard (sound); Wardrobe Supervisor (Jenna Glendye); Production Assistant, Kate Prendergast; Technical Director, Chris Haag; Assistant Production Manager, Catherine Barricklow; Electrician, The Lighting Syndicate; Filmography, Erik Pearson; **Cast:** Annie Golden (Marla), Amber Gray (Simi), Alexandra Henrikson (Provocatrix), Irene Sofia Lucio (Susan), Erika Rolfsrud (Lisa)

Cherry Lane Theatre; First Preview: June 1, 2012; Opening Night: June 11, 2012; Closed June 23, 2012; 8 previews, 14 performances. Setting: Right here; right now. World premiere of a new play presented without intermission. Synopsis: The copier coughs. The air conditioner stutters. Your Post-It supply is running low. Don't dismiss the notion that you may be reckoning with forces divine. In *We Play for the Gods*, four women go to work on a seemingly ordinary day only to find that a trickster god has slid through the cracks and cubicles of their office to take them on a journey to the other side of ordinary. Who knows? Today, the same could happen to you.

Alexandra Henrikson and Amber Gray in We Play for the Gods *(photo by Chasi Annexy)*

York Theatre Company

Forty-third Season

Artistic Director, James Morgan; Managing Director, Geoff Cohen; Director of Development, Andrew Levine; Marketing Manager, Phil Haas; Company Manager, Carolyn Kuether; Audience Services Manager, Cristin Whitley; Development and Communications, Kerry Watterson; Associate Artistic Director, Brian Blythe; Development Associate, Ana Sofia Hernandez; Administrative Assistant, Stefanie Wagner; Reading Series Coordinators, Stefanie Wagner, Seth Christenfeld; Graphics Associate, Ted Stephens III, The Numad Group; Business Partnership Coordinator, Robert Goldberg; Artistic Advisors, John Newton, Mary Jo Dondlinger, Michael Montel, Janet Watson; Educational Materials, William Prante; Founding Director F. Janet Hayes Walker; Press, O+M Company, Rick Miramontez, Philip Carrubba, Sam Corbett

Ionescopade *A Musical Vaudeville* Adapted from the plays and journals of Eugene Ionesco; Music and lyrics by Mildred Kayden; Originally conceived by Robert Allan Ackerman; Director/Choreography, Bill Castellino; Music Direction, Christopher McGovern; Sets, James Morgan; Costumes, Nicole Wee; Lighting, Mary Jo Dondlinger; Sound, Alex Neumann; Technical Director, Wyatt Kuether; Casting, Carol Hanzel; Marketing Consultant, HHC Marketing; PSM, Paul O'Toole; ASM, Stefanie Wagner; Props, Alix Martin; Wigs, J. Jared Janas; Rob Greene; Master Electrician, Chris Robinson; Master Carpenter, Michael Hetzer; Wardrobe Supervisor, Chadd McMillan; Light Board Operator, Kia Rogers; Spot Ops, Michael Hetzer, Martin Peacock; Assistant to the Director, Michael Kinnan; Choreography Assistant, Liz Piccoli; Costume Assistant, Dina Perez; Production Assistant, Carly Flint; Scenic Crew, Daniel Blondet, Chris Ford, Martin Peacock, Greg Westby, Lucas Womack; Lighting Crew, Lois Catanzaro, Jeff Gordon, Kia Rogers; Scenic Painters, Matthew Allamon, Nicole Carroll, Ricola Wille; **Cast:** Nancy Anderson, Paul Binotto, Samuel Cohen, David Edwards, Leo Ash Evens, Susan J. Jacks, Tina Stafford; Band: Christopher McGovern (Conductor/Piano), Jason Curry (Reeds), Greg Landes (Drums)

David Edwards and Samuel Cohen in Ionescopade

Program/Musical Numbers: Salutations; Surprising People; Voyage; Everyone Is Like Us; The Cooking Lesson; Mother Peep; Frenzy For Two (excerpt); Madelleine; The Leader; Knocks; The Killer; Bobby Watson and Family; Ginger Wildcat; In Time; The Saga of the Prima Ballerina; Josette; The Peace Conference; Fire; The Best Is Yet to Be; Flying; Wipe Out Games

Theatre at St. Peter's Church; First Preview: January 23, 2012; Opening Night: February 2, 2012; Closed: February 26, 2012; 9 previews, 27 performances. Revival of a vaudeville musical entertainment with plays and songs presented in two acts. Originally presented Off-Broadway at Theatre Four April 25–May 5, 1974 playing 13 performances (see *Theatre World* Vol. 30, page 88). Synopsis: The

York Theatre celebrates Off-Broadway this season with the first New York revival of *Ionescopade*. The York production takes a new look at the works of the prolific and influential absurdist playwright Eugene Ionesco, famous for his plays *The Bald Soprano*, *Rhinoceros*, *The Chairs* and *Exit the King*. Plays, playlets, and poetry by this master of the absurd transport audiences into a zany musical vaudeville where humor is the antidote to the world's realities.

David Edwards, Nancy Anderson, Tina Stafford, Leo Ash Evans, and Paul Binotto in Ionescopade *(photos by Carol Rosegg unless noted)*

Closer Than Ever Lyrics by Richard Maltby Jr., music by David Shire; Conceived by Richard Maltby Jr. and Steven Scott Smith; Co-produced by Edward Negley, Neil Berg, and Adam Friedson; Director, Richard Maltby Jr.; Co-Director, Steven Scott Smith; Associate Director/Choreography, Kurt Stamm; Music Director, Andrew Gerle; Vocal Arrangements, Patrick Scott Brady; Set, James Morgan; Costumes, Nicole Wee; Lighting, Kirk Bookman; Technical Director, Wyatt Kuether; Associate Choreographer, Emily Morgan; Casting, Mungioli Theatricals, Arnold J. Mungioli; Marketing Red Rising Marketing; PSM, Bernita Robinson; ASM, Niki Armato; Master Electrician, Chris Robinson; Props and Wardrobe Supervisor, Stefanie Wagner; Costume Assistant, Sara Hinkley; Light Board, Chris Robinson, Kia Rogers; Production Graphic, James Morgan; Electricians, Lois Catanzaro, Chris Ford, Jeff Gordon, Martin Peacock, Kia Rogers, Jay Scott, Lucas Womack; Scenic Carpenters, Daniel Blondet, Chris Ford, Martin Peacock, Jordan Reeves, Greg Westby, Lucas Womack; Scenic Painters, Nicole Carroll, Carolyn Kuether; Scenic Assistant, Matthew Allamon; Cast recording: Jay Records 1427; **Cast:** Jenn Colella[*1], George Dvorsky[*2], Christiane Noll[*3], Sal Viviano; Understudies: Rita Harvey, Jamie LaVerdiere; Musicians: Andrew Gerle (Conductor/Piano), Alan Stevens Hewitt or Danny Weller (Bass); *Succeeded by: 1. Julia Murney (8/6/12), Anika Larsen (8/28/12) 2. James Moye (9/25/12-10/7/12) 3. Jacquelyn Piro Donovan (8/6/12), Marya Grandy (10/13/12)

Musical Numbers: Doors; She Loves Me Not; You Wanna Be My Friend; What Am I Doin'?; The Bear, the Tiger, the Hamster and the Mole; I'll Get Up Tomorrow Morning; Miss Byrd; Dating Again; One of the Good Guys; There's Nothing Like It; Life Story; Next Time/I Wouldn't Go Back; Three Friends; Fandango; There; Patterns; There Is Something in a Wedding; Another Wedding Song; If I Sing; Back on Base; The March of Time; Fathers of Fathers; It's Never That Easy/I've Been Here Before; Closer Than Ever

Theatre at St. Peter's Church; First Preview: June 5, 2012; Opening Night: June 20, 2012; Closed November 4, 2012; 15 previews, 150 performances. Revival of a musical revue with new material presented in two acts. The original New York production was presented Off-Broadway at the Cherry Lane Theatre October 17, 1989–July 1, 1990, produced by Janet Brenner, Michael Gill, and Daryl Roth, playing 24 previews and 288 performances (see *Theatre World* Vol. 46, page 57).

Originally developed and first produced at the Williamstown Theatre Festival July 11-22, 1989. Synopsis: Maltby and Shire's treasure *Closer Than Ever* is back with an exciting new cast and fresh additions to the timeless score. When it premiered in 1989, the show spoke to a generation of theater-goers and featured one finest American theater scores of the decade. An intimate musical about love, friendship, security, happiness – and holding onto those essentials in a world that pulls us in a hundred directions at once – *Closer Than Ever* at the York is the homecoming of an Off-Broadway classic.

George Dvorsky, Jacquelyn Piro Donovan, Sal Viviano, and Julia Murney in Closer Than Ever

Sal Viviano, Jenn Collela, Christiane Noll, and George Dvorsky in Closer Than Ever

Musicals in Mufti– Musical Theatre Gems in Staged Concert Performances

TWENTY-SIXTH SERIES – OFF-BROADWAY SERIES

I'm Getting My Act Together and Taking It on the Road Music by Nancy Ford, book and lyrics by Gretchen Cryer; Director, West Hyler; Lighting, Lois Catanzaro; Casting, Geoff Josselson; Music Director, John DiPinto; PSM, Lori Amondson; ASM, Paul O'Toole; Movement Coordinator, Antoinette DiPietropolo; Technical Director, Wyatt Kuether; **Cast:** John DiPinto (Ken/Pianist), Louis Tucci (Lee/Bassist), Jeremy Yaddaw (Bobby/Drummer), Erik Hayden (Jake/Guitarist), Jillian Louis (Cheryl), Lisa Birnbaum (Alice), Daniel Robert Sullivan (Joe), Jenn Colella (Heather)

Musical Numbers: Feel the Love; Natural High; Smile; In a Simple Way I Love You; Miss America; Strong Woman Number; Dear Tom; Old Friend; In a Simple Way I Love You (reprise), Put in a Package and Sold; If Only Things Was Different; Feel the Love (reprise), Happy Birthday; Natural High (reprise)

Theatre at St. Peter's Church; June 19-26, 2011; 8 performances. Setting: A rehearsal studio. 1978. Staged concert version of a revival of a musical presented without intermission in repertory with *Still Getting My Act Together*. The original production opened at the Public Theater June 14, 1978, and later transferred to the downtown's Circle in the Square Theatre December 16, 1978, playing 1,165 performances (see *Theatre World* Vol. 35, page 129). Synopsis: The story follows fictional cabaret singer, Heather Jones, as she evolves her traditional act of romantic pop tunes to a bold new act full of emancipating, feminist pieces. As she performs the new show, song by song, Heather fights to achieve an artistic metamorphosis while her dominating manager, Joe, tries to keep her act in the past.

Still Getting My Act Together Music by Nancy Ford, book and lyrics by Gretchen Cryer; Director, West Hyler; Lighting, Lois Catanzaro; Casting, Geoff Josselson; Music Director, Christopher McGovern; PSM, Sarah Butke; ASM, Colleen M. Sherry; Arrangements, Jeffrey Klitz, Christopher McGovern, Nancy Ford; Technical Director, Wyatt Keuther; **Cast:** Christopher McGovern (Ethan/Pianist), Dennis Michael Keefe (Leo/Bassist), Greg Landes (Bobby/Drummer), Gretchen Cryer (Heather), Betty Aberlin (Cheryl), Scott Wakefield (Jake/Guitarist), Margot Rose (Alice), John Hillner (Joe), Lynne Halliday (Bonnie)

Musical Numbers: Hello, World; Here to Say I Love You; Joy; Timing is Everything; Starting Over; Natural High; The Road Not Taken; Window of Opportunity; Easy Love; Think Outside the Box; Friday Night You're Mine; Never There; Grey-Haired Daddy; Timing is Everything (reprise); Here to Say I Love You (reprise); Finale; Hang On to the Good Times

Theatre at St. Peter's Church; June 19-26, 2011; 8 performances. Setting: A rehearsal studio. Present day. World premiere of a staged concert version of a musical presented without intermission in repertory with *I'm Getting My Act Together and Taking It on the Road*. Synopsis: The never-before-seen-or-heard sequel, *Still Getting My Act Together*, takes place 30 years after the original. In this new show, Heather and her daughter take center stage and will uncover just what happened in the three decades since Heather got her act together and took it on the road. The production features three cast members from the original production: Gretchen Cryer, Betty Aberlin and Margot Rose.

Oh, Coward! Words and music by Noël Coward, devised by Roderick Cook; Director, Michael Montel; Music Director, Greg Pliska; Lighting, Chris Robinson; Casting, Geoff Josselson; PSM, Sarah Hall; ASM, Paul O'Toole; Movement Consultant, Keith Roberts; Technical Director, Wyatt Kuether; **Cast:** KT Sullivan (Woman), Jim Stanek (Man 1), Peter Land (Man 2)

Musical Numbers: Oh, Coward!; England; Family Album; Music Hall; If Love Were All; Travel; Mrs. Worthington; Mad Dogs and Englishmen; A Marvelous Party; Design for Dancing; You Were There; Theatre; Love; Women; World Weary; Let's Do It; Finale

Theatre at St. Peter's Church; July 15-17, 2011; 5 performances. Staged concert version of a revival of a musical revue presented in two acts. The original production played at The New Theatre (located where St. Peter's church currently stands) October 4, 1972–June 17, 1973 playing 294 performances (see *Theatre World* Vol. 29, page 98). A revival played Broadway years later at the Helen Hayes Theatre November 17, 1986–January 3, 1987 (see *Theatre World* Vol. 43, page 21). Synopsis: Interspersed with songs, biographical anecdotes, and sketches from his writings, *Oh, Coward!* celebrates the life and work of British legend Noël Coward.

The Mad Show Book by Larry Siegel and Stan Hart, lyrics by Marshall Barer, Larry Siegel, and Steven Vinaver, music by Mary Rodgers; Based on MAD Magazine; Director, Carl Andress; Music Director, Matt Castle; Lighting, Chris Robinson; Projections, Chris Kateff; Sound, Shannon Slaton; Casting, Geoff Josselson; PSM, Sarah Hall; ASM, Paul O'Toole; **Cast:** Stephanie D'Abruzzo, Chris Hoch, Christine Pedi, Tally Sessions, Steven Strafford; Musicians: Matt Castle (Piano), Jay Mack (Percussion)

Musical Numbers: Opening; Academy Awards; You Never Can Tell; Getting to Know You; Eccch!; Handle with Care; The Real Thing; Primers; Well It Ain't; Misery Is; Football in Depth; Hate Song; Kiddie TV; Looking for Someone; Strainer; The Gift of Maggie (and others); Interview; TV Nik; Transistors; The Boy From; The Irving Irving Story

Theatre at St. Peter's Church; July 29-31, 2011; 5 performances. Staged concert version of a revival of a musical revue presented in two acts. The original production played the New Theatre January 9, 1966–September 10, 1967 playing 871 performances (see *Theatre World* Vol. 22, page 145). Synopsis: *The Mad Show* is a comic revue filled with songs, sketches and the irreverent humor in the style of the ever-popular *Mad* magazine, spoofing everything from television commercials to the generation gap. The original production featured Linda Lavin and Jo Anne Worley.

The Housewives' Cantata Music by Mira J. Spektor, lyrics by June Siegel, additional lyrics by Mira J. Spektor, Charline Spektor, and Lynne Odgers; Director, Karen Carpenter; Music Director, Bob Goldstone; Lighting, Chris Robinson; Technical Director, Wyatt Kuether; Casting, Geoff Josselson; PSM, Lori Amondson; ASM, Lauren McArthur; **Cast:** Anne Tolpegin (Nora), Jennifer Hughes (Flora), Kerry Conte (Dora), Mark Campbell (Men)

Musical Numbers: Dirty Dish Rag; Sex; Guinevere; Little Women; Daughter's Lullaby; Someday Blues; Legs; M.C.P.; Bourgeoisie Beatnik; Mr. Fixer; Our Apartment; Open Road; Suburban Rose; Adultery Waltz; Divorce Lament; The Other One: Revenge; Have Song, Will Travel; Take Me Home Tonight; Hey, All You Doctors; Middle-Aged; What Is a Woman; Ladies of Romance; Sex (reprise); White House Resident; Give Me Time; New Song

Theatre at St. Peter's Church; October 21-23, 2011; 5 performances. Staged concert version of a revival of a musical revue presented without intermission. The original production played Theater Four (Julia Miles Theater) February 18–March 9, 1980 playing 24 performances (see *Theatre World* Vol. 36, page 106). An earlier version was presented in 1973 at St. Peter's Church. Synopsis: *The Housewives' Cantata* is an empowering cabaret-style revue that follows the stories of three women one of whom takes a tremendous journey to become the first female President of the United States.

Tomfoolery Words and music by Tom Lehrer, adapted by Cameron Mackintosh and Robin Ray; Music Arrangements, Chris Walker and Robert Fisher; Director, Pamela Hunt; Music Director, Michael Rice; Lighting, Chris Robinson; Projections, Chris Kateff; Technical Director, Wyatt Kuether; Casting, Geoff Josselson; PSM, Lori Amondson; ASM, Lauren McArthur; **Cast:** Stephanie D'Abruzzo, Josh Grisetti, Ben Liebert, Michael McCormick; Musicians: Michael Rice (Piano), Barbara Merian (Drums)

Musical Numbers: Be Prepared; Poisoning Pigeons in the Park; I Wanna Go Back to Dixie; My Home Town; Pollution; Bright College Days; Fight Fiercely, Harvard; The Elements; The Folk Song Army; In Old Mexico; She's My Girl; When You are Old and Gray; Wernher Von Braun; Who's Next?; National Brotherhood Week; So Long, Mom; The Hunting Song; The Irish Ballad; Smut; Silent E/New Math; Oedipus Rex; I Hold Your Hand in Mine; The Masochism Tango; The Old Dope Peddler; The Vatican Rag; We Will All Go Together When We Go

Theatre at St. Peter's Church; October 28-30, 2011; 5 performances. Staged concert version of a revival of a musical revue presented in two acts. The original production opened in Brighton, England May 13, 1980, and transferred to London's Criterion Theatre June 5, 1980 playing 400 performances. The New York engagement played the Village Gate Upstairs December 14, 1981–March 28, 1982 playing 27 previews and 120 performances (see *Theatre World* Vol. 38, page 58). Synopsis: *Tomfoolery* offers a witty and wicked look at the works of famed satirical songwriter (and Harvard math professor) Tom Lehrer. Pushing boundaries in a playful way, Lehrer's songs have delightfully skewered the world for over fifty years.

TWENTY-SEVENTH SERIES – TOM JONES SERIES

The Show Goes On Book and lyrics by Tom Jones, music by Harvey Schmidt; Director, Pamela Hunt; Music Director, Michael Rice; Lighting, Chris Robinson; Casting, Geoff Josselson; Technical Director, Wyatt Kuether; Assistant to the Director, Carly Flint; PSM, Paul O'Toole; ASM, Sarah Butke; **Cast:** Tom Jones, Stephanie Umoh, Susan Watson, Graham Rowat

Musical Numbers: Come on Along; Try to Remember; Mr. Off-Broadway; Everyone Looks Lonely; I Know Loneliness; The Story of My Life; The Holy Man & The New Yorker; Overhead; I Can Dance; Desseau Dance Hall; Flibberty-Gibbet; Melisande; Simple Little Things; I Do! I Do!; Honeymoon Is Over; My Cup Runneth Over; Celebration; Orphan in the Storm; Survive; Under the Tree; Decorate the Human Face; Where Did It Go?; Wonderful Way to Die; The Room Is Filled With You; Growing Older; Joy; The Show Goes On

Theatre at St. Peter's Church; March 16-18, 2012; 5 performances. Staged concert version of a revival of a musical revue presented in two acts. The York presented the original production December 10, 1997–March 1, 1998 playing 88 performances (see *Theatre World* Vol. 54, page 141). Synopsis: *The Show Goes On* is a portfolio of theatre songs from Tom Jones and longtime collaborator Harvey Schmidt, featuring music from timeless classics such as *The Fantasticks*, *110 in the Shade*, *I Do! I Do!*, *Celebration*, and many more. In a rare treat, Tom Jones himself guides the audience through the onstage revels.

Roadside Book and lyrics by Tom Jones, music by Harvey Schmidt; Based on the play by Lynn Riggs; Director, David Glenn Armstrong; Music Director, Christopher McGovern; Lighting, Chris Robinson; Casting, Geoff Josselson; Technical Director, Wyatt Kuether; Assistant to the Director, Nathan Cohen; PSM, Sarah Butke; ASM, Stefanie Wagner; **Cast:** Ryan Alexander (Black Ike, Mix Foster, Deputy #2), Erick Devine (Pap Raider), Janine DiVita (Hannie Raider), Jamie LaVerdiere (Amos K. 'Buzzey' Hale), Daniel C. Levine (Red Ike, Miz Pritchett, Deputy #1), Ed Watts (Texas), Nick Wyman (The Veridgree Marshal); Musicians: Christopher McGovern (Music Director/Piano), Chuck Pierce (Guitar/Mandolin/Percussion), Marc Schmied (Bass), Justin Smith (Violin/Mandolin/Percussion)

Musical Numbers: Roadside; Here I Am; I Don't Want to Bother Nobody; Smellamagoody Perfume; Lookin' at the Moon; I'm Through with You; Peaceful Little Town; I Toe the Line; I'm Through with You (reprise); Personality Plus; Another Drunken Cowboy; The Way It Should Be; My Little Prairie Flower; All Men Is Crazy; Ain't No Womern But You; Borned; Wild and Reckless; Peaceful Little Town (reprise); The Way It Should Be (reprise); Roadside

Theatre at St. Peter's Church; March 30–April 1, 2012; 5 performances. Setting: The Oklahoma territory, early 1900s. Staged concert version of a revival of a musical presented in two acts. The York presented the original production

Ed Watts and Janine DiVita in Roadside *(photo by Ben Strothman)*

November 29–December 23, 2001 playing 29 performances (see *Theatre World* Vol. 58, page 124). Synopsis: *Roadside* is a melodic, rip-roaring musical based on a play by Lynn Riggs, whose *Green Grow the Lilacs* became *Oklahoma! Roadside* is a Southwestern love story of mythic proportions about two kissin', punchin', cussin', larger-than-life characters who refuse to settle down and be "house-broke" by the arrival of fences and laws.

Harold and Maude Book and lyrics by Tom Jones, music by Joseph Thalken; Based on the screenplay by Colin Higgins; Presented in association with James Cass Rogers and Mildred and Edward Lewis; Director, Carl Andress; Music Director, John Bell; Lighting, Jay Scott; Projections, Chris Kateff; Orchestrations, Joseph Thalken; Casting, Geoff Josselson; Technical Director, Wyatt Kuether; Assistant to the Director, Greg Santos; PSM, Paul O'Toole; ASM, Niki Armato; **Cast:** Matt Dengler (Harold Chasen), Donna English (Mrs. Chasen), Steve Routman (Man), Donna Lynne Champlin (Woman), Cass Morgan (Maude); Musicians: John Bell (Music Director/Piano), Damien Bassman (Drums), Harry Hassell (Woodwinds), Vivian Israel (Cello), Greg Jarrett (Piano)

Musical Numbers: Dearest Mother; Self, Self, Self; Woe; Round & Round (The Cosmic Dance); If You Can't Feel It; Woe (reprise); On the Road; Two Sides of a River; The Real Thing; Montezuma; Song in My Pocket; Maude's Waltz; The Real Thing (reprise); The Chance to Sing; Song In My Pocket (reprise)

Theatre at St. Peter's Church; April 13-15, 2012; 5 performances. Setting: Suburban America in the early 1970s. New York premiere of a staged concert version of a musical presented without intermission. The original production was presented at Paper Mill Playhouse (featuring Ms. Champlin and Ms. English) January 5–February 6, 2005 (see *Theatre World* Vol. 61, page 280). Synopsis: The musical adaptation of the 1971 cult-classic film *Harold and Maude* comes to life in a new version by Jones and Thalken. In what some call the quintessential May-December romance, death-obsessed teenager, Harold, meets Maude, 79, at a funeral and thus begins one of the most unusual, yet truly touching romantic sagas in American pop-culture history.

Colette Collage Book and lyrics by Tom Jones, music by Harvey Schmidt; Director, Michael Montel; Music Director, Robert Felstein; Lighting, Chris Robinson; Movement Consultant, Tom Gold; Casting, Geoff Josselson; Technical Director, Wyatt Kuether; PSM, Stefanie Wagner; ASM, Niki Armato; **Cast:** Christine Andreas (Colette), Jo Ann Cunningham (Sido), Peter Land (Jacques), Patrick Lane (De Jouvenal, Government Official, Photographer, Collaborator), Anne Markt (Nita, Claudine, Colette de Jouvenal), Bill Nolte (Willy), Nicholas Rodriquez (Maurice), Vanessa Reseland (Claudine, Missy, Pompous Lady, Reporter), Carrington Vilmont (Priest, Reporter, German Officer), Sasha Weiss (Polaire, Pauline, Reporter), Scott Willis (Captain Colette, Boudow, Major Domo, Photographer)

Musical Numbers: Joy; Come to Life; Just a Simple Country Wedding; Do It for Wiily; Willy Will Grow Cold; The Claudines; Why Can't I Walk Through That Door?; Love Is Not a Sentiment Worthy of Respect; The Music Hall; I Miss You; La Vagabonde; Autumn Afternoon; Rivera Nights; Oo-La-La; Something for the Summer; Be My Lady; The Room is Filled with You; Growing Older; Joy

Theatre at St. Peter's Church; April 27-29, 2012; 5 performances. Setting: 1890s to 1950; various places in France. Staged concert version of a revival of a musical presented in two acts. The original production played the York March 31–April 17, 1983 playing 20 performances (see *Theatre World* Vol. 39, page 122). An earlier version of the show entitled *Colette* was presented at The Ellen Stewart Theatre May 6–August 2, 1970 playing 14 previews and 101 performances (see *Theatre World* Vol. 26, page 135). Synopsis: The joys, fears and loves of the celebrated French writer Colette are at the center of the insightful bio-musical *Colette Collage*. Sensual, witty, and entirely unconventional, this intimate, highly theatrical musical captures the essence of one of the most liberated women of all time.

The Game of Love Book and lyrics by Tom Jones, music by Jacques Offenbach, arrangements and additional music by Nancy Ford; Based on the *Anatol* plays by Arthur Schnitzler, translated by Lilly Lessing; Director, West Hyler; Music Director, Nancy Ford; Lighting, Chris Robinson; Choreography, Matthew Hardy; Casting, Geoff Josselson; Technical Director, Wyatt Kuether; Assistant to the Director, Michael Kinnan; PSM, Paul O'Toole; ASM, Stefanie Wagner; **Cast:** Steve Routman (Max), Santino Fontana (Anatol), Erin Davie (Cora), Rob Sapp (Fritz, Flieder), Jillian Louis (Annie), Glory Crampton (Gabrielle), Tom Aulino (Franz, Baron Diebel), Janet Dacal (Illona), Ramona Mallory (Annette); Musicians: Nancy Ford (Music Director/Piano), Erin Benim (Violin), Summer Boggess (Cello)

Musical Numbers: Overture; In Vienna; I Love to Be in Love; The Hypnotism Song; The Music of Bavaria; Finishing With an Affair; The Oyster Waltz; Come Buy a Trinket; I Know Just the Place; There's Room; In Vienna (reprise); Entr'acte; Over There; Love Conquers All; Listen to the Rain; Illona's Rampage; Seasons; It's For the Young; Menage-A-Trois; There's a Flower I Wear; The Game of Love

Theatre at St. Peter's Church; May 11-13, 2012; 5 performances. Setting: Vienna; late 19th century. New York premiere of a staged concert version of a musical presented in two acts. Synopsis: *The Game of Love* is deliciously romantic musical about the frivolities and foibles of Anatol, a playful Lothario, whose rendezvous with five unique women unfold over the course of this sensuous, melodic romp.

ADDITIONAL EVENTS

Now or Never Written and performed by Peter Land; Director, Gillian Lynne; Theatre at St. Peter's; February 12, 19, & 26, 2012

NEO 8 (New, Emerging, Outstanding) Annual Benefit Concert featuring new songs by emerging writers; Director, Daniel Goldstein; Music Directors, Matt Castle, David Gardos, Michael Borth; Writers: Andrew Gerle, Jenny Giering, Joe Kinosian & Kellen Blair, Marisa Micelson, Ryan Scott Oliver; Performers: Whitney Bashor, Ben Crawford, Matt Doyle, Jake Kitchin, Theresa McCarthy, Catherine Porter, Margo Seibert, Betsy Wolfe; Mentors: Adam Guettel, Tom Jones, Sheldon Harnick, Maury Yeston; Theatre at St. Peter's; May 21, 2012

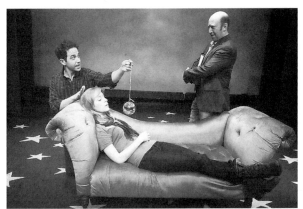

Santino Fontana, Erin Davie, and Steve Routman in The Game of Love *(photo by Ben Strothman)*

The Company of Roadside *(photo by Ben Strothman)*

Donna Lynne Champlin and Matt Dengler in Harold and Maude *(photo by Ben Strothman)*

The Company of Colette Collage *(photo by Ben Strothman)*

Gordon Clapp, Claire van der Boom, Theo Stockman, Dennis Staroselsky, and Jonny Orsini in the New Group production of An Early History of Fire (photo by Monique Carboni)

Eddie Cahill, Anna Chlumsky, Hannah Cabell, and Jake Silbermann in 3C at Rattlestick Playwrights Theater (photo by Joan Marcus)

Virginia Kull, Beth Dixon, and Amy Brenneman in Playwrights Horizons' Rapture, Blister, Burn (photo by Carol Rosegg)

Zach Grenier, Bob Dishy, Tonya Pinkins, Jordan Lage, Giancarlo Esposito, and Ron Cephas Jones in Storefront Church at the Atlantic Theater Company (photo by Kevin Thomas Garcia)

Angela Pierce and Heidi Armbruster in The Mint Theatre's Love Goes to Press (photo by Richard Termine)

Stephen Kunken and Marin Hinkle in the Primary Stages production of Rx (photo by James Leynse)

OFF-OFF-BROADWAY

June 1, 2011–May 31, 2012

Top: Cast in Nia Theatrical Production Company's production of Marry Me?!

Center: Cast in Lesser America's production of Too Much Too Soon
(photo by Hunter Canning)

Bottom: Cast in GoAlleyCat's production of It Is Done

The Off-Off-Broadway Season:
A Season of Inspiration

Shay Gines, Co-Executive Director,
New York Innovative Theatre Foundation

Off-Off-Broadway (OOB) draws inspiration from many sources. Anything from video games to politics could be fodder for OOB productions. This season the creations of New York City's independent theatre community reflected a continued experimentation with evolving technology, a desire to make a personal impression on audiences, an attraction to popular interests, and a strong sense of practicality that shaped artistic trends and decisions. This season there were some interesting trends and themes that were resourceful manifestations of these influences.

Modest resources, shoestring budgets, and—in recent years—limited performance venues are persistent practical challenges OOB producers face today. One of the most impressive and endearing characteristics of Off-Off-Broadway artists, however, is the ability to transform these challenges into unique creative opportunities. A lack of affordable performance venues, for example, has lead to both surprising collaborations and inventive venue choices.

Theatre festivals are on the rise, not only because they allow cash-strapped productions to share venues and pool resources, but they are also conducive to cultivating new audiences and creating community bonds. The New York International Fringe Festival is the largest, presenting over 200 companies from all over the world performing for sixteen days in more than twenty venues. However, many other festivals such as the FRIGID Festival or the Midtown International Theatre Festival also create opportunities that individual artists and companies may not otherwise be able to produce on their own. Even niche genres have found strength in numbers, with the Clown Theatre Festival and the Comic Book Festival (both at the Brick Theater); the New York Musical Theatre Festival; The Samuel French Festival (which focuses on new works); the soloNOVA Festival; and the EstroGenius Festival (which highlights works by women) all becoming mainstays within the community.

This season a theatre partnership called the BFG Collective found its own innovative solution to the space shortage. "BFG" stands for the three companies involved: Boomerang Theatre Company, Flux Theatre Ensemble, and Gideon Productions. These three organizations banded together to secure a six-month lease at a discounted rate at the Secret Theatre in Queens. The three companies presented seven productions during this time. In addition to a lower rent, they also benefitted from shared storage, collective marketing, and audience development—all conducted simultaneously by each company continuously throughout the season. It was a classic win-win situation: the three companies reduced their overhead and increased their audience numbers, while the Secret Theatre secured a solid six-month rental. In addition, the community was not only gifted with seven great productions, but also witnessed the successful proof of concept for a collaborative business model that could be a viable alternative for many OOB productions going forward.

Meanwhile, other artists dealt with the lack of space by presenting their work in non-traditional venues. While site-specific productions are nothing new to the Indie community, this season saw a remarkable number of notable works performed in unexpected spaces. Mariah MacCarthy's *The Foreplay Play* brought audiences to a Brooklyn apartment for this exhilarating and honest work about sex and relationships. The realistic setting added to the intimacy and excitement of the performance. Theatre in a Van is literally taking theatre to the people on the streets, presenting works in a parked van. Their production of *Luminescent Blues* offered an uncommon theatre-going event. Carrie Ahern presented her work *Borrowed Prey*, about the farm-to-table processing of animals, in the Dickson's Farmstand Butcher Shop in Chelsea Market. The Artful Conspirators presented *Brooklyn Underground: Theatrical Stories from the Green-Wood Cemetery* on the grounds of the Green-Wood Cemetery. And Sister Sylvester performed *Hugh Cox Gets the Pink Slip* at an art gallery in Brooklyn. Taking audiences out of the traditional theatre and into unexpected spaces gave them an alternative viewpoint of the work and a memorable, unique experience.

Many OOB innovators are searching for inspiration in the newest gadgets or multimedia tools, experimenting with how they can be manipulated and incorporated into the art. Projections have been around for years and can be a creative alternative to costly sets, but can also serve as visual allegory for the work, or create an iconic design element for the production. Some of the most successful and profound uses of video and mixed media this season included Black Moon Theatre Company's production of *Salome*, with provocative projections and video enhancing the performance about decadence and desire. Video design by Room 404 Media added a striking element for Built for Collapse's production of *Nuclear Love Affair*, which examined America in the Atomic Age. Sometimes disturbing and sometimes comical, the images brought dimension and perspective to historical events. And projections provided a visual representation of body dysmorphic disease to Liat Ron's production of *Guts*, which helped audience members have a deeper understanding of the character's journey through illness.

While technology can enhance the theatre-going experience and even bring heightened emotion or a broader perspective of the work, some of the most exciting productions this season used emerging technology to shift the theatrical paradigm altogether. In these productions theatre is no longer passive or even traditionally interactive, but requires audiences to be active decision makers and participants. These productions got audiences out of their seats, on their feet, and into the streets.

For the last few years, Gyda Arber has been pioneering technology-driven theatre. *Red Cloud Rising*, her most recent endeavor, was cowritten with Wendy Coyle. Part walking tour, part game, and part performance art, this work incorporated phone and text design to guide audience members through lower Manhattan, discovering landmarks, or uncovering clues within the Financial District as they followed a tale of Wall Street power. It delivered a compelling, enlightening, and personal experience for participants.

Endure: A Run Woman Show by Melanie Jones, used synchronized MP3 players to lead audiences through the internal monologue of woman as she prepared for her first marathon. Attendees followed the performer on jogging paths throughout a number of New York City parks. It was an inspirational story that engaged each audience member and literally had them walking in the character's footsteps.

Not only is technology being used to enhance the performances themselves, Indie theatre has also discovered some innovative ways to employ the power of the Internet to reach a broader audience and increase awareness of the sector.

Off-Off the Webseries launched in the spring of 2012 and turned the cameras on the often comical life of creating and surviving Off-Off-Broadway. It follows a fictional theatre company as it struggles to mount a production. Series creators Stephen Bittrich, Dave Marantz, Dan Teachout, and Rob A. Wilson are all well-known Indie Theatre artists and bring a knowing understanding of the work, madness, joy, heartache, and absurdity that is Off-Off-Broadway. The website is: offoffwebseries.com.

This last season the New York Theatre Experience launched Indie Theatre Now (www.indietheaternow.com), which is a searchable online library of new plays by Indie Theatre playwrights. It is sort of an "iTunes for Plays," according to founder Martin Denton. For $1.29 users can download scripts by your favorite independent playwrights to your computer, phone, or e-reader. This important new resource helps artists reach new audiences, share their work with thousands of new readers, and make a few bucks.

Crowdfunding sites like IndieGoGo and Kickstarter have been a boon for OOB theatre companies. Providing the infrastructure to collect small donations that add up to a significant amount on a fixed timeline, these services allow artists to accept funds, share stories, and track progress with friends, family, and strangers around the world. They are an ideal tool for the Indie community since the campaigns are designed to raise funds for a specific project (such as a production), and many productions this past season were funded in part due to successful crowdfunding campaigns.

When reviewing productions from the past season, some predominant themes became evident. Fantasy, science fiction, horror, comics, and super heroes have all been very popular subject matter for the OOB sector over the last few seasons. It is no coincidence that these same themes were also staples for early pulp novels. Pulp magazines were made inexpensively and lacked the sophisticated illustrations or slick binding of their more expensive counterparts. Pulp novels were also produced quickly to reflect current fashionable interests and they were often underappreciated as a legitimate art form. The same can be said of Off-Off-Broadway productions. It is not surprising that both would gravitate to similar source material.

Productions based around comic books and super heroes have become such a trend that they now have their own festival. The Comic Book Festival included playwright Crystal Skillman's *Action Philosophers*, which reimagines the world's greatest philosophers as superheroes, and Jon Hoche's play *Galactic Girl in: Attack of the Starbarians*, a tongue-in-cheek sci-fi adventure. Mark Harvey Levine's play *Superhero*, about overcoming personal fear, was a finalist in the Sam French Off-Off-Broadway Short Play Festival this year. And *Superman 2050* by Theater Un-Speak-Able was presented at the Time Square International Theatre Festival.

Likewise, productions that incorporate horror and gore continue to grow in popularity (and not just around Halloween). The Blood Brothers, which presents short vignettes of gruesome tales, have become a perennial favorite with a devout following. Productions also currently flourish based on the Grand Guignol style of theatre and work based on horror writer H.P. Lovecraft. The Impetuous Theater Group's production of *12th Night of the Living Dead* set Shakespeare's classic in the middle of a zombie apocalypse. *The Tragedy of Maria Macabre*, by Rachel Klein, was inspired by silent horror films; *Vampure*, by Mary Ann Hedderson & LJ Regine; *Brew of the Dead II: Oktoberflesh* by the Dysfunctional Theatre Company; and *NightoftheLivingDead the Musical*, by Musically Human Theatre Productions, were all on the boards this season.

Science fiction live on stage has become a prevailing fad this season. In the Mad One's production of *Samuel and Alasdair: A Personal History of the Robot War*, the audience watches what is perhaps the last transmission from a makeshift radio station as humanity faces its eminent demise by rampaging robots. *Anna & The Annandroids: Memoirs of a Robot Girl,* by Anna Sullivan, is billed as "futuristic performance art" and employs aerial dance and multimedia technology to introduce Anna the android, who is made of "pure synthetic organic flesh"

and struggles to resolve conflicting programming with human emotions. And yet again there is a festival specifically celebrating these genres: *End Times: Vignettes for the Apocalypse*, the 5th annual edition of New York's oldest and largest sci-fi/horror themed theatre festival offered thirty-four plays including: *The Lunar Academy of St. Augustine* by Andrew Turner, *Maybe In Another Universe* by Stacie A. Shellner, and *Smart* by Robert Fieldsteel.

In fact, the most heralded and talked about production of the year was Gideon Production's ambitious science fiction series, the *Honey Comb Trilogy*, by Mac Rogers. These dramas are set in a Florida track home that becomes the center of the resistance movement in a post-alien colonized world. All three productions appropriately take place on the same unassuming domestic living room set. The set itself represents the embodiment of the family unit and transforms throughout the series to reflect the evolution of the conquered world. While Earth is occupied by giant insect aliens that enslave the human race, the tale here is really about the relationship of a brother and sister and the strength of familial bonds.

Each of these genres involves larger-than-life situations and capitalizes on pop culture trends that appeal to an audience through recognizable archetypal characters or familiar premises. However, (and this may be where the lack of large budgets or expensive resources is ultimately an asset), most of these productions avoid the big-budget action, grand-scale spectacle of their counterparts, and instead focus on the personal experiences and interpersonal relationships of the characters caught up in a world in chaos. In the final blackout of *Samuel and Alasdair*... the audience listens to the actors' shallow and guarded breathing while just outside are sounds of what you imagine to be the violent and final destruction of the world. In the end it is this simple, highly human, and intimate perspective that leaves the most lasting and thought-provoking impression.

While Off-Off-Broadway continues to find inspiration from unexpected sources, Off-Off-Broadway itself is a source of inspiration. The ability of this community to meet challenges with creative optimism, to solve problems by working together, and with the courage to continually explore new tools and redefine the theatrical form has resulted in some truly groundbreaking productions this season. There is every indication that Off-Off-Broadway will continue to offer some of the most exciting performances and productions well into the future.

Sources for this section: New York Innovative Theatre Awards (www.nyitawards.com); New York Theatre Experience (www.nytheatre.com); OffOffOnline; TheatreMania (www.theatremania.com)

Krista Amigone, Angela Atwood Perri, Will W. Warren, Mike James, and Mikaal Bates in Cart Before Horse Productions' production of Trifles and Hughie *(photo by Colleen Katana)*

Cast in Funny...Shesh Productions' production of Doubles Crossed

3GRACES THEATER CO.

www.ThreeGracesTheater.org

As It Is In Heaven by Arlene Hutton; Directed by Ludovica Villar-Hauser; Stage Manager, Gary Adamsen; Lighting Designer, Joshua Scherr; Costume Designer, Shelly Norton & Veneda Truesdale; Cast: Margot Avery, Kathleen Bishop, Rachel Cantor, Carla Cantrelle, Kelli Lynn Harrison, Kate Kearney-Patch, Annie McGovern, Megan Tusing, and DeWanda Wise; Cherry Lane Theatre; May 20 – June 11, 2011

3-LEGGED DOG (3LD)

www.3leggeddog.org

Executive Director, Kevin Cunningham; Media Director, Aaron Harrow; Company Manager, Joellen Dolan; Technical Director, David Ogle; Media Designer, Jared Mezzocchi; Program Associate, James Scruggs

The Germ Project by Kara Lee Corthron, Lynn Rosen, Kathryn Walat and Anna Ziegler; Produced by New Georges; 3LD Art & Technology Center; May 23 – July 10, 2011

Photograph 51 by Anna Ziegler; Directed by Lindsay Firman; Produced by Ensemble Studio Theatre; 3LD Art & Technology Center; June 3 – 4, 2011

Battery Dance Choreographed and Directed by Jonathan Hollander; Production Designer, Barry Steele; Composer, Polarity/1; Performers: Robin Cantrell, Mira Cook, Bafana Matea, Carmen Nicole, Sean Scantlebury; Produced by the Battery Dance Company; 3LD Art & Technology Center; June 29, 2011

Botanica by Jeff Jackson and Jim Findlay; Directed by Jim Findlay; Stage Manager, Maurina Lioce; Lighting Designer, Jeff Sugg; Set Designer, Peter Ksander; Costume Designer, Normandy Sherwood; Sound Designer, Jamie McElhinney; AudioVisual Designer, Jeff Sugg; Producer, Joel Bassin; Plant Designer, Rob Besserer; Composer, Jim Dawson; Cast: Ilan Bachrach, Liz Sargent, and Chet Mazu; 3LD Art & Technology Center; September 18 – December 14, 2011 and January 28 - February 25, 2012

Madame Bovary Adapted from Gustave Flaubert; Adapted and Directed by Katherine M. Carter; Set Designer, Julia Noulin-Merat; Projection Designer, Colleen Toole, John Jalandoni; Lighting Designer, Ben Weill; Costume Designer, Caitlin Cisek; Casting, Chelsea Ignagni; Assistant Director, Ellie MacPherson; Photographer, Nick Ronan; Cast: Amy Young, James Parenti, Sam Dash, Brad Thomason, and Logan James Hall; Produced by The Other Mirror; 3LD Art & Technology Center; November 20 – December 12, 2011

WORKSHOPS

Making Up the Truth Written and Performed by Jack Hitt; Directed by Jessica Bauman; Producer Aaron Louis; Video Designer, Aaron Harrow; Set Designer, Neal Wilkinson; Lighting Designer, Laura Mroczkowski; Graphic Designer, Piama Habibullah; 3LD Art & Technology Center; April – June 2011

Paris Orgy by Kevin Cunningham and Charles Mee

Education of the Girlchild by Meredith Monk; Performers: Meredith Monk, Katie Geissinger, Ellen Fisher and Allison Sniffin; Produced by NY Live Arts; 3LD Art & Technology Center; June 5 – 11, 2011

Sontag: Reborn Based on the book by Susan Sontag and edited by David Rieff; Produced by The Builder's Association; 3LD Art & Technology Center; December 7 – 16, 2011

FESTIVALS

Ice Factory Festival 2011 (See Festival listing) Produced by SoHo Think Tank; 3LD Art & Technology Center; June 22 - July 29, 2011

13P

13p.org

A Map of Virtue by Erin Courtney; Directed by Ken Rus Schmoll; Lighting Designer, Tyler Micoleau; Set and Costume Designer, Marsha Ginsberg; Sound Designer, Daniel Kluger; Original Music, Jesse Lenat; Cast: Alex Draper, Birgit Huppuch, Jesse Lenat, Annie McNamara, Hubert Point-Du Jour, Jon Norman Schneider, Maria Striar; 4th Street Theater; February 6 - 25, 2012

59E59 Theaters

www.59e59.org

David Lee Nelson...Status Update by David Lee Nelson; Directed by Adam Knight; Produced in association with East of Edinburgh Festival; 59E59 Theaters; July 15 - 23, 2011

One Thousand Blinks by Nick Starr; Directed by Malinda Sorci; Stage Manager, Debra Stunich; Lighting and Set Designer, Al Roundtree; Costume Designer, Jessa-Raye Court; Sound Designer, Matt Sherwin; Properties Designer, Samantha Shechtman; Cast: Estelle Bajou, Mark Cajigao, Rachel Cornish and Drew Hirshfield; 59E59 Theater; January 12 - 29, 2012

The Active Theater

www.theactivetheater.com

The Violet Hour by Richard Greenberg; Directed by Nathaniel Shaw; Stage Manager, Kerri J. Lynch; Lighting Designer, Mike Inwood; Set Designer, Craig Napoliello; Costume Designer, Bobby Pearce; Sound Designer, Jacob Subotnick; Special Effect, David Ojala; Cast: Cheryl Freeman, Heather Lee Harper, John P. Keller, Andrew Sellon, Lincoln Thompson; The WorkShop Theater | Mainstage; March 9 – 25, 2012

Body Language by Jennie Contuzzi; Directed by Nathaniel Shaw; Stage Manager, Kerri J. Lynch; Lighting Designer, Victoria Miller; Set and Costume Designer, Craig Napoliello; Sound Designer, Jacob Subotnick; Cast: Tim Barker, Christian Campbell, Daniel Damiano, Jeb Kreager, Mary Jo Mecca, Lucy Owen; The WorkShop Theater | Mainstage; May 25 – June 10, 2012

Actors and Directors Living in Brooklyn

www.niany.com

Curse of the Starving Class by Sam Shepard; Directed by Jim Williams; Stage Manager, Maggie Scott; Costume Designer, Josie Williams; Cast: Randy Miles, Michael Venzor, Elizabeth Swearingen, Kam Metcalf, Kirk Miller, Stephen Gleason; The Bridge Theater; October 27 – November 13, 2011

Adam Roebuck Productions

Up To Date by Laura Shamas; Directed by Alice Camarota; Lighting Designer, Bobby Wolfe; Roy Arias Theatre Center at Time Square Art Center; June 21 – July 3, 2011

Nothing Serious by Rich Orloff; Roy Arias Theatre Center at Time Square Art Center; June 25 & 26, 2011

Reefer Madness by Sean Abley; Directed by Mickey McGuire; Lighting Designer, Bobby Wolfe; Roy Arias Theatre Center at Time Square Art Center; June 22 – July 1, 2011

Scared Skinny: A One (Hundred Pound Lighter) Woman Show Written and Performed by Mary Dimino; Directed by Christine Renee Miller; Roy Arias Theatre Center at Time Square Art Center; July 3, 2011

The Adaptations Project

www.AdaptationsProject.org

Kaddish (or The Key in the Window) Created & Performed by Donnie Mather; Directed by Kim Weild; Based on a Poem by Allen Ginsberg; Lighting and Set Designer, Brian H Scott; Costume Designer, Terese Wadden; Sound Designer, Darron L West; Projection Design, C. Andrew Bauer; Cast: Donnie Mather; New York Theatre Workshop's 4th Street Theatre; September 30 – October 9, 2011

AirPort Bar Productions

lovesicknyc.com

Love Sick by K. Poe; Directed by Sturgis Warner; Stage Manager, Marina Steinberg; Lighting Designer, Burke Brown; Set Designer, Raul Abrego; Costume Designer, Meaghane Healey; Sound Designer, Andre Fratto; Original Music, Andre Fratto; Cast: Cara Akselrad, Maggie Burke, Elizabeth Canavan, J. Eric Cook, Charles Goforth, Michael Puzzo, Justin Reinsilber; Theater for the New City; February 3 – 25, 201

All In Black And White Productions

www.allinblackandwhite.com

Flowers: A Thorny Romance Story by Carolyn M. Brown and D. E. Womack; Directed by D.E. Womack; Lighting Designer, Yuriy Nayer; Set Designer, Jennifer Varbalow; Cast: Vanessa Verduga, Shira Kobren, Sarah Joyce, Tiffany Rothman, Cory Tiesel, Nicole Rose, Jillian Joseph, Isaiah Baez; WorkShop Theater Mainstage; July 17 - 31, 2011

All Out Arts, Inc.

Garbo by Joe Gulla; Directed by Brian Rardin; Cast: Joe Gulla, Ari Myrtaj, Nora-Jane Wiliams; Barrow Group Theater; July 23 - 24, 2011

Alternating Incoherence Productions, LLC

www.blahblahtheatre.com

Cocktails on Mars by Maureen FitzGerald; Directed by Andrew Shulman; Stage Manager, Lighting and Sound Designer, Izze Gibson; Costume Designer, Maureen FitzGerald; Cast: Andrew Shulman, Maureen FitzGerald; Brooklyn Lyceum; March 13 – 15, 2012

Altruistic Theatre Company

www.altruistichtheatre.com

Civilization! by Maximilian Avery Clark; Directed by Brock H. Hill; Stage Manager, Keri Taylor; Sound Designer, Adam Schaper; Cast: Don James, Amber Bloom, Claire Gresham, Peter McElligott, Jordon Villines, Joseph Garner, Celeste Sexton, Evan Kincade, Jake Blagburn; Roy Arias Off Broadway Theatre; June 16 – 26, 2011

American Bard Theater Company

www.americanbard.org

Pericles, Prince of Tyre by William Shakespeare; Directed by Natalie Doyle Holmes and Jack Herholdt; Stage Manager, Olivia Gemelli; Lighting Designer, Mark Hankla; Set Designer, Mark Hankla; Costume Designer, Sarah Thea Swafford; Sound Designer, Jeanne Travis; Puppet & Projection Design, Emily Hartford and Justin West; Original Music, Will TN Hall; Choreographer, Kikau Alvaro; Cast: Bryan L. Cohen, Robert Dyckman, Elizabeth Galalis, Erin Gilbreth, Timothy C. Goodwin, Ross Hewitt, Jack Herholdt, Natalie Doyle Holmes, Lily Warpinski, Cheri Wicks and Tom Wolfson; American Globe Theater; March 9 – April 1, 2012

American Indian Arts, Inc. - AMERINDA

www.amerinda.org

Thieves by William S. YellowRobe, Jr.; Directed by Steve Elm; Stage Manager, Neal Kowalsky; Lighting and Set Designer, Nick Francone; Costume Designer, Holly Rihn and Meryl Pressman; Sound Designer, Daniel Kluger; Cast: Veracity Butcher, Dylan Carusona, Neimah Djourabchi, James Fall, Sheri Graubert, Andy Kirtland, Nancy McDoniel, Gloria Miguel, Elizabeth Rolston, Elizabeth Ruelas and Christopher Salazar; The Public Theater; August 3 – 14, 2011

American Thymele Theatre

Medea by Euripides; Directed by Nichole Hamilton; Cast: Danijela Popovic, Andrew Block, Luke Vedder, Eric Liu, Ruth Priscilla Kirstein, Vassilea Terzaki, Debby Skaler, Hollis Beck, Kimberly DiPersia, Emily Eden, Alexandra Milne, Zenon Zeleniuch, Leo Goodman, Bryce Andrew Walsh and Marcus Watson; Chernuchin - American Theater of Actors; July 12 – 17, 2011

aMios Theatre

amiosnyc.org

In the Meantime by David L. Williams; Directed by Rachel Dart; Cast: Lauren Berst, Eddie Boroevich and Jillian LaVinka; Under St Marks; May 3 – 19, 2012

AnimalParts theatre co.

www.tenderpits.com

Tenderpits Written and Performed by Anthony Johnston; Directed by Nathan Schwartz; Sound Designer, Nathan Schwartz; Under St Marks; September 22 – October 16, 2011

AntiMatter Collective

antimattercollective.org

Death Valley by Adam Scott Mazer; Directed by Dan Rogers; Stage Manager, Alex Lubensky; Lighting Designer, Alana Jacoby; Costume Designer, Bevan Dunbar and Karen Boyer; Sound Designer, Will Fulton; Properties Designer, Allison LaPlatney; Assistant Stage Manager, Emily Asaro; Special Effects Designer, Stephanie Cox-Williams; Fight Choreographer, Adam Scott Mazer; Scenic Painting, Geddes Levenson; Graphic Designer, Emily Friend Roberts; Publicity, Emi; Cast: Patrick Harrison, Will Cespedes, Alexandra Arnoldi Panzer, Jessie Hopkins, James Rutherford, Casey Robinson, Kyle Page, Joshua C. Payne, Bryce Henry, Alexandra Hellquist, Caroline Bloom, Caitlin Johnston; Bushwick Starr; June 23 - July 10, 2011

The Dreams in the Witch House Written and Directed by Will Fulton; Set Designer, Danielle Baskin; Sound Designer, Colin Fulton; Adapted from story by H.P. Lovecraft; Puppet Designer, Roxanne Palmer; Cast: James Rutherford, Allison LaPlatney, Dan Rogers; The Brick Theater; October 21 & 22, 2011

sixsixsix by Gregory S. Moss; Directed by Dan Rogers; Production Designer, Pete Fallon; Sound and Graphic Designer, Will Fulton; Cast: Scott Mazer & Eileen Meny; Hotel AXA in Prague; December 2 & 3, 2011

Apple a Day Repertory Company

Second Samuel by Pamela Parker; Stage Manager, Megan Curet; Lighting and Sound Designer, Greg Indelicato; Set and Costume Designer, Dennis DelBene; Original Music, Greg Indelicato; Cast: Orlando Iriarte, Dennis Delbene; Urban Stages; October 20-November 13, 2011

Apple Core Theater Company

www.applecoretheatercompany.org

By The Dawn's Early Light by Mel Nieves; Directed by Walter J. Hoffman; Stage Manager, Farin Rebecca Loeb; Set Designer, Adam Kaynan; Costume Designer, David L. Zwiers; Sound Designer, Joemca; Producing Artistic Director, Allison Taylor; Associate Producer, Barbara Harrison; Cast: Camilo Almonacid, Arturo Castro, Alicia Fitzgerald, Wynn Hall, Mike Havok, Gustavo Heredia, Jorge Humberto Hoyos, Flor De Liz Perez, Kevin Prowse, Gordon Silva, Karen Sours and Damian Thompson; Theatre Row - The Studio Theatre; August 12 - 28, 2011

A Modest Suggestion by Ken Kaissar; Directed by Walter J. Hoffman; Cast: Jeff Auer, Bob Greenberg, Ethan Hova, Russell Jordan, Jonathan Marballi and Robert W. Smith; Studio Theatre; May 10 - 27, 2012

ARLA Productions LLC & Rosalind Productions Inc.

www.rosalindproductions.com

A Splintered Soul by Alan Lester Brooks; Directed by Daisy Walker; Stage Manager, Hannah Woodward; Lighting Designer, Patricia M. Nichols; Set Designer, Kevin Judge; Costume Designer, Valerie Marcus Ramshur; Sound Designer and Original Music, Nathan Leigh; Cast: John Michalski, Anya Migdal, Kenny Morris, Sid Solomon, David Lavine, Michael Samuel Kaplan, Lisa Bostnar, Ella Dershowitz; Theater Three; October 21 – November 13, 2011

ArtEffects Theatre Company

www.arteffectstheatre.org

The Birthday Boys by Aaron Kozak; Directed by Montserrat Mendez; Stage Manager, Mary Spadoni; Set Designer, Jason Bolen; Cast: Zach McCoy, Lowell Byers, Walker Hare, Abraham Makany, Roland Lane, Jevon McFerrin, Patrick Cann; Access Theater Black Box; September 15 – 25, 2011

The Artful Conspirators

www.artfulconspirators.org

Brooklyn Underground: Theatrical Stories from the Green-Wood Cemetery by The Artful Conspirators; Directed by David A. Miller; Stage Manager, Barbara Dente; Lighting Designer, Sam Gordon; Cast: Dorothy Abrahams, John Gardner, Robert James Grimm III, Lauren Sowa, Miranda Shields, and Andrew Zimmerman; Green-Wood Cemetery; September 23 – October 2, 2011

Artists on the Brink

www.someonestryingtokillme.com

someone's trying to kill me Written and Directed by Bryan Santiago; Lighting Designer, Brandon Baruch; Set Designer, Starlet Jacobs; Cast: Osa Wallander, Rachelle Guiragossian, and Ryan Colwell; HERE Arts Center; November 19 – December 4, 2011

Astoria Performing Arts Center

www.apacny.org

A Hard Wall at High Speed by Ashlin Halfnight; Directed by May Adrales; Stage Manager, Lizzy Lee; Lighting Designer, Cat Tate Starmer; Set Designer, Stephen K. Dobay; Costume Designer, Becky Bodurtha; Sound Designer, Nathan A. Roberts; Original Music, Roberts; Properties Designer, Ashley Cavadas; Casting, wojcik|seay casting; Press Representative, Katie Rosin/Kampfire PR; Assistant Director, Liza Renzulli; Associate Set Designer, Michael Minahan; Associate Lighting Designer, Annie Wiegand; Assistant Costume Designer, Nina Bova; Fight Director, Lisa Kopitsky; Technical Director, Drew McCollum; Associate Production Manager, Jenny Herdman Lando; 1st Assistant Stage Manager, Jenna R. Lazar; 2nd Assistant Stage Manager, Alex Fletcher; Graphic Designer, Paul Thureen; Cast: Sarah Kate Jackson, Tom O'Keefe, Johnny Pruitt, Ryan Templeton; Good Shepherd United Methodist Church; November 3 - 19, 2011

The Secret Garden Book & Lyrics by Marsha Norman, Music by Lucy Simon, Based on the novel by Frances Hodgson Burnett; Directed by Tom Wojtunik; Musical Director, Jeffrey Campos; Stage Manager, Jessa Nicole Pollack; Lighting Designer, Dan Jobbins; Set Designer, Michael P. Kramer; Costume Designer, Ryan J. Moller; Sound Designer, Colin Whitely; Musical Staging, Christine O'Grady; Properties Designer, Ashley Cavadas; Dialect/Accent Coach, Kenneth Garner; Dramaturg, Jennifer Lane; Casting, wojcik|seay casting; Press Representative, Katie Rosin/Kampfire PR; 1st Assistant Stage Manager, Kristine Schlachter; 2nd Assistant Stage Manager, Alex Gurevich; Graphic Designer, Paul Thureen; Cast: Jane Bunting, Mario Castro, Marisa Devetta, Jennifer Evans, Britain Gebhardt, Jonathan Gregg, Clint J. Hromsco, Jaimie Kelton, Hannah Lewis, Michael Jennings Mahoney, Benjamin J. McHugh, Mary-Elizabeth Milton, Eric Morris, Jan-Peter Pedross, Lia Peros, Jason Pintar, Sam Poon, Patrick Porter, Spencer Robinson, Jacqueline Sydney, Richard Vernon, Elizabeth Wharton; Good Shepherd United Methodist Church; May 3 - 26, 2012

Athena Theatre

www.athenatheatre.com

President and Artistic Director, Veronique Ory; Vice-President, Technical Director, Kevin Jordan; Associate Artistic Producer, Brionne Davis; Literary Manager, Patrick Varon; Communications Coordinator, Steve Wertheimer; Historian, Peter DiCicco

Beirut by Alan Bowne; Directed by The Zoppa Brothers; Stage Manager, Cassie Dorland; Lighting Designer, Ross Graham; Set Designer, Joseph C. Heitman; Costume Designer, Hadas Tzur; Sound Designer, Colin J. Whitely; Technical Director, Chimmy Anne Gunn; Assistant Stage Managers, Ruth Gersh and James W. Guido; Scenic Artist and Properties Designer, Jon Knust; Fight Choreographer, Robert Tuftee; Producer, Athena Theatre Company, Exhibit Z & Stephen P. Palmese; Publicity Photographer, Bob Johnson; Graphic Designer, Jonna Mayer; Set Builders, Rhea Bundrant, Nicolo DePierro; Cast: Meital Dohan, Sammi Rotibi, Tony Ray Rossi, Paul Bomba, Veronique Ory, Russell Jordan; Theatre Row; January 5-22, 2011

Attic Theater Company

www.theattictheaterco.com

The Time of Your Life by William Saroyan; Directed by Laura Braza; Stage Manager, Katie Kavett; Lighting Designer, Ben Pilat; Set Designer, Julia Noulin-Merat; Costume Designer, Emily Rosenberg; Sound Designer, Colleen Toole; Properties Designer, Kelly Kuykendall; Choreographer, Cody Smith; Cast: Teddy Alvaro, Haley Bond, Rockey Bostick, Seth Andrew Bridges, Ted Caine, Mary Christopher, Anthony Comis, Alexandra Dickson, Kyle Eberlein, Benjamin Fisher,

Ryan Garbayo, Rachel Garis, Chris Gebauer, Monica Hammond, Joshua Everett Johnson, Kevin Jones, Brad Makarowski, Kate Manfre, Henry Packer, Matt Palmer, Geoffrey Parrish, Lauren Shannon; Connelly Theater; February 10 – 25, 2012

The Tutors by Erica Lipez; Directed by Laura Braza; Lighting Designer, Dave Upton; Set Designer, Julia Noulin-Merat; Costume Designer, Travis Chinick; Sound Designer, Colleen Toole; Cast: Dana Berger, Ted Caine, Tommy Heleringer, Ruy Iskandar and Michael Shantz; The Access Theater; May 18-26, 2012

Autonomous Collective

www.autonomous-collective.org

Mic. by Brenton Lengel; Directed by Melinda Prom; Musical Director, Zach Villa; Stage Manager, Lee Goffin-Bonenfant; Lighting Designer, Jake Fine; Set Designer, Brenton Lengel, Melinda Prom; Costume Designer, Melanie Clark; Sound Designer, Kris Alfred; Original Music, Joe Yoga, Kelly B. Dwyer, Brian Douglas, Mike Ogletree, Ed Bernstein; Cast: Jacob A Ware, Daniel Graff, Amanda Sayle, Ed Bernstein, Ben Prayz, Brian Douglas, James Reese, Anthony Mead, Lauren Ferebee, Pedro Rezende, Sonseray Talbot; Choreographer, Melinda Prom; Manhattantheatresource; August 31 – September 17, 2011

Axis Company

www.axiscompany.org

Hospital 2011 Directed by Randy Sharp; Stage Manager, Edward Terhune; Lighting Designer, David Zeffren; Costume Designer, Elisa Santiago; Sound Designer, Steve Fontaine; Assistant Lighting Designer, Amy Harper; Set Construction, Chad Yarborough; Properties Designer and Film Art Director, Lynn Mancinelli; Dramaturge, Christopher Swift; Cinematographer, Adrian Correia, Sean Martin, Ben Wolf; Film Editor, Nicole Turney; Film; Cast: Paul Marc Barnes, Brian Barnhart, Regina Betancourt, David Crabb, George Demas, Britt Genelin, Laurie Kilmartin, Lynn Mancinelli, Matt McGorry, Jason Nahum, Edgar Oliver, Brian Sloan, Jim Sterling; Axis Theatre; July 8 - August 30, 2011

Bad Kid by David Crabb and Josh Matthews; Directed by Josh Matthews; Lighting Designer, David Zeffren & Amy Harper; Sound Designer, Steve Fontaine; Cast: David Crabb; Axis Theatre; October 28 - November 12, 2011

Seven in One Blow Written and Directed by Randy Sharp; Lighting Designer, David Zeffren; Costume Designer, Elisa Santiago; Sound Designer, Steve Fontaine; Original Music, Randy Sharp; Assistant Lighting Designer, Jamie Crocket; Set Construction,Brian Sloan, Lynn Mancinelli; Properties Designer, Lynn Mancinelli; Production Design, Kate Aronsson-Brown; Sound Technician, David Balutanski; Website & Graphic Des; Cast: Marc Palmieri, David Crabb, Lynn Mancinelli, Jim Sterling, Brian Barnhart, George Demas, Britt Genelin, Spencer Aste, Edgar Oliver, Laurie Kilmartin, Regina Betancourt, Marlene Berner; Axis Theatre; December 2 - 18, 2011

Backyart Productions

antenoraplay.wordpress.com

Antenora by Mike Poblete; Directed by Jessica Creane; Cast: Max Woertendyke and Ben Williams; 440 Studios; June 2 - 20, 2011

Ballybeg

www.ballybeg.org

Empanada For A Dream Written and Performed by Juan Francisco Villa; Directed by Alex Levy; The New Ohio Theatre; April 21 – June 6, 2012

Bandwagon Productions

www.baltimoreinblackandwhite.com

Baltimore in Black and White by Jason Odell Williams; Directed by Charlotte Cohn; Lighting Designer, Lauren Parrish; Set Designer, David L. Arsenault; Costume Designer, Carolyn Hoffmann-Schneider; Sound Designer, Asa Wember; Cast: Christopher Burris, Judy Jerome, Paul Perroni, Chris Burke, Anthony Vaughn Merchant, Charleigh E. Parker, Catia Ojeda, Sdrina Renee; Choreographer, Tocarra Cash; the cell; May 11 – 21, 2011

Barefoot Theatre Company

www.barefoottheatrecompany.org

Producing Artistic Director, Francisco Solorzano; Managing Director, Victoria Malvagno; Program Director, Molly Marinik; Company Manager, Sol Crespo; Producing Director, Christopher Whalen

Revised Version of Raft Of The Medusa by Joe Pintauro by Joe Pintauro; Directed by Francisco Solorzano; Stage Manager, Morgan Eisen; Lighting Designer, Niluka Hotaling; Sound Designer, Michael Mallard; Costume Designer, Victoria Malvagno; Sound Designer, John Beverly; Audio/Visual Designer, Francisco Solorzano; Cast: Jeremy Brena, Gillian Rougier, Andrew MacLarty, Charles Everett, Samantha Fontana, John Gazzale, Gil Ron, Mark G. Cisneros, Maia Sage, Christopher Whalen, Michael Pierre Louis; Presented as part of the STRIPPED FESTIVAL in co-production with East 3rd Productions; Cherry Lane Theatre; October 5 - 22, 2011

Verse Chorus Verse by Verse Chorus Verse; Directed by Ricardo Riethmuller; Stage Manager, Charles Casano; Lighting Designer, Eric Nigthengale; Set Designer, Michael Mallard; Costume Designer, Jennie West; Sound Designer, Sidiq Alexander; Audio/Visual Designer, Zoe Sarnak; Cast: Lorraine Rodriguez, Michael Mallard, Kristy Powers, Michael Byran Hill, Forbes March, Joshua Coomer, Singh Birdsong; Presented as part of the STRIPPED FESTIVAL in co-production with East 3rd Productions; Cherry Lane Theatre; October 26 - November 12, 2011

Gloucester Blue Written and Directed by Israel Horovitz; Stage Manager, Samantha Fontana; Lighting and Set Designer, Niluka Hotaling; Costume Designer, Victoria Malvagno; Sound Designer, Francisco Solorzano; Cast: Christopher Whalen, Francisco Solorzano, Therese Plahen, Robert Walsh; Presented as part of the STRIPPED FESTIVAL in co-production with East 3rd Productions; Cherry Lane Theatre; November 16 - December 3, 2011

READINGS

FKing Vigwan (or swag)** by Kristoffer Diaz; Directed by Francisco Solorzano; Cherry Lane Theatre; November 29 - December 3, 2011

bareNaked LA Reading Series by Kristoffer Diaz, Jose Rivera, Mike Reiss, Tyler Fascett, Jason Furlani, Trish Harnetiaux; Directed by Francisco Solorzano, Joyce DeWitt, Nicole Haran, Scott Illingworth; Art Of Acting Studio, Los Angeles, CA; February 20-26, 2012

Beautiful Soup Theater Collective

www.beautifulsouptheatercollective.org

Artistic Director, Steven Carl McCasland; Executive Director, Orlando Iriarte; Technical Director, Chasmin Hallyburton; Talent Director, Samantha Mercado Tudda

Alice Written and Directed by Steven Carl McCasland; Costume and Sound Designer, Steven Carl McCasland; Cast: Emily Floyd, Mallory Berlin, Anne Richmond, Steven Carl McCasland, Courtney de la Rigaudiere, Tracy Jennissen, Rory Allan Meditz, Stephanie Streisand, Allison Wimer, Patrick Whitehead; SoHo Playhouse Theatre; July 30 – October 15, 2011

Ryan Mikita, Lora Nicholas, Madison Turner, AJ Patton, Bryce Payne in Vital Theatre Company's production of StinkyKids the Musical *(photo by Steven Rosen)*

Frank Zilinyi, Eric Whitten in RadioTheatre's production of Reanimator *(photo by Dan Bianchi)*

The Company in Astoria Performing Arts Center's production of The Secret Garden *(photo by Lori McFadden)*

Sarah Wharton & Audience in Organs of State's production of In Memoriam *(photo by Benjamin Lundberg)*

The Company in Fault Line Theatre's production of Frogs

Jillaine Gill in Junta Juleil Productions' production of
Dreams of the Clockmaker *(photo by Joe Stipek)*

*Abigail Hawk and the Company in The Rachel Klein Theater Ensemble's
production of* The Tragedy of Maria Macabre *(photo by Michael Blase)*

*John Ellison Conlee, Kelly Mares, Gibson Frazier and Bobby Moreno in Clubbed
Thumb's production of* Luther *(photo by Heather Phelps-Lipton)*

Macbeth by William Shakespeare; Directed by Steven Carl McCasland; Sound Designer, Steven Carl McCasland; Fight Choreographer, Ellyn Stein; Cast: Lena August, Mallory Berlin and Courtney de la Rigaudiere; 13th Street Repertory Theatre Company; October 19 – 31, 2011

A Doll's House by Henrik Ibsen; Directed by Cristina Carrion; Stage Manager, Tracey Fess; Lighting Designer, Steven Carl McCasland; Cast: Patrick Pizzolorusso, Kymberly Tuttle, Daniel Mian, Frank Van Putten, Shannon Munley; The New Ohio Theatre; January 25 – February 5, 2012

A Doll's Life Music by Larry Grossman; Book & Lyrics by Betty Comden and Adolph Green; Directed and Choreographed by Steven Carl McCasland; Stage Manager, Paul Alexander Hughes; Lighting Designer, Steven Carl McCasland; Cast: Mario Castro, Joseph da Fonseca, Margaret Dietrich, Jordan Shaner, Lisa Crosby Wipperling and Tal Yardeni; The New Ohio Theatre; January 26 – February 5, 2012

neat & tidy Written and Directed by Steven Carl McCasland; Lighting and Sound Designer, Steven Carl McCasland; Cast: Kristi Barron, Emily Floyd, Orlando Iriarte, Anna Kirkland, Rory Allan Meditz, Samantha Steinmetz and Jordan Tierney; Gene Frankel Theatre; May 15 – 27, 2012

READINGS & WORKSHOPS

Goodtime Charley Music by Larry Grossman; Lyrics by Hal Hackady; Book by Sidney Michaels; Directed by Steven Carl McCasland; Joria Theatre; March 25, 2012

Bello Productions

Lift by Leonel Giacometto & Patricia Suarez; Directed by Irma Bello; Cast: Antonio Minino, Irma Bello; Roy Aria Off Broadway Theatre; October 7 – 15, 2011

Beyond Theatre Ensemble

The Two Gentlemen of Verona by William Shakespeare; Directed by Jay Painter and Jeffrey Golde; Cast: Jay Painter, Jeffrey Golde, Diana Johannesson, Courtnay Griswold, Joe Tex, Eric Robinson; produced in association with Face Off Unlimite & The Secret Theatre The Secret Theatre; August 5 – 13, 2011

Big Rodent

www.bigrodent.info

Rosencrantz and Guildenstern Are Dead by Tom Stoppard; Directed by Cora Weissbourd; Stage Manager, Cait Keane; Lighting Designer, Andrew Lu; Costume Designer, Jessa-Raye Court; Sound Designer, Chrissy Farrell; Cast: Jordan Gray, Adam Aguirre, Jeremy Weber, Nick Monroy, Ian Heitzman, Leigh Poulos, Kym Smith, Katie-Rose Spence; Abingdon Theatre Complex; June 3 – 12, 2011

Big Sky Theatre Company

www.marysheridan.net

Producer, Mary Sheridan; Director, Megan Cooper; Stage Manager, Maxwell Waters; Designer, Carissa Cordes

The Dreamer Examines His Pillow by John Patrick Shanley; Directed by Megan Cooper; Stage Manager, Maxwell Waters; Lighting, Set and Sound Designer, Carissa Cordes; Costume Designer, Megan Cooper; Cast: Mary Sheridan, Donna, Jacob Saxton, Tommy, Todd Conner; Under Saint Marks Theatre; March 8-10 & July 15-20, 2012

Bizarre Noir Theatre Company

Miss Robusta Goes to the Movies Conceived and Directed by P. William Pinto; AudioVisual Designer, Marcus Cooper; Choreographer, Fernando Contreras and Jovier Sanchez; Cast: Robusta Capp, Ambar Aranaga, Alexis Braxton, Fernando Contreras, Vincent DiGeronimo, Monica Hernandez, Casey McAuliffe, Nancy Reinstein, Camellia Tatara, Zachary Theis, Ian Wehrle; Players Theatre; July 14 – 16, 2011

Black Moon Theatre Company

www.blackmoontheatrecompany.org

Salome by Oscar Wilde; Directed by Rene Migliaccio; Lighting Designer, Jason Sturm; Set Designer, India Evans; Costume Designer, Hope Governali; Sound Designer, Rene Migliaccio; Video Design & Mixed Media Design, India Evans and Rene Migliaccio; Original Music, Amaury Groc; Choreographer, Natasa Trifan; Cast: Alessio Bordoni, Karina Fernicola-Ikezoe, John Graham, Tatyana Kot, Olgierd Minkiewicz, Marc Thomas Engberg, Chris Ryan; Flea Theatre; July 9 – 23, 2011

Blessed Unrest

www.blessedunrest.org

The Storm by Laura Wickens; Directed by Jessica Burr; Stage Manager, Jaimie Van Dyke; Lighting and Set Designer, Benjamin C. Gevelow; Set Costume Designer, Summer Lee Jack; Sound Designer, Dave Edson, Damen Scranton, and Jaimie Van Dyke; Cast: Sora Baek, Zenzelé Cooper, Andrew Dahl, Dave Edson, Tim Eliot, Jason Griffin, Terria Joseph, Darrell Stokes, and Laura Wickens; Interart Annex; April 13 – May 7, 2012

Boomerang Theatre Company

www.boomerangtheatre.org

Much Ado About Nothing by William Shakespeare; Directed by Daniel Talbott; Stage Manager, Jessica Pecharsky Morales; Costume Designer, Carolyn Pallister; Cast: Nate Miller, Brad Lewandowski, Sara Thigpen, Laura Ramadei, Sid Solomon, Colby Chambers, John Egan; Choreographer, Becky Byers; Central Park Lawn; June 18 – July 17, 2011

The Real Thing by Tom Stoppard; Directed by Cailin Heffernan; Stage Manager, Michelle Foster; Lighting Designer, Kia Rogers; Set Designer, Nikki Black; Costume Designer, Cheryl McCarron; Sound Designer, Jay Spriggs; Cast: Zack Calhoon, Douglas B. Giorgis, Kate Kenney, Synge Maher, David Nelson, Aidan Redmond, Valerie Stanford; The Secret Theatre; March 4 – 24, 2012

Spring Tides by Melissa Gawlowski; Directed by Jeff Woodbridge; Stage Manager, Alicia Thompson; Lighting Designer, Kia Rogers; Set Designer, Nikki Black; Costume Designer, Cheryl McCarron; Sound Designer, Jay Spriggs; Special Effects, Sara Slagel and Evan Hill; Cast: Susan Atwood, Jason Liebman, Michael Mraz, Patricia Santomasso; Choreographer, Joe Mathers; The Secret Theatre; March 10 – 25, 2012

READINGS & WORKSHOPS

Precedence by Michael Champness; Directed by Luke Harlan; ART/NY; December 12, 2011

The Firebird by Tim Errickson; Directed by Christopher Thomasson; ART/NY; December 19, 2011

The Bower Group

This Is For You by Brittany Crowell, Mara Measor, Zach Szofer, Connor Unger; Directed by Jon Cicoski; Lighting Designer, Erik Olson; Set Designer, Ellie Johnson; Costume Designer, Jamie Bock; Sound Designer, Ryan Ettinger; Properties Designer, Ellie Johnson; Original Music, Mara Measor and Daniel Tepper; Cast: Justin Danforth, Chris Davis, Jess Loudon, Rachel Lyle, Daniel Tepper, Jamie Wolfe; New York Theatre Workshop; August 30 – September 3, 2011

BrainSpunk Theater

www.brainspunktheater.com

Artistic Director, Elmer Christopher King

The Shadow Box by Michael Cristofer; Directed by Elmer King; Stage Manager, Estie Sarvasy; Lighting Designer, Rachel Sevedge; Sound Designer, Rachel Sevedge; Cast: David Michael Kirby, Gisela Garbezza, Lance Marshall, David Wesley Cooper, Eileen Maher, Larry Saperstein, Marilyn Duryea, Kathleen Leisure, Tamara Kingston; The Turtle's Shell Studio; September 7 – 18, 2011

Southern Baptist Sissies by Del Shores; Directed by Elmer King; Stage Manager, Amanda Sevedge; Lighting and Sound Designer, Rachel Sevedge; Set Designer, Timothy Meola; Costume Designer, Casey Malone; Properties Designer, Taylor Derwin; Choreographer, Sean Roschman; Cast: Tyler Etheridge, Anthony Orneta, Aaron Wester, Jack Moore, Collin Biddle, Daniel McHenry, Rebecca Smith, Eileen Maher, Evan Closser, Lamar Lewis, Gaston Franco; June Havoc Theatre; May 11 – 27, 2012

READINGS & WORKSHOPS

Three Sheets (*Three Pillows* by Jim Dalglish; *Closet Madness* by Murray Schisgal; *Pillow Talk* by Peter Tolan); Directed by Elmer King; Technical Director, Rachel Sevedge; Stage Manager, Allyson Davis; House Manager, Kimberly Knutsen; Producer, Jonathan Clayton; Cast: Leo Giannopoulos, Sarah Miller, German Rodriguez, Emily Kuckuk, Collin Biddle, Edward Carnevale, Michael Komala, Dylan Uremovich; January 11 – 15, 2012

The Brick Theater, Inc.

www.bricktheater.com

Co-Founder & Artistic Director, Michael Gardner; Co-Founder, Robert Honeywell; Managing Director, Gyda Arber; Associate Artistic Director, Hope Cartelli; Associate Artistic Director, Jeff Lewonczyk; Technical Director, Ian W. Hill; Technical Director, Berit Johnson; Director of Development, Patrice Miller; Box Office Manager, Roger Nasser

Red Cloud Rising by Gyda Arber & Wendy Coyle; Directed by Gyda Arber; Sound Designer, Gyda Arber; Phone & Text Designer, Gyda Arber & Aaron Baker; Cast: Gyda Arber, Danny Bowes, Art Wallace; Bydder Financial; July 9 – September 25, 2011

Little Lord's Babes in Toyland Written and Directed by Michael Levinton; Musical Director, Kate Marvin; Stage Manager, Dina Paola Rodriguez; Cast: Corinne Donly, Das Elkin, Michael Levinton, Tina Shepard, Laura von Holt; co-produced by Little Lord; The Brick; November 30 – December 10, 2011

Bunny Lake Is Missing Written and Directed by Ken Simon; Musical Director, Chris Chappell; Stage Manager, Taylor Marun; Lighting Designer, Amanda Woodward; Set Designer, Matt Brogan; Costume Designer, Candace Lawrence, Alaine Livingston; Sound Designer, Chris Chappell; Assistant Director, Andrew Klein; Consultant, Patrice Miller; Puppet Designer, Fergus J. Walsh; Cast: Olivia Baseman, Walter Brandes, Josephine Cashman, Vanessa Fitzgerald, Justin R.G. Holcomb, Victoria Anne Miller, Christopher Norwood, and Ken Simon; The Brick; January 5 – 14, 2012

Flying Snakes in 3D!!! by Leah Nanako Winkler and Teddy Nicholas; Directed by Leah Nanako Winkler; Stage Manager, Raffaela Vergata; Lighting and Set Designers, Barbara Elderidge, Matt Taylor; Sound and AudioVisual Designer, Chase Voorhees; Co-Direction and Choreography, Lindsay Mack; Cast: Kim Gainer, Lindsay Mack, Cory Hibbs, Jen Kwok, Peter Mills-Weiss, T Ramon Campbell, Chris Tyler, Eevin Hartsough, Heather Lee Rogers, Molly Gray, Brett Hunter, David Weinheimer, Tim Platt and Tricia Cramer; co-produced with Everywhere Theatre Group; The Brick; January 18 – 28, 2012

Piper McKenzie's Dainty Cadaver by Gyda Arber, Julia Lee Barclay, Nat Cassidy, Joshua Conkel, Tim Errickson, Kelly Jean Fitzsimmons, Nina Mansfield, Adam Scott Mazer, Chance Muehleck, Roger Nasser, Timothy Reynolds, Laura Rohrman, Trav S.D., Jen Silverman, Marc Spitz, Adam Szymkowicz, Tema; Directed by Pete Boisvert, Jeff Lewonczyk and Patrice Miller; co-produced with Piper McKenzie; The Brick; February 3 – 5, 2012

Mother Tongue by Jillian Lauren; Directed by D.J. Mendel; Cast: Jillian Lauren; The Brick; February 6 – 7, 2012

VCR Love Written and Performed by David Lawson; The Brick; February 17 – 18, 2012

All the Indifferent Children of the Earth Written and Directed by Eric Bland; Lighting Designer, Morgan Anne Zipf; AudioVisual Designer, Asa Gauen; Sculpture-Arts/Illustration, Abernathy Bland; Cast: Sarah Dahlen, Kathleen Heverin, Daniel Kublick, and Hollis Witherspoon; co-produced by Old Kent Road Theater; The Brick; February 16 – March 3, 2012

The House of Fitzcarraldo Directed by Nikolas Weir; Musical Director, Christopher Luxem & Casey Mraz; Lighting and Set Designer, Nick Kostner; Lyrics, Henry Bial & Adam R. Burnett; Cast: Henry Bial, Brady Blevins, Adam R. Burnett, Jud Knudsen, Hilary Kelman, Christopher Luxem, Geraldo Mercado, and Casey Mraz; co-produced by Buran Theatre Company; The Brick; March 7 – 17, 2012

Monkeys by James Comtois; Directed by John Hurley; Cast: Alexis Black, Pete Boisvert, James Comtois, Shashanah Newman, Gavin Starr Kendall, Brian Pracht, C.L. Weatherstone, Christopher Yustin; co-produced with Nosedive Productions in association with Impetuous Theater Group; The Brick; March 23 – 31, 2012

The Gospel of Judas by Justin Lamb; Directed by Will Storie; Cast: Michelle Ciotta, Dave Ebert, Nathan Gregory, Chris Griswold, Keith Kingbay, Justin Lamb, Sean O'Reilly and Jacqueline Sneyers; The Brick; May 11 – 12, 2012

Antigone Unearthed Written and Directed by Rachel Broderick; Stage Manager, Dana Caputo; Lighting Designer, Juliet Smith; Sound Designer, Katie Pipal; AudioVisual Designer, Adam Gundersheimer; Cast: Sophia Treanor, Katie Helde, Maggie McDowell, Stephanie Hsu, and Joelle Golda; co-produced with Our Ladies of South 4th Street; The Brick; May 18 – 19, 2012

The Collected Rules of Gifted Camp by Valerie Work; Directed by Annie Tippe; Lighting Designer, Juliet Smith; Set Designer, Tyler Mercer; Costume Designer, Eleot Reich; Sound Designer, Eric Biel; Cast: Hollis Beck, Andrew R. Butler, Lena Hudson, & Ryann Weir; co-produced with Glasswork Productions; The Brick; May 16 – 26, 2012

Death Boogie by Darian Dauchan; Directed by Jennifer McGrath; Music by The Mighty Third Rail; Cast: Darian Dauchan co-produced with DDNMB; The Brick; August 22 – 23, 2011

Theater of the Arcade: Five Classic Video Games Adapted for the Stage by Jeff Lewonczyk; Directed by Gyda Arber; Musical Director, Frank Padellaro and Chris Chappell; Lighting Designer, Ian W. Hill; Costume Designer, Hope Cartelli and Jeff Lewonczyk; Cast: Fred Backus, Hope Cartelli, Stephen Heskett, Josh Mertz, Shelley Ray, Timothy McCown Reynolds; The Brick; September 3, 2011

in the great expanse of space, there is nothing to see but More, More, More Written and Directed by Matthew Freeman; Musical Director, Benjamin Warfield; Cast: with Lindsey Carter, Maggie Cino, Stephanie Cox-Williams, Rebecca Davis, Alexis Sottile, Stephanie Willing, and Morgan Anne Zipf; The Brick; September 29 – October 1, 2011

Action Philosophers! by Crystal Skillman; Directed by John Hurley; adapted from the comic book by Fred Van Lente & Ryan Dunlavey; Cast: Neimah Djourabchi, Joseph Mathers, Timothy McCown Reynolds, Matthew Trumbull, Kristen Vaughn, & C.L. Weatherstone; The Brick; October 6 – 16, 2011

Doctor Faustus by Christopher Marlowe; Directed by John Kurzynowski; Lighting and Set Designer, Jonathan Cottle; Sound Designer, Kate Marvin; Cast: Celeste Arias, Hunter Canning, Matt Carr, Matt Connolly, Nathaniel Kent, Emily Marro, Anastasia Olowin, Jon Riddleberger, Eugene Michael Santiago and Tina Shepard; co-produced with Theater Reconstruction Ensemble; The Brick; November 2 – 12, 2011

slut (r)evolution: no one gets there overnight Written and Performed by Cameryn Moore; co-produced with Little Black Book Productions; The Brick; November 18 – 19, 2011

FESTIVALS

The Comic Book Theater Festival; *Carousel*, hosted by Bob Sikoyak, Cast: Emily Flake, Sam Henderson, Doug Skinner, Matthew Thurber, Lauren R. Weinstein; *Mastermind* by Jason Robert Bell and Joe Infurnari; *Action Philosophers!* by Fred Van Lente, Ryan Dunlavey, and Crystal Skillman, Directed by John Hurley; *All I Want Is One More Meanwhile* by Kelly Jean Fitzsimmons, Directed by Ivanna Cullinan; *Batz* by Josh Mertz and Erik Bowie, Cast: Lynn Berg, Melissa DeLancey, Matt Foster, Matt Gray, Bob Laine, Dan Maccarone, Josh Mertz, Sarah Mertz, and Harrison Unger; *The Bubble of Solace* by Jeff Lewonczyk, Cast: Fred Backus, Esther Crow, Gavin Starr Kendall, Roger Nasser and Melissa Roth; *Captain Moonbeam and Lynchpin* by James Comtois, Directed by Leigh Hile; *Death Boogie* by Darian Dauchan, Directed by Jennifer McGrath, Cast: The Mighty Third Rail; *The DEEP*, created by Adrian Jevicki; *Drawn Out Storytelling*, Directed by Nisse Greenberg; *Five Things* by Jillian Tully, Directed by Amy Overman, Cast: Sarah Eliana Bisman, Jillian Tully, Rob Brown, Mim Granahan, and Cedric Jones; *Funnybook/Tragicbook* by Adam McGovern, Directed by Ian W. Hill, Cast: Ian W. Hill, Rasheed Hinds, Gavin Starr Kendall, Amy Overman, Shelley Ray, Tom Reid, and Adam Swiderski; *Galactic Girl in: Attack of the Starbarians* by Jon Hoche, Cast: Erica Swindell, Jamie Dunn, Becky Byers, Temar Underwood, Stephen Heskett, Tim O'Leary & Jon Hoche; *Gutter Space* by Keith Boynton, Directed by Ben Kamine; *Manifesto* by Jasper Patterson and Sarah Al-Kassab, Directed by Jasper Patterson; *Mrs. Perfect! A 10-Minute Episodic Rock Musical in a Van - Episode One: "Mrs. Perfect and the Unexpected Visit of Evil!"* by Crystal Skillman, Directed by James David Jackson; *Our Greatest Year* by Robert Attenweiler, Directed by Anna Brenner; *Reporter Girl* by Laura Rohrman, Directed by Erica Gould; *Savage Radio Plays* by Daniel P. Fay and Andrew Livingston; *Savior* by Brian Silliman, Directed by Jordana Williams, Cast: Mac Rogers and Kristen Vaughan; *Spaceship Alexandria* by Dan and Jon Cottle; *Afternoon Playland Presents: The Confetti Myth* by Gavin Starr Kendall, Directed by Gavin Starr Kendall, John Ivy and Shawn Wickens, Cast: Jaqueline Fouasnon, Eden Gauteron, John Ivy, Starr Kendall, Roy Koshy and Shawn Wickens; The Brick; June 2 - July 18, 2011

Game Play 2011; *BrainExplode!* by Sneaky Snake Productions; *foci + loci* by Chris Burke and Tamara Yadao; *Mastermind* by Jason Robert Bell and Joe Infurnari; *Modal Kombat* by David Hindman and Evan Drummond; *Red Cloud Rising* by Gyda Arber and Wendy Coyle, Directed by Gyda Arber, Technical Effects by Aaron Baker, Cast: Tom Reid and Art Wallace; *Romeoo and Julietet*, Adapted and Directed by Eddie Kim; *Son of Pong* by John DeVore; The Brick; July 7 – 31, 2011

Amuse Bouche 2011: A NY Clown Theatre Festival Hors d'Oeuvre; *Bezinkule* by Christopher Rozzi, Directed by Tasha Gordon-Solmon; *Flocked* by Audrey Crabtree and Gabriela Muñoz, Directed by Hilary Chaplain; *I Have Never Done This Before* by Joel Jeske; *Morro and Jasp Gone Wild* by Heather Marie Annis and Amy Lee, Directed by Byron Laviolette; *Odessey Schodyssey* by Hew Parham; *TiVo La Resistance!* by Logic LIMITED LTD, additional direction by Matt Steiner and Jane Nichols, Cast: Chris Arruda, Sandi Carroll, and Brad Fraizer; *Wing-Man* by Mark Gindick, Direction by David Shiner and Barry Lubin; *Channel One* by Emily James and Ishah Janssen-Faith; *Neon Lights* by Chris Manley and Jeff Seal, Directed by Danny Manley; The Brick; September 7 – 25, 2011

Tiny Theater 2011; *Boldly Go* by Matt Barbot, Cast: Matt Barbot and Kelly Rogers; *Brown Clown* by Art Wallace, Cast: Josephine Cashman, Timothy McCown Reynolds, Trav S.D., Art Wallace, Victoria Miller, and Sarah Engelke; *The Dreams in the Witch House* by Will Fulton, Cast: James Rutherford; *Fear and Loathing in Brooklyn* by Lynn Berg, Directed by Dan Krumm; *It's a 10-Minute Life* by Animal Engine, Cast: Karim Muasher, Carrie Brown, Katie Middleton, Nora Williams, Becca Bernard, Emily Althaus, Megan Venzin; *Mercy* by Tanya Khordoc and Barry Weil; *Roger Nasser is The One-Man Ten-Minute The Crucible* by Roger Nasser, Directed by Melissa Roth; *Yes It Did* by Richard Lovejoy, Directed by Paige Blansfield; The Brick; October 21 – 22, 2011

The Bridge Theatre Company

www.anynighttheplay.com

Any Night by Daniel Arnold & Medina Hahn; Directed by Ron Jenkins; Stage Manager, Jennifer Swan; Lighting Designer, David Fraser; Set Designer, Peter Pokorny; Costume Designer, Erin Macklem; Sound Designer, Gord Heal; Proptperties Designer, Peter Pokorny; Cast: Daniel Arnold and Medina Hahn, Brian Linds; produced in association with DualMinds Productions & Starry Night Entertainment; 14th Street Y Theater; June 8 - 19, 2011

Broken Glass

www.brokenglasstheatre.org

Cymbeline by William Shakespeare; Directed by Nathan Zebedeo; Assistant Director, Terence Stone; Cast: Alton Alburo, Robbie Baum, Emily Ciotti, Courtney Fitzgerald, Julia Giolzetti, Patrick Harvey, Tommy Nelms, Stacy Osei-Kuffour, Reynaldo Piniella, Christina Stone and Alan Tyson; The Secret Theatre; August 17 - 21, 2011

Built for Collapse

Nuclear Love Affair Written, Directed and Choreographed by Sanaz Ghajarrahimi & Ben Hobbs; Lighting Designer, Jenny Beth Snyder; Costume Designer, Michael Krass; Sound Designer, Amy Yourd; Video Design, Room 404 Media; Cast: Emily Brazee, Sanaz Ghajarrahimi, Ben Hobbs, Sophie Labelle, Vincent Santvoord, Soren Stockman; Theater for the New City; May 9 – September 3, 2011

Bull Moose Party

Woody Guthrie Dreams by Michael Patrick Flanagan Smith; Directed by Isabel Milenski; Stage Manager, Kasey Burgess; Lighting Designer, Tim Cryan; Set Designer, Jian Jung; Costume Designer, Sarah Cubbage; Cast: Michael Patrick Flanagan Smith, Jennifer Restivo, Caleb Stine, Ben Curtis, Kelvin Hale, Benjamin Jaeger-Thomas, Erica Lutz, Stephanie Wright Thompson, Aimée Laurence, Oona Laurence; Theater for the New City; September 8 – October 1, 2011

Buran Theatre Company

burantheatreco.weebly.com

The House of Fitzcarraldo by Buran Company; Directed by Nikolas Weir; Stage Manager, Amy Bourque; Set Designer, Nick Kostner; Costume Designer, Christy Artzer; Original Music, C.S. Luxem, Casey Mraz, Adam R. Burnett & Henry Bial; Cast: Henry Bial, Adam R. Burnett, Hilary Kelman, Jud Knudsen, CS Luxem, Geraldo Mercado, Casey Mraz; Brick Theater; March 7 – 17, 2012

The Bushwick Starr

www.thebushwickstarr.org

Gonna See A Movie Called Gunga Din by Mark Sitko, Erica Rippy, and Ned Buskirk; Directed by Mark Sitko; Stage Manager, Liz Nielsen; Lighting Designer, David Roy; Set Designer, Chris Morris; Dramaturge, Erica Rippy; Assistant Director, Michael Newton; Cast: Noel Joseph Allain, Mary Jane Gibson, Danny Bret Krueger, Mary Rasmussen, Monica Salazar, and Samuel Traylor; Co-produced with Van Cougar; The Bushwick Starr Theater; January 24 - February 11, 2012

Cake Productions

www.cakeproductions.org

Founders & Executive Producers, Francesca Day, Marta Kuersten; Associate Producers, Brooke Berry, Sarah Brill; Resident Stage Manager, Courtney Ferrell; Artistic Associate, Amir Darvish; Social Media Manager, Christina Romito

Swimming in the Shallows by Adam Bock; Directed by Maria Aladren; Stage Manager, Courtney Ferrell; Lighting Designer, Jessica Burgess; Set Designer, Chien-Yu Peng; Costume Designer, Carollyn Hoffman; Sound Designer, Louis Wells; Audiovisual Designer, Maria Aladren; Choreographer, Cleo Mack; Cast: Jason Cicci, Moti Margolin, Stephen Ward, Sarah Brill, Francesca Day, Marta Kuersten; Medicine Show Theatre; October 13 – 22, 2011

In the Company of Jane Doe by Tiffany Antone; Directed by Paul Urcioli; Stage Manager, Courtney Ferrell; Lighting Designer, Dante Olivia Smith; Set Designer, Sara Walsh; Costume Designer, Amy Pedigo-Otto; Sound Designer, Louis Wells; Choreographer, Alison Beatty; Cast: Brooke Berry, Sarah Brill, Francesca Day, Jason Guy, Marta Kuersten, Robert Maxwell, Elizabeth Neptune, Joe Stipek; New York Theatre Workshop's 4th Street Theatre; May 17 – June 2, 2012

Calliope Theatre Company

www.calliopetheatrecompany.org

Children of The Future Age Written and Directed by Knud Adams; Lighting Designer, Nick Houfek; Set Designer, D. Schuyler Burks; Costume Designer, Mia Bienovich; Sound Designer and Original Music, Nick Lerangis; Assistant Director, Lydian Blossom; Producer, Kevin Holloway; Cast: Raphael Sacks, Will Dagger, Molly McAdoo; Theaterlab; March 28 – April 1, 2012

Camisade Theatre Company

www.camisadetheatre.com

Derby Day by Samuel Brett Williams; Directed by Michole Biancosino; Stage Manager, Patrick Bernard Clayton; Lighting Designer, Shawn E. Boyle; Set Designer, Alfred Schatz; Costume Designer, Erin Schultz; Sound Designer, Amit Prakash; Choreographer, Alberto Bonilla; Cast: Jared Culverhouse, Malcolm Madera, Jake Silbermann, Beth Wittig; Clurman Theatre; November 30 – December 17, 2011

Canal Park Playhouse

www.canalparkplayhouse.com

Inadmissible by D.B. Gilles; Directed by Sherri Eden Barber; Cast: Charise Greene, Richard Hoehler, and Kathryn Kates; Canal Park Playhouse; January 25 - February 18, 2012

CAP21 Theatre Company

www.cap21.org

Marrying George Clooney: Confessions from a Midlife Crisis by AmyFerris, Ken Ferris, Krista Lyons; Directed by Frank Ventura; Stage Manager, Catherine Digirolamo; Lighting Designer, Clark Gaesser; Set Designer, Jon Kknust; Costume Designer, Julia Broer; Sound Designer, Emmett O'Brien; AudioVisual Designer, Grant McDonald; Production Manager, Becca Doyle; CAP21 Theatre; March 1 - 24, 2012

Caps Lock Theatre

capslocktheatre.com

The Foreplay Play by Mariah MacCarthy; Directed by Leta Tremblay; Stage Manager, Sydney Rainville-Thomson; Cast: Lindsey Austen, Nic Grelli, Parker Leventer, Diana Oh; Kingsland Kastle; April 19 – May 6, 2012

Carrie Ahern Dance

www.carrieahern.com

Borrowed Prey Choreographed and Performed by Carrie Ahern; Stage Manager, Katie Kavett; Lighting Designer, Jay Ryan; Costume Designer, Naoko Nagata; Sound Designer, Anne Hege; Original Music, Anne Hege; Dickson's Farmstand Meats; April 26 – May 13, 2012

Cart Before Horse Productions

Producers, Krista Amigone and Patrick Bonck

Trifles/Hughie by Susan Glaspell and Eugene O'Neill; Directed by S. Quincy Beard; Stage Manager, Yvonne Hartung; Lighting Designer, Patrick Bonck; Set Designer, Dave Powers; Costume Designer, Nicole Tobolski; Sound Designer, Mark Parenti; Executive Producer, Mary C. Healy; Executive Producer, Daniel O'Shea; Cast: Krista Amigone, Angela Atwood Perri, Mikaal Bates, Mike James, Will W. Warren, Daniel O'Shea, Patrick Bonck; Dorothy Strelsin Theatre; November 3 - 20, 2011

Anna Abock by Krista Amigone; Directed by Karen Chamberlain; Cast: Booker Garrett, Robert Z. Grant; As part of The Network's One-Act Festival; The Barrow Group Theatre; March 7-21, 2012

Castillo Theatre

www.castillo.org

Court-Martial At Fort Devens by Jeffrey Sweet; Directed by Mary Beth Easley; Lighting Designer, Shirley Prendergast; Set Designer, John Scheffler; Costume Designer, Ali Turns; Sound Designer, Mark Bruckner; Cast: Alia Chapman, Evander Duck, Gillian Glasco, Nambi E. Kelley, Frank Mayers, Emma O'Donnell, Bill Tatum, Keona Welch, Eboni Witche; Castillo Theatre; March 18 - April 1, 2012

Cat on My Head Productions LLC

Two Intimate (*The Lover* by Harold Pinter and *Eden* by Eugene O'Brien); Directed by Kathy Gail MacGowan; Stage Manager, Laura Hirschberg; Lighting and Set Designer, Lauren Parrish; Sound Designer, Juian Evans; Cast: Dan Patrick Brady, Anna Emily Wood, Robert Lyons; Abingdon Theatre Complex; May 24 – June 9, 2012

The Cell Theatre

www.thecelltheatre.org

A Midsummer Night's Dream by William Shakespeare; Directed by Matthew A. J. Gregory; Stage Manager, Lauren Williams; Lighting Designer, Nick Gonsman; Set Designer, Justin Couchara; Costume Designer, Christina Kim; Sound Designer, Justin Stasiw; Cast: Meghan Grace O'Leary, Ashley Denise Robinson, Ashley Denise Robinson, Shira Gregory, Ron Bopst, Fernando Gambaroni, Glenn Quentin, Guy Rader, Marissa Parness; the cell; July 5 – 31, 2011

Bad Evidence by Terry Quinn; Directed by Kira Simring; Stage Manager, Jessica Biggert; Lighting Designer, Nick Gonsman; Set Designer, Justin Couchara; Costume Designer, Christina Kim; Sound Designer, Justin Stasiw; Cast: Armand Anthony, Carmit Levité, Ryan Lee, Gary Lee Mahmoud, Len Rella, Ana Grosse; the cell; July 7 – 31, 2011

Heroes and Other Strangers Written and Performed by Zac Jaffee; Directed by Christian Haines; Stage Manager, Scott Andrews; Lighting Designer, Lee Terry; Sound Designer, Yvette Jackson; Original Music, Luke Westbrook; the cell; November 1 – 19, 2011

CEO Theatre

www.ceotheatre.org

The Complaint by Randy Noojin; Directed by Bryn Boice; Stage Manager, Joan Wilkerson; Lighting Designer, Amanda Woodward; Sound Designer, Steve Ryan; Cast: Amanda Ladd, Randy Noojin, Nicholas Alexiy Moran, Josh Adler, Michael Poignand; 45th Street Theatre – Upstairs; October 27 – November 13, 2011

Charles Mandracchia/Frizzi & Lazzi Music Theatre Company

www.hushthemusical.com

Producer, Charles Mandracchia and Frizzi & Lazzi/Emelise Aleandri

Hush The Musical Adapted by Emelise Aleandri from Etta Cascini's play SHHHH; Composed and Directed by Charles Mandracchia; Cast: Madelyn Schwartz, Diana Falzone, Seth Blum, Tommy J. Dose & Emelise Aleandri, Mitch Marcus MD, Alisa Horn, Yuiko Kamakari, Blair Anderson, Emily Billig, Isabel Cristina Obando & Jim Roumeles; Co-Produced with The Olde Time Italian-American Music & Theatre Company; Le Poisson Rouge; August 21st - 28, 2011

Clowns Ex Machina

www.ClownsExMachina.com

Clowns Full-Tilt: A Musing on Aesthetics Directed by Kendall Cornell; Lighting Designer, Carla T Bosnjak; Set Designer, Sean Ryan; Costume Designer, Clowns Ex Machina; Cast: Amanda Barron, Carla T. Bosnjak, Kendall Cornell, Julie Kinkle, Michaela Lind, Diana Lovrin, Lucia Rich, Maria Smushkovich, Virginia Venk; Co-Produced with La Mama ETC; La MaMa Experimental Theatre; November 4 – 20, 2011

Clubbed Thumb

www.clubbedthumb.org

Producing Artistic Director, Maria Striar; Managing Director, Nora DeVeau-Rosen

Enfrascada by Tanya Saracho; Directed by Jerry Ruiz; Stage Manager, Mary Spadoni; Lighting Designer, Christian DeAngelis; Set Designer, Steven C. Kemp; Costume Designer, Emily DeAngelis; Sound Designer, Jana Hoglund; Cast: Flora Diaz, Annie Henk, Anna Lamadrid, Jessica Pimentel, Christina Pumariega; HERE Arts Center; June 5-11, 2011

Our Lot by Kristin Newbom and W. David Hancock; Directed by May Adrales; Stage Manager, Lizzy Lee; Lighting Designer, Gina Scherr; Set Designer, Timothy Mackabee; Costume Designer, Alixandra Gage Englund; Sound Designer, Ryan Maeker; Cast: Joanna P. Adler, Nathan Hinton, Mariann Mayberry, Paul Niebanck; HERE Arts Center; June 12-18, 2011

Civilization (All You Can Eat) by Jason Grote; Directed by Seth Bockley; Stage Manager, Sunneva Stapleton; Lighting Designer, Raquel Davis; Set Designer, Laura Jellinek; Costume Designer, Jessica Pabst; Sound Designer, Shane Rettig; Choreographer, Dan Safer; Cast: Jeff Biehl, Reyna de Courcy, Melissa Miller, Andres Munar, Melle Powers, Elizabeth Rich, Tony Torn; HERE Arts Center; June 19-25, 2011

Tarazuka!!! by Susan Soon He Stanton; Directed by Lear deBessonet; Stage Manager, Megan Schwarz Dickert; Lighting Designer, Tyler Micoleau; Set Designer, Mimi Lien; Sound Designer, Dave Malloy; Choreographer, Tracy Bersley; Cast: Jennifer Ikeda, Brooke Ishibashi, Paul Juhn, Glenn Kubota, and Angela Lin; HERE Arts Center; May 26-June 4, 2012

Luther by Ethan Lipton; Directed by Ken Rus Schmoll; Stage Manager, Mary Spadoni; Lighting Designer, Lucrecia Briceno; Set Designer, Arnulfo Maldonado; Costume Designer, Jessica Pabst; Sound Designer, Brandon Wolcott; Fight Choreographer, Dan Safer; Cast: John Ellison Conlee, Crystal Finn, Gibson Frazier, Kelly Mares, Bobby Moreno, and Pete Simpson; HERE Arts Center; June 8-17, 2012

Motel Cherry by Peggy Stafford; Directed by Meghan Finn; Stage Manager, Travis Brendle; Lighting Designer, Brian Aldous; Set Designer, Daniel Zimmerman; Costume Designer, Tilly Grimes; Sound Designer, Shane Rettig; Cast: Noel Allain, Francis Benhamou, Eboni Booth, Steven Boyer, Boo Killebrew, Linda Marie Larson, DJ Mendel, Mike Shapiro, and Monique Vukovic; co-produced with New Georges; HERE Arts Center; June 21-30, 2012

READINGS & WORKSHOPS

The Blood Play Created by The Debate Society, as part of the SuperLab Development Program; Playwrights Horizons

Stockholm Pennsylvania by Nikole Beckwith; Directed by Jo Bonney; As part of the SuperLab Development Program; Playwrights Horizons

Takarazuka!!! by Susan Soon He Stanton; Directed by Chay Yew; As part of the SuperLab Development Program; Playwrights Horizons

Somewhere Fun by Jenny Schwartz; Directed by Anne Kauffman; As part of the SuperLab Development Program; Playwrights Horizons

Co-Op Theatre East

www.cooptheatreeast.org

Twelfth Night: Wall Street by William Shakespeare; Directed by Casey Cleverly; Stage Manager, Rebecca Perlman; Lighting Designer, Nick Solyom; Set Designer, Michael Simmons; Costume Designer, Lizzy Elkins; Sound Designer, Robert A. K. Gonyo and Todd Meredith; Cast: Dana Hunter, Haleigh Ciel, Amanda Renee Baker, Sam Williams, Charles Hinshaw, Mike Rehse, Tyrus Holden, Samantha Bruce, Kerrie Bond, Ramon Torres, Myles Rowland, Rose Kearns; Looking Glass Theatre; February 23 - March 11, 2012

CollaborationTown

www.collaborationtown.org

Artistic Core Members, Jordan Seavey, Boo Killebrew, Geoffrey Decas O'Donnell, TJ Witham; Resident Director, Lee Sunday Evans; Managing Director, Amanda Feldman

The Play About My Dad by Boo Killebrew; Directed by Lee Sunday Evans; Stage Manager, Kelly "Kiki" Hess; Lighting Designer, Nick Houfek; Set Designer, Kate Sinclair Foster; Costume Designer, Beth Goldenberg; Sound Designer, Brandon Wolcott; Associate Director, Jack Nicholas; Dramaturg, Jill Rafson; Associate Costume Designer, Amanda Shafran; Assistant Stage Manager, Kaitlin Nemeth; Artistic Advisors, Jordan Seavey and Geoffrey Decas O'Donnell; Creative Line Producer, Amanda Feldman; Cast: Jay Potter, Anna Greenfield, TJ Witham, Jay Mahome, David Rosenblatt, Annie Henk, Juan Francisco Villa, Geany Masai, Tracey Gilbert; 59e59, Theatre C; June 16 - July 2

The Deepest Play Ever: The Catharsis of Pathos by Geoffrey Decas O'Donnell; Directed by Lee Sunday Evans and Jordan Seavey; Musical Director, Michael Wells; Stage Manager, Kaitlin Nemeth; Lighting Designer, Nick Houfeck; Set Designer, Deb O; Costume Designer, Nichol V. Moody; Sound Designer, Brandon Wolcott; Composer, Michael Wells; Properties and Puppet Designer, Deb O; Associate Music Director, Nicholas Williams; Assistant Stage Manager, Shelby Alison Hibbs Technical Director, Matthew Vieira; Publicist, Ron Lasko/Spin Cycle; Creative Line Producer, Amanda Feldman; Cast: Jordan Barbour, Carly Cioffi, Nick Choksi, John Halbach, Boo Killebrew, Geoffrey Decas O'Donnell, Chinasa Ogbuagu, Phillip Taratula, Emily Watson, TJ Witham; The New Ohio; March 9 – 24

READINGS & WORKSHOPS

The Funny Pain by Jordan Seavey; Directed by May Adrales; Cast, Jenny Seastone Stern, Boo Killebrew, Geoffrey Decas O'Donnell, Jennifer Dorr White; Fight Director, Lisa Kopitsky; Costume Consultation, Becky Bodurtha; Stage Management, Bekah Wachenfeld; IRT Theater; November 19 - 20, 2011

Collaborative Stages

Orpheus and Euridice by Ricky Ian Gordon; Directed by Brian Letchworth; Stage Manager, Griffin Parker; Lighting Designer, Dan Jobbins; Video and Projection Designer, Brian Letchworth & Zhuojie Chen; Cast: Heather Dudenbostel, Ryan Dudenbostel, Jad Bernardo; The DUO Theater; June 2 – 12, 2011

Collision Productions

www.collision-productions.com

Endure: A Run Woman Show Written and Performed by Melanie Jones; Interactive Technology, Suchan Vodoor; Original Music, Christine Owman; The Old Stone House; September 24 – October 30, 2011

Colt Coeur

www.coltcoeur.org

Fish Eye by Lucas Kavner; Directed by Adrienne Campbell-Holt; Stage Manager, Trisha Henson; Lighting Designer, Grant Yeager; Set Designer, John McDermott; Costume Designer, Jessica Pabst; Sound Designer, Daniel Kluger; Properties Designer, Amelia Freeman-Lynde; Technical Director, Markus Paminger; Cast: Katya Campbell, Ato Essandoh, Betty Gilpin, and Joe Tippett; HERE Arts Center; May 27 - June 18, 2011

The Common Tongue

www.tctnyc.org

Artistic Director, Lila Dupree; Development Director, Shawn Kathryn Kane

What The Sparrow Said by Danny Mitarotondo; Directed by Jenna Worsham; Stage Manager, Ellen Mezzera; Lighting Designer, Jamie Roderick; Set Designer, Daniel A. Krause; Sound Designer, Eben Hoffer; Assistant Stage Manager, Alyssa Joy Olson; Fight Choreographer, Casey Robinson; Dramaturg, Jay Jaski;

Photographer, Suzi Sadler; Graphic Designer, Houston Kraft; Producers, Lila Dupree, Alona Fogel, Danny Mitarotondo; Cast: Brenda Currin, Lila Dupree, Matthew Michael Hurley, Kevin Mannering, Heather Oakley, Ruby Ruiz; Presented as part of the 2012 New York International Fringe Festival; Teatro La Tea, The New York International Fringe Festival; August 12-28, 2011

READINGS & WORKSHOPS

Grenadine by Neil Wechsler; Directed by Hal Brooks; Cast: Bob Adrian, Larry Block, Brennan Brown, Bruce Dow, Melissa Miller, Jonathan Randell Silver, Monique Vukovic, John Warren, Margaret Woodard; Producer, Lila Dupree; Stage Manager, Margaret Woodard; Theater for the New City, The Johnson Theater; September 26, 2011

Dancing for Krumholtz by Tom Cudworth; Directed by Eric Bross; Cast: Ali Cobrin, Lila Dupree, Greg Felden, John Harnagel, Houston Rhines, Shawn Kathryn Kane; Producers, Shawn Kathryn Kane and Lila Dupree; The Elephant Theatre, Los Angeles; May 6, 2012

Community Garden Project

Communal Space: a play series in four gardens by Tommy Smith, Angela Santillo, Jason Platt, Lucy Gillespie; Directed by Lillian Meredith; Assistant Director, Tom Meredith; Cast: ; Various Gardens; June 24 - July 24, 2011

Compass Theatrical

www.compasstheatrical.com

Nightfall on Miranga Island by Justin Moran and Jonathan Roufaeal; Directed by Justin Moran; Stage Manager, Erin Coulter; Lighting Designer, Jake DeGroot; Set Designer, Sarah Schetter; Original Music, Adam Podd and Matt Podd; Cast: Ryan Nelson, Jamie Cummings, Nick Kanellis, Robin Rothman, Claire Nuemann, Elana Fishbein; Choreographer, Liz Bachman; The Magnet Theater; October 21 – December 16, 2011

Conni's Avant Garde Restaurant

www.avantgarderestaurant.com

Conni's Avant Garde Restaurant Returns in: The Mothership Landing by the Ensemble; Directed by Paul Bargetto; Stage Manager, Jennifer Caster; Lighting Designer, Jeanette Yew; Set Designer, David Barber; Cast: Melody Bates, Stephanie Dodd, Connie Hall, Deborah Philips, Jeffrey Fracé, Jerusha Klemperer, Justin Badger, Kelly Hayes, Peter Lettre, Peter Richards, Rachel Murdy, David Barber; Irondale Center; September 15 – 25, 2011

Core Creative Productions

www.corecreativeproductions.com

Dia de los Muertos by Anthony P. Pennino; Directed by Alberto Bonilla; Stage Manager, Katy Moore; Costume Designer, Yakima Levy; Fight Choreographer, Alberto Bonilla; Cast: Alberto Bonilla, Ryan Wesley Brown, Ariel Bonilla, Elizabeth Inghram, Javier E. Gómez, Michael Poignand, Robert C. Raicch, Alexander Stine, Adyana de la Torre, Eevin Hartsough, Ydaiber Orozco, Maria Stamenkovic Herranz; Clemente Soto Velez Cultural Center; July 14 – 31, 2011

Coryphaeus Theater Company

References to Salvador Dali Make Me Hot by Jose Rivera; Directed by Patrice Miller; Stage Manager, Jennifer Kern; Set Designer, Jessica J Emerson; Cast: Patrick Cann, Mia Romero, Jason Vance, Sergio Martinez, Osvaldo Hernandez Chavez, Cat Widdifield; Gene Frankel Theatre; September 6 – 11, 2011

Cross-Eyed Bear Productions

www.duncanpflaster.com

Sweeter Dreams Written and Directed by Duncan Pflaster; Stage Manager, Adam Samtur and Jenna Lazar; Multimedia/Film Direction & Editing, Christopher Cariker; Cast: Scott Freeman, Clara Barton Green, Heather Lee Rogers, Doug Rossi; Gene Frankel Theatre; June 2 – 25, 2011

crosshatch theatre company

crosshatchtheatre.com

Einstein and Mileva by Caitlin Shannon; Directed by Emma Canalese; Set Designer, Geoffrey Bryant; Cast: Sarah Manton, Greg Lay, Matthew Baldiga, Sid Solomon; Clurman Theatre; August 18 – September 3, 2011

Crossroads Theatre Project

Tulpa, or Anne&Me by Shawn C. Harris; Directed by Sara Lyons; Lighting Designer, Lauren Bremen; Set Designer, Lauren Bremen; Sound Designer, Peter Weiss; Assistant Director Alexa Gruber; Cast: Starr Kirkland, Rachel Lambert, Mia Y. Anderson and Ayo Cummings; 440 Studios; June 2 – 19, 2011

Culture Project

cultureproject.org

The Wild Finish by Monica Hunken; Directed by Melissa Chambers; Lighting Designer, Evan True; Sound Designer, Xana Chambers and Benjamin Cerf; Cast: Monica Hunken; Produced in association with The Polish Cultural Institute; ABC No Rio Theatre; January 25 - February 11, 2012

Curious Frog Theatre Company

Two Gentlemen of Verona by William Shakespeare; Directed by Renee Rodriguez; Stage Manager, Gae Song; Costume Designer, Samantha Guinan; Fight Choreographer, Rocio Mendez; Cast: Angela Sharp, Justin Maruri, Emilio Aquino, Bushra Laskar, Umi Shakti, Robert Dyckman, James Ware, Krystine Summers;NYC Parks; August 12 – September 4, 2011

Julius Caesar by William Shakespeare; Directed by Robert J. Dyckman; Stage Manager, Shira Segal; Costume Designer, Samantha Guinan; Sound Designer, Manual de la Portilla; Original Music, Manuel de la Portilla; Fight Choreographer, Rocio Mendez; Cast: Nicholas Urda, Renee Rodriguez, Robert J. Dyckman, James Ware, Emilio Aquino, Angela Sharp, Krystine Summers, Kimberley Wong, Manuel de la Portilla, Al Patrick Jo, D. Carlton, Shae Orrick, Holly Dortch; NYC Parks; August 20 – September 10, 2011

Czechoslovak-American Marionette Theatre

czechmarionettes.org

Artistic Director, Vit Horejs; Associate Director, Theresa Linnihan; Executive Director, Bonnie Sue Stein, Set and Costume Designer, Michelle Beshaw

Kacha and the Devil Written and Directed by Vit Horejs; Set Designer, Vit Horejs; Costume Designer, Marika Blossfeldt; Producer, Bonnie Sue Stein; Cast: Vit Horejs; NYPL; July 6, 2011 - June 9, 2012

Kochicka & Pejsek Written and Directed by Vit Horejs; Costume Designer, Marika Blossfeldt; Marionette Maker, Milos Kasal; Producer, Bonnie Sue Stein; Cast: Vit Horejs, Suleiman, Kidville, Oval Lounge, Matthias; Taos; September 4, 2011 - June 1, 2012

Golem Written and Directed by Vit Horejs; Musical Director, Jonathan Singer; Stage Manager, Michael Collins; Lighting Designer, Federico Restrepo; Set Designer, Roman Hladik; Costume Designer, Boris Caksiran; Composer, Frank London; Choreographer, Naomi Goldberg Haas; Marionettes, Jakub Krejci; Cast: Janelle Barry, Deborah Beshaw, Fang Du, Miron Gusso, Alan Barnes Netherton, Steven Ryan, Alex Megan Shell, Bridget Struthers, Ronny Wasserstrom; La Mama Ellen Stewart Theatre; November 17-December4

A Christmas Carol, Oy! Hanukkah, Merry Kwanzaa (Happy Ramadan) Written and Directed by Vit Horejs; Musical Director, Judith Barnes; Stage Manager, Rocky Bostick; Set and Costume Designer, Michelle Beshaw; Puppet Maker, Milos Kasal; Producer, Bonnie Sure Stein; Cast: Judith Barnes, Hayden DeWitt; Clockworks Puppet Theatre; December 15, 2011 - January 1, 2012

Dancing Crane, Inc.

Sarke by Lia Bakhturidze Sirelson; Directed by Ramaz Zurabashvili; Cast: Irma Gachechiladze, Natalia Goderdzishvili, Khatuna Ioseliani, Tsitsino Kapanadze, Irina Khutsurauli, Nika Muradeli, Giorgi Potskhveria, Irakli Shengelia, Ramaz Zurabashvili; WorkShop Theater Mainstage; July 19 – 24, 2011

The Dead Copycats

Ghost in the Machine by Mike Leon; Directed by Nathaniel Basch-Gould; Set Designer, Kate Foster; Sound Designer, Eben Hoffer; Cast: Aspen Lee Jordan, Peter Drivas, Ryan Pavano; Theater for the New City; October 13 – 22, 2011

Desipina & Company

www.desipina.org

Barriers by Rehana Lew Mirza; Directed by Colette Robert; Stage Manager, John Nehlich; Lighting Designer, Marie Yokoyama; Set & Costume Designer, Katherine A. Day; Sound Designer, Colin Whitely; Cast: Pooja Kumar, Sunkrish Bala, Joe Petrilla, Eileen Rivera, Jon Norman Schneider, Rajeev Varma; HERE Arts Center; September 8 – 17, 2011

Dive Theatre

www.divetheatre.com

Garage by Dive Theatre; Directed by Michael Hogwood; Stage Manager, Matthew Rosario; Lighting Designer, Lance Darcy; Set Designer, Ian Belton; Costume Designer, Ruby Kemph; Sound Designer, Mike Harkins; Fight Choreographer, Jason Cutler; Cast: Bryce Kemph, Jenna Kirk, Nathan Riley; Richmond Shepard Theatre; July 7 - 23, 2011

Dixon Place

www.dixonplace.org

3 2's; or Afar; October 6 - 29, 2011

Alien Suns Inspired by H.P. Lovecraft; September 15, 2011

Anna & The Annadroids: Memoirs of a Robot Girl; August 18 - 22, 2011

Artificial Afrika; February 10 - 25, 2012

Belladonna Poetry by Erica Kaufman and Uljana Wolf; October 11, 2011

Belladonna Poetry by Ana Božievi and Caroline Crumpacker and others; Produced by Girls Write Now; September 13, 2011

Bindlestiff Family Cirkus Cabaret; March 1 - 29, 2012

Cohen & Sturman by Davi Cohen and Pete Sturman; September 21, 2011

Cow Play; Produced by Less Than Rent; August 13 - 27, 2011

Dead Spot Cast: Julie Fotheringham and Jarryd Lowder; September 15, 2011

Destructo Snack, USA; September 17, 2011

The Dog and Pony Show; June 3 - 18, 2011

Dystopia Gardens; August 13 - 27, 2011

El Trac; Septeber 7, 2011

Experiments & Disorders Curated by Christen Clifford and Tom Cole; Created by Patty Powers and McKenzie Wark; September 20, 2011

Flaccid Penis Seeks Vaginal Dryness; August 13 - 25, 2011

From The Front Porch: An Evening With David Mixner; July 11 - 18, 2011

Genet Porno Directed by Yvan Greenberg; Performers: Corey Dargel, Oleg Dubson, Wil Smith; September 20, 2011

Girl Crush Written and Performed by Laura Pruden; March 24, 2012

Herringbone; May 21 - 22, 2012

The Homophobes: A Clown Show Written and Directed by Susana Cook; Sptember 9 - 24, 2011

I Light Up My Life: The Mark Sam Celebrity Autobiography; August 12 - 26, 2011

I've Been Elvita Adams; August 19 - 28, 2011

Leakey's Ladies by Erin Courtney, Rachel Hoeffel and Crystal Skillman; Directed by Gretchen Van Lente; Lighting Designer, Jeanette Yew; Sound Designer, Kate Brown; Puppets & Mask Design, David Valentine; Original Music, Stephanie Richards; Cast: Tatiana Pavela, Amy Carrigan, Meghan Williams, Scott Weber, Patrick Shearer; Dixon Place; January 13 – February 4, 2012

Lipshtick; August 12 - 24, 2011

Little Theatre Performers: Scott Adkins, Rob Erickson, Jeff Jones, Tina Satter, Normandy Sherwood; September 12, 2011

Lunatic Cunning by James Godwin and Tom Burnett; Cast: James Godwin; Dixon Place; April 6 - 21, 2012

Mawu Group; September 8, 2011

Moving Men; September 19, 2011

Mr. Aviner's Variety Hour; September 1, 2011

The Mystory of an Angry "Black"; September 14, 2011

Nils' Fucked Up Day; August 14 - 22, 2011

The Peripherals; May 11 - 19, 2012

Pitch!; August 1, 2011

Puppet Block Gets Punched Co-produced by PUNCH-NYC; September 14, 2011

Puppet Blok! ; September 16, 2011

Puppet Blok! An Existential Sing-Along and Three Cheers For America! Featuring *Three Cheers for America!* and *History! Limited Dancing! Maybe a song or two?!*; September 15, 2011

Rollerblading in Gaza; August 14 - 26, 2011

Spring Alive Written and Performed by Spring Groove; March 2 - 25, 2012

The Tom Judson Show; June 24 - 25, 2011

The Underbelly Diaries Redux; August 18 - 28, 2011

The Ventriloquist Circle by Matt Wilson; January 6 - 28, 2012

Wallstories; August 12 - 28, 2011

When the Sky Breaks 3D; August 18 - 26, 2011

White Like Me: A Hunky Dory Puppet Show by Paul Zaloom and Lynn Jeffries; Directed by Randee Trabitz; Cast: Paul Zaloom; Dixon Place; May 25 - June 2, 2012

FESTIVALS

The 20th Annual HOT! Festival (see Festivals); June 24 - August 4, 2011

Down Payment Productions

www.downpaymentproductions.org

Yes We Can by Daniella Shoshan; Directed by Alec Strum; Stage Manager, Andrea Wales; Lighting Designer, Grant Wilcoxen; Set Designer, Tristan Jeffers; Costume Designer, Franny Bohar; Sound Designer, Janie Bullard; Cast: Duane Cooper, Makeda Declet, Judith Dry, Gina Marie Jamieson, Meera Rohit Kumbhani, Jeffrey Omura, Stephen Stout, Ronald Washington, Dax Valdes, Jehan O. Young; Walkerspace; June 17 – July 2, 2011

Downtown Art

www.downtownart.org

The Bowery Wars, Part 2 Written and Directed by Ryan Gilliam; Original Music, Michael Hickey; Cast: Lily Abedin, Zen Anton, Mamadou Barry, Joshua Diaz, Lily Fremaux, Andrew Gangaram, Michela Garabedian, Nick Geisler, Lena Feliciano Hansen, Mae Hardman-Hill, Jeanne Kessira, India Kotis, Tori Matos, Lila Meretzky, Alma Moos-Nunez, Steven Paul, Olivia Rein; Downtown Art; April 28 – May 20, 2012

Drama of Works

www.dramaofworks.com

Leakey's Ladies by Erin Courtney, Rachel Hoeffel and Crystal Skillman; Directed by Gretchen Van Lente; Lighting Designer, Jeanette Yew; Sound Designer, Kate Brown; Puppets & Mask Design, David Valentine; Original Music, Stephanie Richards; Cast: Tatiana Pavela, Amy Carrigan, Meghan Williams, Scott Weber, Patrick Shearer; Dixon Place; January 13 – February 4, 2012

Dreamcatcher Entertainment

www.dreamcatcherentertainment.biz

East in Red by Ryan Sprague; Gore Designer, Emma Servant; Off-Off-Broadway Playhouse at Roy Arias Theaters; October 20 – 30, 2011

Dysfunctional Theatre Company

www.dysfunctionaltheatre.org

Artistic Director, Amy Overman; Director of Development, Justin Plowman; Director of Development, Dysfunctional Classics Series, Peter Schuyler; President of the Board, Paul Wells; Vice President, Rick Vorndran; Secretary, Rob Brown; Treasurer, Jennifer Gill We

Unlicensed Episode 1: The Pilot by Josh Hartung; Directed by Jazz Schuyler; AudioVisual Designer, Justin Plowman; Cast: Nicole Lee Aiossa, Adam Files, Cara Moretto, Tom O'Connor, Amy Overman, Amy Beth Sherman, Jason Unfried, Theresa Unfried, Kathleen Boddington, Rob Brown, Jennifer Gill, Kurt Kingsley Unlicensed was an eight-part episodic theater production; UNDER St. Marks; September 18-19, 2011

Unlicensed Episode 2: Community by Josh Hartung; Directed by Jazz Schuyler; AudioVisual Designer, Justin Plowman; Cast: Nicole Lee Aiossa, Adam Files, Rachel Grundy, Stephen Heskett, Bob Laine, Cara Moretto, Tom O'Connor, Amy Overman, Amy Beth Sherman, Jason Unfried, Theresa Unfried, Josephine Cashman, Eric Chase, Brian Patrick Faherty, Catherine McNelis, Dan Renkin, Peter Schuyler; UNDER St. Marks; October 16-17, 2012

Brew of the Dead II: Oktoberflesh by Patrick Storck; Directed by Justin Plowman; Lighting, Sound and AudioVisual Designer, Justin Plowman; Gore effects by Stephanie Cox Williams; Original Music, Coyote Love; Cast: Nicole Lee Aiossa, Rob Brown, Eric Chase, Tom O'Connor, Amy Beth Sherman, Kathy Stakenas; UNDER St. Marks; November 3-19, 2012

Unlicensed Episode 3: Cheers by Josh Hartung; Directed by Jazz Schuyler; AudioVisual Designer, Justin Plowman; Fight Choreographer: Stephen Heskett; Cast: Nicole Lee Aiossa, George Bronos, Lindsey Carter, Adam Files, Cara Moretto, Tom O'Connor, Amy Overman, Amy Beth Sherman, Jason Unfried, Theresa Unfried, Kathleen Boddington, Kurt Kingsley, Catherine McNelis, Vivian Meisner, Patrick Storck; UNDER St. Marks; November 20-21, 2012

Unlicensed Episode 4: Prison Break by Josh Hartung; Directed by Jazz Schuyler; AudioVisual Designer, Justin Plowman; Choreographer, Nicole Lee Aiossa; Original Music, John Gideon, Andrew Neesley; Cast: Gyda Arber, Nicole Lee Aiossa, Rob Brown, Lindsey Carter, Emily Edwards, Adam Files, Rachel Grundy, Julie Aubin Heller, Cedric Jones, Saidu Marko, Cara Moretto, Tom O'Connor, Amy Overman, Amy Beth Sherman, Kathleen Boddington, Stephanie Cox-Williams, Jennifer Gill, Bob Laine; UNDER St. Marks; December 18-19, 2012

Unlicensed Episode 5: Quantum Leap by Josh Hartung; Directed by Jazz Schuyler; AudioVisual Designer, Justin Plowman; Assistant Director, Eric Chase; Fight Choreographer, Stephen Heskett; Original Music, John Gideon; Cast: Nicole Lee Aiossa, Rob Brown, Lindsey Carter, Adam Files, Cara Moretto, Tom O'Connor, Amy Overman, Amy Beth Sherman, Wayne Willinger; UNDER St. Marks; January 15-16, 2012

Unlicensed Episode 6: by Josh Hartung; Directed by Jazz Schuyler; Musical Director, John Gideon; AudioVisual Designer, Justin Plowman; Assistant Director, Gyda Arber; Cast: Nicole Lee Aiossa, David Berent, George Bronos, Michael DeRensis, Adam Files, Josh Mertz, Cara Moretto, Tom O'Connor, Amy Overman, Amy Beth Sherman, Jillian Tully, Jason Unfried, Theresa Unfried, Sarah Malinda Engelke, Bobby Oahu, Timothy McCown Reynolds; UNDER St. Marks; February 19-20, 2012

Unlicensed Episode 7: The Dating Game by Josh Hartung; Directed by Jazz Schuyler; AudioVisual Designer, Justin Plowman; Assistant Director, Nicole Lee Aiossa; Cast: Nicole Lee Aiossa, Rob Brown, Lindsey Carter, Michael DeRensis, Adam Files, Stephen Heskett, Josh Mertz, Cara Moretto, Tom O'Connor, Amy Overman, Amy Beth Sherman, Jason Unfried, Theresa Unfried; UNDER St. Marks; March 18-19, 2012

Unlicensed Episode 8: The Greatest American Heroes by Josh Hartung; Directed by Jazz Schuyler; AudioVisual Designer, Justin Plowman; Assistant Director, Eric Chase; Assistant Director, Stephen Heskett; Choreographer, Nicole Lee Aiossa; Additional music by John Gideon and Andrew Neesley; Cast: Nicole Lee Aiossa, George Bronos, Michael DeRensis, Emily Edwards, Adam Files, Rachel Grundy, Cedric Jones, Bob Laine, Josh Mertz, Cara Moretto, Tom O'Connor, Amy Overman, Amy Beth Sherman, Jason Unfried, Theresa Unfried, David Berent, Rob Brown, Lindsey; UNDER St. Marks; April 15-16, 2012

E-Merging Writers

www.emergingwriters.com

Stabilized Not Controlled by Frank Blocker; Directed by Jeffrey Edward Peters; Lighting Designer, Jeremy Neal; Set Designer, Edward Morris; Costume Designer, Murray Scott Changar; Sound Designer, Kenneth Allen and Kathy Kelly Christos; Cast: Frank Blocker; Choreographer, Kathy Kelly Christos; Stage Left Studios; May 6-August 12. 2012

Edge In Motion Theatre Company

The Meeting with Stanley by Lloyd Pace; Directed by Shelby-Allison Hibbs; Stage Manager, Elize Simon; Lighting Designer, Phil Waller; Costume Designer, Toni Portacci; Sound Designer, Toni Portacci; Cast: Lindsay-Elizabeth Hand, Justin Waldo, Keith Chandler, Alex Estrada, Christy Richardson, Rachel Riendeau; ; Urban Stages; January 12 – 22, 2012

Ego Actus

www.EgoActus.com

Co-Artistic Directors, Bruce A. Kraemer and Joan Kane

i-Pod by Natalie Menna; Directed by Joan Kane; Stage Manager, Shawn Banerjee; Lighting Designer, Bruce A. Kraemer; Set Designer, Starlet Jacobs; Costume Designer, Cat Fisher; Sound Designer, Bruce A. Kraemer; Cast: Nandita Chandra; Jewel Box; July 19 - 31, 2011

Aliens with Extraordinary Skills by Saviana Stanescu; Directed by Joan Kane; Stage Manager, Jennifer Ainsworth; Lighting Designer, Bruce A Kraemer; Set Designer, Starlet Jacobs; Costume Designer, Erica E. Evans; Sound Designer, Ian Wehrle; Assistant Set Designer Jara Belmonte; Assistant Lighting Designer Melissa Joakim; Balloon Consultant Cat Migliaccio; Pole Dance Consultant Carolyn Chiu; Audition Readers Emma Myers & Jenny Vallencourt; Box Office Staff Jenny Fersch & Gus Ferrari; Cast: Viet Vo, Debby Brand, Gabrielle Young, Richard Zekaria, Abby Rockwell Savage, Doug Rossi; Theatre 54; November 2–20, 2011

New York City Icon Plays; *Francine* by Robin Rice Lichtig, Directed by Rob Weinstein; *Charlie in Central Park* by Penny Jackson, Directed by Sebastian Agdur Nyman; *6 Train to Vermeer* by Marc Lamberg, directed by Evan T. Cummings; *Let Bygones Be* by Zanne Hall, Directed by Emily Cornelius; *Aboard the Molinari* by Bara Swain, Directed by Bara Swain; *Pizza for Life* by Melissa Skirboll, Directed by Melissa Skirboll; Set Designer, Starlet Jacobs; Lighting Designer, Melissa Joakim; Sound Designer, Ian Wehrle; Stage Manager, Katie Quigley; Press Representative, Michael Martinez; Box Office Staff, Jenny Fersch & Gus Ferrari; Theater 54; November 6-19

Pizza Man by Darlene Craviotto; Directed by Joan Kane; Stage Manager, Mary Elsey; Lighting Designer, Bruce A. Kraemer; Set Designer, Stephanie Fallone; Costume Designer, Erica E. Evans; Sound Designer, Ian Wehrle; Press Representative, Michael Martinez; Scene Painter, Chantale Bourdages; Master Carpenter, Jessica Phillips; Cast: Jillian Severin, Danielle Beckmann, Richard Zekaria; Bridge Theatre; January 16 - 29, 2012

Ensemble Studio Theatre

www.ensemblestudiotheatre.org

Personal History Volumes I-V: abridged by Rachel Bonds, Joshua Conkel, Patrick Link, Anna Moench & Jason Gray Platt; Directed by Jason Bruffy, Jessica Fisch, Morgan Gould, Heidi Handelsman & Pirronne Yousefzadeh; Stage Manager, Anna Kroup; Lighting Designer, Lois Catanzaro; Set Designer, Brett Banakis; Costume Designer, Melissa Trn; Sound Designer, Anthony Spinelli;

Cast: Allison Altman, Denny Bess, Evan Enderle, Timur Kocak, Kate Levy, Maria McConville, Anna O'Donoghue, Katie Schorr, Kim Tolksdorf, Amanda Tudesco, Amir Wachterman; Ensemble Studio Theatre; June 29 – 30, 2011

ETdC Projects' Lab

www.etdcprojects.org

Producing/Artistic Director, Roi Escudero; Production Manager, Andy Chmelko

The Matra India (Matinee, Ah Muzen Cab and the Bees, and **The Matra India)** Written and Directed by Roi Escudero; Stage Manager, Valentin Ewan; Lighting, Set, Costume, Sound and AudioVisual Designer, Roi Escudero; Production Manager, Andy Chmelko; Technical Director, James Holland; Assistant Designer, Mika Oyaizu; Tango and Swing Choreographers, Mika Oyaizu and Alex Orzeck Byrnes; Atmospheric Virtual Painting, James Ewan; Infrared Image, Bob Trongone; House Manager, Jenny Huang; Cast: Roi Escudero, Andy Chmelko, Mika Oyaizu, Alex Orzeck-Byrnes, and special video appearance by Rubén Celiberti; Presented as part of Planet Connections Theatre Festivity 2011; The Robert Moss Theater; June 8 - 24, 2012

ETHOS Performing Arts

www.ethosperformingarts.org

The Family Room by Aron Eli Coleite; Directed by Gwenyth Reitz; Stage Manager, Shelby Taylor Love; Lighting Designer, Jeanette Yew; Set Designer, Jian Jung; Costume Designer, Amanda Seymour; Sound Designer, Culley Johnson; Cast: Tyler Lea, David M. Pincus, Nancy Stone, Coco Medvitz, Jonathan Tindle, Jacqueline Sydney, Leah Barker; ArcLight Theatre; September 30 – October 23, 2011

Extant Arts

www.extantarts.org

Corner Pocker by Andy James Hoover; Directed by Bridget R. Durkin; Stage Manager, Anna Burnham; Lighting Designer, Elizabeth Coco; Set Designer, Jeremy Doucette; Costume Designer, Tristan Raines; Sound Designer, Jared Singer; Puppets Design, Chana Porter; Cast: Alexandra Hellquist, James Liebman, Virginia Logan, Kari Swenson Riely, Mary Schneider, Eric Sutton; Gene Frankel Theatre; October 8 – 23, 2011

F*It Club

www.f-itclub.tumblr.com

The Spring Fling: My Best/Worst Date Ever by Lucy Boyle; Directed by Stephen Brackett, Tamara Fisch, Victor Maog, Kate Pines, & Jerry Ruiz; Stage Manager, Joe Mulica; Set Designer, Sarah Martin & Sara Nelson; Lighting Designer, David Sexton; Sound Designer, Mark Parenti; Costume Designer, Whitney Anne Adams; Cast: Jon Bass, Paul Coffey, Allyson Morgan, Topher Mikels, Emily Young, Bobby Moreno, Kevin Dwyer, Amanda Duarte, Stephen Graybill, Kate Dearing, Marty Brown, Mara Kassin, & Yuval Boim; IRT Theatre; April 26 – May 13, 2012

Fault Line Theatre

www.faultlinetheatre.com

Artistic Director, Aaron Rossini; Associate Artistic Director, Craig Wesley Divino; Associate Artistic Director, Tristan Jeffers; Communications Director, Matt Clevy

Frogs by Aristophanes; Directed by Aaron Rossini; Musical Director, Eric Thomas Johnson; Stage Manager, Jamie Steffen; Lighting Designer, John Eckert; Set Designer, Tristan Jeffers; Costume Designer, Allison Crutchfield; Dramaturg and Assistant Director, Brandt Adams; Intern and House Manager, John Racioppo; Backstage Crew, Nina Alexander and Matthew Keating; Lighting Assistant, Mitch Ost; Cast: Matt Clevy, Rachel Christopher, Craig Wesley Divino, Rebecca Gibel, Karl Gregory, Scott Raker, Haas Regen, Blake Segal, Rudi Utter; Understudies: John Tracey and Rich Williams; 4th Street Theatre; November 4 - 19, 2011

From the Same Cloth by Megan Auster-Rosen; Directed by Aaron Rossini; Stage Manager, Jamie Steffen; Lighting Designer, John Eckert; Set Designer, Tristan Jeffers; Costume Designer, Sarita Fellows; Voice and Speech Coach, Craig Wesley Divino; House Manager, Matt Clevy; Intern, John Racioppo; Cast: Megan Auster-Rosen, Jacques Roy; The Shell Theatre; April 5 - 15, 2012

From White Plains Written and Directed by Michael Perlman; Stage Manager, Kevin Clutz; Lighting Designer, John Eckert; Set Designer, Tristan Jeffers; Sound Designer, Chad Raines; AudioVisual Designer, John Racioppo; House Manager, Matt Clevy; Intern, John Racioppo; Cast: Craig Wesley Divino, Karl Gregory, Jimmy King, Aaron Rossini; La Tea Theater; May 31 - June 10, 2012

Femme Fatale Theater

Artistic Director, Robert Ribar; Producing Director Stephen Gribbin

Salome by Oscar Wilde; Directed by Robert Ribar; Stage Manager, Paul Xuereb; Lighting Designer, William Noguchi; Set Designer, Jason Sherwood; Costume Designer, Danielle Mahoney; Sound Designer, Robert Ribar; Original Music, Ryan Marino, Brian Chillemi; Choreographer, Ben Hobbs; Cast: Davi Santos, John C. Hume, Danny Baird, Daniel Destefano, Francisco Huergo, Frankie Lapace, Nick Moore, Eugene Michael Santiago, Ian Schulz; The Secret Theatre; October 6 – 16, 2011

Firebrand Theory Theater Company

Coat Check Casanova by Jaime Robert Carrillo; Directed by Joshua Benson; Stage Manager, Cate DiGirolamo; Lighting Designer, Justin Hoffecker; Set Designer, Jenn Tash; Costume Designer, Kelly Kasper; Sound Designer, Amy Yourd; Associate Producers, Vincent Graham, Ashley Adelman; Choreographer, Sean Scantelbury; Assistant Stage Manager, Laura Meltzer; Cast: Greg Bornstein, Jaime Robert Carrillo, Keldrick Crowder, Julia Falamas, Laura Ferland, Isa Frias, Ellie Jameson, Lindsey Larkin, Jill Maybruch, Matt McAllister; The Living Theatre; Jun 24 - July 9, 2011

Firework Theater

firework theater.com

The Pillow Book by Anna Moench; Directed by David F. Chapman; Stage Manager, Meredith Brown; Lighting & Set Designer, Maruti Evans; Costume Designer, Heather Klar; Original Music, Michael Wall & Darren Morze; Cast: Eric Bryant, Julie Fitzpatrick, Vanessa Wasche; 59 E 59 Theaters; August 4 – 20, 2011

The Flea Theater

www.theflea.org

Artistic Director, Jim Simpson; Producing Director, Carol Ostrow; Managing Director, Beth Dembrow; Technical Director, Liz Blessing

Encyclopedia Performed and Created by Molly Chanoff, Rose Calucchia, Sarah Dey Hirshan, Calia Marshall, Laura Montgomery Sarah East Johnson, Lollo Romanski, Allison Schnur; Visual and Sound Designers, Nancy Brooks Brody,

DJ Tikka Masala, Alison May, Jocelyn Davis, Wayne Schrengohst and Gretchen Hildebran; Produced by LAVA – www.lavabrooklyn.org; The Flea; June 2 – 12, 2011

She Kills Monsters by Qui Nguyen; Directed by Robert Ross Parker; Set & Lighting Designer, Nick Francone, Costume Designer, Jessica Pabst, Sound Designer, Shane Rettig, Puppet Designer, David Valentine, Properties and Assistant Set Designer, Kate Sinclair Foster, Fight Director, Mike Chin, Choreographer, Emily Edwards, Assistant Sound Designer, Patrick Metzger, Stage Manager, Michelle Kelleher; Cast: Satomi Blair, Allison Buck, Ugo Chukwu, Jack Corcoran, Edgar Eguia, Cleo Grey, Raul Sigmund Julia, Annabel Lalonde, Bruce A. Lemon, Sean McIntyre, Megha Nabe, Margaret Odette, Brett Ashley Robinson, and Nicky Schmidlein; The Flea; November 4 – December 23, 2011

Working on a Special Day by Jonas Hassen Khemiri and Toshiki Okada; Lighting Designer, Gabriel Pascal; Sound Designer, Rodrigo Espinosa; Costume Designer, Ana GrahamProduced by The Play Company - www.playco.org; The Flea; January 5 – 15, 2012

The Electric Lighthouse by Ed Hime; Directed by Kristan Seemel; Stage Manager, Michelle Foster; Lighting Designer, Jonathan Cottle; Set Designer, Kate Foster; Costume Designer, Lara de Bruijn; Sound Designer, Colin Whitely; Cast: Seth Moore, Stephen Stout, Jack Corcoran, Allison Buck, Margaret Odette, Glenna Grant, Morgan Everitt; Flea Theatre; May 1 – 15, 2012

The Wundelsteipen (and Other Difficult Roles for Young People) by Nick Jones; Directed by Tom Costello; Stage Manager, Laura Been; Lighting Designer, Jonathan Cottle; Set Designer, Kate Foster; Costume Designer, Nicole Wee; Sound Designer, Stowe Nelson; Puppet Design, Robin Frohardt; Original Music, Corn Mo; Cast: Hannah Corrigan, Tommy Crawford, Eric Folks, Alex Herrald, Maren Langdon, Briana Pozner, Donaldo Prescod, Dominic Spillane; Flea Theatre; May 2 – 23, 2012

A Letter From Omdurman by Jeffrey M. Jones; Directed by Page Burkholder; Stage Manager, JuLondre Brown; Lighting Designer, Jonathan Cottle; Set Designer, Kate Foster; Costume Designer, Whitney Locher; Sound Designer, Colin Whitely; Cast: Matt Barbot, Veracity Butcher, Eric Folks, Will Turner, Wilton YYeung; Flea Theatre; May 5 – 27, 2012

WORKSHOPS

Mark of Cain by Matthew Harris and Terry Quinn; Directed by Eugenia Arsenis; Music Director, Kelly Horsted; Part of the NewOp Week: CCO Development Series; The Flea; March 27, 2012

The Human Zoo by Mark N. Grant; Directed by Eugenia Arsenis; Music Director, Kelly Horsted; Part of the NewOp Week: CCO Development Series; The Flea; March 27, 2012

ADA Music by Kim Sherman; Libretto by Margaret Vandenburg; Directed by Lisa Rothe; Music Director, Kimberly Grigsby; Pianist, Michael Pilafian; Part of the NewOp Week: CCO Development Series; The Flea; March 28, 2012

Big Jim and the Small-Time Investors Music by Eric Salzman; Libretto adapted by Eric Salzman from a work by Ned Jackson; Directed by Antoine Laprise; Music Director, Michael Fennelly Part of the NewOp Week: CCO Development Series; The Flea; March 29, 2012

Flux Theatre Ensemble

www.fluxtheatre.org

Artistic Director, August Schulenburg; Producing Director, Heather Cohn; Communications Director, Kelly O'Donnell; Marketing Director, Isaiah Tanenbaum; Creative Partners: Matthew Archambault, Will Lowry, Kia Rogers, Tiffany Clementi

Ajax in Iraq by Ellen McLaughlin; Directed by August Schulenburg; Stage Manager, Jodi Witherell; Lighting Designer, Kia Rogers; Set Designer, Will Lowry; Costume Designer, Lara de Bruijn; Sound Designer, Asa Wember; Cast: Matthew Archambault, Tiffany Clementi, Sol Crespo, Joshua Koopman, Mike Mihm, Stephen Conrad Moore, Lori E. Parquet, Anna Rahn, Christina Shipp, Raushanah Simmons, Chudney Sykes, Chinaza Uche; Flamboyan Theatre - CSV Cultural Center; June 3 – 25, 2011

Menders by Erin Browne; Directed by Heather Cohn; Stage Manager, Jodi Witherell; Lighting Designer, Kia Rogers; Set Designer, Cory Rodriguez; Costume Designer, Will Lowry; Sound Designer, Asa Wember; Video Design, Trevor James Martin; Cast: Matt Archambault, Isaiah Tanenbaum, Sol Crespo, Mike Mihm, Vivia Font, Raushanah Simmons, Ingrid Nordstrom; The Gym at Judson; January 20 – February 11, 2012

DEINDE by August Schulenburg; Directed by Heather Cohn; Stage Manager, Jodi Witherell; Lighting Designer, Kia Rogers; Set Designer, Will Lowry; Costume Designer, Stephanie Levin; Sound Designer, Martha Goode; Cast: Ken Glickfeld, David Ian Lee, Isaiah Tanenbaum, Rachael Hip-Flores, Nita Vidyasagar, Matthew Murumba, Matthew Trumbull, Sol Crespo, Alyssa Simon; The Secret Theatre; April 28 – May 12, 2012

Foolish Theatre Company

www.foolishtheatre.org

Executive Producing Artistic Director, Rick Tormone; Relatively Artistic Director, Rich Orloff

HA! by Rich Orloff; Directed by Ric Sechrest; Stage Manager, Kate Dial; Lighting Designer, Richard Kent Green; Set Designer, Meagan Miller-McKeever; Costume Designer, Holly Rihn; Sound Designer, Bessimka Bessinovna; Production Manager, Jessi Blue Gormezano; Cast: Jarel Davidow, Anne Fizzard, Gerrianne Raphael, Mike Smith Rivera, Evan Thompson; Co-production with WorkShop Theater Company; The Jewel Box Theatre; March 30 – April 15, 2012

Fn Do it Productions

Vampure by Mary Ann Hedderson & LJ Regine; Directed by Joshua John McKay; Stage Manager, Justine Harrison; Cast: Mary Ann Hedderson, Scott Jernigan, Joe Kurtz, Mark Merritt, Edie Monroy, Rachel Myers, Abigail Raye, LJ Regine, Robert Stubbs and Cristina Velez; Richmond Shepard Theatre; October 8 – December 17, 2011

Foxhole Productions

www.kingsriverplay.com

King's River by Andrew Rosenberg and Ean Miles Kessler; Directed by David Delaney; Stage Manager, Cassandra Levey; Lighting Designer, Jeff Carr; Costume Designer, Courtney Wheeler; Cast: Gwynneth Bensen, Jasmine Carmichael, Mara Gannon, Ean Miles Kessler, Ruffin Prentiss, Andrew Rosenberg, Terrell Wheeler, Tim Giles, Dalton Grey and Landon Woodson; Medicine Show Theatre; May 22 – June 10, 2012

Freshly Squeezed Juices Theatre Company

www.gutstheplay.com

Director/Producer, Shoshona Currier; Associate Producer, Kelcie Beene

Guts: A Multi-Media Fantasia Written and Performed by Liat Ron; Directed by Shoshona Currier; Stage Manager, Zhenesse Heinemann; Lighting Designer, Jason Jeunnette; Set Designer, Eric Beauzay; Costume Designer, Sydney Maresca; Sound Designer, Elisabeth Rhodes; Video Design, Kaz Phillips; Choreographer, Liat Ron; 9th Space; November 3-20, 2011

FullStop Collective

www.fullstopcollective.org

Unville Brazil by Patrick Shaw; Directed by Brian Hashimoto; Lighting Designer, Lois Catanzaro; Set Designer, Jacquelyn D. Marolt; Costume Designer, Abbie Chase; Original Music, Patrick Shaw; Cast: Elizabeth Seldin, Lauren Weinberg, Charity Schubert; Drilling Company Theatre Lab; June 1 – 11, 2011

Funny...Shesh Productions

www.funnysheesh.com

Artistic Director, Jason S. Grossman; Managing Director, Amber Gallery; Founder, Karen Christie Ward; Video Directors, Ryan Stadler and Keith Chandler; Actors, Tori Watson, Kaira Klueber, Allen Warnock, Andrea Big

Doubles Crossed by Jason S. Grossman; Directed by Amber Gallery; Musical Director, Sharon Fogarty; Stage Manager, Joshua Levin; Lighting Designer, Ryan Metzler; Set Designer, Giovanni Villari; Costume Designer, Catherine Siracusa & Sidney Levitt; Sound and AudioVisual Designers, Giovanni Villari & Amber Gallery; Assistant Director, Jaq Sarah French; Postcard/Image Designer, Nick Dransfield; Video Director, Keith Chandler; Piano, Peter Dizozza; Cast: Gregory Cohan, Steve Deighan, Victoria Guthrie, Jim Heaphy, James Holden, Cindy Keiter, Monica Blaze Leavitt, Ron Roth, Ryan Stadler, Allen Warnock, Tori Watson; The Robert Moss Theater; June 1 - 13, 2012

G- Money Productions

www.planetconnections.org

Alba; Directed by Glory Kadigan; Stage Manager, Jenna Dolittle and Shawn Banerjee; Lighting Designer, Christopher Weston; Set Designer, Cory Rodriguez; Costume Designer, David Thompson; Sound Designer, Jacob Subotnick; Fight Choreographer, Nicholas Santasier; Choreographer, Joe Barros, Laura Brandel and Glory Kadigan; Cast: Mariel Matero, Kelly Zekas, Dana Hunter, Tatiana Gomberg, Susan Wallack, Sarah Doudna, Sharon Hunter, Barbara Mundy, Jessica Cermak, Janelle Zapata, Amada Anderson, Tania Jeudy, Danielle Patsakos, Natalia Duong, Mary Sheridan, Victoria Lauzun, Rebecca Joh; Gene Frankel Theatre; November 5 – 20, 2011

The Gallery Players

www.galleryplayers.com

Macbeth by William Shakespeare; Directed by Mark Harborth; Stage Manager, Becky J. Doster; Lighting Designer, Christopher Weston; Costume Designer, Beverly Bullock; Sound Designer, Jacob Subotnick; Assistant Director, Sidney Fortner; Fight Choreographer, Joe Travers; Scenic Artist, Jackie McCarthy; Assistant Stage Manager, Tim Sheridan; Cast: Graham Stuart Allen, Dave Benger, Bryn Carter, Brendan Cataldo, David Patrick Ford, Sidney Fortner, Joel Fullerton, Marcus Denard Johnson, Jara Jones, Mark Kinch, Arthur Koster, James Meneses, Seth D. Rabinowitz, Dan Snow, Minna Taylor, and Hannah Timmons; produced in association with Dominic Cuskern Gallery Players; July 21 – 31, 2011

The Little Dog Laughed by Douglas Carter Beane; Directed by Patrick Vassel; Stage Manager, Matt Remington; Lighting Designer, Heather Sparling; Set Designer, Chris Minard; Costume Designer, Ryan Moller; Cast: Brian Siebert, Maeve Yore, Jake Mendes, Tania Verafield; Gallery Players of Park Slope; September 10 – 25, 2011

Little Shop of Horrors Book and Lyrics by Howard Ashman; Music by Alan Menken; Directed by Joe Barros; Stage Manager, Katharine S. Fergerson; Lighting Designer, Dan Jobbins; Set Designer, Harlan Penn; Costume Designer, Ryan Moeller; Sound Designer, Julianne Merrill & Brett Jarvis; Puppet Design, Fergus J. Walsh and Michael Bush; Choreographer, Joe Barros; Cast: Tamala Baldwin, Thomas Bradfield, Debra Thais Evans, Ryan Hilliard, Emily McNamara, Vasthy Mompoint, Babs Rubenstein, Paul Sadlik, Philip Jackson Smith; Gallery Players of Park Slope; October 22 – November 13, 2011

Reckless by Craig Lucas; Directed by Heather Siobhan Curran; Stage Manager, Ashley Nelson; Lighting Designer, Annie Wiegand; Set Designer, Jason Sherwood; Costume Designer, Kristina Sneshkoff; Sound Designer, Julianne Merrill; Cast: Carey Van Driest, Jan-Peter Pedross, Lauren Roth, Zac Hoogendyk, Lara Knox, Allison Moody, Jason Jacoby; Gallery Players of Park Slope; December 3 – 18, 2011

A Man of No Importance Music by Stephen Flaherty; Lyrics by Lynn Ahrens; Book by Terrence McNally; Directed by Hans Friedrichs; Stage Manager, Andrew Goddard; Lighting Designer, Dan Jobbins; Set Designer, Kate Rance; Costume Designer, Sarah Cogan; Sound Designer, Julian Evans; Projection Designer, Daniel Heffernan; Choreographer, Christine O'Grady; Cast: Charlie Owens, Renee Claire Bergeron, Eric Morris, Julianne Katz, Katie Bruestle, Greg Horton, Danny Randerson, John Weigand, Eric Folks, Megan Opalinski, Lorinne Lampert, Rachel Green, Spencer Robinson, Adam Kee, Eric William Love, Jake Mendes, Sean Patrick Murtagh; Gallery Players of Park Slope; January 28 – February 19, 2012

A Raisin in the Sun by Lorraine Hansberry; Directed by Reginald L. Douglas; Stage Manager, Kristine Schlachter; Lighting Designer, Jake Fine; Set Designer, Casha Jacot-Guillarmod; Costume Designer, Roejendra Adams; Sound Designer, Jacob Subotnick; Cast: Sameerah Luqmaan-Harris, Ross Johnson, Kwaku Driskell, Hope Harley, Brittany Bellizeare, Arthur James Solomon, Gregory Cohan, Gil Charleston, Shawn Herb; Gallery Players of Park Slope; March 17 – April 1, 2012

Wonderful Town Music by Leonard Bernstein; Lyrics by Betty Comden and Adolph Green; Book by Joseph Fields and Jerome Chodorov; Directed by Mark Harborth; Stage Manager, Becky J. Doster; Lighting Designer, Scott Cally; Set Designer, William Davis; Costume Designer, Jevyn Nelms; Sound Designer, Josh Millican; Choreographer, Trey Mitchell and Elyse Daye Hart; Cast: Brian Bailey, Monica Bradley, Ronn Burton, Brad Giovanine, A J Hughes, Maureen Kelley, Matt Kiernan, Maggie Marino, Alida Michal, Lindsay Sutton; Gallery Players of Park Slope; April 28 – May 20, 2012

Gemini CollisionWorks

collisionwork.livejournal.com

Arts, Ian W. Hill; Crafts, Berit A. Johnson

Funnybook/Tragicbook by Adam McGovern; Directed by Ian W. Hill; Stage Manager, Berit Johnson; Lighting and Sound Designer, Ian W. Hill; Projections & Graphics, Stefano Pavan; Mirko Benotto; Giuseppe Palumbo; Cast: Ian W. Hill, Rasheed Hinds, Gavin Starr Kendall, Amy Overman, Shelley Ray, Tom Reid, Adam Swiderski; The Brick; June 4-19, 2011

Antrobus Written and Directed by Ian W. Hill; Stage Manager, Berit Johnson; Lighting and Sound Designer, Ian W. Hill; Costume Designer, Karen Flood; Cast: David Arthur Bachrach, Michael McKim, Patrice Miller, Victoria Miller, William Webber, Bill Weeden, Brian Miskell; The Brick; August 13 - 28, 2011 and January 27 - February 11, 2012

Gone Written and Directed by Ian W. Hill; Stage Manager, Berit Johnson; Lighting Designer, Ian W. Hill; Costume Designer, Karen Flood; Cast: Ivanna Cullinan, Alyssa Simon; The Brick; August 13 - September 1, 2011 and January 27 - February 11, 2012

ObJects Written and Directed by Ian W. Hill; Stage Manager, Berit Johnson; Lighting and Sound Designer, Ian W. Hill; Cast: George Bronos, Josephine Cashman, Samantha Erenberger, Saara Falk, Arthur Griffith, Cara Moretto, Nicholas Miles Newton, Leila Okafor, Justin Plowman, Jack Schaub, Rokia L. Shearin, Joy Song, Anna Stefanic, Gyda Arber, Patrick Thomas Cann, Lindsey Carter, Michael Jefferson, Christian Toth; co-produced with The Brick Theater, Inc.; The Brick; August 11-28, 2011 and January 29 - February 11, 2012

Gideon Productions

gideonth.com

Advance Man by Mac Rogers; Directed by Jordana Williams; Stage Manager, Devan Hibbard; Lighting Designer, Sarah Lurie; Set Designer, Saundra Yaklin; Costume Designer, Amanda Jenks; Sound Designer, Jeanne Travis; Cast: Shaun B. Wilson, Becky Beyers, Becky Comtois, Amanda Duarte, Brian Silliman, Abraham Makany, Jason Howard, David Rosenblatt, Kristen Vaughan, Sean Williams; Secret Theatre; January 12 – 29, 2012

Blast Radius by Mac Rogers; Directed by Jordana Williams; Stage Manager, Devan Hibbard; Lighting Designer, Jennifer Wilcox; Set Designer, Sandy Yaklin; Costume Designer, Amanda Jenks; Sound Designer, Jeanne Travis; Special Effects, Zoe Morsette; Cast: Becky Byers, David Rosenblatt, Jason Howard, Kristen Vaughan, Nancy Sirianni, Adam Swiderski, Cotton Wright, Alisha Spielmann, Seth Shelden, Amy Lee Pearsall, Felicia Hudson, Joe Mathers; Secret Theatre; March 30 – April 14, 2012

GO AlleyCat Productions

www.goalleycat.com

Co-Producing Directors, Alex Goldberg and Catia Ojeda

It is Done by Alex Goldberg; Directed by Tom Wojtunik; Stage Manager, Amanda-Mae Goodridge; Lighting Designer, Christopher Thielking; Set Designer, Tim McMath; Sound Designer, Colin Whitely; Assistant Stage Manager, Lisa Haedrich; Cast: Matt Kalman, Catia Ojeda, Ean Sheehy Co-produced with 22Q Entertainment, this was a site-specific production set in a bar; The Mean Fiddler; November 7, 2011 - January 24, 2012

Go Into Her Room Productions

www.inthesummerpavilion.com

In The Summer Pavilion by Paul Young; Directed by Kathy Mc Gowan; Cast: Meena Dimian, Ryan Barry and Julie Taylor Ross; produced in association with The Present Company; The Living Theatre; August 13 - 22, 2011

GOH Productions

www.gohproductions.org

Executive and Artistic Director, Bonnie Sue Stein

Golem Written and Directed by Vit Horejs; Stage Manager, Michael; Lighting Designer, Federico Restrepo; Set Designer, Roman Hladik; Costume Designer, Boris Caksiran; Marionette Desginer, Jakub Krejci; Original Music, Frank London; Cast: Alan Barnes Netherton, Deborah Beshaw, Ronnie Wasserstrom; Choreographer, Naomi Goldberg Haas; produced in association with La MaMa ETC; La MaMa Experimental Theatre; November 11 – December 4, 2011

Going to Tahiti Productions

www.goingtotahitiproductions.com

Skin Flesh Bone by Camilla Ammirati; Directed by Jessica Ammirati; Stage Manager, Laura Bultman; Lighting Designer, Sam Gordon; Set Designer, Duc Le; Sound Designer, Patrick Metzger; Original Music, Camilla Ammirati; Cast: Kiwi Callahan, David Eiduks, Gavin Alexander Hammon, Laurel Lockhart, Maria Silverman; Choreographer, Dana Boll; Secret Theatre; June 15 – 25, 2011

Full Disclosure by Ruth McKee; Directed by Jessica Ammirati; Set Designer, Becky Sagen; Cast: Kiwi Callahan; The Secret Theatre; December 7 – 18, 2011

Cat Lady Without A Cat Created and Performed by Carrie Keskinen; Directed by Scotty Watson; The Secret Theatre; March 9 – 10, 2012

Gracye Productions

www.gracyproductions.org

Artistic Director, Todd Michael; Resident Director, Lawrence Lesher; Costume & Set Designer, David L. Zwiers; Lighting & Sound Designer, Louis Lopardi

The Asphalt Christmas by Todd Michael; Directed by Lawrence Lesher; Stage Manager, Samantha Kennedy; Lighting and Sound Designer, Louis Lopardi; Set Designer, Lawrence Lesher and David L. Zwiers; Costume Designer, David L. Zwiers; Cast: Courtney Cook, Timothy J. Cox, Nancy Kellogg Gray, Matt Harris, Brian Hopson, Chris Kateff, Jessica Luck, Todd Michael, David L. Zwiers; Theatre Row Studio Theatre; December 8 - 18, 2012

The Great Recession Theatre

www.greatrecessiontheatre.com

Director/Producer, Dorota Krimmel; Executive Producer, Janusz Marecki; Production Manager, Melanie Derblich

The Confusions of Young Torless Based on the novel by Robert Musil; Adapted by Dorota Krimmel; Directed by Dorota Krimmel and Frank-Thomas Grogan; Stage Manager, Troy Bedik; Lighting Designer, Casey Rowe; Set Designer, The Great Recession Theatre; Costume Designer, Cat Fisher; Sound Designer, Karol Nowicki; Sound Effects, Grzegorz Swirszcz; Fight Director, Ben Rezendes; Cast: Ryan Wesley Brown, Ben Rezendes, David Delaney, Logan Reed, Kathi Carlson, Dean Schildkraut, Brian Hendricks, Mark Belnick, Dorota Krimmel, Troy Bedik; The Looking Glass Theatre; January 21- February 11, 2012

Ground Up Productions

www.GroundUpProductions.org

Pratfalls by Holly Webber; Directed by Jenn Thompson; Stage Manager, Devan Elise Hibbard; Lighting Designer, Travis McHale; Set Designer, Travis McHale; Costume Designer, Amanda Jenks; Cast: Victor Verhaeghe, Kate Middleton, Matthew Baldiga, Amelia White; Abingdon Theatre Complex; April 29 – May 19, 2012

The Group Theatre Too

www.grouptheatretoo.org

Artistic Director, Michael Blevins; Executive Producer, Justin Boccitto

Career by James Lee; Directed by Justin Boccitto; Cast: Nicky Romaniello, Cristina Vivenzio, Ariel Frenkel, Suzanne Lenz, Christine De Frece, Steven Bidwell, Dan Mian, Curtis Roth, Michael Mulligan, Isaac Dayley; The Drilling Company Theater; Monday, June 13, 2011

New York by David Rimmer; Directed by David Rimmer; Stage Manager, Allison Schneider; Lighting, Set and Sound Designer, Tim Ruppen; Costume Designer, Ramona Ponce; Producer, Justin Boccitto; Interior Designer, Alexandra Bocon; Assistant to Producer, Jenna Dioguardi; Casting Consultant, Philip Jostrom; Technical Assistant, Eric Barron; Photographer, Vanessa Gualdron; Cast: Polly Adams, Megan Berg, Steven Bidwell, Elaine Bromka, Bob Ferreira, Catherine Hyland, Lauren Leland, Michelangelo Milano, Kathleen Peirce, Skyler Pinkerton, Scott Price, Jen Ryan, Tom Tinelli, Kaylee Torres, Jennifer Laine Williams; Hudson Guild Theater; September 8 - 11, 2011

Provincetown 2012 by Eugene O'Neill, Louise Bryant, Floyd Dell, Pendleton King; Directed by Victor Avila, Jeff Brelvi, Stephanie Sine, Justin Boccitto; Stage Manager, Allison Schneider; Lighting Designer, Cristina Vivenzio; Assistant Director, Michelle Kuchuk; Cast: Cristina Marie, Christine de Frece, Lexie Speirs, Crystal Chapman, Brittany Jeffrey, Dylan Paige, Jennifer Avila, Alex Maxwell, Nicky Romaniello, Justin Boccitto, Steven Bidwell & Michael Hoyt; The Drilling Company Theater; March 27 & April 3, 2012

Choreographer's Canvas 2012 Directed by Justin Boccitto; Stage Manager, Cristina Vivenzio; Lighting Designer, Tim Ruppen; Production Assistant, Shannon Chapman; Graphic Designer, Alex Maxwell; Cast: Michael Blevins, Bob Boross, Lou Brock, Crystal Chapman, Ginger Cox, Karen Gayle, David Guggino, Bobby Hedglin, Taylor, Becky Moyer, Lainie Munro, Sue Samuels, Caleb Teicher, Aaron Tolson, Sidney Erik Wright, Hee Ra Yoo, Eryn Renee Young, Broadway Dance Center's AIM & Tony Stevens; Manhattan Movement and Arts Center; May 10, 2012

Haberdasher Theatre Inc.

www.haberdashertheatre.com

Adam of the Apes by Oliver Thrun; Directed by Joshua M. Feder; The Drilling Company Theatre; June 16 - 25, 2011

Hard Sparks

www.hardsparks.com

Artistic Director, J.Stephen Brantley; Executive Producer, Robert M. Lohman

Eightythree Down by J.Stephen Brantley; Directed by Daniel Talbott; Stage Manager, Amanda Michaels and Alex Mark; Lighting Designer, Brad Peterson; Set Designer, Eugenia Furneaux; Costume Designer, Tristan Raines; Sound Designer, Janie Bullard; Cast: Melody Bates, Ian Holcomb, Bryan Kaplan, Brian Miskell; produced in association with Horse Trade Theatre Group; UNDER St. Marks; September 1-9, 2011

Love In The Time Of Chlamydia Written and Performed by Nicole Pandolfo; Directed by Jonathan Warman; Stage Manager, Alison Carroll; Sound Designer, Janie Bullard; AudioVisual Designer, J.Stephen Brantley; Presented by Frigid NYC; UNDER St. Marks; February 22 - March 4, 2012

Harry Diesel Productions

www.boygetsgirltheplay.com

Artistic Directors, Kate Dulcich and Shaun Gunning

Boy Gets Girl by Rebecca Gilman; Directed by Michael Menger; Musical Director, Jessa; Stage Manager, Connor Davis; Lighting Designer, Max Doolittle; Set Designer, David Menard; Costume Designer, Jessa-Raye Court; Sound Designer, Shaun Gunning; Cast: Kate Dulcich, Talisa Friedman, David Hudson, Kellie Johnson, William Peden, Gregory Ryan, Robert W. Smith; Access Theatre; November 3 - 20, 2011

Heiress Productions, Inc.

www.heiressproductions.org

Thirds by Jacob M. Appel; Directed by Zac Hoogendyk; Stage Manager, Karen Hashley; Lighting Designer, Andy Fritsch; Set Designer, Josh Zangen; Costume Designer, Ashley Rose Horton; Sound Designer, Anthony Mattana; Properties Designer, Dan Giesecke and Josh Zangen; Original Music, Anthony Mattana; Cast: Laura Faith, Jenna Panther, Kelly Strandemo, Leigh Williams; Lion Theatre; March 2 - 18, 2012

HERE Arts Center

www.here.org

Artistic Director, Kristin Marting; Producing Director, Kim Whitener

64 Directed by Robert Prichard; AudioVisual Designer, Ashliegh Nankivell, Alex Brook Lynn, Ann Enzminger; Created by Timothy Braun, Jennilie Brewster, Robert Prichard, Tom Tenney; Producer, Robert Prichard; Co-Producers, Tom Tenney, Ann Enzminger; Words, Timothy Braun; Painter, Jennilie Brewster; Soundscape Designer, Tom Tenney; Original Music, Brief View of the Hudson & Sean T. Hanratty; Cast: Diane O'Debra, Jeff Grow, Sean T. Hanratty, Milton Katz, Jim Melloan and Stephanie Sabelli; HERE Arts Center; March 15 - 17, 2012

Chimera by Suli Holum & Deborah Stein Lighting Designer, James Clotfelter; Set Designer, Jeremy Wilhelm; Costume Designer, Tara Webb; Sound Designer, James Sugg; AudioVisual Designer, Kate Freer & Dave Tennant; Cast: Suli Holum; HERE Arts Center; January 5 - 28, 2012

Floating Point Waves Created, Directed & Choreographed by Ximena Garnica and Shige Moriya; Lighting Designer, Shige Moriya and Solomon Weisbard; Set Designer, Ximena Garnica and Shige Moriya; Sound Designer, Jeremy Slater; Video Design, Shige Moriya; Original Music, Jeremy D. Slater; Cast: Ximena Garnica; Co-Produced with Leimay; HERE Arts Center; April 6 – 14, 2012

Lush Valley by Kristin Marting, Mahayana Landowne and Tal Yarden; Original and Adapted Text by Robert Lyons& Qui Nyguen; Direction by Kristin Marting; Video Designer, Tal Yarden; Dramaturge, Mahayana Landowne; Production Designers Oana Botez-Ban, Clint Ramos, Jane Shaw; Marc Bovino, Irene Longshore, Rudy Mungaray, Mariana Newhard, Abigail Ramsay, Suzi Takahashi, Dax Valdes, Reed Whitney & Karyn De Young; HERE Arts Center; September 8 – 24, 2011

Miranda by Kamala Sankaram, Rob Reese; Directed by Rob Reese; Musical Director, Kamala Sankaram; Stage Manager, Christine Liz Pynn, Heather Smaha; Lighting and Set Designer, Nick Francone; Costume Designer, Jacci Jaye; Audio Mixer and Sound Designer, Matt Schloss; Video Designer, Matt Tennie; Choreographer, Lauren Yalango with Christopher Grant; -Master Electrician and Light Board Operator, Heather Smaha; Live Video Mixer, Spike McCue; Video Operator, Matt Tennie; Technical Director, Nolan Kennedy; Cast: Kamala Sankaram, Drew Fleming, Pat Muchmore, Rima Fand, Ed Rosenberg, Jeff Hudgins, Jerry Miller, Eric Brenner Co-Produced with MirandaCo; HERE Arts Center; January 12 - 21, 20012

Sonnambula by Michael Bodel in collaboration with soprano Casey Cole; Arrangements by Malina Rauschenfels; Lighting Designer, Ayumu Saegusa; Puppet Designer, Lindsay Abromaitis-Smith, Kate Brehm, Kirsten Kammermeyer, Katie Sasso, Michael Bodel; Choreographer, Cheri Paige Fogleman & Katherine Lung; Original Music, Vincenzo Bellini; Musical Director, Casey Cole; Costume Designer, Hunter Kaczorowski; AudioVisual Designer, Hannah Wasileski; Additional Puppet Choreography, Lindsay Abromaitis-Smith; Additional Puppet Designer, Diana Ho; HERE Arts Center; November 10 – 19, 2011

The Three Seagulls, or MashaMashaMasha! by Jaclyn Backhaus; Directed by John Kurzynowski; Stage Manager, Dina Rodriguez; Set Designer, Marika Kent; Costume Designer, Jonathan Cottle; Sound Designer, Kate Marvin; Producer, Sydney Matthews and Reed Whitney; Cast: Celeste Arias, Jaclyn Backhaus, Michael Barringer, Robbie Baum, Caitlin Bebb, Scarlett Bermingham, Andrew Butler, Matt Carr, Matt Connolly, Nick Fesette, Leigh Jones, Nathaniel Kent, Alex Kveton, Whit Leyenberger, Christopher Norwood, Josh Odsess-Rubin, A; HERE Arts Center; March 1 - 10, 2012

Wooden by Laura Peterson; Production Manager, Jon Pope; Lighting Designer, Amanda K. Ringger; Sound Designer, Soichiro Migita; Performers: Laura Peterson, Kate Martel, Edward Rice, Janna Diamond; HERE Arts Center; November 4 – 12, 2011

FESTIVALS

CultureMart 2012: *You Are Dead. You Are Here.* by Christine Evans, Joseph Megel, Jared Mezzocchi; *City Council Meeting* by Aaron Landsman; *Botch* by

Joe Diebes; *A Marriage: 1* by Jake Margolin, Nick Vaughan; *Epyllion* by Lindsay Abromaitis-Smith; *Weights and Balances* by Bora Yoon; *Parts are Extra* by Christina Campanella & Peter Norrman; *The Strangest* by Betty Shamieh; *The Scarlet Ibis* by Stefan Weisman, David Cote; *Science Fair* by Hai-Ting Chinn; *Keep Your Electric Eye On Me* by Shaun Irons, Lauren Petty, Mei-Yin Ng; *other stories* by Alexandra Beller; HERE Arts Center; January 24 – February 11, 2012

Hit and Run Productions

You'll Be Happy When I'm Dead by Bill Rutkoski; Directed by Don Creedon; Cast: Nina Rochelle, Bill Rutkoski, Mike Rutkoski, Joan Porter and Pamela Scott; produced in association with Aching Dogs Theater Producers Club Crowne Theatre; June 8 - 19, 2011

Home Productions

Women and Guns by Steve Gold; Directed by Marc Eardley; Cast: Ramona Mallory, Lucas Van Engen, Malcom Madera and Karen Elliot; TBG Theatre; July 11 - 16, 2011

Homunculus Mask Theater

homunculusmasktheater.com

Homunculus: Reloaded Written and Choreographed by Joe Osheroff & Evan Zes; Directed by Joe Osheroff; Lighting Designer, Cat Tate Starmer; Set Designer, Jeff Wise; Costume Designer, Ghislaine Sabiti; Mask Designer, Joe Osheroff; Cast: Adriana Chavez, David DeSantis, Lauren Elder, Regina Gibson, Mel House, Jennifer Luong, Eeva Semerdjiev, William Silva, and Brett Teresa; Shetler Studio 54; April 5 – 15, 2012

Horizon Theatre Rep

www.htronline.org

Artistic Director, Rafael De Mussa; Managing Director, Andrew Cohen

Benito Cereno by Robert Lowell; Directed by Woodie King Jr.; Stage Manager, Mayra Amaya; Lighting Designer, Joyce Liao; Costume Designer, Cathy Small; Sound Designer, Jonathan Bremner; House Manager: Heesuk Chae; Dance Choreographer, Bruce Heath; Fight Choreographer, Michael Chin; Cast: With Reynaldo Piniella, Frank Mayers, Mutiyat Ade-Salu, Jaymes Jorsling, Arthur Bartow, Benjamin Thys, Abdi Ismail, Pedro Rezende, Osvaldo Chavez, Ama Birch, Uchenna Onyia, Akintunde Sogunro, Rafael De Mussa , Rowan Meyers, and Sean Christian Taylor; The Flea Theater; September 22 - October 16, 2011

Horse Trade Theater Group

www.horsetrade.info

Managing Director, Erez Ziv; Artistic Director, Heidi Grumelot; Office Manager, Marlee Walters; Artistic/Technical Liaison, Ilaria Amadasi; Technical Director, Eduardo Ramirez; Bookkeeper/Bar Manager, Shula Kaplan

Ambrosia by Kelley Nicole Girod; Directed by Nicole A. Watson; Lighting Designer, Justin King; Set Designer, Courtnay Drakos; Cast: Nick Maccarone, Sarah Stephens; The Red Room; August 11-27, 2011

Breakfast by Yusef Miller; Directed by Zoey Martinson; Cast: Juliette Jeffers, Sean C. Turner; The Red Room; August 11-27, 2011

Claire Went To France by Ben Clawson; Directed by Artem Yatsunov; Lighting Designer, Sarah Abigail Hoke-Brady; Set Designer, Jessica Parks, Sara

Sciabbarrasi; Cast: Tony Knotts,Gary Martins, Shannon Sullivan, Scott Cagney, Aliee Chan; Kraine Theatre; May 24 - 31, 2012

Dime Heroes by Eric Kingrea; Directed by Kimberly Faith Hickman; Lighting Designer, Lauren Arneson; Set Designer, Emily Suzanne Sumner; Costume Designer, Alicia Oas; Cast: Brett Dameron, Ashley Dilard, Kelvin Osaze Ehigie, and Steven Solomon; Under St. Mark's Theatre; March 15 - 31, 2012

The Flower Thief by Pia Wilson; Directed by Heidi Grumelot; Stage Manager, Katelyn Martin; Lighting Designer, Justin W. King; Set Designer, Janne Larsen; Costume Designer, Cassandra Andrus; Sound Designer, Maurice Williams; Producer, Jesse Cameron Alick; Assistant Stage Manager, Cassidy Liebman; Production Dramaturg, Heather J. Violanti; Cast: Keona Welch, Allyson Morgan, Erwin E. A. Thomas, Lisa Strum, Larry Powell; Red Room; August 2 - 18, 2012

In The Meantime by David L. Williams; Directed by Rachel Dart; Cast: Lauren Berst, Jillian LaVinka, Eddie Boroevich; Under St. Marks; May 11 - 19, 2012

Memory is a Culinary Affair by Graciela Berger Wegsman; Directed by Fabian Gonzalez; Cast: George Bass, Ben Bucher, Michelle Concha, Ydaiber Orozco, Mariana Parma, and Ron Sarcos; Red Room; June 9 – 17, 2011

Lines by Terence Patrick Hughes; Directed by Heidi Grumelot; produced in association with Ice & Fire Theatre of London Red Room; August 11 – 27, 2011

Oh, That Wily Snake! by Martin Dockery; Cast: Martin Dockery, Vanessa Quesnelle; Under St. Marks; January 26 - February 10, 2012

Tin Bucket Drum by Neil Coppen; Directed by Karen Logan; Produced by The Imbewu Trust; Kraine Theatre; July 26 - August 3, 2012

The Virilogy by Ben Clawson; Directed by Artem Yatsunov; Cast: Alejandro Hernandez, David Murgittroyd, Scott Cagney; Under St. Marks; July 5 - 14, 2012

Your Boyfriend May Be Imaginary by Larry Kunofsky; Directed by Meg Sturiano; Stage Manager, Kelly Ruth Cole; Lighting Designer, Grant Wilcoxen; Set Designer, Kyle Dixon; Costume Designer, Megan Hill; Sound Designer, Meg Sturiano; Assistant Stage Manager, Mauli Delaney; Cast: Quinlan Corbett, Zach Evenson, Darcy Fowler, Geoffrey Hillback, Kirsten Hopkins, Maya Lawson, Jordan Mahome, Penny Middleton, Kunal Prasad, Danielle Slavick, Risa Sarachan, Debargo Sanyal; Under St. Matks; April 5 - 26, 2012

FESTIVALS

Burlesque Blitz; *Bastardpiece Theater* with Bastard Keith and Madame Rosebud; *Hotsy Totsy* with Joe the Shark, Calamity Chang, Gal Friday, Jenny C'est Quoi; *Bare* with Rory School, Dangrr Doll, Brad Lawrence, Jenny C'Est Quoi, Jen Lee, BB Heart, Peter Aguero, Mary Cyn; *Socks and Co*ks* with Tigger!, Mat Fraser, Hard Cory, Ferro and host Jonny Porkpie; *Storybook Burlesque*; Kraine Theatre; December 27 - 30, 2011

Fire This Time; *Four* by Jocelyn Bioh, Directed by Nicole Watson; *The Crisis of the Negro Intellectual: Dream One* by Kevin R. Free, Directed by Christopher Burris; *Little Louise* by Patricia Ione Lloyd, Directed by Donya K. Washington; *The Pitch* by Zoey Martinson, Directed by Brandon Gardner; *Vanna White Must Die* by Antoinette Nwandu, Directed by Dan Rogers; *DIG* by Jerome Parker, Directed by LA Williams; *The Talk* by France-Luce Benson, Directed by Jamie Robinson; Kraine Theatre and Red Room; January 16 - 25, 2012

FRIGID Festival 2011 (see Festivals) Horse Trade Theatres; Feb 22 - Mar 04, 2012

HT Encores; *The Complete and Condensed Stage Directions of Eugene O'Neill Volume 1: Early Plays/Lost Plays* by the New York Neo-Futurists; *Paradise Lost* Created & Performed by Paul Van Dyck; *Creating Illusion* Written & Performed by Jeff Grow, Directed by Jessi D. Hill; *The Star of Happiness: Helen Keller on Vaudeville?!* Written & Performed by Michelle-Leona Godin, Assisted by Igor, Directed by Randi Rivera; *One Man Hamlet* Performed & Adapted by Michael Birch, Directed by Bricken Sparacino; *Radio Star* Written & Performed by Tanya O'Debra, Original Music by Andrew Mauriello; Kraine Theatre; January 5 - 14, 2012

Hub Theatricals

Mistakes: a dark comedy in 5 parts by Mark Levy; Directed by Michael Hagins; Cast: Doug Sharf, Jarrod Luke, Kim Kalish, Christopher Fahmie, Rebecca Klco, Barry Shepperd; Manhattan Repertory Theatre; August 6 – 16, 2011

Hudson Warehouse

Merry Wives of Windsor by William Shakespeare; Directed by Eric Nightengale; Stage Manager, Anna Demenkoff; Costume Designer, Drew Rosene; Managing Director, Susane Lee; Fight Director, Jared Kirby; Properties Master, Chris Behan; Cast: Ruth Nightengale, Brad Makarowski, Corey Tazmania, Michael Selkirk, Jesse Michael Mothershed, Abra Bigham, Demetri Bonaros, George Wells, Drew Rosene, Robert Colpitts, Chelsie Shipley, Nathan Oesterle, James Nightengale, Emma Lee Miller, Anna Richi; Soldiers and Sailors Monument; June 3 – 26, 2011

The Seagull by Anton Chekhov; Directed by Tom Demenkoff; Stage Manager, Anna Demenkoff; Costume Designer, Emily Rose Parman; Producing Artistic Director, Nicholas Martin-Smith; Managing Director, Susane Lee; Music Composers, Tom Demenkoff & Emily Rose Parman; Cast: Amanda Renee Baker, Chris Behan, David Palmer Brown, Margie Catov, Brad Coolidge, Nick DeVita, David Allison DeWitt, Roxann Kraemer, Emily Rose Parman, Michael Selkirk, Roger Stude, Alex Viola, David Martin, Griffin Lee Miller; Soldiers and Sailors Monument; July 8 – 31, 2011

Imagine This Scenario Productions

Moshe Feldstein, Icon of Self-Realization by Alexander Nemser, Angel Beyde & Joseph Shragge; Directed by Joseph Shragge; Cherry Lane Theatre; August 12 – 25, 2011

Impetuous Theater Group

www.impetuoustheater.org

Action Philosophers! by Crystal Skillman; Directed by John Hurley; Stage Manager, Audrey Marshall; Lighting & Set Designer, Olivia Harris; Costume Designer, Meryl Pressman & Holly Rihn; Sound Designer, John Hurley; Properties Designer, Gretchen Van Lente; Original Music, Neimah Djourabchi and Joseph Mathers; Cast: C.L. Weatherstone, Kristen Vaughan, Neimah Djourabchi, Matthew Trumbull, Joseph Mathers, Timothy McCown Reynolds; Co-Produced with the Brick Theater; The Brick Theater; October 6 – 16, 2011

Inspired Artists Theatre Co., Inc.

The Unmitigated Consequence Written and Directed by K.R. Boxberger; Cast: John Leone, Jaclyn Rene Tokos, Sue Anne Dennehy, Patricia d'Accolti and Nicholas F. Cariello; Roy Arias Theatre Center at Time Square Art Center; July 15 – August 21, 2011

Interborough Repertory Theatre

irttheater.org

WORKSHOP

An Evening of Reckonings by Josh Billig, Todd Pate; Directed by Larry Singer, Todd Pate; Cast: Tim Wersan, Marianna McClellan, Chris Hurt; produced in association with 3B Development Series and MadIris Productions Interborough Repertory Theatre; June 22 - 26, 2011

Josiah Theatre Works, LLC

www.josiahtheatreworks.wordpress.com

ExecutiveProducer, Director and Playwright-at-Large, Nickolas Long, III; Chairman of the Board of Investors, Nickolas Long; Make and Hair Department Head, Chanel Silky Golden Brown; Executive Assistant to Nickolas Long, Chadina Marough; Lady Hazel Burkes

Lena (Black Cinderella) Written and Directed by Nickolas Long, III; Musical Director, Andrea Womack; Stage Manager, Andrea Womack; Lighting, Set and Sound Designer, Verinia Taylor; Cast: Noell Lusane Andrea Womack Tangi Guinn Jessica Dunker Dustin Ross; Lafayette Grill, Theatre with Fine Dining; April 4 – 30, 2011

More Then A Dream Written and Directed by Nickolas Long, III; Stage Manager, Andrea Womack; Cast: Whitney G. Shalimah Zahra Omar Knight Jennifer Rebecca Boyd; Ripley Grier Studios; February 3 – 28, 2012

Tribute (Forget Me Not) Written and Directed by Nickolas Long, III; Musical Director, Ckelly Wright; Lighting Designer, Oliver Tucker; Sound and AudioVisual Designer, Thomas; Cast: Michael Marcel, Lisa Golsby , Stefan Harris; Iguana, Theatre with Fine Dining; April 14, 2012

Judith Shakespeare NYC

www.judithshakespeare.org

Artistic Director and Producer, Joanne Zipay; Associate Artistic Director, Jane Titus; Associate Producer, Ginny Hack

READINGS & WORKSHOPS

Shakespeare-A-Thon II: "Comedy Tomorrow! Tragedy Tonight!" *Coriolanus, Julius Caesar, Titus Andronicus, Macbeth, All's Well That Ends Well, Love's Labors Lost, Comedy of Errors* and *Two Gentlemen of Verona* by William Shakespeare; Directed by Joanne Zipay; In honor of Shakespeare's Birthday, over 70 actors reading 8 plays in 24 hours; Irish Times Pub; April 21 - 22, 2012

Junta Juleil Theatricals

www.seangillfilms.com

Co-Executive Producer, Sean Gill; Artistic Director, Sean Gill; Co-Executive Producer, Jillaine Gill

Dreams of the Clockmaker Written and Directed by Sean Gill; Stage Manager, Brandy Rowell; Lighting Designer, Ben Kato; Costume Designer, Jillaine Gill, Rachel Klein; Sound & AudioVisual Designer, Sean Gill; Photography, Joe Stipek; Cast: Jillaine Gill; The Wild Project; October 17-30, 2011

Phsycho Space Laboratory; *Giant Easter Mess, Holy Cuckoos What Has Happened to My Life, Night of the Living Dolls, Ren is a Total Fox: A Tribute to 80s Dance Movies, Giant Oscar Mess,* and *Batshit Crazy Blowout*; co-produced by Junta Juleil Productions, Rachel Klein Productions and Blue Box Productions in association with the Bowery Poetry Club; Bowery Poetry Club; Febuary 27, 2011-March 25, 2012

KADM Productions

Angry Young Women In Low Rise Jeans With High Class Issues Written and Directed by Matt Morillo; Lighting Designer, Amith A. Chandrashaker; Set Designer, Mark Marcante; Sound Designer, Matt Richter; Cast: Zachary Harrison, Peter Buck Dettman, Jessica Durdock Moreno, Jess Loudon, Chris LaCour, Jon Sprik, Christine Cartell, Kelly Lockwood, Jenni Halina; Theater for the New City; December 1 – 18, 2011

Kim Katzberg

www.cheerfulinsanityshows.com

Penetrating the Space Written and Performed by Kim Katzberg; Directed by John Harlacher; Lighting& Set Designer, Josh Iacovelli; Costume Designer, Kim Katzberg; Animation and Sculpture, Maia Cruz Palileo; Original Music, Kim Katzberg; HERE Arts Center; September 27 – October 16, 2011

Knife Edge Productions

Tape by Stephen Belber; Directed by Sam Helfrich; Stage Manager, Heather Arnson; Lighting Designer, Kate Ashton; Set Designer, Laura Jellinek; Costume Designer, Nancy Leary; Sound Designer, Jack Kennedy; Cast: Neil Holland, Don DiPaolo, & Therese Plaehn; Abingdon Theatre Complex; September 9 – 24, 2011

La Criatura Theater

www.lacriatura.org

Artistic and Executive Director, Producer, Karina Casiano

The Orphans by Karina Casiano; Directed by Karina Casiano and Daniel Irizarry; Musical Director, Andrés Rotmistrovsky; Stage Manager, Edna Lee Figueroa; Lighting Designer, María Cristina Fusté; Set Designer, Jorge Dieppa; Costume Designer, Awymarie Riollano; Sound Designer, Karina Casiano; Properties Desiger, Antonio Lago; Choreographer, Daniel Irizarry and Karina Casiano; Technical Director, Miguel Ángel Valderrama; Cast: Karina Casiano, Renzo Ampuero; Connelly Theater; June 9 – 12, 2011

LaMaMa Experimental Theater Club

www.lamama.org

Alexix: A Greek Tragedy Directors: Enrico Casagrande and Daniela Nicolò; Under the Radar Festival; January 4-14, 2012

An Evening with Joseph Keckler Music by Joseph Keckler; November 18 - 20, 2011

Angels of Swedenborg by Great Jones Repertory Company; Directed by Ping Chong; October 27 - November 13, 2011

Beauty as God(dess) by Our Lady J; May 25 - 27, 2012

Body Duet by John Scott's Irish Modern Dance Company; January 7 -10, 2011

Buddha by Company EAST; Director/Choreographer: Kenji Kawaraski; March 2 - 11, 2012

Christmas in Nickyland by Curator and Host: Nicky Paraiso; Dec 17 - 18, 2011

Clowns Full-Tilt:A Musing on Aesthetics by Clowns Ex Machina; Directed by Kendall Cornell; November 4 - 20, 2011

Coffeehouse Chronicles: Dedicated to the Playwright (#103) by Curator: Chris Kapp; October 19, 2011

Coffeehouse Chronicles: Mink Stole and Joe E. Jeffreys (#104) by Curator: Chris Kapp; November 12, 2011

Coffeehouse Chronicles: George Ferencz (#105) by Curator: Chris Kapp; January 28, 2012

Coffeehouse Chronicles: Marsha Johnson (#106) by Curator: Chris Kapp; February 11, 2012

Coffeehouse Chronicles: Candy Darlin (#107) by Curator: Chris Kapp; March 31, 2012

Coffeehouse Chronicles: Café Cino Reunion (#108) by Curator: Chris Kapp; April 28, 2012

Coffeehouse Chronicles: Chris Tanner (#109) by Curator: Chris Kapp; June 30, 2012

Erosion: A Fable Directed by Tomi Tsunoda; Stage Manager, Jes Levine; Lighting Designer, Kayla Goble; Set Designer, Morgen Fleisig; Costume Designer, Hannah Richey; Original Music, Sasha Bogdanowitsch; Choreographer, Neva Cockrell; Cast: Raphael Sacks, Mike O'Bauer, Sasha Bogdanowitsch, Neva Cockrell, Tomi Tsunoda, Katherine Pardue, Zoe Anastassiou, Andrew Broaddus, Kate Hamilton, Helen Joyce; La MaMa Experimental Theatre; February 17 - 26, 2012

Escape by by Susan Mosakowski; Directed by Gaye Taylor Upchurch; Creation Production Company; June 7 - 24, 2012

Eugene Lang College: The New School Showcase Curator: Zishan Ugurlu; Dec 13 - 14, 2011

Experiments: Celestial Hurl by Kimberly Shelby-Szyszko; Directored by George Ferencz; June 19, 2012

Experiments: Chemistry of Love by Jill Campbell; Directed by George Ferencz; January 23, 2012

Experiments: Golem and a Half by Elena Zucker; Directed by George Ferencz; March 12, 2012

Experiments: Shadow Curated & Directed by George Ferencz; Featuring: *Ain't Ethiopia* by Michael Bettencourt; *Louise Alone* by Leslee Warren; *Poles Apart* by John Byrd, Directed by Jasper McGruder; *Kleitos Agoniste* by Owa; February 2 - 5, 2012

Full Beaver Moon Show by Lucy Sexton & Tom Murrin; Guest Artist: Salley Mae; November 8, 2011;

Golem by The Czechoslovak-American Marionette Theatre; Directed by Vit Horejs; November 17 - December 4, 2011

Haunts Directed by Geo Wyeth; June 1 -10, 2012

Hieronymus Written and Directed by Nic Ularu; January 20- 29, 2012

Hot Lunch Apostles by Sidney Goldfarb; Directed by Paul Zimet; Stage Manager, Lisa McGinn; Lighting Designer, Lenore Doxsee; Set Designer, Nic Ularu; Costume Designer, Kiki Smith; Original Music, Sybille Hayn, Ellen Maddow & Harry Mann; Choreographer, James Ferguson; Cast: Will Badgett, Nichi Douglas, Ellen Maddow, Ed Rosenberg, Tina Shepard, Loudon Wainwright, Jack Wetherall; Co-Produced with The Talking Band; La MaMa Experimental Theatre; March; 1 - 17 , 2012

How and Why I Robbed My First Cheese Store by Mike Gorman; Directed by Dave Bennettd; Stage Manager, Ashley Rossetti; Lighting Designer, John Eckert; Set Designer, Donald Eastman; Costume Designer, Gabriel Berry; Sound Designer, Tim Schellenbaum; Art Installation, Gregory de la Haba; Cast: Melody Bates, Mary Notari, Joe Mullen, Alan B. Netherton, Thomas Piper, Travis York; La MaMa Experimental Theatre; May 26 – June 5, 2011

Human Beatbox Festival Curator: Kid Lucky; May 3 - 6, 2012;

I Killed My Mother by Andras Visky; Directed by Karin Coonrod; Stage Manager, Ashley Zednick; Lighting Designer, Peter Ksander; Set Designer, Peter Ksander; Costume Designer, Oana Botez Ban; Original Music, Andrew Livingston; Cast: Melissa Lorraine Hawkins, Andrew Hampton Livingston; La MaMa Experimental Theatre; February 10 - March 4, 2012

In the Solitude of Cotton Fields by Stefan Zeromski Theatre; Directed by Radoslaw Rychcik; Under the Radar Festival; Janary 5-14, 2012

Jukebox Jackie: Snatches of Jackie Curtis Directed by Scott Wittman; May 24 - June 10, 2012;

La MaMa 50th Anniversary Gala October 17, 2011

La MaMa 50th Block Party by Co-Naming "Ellen Stewart Way;" an Outdoor Block Party; October 16, 2011

La MaMa Big Bash Directed by Michael Mayer; Master of Ceremonies: André DeShields; June 24, 2012

La MaMa Cantata Writer, Director, Composer: Elizabeth Swados; November 7 - 8, 11, 2011 & December 29 - 30, 2011

Lick But Don't Swallow by Ozen Yula; Directed by Biriken; Under the Radar Festival; January 4 -15, 2012

Lost in Staten Island, More Tales of Modern Living by Richard Sheinmel; Music and Lyrics by Clay Zambo; Directed by Jason Jacobs; June 15 - July 1, 2012

Macbeth After Shakespeare by Mini Teater Ljubljana and Novo Kazaliste Zagreb; Directed by Ivica Buljan; December 8 - 11, 2011

Mad Women Written and Performed by John Fleck; Directed by Ric Montejano; La MaMa Experimental Theatre; December 1-11, 2011

Monday Nights at La MaMa: Andrei Serban and F; Murray Abraham Conversation with Andrei Serban and F; Murray Abraham; April 23, 2012

Monday Nights at La MaMa: Manu Delago by Conversation with Manu Delago; February 27, 2012

Monday Nights at La MaMa: Meredith Monk by Conversation and Music with Meredith Monk; January 23, 2012

Monday Nights at La MaMa: Julie Taymor by Conversation with Julie Taymor; June 4, 2012

Now the Cat With Jewelled Claws by Tennessee Williams; Directed by Jonathan Warman; Stage Manager, Alison Carroll; Lighting Designer, Yuriy Nayer; Set Designer, Jonathan Collins; Costume Designer, Karl Ruckdeschel; Original Music, Trystan Trazon; Cast: Regina Barkoff, Joseph Keckler, Erin Markey, Everett Quinton, Charles Schick, Max Steele, Mink Stole; Choreographer, Liz Piccoli; La MaMa Experimental Theatre; October 27 - November 13, 2011

Obama44 by Mario Fratti; Directed by Wayne Maugans; Stage Manager, Emily Goforth; Lighting Designer, Paul Bartlett; Set Designer, Tatsuki Nakamura; Costume Designer, Peri Grabin Leong; Sound Designer, Ien DeNio; Cast: Julia Motyka, Thomas Poarch, Richard Ugino, Dennis Ostermaier, Rob Sedgwick; Co-Produced with Voyage Theater Company La MaMa Experimental Theatre; March 29 - April 15, 2012

Oyster Orgasms Obituaries Written and Performed by Raina von Waldenburg; Directed by Zishan Ugurlu; Stage Manager, Paola Di Tolla; Lighting Designer, Tsubasa Kamei; Set Designer, Zishan Ugurlu; Sound Designer, Tim Schellenbaum; Original Music, Fernando Arruda; La MaMa Experimental Theatre; December 1-18, 2011

Poetry Electric 12: Women's Poetry Series Directed by William Electric Black; December 5, 2011

Poetry Electric 12: Meanie Series Directed by William Electric Black; December 19, 2011

Poetry Electric 12: Black History Month Series Directed by William Electric Black; Featuring: Levern Williams, The Tevon Thomas Trio; February 20, 2012

Poetry Electric 12: Zounds Series Directed by William Electric Black; Featuring: Jeffrey Cyphers Wright, Linda Griggs, Tod Thilleman, Alan Gilbert, Michele Madigan Somerville, Leslie Graves, Madison Hatta, and Tamara Gonzales; April 23, 2012

Poetry Electric 12: Jane LeCroy, Tom Abbs and Kid Lucky are Transmitting Series Directed by William Electric Black; May 21, 2012

Poetry Electric 12: Write On Series Directed by William Electric Black; David Mils; June 11, 2012

Poetry Electric 12: That Beast of Festival Skin Series Directed by William Electric Black; Alexandra Tatarsky; June 25, 2012

Poor Baby Bree in I Am Going to Run Away Conceived and Performed by Bree Benton; Directed by David Schweizer; Costume Designer, Ramona Ponce; La MaMa Experimental Theatre; April 13 - 29, 2012

Promethes Within Written and Directed by Theodora Skipitares; Stage Manager, Karen Oughtred; Lighting Designer, Jeff Nash; Set Designer, Donald Eastman; Costume Designer, Theodora Skipitares; Sound Designer, Tim Schellenbaum; Puppet Designer, Catherine Jane Shaw & Theodora Skipitares; Original Music, Sxip Shirey; Choreographer, Hillary Spector; Cast: Black-Eyed Susan, Jonathan Nosan, Eliza McKelway, Alice Tolan-Mee, Trevor Wilson, Allison Plamondon, Jane Catherine Shaw, Britt Moseley, Sarah Grace Holcomb, Dena Paige-Fischer, Rebecca Leigh Silverman; Co-Produced with Skysaver Productions; La MaMa Experimental Theatre; April 13 - 29, 2012

Pua Ali`I `Ilima by Vicky Holt Takamine, and Jeff Takamine; June 19, 2012

RE: Definition Written & Performed by Glenn Gordon; Directed by Chadwick Boseman; Hip Hop Theater Festival; October 28 - 29, 2011

S 16- Luna Nera Written & Directed by Gian Marco Lo Forte; April 6 - 8, 2012

Single Reflex by Kompany Malakh; Artistic Directed by Kwesi Johnson; Hip Hop Theater Festival; October 28 - 29, 2011

Stopped Bridge of Dreams Written & Directed by John Jesurun; January 19 - Feb 4, 2012

Teatro Patologico Festival Directed by Dario D'ambrosi; Dec 15 - 22, 2011

That Beautiful Laugh Created & Directed by Orlando Pabotov; Stage Manager, Cristina Sison; Lighting Designer, Peter West; Set Designer, Scott Tedmon-Jones; Costume Designer, Tilly Grimes; Original Music, Harrison Beck; Choreographer, Byron Easly; Cast: Alan Tudyk, Carlton Ward, Julia Ogilve, Harrison Beck; La MaMa Experimental Theatre;March 15 - 25, 2012

The Etiquette of Death by Chris Tanner Production; Directed by Everett Quinton; Choreographer, Julie Atlas Muz; June 14 - July 1, 2012

The Judith of Shimoda Directed & Designed by Zishan Ugurlu; In collaboration with Hella Wuolijoki May 3 - 6, 2012

The Kreutzer Sonata by The Gate Theatre; Based on the novella by Leo Tolstoy; Adapted by Nancy Harris; Directed by Natalie Abrahami; March 8 - 25, 2012

The Lady and the Peddler; Gimpel the Fool by Howard Rypp; Directed by Geula Jeffet-Attar; The Lady and the Peddler, January 19-29, 2012

The Plot is the Revolution Directors: Enrico Casagrande and Daniele Nicolò; Under the Radar Festival; January 9 - 11 2012

The Star Medicine Hosted by Mia Yoo; Novel by Murielle Bost Tarrant; Ebook launch; November 14, 2011

The Table by Blind Summit (UK); Under the Radar Festival; January 5 - 8, 2012

the-π-roject Directed & Designed by Zishan Ugurlu; Asstistant Director Sofia Tsekoura; March 30 - April 1, 2012

Three by La MaMa Playwrights: Fornes, Shepard & Wilson Cast: Niko Papastefanou, Spencer Bazzano, Lauren Morra, Jonathan Gabrielson, Nicole Madriz, Turquoise Olezene, Courtney Taylor, Kaleb Wells, Matthew Curiano, Patrick Pribyl; Co-Produced with InterArt & Pace University; La MaMa Experimental Theatre February 2 - 12, 2012

Urban Odyssey by Elias Khoury; Directed by Federico Restrepo; Stage Manager, Kevin Hourigan; Lighting, Costume & Set Designer, Federico Restrepo; Sound Designer, Tim Schellenbaum; Video Designer, Federico Restrepo, Angela Sierra; Original Music, Elizabeth Swados; Choreographer, Federico Restrepo; Cast: Penelope Armstead-Williams, Ching-I Chang, Maura Donohue, Denise Greber, Federico Restrepo, Gilbert Reyes, Kayla Schetter, Rocky Bostick, Kiku Sakai; Co-Produced with LOCO7 Dance Puppet Theatre Company;La MaMa Experimental Theatre; March 22 - Apr 8, 2012

When Clowns Play Hamlet by H. M. Koutoukas; Directed by Ozzie Rodriguez; Stage Manager, G. Garrett Ellison; Lighting Designer, Jeff Nash; Set Designer, P. Ginal & G. Granger; Costume Designer, Sally Lesser; Original Music, Joseph Blunt; Cast: Ching Valdes-Aran, Matt Nasser, Sara Galassini; La MaMa Experimental Theatre; May 24 - June 3, 2012

You, My Mother by Kristen Kosmas, Karinne Keithley Syers; Directed by Brooke O'Harra; Stage Manager, Lisa McGinn; Lighting Designer, Chris Kuhl & Justin Townsend; Set Designer, Chris Kuhl & Justin Townsend; Costume Designer, Alice Tavener; Projection Designer, Ahram Jeong & Yoonkyung Lim; Original Music, Rick Burkhardt & Brendan Connelly; Choreographer, Barbara Lanciers; Cast: Beth Griffith, Laryssa Husiak, Mike Mikos, Kate Soper; La MaMa Experimental Theatre; Co-Produced with Two-Headed Calf; February 9 - 20, 2012

READINGS & WORKSHOPS

Experiments: Welcome Home, Sonny T. by William Electric Black; Directed by George Ferencz; November 7, 2011

FESTIVALS

La Mama Moves! Dance Festival – April 27 – 20, 2012

Beauty by Jane Comfort and Company; May 17 - 20, 2012

Chamber Works I by Juliette Mapp, Maura Nguyen Donohue, Vicky Schick; May 11 - 13, 2012

Chamber Works II by Yuko Takahashi Dance Company; Risa Jaroslow, Dancers, Eunhee Lee; May 18 - 20, 2012

Digital Duets by Culturehub; May 19, 2012

Dream Bridge by Yara Arts Group; Directed by Virlana Tkacz; April 27 - May 13, 2012

East Village Dance Project by East Village Dance Project; May 20, 2012

Love Story, Palestine by Yoshiko Chuma; May 9 - 12, 2012

Mermaid Show by Ann Liv Young; May 17 - 20, 2012

Lauren Rayner Productions

www.laurenrayner.com

A Night of Deadly Serious Comedies: Ionesco's 'The Future is in Eggs' & Pirandello's 'Sicilian Limes' by Eugene Ionesco; Directed by Joseph Hendel; Stage Manager, Samantha Gallardo; Lighting Designer, Evan Gannon; Set Designer, Charlie Gaidica; Sound Designer, Nick Engel; Audience Audio Technology Integration, ADEV Inc.; Cast: Adam Hocherman, Bradley Sumner, Brendan Sokler, Frankie Johnson, Grace Folsom, Joel Malazita, Lisa Hickman, Meaghan Sloane, Skylar Saltz; Turtle's Shell Theater; June 17 – 26, 2011

Leimay

www.leimay.org

Floating Point Waves Created, Directed & Choreographed by Ximena Garnica and Shige Moriya; Lighting Designer, Shige Moriya and Solomon Weisbard; Set Designer, Ximena Garnica and Shige Moriya; Sound Designer, Jeremy Slater; Video Design, Shige Moriya; Original Music, Jeremy D. Slater; Cast: Ximena Garnica; Co-Produced with HERE Arts Center; HERE Arts Center; April 6 – 14, 2012

Less Than Rent Theatre

www.lessthanrent.org

The Private Sector by Cory Finley; Directed by Charlie Polinger; Theatre for the New City; June 25 – July 3, 2011

Friends Don't Let Friends by James Presson; Directed by Rachel Buethe; Stage Manager, Lindsey Alexander; Lighting Designer, Ryan Seelig; Set Designer, Caite Hevner; Costume Designer, Amanda Brooklyn; Sound Designer, Gifford Williams; Cast: Becca Ballenger, Will Turner, Cory Asinofsky, Jason Zeren, Emma March Barash, Jenna Grossano, Ashlynn Alexander, Tommy Hettrick; Walkerspace; December 2 – 18, 2011

Lesser America

lesseramerica.com

Founding Members: Daniel Abeles, Nate Miller, and Laura Ramadei

Squealer by Jonathan Blitstein; Directed by Stephen Brackett; Stage Manager, Michael Bradley Block; Lighting Designer, Brad Peterson; Set Designer, Eugenia Furneaux; Costume Designer, Tristan Scott Barton Raines; Sound Designer, Janie Bullard; Cast: Daniel Abeles, Jamie Law, Nick Lawson, Sarah Lemp, Nate Miller and Laura Ramadei; Theater for the New City; May 5 - 21, 2011

Too Much Too Soon by Nikole Beckwith, Dean Imperial, Nick Jones, Ken Urban, Melissa Ross, Emily Schwend; Directed by Stephen Brackett, Portia Krieger; Stage Manager, Michele Ebel; Lighting Designer, Steven Maturno; Set Designer, Deb O; Costume Designer, Campbell Ringel; Sound Designer, Daniel Kluger and Brandon Wolcott; Fight Director, Casey Robinson; Technical Director, Sean Bauer; Cast: Daniel Abeles, Liesel Allen Yeager, Craig Jorczak Nate Miller, Anna O'Donoghue, Laura Ramadei; co-produced with Red Elevator Productions; Theater for the New City; September 29 - October 9, 2011

American River by Micheline Auger; Directed by Stephen Brackett; Stage Manager, Amy Groeschel; Lighting Designer, Marie Yokoyama; Set Designer, Daniel Zimmerman; Costume Designer, Jessica Pabst; Sound Designer, David Corsello; Producers: Daniel Abeles, Nate Miller and Valerie Steinberg; Fight Director, Casey Robinson; Properties Master, Haley Traub; Technical Director, Kevin Rees; Dramaturg, Claire Siebers; Production Intern, Steph Malove; Cast: John Patrick Doherty, Laura Ramadei, Brendan Spieth, Robbie Collier Sublett; Theater for the New City; July 12 - 22, 2012

Leviathan Lab

www.leviathanlab.com

Leviathan Lab's 12N (Twelfth Night) by William Shakespeare; Directed by Nelson T. Eusebio III; Stage Manager, Natalie Zhang; Lighting Designer, Melissa Mizell; Set & Costume Designer, Maiko Chii; Sound Designer, Sam Kusnetz; ; Original Music, Jason Ma; Choreographer, Dax Valdes; Cast: Ka-Ling Cheung, Tina Chilip, Chris Doi, Andrew Eisenman, Jojo Gonzalez, Marcus Ho, Karen Tsen Lee, Eugene Oh, Eileen Rivera, John Roque, Kurt Uy, and Roger Yeh; ArcLight Theatre; November 3-19, 2011

Libra Theater Company

www.libratheater.org

12th Night by William Shakespeare; Directed by Evan Mueller; Costume Designer, Travis Boatright; Original Music, Jeff Raab; Cast: Victoria Weinberg, Jeff Raab, Angela Cristantello, Jeremy Morse, Roy Richardson, Emily Rose Prats, Ryder McNair, Joe Fellman, Nick Moore, Ashley Grombol, Steven Cuevas, Alex Mandell, and Will Gallacher; The Underground Lounge; April 30 – May 12, 2012

Literally Alive Theatre Company

literallyalive.com

Stone Soup Written and Directed by Brenda Bell; Stage Manager, KeriAnne Murphy; Lighting Designer, Amanda Sevedge; Set Designer, Christian Amato; Costume Designer, Grace Trimble; Original Music, Michael Sgouros; Choreographer, Stefanie Smith; Cast: Eric Fletcher, Clare Solly, Timothy Bartlett, Brianna Hurley, Rebecca Hoffman; Players Theatre & Players Loft; September 18 – November 5, 2011

A Christmas Carol Written and Directed by Brenda Bell; Stage Manager, KeriAnne Murphy; Lighting Designer, Amanda Sevedge; Set Designer, Christian Amato; Costume Designer, Grace Trimble; Original Music, Michael Sgouros; Choreographer, Stefanie Smith; Cast: Eric Fletcher, Stefanie Smith, Robert Hoogkirk, Cory Holovach, Doug Sharf, Pasqualino Beltempo, Jennifer Ambler, Victoria Weinberg, Rebecca Hoffman, Catherine A. Nelson; Players Theatre & Players Loft; November 27 – December 30, 2011

Alice in Wonderland by Brenda Bell; Directed by Christian Amato; Stage Manager, KeriAnne Murphy; Lighting Designer, Amanda Sevedge; Set Designer, Christian Amato; Costume Designer, Grace Trimble; Original Music, Michael Sgouros; Cast: Eric Fletcher, Tyler Rebello, Brianna Hurley, Jovanni Guzman, Victor Albaum, Doug Sharf, Jonathan Bethea, Victoria Weinberg, Carolyn Purcell, Jillian Pregach; Choreographer, Stefanie Smith; Players Theatre & Players Loft; February 12 – May 20, 2012

Little Lord (a theater company)

www.littlelord.org

Little Lord's Babes in Toyland Written and Directed by Michael Levinton; Stage Manager, Dina Paola Rodriguez; Lighting Designer, Christina Watanabe; Set Designer, Jason Simms; Costume Designer, Karen Boyer & Bevan Dunbar; Cast: Corinne Donly, Das Elkin, Michael Levinton, Tina Shepard, Laura von Holt & Nicholas Williams; Brick Theater; November 30 – December 10, 2011

The Living Theatre

www.livingtheatre.org

History Of The World Written and Directed by Judith Malina; Set Designer, The Living Theatre; Original Music, Sheila Dabney; Cast: The Living Theatre Ensemble; Living Theatre; December 31, 2011 - February 25, 2012

Local Celebrity Theatre

www.localcelebritytheatre.com

Beyond Therapy by Christopher Durang; Directed by Torrey Rodriguez; Cast: Lou Ellen Howell, Matt Morel, Chris Manetakis, Karen Andronico, Denis Zepeda, Adonis Cruz; I.S. 192; June 16 - 17, 2011

Could've Been Broadway: A Musical Revue Directed by Chris Manetakis & Kimberly Cuellar; P.S. 192; August 26 - 28, 2011

The Longest Lunch

A Week at the NJ Shore by Valerie Work; Directed by Meghan Finn; Cast: Maxwell Cramer, Joseph Gregori, Daliya Karnofsky, Sarah Painter, Chuja Seo; Manhattan Repertory Theatre; July 27 - 30, 2011

Look at the Fish Theatre

Seascape with Sharks and Dancer by Don Nigro; Directed by Thomas James Lombardo & Scott Lakoff; Lighting Designer, Mary Ellen Stebbins; Set Designer, James Fenton; Costume Designer, Toni-Ann Gardiner; Sound Designer, Chris Barlow; Cast: Thomas James Lombardo, Toni-Ann Gardiner; Red Room; November 3 – 20, 2011

Looking Glass Theatre

www.lookingglasstheatrenyc.com

Calamity Jane Battles the Horrible Hoopsnakes by E. J. C. Calvert; Directed by Jacquelyn Honeybourne; Lighting Designer, Daisy Long; Set Designer, Nicole Carroll; Costume Designer, Kristina Sneshkoff; Cast: Abraham M. Adams, Gianna Cioffi, Jessica Kelly, David Mangiamele, Monica O'Malley, Katie Proulx and Sarah Pullman; Looking Glass Theatre; October 15 – November 20, 2011

The Angel Play by Bella Poynton; Directed by Amanda Thompson; Lighting Designer, Libby Jensen; Set Designer, Elle Kunnos De Voss; Costume Designer, Steve Buechler; Sound Designer & Original Music, Lucas Segall; Cast: Julie Ek, Margie Ferris, Dan Lovley, Joey Lozada, Rebecca Nerz and Zachary Zimbler; Looking Glass Theatre; March 16 – April 1, 2012

East of the Sun, West of the Moon by Frankie Little Hardin; Directed by Naima Warden; Lighting Designer, Porsche McGovern; Set Designer, Joseph Lark-Riley; Costume Designer, Karim Rivera; Sound Designer, Sarah M Chichester; Cast: Samantha Cains, Melody Harnish, Lauren Hart, Irina Kaplin, Natalie Kropf and Kevin Russo; Looking Glass Theatre; April 14 – May 20, 2012

Loom Ensemble

Loomensemble.com

Erosion: a Fable by The Loom Ensemble; Directed by Tomi Tsunoda; Stage Manager, Jess Levine; Lighting Designer, Kayla Goble; Set Designer, Morgan Fleisig; Costume Designer, Hanna Richey; Original Music, Sasha Bogdanowitsch; Choreographer, Neva Cockrell; Cast: Sasha Bogdanowitsch, Mike O'Bauer, Neva Cockrell, Raphael Sacks, Zoe Anastassiou, Andrew Broddus, Helen Joyce, Kate Hamilton; La MaMa Experimental Theatre; February 17 – 26, 2012

Loretta Michael Productions

The Other Day by Mark Jason Williams; Directed by Valentina Fratti; Cast: Lars Drew, Amadeo Fusca, Zach Wegner and Elena Zazanis; 440 Studios; June 2 – 22, 2011

The Lost & Found Project

www.lostandfoundprod.com

Founder/Producer, Anna Zicer; Co-producer, Marina Reydler; Artistic Director, Ben Sargent; Honorary Artistic Director, Bryna Wasserman; Score Composer, Dmitri 'Zisl' Slepovitch; Multi-Media Designer, Yevgeniy Klig; Lighting Designer, Evgheni Goncear; Ances

ДOROGA Written by Ensemble; Edited by Ruvym Gilman, Boris Zilberman; Directed by Ben Sargent, Bryna Wasserman; Musical Director, Dmitri 'Zisl' Slepovitch; Stage Manager, Estie Sarvasy; Lighting Designer, Evgheni Goncear; Set Designer, Anna Roz; Costume Designer, Anna Umanskaya; Sound Designer, Dmitri 'Zisl' Slepovitch; AudioVisual Designer, Yevgeniy Klig; House Manager, Jane Strumba, Jael Golad; Properies Manager, Ilya Medvinsky; Cast: Alya Adelman, Anna Zicer, Boris Zilberman, Jane Tuv, Jordan Elizabeth Gelber, Marina

Reydler, Mariya King, Ruslan Verkhovsky, Ruvym Gilman, Sergey Nagorny; Premiered at The JCC of Manhattan on March 8, 2012; moved to The Gene Frankel Theatre; March 14-18 2012; May 29-June 3, 2012

Love Street Theatre

www.lovestreettheatre.org

Artistic Director, Julie S. Halpern; Designer, Seth Weine; Technical Director, Jay Reisberg; Stage Manager, John Simmons

Diminished Fifth Written and Directed by Julie S. Halpern; Stage Manager, John Simmons; Lighting Designer, Jason L. Miller; Set Designer, Seth Weine; Costume Designer, Virginia Seidel; Sound Designer, Jay Reisberg; Cast: Elaine LeGaro, Jacquelyn Poplar, Stacey Scotte, Mary McGloin, Ronalda Ay Nicholas; Producers Club; June 22-July 3, 2011

Bloody Fire...Unchaste Desire by William Shakespeare; Directed by Julie S. Halpern; Musical Director, Tamara Cashour; Stage Manager, John Simmons; Lighting Designer, Pei- Wen Huang; Set Designer, Seth Weine; Costume Designer, Joanne Rogers; Cast: Sarah Arikian, Aron Bederson, Tamara Cashour, Julie S. Halpern, Susan O'Dea, Nathalie Parker, Kevin L. Peters, Mark Peters, Amy Prothro; Co-production with Oper'Avant; Theaterlab; January 11-14, 2012

Lunar Energy

www.lunarenergyproductions.com

Christopher Marlowe's Chloroform Dreams by Katharine Sherman; Directed by Philip Gates; Lighting Designer, Alana Jacoby; Set Designer, Joshua David Bishop; Costume Designer, Kalere Payton; Sound Designer, Will Fulton; Cast: Christopher Fahmie, Sheila Joon, Michael Markham, Valerie Redd, Curry Whitmire; Red Room; April 19 – May 5, 2012

M-34

james-rutherford.com

Letter To My Father by Franz Kafka; Directed by James Rutherford; Original Music, Dave Harrington; Cast: Michael Guagno; Magic Futurebox; May 11–27, 2012

4.48 Psychosis by Sarah Kane; Directed by James Rutherford; Lighting Designer, Oona Curley; Set Designer, Oona Curley; Cast: Emily Gleeson, Lizzie Vieh; Magic Futurebox; May 11 – 27, 2012

Mad Dog Theatre Company

This is Not the Play by Chisa Hutchinson; Directed by Joel Waage; Lighting Designer, Richard Chamblain; Cast: Chisa Hutchinson, Heather Kelley, Jennifer Logue, Kevin O'Callaghan, Nicole Samsel; Theaterlab; June 22–July 3, 2011

The Thrill of the Chase by Philip Gawthorne; Directed by Joel Waage; Stage Manager, Sarah Gleissner; Lighting Designer, Joey Bennett; Cast: Kevin O'Callaghan, Jenna D'Angelo, Ryan Barrentine, Nicole Samsel; Drilling Company Theatre Lab; February 16 – March 4, 2012

Magic Futurebox

www.magicfuturebox.com

Demon Dreams by Tommy Smith; Directed by Kevin Laibson; Stage Manager, Laura Merforth; Lighting Designer, Joseph Cantalupo; Costume Designer, Suzan

Eraslan; Sound Designer, DJ Spooky; Original Music, DJ Spooky; Cast: Celeste Arias, Veracity Butcher, Jeanette Bonner, Dylan Lamb, Joe Burch, Brian Walters; Gene Frankel Theatre; July 8–17, 2011

Maieutic Theatre Works (MTWorks)

www.mtworks.org

Costa Rehab by Rich Rubin; Directed by Shelly Feldman; Stage Manager, London Griffith; Lighting Designer, Dan Gallagher; Set & Costume Designer, Craig Napoliello; Sound Designer, Martha Goode; Cast: Nicholas Urda, Jacob Thornhill, Sarah Chaney, Louise Flory, Peter Cappello, Rachel McPhee; Workshop Theater; November 3 – 19, 2011

Parts of Parts & Stitches by Riti Sachdeva; Directed by Cat Parker; Stage Manager, Sarah E. Ford; Lighting Designer, Carl Faber; Set Designer, George Allison; Costume Designer, Karen Ann Ledger; Sound Designer, Martha Goode; Cast: Sarah Baskin, Purva Bedi, Jaspal Binning, Sergei Burbank, Mariam Habib, Ashok Kumar, Bushra Laskar, Antonio Miniño, Eric Percival, Anil Ramani, Shetal Shah, Imran W. Sheikh and Dathan B. Williams; The 14th Street Y; March 15 – 31, 2012

The Management

managementtheatercompany.com

Your Boyfriend May Be Imaginary by Larry Kunofsky; Directed by Meg Sturiano; Stage Manager, Kelly Ruth Cole; Lighting Designer, Grant Wilcoxen; Set Designer, Kyle Dixon; Sound Designer, Joseph Varca; Cast: Darcy Fowler, Maya Lawson, Danielle Slavick, Risa Sarachan, Kirsten Hopkins, Jordan Mahome, Debargo Sanyal, Zach Evenson, Quinlan Corbett, Kunal Prasad, Geoffrey Hillback, Penny Middleton; Under St Marks; April 5 – 28, 2012

Manhattan Repertory Theatre

Ray's Delay by Barry Ernst; Directed by Robert Previto; Stage Manager, Alex Nartowicz; Properties Designer, Sara Ernst; Cast: Chris Tyrrko, Maria Russo-Schwartz, Douglas Gerbino, Ted Firetog, Lysane Sanchez, Richie Appelbaum, Trevor Firetog, Alyssa Kirel; Manhattan Repertory Theatre; August 13 – 17, 2011

The Mulberry Bush Written and Directed by Jeff Ronan; Cast: Jeff Ronan, Audra Taliercio; Manhattan Repertory Theatre; June 15 – 23, 2011

Mass Bliss Productions

Brave Ducks by Andrew Belcher; Directed by Simón Adina Hanukai; The Living Theatre; August 19 - 26, 2011

Metropolitan Playhouse

www.metropolitanplayhouse.org

Producing Artistic Director, Alex Roe; Associate Producer, Stephen Pelletier; Promotions Coordinator, Rachael Kosch; Associate Director, Michael Hardart; Costumes Coordination, Sidney Fortner; Assistants to the Artistic Director: Rhys Evans, Tori Sicklick, Dana Sumner-Pritchar

From Rags to Riches by Charles A. Taylor; Directed by Alex Roe; Stage Manager, Heather Olmstead; Lighting Designer, Christopher Weston; Costume Designer, Sidney Fortner; Cast: Danny Makali'i Mittermeyer, Erin Leigh Schmoyer, Ralph Petrarca, Tod Mason, Richard Cottrell, Erwin Falcon, Josh Gulotta, Peter Judd, V. Orion Delwaterman, Carol Lambert, Paul Bomba, Ingrid Saxon, Peter

Judd, Claire Warden, V. Orion Delwater, Josh Gulatta; Metropolitan Playhouse; September 17 - October 16, 2011

The Jazz Singer by Samson Raphaelson; Directed by Laura Livingstone; Stage Manager, Niki Armato; Lighting Designer, Christopher Weston; Set Designer, Alex Roe; Costume Designer, Sidney Fortner; Sound Designer, Michael Hardart; Cast: Justin Flagg, Michael Durkin, Andrew Clateman, Christine Claiborne Bullen, Nona Pipes, Charles E. Gerber, Bob Greenberg, John William Rhea, John Russell; Metropolitan Playhouse; November 16 – December 11, 2011

Deep Are The Roots by Arnad d'Usseau and James Gow; Directed by Michael Hardart; Stage Manager, Niki Armato; Lighting Designer, Christopher Weston; Set Designer, Emily Inglis; Costume Designer, Sidney Fortner; Choreographer, Scott Barrow; Cast: R.J. Foster, J.M. McDonough, Michael James Anderson, Teresa Kelsey, Caitlin McEwan, Gloria Sauvé, Stephen Pelletier, David Burfoot, William J. Allgood, John Detty, Nirayl Wilcox; Metropolitan Playhouse; March 9 – April 1, 2012

The House of Mirth by Edith Wharton and Clyde Fitch; Directed by Alex Roe; Stage Manager, William Carlton; Lighting Designer, Christopher Weston; Set & Sound Designer, Alex Roe; Costume Designer, Sidney Fortner; Cast: Oliver Conant, Jane Cortney, Rick Delaney, Suzanne Du Charme, Erik A. Gullberg, Jonathan Horvath, Amanda Jones, Kelly King, Kerry Malloy, Marie Marshall, Laura Sametz, Maria Silverman, Peter Tedeschi; Metropolitan Playhouse; April 21 – May 20, 2012

FESTIVAL

The East Village Theater Festival by Robert Anthony, Claudia Barnett, Alberto Bonilla, Lawrence DuKore, Bryce Richardson, Michael Ian Walker, Kathleen Warnock, Larry R. Yates; Directed by Andrew Firda, Laura Livingstone, Derek Jamison; Cast: Paul Bomba, John Fennessy, Sidiki Fofana, Kate Geller, Emily Gittelman, Ralph Pochoda, Russell Jordan, Gordon Kupperstein, Rob Maitner, Teresa Stephenson, Clare Barron, Keri Setaro, Abraham Sparrow, Me'Lisa Sellers, Jane O'Leary, Joel Putnam, Liz Elise Richards; Metropolitan Playhouse; June 6 – 26, 2011

Mind The Art Entertainment

www.MindTheArtEntertainment.com

Die: Roll to Proceed by Joe Kurtz; Directed by Christian De Gre; Lighting Designer, Sarah Arnold; Set, Sound & Properties Designer, Christian De Gre; Costume Designer, Cora Levin; Cast: Joe Kurtz, Justin Anselmi, Amanda Kay Schill, Robb Moreira, Joseph Reese, David Williams, R. Patrick Alberty, Phillip James, Ed Buck, Emily Meier, Jonathon Siregar; The Red Room; March 30 – October 19, 2012

Mind The Gap Theatre

www.mindthegaptheatre.com

Artistic Director, Paula D'Alessandris

The Average-Sized Mermaid by Jessica Fleitman; Directed by Paula D'Alessandris; Stage Manager, Katy Moore; Lighting Designer, Joyce Liao; Costume Designer, Ghislaine Sabiti; Sound Designer, Nick Robertson; Choreographer, Melissa Riker; Cast: Dawn McGee, Vinnie Penna, David J. Goldberg, Erika Myers, Shannon Munley, Daniel Cibener; Co-produced with Early Bird Theatricals and Robin Rothstein; Connelly Theater, NY Fringe Festival; August 12-28, 2011

The World Is My Cheesecake by Daniel Damiano; Directed by Paula D'Alessandris, Daniel Damiano and Stephanie Staes; Stage Manager, Joshua Quinn; Assistant Stage Manager, Christopher Hlinka; Cast: Judy Alvarez, Sue Glausen, Emma Gordon, Richard Kent Green, Kate Greer, Justin Herfel, Michael

Janove, DH Johnson, Simon Pearl, George Stavropoulos, Stuart Williams, Anna Emily Wood; Co-produced with fandango4 productions; The Workshop Theater; September 6-17, 2012

adrenalin...heart by Georgia Fitch; Directed by Paula D'Alessandris; Cast: Mia Moreland, Lain Gray; Space on White; April 26 - May 20, 2012

Deuteranomaly by Jessica Fleitman; Directed by Paula D'Alessandris; Stage Manager, John Michael Crotty; Lighting Designer, Artem Kreimer; Cast: Vinne Penna, Dee Dee Friedman, David J. Goldberg, Erika Lee; produced as part of the 2012 Planet Connections Festivity; 45 Bleecker; May 30 - June 24, 2012

Miranda Co.

www.miranda-opera.com

Co-Artistic Directors, Kamala Sankaram, Rob Reese

Miranda by Kamala Sankaram, Rob Reese; Directed by Rob Reese; Musical Director, Kamala Sankaram; Stage Manager, Christine Liz Pynn, Heather Smaha; Lighting and Set Designer, Nick Francone; Costume Designer, Jacci Jaye; Audio Mixer and Sound Designer, Matt Schloss; Video Designer, Matt Tennie; Choreographer, Lauren Yalango with Christopher Grant; -Master Electrician and Light Board Operator, Heather Smaha; Live Video Mixer, Spike McCue; Video Operator, Matt Tennie; Technical Director, Nolan Kennedy; Cast: Kamala Sankaram, Drew Fleming, Pat Muchmore, Rima Fand, Ed Rosenberg, Jeff Hudgins, Jerry Miller, Eric Brenner; Co-Produced with HERE Arts Center; HERE Arts Center; January 12-21, 20012

Mississippi Mud Productions

www.mississippimudproductions.com

Orson's Shadow by Austin Pendleton; Directed by Lauren Reinhard; Stage Manager, Bethany Briggs; Lighting Designer, Alexander Bartenieff; Set Designer, Michele Spadaro & Stephen Dobay; Costume Designer, Catherine Siracusa & Sidney Levitt; Sound Designer, Lisa Raymond; Hair & Makeup Designer, Catherine Zubkow; Choreographer, Turner Smith; Cast: Jen Danby, Dana Jesberger, Andy McCutcheon, Adam Newborn, Stephen Peabody, Eric Rice; Studio Theater @ Theatre Row; October 6–19, 2011

Mixed Phoenix Theatre Group

www.mptg.org

Muzungu by David Myers; Directed by Robert A. K. Gonyo; Lighting Designer, Isabella F. Byrd; Set Designer, Joshua David Bishop; Cast: Ryan Victor Pierce, Nneoma Nkuku; New York Theatre Workshop's 4th Street Theatre; October 14–30, 2011

Modern-Day Griot Theatre Company

www.moderndaygriot.org

Founder and Artistic Director, Pharah Jean-Philippe; Associate Artistic Director, Jamila Sockwell; Managing Producer, Liza Bulos; Managing Director, Zenobia Connor

Lyrics in Motion by Whitney Greenaway, Kevantae Idlett, Rainmaker and Zook; Directed by Pharah Jean-Philippe; Stage Manager, Latia Kirby; House Managers, Zenobia Connor, Jamila Sockwell, Loresa Lanceta; Event Coordinator, Liza Bulos; Cast: Whitney Greenaway, Kevantae Idlett, Rainmaker, Zook, Jessica Isa Burns, Jessica Cruz, Yizhen Lim, and Francesca Cecala; South Oxford Space; October 14 - 15, 2011

for black boys who have considered homicide when the streets were too much by Keith Antar Mason; Directed by Pharah Jean-Philippe; Stage Manager, Surayah Davis; Lighting Designer, Matthew Brookshire; Set and Sound Designer, Pharah Jean-Philippe; Costume Designer, Ayanna Siverls-Streater; Dramaturg, Zenobia Connor; Choreographer, Jessica Isa Burns; Lighting Board Operator; Cassandra Powell; Event Coordinator & Marketing, Liza Bulos; House Managers, Hugh Anderson, Loresa Lanceta, Latia Kirby; Cast: Loren Amos, Alexis Francisco, Anthony Gaskins, Robert Siverls, Zook, Moe Felican, Michael Alexis Palmer, David Roberts and Duane Boutte; The Actors Fund Arts Center at The Schermerhorn; December 1- 18, 2011

Spiraling Into Place by Tremane Nicholson; Directed by Pharah Jean-Philippe; Stage Manager, Yvonne Facey; Lighting and Costume Designer, Pharah Jean-Philippe; Cast: Tremane Nicholson; South Oxford Space; February 17 - 19, 2012

READINGS & WORKSHOPS

See, Hear, Taste Touch by Pharah Jean-Philippe, Stephanie Bok, Kay Poiro, Irene Zeigler, Jamie Pachino; Directed by Liza Bulos; Kyle Nunn, Pharah Jean-Philippe, Stacey Hardke, Colin Walker, Alice Renier, Alexis Francisco, China Colston, Scott Hinson; South Oxford Space; May 25, 2012

A Song for Coretta by Pearl Cleage; Directed by Pharah Jean-Philippe; Angela McKee, Kari Hinkson, Yvonne Facey, Latia Kirby, Felecia Mathis and Pharah Jean-Philippe; South Oxford Space; March 17, 2012

Molly Dykeman Productions

mollyequalitydykeman.com

The F*cking World According To Molly Written and Performed by Andrea Alton; Directed by Mark Finley; Stage Manager, Jennifer Russo; Lighting Designer, Daniel Winters; Costume Designer, Anthony Catanzaro; Sound Designer, David Crabb; Choreographer, John Paolillo; Laurie Beechman Theatre/West Bank Cafe; August 13 – September 2, 2011

Moose Hall Theatre Company/ Inwood Shakespeare Festival

www.moosehallisf.org

Producing Artistic Director, Ted Minos; Technical Director/Educational Outreach, Catherine Bruce. Music/Sound Director, Luke St. Francis. Art/Graphics Director, Lee Kaplan. Fight Director, Ray A. Rodriguez. Associate Producer, Aaron Simms. Opera Production

Othello by William Shakespeare; Directed by Chaya Gordon-Bland; Musical Director, Luke St. Francis; Lighting Designer, Catherine Bruce; Costume Designer, Marie Gallas-Suissa & Catherine Bruce; Sound Designer, Luke St. Francis; Technical Director, Catherine Bruce; Fight Choreographer, Chaya Gordon-Bland; Assistant to the director, Samantha Bruce; Associate Producer, Aaron Simms; Producing Artistic Director, Ted Minos; Cast: Andrew Ash, Samantha Rivers Cole, Ben Coleman, Michael Lawrence Eisenstein, Frank Franconeri, Shannon Harris, Per Janson, Ted Minos, Sean MacBride Murray, Ray A. Rodriguez, Jennifer R. Terrell, Johnny Viel; Inwood Hill Park Peninsula; June 8-25 2011

War of the Worlds Written and Directed by Ted Minos; Musical Director, Luke St. Francis; Lighting Designer, Catherine Bruce; Costume Designer, Marie Gallas-Suissa and Catherine Bruce; Sound Designer, Luke St. Francis; Technical Director, Catherine Bruce; Fight Choreographer, Ray A. Rodriguez; Cast: Amanda Griemsmann, Doc Holliday, Randall Marquez, Ted Minos, Marissa Molnar, Alexa Mullen, George Pappas, Ross Pivec, Michael Propster, Max Robkoff, Elliot Wadsworth, Kelly Wallace-Barnhill, Karen Wexler; Inwood Hill Park Peninsula; July 20-August 6, 2011

Mortal Folly Theatre

Merely Players: Princes to Act by William Shakespeare; Directed by Katherine Harte-DeCoux; Cast: Alyssa Borg, Katie Braden, Erik Cheski, Nathan DeCoux, Charlotte Dunn, Cheri Paige Fogelman, Jacqueline Holloway, Laura King, Cary Patrick Martin, Jake Mosser, Marcus Petersen, Emma Servant, John Short; produced in association with Bushwick Shakespeare Repertory Looking Glass Theatre; July 17 – 25, 2011

MultiStages

www.eljallartsannex.com/Multistages

Artistic Director and Founder, Lorca Peress

Temple of the Souls by Anita Velez-Mitchell; Directed by Lorca Peress; Musical Director, Bruce Baumer; Stage Manager, Jessica V. Urtecho; Lighting Designer, Alex Moore; Set Designer, Lorca Peress; Costume Designer, Mark Richard Caswell; Sound Designer, Josh Millican; Producer, Lorca Peress; Composer, Orchestrations, Arrangements, Dean Landon; Composer and Additional Lyrics, Anika Paris; Choreographer, Milteri Tucker; Mask/ Puppetry Designer, Kyla McHale; Conductor/Pianist, Evan Closser; Assistant to Director, Liz Wexler; Assistant Costume Designer, Jessa-Raye Court; Cast: Jen Anaya, Theresa Burns, Victor Cervantes, Raquel Faria, Bradley D. Gale, Giselle Gastell, Randall Marquez, Kenneth Kyle Martinez, Robmariel Olea, Ricardo Puente, Laura Riveros, Laura Lebron-Rojas, Alexis Sweeney, Joshua Torrez, Patrick Valley; West End Theatre; December 8-23, 2011

READINGS & WORKSHOPS

Appetite by Arden Kass; Directed by Lorca Peress; Music Composed by Rob Redei; Cast: Mark Alhadeff, Molly Carden, Ron Cohen, Lynn Cohen, Tovah Feldshuh, Kathryn Layng, Romy Nordlinger, Anna O'Donough, Mikel Sarah Lambert, Tracy Sallows, Marina Squerciati, Susan Wallack, Piano Accompanist, Evan Closter; Assistants to the Director, Jaki Silver, Erin McGuff; Pearl Studios; October 3, 2011

Cenote by Isabella Russell-Ides; Directed by Lorca Peress; Cast: Jen Anaya, Denia Brache, Gabriel Guttierrez, Robmariel Olea, Lillian Rodriguez, Laura Lebron Rojas, Miguel Sierra, Joshua Torrez, Fidel Vicioso; Director's Assistant Timothy Licht; Pearl Studios; February 6, 2012

Little Voices by Chris Longo; Directed by Tea Alagic; Cast: Christianna Nelson, Alec Beard, Keoni Scott, Anna O'Donoghue, Richarda Abrams, Michele LaRue; Assistants Timothy Licht, Lillian Rodriguez; Pearl Studios; February 13, 2012

Remembrance by Jeffrey Harper; Directed by Robert Kalfin; Cast: Jason Collins, Ylfa Edelstein, Michael Lawrence Eisenstein, Sam Guncler, Michael-Kennan Miller, Natalie Mosco, Larry Pine, Joseph Urla; Festival Assistant Timothy Licht; Pearl Studios; February 20, 2012

The mush-room theatre design

www.themush-roomtheatre.com

The Father by August Strindberg; Directed by Oscar A. Mendoza; Sound Designer, Gabriel Comrie Pepin; Original Music, Xavier Paez Haubold; Cast: the mush-room theatre design; Robert Moss Theater; June 11 – 25, 2011

Neighborhood Productions

www.neighborhoodproductions.org

Co-Founder & Producers, Dorit Avganim, Amanda Feldman

Lake Water by Troy Deutsch; Directed by Daniel Talbott; Stage Manager, Hannah

Woodward; Lighting Designer, Brad Peterson; Set Designer, Eugenia Furneaux-Arends; Costume Designer, Tristan Raines; Sound Designer, Janie Bullard; Creative Line Producer, Amanda Feldman; Assistant Director, Ashley Monroe; Cast: Troy Deusch, Samantha Soule; IRT Theater; September 17 - October 2, 2011

Prison Light by Austin Flint; Directed by Alice Reagan; Stage Manager, Kaitlin Nemeth; Lighting Designer, Ellie Rabinowitz; Set Designer, Andreea Mincic; Costume Designer, Ramsey Scott; Sound Designer, Elizabeth Rhodes; Cast: Sara Buffamanti, Bernardo Cubria, Tomas Hiltunen, Chad Hoepner, Meg MacCary, and Danielle Slavick; Dorothy B Williams Theater, HERE Arts Center; October 20 - 30, 2011

New Feet Productions

www.leavethebalconyopen.com

Leave the Balcony Open by Maya Macdonald; Directed by Jessica Bauman; Stage Manager, Emily Paige Ballou; Lighting Designer, Cat Tate Starmer; Set Designer, Gabriel Hainer Evansohn; Costume Designer, Sydney Gallas; Sound Designer, Brandon Wolcott; Properties Designer, Timothy Gilligan; Cast: Heidi Armbruster, Jerzy Gwiazdowski, Betsy Hogg, Julie Kline, Jared McGuire, Anna O'Donoghue, Mary Rasmussen; 3ld Art and Technology Center; February 5 – 26, 2012

New Haarlem Arts Theatre

Blues for Mister Charlie by James Baldwin; Directed by Eugene Nesmith; Stage Manager, Tara Nachtigall; Lighting Designer, Brian Aldous; Set Designer, Heather Wolensky; Costume Designer, Mary Myers; Assistant Director, Naya Tabie Johnson; Dramaturg, Chris Rempfer; Cast: Kelvin Hale, Earl Griffin, Dennis Jordan, Billy Lake, Johnnie Mae, and Reginald L. Wilson, Amanda Figueiredo, Brian Reese, Franceli Chapman, Leroy Graham, Johnny Maldonado, Jasmine Romero, Chandler Wild, Lucas Babits-Feinerman, Trevania Campbell, Dorothy Davis, Katherine Guenther, Stephan Macari, Nathaniel Manning, Edwin Polanco, and Tiffany Warren; Aaron Davis Hall; June 25 - July 17, 2011

It Ain't Nothing But The Blues Written and Directed by Charles Bevel, Lita Gaithers, Randal Myler, Ron Taylor, and Dan Wheetman; Lighting Designer, Brian Aldous; Set Designer, Heather Wolensky; Costume Designer, Mary Myers; Cast: Dameka Hayes, Marvel Allen, Jeffrey Bolding, Nathaly Lopez, Shawn Brown and Darilyn Castillo; unknown; July 30 – August 21, 2011

New Ohio Theatre

www.sohothinktank.org

Artistic Director, Robert Lyons; Producing Director, Marc Stuart Weitz ; Artistic Associate, Samuel Buggeln; Technical Director, Marshall Miller; Publicist, David Gibbs/DARR Publicity; Web Master, Art Meets Commerce; Accountant, Rich and Bander, LLP; Lawyer, Margaret B. Grossman, Paul, Weiss; Development Consultant, Anne Erbe; Intern, Lola Jordan

Take What is Yours by Erica Fae and Jill A. Samuels; Directed by Jill A. Samuels; Video Designer, Tal Yarden; Sound Designer, Kristin Worrall; Costume Designer, Alixandra Gage Englund; Lighting Designer, Alison Brummer; Set Design Consultant, Deb O; Cast: Erica Fae, Nathan Guisinger, Kiki Bowman, David Riley, and Taavo Smith; New Ohio Theatre; October 7 – 23, 2011

Two-Man Kidnapping Rule by Joseph Gallo; Directed by Robin A. Paterson; Set Designer, G. Warren Stiles; Lighting Designer, Robin A. Paterson; Sound Designer, Craig Lenti; Cast: Curran Connor, Duane Cooper & Andy Lutz; New Ohio Theatre; October 29 – November 20, 2011

Post Office by David Jenkins; Directed by Josie Whittlesey; Set Designer, Alexis Distler; Lighting Designer, Seth Reiser; Cast: Anney Giobbe, Eric Hoffmann, and David Gelles; Produced by Human Animals; New Ohio Theatre; December 1 – 17, 2011

Samuel and Alasdair: A Personal History of the Robot War by Marc bovino and Joe Curnutte; Co-conceived & Directed by Lila Neugebauer; Set Designer, Laura Jellinek; Costume Designer, Jessica Pabst; Lighting Designer, Mike Inwood; Sound Designer, Stowe Nelson; Cast: Marc Bovino, Joe Curnutte, Michael Dalto and Stephanie Wright Thompson; Created by The Mad Ones; New Ohio Theatre; January 5 – February 18, 2012

The Deepest Play Ever: The Catharsis of Pathos by Geoffrey Decas O'Donnell; Music by Michael Wells; Directed by Lee Sunday Evans and Jordan Seavey; Set, Properties, and Puppet Designer, Deb O; Costume Designer, Nikki Moody; Lighting Designer, Nick Houfek; Sound Designer, Brandon Wolcott; Music Director, Michael Wells; Associate Music Director, Nicholas Williams; Percussion, Teddy Lytle; Stage Manager, Kaitlin Nemeth; Graphic Designer, Derek Rippe; Creative Producer, Amanda Feldman; Cast: Jordan Barbour, Carly Cioffi, Nick Choksi, John Halbach, Boo Killebrew, Geoffrey Decas O'Donnell, Chinasa Ogbuagu, Phillip Taratula, Emily Walton, TJ Witham; Produced by CollaborationTown; New Ohio Theatre; March 9 – 25, 2012

Tiny Lights: Memory's Storehouse/Infinite Miniature Created and Performed by Lenora Champagne and Lizzie Olesker; Dramaturge, Claire MacDonald; Sound Designer and Music Consultant, Ellen Maddow; New Ohio Theatre; May 17 – 20, 2012

New Perspectives Theatre Company

www.newperspectivestheatre.org

Artistic Director, Melody Brooks; General Manager, Catharine Guiher

Women in Transition by Zeno Obi Constance; Directed by Damion Gonzalez and Merlina Rich; Produced by Banana Boat Production; Costume Designer, Athena Roque; Set Designer, Meganne George; Lighting Designer, Liao; Thecnical Consultant, Mario Monreal; Stage Manager, Laura Merforth; Assistant Stage Manager, Jajmi Robinson; Associat Producer, Melody Brooks; Cast: Nixon Cesar, Lindon Ferryman, Shykla Fields, Damion Gonzalez, Shernell Julien, Gabriella Lake, Shereen Macklin, Tessa Martin, David McLeod, Shirley Parkinson-Wright, Adeola Wilson; New Perspectives Studio; October 26 – November 6, 2011

FESTIVALS

Women's Work Original Short Play Festival; *Bright Lights, Tent City* by France-Luce Benson; Directed by Jenny Greeman; *Nothing Left to Steal* by Marisa Petsakos; Directed by Elysa Marden; *Peola's Passing* by Cynthia Robinson; Directed by Melody Brooks; *An Apple A Day* by Heather Violanti; Directed by Celia Braxton; Stage Manager, Shannon Martha; Set Designer, Meganne George; Costume Designer, Athena Roque; Lighting Designer, Deborah Constantine; New Perspectives Studio; September 26 – October 1, 2011

Voices from the Edge 2012; *Lead Follow or Get Out of the Way* by Rafael Jordan; Directed by Jenny Greeman and Marissa Molnar; Cast: Annie Fox, David Jenkins, Brianna Kalisch, Annalisa Ledson, David Marcus, Michele Richardson, Danny Rivera, Omrae Smith, Federico Trigo, Giovanni Varga; *Iced Out, Shackled and Chained: Still Looking for the North Starr* by Kisha T. Spence and Mo Beasley; Directed by Jeffery V. Thompson; Cast: Stephanie Berry and Bianca LaVerne Jones; Lighting Designer, Joyce Liao; Production Design Consultant, Meganne George; Sound Designer, Kyle Bailey and Elliot Lanes; Stage Manager, Elliot Lanes; New Perspectives Studio; April 26 – May 5, 2012

READINGS

Tunnel Vision by Andrea Lepcio, directed by Melissa Maxwell; McGinn-Cazale Theatre; September 25, 2011

Shamhat by Rosebud Ben-Oni; Directed by Melody Brooks, November 7, 2011

Mother of God! by Michele Miller; Directed by Melody Brooks

Marla and Her Prayers by Kim Merrill; Directed by Elysa Marden; October 2, 2011

New Stage Theatre Company

www.newstagetheatre.org

Artistic Director and Founder, Ildiko Nemeth; Principal Administrator, Fabiyan Pemble-Belkin

Hypnotik: The Seer Will Doctor You Now by Colm O'Shea, Marie Glancy O'Shea & Ildiko Nemeth; Directed by Ildiko Nemeth; Lighting Designer, Federico Restrepo; Set Designer, Ildiko Nemeth; Costume Designer, Jessica Sofia Mitrani; Original Music, Jon Gilbert Leavitt; Choreographer, Julie Atlas Muz; Set Construction Kertek Construction Corp; Set Construction Crew, Sean Bauer and Fabiyan Pemble-Belkin; Sound Engineer, Paul Radelat, Costumer, Marguerite Lochard and Kate Jansyn Thaw; Press Representative, DARR Publicity; Sound Operator, Wilson Sherwin; Cast: Dana Boll, Adam Boncz, Kaylin Lee Clinton, Markus Hirnigel, Denice Kondik, Sarah Lemp, Laurence Martin, Brandon Olson, Fabiyan Pemble-Belkin, Jeanne Lauren Smith, Peter B. Schmitz, Chris Tanner, Paula Wilson, Kat Yew; Theater for the New City; December 21, 2011 - January 15, 2012

New Worlds Theatre Project

www.newworldsproject.org

Producing Artistic Director, Ellen Perecman; Managing Director, Scott Shaw Matthews; Associate Producing Director, Stephen Fried; Associate Artist, Bill Clarke; Graphic Designer, Barrett Brown

Under the Cross by I. D. Berkovitch; Directed by David Winitsky; Stage Manager, Jason Pizzi; Lighting Designer, Josh Benghiat; Set Designer, Bill Clarke; Costume Designer, James McDaniel; Sound Designer, Ken Feldman; Producer, Ellen Perecman; Cast: Dan Bielinski, Anthony Laurent, Trish McCall, Marcus Naylor, Jim Nugent, Tim Roselle, Caroline Ryburn, and Sonja Rzepski; Translation and adaptation by Ellen Perecman; Abingdon Theatre Arts Complex, June Havoc Theatre; June 3 - 25, 2011

Welcome to America by H. Leivick; Directed by Stephen Fried; Stage Manager, Laura Lindsay; Lighting Designer, John Kernisky; Costume Designer, Alixandra Gage Englund; Producer, Ellen Perecman; Scenic Designer, Lee Savage; Cast: Alice Cannon, Jessica DiSalvo, Alvin Keith, Claire Kennedy, Josh Odsess-Rubin, Anthony Peeples, Donald Warfield and Dathan B. Williams; Translation and adaptation by Ellen Perecman; 45th Street Theatre; May 2 - 20, 2012

READINGS & WORKSHOPS

Professor Brenner by Dovid Pinski; Directed by Stephen Fried; Translator and Adaptor, Ellen Perecman; Cast: Brian Cade, Gian-Murray Gianino, Jorge Humberto Hoyos, Peter Francis James, Deanne Lorette, Melissa Miller, Philip Mutz, Sarah Schenkkan, Elaine Stritch, Derek Wilson; Brotherhood Synagogue; Octob er 27, 2011

With the Current by Sholem Asch; Directed by Stephen Fried; Translator and Adaptor Ellen Perecman; Actors Anna Kull, Allan Leicht, Yelena Shmulenson, and Derek Wilson; Yiddish Book Center; August 11 - 14, 2011

New York Classical Theatre

www.newyorkclassical.org

Henry V by William Shakespeare; Directed by Stephen Burdman; Castle Clinton in Battery Park; July 6 - 24, 2011

New York Neo-Futurists

www.nynf.org

Managing Director, Rob Neill; Assistant Managing Director, Cecil Baldwin; Technical Director, Lauren Parrish

Too Much Light Makes the Baby Go Blind Written and Directed by the NY Neo-Futurists Ensemble; Stage Manager, Lauren Parrish, Christine Cullen, Shane Reader, Aliee Chan, Daniel Mirsky, Laurel Detkin and Laura Schlachtmeyer; Cast: Cecil Baldwin, Meg Bashwiner, Joe Basile, Jill Beckman, Christopher Borg, Eliza Burmester, Roberta Colindrez, Jeffrey Cranor, Chris Dippel, Cara Francis, Ricky Gamboa, Ryan Good, Eevin Hartsough, Chisa Hutchinson, Kate Jones, Nicole Hill, Jacquelyn Landgr; Specialty Weekends: *30 Half-Nekkid plays in 60 Half-Nekkid minutes*, August 2011; *Fair Use Show*, April 2012; *Too Much Pride Makes the Baby Go Gay*, June 2012; The Kraine Theater; July 1, 2011- June 30, 2012

The Complete & Condensed Stage Directions of Eugene O'Neill: Vol. 1 Early Plays/Lost Plays by Eugene O'Neill and Christopher Loar; Directed by Christopher Loar; Stage Manager and Lighting Designer, Christine Cullen; Set and Costume Designer, Cara Francis; Sound and AudioVisual Designer, Christopher Loar; General Manager, Mikell Korber; Choreographer, Lauren Sharpe; Cast: Danny Burnam, Brendan Donaldson, Cara Francis, Connor Kalista, Jacquelyn Landgraf, Erica Livingston, Lauren Sharpe; The Kraine Theater; September 8 - October 1, 2011

You are in an open field: A Hip Hop Musical Video Game about Identity by Eevin Hartsough, Kevin R. Free, Marta Rainer and Adam Smith; Directed by Chris Dippel; Musical Director, Carl Riehl; Stage Manager, Shane Reader; Lighting Designer, Lauren Parrish; Set and Costume Designers, Chris Dippel and Lauren Parrish; Sound Designer, Carl Riehl; AudioVisual Designer, Liliana Dirks-Goodman; Dramaturgy, Jeffrey Cranor; Choreography, Laurie Berg; Live Band, Carl Riehl, Scott Selig, Patrick Carmichael; Cast: Kevin R. Free, Marta Rainer, Adam Smith, Steve French, Cherylynn Tsushima; HERE Arts Center; April 26 - May 19, 2012

Nia Theatrical Production Company, Inc.

www.niaproduction.org

Artistic Director, L. Earl Ford; Asstitant Atistic Director, Evria Dechane Atwell

Deceit of Truth by Harvey Johnson; Directed by Ronesha Bell; Stage Manager, Morgan Watters; Lighting Designer, Ulric O'Flaherty; Set Designer, Harvey johnson; Costume Designer, Bruce Lewis; AudioVisual Designer, Stefan Tonio; Producer:,L. Earl Ford; Assistant Stage Manager, Eunice Ukwuani; Interns/Production Assistants, Mekael Ben-Levi, Shawanna Dilworth, Brian Eastman, Giovanni Nolberto, and Debbie Thomas; Cast: Reginald L. Barnes, Dyalekt, Kelly Knight, Johanny Paulino, and Michelle Robinson; Co-Producer: Harvey Johnson; Roy Arias Theatres; March 17-27, 2011

Marry Me?! by KUBA; Directed by L. Earl Ford; Stage Manager, Evria Dechane Atwell; Lighting Designer, Ulric O'Flaherty; Set and Sound Designer, L. Earl Ford; Costume Designer, L. Earl Ford, Evria Dechane Atwell; Production Assistants/Interns: Monai Valentine, Jasmin Niles, Alexandra Morel, and Tyrone Francisco; Cast: Regine Mont-Louis, Larry Greenbush, Gary Lawson, Liz peterson, and Flor Bromley; The Actors Fund Arts Center Brooklyn and Roy Arias Theatres; March 28-April 8, 2012

Nicholas Ward Productions

The Table Scene Written and Directed by MacAdam Smith; Stage Manager, Nicholas Ward; Lighting Designer, Mitch Ost; Sound Designer, M.L. Dogg; Video Designer, Russ Kuhner; Cast: Antony Raymond, Bridget Coyne Gabbe, Jordan Coughtry, Deanna Henson, DeVon Jackson; Urban Stages; April 26 – August 26, 2012

Nicu's Spoon

www.spoontheater.org

How the Day Runs Down by John Langan; Directed & Choreographed by Stephanie Barton-Farcas; Stage Manager, Juni Li; Lighting Designer, Steven Wolf; Sound Designer, Stephanie Barton-Farcas; Makeup, Sammy Mena; Original Music, Damon Law; Cast: Mark Armstrong, Elizabeth Bell, Rebecca Lee Lerman, Erwin Falcon, Matt Derogatis, Sammy Mena, Sophie Farcas, Mandy Beltran, Alexis Stowers, Sean Cameron, Jon Rios, Tyler Strickland, Katie Labahn; Spoon Theatre; July 6 – 24, 2011

No Anita No Productions

www.friendsandrelationstheplay.com

Friends and Relations by Marc Castle; Directed by Adam Fitzgerald; Stage Manager, Jessa Nicole Pollack; Lighting Designer, Travis McHale; Set Designer, David L. Arsenault; Costume Designer, Erica Evans; Sound Designer, Ian Wehrle; Cast: Dan Amboyer, Joel T. Bauer, Nigel DeFriez, Matt Golden, Vince Nappo, Ben Roberts, Christopher Sloan; June Havoc Theatre; December 1 – 17, 2011

Northwest Passage

newptheater.com

Romeo and Juliet by William Shakespeare; Directed by Anya Saffir; Lighting & Set Designer, Gabriel Evansohn; Costume Designer, Katja Andreiev; Original Music, Cormac Bluestone; Fight Choreographer, Turner Smith; Cast: Paul Corning, Sam Dash, Clayton Early, Paul Eddy, Chris Hale, Matt Hanson, Glenn Hergenhahn, Will Irons, Dan Jones, Vladimir Margolin, John-Michael Scapin, Scott Walker, Ben Weaver; American Theatre of Actors; March 1 – 17, 2012

Nosedive Productions

www.nosediveproductions.com

Co-Artistic Directors, Pete Boisvert and James Comtois; Company Manager Stephanie Cox-Williams; Artistic Associates: Rebecca Comtois, Marc Landers, Patrick Shearer, Ben VandenBoom and Christopher Yustin

The Blood Brothers Present Freaks from the Morgue by James Comtois, Stephanie Cox-Williams, Mac Rogers, Brian Silliman, Crystal Skillman; Directed by Pete Boisvert, John Hurley, Patrick Shearer; Production Stage Manager, Jenna Dempsey; Rehearsal Stage Managers, Stephanie Cox-Williams & Sandy Yaklin; Costume Designer, Karle Myers; Graphic Designer, Pete Boisvert; Lighting Designer, Jeremy Pape & Russell Dobular; Makeup Designer, Melissa Roth; Sound Designer, Patrick Shearer; Properties & Effects Designer, Stephanie Cox-Williams; Fight Choreographer, Joe Mathers; Carpenter, Chris Connolly; Original Music, Larry Lees; Press Agent, James Comtois & Ron Lasko; Producers: Pete Boisvert, James Comtois, Stephanie Cox-Williams, Patrick Shearer; Associate Producers: Rebecca Comtois, Marc Landers, Ben VandenBoom, Christopher Yustin; Cast: Leah Carrell, TJ Clark, Stephanie Cox-Williams, Stephanie Finn, Marc Landers, Abraham Makany, Samantha Mason, Collin McConnell, Judy Merrick, Ingrid Nordstrom, Ben Schnickel; Kraine Theater; June 9 – July 2, 2011

Infectious Opportunity by James Comtois; Directed by Pete Boisvert; Stage Manager, Stephanie Cox-Williams; Set Designers, Rebecca Comtois & Ben VandenBoom; Sound Designer, Patrick Shearer; Lighting Designer, Jeremy Pape; Properties & Costume Designer, Stephanie Cox-Williams; Original Music, Itai Sol; David Ian Lee, Jessi Gotta, Daryl Lathon, Matthew Trumbull, DR Hanson, Rebecca Comtois, Ingrid Nordstrom; The Living Theatre; August 13 – 26, 2011

Nunya Productions LLC

nunyaproductions.com

Some Girl(s) by Neil Labute; Directed by Roger Delpozo; Stage Manager, Rome Brown; Lighting Designer, Rome Brown & Michael King; Set & Sound Designer, Michael King; Original Music, Itchy Face; Cast: Michael King, Mariya King, Robin Singer, Rebecca De Ornelas, Betty Kaplan, Jody Lyn Flynn; American Theatre of Actors, Sargent Theatre; December 8 – 17, 2011

Nuyorican Poets Cafe

www.nuyorican.org

A Felony in Blue Written and Directed by Daniel Gallant; Original Music, Michael Gallant; Cast: Sonia Hebe, Brian MacDonald, Rommell Sermons, TK Durham, Kymberly Tuttle, Nicol Moeller; Nuyorican Poets Cafe; October 12 – 29, 2011

Nylon Fusion Collective

You Are Here by Jack Karp, Kate Mulley, Alisha Silver, Joseph Samuel Wright; Directed by Jerry Ruiz; Stage Manager, Kaitlin Springston; Lighting Designer, Chris Weston; Set Designer, Thomas George; Costume Designer, Alisha Silver; Sound Designer, David Corsello; Cast: Caroline Bloom, Justin Maruri, Nick Walkonis, Elyssa Jakim, Brandon Hightower, Wheaton Simis, Rebecca Hirota, Mark Souza; Gene Frankel Theatre; November 4 – 20, 2011

Miss Hope's by Alisha Silver, Jack Karp and Joseph Samuel Wright; Directed by David Triacca; Stage Manager, Rachel Gordon; Lighting Designer, Daisy Long; Costume Designer, Chris Clarke; Sound Designer, Gisela Fulla Silvestre; Cast: Katherine Barron, Rachel Buethe, Chris Cardona, Madison Comerzan, Michael Karp, Dave Hanson, Stephanie Heitman , Joshua Hinck, Dustin Kerns, Eileen Lacy, Kelsey Mahoney, Laura Pruden, Fidel Vicioso, Donna Ross, Ivette Dumeng; American Theatre of Actors; May 23 – June 23, 2012

On the Square Productions

www.onthesquareproductions.com

Executive Director, Rachel McPhee Benson; Artistic Director, Jackie LaVanway; Associate Creative Director, Michael Swartz; Director of Development, Rob Benson; Director of Education, Emily Tucker; Marketing Director, Logan Tracey; Literary Manager, Deborah Wolf

READINGS & WORKSHOPS

Suffer the Brink of Us by Delaney Britt Brewer; Directed by Kara-Lynn Vaeni; Cast: Elizabeth Audley, Bettina Bilger, Charles Andrew Callaghan, Emily Ernst, Wyatt Kuether, Zack Robidas, Ari Rossen, Logan Tracey, Amanda Tudor; The Network NYC; September 12, 2011

The Minervae by Steven Bost; Directed by Dev Bondarin; Cast: Rob Benson, Charles Andrew Callaghan, Colleen Horan, Christopher Kloko, Jackie LaVanway, Brad Makarowski, Rachel McPhee, Marnie Schulenburg, Lavita Shaurice & Michael Swartz; The Room at New Georges; November 7, 2011

Somewhere Safer by Lauren Ferebee; Directed by Deborah Wolfson; Cast: Virginia Baeta, Michelle Beck, Katlyn Carlson, Dan Cozzens, Michael Finn, Daniel Graff, John Michalski, Logan Tracey, Timothy Weinert, & Amelia Workman; The Bridge Theatre; February 27, 2012

Raw Stitch by Jacqueline Goldfinger; Directed by David O'Connor; Cast: Becky Chicoine, Rheaume Crenshaw, Susan Ferrara, Louise Flory, Rachel McPhee & Jenson Smith; Time Out NY Lounge @ New World Stages; April 1, 2012

On Wheels Productions

An Enemy of the People by Henrik Ibsen; Translated by Rolf Fjelde; Directed by Ted Thompson; Stage Manager, Debra Workman; Sound Designer, Peter Lopez; Production Assistants: Lucy Keyes, Nelly Rodriguez; Cast: David Conklin, Frank Hendriks, Thomas Kane, Kate Labahn, Tony Palmieri, Franco Pistritto, Martina Potratz, Jeffrey Wisniewski; Brecht Forum; June 17 - 26, 2011

One Year Lease

oneyearlease.org

Pool (No Water) by Mark Ravenhill; Directed by Ianthe Demos; Stage Manager, Shelley Miles; Lighting Designer, Mike Riggs; Set Designer, James Hunting; Costume Designer, Kristen Kopp; AudioVisual Designer, Scott J. Fetterman; Choreographer, Natalie Lomonte and Christopher Baker; Original Score, Estelle Bajou; Dramaturge, Jessica Kaplow Applebaum; Photographer, Emily Raw; Graphic Designer, Tall Paul; Press Representative, Richard Kornberg and Associates; Cast: Estelle Bajou, Christopher Baker, Christina Bennett Lind, Nick Flint, Richard Saudek; PS122; May 9 - 26, 2012

The Open Book

www.openbooktheatre.org

Artistic Director, Marvin Kaye; Director, Educational Division, Kathleen C. Szaj

The Last Christmas of Ebenezer Scrooge Written and Directed by Marvin Kaye; Stage Manager, Michele Payne; Costume Designer, Arjay Entertainment; Cast: Stacey Jenson, Marvin Kaye, H. Clark Kee, Nancy Temple; The Parlour; December 11, 2011

The Lady and/or the Tiger by Frank R. Stockton, Jack Moffett, and Marvin Kaye; Directed by Marvin Kaye; Stage Manager, Michele Payne; Cast: Sissy Denkova, John Harlacher, Stacey Jenson, Marvin Kaye; 78th Street Theatre Lab; February 23 - March 3, 2012

Oracle Theatre Inc.

www.captainferguson.com

Captain Ferguson's School For Balloon Warfare by Isaac Rathbone; Directed by Philip Emeott; Lighting Designer, Jennifer Rathbone; Set Designer, Bradleyville Creative Industries; Projection Design, Philip Emeott & Chris Kateff; Cast: David Nelson; 59 E 59 Theaters; August 23 – September 3, 2011

Organs of State

organsofstate.org

Artistic Director, Guy Yedwab; Co-Artistic Director, Benjamin Lundberg; Production Manager, Marika Kent; Events Coordinator, Will Notini; Marketing Coordinator, Euthymios Logothetis

Fighter Written and Directed by Jose Perez IV; Stage Manager, Olivia Edery; Lighting Designer, Marika Kent; Costume Designer, Elizabeth Denning; Sound Designer, Sarah Lurie; AudioVisual Designer, Euthymios Logothetis; Fight Director, Mitch McCoy; Visual Artist, Melanie Glickman, Carlotta Summers; Cast: Andy Zou, Carissa Matsushima, Carlotta Summers, Casey Deming, Cornelius Franklin, Frankie Alicea, Gabe Green, Jason Suran, John Charles Ceccherelli, José Perez IV, Katie Polin, Keenan Jolliff, Kevin C. Gall, Logan McCoy, Madeline Lewis, Melanie Glickman, Michele Tirondola, Mitch McCoy, Par Juneja, Shannon Foy, Taylor Marsh, Trevor Buteau; The Turtle Shell; October 13-23, 2011

In Memoriam by Organs of State; Directed by Benjamin Lundberg; Set Designer, Joel Fullerton; AudioVisual Designer, Benjamin Lundberg; Social Media Manager, Guy Yedwab; Videographer, Will Notini and Guy Yedwab; Cast: Benjamin Lundberg, Guy Yedwab, Marika Kent, Erin McGuff, Sarah Wharton, Will Notini, Euthymios Logothetis, Joel Fullerton; various venues, February 1-25, 2012

Original Binding Productions

www.originalbinding.com

Artistic Director, Tom Slot; Business Director, Tom Evans; Managing Director, Paul Caron

Killing Time Written and Directed by Tom Slot; Stage Manager, Victoria Grazioli; Lighting Designer, Evan Teich; Set and Sound Designer, Tom Evans; AudioVisual Designer, Maryellen Molfetta; Cast: Claire Nasuti, Sharon Pinney, Bill Bria, Paul Caron, Daron Ross, Kelsey Schelling, Jordan Swisher, Milee Bang, Tatyana Kalko; Payan Theater, Roy Arias; July 18 - July 29, 2011

Dead Guy by Jordan Swisher; Directed by Tom Slot; Lighting and Set Designer, Tom Slot; Cast: Claire Nasuti, Kristi Barron, Bill Bria, Victoria Grazioli, Paul Caron; Manhattan Reportory Theatre; Febuary 15 - March 15, 2012

READINGS & WORKSHOPS

Farewell To Sanity Written and Directed by Tom Slot; Cast: Kristi Baron, Marlene Berner, Bill Bria, Paul Caron, Tom Evans, Stephanie Haring, Maryellen Molfetta, Claire Nasuti, David Stallings, Jordan Swisher, and Matthew Dean Wood; Pearl Studios; April 21, 2012

The Other Mirror

theothermirrortheatre.com

Artistic Director, Katherine M. Carter; Executive Director, Diana Zambrotta; Development Department, Sam Dash and Amy Young; Marketing Director, Ellie MacPherson; Casting Director, Chelsea Ignagni; Technical Director, James Parenti

Madame Bovary by Adapted by Katherine M. Carter from Gustave Flaubert's Novel, Madame Bovary; Directed by Katherine M. Carter; Stage Manager, Katie Kavett; Lighting Designer, Benjamin Weill; Set Designer, Julia Noulin-Merat; Costume Designer, Caitlin Cisek; Sound Designer, Colleen Toole; AudioVisual Designer, John Jalandoni; Casting Director, Chelsea Ignagni; Assistant Director, Ellie MacPherson; Board Operator, Valerie Novakoff; Photographer, Nick Ronan; Cast: Amy Young, Brad Thomason, Sam Dash, James Parenti, Logan James Hall; 3LD Art and Technology Center; December 8-12, 2011

READINGS & WORKSHOPS

May Violets Spring by James Parenti; Directed by Katherine M. Carter; Cast: Michael Goldsmith, Maura Hooper, Sam Dash, Diana Zambrotta, Chris Kateff, Tim Cox; Private Home-Closed Workshop; January 30, 2012

Bite the Apple by Linda Manning; Directed by Katherine M. Carter; Cast: Mel House, Diana Henry, Annette Arnold, Regina Gibson, Linda Manning, Diana Zambrotta; An Beal Bocht Cafe; January 23, 2012

Other Side Productions and 28bars Productions

www.othersideproductions.org

Accidentally, Like a Martyr by Grant James Varjas; Directed by Grant James Varjas; Stage Manager, Michael Friedlander; Lighting Designer, Brian Tovar; Set Designer, Clifton Chadick; Costume Designer, Melinda Basaca; Sound Designer, Roger Anderson; Fight Coordinator, Ben Newman; Graphic Designer, Alex Munson; Press Representative, Sam Rudy Media Relations; Assistant Director, Kate Hodge; Cast: Chuck Blasius, Kevin Boseman, Brett Douglas, Ken Forman, Keith McDermott, Cameron Pow, and Grant James Varjas; Paradise Factory; December 17, 2011 - January 7, 2012

The Artifacts by Steven Fechter; Directed by Thom Fogarty; Cast: Armand Anthony, Lulu Fogarty, Caitlin McMahon, Amy Newhall; The Bridge Theatre; April 18 – April 29, 2012

Desdemona: A Play About a Handkerchief by Paula Vogel; Directed by Thom Fogarty; Cast: Lulu Fogarty, Colista K. Turner and Christine Verleny; The Bridge Theatre; September 21 – October 2, 2011

Out of Line Productions

Mauritius by Theresa Rebeck; Directed by Raymond Zilberberg; Lighting Designer, Temishia Johnson; Set Designer, Dede Ayite; Costume Designer, Heather Lockard; Choreographer, Al Foote III; Cast: Peter D. Michael , Bob Turano, Chris Thorn, Lanene Charters, Frederique Nahmani; Urban Stages; June 10 – 19, 2011

P.O.V. Artists

www.refraintheplay.com

Artistic Directors, Brooke Eddey and Marc Santa Maria

Refrain by Melisa Tien; Directed by Jessi D. Hill; Stage Manager, Jake Simon Gersuk; Lighting Designer, Chad Lefebvre; Set Designer, Caite Hevner; Costume Designer, Emily DeAngelis; Sound Designer, Jeremy Mather, Jake Simon Gersuk, Melisa Tien; Technical Director, Andre Chandler; Properties Master, Serene Chakraverty; Producers:, Karl Santa Maria, Lauren Busener, Carol Marcia Johnson, Jess Gronholm; PR & Marketing, Kelsey Kyro; Cast: Brooke Eddey, Marc Santa Maria; The Wild Project; November 3-19, 2011

Page 73 Productions

www.page73.org

Executive Directors, Liz Jones and Asher Richelli; Associate Director, Michael Walkup; Producing Associates, Julia Blauvelt and Oren Stevens; Casting Director, Jack Doulin; Business Manager, Melanie Hopkins

Lidless by Frances Ya-Chu Cowhig; Directed by Tea Alagic; Stage Manager, Shayna O'Neill; Lighting Designer, Tyler Micoleau; Set Designer, Scott Bradley; Costume Designer, Jessica Pabst; Sound Designer, Daniel Kluger; Fight Choreography, Tom Schall; Press Representation, David Gersten; Casting, Jack Doulin, C.S.A.; Production Supervisor, McBrien Dunbar; General Management, Brierpatch Productions; Cast: Danielle Skraastad, Laith Nakli, Maha Chehlaoui, Thom Rivera, Emma Galvin; Walkerspace; September 20 - October 15, 2011

Panicked Productions

www.PanickedProductions.com

Follow the Leader by Erin Austin, Glenn De Kler, Rob Egginton and Eli Sands; Cast: Kirsten Benjamin, Andrew Broussard, David Fierro, Aida Leguizamon, Jacob Mondry and Brigitte Thieme-Burdette; Triskelion Arts; February 2 - 25, 2012

Parenthesis

parenthesistheater.com

The Lady's Not for Burning by Christopher Fry; Directed by Bryan Close; Stage Manager, Michelle Foster and Brooke Elsinghorst; Lighting Designer, Lucrecia Briceno and Tim Cryan; Set Designer, Michael V. Moore; Costume Designer, Kirche Zeile; Sound Designer, Asa Wember; Cast: Matthew Baldiga, Gwen Ellis, Nick Fesette, Danny Makali'i Mittermeyer, Anna Olivia Moore, Jefferson Slinkard, Rob Skolits, Jean Tafler, Jared Thompson, Isaac Woofter; Walkerspace; May 21 – June 11, 2011

Partial Comfort Productions

partialcomfort.org

After by Chad Beckim; Directed by Stephen Brackett; Stage Manager, Tara M. Nachtigall; Lighting Designer, Greg Goff; Set Designer, Jason Simms; Costume Designer, Whitney Locher; Sound Designer, Daniel Kluger; Fight Director, David Anzeulo; Dramaturge, John M. Baker; Production Manager, Lindsey Austen; Technical Director, Derek Dickinson; Cast: Jackie Chung, Andrew Garman, Alfredo Narciso, Maria-Christina Oliveras, Debargo Sanyal and Jeff Wilburn; Wild Project; September 21 - October 8, 2011

Perf Productions

www.perfproductions.com

Co-Founders and Producers: Meredith Edwards, Leah Bachar, Lin Laurin and Maria Aparo

Degeneration X by Leah Bachar; Directed by Meredith Edwards; Stage Manager, Maria Aparo; Lighting Designer, Michael De Pasquale; Set Designer, Zach Serafin; Costume Designer, Helen Anstis, Randyll Wendle; Sound Designer, Jeff Jowdy; Projection Designer, Mark Costello; Original Music, Timothy Allen; Cast: Micah Chartrand, Meredith Edwards, Leah Bachar, Gordon Gray, Lauren Hennessy, Lin Laurin, Helene Macaulay; The Living Theatre; April 19 - May 25, 2012

Performance Lab 115

pl115.org

The Ring Cycle (Parts 1-4) Adapted from *The Wagner* by Dave Dalton & Jeremy Beck; Directed by Dave Dalton; Stage Manager, Julia La Vault; Lighting Designer, Jeanette Yew; Set Designer, Jian Jung; Costume Designer, Kristina Makowski; Sound Designer, David Roy; Assistant Director, Bonnie Foster; Production Manager & Properties Designer, Liz Nielsen; Fight Choreographer, Casey Robinson; Technical Director & Carpenter, Kieren O'Hara; Cast: Jereny Beck, Amanda Broomell, Sara Buffamanti, Jeff Clarke, Christopher Hirsh, Rachel Jablin, Marty Keiser, Rebecca Lingafelter, Mike Melkovic, Chris Richards; Incubator Arts Project; April 12 - 29, 2012

Performance Space 122

www.ps122.org

ECHO: 30 Years of PS122: A Video Installation by Charles Dennis Performers: Danny Hoch, Spalding Gray, Blue Man Group, Ethyl Eichelberger, DanceNoise, Min Tanaka, Eric Bogosian, D.D Dorvillier, Anthony, Quentin Crisp and Penny Arcade, Meredith Monk, John Leguizamo, Radiohole, Reggie Watts, Temporary Distortion, Young Jean Lee, Justin Bond, Neal Medlyn, Adrienne Truscott, NYC Players and many more; June 11, 2011

RetroFutureSpective Festival; Created and Performed by Tim Miller, Kamelle Mills, Brigham Mosley and Katie O; June 11 – 25, 2011

Old School Benefit Written and Directed by Dona Ann McAdams; Cast: J Julie Atlas Muz, David White, Thurston Moore, John Fleck, the TEAM, Temporary Distortion, LeeSaar The Company, Yoshiko Chuma, Yvonne Meier, Penny Arcade, Okwui Okpokwawasili, Nicky Paraiso, Jeff McMahon, Forced Entertainment, Alien Comic, NTUSA, Vivarium Studio, Tamar Rogoff, Sally Silvers, Young Jean Lee's Theater Company, Maria Hassabi, Eric Bogosian, Reggie Watts, DanceNoise, Richard Move & Friends, Sarah Michelson, Carmine Covelli, Neal Medlyn, Every House Has A Door, Goat Island, Jack Ferver, Deb Margolin, Jennifer Miller, Sarah Maxfield, Banana Bag & Bodice, Mabou Mines, Jonathan Ames, Neal Medlyn, THEM by Ishmael Houston-Jones, Chris Cochrane, and Dennis Cooper, Ain Gordon, Meredith Monk, DJ Duo Team Company LLC, Carmelita Tropicana, Amanda Palmer, David Leslie, New York City Players, The Wooster Group, Elevator Repair Service, John Zorn, Big Art Group, Split Britches, Big Dance Theater, Carmelita Tropicana, Bob Wonder & the Future Ex-Wives; PS122; June 22 – 25, 2011

AGA Wrecking Ball; Performers: Murray Hill, Salley May, Alien Comic, Tigger, John Kelly, Andrew Schneider, The Factress aka Lucy Sexton, The Dazzle Dancers, Julie Atlas Muz, Urban Bushwomen, Joe E Jeffreys, Miss Joan Moosey, Gina Vetro, Jacqueline Zahora, Annabel Sexton Daldry, Louise Belle Ethyl May, Hank & Cupcakes, Rockman, Uncle Jimmy, Lisa Kron, Rose Wood, Peggy Pettitt, Flawless Sabrina, Karen Therese, M Lamar, Koosil-ja with Lance Blisters, Edgar Oliver, Joe E Jeffreys, Miss Joan Moosey, Gina Vetro, Pezzettino, Jacqueline Zahora, Annabel Sexton Daldry, Louise Belle Ethyl May, Bad Buka, Cudzoo & The Faggettes; Produced by Avant-Garde-Arama; June 17 - 18, 2011

The Rehearsal Directed by Cuqui Jerez. Created and Performed by Maria Jerez, Cristina Blanco, Cuqui Jerez, Amaia Urra and Gilles Gentner; Technical Director, Gilles Gentner; August 23, 2011 & October 12 – 15, 2011

Michel Groisman Showcase; Including *Porta das Maos (Door of Hands)*; *Transferencia (Transference)*; *Sirva-se (Serve Yourself)* Co-created with Gabriela Duvivier; *Polvo (Octopus)*; *A Long Table on Proximity* originally developed by performance artist Lois Weaver; September 21 - 25, 2011

Anger at the Movies by David Levine, Kyoung H. Park and Gideon Lewis-Kraus; Lawyer,Rob Cohen; Photographer, Cate Schappert; Architectural Designer, Jo Walker; Cast: Christianna Nelson; November 10 - 12, 2011

The Spring Gala 2012; January 26, 2012

Strange Cargo Choreographed by Pavel Zuštiak; Original Music, Christian Frederickson & Ryan Rumery; Co-produced with Palissimo Company (NYC); May 3 – 13, 2012

Post Plastica by Carmelita Tropicana & Ela Troyano; Production Designer, Aliza Shvarts; Costume Designer, Yali Romagoza; Lighting Designer, Chris Hudacs; Film Photographer Uzi Parnes; Performers: Becca Blackwell, Erin Markey, and Carmelita Tropicana; Co-produced with El Museo del Barrio; May 31 – June 3, 2012

FESTIVAL

UK Festival; *Watch Me Fall* by Chuck Yeager; *The Moment I Saw You I Knew I Could Love You*; *We See Fireworks* by Helen Cole; *Long Table on Live Art vs Performance Art. (UK vs America. A Special or Essential Relationship. Discuss.)* by Lois Weaver; June 1 - 4, 2011

COIL Festival (See Festival listing) January 5 – 29, 2012

Phoenix Theatre Ensemble

www.phoenixtheatreensemble.org

Art by Yasmina Reza; Directed by Gus Kaikkonen; Cast: Brian A. Costello, Joseph J. Menino, Jason O'Connell; The Wild Project; December 8 – 18, 2011

The Toy Maker's Apprentice Adapted by Kathy Ferman-Menino; Original Music and Lyrics by Ellen Mandel; Director and Choreography by Jeremy Williams; December 10 – 17, 2011

Rumpelstiltskin: The Real Story Adapted by Kathy Ferman-Menino; Original Music and Lyrics by Ellen Mandel; Director and Choreography by Jeremy Williams; February 20 – March 31, 2012

Agamemnon Home by Glyn Maxwell; Directed by Amy Wagner; Lighting and Set, Maruti Evans; Costumes, Margaret McKowen; Sound and Original Music, Ellen Mandel; Cast: Joseph J. Menino, Elise Stone, Craig Smith, Kelli Holsopple, Josh Tyson, Brian A. Costello, Amy Fitts, Zoe Watkins, Brittany Pooler; The Wild Project; March 22 – April 1, 2012

STAGED READINGS

Strindberg: Mad Modern Master Plays by August Strindberg; Directed by Amy Wagner and Jeremy Williams; Included: The Father (October 11-16, 2011), The Stronger & Other Shorts (February 21-26, 2012), The Dance of Death (May 1-6, 2012)

PIECE Theatre

www.theatreinpieces.org

Cracked (upon a time) Written and Directed by Josiah Houston; Lighting Designer, Dean Palmer Jr.; Sound Designer, Michael Vincent Skinner; Cast: Brent Wellington Barker III, Zebedee J Row; Theaterlab; October 12 – 22, 2011

Piehole

www.pieholed.com

2 Stories that End in Suicide by Piehole; Directed by Tara Ahmadinejad and Elliot B. Quick; Stage Manager, Alex Lubensky; Lighting Designer, Anna Carhart; Set Designer, Alexandra Panzer and Jeff Wood; Costume Designer, Vlada Kaganovskaya; Sound Designer, Josie Holtzman, Rachel Quimby, Laura Vitale; AudioVisual Designer, Emily Friend Roberts; Puppet Designer, Alexandra Panzer, Jeff Wood, Allison LaPlatney, Alice Winslow and Tara Ahmadinejad; Original Music, Gocha Tsinadze and Ben Cohen; Video Technician, Sara Wentworth; Graphic Designer, Michelle Snow; Cast: Tara Ahmadinejad, Jessie Hopkins, Allison LaPlatney, Alexandra Panzer, Alice Winslow and Jeff Wood; HERE Arts Center; August 31 - September 4, 2011

Pipe Dream Theatre

pipedreamtheatre.com

3 Ghosts by Music by Collin Simon Lyrics by Liz Muller; Directed by Liz Muller; Stage Manager, Stephanie Goldman; Lighting Designer, Will Murphy; Set Designer, Peter Muller; Costume Designer, Vanessa Price and Liz Muller; Based on *Charles Dickens's A Christmas Carol*; Choreographer, Stefanie Raccuglia; Hair and Makeup Designer, Nicole Finnegan; Cast: Elio Lleo, Liz Muller, Brady Lynch; Beckett Theatre; December 8 – 23, 2011

Pipeline Theatre Company

www.pipelinetheatre.org

Artistic Director, Daniel Johnsen; Executive Director, Arielle Siegel; Managing Director, Fernando Contreras; General Manager, Nicole Spiezio; Marketing Director, Katelyn Manfre; Literary Manager, Meagan Kensil

Bubble & Squeak by Evan Twohy; Set Designer, Andy Yanni; Costume Designer, Meagan Kensil; presented as part of the Samuel French Off-Off-Broadway Play Festival; Theater Row; July 19 - 24, 2011

Felix & The Diligence, or A Play About Fishermen in the 1940's by Colby Day; Directed by Daniel Johnsen; Stage Manager, Kevin C. Gall; Lighting Designer, Erik Olsen; Set Designer, Andy Yanni; Costume Designer, Stacey Juengling; Sound Designer, Seth Clayton; Producer, Burton T. Frey Jr.; Assistant Director, Jessika Doyel; Fight Director, Seth Andrew Bridges; Cast: Willy Appelman, Samuel Chapin, Fernando Contreras, Glenn Apollo Hergenhahn, Nathaniel Katzman, Meagan Kensil, Katelyn Manfre, Brad Mielke, Benj Mirman, Edward Raube-Wilson, Arielle Siegel, Allison Smith, Nicole Spiezio, Mike Steinmetz; The Connelly; September 24-October 8, 2011

The Ash Girl by Timberlake Wertenbaker; Directed by Jessika Doyel; Stage Manager, Kevin C Gall; Lighting Designer, Jeff Toombs; Set Designer, Andy Yanni; Costume Designer, Abbey Steere; Sound Designer, Seth Clayton & Griffin Sherbert; Cast: Sam Chapin, Jenny Donheiser, Meagan Kensil, Ian Lassiter, Megan Linde, Katelyn Manfre, Sydney Matthews, Dawn Newman, Shane O'Grady, Teddy Rodger, Rebecca Schoffer, Ari Schrier, Arielle Siegel, Erica Smith, Jordan Smith, Nicole Spiezio, Camille St. James, Josh Woodard, Zachary Zimbler; The Connelly; April 18-May 5, 2012

READINGS & WORKSHOPS

I's Twinkle by Nate Wieda; Directed by Saheem Ali; Judson Memorial Church

Clown Bar by Adam Szymokowicz; Directed by Andrew Neisler; The Connelly Theater

Friend of the Devil by Forrest Leo; Directed by Saheem Ali; The Connelly Theater

Piper Theatre

The Miser by Moliere; Adapted by Welker White; Directed by Welker White; Cast: Damian Young, Jan Leslie Harding; unknown; July 7 – 22, 2011

The Players Theatre

www. theplayerstheatre.com

Theatre Manager, Courtney Hansen, Kerianne Murphy; Marketing Director, Brenda Bell; Marketing Manager, Niyia Mack; House Manager, Catherine Lamm; Social Media Manager, Christian Amato

FESTIVAL

Short Play Festival - Horror Directed by Christian Amato; Lighting Designer, Rachel Sevedge; Sound Designer, Rachel Sevedge; *True Love Dies* by Ben Monk; *The Fortune Cookie* by Jack Phillips; *Boiled Alive!* by Robert Kilbridge; *Propaganda* by Michael Long; *The Blue Aspic* by Glenn Bassett, Book & Lyrics by Adam Cohen; *A Killer Day* by Neer Asherie; *B.F.F.* by Andrew Rothkin; *A Halloween Fantasy* by Ellis Gaskell; *Tonight Must Be Wednesday* by Tom Burns; *Bad Christmas Sweater* by Mark William Butler; *Death & Deception* by Catherine Lamm; *And Then There Were None* by Larry Hassman; *3 Witches* by Pat Blake; *No Questions Asked* Fidel Fonteboa; *Even Vampires Get the Blues* by Matt Sullivan Players Theatre & Players Loft; September 17 – October 2, 2011

Playing with Reality

www.playingwithreality.org

Give In To Sin by Playing with Reality Ensemble; Directed by Shea Elmore; Cast: Alyssa K Northrop, Amanda Miller, Brian Kendel, Carolyn McCandlish, Eugene Fertelmeyseter, Jennifer Kent, Julio Peña, Mateo Prenderast, Matthew Jenifer, Sarah-Doe Osborne; TBG Theatre; July 15 – 31, 2011

PLG Arts

www.plgarts.org

Daydream Adaptation of William Shakespeare's *A Midsummer Night's Dream*; Directed by Rohana Elias-Reyes; Stage Manager, Gloria Yetter; Costume Designer, Matthew Z. Kessler; Puppet Desgin, Sean and Rohana Elias-Reyes; Original Music, Leslie Ward; Choreographer, Judi Lewis Ockler & Penelope McCourty; Cast: Sean Kenin, T. Scott Lilly, Shequan Datts, Basil Rodericks, Joe Space, Laura Frenzer, Courtney Boddie; Prospect Park's Imagination Playground; June 4 – 26, 2011

Pluck Productions

pluckthedaynyc.com

Pluck the Day by Steven Walters; Directed by Michael O'Donnell; Stage Manager, James Weirich; Lighting Designer, Evan Gannon; Set Designer, Sean McIntosh; Costume Designer, Mo Geiger; Cast: Chris Dall'au, Danny Skinner, Jake Keefe, Lucy Sheftall; American Theatre of Actors; September 8 – 18, 2011

Plugged In Productions

Unplugged In by Brian Pracht; Directed by Michelle Bossy; Stage Manager, Jess Johnston; Lighting Designer, Nicole Pearce; Set Designer, Michael P. Kramer; Costume Designer, Joey Blaha; Sound Designer, Janie Bullard; Cast: Devin Norik, Joe Curnutte, Athena Masci; The Lion @ Theatre Row; May 25 – June 9, 2012

Poetic Theater Productions

www.poetictheater.com

Co-Artistic Directors, Jeremy Karafin and Alex Mallory

Love, Redefined by Aziza Barnes, Mahogany L. Browne, Lorraine Currelley, Darian Dauchan, Brian Dillon, Ishmael Islam, Joell Jackson, Iris A. Law, Mindy Levokove, Hjordy Matos, Kelly Zen-Yie Tsai, William Lowell Von Hoene, Leal Vona, Mickey Bolmer, Megan Cohen; Directed by Nicolette Dixon, Natalia Duong, Jeremy Karafin, Rachel Klein, Sara Lyons, Alex Mallory, and Daniel Roberts; Stage Manager, Sarah Livant and Liesl Spitz; Lighting Designer, Brad Peterson; Composers, Jeremiah Bornfield and Thomas Deneuville; Violinist, Josh Henderson; Flautist, Ashley Bozian-Murtha; Artwork, Courtney Malka'i Chung; Producers, Jeremy Karafin and Alex Mallory; Cast: Kilusan Bautista, Dana Berger, Ashley Bozian-Murtha, Andrew Casanova, Samantha Cooper, April Dayok, Flor De Liz Perez, Dontonio Demarco, Eden Foster, Teniece Divya Johnson, Joe Munley, Brisa Areli Munoz, Robyn Neilsen, Sara Hunter Orr, Wade Ray, Jennifer; The Wild Project; February 25, 2012

faith by Caroline Rothstein; Directed by Alex Mallory; Stage Manager, Sarah Livant; Lighting Designer, Brad Peterson; Sound Designer, Sean Hagerty; Producers, Jeremy Karafin, Alex Mallory; Associate Lighting Designer, Kenneth Wills; Assistant Producer, Leonie Ettinger; Cast: Caroline Rothstein; Co-Presented with Culture Project's Women Center Stage 2012 Festival; The Living Theater, Culture Project; April 3-4, 2012

Veronique Ory, Paul Bomba in Athena Theatre's production of Beirut
(photo by Bitten by a Zebra Photography)

The Company in Gracye Productions' production of The Asphalt Christmas

The Company in Regina Nejman & Company's production of
I Don't have a Title Yet! *(photo by Rodney Zagury)*

*Gerrianne Raphael, Mike Smith Rivera in The Foolish Theatre Company's
production of* HA! *(photo by Gerry Goodstein)*

*Kate Dulcich and David Hudson in Harry Diesel Productions'
production of* Boy Gets Girl *(photo by Gary Wong)*

Mary Sheridan and Jacob Saxton in Big Sky Theatre Company's production of The Dreamer Examines His Pillow *(photo by Ellen Lindsay)*

Cast in The Storm Theatre's production of The London Merchant *(photo by Michael Abrams)*

Lulu Fogarty and Christine Verleny in Thom Fogarty Presents' production of Desdemona: A Play About a Handkerchief *(photo by Carolina Kroon)*

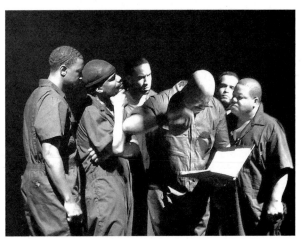

Anthony Gaskins, Zook, Loren Amos, Michael Alexis Palmer, Alexis Francisco, and Robert Siverls in Modern-Day Griot Theatre Company's production of for black boys who have considered homicide when the streets were too much *(photo by Pharah Jean-Philippe)*

Amanda Griemsmann in Moose Hall Theatre Company / Inwood Shakespeare Festival's production of War of the Worlds *(photo by Ted Minos)*

Foreign Bodies by Eboni Hogan; Directed by Nicole A. Watson; Stage Manager, Sarah Livant, Courtney Ulrich; Lighting Designer, Brad Peterson; Set Designer, Raphael Mishler; Costume Designer, Sierra Beth Ryan; Sound Designer, Sean Hagerty; AudioVisual Designer, Brad Peterson; Assistant Director, Courtney Ulrich; Producers, Jeremy Karafin and Alex Mallory; Cast: Samantha Cooper, Eboni Hogan, Joell Jackson, Karma Mayet Johnson, and Teniece Divya Johnson; Co-Presented with Culture Project's Women Center Stage 2012 Festival; A reading of Foreign Bodies was presented by Poetic Theater Productions as part of Poetic License; The Living Theater; April 3-4, 2012

Goliath by Takeo Rivera; Directed by Alex Mallory; Stage Manager, Sarah Livant; Lighting Designer, Brad Peterson; Producers, Jeremy Karafin and Alex Mallory; Dramaturg, Becca Poccia; Fight Choreographer, Jim Cairl; Costume Consultant, Sydney Gallas; Associate Producer, Leonie Ettinger; Cast: Samantha Cooper, Dontonio Demarco, Natalia Duong, Edgar Eguia, Iliana Inocencio, Teniece Divya Johnson, Kenneth Heaton, Monique Paige, and Nabil Viñas; Poetry by Drew Cameron, Cloy Richards, Aaron Hughes, Nicole Goodwin, Paul Wasserman, Jen Pacanowski, James A. Moad and Larry Winters, and spoken word poets Joanna Hoffman, Brian Dillon, Caroline Roths; The Wild Project; May 23 - June 3, 2012

Underground by Edward McWilliams; Directed by Axel Avin Jr.; Stage Manager, Shannon Lippert; Lighting Designer, Brad Peterson; Set Designer, Christopher Thompson; Sound Designer, Enrico DeTrizio; AudioVisual Designer, Brad Peterson; Additional Poetry by D'Janau Morales, Reynaldo Melendez, David Scott, and Daniel Silber-Baker; Choreographer, Ezra Ezzard; Associate Producer & Assistant Director, Dontonio Demarco; Original Composition, Ezra Ezzard and Oliver Reed; Assistant Stage Manager, Curtis Shaw; Cast: Makeda Abraham, Nikia Acy, Keith Alexander, Charles Coleman, Dontonio Demarco, Khadim Diop, Karen Eilbacher, Dave Goldberg, Joell Jackson, Ryan F. Johnson, Teniece Johnson, Allyson Lynch, Wade Ray, Ronnetta Renay, Bheesma Salassie, Bharatta Salassie, Candace Tabbs, Temesgen Tocruray and Leal Vona; The Wild Project; May 23 - June 3, 2012

READINGS & WORKSHOPS

Poetic Theater Productions Presents… by Akua Doku, Kate Foster, Keelay Gipson, Angela Kariotis, Takeo Rivera, Edward McWilliams, Sita Sarkar, Elliott D. SMith, Saviana Stanesc,u and Samantha Toh; Producers, Jeremy Karafin and Alex Mallory; Associate Producers, Barbara Harrison and Chinasa Ogbuagu; Cast: Dontonio Demarco, Akua Doku, Natalia Duong, Edgar Eguia, Scott Frank, Keelay Gipson, Temi Hasen, Angela Kariotis, Elmer King, Rachel Lin, Monique Paige, Marisel Polanco, Wade Ray, Leo Ignacio Rodriguez, and Elliott D. Smith; The Wild Project; May 11, 2012

Polybe + Seats

www.polybeandseats.org

Alice, or the Scottish Gravediggers by René-Charles Guilbert de Pixérécourt; Directed by Jessica Brater; Stage Manager, Alyson Fortner; Lighting Designer, Natalie Robin; Set Designer, Danielle Baskin; Costume Designer, Karen Boyer and Bevan Dunbar; Sound Designer, Kate Marvin; Original Music, Kate Marvin; Choreographer, Lindsay Torrey; Cast: Elaine O'Brien, Avi Glickstein, Kate Reilly, Sarah Sakaan, Lindsay Torrey, and Ari Vigoda; The Old Stone House; October 20 – November 13, 2011

Potomac Theatre Project NYC

www.potomactheatreproject.org

Co-Artistic Directors, Cheryl Faraone, Jim Petosa, Richard Romagnoli; Producing Director, Cheryl Faraone

Spatter Pattern by Neal Bell; Directed by Jim Petosa; Stage Manager, Michael Block; Lighting Designer, Mark Evancho; Set Designer, Hallie Zieselman; Costume Designer, Emma Ermotti; Press Representative, David Gibbs; Marketing, The Pekoe Group; Running Crew: Gillian Durkee, Christo Grabowski, Michael Kessler, Michaela Lieberman, Willy McKay, Mat Nakitare, Lilli Stein, Lucy Van Atta, Ele Woods; Cast: Jeffries Thaiss, Adam Ludwig, Christo Grabowski, Lucy Van Atta; Atlantic Stage 2; July 5-31, 2011

Territories by Steven Dykes; Directed by Cheryl Faraone; Musical Director and Composer, Paul Englosbhy; Stage Manager, Alex Mark; Lighting Designer, Mark Evancho; Set Designer, Hallie Zieselman; Costume Designer, Emma Ermotti; Sound Designer, Hallie Zieselman; AudioVisual Designer, Mark Evancho; Press Representative, David Gibbs; Marketing, The Pekoe Group; Running Crew, Gillian Durkee, Christo Grabowski, Cori Hundt, Michael Kessler, Michaela Lieberman, Willy McKay, Mat Nakitare, Lilli Stein, Lucy Van Atta, Ele Woods; Cast: Alex Draper, Megan Byrne, Stephanie Janssen, Nesba Crenshaw Lilli Stein, Gillian Durkee, Cori Hundt; Atlantic Stage 2; July 6-31, 2011

Victory: Choices in Reaction by Howard Barker; Directed by Richard Romagnoli; Stage Manager, Melissa Nathan; Lighting Designer, Mark Evancho; Set Designer, Hallie Zieselman; Costume Designer, Jule Emerson & Carlie Crawford; Sound Designer, Allison Rimmer; AudioVisual Designer, Hallie Zieselman; Fight Director, Paul Ugalde; Press Representative, David Gibbs; Marketing, The Pekoe Group; Running Crew: Gillian Durkee, Christo Grabowski, Cori Hundt, Michael Kessler, Michaela Lieberman, Willy McKay, Mat Nakitare, Lilli Stein, Lucy Van Atta, Ele Woods; Cast: Jan Maxwell, Steve Dykes, David Barlow, Robert Emmet Lunney, Alex Cranmer, Robert Zukerman, Edelen McWilliams, Willy McKay, Michael Kessler, Mat Nakitare, Michaela Lieberman, Ele Woods; Atlantic Stage 2; July 12-31, 2011

READINGS & WORKSHOPS

Monster Story Written and Directed by Marissa Molnar; Atlantic Stage 2; July 14, 2011

The Last Year Written and Directed by Michael Bradley; Atlantic Stage 2; July 30, 2011

Project Y Theatre Company

www.projectytheatre.org

LoveSick (or Things That Don't Happen) by Lia Romeo; Directed by Michole Biancosino; Stage Manager, Lizzy Lee; Lighting Designer, Ben Hagen and Joe Skowronski; Set Designer, Kevin Judge; Costume Designer, Emily deAngelis; Original Music, Tony Biancosino; Cast: Michael Nathanson, Andrew William Smith, Lisa Velten Smith, Aidan Sullivan, Teresa Stephenson, Pat McRoberts, Joachim Boyle, Jessica Varley, Barrett Hall, Melissa Hammans, Elizabeth Elkins, Joseph Varca, Rian Alfiero, Jeff Tuohy; Choreographer, Doug Hall; 59 E 59 Theaters; Fevruary 3–25, 2012

Project: Theater

www.projecttheater.org

Mangella by Ken Ferrigni; Directed by Joe Jung; Lighting Designer, Alex Goldberg; Set Designer, J.J. Bernard & Francois Portier; Sound Designer, Nick Borisjuk & Joe Jung; Projection Design, Joe Jung & Ken Ferrigni; Cast: Anthony Manna, Bob Austin McDonald, Ali Perlwitz, Hannah Wilson; Drilling Company Theatre Lab; October 6–23, 2011

Pug Skirt Players

lastchanceromance.net

Last Chance Romance by Sam Bobrick; Directed by Susan Pilar; Cast: Athos Cakiades, Krysten Kimmett; produced in association with Write Act Eastside Rep; Richmond Shepard Theatre; June 13 - 21, 2011

Pulse Ensemble Theatre

www.pulseensembletheatre.org

As You Like It by William Shakespeare; Directed by Alexa Kelly; Lighting Designer, Steve O'Shea; Costume Designer, Bob Miller; Sound Designer, Brian Richardson; Cast: Elliot Mayer, David Carlyon, Bill Galarno, Josh Odsess-Rubin, Stella Kammel, Iris McQuillan-Grace, Vincent Bagnall, Cherish Monique Duke, Stuart Rudin, Jacob Heimer, Robert Dyckman, Shawn Williams, Emily McGowan and Deaon Pressley; Riverbank State Park; July 21 - August 13, 2011

Purple Rep

www.purplerep.com

Ampersand: A Romeo & Juliet Story by Mariah MacCarthy, Original Music, Brian Kirchner; Directed by Amanda Thompson; Producer, Leta Tremblay; La MaMa First Floor Theater; August 12 - 27, 2011

The Myths We Need-Or- How to Begin by Larry Kunofsky; Directed by Jose Zayas; Stage Manager, Michal Mendelson; Lighting Designer, Derek Wright; Set Designer, Caite Hevner; Costume Designer, Carla Bellisio; Sound Designer, David Lawson; Cast: Anna Lamadrid, Annie Henk, Luke Forbes, Hugh Sinclair; Choreographer, E. Calvin Ahn; The Monkey NYC; October 2–18, 2011

Rabbit Hole Ensemble

www.rabbitholeensemble.com

Artistic Director, Edward Elefterion; Director of Development, Emily Hartford; PR Representative, Nikki Dillon; Board Members: Scott Loane, Jessica Baker, Jessica Quimby

The Tale of Frankenstein's Daughter by Stanton Wood; Directed by Edward Elefterion; Lighting Designer, Edward Elefterion; Set Designer, Pei-Chi Su & Edward Elefterion; Costume Designer, Pei-Chi Su; Sound Designer, Edward Elefterion; Graphic Designer, Dave Liao; Press Representative, Nikki Dillon; Special Event Planner, Jessica Quimby; Intern, Barbara Ely; Cast: Arthur Aulisi, Kati Delaney, Nikki Dillon, Emily Hartford, Elyse Knight, Jocelyn O'Neil; BAX/Brooklyn Arts Exchange; October 13 - 29, 2011

READINGS & WORKSHOPS

Alone Written and Directed by Edward Elefterion; Cast: Edward Elefterion, Adam Griffith, Emily Hartford, Chelsea Lando, Annalisa Ledson; BAX/Brooklyn Arts Exchange; June 22 - 30, 2012

Rachel Klein Theater Ensemble (RKP)

www.rachelkleinproductions.com

Artistic Director and Executive Producer, Rachel Klein

The Tragedy of Maria Macabre by Rachel Klein with Sean Gill; Directed by Rachel Klein; Stage Manager, Marina Steinberg; Lighting Designer, Ben Kato; Costume Designer, Rachel Klein; Sound Designer, Sean Gill; Makeup Designer, Anita Rundles; Wig Designer and Choreographer, Rachel Klein; Associate Costume Designer, Kae Burke; Additional Choreography, Danielle Marie Fusco and Preston Burger; Cast: Abigail Hawk, Elizabeth Stewart, Michael Porsche, Danielle Marie Fusco, Preston Burger, Megan O'Connor, Eric Schmalenberger, Brian Rubiano, Freddy Mancilla, Scooter Pie, Daniel Mendoza, and Ethan Horsefeathers O'Hara; The Wild Project; October 20-30, 2011

FESTIVALS

House of Yes Christmas Spectacular; *The Land of Misfit Toys* Created and Directed by Juanita Cardenas and Elena Delgado, featuring the HoY Company; *Under the Sea*, Created and Directed by Anya Sapozhnikova, featuring the HoY Company; *The Nativity Scene*, Created and Directed Kae Burke, featuring the HoY Company and the Rachel Klein Theater Ensemble; *The Nightmare Before Christmas*, Created, Choreographed and Directed by Rachel Klein, featuring the Rachel Klein Theater Ensemble; The House of Yes; December 8, 2011-December 17, 2011

Oh You Pretty Things; *March of the Black Queen* Created and Directed by the Rachel Klein Theater Ensemble; *Time* Created and Performed by the Rachel Klein Theater Ensemble; *Dance Magic Dance* Created and Performed by Lady Circus; *Jailhouse Rock* Created and Performed by Bro Circus; *Space Oddity* Created and Performed by Angela Harriell, David Slone, and the Love Show; *Rocky Horror*, Created by Michael T. and Performed by Michael T. and the Rachel Klein Theater Ensemble; *Heros*, Performed by this Ambitious Orchestra; *I want to Break Free* Created by Rachel Klein, featuring this Ambitious Orchestra and the rachel Klein Theater Ensemble; (le) Poisson Rouge; Ongoing

NON-RESIDENT PRODUCTIONS

Phsycho Space Laboratory; *Giant Easter Mess, Holy Cuckoos What Has Happened to My Life, Night of the Living Dolls, Ren is a Total Fox: A Tribute to 80s Dance Movies, Giant Oscar Mess*, and *Batshit Crazy Blowout*; produced by Junta Juleil Productions, Rachel Klein Productions and Blue Box Productions in association with the Bowery Poetry Club; Bowery Poetry Club; Febuary 27, 2011-March 25, 2012

Radiotheatre

www.radiotheatrenyc.com

Artistic Director/Producer, Dan Bianchi; Co-Producer at Horse Trade Theater Group, Erez Ziv

Herbert West, Reanimator Written and Directed by Dan Bianchi; Lighting, Set, Sound and AudioVisual Designer, Dan Bianchi; Audio Engineer, Sean Burns; Cast: Frank Zilinyi, Eric Whitten; UNDER St.Marks Theater; July 7-31, 2011

The Call Of Cthulhu Written and Directed by Dan Bianchi; Lighting, Set, Sound and AudioVisual Designer, Dan Bianchi; Audio Engineer, Sean Burns; Cast: Frank Zilinyi, Eric Whitten; UNDER St.Marks theater; July 7-31, 2011

The Shadow Over Innsmouth by Dan Bianchi; Directed by Frank Zilinyi; Lighting, Set, Sound and AudioVisual Designer, Dan Bianchi; Lightboard Operator, Eduardo Ramirez; Audio Engineer, Alex Hurst; Cast: Frank Zilinyi, R.Patrick Alberty, Kevin Gilligan; Kraine Theater; April 19-May 20, 2011

The Moon Bog by Dan Bianchi; Directed by Frank Zilinyi; Lighting, Set, Sound and AudioVisual Designer, Dan Bianchi; Lightboard Operator, Eduardo Ramirez; Sound Engineer, Alex Hurst; Cast: Frank Zilinyi, R.Patrick Alberty, Kevin Gilligan; Kraine theater; April 19-May 20, 2012

The Lurking Fear by Dan Bianchi; Directed by Frank Zilinyi; Lighting, Set, Sound and AudioVisual Designer, Dan Bianchi; Lightboard Operator, Eduardo Ramirez; Sound Engineer, Alex Hurst; Cast: Frank Zilinyi, R.Patrick Alberty, Kevin Gilligan; Kraine Theater; April 19-May 20, 2012

The Statement Of Randolph Carter by Dan Bianchi; Directed by Frank Zilinyi; Lighting, Set, Sound and AudioVisual Designer, Dan Bianchi; Cast: Frank Zilinyi, R,Patrick Alberty, Kevin Gilligan; Kraine Theater; April 19-May 20, 2012

The Horror At Martin's Beach by Dan Bianchi; Directed by Frank Zilinyi; Lighting, Set, Sound and AudioVisual Designer, Dan Bianchi; Lightboard Operator, Eduardo Ramirez; Sound Engineer, Alex Hurst; Cast: Frank Zilinyi, R.Patrick Alberty, Kevin Gilligan; Kraine Theater; April 19 - May 20, 2012

The Evil Clergyman by Dan Bianchi; Directed by Frank Zilinyi; Lighting, Set, Sound and AudioVisual Designer, Dan Bianchi; Lightboard Operator, Eduardo Ramirez; Sound Engineer, Alex Hurst; Cast: Frank Zilinyi, R.Patrick Alberty, Kevin Gilligan; Kraine Theater; April 19- May 20, 2012

Random Access Theatre

www.randomaccesstheatre.com

Artistic Director, Jennifer Sandella; Managing Director, Jessica Ko; Marketing and PR Director, Martin Meccouri; Director of Development, Christopher Shepard; Social Media/Resident Costume Designer, Lisa Jane Wright; Resident Lighting Designer, Sarah Abig

Rope by Patrick Hamilton; Directed by Christopher Shepard; Stage Manager, Anna Grace Carter; Lighting Designer, Sarah Abigail Hoke-Brady; Set Designer, Andrew Chandler; Costume Designer, Anthony Manfredonia; Sound Designer, Andrew Grimm; Assistant Stage Manager, Lisa Jane Wright; Dramaturge, Stuart Weinstock; Cast: Wydham Brandon, Nate Grams; Charles Granillo, Martin Meccouri; Rupert Cadell, Alex Birnie; Leila Arden, Laura King; Kenneth Raglan, Teddy Lytle; Sabot, Joshua Tewell; Mrs. Debenham, Liz Wasser, Johnstone Kentley, Lincoln L. Hayes; Access Theater; January 26 - February 12, 2012

Twelfth Night by William Shakespeare; Directed by Lawrence Lesher; Stage Manager, Chrislie Francios; Set Designer, Samantha Shoffner; Costume Designer, Lisa Jane Wright; Runing Crew/ASM - Samantha Sandella; Cast: Jessica Ko, Javan Nelson, Kelly Rogers, Chris Kateff, Sean MacBride Murray, Jonathan Craig, Courtney Cook, Matt Harris; Various Locations; May 11-20, 2012

Red Fern Theatre Company

www.redferntheatre.org

We in Silence Hear a Whisper by Jon Kern; Directed by Melanie Moyer Williams; Stage Manager, Laura Luciano; Lighting Designer, Marie Yokoyama; Set Designer, Katherine Akiko Day; Costume Designer, Elizabeth Groth; Sound Designer, Colin J. Whitely; Puppet Design, Amy Mathews; Cast: Marcy Agreen, Crystal Beth, Parker Leventer, Stephen Conrad Moore, Matthew Park, Devere Rogers, Hansel Tan, Keona Welch; 14th Street Y, The; October 5 – 23, 2011

March by Sharyn Rothstein; Directed by Kel Haney; Stage Manager, Michal V. Mendelson; Lighting Designer, Marie Yokoyama; Set Designer, Caite Hevner; Costume Designer, Sydney Maresca; Sound Designer, Anthony Mattana; Projection Design, Caite Hevner; Original Music, Anthony Mattana; Cast: Andrew Ash, Frank Deal, Rachel Geisler, Annie Henk, Ashley Marie Ortiz, Thom Rivera, John-Michael Scapin, and Melissa Teitel; 14th Street Theatre; April 12 – 29, 2012

Redd Tale Theatre Company

www.reddtale.org

Artistic Director, Will Le Vasseur; Co-Artistic Director, James Stewart

Gabriel by Will Le Vasseur; Directed by Lynn Kenny; Stage Manager, Brittany Ray; Lighting, Set, Costume, Sound and AudioVisual Designer, Will Le Vasseur; Producer, James Stewart; Cast: Will Le Vasseur, Michael Wetherbee, Michael Komala, Cameran Hebb, James Stewart; Nicu's Spoon Theatre; August 4 - 27, 2011

Frankenstein With Mary Shelley by Virginia Bartholomew; Directed by Will Le Vasseur; Stage Manager, Brittany Ray; Lighting, Set, Costume, Sound and AudioVisual Designer, Will Le Vasseur; Producer, James Stewart; Cast: Virginia Bartholomew; Nicu's Spoon Theatre; August 4 - 27, 2011

Regina Nejman & Company

reginanejmancompany.blogspot.com

Artistic Director/ Choreographer, Regina Nejman

I Don't Have A Title Yet! Written and Directed by Regina Nejman; Musical Director, Mio Morales; Stage Manager, Gwendolyn Kay; Lighting Designer, Christopher Brown; Costume Designer, Carolyn Hoffman with Regina Nejman; Sound Designer, Mio Morales; Photographer, Rodney Zagury; Cast: Dancers: Amy T. Adams, Zachary Denison, Kristin Licata and Regina Nejman; Presented by Theater for The New City's 2nd Dream Up Festival; Theater for The New City; August 14-21, 2011

Resonance Ensemble

www.resonanceensemble.org

Shakespeare's Slave by Steven Fechter; Directed by Eric Parness; Stage Manager, Sean McCain; Lighting Designer, Joe Doran; Set Designer, Sarah B. Brown; Costume Designer, Mark Richard Caswell; Sound Designer & Original Music, Nick Moore; Cast: Chris Ceraso, Zack Calhoon, Lucille Duncan, Nancy Nagrant, Romy Nordlinger, Steven Pounders, David L. Townsend, Stewart Walker, Shaun Bennet Wilson; Clurman Theatre; May 24 – June 18, 2011

H4 Adaptation of William Shakespeare's *Henry IV*; Directed by Allegra Libonati; Stage Manager, Jessie Vacchiano; Lighting Designer, Joe Doran; Set Designer, Sarah B. Brown; Costume Designer, Brenda Abbandandolo; Sound Designer, David Hancock Turner; Media Design, Johnathan Carr; Original Music, David Hancock Turner; Cast: Dorothy Abrahams, Alice Bahlke, Joie Bauer, Michael Chmiel, Brian D. Coats, Joe Jung, Michael Nathanson, Jensen Olaya, Steven Pounders, Timothy McCown Reynolds, Brian Silliman; Clurman Theatre; May 27 – June 18, 2011

Retro Productions

www.retroproductions.org

Producing Artistic Director, Heather Cunningham

The Runner Stumbles by Milan Stitt; Directed by Peter Zinn; Stage Manager, Jeanne Travis; Lighting Designer, Jacqueline Reid; Set Designer, Jack and Rebecca Cunningham; Costume Designer, Kathryn Rohe; Sound Designer, Jeanne Travis; Properties Designer, Heather Cunningham; Special Effects Designer and Fight Choreographer, Joe Mathers; Assistant Stage Manager, Veronica Gheller; Cast: Jim Boerlin, Becky Byers, Nat Cassidy, Heather E. Cunningham, Casandera M.J. Lollar, Joe Mathers, Christopher Patrick Mullen, Alisha Spielmann and Ric Sechrest; The Richmond Shepard Theatre; November 7-20, 2012

The Runner Stumbles by Milan Stitt; Directed by Peter Zinn; Stage Manager, Ricardo Rust; Lighting Designer, Jacqueline Reid; Set Designer, Jack and Rebecca Cunningham; Costume Designer, Kathryn Rohe, Rebecca Cunningham and Viviane Galloway; Sound Designer, Jeanne Travis; Properties Designer, Heather Cunningham; Special Effects Designer and Fight Choreographer, Joe Mathers; Assistant Stage Manager, MIchael Friedlander; Cast: Becky Byers, Nat Cassidy, Heather E. Cunningham, Casandera M.J. Lollar, Joe Mathers, Christopher Patrick Mullen, Alisha Spielmann, Ric Sechrest and Richard Waddingham; Co-produced with The Bleecker Company in association with the Arclight Theatre; The Arclight Theatre; May 3-20, 2012

Rich Ryan Productions, LLC.

Lemon Meringue by Rich Ryan; Directed by Terri Muuss; Stage Manager, Carly Levin; Lighting Designer, Sam Gordon; Set Designer, Carly Levin; Sound Designer, Craig Mallone; Original Music, Athena Reich; Choreographer, Tracey Katof; Cast: Joe DeGise, James Koroni, Logan Riley Bruner, Ann McCormack, Athena Reich, Maureen Van Trease, Rhett Hackett, Keith Smith, Carly Fox and Shelley McCaughlin; TADA! Theater; July 8 – 10, 2011

Richmond Shepard

Oswald by Dennis Richard; Directed by Richmond Shepard; Lighting Designer, Brett Maughan; Set Designer, Kirk Larsen; Producer John P. Greene; Cast: Tim Intravia, Jonathan Miles, Dan Burkarth, Daniel Hicks, Sky Adams, Josh Rhett Noble, Matt McClure and Ken Driesslein; Richmond Shepard Theatre; Jun 4 – 18, 2011

Rising Phoenix Repertory

www.risingphoenixrep.org

Elective Affinities by David Adjmi; Directed by Sarah Benson; Stage Manager, Tom Taylor; Lighting Designer, Mark Barton; Set Designer, Louisa Thompson; Costume Designer, Susan Hilferty; Sound Designer, Matt Tierney; General Management, Snug Harbor Productions, Steven Chaikelson, Kendra Bator; Casting Director, Jack Doulin, C.S.A.; Cast: Zoe Caldwell; Upper East Side townhouse; November 17 – December 18, 2011

Rising Sun Performance Company

Mash Up! A 10th Anniversary Celebration Directed by Akia, Maura Kelly, Lindsay Beecher & Ted Gorodetzky; Stage Manager, Nzinga Williams; Costume Designer, Barbara Erin Delo; AudioVisual Designer, Derek Shore; Production Manager, Lindsay Beecher; Literary Managers, Michael Ross Albert &John Patrick Bray; Photographer/Videographer, David Anthony & Jason LeMaster; Fundraising Coordinator, Tiffini Minatel; Kraine Theater; June 22, 2011

Romanian Cultural Institute in New York

www.icrny.org

The Window:4 Alice by Saviana Stanescu; Directed by Ana Margineanu; Stage Manager, Patricia Masera; Lighting Designer, Stephen Arnold; Set & Costume Designer, Daniela Codarcea Kamiliotis; Video Designer, Igor Molochevski & Masha Pekurovsky; Choreographer, Melanie S. Armer; Cast: Robin Johnson, Nick Smerkanich, Inés Garcia; Romanian Cultural Institute in New York; May 23 – June 18, 2012

Roots and Wings Theatrical

www.rawtheatrical.org

Producing Artistic Director, Joseph Samuel Wright; Marketing Director, Lauren Rayner; Programs and Casting Director, Caralie Chrisco; Development Director, Maggie Albert

Bck t th Grnd by Joseph Samuel Wright; Directed by Alex Beck; Stage Manager, Sarah Ford; Lighting Designer, Lauren Bremen; Set Designer, Alex Beck; Sound Designer, Alex Beck and Justin Henry; Choreography by Justin Henry; Cast: Tim Abrams, Garrett Bruce, Stacie Capone, Rachel Casparian, Paul Corning, Brenden Rogers, and Michael Sheehan; Bridge Theatre; May 16 - 20, 2012

The Wedding Thieves by Collette La Pointe; Directed by Lauren Rayner; Stage Manager, Sarah Ford; Lighting Designer, Lauren Bremen; Cast: Mackenzie Hawkins, Lauren Rayner; Bridge Theatre; May 16 - 20, 2012

It Got Loud by Sarah Babin; Directed by EJ Marotta; Stage Manager, Sarah Ford; Lighting Designer, Lauren Bremen; Sound Designer, EJ Marotta; Cast: Caralie Chrisco, Tom McVey; Bridge Theatre; May 16 - 20, 2012

Two Shall Meet by Caralie Chrisco; Directed by Roxane Revon; Stage Manager, Sarah Ford; Lighting Designer, Lauren Bremen; Set Designer, Roxane Revon; Sound Designer, Caralie Chrisco; Cast: Leslie Fray, Zach Tirone; ; Bridge Theatre; May 16 - 20, 2012

Logan's Hollow by Bradley Troll; Directed by Daniel LeBlanc; Stage Manager, Sarah Ford; Lighting Designer, Lauren Bremen; AudioVisual Designer, Daniel LeBlanc; Cast: Jeffrey Welk; Bridge Theatre; May 16 - 20, 2012

HUD by Daniel Carroll; Directed by Barbara Harrison; Stage Manager, Sarah Ford; Lighting Designer, Lauren Bremen; Cast: Josh Evans, Christine Mottram; Bridge Theatre; May 16 - 20, 2012

Roy Arias Studios

www.royariasstudios.com

NON-RESIDENT PRODUCTIONS

Up to Date; Roy Arias Theatre 2; June 21 – July 3, 2011

Reefer Madness; Roy Arias Theatre 2; June 22 – July 1, 2011

Nothing Serious by Rich Orloff; Roy Arias Theatre 2; June 25 – 26, 2011

The Wizard of Oz; Roy Arias Theatre 2; June 25 – July 3, 2011

Girls Gone Funny – 1 Night, 7 Women; Roy Arias Theatre 2; July 3 2011

Scared Skinny: A One (Hundred Pound Lighter) Woman Show Written and Performed by Mary Dimino; Roy Arias Theatre 2; July 3, 2011

TRU Voices New Musicals Reading Series; *Oklahomo* by Jesse Gage, Produced by Reed Ridgley; *Famous* by Yvonne Adrian, Cheryl Stern and Tom Kochan, Produced by Jamibeth Margolis and Chris Massimine in association with Cate Cammarata; *Through the Door* by Judy Freed and Laurence Mark Wythe, Produced by Kenny Howard; Presented by Theater Resources Unlimited; Roy Arias Theatre 2; December 5 – 19, 2011

Pune Highway by Rahul Da Cunha; Produced by The Indo-American Arts Council; Roy Arias Times Square Arts Center; June 7 – 12, 2011

The Unmitigated Consequence; Roy Arias Times Square Arts Center; July 15 – August 21, 2011

Comedy Magic Cabaret by Randy Masters; Roy Arias Times Square Arts Center; September 24 – 25, 2011

Love Happened by Chance by Twana Lawler; Music by Jerome Brooks Jr.; Directed by Dwight Ali Williams; Roy Arias Times Square Arts Center; September 29 – October 2, 2011

Holy Child; Roy Arias Times Square Arts Center; February 2 – 11, 2012

Love's Gonna Get You; Roy Arias Times Square Arts Center; February 11 – 12, 2012

Animal Kingdom by Laura Zlatos; Directed by Francesca Mantani Arkus Roy Arias Times Square Arts Center; February 29 – March 4, 2012

Central Park; Roy Arias Times Square Arts Center; April 2 – 15, 2012

Two Sides of Love; Roy Arias Times Square Arts Center; April 5 – 12, 2012

Do You Still Dream?; Roy Arias Times Square Arts Center; April 5 – 15, 2012

13 Fat Girls and the Dead Cat; Roy Arias Times Square Arts Center; April 6 – 9, 2012

Five by Five; Roy Arias Times Square Arts Center; April 7 – 15, 2012

Visiting Hours; Roy Arias Times Square Arts Center; April 11 – 15, 2012

The Emancipation of the Sassy Jewish Woman; Roy Arias Times Square Arts Center; April 14 – 15, 2012

FESTIVALS

Midwinter Madness Short Play Festival; *Circo Poeira (Dust Circus)*, Written and Directed by Caio Stolai; Produced by Milena Nascimento; *One Out of Ten* Created by Laertis Vasiliou; Translated and Directed by Aktina Stathak; *Coffee House, Greenwich Village* by John Doble; *Never Underestimate Karma* by Mike Durell; *The Toupee* by Tom Dunn; *A Month of Sundays* by Tearrance A. Chisholm; *Norma Jeane Enlightened* by Joanne de Simone; *Holiday in Heaven a musical* by Demetria Daniels; *Hungry People, The Musical* by Jung Han Kim; *The Walls Came Tumbling Down* and *The Tower* by Paulanne Simmons; *Jimmy and Janice* by Jason Cicci; *Rest* by Leonard D. Goodisman; *The Seven Stages of Grief* by Dimitri C. Michalakis; *The Babbler* by Jeffrey Fiske; *Hiroshi-Me, Me, Me* by Natalie Menna; *Once* by Dan Bocchino; *Out of the Cradle Endlessly Rocking* by Nikola Tesla Gojcaj; *Red All Over* by Mike Fresta; *Dictators for Hire* by Joe Beck; *Without a Net 5 short plays* by Meri Wallace; *Fetal Attraction* by Sarah M Chichester; *Waiting for Dr. Hoffman* by Michele Willens; *Meredith's Ring* by Andrew Rothkin; *Strawberry Fields* by Ashley Nicole Audette; *La Petite Mort* by Joshua R. Pangborn; *The Brink* by Eugenie Carabatsos; *Social Anxiety* by Gwen Baer; *Animal Kingdom* by Laura Zlatos; *The Man in the Window: The Building of the Brooklyn Bridge* by Donald Orwald and Linda Harvey-Burkley; Produced by the Midtown International Theatre Festival; Roy Arias Times Square Arts Center; February 13 – March 4, 2012

Times Square International Theatre Festival; (See Festival Listing) Produced by Roy Arias Studios; Roy Arias Off Broadway Theatre; January 16 – 22, 2012

Sanguine Theatre Company

sanguinenyc.com

The Last Days of Judas Iscariot by Stephen Adly Guirgis; Directed by Jillian Robertson; Stage Manager, Aaron Salley; Lighting Designer, Jake Fine; Set Designer, Nicholas Schwartz; Costume Designer, Nickey Frankle; Sound Designer, Matt Nelson; Dramaturg, Kate McConnell; Producer, Karly Fischer; PR, Sarah Whalen; Cast: Ray Amell, Sebastian Cintron, Monica Gonzalez, Alex Haynes, Ashley Klanac, Sergio LoDolce, Kaitlin Myers, Jeff Ronan, Mike Roush, Tai Verley, Curry Whitmire; The Drilling Company Theatre; August 18 – 21, 2011

Bees and Lions by Sarah M. Duncan; Directed by Jillian Robertson; Stage Manager, Tracey Fess; Lighting Designer, Carla Linton; Set Designer, Nicholas Schwartz; Costume Designer, Kerry Gibson; Sound Designer, Matt Nelson; Cast: Michael Roush, Kristina Doelling, Mitch Tebo, Daryl Brown, Steven Hajar, Emily Grosland; WOW Cafe Theater; April 19 – 29, 2012

Sans A Productions

www.exitcarolyn.org

Exit Carolyn by Jennie Berman Eng; Directed by Adam Knight; Stage Manager, Austin Vaclavik; Lighting Designer, Austin Bransgrove; Set Designer, Ashlee Springer; Costume Designer, Steven Manuel; Sound Designer, Toby Jaguar; Cast: Anna O'Donoghue, Laura Ramadei, Lauren Blumenfeld, Jake Loewenthal; Drilling Company Theatre Lab; December 2–17, 2011

Saving Grace Productions

Trouble - a new pop/rock Musical Book by Michael Alvarez; Music and Lyrics by Ella Grace; Musical Arrangements, Joss Nightingale; Directed by Michael Alvarez; Musical Director, Brenna Sage; Lighting Designer, Yuriy Nayer; Set Designer, Xiaopo Wang; Choreorapher, Jennifer Weber; The June Havoc Theatre; July 28 – 31, 2011

The Secret Theatre

www.secrettheatre.com

Two Gentlemen of Verona by William Shakespeare; Directed by Jay Painter and Jeffrey Golde; Cast: Jay Painter, Jeffrey Golde, Diana Johannesson, Courtnay Griswold, Joe and Eric Robinson; Co-Produced with Beyond Theatre Ensemble and Face Off Unlimited; The Secret Theatre; August 5 – 13, 2011

Poe: An Imaginary Waltz by Edgar Allan Poe; Produced & Directed by Richard Mazda; Costume Designer, Tom Kleinert; Installation Artist, Eliot Lable; Cast:Alex Cape & Katie Braden as 'Edgar and Virginia Poe; The Secret Theatre; October 27 – 31, 2011

Little Women: The Musical Based on Louisa May Alcott's novel; Directed by Taryn Turney; Producers, Richard Mazda, Alyssa Van Gorder; The Secret Theatre; December 8 – 17, 2011

2011 Secret Christmas Show; Performers: Devyn Rush, Courtnay Griswold, Eric Robinson, Christine Cherry, Danielle Orlando; The Secret Theatre; December 21, 2011

Pirate Pete's Parrot by Richard Mazda; The Secret Theatre; May 5 – 16, 2012

NONRESIDENT PRODUCTIONS

Grindhouse Musical Music by Jason Anderson; Book & Lyrics by Kyle McCoy; Cast: Drew St. Aubin, Caitlin Fillers, Marty Allen, Jessi Cimafonte, Langston Belton, Rebecca Gray Davis, Marty Allen, Mark Schatzel, Kyle McCoy, Becky FerreiraProduced by Midnight Buffet; The Secret Theatre; June 29 – July 2, 2011

ReVision; Performers: Blue Muse Dance, Kyoungin Jung, Hyunsuk Kim, Kraven Seneca: Dance Company and KRAVe Sound, Studio Green Penguin, Codice Rosso Theatre, ActivePhaze, Gessica Paperini, Valentina Priolo, Through the Looking Glass, Visual HornHonkinG, Urban Wash Dance Company, and Micah Produced by Forward Motion Theater; The Secret Theatre; July 7 – 8, 2011

Side Show Book and Lyrics by Bill Russell; Music By Henry Krieger; The Secret Theatre; August 5 – September 10, 2011

Ghosts Produced by the Queens Players; The Secret Theatre; Aug 25 - Sep 24, 2011 *Salome* by Oscar Wilde; Directed by Robert Ribar; Stage Manager, Paul Xuereb; Lighting Designer, William Noguchi; Set Designer, Jason Sherwood; Costume Designer, Danielle Mahoney; Sound Designer, Robert Ribar; Original Music, Ryan Marino, Brian Chillemi; Choreographer, Ben Hobbs; Cast: Davi Santos, John C. Hume, Danny Baird, Daniel Destefano, Francisco Huergo, Frankie Lapace, Nick Moore, Eugene Michael Santiago, Ian Schulz; Produced by Femme Fatale Theater; The Secret Theatre; October 6 – 16, 2011

Othello by William Shakespeare; Directed by Leta Tremblay; Produced and Conceived by Joseph Mitchell and Valerie Redd; Adapted by Valerie Redd; Assistant Director, Christopher Diercksen; Production Stage Manager, Adrienne Buenzli; Assistant Stage Manager, Catharine Crow; Scenic Designer, Jacquelyn D. Marolt; Lighting Designer and Fight Choreographer, Brian Henderson; Costume Designer, Katharine Heath; Original Music and Sound Designer, Jay Spriggs; Video Designer, Kate Eminger; Lighting Assistant, Kaitlin MacKenzie; Producer, Jack Sharkey; Cast: Maggie Blumer, Alan Brincks, Wayne T. Carr, David M. Gallagher, Jacob Green, Abbi Hawk, Peter Herrick, David Muhs, Joseph Mitchell Parks, Valerie Redd; Produced by The Wandering Bark Theatre Company - www.wanderingbarktheatrecompany.org; The Secret Theatre; October 25 – 30, 2011

Gutenberg! The Musical! By Scott Brown and Anthony King; Directed by Ken

Neil Hailey; Costume and Properties Designer, Tom Klieinert; Cast: Matt Swanston and Dalles Wilie; Produced by RepALLIANCE Theatre; The Secret Theatre; November 10 – 20, 2011

Skin Flesh Bone by Camilla Ammirati; Directed by Jessica Ammirati; Stage Manager, Laura Bultman; Lighting Designer, Sam Gordon; Set Designer, Duc Le; Sound Designer, Patrick Metzger; Original Music, Camilla Ammirati; Cast: Kiwi Callahan, David Eiduks, Gavin Alexander Hammon, Laurel Lockhart, Maria Silverman; Choreographer, Dana Boll; Produced by Going to Tahiti Productions - www.goingtotahitiproductions.com; Secret Theatre; June 15 – 25, 2011

Full Disclosure by Ruth McKee; Directed by Jessica Ammirati; Set Designer, Becky Sagen; Cast: Kiwi Callahan; Produced by Going to Tahiti Productions - www.goingtotahitiproductions.com; The Secret Theatre; December 7 – 18, 2011

Advance Man by Mac Rogers; Directed by Jordana Williams; Stage Manager, Devan Hibbard; Lighting Designer, Sarah Lurie; Set Designer, Saundra Yaklin; Costume Designer, Amanda Jenks; Sound Designer, Jeanne Travis; Cast: Shaun B. Wilson, Becky Beyers, Becky Comtois, Amanda Duarte, Brian Silliman, Abraham Makany, Jason Howard, David Rosenblatt, Kristen Vaughan, Sean Williams; Produced by Gideon Productions - gideonth.com; Secret Theatre; January 12 – 29, 2012

Henry V by William Shakespeare; Directed by Lenny Banovez; Stage Manager, Julia LaVault; Assistant Director, Kirsten Benjamin; Lighting Designer, Jason Fassl; Sound Designer, Jason Fassl; Fight Choreographer, Alexis Black; Fight Captain, Jordan McArthur; Cast: Laura Frye, Brendan Marshall Rashid, Duane Allen Robinson, Garen McRoberts, Andrew Goldwasser, Michael Selkirk, Jordan MacArthur, Jake Russo, Jon Sprik, Susan Maris, Celeste Moratti, Alexis Black, Tristan Colton, John Hicks, Celia Ann Smith; Produced by Titan Theatre Company - www.titantheatrecompany.com; The Secret Theatre; February 3 – 18, 2012

Cat Lady Without A Cat Created and Performed by Carrie Keskinen; Directed by Scotty Watson; Produced by Going to Tahiti Productions - www.goingtotahitiproductions.com; The Secret Theatre; March 9 – 10, 2012

Spring Tides by Melissa Gawlowski; Directed by Jeff Woodbridge; Stage Manager, Alicia Thompson; Lighting Designer, Kia Rogers; Set Designer, Nikki Black; Costume Designer, Cheryl McCarron; Sound Designer, Jay Spriggs; Special Effects, Sara Slagel and Evan Hill; Cast: Susan Atwood, Jason Liebman, Michael Mraz, Patricia Santomasso; Choreographer, Joe Mathers; Produced by Boomerang Theatre Company - www.boomerangtheatre.org; The Secret Theatre; March 10 – 25, 2012

The Real Thing by Tom Stoppard; Directed by Cailin Heffernan; Stage Manager, Michelle Foster; Lighting Designer, Kia Rogers; Set Designer, Nikki Black; Costume Designer, Cheryl McCarron; Sound Designer, Jay Spriggs; Cast: Zack Calhoon, Douglas B. Giorgis, Kate Kenney, Synge Maher, David Nelson, Aidan Redmond, Valerie Stanford; Produced by Boomerang Theatre Company - www.boomerangtheatre.org; The Secret Theatre; March 4 – 24, 2012

Blast Radius by Mac Rogers; Directed by Jordana Williams; Stage Manager, Devan Hibbard; Lighting Designer, Jennifer Wilcox; Set Designer, Sandy Yaklin; Costume Designer, Amanda Jenks; Sound Designer, Jeanne Travis; Special Effects, Zoe Morsette; Cast: Becky Byers, David Rosenblatt, Jason Howard, Kristen Vaughan, Nancy Sirianni, Adam Swiderski, Cotton Wright, Alisha Spielmann, Seth Shelden, Amy Lee Pearsall, Felicia Hudson, Joe Mathers; Produced by Gideon Productions - gideonth.com; Secret Theatre; March 30 – April 14, 2012

The Mermaid's Tale adapted from L. Frank Baums' The Sea Fairies; Book and Lyrics by Jack Dyville; Music and Lyrics by John Stutte; Cast: David Gillam Fuller, Amy Marie Stewart, Kacey Cardin, Nicole DiMattei, Vicki Oceguera, Maren Fischer, Charles Moran, Kyle Torrence, Marjorie Conn; Produced by FACT Theatre - www.facttheatre.com; The Secret Theatre; April 28 – June 9, 2012

DEINDE by August Schulenburg; Directed by Heather Cohn; Stage Manager, Jodi Witherell; Lighting Designer, Kia Rogers; Set Designer, Will Lowry; Costume Designer, Stephanie Levin; Sound Designer, Martha Goode; Cast: Ken Glickfeld, David Ian Lee, Isaiah Tanenbaum, Rachael Hip-Flores, Nita Vidyasagar, Matthew Murumba, Matthew Trumbull, Sol Crespo, Alyssa Simon; Produced by Flux Theatre Enxemble; The Secret Theatre; April 28 – May 12, 2012

The Umbrella in the Snow Written and Directed by Jack Dyville; Dramaturg Lynn Manuell; Stage Manager, Eric Pagen; Cast: Lucy Sorlucco, Guss Ferrari, David Gillam Fuller, Kacey Cardin; Produced by FACT Theatre - www.facttheatre.com; The Secret Theatre; May 1 – 6, 2012

Treasures; *Inscriptions* by Mark-Eugene Garcia; *Reluctant Savior* by Marjorie Conn; *Elaine* by Julia Genoveva; *Treasure* by Katie Labahan; Directed by Rodrigo E. Bolanos; Original Music by Mark McDaniels; Cast: Betty Hudson, Mark-Eugene Garcia, Suellen Rubin, Marjorie Conn, Lynn Manuell, Madalyn McKay, Julia Genoveva, Charles Moran, Stephanie Schwartz, Jillian Jacobs, Andrew Pollard, Vicki Oceguera Produced by FACT Theatre - www.facttheatre.com; The Secret Theatre; May 2 – 6, 2012

FESTIVALS

Suite Summer Festival; Produced by In-Sight Dance Company - www.insightdance.org; The Secret Theatre; July 28 – 31, 2011

Seeing Place Theater

www.seeingplacetheater.com

Founding Artistic Director, Brandon Walker; Managing Director, Erin Cronican

Closer by Patrick Marber; Directed by Alan Gordon; Stage Manager, Preesa Adeline Bullington; Lighting Designer, Zach Pizza; Cast: Erin Cronican, Elyse Fisher, Nick Velkov, Brandon Walker; American Theatre of Actors, Sargent Theatre; September 21 – October 9, 2011

Scotch Kiss by Brandon Walker; Directed by Reesa Graham & Brandon Walker; Stage Manager, Nicholas Linnehan; Lighting Designer, Zach Pizza; Cast: Mary Anisi, Amanda Baker, Kathleen Brower, Michael Stephen Clay, Debbie Friedlander, Ned Baker Lynch, Rhonda Musak, David Sedgwick; American Theatre of Actors, Sargent Theatre; September 26 – October 9, 2011

Three Sisters by Brian Friel; Adapted from Anton Chekhov; Directed by Brandon Walker; Stage Manager, Livia Hill; Lighting Designer, Zach Pizza; Set Designer, Michael Minahan; Costume Designer, Preesa Bullington; Cast: Alan Altschuler, Kathleen Brower, Brian Byus, Lee Cavellier, Michael Stephen Clay, Erin Cronican, Mary Lahti, Justin Kress, Ned Baker Lynch, Daniel Perez, Elisa Pupko, David Sedgwick, Daniela Thome, Brandon Walker; American Theatre of Actors, Sargent Theatre; March 1 – 25, 2012

Shakespeare's Sister Company

www.shakespearessister.org

President, Founder, Artistic Directo,r Kris Lundberg; Resident Director, Misti Wills; Director of College Tours, Celest Woo; Outreach Associate,Tess Brenner

Sunday on the Rocks by Theresa Rebeck; Directed by Rachel Wohlander; Stage Manager, Uriel Mendelson; Choreographer, Kris Lundberg; Cast: Kris Lundberg, Maggie Carr, Rain Patterson, Kate Kertez; Red Room; September 29 – October 9, 2011

Shakespeare in the Parking Lot

www.shakespeareintheparkinglot.com

Comedy of Errors by William Shakespeare; Directed by Kathy Curtiss; Cast: Ian Biesinger, Nina Burns, Garret Burreson, Sergio Diaz, Michael at, Lauren Hayden, Jack Herholdt, Thomas Machell, Shane Mitchell, Lisa Pettersson and Drew Valins; Co-Produced with The Drilling Company; Municipal Parking Lot at the corner of Ludlow and Broome Streets, Manhattan; July 7 - July 23, 2011

Hamlet by William Shakespeare; Directed by Hamilton Clancy; Set Designer, Rebecca Lord-Surratt; Fight Choreographer, Kathy Curtiss; Cast: Allesandro Colla, Amanda Dillard, McKey Carpenter, Paul Guskin, Karla Hendrick, David Sitler, Bill Green, Jennifer Fouche, Jed Peterson, Miguel Govea, Graciany Miranda, Andrew Markert, Kate Garfield, James Butler, Dan Teachout, Eric P. Harper, Lulu Costan; Co-Produced with The Drilling Company; Municipal Parking Lot at the corner of Ludlow and Broome Streets, Manhattan; July 28 - August 13, 2011

Sick Little Productions

Awkward Levity by Richard Hinojosa; Directed by Jason Griffith, Sheila Garson & Richard Hinojosa; Cast: Rebecca Nerz, Jonathan Harford, Lindsay MacNaughton and Jesse Presler; Under St. Marks Theatre; January 12 - 21, 2012

Sidekick Productions

Don Gio by Joshua R. Pangborn; Cast: Chris Morris, Drew Moerlein, Emily Gittelman, Jennifer Kent, Jimmy Brooks Jr., Kimberley Shoniker, Linda Blackstock, Michael Thieling; Workshop Mainstage; July 16 - 31, 2011

Sink or Swim Rep

www.sinkorswimrep.org

The Crucible by Arthur Miller; Directed by Wendy Merritt; Stage Manager, Heather Olmstead & Melissa Farinelli; Lighting Designer, Wolfram Ott; Set Designer, Wendy Merritt; Costume Designer, Rachel Guilfoyle; Choreographer, Stephanie Bonner & Dan Renkin; Cast: Ariel Rosen-Brown, Michael Hardart, Natalie Hollins, Kristin Parker, Ellen Laura White, Rachel Charlop-Powers, Richard James Porter, Lena Hudson, Lauren Sowa,Seth McNeill, Mary Looram, Ashton Crosby, Aaron Gaines, Whitney Kaufman, Howard Thoresen, Aaron D; Paradise Factory Theatre; July 13 – 31, 2011

Romeo and Juliet by William Shakespeare; Directed by Eric Smith; Stage Manager, Ed Herman & Melissa Farinelli; Lighting Designer, Wolfram Ott; Set Designer, Wendy Merritt; Costume Designer, Rachel Guilfoyle; Original Music, Kathleen Kenning; Choreographer, Dan Renkin & Stephanie Bonner; Cast: Christopher Chirdon, Bradley Rose, Kane Prestenback, Rachel Charlop-Powers, Nick LaMedica, Deven Anderson, Jonathan Crimeni, Aidan Sank, Daren Kelly, Leah Gabriel, Kristin Parker, Brandon Alan Smith, Kathleen Huber, Aaron David Kapner, Reynaldo Piniella; Paradise Factory Theatre; July 15 – 31, 2011

Sister Sylvester

www.sistersylvester.org

Hugh Cox Gets the Pink Slip by Matt Wilson; Directed by Kathryn Hamilton; Stage Manager, Arienne Pelletier; Lighting Designer, Bruce Steinberg; Costume Designer, Marina Porter; Sound Designer & Original Music, Manolo Moreno; Choreographer, Kathryn Hamilton; Cast: Daniel Kublick, Terence Mintern, Manolo Moreno, Christine Bullen, Colin Cramer, Kyle Knauf, Lillie Jayne, Greg Bosse, Chris Anderson, Ingrid Gillming, Arooj Majid, James Face Yu, Lilianna Velásquez, Stephen Lean, Julien Marcland, & Tessa Skara; Kenny Scharf's Cosmic Cavern; August 18 – 28, 2011

The Ventriloquist Circle

by Matt Wilson; Directed by Kathryn Hamilton; Lighting Designer, Damon Pelletier; Costume Designer, Marina Porter; Sound Designer, Manolo Moreno; AudioVisual Designer, Jesse Garrison; Cast: Daniel Kublick, Terence Mintern, Manolo Moreno, Christine Bullen, Colin Cramer, Kyle Knauf, Lillie Jayne, Greg Bosse, Chris Andersen, Ingrid Gillming, Arooj Majid, James Yu, Lilianna velzquez, Stephen Lean, Julien Marcland, Tessa Skara, Jason Martin; Dixon Place; January 6 - 28, 2012

Small Pond Enterprises

www.midtownfestival.org

Out of Askja by Drew Larimore; Directed by Jesse Edward Rosbrow; Cast: Curt Bouril, Jillian Crane and Peter Reznikoff; 440 Studios; June 4 – 23, 2011

Dad Doesn't Dance by Nora Brown; Directed by Karen Case Cok; Dorothy Strelsin Theatre; July 12 - 30, 2011

Smith Street Stage

www.smithstreetstage.com

Macbeth by William Shakespeare; Directed by Jonathan Hopkins; Stage Manager, Debbie Hoodiman Beaudin; Costume Designer, Campbell Ringel; Original Music, Ruark Downey; Cast: Patrick Harvey, Leal Vona, Beth Ann Leone; Carroll Park; July 13 – 24, 2011

Sneaky Snake Productions

BrainExplode! by Richard Lovejoy, Stephen Aubrey, Danny Bowes; Directed by Paige Blansfield; Stage Manager, Teresa Fellion; Set Designer, Jes Hinkle; Costume Designer, Jim Hammer; Sound Designer & Original Music, Chris Chappell; Production Designer, Jes Hinkle; Cast: Stephen Heskett, Megan Melnyk, Jesse Wilson; Brick Theater; July 14 – 30, 2011

Something/Nothings

3 2's; Or Afar by Mac Wellman; Directed by Meghan Finn; Lighting Designer, Bryan Aldous; Set Designer, Kyle Chepulis; Costume Designer, Normandy Sherwood; Sound Designer, Chris Giarmo; Original Music, Cesar Alvarez; Properties and Masks Designer, Jan Leslie Harding; Assistant Director, Sarah Painter; Producer Leslie Strongwater; Cast: Quinlan Corbett, Jocelyn Kuritsky, Sophie Nimmannit, Jan Leslie Harding, Chuja Seo; Dixon Place; October 9-29, 2011

Spleen Theatre

www.spleentheatre.org

Bound by Laura Tesman and Gene Gillette; Directed by Laura Tesman; Stage Manager, Rekima Cummins; Lighting Designer, Hae Jin Han; Set Designer, Christopher Hoyt; Costume Designer, Jennifer Stimple; Sound Designer & Original Music, George Brunner; Cast: Gene Gillette, Sara Hogrefe, Alenka Kraigher, Maeve Yore, Megan Channell, Kyle Minshew, Christopher Cohen, Jacob A. Ware; NYTW's 4th Street Theatre; June 8 – 18, 2011

Squeaky Bicycle Productions

www.squeakybicycleproductions.com

Reputation Control: Emerging Playwrights' Rep by Jane Miller & Ben Bartolone; Directed by Laura Pestronk & Kathryn McConnell; Cast: Alison Mahoney, Jessica Mortellaro, Kyla Schoer, Sergio LoDolce, Leah Maddrie, Jeff Ronan, John Say, Jeff Johnson, Brandi Varnell, Kelly Kay Griffith and Paul Sabala; The Drilling Company Theatre; July 21 – 31, 2011

Poisoned by J. Boyett; Directed by Kathryn McConnell; Stage Manager, Lori Mannette; Lighting Designer, Tracy Lynn Wertheimer; Sound Designer, Freddie Mac; Cast: Kelly Kay Griffith, Dennis Brito, Kate Eastman; Theater Three; November 19 – December 10, 2011

StageLeft

www.stageleftstudio.net

Grapefruit by Sally Lambert; Directed by Theresa Gambacorta; Sound Designer, Joe Hutcheson; Cast: Cheryl King; StageLeft Studios; September 28, 2011 – ongoing

Stages on the Sound

Nine/Twelve Tapes by Leegrid Stevens; Directed by Ryan Pointer; Theater for the New City; August 31 – September 4, 2011

Stas&Stas

Four Dogs and a Bone by John Patrick Shanley; Directed by Jennifer Gelfer; Stage Manager, Bettiann Fishman; Lighting Designer, Rachael Harris; Sound Designer, Rachael Harris; Jennifer Gelfer; Cast: Taso Mikroulis, Samantha Strelitz, Chase Coleman, Anastasia Morozova; Wild Project; April 5–May 7, 2012

Stasz/Pruitt Productions

staszpruitt.com

Woyzeck by Georg Buchner; Directed by Zach Stasz; Original Music, Jara Jones; Fight Choreographer, Ray A. Rodriguez; Cast: Mark Lindberg, Jessica O'Hara-Baker, Adam Adrianopoulos, Emily Kaplan, Jara Jones, AJ Ditty, Evan Maltby, Jes Levine and Ben Leasure; Space on White; January 26 – February 12, 2012

Stolen Chair

www.stolenchair.org

The Bachelors' Tea Party by Kiran Rikhye; Directed by Jon Stancato; Costume Designer, Julie Schworm; Properties and Graphic Designer, Aviva Meyer; Cast: Liz Eckert & Jody Flader or Amanda Sykes & Natalie Hegg; Lady Mendl's Tea Salon; September 2 - November 25, 2011

The Storm Theatre

www.stormtheatre.com

Artistic Director, Peter Dobbins; Associate Artistic Director, Stephen Logan Day; Producing Director, Chance Michaels; Director of Development, Robert Carroll

The London Merchant by George Lillo; Directed by Peter Dobbins; Stage Manager, Charles Casano; Lighting Designer, Michael Abrams; Set Designer, Ken Larson; Costume Designer, Maria Kousoulous; Sound Designer, David A. Thomas; Cast: Spencer Aste, Joe Danbusky, Michelle Kafel, Jessica Myhr, Megan Stern, Patrick Woodall, Harlan Work; Produced with Blackfriars Repoertory Theatre; The Storm Theatre at the Theater at the Church of Notre Dame; January 6 - February 4, 2012

The President by By Ference Molnár; Adapted by Morwyn Brebner; Directed by Peter Dobbins; Stage Manager, Charles Casano; Lighting Designer, Michael Abrams; Set Designer, Ken Larson; Costume Designer, Meagan Miller-McKeever; Sound Designer, Amy Altadonna; Choreographer, Tiffiny Gulla; Graphic Design, Michelle Malavet; Cast: Spencer Aste, David Bodenschatz, Brian J. Carter, Laura Michelle Cleary, Brian J. Coffey, Gregory Couba, Ashton Crosby, Joe Danbusky, Meaghan Bloom Fluitt, Cheri Paige Fogleman, Robert Ierardi, Benjamin Jones, Hugh Brandon Kelly, Jessica Levesque, Sawyer Mastrandrea, Ted McGuinness, Yukiko Miyawaki, Becca Pesce, Edward Prostak, Josh Vasquez, Matthew Waterson; The Storm Theatre at the Theater at The Church of Notre Dame; April 27 - May 28, 2012

Subjective Theatre Company

No Poem No Song by Jesse Cameron Alick; Directed by David F. Chapman; produced in association with Horse Trade Theater Group; Kraine Theater; May 29 – June 14, 2011

SweetPea Productions

www.sweetpea-nyc.com

Dream Walker by August Schulenburg; Directed by Marielle Duke; Stage Manager, Emily Thomas; Lighting Designer, Olivia Harris; Sound Designer, Jessica Lechtenberg; Graphic Artwork, Alley Scott; Cast: Collin Smith, Matthew Archambault, Jennifer Somers Kipley; Kraine Theater; November 9–19, 2011

T. Schreiber Studio

www.tschreiber.org

You Never Can Tell by George Bernard Shaw; Directed by Robert Verlaque; Stage Manager, Victoria Loye; Lighting Designer, Eric Cope; Set Designer, Chris Minard; Costume Designer, Steven Daniels; Sound Designer, Andy Cohen; Choreographer, Jessica Osborne; Cast: Helen Abell, Townsend Ambrecht, Lucy Avery Brooke, Lowell Byers, Laurence Cantor, Seth James, Peter Judd, Randy Miles, Marilyn Mineo, Jessica Osborne, Edwin Sean Patt; T. Schreiber Studio; May 12 – June 19, 2011

Lobby Hero by Kenneth Lonergan; Directed by Peter Jensen; Stage Manager, Victoria Loye; Lighting Designer, Lois Catanzaro; Set Designer, Matt Brogan; Costume Designer, Anne Wingate; Sound Designer, Andy Cohen; Cast: Nasay Ano, Michael Black, Olivia Rorick and Joshua Sienkiewicz; Gloria Maddox Theatre; October 13 – December 3, 2011

The Last Days of Judas Iscariot by Stephen Adly Guirgis; Directed by Terry Schreiber; Stage Manager, Andrew Slater; Lighting Designer, Dennis Parichy; Set Designer, Hal Tine; Costume Designer, Sherry Martinez; Sound Designer, Andy Cohen; Cast: Tommy Buck, Omar Bustamante, Steven Carrieri, Michael J. Connelly, Adyana De La Torre, Benjamin Jones, Eliud Kauffman, Julia Kelly, Morgan McGuire, Erica Lauren McLaughlin, George Mouriadis, Ben Prayz, Alex Crow Reimers, Rebecca Spiro, Bud Stafford, Julie Szabo, Alexan; Gloria Maddox Theatre; February 22 – April 8, 2012

Jack's Back! by book by Elmer L. Kline with Leo Cardini and Tom Herman; Directed by John Gould Rubin; Lighting Designer, Lois Catanzaro; Set Designer, Andreea Mincic; Costume Designer, Sherry Martinez; Sound Designer, Chris Barlow; Original Music, Tom Herman; Choreographer, Bronwen Carson; Cast:

Megan Abell, Matthew Boyce, Bonnie Cannon-Brown, Emily Cannon-Brown, David Donahoe, Warren Douglas, Alexa Erbach, Shane Lacoss, Kevin Maleike, Lance Olds, Chloë Patellis, Romain Rachline, Casey Shane, Maxine Stewart, Arley Tapirian, Julia Udine; Gloria Maddox Theatre; May 9 – June 22, 2012

TADA! Youth Theater

www.tadatheater.com

Executive & Artistic Director, Janine Nina Trevens; Managing Director, Amy Fiore; Associate Artistic Director/Resident Choreographer, Joanna Greer; Director of Education, Rod Christensen; Director of Development, Jennifer Beirne; Business Manager, Carl Jaynes

History Mystery Written and Directed by Janine Nina Trevens; Musical Director, Eric Rockwell; Stage Manager, Angie McCormack; Lighting, Set and Sound Designer, Steve O'Shea; Costume Designer, Virginia Monte; AudioVisual Designer, Norman Franklin; Choreographer, Joanna Greer; Musical Director, Jim Colleran; Cast: Maddy Abrahams, Romello Rodriguez, Elsa Chung, Martin Lewis, Amanda Prescod, Alex Costello, Tristan Hickey, Subiya Mboya, Nataki Purvis, Annalee Tai, Brian Ward, Nathan Love, Chloe Pae, Milo Bernfield Millman, Austin Tipograph, Maddie Rubin, Donna Falzon; TADA! Youth Theater; January 20-February 19, 2012

Up to You by Eric Rockwell; Directed by Janine Nina Trevens; Musical Director, Jim Colleran; Stage Manager, Angie McCormack; Lighting and Set Designer, Steve O'Shea; Costume Designer, Virginia Monte; Choreographer: Joanna Greer; Cast: Alec Cohen, Gabby Gross, Annalee Tai, Shelley Zoey Schorsch, Meaghan Turner, Ceanna Bryant, Danielle Palmer, Nikki Zivkovic, Romello Rodriguez, Brian Ward, Martin Lewis, Austin Tipograph, Anthony Raddi, Brielle Raddi, Sammy Grob, Georgia O'Leary, Leann Martin, Sawyer Smith, Ondine Atwell Hudson, Victoria Cotton, Nicole Rosengurt, Kristin Callahan, Diego Arellano, Thomas Vaethroeder, Priscilla Estevez, K.K. Pohly, Jaden Jordan, Martine Bowman, Olivia Estevez, Jonah Levinowitz, Nathan Love; TADA! Youth Theater; April 27-May 20, 2012

Take Wing And Soar Productions, Inc.

www.takewingandsoar.org

Producing Artistic Director, Debra Ann Byrd; Associate Artistic Director, Timothy D. Stickney

Saviour? by Esther Armah; Directed by Passion; Stage Manager, William J. Vila; Lighting Designer, Joyce Liao; Set Designer, Pavlo Bosyy; Costume Designer, Gail Cooper Hecht; Sound Designer, Sean O'Halloran; Producers, Voza Rivers and Debra Ann Byrd; Assistant Stage Manager, Annette Nelson-Wright; Marketing, Shabazz Communications; Cast: Michael Green, Jimmy Aquino; Co-produced with New Heritage Theatre Group; Dwyer Cultural Center; October 7 - 30, 2011

Massinissa And The Tragedy of the House of Thunder Written and Directed by Lorey Hayes; Stage Manager, Debra Ann Byrd; Lighting Designer, James Carter; Set Designer, Chris Cumberbatch; Costume Designer, Gail Cooper-Hecht; Sound Designer, David D. Wright; Producers, Debra Ann Byrd and Voza Rivers; Choreographer, Phillip de la Cal; Casting, Sara Koch Casting; Assistant Stage Manager, Abagail Ramsay; House Management, Aixa Kendrick; Production Support, Joshua Glenn & Mark Benavides; Cast: Elijah Black, Phillip Burke, Debra Ann Byrd, Bryant Carroll, Tino Christopher, Lodric D. Collins, Phillip de la Cal, Treasure Davidson, Dianne Dixon, Stacey J. Dotson, Michal Fraser, Kirt A. Harding, Dennis Jordan, Anja Lee, Tom Martin, Dayo Olatokun, Michael Raimondi, Brendan Sokler, Lawrence Winslow, Natasha Yannacañedo; Co-produced in partnership with New heritage Theatre Group; Poet's Den Theatre; December 7 - 18, 2011

READINGS & WORKSHOPS

Hay Fever by Noel Coward; Directed by Dawn Scibilia; Producer, Debra Ann Byrd; Lighting Design, James Carter; Poet's Den Theatre; October 10, 2011

The Talking Band

The Peripherals by Ellen Maddow; Directed by Ken Rus Schmoll; Stage Manager, Lisa McGinn; Lighting Designer, Alan C. Edwards; Set Designer, Sue Rees; Costume Designer, Olivera Gajic; AudioVisual Designer, Sue Rees; Additional Videos Designer, David Dawkins and Ruth Marantz; Cast: Viva DeConcini, Michael Evans, Kim Gambino, Sam Kulik, Ellen Maddow, Kamala Sankaram, and Paul Zimet; Dixon Place; May 3 - 19, 2012

Tall Tales Theatre Company, Solstice Arts Centre, and Irish Arts Center

Bogboy by Deirdre Kinahan; Directed by Jo Mangan; Production Designer, Ciaran Bagnall; Cast: Noelle Brown, Emmet Kirwan, Sorcha Fox, Steve Blount; Irish Arts Center; September 7 - 25, 2011

TeaCup Productions LLC

www.teacupproductions.com

The Alexis & Destiny Chronicles: Love Sick & Sick of Love by Eudora Tucker; Directed by James Booney; Producer's Club; May 20 – June 11, 2011

Ted Mozino Productions LLC

www.boomersthemusical.com

Boomers, the Musical of a Generation by Peter Baron & Meridee Stein; Directed by Gerald vanHeerden; Cast: Katy Blake, Peter Davenport, Kelly Lynn Dorney, David Eiduks, Wade Elkins, Erik Gullberg, Laurie Hymes, Charles Karel, Marvin Riggins, Mattew Schmidt; The June Havoc Theatre; July 15 - 30, 2011

Ten Years Productions

A Hole In His Heart by Jon Kakaley; Directed by Jake Turner; Lighting and Sound Designer, Margaret Christie; Set Designer, Margaret Christie/Jon Kakaley; Costume Designer, Jon Kakaley; Cast: Jon Kakaley, Ydaiber Orozco, Daniel Genalo, Arthur Gerunda, Mark Hennessy, Brian Podnos; Atlantic Stage 2; January 20-28, 2012

Tenement Street Workshop

www.tenementstreet.org

Dust by John MacDonald; Directed by Patrick Letterii & John MacDonald; Lighting and Set Designer, Jonathan Cottle; Costume Designer, Tara DeVincenzo; Sound Designer, Christopher Barlow; Cast: Peter Albrink, Adam Barrie, Nicholas Bonnar, Hunter Canning, Lindsay Teed, Haley Rawson; Incubator Arts Project; September 15-24, 2011

terraNOVA Collective

www.terranovacollective.org

Producing Artistic Director, Jennifer Conley Darling; Associate Artistic Director, Jessi D. Hill; Associate Producers, Elizabeth Carlson, Jo Cattell, Eva Scanlan; Casting Director, Kimberly Faith Hickman

When Thoughts Attack by Kelly Kinsella; Directed by Padraic Lillis; Cast: Kelly Kinsella; The New Ohio Theatre; May 30 – June 6, 2011

Baby Redboots' Revenge by Philip-Dimitri Galás; Directed by Anne Meighan; Production Designer, Anne Meighan; Producer, Lynne Griffin; Cast: Sean Sullivan; New Ohio Theatre; May 29 - June 5, 2012

FESTIVALS

soloNOVA Arts Festival 2011; *Santa Claus is Coming Out… or How the Gay Agenda Came Down My Chimney* Written and Performed by Jeffrey Solomon, Directed by Joe Brancato; *Woman of Leisure and Panic* Created, Choreographed and Performed by Charlotte Bydwell; *…and stockings for the ladies* by Attila Clemann, Directed by Zach Fraser, Performed by Brendan McMurtry-Howlett; *Polanski Polanski* by Saviana Stanescu, Directed by Tamilla Woodard, Performed by Grant Neale, Produced by Nomad Theatrical Company; *Questions My Mother Can't Answer* Written & Performed by Andrea Caban, Directed by Rachel Eckerling; *Tar Baby* Written & Performed by Desiree Burch, Co-Written by Dan Kitrosser, Directed by Isaac Byrne; *Jobz* Written & Performed by Joseph Keckler, Directed by Josh Hecht, Violinist Dan Bartfield; PS122; May 11 – 28, 2011

WORKSHOPS

Pig Shit & The Frozen City by Robert Askins; Directed by José Zayas; Cast: Denny Bess, Steven Boyer, Geneva Carr, Jackie Collier, Matt Huffman, Preston Martin, Chinasa Ogbuagu, Shawn Randall, Scott Sowers, Meg Wolf, Karin Wolfe; New Ohio Theatre; April 10, 2012

Animals Commit Suicide by J. Julian Christopher; Directed by José Zayas; Cast: David Anzuelo, Nic Grelli, Vincent Ingrisano, Armando Riesco, Yolonda Ross; New Ohio Theatre; April 11, 2012

The Death of the Slow'Dying Scuba Diver by Matthew Paul Olmos; Directed by May Adrales; Cast: Jackie Chung, Crystal Finn, Anna Kull, Jose Joaquin Perez, Steven Rishard, Juan Villa, Colleen Werthman; New Ohio Theatre; April 12, 2012

Me You Us Them by Andrea Lepcio; Directed by Jo Cattell; Cast: Carlo Alban, Angelina Fiordellisi, Daniel Irizarry, James Kraft, Eric Lockley; New Ohio Theatre; April 13, 2012

The Seer and the Witch by Jennifer Lane; Directed by Kimberly Faith Hickman; Cast: Megan Channell, Jed Dickson, Sofia Jean Gomez, Maria Maloney, Jens Rasmussen, Carly Robins; New Ohio Theatre; April 14, 2012

4Edges by Crystal Skillman; Directed by John Hurley; Cast: Reyna DeCourcy, Dion Mucciacito, Susan Louise O'Connor, Timothy McKown Reynolds; New Ohio Theatre; April 14, 2012

The Absence of Weather by Ken Urban; Directed by Stephen Brackett; Cast: Kevin Geer, Polly Lee, Scott Sitman; New Ohio Theatre; April 15, 2012

Unhinged: A Silent Opera by Krista Knight; Directed by Jessi D. Hill; Cast: Michael Early, Lanna Joffrey, Aaron Roman Weiner, Jennifer Dorr White; New Ohio Theatre; April 15, 2012

Theater 2020

www.theater2020.com

Romeo & Juliet by William Shakespeare; Directed by David Fuller; Stage Manager, Cynthia Hennon Marino; Lighting and Set Designer, Giles Hogya; Costume Designer, Lynn Marie Macy; Sound Designer, David Fuller; Choreographer, Judith Jarosz & Poonam Basu; Cast: Poonam Basu, Justin Bennett, Vandit Bhatt, Marc Andrew Hem Lee, Kareem M. Lucas, Lynn Marie Macy, Brandie Moore, Nicholas Pollifrone; Saint Charles Borromeo; July 14 – 24, 2011 and Brooklyn Bridge Park; July 30 – 31, 2011

The Comedy of Errors by William Shakespeare; Directed by David Fuller; Stage Manager, Heather Puchalski; Lighting Designer, Giles Hogya; Costume Designer, Roejendra Adams; Puppet Designer, Eric Engelhardt; Cast: Lauren Briggeman, David Fuller, Kristin Rose Kelly, Annalisa Loeffler, Katie Mack, Evan Maltby, Anton Rayn, Elise Reynard, David Weinheimer, Wayne Willinger; Cranberry Street Theater; May 4 – June 2, 2012

Theater for the New City

www.theaterforthenewcity.net

Executive Director, Crystal Field; Development Director, Courtney Harge; Administrator, Jon Weber; Production Manager, Mark Marcante; Lighting Director, Alexander Bartenieff; Technical Director, Sarah Harris; Literary Manager, Michael Scott-Price

The Empress of China Written and Directed by Joanna Chan; Stage Manager, Sheena L. Young; Lighting Designer, Joyce Liao; Set Designer, Lauren Rockman; Costume Designer, Xu HaoJian & Edmond Wong; Fencing Master, James Gitsham; Choreographer, David ChienHui Shen; Original Music, Yuen Cheuk-Wa; Musical Consultant, Su Sheng; Production Assistant, Lin Ying; Cast: Andrei Drooz, Annie Q, William Allgood, Sergio Mauritz Ang, Jason DeShen Cao, Harris Diano, Teresa Du, Bill Engst, Stephan Goldbach, Kwan ShuMei, Arthur Lai, Lin Ying, Joanne Liu, Mike J. McNulty, Katelynn Mory, B J Peterson, Craig Kelton Peterson, Wilson; Produced by Yangtze Rep Theatre; Theater for the New City; June 3 – 26, 2011

Quartet; Theater for the New City; June 5 – 19, 2011

The Private Sector by Cory Finley; Directed by Charlie Polinger; Theatre for the New City; June 25 – July 3, 2011

Bamboozled, or, The Real Reality Show; Various Locations; August 6 – September 18, 2011

Blood/Nectar/Glitter Written and Directed by Suzana Stanković; Lighting Designer, Joshua H. Chen; Costume Designer, Suzana Stanković; Sound Designer, Andy Altman; Cast: Suzana Stanković; Theater for the New City; August 25 - September 1, 2011

La Manao: Tales of the End of the World; Produced by Casa Cruz De La Luna - www.casacruzdelaluna.com; Theater for the New City; August 31 – September 4, 2011

Too Much Too Soon by Nikole Beckwith, Dean Imperial, Nick Jones, Ken Urban, Melissa Ross, Emily Schwend; Directed by Stephen Brackett, Portia Krieger; Stage Manager, Michele Ebel; Lighting Designer, Steven Maturno; Set Designer, Deb O; Costume Designer, Campbell Ringel; Sound Designer, Daniel Kluger and Brandon Wolcott; Fight Director, Casey Robinson; Technical Director, Sean Bauer; Cast: Daniel Abeles, Liesel Allen Yeager, Craig Jorczak Nate Miller, Anna O'Donoghue, Laura Ramadei; Produced by Lesser America and Red Elevator Productions; Theater for the New City; September 29 - October 9, 2011

Siren's Heart (Marilyn in Purgatory) by Walt Stepp; Directed by Lissa Moira; Cast: Louisa Bradshaw; Theater for the New City; October 5 – 23, 2011

The Capitalist Ventriloquist Music and Lyrics by Tom Attea; Music by Arthur Abrams; Directed by Mark Marcante; Theater for the New City; October 6 – 23, 2011

The Poe Project; Produced by the Chekhov Theatre Ensemble; Theater for the New City; October 6 – 9, 2011

The Boxer's Son by Mario Golden; Directed by Andreas Robertz; Set Designer, Yanko Bakulic; Cast: Teodorina Bello, Elle De Amor, Mario Golden, Jonathan Lara, Alban Merdani, Carlos Navedo, and Yvette Quintero; Theater for the New City; October 13 - 23, 2011

Dogmouth by John Steppling; Directed by Stephan Morrow; Lighting Designer, Alex Bartenieff; Set Designer, Zen Mansley; Cast: Stephan Morrow, Ray Wasik, LB Williams, Courtney Pierchoski; Theater for the New City; November 22 – 27, 2011

Hypnotik: The Seer Will Doctor You Now by Colm O'Shea, Marie Glancy O'Shea & Ildiko Nemeth; Directed by Ildiko Nemeth; Lighting Designer, Federico Restrepo; Set Designer, Ildiko Nemeth; Costume Designer, Jessica Sofia Mitrani; Original Music, Jon Gilbert Leavitt; Choreographer, Julie Atlas Muz; Set Construction Kertek Construction Corp; Set Construction Crew, Sean Bauer and Fabiyan Pemble-Belkin; Sound Engineer, Paul Radelat, Costumer, Marguerite Lochard and Kate Jansyn Thaw; Press Representative, DARR Publicity; Sound Operator, Wilson Sherwin; Cast: Dana Boll, Adam Boncz, Kaylin Lee Clinton, Markus Hirnigel, Denice Kondik, Sarah Lemp, Laurence Martin, Brandon Olson, Fabiyan Pemble-Belkin, Jeanne Lauren Smith, Peter B. Schmitz, Chris Tanner, Paula Wilson, Kat Yew; Produced by New Stage Theatre Company - www. newstagetheatre.org; Theater for the New City; December 21, 2011 - January 15, 2012

Unreachable Eden by Barbara Kahn; Directed by Barbara Kahn and Robert Gonzales, Jr.; Stage Manager, Bill Bradford; Lighting and Set Designer, Mark Marcante; Costume Designer, Carla Gant; Sound Designer, Joy Linscheid; Original Music, Arthur Abrams; Choreographer, Robert Gonzales, Jr.; Cast: Zina Anaplioti, Christopher Ben Comeaux, Benjamin Davis, Claire Epstein, Robert Gonzales, Jr., Gusta Johnson, Franco Pedicini and Steph Van Vlack; Theater for the New City; February 9 – 26, 2012

Cirque Le Jazz; Produced by 2 Ring Circus - www.2ringcircus.com; Theater for the New City; February 23 – 26, 2012

Satan's Whore, Victoria Woodhull; Theater for the New City; March 22 – April 8, 2012

Just Sex by Brant Johnson; Directed by Alex Kilgore; Cast: Brant Johnson, Alex Kilgore, Tasha Lawrence, Meghan Miller; Theater for the New City; March 22 – April 15, 2012

Judith of Bethulia by Charles Busch; Theater for the New City; March 302 – April 28, 2012

Pinocchio's Ashes; Theater for the New City; April 13 – April 29, 2012

A Midsummer Night's (Queer) Dream by William Shakespeare; Theater for the New City; April 25 – May19, 2012

The Chalk Circle by Li QienFu; Adapted and Directed by Joanna Chan; Stage Manager, Kristofer Aigner; Lighting Designer, Joyce Liao; Set and Costume Designer, K. K. Wong; Sound Designer, KwanFai Lam; Cast: Denver Chiu,Viet Vo,Hannah Scott,Mayu Iwasaki,Hugh Cha,Shang-Ho Huang ShuMei Kwan,Sajeev Pillai,Bill Engst,Karen Stefano,Kevin Taejin, ary Shiyan Lao, A Patrick Jo,Phillip Lung; Produced by Yangtze Rep Theatre; Theater For The New City; May 3 - 20, 2012

Hoaxocaust! Written and Performed by Barry Levey; Theater For The New City; May 29 – June 17, 2012

Theater Resources Unlimited

www.truonline.org

READINGS & WORKSHOP

2011 TRU Voices New Plays Reading Series by Hal Ackerman, Richard Manley, Zan Skolnick; Directed by Linda Selman, Eric Parness, Richard Manichello; Roy Arias Theatre (Times Square Arts Center); June 13 - 27, 2011

Theater Three Collaborative

www.theaterthreecollaborative.org

Co-Founders, Karen Malpede, George Bartenieff, the late Lee Nagrin; Co-Artistic Directors, Karen Malpede & George Bartenieff

Another Life Written and Directed by Karen Malpede; Musical Director, Arther Rosen; Stage Manager, Kathleen Purcell; Lighting Designer, Tony Gionvannetti; Set Designer, Robert Eggers; Costume Designer, Sally Ann Parsons; Sound Designer, Arthur Rosen; AudioVisual Designer, Luba Lukova; Producer, George Bartenieff; Cast: Abbas Noori Abbood, George Bartenieff, Christen Clifford, Abraham Makany, Susan Hyon, Andrew Guilarte; Irondale Center; March 8-24, 2012

FESTIVAL

The 9/11 Performance Project Produced by Seth Baumrim; Included: *Another Life* by Karen Malpede, Directed by Karen Malpede, Cast: George Bartenieff, Christen Clifford, Omar Koury, Dorien Makhloghi, Ariel Shaffir, Eunice Wong; *The Domestic Crusaders* by Wajahat Ali, Directed by Carla Blank, Cast: Adeel Ahmed, Deepti Gupta, Imran Javaid, Kamran Khan, Monisha Shiva, Abbas Zaidi; *The Demolition of the Eiffel Tower*, by Jeton Neziraj; Gerald W. Lynch Theater, John Jay College; September 8-11, 2011

TheaterSmarts

maurakelley.net

Dog Park Written and Directed by Maura Kelley; Stage Manager, Kristine Schlachter; Lighting Designer, Jeff Greenberg; Set Designer, Maura Kelley; Costume Designer, Rachel Soll; Sound Designer, Tyler Easter; Cast: Walter Cline, Zander Meisner, Willy Alvarez, Cem Uyanik, Kali Katzman, Adam Zuniga, Denise Poirier, Ken Bolander, Channing Brauer; Drilling Company Theatre Lab; January 25 – February 12, 2012

Theatre 167 and Queens Theatre

www.theatre167.org

Jackson Heights, 3am by Jenny Lyn Bader, J. Stephen Brantley, Ed Cardona Jr., Les Hunter, Tom Miller, Melisa Tien and Joy Tomasko; Directed by Ari Laura Kreith; Stage Manager, Sean McCain; Lighting Designer, Kimberly Dowd; Set Designer, Michael Wilson Morgan; Costume Designer, Georgie Landy; Sound Designer, Ben Rodman; Projection Design, Andrew Lazarow; Cast: Roberto Araujo, Varin Ayala, Farah Bala, Cynthia Bastidas, Rajesh Bose, J. Stephen Brantley, Arlene Chico-Lugo, Ross DeGraw, Nick Fehlinger, Marcelino Feliciano, Andrew Guilarte, Kevin Hoffman, John P. Keller, Alex Kip, Ephraim Lopez, Neal Mayer; P.S. 69; January 13 – February 5, 2012

Theatre in a VAN!

www.theatreinavan.com

Mrs.Perfect! and the Unexpected Visit of Evil! by Crystal Skillman; Directed by James David Jackson; Original Music, Dave Strumfeld and Leon Pease; Cast: Jody Christopherson, Leon Pease, Samantha Barrett; The Brick Theater; June 10 – July 1, 2011

Luminescent Blues by Leon Pease; Directed by Sarah Semlear; Cast: Katie Spence, Chandler Wild, Paul Eddie, Star Kirkland, Daniel Jimenez, Aron Christopher, Olivia Osol, Rachel Troy; Theater for the New City; August 25 – September 4, 2011

The Theatre Project

www.thetheatreproject.org

B*tch by Sean Pomposello; Directed by Christian Amato; Stage Manager, KeriAnne Murphy; Lighting Designer, Rachel Sevedge; Set Designer, Christian Amato; Original Music, Danny Gray; Cast: Michael Neithardt, Benjamin Weaver, Brian Cheng, Gina LeMoine, Arthur Aulisi; Players Theatre & Players Loft; January 5 – 28, 2012

Thom Fogarty Presents

Artistic Director, Thom Fogarty

Desdemona: A Play About a Handkerchief by Paula Vogel; Directed by Thom Fogarty; Lighting, Set, Costume and Sound Designer, Thom Fogarty; Cast: Lulu Fogarty, Colista K. Turner, Christine Verleny; Co-production with Other Side Productions; The Bridge Theater @ Shetler Studios; September 21 - October 2, 2011

Ten Tall Tales About The Men I Love Written and Directed by Thom Fogarty; Adapted from a short story by Ronn Smith; Stage Manager, Scott Munsen; Lighting Designer, Bill Stabile; Set Designer, Bill Stabile and Thom Fogarty; Costume, Sound and AudioVisual Designer, Thom Fogarty; Cast: Armand Anthony, Micah Bucey, Quincy Ellis, Ken Kidd, Christopher Michael McLamb, Jeff McMahon, Aidan O'Shea, Adam Patterson, Carlton Tanis, and Dustye Winniford; Judson Memorial Church; February 24 - 25, 2012

The Artifacts by Steven Fechter; Directed by Thom Fogarty; Stage Manager, Scott Munsen; Lighting, Set, Costume and Sound Designer, Thom Fogarty; Cast: Lulu Fogarty, Caitlin Rose McMahon, Amy Newhall and Armand Anthony; Co-produced by Other Side Productions; The Bridge Theater @ Shetler Studios; April 18-29, 2012

READINGS & WORKSHOPS

In the Name of God by Peter-Adrian Cohen; Directed by Thom Fogarty; Based on the PBS/Frontline documentary Faith and Doubt at Ground Zero by Helen Whitney; Cast: Frank Anderson, Michael Ellick, Diane Kagan, George Kareman, Joseph Melendez, Grace Zandarski and Lulu Fogarty; Judson Memorial Church; September 11, 2011

Tongue in Cheek Theater Productions

www.tictheater.com

Humans Anonymous by Kate Hewlett; Directed by Brock H. Hill; Stage Manager, Allison Lemel; Sound Designer, Philip Rothman; Cast: Amanda Bruton, Gusta Johnson, Jake Lipman, Kyle Minshew, Geoffrey J.D. Payne; The Bridge Theater; May 2 – 12, 2012

Toy Box Theatre Company

www.toyboxtheatre.org

The Short Fall by David Caudle; Directed by David Michael Holmes; Stage Manager, Sara Troficanto; Lighting Designer, Jill Nagle; Set Designer, Gian Marco Lo Forte and Ana Popescu; Costume Designer, Kate Mincer; Sound Designer, James Sparber; Original Music, Brady Bagger and James Sparber; Cast: Ron Bopst, Ryan Colwell, Kally Duling, Dori Legg, Ryan Reilly, Karen Stanion; Teatro IATI; June 3 – 18, 2011

The Empress and El Diablo Written and Directed by Jonathan Barsness; Stage Manager, Rebecca Bezaire and Sara Troficanto; Lighting Designer, Tony Galaska; Set Designer, Kacie Hultgren; Costume Designer, Kate R. Mincer; Sound Designer, James Sparber; Original Music, Colonna Sonora; Choreographer, Wyatt Kuether;

Cast: Juan Luis Acevedo, Gary Ray Bugarcic, Glory Gallo, Jessica Giannone, Jake Paque, and Karen Stanion; The Fourth Street Theater; March 16 – 31, 2012

Treehouse Theatre Company

Home Movies by Frank Winters; Directed by Steven Laing; Cast: Jason Ralph, Sofia Lauwers, Morgan Auld, Alice Wiesner; Dorothy Strelsin Theatre; July 16 - 30, 2011

TXC Heavy Industries

www.tomxchao.com

Callous Cad by Tom X. Chao; Directed by John Harlacher; Lighting Designer, Josh Iacovelli; Set Designer, Josh Iacovelli; Cast: Tom X. Chao, Charlotte Pines, Amy Virginia Buchanan; HERE Arts Center; September 30 – October 16, 2011

United Broadcasting Theater Company

unitedbroadcastingtheater.com

Arcane Game Created by United Broadcasting Theater Company; Directed by Jamie Poskin; Stage Manager, Rosalie Lowe; Lighting Designer, Daisy Long; Sound Designer, Chip Rodgers, Matt Schloss; AudioVisual Designer, Chase Voorhees; Administrative Assistant, Olivia Jorgensen; Dramaturge, Tim Youker; Associate Director, Andrew Gilchrist; Cast: Louiza Collins, Gwen Ellis, Andrew Gilchrist, Arielle Lever, and Henry Vick; Incubator Arts Project; October 27-30, 2011

Michael Created by United Broadcasting Theater Company; Director Jamie Poskin; Assistant Director, Andrew Gilchrist, Sound Designer & Original Music, Matt Schloss; Cast: Andrew Gilchrist, Aaron Heron, Rashid Lacario, Isaac Martinez, Wilda Martinez, Eric Rivera, and Kasia Robertson; MIMA; May 30-31, 2012

Unity Stage Company

Museum by Tina Howe; Directed by Dylan Levers; Stage Manager, Shaina Hurst; Lighting Designer, Marika Kent; Set Designer, Amy Vlastelica; Sound Designer, Kevin Brouder; Cast: Stephanie Barton-Farcas, Jimmy Brooks, Willi Burke, Christian T. Chan, Chaunice Chapman, April Evans, Bari Hyman, Fenton Li, Aaron Matteson, Stephanie Miller, Graciany Miranda, Sarah Natochenny, Carolina Reiter, Peter Rothbard, Jonathan Randell Silver, Cesar J. Rosado, Rachel H. Troy, Guy Ventoliere; PaintCan Studios; May 12 – 20, 2012

Untitled Theater Company #61

www.untitledtheater.com

Artistic Director, Edward Einhorn; Associate Artistic Director, Henry Akona

Pangs of the Messiah by Motti Lerner; Directed by Edward Einhorn; Translation byAnthony Berris; Original Music, Henry Akona; Set Designer, Jane Stein; Costume Designer, Carla Gant; Lighting Designer, Jeff Nash; Dramaturg, Sarah Ollove; Assistant Director, Patrice Miller; Stage Manager, Becky J. Doster; Assistant Stage Manger, Elizabeth Irwin; Musician, Jenny Lee Mitchell; Cast: Sidney Fortner, David J. Goldberg, Gusta Johnson, Elliott Mayer, J. M. McDonough, Paul Muriillo, Yvonne Roen, Max Wolkowitz; Theater at the 14th Street Y; October 27– November 20, 2011

The Pig, or Václav or Havel's Hunt for a Pig by Václav Havel; Adapted by Vladimir Morávek; Translation and Additional Text by Edward Einhorn; Directed by Henry Akona; Choreographer and Assistant Producer, Patrice Miller, Set Designer, Jane Stein; Costume Designer, Carla Gant; Lighting Designer, Jeff Nash; Video Designer, Kate Freer and David Tennent, Dramaturge, Karen Lee Ott; Assistant Director, Joe Pikowski; Stage Manager, Elizabeth Irwin; Graphic Designer, Clinton Corbett; Cast: Katherine Boynton, Elizabeth Figols Galagarza, John Gallop, Andrew Goldsworth, Robert Honeywell, Michael Hopewell, Jenny Lee Mitchell, Mateo Moreno, Phoebe Silva, Moira Stone, Terence Stone, Michael Whitney, Sandy York, Melissa Elledge, Michael Midlarsky, Amanda Lo; 3LD Art & Technology Center; June 29 - Sat July 2, 2011

Variations Theatre Group

www.variationstheatregroup.com

Prisoner of Love by Jay Prasad; Directed by Rich Ferraioli; Lighting and Sound Designer, Greg Solomon; Set and Costume Designer, R. Allen Babcock; Cast: Roger Yeh, Whitney Brown, Kelly Johnston, Jamie Geiger, Leo Goodman, Jael Golad, Tara Lynn Gillfillan; 45th Street Theatre; April 6 – 21, 2012

Vital Theatre Company

www.vitaltheatre.org

Artistic Director, Stephen Sunderlin; Education Director, Linda Ames Key; General Manager, Karron Karr; Company Manager, Stephanie Usis; Production Manager, Matt Wharton; Finance Manager: Rennie Matias; Box Office Manager, Monet Hurst-Mendoza; Education Associate, Sage Clemenco; Booking Director, Kathleen Toner; Booking Assistant, Nancy McDonald; Casting Director, Holly Buczek

Uncle Pirate Book by Ben H. Winters, Music & Lyrics by Drew Fornarola; Directed by Marshall Pailet; Musical Director, Jesse Kissel; Stage Manager, Ashley Scoles; Lighting Designer, Josh Bradford; Set Designer, Kyle Dixon; Costume Designer, Amanda Jenks; Assistant Director, Nora Ives; Choreographer, Kyle Mullins; Cast: Kevin Hoffman, Pep Speed, Hannah Owens, Quinn Shadko, Alison Schmidt, Joshua Houghton; McGinn/Cazale Theatre; September 24-November 13, 2011

Angelina Ballerina The Very Merry Holiday Musical Book & Lyrics by Susan DiLallo, Music by Ben Morss; Directed by Sam Viverito; Musical Director, Cody Wymore; Stage Manager, Shani Colleen Murfin; Lighting Designer, Josh Bradford; Set Designer, Kyle Dixon; Costume Designer, Amanda Jenks; Orchestrator, Julian Blackmore; Cast: Carole Ashley, Roberto Araujo, Jennifer Margulis, Lauren Nestor, Stefanie O'Connell, Joyce Paulino, Amanda Varcelotti, John-Michael Lyles, Matthew Paessler, Mallory Schlossberg; McGinn/Cazale Theatre; November 19, 2011-January 8, 2012

The Bully Music & Lyrics by John Gregor, Book by David L. Williams; Directed by Linda Ames Key; Musical Director, Mark T Evans; Stage Manager, Ashley Scoles; Lighting Designer, Josh Bradford; Set Designer, Kyle Dixon; Costume Designer, Sarah Riffle; Assistant Director, John Magalhaes; Assistant to Director, Chernice Miller; Choreographer, Bethany M. White; Cast: Kathleen Choe, Hilary Fingerman, Justin Grascia, Matthew Krob, Cameron Perry, Riley Thomas; McGinn/Cazale Theatre; January 14-February 26, 2012

StinkyKids the Musical Book & Lyrics by Sammy Buck; Music by Daniel S. Acquisto; Directed by Tim Drucker; Musical Director, Kevin Lawson; Stage Manager, Robert Funk; Lighting Designer, Josh Bradford; Set Designer, Kyle Dixon; Costume Designer, Amanda Jenks; Choreographer, J. Austin Eyer; Assistant to Choreographer, Halden Michaels; Cast: Ryan Mikita, Lora Nicholas, AJ Patton, Bryce Payne, Madison Turner, Laura Weiner; McGinn/Cazale Theatre; March 10-April 22, 2012; Extended at Theatre 80; May 12-May 26, 2012

warner | shaw

Six Seeds: The Persephone Project Written and Directed by Annie G. Levy; Cast: Haley Channing, Ean Sheehy, Emily Asaro, Emily Taplin Boyd, Joya Mia Italiano, Franny Silverman, Emily Warshaw; The Tank; June 2 – 11, 2011

Wayfinder Films

Down the Road by Dale Whisman; Directed by Juan Reinoso; Lighting Designer, Scott Franklin; Set Designer, Reynaldo Davis Carter; Costume Designer, Catherine Siracusa & Sid Levitt; Cast: Renée-Michele Brunet, Renée Petrofes, Vincent Petrosini, Kyla Schoer, Kaylee Souther, Autumn Stein & Kristina Thompson; ; ArcLight Theatre; June 16 – 26, 2011

WE Theater

Brilliant Traces by Cindy Lou Johnson; Directed by Adam Fitzgerald; Lighting Designer, Scott Franklin; Set Designer, David L. Arsenault; Sound Designer, Ian Wehrle; Cast: William W. Warren, Erica Linderman; ArcLight Theatre; July 7 – 24, 2011

White Fence Productions

Holy Child by Joe Lauinger; Directed by Sue Glausen; Cast: John Blaycock, Dono Cunningham, Jerry Ferris, Paul Montagna, and Annie Paul; Roy Arias Off-Off Broadway Theatre; February 2 - 11, 2012

White Horse Theater Company

www.whitehorsetheater.com

Producing Artistic Director, Cyndy A. Marion; Managing Director, Vanessa B. Bombardieri; Director of Marketing & Development, Loretta H. Marion; Founding Artistic Director, Rod Sweitzer

Suddenly Last Summer by Tennessee Williams; Directed by Cyndy A. Marion; Musical Director, Joe Gianono; Stage Manager, Elliot Lanes; Lighting Designer, Debra Leigh Siegel; Set Designer, John C. Scheffler; Costume Designer, David B. Thompson; Sound Designer, Colin Whitely; Dramaturg, Vanessa B. Bombardieri; Assistant Director, Michelle Karst; Assistant Stage Manager, Surayah Davis; Dialect Coach, Julie Foh; Fight Director, Michael G. Chin; Illustrator, Serena Huang; Graphics, Melissa Lin; Program Design, eslie Feffer; Set Builder, Randall Parsons; Master Electrician, Shawn Wysocki; Marketing, The Pekoe Group; Cast: Elizabeth Bove, Lacy J. Dunn, Douglas Taurel, Lue' McWilliams, Haas Regen, Heather Lee Rogers & Carol Ann Foley; Hudson Guild Theatre; September 16-October 2, 2011

Wide Eyed Productions

www.wideeyedproductions.com

The Trojan Women by Euripides; Directed by Kristin Skye Hoffmann; Stage Manager, Lesley Stone; Lighting Designer, Dante Olivia Smith; Set Designer, Alfred Schatz; Costume Designer, Olivia Warner and Jaco Connelly; Sound Designer, Trevor Dallier; Original Music, Sky Seals; Cast: Savannah Clement, Anthony Dogaj, Elizabeth Dogaj, Molly Gilman, Jael Golad, Suzanne Hepker, Melissa Johnson, Lisa Mamazza, Judy Merrick, Justin Ness, Amy Lee Pearsall, Kirsta Peterson, William Reid, and Rachel Riendeau; Kraine Theater; July 7 – 23, 2012

The Wild Project

www.thewildproject.com

NON-RESIDENT PRODUCTIONS

Wax Wings by Matthew Maguire; Directed by Michael Kimmel; Set and Light Designer, Ben Kato; Costume Designer, Christina Bullard; Stage Manager, Elizabeth Huber; Assistant Director, Sarah Esmi; Assistant Costume Designer, Nina Bova: Cast: Eliza Baldi, Jack Marshall, Colleen Werthmann, Amirh Vann Rosario; Produced by Creation Production – www.creationproduction.org; The Wild Project; June 1 – 11, 2011

Little Town Blues by James Presson and Rachel Buethe; Directed by James Presson; Produced by Less Than Rent Theatre; The Wild Project; July 23 – August 23, 2011

Between the Seas Festival of Mediterranean Performing Arts; betweentheseas.org; August 29 – September 4, 2011

Wilson Exclusive Talent Productions

www.wetprods.com

Actor/Writer/Producer/Director, Stephanie Lynn Wilson

Blood Makes The Red River Flow Written and Directed by Stephanie Lynn Wilson; Stage Manager, David Brooks; Lighting Designer, Richard Abrams; Set Designer, David Brooks; Costume Designer, Angelina Scantlebury; Sound Designer, Stephanie Lynn Wilson; Assistant Stage Manager, Fabian Zarta; Cast: Christiana Blain, Ron Rivera, Stephanie Lynn Wilson, Candace Purcell, Al Roffe, Harold Mathieu; Roy Aria Theatre; February 21-27, 2012

A Wound In Time Written and Directed by Stephanie Lynn Wilson; Set and Sound Designer, Stephanie Lynn Wilson; Costume Designer, Angelina Scantlebury; Original Music, Wil Milton & Rodney Carter; Cast: Ron Rivera, Soleidy Mendez, Star Davis, Darryl Reilly, Richard Graff, Irma Cadiz; Looking Glass Theatre; May 4 – June 2, 2012

Winners at Life

Other People's Problems by DeAnne Smith, Sarah Quinn & Samuel Booth; Directed by Sarah Quinn; Stage Left Studio; June 16 – 24, 2011

Wolf 359

wolf359.org

Executive Director, Michael Crowley; Artistic Director, Michael Rau; Producing Director, Chas Carey

Song of Convalescent Ayn Rand Giving Thanks to the Godhead in the Lydian Mode by Michael Yates Crowley; Directed by Michael Rau; Producer: Chas Carey; Cast: Michael Yates Crowley, Michael Rau ; Dixon Place; October 13, 2011

Righteous Money by Michael Yates Crowley; Directed by Michael Rau; Stage Manager, Jenny Ainsworth; Lighting Designer, Elizabeth Coco; Set Designer, Sara C Walsh; Sound and AudioVisual Designer, Asa Wember; Producer: Chas Cary; Assistant Director: Nicole Gehring; Cast: Michael Yates Crowley; Red Room; January 13-21,2012 and 3LD; January 4- 21, 2012

WorkShop Theater Company

www.workshoptheater.org

Fabulous Darshan by Bob Stewart; Directed by Susan Izatt; Stage Manager, Michael Palmer; Lighting Designer, Diana Duecker; Set Designer, Sofia Palacios Blanco; Costume Designer, Chris Hlinka; Sound Designer, Quentin Chiapetta; Production Manager, Kelly Anne Burns; Assistant Costumer, Alexa Devin; Cast: Tim Cain, Spencer Scott Barros, Evan Bernardin, Mike Smith Rivera, Ben Sumrall; Workshop Theatre; June 2 - 25, 2011

Tarragona by Gary Giovannetti; Directed by Elysa Marden; Lighting Designer, Deborah Constantine; Set Designer, Meganne George; Cast: Timothy Scott Harris, Loriu Faiella, Shelly McPherson, Christopher Homer, C.K. Allen, Cecily Benjamin Hughes; The Workshop Theater/ The Jewel Box; June 9 – 18, 2011

Beneath the Hush, A Whisper by Abigail Somma; Directed by Thomas Herman; Stage Manager, Miriam Hyfler; Lighting Designer, Diana Duecker; Set Designer, Jennifer Varbalow; Costume Designer, Cathy Small; Sound Designer, John McKinney; Cast: Greg Oliver Bodine, Jed Dickson, Joseph Franchini, Heather Massie, Shelley McPherson, Mia Moreland; Workshop Theater; September 17 – October 8, 2011

Poe, Times Two Written and Performed by Greg Oliver Bodine; Directed by DeLisa M. White; Lighting Designer, Richard Kent Green; Costume Designer, Jeanette Aultz; Sound Designer, Charles Jeffreys; Painting, Richard T. Scott; Workshop Theater; October 26 – November 5, 2011

Beat Chick by Prudence Wright Holmes and Joanne Joseph; Directed by DeLisa M. White; Stage Manager, Laura Schlachtmeyer; Lighting and Set Designer, Lauren Parrish; Costume Designer, Annalisa Loeffler; Sound Designer, DeLisa M. White; Cast: Dan Patrick Brady, Richard Kent Green, Meredith Riley Stewart, Kevin Stanfa, Tom Pennachini, George Carruth, Anne Fizzard; Workshop Theater; March 1 – 10, 2012

HA! by Rich Orloff; Directed by Ric Sechrest; Stage Manager, Kate Dial; Lighting Designer, Richard Kent Green; Set Designer, Meagan McKeever-Miller; Costume Designer, Holly Rihn; Cast: Jarel Davidow, Anne Fizzard, Gerrianne Raphael, Mike Smith Rivera, Evan Thompson; The Workshop Theater/ The Jewel Box; March 30 – April 15, 2012

Protected by Timothy Scott Harris; Directed by Thomas Coté; Stage Manager, Lindsay M. Stringfellow; Lighting Designer, Diana Duecker; Set Designer, Craig Napoliello; Costume Designer, Joanie Schumacher; Sound Designer, Sean Singer; Cast: Jeff Paul, Cam Kornman, Dee Dee Friedman, Matt Walker, Bill Tatum; The WorkShop Theater | Mainstage; April 26 – May 19, 2012

Write Act Rep Eastside

www.writeactrep.org

Look For The Woman by Christie Perfetti; Directed by Matilda Szydagis; Cast: Michael Borne, Elizabeth Bove, John Carey, Stephanie Anne Ervin, Niae Knight, Lynn Mancinelli, Paul Murillo, Melanie Ryan, Ric Sechrest; Richmond Shepard Theatre; March 5 – 25, 2012

Xoregos Performing Company

Anna Nicole: Blonde Glory by Grace Cavalieri; Directed by Shela Xoregos; Lighting Designer, Don Cate; Costume Designer, Rayneese Primrose; Cast: Mary Riley, Amanda Elizabeth Sawyer, John Sarno,Jason Altman Bong Dizon and William Kozy; Theater for the New City; August 21 - 28, 2011

Yangtze Repertory Theatre of America, Inc.

www.yangtze-rep-theatre.com

Artistic Director/Co-founder, Joanna Chan; Technical Director, K. K. Wong; Acting Executive Director, Jason HaoWen Wang

The Empress of China Written and Directed by Joanna Chan; Stage Manager, Sheena L. Young; Lighting Designer, Joyce Liao; Set Designer, Lauren Rockman; Costume Designer, Xu HaoJian & Edmond Wong; Fencing Master, James Gitsham; Choreographer, David ChienHui Shen; Original Music, Yuen Cheuk-Wa; Musical Consultant, Su Sheng; Production Assistant, Lin Ying; Cast: Andrei Drooz, Annie Q, William Allgood, Sergio Mauritz Ang, Jason DeShen Cao, Harris Diano, Teresa Du, Bill Engst, Stephan Goldbach, Kwan ShuMei, Arthur Lai, Lin Ying, Joanne Liu, Mike J. McNulty, Katelynn Mory, B J Peterson, Craig Kelton Peterson, Wilson; Theater for the New City; June 3 – 26, 2011

The Chalk Circle by Li QienFu; Adapted and Directed by Joanna Chan; Stage Manager, Kristofer Aigner; Lighting Designer, Joyce Liao; Set and Costume Designer, K. K. Wong; Sound Designer, KwanFai Lam; Cast: Denver Chiu,Viet Vo,Hannah Scott,Mayu Iwasaki,Hugh Cha,Shang-Ho Huang ShuMei Kwan,Sajeev Pillai,Bill Engst,Karen Stefano,Kevin Taejin, ary Shiyan Lao, A Patrick Jo,Phillip Lung; Theater For The New City; May 3 - 20, 2012

READINGS & WORKSHOPS

My Brother My Hero by Jisen John Ho; Directed by Wayne Chang; Richmond Sheperd Theatre; February 4, 2012

ADDITIONAL PRODUCTIONS

Bait N' Swish by David Sisco; Directed by Laura Josepher; Cast: David Sisco, Tom Gualtieri; Stage Left Studio; October 13 - November 18, 2011 & January 19 - February 10, 2012

Banshee by Brian C. Petti; Directed by Mary Ellen Nelligar; Assistant Director, Jim Pillmeier; Cast: Brian Christopher, Elisabeth Henry-Macari, Matt Meinsen, Ron Morehead and Lauren Murphy; Flamboyan Theater (CSV Cultural Arts Center); August 21 - 27, 2011

DICTEE: Bells Fall a Peal to Sky by Soomi Kim; Directed by Suzi Takahashi; Stage Manager, Leta Tremblay; Lighting Designer, Lucrecia Briceno; AudioVisual Designer, Eric Jiaju Lee; Original Music, Jen Shyu; Cast: Soomi Kim, Kiyoko Kashiwagi and Diana Oh; The Living Theatre; March 20 - 25, 2012

Drawn and Quartered by Maggie Bofill; Directed by Lou Moreno; Stage Manager, Ruby Ruiz; Lighting Designer, Maria Cristina Fuste; Set Designer, Raul Abrego; Costume Designer, Meghan E. Healey; Assistant Director, Gerardo Rodriguez; Fight Director, David Anzuelo; Press Representatives, David Gernsten & Associates; Cast: Liza Fernandez, Jos Joaquin Perez; INTAR Theatre; June 1 - 26, 2011

The Emperor's New Codpiece by Linda Simpson; Directed by Tim Cusack; Set Designer, Steven Hammel; Costume Designer, Becky Hubbert; Cast: Linda Simpson, Buenaventura Rodriguez, Nicholas Gorham, Patrick Johnson, and Michelle Ojeda; The Laurie Beechman Theatre; June 10 – July 15, 2011

Harrison Greenbaum: What Just Happened? Written, Designed and Performed by Harrison Greenbaum; harrisongreenbaum.com; Dan Sperry Theater @ Times Scare; January 17 – April 5, 2012

Heads by Evan Twohy; Directed by Will Storie; Producer, Stephanie Ward; www.headsplay.com; Teatro SEA at Kabayitos Puppet & Children's Theatre; August 12 - 26, 2011

Instinct by Matthew Maguire; Directed by Michael Kimmel; Stage Manager, Christine D'Amore; Lighting Designer, Ben Kato; Set Designer, Ben Kato; Costume Designer, Christina Bullard; AudioVisual Designer, Aaron Rhyne; Original Music, Andrew Ingkavet; Press Representative, Andy Snyder, O+M; Associate Costume Designer Nina Bova; Technical Director John Ralston; Assistant Stage Manager Michelle Heller; Cast: Kim Blair, Maggie Bofill, Amirh Vann, and Jeffrey Withers; The Lion Theatre; January 13 - February 4, 2012

Minq Vaadka's Narcischism by Adam Cochran; Directed by Chantel Pascente; Cast: Minq Vaadka, Barrie McLain, Ryan Maeker, DoctorPrincess Lady Scoutington, Peter Aguero,Dane Johanson; Produced by Patrick Terry and Te Ilum; 440 Studios; August 26 – September 3, 2011

Obama in Naples by Claudio Angelini; Directed by Stephan Morrow; Musical Director, Charles Czarnecki; Lighting Designer, Alexander Bartenieff; Set Designer, Lello Esposito; Paintings, Lello Esposito; Set Design Consultant, Mark Marcante; Composer/Musician Marco Cappelli; Cast: Beau Allen, Toby Blackwell, Brian Childers, Lin Tucci, John Fennessy, Scott Raymond Johnson, Lauren Maslanik, David Goldyn, Jenna Dallacco and Sam Charny; June Havoc Theatre; April 25 - May 6, 2012

The Orange Person by Jeremy Bloom, Brian Rady, Laura Dunn; Directed by Jeremy Bloom; Stage Manager, Erika Bracy; Lighting Designer, Christopher Weston; Set Designer, Chris Morris; Costume Designer, Olga Mill; Cast: Mikey Barringer, Ashley Biel, Laura Dunn, Dana Kaplan-Angle, Robert Lavenstein, Ellen O'Meara, Madalyn McKay, Justin Neal, Jose Paz, Brian Rady, Kirk Siee, Catherine Sullivan and Joe White; Gene Frankel Theatre; November 2 - 18, 2011

Peter & I by Matte O'Brien & Matt Vinson; Directed by Matte O'Brien; Stage Manager, Ashley Nelson; Lighting Designer, Brian Barnett; Set Designer, Billy Davis; Costume Designer, Ryan Moller; Sound Designer, Zachary Duax; Original Music, Matt Vinson; Cast: Aynsley Bubbico, Chris Dwan, Ben Hart, Geoffrey Kidwell, Emily Padgett, and Jared Zirilli; peterandi.com; American Theatre of Actors; October 6 – 16, 2011

A (Radically Condensed and Expanded) Supposedly Fund Thing I'll Never Do Again (After David Foster Wallace) Written and Directed by Daniel Fish; Lighting Designer, Thomas Dunn; Set Designer, Laura Jellinick; Costume Designer, Andrea Lauer; Sound Designer, Daniel Kluger; Cast: John Amir, Efthalia Papacosta, Therese Plaehn, Mary Rasmussen, Jenny Seastone Stern; The Chocolate Factory; March 22 - April 7, 2012

The Scene by Ks Stevens; Directed by Georgia Sanford; Cast: Essence Alexander, Sharon Jane Smith, Sweet Lorraine, Gayle Robbins and Ks Stevens; WOW Cafe; June 15, 2011

Sistas The Musical Written and Produced by Dorothy Marcic; Directed by Christopher Burris; Musical Arrangement, Germono Toussaint; General Manager, Felicia Bass; Abingdon Theater Mainstage; July 11 – 31, 2011

Speargrove Presents Book and lyrics by Sammy Buck; Music by Brandon James Gwinn; Conceived by Joe Barros, Laura Brandel, Sammy Buck, Karen Marshall, Reed Prescott, Samuel Willmott; Produced by New York Theatre Barn; Directors, Joe Barros and Laura Brandel; Music Director, Jason Wetzel; Casting/Producer, Jason Najjoum; Stage Manager, Caitlin Lyons; Assistant Stage Manager, Mackenzie Meeks; Cast: Noah Galvin, Kristen da Costa, Alexa Green, Carolyn Mignini, Erin Leigh Peck, Michael Pesce, Jessica Kent, Babs Rubenstein, Anthony Romeo, Jake Odmark, Ariela Morgenstern, Charlie Owens, Scott Denny, Shorey Walker; The Cell Theatre; May 14-16, 2012

Truth by Ellis Gaskell; Directed by Catherine Lamm; Cast: Tom Leverton, Orion Delwaterman, David Mead; Dorothy Strelsin Theatre; July 16 – 26, 2011

What Are You Doing Here? by Maria Alexandria Beech; Directed by Michelle Bossy; Stage Manager, Katie Fergerson; Lighting Designer, Emily McGillicuddy; Set Designer, Timothy Greenway; Costume Designer, Sophia Lidz; Composer and Sound Design, Benjamin Bonnema; Projection Designer, Patrick Lovejoy; Cast: Maggie Surovell & Kelley Jackson Garcia; Gene Frankel Theatre; June 4 – 12, 2011

What the Time Traveler Will Tell Us by Jeffrey Cranor & Joseph Fink; Directed by Eevin Hartsough; Stage Manager, Randi Rivera; Lighting Designer, Lauren Parrish; Set Designer, Eevin Hartsough; Sound Designer, Christopher Loar; Cast: Jeffrey Cranor, Joseph Fink; Produced by Jeffrey Cranor & Joseph Fink; Incubator Arts Project; August 4 – 13, 2011

FESTIVALS

All For One Theater Festival

www.afofest.org

Theatre 80 St. Marks; November 11 – 20, 2011

23 Feet in 12 Minutes by Mari Brown, Performed by Deanna Pacelli

Creating Illusion Written and Performed by Jeff Grow; Directed by Jessi D. Hill

Good Morning Anita Hill... Written and Performed by Deb Margolin; Directed by Merri Milwe

Hamlet (solo) by William Shakespeare, Performed by Raoul Bhaneja; Directed by Robert Ross Parker

Happiness Written and Performed by Heather Harpham

Masquerade: Calypso & Home Written and Performed by Roger Bonair-Agard; Directed by Kamilah Forbes

Monster Written by Daniel MacIvor, Performed by Avery Pearson; Directed by Steve Cook

Over There – Comedy is His Best Weapon *Written and Performed by PJ Walsh; Directed by Dion Flynn*

RASH Written and Performed by Jenni Wolfson; Directed by Jen Nails

Scared Skinny Written and Performed by Mary Dimino; Directed by Christine Renee Miller

Shadowboxing Written and Performed by Grant Sullivan; Directed by Sal Romeo

Summer in Sanctuary Written and Performed by Al Letson; Directed by Rob Urbinati

Truth Values: One Girl's Romp Through M.I.T.'s Male Math Maze Written and Performed by Gioia De Cari; Directed by Miriam Eusebio

unFRAMED Written and Performed by Iyaba Ibo Mandingo; Directed by Brent Buell

Wanderlust Written and Performed by Martin Dockery; Directed by Jean-Michele Gregory

An Evening of Excerpts; *The Gospel According to Josh* Written and Performed by Josh Rivedal, *Panic Diaries* Written and Performed by Katie Northlich, and *They Call Me Mister Fry* Written and Performed by Jack Fry

New Works Series; *The Three Chords of the Apocalypse* Written and Performed by Joanna Parson, *The Purpose Project: Thao's Library* Written and Performed by Elizabeth Van Meter, and *Death and Taxes; Mourning America* Written and Performed by Zero Boy

The Bococa Arts Festival

bococaartsfestival.com

Various Locations; June 17 – 26, 2011

Will Work For... by Lea Leneskie-Kotte and Charlene A. Donaghy; Directed and Produced by Sarah V. Michelson and Lea Leneskie-Kotte; Cast: Valentina Arena, Jessica Vera, Mateo Moreno, Crystal Domsher

Brooklyn Labyrinth by Isaac Rathbone, Kate Kertez and Sergei Burbank; Directed by Sara Wolkowitz; Cast: Lauren Roth, Justy Kosek

Barnaby by Liza Birkenmeier; Directed by Dara Malina; Lighting Designer, Christopher Weston; Sound Designer, Victoria Pollack; Costume Designer Julia Mancini; Producer Valentine Lysikatos; Cast: David Riley, Matt McDonald, Julia Bentz, Patrick Avella

Island by Ben Ellentuck; Directed by Amanda Junco; Lighting Designer, John Eckert, Costume Designer, Hilary Walker; Cast: Meg Massalone, Jovan A. Davis

Turtleback High by Kevin Dedes; Directed by Jay Marks; Cast: Lauren Tyrrell, Jason Suran, Edward Raube-Wilson, Greg Ramsey, Laura Quackenbush, Emma Myers, Tyler Gilliam; Caroline Gart, Lex Friedman, Brian Fiddyment, Raife Baker

What's in a Name by Timothy Nolan; Cast: Christine Goodman, Chantal Gagnon, Rory Clarke

COIL Festival 2012

Produced by PS122; January 5 – 29, 2012

Anger at the Movies by David Levine, Kyoung H. Park and Gideon Lewis-Kraus; Lawyer,Rob Cohen; Photographer, Cate Schappert; Architectural Designer, Jo Walker; Cast: Christianna Nelson; November 10 - 12, 2011

Choreography for Blackboards by Michael Kliën and Steve Valk; Performers: Brian Schwartz, Paul Muldoon, Jeffrey Gormly, Frank Hentschker, Ivan Martinez, Eugenia Manwelyan, Tal Beery, Emma Fitzgerald, Aine Stapleton, Tony Schultz, Leina Bocar; January 8 – 11, 2012

Let us think of these things always. Let us speak of them never.; January 5 - 9, 2012

Looking For a Missing Employee & The Pixelated Revolution by Rabih Mroué; January 6 - 9, 2012

Mission Drift by TEAM in collaboration with Heather Christian and Sarah Gancher; Directed by Rachel Chavkin; Set Designer, Nick Vaughan; Costume Designer, Brenda Abbandandolo; Lighting Designer, Jake Heinrichs; Sound Designer, Matt Hubbs; Associate Lighting Designer, Seá n Linehan; Dramaturg, Paz Pardo; Stage Manager, Dave Polato; Original Music, Heather Christian; Cast: Heather Christian, Amber Gray, Brian Hastert, Libby King, Ian Lassiter, Matt Bogdanow, Sasha Brown, Gabe Gordon; January 8 – February 4, 2012

newyorkland by Kenneth Collins and William Cusick; January 12 – February 4, 2012

The Past is Grotesque Animal by Mariano Pensotti; January 7 – 15, 2012

too shy to stare by Davis Freeman; Performers: Brian McCorkle, Ed RosenBerg, Hahn Rowe, Maya Orchin, Nora Petroliunas, Lauren Garson, Andrew Broaddus, Matthew Morris, Hope Davis, Megan Harrold, Winnie Ho, Laura Hicks and Paul Singh; Co-produced by Random Scream; January 6 – 14, 2012

Untitled Feminist Show Conceived and Directed by Young Jean Lee; Cast: Becca Blackwell, Amelia Zirin-Brown, Hilary Clark, Katy, Pyle & Regina Rocke; Choreographer, Faye Driscoll, Morgan Gould and Young Jean Lee; January 12 – February 4, 2012 and Merrill Wright Mainstage Theater; April 4 - 7, 2012

Waking Things by Melika Bass; January 07, 2012

Comic Book Theater Festival

Produced by The Brick Theater; June 2 - July 18, 2011 (See listing for the Brick Theater)

Dream Up Festival 2011

www.theaterforthenewcity.net

Sound Designer, Jonah Rosenberg; Animations, Lotte Marie Allen; Festival Director/Curator, Michael Scott-Price; Administrator, Jonathan Weber; Festival Administrator, Roger Brown; Publicist is Jonathan Slaff

Produced by Theatre for the New City; Theatre for the New City; August 14 - September 4, 2011

Buried Alive! A Matchbox Theatre by Deborah Kaufmann

The Choice by Riccardo Costa; Director, Andre Hereford

Dogmouth by John Steppling; Directed by Stephan Morrow

The Fourth State of Matter by Joseph Vitale; Director, Robert Angelini; Cast: Samantha Glovin, Andrew W. Hsu, Ed Heavey, Terrance Montgomery

Love Masters Created and Performed by Erick Paiva-Noguch

Nine/Twelve Tapes by Leegrid Stevens; Director, Ryan Pointer; Cast: Andres Munar, Lynne McCollough, Guy Stroman, Lori Prince and Erin Treadway

Nuclear Love Affair by Sanaz Ghajarahimi & Ben Hobbs; Director, Sanaz Ghajarahimi & Ben Hobbs

Own, Owned Choreographer, Jesse Phillips-Fein

EstroGenius Festival

estrogenius.org

Producers, Catie Choate and Jen Thatcher; Assistant Producers, Ellen Lanese-Spaldo, Helene Galek, Anne Carlino; Sound Designers, Kia Rogersr and Sarah Chichester; Lighting Designers, Micheal Clark Wonson and Karen Sweeney; Stage Manager, Sarah Chichester; Assistant Stage Manager, Earline Stephen; Manhattan Theatre Source; October 5 - November 5, 2011

Goodbye Avis by Celeste Koehler; Directed by Kathleen O'Neill; Cast: Donna Barkman, Susan Scudder, Vincent Marano, Nicholas Radu

Glutton for Punishment by Catherine Noah; Directed by Sandy Yaklin; Cast: Vanessa Shealy, Alan Hasnas

Escape to Wonderland by Patrick Gabridge; Directed by Mary Hodges; Cast: Sheila Joon, Darnelle Williams

Dinner For Who by Gabrielle Compton; Directed by Jennifer Bronstein; Cast: Alex Engquist, Lillith Fallon, Patricia Lynn

Origin by Elizabeth Irwin; Directed by Malini Singh McDonald; Cast: Joane Cajuste, Nicholas Radu

Spinal Alignment by Deborah Yarchun; Directed by Deborah Savadge; Cast: Jed Peterson, Irene Lucio

My Beautiful Grandmother by Amina Henry; Directed by Matilda Szydagis; Susan McBrien, Ben Schnickel

Status Update by Jamie Pachino; Directed by Andrea Finlayson; Cast: Kyle Page, Jane Finlayson

Attendant by Caron Levis; Directed by Irene Carroll; Leigh Adel-Arnold, Zachary Le Vey, Gloria Boucher

Me by Maia Akiva; Directed by Yudelka Heyer; Cast: Thia Stephan, Anna Wallace-Deering

Green Dating by Chantal Bilodeau; Directed by Barbara Harrison; Cast: Quinn Warren, Eugene Oh

Bones of Home by Charlene A. Donaghy; Directed by Pat Golden; Cast: Brent Hunter, Jane Cronin

Supernova by Gemma Irish; Directed by Kathryn McConnell; Cast: Lindsay Schwak, Sergio LoDolce, Christoper Chwee

Black Boys Don't Dance by Philana Omorotionmwan; Directed by Sandra Alexander; Cast: Tom Martin, Sandra Parris, Alfonso Johnson

Tough Love by John C. Davenport; Directed by Delisa M. White; Cast: Shaun Bennet Wilson, Beth Ann Leone

Hand-Me-Downs Written & Performed by Donna Barkman

Lace Curtain Irish by Carolyn Gage; Cast: Denise Poirier
The Pain of Pink Evenings by Rosemary Moore; Directed by Nancy Gabor; Cast: Wendy Allegaert

Listen, Can You Hear Me Now? Written & Performed Gloria Rosen; Directed by Peter Flint

Formerly Known as Sarah Written & Performed by Joyce Griffen

Pelican Girls Written & Directed by Richard Ballon; Cast: Kate Hare

Stand Clear of the Closing Doors, Please Written & Performed by Emily Kunkel

Call Me Written & Performed by Katherine Williams; Directed by Megan Cooper

FRIGID Festival 2011

www.frigidnewyork.info

Produced by Horse Trade Theater Group; Horse Trade Theatres; February 22 - March 04, 2012

Aerial Allusions Performed by Jaz Morneau and Azana; Produced by Agawa Sapphire and Azana Productions

Afternoon Tea with Jane Austen Directed by Bruce Lambie

Big Girls Don't Cry by Rachelle Elie; Produced by Crowning Monkey Productions

Big Plastic Heroes Produced by Plastic Thunder

Blind to Happiness Produced by Better To Burn Out Productions

Breathe, Love, Repeat: A near-life experience Directed by Ching Valdes Valdes; Produced by Mustique Projects

Coosje Directed by Ryan Emmons; Produced by No. 11 Productions

Daughters of Lot Directed by Rachel Kerry and Molly Ballerstein; Produced by Brain Melt Consortium

Death, it happens: A girl's guide to death Directed by Lori Kee; Produced by Bricken and Birch Productions

Drowning Ophelia: A New Rock Musical Directed by JD Cannady; Produced by RIFF Collective

Fear Factor: Canine Edition by John Grady

I Married A Nun! Written and Performed by D'yan Forest

I'm Only Explaining This Once Written and Performed by Moe Rosen

Initium/Finis by Kristin Arnesen and Radoslaw Konopka; Produced by Theatre Reverb

Judge, Yuri, & Executioner Directed by DeLisa White; Produced by Temerity Theatre Company

Little Lady Directed by John Turner

LOL: The End. Directed by Moises Belizario and Una Aya Osato; Produced by Keep it Movin' Productions

Love in the Time of Chlamydia Directed by Jonathan Warman; Produced by Hard Sparks

Man Saved by Condiments! Directed by Bill Stiteler and Matthew Foster; Produced by Theatre Alro

Missed Connections: An Exploration into the Online Postings of Desperate Romantics Directed by, Ricky Dunlop; Produced by Royanth Productions

Musical Pawns Directed by Lindi G. Papoff; Produced by Lost Music Productions

Poe-Dunk: A Matchbox Entertainment Directed by John Pieza; Produced by Playlab NYC

Rabbit Island Directed by Aimee Todoroff; Produced by Elephant Run District

Scratch & Pitz: Burlesque Variety Hour Directed by Cyndi Freeman and Brad Lawrence; Produced by Heroics in Hotpants

Stripper Lesbians Directed by Jeff Woodbridge; Company, Rising Sun Performance

The Rope in Your Hands Directed by Danielle Skraastad

The Stranger to Kindness Directed by Heather Cohn; Produced by D&A Productions

The Terrible Manpain of Umberto MacDougal Directed by Bricken Sparacino

The Traveling Musicians (formerly Borderlines) Produced by 3 Sticks

Til Love Do Us Part Directed by Cameron J. Marcotte; Produced by High Frequency Theatre

HOT Festival 2011

www.hotfestival.org

Dixon Place; June 24 - August 4, 2011

America Ain't Ready AND HOMEbody; July 12, 2011

Bards; July 1, 2011

Burlesque With Essence Revealed And Friends; July 2, 2011

Butch Burlesque: An Evening Of Swagger Co-curated and Hosted by Victoria Libertore and Lea Robinson; Cast: Moe Angelos, Crystal Balls, Drae Campbell, Molly Equalty Dykeman, Luscious von Dykester, Tina Richerson, Jessica Lurie Alto, Lee Frisari; Produced by L Boogie Productions; August 4, 2011

Christian Von Howard -and- Alberto Denis/[QuA²D] -and- Vincent E. Thomas; July 16, 2011

Coby Koehl In Concert; June 30, 2011

Coffee Grindr (work In Progress); July 7, 2011

Disembodied- A Memoir -and- El Ensayo; July 13, 2011

Dyke-opalypse: Laughing At The End Of The World; July 8, 2011

Ejercicios De Belleza/Beauty Exercises; June 29, 2011

Fuck Your Musical; June 28, 2011

He Who Laughs: Live; June 30, 2011

How Brief Eternity and The Matthew Shepard Dance; July 1, 2011

Jessica Halem: Bad Feminist; July 13 - 19, 2011

Lauren M Feldman & Diana Y Greiner/Maria Bauman/Ephrat Asherie/ Jen Abrams; July 5, 2011

MaDHaTters CabArEt's: Give 'em Fiya!; July 15, 2011

Micia Mosely & Friends: The Hotter Than July Edition; July 14, 2011

Molly "Equality" Dykeman's Comedy Extravaganza!; July 15, 2011

Night Mother Cast: Erin Markey and Cole Escola; August 4, 2011

Pete Sturman: Live in The Lounge; June 30, 2011

Pitch!; June 29 - July 27, 2011

Self-Taut -and- Hard Wear Soft Drive; July 6, 2011

Steve Hayes: Tired Old Queen at the Movies LIVE! Movie Stars Sing at Last!; August 6, 2011

Summer & Tokes Cast: Bradford Scobie, Steve Hayes, Gina Vetro, David Ilku, Colleen O'Neill, Joseph Keckler, Judith Greentree and Wes Urish; Costume Designer, Ramona Ponce; Directed by Kevin Malony; Produced by TWEED Fractured Classicks Series; August 4 - 5, 2011

Take the Mic Hosted By Marti Gould Cummings; June 27, 2011

The Body Blend Series: Remixed N' Homotized; June 25, 2011

Tickets to Manhood - A Mondo Cane! Commission; July 14 - 30, 2011

Volcano's Birthright(s); July 1, 2011

Ice Factory Festival

Produced by SoHo Think Tank; 3LD Art & Technology Center; June 22 - July 29, 2011

Struck by Robert Saietta and Rebecca Hart; Directed by D.J. Mendel; Original Music: Rebecca Hart; June 22 - 25, 2011

The Pig or Vaclav Havel's Hunt for a Pig by Vaclav Havel; Adapted by Vladimir Moravek; Translated by Edward Einhorn; Untitled Theater Company #61; June 29 - July 2, 2011

Pontiac Firebird Variations by Casey Wimpee; Directed by Matthew Hancock; Aztec Economy; July 6 - 9, 2011

An Impending Sense of Doom by Ensemble with Julia Hollerman; Directed by Jeffrey Whitted; Subjective Theatre Company; July 13 - 16, 2011

Three Graces Libretto and Lyrics by Ruth Margraff; Directed by Marcy Martin; Original Music: Nikos Brisco; Café Antarsia Ensemble & Immigrants Theatre Project; July 20 - 23, 2011

Sometimes in Prague Created by Joshua William Gelb and Stephanie Johnstone; Magic Futurebox and Rusty Ring Thelin; July 27 - 30, 2011

WORKSHOPS

Commedia dell'Artemisia by Kiran Rikhye; Directed by John Stancato; Stolen Chair Theatre Company; June 23 - 24, 2011

Be Story Free by Kirk Wood Bromley; Inverse Theater; June 30 - July1, 2011

The Love Letter You've Been Meaning to Write to New York by Wirtten and Directed by Jonathan Solari; July 7 - 8, 2011

Dead People Everywhere Theatre Group; July 14 - 15, 2011

Americans 'N' Indians by Matthieu Sys & Yahya Terryn; Directed by Kevin Doyle; Sponsored by Nobody in association with het GEIT (Gent, Belgium); July 21 - 22, 2011

Will Sing by Samantha Chanse, Carla Ching, Mia Chung, Michael Lew, & Qui Nguyen; Directed by Ralph Pena; Ma-Yi Theater Co.; July 28 - 29, 2011

Left Out Festival

www.stageleftstudio.net

Produced by Stage Left Studios; April 14 - 25, 2012

Getting Away with Mother by Topher Cusumano; Directed by Toni Silver; Cast: Gaby Gold, Joe Hutcheson, Cheryl King, Michelle Ramoni and Don Rider

Home In Her Heart by Margaret Morrison; Directed by Cheryl King; Cast: Ericka Hart and Margaret Morrison

Left Out Shorts by Selections from *June & Nancy* by Michelle Ramoni; *The Angel of Wishes* by Robin Goldfin; *...and Scene* by William LoCasto; *Selections from Stabilized Not Controlled* Written and Performed by Frank Blocker; *Things that go Bump* by Richard Ballon; *The Garden Plot* by Karen Thibodeau

A Mad Person's Chronicle of a Miserable Marriage by Sinan Unel; Cast: John Andert;

Southern Gothic Novel by Frank Blocker; Cast: Frank Blocker;

That Play: A Solo Macbeth by Tom Gualtieri & Heather Hill; Directed by Heather Hill; Original Music & Sound by Erin Hill; Cast: Tom Gualtieri

Manhattan Repertory Theatre Festivals

Spring PlayFest 2011 - Manhattan Repertory Theatre; April 10 - June 12, 2011

The Third Pulpit by Ed Stever

The Fireplace by Nancy Bakinde

The File on J. Edgar Hoover by Steve Gold

To the New from the Former Mrs. Girl: Sound advice for my husband's new wife or mistress by Samantha Macher

Killing Time by Tom Slot

Pro Patria Mori by Simone Marie Martelle

Twitter This... Facebook That... Text Me Later.. by Richard Thomas Henle

Prisoner of Illusion by Aileen Kilburn

SUMMER FEST 2011 - MANHATTAN REPERTORY THEATRE; JUNE 18 - AUGUST 17, 2011

1 Only Fuck Stupid 1 Whores by Olivia Peterson

Benny the Baboon by Molly Summer; Original Music by Pumashock

The Bodhisattva of Broadway by Daniel Grove

Daffodils in Deutchland by Dray Rigg

Defences by Ariane Campbell

The Erlenring Song by Pamela Robbins

Feeling Good by Paul Testagrossa

Men by Ken Wolf; Directed by Lori Mannette; Cast: Samantha Ciavarella, Lindsay Davis, Sarah Elizondo, Kate Morris, Thami Moscovici, Mary Regan, Jordan Anna Siegel

Mulberry Bush by Jeff Ronan

My Night with Frida by Rob Santana; Directed by Mark Cisneros

Ray's Delay by Barry Ernst; Directed by Robert Prerito

Same Time, Same Bench by Joseph Lizardi

Sex in Mommyville: The Battle for Who's on Top! by Anna Fishbeyn

The Tide by Paulina Barros Reyes-Retana

Unburdened by Gregory Paul Thomas

The Value of Empty Boxes by Aaron M. Leventman

A Week at the NJ Shore by Valerie Work

When Yellow Were the Stars on Earth by Franco Moschetti

SUMMER ONE ACT PLAY SERIES 2011 - MANHATTAN REPERTORY THEATRE; JULY 7 - SEPTEMBER 2, 2011

Black Girl Lost by Mary McCallum

The Bug Collector by Anthony Smith

Dog House by Andrew Greer

Love in all the right places by Juan Ramirez

The 12 Dates of Christmas by Ginna Hoben

The Actress by Prudence Kahn

The C.L.U.B. by Nicole Diaz and Richard Thomas

Mistakes by Mark Levy

5 Meter Spread. We Move. No Sound. by Suzanne Goldish

Sexual Chemistry 911 by Kathleen Potts

FALL ONE ACT PLAY SERIES 2011 - MANHATTAN REPERTORY THEATRE; SEPTEMBER 14 - SEPTEMBER 17, 2011

At the Ringing of the Bell by Megan Sass

After the Great Chaos by Charles Lear

Attack of the Dorothys by J.E. Phelan

Bear in the Bathroom by Rose Bochner

Broke & Broker by Rachel Blithe

A Cable Situation by Pat O'Connor

Departures by Matt Jacobs

Douche by Chad Chenall

Dust in the Wind by Dorit Katzenelenbogen

Falling Star by Jeanne Chenault Porter

Family Story of Nothing by Anthony J. Fuller

The First Line of Defence by Tariq Hamam

Food Chain by Jack Spagnola

GoodBadUgly by Robin Parrish

Got to Get to the Savoy by Tamu Favorite

How to Cook Adobo by Jorshinelle Taleon-Sonza

If You See Something, Say Something by Liz Magee

Italian Ices by The Default Theater Company

Manhattan Skyline by Richard Thomas Henle

The Mechanicals by Andrew Greer

More Than Strangers by Josheph Lizardi

Muse by Walter Thinnes

A New Game by Leah Dashe

A New Life by Andrew Houlihan

Never Let Go by Raven Petretti

Obello by The Default Theater Company

Off the Bridge by Akua Doku

On the Floor by Julia Gytri

On the Rocks with Mickey & Minnie Mouse by Sharon Goldner

The One by Bonnie Pompili

The Park by Glenn Adkins

Patrick and Lisa's Wedding by Duncan Pflaster

The Pitch by Kathryn Funkhouser

Prescriptions by Ellen Orchid

Scrambled by Tom Lacy

Succession by Charles White

The Waiting Room by Steven A. Shapiro

Underdeveloped by Rachael Solomon

**FALL FEST 2011 - MANHATTAN REPERTORY THEATRE;
OCTOBER 12 - DECEMBER 16, 2011**

Cruelty to Animals by Jerry Lieblich

Game Point by Julia Gytri

Hiding in the Girls' Bathroom by Andrea Macy & Mallory Schlossberg

Josefina & Minerva by Yolanda Rodriguez

L.A. Lights Fire by Eric Czuleger

Legacy A New Musical

Love without Law by Kathleen Wiloe

The Placebo Effect by Helene Montagna

Redemption of the Vampyre by Jeffrey Potter-Watts

Same Time Same Bench by Joe Lizardi

Spirits, Angels and Things That Fly by Pamela L. Robbin

Starts with a Sneeze by Caroline O'Meara

Tact: An Apocalyptic Love Story by Jan Rosenberg

The Tampon Play by Hope Weiner

Waking Kya by Siobhan Fitzpatrick

What Would Sam Spade Do? by David J. Glover

**WINTER ONE ACT PLAY SERIES 2012 - MANHATTAN REPERTORY
THEATRE; JANUARY 10 - JANUARY 28, 2012**

The Beginning of the End without the Beginning by Jennifer Sandella

Bobo, BooBoo, Bibi & Bourbon by Terry M. Sandler

Bombs by Sharon Mathis

Bridge to Baraka by Yvette X

Brooklyn Brownstone by Jeremy Kruse

Bryan And Kim by Adam Delia

Coffee House, Greenwich Village by John Doble

The Confession by D.A.G. Burgos

Downsizing by JoanMarie Maniaci

A Dream by Bryan Quick

FingerPrint Free by Terry Sidney

The Great Gambit by Jodi Van Der Horn-Gibson

The Hostile, The Holy, + The Holding by Nelson Diaz-Marcano

Jake's Inferno by Tom Rizzuto

James Killed A Guy by Van Corona

Lady's Rack by Kimberly Aboltin

Let's Order by Bonnie Rosenbaum

A Long Came Some Spiders by Debbie Workman

Mott by Justin Vibbert

One Night Stand by Race Brown

Outside The Lines by Meredith Allen

Potential by Emily Daly

Protest by Adam Meyer

Right Time to Say I Love You by Cindy Wolfe Boynton

Sexpectations by Stephanie Gardner

Subtext by Jenny Lynn Christofferson

Sudden Improvement by Roy Robbins

Suidice Gal by J. Boyer

Switch 96 by Mike Fresta

Table for Three by Matthew Klein

Teddy and the Tin Foil Hat by Keaton Weiss

Trails of a Scientific Mind by Will Lacker

**WINTER FEST 2012 - PRODUCED BY MANHATTAN REPERTORY
THEATRE; FEBRUARY 8 - MARCH 17, 2012**

Almost Adults by Aaron Leventman

Carry-on Baggage by Debbie Slevin

Danny and the Deep Blue Sea by John Patrick Shanley

Dead Guy by Jordan Swisher

Die Happy by Mary Stewart-David

From the Inside by Richard Thomas Henle

The House of Yes by Wendy MacLeod

It Happened on a Monday by Carrie Lynette Stringfellow

Justice for Walter Weinberg by Ellen Mausner

Reach by Ryan Sprague

The Key to All Mythologies by Jonathan Wallace

Waiting for the Big O by Daniel Huntley Solon

Women in Motion by Donald Margulie

Midtown International Theatre Festival

midtownfestival.org

Various Locations; July 16 - 30, 2011

Alice: A New Musical by Book, Music/Lyrics by Andrew Barbato and Leslie Desantis; Directed by Andrew Barbato; Cellar Door Stage and Erica Ruff Productions; The June Havoc Theatre

Banana Monologues, The by John R. Brennan, Jason C. Cooper and Mary Cimino; Directed by Debra Whitfield; Cast: John R. Brennan; Gregory Taft Gerard in association with Jason C. Cooper; The Dorothy Strelsin Theatre

Between The Bricks by Anthony Giorgio, Cecilia Ceresa; Directed by Anthony Giorgio; Lyricist/Composer, Davey Patterson; Cast: Mathew S. Morgan, Anna Suzuki, Kristen Gheling, Amanda Huxtable, Rori Nogee, Barbara Ceannt, Gregory Pember, Sara Kliger, John Wascavage, Christopher Timson, Charlie Duncan, Blaine Morris; Blair Hotchner; The June Havoc Theatre

Boomers, The Musical of a Generation by Book, Music, and Lyrics by Peter Baron; Directed by Gerald vanHeerden; Arrangements & Orchestrations, Mark Sensinger; The June Havoc Theatre

Children of God Book, Music and Lyrics by Charles Murray; Directed by Ben Harney; Choreographer, Daryl Richardson; Music Supervisor, Charles Czarnecki; Cast: Nathan Lucrezio, Ashley Taylor, Jennie Harney, Keith Antone, Starlett Brown, Paul Geiger, Stephen Glavin and Charles Bernard Murray; Charles Murray; The June Havoc Theatre

Dad Doesn't Dance Written and Performed by Nora Brown; Small Pond Enterprises; The Dorothy Strelsin Theatre

Dickening, The by Ben Ferber and Donald McEwan; Directed by Ben Ferber; Cast: Anna Van Valin, Billy Ferrer, Mieko Gavia, William Passannante, Sarah Rosengarten; Fop! Productions; The MainStage Theater

Dirty Paki Lingerie by Aizzah Fatima; Directed by Erica Gould; Lighting Designer, Evan True; Cast: Aizzah Fatima; Aizzah Fatima; The Dorothy Strelsin Theatre - www.dirtypakilingerie.com

Don Gio Written and Directed by Joshua R. Pangborn; Assistant Director, Jennifer Kent; Cast: Chris Morris, Drew Moerlein, Emily Gittelman, Jennifer Kent, Jimmy Brooks Jr., Kimberley Shoniker, Linda Blackstock, Michael Thieling; Sidekick Productions; The MainStage Theater

Ethan's People by Richard L. Gaw; Cast: Daniel Fox, Luis Alberto Gonzalez, Missy Hernandez, Chloe Lenihan; Buds of May Productions; The Dorothy Strelsin Theatre

Flowers: A Thorny Romance Story by Carolyn M. Brown and D.E. Womack; All in Black and White Productions; The MainStage Theater

Fuel: A Presidential Fantasy by Joe Beck; The June Havoc Theatre

Gated by Marisa Marquez; Directed by Danny Williams; Cast: Erin Adams, Andrew Eisenman, Christopher Kloko, Marisa Marquez, Austin Mitchell, Megha Nabe and Susan Quinn; The Isa Company; The MainStage Theater

Georgia & Me by Sarah Ford; Directed by Zoya Kachadurian; Choreographer, Sarah Ford; Small Pond Enterprises; The Dorothy Strelsin Theatre

Hanky Panky by Vicki Vodrey; Director, Richard Dines; Cast: Rusty Sneary, Craig Benton, Herman Johansen, Peggy Friesen, Jennifer Mays, Cynthia Hyer, Evan White, Diane Bulan, Christina Parke, Bob Vega; Lot In Life Productions, LLC; The MainStage Theater

Home Movies by Frank Winters; The Treehouse Theatre Company / Stephen Brown; The Dorothy Strelsin Theatre

Kelly and Lindsey Do New York by Kelly Wallace-Barnhill and Lindsey Gentile; Directed by Ross Evans; Cast: Kelly Wallace-Barnhill and Lindsey Gentile; Kelly Wallace-Barnhill; The Jewel Box Theater

Lavender Shore by Lawson Caldwell; Directed by Lenny Leibowitz; Managing Producer, Richard Manichello; Artwork, Scott Williams; Cast: Loni Ackerman, Markus Potter, Katie Yamulla, Colin Pritchard, Marc Geller, Rachel Claire, Patrick James Lynch, Alison Phillips; Lawson Caldwell; The MainStage Theater

Mad Mel And The Marradians by Gary Morgenstein; Directed by Carlo Fiorletta; Cast: Jordan Auslander, William Beckwith, Rachel Caccese, Rob Gaines, Mary Riley; Gary Morgenstein; The MainStage Theater

Making God by Book, Music and Lyrics by Rodney Dickerman; Directed by Coco Cohn; Cast: Cara Noel Antosca, Wayne Petro, Angela Shultz, and Rodney Dickerman; The Jewel Box Theater

Mother Eve's Secret Garden of Sensual Sisterhood by Uma Incrocci,

Erica Jensen, Kirk McGee; Directed by Erica Jensen; Choreographer, Ashley Wren Collins; Lyricist, Uma Incrocci, Kirk McGee, Christian Pedersen; Composer, Christian Pedersen; Cast: Ashley Wren Collins, Uma Incrocci, Maitely Weismann, Alena Acker, Danielle Montezinos, Amy Dannenmueller, Benita Robledo, Dan Domingues, Christian Pedersen; Co-Executive Producers, Erica Jensen and Ashley Wren Collins; Mother Eve LLC; The MainStage Theater

Ocean In A Tea Cup by Music by Joel Krantz, Book and Lyrics by Joel Krantz and Neil Selden; Directed by Rozz Morehead; JK Entertainment; The June Havoc Theatre

Peg O' My Heart by Karin Baker; Adapted as a Musical, Original play by J Hartley Manners; Directed and Choreograped by James Gray; Musical Director, David Hancock Turner; Associate Musical Director, Brad Gardner; Producer, Gwen Arment; Cast: Ethan Angelica, David Arthur, Jeremy Benton, Kelly Jeanne Grant, Brittney Lee Hamilton, Allen E. Read, Jennifer Smith, Scott Willis, and Minnie, the dog, trained by Bill Berloni; Hell's Kitchen Musicals; The June Havoc Theatre

Picture Plane, The Written and Performed by Bruce Colbert; The Dorothy Strelsin Theatre

Rip! Music, Lyrics, & Book by Dan Furman, Additional lyrics by Mary-Liz McNamara; Executive Producer, Christopher Massimine; Massimine/Roytman/ Presentations and Wildly Productive Productions; The June Havoc Theatre

Rosencrantz and Guildenstern Are Dead by Tom Stoppard; Panicked Productions; The Dorothy Strelsin Theatre

Royal Weight Watcher, The by Franziska Huber and Brian J. Borkowski; Director, Susan Batson; Franziska Huber and Susan Batson; The Jewel Box Theater

Sarke by Lia Bakhturidze Sirelson; Dancing Crane, Inc.; The MainStage Theater

Sex Curve by Merridith Allen; The Dorothy Strelsin Theatre

Sistas: The Musical by Dorothy Marcic; Directed by Kenneth Ferrone; Dr. Dorothy Productions; The June Havoc Theatre

Surviving Love by Robert Chionis; Directed by Stephan Perdekamp; Original Music, William Bolcom, John Bucchino, William Finn, Ricky Ian Gordon, Adam Guettel, Brian Lasser, Duncan Sheik, Charles Strouse; Cast: Robert Chionis, Timothy Long; Daniel Wolfsbauer & the Open Acting Academy Hamburg-Wien; The MainStage Theater; July 20 – 24, 2011

Tea In A Tempest Written and Performed by James V. O'Connor; The June Havoc Theatre

Trouble: A New Rock Musical by Book by Michael Alvarez; Music & Lyrics by Ella Grace; Directed by Michael Alvarez; Musical Directo,: Brenna Sage; Choreographer, Jennifer Weber; Cast: Elanna White , Lara Hillier, David Errigo, John Wascavage, David Ryan, Jordan Wolfe, Zoe Rosario; Saving Grace Productions; The June Havoc Theatre

Truth by Ellis Gaskell; The Dorothy Strelsin Theatre

Women and Guns by Steve Gold; Maxwell Arts Group; The MainStage Theater

Always Be Ready by Peter Turo

Apartment Haunting by Val Sherman; East Park Productions

Broken Wing by Rachel White

Call Me / Swamp Girl by Katherine Williams & Debra Castellano

Final Discussion by Vincent A. Apollo

I-Pod by Natalie Menna; Ego Actus

Lost and Found by Marsha Lee Sheiness

Mistress Ilsa by N.G. McClernan; Mergatroyd Productions

Moon Orphans: Orphans on the Moon by Mitch Edmond by Alex Fischer; Camille Harris

Perfect by Rebekah L. Pierce

Prescriptions by Ellen Orchid

Rachel and Ruthie by Karen Sokolof Javitch; Norma Johnson

Sweet by Jan Rosenberg

Un-Silenced by Bella Starr; Bella Starr Productions

Windmills by Meri Wallace

READINGS

Naked in Encino by Wendy Kout; Director, Jamibeth Margolis; The June Havoc Theater

Utility Monster by Marina KeeganA Thread Collective; The June Havoc Theater

New York International Fringe Festival

www.fringenyc.org

Various Locations; August 12 – 28, 2011

Producing Artistic Director , Elena K. Holy; President, Board of Directors, Shelley Burch; Festival Administrator, Britt Lafield; Festival Technical Director, Gregg Bellon; Venue Production Coordinator, Scott D. Mancha; Venue Production Coordinator, Maggie Sinak; FringeCENTRAL / Operations Manager, John Trevellini; Technical Directors, Eric Biel, Bryan Hairston, Lily Jimenez, Tsubasa Kamei, Nancy Valladares

...unwanted Choreographer, Carlos A. Cruz Velázquez; colectivodoszeta / carlos a. cruz velázquez - www.colectivodoszeta.kk5.org; 4th Street Theatre; August 13 - 27, 2011

2 Burn by Alex DeFazio; Directed by Jennifer Joyce & Jody P. Person; Elixir Productions Theatre company - www.elixirproductions.org; The Living Theatre; August 13 - 25, 2011

22 Stories by Sofia Johnson; Directed by Anna Foss Wilson; Kelfia Productions - www.22-Stories.blogspot.com; IATI Theater; August 12 - 28, 2011

74 Minutes of Stereo Radio Theater by Maureen FitzGerald; Stereo Radio Theater in Association with Alternating Incoherence Productions, LLC - www.stereoradiotheater.com; Studio at Cherry Lane; August 13 - 27, 2011

A. Chekhov's The Darling by Anton Chekhov, Translation by Victor S. Tkachenko with Lisa Dalton; Directed by Victor S. Tkachenko; Two Chekhovs Productions - www.thedarling.org; IATI Theater; August 13 - 27, 2011

After Anne Frank by Written and Performed by Carol Lempert; Directed by Janice L. Goldberg; Artistic New Directions - www.CarolLempert.com; Connelly Theater; August 12 - 23, 2011

All Atheists Are Muslim by Zahra Noorbakhsh; Directed by W. Kamau Bell; Choreographer, Coke Nakamoto; Cast: ; Zahra Comedy - www.ZahraComedy.com; Studio at Cherry Lane; August 12 - 23, 2011

All the Windows On Alcatraz by Rebecca Poulson; Directed by Dina Vovsi; Whiskey Rebellion; Teatro SEA; August 19 - 27, 2011

American Mud by Jackie RuggieroJacobson; Directed by Jose Aviles; Straw Flower Productions - www.strawflower.org; IATI Theater; August 20 - 27, 2011

American Vaudeville Theatre 15th Anniversary ExTRAVaganza by Written and Directed by Trav S.D.; Choreographer, Becky Byers; Trav S.D. & Mountebanks - travsd.wordpress.com; Bleecker Theatre; August 13 - 27, 2011

Ampersand: A Romeo & Juliet Story by Mariah MacCarthy; Directed by Amanda Thompson; Purple Rep - www.purplerep.com; The Ellen Stewart Theatre @ LaMaMa; August 12 - 27, 2011

An Improvised Explosive Device: an MTV War Story by Daniella Shoshan; Creative Infantry - www.AnIED.com; Teatro SEA; August 17 - 28, 2011

Anna & The Annadroids: Memoirs of a Robot Girl by Written; Directed and Choreographed by Anna Sullivan; Original Music, Forest Christenson and David Morneau; Illustrations, Grace Passerotti and Natalya Kolosowsky; Video Design, Brent Haley and James Pryor; Amerifluff Corporation - www.amerifluff.com; Dixon Place; August 18 - 22, 2011

Apartment: A Play With Four Sides, The by Sorrel Barnard, Melissa Moran, Lindsay Joy Murphy and David Scott; Directed by Adam Blanshay; Kate Russo - www.playwith4sides.com; Teatro SEA; August 13 - 27, 2011

Araby by Chris Rael, based on stories by James Joyce; Directed by Daniel Spector; Christopher Rael - www.myspace.com/ChrisRaelAraby; The Ellen Stewart Theatre @ LaMaMa; August 13 - 21, 2011

As the Boat Approaches by Written and Directed by Justin Kuritzkes; The Boat in Association with Production Workshop - www.astheboatapproaches.tumblr.com; The Kraine Theater; August 12 - 20, 2011

Average-Sized Mermaid, The by Jessica Fleitman; Directed by Paula D'Alessandris; Mind the Gap Theatre - www.avgmermaid.blogspot.com; Connelly Theater; August 13 - 27, 2011

Back to the Garden by Albi Gorn; Directed by Robin Anne Joseph; M&M Productions Acting Company, Inc. - www.albigorn.com; Connelly Theater; August 13 - 18, 2011

Bad Arm - Confessions of a Dodgy Irish Dancer, The by Written and Choreographed by Maire Clerkin; Directed by Dan O'Connor; Clerkin Dagger - www.maireclerkin.com; Bowery Poetry Club; August 13 - 20, 2011

Ballad of Rusty and Roy, The by Jonny and Troy Schremmer, with Music by Dusty Brown; Directed by Shana Gold; Smokin' Holes - www.rustyandroy.com; IATI Theate; August 17 - 28, 2011

Banshee by Brian C. Petti; Directed by Mary Ellen Nelligar; pettiplays.wikispaces.com; CSV Flamboyan; August 21 - 27, 2011

Bardy Bunch: The War of the Families Partridge and Brady, The by Stephen Garvey; Silverhair Productions - www.thebardybunch.com; The Ellen Stewart Theatre @ LaMaMa; August 13 - 24, 2011

Be Careful! The Sharks Will Eat You! by Jay Alvarez; Directed by TheresaGambacorta; www.sharkswilleatyou.com; Studio at Cherry Lane Theatre; August 17 - 26, 2011

Before Placing Me On Your Shelf Adapted from poems by James Tate; Directed by Philip Gates; Lunar Energy - www.lunarenergyproductions.com; The Kraine Theater; August 13 - 21, 2011

Bella and the Pool Boy by Dennis Flanagan; Directed by Shawn Renfro; Apothecary Theatre Company - www.apothecarytheatrecompany.org; 4th Street Theatre; August 13 - 26, 2011

Bette Davis Ain't for Sissies by Jessica Sherr; Directed by Theresa Gambacorta; www.BetteDavisAintForSissies.net; CSV Kabayitos; August 12 - 28, 2011

Big ''A', The by Dan Horrigan; Directed by Matthew DiCarlo; At Hand Theatre Company - www.danhorriganiscute.com; Studio at Cherry Lane Theatre; August 13 - 28, 2011

Blank by Brian Stanton; Directed by McKerrin Kelly; BLANK Productions - www.thebrianstanton.com; Manhattan Theatre Source; August 12 - 27, 2011

Bobbed-Haired Bandit, The Book and Lyrics by Anna Marquardt, Music by Britt Bonney; Directed by Deborah Wolfson; Gus T.T. Showbiz Productions, LLC - www.thebobbedhairedbanditmusical.com; Bleecker Theatre; August 13 - 27, 2011

Bobby and Matt Written and Directed by Kevin Cochran; Grove Theater Center - www.gtc.org; Players Theatre; August 13 - 27, 2011

Bongani by Gabrielle Maisels; Directed by Kate Holland; Gabrielle Maisels - gabriellemaisels.blogspot.com; Manhattan Theatre Source; August 18 - 28, 2011

Booby Prize, The by Lizzie Czerner; Directed by Jeffrey Wylie; Cast: ; Booby Prize Productions - www.LizzieBoobyPrize.com; Players Theatre; August 13 - 21, 2011

Books on Tape by William Missouri Downs; Directed by Brock H. Hill; Cast: ; Tongue in Cheek Theater Productions - www.tictheater.com; Connelly Theater; August 18 - 28, 2011

Brave Ducks by Andrew Belcher; Directed by Simón Adinia Hanukai; MassBliss Productions - www.braveducks.com; The Living Theatre; August 19 - 26, 2011

Break by Louise Rozett; Directed by Tracy Middendorf; LouLou Productions and February 29 Films - www.louiserozett.com; Teatro SEA; August 14 - 27, 2011

Broken Box Mime Presents Words Don't Work by The Broken Box; Broken Box Mime Theater - www.brokenboxmime.com; Bleecker Theatre; August 14 - 27, 2011

Brownsing by Danna Call, Mari Gorman, Craig Pospisil; Directed by Mari Gorman; Glass Beads Theatre Ensemble - www.glassbeadstheatre.org; Teatro SEA; August 14 - 27, 2011

Buried Words by Karen Smith Vastola; Directed by Johanna Gruenhut; Stark Theatre Company - www.buriedwords.org; The Kraine Theater; August 15 - 28, 2011

Butoh Electra by Jordan Rosin; Directed by Jordan Rosin & Christian Leadley; The Ume Group, a division of the Auburn Regional Theatre - www.butohelectra.com; 4th Street Theatre; August 12 - 27, 2011

Call Mr. Robeson by Tayo Aluko; Directed by Olusola Oyeleye; Tayo Aluko & Friends - www.callmrrobeson.com; Bowery Poetry Club; August 14 - 28, 2011

Carnival Knowledge: Love, Lust, and Other Human Oddities by Naomi Grossman; Directed by Richard Embardo; Choreographer, Rodrigo Guzman; Red Meat Entertainment - www.naomigrossman.net; The Kraine Theater; August 18 - 26, 2011

Cassanova Was A Woman Written and Directed by Jezabel Montero; Assitant Director, Paula Ohaus; No Clout Productions - www.nocloutprods.com; The Living Theatre; August 22 - 28, 2011

Chagrin by Michael Ross Albert; Directed by Adam Levi; Outside Inside - www.michaelrossalbert.com; The First Floor Theatre @ La MaMa; August 12 - 20, 2011

Chamber, The by William Grayson; Directed by Gabe Templin; The Step 1 Theatre - www.step1theatre.org; The Kraine Theater; August 14 - 25, 2011

Chasing Heaven Written and Directed by Leah Maddrie; Original Music, Peter Dizozza and Jasper McGruder; MiddleMaddle Company - www.chasingheaven.com; CSV Flamboyan; August 13 - 26, 2011

Chela by Dulce Maria Solis; Directed by Todd Blakesley; Dulce Maria Solis - www.thechelawebsite.com; The First Floor Theatre @ La MaMa; August 20 - 27, 2011

Chien de Moi Written and Directed by Sophia Schrank; Choreographer, Marquis Wood; In the Basement Theater Company - inthebasementtheater.com; The Ellen Stewart Theatre @ LaMaMa; August 20 - 26, 2011

Civilian Written and Directed by Herman Daniel Farrell III; UK Theatre - www.civilianplay.com; Bleecker Theatre; August 14 - 28, 2011

Classroom, The by Craig Clary; Directed by Lori Wolter Hudson; Rebel Collective Theatre and Slant Theatre Project - www.slanttheatreproject.org; Teatro LATEA; August 20 - 26, 2011

COBU - Dance like Drumming, Drum like Dancing Directed and Choreographed by Yako Miyamoto; COBU Inc. - www.facebook.com/COBUNY; Bleecker Theatre; August 12 - 25, 2011

Courtney and Kathleen: A Riot Act Written and Directed by Liz Thaler; In Extremis Theater Company - www.inextremistheater.org; The First Floor Theatre @ La MaMa; August 13 - 22, 2011

Cow Play by Matthew George; Directed by Charlie Polinger; Less Than Rent Theatre - www.lessthanrent.org; Dixon Place; August 13 - 27, 2011

Craving by Delphine Brooker; Directed by Doug Curtis and Heather Moore; Delphine Brooker - www.cravingnyc.ca; Studio at Cherry Lane Theatre; August 12 - 17, 2011

Crawling with Monsters by Anonymous; The Sleepy Border Town Insomniacs - www.crawlingwithmonsters.com; The Living Theatre; August 19 - 24, 2011

Custodian, The Written and Directed by Will Lacker; Five Flights Theater Company - www.fiveflightstheatercompany.org; The Living Theatre; August 13 - 27, 2011

Daja Vu by Aja Nisenson; Directed by Michael Aman; Daja Vu Productions - www.ajanisenson.com; Bowery Poetry Club; August 20 - 27, 2011

Dancing In The Garden by Michael Walker; The Festival Theatre Company in Association with Paul Gregory and Gary Verrill - www.dancinginthegardenplay.com; The Living Theatre; August 12 - 25, 2011

Day the Sky Turned Black, The by Ali Kennedy Scott; Directed by Adrian Barnes; AKS Productions - www.thedaytheskyturnedblack.com; IATI Theater; August 14 - 28, 2011

Destinations Book by Dawn Eaton, Music and Lyrics by RS Rodkin; Directed by Gregory Fletcher, Musical Direction by RS Rodkin; www.desinations.us.com; Le Poisson Rouge; August 14 - 28, 2011

Disorientation of Butterflies, The Written and Directed by Alaska Reece Vance; Music Director, Nathan A. Schmidt; Original Music, Nathan A. Schmidt; The Drifting Theatre - thedriftingtheatre.com; CSV Flamboyan; August 17 - 27, 2011

Donna /Madonna by John Paul Karliak; Directed by Tiger Reel, Matthew Craig;Musical Direction, Billy Thompson, DJ ChocliXxX; Rizzo 39 Productions - www.donnamadonnashow.com; Players Theatre; August 18 - 25, 2011

Dreaming, The by Sheila Ward and Octavia Cup; Original Music, Michel Ayello; Choreographer, Laura Ward; Laura Ward/Octavia Cup Dance Theatre - www.octaviacup.org; 4th Street Theatre; August 13 - 24, 2011

Dreamplay Written and Directed by Joseph Jonah Therrien; Based on "A Dream Play" by August Strindberg; Oh, Yes! Yes! Productions - yesyesdreamplay.com; CSV Flamboyan; August 15 - 27, 2011

Dystopia Gardens by Jerry Miller & Will Nunziata; Directed by Paul Stancato; dystopiagardens.tumblr.com; Dixon Place; August 13 - 27, 2011

Echoes from Home Conceived and Choreographed by Elissaveta Iordanova; Elea Gorana Dance Collective - elissaveta.com; 4th Street Theatre; August 12 - 20, 2011

Elysian Fields by Chris Phillips; Directed by John Michael Beck and Chris Phillips; Revolve Productions - www.elysianfieldstheplay.com; The Kraine Theater; August 22 - 28, 2011

Em O'Loughlin was a Big Fatty Boombah! Written; Directed and Performed by Em O'Loughlin; BLM - www.emoloughlin.com; Players Theatre; August 14 - 27, 2011

Eternal Husband, The Written and Directed by Nat Cassidy; Based on the novella by Fyodor Dostoevsky; Sid & Nancy Productions in Association with Triumvirate Productions - www.eternalhusband.info; The First Floor Theatre @ La MaMa; August 13 - 26, 2011

F*cking World According To Molly, The Written and Performed by Andrea Alton; Directed by Mark Finley; ; Choreographer, John Paolillo; Molly Dykeman - mollyequalitydykeman.com; Players Theatre; August 13 - 28, 2011

Facebook Me by Katie Cappiello; Directed by Katie Cappiello & Meg McInerney; Created by The Arts Effect All-Girl Theater Company; The Arts Effect - www.TheArtsEffectNYC.com; Teatro SEA; August 22 - 28, 2011

Felony Friday by Scott Decker; Directed by Rebecca Yarsin; Manhattan Project Productions - www.felonyfridaytheplay.com; Connelly Theater; August 20 - 28, 2011

Fit by Erin Austin; Directed by Ross Evans; Music Director, Jonathan Cody White; Plastic Flamingo Theatre Company - www.plasticflamingo.org; Teatro LATEA; August 17 - 27, 2011

Flaccid Penis Seeks Vaginal Dryness by Mike Poblete; Directed by Rebecca A. Hengstenberg; Limp Productions - www.flaccidplay.wordpress.com; Dixon Place; August 13 - 25, 2011

Flowers of Fantastico, The Written and Directed by Rachel Kerry; Brain Melt Consortium - www.brainmeltconsortium.com; The Ellen Stewart Theatre @ LaMaMa; August 14 - 27, 2011

Fourteen Flights by Ryan Campbell; Directed by Joshua Brody; The Cadre - www.fourteenflights.com; CSV Kabayitos; August 15 - 27, 2011

Fundamentalist, The by Juha Jokela; Directed by Sebastian Nyman Agdur; Choreographer, Vigdis Hentze Olsen; Scandinavian American Theater Company - www.satcnyc.org; IATI Theater; August 13 - 25, 2011

Gin and Milk Written and Directed by Antony Raymond; Lucky Devil Theater Company - www.ginandmilk.com; CSV Flamboyan; August 13 - 24, 2011

Gleeam by Andrew Lloyd Baughman, with Lyrics by Phil Close; Directed by Emily Jablonski; The Landless Theatre Company - landlesstheatrecompany.org; Le Poisson Rouge; August 13 - 26, 2011

Goldilocks and the Three Polar Bears by Jerrod Bogard, Music by Sky Seals; Wide Eyed Productions with Playlab NYC - www.wideeyedkids.net; CSV Flamboyan; August 14 - 26, 2011

Greenland by Nicolas Billon; Directed by Ravi Jain; The Bridge Theatre Company - www.thebridgetheatrecompany.com; Players Theatre; August 12 - 19, 2011

Hamlet by William Shakespeare; Directed by Greg Foro; Assistant Director, Sarah Walker; BAMA Theatre Company - www.bamatheatrecompany.org; Connelly Theater; August 12 - 22, 2011

Happily Ever After Written and Directed by Cody Lucas; Developed by Cody Lucas and Travis Stuebing; Music Director and Composer, Patrick Emile; Choreographer, George Ferrie; Sundown Collaborative Theatre; CSV Flamboyan; August 22 - 28, 2011

Happy Worst Day Ever by Arlene Hutton; Directed by Mark Lutwak; The Journey Company and Cincinnati Playhouse in the Park - www.sundowntheatre. org; 4th Street Theatre; August 13 - 21, 2011

Hard Travelin' with Woody Based on the music of Woody Guthrie; Directed by Richard Mover; Adapted by Randy Noojin; Rooster Productions - www. hardtravelinshow.com; CSV Flamboyan; August 13 - 25, 2011

Heads by Evan Twohy; Directed by Will Storie; www.headsplay.com; Teatro SEA; August 12 - 26, 2011

Hello, My Name Is Billy by Tim Aumiller and Scott Schneider; Directed by Tim Aumiller; No Hope Productions - www.nohopeproductions.com; Le Poisson Rouge; August 13 - 24, 2011

Heroes and Other Strangers by Zac Jaffee; Directed by Christian Haines; www.heroesandotherstrangers.com; Manhattan Theatre Source; August 13 - 26, 2011

Hip.Bang! Improv www.hipbang.ca; The Kraine Theater; August 12 - 21, 2011

How I Learned to Stop Worrying and Lost My Virginity by Aileen Clark and John Caldon; Directed by Claire Rice; Guerrilla Rep and Ann Marie Productions - www.guerrillarep.org; Manhattan Theatre Source; August 13 - 25, 2011

Hush The Musical Adapted by Emelise Aleandri, based on Shhhh by Etta Cascini; Conceived and Composed by Charles Mandracchia; Charles Mandracchia in Association with Frizzi & Lazzi Music Theatre Company - www.hushthemusical. com; Le Poisson Rouge; August 13 - 25, 2011

I Light Up My Life: The Mark Sam Celebrity Autobiography Written and Performed by Mark Sam Rosethal; Directed by Todd Parmley; Jim Bredeson - www.ILightUpMyLife.com; Dixon Place; August 12 - 26, 2011

I Might Be Edgar Allan Poe by Dawson Nichols; Directed by Tim Vasen; CPM Productions; Manhattan Theatre Source; August 12 - 26, 2011

I Will Be Good by Tricia Rose Burt; Directed by Judith Stone; I Will Be Good Productions - www.triciaroseburt.com; Players Theatre; August 12 - 27, 2011

In the Summer Pavilion by Paul David Young; Directed by Kathy Gail MacGowan; Go In Her Room Productions - www.inthesummerpavilion.com; The Living Theatre; August 13 - 22, 2011

Infectious Opportunity by James Comtois; Directed by Pete Boisvert; Nosedive Productions - www.nosediveproductions.com; The Living Theatre; August 13 - 27, 2011

Interim, The by Gregory Cioffi; Directed by Daniel Capalbo Jr; www.playsbygreg. com; The Kraine Theater; August 12 - 25, 2011

ISTWA! Storytime for a small world by Tom Marion; York College Theatre - The Istwa! Ensemble; The Living Theatre; August 15 - 27, 2011

I've been Elvita Adams by Ashley Smith; Directed by Garth Laughton & Andrew Martyn Sugars; Comfortism - www.elvitaadams.com; Dixon Place; August 19 - 28, 2011

Jeffrey Dahmer Live by Avner Kam; Directed by Jonathan Warman; Musical Director, Peter Fish; www.JeffreyDahmerLive.com; Bowery Poetry Club; August 16 - 23, 2011

Jersey Shoresical: A Frickin' Rock Opera Book, Music & Lyrics by Daniel Franzese and Hanna LoPatin; Directed by Drew Droege; GymTanLibretto - www. jerseyshoresical.com; Bleecker Theatre; August 23 - 28, 2011

Keepers by Spencer LaVallee, Nicco Franklin, Paul Daniel Cloeter & Molly C. Blau; Music and Lyrics by Daniel Wolpow and Paul Daniel Cloeter; Directed by Chris Causer; Musical Director, Paul Daniel Cloeter; What's The Benefit? inc. - www.whatsthebenefit.org; CSV Flamboyan; August 13 - 28, 2011

Killing John Grisham by Jack Moore; Directed by Nicole A. Watson; killingjohngrisham.com; Teatro SEA; August 13 - 21, 2011

Killing Nellie Written and Directed by Oda Aunan and Mark Storen; theMOXYcollective - www.themoxycollective.com; Bowery Poetry Club; August 13 - 27, 2011

Lady Drug Dealer and the Heis, The Written and Directed by Temar Underwood; I Mean! Productions - www.theladydrugdealer.com; Connelly Theater; August 15 - 27, 2011

Le Gourmand or Gluttony! by Nick Ryan; Directed by Jason Bohon; 3 Sticks Theatre Company - www.3sticks.org; Connelly Theater; August 12 - 24, 2011

Legend of Julie Taymor, or The Musical That Killed Everybody!, The Book and Lyrics by Travis Ferguson, Music and Lyrics by Dave Ogrin; Directed by Joe Barros; Choreographer, Joe Barros; www.LegendOfJulie.com; Bleecker Theatre; August 12 - 24, 2011

Leonard Cohen Koans Poetry, Prose and Lyrics by Leonard Cohen; Directed and Musical Directed by Daryl Wallis; Arrangements by Ali & the Thieves; Ali & the Thieves - www.aliandthethieves.com; Le Poisson Rouge; August 21 - 27, 2011

Life Insurance by Joel Jones; Directed by Boomie Pedersen; The Hamner Theater - www.hamnertheater.com; Manhattan Theatre Source; August 13 - 27, 2011

Lipshtick by Romy Nordlinger & Adam Burns; Directed by Bricken Sparacino; Video Designer, Adam Burns; Agent Provocateur Theatre Company - www. lipshtickbaby.com; Dixon Place; August 12 - 24, 2011

Little Girl Blue Written and Directed by Pheralyn Dove; Original Music, Warren Oree; Cast: ; Dove Culture - www.ladydoveslittlegirlblue.blogspot.com; Bowery Poetry Club; August 19 - 21, 2011

Lola-Lola by Peter Michalos; Directed by Rebecca Hengstenberg; www. PeterMichalos.com; The Living Theatre; August 13 - 27, 2011

Lost and Found, The by Hans Augustave; Directed by Tom McNeill and Scott Reagan; www.thelostandfoundplay.com; Manhattan Theatre Source; August 13 - 27, 2011

Lou; Lou Lives! by John Carter; www.loulives.com; Manhattan Theatre Source; August 20 - 28, 2011

Love In A Tub by James Manzello and Oliver Wason; Directed by James Manzello, Oliver Wason, and Joel Bassin; based on a play by Sir George Etherege; Dot The Connective - www.loveinatub.tumblr.com; The Ellen Stewart Theatre @ LaMaMa; August 15 - 25, 2011

Male Matriarch by Amir Lev; Directed by Shauna Horn; Choreographer, Megan Sipe; Inventing Room Productions, LLC and Jason Najjoum - www.malematriarch. com; CSV Kabayitos; August 18 - 25, 2011

Mama Juggs Written and Directed by 'rie Shontel; Princess Dragon Productions - www.mamajuggs.com; Players Theatre; August 13 - 24, 2011

Meanest Guy That Ever Lived, The Written and Produced by Lily Spottiswoode; Directed by Jenny Sullivan; IATI Theater; August 18 - 27, 2011

Mic. by Brenton Lengel; Directed by Melinda Prom; Original Music, Beezy Douglas, Kelly Dwyer, Mike Ogletree and Joe Yoga; Autonomous Collective - www.brentonlengel.com; CSV Flamboyan; August 13 - 18, 2011

Miss Teen Jesus Pageant, The by Patrick DiBattista and Anne Laffoon; Original Music, Ben Camp; LaGoDi - lagodi.com; 4th Street Theatre; August 18 - 27, 2011

More Loving One, The by Cory Conley; Directed by Craig Baldwin; Unincorporated Theater - www.themorelovingone.com; The First Floor Theatre @ La MaMa; August 17 - 28, 2011

Moshe Feldstein, Icon of Self- Realization by Alexander Nemser, Joseph Shragge; Imagine This Scenario - www.moshefeldstein.com; Studio at Cherry Lane Theatre; August 12 - 25, 2011

Mother She's With You Wherever You Go Written and Produced by Mary-Beth Manning; www.motherthesoloshow.com; IATI Theater; August 12 - 19, 2011

Mountain Song, The by Alex Falberg, Arya Shahi, Ben Ferguson, Curtis Gillen, Dan Weschler, Matt Nuernberger, Ryan Melia; PigPen Theatre Co. - www. PigPenTheatre.com; 4th Street Theatre; August 13 - 27, 2011

Much Ado About Nothing by William Shakespeare; Abridged by Kelly Johnston; Red Shark Productions Washington Square Park; August 16 - 21, 2011

Mush Written and Produced by Jim Tierney; Directed by Dina Epshteyn; www. mushtheplay.com; The First Floor Theatre @ La MaMa; August 13 - 27, 2011

Never Look in the Mirror When You're Dancing by Kay Scorah; Directed by David Keating; Choreographer, Jessica Kennedy, Megan Kennedy, Paul Loper; HaveMoreFun - www.havemorefun.org; 4th Street Theatre; August 22 - 28, 2011

Nils' Fucked Up Day Writtena nd Directed by Peca Stefan; Monday Theatre @ Green Hours - www.nilsfuckedup.com; Dixon Place; August 14 - 22, 2011

No-Fault: A tale about the Big D in the Big Apple by Christie Perfetti; Directed by Bryn Boice; Carnival Girls - www.christieperfetti.com; The Kraine Theater; August 13 - 27, 2011

Noir by Stan Werse; Directed by SuzAnne Barabas; Stan Werse in Association with N.J. Rep; Connelly Theater; August 17 - 25, 2011

One, Two, Whatever you do . . . by Vanessa Shealy; Directed by Melissa Attebery; Younger Child Productions - www.YoungerChildProductions.com; 4th Street Theatre; August 14 - 28, 2011

Only Child, The by Jessica Hinds; Directed by Elizabeth Carlson; New York Artists' Community - www.theonlychildtheplay.com; The First Floor Theatre @ La MaMa; August 12 - 28, 2011

Panic Diaries, The Written and Produced by Katie Northlich; Directed by Joe Ricci; www.thepanicdiaries.com; Studio at Cherry Lane Theatre; August 16 - 28, 2011

Paper Cut by Yael Rasooly and Lior Lerman; Directed and Produced by Yael Rasooly; www.yaelrasooly.com; CSV Kabayitos; August 19 - 27, 2011

Parker & Dizzy's Fabulous Jorney to the End of the Rainbow Book by Peter Zachari, Music and Lyrics by Damon Maida and Peter Zachari; Directed by Peter Zachari; Music Director, Douglas Maxwell; Choreographer, Joey Mirabile; Zachari Productions - www.parkeranddizzy.com; The Ellen Stewart Theatre @ LaMaMa; August 12 - 27, 2011

Pawn Written and Directed by Karmia Chan Cao; Choreographer, Alisha Mitchell; Pawn - www.pawnthemusical.com; The Ellen Stewart Theatre @ LaMaMa; August 13 - 28, 2011

Pearl's Gone Blue by Leslie Kramer; Directed by Julie Kramer; Original Music, Gabriel Gordon; Eben Music Productions - www.pearlsgoneblue.com; Teatro LATEA; August 12 - 28, 2011

Poe-Dunk – A Matchbox Entertainment by Kevin P. Hale; Directed by John Pieza; Playlab NYC - www.playlabnyc.org; CSV Kabayitos; August 12 - 27, 2011

Portrait and a Dream by Jacob Marx Rice; Directed by Katie Lupica; Cabbages and Kings Theatre Company - www.portraitandadream.tumblr.com; The First Floor Theatre @ La MaMa; August 15 - 27, 2011

Poteet Girls by Leslie Collins; Directed by Erick Devine; www.poteetgirls.com; Players Theatre; August 12 - 27, 2011

Power of the Crystals, The by James Call and Greg Travis; Directed by Quin Gordon; Mishap Productions - www.power-of-the-crystals.com; CSV Flamboyan; August 12 - 28, 2011

Rachel Calof by Ken LaZebnik, Music & Lyrics by Leslie Steinweiss; Directed by Ellen S. Pressman; Stephens Lake Productions - www.rachelcalof.net; CSV Flamboyan; August 12 - 27, 2011

Recovery by Mark Jason Williams; Directed by Andrew Block; Loretta Michael Productions - www.markjasonwilliams.com; The Kraine Theater; August 21 - 27, 2011

Rollerblading in Gaza by Brian J. Borkowski; Directed by Kyle Wood; Birdstrike - www.rollerbladingingaza.com; Dixon Place; August 14 - 26, 2011

Romeo & Juliet: Choose Your Own Ending by William Shakespeare and Ann and Shawn Fraistat; Directed by Ann Fraistat; The Impressionable Players - www.impressionableplayers.com; Teatro SEA; August 13 - 26, 2011

Rubber Room, The by Ariadne Blayde; Directed by Daniel Winerman; Unless Productions - www.therubberroomplay.com; Teatro LATEA; August 18 - 27, 2011

Salamander Stew by Michael Fixel; Directed by Juliet Fixel and Ron Shreve; The STU Theatre Co - www.facebook.com/salamanderstew; 4th Street Theatre; August 15 - 28, 2011

Sammy Gets Mugged! by Sammy; Directed by Noah Himmelstein; Dan Heching & The Brownstone Project - www.danheching.com; The Living Theatre; August 15 - 28, 2011

Sanyasi2011 by Rabindranath Tagore; Directed by Ameneh Bordi; Original Music, Keith Adams; Namayesh Productions - www.sanyasi2011.blogspot.com; The Kraine Theater; August 18 - 28, 2011

Scared of Sarah by Laura Brienza; Directed by Reginald L. Douglas; Lark Play Development Center and the Kennedy Center Page-to-Stage Festival - www. scaredofsarahplay.com; The First Floor Theatre @ La MaMa; August 12 - 17, 2011

Seed of Abraham, The by Book by Bob Zaslow, Music & Lyrics by Kenny Karen; Directed by Sally Burtenshaw; Kenny Karen and Bob Zaslow - www. seedofabrahamusical.com; Bleecker Theatre; August 14 - 25, 2011

Smiley - How about some emotional pornography? by Eyal Weiser; Directed by Allon Cohen; IATI Theater; August 17 - 22, 2011

Smoke The New Cigarette by Kirk Wood Bromley; Inverse Theatre Company - thenewcigarette.org; Bowery Poetry Club; August 12 - 25, 2011

Smoking Section by Brian Pollock; Directed by Robert Mark and Phil Russo; Two Beard Productions - www.two-beard-productions.com; Teatro LATEA; August 13 - 27, 2011

Star Debate: Trek vs. Wars, The Written and Directed by Nelson Lugo and Mark Schaffer; Epic Win Burlesque - epicwinburlesque.com; The Ellen Stewart Theatre @ LaMaMa; August 17 - 27, 2011

Stimulated! by Les Enfants Terribles Ensemble; Les Enfants Terribles - www.enfantsterribles.org; Teatro SEA; August 12 - 19, 2011

Submitted by C. Randall McCloskey by Ian August; Directed by Paul Whelihan; Quorum Theatre - www.crandallmccloskey.com; Teatro LATEA; August 14 - 24, 2011

Swarupa: Infinite Form Choreographer, Sonali Skandan; Sonali Skandan & Jiva Dance - www.jivaperformingarts.org; 4th Street Theatre; August 12 - 21, 2011

Technodoulia Dot Com Directed by Kate Gagnon; Technoplay Company - www.technodoulia.com; The Living Theatre; August 12 - 22, 2011

Theater of the Arcade: Five Classic Video Games Adapted for the Stage by Jeff Lewonczyk; Directed by Gyda Arber; Piper McKenzie and The Fifth Wall - www.theaterofthearcade.com; Bleecker Theatre; August 13 - 27, 2011

There Was An Old Woman Who Swallowed A Fly And Other Heroines That Reach For The Sky! Written; Directed and Choreographed by Jeanne Beechwood; Original Music and Musical Direction by Jon Copeland; Martin City Melodrama Jr. - www.martincitymelodrama.org; Studio at Cherry Lane Theatre; August 12 - 18, 2011

This One Time in Last Chance by Sam Gooley; Directed by Laura Braza; The Attic Theater Company - www.theatticpresents.org; Teatro LATEA; August 13 - 25, 2011

Three Times She Knocked, The by A.D. Penedo; Flying Squirrel Theatricals; Manhattan Theatre Source; August 13 - 25, 2011

Top Drawer by Adelaide Mestre; Directed by Lauren Cohn; Top Drawer Productions - www.adelaidemestre.com; Bowery Poetry Club; August 18 - 28, 2011

Toughest Girl Alive!, The Written and Produced by Javier Velasco and Candye Kane; Directed by Javier Velasco; Music and Lyrics by Candye Kane; www.candyekane.com; Le Poisson Rouge; August 17 - 27, 2011

Town of No One, The by Tariq Hamami; Directed by Leah Bonvissuto; Playsmiths - www.townofnoone.com; Teatro LATEA; August 21 - 28, 2011

Tutor, The by Kate Mulley; Directed by Ben Gougeon & Doug Spagnola; eXit Productions - www.thetutorplay.com; The Living Theatre; August 12 - 20, 2011

Two Alone/Too Together by Peter Welch; Directed by Vincent Scott; Accidental Repertory Theater (ART) - www.twoalonetootogether.com; Players Theatre; August 14 - 28, 2011

Underbelly Diaries Redux, The by Aaron Berg; Directed by Dwight McFee; APB Productions - www.aaronberg.com; Dixon Place; August 18 - 28, 2011

Unhappiness Plays, The by Greg Kotis; Directed by Bob Fisher; Space 55 Theatre Ensemble - www.space55.org; IATI Theater; August 12 - 15, 2011

Unsung Diva, The by Angela Dean- Baham; Directed by Michael Mohammed; Original Music, Rossini, Gounod, American Folk; Angela Dean Baham Productions - www.angeladeanbaham.com; Bowery Poetry Club; August 12 - 16, 2011

Victor and Victoria's Terrifying Tale of Terrible Things by Nathan Cuckow and Beth Graham; Directed by Kevin Sutley; Kill Your Television - www.facebook.com/ killyourtelevisiontheatre; Teatro LATEA; August 13 - 22, 2011

Vignettes of an Italian American Girl! by Maria Baratta; Directed by Anthony Patellis; IAM Productions - www.maria-baratta.com; The Kraine Theater; August 14 - 25, 2011

Virgie by Renee Newman-Storen; Directed by Mark Storen and Emily McLean; the MOXYcollective - www.themoxycollective.com; Bowery Poetry Club; August 14 - 27, 2011

Virtual Solitaire by Dawson Nichols; Mycelium - facweb.northseattle.edu; Players Theatre; August 17 - 26, 2011

Walls and Bridges by Scott Murphy; Directed by Pauline Daniels & Scott Murphy; The Liverpool Actors Studio - www.theliverpoolactorsstudio.com; Teatro SEA; August 17 - 24, 2011

Wallstories Choreographer, Nejla Y. Yatkin; Nejla Y. Yatkin Dance (NY2Dance) - www.berlinwallproject.com; Dixon Place; August 12 - 28, 2011

Waterlogged by Anais Alexandra Tekerian; Directed by Kevork Mourad; Tangled Lines Productions - www.tangledyarn.net; The First Floor Theatre @ La MaMa; August 19 - 28, 2011

Way of Man, A by Caja van der Poel; Directed by Michael Driebeek van der Ven; Based on the book by F. van Eeden; Michael&Caja - www.michaelandcaja.com; CSV Kabayitos; August 13 - 28, 2011

Welcome to Eternity by Matt Saldarelli; Directed by Laura Konsin; Self Fulfilling Productions - www.welcometoeternitytheplay.com; CSV Flamboyan; August 12 - 25, 2011

Whale Song or: Learning to Live With Mobyphobia by Claire Kiechel; Directed by Brad Raimondo; The Dreamscape Theatre - dreamscapetheatre.org; The First Floor Theatre @ La MaMa; August 14 - 27, 2011

What The Sparrow Said by Danny Mitarotondo; Directed by Jenna Worsham; The Common Tongue - www.tctnyc.org; Teatro LATEA; August 17 - 26, 2011

When the Sky Breaks 3D by Jennifer Weber; Choreographer, Decadancetheatre; Decadancetheatre - www.decadancetheatre.com; Dixon Place; August 18 - 26, 2011

Who Loves You, Baby? by Hunter Nelson; Directed by Taylor Negron; DiMenna & Nelson - www.tellysavalaslive.com; Bowery Poetry Club; August 12 - 28, 2011

Wilhemstrasse by Stuart Caldwell; Directed by Andrew Block; Goldart Productions - www.stuartsvault.com; The First Floor Theatre @ La MaMa; August 13 - 26, 2011

Winner Take All (A Rock Opera) by Claudia Brevis & Skip Brevis; Directed by John Carrafa; Musical Director, Skip Brevis; Choreographer, John Carrafa; www.winnertakeallmusical.com; Bleecker Theatre; August 12 - 26, 2011

Women Of Tu-Na House, The by Nancy Eng; Directed by Ernest Abuba; Mad Cat Productions In Association with Leviathan Lab - www.womenoftunahouse.com; Manhattan Theatre Source; August 12 - 27, 2011

Ya Mama! by Nina Domingue; Directed by Cathy Hartenstein; Choreographer, Kenya Woods; yamama-ndglo.blogspot.com; CSV Kabayitos; August 12 - 20, 2011

Yeast Nation (the triumph of life) Music & Lyrics by Mark Hollmann, Book & Lyrics by Greg Kotis; Directed by Greg Kotis; Choreographer, Wendy Seyb; John Arthur Pinckard and Ryan Bogner - www.yeastnation.com; The Ellen Stewart Theatre @ LaMaMa; August 13 - 25, 2011

You Only Shoot the Ones You Love by Jeffrey Sweet; Directed by Patricia Birch; Artistic New Directions - www.artisticnewdirections.org; Studio at Cherry Lane Theatre; August 13 - 27, 2011

You've Ruined a Perfectly Good Mystery! by Christian Neuhaus and Rick Stemm; Directed by Sam D. White; Choreographer, Rick Stemm; Mercury Players Theatre - www.ruinedmystery.com; Teatro LATEA; August 12 - 18, 2011

Zombie Wedding by Daniel Sturman and R.C. Staab, Music by Daniel Sturman, Lyrics and Libretto by R.C. Staab; UpMarket Productions - www.zombiewedding.co.uk; The Ellen Stewart Theatre @ LaMaMa; August 15 - 26, 2011

New York Musical Theatre Festival

www.nymf.org

Various Locations; September 26 – October 16, 2011

Blood Book, Music, and Lyrics by [By The Mummers]; October 4 – 16, 2011

The Brain That Wouldn't Die! In 3D!!! Book and Lyrics by T. Sivak and E. Gelman; Music by T. Sivak; October 6 – 16, 2011

Date of a Lifetime Book and Lyrics by Carl Kissin; Music by Robert Baumgartner Jr.; October 3 – 16, 2011

Fucking Hipsters! Book by Keythe Farley; Music by Lori Scarlett and John Ballinger; Lyrics by Lori Scarlett; September 27 – October 5, 2011

Jack Perry is Alive (and Dating) Book and Lyrics by Harrison David Rivers and Daniella Shoshan; Music by Julia Meinwald; October 4 – 15, 2011

Jane Austen's Pride and Prejudice, A Musical Book, Music, and Lyrics by Lindsay Warren Baker and Amanda Jacobs; September 29 – October 11, 2011

The Kid Who Would Be Pope Book, Music and Lyrics by Tom Megan and Jack Megan; The Theater at St. Clements; September 26 – October 4, 2011

Madame X -The Musical Book, Music, and Lyrics by Gerard Alessandrini and Robert Hetzel; September 26 – October 13, 2011

Man of Rock Book and Lyrics by Daniel Heath; Music by Kenneth Flagg; September 26 – October 5, 2011

Outlaws Book by Perry Liu, Joe Calarco and Alastair William King; Music by Alastair William King and Perry Liu; Lyrics by Perry Liu; Conceived by Alastair William King and Perry Liu; September 26 – October 9, 2011

Time Between Us Music by Brett Schrier; Book and Lyrics by Tess Barker and Brett Schrier; September 29 – October 12, 2011

The Big Bank by The Seligmann Brothers; Directed by David Glenn Armstrong; The Theater at St. Clements; September 27 – October 4, 2011

Central Avenue Breakdown Music & Lyrics by Kevin Ray; Book by Kevin Ray & Josh Sohn; Additional Story by Suellen Vance; October 10 – 16, 2011

Crazy, Just Like Me Music & Lyrics by Drew Gasparini; Book by Drew Gasparini and Louis Sacco; Directed by Stephen Agosto; September 27 – October 5, 2011

Cyclops: A Rock Opera Book by Chas LiBretto and Louis Butelli; Score by Jayson Landon Marcus with Benjamin Sherman; Conceived by Psittacus Productions; Directed by Louis Butelli; Inspired by Percy Bysshe Shelley's translation of Euripides' *Cyclops*; September 29 – October 9, 2011

ENNIO: The Living Paper Cartoon Written and Performed by Ennio Marchetto; Directed and Designed by Ennio Marchetto and Sosthen Hennekam; September 27 – October 12, 2011

Ghostlight Book, Music and Lyrics by Matthew Martin and Tim Realbuto; Choreography by Michael Kidney; Directed by Matthew Martin and Tim Realbuto; September 26 – October 9, 2011

Greenwood Book, music and lyrics by Tor Hyams & Adam LeBow; October 6 – 16, 2011

Kiki Baby Book by Lonny Price and Kitt Lavoie; Lyrics by Lonny Price and Grant Sturiale; Music by Grant Sturiale; Directed by Lonny Price and Matt Cowart; Based on the novel Sing, Brat, Sing by Rene Fulop-Miller; The Theater at St. C

Kissless Book, Music, and Lyrics by Chance McClain; The Theater at St. Clements; September 28 – October 8, 2011

Les Enfants De Paris Music and Lyrics by David Levinson; Book by Stacey Weingarten; Additional Development by Donna Drake; October 3 – 15, 2011

My History of Marriage Book and Lyrics by Lee Kalcheim; Music and Lyrics by David Shire; October 4 – 14, 2011

This One Girl's Story Music and Lyrics by Dionne McClain-Freeney; Book and Additional Lyrics by Bil Wright; September 27 – October 9, 2011

Tour de Fierce Created by Hollie Howard; Conceived by Hollie Howard and Joey Murray; Performer: Rob Baumgartner; October 11 – 16, 2011

Tut The Theater at St. Clements; October 12 – 15, 2011

WORKSHOPS

Gotta Getta Girl! Book and Lyrics by Peter Charles Morris; Music by David Caldwell; October 11, 2011

Huckleberry Haywood Book, Music, and Lyrics by Stephen Tyler Davis; Music and Lyrics by Taylor Bridges; Additional Story by Kristine Bogan, Abby Burke, Renée McCurry, and Heather Shields; Directed by David Glenn Armstrong; October 14, 2011

Many Happy Returns Book by Carey Ramos; Based on an original story by Carey Ramos and Catrina Bentley; Music and Lyrics by Lamont Dozier; The Theater at St. Clements; September 29 – 30, 2011

Marry Me! Book by Daniel Korb; Lyrics by Daniel Korb and Darren Korb; Music by Darren Korb; October 13, 2011

Matchmaker Matchmaker I'm Willing To Settle Book by Kelvin Moon Loh and Nikki MacCallum; Music and Lyrics by Brandon James Gwinn; October 14 – 16, 2011

The Pigeon Boys Book and Lyrics by Anne Berlin; Music by Andrew Bleckner; Directed by Valentina Fratti; September 30, 2011

CONCERTS

A Flower Is... by Se Jung Kook; The Theater at St. Clements; October 9 – 10, 2011

Gatsby: The Songs in Concert Book by Hugh Wheeler; Music by Lee Pockriss; Lyrics by Carolyn Leigh; Inspired by the novel by F. Scott Fitzgerald; September 30, 2011

Ma Femme, Ma Blonde, et Ma Roulotte Book by Betsy Kelso; Music and Lyrics by David Nehls; Translated by Stephen Pietrantoni, David Laurin, and Patrick Olafson; October 8 – 9, 2011

Three Rounds with Joe Iconis and Family by Joe Iconis; Presented by NYMF and Sh-K-Boom Records; October 10, 2011

Balls...the Musical? Book and Lyrics by Bret Carr, Mick Bonde, Brandon Ellis; Michael "Tuba" McKinsey, and Nick Verina; Music by Various Composers; October 12 – 15, 2011

Blanche: The Bittersweet Life Of A Wild Prairie Dame Book and Lyrics by Onalea Gilbertson; Music by Onalea Gilbertson, Jonathan Lewis and Morag Northey; October 6 – 7, 2011

Just Like Magic Music by Ryan Mercy; Book and Lyrics by Christopher W. Barnes; Book by Cameron Cole; October 7 – 13, 2011

Step Show Written and Choreographed by Maxine Lyle; Directed by Martin Damien Wilkins; October 8, 2011

Tempest Toss'd Conceived by Sarah Rosenberg and Luis Reyes Cardenas; Adaptation by Sarah Rosenberg; Music and Lyrics by Eric Luke and William Shakespeare; Theater at St. Clements; October 7 – 9, 2011

Planet Connections Theatre Festivity 2011

planetconnections.org

Robert Moss Theater and the Gene Frankel Theatre; June 1 - 26, 2011

Antenora by Mike Poblete; Directed by Ruis Woertendyke; Robert Moss Theater

Becoming Emma Goldman Written and Directed by Maggie Surovell; Gene Frankel Theatre

Bomb Shelter by Kimberly Pau; Directed by Eric Mercado; Gene Frankel Theatre

Carry On by Jim Tierney; Directed by Diánna Martin; Gene Frankel Theatre

Cecile by Jean Anouilh; Directed by Victoria Crutchfield; Gene Frankel Theatre

Code Name: Operation Lysistrata! by Yvette Heyliger; Original Music, Larry Farrow; Choreographer, Yvonne Farrow; Produced by Twinbiz; Robert Moss Theater

A Cordial Invitation Written and Directed by J.C. Svec; Produced by Tribe Productions; Gene Frankel Theatre

The Declaration Written and Directed by Rick Leidenfrost-Wilson; Produced by Off Sides Entertainment; Robert Moss Theater

Ethan's People by Richard L. Gaw; Directed by Rose Ginsberg; Gene Frankel Theatre

An Evening of One Acts; *Galileo the Musical* by Marisol Tirelli Rivera; Directed by Jenny Fersch; *The God Particle* by Christina Gorman; Directed by Joan Kane; *The Matra India* Translated, Adapted and Directed by Roi Escudero; Robert Moss Theater

Face Divided by Edward Allen Baker; Directed by Karen Giordano

The Father by August Strindberg; Directed by Oscar Mendoza; Produced by The Mush-Room Theatre; Robert Moss Theater

Fidelity Written and Directed by Larry Schwartz; Gene Frankel Theatre

Finding Elizabeth Taylor by Elizabeth Taylor; Directed by Morgan Gould; Gene Frankel Theatre

Freedom Tower by Gabrielle Fox; Robert Moss Theater

Goliath by Rivera Takeo; Directed by Alex Mallory; Produced by Poetic Theater; Robert Moss Theater

He's Not Himself by Marc Silverberg; Directed by Michael Pantone; Robert Moss Theater

Hell is Where the Heart Is by Melissa Skirboll; Directed by Thom Fogarty; Gene Frankel Theatre

Hold by Ruben Carabajal; Directed by Kelly Johnston; Gene Frankel Theatre

Hummingbirds by Jonathan Wallace; Directed by Karen Raphaeli; Gene Frankel Theatre

I Am Single by Michelle Slonim and Adrienne Sterm; Directed by Michael Schiralli; Produced by A Date My Jewish Friend, Inc.; Robert Moss Theater

Influences by Fidel Fontenboa

Jew Wish Written and Performed by Rachel Evans; Directed by Rachel Eckerling; Gene Frankel Theatre

Loose Women of Low Character by Mary Belmont; Directed by Shauna Horn; Gene Frankel Theatre

Monster by Sabrina M. Patterson; Directed by Gregory Allen

The Mutilation of St. Barbara Written and Directed by Mark Borkowski; Robert Moss Theater

The Other Day by Mark Jason Williams; Directed by Valentina Fratti; Robert Moss Theater

Out of Askja by Drew Larimore; Directed by Jesse Edward Rosbrow; Produced by Small Pond Entertainment; Robert Moss Theater

Rope of Sands by Toni Seger; Directed by Reneé Rodriguez; Robert Moss Theater

The Slow, Torturous Love Affair of Staten Island & Perth Amboy by Alexis Kozak; Directed by Jesse Edward Rosbrow; PCTF intern production; Robert Moss Theater

The Stranger to Kindness by David Stallings; Directed by Heather Cohn

Sweeter Dreams Written and Directed by Duncan Pflaster; Gene Frankel Theatre

The Tramaine Experience: An Urban Dramedy by Tramaine Montell Ford; Directed by Bill Johnson; Gene Frankel Theatre

Tulupa, or Anne & Me by Shawn C. Harris; Directed by Sara Lyons; Produced by Crossroads Theatre Project; Robert Moss Theater

Two Days 'Til Dawn by Tyler Ham Pong; Directed by Laura Sisskin-Fernandez; Gene Frankel Theatre

Wanderlust Written and Directed by Leslie Guyton; Produced by Movement Workshop Group; Robert Moss Theater

What Are You Doing Here by Maria Alexandra Beech; Directed by Michelle Bossy; Gene Frankel Theatre

Woman in the Dark by Elizabeth Murray; Directed by Erika Iverson

READINGS

All's Fair (Six Western) by Sergei Burbank; Directed by Leah Bonvissuto; Produced by Conflict of Interest Theater Company

Becky Needs to Get Laid by Olivia Lilley

Dialing for Donna by Pam Monk and Stacy Glen Tibbetts; Directed by Music Director, Markus Hauck; Produced by Original Theatre Works

Disenchanted Book, Lyrics and Music by Nikki M. Jenkins; Directed by Aaron M. Pratt; Music Director, Brad Gardne

Frack You! by Laura Jacobs Cunningham; Directed by Katherine Bacon; Produced by Parlor City's Players

Frontier by Robin Rice Lichtig; Directed by Joan Kane; Produced by Ego Actus

Fulana by Felippe Ossa; Directed by Leah Bonvissuto

Howling Hilda Book and Lyrics by Anne Berlin; Directed by Valentina Fratti

Inversion of the Baby Snatchers by Ed Malin

Late Nights with the Boys: Confessions of a Leather Bar Chanteuse by Alex Bond; Directed by Steven Yuhasz

Martirio Adapted from Federico Garcia Lorca's *The House of Bernarda Alba* and Directed by Glory Kadigan; Produced by G-Money Productions

Mayday! Mayday! Written and Directed by Dale Wakonen

The Orange Person by Brian Rady; Directed by Jeremy Bloom

Pieces by Kristen Penner and Lorelel Mackenzie; Produced by Violet Productions

Pushing Daisy by Lauren Epsenhar

The Recession Club by Christina Quintana; Directed by Tyne Rafaeli

Stanley's World by Alexandra Klausner; Directed by Ryan Emmons

Sweet, Sweet Spirit by Carol Carpenter; Directed by Cristina Alicea

Samuel French Short Play Festival

oob.samuelfrench.com
Lion Theatre; July 19 - 24, 2011

Assisted Living by Jeffrey Neuman; Produced by Emerging Artists Theatre

Beautiful Hands by Ean Miles Kessler

Bedfellows by Adam Peltzman

Blood Grass by J.Stephen Brantley; Produced by Hard Sparks

The Body Washer by Rosemary Frisino Toohey

Bubble and Squeak by Evan Twohy; Produced by Pipeline Theatre Co.

The Burglar by Kevin V. Mead; Produced by Melge Media

Cabfare for the Common Man by Mark Harvey Levine; Produced by Sweet And Tart Productions

Chun Li by Camilla Maxwell; Produced by Boat Drinks Ink, LLC

Create Me Pegasus by Amy E. Witting; Produced by Awe Creative Group

Dead-Nosed by Oliver Thrun; Produced by Theater For The New City

The Empirical Eskimo by Arlitia Jones; Produced by Lucy Tyger Productions

First Breath After Total Devastation by Victor Lesniewski; Produced by New York Artist's Community

Flight Risk by Caron Levis; Produced by Infinite Nutshell Productions

Girls Play by Masha Obolensky; Produced by The Huntington Theatre

The Golden Ticket by Jennifer Barclay; Produced by A Collection Of Shiny Objects

Grapple by Sarah Young; Produced by The Opposite Of People Theatre Company & Plaid Couch Productions

Hanksylvania by Travis Helwig

Hiding From Adults by Greg Kalleres; Produced by Fusion Theatre Company

HMS Headwind by Michael Gordon Shapiro

Honey Mushroom by Gabrielle Reisman; Produced by The NOLA Project

Mountain Song by Josh Beerman; Produced by The New School For Drama

Mr. Crossover by Mohammad Yousuf

The Muse by Cassie M. Seinuk

My Name Is Yin by Tom Swift

The Painter by Stacy Osei-Kuffour

The Perfect Cup of Coffee by David Loughlin; Produced by HB Studio

Pluck & Tenacity by Daniella Shoshan

Queen Elizabeth of Factory Fifteen by Tariq Hamami; Produced by Marmaduke Theatre Co.

Run. Run. Stop. by Stacy Davidowitz

Screen by Nick Gandiello; Produced by The New School For Drama

Spats by Adrian Singleton

The Story Of Oh (Revised and Abridged) by James Colgan

The Sun Turns Black by Margaret Hoffman

Taking the Plunge by Greg Edwards and Amanda Louise Miller; Produced by Lively Productions

Tower of Toys by Jackob G. Hofmann; Produced by The Aurora Theatre Ensemble

The Truth About Christmas by Daniel Pearle; Produced by The New School For Drama

We Happy Animals by Andrew Kramer; Produced by Factory 81

Why Pluto is a Planet by Darragh Martin

With a Shrug by Nicholas Priore; Produced by Pamela Scott/Aching Dogs Theatre Co.

soloNOVA Arts Festival 2011

Produced by terraNOVA Collective; PS122; May 11 – 28, 2011 (See Listing for terraNOVA Collective)

Strawberry One-Act Festival Winter 2012

www.therianttheatre.com

Produced by The Riant Theatre; Hudson Guild Theatre; March 1 – 11, 2012

Double Guilt Written & Directed by Joseph Lizardi; March 1, 2012
Best Friends by Mary Ryzuk; Directed by JoAnn Oakes; March 1, 2012

Vengeance Once-Removed Written & Directed by Laurence C. Schwartz; March 1, 2012

Monette by Kymberle Joseph; Directed by Jesse Wooden; March 1, 2012
Foreclosure by George Cameron Grant; Directed by Liz Amadio; March 1, 2012

If You See Something, Say Something by Liz Magee; Directed by Michael Kinnan; March 1, 2012

Everybody Wants Me by Stan Fine; Directed by Ted Mornel; March 2, 2012

The Exit Interview Written and Directed by Betsy Kagen & MK Walsh; March 2, 2012

True Love by Paul Testagrossa & Kelsey Moore; Directed by Jaclyn Biskup; March 2, 2012

Perfect by Rebekah L. Pierce; Directed by Gene Hughes; March 3, 2012

Creation by Paul Trupia; Directed by Becky Copley; March 3, 2012

Blood Orange Sorbet by Bradley B. Custer; Directed by Samantha Else; March 3, 2012

Kindergarten Philosophy by Andrew Baer; Directed by Guil Fisher; March 3, 2012

Another Life by Anthony Esposito; Directed by Johnny Culver; March 3, 2012

The Importance of Being Hairy by George R. Johnson; Directed by A. Gilligan; March 3, 2012

Is He or Isn't She? by Will Sevedge; Directed by Taryn Turney; March 3, 2012

Rest in Pieces, A Stand-Up Tragedy by Ellen L. Weinberg; Directed by Ben Prusiner; March 3, 2012

Ideas in Lowercase Written & Directed by Ben Bergin; March 3, 2012

25 on the 405, or, What We Talk About When We Talk About Acting by Travis Leland; Directed Taryn Turney; March 4, 2012

Nobody But Somebody by Davon Clark; Directed by Sarah Mitteldorf; March 4, 2012

An Analysis of Suspense & Dramatic Tension by Hansen Wetsel; Directed by Chad Chenail; March 4, 2012

You Can't Go Swimming with Your Ex Husband Written & Directed by Zoë Cooper; March 4, 2012

Uffizi by Britton Buttrill; Directed by Dustin Brown; March 4, 2012

Like Them? by Rick Charles Mueller; Directed by Rick Charles Mueller & Cameron McIntosh; March 4, 2012

ENCORE SERIES

Crossing Verrazano Written & Directed by Anthony Fusco; March 2 – 4, 2012

Push by George Cameron Grant; Directed by Liz Amadio; March 2 – 4, 2012\

It's Greek to Me by Shelley Bromberg; Directed by Will Budnikov; March 2 – 4, 2012

The Video Diaries Project: A Short Film Series; *It's About Time* by Miguel LaCruz; *Finding Perfection Through Art* by Shantell Cargle & Christina Weathersby; *Act Like a Writer* by Rork Brown; *Thinking About Forever: "Chronicles Of Innocence"* by Jason Ruan; *Behind the Lie: A Diary of a Playwright* by Freedom H. Weeks; March 3 – 4, 2012

Times Square International Theatre Festival

www.royariasstudios.com

Producers, Roy Arias and Stalin Urbano; Cruators, Alfred Preisser and Irma Bello; Produced by Roy Arias Studios; Various Locations; January 16 – 22, 2012

The Night of the Assasins by Jose Triana; Directed by Orestes Amador; Production Designer, Christian Martinez; Cast: Mileny Estévez, Wilson Ureña, Yorlla Lina Castillo; Produced by National Theater Company of the Dominican Republic; Theatre 500; January 17 – 22, 2012

Match Written and Directed by László Kocsis; Produced by The Human Natural Theater; Little Times Square Theatre; January 17 – 21, 2012

Alita the Show Written and Performed by Freia Canals and Denise Kornitz; www. alitatheshow.com; Theatre 500; January 18 – 22, 2012

Breve Temporada de Invierno by Nicolas Dorr; Directed by Josean Ortiz Maranao; Produced by Theater Company; Theatre 500; January 16 – 22, 2012

A Time to Dance Written and Performed by Libby Skala; atimetodance. homestead.com; Theatre 500; January 17 – 20, 2012

Horripilation! Written and Performed by John Sowle; Produced by Kaliyuga Arts - www.kaliyuga.com; Little Times Square Theatre; January 16 – 21, 2012

Legacy of the Tiger Mother Book and Lyrics by Angela Chan & Michael Manley; Music by Angela Chan; Directed by Lysander Abadia; Production Designer, Angela Chan; www.TigerMotherTheMusical.com; Little Times Square Theatre; January 16 – 19, 2012

Melting in Madras: Seeking, Singing and Sickness in India, 1995 Written and Performed by H.R. Britton; Directed by Rajeev Varma; www. OvercoatTheater.com; Various Locations; January 17 – 22, 2012

One Thousand Nine Hundred and Thirty Four Days Conceived by Sivan Hadari and Charlotte Cohn; Directed by Charlotte Cohn; Isramerica Productions; Little Times Square Theatre; January 18 – 22, 2012

Sanctuary by Susanne Sulby; www.sanctuarytheplay.com; Theatre 500; January 16 – 20, 2012

Seasons Lyrics and Book by Katie Hammond; Music by Elaine Pechacek; Directed by Danny Williams; Cast: Kristyn Chalker, Kyle Szen, Katie Hammond and Amy Arbizzani; www.pechacekhammond.com; Little Times Square Theatre; January 16 – 22, 2012

Superman 2050 by Theater Un-Speak-Able; Directed by Marc Frost; superman2050.com; Theatre 500; January 19 – 22, 2012

The Knocking Within Choreographed by Wendy Jehlen; Production Designer Holly Ko; Cast: Wendy Jehlen and Pradhuman Nayak; Produced by ANIKAI Dance Theater - www.akhra.org/anikaiweb/shakes.html; Little Times Square Theatre; January 17 – 22, 2012

Woyzeck Musical Deathmetal Written and Directed by Christopher Carter Sanderson Gorilla Repertory Theater Company - www.gorillarep.org; Little Times Square Theatre; January 18 – 22, 2012

READINGS

Garbo by Joe Gulla; Directed by Brian Rardin; Roy Arias Studios; January 20 – 21, 2012

Times Square Pinero Written and Directed by Antone Pagan; Cast: Luis Salgado, Enrique Cruz De Jesus, Ned Eisenberg, Susan Rybin, Jacqueline Ramos, Malachy Murray, Patrick Michael Wickham, O.G. MacLean and Rick Reid; Roy Arias Studios; January 20 – 21, 2012

Under the Radar Festival 2012

www.undertheradarfestival.com

The Public Theater; January 4 – 28, 2012

Alexis. A Greek Tragedy Directed by Enrico Casagrande and Daniela Nicolò; Motus

The Bee Co-written & Directed by Hideki Noda; Tokyo Metropolitan Theatre

Chimera by Suli Holum & Deborah Stein Lighting Designer, James Clotfelter; Set Designer, Jeremy Wilhelm; Costume Designer, Tara Webb; Sound Designer, James Sugg; AudioVisual Designer, Kate Freer & Dave Tennant; Cast: Suli Holum; HERE Arts Center; January 5 - 28, 2012

El pasado es un animal grotesco (The past is a grotesque animal) by Mariano Pensotti

Feel by Camille O'Sullivan

Goodbar Created by Bambï & Waterwell; Based on Looking for Mr. Goodbar by Judith Rossner; Directed by Arian Moayed and Tom Ridgely; Cast: Bambï: Hanna Cheek, Cara Jeiven, Jimmie Marlowe, Tobi Parks and Kevin Townley

Hot Pepper, Air Conditioner, and the Farewell Speech Written and Directed by Toshiki Okada; Chelfitsch Theater Company

In the Solitude of Cotton Fields Directed by Radosław Rychcik; Stefan Zeromski Theatre

Lick But Don't Swallow by Özen Yula; Directed by Melis Tezkan and Okan Urun; Biriken & Ayça Damgaci

The Plot is the Revolution Directed by Enrico Casagrande and Daniele Nicolò; Cast: Silvia Calderoni and Judith Malina; Motus and The Living Theatre

Sontag: Reborn Based on the book by Susan Sontag and edited by David Rieff; The Builders Association

Super Night Shot by Gob Squad Arts Collective

The Table by Blind Summit Theatre

Word Becomes Flesh Conceived and Directed by Marc Bamuthi Joseph and The Living Word Project; 651 ARTS

Vignettes for the Apocalypse: 5th Annual Sci-fi/Horror Theater Festival

www.endtimesproductions.org

Produced by EndTimes Productions; Kraine Theater; June 9 – July 2, 2011

Downtown Theater by Toby Scales

Wardrobe of the Living Dead by Maximilian Clark

The You Knows Know by Derek Ahonen

Dating Sucks by Mike Poblete

The Madhouse by Jerrod Bogard

Entranced by Ron Burch

Void by Paul Moulton

Hitchhikers May Be Escaping Convicts by Susie Kahlich

Spoken For by S.L. Daniels

X-Boyfriend by Steve Strangio

The Texas Textbook Massacre by Micah McCoy

With You by Chris Van Strander

The Girls In Their Hitler T-Shirts by Peter Rout and Joe Muscara

The Kids Are Awake by Mark Borkowski

The Wolf Manhood by David L. Williams

The Black Market of Memories by Dwayne Yancey

Passenger by Ignacio Zulueta

Night of the Living Relatives by Judy Klass

Seed by Adam Tullis and Leal Vona

Freaks From the Morgue -- one acts by James Comtois, Mac Rogers, Brian Silliman & Crystal Skillman

If You Could Would You by Arthur Jolly

Innsmouth by Michael Jalber

The Lunar Academy of St. Augustine by Andrew Turner

Maybe In Another Universe by Stacie A. Shellner

Zombie Girl by Paco Mad

Smart by Robert Fieldsteel

Megan Opalinski, Eric Morris, Spencer Robinson, Charlie Owens, Adam Kee, Eric William Love, and Rachel Green in The Gallery Players' A Man of No Importance (photo by Bella Muccari)

Ian Holcomb, Melody Bates, Brian Miskell in Hard Sparks' production of Eightythree Down (photo by Hunter Canning)

Josephine Cashman and Leila Okafor in Gemini CollisionWorks' production of ObJECTS (photo by Ian W. Hill)

MJ Lollar and Christopher Patrick Mullen in Retro Productions' production of The Runner Stumbles (photo by Kristen Vaughan)

PROFESSIONAL REGIONAL COMPANIES

Top: Constantine Maroulis as The Toxic Avenger in the Alley Theatre's
production of The Toxic Avenger (photo by Jann Whaley)

Center: Cora Vander Broek and Grant Goodman in Actors Theatre of Louisville's
production of In The Next Room (or the vibrator play) (photo by Alan Simons)

Bottom: The Company of The Scottsboro Boys at
The American Conservatory Theater (photo by Henry DiRocco)

2011-2012 Regional Theatre Season:
Locally Grown Theatre

By Rob Weinert-Kendt, Associate Editor, *American Theatre* magazine

It is a lament you hear periodically about the American regional theatre movement: that, following an idealistic beginning in the 1960s as a way to move the center of gravity away from New York and to nurture local talent and local audiences all around the country, it has become little more than a Broadway touring circuit, with the latest New York hits (critical or financial, not always both) showing up in a spate of new productions, or even in roughly the same productions that bowed last season in Manhattan. A corollary complaint: that the traffic going the other way, with Broadway producers showering "enhancement money" on nonprofit theatres to develop commercial properties, has turned many regional theatres into New York's out-of-town houses.

Certainly, if you use Theatre Communications Group's "Top Ten" list—a survey of most-produced shows at America's nonprofits in a given season—as a guide, with few exceptions in 2011-2012, shows ratified by New York dominate. Roughly in order, there was *Red*, John Logan's play about Mark Rothko; Yasmina Reza's virtuoso four-hander, *God of Carnage*; the vaudevillian movie adaptation *The 39 Steps*, a hit both on Broadway and Off- (oddly enough, in that order); Donald Margulies' war-haunted domestic drama *Time Stands Still*; Duncan Sheik and Steven Sater's angsty-teen musical *Spring Awakening*; Geoffrey Nauffts' tender coming-out play *Next Fall*; Bruce Norris' coruscating examination of race and real estate, *Clybourne Park*, which won the 2011 Pulitzer Prize after premiering Off-Broadway and playing in London (its Broadway homecoming would not come until the following season); David Mamet's tendentious legal drama *Race*; and two plays that had their start at regional theatres before heading to successful runs on Broadway, Sarah Ruhl's bit of revisionist Victoriana, *In the Next Room (or The Vibrator Play)*, and Tracy Letts' fierce family saga *August: Osage County*.

Those last two examples, though, hint at a different reality. While New York stages may still exert both centrifugal and centripetal forces on American theatre, and while Gotham shows no signs of surrendering its status as the medium's commercial capital, dig a little deeper into the regional theatre season lists of 2011-2012 and you will find more than enough local-grown theatre to go around—premieres, adaptations, co-productions, and revivals with distinctive spins that could never show up on a national "most-produced" list precisely because they were not duplicated in lockstep nationwide.

At San Francisco's flagship American Conservatory Theater, for example, artistic director Carey Perloff unveiled her fourth work as a playwright, the architectural drama *Higher*, in February. That same month on ACT's mainstage, Wajdi Mouawad's international thriller *Scorched*, starring David Straithairn, had its West Coast premiere after runaway success in Canada. Meanwhile, in Ohio, the Cleveland Play House kicked off its glistening new downtown space in the city's historic PlayhouseSquare complex with a lavish new September production of Brecht's *The Life of Galileo*, helmed by Michael Donald Edwards.

Edwards, himself artistic director of Asolo Repertory Theater in Sarasota, Florida, directed a bilingual, culturally specific Shakespeare adaptation by playwright Eduardo Machado, *Hamlet, Prince of Cuba*, in February. Putting another fresh take on the Bard, Chicago's movement-based Redmoon Theater mounted a three-actor, puppet-assisted hybrid piece called *The Feast: an intimate Tempest* in January at Chicago Shakespeare Theater.

At Los Angeles' Center Theatre Group, a major beachhead for New York-based or New York-directed productions, there were some encouraging local signs: A homegrown revival of Beckett's *Waiting for Godot*, starring one of the playwright's favored, West Coast-based actors, Alan Mandell, was something of a hit in the spring. And earlier in the season, at CTG's newest space in Culver City, the Kirk Douglas Theater, *I've Never Been So Happy*, a commissioned work from Austin, Texas' Rude Mechanicals, solidified the companies' connection.

Meanwhile, at the historic Ford's Theatre in Washington, D.C.—yes, the one at which our 16th president met his untimely end—the season began in September with a new production of Jason Robert Brown's stark musical about a lynching, *Parade*, and continued in February with *Necessary Sacrifices*, a new play by Richard Hellesen about the relationship between President Lincoln and author/activist Frederick Douglass.

Also in the nation's capital, Arena Stage tended to American theatrical heritage in two distinctly different ways: By mounting an ambitious spring festival of Eugene O'Neill in conjunction with other area theatres, including the Shakespeare Theatre, and in the fall by reviving *Trouble in Mind*, a little-performed play from 1955 by the African-American playwright Alice Childress, which depicts the backstage friction between a white director and the black cast of a Broadway production.

Chicago's Goodman Theatre also tackled O'Neill, in a starry spring revival of *The Iceman Cometh* featuring Nathan Lane and Brian Dennehy, while two Minneapolis troupes, the Penumbra Theatre Company and the Guthrie Theater, brought back another infrequently revived work from the mid-century African-American canon, James Baldwin's *The Amen Corner*, about a troubled Harlem church, also in the spring.

Earlier in the spring, the Guthrie had mounted an intriguing literary adaptation: a three-character staging of Daphne Du Maurier's *The Birds*, which formed the basis of Alfred Hitchcock's 1963 film, but was here conceived by Irish playwright Conor McPherson as a claustrophobic domestic thriller.

Indeed, there were enough distinctive literary adaptations at theatres nationwide to call it a trend, or at least a trendlet. While *GATZ*, the Elevator Repair Service's eight-hour read-through of F. Scott Fitzgerald's *The Great Gatsby*, had thrilled New York and Boston audiences in the previous season (and would go on to an acclaimed run in Los Angeles in the following season), a more traditionally conceived adaptation by Simon Levy, of Los Angeles' Fountain Theatre, bowed in March at the Arizona Theatre Company. And Michael John LaChiusa's musical of Edna Ferber's sprawling oil drama *Giant* had a Texas homecoming at the Dallas Theatre Center in January.

Living authors also saw their work come to life on the stage: Toni Morrison's Harlem Renaissance saga *Jazz* was theatricalized by director Marion McClinton for Baltimore's CENTERSTAGE in January; E.L. Doctorow's Civil War epic *The March*, about Gen. Sherman's devastating 1864 campaign, was staged by seasoned adaptor Frank Galati (*The Grapes of Wrath*, *Ragtime*) at Steppenwolf Theatre Company; and American Repertory Theatre in Boston brought together playwright Alexandra Wood and memoirist Jung Chang to adapt the latter's bestselling book *Wild Swans: Three Daughters of China* in February.

At least one living author wrote was coaxed into writing expressly for the stage: Stephen King collaborated with roots rocker John Mellencamp on the horror musical *The Ghost Brothers of Darkland County*, opening in April. In March, another celebrity from outside the theatre, chef Rick Bayless, helped create a savory, flamenco-flecked show called *Cascabel* with Chicago's Lookingglass Theatre Company; Bayless even appeared in the show and cooked a meal for patrons each night.

One state over, Indiana Repertory Theatre had its own celebrity cooking play, though it could not offer the actual chef on the menu: In resident playwright James Still's *I Love To Eat*, actor Robert Neal embodied the late, great American gourmet James Beard.

In With the New

Developing new plays and nurturing playwights' careers was a recurring theme this season, with Seattle Repertory Theatre debuting its Writers Group and Philadelphia's Arden Theatre its Writers Room. CENTERSTAGE hosted the WordBRIDGE Playwrights Laboratory in September, and Southern California's South Coast Repertory staged its 15th annual Pacific Playwrights Festival in the spring, the same month that the Actors Theatre of Louisville celebrated its 36th annual Humana Festival of New American Plays.

New-play fests fairly dot the map: Centre Stage in Greenville, South Carolina, held one in September; Denver Center Theatre Company played host again in February for the annual Colorado New Play Summit; and the Great Plains Theatre Conference's PlayFest unfolded in the late spring at Omaha, Nebraska's Metropolitan Community College. Highlighting more ensemble-based work were Portland, Oregon's annual Fertile Ground Festival in January and Austin, Texas' Fusebox Festival in April.

While there is understandable excitement about such ensemble-devised work injecting new blood into the theatre, individual playwrights were by rights at the center of much substantial work on regional stages in the past year. At the McCarter Theatre of Princeton, New Jersey, one of American theatre's *eminences grises*, John Guare, premiered a new work in May—the gnarled family comedy *Are You There, McPhee?*—and so did an up-and-comer, actor/writer Danai Gurira, with *The Convert*, her tale of post-colonial Africa, which bowed there in January before going on to the Goodman Theatre in March and Center Theatre Group in April.

Up-and-coming playwright Kirsten Greenidge had two auspicious premieres on opposite sides of the country: In September, her look at teenage materialism, *Milk Like Sugar*, opened at La Jolla Playhouse (en route to an Off-Broadway run at Playwrights Horizons), and in April, her cross-generational drama *The Luck of the Irish*, which examined Boston's history of racialized real estate, hit close to home at the Huntington Theatre Company. In November, the Huntington debuted a charged new play by playwright Evan M. Weiner titled *Captors*, about the trial of Nazi mastermind Adolph Eichmann.

Another historical drama with contemporary relevance was Elizabeth Egloff's *Ether Dome*, about the beginnings of medical anesthesia, which opened at Houston's Alley Theatre in October. In the spring, the Alley played host to Theresa Rebeck—a playwright now more popularly known for creating the theatre-themed TV series *Smash*—for the premiere of a new play about workplace sexism titled *What We're Up Against*.

Indeed, plays with a political edge or agenda were everywhere, and not only when the season calendar turned to 2012, a major election year. Culture Clash's immigration-themed comic revue, *American Night*, which had its debut the previous year at the Oregon Shakespeare Festival, turned up all over: at Denver Center Theatre in October, La Jolla Playhouse in February, and Centre Theatre Group in March. In the fall, Oregon Shakes teamed with Berkeley Repertory Theatre for *Ghost Light*, Jonathan Moscone's *Hamlet*-tinged recollection of his own father's political assassination (his father was San Francisco Mayor George Moscone, notoriously slain alongside councilman Harvey Milk in 1978).

Activism-oriented Jesuit priest/playwright Bill Cain brought forth two new plays with multiple productions: an autobiographical look at grief, *How To Write a New Book for the Bible*, at Berkeley Repertory Theatre in October and Seattle Repertory Theatre in January; and *9 Circles*, about an Iraq War soldier on trial, at L.A.'s Bootleg Theatre in October and at Denver Center Theatre in January. Also at the Denver Center was Lisa Loomer's explosive comedy *Two Things You Don't Talk About at Dinner*, in February (the taboo topics being religion and politics, in case you are wondering—and particularly one subject that uneasily weds them, the Middle East conflict). And bringing a bracing authenticity to its exposé of Chicago police brutality, the Timeline Theatre's *My Kind of Town* was written by John Conroy, a veteran investigative journalist who originally uncovered much of the most incendiary material.

Arguably the season's most notable plays—all of which would eventually find their way to major Off-Broadway runs—were Matthew Lopez's unique drama *The Whipping Man*, about a Jewish family's plantation in the immediate aftermath of the Civil War, which played at Connecticut's Hartford Stage Company in October, at Arden Theatre in November, and at CENTERSTAGE in April; Samuel D. Hunter's tender, unflinching *The Whale*, about a morbidly obese man's final days, at Denver Center in January; and Quiara Alegria Hudes' *Water by the Spoonful*, a drama about an Iraq War veteran which had its premiere at Hartford Stage, and later took the 2012 Pulitzer Prize.

Regional theatres are not all plays all the time; they are also known to break into a song now and again. At the McCarter in September, director John Doyle built a new show around Rodgers & Hart standards and called it *Ten Cents a Dance*. In November La Jolla Playhouse was the site of a glossy new version of *Jesus Christ Superstar*, which soon made its way to Broadway under the able hands of director Des McAnuff (*Tommy*, *Jersey Boys*). Also at La Jolla, in May, was *Hands on a Hardbody*, a new tuner with songs by Phish frontman Trey Anastasio and lyricist Amanda Green. And at Paper Mill Playhouse in Millburn, New Jersey, a new version of the Disney musical *Newsies*, with music by Alan Menken and a book by Harvey Fierstein, opened in September and was delivered to Broadway in March.

Long Wharf Theatre in New Haven, Connecticut premiered Gabriel Kahane and Seth Bockley's unconventional historical musical *February House*, about a house in Brooklyn Heights that played host to everyone from W.H. Auden to Gypsy Rose Lee. And Boston's American Repertory Theater staged two very different kinds of nontraditional musicals: It kicked off its season in September with Gershwin's *Porgy and Bess*, in a new version shaped by director Diane Paulus and playwright Suzan-Lori Parks, which, despite some controversy—including a nasty public tiff in the *New York Times* with composer/lyricist Stephen Sondheim, who was skeptical of changes being made to the original work—quickly went to Broadway headlined by stars Audra McDonald and Norm Lewis. And in March, in its club-like Oberon space, A.R.T. produced *Futurity*, a steampunk rock musical written and performed by indie band The Lisps.

Defying easy genre classification but no less significant in the overall picture of the season were works like *Beertown*, an immersive, interactive urban-issues excavation by Washington, D.C.'s dog & pony; two site-specific works at La Jolla Playhouse, *Susurrus* and *The Car Plays*, the latter literally staged inside various cars in a nearby parking lot; KJ Sanchez and Emily Ackerman's docutheatre piece about returning veterans, *ReEntry*, at the Actors Theatre of Louisville in November; a radical new vision by Spanish auteur Calixto Bieto of Tennessee Williams' phantasmagorical *Camino Real*, at the Goodman Theater in March; the return of beloved commedia dell' arte master Steven Epp (formerly artistic director of Minneapolis' late, beloved Theatre de la Jeune Lune) at the helm of a Moliere farce, *The Doctor in Spite of Himself*, at Berkeley Rep in February; *The Great Immensity* at Kansas City Repertory Theatre in February, a show about climate change by the New York-based ensemble The Civilians; *Mr. Burns*, playwright Anne Washburn's conjuring of a future dystopia built around collective memories of characters from *The Simpsons*, at Washington, D.C.'s Woolly Mammoth Theatre Compay in May; and at Chicago's Victory Gardens in April, Jackie Sibblies Drury's meta-theatrical, interminably titled *We Are Proud To Present a Presentation About the Herero of Namibia, Formerly Known as South-West Africa, From the German Sudwestafrika, Between the Years 1884-1915*.

Finally, one clear trend across the nation was the adapting of ancient texts about war and family dysfunction to reflect the same pathologies in our present day. At Alabama Shakespeare Festival in January, playwright John Walch recast the Book of Ruth as the uneasy homecoming tale of a U.S. Army lieutenant and her Afghani interpreter in *In the Book of...* Elsewhere, it was the Greeks who supplied the raw material. Two separate contemporary reimaginings of the Phaedra myth came in the same month, October: At Berkeley's Shotgun Players, Adam Bock's *Phaedra* set the tale of sex and death in the present-day American suburbs, while Irish playwright Marina Carr's *Phaedra Backwards* at the McCarter Theatre also updated the story, albeit in a less linear fashion.

At the American Players Theatre in Spring Green, Wisconsin, an August staging of Seamus Heaney's *The Cure at Troy: A Version of Sophocles' Philoctetes* made its wartime themes accessible with contemporary if non-specific military styling, and in October at the Guthrie, another Heaney take on Sophocles, *Burial at Thebes* (based on *Antigone*), made similar acute references. These were potent reminders, if any were needed, that since its beginning theatre has never flinched from wrestling with the most urgent problems of the age.

Offstage Drama

Of course, not all the drama at the nation's regional theatres this past season was confined to the stage. The economy, still not fully recovered from its recessionary doldrums, claimed a few more victims, with Fairfax, Virginia's Theatre of the First Amendment shuttering in March, the Arizona Jewish Theatre Company folding in June, and the Illinois Theater Center in Park Forest closing at the end of the season, in large part due to the death of its founder, Ed Billig.

In better news, three Houston troupes—Naked Theatre Company, Mildred's Umbrella Theatre Company, and Classical Theatre Company—consolidated their efforts and helped assure their future survival by moving into a single space in January. In the same month, Chicago's National Pastime Theatre moved to the city's Uptown neighborhood, leaving room in their old space for the nearby Profiles Theatre to expand. And in Miami in May, the PlayGround Theatre, which had a strong reputation as a first-class theatre for young audiences, announced a name change to the Miami Theatre Center, to better reflect its broad-based programming, which includes work for adult audiences as well.

In still better news, the historic Bucks County Playhouse in New Hope, Pennsylvania, announced a reopening after having served as an amateur theatre for decades and finally closing in 2010. The leadership of a seasoned New York producer, Jed Bernstein, was another encouraging sign. A Contemporary Theatre in San Francisco opened a new space, The Costume Shop, in the city's mid-Market neighborhood. As noted above, Cleveland Play House kicked off a season

in beautiful new digs in downtown Cleveland's PlayhouseSquare complex, and Juneau, Alaska's Perseverance Theatre began a "satellite" season at a second stage in Anchorage.

Berkeley Rep opened a play-development wing called the Ground Floor, D.C.'s Woolly Mammoth expanded its company members to include not only actors but directors, playwrights, and designers, and, in one of the season's most memorable gestures, Minneapolis' Mixed Blood Theatre began a program called Radical Hospitality, in which a subsidy makes nearly all the seats for all its shows entirely free of charge.

Another significant offstage development was the April opening of the Center for Theater Commons in Boston. Though not a producing theatre itself, it is closely affiliated with ArtsEmerson, a hybrid producing/presenting organization under the wing of Emerson College. With its combined academic and producerial knowledge base, the Center promises to be a hub and clearinghouse of practical and aesthetic information, research, and advocacy for all of America's regional theatres.

These are a few small but encouraging signs of health for a national theatre that no longer takes all its cues from New York. While a Gotham stamp of approval can inarguably extend the life and reach of a show, live theatre is an inherently local phenomenon, and this past season on American stages proved again that the nation's theatre remains as dispersed, diverse, and idiosyncratic as the United States itself.

Stephen Yoakam, Ernest Bentley, Joseph Turner, and T. Mychael Rambo in the Guthrie Theater's production of The Burial at Thebes *(photo by Michael Brosilow)*

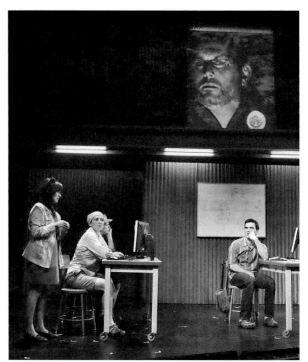

Rebecca Hart, Meghan McGeary, Eddie Korbich, and Dan Domingues in the World Premiere of The Great Immensity *at Kansas City Repertory (photo by Don Ipock)*

Liam Craig, Renata Friedman, Steven Epp, and Julie Briskman in A Doctor in Spite of Himself *at Berkeley Repertory (photo by Kevin Berne)*

ACT - A Contemporary Theatre

Seattle, Washington

Forty-eighth Season

Artistic Director, Kurt Beattie; Executive Director, Gian-Carlo Scandiuzzi; Artistic Associate and Casting Director, Margaret Layne; Literary Manager, Anita Montgomery; Artistic Manager, Nicole Boyer Cochran; Producing Director, Joan Toggenburger; PSM, Jeffrey K. Hanson; Costume Director, Carolyn Keim; Technical Director, Steve Coulter

First Date: A New Musical (a co-production between ACT - A Contemporary Theatre and The 5th Avenue Theatre); Book by Austin Winsberg; Music and lyrics by Alan Zachary and Michael Weiner; Director, Bill Berry; Music Director, R.J. Tancioco; Musical Stager, Josh Prince; Sets, Matthew Smucker; Costumes, Frances Kinney; Lighting, Alex Berry; Sound, Kai Harada; Cast: Kelly Karbacz (Casey), Erik Ankrim (Aaron), Benjamin Harris, Vicki Noon, Sonya Meyer, Brandon O'Neill, Rich Gray, Greg McCormick Allen (Ensemble/Multiple Roles); March 10–May 20, 2012

The Pitmen Painters by Lee Hall inspired by a book by William Feaver; Director, Kurt Beattie; Sets, Carey Wong; Costumes, Cathy Hunt; Lighting, Ben Zamora; Sound, Brendan Patrick Hogan; Cast: Daniel Brockley (Young Lad/Ben Nicholson), Christine Marie Brown (Susan Parks), Frank Lawler (Robert Lyon), Charles Leggett (George Brown), Jason Marr (Oliver Kilbourn), Joseph P. McCarthy (Jimmy Floyd), Morgan Rowe (Helen Sutherland), R. Hamilton Wright (Harry Wilson); April 20–May 20, 2012

One Slight Hitch by Lewis Black; Director, Joe Grifasi; Sets, Robert Dahlstrom; Costumes, Susan Hilferty; Rick Paulsen, Lighting; Lighting, Rick Paulsen; Sound, Brendan Patrick Hogan; SM, JR Welden; Cast: Katherine Grant-Suttie (P.B. Coleman), Marianne Owen (Delia Coleman), Kirsten Potter (Melanie Coleman), Kimberley Sustad (Courtney Coleman), Shawn Telford (Ryan), John Ulman (Harper), R. Hamilton Wright (Doc Coleman) June 8–July 8 2012

THE PINTER FESTIVAL 4 plays by Harold Pinter; Producer, Frank Corrado

Celebration Director, John Langs; Sets, Robert Dahlstrom; Costumes, Sarah Nash Gates; Lighting, Rick Paulsen; Sound, Brendan Patrick Hogan; SM, Erin B. Zatloka, Jeffrey K. Hanson; Alyssa Keene, Dialect; Cast: Anne Allgood (Prue), Julie Briskman (Julie), Cheyenne Casebier (Sonia), Frank Corrado (Lambert), Peter Crook (Richard), Jeffrey Fracé (Russell), Darragh Kennan (The Waiter), Randy Moore (Matt), Mariel Neto (Suki), Benjamin Harris (ensemble), Charles Leggett (ensemble)

Dumb Waiter Director, John Langs; Sets, Robert Dahlstrom; Costumes, Sarah Nash Gates; Lighting, Rick Paulsen; Sound, Brendan Patrick Hogan; SM, Erin B. Zatloka, Jeffrey K. Hanson; Alyssa Keene, Dialect; Cast: Darragh Kennan (Gus), Charles Leggett (Ben)

Old Times Director, Victor Pappas; Sets, Robert Dahlstrom; Costumes, Sarah Nash Gates; Lighting, Rick Paulsen; Sound, Brendan Patrick Hogan; SM, Erin B. Zatloka, Jeffrey K. Hanson; Alyssa Keene, Dialect; Cast: Anne Allgood (Anna), Cheyenne Casebier (Kate), Jeffrey Fracé (Deeley)

No Man's Land Director, Penny Cherns; Sets, Robert Dahlstrom; Costumes, Sarah Nash Gates; Lighting, Rick Paulsen; Sound, Brendan Patrick Hogan; SM, Erin B. Zatloka and Jeffrey K. Hanson; Alyssa Keene, Dialect; Cast: Frank Corrado (Hirst), Peter Crook (Briggs), Benjamin Harris (Foster), Randy Moore (Spooner) July 20–August 26, 2012

Uncle Ho To Uncle Sam by Trieu Tran and Robert Egan; Director, Robert Egan; Sets, Carey Wong; Costumes, Rose Pedersen, Lighting, Rick Paulsen; Sound, Brendan Patrick Hogan; Cast: Trieu Tran; September 7–October 7

Ramayana Adapted by Yussef El Guindi, Stephanie Timm, and the ACT Affiliate Artist Working Group; Directors, Kurt Beattie, Sheila Daniels; Sets, Matthew Smucker; Costumes, Melanie Taylor Burgess; Choreographer, Maureen Whiting; Composition/Sound, Brendan Patrick Hogan; SM, JR Welden; Cast: Anne Allgood (Kausalya/Soorpanaka/Trijata), Cheyenne Casebier (Kaikeyi/Mithila/Indrajit), Khanh Doan (Sita/Manthara), John Farrage (Viswamithra/Ravana), Jim Gall (Das/Mareecha/Vali), Tim Gouran (Lakshmana), Todd Jefferson Moore (Janaka/Court Attendant/Sugreeva), Brandon O'Neill (Vashishta/Hanuman), Tikka Sears (Ensemble), Richard Nguyen Sloniker (Vibishna/Indra), Ray Tagavilla (Bharata), Rafael Untalan (Rama), Akhi Vadari (Ensemble), Belle Wolf (Ensemble) October 12–November 11, 2012

Actors Theatre of Louisville

Louisville, Kentucky

Forty-eighth Season

Artistic Director, Marc Masterson; Managing Director, Jennifer Bielstein

Sense & Sensibility Adapted and directed by Jon Jory from the novel by Jane Austen; Director, Jon Jory; Sets, Thomas Burch; Costumes, Rachel Laritz; Lighting, Brian J. Lilienthal; Sound, original music and composition, Joe Cerqua; Props, Mark Walston; Wigs, Heather Fleming; SM, Paul Mills Holmes; ASM, Kathy Preher; Dramaturg, Sarah Lunnie; Choreographer, Delilah Smyth; Dialect, Rocco Dal Vera; Directing Assistant, Brian Owen; PA, Katie Shade; Casting, Lynn Baber, Zan Sawyer-Dailey; Cast: Justin Blanchard (Willoughby), Colette Delaney (Lady Middleton/Mrs. Ferrars), Jonathan Finnegan (Robert Ferrars), Nancy Lemenager (Elinor Dashwood), Franette Liebow (Mrs. John Dashwood), Diane Mair (Lucy Steele), Si Osborne (Mr. John Dashwood), David Pichette (Sir John Middleton/Doctor), Alex Podulke (Colonel Brandon), Geoff Rice (Edward Ferrars), Wendy Robie (Mrs. Jennings), Helen Sadler (Marianne Dashwood), Penny Slusher (Mrs. Henry Dashwood); Ensemble: Rivka Borek, J. Alexander Coe, Erika Diehl, Kanomé Jones, Alexander Kirby, Katie Medford, Amir Wachterman; August 30–September 24, 2011

Dracula Originally dramatized by John L. Balderston and Hamilton Deane from Bram Stoker's *Dracula*; Adapted and directed by William McNulty; Sets, Paul Owen; Costumes, Lorraine Venberg; Lighting, Tony Penna; Sound, Benjamin Marcum; Props, Joe Cunningham; Video, Philip Allgeier; Wigs/Makeup, Heather Fleming; SM, Kimberly J First; ASM, Stephen Horton; Dramaturg, Adrien-Alice Hansel; Fight Director, k. Jenny Jones; Fight Captain, Nick Vannoy; Dialect, Rinda Frye; Casting, Zan Sawyer-Dailey; Directing Assistant, Lillian Meredith; Literary Consultant, Dominic Finocchiaro; Cast: Alex Morf (Renfield), Rufio Lerma (Count Dracula), Sabrina Conti (Ms. Sullivan), William McNulty (Van Helsing), Christopher Kelly (Dr. Seward), Nick Vannoy (Mr. Briggs), Gisela Chipe (Lucy), Joseph Midyett (Jonathan Harker), Eleanor Ickes (Undead Ensemble), Faith Oukrop (Undead Ensemble), Marianna McClellan (Undead Ensemble), Maggie Raymond (Undead Ensemble), Calvin Smith (Undead Ensemble); September 16–October 30, 2011

The Adventures of Tom Sawyer by Laura Eason; Adapted from the novel by Mark Twain; Director, Jeremy B. Cohen; Sets, Dan Ostling; Costumes, Lorraine Venberg; Lighting, Robert M. Wierzel; Original Music/Sound, Broken Chord; Props, Mark Walston; SM, Paul Mills Holmes; Fight/Movement Director, Tommy Rapley; Dramaturg, Amy Wegener; Directing Assistant, Caitlin O'Connell; Assistant Sets, Daniel Stratton; Assistant Lighting, Adam Greene; Assistant Costumes, Lindsay Chamberlin; PA, Jessica Potter; Casting, Stephanie Yankwitt; Assistant Dramaturg, Molly Clasen; Cast: Joseph Adams (Muff Potter/Ensemble), Justin Fuller (Joe Harper/Ensemble), Tim McKiernan (Tom Sawyer), Michael D. Nichols (Injun Joe/Ensemble), Robbie Tann (Huckleberry Finn/Ensemble), Hayley Treider (Becky Thatcher), Nate Trinrud (Sid/Doc Robinson/Ensemble), Nance Williamson (Aunt Polly/Ensemble); October 4–29, 2011

A Christmas Story by Philip Grecian; Based on the motion picture *A Christmas Story* (© 1983 Turner Entertainment Co., distributed by Warner Bros.), written by Jean Shepherd, Leigh Brown and Bob Clark; and on the book *In God We Trust, All Others Pay Cash* by Jean Shepherd; Director, Drew Fracher; Sets, Scott Bradley; Costumes, Lorraine Venberg; Lighting, Brian J Lilienthal; Sound,

Matt Callahan; Props, Mark Walston; Properties Master, Joe Cunningham; Wigs, Heather Fleming; SM, Kathy Preher; Dramaturg, Amy Wegener; Associate Lighting, Rachel Szymanski; Directing Assistant, Caitlin O'Connell; Casting, Zan Sawyer-Dailey; Assistant Dramaturg, Dominic Finocchiaro; Assistant Costumes, Lindsay Chamberlin; PA, Katie Shade; Cast: Katie Blackerby (Miss Shields), Larry Bull (Ralph Parker), Carter Caldwell (Scut Farkas), Marty Chester (Schwartz), Will DeVary (Flick), Justin R. G. Holcomb (The Old Man), Arabella Paulovich (Esther Jane Alberry), Henry Miller (Ralphie Parker), Kylie McGuffey (Helen Weathers), Gabe Weible (Randy Parker), Jessica Wortham (Mother), Lisa Dring (Elf), Jonathan Finnegan (Elf), Marianna McClellan (Elf), Maggie Raymond (Elf), Keaton Schmidt (Elf), Calvin Smith (Elf), Trent Stork (Elf), Amir Wachterman (Elf); November 8–27, 2011

ReEntry by Emily Ackerman and KJ Sanchez; Director, KJ Sanchez; Sets, Marion Williams; Costumes, Marion Williams; Lighting, Russell Champa and Dani Clifford; Sound, Zach Williamson; Video, Alex Koch; SM, Stephen Horton; ASM, Kimberly J. First; Dramaturg, Amy Wegener; Directing Assistant, Lillian Meredith; PA, Jessica Potter; Assistant Dramaturg, Dominic Finocchiaro; Movement Coordinator, Sameerah Luqmaan-Harris; Cast: Jessi Blue Gormezano (Liz/Rebecca/Suzanne), Brandon Jones (John/Pete), Samerrah Luqmaan-Harris (Mom/Maria/Lisa), Larry Mitchell (C.O.), Ben Rosenblatt (Charlie/Tommy); November 15–December 17, 2011

A Christmas Carol by Charles Dickens; Adapted by Barbara Field; Director, Drew Fracher; Sets, Paul Owen; Costumes, Lorraine Venberg; Lighting, Brian J. Lilienthal; Sound, Matt Callahan; Props, Mark Walston; Properties Master, Joe Cunningham; Media, Phillip Allgeier; Wigs, Heather Fleming; Music Supervisor, David Keeton; Movement Supervisor, Delilah Smyth; SM, Paul Mills Holmes; ASM, Kimberly J. First; Dramaturg, Sarah Lunnie; Dialect, Rinda Fry; Stage Management Intern, Suzanne Spicer; PA, Amelia Vanderbilt; Dramaturg Assistant, Molly Clasen; Directing Intern, Lillian Meredith; Casting, Zan Sawyer-Dailey; Cast: Jonah McElya-LaStrange (Boy Scrooge/Simon/Tom Cratchit), Alexis Broncovic (Belle/Mrs. Fred), Caroline Siegrist (Marjoram/Caroler/Fezzi Guest), Elise Coughlin (Caroler/Fezzi Guest), John Gregorio (Fred/ Mr. Fezziwig), Sean Mellott (Peter/Puss in Boots/Townsperson/Party Guest), Geoff Rice (Bob Cratchit), Ann Hodapp (Mrs. Grigsby/Cook), David Keeton (Grasper/Townsperson), Ruby McElya-LeStrange (Belinda/Fezzi Guest), Alec DeLaney (Tiny Tim/Ensemble), Brad DeLaney (Tiny Tim/Ensemble), William McNulty (Scrooge), Tyrone Mitchell Henderson (Ghost of Christmas Present/Forrest), Larry Bull (Marley/Old Joe), Celina Dean (Mrs. Cratchit), Navida Stein (Mrs. Fezziwig), Lauren Hirte (Ghost of Christmas Past/Mrs. Blakely); Allen Julien (Fezziwig Guest), J. Alexander Coe (Young Ebenezer/Pall Bearer), Erika Diehl (Dorothea/Marigold), Lisa Dring (Fan/Fezziwig Guest/Fred Party Guest), Jonathan Finnegan (Ghost of Christmas Future/Ali Baba/Townsperson/Party Guest), Elijah Foye (Caroler/Fezziwig Guest), VC Heidenreich (Narrator), Katie Medford (Sophia/Petunia), Calvin Ramirez (Artful Dodger), Maggie Raymond (Martha Cratchit/Party Guest), Calvin Smith (Edwards/Townsperson/Undertaker/Party Guest), Trent Stork (Dick Wilkins/Topper/Snarkers/Pall Bearer), Nick Vannoy (Poulterer/McFezzi/Krookings/Pall Bearer); December 6–23, 2010

The Elaborate Entrance of Chad Deity by Kristoffer Diaz; Director, KJ Sanchez; Sets, Michael B. Raiford; Costumes, Lorraine Venberg; Lighting, Brian J. Lilienthal; Sound, Matt Callahan; Props, Joe Cunningham; Wigs, Heather Fleming; Media, Philip Allgeier; SM, Kathy Preher; Dramaturg, Hannah Rae Montgomery; Assistant Dramaturg, Dominic Finocchiaro; Fight Director, Al Snow; Assistant Fight Director, Joe Isenberg; Fight Captain, Jamin Olivencia; Dance Captain, Liz Malarkey; Casting, Judy Bowman; Directing Assistant, Caitlin Ryan O'Connell; PA, Katie Shade; Assistant Costumes, Lindsay Chamberlin; Assistant Media, Chris Owens; Assistant Lighting, Rachel Szymanski; Cast: Kamal Angelo Bolden (Chad Deity), Ramiz Monsef (Vigneshwar Paduar), Jamin Olivencia (The Bad Guy), Alex Hernandez (Macedonio Guerra), Lou Sumrall (Everett K. Olson, Ring Announcer); J. Alexander Coe, Lisa Dring, Zoë Garcia, Doug Harris, Kanomé Jones, Liz Malarkey, Chris Reid, Nick Vannoy (Bodyguards, Wrestlers, Entourage); January 3–February 4, 2012

In the Next Room (or the vibrator play) by Sarah Ruhl; Director, Laura Gordon; Sets and Props, Philip Witcomb; Costumes, Lorraine Venberg; Lighting, Brian J. Lilienthal; Composer and Sound, Barry G. Funderburg; Wigs, Heather Fleming; SM, Paul Mills Holmes; ASM, Kimberly J. First; Dramaturg, Sarah Lunnie; Casting, Claire Simon, Simon Casting; Directing Assistant, Lillian Meredith; Assistant Dramaturg, Molly Clasen; Associate Lighting, Rachel Szymanski; Assistant Lighting, Kevin Frazier; Assistant Costumes, Danny Chihuahua; Stage Management Intern, Kevin Paul Love; Cast: Tyla Abercrumbie (Elizabeth), Cassandra Bissell (Sabrina Daldry), Cora Vander Broek (Catherine Givings), Matthew Brumlow (Leo Irving), Grant Goodman (Dr. Givings), Jenny McKnight (Annie), Jonathan Smoots (Mr. Daldry); January 24–February 18, 2012

HUMANA FESTIVAL

Death Tax by Lucas Hnath; Director, Ken Rus Schmoll; Sets, Philip Witcomb; Costumes, Kristopher Castle; Lighting, Brian H. Scott; Sound, Matt Hubbs; Props, Joe Cunningham; SM, Christine Lomaka; Dramaturg, Sarah Lunnie; Casting, Judy Bowman; Directing Assistant, Caitlin Ryan O'Connell; Assistant Lighting, Kevin Frazier; Assistant Dramaturg, Dominic Finocchiaro; PA, Leslie Cobb; Assistant Costumes, Lisa Weber; Cast: Quincy Tyler Bernstine (Nurse Tina), T. J. Kenneally (Todd), Judith Roberts (Maxine), Danielle Skraastad (Daughter); March 20–April 1, 2012

Eat Your Heart Out by Courtney Baron; Director, Adam Greenfield; Sets, Tom Tutino; Costumes, Connie Furr-Soloman; Lighting, Kirk Bookman; Sound, Benjamin Marcum; Props, Joe Cunningham; SM, Kimberly J. First; Dramaturg, Amy Wegener; Casting, Kelly Gillespie; Directing Assistant, Michael Whatley; Assistant Dramaturg, Dominic Finocchiaro; PA, Kristen Mun; Assistant Costumes, Daniel Chihuahua; Cast: Kate Eastwood Norris (Nance), Alex Moggridge (Tom), Sarah Grodsky (Evie), Jordan Brodess (Colin), Kate Arrington (Alice), Mike DiSalvo (Gabe); March 9–31, 2012

The Hour of Feeling by Mona Mansour; Director, Mark Wing-Davey; Sets, Michael B. Raiford; Costumes, Lorraine Venberg; Lighting, Brian J. Lilienthal; Sound, Matt Callahan; Media, Philip Allgeier; Props, Mark Walston; Wigs, Heather Fleming; SM, Kathy Preher; Dramaturg, Ismail Khalidi, Sarah Lunnie; Casting, Judy Bowman; Directing Assistant, Lillian Meredith; Assistant Dramaturg, Molly Clasen; PA, Katie Shade; Assistant Lighting, Kevin Frazier; Assistant Media, Chris Owens; Assistant Costumes, Megan Shuey; Cast: Hadi Tabbal (Adham), Judith Delgado (Beder), Rasha Zamamiri (Abir), David Barlow (George), William Connell (Theo), Marianna McClellan (Diana); March 6–April 1, 2012

How We Got On by Idris Goodwin; Director, Wendy C. Goldberg; Sets, Tom Tutino; Costumes, Connie Furr-Soloman; Lighting, Kirk Bookman; Sound, Matt Hubbs; Props, Sean McArdle; SM, Bret Torbeck; Dramaturg, Hannah Rae Montgomery; Casting, Harriet Bass; Assistant Dramaturg, Molly Clasen; PA, Caitlin O'Rourke; Directing Assistant, Jane B. Jones; Assistant Costumes, Daniel Chihuahua; Fight Supervisor, Nick Vannoy; Cast: Terrell Donnell Sledge (Hank), Brian Quijada (Julian), Deonna Bouye (Luann), Crystal Fox (Selector); March 2–April 1, 2012

Michael von Siebenburg Melts Through the Floorboards by Greg Kotis; Director, Kip Fagan; Sets, Michael B. Raiford; Costumes, Lorraine Venberg; Lighting, Brian J. Lilienthal; Sound, Matt Callahan; Props, Sean McArdle; Wigs, Heather Fleming; Fight Director, Joe Isenberg; Dialect, Rinda Frye; SM, Paul Mills Holmes; Dramaturg, Zach Chotzen-Freund; Casting, Laura Stanczyk; Directing Assistant, Lillian Meredith; Assistant Dramaturg, Dominic Finocchiaro; PA, Lizzy Lee; Assistant Lighting, Kyle Grant; Assistant Costumes, Megan Shuey; Cast: John Ahlin (Otto), Rufus Collins (Michael von Siebenburg), Ariana Venturi (Jane/Officer Lee), Micah Stock (Sammy), Laura Heisler (April/Officer Claire), Caralyn Kozlowski (Maria/Angela), Rita Gardner (Mrs. Rosemary); March 22–April 15, 2012

The Veri**on Play by Lisa Kron; Director, Nicholas Martin; Original Music, Jeanine Tesori; Sets, Tom Tutino; Costumes, Kristopher Castle; Lighting, Kirk Bookman; Sound, Benjamin Marcum; Music Supervisor, Scott Anthony; Props, Joe Cunningham; Wigs, Heather Fleming; Movement Director, Delilah Smyth;

SM, Stephen Horton; Dramaturg, Amy Wegener; Directing Assistant, Caitlin Ryan O'Connell; Assistant Dramaturg, Molly Clasen; PA, Jessica Potter; Fight Supervisor, Nick Vannoy; Assistant Costumes, Lindsay Chamberlin; Cast: Lisa Kron (Jenni), Carolyn Baeumler (Anissa), Joel Van Liew (Jerry Nyberg, et al.), Kimberly Hebert-Gregory (Wanda, et al.), Ching Valdes-Aran (Carol K. Anderson, et al.), Clayton Dean Smith (Steve, et al.), Calvin Smith (Bryce/Lars), Hannah Bos (Ingrid/Cydney), Sabrina Conti (Ensemble), Chris Reid (Ensemble); February 26 – April 1, 2012

The following short plays were presented under the title *Oh Gastronomy!*, and were performed March 16–April 1, 2012:

Oh Gastronomy (The Apprentice Showcase) by Michael Golamco, Carson Kreitzer, Steve Moulds, Tanya Saracho and Matt Schatz; Director, Amy Attaway; Co-conceived and developed with Sarah Lunnie; Sets, Tom Burch; Costumes, Lindsay Chamberlin; Lighting, Brian J. Lilienthal; Sound, Paul Doyle; Wigs, Hannah Wold; Music, Scott Anthony; Props, Mark Walston; SM, Travis Harty; Dramaturg, Sarah Lunnie; Assistant Dramaturgs, Molly Clasen and Dominic Finocchiaro; Assistant Directors, Lillian Meredith and Caitlin Ryan O'Connell; Assistant Lighting, Rachel Fae Szymanski; Production Manager, Michael Whatley

On Your Mark, Get Set, Eat! / "I Am Good at Eating a Lot" by Matt Schatz; Cast: Daniel Kopystanski (Competitor 1), Nick Vannoy (Host), Erika Diehl (Hostess); J. Alexander Coe, Jonathon Finnegan, Alexander Kirby, Liz Malarkey, Katie Medford, Maggie Raymond, Trent Stork (Other Competitors)

Ingredients by Steve Moulds; Cast: Calvin Smith (Master Baker) and Zoë Sophia Garcia (Apprentice)

Fear and Loathing at the Food Truck by Carson Kreitzer; Cast: Marianna McClellan (Adrian), Maggie Raymond (Jeannine), Rivka Borek (Lana), Sean Mellott (Jimmy)

The Family Feast / "Do You Want Something to Eat?" by Matt Schatz; Cast: Lisa Dring (Sally) and Sabrina Conti (Mary)

Artisanal Foods Anonymous by Steve Moulds; Cast: Doug Harris (Charles), Kanomé Jones (Dorothy), Keaton Schmidt (Jack), Amir Wachterman (Random Attendee); Erika Diehl, Zoë Sophia Garcia, Marianna McClellan, Nick Vannoy (Attendees)

Code Fries by Tanya Saracho; Cast: Trent Stork (Grrl) and Sabrina Conti (Roommate)

The Game by Carson Kreitzer; Cast: J. Alexander Coe (One), Keaton Schmidt (Two), Liz Malarkey (Three), Alexander Kirby (Four), Amir Wachterman (Five)

ORDERING: Memories by Michael Golamco; Cast: Chris Reid (Rick), Lisa Dring (Zelda), Sean Mellott (Poe), Daniel Kopystanski (Herb), Amir Wachterman (Waiter)

"Tastes Like Home" by Matt Schatz; Cast: Katie Medford (Woman), Alexander Kirby (Man), J. Alexander Coe, Jonathan Finnegan, Liz Malarkey (The Band)

In the Line by Tanya Saracho; Cast: Chris Reid (Ian) and Zoë Sophia Garcia (Annie)

The Mix by Steve Moulds; Cast: Calvin Smith (Master Baker) and Zoë Sophia Garcia (Apprentice)

My Mom Won't Let Me Eat That by Michael Golamco; Cast: Daniel Kopystanski (Billy) and Katie Medford (Mrs. Shriver)

Banana Girl by Tanya Saracho; Cast: Lisa Dring (Banana Girl), J. Alexander Coe (Jay), Kanomé Jones (Co-worker), Sabrina Conti (Co-worker 2), Nick Vannoy (Male co-worker)

A Numbers Game by Tanya Saracho; Cast: Liz Malarkey (One), Katie Medford (Two), Amir Wachterman (Three)

"How Do You Know?" by Matt Schatz; Cast: Erika Diehl (Girl)

"ORDERING: Eat What You Kill" by Michael Golamco; Cast: Rivka Borek (Chloe), Sean Mellott (Zack), Amir Wachterman (Waiter)

Tomatoes by Carson Kreitzer; Cast: Nick Vannoy (Farmer), Maggie Raymond (Woman), Kanomé Jones (Girl)

CSA Battle by Matt Schatz; Cast: Liz Malarkey (Female farmer), Trent Stork (Male farmer), Lisa Dring (Patron 1), Katie Medford (Patron 2); J. Alexander Coe, Sabrina Conti, Erika Diehl, Jonathan Finnegan, Zoë Sophia Grace, Doug Harris, Alexander Kirby, Daniel Kopystanski, Calvin Smith (Patrons)

Ordering: Free Lunch by Michael Golamco; Cast: Chris Reid (Mack), Keaton Schmidt (Dennis), Amir Wachterman (Waiter)

"Not Always So Good" by Matt Schatz; Cast: Daniel Kopystanski (Competitor 1); J. Alexander Coe, Jonathan Finnegan, Liz Malarkey (The Band)

Last Supper by Michael Golamco; Erika Diehl (Samantha), Doug Harris (Gil), Alexander Kirby (Chris)

First Taste by Steve Moulds; Cast: Calvin Smith (Master Chef) and Zoë Sophia Grace (Apprentice)

TEN-MINUTE PLAYS

The Dungeons and the Dragons by Kyle John Schmidt; Director, KJ Sanchez; Sets, Tom Burch; Costumes, Lindsay Chamberlin; Lighting, Nick Dent; Sound, Paul Doyle; Props, Mark Walston; Wigs, Hannah Wold; SM, Kathy Preher; Dramaturg, Hannah Rae Montgomery; Casting, Zan Sawyer-Dailey; PM, Michael Whatley; PA, Katie Shade; Cast: Jordan Brodess (Brett), Sean Mellott (Jean Verlaine), Sarah Grodsky (Marlin Bricks), Trent Stork (Felicity Hydrangea Karmikal); March 31–April 1, 2012

Hero Dad by Laura Jacqmin; Director, Sarah Rasmussen; Sets, Tom Burch; Costumes, Lindsay Chamberlin; Lighting, Nick Dent; Sound, Paul Doyle; Props, Mark Walston; Wigs, Hannah Wold; SM, Kathy Preher; Dramaturg, Hannah Rae Montgomery; Casting, Zan Sawyer-Dailey; PM, Michael Whatley; PA, Katie Shade; Cast: Marianna McClellan (Female Tenant/Female Jogger/Seated Female), William Connell (Vincent), Alex Moggridge (Billy), Mike DiSalvo (Mike); March 31–April 1, 2012

The Ballad of 423 and 424 by Nicholas C. Pappas; Director, Sarah Rasmussen; Sets, Tom Burch; Costumes, Lindsay Chamberlin; Lighting, Nick Dent; Sound, Paul Doyle; Props, Mark Walston; Wigs, Hannah Wold; SM, Kathy Preher; Dramaturg, Hannah Rae Montgomery; Casting, Zan Sawyer-Dailey; PM, Michael Whatley; PA, Katie Shade; Cast: David Barlow (Roderick), Kate Eastwood Norris (Ellen); March 31–April 1, 2012

Alley Theatre

Houston, Texas

Sixty-fifth Season

Artistic Director, Gregory Boyd; Managing Director, Dean R. Gladden

Agatha Christie's And Then There Were None by Agatha Christie; Director, Gregory Boyd; Scenic Design, Linda Buchanan; Costume Design, Blair Gulledge; Lighting Design, Michael Lincoln; Sound Design, Pierre Dupree; SM, Elizabeth M. Berther; SM, Terry Cranshaw; Cast: James Black (Judge Wargrave), Jeffrey Bean (William Blore), James Belcher (General Mackenzie), Josie de Guzman (Vera Claythorne), Jennifer Harmon (Emily Brent), Anne Quackenbush (Mrs. Rogers), David Rainey (Rodgers), John Tyson (Doctor Armstrong), Adam Van Wagoner (Anthony Marston), Todd Waite (Philip Lombard); Hubbard Stage; June 29–July 31, 2011

Ether Dome by Elizabeth Egloff; Director, Michael Wilson; Scenic Design, James Youmans; Costume Design, David C. Woolard; Lighting Design, David Lander; Sound Design, Alex Neumann; Original Music, John Gromada; New York Casting, Stephanie Klapper; Assistant Director, Rachel Alderman; SM, Elizabeth M. Berther; Dialect Coach, Sara Becker; Fight Direction, Brian Byrnes; Movement Consultant, Melissa Pritchett; Cast: Michael Bakkensen (Dr. Horace Wells), Jeffrey Bean (Dr. Charles Jackson), Elizabeth Bunch (Elizabeth Wells), James Belcher

(Gardner Colton/Gilbert Abbot/R.H. Eddy, Esq./Phineas Cook), Joshua Estrada (Inman/Messenger/Eben Frost), Adam Gibbs (Medical Student, Citizen of Hartford, Boston, New York, and Washington, D.C.), Dylan Godwin (George Livingston), Chris Hutchison (Dr. Henry Bigelow), Philip Lehl (Dr. George Hayward/Albert Tenney), Sean Lyons (William Morton), Kalob Martinez (Medical Student, Citizen of Hartford, Boston, New York, and Washington, D.C.), Melissa Pritchett (Elizabeth Whitman Morton), Anne Quackenbush (Mrs. Wadsworth/Miss Lanakova/Nurse/Jane White), Rebekah Stevens (Scheherazade/Young Woman in White/Ms. Mary Pierce), John Tyson (Dr. John Warren), Todd Waite (Dr. Augustus Gould/Assistant Secretary of War); Neuhaus Stage; September 9–October 9, 2011

Dividing the Estate by Horton Foote; Director, Michael Wilson; Scenic Design, Jeff Cowie; Costume Design, David C. Woolard; Lighting Design, Rui Rita; Original Music and Sound Design, John Gromada; New York Casting, Stephanie Klapper; Assistant Director, Rachel Alderman; SM, Marisa Levy; ASM, Terry Cranshaw; Cast: Devon Abner (Son), Elizabeth Ashley (Stella Gordon), James Black (Lewis Gordon), Pat Bowie (Mildred), James DeMarse (Bob), Ellen Dyer (Irene Ratliff), Hallie Foote (Mary Jo), Penny Fuller (Lucille), Maggie Lacey (Pauline), Nicole Lowrance (Sissie), Jenny Dare Paulin (Emily), Keiana Richárd (Cathleen); Roger Robinson (Doug); Hubbard Stage; October 7–30, 2011

A Christmas Carol – A Ghost Story of Christmas by Charles Dickens; Adapted and Originally Directed by Michael Wilson; Director, James Black; Scenic Design, Tony Straiges; Costume Design, Alejo Vietti; Lighting Design, Rui Rita; Original Music, John Gromada; PSM, Terry Cranshaw; ASM, Rebecca R.D. Hamlin; Dialect Coach, Jim Johnson; Cast: Jeffrey Bean (Ebenezer Scrooge), James Belcher (Bert/Spirit of Christmas Present), Elizabeth Bunch (Mrs. Fezziwig/Mrs. Cratchit), Joshua Estrada (Medieval Apparition/First Solicitor/Party Guest), Adam Gibbs (Henry V Apparition/Travis), Jennifer Gilbert (12th Century Apparition/Rich Lady/Patricia), Dylan Godwin (Mr. Marvel), Paul Hope (Second Solicitor/Mr. Fezziwig), Chris Hutchison (Bob Cratchit), John Johnston (18th Century Apparition/Dick Wilkins/Mr. Topper), Charles Krohn (Undertaker/Old Joe), Julia Krohn (Mary Pidgeon/Spirit of Christmas Past), Melissa Pritchett (Mary Stuart Apparition/Fred's Sister-in-Law), David Rainey (Mrs. Dilber/Jacob Marley), Rebekah Stevens (Restoriation Apparition/Wendy/Martha Cratchit), Adam Van Wagoner (Fred/Scrooge at Twenty-One), Bree Welch (Belle/Fred's Wife); Hubbard Stage; November 18–December 27, 2011

The Santaland Diaries by David Sedaris; Adapted for the stage by Joe Mantello; Director, David Cromer; Scenic Design, Karin Rabe; Lighting Design, Kevin Rigdon; Costume Design, Blair Gulledge; Sound Design, Pierre Dupree; SM, Elizabeth M. Berther; Cast: Todd Waite (Crumpet), Paul Hope (Alternate Crumpet); Neuhaus Stage; November 25–December 31, 2011

The Toxic Avenger; Book & Lyrics by Joe DiPietro; Music & Lyrics by David Bryan; Based on "The Toxic Avenger" by Lloyd Kaufman; Director, John Rando; Scenic Design, Beowulf Boritt; Costume Design, David C. Woolard; Lighting Design, Jason Lyons; Sound Design, Robert Kaplowitz; Mask Design & Prothetics, Louis Zakarian; Fight Direction & Special Effects, Waldo Warshaw/Fusion Special Effects; Hair & Make-up Design, Mark Adam Rampmeyer; Casting, Pat McCorkle/McCorkle Casting LTD.; Music Direction, Orchestrations, Conductor & Keyboards, Doug Katsaros; Choreography, Kelly Devine; Guitar, Stephan Badreau; Bass, Thomas Helton; Drums, Adam Wolfe; Tenor Saxophone, Johnny Gonzales; PSM, Tom Bartlett; ASM, Terry Cranshaw; ASM, Marisa Levy; Associate Choreographer, Dontee Kiehn; Cast: Mara Davi (Sarah), Mitchell Jarvis (White Dude), Nancy Opel (Mayor Babs Belgoody/Ma Fred/Nun), Constantine Maroulis (Melvin Fred the Third/The Toxic Avenger), Antoine L. Smith (Black Dude); Hubbard Stage; January 13–February 12, 2012

The Seagull by Anton Chekhov; Director, Gregory Boyd; Scenic Design, Kevin Rigdon; Costume Design, Alejo Vietti; Lighting Design, Pat Collins; Music Composition and Sound Design, Rob Milburn and Michael Bodeen; Hair and Wig Design, David H. Lawrence; NY Casting, Laura Stanczyk, CSA; Assitant Director and Dramaturg, Jacey Little; SM, Tree O'Halloran; Cast: Jeffrey Bean (Sorin), James Belcher (Shamreyev), James Black (Boris Trigorin), Josie de Guzman (Irina Arkadina), Ellen Dyer (Housemaid), Karl Glusman (Konstantin Treplev),

David Gorena (Yakov), Chris Hutchison (Medvedenko), Kimberly King (Paulina), Erica Lutz (Nina), Kalob Martinez (Cook), Rebekah Stevens (Housemaid), Rachael Tice (Masha), Todd Waite (Dorn); Neuhaus Stage; February 3–March 4, 2012

Red by John Logan; Director, Jackson Gay; Scenic Design, Takeshi Kata; Costume Design, Jessica Ford; Lighting Design, Paul Whitaker; Sound Design, Matt Tierney; Dramaturg, Jacey Little; SM, Terry Cranshaw; ASM, Rebecca R.D. Hamlin; Cast: Jay Sullivan (Ken), Scott Wentworth (Rothko); Hubbard Stage; March 2—25, 2012

The Seafarer by Conor McPherson; Director, Gregory Boyd; Scenic Designer, Hugh Landwehr; Costume Designer, Judith Dolan; Lighting Designer, Rui Rita; Sound Designer, Jill BC DuBoff; Dialect Coach, Stephen Gabis; Assistant Director, Elizabeth Bunch; Fight Director, Brian Byrnes; Dramaturg, Jacey Little; SM, Elizabeth M. Berther; ASM, Rebecca R.D. Hamlin; Cast: Jeffrey Bean (Ivan Curry), James Black (James "Sharky" Harkin), Chris Hutchison (Nicky Gilbin), Declan Mooney (Ivan Curry), John Tyson (Richard Harkin), Todd Waite (Mr. Lockhart); Hubbard Stage; April 6–May 5, 2012

What We're Up Against by Theresa Rebeck; Director, Scott Schwartz; Scenic and Lighting Design, Kevin Rigdon; Costume Design, Alejo Vietti; Sound Design, Josh Schmidt; NY Casting, Laura Stanczyk, CSA; Dramaturg, Jacey Little; SM, Terry Cranshaw; Cast: Chris Hutchison (Weber), Nancy Lemenager (Janice), David Andrew Macdonald (Stu), Julia Motyka (Eliza), David Rainey (Ben); Neuhaus Stage; May 11–June 10, 2012

Noises Off by Michael Frayn; Director, Gregory Boyd; Scenic Design, Hugh Landwehr; Costume Design, Alejo Vietti; Lighting Design, Pat Collins; Sound Design, Rob Milburn and Michael Bodeen; Movement Director, Brian Byrnes; Dialect, Voice and Text Coach, Pamela Prather; NY Casting, Pat McCorkle/McCorkle Casting LTD.; SM, Elizabeth M. Berther; ASM, Rebecca R.D. Hamlin; Cast: James Black (Lloyd Dallas), Josie de Guzman (Belinda Blair), Ben Diskant (Tim Allgood), Kimberly King (Dotty Otley), Allison Guinn (Poppy Norton-Taylor), Mic Matarrese (Garry Lejeune), Melissa Pritchett (Brooke Ashton), John Tyson (Selsdon Mowbray), Todd Waite (Frederick Fellowes); Hubbard Stage; May 25–June 24, 2012

Alliance Theatre

Atlanta, Georgia

Forty-third Season

Artistic Director, Susan V. Booth

ALLIANCE STAGE

Into the Woods Music & Lyrics by Stephen Sondheim; Book by James Lapine; Director, Susan V. Booth; Sets, Todd Rosenthal; Costumes, Lex Liang; Lighting, Ken Yunker; Sound, Clay Benning; Music Director, Helen Gregory; PSM, Pat Flora; ASM, R. Lamar Williams; ASM, Liz Campbell; Dramaturg, Celise Kalke; Casting, Jody Feldman & Alan Filderman, CSA; Choreographer, Daniel Pelzig; Cast: Courtney Balan (Baker's Wife), Courtenay Collins (Jack's Mother), Chandra Currelley (Cinderella's Stepmother), Jill Ginsberg (Cinderella), Walter Hudson (Narrator/Mysterious Man), Jeannette Illidge (Florinda/Snow White), Amber Iman (Lucinda/Sleeping Beauty), Jamie Wood Katz (Rapunzel/Dance Captain), Barbara Marineau (Cinderella's Mother/Granny/Giant), Jeff McKerley (Steward), Brandon O'Dell (Cinderella's Father), Mark Price (Baker), Angela Robinson (Witch), Diany Rodriguez (Little Red Ridinghood), Hayden Tee (Wolf/Cinderella's Prince), Jeremy Wood (Jack), Corey James Wright (Rapunzel's Prince); August 31–October 2, 2011

Golda's Balcony by William Gibson; Originally Directed by Scott Schwartz; Sets, Anna Louizos; Costumes, Jess Goldstein; Lighting, Jeff Croiter; Sound, Alex Hawthorn; Original Broadway Sound Design, Mark Bennett; Props, Kathy Fabian; Projections, Batwin & Robin Productions, Inc.; Wigs, Paul Huntley; General Manager, KL Management, Richard Martini/Sharon Tinari Pratt; PSM, Zoya

Kachadurian; ASM, Erin Sanchez; Cast: Tovah Feldshuh (Golda Meir); October 12–30, 2011

The Real Tweenagers of Atlanta Conceived by Rosemary Newcott; Written and Created by the Cast of The Real Tweenagers of Atlanta; Director, Rosemary Newcott; Music Composed by Justin Ellington; Lighting, Sean Hamilton; Projections, Jeanette Matte; Costumes, Emily Kramer; Sound, Brian Smith; Music Director, Keith A. Hale; PSM, Amy Radebaugh; Theatre for Youth and Families ASM, Barbara Gantt; Dramaturg Intern, Kate Wicker; Casting, Jody Feldman; Cast: Danielle Deadwyler (August March), Keith A. Hale (Dr. K), Bernard D. Jones (JB March), Claire Rigsby (Chloe Lowenstein-O'Malley-Garcia-Smith), Jacob York (Brandon Tubbs); World Premiere; October 29–November 13, 2011

A Christmas Carol by Charles Dickens; Adapted by David H. Bell; Director, Rosemary Newcott; Sets, D. Martyn Bookwalter; Costumes, Mariann S. Verheyen; Lighting, Diane Ferry Williams; Associate Lighting, Pete Shinn; Children's Backstage Chaperone, Rebecca Brandy; Movement Consultant, Henry Scott; Dialect, Freddie Ashley; Sound, Clay Benning; Music Director, Michael Fauss; PSM, Pat Flora; ASM, Liz Campbell; ASM, Wendy Palmer; Apprentice SM, Erin Sanchez; Casting, Jody Feldman, CSA; Cast: Jade Bacon (Want/Ensemble), Christy Baggett (Peg/Ensemble), Cynthia D. Barker (Mrs. Cratchit/Ensemble), Elizabeth Wells Berkes (Christmas Past/Ensemble), Corey Bradberry (Young Scrooge/Ensemble), David de Vries (Jacob Marley/Ensemble), Je Nie Fleming (Mrs. Fezziwig/Mrs. Dilber/Ensemble), Neal A. Ghant (Bob Cratchit), Jill Ginsberg (Belle/Ensemble), Bart Hansard (Mr. Fezziwig/Christmas Present/Ensemble), Bernard D. Jones (Peter Cratchit/Ensemble), Chris Kayser (Ebenezer Scrooge), Tendal Mann (Daniel Cratchit/Turkey Boy/Ensemble), Daniel Thomas May (Fred/Ensemble), Sinatra Osm (Dick Wilkins/Ensemble), Glenn Rainey (Ensemble), Brad Raymond (Topper/Ensemble), Ivy Catherine Rogers (Melinda Cratchit/Ensemble), Nicholas Sanders (Tiny Tim/Ensemble), Jordan Shoulberg (Belinda Cratchit/Ensemble), Allie Startup (Fan/Martha Cratchit/Ensemble), Bradley Washington (Wyatt Cratchit/Ignorance/Ensemble), Laurie Williamson (Bess/Ensemble); November 25–December 24, 2011

God of Carnage by Yasmina Reza; Translated by Christopher Hampton; Director, Kent Gash; Assistant Director, David Koté; Sets, Edward E. Haynes, Jr.; Costumes, Kara Harmon; Lighting, Liz Lee; Sound, Clay Benning; PSM, Amy L. Gilbert; Assistant SM, Libby Mickle; Apprentice SM, Barbara Gantt; Dramaturgical Assistance, Jireh Holder; Casting, Jody Feldman, CSA; Cast: Crystal Fox (Annette Raleigh), Jasmine Guy (Veronica Novak), Keith Randolph Smith (Michael Novak), Geoffrey Darnell Williams (Alan Raleigh); January 11–29, 2012

The Wizard of Oz by Frank L. Baum; Music & Lyrics by Harold Arlen & E.Y. Harburg; Book Adaptation by John Kane; Director, Rosemary Newcott; Sets, Kat Conley; Costumes, Sydney Roberts; Lighting, Pete Shinn; Sound, Clay Benning; Music Director, Christopher Cannon; Choreographer, Henry Scott; Puppetry Consultant, Michael Haverty; Puppetry Consultant, Reay Kaplan; PSM, Liz Campbell; ASM, Brandon O'Dell; Stage Management PA, Amy Radebaugh; Casting, Jody Feldman; Cast: Lowrey Brown (Scarecrow/Hunk/Munchkin Tough Kid/Munchkin Citizen), Jordan Craig (Tin Woodsman/Hickory/Munchkin Tough Kid/Munchkin Citizen), Je Nie Fleming (Wicked Witch of the West/Miss Almira Gulch), Reay Kaplan (Nikko/The Crow/Munchkin Barrister/Munchkin Tot/Munchkin Citizen), Patrick McColery (Uncle Henry Gale/Lead Winkie/Munchkin Mayor/Munchkin Citizen/Apple Tree), Erin Meadows (Glinda Good Witch of the North/Aunt Em/Munchkin Tot), Brandon O'Dell (Wizard of Oz/Professor Chester Marvel/Guard/Munchkin Coroner/Munchkin Citizen), Brad Raymond (Cowardly Lion/Zeke/Munchkin Tough Kid/Munchkin Citizen), Sharisa Whatley (Dorothy Gale/Munchkin Tot); February 25–March 11, 2012

Ghost Brothers of Darkland County Book by Stephen King; Music and lyrics by John Mellencamp; Music Direction by T Bone Burnett; Director, Susan V. Booth; Assistant Director, William Illg; Sets, Todd Rosenthal; Costumes, Susan E. Mickey; Lighting, Robert Wierzel; Associate Lighting, Paul Hackenmueller; Sound, Clay Benning; Assistant Sound, Brian P. Smith; Projections, Adam Larson; Assistant Projections, Shane Meador; Music Supervisor/Arranger, Andy York; Band Leader, Andy York; Fight Choreographer, Scot Mann, Kelly Martin;

Dramaturg, Celise Kalke; Special Effects, Steve Tolin; Dialect, Elisa Carlson; Copyist/Vocal Coach, Peggy Still Johnson; Dance Captain, Lori Beth Edgeman; Fight Captain, Travis Smith; Crash Pad Rental, A.A. Martin Properties; PSM, Pat A. Flora; ASM, R. Lamar Williams; Apprentice Stage Manager, Jayson T. Waddell; SDC Observer, Sidney Erik Wright; Cast: Jeremy Aggers (Ensemble), Peter Albrink (Jack McCandless), Kylie Brown (Anna Wicklow), Lori Beth Edgeman (Ensemble), Kate Ferber (Jenna Farrell), Justin Guarini (Drake McCandless), Shuler Hensley (Joe McCandless), Gwen Hughes (Ensemble), Joe Jung (Newt/Ensemble), Lucas Kavner (Frank McCandless), Joe Knezevich (Record Company Man/Ensemble), Jake La Botz (The Shape), Rob Lawhon (Ensemble), Royce Mann (Young Joe), Christopher L. Morgan (Dan Coker), Emily Skinner (Monique McCandless), Travis Smith (Andy McCandless), Dale Watson (Deejay/Zydeco Cowboy/Ensemble), Ryan Wotherspoon (Ensemble); World Premiere; April 4–May 13, 2012

HERTZ STAGE

Broke by Janece Shaffer; Director, Jason Loewith; Sets, Jack Magaw; Costumes, Janice Pytel; Lighting, Pete Shinn; Sound, Kendall Simpson; PSM, lark hackshaw (all lowercase) & R. Lamar Williams; ASM, Jayson T. Waddell; Dramaturg, Celise Kalke; Casting, Jody Feldman & Harriet Bass; Cast: Galen Crawley (Missie Eliason), Tess Malis Kincaid (Liz Eliason), James M. Leaming (Jonathan Eliason), Elisabeth Omilami (Evalyn Rentas); World Premiere; September 23–October 23, 2011

Sex and The Second City: A Romantic Dot Comedy Created by the Casts of The Second City; Adapted by and featuring original material by Kirk Hanley and Maribeth Monroe with Jimmy Carlson; Director, Jimmy Carlson; Video Direction, Jeff Hadick; Video Editing, Greg Mulvey; Costumes, Matt Guthier; Composer, Scott Stevenson; PSM, Shawn Pace; SM Apprentice, Jason Waddell; Casting, Beth Kligerman; Cast: Angela Dawe (Allie/Ensemble), Ed Kross (Edrick/Ensemble), Zach Muhn (Travis/Ensemble), Amy Roeder (Dorinda/Ensemble); November 11–December 18, 2011

The Fairytale Lives of Russian Girls (or девушки) by Meg Miroshnik; Director, Eric Rosen; Assistant Director, Molly Richards; Sets, Collette Pollard; Costumes, Ivan Ingermann; Lighting, Howell Binkley; Assistant Lighting, Amanda Zieve; Sound, Clay Benning; Original Music, Joshua Horvath; PSM, R. Lamar Williams; Stage Management PA, Jayson Waddell; Russian Language Consultant, Mila Fesenko; Casting, Jody Feldman and Harriet Bass; Dramaturg, Celise Kalke; Cast: Kate Goehring (Olga/Passport Officer/Professor/Valentina), Alexandra Henrikson (Katya), Judy Leavell (Baba Yaga/Auntie Yaroslava), Diany Rodriguez (Masha), Bree Dawn Shannon (The Other Katya/Nastya), Sarah Elizabeth Wallis (Annie); World Premiere; February 3–26, 2012

I Just Stopped By to See the Man by Stephen Jeffreys; Director, Ron OJ Parson; Assistant to the Director, Elliott Dixon; Sets, Jack Magaw; Costumes, Sydney Roberts; Lighting, Kathy A. Perkins; Sound, Kendall Simpson & Adair Mallory; Fight Choreographer, Scot Mann; Dialect, Elisa Carlson; PSM, Amy L. Gilbert; Stage Management PA, Barbara Gantt; Casting, Jody Feldman; Cast: Mississippi Charles Bevel (Jesse), Dieterich Gray (Karl), Bakesta King (Della); March 9–April 8, 2012

American Conservatory Theater

San Francisco, California

Forty-fifth Season

Artistic Director, Carey Perloff; Executive Director, Ellen Richard

Once in a Lifetime by Moss Hart and George S. Kaufman; Director, Mark Rucker; Sets, Daniel Ostling; Costumes, Alex Jaeger; Video, Alexander V. Nichols; Dramaturg, Michael Paller; Lighting, James F. Ingalls; Sound, Cliff Caruthers; SM, Elisa Guthertz; ASM, Megan Q. Sada; Cast: René Augesen (Helen Hobart), Julia Coffey (May Daniels), Alexander Crowther (Lawrence Vail), Nick Gabriel (Miss Leighton), Margo Hall (Mrs. Walker), Jessica Kitchens (Florabel Leigh), Patrick Lane (George Lewis), Will LeBow (Herman Glogauer), Kevin Rolston (Rudolph

Kammerling), John Wernke (Jerry Hyland), Ashley Wickett (Susan Walker); September 22–October 16, 2011

Race by David Mamet; Director, Irene Lewis; Sets, Christopher Barreca; Costumes, Candice Donnelly; Lighting, Rui Rita; Sound, Cliff Caruthers; Dramaturg, Michael Paller; SM, Kimberly Mark Webb; ASM, Stephanie Schliemann; Cast: Chris Butler (Henry Brown), Anthony Fusco (Jack Lawson), Susan Heyward (Susan), Kevin O'Rourke (Charles Strickland); October 21–November 13, 2011

A Christmas Carol Adapted by Carey Perloff and Paul Walsh from the story by Charles Dickens; Director, Domenique Lozano; Composer, Karl Lundeberg; Répétiteur, Nancy Dickson; Music Director, Robert K. Rutt; Sets, John Arnone; Costumes, Beaver Bauer; Lighting, Nancy Schertler; Sound, Jake Rodriguez; Dramaturg, Michael Paller; SM, Karen Szpaller; ASM, Danielle Callaghan; Cast: Elizabeth Abbe (Gang Member), Matthew Avery (Ned Cratchit), Graham Bennett (Tiny Tim Cratchit), Samuel Berston (Boy Scrooge), Alexander Bires (Boy in Sunday Clothes), Matt Bradley (Young Scrooge/Businessman), James Carpenter (Ebenezer Scrooge), Nathaniel Barrett Correll (Clerk/Boy Dick/Ignorance), Isabella Carlucci (Sally Cratchit), Alexander Crowther (Dick Wilkins/Thomas/Businessman), Penelope Devlin (Spanish Onion), Emma Rose Draisin (Want), Christina Elmore (Belle/Young Wife/Gang Member), Maddie Eisler (Spanish Onion), Manoel Felciano (Bob Cratchit/Giles the Fiddle), Dashiell Ferrero (Rory Wilkins), Anthony Fusco (Ebenezer Scrooge), Jason Frank (Fred/Jim), Gabriel Giacoppo (Edward), Cindy Goldfield (Charitable/Ruth/Ghost of Christmas Future/Produce Seller), Omozé Idehenre (Ghost of Christmas Present), Ben Kahre (Ghost of Christmas Past/Topper), Jessica Kitchens (Felicity/Beth), Alexandra Lee (Little Fan), Shalan Lee (French Plum), Maggie Leigh (Ermengarde/Mary), Elsie Lipson (Turkish Fig), Sharon Lockwood (Mrs. Dilber/Mrs. Fezziwig), Shelby Lyon (Sarah Wilkins), Delia MacDougall (Anne Cratchit), Sarah Magen (Belinda Cratchit), Jarion Monroe (Mr. Fezziwig/Businessman), Evelyn Ongpin (Child of Alan and Ruth), Caroline Pernick (Martha Cratchit), Quinn Poseley (Davey), Annie Purcell (Mrs. Filcher/Gang Member/Produce Seller), Rachel Share-Sapolsky (French Plum), Tony Sinclair (Peter Cratchit), William David Southall (Clerk/Alfred/Ghost of Christmas Future), Emily Spears (Turkish Fig), Sasha Steiner (Precious Wilkins), Howard Swain (Charitable/Alan/Ghost of Christmas Future), Courtney Thomas (Dorothy/Annabelle), Liam Vincent (Burt/Businessman/Young Husband), Jack Willis (Ghost of Jacob Marley); December 1–24, 2011

Humor Abuse by Lorenzo Pisoni and Erica Schmidt; Director, Erica Schmidt; Lighting, Ben Stanton; Sound, Bart Fasbender; SM, Hannah Cohen; ASM, Kimberly Mark Webb; Assistant to Mr. Stanton, Ben Krall; Photographic Images, Terry Lorant; Set Coordinator, Brian Fauska; Costume Coordinator, Denise Damico; Cast: Lorenzo Pisoni (Himself); January 12–February 5, 2012

Higher by Carey Perloff; Director, Mark Rucker; Sets, Erik Flatmo; Costumes, David F. Draper; Lighting, Gabe Maxson; Sound, Will McCandless; Dramaturg, Zohar Tirosh-Polk; SM, Danielle Callaghan; Cast: René Augesen (Elena Constantine), Alexander Crowther (Jacob Stein), Ben Kahre (Isaac Friedman), Andrew Polk (Michael Friedman), Concetta Tomei (Valerie Rifkind); February 1–25, 2012

Scorched by Wadji Mouawad; Translator, Linda Gaboriau; Director, Carey Perloff; Sets, Scott Bradley; Costumes, Sandra Woodall; Lighting, Russell H. Champa; Sound, Jake Rodriguez; Projections, Alexander V. Nichols; Dramaturg, Beatrice Basso; SM, Elisa Guthertz; ASM, Megan Q. Sada; Cast: Jacqueline Antaramian (Jihane/Nawal at 60/Abdessamad), Apollo Dukakis (Nazira/Janitor/Malak/Chamssedine), Manoel Felciano (Ralph/Antoine/Militiaman/Photographer), Nick Gabriel (Nihad/Wahab), Omozé Idehenre (Elhame/Sawda), Marjan Neshat (Nawal 14–40), Annie Purcell (Janine), David Strathairn (Alphonse Lebel/Doctor), Babak Tafti (Simon/Guide); February 16–March 11, 2012

Maple and Vine by Jordan Harrison; Director, Mark Rucker; Sets, Ralph Funicello; Costumes, Alex Jaeger; Lighting, Russell H. Champa; Sound, Jake Rodriguez; Dramaturg, Michael Paller; SM, Karen Szpaller; ASM, Danielle Callaghan; Cast: Danny Bernardy (Omar/Roger), Julia Coffey (Ellen/Jenna), Emily Donahoe (Katha), Jamison Jones (Dean), Nelson Lee (Ryu); March 29–April 22, 2012

Play by Samuel Beckett; Director, Carey Perloff; Sets, Daniel Ostling; Costumes, Candice Donnelly; Lighting, Alexander V. Nichols; Sound, Fabian Obispo; Dramaturg, Michael Paller; Casting, Janet Foster; SM, Elisa Guthertz; ASM, Megan Q. Sada; Cast: René Augesen (W1), Anthony Fusco (M), Annie Purcell (W2); May 9–June 2, 2012. *Play* was presented together with *Endgame*.

Endgame by Samuel Beckett; Director, Carey Perloff; Sets, Daniel Ostling; Costumes, Candice Donnelly; Lighting, Alexander V. Nichols; Sound, Fabian Obispo; Dramaturg, Michael Paller; Casting, Janet Foster; SM, Elisa Guthertz; ASM, Megan Q. Sada; Cast: Nick Gabriel (Clov), Giles Havergal (Nagg), Bill Irwin (Hamm), Barbara Oliver (Nell); May 9–June 2, 2012. *Endgame* was presented together with *Play*.

The Scottsboro Boys Music and lyrics by John Kander and Fred Ebb; Book by David Thompson; Director and Choreographer, Susan Stroman; Associate Director and Choreographer, Jeff Whiting; Sets, Beowulf Boritt; Costumes, Toni-Leslie James; Lighting, Ken Billington; Sound, John Weston; Music Director, Eric Ebbenga; Fight Director, Rick Sordelet; Casting, Janet Foster; SM, Joshua Halperin; ASM, Elisa Guthertz; Cast: David Bazemore (Olen Montgomery), Nile Bullock (Eugene Williams), Clifton Duncan (Haywood Patterson), Jared Joseph (Mr. Bones), Hal Linden (The Interlocutor), Clifton Oliver (Charles Weems), C. Kelly Wright (The Lady), Cornelius Bethea (Willie Roberson), Christopher James Culberson (Andy Wright), Eric Jackson (Clarence Norris), James T. Lane (Ozie Powell), JC Montgomery (Mr. Tambo), Clinton Roane (Roy Wright); June 21–July 22, 2012

American Repertory Theater (A.R.T.)

Cambridge, Massachusetts

Thirty-third Season

Diane Paulus, Artistic Director and CEO

The Gershwins' Porgy and Bess by George Gershwin, Dubose and Dorothy Heyward and Ira Gershwin; Adapted by Suzan-Lori Parks and Diedre L. Murray; Director, Diane Paulus; Sets, Riccardo Hernandez; Costumes, ESosa; Lighting, Christopher Akerlind; Sound, Acme Sound Partners; PSM, Nancy Harrington; SM, Julie Baldauff; Cast: Nikki Renee Daniels (Clara), Natasha Yvette Williams (Maria), Cedric Neal (Frazier), Heather Hill (Lily), Joshua Henry (Jake), J.D. Webster Mingo, David Alan Grier (Sporting Life), Nathaniel Stampley (Robbins), Bryonha Marie Parham (Serena), Norm Lewis (Porgy), Phillip Boykin (Crown), Audra McDonald (Bess), Phumile Sojola (Peter), Christopher Innvar (Detective), Joseph Dellger (Policeman), Andrea Jones-Sojola (Strawberry Woman), Roosevelt André Credit, Trevon Davis, Wilkie Ferguson (Fishermen), Allison Blackwell, Alicia Hall Moran, Lisa Nicole Williamson (Woman of Catfish Row); August 17–October 2, 2011

Three Pianos by Rick Burkhardt, Alec Duffy, and Dave Malloy; with music from Franz Schubert's Winterreise, Op. 89 (1828); Directed by Rachel Chavkin; Sets, Andrea Mincic; Costumes, Jessica Pabst; Lighting, Austin R. Smith; Sound, Matt Hubbs; PSM, Jesse Vacchiano; Cast: Rick Burkhardt, Alec Duffy, Dave Malloy; December 11–January 8, 2012

As You Like It by William Shakespeare; Directed by David Hammond; Sets, J. Michael Griggs; Costumes, Mallory Freers; Lighting, Margo Caddell; Sound, Clive Goodwin; PSM, Taylor Adamik; Cast: Matthew Christian (Orlando), Scotty Ray (Old Adam/Silvius), Luke Lehner (Oliver), Carl James (Dennis/Jaques), Lucas Woodruff (Charles/Corin/Jacques de Boy), Alexandra Wright (Rosalind), Rose Hogan (Celia), Rolland Walsh (Touchstone), Michael Kane (Le beau/Duke Senior/William), Dustyn Gulledge (Duke Frederic/Amiens/Sir Oliver), Liza Dickinson (Phebe), Alison Gregory (Audrey), Lanise Shelley (Hymen), Milia Ayache, Teri Gamble (Pages); January 18–29, 2012

Wild Swans by Jung Chang; Adaptation, Alexandra Wood; Director, Sacha Wares; Sets, Miriam Buether; Costumes, Tom Rand; Lighting, DM Wood; Sound, Gareth Fry; Video Wang GongXin; Movement, Leon Baugh; Puppetry, Michael

Fowkes; Associate Director, Ramin Gray; PSM, Christopher DeCamillis; Cast: Julyana Soelistyo (Yu-Fang), Ka-Ling Cheung (De-Hong), Orion Lee (Shou-Yu), Celeste Den (Ting), Jon Kit Lee (Bolin), Victor Chi (Heng), Joanna Zenghui Qiu (Zhen), Joanne Fong (Huifen), Eric Chan (Dr Wan), Ron Nakahara (Governor Lin), Les J.N. Mau (Team Leader Chi), Jennifer Lm Ai Hua (Teacher Shu), Emme Fuzhen Ricci (Er-Hong/child), Nekhebet Kum Juch (Niu), Annie Chang (Dai), Oliver Biles (Weimin), Katie Leung (Er-Hong); February 11–March 11, 2012

Futurity: A Musical by the Lisps Music by Cesar Alvarez with The Lisps; Lyricist, Cesar Alvarez; Book, Molly Rice and Cesar Alvarez; Director, Sarah Benson; Choreogrphy, Annie-B Parson; Production Design, Emily Orling; Sets/ Costumes, David Israel Reynoso; Lighting, Austin R. Smith; Sound, Matt Tierney; Music Director, Debra Barsha; Mechanical Percussion Design, Eric Farber; Associate Director, Meghan Finn; Assistant Choreographer, Chris Giarmo; SM, Katie Ailinger. Cast: Cesar Alvarez (Julian Munro), Sammy Tunis (Ada Lovelace), Edwin Lee Gibson (The General), Anne Gottlieb (Lady Byron), Aaron Schroeder (The Sergeant), Chelsey Donn (Vincent), Eric Farber, Ben Simon, Lorenzo Wolff (Steam Brain Engineers/Musicians), Carl James (Ezra/Scientist), Michael Kane (Japhy/Scientist), Milia Ayache (Miles/Scientist), Matthew Christian, Liza Dickinson, Teri Gamble, Rose Hogan, Lindsey Liberatore (Soldiers/Scientists/ Others); March 16–April 15, 2012

Woody Sez Words and music by Woody Guthrie; Devised by David M. Lutken with Nick Corley, Darcie Deaville, Helen J. Russell, Andy Teirstein; Sets, Luke Hegel-Cantarella; Costumes, Jeffrey Meek; Lights, Matt Frey; Music Director, David M. Lutken, Director, Nick Corley; Cast: David M. Lutken, Darcie Deaville, Helen J. Russell, Andy Teirstein; May 5–June 3, 2012

Arden Theatre Company

Philadelphia, Pennsylvania

Twenty-fourth Season

Managing Director, Amy L. Murphy; Artistic Director, Terrence J. Nolen

August: Osage County by Tracy Letts; Director, Terrence J. Nolen; Assistant Director, Sarah Ollove; Dramaturg, Ed Sobel; Sets, Dan Conway; Costumes, Alison Roberts; Lighting, Thom Weaver; Sound, James Sugg; PSM, Alec E. Ferrell; ASM, John Grassey; Cast: Elena Araoz (Johnna Monevata), Carla Belver (Violet Weston), Kevin Bergen (Sheriff Deon Gilbeau), Corinna Burns (Ivy Weston), Charlie DelMarcelle (Little Charles Aiken), Dylan Gelula (Jean Fordham), Grace Gonglewski (Barbara Fordham), Eric Hissom (Bill Fordham), David Howey (Beverly Weston), Anthony Lawton (Steve Heidebrecht), Mary Martello (Mattie Fae Aiken), Paul L. Nolan (Charlie Aiken), Kathryn Petersen (Karen Weston); September 29–October 30, 2011

The Whipping Man by Matthew Lopez; Director, Matt Pfeiffer; Assistant Director, Eric Wunsch; Sets, David P. Gordon; Costumes, Alison Roberts; Lighting, Thom Weaver; Sound, Christopher Colucci; PSM, Stephanie Cook; ASM, Alan Paramore; Cast: Johnnie Hobbs Jr. (Simon), Cody Nickell (Caleb), James Ijames (John); October 27–December 18, 2011

Charlotte's Web Adapted from the book by E.B. White by Joseph Robinette; Director, Whit MacLaughlin; Assistant Director, Mark Kennedy; Sets, David P. Gordon; Costumes, Rosemarie E. McKelvey; Lighting, Drew Billiau; Sound and Original Music, Christopher Colucci; PSM, Alec E. Ferrell; ASM, Ryan Pendergast; Cast: Emilie Krause (Fern, Ensemble), Leah Walton (Martha Arable, Goose, Ensemble), Charlie DelMarcelle (John Arable, Gander, Ensemble), Aubie Merrylees (Wilbur, Ensemble), Brandon Pierce (Avery Arable, Reporter, Announcer, Ensemble), Amanda Schoonover (Edith Zuckerman, Lamb, Ensemble), Brian Anthony Wilson (Homer Zuckerman, Sheep, Uncle, Ensemble), Anthony Lawton (Templeton, Lurvy, Ensemble), Sarah Gliko (Charlotte); November 30, 2011–January 29, 2012

Clybourne Park by Bruce Norris; Director, Edward Sobel; Assistant Director, Jill Harrison; Sets, James Kronzer; Costumes, Rosemarie E. McKelvey; Lighting,

Joshua L. Schulman; Sound, Jorg Cousineau; PSM, Katherine M. Hanley; ASM, Zach Trebino; Cast: Julia Gibson (Bev/Kathy), David Ingram (Russ/Dan), Maggie Lakis (Betsy/Lindsey), Steve Pacek (Jim/Tom/Kenneth), Ian Merrill Peakes (Karl/ Steve), Erika Rose (Francine/Lena), Josh Tower (Albert/Kevin), Beth Hylton (Elvira); January 26–March 25, 2012

Robin Hood By Greg Banks; Director, Matthew Decker; Assistant Director, Amber Emory; Fight Choreographer, Jenn Rose; Sets, Tom Gleeson; Costumes, Rosemarie E. McKelvey; Lighting, Justin Townsend; Sound, Original Music, Music Director, Dan Perelstein; PSM, Alec E. Ferrell; ASM, Kaleigh Malloy; Cast: Cast Carl Clemons-Hopkins (Little John), Charlotte Ford (Maid Marian), Sean Lally (Robin Hood), Steve Pacek (Will Scarlet/Prince John), Ian Merrill Peakes (Sheriff of Nottingham), April 25–June 24, 2012

Tulipomania Book, music and lyrics by Michael Ogborn; Director, Terrence J. Nolen; Assistant Director, Sarah Ollove; Music Director and Orchestrator, Dan Kazemi; Sets, James Kronzer; Costumes, Rosemarie E. McKelvey; Lighting, John Stephen Hoey; Sound, Jorge Cousineau; PSM, John Grassey; ASM, Samantha Pedings; Cast: Billy Bustamante (Waiter), Jeff Coon (Owner), Ben Dibble (Painter), Joilet F. Harris (Woman), Adam Heller (Man), Alex Keiper (Young Woman), May 24–July 1, 2012

Arena Stage

Washington, D.C.

Sixty-second Season

Artistic Director, Molly Smith; Executive Director, Edgar Dobie

FICHANDLER STAGE

Oklahoma! Music by Richard Rodgers; Book and lyrics by Oscar Hammerstein II; Based on the play *Green Grow the Lilacs* by Lynn Riggs; Original dances by Agnes de Mille; Director, Molly Smith; Choreographer, Parker Esse; Music Director, George Fulginiti-Shakar; Sets, Eugene Lee; Costumes, Martin Pakledinaz; Lighting, Michael Gilliam; Sound, Timothy M. Thompson; Hair/ Wigs, Paul Huntley; Fight Director, David Leong; Assoc. Director/Dialects, Anita Maynard-Losh; Assistant Choreographer, Ashley Yeater; SM, Susan R. White, Jenna Henderson; ASM, Taryn Friend; Cast: E. Faye Butler (Aunt Eller), Terry Burrell (Aunt Eller), Aaron Ramey (Jud Fry), Nicholas Rodriguez (Curly), Eleasha Gamble (Laurey), Lucas Fedele (Ike Skidmore), Andrew Hodge (Slim), Cody Williams (Will Parker), Philip Michael Baskerville (Cord Elam), Vincent Rodriguez III (Sam), Alvon Reed (Jess), Shane Rhoades (Fred), June Schreiner (Ado Annie Carnes), Nehal Joshi (Ali Hakim), Cara Massie (Gertie Cummings), Emilee Dupre (Vivian), Cyana Paolantonio (Ellen), Jessica Wu (Kate), Annie Petersmeyer (Virginia), Kristyn Pope (Aggie), Hugh Nees (Andrew Carnes), Hollie E. Wright (Dream Laurie/Sylvie), Kyle Vaughn (Dream Curly/Mike), Aaron Umsted (Male Swing), Jessica Hartman (Female Swing); July 8–October 2, 2011

You, Nero by Amy Freed; Director, Nicholas Martin; Sets, James Noone; Costumes, Gabriel Berry; Lighting, Matthew Richards; Sound, Drew Levy; Original Music, Mark Bennett; Assistant to the Director, Bryan Hunt; Hair/Wigs/Makeup, Cookie Jordan; Movement Coach, Brooks Ashmanskas; SM, Jenna Henderson; ASM, Christi B. Spann; Cast: Danny Scheie (Nero), Jeff McCarthy (Scribonius), Nancy Robinette (Agrippina), Susannah Schulman (Poppaea), Laurence O'Dwyer (Burrus), John C. Vennema (Seneca), Kasey Mahaffy (Fabiolo), Jonathan W. Colby, Leigh Marie Marshall, Philip McLeod, Sarah Moser, Marlon Russ, Nicholas Yenson (Ensemble); November 25, 2011–January 1, 2012

Ah, Wilderness! by Eugene O'Neill; Director, Kyle Donnelly; Sets, Kate Edmund; Costumes, Nan Cibula-Jenkins; Lighting, Russel Champa; Composer/Music Director/Arranger , Michael Roth; Hair/Makeup, Christal Schanes; SM, Jenna Henderson; ASM, Christi B. Spann; Cast: Rick Foucheux (Nat Miller), Nancy Robinette (Essie), Davis Chandler Hasty (Arthur), William Patrick Riley (Richard), Talisa Friedman (Mildred), Thomas and T.J. Langston (Tommy), Jonathan Lincoln Fried (Sid Davis), Kimberly Schraf (Lily Miller), Leo Erickson/Salesman (David

David Strathairn and Babak Tafti in Scorched at The American Conservatory Theater (photo by Kevin Berne)

The Company of Arena Stage at the Mead Center for American Theater's production of The Music Man (photo by Joan Marcus)

Patrick Breen and Luke Macfarlane in The Normal Heart at Arena Stage at the Mead Center for American Theater (photo by Scott Suchman)

James Ijames, Cody Nickell, and Johnnie Hobbs, Jr. in Arden Theatre Company's production of The Whipping Man (photo by Mark Garvin)

Jane Summerhays, Bret Lada, and Jean Lichty in Arkansas Repertory Theatre's production of A Loss of Roses (photo by Stephen Thornton)

Taylor Trensch and Adam Monley in Mormons, Mothers and Monsters at Barrington Stage Company (photo by Kevin Sprague)

Michael Poisson and Jasper McGruder in Sunset Limited at Barter Theatre (photo by Nathan Wampler)

Leslie Kritzer and the Company in Guys and Dolls at Barrington Stage Company (photo by Kevin Sprague)

Mikhail Baryshnikov in Berkeley Repertory Theatre's special presentation of In Paris (photo by Maria Baranova)

The Company of Tarzan: The Stage Musical at Barter Theatre (photo by Nathan Wampler)

The Company of A Chorus Line at Berkshire Theatre Group: Berkshire Theatre Festival (photo by Chris Reis)

McComber), June Schreiner (Muriel McComber); James Flanagan (Wint Selby/Bartender), Pearl Rhein (Belle), Allison Leigh Corke (Norah); March 9–April 8, 2012

The Music Man Book, music and lyrics by Meredith Willson; Story by Meredith Willson and Franklin Lacey; Director, Molly Smith; Choreographer, Parker Esse; Music Director, Lawrence Goldberg; Sets, Eugene Lee; Costumes, Judith Bowden; Lighting, Dawn Chiang; Sound, Timothy M. Thompson; Wigs, Anne Nesmith; Associate Director, Anita Maynard-Losh; Assistant Choreographer, Ashley Yeater; Assistant Music Director, Jose C. Simbulan; SM, Susan R. White; ASM, Jenna Henderson; Cast: Burke Moses (Harold Hill), Kate Baldwin (Marian Paroo), Janet Aldrich (Maud Dunlop), Ian Berlin (Winthrop Paroo), Will Burton (Tommy Djilas), Michael Brian Dunn (Jacey Squires/Traveling Salesman), Juliane Godfrey (Zaneeta Shinn), Rayanne Gonzales (Mrs. Squires), Jamie Goodson (Gracie Shinn), Nehal Joshi (Marcellus Washburn), Heidi Kaplan (Amaryllis), John Lescault (Mayor Shinn), Donna Migliaccio (Mrs. Paroo), Justin Lee Miller (Olin Britt/Traveling Salesman), Sasha Olinick (Charlie Cowell/Constable Locke), Katerina Papacostas (Ethel Toffelmier), Joe Peck (Ewart Dunlop/Conductor), Lawrence Redmond (Traveling Salesman), Tina Stafford (Alma Hix), Barbara Tirrell (Eulalie Mackecknie Shinn), Alissa Alter (Female Swing), Kurt Domoney (Male Swing), Tony Lawson (Harold Hill Alternate), Christina Kidd, Scott Shedenhelm, Eric Shorey, Kristen J. Smith, Jessica Wu, Nicholas Yenson (River City Townspeople), Colin J. Cech, Mia Alessandra Goodman (River City Kids); May 11–July 22, 2012

KREEGER THEATER

Trouble in Mind by Alice Childress; Director, Irene Lewis; Sets, David Korins; Costumes, Catherine Zuber; Lighting, Rui Rita, Carl Faber; Sound, David Budries; Hair/Makeup, Jon Carter; SM, Amber Dickerson; ASM, Kurt Hall; Cast: E. Faye Butler (Wiletta Mayer), Laurence O'Dwyer (Henry), Brandon J. Dirden (John Nevins), Starla Benford (Millie Davis), Thomas Jefferson Byrd (Sheldon Forrester), Gretchen Hall (Judy Sears), Marty Lodge (Al Manners), Garrett Neergaard (Eddie Fenton), Daren Kelly (Bill O'Wray), T. Anthony Quinn (Stagehand); September 9–October 23, 2012

Equivocation Oregon Shakespeare Festival's production by Bill Cain; Director, Bill Rauch; Sets, Christopher Acebo; Costumes, Deborah M. Dryden; Lighting, Christopher Akerlind; Compositions/Sound, Andrew Pluess; Movement Director, John Supes, U. Jonathan Toppo; Voice/Text Director, Rebecca Clark Carey; SM, Randall K. Lum; ASM, Mandy Younger; Cast: Anthony Heald (Shag), Jonathan Haugen (Nate), John Tufts (Sharpe), Richard Elmore (Richard), Gregory Linington (Armin), Christine Albright (Judith); November 18, 2011–January 1, 2012

Red by John Logan; In association with Goodman Theatre; Director, Robert Falls; Sets, Todd Rosenthal; Costumes, Birgit Rattenborg Wise; Lighting, Keith Parham; Original Composition and Sound, Richard Woodbury; SM, Kurt Hall; ASM, Keri Schultz; Cast: Edward Gero (Mark Rothko), Patrick Andrews (Ken); January 20–March 11, 2012

Long Day's Journey into Night by Eugene O'Neill; Director, Robin Phillips; Sets, Hisham Ali; Costumes, Susan Benson; Lighting, Michael Whitfield; Sound, James Sugg; Wigs, Paul Huntley; SM, Martha Knight; ASM, Marne Anderson; Cast: Helen Carey (Mary), Peter Michael Goetz (James Tyrone Sr.), Andy Bean (James Tyrone Jr.), Nathan Darrow (Edmund), Helen Hedman (Cathleen); March 30–May 6, 2012

The Normal Heart by Larry Kramer; Presented by special arrangement with Daryl Roth; Director, George C. Wolfe; Sets, David Rockwell; Costumes, Martin Pakledinaz; Lighting, David Weiner; Original Music/Sound, David Van Tieghem; Projections, Batwin & Robin Productions; Restaging Director, Leah C. Gardiner; SM, Amber Dickerson; ASM, Kurt Hall; Cast: Tom Berklund (Craig Donner/Grady), Michael Berresse (Mickey Marcus), Patrick Breen (Ned Weeks), Chris Dinolfo (David), Patricia Wettig (Dr. Emma Brookner), Nick Mennell (Bruce Niles), Luke Macfarlane (Felix Turner), John Procaccino (Ben Weeks), Christopher J. Hanke (Tommy Boatwright), Jon Levenson (Hiram Keebler/Examining Doctor); June 8–July 29, 2012

ARLENE AND ROBERT KOGOD CRADLE

The Book Club Play by Karen Zacarías; Director, Molly Smith; Sets, Donald Eastman; Costumes, Linda Cho; Lighting, Nancy Schertker; Sound, Cricket S. Myers; Projections, Adam Larsen; SM, Susan R. White; Kate Eastwood Norris (Ana), Eric M. Messner (Rob), Tom Story (Will), Ashlie Atkinson (Jen), Rachael Holmes (Lily), Fred Arsenault (Alex); October 7–November 6, 2011

Elephant Room by Steve Cuiffo, Trey Lyford and Geoff Sobelle; Director, Paul Lazar; Sets, Mimi Lien; Costumes, Christal Weatherly; Lighting, Christopher Kuhl; Sound, Nick Kourtides; SM, Thomas E. Shotkin; ASM, Zane Johnston; Cast: Dennis Diamon, Daryl Hannah, Louie Magic; January 20–February 26, 2012

Arkansas Repertory Theatre

Little Rock, Arkansas

Thirty-sixth Season

Executive Director, Robert Hupp

Ring of Fire, The Music of Johnny Cash by Richard Maltby Jr. & William Meade; Director, Jason Edwards; Sets, John Iacovelli; Costumes, Trish Clark; Lighting, Kenton Yeagre; Sound, M. Jason Pruzin; PSM, Patrick Lanczki; Cast: Trenna Barnes, Troy Burgess, Jason Edwards, Kelli Provart; September 16–October 9, 2011

The Second City Director, Ryan Bernier; PSM, Barry Branford; Music Director, Ben Harris,; Cast: Lyndsay Hailey, Nicole C. Hastings, Barry Hite, Tim Stoltenberg, Chris Witaske; October 12–23, 2011

A Christmas Carol by Alan Menken, Lynn Ahrens; Book by Mike Ockrent & Lynn Ahrens; Director, Alan Souza; Sets, E. Mike Nichols; Costumes, Michael Bottari and Ronald Case; Lighting, Cory Pattak; Sound, M. Jason Pruzin; PSM, CJ LaRoche; Cast: David Benoit (Ebenezer Scrooge), Michael J. Borges (Ensemble/Fezziwig/Christmas Present/Marley u/s), Monica Clark-Robinson (Mrs. Fezziwig/Mrs. Mops), Ryan G. Dunkin (A Beadle/Marley/Mr. Fezziwig/Scrooge u/s), Lacy J. Dunn (Mrs. Crachit/Ensemble), Katie Emerson (Sally/Mrs. Cratchit u/s), Hannah Fairman (Female Swing), Stacy Hawking (Ensemble), Brody Hessin (Ensemble/Bob Cratchit u/s/Christmas Past u/s), Adam Hose (Bob Crachit), Chaz Jackson (Ensemble), Marisa Kirby (Dance Captain/Ghost of Christmas Future/Ensemble/Mrs. Fezziwig u/s/Mrs. Mops u/s), Laura Medford (Emily), Shua Potter (Christmas Past), Taylor Quick (Ensemble/Emily u/s), Johnny Stellard (Fred/Ensemble/Young Scrooge u/s), Dennis Stowe (Ghost of Christmas Present/Ensemble), Kirt Thomas (Young Scrooge), Ryan Whitfield (Male Swing), Drew Clark (Jonathon/Young Ebenezer), Price Clark (Tiny Tim), Maddie Lentz (Swing), Joe McCurdy (Boy), Ella Moody (Fan/Want), Marina Redlich (Grace), Abby Shourd (Martha Cratchit); December 2– 25, 2011

To Kill a Mockingbird by Christopher Sergel based on the novel by Harper Lee; Director, Robert Hupp; Sets, E. Mike Nichols; Costumes, Marianne Custer; Lighting, Mike Eddy; Sound, M. Jason Pruzin; PSM, Danny Kuenzel; Fight Choreographer D.C. Wright; Cast: Camron Bradford (Townperson), Jason Collins (Bob Ewell), Verda Davenport (Helen Robinson), Spencer Davis (Dill), John-Patrick Driscoll (Boo Radley/Mr. Gilmer), John Feltch (Atticus), Will Frueauff (Jem u/s/Dill u/s), Kenneth Gaddie (Townperson), Nisheeda Devre Golden (Townperson), Lawrence Hamilton (Reverend Sikes), Laura E. Johnston (Calpurnia), Michael Jones (Tom Robinson); Janurary 27–February 12, 2012

The Wiz by William F. Brown and Charlie Smalls; Director, Rajendra Ramoon Maharah; Music Director, Charles Creath; Choreographer, James Harkness; Sets, E. Mike Nichols; Costumes, Rafael Castanera; Lighting, Douglas Cox; Sound, M. Jason Pruzin; PSM, Danny Kuenzel; Cast: Nik Alexzander (Scarecrow), Kayla Rose Aimable (Ensemble), Sydney Alise (Ensemble/Aunt Em Glinda u/s), Esther M. Antonie (Ensemble), Anthony Bryant (Ensemble), DeVon Wycovia Buchanan (Ensemble/Lion u/s), Myriam Gadri (Ensemble), LaTrisa A. Harper (Ensemble/Dorothy u/s/Addaperle u/s/Evilene u/s/Dance Captain), Bran Hernandez

(Ensemble/Tin man u/s), Jesse Jones (Ensemble/Uncle Henry u/s/The Wiz u/s), Tony Melson (Tin Man), Sinclair Mitchell (The Wiz), Zoie Morris (Aunt Em/Glinda), Christopher Eric Smith (Ensemble), Carla Stewart (Dorothy), Satia Spencer (Pit Singer), Christopher B. Straw (Pit Singer), Torya (Ensemble), Rickey Tripp (Ensemble/Scarecrow u/s), Jennifer Leigh Warren (Addaperle/Evilene); March 9–April1 1, 2012

Next to Normal by Brian Yorkey and Tom Kitt; Director, Nicole Capri; Sets, E. Mike Nichols; Costumes Shelly Hall; Lighting, Mike Eddy; Sound, M. Jason Pruzin; PSM, Steve Emerson; Props, Lynda J. Kwallek; Cast: Will Holly (Gabe), Deb Lyons (Diana), Krisin Parker (Natalie), Jonathan Rayson (Dan), Mo Brady (Henry), Peter James Zielinski (Doctor Fine/Doctor Madden). May 4–20, 2012

A Loss of Roses by William Inge; Director, Austin Pendleton; Sets, Stephen Dobay; Costumes, Marianne Custer; Lights, Keith Parham; Props, Lynda J. Kwallek; PSM, Erin Albrecht; Cast: Sara Croft (Olga St. Valentine), Katye Dunn (Mrs. Mulvaney), Todd Gearhart (Ricky), Max Jenkins (Ronny Cavendish), Bret Lada (Kenny), Jean Litchy (Lila Green), Keegan McDonald (Geoffrey "Jelly" Beamis), Jane Summerhays (Helen), Sydni Whitfield (Sandra Mulvaney); June 15–July 1, 2012

Barrington Stage Company

Pittsfield, Massachusetts

Seventeenth Season

Artistic Director, Julianne Boyd; Tristan Wilson, Managing Director

MAINSTAGE

Guys and Dolls Based on a story and characters by Damon Runyon; Music and lyrics by Frank Loesser; Book by Jo Swerling and Abe Burrows; Director, John Rando; Choreographer, Joshua Bergasse; Music Director, Darren Cohen; Sets, Alexander Dodge; Costumes, Alejo Vietti; Lighting, Rui Rita; Sound, Ed Chapman; Production Director, Jeff Roudabush; Press Representative, Charlie Siedenburg; Casting, Pat McCorkle CSA; PSM, Renee Lutz; Cast: Michael Thomas Holmes (Nathan Detroit), Morgan James (Sarah Brown), Leslie Kritzer (Adelaide), Matthew Risch (Sky Masterson), Daniel Marcus (Nicely-Nicely Johnson), Timothy Shew (Benny Southstreet), Gordon Stanley (Arvide Abernathy), Peggy Pharr Wilson (General Cartwright), Taylor Anderson (Ensemble), Chelsey Arce (Ensemble), Evan Autio (Ensemble), Tommy Bracco (Harry the Horse), Sharona D'Ornellas (Ensemble), Sean Patrick Folster (Detective Brannigan), Michael Hewitt (Ensemble), Steve Konopelski (Ensemble), Chris LeBeau (Ensemble), Brooke Marinovich (Ensemble), Michael Nichols (Big Jule), Hannah Richter (Ensemble), Kellyn Uhl (Ensemble), Nicky Venditti (Ensemble), Michael Wessells (Ensemble), Correy West (Rusty Charlie); June 15–July 16, 2011

The Best of Enemies by Mark St. Germain; Inspired by *The Best of Enemies* by Osha Gray Davidson; Director, Julianne Boyd; Sets, David M. Barber; Costumes, Kristina Lucka; Lighting, Scott Pinkney; Sound, Brad Berridge; Production Director, Jeff Roudabush; Press Representative, Charlie Siedenburg; Casting, Pat McCorkle CSA; PSM, Michael Andrew Rodgers; Cast: John Bedford Lloyd (C.P. Ellis), Aisha Hinds (Ann Atwater), Clifton Duncan (Bill Riddick), Susan Wands (Mary Ellis); July 21–August 6, 2011

The Game Book and lyrics by Amy Powers & David Topchik; Music by Megan Cavallari; Director, Julianne Boyd; Choreographer, Daniel Pelzig; Music Director, Darren R. Cohen; Sets, Michael Anania; Costumes, Jennifer Moeller; Lighting, Jeff Croiter, Grant Yeager; Sound, Ed Chapman; Production Director, Jeff Roudabush; Orchestrator, Mike Morris; Fight Choreographer, Ryan Winkles; Press Representative, Charlie Siedenburg; Casting, Pat McCorkle CSA; PSM, Renee Lutz; Cast: Rachel York (Marquise de Merteuil), Graham Rowat (Vicomte de Valmont), Joy Franz (Madame de Rosemonde), Amy Decker (Madame de Tourvel), Christianne Tisdale (Madame de Volanges), Sarah Stevens (Cecile), Chris Peluso (Danceny), Analisa Leaming (Emilie/Ensemble), Taylor Anderson (Ensemble), Michael Hewitt (Ensemble), Stephen Horst (Ensemble), Hannah

Richter (Ensemble), Amanda Salvatore (Ensemble), Michael Wessells (Ensemble); August 11–28, 2011

The Best of Enemies by Mark St. Germain; Inspired by *The Best of Enemies* by Osha Gray Davidson; Director, Julianne Boyd; Sets, David M. Barber; Costumes, Kristina Lucka; Lighting, Scott Pinkney; Sound, Brad Berridge; Production Director, Jeff Roudabush; Press Representative, Charlie Siedenburg; Casting, Pat McCorkle CSA; PSM, Michael Andrew Rodgers; Cast: John Bedford Lloyd (C.P. Ellis), Aisha Hinds (Ann Atwater), Don Guillory (Bill Riddick), Susan Wands (Mary Ellis); October 5–16, 2011

STAGE 2

Going to St. Ives by Lee Blessing; Director, Tyler Marchant; Sets, Brian Prather; Costumes, Kristina Sneshkoff; Lighting, Scott Pinkney; Sound, Allison Smartt; Production Director, Jeff Roudabush; Press Representative, Charlie Siedenburg; Casting, Pat McCorkle CSA; Associate Producer, Natasha Sinha; PSM, Michael Andrew Rodgers; Cast: Gretchen Egolf (Dr. Cora Gage) and Myra Lucretia Taylor (May N'Kame); June 22–July 9, 2011

Mormons, Mothers and Monsters Book and lyrics, Sam Salmond; Music, Will Aronson; Director and Choreographer, Adrienne Campbell-Holt; Assistant Choreographer, Shakina Nayfack; Music Director, Vadim Feichtner; Sets, Brian Prather; Costumes, Paloma Young; Lighting, Grant Yeager; Sound, Ryan Peavey; Production Director, Jeff Roudabush; Press Representative, Charlie Siedenburg; Casting, Pat McCorkle CSA; Associate Producer, Natasha Sinha; PSM, Rose Marie Packer; Musical Theatre Lab Artistic Producer, William Finn; Cast: Jill Abramovitz/Christianne Tisdale (Mother), Stanley Bahorek (Me), Adam Monley (Monster), Taylor Trensch (Mormon); July 14–31, 2011

My Name Is Asher Lev Written and directed by Aaron Posner; Adapted from the novel by Chaim Potok; Sets, Daniel Conway; Costumes, Olivera Gajic; Lighting John Hoey; Sound, James Sugg; Production Director, Jeff Roudabush; Press Representative, Charlie Siedenburg; Casting, Pat McCorkle CSA; PSM, Rose Marie Packer; Cast: Daniel Cantor (The Men); Renata Friedman (The Women), Adam Green (Asher Lev); August 18–September 11, 2011

ST. GERMAIN STAGE

Lungs Written by Duncan MacMillan; Director, Aaron Posner; Sets, Luciana Stecconi; Lighting, Zach Blane; Production Director, Jeff Roudabush; Press Representative, Charlie Siedenburg; Casting, Pat McCorkle CSA; PSM, Kate J. Cudworth; Associate Producer, Shakina Nayfack; Brooke Bloom (W), Ryan King (M); May 18–June 10, 2012

Barter Theatre

Abingdon, Virginia

Eightieth Season

Producing Artistic Director, Richard Rose; Director of Production, Nicholas Piper; Managing Director, Jeremy Wright

BARTER THEATRE

9 To 5: The Musical by Patricia Resnick; Director, Richard Rose; Choreographer, Amanda Aldridge; Music, Steve Sensenig; Sets, Michael Allen; Costumes, Kelly Jenkins; Lighting, Dale F. Jordan; Sound, Miles Polaski; Props, Ricky Hesson; Wigs/Makeup, Ryan Fischer; Dance Captain, Abbey C. Elliot; SM, Cindi A. Raebel; ASM, Beth Crock; Cast: Tricia Matthews (Violet Newstead), Logan Fritz (Josh), Erin Parker (Doralee Rhodes), Rick McVey (Dwayne/Others), Ashley Campos (Judy Bernly), Abbey C. Elliot (Kathy/Missy/Evil Queen), Hollie Williams (Maria/Intern/Evil Queen), Wendy Piper (Roz Keith), Mary Lucy Bivins (Margaret/Candy Striper), Nick Koesters (Franklin Heart), Matthew Bivins (Joe), Keith Richards (Bob Enright/Doctor/Others), Nicholas Piper (Dick/Others), Michael Poisson (Tinsworth/The Detective/Others); February 23–May 12, 2012

A Tale of Two Cities by Charles Dickens; Adapted by Richard Rose; Director, Richard Rose; Dramaturgical Assistants, Nicholas Piper, Katy Brown; Sets, Derek Smith; Costumes, Adrienne Webber; Props, Ricky Hesson; Wigs/Makeup, Ryan Fischer; Lighting, Dale F. Jordan; Sound, Miles Polaski; SM, Cindi A. Raebel; Cast: Nicholas Piper (Charles Darnay/Others), Nick Koesters (Sydney Carton/Others), Keith Richards (Jarvis Lorry/Others), Mary Lucy Bivins (Madame Defarge/Others), David Alford (Marquis St. Everémonde/Others), Holly Williams (Lucie Manette/Others), Rick McVey (Doctor Manette/Others); March 8–May 12, 2012

Legally Blonde: The Musical Music and lyrics by Laurence O' Keefe and Nell Benjamin; Book by Heather Hach; Director, Richard Rose; Choreographer, Amanda Aldridge; Music, Steve Sensenig; Sets, Daniel Ettinger; Costumes, Amanda Aldridge; Dance Captain/Assistant Choreographer, Ashley Campos; Assistant Music Director, Lee Harris; Lighting, Richard T. Chamberlin II; Sound, Miles Polaski; Assistant Dance Captain, Abbey C. Elliott; Props, Helen Stratakes; Wigs/Makeup, Ryan Fischer; SM, Cindi A. Raebel; ASM, Beth Crock; Cast: Ashley Campos (Margot/Others), Abbey C. Elliott (Serena/Others), Parris Cromer (Pilar/Others), Wendy Piper (Kate/Whitney/Others), Erin Parker (Erin/Enid Hoopes), Holly Williams (Lellani/Vivienne Kensington), Audrey Layne Crocker (Gaelen/Others), Cami René Philgreen (Cami/Stenographer/Others), Ellie Mooney (Elle Woods), Hannah Ingram (Saleswoman/Brooke Wyndham/Others), Tricia Matthews (Store Manager/Phorzheimer/D.A. Joyce Riley/Others), Justin Tyler Lewis (Warner Huntington III), Andrew Slane (Waiter/Nikos/Others), Nicholas Piper (Elle's Dad/Grandmaster Chad/Lowell/Dewey/Judge), Sean Campos (Emmett), Jay Reynolds Jr. (Jet Blue Pilot/Sundeep Padamadan/Carlos), David Alford (Winthrop/Kyle Brendan O'Boyle), Samuel Floyd (Aaron Shultz), Nick Koesters (Professor Callahan), Lacretta Nicole (Paulette Bonafonté/Others), Anna Davis (TV Reporter); May 19–August 19, 2012

The Red Velvet Cake War by Jessie Jones, Nicholas Hope, Jamie Wooten; Director, Nicholas Piper; Sets, Cheri Prough DeVol; Costumes, Megan Schuler; Lighting, Richard T. Chamblin III; Sound, Miles Polaski; Props, Helen Stratakes; Wigs/Makeup, Ryan Fischer; SM, Cindi A. Raebel; Cast: Holly Williams (Cee Cee Windham/Mama Doll Hargis), Erin Parker (Gaynelle Verdeen Bodeen), Mary Lucy Bivins (LaMerle Verdeen Minshew), Michael Poisson (Aubrey Verdeen), Wendy Piper (Jimmie Wyvette Verdeen), Ashley Campos (Peaches Verdeen Belrose), Tricia Matthews (Bitsy Hargis), Rick McVey (Newt Blaylock), Jasper McGruder (Sherriff Grover Lout), Rebekah Anwyll (Elsa Dowdall), Sam McCalla (Purvis Verdeen); May 31–August 18, 2012

Tarzan: The Stage Musical Music and lyrics by Phil Collins; Book by Henry Hwang; Based on the story *Tarzan of the Apes* by Edgar Rice Burroughs and the Disney film *Tarzan*; Originally presented on Broadway by Disney Theatrical Productions; Director, Richard Rose; Choreographer, Amanda Aldridge; Music, Steve Sensenig; Sets, Derek Smith; Costumes, Howard Tsvi Kaplan; Dance Captain, Abbey C. Elliott; Assistant Music Director, Lee Harris; Lighting, Michael Barnett; Sound, Miles Polaski; Assistant Dance Captain, Andrew Slane; Fight Choreographers, Richard Rose, Nick Koesters; Props, Helen Stratakes; SM, John "JP" Pollard; Fight Captain, Nick Koesters; ASM, Beth Crock; Cast: Nicholas Piper (Victorian Father/Clayton/The Creature), Holly Williams (Victorian Mother/Jane), Nick Koesters (Kerchak), Hannah Ingram (Kala), Andrew Slane (The Leopard/Snipes/Shrewdness of Apes/Flora), Alex Vanburen (Young Tarzan), Stephen Scott Wormley (Terk), Sean Campos (Tarzan), Eugene Wolf (Professor Porter), Ashley Campos (Shrewdness of Apes/Flora), Paris Cromer (Shrewdness of Apes/Flora), Abbey C. Elliott (Shrewdness of Apes/Flora), Wendy Piper (Shrewdness of Apes/Flora), Micah Hein (Shrewdness of Apes/Flora), Ginny Osborne (Shrewdness of Apes/Bugs), Teddy Pillion (Shrewdness of Apes/Bugs), Virginia Pillion (Shrewdness of Apes/Bugs); September 14–November 17, 2012

October, Before I Was Born by Lori Tate Matthews; Director, Mary Lucy Bivins; Sets, William Buck; Costumes, Amanda Aldridge; Lighting, Michael Barnett; Sound, Miles Polaski; Props, Helen Stratakes; SM, Cindi A. Raebel; Cast: Ashley Campos (Anne), Nicholas Piper (Houston), Tricia Matthews (Martha); September 27–November 17, 2012

A Christmas Story by Philip Grecian; based on the motion picture *A Christmas Story* written by Jean Shepherd, Leigh Brown and Bob Clark; Director, Katy Brown; Sets, Derek Smith; Costumes, Amanda Aldridge; Lighting, Richard T. Chamblin III; Sound, Miles Polaski; Props, Helen Stratakes; SM, Cindi A. Raebel; Cast: Nicholas Piper (Adult Ralph), Micah Hein (Schwartz/Desperado), Sam McCalla (Flick/Desperado), Hannah Ingram (Helen Weathers), Abbey C. Elliott (Esther Jane Alberry), Wendy Piper (Mother), Justin Tyler Lewis (Young Ralphie), Erin Parker (Randy), Michael Poisson (The Old Man/Santa Claus/ Radio Announcer), Barrett Guyton (Scut Farkas/Black Bart), Ashley Campos (Miss Shields/Elf); November 23–December 30, 2012

BARTER STAGE II

Alfred Hitchcock's The 39 Steps Adapted by Patrick Barlow from the novel by John Buchan from the movie of Alfred Hitchcock; Director, Katy Brown; Sets, Derek Smith; Costumes, Karen Brewster; Lighting, Andrew Morehouse; Props, Ricky Hesson; Wigs/Makeup, Ryan Fischer; Sound, Bobby Beck; SM, John "JP" Pollard; ASM, Beth Crock; Cast: Ben Mackel (Clown #1), Sean Campos (Clown #2), Nathan Whitmer (Richard Hannay), Hannah Ingram (Annabella Schmidt/Pamela/Margaret); February 2–March 4, 2012

Swamp Gas and Shallow Feelings by Jack Eric Williams and Randy Buck; Music by Jack Eric Williams; Based on material by Jack Eric Williams and Shirley Strother; Director, Eugene Wolf; Choreographer, Amanda Aldridge; Music, Steve Sensenig; Sets, Derek Smith; Costumes, Megan Schuler; Orchestration, H. Drew Perkins, Anthony Smith; Props, Ricky Hesson; Wigs/Makeup, Ryan Fischer; Vocal Arranger, Eugene Wolf; Lighting, Andrew Morehouse; Dance Captain, Wendy Piper; Sound, Miles Polaski; SM, John "JP" Pollard; Cast: Sean Campos (Vydell C. Harnet), Hannah Ingram (Tulip-Ann Pardue), Tricia Matthews (Sharmayne Blickett), Abbey C. Elliott (Shirleene Blickett), Wendy Piper (Shirlynne Blickett), Ashley Campos (Shirlayne Blickett), Matthew Bivins (Crash Watson), Erin Parker (Bethelle Blazedale), Michael Poisson (Erman H. Herman); March 15–May 6, 2012

Looking Over The President's Shoulder by James Still; Director, Tricia Matthews; Sets, Derek Smith; Costumes, Amanda Aldridge; Lighting, Camille Davis; Sound, Miles Polaski; Props, Helen Stratakes; SM, John "JP" Pollard; Cast: Jasper McGruder (Alonzo Fields); May 11–July 21, 2012

Avenue Q Music and lyrics by Robert Lopez and Jeff Marx; Book by Jeff Whitty; Based on concept by Robert Lopez and Jeff Max; Director, Katy Brown; Choreographer, Katy Brown; Music, Steve Sensenig; Sets, Derek Smith; Costumes, Kelly Jenkins; Assistant Music Director, Lee Harris; Lighting, Andrew Morehouse; Sound, Miles Polaski; Video, Karahann Kiser; Props, Helen Stratakes; Wigs/Makeup, Ryan Fischer; Puppetry, Russ Walko; Puppetry Consultants, Nick Koesters, Michael Faulkner; SM, John "JP" Pollard; ASM, Beth Crock; Cast: Jay Reynolds Jr. (Princeton/Others), Hannah Ingram (Kate Monster/Others), Justin Tyler Lewis (Brian), Andrew Slane (Rod/Others), Nick Koesters (Nicky/Trekkie Monster/Bad Idea Bear/Others), Sean Campos (Christmas Eve), Lacretta Nicole (Gary Coleman), Audrey Layne Crocker (Bad Idea Bear/Others), Abbey C. Elliott (Mrs. T/Lucy/Others), Parris Cromer (Ricky/Newcomer/Others); June 8–August 12, 2012

Two Jews Walk Into a War by Seth Rozin; Director, Mary Lucy Bivins; Sets, Derek Smith; Costumes, Adrienne Webber; Lighting, Camille Davis; Sound, Miles Polaski; Props, Helen Stratakes; Wigs/Makeup, Ryan Fischer; SM, John "JP" Pollard; Cast: Rick McVey (Zeblyan), Michael Poisson (Ishaq); June 20–August 10, 2012

Zombie Prom Book and lyrics by John Dempsey; Music by Dana P. Rowe; Based on a story by Mr. Dempsey & Hugh M. Murphy; Director, Richard Rose; Choreographer, Amanda Aldridge; Music, Steve Sensenig; Sets, Richard Rose; Costumes, Kelly Jenkins; Dance Captain, Abbey C. Elliott; Assistant Music Director, Lee Harris; Lighting, Andrew Morehouse; Sound, Miles Polaski; Assistant Dance Captain, Sean Campos; Props, Helen Stratakes; Wigs/Makeup, Ryan Fischer; SM, John "JP" Pollard; Production, Karahann Kiser; ASM, Beth

Crock; Cast: Hannah Ingram (Miss Delilah Strict), Holly Williams (Toffee), Parris Cromer (Candy), Wendy Piper (Ginger), Abbey C. Elliot (Coco), Stephen Scott Wormley (Jonny Warner), Justin Tyler Lewis (Josh), Andrew Slane (Jake), Sean Campos (Joey) Nick Koesters (Eddie Flagrante); September 6–November 10, 2012

The Sunset Limited by Cormac McCarthy; Director, Tricia Matthews; Sets, Derek Smith; Costumes, Amanda Aldridge; Lighting, Camille Davis; Sound, Miles Polaski; Props, Helen Stratakes; SM, Cindi A. Raebel; Cast: Jasper McGruder (Black), Michael Poisson (White); September 11–October 7, 2012

The Wind Farmer by Dan O'Neil; Director, Katy Brown; Sets, Derek Smith; Costumes, Adrienne Webber; Lighting, Camille Davis; Sound, Miles Polaski; Props, Helen Stratakes; SM, Cindi A. Raebel; Cast: Justin Tyler Lewis (Leo), Emily Grove (Ramona), Michael Poisson (Palmer); October 11–November 11, 2013

Sherlock Holmes And The Christmas Goose by V. Cate and Duke Ernsberger; Adapted from the short story "The Adventure of the Blue Carbuncle" by Arthur Conan Doyle; Director, Richard Rose; Sets, Derek Smith; Costumes, Amanda Aldridge; Lighting, Camille Davis; Sound, Miles Polaski; Props, Helen Stratakes; SM, John "JP" Pollard; Cast: Holly Williams (Woman With Goose/Betsy/Streetwalker), Eugene Wolf (Dr. Watson), Sean Campos (Eric Robbins/Others), Rick McVey (Officer Peterson), Nick Koesters (Sherlock Holmes), Tricia Matthews (Mrs. Hudson/Beggar/Others), Mary Lucy Bivins (Countess/Charwoman); November 20–December 23, 2012

Berkeley Repertory Theatre

Berkeley, California

Forty-third Season

Artistic Director, Tony Taccone; Managing Director, Susan Medak; Associate Artistic Director, Les Waters; General Manager, Karen Racanelli

MAIN SEASON: RODA THEATRE

Rita Moreno: Life Without Makeup Written by Tony Taccone; Developed by Rita Moreno & Tony Taccone; Staged & directed by David Galligan; Choreographer, Lee Martino; Sets, Anna Louizos; Costumes, Annie Smart; Projections/Lighting, Alexander V. Nichols; Sound, Philip G. Allen; Dramaturg, Madeleine Oldham; SM, Michael Suenkel; ASM, Rachel Motz , Kathy Rose; Music Director, César Cancino; Cast: Rita Moreno (herself), Ray Garcia (Dancer/Dance Captain), Salvatore Vassallo (Dancer), César Cancino (Piano/Conductor), Sascha Jacobsen (Bass), Alex Murzyn (Reeds), David Rokeach (Percussion); World Premiere; September 2–October 30, 2011 (extended to November 13)

A Doctor in Spite of Himself A co-production with Yale Repertory Theatre; Written by Molière; Adapted by Christopher Bayes & Steven Epp; Director, Christopher Bayes; Composer/Music Director, Aaron Halva; Sets, Matt Saunders; Costumes, Kristin Fiebig; Lighting, Yi Zhao; Sound, Ken Goodwin; Dramaturg, Benjamin Fainstein; Vocal Coach, Walton Wilson; SM, Cynthia Cahill; Casting, Tara Rubin Casting; Assistant Director, Jen Wineman; Cast: Julie Briskman (Jacqueline), Liam Craig (Lucas/Thibaut), Steven Epp (Sganarelle), Renata Friedman (Lucinde/Puppeteer), Allen Gilmore (M. Robert/Géronte), Chivas Michael (Léandre /Old Man [February 10–March 10]), Tyler Kent (Léandre/Old Man [March 11–25]), Greg C. Powers (Trombone/Tuba/Ukulele), Jacob Ming-Trent (Valère/Cherub [February 10–March 18]), Rob Seitelman (Valère/Cherub [March 20–25]), Justine Williams (Martine/Perrin), Robertson Witmer (Accordion/Clarinet/Drums); February 10–March 25, 2012

MAIN SEASON: THRUST STAGE

How to Write a New Book for the Bible A co-production with Seattle Repertory Theatre; Written by Bill Cain; Director, Kent Nicholson; Sets, Scott Bradley; Costumes, Callie Floor; Lighting, Alexander V. Nichols; Sound, Matt Starritt; Dramaturg, Madeleine Oldham; SM, Kathy Rose; Casting, Amy Potozkin,

Erin Kraft; PA, Megan McClintock; Assistant Costumes, Jocelyn Leiser Herndon; Cast: Aaron Blakely (Paul), Linda Gehringer (Mary), Leo Marks (Pete), Tyler Pierce (Bill); World Premiere; October 7–November 20, 2011

Ghost Light A co-production with Oregon Shakespeare Festival; Conceived & developed by Jonathan Moscone & Tony Taccone; Written by Tony Taccone; Director, Jonathan Moscone; Sets, Todd Rosenthal; Costumes, Meg Neville; Lighting, Christopher Akerlind; Sound, Andre Pluess; Video/Projections, Maya Ciarrocchi; Dramaturg, Alison Careyam; SM, Michael Suenkel; ASM, Leslie M. Radin; Casting, Nicole Arbusto, Joy Dickson, Amy Potozkin; Cast: Danforth Comins (Loverboy), Ted Deasy (Basil), Peter Frechette (Film Director), Bill Geisslinger (Prison Guard), Isaac Kosydar (Ensemble), Peter Macon (Mister), Christopher Liam Moore (Jon), Tyler James Myers (Boy), Sarita Ocón (Ensemble), Robynn Rodriguez (Louise); World Premiere; January 6–February 19, 2012

Red Written by John Logan; Director, Les Waters; Sets, Louisa Thompsons; Costumes, Anna Oliver; Lighting, Alexander V. Nichols; Sound, Bray Poor; Dramaturg, Julie McCormick; SM, Michael Suenkel; ASM, Kimberly Mark Webb; Casting, Amy Potozkin, Stephanie Klapper; Casting Assistants, Tyler Albright, Lauren O'Connell; Casting Intern, Katja Zarolinski; Associate Lighting, Stephanie Buchner; Cast: John Brummer (Ken), David Chandler (Mark Rothko); March 16–April 29, 2012 (extended to May 12)

LIMITED SEASON

The Wild Bride Presented by Kneehigh Theatre; Adapted by Emma Rice; Director, Emma Rice; Text & Lyrics, Carl Grose; Music, Stu Barker; Choreographer, Etta Murfitt; Sets, Bill Mitchell; Costumes, Myriddin Wannell; Lighting, Malcolm Rippeth; Sound, Simon Baker; Associate Sound, Andy Graham; Producer, Paul Crewes; Assistant Director, Simon Harvey; Additional Dance, Éva Magyar; SM, Steph Curtis; ASM, Cynthia Cahill; PM, David Harraway; Re-lights/Lighting Operator, Ben Nichols; Props/Puppetry, Sarah Wright; Carpenter, Alex Crombie-Rodgers; Cast: Audrey Brisson (The Girl), Stuart Goodwin (The Father and The Prince), Patrycja Kujawska (The Wild), Éva Magyar (The Woman), Stuart McLoughlin (The Devil), Ian Ross (The Musician); Roda Theatre; American Premiere; December 2, 2011–January 1, 2012 (extended to January 22)

Black n Blue Boys / Broken Men A co-production with Goodman Theatre; Written by Dael Orlandersmith; Director, Chay Yew; Sets, Daniel Ostling; Costumes, Anita Yavich; Lighting, Ben Stanton; Sound, Mikhail Fiksel; Dramaturg, Madeleine Oldham; Dialect, Lynne Soffer; SM, Leslie M. Radin; Associate Lighting, Stephanie Buchner; Cast: Dael Orlandersmith; Thrust Stage; World Premiere; May 25–June 24, 2012

SPECIAL PRESENTATIONS

In Paris A production of Baryshnikov Arts Center, Dmitry Krymov Laboratory and Russian Century Foundation in association with Korjaamo Theater, Helsinki; Adapted from the short story by Ivan Bunin; Composition/Director, Dmitry Krymov; Sets/Costumes, Maria Tregubova; Composer, Dmitry Volkov; Lighting, Damir Ismagilov; Audio/Video, Tei Blow; Movement Coach, Andrey Shchukin; Choreographer, Alexei Ratmansky; PM, Will Knapp; Video/Sound Supervisor, Tei Blow; Company Manager, Kathryn Luckstone; Lighting Supervisor, Valentina Migoulia; Technical Director, Anthony Cerrato; Wardrobe/Props, Mariya Masalskaya; Vocal Coach, John-Elliot Kirk; Cast: Mikhail Baryshnikov, Anna Sinyakina, Polina Butko, Maria Gulik, Maxim Maminov, Lasse Lindberg, Ossi Makkonen; Roda Theatre; April 25–May 15, 2012

Emotional Creature Written by Eve Ensler; Director, Jo Bonney; Sets/Costumes, Myung Hee Cho; Lighting, Lap Chi Chu; Sound, Jake Rodriguez; Projections, Shawn Sagady; Music/Music Director, Charl-Johan Lingenfelder; Choreographer, Luam; SM, Michael Suenkel; Associate Director, Pesha Rudnick; Casting, Amy Potozkin, Stephanie Klapper; Assistant Projections, Daniel Mueller; Sets/Costumes Assistant, Sara Clement, Desirae Hepp, Chika Shimizu; Casting Assistant, Tyler Albright, Lauren O'Connell; Cast: Ashley Bryant, Molly Carden, Emily S. Grosland, Joaquina Kalukango, Sade Namei, Olivia Oguma; Roda Theatre; World Premiere; June 14–July 15, 2012

Berkshire Theatre Group and Festival

Stockbridge and Pittsfield, MA

Eighty-fourth Season; Second Season as a merged organization with The Colonial Theatre

Artistic Director/CEO, Kate Maguire

THE UNICORN THEATRE

The Puppetmaster of Lodz by Gilles Ségal; Translated by Sara O'Connor; Director, Brian Roff; Sets, Jason Simms; Costumes, Antonia Ford-Roberts; Lighting, Japhy Weideman; Sound, Scott Killian; Puppetry, Emily DeCola; SM, Peter Durgin; Cast: Joby Earle (Finkelbaum), Tara Franklin (The Concierge), Matt R. Harrington (Weissmann), Jesse Hinson (Schwartzkopf); June 21-July 07, 2012 and September 13–October 06, 2012

A Class Act Music and lyrics by Edward Kleban; Book by Linda Kline and Lonny Price; Director, Robert Moss; Music Director, Mark Gionfriddo; Sets, Brett J. Banakis; Costumes, David Murin; Lighting, Solomon Weisbard; Sound, Brendan Doyle; SM, Kate Johnson; Cast: Rachael Balcanoff (Lucy), Ross Baum (Ed Kleban), Marie Eife (Mona), Brian Scannell (Charley, Marvin, Dr. Nodine, Jean-Claude), Eddie Shields (Bobby, Michael Bennet), Robbie Simpson (Lehman), Tessa Hope Slovis (Felicia), Anya Whelan-Smith (Sophie); July 11–August 04, 2012

Homestead Crossing by William Donnelly; Director, Kyle Fabel; Sets, Anita Stewart; Costumes, Lara De Bruijn; Lighting, Paul Hackenmueller; Sound, Shane Rettig; SM, Shane Van Vliet; Cast: David Adkins (Noel), Ross Cowan (Tobin), Corinna May (Anne), Lesley Shires (Claudia); August 07–September 01, 2012

THE COLONIAL THEATRE

A Chorus Line Book by James Kirkwood and Nicholas Dante; Music by Marvin Hamlisch; Lyrics by Edward Kleban; Director, Eric Hill; Music Director, Steven Freeman; Choreographer, Gerry McIntyre; Sets, Gary English; Costumes, David Murin; Lighting, Michael Chybowski; SM, Jason Hindelang; Cast: Sara Andreas (Judy), Ashley Arcement (Val), Nili Bassman (Cassie), Matthew Bauman (Mike), Giovanni Bonaventura (Mark), Natalie Caruncho (Diana), Alex Chester (Connie), Chris Chianesi (Greg), Warren Curtis (Don), Eddie Gutierrez (Paul), Andrew Hodge (Bobby), Bryan Thomas Hunt (Larry), Julianne Katz (Bebe), Tim McGarrigal (Al), Noah Racey (Zach), Neil Totton (Richie), Margaret Wild (Kristine), Karley Willocks (Maggie), Dana Winkle (Sheila); July 02–July 21, 2012

THE FITZPATRICK MAIN STAGE

A Thousand Clowns by Herb Gardner; Director, Kyle Fabel; Sets, Randall Parsons; Costumes, Olivera Gajic; Lighting, Dan Kotlowitz; Sound, J Hagenbuckle; SM, Laura Wilson; Cast: James Barry (Albert Amundson), Rachel Bay Jones (Sandra Markowitz), Jordan Gelber (Leo Herman), Andrew Polk (Arnold Burns), Russell Posner (Nick Burns), CJ Wilson (Murray Burns); July 16–July 28, 2012

Edith by Kelly Masterson; Director, Michael Sexton; Sets, Brett J. Banakis; Costumes, David Murin; Lighting, Paul Gallo and Craig Stelzenmuller; Sound, Jill BC Du Boff; SM, Stephen Horton; Cast: Jayne Atkinson (Edith Bolling Galt Wilson), Dan Butler (Thomas Marshall), Jack Gilpin (Woodrow Wilson), RJ Hatanaka (Edmund Starling), Walter Hudson (Henry Cabot Lodge), Peter Rini (Joseph Tumulty), Steven Skybell (Cary Grayson), Samantha Soule (Margaret Wilson); July 31–August 11, 2012

Brace Yourself by David Epstein; Director, James Naughton; Sets, Hugh Landwher; Costumes, David Murin; Lighting, Paul Gallo and Craig Stelzenmuller; Sound, Scott Killian; SM, John Grassey; Cast: Clea Alsip (Kitty), Jill Eikenberry (Sunny), Tara Franklin (Nina), Jackie Hoffman (Jeanette), David Ross (Andy), Michael Tucker (Milt); August 14–August 25, 2012

Bristol Riverside Theatre

Bristol, Pennsylvania

Twenty-sixth Season

Founding Director, Susan D. Atkinson; Artistic Director, Keith Baker; Managing Director, Amy Kaissar

Dr. Jekyll and Mr. Hyde Adapted by Jeffery Hatcher; Director/Artistic Director, Keith Baker; Sets, Roman Tatarowicz; Costumes, Linda Bee Stockton; Lighting, Deborah Constantine; Sound, William Neal; Cast: Sean Gormley (Actor 3), Robert Ian McKenzie (Actor 2), Michael Sharon (Jekyll), Eileen Ward (Actor 5), and Debra Whitfield (Actor 6); September 28–October 17, 2010

Old Wicked Songs by Jon Marans; Director/Artistic Director, Keith Baker and David Kenner; Lighting, Charles Reece; Sets, Bill Clark; Cast: Keith Baker (Professor Josef Mashkan), David Kenner (Stephen Hoffman); November 16–December 5, 2010

The Little Prince Adaptor and Director, Scott Hitz; Script, John Scoullar and Rick Cummins; Sets, Tom Gleeson; Lighting, Ryan O'Gara; Costumes, Millie Hiibel; Sound, William Neal; Cast: Leila Ghaznavi (The Little Prince), Lenny Haas (Aviator), Marc Petrosino (Screen Puppeteer), Carole Anne Raffa (Rose), Michael Schupback (the Fox); January 25–February 13, 2011

The Eyes of Babylon Written and performed by Jeff Key; Director, Yuval Hadadi; Sets, Nels Anderson; Costumes, Brick Williamson; Lighting, Evan Purcell; Sound, Chris Comfort; Video, Jennilyn Merten and Yuval Hadadi; March 15–April 3, 2011

Little Women Original novel by Louisa May Alcott; Book, Allan Knee; Director, Susan D. Atkinson; Costumes, Millie Hiibel; Sets, Roman Tatarowicz; Lighting, Deborah Constantine; Choreographer, Karen Getz; Music Director, Mark Yurkanin; Music, Jason Howland; Lyrics, Mindi Dickstein; Cast, Lesli Becker (Marmee March/Hag), Kim Carson (Beth March/Rodrigo 2), Kara Dombrowski (Amy March/Troll), Jennie Eisenhower (Jo March), Elisa Matthews (Meg March/Clarissa), Cathy Newman (Aunt March/Mrs. Kirk), Steven Nicholas (Mr. John Brooke/Braxton), Stephen Schellhardt (Laurie Laurence/Rodrigo), Michael Sharon (Professor Bhaer); James Van Trueren (Mr. Laurence/Knight); May 3–22, 2011

California Shakespeare Theater

Orinda, California

Thirty-ninth Season

Artistic Director, Jonathan Moscone; Managing Director, Susie Falk

The Tempest by William Shakespeare; Director, Jonathan Moscone; Choreographer, Erika Chong Shuch; Sets, Emily Greene; Costumes, Anna Oliver; Lighting, Gabe Maxon; Sound, Cliff Caruthers; Vocal/Text Coach, Domenique Lozano; Dramaturg, Philippa Kelly; SM, Corrie Bennett; Fight Director, Dave Maier; Cast: James Carpenter (Alonso), Catherine Castellanos (Caliban/Antonio), Emily Kitchens (Miranda/Sebastian), Nicholas Pelczar (Ferdinand/Trinculo), Erika Chong Shuch (Ariel/Boatswain), Michael Winters (Prospero/Stephano), Melanie Elms (Sprite), Aaron Moreland (Sprite), Travis Santell Rowland (Sprite), Bruns Memorial Amphitheater, May 30–June 24, 2012

Spunk: Three Tales by Zora Neale Hurston; Adapted by George C. Wolfe; Music, Chic Street Man; Director, Patricia McGregor; Sets, Michael Locher; Costumes, Callie Floor; Lighting, York Kennedy; Sound, Will McCandless; Additional Music, Anthony Michael Peterson, a.k.a. Tru; Movement Director, Paloma McGregor; Dialect/Text Coach, Lynne Soffer; Vocal Coach, Bryan S. Dyer; Fight Consultant, Dave Maier; Dance Captain, Omoze Idenehre; SM, Laxmi Kumaran; Assistant Director, Rebecca Frank; Cast: Aldo Billingslea (Sweet Back/Joe). L. Peter Callender (Sykes/Slang Talk Man), Margo Hall (Delia), Omoze Idehenre (Missy May), Anthony Michael Peterson, a.k.a. Tru (Guitar Man), Tyee Tilghman (Jelly/Slemmons), Dawn L. Troupe (Blues Speak Woman), Bruns Memorial Amphitheater, July 4–29, 2012

Blithe Spirit by Noël Coward; Director, Mark Rucker; Sets, Annie Smart; Costumes, Katherine Roth; Lighting, York Kennedy; Sound, Will McCandless; Dialect, Lynne Soffer; Resident Dramaturg, Philippa Kelly; SM, Corrie Bennett; Assistant Director, Megan Sada; Cast: Rene Augesen (Ruth), Anthony Fusco (Charles), Jessica Kitchens (Elvira), Domenique Lozano (Madame Arcati), Kevin Rolston (Dr. Bradman), Melissa Smith (Mrs. Bradman), Rebekah Brockman (Edith), Bruns Memorial Amphitheater; August 8–September 2, 2012

Hamlet by William Shakespeare; Director, Liesl Tommy; Sets, Clint Ramos; Costumes, Clint Ramos; Lighting, Peter West; Sound, Jake Rodriguez; Resident Dramaturg, Philippa Kelly; Vocal/Text Coach, Nancy Carlin; Fight Director, Dave Maier; SM, Laxmi Kumaran; Cast: Julie Eccles (Gertrude), Nick Gabriel (Horatio), Dan Hiatt (Polonius/Gravedigger), Zainab Jah (Ophelia), Jessica Kitchens (Rosenkrantz/Ensemble), LeRoy McClain (Hamlet), Nicholas Pelczar (Laertes/Lucianus), Brian Rivera (Guildenstern/Bernardo/Ensemble), Adrian Roberts (Claudius/Ghost), Danny Scheie (Osric/Player King/Ensemble), Mia Tagano (Player Queen/Doctor/Ensemble), Joseph Salazar (Marcellus/Ensemble), Bruns Memorial Amphitheater; September 19–October 21, 2012

CENTERSTAGE

Baltimore, Maryland

Fiftieth Season

Artistic Director, Kwame Kwei-Armah OBE; Managing Director, Stephen Richard

THE HEAD THEATER

The Second City Charmed and Dangerous by The Second City, Ed Furman, and Tim Sniffen; Music composed by Matthew Loren Cohen; Director, Matt Hovde; Music Director, Matthew Loren Cohen; Sets, Daniel Ettinger; Lighting, Lesley Boeckman; Sound, Amy C. Wedel; Video, Jeff HAdick; Dramaturg, Gavin Witt; SM, Meghan Teal; Cast: Ryan Archibald (Ensemble), Brooke Breit (Ensemble), Lili-Anne Brown (Ensemble), Chelsea Devantez (Ensemble), Cody Dove (Ensemble), Ric Walker (Ensemble); September 15–October 16, 2011

American Buffalo by David Mamet; Director Liesl Tommy; Sets, Neil Patel; Costumes, Kathleen Geldard; Lighting, Lap Chi Chu; Sound, Broken Chord; Dramaturg, Kellie Mecleary; Fight Choreographer, J. Allen Suddeth; SM, Captain Kate Murphy; ASM, Raine Bode, Laura Smith; Casting, Janet Foster; Cast: William Hill (Don), Rusty Ross (Bob), Jordan Lage (Teach); November 2–December 11, 2011

A Skull in Connemara by Martin McDonagh; Director, BJ Jones; Sets, Todd Rosenthal; Costumes, David Burdick; Lighting, Michelle Habeck; Sound, Andre Pluess; Dramaturg, Kellie Mecleary; Fight Choreographer, Lewis Shaw; Dialect, Gillian Lane Plescia; SM, Captain Kate Muphy; SM, Matthew Melchiorre; Casting, Stephanie Klapper; Cast: Jordan J. Brown (Mairtin Hanlon), Barbara Kingsley (Maryjohnny Rafferty), Si Osborne (Mick Dowd), Richard Thieriot (Thomas Hanlon); January 25–March 4, 2012

The Whipping Man by Matthew Lopez; Director, Kwame Kwei-Armah; Sets, Neil Patel; Costumes, David Burdick; Lighting, Michelle Habeck; Sound, Sean Rettig; Dramaturg, Faedra Chatard Carpenter; Fight Director, J. Allen Suddeth; Dialect, Gillian Lane-Plescia; Casting, Stephanie Klapper; SM, Laura Smith; ASM, Katie Ambrose; Cast: Michael Micalizzi (Caleb), Kevyn Morrow (Simon), Johnny Ramey (John); The Head Theater; April 4–May 13, 2012

THE PEARLSTONE THEATER

The Rivals by Richard Brinsley Sheridan; Director, David Schweizer; Sets, Caleb Wertenbacker; Costumes, David Burdick; Lighting, Russel H. Champa; Original Music, Ryan Rumery; Sound, M. Florian Staab; Assistant Sets, Jen Stearns; Dialect, Ashley Smith; Fight Choreographer, Lewis Shaw; Dramaturg, Whitney Eggers; SM, Laura Smith; ASM, Raine Bode, Captain Kate Murphy; Casting, Janet Foster; Cast: Clifton Duncan (Faukland), Danny Gavigan (Fag/David), Caroline Hewitt (Julia Melvills), Jimmy Kieffer (Bob Acres), David Margulies

(Sir Anthony Absolute), Manu Narayan (Captain Jack Absolute), Kristine Nielsen (Mrs. Malaprop), Libya Pugh (Lucy), Owen Scott (Thomas), Zoe Winters (Lydia Languish), Evan Zes (Sir Lucius O'Trigger); September 28–October 30, 2011

Gleam by Bonnie Lee Moss Rattner, based on the novel *Their Eyes Were Watching God* by Zora Neale Hurston; Director, Marion McClinton; Sets, David Gallo; Costumes, ESosa; Lighting, Michael Wangen; Music/Sound, Rob Milburn, Michael Bodeen; Dramaturg, Gavin Witt; Fight Choreographer, Lewis Shaw; Dialect, Evamarii Johnson; SM, Laura Smith; ASM, Captain Kate Murphy; Casting, Pat McCorkle; Cast: Axel Avin, Jr. (Jody Starks/Ed Dockerty), Stephanie Berry (Pheoby Watson), Brooks Edward Brantly (Tea Cake), Thomas Jefferson Byrd (Logan Killicks/Sam Watson), Christiana Clark (Janie), Erik LaRay Harvey (Hezekiah/Sop-de-Bottom), Tonia M. Jackson (Lulu Moss/Nanny), Celeste Jones (Daisy Blunt/Nunkie), Gavin Lawrence (Amos Hicks/Johnny Taylor/Lias), Jaime Lincoln Smith (Lige Moss/Bootny); January 4–February 5, 2012

Into the Woods Music and lyrics by Stephen Sondheim; Book by James Lapine; Director, Mark Lamos; Music Director, Wayne Barker; Choreographer, Seán Curran; Sets, Allen Moyer; Costumes, Candice Donnelly; Lighting, Robert Wierzel; Sound, Zachary Williamson; Hair/Wigs, Denise O'Brien; Dramaturg, Gavin Witt; SM, Matthew Melchiorre; ASM, Amanda Spooner; Casting, Tara Rubin Casting; Music Contractor, Chris Hofer; Cast: Jeffry Denman (Narrator), Dana Steingold (Little Red Ridinghood), Jenny Latimer (Cinderella), Lauren Kennedy (Witch), Justin Scott Brown (Jack), Alma Cuervo (Stepmother/Granny/Giant), Cheryl Stern (Jack's Mother), Nik Walker (Wolf/Cinderella's Prince), Erik Liberman (Baker), Britney Coleman (Cinderella's Mother/Rapunzel), Danielle Ferland (Baker's Wife), Robert Lenzi (Cinderella's Father/Rapunzel's Prince), Nikka Lanzarone (Florinda), Jeremy Lawrence (Mysterious Man), Eleni Delopoulos (Lucinda); Co-production with Westport Country Playhouse; March 7–April 15, 2012

Center Theatre Group

Los Angeles, California

Forty-fifth Season

Artistic Director, Michael Ritchie; Managing Director, Edward L. Rada

KIRK DOUGLAS THEATRE

I've Never Been So Happy Book/lyrics, Kirk Lynn; Music/lyrics, Peter Stopschinski; Created by Rude Mechs; Directors, Thomas Graves, Lana Lesley; Sets, Leilah Stewart; Costumes, Laura Cannon; Lighting, Brian H. Scott; Music Director/Sound, Peter Stopschniski; Animation, Miwa Matreyek; Choreographer, Dayna Hanson; Shindig, Sandra Burns; Associate Producer, Diane Rodriguez; PSM, Denise Martel; Cast: Cami Alys (Julie/Background Vocals), Kerri Atwood (Sheriff), Lowell Bartholomee (Brutus), Liz Cass (Background Vocals), Noel Gaulin (Dancer), Thomas Graves (Dancer), Hannah Kenah (Dancer), Jenny Larson (Sigmunda), Lana Lesley (Dancer), E. Jason Liebrecht (Jeremy), Michael Mergen (Background Vocals), Erin Meyer (Dancer), Eric Roach (Guitars), Paul Soileau (Sigfried), Peter Stopschinski (Keyboards/Mountain Lion), Meg Sullivan (Annabellee); World Premiere; October 6–23, 2011

The Night Watcher Written and performed by Charlayne Woodard; Director, Daniel Sullivan; Sets, Thomas Lynch, Charlie Corcoran; Costumes, Jess Goldstein; Lighting, Geoff Korf; Original Music and Sound, Obadiah Eaves; Original Projections, Tal Yarden; Associate Artistic Director, Neel Keller; PSM, Mary K. Klinger; November 17–December 18, 2011

A Raisin in the Sun The Ebony Repertory Theatre Production; by Lorraine Hansberry; Director, Phylicia Rashad; Sets, Michael Ganio; Costumes, Ruth E. Carter; Lighting, Elizabeth Harper; Sound, Bob Blackburn; Wigs/Hair, Carol F. Doran; Casting, Victoria Thomas; PSM, David Blackwell; SM, Elle Aghabala; Associate Artistic Director, Kelley Kirkpatrick; Cast: Kenya Alexander (Beneatha Younger), Keith Arthur Bolden (Moving Man), Brandon David Brown (Travis Younger), Kevin T. Carroll (Walter Lee Younger), Jason Dirden (George Murchison), Deidrie Henry (Ruth Younger), Amad Jackson (Joseph Asagai); Scott

Brendan Griffin, Damon Gupton, Annie Parisse, Crystal A. Dickinson, and Jeremy Shamos in Clybourne Park at Center Theatre Group (photo by Craig Schwartz)

Robert Eli, Maia DeSanti, and Jered Mclenigan in All My Sons at Delaware Theatre Company (photo by Matt Urban)

Francesca Choy-Kee, Sarah Dandridge, and Alvin Keith in the Cincinnati Playhouse in the Park's production of As You Like It (photo by Sandy Underwood)

Merritt Janson and Mike Hartman in the Denver Center Theatre Company's production of Great Wall Story (photo by Terry Shapiro)

Susan McKey, Kevin Kelly, Bruce Graham, and Megan McDermott in Time Stands Still at Delaware Theatre Company (photo by Matt Urban)

Maren Bush and Dominic Comperatore in Talley's Folly at Florida Studio Theatre (photo by Maria Lyle)

Brooks Ashmanskas and the Company of the Ford's Theatre production of 1776 *(photo by Carol Rosegg)*

Edward Gero and Patrick Andrews in Goodman Theatre's production of Red *(photo by Liz Lauren)*

The Company of Georgia Shakespeare's The Tempest *(photo by Bill DeLoach)*

The Company of Goodspeed Musicals' City of Angels *(photo by Diane Sobolewski)*

Jodi Dominick and the Company in Great Lakes Theater's production of Cabaret *at Great Lakes Theater (photo by Roger Mastroianni)*

Bowman Wright and Lynda Gravatt in A Raisin in the Sun *at Geva Theatre Center (photo by Ken Huth)*

Mosenson (Mr. Karl Linder), Kem Saunders (Moving Man), Kim Staunton (Lena Younger), Ellis E. Williams (Bobo); January 19–February 19, 2012

American Night: The Ballad of Juan Jose by Richard Montoya; Developed by Culture Clash and Jo Bonney; Director, Jo Bonney; Sets, Neil Patel; Costumes, ESosa; Lighting, David Weiner; Sound, Darron L West; Projections, Shawn Sagady; Choreographer, Ken Roht; Casting Consultants, Nicole Arbusto, Joy Dickson; Associate Artistic Director, Neel Keller; PSM, Randall K. Lum; SM, Tarin Hurstell; Cast: Stephanie Beatriz (Lydia/Ensemble), Rodney Gardiner (Ben Pettus/ Ensemble), David Kelly (Harry Bridges/Ensemble), Terri McMahon (Ms. Finney/ Ensemble), René Millán (Juan José/Fight Captain), Richard Montoya (Juan José the First/Ensemble), Kimberly Scott (Viola Pettus/Ensemble), Herbert Siguenza (Neil Diamante/ Ensemble), Daisuke Tsuji (Johnny/Dance Captain/Ensemble); Co-production with La Jolla Playhouse; March 9–April 1, 2012

The Convert by Danai Gurira; Director, Emily Mann; Sets, Daniel Ostling; Costumes, Paul Tazewell; Lighting, Lap-Chi Chu; Sound, Darron L. West; Dramaturg, Carrie Hughes; Casting, Adam Belcuore, Erika Sellin; Associate Artistic Director, Kelley Kirkpatrick; PSM, Alison Cote; Associate Director, Adam Immerwahr; SM, Brooke Baldwin; Fight Director, J. Steven White; Dialect/ Vocal Coach, Beth McGuire; Cast: Pascale Armand (Jekesai/Ester), Cheryl Lynn Bruce (Mai Tamba), Zainab Jah (Prudence), Kevin Mambo (Chancellor), LeRoy McClain (Chilford), Warner Joseph Miller (Tamba), Harold Surratt (Uncle); World Premiere; A co-production with McCarter Theatre Center and Goodman Theatre; Commissioned by Center Theatre Group; April 17–May 19, 2012

AHMANSON THEATRE

Bring It On: The Musical Libretto, Jeff Whitty; Music, Tom Kitt, Lin-Manuel Miranda; Lyrics, Amanda Green, Lin-Manuel Miranda; Inspired by the motion picture "Bring It On" written by Jessica Bendinger; Director/ Choreographer, Andy Blankenbuehler; Music Supervisor/Dance Arranger, Alex Lacamoire; Sets, David Korins; Costumes, Andrea Lauer; Lighting, Jason Lyons; Sound, Brian Ronan; Video, Jeff Sugg; Hair/Wigs, Charles G. LaPointe; Casting, Telsey + Company; PSM, Bonnie Panson; Technical Supervisor, Jake Bell; Production Supervisor, Lisa Dawn Cave; General Management, 321 Theatrical Management; Arranger/ Orchestrator, Tom Kitt, Alex Lacamoire; Music Coordinator, Michael Keller; Music Director, Dave Pepin; Cast: Taylor Louderman (Campbell), Adrienne Warren (Danielle), Jason Gotay (Randall), Elle McLemore (Eva), Ryann Redmond (Bridget), Ariana DeBose (Nautica), Gregory Haney (La Cienega), Neil Haskell (Steven), Janet Krupin (Kylar), Kate Rockwell (Skylar), Nicolas Womack (Twig), Calli Alden (Burger Pagoda Girl), Nicki Blaemire ("Cross the Line" Soloist), Shonica Gooden ("Don't Drop" Soloist), Haley Hannah (Burger Pagoda Girl), Dominique Johnson (Cameron), Michael Mindlin (Cheer Camp Leader), Alysha Umphress ("Legendary" Soloist); Ensemble/Understudies/Swings: Antwan Bethea, Nikki Bohne, Danielle Carlacci, Dexter Carr, Courtney Corbeille, Dahlston Delgado, Brooklyn Alexis Freitag, Rod Harrelson, Casey Jamerson, Melody Mills, Michael Naone-Carter, Adrianna Parson, David Ranck, Bettis Richardson, Billie Sue Roe, Sheldon Tucker, Lauren Whitt; West Coast Premiere; October 30– December 10, 2011

Fela! Based on the *Life of Fela Anikulapo-Kuti*; Book, Jim Lewis, Bill T. Jones; Music/Lyrics, Fela Anikulapo-Kuti; Additional Lyrics, Jim Lewis; Additional Music, Aaron Johnson, Jordan McLean; Conceived by Bill T. Jones, Jim Lewis, Stephen Hendel; Inspired by the authorized biography *Fela: This Bitch of a Life* by Carlos Moore; Director/Choreographer, Bill T. Jones; Set/Costumes, Marina Draghici; Lighting, Robert Wierzel; Sound, Robert Kaplowitz; Projections, Peter Nigrini; Wigs/Hair/Makeup, Cookie Jordan; PSM, John M. Atherlay; Casting, Arnold J. Mungioli, CSA, Pippa Ailion, CDG; Technical Supervisor, Todd Frank; General Manager, Roy Gabay; Music Director/Coordinator/Orchestrator/Arranger, Aaron Johnson; Tour Presentation, Cami Spectrum/Columbia Artist Theatricals; Music Arranger, Jordan McLean; Music Consultant, Antibalas; Creative Director/ Associate Choreographer, Maija Garcia; Associate Director, Niegel Smith; Cast: Sahr Ngaujah (Fela Anikulapo-Kuti), Adesola Osakalumi (Fela Anikulapo-Kuti), Melanie Marshall (Funmilayo), Paulette Ivory (Sandra), Rasaan-Elijah "Talu" Green (Djembe-'Mustafa'), Ismael Kouyaté (Ismael), Gelan Lambert (J.K. Braimah/

Egungun); Ensemble: Sherinne Kayra Anderson, Jonathan Andre, Cindy Belliot, Nandi Bhebhe, Catia Mota Da Cruz, Nicole Chantal De Weever, Jacqui Dubois (Funmilayo u/s), Poundo Gomis, Oneika Phillips (Sandra u/s), Thierry Picaut, Jermaine Rowe (Assistant Dance Captain), Daniel Soto, Jill Marie Vallery (Dance Captain), Iris Wilson, Aimee Graham Wodobode; Swings: Wanjiru Kamuyu (Dance Captain), Adé Chiké Torbert; December 13, 2011–January 22, 2012

American Idiot Music, Green Day; Lyrics, Billie Joe Armstrong; Book, Billie Joe Armstrong, Michael Mayer; Director, Michael Mayer; Choreographer, Steven Hoggett; Music Supervisor/Arranger/Orchestrator, Tom Kitt; Sets, Christine Jones; Costumes, Andrea Lauer; Lighting, Kevin Adams; Sound, Brian Ronan; Video/ Projections, Darrel Maloney; Casting, Jim Carnahan, CSA, Carrie Gardner, CSA, Jillian Cimini; PSM, Monica Dickhens; Technical Supervisor, Technical Theater Solutions, LLC, Rhys Williams; General Management, Work Light Productions; Booking & Engagement Management, AWA Touring; Music Director, Jared Stein; Associate Choreographer, Lorin Latarro; Associate Director, Johanna McKeon; Associate Producers, Tracy Strauss & Barney Strauss, John Pinckard, Christopher Maring; Cast: Van Hughes (Johnny), Scott J. Campbell (Tunny), Jake Epstein (Will), Gabrielle McClinton (Whatsername), Nicci Claspell (The Extraordinary Girl), Leslie McDonel (Heather, Dance Captain), Joshua Kobak (St. Jimmy); Ensemble/Understudies: Talia Aaron, Krystina Alabado, Gabriel Antonacci, Larkin Bogan, Jennifer Bowles, Matt DeAngelis, Dan Gleason, Kelvin Moon Loh, Jarran Muse, Okieriete Onaodowan; Swings: Tommy McDowell, Jillian Mueller, Vince Oddo (Assistant Dance Captain); March 13–April 22, 2012

Follies The Kennedy Center Production; Book, James Goldman; Music/Lyrics, Stephen Sondheim; Director, Eric Schaeffer; Choreographer, Warren Carlyle; Music Director, James Moore; Orchestrator, Jonathan Tunick; Sets, Derek McLane; Costumes, Gregg Barnes; Lighting, Natasha Katz; Sound, Kai Harada; Hair/Wigs, David Brian Brown; Make-Up, Joseph Dulude II; PSM, Ray Gin; Associate Director, David Ruttura; Dance Music Arranger, John Berkman; Music Coordinator, John Miller; Casting, Laura Stanczyk Casting; PM, Juniper Street Productions; General Managers, Alan Wasser-Allan Williams, Mark Shacket; Cast: Jan Maxwell (Phyllis Rogers Stone), Victoria Clark (Sally Durant Plummer), Danny Burstein (Buddy Plummer), Ron Raines (Benjamin Stone), Elaine Paige (Carlotta Campion), Obba Babatundé (Max Deems), Christian Delcroix (Young Buddy), Colleen Fitzpatrick (DeeDee West), Lora Lee Gayer (Young Sally), Michael Hayes (Roscoe), Leah Horowitz (Young Heidi), Jayne Houdyshell (Hattie Walker), Florence Lacey (Sandra Crane), Carol Neblett (Heidi Schiller), Mary Beth Peil (Solange LaFitte), David Sabin (Dimitri Weismann), Kristen Scott (Young Phyllis), Nick Verina (Young Ben), Susan Watson (Emily Whitman), Terri White (Stella Deems), Sammy Williams (Theodore Whitman); Ensemble/Understudies/Swings: Alison Briner, John Carroll, Matthew deGuzman (Dance Captain), Sara Edwards (Dance Captain), Nathaniel Flatt, Leslie Donna Flesner, Jennifer Foote, Danielle Jordan, Amanda Kloots-Larsen, Joseph Kolinski, Joe Komara, Erin N. Moore, Pamela Otterson, Jessica Perrizo, Andrew Pirozzi, Angel Reda, Clifton Samuels, Becky Elizabeth Stout, Sam Strasfeld, Sarrah Strimel; May 3–June 9, 2012

War Horse National Theatre of Great Britain production; Based on the novel by Michael Morpurgo; Adaptation, Nick Stafford; In association with Handspring Puppet Company; Original Co-Directors, Marianne Elliott, Tom Morris; U.S. Tour Director, Bijan Sheibani; Sets/Costumes/Drawings, Rae Smith; Puppet Designer/Fabricator/Director, Adrian Kohler with Basil Jones for Handspring Puppet Company; Original Lighting, Paul Constable; Additional Lighting and Adaptation, Karen Spahn; Director of Movement and Horse Choreographer, Toby Sedgwick; Animation/Projections, 59 Productions; Artistic Associate, Samuel Adamson; Creative Associate, Mervyn Millar; Music, Adrian Sutton; Songmaker, John Tams; Sound, Christopher Shutt; Additional Sound and Adaptation, John Owens; Music Director, Greg Pliska; PSM, Eric Insko; Company Manager, Darren E. Doutt; Casting, Daniel Swee; Associate Director, Sarna Lapine; Associate Puppetry Director, Matthew Acheson; Associate Director of Movement and Horse Choreographer, Adrienne Kapstein; Fight Director, Tom Schall; NT Technical Producer, Katrina Gilroy; NT Administrative Producer, Robin Hawkes; NT International GM, Samuel Burgess; NT Marketing, Karl Westworth; Tour Booking, Engagement Management Press and Marketing, Broadway Booking

Office NYC; National Tour Press, The Hartman Group; Executive Producer, Seth Wenig; GM, Gregory Vander Ploeg/Gentry & Associates; PM, Steven Ehrenberg/Eberg Stage Solutions; Cast: Michael Stewart Allen (Allan/Private Klausen), Danny Beiruti (Topthorn/Coco/John Greig), Laurabeth Breya (Joey as a foal/Annie Gilbert), Brian Robert Burns (Joey/Topthorn/Coco/John Greig), Jason Alan Carvell (Thomas Bone/Private Schnabel/Sergeant Fine), Todd Cerveris (Ted Narracott/Colonel Strauss), Michael Wyatt Cox (Billy Narracott/Ludwig), Grayson DeJesus (Captain Charles Stewart/Heine), Catherine Gowl (Joey as a foal/Matron Callaghan), Aaron Haskell (Topthorn/Coco), Jon Hoche (Topthorn/Goose), Mat Hostetler (Veterinary Officer Martin), Chad Jennings (Chapman Carter/Corporal Klebb/Manfred), Brian Keane (Arthur Narracott/Sergeant Thunder), Nathan Koci (Song Man–Instrumental), Jessica Krueger (Joey/Topthorn/Coco/Goose), Nick LaMedica (Joey as a foal), Rob Laqui (Joey/Coco), Megan Loomis (Paulette), Jason Loughlin (Lieutenant James Nicholls/Heine/Doctor Schweyk, Paddy), Christopher Mai (Joey), Gregory Manley (Joey/Topthorn/Coco/ Goose), Andrew May (Captain Friedrich Muller/Priest), John Milosich (Song Man–Vocal), Alex Morf (Private David Taylor), Patrick Osteen (Joey/Topthorn/ Coco/John Greig), Angela Reed (Rose Narracott), Jon Riddleberger (Joey/Topthorn), Lavita Shaurice (Emilie), Derek Stratton (Joey/Coco/John Greig), Andrew Veenstra (Albert Narracott), Danny Yoerges (Joey/Topthorn); Understudies: Brooks Brantly, Mike Heslin; June 14–July 29, 2012

MARK TAPER FORUM

Vigil The American Conservatory Theater production; Writer/Director, Morris Panych; Sets/Costumes, Ken MacDonald; Lighting, Alan Brodie, Robert Hahn; Original Music/Sound, Meg Roe, Alessandro Juliani; Sound, Cricket S. Myers; Original Casting, Meryl Lind Shaw; Associate Artistic Director, Neel Keller; PSM, David S. Franklin; SM, Michelle Blair; Cast: Marco Barricelli (Kemp), Olympia Dukakis (Grace); Understudies: Gregory North, Mary Eileen O'Donnell; November 2–December 18, 2011

Clybourne Park The Playwrights Horizons Production; by Bruce Norris; Director, Pam MacKinnon; Sets, Daniel Ostling; Costumes, Ilona Somogyi; Lighting, Allen Lee Hughes; Sound, John Gromada; Hair/Wigs, Charles Lapointe; Casting, Alaine Alldaffer; Associate Artistic Director, Kelley Kirkpatrick; PSM, C.A. Clark; Cast: Crystal A. Dickinson (Francine/Lena), Brendan Griffin (Jim/Tom/Kenneth), Damon Gupton (Albert/Kevin), Christina Kirk (Bev/Kathy), Annie Parisse (Betsy/Lindsey), Jeremy Shamos (Karl/Steve), Frank Wood (Russ/Dan); Understudies: Tanya Alexander, Roger Bridges, Barnaby Carpenter, Matthew Jaeger, Kate Steele; January 11–February 26, 2012

Waiting for Godot by Samuel Beckett; Director, Michael Arabian; Sets, John Iacovelli; Costumes, Christopher Acebo; Lighting/Projections, Brian Gale; Casting, Erika Sellin; Dramaturg, Joy Meads; Associate Artistic Director, Neel Keller; PSM, David S. Franklin; SM, Susie Walsh; Consultant to the production, Rick Cluchey; Cast: Alan Mandell (Estragon), Barry McGovern (Vladimir), James Cromwell (Pozzo), Hugo Armstrong (Lucky), LJ Benet (Boy); Understudies: Mark Bramhall, Jan Munroe, Jarid Root; March 14–April 22, 2012

Los Otros Book/Lyrics, Ellen Fitzhugh; Music, Michael John LaChiusa; Director, Graciela Daniele; Sets, Christopher Barreca; Costumes, Ann Hould-Ward; Lighting, Jules Fisher, Peggy Eisenhauer; Sound, Jon Weston; Orchestrator, Bruce Coughlin; Music Director, Chris Fenwick; Casting, Mark Simon; Associate Artistic Director, Kelley Kirkpatrick; PSM, David S. Franklin; SM, Michelle Blair, Matthew Silver; Cast: Julio Monge (Man), Michelle Pawk (Woman); Understudies: Susann Fletcher, Joseph Melendez; World Premiere; Commissioned by Center Theatre Group; May 23–July 1, 2012

Chicago Shakespeare Theater

Chicago, Illinois

Twenty-fifth Anniversary Season

Artistic Director, Barbara Gaines; Executive Director, Criss Henderson; Creative Producer, Rick Boynton; Associate Artistic Director, Gary Griffin; Artistic Associate/Casting Director, Bob Mason

Murder for Two—A Killer Musical A CST New Classic developed by Rick Boynton; Book and music by Joe Kinosian; Book and lyrics by Kellen Blair; Director, David H. Bell; Sets, Scott Davis; Costumes, Jeremy W. Floyd; Lighting, Jesse Klug; Sound, James Savage; Music Director, Roberta Duchak; PSM, Claire E. Zawa (May 12–June 5, September 5–November 27), Rebecca Green (June 6–September 4); ASM, Amanda Davis; Cast: Joe Kinosian (The Suspects), Alan Schmuckler (Officer Marcus Moscowicz [May 12–October 16]), Adam Overett (Officer Marcus Moscowicz [October 17–November 27]); Upstairs at Chicago Shakespeare; May 12– November 27, 2011

The Adventures of Pinocchio A CST Family Production developed by Rick Boynton; Music and lyrics by Neil Bartram; Book by Brian Hill; Director/Choreographer, Rachel Rockwell; Sets, Kevin Depinet; Costumes, Rachel Anne Healy; Lighting, Jesse Klug; Sound, James Savage; Puppetry, Meredith Miller; Wigs/Make-up, Melissa Veal; PSM, Deborah Acker; ASM, Sheila Schmidt, Angela M. Adams; Cast: Skyler Adams (Pinocchio), Don Forston (Geppetto), Melody Betts (Storyteller), Derek Hasenstab (Fox), Heidi Kettenring (Cat, July 13-31), Ericka Mac (Cat, August 3–28), Liz Pazik (Driver), Ron Rains (Puppet Master), Dylan Saunders (Lampwick), Hannah Sielatycki (Mary), Katie Spelman (Annette); Chicago Shakespeare Theater's Courtyard Theater; July 13–August 28, 2011

Follies Book by James Goldman; Music and lyrics by Stephen Sondheim; Director, Gary Griffin; Produced originally on Broadway by Harold Prince; Orchestrations by Jonathan Tunick; by special arrangement with Cameron Mackintosh; Choreographer, Alex Sanchez; Music Director, Brad Haak; Associate Music Director/Conductor, Valerie Maze; Sets, Kevin Depinet; Costumes, Virgil C. Johnson; Lighting, Christine Binder; Sound, Joshua Horvath and Ray Nardelli; Wigs/Make-up, Melissa Veal; Orchestral Reductions, David Siegel; PSM, Deborah Acker; ASM, Sharon Wilson Miller, Angela M. Adams; Cast: Adrian Aguilar (Young Ben), Devin Archer (Ensemble), Brent Barrett (Benjamin Stone), Marilynn Bogetich (Hattie Walker), Rachel Cantor (Young Phyllis), Julius C. Carter (Ensemble), Bill Chamberlain (Roscoe), L.R. Davidson (Young Sally), Jen Donohoo (Showgirl), David Elliott (Max Deems), Jenny Guse (Ensemble), Rhett Guter (Kevin), Dennis Kelly (Theodore Whitman), Andrew Keltz (Young Buddy), Amanda Kroiss (Young Solange), Nate Lewellyn (Ensemble), Susan Moniz (Sally Durant Plummer), Christina Myers (Young Stella), Mike Nussbaum (Dimitri Weismann), Caroline O'Connor (Phyllis Rogers Stone), Robert Petkoff (Buddy Plummer), Hollis Resnik (Carlotta Campion), Ami Silvestre (Emily Whitman), Tanner Smale (Ensemble), Kari Sorenson (Young Heidi), Linda Stephens (Heidi Schiller), Amanda Tanguay (Margie/Young Carlotta), Kathy Taylor (Solange LaFitte), Nancy Voigts (Stella Deems); Chicago Shakespeare Theater's Courtyard Theater; October 4–November 13, 2011

Elizabeth Rex Written by Timothy Findley; Director, Barbara Gaines; Sets, Daniel Ostling; Costumes, Mariann S. Verheyen; Lighting, Philip S. Rosenberg; Sound, Lindsay Jones; Original Music, Jenny Giering; Wigs/Make-up, Melissa Veal; Dialect, Eva Breneman; Choreographer, Tammy Mader; Fight Director, John McFarland; Bear Movement Coach, Janet Louer; PSM, Deborah Acker; ASM, Calyn P. Swain, Amy M. Bertacini; Cast: Bradley Armacost (Percy Gower), Brenda Barrie (Mary Stanley), Diane D'Aquila (Queen Elizabeth I), Matt Farabee (Harry Pearle), Kevin Gudahl (William Shakespeare), Torrey Hanson (Lord Robert Cecil), Anthony Kayer (Ensemble Intern), Eric Parks (Matthew Welle), Chase Pavlick (Ensemble Intern), Roderick Peeples (Luddy Beddoes), Jude Roche (The Bear), Andrew Rothenberg (Jack Edmund), Steven Sutcliffe (Ned Lowenscroft), Mary Ann Thebus (Kate Tardwell); Chicago Shakespeare Theater's Courtyard Theater; November 29, 2011–January 22, 2012

The Feast: an intimate Tempest A CST New Classic developed by Rick Boynton; Co-created and co-directed by Jessica Thebus and Frank Maugeri; Adaptation, Jessica Thebus; Designer, Frank Maugeri; based on the play by William Shakespeare; Scenic Engineer, Neil Verplank; Art Director/2D and Silhouette Puppetry, Andrea Everman; 3D Puppetry, Jesse Mooney-Bullock; Co-Costumes, Sue Haas and Anna Glowacki; Sound/Composer, Jefferey Allen Thomas; Projections, Mike Tutaj; Lighting, Andrew H. Myers; PSM, Angela M. Adams; Cast: Adrian Danzig; (Caliban), John Judd (Prospero), Samuel Taylor (Ariel), Sarah Addison Ely (Puppeteer), Dustin Valenta (Puppeteer); Upstairs at Chicago Shakespeare; January 18–March 11, 2012

A Midsummer Night's Dream Written by William Shakespeare; Director, Gary Griffin; Sets, Daniel Ostling; Costumes, Mara Blumenfeld; Lighting, Philip S. Rosenberg; Projections, Mike Tutaj; Composer, Sound and Music Directors, Rob Milburn, Michael Bodeen; Wigs/Make-up, Melissa Veal; Fight Director, David Woolley; Choreographer, Matt Raftery; Verse Coach, Kevin Gudahl; PSM, Deborah Acker; ASM, Sheila Schmidt, Angela M. Adams; Cast: Matthew Abraham (Changeling Boy), Tracy Michelle Arnold (Hippolyta/Titania), Heidi Buyck (Ensemble Intern), Kurt Ehrmann (Egeus), Tim Gittings (Ensemble), Laura Huizenga (Helena), Chase Jones (Changeling Boy), Timothy Edward Kane (Theseus/Oberon), Tim Kazurinsky (Peter Quince), Elizabeth Ledo (Puck), Michael Aaron Linder (Snout/Mustardseed), Richard Manera (Snug/Cobweb), Evan Michalic (Ensemble Intern), Christina Nieves (Hermia), Ron Orbach (Bottom), Sean Parris (Philostrate/Thistle), Levenix Riddle (Flute/Peaseblossom), Matt Schwader (Demetrius), Rod Thomas (Starveling/Moth), Andy Truschinski (Lysander), Emma van Ommeren (Ensemble Intern); Chicago Shakespeare Theater's Courtyard Theater; February 7–April 8, 2012

Short Shakespeare! The Taming of the Shrew Written by William Shakespeare; Adapted and directed by Rachel Rockwell; Sets, Kevin Depinet; Costumes, Jacqueline Firkins; Lighting, Jesse Klug; Sound, James Savage; Composer, Kevin O'Donnell; Wigs/Make-up, Melissa Veal; Verse Coach, Kevin Gudahl; PSM, Claire E. Zawa; ASM, Amy M. Bertacini; Cast: Jeffrey Baumgartner (Vincentio/Peter), Tiffany Yvonne Cox (Bianca), Jessie Fisher (Biondella), Don Forston (Baptista Minola), José Antonio García (Curtis), Alex Goodrich (Tranio), Nicholas Harazin (Lucentio), Eric Leonard (Pedant/Widow), Terrence Mosley (Grumio), Matt Mueller (Petruchio), Ericka Ratcliff (Katharina), Matthew Sherbach (Hortensio), Mick Weber (Gremio); Chicago Shakespeare's Courtyard Theater; February 25–April 7, 2012

Othello: The Remix Developed with CST Creative Producer Rick Boynton; Written, directed, and music by GQ and JQ; Costumes/Sets, Scott Davis; Wigs, Melissa Veal; Additional Vocals, Sophie Grimm; PSM, Angela M. Adams; Cast: Jackson Doran (Cassio/Emilia), GQ (Iago/Brabantio), JQ (Roderigo/Loco Vito/Bianca), Postell Pringle (Othello), Clayton Stamper (DJ); On tour in London at the Globe Festival; May 5–6, 2012

Timon of Athens Written by William Shakespeare; Director, Barbara Gaines; Sets, Daniel Ostling; Costumes, Susan E. Mickey; Lighting, Robert Wierzel; Projections, Mike Tutaj; Original Music/Sound, Lindsay Jones; Wigs/Make-up, Melissa Veal; Fight Director, James Newcomb; Choreographer, Nicolas Blanc; Verse Coach, Kevin Gudahl; PSM, Deborah Acker; ASM, Calyn P. Swain; Cast: Sean Blake (Timander/Ensemble), John Byrnes (Caphis/Ensemble), Danforth Comins (Alcibiades), Wesley Daniel (Ensemble Intern), William Dick (Jeweller/Senator), Jen Donohoo (Dancer/Dance Captain/Ensemble), Sean Fortunato (Flavius), Kevin Gudahl (Writer/Judge), Terry Hamilton (Old Senator/Ventidius/Senator), Robert Hope (Leonatus/Ensemble), Timothy Edward Kane (Artist), Noelle Kayser (Dancer/Ensemble), David Lively (Sempronius), Luke Manley (Dancer/Ensemble), Ian McDiarmid (Timon), James Newcomb (Apemantus), Bianca L. Sanders (Dancer/Ensemble), David Schlumpf (Ensemble Intern/Antonius), Malachi Squires (Dancer/Ensemble), Samuel Taylor (Lucius/Mercenary/Ensemble), Demetrios Troy (Banker/Varro/Mercenary/Ensemble), Bruce A. Young (Lucullus); Chicago Shakespeare Theater's Courtyard Theater; April 24–June 10, 2012

Cincinnati Playhouse in the Park

Cincinnati, Ohio

Fifty-second Season

Producing Artistic Director, Edward Stern; Executive Director, Buzz Ward

ROBERT S. MARX THEATRE

God of Carnage by Yasmina Reza, translated by Christopher Hampton; Director, Edward Stern; Sets, Narelle Sissons; Costumes, Gordon DeVinney; Lighting, Kirk Bookman, Steve O'Shea; Fight Director, Drew Fracher; PSM, Jenifer Morrow; Cast: Eva Kaminsky (Veronica Novak), Anthony Marble (Alan Raleigh), Triney Sandoval (Michael Novak), Susan Louise O'Connor (Annette Raleigh); September 3–October 1, 2011

Red by John Logan; Director, Steven Woolf; Sets, Michael Ganio; Costumes, Dorothy Marshall Englis; Lighting, Phil Monat; Sound, Rusty Wandall; Music Consultant, Jeffrey Richard Carter; SM, Joseph Millett; Cast: Brian Dykstra (Mark Rothko), Matthew Carlson (Ken); October 15–November 12, 2011

A Christmas Carol by Charles Dickens; Adapted by Howard Dallin; Director, Michael Evan Haney; Sets, James Leonard Joy; Costumes, David Murin; Lighting, Kirk Bookman; Sound/Composer, David B. Smith; Lighting Contractor, Susan Terrano; Costume Coordinator, Cindy Witherspoon; Music Director, Rebecca N. Childs; Choreographer, Dee Anne Bryll; SM, Andrea L. Shell; Cast: Bruce Cromer (Ebenezer Scrooge), Nick Rose (Mr. Cupp/Percy/Rich Man at Fezziwig's), Stephen Skiles (Mr. Sosser/Topper/Man with Shoe Shine/Guest at Fezziwig's), Andy Prosky (Bob Cratchit/Schoolmaster Oxlip), Craig Wesley Divino (Fred), Gregory Procaccino (Jacob Marley/Old Joe), Dale Hodges (Ghost of Christmas Past/Mrs. Peake), Noah Lentini (Boy Scrooge/Guest at Fezziwig's/Bootblack/Streets), Isabella Siska (Fan/Rich Daughter at Fezziwig's/Streets), Keith Jochim (Mr. Fezziwig/Ghost of Christmas Present), Amy Warner (Mrs. Fezziwig/Patience/Streets), Greg Mallios (Dick Wilkins/Streets), Lormarev Jones (Scrubwoman[Mary] at Fezziwig's/Caroler/Streets), Avery Clark (Young and Mature Scrooge/Ghost of Christmas Future), Joy Farmer-Clary (Belle/Catherine Margaret), Carlos Saldaña (Constable at Fezziwig's/Poulterer/Streets), Regina Pugh (Mrs. Cratchit/Laundress at Fezziwig's/Streets), Jack Johnson (Peter Cratchit/Gregory/Apprentice at Fezziwig's/Streets), Allison Edwards (Belinda Cratchit/Guest at Fezziwig's/Streets), Naomi Stoner (Martha Cratchit/Guest at Fezziwig's/Streets), Von Eric Huhn (Tiny Tim), Lara Miller (Rose/Guest at Fezziwig's/Streets), Riley Nattermann (Ignorance/Matthew/Rich Son at Fezziwig's/Streets), N'Doumbe Ngom (Want/Guest at Fezziwig's/Streets), Ben Sullivan (Man with Pipe/Guest at Fezziwig's/Streets), Margaret Ivey (Mrs. Dilber/Caroler/Guest at Fezziwig's/Streets), Aram Monisoff (Undertaker/Caroler/Guest at Fezziwig's/Streets), Carrington Shropshire (George/Charles/Apprentice at Fezziwig's/Streets), Katherine Leigh (Caroler/Guest at Fezziwig's/Streets); December 1–30, 2011

Dead Accounts by Theresa Rebeck; Director, Giovanna Sardelli; Sets, Scott Bradley; Costumes, Clint Ramos; Lighting, Japhy Weideman; Sound/Composer, Jeremy J. Lee; SM, Joseph Millett; Cast: Stephen Barker Turner (Jack), Carly Street (Lorna), Susan Greenhill (Barbara), Haynes Thigpen (Phil), Victoria Mack (Jenny); World Premiere; January 14–February 11, 2012

Merrily We Roll Along Music and lyrics by Stephen Sondheim; Book by George Furth, based on the original play by George S. Kaufman and Moss Hart; Orchestrations by Jonathan Tunick; Director, John Doyle; Music Supervisor/Orchestrator, Mary-Mitchell Campbell; Music Director, Matt Castle; Sets, Scott Pask; Costumes, Ann Hould-Ward; Lighting, Jane Cox; Sound, Dan Moses Schreier; SM, Andrea L. Shell; Cast: Becky Ann Baker (Mary Flynn), Matt Castle (Scotty), Matthew Deming (Ru), Ben Diskant (Frank, Jr.), David Garry (Jerome), Malcolm Gets (Franklin Shepard), Lee Harrington (Meg), Daniel Jenkins (Charley Kringas), Jane Pfitsch (Beth), Leenya Rideout (Gussie Carnegie), Fred Rose (Tyler), Bruce Sabath (Joe Josephson), Jessica Tyler Wright (K.T.); March 3–31, 2012

Thunder Knocking on the Door by Keith Glover; Music and lyrics by Keb' Mo' and Anderson Edwards; Additional music and lyrics by Keith Glover; Director, Keith Glover; Choreographer, Kenneth L. Roberson; Music Director, Michael Leroy Peed; Sets, David Gallo; Costumes, Paul Tazewell; Lighting, Thomas C. Hase; Sound, David B. Smith; Illusions, James Steinmeyer; Costume Coordinator, Kara Harmon; PSM, Jenifer Morrow; Cast: David St. Louis (Marvell Thunder), Terry Burrell (Good Sister Dupree), Timothy Ware (Jaguar Dupree, Jr.), Jennie Harney (Glory Dupree), Trent Armand Kendall (Jaguar Dupree, Sr./Dregster Dupree); Steve Ditzell (Guitar), Billy Thompson (Guitar, Harmonica), Michael Leroy Peed (Keyboards), Art Gore (Drums), Larry C. Humphrey (Bass); April 21–May 20, 2012

THOMPSON SHELTERHOUSE THEATRE

As You Like It by William Shakespeare; Co-Directors, Edward Stern, Michael Evan Haney; Sets, Joseph P. Tilford; Costumes, Susan Tsu; Lighting, Thomas C. Hase; Composers, Douglas Lowry and Michael Murnoch; Voice/Text Consultant, Phillip Thompson; Fight Director, Drew Fracher; SM, Andrea L. Shell; Cast: Alvin Keith (Orlando), Joneal Joplin (Adam/Sir Oliver Martext), Michael Gabriel Goodfriend (Oliver), Aram Monisoff (Dennis/Lord at the Court/Duke Senior's Lord/William), Brendan Averett (Charles/Corin), Francesca Choy-Kee (Celia), Sarah Dandridge (Rosalind), David Graham Jones (Touchstone), Bob Braswell (Le Beau/Silvius), Chris Hietikko (Duke Frederick), Carlos Saldaña (Lord at the Court/Duke Senior's Lord/Jaques de Boys), Ben Sullivan (Lord at the Court/Duke Senior's Lord), Duke Senior (Christopher McHale), Michael Murnoch (Amiens), Matt D'Amico (Jaques), Katherine Leigh (Audrey), Rebeca Miller (Phoebe); October 1–November 6, 2011

Always … Patsy Cline Written and originally directed by Ted Swindley; Director, Randal Myler; Music Director, Michael Sebastian; Sets, Vicki Smith; Costumes, Gordon DeVinney; Lighting, Betsy Adams; Sound, Timothy J. Ryan; PSM, Jenifer Morrow; SM, Suann Pollock; Cast: Carter Calvert (Patsy), Kathleen M. Brady (Louise); November 19, 2011–January 22, 2012

Speaking in Tongues by Andrew Bovell; Director, Michael Evan Haney; Sets, Paul Shortt; Costumes, Kristine Kearney; Lighting, Kirk Bookman; Sound/Composer, Fabian Obispo; Choreographer, Mario de la Nuez; PSM, Jenifer Morrow; Cast: R. Ward Duffy (Leon/Nick), Amy Warner (Sonja/Valerie), Henny Russell (Jane/Sarah), Bruce Cromer (Pete/Neil/John); February 4–March 4, 2012

Tigers Be Still by Kim Rosenstock; Director, Rob Ruggiero; Sets, Michael Schweikardt; Costumes, Gordon DeVinney; Lighting, John Lasiter; Sound, Vincent Olivieri; SM, Joseph Millett; Cast: Lindsey Kyler (Sherry), Darrin Baker (Joseph), Eric Nelsen (Zack), Joanne Tucker (Grace); March 17–April 15, 2012

The Second City 2: Less Pride … More Pork by Ed Furman and Dana Quercioli, with additional material created by the casts of The Second City; Director, Mick Napier; Music Director, Matthew Loren Cohen; Lighting, Mark C. Williams; SM, Andrea L. Shell; Ensemble: Cody Dove, Sayjal Joshi, Amy Roeder, John Sabine, Tim Stoltenberg, Travis Turner; World Premiere; April 29–July 1, 2012

Cleveland Play House

Cleveland, Ohio

Ninety-sixth Season

Artistic Director, Michael Bloom; Associate Artistic Director, Laura Kepley; Managing Director, Kevin Moore; Director of Administration, Kevin Kruse

ALLEN THEATRE

The Life of Galileo by Bertolt Brecht (Translation by David Edga); Director, Michael Donald Edwards; Sets/Costumes, Clint Ramos; Lighting, Peter West; Projections, Dan Scully; Sound, Fabian Obispo; Movement Specialist, Pandora Robertson; Assistant Director, Nathan Motta; Child Wrangler, Jamie Benetto; Cast: Sheldon Best (Andrea Sarti), Stephen Caffrey (Sagredo), Robert Ellis (Federzoni/

Vanni/Old Cardinal), Aric Floyd (Andrea Sarti, as boy), Eva Gil (Masked Guest #4/Lead F Performer), Philip Goodwin (Cardinal Inquisitor), Andrew Gorell (Senator #3/Prelate/Sec #1), Jeffrey Grover (Doge of Venice/Rector), Dan Hendrock (Senator #1/Masked Guest #3), Michael Herbert (Roman Monk/Masked Guest #4), Alex Hernandez (Ludovico), Charles Kartali (Bursar/Cardinal Barberini), Jeremy Kendall (Little Monk) Kim Krane (Woman #1/Virginia Galilei), Christian Prentice (Lord Chamberlain/2nd Astronomer), Jonathan Ramos (Angel Singer/1st Astronomer), Kelli Ruttle (Masked Guest #3/Street Performer), Myra Lucretia Taylor (Signora), Yan Tual (Theologian, Scholar, Secretary #2), Thomas Weil (Cosimo de Medici, as boy), Paul Whiteworth (Galileo Galilei); September 17–October 9, 2011

Daddy Long Legs by John Caird (Adapted from the novel by Jean Webster); Music and lyrics by Paul Gordon; Associate Director, Nell Balaban; Music Director, Laura Bergquist; Lighting, Paul Toben; Assistant Lighting, Cory Pattak; Technical Director, David King; Cast: Robert Adelman Hancock (Jervis Pendleton), Megan McGinnis (Jerusha Abbott); October 21–November 13, 2011

The Game's Afoot by Ken Ludwig; Director, Aaron Posner; Assistant Director, Marie Sproul; SM, Shannon Habenicht; PA, Katy Herman; Lighting, Dan Conway, Whom Weaver; Costumes, Linda Roethke; Sound, James Swonger; Cast: Lise Bruneau (Madge Geisel), Sarah Day (Inspector Goring), Mattie Hawkinson (Aggie), Eric Hissom (Felix), Patricia Kilgarriff (Martha Gillette), Donald Sage Mackay (William Gillette), Rob McClure (Simon Bright), Erika Rolfsrud (Daria Chase); December 2–24, 2011

Radio Golf by August Wilson; Director, Lou Bellamy; Lighting, Don Darnutzer; Assistant Lighting, Jane Spencer; Sets, Vicki Smith; Costumes, Karen Perry; Cast: David Alan Anderson (Roosevelt Hicks), Terry Bellamy (Sterling Johnson), James Craven (Harmond Wilks), Abdul Salaamel Razzac (Elder), Austene Wan (Mame Wilks); Co-Production with Indiana Repertory Theatre; February 11–29, 2012

Red Written by John Logan; Director, Anders Cato; Sets, Lee Savage; Costumes, Jennifer Moeller; Lighting, Dan Kotlowitz; Sound, Scott Killian; Cast: Bob Ari (Mark Rothko), Randy Harrison (Ken); March 23–April 4, 2012

SECOND STAGE

Ten Chimneys by Jeffrey Hatcher; Director, Michael Bloom; Sets, Lee Savage; Costumes, David Mickelsen; Lighting, Michael Lincoln; Sound, Lindsay Jones; Assistant Lighting, Carolyn Voss; Cast: Jordon Baker (Lynn Fontanne), Donald Carrier (Alfred Lunt), Mariette Hartley (Hattie Sederholm), Jeremy Kendall (Carl Sederholm), Michael McCarty (Sydney Greenstreet), Gail Rastorfer (Louise Greene), Kelli Ruttle (Uta Hagen); January 19–February 1, 2012

In The Next Room, (or the vibrator play) Written by Sarah Ruhl; Director, Laura Kepley; Lighting, Michael Boll; Sets, Michael Raiford; Costumes, David K. Mickelsen; Sound, Jane Shaw; Cast: Donald Carrier (Mr. Daldry), Zac Hoogendyk (Leo Irving), Birgit Huppuch (Mrs. Daldry), Rachel Leslie (Elizabeth), Gail Rastorfer (Annie), Nini Sturgis (Mrs. Givings), Jeremiah Wiggins (Dr. Givings); April 12–May 13, 2012

Dallas Theater Center

Dallas, Texas

Fifty-third Season

Artistic Director, Kevin Moriarty; Managing Director, Heather Kitchen

The Tempest by William Shakespeare; Director, Kevin Moriarty; Sets, Beowulf Boritt; Costumes, Beowulf Boritt; Lighting, Clifton Taylor; Sound, Broken Chord; PSM, Kevin Bertolacci; ASM, Megan Winters; Cast: J. Brent Alford (Antonio), Christopher Carlos (Sebastian), Chamblee Ferguson (Prospero), John Paul Green (Adrian), Hunter Ryan Herdlicka (Ariel), John Dana Kenning (Francisco), Cliff Miller (Trinculo), Joe Nemmers (Caliban), David Price (Boatswain/Master of the King's ship), Jerry Russell (Gonzalo), Abbey Siegworth (Miranda), Matthew Tomlanovich (Alonso), Lee Trull (Stephano), Steven Michael Walters (Ferdinand); September 9–October 9, 2011

To Kill a Mockingbird Adapted by Christopher Sergel from the novel by Harper Lee; Director, Wendy Dann; Sets, Donna Marquet; Costumes, Jennifer Ables; Lighting, Brian Sidney Bembridge; Sound, Sarah Pickett; PSM, Leigh'Ann Andrews; ASM, Jordan Kelly Andrews; Cast: Akin Babatunde (Reverend Sikes), Pam Dougherty (Mrs. Dubose), Greg Dulcie (Judge/Cunningham), James Dybas (Bob Ewell), Matthew Gray (Heck Tate), Bob Hess (Mr. Gilmer), Dawson Holder (Walter/David Allen Norton u/s), Aidan Langford (Dill), Denise Lee (Calpurnia), Hayley Lenamon (Morgan Richards u/s), Anastasia Munoz (Mayella), David Allen Norton (Jem), Van Quattro (Boo Radley), Bob Reed (Doctor/Clerk), Morgan Richards (Scout), Cuatro Roman (Aidan Langford u/s/Dawson Holder), Sally Nystuen Vahle (Miss Maudie/Dialect Coach), Akron Watson (Tom Robinson); October 21–November 20, 2011

A Christmas Carol by Charles Dickens; Adapted by Richard Hellesen; Director and Choreographer, Joel Ferrell; Music Director, Lindy Heath Cabe; Sets, Bob Lavallee; Costumes, Wade Laboissonniere; Lighting, Matthew Richards; Sound, Curtis Craig; PSM, Caron Gitelman Grant; ASM, Korey Kent; Cast: Tatiana Angustia (Belinda Cratchit/Ensemble), Wendy Blackburn (Fan/Martha Cratchit/Ensemble), Jonathan Brooks (The Ghost of Jacob Marley/Topper/Ensemble), Trey Cheatham (Edward Cratchit/Ensemble), Drew Favors (Edward Cratchit/Ensemble), Mark Fisher (Ebenezer the Child/Tiny Tim/Ensemble), Vanessa Gibens (Belle/The Laundress/Ensemble), Emily Gray (Mrs. Fezziwig /The Charwoman/Ensemble), Ashley Puckett Gonzales (Fred's Wife/Ensemble), Brian Gonzales (Fezziwig/Second Subscription Gentleman/Old Joe/Ensemble), Nathan May (Peter Cratchit/Ensemble), Jason Moody (Dick Wilkins/The Undertaker's Man/Ensemble/Assistant Director), Marlhy Murphy (Beggar Child/Ensemble), Kuran Patel (Ebenezer the Child/Tiny Tim/Ensemble), Paloma Renteria (Belinda Cratchit/Ensemble), Kurt Rhoads (Ebenezer Scrooge), Lauren Riley (Beggar Child/Ensemble), Alex Ross (Ebenezer the Apprentice/Ensemble), Joanna Schellenberg (Mrs. Cratchit/Ensemble), Abbey Siegworth (Ghost of Christmas Past/Fred's Wife's Sister/Ensemble), David Ryan Smith (Ghost of Christmas Present/First Subscription Gentleman/ Ensemble), Lee Trull (Bob Cratchit/Belle's Husband/Ensemble), Ben Villaseñor (Peter Cratchit/Ensemble), Steven Michael Walters (Fred/A Fiddler/Ensemble); November 25–December 24, 2011

Giant by Edna Ferber; Music and lyrics by Michael John Lachiusa; Book by Sybille Pearson; Director, Michael Greif; Choreographer, Alex Sanchez; Music Director/Conductor, Chris Fenwick; Orchestrator, Brusce Coughlin; Sets, Allen Moyer; Costumes, Jeff Mahshie; Lighting, Kenneth Posner; Sound, Brian Roman; Fight Choreographer, Chris Hury; PSM, Judith Schoenfeld; ASM, Allison Cotrell; ASM, Eric Tysinger; Cast: Enrique Acevedo (Miguel/Others), Raul Aranas (Polo/Others), Mary Bacon (Adarene/Mrs. Nancy Lynnton/Others), Kate Baldwin (Leslie Lynnton Benedict), Miguel Cervantes (Angel Obregón/Jr & Sr/Others), Natalie Cortez (Juana Guerra Benedict/Others), Rocio Del Mar Valles (Analita/Others), John Dossett (Uncle Bawley Benedict), Matt Doyle (Jordy Bendict/Jr/Others), Andrea Lynn Green (Lil' Luz Benedict/Others), PJ Griffith (Jett Rink), Michael Halling (Lord Karfrey/Others), Jason Hite (Bobby Dietz/Jr & Sr/Others), Dee Hoty (Luz Benedict), Aaron Lazar (Jordan 'Bick' Benedict), Brian Mathis (Uncle Bawley u/s), Doreen Montalvo (Lupe/Others), Allison Rogers (Heidi/Lady Karfrey/Others), Isabel Santiago (Mrs. Obregon/Petra/Others), Martín Sola (Dimodeo/Others), Matthew Stocke (Mike/Others), Katie Thompson (Vashti Snythe/Others), William Youmans (Morty 'Pinkie' Snythe/Others); January 18–February 19, 2012

Tigers Be Still by Kim Rosenstock; Director, Hal Brooks; Sets, John Arnone; Costumes, Claudia Stephens; Lighting, Seth Riser; Sound, Ryan Rumery; PSM, Megan Winters; Cast: Chamblee Ferguson (Joseph), Aleisha Force (Grace), Abbey Siegworth (Sherry), Christopher Sykes (Zack); March 2–May 13, 2012

Next Fall by Geoffrey Nauffts; Director, Kevin Moriarty; Sets, John Arnone; Costumes, Thomas Charles LeGalley; Lighting, Natalie Rubin; Sound, Bruce Richardson; PSM, Laura Maerz; Cast: Lynn Blackburn (Holly), Candy Buckley (Arlene), Kieran Connolly (Butch), Terry Martin (Adam), Lee Trull (Brandon), Steven Michael Walters (Luke); April 13–May 6, 2012

God Of Carnage by Yasmina Reza; Director, Joel Ferrell; Sets, John Arnone;

Costumes, Thomas Charles LeGalley; Lighting, Natalie Rubin; Sound, Bruce Richardson; PSM, Kathryn Davies; Cast: Hassan El-Amin (Michael), Chris Hury (Alan), Sally Nystuen-Vahle (Annette), Christie Vela (Veronica); May 11–June 17, 2012

A Christmas Carol Lyrics by Tim Rice; Music by Andrew Lloyd Webber; Director and Choreographer, Joel Ferrell; Sets, Bob Lavallee; Music Director, Eugene Gqotzdz; Costumes, Wade Laboissonniere; Lighting, Grant Yaeger and Jeff Croiter; Sound, Charles Parsely II; PSM, Eric Tysinger; ASM, Chris Wathen; Cast: Josh A. Dawson (Zebulon/Baker/Ensemble), Jeremy Dumont (Gad/Ensemble/Youth Director), Chamblee Ferguson (Jacob/Potiphar/Pharaoh), Alyssa Franks (Ensemble), Kayla Grizzard (Wife/Ensemble), Jacob Gutierrez (Dan/Ensemble), Sydney James Harcourt (Joseph), Tiffany Hobbs (Wife/Ensemble), Shannon Hucker (Wife/Ensemble), Chavis Humphrey (Ensemble), Rashan James II (Naphthali/Ensemble), Tiffany Mann (Wife/Ensemble), Liz Mikel (Narrator), Jp Moraga (Levi/Ensemble), Tanner Murray (Ensemble), Bob Reed (Reuben/Butler), Jamard Richardson (Judah/Ensemble) Alex Ross (Issachar/Ensemble) Michael Anthony Sylvester (Asher/Ensemble) Liam Taylor (Benjamin/Ensemble) Christie Vela (Jacob's wife/Potiphar's wife) Ben Villaseñor (Benjamin/Ensemble) Ruby Westfall (Ensemble) Kent Zimmerman (Simeon/Ensemble/Associate Choreographer); June 22–August 12, 2012

Delaware Theatre Company

Wilmington, Delaware

Thirty-Third Season

Executive Director, Mary Ann Ehlshlager

All My Sons by Arthur Miller; Director, David Stradley; Sets, Matthew Myhrum; Costumes, Jessica Risser-Milne; Lighting, Shelley Hicklin; Sound, Michael Kiley; PSM, Jessica Simkins; ASM, Bayla Rubin; Cast: P.J. Benjamin (Joe Keller), Anne-Marie Cusson (Kate Keller), Robert Eli (Chris Keller), Maia DeSanti (Ann Deever), Jered McLenigan (George Deever), Fran Prisco (Dr. Jim Bayliss), Christie Parker (Sue Bayliss), Jared Michael Delaney (Frank Lubey), Maggie Lakis (Lydia Lubey), Elijah Shepphard (Bert); October 19–November 6, 2011

A Capella Humana A World Premiere Musical Created by Kevin Ramsey; Co-Writer, Pearl Ramsey; Director, Kevin Ramsey; Music Direction, Jeremy Cohen; Sets, Matthew Myhrum; Costumes, Janus Stefanowicz; Lighting, Joshua Schulman; Sound, Joel Farley; Vocal Arranger, Jeremy Hitch, Raimundo Santos, Randi Stanley; PSM, Jessica Simkins; ASM, Tanya Leppert; Dance Captain, Clinton Derricks-Carroll; Cast: Daniella Dalli (Balthazar Republic), Clinton Derricks-Carroll (Joseph), Jannie Jones (Melchior Democratic), Mykal Kilgore (Emmanuel), David Marmanillo (Gaspar Free Nation), Chesney Snow (Lil Drummer B-Boi), Katie Zaffrann (Mary), Daniel Delaney (Cellist); November 30–December 18, 2011

Time Stands Still by Donald Margulies; Director, Bud Martin; Sets, Dirk Durossette; Costumes, Brian Strachan; Lighting, James Leitner; Sound, David O'Connor; PSM, Marguerite Price; ASM, Allie Steele; Asst. Director, Bill D'Agostino; Cast: Kevin Kelly (James Dodd), Susan McKey (Sarah Goodwin), Bruce Graham (Richard Ehrlich), Megan McDermott (Mandy Bloom); Delaware Theatre Company, January 18–February 5, 2012; Co-production with Act II Playhouse, February 14–March 11, 2012

Crowns Adapted from the book by Michael Cunningham & Craig Marberry; Written by Regina Taylor; Director/Choreographer, Kevin Ramsey; Music Director, e'Marcus Harper; Sets, Daniel P. Boylan; Costumes, Brian Strachan; Lighting, Joshua Shulman; Sound, Joel Farley; PSM, Jessica Simkins; ASM, Debby Lau; Cast: Lauren Blackwell (Jeanette), Ashlei Dabney (Yolanda), Doug Eskew (Man), Kimberly S. Fairbanks (Wanda), Joilet Harris (Mabel), Donna Jones (Velma), Barbara D. Mills (Mother Shaw); April 11–29, 2012

Denver Center Theatre Company

Denver, Colorado

Thirty-third Season

Producing Artistic Director, Kent Thompson

The Liar by David Ives; Adapted from the comedy by Pierre Corneille; Director, Kent Thompson; Sets, Lisa M. Orzolek; Costumes, David Kay Mickelsen; Lighting, Charles R. MacLeod; Sound, Jason Ducat; Original Music, Greg Coffin; Dramaturg; Ely Bowlby; Voice/Text, Michael Cobb; Fight Director, Geoffrey Kent; SM, Kurt Van Raden; ASM, Rachel Ducat; Cast: Drew Cortese (Dorante), Robert Sicular (Geronte), Matt Zambrano (Cliton), Amelia Pedlow (Clarice), Jeanine Serralles (Lucrece), John-Michael Marrs (Alcippe), Jonathan C. Kaplan (Philiste), Amy Kersten (Isabelle/Sabine); September 16–October 16, 2011

To Kill a Mockingbird by Christopher Sergel; Based upon the novel by Harper Lee; Director, Sabin Epstein; Sets, James Kronzer; Costumes, Angela Balogh Calin; Lighting, Don Darnutzer; Sound, Craig Breitenbach; Original Music, Gary Grundei; Voice/Dialect, Kathryn G. Maes Ph.D; Fight Director, Gregory Hoffman; SM, Christopher C. Ewing; ASM, Matthew Campbell; Cast: Kathleen McCall (Jean Louise Finch), Matthew Gary (Jem), Caroline Rosenbaum (Scout), Philip Pleasants (Walter Cunningham/Judge Taylor), John Hutton (Atticus Finch), Kim Staunton (Calpurnia), Kathleen M. Brady (Mrs. Dubose), Thomas Russo (Dill), Mike Hartman (Mr. Radley/Bob Ewell), Jeffrey Roark (Heck Tate), Charles Weldon (Rev. Sykes), Lawrence Hecht (Mr. Gilmer), Courtney Esser (Mayella Ewell), Tyrien Obahnjoko (Tom Robinson), Kimberly McWilliams (Mrs. Robinson), William Hahn (Boo Radley); September 30–October 30, 2011

American Night: The Ballad of Juan José by Lois Lowry; Dramatized by Eric Coble; Director, Christy Montour-Larson; Sets, Robert Mark Morgan; Costumes, Meghan Anderson Doyle; Lighting, Jane Spencer; Sound, Tyler Nelson; Projections, Charlie I. Miller; Music Composition, Gary Grundei, Dramaturg, Allison Horsley; Voice/Dialect, Hilary Blair; SM, Rachel Ducat; Cast: Timothy McCracken (Father), Diana Dresser (Mother), Aliza Fassett (Lily), Amelia Modesitt (Lily), Jackson Garske (Jonas), Alastair Hennessy (Jonas), Gabe Koskinen-Sansone (Asher), Evan Sullivan (Asher), Brynn Gauthier (Fiona), Isabel Sabbah (Fiona), Billie McBride (The Chief Elder), Philip Pleasants (The Giver), Caroline T. Bennet (Rosemary), Hilary Blair (Voice of Speaker); September 28–November 18, 2012

The Adventures of Tom Sawyer by Laura Eason from the novel by Mark Twain; Director, Jane Page; Sets, Vicki Smith; Costumes, David Kay Mickelsen; Lighting, Charles R. MacLeod; Sound, Jason Ducat; Projections, Charlie I. Miller; Dramaturg, Douglas Langworthy; Voice/Dialect, Kathryn G. Maes Ph.D; PSM, Christopher C. Ewing; ASM, Matthew Campbell; Fight Director, Geoffrey Kent; Cast: Stanton Nash (Tom Sawyer), Caitlin Wise (Becky Thatcher), Blake Lowell (Huckleberry Finn), Nick Abeel (Joe Harper), Andrew Schwartz (Sid Sawyer), Rachel Fowler (Aunt Polly), Drew Cortese (Injun Joe), Stephen Weitz (Muff Potter); November 11–December 18, 2011

A Christmas Carol by Charles Dickens; Adapted by Richard Hellesen; Music by David de Berry; Director, Bruce K. Sevy; Sets, Vicki Smith; Costumes, Kevin Copenhaver; Lighting, Don Darnutzer; Sound, Craig Breitenbach; Music Director/Orchestrator, Gregg Coffin; Choreographer, Christine Rowan; Voice/Dialect, Kathryn G. Maes, Ph.D; SM, Christopher C. Ewing; ASM, Kurt Van Raden, Matthew Campbell; Cast: Philip Pleasants (Ebenezer Scrooge), Jeff Cribbs (Bob Cratchit), Douglas Harmsen (Fred), Mike Hartman (Ghost of Jacob Marley), Stephanie Cozart (Ghost of Christmas Past), Michael Fitzpatrick (Fezziwig), Leslie O'Carroll (Mrs. Fezziwig), Harvy Blanks (Ghost of Christmas Present), Leslie Alexander (Mrs. Cratchit), Charlie Korman (Tiny Tim), Zachary Andrews (Ghost of Christmas Yet To Come); November 25–December 24, 2011

The Whale by Samuel D. Hunter; Director, Hal Brooks; Sets, Jason Simms; Costumes, Kevin Copenhaver; Lighting, Seth Reiser; Sound, William Burns; Dramaturg, Mead Hunter; Fight Director, Geoffrey Kent; SM, A. Phoebe Sacks; Cast: Tom Alan Robbins (Charlie), Angela Reed (Liz), Cory Michael Smith (Elder Thomas), Nicole Rodenburg (Ellie), Tasha Lawrence (Mary); World Premiere; January 13–February 19, 2012

Two Things You Don't Talk About At Dinner by Lisa Loomer; Director, Wendy C. Goldberg; Sets, Kevin Depient; Costume, Anne Kennedy; Lighting, Charles R. MacLeod; Sound, Jason Ducat; Dramaturg, Doug Langworthy; SM, Rachel Ducat; Cast: Mimi Lieber (Myriam), Lenny Wolpe (Jack), Karen Pittman (Nikki), Catherine E. Coulson (Ginny), Ben Morrow (Christopher), John Hutton (Josh), Sala Iwamatsu (Kimiko), Shana Dowdeswell (Rachelle), Sam Gregory (Dan), Caitlin O'Connell (Alice), Sophia Espinosa (Mable), Gabriella Cavallero (Lupe), Nasser Faris (Sam); World Premiere; January 20–February 19, 1012

The Taming of the Shrew by William Shakespeare; Director, Kent Thompson; Sets, Michael Ganio; Costumes, Christina Poddubiuk; Lighting, Peter West; Sound, Craig Breitenbach; Fight, Geoffrey Kent; Voice/Dialect, Kathryn G. Maes Ph.D; SM, Kurt Van Raden; ASM, Matthew Campbell; Cast: Drew Cortese (Lucentio), Matt Zambrano (Tranio), Robert Sicular (Baptista Minola), Randy Morre (Gremio), Kathleen McCall (Katherine), John-Michael Marrs (Hortensio), Christy McIntosh (Bianca), Patrick Halley (Biondello, Joseph), John G. Preston (Petruchio), Andrew Schwartz (Grumio), Courtney Esser (Sophia/Walter), Biko Eisen-Martin (Curtis/Police Officer), Mike Hartman (Nathaniel/Vincentio), Chiara Motley (Philip/A Haberdasher), ZZ Moor (Nicholas), Maurice Jones (Peter/A Tailor), Philip Pleasants (Sugarsop/Merchant of Mantua), Amy Kersten (Gabriel), Leslie Alexander (A Widow); January 27–February 26, 2012

Great Wall Story by Lloyd Suh; Director, Art Manke; Sets, Lisa M. Orzolek; Costumes, Angela Balogh Calin; Lighting, Jane Spencer; Sound, William Burns; Projections, El Armstrong; Music Composition, Gary Grundei; Dramaturg, Doug Langworthy; Voice/Dialect, Kathryn G. Maes Ph.D; SM, A. Phoebe Sacks; ASM, Amy M. Scura; Cast: Christopher Kelly (Jack Tournay), Jacob Knoll (Al Stevens), Mike Hartman (John King), John Hutton (Joseph Pulitzer), Merrit Janson (Harriet Sparrow), Gabe Koskinen-Sansone (Charles Tournay), Larry Paulsen (Morris/Simone/Douglas/Johnson/Editor in Chief/Eddie Gardner); World Premiere; March 16–April 22, 2012

Ring of Fire: The Music of Johnny Cash Created by Richard Maltby, Jr.; Conceived by William Meade; Orchestrations by Steven Bishop and Jeff Lisenby; Director, Jason Edwards; Assistant Director/Choreographer, Jane Lanier; Sets, John Iacovelli; Costumes, Kevin Copenhaver; Lighting, Charles R. MacLeod; Sound, Craig Breitenbach; Projections, Charlie I. Miller; Music Director, Jeff Lisenby; Cast: Trenna Barnes (Principal), Troy Burgess (Principal), Jason Edwards (Principal), Kelli Provart (Principal), Bratley Kearns (Fiddle/Guitar), Jeff Lisenby (Keyboards/Accordion), Brent Moyer (Guitars/Cornet), John Marshall (Bass fiddle), Walter Hartman (Drums), John Foley (Guitar/Mandolin/Harmonica/Dobro); March 23–May 13, 2012

Heartbreak House by George Bernard Shaw; Director, Kent Thompson; Sets, Vicki Smith; Costumes, Bill Black; Lighting, Don Darnutzer; Sound, Jason Ducat; Music Composition, Gregg Coffin; Dramaturg, Doug Langworthy; Voice/Dialect, Kathryn G. Maes Ph.D; PM, Edward Lapin; SM, Rachel Ducat; ASM, Matthew Campbell; Cast: Sarah Nealis (Ellie Dunn), Kathleen M. Brady (Nurse Guiness), Philip Pleasants (Captain SHotover), Kathleen McCall (Lady Utterwood), Lise Bruneau (Hesione Hushabye), Randy Moore (Mazzini Dunn), J. Paul Boehmer (Hector Hushabye), Robert Sicular (Boss Mangan), Sam Gregory (Randall Utterwood), Brad Bellamy (William "Billy" Dunn), John Arp (Servant), Crystal Verdon (Servant), Kate Gleason (Servant), Jeffrey Roark (Servant); March 30–April 29, 2012

The Company of The Huntington Theatre Company's Candide
(photo by T. Charles Erickson)

Merle Moores in Kansas City Repertory Theatre's production of
August: Osage County (photo by Don Ipock)

Johanna Day, Brooks Ashmanskas, Stephen Bogardus, and Christy Pusz in God
of Carnage at Huntington Theatre Company (photo by T. Charles Erickson)

Paul Nolan and the Company of La Jolla Playhouse's presentation of Jesus
Christ Superstar (photo by David Hou)

Marlon Washington, Razz Jenkins, and Jonah Taylor in Broke-Ology at
Illinois Theatre Center (photo by Warren Skalski)

Danny Gavigan, Kate Cullen Roberts, Luis Moreno, Evan Zes, and Birgit Huppuch
in La Jolla Playhouse's production of Peer Gynt (photo by Don Ipock)

Brian Dennehy in Krapp's Last Tape *at Long Wharf Theatre (photo by T. Charles Erickson)*

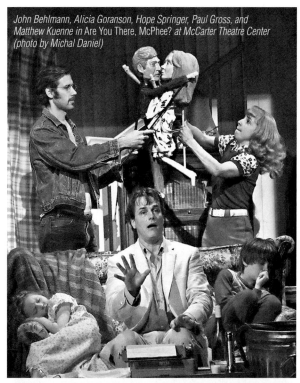

John Behlmann, Alicia Goranson, Hope Springer, Paul Gross, and Matthew Kuenne in Are You There, McPhee? *at McCarter Theatre Center (photo by Michal Daniel)*

Jack Vangorden, Clayton Slee, Jonathan Beck Reed in Lyric Stage's production of Oliver *(photo by Michael Foster)*

Jacob Gutierrez, Karen Robu, and Cody Davis in Music Theatre of Wichita's production of Disney's The Little Mermaid (photo by Christopher Clark)

Beth Wittig and Christina Pumariega in The Persian Quarter *at Merrimack Repertory Theatre (photo by Meghan Moore)*

The Company of New Line Theatre's Passing Strange *(photo by Jill Ritter Lindberg)*

The 5ᵗʰ Avenue Theatre

Seattle, Washington

Twenty-third Season

Executive Producer and Artistic Director, David Armstrong; Managing Director, Bernadine C. Griffin; Producing Director, Bill Berry

Les Misérables A musical based on the novel by Victor Hugo; Music by Claude-Michel Schönberg; Lyrics by Herbert Kretzmer; Original French text by Alain Boublil and Jean-Marc Natel; Additional material by James Fenton; Original production adapted and directed by Trevor Nunn and John Caird; Music Director, Robert Billig; Original orchestrations by John Cameron; New orchestrations by Chris Jahnke; Additional orchestrations by Stephen Metcalfe and Stephen Brooker; Musical staging by Michael Ashcroft; Projections realized by Fifty-Nine Productions; Additional costumes by Christine Rowland; Sound, Mick Potter; Lighting, Paule Constable; Costumes, Andreane Neofitou; Sets, Matt Kinley; Cast: J. Mark Mcvey (Jean Valjean), Andrew Varela (Javert), John Rapson (Farmer), Max Quinlan (Laborer), Julie Benko (Innkeeper's Wife), Joseph Spieldenner (Innkeeper), Benjamin Magnuson (The Bishop Of Digne), Ian Patrick Gibb, Alan Shaw (Constables), Richard Todd Adams (Factory Foreman), Betsy Morgan (Fantine), Lucia Giannetta (Factory Girl), Beth Kirkpatrick (Old Woman), Cornelia Luna (Wigmaker), John Rapson (Bamatabois), Eric Van Tielen (Fauchelevent), Joe Tokarz (Champmathieu), Maya Jade Frank, Juliana Simone (Little Cosette), Shawna M. Hamic (Madame Thénardier), Maya Jade Frank, Juliana Simone (Young Éponine), Michael Kostroff (Thénardier), Sarah Shahinian (Young Whore), Siri Howard (Crazy Whore), Colin Depaula, Ethan Paul Khusidman (Gavroche), Chasten Harmon (Éponine), Jenny Latimer (Cosette), Max Quinlan (Montparnasse), Benjamin Magnuson (Babet), Joe Tokarz (Brujon), John Rapson (Claquesous), Jeremy Hays (Enjolras), Justin Scott Brown (Marius), Eric Van Tielen (Combeferre), Jason Forbach (Feuilly), Cole Burden (Courfeyrac), Alan Shaw (Joly), Joseph Spieldenner (Grantaire), Richard Todd Adams (Lesgles), Ian Patrick Gibb (Jean Prouvaire), Joe Tokarz (Loud Hailer), Joseph Spieldenner (Major Domo), Julie Benko, Briana Carlson-Goodman, Casey Erin Clark, Lucia Giannetta, Siri Howard, Beth Kirkpatrick, Cornelia Luna, Kylie Mcvey, Sarah Shahinian (Ensemble), Richard Barth, Ben Gunderson, Jason Ostrowski, Rachel Rincione, Natalie Weiss (Swings), Jason Ostrowski (Dance Captain), Benjamin Magnuson (Fight Captain), Heather Chockley (Assistant Fight Captain); Understudies: Richard Todd Adams, Joe Tokarz (Jean Valjean); Richard Todd Adams, Benjamin Magnuson (Javert); Julie Benko, Siri Howard (Cosette); Casey Erin Clark, Cornelia Luna (Fantine); Benjamin Magnuson, John Rapson (Thénardier); Lucia Giannetta, Beth Kirkpatrick (Madame Thénardier); Briana Carlson-Goodman, Sarah Shahinian (Éponine); Ian Patrick Gibb, Max Quinlan (Marius); Jason Forbach, Alan Shaw (Enjolras); Kylie Mcvey (Little Cosette/Young Éponine); John Rapson, Joseph Spieldenner (The Bishop Of Digne); Jason Ostrowski, Joseph Spieldenner (The Factory Foreman); Casey Erin Clark, Rachel Rincione (The Factory Girl); Cole Burden, Joseph Spieldenner (Bamatabois); John Rapson, Eric Van Tielen (Grantaire); August 9–27, 2011

Saving Aimee Book & lyrics by Kathie Lee Gifford; Music by David Pomeranz and David Friedman; Additional music by Kathie Lee Gifford; Director, David Armstrong; Choreographer, Lorin Latarro; Music Director/Vocal Arranger, Joel Fram; Sets, Walt Spangler; Costumes, Gregory A. Poplyk; Lighting, Tom Sturge; Sound, Ken Travis; Hair/Makeup, Mary Pyanowski; Associate Director, Brandon Ivie; Associate Choreographer, Sean McKnight; Casting Director, Tara Rubin Casting; PSM, Amber Wedin; ASM, E. Sara Barnes, Libby Unsworth; Cast: Carolee Carmello (Aimee Semple McPherson), Judy Kaye (Minnie Kennedy), Roz Ryan (Emma Jo Schaefer), Charles Leggett (Asa Keyes), Ed Dixon (Brother Bob Bueler), Ed Dixon (James Kennedy), Ed Watts (Robert Semple), Brandon O'Neill (Harold McPherson), Ed Watts (David Hutton), Brandon O'Neill (Kenneth Ormiston), Richard Gray (Bailiff/London Host), Matt Wolfe (Dr. Samuels), Cheryl Massey-Peters (Waitress/Louella Parsons), Tim Shew (Boxing Announcer/Mayor/Hearst/Judge), Billie Wildrick (Eve/Tango Dancer/Myrtle), Mara Solar (Serpent/Tango Dancer), Jared Michael Brown (Tango Dancer/Lawyer), Christian

Duhamel (Charlie Chaplin); Ensemble: Jared Michael Brown, Christian Duhamel, Richard Gray, Cayman Ilika, Corinna Lapid-Munter, Brandi Chavonne Massey, Cheryl Massey-Peters, Heath Saunders, Aaron Shanks, Tim Shew, Mara Solar, Billie Wildrick, Matt Wolfe; Christian Duhamel (Dance Captain); Billie Wildrick (u/s); Charissa Bertels (Swing); September 30–October 29, 2011

Cinderella Music by Richard Rodgers; Book & lyrics by Oscar Hammerstein; Adapted for the stage by Tom Briggs; From the teleplay by Robert L. Freedman; Director, Brandon Ivie; Choreographer, Noah Racey; Music Director, Bruce Monroe; Sets, David Gallo; Costumes, Renato Balestra; Lighting, Tom Sturge; Sound, Tony Smolenski IV; Hair/Makeup, Mary Pyanowski; Orchestrator, Robert Russell Bennett; Associate Choreographer, David Alewine; Associate Music Director, Faith Seetoo; PSM, Bret Torbeck; ASM, Stina Lotti, Shellie Stone; Cast: Kendra Kassebaum (The Godmother), Greg McCormick Allen (Lionel), Suzanne Bouchard (The Stepmother), Nick Garrison (Joy), Sarah Rudinoff (Grace), Jennifer Paz (Cinderella), Allen Fitzpatrick (King Maximillian), Cynthia Jones (Queen Constantina), Brandon O'Neill (Prince Christopher); Ensemble: David Alewine, Jordon Anthony Bolden, Jared Michael Brown, Daniel Cruz, Antonia Darlene, Sarah Rose Davis, Nick Desantis, Erin Herrick, Danny Kam, Corinna Lapid-Munter, Matthew Steven Lawrence, Nikki Long, Cheryl Massey-Peters, Trina Mills, Naomi Morgan, Heath Saunders, Aaron Shanks, Jessica Skerritt, Fune Tautala, Indeah Thomaier, Carolyn Willems Van Dijk; Victoria Alkin, Brayden Daher, Olivia Elliott, Anna Ostrem, Akhilesh Vadari, Deché Washington, Christian West, Noelle Whitman, Samantha Yee (Children's Chorus); David Alewine (Dance Captain); Danny Kam, Carolyn Willems Van Dijk (Swings); September 30–October 29, 2011; November 25–December 31, 2011

Oklahoma! Music by Richard Rodgers; Book & lyrics by Oscar Hammerstein; Based on the play *Green Grow the Lilacs* by Lynn Riggs; Director, Peter Rothstein; Choreographer, Donald Byrd; Music Director, Ian Eisendrath; Sets, Matthew Smucker; Costumes, Lynda L. Salsbury; Lighting, Tom Sturge; Sound, Ken Travis; Hair/Makeup, Mary Pyanowski; Fight Director, Geoffrey Alm; Orchestrator, Robert Russell Bennett; Associate Music Director, Faith Seetoo; PSM, Jeffrey K. Hanson; ASM, Jessica C. Bomball, Erin B. Zatloka; Cast: Eric Ankrim (Curly); Anne Allgood (Aunt Eller); Alexandra Zorn (Laurey); Kyle Scatliffe (Jud Fry); Matt Owen (Will Parker); Kirsten deLohr Helland (Ado Annie Carnes); Daniel C. Levine (Ali Hakim); Sonya Meyer (Gertie Cummings); Allen Fitzpatrick (Andrew Carnes); Kara Walsh (Dream Laurey); Josh Spell (Dream Curly); Donald Jones Jr. (Dream Jud); David Pichette (Ike Skidmore); Jared Michael Brown, Blaine Boyd, Jeroboam Bozeman, Ty Alexander Cheng, Zane Cimino, Derek Crescenti, Jade Solomon Curtis, Jeannette d'Armand, Sarah Rose Davis, Kevin Douglass, Mary Jo duGaw, Eric Esteb, Kassandra Haddock, Mallory King, Jonathan Paul Lee, Vincent Michael Lopez, Amber Nicole Mayberry, Shadou Mintrone, Kate Monthy, Christie Murphy, Briley Neugebauer, Daniel Oakden, Ben Sasnett, Carolyn Willems Van Dijk (Ensemble); Nicholas Hayes, Cameron Renee Washington, DeChé Washington (Children's Ensemble); Jared Michael Brown (Curly u/s); Sonya Meyer (Laurey u/s); February 3–March 4, 2012

First Date Produced in partnership with ACT–A Contemporary Theatre; Book by Austin Winsberg; Music and lyrics by Alan Zachary and Michael Weiner; Director, Bill Berry; Musical Stager, Josh Prince; Music Supervisor/Arranger, Dominick Amendum; Sets, Matthew Smucker; Costumes, Frances Kenny; Lighting, Alex Berry; Sound, Kai Harada; Orchestrator, August Eriksmoen; Associate Music Director, R.J. Tancioco; Associate Sound, Brendan Patrick Hogan; SM, Michael B. Paul; ASM, Whitney Breite; Cast: Eric Ankrim (Aaron), Richard Gray (Man #3/Waiter/Others [March 10-April 13]), Greg McCormick Allen (Man #3/Waiter [April 14-May 20]), Benjamin Harris (Man #2/Reggie), Kelly Karbacz (Casey), Vicki Noon (Woman #2/Allison/Others), Brandon O'neill (Man #1/Gabe/Others), Billie Wildrick (Woman #1/Lauren/Others), Vicki Noon (Casey u/s), Danielle Barnum (Female u/s), Jared Michael Brown (Male u/s), Danielle Barnum (Dance Captain), ACT–A Contemporary Theatre; March 10–May 20, 2012

Damn Yankees Produced in partnership with Paper Mill Playhouse; Words and music by Richard Adler and Jerry Ross; Book by George Abbott and Douglas Wallop; Based on the novel *The Year the Yankees Lost the Pennant* by Douglas

Wallop; Director, Mark S. Hoebee; Choreographer, Denis Jones; Music Director, Ben Whiteley; Sets, Rob Bissinger; Costumes, Alejo Vietti; Lighting, Tom Sturge; Sound, Andrew G. Luft; Wigs, Charles Lapoint; Hair/Makeup, Mary Pyanowski; New Orchestrations and Additional Arrangements by Bruce Monroe; Associate Music Director, Matt Hohensee; Associate Director, Brandon Ivie; Associate Choreographer, Kim Craven; PSM, Amy Gornet; ASM, Jessica C. Bomball, Erin B. Zatloka; Cast: Paul Silvi (TV Announcer), Hugh Hastings (Joe Boyd), Patti Cohenour (Meg Boyd), Hans Altwies (Applegate), Carol Swarbrick (Sister), Julie Briskman (Doris), Christopher Charles Wood (Joe Hardy), Christian Duhamel (Sohovik), Matthew Posner (Smokey), Allen Fitzpatrick (Coach Van Buren), Dane Stokinger (Rocky), Vaden Thurgood (Vernon), Daniel Cruz (Bouley), Scott Brateng (Lowe), Michael Ericson (Henry), David Alewine (Mickey), Eric Esteb (Bryan), Gabriel Corey (Linville), Nancy Anderson (Gloria Thorpe), Richard Ziman (Mr. Welch), Chryssie Whitehead (Lola), Beth Devries (Miss Weston), Bob De Dea (The Commissioner); Ensemble: David Alewine, Blaine Boyd, Scott Brateng, Gabriel Corey, Daniel Cruz, Sarah Rose Davis, Christian Duhamel, Michael Ericson, Eric Esteb, Kasey Nusbickel, Matthew Posner, Dane Stokinger, Vaden Thurgood; David Alewine (Dance Captain); Blaine Boyd (Swing); April 21–May 20, 2012

RENT Book, music, and lyrics by Jonathan Larson; Music Arrangements by Steve Skinner; Original Concept/Additional Lyrics by Billy Aronson; Music Supervision and Additional Arrangements by Tim Weil; Dramaturg, Lynn Thomson; Director, Bill Berry; Choreographer, Daniel Cruz; Music Director, R.J. Tancioco; Sets, Martin Christoffel; Costumes, Pete Rush; Lighting, Tom Sturge; Sound, Kai Harada; Hair/ Makeup, Mary Pyanowski; Associate Lighting, Christian DeAngelis; Electronic Music Programming, Dave Pascal; Assistant Director, Adam Quinn, Associate Director/Film Sequence Producer, Eric Ankrim; Assistant Choreographer, Trina Mills; PSM, Jessica C. Bomball; ASM, Shellie Stone; Cast: Andi Alhadeff (Joanne Jefferson), Logan Benedict (Benjamin Coffin III), Daniel Berryman (Mark Cohen) Aaron C. Finley (Roger Davis), Jerick Hoffer (Angel Dumont Schunard), Naomi Morgan (Mimi Marquez), Ryah Nixon (Maureen Johnson), Brandon O'Neill (Tom Collins), Eric Ankrim, Antonia Darlene, Sarah Rose Davis, Bryan Gula, Kirsten deLohr Helland, Lindsey Hedberg, Jimmie D. Herrod Jr., Diana Huey, Andrew Leonard, Trina Mills, Henry Nettleton, Patrick Shelton, Heath Saunders, Sarah Russell, Casey Raiha (East Villagers), Trina Mills (Dance Captain); Trina Mills, Casey Raiha (Swings); Eric Ankrim, Antonia Darlene, Kirsten deLohr Helland, Jimmie D. Herrod Jr., Diana Huey, Andrew Leonard, Patrick Shelton, Heath Saunders (Covers/Understudies); July 21–August 19, 2012

Florida Studio Theatre

Sarasota, Florida

Thirty-eighth Season

Executive Director, Richard Hopkins

Next to Normal Music by Tom Kitt; Lyrics by Brian Yorkey; Director, Richard Hopkins; Sets, April Soroko; Costumes, Sara J. Hinkley; Lighting, David M. Upton; Sound, Eric Stahlhammer; PSM, Kelli Karen; Cast: Stacia Fernandez (Diana), Mike Backes (Gabe), Leo Daignault (Dan), Ashley Picciallo (Natalie), James LaRosa (Henry), Scott Guthrie (Dr. Madden/Dr. Fine); Keating Theatre and Gompertz Theatre; November 2, 2011–January 7, 2012

The Last Romance by Joe DiPietro; Director, Russell Treyz; Sets, April Soroko; Costumes, April Soroko; Lighting, Robert Perry; PSM, Kelli Karen; Cast: Barbara Broughton (Carol), David S. Howard (Ralph), Marina Re (Rose), Dane Reese (The Young Man); Gompertz Theatre; December 7, 2011–March 2, 2012

Next Fall by Geoffrey Nauffts; Director, Kate Alexander; Sets, Michael Schweikardt; Costumes, Sara J. Hinkley; Lighting, Micheal Foster; PSM, Kelli Karen; Cast: Kenajuan Bentley (Brandon), Phillip Clark (Butch), Kevin Cristaldi (Luke), Judith Hawking (Arlene), Jason O'Connell (Adam), Katherine Michelle Tanner (Holly); Keating Theatre; January 25–April 14, 2012

Jericho by Jack Canfora; Director, Kate Alexander; Sets, Bob Phillips; Costumes, Sara J. Hinkley; Lighting, Byron Winn; PSM, Kelli Karen; Cast: Eleanor Handley (Beth), Will Little (Dr. Kim/Alec), Michael Satow (Ethan), Rachel Moulton (Jessica), Mark Light-Orr (Josh), Diane Ciesla (Rachel); Keating Theatre; April 6–June 3, 2012

Das Barbecü by Jim Luigs and Scott Warrender; Director, Dennis Courtney; Sets, Rob Eastman-Mullins; Costumes; April Soroko; Lighting, Joseph P. Oshry; PSM, Kelli Karen; Cast: Maria Couch, Joanna Parson, Billie Wildrick, Stephen Hope, Joshua Carter; Keating Theatre; June 13–July 15, 2012

Talley's Folly by Lanford Wilson; Director, Kate Alexander; Sets/Costumes, April Soroko; Lighting, Robert Perry; PSM, Kayliane Burns; Cast: Dominic Comperatore (Matt Friedman), Maren Bush (Sally Talley); Keating Theatre; July 25–August 26, 2012

Perfect Wedding by Robin Hawdon; Director, Bruce Jordan; Sets, Michael Lasswell; Costumes, Sarah Bertolozzi; Lighting, Jeffrey Cady; PSM, Kelli Karen; Cast: Graham Stuart Allen (Bill), Daryl Embry (Tom), Lisa McMillan (Daphne), Faith Sandberg (Rachel), Kate Siepert (Julie), Jenny Strassburg (Judy); Gompertz Theatre; August 8–September 9, 2012

Reel Music Developed by Richard Hopkins, Rebecca Hopkins, and Jim Prosser with additional assistance from Amanda Cayo and Jessica Mingoia; Director, Bill Castellino; Music Director, David Nelson; Sets/Costumes, Nicole Wee; Lighting, David Nelson; Sound, David M. Corsello; PSM, Kristin Kerr; Cast: Gil Brady, L.R. Davidson, Matt Mundy, Liz Power; Goldstein Cabaret; March 28–June 17, 2012

Shake, Rattle, and Roll Developed by Richard Hopkins, Rebecca Hopkins and Jim Prosser; Director, Dennis Courtney; Music Director, John Franceschina; Sets/ Costumes, Susan Angermann; Lighting, Jeffrey Cady; Sound, John Valines; PSM, Tommy Rosati; Cast: Eric Scott Anthony, Jonathan Brown, Dominick Cicco, Casey Gensler, Tony Bruno; Goldstein Cabaret; January 4–March 25, 2012

That's Life Again Developed by Richard Hopkins, Rebecca Hopkins, and Jim Prosser; Director/Choreographer, Dennis Courtney; Music Director, John Franceschina; Sets/Costumes, Susan Angermann; Lighting, Micheal Foster; Sound, Tom Jones; PSM, Tommy Rosati; Cast: Eric Collins, Stacey Harrism, Stephen Hope, Arthur W. Marks; Goldstein Cabaret; October 12, 2011–January 1, 2012

Ford's Theatre

Washington, D.C.

Forty-Third Season

Director, Paul R. Tetreault

Parade Book by Alfred Uhry; Music and lyrics by Jason Robert Brown; Co-conceived by Harold Prince; Director, Stephen Rayne; Music Directior, Steven Landau; Choreographer, Karma Camp; Sets, Tony Cisek; Costumes, Wade Laboissonniere; Co-Sound, David Budries and Charles Coes; Fight Director, Brad Waller; Wigs/Make-up, Anne Nesmith; Dialect, Lynn Watson; PSM, Brandon Prendergast; ASM, Kate Killbane; Cast: Carolyn Agan (Monteen), Sandy Bainum (Mrs. Phagan/Sally Slaton), Christopher Bloch (Judge Roan/Old Soldier/Peavy), Michael Bunce (Luther Rosser/ Office Starnes), Erin Driscoll (Essie), Jenny Fellner (Lucille Frank), Will Gartshore (Officer Ivey/Tom Watson), Kellee Knighten Hough (Angela/Minola McKnight), Matthew John Kacergis (Young Soldier/ Frankie Epps), James Konicek (Hugh Dorsey), Kevin McAllister (Newt Lee/Jim Conley/Riley), Euan Morton (Leo Frank), Stephen F. Schmidt (Governor Slaton), Chris Sizemore (Britt Craig/Mr. Turner), Bligh Voth (Iola Stover), Lauren Williams (Mary Phagan/Lila). Understudies: Peter Boyer, Christina Kidd, Deborah Lubega, Sean-Maurice Lynch; September 23–October 30, 2011

A Christmas Carol by Charles Dickens; Adaptor, Michael Wilson; Director, Michael Baron; Sets; Lee Savage; Costumes, Alejo Vietti; Lighting, Rui Rita; Original Music and Sound, Josh Schmidt; Choreographer, Shea Sullivan; Wigs,

Charles G. LaPointe; Choral Director, Jay Crowder; Dialect, Leigh Wilson Smiley; Associate Directors, Craig A. Horness and James D. Gardiner; PSM, Craig A. Horness, Carey Lawless; ASM, Martita Lee Slayden; Cast: Carolyn Agan (Belle), Christopher Bloch (Bob Cratchit), Michael Bunce (Solicitor #2/Undertaker), Steven Carpenter (Solicitor #1), Felicia Curry (Doll Vendor/Ghost of Christmas Past), Drew Eshelman (Jacob Marley/Old Joe), Edward Gero (Scrooge), Rick Hammerly (Mr. Fezziwig), Helen Hedman (Mrs. Dilber/Mrs. Fezziwig/Mother at Doll Stand), Kellee Knighten Hough (Mrs. Fred), Gregory Maheu (Topper/Young Marley), Amy McWilliams (Mrs. Cratchit), Stephen F. Schmidt (Clock Vendor), Anne Stone (Fruit Vendor/Ghost of Christmas Present), Tom Story (Fred/Young Scrooge), Bligh Voth (Mrs. Fred's Sister/Beggar Woman); Understudies: Kristen Garaffo, Vishal Vaidya; November 18–December 31, 2011

Necessary Sacrifices by Richard Hellesen; Director, Jennifer L. Nelson; Sets, James Kronzer; Costumes, Helen Huang; Lighting, Dan Covey; Original Music and Sound, John Gromada; Wigss/Make-up, Anne Nesmith; Dialect, Kim James Bey; PSM, Brandon Prendergast; ASM, Kate Killbane; Cast: Michael Kramer (George Stearns), David Selby (Abraham Lincoln), Craig Wallace (Frederick Douglass); January 25–February 18, 2012

1776 Music and lyrics by Sherman Edwards; Book by Peter Stone; Concept by Sherman Edwards; Director, Peter Flynn; Music Director, Jay Crowder; Choreographer, Michael Bobbitt; Sets, Tony Cisek; Costumes, Wade Laboissonniere; Lighting, Nancy Schertler; Sound, David Budries; Wigs/Make-up, Cookie Jordan; Orchestrator, Kim Scharnberg; Dialect, Susanne Sulby; PSM, Craig A. Horness; ASM, Taryn Friend; Cast: Patrick A'Hearn (Joseph Hewes), Matthew A. Anderson (Lewis Morris), Brooks Ashmanskas (John Adams), Christopher Bloch (Benjamin Franklin), Peter Boyer (Dr. Josiah Bartlett), Michael Bunce (Samuel Chase), Steven Carpenter (Dr. Lyman Hall), Robert Cuccioli (John Dickinson), William Diggle (Thomas Jefferson), Drew Eshelman (Andrew McNair), Kate Fisher (Abigail Adams), Rick Hammerly (Roger Sherman), Matthew John Kacergis (Leather Apron/Painter), Floyd King (Stephen Hopkins), James Konicek (John Hancock), Erin Kruse (Martha Jefferson), Sam Ludwig (Courier), Gregory Maheu (Edward Rutledge), Dan Manning (Robert Livingston), Buzz Mauro (Caesar Rodney), Richard Pelzman (Colonel Thomas McKean), Stephen F. Schmidt (Richard Henry Lee), Thomas Adrian Simpson (Reverend John Witherspoon), Chris Sizemore (George Read), Bobby Smith (James Wilson), Tom Story (Charles Thompson); Understudies: Carolyn Agan, Evan Hoffmann. March 9–May 19, 2012

Geffen Playhouse

Los Angeles, California

Sixteenth Season

Artistic Director, Randall Arney; Managing Director, Ken Novice

GIL CATES THEATER

The Elaborate Entrance of Chad Deity by Kristoffer Diaz; Director, Edward Torres; Sets, Brian Sidney Bembridge; Costumes, Christina Haatainen Jones; Lighting, Jesse Klug; Sound, Mikhail Fiksel; Projections, Peter Nigrini; Fight Director, David Woolley; PSM, Young Ji; ASM, Gary J. Breitbach; Cast: Usman Ally (Vigneshwar Paduar), Terence Archie (Chad Deity), Desmin Borges (Macedonio Guerra), Justin Leeper (The Bad Guy), Timothy Talbot (Billy Heartland/Old Glory), Steve Valentine (Everett K. Olson); August 30–October 9, 2011

Next Fall by Geoffrey Nauffts; Director, Sheryl Kaller; Sets, Wilson Chin; Costumes, Kate Bergh; Lighting, Jeff Croiter; Sound, John Gromada; PSM, James T. McDermott; ASM, Jennifer Brienen; Cast: Ken Barnett (Brandon), Betsy Brandt (Holly), Jeff Fahey (Butch), Geoffrey Nauffts (Adam), Lesley Ann Warren (Arlene), James Wolk (Luke); October 25–December 4, 2011

Red Hot Patriot: The Kick Ass Wit of Molly Ivins by Margaret Engel and Allison Engel; Director, David Esbjornson; Sets, John Arnone; Costumes, Beth Clancy; Lighting, Daniel Ionazzi; Sound, Robert Milburn and Michael Bodeen;

Projections, Maya Ciarrocchi; Wigs, Paul Huntley; PSM, Mary Michele Miner; ASM, Susie Walsh; Cast: Kathleen Turner (Molly Ivins), Helper (Matthew Van Oss); January 3, 2011–February 19, 2012

Good People by David Lindsay-Abaire; Director, Matt Shakman; Sets, Craig Siebels; Costumes, E.B. Brooks; Lighting, Elizabeth Harper; Sound, Jonathan Snipes; PSM, Jill Gold; ASM, Kyra Hansen; Cast: Cherise Boothe (Kate), Sara Botsford (Jean), Marylouise Burke (Dottie), Brad Fleischer (Stevie), Jane Kaczmarek (Margie), Jon Tenney (Mike); April 3– May 13, 2012

The Exorcist by John Pielmeier; Adapted from the novel by William Peter Blatty; Director, John Doyle; Sets/Costumes, Scott Pask; Lighting, Jane Cox; Sound, Dan Moses Schrier; Music, Sir John Tavener; Creative Consultant, Teller; PSM, Adam John Hunter; ASM, Young Ji; Cast: David Wilson Barnes (Father Damien Karras), Stephen Bogardus (Dr. Strong), Richard Chamberlain (Father Merrin), Manoel Felciano (Father Joe), Harry Groener (Burke Dennings), Tom Nelis (Dr. Klein), Roslyn Ruff (Carla), Brooke Shields (Chris MacNeil), Emily Yetter (Regan MacNeil); World Premiere; July 3–August 12, 2012

AUDREY SKIRBALL KENIS THEATER

Radiance: The Passion of Marie Curie by Alan Alda; Director, Daniel Sullivan; Sets, Tom Lynch; Costumes, Rita Ryack; Lighting, Daniel Ionazzi; Sound, Jon Gottlieb; PSM, Young Ji; ASM, Kyra Hansen; Cast: Hugo Armstrong (Émile), John de Lancie (Pierre), Dan Donohue (Paul), Anna Gunn (Marie Curie), Leonard Kelly-Young (Terbougie /Törnebladh), Natacha Roi (Marguerite), Sarah Zimmerman (Jeanne); November 1–December 18, 2011

The Jacksonian by Beth Henley; Director, Robert Falls; Sets, Walt Spangler; Costumes, Ana Kuzmanic; Lighting, Daniel Ionazzi; Sound, Richard Woodbury; PSM, Young Ji; Cast: Ed Harris (Bill Perch), Glenne Headly (Eva White), Amy Madigan (Susan Perch), Bill Pullman (Fred Weber), Bess Rous (Rosy Perch); February 15–March 25, 2012

Mona Golabek in The Pianist of Willesden Lane Adapted and directed by Hershey Felder; Based on the book *The Children of Willesden Lane* by Mona Golabek and Lee Cohen; Sets, David Buess, Trevor Hay; Lighting, Chris Rynne; Sound, Erik Carstensen; Projections, Greg Sowizdrzal, Andrew Wilder; Scenic Construction, Christian Thorsen; Production Manager, Trevor Hay; PSM, Young Ji, Gary Breitbach, Nate Genung; ASM, Brett Taylor; Cast: Mona Golabek (Lisa Jura); April 17–September 15, 2012

Georgia Shakespeare

Atlanta, Georgia

Twenty-sixth Season

Producing Artistic Director, Richard Garner; Managing Director, Lauren Morris

CONANT PERFORMING ARTS CENTER

The Tempest by William Shakespeare; Director, Sharon Ott; Sets, Tyler Tunney; Costumes, Leslie Taylor; Lighting, Ruth Hutson; Sound, Stephen LeGrand; Choreographer, Ivan Pulinkala; Dramaturg, Andrew J. Hartley; SM, Margo Kuhne; ASM, David S. Cohen; Cast: Allan Edwards (Alonso), Joe Knezevich (Sebastian), Carolyn Cook (Prospera), Brad Sherrill (Antonio), Casey Hoekstra (Ferdinand), Allen O'Reilly (Gonzalo), Mark Cabus (Trinculo), Bruce Evers (Stephano), Scott Warren (Boatswain), Caitlin McWethy (Miranda), Chris Kayser (Ariel), Neal A. Ghant (Caliban), Tess Malis Kincaid (Ceres), Kyle Brumley (Mariner/Spirit/Others), Cordell Cole (Mariner/Spirit/Others), Jordan Craig (Mariner/Spirit/Others), Ann Marie Gideon (Mariner/Spirit/Others), Brian Harrison (Mariner/Spirit/Others), Elizabeth Lanier (Mariners/Spirit/Others); June 8–July 23, 2011

Antony and Cleopatra by William Shakespeare; Adaptor, Amlin Gray; Director, John Dillon; Sets, Kat Conley; Costumes, Sydney Roberts; Lighting, Mike Post; Composer, Klimchak; Sound, Clay Benning; Fight Directors, Scot J. Mann and Kelly Martin; Dramaturg, Amlin Gray; SM, Robert Schultz; ASM, Katie Pfohl; Cast: Chris Kayser (Mark Antony), Joe Knezevich (Octavius Caesar), Allen

O'Reilly (Marcus Lepidus/A Schoolmaster/Proculeius), Tess Malis Kincaid (Cleopatra), Caitlin McWethy (Charmian), Elizabeth Lanier (Iras), Kyle Brumley (Alexas/Soldier/Servant/Messenger/Others), Neal A. Ghant (Mardian), Brian Harrison (A Messenger), Ann Marie Gideon (Octavia/Soldier/Servant/Messenger/Others), Allan Edwards (Domitius Enobarbus), Cordell Cole (Canidius/Dercetus), Bruce Evers (Scarrus/Sextus Pompeius), Casey Hoekstra (Eros), Mark Cabus (Maecenas), Brad Sherrill (Agrippa), Jordan Craig (Thidias/Soldier/Servant/Messenger/Others), Brian Harrison (Dolabella/Soldier/Servant/Messenger/Others), Scott Warren (Menas/An Egyptian Rustic/Soldier/Servant/Messenger/Others), Carolyn Cook (A Soothsayer/Soldier/Servant/Messenger/Others), Ben Carbo (Soldier/Servant/Messenger/Others); June 23–July 22, 2011

The Jungle Book Based on Rudyard Kipling's *Jungle Book*; Book and lyrics by April-Dawn Gladu; Music and lyrics by Daniel Levy; Director, Allen O'Reilly; Sets, Alexander K; Costumes, Katy Munroe; Lighting, Katie McCreary; Sound, Thomas Sowers; Choreographer, Ann Marie Gideon; Music Director, Kyle Brumley; SM, Katie Pfohl; ASM, Seth Langer; Cast: Kyle Brumley (Mowgli/Villager), Cordell Cole (Shere Kahn/Chil), Jordan Craig (Baloo/Villager #1), Ann Marie Gideon (Raksha/Bainghan/Villager #5), Brian Harrison (Bagheera/Villager #2), Casey Hoekstra (Bandar Log King/Brother Wolf/Villager #4), Elizabeth Lanier (Messua/Bhopla), Caitlin McWethy (Kaa/Sister Wolf/Villager #3); July 6–22, 2011

Noises Off by Michael Frayne; Director, Richard Garner; Sets, Kat Conley; Costumes, Doug Koertge; Lighting, Mike Post; Sound, Clay Benning; SM, Margo Kuhne; ASM, David S. Cohen; Cast: Chris Kayser (Lloyd Dallas/Director), Carolyn Cook (Dotty Otley/Mrs. Clackett), Joe Knezevich (Garry Lejeune/Roger Trampleman), Ann Marie Gideon (Brooke Ashton/Vicki), Mark Cabus (Frederick Fellowes/Philip Brent/Sheikh), Tess Malis Kincaid (Belinda Blair/Flavia Brent), Allan Edwards (Selsdon Mowbray/Burglar), Scott Warren (Timothy Allgood/SM), Caitlin McWethy (Poppy Norton-Taylor/ASM); July 28–August 14, 2011

The Glass Menagerie by Tennessee Williams; Director, Richard Garner; Sets, Kat Conley; Costumes, Sydney Roberts; Lighting, Mike Post; Sound, Clay Benning; Composer, Kendall Simpson; SM, Margo Kuhne; ASM, Katie Pfohl; Cast: Mary Lynn Owen (Amanda Wingfield), Joe Knezevich (Tom Wingfield), Bethany Anne Lind (Laura Wingfield), Travis Smith (Jim O'Connor); October 5–30, 2011

PIEDMONT PARK

Shakespeare in the Park: The Tempest by William Shakespeare; Director, Sharon Ott; Sets, Tyler Tunney; Costumes, Leslie Taylor; Lighting, Ruth Hutson; Sound, Stephen LeGrand; Choreographer, Ivan Pulinkala; Dramaturg, Andrew J. Hartley; SM, Karen S. Martin; Cast: Mark Kincaid (Alonso), Brian Kurlander (Sebastian), Carolyn Cook (Prospera), Andrew Benator (Antonio), Nick Arapoglou (Ferdinand), Allen O'Reilly (Gonzalo), Mark Cabus (Trinculo), Bruce Evers (Stephano), Sean Moreno (Boatswain), Caitlin McWethy (Miranda), Chris Kayser (Ariel), Neal A. Ghant (Caliban), Tess Malis Kincaid (Ceres), Kyle Brumley (Sprite), Cordell Cole (Sprite), Brian Harrison (Sprite), Elizabeth Lanier (Sprite), Alexander Nathan (Sprite), Karen Thorla (Sprite); May 9–13, 2012

Geva Theatre Center

Rochester, NY

Thirty-ninth Season

Artistic Director, Mark Cuddy; Executive Director, Tom Parrish

ELAINE P. WILSON MAINSTAGE

Second City Summer Spectacular Created by the casts of The Second City; Director, Ryan Bernier; Music Director, Alex Kliner; Lighting, Derek Madonia; Sound, Ian Hildreth; SM, Laura Hum; Cast: Michael Kosinski, Rachel Miller, Eileen Montelione, Tawny Newsome, Tim Ryder; July 6–July 31, 2011

On Golden Pond by Ernest Thompson; Director, Skip Greer; Sets, Robert Koharchik; Costumes, B. Modern; Lighting, Kendall Smith; Sound, Dan Roach; Dramaturg, Eric Evans; SM, Kirsten Brannen, ASM, Veronica Aglow, Julia A.

Madonia; Casting Directors, Elissa Myers & Paul Fouquet, CSA; Cast: Kati Brazda (Chelsea Thayer Wayne), Larry Bull (Bill Ray), Eoin Dennis (Billy Ray, Jr.), Beth Dixon (Ethel Thayer), Patrick Noonan (Charlie Martin), Kenneth Tigar (Norman Thayer, Jr.); September 6–October 2, 2011

Dracula by Steven Dietz; Director, Peter Amster; Sets, Robert Mark Morgan; Costumes, Tracy Dorman; Lighting, Christine Binder; Composer, Gregg Coffin; Sound, Todd Mack Reischman; Dramaturg, Richard J. Roberts; Assistant Director, Michael Burke; Associate Lighting, Josh Beghiat; Associate Sound, Ian Hildreth; SM, Veronica Aglow; ASM, Frank Cavallo, Julie A. Madonia; Casting Director, Claire Simon Casting; Cast: Andrew Antao (Attendant), Jason Bradley (Harker), Chester Brassie (Attendant), Dieterich Gray (Renfield), Erik Hellman (Seward), Katy Kepler (Ensemble), Wade McCollum (Dracula), Tom McElroy (Van Helsing), Bianca S. Rogers (Ensemble), Lee Stark (Mina), Jennifer Joan Thompson (Lucy); October 11–November 13, 2011

A Christmas Carol by Charles Dickens; Adapted for the stage by Mark Cuddy; Music and lyrics by Gregg Coffin; Director, Mark Cuddy; Music Director, Don Kot; Choreographer, Meggins Kelley; Sets, Adam Koch; Costumes, Devon Painter; Lighting, Paul Hackenmueller; Sound, Lindsay Jones; Projections, Dan Scully; Associate Sound, Will Pickens; Assistant Projections, C. Andrew Bauer; Dramaturg, Jean Gordon Ryon; SM, Veronica Aglow, Frank Cavallo; ASM, Julie A. Madonia; Casting Directors, Elissa Myers & Paul Fouquet, CSA; Cast: Melissa Rain Anderson (Mrs. Cratchit/Mrs. Fezziwig/Mrs. Dilber), Andrew Antao (Ensemble), Michael Bennett (The Child Ebenezer/Boy Cratchit/Ignorance), Chester Brassie (Ensemble), Vincent Carbone (Ensemble) Isabel Hartzell (Fan/Miss Fezziwig), Silas Holtz (Ensemble), Natalia Hulse (The Ghost of Christmas Past/Turkey Girl), Katy Kepler (Ensemble), Kara Lindsay (Belle/Fred's Wife/Martha Cratchit/Young Wife), Colin Borden McGory (The Young Ebenezer/Peter Cratchit), Delaney McManus (Girl Cratchit/Want/Turkey Girl), Sierra Morabito (Miss Fezziwig/Servant Girl), Erin Mueller (Tiny Tim), Johnathan Mueller (The Young Ebenezer/Peter Cratchit), Kyle Mueller (The Child Ebenezer/Boy Cratchit/Ignorance), Megan Mueller (Girl Cratchit/Want/Turkey Girl), Ned Noyes (Fred, Apprentice Ebenezer, Young Husband), Emily Osinski (Fiddler), Christian Palmer (Ensemble), Guy Paul (Ebenezer Scrooge), Jim Poulos (Bob Cratchit/Dick Wilkins/Sailor/Undertaker's Man), Kilty Reidy (Businessman/Fezziwig/The Ghost of Christmas Present), Hailey Rene (Miss Fezziwig/Belinda Cratchit), Bianca Rogers (Ensemble), Julie Sandler (Miss Fezziwig/Belinda Cratchit), Remi Sandri (The Ghost of Jacob Marley/Schoolmaster/Miner/Topper/Businessman), Adriana Scalice (Fan/Miss Fezziwig), Carina Scalice (Miss Fezziwig/Servant Girl), Michael Sheehan (Ensemble), Rebekah Stein (Ensemble), Madison Strelick (Tiny Tim), Rachael Yoder (Ensemble), Alizabeth York (The Ghost of Christmas Past/Turkey Girl); November 25–December 24, 2011

Perfect Wedding by Robin Hawdon; Director, Bruce Jordan; Sets, Bill Clarke; Costumes, Mimi Maxmen; Lighting, Derek Madonia; Sound, Dan Roach; Dramaturg, Jean Gordon Ryon; SM, Frank Cavallo; ASM; Veronica Aglow, Julia A. Madonia; Casting Directors, Elissa Myers & Paul Fouquet, CSA; Cast: Tom Coiner (Tom), Cary Donaldson (Bill), Brigitt Markusfeld (Daphne), Kristen Mengelkoch (Julie), Kate Middleton (Judy), Teri Watts (Rachel); January 10–February 12, 2012

A Raisin in the Sun by Lorraine Hansberry, Director Robert O'Hara; Sets/Costumes, Clint Ramos; Lighting, Japhy Weideman; Sound, Lindsay Jones; Dramaturg, Jenni Werner; SM, Veronica Aglow; ASM, Frank Cavallo, Julie A. Madonia; Casting Directors, Elissa Myers & Paul Fouquet, CSA; Cast: Brian D. Coats (Bobo/Big Walter/Moving Man), Arthur Peter Dilbert III (Travis Younger), Jessica Frances Dukes (Beneatha Younger), David Paul Eve (Travis Younger), Keith D.Gallagher (Karl Lindner), Perri Gaffney (Mrs. Johnson), Daphne Gaines (Ruth Younger), Lynda Gravatt (Lena Younger), Tyrien Andre Obahnjoko (Joseph Asagai/George Murchison), Bowman Wright (Walter Lee Younger, Jr.); February 25–March 25, 2012

Superior Donuts by Tracy Letts; Director, Mark Cuddy; Sets, Jack McGaw; Costumes, Christina Selian; Lighting, Matthew Reinert; Fight Choreographer, David Leong; Dramaturg, Jenni Werner; Associate Sound, Ian Hildreth; SM, Frank Cavallo; ASM, Veronica Aglow, Julie Ann Madonia; Cast: Jamal Abdunnasir (Kevin

Magee), Christopher Burns (Luther Flynn), Skip Greer (Arthur Przybyszewski), Daryll Heysham (Max Tarasov), James Holloway (Franco Wicks), Patricia Lewis (Lady Boyle), Mary Jo Mecca (Officer Randy Osteen), Ron Scott (Officer James Bailey), Jeffrey Evan Thomas (Kiril Ivakin); April 3–29, 2012

Company Music and lyrics by Stephen Sondheim; Book by George Furth; Director, Mark Cuddy; Music Director, Don Kot; Sets, G.W. Mercier; Costumes, Pamela Scofield; Lighting, Joel Moritz; Sound, Will Pickens; Musical Staging Associate, Meggins Kelley; Dramaturg, Jean Gordon Ryon; SM, Veronica Aglow; ASM, Frank Cavallo; Casting Directors, Elissa Myers & Paul Fouquet, CSA; Cast: Ann Allgood (Joanne), Bobby Daye (David), Nicolette Hart (Marta/Dance Captain), Leslie Henstock (Kathy), Jessie Hooker (Jenny), Kristen Mengelkoch (Amy), Jim Poulos (Bobby), Michele Ragusa (Sarah), Ben Roseberry (Paul), Bruce Sabath (Harry), Emily Stockdale (April), Elisa Van Duyne (Susan), Kevin Vortmann (Peter), Jeff Williams (Larry); May 9–June 10, 2012

RON AND DONNA FIELDING NEXTSTAGE

Girl Talk by Louise Roche, Tim Flaherty & Sonya Carter; Conceived by Tim Flaherty with additional contributions by Betsy Kelso; Director, Sonya Carter; Music Director/Choreographer, Amy Jones; Technical Advisor/PSM, Jennifer Kules. Cast: Priscilla Fernandez (Laura), Angela Foley (Barbara), Laurie Elizabeth Gardner (Janice), Nidia Medina (Laura), Amber Nelson (Janice), Wilma Cespedes-Rivera (Laura); July 25–August 27, 2011

I Got Sick Then I Got Better by Jenny Allen; Directors, James Lapine and Darren Katz; Cast: Jenny Allen; March 7–11, 2012

Voices of the Spirits in My Soul by Nora Cole; Sets, Bob Ritz; Lighting, Richard Winkler; SM, Candace Lunn; Creative Consultant, Imani; Cast: Nora Cole; April 12–15, 2012

Two Jews Walk Into a War... by Seth Rozin; Director, Melia Bensussen; Lighting, Emily Stork; Sets and Costumes, Judy Gailen; Sound, David Remedios; SM, Jenn Lyons; Cast: Jeremiah Kissel (Zeblyan), Will LeBow (Ishaq); April 27–May 20, 2012

Goodman Theatre

Chicago, Illinois

Eighty-seventh Season

Artistic Director, Robert Falls; Executive Director, Roche Schulfer

ALBERT THEATRE

Red by John Logan; Director, Robert Falls; Sets, Todd Rosenthal; Costumes, Birgit Rattenborg Wise; Lighting, Keith Parham; Music Composition and Sound, Richard Woodbury; Casting, Adam Belcuore; Dramaturg, Neena Arndt; PSM, Joseph Drummond; SM, T. Paul Lynch; Cast: Edward Gero (Mark Rothko), Patrick Andrews (Ken); September 17–October 30, 2011

A Christmas Carol by Charles Dickens; Adapted by Tom Creamer; Director, Steve Scott; Sets, Todd Rosenthal, Costumes, Heidi Sue McMath; Lighting, Robert Christen; Sound, Cecil Averett; Music, Andrew Hansen; Casting, Adam Belcuore; PSM, Alden Vasquez; SM, Jamie Wolfe; Music Director, Andrew Hansen; Vocal Music Director, Malcolm Ruhl; Choreographer, Susan Hart; Dance Captain, Jon Hudson Odhom; Young Performer Supervisor, Meg Grgurich; Dialect, Christine Adaire; Cast: Larry Yando (Ebenezer Scrooge), Ron Rains (Bob Cratchit), Michael Perez (Mr. Ortle), Lisa Tejero (Miss Crumb), Joe Minoso (Fred), Ross Lehman (Poulterer/Mr. Fezziwig), Oscar Vasquez (Child in Doorway/Ignorance), Ora Jones (Charwoman/Mrs. Fezziwig/Catherine), Nathan Hosner (Ghost of Jacob Marley), Elizabeth Ledo (Ghost of Christmas Past/Philomena), Tim Gittings (Schoomaster/Chestnut Seller/Old Joe), Ryan Byrne (Scrooge as Boy/Peter Cratchit), Shanequa Beal (Fan/Belinda Cratchit), Emma Gordon (Pratt/Emily Cratchit/Want), Jarrod Zimmerman (Scrooge as Young Man/Ghost of Christmas Future), Jon Hudson Odom (Dick Wilkins/Tree Seller/Young Man), Nora Fiffer (Belle/Nora Fiffer), Penelope Walker (Ghost of Christmas Present), Karen Janes Woditsch (Mrs.

Cratchit), Emjoy Gavino (Martha Cratchit), Roni Akurati (Tiny Tim Cratchit), Sandra Delgado (Abby/Mrs. Dilber), Nathan Hosner (Topper), Ted Hoerl (Percy/Undertaker), Greg Hirte (Mr. Spinet/Violin/Mr. Sawyer), Justin Amolschd (French horn/Mr. French), Gregory Hirte (Violin/Mr. Sawyer), Malcolm Ruhl (Accordion/Guitar/Mr. Keys), Ben Change (Violin); November 18–December 31, 2011

Race by David Mamet; Director, Chuck Smith; Sets, Linda Buchanan; Costumes, Birgit Rattenborg Wise; Lighting, Robert Christen; Sound, Ray Nardelli, Joshua Horvath; Casting, Adam Belcuore; Dramaturg, Tanya Palmer; Casting, Logan Vaughn; PSM, Joseph Drummond, SM, Tina Jach; Cast: Geoffrey Owens (Henry Brown), Patrick Clear (Charles Strickland), Marc Grapey (Jack Lawson), Tamberla Perry (Susan); January 14–February 19, 2012

Camino Real by Tennessee Williams; New version by Calixto Bieito and Marc Rosich; Director, Calixto Bieito; Sets, Rebecca Ringst; Costumes, Ana Kuzmanic; Lighting, James F. Ingalls; Sound and Composition, Richard Woodbury; Music Director, Andra Velis Simon; Dramaturg, Neena Arndt; Casting, Adam Belcuore; PSM, Jamie Wolfe; SM Alden Vasquez, Rebecca Louise Fischer; Fight Consultant, Nick Sandys; Cast: David Darlow (Jacques Casanova), Matt DeCaro (Gutman), André De Shields (Baron de Charlus), Marilyn Dodds Frank (Marguerite Gautier), Carolyn Ann Hoerdemann (The Gypsy), Antwayn Hopper (Kilroy), Travis A. Knight (The Survivor/Abdullah), Monica Lopez (Esmeralda), Michael Medeiros (The Dreamer), Mark L. Montgomery (Lord Byron), Jonno Roberts (Lobo), Barbara E. Robertson (Rosita), Jacqueline Williams (La Madrecita de los Perdidos); March 3–April 8, 2012

The Iceman Cometh by Eugene O'Neill; Director, Robert Falls; Sets, Kevin Depinet; Costumes, Merrily Murray-Walsh; Lighting, Natasha Katz; Dramaturg, Neena Arndt; Casting, Adam Belcuore; PSM, Joseph Drummond; SM, Alden Vasquez; Cast: Patrick Andrews (Don Parritt), Kate Arrington (Cora), Brian Dennehy (Larry Slade), Marc Grapey (Jimmy Tomorrow), John Hoogenakker (Willie Oban), Salvatore Inzerillo (Rocky Pioggi), John Judd (Piet Wetjoen), Nathan Lane (Theodore "Hickey" Hickman), Loren Lazerine (Moran), Larry Neumann, Jr (Ed Mosher), Stephen Ouimette (Harry Hope), John Reeger (Cecil Lewis), Tara Sissom (Pearl), Lee Stark (Margie), John Douglas Thompson (Joe Mott), Bret Tuomi (Lieb), Lee Wilkof (Hugo Kalmar); April 21–June 17, 2012

Crowns by Regina Taylor; Director, Regina Taylor; Sets, Maruti Evans; Costumes, Karen Perry; Lighting, Kenneth Posner; Sound, Richard Woodbury; Projections, Maya Ciarrochi; Choreographer, Dianne McIntyre; Music, Fred Carl; Casting, Adam Belcuore; Dramaturg, Tanya Palmer; PSM, Alden Vasquez; SM, Jamie Wolfe; Cast: Shari Addison (Ensemble), Melanie Brezill (Ensemble), E. Faye Butler (Mabel), Felicia Fields (Mother Shaw), David Jennings (Man/Preacher), Jasondra Johnson (Velma), Alexis Rogers (Jeanette), Kelvin Roston (Ensemble), Yusha-Marie Sorzano (Ensemble), Laura Walls (Ensemble), Pauletta Washington (Wanda), Marketta P. Wilder (Yolanda); June 30–August 12, 2012

OWEN THEATRE

The Convert by Danai Gurira; Director, Emily Mann; Sets, Daniel Ostling; Costumes, Paul Tazewell; Lighting, Lap Chi Chu; Sound, Darron L. West; Casting, Adam Belcuore, Erika Sellin; Dramaturg, Carrie Hughes; PSM, Alison Cote; Fight Director, J. Steven White; Dialect/Vocal Coach, Beth McGuire; Associate Director, Adam Immerwahr; Cast: Pascale Armand (Jekesai/Ester), Cheryl Lynn Bruce (Mai Tamba), Zainab Jah (Prudence), Kevin Mambo (Chancellor), LeRoy McClain (Chilford Chiredzi), Warner Joseph Miller (Tamba), Harold Surratt (Uncle); Februrary 25–March 25, 2012

Fish Men by Cándido Tirado; Director, Edward Torres; Sets, Collette Pollard; Costumes, Christine Pascual; Lighting, Jesse Klug; Sound, Mikhail Fiksel; Dramaturg, Kristen Leahey, Tanya Palmer; PSM, Kimberly Osgood; Cast: Daniel Cantor (Stuart), Raúl Castillo (Rey Reyes), Ben Chang (Dr. Lee), Mike Cherry (John), Ricardo Gutierrez (Jerome), Kenn E. Head (PeeWee), Cedric Mays (Cash), Howard Witt (Adam Kirchbaum AKA Ninety-Two); April 7–May 6, 2012

Goodspeed Musicals

East Haddam, Connecticut

Forty-eighth Season

Executive Director, Michael P. Price

GOODSPEED OPERA HOUSE

My One and Only Music by George Gershwin; Lyrics by Ira Gershwin, Book by Peter Stone and Timothy S. Mayer; Director, Ray Roderick; Sets, James Youmans; Costumes, Robin L. McGee; Lighting, Paul Miller; Sound, Jay Hilton; PSM, Bradley G. Spachman; ASM, Derek Michael DiGregorio; Projections, Michael Clark; Dialect, Gillian Lane-Plescia; Cast: Trent Armand Kendall (Reverend J.D. Montgomery/Ensemble), Vasthy E. Mompoint (New Rhythms/Ensemble), Victor J. Wisehart (New Rhythms/Ensemble), Richard Riaz Yoder (New Rhythms/Ensemble), Tony Yazbeck (Captain Billy Buck Chandler), Khris Lewin (Prince Nikki/Achmed), Gabrielle Ruiz (Edythe Herbert), Kirsten Wyatt (Mickey), Alde Lewis, Jr. (Mr. Magix); Ensemble: Brian Davis, Deanna Glover, Matthew J. Kilgore, Drew King, Kristyn Pope, Allison Kaye Rihn, Kristen J. Smith; Understudies: Joe Grandy (Billy/Ensemble), Victor J. Wisehart (Nikki/Achmed/Ensemble), Lea Kohl (Edythe/Ensemble), Nancy Renée Braun (Mickey/Ensemble), Jarran Muse (Reverend/Mr. Magix/Ensemble); April 15–June 25, 2011

Show Boat Music by Jerome Kern; Book and lyrics by Oscar Hammerstein II; Based on the novel by Edna Ferber; Director, Rob Ruggiero; Sets, Michael Schweikardt; Costumes, Amy Clark; Lighting, John Lasiter; Sound, Jay Hilton; PSM, Bradley G. Spachman; ASM, Derek Michael DiGregorio; Cast: Lenny Wolpe (Captain Andy), Jennifer Knox (Ellie), Danny Gardner (Frank), Karen Murphy (Parthy), Lesli Margherita (Julie), Rob Richardson (Steve/Ensemble), David Toombs (Pete/Jeb/Ensemble), Andrea Frierson (Queenie), Robert Hannon Davis (Windy/Jim Greene/Ensemble), Greg Roderick (Willy/A Backwoodsman/Ensemble), Ben Davis (Gaylord Ravenal), Jet Thomason (Sheriff Ike/Ensemble), Sarah Uriarte Berry (Magnolia Hawks), David Aron Damane (Joe), Madeleine Berry (Kim as a child), Denise Lute (Mrs. O'Brien/Mother Superior/Old Lady/Ensemble), Robert Lance Mooney (Jake/Ensemble), Richard Waits (Charlie/Ensemble), Elizabeth Ann Berg (Lottie/Ensemble), Elise Kinnon (Dottie/Ensemble), Mollie Vogt-Welch (Kim as an adult/Ensemble); Ensemble: Paule Aboite, Kyle E. Baird, A'Lisa D. Miles, Nicholas Ward; Understudies: Mollie Vogt-Welch (Magnolia/Julie), Rob Richardson (Ravenal), A'Lisa D. Miles (Queenie), Denise Lute (Parthy), Robert Hannon Davis (Captain Andy), Robert Lance Mooney (Frank), Elise Kinnon (Ellie), Nicholas Ward (Joe), Belle Doraz (Kim); July 1–September 17, 2011

City of Angels Book by Larry Gelbart; Music by Cy Coleman; Lyrics by David Zippel; Director, Darko Tresnjak; Sets, David P. Gordon; Costumes, Tracy Christensen; Lighting, John Lasiter; Sound, Jay Hilton; PSM, Bradley G. Spachman; ASM, Derek Michael DiGregorio; Cast: Burke Moses (Stone), Spencer Rowe (Orderly/Sonny/Yamato/Studio Cop), Robert J. Townsend (Orderly/Mahoney/Shoeshine/Sound Engineer), Nancy Anderson (Oolie/Donna), Liz Pearce (Alaura/Carla), Jerry Gallagher (Big Six/Studio Cop), Jeffrey David Sears (Jimmy), Mick Bleyer (Angel City Four/Commissioner Gaines/Cinematographer), Adam West Hemming (Angel City Four), Vanessa Parvin (Angel City Four), Sierra Rein (Angel City Four/Margie/Hairdresser), Danny Bolero (Muñoz/Pancho), Josh Powell (Officer Pasco/Del/Gene), Laurie Wells (Bobbi/Gabby), Jay Russell (Irwin/Buddy), Allen E. Read (Peter/Gerald), Christina Morrell (Margaret/Bootsie/Anna/Carla's Stand-in), Gregor Paslawsky (Luther/Werner), Michael Keyloun (Dr. Mandril/Gilbert), Kathleen Rooney (Mallory/Avril), D.B. Bonds (Stine); Understudies: Robert J. Townsend (Stine/Luther/Mandril), Josh Powell (Stone), Christina Morrell (Bobbi/Gabby/Alaura/Carla), Sierra Rein (Donna/Oolie), Spencer Rowe (Buddy/Irwin/Muñoz/Pancho), Adam Bastien (Jimmy/Peter/Gerald/Gilbert/Party Guest/Buddy's Nephew/Sonny/1st & 2nd Orderly/Yamato/Studio Guard/Pasco/Dacosta/Gene/Butler/Shoeshine Boy/Mahoney/Man in Phone Booth/Sound Engineer), Becca Pesce (Mallory/Avril/Margaret/Anna/Bootsie/Carla's Stand-in/Party Guest), Josh Powell (Big Six/Studio Guard); September 23–November 27, 2011

THE NORMA TERRIS THEATRE

Cutman a Boxing Musical Book by Jared Michael Coseglia; Music and lyrics by Drew Brody; Story by Jared Michael Coseglia and Cory Grant; Director, Jared Michael Coseglia; Sets, Adrian W. Jones; Costumes, Wade Laboissonniere; Lighting, Jason Lyons; Sound, Jay Hilton; PSM, Daniel S. Rosokoff; ASM, Aaron Elgart; Cast: Cory Grant (Ari), Mitch Greenberg (Rabbi Roseman), Dennis Stowe (Moe), Jerold Solomon (Lincoln), Joshua Keith (Killer Karim Karver/Ensemble), Joshua Boone (Quincy/Ensemble), Laura Dean (Edie), Eileen Tepper (Dolores/Ensemble), Haley Hannah (Jo/Ensemble), Ana Nogueira (Olivia), Garrett Long (Cantor Aviva), Ven Daniel (Max/Ensemble), Albert Guerzon (Doctor/Ensemble), Jadi Collado (Ensemble); May 12–June 5, 2011

The Unauthorized Autobiography of Samantha Brown by Kait Kerrigan and Brian Lowdermilk; Director, Daniel Goldstein; Sets, Walt Spangler; Costumes, David C. Woolard; Lighting, Jason Lyons; Sound, Tony Meola; PSM, Dan da Silva; Cast: Meghann Fahy (Samantha), Melissa Benoist (Kelly), Catherine Porter (Mom), Stephen Bogardus (Dad), Andrew Durand (Adam); August 4–28, 2011

Hello! My Baby by Cheri Steinkellner; Director, Ray Roderick; Sets, Michael Scheikardt; Costumes, Robin L. McGee; Lighting, John Lasiter; Sound, Jay Hilton; PSM, Renee Lutz; ASM, Heather Klein; Cast: Justin Bown (Mickey), Stephanie Koenig (Nelly/Ned), Kelly McCormick (Frances), Alex Viola (Violet), Carrington Vilmont (Junior), Jeremy Sevelovitz (Johnny/Ensemble), Michael Warrell (Dickie the Duck/Ensemble), Michael Mendez (Kid Vicious/Ensemble), Matthew Bauman (Albie/Ensemble), Clinton Roane (Noble/Ensemble), Frank Root (Bert/Radio Announcer), Beth McVey (Ethel), Allie Schauer (Marie/Ensemble), Dick Decareau (Stanford), Catherine Blades (Alice/Ensemble); Ensemble: Jessica Azenberg, Zak Edwards, Ashley Wallace; November 3–27, 2011

Great Lakes Theater

Cleveland, Ohio

Fiftieth Season

Producing Artistic Director, Charles Fee; Executive Director, Bob Taylor

HANNA THEATRE

Cabaret Book by Joe Masteroff; Based on the play by John Van Druten; Stories by Christopher Isherwood; Music by John Kander; Lyrics by Fred Ebb; Director, Victoria Bussert; Music Director, Matthew Webb; Choreographer, Gregory Daniels; Sets, Jeff Herrmann; Lighting, Norman Coates; Costumes, Charlotte Yetman; SM, Corrie E. Purdum; Cast: Neil Brookshire (Clifford Bradshaw), Sara M. Bruner (Fraulein Kost), Phillip Michael Carroll (Victor/Max/Sailor), Jodi Dominick (Sally Bowles), Nika Ericson (Ensemble), Danny Henning (Bobby/Gorilla), Jillian Kates (Texas), Andrea Leach (Rosie), Jim Lichtscheidl (Ernst Ludwig), Bailey Carter Moulse (Fritzie), Shannon O'Boyle (Lulu), Eduardo Placer (Master of Ceremonies), Laura Perrotta (Fraulein Schneider), Maggie Roach (Frenchie), Sara Whale (Helga), Rod Wolfe (Customs Official/Rudy), John Woodson (Herr Schultz); September 23–October 30, 2011

The Taming of the Shrew by William Shakespeare; Director, Tracy Young; Additional Staging, Kjerstine Rose Anderson; Sets, Michael Locher; Lighting, Rick Martin; Costumes, Alex Jaeger; Sound, Peter John Still; SM, Tim Kinzel; Cast: Kjerstine Rose Anderson (Bianca), Neil Brookshire (Tranio), Sara M. Bruner (Katherine), Phillip Michael Carroll (Curtis/Coffee Vendor/Cop), Aled Davies (Tourist dad/Vincentio), Jodi Dominick (Ivana/Tailor), Nika Ericson (Map Seller/Waiter/Servant Peter/Haberdasher), Reggie Gowland (Lucentio), Danny Henning (Biondello), Jillian Kates (Tourist Mom/Servant Nathaniel/Bridesmaid), Andrea Leach (Jogger/Servant Phillip/Bridesmaid), Jim Lichtscheidl (Petruchio), Bailey Carter Moulse (Tourist Kid/ Servant Joseph/Bridesmaid), Shannon O'Boyle (Executive/Servant Nicholas/Bridesmaid), Laura Perrotta (The Widow), Eduardo Placer (Hortensio), Dudley Swetland (Autograph Hound/Merchant), M.A. Taylor (Surfer Dude/ Grumio), Rod Wolfe (Gremio), John Woodson (Baptista Minola); September 30–October 29, 2011

The Mousetrap by Agatha Christie; Director, Drew Barr; Sets, Russell Metheny; Lighting, Mary Louise Geiger; Costumes, Kim Krumm Sorenson; Original Music and Sound, Daniel Kluger; Fight Choreographer, Michael Mueller; SM, Corrie E. Purdum; Cast: Sara M. Bruner (Miss Casewell), Aled Davies (Major Metcalf), Jodi Dominick (Mollie Ralston), Kate Duffield (Mrs. Maureen Lyon), Tom Ford (Mr. Paravicini), Paul Hurley (Giles Ralston), Dan Lawrence (Detective Sergeant Trotter), Ryan David O'Byrne (Christopher Wren), Laura Perrotta (Mrs. Boyle); March 9–25, 2012

Romeo and Juliet by William Shakespeare; Director, Charles Fee; Sets, Gage Williams; Lighting, Rick Martin; Costumes, Star Moxley; Sound, Peter John Still; Choreographer, Helene Peterson; Fight Choreographer, Ken Merckx; SM, Tim Kinzel; Cast: J. Todd Adams (Mercutio), Lynn Robert Berg (Friar Laurence), Laurie Birmingham (Nurse), Casey Cott (Balthasar), Aled Davies (Capulet), Jodi Dominick (Sampson/Sister John), Christian Durso (Romeo), Tom Ford (Gregory), Paul Hurley (Benvolio), Dan Lawrence (Tybalt), Betsy Mugavero (Juliet), Melissa Owens (Lady Montague), Laura Perrotta (Lady Capulet), David Anthony Smith (Escalus), Dudley Swetland (Montague), M.A. Taylor (Peter), Jordan Whalen (Paris/Abram); Ensemble: Danielle Dorfman, Mackenzie Duan, Jon Gluckner, Lisa Kuhnen, Cody Zak; April 13–28, 2012

Sondheim on Sondheim Music and lyrics By Stephen Sondheim; Originally conceived and directed by James Lapine; Inspired by a concept by David Kernan; Director, Victoria Bussert; Music Director, Matthew Webb; Choreographer, Gregory Daniels; Projections, Daniel Brodie; Set, Jeff Herrmann; Costumes, Charlotte Yetman; Lighting, Mary Jo Dondlinger; Sound, Richard B. Ingraham; SM, Corrie E. Purdum; ASM, Jamie R. Benetto; Assistant Director, Sara Bruner; Cast: Marie-France Arcilla, Justin Keyes, Pamela Myers, Destan Owens, James Penca, Ciara Renée, Brian Sutherland, Emily Walton; May 16–July 8, 2012

OHIO THEATRE

A Christmas Carol by Charles Dickens; Adapted and directed by Gerald Freedman; Staging, Sara Bruner; Sets, John Ezell, Gene Emerson Friedman; Lighting, Mary Jo Dondlinger, Cynthia Stillings; Costumes, James Scott; Choreographer, David Shimotakahara; Music Adaptator/Arranger, Robert Waldman; Music Director, Matthew Webb; SM, Corrie E. Purdum; ASM, Tim Kinzel; Cast: Lynn Robert Berg (Marley/Lighthouse Man/Man 2/Undertaker), Kayleigh Collins (Master William/Tiny Tim), Jackson Daugherty (James/Robert/Adolescent Scrooge/Ensemble), Aled Davies (Scrooge/Samuels), Jodi Dominick (Jane/Mrs. Cratchit/Charwoman/Ensemble), Mackenzie Dale Durken (Skate Girl/Ensemble), Antwaun Holley (Richard/Peter Cratchit/Dick Wilkins/Ensemble), Cameron Andrew Howell (Delivery Boy/Ensemble), Paul Hurley (Young Scrooge/Nephew Fred/Ensemble), Rachel M. Jones (Elizabeth/Martha Cratchit/Fan/Ensemble), Mia Knight (Swing/Street Child), Darryl Lewis (Charity Man 2/ Mr. Fezziwig/Man 1/Captain), Colleen Longshaw (Cynthia/Mrs. Fezziwig/Laundress/Ensemble), Dougfred Miller (Father/Bob Cratchit/Ensemble), Cameron Danielle Nelson (Sarah/Polly/Want), Carly Marie Nelson (Sled Boy/Ignorance), Cassidy Josephine Nelson (Master William/Tiny Tim), Courtney Anne Nelson (Soloist/Street Child), Laura Perrotta (Mother/Mrs. Fred/Ensemble), Eduardo Placer (Ghost of Christmas Past/Ghost of Christmas Future/Street Singer), Maggie Roach (Debtor's Wife/Belle/Ensemble), David Anthony Smith (Muggeridge/The Ghost of Christmas Present/Debtor/Ensemble), Dudley Swetland (Topper/Man 3/Miner), M.A. Taylor (Charity Man 1/Joe the Keeper/Ensemble), Natalie Welch (Abigail/Belinda); Debember 3–23, 2011

Guthrie Theater

Minneapolis, Minnesota

Forty-ninth Season

Artistic Director, Joe Dowling

WURTELE THRUST STAGE

Much Ado About Nothing by William Shakespeare; Director, Joe Dowling; Sets, Riccardo Hernández; Costumes, Fabio Toblini; Lighting, Christopher Akerlind; Composer, Adam Wernick; Sound, Reid Rejsa; Voice/Language, Andrew Wade; Dramaturg, Michael Lupu; Movement, Joe Chvala; SM, Justin Hossle; ASM, Jason Clusman, Rob Goudy; Assistant Director, Sam Bardwell; Cast: Robert O. Berdahl (Balthasar), Raye Birk (Antonio), Michael Booth (Conrade), Dennis Creaghan (Leonato), Bob Davis (Borachio), Laura Esping (Ursula), Nathaniel Fuller (Verges/Friar Francis), Daniel Gerroll (Benedick), Peter Michael Goetz (Dogberry), Emily Gunyou Halaas (Margaret), H. Adam Harris (Messenger/George Seacoal), David Manis (Don Pedro), Bill McCallum (Claudio), Ron Menzel (Don John/Sexton), Dearbhla Molloy (Beatrice), Michelle O'Neill (Hero), Max Polski (Watchman); September 10–November 5, 2011

A Christmas Carol Adapted by Crispin Whittell from the novel by Charles Dickens; Director, Joe Dowling; Sets, Walt Spangler; Costumes, Mathew J. LeFebvre; Lighting, Christopher Akerlind; Composer, Keith Thomas; Sound, Scott W. Edwards; Dramaturg, Jo Holcomb; Voice/Dialect, D'Arcy Smith; Movement, Joe Chvala; Aerial Flight, John Stead; SM, Michele Harms; ASM, Jason Clusman; Associate Director, James McNamara; Cast: Sam Bardwell (Dick Wilkins/Topper/Jobber), Robert O. Berdahl (Ghost of Christmas Present/Ali Baba/Bull), Virginia S. Burke (Mrs. Cratchit/Robinson Crusoe's Parrot), John Catron (Fred/Daniel/Jobber), J.C. Cutler (Ebenezer Scrooge), Bob Davis (Old Joe/Jacob Marley), Zach Fineblum (Young Scrooge/Broker), Nathaniel Fuller (George/Mr. Sykes/Bear), Stuart Gates (Mr. Wimple/David), Emily Gunyou Halaas (Street Lady/Dora Fezziwig/Jane), Summer Hagen (Daisy Fezziwig/Mabel), Kathryn Lawrey (Wimple's Wife/Belle/Kitty), Tracey Maloney (Ghost of Christmas Past/Mrs. Polkinghorne), Kris L. Nelson (Bob Cratchit/Donald), Lee Mark Nelson (Mr. Fezziwig/Mr. Bones/Scrooge's Priest), Isabell Monk O'Connor (Mrs. Dilber/Bumble), Anna Reichert (Deidre Fezziwig/Sally), Ben Rosenbaum (Belle's Husband/Ghost of Christmas Future), Angela Timberman (Merriweather), Suzanne Warmanen (Bunty/Mrs. Fezziwig); November 19–December 30, 2012

Cat on a Hot Tin Roof by Tennessee Williams; Director, Lisa Peterson; Sets, Rachel Hauck; Costumes, Ilona Somogyi; Lighting, Scott Zielinski; Composer/Sound, Paul James Prendergast; Dramaturg, Carla Steen; Voice/Dialect, Lucinda Holshue; Movement, Marcela Lorca; SM, Susan R. White; ASM, Justin Hossle; Assistant Director, Jennie Ward; Cast: David Anthony Brinkley (Big Daddy), Shá Cage (Sookey), Chris Carlson (Gooper), Stephen D'Ambrose (Rev. Tooker), Peter Christian Hansen (Brick), H. Adam Harris (Lacey), Melissa Hart (Big Mama), Michelle O'Neill (Mae), Reggie Phoenix (Brightie), Emily Swallow (Margaret), Fred Wagner (Dr. Baugh), Joetta Wright (Daisy); January 14–February 26, 2012

Hay Fever by Noël Coward; Director, Christopher Luscombe; Sets/Costumes, Janet Bird; Lighting, Philip S. Rosenberg; Sound, Reid Rejsa; Dramaturg, Carla Steen; Voice/Dialect, D'Arcy Smith; Movement, Marcela Lorca; SM, Chris A. Code; ASM, Michele Harms; Cast: Heidi Bakke (Jackie Coryton), Barbara Bryne (Clara), John Catron (Sandy Tyrell), Anna Hanson (Amy), Harriet Harris (Judith Bliss), Torsten Johnson (William), Charity Jones (Myra Arundel), Simon Jones (David Bliss), John Skelley (Simon Bliss), Matt Sullivan (Richard Greatham), Cat Walleck (Sorel Bliss); March 10–April 22

The Sunshine Boys by Neil Simon; Director Gary Gisselman; Sets/Costumes, John Arnone; Lighting, Don Darnutzer; Sound, Reid Rejsa; Dramaturg, Carla Steen; Voice/Dialect, D'Arcy Smith; Movement, Marcela Lorca; SM, Martha Kulig; ASM, Justin Hossle; Assistant Director, Dionne Laviolette; Cast: Robert O. Berdahl (Ben Silverman), Raye Birk (Al Lewis), Nathaniel Fuller (Television Director), Peter Michael Goetz (Willie Clark), Jennifer Maren (Sketch Nurse), Greta Oglesby (Registered Nurse), Samuel Finnegan Pearson (Eddie), Dudley Riggs (Sketch Patient); July 7–September, 2012

MCGUIRE PROSCENIUM STAGE

The Burial at Thebes by Seamus Heaney based upon Sophocles' *Antigone*; Director, Marcela Lorca; Sets, Monica Frawley; Costumes, Elizabeth Caitlin Ward; Lighting, Christopher Akerlind; Composer, J.D. Steele; Sound, Scott W. Edwards; Dramaturg, Jo Holcomb; Voice/Language, Lucinda Holshue; SM, Martha Kulig; ASM, Michele Harms; Assistant Director, Dario Tangelson; Cast: Ansa Akyea (Messenger), Ernest Bentley (Haemon), Sun Mee Chomet (Antigone), Greta Oglesby (Tiresias), Robert Robinson (Chorus/Vocalist), Brian Sostek (Guard), Prentiss Standridge (Ismene), Regina Marie Willams (Eurydice), Stephen Yoakam (Creon), Morgan Guinta/Ryan McCormick (Tiresias' Boy, alt. performances), Chorus: Lee Mark Nelson, Richard Ooms, T. Mychael Rambo, Joe Nathan Thomas; September 24–November 6, 2011

Charley's Aunt by Brandon Thomas; Director, John Miller-Stephany; Sets, John Coyne; Costumes, Jess Goldstein; Lighting, Marcus Dilliard; Sound, Reid Rejsa; Dramaturg, Michael Lupu; Voice/Language, Lucinda Holshue; Movement, Marcela Lorca; SM, Chris A. Code; ASM, Meaghan Rosenberger; Associate Director, Brian Sostek; Cast: Matthew Amendt (Jack Chesney), Charles Hubbell (Brassett), Ben Mandelbaum (Charles Wykeham), Colin McPhillamy (Stephen Spettigue), Ashley Rose Montondo (Amy Spettigue), Valeri Mudek (Kitty Verdun), Thallis Santesteban (Ela Delahay), John Skelley (Lord Fancourt Babberley), Peter Thomson (Sir Francis Chesney), Sally Wingert (Donna Lucia d'Alvadorez); November 26, 2011–January 15, 2012

End of the Rainbow by Peter Quilter; Director, Terry Johnson; Sets/Costumes, William Dudley; Lighting, Christopher Akerlind; Sound, Gareth Owen; Music Director/Conductor, Jeff Harris; Music Arranger, Chris Egan; Voice/Dialect, Kate Wilson; SM, Mark Dobrow; ASM, Rachel Zack; Assistant Director, Benjamin Shaw; Cast: Tracie Bennett (Judy Garland), Michael Cumpsty (Anthony), Tom Pelphrey (Mickey Deans), Jay Russell (Radio Interviewer/Porter/ASM); January 28–March 11, 2012

Time Stands Still by Donald Margulies; Director, Joe Dowling; Sets, Walk Spangler; Costumes, Christine A. Richardson; Lighting, Tom Mays; Sound, Scott W. Edwards; Dramaturg, Jo Holcomb; Voice/Dialect, D'Arcy Smith; Movement, Marcela Lorca; SM, Martha Kulig; ASM, Meaghan Rosenberger; Assistant Director, Jon Ferguson; Cast: Sarah Agnew (Sarah Goodwin), Bill McCallum (James Dodd), Mark Benninghofen (Richard Ehrlich), Valeri Mudek (Mandy Bloom); April 7–May 20, 2012

Roman Holiday Music and lyrics by Cole Porter; Book by Paul Blake based on the Paramount Pictures motion picture; Director, John Miller-Stephany; Choreographer, Alex Sanchez; Music/Conductor, Andrew Cooke; Sets, Todd Rosenthal; Costumes, Mathew J. LeFebvre; Lighting, Donald Holder; Sound, Scott W. Edwards; Projections, Wendell K. Harrington; Dramaturg, Jo Holcomb; Voice/Dialect, D'Arcy Smith; Fight Director, Robin H. McFarquhar; Orchestrator, Larry Blank, Doug Besterman; Vocal Arranger/Associate Music Director, Michael Horsley; Dance, Samuel S. Davis; SM, Chris A. Code; ASM, Jason Clusman, Michele Harms; Assistant Director, Brian Sostek; Assistant Choreographer, Lanie Sakakura; Cast: Christina Baldwin (Francesca Scabulo), Michelle Barber (Countess), Stephanie Rothenberg (Princess Anne), Jim Stanek (Irving Radovich), Edward Watts (Joe Bradley); Ensemble: David Anders, Matt Baker, Liam Benzvi, Joseph Bigelow, David Anthony Brinkley, David Colacci, Drew Franklin, Gabriela Garcia, Michael Gruber, Linda Talcott Lee, Ann Michels, Jared Oxborough, Aaron Lloyd Pomeroy, Laura Rudolph, Lainie Sakakura, John Skelley, Alan Sorenson, Peter Thomson, Angela Timberman, Tony Vierling, Alexandra Zorn, Swings: Christian DeMarais, Carolyn Doherty, Lee Mark Nelson, Marc Oka, Janet Hayes Trow; June 9–August 19, 2012

DOWLING STUDIO

The Edge of Our Bodies by Adam Rapp; Director, Benjamin McGovern; Sets, Michael Hoover; Costumes, Christine A. Richardson; Lighting, Ryan Connealy; Sound, C. Andrew Mayer; Voice, Lucinda Holshue; SM, Tree O'Halloran; PA, Sarah Howell; Assistant Director, Cristina Castro; Cast: Ali Rose Dachis (Bernadette), Steve Sweere (Maintenance Man); October 22–November 20, 2011

The Birds by Conor McPherson from the short story by Daphne du Maurier; Director, Henry Wishcamper; Sets, Wilson Chin; Costumes, Jenny Mannis; Lighting, Matthew Richards; Sound, Scott W. Edwards; Dramaturg, Michael Lupu; Fight Director, Peter Moore; SM, Jason Clusman; PA, Sarah Howell; Assistant Director, Amanda Friou; Cast: J.C. Cutler (Nat), Angela Timberman (Diane), Summer Hagen (Julia), Stephen Yoakam (Tierney); February 25–April 8, 2012

Huntington Theatre Company

Boston, Massachusetts

Thirtieth Season

Artistic Director, Peter DuBois; Managing Director, Michael Maso

AVENUE OF THE ARTS / BU THEATRE

Candide Book adapted from Voltaire by High Wheeler; Director/Adaptor, Mary Zimmerman; Choreographer, Daniel Pelzig; Music Direction/Additional Arrangements and Orchestrations by Doug Peck; Sets, Daniel Ostling; Lighting, TJ Gerckens; Sound, Richard Woodbury; PSM, M. William Shiner; Cast: Larry Yando (Pangloss/Others), Geoff Packard (Candide), Lauren Molina (Cunegonde), Erik Lochtefeld (Maximillian/Others), McCaela Donovan (Paquette/Others), Travis Turner (Servant/Others), Emma Rosenthal (Bird/Others), Joey Stone (Soldier/Others), Alexander Elisa (Soldier/Others), Evan Harrington (Orator/Others), Abby Mueller (Orator's Wife/Others), Jeff Parket (Anabaptist/Others), Cheryl Stern (Old Lady), Jesse J. Perez (Cacambo/Others), Timothy John Smith (Governor/Others), Tempe Thomas (Queen of El Dorado/Others), Spencer Curnutt (Sailor/Others), Rebecca Finnegan (Vanderdendur/Other)s, Tom Aulino (Martin/Others); September 10–October 16, 2011

Captors by Evan M. Weiner; Director, Peter DuBois; Sets, Beowulf Boritt; Costumes, Bobby Frederick Tilley II; Lighting, Russel H. Champa; Sound, M.L. Dogg; PSM, Marti McIntosh; Cast: Daniel Eric Gold (Cohn), Louis Cancelmi (Malkin), Christopher Burns (Hans), Michael Cristofer (Eichmann), Ariel Shafir (Uzi); World Premiere; November 11–December 11, 2011

God of Carnage by Yasmina Reza; Director, Daniel Goldstein; Sets, Dane Laffrey; Costumes, Charles Schoonmaker; Lighting, Tyler Micoleau; Sound, Brett R. Jarvis; PSM, Kevin Robert Fitzpatrick; Cast: Johanna Day (Veronica Novak), Brooks Ashmanskas (Alan Raleigh), Stephen Bogardus (Michael Novak), Christy Pusz (Annette Raleigh); January 6–February 5, 2012

Ma Rainey's Black Bottom by August Wilson; Director, Liesl Tommy; Sets, Clint Ramos; Costumes, Clint Ramos; Lighting, Marcus Doshi; Original Music, Sound/Music Director, Broken Chord; PSM, Leslie Sears; Cast: Thomas Derrah (Sturdyvant), Will LeBow (Irvin), G. Valmont Thomas (Cutler), Charles Weldon (Toledo), Glenn Turner (Slow Drag), Jason Bowen (Levee), Yvette Freeman (Ma Rainey), Joniece Abbot-Pratt (Dussie Mae), Timothy John Smith (Policeman), Corey Allen (Sylvester); March 9–April 8, 2012

Private Lives by Noël Coward; Director, Maria Aitken; Sets, Allen Moyer; Costumes, Candice Donnelly; Lighting, Philip S. Rosenberg; Sound, Rob Milburn and Michael Bodeen; Choreographer; Daniel Pelzig; Dialect Coach, Stephen Gabis; PSM, Leslie Sears; Cast: Autumn Hurlbert (Sibyl), James Waterston (Elyot), Bianca Amato (Amanda), Jeremy Webb (Victor), Paula Plum (Louise); May 25–June 24, 2012

SOUTH END / CALDERWOOD PAVILION AT THE BCA

Before I Leave You by Rosanna Yamagiwa Alfaro; Director, Jonathan Silverstein; Sets, Allen Moyer; Costumes, Michael Krass; Lighting, David Lander; Original Music and Sound, David Remedios; PSM, Carola Morrone LaCoste; Cast: Kippy Goldfarb (Emily), Ross Bickell (Jeremy), Glenn Kubota (Koji), Karen MacDonald (Trish), Alexis Camins (Peter); World Premiere; October 14–November 13, 2011

The Luck of the Irish by Kirsten Greenidge; Director, Melia Bensussen; Sets, James Noone; Costumes, Mariann S. Verheyen; Lighting, Justin Townsend; Original Music and Sound, David Remedios; PSM, Marti McIntosh; Cast: Shalita

The Company of Hairspray at North Carolina Theatre
(photo by North Carolina Theatre)

Daniel José Molina and Alejandra Escalante in Oregon Shakespeare Festival's
production of Romeo and Juliet (photo by Jenny Graham)

Sydney James Harcourt and the Company of The Rocky Horror Show
at The Old Globe (photo by Henry DiRocco)

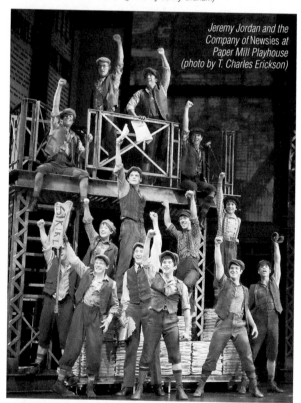

Jeremy Jordan and the
Company of Newsies at
Paper Mill Playhouse
(photo by T. Charles Erickson)

Horton Foote Jr., Penny Fuller, Elizabeth Ashley, Jenny Dare Paulin,
Nicole Lowrance, Hallie Foote, James DeMarse, Kelly McAndrew, and
Devon Abner in the West Coast premiere of Dividing the Estate at The Old Globe
(photo by Henry DiRocco)

Darius de Haas, Saycon Sengbloh, Jerold E. Solomon, Kenita R. Miller, Aurelia Williams, Alan Mingo Jr., Syesha Mercado, and Courtney Reed in Once On This Island at Paper Mill Playhouse (photo by Jerry Dalia)

Don DiGiulio, David Bielewicz, Daniel Krell, Lindsay Smiling, and David Whalen in As You Like It at Pittsburgh Public Theater (photo by Pittsburgh Public Theater)

Bradley Whitford, Roger Bart, and Michael O'Keefe in Art at The Pasadena Playhouse (photo by Jim Cox)

Shawn Fagan and the Ensemble in PlayMakers Repertory Company's production of The Making of a King: Henry IV & Henry V (photo by Jon Gardiner)

The Company of Ruined at Philadelphia Theatre Company (photo by Mark Garvin)

The Company of Sunday in the Park with George at The Repertory Theatre of St. Louis (photo by Jerry Naunheim, Jr.)

Grant (Nessa Charles), Francesca Choy-Kee (Hannah Davis), Nikkole Salter (Lucy Taylor), Victor Williams (Rex Taylor), Marianna Bassham (Patty Ann Donovan), McCaleb Burnett (Joe Donovan), Richard McElvain (Mr. Donovan), Curtis McClarin (Rich Davis), Antione Gray Jr. and Jahmeel Mack (Miles Davis), Nancy E. Carroll (Mrs. Donovan); World Premiere; March 30–April 29, 2012

Illinois Theatre Center

Park Forest, Illinois

Thirty-sixth Season

Producing Director, Etel Billig

The Spitfire Grill Music and book by James Valcq; Lyrics and book by Fred Alley; Director, Etel Billig; Music Director, Jonathan R. Billig; Cast: Danielle Scampini (Percy), Michellle McKenzie-Voigt (Hannah) Jeny Wasilewski (Shelby), Scott Mills (Joe), Ernest W. Ray (Caleb), Jeannie Rega-Markionni (Effy), Robert McConnell (Visitor); September 23–October 9, 2011

Heroes by Tom Stoppard; Adapted from the play *Le Vent des Peuplier* by Gerard Sibleyras; Director, David Perkovich; Cast: Jack Hickey (Gustave), Michael LaGue (Phillipe), David Perkovich (Henri); October 28–November 11, 2011

Greetings by Tom Dudzick; Director, Etel Billig; Cast: Iris Lieberman (Emily), John LiBrizzi (Phil), Robert McConnell (Andy), Lucy Zukaitis (Randi), Jeremy Keene (Mickey); December 2–18, 2011

Broke-Ology by Nathan Louis Jackson; Director, Etel Billig; Cast: Razz Jenkins (William), Jonah Taylor (Ennis), Marlon Washington (Malcolm), Vallea Woodbury (Sonia); January 27–February 12, 2012

The Cocktail Hour by A.R. Gurney; Director, Etel Billig; Cast: David Boettcher (Bradley), Peter Robel (John), Jean Roberts (Ann), Kelly Anne Clark (Nina); March 2–18, 2012

Showtune Music and lyrics by Jerry Herman; Conceived by Paul Gilger; Director, Frank Roberts; Music Director, Jonathan R. Billig; Cast: Joe Lehman, Jeny Wasilewski, Frank Roberts, Caron Buinis, Steve Greist, Khaki Pixley; Apri18–29, 2012

Indiana Repertory Theatre

Indianapolis, Indiana

Fortieth Season

Janet Allen, Artistic Director; Steven Stolen, Managing Director

ONEAMERICA STAGE

Dracula by Steven Dietz; Director, Peter Amster; Sets, Robert Mark Gordon: Costumes, Tracy Dorman; Lighting, Christine Binder; Composer, Gregg Coffin; Sound, Todd Mack Reischman; Dramaturg, Richard J. Roberts; SM, Nathan Garrison; Cast: Jason Bradley (Harker), Dieterich Gray (Renfield), Erik Hellman (Seward), Wade McCollum (Dracula), Tom McElroy (Van Helsing), Lee Stark (Mina), Jennifer Joan Thompson (Lucy), Leah DeWalt (Maid/Vixen/Attendant), Lisa Ermel (Vixen/Nurse/Attendant), Sam Fain (Attendant), John Michael Goodson (Attendant); September 7–October 1, 2011

Julius Caesar by William Shakespeare; Director, Janet Allen; Sets, Gordon Strain; Costumes, Linda Pisano; Lighting, Betsy Cooprider-Bernstein; Sound, Todd Mack Reischman; Fight Choreographer, Rob Johansen; Dramaturg, Richard J. Roberts; SM, Nathan Garrison, Amy K. Denkmann, Delia Neylon; Cast: Andrew Ahrens (Mark Antony), David Alan Anderson (Julius Caesar), Ryan Artzberger (Brutus), Jennifer Johansen (Portia), Rob Johansen (Cassius), Michael Shelton (Casca), Bill Simmons (Decius), Christopher Staley (Soothsayer/Octavius Caesar), Ben Tebbe (Metellus Cimber), Milicent Wright (Calpurnia); October 18–November 5, 2011

A Christmas Carol by Charles Dickens; Adapted by Tom Haas; Director, Richard J Roberts; Sets, Russell Metheny; Costumes, Murell Horton; Lighting, Michael Lincoln; Composition and Sound, Andrew Hopson; Choreographer, David Hochoy; Music Director, Christopher Ludwa; SM, Nathan Garrison; Cast: David Alan Anderson (Fezziwig/Topper/Old Joe), Ryan Artzberger (Ebenezer Scrooge), Matthew Brumlow (Fred/Young Scrooge/Broker), Minita Gandhi (Belle/Fan/Martha Cratchit) Mark Goetzinger (Portly Gentleman/Schoolmaster/Nutley), Jennifer Johansen (Sister of Mercy/Roses Sister/Charwoman), Constance Macy (Mrs. Cratchit/Mrs. Fezziwig/Plump Sister), Rob Johansen (Bob Cratchit/Postboy, Broker), Robert Neal (Marley/Ghost of Christmas Present/Undertaker/Poulterer's Man), Ben Tebbe (Waiter/Young Marley, Lamplighter/Ghost of Christmas Future), Cora Vander Broek (Felicity/Ghost of Christmas Past/Laundress), Anthony Boler, Cullen Oakes (Cratchit/Adolescent Scrooge/Dick Wilkins), Victoria Martine, MacKenzie Isaac (Belinda Cratchit/Young Fan), J. P. Suarez, Nolan Oakes (Henry Cratchit/Ignorance/Turkey Boy), Bronwyn Doebbeling, Sally Root (Betsy Cratchit/Want), Gracie Evans, Kalea Spurlock (Tiny Tim/Boy Scrooge); November 21–December 24, 2011

Radio Golf by August Wilson; Director, Lou Bellamy; Sets, Vicki Smith; Costumes, Karen Perry; Lighting, Don Darnutzer; Sound, Todd Mack Reischman; Dramaturg, Richard J. Roberts; SM, Nathan Garrison; Cast: David Alan Anderson (Roosevelt Hicks), Terry Bellamy (Sterling Johnson), James Craven (Harmond Wilks), Abdul Salam El Razzac (Elder Joseph Barlow), Austene Van (Mame Wilks); January 10–29, 2012

God of Carnage by Yasmina Reza, translated by Christopher Hampton; Director, James Still; Sets, Russell Metheny; Costumes, Guy Clark; Lighting, Michael Lincoln; Sound, Todd Mack Reischman; Dramaturg, Richard J Roberts; SM, Nathan Garrison; Cast: Ryan Artzberger (Alan Raleigh), Tim Grimm (Michael Novak), Shannon Holt (Veronica Novak), Constance Macy (Annette Raleigh); February 28–March 24, 2012

The Miracle Worker by William Gibson; Director, David Bradley; Sets, Robert M. Koharchik; Costumes, Devon Painter; Lighting, Ann. G. Wrightson; Composition and Sound, Fabian Obispo; Sign Language/Culture Consultant, Chuck Daube; Fight Choreographer, Rob Johansen; Dialect, Nancy Lipschultz; Dramaturg, Richard J. Roberts; SM, Nathan Garrison; Cast: Andrew Ahrens (James Keller), Ryan Artzberger (A Doctor/Michael Anagnos), Nora Fiffer (Annie Sullivan), Lauren Graves (Martha), David House (Percy), Diane Kondrat (Aunt Ev), Ciarrah Krohne (Helen Keller), Robert Neal (Captain Keller), Dorcas Sowunmi (Viney), Rebekah Ward (Kate Keller), Rachel Bowling, Charlie Demetris, Ryleigh Mill, Ankia Webster, Kelly Webster, MacKenzie Wilson, Zoe Wilson (Perkins Students); April 17–May 20, 2012

UPPERSTAGE

Lost—A Memoir Adapted for the stage by Cathy Ostlere & Dennis Garnhum; Based on the book by Cathy Ostlere; Director, Jennifer Blackmer; Sets, Robert M. Koharchik; Costumes, Beth Bennett; Lighting, Ryan Koharchik; Sound, Jen Groseth; Dramaturg, Richard J. Roberts; SMs, Amy K. Denkmann, Joel Grynheim; Cast: Constance Macy (Cathy); September 20–October 15, 2011

Nobody Don't Like Yogi by Tom Lysaght; Director, Tim OCel; Sets, Robert M. Koharchik; Costumes, Beth Bennett; Lighting, Ryan Koharchik; Sound, Rustay Wandall; Dramaturg, Richard J. Roberts; SM, Amy K. Denkmann, Joel Grynheim; Cast: Mark Goetzinger (Yogi Berra); September 23–October 23, 2011

I Love to Eat: Cooking with James Beard by James Still; Director, James Still; Sets, Robert M. Koharchik; Costumes, Guy Clark; Lighting, Ryan Koharchik; Sound, Rick Thomas; Dramaturg, Richard J. Roberts; SM, Joel Grynheim; Cast: Robert Neal (James Beard); September 27–October 22, 2011

Fallen Angels by Noël Coward; Director, William Brown; Sets, Kevin Depinet; Costumes, Rachel Anne Healy; Lighting, Jesse Klug; Composition and Sound, Andrew Hansen; Dramaturg, Richard J. Roberts; SM, Amy K. Denkmann; Casting, Claire Simon Casting; Cast: Kelsey Brennan (Jane Banbury), Susan Felder (Saunders), Steve Haggard (Fred Sterroll), Cristina Panfilio (Julia Sterroll), Eric Parks (Willy Banbury), Martin Yurek (Maurice Duclos); March 13–April 15, 2012

Kansas City Repertory Theatre

Kansas City, Missouri

Forty-seventh Season

Artistic Director, Eric Rosen; Managing Director, Cynthia Rider; Producing Director, Jerry Genochio

August: Osage County by Tracy Letts; Director, Eric Rosen; Associate Director, Kyle Hatley; Sets, Donald Eastman; Costumes, Megan Turek; Lighting, Mark Kent Varns; Sound, Andre Pleuss; PSM, Brooke Redler; Cast: Kip Niven (Beverly Weston); Vanessa Severo (Johanna Monevata); Merle Moores (Violet Weston); Kathleen Warfel (Mattie Fae Aiken; Manon Halliburton (Ivy Weston); Gary Neal Johnson (Charlie Aiken); Cheryl Weaver (Barbara Fordham); Craig Benton (Bill Fordham); Katie Hall (Jean Fordham); John Redmond (Sheriff Dean Gilbeau); Jennifer Mays (Karen Weston); David Fritts (Steve Heidebrecht); Rusty Sneary (Little Charles Aiken); September 16–October 9, 2011

The History of Kisses Written, directed and performed by David Cale; Sets, Eric Southern; Costumes, Laura Bauer; Lighting, Beverly Emmons; Sound, Andre Pleuss; Songs by David Cale; October 21–November 27, 2011

A Christmas Carol by Charles Dickens; Adapted for the stage by Barbara Field; Director, Kyle Hatley; Sets, John Ezell; Costumes, Allison Dillard; Projections/Lighting, Jeffrey Cady; Music Director, Eryn Bates Preston; Sound, John Story; Movement Coach, Jennifer Martin; Associate Sets, Gene Emerson Friedman; Vocal Coach, Erika Bailey; PSM, Brooke Redler; Equity Cast: Allan Boardman (Old Joe); Walter Coppage (Bob Cratchit); Jerry Jay Cranford (Topper); Peggy Friesen (Mrs. Fezziwig/Harp Accompanist); Charles Fugate (Charles Dickens); Jim Gall (Solicitor/Mr. Fezziwig/Ghost of Christmas Present); Gary Neal Johnson (Ebenezer Scrooge); Sarah LaBarr (Aunt Fezziwig); Mark Robbins (Ghost of Jacob Marley); Vanessa Severo (Belle/Mrs. Fred); Kathleen Warfel (Grandma/Charwoman); Cheryl Weaver (Mrs. Cratchit); November 19–December 26, 2011

The Adventures of Tom Sawyer Based on the novel by Mark Twain; Adapted for the stage by Laura Eason; In association with Hartford Stage; Co-production with Actors Theatre of Louisville and The Repertory Theatre of St. Louis; Directed by Jeremy B. Cohen; Sets, Dan Ostling; Costumes, Lorraine Venberg; Lighting, Robert Wierzel; Sound/Original Music, Broken Chord; Fight/Movement Director, Tommy Rapley; PSM, Mary R. Honour; Cast: Joseph Adams (Muff Potter); Justin Fuller (Joe Harper); Tim McKiernan (Tom Sawyer); Michael Nichols (Injun Joe/School Master); Robbie Tann (Huckleberry Finn); Hayley Treider (Becky Thatcher); Nate Trinrud (Sid Sawyer/Doc Robinson); Nance Williamson (Aunt Polly/Widow Douglas); January 20–February 12, 2012

The Great Immensity Music and lyrics by Michael Friedman; Book by Steven Cosson; Directed by Steven Cosson; Music Director/Pianist, Daniel Doss; Sets, Mimi Lien; Costumes, Sarah Beers; Lighting, Tyler Micoleau; Projections, Jason H. Thompson; Sound, Ken Travis; Choreographer, Tracy Bersley; PSM, Bonnie Brady; Csting, Stephanie Klapper; Mollie Carden (Julie); Todd Cerveris (Rob/Ship Spotter/Dr. Medvedkov); Dan Domingues (Marcos/Charlie); Rebecca Hart (Phyllis/Polly); Eddie Korbich (Harold/Pete); Meghan McGeary (Allie/Emmanuelle); February 17–March 18, 2012

The Whipping Man by Matthew Lopez, Directed by Eric Rosen; Sets, Jack Magaw; Costumes, Alison Heryer; Sound, Andre Pleuss; Lighting, Victor En Yu Tan; PSM, Brooke Redler; Casting, Stephanie Klapper; Josh Breckenridge (John); Michael Genet (Simon); Kyle Hatley (Caleb). March 16–April 8, 2012

Little Shop of Horrors Book and lyrics by Howard Ashman; Music by Alan Menken; Based on the film by Roger Corman; Screenplay by Charles Griffith; Directed by Kyle Hatley; Music Director, Anthony T. Edwards; Sets/Costumes, Meghan Raham; Lighting, Jason Lyons; Sound, Joshua Horvath; Associate Director, Richard J. Hinds; Associate Costumes, Megan Turek; Assistant Music Director, Eryn Bates Preston; Audrey II Design and Engineering, Grace Hudson; PSM, Mary R. Honour; Casting, Stephanie Klapper; Cast: Ashley Blanchet (Audrey); Nick Cordero (Orin); Eboni Fondren (Ronette); Colleen Grate (Chiffon);

Jennie Greenberry (Crystal); Gary Neal Johnson (Mushnik); Michael James Leslie (Audrey II, voice); Joseph Medeiros (Seymour); April 20–May 20, 2012

La Jolla Playhouse

La Jolla, California

Forty-second Season

Artistic Director, Christopher Ashley; Managing Director, Michael S. Rosenberg

SUBSCRIPTION SHOWS

A Dram of Drummhicit by Arthur Kopit & Anton Dudley; Director, Christopher Ashley; Sets, David Zinn; Costumes, David C. Woolard; Lighting, Philip Rosenberg; Projections, Tara Knight; Sound, John Gromada; Dramaturg, Gabriel Greene; Cast: Kelly AuCoin, John Ahlin, Natalie Birriel, Ron Choularton, Joseph Culliton, Murphy Guyer, Lucas Hall, Polly Lee, Alan Mandell, Kathryn Meisle, Larry Paulson, Jenni Putney, Megan Robinson, Daniel Rubio and Taylor Shurte; Mandell Weiss Theatre; World Premiere; May 17–June 12, 2011

Peer Gynt by Henrik Ibsen; Adapted and directed by David Schweizer; Sets, David Zinn; Costumes, Christina Wright; Lighting/Projections, Darrel Maloney; Sound, Ryan Rumery; Dramaturg, Shirley Fishman; Cast: Danny Gavigan, Birgit Huppuch, Luis Moreno, Kate Cullen Roberts and Evan Zes; A co-production with Kansas City Repertory Theatre; Sheila and Hughes Potiker Theatre; June 28–July 24, 2011

Sleeping Beauty Wakes by Rachel Sheinken; Music and Arrangements by Brendan Milburn; Lyrics, Valerie Vigoda; Director, Rebecca Taichman; Sets, Riccardo Hernandez; Costumes, Miranda Hoffman; Lighting, Christopher Akerlind; Projections, Peter Nigrini; Sound, Leon Rothenberg; Dramaturg, Mara Isaacs; Cast: Adinah Alexander, Jimmy Ray Bennett, Kecia Lewis-Evans, Steve Judkins, Carrie Manolakos, Bryce Ryness, Bob Stillman and Aspen Vincent; A co-production with McCarter Theatre Center; Mandell Weiss Theatre; August 19–28, 2011

Milk Like Sugar by Kirsten Greenidge, Director, Rebecca Taichman; Sets, Mimi Lien; Costumes, Toni-Leslie James; Lighting, Justin Townsend; Composition and Sound, Andre Pluess; Dramaturg, Gabriel Greene; Cast: Cherise Booth, Angela Lewis, Nikiya Mathis, LeRoy McClain, J. Mallory-McCree, Adrienne C. Moore and Tonya Pinkins; Co-commissioned with Theater masters, Produced in Association with Playwrights Horizons and Women's Project Productions; Sheila and Hughes Potiker Theatre; August 30–September 25, 2011

Jesus Christ Superstar Music by Andrew Lloyd Webber; Lyrics by Tim Rice; Director, Des McAnuff; Choreographer, Lisa Shriver; Music Director, Rick Fox; Sets, Robert Brill; Costumes, Paul Tazewell; Lighting, Howell Binkley; Video, Sean Nieuwenhuis; Sound, Jim Neil; Dramaturg, Chad Sylvain; Cast: Matt Alfano, Mary Antonini, Karen Burthwright, Jacqueline Burtney, Mark Cassius, Bruce Dow, Ryan Gifford, Kaylee Harwood, Chilina Kennedy, Jeremy Kushnier, Mike Nadajewski, Marcus Nance, Paul Nolan, Melissa O'Neil, Laurin Padolina, Stephen Patterson, Katrina Reynolds, Matthew Rossoff Jennifer Rider-Shaw, Jaz Sealey, Jason Sermonia, Julius Sermonia, Lee Siegel , Aaron Walpole, Jonathan Winsby, Sandy Winsby and Josh Young; A Stratford Shakespeare Festival Production; November 18–December 31, 2011

American Night: The Ballad of Juan José by Richard Montoya; Developed by Culture Clash & Jo Bonney; Director, Jo Bonney; Sets, Neil Patel; Costumes, ESosa; Lighting, David Weiner; Sound, Darron L. West; Projections, Shawn Sagady; Choreographer, Ken Roht; Cast: Stephanie Beatriz, Rodney Gardiner, David Kelly, Terri McMahon, René Millán, Richard Montoya, Kimberly Scott, Herbert Siguenza and Daisuke Tsuji; A co-production with Center Theatre Group; Originally produced by Oregon Shakespeare Festival; Sheila and Potiker Hughes Theatre; Mandell Weiss Theatre; January 27–February 26, 2012

A WITHOUT WALLS PRODUCTION

Susurrus by David Leddy; San Diego Botanical Garden; September 16–October 23, 2011

The Car Plays: San Diego Conceived by Paul Stein; Written by Jennifer Barclay, Michael David, Lila Rose Kaplan, Alex Lewin, EM Lewis, Steve Lozier, David Myers, Kiff Scholl, Michael Shutt, Jessica Smith, Paul Stein, JJ Strong, Stephanie Alison Walker and Lee Wochner; Directed by Lisa Berger, Matt Bretz, Robert Castro, Jason Duplissea, Richard Martin Hirsch, Claudi Raygoza, Dana Schwartz, Kiff Scholl, Casey Stangl, Paul Stein, Seema Sueko, Matt Thompson, Delicia Turner-Sonnenberg, Sara Wagner and Sam Woodhouse; Cast: Wendy Elizabeth Abraham, Rhianna Basore, Judy Bauerlein, Laura Buckles, Kevane La'Marr Coleman, Rebecca Davis, Tony DeCarlo, Charles Evans Jr., Samantha Ginn, Lisa Goodman, Thomas Hall, D.J. Harner, Zachary Martens, Charles Maze, Cashae Monya, Ron Morehouse, Trey Nichols, Albert Park, John Polak, Donald Rizzo, Michael Shutt, Peter James Smith, Will Tulin, Sean Tweedale, Wendy Waddell, Sara Wagner, Reed Willard, Eddie Yaroch, David Youse, Michael Zlotnik; La Jolla Playhouse; February 23–March 11, 2012

EDUCATIONAL TOURING PRODUCTION

Recipe for Disaster by Barry Kornhauser; Director, David Saar; Music, Deborah Wicks La Puma; Sets, Ian Wallace; Costumes, Ingrid Helton; Puppetry, Lynne Jennings; Cast: Ricky Araiza, David Dickinson, Rae Henderson and Steven Lone; January 30–March 30, 2012

Long Wharf Theatre

New Haven, Connecticut

Forty-seventh Season

Artistic Director, Gordon Edelstein; Managing Director, Joshua Borenstein

MAINSTAGE

Ain't Misbehavin' Book by Murray Horwitz and Richard Maltby Jr., Music by Thomas Wright "Fats" Waller; Director, Richard Maltby Jr.; Co-director/ Choreographer, Arthur Faria; Music Director, Phillip Hall; Sets, John Lee Beatty; Costumes, Gail Baldoni; Lighting, Pat Collins; Sound, Tom Morse; SM, Bonnie Brady; Cast: Eugene Barry-Hill, Doug Eskew, Kecia Lewis-Evans, Cynthia Thomas, Debra Walton; October 26–November 20, 2011

It's A Wonderful Life – A Live Radio Play by Joe Landry; Director, Eric Ting; Sets, Mikiko Macadams; Costumes, Jessica Ford; Lighting, Stephen Strawbridge; Sound, John Gromada; Foley Artist/Associate Sound; Nathan Roberts. Cast: Dan Domingues, Kate Maccluggage, Alex Moggridge, Kevyn Morrow, Ariel Woodiwiss; December 7–30, 2011

Macbeth 1969 by William Shakespeare Conceived and adapted by Eric Ting; Director, Eric Ting; Sets, Mimi Lien; Costumes, Toni-Leslie James; Lighting, Tyler Micoleau; Soubnd, Ryan Rumery; Fight Director David Anzuelo; SM, Lisa Ann Chernoff; Cast: Shirine Babb, McKinley Belcher III, Jackie Chung, George Kulp, Barret O'Brien, Socorro Santiago; January 18–February 12, 2012

Bell, Book & Candle by John Van Druten; Director, Darko Tresnjak; Sets, Alexander Dodge; Costumes, Fabio Toblini; Lighting, Matt Richards; Sound, Lindsay Jones; PSM, Susie Cordon; Cast: Kate MacCluggage (Gillian Holroyd), Michael Keyloun (Nicky Holroyd), Robert Eli (Shep Henderson), Gregor Paslawsky (Sidney Redlitch), Ruth Williamson (Aunt Queenie); Co-produced with Hartford Stage; March 7–April 1, 2012

My Name is Asher Lev by Aaron Posner; Director, Gordon Edelstein; Sets, Eugene Lee; Costumes, Ilona Somogyi; Lighting, Christopher Akerlind; Sound, John Gromada; SM, Bonnie Brady; Cast: Ari Brand (Asher Lev), Melissa Miller (Rivkeh, Others), Mark Nelson (Ariyeh/Others); May 2–27, 2012

STAGE II

Molly Sweeney by Brian Friel; Director, Charlotte Moore. Sets, James Morgan; Costumes, Linda Fisher; Lighting, Richard Pilbrow, Michael Gottlieb; Sound, Zachary Richardson; SM, Katrina Lynn Olsen; Cast: Jonathan Hogan (Mr. Rice), Simone Kirby (Molly Sweeney), Ciaran O'Reilly (Frank Sweeney); In conjunction with Irish Repertory Theatre; September 14–October 16, 2011

Krapp's Last Tape by Samuel Beckett; Director, Jennifer Tarver; Sets/Costumes, Eugene Lee; Lighting, Stephen Strawbridge; Sound, Richard Woodbury; SM, Katrina Lynn Olsen; Cast: Brian Dennehy (Krapp). November 29–December18, 2011

February House Songs and lyrics by Gabriel Kahane; Book by Seth Bockley; Director, Davis McCallum; Sets, Riccardo Hernandez; Costumes, Jess Goldstein; Lighting, Mark Barton; Sound, Leon Rothenberg; Music Director, Andy Boroson; PSM, Cole Bonenberger; Cast: Stanley Bahorek (Benjamin Britten), Ken Barnett (Peter Pears), Ken Clark (Reeves McCullers), Julian Fleisher (George Davis), Stephanie Hayes (Erika Mann), Erik Lochtefeld (W.H. Auden), Kacie Sheik (Gypsy Rose Lee), A.J. Shively (Chester Kallman), Kristen Sieh (Carson McCullers); Co-produced with the Public Theater; February 15–March 18, 2012

Lyric Stage

Irving, Texas

Nineteenth Season

Founding Producer, Steven Jones

Oliver Book, music and lyrics by Lionel Bart based on *Oliver Twist* by Charles Dickens; Director, Cheryl Denson; Music Director, Jay Dias; Choreographer, Ann Nieman; Sets, Mark Morton; Costumes, Drenda Lewis; Lighting, Julie N Moroney; Sound, Bill Eickenloff; Props, Jane Quetin; PSM, Margaret J. Soch; Cast: Jack Vangorden (Oliver), Mike Gallagher (Mr. Bumble), Christine Chambers (Widow Corney), Gordon Fox (Mr. Sowerberry), Kelley Murphy Perlstein (Mrs. Sowerberry/Old Sally), Amber Nicole Guest (Charlotte), Cayman Mitchell (Noah Claypole), Clayton Slee (Artful Dodger), Jonathan Beck Reed (Fagin), Catherine Carpenter Cox (Nancy), Rebekah Wheeler (Bet), Daylon Walton (Bill Sykes), Sarah Comley Caldwell (Mrs. Bedwin), Tom DeWester (Mr. Brownlow), Shane Strawbridge (Dr. Grimwig), Vicki Dean (Old Lady); Ensemble: Caleb Atkinson, Jeff Bailey, Avian Broach, Andew Byerly, Benjamin Byerly, Xavier Carrilo, Claire, Cuny, Mark Fisher, Lindsey Gallegos, Ryan Glen, Everett Golenski, Hunter Hall, Skyler Halliday, Trevor Haueisen, Dawson Holder, Isaac Jarrell, Logan Macaulay, Hunter Martin, Jacob Matheny, Jeff McGee, Ashton Miramontes, Chet Monday, Scott Montgomery, Ashton Morales, Joey Morris, Kuran Patel, Diane Powell, Tyler Rouse, Ty Taylor, Caleb Terlouw, Sam Ward, Keith Warren; June 10–19, 2011

Gypsy Book by Arthur Laurents; Music by Jule Styne; Lyrics by Stephen Sondheim, Original Choreography by Jerome Robbins; Director, Len Pfluger; Music Director, Jay Dias; Sets, Michael Anania; Costumes, Drenda Lewis; Lighting, Julie N. Simmons; Sound, Bill Eickenloff; PSM, Margaret J. Soch; Properties, Jane Quetin; Cast: Sue Mathys (Rose), Kristin Wright (Baby June), Taylor Hennings (Baby Louise), Keith J. Warren (Uncle Jocko/Pastey), Ben Giddings (Georgie/Kringelien/Willy), Bella Murphy (Balloon Girl), Neil Rogers (Pop/Phil), James Williams (Weber/Cigar), Sonny Franks (Herbie), Ashton Smalling (Dainty June), Mary McElree (Louise), Caitlin Carter (Tessie Tura), Sara Shelby-Martin (Mazeppa), Shannon McGrann (Mrs. Cratchitt/Electra), Michael Whitney (Tulsa/Farmboy), Luke Boyce (Newsboy), Hunter Hall (Newsboy), Logan Macaulay (Newsboy), Chet Monday (Newsboy), Douglas Skyler Halliday (Newsboy), Thomas Christopher Renner (Yonkers/Farmboy), Stephen Raikes (LA/ Farmboy/Photographer), Brian Boyce (Angie/Farmboy), Kevin Acosta (Farmboy), Brendan Cyrus (Farmboy), Alex Altshuler (Toreadorable), Mallory Michaellan Brophy (Toreadorable/Showgirl), Caitlin Darby (Toreadorable/Showgirl), Michelle Foard (Toreadorable/Showgirl), Katharine Gentsch (Toreadorable/Showgirl), Chloe Voreis (Toreadorable/Showgirl), Lisa D. Ward (Renee/Showgirl); September 9–19, 2011

Rags Book by Joseph Stein; Music by Charles Strouse; Lyrics by Stephen Schwartz Director, Cheryl Denson; Music Director, Jay Dias; Choreographer, Ann Nieman; Sets, Mamie Trotter; Costumes, Drenda Lewis; Lighting, Julie N. Simmons; Properties, Jane Quetin; PSM, Margaret J. Soch; Cast: Amanda Passanante (Rebecca), Brian Hathaway (Saul), Chet Monday (David), Jackie L. Kemp (Avram), Jonathan Bragg (Ben), Kristin Dausch (Bella), Lois Sonnier Hart (Rachel), G Shane Peterman (Nathan), Martin Antonio Guerra (Jack), Lucia A. Welch (Rosa), Mary-Margaret Pyeatt (Anna), Sahara Glasener-Boles (Esther/Gertrude), Daniel Saroni (Sam), J. Alan Hanna (Big Mike), Joseph Holt (Klezmer/Rosencrantz), Keith J. Warren (Klezmer), Tome Grugle (Bronstein), Max Swarner (Hamlet), Amber Nicole Guest, (Ophelia), Mikey Abrams (Guildenstern), Stephen Bates (Big Tim Sullivan/Gramophone Tenor); Emsemble: Brendan Cyrus, Randy Dobbs, Michelle Foard , Emily Ford, Carlos Gomez, Maranda Harrison, Morgan Mabry Mason, Preston David Pickett, Diane Powell, Scott Taylor, Isaac Jarrell, Lily Monday, Ashton Morales; October 28–November 6, 2011

Kismet Music and lyrics by Robert Wright and George Forrest; Book by Charles Lederer and Luther Davis based on the play by Edward Knoblock; Director/Choreographer, Len Pfluger; Music Director, Jay Dias; Lighting, Julie N. Simmons; Sound, Bill Eickenloff; Props, Jane Quetin; PSM, Margaret J. Soch; Cast: Stephen Bates (Inam of the Mosque/Bangle Man), Martin Guerra (Muezzin/Pearl Merchant), Michael Gasparro (Muezzin/Silk Merchant), Peter DiCesare (Muezzin), Shane Strawbridge (Muezzin/Slave Master), Scott Sutton (Beggar/Silk Merchant), Akron Watson (Beggar/Guard), Doug Fowler (Beggar), Jackie L. Kemp (Omar Khayyam), Christopher Carl (Hajj), Cecily Ellis-Bills (Marsinah), Tom Grugle (Hassan-Ben/Guard), Mark Oristano (Jawan), James Williams (Chief of Police), Brian Mathis (The Wazir of Police), Tyler Donohue (Guard), Daniel Saroni (Guard/Orange Merchant), Margaret Shafer (Lalume), Mallory Brophy (Princess of Ababu), Alex Altshuler (Princess of Ababau), Maranda Harrison (Princess of Ababu), Amber Nicole Guest (Ayah to Princesses of Ababu), Jonathan Bragg (The Caliph), Miriam Baron (Slave Girl), Michelle Foard (Slave Girl), Danielle Estes (Slave Girl), Vernicia Vernon (Slave Girl), Carlos Gomez (Servant), Stephen Raikes (Informer), Delynda Johnson Moravec (Woman in the Garden), Sahara Glasener-Boles (Attendant), Lisa D. Ward (Princess Zubbediya of Damascus), Vicki Dean (Ayah to Zubbediya), Emily Ford (Princess of Samahris of Bangalore), Lee Jamison (Ayah to Samahris); Emsemble: Kevin Acosta, Kristen Blair, Megan Burks, John Campione, Gary Eoff, Doug Fowler, Lindsey Gallegos, Mandy Rausch, Kristin Spires, Natasha Well; January 26–29, 2012

McCarter Theatre Center

Princeton, New Jersey

Thirty-ninth Season

Artistic Director, Emily Mann; Managing Director, Tim Shields; Producing Director, Mara Isaacs; Director of Production, David York

Ten Cents A Dance The Music and Lyrics of Rodgers and Hart Conceived and directed by John Doyle; Music Director/Orchestrator, Mary-Mitchell Campbell; Sets, Scott Pask; Costumes; Ann-Hould-Ward; Lighting, Jane Cox; Sound, Dan Moses Schreier; Wigs, Paul Huntley; Casting, Calleri Casting; PSM, Lauren Kurinskas, Eileen Ryan Kelly; Produced in association with Williamstown Theatre Festival; Cast: Malcolm Gets, Donna McKechnie, Diana DiMarzio, Jessica Tyler Wright, Jane Pfitsch, Elisa Winter; September 9–October 9, 2011

Phaedra Backwards by Marina Carr; Director, Emily Mann; Sets, Rachel Hauck; Costumes, Anita Yavich; Lighting, Jeff Croiter; Original Music/Sound, Mark Bennett; Projects, Peter Nigrini; Movement, Peter Pucci; Casting, Laura Stanczyk, CSA, PSM, Cheryl Mintz; Cast: Stephanie Roth Haberle (Phaedra), Randall Newsome (Theseus), Angel Desai (Pasiphae), Susan Blommaert (Nanny), Christopher Coucill (Inventor), Julio Monge (Minotaur), Julienne Hanzelka Kim (Aricia), Jake Silbermann (Hippolytus), Elsa Rodriguez (Girl), Hope Springer (Child Phaedra), Alexandra Erickson (Child Ariandne), Sean Haberle (Minos), Noah Hinsdale (Child Minotaur), Mariann Mayberry (Ariadne); World Premiere; October 18–November 6, 2011

A Christmas Carol by Charles Dickens; Adaptation, David Thompson; Director, Michael Unger; Music/Lyrics, Michael Starobin; Choreographer, Rob Ashford; Sets, Ming Cho Lee; Costumes, Jess Goldstein; Lighting, Stephen Strawbridge; Sound, Brian Ronan; Music Director, Charles Sundquist; Choreography Supervisor, Jennifer Paulson Lee; Dialect, Gillian Lane-Plescia; Casting, Laura Stanczyk, CSA; Supervising SM, Cheryl Mintz; Cast: Justin Blanchard (Jacob Marley/Mr. Stocks), Tom Riis Farrell (Mr. Fezziwig/Old Joe), Piper Goodeve (Fan/Mrs.Bonds), Andrea Goss (Lily/Belle), David Kenner (Young Scrooge/Mr. Bonds), James Ludwig (Fred/Schoolmaster/Undertaker), Graeme Malcolm (Ebenezer Scrooge), Anne O'Sullivan (Mrs. Dilber), Ronica Reddick (Christmas Present), Christina Rouner (Mrs. Cratchit), Michele Tauber (Mrs. Fezziwig/Mrs. Stocks/Laundress), Price Waldman (Bob Cratchit); Ensemble: William Carlos Angulo, Rachel Baker, Eric Brathwaite, Mike Faist, Justin Henry, Stacey Jackson, Emma Ritchie, Arianna Rosario, Ryan Steer, Jessi Trauth, J. Morgan White; Young Ensemble: Kate Fahey, Annika Goldman, Danny Hallowell, Noah Hinsdale, Matthew Immordino, Samantha Johnson, Matthew Kuenne, Adam LeCompte, Natalie Mehl, Benjamin Palmer, Jackie Patterson, Sophia Sharma, Olivia Sheridan, Emma Ventola; December 4–24, 2011

The Convert by Danai Gurira; Director, Emily Mann; Sets, Daniel Ostling; Costumes, Paul Tazewell; Lighting, Lap Chi Chu; Sound, Darron L. West; Fight Director, J. Steven White; Dialect/Vocal Coach, Beth McGuire; Dramaturg, Carrie Hughes; Casting Directors, Adam Belcuore; Erika Sellin, CSA; PSM, Alison Cote; Produced in association with Center Theatre Group and Goodman Theatre; Cast: Pascale Armand (Jekesai/Ester), Cheryl Lynn Bruce (Mai Tamba), Zainab Jah (Prudence), Kevin Mambo (Chancellor), LeRoy McClain (Chilford), Warner Joseph Miller (Tamba), Harol Surratt (Uncle); World Premiere: January 13–February 12, 2012

Travesties by Tom Stoppard; Director, Sam Buntrock; Sets/Costumes, David Farley; Lighting, David Weiner; Sound, Fitz Patton; Composer, David Shire; Dialect, Deborah Hecht; Movement consultant, Daniel Stein; Casting, Laura Stanczyk, CSA; PSM, Cheryl Mintz; Cast: Fred Arsenault (James Joyce), Demosthenes Chrysan (Lenin), Christian Coulson (Tristan Tzara), Susannah Flood (Gwendolyn), Everett Quinton (Bennett), Lusia Strus (Nadya), Sara Topham (Cecily), James Urbaniak (Henry Carr); March 13–April 1, 2012.

Are You There, McPhee? by John Guare; Director, Sam Buntrock; Sets/Costumes, David Farley; Lighting, Ken Billington; Sound, Jill BC Du Boff; Composer, Justin Ellington; Movement Director/Puppet Consultant, Lisa Shriver; Casting, Laura Stanczyk, CSA; PSM, Cheryl Mintz; Cast: Gideon Ganner (Peter), John Behlmann (McPhee), Jeremy Bobb (Andrew), Molly Camp (Wendy), Patrick Carroll (The Cop), Alicia Goranson (Alice), Paul Gross (Mundie), Matthew Kuenne (Poe), Jenn Lyon (Elsie), Danny Mastrogiorgio (Schuyler), Hope Springer (Lilac), Lusia Strus (Bitsy); World Premiere; May 4–June 3, 2012

Merrimack Repertory Theatre

Lowell, Massachusetts

Thirty-third Season

Artistic Director, Charles Towers; Executive Director, Steven Leon

The Persian Quarter by Kathleen Cahill; Director, Kyle Fabel; Sets, Campbell Baird; Costumes, Theresa Squire; Lighting, Brian Lilienthal; Sound, J Hagenbuckle; SM, Emily F. McMullen; Cast: Barzin Akhavan (Rumi/Pool Attendant/Persian Man); Jason Kolotouros (Mike/Kermit Roosevelt); Christina Pumariega (Shirin/Azadeh); Beth Wittig (Ann Gillies/Emily Gillies); East Coast Premiere; September 15–October 9, 2011

This Verse Business by A.M. Dolan; Director, Gus Kaikkonen; Sets, Gus Kaikkonen; Scenic Assistant, Rob Shearin; Costumes, A. Lee Viliesis; Lighting, John Eckert; Sound, Jason Weber; SM, Emily F. McMullen; Cast: Gordon Clapp (Robert Frost); October 20–November 13, 2011

The Reduced Shakespeare Company The Ultimate Christmas Show (abridged) by Reed Martin and Austin Tichenor; Director, Reed Martin, Austin Tichenor; Sets, Tim Holtslag; Costumes, Skipper Skeoch; Sound, Mark Osten, Matthew Cowell; Props, Jenn Rugyt, Tim Holtslag, Mike Barny, Alli Bostedt; GM, Jane Martin; Office Manager, Alli Bostedt, SM, Emily F. McMullen; Legal Counsel, Sharon Colchamiro, Esq.; Creative Cash Control, Joanne Nagel; Company Founder, Daniel Singer; Cast: Reed Martin (Reed), Austin Tichenor (Austin), Matt Rippy (Matt); East Coast Premiere; November 25–December 18, 2011

The Voice of the Turtle by John Van Druten; Director, Carl Forsman; Sets, Bill Clarke; Costumes, Theresa Squire; Lighting, Josh Bradford; SM, Emily F. McMullen; Cast: Hanley Smith (Sally Middleton), Megan Byrne (Olive Lashbrooke), and William Connell (Bill Page); January 5–29, 2012

Daddy Long Legs Book by John Caird; Music and lyrics by Paul Gordon; Based on the novel by Jean Webster; Director, John Caird, Assistant Director, Nell Balaban; Music Director, Laura Berquist; Sets/Costumes, David Farley; Lighting, Paul Design; Sound, Jonathan Burke; SM, Emily F. McMullen; Cast: Megan McGinnis (Jerusa Abbot); Robert Adelman Hancock (Jervis Pendleton); February 9–March 4, 2012

Mrs. Whitney by John Kolvenbach; Director, Kyle Fabel; Sets, Campbell Baird; Costumes, Deb Newhall; Lighting, Paul Hackenmueller; SM, Emily F. McMullen; Cast: Deirdre Madigan (Margaret Whitney); Joel Colodner (Francis); Rebecca Harris (Louisa); Jay Ben Markson (Fin) and Dennis Parlato (Tom Whitney); March 15–April 8, 2012

Ghost-Writer by Michael Hollinger; Director, Charles Towers, Sets, Bill Clarke; Costumes, Deb Newhall; Lighting, Dan Kotlowitz; Sounds, Jason Weber; SM, Emily F. McMullen; Cast: Rebecca Harris (Myra Babbage); Dan Kremer (Franklin Woolsey); Maureen Garrett (Vivian Woolsey); SM, Emily F. McMullen; April 19–May 13, 2012

Music Theatre of Wichita

Wichita, Kansas

Fortieth Season

Producing Artistic Director, Wayne Bryan

Meredith Willson's The Music Man Book, music and lyrics by Meredith Willson; Story by Meredith Willson and Franklin Lacey; Director, Mark Madama; Choreographer, Peggy Hickey; Music Director, Thomas W. Douglas; Sets, Kenmark Studios, J Branson, Tara A. Houston, Daniel Williams, David Neville, Ray Wetmore; Costumes, Cathleen Edwards; Lighting, David Neville; Hair/Wigs, Alena Sellers; Props, Ray Wetmore; Sound, David Muehl; Technical Director, Jeff Taylor; PSM, Emily F. McMullen; SM, Tiffany K. Orr; Company Manager, Nancy Reeves; Production Manager, David Neville; Cast: Edward Watts (Harold Hill), Jessica Tyler Wright (Marian Paroo), Justin Robertson (Marcellus), Deb Campbell (Mrs. Paroo), Karen L. Robb (Eulalie Shinn), Timothy W. Robu (Mayor Shinn), Marak Gann (Winthrop), Max Clayton (Tommy Djilas), Eloise Kropp (Zaneeta), Michael Parker (Charlie Cowell), Matthew Elliott (Olin Britt), Paul Jackson (Jacey Squires), John Keckeisen (Ewart Dunlop), Arri Simon (Oliver Hix), Sally Olmstead (Amaryllis), Injoy Fountain (Alma Hix), Gail Pilgrim (Maud Dunlop), Emily Christ (Ethel Toffelmier), Marilyn Heffner (Mrs. Squires), Emily Smith (Gracie), Adrian Baidoo (Ensemble), Jordan Barrow (Ensemble), Connor Bourland (Ensemble), Jacob Chancellor (Ensemble), Erin Clemons (Ensemble), Cody Davis (Featured Dancer), Jacob Gutierrez (Featured Dancer), Daniel Horn (Featured Dancer), Shannon Hucker (Ensemble), Hannah Meredith Killebrew (Ensemble), Keaton Jadwin (Ensemble), Jacob January (Ensemble), Ben Lanham (Featured Dancer), Elliott Mattox (Featured Dancer), Ross McCorkell (Ensemble), Emily Mechler (Ensemble), Kassiani Menas (Ensemble), Sophie Menas (Featured Dancer), Maggie Mial (Featured Dancer), Larry D. Mullen (Constable Locke), Nick Palmquist (Featured Dancer), Sarah Quinn (Ensemble), Lyonel Reneau (Ensemble), Molly Rushing (Featured Dancer), Natasha Scearse (Featured Dancer), Sarah Shelton (Featured Dancer), Ethan Spell (Ensemble), Alexis Paige Tedder (Ensemble), Brydan Akin (Youth), Lucy Anderson (Youth), Dominic Bacha (Youth), Anna Bahr (Youth), Clara Broberg (Youth), Holly Broberg (Youth), Daniel Carney (Youth), Reylynn Caster (Youth), Zoe Crowdus (Youth), Nick Falo (Youth), Chase Farha (Youth), Hailey Faust (Youth), Tyler Faust (Youth), Julia Glunt (Youth), Rebekah Glunt (Youth), Hannah Gonzalez (Youth), Alyssa Hershey (Youth), Paige Hidley (Youth), Matthew Janssen (Youth), Emily Jensen (Youth), Hannah Kintzel (Youth), Carson Lee (Youth), Schyler Merrills (Youth), Noah Montgomery (Youth), Chandler Moore (Youth), Gavin Myers (Youth), Drew Mullin (Youth), Brennan O'Rourke (Youth), Kit Riffel (Youth), Katie Robu (Youth), Meggie Schafer (Youth), Ashleigh Sizemore (Youth), Laura Smith (Youth), Edward Sturm (Youth), Alannah Templon (Youth), Tyler Treat (Youth), Caitlin Wagner (Youth), Tony Wilson (Youth), Catherine Vessey (Youth), Lauren Voigt (Youth), Amanda Yoder (Youth), Becca Yoder (Youth); Jennifer Fisher (signing interpreter at certain performances); June 8–12 , 2011

Finian's Rainbow Music by Burton Lane; Book by E.Y. Harburg and Fred Saidy; Lyrics by E.Y. Harburg; Director, Wayne Bryan; Choreographer, Lyndy Franklin Smith, Jeromy Smith; Music Director, Thomas W. Douglas; Sets, Bruce Brockman; Costumes, Sarah Reever; Lighting, David Neville; Hair/Wigs, Alena Sellers; Props, Ray Wetmore; Sound, David Muehl; Technical Director, Jeff Taylor; PSM, Tiffany K. Orr; SM, Emily F. McMullen; Company Manager, Nancy Reeves; Production Manager, David Neville; Cast: Kim Huber (Sharon McLonergan), Edward Watts (Woody Mahoney), Stanley Bahorek (Og), John Boldenow (Finian McLonergan), Reggie Burrell (Bill Rawkins), Timothy W. Robu (Senator Rawkins), Molly Rushing (Susan Mahoney), Betti O. (Dolores), Arri Simon (Preacher/First Gospeleer), Lyonel Reyneau (Black Geologist/Second Gospeleer), Jordan Barrow (Sunny/Third Gospeleer), Adrian Baidoo (Howard), John Keckeisen (Buzz Collins), Michael Parker (Sheriff), Jaiden Armstrong (Henry), Faith Northcutt (Diana), Daniel Horn (White Geologist), Deputy (Ethan Spell), Cody Davis (Mr. Shears), Elliott Mattox (Mr. Robust), Jacob January (2nd Deputy), Wedding Preacher (Ross McCorkell), Jaslyn Alexander (Sharecropper), Connor Bourland (Sharecropper), Audra Bryant (Sharecropper), Jacob Chancellor (Sharecropper), Emily Christ (Sharecropper), Max Clayton (Sharecropper), Erin Clemons (Sharecropper), Hayden Clifton (Sharecropper), Jacob Gutierrez (Sharecropper), Shannon Hucker (Sharecropper), Hannah Meredith Killebrew (Sharecropper), Ben Lanham (Sharecropper), Trevor McChristian (Sharecropper), Emily Mechler (Sharecropper), Sophie Menas (Sharecropper), Maggie Mial (Sharecropper), Nick Palmquist (Sharecropper), Sarah Quinn (Sharecropper), Jean Rust (Sharecropper), Natasha Scearse (Sharecropper), Sarah Shelton (Sharecropper), Zachary James Wilhelm (Sharecropper), Alexandra Adkins (Teen), Ashton Bloomer (Teen), Emily Bruggeman (Teen), Dylan Harris (Teen), Anne Hickerson (Teen), Nathan Hilger (Teen), Liz Jarmer (Teen), Gavin Myers (Teen), Taryn Northcutt (Teen), Colleen Richey (Teen), Kit Riffel (Teen), Katie Sites (Teen), Kelly Ufford (Teen), Maria Collins (Child), Emma Gunderson (Child), Greta Hicks (Child); Jennifer Fisher (signing interpreter at certain performances); June 22–26, 2011

Sunset Boulevard Music by Andrew Lloyd Webber; Book and lyrics by Don Black and Christopher Hampton; Based on the Billy Wilder film; Director, Mark Madama; Choreographer, Lyndy Franklin Smith, Jeromy Smith; Music Director, Thomas W. Douglas; Sets, J Branson; Costumes, George T. Mitchell; Lighting, David Neville; Hair/Wigs, Alena Sellers; Props, Ray Wetmore; Sound, David Muehl; Technical Director, Jeff Taylor; PSM, Emily F. McMullen; SM, Tiffany K. Orr; Company Manager, Nancy Reeves; Production Manager, David Neville; Cast: Ann Morrison (Norma Desmond), Chris Peluso (Joe Gillis), Nicholas F. Saverine (Max von Mayerling), Kaleigh Cronin (Betty Schaefer), Charles Parker (Cecil B. DeMille), Cody Davis (Artie Green), Timothy W. Robu (Sheldrake), Bonnie Bing (Hedda Hopper), Ross McCorkell (Mr. Manfred/Ensemble); Ensemble: Adrian Baidoo, Jordan Barrow, Jacob Chancellor, Emily Christ, Max Clayton, Erin Clemons, Hayden Clifton, Matthew Elliott, Jacob Gutierrez, Daniel Horn, Shannon Hucker, Jacob January, John Keckeisen, Hannah Meredith Killebrew, Ben Lanham, Elliott Mattox, Emily Mechler, Sophie Menas, Maggie Mial, Nick Palmquist, Michael Parker, Lyonel Reneau, Molly Rushing, Natasha Scearse, Sarah Shelton, Arri Simon, Ethan Spell, Zachary James Wilhelm; Jennifer Fisher (signing interpreter at certain performances); July 6–10, 2011

Xanadu Book by Douglas Carter Beane; Music by Jeff Lynne & John Farrar; Lyrics by Jeff Lynne & John Farrar; Based on the Universal Pictures film; Screenplay by Richard Danus & Marc Rubel; Director/Choreographer, Roger Castellano; Music Director, Thomas W. Douglas; Sets, Robert A. Kovach; Costumes, Tiia E. Torchia; Lighting, David Neville; Hair/Wigs, Alena Sellers; Props, Ray Wetmore; Sound, David Muehl; Technical Director, Jeff Taylor; PSM, Tiffany K. Orr; SM, Emily F. McMullen; Company Manager, Nancy Reeves; Production Manager, David Neville; Cast: Emily Mechler (Kira / Clio), Josh Sassanella (Sonny Malone), Kevyn Morrow (Danny Maguire/Zeus), Betti O. (Melpomene/Medusa), Patty Reeder (Calliope/Aphrodite), Natasha Scearse (Thalia), Sophie Menas (Euterpe/Siren), Maggie Mial (Erato), Erin Clemons (Terpsicore), Hannah Meredith Killebrew (Polyhymnia), Sarah Shelton (Urania/Siren), Adrian Baidoo (Young Danny), Shannon Hucker (Siren), Molly Rushing (Siren/Hera), Elliott Mattox (Eros), Lyonel Reyneau (Hermes), Emily Christ (Thetis), Jacob January (Cyclops), Hayden Clifton (Centaur), Satyr (Jordan Barrow): Ensemble: Jacob Chancellor, Max Clayton, Cody Davis, Matthew Elliott, Jacob Gutierrez, Daniel Horn, Ben Lanham, Ross McCorkell, Nick Palmquist, Ethan Spell, Zachary James Wilhelm; Anna Cooper (Teen), Dylan Harris (Teen), Kassiani Menas (Teen), Alexis Paige Tedder (Teen), Kelly Ufford (Teen), Jennifer Fisher (signing interpreter at certain performances); July 20–24, 2011

Disney's The Little Mermaid Music by Alan Menken; Lyrics by Howard Ashman and Glenn Slater; Book by Doug Wright; Based on the Hans Christian Andersen story and the Disney film produced by Howard Ashman & John Musker, and written and directed by John Musker and Ron Clements; Originally produced by Disney Theatrical Productions; Director, Wayne Bryan; Choreographer, Linda Goodrich; Music Director, Thomas W. Douglas; Sets, J Branson; Costumes, Leon Dobkowski; Lighting, David Neville; Hair/Wigs, Alena Sellers; Props, Ray Wetmore; Sound, David Muehl; Technical Director, Jeff Taylor; Projections, David Neville and Sandell Stangl; PSM, Emily F. McMullen; SM, Tiffany K. Orr; Company Manager, Nancy Reeves; Production Manager, David Neville; Cast: Desi Oakley (Ariel), Christopher Charles Wood (Prince Eric), Lawrence Cummings (Sebastian), Kevyn Morrow (King Triton), Karen L. Robu (Ursula), Justin Robertson (Scuttle), Addison Baker (Flounder), Timothy W. Robu (Grimsby), Michael Parker (Chef Louis), Jacob Gutierrez (Flotsam), Cody Davis (Jetsam), Emily Christ (Carlotta), Erin Clemons (Mersister), Hannah Meredith Killebrew (Mersister), Emily Mechler (Mersister), Sophie Menas (Mersister), Maggie Mial (Mersister), Molly Rushing (Mersister), Zachary James Wilhelm (Pilot), Gavin Myers (Cabin Boy); Ensemble: Adrian Baidoo, Jordan Barrow, Audra Bryant, Jacob Chancellor, Max Clayton, Hayden Clifton, Matthew Elliott, Daniel Horn, ShannonHucker, Jacob Lanham, Elliott Mattox, Trevor McChristian, Ross McCorkell, Nick Palmquist, Sarah Quinn, Jean Rust, Natasha Scearse, Sarah Shelton, Ethan Spell; Gavin Myers (Teen), Sally Olmstead (Teen), Brennan O'Rourke (Teen), Maddie Razook (Teen), Colleen Richey (Teen), Kit Riffel (Teen), Charlie Rippy (Teen), Jacob Wasson (Teen), Talia Bauchmoyer (Child), Caroline Boesen (Child), Hannah Brock (Child), Kathryn Bunting (Child), Sydney Dahlgren (Child), Abigail Grier (Child), Eden Hadley (Child), Lizzy Hadley (Child), Rebecca Jensen (Child), Gabbe Meloccaro (Child), Faith Northcutt (Child), Morgan Purdy (Child), Olivia Thornton (Child), Lauren Voigt (Child), Lacey Wellemeyer (Child); Jennifer Fisher (signing interpreter at certain performances); August 5–14, 2011

New Line Theatre

St. Louis, Missouri

Twenty-Second Season

Artistic Director, Scott Miller; Associate Artistic Director, Mike Dowdy

Passing Strange Book and lyrics by Stew; Music by Stew and Heidi Rodewald; Originally created in collaboration with Annie Dorsen; Director, Scott Miller; Assistant Director, Nikki Glenn; Costumes, Amy Kelly; Sets, Todd Schaefer; Lighting, Kenneth Zinkl; Sound, Donald Smith, SM, Trisha Bakula; House Manager, Ann Stinebaker; Box Office Manager, Vicki Herrmann; Lighting, Trisha Bakula; Graphics, Matt Reedy; Photographer, Jill Ritter Lindberg; Cast: Charles

Glenn (Narrator), Keith Parker (Youth), Talichia Noah (Mother), Jeanitta Perkins (Sherry/Renata/Desi), Andrea Purnell (Edwina/Marianna/Sudabey), John Reed II (Rev Jones/Franklin/Joop/Venus), Cecil E. Washington Jr. (Terry/Christophe/Hugo); September 22–October 15, 2011

Cry-Baby (revised) Based on the Universal Pictures film written and directed by John Waters; Music and lyrics by David Javerbaum, Adam Schlesinger; Book by Mark O'Donnell, Thomas Meehan; Director, Scott Miller; Choreographer, Robin Michelle Berger; Costumes, Amy Kelly; Lighting, Sean M. Savoie; Sets, Scott L. Schoonover; Sound, Donald Smith; SM, Trisha Bakula; Dance Captain, Taylor Pietz; Props Master, Alison Helmer; Specialty Props, Pat Edmonds; House Manager, Ann Stinebaker; Box Office Manager, Vicki Herrmann; Lighting Technician, Trisha Bakula; Graphics, Matt Reedy; Photographer, Jill Ritter Lindberg; Cast: Ryan Foizey (Wade "Cry-Baby" Walker), Taylor Pietz (Allison Vernon-Williams), Mike Dowdy (Baldwin Blandish), Cindy Duggan (Mrs. Cordelia Vernon-Williams), Marcy Wiegert (Pepper Walker), Chrissy Young (Wanda Woodward), Sarah Porter (Mona "Hatchet Face" Malnorowski), Ari Scott (Dupree W. Dupree), Terrie Carolan (Lenora Frigid), Zachary Allen Farmer (Judge Igneous Stone and Everybody Else), Evan Fornachon (Whiffle/Drape), Devon A. A. Norris (Whiffle/Drape), Christopher Strawhun (Whiffle/Drape), Jenifer Sabbert (Square Girl/Drape Girl), Alexandra Taylor (Square Girl/Drape Girl); March 1–24, 2012

High Fidelity Based on the novel by Nick Hornby; Book by David Lindsay-Abaire; Music by Tom Kitt; Lyrics by Amanda Green; Director, Scott Miller; Choreographer, Robin Michelle Berger; Costumes, Amy Kelly; Sets, Scott L. Schoonover; Lighting, Kenneth Zinkl; Sound, Donald Smith; SM, Trisha Bakula; Dance Captain, Taylor Pietz; Props Master, Alison Helmer; House Manager, Ann Stinebaker; Box Office Manager, Vicki Herrmann; Lighting Technician, Trisha Bakula; Graphics, Matt Reedy; Photographer, Jill Ritter Lindberg; Cast: Jeffrey M. Wright (Rob), Kimi Short (Laura), Mike Dowdy (Dick), Zachary Allen Farmer (Barry), Aaron Allen (Ian), Talichia Noah (Liz/Jackie), Terrie Carolan (Anna/Alison), Margeau Baue Steinau (Marie LaSalle), Todd Micali (TMPMITW/Bruce Springsteen), Nicholas Kelly (Klepto-Boy), Keith Thompson (Futon Guy/Skid), Ryan Foizey (Hipster/Neil Young/Skid), Chrissy Young (Charlie), Taylor Pietz (Penny), Sarah Porter (Sarah/Marie's back-up singer); May 31–June 23, 2012

North Carolina Theatre

Raleigh, North Carolina

Twenty-eighth and Twenty-ninth Season

President and CEO, Lisa Grele Barrie; Artistic Director, Casey Hushion; Producer, Carolee Baxter

Hairspray by Mark O'Donnell & Thomas Meehan; Music by Marc Shaiman; Lyrics by Scott Wittman and Marc Shaiman; Director, John Simpkins; Choreographer, Josh Rhodes; Music Director/Conductor/Orchestra Contractor, Nancy Whelan; SM, William Alan Coats; ASM, Tyler W. Rhodes; Lighting, Craig Stelzenmuller; Sound, Brian L. Hunt; Costumes, Ann M. Bruskiewitz; Hair/Make-up, Patricia DelSordo; Props, Aline Johnson; Associate Sound, Eric Collins; Wardrobe, Meredith Scott; Master Carpenter, Tommy Reed; Master Electrician, Craig Mowery; Associate Choreographer, Ariana DeBose; Rehearsal Pianist, Andre Cerullo; Properties Assistant, Ashley Laughter; Sound Assistant, Eric Feuerstein; Hair/Wigs/Make-up Assistant, Kimberly Genna, Joyce Hawkins; Director's Assistant, Andrew Britt; PA, Michael McKeever; Production Photographer, Curtis Brown Photography; Cast: Dale Hensley (Edna), Jennifer Foster (Tracy Turnblad), Dirk Lumbard (Wilbur), Jannie Jones (Motormouth Maybelle) Jason Kappus (Link Larkin), Dana Steingold (Penny Pingleton), Rhiannon Hansen (Amber), Christopher Sloan (Corny Collins), Donell James Foreman (Seaweed), Christine Hunter (Velma), Lisa Jolley (Female Authority Figure), J. Michael Beech (male Authority Figure), Marja Harmon (Dynamite/Ensemble), Crystal Sha'nae (Dynamite/Ensemble), Roy Anothony (Brad/Ensemble), Seth Eliser (Fender/Ensemble), Ariana Debose (Little Inez/Dance Captain/Ensemble), English Bernhardt (Tammy/Ensemble), Katie Bottomley (Lou Ann/Ensemble), Christopher Brasfield (Duane/Ensemble), Carlita

V. Ector (Lorraine/US Little Inez/Ensemble), Charlie Johnson (Sketch/Ensemble), Caroline Jordan (Shelley/Ensemble), Christopher C. Minor (Thad/Ensemble), Ryan Naimy (IQ/Ensemble), Justin Showell (Gilbert/Ensemble), Adrienne C. Sulkey (Dynamite/Ensemble), Kelsey Walston (Brenda/Ensemble); July 23–31, 2011

Evita by Tim Rice; Music by Andrew Lloyd Webber; Director/ Choreographer, Tito Hernandez; Music Director/Conductor, Julie Bradley; SM, Eric Lee Tysinger; ASM, Candace E. Hoffman; Lighting, John Bartenstein; Sound, Brian L. Hunt, Eric Collins; Costumes, Ann M. Bruskiewitz; Hair/Make-Up, Patricia DelSordo; Sets/ Set Supervisor, Chris Bernier; Associate Music Director/Contractor/Rehearsal Pianist, Nancy Whelan; Assistant Director/Choreographer, Sherry Lee Allen; Props, Ashley Laughter; Wardrobe, Meredith Scott; Master Electrician, Craig Mowery; Sound Assistant, Eric Feuerstein; Director's Assistant, Meredith Davis; Production Photographer, Curtis Brown Photography; Cast: Lauren Kennedy (Eva Peron), Ray Walker (Che), Jonathon Hammond (Juan Peron), Mary Adamek (Chorus), Sherry Lee Allen (Chorus/Dance Captain), Julian Alvarez (Chorus), Laurena Barros (Chorus), Enclish Bernhardt (Mistress/Chorus), Amanda Blaire Callaghan (Chorus), Nick Duckart (Magaldi/Chorus/Che u/s), Jason Mark Durst (Chorus), Erik Floor (Chorus), Sean Cargan (Chorus), Elgin Giles (Chorus), Heather Patterson King (Chorus/Eva u/s), Carissa Lopez (Chorus), Christopher C. Minor (Chorus), Ryan Naimy (Chorus), Vincent Ortega (Chorus/Peron u/s), Haley Richardson (Acting Intern Chorus), Jonathon Stahl (Chorus/Tango Dancer), Johnny Stellard (Chorus), Selina Verastigui (Chorus), Mackenzie Warren (Chorus), Matthew-Jason Willis (Chorus), Chloe Renee Calhoun (Children's Chorus), Mary Kate Englehardt (Children's Chorus), William Fergusson (Children's Chorus), Carly Grissom (Children's Chorus), Joshua Keen (Children's Chorus), Mary Callan Kelso (Children's Chorus), Nicholas Kraft (Children's Chorus), Caroline Lipson (Children's Chorus), Michael Raul Perez (Children's Chorus), Cady Van Venrooy (Children's Chorus); October 22–30, 2011

Steel Magnolias by Robert Harling; Director, Eric Woodall; SM, Eric Lee Tysinger; ASM, Tiffany Owle; Lighting, John Bartenstein; Sound, Eric Alexander Collins; Costumes, Ann M. Bruskiewitz; Hair/Make-up, Patricia DelSordo; Sets, Chris Bernier; Set Construction, Bill Yates, Jr.; Props, Ashley Laughter; Wardrobe, Kimberly Genna; Master Electrician, Jennifer Sherrod; Carpenter, James W. Pegram; Director's Assistant, Andrew Britt; Lighting Assistant, Caroline Reilly; Props Assistant, Lorraine Mancuso; Production Photographer, Curtis Brown Photography; Cast: Beth Leavel (M'Lynn), Jenn Colella (Truvy), Diane J. Findlay (Ouiser), Anne Horak (Shelby), Darrie Lawrence (Clairee), Madeline Chloe Taylor (Annelle); April 20–29, 2012

Northlight Theatre

Skokie, Illinois

Thirty-seventh Season

Artistic Director, BJ Jones; Executive Director, Timothy J. Evans

Snapshots Book by David Stern, Music and lyrics by Stephen Schwartz; Director, Ken Sawyer; Sets, Jack Magaw; Costumes, Elizabeth Flauto; Lighting, Jesse Klug; Sound, Lindsay Jones; Projections, Mike Tutaj; Stage Manager, Rita Vreeland; Music Director, Musical Supervisor and Arranger, Steve Orich; Cast: Tony Clarno, Nick Cosgrove, Jess Godwin, Megan Long, Susie McMonagle, Gene Weygandt; September 16–October 23, 2011

Season's Greetings by Alan Ayckbourn; Director, BJ Jones; Sets, Keith Pitts; Costumes, Rachel Laritz; Lighting, JR Lederle; Sound, Andre Pluess; Cast: John Byrnes (*Eddie*), Amy J. Carle (Phyllis), Francis Guinan (Bernard), Steve Haggard (Clive), Heidi Kettenring (Belinda), Maggie Kettering (Pattie), Ginger Lee McDermott (Rachel), Rob Riley (Harvey), Matt Schwader (Neville); November 11–December 18, 2011

Black Pearl Sings by Frank Higgins; Director, Steve Scott; Sets, Jack Magaw; Costumes, Emily McConnell; Lighting, Sarah Hughey; Sound, Christopher Kriz; Cast: E. Faye Butler (Pearl), Susie McMonagle (Susannah); January 13–February 19, 2012

Ten Chimneys by Jeffrey Hatcher; Director, BJ Jones; Sets, Tom Burch; Costumes, Rachel Laritz; Lighting, JR Lederle; Sound, Joe Cerqua; Cast: Lance Baker (Carl), Janet Ulrich Brooks (Louise), Sara Griffin (Uta Hagen), V Craig Heidenreich (Alfred Lunt), Lia Mortensen (Lynn Fontanne), Linda Kimbrough (Hattie), Steve Pringle (Sydney Greenstreet); March 9–April 15, 2012.

[title of show] Music and lyrics by Jeff Bowen and book by Hunter Bell; Director, Peter Amster; Sets, Christopher J. Fitzgerald; Costumes, Rachel Laritz; Lighting, Chris Binder; Sound, Victoria Delorio; Stage Manager, Rita Vreeland; Cast: McKinley Carter (Susan), Matthew Crowle (Hunter), Stephen Schellhardt (Jeff), Christine Sherrill (Heidi), Doug Peck (Piano/Conducter); May 4–June 10, 2012

The Old Globe

San Diego, California

Seventy-seventh Season

Managing Director, Michael G. Murphy

LOWELL DAVIES FESTIVAL THEATRE

Much Ado About Nothing by William Shakespeare; Director, Ron Daniels; Sets, Ralph Funicello; Costumes, Deirdre Clancy; Lighting, Alan Burrett; Original Music and Sound, Dan Moses Schreier; Music Director, Charlie Reuter; Fight Director, Steve Rankin; Movement, Liz Shipman; Dialect, Jan Gist; SM, Bret Torbeck; Cast: Michael Stewart Allen (Borachio), John Cariani (Dogberry), Donald Carrier (Don Pedro), Anthony Cochrane (Friar Francis, Sexton), Winslow Corbett (Hero), Kevin Alan Daniels (Claudio), Ben Diskant (Balthasar), Georgia Hatzis (Beatrice), Charles Janasz (Antonio, Verges), Deborah Radloff (Ursula), Jonno Roberts (Benedick), Ryman Sneed (Margaret), Adrian Sparks (Leonato), Jonathan Spivey (Conrade), Jay Whittaker (Don John); Ensemble: Shirine Babb, Adam Daveline, Grayson DeJesus, Christian Durso, Andrew Hutcheson, Rachael Jenison, Jesse Jensen, Jason Maddy, Allison Spratt Pearce; May 29–September 22, 2011

The Tempest by William Shakespeare; Director, Adrian Noble; Sets, Ralph Funicello; Costumes, Deirdre Clancy; Lighting, Alan Burrett; Sound, Dan Moses Schreier; Original Music, Shaun Davey; Music Director, Charlie Reuter; Puppet Advisor, Joe Fitzpatrick; Fight Director, Steve Rankin; Dialect, Jan Gist; SM, Bret Torbeck; Cast: Michael Stewart Allen (Sebastian), Miles Anderson (Prospero), Shirine Babb (Iris), John Cariani (Trinculo), Donald Carrier (Alonso), Anthony Cochrane (Antonio), Winslow Corbett (Miranda), Kevin Alan Daniels (Ferdinand), Adam Daveline (Shipmaster), Grayson DeJesus (Francisco), Ben Diskant (Ariel), Christian Durso (Adrian), Andrew Hutcheson (Boatswain), Charles Janasz (Gonzalo), Allison Spratt Pearce (Ceres), Deborah Radloff (Juno), Jonno Roberts (Caliban), Adrian Sparks (Stephano), Rachael Jenison, Jesse Jensen, Jason Maddy, Ryman Sneed and Jonathan Spivey (Spirits); June 5–September 22, 2011

Amadeus by Peter Shaffer; Director, Adrian Noble; Sets, Ralph Funicello; Costumes, Deirdre Clancy; Lighting, Alan Burrett; Sound, David Bullard; Fight Director, Steve Rankin; Dialect, Jan Gist; SM, Bret Torbeck; Cast: Michael Stewart Allen (Baron van Swieten), Miles Anderson (Antonio Salieri), Shirine Babb (Teresa Salieri), Donald Carrier (Joseph II, Emperor of Austria), Anthony Cochrane (Count Orsini-Rosenberg), Winslow Corbett (Constanze Weber), Adam Daveline (Salieri's Cook), Christian Durso (A Majordomo), Georgia Hatzis (Venticella), Andrew Hutcheson (Salieri's Valet), Charles Janasz (Count von Strack), Allison Spratt Pearce (Katherina Cavalieri), Ryman Sneed (Venticella), Jonathan Spivey (Kapellmeister Bonno), Jay Whittaker (Wolfgang Amadeus Mozart); Ensemble: Grayson DeJesus, Ben Diskant, Rachael Jenison, Jesse Jensen, Jason Maddy and Deborah Radloff; June 12–September 22, 2011

Odyssey Music, lyrics and book by Todd Almond; Conceived and Directed by Lear deBessonet; Movement, Tony Caligagan, Maria Caligagan; Sets/Lighting, Justin Townsend; Costumes, Paul Carey; Sound, Paul Peterson; SM, Evangeline Rose Whitlock; Cast: Alvin Crawford (Odysseus), Shelley Thomas (Penelope), Todd Almond (The Singer), Darlene Gould Davies (Eurynome), Kim Duclo (Penelope's First Suitor), Michael Garcia (Prince), Dylan Hoffinger (Odysseus' Captain), Troy Johnson (Cyclops), Martín Martiarena (Dude with Guitar), Alex Monge (Telemachus), Davina Van Dusen (Nausicaa), Victoria Matthews, Jordon Scowcroft, Katie Ward (The Calliopes), Diana Bahena, Anay Barajas, Jessica Brandon, Dalaysia Cannon, Ashley Dixon, Richard Dobbs, Deja Fields, Renée Gándola, Zyanya Hernandez-Grant, Carson McCalley, Karen Olinga, Elliott Sephus, Al Simmons, Hannah Trujillo, Katherine Zamora and Ayerton Zoutendijk (Ithacans), Karen Bahena, Lina Bien, Katleen Dugas, Paola Kubelism, Stephanie Plascencia (Penelope's Women); Eduardo Bravo, Kenn Burnett, Leland Campbell, Eduard Cao, André A. Carter, William Herrera, Lorenzo Martinez, Leonel Roman, Lamine Thiam (Odysseus' Men); Members of Salsa Inferno (Circe's Lair), Donna Blochwitz, Jane Klofkorn, Yvonne Lindroth Silva, Amara Marsden (Sirens), Kim Dulco, Kent Gándola, Craig Hunter, Terrence Johnson, Mark Keller (Penelope's Suitors); September 30–October 1, 2011

OLD GLOBE THEATRE

Hershey Felder as George Gershwin Alone Music by George Gershwin; Written by Hershey Felder; Director, Joel Zwick; Cast: Hershey Felder (George Gershwin); July 1–July 10, 2011

Hershey Felder in Concert: The Great American Songbook Text by Hershey Felder; Cast: Hershey Felder (Himself); July 11–July 17, 2011

Hershey Felder in Maestro: The Art of Leonard Bernstein Music by Leonard Bernstein; Written by Hershey Felder; Director, Joel Zwick; Cast: Hershey Felder (Leonard Bernstein); July 22–August 28, 2011

Engaging Shaw by John Morogiello; Director, Henry Wishcamper; Sets, Wilson Chin; Costumes, Alejo Vietti; Lighting, Matthew Richards; Sound, Paul Peterson; SM, Lavinia Henley; Cast: Rod Brogan (George Bernard Shaw), Natalie Gold (Beatrice Webb), Angela Pierce (Charlotte Payne-Townshend), Michael Warner (Sidney Webb); July 29–September 4, 2011

Richard O'Brien's The Rocky Horror Show Book, music and lyrics by Richard O'Brien; Director, James Vásquez; Musical Stager/Choeographer, JT Horenstein; Music Director, Mike Wilkins; Sets, Donyale Werle; Costumes, Emily Rebholz; Lighting, Rui Rita; Sound, Kevin Kennedy; Projections, Aaron Rhyne; Casting, Carrie Gardner, CSA; SM, Anjee Nero; Cast: Andrew Call (Eddie, Phantom), Jeanna de Waal (Janet), Sydney James Harcourt (Rocky), Nadine Isenegger (Columbia), Lauren Lim Jackson (Phantom), Kelsey Kurz (Brad), David Andrew Macdonald (Narrator, Dr. Scott), Matt McGrath (Frank 'N' Furter), Anna Schnaitter (Phantom), Laura Shoop (Magenta, Usherette), Kit Treece (Phantom), Jason Wooten (Riff Raff, Usher); September 15–November 16, 2011

Dr. Seuss' How The Grinch Stole Christmas! Book and lyrics by Timothy Mason; Music by Mel Marvin; Original Production Conceived and Directed by Jack O'Brien; Director, James Vásquez; Original Choreography, John DeLuca; Additional Choreography, Bob Richard; Music Director, Ron Colvard; Sets, John Lee Beatty; Costumes, Robert Morgan; Lighting, Pat Collins; Sound, Paul Peterson; Orchestrator, Anita Ruth; Vocal Arranger/Incidental Music, Joshua Rosenblum; Dance Music Arranger, David Krane; SM, Leila Knox; Cast: Steve Blanchard (The Grinch), Logan Lipton (Young Max), Steve Gunderson (Old Max), Remy Margaret Corbin, Caitlin McAuliffe (Cindy-Lou Who), Geno Carr (Papa Who), Kelsey Venter (Mama Who), Phil Johnson (Grandpa Who), Amanda Naughton (Grandma Who), Annie Buckley, Madison Pyle (Annie Who), Gabriela Leibowitz, Natasha Partnoy (Betty-Lou Who), Luke Babbitt, Dylan Nalbandian (Boo Who), Aaron Acosta, Jonas McMullen (Danny Who); Emsemble: Liam James Brandt, Jacob Caltrider, Nancy Snow Carr, Nikki Castillo, Kevin Davison, Danielle Dawson, Julia Dawson, Madi Rae DiPietro, Randall Dodge, A.J. Foggiano, Meredith Inglesby, Kyle J. Jackson, Dylan Mulvaney, Carly Nykanen, Emma Rasse, Blue Schroeder; November 19–December 31, 2011

Dividing the Estate by Horton Foote; Director, Michael Wilson; Sets, Jeff Cowie; Costumes, David C. Woolard; Lighting, Rui Rita; Original Music and Sound, John Gromada; New York Casting Director, Stephanie Klapper; SM, Marisa Levy; Cast: Devon Abner (Son), Elizabeth Ashley (Stella Gordon), Pat Bowie (Mildred), James DeMarse (Bob), Hallie Foote (Mary Jo), Horton Foote Jr. (Lewis Gordon), Penny Fuller (Lucille), Nicole Lowrance (Sissie), Kelly McAndrew (Pauline), Jenny Dare Paulin (Emily), Keiana Richàrd (Cathleen), Roger Robinson (Doug), Bree Welch (Irene Ratliff); January 14–February 12, 2012

The Scottsboro Boys Music and lyrics by John Kander & Fred Ebb; Libretto by David Thompson; Director/Choreographer, Susan Stroman; Music Director, Eric Ebbenga; Associate Director/Choreographer, Jeff Whiting; Sets, Beowulf Boritt; Costumes, Toni-Leslie James; Lighting, Ken Billington; Sound, Jon Weston; Assistant Choreographer, Eric Santagata; Orchestrations by Larry Hochman; Music Arranger, Glen Kelly; Vocal Arranger, David Loud; Fight Director, Rick Sordelet; Casting by Janet Foster, CSA; SM, Joshua Halperin; Cast: David Bazemore (Olen Montgomery), Cornelius Bethea (Willie Roberson), Nile Bullock (Eugene Williams), Christopher James Culberson (Andy Wright), Clifton Duncan (Haywood Patterson), Ron Holgate (The Interlocutor), Eric Jackson (Clarence Norris), Jared Joseph (Mr. Bones), James T. Lane (Ozie Powell), JC Montgomery (Mr. Tambo), Clifton Oliver (Charles Weems), Clinton Roane (Roy Wright), C. Kelly Wright (The Lady), Audrey Martells (The Lady u/s), Shavey Brown, Max Kumangai (Swings); April 29–June 10, 2012

A Room with a View Book by Marc Acito; Music and lyrics by Jeffrey Stock; Additional Lyrics by Marc Acito; Based on the Novel by E.M. Forster; Director, Scott Schwartz; Music Director, Boko Suzuki; Sets, Heidi Ettinger; Costumes, Judith Dolan; Lighting, David Lander; Sound, Jon Weston; Orchestrations, Bruce Coughlin; Arranger, Jeffrey Stock; Musical Stager, Michael Jenkinson; Vocal/Dialect, Jan Gist; Casting, Tara Rubin Casting; SM, Anjee Nero; Cast: Ephie Aardema (Lucy Honeychurch), Glenn Seven Allen (Italiano, Albert), Etai BenShlomo (Freddy Honeychurch), Gina Ferrall (Miss Lavish, Mrs. Honeychurch), Jacquelynne Fontaine (Ragazza, Minnie), Kyle Harris (George Emerson), Will Reynolds (Cecil Vyse), Edward Staudenmayer (Reverend Mr. Beeber), Karen Ziemba (Charlotte Bartlett), Kurt Zischke (Mr. Emerson); March 2–April 15, 2012

SHERYL AND HARVEY WHITE THEATRE

Somewhere by Matthew Lopez; Director, Giovanna Sardelli; Choreographer, Greg Graham; Sets, Campbell Baird; Costumes, Charlotte Devaux; Lighting, Lap Chi Chu; Sound, Jeremy J. Lee; SM, Elizabeth Stephens; Cast: Juan Javier Cardenas (Francisco Candelaria), Leo Ash Evens (Jamie MacRae), Priscilla Lopez (Inez Candelaria), Benita Robledo (Rebecca Candelaria), Jon Rua (Alejandro Candelaria); September 24–October 30, 2011

Some Lovers Book and lyrics by Steven Sater; Music by Burt Bacharach; Director, Will Frears; Music Supervisor, Lon Hoyt; Musical Stager, Denis Jones; Sets, Takeshi Kata; Costumes, Jenny Mannis; Lighting, Ben Stanton; Sound, Leon Rothenberg; Orchestrator, Jonathan Tunick; Vocal, AnnMarie Milazzo; Casting, Jim Carnahan, CSA; SM, Matthew Silver; Cast: Jenni Barber (Young Molly), Jason Danieley (Ben), Michelle Duffy (Molly), Andrew Mueller (Young Ben); November 26–December 31, 2011

The Recommendation by Jonathan Caren; Director, Jonathan Munby; Sets, Alexander Dodge; Costumes, Linda Cho; Associate Costumes, Erick Sundquist; Lighting, Philip S. Rosenberg; Original Music and Sound, Lindsay Jones; Movement, Tony Caligagan; Casting by Calleri Casting; SM, Diana Moser; Cast: Jimonn Cole (Dwight Barnes), Brandon Gill (Iskinder Iudoku); Evan Todd (Aaron Feldman); January 21–February 26, 2012

Anna Christie by Eugene O'Neill; Director, Daniel Goldstein; Sets, Wilson Chin; Costumes, Denitsa Bliznakova; Lighting, Austin R. Smith; Sound, Paul Peterson; Original Music by Chris Miller; Vocal/Dialect, Jan Gist; Casting, Calleri Casting; SM, Annette Yé; Cast: Bryan Banville (Longshoreman), Bill Buell (Chris Christopherson), Chance Dean (Longshoreman, Johnson), Austin Durant (Mat Burke), John Garcia (Johnny-the-Priest), Brent Langdon (Larry), Jessica Love (Anna Christopherson), Jason Maddy (Postman), Kristine Nielsen (Marthy Owen); March 10–April 15, 2012

Jason Hite and the Company of San Jose Repertory's production of Spring Awakening (photo by Kevin Berne)

David Elder and the Company of A Chorus Line at Stages St. Louis (photo by Peter Wochniak)

Floyd King and Carson Elrod in Shakespeare Theatre Company's production of The Heir Apparent (photo by Scott Suchman)

Cliff Chamberlain, Karen Aldridge, Stephanie Childers, James Vincent Meredith, and Brendan Marshall-Rashid in Steppenwolf Theatre Company's production of Clybourne Park (photo by Michael Brosilow)

Dana Green, Kalie Quñones, Joel J. Gelman, Kandis Chappell, Corey Brill, Cate Scott Campbell, and Scott Drummond in South Coast Repertory's production of Pride and Prejudice (photo by Henry DiRocco)

James Vincent Meredith and Alana Arena in Steppenwolf Theatre Company's world premiere production of The March (photo by Michael Brosilow)

Joseph Graves and Matthew Amendt in Red at Syracuse Stage
(photo by Michael Davis)

Stephen Thorne, Brough Hansen, Stephen Berenson, and Phyllis Kay in
His Girl Friday at Trinity Repertory Company (photo by Mark Turek)

Stephen Thorne and Joe Wilson, Jr. in The Merchant of Venice at Trinity
Repertory Company (photo by Mark Turek)

Joshua Elijah Reese in The Brothers Size at Syracuse Stage
(photo by T. Charles Erickson)

J. Bernard Calloway, James A. Williams, Allie Woods Jr., Harvy Blanks,
Anthony Chisholm, and Brandon J. Dirden in Jitney at Two River Theater
(photo by T. Charles Erickson)

Nobody Loves You Music and lyrics by Gaby Alter; Book and lyrics by Itamar Moses; Director, Michelle Tattenbaum; Music Director, Vadim Feichtner; Choreographer, Mandy Moore; Sets, Michael Schweikardt; Costumes, Emily Pepper; Lighting, Tyler Micoleau; Sound, Paul Peterson; Orchestrator/Vocal Arranger, Gaby Alter; Casting, Stephanie Klapper, CSA; SM, Peter Van Dyke; Cast: Jenni Barber (Jenny), Alex Brightman (Chazz, Dominic, Evan), Heath Calvert (Byron), Kate Morgan Chadwick (Samantha, Bonnie), Adam Kantor (Jeff), Kelsey Kurz (Christian, Steve), Nicole Lewis (Tanya, Nina, Zenobia), Lauren Molina (Megan); May 9–June 17, 2012

Olney Theatre Center

Olney, Maryland

Seventy-third Season

Artistic Director, Jim Petosa

Opus by Michael Hollinger; Director, Jim Petosa; Costumes, Kathleen Geldard; Sets, Cristina Todesco; Lighting, Daniel MacLean Wagner; Sound, GW Rodriguez; SM, Josiane M. Lemieux; Cast: Ben Evett (Dorian); Michael Kaye (Elliot); Paul Morella (Carl); Becky Webber (Grace); Shelley Bolman (Alan); June 8–July 10, 2011

Grease Musical by Jim Jacobs and Warren Casey; Director, Bobby Smith; Choreographer, Ilona Kessell; Music Director, Aaron Broderick; Sets, Robert Klingelhoefer; Costumes, Seth Gilbert; Co-Lighting, Charlie Morrison, Sonya Dowhaluk; Sound, GW Rodriguez; Cast: Matthew Anderson (Vince Fontaine), Jessica Lauren Ball (Sandy Dumbrowski), Caroline Bowman (Betty Rizzo), Patrick Cragin (Kenickie Murdock), Parker Drown (Sonny La Tierri), Abby Hart (Patty Simcox), David Bryant Johnson (Danny Zuko), Vincent Kempski (Teen Angel), Ashleigh King (Cha-Cha), Jennie Lutz (Female Swing), Gannon O'Brien (Male Swing), Jamie Ogden (Female Ensemble), Allie Parris (Jan), Maria Rizzo (Marty), Casey Rogers (Female Ensemble), Kyle Schliefer (Eugene Florczyk), Caitlin Shea (Frenchy), Andrew Sonntag (Male Ensemble), Dan Van Why (Roger), Alan Wiggins (Doody), Delores King Williams (Miss Lynch), Carl Michael Wilson (Male Ensemble); July 27–September 4, 2011

Witness for the Prosecution by Agatha Christie; Director, John Going; Sets, James Wolk; Lighting, Dennis Parichy; Sound, Matt Rowe; Costumes, Liz Covey; Wigs, Anne Nesmith; Cast: Bob Ari (Sir Wilfrid Robarts), DC Cathro (Plainclothes Det/Police), Andrea Cirie (Romaine), Jenny Donovan (The Other Woman), Alan Hoffman (Clerk-Usher), Drew Kopas (Mr. Clegg), Monica Lijewski (Janet Mackenzie), Paul Morella (Inspector Hearne), Carolyn Myers (Greta/Stenographer), Joe Palka (Mr. Wyatt), Jim Scopeletis (Judge Wainwright), James Slaughter (Mr. Mayhew), Jeffries Thaiss (Leonard Vole), Greg Twomey (Warder), Alan Wade (Mr. Myers), R. Scott Williams (Carter/Barrister); September 28–October 23, 2011

The Sound of Music by Richard Rodgers and Oscar Hammerstein II; Director, Mark Waldrop; Music Director, Christopher Youstra; Sets, James Fouchard; Costume Coordinators, Jeanne Bland, Seth Gilbert; Lighting, Charlie Morrison; Sound, Jeffrey Dorfman; SM, Josiane M. Lemieux; Cast: Donna Migliaccio (Sister Berthe, Ensemble), Tracy Lynn Olivera (Sister Sophia, Ensemble), Maria Egler (Sister Rafaela, Ensemble, performed by Melynda Burdette), Channez McQuay (Sister Margaretta, Ensemble, performed by Maria Egler), Monica Lijewski (Mother Abbess, performed by Channez McQuay), Jessica Lauren Ball (Maria Rainer), George Dvorsky (Captain Georg von Trapp), Peter Boyer (Franz), Karen Paone (Frau Schmidt, Ensemble), Maggie Donovan (Liesl), Brendan Debonis (Friedrich), Ari Goldbloom-Helzner (Friedrich), Caitlin Deerin (Louisa), Carolyn Youstra (Louisa), Austin Lemere (Kurt), Jake Foster (Kurt), Julia Laje (Marta), Ella Gatlin (Marta), Svea Johnson (Gretl), Heidi Kaplan (Gretl), Caroline Coleman (Brigitta), Sydney Maloney (Brigitta), Danny Yoerges (Rolf Gruber), Jenna Sokolowski (Elsa Schraeder, Ensemble), Bobby Smith (Max Detweiler, Dance Captain), DC Cathro (Baron Elberfeld, Ensemble), Ethan Watermeier (Herr Zeller, Ensemble), Tracy McMullan (Baroness Elberfeld, Ensemble, Elsa u/s), Gracie Jones (A

Postulant, ensemble, Maria u/s), William Diggle (Admiral von Schreiber), David Frankenberger, Jr. (Ensemble), John Fritz (Male Swing), Christine Lacey (Female Swing); November 17, 2011–January 22, 2012

You're A Good Man, Charlie Brown by Clark Gesnar; Director, Stephen Nachamie; Music Director, Christopher Youstra; Sets, Robert Andrew Kovach; Costumes, Seth Gilbert; Lighting, Andrew Griffin; Sound, Jeffrey Dorfman; SM, Josiane M. Lemieux; Cast: Zach Colonna (Charlie Brown), James Gardiner (Snoopy), Jaimie Kelton (Sally), Patrick Prebula (Male Swing), Maria Rizzo (Female Swing), Janine Sunday (Lucy), Vishal Vaidya (Schroeder), Paul Wyatt (Linus); February 22–March 25, 2012

The 39 Steps Adapted by Patrick Barlow, from the novel by John Buchan, from the movie of Alfred Hitchcock; Director, Clay Hopper; Sets, Cristina Todesco; Costumes, Pei Lee; Lighting, Nicholas Houfek; Sound, Alex Neumann; Projections, JJ Kaczynski; Assistant to the Director, Ashleigh Millett; Cast: Evan Casey (Clown Two), Jason Lott (Clown One), Susan Lynskey (Annabella, Pamela, Margaret), Jeffries Thaiss (Richard Hannay); April 18–May 27, 2012

Oregon Shakespeare Festival

Ashland, Oregon

Seventy-seventh season

Artistic Director, Bill Rauch; Executive Director, Paul Nicholson

ANGUS BOWMER THEATRE

Romeo and Juliet by William Shakespeare; Director, Laird Williamson; Sets, Michael Ganio; Costumes, Susan Tsu; Lighting, Don Darnutzer; Original Music and Sound, David Reiffel; Choreographer, Alonzo Lee Moore IV; Dramaturg, Lydia G. Garcia; Voice/Text, David Carey; Fight Choreographer, U. Jonathan Toppo; SM, Moira Gleason; PA, Roxana Khan; Cast: Elijah Alexander (Don Capulet), Vilma Silva (Doña Capulet), Alejandra Escalante (Juliet), Fajer Al-Kaisi (Tybalt), Isabell Monk O'Connor (Nurse), Tony DeBruno (Friar Laurence/Ensemble), Barzin Akhavan (Don Montague/Ensemble), DeLanna Studi (Doña Montague, Apothecary an Ohlone), Daniel José Molina (Romeo), Rex Young (General Prince), Miles Fletcher (Captain Paris), Danielle Chaves (Valentina/Ensemble), Jason Rojas (Mercutio), Kevin Fugaro (Benvolio/Ensemble), Joe Wegner (Peter Capulet's servant/ Ensemble), Jim L. Garcia (Sansón a vaquero/Ensemble), Heath Koerschgen (Gregorio a vaquero/ Ensemble), Mikkei Fritz (Balthazar/Ensemble), David Salsa (Abram a vaquero/Friar John/Esemble), Brittany Brook (Ensemble), Shadee Vossoughi (Ensemble); February 17–November 4, 2012

Animal Crackers by George S. Kaufman & Morrie Ryskind; Music and lyrics by Bert Kalmar & Harry Ruby; Adapted by Henry Wishcamper; Director, Allison Narver; Sets, Richard L. Hay; Costumes, Shigeru Yaji; Lighting, Geoff Korf; Sound, Matt Callahan; Dramaturg, Lue Morgan Douthit; Voice/Text, Scott Kaiser; Fight Choreographer, U. Jonathan Toppo; SM, Gwen Turos; ASM, D. Christian Bolender; Cast: Jonathan Haugen (Roscoe W. Chandler/Hives/Chorus), K. T. Vogt (Mrs. Rittenhouse/Chorus), Mandie Jenson (Arabella Rittenhouse/Chorus), Kate Mulligan (Mrs. Whitehead/Chorus), Jeremy Peter Johnson (Wally Winston/M. Doucet /Sgt. Hennessey/Chorus), Laura Griffith (Grace Carpenter /Mary Stewart /Chorus), Eddie Lopez (John Parker/Horatius Jamison/Butler/Chorus), Mark Bedard (Captain Jeffrey T. Spaulding/Chorus), John Tufts (Emanuel Ravelli/Chorus), Daisuke Tsuji (Emanuel Ravelli/Chorus), Brent Hinkley (The Professor/Chorus); February 19–November 4, 2012

The White Snake Adapted from the classic Chinese fable by Mary Zimmerman; Director, Mary Zimmerman; Sets, Daniel Ostling; Costumes, Mara Blumenfeld; Lighting, T.J. Gerckens; Original Music and Sound, Andre J. Pluess; Flutes, Tessa Brinckman; Plucked strings; Percussion, Ronnie Malley; Cello, Michal Palzewicz; Projections, Shawn Sagady; Voice/Text, Rebecca Clark Carey; SM, Amy Miranda Warner; ASM, Karl Alphonso; Cast: Amy Kim Waschke (White Snake/Ensemble), Christopher Livingston (Xu Xian/Ensemble), Tanya McBride (Green Snake/Ensemble), Jack Willis (Fa Hai/Ensemble), Cristofer Jean (Brother-in-Law/

Ensemble), Lisa Tejero (Sister/Ensemble); Ensemble: Ako, Gina Daniels, Richard Howard, Emily Sophia Knapp,Vin Kridakorn; February 18–July 8, 2012

Madea / MacBeth / Cinderella Adapted by Bill Rauch and Tracy Young from Euripides' *Medea*, Translated by Paul Roche; Music and lyrics by Shishir Kurup; William Shakespeare's *Macbeth*; Rodgers & Hammerstein's *Cinderella*; Music by Richard Rodgers; Book and lyrics by Oscar Hammerstein II; Directors, Bill Rauch, Tracy Young; Choreographer, Sabrina Peck; Music Director, Mathew Aument; Sets, Rachel Hauck; Costumes, Deborah M. Dryden; Lighting, Christopher Akerlind; Sound, Darron L. West; *Medea* Songs Arrangement and Additional Music, David Markowitz; Mask Director, Jared Sakren; Associate Music Director, Darcy Danielso; Co-Orchestrators/Arrangers, Matthew Aument, Andy Einhorn; Woodwinds, Lori Calhoun; Bas/Tambura, Bruce McKern; Cello, Michal Palzewicz; Drums/Percussion, Jacob Phelps-Ransom; Violin, Arlene Tayloe; Phil Killian; Directing Fellow, Nelson Eusebio III; Fight Choreographer, U. Jonathan Toppo; Dramaturg, Lydia G. Garcia; Voice/Text, David Carey; SM, D. Christian Bolender, Jill Rendall; ASM, Karl Alphonso/Mandy Younger; Cast: Mark Bedard (Stagehand/Ensemble), Miriam A. Laube (Medea /Ensemble), Dee Maaske (Nurse/Esemble), Kate Mulligan (Chorus Leader/Ensemble), Lisa Wolpe (Jason/Chorus/Ensemble), Robynn Rodriguez (Tutor/Creon/Chorus/Ensemble), Gahl Falkner, Jada Rae Perry (Medea's sons), Jeffrey King (Macbeth/Ensemble), Christopher Liam Moore (Lady Macbeth/Ensemble), Al Espinosa (Macduff /Ensemble), Ted Deasy (Banquo/Ensemble), Tasso Feldman (Fleance/Ensemble), Armando Durán (Duncan/Ensemble), Daniel José Molina (Malcolm/Ensemble), Daniel T. Parker (First Witch/Ensemble), U. Jonathan Toppo (Second Witch/Ensemble), Eddie Lopez (Third Witch/Ensemble), K. T. Vogt (Godmother/Ensemble), Laura Griffith (Cinderella/Ensemble), Robin Goodrin Nordli (Stepmother/Ensemble), Nell Geisslinger (Portia/Ensemble), Kate Hurster (Joy/ Ensemble), Robert Vincent Frank (The King/Ensemble), Vilma Silva (The Queen/Ensemble), Jeremy Peter Johnson (The Prince/Ensemble); April 18–November 3, 2012

All The Way by Robert Schenkkan; Director, Bill Rauch; Sets, Christopher Acebo; Costumes, Deborah M. Dryden; Lighting, Mark McCullough; Original Music/Sound, Paul James Prendergast; Projections, Shawn Sagady; Dramaturg, Tom Bryant; Voice/Text, Rebecca Clark Carey; Fight Choreographer, U. Jonathan Toppo; SM, D. Christian Bolender; ASM, Mandy Younger; Cast: Jack Willis (President Lyndon Baines Johnson), Richard Elmore (J. Edgar Hoover/Sen. Robert Byrd/Ensemble), Peter Frechette (Sen. Hubert Humphrey/Sen. Strom Thurmond/Ensemble), Mark Murphey (Robert McNamara/Sen. James Eastland/Gov. Paul B. Johnson/Ensemble), Jonathan Haugen (Gov. George Wallace/Sen. Paul Douglas/Walter Reuther /Ensemble), David Kelly (Cartha "Deke" DeLoach/Rep. Howard "Judge" Smith/Sen. Everett Dirksen/Gov. Carl Sanders/Ensemble), Douglas Rowe (Sen. Richard Russell/Jim Martin /Ensemble), Christopher Liam Moore (Walter Jenkins/Rep. William Colmer/Ensemble), Daniel T. Parker (Stanley Levison/Seymore Trammell/Rev. Edwin King/Ensemble), Kenajuan Bentley (Rev. Martin Luther King Jr./Ensemble), Tyrone Wilson (Rev. Ralph Abernathy/Ensemble), Derrick Lee Weeden (Roy Wilkins/Ensemble), Kevin Kenerly (Bob Moses/David Dennis/Ensemble), Wayne T. Carr (James Harrison/Stokely Carmichael/James Chaney/Ensemble), Terri McMahon (Lady Bird Johnson/Katherine Graham/Ensemble), Erica Sullivan (Secretary/Lurleen Wallace/Muriel Humphrey/Ensemble), Gina Daniel (Coretta Scott King/Fannie Lou Hamer/Ensemble); World Premiere; July 25–November 3, 2012

NEW THEATRE

Seagull by Anton Chekhov; Adapted by Libby Appel; Literal Translation by Allison Horsley; Director, Libby Appel; Sets, Christopher Acebo; Costumes, Deborah M. Dryden; Lighting, Alexander V. Nichols; Composition/Sound, Todd Barton; Dramaturg, Allison Horsley; Voice/Text, Rebecca Clark Carey; Fight Choreorgrapher, U. Jonathan Toppo; SM, Heath Belden, Amy Miranda Warner; PA, Karen Hill; Phil Killian Directing Fellow, Nelson Eusebio III; Cast: Kathryn Meisle (Irina Nikolayevna Arkadina), Tasso Feldman (Konstantin Gavrilovich Treplyov - Kostya), Michael J. Hume (Pyotr Nikolayevich Sorin), Nell Geisslinger (Nina Mikhailovna Zarechnaya), John Pribyl (Ilya Afanasyevich Shamrayev), Lisa Wolpe (Polina Andreyevna), Kate Hurster (Marya Ilyinichna - Masha), Al Espinosa (Boris Alekseyevich Trigorin), Armando Durán (Yevgenii Sergeyevich Dorn), Jonathan

Dyrud (Semyon Semyonovich Medvedenko), Cory Davison (Yakov), Ako (A Cook), Kate Torcom (A Housemaid); February 23–June 22, 2012

Troilus and Cressida by William Shakespeare; Director, Rob Melrose; Sets, Michael Locher; Costumes, Christal Weatherly; Lighting, Jiyoun Chang; Original Music/Sound, Cliff Caruthers; Dramaturg, Lue Morgan Douthit; Voice/Text, Rebecca Clark Carey; Fight Choreographer, Christopher DuVal; SM, Heath Belden; PA, D Westerholm; Cast: Brooke Parks (Prologue/Andromache/Helen/Ensemble), Tony DeBruno (Priam/Nestor/Ensemble), Bernard White (Hector/Calchas/Ensemble), Ramiz Monsef (Paris/Patroclus/Ensemble), Raffi Barsoumian (Troilus/Ensemble), Fajer Al-Kaisi (Helenus/Aeneas/Margareton/Ensemble), Elijah Alexander (Antenor/Ajax/Ensemble), Tala Ashe (Cressida/Caassandra/Esemble), Barzin Akhavan (Pandarus/Menelaus/Ensemble), Michael Elich (Alexander/Thersites/Ensemble), Rex Young (Agamemnon/Ensemble), Peter Macon (Achilles/Ensemble), Mark Murphey (Ulysses/Ensemble), Kevin Kenerly (Diomedes/Ensemble); March 28–November 4, 2012

Party People by UNIVERSES (Mildred Ruiz-Sapp, Steven Sapp, William Ruiz, A.K.A. NINJA); Developed and Directed by Liesl Tommy; Sets, Clint Ramos; Costumes, ESosa; Lighting, Marcus Doshi; Original Music/Sound/Vocal Direction, Broken Chord; Video, Pablo N. Molina; Dramaturg, Julie Felise Dubiner; Voice/Text, David Carey; Choreographer, Millicent Johnnie; Fight Choreographer, U. Jonathan Toppo; SM, Mara Filler; ASM, Karl Alphonso; Cast: G. Valmont Thomas (Blue/Ensemble), Mildred Ruiz-Sapp (Helita/Ensemble), William Ruiz, a.k.a. Ninja (Jimmy/Ensemble), Jadele McPherson (Clara/Ensemble), Mateo Gomez (Tito/ Ensemble), Peter Macon (Solias/Ensemble), Steven Sapp (Omar/Ensemble), Michael Elich (Marcus/Ensemble), Kimberly Scott (Amira/Ensemble), Robynn Rodriguez (Donna/Ensemble), Christopher Livingston (Malik/Ensemble), Mariam A. Laube (Maruca/Ensemble); World Premiere; July 3–November 3, 2012

ELIZABETHAN STAGE

Henry V by William Shakespeare; Director, Joseph Haj; Sets, Richard L. Hay; Costumes, Jan Chambers; Lighting, Justin Townsend; Music/Sound, Todd Barton; Music, Kelvin Underwood; Dramaturg, Alan Armstrong; Voice/Text, David Carey; Fight Choreographer, U. Jonathan Toppo; SM, Gwen Turos/Heath Belden/ Kimberley Jean Barry; Cast: John Tufts (King Henry V), Shayne Hanson (Duke of Gloucester), Darek Riley (Duke of Bedford), Howie Seago (Duke of Exeter), Russell Lloyd (Earl of Westmoreland), Richard Howard (Archbishop of Canterbury / Duke of Burgundy), Bernard White (Bishop of Ely/Charles VI/Sir Thomas Erpingham), Ted Deasy (Earl of Cambridge/The Constable of France/Alexander Cour), Raffi Barsoumian (Lord Scroop/Duke of Bourbon/John Bates), Rodney Gardiner (Sir Thomas Grey/Duke of New Orleans /Michael Williams), Robert Vincent Frank (Gower), Jeffrey King (Fluellen), Brent Hinkley (Bardolph/Macmorris), Ramiz Morsef (Nym/Jamy/French Soldier), U. Jonathan Toppo (Pistol), Judith-Marie Bergan (Hostess Quickly/Alice), Christine Albright (Boy), Lisa Tejero (Isabel), Brooke Parks (Katherine), Daisuke Tsuji (Lewis the Dauphin), Josh Bowen (Governor of Harfleur), Cristofer Jean (Montjoy), Kelvin Underwood (Percussionist); June 5–October 12, 2012

The Very Merry Wives of Windsor, Iowa by Alison Carey; Adapted from the play by William Shakespeare; Director, Christopher Liam Moore; Choreographer, Ken Roht; Sets, Christopher Acebo; Costumes, Alex Jaeger; Lighting, Jane Cox; Composer/Sound, Paul James Prendergast; Puppetry, Lynn Jeffries; Dramaturg, Leslie Cross; Voice/Text, Rebecca Clark Carey; Fight Choreographer, U. Jonathan Toppo; SM, Jill Rendall; PA, Monica Keaton, D Westerholm. Cast: Judith-Marie Bergan (Manager of the Come On Inn), David Kelly (Senator John Falstaff), Joe Wegner (Pistol), Delanna Studi (Nym), Isabell Monk O'Connor (Roberta Shallow), Kjerstine Rose Anderson (Slender Shallow), Ted Deasy (George Page), Terri McMahon (Margaret Page), Tala Ashe (Anne Page), Robin Goodrin Nordli (Francie Ford), Gina Daniels (Alice Ford), Daniel T. Parker (Rev. Hugh Evans), Brooke Parks (Doctor Kaya), Catherine E. Coulson (Miss Quickly), Miles Fletcher (Fenton), Brittany Brook (Cheerleader), Mikkei Fritz (Cheerleader), Nikolas Horaites (Cheerleader); June 6–October 13, 2012

As You Like It by William Shakespeare; Director, Jessica Thebus; Sets, Todd Rosenthal; Costumes, Linda Roethke; Lighting, Jane Cox; Composer/Sound,

Andre J. Pluess; Choreographer, Sarah Goldberg; Dramaturg, Lezlie Cross; Voice/ Text, Sara Becker; Fight Choreographer, U. Jonathan Toppo; SM, Mandy Younger, Moira Gleason, Mara Filler; Cast: Wayne T. Carr (Orlando de Boys), Kenajuan Bentley (Oliver de Boys/Ensemble), Ray Fisher (Jack de Boys/Ensemble), Howie Seago (Duke Senior/Ensemble), Michael J. Hume (Duke Frederick/Ensemble), Erica Sullivan (Rosalind), Christine Albright (Celia), Peter Frechette (Touchstone), Douglas Rowe (Adam), Kimberly Scott (Charles the Wrestler/Winter Grace/ Ensemble), Kathryn Meisle (Jacques), John Pribyl (Le Beau/Ensemble), Rodney Gardiner (Amiens/Ensemble), Richard Elmore (Corin/Ensemble), Daisuke Tsuji (Silvius/Ensemble), Alejandra Escalante (Phoebe/Ensemble), Kjerstine Rose Anderson (Audrey/Ensemble), Tyrone Wilson (William/First Lord/Ensemble), Jason Rojas (Second Lord/Ensemble), Mandie Jenson (Spring Grace/Ensemble), Liisa Ivary (Summer Grace/Ensemble), Catherine E. Coulson (Autumn Grace/ Ensemble); June 7–October 14, 2012

Paper Mill Playhouse

Millburn, New Jersey

Seventy-third Season

Producing Artistic Director, Mark S. Hoebee; Managing Director, Todd Schmidt

Newsies Based on the Disney film written by Bob Tzudiker and Noni White; Book, Harvey Fierstein; Music, Alan Menken; Lyrics, Jack Feldman; Director, Jeff Calhoun; Choreographer, Christopher Gattelli; Dance Arranger, Mark Hummel; Music Supervisor, Michael Kosarin; Music Director, David Holcenberg; Orchestrator, Danny Troob; Sets, Tobin Ost; Costumes, Jess Goldstein; Lighting, Jeff Croiter; Sound, Randy Hansen; Projections, Sven Ortel; Hair, Charles Lapointe; Fight Director, J. Allen Suddeth; PSM, Thomas J. Gates; Cast: Jeremy Jordan (Jack Kelly), John Dossett (Joseph Pulitzer), Kara Lindsay (Katherine Plumber), Ben Fankhauser (Davey), RJ Fattori (Les), Vincent Agnello (Les), Andrew Keenan-Bolger (Crutchie/Roger), Tommy Bracco (Spot Conlon/Ensemble), Brendon Stimson (Oscar Delancey/Ensemble), Mike Faist (Morris Delancey/Ensemble), Ryan Breslin (Newsie/Ensemble/u/s Davey), Max Ehrich (Newsie/Jack u/s [Jack October19–23]); Ensemble: Aaron J. Albano, Kyle Coffman, JP Ferreri, Garett Hawe, Corey Hummerston, Evan Kasprzak, Andy Richardson, Scott Shedenhelm and Ryan Steele, Mark Aldrich (Seitz/Ensemble), Helen Anker (Medda/Ensemble/ Mrs. Baum u/s), John E. Brady (Wiesel/Ensemble/Pulitzer u/s), Kevin Carolan (Roosevelt/Ensemble/Wiesel u/s/ Snyder u/s), Julie Foldesi (Ms. Baum/ Ensemble/Medda u/s/Hannah u/s), Stuart Marland (Snyder/Ensemble), Michael McArthur (Swing), Jack Scott (Swing), Nick Sullivan (Bunsen/Ensemble), Laurie Veldheer (Hannah/Ensemble/Katherine u/s); September 15–October 16, 2011

White Christmas Based on the Paramount Pictures film written by Norman Krasna, Norman Panama and Melvin Frank; Book, David Ives and Paul Blake; Music and Lyrics, Irving Berlin; Director, Marc Bruni; Choreographer, Randy Skinner; Musical Director, Steven Freeman; Orchestrator, Larry Blank; Vocal/ Dance Arranger, Bruce Pomahac; Sets, Anna Louizos; Lighting, Ken Billington; Sound, Randy Hansen; Costumes, Carrie Robbins; Hair, Mark Adam Rampmeyer; PSM, Peter Wolf; Cast: Lorna Luft (Martha Watson), James Clow (Bob Wallace), Tony Yazbeck (Phil Davis), Jill Paice (Betty Haynes), Meredith Patterson (Judy Haynes), Edward James Hyland (General Waverly), Jacob ben Widmar (Jimmy/ Ensemble), Cliff Bemis (Ezekiel/General Waverly u/s), Beth Glover (Ensemble/ Martha u/s), Drew Humphrey (Ensemble/Train Conductor/Phil u/s/Ezekial u/s/ Mike u/s), Samantha Kelleher (Susan Waverly u/s), Kristie Kerwin (Ensemble/Rita u/s/ Rhoda u/s), Andie Mechanic (Susan Waverly), Pilar Millhollen (Ensemble/ Rita), Beth Johnson Nicely (Ensemble/Rhoda), Peter Reardon (Ralph Sheidrake/ Bob Wallace u/s), Anthony Reimer (Mike/Sheidrake u/s), Lauren Elaine Taylor (Ensemble/Tessie/Betty u/s), Anna Aimee White (Ensemble/Judy u/s); Ensemble: Luke Hawkins, Leeds Hill, Bryan Thomas Hunt, Megan Kelley, Matthew J. Kilgore, Jason Luks, Sara Michelle Reardon, Swing: Laurie DiFilippo, Drew King; November 16–December 24, 2012

Boeing-Boeing by Marc Camoletti; Director, James Brennan; Sets, Ray Klausen; Costumes, Brian Hemesath; Lighting, F. Mitchell Dana; Sound, Randy Hansen; Hair, Bettie O. Rogers; PSM, Becky Fleming; Cast: Anne Horak (Gretchen), Brynn O'Malley (Gabriella), Heather Parcells (Gloria), John Scherer (Robert), Matt Walton (Bernard), Beth Leavel (Berthe); January 18–February 12, 2012

Damn Yankees Based on the novel *The Year The Yankees Lost the Pennant* by Douglass Wallop; Book, George Abbott and Douglass Wallop; Music and Lyrics, Richard Adler and Jerry Ross; Orchestrator, Bruce Monroe; Director, Mark S. Hoebee; Choreographer, Denis Jones; Music Director, Ben Whiteley; Sets, Rob Bissinger; Costumes, Alejo Vietti; Lighting, Tom Sturge; Sound, Randy Hansen; Hair, Charles Lapointe; PSM, Kathy J. Faul; Cast: Howard McGillin (Applegate), Chryssie Whitehead (Lola), Nancy Anderson (Gloria Thorpe), Jill Abramovitz (Doris/Sister u/s), Mike Cannon (Smokey), Pattie Cohenhour (Meg Boyd), Steve Czarnecki (Rocky/Joe Hardy u/s), Dick Decareau, (Lynch/Commissioner/ Ensemble/Applegate u/s/Van Buren u/s), Ray DeMattis (Van Buren), Joseph Kolinski (Joe Boyd), Susan Mosher (Sister), Christopher Charles Wood (Joe Hardy), Vaden Thurgood (Vernon/Ensemble), Anna Aimee White (Ensemble/ Lola u/s/Gloria u/s), Ryan Steer (Ballplayer/Sohovik/Postmaster/Ensemble), Robbie Roby (Ballplayer/Ensemble/ Smokey u/s/ Rocky u/s), Grady Mclead Bowman (Ballplayer/Ensemble/Welch u/s/ Commissioner u/s), Robin Lounsbury (Ensemble/Meg u/s/Doris u/s/ Miss Weston u/s), Gary Lunch (Welch/Ensemble/ Joe Boyd u/s), Lauren Elaine Taylor (Ensemble); Ballplayer/Ensemble: Scott Brateng, Taurean Everett, Cory Hummerston; Justin Henry (Swing/Sohovik u/s/ Lynch u/s/ Postmaster u/s); March 7–April 1, 2012

Once on this Island Based on the novel *My Love, My Love* by Rosa Guy; Book and Lyrics, Lynn Ahrens; Music, Stephen Flaherty; Music Director/Orchestrator, Lynne Shankel; Director, Thomas Kail; Choreographer, Bradley Rapier; Sets, Donyale Werle; Costumes, Jessica Jahn; Lighting, Kenneth Posner; Sound, Randy Hansen; Hair, Bettie O. Rogers; PSM, Lisa Dawn Cave; Cast: Syesha Mercado (Ti Moune), Kenita Miller (Mama Euralie), Alan Mingo Jr. (Papa Ge), Darius de Haas (Agwe), Kevin R. Free (Tonton Julian), Adam Jacobs (Daniel), Courtney Reed (Andrea), Saycon Sengbloh (Erzulie), Jerold E. Solomon (Armand/Daniel's father), Aurelia Williams (Asaka), Courney Harris (Little Ti Moune), Montana Byne (Little Ti Moune Standby); May 30–June 24, 2012

The Pasadena Playhouse

Pasadena, California

Artistic Director, Sheldon Epps; Executive Director, Elizabeth Doran

Twist – An American Musical Book by William F. Brown & Tina Tippit; Lyrics by Tena Clark; Music by Tena Clark & Gary Prim; Director/Choreographer, Debbie Allen; Executive Producer, Forbes Candlish; Sets, Todd Rosenthal; Lighting, Howell Binkley; Sound, Peter Fitzgerald; PSM, David Blackwell; Cast: Paula Aguirre (Potlatch/Ensemble), Cliff Bemis (Mr. Prudhomme), Joshua Bolden (Pistol), Alaman Diadhiou (Twist), Coco Monroe (Twist at certain performances), Kyle Garvin (Skillet/Ensemble), Jared Grimes (Roosevelt/Ensemble), Diane Delano (Miss Cotton/Ensemble), Matthew Johnson (Boston), Tamyra Gray (Della), Cleavant Derricks (Crazah Chesterfield), Ava Gaudet (Angela/Ensemble), Pat McRoberts (Lucius Thatcher), Angela Wildflower Polk (Naomi/Ensemble), Chase Maxwell (Yancy/Ensemble); Ensemble: John Fisher, Chantel Heath, Holly Hyman, Olivia-Diane Joseph, Vivian Nixon, Malaiyka Reid, Terrance Spencer, Dougie Styles, Armando Yearwood, Nickolas Eibler, Joshua Horton, Wayne Mackins, Julianna Rigoglioso, Issac Spector, Dempsey Tonks; June 14–July 24, 2011

Ennio Marchetto: The Living Paper Cartoon Original Concept, Ennio Marchetto; Producers, Glynis Henderson Productions & Jonathan Reinis Productions; Sound/Lighting, Sosthen Hennekam; Photography, Manuel Bergamin; Designer/Directors, Ennio Marchetto & Sosthen Hennekam; Cast: Ennio Marchetto; August 23–28, 2011

South Street Music and lyrics by Richard Addrisi; Book by Craig Carlisle; Director, Roger Castellano; Producer, Kathleen K. Johnson; Choreographer, Dana Solimando; Music Director, Michael Borth; Sets, Andy Walmsley; Lighting, Brian Monahan; Sound, Julie Ferrin; Costumes, Kate Bergh; PSM, Susie Walsh; ASM, TJ Kearney; Cast: Maria Eberline (Cloe), Brent Schindele (Johnny), Tom Shelton (Sammy), Valerie Perri (Sybil), Ezra Buzzington (Arnie), Lowe Taylor (Lydia), Matthew Patrick Davis (Norton), Andy Scott (Young Norton), Cassie Silva (Crystal), Harrison White (Lou), Jim Holdridge (Tony), Benjamin Goldsmith (Rico), Peter Siragusa (Papa Pachagalope); Ensemble: Anika Bobb, Nigel Columbus, Susann Fletcher, Sylvie Gosse, Kat Liz Kramer, Scott Kruse, John Massey, Jacqueline Nguyen, Stefan Raulston (Dance Captain), Hannah Simmons, Ali Spuck, Estevan Valdes, Corey Wright, Debbie Zaltman; September 20–October 16, 2011

Blues for an Alabama Sky by Pearl Cleage; Director, Sheldon Epps; Sets, John Iacovelli; Costumes/Wigs, Karen Perry; Lighting, Jared A. Sayeg; Sound, Marc Anthony Thompson; PSM, Hethyr Verhoef; ASM, Jessica Aguilar; Cast: Robin Givens (Angel Allen), Kevin T. Carroll (Guy Jacobs), Robert Ray Manning, Jr. (Leland Cunningham), Tessa Thompson (Delia Patterson), Kadeem Hardison (Sam Thomas); November 1–27, 2011

Art by Yasmina Reza; Translated by Christopher Hampton; Director, David Lee; Sets, Tom Buderwitz; Costumes, Kate Bergh; Lighting, Jared A. Sayeg; Sound, Philip G. Allen; PSM, Jill Gold; ASM, Hethyr Verhoef; Cast: Roger Bart (Yvan), Michael O'Keefe (Serge), Bradley Whitford (Marc); January 24–February 19, 2011

Monsieur Chopin Music by Fryderyk Chopin; Book by Hershey Felder; Director, Joel Zwick; Producers, Eighty Eight Entertainment and Samantha F. Voxakis, Stephen Eich; Sets, Yael Pardess; Costumes, Theatr' Hall, Paris; Sound, Benjamin Furiga; Lighting, Margaret Hartmann; Projections, John Boesche; PSM, GiGi Garcia & Nate Genung; Cast: Hershey Felder (Fryderyk Chopin); February 8–March 7, 2012

Maestro: The Art Of Leonard Bernstein Music and lyrics by Leonard Bernstein; Book by Hershey Felder; Director, Joel Zwick; Producers, Eighty Eight Entertainment and Samantha F. Voxakis, Stephen Eich; Sets/Lighting/Projections, François-Pierre Couture; Sound, Erik Carstensen; Lighting, Margaret Hartmann; PSM, GiGi Garcia & Nate Genung; Cast: Hershey Felder (Leonard Bernstein); March 10–18, 2012

Lincoln – An American Story Written, composed and arrranged by Hershey Felder; Director, Joel Zwick; Producers, Eighty Eight Entertainment and Samantha F. Voxakis, Stephen Eich; Orchestra Conductor, Alan Heatherington; Sets, David Buess & Trevor Hay; Costumes, Abigail Caywood; Sound, Erik Carstensen; Lighting, Chris Rynne; Projections, Greg Sowizdrzal & Andrew Wilder; Special Effects, Pat Cain; PSM, Nate Genung; Cast: Hershey Felder (Dr. Charles Augustus Leale); March 27–April 7, 2012

The Heiress by Ruth Goetz and Augustus Goetz; Director, Dámaso Rodriguez; Sets, John Iacovelli; Costumes, Leah Piehl; Sound, Doug Newell; Lighting, Brian L. Gale; PSM, Heathyr Verhoef; SM, Mary Michele Miner; Cast: Richard Chamberlain (Dr. Austin Sloper), Heather Tom (Catherine Sloper), Julia Duffy (Lavinia Penniman), Gigi Bermingham (Elizabeth Almond), Steve Coombs (Morris Townsend), Chris Reinacher (Arthur Townsend), Elizabeth Tobias (Maria), Anneliese van der Pol (Marian Almond), Jill Van Velzer (Mrs. Montgomery), Dale Sandlin (Dr. Sloper u/s); April 24–May 20, 2012

Jitney by August Wilson; Director, Ron OJ Parson; Producer, South Coast Repertory; Sets, Shaun Motley; Costumes, Dana Rebecca Woods; Sound, Vincent Olivieri; Lighting, Brian J. Lilienthal; Fight Choreographer, Ken Marckx; PSM, Jamie A. Tucker; Cast: Larry Bates (Youngblood/Darnell), Ellis E. Williams (Turnbo), David McKnight (Fielding), James A. Watson, Jr. (Doub), Rolando Boyce (Shealy), Gregg Daniel (Philmore), Charlie Robinson (Becker), Kristy Johnson (Rena), Montae Russell (Booster); June 21–July 15, 2012

Philadelphia Theatre Company

Philadelphia, Pennsylvania

Thirty-sixth Season

Producing Artistic Director, Sara Garonzik

The 25th Annual Putnam County Spelling Bee Adapted by Rebecca Feldman from the book by Rachel Sheinkin; Director, Marc Bruni; Sets, Anna Louizos; Costumes, Alejo Vietti; Lighting, David Lander; Sound, Nick Kourtides; Music Director, Andy Einhorn; Music and Lyrics, William Fin; Choreographer, Wendy Seyb; Cast: Ephie Aardema (Logainne), Will Blum (Barfee), Lyle Mackston (Leaf), Marla Mindelle (Rona), Olivia Oguma (Marcy), Jerold Solomon (Mitch), Ali Stroker (Olive), David Volin (Panch), and Brandon Yanez (Chip); November 12–December 12, 2010

Race by David Mamet; Director, Scott Zigler; Costumes, Teresa Squires; Lighting/Sets, Kevin Rigdon; Cast: Jordan Lage (Jack), Nicole Lewis (Susan), John Preston (Charles), and Ray Anthony Thomas (Henry); January 21–February 20, 2011

Let Me Down Easy Author, playwright and actress, Anna Deavere Smith; Adapted from the original work of Jules Fisher and Peggy Eisenhauer; Director, Leonard Foglia; Costumes, Ann Hould-Ward; Lighting, Dan Ozminkowski; Sets, Riccardo Hernandez, Sound, Ryan Rumery; March 18–April 10, 2011

Ruined by Lynn Nottage; Director, Maria Mileaf; Sets, Antje Ellermann; Costumes, Janus Stefanoqicz, Lighting, Russell H. Champa; Sound, Bart Fasbender; Cast: Oberon K.A. Adjepong (Christian), Sean-Michael Bowles (Simon), Kris Davis (Rebel Soldier), James Ijames (Fortune), Jamil A. C. Mangan (Osembrnga), Paul Meshejian (Mr. Harari), U.R (Kisembe), Erika Rose (Salima), Heather Alicia Simms (Mama), Chandra Thomas (Josephine), Keona Welch (Sophie). May 20–June 12, 2011

Pittsburgh Public Theater

Pittsburgh, Pennsylvania

Thirty-seventh Season

Ted Pappas, Producing Artistic Director

Electra by Sophocles; Aadapted by Frank McGuinness; Director, Ted Pappas; Sets, James Noone; Costumes, Gabriel Berry; Lighting, Kirk Bookman; Sound, Zach Moore; PSM, Ruth E. Kramer; ASM, Fredric H. Orner; Cast: Edward James Hyland (Servant to Orestes), Michael Simpson (Orestes), David Bielewicz (Pylades), Catherine Eaton (Electra), Glynis Bell (Chorus), Shinnerrie Jackson (Chorus), Amy Landis (Chorus), Catherine Gowl (Chrysothemis), Lisa Harrow (Clytemnestra), David Whalen (Aegisthus); September 29–October 30, 2011

Red by John Logan; Director, Pamela Berlin; Sets, Michael Schweikardt; Costumes, Kate Mitchell; Lighting, Rui Rita; Sound, Zach Moore; PSM, Fred Noel; ASM, Alicia DeMara; Cast: Jack Cutmore-Scott (Ken), Jeff Still (Mark Rothko); November 10–December 11, 2011

As You Like It by William Shakespeare; Director, Ted Pappas; Composer, Michael Moricz; Sets, James Noone; Costumes, Gabriel Berry; Lighting, Kirk Bookman; Sound, Zach Moore; Fight Director, Randy Kovitz; PSM, Ruth E. Kramer; ASM, Fredric H. Orner; Cast: Christian Conn (Orlando), Noble Shropshire (Adam/Sir Oliver Mar-Tex), David Whalen (Oliver), Don DiGiulio (Dennis/Forester), Lindsay Smiling (Charles/William/Hyman), Julia Coffey (Celia), Gretchen Egolf (Rosalind), Douglas Harmsen (Touchstone), Daniel Krell (Le Beau/Amiens), Ross Bickell (Duke Frederick/Duke Senior), Chris Landis (Silvius), Alex Coleman (Corin), Anderson Matthews (Jaques), Theo Allyn (Phoebe), Lisa Ann Goldsmith (Audrey), David Bielewicz (Jaques De Boys); January 19–February 19, 2012

Freud's Last Session by Mark St. Germain; Director, Mary B. Robinson; Sets/Costumes, Allen Moyer; Lighting, Phil Monat; Sound, Zach Moore; Dialect, Don Wadsworth; PSM, Fred Noel; ASM, Adrienne Wells; Cast: David Wohl (Sigmund Freud), Jonathan Crombie (C.S. Lewis); March 1–April 1, 2012

Around the World in 80 Days by Mark Brown; Based on the novel by Jules Verne; Director, Marcia Milgrom Dodge; Sets, Michael Schweikardt; Costumes, Martha Bromelmeier; Lighting, Kirk Bookman; Sound, Zach Moore; Dialect Coach, Don Wadsworth; PSM, Ruth E. Kramer; ASM, Alicia DeMara; Cast: Tom Beckett (Gauthier Ralph/British Consul/Director of Police/Priest/Sir Francis/Judge Obadiah/Chinese Broker/Ship Clerk/Bunsby/Proctor/Engineer/Mudge/Clerk/Speedy/Ship Engineer/Train Clerk), Ron Bohmer (Phileas Fogg), Jeffrey Kuhn (Passepartout), Meera Rohit Kumbhani (James Forster/John Sullivan/Newspaperman (Nellie Bly)/Priest/Aouda), Richard B. Watson (Andrew Stuart/Detective Fix/Priest/U.S. and Indian Train Conductors/Elephant Owner/Young Parsi/OysterPuff/Reverend Wilson's Servant); April 12–May 13, 2012

Private Lives by Noel Coward; Director, Ted Pappas; Sets, James Noone; Costumes, Andrew B. Marlay; Lighting, Phil Monat; Sound, Zach Moore; Fight Director, Randy Kovitz; Dialect, Don Wadsworth; PSM, Fred Noel; ASM, Adrienne Wells; Cast: Amanda Leigh Cobb (Sibyl Chase), Michael Brusasco (Elyot Chase), Laird Macintosh (Victor Prynne), Victoria Mack (Amanda Prynne), Elena Alexandratos (Louise); May 24–June 24, 2012

PlayMakers Repertory Company

Chapel Hill, North Carolina

Thirty-Sixth Season

Producing Artistic Director, Joseph Haj; Managing Director, Hannah Grannemann

KENAN THEATRE

A Number by Caryl Churchill; Director, Mike Donahue; Sets/Costumes, Jan Chambers; Lighting, Burke Brown; Sound, Ryan J. Gastelum; PSM, Sarah Smiley; Cast: Josh Barrett (Bernard 1/Bernard 2/Michael Black), Ray Dooley (Salter); September 7–11, 2011

No Child by Nilaja Sun; Director, Hal Brooks; PSM, Whitney McAnally; Cast: Nilaja Sun; January 11–15, 2012

PAUL GREEN THEATRE

In the Next Room (or the vibrator play) by Sarah Ruhl; Director, Vivienne Benesch; Sets, Marion Williams; Costumes, Anne Kennedy; Lighting, Scott Bolman; Sound, Ryan J. Gastelum; PSM, Charles K. Bayang; ASM, Sarah Smiley; Cast: Dee Dee Batteast (Elizabeth), Jeffrey Blair Cornell (Mr. Daldry), Kelsey Didion (Mrs. Givings), Julie Fishell (Annie), Matt Garner (Leo), Matthew Greer (Dr. Givings), Katie Paxton (Mrs. Daldry); September 21–October 9, 2011

The Parchman Hour: Songs & Stories of the '61 Freedom Riders by Mike Wiley; Director, Mike Wiley; Sets, McKay Coble; Costumes, Rachel E. Pollock; Lighting, Kathy A. Perkins; Sound, Ryan J. Gastelum; PSM, Sarah Smiley; ASM, Charles K. Bayang; Cast: Dee Dee Batteast (Lucretia Collins), Doug Bynum (John Lewis), Nathaniel Claridad (Carol Silver); David Aron Damane (Pee Wee); Kelsey Didion (Bill Svanoe), John Dreher (Papa Forsyth), Matt Garner (Stephen Green), Kathryn Hunter-Williams (Jim Farmer), Rasool Jahan (Mimi Real), Nilan Johnson (Billy), Randa McNamara (Tyson), J. Alphonse Nicholson (Freddy Leonard), Kashif Powell (Stokely Carmichael), Jessica Sorgi (Janie), Allen Tedder (Ensemble/Patron/Young Tough); October 26–November 13, 2011

Who's Afraid of Virginia Woolf? by Edward Albee; Director, Wendy C. Goldberg; Sets, Alexander Dodge; Costumes, Jade Bettin; Lighting, Josh Epstein; Sound, Ryan J. Gastelum; PSM, Charles K. Bayang; ASM, Sarah Smiley; Cast: Brett Bolton (Nick), Ray Dooley (George), Julie Fishell (Martha), Katie Paxton (Honey); November 30–December 18, 2011

The Making of a King: Henry IV & V by William Shakespeare; Co-Directors, Mike Donahue, Joseph Haj; Assistant Director, Desdemona Chiang; Sets, Jan Chambers; Costumes, Jennifer Caprio; Lighting, Jennifer Tipton; Sound, Ryan J. Gastelum; Composer/Musician, Mark Lewis; PSM, Charles K. Bayang; ASM, Sarah Smiley; Cast for Henry IV: Jeffrey Blair Cornell (King Henry IV/Pistol), Shawn Fagan (Prince Henry), David McClutchey (Earl of Westmoreland), Josh Tobin (John of Lancaster/Snare), J. Alphonse Nicholson (Thomas of Clarence), John Dreher (Humphrey of Gloucester/Lord Edmund Mortimer), Harry Harris (Sir Walter Blunt/Silence/Earl of Northumberland/Owen Glendower), David Adamson (Lord Chief Justice), Dee Dee Batteast (Earl of Surrey), Matt Garner (Earl of Warwick/Morton), Michael Winters (Sir John Falstaff), Patrick McHugh (Ned Poins), John Allore (Bardolph), Nathaniel P. Claridad (Nym), Kathryn Hunter-Williams (Mistress Quickly), Tania Chelnov (Davy), Katie Paxton (Doll Tearsheet/Lady Mortimer), Ray Dooley (Shallow/Fang/Earl of Worcester), Cody Nickell (Henry "Hotspur" Percy), Brett Bolton (Earl of Douglas), Nilan Johnson (Sir Richard Vernon), Kelsey Didion (Lady Percy), Brandon Garegnani (Servant), Maren Searle (Servant); Cast for Henry V: Michael Winters (Chorus), Shawn Fagan (King Henry V), Josh Tobin (Duke of Bedford/MacMorris), John Dreher (Humphrey of Gloucester), Harry Harris (Duke of Exeter), David McClutchey (Earl of Westmoreland), Ray Dooley (Archbishop of Canterbury/Jamy/Duke of Burgundy), Michael Winters (Bishop of Ely/Sir Thomas Erpingham/Governor of Harfleur), Patrick McHugh (Scroop/Duke of Orleans), Nilan Johnson (Earl of Cambridge/Duke of Bourbon), Brett Bolton (Sir Thomas Grey/Constable of France), Brandon Garegnani (English Attendant/Alexander Court), John Allore (Bardolph), Nathaniel P. Claridad (Nym), Jeffrey Blair Cornell (Pistol/King Charles of France), Tania Chelnov (Davy/Alice), Kathryn Hunter-Williams (Mistress Quickly/Queen Isabel of France), Cody Nickell (Fluellen), David Adamnson (Gower), Katie Paxton (John Bates), J. Alphonse Nicholson (Michael Williams), Matt Garner (The Dauphin), Kelsey Didion (Katherine/French Solider), Dee Dee Batteast (Montjoy), Maren Searle (French Attendant); January 28–March 4, 2012

Noises Off by Michael Frayn; Director, Michael Michetti; Assistant Director, Lavina Jadhwani; Sets, McKay Coble; Costumes, Daniel Kay Mickelsen; Lighting, Charlie Morrison; Sound, Ryan T. Gastelum; PSM, Sarah Smiley; ASM, Charles K. Bayang; Cast: Susan Cella (Dotty Otley), Andrea Cirie (Belinda Blair), Jeffrey Blair Cornell (Lloyd Dallas), Kelsey Didion (Poppy Norton-Taylor), Ray Dooley (Selson Mowbray), Brandon Garegnani (Tim Allgood), Katie Paxton (Brooke Ashton), Scott Ripley (Frederick Fellowes), Matthew Schneck (Garry Lejeune); April 4–22, 2012

Penelope by Ellen McLaughlin; Director, Lisa Rothe; Composer, Sarah Kirkland Snider; Musical Director, Rinde Eckert; Sets, Mimi Lien; Costumes, Adam M. Dill; Lighting, Mary Louise Geiger; Sound, Ryan J. Gastelum; PSM, Charles K. Bayang; Cast: Ellen McLaughlin (Penelope); April 25–29, 2012

Portland Center Stage

Portland, Oregon

Twenty-Fourth Season

Artistic Director, Chris Coleman; Associate Artistic Director, Rose Riordan

MAINSTAGE

Oklahoma! Music by Richard Rodgers; Book and lyrics by Oscar Hammerstein II; Based on the play *Green Grow the Lilacs* by Lynn Riggs; Original Dances by Agnes DeMille; Director, Chris Coleman; Musical Director/Conductor, Rick Lewis; Choreographer, Joel Ferrell; Sets, William Bloodgood; Costumes, Jeff Cone; Lighting, Ann Wrightson; Sound, Casi Pacilio; Dialect, Mary McDonald-Lewis; Fight Director, John Armour; SM, Mark Tynan; ASM, Emily N. Wells; PA, Kailyn McCord; Cast: Rodney Hicks (Curly), Joy Lynn Matthews-Jacobs (Aunt Eller), Brianna Horne (Laurey), Troy Valjean Rucker (Ike Skidmore), Don Kenneth Mason (Fred/Dream curly/Ensemble), Timothy Ware (Slim/ Ensemble), Jarran Muse (Will Parker), Justin Lee Miller (Jud Fry), Marisha Wallace (Ado Annie Carnes), Jonathan Raviv (Ali Hakim/Fight Captain), Kelcy Griffin (Gertie Cummings/Dance Captain/Ensemble), Sheila Jones (Ellen/Ensemble), Berwick Haynes (Andrew Carnes), Tyron Roberson (Cord Elam/Ensemble), Gregory J. Hanks (Mike/Ensemble), Kemba Anika Shannon (Dream Laurey/Ensemble), Sumayya Ali (Virginia/Ensemble), Bianca Burgess (Ilene/Ensemble) Marlene Villafane (Vivian/Ensemble); September 20–October 30, 2011

A Christmas Story by Phil Grecian; Co-author, Jean Shepherd, Bob Clark, Leigh Brown; Director, Rose Riordan; Sets, Tony Cisek; Costumes, Jeff Cone; Lighting, Nancy Shertler; Sound, Casi Pacilio; Fight Director, Ted deChatelet; SM, Emily N. Wells; PA, Kailyn McCord; Cast: Darius Pierce (Ralph), Jack Clevenger (Ralphie), Dylan Earhart (Flick), Harrison Goyette (Randy), Hannah Baggs (Helen), Matthew Snyder (Ensemble, Boy u/s), Avish Menon (Schwartz), Laura Faye Smith (Miss Shields), Tim True (The Old Man), Valerie Stevens (Mother), Jeff Schell (Scut Farkus), Hannah Wilson (Esther Jane); Olivia Rentz (Ensemble/Girl u/s); November 20–December 24, 2011

The North Plan by Jason Wells; Director, Rose Riordan; Sets, Tony Cisek; Costumes, Deborah Trout; Lighting, Colin K. Bills; Sound, Casi Pacilio; Dialect, Stephanie Gaslin; Fight Director, Ted deChatelet; SM, Jeremy Eisen; PA, Kelsey Daye Lutz Cast: Ashley Everage (Shonda Cox), Kate Eastwood Norris (Tanya Shepke), Brian Patrick Monahan (Carlton Berg), Tim True (Chief Swensen), Blake DeLong (Bob Lee), Frederic Lehne (Dale Pittman); January 10–February 5, 2012

Red by John Logan; Director, Rose Riordan; Sets, Daniel Meeker; Costumes, Jeff Cone; Lighting, Diane Ferry Williams; Sound, Sarah Pickett; Mark Tynan; PA, Lydia Comer; Cast: Daniel Benzali (Mark Rothko), Patrick Alparone (Ken); February 21–March 18, 2012

Anna Karenina by Kevin McKeon; Adapted from the novel by Leo Tolstoy; Director, Chris Coleman; Sets, G. W. Mercier; Costumes, Miranda Hoffman; Lighting, Ann Wrightson; Sound, Casi Pacilio; Composer, Randall Tico; Choreographer, Eric Skinner; Dialect, Mary McDonald-Lewis; Fight Director, John Armour; SM, Jeremy Eisen; PA, Kelsey Daye Lutz; Cast: Kelley Curran (Anna Karenina), Keith Jochim (Karenin/Ensemble), Michael Sharon (Vronsky/Ensemble), R. Ward Duffy (Stiva/Ensemble), Laura Faye Smith (Dolly/Ensemble), James Farmer (Levin/Ensemble), Kayla Lian (Kitty/Ensemble), Matthew Snyder (Seriozha/Ensemble), Leif Norby (Josif/Ensemble), Maureen Porter (Marya/Ensemble), Gretchen Corbett (Mother Shcherbatskaya/Ensemble), Val Landrum (Betsy Tverskaya), Michael Mendelson (Father Shcherbatskaya/Ensemble); Ensemble: Zach Virden, Bob Thomas, Penuel Corbin , Lauren Luiz; April 10–May 6, 2012

It Ain't Nothin but the Blues by Charles Bevel, Lita Gaithers, Randal Myler, Ron Taylor and Dan Wheetman; Director, Randal Myler; Music Director, Dan Weetman; Sets, Robin Sanford Roberta; Costumes, Jeff Cone; Lighting, Don Darnutzer; Sound, Casi Pacilio; Projections, Jeff Cady; SM, Emily N. Wells; PA, Kailyn McCord; Cast: Mississippi Charles Bevel, Eloise Laws, Sally Mayes, Sugaray Rayford, Chic Street Man, Jennifer Leigh Warren, Trevor Wheetman; Band: Mark T. Jordan (Keyboard), Calvin Jones (Bass), DAryll Witlow (Drums), David Milne (Saxophone and Clarinet), Ross Seligman (Guitar); May 22–June 24, 2012

ELLYN BYE STUDIO

The Real Americans by Dan Hoyle; Director, Charlie Varon; Sets/Lighting, Daniel Meeker; Costumes, Jeff Cone; Sound, Casi Pacilio; SM, Jeremy Eisen; PA, Lydia Comer; Cast: Joseph Graves; September 6–November 21, 2011

The Santaland Diaries by David Sedaris; Adaptor, Joe Mantello; Director, Wendy Knox; Sets/Costumes, Jessica Ford; Lighting, Don Crossley; Sound, Sarah Pickett; SM, Mark Tynan; PA, Aubree Lynn; Cast: Jim Lichtscheidl (Crumpet the Elf); November 30, 2011–January 2, 2012

Shakespeare's Amazing Cymbeline by William Shakespeare; A New Adaptation by Chris Coleman; Director, Chris Coleman; Sets, Alan Schwanke; Costumes, Jeff Cone; Lighting, Eric Southern; Sound, Casi Pacilio; Composer, Randall Tico; Fight Director, John Armour; SM, Emily N. Wells; PA, Kailyn McCord; Cast: Michael G. Keck (Actor1), Danny Wolohan (Actor 2), Scott Coopwood (Actor 3), Kelley Curran (Actor 4), Ryan McCarthy (Actor 5), John San Nicolas (Actor 6); January 31–April 8, 2012

Black Pearl Sings! by Frank Higgins; Director, Bill Fennelly; Sets, Andrew Boyce; Costumes, Jeff Cone; Lighting, Thomas Weaver; Sound, Casi Pacilio; Music Director, Rick Lewis; Casting, Harriet Bass; SM, Mark Tynan; PA, Lydia Comer; Cast: Chavez Ravine (Alberta "Pearl" Johnson), Lena Kaminsky (Susannah Mullaly), Lydia Comer (Guard); April 24–June 17, 2012

Portland Stage Company

Portland, Maine

Thirty-eighth Season

Executive and Artistic Director, Anita Stewart

The Morini Strad by Willy Holtzman; Director, Paul Meshejian; Sets, Anita Stewart; Costumes, Kris Hall; Lighting, Phillip S. Rosenberg; Sound, Christopher Colucci; SM, Myles C. Hatch; Cast: Laura Esterman (Erica Morini), John G. Preston (Brian Skarstad), Seoyeon Kim (violinist); September 27–October 23, 2011

God of Carnage by Yasmina Reza; Translated by Christopher Hampton; Director, Sam Buggeln; Sets, Daniel Zimmerman; Costumes, Kathleen P. Brown; Lighting, Philip S. Rosenberg; Sound, Shannon Zura; Composer, Julian Fleisher; SM, Shane Van Vliet; Cast: Scott Barrow (Alain Reille), Amy Bodnar (Annette Reille), Kevin Cutts (Michel Vallon), Kate Udall (Véronique Vallon); November 1–20, 2011

The Santaland Diaries by David Sedaris; Director, Daniel Burson; Sets, Anita Stewart; Costumes, Susan Thomas; Original Lighting and Sound Design, Matthew Cost; Lighting and Sound Design Adaptation, Shannon Zura; Lobby Decorations, Amber Callahan; SM, Shane Van Vliet; Cast: Dustin Tucker (David); Studio Theater; November 25–December 18, 2011

The Snow Queen Adapted by Portland Stage from the book by Hans Christian Andersen; Director, Anita Stewart; Sets, Anita Stewart; Costumes, Susan Thomas; Lighting, Bryon Winn; Composer and Music Director, Hans Indigo Spencer; Sound, Gregg Carville; SM, Myles C. Hatch; Cast: Patricia Buckley (The Snow Queen), Ian Carlsen (Kai), Tom Ford (Inventor/Crow); Daniel Noel (Storyteller/Ba the Reindeer); Lauren Orkus (Gerda); Sally Wood (Princess/Robber Girl); December 2–24, 2011

Raymond Chandler's Trouble Is My Business Adapted by James Glossman from the short stories of Raymond Chandler; Director, James Glossman; Sets, Anita Stewart; Costumes, Bettina Bierly; Lighting, Bryon Winn; Sound/Multimedia, Jeff Knapp; Original Music, Anthony Blaha; SM, Shane Van Vliet; Cast: Anthony Blaha (Bartender/Piano Player), Paul Murphy (Man 1), Ron Botting (Man 2), Dustin Tucker (Man 3), Daniel Noel (Man 4), Leigh Poulos (The Woman), David Mason (Marlowe); January 24–February 19, 2012

Hidden Tennessee (This Property is Condemned, Steps Must Be Gentle, The Field of Blue Children, The Long Stay Cut Short, or, The Unsatisfactory Supper) by Tennessee Williams; Director, Sally Wood; Sets, Anita Stewart; Costumes, Kathleen Brown; Lighting, Bryon Winn; Sound, Shannon Zura; SM, Myles C. Hatch; Cast: Justin Adams (Man), Maureen Butler (Woman I), Sarah Lord (Woman II), Courtney Moors (Woman III); February 28–March 18, 2012

Heroes by Tom Stoppard; Adapted from Gérald Sibleyras' *Le Vent Des Peupliers*; Director, Paul Mullins; Sets, Anita Stewart; Costumes, Hugh Hanson; Lighting, Gregg Carville; Sound, Seth Asa Sengel; SM, Shane Van Vliet; Cast: Edmond Genest (Gustave), Philip Goodwin (Philippe), Munson Hicks (Henri); March 27–April 22, 2012

Marie Antoinette: The Color of Flesh by Joel Gross; Director, Daniel Burson; Sets, Anita Stewart; Costumes, Hugh Hanson; Lighting, Bryon Winn; Sound, Dave Remedios; SM, Myles C. Hatch; Cast: Ellen Adair (Marie), Caroline Hewitt (Elisa), Tony Roach (Alexis); May 1–20, 2012

The Repertory Theatre of St. Louis

St. Louis, Missouri

Forty-fifth Season

Artistic Director, Steven Woolf; Managing Director, Mark Bernstein

VIRGINIA JACKSON BROWNING MAINSTAGE

Red by John Logan; Director, Steven Woolf; Sets, Michael Ganio; Costumes, Dorothy Marshall Englis; Lighting, Phil Monat; Sound, Rusty Wandall; Music Consultant, Jeffrey Richard Carter; Casting, Rich Cole; PSM, Glenn Dunn; ASM, Shannon B. Sturgis; Cast: Brian Dykstra (Mark Rothko), Matthew Carlson (Ken); September 7–October 2, 2011

God of Carnage by Yasmina Reza; Translated by Christopher Hampton; Director, Edward Stern; Sets, Narelle Sissons; Costumes, Gordon DeVinney; Co-Lighting, Kirk Bookman, Steve O'Shea; Casting, Rich Cole; PSM, Glenn Dunn; ASM, Tony Dearing; Cast: Eva Kaminsky (Veronica Novak), Anthony Marble (Alan Raleigh), Triney Sandoval (Michael Novak), Susan Louise O'Connor (Annette Raleigh); October 12–November 6, 2011

The Adventures of Tom Sawyer by Laura Eason; Adapted from the novel by Mark Twain; Director, Jeremy B. Cohen; Sets, Daniel Ostling; Costumes, Lorraine Venberg; Lighting, Robert M. Wierzel; Original Music/Sound, Broken Chord; Props, Mark Walston; Fight/Movement Director, Tommy Rapley; Dramaturg, Amy Wegener; PSM, Glenn Dunn; ASM, Shannon B. Sturgis; Cast: Joseph Adams (Muff Potter/Ensemble), Justin Fuller (Joe Harper/Ensemble), Tim McKiernan (Tom Sawyer), Michael D. Nichols (Injun Joe/Ensemble), Robbie Tann (Huckleberry Finn/Ensemble), Hayley Treider (Becky Thatcher), Nate Trinrud (Sid/Doc Robinson/Ensemble), Nance Williamson (Aunt Polly/Ensemble); November 30–December 23, 2011

Sunday in the Park with George Music and lyrics by Stephen Sondheim; Book by James Lapine; Director, Rob Ruggiero; Music Director, F. Wade Russo; Choreographer, Ralph Perkins; Sets, Adrian W. Jones; Costumes, Alejo Vietti; Lighting, John Lasiter; Sound, Michael Hooker; Casting, Rich Cole; PSM, Champe Leary; ASM, Tony Dearing; Cast: Ron Bohmer (George), Erin Davie (Dot/Marie), Zoe Vonder Haar (Old Lady/Blair Daniels), Kari Ely (Nurse/Harriet Pawling), Jamie LaVerdiere (Franz/Charles Redmond), Jacob Lacopo (Boy Bathing/Waiter), Jordan Parente (Young Man/Waiter), Charlie Ingram (Horn Player/Photographer), Chris Hietikko (Jules/Bob Greenberg), Deanne Lorette (Yvonne/Naomi Eisen), Steve French (Boatman/Dennis), Meggie Cansler (Celeste #1/Elaine), Audrey Rae McHale (Celeste #2/Party Guest), Abbey Friedmann (Louise), Rebecca Watson (Frieda/Mrs./Betty), Mark Emerson (Louis/Billy Webster), Sean Montgomery (Soldier/Alex), Nyssa Duchow (Young Woman in Park), Whit Reichert (Mr./Lee Randolph); January 4–29, 2012

Race by David Mamet; Director, Timothy Near; Sets, John Ezell; Costumes, Myrna Colley-Lee; Lighting, Brian Sidney Bembridge; Sound, Rusty Wandall; Casting, Rich Cole; PSM, Glenn Dunn; ASM, Shannon B. Sturgis; Cast: Morocco Omari (Henry Brown), Mark Elliot Wilson (Charles Strickland), Jeff Talbott (Jack Lawson), Zoey Martinson (Susan); February 8–March 4, 2012

The Comedy of Errors by William Shakespeare; Director, Paul Mason Barnes; Music Director/Arranger, Jack Forbes Wilson; Sets, Erik Paulson; Costumes, Margaret E. Weedon; Lighting, Lonnie Rafael Alcaraz; Sound, Rusty Wandall; Casting, Rich Cole; PSM, Glenn Dunn; ASM, Tony Dearing; Cast: Lenny Wolpe (Egeon), Walter Hudson (Solinus/Duke of Ephesus), Aaron Orion Baker (Jailer/Officer), Jack Forbes Wilson (Merchant/Harry), Chris Mixon (Antipholus of Syracuse), Doug Scholz-Carlson (Dromio of Syracuse), Christopher Gerson (Dromio of Ephesus), Tarah Flanagan (Adriana), Kate Fonville (Luciana), Michael Fitzpatrick (Antipholus of Ephesus), Christopher Hickey (Balthasar/Nell), Evan Fuller (Luce), Jim Poulos (Angelo), Ryan Fonville (Second Merchant), Shanara Gabrielle (Courtesan), Jerry Vogel (Dr. Pinch), Tina Fabrique (Abbess), Kurt Hellerich (Agador), Adrianna Jones (Citizen/Reveler), Dakota Mackey-McGee (Citizen/Reveler), Thomas Eric Morris (Citizen/Reveler), Joey Otradovec (Citizen/Reveler), Christina Ramirez (Citizen/Reveler); March 14–April 8, 2012

IMAGINARY THEATRE COMPANY (ITC)

Puss in Boots by Brian Hohlfeld; Director, Kat Singleton; Music Director, Neal Richardson; Sets, Scott Loebl; Costumes, Susan Byrd; PSM, Danny Maly; Director of Education, Marsha Coplon; Cast: Lakeetha Blakeney (Puss), Alan Knoll (King/Others), Jerome Lowe (John), Laurie McConnell (Princess/Others); Touring October 17, 2011–April 1, 2012

The Elves and the Shoemaker by Sarah Brandt; Composer/Music, Neal Richardson; Director, Bruce Longworth; Choreographer, Ellen Isom; Sets, Scott Loebl; Costumes, Dorothy Marshall Englis; PSM, Danny Maly; Director of Education, Marsha Coplon; Cast: Lakeetha Blakeney (Townsperson/Betty), Alan Knoll (Townsperson/Elf/Cook/Dancer), Jerome Lowe (Shoemaker), Laurie McConnell (Townsperson/Beggar Woman/Elf/Dancer/Queen); World Premiere; Touring November 7, 2011–December 31, 2011

The Sword in the Stone by Kathryn Schultz Miller; Director, Jason Cannon; Composer/Music, Neal Richardson; Sets, Scott Loebl; Costumes, Elizabeth Eisloeffel; PSM, Danny Maly; Director of Education, Marsha Coplon; Cast: Lakeetha Blakeney (Kai/The Dragon), Alan Knoll (Merlin), Jerome Lowe (Arthur), Laurie McConnell (Spike/Guenevere); Imaginary Theatre Company (ITC); Touring January 17, 2012–April 1, 2012

EMERSON STUDIO THEATRE

Circle Mirror Transformation by Annie Baker; Director, Stuart Carden; Sets, Jack Magaw; Costumes, Garth Dunbar; Lighting, Mark Wilson; Sound, Rusty Wandall; Casting, Rich Cole; PSM, Champe Leary; Cast: Kate Middleton (Theresa), John Ottavino (James), Charlotte Mae Jusino (Lauren), Danny McCarthy (Schultz), Lynne Wintersteller (Marty); October 26–November 13, 2011

A Steady Rain by Keith Huff; Director, Steven Woolf; Sets, Robert Mark Morgan; Costumes, Dorothy Marshall Englis; Lighting, Peter E. Sargent; Sound, Rusty Wandall; PSM, Emilee Buchheit; Cast: Joey Collins (Denny), Michael James Reed (Joey); January 18–February 5, 2012

The Invisible Hand by Ayad Akhtar; Director, Seth Gordon; Sets, Scott C. Neale; Costumes, Lou Bird; Lighting, Ann Wrightson; Sound, Rusty Wandall; Casting, Rich Cole; PSM, Champe Leary; Cast: John Hickok (Nick), Ahmed Hassan (Dar), Bhavesh Patel (Bashir), Michael James Reed (Guard/Agent); World Premiere; March 7–25, 2012

San Jose Repertory Theatre

San Jose, California

Thirty-second Season

Artistic Director, Rick Lombardo; Managing Director, Nick Nichols

Spring Awakening Based on the play by Frank Wedekind; Book and lyrics by Steven Sater; Music by Duncan Sheik; Director, Rick Lombardo; Choreographer, Sonya Tayeh; Musical Director, Dolores Duran-Cefalu; Sets, John Iacovelli; Costumes, Rachel Myers; Lighting/Media, David Lee Cuthbert; Sound, Steven Schoenbeck; SM, Stephanie Schliemann; ASM, Deirdre Rose Holland; Cast: Lowell Abellon (Georg/Reinhold), Ernestine Balisi (Thea), Justin Buchs (Otto/Dieter), Miguel Cervantes (Moritz), Cindy Goldfield (Adult Female), Monique Hafen (Anna), Jason Hite (Melchior), Joshua James (Hanschen/Rupert), Todd Alan Johnson (Adult Male), Zarah Mahler (Ilse), Kristen Majetich (Martha), Eryn Murman (Wendla), Manuel Rodriguez-Ruiz (Ernst/Ulbrecht); September 1–25, 2011

The Last Romance by Joe DiPietro; Director, Laird Williamson; Sets, Michael Ganio; Costumes, Elizabeth Poindexter; Lighting, Daniel Meeker; Sound, Steven Schoenbeck; SM, Joshua M. Rose; ASM, Peter Royston; Cast: Joshua Jeremiah (The Young Man), Sharon Lockwood (Rose), Will Marchetti (Ralph), Kitty Winn (Carol); October 13–November 6, 2011

A Christmas Carol by Charles Dickens; Adapted for the stage by Rick Lombardo; Original music by Anna Lackaff and Rick Lombardo; Director, Rick Lombardo; Music Director, Anna Lackaff; Sets, Peter Colao; Costumes, Frances Nelson McSherry; Lighting, Dawn Chiang; Sound, Rick Lombardo; SM, Laxmi Kumaran; ASM, Deirdre Rose Holland; Cast: Paul Baird (Collecting Man 2/Dick Wilkins/John's Attendant/Topper/Ship's Pilo/Businessman 2/Ensemble), Lizzie Calogero (Ghost of Christmas Past/Mrs. Dilbert/Hermione/Ensemble), Fiona Donovan (Belinda/Ensemble), Richard Farrell (Scrooge), Blythe Foster (Belle/Fred's Wife/Molly/Ensemble), Emilio Fuentes (Willie/Youngest Scrooge/Belle's Child/Ensemble), Marvin Greene (Bob Cratchit/Lighthouse Keeper 2/Ensemble), Dan Hiatt (Marley/John/Miner/Businessman 1/Old Joe/Poulterer/Ensemble), Kimberly Mohne Hill (Mrs. Fezziwig/Mrs. Cratchit/Miner's Wife/Ensemble), Lucas Kernan (Young Scrooge/Peter Cratchit/Turkey Boy/Belle's Child/Ensemble), Alison Lubiens (Alice Cratchit/Want/Belle's Child/Ensemble), Seth Margolies (Collecting Man 1/Fezziwig/Ghost of Christmas Present/Businessman 3/Man with Corpse Cart/Ensemble), Kate McCormick (Edna/Ensemble), Everett Meckler (Tiny Tim/Ignorance/Belle's Child/Ensemble), Sam Misner (Fred/Young Scrooge/Lighthouse Keeper 1/Undertaker's Man/Ensemble), Jessica Salans (Fan/Belle's Child/Martha/Ship's Watch/Young Maid/Ensemble); November 23–December 23, 2011

Double Indemnity by James M. Cain; Adapted for the stage by David Pichette and R. Hamilton Wright; Director, Kurt Beattie; Sets, Thomas Lynch; Costumes, Annie Smart; Lighting, Rick Paulsen; Sound, Brendan Patrick Hogan; SM, Stephanie Schliemann; ASM, Kathleen J. Parsons; Cast: John Bogar (Walter Huff), Jessica Martin (Lola Nirlinger/Nettie/Nurse), Carrie Paff (Phyllis Nirlinger), Mark Anderson Phillips (Nino/Jackson/Norton), Richard Ziman (Keyes/Nirlinger); January 12–February 5, 2012

God of Carnage by Yasmina Reza, Translated by Christopher Hampton; Director, Rick Lombardo; Sets, Kent Dorsey; Costumes, Kish Finnegan; Lighting, David Lee Cuthbert; Sound/Original Music, Brian Jerome Peterson; SM, Timothy Toothman; ASM, Laxmi Kumaran; Cast: Amy Resnick (Veronica Novak), Bob Sorenson (Michael Novak), Joey Parsons (Annette Raleigh), Benjamin Evett (Alan Raleigh); March 22–April 15, 2012

The Understudy by Theresa Rebeck; Director, Amy Glazer; Sets, Annie Smart; Costumes, Fumiko Bielefeldt; Lighting, Daniel Meeker; Sound, Steve Schoenbeck; SM, Laxmi Kumaran; ASM, Stephanie Schliemann; Cast: Gabriel Marin (Harry), Craig Marker (Jake), Jessica Wortham (Roxanne); May 10–June 3, 2012

Bill W. and Dr. Bob by Samuel Shem and Janet Surrey; Director, Richard Seer; Sets, Robin Sanford Roberts; Costumes, Cathleen Edwards; Lighting, Trevor Norton; Sound, Paul Peterson; SM, Stephanie Schliemann; ASM, Deirdre Rose Holland; Cast: Ray Chambers (Bill W.), Robert Sicular (Dr. Bob), Carrie Paff (Lois [June 21–July 12]), Rachel Harker (Lois [July 13–15]), Kandis Chappell (Anne), Cindy Goldfield (Waitress/Henrietta/Mrs. Johnson/Myrna/Ruthie/Hen), Mike Ryan (Clerk/Man with rifle/Ebby Thatcher/Dr. Silkworth/T. Henry Williams/Tunks/Norman Shepard/Lloyd/Eddie/Billy Dotson); June 12–July 15, 2012

Seattle Repertory Theatre

Seattle, Washington

Forty-ninth Season

Artistic Director, Jerry Manning; Managing Director, Benjamin Moore

BAGLEY WRIGHT THEATRE

Humor Abuse by Lorenzo Pisoni and Erica Schmidt; Director, Erica Schmidt; Sets, Brian Fauska; Costumes, Denise Damico; Lighting, Ben Stanton; Sound, Bart Fasbender; SM, Hannah Cohen; ASM, Stina Lotti; Cast: Lorenzo Pisoni (himself); September 30–October 23, 2011

Sylvia by A.R. Gurney; Director, R. Hamilton Wright; Sets, Carey Wong; Cpstumes, Melanie, Taylor Burgess; Lighting, L.B. Morse; Sound, Dominic

CodyKramers; Movement, Geoffrey Alm; Music Director/Vocal Arranger, Robert Scherzer; SM, Jessica C. Bomball; ASMs, Michael B. Paul and Erin B. Zatloka; Cast: Linda K. Morris (Sylvia), Alban Dennis (Greg), Mari Nelson (Kate), Darragh Kennan (Tom/Phyllis/Leslie); November 11–December 11, 2011

How to Write a New Book for the Bible by Bill Cain; Director, Kent Nicholson; Sets, Scott Bradley; Costumes, Callie Floor; Lighting, Alexander V. Nichols; Sound, Matt Starritt; Dramaturg, Madeleine Oldham; SM, Michael John Egan; ASM, Lindsay Byrne; Cast: Aaron Blakely (Paul), Linda Gehringer (Mary), Leo Marks (Pete), Tyler Pierce (Bill); January 13–February 5, 2012

Red by John Logan; Director, Richard E. T. White; Sets, Kent Dorsey; Costumes, Rose Pederson; Lighting, Robert Peterson; Composer/Sound, Brendan Patrick Hogan; SM, Lori Amondson; ASM, Shellie Stone; Cast: Denis Arndt (Mark Rothko), Connor Toms (Ken); February 24–March 18, 2012

A Fool's Paradise by Kevin Kling and Simone Perrin; March 31–April 1, 2012

Clybourne Park by Bruce Norris; Director, Braden Abraham; Sets, Scott Bradley; Costumes, Constanza Romero; Lighting, L.B. Morse; Sound, Matt Starritt; Sign Language Consultant, Jason Plourde; Fight Consultant, Geoffrey Alm; SM, Cristine Anne Reynolds; ASM, Shellie Stone; Cast: Aaron Blakely (Jim/Tom), Suzanne Bouchard (Bev/Kathy), Teagle F. Bougere (Albert/Kevin), Peter Crook (Russ/Dan), Ashton Hyman (Kenneth), Marya Sea Kaminski (Betsy/Lindsey), Darragh Kennan (Karl/Steve), Kim Staunton (Francine/Lena); April 20–May 13, 2012

LEO KREIELSHEIMER THEATRE

Circle Mirror Transformation by Annie Baker; Director, Andrea Allen; Sets, Matthew Smucker; Costumes, Christine Meyers; Lighting, Andrew D. Smith; Sound, Matt Starritt; SM, Lindsay Byrne; Cast: Anastasia Higham (Lauren), Peter A. Jacobs (James), Gretchen Krich (Marty), Michael Patten (Schultz), Elizabeth Raetz (Theresa); October 21–November 20, 2011

I Am My Own Wife by Doug Wright; Director, Jerry Manning; Sets, Jennifer Zeyl; Costumes, Erik Andor; Lighting, Robert J. Aguilar; Composer/Sound, Robertson Witmer; Dialect, Gin Hammond; SM, Whitney Breite; Cast: Nick Garrison, Christopher Marlowe Roche (u/s); February 3–March 4, 2012

Or, by Liz Duffy Adams; Director, Allison Narver; Sets, Matthew Smucker; Costumes, Catherine Hunt; Lighting, L.B. Morse; Sound, Christopher Walker; Dialect, Gin Hammond; SM, Stina Lotti; Cast: Kirsten Potter (Aphra), Basil Harris (Charles II, Others), Montana von Fliss (Nell, Others); March 23–April 22, 2012

Shakespeare Theatre Company

Washington, D.C.

Twenty-Fifth Anniversary Season

Artistic Director, Michael Kahn; Managing Director, Chris Jennings

SIDNEY HARMAN HALL

Free For All: Julius Caesar by William Shakespeare; Presented by Target; Director, David Paul; Original Director, David Muse; Sets, James Noone; Costumes, Jennifer Moeller; Original Lighting, Mark McCullough; Lighting Design recreated by Jason Arnold; Composer, Martin Desjardins; Sound, Daniel Baker; Fight Director, Rick Sordelet; Assistant Fight Director, Michael Rossmy; Casting, Stuart Howard and Paul Hardt; Resident Casting Director, Daniel Neville-Rehbehn; Voice/Text, Ursula Meyer; Assistant Director, Gus Heagerty; PSM, Mary K Klinger; ASM, Elizabeth Clewley, Resident PSM, Joseph Smelser; Cast: Tom Hammond (Brutus), Dan Kremer (Julius Caesar), Geoffrey Owens (Caska), Kurt Rhoads (Mark Antony), Aubrey Deeker (Octavius), Chris Genebach (Murellus/Lucillius), Brent Harris (Decius Brutus), Tyrone Henderson (Metellus), Rachael Holmes (Portia), Naomi Jacobson (Calphurnia), Bill Largess (Trebonius/Scarus), Kryztov Lindquist (Soothsayer), Dan Mason (Ligarius/Titinius), Paul Morella (Flavius/Pindarus), Scott Parkinson (Cassius), Paul Reisman (Cinna the Poet),

John Seidman (Lepidus), Jefferson Slinkard (Cinna), Charles Turner (Cicero); Ensemble: Travis Blumer, Clinton Faulkner, Greg Gallagher, Michael Hammond, Anthony Jackson, Emily Joshi-Powell, Dan Lawrence, Jeremy Lister, Steve Nixon, Joe Palka, Brian Riemer, Armand Sindoni, Kevin Stevens, Emily Whitworth, Jacob Yeh; August 18–September 4, 2011

Much Ado About Nothing by William Shakespeare; Director, Ethan McSweeny; Sets, Lee Savage; Costumes, Clint Ramos; Lighting, Tyler Micoleau; Composer/Sound, Steven Cahill; Associate Sound, Elisheba Ittoop; Choreographer, Marcos Santana; Associate Choreographer, Alison Solomon; Casting, McCorkle Casting, Ltd.; Resident Casting Director, Daniel Neville-Rehbehn; Voice/Dialect, Ellen O'Brien; Literary Associate, Drew Lichtenberg; Assistant Director, Jenny Lord; PSM, Joseph Smelser; ASM, Elizabeth Clewley; Directorial Assistant, Gus Heagerty; Cast: David Emerson Toney (Don Pedro), Matthew Saldivar (Don John), Derek Smith (Benedick), Ryan Garbayo (Claudio), Matthew McGee (Balthasar), Ashley Smith (Conrade), Mark Hairston (Borachio), The Household of Leonato: Adrian Sparks (Leonato), Bev Appleton (Antonio), Kate Hurster (Hero), Kathryn Meisle (Beatrice), Rachel Spencer Hewitt (Margaret), Colleen Delany (Ursula), Lawrence Redmond (Friar Francis), Ted van Griethuysen (Dogberry), Floyd King (Verges), Phil Hosford (Hugh Oatcake), Carlos J. Gonzalez (George Seacoal); Ensemble: Aayush Chandan, James Graham, Michael Gregory, Aaryn Kopp, Janel Miley, Jacob Perkins, Andrew Wassenich; November 25, 2011–January 1, 2012

Strange Interlude by Eugene O'Neill; Director, Michael Kahn; Sets, Walt Spangler; Costumes, Jane Greenwood; Lighting; Stephen Strawbridge; Composer/Sound, Fitz Patton; Projections, Aaron Rhyne; Wigs/Hair, Tom Watson; Casting, Laura Stanczyk, CSA; Resident Casting Director, Daniel Neville-Rehbehn; Literary Associate, Drew Lichtenberg; Assistant Director, Jenny Lord; Directorial Observer/Sir John Gielgud Fellow, Elyzabeth Gorman; Associate Costumes, Daniel Urlie; PSM, Joseph Smelser; ASM, Benjamin Royer; Cast: Francesca Faridany (Nina), Tana Hicken (Mrs. Evans), Charles Marsden (Robert Stanton), Ted van Griethuysen (Professor Henry Leeds), Rachel Spencer Hewitt (Madeline Arnold), Ted Koch (Sam Evans), Jake Land (Young Gordon Evans), Joe Short (Gordon Evans), Baylen Thomas (Ned Darrell); March 27–April 29, 2012

The Merry Wives of Windsor by William Shakespeare; Director, Stephen Rayne; Sets, Daniel Lee Conway; Costumes, Wade Laboissonniere; Lighting, Thom Weaver; Composer/Sound, John Gromada; Casting, McCorkle Casting, Ltd.; Resident Casting Director, Daniel Neville-Rehbehn; Voice/Text, Krista Scott; Literary Associate, Drew Lichtenberg; Assistant Director, Gus Heagerty; PSM, Joseph Smelser; ASM, Christi B. Spann; Cast: Veanne Cox (Margaret Page), Michael Mastro (Ford), David Schramm (Falstaff), Bev Appleton (Bardolph), Jarlath Conroy (Shallow), Alyssa Gagarin (Anne Page), Michael Gregory (Rugby), Amy Hohn (Mistress Quickly), Michael Keyloun (Slender), Jimmy Kieffer (Host), Floyd King (Hugh Evans), James Konicek (Pistol), Caralyn Kozlowski (Alice Ford), Matthew McGee (Simple), Hugh Nees (Nym), Kurt Rhoads (Page), Tom Story (Doctor Caius), Mark J. Sullivan (Fenton); Ensemble: Remy Brettell, Aayush Chandan, Caroline Coleman, Aaryn Kopp, Joey LePage, Ian Pedersen, Aidan White; June 12–July 15, 2012

LANSBURGH THEATRE

The Heir Apparent by Jean-François Regnard; Adapted by David Ives; Director, Michael Kahn; Sets, Alexander Dodge; Costumes, Murell Horton; Lighting, Philip Rosenberg; Composer, Adam Wernick; Sound, Christopher Baine; Casting, Stuart Howard and Paul Hardt; Resident Casting Director, Daniel Neville-Rehbehn; Voice/Text, Ellen O'Brien; Literary Associate, Drew Lichtenberg; Assistant Director, Jenny Lord; PSM, Joseph Smelser; SM, Benjamin Royer; Cast: Kelly Hutchinson (Lisette), Carson Elrod (Crispin), Andrew Veenstra (Eraste), Nancy Robinette (Madame Argante), Floyd King (Geronte), Meg Chambers Steedle (Isabelle), Clark Middleton (Scruple); September 6–October 23, 2011

The Two Gentlemen of Verona by William Shakespeare; Director, PJ Paparelli; Sets, Walt Spangler; Costumes, Paul Spadone, Lighting, Howell Binkley; Composer/Sound, Fabian Obispo; Music Director/Vocal Arranger, Jon Kalbfleisch; Fight Director, Paul Dennhardt; Animal Trainer, William Berloni;

Choreographer, Michael J. Bobbitt; Voice/Text; Ellen O'Brien, Assistant Director; Gus Heagerty, Wigs; Dave Bova, New York Casting, McCorkle Casting, Ltd.; Resident Casting Director, Daniel Neville-Rehbehn; Literary Associate, Drew Lichtenberg; PSM, James Latus; ASM, Elizabeth Clewley; Cast: Nick Dillenburg (Proteus), Natalie Mitchell (Silvia), Miriam Silverman (Julia), Andrew Veenstra (Valentine), Euan Morton (Launce), Adam Green (Speed), Inga Ballard (Lucetta), Davis Duffield (Outlaw #1), Chris Genebach (Outlaw #2), Gene Gillette (Thurio), Brent Harris (Duke of Milan), Stephen Patrick Martin (Panthino/Host), Christopher McHale (Antonio), Todd Scofield (Eglamour/Outlaw); Ensemble: Aayush Chandan, Jonathan W. Colby, Michael Gregory, Aaryn Kopp, Matthew McGee, Janel Miley, Jacob Perkins, Jade Wheeler; January 17–March 4, 2012

The Servant of Two Masters by Carlo Goldoni; Adapted by Constance Congdon; Director, Christopher Bayes; Sets, Katherine Akiko Day; Costumes, Valérie Thérèse Bart; Lighting, Chuan-Chi Chan; Composers/Musicians, Chris Curtis, Aaron Halva; Sound, Nathan A. Roberts, Charles Coes; Casting, Tara Rubin Casting; Resident Casting Director, Daniel Neville-Rehbehn; Fight Director, Rick Sordelet; Original Voice/Text, Beth McGuire; Additional Voice/Text, Ellen O'Brien; Literary Associate, Drew Lichtenberg; Assistant Director, Jenny Lord; PSM, Stina Lotti; ASM, Elizabeth Clewley; Cast: Steven Epp (Truffaldino), Danielle Brooks (Clarice), Liam Craig (Brighella), Allen Gilmore (Pantalone), Andy Grotelueschen (Silvio), Rachel Spencer Hewitt (Beatrice), Jesse J. Perez (Florindo), Don Darryl Rivera (Il Dottore), Liz Wisan (Smeraldina); Ensemble: Paul Edward Hope, Paul Reisman; May 15–July 1, 2012

South Coast Repertory

Costa Mesa, California

Forty-eighth season

Artistic Director, Marc Masterson; Managing Director, Paula Tomei; Founding Artistic Directors, David Emmes, Martin Benson

SEGERSTROM STAGE

Pride and Prejudice by Jane Austen; Adapted by Joseph Hanreddy and J.R. Sullivan; Director, Kyle Donnelly; Sets, Kate Edmunds; Costumes, Paloma H. Young; Lighting, Lap Chi Chu; Sound/Original Music, Michael Roth; Choreographer, Sylvia C. Turner; Assistant Sets, Adam Fleming; Dialect, Ursula Meyer, Eva Barnes; PSM, Jamie A. Tucker; ASM, Chrissy Church; Cast: Eva Barnes (Lady Lucas/Mrs. Gardiner), Corey Brill (Mr. Darcy), Cate Scott Campbell (Charlotte Lucas/Mrs. Reynolds), Jane Carr (Mrs. Bennet), Kandis Chappell (Lady Catherine de Bourgh), Scott Drummond (Mr. Collins), Amy Ellenberger (Miss Caroline Bingley), Amalia Fite (Lydia Bennet), Joel J. Gelman (Fitzwilliam/Mr. Denny), Dana Green (Elizabeth Bennet), Brian Hostenske (Mr. Bingley), Rebecca Lawrence (Jane Bennet), James Newcomb (Sir William Lucas/Mr. Gardiner), Michael A. Newcomer (Mr. Wickham), Randy Oglesby (Mr. Bennet), Claire Kaplan (The Girl), Elizabeth Nolan (Catherine Bennet), Kalie Quinones (Miss Anne de Bourgh/Georgiana Darcy), Justin Sorville (Captain Carter), Daniel Sugimoto (Soldier/Servant), Katie Willert (Mary Bennet); September 9–October 9, 2011

The Trip to Bountiful by Horton Foote; Director, Martin Benson; Sets, Thomas Buderwitz; Costumes, Angela Balogh Calin; Lighting, Tom Ruzika, Donna Ruzika; Sound, Cricket S. Myers; PSM, Chrissy Church; ASM, Jamie A. Tucker; Cast: Mark Coyan (Second Ticket Taker), Richard Doyle (Roy), Lyly Holleman (Thelma), Hal Landon Jr. (Sheriff), Jennifer Lyyon (Jessie Mae Watts), Lynn Milgrim (Carrie Watts), Daniel Reichert (Ludie Watts), Tom Shelton (First Ticket Agent); October 21–November 20, 2011

A Christmas Carol by Charles Dickens; Adapted by Jerry Patch; Director, John-David Keller; Assistant Director, Hisa Takakuwa; Sets, Thomas Buderwitz; Costumes, Dwight Richard Odle; Lighting, Donna and Tom Ruzika; Music Arranger/Composer, Dennis McCarthy; Sound, Drew Dalzell; Choreographer, Sylvia C. Turner; PSM, Jamie Tucker; ASM, Chrissy Church; Cast: Christian Barillas (Undertaker/Young Ebenezer), Daniel Blinkoff (Bob Cratchit), Gregg

Daniel (Marley/Gentleman), Richard Doyle (Solicitor/Spirit of Christmas Past/Gentleman), Karen Hensel (Solicitor/Mrs. Fezziwig), John-David Keller (Mr. Fezziwig/Spirit of Christmas Yet-to-Come), Art Kaustik (Joe/Ensemble), Timothy Landfield (Spirit of Christmas Present), Hal Landon Jr. (Ebenezer Scrooge), Ann Marie Lee (Toy Lady/Sally/Scavenger), William Francis McGuire (Fred/Gentleman), Jennifer Parsons (Mrs. Cratchit), Erika Whalen (Lena/Belle/Scavenger), Jordon Bellow (Young Marley/Cop), Matthew Frow (Puppet Show/Mr. Topper), Chariot Jones (Elizabeth Shelley/Pursued Maiden), Daniel Sugimoto (Thomas Shelley); November 26–December 24, 2011

Elemeno Pea by Molly Smith Metzler; Director, Marc Masterson; Sets, Ralph Funicello; Costumes, David Kay Mickelsen; Lighting, Lap Chi Chu; Sound, Cricket S. Myers; PSM, Jamie A. Tucker; ASM, Chrissy Church; Cast: Cassie Beck (Devon), Jamison Jones (Ethan), Katrina Lenk (Michaela), Melanie Lora (Simone), Jonathan Nichols (Jos-B); January 27–February 26, 2012

The Prince of Atlantis by Steven Drukman; Director, Warner Shook; Sets, Thomas Buderwitz; Costumes, Angela Balogh Calin; Lighting, Peter Maradudin; Original Music/Music Direction, Michael Roth; Dialect, Philip D. Thompson; PSM, Chrissy Church; ASM, Jamie A. Tucker; Cast: Matthew Arkin (Kevin Collette), Nike Doukas (Connie Bonfiglio), John Kapelos (Joey Collettei), Brett Ryback (Miles Overton); March 30–April 29, 2012

Jitney by August Wilson; Director, Ron OJ Parson; Sets, Shaun Motley; Costumes, Dana Rebecca Woods; Lighting, Brian Lillienthal; Sound, Vincent Oliveri; Fight Consultant, Ken Merckx; PSM, Jamie A. Tucker; ASM, Chrissy Church; Cast: Larry Bates (Youngblood/Darnell), Rolando Boyce (Shealy), Gregg Daniel (Philmore), Kristy Johnson (Rena), David McKnight (Fielding), Charlie Robinson (Becker), Montae Russell (Booster), James A. Watson Jr. (Doub), Ellis E. Williams (Turnbo); May 11–June 10, 2012

JULIANNE ARGYROS STAGE

How the World Began by Catherine Trieschmann; Director, Daniella Topol; Sets/Costumes, Sara Ryung Clement; Lighting, Paul Whitaker; Sound, Darron L. West; PSM, Jennifer Ellen Butler; Cast: Sarah Rafferty (Susan Pierce), Jarrett Sleeper (Micah Staab), Time Winters (Gene Dinkel); September 25–October 16, 2011

June B. in Jingle Bells, Batman Smells! by Allison Gregory; Adapted from the books by Barbara Park; Director, Casey Stangl; Sets, Keith Mitchell; Costumes, Sara Ryung Clement; Lighting, Tom Ruzika; Sound, Jeff Polunas; PSM, Sue Karutz; Cast: Melody Butiu (June B. Jones), Emily Eiden (May), Brian Hostenske (Mr. Scary), Rudy Martinez (Herb), Tony Sancho (Jose/Mr. Toot), Erika Whalen (Lucille/Elf Ellen), Tobie Windham (Sheldon/Philip Johnny Bob); Theatre for Young Audiences; November 4–20, 2011

Topdog/Underdog by Suzan-Lori Parks; Director, Seret Scott; Sets, Shaun Motley; Costumes, Soojin Lee; Lighting, Jaymi Smith; Sound, Sam Lerner; PSM, Kathryn Davies; Cast: Larry Bates (Booth), Curtis McClarin (Lincoln); January 8–29, 2012

The Borrowers by Mary Norton; Adapted for the stage by Charles Way; Director, Shelley Butler; Sets, Sibyl Wickersheimer; Costumes, Leah Piehl; Lighting, Tom Ruzika; Sound/Composition, John Ballinger; Puppetry, Lynn Jeffries; PSM, Jennifer Ellen Butler; Cast: Wyatt Fenner (the Boy/Uncle Hendreary), Peter Howard (pod), Nicholas Mongiardo-Cooper (Crampfurl/Spiller/Gypsy Boy), Jennifer Parsons (Mrs/Driver/Aunt Lupy), Kalie Quinones (Arietty), Amelia White (Homily); Theatre for Young Audiences; February 10–26, 2012

Sight Unseen by Donald Margulies; Director, David Emmes; Sets, Cameron Anderson; Costumes, Fred Kinney; Lighting, Geoff; Sound, Cricket S. Meyers; PSM, Kathryn Davies; Cast: Erin Anderson (Grete), Nancy Bell (Patricia), Andrew Borba (Nick), Gregory Sims (Johnathan Waxman); March 11–April 1, 2012

Cloudlands Book and lyrics by Octavio Solis; Music and lyrics by Adam Gwon; Director, Amanda Dehnert; Music Director, Dennis Castellano; Orchestrator, Bruce Coughlin; Sets, Christopher Acebo; Lighting, Lap Chi Chu; Sound, Drew Dalzell; Video, John Crawford, Choreographer, Syliva C. Turner; PSM, Jennifer Ellen

Butler; Cast: Adam Kaokept (Kevin), Katrina Lenk (Caroline), Robert Mammana (Gerald), Addi McDaniel (Monica), Joseph Melendez (Victor); April 15–May 6, 2012

Jane of the Jungle Book and lyrics by Karen Zacarias; Music by Deborah Wicks La Puma; Director, Juliette Carillo; Music Director, Deborah Wicks La Puma; Sets, Sara Ryung Clement; Costumes, Garry Lennon; Lighting, Lonnie Rafael Alcaraz; Sound, Sam Lerner; Choreographer, Sheetal Gandhi; PSM, Jennifer Ellen Butler; Cast: Renée Brna (Jane), Eymard Cabling (Milo), Jamey Hood (Mom/Joanne/Samantha), Derek Mason (Steve Collins/Kayla's Dad), Elia Saldana (Kayla), Erika Whalen (Pat/Kelly/Nicolette Miller); May 25–June 10, 2012

PACIFIC PLAYWRIGHTS FESTIVAL STAGED READINGS

Warrior Class by Kenneth Lin; Director, Evan Cabnet

You are Here by Melissa Ross; Director, Matt Shakman

I and You by Lauren Gunderson; Director, Meredith McDonough

The Few by Samuel D. Hunter; Director, Casey Stangl

Smokefall by Noah Haidle; Director, Anne Kauffman

April 27–29, 2012

STAGES ST. LOUIS

Chesterfield, Missouri

Twenty-Fifth Anniversary Season

Executive Producer, Jack J. Lane; Artistic Director, Michael Hamilton; Managing Director, Ron Gibbs

A Chorus Line Conceived and originally directed by Michael Bennett; Book by James Kirkwood & Nicholas Dante; Music by Marvin Hamlish; Lyrics by Edward Kleban; Director, Michael Hamilton; Choreographer, Kim Shriver; Music Direction, Lisa Campbell Albert; Sets, Mark Halpin; Costumes, Brad Musgrove; Lighting, Matthew McCarthy; Orchestrator, Stuart M. Elmore; PSM, Stacy A. Blackburn; Cast: Tony Howell (Roy), Hillary Michael Thompson (Kristine), Kimberly Wolff (Shelia), Vanessa Sonon (Val) Michael McGurk (Mike), Leeds Hill (Butch), Jeffrey Pew (Larry), Laura Oldham (Maggie), Leonard Sullivan (Richie), Taylor Pietz (Tricia), Brandon Haagenson (Tom), Laura E. Taylor (Judy), Julie Kavanagh (Lois), Borris York (Sammy), Seanna Aguinaga (Bebe), Jill Slyter (Carole), Jessica Vaccaro (Diana), David Elder (Zach), Christopher Rice (Mark), Jessica Lee Goldyn (Cassie), Jeffrey Scott Stevens (Al) Tanner Lane (Frank), Sean Patrick Quinn (Greg), Leigh Wakeford (Bobby), William Carlos Angulo (Paul), Becca Andrews (Vicki); June 3–July 3, 2011

Disney's 101 Dalmatians Music and lyrics Mel Leven, Randy Rogel, Richard Gibbs, Brian Smith, Martin Lee Fuller, Dan Root; Book adaptation and additional lyrics by Marcy Heisler; Music adaptation and arrangement by Bryan Louiselle; Based on the screenplay by Bill Peet; Based on the novel *The Hundred And One Dalmatians* by Dodie Smith; Director, Michael Hamilton; Choreographer, Ellen Isom; Music Direction, Lisa Campbell Albert; Sets, James Wolk; Costumes, Brad Musgrove; Lighting, Matthew McCarthy; Orchestrator, Stuart M. Elmore; PSM, Stacy A. Blackburn; Cast: Darin Wood (Roger), Erin Kelley, (Anita), Sean Patrick Quinn (Pongo), Deanna Aguinaga (Perdita), Leigh Wakeford (Cruella De Vil), Taylor Pietz (Nanny), P.J. Palmer (Lucky/Puppie), Ariane Rinehart (Penny/Puppie), Madisom Johnson (Pepper/Puppie), Zach Erhardt (Patch/Puppie), John Flack (Horace), Jeffrey Scott Stevens (Jasper), Patrick Beecher (Boxers & Poodles/Puppie), Kelsie Johnson (Boxers & Poodles/Puppie), Kyle P. Gunby (Scotties & Chihuahas/Puppie), Savannah Light (Scotties & Chihuahas/Puppie), Taylor Edlin (Spot), Sarah Koo (Dot), Christopher Rice (Tibbs), Kelsey Bearman (Puppie), Patrick Beecher (Puppie), Jessika Dahlheimer (Puppie), Jonathan Frazier (Puppie), Tre'von Griffith (Puppie), Sarah Knoblich (Puppie), Jordan Rackley (Puppie), Kyle Twomey (Puppie), Caitlin Webb (Puppie); June 22–July 3, 2011

The Secret Garden Book and lyrics by Marsha Norman; Music by Lucy Simon; Based on the novel by Frances Hodgson Burnett; Director, Michael Hamilton; Choreographer, Dana Lewis; Music Direction, Lisa Campbell Albert; Sets, James Wolk; Costumes, Dorothy Marshall Englis; Lighting, Matthew McCarthy; Orchestrator, Stuart M. Elmore; PSM, Stacy A, Blackburn; ASM, Tara Kelly; Cast: Kelly McCormick (Lily), Alexix Kinney (Mary Lennox), Edward Juvier (Fakir), Elizabeth Gray (Ayah), Leah Berry (Rose), Matthew Charles Thompson (Captain Lennox), Larry Mabrey (Lieutenant Wright), Christopher Deprophetis (Lieutenant Shaw), John Flack (Major Holmes), Lori Barrett-Pagano (Claire), Laura Ernst (Alice), Peter Lockyer (Archibald Craven), Anthony Holds (Dr. Craven), Zoe Vonder Haar (Mrs. Medlock), Julie Cardia (Martha), Joseph Medeiros (Dickon), Joe Vincent (Ben), Jon Olsen (Colin), Kari Ely (Mrs. Winthrop/Nurse), Sean Patrick Quinn (Thomas), Taylor Pietz (Janet), Leigh Wakeford (William), Ellen Isom (Susan), Leeds Hill (Timothy); July 22–August 21, 2011

Victor/Victoria Book by Blake Edwards; Music by Henry Mancini; Lyrics by Leslie Bricusse; Additional music material by Frank Wildhorn; Director, Michael Hamilton; Choreographer, Dana Lewis; Music Director, Lisa Albert Campbell; Sets, Mark Halpin; Costumes, Lou Bird; Lighting, Matthew McCarthy; Orchestrator, Stuart M. Elmore; PSM, Stacy A. Blackburn; ASM, Adam Moser; Cast: David Schmittou (Toddy), Steve Isom (Chez Lui Pianist), Evan Autio (Les Boys/Ensemble), Tony Howell (Les Boys/Ensemble), Melissa Manning (Les Boys/Ensemble), Tim McGarrigal (Les Boys/Ensemble), Michael McGurk (Les Boys/Ensemble), Alida Michal (Les Boys/Ensemble), Leigh Wakeford (Richard Di Nardo/Ensemble), Kim Shriver (Simone Kallisto/Reporter/Ensemble), Darin Wood (Deviant Husband/Reporter/Clam/Ensemble), Zoe Vonder Haar (Socialite/Miss Selmer), Jame Beaman (Henri Labisse), John Flack (Gregor/Male Guest/Juke/Ensemble), Ellen Isom (Madame Roget/Reporter/Ensemble), Janna Cardia (Victoria Grant), Michael D. Jablonski (Choreographer/Les Boys/Ensemble), Whit Reichert (Andre Cassell), Steve Isom (Reporter/Sal Andretti/Ensemble), Melinda Cown (Norma Cassidy), Gary Lynch (King Marchan), Steve Judkins (Squash), Matthew J. Kilgore (Gendarme/Les Boys/Ensemble), Becca Kloha (Ensemble); September 9–October 9, 2011

Steppenwolf Theatre Company

Chicago, Illinois

Thirty-sixth Season

Artistic Director, Martha Lavey; Executive Director, David Hawkanson

MAINSTAGE

Clybourne Park by Bruce Norris; Director, Amy Morton; Sets, Todd Rosenthal; Costumes, Nan Cibula-Jenkins; Lighting, Pat Collins; Sound, Rob Milburn, Michael Bodeen; SM, Deb Styer; ASM, Michelle Medvin; Cast: Karen Aldridge (Francine, Lena), Cliff Chamberlain (Karl, Steve), Stephanie Childers (Betsy, Lindsey), Kirsten Fitzgerald (Bev, Kathy), John Judd (Russ, Dan), Brendan Marshall Rashid (Jim, Tom, Kenneth), James Vincent Meredith (Albert, Kevin); September 8–November 13, 2011

Penelope by Enda Walsh; Director, Amy Morton; Sets, Walt Spangler; Costumes, Ana Kuzmanic; Lighting, James F. Ingalls; Sound, Rob Milburn and Michael Bodeen; SM, Malcolm Ewen; ASM, Christine D. Freeburg; Cast: Ian Barford (Burns), Scott Jaeck (Dunne), John Mahoney (Fitz), Yasen Peyankov (Quinn), Logan Vaughn (Penelope); December 1, 2011–February 5, 2012

Time Stands Still by Donald Margulies; Director, Austin Pendleton; Sets, Walt Spangler; Costumes, Rachel Anne Healy; Lighting, Keith Parham; Sound, Josh Schmidt; SM, Michelle Medvin, Kimberly Osgood; ASM, Kathleen Petroziello; Cast: Francis Guinan (Richard Ehrlich), Sally Murphy (Sarah Goodwin), Randall Newsome (James Dodd), Kristina Valada-Viars (Mandy Bloom); January 19–May 13, 2012

The March Adapted by Frank Galati from the novel by E. L. Doctorow; Director, Frank Galati; Sets, James Schuette; Costumes, Virgil C. Johnson; Lighting,

Jim Ingalls; Sound, Josh Schmidt; SM, Malcolm Ewen; ASM, Christine D. Freeburg; Cast: Will Allan (Lt. Clarke, Sgt. Walsh), Alana Arenas (Wilma), Ian Barford (Arly Wilcox), Phillip James Brannon (Roscoe, Jake Early, Moses Brown, Calvin Harper), Cliff Chamberlain (Maj. Morrison), Patrick Clear (Gen. Wayne, Edwin Stanton, Old Man, Gen. Mower), Carrie Coon (Emily Thompson), K. Todd Freeman (Roscoe, Jake Early, Moses Brown, Calvin Harper), Alex Goldklang (Soldier), Harry Groener (Gen. William Tecumseh Sherman), Stephen Louis Grush (Will B. Kirkland, Albion Simms), Anthony Kayer (Soldier), Martha Lavey (Letitia Pettibone, Nurse), Michael Mahler (Sgt. Malone, Gen. Slocum), Shannon Matesky (Pearl), Mariann Mayberry (Mattie Jameson), James Vincent Meredith (Coalhouse Walker), Luce Metrius (Soldier), Andy Monson (Soldier), John Mossman (Col. Teack), Alex Newkirk (Soldier), Alex Ring (Soldier), Joe Sinopli (Soldier), Philip R. Smith (Dr. Wrede Sartorius), Alex Stage (Soldier), Alan Wilder (Sgt. Baumgartner, John Jameson, Josiah Culp, William B. Hazen), L. J. Slavin (Musician); April 5–June 10, 2012

Three Sisters by Anton Chekhov; Adapted by Tracy Letts; Director, Anna D. Shapiro; Sets, Todd Rosenthal; Costumes, Jess Goldstein; Lighting, Don Holder; Sound, Rob Milburn and Michael Bodeen; Original Music, David Singer; SM, Laura D. Glenn; ASM, Deb Styer; Cast: Usman Ally (Solyony), Alana Arenas (Natasha), Chance Bone (Rodé), B. Diego Colón (Fedotik), Carrie Coon (Masha), Maury Cooper (Ferapont), Mike DiGirolamo (Ensemble), Jennifer Dymit (Ensemble), Luke Fattorusso (Ensemble), Derek Gaspar (Baron Tusenbach), Brandon Holmes (Ensemble), Scott Jaeck (Chebutykin), Ora Jones (Olga), John Judd (Vershinin), Garrett Lutz (Ensemble), Katie Mazzini (Ensemble), Tom McGrath (Ensemble), Bruce Moore (Ensemble), Caroline Neff (Irina), Yasen Peyankov (Kulygin), Rakisha Pollard (Ensemble), Tommy Rivera-Vega (Ensemble), Mary Ann Thebus (Anfisa), Dan Waller (Andrey); June 28–August 26, 2012

STEPPENWOLF FOR YOUNG ADULTS

The Heart is a Lonely Hunter Adapted by Rebecca Gilman from the novel by Carson McCullers; Director, Hallie Gordon; Sets, Collette Pollard; Costumes, Myron Elliot, Jr.; Lighting, J.R. Lederle; Sound, Christopher Kriz; Fight Choreographer, Matt Engle; SM, Rose Marie Packer; Cast: Jessica Honor Carleton (Mick Kelly), Derrick C. Cooper (Willie, Hospital Attendant), Walter Coppage (Dr. Copeland), Ann Joseph (Portia), Loren Lazerine (Jake Blount), Colm O'Reilly (Biff Brannon), Jay Reed (Antonapoulos, Preacher, Millworker 1, Deputy 2), Robert Schleifer (John Singer), Nick Vidal (Harry, Patient 2), Alan Wilder (Charles Parker, Mr. Kelly, Millworker 2, Deputy 1, Patient 1); October 11–November 4, 2011

fml: how Carson McCullers saved my life by Sarah Gubbins; Director, Joanie Schultz; Sets, Chelsea Warren; Costumes, David Hymen; Lighting, Lee Keenan; Sound, Thomas Dixon; SM, Cassie Wolgamott; Cast: Zoe Levin (Emma), Ian Daniel McLaren (Mickey), Lily Mojekwu (Ms. Delaney), Fiona Robert (Jo), Bradley Grant Smith (Reed); February 28–March 18, 2012

FIRST LOOK REPERTORY OF NEW WORK

Man in Love by Christina Anderson; Director, Robert O'Hara; Sets, Chelsea Warren; Costumes, David Hymen; Lighting, J.R. Lederle; Sound, Miles Polaski; SM, Cassie Wolgamott; ASM, Ashley Singh; Cast: Alana Arenas (Darlynn), Tim Frank (Leigh), Keith D. Gallagher (Walker), Ryan Lanning (Bernice), Namir Smallwood (Paul Pare, Jr.), Claire Wellin (Hazel); October 26–November 20, 2011

Want by Zayd Dohrn; Director, Kimberly Senior; AD, Jonathan L. Green; Sets, Chelsea Warren; Costumes, Crystal Jovae Mazur; Lighting, J.R. Lederle; Sound, Miles Polaski; SM, Jonathan Nook; ASM, Kelly Crook; Cast: Audrey Francis (Julia), Janelle Kroll (Marley), Mark L. Montgomery (David), Kendra Thulin (Lee), Mick Weber (Henry); October 26–November 20, 2011

Oblivion by Carly Mensch; Director, Matt Miller; AD, Catherine Allen; Sets, Chelsea Warren; Costumes, Myron Elliot; Lighting, J.R. Lederle; Sound, Miles Polaski; SM, Tess Lauchaire; Cast: Rammel N. Chan (Bernard), Marc Grapey (Dixon), Elizabeth Rich (Pam), Fiona Robert (Julie); October 26–November 20, 2011

GARAGE REP

Oohrah! by Bekah Brunstetter; Director, Brad Akin; Sets, Anders Jacobson, Judy Radovsky; Costumes, Kristin DeiTos; Lighting, Eric Branson; Sound, Stephen Ptacek; SM, Mary Ellen Rieck; ASM, Ryan Nash; Cast: Melissa Engle (Sara), Peter Esposito (Pop Pop), Joel Ewing (Christopher), Josh Odor (Ron), Calliope Porter (Abby), Ian R. Tranberg (Chip); February 2–April 8, 2012

Hit the Wall by Ike Holter; Director, Eric Hoff; Sets, John Holt; Costumes, Coral Gable; Lighting, Jeff Glass; Sound, Joe Court; SM, Ellen Willett; Cast: Walter Owen Briggs (Cop), Manny Buckley (Carson), Daniel Desmaris (Newbie), Desmond Gray (Mika), Steve Lenz (Cliff), Layne Manzer (A-Gay), Shannon Matesky (Roberta), Rania Manganaro (Peg), Arturo Soria (Tano), Mary Williamson (Madeline); February 2–April 22, 2012

He Who by Michael Montenegro; Director, Michael Montenegro; Sets, Michael Montenegro; Costumes, Rachel Birnbaum, Karen Hoyer; Lighting, Jeff Glass; Sound, Jude Mathews; SM, Danielle Love; Cast: Nancy Andria (1st Mother), Karen Hoyer (2nd Mother), Katherine Jones (Puppet Manipulator), Laura Montenegro (3rd Mother), Ellen O'Keefe (Inquisitor, Old Man), Noah Silver Mathews (Puppet Manipulator), Colleen Werle (4th Mother); February 2–April 8, 2012

NEXT UP

Life and Limb by Keith Reddin; Director, Emily Ruth Campbell; Sets, Courtney O'Neill; Costumes, Sally Dolembo; Lighting, Will Kirkham; Sound, Kevin O'Donnell; SM, Rose Marie Packer; ASM, Nora Mally; Cast: Audrey Francis (Doina), Chris Froseth (Tod), Roman Harris-MacDonald (Chris), Tom Hickey (Sam, Eric, Jerry), Jürgen Hooper (Franklin), Leonard J. Kraft (Grandfather), Grace Rex (Effie); June 5–24, 2012

South of Settling by Emily Schwend; Director, Adam Goldstein; Sets, Sarah JHP Watkins; Costumes, Kelsey Ettman; Lighting, Rebecca Jeffords; Sound, Kevin O'Donnell; SM, Jonathan Nook; AMS, Jennifer McClendon; Cast: Joey deBettencourt (Paulie Wheaton), Keith Kupferer (Irwin Deckhouse), Jeff Trainor (Randall), Janet Ulrich Brooks (Kate Deckhouse), Nicole Wiesner (Amy); June 6–23, 2012

The Glass Menagerie by Tennessee Williams; Director, Laley Lippard; Sets, William Boles; Costumes, Sally Dolembo; Lighting, Rebecca Jeffords; Sound, Kevin O'Donnell; SM, Cassie Wolgamott; ASM, Kelly Crook; Cast: Leah Karpel (Laura Wingfield), Kathy Scambiatterra (Amanda Wingfield), Brett Schneider (Jim O'Connor), Aaron Roman Weiner (Tom Wingfield); June 7–24, 2012

Syracuse Stage

Syracuse, New York

Thirty-ninth Season

Producing Artistic Director, Timothy Bond; Managing Director, Jeffrey Woodward

The Turn of the Screw Adapted by Jeffrey Hatcher from the story by Henry James; Director, Michael Barakiva; Sets, Shoko Kambara; Costumes, Suzanne Chesney; Lighting, Thomas C. Hase; PSM, Stuart Plymesser; Cast: Curzon Dobell (The Man), Kristen Sieh (The Governess); September 21–October 16, 2011

The Boys Next Door by Tom Griffin; Director, Timothy Bond; Sets, Michael Vaughn Sims; Costumes, Jessica Ford; Lighting, Dawn Chiang; Sound, Jeremy Lee; SM, Laura Jane Collins; Cast: Timothy Davis-Reed (Mr. Hedges/Mr. Corbin/Senator Clarke), Carey Eidel (Mr. Klemper), Sean Patrick Fawcett (Norman), William Hall Jr. (Lucien), Marie Kemp (Mrs. Fremus/Mrs. Warren/Clara), Michael Joseph Mitchell (Arnold), Alanna Rogers (Sheila), Samuel Taylor (Barry), Demetrios Troy (Jack); October 19–November 6, 2011

The Lion, the Witch and the Wardrobe Dramatized by Adrian Mitchell; Music composed by Shaun Davey; Director, Linda Hartzell; Music Director, Dianne Adams McDowell; Choreographer, Anthony Salatino; Sets, Carey Wong; Costumes, Catherine Hunt; Lighting, Rick Paulsen; Sound, Jonathan R. Herter;

Master Puppet Building, Annett Mateo; SM, Stuart Plymesser, Laura Jane Collins; Cast: Kyle Anderson (Ogre/Ensemble), Benjamin Ashe (Griffin/Ensemble), Jordan Barbour (Aslan/Railway Porter), Tara Carbone (Face on Butt/Young Wolf/Ensemble), LilyAnn Carlson (Maid 1/Pig/Ensemble), Kendall Cooper (Beaky/Ensemble), Stephen Cross (Maugrim/Rumblebuffin/Ensemble/Fight Captain), Mara Dale (Maid 2/Bat/Ensemble), Maclain W. Dassatti (Tumnus), Jacquelyn Piro Donovan (White Witch), Marie Eife (Susan), Aisling Halpin (Dryad/Reindeer/Evil Dance 1/Ensemble), Ben Holtzman (Grumpskin), James Judy (Professor Kirk/Father Christmas), Charlo Kirk (Edmund), Katie Lamark (Snozy Bosch/Ensemble), Eric Leviton (Beaver/Air Raid Warden), Jenaha McLearn (Lucy), Jayne Muirhead (Mrs. Beaver/Mrs. Macready/Ensemble), Micah Nameroff (Satyr/Evil Dancer 3/Ensemble), Erin Nishimura (Bull/Ensemble), Marcelo Pereira (Centaur/Ensemble), Elliot Peterson (Eagle/Ensemble), Dan Reardon (Leopard/Ensemble), Jonalyn Saxer (Nyad/Reindeer/Evil Dancer 2/White Stag/Ensemble), Amos VanderPoel (Peter), Joanne Wilkens (Maid 3/Stretchy/Ensemble); November 25–December 31, 2011

Caroline, or Change Book and lyrics by Tony Kushner; Music by Jeanine Tesori; Director/Choreographer, Marcela Lorca; Music Director, Christopher Drobny; Sets, William Bloodgood; Costumes, Candice Donnelly; Lighting, Paul Hackenmueller; Sound, Jonathan R. Herter; SM, Stuart Plymesser; Cast: Michelle Barber (Grandma Gellman), Larry Block (Mr. Stopnick), Christof Deboni (Noah u/s), Malachi Emmanuel (Joe), Doug Eskew (The Dryer, The Bus), Séamus Gailor (Noah Gellman), Piper Goodeve (Rose Gellman), Caitlainne Rose Gurreri (Radio 1), Emily Jenda (The Moon), Greta Oglesby (Caroline), Christina Acosta Robinson (Radio 2), Levonn L. Owens (Jackie), Gabrielle Porter (Radio 3), Elijah M. Theus (Jackie u/s/Joe), Danielle K. Thomas (The Washing Machine), James Van Treuren (Grandpa Gellman), Stephanie Umoh (Emmie), Price Waldman (Stuart Gellman), Regina Marie Williams (Dotty); February 1–26, 2012

Red by John Logan; Director, Penny Metropulos; Sets, William Bloodgood; Lighting, Thomas C. Hase; Costumes, Gretchen Darrow-Crotty; Sound, Jeremy J. Lee; SM, Laura Jane Collins; Cast: Matthew Amendt (Ken), Joseph Graves (Rothko); March 7–25, 2012

The Brothers Size by Tarell Alvin McCraney; Director, Timothy Bond; Choreographer, Patdro Harris; Sets/Costumes, Jessica Ford; Lighting, Geoff Korf; Composer, Michael G. Keck (Composer); PSM, Stuart Plymesser; Rodrick Covington (Oshoosi), Sam Encarnación (Elegba), Joshua Elijah Reese (Ogun); April 18–May 12, 2012

Trinity Repertory Company

Providence, Rhode Island

Forty-eighth Season

Artistic Director, Curt Columbus; Executive Director, Michael Gennaro; Production Director, Laura E. Smith; Associate Production Director, Mark Turek; General Manager, Pamela Adams; Director of Marketing and PR, Marilyn Busch

THE CHACE THEATER

His Girl Friday adapted by John Guare from *The Front Page* by Ben Hecht and Charles MacArthur and the Columbia Pictures film; Director, Curt Columbus; Sets, Eugene Lee; Lighting, Michael Gottlieb; Costumes, William Lane; Sound, Peter Sasha Hurowitz; Speech/Voice, Thom Jones; PSM, Melissa Rae Miller; ASM, Lauren Bachman-Streitfield; Stephen Berenson (Schwartz/Sheriff), Philippe Bowgen (Woodenshoes/Holub), Angela Brazil (Hildy Johnson), Richard Donelly (Kruger/Mayor), Janice Duclos (Mrs. Baldwin/Minister), Brough Hansen (Sweeney/Carl), Lovell Holder (Wilson/Pinkus), Phyllis Kay (Endicott/Mollie), Brian McEleney (Bensinger/Diamond Louie), Fred Sullivan, Jr. (Walter Burns), Stephen Thorne (McCue/Bruce Baldwin); September 9–October 9, 2011

A Christmas Carol by Charles Dickens; Adapted by Adrian Hall and Richard Cumming; Director/Choreographer, Christopher Windom; Music Director, Jeremy Fenn-Smith; Sets, Michael McGarty; Costumes, William Lane; Lighting, John

Eckert; Sound, Peter Sasha Hurowitz; Speech/Voice, Thom Jones; PSM, Melissa Rae Miller; ASM, Kate Ferdinandi; Cast: Brian McEleney (Ebenezer Scrooge); Company: Peter Matthew Connolly, Ruth Coughlin, D'Arcy Dersham, Richard Donelly, Janice Duclos, Kevaughn Harvey, Lauren Lubow, Brian McEleney, Barbara Meek, Ricky Oliver, Fred Sullivan, Jr., Stephen Thorne; Musicians: Terry Anthony, Jeremy Fenn-Smith and Mike Sartini; The Children's Red Cast: Lily Clurman, Nigel Richards, Maggie Rock, Eva Senerchia, John Spinelli, Benjamin Thornton; The Children's Green Cast: Faith Buckley, Kate Fitzgerald, Drew Parker, Elliot Peters, Phineas Peters, E. Grace Viveiros; November 18–December 30, 2011

The Merchant of Venice by William Shakespeare; Director, Curt Columbus; Choreography, Sharon Jenkins; Sets, Eugene Lee; Lights, Keith Parham; Costumes, Olivera Gajic; Sound, Benji Inniger; Speech/Voice, Thom Jones; PSM, Buzz Cohen; ASM, Lauren Bachman-Streitfield; Music Director, Rachael Warren; Cast: Darien Battle (The Duke of Venice/Salerio/Launcelot Gobbo), Joe Wilson, Jr. (Antonio/The Prince of Morocco), Stephen Thorne (Bassanio), Fred Sullivan, Jr. (Gratiano/Tubal/The Prince of Aragon), Will Austin (Lorenzo), Stephen Berenson (Shylock), Caroline Kaplan (Jessica), Mary C. Davis (Portia), Rachael Warren (Nerissa); February 3–March 11, 2012

Boeing-Boeing by Marc Camoletti; Translated by Beverley Cross and Francis Evans, Director, Fred Sullivan, Jr.; Sets, Patrick Lynch; Lighting, John Ambrosone; Costumes, William Lane; Sound, Peter Sasha Hurowitz; Speech/Voice, Thom Jones; PSM, Captain Kate Murphy; ASM, Keri Schultz Cast: Joe Wilson, Jr. (Bernard), Rebecca Gibel (Gloria), Nance Williamson (Bertha), Stephen Thorne (Robert), Liz Morgan (Gabriella), Amanda Dolan (Gretchen); April 13–May 13, 2012

THE DOWLING THEATER

Clybourne Park by Bruce Norris; Director, Brian Mertes; Sets, Eugene Lee; Costumes, Olivera Gajic; Lighting, Dan Scully; Sound, Peter Sasha Hurowitz; Speech/Voice, Thom Jones; PSM, Kristen Gibbs; Cast: Timothy Crowe (Russ/Dan), Anne Scurria (Bev/Kathy), Mia Ellis (Francine/Lena), Tommy Dickie (Jim/Tom/Kenneth), Joe Wilson, Jr. (Albert/Kevin), Mauro Hantman (Karl/Steve), Rachael Warren (Betsy/Lindsey); October 14– November 20, 2011

It's A Wonderful Life: A Live Radio Play by Joe Landry; Director, Tyler Dobrowsky; Sets, Michael McGarty; Lighting, John Ambrosone; Costumes, Alison Walker Carrier; Sound, Peter Sasha Hurowitz; Speech/Voice, Thom Jones; PSM, Kristen Gibbs; Cast: Timothy Crowe (Old Man Potter/Others), Mauro Hantman (George Bailey/Others), Rachael Warren (Mary Hatch), Anne Scurria (Violet Bick/Others), Joe Wilson, Jr. (Clarence the Angel/Others), Benjamin Inniger (Foley artist); December 9–31, 2011

THREE BY THREE IN REP: THREE WORLD PREMIERES

Sparrow Grass by Curt Columbus, Director, Brian McEleney; Sets, Michael McGarty; Costumes, William Lane; Lighting, Dan Scully; Sound, Peter Sasha Hurowitz; Speech/Voice, Thom Jones; Fight Supervisor, Craig Handel; PSM, Michael Domue; SM, Kristen Gibbs; Cast: Phyllis Kay (Paula); Barbara Meek (Isabelle), Jaime Rosenstein (Teddie), Tyler Lansing Weaks (Nate), Richard Donelly (Ralph); The Dowling Theater; February 16–May 13, 2012

Love Alone by Deborah Salem Smith; Co-Directors, Tyler Dobrowsky, Deborah Salem Smith; Sets, Michael McGarty; Costumes, William Lane; Lighting, Dan Scully; Sound, Peter Sasha Hurowitz; Speech/Voice, Thom Jones; Fight Supervisor, Craig Handel; PSM, Michael Domue; SM, Robin Grady; Cast: Janice Duclos (Nurse/Woman), Anne Scurria (Helen), Angela Brazil (Becca), Mauro Hantman (J.P.), Leah Anderson (Clementine), Richard Donelly (Mr. Rush); The Dowling Theater; February 28–May 27, 2012

The Mourners' Bench by George Brant, Director, Michael Perlman; Sets, Michael McGarty; Costumes, William Lane; Lighting, Dan Scully; Sound, Peter Sasha Hurowitz; Speech/Voice, Thom Jones; PSM, Michael Domue; Cast: Angela Brazil (Melissa), Mauro Hantman (Bobby), Janice Duclos (Wilma), Phyllis Kay (Caroline), Anne Scurria (Sarah), Timothy Crowe (Joe); The Dowling Theater; March 7–May 24, 2012

Two River Theater Company

Red Bank, New Jersey

Eighteenth Season

Artistic Director, John Dias; Managing Director, Michael Hurst; Executive Producer, Robert M. Rechnitz

Much Ado About Nothing by William Shakespeare; Director, Sam Buntrock; Sets, Tony Straiges; Costumes, Mattie Ullrich; Lighting, Brian Tovar; Sound/Composition, Mark Bennett; Vocal Coach, Deborah Hecht; PSM, Whitney McAnally; Cast: John Ahlin (Dogberry), Tom Bloom (Leonato), Connor Carew (Friar Francis/Verges), Michael Cumpsty (Benedick), Sean Dugan (Don John), Christopher Hirsh (Borachio), Tia James (Margaret), Kevin Kelly (Conrade), Nick LaMedica (Balthasar/Watchman), Kathryn Meisle (Beatrice), Aaron Clifton Moten (Claudio), Mary Anne O'Brien (Ursula/Sexton), Steven Skybell (Don Pedro), Annapurna Sriram (Hero), Zeke Zaccaro (Antonio/Watchman); Joan and Robert Rechnitz Theater; September 10–October 2, 2011

Seven Homeless Mammoths Wander New England by Madeleine George; Director, Ken Rus Schmoll; Sets, Arnulfo Maldonado; Costumes, Kirche Leigh Zeile; Lighting, Matt Frey; Sound/Composition, Ryan Rumery; PSM, Julia P. Jones; Cast: Lauren Culpepper (Early Man 2), Mercedes Herrero (Dean Wreen), Jon Hoche (Early Man 1), Deirdre Madigan (Greer), Flor De Liz Perez (Andromeda), Joel Van Liew (The Caretaker); World Premiere; Marion Huber Theater; October 15–November 20, 2011

No Child... Written and performed by Nilaja Sun; Director, Hal Brooks; Original Sets, Narelle Sissons; Sets adapted by Neil Prince; Costumes, Jessica Gaffney; Lighting, Mark Barton; Sound, Ron Russell; PSM, Whitney McAnally; All roles by Nilaja Sun; Joan and Robert Rechnitz Theater; November 1–20, 2011

Honk! A Musical Tale of 'The Ugly Duckling' Music by George Stiles; Book and lyrics by Anthony Drewe; Director Matt Pfeiffer; Music Director/Conductor/Pianist, Wayne Barker; Choreographer, Jenn Rose; Sets, David P. Gordon; Costumes, Olivera Gajic; Lighting/Projections, Jeanette Oi-Suk Yew; Sound, Karin Graybash; PSM, Matthew Melchiorre; Cast: Amanda Butterbaugh (Grace/Dot/Lowbutt), Laura Diorio (Downy/Froglet), Owen Doherty (Billy/Froglet), Aymee Garcia (Maureen/Snowy/Queenie/Mother Swan), Michael Genet (Turkey/Barnacles/Bullfrog/Father Swan), Doug Hara (Cat), Kenita R. Miller (Ida), Paolo Montalban (Ugly), Jim Newman (Drake/Greylag), Olivia Oguma (Henrietta/Maggie Pie/Pinkfoot/Penny), Julian Sarin (Beaky/Froglet), Gabriella Scerbo (Fluff/Froglet); Joan and Robert Rechnitz Theater; December 6, 2011–January 1, 2012

August Wilson's Jitney Director, Ruben Santiago-Hudson; Sets, Neil Patel; Costumes, Karen Perry; Lighting, Rui Rita; Sound, Leon Rothenberg; Composition, Bill Sims Jr; Fight Director, Thomas Schall; PSM, Amanda Michaels; Cast: Harvy Blanks (Shealy), J. Bernard Calloway (Booster), Anthony Chisholm (Fielding), Chuck Cooper (Becker), Brandon J. Dirden (Youngblood), Roslyn Ruff (Rena), Ray Anthony Thomas (Philmore), James A. Williams (Doub), Allie Woods Jr. (Turnbo); Joan and Robert Rechnitz Theater; January 31–February 25, 2012

In This House Music by Mike Reid; Lyrics by Sarah Schlesinger; Book by Jonathan Bernstein, Sarah Schlesinger, Mike Reid; Director, May Adrales; Music Director/Conductor/Pianist, James Sampliner; Orchestrator, Danny Larsen; Sets, Lee Savage; Costumes, Camille Assaf; Lighting, Gina Scherr; Sound, Nevin Steinberg; PSM, Whitney McAnally; Cast: Chuck Cooper (Henry Arden), Suzzanne Douglas (Luisa Arden [March 19–April 8]), Jeff Kready (Johnny D'Amato), Brenda Pressley (Luisa Arden [March 4–18]), Margo Seibert (Annie Friedkin); Marion Huber Theater; World Premiere; March 4–April 8, 2012

Maureen McGovern in Carry It On Conceived and written by Philip Himberg and Maureen McGovern; Director, Philip Himberg; Music Director/Arrangements/Pianist, Jeffrey Harris; Sets, Neil Patel; Costumes, Gayle Susan Baizer; Lighting, David Lander; Projections, Maya Ciarrocchi; Sound, Zachary Williamson; PSM, Robert V. Thurber; Cast: Maureen McGovern; Joan and Robert Rechnitz Theater; April 3–22, 2012

My Wonderful Day by Alan Ayckbourn; Director, Nicholas Martin; Sets, Cameron Anderson; Costumes, Dane Laffrey; Lighting, Philip Rosenberg; Sound, Mark Bennett; Vocal Coach, Deborah Hecht; PSM, Joanne E. McInerney; Cast: Alison Cimmet (Tiffany), Kimberly Hébert Gregory (Laverne), Susan Heyward (Winnie), Kevin Isola (Josh), Danielle Skraastad (Paula), Marc Vietor (Kevin); Joan and Robert Rechnitz Theater; May 15June 3, 2012

Virginia Stage Company

Norfolk, Virginia

Thirty-third Season

Artistic Director, Chris Hanna; Managing Director, Keith Stava

God of Carnage by Yazmina Reza; Translated by Christopher Hampton; Director, Chris Hanna; Sets, Michael Schweikardt; Costumes, Jennifer Caprio; Lighting, A. Nelson Ruger IV; Casting, Harriet Bass; PSM, Matthew G. Marholin; Cast: Sue Cremin (Annette Raleigh), Ward Duffy (Michael Novak), Laurence Lau (Alan Raleigh), Henny Russell (Veronica Novak); September 13–October 2, 2011

Red by John Logan; Director, Chris Hanna; Sets, Bill Clarke; Costumes, Jeni Schaefer; Lighting, John Ambrosone; Sound, Daniel Erdberg; Casting, Harriet Bass; PSM, Matthew G. Marholin; Cast: Robert Dorfman (Mark Rothko), Eric Gilde (Ken); October 18–November 6, 2011

A Christmas Carol by Charles Dickens; Adapted by Patrick Mullins; Director, Patrick Mullins; Sets, Terri Summers-Flint; Costumes, Jeni Schaefer; Lighting, Bradley King; Sound, Daniel Erdberg; Music, Barton Kuebler; PSM, Matthew G. Marholin; Cast: Bryan Austin (Young Scrooge), Jon Bremner (Ensemble), Sam Cooper (Ensemble), Kevin R. Free (Fezziwig), Katie Fridsma (Ensemble), David Graham Jones (Christmas Present), Caitlin McWethy (Belle), Peter Moore (Ebenezer Scrooge), Andy Paterson (Bob Cratchit), Nancy Pope (Mrs. Cratchit), Kenneth J. Ray (Christmas Future), Kim Stauffer (Christmas Past), Chris Van Cleave (Jacob Marley), Evette Marie White (Mrs. Kidgerbury), Jack Whitelaw (Boy Scrooge), John Whitelaw (Ensemble), Colin Wilson (Tiny Tim), Morgan Wilson (Fan); December 2–24, 2011

Black Pearl Sings! by Frank Higgins; A Co-Production with Capital Repertory Theatre; Director, Patrick Mullins; Set, Bill Clarke; Costume, Jennifer Caprio; Lighting, Victor En Yu Tan; Sound, Elisheba Ittoop; Music, Akin'Babatunde'; PSM, Matthew G. Marholin; Cast: Jannie Jones (Pearl), Jessica Wortham (Susannah); January 17–February 5, 2012

Death of A Salesman by Arthur Miller; Director, Chris Hanna; Sets, Narelle Sissons; Costumes, Jeni Schaefer; Lighting, Mary Louise Geiger; Sound, Amy Altadonna; Casting, Harriet Bass; PSM, Matthew G. Marholin; Cast: Tracy Griswold (Willy Loman), Julie Fishell (Linda), Jed Orlemann (Biff), Jeff Barry (Happy), Robert Mack (Bernard), Frances Mitchell (The Woman), Bus Howard (Charley), Michael R. Schaeffer (Uncle Ben), David Meadows (Howard Wagner), Evette Marie White (Jenny), Joshua Gray (Stanley), Caitlin McWethy (Miss Forsythe), KT Fanelli (Letta); February 21–March 11, 2012

The Fantasticks Book and lyrics by Tom Jones; Music by Harvey Schmidt; Director, Jose Zayas; Sets, Michael Schweikardt; Costumes, Jeni Schaefer; Lighting, John Lasiter; Sound, Daniel Erdberg; Choreographer, Jennifer Lent; Music, Eli Zoller; Casting, Harriet Bass; PSM, Matthew G. Marholin; Cast: Mark Campbell (El Gallo), Hanley Smith (Luisa), Chris Ware (Matt), Larry Bull (Hucklebee), Kilty Reidy (Bellomy), Bob Nelson (Henry), Ryan Clemens

Westport Country Playhouse

Westport, Connecticut

Eighty-first, Eighty-second Seasons

Artistic Director, Mark Lamos; Managing Director, Michael Ross

The Circle by W. Somerset Maugham; Director, Nicholas Martin; Sets, Alexander Dodge; Costumes, Gabriel Berry; Lighting, Philip Rosenberg; Sound, Drew Levy; PSM, Jason Kaiser. Cast: Gretchen Hall (Elizabeth), John Horton (Lord Porteous), Marsha Mason (Lady Catherine Champion-Cheney), James Joseph O'Neil, (George, the Butler), Bryce Pinkham (Edward Luton), Christina Rouner (Mrs. Shenstone), Marc Vietor (Arnold Champion-Cheney, MP), Paxton Whitehead (Clive Champion-Cheney); June 7–25, 2011

Lips Together, Teeth Apart by Terrence McNally; Director, Mark Lamos; Sets, Andrew Jackness; Costumes, Candice Donnelly; Lighting, Robert Wierzel; Sound, John Gromada; Fight Director, Mark Silence; PSM, Matthew Melchiorre; Cast: Chris Henry Coffey (John Haddock), John Ellison Conlee (Sam Truman), Jenn Gambatese (Chloe Haddock), Maggie Lacey (Sally Truman); July 12–July 30, 2011

Suddenly Last Summer by Tennessee William; Director, David Kennedy; Sets, Narelle Sissons; Costumes, Ilona Somogyi; Lighting, Matthew Richards; Sound, Fitz Patton; Fight Director, B. H. Barry; PSM, Matthew Melchiorre; Cast: Susan Bennett (Miss Foxhill), Ryan Garbayo (George Holly), Annalee Jefferies (Mrs. Venable), Charlotte Maier (Mrs. Holly), Liv Rooth (Catharine Holly); Lee Aaron Rosen (Dr. Cukrowicz), Tina Stafford (Sister Felicity); August 23–September 10, 2011

Twelfth Night by William Shakespeare; Director, Mark Lamos; Sets, Andrew Boyce; Costumes, Tilly Grimes; Lighting, Robert Wierzel; Sound, John Gromada; Fight Director, B. H. Barry; Dramaturg, Milla Cozart Riggio; PSM, Matthew Melchiorre; Cast: David Adkins (Malvolio), Jordan Coughtry (Sir Andrew Aguecheek), Darius De Haas (Feste), Rick Ford (Captain/Priest), Donnetta Lavinia Grays (Maria), Lucas Hall (Orsino), Mahira Kakkar (Viola), Justin Kruger (Fabian/Valentine), Chris Ryan (Curio), Rachid Sabitri (Sebastian), David Schramm (Sir Toby Belch), Paul Anthony Stewart (Antonio), Susan Kelechi Watson (Olivia); October 11–November 5, 2011

Into the Woods Music and lyrics by Stephen Sondheim; Book by James Lapine; Director, Mark Lamos; Musical Director, Wayne Barker; Choreography, Seán Curran; Sets, Allen Moyer; Costumes, Candice Donnelly; Lighting, Robert Wierzel; Sound, Zachary Williamson; Fight Director, Michael Rossmy; PSM, Matthew Melchiorre; Cast: Justin Scott Brown (Jack), Britney Coleman (Cinderella's Mother/Rapunzel), Alma Cuervo (Cinderella's Stepmother/Granny/Voice of Giant), Eleni Delopoulos (Lucinda), Jeffry Denman (Narrator), Danielle Ferland (Baker's Wife), Lauren Kennedy (Witch), Nikka Graff Lanzarone (Florinda), Jenny Latimer (Cinderella), Jeremy Lawrence (Mysterious Man/Steward), Robert Lenzi (Cinderella's Father/Rapunzel's Prince), Erik Liberman (The Baker), Dana Steingold (Little Red Ridinghood), Cheryl Stern (Jack's Mother), Nik Walker (Cinderella's Prince/The Wolf); May 1–26, 2012

Yale Repertory Theatre

New Haven, Connecticut

Forty-Sixth Season

Artistic Director, James Bundy; Managing Director, Victoria Nolan; Associate Artistic Director, Jennifer Kiger

Three Sisters by Anton Chekhov; New Version by Sarah Ruhl based on a literal translation by Elise Thoron with Matalya Paramonova and Kristin Johnsen-Neshati; Director, Les Waters; Sets, Annie Smart; Costumes, Ilona Somogyi; Lighting, Alexander V. Nichols; Sound, David Budries; Dramaturg, Rachel Steinberg; Vocal Coach, Grace Zandarski; Casting Directors, Amy Potozkin, C.S.A., Janet Foster, C.S.A.; SM, James Mountcastle; Cast: Josiah Bania (Rode), James Carpenter

(Chebutykin), Richard Farrell (Ferapont), Emily Kitchens (Natasha), Bruce McKenzie (Vershinin), Alex Moggridge (Andrei), Barbara Oliver (Anfisa), Natalia Payne (Masha), Keith Reddin (Kulygin), Thomas Jay Ryan (Tuzenbach), Wendy Rich Stetson (Olga), Brian Wiles (Fedotik), Heather Wood (Irina), Sam Breslin Wright (Solyony); Co-production with Berkeley Repertory Theatre; September 16–October 8, 2011

Belleville by Amy Herzog; Director, Anne Kauffman; Sets, Julia C. Lee; Costumes, Mark Nagle; Lighting, Nina Hyun Seung Lee; Sound/Original Compositions, Robert Kaplowitz; Dramaturg, Amy Boratko, Alex Ripp; Vocal/Dialect, Beth McGuire; Fight Directors, Rick Sordelet, Jeff Barry; Casting Director, Tara Rubin Casting; SM, Gina Noele Odierno; Cast: Pascale Armand (Amina), Maria Dizzia (Abby), Greg Keller (Zack), and Gilbert Owuor (Alioune); World Premiere; October 21–November 12, 2011

A Doctor in Spite of Himself by Molière; Adapted by Christopher Bayes and Steven Epp; Director, Christopher Bayes; Composer/Music Director, Aaron Halva; Sets, Matt Saunders; Costumes, Kristin Fiebig; Lighting, Yi Zhao; Sound, Ken Goodwin; Dramaturg, Benjamin Fainstein; Vocal Coach, Walton Wilson; Casting Director, Tara Rubin Casting; SM, Brandon Curtis; Cast: Julie Briskman (Jacqueline), Liam Craig (Lucas, Thibaut), Steven Epp (Sganarelle), Renata Friedman (Lucinde, Puppeteer), Allen Gilmore (M. Robert, Géronte), Chivas Michael (Léandre, Old Man), Jacob Ming Trent (Valère, Cherub), Justine Williams (Martine, Perrin); Co-production with Berkeley Repertory Theatre; November 26–December 17, 2011

Good Goods by Christina Anderson; Director, Tina Landau; Sets, James Schuette; Costumes, Toni-Leslie James; Lighting, Scott Zielinski; Sound, Junghoon Pi; Dramaturg, Amy Boratko, Alexandra Ripp; Vocal/Dialect, Jane Guyer Fujita; Fight Director, Rick Sordelet; Casting, Tara Rubin Casting; SM, Maria Cantin; Cast: Oberon K.A. Adjepong (Waymon as Hunter Priestess, Factory Folk), de'Adre Aziza (Patricia), Kyle Beltran (Wire), Clifton Duncan (Stacey), Marc Damon Johnson (Truth), Angela Lewis (Sunny); World Premiere; February 3–25, 2012

The Winter's Tale by William Shakespeare; Director, Liz Diamond; Composer, Matthew Suttor; Choreographer, Randy Duncan; Sets, Michael Yeargan; Costumes, Jennifer Moeller; Lighting, Matt Frey; Sound, Elizabeth Atkinson; Dramaturg, Catherine Sheehy, Ilinca Tamara Todorut; Vocal/Dialect, Grace Zandarski; Casting Director, Tara Rubin Casting; SM, Catherine Costanzo; Cast: Tim Brown (Lord 2/Florizel), Rob Campbell (Leontes), Tyrone Mitchell Henderson (Camillo/Guard 2), Sheria Irving (Lady/Dorcas), Felicity Jones (Paulina/Shepherdess), Francis Jue (Dion/Gaoler/Mariner/Shepherd 1), Brian Keane (Antigonus/Servant 3), Thomas Kopache (Old Shepherd/Officer/Time), Hoon Lee (Polixenes), Lupita Nyong'o (Perdita), Adam O'Bryne (Cleomenes/Guard 1/Servant 2/Shepherd 2), Luke Robertson (Lord 1/Autolycus), Richard Ruiz (Servant 1/Clown), Susannah Schulman (Hermione), Chris Van Zele (Bear), Adina Verson (Emilia/Mopsa), and Remsen Welsh (Mamillius/Shepherd Boy); Musicians: Paul Brantley (Cello), Michael Compitello (Percussion), Jason May (Woodwinds), Adam Rosenblatt (Percussion); March 16–April 7, 2012

The Realistic Joneses by Will Eno; Director, Sam Gold; Sets/Costumes, David Zinn; Lighting, Mark Barton; Sound, Ken Goodwin; Projections, Paul Lieber; Dramaturg, Amy Boratko, Anne Seiwerath; Casting, Tara Rubin Casting; SM, Jenna Woods; Cast: Johanna Day (Jennifer Jones), Glenn Fitzgerald (John Jones), Tracy Letts (Bob Jones), Parker Posey (Pony Jones); World Premiere; April 20–May 12, 2012

Johanna Day and Tracy Letts in The Realistic Joneses *at Yale Repertory Theatre (photo by Joan Marcus)*

Lauren Kennedy in Into the Woods *at Westport Country Playhouse (photo by T. Charles Erickson)*

THEATRICAL AWARDS

2011–2012

Top: John Cullum presents a 2012 Theatre World Award to Jessie Mueller (photo by Jim Baldassare)

Center: The 2012 Theatre World Awards (photo by Michael Heeney)

Bottom: 2012 Theatre World Award winner Crystal A. Dickinson and her presenter, Leslie Uggams, meet the press (photo by Xanthe Elbrick)

Tracie Bennett of End of the Rainbow

Phillip Boykin of The Gershwins' Porgy and Bess

Crystal A. Dickinson of Clybourne Park

Russell Harvard of Tribes

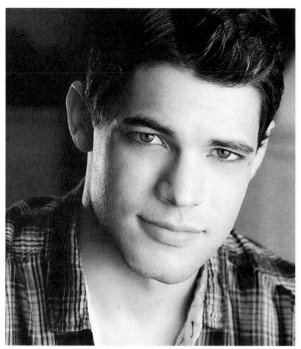

Jeremy Jordan of Bonnie & Clyde

Joaquina Kalukango of Hurt Village

Jennifer Lim of Chinglish

Jessie Mueller of On a Clear Day You Can See Forever

Hettienne Park of Seminar *and* The Intelligent Guide to Capitalism & Socialism with a Key to the Scriptures

Chris Perfetti of Sons of the Prophet

Finn Wittrock of Death of a Salesman

Josh Young of Jesus Christ *Superstar*

68th Annual Theatre World Awards

Tuesday, June 5, 2012 at the Belasco Theatre

Originally dubbed *Promising Personalities* in 1944 by co-founders Daniel Blum, Norman MacDonald, and John Willis to coincide with the first release of *Theatre World*, the definitive pictorial and statistical record of the American theatre, the Theatre World Awards, as they are now known, are the oldest awards given for debut performances in New York City, as well as one of the oldest honors bestowed on New York actors.

Administered by the Theatre World Awards Board of Directors, a committee of current New York drama critics chooses six actors and six actresses for the Theatre World Award who have distinguished themselves in Broadway and Off-Broadway productions during the past theatre season. Occasionally, special Theatre World Awards are also bestowed on performers, casts, or others who have made a particularly lasting impression on the New York theatre scene.

The Dorothy Loudon Foundation in conjunction Theatre World Awards presented the fourth annual Dorothy Loudon Award (formerly known as the *Starbaby Award*) at the ceremony. Dorothy Loudon, a former Theatre World Award winner and repeated presenter at past ceremonies, was an ardent supporter of the Theatre World Awards and a dear friend to John Willis. The Dorothy Loudon Award for Excellence in the Theatre is presented to a performer who made an auspicious Broadway or Off-Broadway performance in the season.

In 2011 the Lunt-Fontanne Award for Ensemble Excellence was introduced and will be presented as deemed worthy by the Theatre World Awards to an outstanding Broadway or Off-Broadway ensemble. This award is sponsored by Aaron Frankel in devoted honor of Alfred Lunt and Lynn Fontanne. The award was not presented this season.

The Theatre World Award is designed by Wade F. Dansby 3 in the spirit of the previous Theatre World Janus statuette, created by internationally recognized artist Harry Marinsky, keeping the Janus tradition with an etching of the original sculpture adapted from the Roman myth of Janus. Janus was the God of Entrances, Exits and All Beginnings - with one face appraising the past and the other anticipating the future.

The Theatre World Award winners are selected by a committee of New York drama critics: David Cote (*Time Out New York* and NY1's *On Stage*), Joe Dziemianowicz (*New York Daily News*), Peter Filichia (*Star-Ledger* and *TheaterMania.com*), Harry Haun (*Playbill*), Matthew Murray (*TalkinBroadway.com*), Frank Scheck (*New York Post*), and Linda Winer (*Newsday*). The Theatre World Awards Board of Directors is: Barry Keating (President), Erin Oestreich (Vice President), Mary K. Botosan & Alden Fulcomer (Secretary), Tabitha Falcone (Treasurer), Dale Badway, Kimothy Cruse, Tom Lynch (Founding Board Member), Lisa Rothe, Stephen Wilde. Board Emeritus: Thom Christopher, Marianne Tatum, Jamie deRoy, Ben Hodges, Walter Willison, Doug Holmes, Patricia Elliott, Leigh Giroux, Scott Denny, Kati Meister; Advisors: Jim Baldassare, Jason Cicci, Christopher Cohen, Wade F. Dansby 3; Randall J. Hemming, Gordon Kelly, Michael Kostel Jon Lonoff, Michael Messina, Barry Monush, Matthew Murray, Flora Stamatiades.

WINNERS Tracie Bennett (*End of the Rainbow*), Phillip Boykin (The Gershwins' *Porgy and Bess*), Crystal A. Dickinson (*Clybourne Park*), Russell Harvard (*Tribes*), Jeremy Jordan (*Bonnie & Clyde*), Joaquina Kalukango (*Hurt Village*), Jennifer Lim (*Chinglish*), Jessie Mueller (*On a Clear Day You Can See Forever*), Hettienne Park (*Seminar* and *The Intelligent Guide to Capitalism & Socialism with a Key to the Scriptures*), Chris Perfetti (*Sons of the Prophet*), Finn Wittrock (*Death of a Salesman*), Josh Young (*Jesus Christ Superstar*); **Dorothy Loudon Award:** Susan Pourfar (*Tribes*)

PRESENTERS John Cullum–*On a Clear Day You Can See Forever* (1966); Victor Garber–*Ghosts* (1973); David Alan Grier–*The First* (1982); Faye Grant–*Singin' in the Rain* (1986); Josh Grisetti– *Enter Laughing, The Musical* (2009); Philip Seymour Hoffman–*True West* (2000); Lizbeth Mackay –*Crimes of the Heart*

(1982); John Rubenstein–*Pippin* (1972); Tony Sheldon–*Priscilla Queen of the Desert* (2011); Wesley Taylor–*Rock of Ages* (2009); Leslie Uggams–*Hallelujah, Baby!* (1967)

PERFORMERS Howard McGillin–*The Mystery of Edwin Drood* (1986): "Something's Coming" from *West Side Story*; Stephanie Umoh–*Ragtime* (2010): "Supper Time" from *As Thousands Cheer*; Brian Stokes Mitchell–*Mail* (1986): "I Was Here" from *The Glorious Ones*; Michael Cerveris–*The Who's Tommy* (1993): "Pinball Wizard" from *The Who's Tommy*

SPECIAL GUESTS Stacy Keach, (Presenter of the The Dorothy Loudon Award); Lionel Larner, Executive Director of the Dorothy Loudon Foundation; Barry Keating, President, Theatre World Awards Board of Directors

THE CEREMONY Writer and Host, Peter Filichia; Producers, Mary K. Botosan & Erin Oestreich; Director, Barry Keating; Music Director/Accompanist, Lawrence Yurman; Associate Director, Jeremy Quinn; Associate Producer, Peter Dagger; Production Stage Manager, Kimothy Cruse; Stage Manager, Alden Fulcomer; Press Agent, Susan L. Schulman; Lighting Consultant, Wendy Luedtke; Photographers, Jim Baldassare, Konrad Brattke, Xanthe Elbrick, Michael Heeney, Michael Kostel; Video Photographer, Michael Kostel; Presented on the set of the *End of the Rainbow*, scenic design by William Dudley, lighting design by Christopher Akerlind, sound design by Gareth Owen

THEATRE WORLD AWARDS STAFF AND CREW Assistant Stage Managers, Stephen Ferri, Michael Mele, Joel Pellini; Graphic Artist, Wade F. Dansby 3; Cover Art/Poster, Justin "Squigs" Robertson; Facebook Administrator, Jim Baldassare; Guest and Volunteer Coordinator, Stephen Wilde; Twitter Administrator, Russell M. Dembin; Legal Counsel, Leigh A. Giroux; ASL Interpretation, Candace Broecker, Lynnette Taylor; Company Manager, Bobby Driggers; Assistant Company Manager, Kendall Booher

2012 THEATRE WORLD AWARD WRANGLERS Emily Rosenfeld and Tyrah Skye Odoms from the cast of next season's revival of *Annie*

VOLUNTEERS Linda Alago, Kate Bader, Tom Bernagozzi, Geoff Botosan, Rebecca Carton, Kelly Childress, Oleg Deyle, Maxwell Eddy, Tiffany Falcone, Josh Fielden, Danny Gordon, Ashley Grombol, Laura Harrison, Sahar Helmy, Jeremiah Hernandez, Keith Hines, Katie Kavett, Emily Kratter, Jon-Michael Miller, Valerie Novakoff, Thomas Ohrstrom, Jenna Panther, Chester Poon, Elisa Pupko, Chuja Seo, James Sheridan, Lisette Silva, Joshua Strone, Jennifer Tsay, Jillian Walker

THE SHUBERT ORGANIZATION INC. Phillip J. Smith (Chairman); Robert E. Wankel (President); Wyche Fowler Jr., Diana Phillips, Lee J. Seidler, Michael I. Sovert, Stuart Subotnick (Board of Directors); Elliot Greene (Chief Financial Officer), David Andrews (SVP, Ticketing); Juan Calvo (VP, Finance); Cathy Cozens (VP, Human Resourses); John Darby (VP, Facilities); Peter Entin (VP, Theatre Operations); Charles Flateman (VP, Marketing); Anthony LaMattina (VP, Audit); Brian Mahoney (VP, Ticket Sales); D.S. Moynihan (VP, Creative Projects); Julio Peterson (VP, Real Estate)

BELASCO THEATRE STAFF Stephanie Wallis (Theatre Manager), Bob Reilly (House Manager)

***END OF THE RAINBOW* PRODUCTION STAFF** Kim Sellon (Company Manager); Mark Dobrow (Production Stage Manager); Joey Parnes, S.D. Wagner, John Johnson, Kim Sellon, Kit Ingui, Nathan V. Koch (General Management); Rachel Zack (Stage Manager); Kit Ingui (Assistant Company Manager)

***END OF THE RAINBOW* CREW FOR THE THEATRE WORLD AWARDS** Mike Smanko (Production Properties), Dan Coey (Production Electrician), Joanna Lynne Staub (Production Sound A1), Liz Coleman (Production Sound A2); Steve Hillis (Followspot Operator), Carlos Jaramillo (House Properties), Joe Luongo (House Flyman), Matt Maloney (House Electrician), Mike Martinez (House Carpenter)

SPONSORSHIP The Dorothy Loudon Foundation, The Shubert Organization Inc., The Alec Baldwin Foundation Inc., Susan S. Channing Trust, Leonard

The Theatre World Awards, Inc. is a 501 (c)(3) nonprofit organization, and our annual presentation is made possible by the generous contributions of previous winners and friends. For more information please visit the website at www. theatreworldawards.org.

Tax-deductible contributions can be sent via PayPay to info@theatreworldawards. org, or checks and money orders sent to:

Theatre World Awards, Inc.
Box 246 Radio City Station
New York, NY 10101-0246

Dorothy Loudon Award

Susan Pourfar of Tribes

Photos by Jim Baldassare (JB), Konrad Brattke (KB), Xanthe Elbrick (XE), Michael Heeney (MH), and Michael Kostel (MK)

Phillip Boykin (MK)

Stephanie Umoh (Winner 2010) entertains the audience with "Supper Time" (MK)

Finn Wittrock (KB)

Hettienne Park and Isabel Keating (MH)

Lionel Larner, Susan Pourfar (Dorothy Loudon Award Winner), and Stacy Keach (KB)

Lizbeth Mackay presents to Chris Perfetti (XE)

Josh Grisetti presents to Josh Young (XE)

Brian Stokes Mitchell (1988 Winner) performs "I Was Here" (MK)

Victor Garber (MK)

Faye Grant and Jennifer Lim (MK)

Wesley Taylor and Jeremy Jordan (KB)

John Rubenstein and Russell Harvard (KB)

Crystal A. Dickinson (JB)

Theatre World Awards Host, Peter Filichia (JB)

Tyrah Skye Odoms and Emily Rosenfeld (KB)

Michael Cerveris (1993 Winner) closes out the ceremony with "Pinball Wizard" (XE)

Keith Boykin and David Alan Grier (KB)

Susan Pourfar (XE)

Philip Seymour Hoffman and Finn Wittrock (KB)

Jessie Mueller (KB)

Jeremy Jordan (MK)

Hettienne Park (KB)

Jennifer Lim (KB)

Russell Harvard (XE)

John Cullum (XE)

Howard McGillin (1986 Winner) performs "Something's Coming" (JB)

Josh Young (KB)

Erin Oestreich (TWA Producer), Barry Keating (TWA Director), Mary Botosan (TWA Producer)

Leslie Uggams (JB)

Tracie Bennett (XE)

Tony Sheldon presents to Tracie Bennett (JB)

Previous Theatre World Award Recipients

1944-45: Betty Comden (*On the Town*), Richard Davis (*Kiss Them For Me*), Richard Hart (*Dark of the Moon*), Judy Holliday (*Kiss Them for Me*), Charles Lang (*Down to Miami* and *The Overtons*), Bambi Linn (*Carousel*), John Lund (*The Hasty Heart*), Donald Murphy (*Signature* and *Common Ground*), Nancy Noland (*Common Ground*), Margaret Phillips (*The Late George Apley*), John Raitt (*Carousel*)

1945-46: Barbara Bel Geddes (*Deep Are the Roots*), Marlon Brando (*Truckline Café* and *Candida*), Bill Callahan (*Call Me Mister*), Wendell Corey (*The Wind is Ninety*), Paul Douglas (*Born Yesterday*), Mary James (*Apple of His Eye*), Burt Lancaster (*A Sound of Hunting*), Patricia Marshall (*The Day Before Spring*), Beatrice Pearson (*The Mermaids Singing*)

1946-47: Keith Andes (*The Chocolate Soldier*), Marion Bell (*Brigadoon*), Peter Cookson (*Message for Margaret*), Ann Crowley (*Carousel*), Ellen Hanley (*Barefoot Boy With Cheek*), John Jordan (*The Wanhope Building*), George Keane (*Brigadoon*), Dorothea MacFarland (*Oklahoma!*), James Mitchell (*Brigadoon*), Patricia Neal (*Another Part of the Forest*), David Wayne (*Finian's Rainbow*)

1947-48: Valerie Bettis (*Inside U.S.A.*), Edward Bryce (*The Cradle Will Rock*), Whitfield Connor (*Macbeth*), Mark Dawson (*High Button Shoes*), June Lockhart (*For Love or Money*), Estelle Loring (*Inside U.S.A.*), Peggy Maley (*Joy to the World*), Ralph Meeker (*Miser Roberts*), Meg Mundy (*The Happy Journey to Trenton and Camden* and *The Respectful Prostitute*), Douglass Watson (*Antony and Cleopatra*), James Whitmore (*Command Decision*), Patrice Wymore (*Hold It!*)

1948-49: Tod Andrews (*Summer and Smoke*), Doe Avedon (*The Young and Fair*), Jean Carson (*Bravo!*), Carol Channing (*Lend an Ear*), Richard Derr (*The Traitor*), Julie Harris (*Sundown Beach*), Mary McCarty (*Sleepy Hollow*), Allyn Ann McLerie (*Where's Charley?*), Cameron Mitchell (*Death of a Salesman*), Gene Nelson (*Lend an Ear*), Byron Palmer (*Where's Charley?*), Bob Scheerer (*Lend an Ear*)

1949-50: Nancy Andrews (*Touch and Go*), Phil Arthur (*With a Silk Thread*), Barbara Brady (*The Velvet Glove*), Lydia Clarke (*Detective Story*), Priscilla Gillette (*Regina*), Don Hanmer (*The Man*), Marcia Henderson (*Peter Pan*), Charlton Heston (*Design for a Stained Glass Window*), Rick Jason (*Now I Lay Me Down to Sleep*), Grace Kelly (*The Father*), Charles Nolte (*Design for a Stained Glass Window*), Roger Price (*Tickets, Please!*)

1950-51: Barbara Ashley (*Out of This World*), Isabel Bigley (*Guys and Dolls*), Martin Brooks (*Burning Bright*), Richard Burton (*The Lady's Not For Burning*), Pat Crowley (*Southern Exposure*), James Daly (*Major Barbara* and *Mary Rose*), Cloris Leachman (*A Story for a Sunday Evening*), Russell Nype (*Call Me Madam*), Jack Palance (*Darkness at Noon*), William Smithers (*Romeo and Juliet*), Maureen Stapleton (*The Rose Tattoo*), Marcia Van Dyke (*Marcia Van Dyke*), Eli Wallach (*The Rose Tattoo*)

1951-52: Tony Bavaar (*Paint Your Wagon*), Patricia Benoit (*Glad Tidings*), Peter Conlow (*Courtin' Time*), Virginia de Luce (*New Faces of 1952*), Ronny Graham (*New Faces of 1952*), Audrey Hepburn (*Gigi*), Diana Herbert (*The Number*), Conrad Janis (*The Brass Ring*), Dick Kallman (*Seventeen*), Charles Proctor (*Twilight Walk*), Eric Sinclair (*Much Ado About Nothing*), Kim Stanley (*The Chase*), Marian Winters (*I Am a Camera*), Helen Wood (*Seventeen*)

1952-53: Edie Adams (*Wonderful Town*), Rosemary Harris (*The Climate of Eden*), Eileen Heckart (*Picnic*), Peter Kelley (*Two's Company*), John Kerr (*Bernardine*), Richard Kiley (*Misalliance*), Gloria Marlowe (*In Any Language*), Penelope Munday (*The Climate of Eden*), Paul Newman (*Picnic*), Sheree North (*Hazel Flagg*), Geraldine Page (*Mid-Summer*), John Stewart (*Bernardine*), Ray Stricklyn (*The Climate of Eden*), Gwen Verdon (*Can-Can*)

1953-54: Orson Bean (*John Murray Anderson's Almanac*), Harry Belafonte (*John Murray Anderson's Almanac*), James Dean (*The Immoralist*), Joan Diener (*Kismet*), Ben Gazzara (*End as a Man*), Carol Haney (*The Pajama Game*), Jonathan Lucas (*The Golden Apple*), Kay Medford (*Lullaby*), Scott Merrill (*The Threepenny Opera*), Elizabeth Montgomery (*Late Love*), Leo Penn (*The Girl on the Via Flaminia*), Eva Marie Saint (*The Trip to Bountiful*)

1954-55: Julie Andrews (*The Boy Friend*), Jacqueline Brookes (*The Cretan Woman*), Shirl Conway (*Plain and Fancy*), Barbara Cook (*Plain and Fancy*), David Daniels (*Plain and Fancy*), Mary Fickett (*Tea and Sympathy*), Page Johnson (*In April Once*), Loretta Leversee (*Home is the Hero*), Jack Lord (*The Traveling Lady*), Dennis Patrick (*The Wayward Saint*), Anthony Perkins (*Tea and Sympathy*), Christopher Plummer (*The Dark is Light Enough*)

1955-56: Diane Cilento (*Tiger at the Gates*), Dick Davalos (*A View from the Bridge*), Anthony Franciosa (*A Hatful of Rain*), Andy Griffith (*No Time for Sergeants*), Laurence Harvey (*Island of Goats*), David Hedison (*A Month in the Country*), Earle Hyman (*Mister Johnson*), Susan Johnson (*The Most Happy Fella*), John Michael King (*My Fair Lady*), Jayne Mansfield (*Will Success Spoil Rock Hunter?*), Sarah Marshall (*The Ponder Heart*), Gaby Rodgers (*Mister Johnson*), Susan Strasberg (*The Diary of Anne Frank*), Fritz Weaver (*The Chalk Garden*)

1956-57: Peggy Cass (*Auntie Mame*), Sydney Chaplin (*Bells Are Ringing*), Sylvia Daneel (*The Tunnel of Love*), Bradford Dillman (*Long Day's Journey Into Night*), Peter Donat (*The First Gentleman*), George Grizzard (*The Happiest Millionaire*), Carol Lynley (*The Potting Shed*), Peter Palmer (*Li'l Abner*), Jason Robards (*Long Day's Journey Into Night*), Cliff Robertson (*Orpheus Descending*), Pippa Scott (*Child of Fortune*), Inga Swenson (*The First Gentleman*)

1957-58: Anne Bancroft (*Two for the Seesaw*), Warren Berlinger (*Blue Denim*), Colleen Dewhurst (*Children of Darkness*), Richard Easton (*The Country Wife*), Tim Everett (*The Dark at the Top of the Stairs*), Eddie Hodges (*The Music Man*), Joan Hovis (*Love Me Little*), Carol Lawrence (*West Side Story*), Jacqueline McKeever (*Oh, Captain!*), Wynne Miller (*Li'l Abner*), Robert Morse (*Say, Darling*), George C. Scott (*Richard III*)

1958-59: Lou Antonio (*The Buffalo Skinner*), Ina Balin (*A Majority of One*), Richard Cross (*Maria Golovin*), Tammy Grimes (*Look After Lulu*), Larry Hagman (*God and Kate Murphy*), Dolores Hart (*The Pleasure of His Company*), Roger Mollien (*French Theatre National Populaire*), France Nuyen (*The World of Suzie Wong*), Susan Oliver (*Patate*), Ben Piazza (*Kataki*), Paul Roebling (*A Desert Incident*), William Shatner (*The World of Suzie Wong*), Pat Suzuki (*Flower Drum Song*), Rip Torn (*Sweet Bird of Youth*)

1959-60: Warren Beatty (*A Loss of Roses*), Eileen Brennan (*Little Mary Sunshine*), Carol Burnett (*Once Upon a Mattress*), Patty Duke (*The Miracle Worker*), Jane Fonda (*There Was a Little Girl*), Anita Gillette (*Russell Patterson's*

The class of 1951: Joy Grunberg, James Daly, William Smithers, Martin Brooks, Jack Palance, Russell Nype, Eli Wallach, Cloris Leachman, Theatre World founder Daniel Blum, Maureen Stapleton, Isabelle Bigley, Marcia Van Dyke, Barbara Ashley, and Pat Crowley

Sketchbook), Elisa Loti (*Come Share My House*), Donald Madden (*Julius Caesar*), George Maharis (*The Zoo Story*), John McMartin (*Little Mary Sunshine*), Lauri Peters (*The Sound of Music*), Dick Van Dyke (*The Boys Against the Girls*)

1960-61: Joyce Bulifant (*Whisper to Me*), Dennis Cooney (*Every Other Evil*), Sandy Dennis (*Face of a Hero*), Nancy Dussault (*Do Re Mi*), Robert Goulet (*Camelot*), Joan Hackett (*Call Me By My Rightful Name*), June Harding (*Cry of the Raindrop*), Ron Husmann (*Tenderloin*), James MacArthur (*Invitation to a March*), Bruce Yarnell (*The Happiest Girl in the World*)

1961-62: Elizabeth Ashley (*Take Her, She's Mine*), Keith Baxter (*A Man for All Seasons*), Peter Fonda (*Blood, Sweat and Stanley Poole*), Don Galloway (*Bring Me a Warm Body*), Sean Garrison (*Half-Past Wednesday*), Barbara Harris (*Oh, Dad, Poor Dad, Mamma's Hung You in the Closet and I'm Feeling So Sad*), James Earl Jones (*Moon on a Rainbow Shawl*), Janet Margolin (*Daughter of Silence*), Karen Morrow (*Sing, Muse!*), Robert Redford (*Sunday in New York*), John Stride (*Romeo and Juliet*), Brenda Vaccaro (*Everybody Loves Opal*)

1962-63: Alan Arkin (*Enter Laughing*), Stuart Damon (*The Boys from Syracuse*), Melinda Dillon (*Who's Afraid of Virginia Woolf?*), Robert Drivas (*Mrs. Dally Has a Lover*), Bob Gentry (*Angels of Anadarko*), Dorothy Loudon (*Nowhere to Go But Up*), Brandon Maggart (*Put It in Writing*), Julienne Marie (*The Boys from Syracuse*), Liza Minnelli (*Best Foot Forward*), Estelle Parsons (*Mrs. Dally Has a Lover*), Diana Sands (*Tiger Tiger Burning Bright*), Swen Swenson (*Little Me*)

1963-64: Alan Alda (*Fair Game for Lover*), Gloria Bleezarde (*Never Live Over a Pretzel Factory*), Imelda De Martin (*The Amorous Flea*), Claude Giraud (*Phédre*), Ketty Lester (*Cabin in the Sky*), Barbara Loden (*After the Fall*), Lawrence Pressman (*Never Live Over a Pretzel Factory*), Gilbert Price (*Jerico-Jim Crow*), Philip Proctor (*The Amorous Flea*), John Tracy (*Telemachus Clay*), Jennifer West (*Dutchman*)

1964-65: Carolyn Coates (*The Trojan Women*), Joyce Jillson (*The Roar of the Greasepaint–The Smell of the Crowd*), Linda Lavin (*Wet Paint*), Luba Lisa (*I Had a Ball*), Michael O'Sullivan (*Tartuffe*), Joanna Pettet (*Poor Richard*), Beah Richards (*The Amen Corner*), Jaime Sanchez (*Conerico Was Here to Stay* and *The Toilet*), Victor Spinetti (*Oh, What a Lovely War*), Nicolas Surovy (*Helen*), Robert Walker (*I Knock at the Door* and *Pictures in the Hallway*), Clarence Williams III (*Slow Dancing on the Killing Ground*)

1965-66: Zoe Caldwell (*Slapstick Tragedy*), David Carradine (*The Royal Hunt of the Sun*), John Cullum (*On a Clear Day You Can See Forever*), John Davidson (*Oklahoma!*), Faye Dunaway (*Hogan's Ghost*), Gloria Foster (*Medea*), Robert Hooks (*Where's Daddy?* and *Day of Absence*), Jerry Lanning (*Mame*), Richard Mulligan (*Mating Dance* and *Hogan's Ghost*), April Shawhan (*3 Bags Full*), Sandra Smith (*Any Wednesday*), Leslie Ann Warren (*Drat! The Cat!*)

1966-67: Bonnie Bedelia (*My Sweet Charlie*), Richard Benjamin (*The Star-Spangled Girl*), Dustin Hoffman (*Eh?*), Terry Kiser (*Fortune and Men's Eyes*), Reva Rose (*You're A Good Man, Charlie Brown*), Robert Salvio (*Hamp*), Sheila Smith (*Mame*), Connie Stevens (*The Star-Spangled Girl*), Pamela Tiffin (*Dinner at Eight*), Leslie Uggams (*Hallelujah, Baby!*), Jon Voight (*That Summer–That Fall*), Christopher Walken (*The Rose Tattoo*)

1967-68: David Birney (*Summertree*), Pamela Burrell (*Arms and the Man*), Jordan Christopher (*Black Comedy*), Jack Crowder–a.k.a. Thalmus Rasulala (*Hello, Dolly!*), Sandy Duncan (*Ceremony of Innocence*), Julie Gregg (*The Happy Time*), Stephen Joyce (*Stephen D.*), Bernadette Peters (*George M*), Alice Playten (*Henry, Sweet Henry*), Michael Rupert (*The Happy Time*), Brenda Smiley (*Scuba Duba*), Russ Thacker (*Your Own Thing*)

1968-69: Jane Alexander (*The Great White Hope*), David Cryer (*Come Summer*), Blythe Danner (*The Miser*), Ed Evanko (*Canterbury Tales*), Ken Howard (*1776*), Lauren Jones (*Does a Tiger Wear a Necktie?*), Ron Leibman (*We Bombed in New Haven*), Marian Mercer (*Promises, Promises*), Jill O'Hara (*Promises, Promises*), Ron O'Neal (*No Place to Be Somebody*), Al Pacino (*Does a Tiger Wear a Necktie?*), Marlene Warfield (*The Great White Hope*)

Theatre World founder Daniel Blum presenting Susan Strasberg with her Theatre World Award for Outstanding Debut performance, 1956, for The Diary of Anne Frank

1969-70: Susan Browning (*Company*), Donny Burks (*Billy Noname*), Catherine Burns (*Dear Janet Rosenberg, Dear Mr. Kooning*), Len Cariou (*Henry V* and *Applause*), Bonnie Franklin (*Applause*), David Holliday (*Coco*), Katharine Houghton (*A Scent of Flowers*), Melba Moore (*Purlie*), David Rounds (*Child's Play*), Lewis J. Stadlen (*Minnie's Boys*), Kristoffer Tabori (*How Much, How Much*), Fredricka Weber (*The Last Sweet Days of Isaac*)

1970-71: Clifton Davis (*Do It Again*), Michael Douglas (*Pinkville*), Julie Garfield (*Uncle Vanya*), Martha Henry (*The Playboy of the Western World*, *Scenes From American Life*, and *Antigone*), James Naughton (*Long Days Journey Into Night*), Tricia O'Neil (*Two by Two*), Kipp Osborne (*Butterflies Are Free*), Roger Rathburn (*No, No, Nanette*), Ayn Ruymen (*The Gingerbread Lady*), Jennifer Salt (*Father's Day*), Joan Van Ark (*School for Wives*), Walter Willison (*Two by Two*)

1971-72: Jonelle Allen (*Two Gentlemen of Verona*), Maureen Anderman (*Moonchildren*), William Atherton (*Suggs*), Richard Backus (*Promenade, All!*), Adrienne Barbeau (*Grease*), Cara Duff-MacCormick (*Moonchildren*), Robert Foxworth (*The Crucible*), Elaine Joyce (*Sugar*), Jess Richards (*On The Town*), Ben Vereen (*Jesus Christ Superstar*), Beatrice Winde (*Ain't Supposed to Die a Natural Death*), James Woods (*Moonchildren*)

1972-73: D'Jamin Bartlett (*A Little Night Music*), Patricia Elliott (*A Little Night Music*), James Farentino (*A Streetcar Named Desire*), Brian Farrell (*The Last of Mrs. Lincoln*), Victor Garber (*Ghosts*), Kelly Garrett (*Mother Earth*), Mari Gorman (*The Hot l Baltimore*), Laurence Guittard (*A Little Night Music*), Trish Hawkins (*The Hot l Baltimore*), Monte Markham (*Irene*), John Rubinstein (*Pippin*), Jennifer Warren (*6 Rms Riv Vu*), Alexander H. Cohen (Special Award)

1973-74: Mark Baker (*Candide*), Maureen Brennan (*Candide*), Ralph Carter (*Raisin*), Thom Christopher (*Noel Coward in Two Keys*), John Driver (*Over Here*), Conchata Ferrell (*The Sea Horse*), Ernestine Jackson (*Raisin*), Michael Moriarty (*Find Your Way Home*), Joe Morton (*Raisin*), Ann Reinking (*Over Here*), Janie Sell (*Over Here*), Mary Woronov (*Boom Boom Room*), Sammy Cahn (Special Award)

1974-75: Peter Burnell (*In Praise of Love*), Zan Charisse (*Gypsy*), Lola Falana (*Dr. Jazz*), Peter Firth (*Equus*), Dorian Harewood (*Don't Call Back*), Joel Higgins (*Shenandoah*), Marcia McClain (*Where's Charley?*), Linda Miller (*Black Picture Show*), Marti Rolph (*Good News*), John Sheridan (*Gypsy*), Scott Stevensen (*Good News*), Donna Theodore (*Shenandoah*), Equity Library Theatre (Special Award)

1975-76: Danny Aiello (*Lamppost Reunion*), Christine Andreas (*My Fair Lady*), Dixie Carter (*Jesse and the Bandit Queen*), Tovah Feldshuh (*Yentl*), Chip Garnett (*Bubbling Brown Sugar*), Richard Kelton (*Who's Afraid of Virginia Woolf?*), Vivian Reed (*Bubbling Brown Sugar*), Charles Repole (*Very Good Eddie*), Virginia Seidel (*Very Good Eddie*), Daniel Seltzer (*Knock Knock*), John V. Shea (*Yentl*), Meryl Streep (*27 Wagons Full of Cotton*), The Cast of *A Chorus Line* (Special Award)

1976-77: Trazana Beverley (*for colored girls…*), Michael Cristofer (*The Cherry Orchard*), Joe Fields (*The Basic Training of Pavlo Hummel*), Joanna Gleason (*I Love My Wife*), Cecilia Hart (*Dirty Linen*), John Heard (*G.R. Point*), Gloria Hodes (*The Club*), Juliette Koka (*Piaf…A Remembrance*), Andrea McArdle (*Annie*), Ken Page (*Guys and Dolls*), Jonathan Pryce (*Comedians*), Chick Vennera (*Jockeys*), Eva LeGallienne (Special Award)

1977-78: Vasili Bogazianos (*P.S. Your Cat Is Dead*), Nell Carter (*Ain't Misbehavin'*), Carlin Glynn (*The Best Little Whorehouse in Texas*), Christopher Goutman (*The Promise*), William Hurt (*Ulysses in Traction, Lulu,* and *The Fifth of July*), Judy Kaye (*On the 20th Century*), Florence Lacy (*Hello, Dolly!*), Armelia McQueen (*Ain't Misbehavin'*), Gordana Rashovich (*Fefu and Her Friends*), Bo Rucker (*Native Son*), Richard Seer (*Da*), Colin Stinton (*The Water Engine*), Joseph Papp (Special Award)

1978-79: Philip Anglim (*The Elephant Man*), Lucie Arnaz (*They're Playing Our Song*), Gregory Hines (*Eubie!*), Ken Jennings (*Sweeney Todd*), Michael Jeter (*G.R. Point*), Laurie Kennedy (*Man and Superman*), Susan Kingsley (*Getting Out*), Christine Lahti (*The Woods*), Edward James Olmos (*Zoot Suit*), Kathleen Quinlan (*Taken in Marriage*), Sarah Rice (*Sweeney Todd*), Max Wright (*Once in a Lifetime*), Marshall W. Mason (Special Award)

1979-80: Maxwell Caulfield (*Class Enemy*), Leslie Denniston (*Happy New Year*), Boyd Gaines (*A Month in the Country*), Richard Gere (*Bent*), Harry Groener (*Oklahoma!*), Stephen James (*The 1940's Radio Hour*), Susan Kellermann (*Last Licks*), Dinah Manoff (*I Ought to Be in Pictures*), Lonny Price (*Class Enemy*), Marianne Tatum (*Barnum*), Anne Twomey (*Nuts*), Dianne Wiest (*The Art of Dining*), Mickey Rooney (*Sugar Babies*–Special Award)

1980-81: Brian Backer (*The Floating Light Bulb*), Lisa Banes (*Look Back in Anger*), Meg Bussert (*The Music Man*), Michael Allen Davis (*Broadway Follies*), Giancarlo Esposito (*Zooman and the Sign*), Daniel Gerroll (*Slab Boys*), Phyllis Hyman (*Sophisticated Ladies*), Cynthia Nixon (*The Philadelphia Story*), Amanda Plummer (*A Taste of Honey*), Adam Redfield (*A Life*), Wanda Richert (*42nd Street*), Rex Smith (*The Pirates of Penzance*), Elizabeth Taylor (*The Little Foxes*–Special Award)

1981-82: Karen Akers (*Nine*), Laurie Beechman (*Joseph and the Amazing Technicolor Dreamcoat*), Danny Glover (*Master Harold…and the Boys*), David Alan Grier (*The First*), Jennifer Holliday (*Dreamgirls*), Anthony Heald (*Misalliance*), Lizbeth Mackay (*Crimes of the Heart*), Peter MacNicol (*Crimes of the Heart*), Elizabeth McGovern (*My Sister in This House*), Ann Morrison (*Merrily We Roll Along*), Michael O'Keefe (*Mass Appeal*), James Widdoes (*Is There Life After High School?*), Manhattan Theatre Club (Special Award)

1982-83: Karen Allen (*Monday After the Miracle*), Suzanne Bertish (*Skirmishes*), Matthew Broderick (*Brighton Beach Memoirs*), Kate Burton (*Winners*), Joanne Camp (*Geniuses*), Harvey Fierstein (*Torch Song Trilogy*), Peter Gallagher (*A Doll's Life*), John Malkovich (*True West*), Anne Pitoniak (*'Night Mother*), James Russo (*Extremities*), Brian Tarantina (*Angels Fall*), Linda Thorson (*Streaming*), Natalia Makarova (*On Your Toes*–Special Award)

1983-84: Martine Allard (*The Tap Dance Kid*), Joan Allen (*And a Nightingale Sang*), Kathy Whitton Baker (*Fool For Love*), Mark Capri (*On Approval*), Laura

Dean (*Doonesbury*), Stephen Geoffreys (*The Human Comedy*), Todd Graff (*Baby*), Glenne Headly (*The Philanthropist*), J.J. Johnston (*American Buffalo*), Bonnie Koloc (*The Human Comedy*), Calvin Levels (*Open Admissions*), Robert Westenberg (*Zorba*), Ron Moody (*Oliver!*–Special Award)

1984-85: Kevin Anderson (*Orphans*), Richard Chaves (*Tracers*), Patti Cohenour (*La Boheme* and *Big River*), Charles S. Dutton (*Ma Rainey's Black Bottom*), Nancy Giles (*Mayor*), Whoopi Goldberg (*Whoopi Goldberg*), Leilani Jones (*Grind*), John Mahoney (*Orphans*), Laurie Metcalf (*Balm in Gilead*), Barry Miller (*Biloxi Blues*), John Turturro (*Danny and the Deep Blue Sea*), Amelia White (*The Accrington Pals*), Lucille Lortel (Special Award)

1985-86: Suzy Amis (*Fresh Horses*), Alec Baldwin (*Loot*), Aled Davies (*Orchards*), Faye Grant (*Singin' in the Rain*), Julie Hagerty (*The House of Blue Leaves*), Ed Harris (*Precious Sons*), Mark Jacoby (*Sweet Charity*), Donna Kane (*Dames at Sea*), Cleo Laine (*The Mystery of Edwin Drood*), Howard McGillin (*The Mystery of Edwin Drood*), Marisa Tomei (*Daughters*), Joe Urla (*Principia Scriptoriae*), Ensemble Studio Theatre (Special Award)

1986-87: Annette Bening (*Coastal Disturbances*), Timothy Daly (*Coastal Disturbances*), Lindsay Duncan (*Les Liaisons Dangereuses*), Frank Ferrante (*Groucho: A Life in Revue*), Robert Lindsay (*Me and My Girl*), Amy Madigan (*The Lucky Spot*), Michael Maguire (*Les Misérables*), Demi Moore (*The Early Girl*), Molly Ringwald (*Lily Dale*), Frances Ruffelle (*Les Misérables*), Courtney B. Vance (*Fences*), Colm Wilkinson (*Les Misérables*), Robert DeNiro (Special Award)

1987-88: Yvonne Bryceland (*The Road to Mecca*), Philip Casnoff (*Chess*), Danielle Ferland (*Into the Woods*), Melissa Gilbert (*A Shayna Maidel*), Linda Hart (*Anything Goes*), Linzi Hateley (*Carrie*), Brian Kerwin (*Emily*), Brian Mitchell (*Mail*), Mary Murfitt (*Oil City Symphony*), Aidan Quinn *A Streetcar Named Desire*), Eric Roberts (*Burn This*), B.D. Wong (*M. Butterfly*), Tisa Chang and Martin E. Segal (Special Awards)

1988-89: Dylan Baker (*Eastern Standard*), Joan Cusack (*Road and Brilliant Traces*), Loren Dean (*Amulets Against the Dragon Forces*), Peter Frechette (*Eastern Standard*), Sally Mayes (*Welcome to the Club*), Sharon McNight (*Starmites*), Jennie Moreau (*Eleemosynary*), Paul Provenza (*Only Kidding*), Kyra Sedgwick (*Ah, Wilderness!*), Howard Spiegel (*Only Kidding*), Eric Stoltz (*Our Town*), Joanne Whalley-Kilmer (*What the Butler Saw*); Pauline Collins of *Shirley Valentine* (Special Award), Mikhail Baryshnikov (Special Award)

1989-90: Denise Burse (*Ground People*), Erma Campbell (*Ground People*), Rocky Carroll (*The Piano Lesson*), Megan Gallagher (*A Few Good Men*), Tommy Hollis (*The Piano Lesson*), Robert Lambert (*Gypsy*), Kathleen Rowe McAllen (*Aspects of Love*), Michael McKean (*Accomplice*), Crista Moore (*Gypsy*), Mary-Louise Parker (*Prelude to a Kiss*), Daniel von Bargen (*Mastergate*), Jason Workman (*Jason Workman*), Stewart Granger (*The Circle*–Special Award), Kathleen Turner (*Cat on a Hot Tin Roof*–Special Award)

1990-91: Jane Adams (*I Hate Hamlet*), Gillian Anderson (*Absent Friends*), Adam Arkin (*I Hate Hamlet*), Brenda Blethyn (*Absent Friends*), Marcus Chong (*Stand-up Tragedy*), Paul Hipp (*Buddy*), LaChanze (*Once on This Island*), Kenny Neal (*Mule Bone*), Kevin Ramsey (*Oh, Kay!*), Francis Ruivivar (*Shogun*), Lea Salonga (*Miss Saigon*), Chandra Wilson (*The Good Times Are Killing Me*); Tracey Ullman (*The Big Love* and *Taming of the Shrew*), Ellen Stewart (Special Award)

1991-92: Talia Balsam (*Jake's Women*), Lindsay Crouse (*The Homecoming*), Griffin Dunne (*Search and Destroy*), Laurence Fishburne (*Two Trains Running*), Mel Harris (*Empty Hearts*), Jonathan Kaplan (*Falsettos* and *Rags*), Jessica Lange (*A Streetcar Named Desire*), Laura Linney (*Sight Unseen*), Spiro Malas (*The Most Happy Fella*), Mark Rosenthal (*Marvin's Room*), Helen Shaver (*Jake's Women*), Al White (*Two Trains Running*), The Cast of *Dancing at Lughnasa* (Special Award), Plays for Living (Special Award)

1992-93: Brent Carver (*Kiss of the Spider Woman*), Michael Cerveris (*The Who's Tommy*), Marcia Gay Harden (*Angels in America: Millennium Approaches*), Stephanie Lawrence (*Blood Brothers*), Andrea Martin (*My Favorite Year*), Liam

Neeson (*Anna Christie*), Stephen Rea (*Someone Who'll Watch Over Me*), Natasha Richardson (*Anna Christie*), Martin Short (*The Goodbye Girl*), Dina Spybey (*Five Women Wearing the Same Dress*), Stephen Spinella (*Angels in America: Millennium Approaches*), Jennifer Tilly (*One Shoe Off*), John Leguizamo and Rosetta LeNoire (Special Awards)

1993-94: Marcus D'Amico (*An Inspector Calls*), Jarrod Emick (*Damn Yankees*), Arabella Field (*Snowing at Delphi* and *4 Dogs and a Bone*), Aden Gillett (*An Inspector Calls*), Sherry Glaser (*Family Secrets*), Michael Hayden (*Carousel*), Margaret Illman (*The Red Shoes*), Audra McDonald (*Carousel*), Burke Moses (*Beauty and the Beast*), Anna Deavere Smith (*Twilight: Los Angeles, 1992*), Jere Shea (*Passion*), Harriet Walter (*3Birds Alighting on a Field*)

1994-95: Gretha Boston (*Show Boat*), Billy Crudup (*Arcadia*), Ralph Fiennes (*Hamlet*), Beverly D'Angelo (*Simpatico*), Calista Flockhart (*The Glass Menagerie*), Kevin Kilner (*The Glass Menagerie*), Anthony LaPaglia (*The Rose Tattoo*), Julie Johnson (*Das Barbecü*), Helen Mirren (*A Month in the Country*), Jude Law (*Indiscretions*), Rufus Sewell (*Translations*), Vanessa Williams (*Kiss of the Spider Woman*), Brooke Shields (Special Award)

1995-96: Jordan Baker (*Suddenly Last Summer*), Joohee Choi (*The King and I*), Karen Kay Cody (*Master Class*), Viola Davis (*Seven Guitars*), Kate Forbes (*The School for Scandal*), Michael McGrath (*Swinging on a Star*), Alfred Molina (*Molly Sweeney*), Timothy Olyphant (*The Monogamist*), Adam Pascal (*Rent*), Lou Diamond Phillips (*The King and I*), Daphne Rubin-Vega (*Rent*), Brett Tabisel (*Big*), The Cast of *An Ideal Husband* (Special Award)

1996-97: Terry Beaver (*The Last Night of Ballyhoo*), Helen Carey (*London Assurance*), Kristin Chenoweth (*Steel Pier*), Jason Danieley (*Candide*), Linda Eder (*Jekyll & Hyde*), Allison Janney (*Present Laughter*), Daniel McDonald (*Steel Pier*), Janet McTeer (*A Doll's House*), Mark Ruffalo (*This Is Our Youth*), Fiona Shaw (*The Waste Land*), Antony Sher (*Stanley*), Alan Tudyk (*Bunny Bunny*), The Cast of *Skylight* (Special Award)

1997-98: Max Casella (*The Lion King*), Margaret Colin (*Jackie*), Ruaidhri Conroy (*The Cripple of Inishmaan*), Alan Cumming (*Cabaret*), Lea Delaria (*On the Town*), Edie Falco (*Side Man*), Enid Graham (*Honour*), Anna Kendrick (*High Society*), Ednita Nazario (*The Capeman*), Douglas Sills (*The Scarlet Pimpernel*), Steven Sutcliffe (*Ragtime*), Sam Trammel (*Ah, Wilderness!*), Eddie Izzard (Special Award), The Cast of *The Beauty Queen of Leenane* (Special Award)

John Cullum, Reva Rose, Russ Thacker at the 1968 party

1998-99: Jillian Armenante (*The Cider House Rules*), James Black (*Not About Nightingales*), Brendan Coyle (*The Weir*), Anna Friel (*Closer*), Rupert Graves (*Closer*), Lynda Gravátt (*The Old Settler*), Nicole Kidman (*The Blue Room*), Ciáran Hinds (*Closer*), Ute Lemper (*Chicago*), Clarke Peters (*The Iceman Cometh*), Toby Stephens (*Ring Round the Moon*), Sandra Oh (*Stop Kiss*), Jerry Herman (Special Award)

1999-2000: Craig Bierko (*The Music Man*), Everett Bradley (*Swing!*), Gabriel Byrne (*A Moon for the Misbegotten*), Ann Hampton Callaway (*Swing!*), Toni Collette (*The Wild Party*), Henry Czerny (*Arms and the Man*), Stephen Dillane (*The Real Thing*), Jennifer Ehle (*The Real Thing*), Philip Seymour Hoffman (*True West*), Hayley Mills (*Suite in Two Keys*), Cigdem Onat (*The Time of the Cuckoo*), Claudia Shear (*Dirty Blonde*), Barry Humphries (*Dame Edna: The Royal Tour*– Special Award)

2000-2001: Juliette Binoche (*Betrayal*), Macaulay Culkin (*Madame Melville*), Janie Dee (*Comic Potential*), Raúl Esparza (*The Rocky Horror Show*), Kathleen Freeman (*The Full Monty*), Deven May (*Bat Boy*), Reba McEntire (*Annie Get Your Gun*), Chris Noth (*The Best Man*), Joshua Park (*The Adventures of Tom Sawyer*), Rosie Perez (*References to Salvador Dali Make Me Hot*), Joely Richardson (*Madame Melville*), John Ritter (*The Dinner Party*), The Cast of *Stones in His Pocket*– Seán Campion & Conleth Hill (Special Awards)

2001-2002: Justin Bohon (*Oklahoma!*), Simon Callow (*The Mystery of Charles Dickens*), Mos Def (*Topdog/Underdog*), Emma Fielding (*Private Lives*), Adam Godley (*Private Lives*), Martin Jarvis (*By Jeeves*), Spencer Kayden (*Urinetown*), Gretchen Mol (*The Shape of Things*), Anna Paquin (*The Glory of Living*), Louise Pitre (*Mamma Mia!*), David Warner (*Major Barbara*), Rachel Weisz (*The Shape of Things*)

2002-2003: Antonio Banderas (*Nine*), Tammy Blanchard (*Gypsy*), Thomas Jefferson Byrd (*Ma Rainey's Black Bottom*), Jonathan Cake (*Medea*), Victoria Hamilton (*A Day in the Death of Joe Egg*), Clare Higgins (*Vincent in Brixton*), Jackie Hoffman (*Hairspray*), Mary Stuart Masterson (*Nine*), John Selya (*Movin' Out*), Daniel Sunjata (*Take Me Out*), Jochum ten Haaf (*Vincent in Brixton*), Marissa Jaret Winokur (*Hairspray*), Peter Filichia, Ben Hodges (Special Awards)

2003-2004: Shannon Cochran (*Bug*), Stephanie D'Abruzzo (*Avenue Q*), Mitchel David Federan (*The Boy From Oz*), Alexander Gemignani (*Assassins*), Hugh Jackman (*The Boy From Oz*), Isabel Keating (*The Boy From Oz*), Sanaa Lathan (*A Raisin in the Sun*), Jefferson Mays (*I Am My Own Wife*), Euan Morton (*Taboo*), Anika Noni Rose (*Caroline, or Change*), John Tartaglia (*Avenue Q*), Jennifer Westfeldt (*Wonderful Town*), Sarah Jones (*Bridge and Tunnel*–Special Award)

2004-2005: Christina Applegate (*Sweet Charity*), Ashlie Atkinson (*Fat Pig*), Hank Azaria (*Spamalot*), Gordon Clapp (*Glengarry Glen Ross*), Conor Donovan (*Privilege*), Dan Fogler (*The 25th Annual Putnam County Spelling Bee*), Heather Goldenhersh (*Doubt*), Carla Gugino (*After the Fall*), Jenn Harris (*Modern Orthodox*), Cheyenne Jackson (*All Shook Up*), Celia Keenan-Bolger (*The 25th Annual Putnam County Spelling Bee*), Tyler Maynard (*Altar Boyz*)

2005-2006: Harry Connick Jr. (*The Pajama Game*), Felicia P. Fields (*The Color Purple*), Maria Friedman (*The Woman in White*), Richard Griffiths (*The History Boys*), Mamie Gummer (*Mr. Marmalade*), Jayne Houdyshell (*Well*), Bob Martin (*The Drowsy Chaperone*), Ian McDiarmid (*Faith Healer*), Nellie McKay (*The Threepenny Opera*), David Wilmot (*The Lieutenant of Inishmore*), Elisabeth Withers-Mendes (*The Color Purple*), John Lloyd Young (*Jersey Boys*)

2006-2007: Eve Best (*A Moon for the Misbegotten*), Mary Birdsong (*Martin Short: Fame Becomes Me*), Erin Davie (*Grey Gardens*), Xanthe Elbrick (*Coram Boy*), Fantasia (*The Color Purple*), Johnny Galecki (*The Little Dog Laughed*), Jonathan Groff (*Spring Awakening*), Gavin Lee (*Mary Poppins*), Lin-Manuel Miranda (*In the Heights*), Bill Nighy (*The Vertical Hour*), Stark Sands (*Journey's End*), Nilaja Sun (*No Child…*), The Actors Fund (Special Award)

2007-2008: de'Adre Aziza (*Passing Strange*), Cassie Beck (*The Drunken City*), Daniel Breaker (*Passing Strange*), Ben Daniels (*Les Liaisons Dangereuses*),

Deanna Dunagan (*August: Osage County*), Hoon Lee (*Yellow Face*), Alli Mauzey (*Cry-Baby*), Jenna Russell (*Sunday in the Park with George*), Mark Rylance (*Boeing-Boeing*), Loretta Ables Sayre (*South Pacific*), Jimmi Simpson (*The Farnsworth Invention*), Paulo Szot (*South Pacific*)

2008-2009: David Alvarez (*Billy Elliot The Musical*), Chad C. Coleman (*Joe Turner's Come and Gone*), Jennifer Grace (*Our Town*), Josh Grisetti (*Enter Laughing The Musical*), Haydn Gwynne *Billy Elliot The Musical*), Colin Hanks (*33 Variations*), Marin Ireland (*reasons to be pretty*), Trent Kowalik (*Billy Elliot The Musical*), Kiril Kulish (*Billy Elliot The Musical*), Susan Louise O'Connor (*Blithe Spirit*), Condola Rashad (*Ruined*), Geoffrey Rush (*Exit the King*), Josefina Scaglione (*West Side Story*), Wesley Taylor (*Rock of Ages*); The Cast of *The Norman Conquests* (Special Award)

2009-2010: Nina Arianda (*Venus in Fur*), Chris Chalk (*Fences*), Bill Heck (*The Orphans' Home Cycle*), Jon Michael Hill (*Superior Donuts*), Scarlett Johansson (*A View from the Bridge*), Keira Keeley (*The Glass Menagerie*), Sahr Ngaujah (*Fela!*), Eddie Redmayne (*Red*), Andrea Riseborough (*The Pride*), Heidi Schreck (*Circle Mirror Transformation*), Stephanie Umoh (*Ragtime*), Michael Urie (*The Temperamentals*); Dorothy Loudon Award: Bobby Steggert (*Yank!* & *Ragtime*)

2010-2011: Ellen Barkin (*The Normal Heart*), Desmin Borges (*The Elaborate Entrance of Chad Deity*), Halley Feiffer (*The House of Blue Leaves*), Grace Gummer (*Arcadia*), Rose Hemingway (*How to Succeed in Business Without Really Trying*), John Larroquette (*How to Succeed in Business Without Really Trying*), Heather Lind (*The Merchant of Venice*), Patina Miller (*Sister Act*), Arian Moayed (*Bengel Tiger at the Baghdad Zoo*), Jim Parsons (*The Normal Heart*), Zachary Quinto (*Angels in America: A Gay Fantasia on National Themes*), Tony Sheldon (*Priscilla Queen of the Desert*); Dorothy Loudon Award: Seth Numrich (*War Horse*); Lunt-Fontanne Award for Ensemble Excellence: The Cast of *The Moherf**ker with the Hat*

Bernadette Peters and Robert Westenberg at the 1984 ceremony

Jason Danieley and Carol Channing at the 1997 ceremony

Mamie Gummer at the 2006 ceremony

Patricia Elliott, Lawrence Guittard, D'Jamin Bartlett, 1973 winners from A Little Night Music

MAJOR NEW YORK THEATRICAL AWARDS

American Theatre Wing's Antoinette Perry "Tony" Awards

Sunday, June 10, 2012 at the Beacon Theatre; 66th annual; Host: Neil Patrick Harris. Presented for distinguished achievement in the Broadway theatre by The American Theatre Wing (Theodore S. Chapin, Chairman; Howard Sherman, Executive Director) and The Broadway League (Paul Libin, Chairman; Charlotte St. Martin, Executive Director); Tony Awards Production General Managers, Alan Wasser and Allen Williams; Executive Producers, Ricky Kirshner and Glenn Weiss/ White Cherry Entertainment; Production Director, Glen Weiss; 2011–2012 Tony Awards Nominating Committee (appointed by the Tony Awards Administration Committee): John Arnone (Scenic Designer), Victoria Bailey (Executive Director, Theatre Development Fund), David Caddick (Music Supervisor), Kathleen Chalfant (Actor), Hope Clarke (Stage Director/Choreographer/Actor), Douglas J. Cohen (Composer/Lyricist/Playwright), André De Shields (Actor), Edgar Dobie (Managing Director, Arena Stage Washington, DC), Gordon Edelstein (Director/ Artistic Director of Long Wharf Theatre), Beverly Emmons (Lighting Designer), Bert Fink (SVP/Communications of Rodgers & Hammerstein), Boyd Gaines (Actor), Michael Greif (Director), Kathryn Grody (Actor/Writer), Paulette Haupt (Director of the Music Theatre Conference at The O'Neill Center), Susan Hilferty (Costume Designer), Mark Hollmann (Composer/Lyricist), Abe Jacob (Sound Designer), Robert Kamlot (Retired General Manager), Anne Kauffman (Director), Moisés Kaufman (Director/Playwright/Artistic Director, Tectonic Theater), Pia Lindström (Former Reporter/Theatre Critic), Todd London (Artistic Director, New Dramatists), Pam MacKinnon (Director), Donna McKechnie (Actor/Choreographer), Susan Rice (Playwright/Screenwriter), Mervyn Rothstein (Retired Writer & Editor *The New York Times*), Susan H. Schulman (Director), Tobie S. Stein (Director, Graduate Program in Performing Arts and Management, Brooklyn College), Rosemarie Tichler (Theatre Executive, Educator/Casting Director), Robert Viagas (Playbill Program Director/Editor), Kevin Wade (Playwright/Screenwriter), Tony Walton (Scenic and Costume Designer), Carol Wasser (Retired AEA Offical/ Company and Stage Manager), Chay Yew (Playwright/Director).

Best Play: *Clybourne Park* by Bruce Norris, Produced Jujamcyn Theaters, Jane Bergère, Roger Berlind/Quintet Productions, Eric Falkenstein/Dan Frishwasser, Ruth Hendel/Harris Karma Productions, JTG Theatricals, Daryl Roth, Jon B. Platt, Center Theatre Group, Lincoln Center Theater, Playwrights Horizons

Nominees: *Other Desert Cities* by Jon Robin Baitz, Produced by Lincoln Center Theater, André Bishop, Bernard Gersten, Bob Boyett; *Peter and the Starcatcher* by Rick Elice, Produced by Nancy Nagel Gibbs, Greg Schaffert, Eva Price, Tom Smedes, Disney Theatrical Productions, Suzan & Ken Wirth/DeBartolo Miggs, Catherine Schreiber/Daveed Frazier & Mark Thompson, Jack Lane, Jane Dubin, Allan S. Gordon/Adam S. Gordon, Baer & Casserly/Nathan Vernon, Rich Affannato/ Peter Stern, Brunish & Trinchero/Laura Little Productions, Larry Hirschhorn/ Hummel & Greene, Jamie deRoy & Probo Prods./Radio Mouse Entertainment, Hugh Hysell/Freedberg & Dale, New York Theatre Workshop; *Venus in Fur* by David Ives, Produced by Manhattan Theatre Club, Lynne Meadow, Barry Grove, Jon B. Platt, Scott Landis, Classic Stage Company

Best Musical: *Once* Produced by Barbara Broccoli, John N. Hart, Jr., Patrick Milling Smith, Frederick Zollo, Brian Carmody, Michael G. Wilson, Orin Wolf, The Shubert Organization, Robert Cole, New York Theatre Workshop

Nominees: *Leap of Faith* Produced by Michael Manheim, James D. Stern, Douglas L. Meyer, Marc Routh, Richard Frankel, Tom Viertel, Steven Baruch, Annette Niemtzow, Daryl Roth, Robert G. Bartner, Steven and Shanna Silva, Endgame Entertainment, Patricia Monaco, Debi Coleman, Dancap Productions, Inc., Steve Kaplan, Relativity Media, LLC, Rich/Caudwell, Center Theatre Group, Michael Palitz, Richard J. Stern, Melissa Pinsly/Celine Rosenthal, Independent Presenters Network, Diana Buckhantz, Pamela Cooper, Vera Guerin, Leading Investment Co., Ltd., Christina Papagjika, Victor Syrmis, Semlitz/Glaser Productions, Jujamcyn Theaters; *Newsies* Produced by Disney Theatrical Productions, Thomas Schumacher; *Nice Work If You Can Get It* Produced by Scott Landis, Roger Berlind, Sonia Friedman Productions, Roy Furman, Standing CO Vation, Candy Spelling, Freddy DeMann, Ronald Frankel, Harold Newman, Jon B. Platt, Raise the Roof 8, Takonkiet Viravan, William Berlind/Ed Burke, Carole L. Haber/Susan Carusi, Buddy and Barbara Freitag/Sanford Robertson, Jim Herbert/ Under the Wire, Emanuel Azenberg, The Shubert Organization

Best Book of a Musical: *Once* by Enda Walsh

Nominees: *Lysistrata Jones* by Douglas Carter Beane; *Newsies* by Harvey Fierstein; *Nice Work If You Can Get It* by Joe DiPietro

Best Original Score (music and/or lyrics) Written for the Theatre: *Newsies* Music by Alan Menken, Lyrics by Jack Feldman

Nominees: *Bonnie & Clyde* Music by Frank Wildhorn, Lyrics by Don Black; *One Man, Two Guvnors* Music and Lyrics by Grant Olding; *Peter and the Starcatcher* Music by Wayne Barker, Lyrics by Rick Elice

Best Revival of a Play: *Death of a Salesman* by Arthur Miller, Produced by Scott Rudin, Stuart Thompson, Jon B. Platt, Columbia Pictures, Jean Doumanian, Merritt Forrest Baer, Roger Berlind, Scott M. Delman, Sonia Friedman Productions, Ruth Hendel, Carl Moellenberg, Scott & Brian Zeilinger, Eli Bush

Nominees: *Gore Vidal's The Best Man*, Produced by Jeffrey Richards, Jerry Frankel, INFINITY Stages, Universal Pictures Stage Productions, Barbara Manocherian/ Michael Palitz, Kathleen K. Johnson, Andy Sandberg, Ken Mahoney/ The Broadway Consortium, Fifty Church Street Productions, Larry Hirschhorn/ Bennu Productions, Patty Baker, Paul Boskind and Martian Entertainment, Wendy Federman, Mark S. Golub & David S. Golub, Cricket Hooper Jiranek, Stewart F. Lane & Bonnie Comley, Carl Moellenberg, Harold Thau, Will Trice; *Master Class* by Terrence McNally, Produced by Manhattan Theatre Club, Lynne Meadow, Barry Grove, Max Cooper, Maberry Theatricals, Marks-Moore-Turnbull Group, Ted Snowdon; *Wit* by Margaret Edson, Produced by Manhattan Theatre Club, Lynne Meadow, Barry Grove

Best Revival of a Musical: The Gershwins' *Porgy and Bess* Produced by Jeffrey Richards, Jerry Frankel, Rebecca Gold, Howard Kagan, Cheryl Wiesenfeld/ Brunish Trinchero/Lucio Simons TBC, Joseph & Matthew Deitch, Mark S. Golub & David S. Golub, Terry Schnuck, Freitag Productions/Koenigsberg Filerman, The Leonore S. Gershwin 1987 Trust, Universal Pictures Stage Productions, Ken Mahoney, Judith Resnick, Tulchin/Bartner/ATG, Paper Boy Productions, Christopher Hart, Alden Badway, Broadway Across America, Irene Gandy, Will Trice, American Repertory Theater

Nominees: *Evita* Produced by Hal Luftig, Scott Sanders Productions, Roy Furman, Yasuhiro Kawana, Allan S. Gordon/Adam S. Gordon, James L. Nederlander, Terry Allen Kramer, Gutterman Fuld Chernoff/Pittsburgh CLO, Thousand Stars Productions, Adam Blanshay, Adam Zotovich, Robert Ahrens, Stephanie P. McClelland, Carole L. Haber, Richardo Hornos, Carol Fineman, Brian Smith, Warren & Jâlé Trepp; *Follies* Produced by The John F. Kennedy Center for the Performing Arts, David M. Rubenstein, Michael M. Kaiser, Max A. Woodward, Nederlander Presentations, Inc., Adrienne Arsht, HRH Foundation, Allan Williams; *Jesus Christ Superstar* Produced by The Dodgers and The Really Useful Group, Latitude Link, Tamara and Kevin Kinsella, Pelican Group, Waxman-Dokton, Joe Corcoran, Detsky/Sokolowski/Kassie, Florin-Blanshay-Fan/Broadway Across America, Rich/Caudwell, Shin/Coleman, TheatreDreams North America, LLC, Stratford Shakespeare Festival

Best Performance by a Leading Actor in a Play: James Corden, *One Man, Two Guvnors*

Nominees: Philip Seymour Hoffman, Arthur Miller's *Death of a Salesman*; James Earl Jones, Gore Vidal's *The Best Man*; Frank Langella, *Man and Boy*; John Lithgow, *The Columnist*

Best Performance by a Leading Actress in a Play: Nina Arianda, *Venus in Fur*

Nominees: Tracie Bennett, *End of the Rainbow*; Stockard Channing, *Other Desert Cities*; Linda Lavin, *The Lyons*; Cynthia Nixon, *Wit*

Best Performance by a Leading Actor in a Musical: Steve Kazee, *Once*

Nominees: Danny Burstein, *Follies*; Jeremy Jordan, *Newsies*; Norm Lewis, The Gershwins' *Porgy and Bess*; Ron Raines, *Follies*

Best Performance by a Leading Actress in a Musical: Audra McDonald, The Gershwins' *Porgy and Bess*

Nominees: Jan Maxwell, *Follies*; Cristin Milioti, *Once*; Kelli O'Hara, *Nice Work If You Can Get It*; Laura Osnes, *Bonnie & Clyde*

Best Performance by a Featured Actor in a Play: Christian Borle, *Peter and the Starcatcher*

Nominees: Michael Cumpsty, *End of the Rainbow*; Tom Edden, *One Man, Two Guvnors*; Andrew Garfield, Arthur Miller's *Death of a Salesman*; Jeremy Shamos, *Clybourne Park*

Best Performance by a Featured Actress in a Play: Judith Light, *Other Desert Cities*

Nominees: Linda Emond, Arthur Miller's *Death of a Salesman*; Spencer Kayden, *Don't Dress for Dinner*; Celia Keenan-Bolger, *Peter and the Starcatcher*; Condola Rashad, *Stick Fly*

Best Performance by a Featured Actor in a Musical: Michael McGrath, *Nice Work If You Can Get It*

Nominees: Phillip Boykin, The Gershwins' *Porgy and Bess*; Michael Cerveris, *Evita*; David Alan Grier, The Gershwins' *Porgy and Bess*; Josh Young, *Jesus Christ Superstar*

Best Performance by a Featured Actress in a Musical: Judy Kaye, *Nice Work If You Can Get It*

Nominees: Elizabeth A. Davis, *Once*; Jayne Houdyshell, *Follies*; Jessie Mueller, *On A Clear Day You Can See Forever*; Da'Vine Joy Randolph, *Ghost the Musical*

Best Direction of a Play: Mike Nichols, Arthur Miller's *Death of a Salesman*

Nominees: Nicholas Hytner, *One Man, Two Guvnors*; Pam MacKinnon, *Clybourne Park*; Roger Rees and Alex Timbers, *Peter and the Starcatcher*

Best Direction of a Musical: John Tiffany, *Once*

Nominees: Jeff Calhoun, *Newsies*; Kathleen Marshall, *Nice Work If You Can Get It*; Diane Paulus, The Gershwins' *Porgy and Bess*

Best Scenic Design of a Play: Donyale Werle, *Peter and the Starcatcher*

Nominees: John Lee Beatty, *Other Desert Cities*; Daniel Ostling, *Clybourne Park*; Mark Thompson, *One Man, Two Guvnors*

Best Scenic Design of a Musical: Bob Crowley, *Once*

Nominees: Rob Howell and Jon Driscoll, *Ghost the Musical*; Tobin Ost and Sven Ortel, *Newsies*; George Tsypin, *Spider-Man Turn Off The Dark*

Best Costume Design of a Play: Paloma Young, *Peter and the Starcatcher*

Nominees: William Ivey Long, *Don't Dress for Dinner*; Paul Tazewell, *A Streetcar Named Desire*; Mark Thompson, *One Man, Two Guvnors*

Best Costume Design of a Musical: Gregg Barnes, *Follies*

Nominees: ESosa, The Gershwins' *Porgy and Bess*; Eiko Ishioka, *Spider-Man Turn Off The Dark*; Martin Pakledinaz, *Nice Work If You Can Get It*

Best Lighting Design of a Play: Jeff Croiter, *Peter and the Starcatcher*

Nominees: Peter Kaczorowski, *The Road to Mecca*; Brian MacDevitt, Arthur Miller's *Death of a Salesman*; Kenneth Posner, *Other Desert Cities*

Best Lighting Design of a Musical: Natasha Katz, *Once*

Nominees: Christopher Akerlind, The Gershwins' *Porgy and Bess*; Natasha Katz, *Follies*; Hugh Vanstone, *Ghost the Musical*

Best Sound Design of a Play: Darron L. West, *Peter and the Starcatcher*

Nominees: Paul Arditti, *One Man, Two Guvnors*; Scott Lehrer, Arthur Miller's *Death of a Salesman*; Gareth Owen, *End of the Rainbow*

Best Sound Design of a Musical: Clive Goodwin, *Once*

Nominees: Acme Sound Partners, The Gershwins' *Porgy and Bess*; Kai Harada, *Follies*; Brian Ronan, *Nice Work If You Can Get It*

Best Choreography: Christopher Gattelli, *Newsies*

Nominees: Rob Ashford, *Evita*; Steven Hoggett, *Once*; Kathleen Marshall, *Nice Work If You Can Get It*

Best Orchestrations: Martin Lowe, *Once*

Nominees: William David Brohn and Christopher Jahnke, The Gershwins' *Porgy and Bess*; Bill Elliott, *Nice Work If You Can Get It*; Danny Troob, *Newsies*

Special Tony Award for Lifetime Achievement in the Theatre: Emanuel Azenberg

Regional Theatre Tony Award: Shakespeare Theatre Company, Washington, D.C.

Isabelle Stevenson Award for Service: Bernadette Peters

Special Tony Awards: Actors' Equity Association; Hugh Jackman

Tony Honor for Excellence in the Theatre: Freddie Gershon; Arthur Siccardi; TDF Open Doors

PREVIOUS TONY AWARD-WINNING PRODUCTIONS Awards listed are Best Play followed by Best Musical and, as awards for Best Revival and the subcategories of Best Revival of a Play and Best Revival of a Musical were instituted, they are listed respectively. **1947:** No award given for musical or play **1948:** *Mister Roberts* (play) **1949:** *Death of a Salesman*; *Kiss Me, Kate* (musical) **1950:** *The Cocktail Party*; *South Pacific* **1951:** *The Rose Tattoo*; *Guys and Dolls* **1952:** *The Fourposter*; *The King and I* **1953:** *The Crucible*; *Wonderful Town* **1954:** *The Teahouse of the August Moon*; *Kismet* **1955:** *The Desperate Hours*; *The Pajama Game* **1956:** *The Diary of Anne Frank*; *Damn Yankees* **1957:** *Long Day's Journey into Night*; *My Fair Lady* **1958:** *Sunrise at Campobello*; *The Music Man* **1959:** *J.B.*; *Redhead* **1960:** *The Miracle Worker*, *Fiorello!* & *The Sound of Music* (tie) **1961:** *Becket*; *Bye Bye Birdie* **1962:** *A Man for All Seasons*; *How to Succeed in Business Without Really Trying* **1963:** *Who's Afraid of Virginia Woolf?*, *A Funny Thing Happened on the Way to the Forum* **1964:** *Luther*, *Hello, Dolly!* **1965:** *The Subject Was Roses*; *Fiddler on the Roof* **1966:** *The Persecution and Assassination of Marat as Performed by the Inmates of the Asylum of Charenton Under the Direction of the Marquis de Sade*; *Man of La Mancha* **1967:** *The Homecoming*; *Cabaret* **1968:** *Rosencrantz and Guildenstern Are Dead*; *Hallelujah Baby!* **1969:** *The Great White Hope*; *1776* **1970:** *Borstal Boy*, *Applause* **1971:** *Sleuth*; *Company* **1972:** *Sticks and Bones*; *Two Gentlemen of Verona* **1973:** *That Championship Season*; *A Little Night Music* **1974:** *The River Niger*, *Raisin* **1975:** *Equus*; *The Wiz* **1976:** *Travesties*; *A Chorus Line* **1977:** *The Shadow Box*, *Annie* **1978:** *Da*; *Ain't Misbehavin*, *Dracula* (innovative musical revival) **1979:** *The Elephant Man*; *Sweeney Todd* **1980:** *Children of a Lesser God*; *Evita*, *Morning's at Seven* (best revival) **1981:** *Amadeus*; *42nd Street*, *The Pirates of Penzance* **1982:** *The Life and Adventures of Nicholas Nickleby*; *Nine*; *Othello* **1983:** *Torch Song Trilogy*, *Cats*; *On Your Toes* **1984:** *The Real Thing*, *La Cage* aux Folles; *Death of a Salesman* **1985:** *Biloxi Blues; Big River, A Day in the Death of Joe Egg* **1986:** *I'm Not Rappaport; The Mystery of Edwin Drood; Sweet Charity* **1987:** *Fences; Les Misérables; All My Sons* **1988:** *M. Butterfly; The Phantom of the Opera; Anything Goes* **1989:** *The Heidi Chronicles; Jerome Robbins' Broadway; Our Town* **1990:** *The Grapes of Wrath; City of Angels; Gypsy* **1991:** *Lost in Yonkers; The Will Rogers' Follies; Fiddler on the Roof* **1992:** *Dancing at Lughnasa; Crazy for You; Guys and Dolls* **1993:** *Angels in America: Millenium Approaches; Kiss of the Spider Woman; Anna Christie* **1994:** *Angels in America: Perestroika; Passion; An Inspector Calls* (play revival); *Carousel* (musical revival) **1995:** *Love! Valour! Compassion!; Sunset Boulevard; The Heiress; Show Boat* **1996:** *Master Class; Rent; A Delicate Balance; King and I* **1997:** *Last Night of Ballyhoo; Titanic; A Doll's House; Chicago* **1998:** *Art; The Lion King; View from the Bridge; Cabaret* **1999:** *Side Man; Fosse; Death of a Salesman; Annie Get Your Gun* **2000:** *Copenhagen; Contact; The Real Thing; Kiss Me, Kate* **2001:** *Proof; The Producers; One Flew Over the Cuckoo's Nest; 42nd Street* **2002:** Edward Albee's *The Goat, or Who Is Sylvia?; Thoroughly Modern Millie; Private Lives; Into the Woods* **2003:** *Take Me Out; Hairspray; Long Day's Journey Into Night; Nine* **2004:** *I Am My Own Wife; Avenue Q; Henry IV; Assassins* **2005:** *Doubt; Monty Python's Spamalot; Glengarry Glen Ross; La Cage aux Folles* **2006:** *The History Boys; Jersey Boys; Awake and Sing!; The Pajama Game* **2007:** *The Coast of Utopia; Spring Awakening; Journey's End; Company* **2008:** *August: Osage County; In the Heights; Boeing-Boeing; South Pacific* **2009:** *God of Carnage; Billy Elliot The Musical; The Norman Conquests; Hair* **2010:** *Red; Memphis; Fences; La Cage aux Folles* **2011:** *War Horse; The Book of Mormon; The Normal Heart; Anything Goes*

Drama Desk Awards

Sunday, June 3, 2012 at Town Hall; 57th annual; Hosts: Brian d'Arcy James and Brooke Shields. Originally known as the Vernon Rice Awards until 1964 (named after the former *New York Post* theatre critic); Presented for outstanding achievement in the 2011–2012 season for Broadway, Off-Broadway, and Off-Off Broadway productions, voted on by an association of New York drama reporters, editors and critics. Ceremony Writer, Bill Rosenfeld; Ceremony Director, Mark Waldrop; Presented by TheatreMania.com; Executive Producers, Gretchen Shugart, Robert R. Blume, David S. Stone; General Management, Joe Parnes; Associate Producer, Renee McCurry; Special Events Director, Randie Levine-Miller; Board of Directors: Isa Goldberg (President), Leslie Hoban Blake (Vice President), Charles Wright (Treasurer and 2nd Vice President), Richard Ridge (Secretary), Arlene Epstein, Elysa Gardner, Randy Gener, John Istel, David Kaufman, William Wolf, Lauren Yarger; Nominating Committee: Barbara Siegel – Chairperson (*TheaterMania.com* and *TalkinBroadway.com*), Suzanna Bowling (Times Square Chronicle), Lawrence Harbison (Senior Editor and Columnists for *Smith & Kraus, Inc.*), Mark Peikert (*Back Stage*), Richard Ridge (*Broadway Beat TV*), Frank Verlizzo (Fraver Design).

Outstanding Play: *Tribes* by Nina Raine

Nominees: David Henry Hwang, *Chinglish*; Dan LeFranc, *The Big Meal*; Members of the Plastic Theatre, *Unatural Acts*; Itamar Moses, *Completeness*; Lynn Nottage, *By the Way, Meet Vera Stark*; Nicky Silver, *The Lyons*

Outstanding Musical: *Once*

Nominees: *Bonnie & Clyde; Death Takes a Holiday; Leap of Faith; Newsies; Nice Work If You Can Get It; Queen of the Mist*

Outstanding Revival of a Play: *Death of a Salesman*

Nominees: *A Little Journey*; Edward Albee's *The Lady from Dubuque*; Gore Vidal's *The Best Man; Lost in Yonkers; Richard III*

Outstanding Revival of a Musical: *Follies*

Nominees: *Carrie; Evita; Jesus Christ Superstar*; The Gershwins' *Porgy and Bess; The Threepenny Opera*

Outstanding Actor in a Play: James Corden, *One Man, Two Guvnors*

Nominees: Hugh Dancy, *Venus in Fur*; Claybourne Elder, *One Arm*; Santino Fontana, *Sons of the Prophet*; Joseph Franchini, *The Navigator*; Philip Seymour Hoffman, *Death of a Salesman*; Kevin Spacey, *Richard III*

Outstanding Actress in a Play: Tracie Bennett, *End of the Rainbow*

Nominees: Sanaa Lathan, *By the Way, Meet Vera Stark*; Linda Lavin, *The Lyons*; Jennifer Lim, *Chinglish*; Kim Martin-Cotton, *A Moon for the Misbegotten*; Carey Mulligan, *Through a Glass Darkly*; Joely Richardson, *Side Effects*

Outstanding Actor in a Musical: Danny Burstein, *Follies*

Nominees: Kevin Earley, *Death Takes a Holiday*; Raúl Esparza, *Leap of Faith*; Jeremy Jordan, *Newsies*; Norm Lewis, The Gershwins' *Porgy and Bess*; Ricky Martin, *Evita*

Outstanding Actress in a Musical: Audra McDonald, The Gershwins' *Porgy and Bess*

Nominees: Miche Braden, *The Devil's Music: The Life & Blues of Bessie Smith*; Jan Maxwell, *Follies*; Kelli O'Hara, *Nice Work If You Can Get It*; Bernadette Peters, *Follies*; Molly Ranson, *Carrie*

Outstanding Featured Actor in a Play: Tom Edden, *One Man, Two Guvnors*

Nominees: Bill Camp, *Death of a Salesman*; Jim Dale, *The Road to Mecca*; Bill Irwin, *King Lear*; Jefferson Mays, *Blood and Gifts*; Will Rogers, *Unnatural Acts*; Morgan Spector, *Russian Transport*

Outstanding Featured Actress in a Play: Judith Light, *Other Desert Cities*

Nominees: Stephanie J. Block, *By the Way, Meet Vera Stark*; Anna Camp, *All New People*; Kimberly Hébert Gregory, *By The Way, Meet Vera Stark*; Lisa Joyce, *The Ugly One*; Joaquina Kalukango, *Hurt Village*; Angela Lansbury, Gore Vidal's *The Best Man*

Outstanding Featured Actor in a Musical: Michael McGrath, *Nice Work If You Can Get It*

Nominees: Phillip Boykin, The Gershwins' *Porgy and Bess*; Matt Cavenaugh, *Death Takes a Holiday*; Michael Cerveris, *Evita*; Patrick Page, *Spider-Man: Turn Off the Dark*; Andrew Samonsky, *Queen of the Mist*

Outstanding Featured Actress in a Musical: Judy Kaye, *Nice Work If You Can Get It*

Nominees: Marin Mazzie, *Carrie*; Jessie Mueller, *On a Clear Day You Can See Forever*; Elaine Paige, *Follies*; Sarah Sokolovic, *The Shaggs: Philosophy of the World*; Melissa van der Schyff, *Bonnie & Clyde*

Outstanding Director of a Play: Mike Nichols, *Death of a Salesman*

Nominees: Jo Bonney, *By the Way, Meet Vera Stark*; David Cromer, *Tribes*; Ed Sylvanus Iskandar, *These Seven Sicknesses*; Sam Mendes, *Richard III*; Tony Speciale, *Unnatural Acts*

Outstanding Director of a Musical: John Tiffany, *Once*

Nominees: Christopher Ashley, *Leap of Faith*; Jack Cummings III, *Queen of the Mist*; Doug Hughes, *Death Takes a Holiday*; Kathleen Marshall, *Nice Work If You Can Get It*; Eric Schaeffer, *Follies*

Outstanding Choreography: Kathleen Marshall, *Anything Goes*

Nominees: Rob Ashford, *Evita*; Warren Carlyle, *Follies*; Breandán de Gallai, *Noctú*; Christopher Gattelli, *Newsies*; Kathleen Marshall, *Nice Work If You Can Get It*; Sergio Trujillo, *Leap of Faith*

Outstanding Music: Alan Menken, *Newsies*

Nominees: Glen Hansard and Markéta Irglová, *Once*; Michael John LaChiusa,

Queen of the Mist; Alan Menken, *Leap of Faith*; Frank Wildhorn, *Bonnie & Clyde*; Maury Yeston, *Death Takes a Holiday*

Outstanding Lyrics: Glen Hansard and Markéta Irglová, *Once*

Nominees: Don Black, *Bonnie & Clyde*; Jack Feldman, *Newsies*; Joy Gregory and Gunnar Madsen, *The Shaggs: Philosophy of the World*; Michael John LaChiusa, *Queen of the Mist*; Maury Yeston, *Death Takes a Holiday*

Outstanding Book of a Musical: Joe DiPietro, *Nice Work If You Can Get It*

Nominees: Douglas Carter Beane, *Lysistrata Jones*; Janus Cercone and Warren Leight, *Leap of Faith*; Joy Gregory, *The Shaggs: Philosophy of the World*; Michael John LaChiusa, *Queen of the Mist*; Thomas Meehan and Peter Stone, *Death Takes a Holiday*

Outstanding Orchestrations: Martin Lowe, *Once*

Nominees: Bill Elliott, *Nice Work If You Can Get It*; Larry Hochman, *Death Takes a Holiday*; John McDaniel, *Bonnie & Clyde*; Michael Starobin, *Queen of the Mist*; Danny Troob, *Newsies*

Outstanding Music in a Play: Grant Olding, *One Man, Two Guvnors*

Nominees: Mark Bennett, *An Illiad*; Mark Bennett, *Richard III*; Tom Kitt, *All's Well That Ends Well*; Gina Leishman, *Septimus and Clarissa*; Suzanne Vega and Duncan Sheik, *Carson McCullers Talks About Love*

Outstanding Revue: *The Best Is Yet to Come: The Music of Cy Coleman*

Nominee: *Newsical The Musical—End of the World Edition*

Outstanding Set Design: Jon Driscoll, Rob Howell and Paul Kieve, *Ghost: The Musical*

Nominees: David Gallo, *The Mountaintop*; Roger Hanna, *A Little Journey*; David Korins, *Assistance*; David Korins, *Chinglish*; Derek McLane, *Follies*

Outstanding Costume Design: Gregg Barnes, *Follies*

Nominees: ESosa, *By the Way, Meet Vera Stark*; William Ivey Long, *Lucky Guy*; Jessica Pabst, *She Kills Monsters*; Martin Pakledinaz, *Nice Work If You Can Get It*; Catherine Zuber, *Death Takes a Holiday*

Outstanding Lighting Design: Brian MacDevitt, *Death of a Salesman*

Nominees: Kevin Adams, *Carrie*; Neil Austin, *Evita*; David Lander, *One Arm*; Kenneth Posner, *Death Takes a Holiday*; Paul Pyant, *Richard III*

Outstanding Sound Design in a Musical: Acme Sound Partners, The Gershwins' *Porgy and Bess*

Nominees: Jonathan Deans, *Carrie*; Clive Goodwin, *Once*; Kai Harada, *Follies*; Steve Canyon Kennedy, *Jesus Christ Superstar*; Jon Weston, *Death Takes a Holiday*

Outstanding Sound Design in a Play: John Gromada, Gore Vidal's *The Best Man*

Nominees: Quentin Chiappetta/mediaNoise, *The Navigator*; Gregory Clarke, *Misterman*; Gareth Fry, *Richard III*; Stowe Nelson, *Samuel and Alasdair: A Personal History of the Robot War*; Shane Rettig, *She Kills Monsters*

Outstanding Solo Performance: Cillian Murphy, *Misterman*

Nominees: Baba Brinkman, *The Rap Guide to Evolution*; Suli Holum, *Chimera*; Jeff Key, *The Eyes of Babylon*; Denis O'Hara, *An Illiad*; Stephen Spinella, *An Illiad*

Unique Theatrical Experience: *Gob Squad's Kitchen (You've Never Had It So Good)*

Nominees: *Give Me Your Hand*; *Noctú*; *The Complete & Condensed Stage Directions of Eugene O'Neill, Vol. 1: Early Plays/Lost Plays*; *The Ryan Cast 1873*; *White*

Outstanding Ensemble Performances: *Sweet and Sad* (Jon DeVries, Shuler Hensley, Maryann Plunkett, Laila Robins, Jay O. Sanders, J. Smith-Cameron)

Special Awards: Mary Testa (Actor); Nick Westrate (Actor); The New Victory Theatre

Sam Norkin Off-Broadway Award: Stephen Karam (Playwright)

PAST DRAMA DESK AWARD-WINNING PRODUCTIONS From 1954–1974, non-competitive awards were presented to various artists: performers, playwrights, choreographers, composers, designers, directors, theatre companies and occasionally to specific productions. In 1975 the awards became competitive, and citations for Outstanding New Play (P)–or in some instances Outstanding New American Play (AP) and Outstanding New Foreign Play (FP), Outstanding Musical (M), Musical Revue (MR), Outstanding Revival, (R)–and later, Outstanding Play Revival (RP) and Outstanding Musical Revival (RM)–were instituted and presented as the season demanded. If year or a specific category within a year is missing, no production awards were presented in that year or specific category. **1955:** *The Way of the World*; *Thieves' Carnival*; *Twelfth Night*; *The Merchant of Venice* **1956:** *The Iceman Cometh* **1963:** *The Coach with Six Insides*; *The Boys from Syracuse* **1964:** *In White America*; *The Streets of New York* **1970:** *Borstal Boy* (P); *The Effect of Gamma Rays on Man-in-the-Moon Marigolds* (AP); *Company* (M) **1975:** *Same Time, Next Year* (AP), *Equus* (FP); *The Royal Family* (R) **1976:** *Streamers* (P); *The Royal Family* (R) **1977:** *A Texas Trilogy* (AP); *The Comedians* (FP); *Annie* (M) **1978:** *Da* (P); *Ain't Misbehavin'* (M) **1979:** *The Elephant Man* (P); *Sweeney Todd, The Demon Barber of Fleet Street* (M) **1980:** *Children of a Lesser God* (P); *Evita* (M) **1981:** *Amadeus* (P); *Lena Horne: The Lady and Her Music* (M) **1982:** *"Master Harold"… and the boys* (P); *Nine* (M); *Entertaining Mr. Sloan* (R) **1983:** *Torch Song Trilogy* (P); *Little Shop of Horrors* (M); *On Your Toes* (R) **1984:** *The Real Thing* (P); *Sunday in the Park with George* (M); *Death of a Salesman* (R) **1985:** *As Is* (P); *A Day in the Death of Joe Egg* (R) **1986:** *A Lie of the Mind* (P); *The Mystery of Edwin Drood* (M); *Lemon Sky* (R) **1987:** *Fences* (P); *Les Misérables* (M) **1988:** *M. Butterfly* (P); *Into the Woods* (M); *Anything Goes* (R) **1989:** *The Heidi Chronicles* (P); *Jerome Robbins' Broadway* (M); *Our Town* (R) **1990:** *The Piano Lesson* (P); *City of Angels* (M); *Gypsy* (R) **1991:** *Lost in Yonkers* (P); *The Secret Garden* (M); *And the World Goes Round* (MR); *A Little Night Music* (R) **1992:** *Lips Together, Teeth Apart* (P); *Crazy for You* (M); *Guys and Dolls* (R) **1993:** *Jeffrey* (P); *Kiss of the Spider Woman* (M); *Anna Christie* (R) **1994:** *Angels in America: Perestroika* (P); *Passion* (M); *Howard Crabtree's Whoop-Dee-Doo* (MR); *An Inspector Calls* (RP); *She Loves Me* (RM) **1995:** *Love! Valour! Compassion!* (P); *Showboat* (M); *The Heiress* (R) **1996:** *Master Class* (P); *Rent* (M); *A Delicate Balance* (RP); *The King and I* (RM) **1997:** *How I Learned to Drive* (P); *The Life* (M); *Howard Crabtree's When Pigs Fly* (MR); *A Doll's House* (RP); *Chicago* (RM) **1998:** *The Beauty Queen of Leenane* (P); *Ragtime* (M); *A View from the Bridge* (RP); *1776* (RM) **1999:** *Wit* (P); *Parade* (M); *Fosse* (MR); (tie) *Death of a Salesman* and *The Iceman Cometh* (RP); *You're a Good Man, Charlie Brown* (RM) **2000:** *Copenhagen* (P); *Contact* (M); *The Real Thing* (RP); *Kiss Me, Kate* (RM) **2001:** *Proof* (P); *The Producers* (M); *Forbidden Broadway 2001: A Spoof Odyssey* (MR); *The Best Man* (RP); *42nd Street* (RM) **2002:** (tie) *The Goat, or Who Is Sylvia?*; *Metamorphoses* (P); *Private Lives* (RP); *Into the Woods* (RM) **2003:** *Take Me Out* (P); *Hairspray* (M); *Long Day's Journey Into Night* (RP); *Nine* (RM) **2004:** *I Am My Own Wife* (P); *Wicked* (M); *Henry IV* (RP); *Assassins* (RM) **2005:** *Doubt* (P); *Monty Python's Spamalot* (M); *Forbidden Broadway: Special Victims Unit* (MR); *Twelve Angry Men* (RP); *La Cage aux Folles* (RM) **2006:** *The History Boys* (P); *The Drowsy Chaperone* (M); *Awake and Sing!* (RP); *Sweeney Todd, The Demon Barber of Fleet Street* (RM) **2007:** *The Coast of Utopia* (P); *Spring Awakening* (M); *Journey's End* (RP); *Company* (RM) **2008:** *August: Osage County* (P); *Passing Strange* (M); *Forbidden Broadway: Rude Awakening* (MR); *Boeing-Boeing* (RP); *South Pacific* (RM) **2009:** *Ruined* (P); *Billy Elliot The Musical* (M); *The Norman Conquests* (RP); *Hair* (RM) **2010:** *Red* (P); *Memphis* (M); Tie: *A View from the Bridge* and *Fences* (RP); *La Cage aux Folles* (RM) **2011:** *War Horse* (P); *The Book of Mormon* (M); *The Normal Heart* (RP); *Anything Goes* (RM)

Village Voice Obie Awards

Monday, May 21, 2012 at Webster Hall; 57th annual; Presented for outstanding achievement in Off- and Off-Off-Broadway theatre in the 2011–2012 season. Founded in 1955 by Village Voice cultural editor Jerry Tallmer; Judges: Brian Parks (*Village Voice* Arts and Cultural Editor), Michael Feingold (Committee Chair and *Village Voice* chief theatre critic), Alexis Soloski (*Village Voice* theatre critic), Annie Baker (Playwright), Anne Kauffman (Director/Instructor), José Rivera (Playwright), Helen Shaw (*Time Out New York* theatre critic). Hosts/Presenters: Eric McCormack, Grace Gummer, Hugh Dancy, Jonathan Pryce, Justin Bartha, Leslie Odom Jr., Lily Rabe, Michael McKean, Tonya Pinkins, Topher Grace, Tracee Chimo, Juliet Rylance; Performances by Joshua Henry and Sumayya Ali from *Porgy and Bess*, David Patrick Kelly and the cast of *Once*, and Ethan Lipton and His Orchestra from *No Place to Go*.

Best New American Play: ($1,000): *4000 Miles* by Amy Herzog (Lincoln Center Theater)

Performance: Cherise Booth, *Milk Like Sugar* (Playwrights Horizons and Women's Project); Steven Boyer, *Hand to God* (Ensemble Studio Theatre/Youngblood); Jon DeVries, Shuler Hensley, Maryann Plunkett, Laila Robins, Jay O. Sanders, *Sweet and Sad* Ensemble (The Public Theater); Gabriel Ebert and Mary Louise Wilson, *4000 Miles* (Lincoln Center Theater); Jim Fletcher, sustained excellence; Santino Fontana, *Sons of the Prophet* (Roundabout Theatre Company); Linda Lavin, *The Lyons* (Vineyard Theatre); Susan Pourfar, *Tribes* (Barrow Street Theatre)

Playwrighting: Kirsten Greenidge, *Milk Like Sugar* (Playwrights Horizons and the Women's Project)

Direction: Richard Maxwell, *Early Plays* (The Wooster Group and St. Ann's Warehouse); Jay Scheib, *World of Wires* (The Kitchen)

Design: Mark Barton, Sustained excellence of lighting design; Mimi Lien, sustained excellence of set design

Special Citations: Mark Barton, Denis O'Hare, Lisa Peterson, and Stephen Spinella, *An Illiad* (New York Theatre Workshop); Erin Courtney and Ken Rus Schmoll, *A Map of Virtue* (13P); Elevator Repair Service, sustained excellence; Ethan Lipton and His Orchestra, *No Place to Go* (The Public Theater/Joe's Pub); Steven Hoggett, Martin Lowe, and John Tiffany, *Once* (New York Theatre Workshop); Daniel Kitson, *It's Always Right Now, Until It's Later* (St. Ann's Warehouse)

Ross Wetzsteon Memorial Award: ($1,000): Youngblood Company (Ensemble Studio Theatre)

Obie Theater Grants ($5,000 divided among winners): The Bushwick Starr and The Debate Society

Lifetime Achievement: Caridad Svich

PAST OBIE AWARD-WINNING BEST NEW PLAYS If year is missing, no award was given that season; multiple plays were awarded in some seasons. **1956:** *Absalom, Absalom* **1957:** *A House Remembered* **1959:** *The Quare Fellow* **1961:** *The Blacks* **1962:** *Who'll Save the Plowboy?* **1964:** *Play* **1965:** *The Old Glory* **1966:** *The Journey of the Fifth Horse* **1970:** *The Effect of Gamma Rays on Man-in-the-Moon Marigolds* **1971:** *The House of Blue Leaves* **1973:** *The Hot L Baltimore* **1974:** *Short Eyes* **1975:** *The First Breeze of Summer* **1976:** *American Buffalo, Sexual Perversity in Chicago* **1977:** *Curse of the Starving Class* **1978:** *Shaggy Dog Animation* **1979:** *Josephine* **1981:** *FOB* **1982:** *Metamorphosis in* Miniature; *Mr. Dead and Mrs. Free* **1983:** *Painting Churches; Andrea Rescued; Edmond* **1984:** *Fool for Love* **1985:** *The Conduct of Life* **1987:** *The Cure; Film Is Evil, Radio Is Good* **1988:** *Abingdon Square* **1990:** *Prelude to a Kiss; Imperceptible Mutabilities in the Third Kingdom; Bad Benny, Crowbar, Terminal Hip* **1991:** *The Fever* **1992:** *Sight Unseen; Sally's Rape; The Baltimore Waltz* **1994:** *Twilight: Los Angeles, 1992* **1995:** *Cryptogram* **1996:** *Adrienne Kennedy* **1997:** *One Flea Spare* **1998:** *Pearls for Pigs and Benita Canova* **2001:**

The Syringa Tree **2004:** *Small Tragedy* **2009:** *Ruined* **2010:** *Circle Mirror Transformation* **2011:** *The Elaborate Entrance of Chad Deity*

Outer Critics Circle Awards

Thursday, May 24, 2012; Sardi's Restaurant; 62nd annual. Presented for outstanding achievement for Broadway and Off-Broadway productions during the 2011–2012 season. Winners are voted on by theatre critics of out-of-town periodicals and media. Executive/Nominating Committee: Simon Saltzman (President), Mario Fratti (Vice-President), Patrick Hoffman (Corresponding Secretary), Stanley L. Cohen (Treasurer), Glenn Loney (Historian & Member-at-Large), Rosalind Friedman (Recording Secretary), Aubrey Reuben, Thomás Gentile, Harry Haun (Members-at-Large); Presenters: Jon Robin Baitz, Josh Gad, Montego Glover, Jerry Stiller, Anne Meara.

Outstanding New Broadway Play: *One Man, Two Guvnors*

Nominees: *Seminar; Stick Fly; The Lyons*

Outstanding New Broadway Musical: *Once*

Nominees: *Bonnie & Clyde; Newsies; Spider-Man: Turn Off the Dark*

Outstanding New Off-Broadway Play: *Sons of the Prophet*

Nominees: *Blood and Gifts; The School for Lies; Tribes*

Outstanding New Off-Broadway Musical: *Queen of the Mist*

Nominees: *Death Takes a Holiday; Lucky Guy; Play It Cool*

Outstanding New Score (Broadway or Off-Broadway)**:** *Newsies*

Nominees: *Bonnie & Clyde; Death Takes a Holiday; Queen of the Mist*

Outstanding Revival of a Play: *Death of a Salesman*

Nominees: *Private Lives; The Best Man; The Lady from Dubuque*

Outstanding Revival of a Musical: *Follies*

Nominees: *Carrie; Evita; Porgy and Bess*

Outstanding Director of a Play: Nicholas Hytner, *One Man, Two Guvnors*

Nominees: David Cromer, *Tribes*; Mark Brokaw, *The Lyons*; Mike Nichols, *Death of a Salesman*

Outstanding Director of a Musical: John Tiffany, *Once*

Nominees: Jeff Calhoun, *Newsies*; Kathleen Marshall, *Nice Work If You Can Get It*; Michael Grandage, *Evita*

Outstanding Choreography: Christopher Gattelli, *Newsies*

Nominees: Kathleen Marshall, *Nice Work If You Can Get It*; Rob Ashford, *Evita*; Steven Hoggett, *Once*

Outstanding Actor in a Play: James Corden, *One Man, Two Guvnors*

Nominees: Hamish Linklater, *The School for Lies*; Philip Seymour Hoffman, *Death of a Salesman*; Russell Harvard, *Tribes*; Santino Fontana, *Sons of the Prophet*

Outstanding Actress in a Play: Tracie Bennett, *End of the Rainbow*

Nominees: Laila Robins, *The Lady from Dubuque*; Linda Lavin, *The Lyons*; Nicole Ari Parker, *A Streetcar Named Desire*; Tyne Daly, *Master Class*

Outstanding Actor in a Musical: Danny Burstein, *Follies*

Nominees: Jeremy Jordan, *Newsies*; Norm Lewis, *Porgy and Bess*; Raúl Esparza, *Leap of Faith*; Steve Kazee, *Once*

Outstanding Actress in a Musical: Audra McDonald, *Porgy and Bess*

Nominees: Cristin Milioti, *Once*; Jan Maxwell, *Follies*; Kelli O'Hara, *Nice Work If You Can Get It*; Marin Mazzie, *Carrie*

Outstanding Featured Actor in a Play: James Earl Jones, *The Best Man*

Nominees: Andrew Garfield, *Death of a Salesman*; Jefferson Mays, *Blood and Gifts*; Tom Edden, *One Man, Two Guvnors*; Will Brill, *Tribes*

Outstanding Featured Actress in a Play: Spencer Kayden, *Don't Dress for Dinner*

Nominees: Angela Lansbury, *The Best Man*; Daphne Rubin-Vega, *A Streetcar Named Desire*; Joanna Gleason, *Sons of the Prophet*; Judith Light, *Other Desert Cities*

Outstanding Featured Actor in a Musical: Michael McGrath, *Nice Work If You Can Get It*

Nominees: Andrew Keenan-Bolger, *Newsies*; Chris Sullivan, *Nice Work If You Can Get It*; Patrick Page, *Spider-Man: Turn Off the Dark*; Phillip Boykin, *Porgy and Bess*

Outstanding Featured Actress in a Musical: Judy Kaye, *Nice Work If You Can Get It*

Nominees: Da'Vine Joy Randolph, *Ghost: The Musical*; Jayne Houdyshell, *Follies*; Melissa van der Schyff, *Bonnie & Clyde*; Rebecca Luker, *Death Takes a Holiday*

Oustanding Book of a Musical: *Once*

Nominees: *Newsies*; *Nice Work If You Can Get It*; *Queen of the Mist*

Outstanding Scenic Design (Play or Musical): George Tsypin, *Spider-Man: Turn Off the Dark*

Nominees: Bob Crowley, *Once*; Christopher Oram, *Evita*; Derek McLane, *Nice Work If You Can Get It*

Outstanding Costume Design (Play or Musical): Eiko Ishioka, *Spider-Man: Turn Off the Dark*

Nominees: Gregg Barnes, *Follies*; Martin Pakledinaz, *Nice Work If You Can Get It*; William Ivey Long, *Don't Dress for Dinner*

Outstanding Lighting Design (Play or Musical): Hugh Vanstone, *Ghost: The Musical*

Nominees: Brian MacDevitt, *Death of a Salesman*; Donald Holder, *Spider-Man: Turn Off the Dark*; Neil Austin, *Evita*

Outstanding Solo Performance: Denis O'Hare, *An Iliad*

Nominees: David Greenspan, *The Patsy*; Judy Gold, *My Life as a Sitcom*; Stephen Spinella, *An Illiad*

John Gassner Playwriting Award: Jeff Talbott, *The Submission*

Nominees: Erika Sheffer, *Russian Transport*; Gabe McKinley, *CQ/CX*; Robert Askins, *Hand to God*

PAST OUTER CRITICS CIRCLE AWARD-WINNING PRODUCTIONS
Awards listed are for Best Play and Best Musical; as other categories were cited, they are indicated as such: (R) Best Revival; (RP) Best Play Revival; (RM) Best Musical Revival; (BP) Best Productions; (OP) Best Off-Broadway Play; (OM) Best Off-Broadway Musical. Beginning with 1990, shows listed are: Best (New) Play, Best (New) Musical, Best Play Revival, Best Musical Revival, Best Off-Broadway Play, Best New Off-Broadway Musical. In 1999, the awards were qualified as "Outstanding" instead of "Best"; if year is missing, no production awards were presented. **1950:** *The Cocktail Party*; *The Consul* **1951:** *Billy Budd*; *Guys and Dolls* **1952:** *Point of No Return*; no musical award **1953:** no play award;

Wonderful Town **1954:** *The Caine Mutiny Court-Martial*; *Kismet* **1955:** *Inherit the Wind*; *Three for Tonight* **1956:** *The Diary of Anne Frank*; *My Fair Lady* **1957:** *Long Day's Journey Into Night*; *My Fair Lady* **1958:** *Look Homeward, Angel*; *The Music Man* **1959:** *The Visit*; no musical award **1960:** *The Miracle Worker*; *Bye Bye Birdie* **1962:** *Anything Goes* (R) **1964:** *The Trojan Women* (R-classic); *The Lower Depths* (R-modern) **1965:** (BP)–*Oh What a Lovely War*, *Tartuffe* **1966:** (BP)–*Wait a Minim!*, *Mame* **1967:** (BP)–*America Hurrah*; *Cabaret*; *You Know I Can't Hear You When the Water's Running*; *You're A Good Man, Charlie Brown* **1968:** (BP)–*Rosencrantz and Guildenstern are Dead*; *The Price*; *George M!*; *Your Own Thing* **1969:** *Dames at Sea* (OM) **1970:** *Child's Play*; *Company*; *The White House Murder Case* (OP); *The Last Sweet Days of Isaac* (OM) **1971:** (BP)–*A Midsummer Night's Dream*; *Follies*; *No, No, Nanette* **1972:** *Sticks and Bones* and *That Championship Season*; no musical award **1974:** *A Moon for the Misbegotten* and *Noel Coward in Two Keys*; *Candide* **1975:** *Equus*; no musical award **1977:** *for colored girls…*; *Annie* **1978:** *Da*; no musical award **1979:** *The Elephant Man*; *Sweeney Todd, the Demon Barber of Fleet Street* **1980:** *Children of a Lesser God*; *Barnum* **1981:** *Amadeus*; *The Pirates of Penzance* (R); *March of the Falsettos* (OM) **1982:** *"Master Harold"…and the Boys*; *Nine*; *A Soldier's Play* (OP) **1983:** *Brighton Beach Memoirs*; *Cats*; *You Can't Take It With You* (RP); *On Your Toes* (RM); *Extremities* (OP); *Little Shop of Horrors* (OM) **1984:** *The Real Thing*; *La Cage aux Folles*; *Death of a Salesman* (R); *Painting Churches* (OP); *A… My Name is Alice* (Revue) **1985:** *Biloxi Blues*; *Sunday in the Park With George*; *Joe Egg* (R); *The Foreigner* (OP); *Kuni-Leml* (OM) **1986:** *I'm Not Rappaport*; *The Mystery of Edwin Drood*; *Loot* (R); *A Lie of the Mind* (OP); *Nunsense* (OM) **1987:** *Fences*; *Les Misérables*; *All My Sons* (R); *The Common Pursuit* (OP); *Stardust* (OM) **1988:** *M. Butterfly*; *The Phantom of the Opera*; *Anything Goes* (R); *Driving Miss Daisy* (OP); *Oil City Symphony* and *Romance, Romance* (OM) **1989:** *The Heidi Chronicles*; *Jerome Robbins' Broadway* **1990:** *The Grapes of Wrath*; *City of Angels*; *Cat on a Hot Tin Roof*; *Gypsy*; *Prelude to a Kiss*; *Closer Than Ever* **1991:** *Lost in Yonkers*; *Miss Saigon*; *Fiddler on the Roof* (R); *The Sum of Us*; *Falsettoland*; *And the World Goes Round* (Revue) **1992:** *Dancing at Lughnasa*; *Crazy for You*; *The Visit*; *Guys and Dolls*; *Marvin's Room*; *Song of Singapore* **1993:** *The Sisters Rosensweig*; *The Who's Tommy*; *Anna Christie*; *Carnival*; *Jeffrey*; *Ruthless!* **1994:** *Angels in America*; *Kiss of the Spider Woman*; *An Inspector Calls*; *She Loves Me*; *Three Tall Women*; *Annie Warbucks* **1995:** *Love! Valour! Compassion!*; *Sunset Boulevard*; *The Heiress*; *Show Boat*; *Camping with Henry and Tom*; *Jelly Roll* **1996:** *Master Class*; *Victor/Victoria*; *Inherit the Wind*; *The King and I*; *Molly Sweeney* and *Picasso at the Lapin Agile*; *Rent* **1997:** *The Last Night at Ballyhoo*; *The Life*; *A Doll's House*; *Chicago*; *How I Learned to Drive*; *Howard Crabtree's When Pigs Fly* **1998:** *The Beauty Queen of Leenane*; *Ragtime*; *A View from the Bridge*; *Cabaret*; *Never the Sinner* and *Gross Indecency: The Three Trials of Oscar Wilde*; *Hedwig and the Angry Inch* **1999:** *Not About Nightingales*; *Fosse*; *The Iceman Cometh*; *Annie Get Your Gun* and *Peter Pan* and *You're a Good Man, Charlie Brown*; *Wit*; *A New Brain* **2000:** *Copenhagen*; *Contact*; *A Moon for the Misbegotten*; *Kiss Me, Kate*; *Dinner With Friends*; *The Wild Party* **2001:** *Proof*; *The Producers*; *The Best Man* and *One Flew Over the Cuckoo's Nest*; *42ⁿᵈ Street*; *Jitney*; *Bat Boy: The Musical* **2002:** *The Goat, or Who Is Sylvia?*; *Urinetown the Musical* and *The Dazzle*; *Morning's at Seven*; *Oklahoma!*; *tick, tick…BOOM!* **2003:** *Take Me Out*; *Hairspray*; *A Day in the Death of Joe Egg*; *Nine*; *The Exonerated*; *A Man of No Importance* **2004:** *I Am My Own Wife*; *Wicked*; *Henry IV*; *Wonderful Town*; *Intimate Apparel*; *Johnny Guitar* and *The Thing About Men* **2005:** *Doubt*; *Monty Python's Spamalot*; *Twelve Angry Men*; *La Cage aux Folles*; *Fat Pig* and *Going to St. Ives*; *Altar Boyz* **2006:** *The History Boys*; *Jersey Boys*; *Awake and Sing!*; *Sweeney Todd, the Demon Barber of Fleet Street*; *Stuff Happens*; *Grey Gardens* **2007:** *The Coast of Utopia*; *Spring Awakening*; *Journey's End*; *Company*; *Indian Blood*; *In the Heights* **2008:** *August: Osage County*; *Xanadu* and *Young Frankenstein*; *The Homecoming*; *South Pacific*; *Dividing the Estate*; *Adding Machine* **2009:** *God of Carnage*; *Billy Elliot The Musical*; *The Norman Conquests*; *Hair*; *Ruined*; *The Toxic Avenger* **2010:** *Red*; *Memphis*; *Fences*; *La Cage aux Folles*; *The Orphans' Home Cycle*; *The Scottsboro Boys* and *Bloody Bloody Andrew Jackson* **2011:** *War Horse*; *The Book of Mormon*; *The Normal Heart*; *Anything Goes*; *Other Desert Cities*; *The Kid*

Lucille Lortel Awards

Sunday, May 6, 2012; NYU Skirball Center; 27th annual; Host: Mario Cantone. Presented by the League of Off-Broadway Theatres and Producers for outstanding achievement Off-Broadway. Lortel Awards Producing and Administrative Committee: Terry Byrne, Denise Cooper, Margaret Cotter, George Forbes, Melanie Herman, Catherine Russell, Steven Showalter, Carl D. White. The 2011–2012 awards voting committee consisted of Randy Anderson (SDC), Terry Berliner (SDC), Jan Buttram (Abingdon Theatre Company), Kia Corthron (Playwright), Peter Filichia (*The Star-Ledger*), Eleanor Goldhar (Guggenheim Foundation), Melanie Herman (MH Productions), Susan Gallin (Susan Gallin Productions), Linda Herring (Tribeca Performing Arts Center), Walt Kiskaddon (AEA), Barbara H Lorber (NYC and Company), Kenneth Naanep (AEA), Eva Price (Maximum Entertainment Productions), Richard Price (TDF), Mark Rossier (New York Foundation for the Arts), David Savran (Graduate Center at CUNY), Helen Shaw (Actor), Philip Taylor (NYU Steinhardt Program in Educational Theatre), Rosemarie Tichler (Tisch School of the Arts), Barbara Toy (American Theatre Wing).

Outstanding Play: *Sons of the Prophet* by Stephen Karam (Roundabout Theatre Company)

Nominees: *Blood and Gifts* by J.T. Rogers (Lincoln Center Theater); *Milk Like Sugar* by Kirsten Greenidge (Playwrights Horizons and Women's Project Theatre); *The Big Meal* by Dan LeFranc (Playwrights Horizons); *The School for Lies* by David Ives (Classic Stage Company)

Outstanding Musical: *Once* Music and Lyrics by Glen Hansard and Markéta Irglová, Book by Enda Walsh (New York Theatre Workshop)

Nominees: *Queen of the Mist* Words and Music by Michael John LaChiusa (Transport Group); *SILENCE! The Musical* Music and Lyrics by Jon and Al Kaplan, Book by Hunter Bell (Victoria Lang, Rich Affannato, Donna Trinkoff in association with Scott Kirschenbaum, Theater Mogul, Kitefliers Studio, Terry Schnuck and John Arthur Pinckard); *The Blue Flower* by Jim Bauer and Ruth Bauer (Second Stage); *The Shaggs: Philosophy of the World* Book and Lyrics by Joy Gregory, Music and Lyrics by Gunnar Madsen, Story by Joy Gregory, Gunnar Madsen, and John Langs (Playwrights Horizons and New York Theatre Workshop)

Outstanding Revival: *The Cherry Orchard* by Anton Chekhov, translated by John Christopher Jones (Classic Stage Company)

Nominees: *Blood Knot* by Athol Fugard (Signature Theatre Company); *The Lady from Dubuque* by Edward Albee (Signature Theatre Company); *Look Back in Anger* by John Osborne (Roundabout Theatre Company); *The Maids* by Jean Genet, translated by Bernard Frechtman (Red Bull Theater)

Outstanding Solo Show: *An Illiad* Written by Denis O'Hare and Lisa Peterson, performed by Denis O'Hare and Stephen Spinella (New York Theatre Workshop)

Nominee: *The Devil's Music: The Life and Blues of Bessie Smith* Written by Angelo Parra and performed by Miche Braden (Penguin Rep Theatre and Edmund Gaynes in association with Lizanne and Don Mitchell)

Outstanding Director: Sam Gold, *The Big Meal*

Nominees: Jo Bonney, *By the Way, Meet Vera Stark*; David Cromer, *Tribes*; Sam Gold, *Look Back in Anger*; John Tiffany, *Once*

Outstanding Choreography: Steven Hoggett, *Once*

Nominees: Chase Brock, *The Blue Flower*; Bill Castellino, *Ionescopade*; Christopher Gattelli, *SILENCE! The Musical*; Annie-B Parson, *The Broken Heart*

Outstanding Lead Actor: Santino Fontana, *Sons of the Prophet*

Nominees: Russell Harvard, *Tribes*; Hamish Linklater, *The School for Lies*; Jefferson Mays, *Blood and Gifts*; Jay O. Sanders, *Titus Andronicus*

Outstanding Lead Actress: Sanaa Lathan, *By the Way, Meet Vera Stark*

Nominees: Cristin Milioti, *Once*; Carey Mulligan, *Through a Glass Darkly*; Molly Manson, *Carrie*; Mary Testa, *Queen of the Mist*

Outstanding Featured Actor: Adam Driver, *Look Back in Anger*

Nominees: David Wilson Barnes, *The Big Meal*; Alvin Epstein, *The Cherry Orchard*; Peter Francis James, *The Lady from Dubuque*; Jeff Perry, *Tribes*

Outstanding Featured Actress: Tonya Pinkins, *Milk Like Sugar*

Nominees: Anita Gillette, *The Big Meal*; Kimberly Hébert Gregory, *By the Way, Meet Vera Stark*; Marin Mazzie, *Carrie*; Mare Winningham, *Tribes*

Outstanding Scenic Design: Lauren Helpern, *4000 Miles*

Nominees: Bob Crowley, *Once*; Andrew Lieberman, *Look Back in Anger*; Adrianne Lobel, *Galileo*; David Zinn, *The Select (The Sun Also Rises)*

Outstanding Costume Design: ESosa, *By the Way, Meet Vera Stark*

Nominees: Toni-Leslie James, *Milk Like Sugar*; William Ivey Long, *The School for Lies*; Ilona Somogyi, *Maple and Vine*; Catherine Zuber, *Death Takes a Holiday*

Outstanding Lighting Design (tie): Natasha Katz, *Once*; David Weiner, *Through a Glass Darkly*

Nominees: Keith Parham, *Tribes*; Justin Townsend, *Unnatural Acts*; Scott Zielinski, *An Illiad*

Outstanding Sound Design: Matt Tierney and Ben Williams, *The Select (The Sun Also Rises)*

Nominees: Mark Bennett, *An Illiad*; Clive Goodwin, *Once*; Daniel Kluger, *Tribes*; David Van Tieghem, *Through a Glass Darkly*

Lifetime Achievement Award: Richard Frankel

Service to Off-Broadway Award: Fire Department of the City of New York (NYFD)

Playwrights' Sidewalk Inductee: Richard Foreman

PAST LUCILLE LORTEL-AWARD WINNING PRODUCTIONS Awards listed are Outstanding Play and Outstanding Musical, respectively, since inception. **1986:** *Woza Africa!*, no musical award **1987:** *The Common Pursuit*, no musical award **1988:** no play or musical award **1989:** *The Cocktail Hour*, no musical award **1990:** no play or musical award **1991:** *Aristocrats*; *Falsettoland* **1992:** *Lips Together, Teeth Apart*; *And the World Goes 'Round* **1993:** *The Destiny of Me*; *Forbidden Broadway* **1994:** *Three Tall Women*; *Wings* **1995:** *Camping with Henry & Tom*; *Jelly Roll!* **1996:** *Molly Sweeney*; *Floyd Collins* **1997:** *How I Learned to Drive*; *Violet* **1998:** (tie) *Gross Indecency* and *The Beauty Queen of Leenane*; no musical award **1999:** *Wit*; no musical award **2000:** *Dinner With Friends*; *James Joyce's The Dead* **2001:** *Proof*; *Bat Boy: The Musical* **2002:** *Metamorphoses*; *Urinetown* **2003:** *Take Me Out*; *Avenue Q* **2004:** *Bug*; *Caroline or Change* **2005:** *Doubt*; *The 25th Annual Putnam County Spelling Bee* **2006:** *The Lieutenant of Inishmore*; *The Seven* **2007:** *Stuff Happens*; (tie) *In the Heights* and *Spring Awakening* **2008:** *Betrayed*; *Adding Machine* **2009:** *Ruined*; *Fela! A New Musical* **2010:** *The Orphans' Home Cycle*; *The Scottsboro Boys* **2011:** *The Elaborate Entrance of Chad Deity*; *Bloody Bloody Andrew Jackson*

New York Drama Critics' Circle Awards

Monday, May 7, 2012; 77th annual. Presented by members of the press in the New York area. New York Drama Critics' Circle Committee: Adam Feldman–President (*Time Out New York*), Elizabeth Vincentelli–Vice President (*New York* Post), Joe Dziemianowicz–Treasurer (*The Daily News*), Eric Grode–Recording Secretary (non-voting), Hilton Als (*The New Yorker*), Melissa Rose Bernardo (*Entertainment Weekly*), Scott Brown (*New York*), David Cote (*Time Out New York*), Michael Feingold (*The Village Voice*), Robert Feldberg (*The Bergen Record*), David Finkle

(TheatreMania.com), Elysa Gardner (USA Today), Jeremy Gerard (Bloomberg News), Eric Haagensen (Back Stage), Mark Kennedy (Associated Press), Jesse Oxford (New York Observer), David Rooney (Hollywood Reporter), Frank Scheck (New York Post), David Sheward (Back Stage), John Simon (Yonkers Tribune), Alexis Soloski (The Village Voice), Marilyn Stasio (Variety), Steven Suskin (Variety), Terry Teachout (Wall Street Journal), Linda Winer (Newsday), Richard Zoglin (Time); Emeritus: Michael Sommers (Newhouse)

Best Play: Sons of the Prophet by Stephen Karam

Best Foreign Play: Tribes by Nina Raine

Best Musical: Once by Enda Walsh, Glen Hansard, and Markéta Irglová

Special Citations: Signature Theatre Company; Mike Nichols for his contribution to the theatre

PAST DRAMA CRITICS' CIRLCE AWARD-WINNING PRODUCTIONS AND CITATIONS From 1936 to 1962, the New York Drama Critics' Circle presented awards for Best American Play, Best Foreign Play, and Best Musical, although some years no awards were given in specific categories. For entries below during those years, the first entry (unless otherwise indicated) is for Best American Play, (F) for Best Foreign Play, and (M) for Best Musical. For listings from 1962 to the present, the first listing (unless otherwise indicated) is for Best Play, and proceeding listings are as follow (depending on which awards were cited): (A) Best American Play; (F) Best Foreign Play; (M) Best Musical. Special Citations, periodically presented, are indicated as (SC). **1936:** Winterset **1937:** High Tor **1938:** Of Mice and Men; Shadow and Substance (F) **1939:** The White Steed (F) **1940:** The Time of Your Life **1941:** Watch on the Rhine; The Corn Is Green (F) **1942:** Blithe Spirit (F) **1943:** The Patriots **1944:** Jacobowsky and the Colonel (F) **1945:** The Glass Menagerie **1946:** Carousel (M) **1947:** All My Sons; No Exit (F); Brigadoon (M) **1948:** A Streetcar Named Desire; The Winslow Boy (F) **1949:** Death of a Salesman; The Madwoman of Chaillot (F); South Pacific (M) **1950:** The Member of the Wedding; The Cocktail Party (F); The Consul (M) **1951:** Darkness at Noon; The Lady's Not for Burning (F); Guys and Dolls (M) **1952:** I Am a Camera; Venus Observed (F); Pal Joey (M); Don Juan in Hell (SC) **1953:** Picnic; The Love of Four Colonels (F); Wonderful Town (M) **1954:** Teahouse of the August Moon; Ondine (F); The Golden Apple (M) **1955:** Cat on a Hot Tin Roof; Witness for the Prosecution (F); The Saint of Bleecker Street (M) **1956:** The Diary of Anne Frank; Tiger at the Gates (F); My Fair Lady (M) **1957:** Long Day's Journey into Night; The Waltz of the Toreadors (F); The Most Happy Fella (M) **1958:** Look Homeward Angel; Look Back in Anger (F); The Music Man (M) **1959:** A Raisin in the Sun; The Visit (F); La Plume de Ma Tante (M) **1960:** Toys in the Attic; Five Finger Exercise (F); Fiorello! (M) **1961:** All the Way Home; A Taste of Honey (F); Carnival (M) **1962:** Night of the Iguana; A Man for All Seasons (F); How to Succeed in Business Without Really Trying (M) **1963:** Who's Afraid of Virginia Woolf?; Beyond the Fringe (SC) **1964:** Luther; Hello Dolly! (M); The Trojan Women (SC) **1965:** The Subject Was Roses; Fiddler on the Roof (M) **1966:** Marat/Sade; Man of La Mancha (M); Mark Twain Tonight - Hal Holbrook (SC) **1967:** The Homecoming; Cabaret (M) **1968:** Rosencrantz and Guildenstern Are Dead; Your Own Thing (M) **1969:** The Great White Hope; 1776 (M) **1970:** Borstal Boy; The Effect of Gamma Rays on Man-in-the-Moon Marigolds (A); Company (M) **1971:** Home; The House of Blue Leaves (A); Follies (M) **1972:** That Championship Season; The Screens (F); Two Gentlemen of Verona (M); Sticks and Bones (SC); Old Times (SC) **1973:** The Changing Room; The Hot L Baltimore (A); A Little Night Music (M) **1974:** The Contractor; Short Eyes (A); Candide (M) **1975:** Equus; The Taking of Miss Janie (A); A Chorus Line (M) **1976:** Travesties; Streamers (A); Pacific Overtures (M) **1977:** Otherwise Engaged; American Buffalo (A); Annie (M) **1978:** Da; Ain't Misbehavin' (M) **1979:** The Elephant Man; Sweeney Todd (M) **1980:** Talley's Folly; Betrayal (F); Evita (M); Peter Brook's Le Centre International de Créations Théâtricales at La MaMa ETC (SC) **1981:** A Lesson from Aloes; Crimes of the Heart (A); Lena Horne: The Lady and Her Music (SC); The Pirate of Penzance at New York Shakespeare Festival (SC) **1982:** The Life and Adventures of Nicholas Nickleby; A Soldier's Play (A) **1983:** Brighton Beach Memoirs; Plenty (A); Little

Shop of Horrors (M); Young Playwrights Festival (SC) **1984:** The Real Thing; Glengarry Glen Ross (F); Sunday in the Park with George (M); Samuel Beckett (SC) **1985:** Ma Rainey's Black Bottom **1986:** A Lie of the Mind; Benefactors (A); The Search for Signs of Intelligent Life in the Universe (SC) **1987:** Fences; Les Liaisons Dangereuses (F); Les Misérables (M) **1988:** Joe Turner's Come and Gone; The Road to Mecca (F); Into the Woods (M) **1989:** The Heidi Chronicles; Aristocrats (F); Bill Irwin: Largely New York (SC) **1990:** The Piano Lesson; Privates on Parade (F); City of Angels (M) **1991:** Six Degrees of Separation; Our Country's Good (F); The Will Rogers Follies (M) Eileen Atkins - A Room of One's Own (SC) **1992:** Dancing at Lughnasa; Two Trains Running (A) **1993:** Angels in America: Millenium Approaches; Someone Who'll Watch Over Me (F); Kiss of the Spider Woman (M) **1994:** Three Tall Women; Twilight: Los Angeles, 1992 - Anna Deavere Smith (SC) **1995:** Arcadia; Love! Valour! Compassion! (A); Signature Theatre Company's Horton Foote Season (SC) **1996:** Seven Guitars; Molly Sweeny (F); Rent (M); New York City Center's Encores! (SC) **1997:** How I Learned to Drive; Skylight (F); Violet (M); Chicago - Broadway revival (SC) **1998:** Art; Pride's Crossing (A); Lion King (M); Cabaret—Broadway revival (SC) **1999:** Wit; Closer (F); Parade (M); David Hare (SC) **2000:** Jitney; James Joyce's The Dead (M); Copenhagen (F) **2001:** The Invention of Love; The Producers (M); Proof (A) **2002:** Edward Albee's The Goat, or Who is Sylvia?; Elaine Stritch: At Liberty (SC) **2003:** Take Me Out; Talking Heads (F); Hairspray (M) **2004:** Intimate Apparel; Barbara Cook (SC) **2005:** Doubt; The Pillowman (F) **2006:** The History Boys; The Drowsy Chaperone (M); John Doyle, Sarah Travis and the Cast of Sweeney Todd (SC); Christine Ebersole (SC) **2007:** The Coast of Utopia; Radio Golf (A); Spring Awakening (M); Journey's End (SC) **2008:** August: Osage County; Passing Strange (M) **2009:** Ruined; Black Watch (F); Billy Elliot The Musical (M); Angela Lansbury (SC); Gerard Alessandrini for Forbidden Broadway (SC); Matthew Warchus and the Cast of The Norman Conquests (SC) **2010:** The Orphans Home Cycle; Lincoln Center Festival (SC); Viola Davis (SC); Annie Baker for Circle Mirror Transformation and The Aliens (SC) **2011:** Good People; Jerusalem (F); The Book of Mormon (M); The Broadway revival of The Normal Heart (SC); Mark Rylance for La Bête and Jerusalem (SC); Direction, design, and puppetry of War Horse (SC)

Drama League Awards

Friday, May 18, 2012; Broadway Ballroom at The Marriott Marquis; 78th annual. Hosts: Stockard Channing and John Larroquette. First awarded in 1922 and formalized in 1935, the Drama League Awards are the oldest theatrical honors in America. Presented for distinguished achievement in the New York theatre, the winners are selected by members of the League. Drama League President, Jano Herbosch; Executive Director, Gabriel Shanks; Honorary Co-Chairs: Nina Arianda, Christian Borle, Norbert Leo Butz, Kathleen Chalfant, Raúl Esparza, Rosemary Harris, Jeremy Jordan, Christine Lahti, Linda Lavin, Norm Lewis, Judith Light, Audra McDonald, Cynthia Nixon, Blair Underwood; Presenters: Philip Seymour Hoffman, Christian Borle, Cynthia Nixon, Kelli O'Hara, John Lithgow, Donna Murphy, Harvey Fierstein, Gavin Creel

Play: Other Desert Cities

Musical: Once

Revival of a Play: Death of a Salesman

Revival of a Musical: Follies

Performance: Audra McDonald, The Gershwins' Porgy and Bess

Julia Hansen Award for Excellence in Directing: Diane Paulus

Achievement in Musical Theatre: Alan Menken

Unique Contribution to Theater: Rosie O'Donnell

Pulitzer Prize Award Winners for Drama

Established in 1917; Administered by the Pulitzer Prize Board, Columbia University; Lee C. Bollinger, President. Winner is chosen by a jury, composed of three to four critics, one academic and one playwright, however the board has final authority over choice. Presented for an outstanding drama or musical presented in New York or regional theater. The award goes to the playwright but production of the play as well as the script, is taken into account.

2012 Winner: *Water by the Spoonful* by Quiara Alegría Hudes; Finalists: *Other Desert Cities* by Jon Robin Baitz; *Sons of the Prophet* by Stephen Karam

PAST PULITZER PRIZE WINNERS If year is missing, no award was presented that year. **1918:** *Why Marry?* by Jesse Lynch Williams **1920:** *Beyond the Horizon* by Eugene O'Neill **1921:** *Miss Lulu Bett* by Zona Gale **1922:** *Anna Christie* by Eugene O'Neill **1923:** *Icebound* by Owen Davis **1924:** *Hell-Bent for Heaven* by Hatcher Hughes **1925:** *They Knew What They Wanted* by Sidney Howard **1926:** *Craig's Wife* by George Kelly **1927:** *In Abraham's Bosom* by Paul Green **1928:** *Strange Interlude* by Eugene O'Neill **1929:** *Street Scene* by Elmer Rice **1930:** *The Green Pastures* by Marc Connelly **1931:** *Alison's House* by Susan Glaspell **1932:** *Of Thee I Sing* by George S. Kaufman, Morrie Ryskind, Ira and George Gershwin **1933:** *Both Your Houses* by Maxwell Anderson **1934:** *Men in White* by Sidney Kingsley **1935:** *The Old Maid* by Zoe Atkins **1936:** *Idiot's Delight* by Robert E. Sherwood **1937:** *You Can't Take It with You* by Moss Hart and George S. Kaufman **1938:** *Our Town* by Thornton Wilder **1939:** *Abe Lincoln in Illinois* by Robert E. Sherwood **1940:** *The Time of Your Life* by William Saroyan **1941:** *There Shall Be No Night* by Robert E. Sherwood **1943:** *The Skin of Our Teeth* by Thornton Wilder **1945:** *Harvey* by Mary Chase **1946:** *State of the Union* by Howard Lindsay and Russel Crouse **1948:** *A Streetcar Named Desire* by Tennessee Williams **1949:** *Death of a Salesman* by Arthur Miller **1950:** *South Pacific* by Richard Rodgers, Oscar Hammerstein II, and Joshua Logan **1952:** *The Shrike* by Joseph Kramm **1953:** *Picnic* by William Inge **1954:** *The Teahouse of the August Moon* by John Patrick **1955:** *Cat on a Hot Tin Roof* by Tennessee Williams **1956:** *The Diary of Anne Frank* by Frances Goodrich and Albert Hackett **1957:** *Long Day's Journey Into Night* by Eugene O'Neill **1958:** *Look Homeward, Angel* by Ketti Frings **1959:** *J.B.* by Archibald MacLeish **1960:** *Fiorello!* by Jerome Weidman, George Abbott, Sheldon Harnick, and Jerry Bock **1961:** *All the Way Home* by Tad Mosel **1962:** *How to Succeed in Business Without Really Trying* by Abe Burrows, Willie Gilbert, Jack Weinstock, and Frank Loesser **1965:** *The Subject Was Roses* by Frank D. Gilroy **1967:** *A Delicate Balance* by Edward Albee **1969:** *The Great White Hope* by Howard Sackler **1970:** *No Place to Be Somebody* by Charles Gordone **1971:** *The Effect of Gamma Rays on Man-in-the-Moon Marigolds* by Paul Zindel **1973:** *That Championship Season* by Jason Miller **1975:** *Seascape* by Edward Albee **1976:** *A Chorus Line* by Michael Bennett, James Kirkwood, Nicholas Dante, Marvin Hamlisch, and Edward Kleban **1977:** *The Shadow Box* by Michael Cristofer **1978:** *The Gin Game* by D.L. Coburn **1979:** *Buried Child* by Sam Shepard **1980:** *Talley's Folly* by Lanford Wilson **1981:** *Crimes of the Heart* by Beth Henley **1982:** *A Soldier's Play* by Charles Fuller **1983:** *'night, Mother* by Marsha Norman **1984:** *Glengarry Glen Ross* by David Mamet **1985:** *Sunday in the Park with George* by James Lapine and Stephen Sondheim **1987:** *Fences* by August Wilson **1988:** *Driving Miss Daisy* by Alfred Uhry **1989:** *The Heidi Chronicles* by Wendy Wasserstein **1990:** *The Piano Lesson* by August Wilson **1991:** *Lost in Yonkers* by Neil Simon **1992:** *The Kentucky Cycle* by Robert Schenkkan **1993:** *Angels in America: Millenium Approaches* by Tony Kushner **1994:** *Three Tall Women* by Edward Albee **1995:** *Young Man from Atlanta* by Horton Foote **1996:** *Rent* by Jonathan Larson **1998:** *How I Learned to Drive* by Paula Vogel **1999:** *Wit* by Margaret Edson **2000:** *Dinner with Friends* by Donald Margulies **2001:** *Proof* by David Auburn **2002:** *Topdog/Underdog* by Suzan Lori-Parks **2003:** *Anna in the Tropics* by Nilo Cruz **2004:** *I Am My Own Wife* by Doug Wright **2005:** *Doubt* by John Patrick Shanley **2007:** *Rabbit Hole* by David Lindsay-Abaire **2008:** *August: Osage County* by Tracy Letts **2009:** *Ruined* by Lynn Nottage **2010:** *Next to Normal* by Tom Kitt and Brian Yorkey **2011:** *Clybourne Park* by Bruce Norris

REGIONAL AND OTHER THEATRICAL AWARDS

American Theatre Critics Association Awards
STEINBERG NEW PLAY AWARD AND CITATIONS

March 31, 2012; Ceremony at the Humana Festival at Actors Theatre Louisville; founded in 1977. The Harold and Mimi Steinberg/ATCA Awards honor new plays that had their world premieres in the previous year in professional productions outside New York City. From 1977–1984 ACTA gave only one play a citation. After 1985, three citations were awarded. Currently the new play award comes with a $25,000 prize and the two other citations are awarded a $7,500 prize.

2012 New Play Award: *Pilgrims Musa and Sheri in the New World*, by Yussef El Guindi (premiered at A Contemporary Theatre in Seattle); **Citations:** *On the Spectrum* (premiered at Mixed Blood Theatre in Minneapolis) & *Edith Can Shoot Things and Hit Them*, by A. Ray Pamatmat (premiered at Actor's Theatre of Louisville/Humana Festival of Plays)

Past Recipients (after 1986, first entry is the principal citation): **1977:** *And the Soul Shall Dance* by Wakako Yamauchi **1978:** *Getting Out* by Marsha Norman **1979:** *Loose Ends* by Michael Weller **1980:** *Custer* by Robert E. Ingham **1981:** *Chekhov in Yalta* by John Driver and Jeffrey Haddow **1982:** *Talking With* by Jane Martin **1983:** *Closely Related* by Bruce MacDonald **1984:** *Wasted* by Fred Gamel **1985:** (no principal citation) *Scheherazade* by Marisha Chamberlain, *The Shaper* by John Steppling, *A Shayna Maidel* by Barbara Lebow **1986:** *Fences* by August Wilson; *Fugue* by Lenora Thuna; *Hunting Cockroaches* by Januscz Glowacki **1987:** *A Walk in the Woods* by Lee Blessing; *The Film Society* by John Robin Baitz; *Back to the World* by Stephen Mack Jones **1988:** *Heathen Valley* by Romulus Linney; *The Voice of the Prairie* by John Olive; *The Deal* by Matthew Witten **1989:** *The Piano Lesson* by August Wilson; *Generations* by Dennis Clontz; *The Downside* by Richard Dresser **1990:** *2* by Romulus Linney; *Pick Up Ax* by Anthony Clarvoe; *Marvin's Room* by Scott McPherson **1991:** *Two Trains Running* by August Wilson; *Sincerity Forever* by Mac Wellman; *The Ohio State Murders* by Adrienne Kennedy **1992:** *Could I Have This Dance* by Doug Haverty; *American Enterprise* by Jeffrey Sweet; *Miss Evers' Boys* by David Feldshuh **1993:** *Children of Paradise: Shooting a Dream* by Steven Epp, Felicity Jones, Dominique Serrand, and Paul Walsh; *Black Elk Speaks* by Christopher Sergel; *Hurricane* by Anne Galjour **1994:** *Keely and Du* by Jane Martin **1995:** *The Nanjing Race* by Reggie Cheong-Leen; *Rush Limbaugh in Night School* by Charlie Varon; *The Waiting Room* by Lisa Loomer **1996:** *Amazing Grace* by Michael Cristofer; *Jungle Rot* by Seth Greenland; *Seven Guitars* by August Wilson **1997:** *Jack and Jill* by Jane Martin; *The Last Night of Ballyhoo* by Alfred Uhry; *The Ride Down Mount Morgan* by Arthur Miller **1998:** *The Cider House Rules, Part II* by Peter Parnell; *Jitney* by August Wilson; *The Old Settler* by John Henry Redwood **1999:** *Book of Days* by Lanford Wilson; *Dinner With Friends* by Donald Margulies; *Expecting Isabel* by Lisa Loomer **2000:** *Oo-Bla-Dee* by Regina Taylor; *Compleat Female Stage Beauty* by Jeffrey Hatcher; *Syncopation* by Allan Knee **2001:** *Anton in Show Business* by Jane Martin; *Big Love* by Charles L. Mee; *King Hedley II* by August Wilson **2002:** *The Carpetbagger's Children* by Horton Foote; *The Action Against Sol Schumann* by Jeffrey Sweet; *Joe and Betty* by Murray Mednick **2003:** *Anna in the Tropics* by Nilo Cruz; *Recent Tragic Events* by Craig Wright; *Resurrection Blues* by Arthur Miller **2004:** *Intimate Apparel* by Lynn Nottage; *Gem of the Ocean* by August Wilson; *The Love Song of J. Robert Oppenheimer* by Carson Kreitzer **2005:** *The Singing Forest* by Craig Lucas; *After Ashley* by Gina Gionfriddo; *The Clean House* by Sarah Ruhl; *Madagascar* by J.T. Rogers **2006:** *A Body of Water* by Lee Blessing; *Red Light Winter* by Adam Rapp; *Radio Golf* by August Wilson **2007:** *Hunter Gatherers* by Peter Sinn Nachtrieb; *Opus* by Michael Hollinger; *Guest Artist* by Jeff Daniels **2008:** *33 Variations* by Moises Kaufman; *End Days* by Deborah Zoe Laufer; *Dead Man's Cell Phone* by Sarah Ruhl **2009:** *Song of Extinction* by E.M. (Ellen) Lewis; *Great Falls* by Lee Blessing; *Superior Donuts* by Tracy Letts **2010:** *Equivocation* by Bill Cain; *Time Stands Still* by Donald Margulies; *Legacy of Light* by Karen Zacarias **2011:** *Nine Circles* by Bill Cain; *The Good Counselor* by Kathryn Grant; *The History of Invulnerability* by David Bar Katz

M. ELIZABETH OSBORN AWARD

March 31, 2012: Ceremony at the Humana Festival at Actors Theatre Louisville; established in 1993. Presented by the American Theatre Critics Association in memory of Theatre Communications Group and American Theatre play editor M. Elizabeth Osborn to an emerging playwright who has not received other major national awards, has not had a significant New York production, and whose work has not been staged widely in regional theatres; $1,000 prize and recognition in the *Best Plays Theater Yearbook* edited by Jeffrey Eric Jenkins.

2012 Winner: Darren Canady, *Brothers of the Dust* (premiered at Congo Square Theatre Company in Chicago)

Past Recipients: 1994: *Hurricane* by Anne Galjour **1995:** *Rush Limbaugh in Night School* by Charlie Varon **1996:** *Beast on the Moon* by Richard Kalinoski **1997:** *Thunder Knocking On the Door* by Keith Glover **1998:** *The Glory of Living* by Rebecca Gilman **1999:** *Lamarck* by Dan O'Brien **2000:** *Marked Tree* by Coby Goss **2001:** *Waiting to Be Invited* by S.M. Shephard-Massat **2002:** *Chagrin Falls* by Mia McCullough **2003:** *The Dinosaur Within* by John Walch **2004:** *The Intelligent Design of Jenny Chow* by Rolin Jones **2005:** *Madagascar* by J.T. Rogers **2006:** *American Fiesta* by Steven Tomlinson **2007** *Vestibular Sense* by Ken LaZebnik **2008:** *Gee's Bend* by Elyzabeth Wilder **2009:** *Our Enemies: Lively Scenes of Love and Combat* by Yusseff El Guindi **2010:** *Perfect Mendacity* by Jason Wells; **2011:** *When January Feels Like Summer* by Cori Thomas

AUDELCO Awards - The "VIVS"

Monday, November 14, 2011; Harlem Stages/Aaron Davis Hall – Marion Anderson Theatre; 39th annual. Presented for excellence in Black Theatre for the 2010–2011 season by the Audience Development Committee, created by Vivian Robinson. Honorary Co-Chairs: Samuel L. Jackson and LaTanya Richardson; Co-Chairs: Hattie and Tony Winston; Co-hosts: Cheryl Willis and Danny Simmons

Outstanding Dramatic Production of the Year: *Knock Me a Kiss* (New Federal Theatre/Legacy Creative Arts Co.)

Outstanding Musical Production of the Year: *It Ain't Nothin' But the Blues* (New Harlem Arts Theatre)/*The Widow and Miss Mamie* (Harlem School of the Arts)

Outstanding Director/Dramatic Production: Chuck Smith, *Knock Me a Kiss* (New Federal Theatre/Legacy Creative Arts Co.)

Outstanding Director/Musical Production: Lee Kirk, *Knock Me a Kiss* (New Federal Theatre/Legacy Creative Arts Co.)

Outstanding Choreographer: Tracy Jack, *It Ain't Nothing' But the Blues* (New Harlem Arts Theatre)

Outstanding Playwright: Charles Smith, *Knock Me a Kiss* (New Federal Theatre/Legacy Creative Arts Co.)

Outstanding Lead Actor: Andre DeShields, *Knock Me a Kiss* (New Federal Theatre/Legacy Creative Arts Co.)

Outstanding Lead Actress: Sanaa Lathan, *By the Way, Meet Vera Stark* (Second Stage Theatre) Kimberlee Monroe, *Nobody Knew Where They Was* (H.A.D.L.E.Y. Players)

Outstanding Supporting Actor: Andre Holland, *The Whipping Man* (City Center Stage I)

Outstanding Supporting Actress: Marie Thomas, *Knock Me a Kiss* (New Federal Theatre/Legacy Creative Arts Co.)

Outstanding Performance in a Musical/Female: Toni Seawright, *The Widow and Miss Mamie* (Harlem School of the Arts)

Outstanding Performance in a Musical/Male: Tommie Thompson, *The Widow and Miss Mamie* (Harlem School of the Arts)

Outstanding Ensemble Performance: *Playing with Heiner Muller* (Castillo Theatre)

Outstanding Solo Performance: Stephanie Berry, *The Shaneequa Chronicles* (Ensemble Studio Theatre)

Outstanding Set Design: Anthony Davidson, *Knock Me a Kiss* (New Federal Theatre/Legacy Creative Arts Co.)

Outstanding Costume Design: Ali Turns, *Knock Me a Kiss* (New Federal Theatre/Legacy Creative Arts Co.)

Outstanding Lighting Design: Shirley Prendergast, *Knock Me a Kiss* (New Federal Theatre/Legacy Creative Arts Co.)

Outstanding Sound Design: Bill Toles, *Knock Me a Kiss* (New Federal Theatre/Legacy Creative Arts Co.)

Outstanding Pioneer Awards: Felix E. Cochren, James Pringle, Mary Alice

Board of Directors Awards: Jackie Jeffries, Jacquetta I. McMurray, Rome Neal

Rising Star Award: Eden Sanaa Duncan Smith

Special Achievement Awards: Hazel Rosetta Smith; Clifford B. Simmons; Blue Nile Passage, Inc.; The Significant Elders

Barrymore Awards

October 3, 2011; Walnut Street Theatre; 17th annual. Presented by the Theatre Alliance of Greater Philadelphia for excellence in theatre in the greater Philadelphia area for the 2010-2011 season.

Outstanding Production of a Play: *In the Next Room, or the vibrator play* (Wilma Theater)

Outstanding Production of a Musical: *The Flea and the Professor* (Arden Theatre Company)

Outstanding Direction of a Play: Blanka Zizka, *In the Next Room, or the vibrator play* (Wilma Theater)

Outstanding Direction of a Musical: Matthew Decker, *The 25th Annual Putnam County Spelling Bee* (Theatre Horizon)

Outstanding Leading Actor in a Play: Dan Hodge, *Around the World in 80 Days* (Delaware Theatre Company)

Outstanding Leading Actress in a Play: Anna Deavere Smith, *Let Me Down Easy* (Philadelphia Theatre Company)

Outstanding Leading Actor in a Musical: Rob McClure, *The Flea and the Professor* (Arden Theatre Company)

Outstanding Leading Actress in a Musical: Melinda Chua, *Miss Saigon* (Walnut Street Theatre)

Outstanding Supporting Actor in a Play: James Ijames, *Superior Donuts* (Arden Theatre Company)

Outstanding Supporting Actress in a Play: Krista Apple, *In the Next Room, or the vibrator play* (Wilma Theater)

Outstanding Supporting Actor in a Musical: Michael Doherty, *The 25th Annual Putnam County Spelling Bee* (Theatre Horizon)

Outstanding Supporting Actress in a Musical: Rachel Camp, *The 25th Annual Putnam County Spelling Bee* (Theatre Horizon)

Outstanding Set Design: Alexis Distler, *In the Next Room, or the vibrator play* (Wilma Theater)

Outstanding Lighting Design: Thom Weaver, *In the Next Room, or the vibrator play* (Wilma Theater)

Outstanding Costume Design: Oana Botez-Ban, *In the Next Room, or the vibrator play* (Wilma Theater)

Outstanding Sound Design: Christopher Colucci, *In the Next Room, or the vibrator play* (Wilma Theater)

Outstanding Music Direction: Alex Bechtel, *My Way: A Musical Tribute to Frank Sinatra* (Walnut Street Theatre)

Outstanding Choreography/Movement: Waldo Warshaw & Aaron Cromie, *The Lieutenant of Inishmore* (Theatre Exile)

Outstanding New Play: *Ghost-Writer* (Arden Theatre Company)

Outstanding Ensemble in a Play: *In the Next Room, or the vibrator play* (Wilma Theater)

Outstanding Ensemble in a Musical: *The 25th Annual Putnam County Spelling Bee* (Theatre Horizon)

Ted & Stevie Wolf Award for New Approaches to Collaborations: Robert Smythe and the Chamber Orchestra of Philadelphia — Stravinsky's *l'Histoire du Soldat* — Kimmel Center for the Performing Arts

F. Otto Haas Award for Emerging Philadelphia Theatre Artist: James Ijames

Brown Martin Philadelphia Award: *Love and Communication* (Passage Theatre)

Excellence in Theatre Education and Community Service Award: Otis D. Hackney III — Principal, South Philadelphia High School — The Wilma Theater/1812 Productions/Philadelphia Young Playwrights

Lifetime Achievement Award: Harry Dietzler, Executive Director, Upper Darber Summer Stage

Barrymore Tribute for a Distinguished Artist in the Theatre: Terrence McNally

Bay Area Theatre Critics Circle Awards

April 2, 2012; Palace of the Fine Arts Theatre Lobby; 36th Annual. Presented by members of the print and electronic media for outstanding achievement in theatre in the San Francisco Bay Area for the 2011 calendar year.

THEATRES OVER 300 SEATS: DRAMA

Entire Production: *Ruined* (Berkeley Repertory Theatre)

Principal Performance, Female: Tonye Patano, *Ruined* (Berkeley Repertory Theatre)

Principal Performance, Male: James Carpenter, *Titus Andronicus* (California Shakespeare Theater)

Supporting Performance, Female: Carla Duren, *Ruined* (Berkeley Repertory Theatre)/Zainab Jah, *Ruined* (Berkeley Repertory Theatre)

Supporting Performance, Male: Rob Campbell, *Titus Andronicus* (California Shakespeare Theater)

Direction: Jonathan Moscone, *Candida* (California Shakespeare Theater)

Set Design: J.B. Wilson, *Clementine in the Lower Nine* (TheatreWorks)

Costume Design: Paloma H. Young, *Titus Andronicus* (California Shakespeare Theater)

Lighting Design: Alexander V. Nichols, *Clybourne Park* (American Conservatory Theater)

Sound Design: Will McCandless, *Candida* (California Shakespeare Theater)

Specialties: Randy Duncan, *Ruined* (Berkeley Repertory Theatre)

Original Script: Bill Cain, *How to Write a New Book for the Bible* (Berkeley Repertory Theatre)

Solo Performance: Rita Moreno, *Rita Moreno: Life Without Makeup* (Berkeley Repertory Theatre)

Ensemble: *The Dresser* (San Jose Repertory Theatre)

Touring Production: *The Wild Bride* (Berkeley Repertory Theatre & Kneehigh Theatre Company)

Theatres Over 300 Seats: Musicals

Entire Production: *Seussical: The Musical* (Berkeley Playhouse)

Principal Performance, Female: Nandi Drayton, *Seussical: The Musical* (Berkeley Playhouse)

Principal Performance, Male: Jason Hite, *Hairspray* (Contra Costa Musical Theatre)

Supporting Performance, Female: Rebecca Pingree, *Seussical: The Musical* (Berkeley Playhouse)

Supporting Performance, Male: Marcus Klinger, *Hairspray* (Contra Costa Musical Theatre)

Direction: Jason Moore, *Tales of the City* (American Conservatory Theater)

Music Direction: Tal Ariel, *Suessical: The Musical* (Berkeley Playhouse)

Set Design: Douglas W. Schmidt, *Tales of the City* (American Conservatory Theater)

Costume Design: Beaver Bauer, *Tales of the City* (American Conservatory Theater)

Lighting Design: Robert Wierzel, *Tales of the City* (American Conservatory Theater)

Sound Design: John Shivers, *Tales of the City* (American Conservatory Theater)

Original Script: Jeff Whitty, *Tales of the City* (American Conservatory Theater)

Specialties: Jennifer Perry (choreography), *Hairspray* (Contra Costa Musical Theatre)

Solo Performance: No award presented this season

Ensemble: *Seussical: The Musical* (Berkeley Playhouse)

Touring Production: *The Wild Bride* (Berkeley Repertory Theatre & Kneehigh Theatre Company)

THEATRES 100 – 300 SEATS: DRAMA

Entire Production: *Metamorphosis* (Aurora Theatre Company)

Principal Performance, Female: Susi Damilano, *Harper Regan* (San Francisco Playhouse)

Principal Performance, Male: Alexander Crowther, *Metamorphosis* (Auora Theatre Company)

Supporting Performance, Female: Omoze Idehenre, *Seven Guitars* (Marin Theatre Company)

Supporting Performance, Male: (tie) Charles Dean, *A Delicate Balance* (Aurora Theatre Company); Craig Barker, *The Glass Menagerie* (Marin Theatre Company)

Direction: Mark Jackson, *Metamorphosis* (Aurora Theatre Company)

Set Design: Nina Ball, *Metamorphosis* (Aurora Theatre Company)

Costume Design: (tie) Lindsay W. Davis, *The Lily's Revenge* (Magic Theatre); Callie Floor, *Seven Guitars* (Marin Theatre Company)

Lighting Design: Kurt Landisman, *Seven Guitars* (Marin Theatre Company)

Sound Design: Matthew Stines, *Metamorphosis* (Aurora Theatre Company)

Specialties: Stef Baldwin, Cher Simnitt (Doll Designers), *Reborning* (San Francisco Playhouse)

Original Script: David Faar, Gisli Orn Gardarsson, *Metamorphosis* (Aurora Theatre Company)

Solo Performance: David Cale, *Palomino* (Aurora Theatre Company)

Ensemble: *Seven Guitars* (Marin Theatre Company)

THEATRES 100 – 300 SEATS: MUSICALS

Entire Production: *Assassins* (Ray of Light Theatre)

Principal Performance, Female: Anna Ishida, *Beardo* (Shotgun Players)

Principal Performance, Male: Ashkon Davaran, *Beardo* (Shotgun Players)

Supporting Performance, Female: Lisa-Marie Newton, *Assassins* (Ray of Light Theatre)

Supporting Performance, Male: Gregory Sottolano, *Assassins* Ray of Light Theatre)

Direction: Jason Hoover, *Assassins* (Ray of Light Theatre)

Musical Direction: David Möschler, *Assassins* (Ray of Light Theatre)

Set Design: Maya Linke, *Assassins* (Ray of Light Theatre)

Costume Design: Christine Crook, *Beardo* (Shotgun Players)

Lighting Design: Cathie Anderson, *Assassins* (Ray of Light Theatre)

Sound Design: Brendan West, *Beardo* (Shotgun Players)

Specialties: Chris Black (choreographer), *Beardo* (Shotgun Players)

Original Script: Jason Craig, *Beardo* (Shotgun Players)

Ensemble: *Assassins* (Ray of Light Theatre)

THEATRES UNDER 99 SEATS: DRAMA

Entire Production: *Pelleas & Melisande* (Cutting Ball Theater)

Principal Performance, Female: Ann Kendrick, *Driving Miss Daisy* (Diablo Actors Ensemble)

Principal Performance, Male: (tie) L. Peter Callender, *Driving Miss Daisy* (Diablo Actors' Enemble); Don DeMico, *Death of a Salesman* (The Pear Avenue Theatre); Michael Phillis, *Wish We Were Here* (New Conservatory Theatre Center)

Supporting Performance, Female: Michelle Ianiro, *Clue* (Boxcar Theatre)

Supporting Performance, Male: Paul Stout, *Indulgencies in the Louisville Harem* (Off-Broadway West Theatre Company)

Direction: Richard Harder, *Master Harold and the Boys* (Off-Broadway West Theatre Company)

Original Script: Geoff Hoyle, *Geezer* (The Marsh)

Ensemble: *Pelleas & Melisandre* (Cutting Ball Theater)

Costume Design: (tie) Ann Kuchins, *Death of a Salesman* (The Pear Avenue Theatre); Tammara Plankers, Jacki Medernach, *The Mystery of Irma Vep* (Masquers Playhouse)

Lighting Design: Christian Mejia, Alexander Sanchak, *Into the Clear Blue Sky* (Sleepwalkers Theatre)

Specialties: Bert van Aalsburg (Set Design), *How the Other Half Loves* (Off Broadway West Theatre Company)

THEATRES UNDER 99 SEATS: MUSICALS

Entire Production: *The Musical of Musicals* (Masquers Playhouse)

Principal Performance, Female: Leigh Crow, *Vice Palace* (Thrillpeddlers)

Principal Performance, Male: No award presented this season

Supporting Performance, Female: Bonnie Suval, *Vice Palace* (Thrillpeddlers)

Supporting Performance, Male: Eric Tyson Wertz, *Vice Palace* (Thrillpeddlers)

Direction: Jeremy Messmer, *Side by Side by Sondheim* (Hapgood Theatre Company)

Musical Direction: Ted Bigornia, Pat King, *The Musical of Musicals* (Masquers Playhouse)

Costume Design: Kära Emry, *Vice Palace* (Thrillpeddlers)

Lighting Design: Nicholas Torre, *Vice Palace* (Thrillpeddlers)

Original Script: Margery Fairchild, *Eleanor* (Dark Porch Theatre & DIVAfest)

Ensemble: *The Musical of Musicals* (Masquers Playhouse)

Specialties: John LeFan (choreographer), *Vice Palace* (Thrillpeddlers

SPECIAL AWARDS

Paine Knickerbocker Award: Shotgun Players

Jerry Friedman Award (former the Barbara Bladen Porter Award): James Dunn, longtime faculty member of Marin College, Artistic Director of the Mountain Play

Gene Price Award: Tom Kelly, longtime *San Francisco Bay Times* Arts Editor

Bistro Awards

April 23, 2012; Gotham Comedy Club; 27th annual. Presented by *Back Stage* for outstanding achievement in the cabaret field; Winners selected by a committee consisting of Elizabeth Ahlfors (*Cabaret Scenes*), David Finkle (*Back Stage's* "Bistro Bits" columnist), Kevin Scott Hall (Edge Media Network, BistroAwards.com), Rob Lester (*Cabaret Scenes* & *TalkinBroadway.com*), Erv Raible (Executive/Artistic Director of the Cabaret Conference – Yale University), Roy Sander (former "Bistro Bits" columnist) and Sherry Eaker (*Back Stage* Editor at Large); Produced by Sherry Eaker; Directed by Sara Louise Lazarus; Musical Direction by Lenny Babbish; Originally created by the late *Back Stage* cabaret critic Bob Harrington.

Outstanding Vocalist: Amy Beth Williams (Metropolitan Room)

Outstanding Vocalist: Nicholas King (Don't Tell Mama, Iridium, Metropolitan Room)

Outstanding Musical Series: *If It Only Runs a Minute*, Created and produced by Jennifer Ashley Tepper and Kevin Michael Murphy; Musical Direction by Caleb Hoyer (Le Poisson Rouge, Caroline's on Broadway)

Outstanding Debut: Lauren Fox (Metropolitan Room)

Ira Eaker Special Achievement Award: Aaron Weinstein

Outstanding Major Engagement: Rita Gardner, *Try to Remember: A Look Back at Off-Broadway* (Metropolitan Room)

Outstanding Recording: Parker Scott, Wells Hanley, *Selecting Souvenirs*

Outstanding Ongoing Excellence as Jazz Instrumentalist: Warren Vaché

Outstanding Theme Show: Billie Roe, *Dangerous Women—Life in Film Noir* (Don't Tell Mama)

Outstanding Tribute Show: Jean Brassard, *The Kid from Paris: Jean Brassard Sings Yves Montand* (The Triad); Terese Genecco, Shaynee Rainbolt, Billy Stritch, Russ Garcia, *Russ Garcia's 95th Birthday Show* (Iridium)

Outstanding Musical Comedy: *Max & Maxine: Together Again!* Conceived, written and performed by Gary Adler, Bryan Scott Johnson, Jen Perry (Don't Tell Mama)

Outstanding Ongoing Artistry in Jazz: Dee Dee Bridgewater

Outstanding Ongoing Vocal Artisty: Joyce Breach

Outstanding Comedy Artisty: Justin Sayre, *The Meeting* (The Duplex)

Outstanding Musical Director: Jon Weber

Outstanding Contributions to American Popular Music: Melissa Manchester

Bob Harrington Lifetime Achievement Award: Kaye Ballard

Broadway.com Audience Choice Awards

May 13, 2012; Allen Room at Jazz at Lincoln Center; 13th annual. Host: Darren Criss. The Broadway.com Audience Awards give real theatergoers a chance to honor their favorite Broadway and Off-Broadway shows and performers.

Favorite Musical: *Newsies*

Favorite Play: *Peter and the Starcatcher*

Favorite Musical Revival: *Godspell*

Favorite Play Revival: *Death of a Salesman*

Favorite Actor in a Musical: Jeremy Jordan, *Newsies*

Favorite Actress in a Musical: Laura Osnes, *Bonnie & Clyde*

Favorite Actor in a Play: Alan Rickman, *Seminar*

Favorite Actress in a Play: Celia Keenan-Bolger, *Peter and the Starcatcher*

Favorite Diva Performance: Patti LuPone, *An Evening with Patti LuPone*

Favorite Funny Performance: Christian Borle, *Peter and the Starcatcher*

Favorite Onstage Pair: Jeremy Jordan & Kara Lindsay, *Newsies*

Favorite Breakthrough Performance: Andrew Garfield, *Death of a Salesman*

Breakthrough Performance (Female): Krysta Rodriguez, *The Addams Family*

Favorite Replacement: Darren Criss, *How to Succeed in Business Without Really Trying*

Favorite New Broadway Song: "Something to Believe In," *Newsies*

Favorite Long-Running Broadway Show: *Wicked*

Favorite Tour: *Wicked*

Carbonell Awards

April 2, 2012; Broward Center for the Performing Arts – Amaturo Theatre; 36th annual. Presented for outstanding achievement in South Florida theatre during the 2011 calendar year.

Best New Work: *Stuff*, Michael McKeever, Caldwell Theatre Company

Best Production of a Play: *All My Sons* (Palm Beach Dramaworks)

Best Director, Play: J. Barry Lewis, *All My Sons* (Palm Beach Dramaworks)

Best Actor, Play: Kenneth Tigar, *All My Sons* (Palm Beach Dramaworks)

Best Actress, Play: Deborah Sherman, *Side Effects* (Mosaic Theatre)

Best Supporting Actor, Play: Marckenson Charles, *Superior Donuts* (Gablestage)

Best Supporting Actress, Play: Angie Radosh, *Stuff* (Caldwell Theatre Company)

Best Production of a Musical: *Crazy for You* (Maltz Jupiter Theatre)

Best Director, Musical: Mark Martino, *Crazy for You* (Maltz Jupiter Theatre)

Best Musical Director: Helen Gregory, *Crazy for You* (Maltz Jupiter Theatre)

Best Actor, Musical: Matt Loehr, *Crazy for You* (Maltz Jupiter Theatre)

Best Actress, Musical: Katherine Walker, *The Sound of Music* (Maltz Jupiter Theatre)

Best Supporting Actor, Musical: Avi Hoffman, *Hairspray* (Actor's Playhouse)

Best Supporting Actress, Musical: Julie Kleiner, *Hairspray* (Actors' Playhouse)

Best Musical Direction: Eric Alsford, *Miss Saigon* (Actors' Playhouse at the Miracle Theatre)

Best Choreography: Shea Sullivan, *Crazy for You* (Maltz Jupiter Theatre)

Best Scenic Design, Play or Musical: Tim Bennett, *Stuff* (Caldwell Theatre Company)

Best Lighting, Play or Musical: Patrick Tennent, *Jacob Marley's Christmas Carol* (Actor's Playhouse)

Best Costume Design, Play or Musical: José M. Rivera, *Joseph and the Amazing Technicolor Dreamcoat* (Maltz Jupiter Theatre)

Best Sound Design: Alexander Herrin, *Jacob Marley's Christmas Carol* (Actor's Playhouse)

Best Ensemble, Play or Musical: *The Irish Curse* (Mosaic Theatre)

Special Awards

George Abbott Award: Jay H. Harris, Producer, Board Member, Carbonell Awards

Howard Kleinberg Award: Mary Brecht, Director, Broward Cultural Division

Bill Von Maurer Award: Maltz Jupiter Theatre

Carbonell Scholarship Winners: Abby Jaras, Boca Raton Community High School; Jennifer Jaroslavsky, American Heritage School of Boca/Delray; Kimberlee Johnson, JP Taravella High School; Valerie Novakoff, Pine Crest School; and Mario Pavón, Boca Raton Community High School

Clive Barnes Award

December 5, 2011; Walter Reade Theatre; 2nd Annual. Presented by the Clive Barnes Foundation in honor of the late theatre and dance critic who died in 2008, and who also served as a member of the Theatre World Awards Voting Committee for several years. Awarded to a young actor and a young dancer for outstanding achievement.

Award for Theatre: MJ Rodriguez, *Rent*

Award for Dance: Isabella Boyston (American Ballet Theatre)

Connecticut Critics' Circle Awards

June 24, 2012; Mark Twain House and Museum, Hartford, Connecticut; 22nd annual. Presented for outstanding achievement in Connecticut theatre, selected by statewide reviews, feature writers, columnists, and broadcasters, for 2011–2012 season.

Outstanding Production of a Play: *Water by the Spoonful* (Hartford Stage)

Outstanding Production of a Musical: *Into the Woods* (Westport Country Playhouse); *Show Boat* (Goodspeed Musicals)

Outstanding Actress in a Play: Brenda Thomas, *Sty of the Blind Pig* (TheaterWorks of Hartford); Annalee Jeffries, *Suddenly Last Summer* (Westport Country Playhouse)

Outstanding Actor in a Play: Steve Epp, *A Doctor in Spite of Himself* (Yale Repertory Theatre, in coproduction with Berkeley Repertory Theatre); Sam Tsoutsouvas, *The Crucible* (Hartford Stage); John Horton, *The Circle* (Westport Country Playhouse)

Outstanding Actress in a Musical: Jacqueline Petrocccia, *Always, Patsy Cline* (Ivoryton Playhouse); Sara Uriarte Berry, *Show Boat* (Goodspeed Musicals); Dana Steingold, *Into the Woods* (Westport Country Playhouse); Kirsten Wyatt, *Mame* (Goodspeed Musicals); Claire Brownell, *Boeing, Boeing* (Hartford Stage)

Outstanding Actor in a Musical: Stanley Boherek, *February House* (Long Wharf Theatre); Ken Barnett, *February House* (Long Wharf Theatre); Erik Lochtefeld, *February House* (Long Wharf Theatre)

Outstanding Direction of a Play: David McCallum, *Water by the Spoonful*; Sam Gold, *The Realistic Joneses* (Yale Repertory Theatre); Christopher Bayes, *A Doctor in Spite of Himself* (Yale Repertory Theatre)

Outstanding Direction of a Musical: Rob Ruggiero, *Show Boat*; Mark Lamos, *Into the Woods*

Outstanding Choreography: Noah Racey, *Show Boat*

Outstanding Set Design: Alexander Dodge, *The Tempest* (Hartford Stage) and *The Circle* (Hartford Stage)

Outstanding Lighting Design: Jon Lasiter, *City of Angels* (Goodspeed Musicals)

Outstanding Costume Design: Robin L. McGee, *My One and Only* (Goodspeed Musicals); Fabio Toblini, *Bell, Book and Candle* (Hartford Stage in collaboration with Long Wharf Theatre)

Outstanding Sound Design: John Gromada, *Lips Together, Teeth Apart* (Westport Country Playhouse)

Outstanding Ensemble Performance: *Into the Woods*; *Water by the Spoonful*; *The Realistic Joneses*

Outstanding Debut Awards: Carey Cannata, *Over the Tavern* (Seven Angels Theatre); Ben Cole, *The Tempest* (Hartford Stage)

Tom Killen Memorial Award: Jacqueline Hubbard, Artistic Director, Ivorytown

Special Recognition: Mike Reiss, *I'm Connecticut* (Connecticut Repertory Theatre)'

Craig Noel Awards

February 6, 2012; Museum of Contemporary Art; 10th annual. Presented by the San Diego Theatre Critics Circle for outstanding achievement in the greater San Diego theatre in the 2011 calendar year.

Outstanding Resident Musical: *Jane Austen's Emma* (The Old Globe)

Outstanding Direction of a Musical: Sean Murray, *Cabaret* (Cygnet Theatre)

Outstanding Musical Direction: Steve Funderson, *The Who's Tommy* (San Diego REPertory Theatre)

Outstanding Music for a Play: Shaun Davey, *The Tempest* (The Old Globe)

Outstanding Lead Performance in a Musical, Female: Linda Libby, *Gypsy* (ion Theatre); Karson St. John, *Cabaret* (Cygnet Theatre)

Outstanding Lead Performance in a Musical, Male: B. Slade, *The Who's Tommy* (San Diego REPertory Theatre)

Outstanding Featured Performance in a Musical, Male: Randall Hickman, *Hairspray* (Moonlight Stage)

Outstanding Featured Performance in a Musical, Female: Katie Whalley, *Gypsy* (ion Theatre)

Outstanding Choreography: David Brannen, *Cabaret* (Cygnet Theatre)

Outstanding Direction of a Play: Sam Gold, *August: Osage County* (The Old Globe)

Outstanding Sound Design: Melanie Chen, *Angels in America* (ion Theatre); Deborah Gilmour Smyth, *The Book of the Dun Cow* (Lamb's Players Theatre)

Outstanding Costume Design: Jennifer Brawn Gittings, *In the Next Room* (or the vibrator play) (San Diego REPertory Theatre); Jeanne Reith, *The Servant of Two Masters* (Lamb's Players Theatre)

Outstanding Lighting Design: Michael Gilliam, *Jane Austen's Emma* (The Old Globe); Karen Filijan, *Angels in America* (ion Theatre)

Outstanding Set Design: Tobin Ost, *Jane Austen's Emma* (The Old Globe)

Outstanding Projection Design: Peter Nigrini, *Sleeping Beauty Wakes* (La Jolla Playhouse)

Outstanding Ensemble: *August: Osage County* (The Old Globe)

Outstanding Featured Performance in a Play, Female: Catalina Maynard, *Angels in America*; Diana Reasonover, *Stick Fly* (Mo' olelo Performing Arts)

Outstanding Featured Performance in a Play, Male: David Ellenstein, *My Name is Asher Lev* (North Coast Repertory Theatre)

Outstanding Lead Performance in a Play, Male: Manny Fernandes, *Of Mice and Men* (New Village Arts Theatre); Robert Foxworth, *Superior Donuts* (San Diego REPertory Theatre)

Outstanding Lead Performance in a Play, Female: Lois Markle, *August: Osage County* (The Old Globe); Rosina Reynolds, *The Glass Menagerie* (Cygnet Theatre)

Outstanding Touring Production: *Jesus Christ Superstar* (La Jolla Playhouse)

Outstanding Dramatic Production: *August: Osage County* (The Old Globe)

Outstanding New Play: *Milk Like Sugar*, by Kirsten Greenidge (La Jolla Playhouse)

Outstanding Young Artist/Sandra Ellis-Troy Scholarship: Lucia Vecchio, *The Diary of Anne Frank* (Onstage Playhouse)

Outstanding Special Event: *Susurrus* (produced by La Jolla Playhouse and presented at San Diego Botanic Garden)

Special Awards

Producer of the Year: Ion Theatre, Claudio Raygoza & Glenn Paris

Actor of the Year: Brian Mackey, *The Woolgatherer* (ion Theatre), *Bash: Latter Day Plays* (ion Theatre); *In the Next Room (or the vibrator play)*(San Diego REPertory Theatre); and *The Glass Menagerie* (Cygnet Theatre)

Don Braunagel Award for Outstanding Work at a Small Theater: *Angels in America* (ion Theatre)

Dramatist Guild Awards

November 14, 2011; The Players Club; Host: David Henry Hwang; Established in 2000, these awards are presented by the Dramatists Guild of America to outstanding writers at the Dramatists Guild Annual Benefit and Awards Gala.

Elizabeth Hull-Kate Warriner Award (to the playwright whose work deals with social, political or religious mores of the time): Bruce Norris, *Clybourne Park*

Frederick Loewe Award for Dramatic Composition: John Kander, Fred Ebb, and David Thompson, *The Scottsboro Boys;* Robert Lopez, Trey Parker & Matt Stone, *The Book of Mormon*

Flora Roberts Award: Christopher Durang

Lifetime Achievement: Paula Vogel

Ed Kleban Prize

May 14, 2012; BMI; 22ⁿᵈ annual. Presented by New Dramatists in honor of Edward Kleban; award is given annually to both a librettist and a lyricist ($100,000 to each recipient payable over two years); Final decisions this year made by: Ted Chapin, Director of the Rodgers and Hammerstein Organization, Marshall Brickman, Tony Award-winning librettist, and Tony Award-winning actress Debra Monk. Board of Directors: Andre Bishop, Elliot H. Brown, Sheldon Harnick, Richard Maltby Jr., John Weidman, and Maury Yeston.

2012 Winners: Most Promising Musical Theatre Lyricist: Marcy Heisler; Most Promising Musical Theatre Librettist (Tie): Andrew Gerle & Matt Shatz

Elliot Norton Awards

May 21, 2012; Paramount Theatre; 30ᵗʰ annual. Presented for outstanding contribution to the theater in Boston from April 2011 to March 2012; selected by a Boston Theater Critics Association selection committee comprising of Don Aucoin, Jared Bowen, Terry Byrne, Carolyn Clay, Nick Dussault, Iris Fanger, Joyce Kulhawik, Sandy MacDonald, Robert Nesti, Jenna Sherer, and Ed Siegel.

Visiting Production: Mabou Mines Dollhouse (ArtsEmerson)

Outstanding Production, Large Company: *All's Well That Ends Well* (Commonwealth Shakespeare Company),

Outstanding Production, Midsized Company: *Red* (SpeakEasy Stage Company)

Outstanding Production, Small Company: *Twelfth Night* (Actors' Shakespeare Project)

Outstanding Production, Fringe Company: *Love Song* (Orfeo Group)

Outstanding Musical Production, Large Company: *The Gershwin's Porgy and Bess* (American Repertory Theater)

Outstanding Musical Production, Small/Midsize Company: *The Drowsy Chaperone* (SpeakEasy Stage Company)

Outstanding New Script: Stephen Sachs, *Bakersfield Mist* (New Repertory Theatre, Wellfleet Harbor Actors Theater)

Outstanding Director, Large Company: Mary Zimmerman, *Candide* (Huntington Theatre Company)

Outstanding Director, Midsized Company: Larry Coen, *The Divine Sister* (SpeakEasy Stage Company)

Outstanding Director, Small/Fringe Company: Danielle Fauteux Jacques, *Uncle Vanya* (Appolinaire Theatre Company)

Outstanding Solo Performance: Yves Jacques, *The Anderson Project* (ArtsEmerson)

Outstanding Actor, Large Company: Richard Clothier, *Richard III* (Propellor, presented by Boston University School of Theatre in association with the Huntington Theatre Company)

Outstanding Actor, Midsized Company: Thomas Derrah, *Red* (SpeakEasy Stage Company)

Outstanding Actor, Small/Fringe Company: Hampton Fluker, *The Brother/Sister Plays* (Company One)

Outstanding Actress: Large Company: Maude Mitchell, *Mabou Mines DollHouse* (ArtsEmerson)

Outstanding Actress, Midsized Company: Kathy St. George, *The Divine Sister*

Outstanding Actress, Small/Fringe Company: Erin Markey, *Green Eyes* (Company One)

Outstanding Musical Performance by an Actress, Small/Midsized Company: Megan McGinnis, *Daddy Long Legs* (Merrimack Repertory Theatre)

Outstanding Musical Performance by an Actor, Small/Midsized Company: Michael Tacconi, *Next to Normal* (SpeakEasy Stage Company)

Outstanding Musical Performance by an Actress, Large Company: Audra McDonald, The Gershwins' *Porgy and Bess* (American Repertory Theater)

Outstanding Musical Performance by an Actor, Large Company: Christopher Sieber, *La Cage aux Folles* (Broadway in Boston)

Outstanding Design, Large Company: *The Andersen Project* (ArtsEmerson: Jean Le Bourdais [set]; Catherine Higgins [costumes]; Nicolas Marois [lighting], Jean Sébastien Côte [sound]; Marie-France Lanviére[Properties]; Jean-Nicholas Marquis [puppetry]; and Jacques Collin, Véronique Couterier, and David Leclerc [images]

Outstanding Design, Fringe/Small/Medium Company: *Twelfth Night* (Actor's Shakespeare Project: Cristina Todesco [sets], Molly Trainer [costumes], Jason Ries [lighting], and Arshan Gailus [sound])

The Elliot Norton 30ᵗʰ Anniversary Lifetime Achievement Award: Tommy Tune

The Elliot Norton 30ᵗʰ Anniversary Award: Spring Sirkin

Norton Prize for Sustained Excellence: Kate Snodgrass

Special Citation: Charlestown Working Theatre

Special Citation to Emerging Artists: The Factory Theatre

The Equity Awards

St. Clair Bayfield Award Established in 1973 in memory of Equity member St. Clair Bayfield, the Award honors the best performance by an actor in a Shakespearean play in the New York metropolitan area. **2011 Winner:** Nick Westrate, *Love's Labour's Lost* (The Public Theater)

Joe A. Callaway Award Established by Equity member Joe A. Callaway in 1989 to encourage participation in the classics and non-profit theatre. **2011 Winners:** Danai Gurira, *Measure for Measure* (The Public Theater); Derek Smith, *The Witch of Edmonton* (Red Bull Theater)

Clarence Derwent Awards 68th annual; Presented to honor the most promising female and male performers on the New York metropolitan scene. **2012 Winners:** Susan Pourfar, *In the Wake* (The Public Theater); Finn Wittrock, *Death of a Salesman* (Barrymore Theatre)

Alan Eisenberg Award 6th created by former AEA Executive Director, this award is presented to an outstanding graduating senior of the University of Michigan Musical Theatre program, Mr. Eisenberg's alma mater. **2012 Winner:** Sam Lips, Class of 2012

Lucy Jordan Award Established in 1992 to honor the legacy of Lucy Finney Jordan, a former ballerina and chorus "gypsy" who, for many years, was the "face" of Actors' Equity in the Western Region as the Union's Outside Field Rep. The award is given to those who demonstrate a lifetime commitment to the theatre and especially, helping other theatre artists. **2012 Winner:** Connie McMillan, theatre supporter

Rosetta LeNoire Award Established in 1988, the award was named in honor of the actress Rosetta LeNoire, who was also the first recipient, not only because of her body of work in the theatre—and her work with the then titled Actors' Equity Association's Ethnic Minorities Committee—but also for founding the AMAS Repertory Theatre Company. **2011 Winner:** Philadelphia InterAct Theatre Company (Founding/Producing Director, Seth Rozin)

Paul Robeson Award Established in 1974 to recognize a person who best exemplified the principles by which Mr. Robeson lived. It was created by donations from members of the acting profession. **2011 Winner:** James Earl Jones

Richard Seff Award Established in 2003, this annual award is given to a male and female character actor who is 50 years old or older and who has been a member of the Actors' Equity for 25 years or longer, for the best performance in a featured or unfeatured supporting role in a Broadway or Off-Broadway production. **2011 Winners:** Patrick Page, *Spider-Man: Turn Off the Dark* (Foxwoods Theatre); Laila Robbins, *The Lady from Dubuque* (Signature Theatre)

Roger Sturtevant Musical Theatre Award 8th annual; established in 2005 in memory of Roger Sturtevant, a beloved box office treasurer and part-time casting director. This award is presented to Equity Membership Candidates who have demonstrated outstanding abilities in the musical theatre field. **2012 Winners:** Emelie Faith Thompson; Matthew Elliott

ACCA Award 5th annual; Presented to an outstanding Broadway chorus. **2011 Winner:** *The Scottsboro Boys*

Diversity on Broadway Award Presented by AEA's Equal Employment Opportunity Committee for extraordinary excellence in diversity on Broadway. **2011 Winner:** Oskar Eustis (*The Merchant of Venice*, The Public Theater)

Fred and Adele Astaire Awards

June 4, 2012; New York University's Skirball Center for the Performing Arts; 30th Annual; Hosts: Ava Astaire and Patricia Watt. Originally known as the Astaire Awards these awards were founded by the Anglo-American Contemporary Dance Foundation and have been administered by Theatre Development Fund since 1991. These awards recognize outstanding achievement in dance on Broadway and in film.

Outstanding Choreographer for a Broadway Musical: Ron Brown, *Porgy & Bess*

Outstanding Feature Film (Fictional): *The Artist*

Outstanding Dance Documentary: *Pina*

Outstanding Male Dancer in a Broadway Musical: Leslie Odom, Jr., *Leap of Faith*

Outstanding Female Dancer in a Broadway Musical: Lisa Nicole Wilkerson, *Porgy & Bess*

Douglas Watt Lifetime Achievement Award: Liza Minnelli

Special Award: Kathleen Raitt, for her efforts in helping establish the Astaire Awards

Adele Astaire Scholarship: Shannen O'Neill

Fred Ebb Award

November 28, 2011; American Airlines Theatre Penthouse Lounge; 7th annual. The Fred Ebb Award recognizes excellence in musical theatre songwriting, by a lyricist, composer, or songwriting team that has not yet achieved significant commercial success. The award is meant to encourage and support aspiring songwriters to create new works for the musical theatre. The selection panel includes Mitchell S. Bernard, Sheldon Harnick, David Loud, Marin Mazzie, Tim Pinckney, and Arthur Whitelaw. Presenter, Eric Bebe Neuwirth; The prize includes a $50,000 award.

2011 Winner: Jeff Blumenkrantz

Past Recipients: 2005: John Bucchino **2006:** Robert L. Freedman and Steven Lutvak **2007:** Peter Mills **2008:** Adam Gwon **2009:** Marcy Heisler and Zina Goldrich **2010:** Douglas J. Cohen

George Freedley Memorial Award

Established in 1968 to honor the late George Freedley, theatre historian, critic, author, and first curator of the New York Public Library Theatre Collection, this award honors a work about live theatre published in or distributed in the United States during the previous year. Presented by authors, publishers and members of the Theatre Library Association.

2011 Winner: James Shapiro, *Contested Will: Who Wrote Shakespeare?* (Simon & Shuster, 2010); Special Jury Prize: Stephen Sondheim, *Finishing the Hat: Collected Lyrics (1954-1981)* (Knopf, 2010).

George Jean Nathan Award

With his preamble "it is my object and desire to encourage and assist in developing the art of drama criticism and the stimulation of intelligent playgoing," the late George Jean Nathan provided in his will for a prize known as the George Jean Nathan Award for Dramatic Criticism. The prize consists of the annual net income of half of Mr. Nathan's estate, which "shall be paid to the American who has written the best piece of drama criticism during the theatrical year (July 1 to June 30), whether it is an article, an essay, treatise, or book. The award now amounts to $10,000 and in addition, the winner receives a trophy symbolic of, and attesting to, the award. **2012 Winner for 2009-2010:** Jill Dolan, the Annan Professor in English and Professor of Theater at Princeton University

GLAAD Media Awards

New York: March 24, 2012 in New York at the Marriott Marquis; 23rd annual. Presented by the Gay and Lesbian Alliance Against Defamation for fair, accurate and inclusive representations of gay individuals in the media as a means of eliminating homophobia and discrimination based on gender identity and sexual orientation.

2011 Winners in Theater: New York Theater—Broadway & Off-Broadway: *The Intelligent Homosexual's Guide to Capitalism and Socialism with a Key to the Scriptures*, by Tony Kushner; Off-Off-Broadway: *Southern Comfort* Book and Lyrics by Dan Collins, Music by Julianne Wick Davis; Los Angeles Theatre: *No Word in Guyanese for Me* by Wendy Graf

Grammy Awards

February 12, 2012; Staples Center, Los Angeles; 54th annual. Presented by the Recording Academy for excellence in the recording industry for albums released October 1, 2010–September 30, 2011.

Best Musical Show Album: *The Book of Mormon*: Original Broadway Cast Recording (Anne Garefino, Robert Lopez, Trey Parker & Matt Stone, composers/lyricists); Robert Lopez, Stephen Oremus, Trey Parker, Scott Rudin & Matt Stone, producers; Josh Gad and Andrew Rannells, principal soloists

Nominees: *Anything Goes; How to Succeed in Business Without Really Trying*

Helen Hayes Awards

April 23, 2012; The Warner Theatre; 28th annual; Hosts, Holly Twyford and Felicia Curry; Presented by the Washington Theatre Awards Society in recognition of excellence in Washington, D.C., area, including Maryland and Virginia, for the 2011 season.

Outstanding Resident Play: *Ruined*, Arena Stage

Outstanding Resident Musical: *Hairspray*, Signature Theatre

Outstanding Lead Actress, Resident Musical: Carolyn Cole, *Hairspray* (Signature Theatre Company)

Outstanding Lead Actor, Resident Musical: Euan Morton, *Parade* (Ford's Theatre and Theatre J)

Outstanding Lead Actress, Resident Play: (tie) Erica Sullivan, *Venus in Fur* (Studio Theatre); Rena Brown, *Wit* (Bay Theatre Company)

Robert Prosky Award for Outstanding Lead Actor, Resident Play: Mitchell Hebert, *After the Fall* (Theatre J.)

Outstanding Supporting Actress, Resident Musical: Nova Payton, *Hairspray* (Signature Theatre)

Outstanding Supporting Actor, Resident Musical: Matthew Delorenzo, *Pop!* (Studio Theatre 2ndStage)

Outstanding Supporting Actress, Resident Play: Gabriela Fernandez-Coffey, *After the Fall* (Theater J)

Outstanding Supporting Actor, Resident Play: Ted van Griethuysen, *Much Ado About Nothing* (Shakespeare Theatre Company)

Outstanding Director, Resident Play: Aaron Posner, *Cyrano* (Folger Theatre)

Outstanding Director, Resident Musical: Michael Baron, *A Year With Frog and Toad* (Adventure Theatre)

Outstanding Set Design, Resident Production: Lee Savage, *Much Ado About Nothing* (Shakespeare Theatre)

Outstanding Costume Design, Resident Production: Kendra Rai, *Green Bird* (Constellation Theatre Company)

Outstanding Lighting Design, Resident Production: Andrew Griffin, *King Lear* (Synetic Theater)

Outstanding Sound Design, Resident Production: (tie) Konstantine Lortkipanidze and Irakli Kavsadze, *King Lear* (Synetic Theater); Chris Baine, *A Bright New Boise* (Woolly Mammoth Theatre Company)

Outstanding Musical Direction, Resident Production: Jon Kalbfleisch, *Hairspray* (Signature Theatre)

Outstanding Choreography, Resident Production: Ben Cunis and Irina Tsikurishvili, *King Lear* (Synetic Theater)

Outstanding Ensemble, Resident Musical: *Hairspray* (Signature Theatre)

Outstanding Ensemble, Resident Play: *King Lear* (Synetic Theater)

Outstanding Non-Resident Production: *Edward Albee's Who's Afraid of Virginia Woolf?* (Arena Stage)

Outstanding Production, Theatre for Young Audiences: *Charlotte's Web* (Adventure Theatre)

Outstanding Lead Actress, Non-Resident: Cate Blanchett, *Uncle Vanya* (The Kennedy Center)

Outstanding Lead Actor, Non-Resident: Sahr Njaujah, *FELA!* (Shakespeare Theatre Company)

Outstanding Supporting Performer, Non-Resident: Hugo Weaving, *Uncle Vanya* (The Kennedy Center)

Charles MacArthur Award for Outstanding New Play or Musical: Marc Acito, *Birds of a Feather* (Hub Theatre)

John Aniello Award for Outstanding Emerging Theatre Company: Faction of Fools Theatre Company

Helen Hayes Tribute: Kevin Spacey

Washington Post Award for Innovative Leadership in the Theatre Community: Jane Lang (Founder and Chair of the Board), and Paul Sprenger (Cofounder and Trustee)

Henry Hewes Design Awards

October 29, 2012; 47th annual. Sponsored by the American Theatre Wing, these awards are presented for outstanding design originating in the U.S. for the 2010-2011 theatre season. The award (formerly known as the Maharam Theatre Design Award up until 1999) is named after the former theatre critic for the *Saturday Review* who passed away July 20, 2006. The awards are selected by a committee comprising of Jeffrey Eric Jenkins (chair), Dan Bacalzo, David Barbour, David Cote, Glenda Frank, Mario Fratti, and Joan Ungaro.

Scenic Design: John Lee Beatty, *The Whipping Man* (Manhattan Theatre Club)

Lighting Design: Jeffrey Coiter, *Peter and the Starcatcher* (NY Theatre Workshop)

Costume Design: William Ivey Long, *The School for Lies* (Classic Stage Company)

Notable Effects/Production Design: (Scenery and Projections): David Rockwell, *The Normal Heart*; Batwin + Robin, *The Normal Heart*

IRNE Awards

April 24, 2012; Boston Center for the Arts. Founded in 1997 by Beverly Creasey and Larry Stark. Presented by The Independent Reviewers of New England for extraordinary theatre in the Boston area during the 2011 calendar year.

LARGE THEATRE

Best New Play: *Sons of the Prophet* by Stephen Karam (Huntington Theatre Company of Boston)

Best Play: *Ruined* (Huntington Theatre Company of Boston)

Best Musical: *Candide* (Huntington Theatre Company of Boston)

Best Director, Play: Liesl Tommy, *Ruined* (Huntington Theatre Company of Boston)

Best Director, Musical: Mary Zimmerman, *Candide* (Huntington Theatre Company of Boston)

Best Music Director: Doug Peck, *Candide* (Huntington Theatre Company of Boston)

Best Choreography: Daniel Pelzig, *Candide* (Huntington Theatre Company of Boston)

Best Solo Performance: Thomas Derrah, *R. Buckminster Fuller: The History and Mystery of the Universe—American Repertory Theater*

Best Ensemble: *Candide* (The Huntington Theatre Company of Boston)

Best Actress, Play: Tonye Patano, *Ruined* (Huntington Theatre Company)

Best Actor, Play: Fred Sullivan Jr., *His Girl Friday* (Trinity Repertory Company)

Best Supporting Actress, Play: Pascale Armand, *Ruined* (Huntington Theatre Company of Boston)

Best Supporting Actor, Play: Oberon K.A. Adjepong, *Ruined* (Huntington Theatre Company of Boston)

Best Actress, Musical: Audra McDonald, The Gershwins' *Porgy and Bess* (American Repertory Theater)

Best Actor, Musical: Geoff Packard, *Candide* (Huntington Theatre Company of Boston)

Best Supporting Actress, Musical: Cheryl Stern, *Candide* (Huntington Theatre Company of Boston)

Best Supporting Actor, Musical: Philip Boykin, The Gershwins' *Porgy and Bess* (American Repertory Theater)

Best Set Design: Daniel Ostling, *Candide* (Huntington Theatre Company of Boston)

Best Lighting Design: T.J. Gerckens, *Candide* (Huntington Theatre Company of Boston)

Best Costume Design: Mara Blumenfeld, *Candide* (Huntington Theatre Company of Boston)

Best Sound Design: Richard Woodbury, *Candide* (Huntington Theatre Company of Boston)

Most Promising Performance by a Young Performer: Ellis Gage, *The King and I* (North Shore Music Theatre)

Best Visiting Production: *Hair* (Broadway Across America Boston)

Best Visiting Performer: Christopher Sieber, *La Cage aux Folles* (Broadway Across America Boston)

MIDSIZE-SMALL THEATRE

Best New Play: *Hotel Nepenthe* by John Kuntz (Actors' Shakespeare Project)

Best Play (Fringe/Small): *Arcadia* (Bad Habit Productions)

Best Play (Midsize): *The Brother/Sister Plays* (Company One)

Best Musical: *The Drowsy Chaperone* (SpeakEasy Stage Company)

Best Director, Play (Small): Daniel Morris, *Arcadia* (Bad Habit Productions)

Best Director, Play (Midsize): (tie) Daniel Gordon, *Arabian Nights* (The Nora Theatre Company & Underground Railway)

Best Director, Musical: David Connolly, *The Drowsy Chaperone* (SpeakEasy Stage Company)

Best Music Director: Steven Bergman, *Spring Awakening* (F.U.D.G.E. Theatre Company)

Best Choreography: Ilyse Robbins, *42nd Street* (Stoneham Theatre)

Best Solo Performance: Jeff Gill, *The Auerbach Dynasty*, Ken Dooley, Producer

Best Ensemble: *Arabian Nights* (The Nora Theatre Company & Underground Railway Theater)

Best Actress, Play: Bobbie Steinbach, *Collected Stories* (New Repertory Theatre)

Best Actor, Play: Allyn Burrows, *Breaking the Code* (Underground Railway Theater & Catalyst Collaborative @ MIT)

Best Supporting Actress, Play: Alycia Sacco, *Arcadia* (Bad Habit Productions)

Best Supporting Actor, Play: Hampton Fluker, *The Brother/Sister Plays* (Company One)

Best Actress, Musical: Jennifer Ellis, *The Most Happy Fella* (Gloucester Stage Company)

Best Actor, Musical: Will McGarrahan, *The Drowsy Chaperone* (SpeakEasy Stage Company)

Best Supporting Actress, Musical: Aimee Doherty, *Nine* (SpeakEasy Stage Company)

Best Supporting Actor, Musical: Thomas Derrah, *The Drowsy Chaperone* (SpeakEasy Stage Company)

Best Set Design: James Fluhr, *The Road to Mecca* (Boston Center for American Performance)

Best Lighting Design: Jeff Adelberg, *Hotel Nepenthe* (Actors' Shakespeare Project)

Best Costume Design: Leslie Held, *Arabian Nights* (The Nora Theatre Company & Underground Railway Theater)

Best Puppetry: David Fichter & Will Cabell, *Arabian Nights* (The Nora Theatre Company & Underground Railway Theater)

Best Sound Design: David Remedios, *Afterlife: A Ghost Story* (New Repertory Theatre)

Best Promising Performance by a Young Performer: Hyacinth Tauriac, *My Wonderful Day* (Zeitgeist Stage Company)

Best Visiting Production: *The Mountain Song—Pig Pen Theatre at Company One*

SPECIAL RECOGNITION

Kenneth A. MacDonald Award for Theater Excellence: Danielle Fauteux Jacques

The Hubbie Award: Danny Bryck, *No Room for Wishing*, a documentary play about Occupy Boston

ITBA Awards – Patrick Lee Theater Blogger Awards

June 5, 2012; 4th Annual; Founded by Ken Davenport, the Independent Theater Bloggers Association was created to provide structure to the quickly growing theatrical blogosphere, and give the new media voices a chance to recognize excellence for Broadway, Off-Broadway, and Off-Off Broadway productions. The Award was renamed the Patrick Lee Theater Blogger Award in honor of Patrick Lee who passed away in June 2010.

Outstanding New Broadway Play: *Peter and the Starcatcher*

Outstanding Broadway Play Revival: *Death of a Salesman*

Outstanding New Broadway Musical: *Once*

Outstanding Broadway Musical Revival: *Follies*

Outstanding New Off-Broadway Play: *Sons of the Prophet*

Outstanding New Off-Broadway Musical: *Now. Here. This.*

Outstanding Off-Off Broadway Unique Theatrical Experience: *The Tenant*, by Woodshed Collective

Outstanding Solo Show: Hugh Jackman in *Back on Broadway;* Denis O'Hare, *An Iliad* (New York Theatre Workshop); Zoe Caldwell, *Elective Affinities* (Soho Rep); Juan Villa, *Empanada for a Dream* (Ballybeg at Barrow Group); *Stephen Spinella, An Iliad* (New York Theatre Workshop); Daniel Kitson, *It's Always Right Now Until It's Later*; Lorinda Lisitza, *Triumphant Baby*

Outstanding Ensemble Performance: *Peter and the Starcatcher*

Citations for Outstanding Off-Off Broadway Show: *Samuel & Alasdair: A Personal History of the Robot War* by the Mad Ones, at The New Ohio; *She Kills Monsters* at the Flea

Citation for Excellence in Off-Off Broadway Theatre: The Flea

Citations for Excellence by Individual Performances: Nina Arianda, *Venus in Fur*; Christian Borle, *Peter and the Starcatcher;* Philip Boykin, The Gershwins' *Porgy & Bess;* Danny Burstein, *Follies;* James Corden, *One Man, Two Guvnors;* Santino Fontana, *Sons of a Prophet;* Judy Kaye, *Nice Work If You Can Get It;* Judith Light, *Other Desert Cities;* Jan Maxwell, *Follies;* Lindsay Mendez, *Godspell;* Terri White, *Follies*

Jonathan Larson Performing Arts Foundation Awards

March 29, 2012; Jonathan Larson's dream was to infuse musical theatre with a contemporary, joyful urban vitality. After 12 years of struggle as a classic "starving artist," his dream came true with the phenomenal success of *Rent*. To celebrate his creative spirit and honor his memory, Jonathan's family and friends created the Jonathan Larson Performing Arts Foundation. The mission of the Foundation is to provide financial support and encouragement to a new generation of musical theatre composers, lyricists and bookwriters, as well as nonprofit theatre companies that develop and produce their work.

2012 Recipients: Dan Collins (book/lyrics) and Julianne Wick (composer), *Southern Comfort*

Joseph Jefferson Awards
EQUITY WING AWARDS

November 7, 2011; Drury Lane Oakbrook Terrace; 43rd annual. Presented for achievement in Chicago Equity theater from August 1, 2010–July 31, 2011; given by the Jefferson Awards Committee.

Production – Play – Large: *The Madness of King George III* (Chicago Shakespeare Theater)

Production – Play – Midsize: *Edward Albee's The Goat or, Who is Sylvia?* (Remy Bumppo Theatre Company)

Production – Musical – Large: *Candide* (Goodman Theatre in collaboration with Shakespeare Theatre Company of Washington, D.C.)

Production – Revue: *Sky's the Limit (Weather Permitting)* (The Second City e.t.c.)

Ensemble: *The Big Meal* (American Theater Company)

Director – Play: Penny Metropulos, *The Madness of George III* (Chicago Shakespeare Theater)

Director – Musical: Charles Newell, The Gershwins' *Porgy and Bess* (Court Theatre)

New Work – Play: Bruce Graham, *The Outgoing Tide* (Northlight Theatre); David Henry Hwang, *Chinglish* (Goodman Theatre)

New Work – Play or Musical: Tim Baltz, Aidy Bryant, Jesse Case, Matt Hovde, Brendan Jennings, Jessica Joy, Michael Lehrer and Mary John, *Sky's the Limit (Weather Permitting)* (The Second City e.t.c.); Joe Kinosian and Kellan Blair, *Murder for Two—A Killer Musical* (Chicago Shakespeare Theater)

Solo Performance: Barbara Robertson, *The Detective's Wife* (Writers' Theatre)

Actress in a Principal Role – Play: Annabel Armour, *Edward Albee's The Goat or, Who is Sylvia?* (Remy Bumppo Theatre Company)

Actor in a Principal Role – Play: Harry Groener, *The Madness of King George III* (Chicago Shakespeare Theater)

Actress in a Supporting Role – Play: Diana Simonzadeh, *Scorched* (Silk Road Theatre Project)

Actor in a Supporting Role – Play: Mike Nussbaum, *Broadway Bound* (Drury Lane Productions)

Actress in a Principal Role – Musical: Jessie Mueller, *She Loves Me* (Writers' Theatre)

Actor in a Principal Role – Musical: Geoff Packard, *Candide* (Goodman Theatre in collaboration with Shakespeare Theatre Company of Washington, D.C.)

Actress in a Supporting Role – Musical: Hollis Resnik, *Candide* (Goodman Theatre in collaboration with Shakespeare Theatre Company of Washington, D.C.)

Actor in a Supporting Role – Musical: Larry Yando, *Candide* (Goodman Theatre in collaboration with Shakespeare Theatre Company of Washington, D.C.)

Actor or Actress in a Revue: Tim Baltz, *Sky's the Limit (Weather Permitting)* (Writers' Theatre)

Scenic Design – Large: David Korins, *Chinglish* (Goodman Theatre)

Scenic Design – Midsize: Collette Pollard, *The Front Page* (TimeLine Theatre Company)

Costume Design – Large: Susan E. Mickey, *The Madness of George III* (Chicago Shakespeare Theater)

Costume Design – Midsize: Bill Morey, *The King and I* (Porchlight Music Theatre)

Lighting Design – Large: Jason Lyons, *White Noise* (Royal George Theatre)

Lighting Design – Midsize: Sarah Hughey, *Scorched* (Silk Road Theatre Project)

Sound Design – Large: Mikhail Fiksel, *Travels with My Aunt* (Writers' Theatre)

Sound Design – Midsize: Peter J. Storms, *Scorched* (Silk Road Theatre Project)

Choreography: Tammy Mader, *42nd Street* (Marriott Theatre)

Fight/Movement Direction: Rick Sordelet, *Romeo and Juliet* (Chicago Shakespeare Theater)

Original Incidental Music: Andrew Hansen, *To Master the Art* (TimeLine Theatre Company)

Musical Direction: Doug Peck, The Gershwins' *Porgy and Bess* (Court Theatre)

Projections/Video Design: John Boesche, *A Twist of Water* (Route 66 Theatre Company); Mike Tutaj, *In Darfur* (TimeLine Theatre Company)

Artistic Specialization: Tracy Otwell, Toy Theatre Design, *The Last Act of Lilka Kadison* (Lookingglass Theatre Company); Melissa Veal, Wig and Makeup Design, *The Madness of King George III*

Special Award: *Chicago Sun-Times* theatre critic Hedy Weiss in recognition of her contributions to Chicagoland theatre

Tribute Award: Kathryn V. Lamkey, recently retired executive director/central regional director, Actors Equity Association

NON-EQUITY AWARDS

June 4, 2012; Park West; 39th annual. Formerly called the Citations, the Non-Equity Awards are for outstanding achievement in professional productions which played at Chicago theaters not operating under union contracts from April 1, 2011–March 31, 2012; given by the Jefferson Awards Committee.

Production – Play: *Sophocles: Seven Sicknesses* (The Hypocrites)

Production – Musical or Revue: *The Light in the Piazza* (Theo Ubique Cabaret Theatre)

Ensemble: *Punk Rock* (Griffin Theatre Company)

Director – Play: Jonathan Berry, *Punk Rock* (Griffin Theatre Company); Sean Graney, *Sophocles: Seven Sicknesses* (The Hypocrites)

Director – Musical or Revue: Fred Anzevino and Brenda Didier, *The Light in the Piazza* (The Cabaret Theatre)

New Work: Shepsu Aakhu, *Speaking in Tongues: The Chronicles of Babel* (MPAACT); Deirdre O'Connor, *Assisted Living* (Profiles Theatre)

New Adaptation: Sean Graney, *Sophocles: Seven Sicknesses* (The Hypocrites); Blake Montgomery, *Moby-Dick* (The Building Stage)

Actress in a Principal Role – Play: Jacqueline Grandt, *Bug* (Redtwist Theatre); Melanie Keller, *East of Berlin & The Russian Play* (Signal Ensemble Theatre)

Actor in a Principal Role – Play: Joey DeBettencourt, *Punk Rock* (Griffin Theatre Company)

Actress in a Supporting Role – Play: Sasha Gioppo, *Red Light Winter* (Mary-Arrchie Theatre Co.)

Actor in a Supporting Role – Play: Aaron Kirby, *Dark Play for Boys* (Theo Ubique Cabaret Company)

Actress in a Principal Role – Musical or Revue: Kelli Harrington, *The Light in the Piazza* (The Cabaret Theatre)

Actor in a Principal Role – Musical or Revue: Chuck Sisson, *The Baker's Wife* (Circle Theatre)

Actress in a Supporting Role – Musical or Revue: Dana Tretta, *Pippin* (Bohemian Theatre Ensemble)

Actor in a Supporting Role – Musical or Revue: Justin Adair, *The Light in the Piazza* (The Cabaret Theatre)

Scenic Design: Amanda Rozmiarek, *The Price* (Raven Theatre)

Lighting Design: Jared Moore, *Sophocles: Seven Sicknesses* (The Hypocrites)

Costume Design: Jesus Perez, *Urinetown the Musical* (Circle Theatre)

Sound Design: Christopher Kriz, *Opus* (Redtwist Theatre)

Choreography: Kevin Bellie, *Urinetown the Musical* (Circle Theatre)

Fight Design: Matt Hawkins, *Cyrano* (The House Theatre of Chicago)

Dialect Coaching: Eva Breneman, *The Light in the Piazza* (Theo Ubique Cabaret Theatre)

Original Incidental Music: Ovidiu Iloc, *The Word Progress on My Mother's Lips Doesn't Ring True* (Trap Door Theatre); Kevin O'Connell, *Moby Dick* (The Building Stage)

Musical Direction: Jeremy Ramey, *The Light in the Piazza* (The Ubique Cabaret Theatre)

Artistic Specialization: Casey Baker, Kevin O'Donnell and Mike Przygoda, Percussion, *Moby Dick* (The Building Stage); Zhanna Bullock, Music, *Opus* (Redtwist Theatre)

Kennedy Center

Honors 34th annual; presented December 3, 2011 (honored with broadcast on CBS December 27, 2011); for distinguished achievement by individuals who have made significant contributions to American culture through the arts: Barbara Cook, Neil Diamond, Yo-Yo Ma, Sonny Rollins, and Meryl Streep.

Mark Twain Prize 14th annual; October 23, 2011 (Broadcast on PBS October 31, 2011); for American humor: Will Ferrell

Kevin Kline Awards

April 2, 2012; Loretto-Hilton Center for the Performing Arts; 7th annual. Presented for outstanding achievement in professional theatre in the Greater St. Louis area for the 2011 calendar year; produced by The Professional Theatre Awards Council; Winners were selected by a floating pool of 45 judges.

Outstanding Production of a Play: (tie) *Red* (The Repertory Theatre of St. Louis); *Awake and Sing!* (The New Jewish Theatre)

Outstanding Director of a Play: Steven Woolf, *Red* (The Repertory Theatre of St. Louis)

Outstanding Production of a Musical: *Singin' in the Rain,* (The Muny)

Outstanding Director of a Musical: Deanna Jent, *Godspell* (Mustard Seed Theatre)

Outstanding Lead Actress in a Play: Brooke Edwards, *Danny and the Deep Blue Sea* (The Non-Prophet Theatre Company)

Outstanding Lead Actor in a Play: Bob Thibaut, *The Immigrant* (The New Jewish Theatre)

Outstanding Lead Actress in a Musical: Alexis Kinney, *The Secret Garden* (Stages St. Louis)

Outstanding Lead Actor in a Musical: Leigh Wakeford, *Disney's 101 Dalmatians* (Stages St. Louis)

Outstanding Supporting Actress in a Play: Peggy Billo, *The Immigrant* (The New Jewish Theatre)

Outstanding Supporting Actor in a Play: Gary Wayne Baker, *The Immigrant* (The New Jewish Theatre)

Outstanding Supporting Actress in a Musical: Melinda Crown, *Victor/Victoria* (Stages St. Louis)

Outstanding Supporting Actor in a Musical: Curtis Holbook, *Singin' in the Rain* (TheMury)

Outstanding Musical Direction: (tie) Lisa Campbell-Albert, *The Secret Garden* (Stages St. Louis); Joe Schoen, *Godspell* (Mustard Seed Theatre)

Outstanding Choreography: Pepper Clyde, *Seven Brides for Seven Brothers* (The Muny)

Outstanding Costume Design: Dorothy Marshall Englis, *The Secret Garden* (Stages St. Louis)

Outstanding Lighting Design: Robert M. Wierzel, *The Adventures of Tom Sawyer* (The Repertory Theatre of St. Louis)

Outstanding Set Design: (tie): Gianni Downs, *In the Next Room (or the vibrator play)* (The Repertory Theatre of St. Louis); Scott C. Neale, *Awake and Sing!* (The New Jewish Theatre); Michael Ganio, *Red* (The Repertory Theatre of St. Louis)

Outstanding Sound Design: Daniel Baker & Aaron Meicht, *The Adventures of Tom Sawyer* (The Repertory Theatre of St. Louis)

Outstanding Ensemble in a Play: (tie) *The Immigrant* (The New Jewish Theatre) *Circle Mirror Transformation* (The Repertory Theatre of St. Louis)

Outstanding Ensemble in a Musical: *Seven Brides for Seven Brothers* (The Muny)

Production for Young Audiences: *The Giver* (Metro Theater Company and Edison Theatre)

Outstanding New Play or Musical: Deanna Jent, *Till We Have Faces* (Mustard Seed Theatre)

Los Angeles Drama Critics Circle

March 19, 2012; A Noise Within in Pasadena; 43rd annual. Hosted by Jason Graae and Leslie Margherita; Presented for excellence in theatre in the Los Angeles and Orange County during the 2011 calendar year; Voting members: F. Kathleen Foley (*L.A. Times*), Shirle Gottlieb (*Gazette Newspapers*, StageHappenings.com), Hoyt Hilsman (*Back Stage*, The Huffington Post), Mayank Keshaviah (*L.A. Weekly*), Amy Lyons (*Back Stage, L.A. Weekly*), Dany Margolies (*Back Stage*), Terry Morgan (*Variety*), Steven Leigh Morris (*L.A. Weekly*), David C. Nichols (*L.A. Times, Back Stage*), Sharon Perlmutter (TalkinBroadway.com), Melinda Schupmann (*Back Stage*, ShowMag.com), Madeleine Shaner (*Park La Brea News/Beverly Press, Back Stage*), Les Spindle (*Back Stage*), Bob Verini (*Variety*), and Neal Weaver (*Back Stage*). Joining for 2012 is Pauline Adamek (*L.A. Weekly*).

Productions: *Margo Veil* (The Odyssey Theatre Ensemble and Evidence Room, Odyssey Theatre); *Small Engine Repair* (Rogue Machine, Theatre/Theater)

T.H. McCulloh Award for Best Revival: *A Raisin in the Sun* (Ebony Repertory Theatre; Nate Holden Performing Arts Center); *Cabaret* (Reprise Theatre Company, Freud Playhouse); *The Crucible* (Theatre Banshee)

Direction: Andrew Block, *Small Engine Repair* (Rogue Machine at Theatre/Theater); Sean Branney, *The Crucible* (Theatre Banshee); Bart DeLorenzo, *Margo Veil* (The Odyssey Theatre Ensemble and Evidence Room at the Odyssey Theatre)

Writing: David Harrower, *Blackbird* (Rogue Machine at Theatre/Theater; John Pollono, *Small Engine Repair* (Rogue Machine at Theatre/Theater)

Adaptation: Dakin Matthews, *The Capulets & The Montagues* (Andak Stage Company at NewPlace Studio Theatre)

Musical Direction: Gerald Sternbach, *The Robber Bridegroom* (International City Theatre); Mike Wilkins, *Jerry Springer: The Opera* (Chance Theater)

Musical Score: Mark Nutter, *Re-Animator: The Musical* (Steve Allen Theater)

Choreography: Andy Blankenbuehler, *Bring It On: The Musical* (Center Theatre Group at the Ahmanson Theatre)

Lead Performance: Sam Anderson, *Blackbird* (Rogue Machine at Theatre/Theater; Anne Gee Byrd, *All My Sons* (Matrix Theatre); L. Scott Caldwell, *A Raisin in the Sun* (Ebony Repertory Theatre at the Nate Holden Performing Arts Center); Edi Gathegi, *Superior Donuts* (Geffen Playhouse); Lisa O'Hare, *Cabaret* (Reprise Theatre Company at Freud Playhouse)

Featured Performance: Anna Gee Byrd, *I Never Sang for My Father* (The New American Theatre at the McCadden Theatre); Dermot Crowley, *The Cripple of Inishmaan* (Center Theatre Group and Druid and Atlantic Theater Company at the Kirk Douglas Theatre); Deidre Henry, *A Raisin in the Sun* (Ebony Repertory Theatre at the Nate Holden Performing Arts Center); Casey Kramer, *Dolly's West Kitchen* (Theatre Banshee)

Ensemble Performance: *A Raisin in the Sun* (Ebony Repertory Theatre at the Nate Holden Performing Arts Center); *Margo Veil* (The Odyssey Theatre Ensemble and Evidence Room at the Odyssey Theatre)

Solo Performance: Tom Dugan, *Nazi Hunter—Simon Wiesenthal* (Theatre 40 at the Reuben Cordova Theatre); Charlayne Woodard, *The Night Watcher* (Center Theatre Group at the Kirk Douglas Theatre)

Set Design: Richard Hoover, *House of the Rising Son* (Ensemble Studio Theatre—LA at the Atwater Village Theatre)

Lighting Design: Paule Constable, *Les Misérables* (Center Theatre Group at the Ahmanson Theatre); Jeremy Pivnick, *House of the Rising Son* (Ensemble Studio Theatre—LA at the Atwater Village Theatre)

Costume Design: Philippe Guillotel, *Iris* (Cirque du Soleil at Kodak Theatre)

Sound Design: John Zalewski, *Margo Veil* (The Odyssey Theatre Ensemble and Evidence Room at Odyssey Theatre)

Specialty: Eric Anderson (fight choreography), *Gospel According to First Squad* (The Los Angeles Theatre Ensemble at The Powerhouse Theatre); John Boesche (projection design), *Radiance: The Passion of Marie Curie* (Geffen Playhouse); Tony Doublin, John Naulin, John Buechler, Tom Devlin, & Greg McDougall (special effects), *Re-Animator: The Musical* (Steve Allen Theater); Shana Carroll, Boris Verkhovsky, Pierre Masse (acrobatic performance design), *Iris* (Cirque de Soleil at Kodak Theatre)

Unique Theatrical Event: *Standing on Ceremony*, Joan Stein and Stuart Ross in association with the L.A. Gay & Lesbian Center's Lily Tomlin/Jane Wagner Cultural Arts Center at The Renberg Theatre

SPECIAL AWARDS

Ted Schmitt Award (for the world premiere of an outstanding new play, accompanied by offer to publish by Samuel French, Inc.): David Wiener, *Extraordinary Chambers*

Margaret Harford Award (for Sustained Excellence in Theatre, accompanied by honorarium, funded by contributions from the theatrical community): Odyssey Theatre

Polly Warfield Award (for outstanding single season by a small to mid-sized theatre, accompanied by honorarium from Nederlander Organization): Rogue Machine

Angstrom Award (for career achievement in lighting design, accompanied by an honorarium, funded by Angstrom Lighting): Lap Chi Chu

Joel Hirschhorn Award (for outstanding achievement in musical theatre, accompanied by an honorarium, funded an anonymous donor): Lee Martino

Bob Z Award (for career achievement in set design): Kurt Boetcher

Milton Katseals Award (for career or special achievement in direction, accompanied by an honorarium, funded by The Katselas Theatre Company): Matt Shakman

MAC Awards

March 29, 2012; B.B. King's; 26ᵗʰ annual. Presented by the Manhattan Association of Cabarets and Clubs to honor achievements in cabaret, comedy, jazz, and live entertainment in the previous year. Producer, Julie Miller; Director, Lennie Watts; Musical Director, Tracy Stark; Host, Jason Graae.

Show of The Year: Terese Genecco, *Terese Genecco & Her Little Big Band* (Iridium)

Female Vocalist: Janice Hall, *Grand Illusions: The Music of Marlene Dietrich* (Urban Stages)

Male Vocalist: Craig Pomranz, *Love and the Weather* (Metropolitan Room)

Major Artist–Female or Duo: Terese Genecco, *Terese Genecco & Her Little Big Band* (Iridium)

Major Artist–Male: Eric Michael Gillett, *Cast of Thousands: Gillett Sings Carnelia* (Laurie Beechman Theatre)

New York Debut–Female: Lauren Fox, *Here's to Love; Love, Lust, Fear & Freedom: The Songs of Joni Mitchell and Leonard Cohen*

New York Debut–Male: T. Oliver Reid, *This Love I Know* (Metropolitan Room)

Celebrity Artist: Marilyn Maye, *It's Maye in May* (Feinstein's)

Comedy/Musical Comedy Performer: Joan Jaffe, *Joan Jaffe's MAN-ha-ha-ha-TAN* (Don't Tell Mama)

Vocal Duo/Group: Tommy Femia & Rick Skye, *Judy Garland and Liza Minelli Live!* (Don't Tell Mama)

Revue/Special Production: *Metrostar Talent Challenge*, Produced by The Metropolitan Room; Hosted by Tom Gamblin (Metropolitan Room)

Variety Production/Recurring Series: *Wednesday Night at the Iguana*, Produced and hosted by Dana Lorge (Iguana)

Open Mic: *Salon*, Created and hosted by Mark Janas, produced by Tanya Moberly (Etcetera Etcetera)

Host – Variety Show/Series or Open Mic: Dana Lorge, *Wednesday Night at the Iguana* (Iguana)

Benefit: *Cabaret Cares*, Produced by Joseph Macchia; to benefit Help Is On The Way

Piano Bar/Restaurant Singing Entertainer: Alison Nusbaum (Don't Tell Mama)

Piano Bar/Restaurant Instrumentalist: Bill Zeffiro (La Mediterranée)

Director: Peter Napolitano, for: Barbara Poretus & Barry Levitt (Feinstein's, Metropolitan Room, Laurie Beechman), *A Tribute toe Donald Smith* (Urban Stages), *Janice Hall: I'd Rather Be Doing this* (Urban Stages), David Vernon (Laurie Beechman)

Technical Director: Jean Perraux, for: Barb Jungr, Amanda McBroom, Marilyn Maye (Metropolitan Room)

Musical Director: Tracy Stark, for: Barb Jungr (The Metropolitan Room), Gay Feinstein (Feinstein's, Urban Stages), Marcus Simeone (Metropolitan Room), Gretchen Reinhagen (Urban Stages, Don't Tell Mama)

Recording (LaMott Friedman Recording Award): H2 (Sean Harkness, Mike Herriott), "Home for the Holidays"

Song: "He's On His Way" (Music by Robby Stamper/Lyrics by Arianna Rose)

Special Musical Material: "Universal Truth," Music and Lyrics by Bill Zeffiro

Hanson Award: Rosemary Loar

Board of Directors Awards: Francesca Blumenthal, John Bucchino, and Julie Gold

Lifetime Achievement Award: Ervin Drake, David Friedman

Margo Jones Citizen of the Theater Medal

Presented by the Ohio State University Libraries and College of the Arts to a citizen of the theater who has made a lifetime commitment to the theater in the United States and has demonstrated an understanding and affirmation of the craft of playwriting. The Medal Committee is comprised of Deborah Robison for the family of Jerome Lawrence, Janet Waldo Lee and Lucy Lee for the family of Robert E. Lee, Alan Woods, Mary Taratino and Nena Couch (from the Jerome Lawrence Institute).

2012 Winner: Tony Taccone, Berkeley Repertory Theatre

Past Recipients: 1961: Lucille Lortel **1962:** Michael Ellis **1963:** Judith Rutherford Marechal; George Savage (university award) **1964:** Richard Barr; Edward Albee; and Clinton Wilder; Richard A. Duprey (university award) **1965:** Wynn Handman; Marston Balch (university award) **1966:** Jon Jory; Arthur Ballet (university award) **1967:** Paul Baker; George C. White (workshop award) **1968:** Davey Marlin-Jones; Ellen Stewart (workshop award) **1969:** Adrian Hall; Edward Parone and Gordon Davidson (workshop award) **1970:** Joseph Papp **1971:** Zelda Fichandler **1972:** Jules Irving **1973:** Douglas Turner Ward **1974:** Paul Weidner **1975:** Robert Kalfin **1976:** Gordon Davidson **1977:** Marshall W. Mason **1978:** Jon Jory **1979:** Ellen Stewart **1980:** John Clark Donahue **1981:** Lynne Meadow **1982:** Andre Bishop **1983:** Bill Bushnell **1984:** Gregory Mosher **1985:** John Lion **1986:** Lloyd Richards **1987:** Gerald Chapman **1988:** no award **1989:** Margaret Goheen **1990:** Richard Coe **1991:** Otis L. Guernsey Jr. **1992:** Abbot Van Nostrand **1993:** Henry Hewes **1994:** Jane Alexander **1995:** Robert Whitehead **1996:** Al Hirschfield **1997:** George C. White **1998:** James Houghton **1999:** George Keathley **2000:** Eileen Heckart **2001:** Mel Gussow **2002:** Emilie S. Kilgore **2003-2004:** Christopher Durang and Marsha Norman **2005-2006:** Jerome Lawrence and Robert E. Lee **2007-2008:** David Emmes and Martin Benson **2009:** Bill Rauch **2010:** No Award **2011:** Anne Cattaneo

National Arts Club Awards

JOSEPH KESSELRING FELLOWSHIP AND HONORS

National Arts Club member Joseph Otto Kesselring was born in New York in 1902. He was an actor, author, producer, and playwright. Mr. Kesselring died in 1967, leaving his estate in a trust, which terminated in 1978 when the life beneficiary died. A bequest was made to the National Arts Club "on condition that said bequest be used to establish a fund to be known as the Joseph Kesselring Fund, the income and principal of which shall be used to give financial aid to playwrights, on such a basis of selection and to such as the National Arts Club may, in its sole discretion, determine." A committee appointed by the president and the governors of the National Arts Club administers the Kesselring Prizes. It approves monetary prizes annually to playwrights nominated by qualified production companies whose dramatic work has demonstrated the highest possible merit and promise and is deserving of greater recognition, but who as yet has not received prominent national notice or acclaim in the theater. The winners are chosen by a panel of judges who are independent of the Club. In addition to a cash prize, the first-prize winner also receives a staged reading of a work of his or her choice. In the fall of 2007, the Club redefined the award to consist of the Kesselring Fellowship, and created a new category called the Kesselring Honors.

Previous Fellowship Recipients: 1980: Susan Charlotte **1981:** Cheryl Hawkins **1982:** No Award **1983:** Lynn Alvarez **1984:** Philip Kan Gotanda **1985:** Bill Elverman **1986:** Marlane Meyer **1987:** Paul Schmidt **1988:** Diane Ney **1989:** Jo Carson **1990:** Elizabeth Egloff, Mel Shapiro **1991:** Tony Kushner **1992:** Marion Isaac McClinton **1993:** Anna Deavere Smith **1994:** Nicky Silver **1995:** Amy Freed, Doug Wright **1996:** Naomi Wallace **1997:** No Award **1998:** Kira Obolensky **1999:** Heather McDonald **2000:** David Auburn **2001:** David Lindsay-Abaire **2002:** Melissa James Gibson **2003:** Bridget Carpenter **2004:** Tracey Scott Wilson **2005:** Deb Margolin **2006:** Mark Schultz **2007:** Jordan Harrison **2009:** Rajiv Joseph, David Adjmi **2010:** No Award **2011:** No Award

Previous Honors Recipients (if year is missing none were presented): **1980:** Carol Lashof **1981:** William Hathaway **1983:** Constance Congdon **1985:** Laura Harrington **1986:** John Leicht **1987:** Januzsz Glowacki **1988:** Jose Rivera, Frank Hogan **1989:** Keith Reddin **1990:** Howard Korder **1991:** Quincy Long, Scott McPherson **1992:** José Rivera **1993:** Han Ong **1996:** Nilo Cruz **1997:** Kira Obolensky, Edwin Sanchez **1998:** Erik Ehn **1999:** Steven Dietz **2000:** Jessica Hagedorn **2001:** Dael Orlandersmith **2002:** Lydia Diamond **2003:** Lynn Nottage **2004:** John Borello **2005:** Tanya Barfield **2006:** Bruce Norris **2007:** Will Eno, Rinne Groff, Marcus Gardley **2009:** Jenny Schwartz, Tarrel Alvin McCraney **2010:** No Award **2011:** No Award

National Medals of the Arts

February 13, 2012; East Room at the White House. Presented to individuals who and organizations that have made outstanding contributions to the excellence, growth, support, and availability of the arts in the United States, selected by the President of the United States from nominees presented by the National Endowment of the Arts. **2011 Individual Winners**: Will Barnett, Painter/Printmaker (New York, NY); Rita Dove, Poet/Author (Charlottesville, VA); Al Pacino, Actor (Palisades, CA); Emily Rauh Pulitzer, Contemporary Arts Patron/Philanthropist (St. Louis, MO); Martin Puryear, Contemporary Sculptor (Accord, NY); Mel Tillis, Singer/Songwriter (Silver Springs, FL); Classical Pianist (Park City, NJ) **2011 Organization Winner:** USO (United Service Organizations, accepted by Sloan Gibson, USO President and CEO); André Watts

New Dramatists Lifetime Achievement Award

May 24, 2012; Marriott Marquis; 63rd annual. Presented to an individual who has made an outstanding artistic contribution to the American theater. **2012 Winner:** Bernadette Peters

New York Innovative Theatre Awards

September 19, 2011; Cooper Union Great Hall; 7th annual; Host: Harrison Greenbaum. Presented to honor individuals and organizations who have achieved artistic excellence in Off-Off-Broadway theatre for the 2010-2011 season. The New York IT Awards committee recognizes the unique and essential role Off-Off-Broadway plays in contributing to American and global culture, and believes that publicly recognizing excellence in independent theatre will expand audience awareness and appreciation of the full New York theatre experience. Staff: Jason Bowcutt, Shay Gines, Nick Micozzi, Executive Directors; Awards Committee: Co-chairs: Cat Parker (Director), Abby Marcus (Vampire Cowboys); Paul Adams (Artistic Director, Emerging Artists Theatre), Dan Bacalzo (*TheatreMania.com*), Christopher Borg (Actor/Director), Tim Errickson (Artistic Director, Boomerang Theatre Company), Shay Gines (New York IT Awards), Ben Hodges (*Theatre World*), Bob Lee, Rehana Mirza (Artistic Director, Desipina & Company), Nicky Paraiso (La MaMa E.T.C.), Cat Parker (Director), Aaron Riccio (Editor, That Sounds Cool), James Scruggs (Actor), Akia Squiterri (Artistic Director, Rising Sun Performance Company), Daniel Talbott (Artistic Director, Rising Phoenix Rep), Kathleen Warnock (Playwright) Lanie Zipoy (Freelance Publicist)

Outstanding Ensemble: Whitney Branan, Jennifer DiDonato, Tauren Hagans, Robert Anthony Jones, Edward Juvier, Lorinne Lampert, Aaron J. Libby, Jake Mendes, Trey Mitchell, Jan-Peter Pedross, Colin Pritchard, Megan Rosenblatt, Chloe Sabin, Dawn Trautman, Craig Treubert, Tyler Wallach, Eric Weaver, *The Drowsy Chaperone* (The Gallery Players)

Outstanding Solo Performance: Nat Cassidy, *I Am Providence* from *Things At The Doorstep: An Evening Based on the works of H.P. Lovecraft* (Manhattan Theatre Source, Greg Oliver Bodine and Nat Cassidy)

Outstanding Actor in a Featured Role: David Darrow, *The Revival* (Project Y Theatre Company)

Outstanding Actress in a Featured Role: Deanna McGovern, *An Impending Rupture of the Belly* (The Godlight Theatre Company)

Outstanding Actor in a Lead Role: Nick Paglino, *An Impending Rupture of the Belly* (Godlight Theatre Company)

Outstanding Actress in a Lead Role: Kristen Vaughan, *Benefactors* (Retro Productions)

Outstanding Choreography/Movement: Christine O'Grady, *The Drowsy Chaperone* (The Gallery Players)

Outstanding Director: Leslie Kincaid Burby, *The Navigator* (Workshop Theater Company)

Outstanding Set Design: Kevin Judge, *The Revival* (Project Y Theatre Company)

Outstanding Costume Design: Ryan J. Moller, *The Drowsy Chaperone* (The Gallery Players)

Outstanding Lighting Design: Duane Pagano, *The Navigator* (Workshop Theater Company)

Outstanding Sound Design: Aldo Perez, *Radio Purgatory* (Theatre THE)

Outstanding Innovative Design: Kae Burke, Aerial & Circus Rigging Design, *Circus of Circus, The House of Yes*

Outstanding Original Music: Cormac Bluestone, *The Caucasian Chalk Circle* (Pipeline Theatre Company)

Outstanding Original Full-Length Script: Jonathan Blitstein, *Keep Your Baggage With You (at all times)* (Artists Empire)

Outstanding Original Short Script: Isaac Oliver, *Come Here* from *The Spring Fling, F*lt Club*

Outstanding Stage Manager: Laura Schlachtmeyer, *Things at the Doorstep* (Manhattan Theatre Source, Greg Oliver Bodine and Nat Cassidy, and *(un)afraid*, New York Neo-Futurists)

Outstanding Performance Art Production: *Locker #4173b* (New York Neo-Futurists)

Outstanding Production of a Musical: *The Drowsy Chaperone* (The Gallery Players)

Outstanding Production of a Play: *Balm in Gilead* (T. Schreiber Studio)

Artistic Achievement Award: Robert Patrick

Ellen Stewart Award: Horse Trade Theater Group

Caffé Cino Fellowship Award ($1,000 grant): Flux Theatre Ensemble

Off Broadway Alliance Awards

June 19, 2012; Sardi's Restaurant; 2nd Annual. Presented by the Off Broadway Alliance to honor commercial and not-for-profit productions that opened Off-Broadway during the 2011–2012 season. The Off Broadway Alliance is a non-profit corporation organized by theater professionals dedicated to supporting, promoting and encouraging the production of Off-Broadway theater and to making live theater increasingly accessible to new and diverse audiences.

Best New Musical: *SILENCE! The Musical*

Best New Play: *Tribes*

Best Play Revival: *Cymbeline*

Best Musical Revial: *Carrie*

Best Special Event: *Traces*

Best Family Show: *StinkyKids, The Musical*

Legends of Off-Broadway Honorees: Edward Albee, Gerard Alessandrini, Kathleen Chalfant, Catherine Russell, Mary Louise Wilson

Off Broadway Alliance Hall of Fame Honorees: Howard Kissel (posthumous), Theodore Mann (posthumous)

Friend of Off Broadway Award: Roni and Sol Cohen of Genie Printing

Otto René Castillo Awards

May 20, 2012; Castillo Theatre All Stars Project; 14th annual. Presented to artists for and theatres from around the world in recognition for contributions to Political Theatre. The Otto Award is named for the Guatemalan poet and revolutionary Otto Rene Castillo, who was murdered by that country's military junta in 1968. **2012 Winners:** Ajoka Theatre; Hector Aristizábal; John O'Neal; Sistern Theatre Collective; Urban Bush Women

Ovation Awards

November 14, 2011; Thousand Oaks Civic Arts Plaza; 22nd annual. Established in 1989, the L.A. Stage Alliance Ovation Awards are Southern California's premiere awards for excellence in theatre. Winners were selected by a 190 member voting pool of theatre professionals working in the Los Angeles theatre community for productions that played September 1, 2010–August 31, 2011.

Best Season: Troubadour Theater Company

Production of a Play–Intimate Theatre: *Small Engine Repair* (Rogue Machine)

Production of a Musical–Intimate Theatre (Franklin R. Levy Memorial Award): *Jerry Springer: The Opera* (Chance Theater)

Production of a Play–Large Theatre: *A Raisin in the Sun* (Ebony Repertory Theatre)

Production of a Musical–Large Theatre: *Kiss Me Kate* (Reprise Theatre Company)

Playwriting for an Original Play: Stefan Marks, *Hello* (Stella Adler Theatre)

Book for an Original Musical: William Norris, Stuart Gordon, and Dennis Paoli, *Re-Animator: The Musical* (Steve Allen Theater)

Lyrics/Music for an Original Musical: Gregory Nabours, *The Trouble With Words* (Coeurage Theatre Company)

Director of a Play: Andrew Block, *Small Engine Repair* (Rogue Machine)

Director of a Musical: Matt Walker, *A Wither's Tale* (Troubadour Theater Company)

Musical Direction: Paul Litteral, *Hoboken to Hollywood* (Edgemar Center for the Arts)

Choreographer: Cate Caplin, *Fascinating Rhythms* (Rubicon Theatre)

Ensemble Performance (Play): *Small Engine Repair* (Rogue Machine)

Ensemble Performance (Musical): *A Wither's Tale* (Troubadour Theater Company)

Lead Actor in a Play: Stefan Marks, *Hello* (Stella Adler Theatre)

Lead Actress in a Play: Laurie Metcalf, *Voice Lessons* (Sacred Fools Theater Company)

Lead Actor in a Musical: Raul Esparza, *Leap of Faith* (Ahmanson Theatre)

Lead Actress in a Musical: Lesli Margherita, *Kiss Me Kate* (Reprise Theatre Company)

Featured Actor in a Play: Henry Dittman, *The Last Great Tale of the Legendary Sherlock Holmes* (Sacred Fools Theatre Company)

Featured Actress in a Play: Deirdre Henry, *A Raisin in the Sun* (Ebony Repertory)

Featured Actor in a Musical: Matt Walker, *A Wither's Tale* (Troubadour Theater Company)

Featured Actress in a Musical: Beth Kennedy, *A Wither's Tale* (Troubadour Theater Company)

Set Design–Intimate Theatre: Joel Daavid, *Skeleton Stories* (Theatre of NOTE)

Set Design–Large Theatre: Todd Rosenthal, *Twist—An American Musical* (Pasadena Playhouse)

Costume Design–Intimate Theatre: A. Jeffrey Schoenberg, *The Malconent* (Antaeus Company)

Costume Design–Large Theatre: Emilio Sosa, *Twist—An American Musical* (Pasadena Playhouse)

Lighting Design–Intimate Theatre: Christopher Kuhl, *How to Disappear*

Completely and Never Be Found (The Theatre @ Boston Court). Kuhl was also this year's winner of the $10,000 Richard E. Sherwood Award, given by Center Theatre Group for early career artists living and working in Los Angeles.

Lighting Design–Large Theatre: David Weiner, *Venice* (Kirk Douglas Theatre)

Sound Design–Intimate Theatre: Alyssa Ishii, *Awake* (Bootleg Theater)

Sound Design–Large Theatre: Joshua Horvath, *Venice* (Kirk Douglas Theatre)

OVATION HONORS

Video Design: Jason Thompson, *Venice* (Kirk Douglas Theatre)

Music Composition for a Play: Brian Joseph, Lyle Lovett, Fred Sanders, Sara Watkins and Sean Watkins, *Much Ado About Nothing* (Shakespeare Center of Los Angeles)

Puppet Design: Kristopher Bicknell, Gwyneth Conaway Bennison and Miles Taber, *Di is for Dog* (Rogue Artists Ensemble)

Fight Choreography: Brian Danner, *The Walworth Farce* (Theatre Banshee)

Pittsburgh Civic Light Opera's Richard Rodgers Award

Founded in 1988. Recognizes the lifetime contributions of outstanding talents in musical theatre; Presented by The Pittsburgh Civic Light Opera in conjunction with the families of Richard Rodgers and Oscar Hammerstein II.

Past Recipients: 1988: Mary Martin **1989:** Dame Julie Andrews **1991:** Harold Prince **1992:** Sir Cameron Mackintosh **1993:** Stephen Sondheim **1996:** Lord Andrew Lloyd Webber **2000:** Gwen Verdon **2002:** Bernadette Peters **2007:** Shirley Jones **2008:** Rob Marshall and Kathleen Marshall **2009:** Stephen Schwartz **2010:** No Award given **2011:** No Award given

Princess Grace Awards

November 1, 2011; Cipriani on 42nd Street, New York; Presented by the Princess Grace Foundation – USA for excellence in theatre, dance, and film across the United States. 2011 Awards: **Statue Award:** John M. Chu (*Justin Bieber: Never Say Never, The League of Extraordinary Dancers*); **Pierre Cardin Theater Award**: Sarah Rasmussen (Oregon Shakespeare Festival); **Fabergé Theater Award**: Hana Sooyen Kim (University of California—Los Angeles); **Robert and Gloria Houseman Theater Award:** Matt Jones (Alterenative Theater Ensemble –Theater Apprenticeship); **Gant Gaither Theater Award:** Sadieh Rifai (American Theatre Company); **George C. Wolfe Award:** Miram A. Hyman (Yale School of Drama–Theatre Scholarship; **Grace Le Vine Theater Award:** Carlos Alexis Cruz (Miracle Theatre Group)–Theatre Fellowship); **Playwrighting Fellowship:** Johanna Adams (New Dramatists Inc.); **Theater Honorarium:** R. Davis MCCallum (The Public Theater); **Works-in-Progress Residency:** Jacobs-Jenkins, *Neighbors, The Octoroon*

Richard Rodgers Awards

For staged readings of musicals in nonprofit theaters, administered by the American Academy of Arts and Letters and selected by a jury including Stephen Sondheim (chairman), Lynn Ahrens, John Guare, Sheldon Harnick, David Ives, Richard Maltby Jr., and Lin-Manuel Miranda.

2012 Winners: *Witness Uganda*, by Matt Gould and Griffin Matthews

Robert Whitehead Award

March 13, 2012; Sardi's, New York New York; Founded in 1993. Presented for outstanding achievement in commercial theatre producing, bestowed on a graduate of the fourteen-week Commercial Theatre Institute Program who has demonstrated a quality of production exemplified by the late producer, Robert Whitehead. The Commercial Theatre Institute (Jed Bernstein, Director) is the nation's only formal program that professionally trains commercial theatre producers. It is a joint project of the League of American Theatres and Producers, Inc., and Theatre Development Fund. **2012 Winner:** Jon B. Platt

Previous Recipients: **1993:** Susan Quint Gallin; Benjamin Mordecai **1994:** Dennis Grimaldi **1995:** Kevin McCollum **1996:** Randall L. Wreghitt **1997:** Marc Routh **1998:** Liz Oliver **1999:** Eric Krebs **2000:** Anne Strickland Squadron **2001–2003:** No Award **2004:** David Binder **2005–2007:** No Award **2008:** Nick Scandalios **2009:** Dori Bernstein **2010:** Stuart Thompson **2011:** Jill Furman

Stage Director and Choreographers (SDC) Foundation Awards

MR. ABBOT AWARD

October 3, 2011; Edison Ballroom; Named in honor of the legendary director George Abbot, this award is presented exclusively for directors and choreographers in recognition of lifetime achievement in the American Theatre.

2011 Winner: George C. Wolfe

Previous Recipients: 1985: Harold Prince **1986:** Bob Fosse **1987:** Mike Nichols **1988:** Agnes de Mille **1989:** Michael Bennet **1990:** Gene Saks **1991:** Tommy Tune **1992:** Arvin Brown **1993:** Trevor Nunn **1994:** Jerry Zaks **1995:** Gordon Davidson **1996:** Lloyd Richards **1997:** Garson Kanin **1998:** Graciela Daniele **1999:** Vinnette Carrol, Zelda Fichandler, Peter Gennaro, Gillian Lynne, Marshall W. Mason, Andrei Serban **2000:** Cy Feuer **2001:** Susan Stroman **2002:** Jack O'Brien **2003:** Lynne Meadow **2005:** Kathleen Marshall and Rob Marshall **2007:** Daniel Sullivan **2009:** Donald Saddler **2010:** No Award

JOE A. CALLAWAY AWARDS

Also known as the "Joey," this award, created in 1989, is issued for excellence in the craft of direction and/or choreography for during the New York City theatre season from September 1, 2009 through August 31, 2010.

2011 Winners: Director: Carolyn Cantor, *After the Revolution;* Choreographer: Larry Keigwin, *Rent*

Previous Winners: 1989: Gloria Muzio **1990:** Frank Galati **1991:** Susan Stroman **1992:** George C. Wolfe, Hope Clark **1993:** Harold Prince **1994:** Gerald Gutierrez **1995:** Joe Mantello, Scott Elliott **1996:** Julie Taymor **1997:** Moisés Kaufman **1998:** Frank Galati, Graciela Daniele **1999:** Trevor Nunn **2000:** Gabriel Barre, Mark Dendy **2001:** Jack O'Brien **2002:** Bartlett Sher **2003:** Devanand Janki, Doug Hughes **2004:** Daniel Sullivan **2005:** Doug Hughes, Christopher Gattelli **2006:** Bill T. Jones, Peter DuBois **2007:** Thomas Kail, Andy Blankenbuehler **2008:** Giovanna Sardelli, Lynne Taylor-Corbett **2009:** Garry Hynes, Martha Clarke **2010:** Ciaran O'Reilly, Byron Easley

Steinberg Playwright Award

November 14, 2011; Vivian Beaumont Theatre; 2nd presentation; Created by the Harold and Mimi Steinberg Charitable Trust, this award recognizes playwrights at various stages of their early careers whose profession works show great promise. This award is presented on alternate years with the Steinberg Distinguished Playwright Award which recognizes an established American playwright whose body of work has made significant contributions to the American theater. The

2011 Advisory Committee is comprised of Susan Booth, Artistic Director of the Alliance Theater; Polly Carl, Director of Artistic Development, Steppenwolf Theater Company; Jeremy Cohen, Producing Artistic Director, The Playwrights' Center; David Emmes, Producing Artistic Director, South Coast Repertory; Oskar Eustis, Artistic Director, The Public Theater; Todd London, Artistic Director of New Dramatists; and Lynne Meadow, Artistic Director, Manhattan Theater Club. The winners receive 'The Mimi,' a statue designed by David Rockwell, and a cash prize (a share of $100,000 for playwrights in early stages of their careers and $200,000 for established playwrights), making the award the largest ever created to honor and encourage artistic achievement in the American Theatre.

2011 Recipients: Lisa D'Amour, Melissa James Gibson

Previous Distinguished Recipients: 2008: Tony Kushner **2010:** Lynn Nottage

Previous Steinberg Playwright Recipient: 2009: Bruce Norris, Tarrell Alvin McCraney & David Adimi

Susan Smith Blackburn Prize

February 28, 2012; London, England; 34th annual; Presenter: Imogene Stubs. Presented to women who have written works of outstanding quality for the English-speaking theater. The Prize is administered in Houston, London, and New York by a board of directors who choose six judges each year and submitted by various theatres. 2011–2012 Judges included US judges Randy Gener, award-winning writer/editor/critic; Martha Lavey, artistic director of the Steppenwolf Theatre (Chicago); and Frances McDormand, Oscar and Tony Award-winning film and stage star. Judges from the UK are Jonathan Church, artistic director of the Chichester Festival Theatre; Ben Power, associate director of the National Theatre; and Imogen Stubbs, actress/writer/director and stage and screen star. The winner receives a $20,000 cash prize and a signed and numbered print by artist Willem de Kooning. The Special Commendation winner receives a $5,000 cash prize, and each finalist receives $1,000.

2012 Winner: Jennifer Haley, *The Nether*

Special Commendation: Not presented this year

Finalists: Johnna Adams, *Gideon's Knot* (The Repertory Theatre St. Louis)(U.S.); Alice Birch, *Many Moons* (Theatre 503)(U.K.); Madeline George, *Seven Homeless Mammoths Wander New England* (Clubbed Thumb)(U.S.); Nancy Harris, *No Romance* (Abbey Theatre)(Ireland); Zinnie Harris, *The Wheel* (National Theatre of Scotland)(U.K.); Jaki McCarrick, *Belfast Girls* (King's Head Theatre)(U.K.); Molly Smith Metzler, *Close Up Space* (Manhattan Theatre Club)(U.S.); Meg Miroshnik, *The Fairytale Lives of Russian Girls*, (Alliance Theatre)(U.S.); Alexis Zegerman, *The Steingolds* (Playful Productions)(U.K.)

Theatre Development Fund Awards

IRENE SHARAFF AWARDS

May 4, 2012: Hudson Theatre; 17th annual. Founded in 1993, this award has become an occasion for the costume design community to come together to honor its own and pays tribute to the art of costume design. Named after the revered costume designer, the awards are and now underwritten by the Tobin Theatre Arts Fund. The Awards are decided upon by the TDF Costume Collection Advisory Committee: Kitty Leech, Gregg Barnes, Suzy Benzinger, Dean Brown, Stephen Cabral, Linda Fisher, Lana Fritz, Rodney Gordon, Desmond Heeley, Allen Lee Hughes, Holly Hynes, Carolyn Kostopoulous, Anna Louizos, Mimi Maxmen, David Murin, Sally Ann Parsons, Robert Perdziola, Gregory A. Poplyk Carrie Robbins, Tony Walton, Patrick Wiley, David Zinn.

Lifetime Achievement Award: Carrie Robbins

Young Master Award: Matthew LeFebvre

Artisan Award: Lynn Pecktal

The Robert L.B. Tobin Award for Sustained Excellence in Theatrical Design: Lloyd Burlingame

Memorial Tribute: William and Jean Eckart

The Theater Hall of Fame

January 30, 2012; Gershwin Theatre North Rotunda; 41st annual; The Theater of Hall of Fame was created in 1971 to honor those who have made outstanding contributions to the American theater in a career spanning at least twenty-five years, with at least five major credits.

2012 Inductees (for the year 2011)**:** Tyne Daly, Woodie King Jr., Elliot Martin, Ann Roth, Paul Sills, Daniel Sullivan, Ben Vereen

Previous Inductees: George Abbott, Maude Adams, Viola Adams, Stella Adler, Edward Albee, Theoni V. Aldredge, Ira Aldridge, Jane Alexander, Mary Alice, Winthrop Ames, Judith Anderson, Maxwell Anderson, Robert Anderson, Julie Andrews, Margaret Anglin, Jean Anouilh, Harold Arlen, George Arliss, Boris Aronson, Adele Astaire, Fred Astaire, Eileen Atkins, Brooks Atkinson, Alan Ayckbourn, Emanuel Azenberg, Lauren Bacall, Pearl Bailey, George Balanchine, William Ball, Anne Bancroft, Tallulah Bankhead, Richard Barr, Philip Barry, Ethel Barrymore, John Barrymore, Lionel Barrymore, Howard Bay, Nora Bayes, John Lee Beatty, Julian Beck, Samuel Beckett, Brian Bedford, S.N. Behrman, Barbara Bel Geddes, Norman Bel Geddes, David Belasco, Michael Bennett, Richard Bennett, Robert Russell Bennett, Eric Bentley, Irving Berlin, Roger Berlind, Sarah Bernhardt, Leonard Bernstein, Patricia Birch, Earl Blackwell, Michael Blakemore, Kermit Bloomgarden, Jerry Bock, Ray Bolger, Edwin Booth, Roscoe Lee Brown, Junius Brutus Booth, Shirley Booth, Philip Bosco, Dion Boucicault, Alice Brady, Bertolt Brecht, Fannie Brice, Peter Brook, John Mason Brown, Robert Brustein, Billie Burke, Abe Burrows, Richard Burton, Mrs. Patrick Campbell, Zoe Caldwell, Eddie Cantor, Len Cariou, Morris Carnovsky, Mrs. Leslie Carter, Joseph Chaikin, Gower Champion, Frank Chanfrau, Carol Channing, Stockard Channing, Ruth Chatterton, Paddy Chayefsky, Anton Chekhov, Caryl Churchill, Ina Claire, Bobby Clark, Harold Clurman, Lee. J. Cobb, Richard L. Coe, George M. Cohan, Alexander H. Cohen, Jack Cole, Cy Coleman, Constance Collier, Alvin Colt, Betty Comden, Marc Connelly, Barbara Cook, Thomas Abthorpe Cooper, Katherine Cornell, Noel Coward, Jane Cowl, Lotta Crabtree, Cheryl Crawford, Hume Cronyn, Rachel Crothers, Russel Crouse, John Cullum, Charlotte Cushman, Jim Dale, Jean Dalrymple, Augustin Daly, Graciela Daniele, E.L. Davenport, Gordon Davidson, Ossie Davis, Owen Davis, Ruby Dee, Alfred De Liagre Jr., Agnes DeMille, Brian Dennehy, Colleen Dewhurst, Howard Dietz, Dudley Digges, Melvyn Douglas, Eddie Dowling, Alfred Drake, Marie Dressler, John Drew, Mrs. John Drew, William Dunlap, Mildred Dunnock, Charles Durning, Eleanora Duse, Jeanne Eagles, Richard Easton, Fred Ebb, Ben Edwards, Florence Eldridge, Lehman Engel, Maurice Evans, Abe Feder, Jose Ferber, Cy Feuer, Zelda Fichandler, Dorothy Fields, Herbert Fields, Lewis Fields, W.C. Fields, Harvey Fierstein, Jules Fisher, Minnie Maddern Fiske, Clyde Fitch, Geraldine Fitzgerald, Henry Fonda, Lynn Fontanne, Horton Foote, Edwin Forrest, Bob Fosse, Brian Friel, Rudolf Friml, Charles Frohman, Daniel Frohman, Robert Fryer, Athol Fugard, John Gassner, Larry Gelbart, Paul Genignani, Peter Gennaro, Grace George, George Gershwin, Ira Gershwin, Bernard Gersten, William Gibson, John Gielgud, W.S. Gilbert, Jack Gilford, William Gillette, Charles Gilpin, Lillian Gish, Susan Glaspell, John Golden, Max Gordon, Ruth Gordon, Adolph Green, Paul Green, Charlotte Greenwood, Jane Greenwood, Joel Grey, Tammy Grimes, George Grizzard, John Guare, Otis L. Guernsey Jr., A.R. Gurney, Mel Gussow, Tyrone Guthrie, Uta Hagen, Sir Peter Hall, Lewis Hallam, T. Edward Hambleton, Marvin Hamlisch, Oscar Hammerstein II, Walter Hampden, Otto Harbach, E.Y. Harburg, Sheldon Harnick, Edward Harrigan, Jed Harris, Julie

Harris, Rosemary Harris, Sam H. Harris, Rex Harrison, Kitty Carlisle Hart, Lorenz Hart, Moss Hart, Tony Hart, June Havoc, Helen Hayes, Leland Hayward, George Hearn, Ben Hecht, Eileen Heckart, Theresa Helburn, Lillian Hellman, Katharine Hepburn, Victor Herbert, Jerry Herman, James A. Herne, Henry Hewes, Gregory Hines, Al Hirschfeld, Raymond Hitchcock, Hal Holbrook, Celeste Holm, Hanya Holm, Arthur Hopkins, De Wolf Hopper, John Houseman, Eugene Howard, Leslie Howard, Sidney Howard, Willie Howard, Barnard Hughes, Henry Hull, Josephine Hull, Walter Huston, Earle Hyman, Henrik Ibsen, William Inge, Dana Ivey, Bernard B. Jacobs, Elise Janis, Joseph Jefferson, Al Jolson, James Earl Jones, Margo Jones, Robert Edmond Jones, Tom Jones, Jon Jory, Raul Julia, Madeline Kahn, John Kander, Garson Kanin, George S. Kaufman, Danny Kaye, Elia Kazan, Gene Kelly, George Kelly, Fanny Kemble, Jerome Kern, Walter Kerr, Michael Kidd, Richard Kiley, Willa Kim, Sidney Kingsley, Kevin Kline, Florence Klotz, Joseph Wood Krutch, James Lapine, Bert Lahr, Burton Lane, Frank Langella, Lawrence Langner, Lillie Langtry, Angela Lansbury, Nathan Lane, Charles Laughton, Arthur Laurents, Linda Lavin, Gertrude Lawrence, Jerome Lawrence, Eva Le Gallienne, Canada Lee, Eugene Lee, Ming Cho Lee, Robert E. Lee, Lotte Lenya, Alan Jay Lerner, Sam Levene, Robert Lewis, Beatrice Lillie, Howard Lindsay, John Lithgow, Andrew Lloyd Webber, Frank Loesser, Frederick Loewe, Joshua Logan, William Ivey Long, Santo Loquasto, Pauline Lord, Lucille Lortel, Charles Ludlam, Dorothy Loudon, Alfred Lunt, Patti LuPone, Charles MacArthur, Steele MacKaye, Judith Malina, David Mamet, Rouben Mamoulian, Ted Mann, Richard Mansfield, Robert B. Mantell, Frederic March, Nancy Marchand, Julia Marlowe, Ernest H. Martin, Mary Martin, Raymond Massey, Elizabeth Ireland McCann, Ian McKellen, Siobhan McKenna, John McMartin, Terrence McNally, Sanford Meisner, Helen Menken, Burgess Meredith, Ethel Merman, David Merrick, Jo Mielziner, Arthur Miller, Marilyn Miller, Liza Minnelli, Helena Modjeska, Ferenc Molnar, Lola Montez, Victor Moore, Robert Morse, Zero Mostel, Anna Cora Mowatt, Paul Muni, Brian Murray, Tharon Musser, George Jean Nathan, Mildred Natwick, Alla Nazimova, Patricia Neal, James M. Nederlander, Mike Nichols, Elliot Norton, Jack O'Brien, Sean O'Casey, Clifford Odets, Donald Oenslager, Laurence Olivier, Eugene O'Neill, Jerry Orbach, Geraldine Page, Joseph Papp, Estelle Parsons, Osgood Perkins, Bernadette Peters, Molly Picon, Harold Pinter, Luigi Pirandello, Christopher Plummer, Cole Porter, Robert Preston, Harold Prince, Jose Quintero, Ellis Rabb, John Raitt, Tony Randall, Lynn Redgrave, Michael Redgrave, Ada Rehan, Elmer Rice, Lloyd Richards, Ralph Richardson, Chita Rivera, Jason Robards, Jerome Robbins, Paul Robeson, Richard Rodgers, Will Rogers, Sigmund Romberg, Harold Rome, Billy Rose, Lillian Russell, Donald Saddler, Gene Saks, Diana Sands, William Saroyan, Joseph Schildkraut, Harvey Schmidt, Alan Schneider, Gerald Shoenfeld, Arthur Schwartz, Maurice Schwartz, Stephen Schwartz, George C. Scott, Marian Seldes, Peter Shaffer, Irene Sharaff, George Bernard Shaw, Sam Shepard, Robert F. Sherwood, J.J. Shubert, Lee Shubert, Herman Shumlin, Neil Simon, Lee Simonson, Edmund Simpson, Otis Skinner, Lois Smith, Maggie Smith, Oliver Smith, Stephen Sondheim, E.H. Sothern, Kim Stanley, Jean Stapleton, Maureen Stapleton, Joseph Stein, Frances Sternhagen, Roger L. Stevens, Isabelle Stevenson, Ellen Stewart, Dorothy Stickney, Fred Stone, Peter Stone, Tom Stoppard, Lee Strasburg, August Strindberg, Elaine Stritch, Charles Strouse, Jule Styne, Margaret Sullivan, Arthur Sullivan, Jessica Tandy, Laurette Taylor, Ellen Terry, Sada Thompson, Cleon Throckmorton, Tommy Tune, Jonathan Tunick, Gwen Verdon, Robin Wagner, Nancy Walker, Eli Wallach, James Wallack, Lester Wallack, Tony Walton, Douglas Turner Ward, David Warfield, Wendy Wasserstein, Ethel Waters, Fritz Weaver, Clifton Webb, Joseph Weber, Margaret Webster, Kurt Weill, Orson Welles, Mae West, Robert Whitehead, Richard Wilbur, Oscar Wilde, Thorton Wilder, Bert Williams, Tennessee Williams, August Wilson, Elizabeth Wilson, Lanford Wilson, P.G. Wodehouse, Peggy Wood, Alexander Woollcott, Irene Worth, Teresa Wright, Ed Wynn, Vincent Youmans, Stark Young, Florenz Ziegfeld, Patricia Zipprodt

THEATER HALL OF FAME FOUNDERS AWARD

Established in 1993 in honor of Earl Blackwell, James M. Nederlander, Gerald Oestreicher and Arnold Weissberger. The Theater Hall of Fame Founders Award is voted by the Hall's board of directors and is presented to an individual for his of her outstanding contribution to the theater.

Past Recipients: (if year is missing, no award was presented) **1993:** James M. Nederlander **1994:** Kitty Carlisle Hart **1995:** Harvey Sabinson **1996:** Henry Hewes **1997:** Otis L. Guernsey Jr. **1998:** Edward Colton **2000:** Gerard Oestreicher; Arnold Weissberger **2001:** Tom Dillon **2003:** Price Berkley **2004:** No Award **2005:** Donald Seawell **2007:** Roy Somlyo **2009:** Shirley Herz **2010:** No Award **2011:** No Award

William Inge Theatre Festival Awards

April 18-21, 2012; 31st annual. The Inge Festival brings some of the world's most beloved playwrights to America's heartland in Independence, Missouri. During the four-day festival, honorees are chosen for distinguished achievement in American theater. Also, the festival selects a winner of the Otis Guernsey New Voices Playwriting Award, which recognizes contemporary playwrights whose voices are helping shape the American theater of today. It is named for the late Otis L. Guernsey Jr., beloved theater writer and editor who was a frequent guest at the William Inge Theatre Festival and a champion of exciting new plays.

2012 Distinguished Achievement in the American Theatre Award: David Henry Hwang

20th Annual Otis Guernsey New Voices in Playwrighting Award: Catherine Treischmann

Previous Festival Honorees: 1982: William Inge Celebration; **1983:** Jerome Lawrence **1984:** William Gibson **1985:** Robert Anderson **1986:** John Patrick **1987:** Garson Kanin **1988:** Sidney Kingsley (in Independence), Robert E. Lee (on the road) **1989:** Horton Foote **1990:** Betty Comden & Adolph Green **1991:** Edward Albee **1992:** Peter Shaffer **1993:** Wendy Wasserstein **1994:** Terrence McNally **1995:** Arthur Miller **1996:** August Wilson **1997:** Neil Simon **1998:** Stephen Sondheim **1999:** John Guare **2000:** A.R. Gurney **2001:** Lanford Wilson **2002:** John Kander & Fred Ebb **2003:** Romulus Linney **2004:** Arthur Laurents **2005:** Tina Howe **2006:** 25th Anniversary retrospective **2007:** Jerry Bock & Sheldon Harnick **2008:** Christopher Durang **2009:** Tom Jones and Harvey Schmidt **2010:** Paula Vogel **2011:** Marsha Norman

Previous New Voices Recipients: 1993: Jason Milligan **1994:** Catherine Butterfield **1995:** Mary Hanes **1996:** Brian Burgess Cross **1997:** Joe DiPietro **1998:** David Ives **1999:** David Hirson **2000:** James Still **2001:** Mark St. Germain **2002:** Dana Yeaton **2003:** Theresa Rebeck **2004:** Mary Portser **2005:** Lynne Kaufman **2006:** Melanie Marnich **2007:** JT Rogers **2008:** Adam Bock **2009:** Carlos Murillo **2010:** Katori Hall **2011:** Dael Orlandsmith

Top: The Company of Avenue Q *(photo by Carol Rosegg)*

Center: Ann Miller and Mickey Rooney in Sugar Babies
(photo by Martha Swope)

*Bottom: Robert Morse as Finch, with members of the Company
in* How to Succeed in Business Without Really Trying

Broadway

The Phantom of the Opera*
10,126 performances
Opened January 26, 1988

Cats
7,485 performances
Opened October 7, 1982
Closed September 10, 2000

Les Misérables
6,680 performances
Opened March 12, 1987
Closed May 18, 2003

Chicago* (revival)
6,451 performances
Opened November 19, 1996

A Chorus Line
6,137 performances
Opened July 25, 1975
Closed April 28, 1990

The Lion King*
6,038 performances
Opened November 13, 1997

Oh! Calcutta (revival)
5,959 performances
Opened September 24, 1976
Closed August 6, 1989

Beauty and the Beast
5,464 performances
Opened April 18, 1994
Closed July 29, 2007

Rent
5,124 performances
Opened April 29, 1996
Closed September 7, 2008

Mamma Mia!*
4,403 performances
Opened October 12, 2001

Miss Saigon
4,097 performances
Opened April 11, 1991
Closed January 28, 2001

Wicked*
3,560 performances
Opened October 30, 2003

42nd Street
3,486 performances
Opened August 25, 1980
Closed January 8, 1989

Grease
3,388 performances
Opened February 14, 1972
Closed April 13, 1980

Fiddler on the Roof
3,242 performances
Opened September 22, 1964
Closed July 2, 1972

Life With Father
3,224 performances
Opened November 8, 1939
Closed July 12, 1947

Tobacco Road
3,182 performances
Opened December 4, 1933
Closed May 31, 1941

Hello, Dolly!
2,844 performances
Opened January 16, 1964
Closed December 27, 1970

My Fair Lady
2,717 performances
Opened March 15, 1956
Closed September 29, 1962

Jersey Boys*
2,714 performances
Opened November 6, 2006

Hairspray
2,641 performances
Opened August 15, 2002
Closed January 4, 2009

Avenue Q
2,534 performances
Opened July 31, 2003
Closed September 13, 2009

The Producers
2,502 performances
Opened April 19, 2001
Closed April 22, 2007

Cabaret (revival)
2,378 performances
Opened March 19, 1998
Closed January 4, 2004

Annie
2,377 performances
Opened April 21, 1977
Closed January 22, 1983

Man of La Mancha
2,328 performances
Opened November 22, 1965
Closed June 26, 1971

Abie's Irish Rose
2,327 performances
Opened May 23, 1922
Closed October 21, 1927

Mary Poppins*
2,306 performances
Opened November 16, 2006

Oklahoma!
2,212 performances
Opened March 31, 1943
Closed May 29, 1948

Smokey Joe's Café
2,036 performances
Opened March 2, 1995
Closed January 16, 2000

Pippin
1,944 performances
Opened October 23, 1972
Closed June 12, 1977

South Pacific
1,925 performances
Opened April 7, 1949
Closed January 16, 1954

The Magic Show
1,920 performances
Opened May 28, 1974
Closed December 31, 1978

Aida
1,852 performances
Opened March 23, 2000
Closed September 5, 2004

Gemini
1,819 performances
Opened May 21, 1977
Closed September 6, 1981

Deathtrap
1,793 performances
Opened February 26, 1978
Closed June 13, 1982

Harvey
1,775 performances
Opened November 1, 1944
Closed January 15, 1949

Dancin'
1,774 performances
Opened March 27, 1978
Closed June 27, 1982

La Cage aux Folles
1,761 performances
Opened August 21, 1983
Closed November 15, 1987

Hair
1,750 performances
Opened April 29, 1968
Closed July 1, 1972

The Wiz
1,672 performances
Opened January 5, 1975
Closed January 29, 1979

Born Yesterday
1,642 performances
Opened February 4, 1946
Closed December 31, 1949

The Best Little Whorehouse in Texas
1,639 performances
Opened June 19, 1978
Closed July 24, 1982

Barry Bostwick and Carole Demas in Grease *(photo by Friedman-Abeles)*

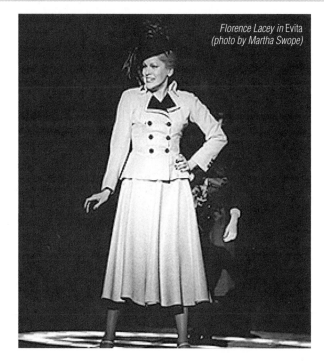

Florence Lacey in Evita *(photo by Martha Swope)*

Crazy for You
1,622 performances
Opened February 19, 1992
Closed January 7, 1996

Ain't Misbehavin'
1,604 performances
Opened May 9, 1978
Closed February 21, 1982

Monty Python's Spamalot
1,575 performances
Opened March 17, 2005
Closed January 11, 2009

Mary, Mary
1,572 performances
Opened March 8, 1961
Closed December 12, 1964

Evita
1,567 performances
Opened September 25, 1979
Closed June 26, 1983

The Voice of the Turtle
1,557 performances
Opened December 8, 1943
Closed January 3, 1948

Jekyll & Hyde
1,543 performances
Opened April 28, 1997
Closed January 7, 2001

Barefoot in the Park
1,530 performances
Opened October 23, 1963
Closed June 25, 1967

Brighton Beach Memoirs
1,530 performances
Opened March 27, 1983
Closed May 11, 1986

42nd Street (revival)
1,524 performances
Opened May 2, 2001
Closed January 2, 2005

Dreamgirls
1,522 performances
Opened December 20, 1981
Closed August 11, 1985

Mame
1,508 performances
Opened May 24, 1966
Closed January 3, 1970

Grease (revival)
1,505 performances
Opened May 11, 1994
Closed January 25, 1998

Same Time, Next Year
1,453 performances
Opened March 14, 1975
Closed September 3, 1978

Arsenic and Old Lace
1,444 performances
Opened January 10, 1941
Closed June 17, 1944

The Sound of Music
1,443 performances
Opened November 16, 1959
Closed June 15, 1963

Me and My Girl
1,420 performances
Opened August 10, 1986
Closed December 31, 1989

How to Succeed in Business Without Really Trying
1,417 performances
Opened October 14, 1961
Closed March 6, 1965

Hellzapoppin'
1,404 performances
Opened September 22, 1938
Closed December 17, 1941

The Music Man
1,375 performances
Opened December 19, 1957
Closed April 15, 1961

Funny Girl
1,348 performances
Opened March 26, 1964
Closed July 15, 1967

Mummenschanz
1,326 performances
Opened March 30, 1977
Closed April 20, 1980

Oh! Calcutta!
1314 performances
Opened June 17, 1969
Closed August 12, 1972

Billy Elliot The Musical
1,312 performances
Opened November 13, 2008
Closed January 8, 2012

Movin' Out
1,303 performances
Opened October 24, 2002
Closed December 11, 2005

Angel Street
1,295 performances
Opened December 5, 1941
Closed December 30, 1944

Lightnin'
1,291 performances
Opened August 26, 1918
Closed August 27, 1921

Promises, Promises
1,281 performances
Opened December 1, 1968
Closed January 1, 1972

The King and I
1,246 performances
Opened March 29, 1951
Closed March 20, 1954

Cactus Flower
1,234 performances
Opened December 8, 1965
Closed November 23, 1968

Jeff Fenholt and Ben Vereen in Jesus Christ Superstar *(photo by Friedman-Abeles)*

Rock of Ages*
1,229 performances
Opened April 7, 2009

Sleuth
1,222 performances
Opened November 12, 1970
Closed October 13, 1973

Torch Song Trilogy
1,222 performances
Opened June 10, 1982
Closed May 19, 1985

1776
1,217 performances
Opened March 16, 1969
Closed February 13, 1972

Equus
1,209 performances
Opened October 24, 1974
Closed October 7, 1977

Sugar Babies
1,208 performances
Opened October 8, 1979
Closed August 28, 1982

Guys and Dolls
1,200 performances
Opened November 24, 1950
Closed November 28, 1953

In the Heights
1,184 performances
Opened March 9, 2008
Closed January 9, 2011

Amadeus
1,181 performances
Opened December 17, 1980
Closed October 16, 1983

Cabaret
1,165 performances
Opened November 20, 1966
Closed September 6, 1969

Mister Roberts
1,157 performances
Opened February 18, 1948
Closed January 6, 1951

Annie Get Your Gun
1,147 performances
Opened May 16, 1946
Closed February 12, 1949

Guys and Dolls (revival)
1,144 performances
Opened April 14, 1992
Closed January 8, 1995

The Seven Year Itch
1,141 performances
Opened November 20, 1952
Closed August 13, 1955

The 25th Annual Putnam County Spelling Bee
1,136 performances
Opened May 2, 2005
Closed January 20, 2008

Bring in 'da Noise, Bring in 'da Funk
1,130 performances
Opened April 25, 1996
Closed January 19, 1999

Butterflies Are Free
1,128 performances
Opened October 21, 1969
Closed July 2, 1972

Pins and Needles
1,108 performances
Opened November 27, 1937
Closed June 22, 1940

Plaza Suite
1,097 performances
Opened February 14, 1968
Closed October 3, 1970

Fosse
1,093 performances
Opened January 14, 1999
Closed August 25, 2001

Memphis*
1,088 performances
Opened October 19, 2009

They're Playing Our Song
1,082 performances
Opened February 11, 1979
Closed September 6, 1981

Kiss Me, Kate
1,070 performances
Opened December 30, 1948
Closed July 25, 1951

Don't Bother Me, I Can't Cope
1,065 performances
Opened April 19, 1972
Closed October 27, 1974

The Pajama Game
1,063 performances
Opened May 13, 1954
November 24, 1956

Shenandoah
1,050 performances
Opened January 7, 1975
Closed August 7, 1977

Annie Get Your Gun (revival)
1,046 performances
Opened March 4, 1999
Closed September 1, 2001

The Teahouse of the August Moon
1,027 performances
Opened October 15, 1953
Closed March 24, 1956

Damn Yankees
1,019 performances
Opened May 5, 1955
Closed October 12, 1957

Grand Hotel (musical)
1,017 performances
Opened November 12, 1989
Closed April 25, 1992

Contact
1,010 performances
Opened March 30, 2000
Closed September 1, 2002

Never Too Late
1,007 performances
Opened November 26, 1962
Closed April 24, 1965

Big River
1,005 performances
Opened April 25, 1985
Closed September 20, 1987

South Pacific (revival)
996 performances
Opened April 3, 2008
Closed August 22, 2010

The Will Rogers Follies
983 performances
Opened May 1, 1991
Closed September 5, 1993

Any Wednesday
982 performances
Opened February 18, 1964
Closed June 26, 1966

Sunset Boulevard
977 performances
Opened November 17, 1994
Closed March 22, 1997

Urinetown the Musical
965 performances
Opened September 20, 2001
Closed January 18, 2004

A Funny Thing Happened on the Way to the Forum
964 performances
Opened May 8, 1962
Closed August 29, 1964

Dorothy Collins and Alexis Smith in Follies *(photo by Friedman-Abeles)*

The Odd Couple
964 performances
Opened March 10, 1965
Closed July 2, 1967

Anna Lucasta
957 performances
Opened August 30, 1944
Closed November 30, 1946

Kiss and Tell
956 performances
Opened March 17, 1943
Closed June 23, 1945

Show Boat (revival)
949 performances
Opened October 2, 1994
Closed January 5, 1997

Dracula (1977 revival)
925 performances
Opened October 20, 1977
Closed January 6, 1980

Bells Are Ringing
924 performances
Opened November 29, 1956
Closed March 7, 1959

The Moon Is Blue
924 performances
Opened March 8, 1951
Closed May 30, 1953

Beatlemania
920 performances
Opened May 31, 1977
Closed October 17, 1979

Proof
917 performances
Opened October 24, 2000
Closed January 5, 2003

The Elephant Man
916 performances
Opened April 19, 1979
Closed June 28, 1981

The Color Purple
910 performances
Opened December 1, 2005
Closed February 24, 2008

Kiss of the Spider Woman
906 performances
Opened May 3, 1993
Closed July 1, 1995

Thoroughly Modern Millie
904 performances
Opened April 18, 2002
Closed June 20, 2004

Luv
901 performances
Opened November 11, 1964
Closed January 7, 1967

The Who's Tommy
900 performances
Opened April 22, 1993
Closed June 17, 1995

Chicago
898 performances
Opened June 3, 1975
Closed August 27, 1977

Applause
896 performances
Opened March 30, 1970
Closed July 27, 1972

Can-Can
892 performances
Opened May 7, 1953
Closed June 25, 1955

Carousel
890 performances
Opened April 19, 1945
Closed May 24, 1947

I'm Not Rappaport
890 performances
Opened November 19, 1985
Closed January 17, 1988

Hats Off to Ice
889 performances
Opened June 22, 1944
Closed April 2, 1946

Fanny
888 performances
Opened November 4, 1954
Closed December 16, 1956

Children of a Lesser God
887 performances
Opened March 30, 1980
Closed May 16, 1982

Follow the Girls
882 performances
Opened April 8, 1944
Closed May 18, 1946

Kiss Me, Kate (revival)
881 performances
Opened November 18, 1999
Closed December 30, 2001

City of Angels
878 performances
Opened December 11, 1989
Closed January 19, 1992

Angela Lansbury and Len Cariou in Sweeney Todd *(photo by Martha Swope)*

Camelot
873 performances
Opened December 3, 1960
Closed January 5, 1963

I Love My Wife
872 performances
Opened April 17, 1977
Closed May 20, 1979

The Bat
867 performances
Opened August 23, 1920
Closed Unknown closing date

My Sister Eileen
864 performances
Opened December 26, 1940
Closed January 16, 1943

No, No, Nanette (revival)
861 performances
Opened January 19, 1971
Closed February 3, 1973

Ragtime
861 performances
Opened January 18, 1998
Closed January 16, 2000

Song of Norway
860 performances
Opened August 21, 1944
Closed September 7, 1946

Spring Awakening
859 performances
Opened December 10, 2006
Closed January 18, 2009

Chapter Two
857 performances
Opened December 4, 1977
Closed December 9, 1979

A Streetcar Named Desire
855 performances
Opened December 3, 1947
Closed December 17, 1949

Barnum
854 performances
Opened April 30, 1980
Closed May 16, 1982

Comedy in Music
849 performances
Opened October 2, 1953
Closed January 21, 1956

Raisin
847 performances
Opened October 18, 1973
Closed December 7, 1975

Blood Brothers
839 performances
Opened April 25, 1993
Closed April 30, 1995

You Can't Take It With You
837 performances
Opened December 14, 1936
Unknown closing date

La Plume de Ma Tante
835 performances
Opened November 11, 1958
Closed December 17, 1960

Three Men on a Horse
835 performances
Opened January 30, 1935
Closed January 9, 1937

The Subject Was Roses
832 performances
Opened May 25, 1964
Closed May 21, 1966

Black and Blue
824 performances
Opened January 26, 1989
Closed January 20, 1991

The King and I (revival)
807 performances
Opened April 11, 1996
Closed February 22, 1998

Inherit the Wind
806 performances
Opened April 21, 1955
Closed June 22, 1957

Anything Goes (revival)
804 performances
Opened October 19, 1987
Closed September 3, 1989

Titanic
804 performances
Opened April 23, 1997
Closed March 21, 1999

No Time for Sergeants
796 performances
Opened October 20, 1955
Closed September 14, 1957

Fiorello!
795 performances
Opened November 23, 1959
Closed October 28, 1961

Where's Charley?
792 performances
Opened October 11, 1948
Closed September 9, 1950

The Ladder
789 performances
Opened October 22, 1926
Unknown closing date

Fiddler on the Roof (revival)
781 performances
Opened February 26, 2004
Closed January 8, 2006

Forty Carats
780 performances
Opened December 26, 1968
Closed November 7, 1970

Lost in Yonkers
780 performances
Opened February 21, 1991
Closed January 3, 1993

The Prisoner of Second Avenue
780 performances
Opened November 11, 1971
Closed September 29, 1973

M. Butterfly
777 performances
Opened March 20, 1988
Closed January 27, 1990

The Tale of the Allergist's Wife
777 performances
Opened November 2, 2000
Closed September 15, 2002

Oliver!
774 performances
Opened January 6, 1963
Closed November 14, 1964

The Pirates of Penzance (revival)
772 performances
Opened January 8, 1981
Closed November 28, 1982

The 39 Steps
771 performances
Opened January 15, 2008
Closed January 10, 2010

The Full Monty
770 performances
Opened October 26, 2000
Closed September 1, 2002

Woman of the Year
770 performances
Opened March 29, 1981
Closed March 13, 1983

My One and Only
767 performances
Opened May 1, 1983
Closed March 3, 1985

Sophisticated Ladies
767 performances
Opened March 1, 1981
Closed January 2, 1983

Bubbling Brown Sugar
766 performances
Opened March 2, 1976
Closed December 31, 1977

Into the Woods
765 performances
Opened November 5, 1987
Closed September 3, 1989

State of the Union
765 performances
Opened November 14, 1945
Closed September 13, 1947

Starlight Express
761 performances
Opened March 15, 1987
Closed January 8, 1989

The First Year
760 performances
Opened October 20, 1920
Unknown closing date

A Chorus Line (revival)
759 performances
Opened October 5, 2006
Closed August 17, 2008

Broadway Bound
756 performances
Opened December 4, 1986
Closed September 25, 1988

You Know I Can't Hear You When the Water's Running
755 performances
Opened March 13, 1967
Closed January 4, 1969

Two for the Seesaw
750 performances
Opened January 16, 1958
Closed October 31, 1959

West Side Story (2009 revival)
748 performances
Opened March 19, 2009
Closed January 2, 2011

Joseph and the Amazing Technicolor Dreamcoat
747 performances
Opened January 27, 1982
Closed September 4, 1983

Death of a Salesman
742 performances
Opened February 10, 1949
Closed November 18, 1950

for colored girls who have considered suicide/when the rainbow is enuf
742 performances
Opened September 15, 1976
Closed July 16, 1978

Sons o' Fun
742 performances
Opened December 1, 1941
Closed August 29, 1943

Candide (revival)
740 performances
Opened March 10, 1974
Closed January 4, 1976

Gentlemen Prefer Blondes
740 performances
Opened December 8, 1949
Closed September 15, 1951

The Man Who Came to Dinner
739 performances
Opened October 16, 1939
Closed July 12, 1941

Nine
739 performances
Opened May 9, 1982
Closed February 4, 1984

Call Me Mister
734 performances
Opened April 18, 1946
Closed January 10, 1948

Victor/Victoria
734 performances
Opened October 25, 1995
Closed July 27, 1997

Next to Normal
733 performances
Opened April 15, 2009
Closed January 16, 2011

West Side Story
732 performances
Opened September 26, 1957
Closed June 27, 1959

High Button Shoes
727 performances
Opened October 9, 1947
Closed July 2, 1949

The Addams Family
725 performances
Opened April 8, 2010
Closed December 31, 2011

Finian's Rainbow
725 performances
Opened January 10, 1947
Closed October 2, 1948

Claudia
722 performances
Opened February 12, 1941
Closed January 9, 1943

The Gold Diggers
720 performances
Opened September 30, 1919
Unknown closing date

Jesus Christ Superstar
720 performances
Opened October 12, 1971
Closed June 30, 1973

Carnival!
719 performances
Opened April 13, 1961
Closed January 5, 1963

The Miracle Worker
719 performances
Opened October 19, 1959
Closed July 1, 1961

The Diary of Anne Frank
717 performances
Opened October 5, 1955
Closed June 22, 1955

**A Funny Thing Happened on the
Way to the Forum** (revival)
715 performances
Opened April 18, 1996
Closed January 4, 1998

I Remember Mama
714 performances
Opened October 19, 1944
Closed June 29, 1946

Tea and Sympathy
712 performances
Opened September 30, 1953
Closed June 18, 1955

Junior Miss
710 performances
Opened November 18, 1941
Closed July 24, 1943

Footloose
708 performances
Opened October 22, 1998
Closed July 2, 2000

Last of the Red Hot Lovers
706 performances
Opened December 28, 1969
Closed September 4, 1971

The Secret Garden
706 performances
Opened April 25, 1991
Closed January 3, 1993

Company
705 performances
Opened April 26, 1970
Closed January 1, 1972

Seventh Heaven
704 performances
Opened October 30, 1922
Unknown closing date

Gypsy
702 performances
Opened May 21, 1959
Closed March 25, 1961

That Championship Season
700 performances
Opened September 14, 1972
Closed April 21, 1974

The Music Man (revival)
698 performances
Opened April 27, 2000
Closed December 30, 2001

Da
697 performances
Opened May 1, 1978
Closed January 1, 1980

Cat on a Hot Tin Roof
694 performances
Opened March 24, 1955
Closed November 17, 1956

Li'l Abner
693 performances
Opened November 15, 1956
Closed July 12, 1958

Jonathan Hadary and Tyne Daly in the 1990 revival of Gypsy
(photo by Robert G. Ragsdale)

The Children's Hour
691 performances
Opened November 20, 1934
Unknown closing date

Purlie
688 performances
Opened March 15, 1970
Closed November 6, 1971

Dead End
687 performances
Opened October 28, 1935
Closed June 12, 1937

The Lion and the Mouse
686 performances
Opened November 20, 1905
Unknown closing date

White Cargo
686 performances
Opened November 5, 1923
Unknown closing date

The Little Mermaid
685 performances
Opened January 10, 2008
Closed August 30, 2009

Dear Ruth
683 performances
Opened December 13, 1944
Closed July 27, 1946

East Is West
680 performances
Opened December 25, 1918
Unknown closing date

Come Blow Your Horn
677 performances
Opened February 22, 1961
Closed October 6, 1962

The Most Happy Fella
676 performances
Opened May 3, 1956
Closed December 14, 1957

The Drowsy Chaperone
672 performances
Opened May 1, 2006
Closed December 30, 2007

Mary Beth Hurt, Lizbeth Mackay and Mia Dillon in Crimes of the Heart
(photo by Gerry Goodstein)

Defending the Caveman
671 performances
Opened March 26, 1995
Closed June 22, 1997

The Doughgirls
671 performances
Opened December 30, 1942
Closed July 29, 1944

The Impossible Years
670 performances
Opened October 13, 1965
Closed May 27, 1967

Irene
670 performances
Opened November 18, 1919
Unknown closing date

Boy Meets Girl
669 performances
Opened November 27, 1935
Unknown closing date

The Tap Dance Kid
669 performances
Opened December 21, 1983
Closed August 11, 1985

Beyond the Fringe
667 performances
Opened October 27, 1962
Closed May 30, 1964

Who's Afraid of Virginia Woolf?
664 performances
Opened October 13, 1962
Closed May 16, 1964

Blithe Spirit
657 performances
Opened November 5, 1941
Closed June 5, 1943

A Trip to Chinatown
657 performances
Opened November 9, 1891
Unknown closing date

The Women
657 performances
Opened December 26, 1936
Unknown closing date

Bloomer Girl
654 performances
Opened October 5, 1944
Closed April 27, 1946

The Fifth Season
654 performances
Opened January 23, 1953
Closed October 23, 1954

August: Osage County
648 performances
Opened December 4, 2007
Closed June 28, 2009

Rain
648 performances
Opened September 1, 1924
Unknown closing date

Witness for the Prosecution
645 performances
Opened December 16, 1954
Closed June 30, 1956

Call Me Madam
644 performances
Opened October 12, 1950
Closed May 3, 1952

Janie
642 performances
Opened September 10, 1942
Closed January 16, 1944

The Green Pastures
640 performances
Opened February 26, 1930
Closed August 29, 1931

Auntie Mame
639 performances
Opened October 31, 1956
Closed June 28, 1958

A Man for All Seasons
637 performances
Opened November 22, 1961
Closed June 1, 1963

Jerome Robbins' Broadway
634 performances
Opened February 26, 1989
Closed September 1, 1990

The Fourposter
632 performances
Opened October 24, 1951
Closed May 2, 1953

Dirty Rotten Scoundrels
627 performances
Opened March 3, 2005
Closed September 3, 2006

The Music Master
627 performances
Opened September 26, 1904
Unknown closing date

Two Gentlemen of Verona
(musical)
627 performances
Opened December 1, 1971
Closed May 20, 1973

The Tenth Man
623 performances
Opened November 5, 1959
Closed May 13, 1961

The Heidi Chronicles
621 performances
Opened March 9, 1989
Closed September 1, 1990

Is Zat So?
618 performances
Opened January 5, 1925
Closed July 1926

Anniversary Waltz
615 performances
Opened April 7, 1954
Closed September 24, 1955

The Happy Time (play)
614 performances
Opened January 24, 1950
Closed July 14, 1951

Separate Rooms
613 performances
Opened March 23, 1940
Closed September 6, 1941

Affairs of State
610 performances
Opened September 25, 1950
Closed March 8, 1952

Star and Garter
609 performances
Opened June 24, 1942
Closed December 4, 1943

The Mystery of Edwin Drood
608 performances
Opened December 2, 1985
Closed May 16, 1987

The Student Prince
608 performances
Opened December 2, 1924
Unknown closing date

Sweet Charity
608 performances
Opened January 29, 1966
Closed July 15, 1967

Bye Bye Birdie
607 performances
Opened April 14, 1960
Closed October 7, 1961

Riverdance on Broadway
605 performances
Opened March 16, 2000
Closed August 26, 2001

Irene (revival)
604 performances
Opened March 13, 1973
Closed September 8, 1974

Sunday in the Park With George
604 performances
Opened May 2, 1984
Closed October 13, 1985

Adonis
603 performances
Opened 1884
Unknown closing date

Broadway
603 performances
Opened September 16, 1926
Unknown closing date

Peg o' My Heart
603 performances
Opened December 20, 1912
Unknown closing date

Master Class
601 performances
Opened November 5, 1995
Closed June 29, 1997

Street Scene (play)
601 performances
Opened January 10, 1929
Unknown closing date

Flower Drum Song
600 performances
Opened December 1, 1958
Closed May 7, 1960

Kiki
600 performances
Opened November 29, 1921
Unknown closing date

A Little Night Music
600 performances
Opened February 25, 1973
Closed August 3, 1974

Art
600 performances
Opened March 1, 1998
Closed August 8, 1999

Agnes of God
599 performances
Opened March 30, 1982
Closed September 4, 1983

Don't Drink the Water
598 performances
Opened November 17, 1966
Closed April 20, 1968

Wish You Were Here
598 performances
Opened June 25, 1952
Closed November 28, 1958

Sarafina!
597 performances
Opened January 28, 1988
Closed July 2, 1989

A Society Circus
596 performances
Opened December 13, 1905
Closed November 24, 1906

Legally Blonde
595 performances
Opened April 29, 2007
Closed October 19, 2008

Absurd Person Singular
592 performances
Opened October 8, 1974
Closed March 6, 1976

A Day in Hollywood/
A Night in the Ukraine
588 performances
Opened May 1, 1980
Closed September 27, 1981

The Me Nobody Knows
586 performances
Opened December 18, 1970
Closed November 21, 1971

The Two Mrs. Carrolls
585 performances
Opened August 3, 1943
Closed February 3, 1945

Kismet (musical)
583 performances
Opened December 3, 1953
Closed April 23, 1955

Gypsy (revival)
582 performances
Opened November 16, 1989
Closed July 28, 1991

Brigadoon
581 performances
Opened March 13, 1947
Closed July 31, 1948

Detective Story
581 performances
Opened March 23, 1949
Closed August 12, 1950

No Strings
580 performances
Opened March 14, 1962
Closed August 3, 1963

Brother Rat
577 performances
Opened December 16, 1936
Unknown closing date

Blossom Time
576 performances
Opened September 29, 1921
Unknown closing date

Pump Boys and Dinettes
573 performances
Opened February 4, 1982
Closed June 18, 1983

Show Boat
572 performances
Opened December 27, 1927
Closed May 4, 1929

The Show-Off
571 performances
Opened February 5, 1924
Unknown closing date

Sally
570 performances
Opened December 21, 1920
Closed April 22, 1922

Jelly's Last Jam
569 performances
Opened April 26, 1992
Closed September 5, 1993

Golden Boy (musical)
568 performances
Opened October 20, 1964
Closed March 5, 1966

One Touch of Venus
567 performances
Opened October 7, 1943
Closed February 10, 1945

The Real Thing
566 performances
Opened January 5, 1984
Closed May 12, 1985

Happy Birthday
564 performances
Opened October 31, 1946
Closed March 13, 1948

Look Homeward, Angel
564 performances
Opened November 28, 1957
Closed April 4, 1959

Morning's at Seven (revival)
564 performances
Opened April 10, 1980
Closed August 16, 1981

The Glass Menagerie
561 performances
Opened March 31, 1945
Closed August 3, 1946

I Do! I Do!
560 performances
Opened December 5, 1966
Closed June 15, 1968

Wonderful Town
559 performances
Opened February 25, 1953
Closed July 3, 1954

The Last Night of Ballyhoo
557 performances
Opened February 27, 1997
Closed June 28, 1998

Mandy Patinkin and the Company of Sunday in the Park With George
(photo by Martha Swope)

Rose Marie
557 performances
Opened September 2, 1924
Unknown closing date

Strictly Dishonorable
557 performances
Opened September 18, 1929
Unknown closing date

Sweeney Todd, the Demon Barber of Fleet Street
557 performances
Opened March 1, 1979
Closed June 29, 1980

The Great White Hope
556 performances
Opened October 3, 1968
Closed January 31, 1970

A Majority of One
556 performances
Opened February 16, 1959
Closed June 25, 1960

The Sisters Rosensweig
556 performances
Opened March 18, 1993
Closed July 16, 1994

Sunrise at Campobello
556 performances
Opened January 30, 1958
Closed May 30, 1959

Toys in the Attic
556 performances
Opened February 25, 1960
Closed April 8, 1961

Jamaica
555 performances
Opened October 31, 1957
Closed April 11, 1959

Stop the World—I Want to Get Off
555 performances
Opened October 3, 1962
Closed February 1, 1964

Grease (revival)
554 performances
Opened August 19, 2007
Closed January 4, 2009

Florodora
553 performances
Opened November 10, 1900
Closed January 25, 1902

Noises Off
553 performances
Opened December 11, 1983
Closed April 6, 1985

Ziegfeld Follies (1943)
553 performances
Opened April 1, 1943
Closed July 22, 1944

Dial "M" for Murder
552 performances
Opened October 29, 1952
Closed February 27, 1954

Good News
551 performances
Opened September 6, 1927
Unknown closing date

Peter Pan (revival)
551 performances
Opened September 6, 1979
Closed January 4, 1981

How to Succeed in Business Without Really Trying (revival)
548 performances
Opened March 23, 1995
July 14, 1996

Let's Face It
547 performances
Opened October 29, 1941
Closed March 20, 1943

Milk and Honey
543 performances
Opened October 10, 1961
Closed January 26, 1963

Within the Law
541 performances
Opened September 11, 1912
Unknown closing date

Pal Joey (revival)
540 performances
Opened January 3, 1952
Closed April 18, 1953

The Sound of Music (revival)
540 performances
Opened March 12, 1998
Closed June 20, 1999

What Makes Sammy Run?
540 performances
Opened February 27, 1964
Closed June 12, 1965

The Sunshine Boys
538 performances
Opened December 20, 1972
Closed April 21, 1974

What a Life
538 performances
Opened April 13, 1938
Closed July 8, 1939

Crimes of the Heart
535 performances
Opened November 4, 1981
Closed February 13, 1983

Damn Yankees (revival)
533 performances
Opened March 3, 1994
Closed August 6, 1995

The Unsinkable Molly Brown
532 performances
Opened November 3, 1960
Closed February 10, 1962

The Red Mill (revival)
531 performances
Opened October 16, 1945
Closed January 18, 1947

Rumors
531 performances
Opened November 17, 1988
Closed February 24, 1990

A Raisin in the Sun
530 performances
Opened March 11, 1959
Closed June 25, 1960

Godspell
527 performances
Opened June 22, 1976
Closed September 4, 1977

Fences
526 performances
Opened March 26, 1987
Closed June 26, 1988

The Solid Gold Cadillac
526 performances
Opened November 5, 1953
Closed February 12, 1955

Doubt
525 performances
Opened March 9, 2005
Closed July 2, 2006

Biloxi Blues
524 performances
Opened March 28, 1985
Closed June 28, 1986

Irma La Douce
524 performances
Opened September 29, 1960
Closed December 31, 1961

The Boomerang
522 performances
Opened August 10, 1915
Unknown closing date

Follies
521 performances
Opened April 4, 1971
Closed July 1, 1972

Rosalinda
521 performances
Opened October 28, 1942
Closed January 22, 1944

The Best Man
520 performances
Opened March 31, 1960
Closed July 8, 1961

Chauve-Souris
520 performances
Opened February 4, 1922
Unknown closing date

Hair (revival)
519 performances
Opened March 31, 2009
Closed June 27, 2010

Blackbirds of 1928
518 performances
Opened May 9, 1928
Unknown closing date

The Gin Game
517 performances
Opened October 6, 1977
Closed December 31, 1978

Side Man
517 performances
Opened June 25, 1988
Closed October 31, 1999

Sunny
517 performances
Opened September 22, 1925
Closed December 11, 1926

Victoria Regina
517 performances
Opened December 26, 1935
Unknown closing date

Xanadu
512 performances
Opened July 10, 2007
Closed September 28, 2008

Curtains
511 performances
Opened March 22, 2007
Closed June 29, 2008

Fifth of July
511 performances
Opened November 5, 1980
Closed January 24, 1982

Half a Sixpence
511 performances
Opened April 25, 1965
Closed July 16, 1966

The Vagabond King
511 performances
Opened September 21, 1925
Closed December 4, 1926

The New Moon
509 performances
Opened September 19, 1928
Closed December 14, 1929

The World of Suzie Wong
508 performances
Opened October 14, 1958
Closed January 2, 1960

The Rothschilds
507 performances
Opened October 19, 1970
Closed January 1, 1972

On Your Toes (revival)
505 performances
Opened March 6, 1983
Closed May 20, 1984

Sugar
505 performances
Opened April 9, 1972
Closed June 23, 1973

The Light in the Piazza
504 performances
Opened March 17, 2005
Closed July 2, 2006

Shuffle Along
504 performances
Opened May 23, 1921
Closed July 15, 1922

Up in Central Park
504 performances
Opened January 27, 1945
Closed January 13, 1946

Carmen Jones
503 performances
Opened December 2, 1943
Closed February 10, 1945

Saturday Night Fever
502 performances
Closed Opened October 21, 1999
December 30, 2000

The Member of the Wedding
501 performances
Opened January 5, 1950
Closed March 17, 1951

Panama Hattie
501 performances
Opened October 30, 1940
Closed January 13, 1942

Personal Appearance
501 performances
Opened October 17, 1934
Unknown closing date

Bird in Hand
500 performances
Opened April 4, 1929
Unknown closing date

Room Service
500 performances
Opened May 19, 1937
Unknown closing date

Sailor, Beware!
500 performances
Opened September 28, 1933
Unknown closing date

Tomorrow the World
500 performances
Opened April 14, 1943
Closed June 17, 1944

Off-Broadway

The Fantasticks
17,162 performances
Opened May 3, 1960
Closed January 13, 2002

Blue Man Group*
11,269 performances
Opened November 17, 1991

Perfect Crime*
10,281 performances
Opened April 18, 1987

Stomp*
7,681 performances
Opened February 27, 1994

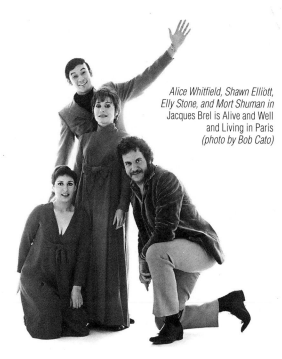

*Alice Whitfield, Shawn Elliott,
Elly Stone, and Mort Shuman in*
Jacques Brel is Alive and Well
and Living in Paris
(photo by Bob Cato)

Tony 'n' Tina's Wedding
5,901 performances
Opened February 6, 1988
Closed June 2, 2011

**I Love You, You're Perfect,
Now Change**
5,003 performances
Opened August 1, 1996
Closed July 29, 2008

Nunsense
3,672 performances
Opened December 12, 1985
Closed October 16, 1994

Naked Boys Singing
3,069 performances
Opened July 22, 1999
Closed January 28, 2012

The Threepenny Opera
2,611 performances
Opened September 20, 1955
Closed December 17, 1961

De La Guarda
2,475 performances
Opened June 16, 1998
Closed September 12, 2004

Forbidden Broadway (original)
2,332 performances
Opened January 15, 1982
Closed August 30, 1987

The Fantasticks* (revival)
2,305 performances
Opened August 23, 2006

Little Shop of Horrors
2,209 performances
Opened July 27, 1982
Closed November 1, 1987

Godspell
2,124 performances
Opened May 17, 1971
Closed June 13, 1976

The Gazillion Bubble Show*
2,101 performances
Opened February 15, 2007

Altar Boyz
2,032 performances
Opened March 1, 2005
Closed January 10, 2010

Vampire Lesbians of Sodom
2,024 performances
Opened June 19, 1985
Closed May 27, 1990

Teller and Penn Jillette in Penn and Teller *(photo by Gerry Goodstein)*

Jacques Brel is Alive and Well and Living in Paris
1,847 performances
Opened January 22, 1968
Closed July 2, 1972

Forever Plaid
1,811 performances
Opened May 20, 1990
Closed June 12, 1994

Vanities
1,785 performances
Opened March 22, 1976
Closed August 3, 1980

The Donkey Show
1,717 performances
Opened August 18, 1999
Closed July 16, 2005

Menopause the Musical
1,712 performances
Opened April 4, 2002
Closed May 14, 2006

Fuerza Bruta: Look Up*
1,604 performances
Opened October 24, 2007

You're A Good Man, Charlie Brown
1,597 performances
Opened March 7, 1967
Closed February 14, 1971

The Blacks
1,408 performances
Opened May 4, 1961
Closed September 27, 1964

The Vagina Monologues
1,381 performances
Opened October 3, 1999
Closed January 26, 2003

One Mo' Time
1,372 performances
Opened October 22, 1979
Closed 1982–83 season

Grandma Sylvia's Funeral
1,360 performances
Opened October 9, 1994
Closed June 20, 1998

Let My People Come
1,327 performances
Opened January 8, 1974
Closed July 5, 1976

Late Nite Catechism
1,268 performances
Opened October 4, 1995
Closed May 18, 2003

Driving Miss Daisy
1,195 performances
Opened April 15, 1987
Closed June 3, 1990

The Hot L Baltimore
1,166 performances
Opened September 8, 1973
Closed January 4, 1976

I'm Getting My Act Together and Taking It on the Road
1,165 performances
Opened May 16, 1978
Closed March 15, 1981

Little Mary Sunshine
1,143 performances
Opened November 18, 1959
Closed September 2, 1962

Steel Magnolias
1,126 performances
Opened November 17, 1987
Closed February 25, 1990

El Grande de Coca-Cola
1,114 performances
Opened February 13, 1973
Closed April 13, 1975

The Proposition
1,109 performances
Opened March 24, 1971
Closed April 14, 1974

Our Sinatra
1,096 performances
Opened December 8, 1999
Closed July 28, 2002

Avenue Q* (transfer from Broadway)
1,089 performances
Closed Opened October 9, 2009

Beau Jest
1,069 performances
Opened October 10, 1991
Closed May 1, 1994

Jewtopia
1,052 performances
Opened October 21, 2004
Closed April 29, 2007

Tamara
1,036 performances
Opened November 9, 1989
Closed July 15, 1990

One Flew Over the Cuckoo's Nest (revival)
1,025 performances
Opened March 23, 1971
Closed September 16, 1973

Love, Loss, and What I Wore
1,013 performances
Opened October 1, 2009
Closed March 25, 2012

Slava's Snowshow
1,004 performances
Opened September 8, 2004
Closed January 14, 2007

The Boys in the Band
1,000 performances
Opened April 14, 1968
Closed September 29, 1985

Fool For Love
1,000 performances
Opened November 27, 1983
Closed September 29, 1985

Forbidden Broadway: 20th Anniversary Celebration
994 performances
Opened March 20, 2002
Closed July 4, 2004

Other People's Money
990 performances
Opened February 7, 1989
Closed July 4, 1991

Cloud 9
971 performances
Opened May 18, 1981
Closed September 4, 1983

Secrets Every Smart Traveler Should Know
953 performances
Opened October 30, 1997
Closed February 21, 2000

Sister Mary Ignatius Explains It All for You & The Actor's Nightmare
947 performances
Opened October 21, 1981
Closed January 29, 1984

Your Own Thing
933 performances
Opened January 13, 1968
Closed April 5, 1970

Curley McDimple
931 performances
Opened November 22, 1967
Closed January 25, 1970

Leave It to Jane (revival)
928 performances
Opened May 29, 1959
Closed 1961–62 season

The Mad Show
871 performances
Opened January 9, 1966
Closed September 10, 1967

Hedwig and the Angry Inch
857 performances
Opened February 14, 1998
Closed April 9, 2000

Forbidden Broadway Strikes Back
850 performances
Opened October 17, 1996
Closed September 20, 1998

When Pigs Fly
840 performances
Opened August 14, 1996
Closed August 15, 1998

Scrambled Feet
831 performances
Opened June 11, 1979
Closed June 7, 1981

The Effect of Gamma Rays on Man-in-the-Moon Marigolds
819 performances
Opened April 7, 1970
Closed June 1, 1973

Forbidden Broadway SVU
816 performances
Opened December 16, 2004
Closed April 15, 2007

Over the River and Through the Woods
800 performances
Opened October 5, 1998
Closed September 3, 2000

A View from the Bridge (revival)
780 performances
Opened January 28, 1965
Closed December 11, 1966

The Boy Friend (revival)
763 performances
Opened January 25, 1958
Closed 1961–62 season

True West
762 performances
Opened December 23, 1980
Closed January 11, 1981

Forbidden Broadway Cleans Up Its Act!
754 performances
Opened November 17, 1998
Closed August 30, 2000

Isn't It Romantic
733 performances
Opened December 15, 1983
Closed September 1, 1985

Dime a Dozen
728 performances
Opened June 13, 1962
Closed 1963–64 season

The Pocket Watch
725 performances
Opened November 14, 1966
Closed June 18, 1967

The Connection
722 performances
Opened June 9, 1959
Closed June 4, 1961

Freud's Last Session*
715 performances
Opened July 9, 2010

The Passion of Dracula
714 performances
Opened September 28, 1977
Closed July 14, 1979

Love, Janis
713 performances
Opened April 22, 2001
Closed January 5, 2003

Adaptation & Next
707 performances
Opened February 10, 1969
Closed October 18, 1970

Oh! Calcutta!
704 performances
Opened June 17, 1969
February 12, 1971

Scuba Duba
692 performances
Opened November 11, 1967
Closed June 8, 1969

The Foreigner
686 performances
Opened November 2, 1984
Closed June 8, 1986

The Knack
685 performances
Opened January 14, 1964
Closed January 9, 1966

My Mother's Italian, My Father's Jewish & I'm in Therapy
684 performances
Opened December 8, 2006
Closed August 24, 2008

Fully Committed
675 performances
Opened December 14, 1999
Closed May 27, 2001

The Club
674 performances
Opened October 14, 1976
Closed May 21, 1978

The Balcony
672 performances
Opened March 3, 1960
Closed December 21, 1961

Adam Arian, Anne Bobby, Ron Bohmer, and Jodie Langel in I Love You, You're Perfect, Now Change *(photo by Carol Rosegg)*

Penn & Teller
666 performances
Opened July 30, 1985
Closed January 19, 1992

Newsical the Musical*
655 performances
Opened January 9, 2011

Dinner With Friends
654 performances
Opened November 4, 1999
Closed May 27, 2000

Our Town (revival)
644 performances
Opened February 26, 2009
Closed September 12, 2010

America Hurrah
634 performances
Opened November 7, 1966
Closed May 5, 1968

Cookin'
632 performances
Opened July 7, 2004
Closed August 7, 2005

Oil City Symphony
626 performances
Opened November 5, 1987
Closed May 7, 1989

The Countess
618 performances
Opened September 28, 1999
Closed December 30, 2000

The Exonerated
608 performances
Opened October 10, 2002
Closed March 7, 2004

The Dining Room
607 performances
Opened February 11, 1982
Closed July 17, 1983

Hogan's Goat
607 performances
Opened March 6, 1965
Closed April 23, 1967

Drumstruck
607 performances
Opened June 16, 2005
Closed November 16, 2006

Beehive
600 performances
Opened March 30, 1986
Closed August 23, 1987

Criss Angel Mindfreak
600 performances
Opened November 20, 2001
Closed January 5, 2003

The Trojan Women
600 performances
Opened December 23, 1963
Closed May 30, 1965

The Quantum Eye*
597 performances
Opened February 9, 2007

The Syringa Tree
586 performances
Opened September 14, 2000
Closed June 2, 2002

Janet Dickinson, Michael West, Jared Bradshaw, and Valerie Fagan in Forbidden Broadway: SVU (photo by Carol Rosegg)

The Musical of Musicals (The Musical!)
583 performances
Opened December 16, 2003
Closed November 13, 2005

Krapp's Last Tape & The Zoo Story
582 performances
Opened August 29, 1960
Closed May 21, 1961

Three Tall Women
582 performances
Opened April 13, 1994
Closed August 26, 1995

The Dumbwaiter & The Collection
578 performances
Opened January 21, 1962
Closed April 12, 1964

Forbidden Broadway 1990
576 performances
Opened January 23, 1990
Closed June 9, 1991

Dames at Sea
575 performances
Opened April 22, 1969
Closed May 10, 1970

The Crucible (revival)
571 performances
Opened 1956-57 Season
Closed 1957-58 Season

The Iceman Cometh (revival)
565 performances
Opened May 8, 1956
Closed February 23, 1958

Forbidden Broadway 2001: A Spoof Odyssey
552 performances
Opened December 6, 2000
Closed February 6, 2002

The Hostage (revival)
545 performances
Opened October 16, 1972
Closed October 8, 1973

The Marvelous Wonderettes
545 performances
Opened September 14, 2008
Closed January 3, 2010

Wit
545 performances
Opened October 6, 1998
Closed April 9, 2000

What's a Nice Country Like You Doing in a State Like This?
543 performances
Opened July 31, 1985
Closed February 9, 1987

Forbidden Broadway 1988
534 performances
Opened September 15, 1988
Closed December 24, 1989

Gross Indecency: The Three Trials of Oscar Wilde
534 performances
Opened September 5, 1997
Closed September 13, 1998

Frankie and Johnny in the Claire de Lune
533 performances
Opened December 4, 1987
Closed March 12, 1989

Six Characters in Search of an Author (revival)
529 performances
Opened March 8, 1963
Closed June 28, 1964

All in the Timing
526 performances
Opened November 24, 1993
Closed February 13, 1994

Oleanna
513 performances
Opened October 3, 1992
Closed January 16, 1994

Making Porn
511 performances
Opened June 12, 1996
Closed September 14, 1997

The Dirtiest Show in Town
509 performances
Opened June 26, 1970
Closed September 17, 1971

Happy Ending & Day of Absence
504 performances
Opened June 13, 1965
Closed January 29, 1967

Greater Tuna
501 performances
Opened October 21, 1982
Closed December 31, 1983

A Shayna Maidel
501 performances
Opened October 29, 1987
Closed January 8, 1989

The Boys from Syracuse (revival)
500 performances
Opened April 15, 1963
Closed June 28, 1964

* Production is still running as of May 31, 2012; count includes performances up to and including that date. Performance counts do not include previews.

Blue Man Group *(photo by Darbe Rotach)*

OBITUARIES
June 1, 2011–May 31, 2012

Broadway Dims Its Lights*

Broadway dimmed the marquee lights upon the deaths of the following theatre luminaries, and did so on the following dates:

THEODORE MANN, theatre producer and director: February 24, 2012

HOWARD KISSEL, longtime theatre critic: February 28, 2012

Disney theatres dimmed their lights in honor of **Robert Sherman,** American songwriter whose songs were incorporated into both the film and musical stage productions of *Mary Poppins.*

*NOTE: Dates following productions indicate the year in which that theatrical production was revived. If no date follows the name of a production, then it may be assumed that it was the original run.

TOM ALDREDGE (Thomas Ernest Aldredge), 83, Dayton, Ohio-born actor, died Jul. 22, 2011, in Tampa, FL, of lymphoma. A Tony Award nominee for his roles in *Sticks and Bones; Where's Charley; On Golden Pond; The Little Foxes; Passion;* and *Twentieth Century,* he won a Drama Desk Award for *Sticks and Bones* and gained another Drama Desk nomination for *Incommunicado.* His other Broadway credits include *The Nervous Set; UTBU; Slapstick Tragedy; Everything in the Garden; Indians; The Engagement Baby; How the Other Half Loves; The Iceman Cometh; The Leaf People; Rex; Vieux Carré; Saint Joan; Stages; Strange Interlude; Into the Woods; Two Shakespearean Actors; Inherit the Wind; The Three Sisters; 1776; The Adventures of Tom Sawyer; The Crucible; Twelve Angry Men;* and the 1997 *Into the Woods* benefit. Off-Broadway credits include many with Joseph Papp's Public Theater and Shakespeare in the Park, including *Love's Labor's Lost; Troilus and Cressida; Ergo; Romeo and Juliet; Twelfth Night; The Happiness Cage; Sticks and Bones; Hamlet; The Orphan; King Lear;* and *Richard II.* Other Off-Broadway credits include *The Butter and Egg Man; The Boys in the Band; Black Angel; Neon Palms; The Last Yankee; La Terrasse; The Time of the Cuckoo;* and *Mimi le Duck.* He won a Daytime Emmy Award for his performance as Shakespeare in *Henry Winkler Meets William Shakespeare* (an episode of *The CBS Festival of Lively Arts for Young People),* and his other television credits include *The Sopranos; Ryan's Hope;* and *Damages.* His numerous film roles include *The Mouse on the Moon; Who Killed Teddy Bear; The Boston Strangler; The Rain People; *batteries not included; See You in the Morning; Other People's Money; The Adventures of Huck Finn; Lawn Dogs; Rounders; Intolerable Cruelty; What About Bob?;* and *Cold Mountain.* In the early 1960s he performed with Gene Hackman and Buck Henry in a Greenwich Village improvisational troupe. A longtime resident of Stamford, CT, his wife of fifty-seven years, Tony Award-winning designer Theoni V. Aldredge, predeceased him by six months.

JEFFREY ASH, 65, theatrical advertising executive/producer, died Aug. 8, 2011, in Manhattan, NY, having suffered for a long time from inclusion body myositis. His Broadway credits as a theatrical advertising executive include *Paul Sills' Story Theatre; And Miss Reardon Drinks a Little; Solitaire/Double Solitaire; 6 Rms Riv Vu; Pippin; A Little Night Music; Ulysses in Nighttown;* and *We Interrupt This Program.* Under the imprint of his own theatrical agency Ash/LeDonne, his numerous Broadway credits include *Pacific Overtures; A Memory of Two Mondays/27 Wagons Full of Cotton* (1976); *They Knew What They Wanted* (1976); *Secret Service; Boy Meets Girl; Rex; Siamsa; Comedians; Music Is; American Buffalo; Anna Christie* (1977); *I Love My Wife; Side by Side by Sondheim; Annie; An Almost Perfect Person; Deathtrap; Hello, Dolly!* (1978); *13 Rue de l'Amour; Stages; Dancin'; Da; Ain't Misbehavin'; Working; The American Dance Machine; Once in a Lifetime* (1978); *The Best Little Whorehouse in Texas; The Inspector General; St. Mark's Gospel; The Playboy of the Western World; The Kingfisher; Man and Superman* (1978); *A Broadway Musical; Whoopee!* (1979); *On Golden Pond; Spokesong; Zoot Suit; Manny; Break a Leg; The Goodbye People; The Utter Glory of Morrissey Hall; I Remember Mama* (1979); *Bruce Forsyth on Broadway!; The Madwoman of Central Park West; Evita; Devour the Show; Strider; Bent; Oklahoma!; Teibele and Her Demon; Comin' Uptown; Watch on the Rhine* (1980); *The Lady from Debuque; Canterbury Tales* (1980); *West Side Story* (1980);

Charlotte; Censored Scenes from King Kong; Heartaches of a Pussycat; Children of a Lesser God; Happy New Year; Nuts; Barnum; A Day in the Hollywood/A Night in the Ukraine; The Roast; The Suicide; Brigadoon (1980); *Banjo Dancing; A Life; Tricks of the Trade; Lunch Hour; Perfectly Frank; Onward Victoria; Amadeus; Mixed Couples; Frankenstein; Emlyn Williams as Charles Dickens* (1981); *Heartland; Sophisticated Ladies; Bring Back Birdie; Lolita; Woman of the Year; The Father; The Moony Shapiro Songbook; The Little Foxes* (1981); *St. Mark's Gospel; Wally's Café; Ned & Jack; Oh, Brother; Merrily We Roll Along; The First; The Little Prince and the Aviator; Joseph and the Amazing Technicolor Dreamcoat; Macbeth* (1982); *Eminent Domain; Is there life after high school?; Nine; Do Black Patent Leather Shoes Really Reflect Up?; The Best Little Whorehouse in Texas* (1982); *Cleavage; Play Me a Country Song; Seven Brides for Seven Brothers; The Queen and the Rebels; Foxfire; 84 Charing Cross Road; Steaming; Monday After the Miracle; A Little Family Business; Almost an Eagle; Angels Fall; The Misanthrope* (1983); *A View From the Bridge* (1983); *On Your Toes* (1983); *The Caine Mutiny Court-Martial* (1983); *Private Lives* (1983); *The Flying Karamazov Brothers; La Cage aux Folles; The Corn Is Green* (1983); *Edmund Kean; American Buffalo* (1983); *Brothers; La Tragedie de Carmen; Marilyn; Doonesbury; Noises Off; Peg; Ian McKellen: Acting Shakespeare* (1984); *Open Admissions; Glengarry Glen Ross; The Golden Age; Play Memory; The Babe; Design for Living* (1984); *Much Ado About Nothing* (1984); *Cyrano de Bergerac* (1984); *Doug Henning & His World of Magic; Home Front; Requiem for a Heavyweight; Leader of the Pack; Grind; Singin' in the Rain; Tango Argentino; La Bête; Falsettos; Love! Valour! Compassion!; Buttons On Broadway; An Ideal Husband* (1996); *Chicago* (1996); *Present Laughter* (1996); *David Copperfield: Dreams and Nightmares; The Last Night of Ballyhoo; The Young Man from Atlanta; A Doll's House* (1997); *The Chairs* (1998); *Colin Quinn—An Irish Wake; Aznavour; Electra* (1998); *Marlene;* and *It Aint' Nothin' But the Blues.* As a producer, his Broadway credits include *Fool Moon* (1993 [Drama Desk Award, Unique Theatrical Experience]; 1995, and 1998); and *The Crucible* (Tony Award nomination and Drama Desk nomination). His Off-Broadway credits as a producer include *Three Tall Women* (Drama Desk Award nomination); *Other People's Money; Old Wicked Songs; The Rothschilds; Mrs. Klein; Mindgames;* and *Wrong Turn at Lungfish.* He was responsible for the first live action television spot for *Pippin.* His daughters, Nicole Ash, Danielle Ash, and Heather Ash; and son-in-law Rene Hidalgo, all of New York City; brother and sister-in-law, Steve and Mariah Ash; and niece, Emily Ash, all of Scituate, MA; and longtime companion, Melly Garcia, of New York City, survive him.

DORIS BELACK, 85, New York City, NY-born actress died Oct. 4, 2011, in Manhattan, NY, of natural causes. Her Broadway credits include *Semi-Detached; The Heroine; Nathan Weinstein, Mystic, Connecticut; The Ninety Day Mistress; Last of the Red Hot Lovers; Bad Habits; The Trip Back Down; Cheaters; Social Security;* and *The Cemetery Club.* Her Off-Broadway credits include *P.S. 193; Letters Home; Emerald City; Surviving Grace;* and *The Right Kind of People.* Perhaps best known for her role as a judge on the long-running television program *Law & Order,* her other television credits include *The Patty Duke Show; The Defenders; Barney Miller; Family Ties;* and *The Cosby Show.* Her movie credits include *The Black Marble; Hanky Panky; Tootsie; Fast Forward; *batteries not included; The Luckiest Man in the World; She-Devil; What about Bob?; Naked Gun 33 1/3: The Final Insult; Krippendorf's Tribe;* and *Prime.* Her husband of sixty-five years, theater producer Philip Rose, predeceased her by four months.

PRICE BERKLEY (Price Berkowitz), 92, Philadelphia, PA-born founder of *Theatrical Index,* died Aug. 21, 2011, in Manhattan, NY. Publishing the first edition of *Theatrical Index* on Nov. 9, 1964, he began with a mere sixteen subscribers, but the publication became an indispensable resource for the theatre industry. Prior to establishing *Theatrical* Index, he worked for Celebrity Service International, providing contact information for stars. A longtime member of the Tony Awards nominating committee, he was awarded the Theatre Hall of Fame Founders Award in 2003. He was a veteran of W.W. II. His niece, Linda Berman; and nephew, Michael Golden, survive him.

ROBERTS BLOSSOM, 87, New Haven, CT-born actor, died Jul. 8, 2011, in Santa Monica, CA, of natural causes. His Broadway credits include *The Infernal Machine; A Cook for Mr. General; The Ballad of the Sad Café; The Physicists;*

Operation Sidewinder; and *Status Quo Vadis.* His Off-Broadway credits include *Excerpts from Shaw/Village Wooing; The Infernal Machine; Victims of Duty; Bartleby; The American Dream/The Death of Bessie Smith; Whisper into My Good Ear/Mrs. Dally Has a Lover; Do Not Pass Go* (Obie Award); *Sunset; Siamese Connections;* and *A Midsummer Night's Dream.* His television credits include *Naked City; Another World; Moonlighting; Northern Exposure;* and *In the Heat of the Night.* His movie credits include *The Hospital; Slaughterhouse-Five; Deranged; The Great Gatsby; Handle with Care* (Citizens Band); *Close Encounters of the Third Kind; Escape from Alcatraz; Resurrection; Christine; Reuben Reuben; The Last Temptation of Christ; Home Alone; Doc Hollywood;* and *The Quick and the Dead.* His daughter, Deborah, and a son, Michael, survive him.

Roberts Blossom

PHIL BRUNS, 80, Pipestone, MN-born actor, died Feb. 8, 2012, in Los Angeles, CA, of natural causes. His Broadway credits include *The Deputy; King Henry V; Blood Red Roses;* and *Lysistrata.* His Off-Broadway credits include *The Butter and Egg Man; The Moths;* and *A Dream Out of Time.* His film credits include *The Great Waldo Pepper; Harry and Tonto; Flashdance; The Stunt Man; My Favorite Year;* and *Return of the Living Dead II.* His television credits include *Columbo; Night Court; Just Shoot Me!; Mary Hartman, Mary Hartman;* and *M*A*S*H*.* He also published *The Character Actor's Do's, Don'ts, And Anecdotes,* with foreword by Peter O'Toole. He also established the largest private school library in the Bahamas. His wife, actress Laurie Franks, survives him.

GILBERT CATES (Gilbert Lewis Katz), 77, New York, NY-born director/producer, died Oct. 31, 2011, after collapsing in a parking lot on the campus of UCLA. He had recently undergone heart surgery. His theatrical directing credits include *I Never Sang for My Father; Summer Wishes Winter Dreams; The Promise;* and *The Last Married Couple in America.* On television, in addition to directing and producing several movies, he served as producer of fourteen Academy Award ceremonies over an eighteen-year period (1990-2008), and for many years ran the Geffen Playhouse. His wife; three sons; two stepdaughters; and five grandchildren survive him.

DIANE CILENTO, 78, Brisbane, Australia-born actress, died Oct. 6, 2011, in Cairns, Queensland, Australia. Her Broadway credits include *Tiger at the Gates* for which she received a 1956 Theatre World Award; *Heartbreak House;* and *The Good Soup.* She earned an Academy Award nomination playing the slatternly Molly in the 1963 Academy Award-winner *Tom Jones,* and her other film credits include *Stop Me before I Kill!; The Naked Edge; I Thank a Fool; The Third Secret; Rattle of a Simple Man; The Agony and the Ecstasy; Hombre; Negatives; Z.P.G.; Hitler: The Last Ten Days;* and *The Wicker Man* (1973; later marrying its writer, Anthony Shaffer). Her daughter from her first marriage; and her son, actor Jason Connery, from her second marriage to actor Sean Connery), survive her.

SHELAGH DELANEY, 71, Salford, England-born writer, best known for her breakthrough play, *A Taste of Honey,* produced in the West End when she was

Diane Cilento

only nineteen years old, died Nov. 20, 2011, in Suffolk, England, of heart failure and breast cancer. In addition to adapting *A Taste of Honey* to the screen in 1961, her other film credits include *Charlie Bubbles* and *Dance with a Stranger.* She also wrote a collection of stories and nonfiction pieces, *Sweetly Sings the Donkey.* Her daughter and three grandchildren survive her.

STEPHEN DOUGLASS (Stephen Fitch), 90, Mt. Vernon, OH-born actor, died Dec. 27, 2011, of complications of leukemia. His Broadway credits include *Carousel; Make a Wish; The Golden Apple; The Pajama Game; Damn Yankees* (Tony nomination); *Rumple; 110 in the Shade;* and *I Do! I Do!.* He was married to singer Christine Yates.

WILLIAM DUELL (George William Duell), 88, Corinth, NY-born actor, died Dec. 22, 2011, in Manhattan, NY, of respiratory failure. His Broadway credits include *Threepenny Opera* (and 1955 and 1976 revivals); *A Cook for Mr. General; The Ballad of the Sad Café; Illya Darling; 1776; Kings; Stages; The Inspector General; The Marriage of Figaro;* and *A Funny Thing Happened on the Way to the Forum* (and 1996 revival); *The Man Who Came to Dinner* (2000 revival). His Off-Broadway credits include *Threepenny Opera; A Portrait of the Artist as a Young Man/The Barroom Monks; The Memorandum; Romeo and Juliet; Romance Language; Hamlet; Henry IV Part I; Henry IV Part II; On the Bum; The Underparents;* and *Comedians.* His film credits include *The Hustler.* He was a veteran of W.W. II, and his wife, Mary Barto survives him.

PETER FALK (Peter Michael Falk), 83, New York, NY-born actor, died Jun. 23, 2011, at his home in Beverly Hills, CA, after having suffering from Alzheimer's disease. His Broadway credits include *Saint Joan; Diary of a Scoundrel; The Passion of Josef D;* and *The Prisoner of Second Avenue.* His Off-Broadway credits include *Don Juan; The Iceman Cometh; Purple Dust; The Lady's Not For Burning;* and *Bonds of Interest.* He received Academy Award nominations for his performances in *Murder, Inc.* and *Pocketful of Miracles.* His other films include *Wind Across the Everglades* (debut, 1958); *Pretty Boy Floyd; Pressure Point; The Balcony; It's a Mad, Mad, Mad, Mad, World; Robin and the 7 Hoods; The Great Race; Penelope; Luv; Anzio; Machine Gun McCain; Castle Keep; Husbands; A Woman Under the Influence; Murder by Death; Mikey and Nicky; The Cheap Detective; The Brink's Job; The In-Laws* (1979); *The Great Muppet Caper; All the Marbles; Wings of Desire; Happy New Year; The Princess Bride; Cookie, In the*

Spirit; Tune in Tomorrow...; Roommates; Lake Boat; Made; Checking Out; and *Next.* On television he was best known for his starring role on the series *Columbo* for which he won four Emmys. He was a veteran of the Merchant Marine and early in his career he studied with Eva Le Gallienne at the White Barn Theater in Westport, CT. His second wife, the former Shera Danese; and two daughters, Jackie and Catherine, survive him.

Peter Falk

JAMES FARENTINO, 73, Brooklyn, NY-born actor, died Jan. 24, 2012, in Los Angeles, CA, of heart failure following a broken hip. A 1973 Theatre World Award winner for his role in *A Streetcar Named Desire* (1973), his other Broadway credits include *The Night of the Iguana* and *Death of a Salesman* (1975). His numerous television credits include *Dynasty; The Bold Ones: The Lawyers; Blue Thunder; Police Story; Jesus of Nazareth* (Emmy nomination); *The Pad and How to Use It* (Golden Globe Award); and *ER.* His film roles include *The Final Countdown.* His four previous marriages, to wives Debrah and actresses Elizabeth Ashley and Michele Lee, all ended in divorce. His wife Stella survives him, as does a son, David, from his marriage to Michele Lee.

MARY FICKETT, 83, Buffalo, NY-born actress, died Sept. 8, 2011, in Callao, VA, of complications from Alzheimer's disease. Best known as the character of Ruth Martin on the television soap opera *All My Children* for nearly thirty years and for which she received a Daytime Emmy Award, her Broadway credits include *I Know My Love; Tea and* Sympathy, for which she won a Theatre World Award; *Sunset at Campobello* (Tony nomination); and *Love and Kisses.* Early in her career she studied acting at the Neighborhood Playhouse School of Theater under Sanford Meisner, and her numerous other television credits include *Armstrong Circle Theater; Kraft Theater; The Untouchables; Have Gun—Will Travel; Naked City;* and *The Edge of Night.* A news program in which she appeared with Harry Reasoner ran from 1961-1963. Her films include *Man on Fire.* Her first two marriages, to James Congdon and Jay Leonard Scheer, ended in divorce. Her third husband

died in 2008. Her daughter, Bronwyn Cogdon, and son, Kenyon Congdon, survive her, as do her eight grandchildren and two great-grandchildren.

LEO FRIEDMAN, 92, Broadway photographer, died Dec. 2, 2011, in Las Vegas, NV, of complications from pneumonia. His over 800 Broadway credits include *Bye Bye Birdie; Advise and Consent; A Cook for Mr. General; The Prime of Miss Jean Brodie; Sheep on the Runway; Irene; Noël Coward in Two Keys; Over Here!; Seascape; My Fair Lady; Barefoot in the Park; Fiddler on the Roof; Cabaret; Bye Bye Birdie; The Entertainer; I Can Get It For You Wholesale; The Music Man; Purlie Victorious; Coco;* and famously, *West Side Story,* the iconic photograph of Carol Lawrence and Larry Kert running down the streets of Hell's Kitchen having graced the cast album of the landmark production. He served as a photographer in the Army Signal Corps in Europe in W.W. II. Following the war, he formed a partnership with fellow photographer Joseph Abeles, which lasted until the 1970s. His wife of over forty years, Doris; son from a previous marriage; and two grandchildren survive him.

BUDDY FREITAG, 80, died May 30, 2012, in New York, from complications of a brain tumor. A Tony and Drama Desk Award winner for *Memphis,* other Broadway credits include *The Homecoming* (2007; Tony nomination); *November; Passing Strange* (Drama Desk Award; Tony nomination); *Blithe Spirit* (2009, Drama Desk nomination); *Memphis; The Miracle Worker* (2010); *Catch Me If You Can; High;* and *Nice Work If You Can Get It.* He was a veteran of W.W. II, a vice-president of advertising at Grey Advertising, and a mortgage banker prior to becoming a theatre producer. His wife, Barbara; and four children, Larry, Eve, Harry, and Liz; and grandchildren survive him.

BEN GAZZARA (Biagio Anthony Gazzara), 81, New York, NY-born actor, died Feb. 3, 2012, in Manhattan, New York, of pancreatic cancer. One of Lee Strasberg's original students at The Actors Studio, his Broadway credits include *End as a Man,* for which he won a Theatre World Award; *Cat on a Hot Tin Roof; A Hatful of Rain* (Tony nomination); *The Night Circus; Strange Interlude* (1963); *Traveller Without Luggage; Hughie/Duet* (1975, Tony nomination, Drama Desk nomination); *Who's Afraid of Virginia Woolf?* (1976, Tony nomination); *Shamada;* and *Awake and Sing!* (2006, Drama Desk Award). His Off-Broadway credits include *Nobody Don't Like Yogi.* He collaborated often with film director John Cassavetes, and film roles include those in *If It's Tuesday This Must Be Belgium; Husbands; The Killing of a Chinese Bookie; Opening Night; Saint Jack; They All Laughed; Bloodline; The Spanish Prisoner; Big Lebowski; Summer of Sam; Tales of Ordinary Madness; Il Camorrista;* and *Bandits.* His numerous television roles include *Run for Your Life* (Two Emmy Award nominations); *An Early Frost* (Emmy nomination); and *Hysterical Blindness* (Emmy Award). His autobiography was entitled *In the Moment* in 2004. His daughter, Elizabeth, from his marriage to actress Janice Rule; and daughter Danja, his wife Elke Stuckmann's daughter from a previous relationship whom he adopted; and brother, Anthony survive him.

DONALD GRODY (Donald Peter Grody), 83, actor/playwright, died Jul. 13, 2011, in Manhattan, NY. His Broadway credits include *Jekyll & Hyde; Caroline, or Change;* and *Grey Gardens.* His national tours include *Wonderful Town; Bells Are Ringing; Happy Hunting; Kismet; Gentleman Prefer Blondes; Guys and Dolls; Parade; Jekyll and Hyde; Caroline, or Change;* and *Grey Gardens.* He also attended Royal Academy of Dramatic Arts in London, England. Having served as executive director of Actors Equity Association from 1973-1980, he was also a graduate of New York Law School. His wife, Judith Anderson; sons, Dion, Gordon, James, Jeremy, and Patrick; and granddaughters Jess, Jo, and Cecily survive him.

ULU GROSBARD, 83, Antwerp, Belgium-born director, died Mar. 18, 2012, in Manhattan, NY. A Tony nominee for *The Subject Was Roses* and *American Buffalo,* his other Broadway credits include *The Investigation; That Summer—That Fall; The Price; The Floating Light Bulb; The Wake of Jamey Foster;* and *The Tenth Man.* His Off-Broadway credits include *A View From the Bridge* (Obie Award, Drama Desk Award); *The Days and Nights of Beebee Fenstermaker; The Woods; Weekends Like Other People;* and *Family Week.* His numerous film credits include *The Subject Was Roses; Who Is Harry Kellerman and Why Is He Saying Those Terrible Things About Me?; Straight Time; Falling in Love; Georgia;* and *The Deep End of the Ocean.* Previously he worked as an apprentice director on *The Hustler;*

Splendor in the Grass; and *The Miracle Worker.* A veteran of W.W. II, his wife, Rose Gregorio, and nephew, Robert Grosbard survive him.

EIKO ISHIOKA, 73, Tokyo, Japan-born costume designer, died Jan. 21, 2012, in Tokyo, Japan, of pancreatic cancer. A three-time Tony nominee for *M. Butterfly* (sets and costumes) and *Spider-Man: Turn Off The Dark,* her other Broadway credits include *David Copperfield: Dreams and Nightmares.* An Academy Award winner for Francis Ford Coppola's *Dracula* in 1993, her other film credits include *Mishima: A Life in Four Chapters;* and *The Call.* Additionally she designed the costumes for the Cirque du Soleil show *Varekai* and several times designed costumes for many countries for the Winter and Summer Olympics. Two books were published about her work, *Eiko by Eiko* in 1993, and *Eiko on Stage* in 2000. She also won a Grammy Award for "Tutu" in 1986. Her husband, Nicholas Soultanakis; mother, Mitsuko Saegusa Ishioka; her brothers, Koichiro and Jun Ishioka; and her sister, Ryoko Ishioka survive her.

CHARLES JAFFE, 94, musical director/conductor, died Aug. 16, 2011, in Warminster, PA. A 1964 Tony nominee for *West Side Story,* his Broadway credits include the original *West Side Story; My Fair Lady;* and *Fiddler on the Roof.* A former violinist with the NBC Symphony Orchestra, he founded the Long Island Symphony Orchestra on his own. He became a conductor of the American Ballet Theater and toured with them internationally. His daughter, Elissa; grandchildren Shara, Ellen, David, and Robyn survive him.

MARKETA KIMBRELL (nee Mareta Nitschova) 82, Czechoslovakian-born theatre producer/teacher, died Jul. 6, 2011, in Sykesville, MD, of Alzheimer's disease. A displaced person in a camp in Germany during W.W. II when she met and married George Kimbrell, she soon emigrated to the United States, where she was cast in several roles, including those in *Playhouse 90; Judgment at Nuremberg;* and the *Armstrong Circle Theater* production of *The Man Who Refused to Die.* She achieved her most notoriety as the cofounder in 1970 of the New York Street Theater Caravan with Robert Levy. She served as artistic director of the Caravan from 1970-1998, and the troupe performed initially only in New York, but eventually performed as far away as Europe. The Caravan received an Obie Award for its work. Her film credits include *The Pawnbroker.* From 1979-2006 she taught film acting and directing at New York University's Tisch School of the Arts. Her sons Andrew and Mark; sister, Marta McCulloch; seven grandchildren; and one great-grandchild survive her.

HOWARD KISSEL, 69, Milwaukee, WI-born theatre critic, died Feb. 24, 2012, following complications from an April 2010 liver transplant. He served as an arts editor of *Women's Wear Daily* and *W Magazine* before the *Daily News,* where he was the chief theatre critic for twenty years, and up until recently he wrote a column known as *The Cultural Tourist* and blogged for *The Huffington Post.* He was a former chairperson of both the New York Film Critics Circle and the New York Drama Critics' Circle as well as a former Pulitzer Prize jurist. He authored *David Merrick: The Abominable Showman; The Art of Acting;* and *New York Theater Walks,* and had a role in Woody Allen's 1980 film, *Stardust Memories.* His sisters, Judy Kissel and Anne Kissel Elliot survive him. The marquis lights of Broadway were dimmed in his honor for one minute on Feb. 28, 2012.

DANIA KRUPSKA, director/performer/choreographer/assistant, died Aug. 27, 2011, in Easthampton, NY. Her Broadway credits include *Oklahoma!; Chauve-Souris 1943; Allegro; Gentlemen Prefer Blondes; Out of This World; The King and I; Seventeen; Can-Can; The Girl in Pink Tights; The Most Happy Fella* (and 1959); *The Happiest Girl in the World; Rugantino;* and *Rex.* She also directed extensively in Scandinavia and northern Europe in the 1970s and 1980s and served on the governing board of the SSDC (precursor to SDS). The wife of actor Ted Thurston, she was survived by a son and a daughter.

JERRY LEIBER, 78, Baltimore, MD-born lyricist and one half of Leiber and Stoller—one of the most successful songwriting teams of all time, died Aug. 22, 2011, in Los Angeles, CA, of cardio-pulmonary failure following a lengthy illness. One of the biggest songwriting teams of the 1950s, Leiber and Stoller's hits include "Hound Dog"; "Jailhouse Rock"; "Kansas City"; and "Stand by Me". Leiber's Broadway credits include *Hail Scrawdykel; Dancin'; Rock 'N Roll! The first*

5,000 Years; Peg; Smokey Joe's Café; All Shook Up; Ring of Fire; and *Million Dollar Quartet.* Leiber and Stoller were inducted into the Songwriters Hall of Fame in 1985, and the Rock & Roll Hall of Fame in 1987, among many other awards and honors. His sons, Jed, Oliver, and Jake survive him.

THEODORE "TED" MANN, 87, Cofounder (with José Quintero) of the Circle in the Square Theatre in 1951, died Feb. 24, 2012, from complications of pneumonia. Off-Broadway was considered to have been born with their production in 1952 of *Summer and Smoke* (starring Geraldine Page). He also served as the artistic director of the Circle In the Square Theatre School for over four decades. In 1972 at the request of Mayor Lindsay, Circle In the Square moved from Greenwich Village to its current house on Broadway. A Tony Award winner for *Long Day's Journey Into Night* in 1957, Circle in the Square also received a Special Tony Award in 1976. His scores of other Broadway credits as a producer include *Once Upon A Tailor; The Innkeepers; General Seeger; Great Day in the Morning; Hughie; And Things Go Bump in the Night; The Royal Hunt of the Sun; The Zulu and the Zayda; Morning, Noon and Night; Trumpets of the Lord; Mourning Becomes Electra* (1972); *Medea* (1972); *Here Are Ladies; Uncle Vanya* (1973, 1995); *The Waltz of the Toreadors* (1973); *The Iceman Cometh* (1973); *An American Millionaire; Scapino; The National Health* (Tony and Drama Desk nominations); *Where's Charley?* (1974); *All God's Chillun Got Wings* (1975); *Death of a Salesman* (1975); *Ah, Wilderness!* (1975); *The Glass Menagerie* (1975); *Geraldine Fitzgerald in Songs of the Street; The Lady from the Sea* (1976); *Pal Joey* (1976); *Days in the Trees* (1976); *The Night of the Iguana* (1976, 1988); *Romeo and Juliet* (1977); *The Importance of Being Earnest* (1977); *Tartuffe* (1977, Tony nomination); *Saint Joan* (1977); *13 Rue de l'Amour; Once in a Lifetime* (1978); *The Inspector General* (1978); *Man and Superman* (1978); *Spokesong; Loose Ends; Major Barbara* (1980, Tony nomination); *Past Tense; The Man Who Came to Dinner* (1980); *The Bacchae; John Gabriel Borkman* (1980); *The Father* (1981); *Scenes and Revelations; Candida* (1981); *Macbeth* (1982); *Eminent Domain; Present Laughter* (1982, Drama Desk nomination); *The Queen and the Rebels* (1982); *The Misanthrope* (1983); *The Caine Mutiny Court-Martial* (1983, Tony and Drama Desk nominations); *Heartbreak House* (1983, Tony and Drama Desk nominations); *Awake and Sing!* (1984); *Design for Living* (1984); *The Loves of Anatol; Arms and the Man* (1985); *The Marriage of Figaro; The Robert Klein Show!; The Caretaker* (1986); *The Boys in Autumn; You Never Can Tell* (1986); *A Streetcar Named Desire* (1988, Tony nomination); *An Evening with Robert Klein; Juno and the Paycock* (1988, Drama Desk nomination); *The Devil's Disciple* (1988); *Ghetto; Sweeney Todd* (1989, Tony nomination); *Zoya's Apartment; The Miser* (1990); *Taking Steps; Getting Married* (1991); *On Borrowed Time* (1991, Tony nomination); *Search and Destroy; Chinese Coffee* (1992); *Salome* (1982); *Anna Karenina* (1992); *Wilder, Wilder, Wilder* (Tony and Drama Desk nominations); *The Shadow Box* (1994); *The Rose Tattoo* (1995, Tony nomination); *Garden District; Holiday* (1995); *Bus Stop* (1996); *Tartuffe* (1996); *Hughie* (1996); *True West* (2000); *Metamorphoses; Life (x) 3; Frozen; The 25*[th] *Annual Putnam County Spelling Bee; Glory Days; The Norman Conquests* (2009); *The Miracle Worker* (2010); *Lombardi;* and *Godspell* (2011). In addition to his Broadway and Off-Broadway credits, he directed *The Turn of the Screw* for the New York City Opera, *La Boheme* for the Julliard School, and *The Night of the Iguana* for Moscow's Maly Theater, as well as many national tours. His memoirs, entitled *Journeys in the Night: Creating a New American Theatre with Circle In The Square,* was published in 2007 by Applause Theatre & Cinema Books. He is survived by his sons, Andrew and Jonathan; and five grandchildren. He was predeceased by his wife, New York City Opera lyric coloratura Patricia Brooks. The marquis lights of Broadway were dimmed in his honor for one minute on Feb. 24, 2012.

HARRY MORGAN (Harry Bratsburg), 96, Detroit, MI-born actor, died Dec. 7, 2011, in Los Angeles, CA, of pneumonia. His Broadway credits as Harry Bratsburg include *Golden Boy; The Gentle People; My Heart's in the Highlands; Thunder Rock; Night Music; Heavenly Express; The Cream in the Well;* and *The Night Before Christmas.* Launching his movie career in 1942 as "Henry Morgan," he was seen in such movies as *The Ox-Bow Incident; The Glenn Miller Story; Inherit the Wind; To the Shores of Tripoli; Happy Land; A Bell for Adano; Dragonwyck; The Big Clock; All My Sons; Yellow Sky; Down to the Sea in Ships; Holiday*

Affair; Madame Bovary; The Blue Veil; Scandal Sheet; Bend of the River; High Noon; Torch Song; About Mrs. Leslie; The Far Country, Not as a Stranger; and *The Teahouse of the August Moon.* Under the name "Harry" his films include *It Started with a Kiss; The Mountain Road; How the West Was Won* (as Ulysses S. Grant*); Frankie and Johnnie; What Did You Do in the War Daddy?; The Flim-Flam Man; Support Your Local Sheriff!; Viva Max!; The Barefoot Executive; The Apple Dumpling Gang; The Shootist,* and *Dragnet* (1987). His many series on television included *December Bride; Dragnet;* and, most notably, *M*A*S*H,* which brought him an Emmy Award. His second wife, Barbara Bushman; three sons from his first marriage to his forty-five year marriage to Eileen Detchon: Christopher, Charles, and Paul; and eight grandchildren survive him.

JOHN NEVILLE, 86, London, England-born actor died on Nov.19, 2011, in Toronto, Canada, after suffering from Alzheimer's disease. His Broadway credits include *King Richard II* (1956); *Romeo and Juliet* (1956); *Macbeth* (1956); *Troilus and Cressida* (1956); *Twelfth Night* (1958); *Hamlet* (1958); *Sherlock Holmes* (1974); *Ghosts* (1982); and *Saint Joan* (1993). Among his films are *Oscar Wilde; I Like Money* (Mr. Topaze); *Billy Budd; A Study in Terror* (as Sherlock Holmes); *The Adventures of Baron Munchhausen; The Road to Wellville; Little Women* (1994); *Dangerous Minds; High School High; The Fifth Element, Sunshine* (1999); *Spider,* and *The Statement.* After moving to Canada in 1972 he became a mainstay in theater there, serving as artistic director of the Stratford Shakespeare Festival from 1986–1989, and largely credited for returning it to financial security. His wife of sixty-two years, their six children, and six grandchildren survive him.

John Neville

PATRICIA NEWAY (Patricia Mary Neway), 92, Kensington, Brooklyn-born soprano and musical theatre actress, died Jan. 24, 2012, in Corinth, VT. A 1960 Tony Award winner for her role as Mother Superior in *The Sound of Music,* her other Broadway credits include *La Vie Parisienne; The Rape of Lucretia; The Consul;* and *Maria Golovin.* But it was her operatic career for which she was mainly distinguished. Making her debut with the New York City Opera in 1951, her many credits there include *The Dybbuk; Six Characters in Search of an Author; Cacalleria rusticana; Amahl and the Night Visitors; The Medium; Tale for a Deaf Ear; Wuthering Heights; The Turn of the Screw;* and *Salome.* Her other credits include *Iphigénie en Tauride* at the Aix-en-Provence Festival; those at the Opêra-Comique, in Paris, including *Tosca* and *Risurrezione; Una lettera d'amore di Lord Byron* in New Orleans, Lousiana; and with NBC Opera she portrayed a role in *Dialogues of the Camelites.* Other credits include *The King and I* at Lincoln Center; and *The Turn of the Screw* and *Rise and Fall of the City of Mahogonny* at San Francisco Opera. Her recordings include those by Menotti and Samuel Barber, and in the '50s and '60s she started her own opera company in New York, which was originally named the Patricia Neway Opera Workshop and later the Neway Opera Theater. Her niece, Michal Twine, and three nephews survive her.

Alice Playten

ALICE PLAYTEN (Alice Plotkin), New York, NY-born actress, 63, died Jun. 25, 2011, in Manhattan, NY, of heart failure, complicated by a lifetime of juvenile diabetes and pancreatic cancer. A 1968 Theatre World Award winner and Tony nominee for her role in *Henry, Sweet Henry;* her other Broadway credits include *Gypsy; Oliver!; Hello, Dolly!; Spoils of War* (Drama Desk nomination); *Rumors; Seussical; Caroline, or Change;* and the benefits *Sondheim: A Musical Tribute* in 1973; and *Funny Girl* in 2002. An Obie Award winner for her roles in *National Lampoon's Lemmings* and *First Lady Suite,* her Off-Broadway credits include *Promenade; The Last Sweet Days of Isaac; Up from Paradise; Sister Mary Ignatius Explains It All for You; Four Short Opens; First Lady Suite; A Flea in Her Ear;* and *Shlemiel the First.* Her many film and television credits include *Ladybug Ladybug; Who Killed Mary What'sername?; California Dreaming; Legend; For Love or Money* (1993); *I.Q.; The Lost Saucer; Frasier;* and *As the World Turns.* Her husband, Joshua White; and brother, Stephen Plotkin survive her.

CLIFF ROBERTSON (Clifford Parker Robertson III), 88, La Jolla, CA-born actor, who won the Academy Award for his portrayal of a mentally handicapped man who temporarily becomes a genius in the 1968 movie Charly, died Sept. 10, 2011, one day after his birthday, in Stony Brook, NY, of natural causes. A 1957 Theatre World Award winner for Orpheus Descending, his other Broadway credits include Late Love; The Wisteria Trees; and Love Letters. Following his 1955 film debut in Picnic, he was seen in such other pictures as Autumn Leaves; The Girl Most Likely; The Naked and the Dead; Gidget; The Big Show; All in a Night's Work; Underworld U.S.A.; The Interns; PT 109 (as John F. Kennedy), Sunday in New York; The Best Man; 633 Squadron; Masquerade; The Honey Pot; The Devil's Brigade; Too Late the Hero; J.W. Coop (which he also directed, produced, and wrote); The Great Northfield Minnesota Raid; Ace Eli and Rodger of the Skies; Man on a Swing; Three Days of the Condor; Midway; Obsession; The Pilot (also director, writer); Star 80; Class; Brainstorm (1983); Wild Hearts Can't Be Broken; Wind; Renaissance Man; Escape from L.A.; 13th Child (also writer); and Spider-Man. An avid pilot (including balloon races), he was actually flying over the World Trade Center during the 9/11 attacks. He also was a longtime member of the Experimental Aircraft Association, and founded EAA's Young Eagles program, which he chaired from 1992-1994. Cliff was a close personal friend of the editors of this volume, its former editor John Willis, and a devoted contributor and attendee of the Theatre World Awards. His daughter, Stephanie, and a granddaughter survive him.

Cliff Robertson

BRADSHAW SMITH (George Bradshaw Smith), Derby, CT-born singer/theatre historian, 56, died Jan. 16, 2012, in Manhattan, New York, of a stroke. Beginning his career as a vocalist, he won a 1985 Backstage Bistro Award for Best Male Vocalist, and was also creator of Cabaret Beat, for which he received a MAC Board of Directors Award in 1990. His Broadway Beat, begun in 1985 and currently hosted by Smith's former partner, Richard Ridge, chronicled nearly thirty years of Broadway and Off-Broadway openings, press events, concerts, and one-nighters, amassing a major archive of theatre footage and presented as a thirty minute cable

program that showcased his footage and interviews. He was a major contributor to Broadway Cares/Equity Fights Aids, and regularly appeared and was a top earner at the annual Broadway Flea Market. A personal friend of the editors of this volume, his coverage of the Theatre World Awards will always be greatly appreciated. His brother, Robert Smith survives him. His longtime companion, John Scoullar, predeceased him in 2011.

TONY STEVENS (Anthony Pusateri), 63, Herculanaeum, MO-born dancer/choreographer/director, died in July 2011, in New York, NY, of Hodgkins' lymphoma. His Broadway credits in any number of capacities include The Fig Leaves are Calling; Billy; Jimmy; Georgy; The Boy Friend (1970); On The Town (1971); Rachael Lily Rosenbloom and Don't You Ever Forget It; Chicago (1975); Rockabye Hamlet; Perfectly Frank; Wind in the Willows; and Chita Rivera: The Dancer's Life; as well as the benefit Sondheim: A Musical Tribute in 1973. Off-Broadway his credits include Zombie Prom; The Body Shop; Sheba; and he earned a Lucille Lortel Award nomination for The Complete Works of Shakespeare (Abridged). He also choreographed many one-woman shows, including those for Chita Rivera; Bernadette Peters; Dolly Parton; Liza Minelli; Debbie Shapiro; and Jane Powell. His film credits include The Great Gatsby; The Best Little Whorehouse in Texas; She's Having a Baby; Johnny Dangerously; and Where the Boys Are (1984). His television credits include The Mary Tyler Moore Show and the People's Choice Awards. Regional credits include over forty shows, and national tours include Dreamgirls and the twentieth anniversary tour of Jesus Christ Superstar.

WARREN STEVENS (Warren Albert Stevens), 92, Clark's Summit, PA-born actor, died Mar. 27. 2012, in Sherman Oaks, CA, of chronic lung disease. An early member of the Actors Studio, his Broadway credits include Galileo; Six O'Clock Theatre; Sundown Beach; The Smile of the World; and Detective Story. Among his forty films were The Barefoot Contessa; Gunpoint; Madigan; Red Skies of Montana; Mr. Belvedere Rings the Bell; and Forbidden Planet. Television roles include Have Gun, Will Travel; Voyage to the Bottom of the Sea; Bonanza; Ironside; Return to Peyton Place; The Twilight Zone; M*A*S*H*; Rawhide; The Man From U.N.C.L.E.; Gunsmoke; The Trail to Hope Rose; and ER. He was a veteran in W.W. II and his wife of forty-three years, Barbara Fletcher; their two sons, Adam and Mathew; and son, Laurence, from a previous marriage to Susan Huntington survive him.

LEONARD STONE, 87, Salem, OR-born actor, died Nov. 2, 2011, in San Diego, CA, after a brief bout with cancer. A Tony Award nominee for his role in Redhead; his other Broadway credits include Look Homeward Angel. His numerous film roles include the memorable role of Sam Beauregarde in Willy Wonka and the Chocolate Factory; Soylent Green; and American Pop. His television credits include The Jean Arthur Show; McHale's Navy; Perry Mason; Gomer Pyle; Dragnet; Mission: Impossible; Hawaii Five-O; Gunsmoke; All in the Family; Falcon Crest; L.A. Law; The Outer Limits; Lost in Space; M*A*S*H*; and Dorothy. He studied acting at the Royal Academy of Dramatic Art in London, England before serving in the U.S. Navy during W.W. II. His wife, Carole Kleinman; four children; and eight grandchildren survive him.

ALAN SUES (Alan Grigsby Sues), 85, Ross, CA-born actor, died Dec. 1, 2011, at his home in Los Angeles, CA, of an apparent heart attack. Perhaps best known for his roles on television's Laugh-In, most notably Uncle Al the Kiddies' Pal, a consistently hung-over children's entertainer; Big Al, an effeminate sportscaster; and his impersonation of fellow cast member Jo Anne Worley, his other Broadway credits include Tea and Sympathy and Sherlock Holmes. His Off-Broadway credits include The Mad Show. Other television roles include the notable "The Masks" episode of The Twilight Zone; Punky Brewster; and Sabrina, the Teenage Witch. He served in the Army in W.W. II and appeared in the one-man play No Flies on Me. His sister-in-law, Yvonne Sues survives him.

BEATRICE TERRY (Beatrice Terry Lopez), 51, director, died May 15, 2011, in New York, NY, of cancer. An associate director for several Broadway musicals, her credits include Memphis; God of Carnage; La Bête; and Leap of Faith. She was an assistant director on Spring Awakening as well as for its national tour. Her other Off-Broadway credits include Measure for Measure and productions at Ensemble

Studio Theatre, HERE Arts Center, and Pearl Theatre Company. For her work she received an NEA/TCG Career Development Program for Directors and a Drama League Fellowship. Her wife, playwright Gretchen M. Michelfeld and son, Beckett survive her; as do her parents; her sisters; and their families, all of Texas.

Matgaret Tyzack

MARGARET TYZACK, 79, London, England-born actress, died Jun. 25, 2011, in London, England, after a brief battle with cancer. A 1990 Tony winner for her role in *Lettice and Lovage,* her other Broadway credits include *All's Well that Ends Well* (Tony nomination). Her Off-Broadway credits include *Tom and Viv* (Drama Desk nomination). She won an Olivier Award for her role as Martha in *Who's Afraid of Virginia Woolf?,* among many other roles in Britain. Her motion pictures include *The Whisperers; 2001: A Space Odyssey; Thank You All Very Much; A Clockwork Orange; The Legacy; Prick Up Your Ears; Mrs. Dalloway; Bright Young Things;* and *Match Point.* On television she was known for her roles in *The Forsyte Saga* and *Claudius.* Her husband, mathematics professor Alan Stephenson; and son, Matthew survive her.

BERENICE WEILER, 88, producer/theatrical manager, died Apr. 28, 2012, in Manhattan. Her Broadway credits include *Henry V* (1969); *Othello* (1970); *A Broadway Musical; Marlowe; Nine; Wind in the Willows; Stardust;* and *Meet Me in St. Louis.*

JANE WHITE, 88, New York, NY-born actress, died Jul 11, 2011, in New York, NY, of cancer. Her Broadway credits include *Strange Fruit; The Insect Comedy; Razzle Dazzle; The Climate of Eden; Take a Giant Step; Once Upon a Mattress; Jane Eyre; The Power and the Glory; The Cuban Thing;* and *Follies* (2001). Her Off-Broadway credits include *Hop, Signor; The Living Room; The Trojan Women; Love's Labor's Lost; Coriolanus* (Obie Award)*; Troilus and Cressida; The Tale of Cymbeline; The Burnt Flowerbed; Rosmersholm; The Madwoman of Chaillot; Viva! Vivat Regina!; King John; Iphigenia in Aulis; The Taming of the Shrew;* and *The Petrified Prince.* She received an Obie in 1971 for Sustained Excellence, and won a 1988-1989 Los Angeles Critics Circle Award for *Blood Wedding.* Her film roles include those in *Beloved.*

DICK ANTHONY WILLIAMS, 77, Chicago, IL-born actor, died Feb. 16, 2012, in Los Angeles, CA. An original member of the singing group Williams Brothers Quartet, he eventually moved to Los Angeles, and performed roles including *Big Time Buck White.* A Tony nominee for *What the Wine-Sellers Buy* (also Drama Desk Award) and *Black Picture Show,* his other Broadway credits include *Ain't Supposed to Die a Natural Death; We Interrupt This Program…;* and *The Poison Tree.* Off-Broadway he received praise for Ron Milner's *What the Wine-Sellers Buy,* the first play by an African-American produced by Joseph Papp's New York Shakespeare Festival. His film roles include those in *The Mack; The Jerk;* and *Mo' Better Blues.* His television credits include *King* and *Homefront.* In the early 1970s, Mr. Williams and Woodie King Jr. were co-founders of the New Federal Theater at the Henry Street Settlement. Artists including David Henry Hwang, Ntozake Shange, Amiri Baraka, Samuel L. Jackson, Morgan Freeman, and Denzel Washington performed there. His daughters, Mona and Mikah; and son, Jason survive him.

JUDD WOLDIN (Edwin Judd Woldin), 86, Somerset, NJ-born composer/writer/lyricist/arranger/musical staffer, died Nov. 27, 2011, in Manhattan, NY, of cancer. A 1974 Tony Award nominee for Best Original Score for *Raisin,* an adaptation of Lorraine Hansberry's groundbreaking drama, his other Broadway credits include *The Beast in Me; The Roar of the Greasepaint—The Smell of the Crowd;* and *Hello, Dolly!* His other works include *King of Schnorrers.* Off-Broadway credits include *Little Ham.* His five children, John, Mark, and Daniel Woldin; Peter Simon and Hadjipopov; life partner of thirty-five years, Amy Seidman; and seven grandchildren survive him.

JOHN WOOD, 81, Derbyshire, England-born actor, died Aug. 6, 2011, in England, in his sleep. A 1976 Tony Award and Drama Desk Award winner for his role in *Travesties,* his other Broadway credits include *Rosencrantz and Guildenstern Are Dead* (Tony nomination); *Sherlock Holmes* (1974, Tony nomination); *Tartuffe; Deathtrap;* and *Amadeus.* Turning from the study of law to theatre while at Oxford, he began his career at the Royal Shakespeare Company with credits including *Julius Caesar; The Tempest; King Lear;* and *Master Builder.* His films include *The Purple Rose of Cairo; Jane Eyre; War Games; Orlando; Shadowlands; An Ideal Husband; Chocolat; The Madness of King George;* and *Richard III.* He was awarded a CBE in 2007 for his contributions to drama. His wife, Sylvia; and four children survive him.

Index

1001 Nights 98
101 Dalmations 399
101 Productions Ltd. 45, 78, 84, 86, 104
12th Night 296
13 Fat Girls and the Dead Cat 313
13P 272
1776 361, 372
2 Guys Productions 102
2 Stories that End in Suicide 306
25th Annual Putnam County Spelling Bee, The 393
3 2's; Or Afar 316
3 Ghosts 306
321 Theatrical Management 71, 109, 111
39 Steps, The 356, 390
3C 250, 268
3Graces Theater Co 272
3-Legged Dog (3LD) 272
4.48 Psychosis 298
4000 Miles 204, 224
47th Street Theatre 181
4Edges 319
4Wall Entertainment 410
59 Productions 110
59E59 Theaters 126, 133, 147, 154-160, 162, 166, 170, 171, 176, 182, 184, 186, 243, 272
5th Avenue Theatre 92, 367
64 291
69°S 211
8 (The Play) 113
8cho Aerial Tango 234
9 to 5 The Musical 355
9/11 Performance Project 320

A
A Capella Humana 366
Aardvark Interiors 50
Aaron Davis Hall 431
Aaron, Caroline 37
Aarons, Michael 40, 68, 87
Abate, Shelagh 68, 101
Abbandandolo, Brenda 82, 77, 261

Abbot, Christopher 94
Abbott, Chip 113
Abbott, Gianne 232
Abbott, James 43, 84, 111, 188
Abboud, Carole 210
Abdul-Rahim, Islah 202
Abel, Larry 54
Abel, Marybeth 111
Abel, Meghan 179
Abel, Ron 117
Abel, Timothy M. 28, 101
Abeles, David 60, 136, 236
Abella, Nanda 149
Abens, Byron F. 135
Abercrombie, Tiffany 163
Aberlin, Betty 265
Abingdon Theatre Company 206
Abner, Devon 378
Above the Title Entertainment 169
Abraham, F. Murray 218
Abraham, Jolly 239, 250
Abrams, Bernie 47, 50, 95
Abramson, Deborah 76
Abramson, Jane 101
Abrazado, Carmen I. 99
Abrego, Raul 146, 249
Abreu, Cesar 113
Abromaitis-Smith, Lindsay 145
Abrons Arts Center 145
Abruzzo, Emanuel 183
Absence of Weather 319
Absolute Uncertainty 182
Abston, Melvin 109
Abt, Meryl 101
Abuba, Auric 238
Abuba, Ernest 238
Abuchovich, Alexander 215
Abueg, Christopher 127
ACCA Award 437
Access Theater 170
Accidental Pervert, The 188
Accidentally, Like a Martyr 305
Accorso, Philip 202
Accurso, Aron 109
Acevedo, Juan Luis 239

Acevedo, Lisa 75
Acheson, Matt 110
Ackerman, Hilary 28, 52
Ackerman, Loni 172
Ackerman, Rob 167
Ackerman, Robert Allan 263
Ackerman, Talon 47, 83
Ackerman, Ted 105
Acme Sound Partners 32, 42, 54, 84, 88, 103, 107, 112, 188, 244-246, 248, 261
ACOM International 198
Acorn Theatre on Theatre Row 135, 137, 143, 230
Acreman, Travis 140, 223
ACT - A Contemporary Theatre 345
Act II Playhouse 147
Act Productions Limited 214
Act Without Words II 259
Acting Company, The 176
Action Philosophers! 280, 293
Active Theater, The 272
Active Theater, The 147, 272
Actman, Jane 172
Actors and Directors Living in Brooklyn 272
Actors Collective, The 195
Actors Company Theatre (TACT), The 207
Actors Fund, The 115, 201, 202, 420
Actors Temple Theatre 125, 142, 171, 172, 189
Actors Theatre of Louisville 233, 241, 341, 345
Actors' Equity Association 410
ADA 288
Adair, Ellen 141
Adam of the Apes 291
Adam Roebuck Productions 272
Adamek, Pauline 442
Adams, Anna 157

Adams, Cameron 78, 95
Adams, Candi 244
Adams, Edie 417
Adams, Jane 419
Adams, Jennifer 28
Adams, Joseph 233
Adams, Kevin 32, 35, 50, 139, 165, 226
Adams, Knud 258
Adams, Margot 116
Adams, Nia 239
Adams, Nick 106, 114, 115, 198, 202
Adams, Paul 444
Adams, Phij 75
Adams, Randy 102
Adams, Tim 163
Adams, Tony 28
Adams, Warren 253
Adams, Whitney 237
Adamson, Evan 36, 49, 86, 185
Adamy, Julia 146
Adamy, Paul 100
Adaptations Project, The 273
Addams Family, The 84, 116
Addams, Charles 84
Adderly, Konrad 111
Addiss, Pat Flicker 190
Adelizzi, Susan 174
Adelman, Adam 68
Ader, Bob 259
Adinolfi, Carlo 157
Adjmi, David 250, 258
Adkisson, Shaleah 32, 140
Adler, Brian 149
Adler, Dara 105
Adler, Gary 188, 200
Adler, Jessica 31, 42, 57, 80, 227
adrenalin...heart 299
Aduba, Uzo 40
Aduro Productions 262
Advance Man 290, 315
Adventures of Pinocchio, The 363
Adventures of Tom Sawyer, The 233, 345, 367, 381, 396
Aeschylsus 130
Affannato, Rich 71, 132
After 305
Afterglow Group LLC 82
Afton, Emily 32

AGA Wrecking Ball 306
Agamemnon Home 306
Agbuya, George Anthony 129
Agee, Martin 43
Aggarwal, Ujju 127
Agger, Henrik 215
Aghabekian, Kara 255
Aghayere, Itohan 219
Agins, Suzanne 223
Agony and the Ecstasy of Steve Jobs, The 245
Agosta, Alexandra 132
Agosta, Micka 106
Agraz, Raul 90
Aguilar, Alexander 16, 52, 124
Aguilar, Carlos 157, 240
Aguinaga, Deana 100
Aguirre, Michael 239, 240
Aguirre-Sacasa, Roberto 28
Ah Muzen Cab and the Bees 287
Ah, Wilderness! 351
Ahearn, Scott 113
Ahhh HA! 233
Ahlfors, Elizabeth 433
Ahmed, Adeel 239
Ahn, Ali 156
Ahonen, Derek 138
Ahrens, Elisabeth 207
Ahrens, Lynn 446
Ahrens, Robert 68
Aibel, Douglas 115, 261
Aidem, Betsy 208
Aiello, Danny 135, 419
Aigner, Peter 212
Ailion, Pippa 89
Ainge, Christina 33
Ainge, Christine 73
Ainge, Patrick 106
Ain't Misbehavin' 382
AirPort Bar Productions 273
Aitken, Bobby 75, 100
Aitken, Charles 197
Aitken, Maria 35
Aives, Dyana 117
Ajax 163
Ajax in Iraq 288
aka 44, 49, 67, 74, 77, 89, 90, 94, 98, 102, 103, 108, 109, 115, 133, 138, 147, 169
Akazawa, Kaori 239

Akbar, Gabby 215
Akerlind, Christopher 54, 67, 245, 409
Akers, Karen 419
Akimova, Natalia 215
Akins, Meredith 100, 113
Al Ameeri, Faisal 210
Al Eskanazy Productions 133
Al Fraheen, Wafa 210
Al Hadad, Hana 232
Al Hirschfeld Theatre 95, 117
Al Nassar, Nassar 210
Alacon, Ameyalli Ruiz 244
Alagi , Tea 146
Alago, Linda 409
Alan Eisenberg Award 437
Alan Wasser Associates 52, 113
Alba 289
Albano, Aaron J. 64, 111
Al-Bassam, Sulayman 210
Albee, Edward 255, 257
Albers, Ryan 195
Albery, Shana 95, 153
Albiges, Aude 210
Alboher, Olivia 89
Albrecht, Erin 239, 240
Albright, Alicia 111
Albright, Tim 43, 68
Alchemy Production Group 102
Alchemy Theatre Company 170
Alchimia Public Relations and Marketing 171
Alda, Alan 418
Alden, Michael A. 47, 54, 112
Alden-Badway-Podell 47
Aldous, Brian 189
Aldredge, Tom 464
Aldrich, Mark 64
Aldridge, Karen 388
Alec Baldwin Foundation Inc. 410
Alemu, Yonas 187
Aleshina, Ekaterina 129
Alessandrini, Gerard

202
Aletaha, Sherz 162
Alex, Timothy J. 95
Alexander, C. Renee 127, 135, 137, 186
Alexander, Graham 107
Alexander, Jane 205, 257, 418
Alexander, Jennie West 180
Alexander, Lawrence 33, 85
Alexander, Lindsey 179, 226
Alexander, Nina 249
Alexander, Ryan 133, 266
Alexander, Terence Orleans 101, 115, 118
Alexandrov, Mikhail 215
Alexis & Destiny Chronicles, The 318
Alexix: A Greek Tragedy 294
Alfano, Matt 62
Alfred Hitchcock's *The 39 Steps* 356, 390
Alfred P. Sloan Foundation Science & Technology Project 182
Algya, Toby 207, 237
Alhadeff Productions 36, 67
Alhadeff, Aaron 102
Alhadeff, Alison 102
Alhadeff, Andi 102
Alhadeff, Emily 102
Alhadeff, Kenny 36, 102
Alhadeff, Mark 42, 207
Alhadeff, Marleen 36, 102
Ali Forney Center 202
Ali, Sumayya 54, 118, 426
Alia, Lily 49, 74, 177, 410
Alianiello, Diane 146
Alice Griffin Jewel Box Theatre 255, 256
Alice in Wonderland 297
Alice, or the Scottish Gravediggers 310
Aliens with Extraordinary Skills 286
Alifanz, Michael 157, 171, 209
Alisson, Igor 232
Alix, John 113
Al-Juburi, Faisal 200
Al-Kaisi, Fajer 88
Alkestis 212
All For One Theater

Festival 325
All in Black and White Productions 273
All My Sons 360, 366
All Out Arts, Inc. 273
All the Indifferent Children of the Earth 279
All the Way 391
All's Well That Ends Well 244
Alladin, Opal 228
Allain, Noel Joseph 151
Allam, Charlotte 156
All-American 225
Allamon, Matthew 143, 169, 263, 264
Allan, Jo 214
Allan, Laurena 247
Allard, Martine 419
Alldaffer, Alaine 73, 241, 262
Allen, Donald M. 239
Allen, Eddie 164
Allen, Ian 226
Allen, Jennifer 109
Allen, Jenny 192
Allen, Joan 419
Allen, Jonathan 100
Allen, Jonelle 418
Allen, Karen 419
Allen, Matthew 201
Allen, Megan 113
Allen, Michael 64
Allen, Mike 96
Allen, Nicholas 124
Allen, Rin 57
Allen, Woody 37
Allenberg, Robert 31, 42, 57, 80, 227
Allers, Roger 99
Alley Theatre 341, 347
Alliance Theatre 348
Allied Live 32, 89, 103, 129, 139
Allis, Andy 167
Allison, Drayton 90
Allison, Thom 106
Allred, John 95
Almeida, Aldredo 213
Aloise, Anthony 112
Alone 311
Alony, Rinat 133
Alós, Karina 149
Alpert, David 66
Alpyspaev, Armand 112
Als, Hilton 428
Alston, Shani 199
Altadonna, Amy 165
Altbaum, Michael 33, 62
Altenburg, Gerry 62
Alterman, Charlie 40
Alternating Incoherence

Productions LLC 273
Altinay, Tia 101, 118
Altman, Allison 249
Altomare, Christy 227
Altruistic Theatre Company 273
Altschuler, Alan 170
Alu, Maria 184
Alvarado, Mando 135
Alvarez, David 421
Alvarez, Lauren 84, 90, 94
Alves, Clyde 78, 85
Alves, Tessa 108
Alvin Ailey Citigroup Theatre 130
Alvord, Megan J. 143, 245, 256
Always…Patsy Cline 365
Amadeus 386
Amália Hoje 213
Aman, Brian 68
Amato, Bianca 86, 260
Ambassador Theatre 93, 115
Ambassador Theatre Group 36, 47, 214
Amber, Ashley 68
Ambrose, Kathryn 109
Ambrosia 292
Amendola, Dana 64
Amendt, Matthew 389
Amendum, Dominick 253
American Airlines Theatre 35, 56, 81, 96, 437
American Bard Theater Company 273
American Buffalo 359
American Conservatory Theater 341, 349
American Foundation for Equal Rights 113
American Idiot 362
American Indian Arts, Inc. 273
American Irish Historical Society 258
American Jornalero 183
American Night: The Ballad of Juan Jose 359, 67, 381
American Pop Anthology 87, 103, 136
American Repertory Theater 54, 236, 253, 259, 350
American River 296
American Theater Company 242
American Theatre Critics

Association Awards 430
American Theatre of Actors 181
American Theatre Wing 422, 438
American Thymele Theatre 273
Americas Off Broadway Festival 126
Amerling, Victor 101
Ames, Mason 138
Amigone, Krista 271
aMios Theatre 273
Amiot, Dominique 238
Amis, Suzy 419
Amondson, Lori 141, 264, 265
Amoralists, The 138
Amos, Loren 309
Ampersand: A Romeo & Juliet Story 311
Amundsen, Cressa 222
Amuse Bouche 2011 280
Amuse Inc. 92
Anastasia, Nick 133
Anastasio, Matthew 137
Anatol 267
Ancheta, Susan 238
Anctil, Matt 113
And God Created Great Whales 120, 165
And Then There Were None 347
Anderman, Maureen 214, 418
Andersen, Hans Christian 233
Anderson, Alex 249
Anderson, Anna 72
Anderson, Cailin 60, 124, 202, 236
Anderson, Cherine 49, 74
Anderson, D.C. 153
Anderson, Dave 176
Anderson, David 164
Anderson, Gillian 419
Anderson, J. David 160
Anderson, Jack 28, 219
Anderson, Jennifer 238
Anderson, Jillian 253
Anderson, Kaitlyn 104
Anderson, Kevin 419
Anderson, Lisa 249, 250
Anderson, Mark 118
Anderson, Nancy 263
Anderson, Peta 219
Anderson, Rachel 255
Anderson, Randy 428
Anderson, Rebecca 234
Anderson, Scot Charles

178
Anderson, Stephen Lee 214
Anderson, Stig 100
Anderson, Thomas 45
Anderson, Todd 111
Anderson, Wendy 172
Andersson, Benny 100
Andersson, Helena 215
Andes, Keith 417
Ando, Yoko 211
Andolfi, Francesco 155
Andos, Randy 90, 192, 216, 217
Andreas, Christine 266, 419
Andreas, Sara 92, 113
Andreev, Michail 215
Andreiev, Katja 208, 209
Andress, Carl 115, 265, 266
Andrews, Beckley 113
Andrews, David 410
Andrews, George Lee 68, 105
Andrews, Julie 417
Andrews, Nancy 417
Andrews, Patrick 361
Andrews, Scott 185
Andrews, Steve 98
Andrews, Stuart 68, 101
Andrews, Tod 417
Andron, Jim 143
Andros, Andrea 235
Andrus, Cody 261
Andrusko, Robert John 28
Andújar, Victoria 130, 159, 165
anecdota 184
Angel Play, The 297
Angela, Moya 76
Angeles, John 196
Angelina Ballerina the Musical 125
Angelina Ballerina: The Very Merry Holiday Musical 322
Angelo Fraboni Productions 128, 197
Anger at the Movies 306
Angiel, Brenda 234
Angleflod, Alex 215
Anglim, Philip 419
Angry Young Women in Low Rise Jeans With High Class Issues 293
Anhorn, Naomi 133
Aniello, Chris 74, 108, 143, 177
Animal Crackers 390
Animal Kingdom 313
Animals & Plants 138

Animals Commit Suicide 319
Anita Dloniak and Associations 159
Anixter Rice Music Services 50, 64, 83, 95, 226
Anixter, Russell 82, 109
Anna Abock 281
Anna Christie 221, 387
Anna Karenina 395
Anna Nicole: Blonde Glory 323
Anndee Productions 193
Annerin Production 107
Anni Dori Public Relations 175
Another Life 320
ANPU Theatre 129
Anschutz, Sue 100
Anselmo, John, Jr. 125, 133, 138, 141, 146, 147, 164, 172, 177, 236, 237
Anspacher Theater 247, 248
Antaramian, Jacqueline 31
Antenora 275
Anthonissen, Peter 232
Anthony, Byron 138
Anthony, La La 192
Anthony, Stephen James 110
Antico, Tommaso 193
Antidote 223
Antigone 163
Antigone Unearthed 279
AntiMatter Collective 273
Antkowiak-Maier, Sara 113
Antoinette Perry "Tony" Awards 422
Antonini, Mary 62
Antonio, Lou 410, 417
Antony and Cleopatra 219, 372
Antony, John 128
Antrim, Chelsea 94
Antrobus 289
Any Given Monday 147
Any Night 280
Anything Goes 85, 116, 118
Anzuelo, David 172, 181, 183, 223, 230, 249
Aomori, Hideaki 76
Apesteguia, Joaquin 234
Apichell, David 183
Apostoulou, Sharin 184
Appelman, Zach 110

Appetite 300
Applause Books 410
Apple a Day Repertory
 Company 274
Applegate, Christina 420
Applegate, Fred 109
Apples and Oranges
 Productions 102
Apps, William 139
Apuzzo, Michael 113
Aquila Theatre 179
Aquino, Caroline 241
Aquino, Jim 36
Araca Group, The 92,
 94, 111, 410
Arambulo, Jeremy 166
Arana, Carlos 50
Aranas, Raul 239
Arango, Julian Andres
 67
Aranzasti, Inigo 212
Araujo, Roberto 125
Arbisser, Lily 184
Arboleda, Steve 103
Arbuckle, Sean 96
Arbus, Arin 259, 260
Arcade, Penny 187
Arcadia 86
Arcane Game 321
Arcangeli, Juan Pablo
 234
Arce, Kimberly 149
Arcelus, Sebastian 205,
 253
Arcement, Ashley 113
Arch, David 43, 52,
 75, 87, 89, 90, 102,
 112, 136
Archbold, Mary Theresa
 178
Archer, Kelly 99
Archer, Laura 185
Archer, Nicholas 217
Archer, Pascal 184
Archuletta, Dave 211
ArcLight Theatre 164
Arden Theatre Company
 351
Arditti, Paul 72, 89
Arditti, Stephanie 68
Are You There, McPhee?
 369, 383
Arena Stage 351
Arena, Andrew 189
Arent, Arthur 127
Argue, Darcy James 212
Ari, Bob 125
Arian, Adam 461
Arianda, Nina 13, 42,
 91, 118, 198, 421, 429
Arias with a Twist Deluxe
 145
Arias, Joey 145

Arias, Roy 124
Arima, Stafford 226
Arkansas Repertory
 Theatre 352, 354
Arkin, Adam 419
Arkin, Alan 418
Arkin, Anthony 257
Arkley, Joseph 197
ArKtype 130, 211
ARLA Productions LLC
 274
Arlen, Harold 199
Armato, Niki 264, 266
Armbruster, Heidi 229,
 268
Armenante, Jillian 420
Armfield, Neil 234
Armitage, Karole 32
Armitage, Stephanie 184
Armon, Faye 73, 110,
 125, 224, 225, 232,
 243
Armstrong, David Glenn
 266
Armstrong, Jim 177
Armstrong, Karen 104
Army, Bill 37, 185, 245
Arnal, Estelle Woodard
 212
Arnaz, Lucie 419
Arnet, Marie 212
Arnette, Crystal 163
Arnold, Andy 176
Arnold, Damian 81
Arnold, David A. 208,
 209, 230, 243, 244,
 261
Arnold, Eileen 115,
 167, 207
Arnold, Hunter 38, 40
Arnold, Jacqueline
 B. 106
Arnold, Lianne 208, 255
Arnold, Michael 89
Arnold, Scott 225
Arnone, John 257, 422
Arnson, Heather 127
Aron, Tracy 104
Aronoff, Matt 187
Aronov, Michael 224
Aronson, Billy 139
Aronson, Gabriel 187
Aronson, Henry 108
Aronson, Letty 37
*Around the World in 80
 Days* 393
Arredondo, Rosa
 Evangelina 74
Arrington, Damon W.
 172
Arroyo, Caesar 219
Arroyo, Elis C. 221, 238
Ars Nova 142

Arsenault, David L. 151,
 167, 206, 252
Arsenault, Fred 91
Arsht, Adrienne 33
Arst, Greg 89
Art 306, 379, 393
Art Meets Commerce
 138
ArtEffects Theatre
 Company 274
Artful Conspirators,
 The 274
Arthur, Ken 135
Arthur, Phil 417
Arthur, Shane 135
Artifacts, The 305, 321
Artists on the Brink 274
Arts Council London
 199
Arvia, Ann 101
As It Is In Heaven 272
As You Like It 197, 311,
 350, 360, 365, 379,
 391, 393
Asbury, Cleve 95
Asbury, Donna Marie 93
Ascenzo, Paul 99
Ash Girl, The 307
Ash, Christopher 160
Ash, Erica 87
Ash, Jeffrey 464
Ash, Larry K. 143
Ash, Simon 75
Ashford, Annaleigh 140,
 254
Ashford, Rob 68, 95
Ashleigh, Nia 99
Ashley, Barbara 417
Ashley, Carole 125
Ashley, Christopher 82,
 102, 241, 262
Ashley, Elizabeth 378,
 418
Ashman, Howard 46,
 202
Ashmanskas, Brooks
 361, 368
Ashton, Paul 85, 116
Ask/Tell 223
Askins, Robert 150
Asnes, Andrew 168
*Asphalt Christmas,
 The* 308
Assael, Deborah 64,
 104, 216, 217
Assistance 242
Assor, Josh 101
Astaire, Ava 437
Astor Place Theatre 189
Astoria Performing Arts
 Center 274
Astrachan, Margot 78
Asuncion 123, 249

Asuncion, Alan 196
At Play Productions 140
Athena Theatre 274, 308
Athens, Jim 68, 95
Atherton, William 418
Atkins, Phil 196
Atkinson, Arthur 112,
 221
Atkinson, Ashlie 420
Atkinson, Helen 156
Atkinson, Nicholas 196
Atkinson, Susan D. 231
Atlantic Stage 2 164,
 208, 209
Atlantic Theater
 Company 208, 268
*Atmosphere of Memory,
 The* 223
Attebury, Melissa 235
Attic Theater Company,
 The 274
Attmore, Phillip 217
Attridge, Rachel 75, 92
Attwood, Alex 175
Auberjonois, Remy 59,
 249
Aubin, Kevin 28, 29
Aubrey, Miles 97
Auburn, David 80
Auciello, Emily 150,
 182, 254
Auclair, Sylvain 129
Aucoin, Don 436
AUDELCO Awards 431
Auerbach, Jeffery 28
Augello, Anthony 188
August Wilson Theatre
 97
August, Dave 113, 116,
 194
August, Kate 190
August: Osage County
 351, 368, 380
Augustine, Thomas 54
Aukin, Daniel 224, 258
Aulino, Tom 267
Aument, Matt 90, 117,
 169
Aurora Productions 35-
 37, 46, 49, 56, 58-60,
 73, 75, 77, 81, 84, 90,
 94, 96, 98, 103, 104,
 109, 113, 185, 251
Aurora, Anup 253
Ausloos, Benoit 210
Auster, David 45
Austin, Aaron 138
Austin, Danny 97
Austin, Hilary 74, 164
Austin, Neil 68
Austrian, Jessie 96, 141
Autonomous Collective
 275

Autonomous Production
 Services 188
Auxier, David 235
Avaliani, Ika 258
Avallone, Angelina 31,
 39, 42, 57, 66, 78, 81,
 82, 84, 85, 96, 102,
 104, 108, 227, 228
Avebe, Katie 200
Avedon, Doe 417
Avenue Q 118, 188, 356
*Average-Sized Mermaid,
 The* 299
Averett, Brendan 250
Avers, Brian 241
Avery Fisher Hall 200
Avery, Gerald 28, 29
Avganim, Dorit 173
Avila Productions LLC
 171
Avner, Janna 213
Awadhi, Abdullah Al 210
Awakening 210
Awesome 80s Prom, The
 116, 118, 188
Awkward Levity 316
Awuart, Bashan 67
Axis Company 275
axis: Ballymun 134
Axness, Ian 168
aya theatre company
 156
Ayala, Marcos 234
Ayala, Varín 260
Ayckbourn, Alan 158
Ayende, Che 246
Ayers, Becca 84, 254
Ayers, Heather 50
Ayers, Kristine 146, 156,
 163, 166, 172
Ayers, Rachel E. 251,
 252
Ayesa, MiG 108
Ayite, Dede 252, 256
Ayling, Dan 199
Ayoub, Hend 88
Ayvazian, Leslie 243
Azab, Sherrine 127, 151
Azaria, Hank 420
Azenberg, Emanuel 78
Aziza, de'Adre 420

B
B Square + 4
 Productions 36
B.B. King's 202, 443
Bååth, Johan 215
Babbish, Lenny 433
Babes in Toyland 297
Babinsky, Jason 76, 89
Baby It's You! 87
Baby Redboots' Revenge
 319

Bac, Benjamin 210
Bacalhau, Ana 213
Bacalzo, Dan 438, 444
Bach, J.S. 210
Bach, Steve 130
*Bachelors' Tea Party,
 The* 317
Bachkönig, Walter 212
Back Stage 433
Backer, Brian 419
Bäcker, Mats 215
Backstrom, Greg 35, 56,
 81, 96, 116, 251
Backus, Richard 418
Backyart Productions
 275
Bacon, Claire 238
Bacon, Mary 207, 243
Bacon, Musa 239
Bad Evidence 282
Bad Feather 258
Bad Guys, The 254
Bad Kid 275
Baden Papa, Leslie 50,
 68, 92, 181, 410
Bader, Kate 409
Badger, Justin 144
Badwagon Productions
 275
Badway, Dale 54, 409
Bae, Ga Hyun 36
Baer, Adriana 176
Baer, Merritt Forrest 59
Baer, Zachary 71, 99,
 116
Bahorek, Stanley 153,
 247
Bai Xi 232
Baiba, Baiba 28
Bailey, Adam 36, 88
Bailey, Chris 68
Bailey, Christopher 95
Bailey, Erika 233
Bailey, Lucy 197
Bailey, Theresa A. 28
Bailey, Victoria 422
Bailey, William 130, 154
Bain, Bob 190
Bainbridge, Veronica
 R. 261
Bair, Heather Lea 113
Baird, Campbell 96
Baird, Derek 202
Baird, Heather 208
Baird, Kimberly 82
Baird, Polly 105
Baisden-Folkes, Akeem
 208, 209
Bait N' Swish 324
Baitz, Jon Robin 39,
 426, 430
Baja, Collin 28, 29
Baker, Annie 255, 258,

426
Baker, Brandon 43
Baker, Daniel 250
Baker, Douglas C. 73
Baker, Dylan 419
Baker, Jordan 104, 410, 420
Baker, Joseph A. 143
Baker, Kathy Whitton 419
Baker, Keith 231
Baker, Mark 418
Baker, Max 98
Baker, Patty 47, 66, 92, 102
Baker, Rosebud 173
Baker, Rozi 47, 101
Baker, Ted 99
Baker, Word 190
Bakkensen, Michael 174, 243
Balaban, Bob 114, 223
Balaban, Japhet 103
Balabanova, Sia 28
Balan, Courtney 119, 169, 188
Balch, Justin 212
Balck, Joe & Sandi 168
Bald Soprano, The 239
Baldassare, Jim 409, 410
Baldauff, Julie 54
Balderrama, Michael 76
Baldonieri, Louis 135
Baldwin, Alec 419
Baldwin, Craig 141, 172, 218, 219, 251
Baldwin, Julia 227
Baldwin, Whit 216
Baldy, Cyril 211
Balfe, Esther 211
Balgord, Linda 115, 118, 164
Balin, Ina 417
Ball, Amy 98
Ball, Cade Cannon 159
Ballad of 423 and 424 347
Ballagh, Robert 134
Ballantine, Erin 230, 243, 252, 254
Ballard, Bill 44
Ballard, Charity 263
Ballard, Glen 75
Ballard, James 78
Ballard, Jamie Lynn 40
Ballard, John W. 107
Ballenger, Travis LeMont 145
Ballew, Meryl 33, 202
Ballou, Emily Paige 148
Balls…the Musical? 158

Ballybeg 275
Balmer, Andrew 187, 247
Balsam, Talia 419
Baltic, Annie 101
Baltimore in Black and White 275
Bamboozled, or The Real Reality Show 319
Banach, Curran 28
Banakis, Brett 33, 50, 88, 95, 139, 207, 219, 248, 253, 254
Bancroft, Anne 417
Banderas, Antonio 420
Bandhu, Pun 57
Banes, Lisa 419
Bank Street Theater 223
Bank, Jonathan 229
Banner, Gideon 189
Banshee 324
Banta, Alden 92
Banta, Martha 100
Bantal, John 91
Banuazizi, Roeya 109
Baptiste, Sean 113
Barabas, Gabor 166
Barabas, SuzAnene 166
Baramzin, Yury 129
Baran, Tiffany Kleeman 239
Barash, Emma March 149
Barati, Joe 50
Barbeau, Adrienne 115, 418
Barber, David 144, 164
Barber, Kortney 253
Barber, Shannon 127
Barber, Sherri Eden 140
Barbican 199, 214
Barbosa, Delano 189
Barbot, Matt 163
Barbour, David 438
Barbour, James 112
Barclay, Kelli 216
Barclay, Shelley 93
Barczys, Mike 146
Bárdos, Anika 210
Bardwil, Kristen 36, 43, 75
Barefoot Theatre Company 180, 275
Barer, Marshall 265
Bargeron, Dave 93
Bargetto, Paul 144
Barisich, Kyle 105
Barker, Abby 141, 255
Barker, Wayne 71, 117, 236
Barkin, Ellen 104, 114, 421
Barksdale, Charles 181

Barlow, Chris 150
Barn Series (Labyrinth Theater) 223
Barna, Mark 28, 52, 136
Barnes, Bruce 112, 160
Barnes, Darius 102
Barnes, David Wilson 242
Barnes, Geoffrey 222
Barnes, Gregg 33, 202, 447
Barnes, Jason 44
Barnes, Jenny 33, 64
Barnes, Julie 101, 115
Barnes, Reginald L. 189
Barnes, Stephen 127
Barnes, William Joseph 32, 72, 113
Barnett, Ken 247
Barnett, Molly 32, 36, 71, 104, 155, 169, 192, 226, 410
Barney, Tom 99
Barnhardt, Scott 90
Barnhill, Hettie 83
Barnum, Collin 156
Barr, Drew 110, 207
Barra, Michael 188
Barras, Susan 52, 124, 208, 209, 253, 254
Barre, Gabriel 201
Barreca, Christopher H. 255
Barreiros, Mario 213
Barrett, Andrew 109, 111
Barrett, Brent 93, 120, 132, 202
Barrett, Felix 196
Barrett, Gregory 209
Barrett, Kelli 87
Barrett, KK 148
Barrett, Leslie 104
Barrett, Mary Caitlin 28
Barrett, Nigel 210
Barrett, Sean 132
Barricklow, Catherine 246-248, 263
Barrie, James M. 159
Barriers 284
Barrineua, David 33
Barrington Stage Company 191, 353, 355
Barrington, Rachel 179
Barrino, Fantasia 420
Barrios, Jessica 219, 220
Barrios, Will 141
Barrow Street Theatre 121, 126, 134, 141, 169, 259
Barrow, Ardis 149

Barrow, Chip 226, 260
Barrow, Scott 237
Barry, B.H. 260
Barry, Brian 115
Barry, Jeff 225
Barry, Kevin 68
Barry-Hill, Eugene 128
Barrymore Awards 431
Barsamian, Tricia 149
Barsha, Debra 148
Barsoum, Sue 28
Bart, Brandon 60
Bart, Roger 379
Bartek, Ann 92, 163
Bartell, Cameron 177
Bartelme, Reid 212
Barter Theatre 353, 355
Bartha, Justin 123, 249, 426
Bartholomew, Virginia 240
Bartlett, Alex 225
Bartlett, D'Jamin 418, 421
Bartlett, Mike 185
Bartlett, Peter 116
Bartlett, Rob 95, 118
Bartley, Meghan 44
Bartley, Robert 117
Bartmus, Russ 40, 92
Bartner, Beverly 98
Bartner, Robert G. 47, 54, 82, 86, 102, 103, 214
Bartner/Jenkins Entertainment 106
Bauchman, John 195
Bartnik, Kelly 196
BAUDELAIRE: La Mort 238
Barton, Cherice 28
Barton, Debi 249
Barton, Mark 126, 134, 236, 242, 247, 248, 251, 258
Barton, Toni 28
Bartosik, Steve 181
Bartz, Paul 32
Baruch Performing Arts Center 141, 152, 176
Baruch, Steven 82, 185
Baryshnikov Arts Center 259
Baryshnikov, Mikhail 353, 419
Basaca, Melinda 226
Bascom, Hugh 261
Bash, Eddie 64
Bashor, Whitney 267
Baskin, Danielle 184
Baskin, Derrick 102
Bass, Brad 97
Bass, Kaolin 178
Bass, Rob 71
Bassett, Angela 11, 36
Bassett, J. Philip 70

Bassi, Maddy 140
Bassman, Damien 84, 227, 244, 266
Bassman, Nili 93
Basso, Robert S. 91
Basten, Scott 222, 244
Bate, Jonathan 214
Bateman, Bill 190
Bates, Cath 98
Bates, Django 197
Bates, Eric 97
Bates, Jerome Preston 49
Bates, Liz 72
Bates, Melody 144, 340
Bates, Mikaal 271
Bates, Stephen 175, 194
Bathroom Bolero 223
Batiuk, Valencia 234
Batman, Jack W. 47, 78, 131
Bator, Kendra 250, 258
Batori, Piroska 212
Batstone, Chris 208, 209
Batt, Bryan 114, 117, 201, 202
Batten, Keith 28
Battery Dance 272
Battis-Reese, Vera 211
Battiste, Francois 70
Battle, Hinton 149
Battye, Eileen 158
Batwin + Robin Productions Inc. 104
Bauchman, John 195
Baudendistel, Karl 85, 104, 116
Bauder, Matthew 187
Bauder, Mike 28
Bauder, Rachel 85, 116
Bauer, C. Andrew 54, 66, 208
Bauer, Jess 244, 248
Bauer, Jim 253
Bauer, Joie 181
Bauer, Monica 173
Bauer, Ruth 253
Bauer, Sean 138
Baum, David 101
Baum, L. Frank 135
Bauman, Jenna 184
Bauman, Matthew 216
Baumwoll, Becky 207
Bausilo, Giuseppe 89
Bausor, Jon 197
Bavaar, Tony 417
Bax, Clifford 184
Baxter, Keith 418
Baxter, Rick 52
Baxter, Robin 80

Bay Area Theatre Critics Circle Awards 432
Bay Bridge Productions 49, 94
Bay, Abbey 239, 262
Bayer, Daniel 259
Bayer, Elisabeth 230
Bayley, Alex 110
Bazadona, Damian 28, 99
Bazemore, Gregory 49
Bazinet & Company 47
Bazinet, René 129
Bazzano, Elizabeth 231
Bck t th Grnd 313
Beach, David 100, 115, 118
Beach, Louise 244
Beach, Sean 38, 46, 60, 70, 94, 95, 103, 108, 117
Beacon Theatre 422
Beal, John 46, 104, 116, 216, 217
Beale, Simon Russell 208
Beamish, Jamie 221
Beamish, Kiki 213
Bean, Orson 417
Bean, Richard 72
Beane, Douglas Carter 52, 109, 124
Beard, Alec 207
Beard, Robert 96
Beardsley, Julia 142, 149, 150, 171, 172, 184, 189, 190
Beasley, Brian 112
Beat Chick 323
Beattie, Laura 44, 66
Beatty, Alison 208, 209
Beatty, John Lee 39, 42, 43, 80, 81, 91, 93, 199, 216, 227
Beatty, Katie 95
Beatty, Warren 417
Beauchamp, Jonny 195
Beaulieu, Kelly 57, 81, 94
Beautiful Soup Theater Collective, The 275
Beauty and the Beast 202
Beauty as God(dess) 294
Beauty Queen of Leenane, The 420
Beauzay, Eric 28, 142
Beaver, Terry 78, 91, 420
Bebout, Steve 84, 109, 116
Becelewski, Thomas 259

Bechtler, Hildegard 86
Beck Lee Media Blitz 124
Beck, Cassie 208, 420
Beck, Matt 29
Beck, Michelle 248
Beck, Mitchell 33, 59
Becker, Bonnie L. 78, 89
Becker, Fabrice 129
Becker, Jim 113
Becker, Leslie 47, 85
Becker, Manuel 37
Becker, Neil 150
Beckerman, Ilene 192
Beckett Theatre on Theatre Row 140, 143, 161, 166, 186, 207
Beckett, Amanda 230
Beckett, Samuel 213, 259
Beckett, Wendy 151
Beckler, Steven 109
Beckman, Jill 173
Becton, Shaylin 99
Becton, Shelton 87
Bedelia, Bonnie 418
Bedford, Brain 96
Bedlam Theatre Company 170
Beebee, Kevin 78
Beecher, Lindsay 179
Beechman, Laurie 419
Beene, Kelcie 138, 140
Beers, Sarah 177
Beers, Steve 85, 116
Beers, Sydney 35, 56, 81, 85, 96, 104, 116, 251
Bees and Lions 314
Beethoven 199
Before I Leave You 377
Beggar's Opera, The 210
Begle, Nate 192
Begole, Web 150, 182
Beguelin, Chad 112
Behlmann, John 226, 369
Behrman, David 213
Beigi, Mickey 232
Beijing Dance Theater 211
Being Shakespeare 214
Beinhaker, Alyssa 410
Beirut 274, 308
Beitzel, Robert 178
Béjanin, Claire 214
Bekerman-Greenberg, Rivka 180
Bekesi, Mishi 154
Bel Geddes, Barbara 417
Belack, Doris 464
Belafonte, Harry 417
Belasco Theatre 67, 409

Belber, Stephen 223
Belcuore, Adam 38
Belenky, Sofia Pia 248
Belgrader, Andrei 218
Belknap, Ian 176
Bell, Alec 113
Bell, Alison 234
Bell, Barbara A. 239
Bell, Book & Candle 382
Bell, Hunter 116, 132, 205, 261
Bell, Jake 74, 105, 111
Bell, Jody 40
Bell, John 220, 221, 266
Bell, Mackenzie 226, 227
Bell, Marion 417
Bell, Patrick 216
Bell, Sean 112
Bellamy, Judah 99
Bellamy, Marcus 28, 29, 115
Belleville 403
Bellin, Marion 138
Bellinger, Samuel J. 206
Belliston, Seth 160
Bello Productions 278
Bello, Sant'gria 99
Belmont, David 167
Belmonte, Jara 258
Belmonte, Pilar 234
Belopede, Robert 28
Belous, Anna Alisa 182
Belsher, Nikki 89
Belton, Nicholas 32
Belushi, Jim 91
Belvoir Street Theatre 234
Bemis, Cliff 221
Benally, Asa 140
Benati, Christy 188
Benavides, Mark 137
Bencivenga, Cathy 207
Ben-David, Adam 90
Bender, Sara 216, 220, 221
Beneath the Hush, A Whisper 323
Bengal Tiger at the Baghdad Zoo 88
Bengel, Harlan 105, 110
Benhamou, Francis 143
Beni, Thomas 210
Benim, Erin 244, 267
Benincasa, Joseph 201, 202
Bening, Annette 419
Benish, Jeff 191
Benito Cereno 292
Benjamin, Ariel 38
Benjamin, P.J. 111
Benjamin, Richard 418
Benken, David 70, 71,

72, 99, 101, 106
Benko, Tina 199
Benner, Carol 235
Bennett, Eddie 93
Bennett, Gabriel 245, 247
Bennett, Jenny 138
Bennett, Mark 74, 208, 214, 237
Bennett, Robert 49, 77
Bennett, Robert Russell 216
Bennett, Susan 94
Bennett, Tracie 20, 67, 406, 409, 410, 416
Bennion, Karl 105
Bennison, Willow 192
Bennu Productions 66
Benoit, Mariusz 178
Benoit, Patricia 417
Benoit, Steve 103
Benoît-Charbonneau, Valérie 138
BenShlomo, Etai 111
Bensinger, Chris 38, 78
Bensky, Danielle Hannah 113
Benson, Meredith 47, 62
Benson, Rob 240
Benson, Sarah 258
Benthal, John 109
Bentley, Ernest 176, 344
Benton, Jeremy 217
Benton, Rosie 49, 229
Benvenuti, Sarah 177
Benzinger, Suzy 243, 447
Beoga 219
Berardi, Dan 239
Berens, Sydney Christopher 113
Berenson, Stephen 389
Berenstain Bears Live! In Family Matters, the Musical, The 130
Berenstain, Stan & Jan 130
Beretta, Selene 139
Berg, Aaron 174
Berg, Alex 148, 151, 160
Berg, Neil 264
Bergamini, Wendi 68
Bergen, Candice 66
Bergen, Erich 201
Bergen, Polly 202
Berger, Barry 80
Berger, Dani 78
Berger, Dave 187
Berger, Glen 28
Berger, Jesse 172
Berger, Matthew roi 181
Berger, Melody Allegra

137
Berger, Michael 139
Berger, Samantha 113
Berger, Stephen 125
Bergère, Jane 73
Bergeret, Albert 235
Bergeron, Nova 111
Bergl, Emily 192
Berglund, Michael 75
Bergman, Evan 166
Bergman, Ingmar 211
Bergman, Teddy 71
Bergmann, Callan 132, 217
Bergmann, Michelle 64, 101, 109, 253
Bergson, Simon 108
Bergson, Stefany 104, 108
Bergstein, Henry Russell 77, 261
Berk, Melinda 231
Berkeley Repertory Theatre 344, 353, 357, 443
Berkeley, Beth 39, 98
Berkeley, Dinah 149
Berkley, Price 464
Berklund, Tom 84
Berkman, John 33
Berkshire Theatre Festival 353, 357
Berkun, Dianne 210
Berlin, Alec 140
Berlind, Roger 59, 72, 73, 78, 86, 90, 98
Berlind, William 78, 185
Berliner Ensemble 210
Berliner Festspiele 199
Berliner, Jay 93, 217
Berliner, Terry 428
Berlinger, Warren 417
Berlyavsky, Vera 230
Berman, Allegra 192
Berman, Ashley 89
Berman, Brooke 243
Berman, Fred 99
Berman, Julia 134, 153
Berman, Rob 216, 217
Bernagozzi, Tom 409, 410
Bernard B. Jacobs Theatre 36, 60
Bernard, Jason E. 199
Bernard, Kevin 89
Bernard, Mitchell S. 437
Bernardi, Mary 200
Bernardo, Jad 195
Bernardo, Melissa Rose 428
Bernbaum, Abby 125
Berney, Brig 36, 66, 91
Bernson, Alexandra 128

Bernstein, Adam 255
Bernstein, David 209
Bernstein, Jed 168, 446
Bernstein, Jonathan 93
Bernstein, Leslie 57
Bernstine, Quincy Tyler 192, 208
Berresse, Michael 261
Berry, Cicely 141
Berry, Dave 71
Berry, Denny 105
Berry, Gabriel 177, 237, 245, 248
Berry, Jonathan 252
Berry, Robbie 172
Berry, Sarah Uriarte 67
Berry, Stephanie 138
Berserker Residents 142
Bert, Stephen 241, 242
Bert, Valerie 226, 253
Bertels, Charissa 217
Bertelsen, Tommy 211
Bertish, Suzanne 57, 419
Bertolazzi, Sarah 221, 223, 226
Bertoluzzi, Jamie 178, 222
Bertoncin, Jarrett 233
Bertsch, Tom 50
Bertschinger, Chasper 246
Berzan, Sheila 188
Berzon, Jeff 183
Bespoke Theatricals 43, 47, 58, 68, 70, 73, 75, 89, 100
Besschetnaya, Irina 129
Besschetnaya, Kristina 129
Besschetnyy, Konstantin 129
Bessette, Mimi 47
Bessey, Sarah 223
Best Man, The 19, 66
Best of Enemies, The 355
Best of Jim Caruso's Cast Party, The 201
Best, Eve 420
Best, Ravi 87
Besterman, Doug 50, 95, 109, 226
BET Networks 74
Beth Morrison Projects 211, 212
Betito, Nicholas 167
Bette Midler's Clams on the Half Shell Revue 202
Better, Ruth 37
Bettis, Valerie 417
Bettridge, Stephen 224

Between You, Me & The Lampshade 223
Betz, Paul 235
Beugre-Tellier, Pascal 210
Bevan, Tim 89
Bevenger, Rob 32
Beverley, Trazana 419
Bevilacqua, Patrick 50, 80, 91
Bewick, Linda 75
Bexon, Pippa 44, 67
Beyer, Mark 107
Beyond the Horizon 220
Beyond Theatre Ensemble 278
Beyond Therapy 297
Beyond Words 148
BGM 47
Bhulai, Dave 220, 221
Bhutia, Lakpa 168
Biales, Lisa 259
Biales, Marc & Lisa 141, 169, 259
Bialy, Sharon 97
Bianchini, Raquel 244
Bianco, Christina 194
Biangone, Gary 33, 64
Bickley, Buist 36, 39, 45, 56, 66, 81, 91, 108, 181, 192
Bidd Group, The 154
Bieber, Brandon 33, 85, 116
Bieber, Justin 197
Biehl, Jeff 230
Bielisnki, Daniel 219
Bielsker, Jason 223
Bienskie, Stephen 132
Bienstock, Amelia 169
Biering, Jeff 116, 194
Bierko, Craig 155, 420
Bierman, Haley 262
Biesinger, Tade 89
Biesterfeldt, Chris 261
Bieundurry, Clifton 43
Big Dance Theater 212
Big Jim and the Small-Time Investors 288
Big Meal, The 242
Big Rodent 278
Big Sky Theatre Company 278, 309
Bigger, Kevin 227, 228
Biggers, Barbara 33
Biggs, Andrea 189
Bigley, Isabel 417
Biglin, Kristi 230
Bikema, Joel 246
Bilbao, Diana 262
Bill W. and Dr. Bob 397
Billeisen, Ward 85, 115
Billet, Don 115

Billings, Curtis 66
Billings, Mike 50, 78, 85
Billington, Ken 43, 58, 81, 93, 216
Billy Elliot 89, 116
Binder, Jay 78, 91, 93, 99, 125, 216
Binder, Jeff 99
Bingham, Margot 140
Bingman, Brett 92
Binion, Sandy 95
Binkley, Howell 62, 70, 87, 95, 97, 102-104, 138, 188
Binnie, Kaitlin 150
Binoche, Juliette 420
Binotto, Paul 263
Bint-Kadi, Haifa 168
Bioh, Jocelyn 145
Biosphere 211
Birch, Patricia 115
Bird, Sarah 37, 50, 103, 218, 255-257
Birds, The 377
Birdsong, Mary 420
Birdwell, Zane 140
Birkelo, Paul 178
Birl, Tanya 95, 199
Birmingham, Laurie 193
Birnbaum, Lisa 264
Birnbaum, Mary 31
Birney, David 418
Birney, Griffin 242
Birney, Reed 208, 258
Birns, Charlie 258
Birthday Boys, The 274
Bisantz, Max 209
Bischoff, Sara-Ashley 95
Bischoff, Sash 209, 230
Bishop, Adam Mark 222
Bishop, André 39, 73, 110, 224, 436
Bishop, Jessica 105
Bishop, Kelly 85
Bisker, Alex 181
Biskup, Jaclyn 248
Bisno, Debbie 32, 106
Bissinger, Rob 28, 179
Bisson, Paul 129
Bistro Awards 433
B*tch 321
Bite the Apple 304
Bithorn, Joe 107
Bittencourt, Guto 113
Bittrich, Stephen 190
Bivone, Joe 101
Bizar, Francine 102
Bizarre Noir Theatre Company 278
Bjelajac, Tijana 28
Björfors, Tilde 215
Björk 219
Björnson, Maria 105

Bjurholm, Louise 215
Black Angels Over Tuskegee 189
Black Box Theatre at the Steinberg Center 174, 252
Black Gents of Hollywood 189
Black Moon Theatre Company 278
Black n Blue Boys / Broken Men 357
Black Pearl Sings 386, 395, 403
Black, Alex 188
Black, Brent 100
Black, Christina 113
Black, Don 47
Black, Dustin Lance 113
Black, James 420
Black, Seneca 212
Blackburn, Scott A. 151
Blacketer, Jack 143, 218
Blackford, Caroline 241, 242
Blackstone, Al 111, 200
Blackwell, Allison 54, 55, 118
Blackwell, Carolyn 242
Blackwell, Dennis 184
Blackwell, Susan 114, 205, 261
Blade, Ethan 259
Blaemire, Nick 40, 254
Blagburn, Jake 177
Blaha, Joseph 52, 181, 217, 243, 244
Blaine, Jason 112
Blair, Jason 40, 87
Blair, Jim 102
Blair, Kellen 267
Blair, Randy 181
Blair, Satomi 163
Blair, Susan 102
Blaise, Kirsten 212
Blake Zidell & Associates 128, 141, 148, 151, 160, 168, 174, 258
Blake, Andrew B. 152
Blake, Leslie Hoban 424
Blake, Marsha Stephanie 256
Blake, Richard H. 111
Blakeley, Karel 182
Blanchard, Justin 260
Blanchard, Tammy 95, 420
Blanchard, Terence 74, 103
Blanchet, Ashley 102
Blanco, Andrew 78
Blanco, Jazmin 149

Blanco, Michael 254
Blanco, Nacho 149
Blanco, R. Michael 214
Bland, Katie 133
Blanding, Walter 199
Blanenbuehler, Andy 104
Blangiardo, Sonia 193
Blank, Larry 50, 92
Blank, Radha 145
Blanken, Hillary 28, 33, 40, 44, 52, 95, 103, 179
Blankenship, Paul 190
Blanks, Harvy 389
Blankson-Wood, Ato 16, 52, 124
Blanshay, Adam 50, 62, 68, 95, 98
Blast Radius 290, 315
Blatt, Michael 113
Blau, Adam 181
Blaustein, Jeremy Scott 38, 47
Blazek, Kira Rae 211
Bledel, Alexis 228
Bleezarde, Gloria 418
Blessed Unrest 278
Blessing, Liz 163, 177
Blethyn, Brenda 419
Bleu, Corbin 40, 118
Blevins, John 152
Blickenstaff, Heidi 84, 198, 205, 261
Blimline, Genson 108
Blinkwolt, Renee 172, 261
Blinn, David 68, 216, 217
Blithe Spirit 358
Bloch, Peter 128
Block, Daniel 32
Block, Michael 49
Block, Sandy 28, 33, 40, 46, 50, 52, 62, 84
Block, Stephanie J. 85, 115, 201
Blocker, Jeremy 142
Blodgett, Adam 124, 258
Blodgett, Sarah 125
Blodgette, Kristen 68, 105, 116
Blommaert, Susan 224
Blondet, Daniel 263, 264
Blood and Gifts 224
Blood Brothers Present Freaks from the Morgue, The 303
Blood Knot 255
Blood Makes the River

Flow 323
Blood/Nectar/Glitter 319
Bloody Fire...Unchaste Desire 298
Bloom, Adam 188
Bloom, Tom 242
Bloom, William 70
Blossom, Lydian 149
Blossom, Robert 464
Blow, Tei 211
Blue Balls Inc. 158
Blue Flower, The 205, 253
Blue Man Group 189
Bluebird 208
Blues for an Alabama Sky 393
Blues for Mister Charlie 301
Bluestone, Darren 188
Blum, Daniel 409, 417, 418
Blum, Mark 227, 253
Blum, Will 90
Blumberg, Kate 208
Blumberg, Sophie 262
Blume, Robert R. 424
Blumenkrantz, Jeff 437
Blumenthal Performing Arts 36
Blumenthal, Adam 174, 243
Blumenthal, Hilarie 156, 180
Blythe, Brian 263
Bo, Liu 211
Boardman, Corey 227
Boat Rocker Entertainment 171
Bob 162
Bob, Pamela 112, 132
Bobb, Dave 158
Bobb, Jeremy 214
Bobbie, Walter 42, 93, 115, 216, 226, 262
Bobby, Anne 188, 461
Bobry, Rita 258
Boccherini, Luigi 212
Bock, Jerry 116
Bockhorn, Craig 246
Bockley, Seth 247
Bococa Arts Festival, The 325
Bodall, Kristin 206, 239, 240
Boddendijk, Florentijn 232
Boddie, Courtney J. 231
Bodeen, Michael 253
Bodel, Michael 258
Bodnar, Bill 108
Bodow, Steve 247
Bodson, Maxime 210

Body Duet 294
Body Language 272
Boecker, Ben 112, 132
Boeing-Boeing 392, 401
Boffey, Mercer 133
Bog Boy 318
Bogaev, Paul 28
Bogan, Larkin 32
Bogardus, Stephen 368
Bogart, Anne 162
Bogart, Matt 97
Bogazianos, Vasili 419
Bogden, Michael 40
Boggess, Sierra 10, 31, 117, 192
Boggess, Summer 55, 117, 253, 267
Bogin, Brian 104
Bogosian, David 222
Bogue, Robert 129
Bogyo, Peter 49
Bohannon, Chris 105, 109
Bohlke, Susannah 175
Bohmer, Ron 461
Bohon, Justin 90, 420
Boka, Kate 35, 96
Bokhour, Raymond 93
Boland, Melanie 178
Boldyreva, Maria 129
Bolen, Jason 133
Bolen, Sam 217
Boles, Ariel 184
Bolet, Adela Marai 149
Bolger, David 198
Bolger, Dermot 134
Boling, Steven 181
Boll, Christopher 241, 262
Boll, Patrick 100
Bollinger, Lee C. 430
Bolli-Thompson, Jordan 198
Bolman, Scott 212, 263
Bologna, Joe 107
Bolt, Sarah 109
Bolton, Guy 78, 85
Bomba, Paul 308
Bomer, Matt 114
Bonan, Marc 80
Bonanni, Caroline 242
Bonanni, Carolyn 241, 242, 255, 261
Bonati, Gina 137
Bond, Clint, Jr. 44
Bond, Justin Vivian 187
Bond, Will 162
Bonde, Mick 158
Bonder, Kyle 36-38, 46, 54, 66
Bonds, D.B. 115
Bondurant, Madelaine 179

Boneau, Chris 31, 37, 42, 49, 57, 59, 78, 80, 82, 90, 94, 98, 103, 113, 185, 208, 227, 255
Boneau/Bryan-Brown 31, 33, 35, 37, 42-44, 46, 49, 56-60, 72, 78, 80-82, 85, 86, 90, 94, 96-98, 100, 103, 104, 106, 113, 115-118, 136, 185, 196, 202, 208, 227, 251, 255, 410
Bonenberger, Cole 247
Bonewits, Lucas 232
Bonino, Ally 164
Bonnell, Wilburn 64, 185, 243, 259
Bonner, Ellen 219
Bonnerna, Benjamin M. 247
Bonnevier, Anna 215
Bonney, Jo 230
Bonnie & Clyde 14, 27, 47, 407, 409
Bonnie Franklin Living Trust 410
Bonny, Francis 105
Bono and The Edge 28
Bontrager, Laura 33
Bonvissuto, Bruce 93, 216, 217
Booher, Kendall 185, 409, 410
Book Club Play, The 354
Book of Everything, The 234
Book of Mormon, The 90, 118, 200, 202
Bookman, Kirk 129, 221, 264
Boomerang Theatre Company 278
Boomers, the Musical of a Generation 318
Boon, Paul 43
Boonstra, Titus 232
Booth Theatre 39
Booth, Geoffrey 258
Booth, Steven 254
Booth, Susan 447
Booth, Terence 158
Booth, Timothy 100
Boothe, Cherise 203, 241, 262
Boras, Annika 260
Borden, Meredith 235
Borders, Carmen Shavone 102
Boren, Katie 52, 119, 124
Borenstein, Joshua 247

Borg, Chirstopher Michael 109
Borg, Chris 248, 444
Borger, Diane 236
Borges, Desmin 421
Borghi, Pablo 234
Borisjuk, Nick 104, 241
Boritt, Beowulf 108, 146, 181, 222, 253
Borle, Christian 71, 429
Born Yesterday 91
Bornstein, David 75
Boronson, Andy 247
Borovay, Zachary 68, 108
Borowitz, Katherine 37
Borowski, Michael S. 40, 45, 84, 105, 241, 410
Borrowed Prey 281
Borrowers, The 399
Borsak, Marc 28
Borstelmann, Jim 46, 84
Borth, Michael 125, 267
Bortolussi, Sophie 196
Borton, Michael 130
Bortright, Bart 253
Borts, Joanne 60
Bortz, Jerad 111
Borys, Renée 82, 86
Bosch, Michelle 97, 198
Bosche, Freddy 191
Bose, Nilanjana 185
Boskind, Paul 50, 66, 104, 106
Bossert, Cameron 37
Bossy, Michelle 243
Bostedt, Alli 231
Bostic, Kathryn 88
Boston Properties 187
Boston Theater Critics Association 436
Boston, Gretha 420
Boston, Matthew 167
Bostwick, Barry 115, 450
Boswell, Felicia 102
Botanica 272
Botchan, Rachel 239, 240
Botchis, Paul 196
Botez-Ban, Oana 141, 143, 212, 218, 219, 248, 250
Botosan, Geoff 409, 410
Botosan, Mary K. 409, 416
Bottomley, Courtney 70
Boucher, Céline 138
Boudreau, John 206
Boulay, Steve 107
Bound 316
Bound East for Cardiff

168
Bourgeois, Paul 171, 172, 184
Bouril, Curt 136, 228
Bourne, Eric 217
Bourne, Matthew 101
Bourne, Miki 131
Bourne, Simon 214
Bouthillier, Donna 168
Boutin, Lucas 138
Bouvy, Harry 132
Bove, Karen 82
Bowcutt, Jason 444
Bowdan, Jack 78, 125, 216
Bowen, Chris 189
Bowen, Dirsten 255
Bowen, Graham 90
Bowen, Grant 208
Bowen, Jared 436
Bowen, Jeff 205, 261
Bowen, Kirsten 255, 256
Bowen, Trevor 247
Bower Group, The 279
Bowers, Bill 148
Bowers, Danya 112
Bowers, Megan 72
Bowers, Meghan 106
Bowery Wars Part 2, The 285
Bowling, Suzanna 424
Bowlmor Lanes 410
Bowman, Caroline 111
Bowman, Grady McLeod 254
Bowman, Judy 164, 223, 249
Bowness, Tim 159
Boxer's Son, The 319
Boy Gets Girl 291
Boyce, Andrew 131, 208
Boyd, Carolyn Rae 196
Boyd, Corky 38 ,54, 66
Boyd, D'Ambrose 90
Boyd, David 193
Boyd, Frank 236, 247
Boyd, Jake 226, 227
Boyd, Jason 128
Boyd, Julianne 191
Boyd, Michael 197
Boyd, Patrick 115
Boyd, Sean 159
Boyer, Karen 250
Boyer, Steven 121, 150, 217, 258
Boyes, Adrian 248
Boyett, Bob 39, 72, 110, 243
Boykin, Keith 413
Boykin, Phillip 54, 406, 409, 411
Boykins, David 189
Boyle, Danielle 33,

38, 54
Boyle, Loraine 92, 102
Boyle, Rob 253
Boyle, Shawn 116
Boyle, Valerie 101
Boys Next Door, The 401
Bracchitta, Jim 94
Bracco, Carly 159, 160
Bracco, Tommy 64, 115
Brace Yourself 358
Bracke, Siobhan 215
Bracken, Fred 196
Bradbury, Colin 183
Bradbury, Peter 140, 179
Braden, Miche 127, 128
Bradfield, Fran 220
Bradfield, Thomas 113
Bradford, Bryan 64
Bradford, Josh 125, 179, 222
Bradford, Melanie 235
Bradford, Tommy 160
Bradley, Alexandria "Brinae Ali" 199
Bradley, Brad 89, 104, 172
Bradley, Corey 32
Bradley, Eric Jackson 196
Bradley, Everett 199, 420
Bradley, Jerry 206
Bradley, Pam 101
Bradley, Paul 223, 236
Bradley, Sara Cox 90, 96, 252, 253
Bradley, Scott 146
Bradley, Will 221
Bradshaw, Jared 97, 462
Bradshaw, Natalie 100, 109
Bradshaw, Thomas 230
Brady, Barbara 417
Brady, John E. 64
Brady, Mo 84, 113
Brady, Patrick Scott 264
Brady-Dalton, Abbie 40
Brae, Karli 138
Bragg, Pete 35, 226
Brain, Devin 248
BrainExplode! 316
BrainSpunk Theater 279
Brake, Brian 43
Bramhall, Kristina 40
Brancato, Joe 127, 162, 184
Brandeberry, Jim 102
Brandenburg, Hans-Jörn 210
Brandford, Jay 78, 89
Brandhagen, Clinton 31

Brandhoff, Ulrich 210
Brando, Marlon 417
Bransford, Patricia 74
Bransford, Thomas 74
Bransgrove, Laurence Austin 230, 243, 244
Branson, Tilly 159
Brattke, Konrad 409, 410
Bratton, Steve 113
Brauer, Jenna 93
Braun, Betsy 192
Braun, Michael 110, 254
Braun, Nancy Renée 130, 181
Brauner, Laura 245
Braunstein, Adam 94, 198
Braunstein, Alan 410
Brave Ducks 298
Braverman, Douglas 202
Braverman, Lindsay 99
Bravo, Amy Elizabeth 135
Brawner, Kenny 179, 248
Bray, Bob 118
Brazil! Brazil 232
Brea, Gonzalo 28
Breaker, Daniel 420
Breakfast 292
Brecht, Bertolt 210, 218
Breckenridge, Rob 229
Breen, Patrick 104, 226, 352
Breglio, John 52
Brenda Angiel Aerial Dance Company 234
Brendle, Travis 226
Brenman, Stephen 156, 168
Brenman, Steven 180
Brenn, Kyle 83
Brennan, Beverly 64
Brennan, Deirdre 220
Brennan, Eileen 417
Brennan, Maureen 418
Brennan, Nick 130
Brennan, Nora 89, 153
Brenneman, Amy 242, 268
Brenner, Anna 213
Brenner, Rob 77
Brescia, Kenny 181
Brescia, Lisa 100, 118
Breshnahan, Alyssa 110
Breslin, Mark 174
Breslin, Ryan 64
Bress, Rachel 104, 168
Bretschneider, Claire 217
Brett, Tom 99
Brettle, Jessica 176

Brew of the Dead II: Oktoberflesh 286
Brewer, Carrie 218
Brewer, Lute 110
Brewer, Nathan 37
Brewster, Kaliswa 176
Brewster, Paul 251
Brians, Sara 89, 116, 217
Brice, Richard 83, 216
Bricendo, Lucrecia 141
Brick Theater, The 279
Brickman, Marshall 84, 97, 436
Bridge Project, The 214
Bridge Theatre Company, The 280
Bridge, Andrew 105
Bridgeford, Nicole 148
Bridgeman, Lukas 236, 237
Bridges, Beau 95
Bridgewater, Nicole 93
Brier, Ali 89
Brière, Daniel 161
Brierley, Tim 159
Brierpatch Productions 124, 147, 158
Brigden, Tracy 244
Briggs, Cassidy 90
Briggs, Christy 130, 171, 262
Brigstocke, Colin 112, 117
Brill, Corey 66, 88, 388
Brill, Robert 62
Brill, Will 169
Brilliant Traces 322
Brimmer, J. David 57, 91, 209, 250, 256
Bring It On: The Musical 362
Brinker, Jen 222
Brinker, Mara 211
Brinkley, Christie 93
Brinkman, Baba 128, 157
Brinkman, Erik 157
Brinks, Alan 222
Briskman, Julie 344
Bristol Riverside Theater 231, 358
Brits Off Broadway 154-160
Britten, Benjamin 184
Britten, Matt 410
Broad, Katie 139, 149
Broadhurst Theatre 43, 74, 87
Broadway Across America 36, 40, 47, 50, 52, 54, 62, 72, 82, 93, 95, 98, 102, 103,

106, 136
Broadway Asia International 232
Broadway Backwards 7 117
Broadway Bares XXI: Masterpiece 112
Broadway Barks 13 198
Broadway Bears XV 202
Broadway Beauty Pageant 202
Broadway Booking Office NYC 32
Broadway Cares/Equity Fights AIDS 112, 114-118, 198-200, 202
Broadway Consortium, The 38, 47, 54, 66
Broadway Fantasy Camp 410
Broadway Flea Market and Grand Auction 114
Broadway Impact 113
Broadway League 422
Broadway Records 47, 52
Broadway Theatre 109
Broadway.com Audience Choice Awards 433
Broadway's Best Shows 38, 47, 54
Brobert, Sara 215
Broccoli, Barbara 60
Brochu, Jim 117, 121, 158
Brock, Chase 28, 253
Brock, Giselle Lorenz 113
Brockman, Jane 116
Broderick, Jack 89
Broderick, Matthew 78, 419
Brodie, Daniel 38, 54, 70, 108, 145, 216
Brody, Benjamin 112
Brody, Noah 141
Broecker-Penn, Candace 169, 409
Broer, Julia 86, 108, 230, 262
Brogan, Rod 220
Brohn, Maggie 43, 47, 58, 68, 70, 73, 75, 100
Brohn, William David 54, 101, 111
Brokaw, Mark 77, 243, 261
Broke 349
Broken Chord 209, 233
Broken Glass Theatre 280
Broken Heart, The 260
Broke-Ology 368, 380

Bromelmeier, Martha 43, 82, 92
Bronfman, Stephen 28
Brontë, Emily 232
Brook, Peter 259
Brook, Susanne 108
Brookes, Jacqueline 410, 417
Brooklyn Academy of Music 204, 210
Brooklyn Babylon 212
Brooklyn Underground 274
Brooklyn Youth Chorus 210
Brooks Atkinson Theatre 37, 71, 107
Brooks, Bill 112
Brooks, Braxton 199
Brooks, Eric 242, 261
Brooks, Hal 126, 239, 254
Brooks, Jeff 259
Brooks, Martin 417
Brooks, Suzy 234
Brooksher, Rebecca 248
Brookshire, Janie 221
Broom, David 207
Broomell, Kevin 28, 95, 103
Brophy, Sara 152
Brosnan, Deane 262
Brosnan, Justen 106
Brotebeck, Stephen 75
Brothers of the Dust 431
Brothers Size, The 389, 401
Brothers, Julia 37
Brotherston, Lez 109
Broughton, Christopher 199
Brouillard, Jason 47, 87
Brouk, Tricia 164
Brouwer, Alex 145
Brouwer, Peter 206
Broward Center for the Performing Arts 433
Brown, Ashely 101
Brown, Avril 99
Brown, Brandon 186
Brown, Brantley 410
Brown, Brennan 217
Brown, Caitlin 185
Brown, Camille A. 127
Brown, Camille M. 99, 116
Brown, Campbell 114
Brown, Charl 109, 116
Brown, Dale 43, 62, 75
Brown, Dave 163
Brown, David Brian 33, 59, 86, 93, 109
Brown, David S. 39,

110, 224
Brown, Dean 447
Brown, Deborah 141, 219, 259, 260
Brown, Debra 129
Brown, Devon 249
Brown, Eddie R., III 248
Brown, Elijah 129
Brown, Elliot H. 436
Brown, Emmanuel 28, 115
Brown, Heidi 78, 103
Brown, Howie 147
Brown, James, III 75, 106
Brown, Jeb 28, 29
Brown, Jessica Leigh 28, 29
Brown, Jocelyn 172
Brown, Kate 156, 166
Brown, Ken 75
Brown, Kristel J. 102
Brown, Krystal Joy 83
Brown, Kyle 106, 217
Brown, Larry W. 28
Brown, Lauren 175
Brown, Leon Addison 255
Brown, Luqman 145, 256
Brown, Matt 162
Brown, Meredith 155
Brown, Nate 101
Brown, Oni 125
Brown, Patrick R. 99
Brown, Rachel 244
Brown, Robin Leslie 239
Brown, Rome 157
Brown, Ronald K. 54
Brown, Scott 428
Brown, Shane Marshall 67
Brown, Shereen 167
Brown, Stephen 150, 182
Brown, Tim 43, 179
Brown, Timothy 146, 256
Brown, Vanessa 47, 64, 115
Brownell, Julia 225
Browning, Diana 140
Browning, Susan 418
Brown-Orleans, James 99
Brown-Sanders, Sylvia 410
Brownsville Bred 133
Broyhill, Summer 113
Brubaker, Jason 112, 220, 221
Bruce, Andrew 100
Bruce, Christy 44

Bruce, Jeff 136, 183
Bruck, Therese 143
Bruckmann-Hiller, Christiane 212
Bruder, Nicholas 196
Brunell, Catherine 101
Brummer, Alison 184
Brunell, Catherine 101
Bruner, Logan Riley 222
Bruni, Marc 78, 85, 185, 216
Brunish, Corey 47, 54, 71
Bruno, Louis 67
Bruns, Phil 465
Brusoski, Pamela 112, 220, 221
Brustein, Robert 259
Brustein, Steve 189
Bryan, David 102
Bryan, Kevin 50
Bryan-Brown, Adrian 33, 35, 43, 44, 46, 56, 58, 60, 62, 72, 81, 85, 86, 96, 103, 104, 106, 116, 410
Bryant, Dean 106
Bryant, John 139
Bryant, Khail Toy 99
Bryant, Kimilee 105
Bryars, Gavin 213
Bryce, Edward 417
Bryce, Karen 177
Bryceland, Yvonne 419
Bryden, Ben 176
Brydon, Angela C. 102
Bryggman, Larry 208
Brzoza, Katarzyna 212
Bubble & Squeak 307
Buccellato, Krista 159
Bucchino, John 201
Buccino, Danielle 156, 166, 182, 236
Buch, René 149
Buchanan, Brian 100
Buchanan, Georgianna 233
Buchanan, Keith 62, 87
Buchanan, Meghan 252, 260
Buchanan, Michael 84, 143, 144, 181
Buchegger, Christopher 246
Buchman, Allan 130, 159, 165, 174, 177
Bu in, Dejan 210
Buck, Allison 163
Buck, Sammy 322, 324
Buckeridge, Corin 86
Buckhantz, Diana 82, 155
Buckley, Betty 117, 202
Buckley, Connor 178

Buckley, Erick 84
Buckley, Lisa 60, 75, 236
Buckley, Melissa 58
Buckley, Michael 106
Buckley, Patricia 182
Buckroyd, Daniel 159
Buczek, Holly 195
Buddeke, Kate 250
Buddha 294
Buddha-Cowboy Productions 125
Buell, Bill 250
Buether, Miriam 185, 245
Buffrey, Catherine 213
Built for Collapse 280
Bujak, Amanda 87, 165
Bulfant, Joyce 418
Bull Moose Party 280
Bullard, Brian 87
Bullard, David 36, 223, 253
Bullard, Janie 57, 70, 131, 163, 182, 208, 227, 243, 249, 250, 257, 258
Bullard, Walter 78
Bulleit, Hallie 191
Bullington, Preesa Adeline 240
Bullock, Jennifer 52
Bullock, Larry 113
Bullock, R. Keith 118
Bullock, Sarah 253, 254
Bully, The 322
Bulos, Yusef 205, 251
Bunham, Charlie 141
Bunny 154
Bunny Lake Is Missing 279
Buntrock, Stephen R. 217
Buran Theatre Company 280
Burcham, Susan 112
Burchill, Geahk 233
Burden, Suzanne 214
Burger-Brujis, Ulrike 109
Burgess, Jessica 131
Burgess, Titus 118
Burial at Thebes, The 344, 376
Burk, Richard 128
Burkart, Dana 28, 62
Burke, Cáitlín 235
Burke, Ed 78
Burke, Geoff 50
Burke, Mary Kate 195
Burke, Marylouise 192, 243

Burke, Rowena 213
Burke, William 258
Burkhardt, Steel 32, 187, 198
Burkland, John 137, 151
Burkle, Jess 147
Burks, D. Schuyler 156, 253
Burks, Donny 418
Burlak, John 154
Burlesque Blitz 292
Burlingame, Lloyd 447
Burmese Days 156
Burnell, Holly 242, 249, 250
Burnell, Peter 419
Burnett, Carol 417
Burney, Christopher 253
Burning 230
Burns, Andréa 202
Burns, Andy 233
Burns, Angie 214
Burns, Catherine 418
Burns, Craig 40
Burns, Heather 257
Burns, Jackie 111
Burns, Joshua 95
Burns, Ralph 93
Burns, Shana 96
Burnt Umber 88, 141, 169, 259
Burrell, Pamela 418
Burridge, Bud 84
Burrows, Abe 95
Burrows, Julia 112
Burse, Denise 419
Burstein, Danny 33, 114, 115, 202
Burstyn, Ellen 223
Burt, Elaine 32
Burthwright, Karen 62
Burtney, Jacqueline 62
Burton, Adam 197
Burton, Arnie 71
Burton, Deb 189
Burton, Kate 419
Burton, Richard 417
Burton, Ronn 125, 152
Burton, Will 75
Burtzos, Alex 207
Burward-Hoy, Kenneth 33
Burwell, Carter 212
Busackino, Barbara 145
Busby, Barry 162
Busch, Charles 114, 117, 243
Buscher, Joshua 106, 113
Busetti, Luana 218
Bush, Eli 59, 90
Bush, Kate 219
Bush, Kristen 252

Bush, Lee C. 222
Bush, Maren 360
Bush, Michael 165
Bush, Nancy 195
Bushmann, Kate 206
Bushwick Starr 281
Bussert, Meg 419
Busted 223
Bustin, Colle 75
Bustos, Brian J. 106
Butcher, Veracity 149
Butchko, Donald Peter 124, 142
Butke, Sarah 155, 185, 265, 266
Butkus, Denis 249, 250, 260
Butler, Ari 166
Butler, Artie 104
Butler, Ben 29
Butler, Dan 117, 243
Butler, Holly Ann 95
Butler, Isaac 212
Butler, John 108
Butler, Kerry 66, 92, 198
Butler, Kimberly 66, 116
Butler, Maeve Fiona 66, 109
Butler, Oliver 142
Buttacavoli, Ronald 32
Buttchereit, Heinrich 210
Butterworth, Jez 98
Buttram, Jan 206, 428
Butts, Cynthia 127
Butz, Norbert Leo 92, 198, 253, 429
Buxbaum, Lisa 45
Buzik, Zachary 181
By the Dawn's Early Light 274
Bydwell, Charlotte 163
Bye, Ellie 242, 247
Byk, Jim 59, 90, 98, 410
Bykovsky, Alexander 215
Byrd, Byan 146
Byrd, Daniel 113
Byrd, Stephen C. 74
Byrd, Thomas Jefferson 420
Byrd-Marrow, David 153, 216
Byrne, Beth 214
Byrne, Erin 91
Byrne, Gabriel 159, 420
Byrne, Terry 428, 436
Byun, Jae Hee 130, 159
Bzymek, Zbigniew 168

C

C.I.C.T/Théâtre des Bouffes du Nord 259

Cabaret 361, 375
Cabell, Hannah 250, 268
Cabnet, Evan 225, 254, 261
Cabral, Stephen 447
Cabrera, Leanne 238
Cabuag, Arcell 54
Caccamise, Craig 46
Caccavo, Nicholas 251, 252
Caccioppoli, Evan 249
Caddell, Dewey 112, 221
Caddick, David 101, 105, 422
Cady, Scott 93
Café Pacific Records 194
Cafero, Chris 189
Caffrey, Roisin 214
Cage, John 213
Caggiano, Keith 28, 50, 108
Cahan, Cora 231
Cahill, Eddie 250, 268
Cahill, Edwin 220
Cahn, Sam J. 102, 113
Cahn, Sammy 418
Cahn, Victor L. 143
Cahoon, Kevin 253
Cai, Congcong 232
Cain, Holly 154, 232
Cain, Marie 175, 194
Cain, Scotty 52, 68, 92
Cain, Stephen 259
Cain, Tim 182
Caine, Neal 50, 95
Caiola, Luigi 40, 155
Caiola, Rose 40, 130, 154
Cairns, Tom 214
Cake 219
Cake Productions 281
Cake, Jonathan 420
Cal Performances 199
Calabretta, Giovanna 82, 85, 92, 153
Calahan, Kathy 101
Calamity Jane Battles the Horrible Hoopsnakes 297
Calderazzo, Diana 28
Calderon, Victoria E. 129
Caldwell, Adam 37, 185, 52
Caldwell, Courtney F. 259
Caldwell, Jaron 28, 202, 226
Caldwell, Zoe 258, 418
Cale, David 248

Calhoun, Jeff 47, 64, 115, 134
Cali, Brian 31
California Shakespeare Theater 358
Call Me Waldo 167
Call of Cthulhu, The 311
Callaghan, Edward 171
Callahan, Bill 417
Callahan, Tom 38, 50, 54
Callaway, Ann Hampton 420
Calleri Casting 144, 222, 249
Calleri, James 42, 191, 218
Callous Cad 321
Callow, Simon 214, 420
Calloway, J. Bernard 102, 389
Calveri, Joey 108
Calvert, Danny 112, 113
Calvo, Juan 410
Calvo, Lian Calvo 213
Camara, Mamadyba 199
Cambell Young Associates 72
Camelot 112
Camera, Frank 152
Cameron, Ian 231
Cameron, Shannon 74
Camille, Amima 125
Camino Real 374
Camisade Theatre Company 281
Camoletti, Marc 81
Camp, Bill 59
Camp, Joanne 419
Camp, Molly 228
Campana, Ashley 189
Campbell Young Associates 28, 44, 75
Campbell, Amelia 74, 162
Campbell, Cate Scott 388
Campbell, David 28
Campbell, Erma 419
Campbell, Jeff 100, 118
Campbell, Mark 265
Campbell, Mary-Mitchell 84, 117, 118, 226, 227, 244
Campbell, Rob 248
Campbell, Robin 43, 217
Campbell, Roy 238
Campbell, Ta'Rae 83, 90
Campbell, Wiliam I. 210
Campey, Daisy 75
Campion, Kieran 252
Campion, Seán 420

Campisi, Tony 224
Campo, Helen 111
Campo, John 111
Campos, Jennifer 243, 244
Camus, Alex 226, 227
Camuzeaux, Jonathan 219
Canada, Ron 182
Canady, Darren 431
Canal Park Playhouse 281
Canale, Tymberly 212, 260
Canaries Sometimes Sing 207
Canavan, Elizabeth 223
Candela, Claire 236
Candela, Peter 118
Candide 368, 377
Candler, Cristy 93, 111
Cane, Jim 95
Cañez, Teddy 209
Canfield, Tiffany Little 40
Canfora, Jack 166
Canidy, Maria 189
Canino, Frank 32
Cannavale, Bobby 103, 114, 198, 223
Cannery Row 216
Canning, Hunter 110
Canning, James 115
Cannon, Mike 76, 84
Cannon, Reuben 49
Cannon, William 224
Cano, Xavier 140
Cantalupo, Joe 148, 177, 185, 226
Canterbury Tales Remixed, The 157
Cantler, Will 40, 66, 74, 226, 255
Cantone, Mario 117, 197, 202, 428
Cantor, Carolyn 228, 446
Canuel, Angie 43
Canuso, Joe 147
Canyon 212
Cao, Andrew 85
CAP21 Theatre Company 281
CAPA 215
Caparelliotis, David 45, 49, 80, 142, 227, 253
Capatasto, Nicole 87, 95, 138
Capie, John 124
Capitalist Ventriloquist, The 319
Caplan, Howard 47
Caplan, Jamie 50

Caplan, Matt 28, 29
Caplan, Megan 208, 219, 259, 260
Caplow, Jane 40
Capo, John 189, 190, 194, 195
Capone, Carla 112
Capone, Steven 168
Caporello, Corradina 31
Cappelli-King, Maximilian 151
Capri, Mark 419
Caprio, Jennifer 174, 202
Caps Lock Theatre 281
Captain Ferfuson's School For Balloon Warfare 304
Captors 377
Car Plays: San Diego, The 381
Carato, Rick 44, 68, 86
Carbone, Kimberly 146
Carbone, Kristin 101
Carbonell Awards 433
Carbonell, Albert 171
Carboni, Monique 223
Carcione, Chris 251
Carden, William 150, 182
Cardona, Christopher 29
Cardona, Ed, Jr. 183
Cardwell, Steven 59, 90
Career 290
Carena, Elizabeth 259
Caretaker, The 215
Carew, Connor 240
Carey, Heather 57
Carey, Helen 420
Carey, Kelly 146
Cargnegie-Brown, Bruce 75
Cariot, James 106
Cariou, Heather A. 410
Cariou, Len 117, 410, 418, 453
Carl, Polly 447
Carlile, Adrienne 177, 221
Carlin, Frances S. 410
Carlin, Paul 229
Carlin, Tony 38, 66
Carlotto, Rafe 44
Carlsen, Michael 249
Carlson, Caleb 176
Carlson, Elizabeth 256
Carlson, Jeffrey 165
Carlson, Sandra 97
Carlson, Trevor 213
Carlucci, Jonathan 192
Carluzzo, Phil 138
Carlyle, Curtis 233
Carlyle, Warren 33,

43, 199
Carlyon, Daniel 254
Carman, Dale 35, 56, 81, 96
Carmané 213
Carmargo, Tania 258
Carmeli, Audrey 218
Carmello, Carolee 109
Carmichael, Patrick 253
Carmody, Brian 60
Carnagie Hill Productions 125
Carnahan, Jim 35, 36, 50, 56, 60, 71, 81, 85, 86, 96, 98, 104, 116, 236, 251
Carnahan, Michael 71, 96
Carney, Adrianne 248
Carney, Jeffrey 85
Carney, John 60, 236
Carney, Liam 198
Carney, Reeve 28, 198
Carney, Sean 84, 116, 184, 254
Carney, Zane 29
Carol Ostrow Productions 410
Carol Tambor Theatrical Foundation 161
Carolan, Kevin 64
Carolan, Marshal Kennedy 32
Caroline, or Change 401
Carpenter, Anthony 152
Carpenter, Dean A. 253
Carpenter, Karen 192, 265
Carpenter, Kim 234
Carpio, T.V. 28
Carr, Allyson 100, 113
Carr, Amy 179
Carr, Bret 158
Carr, David 197
Carr, Geneva 150
Carr, Jonathan 168
Carr, Sharon A. 49
Carr, Wayne T. 239
Carradine, David 418
Carrasco, Stephen 76, 89
Carricart, Robertson 229
Carrie 204, 226
Carrie Ahern Dance 281
Carrière, Berthold 96
Carrington, Gemma 75
Carroll, Alexa 174
Carroll, Alice 220, 221
Carroll, Barbara 39, 110, 224, 410
Carroll, Bridie 181
Carroll, Jade King 74
Carroll, John 33

Carroll, Lisa 132
Carroll, Nicole 263, 264
Carroll, Orit Jacoby 187, 244, 245
Carroll, Patrick 248
Carroll, Peter 234
Carroll, Rocky 419
Carroll, Shana 137, 138
Carrow, Dylan 127, 156, 241, 242
Carrubba, Philip 36, 243, 263
Carsch, Ruth 46
Carsella, Meghan 106
Carson, Anne 212
Carson, Brian T. 192
Carson, Jean 417
Cart Before Horse Productions 271, 281
Cartell, Nick 62, 63
Carter, Aaron 190
Carter, Andrew "Dr. Ew" 199
Carter, Clint 152
Carter, David 138
Carter, Dixie 419
Carter, Jodi Schoenbrun 147, 192
Carter, Jon 224, 250
Carter, Julius C. 29
Carter, Kim 138
Carter, Lauren Ashley 147
Carter, Megan E. 262
Carter, Nell 419
Carter, Rachel 206
Carter, Ralph 418
Carter, Shelley 250
Carter-Parke Productions 190
Cartmell, Selina 260
Carton, John 54
Carton, Rebecca 409
Cartwright, Mark 154
Carty, Orlagh 219
Carusi, Susan 78
Caruso, Anne 91
Caruso, Eileen 193
Caruso, Jim 114, 201
Caruso, Thomas 75
Caruso, Vincent 91
Caruthers, Cliff 176
Carvajal, Celina 146
Carver, Brent 419
Casale, Glenn 159
Case, Daniel 191
Case, Shannon 140, 192
Casella, Carl 37, 87, 128, 132, 135, 143, 150, 164, 179
Casella, Martin 143
Casella, Max 223, 420
Casey, Mary 38

Casey, Peter 198
Cash, Aya 208
Cash, Johnny 103, 136
Cashman, Josephine 340
Caskey, Kristin 137
Caskey, Marilyn 105
Casl, Karyn 40
Casnoff, Philip 419
Caspersen, Dana 211
Cass, Katie 113
Cass, Peggy 417
Cassara, Michael 143, 157, 179, 181, 183, 201
Cassavalle, Quinn 133
Cassel, Anna 138
Casserly, Sean 112
Casserly, Tom 71
Cassidy, Joe 92
Cassidy, Orlagh 203, 220
Cassiopée 129
Cassius, Mark 62, 63
Castaldo, Eric 50, 82
Castañeda, Jaime 208, 209
Castanheira, Maria Joao 213
Castelli, Carol 179
Castelli, Ralph 107
Castellino, Bill 263
Caster, Jennifer 141
Castillo Theatre 152, 167, 281, 445
Castillo, Raúl 223
Castle Talent Inc. 191
Castle, Andrew 187
Castle, Gene 172, 190
Castle, Matt 112, 265, 267
Castner, Fred 90
Castot, Ljuba 164
Castree, Paul 162
Castro, Bernadette 189
Castro, Camilo 192
Castro, Eduardo 64
Castro, Ilia 191
Castro, Lou 64
Caswell, Jeff 101
Caswell, Mark Richard 78, 161
Cat Lady Without a Cat 290, 315
Cat on a Hot Tin Roof 376
Cat on My Head Productions 281
Catanese, Charlie 39
Catanzaro, Lois 246, 247, 263-265
Catch Me If You Can 92
Catenaccio, Claire 237

Cates, Adam 85
Cates, Gilbert 465
Catherine Wheels Theatre Company 231
Cathey, Reg E. 248
Cats 202
Cats Paying Dues Company 201
Cattaneo, Anne 39, 110, 224
Catti, Christine 177
Cattrall, Kim 9, 44, 115, 219
Caudwell, John 62, 82
Caughell, Caitlyn 64
Caulfield, Maxwell 419
Cause Célèbre 135, 137, 186
Caussa, Nina 255
Cavaliere, Virginia 135
Cavanaugh, Kristy 113
Cavanaugh, Maureen 112, 219
Cavari, Jack 50
Cavari, Perry 82, 83
Cavett, Wendy Bobbitt 146
Caza-Cleypool, Damian 90
CD Baby 194
Cearcy, Darlesia 90
Cecchini, Lisa 99
Cecchini, Michael 246, 247
Cefala, Anthony 113
Celada, Valentina 81
Celebration 345
Celebrity Autobiography: Gay Pride Edition 197
Celebrity Charades 223
Cell Theatre, The 282
Cella, Eileen 231
Cendese, Alexander 165
Cenote 300
Centalonza, Richard 93
Centeno, Francisco 63, 87
Center Theatre Group 73, 82, 88, 359, 360
CENTERSTAGE 359
Central Park 313
CEO Theatre 282
Cerato, Richard 46
Cerceo, Susan 72
Cercone, Janus 82
Cermak, Alyson 143, 256
Cernadas, Elisabeth 235
Cerniglia, Ken 71
Cerruti, David 112
Cerullo, John 410
Cervejeira, Luamar 220
Cerveris, Michael 68,

409, 413, 419
Cesa Entertainment 146
Cesa, Jamie 131, 194
Ceustermans, Nele 232
Chacon, Jorge 248
Chadwick, Suzanne 184
Chaifetz, Jill 75
Chaifetz, Richard 75
Chaikelson, Steven 250, 258
Chaikovsky, Petr 215
Chakartash, Enver 168
Chalcraft, Miles 246
Chalfant, Andromache 226, 237, 250, 254
Chalfant, Kathleen 222, 422, 429
Chalk Circle, The 320, 324
Chalk, Chris 421
Chamberlain, Cliff 388
Chambers, Jess 231
Chambers, Lindsay Nicole 52, 119, 124, 162
Chambers, Lucy 231
Chamblin, Richard 142
Champa, Russell H. 241
Champlin, Donna Lynne 155, 266
Chandler, Adam 113
Chandler, Andrew T. 157
Chandler, Zac 84, 112, 117, 263
Chang, Ching-I 196
Chang, Gi Young 198
Chang, Ji-Youn 144, 238
Chang, Tisa 238, 419
Changchien, Louis Ozawa 144, 254
Chang-Ning, Chou 211
Chanler-Berat, Adam 21, 71, 118, 140
Channeling Kevin Spacey 189
Channing, Carol 115, 417, 421
Channing, Stockard 39, 118, 429
Channon, Steve 36, 102, 185, 249
Chanukah Charol, A 200
Chao, Caroline 28, 54, 67, 86, 103, 224, 253
Chao, Wang 211
Chapin, Anika 33, 183
Chapin, Chloe 80
Chapin, Ted 422, 436
Chaplin, Sydney 417
Chapman, Daniel B. 176
Chapman, David 247
Chapman, Ed 73

Chapman, Emma 154
Chapman, Kate 101
Chapman, Linda S. 236
Chapman, Ray 176
Chapman, Samantha 190
Chappel, Tim 106
Chappell, Kandis 388
Chappelle, Andrew 100, 113, 202
Chappelle, Keith Eric 248
Charisse, Zan 419
Charity Case, A 151
Charlap, Moose 159
Charlebois, Catherine 111
Charles, Josh 223
Charles, Marilyn 127
Charles, Melanie 249
Charles, Walter 85
Charley's Aunt 376
Charlier, Cybil 249
Charlotte Wilcox Company, The 40, 50, 92
Charlotte, Susan 135, 137, 186
Charlotte's Web 351
Charlston, Erik 95
Charlton, Amanda 131
Charman, Matt 228
Charpentier, Erica 213
Charrat, Martin 187
Chase, Brian 149
Chase, Crystal 46, 50
Chase, David 68, 78, 85, 89, 95, 112
Chase, Jenna 226
Chase, Laurelyn Watson 235
Chase, Myles 100
Chase, Noah 137
Chase, Will 89, 216
Chasin, Lisa 82
Chasman-Beck, Coby 59
Chassé, Isabelle 137, 138
Chatfield, Ross 214
Chau, Ada 238
Chau, Paul 95
Chaucer 157
Chauncey, Xander 128
Chauspeciale/Astrachan & Jupin 50
Chaves, Richard 419
Chavez, Gena 232
Chavkin, Rachel 218
Chayes, Jess 253
Chazaro, Steve 28, 91
Cheadle, Phil 158
Checklick, Susan 47,

70, 103
Cheek by Jowl 214
Cheeseman, Ken 218
Cheever, John 207
Chehlaoui, Maha 147, 237
Chekhov, Anton 215, 218, 259
Chekhovek 164
Chelimsky, Robert 181
Chelsea Music Services 93
Chen, Erika 130
Chen, Miao Miao 232
Chen, Qi 232
Chen, Sidney 210
Chen, Szu-Feng 28
Chen, Tiffany 239
Cheng, Jessy 167
Cheng, Nicholas 47, 149
Chenoweth, Kristin 420
Chepy, Julie 58
Cher 197
Cheraneva, Katja 211
Cheretun, Debbie 95
Chernevich, Igor 215
Chernick, Jeremy 36, 84, 138, 148, 223, 250
Chernoff, Cathy 38, 68, 92
Chernoff, Lisa Ann 92, 242
Chernus, Michael 227
Chernyy, Valeriy 129
Cherry Lane Studio 180
Cherry Lane Theatre 123, 129, 144, 165, 171, 182, 249, 263
Cherry Orchard, The 218
Chervenka, Bridget 177, 241, 255, 256
Cheryl Dunkin & Company 145
Chesney, Suzanne 171, 182
Chester, Nora 207
Cheung, Alex 191
Cheung, Cindy 156
Chevillot, Patrick 243
Chevron, Damien 210
Chevron, Philip 198
Chevys Fresh Mex 410
Chia-Liang, Lin 211
Chiang, Desdemona 249
Chia-Nung, Li 210
Chiavetta, Carol 103
Chicago 93, 115, 118
Chicago Children's Theatre 209
Chicago Shakespeare Theater 363

Chieftains, The 131
Chien-Hung, Yu 211
Chieu, Aaron 239
Chihaby, Katie 60, 237, 241, 242
Chih-Feng, Chen 210
Chih-Hao, Wang 211
Chii, Maiko 108
Chilana, Meetu 129
Child's Christmas in Wales in Concert, AA 220
Childers, Brian 190
Childers, Stephanie 388
Children 207
Children of the Future Age 281
Childress, Kelly 409
Childs, Casey 243, 244
Childs, Terri & Timothy 44, 106
Chillé, Alessandro 138
Chilton, Eve 168
Chimera 291
Chimichangas and Zoloft 209
Chimo, Tracee 426
Chin, Judy 28
Chin, Kimberly 167
Chin, Michael G. 229, 238, 251
Chin, Sae La 115
Chinault, Alena 171
Ching, Carla 156
Ching, Daniel 199
Ching-Chun, Lee 210, 211
Ching-Ju, Lin 210
Ching-Kai, Lin 211
Chinglish 12, 38, 407, 409
Chirillo, James 199
Chisholm, Anthony 389
Chittick, Joyce 85
Chiu, Vivian 38
Chivu, Michele 182
Chix 6 146
Chlumsky, Anna 250, 268
Cho, Chermaine 191
Cho, Hwee 198
Choi, Joohee 420
Chokachi, Jamil 127, 184, 189
Choksi, Nick 143
Cholot, Tom 129
Chonchubhair, Niamh Ni 134
Chong, Candace 38
Chong, Marcus 419
Choodu, Masha 129
Choquette, Jason 60
Choreographer's Canvas

2012 291
Choroszewski, Joe 112, 188
Chorus Line, A 353, 358, 399, 419
Chou, Holly 163
Chow, Warren 189
Choy-Kee, Francesca 360
Chriqui, Emmanuelle 192
Chris, Oliver 21, 72
Chrisman, Lee 240
Christ, Bill 91, 240
Christenfeld, Seth 263
Christensen, Erica 88
Christensen, Henry, III 259
Christensen, Scott 107
Christensen, Tracy 170
Christian, Eric L. 68
Christian, Lionel A. 133
Christiansen, Ken 171
Christmas Carol, A 200, 297, 346, 348, 349, 350, 354, 364, 366, 367, 371, 373, 374, 376, 380, 381, 396, 398, 401, 403
Christmas Carol, Oy!, A 284
Christmas Eve with Christmas Eve 200
Christmas in Nickyland 294
Christmas Story, A 345, 356, 394
Christopher Hart Productions 32
Christopher Marlowe's Chloroform Dreams 298
Christopher, Jordan 418
Christopher, Joshua 253
Christopher, Nicholas 140, 256
Christopher, Thom 409, 418
Chryst, Gary 93
Chrzczon, Jeffrey 77, 129
Chu, Jenelle 163
Chu, Lap Chi 230
Chua, Damon 222
Chudoba, John 84
Chugg Entertainment 106
Chukwu, Ugo 163
Chung, Catherine 28
Chung, Jamie 138
Chung, Sung Hwa 198
Chungh, Teerth 213
Chunleau, Amelie 208

Chun-Mei, Liang 210
Church, Abby 95, 221
Church, Jeff 233
Church, Jonathan 447
Church, Joseph 99
Churchill, David 129
Chybowski, Michael 176
Chyra, Andrzej 178
Ciaburri, Zachary 141, 156, 225
Cianfichi, Tom 201
Ciannavei, Andrea 223
Cicala, Teresa A. 193
Ciccarone, Rock 99
Cicci, Jason 409
Cichulska, Małgorzata 178
Cielecka, Magdalena 178
Cieslik, Don 157
Cigar Box Studios 50
Cilento, Diane 417, 465
Cilento, Wayne 111
Cimini, Jillian 50, 90
Cimmelli, Gina 218
Cimmet, Alison 47, 87
Cincinnati Playhouse in the Park 360, 364
Cinderella 370
Ciotti, Emily 189
Cipolla, Olivia 113
Circa 1440 Inc. 140
Circle in the Square Theatre 40
Circle Mirror Transformation 396, 397
Circle of Eleven 161
Circque Le Jazz 320
Cirkus Cirkör 215
Cirque du Soleil: Zarkana 129
Cirque Shanghai 232
Cisek, Caitlin 178
CITC 191
Citron, Drew 149
City Center *Encores!* 93, 199, 205, 216
City Center Stage I 227
City Center Stage II 239
City Club, The 179
City Lights 208
City of Angels 361, 375
Civilians, The 177, 241
Civilization (All You Can Eat) 282
Civilization! 273
Claessens, Marq 232
Claflin, Phillip 202
Claire Tow Theater 225
Claire Went to France 292
Claire, Felicity 100

Clancy, Elizabeth Hope 245, 257
Clancy, John 29
Clapp, Benjamin 211
Clapp, Gordon 230, 268, 420
Clare, Ben 109
Clarence Derwent Awards 437
Clarence LLC 84
Clares, Zulema 149
Clark Studio Theater 199
Clark, Amy 78, 109
Clark, C.A. 73, 223
Clark, Dick 89
Clark, Dwayne 28
Clark, Hannah 154
Clark, Jason 37, 59
Clark, Jenny 84
Clark, Jon 197, 199
Clark, Ken 247
Clark, Lindsay 212
Clark, Michael 75, 97, 112
Clark, Sean 202
Clark, Victoria 109, 198
Clarke, Bill 222
Clarke, Hope 422
Clarke, Jocelyn 162
Clarke, Katie Rose 111
Clarke, Lydia 417
Clarkson, Patricia 201
Clarkson, Paula 243, 254
Class Act, A 358
Classic Stage Company 42, 218
Classical Theatre of Harlem 138, 145
Claus, Nathan K. 117, 165
Clause, Zachary 194
Clay, Carolyn 436
Clay, Ken 102
Clay, Thom 78, 106
Clayburgh, Jim 168
Claycomb, Eva 213
Clayton, Jeremy 112, 221
Clayton, Josh 216, 217, 221
Clayton, Richard 214
Cleale, Lewis 90
Cleary, Malachy 161
Clegg, Amada 148
Clemens, Ceili 84, 145
Clemente, Jacob 89, 112
Clements, Lillian 208, 224, 247
Clemmons/Dewing Casting 133

Clendening, Eddie 103, 136
Clennett, Jamie 106
Cleveland Play House 365
Cleveland, James E. 125, 137, 141, 143, 146, 151, 155, 165-169, 172, 177, 185, 212, 218
Clifford, Cameron 89
Clifford, Danielle 225, 252
Clifton, Tina 75
Climer, Jacob A. 39, 45, 88, 164, 227, 241, 242, 251, 254
Cline, Bob 195
Cline, Cathy 33
Clinton, Moria 94, 103, 136, 144, 244, 263
Clive Barnes Award 435
Cloer, Tony 410
Clohesy, Matt 212
Close Up Space 227
Closer 315
Closer Than Ever 204, 264
Clotfelter, James 212
Cloud Gate Dance Theatre 210
Cloudlands 399
Clouston, Keith 197
Cloutier, Mathieu 138
Clow, James 216
Clowns Ex Machina 282
Clowns Full-Tilt: A Musing on Aesthetics 282, 294
Clubbed Thumb 277, 282
Clurman Theatre on Theatre Row 131, 151, 161, 178, 222, 239
Clybourne Park 22, 73, 351, 360, 363, 388, 397, 400, 402, 406, 409
Clyve, Scott 171
Coakley, Vanessa 242
Coartney, Amber 149
Coat Check Cassanova 287
Coates, Carolyn 418
Coats, William Alan 159
Cobb, Amanda Lee 96
Cobbin, Angela 101
Cobham, Geoff 234
Coble, Kurt 105
Cobley, Tom 157
Cocchiara, Christina 68
Cocchiara, Rich 86
Cochran, Jay 232

Cochran, Kevin 170
Cochran, Shannon 420
Cochrane, Anthony 110
Cochrane, Jessica Perlmeter 110, 224
Cock 121, 185
Cocktail Hour, The 380
Cocktails on Mars 273
Coco, Ed 50
Cocoran, Joe 62
Cody, Jen 113
Cody, Karen Kay 420
Cody, Meredith 168
Coe, Johanna 110
Coen, Ethan 37, 208
Coes, Charles 71, 81, 237, 245, 251
Coey, Dan 36, 59, 67, 90, 410
Coffeehouse Chronicles 294
Coffey, Paul L. 141, 260
Coffman, Kyle 64
Cohen, Alexander H. 418
Cohen, Andrew Zachary 140
Cohen, Andy 186
Cohen, Bruce 113, 141, 144, 150, 182, 259, 262
Cohen, Buzz 244, 245
Cohen, Christopher 409
Cohen, David M. 52, 70, 104
Cohen, David S. 199
Cohen, Douglas J. 422
Cohen, Eric 105
Cohen, Geoff 263
Cohen, Hannah 228
Cohen, Jacob Colin 72
Cohen, Jeff 174
Cohen, Jeremy 31, 233, 447
Cohen, Jim 137
Cohen, Joanne Lee Drexler 137
Cohen, Jonathan 94
Cohen, Larry 136, 182, 183
Cohen, Lawrence D. 226
Cohen, Leonard 219
Cohen, Lynn 180
Cohen, Lynne 55
Cohen, Melissa 68
Cohen, Michael Rico 47, 112
Cohen, Michael T. 116
Cohen, Nathan 266
Cohen, Randy 40, 47, 52, 71, 78, 90, 95, 104, 108, 116, 169, 188, 226, 254

Cohen, Rebecca 76
Cohen, Ron 180
Cohen, Samuel 60, 263
Cohen, Sherry 100
Cohen, Stanley L. 426
Cohen, Steve 110
Cohen, Wendy 233
Cohenour, Patti 419
Cohl, Michael 28
Cohn, Ben 111, 115, 118
Cohn, Charlotte 168
Cohn, Heather 181
Cohn, Robert 244
Coid, Marshall 93
COIL Festival 325
Coit, Michael D. 47
Coker, Mark 87
Coker, Tug 70
Colaizzo, Paul Downs 109
Colasanti, Craig 189
Colbert, David Brian 199
Colburn, Danielle 245, 246, 248
Cole, Aidan 189
Cole, Daniel James 137
Cole, Darren Lee 128, 157
Cole, Kay 125
Cole, Kelly Ruth 146, 166, 182, 201
Cole, Michael 40
Cole, Nora 165
Cole, Robert 60
Cole, Rudi 210
Cole, Thomas, Jr. 109
Colella, Jenn 117, 204, 264
Coleman, Amanda 102
Coleman, Brian 241
Coleman, Britney 149
Coleman, Chad C. 421
Coleman, Chase 193
Coleman, Debi 82
Coleman, Elizabeth 33
Coleman, Jackie 189
Coleman, Kris 97
Coleman, Liz 67, 410
Coleman, M. Graham 137, 186
Coleman, Rahn 87
Coleman, Roger 62
Coleman, Rori 28
Coleman, Rosalyn 36
Coleman, Ross 106
Colette Collage 266
Colgan, Michael 213
Colicchio, Tom 223
Colice, Anne 92
Colin, Margaret 24, 80, 86, 420
Colin, Nicholas 244

CollaborationTown 282
Collaborative Stages 283
Collected Rules of Gifted Camp 279
Collette, Toni 420
Collier, Alexandra 263
Collier, Brian 101
Collings, David 214
Collins, Anna 214
Collins, Brian 70
Collins, Brooke 235
Collins, Dan 440
Collins, Dorothy 452
Collins, Jessica 227
Collins, John 236, 247
Collins, Jonathan 50, 52, 139, 219
Collins, Kevin 220
Collins, Pauline 419
Collins, Rufus 197
Collins, Sam 210
Collins, Stephen W. 410
Collision Productions 283
Collis-Scurll, Jonny 154
Collopy, Andy 118
Collura, Jill M. 55
Collwes, Brandon 213
Coloff, Rachel 216
Colom, Alvaro 191
Colombick, Leigh 130
Colombo, Patti 159
Colón, Liza 223
Colón, Rosal 103, 223
Colon, Solimar 253
Color Between the Lines 180
Colosi, Rosie 112, 113
Colt Coeur 283
Columbia Artists Management 196
Columbia Pictures 59
Columbia School for the Arts 219
Columnist, The 24, 80
Comas, Jessica Sadowski 243
Combs, Jacob 253
Comden, Betty 159, 417
Come and Go 259
Come On 186
Comedy of Errors, The 319, 396
Comerford, Joseph 219
Comfort, Bob 254
Comfort, Chris 126
Comic Book Theater Festival 280
Comley, Bonnie 66, 106
Common Pursuit, The 252
Common Tongue, The

283
Communal Space: a play series in four gardens 283
Communicado Productions 176
Community Garden Project 283
Compagnie Thor 210
Company 373
Compass Theatrical 283
Comperatore, Dominic 207, 360
Complaint, The 282
Complete & Condensed Stage Directions of Eugene O'Neill: Vol. 1 Early Plays/Lost Plays 302
Complete Performer, The 190
Complete World of Sports (abridged), The 231
Completeness 241
Compton, James 179
Conacher, William 89
Conci, Caitlin 169, 249
Cone, Lizbeth 88
Confusions of Young Torless, The 290
Conklin, John 248
Conlee, John Ellison 277
Conlin, Sean 184
Conlon, Francesca 151
Conlow, Peter 417
Conn, Didi 150, 192
Connaughton, Lara 198
Connecticut Critics' Circle Awards 435
Conneff, Kevin 131
Connelly Theater 156
Connelly, Brendan 223
Connick, Harry, Jr. 15, 50, 420
Conni's Avant Garde Restaurant: The Mothership Landing 144, 283
Connolly, Eileen 131
Connolly, Keith 168
Connolly, Kristen 245, 246
Connolly, Michael 235
Connolly, Will 60, 236
Connor, Laurie 33, 38, 46, 50, 52
Connor, Nikki 219
Connor, Whitfield 417
Conolly, Patricia 220
Conover, Kate 225
Conrad, Michael 167

Conrad, Moira 74
Conroy, Ruaidhri 420
Consortium Ventures 74
Conspirare 233
Constable, Paule 110
Constantine, Deborah 173
Consuelos, Mark 155
Conte, Kerry 112, 265
Conteras, Edgar 68
Conti, Eva 89
Conti, Nina 155
Contreras, David 113
Contuzzi, Jennie 226
Convert, The 362, 374, 383
Conway, Kevin 410
Conway, Ryan 100
Conway, Shirl 417
Conyers, Sarah K. 251
Cook, Alexander 163
Cook, Alexandra 99
Cook, Barbara 441, 417
Cook, Ben 89
Cook, Carla 199
Cook, Carrie 163
Cook, Casey 112
Cook, Dave 212
Cook, Helen R. 241
Cook, Jason 179
Cook, Nancy 176
Cook, Roderick 265
Cook, Susan E. 82
Cooke, Camron 94
Cooke, Josh 252
Cookson, Peter 417
Coolbaugh, Jennifer 40, 50, 64, 87, 109, 179
Cooley, Ann 146
Coombes, Rosalind 75
Coombs, Holly 92
Coomer, Alastair 72
Cooney, Daniel 47
Cooney, Dennis 418
Cooney, Sarah 112
Coonrod, Karin 248
Co-Op Theatre East 282
Cooper Union 444
Cooper, Anderson 95
Cooper, Brendan 95
Cooper, Cara 97
Cooper, Denise 35, 56, 81, 428
Cooper, Heather 126
Cooper, Jeff 68
Cooper, Kyle 28
Cooper, Max 31, 36
Cooper, Pamela 82
Cooper-Hecht, Gail 184
Copeland, Carolyn Rossi 191
Copeland, Lawrence 82
Copeland, Reagan 146

Copley, Dave 102
Copp, Aaron 194, 213
Coppel, Fernanda 209
Coppel, Michael 75
Corbeil, Ann-Marie 129
Corbett, Clinton 174
Corbett, Quinlan 183
Corbett, Sam 28, 36, 104, 155, 263
Corcoran, Charles 31, 92
Corcoran, Kristina 134, 153
Corden, James 21, 72
Cordle, Jill 59, 98
Cordon, Susie 31
Cordova, Richard 184
Core Creative Productions 283
Corey, Wendell 417
Coria, Lucas 234
Cork, Adam 197
Corker, John S. 139
Corley, Richard 229
Corman, Maddie 125, 192, 170
Corman, Roger 202
Cormican, Peter 229
Cornell, Eric 109
Cornell, Erin 212
Cornell, Michael 92, 75, 107
Corner Pocker 287
Corner Store Fund 108
Cornwell, Chris 240
Cornwell, Eric 46
Couro, Pururu Mao No 232
Corradetti, Greg 33, 38, 40, 46, 52, 54
Corrado, Susan 75
Correia, Don 33
Corren, Donald 174, 185
Correra, Alex 218
Corrigan, Hannah 149
Corrigan, Kevin 223
Corrubia, Lucas Rico 198
Corrubia, Lucas Rico, Jr. 198
Corrubia, Rebecca Heroff 198
Corsello, David 247
Cort Theatre 49, 77, 91
Cortes, Dashira 112
Cortes, J.W. 137
Corthron, Kia 428
Cortright, Bart 147
Corvers, Monique 232
Coryphaeus Theater Company 283
Cosgrave, Peggy 184
Coskunses, Jon Can 46
Cossette, Mary 47

Cosson, Steven 177
Costa Rehab 298
Costabile, Richard 112, 176
Costanzi, Victor 68
Costanzo, Catherine 229
Costea, Monica 75, 85
Costello, Jennifer 103
Costello, Tom 163, 208
Coster, Ritchie 255
Cote, A.J. 239, 249, 250
Cote, David 409, 428, 438
Cote, Michelle 219
Coterie Theatre 233
Cotter, Margaret 428
Cottle, Jonathan 151
Cottle, Matthew 158
Cotton Club Parade 199
Cotton, Julia 234
Cotton, Keith 108
Cottrell, Allison 28, 241, 242, 262
Couch, Maria 152
Couch, Nena 443
Coughlan, Mary 219
Coughlin, Bruce 163
Could've Been Broadway: A Musical Revue 297
Count, Steve 261
Countryman, Michael 57, 208
County, Jayne 187
Couro, Pururu Mao No 232
Courson, Jason 194
Court-Martial at Fort Devens 281
Coutts, Megan E. 40, 171
Cover, Bradford 229, 239, 240
Covert, Kevin 95, 113
Covert, Ralph 209
Covey, David 213
Covey, Jason 101
Covey, Liz 186
Covillo, Kristine 68
Coward, Noël 44, 265
Cowhig, Frances Ya-Chu 146
Cowles, Matthew 260
Cowles, Virginia 229
Cowperthwaite, Janet 210
Cox, Alan 75, 197, 215
Cox, Douglas 107
Cox, Veanne 192
Coyle, Bill 133
Coyle, Brendan 420
Coyne, Nancy 28
Cozart, Stephanie 207

Cozens, Cathy 410
CQ/CX 208
Crabtree, Audrey 149
Cracked (upon a time) 306
Cracking Up Productions 160
Craddock, Clayton 102
Craffey, Paul 410
Craig Noel Awards 435
Craig, Helen 125
Craig, Jason 241, 242
Craig, Joseph 102
Craig, Liam 344
Crain, Todd Alan 173
Cram, Cusi 223
Cramer, Daina 237
Crampton, Glory 267
Crandall, William S. 231
Crane Story 144
Crane, Jillian 174
Crane, Michael 246
Craven, William 85, 116
Crawford, Alvin 99
Crawford, Ben 216, 267
Crawford, Gary & Stephanie 191
Crawford, Kevin 72
Crawford, Lilla 89
Crawford, Richard 110
Crawford, Tommy 163
Craymer, Judy 100
CRC Productions 191
Crea, Michael 38, 47, 54, 66
Creane, Jessica 81
Creative Link 94
Creative Scotland 175
Creators Project, The 148
Credit, Roosevelt André 54
Creeden, Matt 166
Creek, Luther 28, 29
Creel, Gavin 113, 116, 118, 429
Creighton, Robert 85
Creighton, Whitney 33, 46, 50, 52
Crenshaw, Chris 199
Crenshaw, Darius 105
Creskoff, Rebecca 225
Crespo, Sheena 45, 78
Cresswell, Luke 196
Creswell, David 33, 216
Crewe, Bob 97
Cridge, Denise 184
Cries and Whispers 211
Crisara, Ray 158
Criss, Darren 95, 202, 433
Cristina, Vânia 213
Cristofer, Michael 419

Critchlow, Michael 64
Croasdale, Kate 37, 75, 258
Crockett, Stephen 75
Croft-Fraser, Erica 62
Croghan, Robert 256
Croissant, John 75
Croiter, Jeff 64, 71, 127, 132, 135, 165, 185, 192, 242, 261
Croiter, Michael 192
Crokett, Ahsley 256
Crom, Rick 115, 194
Croman, Dylis 93
Cromarty and Company 150
Cromarty, Peter 150, 194, 235
Cromer, David 94, 169
Crommett, David 183
Crompton, Barbara 45
Cronin, Chris 44, 73
Cronin, Christopher 94
Crook, Bryan 90, 115
Crook, Mackenzie 98
Croom, Gabriel 99, 113
Croot, Cynthia 144
Crosby, Aaron 219
Crosby, Julie 241, 262
Crosby, Kim 159
Crose, Kyle 163, 177
Crosland, J. Marvin 74
Cross Cut Productions 154
Cross, Dustin 132, 142, 172, 173
Cross, Lezlie 219
Cross, Richard 417
Cross-Eyed Bear Productions 284
crosshatch theatre company 284
Crossman, Dylan 213
Crossroads Theatre Project 284
Crouch, Julian 84, 250
Crouse, Lindsay 419
Crouse, Russell 85
Crouse, Timothy 85
Crowder, Jack 418
Crowe, Annelies 234
Crowe, Miriam 73, 211
Crowe, Patricia 206
Crowley, Ann 417
Crowley, Bob 60, 101, 236
Crowley, Dennis 64, 99, 101
Crowley, Dermot 221
Crowley, George 258
Crowley, Michael 54, 60
Crowley, Pat 417
Crowns 366, 374

Crowthers, Chris 113
Crozier, Judy 77
Crucible, The 316
Crudup, Billy 86, 420
Cruse, Kimothy 112, 409
Crutchfield, Buddy 154
Cruz, Carla 192
Cruz, Cece 33
Cruz, Christine 183
Cruz, Francisco 138
Cruz, Holly 113
Cruz, Isaac 193
Cruz, Joshua 135
Cruz, Maria Cecilia 62
Cruz, Michael 143
Cruz, Mike 112
Cruz, Rosey 223, 236, 237
Cryan, Tim 141
Cry-Baby 385
Cryer, David 105, 410, 418
Cryer, Gretchen 264, 264
Crystal, Jason 42, 54, 70, 84, 88, 187, 244, 245
Csibi, Joe 219
Cubbage, Sarah 31, 40, 74, 185
Cubría, Bernardo 183
Cudworth, Kate J. 191
Cuervo, Alma 135
Cuevas, Steven 152
Cuiffo, Steve 173, 174
Cuismano, Jeffrey 249
Culkin, Macaulay 420
Cullen, David 68, 105
Cullman, Trip 226, 242, 253
Cullom, Ray 146, 183
Cullum, John 115, 244, 245, 405, 409, 415, 418, 420
Culpepper, Daniel 105
Culture Ireland 134, 159
Culture Project 130, 159, 165, 174, 177, 284
CultureMart 2012 291
Cumming, Alan 420
Cummings, Jack, III 124, 134, 153
Cummings, Patrick 221
Cummins, Cenovia 47, 76
Cummins, Rick 231
Cummins, Stephanie 101
Cumpsty, Michael 20, 67
Cunliffe, Colin 68, 84

Cunningham, Davy 198
Cunningham, Jeremy 52, 139, 260
Cunningham, JoAnn 266
Cunningham, John 222
Cunningham, Mark 214
Cunningham, Merce 213
Cunningham, Nicholas 105, 113, 118
Cunningham, Peter 216
Cunningham, Ryan 40, 50, 52, 62
Cuoco, Monica A. 139
Cupo, Steven 200
Curatolo, Joey 107
Curious Frog Theatre Company 284
Curran, Heather 192
Curran, Kelley 223
Curran, Michael 236, 244
Curren, Megan 90
Currier, Shoshona 138
Curry, Daniel 28, 29
Curry, Felicia 438
Curry, Fran 78
Curry, Jason 263
Curry, Michael 99
Curry, Will 117
Curse of the Starving Class 272
Curtain, Catherine 257
Curtsinger, Jolie 162
Cusack, Carmen 227
Cusack, Joan 419
Cusack, Matt 72, 149
Cusimano, Jeff 256
Cuskern, Dominic 240
Cusson, Anne-Marie 70
Custom Glass Etching 410
Cusumano, Michael 93, 113, 202
Cutler, Duncan 148
Cutman, A Boxing Musical 375
Cutmore-Scott, Jack 86
Cwill, Janice B. 253
Cymbeline 141, 259, 280
Cyrano Players Inc. 146
Czechoslovak-American Marionette Theatre 284
Czerny, Henry 420

D
D'Abruzzo, Stephanie 265, 420
D'Agostino, Bill 147
D'Agostino, Carole 192
d'Amboise, Charlotte 93

D'Ambrosio, Tom 52, 109, 253
D'Amico, Marcus 420
D'Amico, Matt 71
D'Ammassa, Janel 185
D'Amore, Christine 244
D'Amour, Lisa 447
D'Angelo, Christopher 52, 84, 98
D'Angelo, Sabrina 211
D'Angora, Michael 175
D'Angora, Tom 175, 194
D'Aquila, Fabio 191
D'Areinzo, Juan 219
D'Arienzo, Chris 108
d'Auguste, Joseph 112
D'Avonzo, Sylvia 116
d'Orleans, Philip 197
D'Ornellas, Sharona 76
D'Silva, Darrell 197
Da Conceição, Beatriz 213
Da Costa, Kyra 87
da Silva Martins, Pedro 213
Dabbon, David 116, 163
Dacal, Janet 267
Dacey, Kathy 93
Dad Doesn't Dance 316
Dadadi, Yuval 126
Dadap, Laura 133
Daddy Long Legs 365, 383
Dagger, Peter 409
Dagna, Robert 40
Daher, James 124, 212
Dailey, Brandon 71
Daily, Dan 239, 240
Dain, Frank 142, 171
Daisey, Mike 245
Daito, Shunsuke 197
Daitsman, Judith 49
Dal Santo, Paula 143
Dalba, Amy 126, 141, 169
DalCortivo, Rick 109
Daldry, Stephen 89
Dale, Jim 17, 56
Dale, Mary Beth 71, 131, 133
Dale, Terence 215
Dalenberg, Ann-Marie 245, 247, 248
Daley, Bob 135
Daley, Maximillian 144
Dałkowska, Ewa 178
Dall'Ava, Louis 235
Dallas Theater Center 365
Dallos, Chris 182
Dally with the Devil 143
Dalton, Adam 180
Dalton, Penelope 95

Dalton, Steven 35-37, 46, 49, 56, 58, 59, 60, 73, 75, 77, 81, 185
Daly, Christine M. 188
Daly, Emily 249
Daly, James 417
Daly, Patrick 36, 169, 185
Daly, Timothy 419
Daly, Tyne 10, 31, 447, 455
Damane, David Aron 81
Damer, Andrew 67
Damiano, Jennifer 28, 198
Damkjaer, Camilla 215
Damn Yankees 370, 392
Damon, Stuart 418
Damscroder, Caleb 128
Danaher, Colleen 40
Dancap Productions 74, 82, 102
Dancers Responding to AIDS 118
Dancewicz, Mark 100
Dancing at Lughnasa 203, 219, 419
Dancing Crane Inc. 284
Dancing for Krumholtz 283
Dancy, Hugh 13, 42, 118, 426
Dandridge, Sarah 360
Dane, Faith 202
Daneel, Sylvia 417
Danelson, Christine 113
D'Angelo, Beverly 420
Dani'Q 152
Daniel, Ian 177
Daniel, James 212
Daniel, Nicolas 210
Daniele, Graciela 39, 224
Danieley, Jason 114, 420, 421
Danielian, Barry 106
Danielian, Ben 24, 81, 420
Daniels, Cicily 117
Daniels, David 417
Daniels, Kevin 70
Daniels, Nikki Renée 54, 85
Daniels, Sean 147
Daniels, Thaddeus 189
Danis, Amy 190
Dann, Mauro 234
Danner, Andrew 44
Danner, Blythe 410, 418
Dannheisser, Adam 108
Danny and Sylvia: The Danny Kaye Musical 190
Dansby, Daniel 125

Dansby, Wade F. 3 190, 409, 410
Danson, Randy 111
Danz, Marjorie 102
Danz, Ronn 102
Danzansky, Rick 49
Darbourne, Richard 154
Darby, John 410
Darcy, Niamh 219
Dare, Bill 155
Darke, Erin 230
Darling, Peter 89
Darneille, Sara 50, 82
DARR Publicity 138
Darr, Taryn 113
Darrah, James 188
Darrow, Nathan 214
Dart, Iris Rainer 104
Darwin, David 170
Daryl Roth Theatre 191
Daryl Roth Theatrical Management 134, 137, 147, 164, 168, 170, 191
Das Barbecü 371
Dash, Pradeep 214
DaSilva, Emily 67
Dauriac, Jean 259
Daurio, Matt 182
Davalos, Dick 417
D'Avanzo, Sylvia 50, 104
Davenport Theatrical Enterprises 40, 130, 140, 151, 154, 185, 188, 193
Davenport, Ken 38, 40, 185, 188, 193, 440
Davey, Bruce 106
David Bury and Associates 239
David Eden Productions 213, 215
David Gersten and Associates 124, 125, 127, 147, 152, 172, 174, 179, 183, 184, 188, 189, 200, 222, 229
David H. Koch Theater 198
David Nelson...Status Update 272
David, Alan 98
David, Boaz Ben 133
David, Ino Ben 133
David, Michael 62, 97
David, Troy 132
Davidson, Ann 37
Davidson, Anthony 152
Davidson, Brandon 217
Davidson, Jack 39
Davidson, Jeremy 224

Davidson, John 418
Davidson, Kaitlyn 78
Davidson, Patrice 161
Davie, Erin 267, 420
Davies, Aled 419
Davies, Geraint Wyn 166
Davila, Linda 74
Davis, Anita Ali 49, 74
Davis, Barrett 113, 115, 118, 101
Davis, Caitlin 149
Davis, Carol 235
Davis, Clifton 418
Davis, Cody 369
Davis, Daniel 218
Davis, Derrick 99
Davis, Elizabeth A. 60, 143, 236
Davis, Elliot 198
Davis, Eric 76, 85
Davis, Eric C. 55, 112
Davis, Glenn 88
Davis, Hannah 71, 206, 216
Davis, Helene 199, 216
Davis, Holly 109
Davis, Hope T. 196
Davis, J. Alan 214
Davis, Jeremy 76, 89, 104
Davis, Jimmy 94
Davis, Jordyn 159, 160
Davis, Josh 247
Davis, Katelyn 238
Davis, Lloyd, Jr. 74
Davis, Maggie 169, 177
Davis, Mary J. 135, 137, 186
Davis, Michael 106
Davis, Michael Allen 419
Davis, Michelle 230
Davis, Paige 198
Davis, Paul 64, 144
Davis, Paula 108
Davis, Peter J. 181
Davis, Richard 417
Davis, Ryan J. 202
Davis, Sam 117
Davis, Sandra E. 244
Davis, Scott 140
Davis, Stephanie 149
Davis, Sydney 239
Davis, Toni Marie 243
Davis, Trevon 54, 55
Davis, Vicki R. 229
Davis, Viola 420
Davison, Susan 117
Davoy, Napaua 238
Dawson, Brian 95
Dawson, Jared 219
Dawson, Mark 417
Dawson, Michelle 100

Dawson, Trent 241
Day, Christopher 184
Day, Jae 62
Day, Johanna 368, 404
Day, Kaitlyn 229
Day, Katherine Akiko 37, 258
Day, Robert 159
Day, Simon Paisley 44
Daydream 307
Days, Garland 99
Dayton, Aaron 209
DBS Press 195
de Benedet, Rachel 92, 116
de Bruijn, Annemarie 232
de Bruijn, Lara 184
De Burgh, Alison 44
de Courcy, Reyna 230
de Gallaí, Breandán 219
de Gallaí, Seán 219
de Haas, Aisha 192
de Haas, Darius 379
De Jésus, Robin 113, 117
de Jong, Remco 232
De Jonge, Doreien 232
de la Barre, Margot 68, 85
De La Cruz, Jessica 187
de la Cruz, Jordana 183
de La Lombana, Luis Carlos 149
De La Peña, George 218
De La Vega, Fracesca 50
de Lavallade, Carmen 74
de Lesseps, Countess Luann 202
De Lisle, Christine 165
de Loera, Charity 99
De Lottinville, Anne 129
de Luce, Virginia 417
De Lucia, Aurora 112
De Martin, Imelda 418
De Matteo, Danielle 141
De Meur, Tony 179
De Mink, Hanna 232
De Niro, Drea 186
De Oliveira, Manuel 213
De Oliveira, Marco 213
De Prato, Olivia 212
de Quesada, Ana Mari 151
de Saint-Exupéry, Antoine 231
De Salazar, Francisco 171
De Santis, Davin 81, 258
De Shields, André 422
De Silva, Sanjit 110
de Trizio, Enrico 117

De Vega, Lope 223
de Viteri, Robbie Saenz 258
De Waal, Jeanna 227
DeAbreu, Glenda 153
Dead Accounts 364
Dead Copycats, The 284
Dead Guy 304
Deale, Molly 33
Dean, Bradley 68, 190
Dean, David 156, 180
Dean, Erin Hennessy 31, 42, 57, 80, 227
Dean, James 417
Dean, Jordan 100, 219
Dean, Laura 419
Dean, Loren 419
Dean, Paul 78
Dean, Van 92
DeAngelis, Anthony 33, 117
DeAngelis, Christian 47, 78, 177, 229
DeAngelis, Emily 131, 145, 163, 168
DeAngelis, Matt 32, 198
Deans, Jonathan 28, 106, 226
DeArmon, Jill 223
Death Boogie 279
Death of a Salesman 27, 59, 118, 403, 408, 409
Death of the Slow Dying Scuba Diver 319
Death Tax 346
Death Valley 273
Deb O 184
DeBellis, Robert 99
Debenport, Dan 112
Deblinger, David 223, 249
DeBoice, Jenna 107
DeBord, Jason 181
DeBrock, Thad 40
Decarlis, Anthony 113
Decca Broadway Records 84, 89, 95, 111
Decca Theatricals 84
Deceit of Truth 302
DeCesare, Kristin 113
DeCicco, Christina 68, 109
Deckman, Tom 202
Dee, Cat 109
Dee, Catherine 74
Dee, Janie 420
Deep Are the Roots 299
Deep Trees 223
Deepest Play Ever: The Catharsis of Pathos, The 283, 301
Deevy, Teresa 229

Def, Mos 420
Defassio, Danielle 130
DeFrange, Nick 181, 241
Defrin, Carolyn 213
Degaetano, Jon 127
DeGanon, Clint 47, 63, 92
Degefa, Tariku 187
Degeneration X 305
DeGioia, Eric 109, 217
DeGroot, Jake 91
Degros, Cynthia 37
deGuzman, Matthew 33
Dehm, Emily 58
DEINDE 288, 315
Deitch, Joseph 38, 54, 92
Deitch, Matthew 38, 54, 92
Deitweiler, David 233
Deitz, O. David 410
DeJesus, Ron 146
Dekker, Amanda 39, 110, 224, 410
Del Aguila, Kevin 71
Dela Cruz, Joshua 216
Dela Garza, James 68, 89
Delacorte Theater 245
DelaCruz, Scott 175, 194
Delahunt, Suzanne 78, 85
Delahunt, Tara 85
Delaney, Mauli 166, 257
Delaney, Shelagh 465
DeLaria, Lea 174, 420
DeLaurenti, Julie 209
Delaware Theatre Company 360, 366
Delcioppo, Paul 46, 50, 60, 64, 68, 95
Delcroix, Christian 33
Delinois, Alex 168
Della Posta, Sara 116
DellaFera, Kate 28
Dellamonica, Thomas 169
DellaPietra, Steve 410
Dellapina, Matt 261
Dellger, Joseph 54, 55
Dellimore, Alicia 211
Dellimore, Alison 211
Delman, Scott M. 36, 59, 84, 86, 90, 94, 185
Delmore, Marisa 76
Delre, Kylie 239
DeLuca, Jeremy 255, 256
DeLuca, Petra 199
DeLuise, Christopher 117, 118

DeLuise, Joseph 28, 33, 40, 44, 52, 95, 136, 179
DeLustro, John 136
Demand, Cynthia 110
DeMann, Freddy 78
DeMarco, Vincent J. 145
DeMarse, James 378
DeMary, Ava 89
Demas, Carole 115, 450
Demavich, Drew 134
Dembin, Russell M. 409
Dembrow, Beth 163, 177
DeMeester, Amanda 117
DeMent, Elizabeth 212
Demers, Carole 130
Deming, Matthew 115
Demme, Jonathan 132
Demon Dreams 298
Demone, Nikkieli 158, 179
Demos Bizar Entertainment 102
Demos, Nick 102
Dernous, John 43, 81
Dempsey, Ron 177
Dempster, Loren 213
Demyan, Michael 139
Dengel, Liz 38
Dengler, Matt 190, 266
DeNio, Ien 141, 190
DeNiro, Robert 419
Denis, Michael 180, 249, 250
Denison, Zachary 113
Denisov, Dmitry 129
Denkert, Darcie 106
Denman, Jeffry 194, 201, 242
Denmark, Ira 158
Dennehy, Brian 369
Dennis Grimaldi Productions 40
Dennis, Kate 63
Dennis, Sandy 418
Denniston, Leslie 419
Denny, Christopher 202
Denny, Scott 112, 324, 409, 410
Denoff, Douglas 78
Dent, John 89, 216
Dent, Jonathan Louis 205, 251
Dente, Eric 261
Dentz, Shira 126
Denver Center for the Performing Arts 137
Denver Center Theatre Company 360, 366
Deolinda 213
OROGA 297
DePass, Nicolette 199

DePierro, Nicolo 163
Depinet, Kevin 103
DePinto, Jason 78
DePoo, Paul 78, 95
Derasse, Dominic 104, 116
Derby Day 281
Dermody, Jessica 52, 71
DeRosa, Elizabeth 101
DeRossi, Julie 134, 169, 250
deRoy, Jamie 71, 78, 84, 92, 103, 244, 409, 410
Derr, Richard 417
Derrington, Richard 158
DeRuyter, Joel 75
Desai, Angel 125
Desai, Snehal 239
DeSanti, Maia 360
DeSantis, Alison 208, 209
Desantis, Devin 128
Descarfino, Charles 33, 55
Descarfino, Charlie 87
Deschene, Christopher 47, 102
Desdemona 199
Desdemona: A Play About a Handkerchief 305, 309, 321
DeSerio, Michaelangelo 144, 156, 168, 180
Deshmukh, Mayur 150
Desimini, Angelo 28, 84
Desjardins, Emma 213
Desmarais, Manon 137
Desperate Writers 125
Despina & Company 284
Desposito, Mike 153
Detre, Antony 74
Detrick, Charlotte 235
Detsky, Allan 62
Deu, Amerjit 156
Deuteranomaly 299
Deutsch, Allison 229
Devany, Christina 52
Devany, Victoria 235
Devcich, Donald 59
Deverich, Resa 87
Deverna, Charles J. 74
DeVerna, Charlie 87
DeVerna, Scott 38, 49, 77, 91
DeVille, Chris 145
Devil's Music: The Life and Blues of Bessie Smith, The 127
Devine, Erick 266
Devine, Kelly 97, 102, 108, 181
DeVito, Lucy 135

DeVore, Julie 78, 103, 262
DeVos, William 33, 63
DeVries, Jon 218, 247
DeVries, Michael 111
Devyatisilnaya, Olga 148, 173
Dewey, Justin 239
Dewhurst, Colleen 417
Dewing, Joy 133
DeWitt, Joyce 114, 193
Deyle, Oleg 409
Deyo, Aron 168
Di Cesare, Francesca 182
Di de los Muertos 283
Di Dia, Maria 146, 189
Diab, Tina 138
Diabaté, Mamah 199
Diamond, Charles 67
Diamond, Dennis 189
Diamond, Lydia R. 49
Diamond, Neil 441
Diamond, Sasha 262
Diaz, Andrew 249, 250
Diaz, Edward 38, 49, 62, 77, 91
Diaz, Javier 50
Diaz, Mark 47
Diaz, Missy 189
Diaz, Reese Sebastian 101
DiBella, Richard 132, 168, 221, 261
DiBello, Larry 89
Dicapo Opera Theatre 125
DiCarlo, Matthew 108, 112, 117
Dick, Maggie 49
Dickerson, Amber 195
Dickert, Megan Schwarz 177
Dickey, Jessica 57
Dickinson, Crystal A. 22, 73, 360, 405, 406, 409, 413
Dickinson, Derek F. 150, 182
Dickinson, Ian 98
Dickinson, Janet 181, 462
Dickinson, Remmel T. 78, 92, 102
Dickler, Pam 185
Dickson, Matt 110
Dickstein, Rachel 141
DiCrescento, Donna 193
DICTEE: Bells Fall A Peal to Sky 324
Did You Know My Husband? 186
Didier, Brenda 232

Didner, Motl 259
DiDonato, Jennifer 152
Die: Roll to Proceed 299
Diebold, Tracey 68, 92
Diehl, John 223
Dieli, Annette 235
Diener, Joan 417
Dienz, Alexandra 212
Dieterle, Vito 246
Dietz, Zachary 135
Dietzler, Beth 147
DiFabbio, Lianne 134
DiFabbio, Nicholas 112
DiFulvio, Carly 35, 56, 81, 96
DiGiallonardo, Christine 217
DiGiallonardo, Nadia 32
DiGiovanni, Jessica 227
DiGiulio, Don 379
Dignazio, David 78
DiGregorio, Derek 90
DiLallo, Susan 125, 152
Dileo, Lou 236, 237
Dillane, Stephen 199, 420
Dillard, Case 101
Dillard, Robert Lee 113
Dillman, Bradford 417
Dillon, Melinda 418
Dillon, Mia 456
Dillon, Ryan 192
DiLorenzo, Laura 253
DiLoreto, Matt 189
DiMaggio, Stephanie 248
DiMatteo, Sheena 202
Dimbleby, Ed 110
Dime Heroes 292
Diminished Fifth 298
Dimond, Jon 126, 226
Dimou, Fotini 197
Dineen, Joseph 206
Dinklage, Jonathan 76
Dinoia, Jennifer 111
Dinsick, Matt 183
DioGuardi, Kara 93
Dionne, Julie 129
Diop, Khadim 145
DiPietro, Joe 78, 102
DiPietropolo, Antoinette 264
DiPinto, John 264
Dirden, Brandon J. 73, 389
Director, Kim 249
Directors Company, The 166
DiSalvo, Mike 252
DiSanti, Rocco 57, 80, 241
DISASTER! 162
Dishy, Bob 209, 268

Diskant, Ben 218
Disney Theatrical Productions 64, 71, 86, 101, 109
Diss, Eileen 215
Distler, Alexis 108, 146, 253
Ditsky, Stuart 84
Dive Theatre 284
Diversity on Broadway Award 437
Dividing the Estate 348, 378, 387
DiVita, Diane 253, 254
DiVita, Janine 85, 266
Dixon Place 284
Dixon, Ananias 189
Dixon, Beth 242, 268
Dixon, Brandon Victor 140, 199
Dixon, Caitlin 259, 260
Dixon, Ed 85, 101
Dixon, Gayle 105
Dixon, Keisha 74
Dixon, Kyle 125
Dixon, MacIntyre 190
Dixon, Meredith 207
Dixon, Scott 90
Dixon, Troy 74
Dizzia, Maria 258
DJ Tr!p 234
Djourabchi, Neimah 166
Dlamini, Lindiwe 99
Do Jump! 233
Do You Still Dream? 313
Dobay, Stephen 71
Dobbins, Kathleen 92
Dobbs, A.J. 238
Dobell, Curzon 229
Dobie, Edgar 422
Dobie, Paul 111
Dobie, Stephen 196
Dobkowski, Leon 50, 78
Dobrish, Jeremy 168
Dobrow, Mark 67, 101, 410
Dobson, Dan 189
Dobson, Jack 231
Dobsovits, Adrienne 244
Dockett, Bryan 64
Dockhorn, Andrea 177
Doctor Faustus 280
Doctor in Spite of Himself, A 344, 357, 403
Dodd, Stephanie 144
Dodge, Alexander 241, 242
Dodger Theatricals/ Marketing/Management 46, 62, 97, 181
Dodin, Lev 215
Dodson, Jeff 227

Dodson, Ryan 223
Dog Park 320
Dogfight 254
Dogg, M.L. 142, 239, 242, 251, 254
Dogmouth 320
Doherty, Brian 197
Doherty, Madeleine 109
Doherty, Mark 206
Doherty, Patricia E. 127, 162, 166
Dohrn, Zayd 261
Dokton, Tom 62
Dolan, Rick 33, 83, 92
Dolce, Frank 248
Dold, Mark H. 191
Dolhas, Peter 95
Doll, Lauren 36, 102
Dollar, Aubrey 241
Dollison, Trista 99
Doll's House, A 278
Doll's Life, A 278
Dombo, Aimee B. 66, 87, 243
Dombrowski, Amelia 224
Dombrowski, Jill 259
Dombrowski, Wil 54
Domenech, Dan 108
Domiano, Cat 118
Domingo, Colman 255
Domingues, Dan 344
Dominick, Jodi 361
Domi ski, Piotr 178
Dominus, Stephanie Altman 184
Domski, Jude 183
Don Gio 316
Don't Dress for Dinner 24
Donadio, Lisa 73, 262
Donald, Andy 261
Donaldson, Mark 113
Donaldson, Martha 185, 227, 261
Donaldson, Ty 125
Donaldson-Forbes, Jeff 213
Donat, Peter 417
Donatelle, Marc 101
Donato, Kimberly Pau 179
donaufestival Niederoesterreich 246
Dondlinger, Mary Jo 190, 221, 263
Donheiser, Jenny 222
Donica, Jim 162
Donini, Marilynn 148, 151, 160
Donmar Warehouse 199
Donne, Naomi 86, 94,

101
Donnell, Colin 85, 114, 205, 216
Donnellan, Declan 214
Donnelly, Candice 176
Donnelly, Jennifer 156
Donnelson, Carie 259
Donovan, Conor 420
Donovan, Jacquelyn Piro 264
Donovan, Jeffrey 70
Donovan, Peter 101
Donovan, Sheila 135, 226, 227
Donovan, Stephen 40, 50, 92, 125
Donovan, Tate 257
Don't Dress for Dinner 81
Dooley, Wade 116, 118, 189
Door to Door Generations 182
Door, The 157
Doran, Christian 146
Doran, Joe 70, 168
Dorfler, Erica 87
Dorfman, Hannah 28, 85
Dorfman, Robert 218
Dorland, Cassie 37, 38, 49, 50, 74, 256
Dorman, Andrew 135
Dorman, Kathleen 218
Dorman-Phaneuf, Mairi 68, 244
Dorothy Loudon Award 409, 421
Dorothy Loudon Foundation 409, 410
Dorothy Strelsin Theatre 206
Dorr, Ann Marie 147
Dorrance, Michelle 196
Dorsch, Emily 192
Dorst, Susanne 116
Dory, John 36, 68
Dos Santos, Marivaldo 196
Doshi, Marcus 210, 249, 255, 260
Doss, Barrett 230
Doss, Barry 38, 68, 104
Doss, Trisha 112, 115, 117, 118, 199
Dossett, John 64, 100
Dotson, Bernard 216
Double Crossed 271
Double Indemnity 397
Doubles Crossed 289
Doucette, Josh 240
Doughty, Will 181
Douglas, Brett 193

Douglas, Daniel 115
Douglas, Donna 127
Douglas, Latisha 127
Douglas, Michael 418
Douglas, Natalie 112
Douglas, Ned 75
Douglas, Paul 417
Douglas, Reginald L. 227
Douglass, Allison 243
Douglass, Eliot 145
Douglass, Stephen 465
Doulin, Jack 71, 147, 197, 236, 258
Doumanian, Jean 36, 59, 78, 90, 94, 103, 141, 169, 185, 259
Dove, Bernie 135, 137, 154, 151
Dovell, David Lee 129
Dovetail Productions 128
Dow, Bruce 62
Dow, Ken 97
Dow, Kevin 97
Dow, Oliver 208
Dow, Steve 58, 75
Dowdy, Michelle 113
Dowling, Bairbre 229
Dowling, Joe 67, 176
Dowling, Robert W., II 35, 56, 81, 96
Dowling, Sarah 182, 197
Down Payment Productions 285
Down the Road 322
Downing, Steven 64
Downs, Don 29, 59
Downs, Donald 216, 217
Downstairs Cabaret Theatre at Sofia's 193
Downtown Art 285
Doyle, Christopher 198
Doyle, Conor 196
Doyle, Jack 216
Doyle, Lori M. 116
Doyle, Matt 110, 267
Doyle, Maxine 196
Dozier-Ezell, Rachel 138
Dr. Jekyll and Mr. Hyde 358
Dr. Seuss' How the Grinch Stole Christmas 387
DR2 119, 131, 170
Drabek, David 212
Drabicki, Stephen 178
Drabkin, Lois 223
Drachenberg, Andy 38, 57
Dracula 345, 373, 380

Draghici, Marina 237
Dragotta, Robert 151
Drake, Alan 160
Drake, Berlando 87
Drake, Berlando 87
Drake, Donna 192
Dram of Drummhicit, A 381
Drama Desk Awards 424
Drama League Awards 429
Drama of Works 285
Dramatist Guild Awards 436
Draper, Polly 155
Dratch, Rachel 197
Dravnel, Jan 178
Drawn and Quartered 324
Dream Up Festival 326
Dream Walker 317
Dreamcatcher Entertainment 201, 285
Dreamer Examines His Pillow, The 278, 309
Dreams in the Witch House, The 273
Dreams of Flying Dreams of Falling 208
Dreams of the Clockmaker 277, 293
dreamVisible Event Production 410
DreamWorks 92
Dreier, Alex 89
Drennan, Emily 133
Drewe, Anthony 101
Drewes, Glenn 93, 216, 217
Dreyfuss, Laura 32
Driggers, Bobby 146, 185, 409, 410
Driscoll, John-Patrick 129
Driscoll, Jon 75, 214
Driscoll, Sean 199
Drivas, Robert 418
Driver, Adam 9, 35, 251
Driver, John 418
Drucker, Tim 181
Druid Theater Company 198
Drummond, Pete 62, 92
Drummond, Scott 388
Drupla, Dale 257
Drury Lane Oakbrook Terrace 440
Druther, Ritchard 132
Dryda, Yakov 129
Dryer, Karen 133
DSM 47
Duan, Shawn 38, 116
Dubé-Dupuis, Noémie

129
Dubin, Jane 71
Dubin, Peter 150
DuBoff, Jill BC 39, 57, 134, 168, 225, 227, 228, 242, 243, 254, 261
DuBois, Amanda 137, 188
DuBois, Peter 242, 251
DuBon, Beth 248
Duborsarsky, Ursula 234
Dubuc, Stephano 167
Dubuc, Steven 129
Ducey, Therese 28
Duchan, Peter 254
duChateau, Annbritt 89
duChateau, Charles 29, 118
Duda, Kevin 90
Duddy, Joan 178
Dudley, William 67, 197, 409
Dudzick, Tom 184
Duell, William 465
Duffe, Mary 45, 78, 104, 108
Dupré, Ashlee 132
Duffin, Greg 145
Duff-MacCormick, Cara 418
Duffy, Amanda 64
Duffy, Michelle 83
Duffy, Rory 112
Duffy, Xander 169
Duffy, Zara 94
Dugan, Patrick 185
Dugger, Preston W., III 102
Duguid, Lorna 176
Dujardin, Maurice 232
Duke on 42nd Street 121, 134, 185, 225, 231, 232, 260
Duke, Patty 417
Duling, Michael 175, 194
Dulude, Joseph, II 33, 35, 92, 104, 111
Duma, Bongi 99, 116
Dumas, Cadien 195
Dumas, Debra 105
Dumas, Jennifer 194
Dumb Waiter 345
Dumezweni, Noma 197
Dunagan, Deanna 410, 421
Dunaway, Faye 418
Dunbar, Heather 28
Dunbar, McBrien 38, 66, 88, 147
Duncan, Laura Marie 89
Duncan, Lindsay 419
Duncan, Ryan 135

Duncan, Sandy 418
Duncan, Twilla 107
Dune, Carol M. 89
Dungeons and the Dragons, The 347
Dunlap, Jen 59, 252
Dunlop, Christopher C. 259
Dunn, Jamie 166
Dunn, Kate 93
Dunn, Kathryn 89
Dunn, Lindsay 201
Dunn, Loren 137
Dunn, Thomas 182
Dunn, Victoria 36
Dunne, Clare 198
Dunne, Griffin 419
Dunne, Jennifer 93, 113
Dunning, Tessa 77, 244, 261
Dunson, Janet 179
Dunster, Matthew 154
Dunton, Wayne 32
DuPaty, Bjorn 156, 176
Duplication Services 410
Dupré, Emilee 104, 253
Duque, Alejandra 127, 151
Durand, Andrew 110
Durant, Austin 110
Durcan, Paul 221
Durham, Christopher 125
Durham, Ryan C. 144
Durkin, Dan 253
Durkin, Daniel 47
Durond, Lelund 138
Durossette, Dirk 147
Dürrenmatt, Friedrich 115
Durst, Douglas 116
Dusel, Melanie 195
Dussault, Nancy 117, 192, 418
Dussault, Nick 436
Dust 318
Dutiel, Robert 239
Dutt, Hank 210
Dutton, Charles S. 419
Duty, Will 241, 242
Duveneck, Sonya 28
Dvoretskaya, Anastasia 129
Dvoretskaya, Victoria 129
Dvoretskiy, Dmitry 129
Dvorsky, George 204, 264
Dwyer, Kristin 163
Dwyfor, Dyfan 197
Dyer, Adam Ray 29

Dyer, Tom 136, 139, 146, 179, 185, 219, 230, 243, 244, 251, 252
Dykstra, Brian 167
Dymock, Mark 159
Dyrud, Claire 258
Dysfunctional Theatre Company 285
Dziedzic, Wojciech 211
Dziemianowicz, Joe 409, 428

E
Eagan, Daisy 192, 197
Eagan, Jason 142
Eakeley, Benjamin 50
Eaker, Sherry 433
Eaker, Timothy 64, 115
Earle, Joby 110
Early History of Fire, An 230, 268
Early Plays 168
Early, Clayton 208
Early, Michael 138
Earnshaw, Tony 157
Eason, Laura 233
East 13th Street Theatre 188, 208, 209, 218
East 4th Street Theatre 236
East in Red 285
East of the Sun, West of the Moon 297
East Village Theater Festival 299
East, Richard 100
Easter Bonnet Competition 118
Easter, Tyler 126
Eastman, Peter 72, 99
Easton, Richard 181, 417
Eat Your Heart Out 346
Eaton, Sam 195
Eaton, Stephanie 196
Eaves, Obadiah 222, 248
Eavesdropping on Dreams 180
Ebb, Fred 46, 93, 115
Ebel, Michele 150
Ebert, Gabriel 204, 224, 252
Ebner, Hermann 212
Echezaretta, Yurel 113
ECHO: 30 Years at PS122 306
Eckart, William & Jean 447
Eckelman, Laura 182, 259
Eckersley, Rogers 241

Eckert, Desiree 139, 226
Eckert, Ginger 141
Eckert, Rinde 120, 141, 165
Economakos, Christopher 112
Ed Kleban Prize 436
Edden, Tom 21, 72
Eddy, Isaac 189
Eddy, Maxwell 409
Eddy, Paul 209
Edelstein, Barry 244
Edelstein, Gordon 56, 247, 249, 422
Eder, Linda 420
Edge in Motion Theatre Company 286
Edge, Amanda 105
Edgerley, Phillip 197
Edgerton, Annie 100
Edinburgh Fringe Festival 161
Edington, Pamela 154
Edith 358
Edith Can Shoot Things and Hit Them 430
Edlund, Stephen 109
Edmonds, Katharine 78, 85, 87, 90, 104, 116
Edmonds, Shawn 78
Edson, Margaret 57
Education of the Girlchild 272
Edwall, Mattias 215
Edwards, Aimeé-Ffion 98
Edwards, Alan 146, 255
Edwards, Alan C. 247
Edwards, Andrew D. 109
Edwards, Angelica 99
Edwards, Anthony 114
Edwards, Anthony T. 233
Edwards, C.K. 89
Edwards, Daniel J. 85
Edwards, David 263
Edwards, Eboni 89
Edwards, Jim 36, 43, 58, 60, 70, 75
Edwards, John 97
Edwards, Leah 31
Edwards, Sara 33
Edwards, Sarah 208
Effinger, Trevor 113
Efimov, Pavel 215
Egan, Chris 67
Egan, John Treacy 109
Egan, Joseph 136, 182
Egan, Kate 68
Egan, Patrick 64
Egenes, Kirsten 249
Eggers, David 78, 85
Egizi, Diana 144

Ego Actus 286
Egosi, Ornit 133
Eh, Ulrich 210
Eheart, Steven 208
Ehle, Dave 101
Ehle, Jennifer 420
Ehrenberg, Jennifer 124
Ehrenreich, Jake 136, 182
Ehrenreich, Lisa 136, 182
Ehrlich, Stephen 255, 256
Eiben, Gabel 258
Eich, Stephen 87
Eichenberger, Rebecca 68, 116
Eichenhorn, Zach 189
Eichholz, Laura 101
Eidem, Bruce 76, 104, 116
Eifert, Karen L. 78
Eightythree Down 291, 340
Eigsti, Caleb 222
Eilerman, Nick 52
Einhorn, Andrew 68
Einhorn, Edward 171, 174
Einstein and Mileva 284
Eisenberg, Daryl 188, 193
Eisenberg, Jesse 123, 249
Eisenberg, Michael 95, 125
Eisenstein, Mat 33, 64
Eismann, Sarah 219
Ejan, Jasmine 160
Ekhougen, Marte Johanne 150
Ekström, Joakim 215
Ekström, Petter 215
Ekulona, Saidah Arrika 243
El Farraj, Sa'ad 210
El Guindi, Yussef 430
El Shaarawy, Saad 210
Elaborate Entrance of Chad Deity, The 346, 372
Elbrick, Xanthe 409, 410, 420
Elder, Claybourne 47
Elder, David 183
Eldon, Jack 64
Eldor, Oran 117
Elective Affinities 258, 313
Electra 393
Electric Lighthouse, The 288
Elektra 163

Elemeno Pea 398
Elephant Eye Theatrical 84
Elephant Room 173, 354
Elers, Francis 85, 116
Elevator Repair Service 236, 247
Eleven Entertainment 181
Elgart, Aaron 47, 58, 64, 134
Elgort, Ansel 228
Elhai, Robert 99
El-Husseini, Nassib 137, 138
Eli, Robert 137, 360
Elia, Julian 89, 116
Elias, Rosalind 33
Elice, Rick 71, 84, 97
Eliot, T.S. 199
Eliran Murphy Group 192
Elizabeth Hull-Kate Warriner Award 436
Elizabeth Rex 363
Elk, Hilary 102
Elkins, Doug 260
Ellen Stewart Theatre 186
Ellenberger, Jeff 235
Ellerman, Antje 143, 218, 219, 260
Ellert, Kristin 248
Elless, Hannah 40
Ellingsen, Brian 237
Ellington, Duke 199
Ellington, Justin 39
Elliot Norton Awards 436
Elliott, Bill 78, 85
Elliott, Erin 28
Elliott, Hillary 113
Elliott, Katrina 74, 92, 177
Elliott, Marianne 110
Elliott, Matthew 437
Elliott, Nicholas 168
Elliott, Patricia 409, 410, 418, 421
Elliott, Paul 44
Elliott, Scott 230
Elliott, Shawn 171, 459
Elliott, Stephan 106
Ellis, Alex 50, 92, 113
Ellis, Brandon 60, 158
Ellis, Jack 214
Ellis, John 212
Ellis, Joshua Mark 410
Ellis, Laura 36, 60
Ellis, Martyn 72
Ellis, Natalie Charle 169
Ellis, Sam 38, 50, 54, 62, 64, 66, 82

Ellis, Scott 35, 56, 81, 85, 116, 251
Ellison, Bill 55
Ellott, Ken 45
Ellsworth, Ryan 214
Elmalah, Alex 151
Elmaleh, Yaeko Miranda 259
Elman, Andrew 28
Elmer, David J. 33, 52, 68
Elrod, Carson 21, 71, 245, 388
Elrod, Josh 189
ElSaffar, Amir 237
Elsea, Dustin 196
Elsinghorst, Brooke 178
Elves and the Shoemaker, The 396
Emancipation of the Sassy Jewish Woman, The 314
Embry, Daryl 189
Emerald Green Productions 128
E-Merging Writers 286
Emerson, Jessica 134
Emerson, Michael 114
Emery, Lisa 11, 37, 253
Emick, Jarrod 420
Emig, Janna 209
EmilieCharlotte 167
Emillio, Nilton 189
Emily Grishman Music Preparation 78, 89, 90, 101
Emme 192
Emmes, David 447
Emmons, Beverly 49, 422
Emmons, Ryan 75
Emond, Linda 59
Emotional Creature 357
Empanada for a Dream 275
Emperor's New Codpiece, The 324
Empress and El Diablo, The 321
Empress of China, The 319, 324
Emrick, Kevin 59, 90, 185
Emursive 196
End Days 208
End of the Rainbow 20, 67, 377, 406, 409
End Stage Theatre 257
Endara, Robert J., II 58
Ende, Michael 232
Endgame 350
Endgame Entertainment 82

Endure: A Run Woman Show 283
Enemy of the People, An 304
Enfrascada 282
Eng, Randal 54
Engaging Shaw 387
Engel, Georgia 258
Engelbach, Jerry 258
Engelgeer, Rik 232
Engelhart, Jamie 71, 104
Engelke, Sarah 241
Engelsmann, Anke 210
Engen, Faith Annette 128
England, Sarah Brett 238
Englander, Heather 254
Englander, Jeff 151, 230
Englander, Michael 109
Engleman, Arnold 94
English, Bill 85
English, Donna 266
English, Dottie Marshall 231
English, Elizabeth R. 263
Englund, Alixandra Gage 181, 184
Englund, Ulf 215
Ennio Marchetto: The Living Paper Cartoon 392
Eno, Brian 213
Eno, Will 255, 256
Enomoto, Kiku 33
Ensemble Studio Theatre 121, 150, 182, 286, 419
Ensign, Evan 188
Entin, Peter 410
Entwisle, Christine 197
Eonnet, Eloise 163
Epcar, Jon 29
Ephron, Delia 192
Ephron, Nora 192
Epic Theatre Ensemble 126, 181
Epp, Steven 344
Epperson, Brandon 107
Epps, Sheldon 87
Epstein, Aaron 241
Epstein, Adam 58
Epstein, Adam Troy 58
Epstein, Alvin 218
Epstein, Arlene 424
Epstein, Dasha 38
Epstein, Shannon 188, 229
Epstein-O'Brien Adverstising 171, 172, 189

Equity Awards, The 437
Equity Library Theatre 419
Equivocation 354
Erat, Will 92
Erbe, Kathryn 249
Ercole, James 68, 85
Erdberg, Danny 74
Erhan, Yalcin 233
Eriksmoen, August 43, 84, 102, 103, 136
Eriksson, Bo 128
Eriksson, David 215
Ériu Dance Company 219
Erlick, Myles 89
Ernst, Bary 78
Ernst, Emily 260
Erosion: A Fable 294, 297
Errickson, Tim 444
Errico, Melissa 112
Erskine, Danny 198
Erwin, Jon 46
Esbjornson, David 200, 245, 257
Escalante, Alejandra 378
Escape 294
Escatel, Lynann 113
Escobar, Irma 33, 66, 78, 90
Escola, Cole 187
Escott, Colin 87, 103, 136
Esell, Damian 234
Esham, Gavin 192
Eshkar, Shelley 213
Eshleman, Robert 153
Eskandini, Saum 162
Eskelson, Dana 250
Eskin, Simon 213
Esnaola, Juan Kruz de Garaio 161
ESosa 54
Esparza, Audrey 223
Esparza, Raúl 9, 83, 86, 420, 429
Esper, Michael 23, 77, 242
Esposito, Cyrena 102
Esposito, Giancarlo 209, 268, 419
Esposito, Teressa 150
Esse, Parker 168
Essman, Nina 71, 109, 111
Estep, John 37, 49, 50, 243
Estes, Eleanor 209
Esteva, Joaquin 40
Estevez, Winston 149
Estienne, Marie-Hélène 259

EstroGenius Festival 326
ETdC Projects' Lab 287
Eternal Equinox 170
Ethel Barrymore Theatre 46, 59, 86
Ether Dome 347
Ethos Performing Arts 287
Etiquette of Death, The 295
Eugene O'Neill Theater Center 152
Eugene O'Neill Theatre 90, 113
Eunice, Beth 112
Euripides 155, 212
Eusebio, Nelson T., III 244
Eustis, Molly Minor 181, 208
Eustis, Oskar 32, 38, 244, 437, 447
Eva the Chaste 131
Evangelisto, Christie 211, 255-257
Evanko, Ed 418
Evanko, Edward D. 410
Evans, B.J. 163, 187
Evans, Ben 75
Evans, Bridgit Antoinette 145
Evans, C. Barrack 236
Evans, Daniel Lynn 113
Evans, David 111
Evans, Dorothy 50
Evans, Erica 226, 260
Evans, Harvey 117, 202, 410
Evans, Lawrence 152
Evans, Len 194
Evans, Lynorris 83
Evans, Maruti 54, 208, 247
Evans, Paige 39, 110, 224
Evans, Ross 42, 216, 226
Evans, Scott 158
Evans, Scott Alan 207
Evansohn, Gabe 208, 209
Evariste, Mike 32
Evening of Reconings, An 293
Evening with Joseph Keckler, An 294
Evening with Patti LuPone and Mandy Patinkin, An 14, 46
Evens, Leo Ash 263
Everett, Bridget 187
Everett, Dany 215

Everett, Rick 157
Everett, Tim 417
Everidge, Daniel 181
Everitt, Morgan 149
Evil Clergyman, The 312
Eviston, Patrick 71, 101, 106
Evita 20, 68, 385
Evolution 182
Ewwaraye-Griffin, Maia 111
Exit Carolyn 314
Exorcist, The 372
Experiments 294
Explosion, Ananias 232
Extant Arts 287
Extrell, Kirk 134
Eyer, J. Austin 95, 193
Eyes of Babylon, The 126, 358
Eyre, Richard 44, 101
Eyrick, Aiden 98
Ezell, Jeremy 201
Ezralow, Daniel 28

F
Faba, Mike 168
Fabel, Katie 112
Faber, Carl 90
Faber, Mary 95, 188
Fabian, Kathy 37, 38, 49, 50, 74, 78, 94, 104, 169, 243, 256
Fabiani, Carla 184, 235
Fabozzi, Alex 237
Fabricatore, Dan 144
Fabris, Bill 235
Fabris, Richard 87
Fabula Media Partners LLC 103
Fabulous Darshan 323
FACT Theatre 315
Fae, Erica 184
Fagan, Garth 99
Fagan, Kip 249
Fagan, Shawn 379
Fagan, Valerie 84, 462
Fagles, Robert 237
Fahey, Caitlin 54
Fahie, Mike 212
Fahmi, Raida 88
Fahmy, Kareem 236
Fahrner, Kate 111
Fahy, Meghann 201
Fairbanks, Lily 258, 261
Fairhurst, Jimmy 214
Fairytale Lives of Russian Girls, The 349
Faist, Mike 64
Faitelson, Danielle 219
faith 307
Fajans, Pepper 213
Fajardo, Alejandro 177,

242, 261
Fakler, Ken 155
Fakston Productions 92, 95, 155
Falana, Lola 419
Falberg, Alex 147
Falborn, Veronica 112, 115
Falco, Edie 94, 420
Falcon, Rebecca 155
Falcone, Tabitha 409
Falcone, Tiffany 409, 410
Fales, Maggie 240
Falk, Katie 202
Falk, Peter 465
Falk, Yasmine 223
Falkenstein, Eric 49, 73
Fall to Earth, The 162
Fall, Lulu 32
Fallen Angel Theatre Company 131
Fallen Angels 380
Fallon, Susan J. 35, 56, 81, 96
Family Room, The 287
Fan, Lily 38, 62, 193
Fand, Peter 130
Fane, Lisa 262
Fanelli, Henry 105
Fang, Yin 211
Fanger, Iris 436
Fania Records 133
Fankhauser, Ben 64
Fantasticks, The 190, 403
Fanuele, Vincent J. 33
Farber Foundry Theatre Company 130
Farber, Seth 92
Farber, Yael 130
Farbiarz, Elan Wolf 189
Farbrother, Mindy 93
Farcher, Matthew 164
Farcry Production 159
Farentino, James 418, 466
Farewell to Sanity 304
Farfalla, Michael 103
Farfan, Armando, Jr. 112, 113
Fargotstein, Dara 226, 259, 260
Faridany, Francesca 35
Farina, Gina 159
Faris, Nasser 237
Faris, Scott 58
Farley, Kristin 95
Farm Boy 159
Farmer, George 102
Farnworth, John 232
Farquhar, Robert 160
Farr, David 197

Farra, Ashley 253
Farrar, Thursday 158, 228
Farrell, Brian 418
Farrell, Brian D. 410
Farrell, John 257
Farrell, Larry 85
Farrell, Malony 82, 83
Farrell, Matthew 66, 104
Farrell, Tom Riis 162
Farrelly, Leah 137, 143
Farrington, Kate 239
Farris, Ralph 99
Farris, Scott 93
Fartiste, The 151
Fasano, Matthew 84
Fasbender, Bart 143, 209, 230, 249, 253
Fast, Alex 188, 189
Fat Camp 181
Father, The 300
Fatica, Michael 64
Faucher, Matt 207
Faulkenberry, Rebecca 29, 108
Fault Line Theatre Company 276, 287
Fauré, Kimberly 85, 78, 115
Faure, Paige 95
Faust, Kenneth 177, 185
Favorito, Joe 70
Fay, Brendan 198
Fay, Brendan M. 97
Fay, Vincent 92, 179
Fearless Design 195
Feast: an intimate Tempest, The 363
February House 247, 382
Federan, Mitchel David 420
Federer Versus Murray 176
Federman, Wendy 36, 66, 84
Federov, Anthony 117
Fedigan, James 28, 33, 75, 92, 93, 95, 107
Fee, Andrew 231
Feher, Jack 241
Feiffer, Halley 94, 257, 421
Feigenbaum, Michael 133
Feilhauer, Ross 82
Feiner, Harry 157, 239
Feingold, Michael 426, 428
Feirstein, Barry 92, 244
Feist, Gene 35, 56, 81, 85, 96, 116, 251
Fela! 362

Feld, Aneta 58, 59, 60, 75, 142, 166
Feld, Melanie 216
Feldberg, Robert 428
Felder, Abby 238
Feldman, Adam 428
Feldman, Danny 223
Feldman, Jack 64
Feldman, Lawrence 95
Feldman, Susan 148, 151, 160, 168, 173, 178
Feldshuh, Tovah 202, 419
Felix & The Diligence 307
Fellini, Federico 149
Fellman, Ashley 171
Fellner, Eric 89
Fellner, Jenny 111
Fellowes, Julian 101
Felony in Blue, A 303
Felstein, Robert 190, 266
Femenella, Andrew 40
Femme Fatale Theater 287
Feng, Jianbin 232
Fenholt, Jeff 451
Fenkart, Bryan 102
Fenton, James J. 162
Fenwick, Chris 153
Fenwick, Oliver 197
Ferber, Alan 92
Ferbers, Jutta 210
Fergerson, Katharine S. 131, 166
Ferguson, Ben 147
Ferguson, Earlyn Kizzy 127
Ferguson, Lauren 245
Ferguson, Wilkie, III 54, 55, 113, 202
Ferland, Danielle 221, 419
Fernandez, Arianda 140
Fernandez, Kristina 111
Fernandez, Peter Jay 208
Fernandez, Ricardo 153
Fernandez, Stacia 100, 118
Fernhout, Roeland 211
Ferraiuolo, Caroline 234
Ferrall, Gina 116
Ferrante, Frank 419
Ferranti, Gina 188
Ferrara, Julie 116
Ferreira, Carlos 178
Ferrell, Conchata 418
Ferrell, Rachelle 118
Ferrell, Will 441
Ferri, David 234

Ferri, Stephen 409
Ferrin, Julie 159
Ferris, Gretchen 146
Ferris, Jim 99
Ferro, Tim 37, 49, 50, 85, 94
Ferrone, Keneth 149
Ferrone, Richard 207
Ferziger, Sue 178
Festen 178
Festwochen, Wiener 199
Fetela, Monika 178
Feuchtwanger, Peter R. 230, 243
Feustel, Kevin 166, 201
Fiasco Theater 141, 259
Fickett, Mary 417, 466
Fickinger, Steve 64
Fico, John 152
Fidelity Investments 89
Fiedelman, Rosie Lani 113, 183
Fiedler, Joe 192
Fiedler, Josh 252
Fieger, Stephanie 252
Field, Alexis 125
Field, Anita 77
Field, Arabella 420
Field, Melanie 68, 105
Field, Michael 238
Fielden, Josh 409
Fielding, Emma 420
Fields, Dorothy 199
Fields, Felicia P. 420
Fields, Joe 419
Fields, Joseph 217
Fiendel, Colyn 52, 112, 115, 117, 261
Fiennes, Ralph 420
Fierce! 246
Fierstein, Harvey 64, 410, 419, 429
Fifty Church Street Productions 66
Figgins, Dionne 82
Fighter 304
Figueiras, Alberto 191
Filanovsky, Nadia 192
Filerman, Michael 38, 54, 78, 159, 410
Files, Christina 189
Filichia, Peter 409, 413, 420, 428
Filippelli, Jamie 202
Filloux-Bennett, Henry 160
Filomena, Doug 185, 250
Filomena, Douglas 241, 242
Fily-Paré, Yann 138
Fin, Jon 89
Findlay, Elizabeth 115,

147
Findlay, Jim 182, 212
Fine, Lydia 147
Fine, Zachary 176
Fineman, Carol 68
Fineman, Lori 124, 134, 153
Finen, John 211
Finian's Rainbow 384
Fink, Bert 422
Fink, Katherine 55, 59
Finke, Anna 213
Finkelstein, Viviana 234
Finkle, David 433
Finkle, David 428, 433
Finley, Felicia 162
Finley, Shersten 233
Finn, Jeffrey 45
Finno, Tony 47
Fiordellisi, Angelina 129, 144, 165, 171, 249
Fiore, Mark 46
Fiorello, David 190
Fire This Time 292
Fireboat Productions 152
Firebrand Theory Theater Company 287
Firefly Music Service 108, 153
Firework Theater 287
Firman, Linsay 150, 182
First Date: A New Musical 345, 370
Firth, Peter 419
Fisch, Irwin 202
Fischbach, Makenzi Rae 89
Fischer, AraBella 129, 143, 218, 219, 248, 250
Fischer, Desi 218, 219, 255, 256
Fischer, Kim 209
Fischer, Kurt 115
Fischer, Lindsay 233
Fischer, Russell 97, 113, 115
Fish Eye 283
Fish Men 374
Fishburne, Laurence 410, 419
Fishel, Jacob 248, 252, 260
Fisher, A.J. 100
Fisher, Alex 163
Fisher, Alexander 129
Fisher, Layna 144
Fisher, Linda 219, 220, 447
Fisher, Richard 410
Fisher, Rick 89

Fisher, Rob 85, 93, 265
Fisher, Wil 202
Fisher-Wilson, LaVon 52
Fishman, Alan H. 210
Fishman, Carol 73, 241, 262
Fishman, Shai 133
Fitch, Andrew 183
Fitch, Niles 99
Fitzgerald, Adam 151
Fitzgerald, Bill 142, 149, 150, 172, 184
Fitzgerald, Christian 179
Fitzgerald, Ed 259
Fitzgerald, F. Scott 247
Fitzgerald, Kathy 111, 162
Fitzgerald, Kirk 183
Fitzgerald, Lauren P. 231
Fitzgerald, Peter 49, 58, 94, 106, 143, 146, 185
Fitzgibbons, Mark 28
Fitzhugh, Ellen 163
Fitzpatrick, Colleen 33, 216
Fitzpatrick, Paul 231
Fitzpatrick, Sara 36, 43, 60, 76
FitzSimmons, James 39, 113
Five by Five 314
Five Cent Productions 84
Fjelstad, Gary 232
Flachbart, Jack 180
Flack, Eamon 234
Flacks, Niki 146
Flagg, Tom 190
Flaglor, Anna 242
Flaglor, Anna Estelle 262
Flaherty, Tacy 236, 237
Flaiano, Ennio 149
Flanagan, Kate 219
Flanagan, Margian 75
Flanagan, Theresa 112, 134, 153
Flanders, Kristin 224
Flanigan, Lauren 202
Flateman, Charles 410
Flateman, Timothy 60
Flatow, Paula 235
Flatt, Andrew 64
Flauto, Elizabeth 97
Flea Theater 143, 163, 177, 287
Fleck, Charlotte 80, 227
Fleeshman, Richard 22, 76
Flegelman, Rheba 110
Fleischer, Brad 88
Fleischer, Evan 168

Fleisher, Julian 247
Fleming, Adam 113, 200
Fleming, Becky 64
Fleming, Craig 231
Fleming, DeWitt, Jr. 199
Fleming, Jon 173
Fleming, Katie 125
Fleming, Ron 33, 73
Fleming, Sam 105, 240
Flemming, Theresa 159
Fleshler, Glenn 59, 86
Flesner, Leslie Donna 33
Fletcher, Jim 168, 247
Fletcher, John 146
Fletcher, Jon 47
Fletcher, Rebecca Joy 174
Fletcher, Ross 247
Fliakos, Ari 168
Flight 170
Flinn, Lewis 52, 124
Flinn, Nick 115
Flint, Carly 263, 266
Flint, Samantha 42, 245
Floating Point Waves 291, 296
Flockhart, Calista 420
Flora Roberts Award 436
Flora, David 206
Florence, Jocelyn 142
Flores, Alex 223
Flores, Charles 171
Flores, Elizabeth 125, 190
Flores, Eugenio Saenz 35-37, 46, 49, 56, 58-60, 73, 75, 77, 81, 185
Flores, Julia 159
Flores, Wallace 37, 74, 87, 94
Florida Studio Theatre 360, 371
Florin, Jacki Barlia 36, 50, 62, 78, 95, 98
Flower Thief, The 292
Flowers, Cynthia 208
Flowers: A Thorny Romance 273
Floyd, Carmen Ruby 54, 55, 199, 202
Floyd, Jay 87
Floyd, Mike 64, 106
Flux Theatre Ensemble 288
Flying by Foy 106
Flying Snakes in 3D!!! 279
Flynn, George 95
Flynn, Gerard Mannix 159
Flynn, Michael Bradshaw 154
Flynn, Nick 172

Flynn, Rachel 149
Flynn, Tom 111
Flynn, Warren 47, 54
fml: how Carson McCullers saved my life 400
Fn Do it Productions 288
Foa, Barrett 117
Foard, Merwin 84
Focht, Osborn 128
Fodor, Kate 243
Fogarty, Lulu 309
Fogel, Alex 80
Fogler, Dan 420
Foglia, Leonard 104
Foil, Jeremy W. 87
Foister, Breanna 249
Foldesi, Julie 64
Foley, Bobby 163
Foley, Don 40
Foley, Dylan 86
Foley, F. Kathleen 442
Foley, Peter 47
Folk-Sullivan, Katherine 163
Follies 11, 33, 116, 202, 362, 363
Follow the Leader 305
Fomina, Maria 215
Fon, Simon 62
Fonda, Jane 417
Fonda, Peter 418
Fong, Rebecca 138, 149
Fontaine, Bruno 243
Fontaine, Jeff 195
Fontana, Samantha 180
Fontana, Santino 96, 205, 251, 267
Food and Fadwa 237
Foolish Theatre Company 288, 308
Fool's Paradise, A 397
Foote, Hallie 378
Foote, Horton, Jr. 378
Foote, Jenifer 33, 108, 116
for black boys who have considered homicide... 300, 309
Forbes, George 428
Forbes, Kamilah 36, 49, 145
Forbes, Kate 420
Forbrich, Joe 245
Force, Richard 78
Ford, Carin 227
Ford, Chris 263, 264
Ford, Jennie 68
Ford, Jessica 244
Ford, John 214, 260
Ford, Nancy 264, 265, 267

Ford, Paul 46
Ford, Sara Jean 105
Ford, Sarah Elizabeth 151
Ford, Shannon 40
Ford's Theatre 361, 371
Foreign Bodies 310
Foreman, Donell James 164
Foreplay Play, The 281
Forestieri, Gabriel 196
Forlenza, Meredith 225, 241
Fornarola, Andrea 113
Fornier, Robert 85
Forshaw, Jamie 28
Forsman, Carl 222
Forst, Liz 146
Forste, Andrew 85
Forsyth, Julie 234
Forsythe Company 211
Forsythe, William 211
Forte, Alexis 223
Fosse, Bob 93
Fossi, Jim 98
Foster Entertainment 128
Foster, David J. 187
Foster, Fred 258
Foster, Gloria 418
Foster, Herb 246
Foster, Hunter 103, 112, 230
Foster, Jennifer 181
Foster, Kate 177, 258
Foster, Sutton 85, 114, 198
Fouché, Jennifer 149
Foucher, Marie Renee 115
Fouéré, Olwen 260
Foundry Theatre 127, 151
Fountain, Elizabeth 164
Fountain, Trey 32
Four Dogs and a Bone 317
Four Quartets 199
Fowler, Bruce 99
Fowler, David 236
Fowler, Kelsey 47
Fowler, Rana 98
Fowler, Randi 195
Fowler, Wyche, Jr. 410
Fowles, Catherine 142, 149, 150, 171, 172, 184, 189
Fox Theatricals 137
Fox, Alan 174
Fox, Bette-Lee 410
Fox, Eamonn 198
Fox, Elliot 243
Fox, Laurel 151

Fox, Libby 47, 58, 75
Fox, Morgan 152, 163, 172, 223
Fox, Rick 62, 63
Fox, Robert 43
Foxhole Productions 288
Foxwoods Theatre 28
Foxworth, Robert 418
Foy, Harriett D. 248
Fracé, Jeffrey 144
Fragments 259
Fragomeni, Brianna 89
Fraley, Lisa Ann 32
Fram, Joel 117, 217
Francavilla, Anthony 138, 140
Francavilla, Len 177
Franciosa, Anthony 417
Francis, Steve 234
Francisco, Alexis 309
Franck, Alison 40
Franck, Sandra M. 28
Francoise, Jean Houle 145
Francone, Nick 74, 166
Frank Music Corp. 75
Frank, Emmy 216
Frank, Glenda 438
Frank, Laura 75
Frank, Maya Jade 68
Frank, Micha 94
Frank, Todd 50, 82, 103
Franke, Mara 233
Frankel Green Theatrical Management 82, 155, 185
Frankel, Brian 54
Frankel, Jennifer 92, 113
Frankel, Jerry 38, 47, 54, 66
Frankel, Mac 38
Frankel, Mark 189
Frankel, Richard 82, 155, 185
Frankel, Ronald 38, 47, 54, 78
Frankenstein With Mary Shelley 312
Frankl, Lizzie 75
Frankle, Sophie 229
Franklin, Bonnie 418
Franklin, Josh 76, 85
Franklin, Zoe 196
Frankovich, Lauren 235
Franks, Andrew 197
Franks, Jay 108
Franzblau, William 149, 150
Franzetti, Matt 130
Franzgrote, Christoph 216, 217

Fraser, Alexander 104, 131, 192
Fraser, Alison 151, 178, 192
Fraser, Bonnie 112
Fraser, Dominic 214
Fraser, Scott 210
Fratti, Mario 426, 438
Fraver 169
Frazier, Daveed D. 37, 49, 71, 94
Frazier, Gibson 277
Frazier, Jan Price 36, 49
Frech, Kevin R. 173
Frechette, Peter 419
Frechtman, Bernard 172
Freckleface The Musical 154
Fred and Adele Astaire Awards 437
Fred Ebb Award 437
Frederick Loewe Award 436
Frederick P. Rose Hall 197, 199
Frederickson, Christian 218, 219, 226
Free For All: Julius Caesar 397
Freed, Lauren 181
Freedberg, Avram 71, 131, 133
Freedman, Greg 112
Freedman, Katherine 231
Freedom to Marry 155
Freeman, Christopher 99
Freeman, Craig 125
Freeman, Jackie 28
Freeman, Jeff 233
Freeman, Jonathan 101
Freeman, Justin 103
Freeman, K. Todd 114
Freeman, Kate 33
Freeman, Kathleen 420
Freeman, Lindsey 193
Freeman, Morgan 114
Freeman-Lynde, Amelia 247, 248
Freer, Kate 145
Freiburg, Johanna 246
Freitag Productions 54
Freitag, Alexis 410
Freitag, Barbara 36, 67, 78, 92, 102
Freitag, Buddy 36, 67, 78, 92, 102, 466
Freitas, Jessica 125
French, Arthur 161
French, Susan 153
Frener, Samantha 247
Fresh Glory Productions

75
Freshly Squeezed Juices Theatre Company 288
Freshwater, Geoffrey 197
Freud's Last Session 191, 393
Freudendahl, Anders 215
Frew, Matt 230, 248
Frey, Jessica 209
Frey, Matt 227, 253, 258
Frey, Taylor 95
Freymann, Saz 190
Fribo, Louise 212
Fricker, Stephanie 105
Fridell, Lexie 188
Fried and Kowgios Partners 410
Fried, Donald 237, 243, 256
Fried, Jessica 36-38, 46, 54, 66
Fried, Marilyn 129
Friedlander, Michael 207
Friedler, Dina S. 40, 50, 92
Friedman, Dan 152, 167
Friedman, Dana 131
Friedman, Dave 219
Friedman, David 112, 118
Friedman, Leo 466
Friedman, Lyle 223
Friedman, Maria 420
Friedman, Meg 138, 146, 176, 198
Friedman, Melissa 181
Friedman, Michael 260
Friedman, Peter 258
Friedman, Renata 344
Friedman, Rosalind 426
Friedman, Sonia 72
Friedmann, Joyce 73
Friedson, Adam 264
Friel, Anna 420
Friel, Brian 219
Friel, Dierdre 83, 254
Friend, Simon 215
Friends and Relations 303
Friends Don't Let Friends 296
Friends in Theater Company 202
FRIGID Festival 326
Frimer, Danielle 149
Friou, Amanda 253
Frishwasser, Dan 49, 73, 102, 146, 244
Frishwasser, Daniel 95
Frisina, Kyle 253
Fritsch, Andy 32, 71

Fritz Travel 410
Fritz, David 410
Fritz, Lana 447
Frizzi & Lazzi Music
   Theatre Company 282
Froelich, Danielle 113
Frogs 276, 287
From Rags to Riches
   298
From the Same Cloth
   287
From White Plains 287
Froman, Kurt 89
Fromin, Vladimir 129
Froncek, Jesse 225, 227
Frost, Sue 102
Fruge, Lloyd 47
Fry, Gareth 214
Fry, Jake 47, 68
Fry, Katherine 236, 237
Fry, Katie 223
Fry, Peter 125, 169,
   172, 177, 185, 240
Frydman, Ken 131
Frydrychowski, Paul
   143
Fuchs, Andreas 210
Fuchs, Dorian 85, 116
F*lt Club 287
*F*cking World According
   to Molly, The* 300
*Fuente Ovejuna: A
   Disloyal Adaptation*
   223
Fuerza Bruta: Look Up
   191
Fugard, Athol 56, 255
Fugaro, Kevin 158
Fuhr-Carbone, Kim 133
Fujiwara, Sarah 139
Fukuoka, Yutaka 197
Fulbright, Peter 45, 78,
   86, 97, 104, 108
Fulcomer, Alden 409
Fuld, James 54, 68
Full Beaver Moon Show
   294
Full Disclosure 290, 315
Fuller, Justin 233
Fuller, Penny 378
FullStop Collective 289
Fullum, John 31, 80
Fulman, Porter 187
Fulton, Brandalyn 52,
   113
Fulton, Dave 28
Fumusa, Dominic 223
Funke, Annie 132
Funny Pain, The 283
Funny…Shesh
   Productions 271, 289
Funnybook/Tragicbook
   289

Furby, Andrew 214
Furches-Howell, Brie
   170
FUREE 127
Furey, Ben 89
Furiga, Benjamin 224
Furman, Gabriel 129
Furman, Jill 45
Furman, Roy 37, 45, 68,
   78, 84, 90, 94, 106
Furneaux-Arends,
   Eugenia 249
Furnish, David 89
Furnon, Ludivine 187
Furr, David 96
Furth, George 216
Furze, Elizabeth 67
Furze, Liz 77, 147
Fusco, Giuseppe 152
Fusco, Luciano 93
Fusté, María Cristina
   183
Future is in Eggs, The
   296
*Futurity: A Musical by
   the Lisps* 351

G
Gabay, Roy 74, 108,
   177, 177
Gabbard, Tom 36, 137
Gabbard, Tyler 226
Gaber, Meghan 143
Gabis, Stephen 35, 60,
   70, 97, 102, 169, 208,
   220, 221, 236, 251
Gabler, Jolie 103
Gabowski, Charlie 35,
   56, 81, 85, 96, 251
Gabriel 312
Gabriel, Dapne 171
Gabrielle, Clara 171
Gabrielsen, Helen 184
Gacetta, Michael 140
Gachignard, Molly 85
Gad, Josh 90, 114,
   202, 426
Gaddas, James 154
Gaddy, Lonnie 49,
   77, 91
Gaeta, Doug 47, 70, 85
Gaffin, Arthur 33
Gaffney, Jessica 126
Gaffney, Mo 155
Gagliardi, Marg 74
Gagliardi, Mark 143,
   177, 410
Gagne, Olivia 176
Gagnon, Richard 138
Gago, Alejo 234
Gaiger, Lucy 100
Gailus, Arshan 177
Gaines, Bahiyah Sayyed

102
Gaines, Boyd 80, 419,
   422
Gaines, Danielle 195
Gajda, Lisa 92
Galante, Michael 235
Galantich, Tom 81
Galbraith, Sarah 410
Galde, Anthony 111
Gale, David 243
Gale, Gregory 86, 108,
   261
Gale, Mariah 197
Galecki, Johnny 420
Galendeev, Valery 215
Galgano, Frank 112
Galiatsatos, Vicky 410
Galileo 218
Gallagher, Brian 146
Gallagher, Heather 182,
   258
Gallagher, John, Jr. 98
Gallagher, Kathleen 43,
   60, 109
Gallagher, Matt 63
Gallagher, Megan 419
Gallagher, Peter 419
Gallagher, Richard
   77, 96
Gallaher, Jason 128
Gallaher, Tom 117
Gallas, Sydney 245
Gallerani, Allie 255
Gallery Players, The
   289, 340
Galletto, Dardo 81
Galligan-Stierle, Aaron
   105
Gallin, Susan 94, 428
Gallitelli, Lauren 78, 96
Gallo, David 49
Gallo, David 36, 49,
   102, 146, 155, 185,
   223, 256
Gallo, Fred 28, 33, 52
Gallo, Natalie 100
Gallo, Paul 254
Gallo, Suzanne 213
Galloway, Don 418
Galloway, Ian William
   154
Galloway, Kathryn 188
Galvan, Jesse 54
Galvin, Emma 147
Galvin, Noah 203, 249
Gambarose, Jenn 152
Gamble, Eleasha 202
Gamble, Julian 59
Game of Love, The 267
Game Play 2011 280
Game, The 355
Game's Afoot, The 365
Gandolfo, B.J. 128

Gandy, Irene 38, 47, 54,
   66, 410
Ganner, Josephine
   Edwards 149
Gans, Andrew 410
Ganz, Joel Reuben 110
Gao, Jian 232
Gaouette, Deborah 127,
   150
Garage 284
Garber, Brian 236
Garber, Victor 116, 409,
   412, 418
Garbo 273
Garchik, Jacob 210, 211
Garcia, Alejandro 191
Garcia, Ana M. 60
Garcia, Carlos E.
   Fernandes 213
García, Gabriel 149
Garcia, Gabriela 93
Garcia, Kevin 199
Garcia, Martin 28
Garcia-Lee, Paloma
   105, 113
Garci-Suli, Hilda 62
Gardin, Miriam 99, 182
Gardiner, Eric 102
Gardiner, Lizzy 106
Gardiner, Marsi 102
Gardiner, Peter F. 179
Gardner, Brad 116, 117
Gardner, Carrie 50, 81,
   90, 96, 251, 252
Gardner, Cooper 258
Gardner, Earl 85
Gardner, Elysa 424, 429
Gardner, Ian Yuri 99
Gardner, Lori 206
Gardner, Vincent 199
Gardos, David 267
Gare St Lazare Players
   256
Garefino, Anne 90
Garfield, Andrew 59
Garfield, Julie 418
Garfinkle, David 28, 75
Garland, Jim 127
Garman, Andrew 230,
   258
Garner, Andre 118
Garner, Crystal 217
Garner, Crystal 55, 217
Garner, Rosy 148, 169
Garner, Sandra 168
Garnett, Chip 419
Garnett, Kim 44, 98
Garofalo, Janeane 230
Garou 129
Garratt, Geoffrey 101
Garrett, Kelly 418
Garrett, Lou 253
Garrett, Rachel 28

Garrett, Vance 196
Garrison, Daniel 244
Garrison, David 132,
   243
Garrison, Gary 170
Garrison, Sean 418
Garson, Heidi 235
Garver, Jack 235
Garvey-Blackwell,
   Jennifer 115, 261
Garvoille, David 180
Gaschen, David 105
Gaskins, Anthony 309
Gaspard, Charlotte 169,
   244, 246
Gasser, Johnny 130
Gasteyer, Ana 114
Gaswirth, Nick 192
Gate Theatre 213
Gatehouse, Paul 105
Gates, Kyle 241, 242,
   254, 262
Gates, Philip 250
Gates, Sarah 241, 255
Gates, Thomas J. 64
Gatling, Nkrumah 32
Gattelli, Christopher 40,
   64, 132, 254
Gatz 247
Gaudio, Bob 97
Gaughan, John 198
Gauthier, Leslie 149
Gavigan, Danny 368
Gavigan, Jenna 158
Gavin, Rupert 98
Gavrylenko, Anastasiia
   187
Gay Agenda, The 155
Gay, Jackson 250
Gay, John 210
Gayer, Lora Lee 33, 216
Gaynes, Edmund 127,
   142, 149, 150, 171,
   172, 184, 189, 190
Gaynor, Bob 83, 92
Gazillion Bubble Show
   191
Gazzara, Ben 417, 466
Gbeblewoo, Alexandre
   210
Ge, Haiping 232
Geballe, Tony 248
G bska, Karolina 178
Geer, Kevin 257
Geffen Playhouse 372
Gehan, Nathan 68
Gehlfuss, Nick 219
Gehling, Drew 50
Gehring, Nicole 188
Geidel, Paul 235
Geigel, Laurie 130
Geiger, Allie 237
Geiger, Mary Louise

243, 244
Gelber, Jordan 200
Geller, Jeremy 162
Gellhorn, Martha 229
Gelman, Joel J. 388
Gelpe, Leah 177, 225,
   242
Geltman, Tracy 71, 84
Geltman, Zoe 249
Gemignani, Alexander
   104, 182, 420
Gemignani, Paul 104,
   116
Gemini CollisionWorks
   289, 340
Genda, Stefanie 45
Gendron, John E. 52,
   94, 113, 181
Gener, Randy 424, 447
Genet, Jean 172
Genthner, Penn 163,
   177
Gentile, Thomás 426
*Gentlemen Prefer
   Blondes* 217
Gentry, Bob 418
Geoffreys, Stephen 419
George Freedley
   Memorial Award 437
George Is Dead 37
George Jean Nathan
   Award 437
George, Abhilash 191
George, George W. 102
George, Jeff 233
George, Laura 235
George, Madeleine 227
George, Rhett 102
George, Thomas 164
George, Tony 140
Georgia Shakespeare
   361, 372
Geraci, Drew 162, 188
Gerald Lynch Theatre
   202
Gerald Schoenfeld
   Theatre 47, 66, 103
Gerald W. Lynch Theater
   198
Geralis, Tony 116
Gerard, Jeremy 429
Gerasimowicz, Sonny
   148
Gerber, Bill 141, 169
Gerdes, Anna 239, 240
Gere, Richard 419
Gerecitano, Liz 193
Gerhard, Daniel J. 46
Gericke, Joshua 50
Gering, Luc 210
Gerlach, Megan 189
Gerle, Andrew 264,
   267, 436

Germ Project, The 272
Germanacos, Constantine 68
Gero, Edward 361
Gerroll, Daniel 419
Gersh, Geoff 189
Gershwin Hotel 138
Gershwin Theatre 111, 447
Gershwin, George 54, 78
Gershwin, Ira 54, 78
Gershwin, Leonore 54
Gershwins' *Porgy and Bess, The* 16, 54, 118, 350, 406, 409
Gerstel, Leah 113, 193
Gersten, Bernard 39, 73, 110, 224
Gersten, David 172, 194
Gersten, Jenny 32
Gertner, Jared 90
Gertrude and Irving Dimson Theatre 261
Gethers, Peter 185
Gettler, Victoria 28
Geva Theatre Center 361, 373
GFour Productions 136
Ghebremichael, Asmeret 90
Gheesling, Anna 238, 239
Ghersa, Martín 234
Ghetto Klown 94
Ghost Brothers of Darkland County 349
Ghost in the Machine 284
Ghost Light 357
Ghost The Musical 22, 75, 410
Ghosts 314
Ghost-Writer 384
Ghoussaini, Noelle 237
Giamanco, Dusty 191
Giampaolo, Aldo 129
Giancola, Eric 100
Gianino, Antonia 99, 103
Gianino, Jack 207, 262
Giannetta, Lucia 83
Giannini, Maura 216, 217
Giant 366
Giarmo, Chris 212
Giasson, Line 129
Gibbens, Kate Sullivan 113
Gibbons, Sean Patrick 167
Gibbs, Caroline 138
Gibbs, David 108, 139

Gibbs, Kristen 245
Gibbs, Nancy Nagel 71, 109
Giberson, Heidi 190
Gibson, Jane 214
Gibson, Kate Michael 143
Gibson, Lewis 210
Gibson, Matt 221
Gibson, Melissa James 447
Gibson, Michael 43, 85, 115
Gibson, Stephanie 84, 113
Gideon Productions 290
Gieger, Alexandra 130, 208
Giering, Jenny 267
Gifford, Alex 145
Gifford, Ryan 62
Gift Theatre Company 252
Gil, Ramon 238
Gilbert Productions 75
Gilbert, Hayden 213
Gilbert, Karen 72
Gilbert, Melissa 419
Gilbert, Phil 28, 52
Gilbert, William S. 235
Gilbert, Willie 95
Giles, Erica 146, 183, 201
Giles, Nancy 419
Gilewski, Steve 253
Gill, Jaymes 75
Gill, Jillaine 277
Gill, Len 28
Gilleland, Lou Anne 235
Gillen, Curtis 147
Gillespie, Kelly 207
Gillett, Aden 420
Gillette, Anita 192, 242, 410, 417
Gillette, Priscilla 417
Gilliam, Michael 47, 159
Gilliam, Seth 246
Gillibrand, Nicky 89
Gillis, Graeme 150, 182
Gilmore, Rosa 249
Gilner, Jeff 410
Gilpin, Betty 227
Gilpin, Nicholas 100
Gilroy, Katrina 72, 110
Gilvary, Paul 209
Gimaletdinov, Nikolay 212
Gimblett, Sarah 214
Gindele, Joshua 199
Gines, Shay 270, 444
Gingold Theatrical Group 221
Ginino, Gian-Murray

124
Gionfriddo, Gina 242
Giovanni, Kearran 13, 43, 85, 92
Giradet, Adam 68, 92
Girard, François 129
Giraud, Claude 418
Gircha, Denis 129
Girl Talk 374
Girls Gone Funny 313
Giroux, Leigh 409, 410
Girshek, Scott 135
Gisbert, Gregory L. 50, 83
Gisy, Greer 113
Gittins, James 230
Give In to Sin 307
Give Me Your Hand 221
Givens, Cassy 64
Gjoka, Brigel 211
Glaab, Caryl 189
GLAAD Media Awards 438
Glacéau Vitamin Water 410
Gladstone, Lydia 142
Glant, Bruce 102
Glant, Joanne 102
Glant-Linden, Andrew 118
Glaser, Gyula 219
Glaser, Sherry 420
Glasgow, Kelly 226, 248
Glass Menagerie, The 373, 401
Glass, Daniel 201
Glaszek, Andrew 113
Glattstein, Susan 410
Glaub, Jim 33, 38, 46, 50, 52
Glaudini, Bob 223
Glaudini, Lola 223
Gleam 359
Gleason, Anthony 181
Gleason, Joanna 251, 410, 419
Glendye, Jenna 263
Glenna Freedman Public Relations 151, 181, 182
Gless, Sharon 197
Glick, Gideon 226
Glikas, Bruce 410
Glinick, Emily 224
Glorioso, Bess Marie 60, 112, 118, 192, 202, 236
Glöss, Ruth 210
Glotzer, Marci 112
Gloucester Blue 275
Glover, Beth 125
Glover, Danny 419
Glover, Jess 117

Glover, John 59, 223
Glover, Montego 102, 114, 426
Gluck, Christophe Willibald 212
Glur, Christina 191
Glushchenko, Nikolay 129
Glyn, Gruffudd 197
Glynn, Carlin 419
G-Money Productions 289
Gneiting, Chad 124
GO AlleyCat Productions 290
Go Into Her Room Productions 290
GoAlleyCat 269
Gob Squad's Kitchen (You've Never Had It So Good) 246
Gobbel, Wolfgang 197
Gobioff, Neil 132
God of Carnage 349, 364, 366, 368, 377, 380, 395, 397, 402
Godbout, Adam 177
Goddard, Michael 114
Godfrapp 219
Godfrey, Leslie 112
Godineaux, Edgar 82, 102
Godino, Nicole 143
Godley, Adam 85, 114, 198, 420
Godspell 12, 40
Goedken, Jason 223
Goehring, Tom 212, 230
Goelz, Anne Allen 140
Goeres, Lucy 235
Goffman, Andrew 188
Goforth, Charles 223
Goggans, Jennifer 213
Gogin, Bryce 211
GOH Productions 290
Goheen, Marcella 171
Gohl, Teese 28
Gohsman, Ryan 207, 241
Goidel, Emma 262
Goines, Victor 199
Going to St. Ives 355
Going to Tahiti Productions 290
Goland-Van Ryn, Becca 39
Golay, Seth 233
Gold, Alyssa May 86, 222
Gold, Brian 104
Gold, Candy 67
Gold, Judy 119, 131
Gold, Rebecca 32, 54,

106
Gold, Sam 45, 227, 242, 251, 258
Gold, Shana 237
Gold, Tom 266
Golda's Balcony 348
Goldberg, Blair 118, 227
Goldberg, Geoffrey 101
Goldberg, Isa 424
Goldberg, Jessica 243
Goldberg, Jon-Erik 100
Goldberg, Larry 116
Goldberg, Marcia 71, 109, 111
Goldberg, Robert 263
Goldberg, Sarah 251
Goldberg, Suzanne 177
Goldberg, Wendy 108
Goldberg, Whoopi 109, 200, 419
Goldberger, Amy 149
Goldblum, Jeff 45
Golden, Annie 162, 263
Golden, Bob 249
Golden, Pat 74
Goldenberg, Lisa 410
Goldenhersh, Heather 420
Goldfeder, Karen 253
Goldfelder, Laurie 33
Goldhar, Eleanor 428
Goldman, Christine 208, 209
Goldman, Herrick 163
Goldman, James 33
Goldman, Matt 189
Goldman, Maya 104
Goldmann, Anne 187
Goldmark, Sandra 153
Goldner, Justin 199
Goldoni, Carlo 72
Goldsberry, Jason 68
Goldsberry, Renee Elise 248
Goldschneider, Ed 115, 194
Goldsmith, Herbert 38
Goldstein, Daniel 40, 267
Goldstein, Jared 168, 212
Goldstein, Jess 64, 80, 97, 208, 247
Goldstein, Seth A. 137, 147, 164, 168, 192
Goldstein, William 192
Goldstein-Glaze, Rebecca 246
Goldstone, Bob 265
Goldwasser, Andrew 240
Golem 284, 290, 294
Goley, Alex 130
Golia, Nanette 75

Goliath 310
Golijov, Osvaldo 210
Goloshapov, Sergei 28
Golovko, Vilen 129
Golub, David S. 54, 66
Golub, Mark S. 54, 66
Gomes, Nelson 213
Gomes, Paloma 232
Gomez, Daniel V. 81
Gomez, Danny 238
Gomez, Laura Kathryne 183
Gomez, Lino 216
Gonçalves, John 213
Gonçalves, Nuno 213
Gone 289
Gonna See a Movie Called Gunga Din 281
Gonzales, Brian 72
Gonzales, Tony 100
Gonzalez, Aaron 94
Gonzalez, Amancio 211
Gonzalez, Andrea 66
Gonzalez, Jojo 250
Gonzalez, Roberto Bevenger 67
Good Goods 403
Good People 372
Goodell, Mark 182
Goodfriend, Michael Gabriel 170
Goodin, James 145
Goodland, Katherine 170
Goodman Theatre 38, 361, 374
Goodman, Ellis 67
Goodman, Grant 240, 341
Goodman, Matthew 105
Goodman, Rebecca 213
Goodman, Robyn 88, 188, 251, 252
Goodman, Wayne 67, 85, 199
Goodridge, Amanda-Mae 170
Goodrum, Elizabeth 225
Goodsell, Allison 107
Goodsey, Jimmy 244
Goodspeed Musicals 361, 374
Goodtime Charley 278
Goodwin, Clive 60, 236
Goodwin, Deidre 132
Goodwin, Patrick 40
Goodwin, Philip 260
Goold, Rupert 197
Goos, Winfried 210
Goranson, Alicia 369
Goranson, Lindsay 173
Gorczynski, Nicholas 218, 219

Gordon, Adam S. 68, 71
Gordon, Allan S. 54, 68, 71, 139
Gordon, Charles 32
Gordon, Danny 409
Gordon, David 259
Gordon, Glenn 138
Gordon, Howie 151
Gordon, Jack 214
Gordon, Jeff 263, 264
Gordon, Michael 210
Gordon, Michael-David 156, 180
Gordon, Rachel 153
Gordon, Rodney 447
Gordon, Sam 144, 227, 259, 260
Gore Vidal's The Best Man 19, 66
Gore, Hannah 98
Gore, John 36, 52, 54, 82, 102, 103
Gore, Michael 226
Gore, Whitney Holden 50, 68, 181, 410
Górecki, Henryk 211
Gorenc, Gred 195
Gorman, Elyzabeth 243
Gorman, Katie 195
Gorman, Mari 418
Gorski-Wergeles, Kristen Leigh 111
Goslinga, Janni 211
Gosnell, Sarah 45, 224
Gospel of Judas, The 279
Goss, Andrea 60
Goss, Patrick 124
Gosse, Angela 110
Gosset, Bick 154
Gotham Comedy Club 433
Gotschel, Stephan 107
Gottlieb, Andrew C. 89, 256, 257
Gottlieb, Jenna 162
Gottlieb, Jim 31
Gottlieb, Max 108
Gottlieb, Michael 52, 124, 168, 219
Gottlieb, Roy 38
Gottlieb, Shirle 442
Gottschall, Ruth 101
Gough, Louise 261
Gough, Shawn 78, 89
Gough, Toby 232
Gould, Christina 75
Gould, David 216
Gould, Dorothy Ann 130
Gould, James M. 75
Goulet, Adrien 141
Goulet, Robert 418
Goulet, Susan 198

Gourdine, Laura 149
Goutman, Christopher 410, 419
Gowenlock, Kay 87
Gowland, Reggie 224
Goyanes, Maria 244
Gozelski, Sonoka 97
Gozzo, Teresa 208
Graae, Jason 442, 443
Grabb, Patty 146
Grace, Jennifer 421
Grace, Topher 253, 426
Gracey, Patrick 59
Gracye Productions 290, 308
Grade, Tiago 133
Grady, Bill 225-227
Graenzer, Anna 210
Graff, Heather 82, 88
Graff, Randy 243
Graff, Sondra 148
Graff, Todd 419
Graham, Andrew 118, 188
Graham, Bruce 147, 360
Graham, Elain 161
Graham, Enid 246, 420
Graham, Kimberly 230
Graham, Mark 92
Graham, Melissa 219
Graham, Nathan Lee 106
Graham, Ronny 417
Graham, Vicky 154
Graham, Wilbur 70
Grammercy Theatre 197
Grammy Awards 438
Granade, Stephanie 112
Granat, Arny 84
Granath, Bruce 107
Grand Duke, The 235
Grand, Murray 46
Grandage, Iain 234
Grandage, Michael 68
Grande, Frankie James 91, 102
Grandy, Marya 264
Graney, Ben 110
Graney, Sean 163
Granger, Milton 101, 118
Granger, Phil 104
Granger, Stewart 419
Grano, Joseph J. 97
Grant, Aaron 145
Grant, Aubrey 116, 194
Grant, Beth 140
Grant, Cathlene 192
Grant, Christopher Ryan 103, 136
Grant, Faye 409, 410, 412, 419
Grant, Glenna 163
Grant, Jonathan 231

Grant, Kate Jennings 23, 77, 261
Grant, Kelly Jeanne 105
Grant, Maddy 98
Grant, Shalita 240
Grantom, Wes 216
Grapefruit 317
Grassel, Tim 196
Grasso, John 198
Graus, Ramses 232
Gravátt, Lynda 361, 420
Graveline, Veronica 143
Graves, Aaron 128
Graves, Claire 142
Graves, Jennifer R. 32
Graves, Joseph 389
Graves, Karron 240
Graves, Katy 140
Graves, Rupert 420
Gray, Amber 263
Gray, Cleo 163
Gray, David 113
Gray, DJ 216
Gray, Fin 75
Gray, Keisha Laren Clarke 99
Gray, Layon 189
Gray, Nicholas Warren 118, 226, 227
Gray, Simon 197, 252
Graynor, Ari 37
Grazaï, Daudet 210
Graziano, Jacqui 109
Graziano, Michael 112, 114, 115, 117, 118
Grease 115, 390
Great Gatsby, The 247
Great Immensity, The 344, 381
Great Lakes Theater 361, 375
Great Recession Theatre 290
Great Wall Story 360, 367
Greathouse, Jamie 33
Greaves, Danielle Lee 74, 146
Grecki, Victoria 50, 82, 109
Greco, Karen 126, 133, 134, 154-162, 166, 170, 171, 176, 177, 182, 184, 186, 187
Greco, Marco 223
Green, Adolph 159
Green, Alan H. 109, 115
Green, Andy 211
Green, Cat 237
Green, Dan 117, 118
Green, Dana 388
Green, Daniel 130
Green, Demond 109

Green, Heidi 28
Green, Jackie 43, 44, 58, 82, 94, 185, 196
Green, Jake 207
Green, Jenna Leigh 201
Green, Jessica 113
Green, Jodi 47, 68
Green, Laura 185
Green, Rachel 340
Greenan, Corey 100
Greenan, James 219
Greenbaum, Harrison 444
Greenberg, Kimberly Faye 190
Greenberg, Ted 190
Greenberry, Jennie 233
Greene, Adam 233
Greene, Ana Rose 28, 33, 40, 44, 52, 95, 103, 179
Greene, Elliot 410
Greene, Gabriel 102
Greene, R.K. 71, 166
Greene, Rob 54, 132, 194, 263
Greene, Sally 89
Greenfield, Adam 241
Greenfield, Alexander 56, 91
Greenfield, Mandy 31, 42, 57, 80, 227
Greenidge, Kirsten 241, 262
Greenspan, David 134, 219
Greenwald, Tom 36, 43, 58, 60, 70, 75
Greenway, T.J. 92, 208
Greenwood, Daniel 235
Greenwood, Jane 94, 103, 136, 244
Greenwood, Judith 214
Greer, Adam 251
Greer, Dean R. 100
Greer, Jennie 258
Greer, Justin 85
Greer, Matthew 45
Greer, Ryan 50, 52
Greer, Steve 95, 105
Greer, Tim 109
Greetings 380
Gregg, Clark 208
Gregg, Julie 418
Gregor, John 195
Gregory, Chester 109
Gregory, Gavin 55
Gregory, Jean-Michele 245
Gregory, Lynne Gugenheim 35, 56, 81, 85, 96, 116, 251
Gregory, Wanda 68,

109, 113
Gregson, Mary-Susan 232
Gregus, Melissa Mae 249, 250
Gregus, Peter 97
Greif, Michael 139, 422
Greiner, Ken 106
Greiss, Terry 144, 147, 156, 180
Grenadine 283
Grenell-Zaidman, Samantha 192
Grenfell, Colin 215
Grenfell, Katy 113
Grenier, Zach 35, 209, 268
Grenrock, Joshua 125
Grevengoed, David 82
Grey, Andre 70
Grey, Frances 158
Grey, Jane 80
Grey, Joel 85, 104, 114, 198
Grey, Sheila 28
Gribtsov, Alexey 129
Grieco, Charles 95
Griego, Juliet 171
Griemsmann, Amanda 309
Grier, David Alan 16, 54, 409, 413, 419
Grier, Jean Michelle 99
Grieves, Glenn 226
Griffin, Amy 194
Griffin, Ashley 201
Griffin, Brendan 73, 360
Griffin, Casey 258
Griffin, Chad H. 113
Griffin, Holly 49, 187
Griffin, Jakubu 130
Griffin, Jeff 218
Griffin, Jung 241
Griffin, Kelcy 179
Griffin, Robert 66
Griffing, Lois 52, 77
Griffith, Andy 417
Griffith, Khadija 191
Griffith, Kristin 158
Griffith, Marey 99
Griffith, Megan 218
Griffiths, Heidi 32, 38, 103, 244
Griffiths, Rachel 13, 39
Griffiths, Richard 420
Grigg, Jessica 184
Griggs-Cennamo, Jennifer 109
Grigorlia-Rosenbaum, Jacob 71
Grigsby, Kimberly 28, 29
Grillo, Denise J. 72

Grimaldi, Dennis 78, 137
Grimaldi, Gary 109
Grimard, Paige 189
Grimes, Jared 199, 217
Grimes, Peter 31, 42, 57, 80
Grimes, Tammy 417
Grimshaw, Marc 251, 252
Grimshaw, Ron 125, 143, 155, 172, 247
Grimson, Martene 212
Grindhouse Musical 314
Grindrod, David 75
Grindstaff, Jessica 211
Grisan, Bonnie 88
Grisell, Jason 149
Grisetti, Josh 112, 140, 265, 409, 412, 421
Grishman, Emily 67, 75, 85, 87, 104, 116, 188
Grixti, Daniel 221
Grizzard, George 417
Grnya, Isaac 244
Grobengieser, Andy 75, 76
Grode, Eric 428
Grodner, Suzanne 185
Grody, Donald 466
Grody, Kathryn 422
Groener, Harry 419
Groener/Didawick Living Trust 410
Groff, Jonathan 114, 226, 420
Gromada, John 35, 45, 56, 66, 73, 80, 243, 245, 257
Grombol, Ashley 409
Gronningen, Ellen 235
Groom, Corey 235
Groomes, Ron 88
Groove, Spring 162
Grosbard, Ulu 466
Gross, Carson 247
Gross, Dan 144
Gross, Halley Wegryn 219
Gross, Paul 9, 44, 369
Gross, Richard 49
Gross, Steven 117
Grossman, Jason E. 71
Grossman, Marie 40
Grossman, Max 90
Grossman, Rick 142
Grossman, Sarahbeth 49
Grossman, Walt 88
Grosso, Joseph 184
Grosso, Lewis 64, 101
Grotelueschen, Andy 141, 260
Grotke, Abigail 193

Grouard, Sebastien 209, 249
Ground Up Productions 290
Groundswell Theatricals Inc. 46
Group Theatre Too, The 290
Grove Theater Center 170
Grove, Barry 31, 42, 57, 80, 227
Groves, Todd 33, 78, 92, 216
Grovey, Angela 83
Growler, Michael 148
Growney, Bill 169
Grubbs, Alex 163
Gruby, Jenny 113
Grunberg, Joy 417
Grunder, Kay 37, 59, 98
Grundstrem, P. 215
Grunewald, Elizabeth 196
Grupper, Adam 84, 111, 205, 216
Gruse, Stephen R. 40
Grush, Rosalind 177
Guan, Xinyue 167
Guare, John 94, 446
Guarnaccia, Greg 49, 191
Gubin, Ron 78, 104
Guercy-Blue, Tanya 68, 92
Guerematchi, Christian D. 210
Guerin, Kristin 125
Guerin, Vera 82
Guernsey, Peter 47
Guerrero, Brad 171
Guerrero, Rudy 166
Guerrero, Tony 113
Guerzon, Albert 76, 100
Guest, Lance 103, 136
Guettel, Adam 163, 267
Guevara, Zabryna 209
Guggino, Michael 93
Gugino, Carla 17, 56, 420
Guibert, Iliana 261
Guida, Kathryn 72
Guiderdoni, Thierry 211
Guidroz, Lori 94
Guidry, Aaron 130
Guiher, Catharine 253
Guilarte, Andrew Ramcharan 143
Guilfoyle, Rachel 152
Guillarmo, Catherine Jacot 164
Guillory, Don 49
Guinan, Samantha 254

Guinn, Allison 32
Guiod, Kelly 37, 43, 44, 59, 82, 94, 103, 208, 410
Guirgis, Stephen Adly 103, 223
Guittard, Laurence 418, 421
Gujardo, Eliza 187
Gulley, Phillip 151
Gullie, Lee Ann 253
Gumley, Matthew 84, 207
Gummer, Grace 80, 86, 421, 426
Gummer, Mamie 420, 421
Gunhus, Eric 89, 116
Gunn, Einar 158
Gunther, Peter 54
Guo, Jun 129
Gupa, Dennis 156
Gupton, Damon 22, 73, 360
Gurira, Danai 245, 437
Gurney, A.R. 201, 207
Gursky, David 85, 216
Gurtner, Christian 212
Gutenberg! The Musical 315
Guthrie Theater 67, 176, 344, 376
Guthrie, Bruce 214
Guthrie, Scott 112, 113
Gutierrez, Eddie 193, 201
Gutierrez, Jacob 369
Gutierrez, Michelle 233
Guts: A Multi-Media Fantasia 288
Guttenberg, Steve 37
Gutterman, Cindy & Jay 38, 68, 84, 92
Guy, Robert 45, 82, 86
Guyot, Alejandro 234
Guys and Dolls 353, 355
Guzman, Lisa 28
Guzman, Marina 152, 224, 225, 243
Guzman, Natalia Miranda 219
Guzzardi, Autumn 179
Guzzone, Ian 173
Gwitzman, Daniel 259
Gwon, Adam 185
Gwynne, Haydn 214, 421
Gypsy 382
Gypsy of the Year 115

H
H4 312

HA! 288, 308, 323
Ha, Mina 175
Haag, Annabell 203
Haag, Chris 222, 263
Haagensen, Eric 429
Haak, Brad 101
Haas, Leonard C. 231
Haas, Phil 263
Haase, Garry 202
Haaskivi, Olli 201
Habel, Rebecca 96, 104, 261
Haber, Carole L. 68, 78, 98
Haberdasher Theatre Inc. 291
Haberl, Chris 52, 115, 117
Haberle, Stephanie Roth 180, 219, 249
Habib, Barry 108
Habib, Toni 108
Hackett, Joan 418
Hackett, Mandy 32, 244
Hackselmans, An 232
hackshaw, lark 49
Hadary, Jonathan 455
Hadly, Heather 232
Hadsall, Luke 136, 182
Haedrich, Lisa 244
Haft, Simone Genatt 232
Hagen, Ben 179, 252
Hager, Molly 181
Hager, Robert 95
Hagerty, Julie 419
Hagerty, Sean 162, 173
Hägg, Annabel 220
Haggerty, Eileen F. 28
Hagiwara, Jan 105
Hagman, Larry 417
Hague, Thomas 74
Hahn, Abigail 216, 139, 277
Hahn, David 50
Hahn-Gallego, Julia 229
Hailand, Tim 187
Haimes, Tamar 36-38, 46, 54, 66
Haimes, Todd 35, 56, 81, 85, 96, 104, 116, 251
Haines, Sarah 154
Hair 32
Hairspray 378
Hajian, Chris 154
Hal Leonard Company 410
Hale, Mitchell 159
Halem, Jessica 222
Haley, Jennifer 447
Hall, Andy 158
Hall, Carlton 125, 229
Hall, Connie 144

Hall, Freddy 52, 124
Hall, Gretchen 49
Hall, Jake 40
Hall, James 40, 87, 213
Hall, Janice 173
Hall, Justin 78, 85
Hall, Katie 235
Hall, Katori 36, 255, 256
Hall, Kevin Scott 433
Hall, Lee 89
Hall, Lena 187
Hall, Linsey 214
Hall, Lucas 220
Hall, Pamela 142, 149, 150, 171, 172, 184, 190
Hall, Reid 60, 235
Hall, Sally 239, 256
Hall, Sarah 265
Hall, Sarah Melissa 244
Hall, T. Michael 244-248
Hall, Vondie Curtis 248
Hall, Yoji 234
Halladay, Christopher 178
Hallahan, Romo 218
Hallett, Ryan 38, 47, 54, 66
Halliday, Daniel 229
Halliday, Lynne 265
Halliday, Rob 68
Halloran, Pat 102
Hallsworth, Andrew 106
Hally, Martha 239
Halm, Jes 208, 227, 253
Halperin, Joshua 87
Halpern, Lauren 125, 209, 224
Halpin, Adam 254
Halsey, Suzanna 60, 236
Halston, Julie 85, 118, 192, 243
Haltman, Jenn 147
Hamic, Shawna 117
Hamill, Kate 170, 184
Hamilton, Aaron 113
Hamilton, Bonita J. 99
Hamilton, Ed 106
Hamilton, Hilary 106
Hamilton, Josh 218, 257
Hamilton, Kate 149
Hamilton, Paul 197
Hamilton, Sue 109
Hamilton, Victoria 420
Hamilton, William 28
Hamingson, Andrew D. 173
Hamlet 316, 359
Hamlin, Dimitri 129
Hamlin, Jeff 39, 110, 224
Hamlyn, Michael 106

Hamm, Brian 227
Hamm, Melissa 138
Hammann, Joyce 105
Hammarström, Camilla 215
Hammerstein, Dena 185
Hammerstein, Oscar, II 46, 216
Hammond, Blake 109
Hammond, Jonathan 134, 221
Hammond, Richard 29
Hammond, Thomas Michael 59
Hammons, Caleb 147, 258
Hampe, George 228
Hamrick, Mary 195
Han, A Reum 198
Han, Jee 181
Hancock, Carole 99
Hancox, Jesse 106
Hand to God 121, 150
Hand, Mat 246
Handley, Paul 98
Hands Up! 232
Handspring Puppet Company 110
Haney, Carol 417
Haney, Gregory 102
Haney, Kel 57
Hanggi, Kristin 108
Hanke, Christopher J. 95
Hankin, Laura 149
Hankins, Jim 128
Hanks, Colin 421
Hanks, Stephen 151
Hanley, Ellen 417
Hanley, J.C. 128
Hanley, Katie 115
Hanlon, Cassie 106
Hanlon, Colin 201
Hanlon, Robert 87
Hanmer, Don 417
Hann, Kristen 106
Hanna, Roger 135
Hanna, Stephen 89
Hannah, Michael D. 28
Hannah, Zach 111
Hannett, Juliana 76, 102
Hanover, Donna 66
Hansard, Glen 60, 236
Hansell, Dan 256
Hansen, Brough 389
Hansen, Erik 95
Hansen, Melissa 33
Hansen, Will 166
Hanson, Ashley 90
Hanson, Derek 85
Hanson, Peter 85
Hanzel, Carol 263
Hao, Wang 211

Hamm, Brian 227
Happy Hour 208
Haqq, Devin E. 181
Harada, Ann 192, 200
Harada, Kai 33, 103, 136
Haran, Nicole 180
Harber, Katherine 227, 256
Harbison, Lawrence 424
Harburg, Yip 127
Harcourt, Sydney James 378
Hard Sparks Productions 291, 340
Hard Wall at High Speed, A 274
Harden, Marcia Gay 419
Harder, Jennifer 149
Harding, Emily 75
Harding, Jan Leslie 165
Harding, June 418
Harding, Lynnea 182
Hardt, Paul 115, 140
Hardy, KJ 175, 177
Hardy, Matthew 267
Hardy, Melissa 143
Hardyman, Hugh 28
Harelik, Mark 104
Haren, Sam 234
Harewood, Dorian 419
Harkins, Lance 227
Harkness, James 93, 112, 216
Harlan, Luke 166
Harlem Stages 431
Harley, Margot 176
Harma, Alison 58
Harmon, Jennifer 39
Harmon, John 186
Harmon, Kara 70, 102
Harmon, Marja 216
Harms, James 115
Harner, Jason Butler 121, 185
Harnick, Sheldon 116, 267, 436, 437, 446
Harold and Maude 266
Harold and Mimi Steinberg Charitable Trust 446
Harp, Jim 92
Harper, Chris 72, 110
Harper, Courtney 87
Harper, Elliot 198
Harper, Ermiyas 127
Harper, Richard 127
Harper, Rodney 151
Harper, William Jackson 248, 250
Harper, Yosef 127
Harrell, David 178
Harrell, Micheal 90
Harrell, Scott 109

Harrington, Brigid 101
Harrington, David 210, 211
Harrington, Evan 105
Harrington, Jeanette 82, 92
Harrington, Joseph 89
Harrington, Michael 259
Harrington, Nancy 32, 54
Harrington, Patrick 87
Harrington, Wendall K. 128, 157, 216, 230
Harris Karma Productions 72, 73
Harris, Barbara 418
Harris, Brock 225
Harris, Bruce Robert 47, 78, 131
Harris, Cynthia 207
Harris, Dede 98
Harris, Derrick 138
Harris, Ed 419
Harris, Harriet 155
Harris, Jay 49, 149, 150
Harris, Jenn 120, 132, 420
Harris, Jeremiah J. 28
Harris, Joseph P., Jr. 28
Harris, Julie 417
Harris, Kevin Mark 85
Harris, Larry Dean 143
Harris, Laurel 68
Harris, Marilyn 143
Harris, Mel 419
Harris, Neil Patrick 422
Harris, Rosemary 17, 56, 417, 429
Harris, Roy 56, 261
Harris, Sarah 186
Harris, Taifa 180
Harris, Tom 115, 132
Harris, Wood 74
Harrison Greenbaum: What Just Happened? 324
Harrison, Eddie 109
Harrison, Elinor 113
Harrison, Grant 163
Harrison, Howard 100, 101, 197
Harrison, Jordan 155, 241
Harrison, Katie Laine 174
Harrison, Laura 409
Harrison, Stanley 188
Harrison, Tim 244, 247, 248
Harrison, Wayne 187
Harrower, David 176
Harry & Eddie: The Birth of Israel 142

Harry Diesel Productions 291
Harry, Doug 152
Hart, Alyssa 92
Hart, Cecilia 419
Hart, Charles 105
Hart, Christopher 54, 186
Hart, Dolores 417
Hart, Joe 47
Hart, John N., Jr 45, 60
Hart, Linda 92, 410, 419
Hart, Moss 112, 157, 216
Hart, Nicolette 106, 146
Hart, Perry 175, 194
Hart, Rebecca 344
Hart, Richard 417
Hart, Stan 265
Hartenstein, Frank 62
Hartford Stage 233, 243
Hartley, Jan 218, 243, 244
Hartman Group, The 50, 52, 68, 76, 87, 89, 92, 95, 102, 107-109, 111, 124, 138, 253, 410
Hartman, Jessica 52, 124
Hartman, Mark 112, 132, 164, 188
Hartman, Michael 50, 52, 68, 76, 87, 92, 95, 102, 109, 124, 138
Hartman, Mike 360
Hartmann, Eva 246
Hartmann, Teresa 168
Hartrampf, Roe 254
Hartse, Kendal 50
Hartsoe, Katie 138, 147, 148, 225, 226, 242, 249, 253
Hartwell, Robert 78, 102
Hartwig, Randy Lee 166
Hartzell, John 191
Harvard, Russell 121, 169, 406, 409, 412, 415
Harvey Theater 210, 211
Harvey, Ellen 95
Harvey, Emily 101
Harvey, K. Lee 159
Harvey, Laurence 417
Harvey, Rita 112, 264
Harwood, Kaylee 62, 63
Haselböck, Martin 212
Hasenburger, Florian 212
Hashimoto, Matsuri 197
Hashley, Karen 252
Haskins, Daniel 101
Hassell, Alex 215
Hassell, Harry 266

Hassler, Jay 247
Hastings, Bill 183
Hastings, Donald F. 410
Hastings, Leslie 410
Hata, Joyce 258
Hatch, Eric 101
Hatch, Joel 89
Hatcher, Jeffrey 233
Hateley, Linzi 419
Hatem, Noel 253
Hatendi, Nyasha 214
Hathaway, Nathaniel 78, 85, 116
Hatkoff, David 255
Hauck, Rachel 208, 225, 228, 237, 243
Haun, Ellen 149
Haun, Harry 409, 426
Haunts 294
Haupt, Paulette 422
Hauptmann, Elizabeth 210
Hause, Maureen Hur 228
Hauser, Mark 75
Havard, Julien 85
Havlik, Emily 147
Hawaiian Tropic 410
Hawdon, Robin 81
Hawe, Garett 64, 101
Hawk, Abigail 277
Hawkes, Robin 72, 110
Hawkins, Corey 252, 256
Hawkins, Jack 214
Hawkins, Jeffrey C. 207
Hawkins, Joel 90
Hawkins, Kennis 212
Hawkins, Luke 217
Hawkins, Phyre 32
Hawkins, Trish 418
Hawkins, Vicky 214
Hawser, Gillian 28
Hawthorn, Alex 64, 102
Hay Fever 376
Hayashi, T. Rick 92
Hayden, Erik 103, 136, 264
Hayden, Michael 244, 245, 257, 420
Haydn, Franz Joseph 212
Hayes, Bill 85
Hayes, Emily 255
Hayes, Hugh 194
Hayes, Katharine 106
Hayes, Kelly 144
Hayes, Lauren 149
Hayes, Michael 33
Hayes, Stephanie 247
Hayman, Anna 207
Haynes, Jeremiah 199
Haynes, Michail 112

Haynes, Victoria 163
Haynie, F. Michael 227, 254
Hays, Kathleen 58
Hayward, Kalon 138
Hayward-Jones, Michael 115
Haze 211
He Who 400
Headland, Leslye 242
Headly, Glenne 419
Headrick, Genevieve 32
Heads 324
Headstrong 182
Heald, Anthony 219, 419
Healy, Diane 222
Heard, Ethan 131
Heard, John 419
Hearn, Nicole Borrelli 211
Heart is a Lonely Hunter, The 400
Heartbreak House 367
Heat Wave: The Jack Cole Project 183
Heaton, Katherine 112
Heavey, Lorna 197
Hebb, Cameran 163
Hebel, Christian 111, 244
Heberlee, Brad 239
Hecht, Deborah 28, 42, 75, 101, 172, 224, 247, 252
Hecht, Josh 174
Heck, Bill 421
Heckart, Eileen 417
Heckman, Philip 117, 193
Heckman, Rick 33, 78, 89, 92, 110, 216
Hecktman, Jeffrey B. 28, 75
Hector, Fritzlyn 196
Hedglin-Taylor, Bobby 146
Hedison, David 417
Hedley, Nevin 35
Hedstrom, Cynthia 168
Hedwall, Deborah 162
Hedwig and the Angry Inch 199
Heeley, Desmond 96, 447
Heeney, Michael 409, 410
Heflin, Drew 29
Hegarty, Ruth 198
Hegel-Cantarella, Luke 130
Heger, Erik 67
Heggie, Femi 161

Hegner, Julie 206
Heick, Aaron 29
Heidami, Daoud 88, 248
Height, Michael 99
Heilman, Christopher 148
Heindel, June 64
Heinemann, Larry 189
Heinrichs, Jake 127, 143, 255
Heir Apparent, The 388, 398
Heiress, The 393
Heirless Productions Inc. 291
Heiser, Marissa 118
Heishman, Robert 213
Heisler, Marcy 436
Held, Jessica 59
Helen Hayes Awards 438
Helen Hayes Theatre 108
Helfer, Amy Maude 235
Helk, David 101
Helland, J. Roy 77
Heller, Adam 87
Heller, Ariel 110
Heller, Ben 35, 36, 37, 46, 49, 56, 58, 59, 60, 73, 75, 77, 81, 185
Heller, Dale 88, 143, 261
Heller, Laura 140, 151, 154
Heller, Melissa 193
Heller, W. Benjamin, II 90, 109
Hello Entertainment 28, 75
Hello! My Baby 375
Helm, Garth 75, 106
Helman, Joshua 31, 42, 57, 80, 227
Helmy, Sahar 409
Helsing, Tomas 215
Hemesath, Brian 115, 162
Hemesath, Matthew 202
Hemingway, Ernest 236
Hemingway, Rose 95, 114, 421
Hemming, Randall J. 409, 410
Hemminger, Erica 33, 35, 66, 85, 116
Hemphill, David 100
Henckel, Rhett 181
Hendel, Ruth 59, 73, 88, 94, 103, 106
Henderson, Aland 82, 84, 99
Henderson, Bradley 138

Henderson, Celisse 40
Henderson, Geno 87
Henderson, Heather 206
Henderson, Jacqueline 109
Henderson, Judy 143, 151, 166, 230
Henderson, Marcia 417
Henderson, Mark 72
Hendricks, Sam 242
Hendrickson, Barry 145
Hendrickson, Kathy 59
Heneghan, Pádraig 213
Henig, Andi 410
Henke, Rob 168
Henkin, Elyce 50, 52, 68, 95
Henley, Beth 243
Henning, Matthew 214
Henninger, Megan 49, 94, 146, 185
Hennings, Brian 28
Henningsen, Craig 28
Henriet, Gisle 138
Henrikson, Alexandra 263
Henriquez, Carlos 199
Henry Hewes Design Awards 438
Henry V 138, 156, 315, 391
Henry, Buck 178
Henry, Chris 200
Henry, Gregg 223
Henry, Joshua 54, 118, 426
Henry, Martha 418
Henry, Robyn 96
Henry, Savannah 192
Henry, Steve 50, 181
Henry, Susannah 160
Henshaw, Johnson 38, 248
Henshaw, Steve 106
Hensley, Shuler 247
Henson, John 202
Henson, Trisha 56, 147, 167, 243
Hentze, Bobby 44
Hentze, Robert 87
Henze, Sheryl 105
Hepburn, Audrey 417
Herbert West, Reanimator 311
Herbert, Diana 417
Herbert, Jim 78
Herbosch, Jano 429
Herdlicka, Hunter Ryan 202
HERE Arts Center 291
Here I Go 186
Hermalyn, Joy 115
Herman Kline's Midlife

Crisis 140
Herman, Chris 28, 106, 139, 188
Herman, Edward 163
Herman, Jerry 420
Herman, Katarzyna 178
Herman, Melanie 428
Hermann, Katrina 227, 241, 242
Hermann, Peter 110
Hernandez, Ana Sofia 263
Hernandez, Evan 138
Hernández, Jeffrey 137
Hernandez, Jeremiah 409
Hernandez, Joanna 195
Hernandez, Joshua 150
Hernández, Philip 216
Hernandez, Riccardo 54, 104, 208, 247
Hernandez, Victor 47
Hernandez-Adams, Niki 239
Hero Dad 347
Hero Props 88
Hero: The Musical 198
Heroes 377, 395
Heroes and Other Strangers 282
Herold, Paula 52, 92
Herr, Andrea 235
Herrald, Alex 163
Herrera, Manuel 193
Herrick Entertainment 28
Herrick, Norton 28
Herring, Brit 146
Herring, Linda 428
Herron, Mike 206
Hersey, Derek 64
Hersey, Ian 245, 248
Hershberg, Jessica 216
Hershey Felder as George Gershwin Alone 387
Hershey Felder in Concert 387
Hershey Felder in Maestro 387, 393
Hershey, Lowell 105
Hershman, James 78, 216
Hershman, Jim 84, 117
Herskowitz, Erik 150
Hertzer, Michael 125, 263
Hervida, Roma 187
Herz, Shirley 112, 129, 219
Herzog, Amy 224
Hess, Adam 134, 137, 147, 164, 168, 192
Hess, Kelly 158

Hess, Rodger 94
Hesselink, Ray 183
Hester, Richard 97, 112, 198
Hesterman, Angela 129
Heston, Charlton 417
Het Boek van alle dingen 234
Het Filiaal 232
Hettel, Nadine 85
Heulitt, Chad 73
Heus, Edyth 28
Heverin, Nathan 28
Hevia, Flavia 137, 161
Hevner, Caite 141, 146, 177, 187, 249, 256
Hewit, Anna 181
Hewitt, Alan Stevens 52, 124, 264
Hewitt, Gary 107
Hewitt, Tom 62, 159
Hewitt-Roth, Sarah 33, 83
Hewski, Kim 46
Hey Jude Graphics 229
Heyenga, Jefrey 96
Heymann, Dirk 211
Heyward, Dorothy 54
Heyward, DuBose 54
HHC Marketing 97, 124, 131, 137, 143, 191-193, 263
Hibah, Bahiyah 68, 93
Hibbert, Eugene 215
Hickey, Joe 50, 82
Hickey, John Benjamin 104, 198
Hickey, Kaitlyn 151
Hickman, John 97
Hickman, Kimberly Faith 73, 262
Hickok, Hope 213
Hickok, John 35
Hickok, Molly 212
Hicks, Celise 99
Hicks, Daniel 142
Hicks, Greg 197
Hicks, Tiffany 28
Hidden Tennessee 395
Hidlago, Glenn 195
Hieronymus 294
Higgason, Josh 212
Higgins, Clare 420
Higgins, Colin 266
Higgins, Deirdre 112, 219
Higgins, Jennifer 213
Higgins, Joel 419
Higgins, Patience 188
Higgins, Thomas 226
High Fidelity 385
High Performance 214
Higher 350

Highline Ballroom 223
Hightower, Brandon Lavon 259
Hiibel, Millie 231
Hildebrand, Drew 230
Hildreth, Greg 71
Hilferty, Susan 56, 111, 202, 247, 255, 258, 260, 422
Hill, Alan 235
Hill, Andrew 211
Hill, Arlo 217
Hill, Brendan 135, 137, 186
Hill, Cedric 191
Hill, Conleth 420
Hill, Dulé 15, 49
Hill, Erin 219
Hill, Frances 148, 173
Hill, Heather 54, 55, 118
Hill, Jessi D. 237, 262, 263
Hill, Jon Michael 421
Hill, Leeds 183
Hill, Mary 140
Hill, Megan 121, 150
Hill, Michael 59, 67
Hill, Rosena 199
Hiller, Jeff 132
Hillis, Steve 410
Hillman, Richard 177, 207, 249
Hillner, John 195, 265
Hills, Brian D. 167
Hilsman, Hoyt 442
Hilty, Megan 114, 118, 217
Him 173
Himelstein, Aaron 218
Hinchee, Jeffrey 84
Hindelang, Jason 91
Hinderaker, Andrew 252
Hindman, James 101, 116, 118
Hinds, Ciáran 420
Hinds, Richard J. 64
Hines, Afra 75, 76, 113, 420, 444
Hines, Edena 245
Hines, Gregory 419
Hines, Keith 409
Hinkle, Amanda 156, 168, 180
Hinkle, Marin 243, 268
Hinkley, Matt 40, 199
Hinkley, Sara 264
Hinkson, Rick 201
Hinrichs, John 213
Hip-Flores, Rachel 131
Hip-Flores, Rick 183
Hip-Hop Theater Festival 145
Hipp, Paul 419
Hirsch, Julia 149

Hirsch, Melissa 140
Hirsch, Peter 235
Hirsch, Santa Claire 140
Hirschfeld, James 212
Hirschhorn, Larry 66, 71, 84, 168
Hirsh, Lauren 78
Hirst, Kevin 44
Hirzel, Jake 28, 52
His Girl Friday 389, 401
History Mystery 318
History of Kisses, The 380
History of the World 297
Hit and Run Productions 292
HIT Entertainment 125
Hit the Wall 400
Hitchcock, Ken 102
Hite, Jason 388
Hiyama, Kanako 149
Hjelm, Kristina 214
Hoare, Charmian 98
Hoaxocaust! 320
Hobart, Scott 233
Hobbs, Brian 108
Hobbs, Brian Allan 153
Hobbs, Johnnie, Jr. 352
Hobson, Jwyanza Kalonji 171
Hobson, Louis 47, 83, 104
Hoch, Chris 144, 169, 265
Hoch, Danny 37
Hoche, Jon 166
Hochman, Larry 43, 84, 90, 115
Hochstine, Dan 28, 46, 60
Hochwald, Jonathan 196
Hockaday, Lindsay 236, 247
Hodes, Gloria 419
Hodge, Richard A. 148, 169
Hodges, Ben 409, 410, 420, 444
Hodges, Drew 36, 43, 58, 60, 70, 75
Hodges, Eddie 417
Hodges, Matthew 187
Hodges, Matthew Elias (Matt) 33, 35, 56, 60, 187, 236, 251, 255, 256, 257
Hodges, Patricia 91
Hodges, Seena 138
Hodun, Jim 71
Hoeffler, Alex 110
Hoekstra, Joel 108
Hoerauf, Deanna 140
Hoerburger, Peter 36,

56, 60, 94, 116, 181, 222
Hoess, Traute 210
Hoff, Barry 95
Hoffer, Eben 262
Hoffman, Ana 179
Hoffman, Anthony 95
Hoffman, Barbara 410
Hoffman, Cary 124
Hoffman, Clare 184
Hoffman, Dustin 418
Hoffman, Jackie 84, 114, 117, 198, 200, 202, 410, 420
Hoffman, Miranda 40
Hoffman, Patrick 426
Hoffman, Philip 50
Hoffman, Philip Seymour 27, 59, 223, 409, 414, 420, 429
Hoffman, Rachel 40
Hoffman, Sam 185
Hoffmann, Carolyn 179
Hoffner, Mark 206
Hofman, Leah 110
Hofman, Satomi 105
Hofmann, Jackob G. 206
Hofmann, Regan 200
Hofstetter + Partners/ Agency 212 129, 131, 132, 149, 150, 164, 179, 183, 192
Hogan, Robert 224, 229
Hogg, Betsy 71
Hoggett, Steven 60, 71, 236
Hoglund, Jana 33, 62, 136, 241
Hohn, Jennifer 47
Hoke-Brady, Sarah Abigail 150
Holabird, Katharine 125
Holbrook, Curtis 202
Holbrook, Morgan 72, 251
Holcenberg, David 75, 76, 100
Holcomb, Ian 260, 340
Holcomb, Justin R.G. 184, 189
Holden, Sarah 208
Holder, Don 82
Holder, Donald 28, 86, 99, 103, 224, 253
Holder, Jakob 257
Holder, Oslyn 87
Hole in His Heart, A 318
Holiday, Anthony 70
Holland, André 244, 245
Holland, Brad 196
Holland, Michael 40
Holland-Moritz, Shelly 216

Hollenbeck, Franklin 47, 64, 87
Hollick, Michael 191
Holliday, David 418
Holliday, Jennifer 419
Holliday, Judy 417
Holligsworth, Michah 410
Holling, Damion 234
Hollingsworth, Rachael 199
Hollis, Gretchen 138
Hollis, Tommy 419
Hollmann, Mark 422
Hollock, Anthony 202
Holloway, JaMeeka 36
Holloway, Luke 136
Holm, Jeremy Stiles 129
Holman, Matt 212
Holme, Gillie 258
Holmes, Doug 409
Holmes, Mike 173
Holmes, Richard Alan 235
Holmes, Rick 71
Holmes, Rupert 150
Holser, Stephanie 152, 163
Holsinger, E. Cameron 191
Holst, Gustav 184
Holst, Imogen 184
Holst, Rich 244
Holt, B.J. 93, 106
Holton, Alex 68, 89
Holtz, Jürgen 210
Holtzclaw, Matthew 226
Holtzman, Willy 244
Holy Child 313, 322
Holzman, Meredith 59
Holzman, Winnie 111
Home Movies 321
Home Productions 292
Homer 237
Homestead Crossing 358
Homgren, Slate 218
Homunculus Mask Theater 292
Homunculus: Reloaded 292
Honeymoon Motel 37
Hong, Katie 125, 218
Hong, Matt 97
Hong, Sooyean 188, 245, 261
Honk! 402
Honnold, Heather 262
Hoo, Audrey 214
Hood, Andrea 177, 244, 247, 248
Hooks, Robert 418
Hooper, Matthew 154

Hooper, Tom 187
Hop Theatricals LLC 95
Hope, Ben 60
Hope, Roxanna 249
Höpfner-Tabori, Ursula 210
Hopkins, Billy 177, 183
Hopkins, Cynthia 211
Hopkins, Karen Brooks 210
Hopkins, Melanie 141, 187
Hopkins, Reece 231
Hopley, Lizzie 214
Hopper, Antwayn 180
Hopper, Chantel 40, 50
Hopper, Luico 106
Hopper, Tim 208
Hopprich, Tyson 234
Horgan, Con 229
Horizon Theatre Rep 292
Horman, Todd A. 106
Horn, Alan 87
Horn, Alisa 227, 254
Horn, Andrew M. 127, 184
Horn, Ashley 33
Horne, Lance 187
Horner, Ben 110
Hornos, Ricardo 68, 168
Horowitz, Dave 140, 153, 256
Horowitz, Jeffrey 141, 259
Horowitz, Leah 33, 216
Horowitz, Stefanie Abel 249
Horrigan, Ben 37, 62
Horrigan, Joby 75
Horror at Martin's Beach, The 312
Horse Trade Theater Group 292
Horsedreams 249
Horsley, Owen 214
Horst, Thad 245-248
Horton, Ashley Rose 209, 252
Horton, John 85
Horton, Ward 178
Horwith, Sam 249, 250
Hosokawa, Toshio 210
Hospital 2011 275
HOT Festival 327
Hot Lunch Apostles 294
Hotaling, Niluka 180
HotelMotel 138
Hoty, Dee 192
Houben, Gertjan 223
Houben, Jos 259
Houdyshell, Jayne 33, 96, 114, 420
Houfek, Nicholas 212

Houghton, James 255
Houghton, Katharine 137, 418
Hould-Ward, Ann 104, 202, 216, 230, 253
Houle, Sophie 138
Houle, Vincent 138
Houlehen, Colleen 45, 104, 108
Hoult, Jennifer 116
Hounour, Mary R. 233
Hour of Feeling, The 346
House of Blue Leaves, The 94
House of Fitzcarraldo, The 279, 280
House of Mirth, The 299
House of Yes Christmas Spectacular 311
Housel, Ginny 87
Housewives' Cantata, The 265
Houston, Daxfurth 113
Houston, Doug 117
Houston, Mary 112
Hovis, Don 233
Hovis, Joan 417
How and Why I Robbed My First Cheese Store 294
How I Learned to Drive 253
How Much Is Enough? Our Values in Question 151
How the Day Runs Down 303
How the World Began 262, 399
How to Succeed in Business Without Really Trying 95, 116, 202
How to Write a New Book for the Bible 357, 397
How We Got On 346
Howard Gilman Opera House 210, 211
Howard, Arliss 208
Howard, James 197
Howard, Jason 70
Howard, Joanne 212
Howard, Joseph 109
Howard, Ken 418
Howard, Lisa 106
Howard, Peter 93
Howard, Richard 238
Howard, Sherman 66, 88, 248
Howard, Stephen 28
Howard, Steve 191
Howard, Stuart 115, 140

Howard, Tiffany Janene 83, 102
Howden, Lewis 177
Howe, David 44
Howe, Tina 222
Howell, Debbie 127
Howell, Joel 241, 242
Howell, Katherine 184
Howell, Michael 186
Howell, Rob 44, 75
Howell, Sarah 67
Howell, Tony 117
Howgill, Richard 212
Howington, Roy 209
Howland, Jason 47
Howrad, Richard 74
Hoyos, Daniel 255
Hoyt, Lon 92, 112
Hoyt, Tom 111
Hranitelj, Alan 129
HRH Foundation 33
Hruska, Dennis 261
Hrustic, Olja 66
Hsieh, Brian 28
Hsin-Fang, Lin 211
Hsu, Adam Chi 210
Hsu, Emily 216
Hsu, Stephanie 209
Hu, Qing 232
Huang, Jian Min 232
Huang, Mark 253, 254
Huang, Shiting 232
Huang, Xueping 232
Huang, Zhiwei 232
Hub Theatricals 293
Hubbard, Charles 124, 134, 153
Hubbard, Cristin J. 105
Hubbard, Elizabeth 200
Hubbard, Merle 200
Hubbard, Tom 201
Hubbs, Matt 245
Hubert, Melissa 152, 163
Huberth, Jon 136, 182
Hubley, Emily 243
Huckins, George 68, 109
HUD 313
Hudes, Quiara Alegría 430
Hudson Theatre 447
Hudson Theatrical Associates 38, 43, 47, 50, 54, 62, 66, 78, 82, 94
Hudson Warehouse 293
Hudson, Charlie, III 256
Hudson, Damian Lemar 248
Hudson, Richard 99
Hudson, Scott 223
Hudson, Whitney 176

Huff, Justin 40, 64
Huffman, Brent-Alan 82, 83, 109
Huffman, Cady 158
Huffnagle, Melvin 189
Hufford, Jean Marie 169
Hufnagel, Lisa 261
Hugh Cox Gets the Pink Slip 316
Hugh Jackman Back on Broadway 13, 43, 202
Hughes, Allen Lee 73, 447
Hughes, Carly 76
Hughes, Chloe 208
Hughes, Doug 91
Hughes, Geraldine 98
Hughes, Jennifer 265
Hughes, Kirsten 255
Hughes, Langston 199
Hughes, Marika 141
Hughes, Mark 177
Hughes, Maureen 198
Hughes, Mick 158
Hughes, Owen 148, 151, 160
Hughes, Sarah 236, 247
Hughes, Timothy 113
Hughey, David 54, 55
Hui-Ling, Liu 211
Huizenga, Laura 128
Hulbert, Don 167
Hulce, Tom 50
Hulett, Nadia 149
Hull, Charlie 106
Hull, David 95, 111, 116
Hull, Michael 202
Hull, Mylinda 216
Hultgren, Kacie 39, 42, 80, 81, 91, 216, 217, 227
Human Zoo, The 288
Human Beatbox Festival 294
Humana Festival 346
Humans, Anonymous 321
Hume, John C. 218
Hummel, Mark 43, 64, 109
Hummel, Martin 71
Humor Abuse 350, 397
Humphrey, Michelle Eden 143
Humphrey, Tom 214
Humphries, Barry 420
Hundertmark, Joe 130
Hundley, Matt 156, 169,171, 177
Hundred Dresses, The 209
Hungerford, Stephen 231

Hunsader, Caskey 112
Hunt, Kayleigh 159
Hunt, Pamela 265, 266
Hunt, Robb 152
Hunter, Adam John 108
Hunter, Dave 260
Hunter, Erika 108
Hunter, JoAnn M. 50, 116
Hunter, Kathryn 259
Hunter, Kelly 197
Hunter, Renee 74
Hunter, Sophie 211
Huntington Theatre Company 49, 251, 368, 377
Huntley, Paul 31, 35, 39, 56, 57, 78, 81, 82, 85, 92, 96, 100, 104, 110, 153, 218, 227
Huntley, Ralph 233, 234
Hunton, Emma 140
Huppuch, Birgit 368
Hurd, Colin 189
Hurd, Keith 28
Hurder, Robyn 78, 144
Hurley, Jon 136, 186
Hurley, Kevin 168
Hurley, Liam 211
Hurley, Matthew Michael 219
Hurley, Tim 46, 157
Hurley's Saloon 410
Hurlin, Nathan 112, 114, 115, 117, 118, 199
Hurst-Mendoza, Monet 238
Hurt Village 256, 407, 409
Hurt, John 213
Hurt, Mary Beth 94, 456
Hurt, William 419
Hurtado, Christina 249
Hurwitz, Deborah 97
Hush The Musical 282
Hushion, Casey 181
Husinko, Greg 50
Husmann, Ron 418
Hutchings, Sasha 102
Hutchings, Sealy 140
Hutchison, Brian 35, 228
Hutchison, LeeAnne 125, 141
Hutchison, Sarah 235
Huth, Timothy 173
Hutner, Nicholas 39
Hutt, Amanda 60
Hutter, Birgit 212
Hutton, Wendy 35, 56, 81, 251
Huygen, Floor 232
Huynh, Brian Lee 110

Hwai-Min, Lin 210
Hwang, David Henry 38, 436, 448
Hyatt, Jeffrey 195
Hyde, Martha 153
Hyfler, Miriam 174, 239
Hyland, Edward James 86
Hyland, Karen 76
Hylenski, Peter 50, 108
Hylenski, Suzanne 101, 118
Hyler, West 97, 264, 265, 267
Hyman, Earle 417
Hyman, Mike 59
Hyman, Phyllis 419
Hynes, Garry 198
Hynes, Holly 447
Hyon, Susan 144, 208
Hypes, Ken 257
Hypnotik: The Seer Will Doctor You Now 302, 320
Hysell, Hugh 71, 157
Hyslop, David 106
Hytner, Nicholas 72, 110, 224

I
I Am a Tree 187
I Am My Own Wife 397
I don't believe in outer space 211
I Don't Have a Title Yet! 308, 312
I Got Sick Then I Got Better 374
I Just Stopped By to See the Man 349
I Killed My Mother 294
I Love to Eat: Cooking with James Beard 380
I'm Getting My Act Together and Taking It on the Road 264
Iacovelli, John 159, 353, 363, 367, 369, 393, 396
Iacovelli, Josh 125, 127, 132, 142, 149, 150, 171, 172, 173, 184, 189, 190
Iacucci, Lisa 50, 110
Iakovou, Michael 155
Ianculovici, Dan 43
Iannetta, Mario 64
Iannucci, Michael 259
Ibbitson, Thomas 245
Ice Factory Festival 327
Ice, Kelly 112, 193
Iceman Cometh, The 374

I-Chun, Yang 211
Ideal Husband, An 420
Idle Mind Ltd. 140
Iglesias, Juan 234
Igoe, Louis 78, 139
Igoe, Tommy 99
I-Hsuan, Lin 210
Iino, Rika 164, 211
Ijames, James 352
Ikeda, Jennifer 248
Ilardi-Lowy, Mariah 186
Iliad, An 123, 237
Ilku, David 145
Illes, Mary 105
Illingworth, Scott 148, 223, 249
Illinois Theatre Center 368, 377
Illman, Margaret 420
Im, Hee Jung 198
Imagine Ireland 219
Imagine This Scenario Productions 293
ImaginOcean 192
Imasuen, Wanda 127
Imbert, Stefano 229
Imfurst, Mimi 193
Imperial Theatre 78, 89
Impetuous Theater Group 293
Importance of Being Earnest, The 96
Important Musicals LLC 90
In Colonus 163
In Masks Outrageous and Austere 177
In Memoriam 304
In Paris 353, 357
in the great expanse of space… 279
In the Meantime 292
In the Name of God 321
In the Next Room (or the vibrator play) 341, 346, 365, 394
In the Solitude of Cotton Fields 294
In The Summer Pavilion 290
In This House 402
In Trachis 163
Inadmissible 281
Inbrook 175
Inc Lounge in the Time Hotel 410
Indelicato, Lucas 72
Independent Presenters Network 82
Indiana Repertory Theatre 380
Inexplicable Redemption of Agent G, The 166

Infectious Opportunity 303
Infernal Comedy: Confessions of a serial killer, The 212
INFINITY Stages 47, 54, 66
Ingalls, James F. 104, 199, 213, 218
Ingenthron, Blair 40
Inglehart, James Monroe 102
Inglis, Emily 70
Ingraham, Dana Marie 28, 115
Ingram, Ashley 177
Ingram, Carol A. 118, 202
Ingram, Colin 75
Ingram, Glenn 47, 103
Ingram, Kenny 99, 118
Ingram, Zach Law 99
Ingui, Kit 32, 67, 410
Inkley, Fred 84
Innocent Flesh 171
Innovation Arts and Entertainment 58
Innvar, Christopher 54, 104
InProximity Theatre Company 162
Inspired Artists Theatre Co. 293
Instinct 324
Insurgent Media 94
INTAR 183
Intelligent Guide to Capitalism & Socialism with a Key to the Scriptures, The 408, 409
Interart Theatre 182
Interborough Repertory Theatre 293
Interscope Records 28
Into the Woods 348, 359, 403
Invasion! 143
Invisible Hand, The 396
Inwood Shakespeare Festival 300
Inwood, Mike 248, 251, 258
Inzerillo, Salvatore 223
Iolanthe 235
Ionesco, Eugene 239, 263
Ionescopade 263
Iphigenia in Tauris 155
I-Ping, Su 211
i-Pod 286
Ippolito, David 201
Irby, A. Dean 152

Irby, Sherman 199
Ireland, Biran 125
Ireland, Brian 209, 224
Ireland, Marin 241, 421
Irene Diamond Stage 257
Irene Sharaff Awards 447
Irglová, Markéta 60, 236
Irish Repertory Theatre 112, 203, 219
Irish, Katie 28, 40, 62, 98, 106
Irizarry, Courtney 127, 137, 184
Irizarry, Jim 107
IRNE Awards 439
Iron Curtain 152
Irondale Center 127, 144, 147, 156, 168, 180
Irondale Ensemble Project 156, 180
Irons, Jeremy 112
Irons, Shaun 211
Irun, Paola 239
Irvin, A.J. 112
Irving, Amy 227
Irving, Everett 249
Irwin, Aaron 247
Irwin, Bill 246
Irwin, Elizabeth 142
Isaac, Oscar 227
Isaacs, Jessica 74
Isaacs, Mara 237
Isaacson, Mike 137
Isenegger, Nadine 183
Ishibashi, Brooke 166
Ishioka, Eiko 28, 467
Ishmael, Clement 99
Iskandar, Ed Sylvanus 163
Ismagilov, Damir 215
Israel, Robert 259
Israel, Vivian 43, 266
Isreal, Toni 49
Issaq, Lameece 237, 243
Istel, John 424
It Ain't Nothin But the Blues 301, 395
It Got Loud 313
It It Done 269, 290
ITBA Awards 440
Ito, Chihiro 197
It's A Wonderful Life - A Live Radio Play 382, 402
It's Always Right Now, Until It's Later 160
Ivanek, Željko 225
Ivanoff, Felix 176
Ivanov, Sergey 215

Ivanova, Galina 215
I've Never Been So Happy 359
Ives, David 42, 216, 217, 446
Iveson, Mike 236, 247
Ivey, Karine 167
Ivins, Todd 92, 97
Ivory-Castile, Mandy 159
I-Wen, Chiu 211
Iwuji, Chuk 214
Izquierdo, Michael 246
Izumi, Julia 179
Izzard, Eddie 420

J
J Media 222
Jack H. Skirball Center for the Performing Arts 259
Jack, Summer Lee 208
Jackman, Hugh 13, 43, 115, 202, 420
Jackowitz, Michael 95
Jack's Back! 317
Jacks, Demetrius 222
Jacks, Susan J. 263
Jacksina, Judy 188
Jackson Heights, 3am 320
Jackson, A.J. 166, 244-246
Jackson, Adam 111
Jackson, Ali 199
Jackson, Amy Jo 163
Jackson, Ayo 28, 115
Jackson, Cheyenne 114, 420
Jackson, Christopher 102, 253
Jackson, Eddie Ray 219
Jackson, Elaine 152
Jackson, Ernestine 410, 418
Jackson, Jason 78
Jackson, Lauren Lim 102, 113, 149
Jackson, Lora 152
Jackson, Mike 187
Jackson, Nagle 166
Jackson, Pope 149
Jackson, Renee 229
Jackson, Samuel L. 11, 36, 431
Jackson, Tyrone A. 87, 102, 116
Jackson, Warren 138
Jackson, Yasha 153
Jacksonian, The 372
Jacob, Abe 107, 422
Jacob, Askia Won Ling 36

Jacob, Jennifer A. 84, 86
Jacobs, Adam 99
Jacobs, Amy 43, 47, 58, 68, 70, 75, 100
Jacobs, Craig 105
Jacobs, Jim 115
Jacobs, Kelly 101
Jacobs, Sander 88
Jacobs, Starlet 143, 147, 218, 237, 258
Jacoby, Boris 210
Jacoby, Mark 115, 410, 419
Jacoby, Miles 163
Jacoby, Rob 47
Jacqueline Kennedy Onassis Theater 182
Jacquet, Fedna 138
Jaffe, Brandon 247
Jaffe, Charles 467
Jagendorf, Dan 195
Jagoe, Hannah 245
Jahn, Jessica 192
Jahnke, Christopher 54, 102
Jain, Justin 142
JAKK Productions 158
Jakubasz, Sarah 28, 78
Jalac, Anjia 259
Jalandoni, John 163
Jam Theatricals 28, 38, 72, 84
James X 159
James, Adam 81
James, Agustina 191
James, Brian d'Arcy 424
James, Courtney 62, 225, 261
James, Diqui 191
James, Eli 72, 229
James, Erik 172
James, Euston 127
James, Jeremiah 190
James, John 28
James, Marcus Paul 139, 140
James, Mary 417
James, Mike 271
James, Morgan 40
James, Nikki M. 90, 114, 115, 198, 200
James, Peter Francis 245, 257
James, Sara 192, 260
James, Stephen 419
James, Taylor 131, 133
James, Tess 36, 249
James, Toni-Leslie 199, 216, 241, 262
James, Wendy 109
James, Zachary 84, 202
Jamison, Katherine 206

Jamros, Chris 222
Janas, J. Jared 54, 7, 132, 194, 263
Jane of the Jungle 399
Janetopoulos, Elliot 178
Jang, Jamie 191
Janicki, Jay 129, 130, 232, 238, 262
Janiga, Joe 233, 234
Janis, Conrad 417
Janisse, Lindsay 108, 111
Janki, Devanand 130, 135
Jankowski, Cynthia 112, 219
Jannelli, Ronald 43, 85, 217
Janney, Allison 420
Janocko, Rachel Short 28
Janozak Productions 125
Jansen, Fabian 232
Janson, Merritt 360
Janssen, Stephanie 59
January, Shannon M.M. 91
Januszewski, Anthony 154
Jaramillo, Carlos 410
Jarecki, Henry G. 74
Jaris, Dick 92, 208
Jaris, Richard 104
Jarrett, Greg 266
Jarvis, Brett 188, 255
Jarvis, Martin 420
Jarvis, Mitchell 108
Jarzyna, Grzegorz 178
Jaslin, Omar 168
Jason, Rick 417
Jasperse, John 212
Jasperson, Thayne 64
Jawalaprasad, Chandra 167
Jaw-Hwa, Wang 210
Jay Records 264
Jay, Adam 44, 67, 77, 115
Jay, Asher 157
Jaynes, Randall 189
Jazz at Lincoln Center 199, 433
Jazz Singer, The 299
Jbara, Gregory 89
Jean, Valery 127
Jeannot, Christophe 210
Jedström, Joel 215
Jeffers, Tristan 245
Jeffrey Richards Associates 38, 47, 54, 66
Jeffrey, Ben 99

Jeffreys, Joe E. 177
Jeffries, Susan 158
Jellison, John 102
Jeminez, Cory 127
Jenen, Jessica R. 46
Jenkay LLC 149
Jenkins, Ava 167
Jenkins, Beverly 88
Jenkins, Carpathia 64
Jenkins, Christopher 259
Jenkins, Daniel 89, 200
Jenkins, Jeffrey Eric 438
Jenkins, Michael A. 47
Jenkins, Razz 368
Jenks, Amanda 156, 222, 230, 258
Jenness, Morgan 151
Jenness, Sean 47
Jennette, Tyson 90
Jennings, Byron 86
Jennings, Ken 419
Jennino, Nichole 33, 54, 92
Jensen, Ingrid 212
Jenson, David 231
Jentzen, Julie 241, 242
Jeong, Eui Uk 198
Jepson, Howard 44
Jericho 371
Jerome, Tim 77
Jersey Boys 97, 118, 202
Jerusalem 98
Jeseneck, Julie 140
Jesse, Ryan 97
Jessimeg Productions 127, 142, 149, 150, 171, 172, 184, 189, 190
Jesus Christ Superstar 18, 62, 368, 381, 408, 409
Jeter, James 235
Jeter, Michael 419
Jeun, Mi Do 198
Jevicki, Adrian 184
Jew Grows in Brooklyn, A 136, 182
Jhung, Finis 89
Jiang, Han 211
Jiani, Zhong 211
Jiaxin, Yuan 211
Jibson, Carly 181
Jie, Zheng 211
Jill Myers Music 87
Jillette, Penn 460
Jillson, Joyce 418
Jingjing, Qiu 211
Jiranek, Cricket Hooper 66
Jitney 393, 399, 402
Joan Weill Center for

Dance 130
Joann Kane Music Service 40, 92
Jocko Productions 102
Jocobs, Amy 73
Joe A. Callaway Award 437
Joe A. Callaway Awards 446
Joe's Pub 246
Joey Parnes Productions 67
Johanness, Mark 190
Johannsen, Rainer 212
Johansen, Christy 175
Johanson, Charles 170
Johanson, Eric 170
Johansson, Scarlett 421
John Cossette Productions 103, 136
John F. Kennedy Center for the Performing Arts 33
John Golden Theatre 45, 104
John, Elton 89, 99, 129
Johnnie, Millicent 211
Johnny Roscoe Productions 92
Johns, Ernie 225, 227, 260
Johns, Jasper 213
Johns, Kurt 262
Johnsen, Daniel 209
Johnson, Amanda 28
Johnson, Angela 28
Johnson, Anthony 196
Johnson, Berit 174
Johnson, Birch 102
Johnson, Britt 142
Johnson, Bryan 68, 106
Johnson, Bryan Scott 100
Johnson, Burr 212
Johnson, C. David 106
Johnson, Carol Linnea 100
Johnson, Carrie A. 109
Johnson, Catherine 100
Johnson, Chiké 57
Johnson, Chris 141
Johnson, Christina 210
Johnson, Christine Toy 144, 238
Johnson, Clark 90
Johnson, Craig 109
Johnson, Craig Hella 233
Johnson, Dave 142
Johnson, Evan 230
Johnson, Graham 143
Johnson, Heather 184
Johnson, Isaiah 71, 214

Johnson, Jay Armstrong 92, 114
Johnson, Jeffrey 95
Johnson, Jesse JP 111
Johnson, Jessica 35, 56, 72, 81, 85, 96, 104, 116, 251
Johnson, Jill 44, 73
Johnson, Joel Drake 162
Johnson, John 32, 67, 410
Johnson, John (dancer) 211
Johnson, John (musician) 93
Johnson, Jon 157
Johnson, Joshua 74
Johnson, Joshua Paul 229
Johnson, Julie 420
Johnson, Justin 140
Johnson, Kathleen K. 66, 77
Johnson, Kevin 256
Johnson, Kristin 40
Johnson, Laura 113, 199
Johnson, Lisa Helmi 188
Johnson, Max 219
Johnson, Miles 112
Johnson, Nathan 115
Johnson, Nicole Adell 99
Johnson, Page 417
Johnson, Royce 173
Johnson, Ryan 196
Johnson, Sarah 33, 243
Johnson, Scott 50, 62
Johnson, Stephen 74
Johnson, Susan 417
Johnson, Ted 196
Johnson, Temisha 183
Johnson, Terry 67
Johnson, Todd Alan 152
Johnson, Trey 74, 112, 117
Johnson-Liff Associates 105
Johnston, Dennis 99
Johnston, J.J. 419
Johnston, Jess 154, 157, 160, 164, 177
Johnston, Kristen 197
Johnston, Sherra 149, 150, 252
Johnston, Zane 173
Johnstone, Flora 62, 97, 181
Johnstone, Jessica 77, 261
Joines, Howard 76, 89,

95, 261
Jolles, Susan 216
Jolley, David 209
Jonas 134
Jonas, Nick 95, 118, 202
Jonathan Larson Performing Arts Foundation Awards 440
Jones, Adrian W. 171
Jones, Alfie 197
Jones, Alia M. 74
Jones, Amy 192
Jones, Andrea 99
Jones, Andrew 139
Jones, Andy 111
Jones, Basil 110
Jones, Billy Eugene 36
Jones, Bob 128
Jones, Calvin L. 210
Jones, Cari 137
Jones, Christine 50, 256
Jones, Claire 234
Jones, Darius 152
Jones, David Graham 229
Jones, Denis 162
Jones, Gemma 214
Jones, Gregory 70
Jones, James Earl 66, 418, 437
Jones, Jannie 404
Jones, Jay Armstrong 226
Jones, John Christopher 218, 260
Jones, Julia P. 75
Jones, Kara 125, 195
Jones, Ken 410
Jones, Kendrick 199
Jones, Lauren 418
Jones, Lindsay 240, 243, 244
Jones, Liz 146
Jones, Lyle 28, 46
Jones, Michael P. 28, 72, 86, 103, 104, 106, 253
Jones, Patrick Oliver 128
Jones, Paul 156
Jones, Robert 33, 38, 50
Jones, Ron Cephas 103, 209, 248, 256, 268
Jones, S. Brian 181
Jones, Samuel-Moses 112
Jones, Sarah 420
Jones, Simon 207, 217
Jones, Tom 190, 266, 267
Jones, Ty 138, 145, 181

Jones, Tyrick 192
Jones, Zach 72
Jones-Sojola, Andrea 54, 55
Jones-Wilmore, Leilani 410, 419
Jongeneel, Michele 191
Jorczak, Craig 188, 189
Jordan, Cookie 103, 145, 177, 179, 245, 256
Jordan, Danielle 33
Jordan, Jeremy 14, 27, 47, 64, 118, 202, 378, 407, 409, 412, 414, 429
Jordan, John 417
Jordan, Jon 67
Jordan, Kevin 111
Jorgensen, Michael 73, 177
Jornov, Amanda 238
Josefsberg, David 119, 169
Joseph Jefferson Awards 440
Joseph Kesselring Fellowship and Honors 444
Joseph, Aubrey Omari 99
Joseph, Greg 162
Joseph, Melanie 127, 151
Joseph, Rajiv 88
Joshi, Amanda Kate 206
Josiah Theatre Works 293
Josselson, Geoff 141, 264-267
Joubert, Joseph 78, 82, 89
Joy, Christian 148
Joyce, Antoine 167
Joyce, Elaine 410, 418
Joyce, Jennifer 130, 159, 165
Joyce, Lisa 258
Joyce, Stephen 418
Joyner, Andrew 234
JPH Consulatants 211
JS2 Communications 140, 151, 154, 183
JTG Theatricals 73
Ju, Patricia 138
Judd, Elizabeth 29
Judd, General 189
Judge-Russo, Jonathan 220
Judith of Bethulia 320
Judith of Shimoda, The 295
Judith Shakespeare

NYC 293
Judson Memorial Church Gymnasium 124, 153, 179
Judson, Chanon 199
Judy Jacksina Company 179
Judy Katz Public Relations 176, 198
Judy Show: My life as a sitcom, The 119, 131
Jue, Francis 248
Jujamcyn Theatres 73, 82, 113, 410
Jukebox Jackie: Snatches of Jackie Curtis 186, 294
Julius Caesar 176, 197, 284, 380
Jump, Jay Super 232
June B. in Jingle Bells, Batman Smells! 399
June Havoc Theatre 167
June, Cato 49
June, Nicole 49
Junek, Mark 218, 219
Jungle Book, The 372
Juniper Street Productions 28, 33, 40, 44, 52, 95, 102, 103, 136, 179
Junkyard Dog Productions 102
Junta Juleil Productions 277, 293
Jurman, Karl 99
Jusino, Anthony 46, 49, 56, 58, 59, 60, 73, 75, 77, 81, 185
Just Sex 320
Jutagir, Hattie K. 39, 110, 224
Juter, Hy 190

K
Kabia, Ansu 197
Kaburick, Aaron 89
Kacha and the Devil 284
Kachadurian, Zoya 192
Kaczorowski, Peter 42, 56, 57, 78, 85, 91, 116, 199, 217, 230, 244, 245, 253
Kaddish (or The Key in the Window) 273
Kader, Jacob 237
Kadleck, Tony 29, 216
KADM Productions 293
Kagan, Howard 47, 54
Kagel, Bruce 74, 143, 177
Kagy Productions Inc 410

Kahane, Gabriel 247
Kahler, Angela M. 28, 36, 62
Kahn, Alfred R. 174
Kahn, Brandon 190
Kahn, Rosemary 238
Kai, Keiko 184
Kaikkonen, Gus 240
Kail, Thomas 70
Kainuma, Morris 99
Kairis, Lilaia 231
Kaiser, Corey 103, 146
Kaiser, Jaymes 58
Kaiser, Michael M. 33
Kaiser, Paul 213
Kaissar, Amy 231
Kakegawa, Yasunori 197
Kakuk, Naomi 113
Kalarus, Wojciech 178
Kalb, Jonathan 259, 260
Kalbfleisch, Jon 115
Kalember, Patricia 24, 81
Kaley, David 84, 104, 132, 194
Kalfo, Lior 133
Kalin, Brian 47
Kalinina, Elena 215
Kaliski, Stephen 68
Kalita, Antoninia 178
Kalita, Marek 178
Kallman, Dick 417
Kalmbach, Heiko 161
Kalukango, Joaquina 40, 256, 407, 409
Kaluzhskikh, Maria 212
Kam, Chris 208
Kamakari, Yuiko 149
Kambara, Shoko 33, 35, 78, 95, 103, 136, 230, 253
Kamel, Gabriel 47
Kamerer, Carrie 28, 70
Kamine, Ben 163
Kaminsky, Eva 77
Kamlot, Robert 422
Kammermeyer, Kirsten 145
Kamphuis, Marike 232
Kan, Lilah 238
Kanakamedala, Prithi 180
Kandel, Elizabeth 243
Kandel, Paul 223
Kander, John 46, 93, 115, 262
Kane, Donna 419
Kane, Ellen 89
Kane, Paul Manuel 125
Kane, Sean 57
Kanelos, Jenny 113
Kanin, Garson 91
Kann, Elizabeth 195

Kann, Victoria 195
Kansas City Repertory Theatre 233, 244, 268
Kantor, Adam 139, 188
Kantor, Justin 149
Kantor, Kenneth 105
Kaou, Osamu 197
Kapetanis, Brian 91
Kaplan, Al 132
Kaplan, Gary 84
Kaplan, Jon 132
Kaplan, Jonathan 419
Kaplan, Megan 259
Kaplan, Randi 193
Kaplan, Steve 82
Kaplan, Steven Howard 116
Kaplan-Wildmann, Eli 140
Kaplow-Goldman, Laura 231
Kaplowitz, Robert 255, 256
Kapoor, Monica 100, 118
Kapstein, Adrienne 110
Karafin, Jeremy 162
Karam, Stephen 251, 430
Karamon, Cletus 88
Karapetyan, Geo 90
Karasik, Irene 82
Karasu, Bozkurt 168
Karavatakis, Adam 243
Kardana/Hart Sharp Productions 93
Karel, Katie 233
Kareman, Pamela Moller 133
Karen O 148, 149
Karfakis, Stefan 182
Karg, Kendall 130
Karie, Joel 99
Karijord, Rebekka 215
Karl, Andy 97
Karlin, B. Bales 112, 185, 224, 243
Karlin, Lisa 84, 113
Karliner, Danielle 138, 147, 164
Karlson, David 39
Karlstöm, Stefan 215
Karns, Michael 261
Karoff, Claire 246, 260
Karp, Warren 77, 124, 153, 261
Karpati, Arthur 196
Karpoff, Alana 38, 47, 54, 66, 410
Karrer, Peter 82
Karrer, Pitsch 109
Karst, Michelle 152
Kasca, Kevin 238

Kaseluris, Vangeli 35, 54
Kasim, Tunji 197
Kaskeski, Amy 156, 159, 176
Kasper, Glen 206
Kasper, Lee 225, 261
Kasprzak, Evan 64, 115
Kass, Amy 35, 56, 81, 85, 96, 103, 104, 116, 136, 185, 251, 410
Kass, Roger E. 169
Kassebaum, Kendra 83
Kassie, David 62
Kata, Takeshi 208, 209, 249, 261
Kataoka, Masako 145
Kateff, Chris 97, 168, 261, 265, 266
Katell, Gerald 87
Kates, Kathryn 140, 237
Katigbak, Mia 151
Kato, Takahiro 197
Katsaros, Doug 193
Katsuyoshi, Charlaine 99
Katz, Abigail 208
Katz, Amy 107
Katz, Benjamin 209
Katz, Danny 112
Katz, Darren 99
Katz, David Bar 223, 249
Katz, Jeremy 131
Katz, Natasha 33, 60, 84, 109, 236
Katz, Philip 192
Katz, Richard 197
Katz, Sara 108
Katz, Sean 176
Katzanek, Isaac 35, 36, 37, 46, 49, 56, 58, 59, 60, 73, 75, 77, 81, 185
Katzenelenbogen, Dorit 222
Kauffman, Anne 177, 225, 241, 422, 426
Kaufhold, Molly 125, 155, 185
Kaufman, David 108, 424
Kaufman, George S. 157, 216
Kaufman, Kara 163
Kaufman, Marci 62
Kaufman, Moisés 88, 155, 252, 422
Kaufman, Rachel 151
Kaufman, Shelby 154
Kaufman, Tim 244, 245, 246
Kaus, Stephen M. 38
Kautz, James 138
Kauzlaric, Robert 209

Kavanagh, Peter 214
Kavanagh, Ruth 131
Kavett, Katie 253, 409
Kavner, Julie 37
Kawahara, Karl 33, 55
Kawana, Yasuhiro 68, 92
Kay, Phyllis 389
Kayanan, Rafael 28
Kayden, Mildred 263
Kayden, Spencer 24, 81, 420
Kaye, Anne 117
Kaye, Barry 38, 47
Kaye, Carole 38, 47
Kaye, Howard 115, 132
Kaye, Judy 78, 410, 419
Kaye-Houston Music Inc. 43, 84, 139
Kaye-Phillips, Jamie 45
Kazak, Fayez 210
Kazan, Zoe 227
Kazee, Steve 18, 60, 204, 236
Kazman, Matt 28
Ke, Zhu 211
Keach, Stacy 39, 118, 409, 411
Keane, George 417
Keappock, Susan 60
Kearney, T.J. 82
Kearse, Jahi A. 87
Keating, Barry 409, 416
Keating, Isabel 28, 198, 411, 420
Keating, John 131, 260
Keating, Kevin 33, 46, 50, 52
Keating, Matthew 229
Keberle, Ryan 212
Kedem, Sigal 133
Keding, Chelsey 133
Kee, Adam 340
Keefe, Dennis Michael 265
Keeler, Patrick 149
Keeley, Keira 421
Keen Company 222
Keenan-Bolger, Andrew 64, 101, 200
Keenan-Bolger, Celia 71, 118, 205, 216, 420
Keene, Kris 28
Kehoe, Claire 214
Kehr, Donnie 202
Kehrwald, Nicolo 233, 234
Keightley, Benjamin 47, 66, 139, 177
Keigwin, Larry 139, 446
Keilmann, Kurt 54
Keirsey, Jeffrey 233
Keister, Andrew 40, 62, 92, 97

Keith Sherman and Associates 131, 133, 147, 164, 193, 238, 243
Keith, Alvin 360
Keller, Greg 57
Keller, Judy 180
Keller, Laura 113
Keller, Lynn 83
Keller, Michael 84, 89, 90, 99, 100, 102, 103, 111, 136, 139, 254
Kellermann, Susan 419
Kelley, Joshua W. 134
Kelley, Kimberly 33, 62
Kelley, Megan 153
Kelley, Peter 417
Kelley, R.J. 55
Kelley, Rich 182
Kelley, Ryan Patrick 111
Kelley, Thomas 156
Kelley, Thomas Matthew 229
Kelley, Warren 206
Kelly, Aimé Donna 181
Kelly, Carisa 85
Kelly, David Patrick 60, 236, 426
Kelly, Eileen Ryan 228
Kelly, Gerard 32, 198, 229, 240
Kelly, Glen 59, 90
Kelly, Gordon 409
Kelly, Grace 417
Kelly, Jeslyn 110, 191
Kelly, Kevin 247
Kelly, Laura Michelle 101
Kelly, Lorna 114, 202
Kelly, Maeve 163
Kelly, Reed 29, 84, 113
Kelly, Renee 87
Kelly, Rick 33, 64
Kelly, RJ 112
Kelly, Tara 117
Kelly, Tari 85
Kelly, Tom 75
Kelly, Troy 231
Kelly-Sordelet, Christian 165
Kelman, Vic 143
Kelson, Carolyn 103, 136, 262
Kelton, Richard 419
Kelvin Productions LLC 145
Kemmerer, Adam 167
Kemp, Jennifer Hindman 46, 59
Kemp, John 142, 242, 247, 253
Kemp, Steven C. 62, 102, 229

Kempf, Annabelle 89
Ken Larson Company 162, 238, 249, 250
Kendall, Simon 240
Kendell, Devin 43, 47, 58, 68, 70, 73, 75, 89, 100
Kendrick, Anna 420
Kendrick, Michael 156
Keneally, Ken 90
Kenkel, Nick 68, 92, 112, 113
Kenn, Dana 105
Kenn, Dana Lauren 129
Kenna, Greg 254
Kennedy Center Honor 441
Kennedy, Bill 168
Kennedy, Caroline 213
Kennedy, Chilina 62
Kennedy, Debbie 183
Kennedy, Deborah 234
Kennedy, Jack 127
Kennedy, Kevin 47, 82, 109, 157
Kennedy, Lauren 162, 404
Kennedy, Laurie 221, 419
Kennedy, Mark 429
Kennedy, Meghan 247
Kennedy, Nolan 156, 168, 180
Kennedy, R. Lee 153
Kennedy, Steve Canyon 62, 92, 97, 99, 101
Kenny, Dawn 28
Kenrick, Iona 98
Kent, David 93
Kent, Marika 147, 219, 230, 250
Kent, Monroe 199
Kent, Richard 68
Kenyon, Steven 55, 95, 216, 217
Kenzler, Karl 101
Keogh, Valerie 213
Keough, Rosemary 28, 43
Kepley, Nick 101
Keppie, Andrew 231
Kerkvliet, Peter 232
Kern, Benjamin 244
Kern, David 211
Kern, Jerome 46
Kern, Jon 156
Kerns, Scott 181
Kerpel, Gaby 191
Kerr, John 417
Kerrick, Katherine 149
Kerrod, Jacqueline 190
Kershen, Ed 125

Kerwin, Brian 419
Keshaviah, Mayank 239, 442
Keslake, Nicholas 50
Kessler, Chad 193
Kessler, Tommy 108
Kester, Muriel 60
Kesterson, Colleen 86, 108, 195, 261
Kevin Kelly 360
Kevin Kline Awards 441
Key, Jeff 126
Key, Linda Ames 195
Key, Rebecca 261
Keyes, Dave 154
Keyes, Justin 95
Keyes, Seth 58
Keys, Alicia 49
Kfir 105
Khalifah, Omar 143
Khan, Faizul 239
Khemiri, Jonas Hassen 143
Kho, Alan 191
Kholodkov, Sergey 129
Khosrowpour, Amir 207
Kibitzer 207
Kid, Billi 94
Kidman, Nicole 420
Kiehl, David 233
Kiehn, Dontee 84, 112, 181
Kiendl-Samarovski, Diana 212
Kiernan, Sam 101
Kiessel, Angela F. 117, 226
Kieve, Paul 75
Kiggell, Ryan 156
Kilday, Ray 33, 64
Kiley, Ed 183
Kiley, Richard 417
Kilgore, John 211
Kilgore, Matthew 117, 216
Kilian, Leslie Ann 47, 103
Kiliany, Paige 257
Killing Time 304
Kilner, Kevin 222, 420
Kim Carpenter's Theatre of Image 234
Kim Katzberg Productions 294
Kim, A. Ram 56, 181, 254
Kim, Ha-Yang 212
Kim, Ji Yeon 198
Kim, Jin Ho 191
Kim, Jisun 56, 143, 256
Kim, Jonathan 178
Kim, Moon Jyung 198
Kim, Peter 241

Kim, Sanghee 228, 241
Kim, Shinwon 83
Kim, Sue Jean 242
Kim, Sung Gee 198
Kim, Young Wan 198
Kim, Young-Ah 94
Kimball, Chad 102
Kimble, G.D. 35
Kimbrell, Marketa 467
Kimelman, Marc 62, 143
Kimmel, Veronica 143
Kincaid, Wheeler 191
Kinchen, Aaron 177
Kindler, Samantha 227
Kindred, Graham 189, 190, 193
King Displays 410
King Lear 197, 245
King, Bobby C. 88
King, Bradley 207, 223, 237, 262
King, Floyd 388
King, Gabriel 156
King, John 213
King, John Michael 417
King, Lillian 71
King, Mariana Carreño 183
King, Raymond 101
King, Sara 32
King, Sid 38, 260
King, Simon 75
King, Stephen 226
King, Terry 75, 197, 214
King, Woodie, Jr. 152, 447
Kingley, Evangelia 128
King's River 288
Kingsberry, Grasan 50, 83, 92, 113
Kingsley, Susan 419
Kinnaird, Johnny 136
Kinnan, Michael 263, 267
Kinnane, Martin 187
Kinney, Polly Isham 202
Kinoshita, Shuhei 164
Kinosian, Joe 267
Kinsela, Kelly 198
Kinsella, Jo 220
Kinsella, Kevin 62, 97
Kinsella, Tamara 62, 97
Kinter, Rod 240
Kirk Theatre on Theatre Row 175, 194
Kirk, Christina 22, 73
Kirk, Justin 39
Kirkham, Steven 92, 183
Kirkland, Dale 111
Kirkwood, Chris 159
Kirmser Ponturo Group 70
Kirmser, Fran 70

Kirrane, Danny 98
Kirschenbaum, Scott 132
Kirshner, Ricky 422
Kirspel, Laura 191
Kiser, Terry 418
Kishimoto, Masumi 144
Kiskaddon, Walt 428
Kismet 382
Kisor, Ryan 199
Kissel, Jesse 82
Kissell, Howard 464, 467
Kissing Sid James 160
Kitamura, Takemi 211
Kitchen Theater 167
Kitchin, Jake 267
Kitt, Tom 244
Kittel, Hannah 85
Kitzhaber, Amy 251, 252
Kiyan, Kaitlin 32
Kjellman, Cara 89, 216
Kladitis, Manny 77, 107, 129
Klaff, Adam 59, 90
Klapinski, Bridget 142, 230
Klapper, Stephanie 129, 134, 143, 148, 151, 243
Klasko, Dave 219
Klaus, Katie 47
Klausen, Ray 135, 137
Klausner, Patricia 49
Klausner, Terri 201
Klebba, Tom 31
Kleiman, Brandon 62
Klein, Isaac 116, 118
Klein, Kara 105
Klein, Lauren 39
Klein, Matthew 230
Klein, Randall E. 188
Klein, Scott 133
Klein, Tessa 110
Kleinhans, Elysabeth 154-160
Klemons, Stephanie 113, 117
Klemperer, Jerusha 144
Klena, Derek 227, 254
Kleopina, Ekaterina 215
Klezmocracy 234
Klieverik, Mirthe 232
Klijnstra, Redbad 178
Kline, April Ann 220, 239
Kline, Julie 249
Klinger, Bruce 37, 54
Klinger, Kate 160

Klinger, Richard 80
Klitz, Jeffrey 106, 265
Kloha, Becca 115
Kloots-Larsen, Amanda 33
Klores, Dan 249
Kloss, Kristina 68
Kluger, Daniel 147, 169, 233, 252
Kluth, Chris 87
Knapik, Gina 58
Knapp, Andy 247
Knapp, Bob 257
Knapp, Maria 156, 180
Knechtges, Dan 52, 124, 216
Knife Edge Productions 294
Knight, Dudley 239
Knight, Krista 261
Knight, Olive 43
Knight, Shirley 178, 197
Knight, Vin 236, 247
Knoll, Alexandra 101
Knoth, Dale 185
Knowles, Ryan 194
Knox, Bethany 40
Knox, Hilary 109
Knox, Jennifer 162
Knox, Ronald 54
Knust, Jon 162
Kobak, Joshua 28, 29, 191
Koch, Adam 154
Koch, Alex 156
Koch, David 89
Koch, Laura 74
Koch, Martin 89, 100
Koch, Nathan V. 32, 67, 410
Koch, Timothy 88
Kochanov, Nicholas 125
Kochika & Pejsek 284
Kochman, Hannah 167
Kochuba, Courtney 208
Kocis, Stephen 88
Koed, Brad 59
Koehler, Aidan 180
Koenig, Jack 207
Koenig, Jeanne 82, 99
Koenigsberg, Heni 38, 54, 106, 159
Koenigsberg, Josh 140
Koerner, Kati 39, 110, 224
Koffler, Abby 139
Kohler, Adrian 110
Kohler, Joshua 142, 169
Kohler, Terri K. 112
Kohli, Rock 208
Kohn, Nicholas 188
Koka, Juliette 419
Kolek, Jacqueline 36,

37, 38, 46, 54
Koliadenko, Olena 129
Kolibyanov, Anatoly 215
Kolin, Nick 167, 230
Kolinski, Joseph 33
Kolker, Adam 43
Kollen, Ron 64
Koloc, Bonnie 419
Kolpin, James 78
Kolthof, Gercho 232
Kołtonowicz, El bieta 178
Konczewska, Justyna 178
Kondakov, Andrei 238
Kondor, Dillon 227, 254
Kong, Chris 116
Kong, Phil 241
Kono, Ben 43, 97
Koo, Yun Young 198
Koolschijn, Hugo 211
Koonin, Brian 47, 64, 92, 192
Koop Ouellette, Kris 105, 116, 118
Koops, Liz 106
Kopache, Thomas 249
Kopel, Stephen 50, 56, 60, 81, 85, 104, 116, 236, 252
Kopf, Rachel 151
Kopitsky, Lisa 245
Kopko, Tamara 47
Koplovitz, Fay 221
Kops, Jerry 189
Korbich, Eddie 344
Koreshkov, Pavel 129
Korins, David 38, 40, 46, 70, 242
Korley, Debbie 197
Kornfeld, Eric 131
Korol, Ilia 212
Kosack, Amanda 257
Kosaka, Akiko 263
Kosarin, Michael 64, 82, 109
Koshkarev, Alexander 215
Kosi ski, Cezary 178
Kosi ski, Konstanty 178
Kosis, Tom 101, 162
Kostel, Michael 409
Koster, Erin Maureen 181, 208
Kostopoulous, Carolyn 447
Kosugi, Takehisi 213
Kotimsky, Sherri 178, 229
Kotula, Bobbi 152
Kourtides, Nick 173
Koury, Kristine 178, 230
Kouyaté, Fatim 199

Kovach, Robert Andrew 192
Kovich, Matt 40, 193
Kovner, Katherine 144
Kowalik, Trent 421
Kowalsky, Neal 154
Koye, Danny 33, 82, 112
Kozatek, Gregory 211
Kozlark, Kathryn 258
Kozlovsky, Adi 133
Kozlow, Adrian 130, 262
Kozyrev, Sergey 215
Kraft, Kevin 151
Kraish, Mousa 248
Krakowski, Fritz 43
Krakowski, Jane 116
Kramer, Brittany 208, 258
Kramer, Larry 104, 114
Kramer, Terry Allen 28, 68, 84, 106
Kranz, Fran 59
Krapp's Last Tape 213, 369, 382
Krasnow, Neil 253
Krass, Danny 231
Krass, Ellen 74
Krass, Michael 77, 256, 261
Krassner, Meri 194
Krassowski, Laura 166, 244, 245, 247
Kratter, Emily 409
Kraus, Jeremy 28
Kraus, Matt 133, 181, 187
Krause, Caitlin 113
Krause, Joel 252
Krause, Jon 85
Krause, Ryan 240
Krauss, Elaine 36, 78
Kravits, Garth 185
Kravits, Jason 37
Krawczy ski, Krzysztof 178
Krawiec, Matthew W. 40, 50, 92
Kready, Jeff 164
Kreeger, Doug 115
Kreer, Yuri 130
Kreiman-Miller, Perchik 171
Kreis, Levi 103, 136
Kreisler, Katie 94
Kreitzer, Scott 102
Krell, Daniel 379
Krembs, Max 134
Kremer, Dan 240
Kreutzer Sonata, The 295
Krieger, Henry 233
Krieger, Portia 45
Kriegsman, Thomas O.

130, 211
Krigovsky, Jan 212
Krill, Sean Allan 50
Kring, Newell 227
Krise, Cale 181
Krispel, Talia 112, 198
Kristen, Ilene 115, 202
Kritzer, Leslie 194, 353
Kritzerland Records 104
KRL Creative 94
Kroboth, Julian 237
Kroeter, Susan 87
Kroll, Cameron 142
Krometis, Damon 130
Kronberg, Malachy 246-248
Kronenberg, Marisa 177
Kronos Quartet 210, 211
Krop, Eric Michael 40
Krueger, Casey 208, 219
Krug, Ken 137, 186
Krug, Michael 190
Krüger, Dietrich 211
Kruger, Johnny 33
Kruger, Justin 262
Krugley, Eric 249
Krul, Rienus 232
Krumins, Greg 233
Krupp, Judi 141, 169
Krupska, Dania 467
Kruse, Mahlon 106
Ku, Austin 164
Kubly, Riley 236
Kuburick, Aaron 109
Kuchlewska, Andrea 262, 263
Kudisch, Marc 200, 205, 253
Kudlicka, Boris 197
Kuenne, Matthew 369
Kuether, Carolyn 263, 264
Kuether, John 105
Kuether, Wyatt 174, 263, 264, 266, 267
Kuhl, Christopher 173, 241-243
Kuhn, Dave 84
Kuhn, Kevin 99
Kuhn, Natalie 149, 166
Kuhn, Veronica 188
Kuijer, Guus 234
Kukul, Kris 131
Kukva, Dmitry 129
Kulhawik, Joyce 436
Kulick, Brian 218, 219
Kulish, Kiril 421
Kulka, Paweł 178
Kull, Virginia 35, 242, 268
Kumangai, Max 124
Kumbhani, Meera Rohit 240

Kunath, Gerd 210
Kunene, Ron 99, 118, 255
Kuney, Daniel 74, 108, 143, 177
Kuney, Scott 95
Kunis, Rick 64
Kunken, Stephen 80, 207, 243, 268
Kupiszewski, Jakub 230
Kupper, Gary 154
Kupper, Pamela 143
Kurchuk, Michelle 251
Kurinskas, Lauren 208
Kurisu-Chan 189
Kuriyama, Satoshi 197
Kurland, Dan K. 31
Kurlander, Gabrielle L. 167
Kurs, Remy 152
Kurt, Stefan 210
Kurtz, Chris 75
Kurtz, Marcia Jean 243
Kurtzuba, Stephanie 89
Kuryshev, Sergey 215
Kurz, Peggie 75
Kurzner, Jill 130
Kushi, Angelica 191
Kushner, Tony 200
Kushnier, Jeremy 62, 63
Kusinski, Dawn 28, 103
Kusner, Jon 93
Kusnetz, Sam 129, 209, 225, 230, 232, 253, 260
Kuster, Roerita 211
Kuta, Magdalena 178
Kux, Bill 64
Kuykendall, Kelly 49
Kwan, Guy 28, 33, 40, 44, 52, 92, 103, 179
Kwitchoff, Julia 231
Kwon, Cathy 95
Kwon, Cathy 44, 95
Kwon, Do Kyung 198

L
La Criatura Theater 294
La Jolla Playhouse 241, 262, 368
La Manao: Tales of the End of the World 319
La Mirada Theatre for the Performing Arts 159
La Scala, Anita 28, 179
La Strada 149
La Strada Theater Company 149
La Touche, Lisa 196
LaBarre, Deirdre 68, 92
LaBute, Neil 155, 226
Labyrinth Theater Company 103, 223

Lacamoire, Alex 104, 111, 188
Lacavera, Anthony 74
Lacey, Christopher Michael 113
Lacey, CP 189
Lacey, Florence 33, 419
Lacey, Matthew 37, 75, 86
LaChanze 117, 419
LaChiusa, Michael John 43, 153
Lacivita, Anna 173
Lackey, Herndon 151
Lackey, Ty 87, 146
Lacolla, Kyle 116
Lacy, Todd 101
Lada, Bret 352
LaDassor, Ren 96, 192
Ladd, Eliza 149
Ladd, Jenni Schwaner 231
Laderoute, Matthew 143
Lady and the Peddler; Gimpel the Fool, The 295
Lady and/or the Tiger, The 304
Lady from Dubuque, The 205, 257
Lady's Not for Burning, The 305
Laemmie, Nicole 224
Laev, Jim 43
Lafarga, Kelly 111
Laffery, Dane 134, 172
Lage, Jordan 209, 268
Lagerkvist, Anna 215
Lahti, Christine 114, 208, 419, 429
Lai, David 47, 68, 101, 105
Lai, Valerie Lau-Kee 28, 101, 115, 118
Laine, Cleo 419
Laiosa, Matthew 181
Laird, Ashley 192
Laird, Marvin 33
Laird, Trevor 72
Lake Water 300
Lake, Beth 191
Lake, Jim 110
Lakin, Philip 40
Lakshmi, Padma 223
Laliberté, Guy 129
Lalley, Eileen 182
Lalor, Anthony 138
LaMaMa E.T.C 186, 294
Lamarre, Daniel 129
LaMattina, Anthony 410
Lamb, Georgina 197
Lamb, Mary Ann 115
Lambeek, Martin J.A.

211
Lambert, Denis 216
Lambert, Kelly Ann 160
Lambert, Robert 419
Lambrecht, Patricia 28, 75
Lame, Jerry Dee 115
Lamon, Anton Harrison 113
Lamon, Josh 32, 198, 247
Lamontagne, Evelyne 129
Lamothe, Serge 129, 197
Lampanelli, Lisa 118, 201
Lampert, Rachel 167
Lams, Claire 72
Lanasa, John 28
Lancaster, Burt 417
Lancaster, Cody Scott 108
Lancaster, Margaret 184
Lancaster, Mark 213
Land Line Productions 28, 75, 102
Land, Elizabeth Ward 102
Land, Peter 265-267
Landau, Becka 174, 196
Landau, Elie 45, 78
Landau, Leah 113
Landau, Randy 76, 89, 117
Lander, David 31, 77, 88, 252, 257, 261
Lander, Norman 156, 168
Landers, P.J. 142
Landes, Greg 263, 265
Landes, Steve 107
Landesman, Rocco 97
Landing, The 262
Landis, Scott 42, 78, 94
Landon, Amy 121, 158
Landon, Carol 235
Landry, Martin 201
Landwehr, Hugh 220
Lane, Alice 94
Lane, Burton 50
Lane, Daniel 233
Lane, Jack 71
Lane, Liam 191
Lane, Lourds 146
Lane, Patrick 266
Lane, Robin 233
Lane, Saskia 250
Lane, Stewart F. 66, 106
Lane-Piescia, Gillian 106, 110, 261
LaNeve, Tessa 243
Lang, Adam 251, 252

Lang, Charles 417
Lang, David 212
Lang, Heather 29
Lang, John 181
Lang, Stephanie 112
Lang, Victoria 132
Lang, William H. 185, 241, 243, 246
Langdon, Laurie V.. 105
Lange, Jessica 419
Lange, Letitia 207
Langel, Jodie 461
Langella, Frank 9, 35
Langer, Julia 206
Langlitz, Bryan 102
Lanham, Bill 68
Lannan, Nina 43, 47, 58, 68, 70, 73, 75, 100
Lanning, Jerry 115, 418
Lanning, Michael 47
Lansbury, Angela 66, 453
Lansbury, David 110
Lansbury, Edgar 40
Lantzy, Meghan 224
Lanz, Niels 211
Lanzarone, Nikka Graff 93, 113
Lanzarotta, Andrew 90
LaPaglia, Anthony 420
Lap-Cheong, Wong 211
Lapine, James 216
Lapinsky, Michael 222
LaPlatney, Martin 56
LaPointe, Charles G. 36, 47, 64, 70, 73, 74, 80, 97, 102, 179, 209, 219, 228, 241, 245
LaPorte, John Paul 113
Laporte, Manuela 35, 56, 81, 96
Lapp, J. Scott 47
Lapsburgh Layover, The 142
Larche, Megan 138
Large, Dan 214
Largess, John 199
Larimore, Drew 174
Laritz, Rachel 240
Lark Play Development 410
Larkin, Christopher 156
Larkin, Jimmy 125
Larkin, Linda 171, 223
Larner, Lionel 409-411
LaRosa, James 235
Larroquette, John 19, 66, 95, 421, 429
Larry A. Thompson Organization 58
Larsen, Anika 162, 164, 264
Larsen, David 89

Larsen, Gwyneth 191
Larsen, Michael 259
Larson, Cambria 159
Larson, Dick 157
Larson, Jeff 212
Larson, Jonathan 139
Larson, Kalen 177
Larson, Ken 127, 145, 184, 186, 219
Lasalle, Blanca 94
Lasko, Bob 112, 129, 178, 206, 219
Lasko, Ron 163, 170, 177, 197
Lasky, Rebecca 40
Lasser, Ben 208
Lassiter, Ian 110, 258
Last Chance Romance 311
Last Christmas of Ebenezer Scrooge, The 304
Last Days of Judas Iscariot, The 314, 317
Last Romance, The 371, 396
Last Year, The 310
Laster, Dominika 178
Laszlo, Miklos 116
Latarro, Lorin 179
Latessa, Dick 23, 77, 261
Lathan, Sanaa 420
Latitude Link 62, 97, 102
Latus, James 73, 244, 245
Lau, David 191
Lau, Laurence 165
Lauer, Andrea 218, 243, 256
Laughlin, Jason 227
Laughton, Charles 218
Laule, Scott 31, 42, 57, 80, 91, 227
Laura Little Productions 71
Laura Pels Theatre 251
Lauren Rayner Productions 296
Laurence, Aimée 220
Laurence, Michael 244, 249
Laux, Sarah 84, 110, 227
Lavallée, Céline 129
Lavender, James 179
LaVerdiere, Jamie 264, 266
Lavery, Elisa 130, 159
Lavey, Martha 447
Lavidis, Achilles 249, 250

LaVigne, Aaron 140
Lavin, Linda 23, 77, 201, 261, 418, 429
Lavine, Michael 202
LaViolette, Chandra 218
LaVon, Lora 130
Law, Ethan 138
Law, Jude 420
Lawhead, Blair 112
Lawing, Skip 118
Lawler, Julia 224
Lawler, Mike 183
Lawlor, Jimmy 157
Lawrence Weiner and Associates 171
Lawrence, Bailey 117
Lawrence, Blake 222
Lawrence, Carol 417
Lawrence, Darrie 207
Lawrence, David 87, 253
Lawrence, Don 28, 118
Lawrence, Jack 149
Lawrence, Peter 198, 199, 216, 217
Lawrence, Robert 235
Lawrence, Samantha 68, 92
Lawrence, Stephanie 419
Lawrence, Tamika Sonja 90, 140
Lawrence, Tasha 114
Lawrey, Tom 45, 78
Lawson, David 195
Lawson, David Margolin 148, 206
Lawson, James 50, 92
Lawson, Jason 86, 160
Lawson, Jeffory 208
Lawson, Jon 44, 72, 106
Lawson, Kent 161
Lawson, Marty 95
Lawson, Nick 139
Layag, JC 159, 160
Layman, Scott 189
Layon Gray Experience 189
Layton, Charley 222
Layton, Chris 194
Layton, Zachary 211
Lazar, Aaron 217
Lazar, Paul 173, 212
Lazarus, Julia 208
Lazarus, Sara Louise 433
LaZebnik, Claire 243
Lazzaretto, Marina 113
Lazzaro, Nicholas 178, 230
Lazzaro, Segolene Marchand 178
Le Baut, Jerôme 137
Le, Leon 29

Leabo, Matt 145
Leach, Nemo 244
Leachman, Cloris 417
Leadbelly 127
Leading Investment Co. Ltd. 82
League of Off-Broadway Theatres and Producers 428
Leahy, Matt 112
Leak, Bennett 188
Leakey's Ladies 285
Leaming, Analisa 151, 216
Leap of Faith 9, 82
Lear, Kate 92
Lear, Kenny 113, 194
Leary, John 234
Lease, Russ 107
Leave the Balcony Open 301
Leavel, Beth 87, 112, 113, 114, 115, 155, 198
Leavitt, Michael 84
LeBlanc, Jeanne 76
LeBlang, Craig 211
Lebo M 99
LeBon, Pierre 141
Lecat, Jean-Guy 141
Lecesne, James 66, 243
Lechtenberg, Jessica 207
Leckenby, Pip 158
LeCompte, Elizabeth 168
Ledbetter, Sammy 82
Lederer, Amanda A. 259
Ledger, Sydney 244
Ledovskikh, Artem 129
Ledwich, Anna 44
LeGalley, Thomas Charles 52, 124
LeGallienne, Eva 419
Legally Blonde The Musical 356
Leggs, Kingsley 109
Leguillou, Lisa 111
Leguizamo, John 94, 420
Lehne, Fredric 228
Lehrer, Angela 54
Lehrer, Jamie 230
Lehrer, Scott 59, 93, 199, 216, 217, 247
Lehrer, Tom 265
Leiba, Cedric, Jr. 135
Leiber, Jerry 467
Leibman, Ron 418
Leigh, Andrea 195
Leigh, Carolyn 159
Leigh, Steffanie 101
Leight, Warren 82
Leimay 296

Lee, Jennifer Jason 94
Lee, Jeremy 245
Lee, Joanna C. 38
Lee, Joon 191
Lee, Judy Yin-Chi 110
Lee, Katie 192
Lee, Kyu Hyung 191
Lee, Linda 66
Lee, Liz 244
Lee, Lucy 443
Lee, Lulu W.L. 210
Lee, Nelson 261
Lee, Pamela 36
Lee, Ran Young 198
Lee, Raymond J. 85, 118, 200
Lee, Robert E. 443
Lee, Robyn Elizabeth 112
Lee, Stephanie 245, 247
Lee, Steve 191
Lee, Sung Eun 198
Lee, Tom 110
Lee, Tracey Conyer 149
Lee, Tuck 111
Lee, Whitney Kam 238
Lee, Yasmine 60, 236
Leech, Kitty 447
Leeds, Robin 231
Lees, Elizabeth 259
Leese, Jared B. 115
Lefébure, Olivier 129
LeFebvre, Matthew 447
LeFevre, Adam 106, 140, 262
LeFevre, Alex 175
Lefferts, Matt 146
Lefkowich, David 202
Lefrancois, Vanessa 198
Left Out Festival 328

Leis, Krista 62
Leisey, Matt 190
Leishman, Gina 141
Leister, Johanna 220
Leitão, Ze Pedro 213
Leitzel-Reichenbach, Ashley 109
Lejo 232
LeKae, Valisa 90
Leland, Kyle 102
Lelli, Larry 103, 104
Lemen, Amanda 227, 259
Lemme, Christine 112, 187, 221
Lemmond, Rod 38, 46, 70
Lemoine, Robert 129
Lemon Meringue 313
Lemon Sky 222
Lemp, Sarah 138
Lemper, Ute 420
Lena (Black Cinderella) 293
Lendermon, Adam 113
Lenk, Katrina 29
LeNoire, Rosetta 420
Lenox, Adriane 192, 199, 228
Lent, Patricia 213
Lentina, Liza 188
Lenz, Matt 92
Lenzi, Robert 254
Leo 161
Leon, David 107
Leon, Kenny 36, 49
Leonard, Brett C. 223
Leonard, Gates Loren 186
Leonard, John 198
Leonard, Luke 186
Leonard, Natalie 186
Léonard, Patrick 138
Leonard, Robert Sean 91
Leonardis, Tom 109
Leone, Gina 256
Leone, Vivien 28, 44
Leong, David S. 89
Leonidas Loizides Theatre Company 155
LePage, Joey 186
LePage, Tony 108
LeProtto, Jess 64, 118
Lerman, Rebecca Lee 238
Lerner, Alan Jay 50, 112
Lerner, David Gabriel 101
Lerner, Jenny 162
Lerner, Liza 50
Lerner, Myla 32, 67, 106
Lerner, Salomon 135
Leroux, Gaston 105

Leroux, Larry 130
Les 7 Doigts de la Main/7 Fingers 137, 138
Les Gémeaux 214
Les Misérables 367
Lesch, Austin 89
Leslie, Nathan 253
Leslie, Struan 197
Less Than Rent Theatre 296
Lesser America 269, 296
Lessing, Kim 59
Lessing, Lilly 267
Lester, Ketty 418
Lester, Rob 433
Let Me Down Easy 393
Lethridge, Kenyetta 171
Letter From Omdurman, A 288
Letter to My Father 298
Lettre, Peter 144
Letts, Tracy 404
Lettuce, Hedda 193
Leung, Ken 114
Leung, Telly 40, 114, 117, 200
Lev, Elena 187
Levan, Martin 105
Levasseur, Brittany 90
Levasseur, Joe 212
Leve, Gette 118
Leve, Harriet Newman 36, 72, 78, 196
Leveaux, David 86, 208
Leveille, Savan 50
Levels, Calvin 419
Levenberg, Alison 89
Levenberg, David 91
Levengood, Caleb 184, 230, 255, 261
Levenson, Jon 104
Levenson, Keith 159, 160
Leversee, Loretta 417
Leviathan Lab 296
Leville, Savannah 31
Levin, Carl 108
Levin, Carly 140, 170
Levin, Hannah 214
Levin, Stephanie 254
Levine, Andrew 263
Levine, Arnold 239
Levine, Dan 33, 64
Levine, Daniel C. 266
Levine, Jeffrey 153
Levine, Jonathan 55
Levine, Josh 258
Levine, Lindsay 43, 62, 75
Levine, Sarah 157, 179, 253

Levine, Staci 46
Levine-Miller, Randie 424
Levings, Nigel 234
Levinson, Daniel 62
Levinson, David 112
Levinson, Frank 193
Levinson, Gary 239
Levinson, Tamara 191
Levinton, Michael 239
Leviss, Andy 152
Levitch, Leon 174
Levitt, Daniel 219
Levitt, Sidney 206
Levran, Ido 80, 241
Levy, Caissie 22, 76
Levy, Drew 72, 75, 96, 108
Levy, Eben 246
Levy, Julia C. 35, 56, 81, 85, 96, 104, 116, 251
Levy, Marisa 247
Levy, Sharon 128
Levy, Steven M. 198
Levy, Tim 72, 110
Levy, Valery 235
Lewin, Alex 236
Lewis & Fox Casting 128
Lewis, Angela 203, 241, 262
Lewis, Ashley 245-247
Lewis, Barry & Helene 184
Lewis, Brieanna 127
Lewis, Drew 240
Lewis, Jerry Lee 103, 136
Lewis, Jonathan D. 113
Lewis, Lisa 99
Lewis, Mark 107
Lewis, Megan 28, 29
Lewis, Michael Shawn 192
Lewis, Mildred & Edward 266
Lewis, Norm 54, 200, 202, 429
Lewis, R. MacKenzie 130
Lewis, Richard 177
Lewis, Shannon 95, 104
Lewis, Ted 170
Lewis-Evans, Kecia 83
Lewman, Dana 255
Lewter, Harold 112
Lexemberg, Liza 35-37, 46, 49, 56, 58-60, 73, 75, 77, 81, 109, 185
Leynse, Andrew 243
Leyton-Brown, Allison 165

Leyva, Haydee 137
LGBT Community Center 117
Li, Dennis Yueh-Yeh 168
Li, Jun 238
Li, Juni 173
Li, Li Jun 261
Liao, Joyce 151
Liar, The 366
Libby, Aaron J. 113
Libby, David 143, 144
Libertini, Richard 37
Liberto, Ian 89, 95
Libii, Kobi 208
Libin, Paul 113, 115, 422
Libra Theater Company 296
Licea, Todd 125
Lichtenstein, Roy 213
Lichty, Jean 352
Lick But Don't Swallow 295
Liddel, David E. 117
Lidless 146, 305
Lidz, Sarah Sophia 87
Lieber, Mimi 244
Lieberman, Andrew 248, 251, 258
Lieberman, Haley 141, 207, 259
Liebert, Ben 265
Liebert, Josh 37, 87, 179
Liebhart, Vince 196
Lien, Mimi 28, 173, 177, 241, 262
Life and Limb 400
Life of Galileo, The 365
Lifeline 206
Lifsher, Georgia X. 173
Lift 278
Ligeti, Barbara 165
Light, Anna 239
Light, Judith 13, 39, 113, 114, 115, 118, 429
Light, Kate 112
Lightburn, Tom 137
Lightcap, Chris 47
Lighthall, Ricky 146
Lighting Syndicate, The 125, 127, 143, 169, 181, 185, 208, 209, 218, 219, 249, 250, 258, 263
Lightning, Britt 146
Lightswitch 52
Ligon, Kevin 105, 109
Liles, Lance 196
Lilienthal, Erika Ingrid 37

Lillis, Padraic 170, 223
Lilly, Rob 152
Lim, Anderson 189
Lim, Jennifer 12, 38, 407, 409, 412, 415
Lim, Jin Woong 198
Lim, Yong Hee 198
Limberg, Ben 45, 60
Lim-Dutton, Elizabeth 76
Lin, Angela 38, 144
Lin, Christine 38
Lin, Kenneth 254
Lin, Yingshi June 28
Lincoln - An American Story 393
Lincoln Center Festival 197
Lincoln Center Theater 39, 73, 110, 204, 224
Lind, Heather 421
Linda Gross Theater 209
Lindahl, Jason 28, 75
Lindeman, Colby Q. 111
Linden, Daniel 259
Lindquist, Karen 112
Lindqvist, Anna 215
Lindsay, Allan 175
Lindsay, Howard 85
Lindsay, Kara 64
Lindsay, Katie 237
Lindsay, Laura 148
Lindsay, Robert 419
Lindsey, Chad 219
Lindström, Pia 422
Linehan, Sean 255
Lines 292
Link, Patrick 182
Link, Synthia 95
Linke, Paul 124
Linklater, Hamish 14, 45
Linn, Bambi 417
Linnard, T.J. 140
Linney, Laura 419
Linshu, Feng 211
Linton, Carla 229
Lion King, The 99, 116, 118, 202
Lion Theatre on Theatre Row 146, 155, 158
Lion, Margo 92
Lion, the Witch and the Wardrobe, The 401
Lionella Productions LLC 109
Lipman, Jonathan 214
Lippa, Andrew 84
Lippard, Alex 47, 165
Lippitt, Betsy 163
Lippstreu, Kate 188
Lips Together, Teeth Apart 403
Lipscomb, Rhonda 225

Lipstein, Jeff 189
Lipton, Dan 168
Lipton, Ethan 246, 426
Lira, Julie 112
Lisa, Luba 418
Lisboa Soul 213
Liscio, Michael, Jr. 188
Lishman, Tom 215
Lister-Jones, Zoe 45
Literally Alive Theatre Company 297
Lithgow, John 24, 80, 114, 429
Littell, Mary 67
Little Dog Laughed, The 289
Little Lord (a theater company) 297
Little Lord's Babes in Toyland 279
Little Mermaid, The 369, 385
Little Opera Theatre of NY, The 184
Little Prince, The 231, 358
Little Shop of Horrors 202, 289, 381
Little Town Blues 323
Little Voices 300
Little Women: The Musical 314, 358
Little, Brad 68
Little, Christiana 137
Littlefield, Chris 117
Littlemore, Nick 129
Littlestar Services Limited 100
Litvin, Mark 216
Liu, Guangbo 232
Liu, Guangying 232
Liu, Sheryl 185
Liu, Tim 239
Liu, Wenwei 232
Liu, Yunming 232
Live Nation 191
Liverpool Everyman and Playhouse 215
Living for Design 186
Living Theatre, The 297
Livingston, Ben 72
Livingston, Harmony 125
Livolsi, Katherine 68, 244
Livolsi, Vincent 169
Livoti, Gregory T. 70, 227
Liz Caplan Vocal Studios 60, 108, 133, 236
Liz Ulmer Theatricals 201
Ljova 210

Llana, Jose 200
Lloyd Webber, Andrew 46, 62, 68, 105
Lloyd, Mary Rose 231
Lloyd, Pamela 62
Lloyd, Phyllida 100
Lloyd, Robert Langdon 260
Llynn, Jana 132
Lo Forte, Gian Marco 238
Lobby Hero 317
Lobel, Adrianne 218
Lobo, Ritinha 213
Lobsinger, Leon 159
LoBue, Michael 70, 86, 104
Local Celebrity Theatre 297
Locher, Michael 144
Locher, Whitney 140, 141
Lochtefeld, Erik 247
Lockard, Heather 78
Lockhart, June 410, 417
Lockwood, Daniel 235
Lockyer, Melanie 192
Loden, Barbara 418
Lodge, Gavin 106
Loe, Amy Gilkes 31, 42, 57, 80, 227
Loeb, Ari 28, 29, 115
Loebl, Scott 231
Loeffelholtz, J. 93
Loesel, Paul 111, 201
Loesser, Frank 46, 95
Loetterle, Erich 152, 167
Loewald, Kate 143, 258
Loewe, Frederick 112
Lofgren, John 70
Loftis, Keith 128
Logan's Hollow 313
Logsdon, Micah 189
Loiseau, Nehanda 40
Loizides, Leonidis 155
Lojo, Phil 46, 50, 60, 64, 68, 95
Lok, Winnie Y. 42
Lollar, MJ 340
Lomaga, Olena 187
Lombana, Martín Fernandez 149
Lombard, Garrett 198
Lombardo, Jonny 220, 221
Lombardo, Tom 183
Lomonte, Natalie 28, 115
London Merchant, The 309, 317
London Mosquitoes 155
London, Frank 149
London, Todd 422, 447

Lonely, I'm Not 253
Lonergan, Kenneth 255, 256
Loney, Glenn 426
Long Day's Journey Into Night 354
Long Voyage Home, The 168
Long Wharf Theatre 247, 369, 382
Long, Amy 177
Long, Andrew 214
Long, Brian 249
Long, Daisy 181, 222
Long, Garrett 47
Long, Justin 45
Long, Stephen 33, 75
Long, William Ivey 43, 81, 82, 92, 93
Longacre Theatre 38, 70
Longest Lunch, The 297
Lonoff, Jon 409, 410
Lonsdale, Frederick 207
Look at the Fish Theatre 297
Look Back in Anger 251
Look for the Woman 323
Lookadoo (Loucadoux), Michelle 85, 118
Looking Glass Theatre 297
Looking Over the President's Shoulder 356
Loom Ensemble 297
Loomer, Lisa 243
Loomis, Dodd 28, 128
Loomis, Kevin C. 28, 29
Loos, Anita 217
Lopez, John Anthony 112
Lopez, Lauren 201
Lopez, Luis 151
Lopez, Mariangela 148
Lopez, Robert 90, 188
Lopez, Telesh 151
Loquasto, Santo 37, 57, 218
Lorber, Barbara H. 428
Lord Jamar 211
Lord, Brent 113
Lord, Jack 417
Lord-Surratt, Rebecca 150, 237, 254
Loreque, Kevin 162
Loretta Michael Productions 297
Loretto-Hilton Center for the Performing Arts 441
Lorey, Rob 116
Loring, Estelle 417
Lortel, Lucille 419

Lortie, Alain 129
Los Angeles Drama Critics Circle 442
Los Otros 363
Loss of Roses, A 352, 355
Lost - A Memoir 380
Lost & Found Project, The 297
Lost in Staten Island, More Tales of Modern Living 295
Lost in Yonkers 207
Lost on the Natchez Trace 206
Lotito, Mark 97
Loud, David 54, 59, 115, 262, 437
Loudon, Bella 180
Loudon, Dorothy 418
Loughner, David 52, 107
Loughran, Conor 227
Loughton, Amy 158
Louie, Eric 244
Louis, Allan 87
Louis, Jillian 264, 267
Louise, Merle 89
Louizos, Anna 87, 188, 243, 251, 447
Loukas, Leah 47, 64, 73, 102, 169, 185, 209, 226
Loungway, Gianna 105
Louryk, Bradford 241, 242
Love Alone 402
Love Goes to Press 229, 268
Love Happened by Chance 313
Love in the Time of Chlamydia 291
Love Letters 201
Love Sick 273
Love Street Theatre 298
Love, Brian M. 99
Love, Eric 60
Love, Eric William 340
Love, Jessica 227
Love, Loss, and What I Wore 192
Love, Redefined 307
Love's Labor's Lost 248
Love's Gonna Get You 313
LoveSick (or Things That Don't Happen) 310
Lovett, Conor 256
Lovett, Judy Hegart 256
Lovett, Rachel 259
Lowe, Christina 141, 258
Lowe, Gayle 189

Lowe, James 85, 116
Lowe, Kathy 82, 103, 155
Lowe, Leopold 206
Lowe, Martin 60, 236
Lowe, Michele 243
Lowe, Ryan 93, 115
Lowell, John W. 47
Lowell, Robert 238
Lowen, Michael 75
Lowenthal, Josh 224, 225
Lowrance, Nicole 378
Lowrie, Jen 175
Lowry, Craig 112, 194
Lowy, Andrew 59, 90
Loxley, Clare 214
Loyd, Ron 184
Loye, Victoria 187, 240, 247
Lozano, Florencia 223
Lozano, Jaime 135
Lu, Andrew 206
Lu, Qin (Lucy) 28
Lubetzky, Yael 33, 60, 84, 109, 187, 236
Lubinsky, Maya 196
Lubitz, Adam 219
Lucas, Charles Murdoch 216
Lucas, Elizabeth 163
Lucas, Jonathan 417
Lucci, Susan 197
Luce, K.C. 249
Luciani, Anthony 256
Luciani, Kristen 32
Lucille Lortel Awards 428
Lucille Lortel Foundation 135
Lucille Lortel Theatre 135, 202, 226
Lucio, Irene Sofia 57, 263
Lucio, Meredith 54
Luck of the Irish, The 377
Luckenbaugh, Nick 208
Luckett, Nehemiah 54
Lucky Duck 233
Lucrezio, Elizabeth 211
Lucy Jordan Award 437
Ludick, Paul 70, 103
Ludwig, Jessica 62
Luedtke, Wendy 409
Luff, Alison 76, 100
Luff, Darbourne 154
Luff, David 154
Luftig, Hal 68, 92
Lugo, Hector 62
Lugo, Wally 227
Luka, Stiven 213
Lukas, Stephen Mark

193
Luke, Dylan 209
Luker, Rebecca 202
Lukianov, Alex 102
Lukianov, Katya 102
Lukos, Christopher David 133
Luminescent Blues 320
Lunar Energy Productions 298
Lunchtime Theatre 176
Lund, John 417
Lund, Jordan 244, 245
Lundon, Natalie 130
Lundquist, Lori 66, 248
Lungisa, Tandiwe 130
Lungs 355
Lunn, Maggie 214
Lunney, Robert Emmet 91
Lunsford, Erin Kennedy 178, 209, 223, 249, 250, 253, 257, 260
Lunt-Fontanne Award 421
Lunt-Fontanne Theatre 75, 84
Luo, Jiali 232
Luongo, Joe 410
Lupes, Anka 138
Lupi, Scott 147, 169
Lupica, Katie 40
LuPone, Patti 14, 46
LuPone, Robert 226
Lurie, David H. 227, 256, 257
Lurie, Sarah 253, 254, 258
Lurking Fear, The 311
Lush Valley 291
Lustbader, Aaron 28, 33, 44, 52, 87, 95, 113
Lusteck, Jay 216
Lustig, Rebecca 146
Luther 277, 282
Luther, Patti 33
Lutken, David M. 202
Lutkin, Tim 75
Lutwick, Nina 28, 52
Lutz, Matt 47, 70
Lutz, Renee 260
Luxury Worldwide Transportation 410
Lyceum Theatre 42, 94
Lydic, Jeremy 33, 259
Lyford, Trey 173, 174
Lyle, Kim 94
Lympus, Ryan 185, 188
Lyn, Anthony 101
Lynch, Amy 261
Lynch, Brian 87, 88, 139
Lynch, Catherine 140, 170, 209

Lynch, Connor 206, 230
Lynch, Jenny 189
Lynch, Jonathon 179
Lynch, Kerri J. 147
Lynch, Matthew J. 28
Lynch, Patrick 258
Lynch, Sarah 198
Lynch, Thomas 31
Lynch, Tom 409
Lyndon, Nicholas Wolff 251, 252
Lyne, Luci 214
Lynes, James L. 259
Lynley, Carol 417
Lynn, Christopher 112
Lynn, Krik 151
Lynne, Gillian 105, 267
Lyon, Amanda 224
Lyon, Amanda Clegg 141, 184, 243
Lyon, Jeffery 196
Lyon, Rick 188
Lyon, Steve 117
Lyons, Amy 442
Lyons, Douglas 90
Lyons, Jason 108, 181, 208, 256
Lyons, Robert Britton 103, 136
Lyons, Ryan 113
Lyons, Sean 66
Lyons, Steven 104
Lyons, The 23, 77, 261
Lyric Stage 369, 382
Lyrics in Motion 299
Lysistrata Jones 16, 52, 119, 124
Lyster, Pamela 46

M
M. Elizabeth Osborn Award 431
M·A·C Pro Team 112
M-34 Productions 298
Ma Rainey's Black Bottom 377
Ma, Yo-Yo 441
MAAVS 410
Mabardi, Justin 108
Maberry Theatricals 31
MAC Awards 443
Mac, Taylor 219
MacAdams, Mikiko Suzuki 56, 181, 224, 250
Macaggi, Rudi 201
Macaleer, Carey 133
Macaluso, David 235
Macapugay, Jaygee 238
MacArthur, James 418
Macbeth 179, 181, 278, 289, 316
Macbeth 1969 382

Macbeth After Shakespeare 295
Maccarone, Nick 167
Macchiarola, Christina 258
MacDermot, Galt 32
MacDevitt, Brian 36, 38, 59, 90, 94
MacDonald, Gordon 208
MacDonald, James 185, 245
MacDonald, Norman 409
Macdonald, Robert & Wendy 141
MacDonald, Sandy 436
MacDonald, Tim 96
MacDonnell, Theresa 29
MacDowell, Al 127
Macey, Pamela 188
MacFarland, Dorothea 417
MacFarlane, Luke 104, 352
MacGilvray, James P. 91
MacGregor-Conrad, Moira 36, 88
Mach, Corey 40, 202
Machado, Agosto 187
Machesko, Johnny 125
Macias, Brett 115
Maciejewska, Magdalena 178
MacInnis, John 90
Mack, Jay 117, 164, 265
Mack, Kathleen 68
Mack, Victoria 42
Mackay, John 197
Mackay, Lizbeth 251, 409-411, 419, 456
MacKeen, Beverley D. 109
Mackenzie Wood, Barbara 156, 180
Mackessy, John 253
Mackey, Erin 85
Mackiewicz, Zachary 222
Mackinnon, Lucy 64, 226
MacKinnon, Pam 73, 223, 241, 422
Mackintosh, Cameron 101, 105, 265
Mackmin, Scarlett 44
Macks, John 43
Mackston, Lyle Colby 128
MacLaughlin, Sean 105
Maclean, Lara 192
MacLean, Simon W. 133
MacLeod, Mary 109
MacLeod, Terra C. 93

MacLeod, Wendy 155
MacMillan, Jonathan Christopher 110
Macnare, Hunter 138
MacNaughton, Donna 159
MacNeil, Ian 89
MacNicol, Peter 419
MacPhee, Megan 195
MacPherson, Ellie 117
Mad Dog Theatre Company 298
Mad Show, The 265
Mad Women 295
Madame Bovary 272, 304
Maday, Gregg 87
Madden, Donald 418
Madden, Lauren 143, 207
Maddening Rain, The 154
Madea/MacBeth/Cinderella 390
Madeleine 219
Madeley, Anna 44
Madigan, Amy 419
Madison, Emily 248
Madison, Kateria 230
Madison, Louise 109
Madoff, Daniel 213
Madonia, Maggie Gomez 125
Madonna 197
Madore, David John 201
Madsen, Andrew 95
Maeda, Ayako 197
Magdalene, The 128
Magee, Rowan 211
Maggart, Brandon 418
Maghuyop, Mel Sagrado 164
Magic Arts & Entertainment 107
Magic Futurebox 298
Magic/Bird 70
Magliula, Melissa 112
Magnano, Craig 227
Magner, J. Anthony 100
Magni, Marcello 259
Magnus, Bryn 169
Maguire, Gregory 111, 202
Maguire, Michael 419
Mah, Melanie Arii 224
Mahabharata, The 184
Mahan, Sam 64
Maharis, George 418
Maher, Audrey 224
Maher, Brian 44
Maher, Dennis 44, 98
Maher, Matthew 177, 258

Maher, Sheri 224
Mahmoud, Nesreen 95
Mahmoud, Neveen 52
Mahon, Melissa Rae 93, 112, 115, 118
Mahon, Robert G., III 253
Mahoney, Brian 410
Mahoney, John 419
Mahoney, Ken 47, 54, 66
Mahoney, Michael Jennings 112
Mahoney, Sean 201
Mahshie, Jeff 116
Mai, Diana Lea 206
Maids, The 172
Maier, Barbara 248
Maier, Charlotte 80
Maier, Karl 113
Maier, Rachel 82, 112
Maieutic Theatre Works 298
Maines, Sarah E.C. 97
Mainland, Kath M. 161
Mais, Michele 108, 115
Maisonet, Carlos 422, 188, 193
Maitlin, Zachary 89
Maiuri, Brian 35, 56, 66, 81, 96
Maize, Jimmy 218, 219
Majestic Theatre 105
Majzner, Johanna 215
Makarova, Natalia 419
Making of a King: Henry IV & Henry V, The 379, 394
Making Up the Truth 272
Makowski, Kristina 151, 166, 225, 261
Malabanan-McGrath, Alma 231
Malachkin, Vladamir 187
Malanowicz, Zygmunt 178
Malas, Marlena 31
Malas, Spiro 419
Malbuisson, Peter 104
Malcolm, Deborah H. 159
Maldonado, Arnulfo 127
Maldonado, Paula 62
Maley, Peggy 417
Malgeri, Alyssa 112
Maliekel, Lindsey Buller 231
Malinskiy, Vadim 185
Malitz, Leslie 47
Malizia, Juan 234
Malkemes, Becky 146

Malkovich, John 212, 419
Mallare, Rose 191
Mallin, Erika 255
Mallis, Fern 192
Mallory, Alex 165
Mallory, Ramona 267
Mallory, Victoria 112
Malloy, Dearbhla 221
Malloy, Geoffrey 207
Mallue, Lorielle 208
Mallumud, David 201
Malone, Steven 64, 109
Maloney, Darrel 148, 164, 177, 226
Maloney, James 64, 66, 82, 94, 103
Maloney, Janel 192
Maloney, Jennifer 108
Maloney, Jimmy 47, 54, 68
Maloney, Jimmy, Jr. 43, 78
Maloney, John 118
Maloney, Matt 31, 410
Maloney, Peter 260
Maltby, Jordan 128
Maltby, Richard, Jr. 128, 264, 436, 446
Malvagno, Victoria 180
Maly Drama Theatre 215
Mamalimov, Rafael 215
Mamma Mia! 100, 115, 118
Man and Boy 9, 35
Man and Superman 221
Man in Love 400
Man of No Importance, A 289, 340
Man Who Came to Dinner, The 121, 157
Mana, Camille 249
Manabat, Jake 144
Management Theater Company 298
Mancha, Regina 40, 50, 92
Mancillas, Blaze 219
Mancina, Mark 99
Mancuso, Camille 101
Mandel, Ellen 229
Mangella 310
Manhattan Movement and Arts Center 130, 154
Manhattan Repertory Theatre 298, 328, 329
Manhattan Theatre Club 31, 42, 57, 80, 227, 419
Manheim, Michael 82
Manhoff, Dinah 419
Maniar, Sheila 68

Manipulation 129
Manis, David 110, 244, 245
Manley, Andy 231
Mann, David 63, 106
Mann, Dwayne K. 88
Mann, Emily 74, 237
Mann, Erica 261
Mann, Michael 171
Mann, Nalina 113
Mann, Richard 43
Mann, Theodore 464, 467
Mann, Will 102
Mannato, Donovan 75
Manners, Katherine 214
Mannikus, Luke 106
Manning, Jerry 237
Manning, Kara 112, 219
Manning, Robert, Jr. 70
Mannion, Jonathan 211
Mannis, Jenny 226, 253
Manocherian, Barbara 66, 169
Manocherian, Jennifer 36, 78, 169, 188
Manolakos, Carrie 146, 162
Mansfield, Erica 68, 95
Mansfield, Jayne 417
Mansfield, Karl 50, 87, 188
Mansfield, Tom 154
Mansilla, Arthur 232
Mantello, Joe 39, 104, 111, 113, 198, 254
Manton, Sarah 72
Manuel, Bruston Kade 54
ManUnderdog Productions 134
Manus, Bob 146
Manye, Tshidi 99, 118
Manzano, Sonia 192
Manzi, Warren 195
Manzo, Dina 193
Map of Virture, A 272
Maple and Vine 241, 350
Maples, Marla 192
Mara, John, Jr. 70
Marable, Kimberly 109
Marans, Jon 134
Marathon Consulting 239
Marcato, Rob 255
March 312
March, Annie 211
March, Chris 146
March, The 388, 400
Marchant, Chris 112
Marchant, Kyle 249
Marchant, Tyler 191

Marchese, Jesse 229
Marchica, Ray 100
Marchione, Nicholas 55, 95
Marchuk, Andriy 129
Marciano, Eric 177
Marcic, Dorothy 149
Marcin, Brittany 33, 85
Marcoccia, Dawn 82
Marcos, J. Elaine 106
Marcotte, Michael 217
Marcus, Abby 166, 444
Marcus, Leslie 73, 241, 262
Marcus, Michelle 174
Marcus, Pat 47, 73, 87, 113
Marcus, Rachel 262
Marcus, Sarah 62
Marder, Jeff 64, 82, 83, 106
Mares, Kelly 277
Maresca, Sydney 135, 142, 150
Margaroli, Gretchen 152
Margherita, Leslie 442
Margo Jones Citizen of the Theater Medal 443
Margolies, Dany 442
Margolin, Janet 418
Margolis, Jamibeth 149
Margolis, Jason 90, 109
Margoshes, Steve 64
Margulis, Jennifer 125, 152
Maria Project, The 171
Mariani, Mark 191
Maricic, Dragan 191
Marie Antoinette: The Color of Flesh 395
Marie, Julienne 418
Marie, Kristen 202
Marik, Jennifer 111
Maring, Christopher 50
Marino, Jennie 177
Marino, Kasey 158
Marino, Renée 113, 149
Marion Anderson Theatre 431
Marion, Antonio 75
Marion, Seth 255
Marjorie S. Deane Little Theatre 130, 191
Mark of Cain 288
Mark Twain House and Museum 435
Mark Twain Prize 441
Mark, Aaron 199
Mark, Alex 80
Mark, Kimberly 50, 82
Mark, Zane 82
Marketing Division, The 136

Markham, Monte 418
Markham, Shelly 175, 194
Markle, Lois 186
Markley/Manocherian 196
Markoff, Matthew 39, 110
Markos, Louis 155
Marks, Jennie 40
Marks, Ken 28, 29
Marks, Matthew 90, 159
Marks-Moore-Tunbull Group 31
Markt, Anne 190, 266
Marla and Her Prayers 302
Marla Rubin Productions 36
Marland, Stuart 64
Marlot, Jacquelyn 142, 169
Marlowe, Gloria 417
Marlowe, Noah 101
Marotta, Brandon 189
Maroulis, Constantine 200, 341
Marques, Mario 213
Marquette, Josh 66, 90, 100, 251, 254
Marquette, Seth 40, 50, 92
Marquez, David 118
Marquez, Socrates 74
Marquis Theatre 33, 68
Marr, Danny 113
Marrero, Janio 144, 182
Marriott Marquis 429, 438, 444
Marriott, Laura 91
Marroquin, Bianca 93
Marry Me?! 269, 302
Marrying George Clooney: Confessions from a Midlife Crisis 281
MARS Theatricals 190
Marsalis, Branford 36
Marsalis, Wynton 199
Marsellis, Antony 135, 137, 186
Marsh, Ellyn Marie 106
Marsh, Joe 107
Marsh, Judith E. 202
Marsh, Kyla 219
Marsh, Lane 52, 95, 113, 136
Marshal, Heidi Miami 84
Marshall, Ann 142
Marshall, Jerry 71, 106
Marshall, Karen 214
Marshall, Kathleen 78,

85, 216
Marshall, Lee D. 107
Marshall, Patricia 417
Marshall, Sarah 417
Marshall-Rashid, Brendan 388
Marsico, Amy 110
Martello, John 197
Martian Entertainment 50, 66, 104, 106
Martignetti, Stephanie 78
Martin, Alix 263
Martin, Andrea 419
Martin, Andrea Jo 117, 183, 229
Martin, Anna Cecilia 86
Martin, Barrett 78, 95
Martin, Bob 420
Martin, Bud 147
Martin, Clay 75
Martin, DJ 33
Martin, Dorothy 132
Martin, Elliot 197, 447
Martin, Emilia 68
Martin, Hugh 217
Martin, Jane 231
Martin, Jerome 64
Martin, Jesse L. 223
Martin, Jonathan David 110
Martin, Kat 35, 56, 81, 96
Martin, Kristen 28, 29, 179
Martin, Leo A. 144, 237, 242, 252
Martin, Manda 130, 165, 263
Martin, Michael X. 78, 92, 216
Martin, Peter 197
Martin, Raphael 258
Martin, Reed 231
Martin, Ricky 68, 118
Martin, Robert J. 68
Martin, Ron 28
Martin, Trevor 142
Martin-Carter, Paulette 74
Martin-Cotton, Kim 240
Martindale, Kelly A. 62
Martinez, Annel 238
Martinez, Arturo 239
Martinez, John A. 230, 243, 244
Martinez, Mike 90, 410
Martin-Green, Sonequa 261
Martino, Rosanne 410
Martins, Luis Jose 213
Martinson Theater 245, 247

Martinson, Zoey 245
Martinsson, Patric 215
Martos, Caridad 149
Martynov, Vladimir 210
Marun, Taylor 152
Marvel Entertainment 28
Marvel, Elizabeth 39
Marvel, Linda 113, 255, 260
Marwell, David G. 174
Marx, Jeff 188
Marx, Richard 43
Mary Poppins 101, 116, 118
Mary's Hideaway LLC 143
Maryles, Daisy 410
Marz, Caitlin 149
Marzullo, Steve 100, 162
MAS Music Arts & Show 106
Mas, Stephanie 211
Mash Up! A 10th Anniversary Celebration 313
Maso, Michael 49, 251
Mason, Buck 159
Mason, Jared 103
Mason, Marshall W. 410, 419
Mason, Melanie 112, 184
Mass Bliss Productions 298
Massacre (Sing to Your Children) 250
Masse, Paul 55
Massee, Happy 94
Massenheimer, David 118
Massey, Cara 118
Massey, Julia 159
Massey, Kevin 102
Massey, Kyle Dean 111
Massicotte, Robert 129
Massimine, Chris 177
Massimine, Christopher 163
Massinissa and the Tragedy of the House of Thunder 318
Masson, Forbes 197
Masson, Jo 177
Massoud, Christine 178, 194
Masten, Fritz 145
Masten, Matthew 66
Master Class 10, 31
Master Kansuke 164
Masteroff, Joe 116
Masters, Marie 230
Masterson, Jane 137

Masterson, Marc 241, 262
Masterson, Mary Stuart 420
Masterworks Broadway 60, 68, 217, 236
Mastro, Jonathan 260
Mastro, Michael 147
Mastrogiorgio, Danny 230
Mastrone, Frank 105
Masur, Richard 243
Maszle, Josh 52, 124
Matarazzo, Gaten 106
Máté, Balázs 212
Matela, Kimberly 206
Mateo, Jon-Paul 175
Materno, Steven 187
Matheos, Cleopatra 93
Mathers, Joseph 247
Mathews, Andrew 189
Mathie, Alexandra 158
Mathiesen, Heather 85
Mathis, Nikiya 203, 241, 262
Mathis, Samantha 192
Mathis, Stanley Wayne 78
Mathole, Johny 130
Matinee 287
Matland, Michelle 90
Matlock, Victoria 106, 136
Matoli, Jana 146
Matra India, The 287
Matricardi, Lisa 216, 217
Matsheni, Sandile 130
Matson, Justin 177
Matsubara, Ross 151
Mattana, Anthony 243, 244, 254
Matthew, Ed 105
Matthews, Ben 156, 180
Matthews, Dakin 66, 244, 245
Matthews, Elaine 118
Matthews, Jackson 238
Matthews, Josh 189
Matthews, Simon 28
Matthews, Stacy Lane 193
Matthis, April 156
Mattingly, Sam 149
Mattio, Andrea 191
Mattioli, AJ 183
Mattison, Julia 40
Mattocks, Aaron 211, 212
Maturno, Steve 218
Maugans, Wayne 184
Maugham, W. Somerset 207

Maughan, Brett 187
Maulella, Andrea 184
Maureen McGovern in Carry It On 402
Maurer, Desireé 208, 241
Maurer, Gary 110
Mauritius 305
Maury, Nathalie 197
Mauzey, Alli 421
Mawbey, Richard 68, 106
Max, Adam E. 210
Maximum Entertainment Productions 131, 133
Maxmen, Mimi 447
Maxwell, Jan 33, 115, 116, 202
Maxwell, Mitchell 179
Maxwell, Richard 168
Maxwell, Roberta 218, 258
May Violets Spring 304
May, Andrew 240
May, Deven 420
May, Eizabeth 149
May, Elaine 37
May, Imelda 219
May, Maria 89
Maya, Stacey 58
Maybank, Euan 196
Maybee, Kevin 50, 72
Maye, Marilyn 201, 202
Mayer, George 172
Mayer, Michael 50
Mayerson, Frederic H. 75
Mayerson, Rhoda 97
Mayerson/Gould/Hauser/ Tysoe Group 28
Mayes, Sally 144, 419
Ma-Yi Theater Company 156, 166
Mayland, Nathan 63
Maynard, Tyler 50, 101, 420
Mayo, Nick 95, 116
Mays, Jefferson 66, 224, 420
Mazdra, Melissa 35, 36, 37, 46, 49, 56, 58, 59, 60, 73, 75, 77, 81, 90, 109, 185
Mazliah, Fabrice 211
Mazrowski, Peter 89
Mazzarella, Gina 113
Mazzella, Neil A. 38, 43, 47, 54, 62, 64, 66, 78, 82
Mazzie, Marin 114, 204, 227, 437
MB Productions 28
McAdam, Josie 156,

180
McAdoo, Molly 149
McAllen, Kathleen Rowe 419
McAllister, Linda 224
McAnarney, Kevin P. 134, 143, 161, 170
McAndrew, Kelly 207, 378
McAnuff, Des 62, 97
McArdle, Andrea 202, 419
McArdle, Seán 88
McArthur, Lauren 229, 265
McArthur, Michael 201
McBeth, Rachel 236
McBride, Julie 146
MCC Theater (Manhattan Class Company) 226
McCabe, Dan 251
McCabe, Michael 50, 52, 95, 103, 136
McCabe, Patti 189
McCaffrey, Erin 171
McCaffrey, Neil 89
McCain, Sankara 49
McCain, Sean 143
McCall, Barry 177
McCall, Candice Monet 102
McCallum, Davis 247
McCallum, Martin 28, 52
McCallum, Sheryl 99
McCann, Elizabeth Ireland 32
McCann, Mary 208
McCann, Tom 60
McCarter Theatre Center 237, 369, 383
McCarthy, Elaine J. 104, 111, 116
McCarthy, Hollis 170
McCarthy, Matthew 189
McCarthy, Theresa 153, 267
McCartney, Liz 105
McCarty, Mary 417
McCasland, Truman Clarke 184
McCaslin, Greg 35, 56, 81, 85, 96, 251
McCaulley, Darren 107
McClain, Amelia 94
McClain, LeRoy 203, 241, 262
McClain, Marcia 419
McClary, Ron 207
McClelland, Stephanie P. 68, 72, 84, 86, 90, 92, 98
McClernon, Mike 40

McCleskey, Anastacia 106
McClintock, Jodie Lynne 140
McClintock, Justin 109
McClintock, Melanie 90
McCloskey, Angrette 62
McClyde, Nedra 182
McColloch, Shawn 257
McCollum, Jaysin 99
McCollum, Kevin 88, 139, 188
McCollum, Patrick 71, 113
McConnell, James 213
McConnell, Michele 105, 202
McConnell-Wood, Suzu 195
McConney, Kate 107
McCord, Gerry 167
McCorkle, Pat 67, 169, 176, 191
McCormack, Eric 66, 118, 426
McCormack, John 183
McCormick, Eildh 175
McCormick, Michael 265
McCourt, Sean 111
McCoy Rigby Entertainment 159
McCoy, Daniel 253
McCoy, John 33, 37
McCoy, Katie 159
McCoy, Mitchell 57
McCoy, Rebecca 218
McCreary, Brent 71
McCree, J. Mallory 74, 241, 262
McCrimmon, Heather 161
McCrystal, Cal 72
McCue, Spike 166
McCulloch, Jill 44
McCullough, Andrea 152
McCullough, Frank 28, 47, 60, 84, 86, 90, 110, 236
McCurdy, Ryan 60
McCurry, Renee 424
McCutchen, Rachel S. 90
McCutcheon, Cory 28
McCutcheon, Lee 105
McDaniel, Aaron 179
McDaniel, Addi 190
McDaniel, George 195
McDaniel, John 47, 92
McDaniel, Sean 90, 118
McDermott, John 207, 249, 250

McDermott, Megan 360
McDermott, Phelim 84
McDiarmid, Ian 420
McDonald, Audra 54, 118, 410, 420, 429
McDonald, Bryce 35, 96, 252, 253
McDonald, Daniel 420
McDonald, David 102, 258
McDonald, Gregory 112
McDonald, Michael 32
McDonald, Steve 47
McDoniel, Kate 112
McDormand, Frances 447
McDowall, Alison 154
McDowell, Shannon 28
McDuffee, Jennifer 238
McElhatton, Megan 219
McElhinney, Jamie 148, 212
McElver, Bobby 168
McElwaine, Robert 190
McEntire, Reba 420
McEowen, Michael 159
McFadden, Ashlene 219
McFadden, Heather 105
McFadden, Jodi 28, 29
McFadden, Kern 240
McFadden-Herrera, Corinne 111
McFarland, Judy 247, 248
McFarland, Stephen 225
McFarlin, Volney 36
McFee, Dwight 174
McFerrin, Bobby 255
McGarity, Brian GF 71, 74, 87
McGarry, Danielle 91
McGarty, Terry 45
McGaughey, Kathryn 142
McGeary, Meghan 253, 344
McGee, Jason 189
McGee, Kenneth J. 36, 66, 98
McGee, Michael 168, 230
McGee, Pennix 171
McGee, Robin 202
McGee, Tyler 76
McGeehan, J.J. 43, 76, 89
McGeen, Don 50, 104, 116
McGeever, Tim 252
McGill, Emily 76
McGill, Jonathan 111
McGill, Paul 102
McGillin, Howard 220,

409, 410, 419
McGinn, James 212
McGinn, Lisa 229
McGinn/Cazale Theatre 254
McGiver, Boris 110
McGloin, Emil 209
McGoff, Michael 115, 199
McGough, Nick 217
McGovern, Christopher 263, 265, 266
McGovern, Elizabeth 419
McGovern, Porsche 28, 143
McGovney, Jeff 90
McGowan, James 238
McGowan, Marissa 47
McGowan, Mike 106
McGowan, Tom 111
McGrath, Katherine 89
McGrath, Kelly 218
McGrath, Kerry 64
McGrath, Michael 78, 91, 116, 198, 420
McGrath, Thomas B. 54, 102, 103
McGraw, W. Scott 70
McGregor, Patricia 256
McGrory, Francesca 154
McGrory, Jeff 246
McGruder, Jasper 353
McGuckin, Brayn 253
McGuckin, Bryan 253, 254
McGuinness, Paul 28
McGuire, Beth 74
McGuire, Kerry 195
McGuire, Mickey 164, 169
McGuirk, Michael F. 144
McGurk, Colin 162, 242
McHale, Sea 138
McHale, Travis 77, 151, 206, 257
McHugh, Benjamin 164
McHugh, Jimmy 199
Mclenigan, Jered 360
McInerney, Caitlin 62
McInerney, Joanne E. 112, 144, 218
McIntosh, Marcia 75
McIntosh, Sean 128
McIntyre, Kaytlin 243
McIntyre, Nat 110
McIntyre, Sean 163
McKay, Julie 239
McKay, Kristi 182
McKay, Monette 102
McKay, Nellie 420
McKean, Michael 66, 246, 419, 426

McKeaney, Edward 236
McKechnie, Donna 422
McKee, Kathryn 32
McKee, Katie 72
McKee, Michael Roberts 253
McKeever, Jacqueline 417
McKeirnan, Tommy 125
McKelahan, Elana 177
McKenna, Jason 90
McKennon, John 93, 115
McKenny, Stephan 249
McKeon, Johanna 164
McKevitt, Mara 129
McKiernan, Tim 233
McKim, Tod L. 90
McKinley, Gabe 208
McKinley, Philip Wm. 28
McKinney, Charlotte 160
McKinney, Nathan 187
McKinsey, Michael "Tuba" 158
McKittrick Hotel 196
McKnight, Sean 216
McLane, Derek 33, 35, 66, 78, 85, 88, 95, 103, 116, 136, 230, 252, 253
McLane, Judy 100, 198, 202
McLaren, James 171
McLaughlin, Ellen 141
McLean, Carter 140
McLemore, Allison 229
McLeod, Kenn 159
McLerie, Allyn Amm 417
McLinden, Mike 82
McMahon, Brendan 129
McMahon, Maedhbh 159
McMartin, John 85, 198, 410, 418
McMath, Tim 226, 241
McMenamin, James 252, 254
McMillan, Chadd 179, 263
McMillan, Dan 132
McMonagle, Michael 220
McMullan, James 39
McMurran, Kailee 234
McNabb, Barry 219, 221
McNall, Sean 240
McNally, Terrence 31, 92, 115
McNamara, Annie 247
McNamara, Colin 192
McNamara, Emily 188

McNamee, Katherine 105
McNeill, Jared 251
McNenny, Kathleen 59
McNicholas, Steve 196
McNicholl, B.T. 89
McNiff, Katie 129
McNight, Sharon 419
McNulty, Adam 245
McNulty, John 39
McNulty, Lisa 31, 42, 57, 80, 227
McPherson, John 72
McPhillamy, Colin 96
McQueen, Armelia 419
McQueen, Robert 100
McQuinn, Garry 106
McRae, Shane 208
McShane, Neil 40, 58
McStotts, Elijah 247
McSweeney, MaryAnn 192
McSweeny, Ethan 243
McTaggart, Fletcher 83
McTeer, Janet 420
McTernan, Helen 112
McVarish, Matthew 175
McVay, Jessica Rose 66
McVety, Drew 89
McVoy, Jens 49, 91
McWaters, Debra 93
McWilliams, Ryan Hugh 150, 182
McWilliams, Tim 47, 103
Me You Us Them 319
Mead, Chuck 103, 136
Mead, Shepherd 95
Meade, Katie 240
Meadow, Lynne 31, 42, 57, 80, 227, 447
Meadows, Rick 93
Meagher, Emily 31, 42, 49, 57, 62, 80, 86, 227, 255, 410
Means, Charles 45, 103
Means, Jesse 259
Mear, Brian 82
Mear, Stephen 101
Meara, Anne 426
Measor, Mara 208
Measure for Measure 245
Mecchi, Irene 99
Mechanic, Andie 104
Mechler, Emily 68
Meck, Lindsay 410
Medcalf, Harley 155
Medea 273
Medeiros, Joseph 253
Medford, Kay 417
Medieval Play 256
Medina-Cerdeira,

Milagros 109
Medinilla, Erick 68
Mee, Rosa 232
Meeh, Gregory 84
Meehan, Sean 174
Meeker, Andrew 33, 52, 59, 104
Meeker, Ralph 417
Meeker, Richard 113
Meeting with Stanley, The 286
Meffe, Rob 68, 117, 163
Mefford, Danny 247
Megee, Ron 233
Meggat, Jon 160
Mehadi Foundation 126
Mehelba, Marihan 224, 253
Mehlman, Kenneth B. 113
Mehr, Joshua 90
Mehta, Krishen 239
Meier, Aaron 31, 44, 57, 80, 86, 103, 136, 227
Meineck, Desiree Sanchez 179
Meineck, Peter 179
Meir, Naor Ben 133
Meister, Brian 129
Meister, Kati 409
Meister, Katie 245
Meister, Kent 189
Meitzler, Ralph 108
Mei-Ya, Huang 211
Mekenian, Ryan 62
Melançon, Corinne 100
Melane, Sarah 238
MelCap Casting 45, 49, 59, 88, 94, 208, 209, 253
Mele, Michael 409
Mele, Peej 195
Mele, Tim 261
Melia, Careena 196
Melia, Ryan 147
Melillo, Joseph V. 210
Melino, Kienan 219
Mellinger, Matthew 87, 253
Mellits, Marc 182
Melnick, Michael 75
Melrose, Rob 176
Melrose, Ron 97
Meltzer, Julia 225
Memoriam 276
Memory is a Culinary Affair 292
Memphis 102, 116
Memphis Orpheum Group 102
Ménard, Valérie 137
Menchell, Ivan 47
Mendel, D.J. 211

Mendeloff, Dan 85, 116
Menders 288
Mendes, Brian 139, 168
Mendes, Jake 195
Mendes, Paulo 213
Mendes, Sam 214
Mendez, Eric 47
Mendez, Lindsay 40, 114, 118, 254
Mendez, Michael 181
Mendez, Rocio 240
Mendizábal, David 71, 226
Mendoza, Francisca 99
Mendoza, Orville 71
Mendoza, Robert 229
Mendozza, Eliana 99
Menken, Alan 46, 64, 82, 109, 202
Mentor 223
Meola, Tony 52, 99, 111, 124
Mercado, Eric 179
Mercado, Syesha 379
Mercanti-Anthony, Frances 81, 98
Merce Cunningham Dance Company 213
Merce Cunningham: The Legacy Tour 213
Merced, Anthony J. 206
Merced, Jorge 149
Mercedes, Samuel 223
Mercer, Christopher 234
Mercer, Johnny 46
Mercer, Julian 173
Mercer, Marian 418
Mercer, Randy Houston 90
Mercer, Ray 99, 116, 118
Merchant of Venice, The 178, 389, 401
Mercurio, Rich 109
Merder, Jason 58
Meredith, James Vincent 388
Merely Players: Princes to Act 300
Merg, Dorothee 211
Merian, Barbara 265
Meriweather, Emily 85
Merk, Anita 151
Merkel, Andrew 227
Merle Frimark Associates 107
Mermaid's Tale, The 315
Merna, Tyler 101
Meron, Neil 95
Merriam, Mason 181
Merrick, Judy 138, 224, 249
Merrill, Bob 221

Merrill, Scott 417
Merrily We Roll Along 205, 216, 364
Merry Wives of Windsor, The 293, 398
Merry, Lyndall 197
Merten, Jennilyn 126
Mertes, Brian 250
Merwede, Glenn 35, 56, 81, 96
Mesa, Mike 233, 234
Meschter, David 259
Mesh, Kaitlin 85, 113, 179, 201
Mesri, Julian 183
Messina, Charles 188
Messina, Chris 113
Messina, Michael 409, 410
Metcalf, Laurie 419
Metcalf, Troy 188
Methuen Company 195
Metropolitan Museum of Art 197
Metropolitan Playhouse 298
Metters, Mardi 67
Mettler, Marc 43, 60, 76
Metuki, Ella 127
Metzger, Christopher 263
Metzger, David 99
Metzger, Patrick 163, 243
Metzler, Jeff 106
Metzler, Logan 131, 133
Metzler, Molly Smith 227
Metzler, Ryan 169
Meyer, Barry 87
Meyer, David 223
Meyer, Douglas L. 82
Meyer, Steve 234
Meyers, Elliot 165
Meyers, Jeff 222
Meyers, Karle J. 139
Meyers, Laurence 67
Meyrelles, Chip 33, 46, 50, 52
Mezzera, Ellen 112
MGM On Stage 106
Mic. 275
Micalizzi, Marina 89
Micallef, Amy 202
Micchiche, D. 93
Miccucci, Matt 245
Micelson, Marisa 267
Michael 321
Michael Andrews AV Systems 410
Michael Groisman Showcase 306
Michael von Siebenburg

Melts Through the Floorboards 346
Michael, Cory 121, 185
Michael, Sean Day 165
Michael, Taylor 50, 169, 181, 245
Michaels, Amanda 255
Michaels, Brant 113
Michalos, Leah 157, 166
Michaud, Kate 163
Michelson, Michael 213
Mickelson, Gary 102
Mickelson, Jerry 84
Micklin, Lee 33, 68
Micoleau, Tyler 146, 208, 218, 250
Micone, Roger 39, 52
Micozzi, Nick 444
Middlebrook, Coy 47
Middleton, Keith 196
Middleton, Stephanie 196
Middleton, Wesley 141
Midler, Bette 106, 202
Midsummer Night's Dream, A 218, 282, 364
Midsummer Night's (Queer) Dream 320
Midtown International Theatre Festival 329-331
Midtown Theater at HA! 124, 139, 200
Midwinter Madness Short Play Festival 314
Midyett, Joseph 176
Mielziner, Jo 59
Mientus, Andy 227
Mieser, Pamela 255
Miggs, DeBartolo 71
Migliore, Mike 89, 179
Mihalsky, Dennis 183
Mikata, Ryan 276
Mikel, Liz 52, 119, 124, 201
Mikhail, Dana 210
Mikita, Scott 105
Miklas, Brian 206
Mikroulis, Taso 155
Milando, Patrick 99
Milani, Johnny 78, 88, 115
Milazzo, AnnMarie 226
Milazzo, Kate 244
Milburn, Rob 253
Miles, Jermaine 133, 178
Miles, Ruthie Ann 188
Miles, Shelley 66
Milesquare Theatre 182
Milgrom, Irving 43

Milhano, Sergio 213
Milioti, Cristin 18, 60, 204, 236
Milk Like Sugar 203, 241, 262, 381
Milkey, James 216
Millar, Mervyn 110
Miller Advertising 152, 238
Miller, Adam J. 90
Miller, Allan 187
Miller, Amanda 208, 239, 258
Miller, Andrea 211
Miller, Ann 449
Miller, Arthur 59
Miller, Ashley 183
Miller, Austin 200
Miller, Barry 419
Miller, Billy 84, 216, 217
Miller, Brian 101
Miller, Caitlin 177
Miller, Cat 103, 223
Miller, Catherine 184
Miller, Chet 66
Miller, Dan 111
Miller, Denise Marie 113
Miller, Dustienne 115, 118
Miller, Eileen 49, 77
Miller, Gabrielle 165
Miller, James 410
Miller, Jason L. 246
Miller, Jenna 202
Miller, John 33, 40, 50, 54, 60, 62, 64, 82, 87, 92, 97, 106, 108, 109, 179
Miller, Jon-Michael 409
Miller, Julie 443
Miller, Julie Marie 184
Miller, Karl 241
Miller, Katie 259
Miller, Kenita 202, 216, 379
Miller, Larry 237
Miller, Lauren 207
Miller, Linda 419
Miller, Luke 260
Miller, Marshall 222
Miller, Meredith 84
Miller, Patina 109, 112, 113, 114, 198, 421
Miller, Paul 115, 147, 183, 200
Miller, Paul Heesang 100
Miller, Peter R. 111
Miller, PJ 75
Miller, Tim 62
Miller, Todd 40, 193
Miller, Victoria 146

Miller, Winter 130, 159
Miller, Wynne 417
Millhouse, Steve 40, 112
Milligan, Tuck 191
Millikan, Robert 32, 78
Million Dollar Quartet 103, 136
Mills, Andy 102, 113
Mills, Bridget 68
Mills, Charlotte 98
Mills, Dan 103, 136
Mills, G. Riley 209
Mills, Greg 105
Mills, Hayley 420
Mills, James 235
Mills, Jason 196
Mills, Marianne 52
Mills, Oga 229
Mills, Peter 152
Mills, Shanon Mari 159, 160
Milne, Alexandra 179
Milne, George D. 109
Milne, Karen 105
Milo, Roy 133
Miloszewicz, Jeremy 33, 83
Minarik, Michael 108, 181
Mincer, Kate 238
Mincic, Andreea 151
Mind The Art Entertainment 299
Mind The Gap Theatre 299
Mindelle, Marla 109, 113
Mindich, Stacey 92
Mindlin, Matthew 100
Minervae, The 303
Minetta Lane Theatre 140, 155, 179
Minfie, Colby 228
Ming, Xie 211
Mingfu, Guo 211
Mingo, Alan, Jr. 379
Ming-Trent, Christy 253
Minguez, María Luján 234
Ming-Yuan, Tsai 211
Minnelli, Liza 418
Minneman, Carl 213
Minns, Beatrice 196
Minq Vaadka's Narcischism 324
Minskoff Theatre 99, 118
Mint Theater Company 229, 268
Miracle on South Division Street 184
Miracle Worker, The 380

Miramontez, Rick 28, 32, 36, 67, 71, 73, 104, 155, 169, 177, 192, 223, 226, 243, 249, 263
Miranda 291, 299
Miranda, Braulio 206
Miranda, Lin-Manuel 205, 216, 420, 446
Miró Quartet, The 199
Mirren, Helen 420
Mirvish, David 44, 45, 106
Mirza, Rehana 444
Miser, The 307
Mishima, Yuko 197
Mishkin, Chase 67, 102
Mishler, Raphael 145, 246, 247
Miskell, Brian 249, 34000
Miskie, Del 50, 67
Miss Abigail's Guide to Dating, Mating and Marriage! 193
Miss Hope's 303
Miss Ophelia 232
Miss Robusta Goes to the Movies 278
Mississippi Mud Productions 299
Mistakes: a dark comedy in 5 parts 293
Mitall, Duduzile 75
Mitchel, Sarah Rae 117
Mitchell, Allison Mui 231
Mitchell, Billy 143
Mitchell, Brandon D. 227, 228, 253
Mitchell, Brian Stokes 3, 409, 412, 419
Mitchell, Cameron 417
Mitchell, Don 127
Mitchell, James 417
Mitchell, Jerry 92, 106, 112
Mitchell, Jon Cameron 199
Mitchell, Kate 244
Mitchell, Katie 199
Mitchell, Lauren 62, 97
Mitchell, Leah 211, 229
Mitchell, Lizanne 127
Mitchell, Mark 104, 116, 153, 216
Mitchell, Maude 178
Mitchell, Rashaun 213
Mitchell, Ruth 105
Mitchell, Thom 28
Mitchell, Tina 162
Mitsi, Pantelis 155
Mittelman, Arnold 174

Mittenthal, Ellen 229
Mitzi E. Newhouse Theater 224
Miwa, Hitomi 197
Mixed Phoenix Theatre Goup 299
Mixon, Chris 240
Miyamoto, Amon 197
Miyasaki, Brooke 191
Miyashiro, Alex 156, 180
MJE Productions 75
Mlotek, Zalmen 259
Mlyn, Paula 184
Moans, Farrah 193
Moar, Danny 215
Moauro, John 32
Moayed, Arian 88, 237, 246, 421
Moccia, Jodi 86
Mochizuki, Koh 101
Modern-Day Griot Theatre Company 299, 309
Modest Suggestion, A 274
Modrono, Mabel 105
Moe, Barry Lee 139
Moe, Karla 235
Moellenberg, Carl 32, 36, 59, 66, 84, 103
Moeller, Erin 42, 57, 80
Moeller, Jennifer 263
Moench, Dennis 101
Moere, Jamie 253
Mohon, Scott 183
Mohr, Brian 210
Mohrman, Thom 93
Moir, Benjamin 106
Moira Anderson Foundation 175
Mol, Gretchen 420
Moldovan, Trista 105, 118
Molina, Alfred 420
Molina, Daniel José 378
Molina, Ric 111
Mollien, Roger 417
Mollison, Ross 187
Molly Dykeman Productions 300
Molly Sweeney 382
Molnar, Paul 222
Moloney, Aedín 131, 203, 220
Moloney, Paddy 131
Molony, Patrick 44
MoLoRa 130
Mompoint, Vasthy 76, 115
Monaco, John 115
Monaco, Patricia 82
Monahan, James 218

Moncrief, Brianne 228
Moner, Isabela 68
Monferdini, Carole 206
Monheit, Jane 201
Monk, Debra 436
Monkey Boys Productions 231
Monkeys 279
Monks, Chris 158
Monley, Adam 353
Monokian, Brandon 259
Monroe, Ashley 147, 258
Monroe, Josh 130
Monroe, Marcus 201
Monroe, Martine 106
Monroe, Rebecca C. 220
Monroe, Scott 98
Monroy, Nick 249
Monsieur Chopin 393
Monster Story 310
Mont, Ira 37, 75, 86
Montagriff, Kim 233
Montalvo, Leticia 213
Montan, Chris 64, 99
Montano, Meladi 192
Montbertrand, Carine 138
Montclair State University 259
Monteiro, Eddie 68
Montel, Michael 263, 265, 266
Montes, Ulises Avedaño 234
Montgomery, Elizabeth 417
Montgomery, John 93
Montgomery, Richard A., II 223
Monush, Barry 409, 410
Moody, Nick 246
Moody, Nicole 91
Moody, Ron 419
Moon Bog, The 311
Moon for the Misbegotten, A 240
Moon of the Caribbees 168
Moon, Sung Hyuk 198
Mooney, Dana 235
Mooneyham, Joseph 93
Moore, Adrienne C. 241, 262
Moore, Aiden 29
Moore, Allie 90
Moore, Annette 87
Moore, Benjamin 237
Moore, Bethany 28
Moore, Bradley 31
Moore, Brianne 115
Moore, Charlotte 112, 219-221

Moore, Crista 419
Moore, Curtis 214
Moore, Demi 419
Moore, Erin N. 33
Moore, James 33
Moore, Jamie 145
Moore, Jason 188
Moore, Jennifer Rae 224, 243
Moore, Jodie 181
Moore, Julianne 154
Moore, Karen 90
Moore, Karrie 189
Moore, Kim 190, 195
Moore, Mary 165
Moore, Mary Tyler 198
Moore, Max Gordon 37, 221
Moore, Megan 136
Moore, Melba 418
Moore, Michael V. 165
Moore, Nick 143
Moore, Scott A. 67, 77, 147
Moore, Seth 163
Moore, Sharon 93
Moore, Toby Leonard 252
Moore, Tom 115
Moore, Zach 231
Moorehead, Austin 72
Moores, Merle 368
Moorman, Shaun 75
Moose Hall Theatre Company 300, 309
Moradi, David 258
Morahan, Christopher 215
Morales, Carole 36, 66
Morales-Mantos, Rolando 99
Moran, Alicia Hall 54, 55
Moran, Patrick John 177
More Then A Dream 293
Moreau, Elizabeth 246-248, 263
Moreau, Jennie 419
Morelli, Stella 28
Morena, Anna 214
Moreno, Bobby 140, 143, 150, 277
Moreno, Derek 50
Moreno, Lou 183
Moreno, Luis 368
Moreton, Peter 214
Moretti, Eddy 148
Moretton, Lonné 167
Morey, Chris 49, 78, 94
Morfee, Scott 126, 141, 169, 259
Morfogen, George 191
Morgaman, Philip 91

Morgan, Barry 112
Morgan, Cass 102, 266
Morgan, Emily 264
Morgan, Harry 467
Morgan, Ian 230
Morgan, James 221, 263, 264
Morgan, Jim 175, 194, 200
Morgan, Josh 164, 185, 218
Morgan, Matthew S. 99
Morgan, Melanie T. 187
Morgan, Meredith 52, 125
Morgan, Rob 189
Morgan, Terry 442
Moriarty, Michael 418
Morin, Geneviève 138
Morini Strad, The 244, 395
Morisseau, Dominique 263
Morita, Chie 67
Morita, Go 197
Moritz, Joel 249
Morlani, Michael 50
Morley, Jordan 196
Morley, Larry 32, 67, 91
Mormons, Mothers and Monsters 353, 355
Morogiello, John 206
Morohunfola, Tosin 233
Moroney, Molly 146
Morozov, Col. Nikolay 215
Morpurgo, Michael 110, 159
Morris + King Company 193
Morris, Ashley Austin 192
Morris, Ben 242, 261
Morris, Beverly 410
Morris, Bill 182
Morris, David 40
Morris, Eric 340
Morris, Halle 100
Morris, Jennifer R. 177
Morris, John 216
Morris, Jon 191
Morris, Kevin 410
Morris, Kira 191
Morris, Lisa 410
Morris, Shina Ann 85, 115
Morris, Steven Leigh 442
Morris, Sue Endrizzi 165
Morris, Tom 110
Morrisey & Morrisey LLP 410
Morrison, Angela 89

Morrison, Ann 419
Morrison, James 127
Morrison, Nick 259
Morrison, Pauline 214
Morrison, Rob 188
Morrison, Robert 31
Morrison, Toni 199
Morrissey, Eamon 198
Morris-Stan, Hugh 244-248
Morrow, Allison 52
Morrow, David 211
Morrow, Karen 418
Morse, Barbara 82
Morse, Robert 417, 449
Morse, Sally Campbell 62, 97
Morsette, Zoë 202
Morss, Ben 125
Mortal Folly Theatre 300
Mortimer, Vicki 199
Morton, Elizabeth 59
Morton, Euan 420
Morton, Jessica 85, 116
Morton, Joe 418
Morton, Sydney 68, 102
Mosca, Roberta 211
Mosery, Whitney 252
Moses, Burke 420
Moses, Itamar 241
Moses, John 111
Moses, Spencer 169
Moshe Feldstein, Icon of Self-Realization 293
Mosleh, Florian 64, 102, 226
Moss, Heather 124
Moss, Jane 199
Moss, Larry 171
Mossman, Carrie 37, 49, 50, 74, 78, 85, 132, 243
Motel Cherry 282
Moten, Aaron Clifton 74
Mother of God! 302
Mother Tongue 279
Motherf**ker with the Hat, The 103, 421
Motherhood Out Loud 243
Motz, Mike 190
Motz, Rachel 226
Moukarzel, Bush 198
Moulton, Leslie 28
Mountain, Mia 223
Mountaintop, The 11, 36
Mountjoy, Ric 154
Mourners' Bench, The 402
Mousetrap, The 375
Moustakas, George 156
Moutinho, Helder 213
Mouyiaris, Alexis 155

Move, Richard 151
Mowatt, Joe 261
Moy, Jessica 261
Moye, James 103, 136, 216, 254, 264
Moyer, Allen 52, 77, 124, 261
Moyer, Claire 156
Moyle, Sarah 98
Moynihan, D.S. 410
Mozart, Wolfgang Amadeus 212
Mozgala, Gregg 178
Mpayipheli, Tsolwana B. 130
Mr. Abbot Award 446
Mraz, Carolyn 208, 223, 225, 228, 237, 243
Mrs. Dalloway 141
Mrs. Perfect! And the Unexpected Visit of Evil! 320
Mrs. Whitney 384
Much Ado About Nothing 219, 278, 376, 389, 397, 402
Mudge, Jennifer 242
Mueller, Dan 82
Mueller, Jessie 15, 50, 117, 405, 407, 409, 414
Mueller, Kristina 151, 180
Muery, Michael 71
Mugler, Manfred Thierry 145
Mugleston, Linda 85, 216
Muikkonzept 212
Mujaj, Bestar 190
Mukhi, Sunita S. 239
Mulberry Bush, The 298
Mulgrew, Gerry 176
Mulheren, Michael 28, 198
Mulholland, Brad 152
Mulholland, Rory 156, 256, 257
Mullavey, Greg 174
Mullen, Christopher Patrick 340
Mullen, Jan 105
Muller, Annick 410
Muller, Jenni 94
Müller, Rufus 184
Mulligan, Richard 418
Mullins, Antoinette 148, 173
Mullins, Dan 223, 226, 227
Mullins, Kevin 164, 218, 239, 240
Mulryan, Patrick 141

MultiStages 300
Mulvey, Patrick 89
Mulvhill, Faith A. 128
Mumeni, David 214
Mumford, Peter 185
Munar, Andrés 224
Munday, Penelope 417
Mundraby, Nathan 43
Mundy, Meg 417
Mungaray, Rudy 224
Mungavin, Craig 239, 240
Mungioli Theatricals 264
Mungioli, Arnold J. 264
Munhall, Kevin 85
Muniz, Carla 95
Munn, Brian 111
Munnell, Christopher R. 112
Munnerlyn, Marcie 213
Munoz, Michael 116, 194
Munroe, Brian 36
Munroe, Kathleen 117
Mura, Daniel 28
Murania, Sergio 169
Muraoka, Alan 200
Murder for Two - A Killer Musical 363
Murdock, Christel 28
Murdy, Rachel 144
Murfin, Shani Colleen 125
Murfitt, Mary 419
Murin, David 447
Murin, Patti 52, 119, 124
Murney, Julia 153, 201, 262, 264
Murphy, Ann 141
Murphy, Brian Patrick 113
Murphy, Charlie 198
Murphy, Charlie Francis 240, 245
Murphy, Claire 89
Murphy, Donald 417
Murphy, Donna 104, 429
Murphy, Geoffrey Allen 110
Murphy, Joe 154
Murphy, Julia 410
Murphy, Karen 115
Murphy, Luke 196
Murphy, Matt 102, 130
Murphy, Maurice 83
Murphy, McKenzie 57, 71
Murphy, Molly 256
Murphy, Nicola 182
Murphy, Patricia 189

Murphy, Stephen "Spud" 106
Murphy, Walter 38, 54, 66
Murphy, Zach 244-247
Murray, Andy 110
Murray, Brian 96 112, 197 221
Murray, Diedre L. 54
Murray, Gregory 28
Murray, Joey 193
Murray, Jon 92, 155
Murray, Matthew 409
Murray, Patrena 156, 180
Murray, Rich 221
Murray, Sean Michael 140
Murray, Tom 64, 87, 78
Murtaugh, James 207
Musante, Peter 189
Museum 321
Musgrove, Brad 183
mush-room theatre design, The 300
Music Box Theatre 44, 58, 72, 98
Music Ink 47
Music Man, The 352, 354, 384
Music Preparation International 54
Music Theatre of Wichita 369, 384
Musicals in Mufti 264
Musser, Kristina 109, 216, 217
Musto, Michael 202
Mutrux, Ashley 87
Mutrux, Birgitte 87
Mutrux, Floyd 87, 103, 136
Muxlow, Sarah 70
Muzik, Paula 410
Muzungu 299
Mvotyo, Nofenishala 130
Mvotyo, Nokhaya 130
Mvotyo, Nopasile 130
My Big Gay Italian Wedding 193
My Brother My Hero 324
My Children! My Africa! 255
My Husband 155
My Mother's Italian, My Father's Jewish, and I'm Still in Therapy 139
My Name is Asher Lev 355, 382
My Occasion of Sin 173
My One and Only 374

My Sinatra 124
My Wonderful Day 402
Myars, Mark 111, 200
Myers, Cricket S. 88
Mygatt, Thomas 81, 85, 251
Myhrum, Matthew 97
Mykietyn, Paweł 178
Myler, Randal 124
Myrgorodska, Ganna 129
Myths and Hymns 163
Myths We Need-Or-How To Begin 311

N

Naanep, Kenneth 428
nabokov 154
Nachman, Chelsea 71, 223
Nachsin, Larry 124
Nacht, Brad 89
Nachtigall, Tara 194
Nackman, David 167
Nadajewski, Mike 62, 63
Nadal, Harry 183
Nagle, Jill 166
Nagler, Mele 45, 49, 253
Nagler, Niclas 155
Nahodil, Alesandra 155
Najarian, Rob 196
Nakagoshi, Noriko 197
Nakahara, Ron 238
Naked Angels 261
Naked Boys Singing! 116, 175, 194
Nakli, Laith 147, 237
Namoff, Jen 95
Nance, Marcus 62
Nanni, Kathleen 101, 118
Napoliello, Craig 71, 156, 262
Napolitano, Peter 148, 173
Nappi, Samuel 49
Naranjo, Valerie Dee 99
Narayan, Ram 210
Narciso, Alfredo 103, 209, 258
Nash, Brian J. 112, 116, 132
Nash, Kelsey 125
Nash, Ted 199
Naso, Dolores 193
Nason, Brian 220
Nathan, Anne L. 60, 236
Nathanson, Beth 241
National Angels 67, 72
National Arts Club 444
National Arts Club Awards 444

National Basketball Association 70
National Black Theatre 145
National Jewish Theatre 174
National Medals of the Arts 444
National Theatre of Great Britain 72, 110
National Yiddish Theatre – Folksbiene 259
Naughton, James 92, 200, 418
Naughton, Jeannie 68
Nauiokas, Amy 45
Nauman, Audrey 75
Naumann, Ulf 211
Nayer, Yuriy 243
Naylor, Brendan 40, 132
Naylor, James 208
Naylor, Michael 192
Naylor, Rashad 140
Nazario, Ednita 420
Nchako, Chantal 138
Neal Street 214
Neal, Andrew 28
Neal, Cedric 54
Neal, Kenny 419
Neal, Patricia 417
Neal, William 126, 143, 230, 231
Neale, Grant 184
Near, Holly 201
Near-Verbrugghe, Lucas 242, 252
neat & tidy 278
Nebrig, Drew 54
Necessary Sacrifices 371
Nederlander Presentations 32, 33, 47, 62, 92, 107, 159
Nederlander Theatre 64, 103
Nederlander, James L. 28, 68, 84, 103, 106, 136
Nederlander-Browne 146
Neenan, Audrie 109
Neeson, Liam 159, 419
Neff, Laurence 210
Neff, Matthew 201
Negley, Edward 264
Neglin, Anders 100
Negrete, Kim 143
Negro Ensemble Company 161
Nehmer, Kira 182, 242
Neidenbach, Tony 194
Neighborhood Productions 300

Neighbourhood Watch 158
Neil Simon Theatre 62, 92, 107
Neil, Harvey 146
Neiman, Susan 35, 56, 81, 85, 96, 251
Neinenger, Virginia 90
Neither 259
Nejat, Kat 52, 119, 124
Nelis, Tom 141, 260
Nelligan, Liam 124
Nellis, Andrea 244
Nellis, Jeff 229
Nelson, Alex 124
Nelson, Anthony E., Jr. 128
Nelson, Antonio 112
Nelson, Ashley J. 253, 254
Nelson, Daniel Allen 137
Nelson, David 127, 241, 261
Nelson, Dee 251
Nelson, Gene 417
Nelson, Jaime 410
Nelson, James Patrick 219, 229
Nelson, Jeff 109
Nelson, Jessica 112
Nelson, Julie 186
Nelson, Kari 230
Nelson, Krista 213
Nelson, Leah 45, 94
Nelson, Peter 93, 113
Nelson, Richard 213, 247
Nelson, Ruperta 192
Nelson, Stowe 151, 263
Nelson, Sven Henry 218, 220, 221
Nemec, Rachel 96, 139, 219
Nemeth, Matt 90
Nemr, Andrew 201
NEO 8 267
Neodus Company Ltd. 191
Nester, Kathleen 68
Nesti, Robert 436
Nestor, Lauren 125
Neswald, Amy 70
Neto, Jose Manuel 213
Netsky, Aaron 259
Netsky, Hankus 259
Nettles, William 74
Neubauten, Einstürzende 210
Neuer, Kim Dobbie 231
Neugebauer, Lila 148, 227
Neuman, Sam 244

Neumann, Alex 45, 66, 80, 131, 244, 263
Neumann, David 248
Neumann, Kimberly Dawn 221
Neumann, Trevor 33, 43, 64, 92
Neurnberger, Matt 156
Neuwirth, Bebe 84, 219, 198, 437
Neven, Heidi 43, 58, 73
Neville, John 468
Neville, Marcus 181
Nevins, Kristine 158
New Amsterdam Theatre 101, 115
New Dramatists 436
New Dramatists Lifetime Achievement Award 444
New Federal Theatre 152
New Feet Productions 301
New Girl in Town 221
New Group, The 188, 204, 230, 268
New Haarlem Arts Theatre 301
New Jersey Repertory Company 166
New Line Records 108
New Line Theatre 369, 385
New Ohio Theatre 301
New Perspectives Theatre Company 159, 301
New Stage Theatre Company 302
New Victory Theater 231, 232
New Ways 157
New World Stages 120, 133, 136, 139, 188, 191, 192, 194, 199, 200, 201
New Worlds Theatre Project 302
New York 290
New York City Center 199, 216, 227, 239
New York City Icon Plays 286
New York City Players 168
New York Daily News 409
New York Drama Critics' Circle Awards 428
New York Gilbert & Sullivan Players 235
New York Innovative

Theatre Awards 444
New York International Fringe Festival 331–336
New York Live Arts 162
New York Musical Theatre Festival 336
New York Neo-Futurists 302
New York Post 409
New York Sports Clubs 410
New York Stage and Film Company 247
New York Theatre Workshop 60, 71, 123, 204, 236
Neway, Patricia 468
Newell, David 50, 224
Newfield, Anthony 80
Newhall, Anne 206
Newhouse, Caroline 36, 60, 75
Newhouse, Kristin 118
Newirth, Tracy 146
Newkirk, Alicia 33
Newman Theater 246
Newman, Fred 167
Newman, Harold 78
Newman, Jennifer Harrison 99
Newman, Josh 124
Newman, Joy 32
Newman, Paul 417
Newman, Phyllis 202
Newman, Robert 186
Newman, Toby 184
Newman, Tommy 135
Newsday 409
NEWSical the Musical 115, 194
Newsies 19, 27, 64, 202, 37, 392
NewSpace 107
Newton, John 263
Next Fall 366, 371, 372
Next to Normal 355, 371
Next Wave Festival 210
Ney, Christy 111
Ng, Timothy 238
Ngaujah, Sahr 421
Ngema, S'bu 99
Ngqoko Cultural Group 130
Nguyen, Qui 166
Nia Theatrical Production Company 23, 269
Nice Work If You Can Get It 78
Nicholas, J. Paul 224
Nicholas, Lora 276
Nicholaw, Casey 90
Nicholi, Dr. Armand M.,

Jr. 191
Nichols, Alexander V. 43, 78, 177
Nichols, Andrus 170
Nichols, Darius 32
Nichols, David C. 442
Nichols, Dean 214
Nichols, Manna 164
Nichols, Margaret 207
Nichols, Michael 233
Nichols, Mike 59
Nichols, Patricia 97
Nichols, Teff 258
Nicholson, Kent 241
Nicholson, Susan M. 163
Nickell, Cody 352
Nicks, Eugene 90
Nicola, James C. 60, 236
Nicolas Ward Productions 303
Nicole, Lacretta 162
Nicu's Spoon 303
Niebanck, Jessica 224
Niebanck, Paul 224, 243
Nielsen, Jeffrey 157, 166
Niemtzow, Annette 82, 155, 194
Niesen, Jim 144, 147, 156, 180
Nietvelt, Chris 211
Nieuwenhuis, Sean 62
Niewood, Kay 199
Night of Deadly Serious Comedies 296
Night Watcher, The 359
Nightengale, Eric 180, 186, 229
Nightfall on Miranga Island 283
Nightingale, Christopher 75
Nightingale, Colin 196
Nightmare Story, The 147
Nighy, Bill 420
Nigrini, Peter 66, 139, 208
Niklaus, Jill 93
Niko Companies Ltd. 77, 107, 129
Nikoiforov, Evgeny 215
Nikolajeff, Jesper 215
Nikolsky, Stanislav 215
Niles, Sharika 54
Nimmer, Dan 199
Nina Conti: Talk to the Hand 155
Nina Lannan Associates 89
Nine/Twelve Tapes 317

Ninth and Joanie 223
Nious, Jason 129
Nirenberg, Nadav 112
Nishii, Brian 38
Nishimura, Ed 112
Niven, Kip 233
Nixon, April 149
Nixon, Cynthia 17, 57, 419, 429
Nixon-Marinoni Family Foundation Inc. 410
Nkhela, Nteliseng 99
Nkhela, Selloane A. 99
No Anita No Productions 303
No Child… 126, 394, 402
No Man's Land 345
No Place to Go 246
No Poem No Song 317
Nobbs, Keith 222
Noble, Don 67, 195
Noble, Elly 227
Noble, Jennifer 76
Noble, Leslie 182
Noble, Polly 62
Nobody Don't Like Yogi 380
Nobody Loves You 387
Nocciolino, Albert 159
Nochenson, Sarah 170
NO TÚ 219
Nocturne 200
Noelle, Sebastian 212
Noel-Montague, Willa 99
Nogee, Rori 130, 195
Noguchi, William 125, 226, 241
Noises Off 348, 373, 394
Nolan, Christine 32
Nolan, Ernie 233
Nolan, Paul 62, 368
Nolan, Peter 18
Noland, Dave 33, 83, 117
Noland, Nancy 417
Nolfi, Dominic 97
Noll, Christiane 204, 264
Nolte, Bill 266
Nolte, Charles 417
Nolte, Derric 68, 115, 217
Noonan, Patricia 216
Noone, James 177, 221
Noor Theatre 237
Noordhuis, Nadje 212
Norbitz, Bryce 132
Nord, John Patrick 116
Norett, Bill 146
Norige, Sherri 188

Normal Heart, The 104, 352, 354
Norman Conquests, The 421
Normand, Suzie 231
Normand-Jenny, Philippe 138
Norment, Elizabeth 57, 129, 143
Norris, Bruce 73
Norris, Eric 33, 60, 95, 98, 117
Norris, Mike 28
Norter, Kristy 192
North Carolina Theatre 378, 385
North Plan, The 394
North, Alex 59, 75
North, Sheree 417
Northen, Lindsay K. 111
Northington, Philip 183
Northlight Theatre 386
Northwest Passage 303
Nosedive Productions 303
Nostrand, Michael 190
Nosuchinsky, Joanne 189
Noth, Chris 420
Noth, Jennifer 100
Nothing Like a Dame 202
Nothing Serious 272, 313
Notion Music Inc. 159
Nottage, Lynn 127
Nottingham Playhouse 246
Noulin-Merat, Julia 163
Novak, Jason 191
Novakoff, Valerie 409
Novie, Tara 149
Novoa, Mariela 176
Novogorodoff, Danika 138
Now or Never 267
Now the Cat With Jewelled Claws 295
Now. Here. This. 205, 261
Nowicki, Allison 255, 256
Nowinski, Paul 43
Noxon, Hilary 193, 251
Noyes, Ned 229
Ntese, Nosomething 130
Nuccio, Topher 132
Nuclear Love Affair 280
Nudel, Alla 215
Nuemberger, Matt 147
Nugent, Nelle 49, 94
Numad Group, The 263
Number, A 394

Numrich, Seth 110, 114, 202, 203, 249, 421
Nunes, Travis 195
Nunez, Emmanuel 167
Nuñez, Marc Andrew 159
Nunez, Reece 136, 244
Nunez, Ylena 54, 87
Nunley, Stephen 167
Nunya Productions 303
Nupieri, Hernan 191
Nuriddin, Jameelah 171
Nuyen, France 417
Nuyorican Poets Café 303
Nyambi, Nyambi 223
Nyberg, David 100
Nylin, Ulf Poly 215
Nylon Fusion Collective 303
Nype, Russell 417

O

O'Brien, Barret 144
O'Brien, Barry 198
O'Brien, Brian 93, 15, 118
O'Brien, Daniel 131, 139
O'Brien, David 40
O'Brien, Jack 39, 92, 224
O'Brien, Kevin 82, 86
O'Brien, Mark 134
O'Brien, Paul 50, 96, 221
O'Brien, Scott 195
O'Brien, Seán 219
O'Brien, Sonja 235
O'Brien, Stephen 235
O'Brient, Evan 127, 151, 172, 250
O'Carroll, Mike 164
O'Casey, Sean 198
O'Connell, Caitlin 225, 244, 245, 248, 250
O'Connell, Deirdre 70
O'Connell, Heidi 245-247
O'Connell, Jerry 14, 45, 118
O'Connell, John 187
O'Connell, Nick 219
O'Connell, Patricia 37
O'Connell, Stefanie 125
O'Conner, Rachel 137
O'Connor, Bridget 110, 251, 252
O'Connor, Francis 198
O'Connor, Jake 252
O'Connor, James Andrew 81
O'Connor, Jennifer

28, 52
O'Connor, Jeremy 231
O'Connor, Kyle 28
O'Connor, Michael 128, 219, 220
O'Donnell, Addison 174
O'Donnell, Katrina 219
O'Donnell, Kelley Rae 223
O'Donnell, Mimi 103, 223, 242
O'Donnell, Tilman 211
O'Donnell, Tim 410
O'Donnell, Vayu 35, 125
O'Donovan, Gene 35-37, 46, 49, 56, 58-60, 73, 75, 77, 81, 90, 109, 185
O'Driscoll, Dan 57
O'Dwyer, Marion 198
O'Gara, Ryan 62, 70, 87, 95, 103, 117, 134, 136, 146, 188, 231, 232
O'Gleby, Sarah 95
O'Grady, Christine 152
O'Halloran, Sean 152
O'Hara, Kelli 78, 116, 246, 429
O'Hare, Denis 123, 237
O'Hare, Fergus 197
O'Hare, Jane 247
O'Hurley, John 93
O'Keefe, Michael 379, 419
O'Keefe, Nathan 234
O'Keefe, Tom 170
O'Keeffe, Maura 256
O'Lurie, Noodles H. 198
O'Malley, Kerry 50
O'Malley, Rory 90, 113, 114, 116, 118, 198
O'Neal, Brendan 54 95
O'Neal, Cathy 117
O'Neil, Lindsay 217
O'Neil, Melissa 62, 63
O'Neil, Tricia 418
O'Neill, Dustin 62, 208, 209
O'Neill, Emma 234
O'Neill, Eugene 168, 220, 221, 240
O'Neill, Jonjo 197
O'Neill, Meghan Mae 169
O'Neill, Patrick 50, 117, 179
O'Neill, Rebecca 60, 251, 252
O'Neill, Shayna 147
O'Reilly, Ciarán 112, 219, 220
O'Reilly, Donal 219
O'Shea, Steve 129

O'Sullivan, Rebecca 235
O'Toole, Katie 97
O'Toole, Paul 263-267
O'Wyatt, Jane 178
O+M Company 28, 32, 36, 67, 71, 73, 104, 126, 130, 155, 169, 177, 187, 189, 192, 202, 207, 223, 226, 243, 249, 263, 410
Oakley, Brent 70
Oakley, Desi 111
Oaks, Matthew 196
Oates, Kara 101
Obama in Naples 324
Obama44 295
Oberholtzer, Jared 247
Oberman, Brett 131,133, 147, 193, 243
Obermeier, Ryan 175, 194
Oberpriller, Don 47
Oberpriller, Donald J. 68, 92
Oberpriller, Mary Ann 39
Oberstein, Matthew 202
ObJects 289, 340
Oblivion 400
Obremski, Keiko 238
O'Brien, John Emmett 85, 166
O'Bryan, Shannon M. 216, 217
Ochoa, Jules 206
Ockler, Judi Lewis 219
O'Connor, Susan Louise 125, 421
October, Before I Was Born 356
Oda, Naoya 197
Odgers, Lynne 265
Odom, Leslie, Jr. 83, 426
Odoms, Tyrah Skye 409, 413
Odyssey 386
Odze, Warren 106
Oedipus 163
Oei, Kristen Faith 28
Oestreich, Erin 409, 416
Off Broadway Alliance Awards 445
Off Broadway Booking 139
Off The Aisle 162
Offenbach, Jacques 267
Ogden, Leonard 170
Ogilvie, Brian 101
Ogle, Dave 258
Oh You Pretty Things 311
Oh, Coward! 265
Oh, Gastronomy 347

Oh, Julie 59
Oh, Sandra 420
Oh, Sang Joon 198
Oh, That Wily Snake! 292
O'Hara, Jill 418
Ohio State University 197, 443
Ohrstrom, Thomas 409
Ojala, David 130, 145
Ojeda, Martín 234
Okada, Agatha 197
Okafor, Leila 340
Okamoto, Rei 197
Oken, Stuart 84
Okenka, Cassie 47
Oklahoma! 351, 370, 394
Okrent, Daniel 185
Olaya, Jensen 219
Olbrych, Melanie 82
Old Globe, The 378, 386
Old Jews Telling Jokes 185
Old Masters, The 197
Old School Benefit 306
Old Times 345
Old Vic, The 89, 214
Old Wicked Songs 358
Olding, Grant 72
Olds, Lance 235
Olenik, Andrei 46
Olin, Tom 183
Olive and the Bitter Herbs 243
Oliver 369, 382
Oliver, Clark 162
Oliver, Clifton 99
Oliver, David 80
Oliver, Edgar 145
Oliver, Jillian M. 38, 66
Oliver, Ryan Scott 267
Oliver, Susan 417
Oliver-Watts, Guy 179
Olivia, Jay 259
Olm, James 128
Olmos, Edward James 419
Olney Theatre Center 390
Olohan, John 198
Olsen, Ralph 78, 85
Olsen, Shad 128
Olson, Erik 163
Olson, Gordon 98
Olson, Jonathan 64
Olson, Judi 256
Olson, Katrina Lynn 138
Olson, Tricia 28
Olsson, Caroline Lena 44
Olver, Christine 31, 42, 46, 57, 60, 72, 80, 90,

98, 185, 227
Olympus Theatricals 38, 86
Olyphant, Timothy 420
Olyslaegers, Jeroen 232
Omari, Morocco 74
Omneity Entertainment 28
Omnivore 258
Omran, Amal 210
On a Clear Day You Can See Forever 15, 50, 407, 409,
On Facebook 155
On Golden Pond 373
On Location Education 47, 60, 64, 68, 82
On Stage 409
On the Spectrum 430
On the Square Productions 303
On Wheels Productions 304
Onat, Cigdem 420
Onatieva, Alla 215
Onayemi, Prentice 110
Once 60, 118, 204, 236
Once in a Lifetime 349
Once on This Island 379, 392
One Man, Two Guvnors 21, 72
One Slight Hitch 345
One Thousand Blinks 272
One Year Lease 304
O'Neal, Ron 418
Onodera, Shuji 197
Oohrah! 400
Opalinski, Megan 193, 340
Opel, Nancy 102
Open Book Theatre 304
Ophelia's Shadow Theatre 232
Opus 390
O'Quinn, Keith 33, 55
Or, 397
Oracle Theatre Inc. 304
Oram, Christopher 68
Orange Person, The 324
Orbison, Willie 223
Orchestra Wiener Akademie 212
Ordinaire, Mirabelle 172
Oregon Shakespeare Festival 390
Oremus, Stephen 90, 111, 188
Oreskes, Daniel 230
Oresteia 130
Organs of State 276, 304

Orich, Steve 97
Original Binding
 Productions 304
Orihara, Miki 144
Oriol, Jeantique 189
Orlandersmith, Dael 249
Orlemann, Jed 39
Ormerod, Nick 214
Ormond, Michael Joseph
 125
Ornstein, Suzanne 109,
 216, 217
Oropesa, Melissa 113
Orphans, The 294
Orpheum Theatre 196
Orpheus and Euridice
 283
Orrico, Tony 212
Orshan, Wendy 45, 78
Orsher, Glenn 28
Orsini, Jonny 230, 268
Orson's Shadow 299
Ortel, Sven 64, 266
Ortiz, Genevieve 206
Ortiz, John 223
Ortiz, Maria-Elena 142,
 149, 150
Ortiz, Marlyn 94, 191
Ortiz, Victor Joel 163
Ortoll, Jorge Z. 156, 166
Orton, Kevin 176
Orton, Richard 33
Orwell, George 156
Ory, Veronique 308
Orzano, Mary 112
Osborne, Ariel C. 59
Osborne, Georgia 112
Osborne, Jessica 191
Osborne, John 251
Osborne, Julia 253
Osborne, Kipp 418
Oscar, Brad 84, 114,
 198
Osei, Kwasi 138
Osher/Staton/Bell/
 Mayerson Group 97
Oslak, Ryan 62
Osnes, Laura 14, 47, 85,
 114, 201, 202, 216
Osrowitz, Michael 235
Ost, Mitchell 187, 227
Ost, Tobin 47, 64
Ostendorf, Alison 187
Osterhaus, Megan 101
Ostling, Dan 233
Ostling, Daniel 73
Ostopchuck, Kasey 208,
 224
Ostrow, Carol 143,
 163, 177
O'Sullivan, Michael 418
Oswald 313
Oswald, John 210

Othello 300, 314
Othello: The Remix 364
Other Day, The 297
Other Desert Cities 13,
 39, 118, 430
Other Mirror Theatre,
 The 304
Other People's Problems
 323
Other Side Productions
 305
Ott, Francine Elizabeth
 127
Ott, Quinto 235
Otterson, Pamela 33
Otto René Castillo
 Awards 445
Otto, Anne 43
Otto, Driscol A. 68, 108
Otto, Rebecca 184
Oulianine, Anik 153
Our Lot 282
Out of Askja 316
Out of Iceland 174
Out of Line Productions
 305
Outer Critics Circle
 Awards 426
Outside People 261
Ovation Awards 445
Overberg, Ryan 113
Overbey, Kellie 222, 242
Overend, Cambra 168
Overett, Adam 109
Overshown, Howard
 W. 214
Overtree, Lee 133
Owen, Amy M. Ables
 233
Owen, Gareth 67, 409
Owen, Louise 50
Owen, Susan 105
Owens, Amber 101
Owens, Charlie 289,
 324, 340
Owens, Hannah 125
Owens, John 72, 89,
 110
Owens, Jon 111
Owens, Larry 181
Ownbey, Meghan 43,
 54, 60
Oxford, Jesse 429
Oyster Orgasms
 Obituaries 295
Ozono 191

P
P.O.V. Artists 305
Paar, Jennifer 222
Pablo & Andrew at the
 Altar of Words 155
Pabotoy, Orlando 218

Pabst, Jessica 138, 147,
 148, 242, 249, 254
Pace, Atkin 82
Pace, Jenna 188
Pace, Lee 104
Pachtman, Matthew 33,
 35, 52, 59, 66, 71, 90
Pacino, Al 418
Pack, Eugene 197
Packer, Tina 170
Padden, Daniel 176
Padden, Michael 94
Padgett, Emily 108
Padila, Stephanie 211
Padilla, Genny Lis 140
Padilla, Laura 230
Padolina, Laurin 62
Paessler, Matt 125
Paganini, Nicola 215
Pagano, Duane 171, 206
Pagano, Frank 179
Pagano, Lauren 410
Page 73 Productions
 146, 305
Page, Angelica 66,
 137, 165
Page, Elaine 33
Page, Geraldine 417
Page, Gretchen H. 219
Page, Ken 419
Page, Mark 98
Page, Melissa 166
Page, Michael 126,
 141, 169
Page, Patrick 28, 114,
 115, 198, 200, 202,
 437
Paget, Ian 82, 83
Pagula, Marco 71, 84
Pai, Ian 189
Paice, Jill 164
Paige, Amanda Ryan
 188
Paine, Rebekah 236
Painter, Devon 96
Painter, Max 232
Painting Churches 222
Pajeú, Carlinhos 233
Pakledinaz, Martin 31,
 35, 78, 85, 104
Palace Theatre 106
Paladino, Sonny 63, 158
Palame, Emilio 143
Palance, Jack 417
Palitz, Michael 66, 82
Pallas, Ted 107
Pallone, Davina 126
Palm, Michael 112, 202
Palmatier, Nancy A. 38
Palmer, Byron 417
Palmer, Kristen 263
Palmer, Michael 162,
 184

Palmer, Michael Alexis
 309
Palmer, Nicky 215
Palmer, Peter 417
Palmer, Saxon 260
Palmer, Stephanie 255
Palmer-Lane, Charlotte
 229
Palmieri, Gayle 78, 109
Palombo, Rose 70-72,
 106
Palomino, Tony 234
Palumbo, Antonio 35,
 96, 86
Pamatmat, A. Ray 430
Pamela Moller Kareman
 133
Pampin, Edi 191
Pan Asian Repertory
 Theatre 238
Panaro, Hugh 105
Pandaleon, Andrew 179
Pando, Nicole 62
Pandya, Rohi Mirza 143
Panelli, Raymond 72
Pang, Jie 232
Pangs of the Messiah
 321
Panichello, John 179
Panicked Productions
 305
Panke, Ingo 161
Pankov, Denis 129
Pankow, John 257, 260
Panson, Bonnie 28
Panter, Howard 36, 214
Panther, Jenna 409
Pantuso, Christopher 95
Paoluccio, Tricia 134,
 257
Paoppi, Florencia 182
Papadopoulou, Eftychia
 155
Papaelias, Lucas 60,
 236
Papagjika, Christina 82
Pape, Andrew 208, 209
Paper Boy Productions
 54
Paper Mache Monkey Art
 and Design 156, 248
Paper Mill Playhouse
 378, 392
Papp, Joseph 419
Paquin, Anna 420
Paquin, Jaque 28
Parade 371
Paradine, Jason 208,
 245-247
Paradis, Luc 138
Paradise, Grace 95
Paradise, Sandra 52, 92
Paraiso, Nicky 444

Paramount Pictures
 75, 82
Paran, Janice 177, 243
Paraska, Keith 130
Parchman Hour, The
 394
Pardes, Daniel 262
Parenthesis Theater 305
Parenti, Mark 131
Pares, Emiliano 47, 62,
 64, 109
Pareschi, Brian 78, 216
Pargac, Eric 261
Parham, Bryonha Marie
 54
Parham, Keith 138, 141,
 148, 169
Parichy, Dennis 186
Parinello, Al 104
Paris Orgy 272
Parison, Richard M. 191
Parisse, Annie 22, 73,
 244, 245, 360
Park Avenue Armory
 197
Park, Dong Woo 198
Park, Hettienne 14, 45,
 408, 409,411, 414
Park, Joshua 420
Park, Kina 185, 261
Park, Michael 95
Park, Ryan 50, 91, 224
Parker, Alecia 93, 106
Parker, Brittany 149
Parker, Cat 444
Parker, Christian 208
Parker, Fred 66
Parker, John Eric 90
Parker, Katey 209
Parker, Mary-Louise 419
Parker, Nicole 104
Parker, Nicole Ari 22, 74
Parker, Robert Ross 166
Parker, Trey 90, 202
Parks, Ania 28
Parks, Brian 426
Parks, Gregg 161
Parks, Icey 95
Parks, Jessica L. 166
Parks, Joseph 176
Parks, Rachel E. 142
Parks, Suzan-Lori 54,
 244
Parnell, Peter 50
Parnes, Joey 32, 67,
 244, 410, 424
Parness, Eric 143
Parquet, Lori E. 181
Parra, Angelo 127
Parreira, Ricardo 213
Parrish, Hunter 40, 114
Parrish, Timothy 147,
 158, 222, 255, 256

Parrots, Monk 186
Parrott, Cathy 28, 54,
 81, 242
Parry, Charlotte 96,
 208, 251
Parry, Jeff 107
Parry, Marisa 209
Parson, Annie-B 212,
 260
Parsons, Alexis 46
Parsons, Estelle 78, 418
Parsons, Jim 104, 113,
 421
Parsons, Sally Ann 447
Partial Comfort
 Productions 305
Partier, Justin 96, 237,
 241, 251
Parting Glass, The 134
Parton, Dolly 197
Parts of Parts & Stitches
 298
Party People 391
Parva, Michael 166
Parvin, Jeff 62, 97, 181
Pasadena Playhouse 87,
 379, 392
Pasarro, Joe 116
Pasbjerg, Carl 28, 102
Pascal Productions 151
Pascal, Adam 102, 114,
 117, 420
Pascal, Pedro 241, 249
Pasek, Benj 254
Pask, Scott 32, 90, 94,
 113, 132, 169, 186,
 244, 245
Pasquale, Elyse 194
Passaro, Joseph 63, 92
Passaro, Michael J.
 68, 95
Passer, Daniel 129
Passero, Jeffery 165
Passing Strange 369,
 385
Passley, Marcie 112,
 235
Pasternack, Barbara 135
Pastorek, Lauren 235
Patch, Jerry 31, 42, 57,
 80, 227
Patel, Bhavesh 110
Patel, Dharmesh 197
Patel, Neil 162, 176,
 184, 187, 230, 244,
 255, 261
Paterson, Christine 133
Paterson, Victoria 84
Patience 235
Patinkin, Mandy 14,
 46, 457
Patino, Nelson, Jr. 230
Patrick, Dennis 417

Patridge, David 43, 47, 82, 100, 109
Patsy, The 134
Pattak, Cory 46, 64, 71, 127, 135, 242
Patten, Nate 132
Patten, Sean 246
Patten, Wendy 124, 134, 153
Patterson, Billy "Spaceman" 127
Patterson, Carra 57, 245
Patterson, James 152
Patterson, Jay 229
Patterson, Justin 102
Patterson, Mary Michael 85
Patterson, Rebecca 207
Patterson, Rhea 111
Patton, AJ 276
Patton, Fitz 94, 226, 254
Patton, Monica L. 216
Patty, Jessica Lea 68, 84, 104
Paul Robeson Award 437
Paul, Alan 115
Paul, Amber 166
Paul, Daniel 66
Paul, Danny 33, 94
Paul, David 31
Paul, Justin 254
Paul, Pamela 206
Paulin, Jenny Dare 378
Paulino, Joyce 125
Paull, Alexandra 28, 136
Paulson, Doug 209, 230
Paulus, Diane 32, 54, 236
Pavloff, Martin 70
Pavlos, Vivian 244
Paxton, Tom 238
Payne, Bryce 276
Payne, Joe 97
Payne, Robyn 112
Payne, Samuel 222
Payson, S.M. 185
Payton, Kalere A. 249, 257
Payton, Larry 159
Payton, Philip 55
Paz, Jessica 158, 255, 256
Paz, Paulo 213
Pazakis, Kate 113
Peabody, Ross 241
Peacock, Martin 125, 263, 264
Peak Performances 259
Pearce, Bobby 147
Pearce, Liz 89
Pearce, Nicole 229
Pearcy, Benjamin 110

Pearl Theatre Company 239
Pearl, Barry 87
Pearlman, Lindsey Hope 82
Pearson, Anthony 39, 43, 58, 216
Pearson, Beatrice 417
Pearson, Erik 128, 157, 263
Pearson, Ridley 71
Pearson, Thaddeus 167
Pease, Tabitha 49, 256
Peay, Jeramiah 193
Peccadillo Theater Company 121, 157
Peck, Dan 93
Peck, Gail 167
Peck, Justin 105
Peck, Nathan 111
Pecktal, Lynn 447
Pedersen, Christian 170
Pedersen, Susan 68
Pedi, Christine 193, 194, 202, 265
Pedigo-Otto, Amy 157, 173
Pedrosa, Joaa 213
Peel, David 95
Peer Gynt 368, 381
Pegg, Scott 131, 151, 165, 177
Pegram, David 110
Peguero, Natalia 124
Pei, Flora 77
Pei-Hua, Huang 211
Peikert, Mark 424
Peil, Mary Beth 33, 244
Peirano, Marina 112
Pekoe Group, The 125, 128, 146, 151, 165, 187, 191, 229, 243, 250, 262
Pelican Group 62, 97
Pelkey, Melissa L. 112, 219
Pellegrino, Susan 141
Pelletier, Carol A. 239
Pelletier, Damon 28
Pelletier, Dee 174
Pelletier, Monique 235
Pellicano, John 410
Pellick, Andy 191
Pellini, Joel 409
Pell-Walpole, Rob 160
Pelphrey, Tom 67
Pelteson, Ben 113
Pelusio, Jason 86, 98, 112, 198
Pemberton, Robert 190
Pemiakova, Anastasiia 187
Peña, Ralph B. 156, 166

Pendelton, Marcia 241
Pendergraft, Eddie 111
Pendergraft, Jenny 68
Pendergras, Sally & Douglas 140
Pendleton, Austin 178
Pendleton, E. John 211
Penelope 394, 400
Penetrating the Space 294
Penfield, Jay 37, 42, 66, 88, 139, 227, 236
Penford, Adam 72
Peng, Chien-Yu 56, 181, 224
Penguin Rep Theatre 127, 184
Penn, Leo 417
Pennette, Marco 243
Pennewell, Norwood J. 99
Pennington, Gail 154
Pennington, Shawn 111
Pennisi, Stefano 187
Penny, Kristine 410
Pentz, David 133
People in the Picture, The 104
People of *Godspell*, The 40
Pepe, Neil 208
Pepin, Dave 84
Pepper, Ry 185
Peral, Cesar 234
Perayda, Brandon 113
Percefull, Danny 216
Perdziola, Robert 447
Pereira, Israel 213
Perelman, Suzy 68, 116
Pereshkura, Valerii 129
Peretz, Don 136, 221
Perez de Taglé, Anna Maria 40, 114
Perez, Angela 162
Perez, Dina 263
Perez, Jose Joaquin 183
Perez, Mauricio 193
Perez, Rosie 227, 420
Perez, Susana 174
Perf Productions 305
Perfect Crime 195
Perfect Wedding 371, 373
Perfetti, Chris 205, 251, 408, 409, 411
Performance Lab 115 305
Performance Space 122 132, 306
Pericles, Prince of Tyre 273
Perillo, Robert 248
Peripherals, The 318

Perkins, Anthony 417
Perkins, Carl 103, 136
Perkins, Delainah 192
Perkins, Laurie 75
Perkins, Myriah 99
Perlman, David 152
Perlman, Michael 141, 252
Perlmutter, Lily 247, 255, 257
Perlmutter, Sharon 442
Perlov, Naomi 133
Perri, Angela Atwood 271
Perri, Bryan 111, 254
Perri, Matt 95
Perrin, Martin 251, 254
Perron, Francois 89
Perrotta, Joe 37, 106, 136, 196, 208
Perry, Adam 78
Perry, Dawn Marie 206
Perry, Jeff 169
Perry, Jennifer 100
Perry, Jennifer Christine 28
Perry, Karen 255
Perry, Margarett 167
Perry, Marissa 109, 113
Perry, Richard 87
Pershing Square Signature Center 255
Persian Quarter, The 369, 383
Person, Erika 235
Person, Erin 154
Personal History Volumes I-V: abridged 286
Pesce, Vince 85
Peszek, Jan 178
Peter & I 324
Peter and the Starcatcher 21, 71
Peter Jay Sharp Theatre 203, 241, 262
Peter Norton Space 208, 209
Peter Pan 159
Peters, Bernadette 33, 115, 198, 202, 418, 421, 444
Peters, Christine 47, 64, 84, 90, 94
Peters, Clarke 420
Peters, Jennifer 189
Peters, Lauri 418
Peters, Robert 91, 253
Peters, William Michael 113
Petersen, Agnes 212
Petersen, Jeffery 218
Petersen, Leo 232

Petersen, Stefanie 157
Petersmeyer, Annie 113
Peterson, Bob 104
Peterson, David 82
Peterson, Julia 155
Peterson, Julio 410
Peterson, Kurt 202
Peterson, Lisa 123, 237, 243
Peterson, Mary Nemecek 28, 99
Peterson, Matthew 33, 83
Peterson, Rebecca 109
Peterson, Stu 107
Peterson, Valeria A. 230
Peti, Megan 220, 221
Petitjean, Douglas 44, 68, 92
Petkoff, Robert 85
Petrilli, Stephen 239, 240
Petro, Wayne 258
Petrocelli, Richard 223
Petrosino, Joe 208
Petska, Bobby 115
Pettet, Joanna 410, 418
Pettigrew, Bethany 40
Petty, Lauren 211
Pevec, Aleks 68, 92
Peverley, Peter 197
Pevsner, David 175, 194
Peyramaure, María 149
Peyroux 219
Pezzello, Christina 116, 130
Pfaffl, Kate 110
Pfeffer, Lurie Horns 107
Phaedra Backwards 383
Phaneuf, Marc 109
Phantom of the Opera, The 105, 116, 118
Phelan, Andy 218
Phelan, Fred 93
Phelan, Marla 196
Phelps-Lipton, Heather 249
Phifer, Mekhi 49
Philadelphia Theatre Company 379, 393
Philanderer, The 240
Philips, Deborah 144
Phillip, Jackie 127
Phillips, Angela 28
Phillips, Dave 90
Phillips, Diana 410
Phillips, Jeanna 149, 209
Phillips, Jessica 83, 106
Phillips, Kevin 78, 202
Phillips, Lou Diamond 420
Phillips, Margaret 417

Phillips, Mychal 195
Phillips, Simon 106
Phillips, Simon Lee 214
Phillips, Tripp 91
Phillips, Valerie 127
Philoktetes 163
Phoenix Theatre Ensemble 306
Photograph 51 272
Phrasavath, Thavisouk 171
Phsycho Space Laboratory 293
Piacenti, Jennifer 235
Pianist of Williesden Lane, The 372
Piazza, Ben 417
Piazza, Michael R. 209
Picard, Sophie 138
Piccione, Nancy 31, 42, 57, 80, 227
Piccoli, Liz 124, 263
Pickens, Will 59, 96, 182, 240, 247
Pickup, Rachel 203, 220
Picou, Rhonda 208, 223
Picture Box, The 161
piece by piece productions 250, 258
PIECE Theatre 306
Piehole 306
Piemontese, Marco 218
Pierce, Angela 229, 268
Pierce, Chuck 266
Pierce, David Hyde 227, 262
Pierce, Edward 58, 74
Pierce, Greg 225, 262
Pierce, James A. 99
Pierce, Xavier 73
Pierpan, Nicholas 154
Pierzina, Pamela 85
Pig Shit & The Frozen City 319
Pig, The 322
Piggee, Timothy McCuen 92
PigPen Theatre Company 147
Pilat, Ben 31, 88, 261
Pilbrow, Richard 219
Pilgrims Musa and Sheri in the New World 430
Pilieci, Matthew 138, 139
Pilipski, Mike 92
Pilkington, Stephen 72
Pill, Alison 94
Pillet, Jean-Jacques 129
Pillow Book, The 287
Pillow, Charles 50, 83, 84
Pilo Arts 410

Pilote, Joshua 35, 115, 117, 118, 158, 198
Pina, Jorge 213
Pinckard, John 32, 132
Pinckney, Tim 115, 201, 202, 437
Pine, Pamela 175
Pineda, Christopher 38, 54
Pinelli, Tullio 149
Pines, Kate 40
Ping Chong & Co. 127
Pingenot, James 152
Pinion, Jacob 100
Pink Knees On Pale Skin 138
Pinkalicious, The Musical 195
Pinkham, Bryce 76
Pinkins, Tonya 202, 209, 241, 244, 245, 256, 262, 268, 426
Pinkleton, Sam 77, 243, 261
Pinocchio's Ashes 320
Pins and Needles 127
Pinsly, Melissa 82
Pinter, Harold 215
Piotrowicz, Adam 249
Pipe Dream 216
Pipe Dream Theatre 306
Pipeline Theatre Company 307
Piper McKenzie's Dainty Cadavar 279
Piper Theatre 307
Piper, Tom 197, 214
Pirate Pete's Parrot 314
Pirates of Penzance, The 235
Piretti, Ron 88
Piro, Kristin 92, 113, 183
Pisapia, Frederico 129
Piscitelli, Michael 28
Pisoni, Lorenzo 244, 245
Pit Bull Interactive 139
Pita, Arthur 197
Pitcairn, Jessica 182
Pitch Control PR 145
Pitchford, Dean 226
Pitman Painters, The 345
Pitoniak, Anne 419
Pitre, Louise 420
Pittelman, Ira 50
Pittsburgh CLO 68, 84, 92, 446
Pittsburgh Public Theater 379, 393
Pittu, David 208
Pitzer, J. Michael 109

Pitzer, Michael 60, 73
Pivnick, Jeremy 125
Pivot Entertainment Group 40
Pizutti, Paul 50, 95, 116
Pizza Man 286
Pizzarelli, Vera 49, 68
Pizzi, Joey 92, 187
Plachy, Spencer 252
Plamondon, Allison 118
Planalp, Ronnie 36
Planet Connections Theatre Festivity 337
Plantadit, Karine 199, 238
Plasencia, Bobby 183
Platt, Jacob 165, 179
Platt, Jason Gray 168
Platt, Jon B. 42, 46, 59, 73, 78, 90, 94, 98, 103, 111, 185, 446
Platt, Marc 111
Play 350
Play About My Dad, The 283
Play Company, The 143, 258
Play It Cool 143
Playbill 409, 410
Players Club 436
Players Theatre 188, 307
Playful Productions 38
Playing With Reality 307
PlayMakers Repertory Company 379, 394
Plays for Living 419
Playten, Alice 418, 468
Playwrights Horizons 73, 203, 241, 262, 268
Playwrights Realm, The 144
Playwrights' Playground 170
Plaza, Begonya 171
Pleasance Theatre 155
Plesent, Mark 167
Pleßmann, Uli 210
PLG Arts 307
Pliska 110
Pliska, Greg 265
Plop! 234
Ploski, Marisha 82
Plosky, Stuart 124
Plot is the Revolution, The 295
Plotnick, Jack 162
Pluck the Day 307
Pluess, Andre 241, 262
Plugged In Productions 307
Plumb, Eve 192, 193
Plummer, Amanda 419

Plummer, Christopher 417
Plummer, Joe 131
Plumpis, John 207
Plunkett, Maryann 247
Plunkett, Stephen 110
Poarch, Thomas 188
Podschun, Hayley 85
Podsiadlik, Agnieszka 178
Poe Project, The 319
Poe, Kristina 223
Poe, Times Two 323
Poe: An Imaginary Waltz 314
Poet, Bruno 214
Poetic License 166
Poetic Theater Productions 307
Poetry Electric 12 295
Poet's Den Theater 137
Pohlman, Jessica 186
Poignand, Michael 162
Pointer, Ryan 208
Pointet, Heidi 249
Poisoned 317
Poisson, Michael 353
Poitras, Scott "Gus" 33, 95
Polack, Joe 146
Poland, Eric 78
Polato, Dave 222, 256
Polato, David 257
Pold, Erik 246
Pole, Jane 143, 256
Poletskyy, Sergey 129
Poliacik, Susan 233
Polimeni, Marc 31, 33, 40, 72, 104, 115
Polischuck, Geoffrey 43, 78, 109
Polk, Andrew 230
Polk, Matt 35, 56, 60, 81, 85, 96, 104, 116, 251
Polland, Elizabeth 173
Polonsky, Larisa 230
Polybe + Seats 310
Polydor Records 100, 105
Pomahac, Bruce 216
Pomerantz, Will 129, 171, 181, 253
Pompeani, Meredith 245-247, 261
Ponce, Richard 227
Pond, Teresa K. 195
Ponturo, Tony 70, 102
Pool (No Water) 304
Pool, Meghan 113
Poole, Joshua Lee 77
Poole, Richard 105
Poon, Chester 409

Poor Baby Bree in I Am Going to Run Away 295
Poor, Bray 241, 251
Poor, Ted 212
Poorboy Theatre Company 175
Pope, Katie 82, 155
Pope, Kristyn 216, 217
Pope, Nicholas 216, 237, 253
Popławska, Aleksandra 178
Poplyk, Gregory A. 447
Popp, Ethan 108, 115
Poppleton, L. Glenn 159
Porazzi, Arturo E. 102
Porcaro, Mary Ann 107
Porgy and Bess 16, 54, 118, 350, 406, 409
Port, Lauren 49, 253
Portacci, Toni 247
Porte, Suzette 156, 166
Porter, Billy 139
Porter, Catherine 267
Porter, Cole 85
Porter, Dillon 188
Porter, Joan 235
Porter, Leigh 67
Porter, Linda 102
Portland Center Stage 394
Portland Stage Company 395
Porto, Michael 95
Porvaznika, Erin 202, 250
Pos, Reier 232
Posener, Daniel 71
Poskin, Jamie 168
Posner, Kenneth 37, 39, 66, 80, 92, 111
Posner, Russell 207
Post Office 301
Post Plastica 306
Post, Kyle 28, 29
Post, Lisa Lawer 231
Postma, Martin 188
Posvanecz, Éva 212
Pot, Florence 129
Potamkin, Andi 174
Potomac Theatre Project NYC 310
Potter, Bill 102
Potter, Michael Todd 92
Potter, Mick 68
Potter, Mike 148
Potter, Rachel 68, 84
Potter, Shua 101
Potter, Todd 188
Potter-Watts, Jeffrey 152, 182
Potts, Michael 90

Pou, Jimmy 107
Pounds, Raymond 87
Pourfar, Susan 121, 169, 409, 411, 413, 437
Pow, Cameron 99
Powell, Annalie 156
Powell, Arabella 94, 99
Powell, Emily 64
Powell, Gary 214
Powell, Katharine 254
Powell, Miranda 192
Powell, Nick 214
Powell-Jones, Stella 185
Power Arts 95
Power of Duff, The 223
Power, Ben 447
Power, Mark R. 244
Powerhouse Theater 247
Powers, Mary Margaret 239
Powers, Rory 59
Powley, Bel 86
Poyer, Lisa M. 60
Praça, Paulo 213
Pracher-Dix, Tim 181
Pramik, Nick 36, 60, 75, 106
Prante, William 263
Pratfalls 290
Prather, Brian 152, 191
Pratt, Loren 244-247
Pratt, Sydney 136, 183
Pravata, Chris 50, 82
Pregosin, Lexie 50
Preiss, Samantha 28, 50, 71, 112
Preisser, Alfred 124
Premo, Michael 127
Prendergast, Angelina 171
Prendergast, James 207
Prendergast, Kate 262, 263
Prendergast, Shirely 152
Prentice, Kim 37
Prentice, Kimberly 59, 98
President, The 317
Presley, Elvis 103, 136
Presley, Rob 45
Presley, Robert 86
Press, Jessica 113
Press, Nicole 128, 157
Press, Seymour Red 32, 67, 78, 85, 93, 153, 216
Pressgrove, Larry 261
Pressley, Brenda 77, 261
Pressman, Lawrence 418

Pressman, Meghan 255
Presti, Brian 235
Prestini, Paola 210
Preston, Carrie 114
Preston, Lisa 75
Preston, Michelle 162
Preston, Sylvie 137
Preston, Vaughn 31, 80
Pretty Trap, The 137
Preuss, Rob 60, 100, 236, 261
PRF Productions 230
Price, Canara 64
Price, Carly J. 38, 68, 92
Price, Daniel 256
Price, Eva 71, 84, 131, 133, 428
Price, Gilbert 418
Price, Lonny 419
Price, Mack 189
Price, Marguerite 147
Price, Molly 59
Price, Richard 428
Price, Roger 417
Priddy-Barnum, Collin 261
Pride and Prejudice 388, 398
Pridemore, Ashley 249
Pridemore, Patrick 50
Prigogiy, Iakov 215
Primary Stages 243, 268
Prime Blueprint 28
Primis, Damian 253
Primis, Theo 111
Primmerman, Jake 125
Primorac, Ivana 59
Primrose, Rayneese 125
Prince of Atlantis, The 398
Prince, Harold 105, 216
Prince, Zachary 50, 87
Princess Grace Awards 446
Printup, Marcus 199
Prinz, Rosemary 186
Prisand, Scott 108
Priscilla Queen of the Desert 106, 202
Prison Light 301
Prisoner of Love 322
Pritcard, Sean 215
Prittie, David 163
Pritzker, Gigi 103
Private Lives 9, 44, 377, 393
Private Sector, The 296, 319
Probo Productions 71
Procaccino, John 224
Procter, Diane 151

Proctor, Charles 417
Proctor, Philip 418
Production Core 125, 137, 141, 143, 146, 151, 155, 164, 165, 167, 168, 169, 172, 177, 185, 212, 218
Proenca, Carlos Manuel 213
Professor Brenner 302
Profeta, Katherine 236
Profit, Chondra La-Tease 99
Project Publicity 194
Project Y Theatre Company 310
Project: Theater 310
Promethes Within 295
Pronk, André 211
Proper, Linsey 58
Propstar 37, 49, 50, 74, 78, 94, 116, 169, 243
Prospect Pictures 108
Prospect Theater Company 152, 163
Prosser, Peter 43
Protected 323
Protter-Watts, Jeff 184
Proud, Lee 89
Prouty, Deanne 71
Provencale, Jessica 50, 241, 242
Provencher, Tiffany 157
Provenza, Paul 419
Provincetown 2012 291
Provost, Heather 146
Provost, Kyle 134, 147, 164, 168
Pruitt, Richard 216
Pruneda, Ernie 109
Prunoske, Eddie 177
Prusik, Michael 233
Prusiner, Ben 172
Prussack, Alexis R. 118
Pryal, Richard 159
Pryce, Jonathan 215, 419, 426
PS 122 132, 306
PS Classics 33, 54, 216
Psarros, Thanasis 246
Psillas, Avgoustos 214
Psycho Space Laboratory 311
Psycho Therapy 165
Pu, Wang 211
Pua Ali`l `llima 295
Puberty Rites…not a bootleg experience 152
Public Theater, The 32, 106, 244
Publicity Office, The 40, 45, 84, 93, 105, 115,

129, 135, 218, 241, 262, 410
Pucci, Maria 186
Pucci, Stephen 38
Pucci/Hunt PR 186
Puckering, Ruth 158
Puckett, Geoff 99
Puertas, Andrés 234
Puette, Alex 221
Pug Skirt Players 311
Pujols, Betsy 149
Pule, Michael 100, 118
Puleo, Amy 244
Puleo, Peter J. 91
Pulford, Donald 154
Pulitzer Prize Award 430
Pulse Ensemble Theatre 311
Pumariega, Christina 45, 369
Pummill, Patrick 33
Punchdrunk 196
Punia, Sam 241, 242
Pupko, Elisa 409
Puppet Kitchen, The 144, 173, 192
Puppetmaster of Lodz, The 358
Purcell, Evan 243
Purcell, Terri 75
Purdy, Marshall B. 90, 94, 103
Pure Highway 313
Pure Projects Inc. 171
Purple Rep 311
Pursell, Katherine 209
Purviance, Douglas 111
Purvis, Kat 28, 115, 118
Puss in Boots 396
Pusz, Christy 368
Putman, Tracy Lynn 198
Putnam, John 102
Putnam, Nate 139
Putterman, Noah 176
Pyant, Paul 214
Pyle, Stephen 105
Pyzocha, Robert 28

Q
Quackenbush, Karyn 192
Quaid, Amanda 185, 208, 218
Quantum Eye: Magic and Mentalism 195
Quart, Anne 64, 99
Quart, Geoffrey 64
Quartet 319
Queen of the Mist 121, 153
Queens Theatre 136, 146, 183
Queer New York

International Arts Festival 186
Quenqua, Joe 64
Question of God, The 191
Quick, Mary 140
Quigley, Rebecca 109
QUILT – A Musical Celebration and Reflection on 30 Years 200
Quilter, Peter 67
Quinlan, Kathleen 419
Quinn, Aidan 419
Quinn, Doug 100
Quinn, Jason A. 112, 115, 179, 187
Quinn, Jeremy 409
Quinn, Josh 149, 216, 241
Quinn, Kali 239
Quinn, Michael 189
Quint, Stephen 235
Quintet Productions 73
Quinto, Zachary 421
Quiqley, Brendan C. 74, 98
Quiroga, Alexander 111, 113
Quiros, Paulo 138
Quiroz, Jamie 68
Quñones, Kalie 388

R
Raab, Marni 105, 116
Rabbit Hole Ensemble 311
Rabe, David 230
Rabe, Lily 14, 45, 426
Rabello, Dany 129
Rabinowitz, Jason 72
Rabl, Peter 212
Rabon, Eddie 113
Raby, Greg 104, 131
Race 350, 374, 393, 396
Rachel Klein Theater Ensemble 277, 311
Rachel Reiner Productions 143
Rada, Edward L. 73
Rada, Mirena 188
Radcliffe, Daniel 95, 115, 116, 202
Radetsky, Jessica 105
Radiance: The Passion of Marie Curie 372
(Radically Condensed and Expanded) Supposedly Fund Thing I'll Never Do Again (After David Foster Wallace), A 324

Radio City Music Hall 129
Radio Golf 365, 380
Radio Mouse Entertainment 71
Radiohead 213
RadioTheatre 276, 311
Radnor, Josh 116
Rado, James 32
Radtke, Kay E. 410
Rady, Brian 212
Rae, Gregory 104
Raffa, Carol Anne 231
Raffo, Heather 200, 237
Rafson, Jill 252
Rafter, Michael 97
Ragas, Matthew 113
Rager, Stefan 210
Ragni, Gerome 32
Rags 382
Rahn, Christina Rose 195
Raible, Erv 433
Raimone, Antuan 113
Rain: A Tribute to The Beatles on Broadway 107
Rainbow, Clare 106
Raine, Kristen 233
Raine, Nina 169
Raines, Chad 252
Raines, Ron 33, 114
Raines, Tristan 169, 249
Raise the Roof 36, 78
Raisin in the Sun, A 289, 359, 361, 373
Raitt, Jayson 108
Raitt, John 417
Raitt, Kathleen 47
Rak, Rachelle 92, 112, 183
Rakez, Fouzia 215
Rakos, Ruby 89
Raley, John 64
Ralph, Jason 71
Ralske, Amy 50
Ramage, Ghislain 129
Ramayana 345
Rambo, T. Michael 344
Ramessar, Kevin 63
Ramey, Aaron 152
Ramey, Corey 184
Ramm, Leandra 184
Rammo, Tarek 138
Ramos, Clint 134, 156, 165, 230, 252, 256, 262
Ramos, Liz 84
Ramos-Nisita, Mark 149
Rampmeyer, Mark Adam 52, 113, 217
Rampton, Ken 85, 199, 217

Ramsay, Yolanda 96
Ramsey, Kevin 419
Ramsey, Matt 189
Ramsey, Shad 47, 102
Ramshur, Valerie 78, 103
Ramthun, Kendra 255
Ramzi, Ammar 88
Rana, James 239
Randall, Lynne 31, 42, 57, 80, 227
Rando, John 217
Randolph, Beverly 84
Randolph, Da'Vine Joy 22, 76
Randolph, Elaine 231
Randolph, Jim 132, 157, 191
Randolph, Julie 62
Random Access Theatre 312
Ranger, Nancy 235
Rangoon 239
Rankin, Gayle 169
Rankin, John, III 167
Rankin, Steve 47, 97, 102
Rannells, Andrew 90, 114, 117, 198, 202
Ransom, Erik 193
Ranson, Molly 98, 204, 227
Rap Guide to Evolution, The 128
Raphael Benavides Productions 137
Raphael, Blake 150
Raphael, Gerianne 308
Raphali, Nitzan 133
Rapier, Bradley "Shooz" 62
Rapier, Trisha 109
Rapley, Tommy 233
Rapp Reads Rapp: Nocturne 200
Rapp, Adam 138, 148, 200, 208
Rapp, Anthony 114, 200
Rapp, Francis 43, 54, 75, 109
Rapp, Jenn 226
Rapture, Blister, Burn 242, 268
Rardin, Brian 129
Rasbury, Michael 134
Rasche, David 254
Rashad, Condola 49, 421
Rashovich, Gordana 56, 419
Raskin, Gene 127
Raskopf, Jen 28
Rasmussen, Charles

109
Rasmussen, Sarah 263
Rasulala, Thalmus 418
Ratajczak, Dave 101
Rated P for Parenthood 119, 168
Ratelle, Ryan 71, 73, 410
Raterman, John 113
Rathbun, Justin 54, 88
Rathbun, Kristen 36, 60, 75
Rathburn, Roger 418
Ratigan, Terence 35
Ratray, Devin 230
Rattan, Gina 168
Rattazzi, Steven 218
Ratter Productions LLC 151
Rattlestick Playwrights Theater 203, 249, 268
Rauch, Ben 151
Rauhe, Sven 187
Raven-Symoné 109, 118
Raver-Lampman, Emmy 32
Ravet, Stephen 139
Raw Metal Dance 231
Raw Stitch 304
Rawlins, Ted 103
Ray, Reggie 49
Ray, Robin 265
Ray, Will 158
Raymond Chandler's Trouble Is My Business 395
Raymond, Amanda 151, 177, 185
Raymundo, Hazel Ann 188
Rayner, Martin 191
Raynor, Derek 164
Ray's Delay 298
RCA 188
RE: Definition 295
Rea, Chuck 101
Rea, Stephen 420
Read, Richard 92
Ready, Fire, Aim Productions 146
Real Americans, The 395
Real Thing 278, 315
Real Tweenagers of Atlanta, The 349
Realistic Joneses, The 404
Really Useful Group 62, 68, 105
Reaney, Rebecca 179
Reanimator 276
Reaser, Elizabeth 253
Rebecca Gold

Productions 196
Rebeck, Theresa 45, 243, 410
Rebek, Nancy 58
Rebholz, Emily 223, 225-227, 253
Rech, Erin 44, 67, 77
Recipe for Disaster 381
Recker, Christopher A. 99
Reckless 289
Recktenwald, Thomas 52
Recommendation, The 387
Red 348, 354, 357, 361, 364, 365, 374, 389, 393, 395, 397, 401, 402
Red Awning 73
Red Bull Theater 172
Red Cloud Rising 279
Red Fern Theatre Company 312
Red Hart Productions 410
Red Hot Patriot: The Kick Ass Wit of Molly Ivins 372
Red Lion Theatres 160
Red Rising Marketing 62, 264
Red Velvet Cake War, The 356
Redanty, Marisa 161
Redd Tale Theatre Company 312
Redd, Randy 103, 136
Redd, Terita 83
Redden, Nigel 197
Redfield, Adam 419
Redford, Robert 418
Redhouse Arts Center 182
Redler, Zach 237
Redman, Michael 62
Redmayne, Eddie 421
Redmond, Richard 70
Redsecker, John 85
Reduced Shakespeare Company 231
Reed, Courtney 379
Reed, Jonathan Beck 369
Reed, Kevin 115
Reed, Madeline 113
Reed, Marcy 237
Reed, Maxx 29
Reed, Vivian 419
Reeder, Ana 172, 208
Reedy, M. Kilburg 71
Reefer Madness 272, 313

Reel Music 371
ReEntry 346
Rees, James 245
Rees, Kevin 142
Rees, Roger 71, 84, 113, 114, 261
Reese, Harvey 155
Reese, Joshua Elijah 389
Reese, Rob 141, 244
Reever, Sarah 241, 242, 251
Reeves, Jordan 264
References to Salvador Dali Make Me Hot 283
Refrain 305
Regan, Austin 50
Regan, Jennifer 91, 253
Regan, Jessica West 189
Regina Nejman & Company 308, 312
Regrets 228
Rehbein, Amanda 219
Rehearsal, The 306
Rehn, Rita 167
Reiber, Julie 106
Reichel, Cara 152, 163
Reid, Aleque 244, 245
Reid, Corbin 109, 140
Reid, Joe Aaron 76, 92
Reid, John 76
Reid, Joshua 94, 107, 125, 177, 226, 254
Reid, T. Oliver 101, 109, 118, 199
Reidel, Michael 113
Reifsteck, Matthew 142
Reijn, Halina 211
Reilly, Bob 410
Reilly, Hanne 145
Reilly, Liam 215
Reilly, Neil Douglas 54
Reimond, Nick 59
Reiner, Alysia 151
Reiner, Greg 155, 218
Reiner, Michele 113
Reiner, Rob 113, 114
Reinius, Hanna 215
Reinking, Ann 46, 93, 115, 418
Reinking, Megan 104, 136
Reinserman, Anna 50
Reiser, Seth 54, 245, 254
Reit, Peter 105
Reiter, Martina 212
Reitz, Casey 253
Related Companies 187
Relatively Speaking 11, 37
Relativity Media LLC 82

Relevant Theatricals 103, 136
Rembert, Jermaine R. 102
Remembrance 300
Remillard, Paris 32, 198
Remler, Pamela 97
René, Jacqueline 99
Renee, Theresa 125
Renfro, Shaun 103, 227
Reno, Michael 109
Renoni, Brian 46
Renschler, Eric 93
Rent 120, 139, 371
Repertory Theatre of St. Louis 233, 379, 395
Repole, Charles 419
Reppe, Shona 231
Reputation Control: Emerging Playwrights' Rep 317
Reseland, Vanessa 266
Resheff, Rachel 101, 104, 242
Resnick, Andrew 117
Resnick, Jed 118, 188
Resnick, Judith 54
Resnick, Zak 162
Resonance Ensemble 312
Restlessness of Desire, The 223
Restrapo, Karly 171
Reti, Marina 56, 109, 252, 255, 260
Retro Productions 312, 340
RetroFutureSpective Festival 306
Retter, Thommie 89
Rettig, Shane 156, 166
Reuben, Aubrey 426
Reude, Clay 92, 192
Reupert, Michelle 198
Reuter, Greg 93
Revised Version of Raft of the Medusa 275
ReVision 314
Revision, The 155
Reyes, José 142
Reyes, Rainerio J. 92
Reyes, Veronica 135
Reyfel, Dayle 197
Reynaud, Jacques 210
Reynolds, Jeremiah 175
Reynolds, Katrina 62
Reynolds, Marie 143
Reynolds, Timothy 242
Reynolds, Tom 99, 261
Reynoso, David Israel 196
Reza, Chris 164
Rhino Records 97, 102,

106
Rhoades, Lexi 135, 149
Rhoads, Linden 74
Rhoads, Megan 410
Rhodes, Betsy 151
Rhodes, Danielle Erin 220
Rhodes, Elizabeth 170
Rhodes, Josh 112
Rhodes, Paul 112
Rhyne, Aaron 47, 112, 253
Rhys, Matthew 251
Rhythm Carnival 232
Rialto Group, The 92
Rias, Jennifer 108
Ribeiro, Chantal 37
Ricafort, Catherine 100
Riccardi, Rose 166
Ricci, Brett 125
Ricci, Christina 219
Riccio, Aaron 444
Rice, Don 82
Rice, Grant A. 185
Rice, Linda 38, 66, 87
Rice, Luanne 243
Rice, Michael 265, 266
Rice, Paul G. 32
Rice, Sarah 419
Rice, Susan 243, 422
Rice, Tim 46, 62, 68, 99
Rich Entertainment Group 62, 82
Rich Ryan Productions 313
Rich, Geoffrey 230
Rich, Janet Billig 108
Rich, Josh 224
Richard Frankel Productions 196
Richard II 239
Richard III 204, 214
Richard Kornberg and Associates 91
Richard Rodgers Awards 446
Richard Rodgers Theatre 54, 88
Richard Seff Award 437
Richard, Cody Renard 52, 75, 124
Richard, Lysanne 130
Richards, Barry 92
Richards, Beah 418
Richards, Chris 240
Richards, David R. 36-38, 46, 54, 66
Richards, Faye 144, 153
Richards, Jeffrey 38, 47, 54, 66, 410
Richards, Jess 418
Richards, Matthew 143, 150, 209, 243

Richards, Peter 144
Richards, Vincent 255
Richards/Climan Inc. 36-38, 46, 54, 66, 88, 91
Richardson, Andy 64
Richardson, Ian M. 113
Richardson, Joely 420
Richardson, LaTanya 431
Richardson, Nan 130, 165
Richardson, Natasha 420
Richardson, Rick 175
Richardson, Sarah 43
Richelli, Asher 146
Richert, Wanda 419
Richmond Shepard Theatre 313
Richter, Julian Gabriel 211
Ricker, Teddy 239
Rickman, Alan 14, 45
Rickman, Allen Lewis 37
Rickson, Ian 98
Riddick, Jacinto Taras 74
Riddle, Stephanie 152, 255
Rideout, Leenya 110
Ridge, Richard 424
Ridgeway, Fred 72
Ridgley, Reed 226
Ridley, Michelle 218, 243, 244
Riegel, Lisa 112
Riegler, Adam 84, 116
Riehl, Carl 253
Riehl, Karissa 251
Rieling, Dale 101
Riener, Silas 213
Riessett, Scott 92
Riffle, Sarah 183
Rifkin, Jay 99
Rigby, Adam 143, 179
Rigby, Cathy 159
Rigby, Daniel 72
Rigby, Rodney 92
Riggs, Ian M. 246
Riggs, Lynn 266
Righteous Money 323
Rigimbal, Brendon 236
Rigolo 187
Riha, Michael 50
Riley, Andrew 68
Riley, Bridget 154
Riley, David 184
Riley, Kate Wood 189
Riley, Terry 210
Riley, Tom 86
Rilke, Rainer Maria 212
Rimmer, Matthew 93

Rinaldi, John 92
Rinaldi, Joy 115
Rinaldi, Philip 39, 46, 110, 224
Ring Cyle (Parts 1-4), The 305
Ring of Fire 354, 367
Ringel, Campbell 247
Ringham, Ben 214
Ringham, Max 214
Ringler, Alex 113, 175
Ringwald, Molly 419
Rink, Scott 153
Rinker, Troy 184
Rinn, Patrick 93
Riordan, James 98
Riordan, Joseph 128
Riordan, Liam 167
Riordan, Megan 128
Ripe Time 141
Ripka, Joel 183
Ripley, Alice 114, 226
Ripp, Artie 87
Rippey, Anne 33, 37, 50, 52, 68, 87, 95
Rippy, Matt 231
Risch, Matthew 39
Riscica, Anthony 189
Riseborough, Andrea 421
Rising Phoenix Repertory 250, 258, 313
Rising Sun Performance Company 313
Risley, David 198
Rita Moreno: Life Without Makeup 357
Ritchie, Michael 73
Ritenauer, Sean 32
Ritter, Alex 181, 261
Ritter, Jennifer Collins 185, 188
Ritter, John 420
Rittman, Trude 217
Rivals, The 359
Rivera, Chita 115
Rivera, Danny 164
Rivera, José 155, 250, 426
Rivera, Matt 183
Rivera, Michael 245, 246
Rivera, Mike Smith 308
Rivera, Randi 211
Rivera, Scarlet Maressa 156, 180
Rivera, Thom 147
Rivers, Gillian 149
Rivers, Kurtis 141, 143
Rivers, Ramik 167
Rives-Corbett, Gabe 64, 226
Rivieccio, Carlo 188

Rizner, Russ 101, 216, 217
Roach, Kevin Joseph 189
Road Company, The 107
Road Concierge 410
Road to Mecca, The 17, 56
Roadside 266
Robar, Meagan 193
Robards, Jason 417
Robards, Kate 247
Robbins, Carrie 447
Robbins, Jerome 159
Robbins, Krista 182
Robbins, Lois 165
Robbins, Noah 86
Robbins, Tom Alan 99
Robelen, John 45
Roberson, Ken 188
Robert Whitehead Award 446
Robert, Jérmémie 129
Roberts, Adam 29
Roberts, Carrie 118
Roberts, Clark 159
Roberts, Daniel 258
Roberts, David 189, 239
Roberts, Dominic 101
Roberts, Donald 116
Roberts, Eric 419
Roberts, Jonathan 99
Roberts, Josephine Rose 108
Roberts, Kate Cullen 368
Roberts, Keith 265
Roberts, Lance 76, 109, 116
Roberts, Lindsay 217
Roberts, Melissa 160
Roberts, Michael 151
Roberts, Nathan A. 144, 169
Roberts, Olivia 44
Roberts, Rod 159, 160
Roberts, Ronald Jordan 410
Robertson, Brad 47, 64
Robertson, Cliff 417, 469
Robertson, Darren 57
Robertson, Gill 231
Robertson, Justin 'Squigs' 118, 198, 409
Robertson, Sanford 78
Robertson, Scott 173
Robin Hood 351
Robin, Leo 217
Robin, Natalie 184, 224, 227
Robins, Laila 205, 219, 247, 257, 437

Robinson, Amina S. 40
Robinson, Arbender 32, 99
Robinson, Ashley 220
Robinson, Benjamin 184
Robinson, Bernita 125, 186, 264
Robinson, Chris 263-267
Robinson, Daniel 112
Robinson, Earl 127
Robinson, Edward G. 207
Robinson, Hal 104, 115
Robinson, Harvey 98
Robinson, Ian 150
Robinson, James G. 52
Robinson, Janelle Anne 101
Robinson, Joseph 196
Robinson, Ken 87
Robinson, Kristen 128
Robinson, Lance 128
Robinson, Lenox 207
Robinson, Liam 110
Robinson, Margaret Loesser 221, 260
Robinson, Max 219
Robinson, Robin 107
Robinson, Spencer 340
Robinson, Vivian 431
Robison, Deborah 443
Robison, John 254
Roboff, Annie 167
Robu, Karen 369
Robustelli, Patrick 190, 195
Roby, Evan 166
Roby, Robbie 89, 113
Rocca, Mo 197
Rocha, Cesar A. 40
Rock of Ages 108
Rock, Chris 103, 223
Rockaby 259
Rockage, Richard 116
Rockman, Lauren 56, 144
Rockwell, David 92, 104, 208
Rocky Horror Show, The 378, 387
Rodas, Daniel 155
Rodbro, Ashley 66
Roddy, Buzz 206
Roderick, Jamie 181
Roderick, Rhea 99
Rodet, Laird 210
Rodewald, Heidi 248
Rodgers, Gaby 417
Rodgers, Mary 265
Rodgers, Richard 46, 216
Rodibaugh, Anmaree

109
Rodman, Ben 167
Rodrigo 213
Rodriguez, Cory 244, 246
Rodriguez, Desiree 140
Rodriguez, Elizabeth 103, 198, 223
Rodriguez, MJ 140
Rodriguez, Vincent, III 216
Rodriguez, Nicholas 266
Roebling, Paul 417
Roehl, Veleda 211
Roencrantz, Emily 174
Roffe, Mary Lu 38, 84, 94
Roger Sturtevant Musical Theatre Award 437
Roger, Elena 20, 68
Rogers & Cowan Inc. 43, 191
Rogers Eckersley Design 230
Rogers Media Associates 152
Rogers, Alvin E. 105
Rogers, Charles 152
Rogers, Dulcy 187
Rogers, J.T. 224
Rogers, James Cass 266
Rogers, Jen 153
Rogers, Jennifer 112, 115, 179, 198
Rogers, Kia 149, 222, 263, 264
Rogers, Natalie 99
Rogers, Reg 244, 245
Rogers, Ric 70
Rogers, Scott 28
Rogers, Susan Zeeman 141
Rogers, Theodore 259
Rogers, Tim 71, 181
Rogers, Will 226
Roginski, Lindsay 151, 183
Rogow, Andy 139
Rohe, Kathryn 153
Rohm, Carrie 47, 62
Rojas, Marcus 29, 216
Roland, Mark 113
Roland, Richard 202
Rolecek, Charles 108
Rolfe, Phillip 33, 64
Rolfs, Beth 192
Rolfsrud, Erika 143, 263
Rollins, Sonny 441
Rollins, Tremayne 138
Rollison, Scott Taylor 84
Rolph, Marti 419
Rolston, Emily 240
Roly Poly 207

Roman Cultural Institute 313
Rodman, Ben 167 — (see below)
Roman Holiday 377
Román, Eliseo 83
Romanski, Elizabeth 196
Romanyuta, Alexander 129
Romashina, Maxim 215
Rome, Harold 127
Romeo and Juliet 197, 303, 316, 319, 375, 390
Romeo, Anthony 194
Romer, Patrick 197
Romero, Constanza 36
Romero, Xochitl 209
Romick, James 105
Rommen, Ann-Christin 210
Romo, Francesca 211
Rompante, Frederico 213
Romulus Linney Courtyard Theatre 255
Ron Lasko 173
Ronan, Brian 75, 85, 90, 113, 116, 139
Ronan, Jeff 163
Rong, Sun 211
Ronga, Josephine 229
Rooks, Joel 150
Room With a View 387
Rooney, Brian Charles 117
Rooney, David 429
Rooney, Lucas Caleb 228, 245
Rooney, Mickey 419, 449
Rooper, Jemima 72
Rooth, Liv 42, 91, 224
Roots and Wings Theatricals 313
Rope 312
Rós, Sigur 213
Rosado, Roselle 229
Rosalind Productions Inc. 274
Rosco Lighting 410
Rose, Amanda 111
Rose, Anika Noni 420
Rose, Cailan 32
Rose, Erika 49
Rose, Hannah 157
Rose, Jonathan 202
Rose, Margot 265
Rose, Reva 418, 420
Roseland Ballroom 112
Rosen, Charlie 72, 199
Rosen, Cherie 99
Rosen, Lee Aaron 104
Rosen, Marissa 113, 193

Rosen, Sharon 143
Rosen, Steve 208
Rosenbaum, Ari 130
Rosenberg, D.C. 207
Rosenberg, Jan 124
Rosenberg, Michael 241, 262
Rosenberg, Neil 47, 78
Rosenberg, Neuwith & Kuchner 410
Rosenberg, Philip S. 112, 138
Rosenberg, Roger 83
Rosenberg, Stephanie 66
Rosenberg, Steve 254
Rosenblum, Aaron 212
Rosenblum, Joshua 216
Rosencrantz and Guildenstern Are Dead 278
Rosenfeld, Andrew 142
Rosenfeld, Andrew Scott 141
Rosenfeld, Ben 114
Rosenfeld, Bill 424
Rosenfeld, Emily 409, 413
Rosenfeld, Kristen 124, 153
Rosenfield, Steve 190
Rosengarten, Michael 219
Rosengren, Kristen 181
Rosenkranz, Nicholas Quinn 86
Rosensweig, Richard 67, 216
Rosenthal, Celine 82
Rosenthal, Mark 419
Rosenthal, Mimi 195
Rosenthal, Reuben 201
Rosenthal, Samuel 195
Rosenthal, Todd 103, 227
Rosenwald, Lucia 196
Rosenzweig, Rich 33
Rosenzweig, Sara 44, 77, 147
Rosetta LeNoire Award 437
Rosin, Jordon 156
Rosoff, Amy 242
Ross, Alli 196
Ross, Anita 135, 137
Ross, Cilla 215
Ross, Katy 125
Ross, Linda Mason 39, 110, 224
Ross, Matt 95, 138
Ross, Melissa 223
Ross, Philip 181
Ross, Robert 40, 208

Ross, Rusty 184
Ross, Stephen 215
Ross, Stuart 155, 185, 207
Ross, Tanesha 32
Rosse, Morgan 219
Rosser, Tim 117, 227
Rossetti, Ashley 127
Rossetto, Ryan 39
Rossi, Nadia 234
Rossi, Philip 250
Rossi, Tim 54
Rossi, Todd 58
Rossier, Mark 428
Rossmer, David 21, 71, 168
Rossoff, Matthew 62
Rostand, Edmond 190
Roth, Aafje 232
Roth, Ann 59, 66, 90, 447
Roth, Chelsea 33
Roth, Daryl 72, 73, 74, 82, 104, 131, 134, 192, 243
Roth, David (musician) 68, 216
Roth, David (management) 47, 58, 68
Roth, Erin Brooke 109
Roth, Irving 174
Roth, Jordan 113, 410
Roth, Leah 149
Rothchild, Ken 156, 180
Rothe, Lisa 409
Rothenberg, Leon 74, 247
Rothenberg, Stephanie 95
Rothermel, Janet 100, 109
Rothman, Carole 253
Rothstein, Mervyn 422
Rouah, Josh 111
Rough for Theatre I 259
Rouleau, Nic 90
Roumain, Daniel Bernard (aka DBR) 211
Roumanos, Laura 148
Roundabout Theatre Company 35, 56, 81, 85, 96, 104, 116, 205, 251
Rounds, David 418
Rounsaville, Ted 226
Rountree, Bryan 216
Roup, Megan 125
Rourke, Kate 147
Roush, Janette 44, 67,77
Rousouli, Constantine 76, 111

Roussel, Marie Claire 163
Roussos, Christina 178
Routh, Marc 82, 185, 196, 232
Routman, Steve 216, 266, 267
Rovegno, Mia 263
Roven, Glen 202
Rovzar, Billy 28
Rovzar, Fernando 28
Rowan, Tom 150, 182
Rowat, Graham 253, 266
Rowe, Hahn 212
Rowell, Mary 64
Rowen, Scott 78, 89
Rowland, Logan 84
Rowland, William K. 44, 98
Rowley, Cynthia 223
Roy Arias Studios and Theatre 124, 313
Roy Gabay Productions 143
Roy, Jacques 141
Roy, Kevin 111
Roy, Rob Leo 164
Roy, Sarah 139
Roy, Stéphane 129
Royal Court Theatre 98, 185
Royal Family Productions 200
Royal Shakespeare Company 197
Roye, Winston 108
Rozzell, Julian, Jr. 181, 248
Rua, Jon 112
Ruas, Nuno 213
Rubendall, Brandon 28, 29, 85, 113, 118
Rubenstein, David M. 33
Rubenstein, Fran 151
Rubenstein, John 409, 412, 418
Rubin, Alexandra 39
Rubin, Amy 173
Rubin, Barbara 255
Rubin, Bruce Joel 75
Rubin, Celia Mei 113
Rubin, David 197
Rubin, John Gould 151
Rubin, Joseph 235
Rubin, Paul 111, 146, 159
Rubin, Tara 43, 71, 72, 89, 95, 97, 100, 101, 105, 155, 185, 192
Rubinos, Alejandra 28
Rubin-Vega, Daphne 74, 200, 223, 420
Rubio, Julius Anthony

Ruckdeschel, Karl 108, 188
Rucker, Bo 419
Rucker, Lamman 189
Rudetsky, Seth 115, 162
Rudin, Scott 59, 72, 90, 94, 98, 103, 185
Rudko, Michael 214
Rudman, Michael 197
Rudnick, Paul 155
Rudolph, Felicia 49
Rudy, Phillip 238, 239
Rudy, Sam 88
Ruff, Roslyn 192
Ruffalo, Mark 420
Ruffelle, Frances 419
Ruffing, Mac 107
Ruger, Bill 50
Rugg, Carla 159
Ruggiero, Holly-Anne 97
Rühl, Mechthild 211
Rühl, Tanja 211
Ruined 379, 393
Ruivivar, Francis 419
Ruiz, Gabriel 224
Ruiz, Gonzalo 212
Ruiz, Israel 149
Ruiz, Jerry 229
Rukov, Mogens 178
Rule, Christiaan 134, 153
Rumbaugh, Carl 177
Rumery, Ryan 174, 218, 219, 220, 222, 224, 226, 227, 249, 254
Rummage, Michael 87, 136
Rummel, Chris 184
Rumpelstiltskin: The Real Story 306
Rumplestiltskin 232
Runciman, Pip 106
Runge, Christina 246
Runner Stumbles, The 312, 340
Runolfsson, Anne 410
Rupert, Michael 418
Rusalka, Naomi 113, 183
Rush, Cindi 130, 132, 147, 154, 162, 168, 174, 184, 259
Rush, Deborah 217
Rush, Geoffrey 421
Rush, Jessica 97
Rush, William 209
Rushakoff, Sarah 226
Russ, Jonathan 164
Russek, Jim 39
Russell, Amy 223
Russell, Beth 62

Russell, Bill 233
Russell, Catherine 195, 428
Russell, Jay 67
Russell, Jenna 421
Russell, Kimberly 112, 115, 117, 118, 198
Russell, Lucian 235
Russell, Mark 244
Russell, Ron 126, 181
Russell, Sophie 197
Russian Transport 230
Russman, Brian 89
Russo, Glen 118
Russo, James 419
Russo, Jennifer Marie 201
Russo, Mike 95, 113, 193
Russo, Nick 221
Russo, Peter 245, 247
Russo, William 60, 236
Russomano, Joseph 196
Rustin, Sandy 168
Rutberg, Elon 47, 54
Rutherford & Son 229
Rutherford, Jared 222, 240
Rutherford, Neil 214
Rutigliano, Danny 89, 91
Rutkowski, Zsaz 167
Ruttura, David 33, 103, 136
Rux, Carl Hancock 151
Ruyle, Bill 29, 245
Ruymen, Ayn 418
Rx 243, 268
Ryack, Rita 187
Ryall, William 85, 116
Ryan, Aislinn 219
Ryan, Alison 113
Ryan, Ashley 40, 47, 50, 91, 95, 164, 254
Ryan, Cate 161
Ryan, Dorothy 141, 259
Ryan, Golda Kelly 138
Ryan, James Leo 160
Ryan, Jay 124
Ryan, Kate Moira 131
Ryan, Lindsay 188
Ryan, Oliver 197
Ryan, Roz 93
Ryan, Thomas 251
Ryan, Thomas Jay 257
Ryerson, Amy 113
Rylance, Juliet 218, 426
Rylance, Mark 98, 421
Ryness, Bryce 83
Rzepski, Sonja 95

S

S 16 - Luna Nera 295
S Theatre 210
S. Walter Art Department 410
S.R.O. Marketing 194
S2BN Entertainment 28
Saba, James 207
Sabakta-Davis, Brenda 73
Sabaugh, Pamela 178
Sabherwal, Anita 239
Sabin, David 33
Saccente, Patty 198
Sacco, Maegen 256
Sachs, Joyce Hokin 170
Sack, Dominic 190
Sack, Jason 59
Sacks, Jennifer 76
Sacred Flame, The 207
Sadigursky, Sam 212
Sadler, David 214
Sadoski, Thomas 39, 94, 114
Saegusa, Ayuma "Poe" 145
Saffell, Kathryn 260
Saffir, Anya 209
Sag, Lindsey Brooks 31, 42, 57, 80, 227
Sag, Michael 36-38, 46, 54, 66
Sagady, Sandy 102
Sagady, Shawn 82, 176
Sagawa, Tetsuroh 197
Saia, Janet 105
Saint Joan 170
Saint, Eva Marie 417
Saintey, David 233
Sajous, Christina 29, 87
Sakelaris, Yana 130
Sakolsky, Mike 245
Saks, Danielle 47, 58, 70, 75
Salameno, Charles 49
Salas, Veronica 105
Salata, Gregory 207
Salata, Justine 207
Salazar, George 40, 118
Salazar, Hector 89
Salazar, Marcia Otero 171
Saldívar, Matthew 74
Saletnik, Joshua A. 82
Salgado, Paulo 213
Salgado-Ramos, Kepani 191
Salinas, Ivan 183
Salisbury, D.J. 146
Salisbury, Sebastian 197
Salit, Jacqueline 167
Salkin, Edward 67, 89
Sallinen, Aulis 210

Salling, Pamela 245, 247, 255
Sally and Tom (The American Way) 167
Salome 278, 287
Salomons, Ruthlyn 99
Salonga, Lea 419
Salonia, Michal 151, 170, 410
Salt, Jennifer 418
Saltzberg, Sarah 193
Saltzman, Larry 63, 92
Saltzman, Rina L. 93
Saltzman, Samantha 181
Saltzman, Simon 426
Salvador, Gerard 100, 116
Salvio, Robert 418
Salwell, Jennifer 146
Salzman, Katherine 233
Sam Rudy Media Relations 77, 140, 143, 156, 165, 166, 167, 180, 187, 188, 261
Samayoa, Caesar 109
Sambataro, Lauren 100
Sambrato, Robert 169, 209, 227, 252
Same River 168
Samelson, Peter 82
Samonsky, Andrew 153, 216
Sampline, Susan 111
Sam's Romance 125
Samuel and Alassdair: A Personal History of the Robot War 301
Samuel French Short Play Festival 338
Samuel J. Friedman Theatre 31, 42, 57, 80
Samuels, Bruce 85
Samuels, Clifton 33, 201
Samuels, Jill A. 184
Samuels, Ken 176
Samuels, Sean 28, 29
Samuelson, Howerd 94
San Angelo, David 175
San Diego Theatre Critics Circle 435
San Jose Repertory Theatre 388, 396
San Martin, Jone 211
Sanchez, Chris-Ian 235
Sanchez, Jaime 418
Sanchez, Jennifer 76
Sanchez-Diaz, Irmaris 183
Sandberg, Andy 66
Sander, Roy 433
Sander, Ryan 100

Sanders, Chris 109
Sanders, Donald 81, 82, 92, 93
Sanders, Jay O. 247, 248
Sanders, John 71
Sanders, Kristie Dale 68
Sanders, Pete 140, 151, 154, 174, 183
Sanderson, Dave 81
Sanderson, David 77, 86, 91, 104, 168, 228
Sandhu, Rommy 101, 115, 118
Sandler, Zak 164
Sands, Diana 418
Sands, Jason Patrick 93
Sands, Lena 245
Sands, Stark 420
Sandy, Jude 110
Sandy, Julia 31, 42, 45, 57, 80
Sanfilippo, Michael 159
Sanford, Tim 73, 241, 262
Sangaré, Kadiatou 199
Sanger, Jonathan 87
Sanguine Theatre Company 314
Sanko, Erik 211
Sanneh, Alpha 210
Sans A Productions 314
Santagata, Frank 84
Santaland Diaries, The 348, 395
Santana, Marcos 113, 232
Santana, Tedy 233
Santaolalla, Gustavo 210
Santen, Kathy 111
Santeramo, Rob 193
Santiago, Saundra 129
Santiago-Hudson, Ruben 49, 255
Santolis, Marcelo 233
Santore, Stephen 76
Santos, Greg 266
Santos, Jennae Alexa Ruiz 149
Santos, Jonathan 173, 184, 189
Sapenoff, Jill 410
Sapp, Rob 267
Sapper, Wayne 410
Saracena, Robert 231
Saraffian, Andrea O. 92
Sarafin, Peter 35, 36, 56, 66, 81, 90, 96
Sarandon, Chris 410
Sardi's Restaurant 426, 445
Sargent, Elizabeth 178

Sargent, Justin Matthew 47, 108, 202
Sarian, Alex 226
Sarke 284
Sarmiento, Stacy 85
Sarpola, Richard 78, 109
Sarrington, Maralyn 214
Sarrow, Dan 59
Sarvay, Tree 45, 88
Sassanella, Josh 108, 145
Satalof, Stu 85
Satan's Whore, Victoria Woodhull 320
Sato, Atsuko 105
Saudek, Molly 215
Saul, Christopher 197
Saunders, Amanda 158
Saunders, Heath 217
Saunders, Simone 197
Saunier, Matt 232
Sautin, Maksym 129
Sautter, James 173
Savage, Lee 225, 243
Savage, Mark 175, 194
Savelli, Jennifer 85
Saver, Jeffrey 67
Saving Aimee 370
Saving Grace Productions 314
Saviour? 318
Savit, Gavriel 133
S vitri 184
Savran, David 428
Sawada, Yuji 197
Sawyers, Jenny B. 37
Saxe, Gareth 99
Saxner, Robert 170
Saxon, Kelly 33, 59
Saxton, Jacob 309
Say Goodnight Gracie 150
Saye, John 101
Sayegh, Sharone 100
Sayers, Henry 215
Sayre, Loretta Ables 410, 421
Sayre, Mike 184
Sbokou, Anna 156
Scaglione, Dominic, Jr. 97
Scaglione, Josefina 421
Scalin, Noah 143, 147
Scalpone, Michelle 245
Scandal Productions 164
Scandrett, Davison 213
Scanio, Joe 193
Scanlan, Arlene 95
Scanlan, Christie 132
Scanlan, Emily 247
Scanlon, Erik 183

Scannell, Raymond 198
Scarcelle, Michael 184
Scardino, Frank 102
Scared Skinny: A One (Hundred Pound Lighter) Woman Show 272, 313
Scarfuto, Christine 144
Scarlata, Ryan 130
Scarpone-Lambert, Anthony 101
Sceaux 214
Scelsa, Kate 236, 247
Scenario Thailand 50, 52, 95
Scène Nationale 214
Scene, The 324
Schaal, Kaneza 236
Schadl, Meg 181
Schaechter, Ben 175, 194
Schaefer, Celia 164
Schaefer, Laurie 162
Schaefer, Paul A. 105
Schaeffer, Eric 33, 103, 136
Schafer, Kimberly 113
Schafer, Scott 207
Schaffert, Greg 71
Schafler, Lauren 189
Schak, John 200
Schall, Ira 137, 186
Schall, Thomas 42, 59, 77, 80, 81, 94, 110, 111, 147, 224, 226, 227, 228, 244, 245, 248, 249, 251, 252, 254, 258,
Schambelan, Ike 178
Schanzer, Leanne 124, 129, 133, 149, 150, 151, 155, 182, 185, 192
Schapira, Rachel 141
Schatz, Alfred 138
Schatz, Jack 43, 78, 89
Schatz, Stefan 183
Schechter, Matthew J. 64, 249
Scheck, Frank 409, 429
Scheck, Norma 236
Schecter, Amy 229
Schecter, Jeffrey 78, 104, 116
Schecter, LeRoy 37
Scheer, Rachel 110, 224
Scheerer, Bob 417
Scheid, Patrick 127
Scheinman, Norah 240
Schenková, Bela 129
Schepis, Steve 106
Scher, Adam 196
Scherich, Nathan 97

Scherr, Gina 42, 244, 245
Scherr, Joshua 131, 133, 141, 146, 147, 187
Schetter, Sarah 183
Schiappa, John 111
Schiavo, Giuseppe 129
Schiavo, Vincenzo 129
Schierman, Alisa 236
Schilke, Raymond 189
Schill, William 206
Schiller, Jeff 112
Schiller, Sandy 145
Schimmel, Bill 116
Schings, Heather 147, 164, 192
Schiralli, Michael 200
Schiro, Chad Luke 187
Schlachter, Kristine 130
Schlenk, Thomas 99
Schlesinger, Adam 223
Schlict, Ursel 167
Schliefer, Joshua 253
Schlieper, Nick 106
Schlossberg, Julian 37
Schmidinger, Walter 210
Schmidt, Erica 143
Schmidt, Harvey 190, 266
Schmidt, Josh 94
Schmidt, Kiira 33
Schmidt, Sara 97
Schmidt, Timothy 159, 168
Schmidt, Wrenn 220, 229
Schmidtke, Ralph 107
Schmied, Marc 266
Schmittroth, Marc 47
Schmoll, Ken Russ 127, 258
Schnall, Eric 191
Schneid, Megan 47, 106
Schneider, Andrew 168
Schneider, David 244, 246
Schneider, Jacob 133
Schneider, Keith 153
Schneider, Lauren Class 410
Schneider, Mark 89
Schneider, Martin 210
Schneider, Matthew 45
Schneider, Peter 99, 109
Schneider, Robert E. 191
Schneier, Lane 112
Schnetzer, Stephen 57
Schnetzler, Shane 141, 251, 258
Schnitzler, Arthur 267
Schnuck, Terry 32, 47, 54, 132

Schoch, Laura 222
Schochet, Jillian 128
Schoeffler, Paul 108
Schoenfeld, Emilie Bray 192
Schoer, Kyla 195
Schoffer, Rebecca 209
Scholey, Annabel 214
Scholl, Vera Shepps 177
Schondorf, Zohar 76, 84
Schoolhouse Theater, The 133
Schoonheim, Laurens 232
Schorr, Eric 164
Schorr, Sari 151
Schott, Amy Francis 46
Schrader, Benjamin 90
Schrader, David 64
Schreck, Heidi 197, 62, 421
Schreiber, Catherine 49, 71, 125
Schreier, Dan Moses 36, 104, 177, 216, 253
Schrider, Tommy 110, 141
Schriever, Jennifer 36, 59, 94
Schrock, Robert 175, 194
Schroeder, Katelyn 232
Schroeder, Ricky 175
Schroettnig, Steve 109
Schubert-Blechman, Julienne 33, 62
Schuberth, Karl 47, 64
Schuette, James 162
Schulberts, The 151
Schulenburg, Marnie 253
Schuler, Arlene 199, 216
Schuler, Chanteé 99
Schuler, Duane 96
Schuler, Stephen 84
Schull, Rebecca 258
Schulman , Susan H. 422
Schulman , Susan L. 142, 190, 409, 410
Schulman, Charlie 151
Schulteis, Joshua 183
Schultz, Carol 239, 240
Schultz, Erin 168
Schultz, Evan 199
Schultz, Victor 111
Schulz-Eckart, Veronika 212
Schumacher, Ana 247
Schumacher, Thomas 64, 99, 101
Schumeister, David 32
Schupbach, Michael

231
Schupmann, Melinda 442
Schuster/Maxwell Galin/ Sandler 196
Schutter, Laura 101
Schwartz, Alison 189
Schwartz, Chandra Lee 111
Schwartz, Clifford 71
Schwartz, Erica Lynn 226
Schwartz, Heath 33, 49, 78, 94, 97, 103, 255
Schwartz, Jake 90
Schwartz, Jenny 258
Schwartz, Josh 143
Schwartz, Lisa 31, 60, 112, 236
Schwartz, Paul 105
Schwartz, Rebecca 165
Schwartz, Stephen 40, 111, 202
Schwartzbord, Aaron 239
Schwartz-Brown, Francine 73
Schwarzbaum, Nurit 130, 159
Schweikardt, Michael 127
Schwein, Natalia 229
Schweizer, David 165, 177
Schweppe, Brian 47, 64, 109
Schwier, Ronald 43, 82
Schworer, Angie 92
Sciaroni, Rayme 175, 194
Sciascia, Alaina 230
Scieszka, Jon 209
Sci-Fi/Horror Theater Festival 339
Sciorra, Annabella 103, 198
Sciotto, Eric 106
Sciranka, Zachary 189
Scneid, Megan 112
Scoblick, Jessica 75
Scoggins, Cameron 242
Scolari, Peter 70
Scorched 350, 352
Scotch Kiss 315
Scott Mauro Productions 106
Scott Sanders Productions 68
Scott, Adrienne 229
Scott, Alan 106
Scott, Bert 178
Scott, Brian 189
Scott, Brian (stage

manager) 62
Scott, Brian H. 162, 248, 262
Scott, Colin 179, 220, 221, 230, 243, 244, 251, 252
Scott, Ellenore 146
Scott, Felix 154
Scott, Geoffrey Jackson 236
Scott, George C. 417
Scott, Jack 28, 64
Scott, Jamie 213
Scott, Jamison 102
Scott, Jay 160, 174, 264, 266
Scott, Joel 87
Scott, Kevin 245-247
Scott, Kirsten 33
Scott, Les 33
Scott, Matthew 44
Scott, Michael James 90
Scott, Michael Lee 112
Scott, Pippa 417
Scott, Ramsey 153
Scott, Rashidra 109, 112, 113
Scott, Steven 151
Scott, Thom, II 189
Scott, Tim 233
Scott, Vincent 206
Scottsboro Boys, The 341, 350, 387, 437
Scoullar, John 231
Scranton, Damen 156, 168, 180
Scribner, Justin 108
Scrofani, Aldo 146
Scruggs, James 444
Scudder, Jake 244
Scully, Dan 66, 139, 177
Scutt, Tom 197
Seafarer, The 348
Seagull, The 293, 348, 391
Sealey, Jaz 62
Sears, Brian 90, 202
Sears, Jeffrey David 188
Sears, Leslie 251
Seascape with Sharks and Dancer 297
Season's Greetings 386
Seastone, Victor 50, 64
Seaton, Laura 216
Seattle Repertory Theatre 237, 397
Seay, Gayle 146
Sebastain, Jason 236, 247, 258
Sebastian, Maureen 253
Šebek, Christian 105
Sebesky, Don 87
Sebesky, Olivia 148

Sebesta, Ronald 212
Sebouhian, Carly Blake 105
Secada, Jon 200
Sechrest, Marisa 410
Second City - Charmed and Dangerous, The 359
Second City - Less Pride...More Pork, The 365
Second City Summer Spectacular, The 373
Second City, The 354, 359, 365, 373
Second Samuel 274
Second Stage 205, 253
Secret Garden, The 274, 399
Secret Theatre, The 314
Sedgwick, Kyra 419
Sedwick, Toby 110
See, Hear, Taste Touch 300
Seed 145
Seeing Place Theater 315
Seeley, Mark 33, 52
Seelig, Ryan 124, 247, 248
Seer and the Witch 319
Seer, Richard 419
Seery, Florie 31, 42, 57, 80, 227
Sees, Christina 76
Segal, David F. 179
Segal, Martin E. 419
Segal, Tobias 208, 254
Segarra, Josh 52, 124, 254
Segura, Enrique 99
Seib, Chad 101
Seibert, Lara 13, 43
Seibert, Margo 267
Seidel, Kit 106
Seidel, Virginia 419
Seid-Green, Shoshana 238
Seidler, Lee J. 410
Seidman, John 158
Seidner, Allison 84, 112, 167
Seiff, Carolyn 158
Seiler, Roy 62
Seiver, Sarah 55, 59
Sekou, Karim 138
Seldes, Raina 410
Select (The Sun Also Rises), The 236
Selezneva, Natalia 215
Self, Jeffery 202
Seligson, Gary 89
Sell, Janie 418

Sellars, Peter 199
Seller, Jeffrey 88, 139, 188
Sellers, Jamie 146
Sellon, Kim 32, 67, 410
Selman, Betsy 116
Seltzer, Daniel 419
Selya, John 420
Selzer, John Adrian 258
Semaan, Sue 103
Semaphore Projects 126
Sembler, Samantha 182
Seminar 14, 45, 408-410
Semlitz/Glaser Productions 82
Semmes, Allison 90
Semon, Timothy R. 226
Sempey, Yannick 211
Senatore, Marco 129
Senckel, Marina 210
Senechal, Dorothee 142
Senewiratne, Tania 82
Sengbloh, Saycon 256, 379
Senor, Andy, Jr. 139
Sense & Sensibility 345
Seo, Chuja 409
Septimus & Clarissa 141
Serapiglia, Michael 117
Serdioukov, Petr 129
Serino/Coyne 28, 33, 37, 38, 39, 40, 45, 46, 47, 50, 52, 54, 59, 62, 64, 66, 71, 73, 78, 82, 185
Sermonia, Jason 62
Sermonia, Julius 62
Serotsky, Aaron 253
Serralles, Jeanine 172, 241
Serrano, Liana 100
Servais, Libby 52, 111
Servant of Two Masters, The 72, 398
Service, Kevin 31, 42, 57, 80
Sese, Jen 32, 227, 254
Sessions, Tally 94, 153, 265
Sessions, Timothy 83
Seth Rudetsky's DISASTER! 162
Seth, Daniel 192
Setpnik, Sue 93
Settle, Joanna 248
Settle, Keala 106
Setton, Amanda 192
Seven Homeless Mammoths Wander New England 402
Seven in One Blow 275
Seven17 PR 142, 230

Severeid, Krista 192
Sewell, Rufus 420
Sex and The Second City: A Romantic Dot Comedy 349
Sex on the Beach 124
Sexton, David 208, 226, 256
Sexton, Katie 125
Sexton, Michael 248
Sexton, Tom 258
Seyb, Wendy 163
Seymour, Amanda 78, 258
Seymour, Kenny J. 102
Sgambati, Brian 221
Shabazz Center 138
Shackelford, Emily 233
Shacket, Mark 28, 33, 44, 52, 95, 103
Shackner, Jill 151
Shad, Tom 189
Shadow Box, The 279
Shadow Boxing 154
Shadow Over Innsmouth, The 311
ShadowCatcher Entertainment 67, 102
Shaffer, Jeremy 40, 45, 84, 93, 105, 115, 135, 241
Shah, Anita 35, 36, 37, 46, 49, 56, 58, 59, 60, 73, 75, 77, 81, 185
Shahar Productions 75
Shaheen, Dan 190
Shahi, Arya 147
Shaiman, Marc 92
Shaish, Omer 133
Shake Shack 410
Shake, Rattle, and Roll 371
Shakespeare in the Park 244
Shakespeare in the Parking Lot 316
Shakespeare Theatre Company 388, 397
Shakespeare, William 138, 141, 156, 176, 178, 179, 181, 214, 218, 239, 244, 245, 248, 259, 260
Shakespeare's Amazing Cymbeline 395
Shakespeare's Sister Company 315
Shakespeare's Slave 312
Shakun, Melissa 87, 131, 243
Shalina, Margarita 258
Shallenberg, Christine 213

Shamhat 302
Shamos, Jeremy 22, 73, 227, 360
Shane, Stacy 134
Shaner, Madeleine 442
Shanghai Lil's 238
Shankel, Lynn 112
Shanks, Gabriel 429
Shanley, John Patrick 209
Shannon, Bryen 38, 104
Shannon, Michael 258
Shannon, Sidney 152
Shannon, Tad 233
Shanshan, Wu 211
Shaoyuan, Tan 211
Shapiro, Aaron Heflich 184
Shapiro, Anna D. 103
Shapiro, Mike 180
Sharenow, Dean 52
Sharett, Gili 184
Sharian, John 208
Sharkey, Dan 190
Sharkey, Jack 171
Sharman, Clint 78
Sharnell, LaQuet 52, 119, 124, 202
Sharon, Ronen 133
Sharon, Ted 64
Sharp, Kim T. 206
Sharp, Shanna 112, 113
Sharpe, Robby 152
Sharrock, David 154
Sharrow, Roseanna 47, 75
Shatner, William 58, 417
Shatner's World: We Just Live In It... 58
Shatz, Matt 436
Shaud, Grant 37
Shaun, Derek 189
Shaur, Cilda 244
Shaver, Helen 419
Shaw, Andy 147
Shaw, Benjamin 67
Shaw, Byron 129
Shaw, Curtis 184
Shaw, Darryl 93
Shaw, David 230
Shaw, Fiona 420
Shaw, George Bernard 170, 221, 240
Shaw, Helen 426, 428
Shaw, Jane 141, 171, 212, 229, 237, 239, 240
Shaw, Julie 233
Shaw, Kaitlin 43, 62, 75
Shaw, Keith 47, 64
Shaw, Loren 163
Shaw, Lynn 125, 131
Shaw, Nathaniel 147

Shaw, Pamela 178
Shaw, Robert 33, 136
Shaw, Stephen 191
Shaw, Susan 235
Shawhan, April 418
Shay, Jessica Wegener 73, 166, 209, 225, 252, 261
Shayne, Tracy 93
She Kills Monsters 288
She Loves Me 116
Shea, Dave 176
Shea, Ed 64
Shea, Jere 420
Shea, John V. 419
Shea, Katherine 60, 236
Shea, Patrick 109
Shear, Claudia 420
Shechter, Stephanie 247, 259
Sheckler, Aaron 153
Sheehan, Ciarán 112
Sheehan, Dans Maree 223, 236, 247
Sheehan, Joanna 222
Sheehan, Kelly 216, 217
Sheen, Ray 113
Sheffer, Erika 230
Sheik, Kacie 32, 198, 247
Sheldon, Tony 106, 114, 115, 202, 409, 410, 421
Shell, Charles 178, 225
Shell, Roger 109, 116, 216, 217
Shelley, Carole 89
Shelley, Dave 211
Shepard, Brian 33
Shepard, Zack 246
Shepeleva, Tatiana 215
Shepherd, Elizabeth 37
Shepherd, Scott 247, 255
Shepp, Michael 72, 106
Sheppard, John 101
Sheppard, Laurie 112, 113
Shepperd, Michael A. 160
Shepsle, Seth 31
Sher, Antony 420
Sher, Bartlett 39, 224
Sher, Matthew 87
Sherak, Tom 37
Sherba, John 210
Sherbundy, Jason 92
Sherer, Jenna 436
Sheridan, James 409
Sheridan, Jessica 33, 101, 109
Sheridan, John 419
Sheridan, Joseph 82

Sheridan, Mary 309
Sherin, Mimi Jordan 98, 162
Sherline, Stephanie 35-37, 46, 49, 56, 58, 59, 60, 73, 75, 77, 81, 90, 109
Sherlock Holmes and the Christmas Goose 357
Sherman, Bonnie 166
Sherman, Daniel Stewart 226
Sherman, Howard 422
Sherman, Jayne Baron 104
Sherman, Josh 58
Sherman, Laura 111
Sherman, Rebecca 247
Sherman, Robb 113
Sherman, Robert 464
Sherman, Robert B. 101
Sherrell, Kat 117
Sherrill, Robert A. 223
Sherry, Colleen M. 74, 254, 265
She's of a Certain Age 186
Shethar, Eric 258
Shevchenko, Danila 215
Shew, Jonathan 133
Shew, Timothy 68
Sheward, David 429
Shia, Joanne 112
Shields, Brooke 84, 420, 424
Shields, Tim 237
Shier, Joel 33, 40, 75, 84, 187
Shih, David 144
Shilov, Dmitry 129
Shimaji, Yasutake 211
Shimelonis, Eric 138
Shimizu, Chika 249
Shimkin, Becca 112
Shimko, Kevin 240
Shin, Chunsoo 62
Shindle, Kate 114
Shiner, M. William 244, 245, 248
Shingledecker, Matt 140
Shinn, Christopher 101
Shipley, Sandra 96, 217, 229
Shippers, Melissa 142, 143, 218
Shire, David 264
Shirley Herz Associates 178, 206
Shirley, Jennifer 226
Shishkin, A. 215
Shively, A.J. 247
Shivers, John 43, 47, 82, 99, 109

Sh-K-Boom/Ghostlight Records 32, 40, 82, 85, 90, 92, 109, 132, 153, 190, 216, 227, 254, 261
Shlemiel the First 259
Shneiderman, Stacy 251
Shneidman, Philip 184
Shoberg, Richard 195
Shoch, Laura 182
Shoemaker, The 135
Shoenberger, Eric 146
Shoffner, Samantha 36, 49, 124, 223
Shook, Karla 172
Shookhoff, David 31, 42, 57, 80, 227
Shoolin, Emily 29
Shooltz, Emily 142
Shorenstein Hays-Nederlander Theatres LLC 54
Shorsten, Adam 193
Short Fall, The 321
Short Play Festival - Horror 307
Short Shakespeare! The Taming of the Shrew 364
Short, Martin 420
Short, Richard 98
Shorter, Alexis 102
Shout Factory 78
Show Boat 375
Show Goes On, The 266
Showalter, Steven 244, 428
Showtune 380
Shreve, Leslie 410
Shriver, Jon 246
Shriver, Lisa 62
Shubert Organization, The 43, 60, 78, 109, 410
Shubert Theatre 102, 112
Shu-Chen, Wang 210
Shuford, Bret 118
Shugart, Gretchen 424
Shukor, Zak 156
Shulman, Steve 235
Shuman, Mort 459
Shunkey, Mark 111
Shunock, Mark 188
Silver Tassie, The 198
Shupe, Jason 28
Shutt, Christopher 110, 197
Shwartzberg, Tom 133
Siberry, Michael 35
Sibley, John 28
Sicari, Joseph R. 158
Siccardi, Arthur 89, 93, 100, 107

Sicilian Limes 296
Siciliano, Carl 202
Sick Little Productions 316
Side Show 314
Sidekick Productions 316
Sidman, Sarah 127, 170, 256
Sidorenko, Dima 129
Sie, Adrian 134
Sieber, Christopher 93, 113
Siebert, Jeff 117
Siedenberg, Charlie 158
Siegel, Adam 39, 73, 110, 224
Siegel, Barbara 424
Siegel, Chet 250
Siegel, Dave 64
Siegel, Ed 436
Siegel, Evan 113
Siegel, Jamie 187
Siegel, Janis 201
Siegel, June 265
Siegel, Larry 265
Siegel, Lee 62
Siegel, Scott 201
Siegfried, Jake Bennett 262
Sieh, Kristen 247
Siff, Maggie 260
Sigafoose, David 235
Sight Unseen 399
Signature Theatre Company 56, 205, 255
Sikes, Seth 169
Sikora, Megan 95, 217
Silber, Alexandra 31, 192, 198, 202
Silber, Chic 40, 111
Silberman, Adam 28, 75
Silbermann, Jake 250, 268
SILENCE! The Musical 116, 120, 132
Sills, Douglas 420
Sills, Paul 447
Silovsky, Joseph 258
Silva, Cassie 108
Silva, Lisette 409
Silva, Shanna 82
Silva, Steven 82
Silver Tassie, The 198
Silver, Charlie 152
Silver, Joel 32, 50, 71, 164
Silver, Nicky 77, 261
Silver, Rafi 129
Silverman, Adam 248
Silverman, Alexander 196
Silverman, Antoine

29, 29
Silverman, Jen 144
Silverman, Leigh 38, 227, 246
Silverman, Miriam 141
Silverman, Rachel 236
Silverstein, Jonathan 222
Simard, Jennifer 109
Simitzis, Sophia 246
Simko, Kate 126, 231
Simmonds, Jamie 128, 157
Simmons, Brad 52, 124
Simmons, Brian 143
Simmons, Courter 97
Simmons, Danny 431
Simmons, F. Michael 241
Simmons, Fredrick 254
Simmons, Godfrey L., Jr. 181
Simmons, Michael 45, 226, 236, 242
Simmons, Nick 110
Simms, Jason 182, 254
Simon Says Entertainment 74
Simon, Alan 47, 68
Simon, Jill 90
Simon, John 429
Simon, Neil 207, 410
Simonelli, Matthew 45
Simon-Gersuk, Jake 227
Simons, Lake 129, 135
Simonson, Eric 70
Simpson, Angela 52, 62
Simpson, Drew 254
Simpson, Jim 143, 163, 177
Simpson, Jimmi 421
Simpson, Marguerite 125
Simpson, Mark 102, 112
Simpson, Pete 189, 212, 236
Sims, Jennifer 77
Sinato, Vinny 36
Sinclair, Eric 417
Sindall, Jonathan A. 151
Singer, Daniel 231
Singer, Isaac Bashevis 259
Singh, Ashley 115, 209
Singh, Paul 196
Single Reflex 295
Singleton, Christopher A. 147
Singleton, Lori 249
Sink or Swim Rep 316
Sinn, Aubrey 152
Sintes, Daniel 231

Sintes, Matthew 231
Sinton, Josh 212
Sipes, Nicholas 89
Siracusa, Catherine 206
Siren's Heart (Marilyn in Purgatory) 319
Sirkin, Spring 67
Sirola, Joseph 49
Sissons, Narelle 126, 174
Sistas: The Musical 149, 324
Sister Act 109, 116
Sister Sylvester 316
Sisto, Rocco 45
SITI Company 162
Sitler, David 220
Situation Interactive 28, 32, 35, 47, 56, 62, 81, 84, 85, 92, 99
Siverls, Robert 309
Six Seeds: The Persephone Project 322
sixsixsix 273
Skabelkin, Artem 129
Skaff, Greg 111
Skaggs, Corey 101
Skeggs, Emily 112
Skeist, David 259
Skillin, Kyle 166, 256
Skin Flesh Bone 290, 315
Skinner, Ben 40
Skinner, Emily 89
Skinner, Nora 90
Skinner, Randy 217
Skinner, Steve 139
Skinner, Todd 107
Skirball Center 428, 437
Sklar, Matthew 112
Sklar-Heyn, Seth 68, 155
Skolnick, Marci 145, 165, 259
Skolnick, Sara 103
Skolnik, Laura 46
Skovgaard, Erik 263
Skow, Sami 112
Skraastad, Danielle 147
Skrincosky, Matthew 113
Skull in Connemara, A 359
Skura, Jennifer 186
Skybell, Steven 218, 219, 248
Skylight 420
Slack, Jason 164, 239
Slade, Michael 130
Slanina, Ron 182
Slater, Andrew 249
Slater, Glenn 82, 109

Slaton, Juliana 94
Slaton, Shannon 85, 116, 265
Slattery, Jenny 28
Slaven, Rachel 80
Slavin, Martin 197
Slee, Clayton 369
Slee, Paul Alexander 150, 182
Sleep No More 196
Sleeping Beauty Wakes 381
Sleiman, Haaz 237
Slepovitch, Dmitri "Zisl" 259
Sliman, James 137
Slinger, Michaeljon 68, 89, 95, 113
Sloan, Chris 78, 90, 113
Sloan, Sabrina 92
Sloane, Barry 98
Sloat, Hannah 110
Slocum, Melissa 105
Slootskiy, Gary 251
Slotnick, Joey 208
Slow Air, A 176
Slowgirl 225
slut ®evolution: no one gets there overnight 280
SM Communications 149
Smaha, Heather 166, 247, 258
Small Pond Enterprises 316
Small, Cathy 85
Small, Jeffrey 140
Small, Mews 115
Small, Neva 125
Smallcomb, Matt 184
Smalls, Danese C. 60
Smallwood, Chris 107
Smallwood, Dale 239, 240
Smallwood, George 113
Smanko, Mike 32, 67, 410
Smart, Andy 142
Smedes, Tom 71, 125, 131, 132, 194
Smerdon, Vic 89
Smiley, Brenda 418
Smiling, Lindsay 379
Smillie, Ryan 40, 50, 92
Smit, Joris 232
Smith Street Stage 316
Smith, Alena 254
Smith, Alexandra C. 113
Smith, Alexis 452
Smith, Amaker 106
Smith, Angela Christine 235

Smith, Anna Deavere 420
Smith, Antoine L. 102
Smith, Austin 250, 256, 257
Smith, Austin R. 196
Smith, Barry Satchwell 47
Smith, Bob 131
Smith, Bradshaw 469
Smith, Brendan 105
Smith, Brian 68, 92
Smith, Brian J. 80
Smith, C.E. 83
Smith, Cameron 235
Smith, Chad 33, 111
Smith, Christopher C. 68, 92
Smith, Clarence 197
Smith, Cotter 185, 208
Smith, Courtney 219
Smith, Courtney Russell 172
Smith, Dante Olivia 237
Smith, Darrell 128
Smith, David 105
Smith, David Ryan 72
Smith, Derek 437
Smith, Douglas 86, 196
Smith, Dylan Scott 44
Smith, Elaine 150
Smith, Elizabeth 86, 96, 245
Smith, Erica 209
Smith, Garret D. 194
Smith, Grant 259
Smith, Greg 99
Smith, Hillary B. 147
Smith, Howie Michael 200
Smith, Imani Dia 99
Smith, Jaime Lincoln 145
Smith, Jaymi Lee 240
Smith, Jennifer 78, 202
Smith, Jimmie Lee 36
Smith, Jocelyn 85, 116
Smith, Joseph 50, 52, 95, 103, 136
Smith, Justin 133, 266
Smith, Ken 38
Smith, Kristyn R. 148, 151, 160
Smith, Lane 209
Smith, Laura 108
Smith, Luke 86
Smith, MaryAnn D. 84
Smith, Megan 104, 131, 251
Smith, Monique 199
Smith, Natalie 72
Smith, Nicole 260
Smith, Nicole Jescinth

42, 225
Smith, Nicole M. 131
Smith, Niegel 145
Smith, Patrick Milling 45, 60
Smith, Paul J. 47, 58
Smith, Philip J. 43, 60, 78, 410
Smith, Rae 110
Smith, Randee 150, 182
Smith, Rex 419
Smith, Rolt 92, 93
Smith, Sandra 418
Smith, Sarah 38
Smith, Sarah Caldwell 235
Smith, Shannon 85
Smith, Sharon 246
Smith, Sheila 410, 418
Smith, Steven Scott 264
Smith, T. Ryder 110
Smith, T.C. 233
Smith, T.W. 93
Smith, Turner 57, 91
Smith, Wallace 40
Smith, Warren 127
Smith, Wayne 45, 66
Smith, Yeardley 114, 192
Smith-Cameron, J. 172, 247
Smith-Croll, Dana 207
Smithers, William 417
Smith-Marooney, Lila 192
Smithyman, Paul 182, 224
Smits, Thierry 210
Smokler, Elly 149
Smolenski, Tony, IV 68, 89
Smulders, Karina 211
Smyth, Steve 183
Smythe, Robert 231
Snaderson, David 39
Snapple Theater Center 190, 195
Snapshot 223, 386
Sneaky Snake Productions 316
Sneddon, David 177
Snell, Tom 72
Snider, Gypsy 137, 138
Snow Queen, The 395
Snow, Jason 28
Snow, Jason Michael 90, 117, 201
Snowdon, Ted 31, 36, 141, 185, 259, 410
Snug Harbor Productions 250, 258
Snyder, Andy 28, 36, 67, 73, 104, 155, 410

Snyder, Beryl 116
Snyder, Stephen "Hoops" 97
Snyder, Thomas 173
Soap Myth, The 174
Sobelle, Geoff 173, 174
Sobiszewski, Jacqueline 178
Sobo, Ripley 60
Socarides, Charles 251
Sochorakis, Ioannis 256
Soddu, Antonio 77, 222
Soffe, Emilie 248
Sofia's Downstairs Theater 124, 151
Sogliuzzo, Caraline 43
SoHo Playhouse 128, 157, 173, 190
Soho Rep 258
Sojola, Phumzile 54, 55
Sokol, Marilyn 185
Sokol, Susie 236, 247
Sokolovic, Sarah 37
Sokolowski, Howard 62
Sola, Amparo González 234
Solá, Martín 216
Solano, Mateo 181
Soldevila, Sébastien 137, 138
Soldier's Song 137
Soley, Chris 252
Solis, Felix 223
Sollogub, Nathalia 215
Solomon, Abigail Rose 222
Solomon, Dave 118
Solomon, David 85, 116
Solomon, Greg 221, 252
Solomon, Jerold E. 379
Solomon, Mary C. 155
Solomon, Sid 176
Solomon, Steve 139
Solomonova, Elena 215
Solomons, Leeorna 133
soloNOVA Arts Festival 319
Solorzano, Francisco 180
Soloski, Alexis 426, 429
Soloway, Jen 218
Soloway, Leonard 198
Solshay Productions 92
Soltau, Tess 84
Solyom, Nick 80
Some Girl(s) 303
Some Lovers 387
someone's trying to kill me 274
Somerled Charitable Foundation 141, 259
Something/Nothings 316

Somewhere 387
Somewhere Safer 304
Sommers, Allison 31
Sommers, Michael 429
Somogyi, Ilona 73, 228, 241
Son, Yeung Jin 191
Sondheim on Sondheim 376
Sondheim, Stephen 33, 46, 216, 446
Sondiyazi, Vusi 99
Song for Coretta, A 300
Song of Convalescent Ayn Rand Giving Thanks to the Godhead in the Lydian Mode 323
Song, Min 191
Sonia Friedman Productions 36, 44, 59, 78, 86, 86, 90, 94, 98
Sonnambula 291
Sonnleitner, Anna-Maria 212
Sonnleitner, Gerlinde 212
Sonnleitner, Paul J. 92
Sonon, Vanessa 85, 115
Sons of the Prophet 205, 251 408, 409 430
Sontag: Reborn 272
Sony Pictures Entertainment 28
Soper, Sonja 82
Sophocles 163
Sordelet, Rick 74, 104, 129, 179, 191, 206, 216, 226, 250, 255, 256, 257
Sorensen-Jolink, John 196
Sorenson, Garrett 31
Sorg, Kate 40, 54, 87
Sorge, Joey 78, 95
Sosnow, Pat 68, 95
Sosnowski, Stephen 75
Soto, Jerry Nelso 137
Soto-Arbors, Natasha 180
Souhrada, Tom 101, 112, 116, 118
Soules, Dale 229
Soumbonou, Bintou 199
Sound Associates 155, 188, 410
Sound of Music, The 390
Source Communications 131
South Coast Repertory 241, 262, 388, 398

South of Settling 401
South Park Digital Studios 90
South Street 392
Southern Baptists Sissies 279
Southern, Eric 248
Southern, Patrick 70, 169
Souza, Kiko 233
Sovar, Rodd 118
Sovert, Michael I. 410
Sovronsky, Alexander 245
Sowerby, Githa 229
Sowers, Scott 150, 223
Sozo Media 164
Sozzi, Kim 193
Spacey, Kevin 204, 214
Spadaro, Stephen 93, 106
Spahn, Karen 82, 110
Spain, Lucy 126
Spangler, David 156
Spangler, Nick 90
Spangler, Walt 256
Spann, Jack 110
Spara v ski, Stanisław 178
Sparks, Tori 196
Sparling, Vanessa 130, 162, 165
Sparnon, James 154, 155
Sparnon, Jim 177
Sparrow Grass 402
Speakers Progress, The 210
Speaking in Tongues 365
Speakman, Ryan 112, 195
Spear, Jamie 167
Speargrove Presents 324
Speciale, Tony 218
Speck, Jake 97
Spector, Hillary 125
Spector, Jarrod 97
Spector, Morgan 230
Speer, Beau 113
Speers, Adam 214
Spektor, Charline 265
Spektor, Mira J. 265
Spelling, Candy 78, 95
Spellman, Laurence 214
Spencer, Ashley 106, 108
Spencer, Callum 219
Spencer, Cody 78, 139
Spencer, Jonathan 28, 74, 109
Spencer, Rebecca Erwin

88
Spengler, Melissa 28, 183
Sperling, Ted 244
Speyer, Michael 47, 50, 95
Speyerer, Charlene 89
Spicer, Zachary 57, 221
Spider-Man Turn Off the Dark 10, 28 115, 118
Spiegel, Howard 419
Spiegel, Sam 148
Spiegelman, Eric 185
Spiegelworld: Empire 187
Spier, David 97
Spin Cycle 163, 170, 173, 177, 197
Spina, Joanie 75
Spina, Lucia 116, 132
Spinac, Rebecca 70, 167
Spindle, Les 442
Spinella, Stephen 114, 123, 237, 420
Spinello, Shanna 190
Spinetti, Victor 418
Sping Fling: My Best/ Worst Date Ever, The 287
Spinney, Corey 75
Spinozza, David 83
Spiotto, Bob 142
Spiriling Into Place 300
Spirito, Joseph 167
Spirtas, Kevin 106
Spitaliere, Daniel 241, 242
Spitfire Grill, The 377
Spitulnik, Brian 93
Spivey, Aaron 92, 187
Splain, Tim 209
Splatter Pattern 310
Spleen Theatre 316
Splinter Group, The 192
Splintered Soul, A 274
Spohnheimer, Deb 235
Sponseller, Trevor 44
Spore, Heather 111
Sposito, Stephen 95, 217
SpotCo 32, 35, 36, 43, 54, 56, 57, 58, 60, 68, 70, 72, 75, 80, 81, 85, 87, 88, 89, 92, 94
Spradley, Shayla 185
Spring Awakening 388, 396
Spring Tides 278, 315
Springer Associates 74, 130, 135, 137, 139, 146, 148, 157, 162, 173, 191, 200, 201
Springer, Gary 74, 191

Springer, Hope 369
Spry, James 45, 125
Spunk: Three Tales 358
Spybey, Dina 420
Squared, Greg 184
Squeaky Bicycle Productions 317
Squealer 296
Squerciati, Marina 129
Squire, Rosemary 36
Squire, Theresa 135, 151, 156, 208, 221, 230, 258
Squitero, Roger 106
Squiterri, Akia 189, 444
St. Ann's Warehouse 148, 151, 160, 168, 173, 178
St. Clair Bayfield Award 437
St. Germain, Mark 191
St. James Theatre 32, 50, 82
St. Luke's Theatre 127, 142, 149, 150, 175, 184, 189, 190, 193
St. Martin, Charlotte 422
St. Pierre, Derek 113
Staab, M. Florian 174, 185, 218-222, 224, 226, 254
Stabile, Bill 129
Stableized Not Controlled 286
Stack, Andy 247
Stack, Kate 182, 241, 242
Stackle, Steve 101
Stadelmeier-Tresco, Therese 202
Stadlen, Lewis J. 104, 418
Staebell, Christopher 140
Stafford, Nick 110
Stafford, Tina 263
Stage Director and Choreographers (SDC) Foundation Awards 446
Stage Entertainment 109
Stage Ventures Ltd. Partnership 47, 50, 95
StageLeft Studio 317
Stages on the Sound 317
Stages St. Louis 399
Stahel, Michal 212
Stahl, David 67
Stahl, Diana 249
Stair, Marie 222
Stajmiger, Tom 112
Stalker, Naomi 176

Staller, David 221
Stallings, Courtney 184
Stallings, Lawrence 90
Stamatiades, Flora 409, 410
Stamm, Kurt 264
Stampley, Nathaniel 54, 55
Stanczyk, Laura 33, 81, 170, 199
Standing CO Vation 78
Standing On Ceremony: The Gay Marriage Plays 155
Stanek, Jim 125, 191, 265
Stanek, Steph 175
Stang, Eric 136
Stanilav, Tereza 199
Stanislavskaya, Katya 136, 163, 164, 182, 183
Stanisz, Ryan 90, 109
Stanko, Joe 235
Stanley, Elizabeth 117, 216
Stanley, Gordon 152
Stanley, Heather 246
Stanley, Kim 417
Stanois, Valerie 108
Stanton, Ben 45, 177, 208, 227, 228, 242, 246, 249, 256, 261
Stanton, Phil 189
Stanton, Robert 248
Stapleton, Maureen 417
Stapleton, Sunneva 249
Stappenbeck, Stefanie 210
Star Medicine, The 295
Starbucks 410
Stares, Lindsay 232
Starevich, Halina 129
Stark, Tracy 443
Star-Ledger 409
Starmer, Cat Tate 181
St-Arnaud, Mathieu 107
Staroba, Paul 226, 227, 253
Starobin, Michael 82, 104, 116, 153, 254
Staroselsky, Dennis 230, 268
Starr, Crystal 87
Starr, Josh 155, 160, 194
Starr, Meghan 113
Starr, Nick 72, 110
Stas&Stas 317
Stasio, Marilyn 429
Stasz/Pruitt Productions 317
Statement of Randolph

Carter 311
Staub, Joanna Lynne 67, 94, 98, 410
Staudenmayer, Ed 149
Stazewski, Mary 222
Steady Rain, A 396
Stebbins, Mary Ellen 164
Stebbins, Paul 235
Steckel, Chris 254
Ste-Croix, Gilles 129
Steel Magnolias 386
Steel, Liam 75
Steele, James C. 72, 237, 243
Steele, Lucas 163, 164
Steele, Ryan 64, 89
Steele, Sarah 225, 230
Steelman, Larry 143
Steeves, Finnerty 207
Stefaniuk, John 99
Stefano, Georgio 155
Stefany & Simon Bergson Foundation 410
Steffen, David B. 35, 56, 85, 96, 116, 251
Steggert, Bobby 200, 242, 421
Stegman, Beth 209
Stegmeier, Wilheim 248
Steiger, Rick 110
Stein, Billy Jay 29
Stein, Elisa Loti 410, 418
Stein, Jared 32
Stein, Joan 92, 155, 243
Stein, Tobie S. 422
Steinbeck, John 216
Steinberg New Play Award and Citations 430
Steinberg New Works Program (LCT3) 225
Steinberg Playwright Award 446
Steinberg, Nevin 70
Steiner, Daniela 233
Steiner, Rick 97
Steinfeld, Ben 141
Steingold, Dana 115
Steinhagen, Natasha 31, 42, 57
Steinkellner, Bill 109
Steinkellner, Cheri 109
Steinman, Amy 59
Steinmetz, Samantha 170
Steinmeyer, Jim 101
Steinthal, Robin 33, 37
Stella Den Haag 232
Stella Rising 238
Stella, Tim 105

Stellard, Johnny 68
Stelzenmuller, Craig 52, 254
Stenborg, Derek 128
Stenborg, Jackson 158
Stenhouse, Gavin 214
Stenka, Danuta 178
Stephen Joseph Theatre 158
Stephen Sondheim Theatre 85, 116
Stephens, Amanda 40, 70, 242
Stephens, Caitlin Savlor 149
Stephens, J. Paul 410
Stephens, James A. 112
Stephens, Katy 197
Stephens, Ruthie 125
Stephens, Simon 208
Stephens, Ted, III 263
Stephens, Toby 420
Stephenson, Hunter 170
Stephenson, Mia 124
Stephenson, Regina 132
Steppenwolf Theatre Company 388, 400
Sterkel, Jay 255, 256
Sterman, Andrew 109
Stern, Abbi 193
Stern, David J. 70
Stern, James D. 82, 196
Stern, Kimberly 132
Stern, Matthew Aaron 46, 87
Stern, Peter 71
Stern, Richard J. 82
Stern, Sarah 261
Sternbach, Stu 146
Sternberg, Ruth E. 244
Sternberg, Taylor 97, 113
Steven A. & Marianne M Mills Charitable Foundation 410
Stevens, Barney 235
Stevens, Connie 418
Stevens, Fisher 94
Stevens, Jesse 50
Stevens, Oren 147
Stevens, Scott T. 115, 117, 118, 198, 202
Stevens, Tony 469
Stevens, Warren 469
Stevenson, Scott 419
Stevenson, Gerda 176
Stevenson, Jeffrey C. 182
Stew 248
Stewart, Dave 75
Stewart, Donna 179
Stewart, Duncan 93
Stewart, Ellen 419

Stewart, Glenn M. 179
Stewart, Jamie 74
Stewart, John 417
Stewart, Kyle 28
Stewart, Louis 238
Stewart, Molly Winter 113
Stewart, Patrick 200
Stewart, Paul Anthony 104, 262
Stick Fly 15, 49
Stifelman, Leslie 93, 115, 118
Stiff, Barclay 57, 81, 94
Stiles, Danny 83, 109
Stiles, Diane 152, 167
Stiles, George 101
Stiles, Jesse 213
Stiles, Sarah 50
Stilgoe, Richard 105
Still Getting My Act Together 265
Still, Peter John 224
Stiller, Ben 94
Stiller, Jerry 426
Stillman, Bob 164
Stillman, Darin 54, 86
Stillman, Robert 191
Stillwell, Denise 192
Stillwell, Esther 106
Stillwell, Kelly 224
Stimler, Nick 47
Stimson, Brendon 64
Stine, Matt 133
StinkyKids the Musical 276, 322
Stinton, Colin 419
Stiverson, Felicity 118
St-Lean, Raymond 129
Stock, Chelsea Morgan 87, 109
Stockbridge, Gregory 113, 194
Stocke, Matthew 118
Stockler, Michael 200
Stocklynn, Jack 234
Stockman, Theo 230, 268
Stockton, Kendra 40
Stoeke, Shannon 160
Stoessel, Lisi 142
Stokely, Hannah 214
Stoker, Olivia 163
Stokes, Anjeanette 136, 182
Stokes, Matt 62, 63
Stokes, Tilly 214
Stolber, Dean 106
Stolen Chair Theater 317
Stoll, Alex Michael 68
Stolle, Jeremy 105
Stoller, Amy 229, 239,

240
Stoller, Barbara 38, 54
Stoller, David 38, 54
Stoller, Mike 104
Stoller, Molly 125
Stollings, David 59
Stoltz, Eric 419
Stomp 196
Stone Soup 297
Stone, Adam 180
Stone, Amber 221
Stone, Chad 113
Stone, Charles 45, 60
Stone, Dan 155
Stone, Daryl 72
Stone, Daryl A. 75
Stone, David 111, 424
Stone, Elly 459
Stone, Jay 195
Stone, Jessica 85
Stone, Leonard 469
Stone, Matt 90, 202, 253
Stone, Yael 234
Stonefield, Samuel 164
Stop the Silence 175
Stop the Virgens 148
Stoppard, Tom 86
Stopped Bridge of Dreams 295
Storefront Church 209, 268
Storm Theatre 309, 317
Storm, The 278
Story Pirates 202
Story Sound Records 247
Stotts, Michael 243
Stout, Marilyn 106
Stout, Stephen 163
Stovall, Count 74
Stowe, Dennis 83
Straatemeier, Kim 28
Strachan, Nova 127
Strafford, Steven 160, 265
Stram, Henry 141
Strand, Mark 74
Strange and Separate People, A 134
Strange Cargo 306
Strange Fruit 155
Strange Interlude 398
Strangfeld, Jason 95
Strano, Kevin 222
Strasberg, Susan 417, 418
Strasser, Robin 192
Strassheim, Michael 33, 58, 78, 94, 106, 113
Stratford Shakespeare Festival 62, 96
Strathairn, David 352

Strathie, Angus 187
Stratis, Neophytos 155
Stratton, Daniel 233
Stratton, Jay 121, 158
Strauchn, Biti 52, 124
Strausser, Frank 165
Stravinsky, Igor 219
Strawberry One-Act Festival 338
Strawbridge, Stephen 255
Streby, Lee 184
Strecker, Worth 54
Streep, Meryl 419, 441
Street, Carly 73
Streetcar Named Desire, A 22, 74
Streit, Clifford 173
Strelitz, Samantha 249
Stresen-Reuter, Ned 47, 253
Stribling, Barak 202
Stricklyn, Ray 417
Stride, John 418
Strike Anywhere Performance Ensemble 168
Strimaitis, Rebecca 115
Strimel, Sarrah 92, 113
Strindberg: Mad Modern Master Plays 306
Stritch, Billy 201
Stritch, Elaine 202
Strole, Phoebe 242
Stroman, Susan 39, 224
Stromberg, Anna 138
Strone, Joshua 409
Strong, Allison 100
Strong, Edward 97
Strother, Frederick 33
Stroum, Cynthia 47
Strunsky, Jean 54
Strunsky, Michael 54
Struxness, Betsy 83, 102
Stryker-Rodda, Andrea 235
Stuart Thompson Productions 59, 90, 94, 98, 103
Stuart, Hanah 244
Stuart, Laura 104
Stuart, Mark 112, 113
Stuart, Molly Wright 207
Stubbs, Imogen 447
Stuckey, Jack 93
Studio 54 74, 104
Studio Canal 89
Studio Theatre on Theatre Row 134, 174
Stuhr, Greg 73
Stumpf, Berit 246
Stunich, Debra 173

Sturdivant, William 176
Sturgis, Nisi 137
Sturiale, Brandon 152, 209
Sturm, F.P. 238
Sturm, Jason 149
Sturm, Rolf 168
Sturm, Samantha 78, 84
Sturminger, Michael 212
Sturnam, Josh 255
Sturrup, Randolph 74
Stuttmann, Robert 84
Styne, Jule 46, 159, 217
Stys, Mark A. 64
Su, Wenhua 232
Su, Yushi 232
Subias, Mark 148
Subietas, Anthony 170
Subjective Theatre Company 317
Sublett, Robbie Collier 39, 177
Submission, The 226
Subotnick, Jacob 147
Subotnick, Stuart 410
Suc, Thierry 106
Suddenly Last Summer 322, 403
Suddeth, J. Allen 64, 141, 260
Sudduth, Skipp 202
Sues, Alan 469
Suffer the Brink of Us 303
Suga, Shigeko Sara 238
Sugarhouse at the Edge of the Wilderness, The 156
Sugarman, David 112, 115, 118, 198
Sugarman, Merri 43, 62, 75
Sugg, Jeff 38, 70, 169
Suh, Hong Seok 198
Suicide, Incorporated 252
Suisse, Brandon 230
Sulka, Tim 97
Sullivan, Arthur 235
Sullivan, Chris 78, 93
Sullivan, Daniel 31, 39, 42, 57, 80, 224, 244, 447
Sullivan, Daniel Robert 239, 264
Sullivan, Deb 143
Sullivan, J.R. 239, 240
Sullivan, James 166
Sullivan, Jamie Lynne 208, 209, 252
Sullivan, Jay 98
Sullivan, KT 112, 265
Sullivan, Matt 155

Sullivan, Nick 64
Sullivan, Pat 107
Sullivan, Rachel 148
Sullivan, Rory 152
Sullivan, Shea 116
Sullivan, Susan 192
Sullivan, Timothy 117, 118
Summa, Don 91, 124, 134, 139, 153, 236, 250
Summerhays, Jane 352
Sumner, Elly 240
Sumner, Jarid 35-37, 46, 49, 56, 58, 59, 60, 73, 75, 77, 81, 90, 109, 185
Sun, Gloria 49
Sun, Nilaja 126, 420
Sun, Pearl 216
Sunai, Annie 77
Sunday in the Park with George 379, 396
Sunday on the Rocks 315
Sunderlin, Stephen 125, 195
Sundown 186
Sundquist, Erick L. 227
Sung, Milim 255
Sunjata, Daniel 420
Sunset Boulevard 384
Sunset Limited, The 353, 357
Sunshine Boys, The 376
Sunshine, Eylsa 136, 182
Sunshine, Ken 28, 106
Sunshine, Sachs & Associates 28
Supeck, Steve 92
Superior Donuts 373
Supernatural Wife 212
Surfdog Records 76
Surovy, Nicolas 418
Surrey, Sara 229
Susan McKey 360
Susan S. Channing Trust 410
Susan Smith Blackburn Prize 447
Suskin, Steven 429
Susman, Todd 185
Sussman, Darren 145
Susurrus 381
Sutcliffe, Steven 420
Sutherland, Michael 201
Sutton, Adrian 110
Sutton, Charlie 52, 84, 92, 95, 113, 216
Sutton, Eric T. 94
Sutton, Holly 131, 133
Sutton, Maia 87

Suveren, Ayla 246
Suyama, Y. Darius 43
Suzanne Hylenski 33
Suzuki, Pat 417
Suzuki, Tadashi 162
Swain, Bara 206
Swamp Gas and Shallow Feelings 356
Swan, Michael 130
Swanberg, Sara 240, 244, 246, 247
Swann, Phillip 143
Swanson, Margaret E. 410
Swartz, Marlene 189, 258
Sweany, Erica 146
Swee, Daniel 39, 110, 214, 224
Sweeney, Adrian 158
Sweeney, Virginia 130
Sweet and Sad 247
Sweet Thursday 216
Sweeter Dreams 284
Sweetman, Ashley 143
SweetPea Productions 317
Swenson, Inga 417
Swenson, Jesse 84
Swenson, Swen 418
Swenson, Will 106, 198, 202
Swerling, Jo 207
Swift, Michael 138, 148
Swimm, Jesse 101, 115, 118, 202
Swimming in the Shallows 281
Swinburne, Algernon Charles 238
Swing, Maggie 225, 247, 248, 255
Swinsky, Mort 84
Swinston, Robert 213
Swit, Loretta 192
Switser, Austin 108
Switser, Sky 33
Swoboda, Pat 152
Swope, G. Benjamin 209
Sword in the Stone, The 396
Sydney Festival 214
Sykes, Ephraim 64, 102, 140
Sylvia 397
Sylvia, Dan 159
Symphony for the Dance Floor 211
Symphony Space 200, 202, 235
Synthlink LLC 92
Syracuse Stage 389, 401

Syrmis, Victor 82, 177
Szadkowski, Zuzanna 192
Szaflarska, Danuta 178
Szcz niak, Małgorzata 178
Szolovits, Lisa 248
Szor, Terry 235
Szot, Paulo 201, 421
Szu-Chen, Lin 211
Szucs, Nicholas 235
Szymanski, Rachel 229
Szymko, Joan 233

T
T. Schreiber Studio 317
Tabassomi, Yashi 210
Tabeck, James 101, 113, 118
Tabisel, Brett 420
Table Scene, The 303
Table, The 295
Tabnick, Michelle 136, 178
Tabori, Kristoffer 418
Taccone, Tony 211, 443
Tackett, Caren Lyn 32
TADA! Youth Theater 318
Tafti, Babak 352
Tagert, Ron 28
Taggart, Christopher 59, 90
Taguchi, Hiroko 76, 84
Taichman, Rebecca 241, 262
Tait, Jenefer 214
Takacs, Katie 193, 249
Takahashi, Choei 197
Takahashi, Kenichi 242
Takaoka, Sousuke 197
Take What Is Yours 184, 301
Take Wing and Soar Productions 318
Takeda, Mioi 184
Takei, George 117
Tal, Ron 112
Talbott, Daniel 249, 250, 258, 444
Talbott, Jeff 226
Talbott, Jonathan 164
Tale of Frankenstein's Daughter 311
Tale of Two Cities, A 355
Talenfeld, Greg 245
TalkinBroadway.com 409
Talking Band, The 318
Talking Cure 37
Talking Heads 219
Tall Tales Theatre Company 318

Talley, Jessica Disbrow 190
Talley's Folly 360, 371
Tallmer, Jerry 426
Tallon, Robert 188
Talluto, Ashley 125
Tally, Ted 132
Talmadge, Elizabeth M. 38, 72
Tam, Jason 52, 124
Tamagwa, Michelle 102
Tambor, Carol 161
Taming of the Shrew, The 260, 367, 375
Tammi, Marilynn 161
Tamny, Amanda 64
Tams, John 110
Tamura, Ikkou 197
Tan, Dollar 28, 29
Tan, Layhoon 156, 255
Tan, Victor En Yu 239
Tanaka, Anne 28
Tancredi, Liz 163
Tandem Otter Productions 145
Tang, Huiyuan 232
Tang, Liu 211
Tang-Li, Hou 211
Tangredi, Frank 206
Tanji, Lydia 189
Tann, Robbie 233
Tanski, Jeff 47
Tape 294
Tapia, Sheila 208
Tara Rubin Casting 43, 62, 75
Tarantina, Brian 419
Taranto, Joey 28, 29
Tarasova, Ekaterina 215
Taratino, Mary 443
Tarazuka!! 282
Tardy, Jeremy J. 138
Tarján, Gábor 232
Tarpey, Emily 189
Tarr, Frances 208
Tarragona 323
Tartaglia, Jack 47
Tartaglia, John 192, 420
Tartick, Steven 40
Tarzan: The Stage Musical 353, 356
Tassé, Bruno 137
Tatad, Robert 108, 135
Tatarowicz, Roman 148, 173
Tate, Kendra 89
Tate, Mandy 74, 143, 151, 177
Tatoyan, Sona 250
Tatum, Marianne 409, 410, 419
Taub, Shaina K. 149
Tavares, Sonia 213

Taylor, Alaina 242, 248
Taylor, Alex 244, 247, 248
Taylor, Andy 60, 236
Taylor, Bill 109
Taylor, Brian 118
Taylor, Christian Chadd 141, 169, 259
Taylor, Clifton 191
Taylor, Deborah 36, 72
Taylor, Elizabeth 197, 419
Taylor, Holly 89
Taylor, Jamie 231
Taylor, Jen 44, 67, 77, 101
Taylor, Jonah 368
Taylor, Jonathan 187
Taylor, L. Steven 99
Taylor, Lili 149, 223
Taylor, Lucy 236
Taylor, Lynnette 409
Taylor, Matthew 185
Taylor, Millie 145
Taylor, Myra Lucretia 192
Taylor, Patricia 262
Taylor, Philip 428
Taylor, Regina 255
Taylor, Scott 50, 116
Taylor, Tom 126, 250, 258
Taylor, Wesley 409, 412, 421
Taymor, Danya 28, 259, 260
Taymor, Julie 28, 99, 202
Tazewell, Paul 62, 70, 74, 102
TBG Theater 149
TBS Service 95, 103, 136
Teachout, Terry 429
TeaCup Productions 318
Teague-Daniels, Danielle 177
Tear, Peter 154-160
Teatro Patological Festival 295
TeatroStageFest 183
Tebelak, John-Michael 40
Tech Production Services 45, 78, 97, 104, 108
Tecklenburg, Nina 246
Tectonic Theater Project 155
Ted Mozino Productions 318
Tedesco, Amie 222
Tedmon-Jones, Scott 134

Teeley, Tom 107
Tees, John 253, 254
Teeter, Jeff 87
Teller 460
Telsey + Company 28, 38, 40, 47, 54, 64, 66, 68, 70, 74, 82, 84, 87, 92, 102, 103, 104, 106, 108, 109, 113, 136, 139, 208, 226, 241, 243, 255, 262, 362
Telsey, Bernard 40, 111, 226
Temperley, Joe 199
Tempest Entertainmant 213
Tempest, The 358, 361, 372, 373, 389
Temple of the Golden Pavilion, The 197
Temple of the Souls 300
Temporal Powers 229
Ten Cents a Dance 383
Ten Chimneys 365. 386
ten Haaf, Jochum 420
Ten Tall Tales About the Men I Love 321
Ten Years Productions 318
Tenderpits 273
Tenement Street Workshop 318
Tenenbaum, Lara 187
Tenenbaum, Natalie 137
Tennen, Robert 235
Tennent, David 182
Tennessen, Nora 28
Tennie, Matt 166
Teolis, Kara M. 195
Tepe, Heather 89
Tepper, Jennifer Ashley 40
Terentieva, Masha 129
Teresa's Ecstasy 171
Tergesen, Lee 242
Terkel, Paul 138, 139
Terracio, Nate 187
Terrano, Richard 410
terraNOVA Collective 319
Terren, Elisa 156
Terrible Plop, The 234
Terrio, Deney 250
Territories 310
Terry, Alden 164
Terry, Beatrice 82, 102, 469
Terry, Cory 189
Terry, Lee 126, 148
Terwilliger, Kate 58
Terzetto LLC 190
Teschner, Kristina 222
Tessero, Jonathan 77

Testa, Mary 121, 140, 153
Testerman, Sarah 112
Tetlow, George 31, 42, 57, 80, 227
Tétreault, Samuel 138
Tevelow, Ben 143
Tevyaw, Robert 107
Tewksbury, Stephen 105
Thacker, Russ 418, 420
Thake, Shanta 244
Thaler, Jordan 32, 38, 103, 244
Thalken, Joseph 266
Thane, James 64, 101
Tharp, Katherine Gloria 166
That Beautiful Laugh 295
That's Life Again 371
Thau, Harold 66
Thayer, Greg 245, 247
Theater 167 320
Theater 2020 319
Theater Antigone 232
Theater Artemis 232
Theater at Madison Square Garden 159
Theater Breaking Through Barriers 178
Theater for the New City 319
Theater Hall of Fame 447
Theater Hall of Fame Founders Award 448
Theater IATI 149
Theater Mogul 132
Theater of the Arcade 279
Theater Resources Unlimited 320
Theater Three Collaborative 320
TheaterMania.com 409, 424
TheaterSmarts 320
Theatre 80 St. Marks 120, 132, 175, 195
Theatre 808 133
Theatre at 45 Bleecker 120, 159, 165, 177, 195
Theatre at St. Clement's 128, 157, 172, 187
Theatre at St. Peter's Church 263-267
Théâtre de la Place 210
Théâtre de Namur 210
Theatre Development Fund Awards 447
Theatre Exile 147
Theatre for a New

Audience 141, 259
Theatre in a VAN! 320
Theatre Management Associates 146
Théâtre Nanterre-Amandiers 199
Theatre Project, The 321
Theatre Royal Bath 44, 215
Theatre Venture Inc. 74
Theatre World Awards 409-421
TheatreDreams North America LLC 62
Theatreworks USA 135
Theatrical Services Inc. 107
Thelin, Johanna 130
Theodore, Donna 419
Theodorou, Andy 182, 184, 200
Theodosis, Georgia 46
These Seven Sicknesses 163
Theus, Alejandra 232
the-ʊ-roject 295
Thibodeau, Keri 56, 127, 217
Thibodeau, Marc 40, 45, 84, 105, 129, 218, 241
Thielking, Christopher 218, 219, 246-248
Thieme, Jörg 210
Thieriot, Richard 73, 207
Thies, Jeremiah 148
Thieves 273
Thirds 291
Thirlby, Olivia 253
This Flight Tonight 155
This Is For You 279
This is Not the Play 298
This Verse Business 383
Thom Fogarty Presents 309, 321
Thom, C.J., III 193
Thom, Sarah 246
Thomas, Baylen 86
Thomas, Brenna C. 236
Thomas, Carlos 196
Thomas, Cheryl 82
Thomas, Daniel 129, 145
Thomas, Danny 262
Thomas, David 32, 70, 103
Thomas, Dylan 220
Thomas, Eddie Kaye 226
Thomas, Fiona 64
Thomas, Jack 191
Thomas, John 159, 235
Thomas, Julius, III 54, 55

Thomas, Marlo 11, 37
Thomas, Marty 193
Thomas, Matthew James 28
Thomas, Natalie 196
Thomas, Patrice 211
Thomas, Richard 155, 200
Thomas, Sebastian 106
Thomas, Sherry 97
Thompson, Aaron 147, 164
Thompson, Adam J. 167
Thompson, Allison Carter 189
Thompson, April Yvette 73
Thompson, Ben 140, 226, 267
Thompson, Bradley 191
Thompson, Brian 106
Thompson, Christopher 162
Thompson, Danielle 173
Thompson, David 93
Thompson, Emelie Faith 437
Thompson, Heather 38
Thompson, Hilary Michael 43
Thompson, Jared 189
Thompson, Jason 87, 97
Thompson, Jenn 207
Thompson, Jennifer Joan 251
Thompson, Jennifer Laura 78
Thompson, John Douglas 246
Thompson, Kristie 111
Thompson, Larry A. 58
Thompson, Louisa 247, 258
Thompson, Mark 49, 71, 72, 100
Thompson, Nic 101
Thompson, Nicholas 160
Thompson, Ryder 218
Thompson, Stuart 59, 90, 94, 98, 103, 185
Thompson, Trance 175, 194
Thoms, Tracie 15, 49
Thomson, Lynn M. 139
Thomson, Sandy 175
Thorell, Clarke 100, 217
Thorn, Clif 162
Thorne, Jack 154
Thorne, Sean M. 226, 245
Thorne, Stephen 389

Thorne, Wells 135
Thorpe, Ben 130
Thorson, Linda 419
Thorsson, Bryn 236
Thousand Clowns, A 358
Thousand Stars Productions 68
Thrasher, Mark 59, 64, 95
Three British Solos 154
Three Pianos 350
Three Seagulls, or MashaMashaMasha!, The 291
Three Sheets 279
Three Sisters 215, 315, 400, 403
threeASFOUR 211
Threepenny Opera, The 210
Thrill of the Chase, The 298
Thrower, Antoine 179
Thru the Stage Door 192
Thun, Nancy 97, 100
Thunder Knocking on the Door 364
Thurber, Lucy 183, 226
Thurber, Robert V. 207
Thureen, Paul 258
Thymius, Greg 83, 104, 116
Thys, Benjamin 196, 245
Tichenor, Austin 231
Tichler, Rosemarie 422, 428
Tieming, Cai 211
Tien, Melisa 263
Tierney, Christopher W. 28
Tierney, Marie 134
Tierney, Matt 236, 247, 250, 258
Tierney, Paula 198
Tietz, Holger 211
Tietze, Larry 235
Tiffany, John 60, 236
Tiffin, Pamela 418
Tigáná, André 233
Tigers Be Still 365, 366
Tiggeloven, John 62
Tighe, Kelly James 183
Tighe, Susanne 46, 62, 97, 185
Tilkin, Howie 261
Tilley, Bobby Frederick, II 251
Tilley, Jillian 81
Tilli, Tony 33
Tillinger, John 81
Tillmanns, Nora 70, 75

Tilly, Jennifer 81, 420
Timbers, Alex 71, 91
Time of Your Life, The 274
Time Out New York 409
Time Out NY Lounge 200
Time Stands Still 360, 366, 377, 400
Times Square International Theatre Festival 339
TimeWontWait 154
Timm, Rosita 152
Timmons, Wendy 146
Timon of Athens 364
Timpo, Awoye 255
Tin Bucket Drum 292
Tin Pan Alley 172
Tindall, Don 167
Ting, Liuh-Wen 55
Tiny Lights: Memory's Storehouse/Infinite Miniature 301
Tiny Theater 2011 280
Tiplady, Neil 196
Tiplady, Steve 197
Tipton, Jennifer 247, 259
'Tis Pity She's a Whore 214
Tisdale, Christianne 50
Tisdale, Jordan 138
Titcomb, Gordon 47
Titizian, Hrach 88
Title and Deed 256
[title of show] 386
Titley, Brendan 245
Titone, Richard 235
Titus Andronicus 248
Tiwary, Vivek 84
Tix Productions 107
Tkach, Davida 62, 252
To Kill a Kelpie 175
To Kill a Mockingbird 354, 367
To the Ones I Love 210
Toase, Suzie 72
Toback, Jordana 211
Toben, Paul 50, 78, 85, 131
Tobia, Julie 44, 92
Tobias, Ashley 154
Tobias, Michelle 173
Tobin, Becca 108
Tobler, Greg 127
Toblini, Fabio 154, 232
Toboloski, Nicky 216
Todd, David 186
Todd, John J. 160
Todorov, Entcho 90
Togrimson, Kristen 75
Toibin, Fiana 229

Toisuta, Michael 234
Tokarsky, Phillip 260
Tokio Confidential 164
Tokunaga, Yasuko 181
Tolan, Barbara 198
Tolan, Cindy 37, 52, 124, 185, 188
Tolan, RJ 150
Tolchin Family, The 40
Toles, Bill 152
Tollefsen, Elise 33
Tolpegin, Anne 227, 268
Tomaszewski, Tadeusz 178
Tomei, Concetta 192
Tomei, Marisa 419
Tomei, Paula 262
Tomfoolery 265
Tomkins, Steve 152
Tone, Una 33, 83, 112
Toneelgroep Amsterdam 211
Tongue in Cheek Theater 321
Tonke, Laura 246
Tony Awards 422
Too Much Light Makes the Baby Go Blind 302
Too Much Too Soon 269, 296, 319
Toogood, Melissa 213
Toombs, Jeffrey 222
Topdog/Underdog 399
Topol, Daniella 156, 262
Topol, Richard 104, 228, 246
Toporov, Pavel 215
Topper, Jenny 67
Torchia, Tiia E. 241, 242
Toress, Luis 244-248
Torgrimson, Kristen 35, 252
Torn, Rip 417
Torns, Stephanie 111
Toro, Natalie 135
Torre, Frank 155
Torres, Carmen 145
Torres, Daniel 68
Torres, John 165
Torres, Juan 40
Torres, Judy 193
Torres, Wilson 52
Torya 99
Toser, David 135, 137, 207, 220
Tosetti, Sara 40, 74, 85, 172
Tosevski, Kire 173
Tosto, Michael 72
Total Bent, The 248
Totero, Lolly 33, 66, 92
Toth, Paul J. 107
Touchette, Yves 138

Touchstone Pictures 109
Toups, Stephanie 115
Tour Group Ltd 159
Toussaint, Germono 149
Tovar, Brian 142, 202
Town Hall 201, 424
Townsend, Justin 218, 241, 262
Townsend, Robert J. 179
Toxic Avenger, The 341, 348
Toy Box Theatre Company 321
Toy Maker's Apprentice, The 306
Toy, Barbara 428
Toye, Teddy 16, 52, 124
TR Warszawa 178
Traber, Maximillian 60
Traces 120, 137
Tracey Miller & Associates 135
Tracey, Mike 181
Trachtenberg, Michelle 223
Trachtman, Anna 117
Tracking Productions 232
Tracy, John 418
Traditional Wedding, A 155
Trafton, Juliette 190
Tragedy of Maria Macabre, The 277, 311
Traherne, James 197
Train Driver, The 255
Trammel, Sam 420
Tramontozzi, Daniel 92
Transport Group 52, 119, 121, 124, 134, 153
Traoré, Rokia 199
Trapp, Doug 132
Trarbach, Walter 62, 92, 140, 153, 192
Trask, Stephen 199
Traugott, Scott 100
Travelers 184
Travers, P.L. 101
Travesties 383
Travis, Benjamin C. 90, 113
Travis, Ken 64, 102, 128, 230
Traxler, Steve 84
Treasures 315
Treat, Aaron 244-248
Treaton, Kenneth 49, 94
Treehouse Theatre Company 321
Treherne, Nichola 100
Treider, Hayley 233
Tremblay, Line 129

Trensch, Taylor 111, 140, 353
Trentacosta, Joe 74, 130, 137, 139, 143, 146, 148, 157, 162, 166, 173, 191, 200, 201
Trentinella, Anthony 132
Trépanier, Philippe 130
Trepiana, Adolfo Maria 234
Trepinski, Christopher 175
Trepp, Jâlé 68
Trepp, Warren 68, 92
Trese, Adam 230
Trese, Jane 410
Trester, Erik 253
Tretiakov, Vladimir 215
Tretiakova, Svetlana 215
Treusdale, Veneda 90
Trevellini, John 206
Trevigne, Talise 202
Trezza, Mark 78, 92
Triad, The 162
Triano, Tony 158
Tribbey, Amy 66
Tribe Theatricals 84
Tribes 121, 169, 406, 409
Tribute (Forget Me Not) 293
Trice, Will 54, 66
Tricks the Devil Taught Me 140
Trieckel, Sarah 236
Trieschmann, Catherine 262, 448
Trifles and *Hughie* 271, 281
Trigg, Dave 63, 92
Trimble, Deborah Anne 231
Trimble, Grace 183, 258
Trinchero, Brisa 47, 54, 71
Triner, James 72
Trinidad, Kay 112
Trinity Repertory Company 389, 401
Trinkoff, Donna 132
Trinrud, Nate 233
Trip to Bountiful, The 398
Tripp, Rickey 113
Troika Entertainment 64
Troisi, Louis 28, 99
Trojan Women, The 322
Troilus and Cressida 391
Tron Theatre Company 176
Troob, Danny 43, 64, 84

Trost, Bastian 246
Trost, Steven 116
Trouble- a new pop/rock Musical 314
Trouble in Mind 354
Troughton, Sam 197
Troutman, Tara 146
Trow, Andrew 208
Trsek, Thomas 212
TRU Voices New Musicals Reading Series 313
Truax, Keith A. 124, 146
Trubitt, Jason 101, 109, 112, 115, 118
True Love Productions 185
True Story of the 3 Little Pigs!, The 209
True, Evan 130
Trujillo, Sergio 82, 84, 97, 102
Truman, Araina Smart 236, 247
Truman, Joe 222
Trumble, Madeline 64
Trump, Ivana 197
Trupp, Ryan 98
Truppin-Brown, Ben 208, 229, 237, 243, 225, 261
Truskinoff, David 32
Truth 324
Truvillion, Tobias 189
Tsao, Jim 76
Tsay, Jennifer 409
Tschirpke, Sarah 187
Tshabalala, Jabulile 130
Tsivanoglou, Georgios 210
Tsoutsouvas, Sam 219
Tsuji, Yukio 239
Tsypin, George 28
Tubbs, Premik Russell 167
Tubbs, Shaun Patrick 186
Tucci, Louis 264
Tucci, Maria 170
Tucker, Catherine Anne 142
Tucker, Dion 50
Tucker, Eric 170
Tucker, James 197
Tucker, Jeffrey 184
Tucker, Scott 72
Tucker, Sheldon 113
Tudo Isto É Fado 213
Tudor, David 213
Tudyk, Alan 420
Tuft, Diane 116
Tuft, Tom 116
Tulchin, Alice 98

Tulchin, Norman 54, 214
Tulchin, Steven 103
Tulipomania 351
Tulloch, Richard 234
Tulpa, or Anna&Me 284
Tuminelly, Katie 245
Tunick, Jonathan 33, 216
Tunie, Tamara 70
Tunison, Wesley 125, 154
Tunnnel Vision 301
Tuomi, Bret 108
Tupikin, Igor 215
Turn of the Screw, The 401
Turnbull, Kate 222
Turner, Charles M., III 225, 241, 261
Turner, David 15, 50, 59, 86, 90, 98
Turner, Grant 89
Turner, Greg 253
Turner, Jenny 154
Turner, Joseph 344
Turner, Kathleen 419
Turner, Madison 276
Turner, Natalie 99
Turner, Philip W. 99
Turner, Will 163
Turning Star Inc. 50
Turns, Ali 152
Turteltaub, Lindsey 33, 212, 237
Turton, Neil 94
Turturro, John 37, 218, 419
Tushan, Wei 211
Tuszewicz, Andrzej 178
Tuszy ska, Agnieszka 178
Tutalo, John 37, 78, 103
Tutors, The 275
Tveit, Aaron 92, 198
Twain, Mark 233
Twaine, Michael 135
Twelfth Night 296, 312, 403
Twelfth Night: Wall Street 282
Twiggs, Mckayla 60
Twilight: The Musical 201
Twining, Janine 233
Twining, Lily 28
Twist - An American Musical 392
Twist, Basil 84, 145
Two Gentlemen of Verona, The 278, 284, 314, 398
Two Intimate: The

Lover and *Eden* 281
Two Jews Walk Into a War 356, 374
Two Left Feet Productions 95
Two Rivers Theater 389, 402
Two Shall Meet 313
Two Sheps That Pass... 177
Two Sides of Love 313
Two Things You Don't Talk About at Dinner 367
Two-Man Kidnapping Rule 301
Twomey, Anne 419
Twyford, Holly 438
Twyman, Chris 106
Twyman, Richard 221
TXC Heavy Industries 321
Tychinina, Irinia 215
Tyndall, Richard 28
Tynes, Antoinette 152
Tynes, Molly 146
Type A Marketing 33, 37, 50, 52, 68, 84, 87, 91, 95, 105, 136
Tyra, Emily 13, 43, 179
Tyree, Brian 90
Tyrol, Jamie 208
Tyrrell, John 220
Tysoe, Ron 75
Tyson, CJ 146
Tyzack, Margaret 470
Tziouras, Cristina 234
Tzu-Chun, Lee 211
Tzudiker, Bob 64

U
U.K. Festival 306
Uche, Chinaza 213
Udel, Eric 167
U-Dig Dance Academy 256
Uggams, Leslie 216, 405, 409, 415, 416
Ugly Duckling, The 233
Ugly One, The 258
Ullman, Raviv 230, 254
Ullman, Tracey 419
Ulreich, Michael 68
Ultimate Christmas Show (abridged), The 383
Ultz 98
Ulvaeus, Björn 100
Umansky, Anna 237
Umberger, Lea 170
Umbrella in the Snow, The 315
Umhoefer, Adam 113
Umoh, Stephanie 266,

409, 411, 421
Umphress, Alysha 50, 106
Unauthorized Autobiography of Samantha Brown, The 375
Unchinged: A Silent Opera 319
Uncle Frank Productions 171
Uncle Ho To Uncle Sam 345
Uncle Pirate 322
Uncle Vanya 258
UNCLES, LLC 124
Under the Cross 302
Under the Radar Festival 339
Under the Wire 78
Underbelly Diaries, The 174
Underground 310
Underhill, Charles 43, 78
Understudy, The 397
Underwood, Blair 22, 74, 429
Underwood, John 241, 242
Underwood, Sam 178
Underwood, Temar 166
Underwood, Todd 226
Unfit Productions U.K. Ltd 157
Ungaro, Joan 438
Unger, Zachary 216, 245
Union Square Theatre 120, 125, 137
Union, Kaylin 102
Union, Scott 102
United Broadcasting Theater Company 321
United Pies Inc. 187
Uniteus Entertainment 47
Unity Stage Company 321
Universal Music Group 87
Universal Pictures 89, 111
Universal Pictures Stage Productions 54, 66
Unlicensed 286
Unmitigated Consequence, The 293, 313
Uno, Chsato 28
Unplugged In 307
Unreachable Eden 320
Untapped! 231
Untitled Theater

Company #61 321
Unville Brazil 289
Up to Date 313
Up to You 318
Upchurch, Gaye Taylor 208, 214
Updegraff, Bill 148, 151, 160
Uppaluri, Arielle 153
Upstart Theatre 154
Upton, Dave 172
Uranis, Eleni 129
Uranowitz, Brandon 87
Urban Latino Media 133
Urban Odyssey 295
Urban Stages 148, 173
Uremovich, Dylan 227
Urie, Michael 95, 118, 197, 200, 218, 421
Urla, Joe 419
Urlie, Dan 47
Urness, Dan 55, 117
Urrestarazu, Mar 241
Usifer, Brian 90, 117
Utzig, Greg 33

V
Vaccarelli, Bob 211
Vaccari, David 40
Vaccariello, Patrick 43
Vaccaro, Brenda 418
Vaccaro, Dario 191
Vacchiano, Jessie 128
Vache, Vanessa 138
Vahdat, Pej 224
Vail, Willa 253
Valan, Laura 87
Valcarcel, Ali 183, 258
Valdes, Dax 195, 261
Valdés, Jaime 177
Valley, Paul Michael 147
Valli, Frankie 202
Valli, Robert N. 50, 82
Valncy, Maurice 115
Vampire Cowboys 166
Vampure 288
Van Achte, Alain 118
Van Ark, Joan 418
Van Asselt, David 249
van Bommel, Marjolein 232
Van Buren, Ashley 261
Van Buren, Elizabeth 87
van Cauwelaert, Michiel 232

van den Berg, Erna 232
van den Boom, Hans 232
Van Den Ende, Joop 109
van der Boom, Claire 230, 268
van der Schyff, Melissa 47
van Dijsseldonk, Daan 232
Van Dyck, Jennifer 161
Van Dyke, Dick 418
Van Dyke, Elizabeth 150
Van Dyke, Jaimie 138
Van Dyke, Marcia 417
Van Dyke, Will 139, 140
van Genuchten, Nol 137
Van Hare, Mark 176
Van Heese, Tjarko 232
van Hove, Ivo 211
Van Keuren, Lael 109
van Kraaij, Peter 211
Van Laast, Anthony 109, 109
Van Ness, Nancy 64
Van Nest, Michael 43
van Oosterwijk, Joris 232
Van Patten, Joyce 104, 192
Van Pelt, David 229
Van Praag, Alex 36
Van Tassel, Craig 107
Van Tieghem, David 77, 81, 86, 91, 104, 208, 256, 260, 261
Van Veek, Jonathan 156
Van Vlaenderen, Roos 232
Van Welie, Georgina 210
van Wijmen, Joost 232
van Zyll de Jong, David 86
VanAntwerp, Quinn 97
vanBergen, Jim 38, 77, 107
Vance, Bryant 133
Vance, Courtney B. 419
Vand, Sheila 88
vanden Heuvel, Wendy 250, 258
Vander Broek, Cora 341
Vanderbilt, Kayla 89
VanderEnde, Matt 111
Vanderpoel, Mark 140
Vandervliet, David A. 182
Vanderwoude, Jason T. 77, 107, 129
Vandewater, Peter 235
Vanelslader, Jena 183
Vangorden, Jack 369

Vanhorn, Greg 163
Vanilla, Cherry 187
Vann, Liza 166
Vanstone, Hugh 75
VanWinkle, Lindsie 128
Varcelotti, Amanda 125
Varga, Andrea 229
Varga, Ferenc 212
Vargas, Jesse 118, 200
Vargas, Jorge 78, 84, 96
Vargyas, Carmel 37, 72, 91
Variations Theatre Group 322
Varjas, Grant James 252
Vergano, Rina 232
Varon, Susan 158
Vartanian, Nina 140
Vashee, Sita 102
Vashee, Vijay 102
Vasil, Sarah 146
Vasilkov, Yuri 215
Vasilyeva, Nataliya 195
Vasquez, Grace 206
Vasquez, Josh 243
Vassel, Patrick 70
Vassilieva, Ksenia 215
Vass-Rhee, Freya 211
Vastola, Elisabeth 125
Vaswani, Neelam 145
Vatsky, Daniel 68, 139
Vaughan, Brittany 251, 252
Vaughan, David 213
Vaughan, Jennifer F. 97, 181
Vaughan, Livi 196
Vaughn, Donna Michelle 99
Vaughn, Geoffrey 28
Vaughn, Nelson 85, 116
Vaz, Michaela 213
Vázquez, Gerard 149
Vazquez, Michele 129
Vazquez, Victoria 168, 236, 247
Vázquez, Yul 103, 198, 223
VCR Love 279
Veasey, Jason 99
Vega, Kathryn 142, 243, 247
Vega, Tiffany 145
Veillette, Kathryn 241
Velasquez, Andrees 148
Veldheer, Laurie 64
Velez, Ray Navas 130
Velez, Rony Navas 130
Velez, Rudy Navas 130
Venberg, Lorraine 233
Venditti, Nicky 118
Venegas, Janette Valenzo 127
Venito, Lenny 208

Vennera, Chick 419
Ventriloquist Circle, The 316
Ventura, Frank 96
Ventura, Lorna 78
Venus in Fur 13, 42
Venuti, John Paul 218
Vera, Nella 244
Vera, Nikki 224
Verdery, Aaron 144, 146
Verdon, Gwen 417
Vereen, Ben 418, 447, 451
Verel, Maria 192
Vergano, Rina 232
Vergara, Christopher 230
*Veri**on Play, The* 346
Verina, Nick 33, 158
Verini, Bob 442
Verlaet, Claire 50
Verlaet, Claire 59, 91
Verleny, Christine 309
Verlizzo, Frank 424
Vernace, Kim 43
Vernon, Nathan 71
Versailles, Vladimir 230, 249
Verschueren, Luc 28, 44
Verse Chorus Verse 275
Vershbow, Paul 104, 128, 146, 157
Versweyveld, Jan 211
Verve Music Group 87
Very Merry Wives of Windsor, Iowa, The 391
Vesce, Bob 246
Vessey, Reg 60
Vest, Nancy Elizabeth 118, 192
Vestergren-Ahlin, Rebecka 215
Vett, Ilya 202
Viade, Michael 410
Viagas, Robert 422
Vialatte, Philippe 259
Victor/Victoria 399
Victory: Choices in Reaction 310
Vidal, Gore 66
Vidler, Susan 177
Viebeg, Paul 211
Viega, Christine 102
Vieira, Matt 143
Viertel, Bejmamin 252
Viertel, Jack 199, 216
Viertel, Tom 82, 185
Viesta, John 37, 66, 86
Vietti, Alejo 97, 129, 185, 209
Vigil 363
Vilanch, Bruce 117, 175,

194, 200, 202
Villa, Zach 110
Villada, Diego 189
Village Theatre 152
Village Voice Obie Awards 426
Villalobos, Amanda 145
Villamaria, Lisa 238
Villanova, Libby 50
Villar, Elliot 110
Villegas, Francisco 233
Vilmont, Carrington 105, 266
Vilnai-Kalfo, Revital 133
Vinaver, Steven 265
Vincentelli, Elizabeth 428
Vineyard Theatre 77, 115, 188, 205, 261
Vinterberg, Thomas 178
Viola, Kissane 187
Viola, Tom 114, 115, 117, 118, 199
Violanti, Heather J. 229
Violet Hour, The 272
Viravan, Takonkiet 50, 52, 78, 95
Virginia Stage Company 402
Virta, Ray 86
Virtmanis, Arturs 28
Viscardi, John 249
Viselli, Nicholas 178
Visit, The 115
Visiting Hours 314
Vitagliano, Joseph 253
Vital Theatre Company 125, 195, 276, 322
Vitale, Nancy 237
Vitelli, Ronnie 87
Vitlar, Adria 80, 224
Vivaldi, Antonio 212
Viverito, Sam 125
Viveros, Frank 135
Vivian Beaumont Theatre 110, 446
Viviano, Sal 204, 264
Vivier, Judylee 228
Vlasov, Sergey 215
Vo, Tony 163
Voca People 120, 133
Vodicka, Ron 99
Vogel, Paula 253
Vogt, Jon 257
Vogt, Marc 241
Voice of the Turtle, The 383
Voices from the Edge 2012 301
Voices of the Spirits in My Soul 374
Voight, Brandon 244-246

Voight, Jon 418
Vojta, Sandy 50
Volckhausen, Alex Lyu 88, 112, 118
Volksbuehne 246
Volpacchio, Laura 113
Völsch, Gabriele 210
von Arx, Serge 210
von Bargen, Daniel 419
von Drehle, Courtney 233, 234
Von Essen, Max 68
Von Gawinski, Tomke 28
Von Kleist, Erica 84, 212
Von Klug, Theresa 141, 259
von Mayenburg, Marius 258
von Mayrhauser, Jennifer 57
von Mayrhauser, Peter 105
von Stuelpnagel, Mortitz 150
von Weber, Carl Maria 212
Vörös, Mrs. Laszlo Zoltanne 212
Vorse, Alex 52
Vosk, Jessica 116, 216, 217
Vovsi, Dina 167
Voyce, Kaye 224, 249
Vreeland, Martin E. 99, 118, 207
Vrtar, Jack 410

W

Waage, Catherine 60
Wachter, Adam 117, 185, 226, 227
Wacker, Jeanine 125
Wackerman, Dan 157
Waddell, Adam 164
Waddell, Helen 184
Wade, Andrew 98, 176, 259, 260
Wade, Kevin 422
Wade, Lezlie 62
Wade, Michael 208, 252
Wade, William 192
Wadsworth, Alison 82
Wadsworth, Stephen 31
Wages, Matthew 235
Waggoner, Frederick 64
Wagner, Dane 159
Wagner, Darrell 128
Wagner, Elizabeth 28, 32, 169, 223
Wagner, George 40, 87, 88, 139
Wagner, Robin 82
Wagner, S.D. 32, 67,

410
Wagner, Stefanie 263, 264, 266, 267
Wahlers, Jeremy 109
Wailes, Alexandria 169
Waite, John Thomas 220
Waiting for Godot 363
Waitz, Aaron 40
Wakaba, Kouhei 197
Wake Up Marconi 45
Wakefield, Amber 32
Wakefield, Scott 265
Walck, Adam 241, 242
Walcott, Karen 258
Walden, Josh 188
Waldmann, Clem 189
Waldron, Louise 75
Waldrop, Mark 115, 194, 424
Waldrop, William 68
Wales, Andrea 157, 223
Walk Tall Girl Productions 70
Walken, Christopher 418
Walker Arts Center 247
Walker Communications Group Inc 49, 74
Walker, Ally 192
Walker, Chet 183
Walker, Chris 265
Walker, Daniel 68, 89
Walker, Don 43, 116, 217
Walker, F. Janet Hayes 263
Walker, Jasmin 188
Walker, Jillian 409
Walker, Jonathan 170
Walker, Larrington 197
Walker, Leese 168
Walker, Mia 54
Walker, Pernell 145
Walker, Robert 418
Walker, Shonté 82, 117
Walker, Tommy 194
Walker, Travis 188
Walker, Zareen 214
Walkerdance 183
Walker-Kuhne, Donna 49, 74, 145
Walkerspace 146, 174, 258
Walkup, Michael 146
Wall, Cornelia 253
Wall, Matt 68, 95
Wall, Roberta 83, 109
Wallace, Brian 206
Wallace, Katherine 39
Wallace, Rebecca Joy 245
Wallach, Eli 417

Wallach, Jeffrey 60, 236, 237
Walleck, Cat 110
Wallem, Stephen 216
Wallen, Ashley 75
Waller, Jonathan K. 261
Wallerstein, Michael 170
Wallert, James 181
Wallin, Erik 148, 151, 160, 174
Wallis, Stephanie 410
Walls, Marques 52, 124
Walnut Street Theatre 431
Walpole, Aaron 62
Walsh, Brittany 234
Walsh, Emily 45
Walsh, Enda 60, 236
Walsh, Erikka 60, 236
Walsh, John 102
Walsh, Karen 39, 56
Walsh, Matthew 35, 56, 62, 153
Walsh, Michael 167
Walsh, Shannon 125
Walsh, Thomas A. 143
Walson, Edward 37
Walt Disney Theatrical Productions 99, 101
Walter Kerr Theatre 52, 73, 94
Walter Reade Theatre 435
Walter, Harriet 420
Walter, Jessica 85
Walter, Karen 115, 118
Walter, Stephanie 207
Walters, Brian 60, 236
Walters, John 159
Walters, William 54
Walters-Maneri, Lucy 144, 156, 168, 180
Walton, Jim 116
Walton, Leah 142
Walton, Tony 422, 447
Wan-Chun, Ko 211
Wandering Bark Theatre Company 314
Wandering Scholar, The 184
Wanee, Brian 111
Wang, Bruce 99
Wang, Ethan 210
Wang, Irene 38, 54, 62, 64, 66, 78
Wankel, Robert E. 43, 60, 78, 410
Wanlass, Megan 162
Wan-Ling, Lee 210
Wannen, David 235
Wansley, Sarah 163, 177

Want 400
War Horse 110, 202, 362
War of the Worlds 300, 309
Warbeck, Stephen 98
Warchus, Matthew 75
Ward, Amy 140
Ward, Bethe 105
Ward, Beverly 220
Ward, Carlton 211
Ward, Joseph 255
Ward, Kristy Patrick 154
Ward, Max 244, 245, 247
Ward, Michael 99
Ward, Miriam 198
Ward, Molly 242
Ward, Nicholas 216
Ward, Tammie 106
Ward, Tony 80, 228
Ward, Victoria L. 180
Wardell, Brandon 92
Warden, Joel 231
Warden, Karl 95, 216
Wardle, Lynette 184
Ware, Jamie 109
Warfield, Marlene 418
Warhol, Andy 213
Waring, Minouche 238
Warmbrunn, Erika 85, 116
Warmen, Timothy 29
warner | shaw 322
Warner Brothers 254
Warner Brothers Theatre Ventures 87
Warner Theatre 438
Warner, David 420
Warnock, Kathleen 444
Warren, Amy 259
Warren, Christy 58
Warren, Dianna 105
Warren, Jennifer 418
Warren, Jonathan 111
Warren, Leslie Ann 418
Warren, Philip Cruise 256
Warren, Thom Christopher 99, 146
Warren, Will W. 271
Warrior Class 254
Warshavsky, Mark 104
Wartella, Michael 140
Washburn, Nate 163
Washington Theatre Awards Society 438
Washington, Marlon 368
Washington, Pauletta 125
Wasilewski, Jessica 259
Wason, Oliver 125, 263

Wasser, Alan 28, 33, 44, 52, 87, 95, 101, 103, 105, 113, 136, 422
Wasser, Carol 422
Wasserman, Bryna 259
Wasserman, Scott 82
Wassrin, Lars 215
Water by the Spoonful 430
Water Stains on the Wall 210
Waterhouse, Elizabeth 211
Waters, Daryl 102, 199
Waters, Kate 197
Waterston, Elisabeth 218
Waterston, Katherine 208, 218
Waterston, Sam 197, 246
Wathen, Tonya 93
Watkins, James 181
Watkins, Matt 129
Watkins, Maurine Dallas 93
Watkinson, Ryan 95, 113
Watley, Matthew 49
Watley, Shawna 49
Watson, Arlene 28
Watson, Beth 70
Watson, Douglass 417
Watson, Erica 192
Watson, Janet 190, 263
Watson, Joe 155, 185, 196
Watson, Maia 196
Watson, Nicole A. 248, 263
Watson, Samantha 214
Watson, Susan 33, 266
Watson, Tom 50, 84, 91, 94, 95, 103, 108, 111, 136, 216, 244
Watstein, Tema 247
Watt, Michael 50, 75, 92
Watt, Patricia 437
Watters, Aléna 109, 112, 113
Watters, Craig 410
Watters, Vanessa 255
Watterson, Kerry 263
Watts, Daniel J. 76, 199
Watts, Ed 190, 266
Watts, Edward 190
Watts, Lennie 443
Watts, Lloyd 256
Watts, Riley 211
Wax Wings 323
Waxman, Anita 62
Waxman-Pilla, Debra 31, 42, 57, 80, 227

Wayfarer's Inn 208
Wayfinder Films 322
Wayne, Anthony 85, 106, 113, 115, 202
Wayne, David 417
Wayne, Matt 190
We in Silence Hear a Whisper 312
We Live Here 227
We Play for the Gods 263
WE Theater 322
Wear it like a crown 215
Weatherly, Christal 173
Weaver, Fritz 417
Weaver, Hillary 108
Weaver, Matthew 108
Weaver, Neal 442
Weaver, Patrick 115
Weaver, Ves 161
Webb, Brian 59
Webb, Jason Michael 83, 102, 116
Webb, Jeremy 115
Webb, Joseph Monroe 199
Webb, Rema 90, 99
Webb, Rosina 214
Webber, Julian 89
Webber, Katie 92, 108, 113
Webber, Madeleine Lloyd 62
Webel, Betsy 111
Weber, Andrea 213
Weber, Brittany 59
Weber, Bud 111
Weber, Doron 182
Weber, Fredricka 418
Weber, Jason 231
Weber, Jon 108
Weber, Kate 181
Webster Hall 188, 426
Webster, Gordon 212
Webster, J.D. 54
Wechsler, Julie 36, 60, 75
Wedderburn, Junior "Gabu" 99
Wedding Thieves, The 313
Wedge.a&d 107
Wee, Nicole 208, 263, 264
Weed, Barrett Wilbert 52
Weed, Morgan 140
Week at the NJ Shore, A 297
Weeks, Jessica 78, 139
Weeks, Todd 208
Weems, Andrew 91, 224, 260
Wegner, Tobias 161

Wegorzewski, John 171
Wehrle, Ian 151, 206
Wei, Hsiung 210
Wei, Liu 211
Weichers, Guillermo 40
Weida, Nate 209
Weideman, Japhy 156, 224, 225, 237, 251, 254
Weidman, John 85, 436
Weigant, David 169
Weigel, Lauren 143, 258
Wei-Jong, Huang 210
Weil, Raymond 223
Weil, Tim 139
Weiler, Berenice 470
Weiler, Tracy 181
Weill, Benjamin 240
Weill, Kurt 210
Weimer, Paul 32, 75
Weinberg, Jenna 156
Weinberg, Richard G. 28
Weinberger, Ian 85
Weiner, David 40, 104, 226, 241
Weiner, Deanna 82
Weiner, Jim 171
Weiner, Micki 113
Weiner, Miriam 261
Weiner, Randy 196
Weiner, Samantha 247
Weiner, Stephen 152
Weingart, John 39
Weingarten, Stacey 192
Weinman, James 38
Weinman, James 242
Weinperl, Franc 33, 64
Weinstein Company 37, 84, 89
Weinstein, Aaron 201
Weinstein, Arnold 259
Weinstein, Bethany 31, 42, 57, 80, 187
Weinstein, Josh 32
Weinstein, Rachel 70
Weinstock, Adam 194
Weinstock, Jack 95
Weintraub, Gary 159
Weir, Annie Mullaly 113
Weis, David 99
Weisberg, Noah 134, 188
Weisbrod, Nimmy 194
Weiser, Dave 68
Weisman, Annie 243
Weiss, David 217
Weiss, Glen 422
Weiss, Heather J. 108
Weiss, Michele B. 147, 169
Weiss, Norman 105
Weiss, Sasha 266
Weissler, Barry 93

Weissler, Fran 93
Weissman, Gabriel 255
Weissman, Samone B. 229
Weisz, Rachel 420
Weitz, Paul 253
Weitzer, Jim 105
Weitzman, Ira 39, 110, 224
Weitzman, Josh 78, 85
Welch, Chris 40
Welch, Elizabeth 105
Welch, Jared 127
Welcome to America 302
Welder, Brandon Bart 236
Weldon, Charles 161
Weldon, Duncan C. 44
Weller, Danny 164, 264
Weller, Ezra 259
Wells, Dawn 192
Wells, Laura Beth 28, 29
Wells, Laurie 100
Wells, Orlando 55
Wells, Simon Anthony 68
Welsh, Adam 198
Welsh, Steve 187
Welzer, Irving 47
Wendholt, Scott 43, 95
Wendland, Mark 139, 218, 253
Wendt, Angela 139
Wendt, Timothy 112
Wenegrat, Lauren 235
WenLarBar Productions 32
Wenslawski, Steven 113
Wen-Wen, Hsu 211
Wenzelberg, Benjamin Perry 245
Wepper, Chloe 209
Werb, Brett 174
Werle, Donyale 71, 260
Werner, Axel 210
Werner, Eric 235
Werner, Howard 28, 52, 113
Werner, Jennifer 90
Wernke, John 77
Werntz, Mary 179
Wertenbaker, Caleb 130, 165
Wertheimer, Tracy 124, 151
Werthmann, Coleen 247
Werthmann, Colleen 236
Weschler, Daniel 147, 156
Wesley, Rutina 226
West End Theatre 163,

238
West Ocean Quartet 219
West, Blake 226
West, Bryan 106
West, Charles 190
West, Cheryl L. 243
West, Darron L 38, 71, 162, 185, 208, 245, 262
West, Jennifer 418
West, John Walton 194
West, Justin 238
West, Kat 152
West, Michael 194, 462
West, Peter 172
WestBeth Entertainment 94
Westby, Greg 142, 263, 264
Westenberg, Robert 419, 421
Westervelt, Scott 52, 62
Westfeldt, Jennifer 420
Westgate, Chris 157
Westley, Robert 150
Weston, Audrey Lynn 185
Weston, Jon 95, 189
Weston, Mark 142
Westport Country Playhouse 403
Westrate, Nick 218, 248, 437
Westside Theatre 119, 120, 133, 168, 185, 192, 201
Wetherhead, Kate 132
Wever, Merritt 258
Wexner Center for the Arts 212
Wey, Enrico D. 110
Whale, The 367
Whalen, Christopher 180
Whalen, David 379
Whalley-Kilmer, Joanne 419
Wharton, Jennifer 55, 212
Wharton, Philip 184
Wharton, Sarah 276
What Are Yoi Doing Here? 324
What the Sparrow Said 283
What the Time Traveler Will Tell Us 325
What We're Up Against 348
Wheeler, Harold 43
Wheeler, Jedediah 259
Wheeler, Nathan 172, 169, 248

Whelan, Fiona 112, 219
When Thoughts Attack 319
Whipping Man, The 351, 352, 359, 381
Whitaker, Adia 211
Whitaker, Beth 255
Whitaker, Paul 174
Whitaker, William 105
White 231
White Cherry Entertainment 422
White Christmas 392
White Clowns Play Hamlet 296
White Fence Productions 322
White Horse Theater Company 322
White Light Festival 199
White Snake, The 390
White, Adrian 133
White, Adrian 143, 218
White, Al 419
White, Allison Jean 35
White, Alton Fitzgerald 99
White, Amber 226
White, Amelia 419
White, Amy 125
White, Andrew J. 133
White, Anna Aimee 217
White, B.D. 226, 236, 259
White, Bernard 224
White, C. Randall 28
White, Carl D. 194, 428
White, Chip 72, 98
White, Christian Dante 199
White, Conleth 134
White, Evann 214
White, Frances 52, 102
White, Genavieve 219
White, J. Steven 54, 143
White, Jacob 70, 92
White, James 227
White, Jane 470
White, Jennifer Dorr 167
White, Jesse 107
White, Josh 127
White, Karin 226
White, Katie 140
White, Lillias 192
White, Margot 207, 229
White, Matthew 223
White, Meggan 239, 240
White, Noni 64
White, Patricia 152
White, T.H. 112
White, Terri 33, 114
White, Walter 74
Whitehead, Reggie 158

Whitelaw, Arthur 437
Whiteley, Ben 216
Whitely, Colin 169, 222
Whitfield, Alice 459
Whitford, Bradley 114, 379
Whiting, Brendan 64, 109
Whitley, Cristin 263
Whitman, Danny 117, 118
Whitman, Matheiu 195
Whitmore, James 417
Whitney, Belinda 55, 92, 216, 217
Whitney, Janine Safer 86
Whitney, Jim 233, 259
Whitsitt, Lily 218
Whitten, Damon 163
Whitten, Eric 276
Whittet, Matthew 234
Whittle, Brit 206
Whitty, Jeff 188
Whitty, Paul 60, 236
Whoriskey, Kate 253
Who's Afraid of Virgina Woolf? 394
Whylan, Erin 182
Whyte, Blake 100
Wick, Julianne 440
Wicked 111, 202
Wicks, Teal 111, 253
Widdoes, James 419
Wide Eyed Productions 322
Widgren, John 253
Widmann, Thom 111
Widner, Cheryl 28
Wiegand, Annie 176, 227
Wieland, Katie 245
Wiemann, Carl 163
Wierzel, Robert 233
Wiesel, Elisha 165
Wieselman, Doug 141, 212, 255
Wiesend, Tiffany 125
Wiesenfeld, Cheryl 54
Wieser, Michael 163, 218
Wiest, Dianne 218, 419
Wiggans, Gregg 153
Wiggins, Adam 117
Wigginton, Miranda 108
Wiig, Kristen 223
Wilbur, Joel 244
Wilcox, Felicity 151
Wilcox, Margaret 40, 50, 92
Wilcox, Wayne Alan 104, 227
Wilcoxen, Grant 108, 208, 256

Wilcoxen, Webb 223
Wilcozs, Jason 78
Wild Animals You Should Know 226
Wild Bride, The 357
Wild Finish, The 284
Wild Project, The 323
Wild Swans 350
Wild, Jeff 253
Wilde, Oscar 96
Wilde, Stephen 409
Wilder, Andrew 97
Wilder, John 94, 142, 246
Wilder, Stephanie 171
Wildhorn, Frank 47, 201
Wildman, Jesse 76
Wiles, Brannon 50
Wiley, Anissa 118
Wiley, Patrick 447
Wiley, Samira 248
Wilfore, Jeff 63
Wilhemi, Joel 130
Wilhoite, Michael 28, 101
Wilinson, James 87
Wilk, Emma 77, 237, 242, 246, 261
Wilkas, Matthew 29
Wilkerson, Lisa Nicole 54, 118
Wilkerson, Rob 212
Wilkes, Fiona 196
Wilkins, Jacob 175
Wilkins, Lee 112, 113
Wilkinson, Anthony J. 193
Wilkinson, Colm 419
Wilkinson, Hugh 214
Wilkinson, James 54
Wilkinson, Jeanne 168
Wilkinson, Jim 32
Wilkinson, Simon 176
Will, Simon 246
Wille, Ricola 137, 143, 222, 263
Willems, Jasper 232
Willems, Stephen 226
Willems, Thom 211
William Inge Theatre Festival Awards 448
Williams, Allan 28, 33, 44, 52, 87, 95, 103, 105, 113, 136, 422
Williams, Aurelia 379
Williams, Ben 236, 247
Williams, Beth 95, 102
Williams, Brandon 188
Williams, Buddy 202
Williams, Cat 104
Williams, Chandler 214
Williams, Charlie 95
Williams, Christopher

B. 154
Williams, Christopher Brian 89
Williams, Clarence, III 418
Williams, DaRon Lamar 158
Williams, Diane 109
Williams, Dick Anthony 470
Williams, Dolly 90
Williams, Elizabeth 92
Williams, Emily 108
Williams, Gareth 215
Williams, George 74
Williams, Gifford 143
Williams, Hilary A. 52, 67, 95
Williams, J.L. 199
Williams, James A. 255, 389
Williams, Kristen Beth 78, 85, 113
Williams, Lia 86
Williams, Mark 175
Williams, Matt 226
Williams, Maurice 174
Williams, Monica L. 127
Williams, NaTasha Yvette 54
Williams, Robin 88
Williams, Sidney 223, 249
Williams, Skekth 167
Williams, Stephanie 214
Williams, Stephen Tyrone 230, 255
Williams, Tennessee 74, 137, 177
Williams, Tim 185
Williams, Vanessa 420
Williamson, Dan'yelle 102, 202
Williamson, Nance 233
Williamson, Zach 52, 124, 153, 221
Willibanks, Marguerite 118
Willingham, Patrick 244
Willingham, Scot 196
Willis, Cheryl 431
Willis, Dan 47
Willis, John 409
Willis, Richard 72, 98, 106
Willis, Scott 266
Willison, Walter 409, 418
Wilkens, Sean 182
Wills, Louise Gilmour 231
Wills, Misti B. 201
Willson-Broyles, Rachel

143
Wilmes, Gary 12, 38, 247
Wilmore Living Trust 410
Wilmot, David 420
Wilner, Lori 50, 104
Wilner, Robin 111
Wilsman, Lauren 191
Wilson Exclusive Talent Productions 323
Wilson, Akyiaa 163
Wilson, Andrew 160
Wilson, Blythe 101
Wilson, C.J. 225, 257
Wilson, Chandra 419
Wilson, Courtney 234
Wilson, Dougie 214
Wilson, Edward J. 43, 82, 92
Wilson, Jamie 176
Wilson, Jeffrey M. 45, 78
Wilson, Jesse 222
Wilson, Joe, Jr. 389
Wilson, Kate 31, 36, 38, 49, 66, 67, 104, 110, 185, 253, 256
Wilson, Keve 184
Wilson, Lanford 222
Wilson, Lydia 214
Wilson, Maia Nkenge 90
Wilson, Mary 37, 49, 50, 85, 243
Wilson, Mary Louise 204, 224
Wilson, Mathew 90
Wilson, Michael 66, 243
Wilson, Michael G. 60
Wilson, Robert 210
Wilson, Ryn 131
Wilson, Sanford 249
Wilson, Stephanie 138
Wilson, Tad 47, 106
Wilson, Thad Turner 89
Wilson, Tobias 258
Wilson, Tommar 90
Wilson, Wayne 129
Wilson, Willis 219
Wilstein, Matt 43, 76
Wimmer, Paul 45, 78
Win, Shwe Min Thar Than 156
Winbush, Dawn 167
Wind Farmer, The 357
Winde, Beatrice 418
Winder, John 216, 217
Windmill Theatre 234
Windom, Christopher 54
Window: 4 Alice, The 313
Windsor, Sam 231
Windsor-Cunningham,

John 158
Winebold, Kevin B. 112
Winer, Linda 409, 429
Winerib, Franklin 146
Wingate, Anne 226
Wingate, Roger 214
Wing-Davey, Mark 223
Wingert, Andrew 188
Wingfield, Jeffrey 112, 219
Winiarski, Jo 108, 181, 192, 240
Winick, Eric 241
Wink, Chris 189
Winkler, Angela 210
Winkler, Joe 231
Winkler, Mark 143, 175, 194
Winkler, Richard 78, 92, 102
Winner, Nathan 225
Winners at Life 323
Winnicki, Andrzej 178
Winningham, Mare 169
Winokur, Emily 81
Winokur, Marissa Jaret 420
Winsby, Jonathan 62, 63
Winsby, Sandy 62, 63
Winship, Michael J. 410
Winslow, Darryl 112, 259
Winston, Hattie & Tony 431
Winter Garden Theatre 100
Winter, Charlie 209
Winter, Matthias 192
Winter's Tale, The 197, 404
Winters, Marian 417
Winters, Susan 159
Winters, Zoë 224
Winther, Michael 216
Wirth, David 146
Wirth, Jill Melanie 146
Wirth, Ken 71
Wirth, Suzan 71
Wirtshafter, Tom 126, 141, 169, 259
Wisan, Liz 39
Wisdom, Natalie 89
Wise, Arnie 167
Wise, Kathleen 176
Wise, Paula 36
Wisehart, Victor James 216
Wiseman, Jason 112
Wishing Well Productions 165
Wit 17, 57
WiT Media 250
Witek, Krystof 99

With the Current 302
Witherby, Amy 245-247
Witherow, Robert 103, 136
Withers, Louise 75
Withers-Mendes, Elisabeth 420
Witherspoon, Randy 113
Withrow, David 174
Witness for the Prosecution 390
Witter, Terrence J. 93
Witthohn, Leslie 189
Wittig, Beth 369
Wittlin, Michael 108
Wittman, Scott 92, 186, 187
Wittrock, Finn 59, 408, 409, 411, 414, 437
Wittstein, Ed 190
Wiz, The 354
Wizard of Oz, The 313, 349
WME Entertainment 43
Wodehouse, P.G. 78, 85
Woerz, Ashton 106
Wofford, Gail 235
Wojchik, Mike 75
Wojcik, Scott 146
Wojnar, Dann 35, 56, 81, 96
Wojtal, James W., Jr. 192
Wolcott, Brandon 147, 172, 208, 248, 256
Wolcott, Nicole 139
Woldin, Judd 470
Wolensky, Heather 160, 174
Wolf & William Productions 189
Wolf 359 323
Wolf, Amanda 116
Wolf, Gary 116
Wolf, Orin 60, 139
Wolf, Peter 104, 214
Wolf, Steve 183
Wolf, William 424
Wolfe, Betsy 205, 216, 267
Wolfe, George C. 104, 446
Wolfe, Isadora 196
Wolfe, Jamie 249
Wolfe, Wayne 87, 95
Wolff, Amos 33, 93, 116
Wolff, Gia 211
Wolff, Lizz 87
Wolff, Rachel A. 50, 181
Wolfram, Paul 184
Wolfslau, Joseph 142, 262
Wolfson, Courtney 84

Wolfson, Deborah 172
Wolfson, Israel 108
Wolk, James 186
Wolkowitz, Morton 184, 196
Wollensen, Kenny 141
Wolpe, Lenny 185
Wolpert, Harold 35, 56, 81, 85, 96, 104, 116, 251
Woltring, Marielle 232
Womack, Lucas 263, 264
Women and Guns 292
Women in Transition 301
Women's Project Lab 263
Women's Project Theater 203, 241, 262
Women's Work Original Short Play Festival 301
Wonderful Town 289
Wonderful Wizard of Oz, The 135
Wong, Alex 64
Wong, B.D. 419
Wong, Carolyn 28, 106, 224, 253
Wong, Kimberly 240
Wong, Simon 188
Wood, Anja 29, 216
Wood, Bethany 67
Wood, Carrie 213
Wood, D.M. 98
Wood, Evan Rachel 223
Wood, Frank 22, 73, 91, 118, 246
Wood, Gabe 64
Wood, Haneefah 188
Wood, Helen 417
Wood, Jacob 113
Wood, Jody Cole 113
Wood, John 470
Wood, Marjorie Ann 260
Wood, Natalie 75
Wood, Olga 190
Wood, Stephen 158
Wood, The 249
Woodall, Eric 43, 62, 75
Woodard, Jeremy 108
Woodbridge, Libby 98, 203, 249
Woodell, Gregory 77, 261
Wooden 291
Woodhead, David 68
Woodie, Joshua 115
Woodiel, Paul 78
Wooding, John 85
Woodman, Branch 106
Woodruff, Virginia Ann 83

Woods, Alan 443
Woods, Allie, Jr. 389
Woods, Candice Marie 78, 92
Woods, Carol 93
Woods, Denise 54
Woods, James 418
Woods, Jay 68
Woods, Jenna 208, 252, 254
Woods, Remy 33
Woodward, Alexander 152, 191, 241
Woodward, Billy 103
Woodward, Hannah 255
Woodward, Kirsty 197
Woodward, Max A. 33
Woodworth, Kevin 93
Woody Guthrie Dreams 280
Woody Sez 351
Woofter, Isaac 110
Woolard, David C. 52, 124, 179, 181, 217, 243, 244
Woolf, John 197
Woolf, Virginia 141
Woolley, Jim 216, 217
Woolverton, Linda 99
Wooster Group 168
Wopat, Tom 92, 216
Worall, Kristin 125, 184
Wordsworth, Mark 62
Working on a Special Day 288
Working Theater 167
Working Title Films 89
Workman, Camille 99
Workman, Caroline 89
Workman, Jason 419
WorkShop Theater Company 323
Workspace Co Ltd. 191
World Is My Cheesecake, The 299
World Stage Productions 232
Woronov, Mary 418
Worsham, Jenna 253
Worsing, Ryan 93, 113
Wortham, Jessica 404
Wound in Time, A 323
Woyasz, Laura 111
Woyzeck 317
Wozniak, Sarah 239
Wozunk, Theresa 54
Wragg, Barney 62
Wren, Jennifer 112
Wren, Todd 162
Wrenn, Bradley K. 142
Wright, Amra-Faye 93
Wright, Amy 219, 256
Wright, Bowman 361

Wright, Brian 46
Wright, Charles 424
Wright, Chris 240
Wright, Christina 49
Wright, Darcy 202
Wright, Doug 155
Wright, Emily D. 235
Wright, Eric 135
Wright, Heather 62, 85
Wright, Jenna 159
Wright, Jessica Tyler 110
Wright, Lynn 207
Wright, Max 419
Wrights, Raynelle 28
Wrightson, Will 215
Write Act Rep Eastside 323
Wu, Di 129
Wu, Johnny 38
Wu, Raymond 87
Wu, Yizhu 232
Wuest, Catherine 245
Wulfson, Brett 172
Wundelsteipen, The 288
Wuthering Heights, Restless Souls 232
Wuttke, Peter 212
Wyatt, Jayashri 130, 159, 165
Wyatt, Kristen 114
Wyatt, Rosie 154
Wyeth, Christina 186
Wyld, Carolyn 129
Wyman, Nick 92, 151, 266
Wymore, Patrice 417
Wynn, Joceline 233
Wyse, Alex 16, 52, 124
Wysocki, Sonya 28
Wyszniewski, John 145

X
Xanadu 384
Xiaji, Chen 211
Xiaochuan, Zhang 211
Xiaoqiang, Yan 211
Xie, Famin 232
Xoregos Performing Company 323
Xu-Bustin, Elle 38

Y
Yacavone, Briana 111
Yachechak, Amanda 154
Yaddaw, Jeremy 264
Yaeger, Samantha 241, 242
Yahn, Mike 149
Yahui, Lu 211
Yaji, Shigeru 159
Yajima, Mineko 109, 216, 217

Yakata, Hitomi 110
Yale Repertory Theatre 403
Yamakawa, Fuyuki 197
Yamamoto, Koichi 197
Yamashita, Yuri 127
YAMI 213
Yandoli, James 59
Yaney, Denise 56, 80, 261
Yang, Ana 191
Yang, Deni 191
Yang, Fan 191
Yang, Hee Sun 198
Yang, Jano 191
Yang, Melody 191
Yang, Rob 219
Yang, Xle 211
Yangtze Repertory Theatre 324
Yankowy, Adam 235
Yankwitt, Stephanie 62, 75
Yanov-Yanovsky, Dmitri 210
Yarbrough, Chad 111
Yarden, Tal 184, 211
Yarger, Lauren 424
Yarnell, Bruce 418
Yass, Catherine 213
Yau, Cedric 40
Yaukey, Katrina 89, 110
Yavich, Anita 38, 42, 226, 260
Yazbeck, Tony 93
Ybarra, Stephanie 144, 263
Yeager, Grant 71, 132, 192, 209, 261
Yeager, Wayne 229
Yeargan, Michael 56, 224
Yeater, Ashley 33
Yeates, Ray 134
Yee, Ann 197
Yee, Kevin Samuel 101
Yefet, Hana 133
Yeh, Molly 260
Yeh, Roger 245
Yehuda, Yoni-Ben 163
Yekani, Nogcinile 130
Yellow Brick Road, The 135
Yellow Sound Lab 192
Yen, Madeleine Rose 110
Yes We Can 285
Yeshion, Michael 192, 202
Yeston, Maury 267, 436
Yew, Chay 422
Yew, Jeanette 144, 151
Yi-Ling, Liu 210

Yoakam, Stephen 344
Yocom, Joshua 135, 146, 185, 229, 239
Yoder, Billy 193
Yokoyama, Marie 238
Yonally, Katy 143, 155, 169
Yoo, Mia 186
Yoon, Jeena 147, 168
York Theatre Company 204, 263
York, Jaclyn 151, 183
York, Lucy 196
York, Marshall 256, 257
York, Rachel 217
Yosemite 203, 249
Yoshikawa, Yasuaki 187
Yoshioka, Sylvia 45
You Are Here 303
You are in an open field 302
You Better Sit Down: Tales from My Parents' Divorce 177
You Never Can Tell 317
You, My Mother 296
You, Nero 351
You'll Be Happy When I'm Dead 292
Youmans, Vincent 46
Youmans, William 89
Young, Campbell 89, 214
Young, Colin D. 138, 145
Young, Dashaun 99
Young, David 43, 85, 217
Young, Denise 174
Young, Emily 141
Young, Fletcher 188
Young, Georgianna 192
Young, Hannah 197
Young, Ian 149
Young, Joanna 169
Young, John Lloyd 410, 420
Young, Josh 62, 408, 409, 412, 416
Young, Katherine 139, 140
Young, Marion Friedman 177
Young, Nicholas V. 196
Young, Paloma 71, 212
Young, Samantha 197
Young, Zakiya 49
Youngson, Victoria 214
Yount, Bret 215
Younts, Shane Ann 47, 64, 209, 244, 245
Your Boyfriend May Be Imaginary 292, 298

You're a Good Man, Charlie Brown 390
Yousef, Nowar 210
Yousuf, Mohammad 151
Yovany, Roberto Navas 130
Yu, Zhang 211
Yuan-Hsien, Kuo 210
Yuanyuan, Wang 211
Yuen, Michael 218
Yuhasz, Steven 115
Yun, Ho Jin 198
Yurman, Lawrence 50, 117, 409
Yusef, Anatol 250
Yuyama, Daiichiro 197

Z
Zabala, Ander 211
Zaccardi, Chris 32, 72
Zachery, Andre 211
Zack, Rachel 67, 410
Zack, Samantha 95, 113
Zadan, Craig 95
Zade, Maja 258
Zadegan, Necar 88
Zadravec, Stefanie 263
Zagnit, Stuart 64, 104
Zaibek, Randall 28, 33, 75, 92, 95
Zaitsev, Alexandre 129
Zakarian, Louie 28
Zakowska, Donna 37
Zaks, Jerry 84, 109
Zaleski, Michael P. 90
Zalevskiy, Anatoliy 129
Zally, J. Michael 227, 230, 243, 244
Zamansky, Maria 102
Zande, Michael 199, 216
Zander, James 105
Zaneski, Meghan 218
Zanetta, Tony 186, 187
Zang, Neka 108
Zangen, Josh 28, 45, 98, 187
Zapp, Tia Monet 234
Zaret, Hy 75
Zarkana 129
Zarrett, Lee 32
Zatz, Sara 127
Zavelson, Billy 91, 125
Zavyalov, Alexander 215
Zawacki, Benjamin M. 245
Zayas, David 223
Zazzi, Liz 184
Zbornik, Kristine 259
Zeh, Robin 76
Zehrer, Todd 195
Zeigler, Jeffrey 210

Zeigler, Marsha 127
Zeilinger, Brian 59, 88, 92
Zeilinger, Scott 59, 88, 92
Zeitler, Sarah 36, 49, 155, 223
Zen, Danny 129
Zepel, Leah 100
Zepp, Lori Ann 253, 254
Zerrer, Jake 237
Zervoulis, Meg 168, 169
Zes, Evan 368
Zezelj, Danijel 212
ZFX Inc. 111
Zhang, Hailin 232
Zhang, Larry Lei 38
Zhang, Vicky 126
Zhao, Liu 211
Zhengqi, Xia 138
Zhou, Yehai 232
Zhu, Yuhua 232
Zhurbin, Lev 210
Ziadeh, George 237
Ziegenbein, Tim 191
Zieglerova, Klara 97, 109
Zielinski, Scott 237
Zielski, Grzegorz 178
Ziemer, Paul 255
Zien, Chip 104
Ziering, Sarah 50, 95
Zieve, Amanda 62, 95, 102, 103
Zilinyi, Frank 276
Zilles, Carmen 209
Zimmer, Hans 99
Zimmerman, Andrew 259
Zimmerman, Daniel 28, 252
Zimmerman, Matt 217
Zingales, Rosi 202
Zink, Jeff 70, 106
Zinn, David 39, 45, 88, 226, 227, 236, 241, 242, 251, 254, 447
Zinnato, Stephen 221
Zinner, Nick 149
Zinni, Lisa 32, 139
Zipoy, Lanie 190, 444
Zirilli, Jared 16, 52, 181, 201
Zirngibl, Ryan J. 233
Zito, Ronald 93
Zittel, Harry 225
Zlabinger, Michael 125
Zlotnik, Bobbie Clifton 117
Zoback, Eric 173
Zoch, Amanda 70
Zoe, Otis Ramsey 138
Zoem! New Dutch

Theater 232
Zoglin, Richard 429
Zolezzi, Jaclyn 142
Zollicoffer, Diana C. 171
Zollow, Frederick 60
Zombie Prom 356
Zorthian, Doc 99
Zotovich, Adam 68, 84, 93
Zox, Andrew 219
Zubairi, Jamie 156
Zuber, Catherine 50, 91, 95, 214, 224, 259
Zuber, Rebecca 35-37
Zubrycki, Robert 216, 217
Zuckerman, Andrea 410
Zugibe, Meghan 177
Zuiker, John 169
Zumkehr, Florian 138
Zunino, Marco 93
Zweigbaum, Steven 82
Zygo, J. Michael 60, 236

Ben Hodges (Founder, President, and Publisher, Theatre World Media/Screen World; Editor in Chief, Theatre World) served as an editorial assistant for seven years on the 2001 Special Tony Honor Award-winning *Theatre World*, becoming the associate editor to John Willis in 1998 and editor in chief in 2008. *Theatre World*—at sixty-eight—is the only complete annual pictorial and statistical record of the American theatre, including Broadway, Off-Broadway, Off-Off-Broadway, and regional theatre productions, and is referenced daily by students, historians, and industry professionals worldwide.

In 2011, Ben founded Theatre World Media, which publishes both *Theatre World* and its sister publication, *Screen World*—the oldest, annual pictorial and statistical record of the foreign and domestic film seasons, edited by Barry Monush.

Also an assistant for seven years to John Willis for the prestigious Theatre World Awards given for Broadway and Off-Broadway debut performances, Ben was elected to the Theatre World Awards board of directors in 2002 and served as executive producer for the annual ceremony from 2002–2007. In 2003 he was presented with a Special Theatre World Award in recognition of his ongoing stewardship of the event. He currently serves as a member of the board emeritus of the Theatre World Awards. He also served as executive producer for the 2005 LAMBDA Literary Foundation "Lammy" Awards, given for excellence in LGBT publishing.

The Commercial Theater Institute Guide to Producing Plays and Musicals, which Hodges co-edited with late Commercial Theater Institute director Frederic B. Vogel, was released by Applause Theatre and Cinema Books in 2007, and with contributions by twenty-eight Broadway producers, general managers, attorneys, and publicists, has had multiple printings and has become the definitive resource in its field. It has also been adopted as a course book by North Carolina School for the Arts and New York University, among other colleges and universities.

Forbidden Acts, the acclaimed first collected anthology of gay and lesbian plays from the span of the twentieth century, edited and with an introduction by Hodges, was published by Applause Theatre and Cinema Books in 2003 and became a finalist for the 2003 LAMBDA Literary Award for Drama, and has had multiple printings. New York University, Cornell University, Salisbury University, University of Las Vegas, and University of Louisville have adopted it as a course book, among other high schools, colleges and universities.

His *Out Plays: Landmark Gay and Lesbian Plays from the Twentieth Century*, edited and with an introduction by Hodges, featuring a foreword by Harvey Fierstein as well as a new introduction to *The Boys in the Band* by Mart Crowley, was released by Alyson Books in spring 2008. With *Out Plays*, Hodges became the most prolific single anthologist of published gay and lesbian American plays either in or out-of-print.

His highly acclaimed *The American Theatre Wing Presents The Play That Changed My Life: America's Foremost Playwrights on the Plays That Influenced Them*, with essays and interviews by nineteen of America's foremost American playwrights including David Auburn, Christopher Durang, Lynn Nottage, and John Patrick Shanley, was released by Applause Theatre and Cinema Books in fall 2009 and has had numerous printings.

As an actor, director, and/or producer, Ben has appeared in New York with The Barrow Group Theater Company, Origin Theater Company, Daedalus Theater Company, Monday Morning Productions, the Strawberry One-Act Festival, Coyote Girls Productions, Jet Productions, New York Actors' Alliance, and Outcast Productions. Additionally, he has appeared in numerous productions presented by theatre companies that he founded, including the Tuesday Group and Visionary Works. On film, he can be seen in *Macbeth: The Comedy*.

In 2001, Ben became director of development and then served as executive director for Fat Chance Productions Inc. and the Ground Floor Theatre, a New York-based nonprofit theatre and film production company. Fat Chance developed *Prey for Rock and Roll* from their stage production (the first legit production to play CBGBs) into a critically acclaimed feature film starring Gina Gershon and

The Sopranos' Emmy winner Drea de Matteo. *Prey for Rock and Roll* debuted at the Sundance Film Festival in 2003 and won Best Feature at the 2003 Santa Cruz Film Festival. Additionally, Fat Chance produced the American premiere of Tony Award-winning Irish playwright Enda Walsh's *Misterman* Off-Broadway, and a host of readings, workshops, and productions in their Ground Floor Theatre, with Fat Chance's mission statement being to present new works by new artists.

In 2003, frustrated with the increasingly daunting economic prospects involved in producing theatre on a small scale in New York, Ben organized NOOBA, the New Off-Off Broadway Association, an advocacy group dedicated to representing the concerns of expressly Off-Off-Broadway producers in the public forum and in negotiations with other local professional arts organizations—being their chief objective the reformation of the Actors' Equity Basic Showcase Code.

He also serves on the New York Innovative Theatre Awards Committee, selecting outstanding individuals for recognition Off-Off-Broadway, as vice-president of Summer Stage New York, a professional summer theatre program in Fayetteville, New York, and as executive producer of the annual Fire Island Pines Literary Weekend.

In 2005 Ben founded and served for two years as executive director of The Learning Theatre Inc., a 501(c)(3) nonprofit organization incorporating theatre into the development and lives of learning disabled and autistic children.

In support of his projects and publications, Ben has appeared on nationwide radio on *The Joey Reynolds Show*, *The Michael Dresser Show*, *Stage and Screen with Mark Gordon*; and on "Break a Leg with Deborah Sharn and Scott Miller in St. Louis, and on *WCRK* in Morristown, Tennessee. On television, he appeared on New York 1 and *Philly Live* in Philadelphia, PA—the only live televised LGBT call-in show in the United States. Reviews and articles on Ben, his projects, or publications have appeared in the *New York Times*; *New Yorker*; *GQ*, *Elle*; *Genre*; *Back Stage*; *Time Out New York*; *Playbill*; *Next*; *New York Blade*; *Library Journal*; *The Advocate*; *Chicago Free Press*; *Philadelphia Gay News*; *Houston Voice*; *Stage Directions*; *Between the Lines*; *The Flint Journal*; and *Citizen Tribune*; as well as the web sites Broadwayworld.com; CurtainUp.com; Playbill.com; and in Peter Filichia's Diary on Theatermania.com. He has made guest appearances in support of his publications at the Nadine's in the West Village; Good Beans Café in Flint, Michigan; Common Language Bookstore in Ann Arbor, Michigan, A Different Light in both Los Angeles and San Francisco; Michigan Design Center in Birmingham, Michigan; The Open Book in Sacramento; and at Giovanni's Room in Philadelphia, as well as at the DR2 Theatre D-2 Lounge, Barnes and Noble Lincoln Center, the Drama Book Shop, in New York City, Lehman College in Bronx, New York, and Seton Hall University School of Law in Newark, New Jersey.

He holds a BFA in Theatre Acting and Directing from Otterbein College in Westerville, Ohio, is an alumnus of the Commercial Theater Institute, and received his Juris Doctorate in May 2012 from Seton Hall University School of Law in Newark, NJ. He is currently a practicing attorney and a member of the New York City, County, and State Bar Associations. He lives in Jersey City, New Jersey. For more information or to schedule speaking engagements, please visit benhodges.com, or e-mail benjaminahodges@gmail.com.

Scott Denny (Coeditor) is an actor and singer who has worked professionally for over twenty years. Originally from Terre Haute, Indiana, he attended Western Kentucky University in Bowling Green, Kentucky, and holds a degree in performing arts.

The past three years he appeared in the Irish Repertory Theatre's gala concerts of *Brigadoon*, *Camelot*, and *Oliver* at the Shubert Theatre. He also recently appeared in the Off-Off Broadway production of the new musical *Speargrove Presents* and a staged reading of the Gallery Players' *A Man of No Importance*.

His professional theatrical credits include Richard Henry Lee in the Big League Theatricals national tour of *1776*, Uncle Wes in the Las Vegas and national touring production of *Footloose*, and the assistant company manager and swing on the 2001–2002 national tour of Susan Stroman's production of *The Music Man* While on tour he arranged several cast benefit cabarets for local charities.

Regionally he has appeared in *Evita, The Wizard of Oz,* and *The King and I* at Houston's Theatre Under the Stars, *The Mikado* starring Eric Idle at Houston Grand Opera, and in the regional theatre premieres of *Silver Dollar* and *Paper Moon* at Stage One in Wichita, Kansas.

He performed frequently at the Broadway Palm Dinner Theatre in Fort Myers, Florida, as well as Beef and Boards Dinner Theatre (Indianapolis, Indiana); Fireside Theatre (Fort Atkinson, Wisconsin); Miami Valley Dinner Theatre (Springboro, Ohio); Dutch Apple Dinner Theatre (Lancaster, Pennsylvania); Circa 21 (Rock Island, Illinois); and the Crown Uptown (Wichita, Kansas).

He worked six summers at the Galveston Island Outdoor Musicals and at the Sullivan Illinois' historic Little Theatre on the Square. Credits at those theatres include *Me and My Girl; Gypsy; She Loves Me; The Best Little Whorehouse in Texas; The Music Man; Some Like It Hot; Man of La Mancha; The Odd Couple; South Pacific; Oklahoma!; Grease; Wonderful Life! The Musical;* and *How to Succeed in Business Without Really Trying,* among many others.

In New York he has appeared Off-Off-Broadway in *Election Day The Musical, Like You Like It, Vanity Fair,* and in several readings, workshops, and cabaret shows. His screen credits include the independent films *Red Hook, Clear Blue Tuesday,* and *Illegally Yours.*

Scott worked as an assistant editor on *Theatre World Volume 60,* and has been an associate editor on *Volumes 61–65.* In the fall of 2006 Scott served as treasurer on the board of directors of the Theatre World Awards and as the associate producer for the 2006 Theatre World Awards ceremony. He was the coproducer for the Theatre World Awards between 2007–2009.

Scott has worked seasonally for the Macy's Thanksgiving Day Parade and Macy's Annual Events in the production office, and spent one season in the costume operations for the Parade. Since 2003 Scott has also worked as an outside group sales manager specializing in incentive groups for Cruise Everything, a travel agency located in Fort Myers, Florida. He coordinated the entertainment and sales operations for four cruises with two of QVC Network's most known and loved personalities, the Quacker Factory host Jeanne Bice, and Jenniefer Kirk of Kirk's Folly Jewelry, as well as three New York Theatre vacations. In addition to his many other hats, he bartends at the Duplex Cabaret and Piano Bar and Don't Tell Mama's in New York City.

He is honored to help continue the astounding work of the late John Willis, and would like to thank his high school drama teacher Jean Shutt for introducing him to the wonderful theatre world, as well as the former faculties of Western Kentucky University and Indiana State University: Bill Leonard; Jackson Kessler; Beverly Veenker; Steve Probus; Jim Brown; Larry Ruff; Lew Hackleman; Gary Stewart; Glenn and Patti Harbaugh; Don Nigro; David DelColletti; and the late Whit Combs.

Shay Gines (Associate Off-Off-Broadway Editor) graduated from the Actors Training Program at the University of Utah. Since then she has done everything from spackling walls at the Pasadena Playhouse and running follow-spot for the Pioneer Theatre Company to serving as the Artist in Residence for Touchstone Theatre. She has performed in theatres of all sizes from thirty to 1,000 seats and across the country, from Los Angeles to New York City. She is an award-winning producer whose Off and Off-Off-Broadway shows include: *Home Again Home Again Jiggity Jig, What the F**k?!, Hamlet,* and *Muse of Fire.* She was a founding member and the Producing Director for Esperance Theatre Company, served for five years as the Managing Director for Emerging Artists Theatre Company, and is an Executive Director for the New York Innovative Theatre Foundation.

Raj Autencio (Associate Regional Editor) Rommel "Raj" Autencio is a native of Manila, Phillipines, where he graduated with a Bachelor of Arts in Organizational Communication from the University of Phillipines, Manila, in 2000. As a professional singer, he performed in various show bands that travelled throughout the Middle East and Asia, including performances in Hong Kong and Bahrain. In New York, he has studied photography at the International Center of Photography, and has served as a staff photographer for *Theatre World* and the Theatre World Awards and the Fire Island Pines Literary Theater Festival in Pines, New York, since 2008. His first group photography exhibit was held in New York in November 2011, in collaboration with the ElevenEleven Collective. He has additionally exhibited his photography at Jackson Hall Gallery of MCCNY. He is currently studying decorative arts and will complete his training in that regard in July 2013. He lives in Brooklyn, New York.

Heath McCormack (Associate Editor) is a classically trained former dancer whose lifelong passion for ballet and musical theatre has taken him on an amazing journey across the United States. In addition to dancing for three consecutive seasons in the largest outdoor drama in America, *Texas! The Musical Drama,* Heath has also had the opportunity to be seen performing alongside a very eclectic group of entertainers, among them, the Lightcrust Doughboys, the country's oldest Western swing band, the Jim Cullum Jazz band, Canadian illusionist Brian Glow, and countless productions *The Nutcracker,* his favorite being one of the most opulently executed under the direction and original choreography of Mr. Neil Hess with Lone Star Ballet. In recent years Heath has taken his love of entertaining to the friendly skies and can be seen by hundreds of people coast to coast, non-stop, daily.

Adam Feldman (Contributing Editor: Broadway Review) is the associate theater editor at *Time Out New York,* where he is also cabaret editor. Since 2005, he has served as president of the New York Drama Critics' Circle, making him both the youngest and the longest-serving president in the group's seventy-five-year history. His essays and reviews have appeared in Canada's *Globe and Mail* and *National Post,* as well as Broadway.com, *Time Out London, Time Out New York Kids* and the *Gay & Lesbian Review.* He is a frequent commentator on New York's NPR station, WNYC, and has been interviewed on ABC's Nightline, CNN, and CBS News. He has hosted panel events at the 92nd Street Y, the Brooklyn Academy of Music, the Public Theater and Theater Row, among others. He is a graduate of Harvard University, where he received the Helen Choate Bell prize for essays on American literature.

Linda Buchwald (Contributing Editor: Off-Broadway Review) writes monthly features for TDF Stages and is a regular contributor to Backstage.com, StageGrade, Broadway Direct, and the theater site The Craptacular. She is the associate editor of Scholastic MATH Magazine and also runs a (mostly) theater blog, Pataphysical Science, part of the Independent Theater Bloggers Association (ITBA). She is a graduate of the Goldring Arts Journalism Program at Syracuse University. You can follow her on Twitter @PataphysicalSci.

Rob Weinert-Kendt (Contributing Editor: Regional Review) is associate editor at *American Theatre* magazine. He has written features and criticism for the *New York Times,* the *Los Angeles Times, Variety,* the *Sondheim Review,* and *Time Out NY,* among others. He was the founding editor of *Back Stage West.*

Kelley Murphy Perlstein (Assistant Editor) has been working professionally in the theatre for over twenty years. She has her B.F.A. in Theatre from the University of Science and Arts in Oklahoma and an M.F.A. in Music Theatre Performance from Roosevelt University in Chicago. From 2000–2007, she was the Development Director and eventually managing director Praxis Theatre Project, an Off-Off-Broadway theatre company in New York City. She currently resides in Dallas, Texas.